Take 'Five' to Try 572 Short Recipes That Are Long on Flavor

Festive Fillets, p. 59

Onion-Roasted Potatoes, p. 162

Dipped Strawberries, p. 290

PRESSED FOR TIME and don't have much in your pantry? *Taste of Home's 5-Ingredient Cookbook* is packed with 572 fuss-free recipes that are easy to assemble with only five ingredients or less!

Readers of *Taste of Home* and *Quick Cooking* magazines have been begging us to publish a big cookbook full of such family-pleasing, no-nonsense fare...and now it's finally here! Inside you'll find hundreds of simply delicious recipes that call for basic ingredients most cooks keep on hand.

Say you have chicken—and not much else. This handy cookbook has plenty of recipes to put that poultry to satisfying use. Beef, pork, turkey and seafood, too.

WHAT'S INSIDE

With 116 main dishes to choose from, you can make the down-home dinner your family has been looking forward to all day...without a lot of work! Pick from a selection of 76 complementary side dishes and condiments, 56 salads and dressings, and 48 fast from-scratch breads and rolls to serve alongside.

Soups and sandwiches make a hearty supper or lunch all by themselves. So pair any of this book's 48 bowl-filling suggestions and piled-high choices for a winning combination.

Having this *5-Ingredient Cookbook* in your collection means never having to say, "Sorry, no dessert tonight". You won't need a special trip to the supermarket to make any of the 152 short and sweet desserts inside!

And 76 tempting snacks and beverages will control a case of the "munchies" until your next mouth-watering meal.

STAMP OF APPROVAL

Your gang is going to love these great-tasting recipes. How can we be so sure? Because each is already the tried-and-true favorite of a fellow busy cook's family. Our Test Kitchen staff prepared and tasted every easy-to-make dish, too, to guarantee you'll have delicious results when you make them in your own kitchen.

So if the supplies in your cupboard and refrigerator are running low, don't run to the grocery store to feed your hungry family supper. Reach for *Taste of Home's 5-Ingredient Cookbook* and whip up flavorful meals you can fix with only five ingredients or less!

Pictured on back cover: Pizza Chicken Roll-Ups (p. 62) and Chocolate Mousse Pie (p. 270).

Editor: Jean Steiner

Art Director: Lori Arndt

Senior Editor/Books: Heidi Reuter Lloyd

Associate Editor: Beth Wittlinger

Graphic Art Associate: Catherine Fletcher

Editorial Assistant: Barb Czysz

Food Editor: Janaan Cunningham

Associate Food Editors: Coleen Martin, Diane Werner

Assistant Food Editor: Karen Wright

Senior Recipe Editor: Sue A. Jurack

Recipe Editor: Janet Briggs

Test Kitchen Director: Mark Morgan

Food Photography: Rob Hagen, Dan Roberts

Food Photography Artists: Julie Ferron, Sue Myers

Photo Studio Manager: Anne Schimmel

Senior Vice President,
Editor in Chief: Catherine Cassidy

President: Barbara Newton

Chairman and Founder: Roy Reiman

Taste of Home Books
© 2005 Reiman Media Group, Inc.
5400 S. 60th St., Greendale WI 53129
International Standard Book Number: 0-89821-424-6
Library of Congress Control Number: 2004099534
Second Printing, January 2006

To order additional copies of this book, write to:
Taste of Home Books, P.O. Box 908, Greendale WI 53129

To order with a credit card,
call toll-free 1-800/344-2560 or
visit our Web site at *www.reimanpub.com*

Taste of Home's
5-Ingredient Cookbook

|TABLE OF CONTENTS|

Snacks & Beverages

Fruity Sherbet Punch (p. 17), Ham Roll-Ups (p. 6), Turkey Meatballs (p. 8) and Sausage Biscuit Bites (p. 9)

| BEVERAGES |

Blackberry Banana Smoothies, p. 10

Creamy Thyme Spread, p. 12

Ham Roll-Ups

(Pictured on page 4)

Green onions and ripe olives give lively flavor to these bite-size appetizers. They're quick to assemble and can be made the day before they're needed. They're very popular with my friends and family.

—*Kathleen Green, Republic, Missouri*

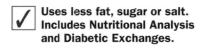 **Uses less fat, sugar or salt. Includes Nutritional Analysis and Diabetic Exchanges.**

- **1 package (8 ounces) cream cheese, softened**
- **1 can (2-1/4 ounces) chopped ripe olives, drained**
- **1/3 cup thinly sliced green onions**
- **8 to 10 thin slices fully cooked ham**

In a mixing bowl, beat cream cheese until smooth; stir in the olives and onions. Spread over ham slices. Roll up, jelly-roll style, starting with a short side. Chill for at least 1 hour. Just before serving, cut into 1-in. pieces. **Yield:** 40 appetizers.

Nutritional Analysis: One serving of 2 roll-ups (prepared with fat-free cream cheese and reduced-fat ham) equals 27 calories, 259 mg sodium, 7 mg cholesterol, 1 g carbohydrate, 4 g protein, 1 g fat. **Diabetic Exchange:** 1/2 meat.

Raspberry Iced Tea

A co-worker of mine from England gave me a tip on making the best iced tea: The sugar should be added first to make a syrup before adding the tea bags. I often serve Raspberry Iced Tea with lemon slices and prepare it with fresh raspberries from my backyard bushes.

—*Christine Wilson*
Sellersville, Pennsylvania

- **8-1/4 cups water, *divided***
- **2/3 cup sugar**
- **5 individual tea bags**
- **3 to 4 cups unsweetened raspberries**

In a large saucepan, bring 4 cups water to a boil. Stir in sugar until dissolved. Remove from the heat; add tea bags. Steep for 5-8 minutes. Discard tea bags. Add 4 cups water.

In another saucepan, bring raspberries and remaining water to a boil. Reduce heat; simmer, uncovered, for 3 minutes. Strain and discard pulp. Add raspberry juice to the tea mixture. Serve over ice. **Yield:** about 2 quarts.

Smoky Bacon Wraps

These cute little sausage and bacon bites are finger-licking good. They have a sweet and salty taste that's fun for an appetizer. I've even served them for breakfast and brunch, and everyone gobbles them up!
—*Cara Flora, Kokomo, Indiana*

1 pound sliced bacon
1 package (16 ounces)
   miniature smoked
   sausage links
1 cup packed brown sugar

Cut each bacon strip in half widthwise. Wrap one piece of bacon around each sausage. Place in a foil-lined 15-in. x 10-in. x 1-in. baking pan. Sprinkle with brown sugar.

Bake, uncovered, at 400° for 30-40 minutes or until bacon is crisp and sausage is heated through. **Yield:** about 3-1/2 dozen.

Salsa Strips

I rely on refrigerated crescent rolls to make these crisp Southwestern appetizers. Choose mild, medium or hot salsa to suit your taste. I often use the hot variety for my own family and a milder salsa when I serve them to guests.
—*Joann Woloszyn*
Fredonia, New York

1 tube (8 ounces)
   refrigerated crescent
   rolls
2 tablespoons Dijon
   mustard
3/4 cup salsa
1 cup (4 ounces) shredded
   mozzarella cheese
Minced fresh cilantro

Unroll crescent roll dough and separate into four rectangles. Place on greased baking sheets. Spread mustard and salsa on each rectangle.

Bake at 350° for 10 minutes. Sprinkle with cheese; bake 8-10 minutes longer or until golden brown. Cool for 10 minutes. Cut each into four strips; sprinkle with cilantro. **Yield:** 16 appetizers.

Glazed Chicken Wings

I received the recipe for these yummy chicken wings from a cousin on Vancouver Island during a visit there a number of years ago. They're an appealing appetizer but also a favorite for Sunday lunch with rice and a salad. We love the glaze that coats each wing. —*Joan Airey*
Rivers, Manitoba

**12 whole chicken wings
(about 2-1/2 pounds)**
1/2 cup barbecue sauce
1/2 cup honey
1/2 cup soy sauce

Cut chicken wings into three sections; discard wing tip section. Place in a greased 13-in. x 9-in. x 2-in. baking dish. Combine barbecue sauce, honey and soy sauce; pour over wings. Bake, uncovered, at 350° for 50-60 minutes or until chicken juices run clear. **Yield:** 4 servings.

Editor's Note: 2-1/2 pounds of uncooked chicken wing sections may be substituted for the whole chicken wings. Omit the first step of the recipe.

Turkey Meatballs

(Pictured on page 4)

I hate to cook, so I'm always looking for fast and easy recipes like this one. A sweet sauce coats these firm meatballs that are made with ground turkey for a nice change of pace. —*Hazel Bates*
Clinton, Oklahoma

 **Uses less fat, sugar or salt.
Includes Nutritional Analysis
and Diabetic Exchanges.**

1 pound ground turkey
1/4 cup oat bran cereal
**1 bottle (14 ounces)
ketchup**
1 cup grape jelly
**3 to 4 tablespoons lemon
juice**

In a bowl, combine turkey and cereal; mix well. Shape into 1-in. balls. In a Dutch oven, combine ketchup, jelly and lemon juice; bring to a boil. Add meatballs. Reduce heat; simmer, uncovered, for 30-35 minutes or until meat is no longer pink, stirring several times. **Yield:** 4-1/2 dozen.

Nutritional Analysis: One serving of 5 meatballs (prepared with ground turkey breast, no-salt-added ketchup and reduced-sugar grape jelly) equals 137 calories, 36 mg sodium, 20 mg cholesterol, 24 g carbohydrate, 11 g protein, 1 g fat. **Diabetic Exchanges:** 1 very lean meat, 1 starch, 1/2 fruit.

Sausage Biscuit Bites

(Pictured on page 4)

I sometimes bake these delightful little morsels the night before, refrigerate them, then put them in the slow cooker in the morning so my husband can share them with his co-workers. They're always gone in a hurry.
—*Audrey Marler, Kokomo, Indiana*

1 tube (7-1/2 ounces) refrigerated buttermilk biscuits
1 tablespoon butter, melted
4-1/2 teaspoons grated Parmesan cheese
1 teaspoon dried oregano
1 package (8 ounces) brown-and-serve sausage links

On a lightly floured surface, roll out each biscuit into a 4-in. circle; brush with butter. Combine Parmesan cheese and oregano; sprinkle over butter. Place a sausage link in the center of each; roll up.

Cut each widthwise into four pieces; insert a toothpick into each. Place on an ungreased baking sheet. Bake at 375° for 8-10 minutes or until golden brown. **Yield:** 40 appetizers.

Fluffy Hot Chocolate

Melted marshmallows provide the frothy texture that you'll savor in this sweet and speedy warm beverage. They're also what makes this hot chocolate different from (and better than) the instant kind you make from a store-bought mix. Chocolaty and comforting, it's our daughter's favorite.
—*Jo Ann Schimcek*
Weimar, Texas

8 teaspoons sugar
4 teaspoons baking cocoa
4 cups milk
1-1/2 cups miniature marshmallows
1 teaspoon vanilla extract

In a saucepan, combine the first four ingredients. Cook and stir over medium heat until the marshmallows are melted, about 8 minutes. Remove from the heat; stir in vanilla. Ladle into mugs. **Yield:** 4 servings.

Blackberry Banana Smoothies

(Pictured on page 5)

I originally began blending up this simple beverage when our young girls shied away from berries. Now they're thrilled whenever I serve it. The thick fruity drink is a refreshing treat no matter what kind of berries you use.
—*Heidi Butts, Streetsboro, Ohio*

 Uses less fat, sugar or salt. Includes Nutritional Analysis and Diabetic Exchanges.

2 cups orange juice
1/3 cup vanilla yogurt
2 medium ripe bananas, cut into thirds and frozen
1/2 cup fresh *or* frozen blackberries

In a blender, combine all ingredients. Cover and process until blended. Serve immediately. **Yield:** 4 servings.

Nutritional Analysis: One 3/4-cup serving (prepared with reduced-fat yogurt) equals 136 calories, 1 g fat (trace saturated fat), 1 mg cholesterol, 14 mg sodium, 32 g carbohydrate, 2 g fiber, 2 g protein. **Diabetic Exchanges:** 1 starch, 1 fruit.

Reuben Roll-Ups

This recipe turns the popular Reuben sandwich into an interesting and hearty snack. We love these roll-ups at our house. Company quickly reaches for them as well. —*Patty Kile Greentown, Pennsylvania*

1 tube (10 ounces) refrigerated pizza dough
1 cup sauerkraut, well drained
1 tablespoon Thousand Island salad dressing
4 slices corned beef, halved
4 slices Swiss cheese, halved

Roll dough into a 12-in. x 9-in. rectangle. Cut into eight 3-in. x 4-1/2-in. rectangles. Combine sauerkraut and salad dressing. Place a slice of beef on each rectangle. Top with about 2 tablespoons of the sauerkraut mixture and a slice of cheese. Roll up.

Place with seam side down on a greased baking sheet. Bake at 425° for 12-14 minutes or until golden. **Yield:** 8 roll-ups.

Cucumber Pita Wedges

I first tasted these delicious snacks at a basket party in a friend's home. (I work as a sales consultant for a hand-crafted basket company.) Of the finger foods she served, this platter was the first to become empty.
—Grace Yaskovic
Branchville, New Jersey

1 package (8 ounces) cream cheese, softened
2 tablespoons Italian salad dressing mix
4 whole pita breads
1 to 2 medium cucumbers, peeled and cut into 1/8-inch slices
Lemon-pepper seasoning

In a mixing bowl, beat cream cheese and salad dressing mix until combined. Split pita breads in half, forming two circles. Spread cream cheese mixture over pita circles; cut each into six wedges. Top with cucumbers. Sprinkle with lemon-pepper. **Yield:** 4 dozen.

Easy Cheese Nachos

There's no need to brown ground beef when fixing this satisfying snack. I simply top crunchy tortilla chips with warm canned chili and melted cheese, then sprinkle it all with chopped tomato and onion for fresh flavor and color.
—Laura Jirasek
White Lake, Michigan

1 package (14-1/2 ounces) tortilla chips
2 cans (15 ounces *each*) chili without beans
1 pound process cheese (Velveeta), cubed
4 green onions, sliced
1 medium tomato, chopped

Divide the tortilla chips between six plates and set aside. In a saucepan, warm chili until heated through. Meanwhile, in another saucepan, heat the cheese over medium-low heat until melted, stirring frequently. Spoon chili over chips; drizzle with cheese. Sprinkle with onions and tomato. **Yield:** 6 servings.

Hot Diggety Dogs

My family has always enjoyed this quick and easy snack. When our children were young, they used to help me fix these. Now they prepare them with their own families. And their kids enjoy them as much if not more!
—Linda Blankenmyer
Conestoga, Pennsylvania

20 **saltine crackers**
5 **slices process American cheese, quartered**
Ketchup, mustard *and/or* pickle relish
2 **hot dogs**

Place crackers on a lightly greased baking sheet. Top with cheese and ketchup, mustard and/or relish. Cut each hot dog into 10 slices; place one slice on each cracker. Bake at 350° for 10-12 minutes or until the cheese is melted. **Yield:** 20 snacks.

Editor's Note: If serving small children, cut hot dog slices in half; double the amount of crackers and cheese.

Creamy Thyme Spread

(Pictured on page 5)

This make-ahead cracker spread showcases thyme and garlic. A neighbor who has an herb garden gave me the recipe. It's simple to stir up and makes a special appetizer for company. It's also great to serve at a party.
—Mary Steiner, West Bend, Wisconsin

1 **package (8 ounces) cream cheese, softened**
1 **tablespoon minced fresh thyme *or* 1 teaspoon dried thyme**
1 **tablespoon minced fresh parsley *or* 1 teaspoon dried parsley flakes**
1 **garlic clove, minced**
Assorted crackers

In a bowl, combine the cream cheese, thyme, parsley and garlic; mix well. Cover and refrigerate until serving. Serve with crackers. **Yield:** about 1 cup.

|IT'S ABOUT THYME| Thyme has a bold earthy taste and a strong aroma. There are many varieties of fresh thyme, including the popular lemon-flavored plant. Use fresh or dried thyme to season fish, potato dishes, soups, stuffing, stews, rice pilaf, wild rice dishes, poultry and meat marinades.

Chocolate Quivers

These smooth, cool snacks are more fun than chocolate pudding! They're a nice make-ahead treat that I keep on hand for kids of all ages.
—*Shirley Kidd, New London, Minnesota*

2 envelopes unflavored gelatin
2 cups milk, *divided*
1/2 cup instant chocolate drink mix
1/4 cup sugar

In a bowl, dissolve gelatin in 1 cup milk. In a small saucepan over medium-high heat, combine drink mix, sugar and remaining milk; bring to a boil, stirring until chocolate and sugar are dissolved. Add to gelatin mixture and mix well.

Pour into an 8-in. square pan. Cool at room temperature for 30 minutes. Cover and refrigerate until firm, about 5 hours (do not freeze). Cut with a knife or cookie cutter. **Yield:** about 1 dozen.

Apricot Wraps

I accumulated a large recipe collection from around the world while my husband served in the Air Force for 25 years. This mouth-watering appetizer is one of our favorites, and we enjoy sharing it with friends.
—*Jane Ashworth, Beavercreek, Ohio*

1 package (14 ounces) dried apricots
1/2 cup whole almonds
1 pound sliced bacon
1/4 cup plum *or* apple jelly
2 tablespoons soy sauce

Fold each apricot around an almond. Cut bacon strips into thirds; wrap a strip around each apricot and secure with a toothpick. Place on two ungreased 15-in. x 10-in. x 1-in. baking pans. Bake, uncovered, at 375° for 25 minutes or until bacon is crisp, turning once.

In a small saucepan, combine jelly and soy sauce; cook and stir over low heat for 5 minutes or until warmed and smooth. Remove apricots to paper towels; drain. Serve with sauce for dipping. **Yield:** about 4-1/2 dozen.

Granola Chip Shakes

Packed with irresistible ingredients and served with a spoon, this shake is a super summertime treat. Treat your family and friends to this blended beverage soon!

—Elaine Anderson
Aliquippa, Pennsylvania

3/4 to 1 cup milk
4 tablespoons butterscotch ice cream topping, *divided*
2 cups vanilla ice cream, softened
1/2 cup granola cereal
2 tablespoons miniature semisweet chocolate chips

In a blender, combine milk, 2 tablespoons butterscotch topping and ice cream; cover and process until smooth. Pour into chilled glasses.

Drizzle with remaining topping; sprinkle with half of the granola and chocolate chips. Use a knife to swirl topping into shake. Top with remaining granola and chips. **Yield:** 2-1/2 cups.

Orange Marmalade Turnovers

A church friend prepares these delicate pastries for gatherings, but they're usually gone before she gets the platter to the serving table.

—Anna Jean Allen
West Liberty, Kentucky

1/2 cup butter, softened
1 jar (5 ounces) sharp American cheese spread
1 cup all-purpose flour
1/3 cup orange marmalade

In a bowl, combine butter and cheese. Add flour; stir until mixture forms a ball. Cover and refrigerate for 1 hour.

On a lightly floured surface, roll dough to 1/8-in. thickness; cut into 2-3/4-in. circles. Place 1/2 teaspoon marmalade on each circle. Fold pastry over and seal edges with a fork. Cut slits in top of pastry.

Place 2 in. apart on ungreased baking sheets. Bake at 350° for 5-9 minutes or until lightly browned. Remove to wire racks to cool. **Yield:** 2-1/2 dozen.

Picnic Fruit Punch

This pink cooler is deliciously thirst-quenching on a warm day. Seeing its color, folks guess it might be pink lemonade. They're pleasantly surprised to discover the bubbly blend includes cranberry, pineapple, orange and lemon juices.
—*Marion Lowery*
Medford, Oregon

2 quarts cranberry juice
3 cups pineapple juice
3 cups orange juice
1/4 cup lemon juice
1 liter ginger ale, chilled
1 medium navel orange, sliced, optional

Combine the juices in a large container. Refrigerate. Just before serving, stir in ginger ale and orange slices if desired. **Yield:** 5 quarts.

Icebox Sandwiches

My mother liked making these cool, creamy treats when I was growing up in the States because they're so quick to fix. Now my three kids enjoy them.
—*Sandy Armijo, Naples, Italy*

1 package (3.4 ounces) instant vanilla pudding mix
2 cups cold milk
2 cups whipped topping
1 cup (6 ounces) miniature semisweet chocolate chips
48 graham cracker squares

Mix pudding and milk according to package directions and refrigerate until set. Fold in whipped topping and chocolate chips.

Place 24 graham crackers on a baking sheet; top each with about 3 tablespoons filling. Place another graham cracker on top. Freeze for 1 hour or until firm. Wrap individually in plastic wrap; freeze. Serve sandwiches frozen. **Yield:** 2 dozen.

Pineapple Orange Drink

Living in the Sunshine State gives me a sunny outlook on life, as this drink deliciously proves! The delightful beverage featuring our famous orange juice is not too sweet but is so easy to make...just throw it in a blender and it's done.
—LaChelle Olivet, Pace, Florida

6 cups orange juice
2 cans (8 ounces *each***)**
crushed unsweetened
pineapple, undrained
16 ice cubes

Place half of the orange juice, pineapple and ice cubes in a blender; cover and process until smooth. Repeat with remaining ingredients. Pour into chilled glasses. Serve immediately. **Yield:** 8 servings.

Grilled Jalapenos

When barbecuing with my friends, I also use the grill to serve up hot appetizers. These crowd-pleasing stuffed peppers have a bit of bite. They were concocted by my son.
—Catherine Hollie
Cleveland, Texas

24 fresh jalapeno peppers
12 ounces bulk pork
sausage
12 bacon strips, halved

Wash peppers and remove stems. Cut a slit along one side of each pepper. Remove seeds; rinse and dry peppers. In a skillet over medium heat, cook sausage until no longer pink; drain. Stuff peppers with sausage and wrap with bacon; secure with a toothpick.

On an uncovered grill over medium heat, grill peppers for about 15 minutes or until tender and bacon is crisp, turning frequently. **Yield:** 2 dozen.

Editor's Note: When cutting or seeding hot peppers, use rubber or plastic gloves to protect your hands. Avoid touching your face.

One of the most common hot peppers, jalapenos are usually moderately to very hot and are sold at their green stage. At the red stage of full maturity, the jalapeno is super hot.

Fruity Sherbet Punch

(Pictured on page 4)

Everybody loves glasses of this sweet fruit punch. When entertaining, I start with a quart of sherbet, then add more later so it all doesn't melt right away.　　—*Betty Eberly, Palmyra, Pennsylvania*

4 cups apple juice, chilled
4 cups pineapple juice,
**　chilled**
4 cups orange juice, chilled
2 liters ginger ale, chilled
1 to 2 quarts orange *or*
**　pineapple sherbet**

Combine juices in a punch bowl. Stir in ginger ale. Top with sherbet. Serve immediately. **Yield:** 15-20 servings (about 5 quarts).

Veggie Dip

I always serve a colorful array of vegetables with this delicious dip. This popular appetizer is a welcome snack just about anytime.
　　—*Sue Schuller*
　　Brainerd, Minnesota

1 cup mayonnaise
1 cup (8 ounces) sour
**　cream**
1 envelope vegetable soup
**　mix**
1 package (10 ounces)
**　frozen chopped spinach,**
**　thawed and squeezed dry**
1 can (8 ounces) water
**　chestnuts, drained and**
**　chopped**

In a bowl, combine mayonnaise, sour cream and soup mix. Stir in spinach and water chestnuts. Cover and refrigerate for at least 2 hours. **Yield:** 3 cups.

Harvest Apple Drink

My family loves this spiced apple drink, especially during the cooler fall months. I like that I can hand out mugfuls of it in a hurry.

—Linda Young, Longmont, Colorado

1 can (46 ounces) apple juice
1/3 cup packed brown sugar
2 cinnamon sticks
6 whole cloves

In a medium saucepan, bring all ingredients to a boil. Reduce heat; simmer for 15 minutes. Strain. Serve warm. **Yield:** 4-6 servings.

Bacon-Broccoli Cheese Ball

Needing a quick appetizer one night when dinner was running late, I combined a few leftovers into this easy cheese ball. For variety, you can shape it into a log or substitute favorite herbs for the pepper. However you make it, it's delicious served with a variety of crackers.

—Tamara Rickard
Bartlett, Tennessee

1 package (8 ounces) cream cheese, softened
1 cup (4 ounces) finely shredded cheddar cheese
1/2 teaspoon pepper
1 cup finely chopped broccoli florets
6 bacon strips, cooked and crumbled

In a mixing bowl, beat cream cheese, cheddar cheese and pepper until blended. Stir in broccoli. Shape into a ball and roll in bacon. Cover and refrigerate. Remove from the refrigerator 15 minutes before serving. **Yield:** 2-1/2 cups.

|SHAPING A CHEESE BALL| To keep your hands and the countertop clean, spoon the cheese mixture onto a piece of plastic wrap. Working from the underside of the wrap, pat the mixture into a ball. Complete the recipe as directed.

Caramel Peanut Butter Dip

When crisp autumn apples are available, I make this quick delicious dip. My family loves the combination of caramel and peanut butter, and the consistency is perfect for dipping. —Sandra McKenzie
Braham, Minnesota

30 **caramels**
1 **to 2 tablespoons water**
1/4 **cup plus 2 tablespoons creamy peanut butter**
1/4 **cup finely crushed peanuts, optional**
Sliced apples

In a microwave-safe bowl, microwave the caramels and water on high for 1 minute; stir. Microwave 1 minute more or until smooth. Add peanut butter and mix well; microwave for 30 seconds or until smooth. Stir in peanuts if desired. Serve warm with apples. **Yield:** 1 cup.

Editor's Note: This recipe was tested in a 700-watt microwave.

Pizza Roll-Ups

Since receiving this recipe through 4-H, it's been a regular after-school snack. These bite-size pizza treats, made with refrigerated crescent rolls, are especially good served with spaghetti sauce for dipping. —Donna Klettke, Wheatland, Missouri

1/2 **pound ground beef**
1 **can (8 ounces) tomato sauce**
1/2 **cup shredded mozzarella cheese**
1/2 **teaspoon dried oregano**
2 **tubes (8 ounces** *each***) refrigerated crescent rolls**

In a skillet, cook beef over medium heat until no longer pink; drain. Remove from the heat. Add tomato sauce, mozzarella cheese and oregano; mix well.

Separate crescent dough into eight rectangles, pinching seams together. Place about 3 tablespoons of meat mixture along one long side of each rectangle. Roll up, jelly-roll style, starting with a long side. Cut each roll into three pieces. Place, seam side down, 2 in. apart on greased baking sheets. Bake at 375° for 15 minutes or until golden brown. **Yield:** 2 dozen.

Mushroom Bacon Bites

This is the perfect appetizer for most any occasion. The tasty bites are easy to assemble and brush with prepared barbecue sauce. When we have a big cookout, they're always a hit...but they make a nice little "extra" for a family dinner, too.
—Gina Roesner, Ashland, Missouri

24 medium fresh
   mushrooms
12 bacon strips, halved
1 cup barbecue sauce

Wrap each mushroom with a piece of bacon; secure with a toothpick. Thread onto metal or soaked bamboo skewers; brush with barbecue sauce.

Grill, uncovered, over indirect medium heat for 10-15 minutes or until the bacon is crisp and the mushrooms are tender, turning and basting occasionally with remaining barbecue sauce. **Yield:** 2 dozen.

|MUSHROOM HINT| Clean mushrooms just before using. Never immerse them in water, as they're very absorbent and become mushy. Simply rinse mushrooms under cold running water and blot dry with paper towels.

Cranberry Quencher

This tart, fruity punch has such a pretty color. I got the recipe while visiting Hawaii, so it's no surprise pineapple juice is a main ingredient. I like to serve it for the holidays.
—Dorothy Smith
El Dorado, Arkansas

1 bottle (1 gallon)
   cranberry-apple juice,
   chilled
1 can (46 ounces)
   pineapple juice, chilled
3/4 cup (6 ounces) lemonade
   or orange juice
   concentrate
Pineapple rings *or* tidbits, fresh
   cranberries *and/or* mint,
   optional

Combine cranberry-apple and pineapple juices in a large container or punch bowl. Stir in lemonade concentrate. Garnish glasses with pineapple, cranberries and/or mint if desired. **Yield:** 6 quarts.

Pineapple Ham Spread

This is a recipe I served my kids when time was short...and so was leftover ham. Spread the sweet ham mixture on rye bread or crunchy crackers for an effortless appetizer. —*Delia Kennedy*
Deer Park, Washington

4 ounces cream cheese, softened
1 can (8 ounces) crushed pineapple, drained
1/2 cup ground fully cooked ham
Crackers *or* snack rye bread

In a bowl, combine the cream cheese, pineapple and ham. Serve with crackers or bread. **Yield:** 1-1/3 cups.

Editor's Note: See your local butcher to purchase ground ham.

Raspberry Lemonade

This crisp, tart beverage is a real thirst-quencher on a hot day. Pretty enough to serve at a bridal shower and refreshing enough to pour at a picnic, it's a fun change from iced tea or regular lemonade.
—*Dorothy Jennings, Waterloo, Iowa*

2 cans (12 ounces *each*) frozen lemonade concentrate, thawed
2 packages (10 ounces *each*) frozen sweetened raspberries, partially thawed
2 to 4 tablespoons sugar
2 liters club soda, chilled
Ice cubes

In a blender, combine lemonade concentrate, raspberries and sugar. Cover and process until blended. Strain to remove seeds. In a 4-1/2-qt. container, combine raspberry mixture, club soda and ice cubes; mix well. Serve immediately. **Yield:** 3-1/2 quarts.

Ham Pickle Pinwheels

My mom introduced me to these appetizers a number of years ago, and I've been serving them for parties ever since. They're easy to make and are always well received by guests. —*Gloria Jarrett*
Loveland, Ohio

1 package (8 ounces)
   cream cheese, cubed
1/4 pound sliced Genoa
   salami
1 tablespoon prepared
   horseradish
7 slices deli ham
14 to 21 okra pickles *or* dill
   pickle spears

Place cream cheese, salami and horseradish in a blender or food processor; cover and process until smooth. Spread over ham slices.

Remove stems and ends of okra pickles. Place two or three okra pickles or one dill pickle down the center of each ham slice. Roll up tightly and wrap in plastic wrap. Refrigerate for at least 2 hours. Cut into 1-in. slices. **Yield:** about 3-1/2 dozen.

|MAKE-AHEAD ADVICE| Ham Pickle Pinwheels can be prepared a day or two before you serve them. Simply store the uncut appetizer in the refrigerator tightly wrapped in plastic wrap.

Frothy Apricot Drink

Four simple ingredients make this drink as refreshing as it is pretty. It's especially great to sip this treat on a hot day. —*Diane Hixon*
Niceville, Florida

1 can (15-1/4 ounces)
   apricot halves, undrained
1/2 cup milk
1/4 cup orange juice
   concentrate
1 pint lemon sherbet

In a blender, place apricot halves with juice, milk and orange juice concentrate. Cover and process until smooth. Add sherbet; cover and process just until combined. Pour into glasses; serve immediately. **Yield:** 4 cups.

Chocolate Cream Fruit Dip

This recipe was truly an accident. While hosting a graduation party, I realized I'd forgotten the fruit dip. So I raided my cabinets and slapped this combination together. It was a surprising success and has since become one of our family's favorites.
—*Debbie Bond, Richwood, West Virginia*

1 package (8 ounces)
    cream cheese, softened
1/4 cup chocolate syrup
1 jar (7 ounces)
    marshmallow creme
Apple wedges, fresh strawberries
and/or banana chunks

In a small mixing bowl, beat cream cheese and chocolate syrup. Fold in marshmallow creme. Cover and refrigerate until serving. Serve with fruit. **Yield:** about 2 cups.

Lunch Box Pizzas

It's a challenge finding lunch fare that both our children enjoy. These mini pizzas are fun to make. They pack nicely in plastic sandwich bags and travel well, so there's no mess. They also make a tasty after-school snack.   —*Rhonda Cliett, Belton, Texas*

1 tube (7-1/2 ounces)
    refrigerated buttermilk
    biscuits (10 biscuits)
1/4 cup tomato sauce
1 teaspoon Italian
    seasoning
10 slices pepperoni
3/4 cup shredded Monterey
    Jack cheese

Flatten each biscuit into a 3-in. circle and press into a greased muffin cup. Combine the tomato sauce and Italian seasoning; spoon 1 teaspoonful into each cup. Top each with a slice of pepperoni and about 1 tablespoon of cheese.

Bake at 425° for 10-15 minutes or until golden brown. Serve immediately or store in the refrigerator. **Yield:** 10 servings.

Creamy Swiss Spinach Dip

A few items and a microwave oven are all you need to throw together this warm cheesy dip. It's always gone at the party's end. My favorite way to serve the dip is in a bread bowl with bread cubes, but it's also good with tortilla chips or French bread slices. —*Heather Millican Fort Myers, Florida*

- 1 package (8 ounces) cream cheese, softened
- 1 teaspoon garlic powder
- 1 package (9 ounces) frozen creamed spinach, thawed
- 2 cups diced Swiss cheese
- 2 unsliced round loaves (1 pound *each*) Italian *or* French bread

In a small microwave-safe mixing bowl, beat cream cheese and garlic powder until smooth. Stir in spinach and Swiss cheese. Cover and microwave on high for 5-8 minutes or until cheese is melted, stirring occasionally.

Meanwhile, cut a 4-in. circle in the center of one loaf of bread. Remove bread, leaving 1 in. at bottom of loaf. Cut removed bread and the second loaf into 1-1/2-in. cubes. Spoon hot spinach dip into bread shell. Serve with bread cubes. **Yield:** 3-1/2 cups.

Editor's Note: This recipe was tested in an 850-watt microwave.

After-School Treats

These delicious no-bake bars satisfy my craving for chocolate and are much easier to whip up than brownies or cookies from scratch. Requiring just five ingredients, they're especially handy for a bake sale or after-school treat. —*Andrea Neilson, East Dundee, Illinois*

- 2 cups (12 ounces) semisweet chocolate chips
- 1/4 cup butter-flavored shortening
- 5 cups crisp rice cereal
- 1 package (10 ounces) Milk Duds
- 1 tablespoon water

In a large microwave-safe bowl, combine chocolate chips and shortening. Cover and microwave on high until chocolate is melted, about 2 minutes; stir until well blended. Stir in cereal until well coated.

In another microwave-safe bowl, combine Milk Duds and water. Cover and microwave on high for 1 minute or until mixture is pourable; mix well. Stir into cereal mixture. Spread into a buttered 13-in. x 9-in. x 2-in. pan. Cover and refrigerate for 30 minutes or until firm. Cut into bars. **Yield:** 2 dozen.

Editor's Note: This recipe was tested in an 850-watt microwave.

Skewered Shrimp

I combine four ingredients to create a ginger mixture that's used as both a marinade and a sauce for these barbecued shrimp. Serve them with toothpicks as an appetizer or stir the shrimp into pasta for an entree.
—*Joan Morris, Lillian, Alabama*

3 tablespoons soy sauce
2 tablespoons lemon juice
1 tablespoon chili sauce
1 tablespoon minced fresh gingerroot
1 pound uncooked medium shrimp, peeled and deveined

In a bowl, combine the soy sauce, lemon juice, chili sauce and ginger; mix well. Pour half into a large resealable plastic bag; add the shrimp. Seal bag and turn to coat; refrigerate for 2 hours. Cover and refrigerate remaining marinade.

Drain and discard marinade from shrimp. Thread onto metal or soaked wooden skewers. Grill, uncovered, over medium heat for 6-8 minutes or until shrimp turn pink, turning once. Serve with reserved marinade. **Yield:** 4 servings.

|PEELING AND DEVEINING SHRIMP| Remove the shell by opening the shell at the underside or leg area and peeling it back. A gentle pull may be necessary to release the shell from the tail area. To remove the black vein, make a slit with a paring knife along the back from the head area to the tail. Rinse shrimp under cold water to remove the exposed vein.

Peach Smoothies

Nothing could be sweeter than starting the day off with this refreshing beverage. But I enjoy the smoothies so much, I make them throughout the day.
—*Dana Tittle, Forrest City, Arkansas*

2 cups milk
2 cups frozen unsweetened sliced peaches
1/4 cup orange juice concentrate
2 tablespoons sugar
5 ice cubes

In a blender, combine all ingredients; cover and process until smooth. Pour into glasses; serve immediately. **Yield:** 4 servings.

Ranch Chicken Bites

These zesty bites are a fun and easy way to serve chicken. Only two simple ingredients make the savory ranch coating.
—*Ann Brunkhorst, Masonville, Iowa*

1 pound boneless skinless
   chicken breasts
1/2 cup ranch salad dressing
2-1/2 cups finely crushed sour
   cream and onion potato
   chips

Cut chicken into bite-size pieces; place in a bowl. Add salad dressing and stir to coat. Let stand for 10 minutes. Add potato chips and toss well. Place on a greased baking sheet. Bake, uncovered, at 350° for 18-20 minutes or until juices run clear. **Yield:** 4 servings.

Fried Cinnamon Strips

I first made these crispy strips for a special family night at our church. Most of them were snapped up before dinner!
—*Nancy Johnson*
Laverne, Oklahoma

1 cup sugar
1 teaspoon ground
   cinnamon
1/4 teaspoon ground nutmeg
10 flour tortillas (8 inches)
Vegetable oil

In a large resealable plastic bag, combine sugar, cinnamon and nutmeg; set aside. Cut tortillas into 3-in. x 2-in. strips. Heat 1 in. of oil in a skillet or electric fry pan to 375°; fry 4-5 strips at a time for 30 seconds on each side or until golden brown. Drain on paper towels.

While still warm, place strips in bag with sugar mixture; shake gently to coat. Serve immediately or store in an airtight container. **Yield:** 5 dozen.

|DEEP-FRYING FACT| It's best to fry food in small batches. Large amounts of food lower the oil's temperature, which means that it's more likely to soak into the food.

Sugar-Coated Pecans

It's impossible to stop snacking on these sweet crispy nuts, so I make several batches over the holidays to keep a supply on hand. They also make a mouth-watering homemade Christmas gift. People tend to eat them by the handful. —*Carol Crowley*
West Haven, Connecticut

1 tablespoon egg white
2 cups pecan halves
1/4 cup sugar
2 teaspoons ground
   cinnamon

In a bowl, beat egg white until foamy. Add pecans and toss until well coated. Combine sugar and cinnamon; sprinkle over pecans and toss to coat.

Spread in a single layer on an ungreased baking sheet. Bake at 300° for 25-30 minutes or until browned, stirring occasionally. Cool on waxed paper. **Yield:** 3 cups.

Nutty Cracker Delights

I always receive compliments when I serve these crispy snacks. Both sweet and salty, they're fun as appetizers or for munching. They freeze well, too, so you can make them ahead if you're planning a party.
—*Carla Lee, Devils Lake, North Dakota*

42 Club crackers (2-1/2
   inches x 1 inch)
1/2 cup butter
1/2 cup sugar
1 teaspoon vanilla extract
1 cup slivered almonds

Place crackers in a single layer in a foil-lined 15-in. x 10-in. x 1-in. baking pan. In a saucepan over medium heat, melt butter. Add sugar; bring to a boil, stirring constantly. Boil for 2 minutes. Remove from the heat; add vanilla. Pour evenly over crackers; sprinkle with nuts.

Bake at 350° for 10-12 minutes or until lightly browned. Immediately remove from the pan, cutting between crackers if necessary, and cool on wire racks. Store in an airtight container. **Yield:** 3-1/2 dozen.

Mozzarella Puffs

These savory cheesy biscuits go over great at my house. Since they're so quick to make, I can whip up a batch anytime. They're full of pizza flavor but are more fun to serve!
—*Joan Mousley Dziuba*
Waupaca, Wisconsin

1 tube (7-1/2 ounces) refrigerated buttermilk biscuits
1 teaspoon dried oregano
1 block (2 to 3 ounces) mozzarella cheese
2 tablespoons pizza sauce

Make an indentation in the center of each biscuit; sprinkle with oregano. Cut the mozzarella into 10 cubes, 3/4 in. each; place a cube in the center of each biscuit. Pinch dough tightly around cheese to seal.

Place seam side down on an ungreased baking sheet. Spread pizza sauce over tops. Bake at 375° for 10-12 minutes or until golden brown. **Yield:** 10 servings.

Simple Guacamole

This homemade guacamole is pretty basic, but it always gets compliments. A jar of salsa makes it a breeze to stir up and serve with crunchy tortilla chips for an effortless appetizer.   —*Heidi Main*
Anchorage, Alaska

2 medium ripe avocados
1 tablespoon lemon juice
1/4 cup chunky salsa
1/8 to 1/4 teaspoon salt

Peel and chop avocados; place in a small bowl. Sprinkle with lemon juice. Add salsa and salt; mash coarsely with a fork. Refrigerate until serving. **Yield:** 1-1/2 cups.

|AVOCADO ADVICE| To peel an avocado half, use the point of a sharp paring knife to make a lengthwise cut down the middle of the skin. At the stem end, grasp one piece of the skin between your thumb and the knife edge; pull the skin down and off the avocado. Repeat with the other strip of skin. For guacamole or other dips, choose slightly over-ripe avocados—they'll mash more easily. Always add lemon juice to guacamole. The acid not only helps keep the avocado from browning, it also brightens the flavor.

Purple Cows

Kids will need only three ingredients to whip up this bright beverage. The sweet blend gets its purple color and refreshing flavor from grape juice concentrate.

—Renee Schwebach
Dumont, Minnesota

1-1/2 cups milk
3/4 cup grape juice concentrate
2 cups vanilla ice cream

In a blender, combine milk and grape juice concentrate. Add ice cream; cover and blend until smooth. Serve immediately. **Yield:** 4 servings.

|WHAT'S IN A NAME?| A Purple Cow consists, basically, of purple grape juice and milk and/or milk products. There are more variations than breeds of real cows! Kids love it, partly because it turns their tongue purple and gives them a violet mustache.

Tiger Tea

"Tee time" was deliciously refreshing when we poured this thirst-quenching iced tea at a golf party we had a few years ago. I enjoyed coming up with the recipe titles for our theme foods. Even non-golfers know this bright beverage is named for famous young pro Tiger Woods.

—Sue Ann O'Buck
Sinking Spring, Pennsylvania

3 quarts water, *divided*
6 individual tea bags
3/4 cup lemonade concentrate
3/4 cup orange juice concentrate
1 cup sugar

In a large kettle, bring 1 quart water to a boil. Remove from the heat; add tea bags. Steep for 5 minutes. Discard the tea bags.

Stir in the lemonade and orange juice concentrates, sugar and remaining water. Serve over ice. **Yield:** about 3 quarts.

Chocolate Malts

I can whip up this decadent ice cream drink in just minutes. It's a favorite with kids after a day in the pool or for dessert after a barbecue.
—*Marion Lowery, Medford, Oregon*

    3/4 cup milk
    1/2 cup caramel ice cream
        topping
      2 cups chocolate ice
        cream, softened
      3 tablespoons malted milk
        powder
      2 tablespoons chopped
        pecans, optional
Grated chocolate, optional

In a blender, combine the first five ingredients; cover and process until blended. Pour into chilled glasses. Sprinkle with grated chocolate if desired. **Yield:** 2-1/2 cups.

|SCOOPING ICE CREAM| Dip your ice cream scoop in hot water before removing ice cream from the carton, and the ice cream will easily slip off the scoop.

Pizza Corn Dog Snacks

I dress up frozen corn dogs to create these tasty bite-size treats. Just slice 'em and spread 'em with pizza sauce and other toppings for a fun snack for kids or an easy appetizer for adults.
—*Linda Knopp*
Camas, Washington

      1 package (16 ounces)
        frozen corn dogs, thawed
    1/2 cup pizza sauce
      3 tablespoons chopped
        ripe olives
      1 jar (4-1/2 ounces) sliced
        mushrooms, drained
    1/4 cup shredded mozzarella
        cheese

Remove stick from each corn dog; cut into 1-in. slices. Place on an ungreased baking sheet. Spread with pizza sauce. Top with olives, mushrooms and cheese.

Bake at 350° for 15-20 minutes or until the cheese is melted and corn dogs are heated through. **Yield:** 30 snacks.

Buttermilk Shakes

These rich shakes taste like liquid cheesecake! With just a few ingredients, they're a snap to prepare at a moment's notice any time of the day.

—Gloria Jarrett, Loveland, Ohio

1 pint vanilla ice cream, softened
1 cup buttermilk
1 teaspoon grated lemon peel
1/2 teaspoon vanilla extract
1 drop lemon extract

Place all ingredients in a blender container. Cover and process on high until smooth. Pour into glasses. Refrigerate any leftovers. **Yield:** 2 servings.

Honey-Glazed Snack Mix

Short and sweet sums up the recipe for this munchable snack mix. It's a cinch to package it in individual snack bags, too.

—Jan Olson
New Hope, Minnesota

8 cups Crispix cereal
3 cups miniature pretzels
2 cups pecan halves
2/3 cup butter
1/2 cup honey

In a large bowl, combine the cereal, pretzels and pecans; set aside. In a small saucepan, melt butter; stir in honey until well blended. Pour over cereal mixture and stir to coat. Spread into two greased 15-in. x 10-in. x 1-in. baking pans.

Bake at 350° for 12-15 minutes or until mixture is lightly glazed, stirring occasionally. Cool in pan for 3 minutes; remove from pan and spread on waxed paper to cool completely. Store in an airtight container. **Yield:** about 12 cups.

Low-Fat Eggnog

Everyone can enjoy a traditional taste of the season with this smooth, creamy eggnog. Although it's made with low-fat ingredients, the easy-to-fix recipe retains the thick and creamy consistency of the classic Christmas beverage. Our kids love it.
—*Paula Zsiray, Logan, Utah*

✓ Uses less fat, sugar or salt. Includes Nutritional Analysis and Diabetic Exchanges.

11 cups cold fat-free milk
2 teaspoons vanilla extract
2 packages (1.5 ounces *each*) instant sugar-free vanilla pudding mix
Artificial sweetener equivalent to 1/3 cup sugar
1/2 teaspoon ground nutmeg

In a large bowl, combine the milk and vanilla. In another bowl, combine dry pudding mix, sweetener and nutmeg. Whisk into milk mixture until smooth. Refrigerate until serving. **Yield:** 12 servings.

Nutritional Analysis: One 1-cup serving equals 105 calories, 408 mg sodium, 4 mg cholesterol, 17 g carbohydrate, 8 g protein, trace fat. **Diabetic Exchanges:** 1 skim milk, 1/2 starch.

|EGGNOG IQ| A takeoff on similar European egg-and-milk drinks, eggnog was a popular wintertime beverage in Colonial America. It was made in large quantities and was nearly always served for social occasions, especially on Christmas.

Cherry Berry Smoothies

We have three young children, so we always have fruit juices on hand to experiment with when making smoothies. I turn cherry juice, fruit and yogurt into this colorful family favorite.
—*Shonna Thibodeau, Fort Huachuca, Arizona*

1 cup cherry juice
1 carton (8 ounces) vanilla yogurt
1 cup frozen unsweetened raspberries
1/2 cup seedless red grapes
3 to 4 teaspoons sugar

In a blender, combine all ingredients. Cover and process until well blended. Pour into glasses; serve immediately. **Yield:** 3 servings.

Reuben Party Spread

This speedy sandwich spread makes an appearance at almost all of our family gatherings. It tastes like a traditional Reuben sandwich, but it's easier to assemble.
—Connie Thompson
Racine, Wisconsin

1 pound fully cooked ham, chopped
4 cups (1 pound) shredded Swiss cheese
1 can (8 ounces) sauerkraut, drained
1/2 cup Thousand Island salad dressing
Cocktail rye bread

In a microwave-safe bowl, combine the ham, cheese, sauerkraut and salad dressing. Cover and microwave on high for 1 to 1-1/2 minutes or until cheese is melted, stirring once. Serve on rye bread. **Yield:** 6 cups.

Editor's Note: This recipe was tested in an 850-watt microwave.

Sweet Pretzel Nuggets

This crowd-pleasing snack has been a tremendous hit both at home and at work. The fun crunchy bites have a sweet cinnamon-toast taste and just a hint of saltiness that make them very munchable.
—Billie Sue Ebinger, Holton, Indiana

1 package (15 to 18 ounces) sourdough pretzel nuggets
2/3 cup vegetable oil
1/3 cup sugar
1 to 2 teaspoons ground cinnamon

Place pretzels in a microwave-safe bowl. In a small bowl, combine the oil, sugar and cinnamon; pour over the pretzels and toss to coat. Microwave, uncovered, on high for 2 minutes; stir. Microwave 3-4 minutes longer, stirring after each minute or until oil is absorbed. Cool to room temperature. **Yield:** 12-16 servings.

Editor's Note: This recipe was tested in an 850-watt microwave.

Salsa Sausage Quiche

A prepared pastry crust hurries along the assembly of this hearty appetizer. Served with sour cream and additional salsa, it's a party favorite in our retirement community. If you're feeding a crowd, bring two—they disappear fast!
—*Dorothy Sorensen, Naples, Florida*

3/4 **pound bulk pork sausage**
1 **unbaked pastry shell (9 inches)**
2 **cups (8 ounces) shredded cheddar cheese,** *divided*
3 **eggs**
1 **cup salsa**

In a skillet, cook the sausage over medium heat until no longer pink; drain. Transfer to the pastry shell. Sprinkle with half of the cheese. In a small bowl, lightly beat the eggs; stir in salsa. Pour over cheese.

Bake at 375° for 30-35 minutes or until a knife inserted near the center comes out clean. Sprinkle with the remaining cheese. Bake 5 minutes longer or until the cheese is melted. **Yield:** 6-8 servings.

|STORING SAUSAGE| Refrigerator storage for sausages depends on the type: uncooked fresh sausages (like pork sausage) are very perishable and should be refrigerated, well wrapped, for no more than 2 days; uncooked smoked (mettwurst) for up to 1 week; cooked smoked (knockwurst) in unopened package for 2 weeks; dry sausage (pepperoni) for up to 3 weeks.

Strawberry Banana Shakes

This very thick, not-too-sweet shake packs a big strawberry and banana taste. It's easy to mix together in the blender. I especially like it topped with whipped cream. —*Grant Dixon Roseburg, Oregon*

1/4 **cup milk**
1 **cup strawberry ice cream**
1 **medium firm banana, sliced**
Whipped cream and two fresh strawberries, optional

Place milk, ice cream and banana in a blender; cover and process until smooth. Pour into glasses. Garnish with whipped cream and a strawberry if desired. **Yield:** 2 servings.

Cheese Wedges

These easy cheesy treats are a hit at evening gatherings. They're a zesty change of pace from mozzarella sticks, plus they're great for dipping in pizza sauce.
—Jennifer Eilts, Omaha, Nebraska

1 package (7 ounces) extra sharp cheddar cheese
1/3 cup seasoned dry bread crumbs
1/2 teaspoon crushed red pepper flakes, optional
1 egg
1 can (8 ounces) pizza sauce, warmed

Cut cheese into 1/2-in. slices; cut each slice in half diagonally. In a shallow bowl, combine bread crumbs and red pepper flakes if desired. In another bowl, beat egg. Dip cheese triangles into egg, then in crumb mixture.

Place on a greased baking sheet. Broil 4 in. from the heat for 2-3 minutes or until browned and cheese begins to melt. Serve cheese wedges warm with pizza sauce for dipping. **Yield:** 6 servings.

Hot Mustard Pretzel Dip

It's a snap to stir together this zippy dip. With its hint of honey, the mixture is great with pretzels...or try it anywhere you'd use a hot-and-spicy sauce.
—Kim Barrick, Lincoln, Illinois

1/4 cup ground mustard
1/4 cup vinegar
1/4 cup sugar
1 egg yolk
2 tablespoons honey

In a small saucepan, combine mustard and vinegar; let stand for 30 minutes. Whisk in the sugar and egg yolk until smooth.

Cook over medium heat, whisking constantly, until mixture just begins to simmer and is thickened, about 7 minutes. Remove from the heat; whisk in honey. Store in the refrigerator. **Yield:** 1/2 cup.

Trail Mix

With nuts, raisins, M&M's and coconut, this is a super snack. In small gingham bags, it made wonderful party favors for each guest at the cowboy-theme wedding shower I hosted a number of years ago. This mix is a tasty treat anytime, so I always keep batches on hand in my cupboard.
— *Sandra Thorn*
Sonora, California

2 pounds dry roasted peanuts
2 pounds cashews
1 pound raisins
1 pound M&M's
1/2 pound flaked coconut

Combine all ingredients in a large bowl. Store in an airtight container. **Yield:** 6 quarts.

|DEFINING RAISINS| Dark raisins are sun-dried for several weeks, thereby gaining their dark color and shriveled appearance. Golden raisins have been treated with sulphur dioxide (to prevent darkening) and dried with artificial heat, which leaves them plumper and moister than dark raisins. Raisins can be stored in a tightly sealed plastic bag at room temperature for several months.

Mock Champagne Punch

Every Christmas, I place holly from our own trees around my punch bowl filled with Mock Champagne Punch. Even the children can enjoy this nonalcoholic beverage. Of all the punch recipes I've tried, I keep coming back to this one. It's so easy to keep the ingredients in the refrigerator and mix as much as needed.
— *Betty Claycomb, Alverton, Pennsylvania*

1 quart white grape juice, chilled
1 quart ginger ale, chilled
Strawberries *or* raspberries

Combine grape juice and ginger ale; pour into a punch bowl or glasses. Garnish with strawberries or raspberries. **Yield:** 16 (1/2-cup) servings.

|PUNCH POINTER| Chill all punch ingredients before mixing so that you don't have to dilute the punch with ice to get it cold. Or garnish a cold punch with an ice ring made from punch ingredients instead of water.

Roasted Mixed Nuts

It's impossible to stop eating these savory nuts once you start. We love to munch on them as an evening snack.
—*Carolyn Zimmerman, Fairbury, Illinois*

1 pound mixed nuts
1/4 cup maple syrup
2 tablespoons brown sugar
1 envelope ranch salad
dressing mix

In a bowl, combine the nuts and maple syrup; mix well. Sprinkle with brown sugar and salad dressing mix; stir gently to coat.

Spread in a greased 15-in. x 10-in. x 1-in. baking pan. Bake at 300° for 20-25 minutes or until lightly browned. Cool. Store in an airtight container. **Yield:** 3 cups.

|STOVETOP SNACK| You can also make cocktail nuts in a skillet. Saute 2 cups nuts in 2 tablespoons oil or melted butter over medium-high heat, stirring often, until they begin to brown. Sprinkle with your choice of seasonings (salt, pepper, cayenne pepper, curry powder, etc.), tossing the nuts with a wooden spoon. Turn out onto paper towels to cool, then store in an airtight container.

Cool Waters Shakes

Ride a wave of approval when you serve this refreshing berry-flavored beverage. Kids will love its pastel blue color and sea-foamy consistency...and with just three simple ingredients, it's a breeze to whip up in the blender.
—*Taste of Home Test Kitchen*

4 cups cold milk
2 packages (3 ounces
***each*) berry blue gelatin**
1 quart vanilla ice cream

In a blender, combine 2 cups of milk, one package of gelatin and 2 cups of ice cream. Cover and process for 30 seconds or until smooth. Repeat. Pour into glasses and serve immediately. **Yield:** 6 servings.

Lemonade Slush

I used to make a similar beverage with orange juice concentrate, but I enjoy lemonade so much that I altered the recipe a bit. My family loved the results and now I fix this lemon version all the time. Not only is the drink fast and refreshing, but it's perfect at breakfast, after school or any time of the day.
—*Tracy Brousseau, Orem, Utah*

✓ **Uses less fat, sugar or salt. Includes Nutritional Analysis and Diabetic Exchanges.**

2/3 cup lemonade
    concentrate, partially
    thawed
1 cup milk
2/3 cup water
1 teaspoon vanilla extract
Yellow food coloring, optional
12 ice cubes, crushed

In a blender, combine lemonade concentrate, milk, water, vanilla and food coloring if desired; cover and process until blended. While processing, slowly add crushed ice. Process until slushy. Serve immediately. **Yield:** 8 servings.

Nutritional Analysis: One 3/4-cup serving (prepared with fat-free milk) equals 56 calories, trace fat (trace saturated fat), 1 mg cholesterol, 17 mg sodium, 13 g carbohydrate, trace fiber, 1 g protein. **Diabetic Exchange:** 1 fruit.

Minted Iced Tea Cooler

This cool rose-colored tea quenches your thirst in the most delightful way. It's a pleasant blend of fruit and mint flavors. It's easy to make but more special than traditional iced tea.
—*Debbie Terenzini Wilkerson*
Lusby, Maryland

3 peppermint-flavored tea
    bags
7 cups boiling water
1 cup cranberry juice
3/4 cup pink lemonade
    concentrate

Steep tea bags in boiling water for 5-10 minutes. Discard tea bags. Pour tea into a pitcher or large bowl; stir in cranberry juice and lemonade concentrate. Cover and refrigerate overnight. Serve over ice. **Yield:** 8 servings.

Cheerio Treats

I use peanut butter, Cheerios and candies to put a tooth-tingling spin on marshmallow-cereal bars. Whether I take them to picnics or bake sales, I'm always asked for the recipe. —*Penny Reifenrath*
Wynot, Nebraska

3 tablespoons butter
1 package (10-1/2 ounces) miniature marshmallows
1/2 cup peanut butter
5 cups Cheerios
1 cup plain M&M's

Place the butter and marshmallows in a large microwave-safe bowl. Microwave, uncovered, on high for 2 minutes or until puffed. Stir in the peanut butter until blended. Add the cereal and M&M's; mix well. Spoon into a greased 13-in. x 9-in. x 2-in. pan; press down gently. Cool slightly before cutting. **Yield:** 15 servings.

Corny Snack Mix

It's hard to stop munching on this yummy snack mix! Melted vanilla chips make a delightful coating for the crisp corn chips, cereal and popcorn. This mix is quick and easy to toss together. I like to keep it on hand for when our five grandchildren visit.
—*Sandy Wehring, Fremont, Ohio*

3 quarts popped popcorn
1 package (15 ounces) Corn Pops
1 package (15 ounces) corn chips
2 packages (10 to 12 ounces *each*) vanilla *or* white chips

In several large bowls, combine the popcorn, Corn Pops and corn chips. In a saucepan over medium-low heat, melt chips; stir until smooth. Pour over popcorn mixture and toss to coat. Spread in two 15-in. x 10-in. x 1-in. pans. Cool. Store in airtight containers. **Yield:** 7-1/2 quarts.

Pineapple Cooler

I stir up this mild and refreshing beverage in a jiffy. Lemon juice cuts the sweetness you might expect from pineapple juice and lemon-lime soda.
—*Michelle Blumberg*
Littlerock, California

✓ Uses less fat, sugar or salt. Includes Nutritional Analysis and Diabetic Exchanges.

1 cup unsweetened pineapple juice, chilled
1 to 2 tablespoons lemon juice
1 can (12 ounces) lemon-lime soda, chilled

Combine all ingredients in a pitcher; stir well. Serve over ice. **Yield:** 2-2/3 cups.

Nutritional Analysis: One 1-cup serving (prepared with diet soda) equals 48 calories, 13 mg sodium, 0 cholesterol, 12 g carbohydrate, trace protein, trace fat. **Diabetic Exchange:** 1 fruit.

Mocha Morning Drink

When I'm sipping this delicious coffee in the morning, I almost feel like I've been to my favorite coffeehouse instead of to my own kitchen to whip it up.
—*Jill Rodriguez, Gonzales, Louisiana*

6 cups hot brewed coffee
3/4 cup half-and-half cream
6 tablespoons chocolate syrup
7 teaspoons sugar
6 cinnamon sticks (3 inches)
Whipped cream in a can, optional

In a saucepan, combine the coffee, cream, chocolate syrup and sugar. Cook and stir over medium heat until sugar is dissolved and mixture is heated through. Ladle into six large mugs. Stir with a cinnamon stick. Garnish with whipped cream if desired. **Yield:** 6 servings.

|COFFEE FACTS| For maximum flavor, grind only as many beans as needed to brew each pot of coffee. Generally, the finer the grind, the fuller the flavor. The flavor of coffee begins to deteriorate within 15 minutes after it's brewed.

Lo-Cal Apple Snack

This quick snack is often requested as an office treat. It's a simple and harvest-fresh way to serve autumn's best apples—kids also love it.
—*Nancy Horan, Sioux Falls, South Dakota*

✓ **Uses less fat, sugar or salt. Includes Nutritional Analysis and Diabetic Exchanges.**

    4 medium Golden Delicious apples, peeled, cored and sliced into rounds
1/2 cup apple juice
1/4 teaspoon ground cinnamon
    1 tablespoon grated lemon peel

In an ungreased 11-in. x 7-in. x 2-in. microwave-safe baking dish, arrange apples in two rows. Pour apple juice over apples. Sprinkle with cinnamon and lemon peel. Cover and microwave on high for 7 minutes or until apples are tender, turning after 3-1/2 minutes. **Yield:** 4 servings.

Nutritional Analysis: One serving equals 88 calories, 1 mg sodium, 0 cholesterol, 23 g carbohydrate, trace protein, trace fat. **Diabetic Exchange:** 1-1/2 fruit.

Editor's Note: This recipe was tested in a 700-watt microwave.

Taco Tidbits

This four-ingredient combination is a great change of pace from typical snack mixes. It's a good thing the crispy treat is so simple to throw together because your family will empty the bowl in no time.
—*Sharon Mensing, Greenfield, Iowa*

    6 tablespoons butter
2 to 3 tablespoons taco seasoning
    8 cups Corn Chex
1/4 cup grated Parmesan cheese

Place butter in an 11-in. x 7-in. x 2-in. microwave-safe dish. Cover and microwave on high for 60-70 seconds or until melted. Add taco seasoning. Stir in the cereal until evenly coated.

Microwave on high for 1 minute; stir. Heat 1 to 1-1/2 minutes longer; stir. Sprinkle with Parmesan cheese; microwave for 1 minute. Stir; heat 1 minute longer. Cool. **Yield:** 8 cups.

Editor's Note: This recipe was tested in an 850-watt microwave.

Banana Pops

Frozen pops, kids and summer just naturally seem to go together. Not only do kids like eating the sweet treats, they also can have fun making them. Making a batch of Banana Pops is easy. My little granddaughter likes scooping the yogurt and pouring in the orange juice. The hardest part for her is waiting for the pops to freeze so she can enjoy one down to the last refreshing lick!

—Elaine Carver, Portland, Maine

1 cup vanilla yogurt
1/2 cup orange juice
1 medium ripe banana, cut into chunks

In a blender, combine the yogurt, orange juice and banana; cover and process until smooth. Pour into Popsicle trays, or pour into small plastic disposable cups and insert Popsicle sticks. Freeze until firm, about 5 hours or overnight. **Yield:** 6 servings.

Sunny Citrus Cooler

The sunny color of this refreshing punch matched the bright yellow sunflower decorations for my theme dinner I hosted a few years ago. It's easy to stir up, too, which is good news because a few sips may quench your thirst, but your taste buds are sure to be asking for more.

—Holly Joyce
Jackson, Minnesota

1 can (46 ounces) pineapple juice
2 cans (12 ounces *each*) frozen orange juice concentrate, thawed
3/4 cup lemonade concentrate
6 cups ginger ale *or* white soda, chilled
Orange slices, optional

In a 1-gal. pitcher, combine pineapple juice, orange juice concentrate and lemonade concentrate. Add ginger ale and mix well. Serve over ice. Garnish with orange slices if desired. Refrigerate leftovers. **Yield:** 1 gallon.

Peanut Butter Popcorn Bars

If you're looking for a fun snack for kids, try these chewy popcorn treats that have a mild peanut butter taste. They're easy to stir up and can be pressed into a pan to form bars or shaped into balls.
—*Kathy Oswald, Wauzeka, Wisconsin*

10 cups popped popcorn
1/2 cup sugar
1/2 cup light corn syrup
1/2 cup creamy peanut
  butter
1/2 teaspoon vanilla extract

Place popcorn in a large bowl; set aside. In a saucepan over medium heat, bring sugar and corn syrup to a boil, stirring constantly. Boil for 1 minute. Remove from the heat.

Stir in peanut butter and vanilla; mix well. Pour over popcorn and mix until well coated. Press into a buttered 13-in. x 9-in. x 2-in. pan. Cool slightly before cutting. **Yield:** 2 dozen.

Cinnamon 'n' Spice Fruit Dip

Cinnamon, nutmeg and brown sugar dress up whipped topping in this extremely easy party pleaser. My gang especially likes the dip with apples and pears, but feel free to try it with pineapple slices, strawberries and other fresh fruit. —*Julie Bertha Pittsburgh, Pennsylvania*

✓ **Uses less fat, sugar or salt. Includes Nutritional Analysis and Diabetic Exchanges.**

2 cups whipped topping
1/4 cup packed brown sugar
1/8 to 1/4 teaspoon ground
  cinnamon
Dash ground nutmeg
Assorted fresh fruit

In a small bowl, combine the whipped topping, brown sugar, cinnamon and nutmeg. Store in the refrigerator. Serve with fruit. **Yield:** about 2 cups.

Nutritional Analysis: 2 tablespoons dip (prepared with reduced-fat whipped topping; calculated without fruit) equals 66 calories, 2 g fat (2 g saturated fat), 0 cholesterol, 3 mg sodium, 11 g carbohydrate, trace fiber, 0 protein. **Diabetic Exchange:** 1/2 starch.

Main Dishes

Bacon Cheeseburger Pasta, p. 47

Tuscan Pork Roast, p. 49

Apricot Round Steak, p. 48

| POULTRY |

Almond-Topped Chicken, p. 52

| SEAFOOD |

Creole Salmon Fillets, p. 46

Creole Salmon Fillets

(Pictured on page 45)

My crusty salmon fillets bake up moist and golden brown. Our grown daughters and grandsons like their food on the spicy side, so I knew Creole seasoning would make this entree a family favorite.
—*Florine Bruns, Fredericksburg, Texas*

4 teaspoons Creole
  seasoning
2 garlic cloves, minced
2 teaspoons pepper
4 salmon fillets (6 ounces
  each)
1/4 cup minced fresh parsley

In a large resealable plastic bag, combine the first three ingredients. Add salmon; shake to coat. Place salmon on a broiler pan or baking sheet. Broil 6 in. from the heat for 10-14 minutes or until fish flakes easily with a fork. Sprinkle with parsley. **Yield:** 4 servings.

Citrus Sirloin Steak

The mild citrus flavor of the marinade offers a nice change of pace from the usual steak seasonings. It's easy to prepare the steak the night before, then throw it on the grill.
—*Carol Towey
Pasadena, California*

2 medium unpeeled
  lemons, quartered
1 medium unpeeled
  orange, quartered
1/2 cup vegetable oil
1 garlic clove, minced
1 boneless sirloin steak
  (about 2-1/2 pounds
  and 1-3/4 inches thick)

In a skillet, cook the lemon and orange wedges in oil over medium heat for 10-15 minutes, stirring often. Add garlic; cook and stir 1-2 minutes longer. Place steak in a shallow glass baking dish; pierce meat every inch with a fork. Pour citrus mixture over meat; turn to coat. Cover and refrigerate overnight, turning three or four times.

Drain and discard marinade. On a covered grill over medium-hot heat, cook steak for 9-10 minutes on each side or until meat reaches desired doneness (for medium-rare, a meat thermometer should read 145°; medium, 160°; well-done, 170°). **Yield:** 6-8 servings.

Apple Kielbasa Coins

The juice, jelly and syrup add sweetness to sliced sausage in this stovetop sensation. My grown children look forward to this breakfast dish on special occasions such as Christmas. Slices of toast are tasty served with it.

—JoAnn Lee
Kerhonkson, New York

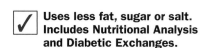 **Uses less fat, sugar or salt. Includes Nutritional Analysis and Diabetic Exchanges.**

1-1/2 pounds fully cooked kielbasa *or* Polish sausage, cut into 1/4-inch slices
1/4 cup apple juice
1/4 cup apple jelly
2 tablespoons maple syrup

In a large skillet, bring sausage and apple juice to a boil. Cover and cook for 5 minutes. Uncover and cook 5 minutes longer. Drain. Add jelly and syrup; cook and stir until jelly is melted and sausage is coated. **Yield:** 6 servings.

Nutritional Analysis: One 4-ounce serving (prepared with smoked turkey sausage) equals 224 calories, 5 g fat (2 g saturated fat), 51 mg cholesterol, 980 mg sodium, 27 g carbohydrate, trace fiber, 14 g protein. **Diabetic Exchanges:** 2 lean meat, 2 fruit.

Bacon Cheeseburger Pasta

(Pictured on page 44)

Children of all ages are sure to enjoy Bacon Cheeseburger Pasta, an effortless entree I concocted to duplicate all the wonderful flavors of my favorite hamburger.

—Melissa Stevens
Elk River, Minnesota

8 ounces uncooked tube *or* spiral pasta
1 pound ground beef
6 bacon strips, diced
1 can (10-3/4 ounces) condensed tomato soup, undiluted
1 cup (4 ounces) shredded cheddar cheese
Barbecue sauce and prepared mustard, optional

Cook pasta according to package directions. Meanwhile, in a skillet, cook beef over medium heat until no longer pink; drain and set aside. In the same skillet, cook bacon until crisp; remove with a slotted spoon to paper towels. Discard drippings.

Drain pasta; add to the skillet. Add soup, beef and bacon; heat through. Sprinkle with cheese; cover and cook until the cheese is melted. Serve with barbecue sauce and mustard if desired. **Yield:** 4-6 servings.

Grilled Wild Turkey Breast

With only two ingredients, this is definitely the easiest recipe I have for cooking the wild turkey that my husband, Richard, brings home during spring hunting season. The grilled meat takes on a wonderful sweet smoky flavor. This recipe is equally delicious made with Italian salad dressing in place of the honey mustard variety.
—*Michelle Kaase*
Tomball, Texas

1 **bone-in wild turkey breast (about 1-1/2 pounds), split**
1 **cup honey mustard salad dressing**

Place turkey in a large resealable plastic bag; add salad dressing. Seal bag and turn to coat; refrigerate overnight, turning occasionally.

Drain and discard marinade. Grill turkey, covered, over indirect medium heat for 45-55 minutes or until juices run clear and a meat thermometer reads 170°. **Yield:** 2 servings.

|GRILLING GUIDE| With the indirect grilling method, foods are not cooked directly over the heat. On a charcoal grill, the hot coals are moved or "banked" to opposite sides of the grill, and a shallow foil pan is placed between the coals to catch the drippings. The food is placed on the center of the grill rack above the pan.

Apricot Round Steak

(Pictured on page 44)

Looking for a fun alternative to traditional steak sauce? Serve tender slices of round steak with a sweet apricot sauce that has a hint of pepper. The broiled entree is a snap to prepare.
—*Bernadine Dirmeyer, Harpster, Ohio*

1-3/4 **pounds boneless top round steak (3/4 inch thick)**
3/4 **cup apricot preserves**
1 **tablespoon lemon juice**
1/2 **teaspoon salt**
1/8 **teaspoon hot pepper sauce**

Place steak on broiler pan rack; broil for 6-8 minutes on each side. Meanwhile, in a saucepan or microwave-safe bowl, combine remaining ingredients. Cook until preserves are melted. Set aside 1/2 cup; brush remaining sauce over steak.

Broil 2-3 minutes longer or until meat reaches desired doneness (for medium-rare, a meat thermometer should read 145°; medium, 160°; well-done, 170°). Slice meat on the diagonal; serve with reserved apricot sauce. **Yield:** 8 servings.

Tuscan Pork Roast

(Pictured on page 44)

Everyone's eager to eat after the wonderful aroma of this roast tempts us all afternoon. This is a great Sunday dinner with little fuss. Since I found this recipe a few years ago, it's become a favorite with our seven grown children and their families. —*Elinor Stabile, Canmore, Alberta*

5 to 8 garlic cloves, peeled
1 tablespoon dried
    rosemary
1 tablespoon olive oil
1/2 teaspoon salt
1 boneless pork loin roast
    (3 to 4 pounds)

In a blender or food processor, combine garlic, rosemary, oil and salt; blend until mixture turns to paste. Rub over the roast; cover and let stand for 30 minutes.

Place roast fat side up on a greased baking rack in a shallow roasting pan. Bake, uncovered, at 350° for 1 to 1-1/4 hours or until a meat thermometer reads 160°. Let stand for 15 minutes before slicing. **Yield:** 10-12 servings.

Stuffed Pasta Shells

These savory shells never fail to make a big impression, even though the recipe is very easy. One or two of these shells makes a great individual serving at a potluck, so a single batch goes a long way. —*Jena Coffey, St. Louis, Missouri*

4 cups (16 ounces)
    shredded mozzarella
    cheese
1 carton (15 ounces)
    ricotta cheese
1 package (10 ounces)
    frozen chopped spinach,
    thawed and drained
1 package (12 ounces)
    jumbo pasta shells,
    cooked and drained
1 jar (28 ounces) spaghetti
    sauce

Combine cheeses and spinach; stuff into shells. Arrange in a greased 13-in. x 9-in. x 2-in. baking dish. Pour spaghetti sauce over the shells. Cover and bake at 350° for 30 minutes or until heated through. **Yield:** 12-14 servings.

|PASTA POINTER| Instead of draining jumbo pasta shells in a colander, which can cause them to tear, carefully remove them from the boiling water with a tongs. Pour out any water inside the shells and drain on lightly greased waxed paper until you're ready to stuff them.

Supreme Roast Beef

This fix-and-forget roast is one of our family's favorite Sunday meals. It's simple to prepare and leaves plenty of leftovers to enjoy later in the week.
—Jackie Holland, Gillette, Wyoming

1 large onion, sliced into rings
2 tablespoons Worcestershire sauce
4 to 5 teaspoons coarsely ground pepper
1 boneless rump roast (4 to 5 pounds)
6 to 8 bay leaves

Place onion in a greased shallow roasting pan. Rub Worcestershire sauce and pepper over the roast. Place over the onion; top with bay leaves.

Cover and bake at 325° for 1-3/4 to 2-1/4 hours or until meat reaches desired doneness (for rare, a meat thermometer should read 140°; medium, 160°; well-done, 170°). Discard bay leaves. Let stand for 10-15 minutes before carving. Thicken pan juices if desired. **Yield:** 8 servings.

Cheesy Chicken

This tender chicken with its cheesy crumb coating is one of my husband's favorites. It's always a hit with company, too, because it comes out juicy and great-tasting every time.
—Joan Ergle
Woodstock, Georgia

5 tablespoons butter, melted, *divided*
1 cup crushed cheese-flavored snack crackers
1/4 teaspoon pepper
4 boneless skinless chicken breast halves
1/2 cup sour cream

Place 1 tablespoon of butter in an 11-in. x 7-in. x 2-in. microwave-safe dish; set aside. Combine cracker crumbs and pepper. Dip chicken in remaining butter, then spread with sour cream. Roll in the crumb mixture.

Place in prepared dish. Cover loosely and microwave on high for 6-7 minutes or until chicken juices run clear. Let stand for 5-10 minutes before serving. **Yield:** 4 servings.

Editor's Note: This recipe was tested in an 850-watt microwave.

Maple French Toast Bake

This scrumptious French toast casserole is a breeze to whip up the night before a busy morning. My family loves the richness it gets from cream cheese and maple syrup.
—Cindy Steffen
Cedarburg, Wisconsin

12 slices bread, cubed
1 package (8 ounces) cream cheese, cubed
8 eggs
1 cup milk
1/2 cup maple syrup
Additional maple syrup

Arrange half of the bread cubes in a greased shallow 2-qt. baking dish. Top with the cream cheese and remaining bread. In a bowl, whisk eggs, milk and syrup; pour over bread. Cover and refrigerate overnight. Remove from the refrigerator 30 minutes before baking.

Cover and bake at 350° for 30 minutes. Uncover; bake 20-25 minutes longer or until golden brown. Serve with additional syrup. **Yield:** 8 servings.

Turkey Stuffing Roll-Ups

When I worked at a local deli, a customer gave me this family-pleasing recipe. After a busy day, I tried it with quicker boxed stuffing mix in place of homemade dressing. It's wonderful with salad and green beans.
—Darlene Ward, Hot Springs, Arkansas

1 package (6 ounces) stuffing mix
1 can (10-3/4 ounces) condensed cream of chicken soup, undiluted
3/4 cup milk
1 pound sliced deli smoked turkey
1 can (2.8 ounces) french-fried onions, crushed

Prepare stuffing mix according to package directions. Meanwhile, in a bowl, combine soup and milk; set aside. Spoon about 1/4 cup stuffing onto each turkey slice. Roll up and place in a greased 13-in. x 9-in. x 2-in. baking dish. Pour soup mixture over roll-ups.

Bake, uncovered, at 350° for 20 minutes. Sprinkle with onions. Bake 5 minutes longer or until heated through. **Yield:** 6 servings.

Editor's Note: 3 cups of any prepared stuffing can be substituted for the stuffing mix.

Almond-Topped Chicken

(Pictured on page 45)

Lemon juice adds a pleasant tartness to the buttery sauce I serve over this chicken. My family loves this easy-to-make entree. I often toss in more almonds for extra crunch. —*Karen Zink*
Grand Island, Nebraska

4 boneless skinless chicken breast halves
5 tablespoons butter, *divided*
1/3 cup slivered almonds
3 tablespoons lemon juice

In a skillet, cook the chicken in 2 tablespoons of butter until juices run clear, about 20 minutes. Transfer to serving plate and keep warm. Add almonds and remaining butter to skillet; cook and stir just until almonds are lightly browned. Stir in lemon juice; heat through. Spoon over chicken. **Yield:** 4 servings.

Salmon with Dill Sauce

This moist, tender salmon is a savory treat draped with a creamy dill sauce. When my daughter served this tempting main dish for dinner, I was surprised to learn how easy the recipe is. —*Janet Painter*
Three Springs, Pennsylvania

 Uses less fat, sugar or salt. Includes Nutritional Analysis and Diabetic Exchanges.

1 salmon fillet (1 pound)
1-1/2 teaspoons dill weed, *divided*
1/2 cup reduced-fat plain yogurt
1/2 teaspoon sugar
1/2 teaspoon salt-free seasoning blend

Place salmon in a 13-in. x 9-in. x 2-in. baking dish coated with nonstick cooking spray; sprinkle with 1/2 teaspoon dill. Cover and bake at 375° for 20-25 minutes or until fish flakes easily with a fork.

Meanwhile, in a small saucepan, combine the yogurt, sugar, seasoning blend and remaining dill. Cook and stir over low heat until warmed. Serve with the salmon. **Yield:** 4 servings.

Nutritional Analysis: One serving equals 227 calories, 12 g fat (3 g saturated fat), 77 mg cholesterol, 76 mg sodium, 3 g carbohydrate, 0 fiber, 24 g protein. **Diabetic Exchanges:** 2-1/2 lean meat, 2 fat.

Hawaiian Pork Roast

Preparing a pork roast with bananas, Liquid Smoke and soy sauce produces a wonderfully tender meat. If you garnish the roast with flowers, as shown in the photo, make sure they are edible and have not been chemically treated; wash and pat dry before using.
—*Mary Gaylord, Balsam Lake, Wisconsin*

1 boneless pork shoulder roast (3 to 4 pounds), trimmed
4 teaspoons Liquid Smoke, optional
4 teaspoons soy sauce
2 unpeeled ripe bananas
1/2 cup water

Place roast on a 22-in. x 18-in. piece of heavy-duty foil; sprinkle with Liquid Smoke if desired and soy sauce. Wash bananas and place at the base of each side of roast. Pull sides of foil up around meat; add water. Seal foil tightly; wrap again with another large piece of foil. Place in a shallow baking pan; refrigerate overnight, turning several times.

Place foil-wrapped meat in a roasting pan. Bake at 400° for 1 hour. Reduce heat to 325°; continue baking for 3-1/2 hours. Drain; discard bananas and liquid. Shred meat with a fork. **Yield:** 8-10 servings.

Garlic Potatoes And Ham

Not even my finicky little eaters can resist the veggies in this main dish when they're seasoned with soup mix. I sometimes replace the ham with cooked kielbasa or smoked sausage for a change of pace.
—*Melody Williamson, Blaine, Washington*

8 small red potatoes, cut into wedges
1 tablespoon vegetable oil
1 package (16 ounces) frozen broccoli cuts, partially thawed
1 cup cubed fully cooked ham
1 envelope herb with garlic soup mix

In a large skillet, cook potatoes in oil over medium-high heat for 10 minutes or until lightly browned. Stir in broccoli, ham and soup mix. Reduce heat; cover and cook for 25 minutes or until potatoes are tender. **Yield:** 4 servings.

Editor's Note: This recipe was tested with Lipton Recipe Secrets Savory Herb with Garlic soup mix.

Reuben Dogs

My husband and children enjoy Reuben sandwiches, and this quick casserole is as close as you can get without the mess.
—*Colleen Hawkins, Monrovia, Maryland*

1 can (27 ounces) sauerkraut, rinsed and drained
1 to 2 teaspoons caraway seeds
8 hot dogs, halved lengthwise
1 cup (4 ounces) shredded Swiss cheese
Thousand Island salad dressing

Place sauerkraut in a greased 2-qt. baking dish. Sprinkle with caraway seeds. Top with hot dogs. Bake, uncovered, at 350° for 15-20 minutes or until heated through. Sprinkle with cheese. Bake 3-5 minutes longer or until cheese is melted. Serve with salad dressing. **Yield:** 4-6 servings.

|SAUERKRAUT SUGGESTIONS| Apples are also delicious with sauerkraut. Simply cut them into chunks and cook with the kraut. Or add chopped apples and onions to cooked and cooled sauerkraut and serve cold as a salad.

Seasoned Flank Steak

I always keep a flank steak in the freezer for unexpected company. This recipe has often saved me when our son appears on the doorstep. The easy marinade provides delicious flavor. —*Betty Graham Sun City, California*

1/4 cup vegetable oil
2 tablespoons water
1 to 2 tablespoons lemon-pepper seasoning
1 to 2 teaspoons seasoned salt
1 beef flank steak (about 1-1/2 pounds)

In a large resealable plastic bag, combine the first four ingredients; add steak. Seal bag and turn to coat; refrigerate for 1-2 hours, turning occasionally.

Grill steak, uncovered, over medium-hot heat for 6-12 minutes or until meat reaches desired doneness (for medium-rare, a meat thermometer should read 145°; medium, 160°; well-done, 170°). **Yield:** 6 servings.

Honey-Lime Grilled Chicken

You don't need a lot of ingredients to stir up my easy marinade. It requires only three items and gives fabulous lime flavor to tender chicken breasts.
—Dorothy Smith
El Dorado, Arkansas

1/2 cup honey
1/3 cup soy sauce
1/4 cup lime juice
4 boneless skinless chicken breast halves

In a resealable plastic bag or shallow glass container, combine the honey, soy sauce and lime juice; mix well. Add chicken and turn to coat. Seal or cover and refrigerate for 30-45 minutes.

Drain and discard marinade. Grill chicken, uncovered, over medium heat for 6-7 minutes on each side or until juices run clear. **Yield:** 4 servings.

Ham and Rice Bake

I can put a satisfying meal on the supper table in a jiffy. I just add a can of soup, rice and a few convenience items to leftover ham for a flavorful no-fuss casserole. —Sharol Binger, Tulare, South Dakota

1 can (10-3/4 ounces) condensed cream of chicken soup, undiluted
1 cup (4 ounces) shredded cheddar cheese, *divided*
1 package (16 ounces) frozen California-blend vegetables, thawed
1 cup cooked rice
1 cup cubed fully cooked ham

In a large saucepan, combine the soup and 1/2 cup cheese; cook and stir until cheese is melted. Stir in the vegetables, rice and ham.

Transfer to a greased 1-1/2-qt. baking dish. Sprinkle with remaining cheese. Bake, uncovered, at 350° for 25-30 minutes or until heated through. **Yield:** 4 servings.

|HAM HINTS| Choose firm, plump ham that is rosy pink and finely grained. When using ham as a flavoring in soups, casseroles, bean dishes or stir-fries, finely chop the meat. You'll get more intense, evenly distributed flavor than with a few large chunks.

Bacon-Wrapped Chicken

Tender chicken gets a special treatment when spread with a creamy filling and wrapped with tasty bacon strips. This easy entree is frequently requested by my bunch. I'm happy to make it for them as often as they like because I keep the ingredients on hand and can have it on the dinner table in less than an hour.

—MarlaKaye Skinner
Tucson, Arizona

6 boneless skinless
    chicken breast halves
1 carton (8 ounces)
    whipped cream cheese
    with onion and chives
1 tablespoon butter, cubed
Salt to taste
6 bacon strips

Flatten chicken to 1/2-in. thickness. Spread 3 tablespoons cream cheese over each. Dot with butter and sprinkle with salt; roll up. Wrap each with a bacon strip. Place, seam side down, in a greased 13-in. x 9-in. x 2-in. baking pan.

Bake, uncovered, at 400° for 35-40 minutes or until juices run clear. Broil 6 in. from the heat for 5 minutes or until bacon is crisp. **Yield:** 6 servings.

|FLATTENING CHICKEN| Place one chicken breast between two pieces of waxed paper. Starting in the center and working out to the edges, pound lightly with the flat side of a meat mallet until the chicken is even in thickness.

Peppy Macaroni

I like to keep an extra box of macaroni and cheese on the pantry shelf to make this fun pizza-flavored casserole for unexpected guests. Because it's a snap to prepare, older kids could assemble it to give Mom and Dad a break from dinner duties.   —Helen Cluts, Sioux Falls, South Dakota

1 package (7-1/4 ounces)
    macaroni and cheese
    dinner
2 eggs, lightly beaten
1 jar (8 ounces) pizza sauce
40 slices pepperoni
    (about 2-1/2 ounces)
2 cups (8 ounces) shredded
    mozzarella cheese

Prepare macaroni and cheese according to package directions. Fold in eggs. Spread into a greased 13-in. x 9-in. x 2-in. baking dish. Top with pizza sauce, pepperoni and mozzarella.

Bake, uncovered, at 350° for 30-35 minutes or until lightly browned and cheese is melted. Let stand for 5 minutes before serving. **Yield:** 4 servings.

Fish Nuggets

My family loves to camp and fish. We developed this different breading made with saltines and graham crackers to coat our "catch of the day". It fries to a tasty golden brown and has become a campground favorite.
—*Deana Brandenburg, Great Bend, Kansas*

2 pounds haddock *or* cod fillets
1 cup finely crushed graham crackers (about 16 squares)
3/4 cup finely crushed saltines (about 25 crackers)
1-1/2 to 2 teaspoons seasoned salt
Oil for deep-fat frying

Cut fish into 1-in. cubes; secure with a toothpick if necessary. Combine cracker crumbs and seasoned salt in a shallow bowl; roll fish in crumb mixture until coated.

In an electric skillet or deep-fat fryer, heat oil to 375°. Fry nuggets, a few at time, for 3 minutes or until browned. Drain on paper towels. **Yield:** 4-6 servings.

Shrimp Newberg

A friend gave me the recipe for this tasty time-saving dish that takes advantage of cooked shrimp. It's a quick company meal when served over rice with a tossed salad and dessert.
—*Donna Souders*
Hagerstown, Maryland

1 can (10-3/4 ounces) condensed cream of shrimp *or* mushroom soup, undiluted
1/4 cup water
1 teaspoon seafood seasoning
1 package (1 pound) frozen cooked medium salad shrimp, thawed
Hot cooked rice

In a saucepan, combine soup, water and seafood seasoning. Bring to a boil. Reduce heat; stir in shrimp. Heat through. Serve over rice. **Yield:** 4 servings.

|RELY ON RICE| Instant rice has been fully or partially cooked, then dehydrated, that's why it only takes a few minutes to prepare. Make a double batch of rice so you can use the leftovers for another night's meal. It will keep in the refrigerator for up to 4 days.

Apricot Sausage Kabobs

Basted with a simple sweet-sour sauce, these tasty kabobs make a quick meal that's elegant enough for company. —*Susie Lindquist, Ellijay, Georgia*

3/4 cup apricot preserves
3/4 cup Dijon mustard
1 pound fully cooked
   kielbasa *or* Polish
   sausage, cut into 12
   pieces
12 dried apricots
12 medium fresh mushrooms
Hot cooked rice, optional

In a small bowl, combine preserves and mustard; mix well. Remove 1/2 cup for serving; set aside. Alternate sausage, apricots and mushrooms on four metal or soaked bamboo skewers.

Grill, covered, over indirect heat for 15-20 minutes or until meat juices run clear. Turn frequently and baste with remaining apricot sauce. Warm the reserved sauce; serve with kabobs and rice if desired. **Yield:** 4 servings.

Taco Chicken Rolls

I always keep the ingredients for this tender and flavorful chicken on hand. The cheese-stuffed rolls are nice with a green salad or plate of fresh vegetables and Spanish rice. —*Kara De la vega Suisun City, California*

1 cup finely crushed
   cheese-flavored crackers
1 envelope taco seasoning
6 boneless skinless
   chicken breast halves
   (about 2 pounds)
2 ounces Monterey Jack
   cheese, cut into
   six 2-inch x 1/2-inch
   sticks
1 can (4 ounces) chopped
   green chilies

In a shallow dish, combine the cracker crumbs and taco seasoning; set aside. Flatten chicken between two sheets of waxed paper to 1/4-in. thickness. Place a cheese stick and about 1 tablespoon of chilies on each piece of chicken. Tuck ends of chicken in and roll up; secure with a toothpick.

Coat chicken with crumb mixture. Place in a greased 13-in. x 9-in. x 2-in. baking dish. Bake, uncovered, at 350° for 35-40 minutes or until chicken juices run clear. Remove toothpicks. **Yield:** 6 servings.

Festive Fillets

(Also pictured on front cover)

When the weather's not right for outdoor cooking and you want an outstanding steak, this recipe is the answer. We like the zippy gravy so much that we don't wait for inclement evenings to fix this. It's a cinch to prepare on the stovetop.

—Donna Cline
Pensacola, Florida

 Uses less fat, sugar or salt. Includes Nutritional Analysis and Diabetic Exchanges.

  1 envelope brown gravy mix
  1 jar (4-1/2 ounces) sliced mushrooms, drained
  2 teaspoons prepared horseradish
  4 beef tenderloin fillets (5 ounces *each***)**
1/8 teaspoon pepper

Prepare gravy according to package directions; add mushrooms and horseradish. Set aside and keep warm. In a nonstick skillet, cook fillets over medium-high heat until meat reaches desired doneness (for rare, a meat thermometer should read 140°; medium, 160°; well-done 170°), turning once. Season with pepper. Serve with the gravy. **Yield:** 4 servings.

Nutritional Analysis: One serving equals 268 calories, 714 mg sodium, 88 mg cholesterol, 7 g carbohydrate, 33 g protein, 11 g fat. **Diabetic Exchanges:** 4 lean meat, 1/2 starch.

Editor's Note: Fillets can be baked. First brown in a skillet for 1 minute on each side, then transfer to an 8-in. square baking pan. Bake, uncovered, at 350° for 10-20 minutes or until meat reaches desired doneness.

Crabby Alfredo

Supper couldn't be easier when you put this quick, creamy entree on the menu. My mother-in-law gave me this wonderful recipe. The whole family loves it and everyone asks for more.

—Tara Kampman, Manchester, Iowa

  4 cups cooked egg noodles
  1 package (16 ounces) imitation crabmeat, chopped
  1 jar (16 ounces) Alfredo sauce
Seafood seasoning *or* **minced chives**

In a large saucepan, combine the noodles, crab and Alfredo sauce. Cook and stir until heated through. Sprinkle with seafood seasoning or chives. **Yield:** 4 servings.

Italian Sausage Skillet

Served over rice or pasta, this skillet is a hearty favorite. This garden-fresh dish gets extra color from a can of stewed tomatoes. The Italian sausage has so many wonderful flavors you don't need to add any other seasonings. *—Eve Gauger Vargas*
Prairie Village, Kansas

1-1/4 pounds uncooked Italian
    sausage links
    3 small zucchini *or* yellow
      summer squash, cubed
1/2 cup chopped onion
    1 can (14-1/2 ounces)
      stewed tomatoes
Hot cooked rice *or* pasta

In a skillet over medium heat, brown the sausage until no longer pink; drain. Cut sausage into 1/4-in. slices; return to the skillet to brown completely.

Add zucchini and onion; cook and stir for 2 minutes. Stir in the tomatoes. Reduce heat; cover and simmer for 10-15 minutes or until the zucchini is tender. Serve over rice or pasta. **Yield:** 4-6 servings.

Perch Fillets

Guests will never guess that lemon-lime soda and pancake mix are the secret ingredients behind these tasty perch fillets in a golden coating. If perch isn't available, try substituting haddock.
—Connie Tibbetts, Wilton, Maine

1-1/2 cups lemon-lime soda
    1 pound perch fillets
    2 cups pancake mix
1/4 teaspoon pepper
Oil for frying

Pour soda into a shallow bowl; add fish fillets and let stand for 15 minutes. In another shallow bowl, combine pancake mix and pepper. Remove fish from soda and coat with pancake mix.

In a large skillet, heat 1/4 in. of oil over medium-high heat. Fry fish for 2-3 minutes on each side or until fish flakes with a fork. Drain on paper towels. **Yield:** 4 servings.

|BREADING FISH| When buying fresh fish fillets, look for firm flesh that has a moist look; don't purchase fish that looks dried out. To bread fish, combine the dry ingredients in a pie plate or shallow bowl. In another pie plate or bowl, whisk egg, milk and/or other liquid ingredients. Dip fish into liquid mixture, then gently roll in dry ingredients. Fry as directed.

Noodle Pepperoni Pizza

My family would eat wedges of this great-tasting skillet dinner without any complaint several nights a week. I love it because it's inexpensive and can be made in a snap.
—*Gayle Lizotte*
Merrimack, New Hampshire

- 4 **packages (3 ounces** *each***) ramen noodles**
- 1 **tablespoon olive oil**
- 1 **cup spaghetti** *or* **pizza sauce**
- 1 **cup (4 ounces) shredded mozzarella cheese**
- 1 **package (3 ounces) sliced pepperoni, cut into strips**

Discard seasoning packets from noodles or save for another use. Cook noodles according to package directions; drain. Heat oil in a 10-in. ovenproof skillet. Press noodles into skillet, evenly covering the bottom of pan. Cook until bottom of crust is lightly browned, about 5 minutes.

Pour spaghetti sauce over the crust. Sprinkle with cheese and pepperoni. Broil 4 to 6 in. from the heat for 3-4 minutes or until heated through and cheese is melted. **Yield:** 4-6 servings.

Marinated Baked Chicken

This tender, flavorful chicken is one of my mom's specialties. Soy sauce and bottled Italian dressing combine in a mouth-watering marinade that nicely complements the meat.
—*Cindy Kufeldt*
Orlando, Florida

- 1/2 **cup Italian salad dressing**
- 1/2 **cup soy sauce**
- 6 **bone-in chicken breast halves**
- 1/8 **teaspoon onion salt**
- 1/8 **teaspoon garlic salt**

Kale and spiced apple rings, optional

In a measuring cup, combine salad dressing and soy sauce. Pour 3/4 cup into a large resealable plastic bag; add chicken. Seal the bag and turn to coat; refrigerate for 4 hours or overnight, turning several times. Refrigerate remaining marinade for basting.

Drain chicken, discarding marinade. Place chicken, skin side up, on a rack in a roasting pan. Sprinkle with onion salt and garlic salt. Bake, uncovered, at 350° for 45-60 minutes or until juices run clear and a meat thermometer reads 170°, brushing occasionally with reserved marinade. Garnish platter with kale and apple rings if desired. **Yield:** 6 servings.

Crumb-Coated Cod

Fish fillets get fast flavor from Italian salad dressing mix and a breading made with seasoned stuffing mix. I serve this baked fish with a tossed salad or relishes. —*Julia Bruce, Tuscola, Illinois*

- **2 tablespoons vegetable oil**
- **2 tablespoons water**
- **1 envelope Italian salad dressing mix**
- **2 cups crushed stuffing mix**
- **4 cod fillets (about 6 ounces *each*)**

In a shallow bowl, combine the oil, water and salad dressing mix. Place the stuffing mix in another bowl. Dip fillets in salad dressing mixture, then in stuffing.

Place on a greased baking sheet. Bake at 425° for 15-20 minutes or until the fish flakes easily with a fork. **Yield:** 4 servings.

Pizza Chicken Roll-Ups

(Also pictured on back cover)

I love the chicken roll-ups my mom made for special occasions, filled with spinach and cream cheese. My own kids wouldn't eat those, so I came up with this pizza-flavored variety the whole family enjoys.
—*Tanja Penquite, Oregon, Ohio*

- **4 boneless skinless chicken breast halves**
- **12 pepperoni slices**
- **8 mozzarella cheese slices, *divided***
- **1 can (15 ounces) pizza sauce**
- **Minced fresh parsley, optional**

Flatten chicken to 1/4-in. thickness. Place three slices of pepperoni and one slice of cheese on each. Roll up tightly; secure with toothpicks. Place in a greased 11-in. x 7-in. x 2-in. baking dish. Spoon pizza sauce over roll-ups.

Cover and bake at 350° for 35-40 minutes. Uncover; top with the remaining cheese. Bake 5-10 minutes longer or until cheese is melted. Sprinkle with parsley if desired. **Yield:** 4 servings.

Thanksgiving In a Pan

This meal-in-one tastes like a big holiday dinner without the work. It's a great way to use up leftover turkey, but I often use thick slices of deli turkey instead with equally delicious results. —*Lynne Hahn*
Temecula, California

1 package (6 ounces) stuffing mix
2-1/2 cups cubed cooked turkey
2 cups frozen cut green beans, thawed
1 jar (12 ounces) turkey gravy
Pepper to taste

Prepare stuffing mix according to package directions. Transfer to a greased 11-in. x 7-in. x 2-in. baking dish. Top with turkey, beans, gravy and pepper. Cover and bake at 350° for 30-35 minutes or until heated through. **Yield:** 6 servings.

Editor's Note: Any poultry, herb seasoned or corn bread stuffing mix would work in this recipe.

Pork Chop Casserole

I rely on orange juice and canned soup to boost the flavor of this tender pork chop and rice bake. It's very good...and a little different from your usual fare. —*Wanda Plinsky, Wichita, Kansas*

4 bone-in pork loin chops (1/2 inch thick)
1 tablespoon vegetable oil
1-1/3 cups uncooked long grain rice
1 cup orange juice
1 can (10-1/2 ounces) condensed chicken with rice soup, undiluted

In a large skillet, brown pork chops in oil; drain. Place the rice in an ungreased shallow 3-qt. baking dish; pour orange juice over rice. Top with pork chops and soup.

Cover and bake at 350° for 40-45 minutes or until pork juices run clear and rice is tender. **Yield:** 4 servings.

|SIZING IT UP| Casserole dishes are measured by volume. If you're unsure of how large a dish is, fill it with water, then measure the liquid. Casserole dishes are most commonly found in the following sizes: 1, 1-1/2, 2 and 3 quarts.

Chili Casserole

I threw together this main dish when my husband unexpectedly invited his hunting buddies for dinner. It was on the table by the time they'd unpacked their gear and washed up. —Karen Bruggman
Edmonds, Washington

1 can (40 ounces) chili
  with beans
1 can (4 ounces) chopped
  green chilies
1 can (2-1/4 ounces)
  sliced ripe olives, drained
2 cups (8 ounces) shredded
  cheddar cheese
2 cups ranch-flavored
  tortilla chips, crushed

In a bowl, combine all ingredients. Transfer to a greased 2-1/2-qt. baking dish. Bake, uncovered, at 350° for 30-35 minutes or until bubbly. **Yield:** 6 servings.

|CRUSHING TORTILLA CHIPS| Place tortilla chips in a resealable plastic bag and seal. Then simply crush the chips with your hands. Crushing them with a rolling pin will produce pieces that are too fine.

Saucy Apricot Chicken

The tangy glaze on this tender chicken entree is just as wonderful with ham or turkey. Leftovers reheat nicely in the microwave. —Dee Gray
Kokomo, Indiana

6 boneless skinless
  chicken breast halves
  (about 1-1/2 pounds)
2 jars (12 ounces *each*)
  apricot preserves
1 envelope onion soup mix
Hot cooked rice

Place chicken in a slow cooker. Combine the preserves and soup mix; spoon over chicken. Cover and cook on low for 4-5 hours or until tender. Serve over rice. **Yield:** 6 servings.

Biscuit Tostadas

Refrigerated biscuits and just four other ingredients make it easy for little hands to assemble these cute kid-size tostadas. I enjoy the time our gang spends together in the kitchen making these Mexican mini main dishes. They're best eaten on a plate with a fork.

—*Terrie Stampor*
Sterling Heights, Michigan

1 pound ground beef
1 jar (16 ounces) salsa, *divided*
1 tube (17.3 ounces) large refrigerated biscuits
2 cups (8 ounces) shredded Colby-Monterey Jack cheese
2 cups shredded lettuce

In a skillet, cook beef over medium heat until no longer pink; drain. Add 1-1/2 cups salsa; heat through.

Split each biscuit in half; flatten into 4-in. rounds on ungreased baking sheets. Bake at 350° for 10-12 minutes or until golden brown. Top with meat mixture, cheese, lettuce and remaining salsa. **Yield:** 16 servings.

Tangy Ham Steak

This glazed ham steak is a yummy quick-and-easy main dish. It tastes especially good heated on the grill but works well in the oven broiler, too. Dad fires up the grill for this tasty steak while my mom heads to the kitchen to prepare the rest of the meal.

—*Sue Gronholz*
Columbus, Wisconsin

1/3 cup spicy brown mustard
1/4 cup honey
1/2 teaspoon grated orange peel
1 fully cooked ham steak (about 2 pounds)

In a small bowl, combine mustard, honey and orange peel. Brush over one side of ham. Broil or grill, uncovered, over medium-hot heat for 7 minutes. Turn; brush with mustard mixture. Cook until well glazed and heated through, about 7 minutes. **Yield:** 6-8 servings.

Saucy Beef Casserole

I rely on canned soups and crunchy chow mein noodles to flavor this hearty ground beef bake. My family gobbles it up!

—Ferne Spielvogel, Fairwater, Wisconsin

1 pound ground beef
1 medium onion, chopped
1 can (10-3/4 ounces) condensed cream of chicken soup, undiluted
1 can (10-3/4 ounces) condensed vegetable soup, undiluted
3/4 cup chow mein noodles

In a skillet, cook beef and onion over medium heat until meat is no longer pink; drain. Stir in soups. Transfer to a greased 8-in. square baking dish.

Cover and bake at 350° for 25-30 minutes or until heated through. Uncover; sprinkle with chow mein noodles. Bake 5 minutes longer or until chow mein noodles are crisp. **Yield:** 4 servings.

Italian Pineapple Chicken

I created this one night when I was in a particular hurry. There is hardly any preparation involved, and everyone who tries it asks for the recipe. The tender five-ingredient entree features skillet-browned chicken breasts and pineapple slices seasoned with bottled salad dressing.

—Becky Lohmiller, Monticello, Indiana

4 boneless skinless chicken breast halves
1/2 cup Italian salad dressing
2 tablespoons olive oil
1 can (8 ounces) sliced pineapple, drained
1/3 cup shredded Swiss cheese, optional

Flatten chicken to 1/2-in. thickness. Pour salad dressing into a shallow bowl; dip chicken in dressing. In a large skillet, heat oil. Add chicken; cook over medium-high heat for 5-7 minutes on each side or until juices run clear. Remove and keep warm.

Add pineapple slices to the skillet; cook for 30 seconds on each side or until lightly browned. Place a slice on each chicken breast half. Sprinkle with cheese if desired. **Yield:** 4 servings.

Fast Baked Fish

I enjoy fixing hearty, home-style meals whenever I can. Time is often tight, though. Our son is a world-record-holding fisherman who keeps us supplied with fresh fish. So I make my Fast Baked Fish often. It's moist, tender and flavorful.

—Judie Anglen
Riverton, Wyoming

1-1/4 pounds fish fillets
1 teaspoon seasoned salt
Pepper to taste
Paprika, optional
3 tablespoons butter, melted

Place fish fillets in a greased 11-in. x 7-in. x 2-in. baking dish. Sprinkle with seasoned salt, pepper and paprika if desired. Drizzle with butter. Cover and bake at 400° for 15-20 minutes or until the fish flakes easily with a fork. **Yield:** 4 servings.

Editor's Note: Orange roughy, haddock, trout or walleye may be used in this recipe.

Colorful Kabobs

We cook out all year long. These kabobs cook up in a snap and taste wonderful. My son likes to help assemble them.
—Janell Aguda, Joelton, Tennessee

12 cherry tomatoes
1 pound fully cooked smoked turkey sausage, cut into 1/2-inch chunks
2 medium green peppers, cut into 1-inch pieces
1 medium onion, cut into wedges
Hot cooked rice

Thread a cherry tomato onto six metal or soaked wooden skewers. Alternate the sausage, green pepper and onion pieces on skewers, ending with another tomato.

Grill, uncovered, over medium-hot heat for 10-15 minutes or until meat is heated through and vegetables are tender. Remove meat and vegetables from skewers and serve over rice. **Yield:** 6 servings.

|SOAKING SKEWERS| To help prevent wooden skewers from burning or splintering while grilling, soak them in water for 15-30 minutes. Remove them from the water and then thread on the ingredients of your choice.

Maple Barbecued Chicken

This tender glazed chicken is so delicious, it will disappear very quickly. The sweet maple sauce is used to baste the chicken while grilling, with additional sauce served alongside for dipping. —*Ruth Lowen Hythe, Alberta*

✓ **Uses less fat, sugar or salt. Includes Nutritional Analysis and Diabetic Exchanges.**

3/4 cup barbecue sauce
3/4 cup maple pancake syrup
1/2 teaspoon salt
1/2 teaspoon maple flavoring
8 boneless skinless
   chicken breast halves
   (2 pounds)

In a bowl, combine the first four ingredients and mix well. Remove 3/4 cup to a small bowl for serving; cover and refrigerate.

Grill chicken, uncovered, over medium heat for 3 minutes on each side. Grill 6-8 minutes longer or until juices run clear, basting with remaining sauce and turning occasionally. Serve with reserved sauce. **Yield:** 8 servings.

Nutritional Analysis: One serving (one chicken breast with 1-1/2 tablespoons sauce) equals 228 calories, 2 g fat (trace saturated fat), 66 mg cholesterol, 436 mg sodium, 26 g carbohydrate, trace fiber, 27 g protein. **Diabetic Exchanges:** 3 lean meat, 1-1/2 fruit.

Fiesta Macaroni

When time is short, I rely on this family-pleasing main dish. It's so easy to fix, and everyone loves the zesty flavor that the salsa and chili beans provide. —*Sandra Castillo, Sun Prairie, Wisconsin*

1 package (16 ounces)
   elbow macaroni
1 pound ground beef
1 jar (16 ounces) salsa
10 ounces process cheese
   (Velveeta), cubed
1 can (15 ounces)
   chili-style beans

Cook macaroni according to package directions. Meanwhile, in a skillet, cook beef over medium heat until no longer pink; drain. Drain macaroni; set aside.

In a microwave-safe bowl, combine salsa and cheese. Microwave, uncovered, on high for 3-4 minutes or until cheese is melted. Stir into the skillet; add the macaroni and beans.

Transfer to a greased 13-in. x 9-in. x 2-in. baking dish. Bake, uncovered, at 350° for 30-35 minutes or until heated through. **Yield:** 6-8 servings.

Quick 'n' Easy Lasagna

I never have leftovers when I prepare this hearty crowd-pleaser. It's my son's favorite, and my husband and I like to make it on nights we have friends over to play cards.
—*Brenda Richardson*
Rison, Arkansas

16 **lasagna noodles**
2 **pounds ground beef**
1 **jar (28 ounces) spaghetti sauce**
1 **pound process cheese (Velveeta), cubed**

Cook noodles according to package directions. Meanwhile, in a large skillet, cook beef over medium heat until no longer pink; drain. Add the spaghetti sauce; heat through. Rinse and drain the noodles.

In a greased 13-in. x 9-in. x 2-in. baking dish, layer a third of the meat sauce and half of the noodles and cheese. Repeat the layers. Top with the remaining meat sauce. Cover and bake at 350° for 35 minutes or until bubbly. **Yield:** 6-8 servings.

Tomato Bacon Pie

This simple but savory pie makes a tasty addition to brunch buffets and leisurely luncheons. I rely on a cheesy mixture for the pie's golden topping and a refrigerated pastry shell for easy preparation.
—*Gladys Gibson, Hodgenville, Kentucky*

1 **unbaked deep-dish pastry shell (9 inches)**
3 **medium tomatoes, cut into 1/4-inch slices**
10 **bacon strips, cooked and crumbled**
1 **cup (4 ounces) shredded cheddar cheese**
1 **cup mayonnaise**

Bake pastry shell according to package directions; cool. Place tomatoes in the crust; sprinkle with bacon. In a bowl, combine the cheese and mayonnaise. Spoon over bacon in the center of pie, leaving 1 in. around edge.

Bake at 350° for 30-40 minutes or until golden brown (cover edges with foil if necessary to prevent overbrowning). **Yield:** 6 servings.

Editor's Note: Reduced-fat or fat-free mayonnaise may not be substituted for regular mayonnaise in this recipe.

Angel Hair Tuna

This recipe came from a dear friend, and it quickly became a favorite standby. Simply toss together a green salad and toast some garlic bread for a complete meal.   —*Collette Burch, Edinburg, Texas*

2 packages (5.1 ounces *each*) angel hair pasta with Parmesan cheese dinner mix
1 can (12 ounces) tuna, drained and flaked
1/2 teaspoon Italian seasoning
3/4 cup crushed butter-flavored crackers (about 15)
1/4 cup butter, melted

Prepare pasta dinner mixes according to package directions. Stir in the tuna and Italian seasoning. Transfer to a serving bowl; cover and let stand for 5 minutes to thicken. Toss cracker crumbs and butter; sprinkle over the top. Serve immediately. **Yield:** 4 servings.

|TUNA TIDBITS| Canned tuna is precooked and can be water- or oil-packed. It comes in three grades, the best being solid or fancy (large pieces), followed by chunk (smaller pieces) and flaked (bits and pieces). Water-packed tuna not only contains fewer calories, but it also has a fresher flavor.

Pork Chops with Apples and Stuffing

The heartwarming blend of cinnamon and apples is the perfect accompaniment to these tender pork chops. This dish is always a winner with my family. It's a main course I can serve with little preparation.
—*Joan Hamilton*
Worcester, Massachusetts

6 boneless pork loin chops (1 inch thick)
1 tablespoon vegetable oil
1 package (6 ounces) crushed stuffing mix
1 can (21 ounces) apple pie filling with cinnamon

In a skillet, brown pork chops in oil over medium-high heat. Meanwhile, prepare stuffing according to package directions. Spread pie filling into a greased 13-in. x 9-in. x 2-in. baking dish. Place the pork chops on top; spoon stuffing over chops.

Cover and bake at 350° for 35 minutes. Uncover; bake 10 minutes longer or until a meat thermometer reads 160°. **Yield:** 6 servings.

Beef in Onion Gravy

I double this super recipe to feed our family of four so I'm sure to have leftovers to send with my husband to work for lunch. His co-workers tell him he's lucky to have someone who fixes him such special meals. It's our secret that it's an easy slow-cooker dinner!

—Denise Albers
Freeburg, Illinois

1 can (10-3/4 ounces)
  condensed cream of
  mushroom soup,
  undiluted
2 tablespoons onion soup
  mix
2 tablespoons beef broth
1 tablespoon quick-cooking
  tapioca
1 pound beef stew meat,
  cut into 1-inch cubes
Hot cooked noodles *or* mashed
  potatoes, optional

In a slow cooker, combine the soup, soup mix, broth and tapioca; let stand for 15 minutes. Stir in the beef. Cover and cook on low for 6-8 hours or until meat is tender. Serve over noodles or mashed potatoes if desired. **Yield:** 3 servings.

|NO PEEKING!| Refrain from lifting the lid while the slow cooker is cooking unless you're instructed in a recipe to stir or add ingredients. The loss of steam can mean an additional 15 to 30 minutes of cooking time each time you lift the lid. Be sure the lid is seated properly, not tilted or askew. The steam during cooking creates a seal.

Chicken Fried Rice

I rely on a fried rice mix to start this speedy skillet supper. It makes the most of leftover cooked chicken and a can of crunchy water chestnuts.
—Kathy Hoyt, Maplecrest, New York

1 package (6.2 ounces)
  fried rice mix
2 cups cubed cooked
  chicken
1-1/2 cups cooked broccoli
  florets
1 can (8 ounces) sliced
  water chestnuts, drained
1 cup (4 ounces) shredded
  mozzarella cheese

Cook rice according to package directions. Stir in chicken, broccoli and water chestnuts; heat through. Sprinkle with cheese. **Yield:** 4 servings.

Tangy Pork Tenderloin

A simple marinade adds sweet flavor and tangy zip to juicy pork tenderloin. No one will ever guess there are only four ingredients in this sauce. For a spicier version, I like to add more chili powder.

—*Christopher Bingham*
Lansing, Michigan

2 pork tenderloins
(1 pound *each*)
2/3 cup honey
1/2 cup Dijon mustard
1/4 to 1/2 teaspoon chili
powder
1/4 teaspoon salt

Place pork tenderloins in a large resealable plastic bag or shallow glass container. In a bowl, combine the remaining ingredients; set aside 2/3 cup. Pour remaining marinade over pork; turn to coat. Seal or cover and refrigerate for at least 4 hours, turning occasionally.

Drain and discard marinade. Grill pork, covered, over indirect medium heat for 8-9 minutes on each side or until meat juices run clear and a meat thermometer reads 160°-170°. In a saucepan, warm the reserved sauce; serve with the pork. **Yield:** 6 servings.

Swiss Tuna Bake

My husband enjoys cooking just as much as I do. One night he tossed together this comforting casserole from meager ingredients we had in our cupboard. It turned out to be the best-tasting tuna casserole I have ever had! Swiss cheese flavors the noodles nicely.

—*Joanne Callahan*
Far Hills, New Jersey

4 cups cooked medium
egg noodles
1-1/2 cups (6 ounces) shredded
Swiss cheese
1 cup mayonnaise
1 can (6 ounces) tuna,
drained and flaked
1 cup seasoned bread
crumbs, *divided*

In a large bowl, combine the noodles, cheese, mayonnaise and tuna. Sprinkle 1/2 cup bread crumbs into a greased 9-in. square baking dish. Spread noodle mixture over crumbs. Sprinkle with the remaining crumbs. Bake, uncovered, at 350° for 20 minutes or until heated through. **Yield:** 4 servings.

Editor's Note: Reduced-fat or fat-free mayonnaise may not be substituted for regular mayonnaise in this recipe.

Artichoke Chicken

A friend agreed to repair some plumbing in exchange for a home-cooked dinner, but he showed up before I could shop for groceries. A can of artichokes in the pantry inspired me to combine a favorite hot dip recipe with a chicken bake. The results were so delicious, he said he'd rush over anytime.
—*Lisa Robisch, Cincinnati, Ohio*

1 can (14 ounces) water-packed artichoke hearts, well drained and chopped
3/4 cup grated Parmesan cheese
3/4 cup mayonnaise
Dash garlic powder
4 boneless skinless chicken breast halves

In a bowl, combine the artichokes, cheese, mayonnaise and garlic powder. Place chicken in a greased 11-in. x 7-in. x 2-in. baking dish. Spread with artichoke mixture. Bake, uncovered, at 375° for 30-35 minutes or until chicken juices run clear. **Yield:** 4 servings.

Editor's Note: Reduced-fat or fat-free mayonnaise may not be substituted for regular mayonnaise in this recipe.

Sweet and Savory Brisket

I like this recipe not only because it makes such tender and flavorful beef, but because it takes advantage of a slow cooker. It's wonderful to come home from work and have this mouth-watering main dish waiting for you. The beef doubles as a warm sandwich filling, too.   —*Chris Snyder, Boulder, Colorado*

1 beef brisket (3 to 3-1/2 pounds), cut in half
1 cup ketchup
1/4 cup grape jelly
1 envelope onion soup mix
1/2 teaspoon pepper

Place half of the brisket in a slow cooker. In a bowl, combine the ketchup, jelly, soup mix and pepper; spread half over meat. Top with the remaining meat and ketchup mixture.

Cover and cook on low for 8-10 hours or until meat is tender. Slice brisket; serve with cooking juices. **Yield:** 8-10 servings.

Editor's Note: This is a fresh beef brisket, not corned beef.

Seasoned Cube Steaks

Soy sauce really wakes up the flavor of these nicely browned cube steaks. I serve this meaty main dish with mixed vegetables and rice or baked potatoes. My family loves this meal.

—Cathee Bethel, Lebanon, Oregon

1 cup soy sauce
1 teaspoon dried minced garlic
1 teaspoon dried minced onion
4 cube steaks (about 1-1/4 pounds)

In a large resealable plastic bag, combine the soy sauce, garlic and onion; add cube steaks. Seal bag; turn to coat. Refrigerate for 30-45 minutes, turning once.

Drain and discard marinade. Place steaks on a greased broiler pan. Broil 4 in. from the heat for about 4 minutes on each side or until meat reaches desired doneness. **Yield:** 4 servings.

Broiled Chicken Cordon Bleu

I serve this meal at least monthly. For variety, I sometimes use different types of cheese, such as Monterey Jack or cheddar. I even replace the ham with other favorite cold cuts.
—Hope Meece
Fowler, Indiana

4 boneless skinless chicken breast halves
1/4 cup butter, melted
4 thin slices fully cooked ham
4 tablespoons honey mustard salad dressing
4 thin slices Swiss *or* mozzarella cheese

Place chicken on the rack of a broiler pan. Broil 4 in. from the heat for 3 minutes; turn and broil 3 minutes on the other side. Brush with butter. Continue turning and basting until juices run clear, about 4 minutes.

Place a ham slice on each chicken breast; broil for 1-2 minutes. Spread 1 tablespoon dressing over each; top with cheese. Broil for 30 seconds or until cheese is melted. **Yield:** 4 servings.

Honey-Dijon Ham

Your family will think you took hours to prepare dinner when you slice servings of this delicious ham. Really, you just put it in the oven and baste it once! The glaze combines honey, brown sugar and mustard for tasty results. —*Karin Young Carlsbad, California*

1 boneless fully cooked
  ham (about 3 pounds)
1/3 cup honey
2 tablespoons Dijon
  mustard
2 tablespoons brown sugar
1 tablespoon water

Place ham on a greased rack in a shallow roasting pan. Bake, uncovered, at 325° for 50-60 minutes. Combine honey, mustard and sugar; brush about 3 tablespoonfuls over ham.

Bake 10-15 minutes longer or until a meat thermometer reads 140° and ham is heated through. Stir water into remaining glaze; heat through and serve with the ham. **Yield:** 8-10 servings.

Easy Meat Loaf

My mother-in-law invented this recipe by mistake, but it was so well received, it became the most popular way for her to make meat loaf. It couldn't be any easier. —*Pat Jensen, Oak Harbor, Ohio*

1 egg, lightly beaten
1 can (10-1/2 ounces)
  condensed French onion
  soup, undiluted
1-1/3 cups crushed
  butter-flavored crackers
  (about 33 crackers)
1 pound lean ground beef
1 can (10-3/4 ounces)
  condensed golden
  mushroom soup,
  undiluted

In a bowl, combine the egg, onion soup and cracker crumbs. Crumble beef over mixture and mix well. Shape into a loaf. Place in a greased 11-in. x 7-in. x 2-in. baking dish. Bake, uncovered, at 350° for 30 minutes.

Pour mushroom soup over loaf. Bake 1 hour longer or until meat is no longer pink and a meat thermometer reads 160°; drain. Let stand for 10 minutes before slicing. **Yield:** 4 servings.

|MMM..MEAT LOAF| When shaping meat loaves, handle the mixture as little as possible to keep the final product light in texture. Combine all of the ingredients except for the ground beef. Then crumble the beef over the mixture and mix well.

Fisherman's Specialty

A friend at work shared some of his fresh catch prepared in this simple way. After one bite, I knew it was the best fried fish I'd ever tasted. Whenever I catch bass, crappie or bluegill, my wife uses this recipe. The fillets come out moist and not fishy-tasting. Our family won't eat fish any other way.

—*Bruce Headley, Greenwood, Missouri*

2 eggs
1 to 2 teaspoons lemon-pepper seasoning, *divided*
6 bluegill *or* perch fillets (2 to 3 ounces *each*)
1 cup crushed saltines (about 30 crackers)
Vegetable oil

In a shallow bowl, beat eggs and 1 teaspoon lemon-pepper. Dip fillets in egg mixture, then coat with cracker crumbs. Sprinkle with remaining lemon-pepper.

In a skillet, heat 1/4 in. of oil. Fry fillets for 3-4 minutes on each side or until fish flakes easily with a fork. **Yield:** 3 servings.

Turkey Broccoli Hollandaise

This delectable dish is a great way to use extra turkey. The original recipe called for Thanksgiving leftovers, but my family loves it so much that I prepare this version all year long.

—*Pamela Yoder, Elkhart, Indiana*

1 cup fresh broccoli florets
1 package (6 ounces) stuffing mix
1 envelope hollandaise sauce mix
2 cups cubed cooked turkey *or* chicken
1 can (2.8 ounces) french-fried onions

Place 1 in. of water and broccoli in a saucepan. Bring to a boil. Reduce heat; cover and simmer for 5-8 minutes or until crisp-tender. Meanwhile, prepare stuffing and sauce mixes according to package directions.

Spoon stuffing into a greased 11-in. x 7-in. x 2-in. baking dish. Top with turkey. Drain broccoli; arrange over turkey. Spoon sauce over the top; sprinkle with onions. Bake, uncovered, at 325° for 25-30 minutes or until heated through. **Yield:** 6 servings.

Chicken Potato Bake

On evenings I'm busy helping our two kids with homework and don't have time to spend in the kitchen, I rely on this easy recipe. Bottled Italian salad dressing, Italian seasoning and Parmesan cheese give fast flavor to the juicy chicken and tender potatoes in this satisfying supper.

—Debbi Mullins, Canoga Park, California

1 broiler/fryer chicken (about 3 pounds), cut up
1 pound red potatoes, cut into chunks
1/2 to 3/4 cup prepared Italian salad dressing
1 tablespoon Italian seasoning
1/2 to 3/4 cup grated Parmesan cheese

Place chicken in a greased 13-in. x 9-in. x 2-in. baking dish. Arrange potatoes around chicken. Drizzle with dressing; sprinkle with Italian seasoning and Parmesan cheese.

Cover and bake at 400° for 20 minutes. Uncover; bake 20-30 minutes longer or until potatoes are tender and chicken juices run clear. **Yield:** 4 servings.

Peachy Pork

Who says you can't make a hearty dinner when you're racing against the clock? This unique combination of peach preserves and salsa makes a heartwarming main dish your family will ask for time and time again.　　—Marilyn Monroe, Erie, Michigan

1 pound pork tenderloin, cut into 1/8- to 1/4-inch slices
1 to 2 tablespoons vegetable oil
3 to 4 garlic cloves, minced
1 jar (16 ounces) salsa
1/4 cup peach preserves
Hot cooked rice, optional

In a large skillet, saute pork in oil for 4 minutes. Add garlic; cook and stir 1 minute longer. Stir in salsa and preserves; bring to a boil. Reduce heat; cover and simmer for 2 minutes or until meat is no longer pink. Serve over rice if desired. **Yield:** 3-4 servings.

Hearty Hamburger Casserole

I love to invent my own recipes. I used convenient stuffing mix and canned vegetable soup to come up with this tasty and satisfying supper. —*Regan Delp, Independence, Virginia*

1 pound ground beef
1 can (19 ounces) ready-to-serve chunky vegetable soup
1 package (6 ounces) instant stuffing mix
1/2 cup shredded cheddar cheese

In a skillet, cook beef over medium heat until no longer pink; drain. Stir in soup and set aside. Prepare stuffing mix according to package directions; spoon half into a greased 2-qt. baking dish. Top with beef mixture, cheese and remaining stuffing. Bake, uncovered, at 350° for 30-35 minutes or until heated through. **Yield:** 4 servings.

|BUY IN BULK| Ground beef is often sold in large economy sizes. These packages are a bargain because you can use some of the meat now and freeze the rest for future use. Ground beef can be frozen for up to 2 weeks in its original packaging.

Tortilla Beef Bake

My family loves Mexican food, so I came up with this simple, satisfying casserole that gets its spark from salsa. We like it so much that there are rarely leftovers. —*Kim Osburn Ligonier, Indiana*

1-1/2 pounds ground beef
1 can (10-3/4 ounces) condensed cream of chicken soup, undiluted
2-1/2 cups crushed tortilla chips, *divided*
1 jar (16 ounces) salsa
1-1/2 cups (6 ounces) shredded cheddar cheese

In a skillet, cook beef over medium heat until no longer pink; drain. Stir in soup. Sprinkle 1-1/2 cups tortilla chips in a greased shallow 2-1/2-qt. baking dish. Top with beef mixture, salsa and cheese.

Bake, uncovered, at 350° for 25-30 minutes or until bubbly. Sprinkle with the remaining chips. Bake 3 minutes longer or until chips are lightly toasted. **Yield:** 6 servings.

Breaded Ranch Chicken

A coating containing corn-flakes, Parmesan cheese and ranch dressing mix adds delectable flavor to the chicken pieces in this recipe and bakes to a pretty golden color. It's a mainstay I can always count on.
—*Launa Shoemaker*
Midland City, Alabama

3/4 **cup crushed cornflakes**
3/4 **cup grated Parmesan cheese**
1 **envelope ranch salad dressing mix**
8 **boneless skinless chicken breast halves (2 pounds)**
1/2 **cup butter, melted**

In a shallow bowl, combine the cornflakes, Parmesan cheese and salad dressing mix. Dip chicken in butter, then roll in cornflake mixture to coat.

Place in a greased 13-in. x 9-in. x 2-in. baking dish. Bake, uncovered, at 350° for 45 minutes or until chicken juices run clear. **Yield:** 8 servings.

Tuna Delight

A handful of ingredients is all it takes to put a meal on the table. This recipe makes a speedy dinner on busy weeknights or a tasty lunch when unexpected guests drop by.
—*Marie Green*
Belle Fourche, South Dakota

 Uses less fat, sugar or salt. Includes Nutritional Analysis and Diabetic Exchanges.

1-3/4 **cups frozen mixed vegetables, thawed**
1 **can (12 ounces) tuna, drained and flaked**
1 **can (10-3/4 ounces) condensed cream of chicken *or* celery soup, undiluted**
Hot cooked rice *or* noodles

In a large saucepan, combine the vegetables, tuna and soup. Cook and stir until heated through. Serve over rice or noodles. **Yield:** 3 servings.

Nutritional Analysis: One 1-cup serving (prepared with water-packed tuna and reduced-fat cream of chicken soup; calculated without rice) equals 260 calories, 4 g fat (1 g saturated fat), 42 mg cholesterol, 1,166 mg sodium, 21 g carbohydrate, 5 g fiber, 34 g protein. **Diabetic Exchanges:** 3 lean meat, 1 starch, 1 vegetable.

Bubble Pizza

A top-ranked food with teens, pizza can quickly quell a growling tummy! This recipe has a no-fuss crust made from refrigerated biscuits. For a jazzed-up version, add any of your favorite toppings such as green pepper, mushrooms, black olives or fresh tomatoes. Anything goes with this easy entree!
—Jo Groth
Plainfield, Iowa

1-1/2 pounds ground beef
1 can (15 ounces) pizza sauce
2 tubes (12 ounces *each*) refrigerated buttermilk biscuits
1-1/2 cups (6 ounces) shredded mozzarella cheese
1 cup (4 ounces) shredded cheddar cheese

In a skillet, cook the beef over medium heat until no longer pink; drain. Stir in pizza sauce. Quarter the biscuits; place in a greased 13-in. x 9-in. x 2-in. baking dish. Top with the beef mixture.

Bake, uncovered, at 400° for 20-25 minutes. Sprinkle with cheeses. Bake 5-10 minutes longer or until cheese is melted. Let stand for 5-10 minutes before serving. **Yield:** 6-8 servings.

Chow Mein Chicken

This basic recipe can be expanded many ways, but it's quite a success by itself. Sometimes I add sliced water chestnuts for extra crunch or a green vegetable for a burst of color.
—Roberta Fall
Paw Paw, Michigan

1 can (10-3/4 ounces) condensed cream of chicken soup, undiluted
1 can (10-1/2 ounces) condensed chicken with rice soup, undiluted
1 can (5 ounces) evaporated milk
2 cups cubed cooked chicken
1 can (3 ounces) chow mein noodles

In a bowl, combine soups and milk. Stir in chicken. Transfer to a greased 8-in. square baking dish. Bake, uncovered, at 350° for 40 minutes; stir. Sprinkle with chow mein noodles. Bake 5-10 minutes longer or until bubbly and noodles are crisp. **Yield:** 4 servings.

Turkey and Stuffing Pie

For a fast and flavorful way to use up Thanksgiving leftovers, try this main-dish pie. This is such a handy recipe during the holidays.

—*Debbi Baker, Green Springs, Ohio*

 Uses less fat, sugar or salt. Includes Nutritional Analysis and Diabetic Exchanges.

3 cups prepared stuffing
2 cups cubed cooked turkey
1 cup (4 ounces) shredded Swiss cheese
3 eggs
1/2 cup milk

Press stuffing onto the bottom and up the sides of a well-greased 9-in. pie plate. Top with turkey and cheese. Beat eggs and milk; pour over cheese. Bake at 350° for 35-40 minutes or until a knife inserted near the center comes out clean. Let stand 5-10 minutes before serving. **Yield:** 8 servings.

Nutritional Analysis: One serving (prepared with reduced-fat Swiss cheese, fat-free milk and egg substitute equivalent to 3 eggs) equals 327 calories, 1,065 mg sodium, 46 mg cholesterol, 39 g carbohydrate, 28 g protein, 6 g fat, 2 g fiber. **Diabetic Exchanges:** 3 lean meat, 2 starch.

Ravioli Casserole

The whole family will love the fun, cheesy flavor of this main dish that tastes like lasagna without all the fuss. Time-saving ingredients, including prepared spaghetti sauce and frozen ravioli, hurry the preparation along.

—*Mary Ann Rothert, Austin, Texas*

1 jar (28 ounces) spaghetti sauce
1 package (25 ounces) frozen cheese ravioli, cooked and drained
2 cups (16 ounces) small-curd cottage cheese
4 cups (16 ounces) shredded mozzarella cheese
1/4 cup grated Parmesan cheese

Spread 1/2 cup of spaghetti sauce in an ungreased 13-in. x 9-in. x 2-in. baking dish. Layer with half of the ravioli, 1-1/4 cups of sauce, 1 cup of cottage cheese and 2 cups of mozzarella cheese. Repeat layers. Sprinkle with the Parmesan cheese.

Bake, uncovered, at 350° for 30-40 minutes or until bubbly. Let stand 5-10 minutes before serving. **Yield:** 6-8 servings.

Editor's Note: 4-5 cups of any style cooked ravioli may be substituted for the frozen cheese ravioli.

Cheesy Beef Macaroni

Little ones will light up the room with smiles when you bring this supper to the table. Crunchy canned corn is an appealing addition to the mild and cheesy combination of ground beef and pasta.

—Dena Evetts, Sentinel, Oklahoma

1 pound ground beef
1 can (15-1/4 ounces) whole kernel corn, drained
1 can (10-3/4 ounces) condensed cream of chicken soup, undiluted
8 ounces process cheese (Velveeta), shredded
2-1/2 cups cooked elbow macaroni

In a large skillet, cook beef over medium heat until no longer pink; drain. Add the corn and soup. Set aside 1/2 cup cheese for topping; stir remaining cheese into meat mixture until melted. Gently stir in macaroni until coated.

Transfer to a greased 8-in. square baking dish. Top with reserved cheese. Bake, uncovered, at 350° for 20-25 minutes or until heated through. **Yield:** 4-6 servings.

Crispy Chicken Strips

This is an easy method for dressing up chicken. Roll strips in a quick coating made with potato flakes and bread crumbs, then cook them for a couple minutes in a skillet.

—Dawn Hart
Lake Havasu City, Arizona

 Uses less fat, sugar or salt. Includes Nutritional Analysis and Diabetic Exchanges.

3/4 pound boneless skinless chicken breasts
1/2 cup mashed potato flakes
1/2 cup seasoned bread crumbs
Egg substitute equivalent to 1 egg
2 tablespoons olive oil

Flatten chicken to 1/2-in. thickness; cut into 1-in. strips. In a shallow bowl, combine the potato flakes and bread crumbs. Dip chicken in egg substitute, then in potato mixture. In a skillet, cook chicken in oil for 4-5 minutes or until golden. **Yield:** 3 servings.

Nutritional Analysis: One serving equals 327 calories, 629 mg sodium, 63 mg cholesterol, 19 g carbohydrate, 28 g protein, 14 g fat. **Diabetic Exchanges:** 3 meat, 1-1/2 starch.

Bean and Beef Skillet

The mix of ground beef, beans and barbecue sauce in this skillet dish is a mainstay for us. I'll often brown the meat with the sauce and freeze it in a resealable bag. Later, I thaw it, add the beans, cook and serve.

—Rose Purrington
Windom, Minnesota

1 **pound ground beef**
1 **medium onion, chopped**
1 **can (28 ounces) baked beans**
1/4 **cup barbecue sauce** *or* **ketchup**
1 **cup (4 ounces) shredded cheddar cheese**

In a large skillet, cook beef and onion over medium heat until meat is no longer pink; drain. Stir in beans and barbecue sauce; heat through. Sprinkle with cheese; cover and cook on low until cheese is melted. **Yield:** 4 servings.

|SERVING ALTERNATIVES| Use this recipe as a dip by scooping it up with tortilla chips. Or you could crumble corn chips over the top. You might even mix the meat and beans with taco sauce, spoon it onto tortillas and roll them up like a burrito.

Mac and Cheese Tuna Casserole

This dish is so easy to fix, and the flavor is better than any tuna helper I've ever tried. It was a staple when I was in college since a box of macaroni and cheese and a can of tuna cost so little.

—Suzanne Zick, Osceola, Arkansas

1 **package (7-1/4 ounces) macaroni and cheese**
1 **can (10-3/4 ounces) condensed cream of celery soup, undiluted**
1 **can (6 ounces) tuna, drained and flaked**
1/2 **cup milk**
1 **cup (4 ounces) shredded cheddar cheese**
Minced fresh parsley, optional

Prepare macaroni and cheese according to package directions. Stir in soup, tuna and milk. Pour into a greased 2-qt. baking dish. Sprinkle with cheese and parsley if desired. Bake, uncovered, at 350° for 20 minutes or until cheese is melted. **Yield:** 4 servings.

Sausage Spaghetti Spirals

My family loves this flavorful casserole with hearty chunks of sausage and green pepper. The recipe makes a big pan, so it's nicely sized for a potluck.
—Carol Carlton
Wheaton, Illinois

✓ Uses less fat, sugar or salt. Includes Nutritional Analysis and Diabetic Exchanges.

1 pound bulk Italian sausage
1 medium green pepper, chopped
5 cups spiral pasta, cooked and drained
1 jar (28 ounces) meatless spaghetti sauce
1-1/2 cups (6 ounces) shredded mozzarella cheese

In a skillet, cook sausage and green pepper over medium heat until meat is no longer pink; drain. Stir in pasta and spaghetti sauce; mix well.

Transfer to a greased 13-in. x 9-in. x 2-in. baking dish. Cover and bake at 350° for 25 minutes. Uncover; sprinkle with cheese. Bake 5-10 minutes longer or until the cheese is melted. **Yield:** 10 servings.

Nutritional Analysis: One 1-cup serving (prepared with turkey Italian sausage and reduced-fat mozzarella) equals 249 calories, 8 g fat (3 g saturated fat), 34 mg cholesterol, 710 mg sodium, 28 g carbohydrate, 2 g fiber, 16 g protein. **Diabetic Exchanges:** 2 starch, 1-1/2 lean meat.

Savory Roast Chicken

Brushing the bird with a savory-seasoned butter makes the meat nice and moist. This roasted chicken is so easy to make and tastes so delicious!
—Connie Moore, Medway, Ohio

1 broiler/fryer chicken (2-1/2 to 3 pounds)
2 tablespoons butter, melted
3 tablespoons lemon juice
1 tablespoon minced fresh savory *or* 1 teaspoon dried savory

Place chicken, breast side up, on a rack in a shallow roasting pan. Combine butter, lemon juice and savory; brush over chicken. Bake, uncovered, at 375° for 1-1/2 hours or until juices run clear, basting occasionally with the pan drippings. **Yield:** 4 servings.

|"SPRING" CHICKEN| As with any poultry, the younger the chicken, the more tender it is. Younger chickens, including broiler/fryers, are best cooked with dry-heat methods like baking, frying, roasting and grilling.

Breakfast Skewers

These brown 'n' serve sausage kabobs are fun, different and delicious. Plus, any egg dish goes well with them.
—*Bobi Raab, St. Paul, Minnesota*

1 package (7 ounces) brown 'n' serve sausage links
1 can (20 ounces) pineapple chunks, drained
10 medium fresh mushrooms
2 tablespoons butter, melted
Maple syrup

Cut sausages in half; alternately thread sausages, pineapple and mushrooms onto metal or soaked bamboo skewers. Brush with butter and syrup.

Grill, uncovered, over medium-hot heat, turning and basting with syrup, for 8 minutes or until sausages are lightly browned and fruit is heated through. **Yield:** 5 servings.

|ANOTHER EYE-OPENER| Turn plain smoked sausage into a breakfast treat by wrapping each slice with half of a bacon strip. Secure it with a toothpick, then place in a baking dish and sprinkle with brown sugar. Bake at 350° for 1 hour.

Salsa Fish

My family loves outdoor activities, especially fishing. I give their catch of the day some unexpected zip with salsa. It dresses up these golden crumb-coated fillets and keeps them moist and tender.
—*Diane Grajewski, North Branch, Michigan*

2 pounds fish fillets (walleye, bass *or* perch)
1 cup seasoned bread crumbs
1 tablespoon vegetable oil
1-1/2 cups salsa
8 ounces shredded *or* sliced mozzarella *or* provolone cheese

Coat fish fillets in bread crumbs. In a skillet, brown fillets in oil. Arrange in a greased 13-in. x 9-in. x 2-in. baking dish. Top with salsa and cheese.

Bake, uncovered, at 400° for 7-10 minutes or until the fish flakes easily with a fork and the cheese is melted. **Yield:** 6 servings.

Turkey Asparagus Casserole

It takes just minutes to assemble this creamy casserole filled with tender turkey. Convenient frozen asparagus lends bright color and garden flavor while a sprinkling of french-fried onion rings provides a yummy crunch.

—*Cheryl Schut, Grand Rapids, Michigan*

    1 package (8 ounces) frozen chopped asparagus
    2 cups cubed cooked turkey
    1 can (10-3/4 ounces) condensed cream of chicken soup, undiluted
1/4 cup water
    1 can (2.8 ounces) french-fried onions

In a small saucepan, cook asparagus in a small amount of water for 2 minutes; drain. Place in a greased 11-in. x 7-in. x 2-in. baking dish. Top with turkey. Combine soup and water; spoon over turkey.

Bake, uncovered, at 350° for 25-30 minutes. Sprinkle with onions. Bake 5 minutes longer or until golden brown. **Yield:** 4 servings.

Editor's Note: Out of turkey? Cooked chicken can be substituted measure-for-measure in this recipe.

French Bread Pizza

This pizza is a great change of pace. It's soft...easy to chew...and just plain fun to eat—the kids feel like they are each getting their own personal pizza. For a garden pizza, cover it with your favorite vegetables in place of the ground beef.

—*Sue McLaughlin, Onawa, Iowa*

1/2 pound ground beef
    1 can (16 ounces) pizza sauce
    1 jar (8 ounces) sliced mushrooms, drained
    1 loaf (1 pound) French bread
    2 cups (8 ounces) shredded mozzarella cheese

In a medium skillet, cook beef over medium heat until no longer pink; drain. Stir in pizza sauce and mushrooms; set aside. Cut bread in half lengthwise, then into eight pieces.

Spread meat sauce on bread; place on a greased baking sheet. Sprinkle with mozzarella. Bake, uncovered, at 400° for 10 minutes or until cheese is melted and bubbly. **Yield:** 6-8 servings.

Sesame Ginger Chicken

Why grill plain chicken breasts when a simple ginger-honey basting sauce can make them extra special? This tempting chicken is a wonderful summer main dish since it's quick and light. We love it.

—Nancy Johnson
Connersville, Indiana

2 tablespoons soy sauce
2 tablespoons honey
1 tablespoon sesame seeds, toasted
1/2 teaspoon ground ginger
4 boneless skinless chicken breast halves
2 green onions with tops, cut into thin strips, optional

In a small bowl, combine the first four ingredients; set aside. Pound the chicken breasts to 1/4-in. thickness. Grill over medium-hot heat, turning and basting frequently with soy sauce mixture, for 8 minutes or until juices run clear. Garnish with onions if desired. **Yield:** 4 servings.

Saucy Spareribs

My husband likes spareribs, so when my mom gave me this stovetop recipe, I knew I had to try it. He loves the tender ribs and barbecue sauce.
—Melanie Sanders, Kaysville, Utah

2 pounds pork spareribs
2 cans (12 ounces *each*) cola
1 cup ketchup
2 tablespoons cornstarch
2 tablespoons cold water

In a large nonstick skillet, brown the ribs; drain. Add the cola and ketchup; cover and simmer for 1 hour or until the meat is tender.

Remove ribs and keep warm. Transfer 2 cups of sauce to a saucepan. Bring to a boil. In a small bowl, combine the cornstarch and cold water; stir into sauce. Bring to a boil; cook for 1-2 minutes or until thickened. Serve over the ribs. **Yield:** 2 servings.

|TAKE IT SLOW| Saucy Spareribs also could be prepared in the slow cooker. Just combine all of the ingredients, set the slow cooker to low and let the ribs cook for 4 to 6 hours.

Honey–Mustard Chicken

I get bored with the same old chicken, so I came up with this simple recipe. The coating adds fast flavor to tender chicken cooked on the stovetop.
—*Laura Theofilis*
Leonardtown, Maryland

✓ **Uses less fat, sugar or salt. Includes Nutritional Analysis and Diabetic Exchanges.**

4 boneless skinless chicken breast halves (1 pound)
1 cup dry bread crumbs
1 teaspoon plus 2 tablespoons Dijon mustard, *divided*
3 tablespoons honey
2 tablespoons butter

Flatten chicken to 1/4-in. thickness. In a shallow bowl, combine bread crumbs and 1 teaspoon of mustard. In another shallow bowl, combine honey and remaining mustard. Dip chicken in honey-mustard mixture, then coat with crumbs.

In a nonstick skillet over medium heat, cook chicken in butter on both sides until juices run clear, about 8 minutes. **Yield:** 4 servings.

Nutritional Analysis: One serving (prepared with reduced-fat margarine) equals 338 calories, 583 mg sodium, 73 mg cholesterol, 34 g carbohydrate, 31 g protein, 9 g fat, 1 g fiber. **Diabetic Exchanges:** 4 very lean meat, 2 starch, 1 fat.

Pineapple Ham Bake

Brunch is a great meal to mark special occasions. At our house, we've celebrated birthdays, confirmations and graduations with a favorite mid-morning menu. I found Pineapple Ham Bake in a church cookbook from my grandfather's hometown. It's simple to fix, and the tangy pineapple flavor goes well with the casserole.
—*Patricia Throlson, Hawick, Minnesota*

2 cans (8 ounces *each*) crushed pineapple, undrained
2/3 cup packed brown sugar
1 tablespoon vinegar
2 teaspoons ground mustard
1 pound fully cooked ham, cut into bite-size pieces

Combine the first four ingredients in an ungreased 2-qt. baking dish; mix well. Stir in ham. Bake, uncovered, at 350° for 30-40 minutes or until heated through. Serve with a slotted spoon. **Yield:** 8 servings.

Mini Sausage Pizzas

I dress up English muffins with sausage and cheese to make these handheld breakfast pizzas. My husband and son really enjoy them in the morning. —*Janice Garvert, Plainville, Kansas*

1 pound bulk pork sausage
2 jars (5 ounces *each*) sharp American cheese spread
1/4 cup butter, softened
1/8 to 1/4 teaspoon cayenne pepper
12 English muffins, split

In a large skillet, cook sausage over medium heat until no longer pink; drain well. In a small mixing bowl, beat the cheese, butter and pepper. Stir in the sausage. Spread on cut sides of muffins.

Wrap individually and freeze for up to 2 months. Or place on a baking sheet and bake at 425° for 8-10 minutes or until golden brown.

To use frozen pizzas: Unwrap and place on a baking sheet. Bake at 425° for 10-15 minutes or until golden brown. **Yield:** 2 dozen.

Italian Flank Steak

Savory and satisfying, this flank steak is nice for entertaining or busy days since it marinates overnight and grills in minutes. Leftovers, if there are any, make super sandwiches the next day.
—*Walajean Saglett, Canandaigua, New York*

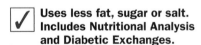 **Uses less fat, sugar or salt. Includes Nutritional Analysis and Diabetic Exchanges.**

2 envelopes (.7 ounce *each*) fat-free Italian salad dressing mix
2 tablespoons vegetable oil
1 tablespoon lemon juice
1 flank steak (1 pound)

Combine salad dressing mix, oil and lemon juice. Brush onto both sides of steak; place in a shallow dish. Cover and refrigerate several hours or overnight.

Grill over hot heat for 4 minutes per side for medium, 5 minutes per side for medium-well or until desired doneness is reached (for rare, a meat thermometer should read 140°; medium, 160°; well-done 170°). **Yield:** 4 servings.

Nutritional Analysis: One serving equals 267 calories, 793 mg sodium, 59 mg cholesterol, 8 g carbohydrate, 24 g protein, 16 g fat. **Diabetic Exchanges:** 3 meat, 1/2 starch.

Dijon Chicken Kabobs

People are always asking for the recipe for these tangy, juicy chicken kabobs. They're a fun and festive way to bake chicken.
—*Earleen Lillegard, Prescott, Arizona*

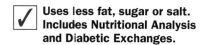
Uses less fat, sugar or salt. Includes Nutritional Analysis and Diabetic Exchanges.

1/2 cup Dijon mustard
1 tablespoon finely chopped green onion
2 cups fresh bread crumbs
1/4 cup minced fresh parsley
1-1/4 pounds boneless skinless chicken breasts, cut into 3/4-inch chunks

In a bowl, combine mustard and onion. In another bowl, combine bread crumbs and parsley. Toss chicken in mustard mixture, then coat evenly with crumb mixture. Line a baking sheet with foil; coat the foil with nonstick cooking spray.

Thread chicken onto metal or soaked wooden skewers, leaving a small space between chunks. Place on the prepared baking sheet. Bake, uncovered, at 450° for 6-8 minutes or until juices run clear. **Yield:** 5 servings.

Nutritional Analysis: One serving equals 222 calories, 762 mg sodium, 73 mg cholesterol, 12 g carbohydrate, 30 g protein, 6 g fat. **Diabetic Exchanges:** 4 very lean meat, 1 starch.

Ribs with Plum Sauce

I found the recipe for this tangy-sweet basting sauce when a surplus of plums sent me searching for new ideas to use all the fruit. In summer, I like to finish the ribs on the grill, brushing on the sauce, after first baking them in the oven.
—*Marie Hoyer*
Hodgenville, Kentucky

5 to 6 pounds pork spareribs
3/4 cup soy sauce
3/4 cup plum jam *or* apricot preserves
3/4 cup honey
2 to 3 garlic cloves, minced

Cut ribs into serving-size pieces; place with bone side down on a rack in a shallow roasting pan. Cover and bake at 350° for 1 hour or until ribs are tender; drain.

Combine remaining ingredients; brush some of the sauce over ribs. Bake at 350° or grill over medium heat, uncovered, for 30 minutes, brushing occasionally with sauce. **Yield:** 6 servings.

Green Chili Burritos

My husband and I love Mexican food, so I usually have the ingredients for these tasy burritos on hand. A woman in our congregation shared the recipe. They soon became a fast favorite in our home, and when I serve them at church potlucks, they disappear quickly.

—Kathy Ybarra
Rock Springs, Wyoming

1 can (16 ounces) refried beans
8 flour tortillas (6 inches)
1/2 pound ground beef, cooked and drained
1 cup (4 ounces) shredded sharp cheddar cheese, *divided*
1 can (4-1/2 ounces) chopped green chilies

Spread refried beans over tortillas. Top each with beef and 2 tablespoons of cheese. Fold ends and sides over filling and roll up; place seam side down in a greased 13-in. x 9-in. x 2-in. baking dish.

Sprinkle with chilies and remaining cheese. Bake, uncovered, at 350° for 20 minutes or until heated through. **Yield:** 4 servings.

Oven Swiss Steak

There's no need to brown the steak first, so you can get this main course into the oven in short order. The fork-tender results are sure to remind you of Swiss steak Grandma used to make, with lots of sauce left over for dipping.
—Sue Call, Beech Grove, Indiana

 Uses less fat, sugar or salt. Includes Nutritional Analysis and Diabetic Exchanges.

2 pounds boneless round steak (1/2 inch thick)
1/4 teaspoon pepper
1 medium onion, thinly sliced
1 can (4 ounces) mushroom stems and pieces, drained
1 can (8 ounces) no-salt-added tomato sauce
Hot cooked noodles, optional

Trim beef; cut into serving-size pieces. Place in a greased 13-in. x 9-in. x 2-in. baking dish. Sprinkle with pepper. Top with the onion, mushrooms and tomato sauce.

Cover and bake at 325° for 1-3/4 to 2 hours or until meat is tender. Serve over noodles if desired. **Yield:** 8 servings.

Nutritional Analysis: One serving (calculated without noodles) equals 209 calories, 112 mg sodium, 68 mg cholesterol, 4 g carbohydrate, 26 g protein, 10 g fat. **Diabetic Exchanges:** 3 lean meat, 1 vegetable.

Sunday Chicken and Stuffing

This hearty entree is a surefire family pleaser. It's easy to prepare because you don't have to brown the chicken. Plus, it looks so nice you can serve it to company.   —Charlotte Kidd, Lagrange, Ohio

- 1 package (6 ounces) instant chicken stuffing mix
- 6 boneless skinless chicken breast halves
- 1 can (10-3/4 ounces) condensed cream of chicken soup, undiluted
- 1/3 cup milk
- 1 tablespoon dried parsley flakes

Prepare stuffing according to package directions; spoon down the center of a greased 13-in. x 9-in. x 2-in. baking dish. Place chicken around stuffing. Combine soup, milk and parsley; pour over chicken.

Cover and bake at 400° for 20 minutes. Uncover and bake 10-15 minutes longer or until chicken juices run clear. **Yield:** 6 servings.

Turkey Tenderloin Supreme

We're a busy hockey and figure skating family, so we're always on the go. Served over rice, this fast skillet supper makes a good home-cooked meal when there's little time.

—Nancy Levin
Chesterfield, Missouri

✓ **Uses less fat, sugar or salt. Includes Nutritional Analysis and Diabetic Exchanges.**

- 6 turkey breast tenderloin slices (3/4 inch thick and 4 ounces *each*)
- 1 tablespoon butter
- 3 green onions, thinly sliced
- 1 can (10-3/4 ounces) condensed cream of chicken soup, undiluted
- 1/4 cup water

In a large skillet, brown turkey in butter. Add onions; cook for 1-2 minutes. Combine soup and water; pour over turkey. Bring to a boil. Reduce heat; cover and simmer for 8-10 minutes or until meat juices run clear. **Yield:** 6 servings.

Nutritional Analysis: One serving (prepared with reduced-fat margarine and reduced-fat soup) equals 175 calories, 264 mg sodium, 81 mg cholesterol, 5 g carbohydrate, 26 g protein, 5 g fat. **Diabetic Exchanges:** 3 very lean meat, 1 vegetable, 1 fruit.

Duck with Cherry Sauce

My mom prepared this golden tender roast duck often for Sunday dinner when I was growing up. It was one of my dad's favorite meals. The cheery cherry sauce stirs up easily and makes this main dish doubly delightful.
—Sandy Jenkins
Elkhorn, Wisconsin

1 domestic duckling (4 to 5 pounds)
1 jar (12 ounces) cherry preserves
1 to 2 tablespoons red wine vinegar
Bing cherries, star fruit and kale, optional

Prick skin of duckling and place, breast side up, on a rack in a shallow roasting pan. Tie drumsticks together. Bake, uncovered, at 325° for 2 hours or until juices run clear and a meat thermometer reads 180°. (Drain fat from pan as it accumulates.) Cover; let stand for 20 minutes before carving.

Meanwhile, for sauce, combine preserves and vinegar in a small saucepan. Cook and stir over medium heat until heated through. Serve with duck. Garnish platter with fruit and kale if desired. **Yield:** 4-5 servings.

Easy and Elegant Ham

I fix this moist, tender ham to serve my large family. It can be readied quickly in the morning, frees up my oven, tastes outstanding and can feed a crowd. Covered with colorful pineapple slices, cherries and orange glaze, its showstopping appearance appeals to all. —Denise DiPace, Medford, New Jersey

2 cans (20 ounces *each*) sliced pineapple
1 fully cooked boneless ham (about 6 pounds), halved
1 jar (6 ounces) maraschino cherries, well drained
1 jar (12 ounces) orange marmalade

Drain pineapple, reserving juice; set juice aside. Place half of the pineapple in an ungreased 5-qt. slow cooker. Top with the ham. Add cherries, remaining pineapple and reserved pineapple juice. Spoon marmalade over ham. Cover and cook on low for 6-7 hours or until heated through.

Remove to a warm serving platter. Let stand for 10-15 minutes before slicing. Serve pineapple and cherries with sliced ham. **Yield:** 18-20 servings.

Spaghetti Carbonara

This is a swift and yummy recipe that I received from a dear friend. My family asks for it often and I'm always happy to oblige.
—*Roni Goodell, Spanish Fork, Utah*

1 package (7 ounces) thin spaghetti
10 bacon strips, diced
1/3 cup butter
2 eggs, lightly beaten
3/4 cup grated Parmesan cheese

Cook spaghetti according to package directions. Meanwhile, in a skillet, cook bacon over medium heat until crisp; drain on paper towels. Add butter to drippings; heat until melted.

Drain spaghetti; toss with eggs and Parmesan cheese. Add to skillet; cook and stir over medium heat for 3-4 minutes or until eggs are set. Sprinkle with bacon. **Yield:** 3-4 servings.

Green 'n' Gold Egg Bake

I need just five ingredients to assemble this pretty casserole. The firm squares have a delicious spinach flavor that's welcome at breakfast or dinner.
—*Muriel Paceleo Montgomery, New York*

 Uses less fat, sugar or salt. Includes Nutritional Analysis and Diabetic Exchanges.

1 cup seasoned bread crumbs, *divided*
2 packages (10 ounces *each*) frozen chopped spinach, thawed and squeezed dry
3 cups (24 ounces) small-curd cottage cheese
1/2 cup grated Romano *or* Parmesan cheese
5 eggs

Sprinkle 1/4 cup bread crumbs into a greased 8-in. square baking dish. Bake at 350° for 3-5 minutes or until golden brown. In a bowl, combine the spinach, cottage cheese, Romano cheese, three eggs and remaining crumbs. Spread over the baked crumbs. Beat remaining eggs; pour over spinach mixture.

Bake, uncovered, at 350° for 45 minutes or until a knife inserted near the center comes out clean. Let stand for 5-10 minutes before serving. **Yield:** 9 servings.

Nutritional Analysis: One 1/2-cup serving (prepared with fat-free cottage cheese and egg substitute) equals 181 calories, 6 g fat (2 g saturated fat), 127 mg cholesterol, 808 mg sodium, 15 g carbohydrate, 2 g fiber, 18 g protein. **Diabetic Exchanges:** 2 lean meat, 1 starch.

Breaded Pork Chops

No matter how busy the day becomes, I strongly believe everyone should sit down together at least once around a meal. My brother-in-law invented this recipe, which is a family favorite. Sometimes I'll make the pork chops Italian-style by adding red sauce and more Parmesan cheese.

—*Ann Ingalls*
Gladstone, Missouri

1 cup Italian-seasoned dry bread crumbs
2 tablespoons grated Parmesan cheese
1/3 cup bottled ranch salad dressing
6 pork chops (1/2 inch thick)

Combine bread crumbs and Parmesan cheese in a shallow dish. Place dressing in another shallow dish. Dip pork chops in dressing, then coat in crumb mixture.

Place in an ungreased 13-in. x 9-in. x 2-in. baking pan. Bake, uncovered, at 375° for 25 minutes or until pork is no longer pink. **Yield:** 4-6 servings.

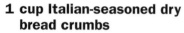 **|PICKING OUT PORK|** When buying pork, look for meat that's pale pink with a small amount of marbling and white fat. If you want succulent chops, choose those that are about 1/2 to 1 inch thick.

Cheeseburger 'n' Fries Casserole

There are only four ingredients in this quick recipe—and you're likely to have them all on hand. Kids love it because, as the name suggests, it combines two of their favorite fast foods.

—*Karen Owen, Rising Sun, Indiana*

2 pounds lean ground beef
1 can (10-3/4 ounces) condensed golden mushroom soup, undiluted
1 can (10-3/4 ounces) condensed cheddar cheese soup, undiluted
1 package (20 ounces) frozen crinkle-cut French fries

In a skillet, cook the beef over medium heat until no longer pink; drain. Stir in soups. Pour into a greased 13-in. x 9-in. x 2-in. baking dish. Arrange French fries on top. Bake, uncovered, at 350° for 50-55 minutes or until the fries are golden brown. **Yield:** 6-8 servings.

Barbecued Chicken Pizza

My pizza starts with a prepared bread shell and barbecue sauce, plus leftover cooked chicken. Then I simply assemble and bake. My daughter, Haley, loves creating smiling pizza "faces" with shredded cheese and fresh veggie toppings.

—Patricia Richardson
Verona, Ontario

1 prebaked Italian bread shell crust (14 ounces)
2/3 cup honey garlic barbecue sauce
1 small red onion, chopped
1 cup cubed cooked chicken
2 cups (8 ounces) shredded mozzarella cheese

Place the crust on a pizza pan. Spread with barbecue sauce; sprinkle with onion, chicken and cheese. Bake at 350° for 10 minutes or until cheese is melted. **Yield:** 4 servings.

|**SERVING ALTERNATIVES**| Cut the pizza into small bite-size pieces and serve it as an appetizer. Or use any thick flat bread for the crust and replace the chicken with round steak.

Pasta with Sausage and Tomatoes

I reach for this recipe whenever I crave spaghetti sauce but don't have the time to make my usual spaghetti and meatballs recipe. This sausage and diced tomatoes blend is fast and very flavorful.

—Michelle Fryer Dommel, Quakertown, Pennsylvania

1 pound bulk Italian sausage
2 cans (16 ounces *each*) diced tomatoes, undrained
1-1/2 teaspoons chopped fresh basil *or* 1/2 teaspoon dried basil
1 package (12 ounces) pasta, cooked and drained

In a skillet, cook sausage over medium heat until no longer pink; drain. Add tomatoes and basil. Simmer, uncovered, for 10 minutes. Serve immediately over pasta. **Yield:** 4 servings.

  Editor's Note: For even more flavor, use cans of diced tomatoes with garlic and onion.

Cheesy Crab Burritos

Everyone who tries this elegant variation on the standard burrito loves it. I'm always asked for the recipe. Serve them with a green salad for a lighter lunch or with traditional rice and beans for supper.

—*Karen Dye, Tempe, Arizona*

1 package (8 ounces)
   cream cheese, softened
2 cups (8 ounces) shredded
   cheddar cheese
1 package (8 ounces)
   imitation crabmeat,
   flaked
8 flour tortillas (10 inches)
Salsa

In a mixing bowl, combine the cream cheese and cheddar cheese. Stir in the crab. Spoon down the center of each tortilla; roll up tightly and place on an ungreased baking sheet. Bake at 350° for 20 minutes or until heated through. Serve with salsa. **Yield:** 4 servings.

Broiled Orange Roughy

The fillets are flaky, moist and mildly flavored. They can be broiled in the oven, but I often cook them on our outdoor grill instead to reduce kitchen cleanup.

—*Judy Bernacki, Las Vegas, Nevada*

 **Uses less fat, sugar or salt.
Includes Nutritional Analysis
and Diabetic Exchanges.**

1-1/2 pounds fresh *or* frozen
   orange roughy, red
   snapper *or* haddock
   fillets, thawed
1 teaspoon garlic powder
1/4 cup butter, melted
1/4 cup lemon juice
1/4 cup soy sauce
Paprika, optional

Place fillets in a shallow dish; sprinkle with garlic powder. Combine butter, lemon juice and soy sauce; pour over fish and turn. Marinate for 10 minutes.

Drain and discard marinade. Place fillets on a broiler pan. Broil 3-4 in. from the heat for 10 minutes or until fish flakes easily with a fork, turning once. Sprinkle with paprika. **Yield:** 4 servings.

Nutritional Analysis: One serving (prepared with orange roughy and reduced-sodium soy sauce) equals 189 calories, 7 g fat (4 g saturated fat), 50 mg cholesterol, 489 mg sodium, 5 g carbohydrate, trace fiber, 26 g protein. **Diabetic Exchanges:** 4 very lean meat, 1 fat.

Pesto Chicken Penne

A convenient pesto sauce mix provides the pleasant basil flavor in this simple chicken and pasta combination. This entree requires little effort, yet seems elegant.

—Beth Martin Sine
Faulkner, Maryland

8 ounces penne *or any medium pasta*
1 envelope pesto sauce mix
3/4 cup milk
1/4 cup olive oil
2 cups cubed cooked chicken *or turkey*
Shredded Parmesan cheese, optional

Cook the pasta according to package directions. Meanwhile, in a large saucepan, whisk together the pesto mix, milk and oil. Bring to a boil. Reduce heat; simmer, uncovered, for 5 minutes.

Add chicken; heat through. Drain pasta. Add to the sauce and toss to coat. Sprinkle with Parmesan cheese if desired. **Yield:** 4-6 servings.

Mock Lobster

My family loves when I serve Mock Lobster with macaroni and cheese or coleslaw. For a change of taste, you can substitute your favorite seafood sauce for the melted butter.

—Gloria Jarrett, Loveland, Ohio

1-1/2 to 2 pounds frozen cod *or* haddock fillets, partially thawed
1-1/2 teaspoons salt
2 teaspoons seafood seasoning *or* paprika
3 tablespoons vinegar
Melted butter

Cut fillets into 2-in. x 2-in. pieces; place in a skillet. Cover with water. Add salt and seafood seasoning; bring to a boil. Reduce heat; simmer, uncovered, for 10 minutes. Drain.

Cover with cold water. Add vinegar and bring to a boil. Reduce heat; simmer, uncovered, for 10 minutes. Drain. Serve with melted butter. **Yield:** 4-6 servings.

Garlic Rosemary Turkey

The house smells so good while this turkey is cooking that my family can hardly wait until it's done! This is a beautiful, succulent main dish that deliciously serves a crowd.

—*Cathy Dobbins*
Rio Rancho, New Mexico

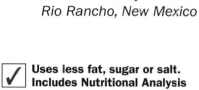 Uses less fat, sugar or salt. Includes Nutritional Analysis and Diabetic Exchanges.

1 whole turkey (10 to 12 pounds)
6 to 8 garlic cloves
2 large lemons, halved
2 teaspoons dried rosemary, crushed
1 teaspoon rubbed sage
Gravy, optional

Cut six to eight small slits in turkey skin; insert garlic between the skin and meat. Squeeze two lemon halves inside the turkey and leave them inside. Squeeze remaining lemon over outside of turkey. Spray the turkey with nonstick cooking spray; sprinkle with rosemary and sage.

Place on a rack in a roasting pan. Bake, uncovered, at 325° for 1 hour. Cover and bake 2-1/2 to 3-1/2 hours longer or until a meat thermometer reads 185°. Serve with gravy if desired. **Yield:** 8-10 servings.

Nutritional Analysis: One serving (4 ounces of white meat without skin; calculated without gravy) equals 144 calories, 57 mg sodium, 88 mg cholesterol, trace carbohydrate, 31 g protein, 1 g fat. **Diabetic Exchange:** 4 very lean meat.

Tender Pork Roast

This is a melt-in-your-mouth, fall-apart-tender pork roast. It's wonderful to serve to company because it never fails to please.
—*LuVerne Peterson, Minneapolis, Minnesota*

1 boneless pork roast (about 3 pounds)
1 can (8 ounces) tomato sauce
3/4 cup soy sauce
1/2 cup sugar
2 teaspoons ground mustard

Cut roast in half; place in a 5-qt. slow cooker. Combine remaining ingredients; pour over roast. Cover and cook on low for 8-9 hours or until a meat thermometer reads 160°-170°. Remove roast to a serving platter and keep warm. If desired, skim fat from pan juices and thicken for gravy. **Yield:** 8 servings.

|TESTING FOR DONENESS| The best way to test a pork roast's doneness is with a meat thermometer. Cutting into it to see if it's still pink lets too many of the juices run out.

Taco Dogs

A taco shell makes a good holder for a hot dog dressed up with a tasty combination of baked beans and cheese...and holds up better than a plain bun. When our children were young, they asked for this meal at least once a week. I was always happy to make it for them because it goes from start to the supper table in less than 30 minutes.

—*Kat Thompson, Prineville, Oregon*

1 package (1 pound) hot dogs
10 slices process American cheese
10 hard taco shells, warmed
1 can (16 ounces) baked beans, warmed

Prepare hot dogs according to package directions. Place a cheese slice and hot dog in each taco shell; top with beans. **Yield:** 10 tacos.

Sweet–Sour Chicken Casserole

Apricot preserves give a different twist to this saucy sweet-and-sour chicken. It's a snap to stir up and serve over rice.

—*Melanie May, Fishers, Indiana*

 Uses less fat, sugar or salt. Includes Nutritional Analysis and Diabetic Exchanges.

2 cups cubed cooked chicken
1 can (20 ounces) unsweetened pineapple chunks, drained
1 jar (12 ounces) apricot preserves *or* spreadable fruit
1 can (10-3/4 ounces) condensed cream of chicken soup, undiluted
1 can (8 ounces) water chestnuts, drained
Hot cooked rice, optional

In a bowl, combine the first five ingredients. Transfer to a greased 2-qt. baking dish. Bake, uncovered, at 350° for 30 minutes or until heated through. Serve over rice if desired. **Yield:** 6 servings.

Nutritional Analysis: One serving (prepared with reduced-fat soup and spreadable fruit; calculated without rice) equals 259 calories, 413 mg sodium, 44 mg cholesterol, 41 g carbohydrate, 16 g protein, 3 g fat, 3 g fiber. **Diabetic Exchanges:** 2 lean meat, 2 fruit, 1/2 vegetable.

Golden Game Hens

I served game hens at a diplomatic dinner when my wife, Ruth, was the defense attaché at the American Embassy in Budapest, Hungary. They were an appealing choice because they filled a plate and garnered many fine comments.
—*Andy Anderson, Graham, Washington*

6 **Cornish game hens (20 ounces** *each***)**
1 **medium tart apple, sliced**
1 **medium onion, sliced**
1/4 **cup butter, melted**
1/4 **cup soy sauce**

Loosely stuff hens with apple and onion. Place on a rack in a shallow baking pan. Combine butter and soy sauce; brush over hens.

Bake, uncovered, at 350° for 50-60 minutes or until a meat thermometer reads 165° and juices run clear, basting occasionally. **Yield:** 6 servings.

|GAME HEN FACTS| Cornish game hens are a cross between Cornish and White Rock chickens and typically weigh 1-1/2 pounds or less. They look elegant, have tender white meat and take less time to prepare than a whole chicken.

Mexicali Pork Chops

These fast and tender pork chops are ready to serve in about 10 minutes! They get their zippy flavor from a packet of taco seasoning. Spoon salsa over the top for even more flavor.
—*Laura Cohen*
Eau Claire, Wisconsin

1 **envelope taco seasoning**
4 **boneless pork loin chops (1/2 inch thick)**
1 **tablespoon vegetable oil**
Salsa

Rub taco seasoning over pork chops. In a skillet, cook chops in oil over medium-high heat until meat is no longer pink and juices run clear, about 9 minutes. Serve with salsa. **Yield:** 4 servings.

Barbecue Beef Patties

I frequently fix these family-pleasing patties that taste like individual meat loaves. Barbecue sauce brushed on top gives them fast flavor.
—*Marlene Harguth, Maynard, Minnesota*

1 egg
1/2 cup barbecue sauce, *divided*
3/4 cup crushed cornflakes
1/2 to 1 teaspoon salt
1 pound ground beef

In a bowl, combine egg, 1/4 cup barbecue sauce, cornflake crumbs and salt. Add beef and mix well. Shape into four oval patties, about 3/4 in. thick. Place in a greased 11-in. x 7-in. x 2-in. baking pan. Spread with remaining barbecue sauce.

Bake, uncovered, at 375° for 25-30 minutes or until meat is no longer pink and a meat thermometer reads 160°; drain. **Yield:** 4 servings.

Chicken Nugget Casserole

Youngsters will need just five ingredients to help prepare this easy entree. Our kids love to eat chicken nuggets this way. It's a satisfying supper with spaghetti and a salad.
—*Tylene Loar, Mesa, Arizona*

1 package (13-1/2 ounces) frozen chicken nuggets
1/3 cup grated Parmesan cheese
1 can (26-1/2 ounces) spaghetti sauce
1 cup (4 ounces) shredded mozzarella cheese
1 teaspoon Italian seasoning

Place chicken nuggets in a greased 11-in. x 7-in. x 2-in. baking dish. Sprinkle with Parmesan cheese. Top with spaghetti sauce, mozzarella cheese and Italian seasoning.

Cover and bake at 350° for 30-35 minutes or until chicken is heated through and cheese is melted. **Yield:** 4-6 servings.

Bean Burritos

My husband and I have two sons. With our demanding careers, main dishes like this one that can be prepared in a flash are essential for us. I always have the ingredients for this recipe on hand. Cooking the rice and shredding the cheese the night before save precious minutes at dinnertime.

—Beth Osborne Skinner
Bristol, Tennessee

1 can (16 ounces) refried beans
1 cup salsa
1 cup cooked long grain rice
2 cups (8 ounces) shredded cheddar cheese, *divided*
12 flour tortillas (6 to 7 inches)

In a bowl, combine the beans, salsa, rice and 1 cup cheese. Spoon about 1/3 cup off-center on each tortilla. Fold the sides and ends over filling and roll up.

Arrange burritos in a greased 13-in. x 9-in. x 2-in. baking dish. Sprinkle with the remaining cheese. Cover and bake at 375° for 20-25 minutes or until heated through. **Yield:** 1 dozen.

Potato Sloppy Joe Bake

I created this speedy sensation while racing against the clock one day. I needed a quick meal that was low on ingredients but high on taste, so I came up with this hearty casserole.

—Ruth Chiarenza, Cumberland, Maryland

1 pound ground beef
1 can (15-1/2 ounces) sloppy joe sauce
1 can (10-3/4 ounces) condensed cream of potato soup, undiluted
1 package (32 ounces) frozen cubed hash brown potatoes, thawed
1 cup (4 ounces) shredded cheddar cheese

In a skillet, cook beef over medium heat until no longer pink; drain. Add sloppy joe sauce and soup. Place hash browns in a greased 13-in. x 9-in. x 2-in. baking dish. Top with beef mixture.

Cover and bake at 450° for 20 minutes. Uncover; bake 10 minutes longer or until heated through. Sprinkle with cheese. **Yield:** 6-8 servings.

Soups & Sandwiches

Fast Fiesta Soup, p. 124

Chuck Wagon Burgers, p. 129

Cucumber Sandwiches

I was introduced to a similar sandwich by a friend many years ago. I sometimes add thinly sliced onions for a change of pace. Along with fruit salad, it makes a light summer lunch.

—*Karen Schriefer, Stevensville, Maryland*

1 carton (8 ounces) cream cheese spread
2 teaspoons ranch salad dressing mix
12 slices pumpernickel rye bread
2 to 3 medium cucumbers

In a bowl, combine cream cheese and dressing mix. Spread on one side of each slice of bread. Peel cucumbers if desired; thinly slice and place on six slices of bread. Top with remaining bread. Serve immediately. **Yield:** 6 servings.

Cran–Orange Turkey Bagel

I adapted the recipe for this tasty turkey sandwich from a deli where I worked. To make it easier to eat, we often dip each bite into the cranberry mixture instead of spreading it inside. —*Tanya Smeins, Kalamazoo, Michigan*

1 can (11 ounces) mandarin oranges, drained
1 can (16 ounces) whole-berry cranberry sauce
6 tablespoons cream cheese, softened
6 onion bagels *or* flavor of your choice, split and toasted
1 pound thinly sliced cooked turkey

In a bowl, mash mandarin oranges with a fork. Stir in cranberry sauce. Spread cream cheese over the bottom of each bagel; top with turkey and cran-orange sauce. Replace bagel tops. **Yield:** 6 servings.

Editor's Note: Poppy, sesame and wheat bagels are also good choices for these sandwiches.

Cheesy Wild Rice Soup

We often eat easy-to-make soups when there's not a lot of time to cook. I replaced the wild rice requested in the original recipe with a boxed rice mix. This creamy concoction is now a family favorite.

—Lisa Hofer
Hitchcock, South Dakota

1 package (6 ounces) quick-cooking long grain and wild rice mix
4 cups milk
1 can (10-3/4 ounces) condensed cream of potato soup, undiluted
8 ounces process cheese (Velveeta), cubed
1/2 pound sliced bacon, cooked and crumbled

In a large saucepan, prepare rice according to package directions. Stir in milk, soup and cheese; mix well. Cook and stir until cheese is melted. Garnish with bacon. **Yield:** 6-8 servings.

Buffalo Chicken Wing Soup

My husband and I love buffalo chicken wings, so we created a soup with the same zippy flavor. It's very popular with guests. Start with a small amount of hot sauce, then add more if needed to suit your family's tastes.

—Pat Farmer, Falconer, New York

6 cups milk
3 cans (10-3/4 ounces each) condensed cream of chicken soup, undiluted
3 cups shredded cooked chicken (about 1 pound)
1 cup (8 ounces) sour cream
1/4 to 1/2 cup hot pepper sauce

Combine all ingredients in a slow cooker. Cover and cook on low for 4-5 hours. **Yield:** 8 servings (2 quarts).

|SHREDDING MEAT| To shred beef, pork or chicken for sandwiches or soups, place it in a shallow pan. Then simply pull the meat into thin shreds using two forks.

Oven–Baked Burgers

A seasoned coating mix and steak sauce dress up these hamburgers that cook in the oven rather than on the grill. I like to use a sweet and spicy steak sauce for the best flavor.
—*Mike Goldman*
Arden Hills, Minnesota

1/4 cup steak sauce
2 tablespoons plus 1/3 cup Shake'n Bake seasoned coating mix, *divided*
1 pound ground beef
4 hamburger buns, split
4 lettuce leaves

In a bowl, combine the steak sauce and 2 tablespoons of coating mix. Crumble beef over mixture and mix until combined. Shape into four 3-1/2-in. patties. Dip both sides of patties in remaining coating.

Place on an ungreased baking sheet. Bake at 350° for 20 minutes or until no longer pink, turning once. Serve on buns with lettuce. **Yield:** 4 servings.

|SHAPING HAMBURGER PATTIES| Use a 1/2-cup measuring cup or ice cream scoop to make equal size patties. Gently form each portion into a patty. For moist light-textured burgers, be careful not to over-mix or over-handle the meat mixture.

Quick Pea Soup

This brightly colored, fresh-tasting soup is one of our daughter's favorites. She purees it in the blender in just seconds, then "zaps" a mugful in the microwave until heated through.   —*Paula Zsiray*
Logan, Utah

 Uses less fat, sugar or salt. Includes Nutritional Analysis and Diabetic Exchanges.

1-1/2 cups frozen peas, thawed
1-1/4 cups milk, *divided*
1/4 teaspoon salt, optional
1/8 teaspoon pepper

Place the peas and 1/4 cup of milk in a blender; cover and process until pureed. Pour into a saucepan; add salt if desired, pepper and remaining milk. Cook and stir for 5 minutes or until heated through. **Yield:** 2 servings.

Nutritional Analysis: One 1-cup serving (prepared with fat-free milk and without salt) equals 137 calories, 200 mg sodium, 3 mg cholesterol, 22 g carbohydrate, 11 g protein, 1 g fat. **Diabetic Exchanges:** 1 starch, 1 skim milk.

Hot Ham 'n' Swiss

I've been preparing these versatile open-faced sandwiches for more than 20 years for different occasions and mealtimes. They're a special beginning to a cozy Sunday brunch.   —Debbie Petrun
Smithfield, Pennsylvania

5 eggs
8 slices Italian bread
  (3/4 inch thick)
1 pound thinly sliced deli
  ham
8 slices Swiss cheese

In a shallow bowl, beat the eggs. Dip both sides of bread in eggs. Cook on a greased hot griddle until lightly browned on both sides. Transfer to a baking sheet; top each slice with ham and cheese. Broil 4 in. from the heat for 5 minutes or until the cheese is melted. **Yield:** 8 servings.

|BROILING BASICS| When a recipe says to "broil 4 inches from the heat", it's referring to the food's surface, not the bottom of the pan. If you measure from the rack on which the pan sits, the food will be too close to the heat and could burn before it cooks through.

Beef Noodle Soup

I take advantage of convenience items to prepare this hearty soup in a hurry. Bowls of the chunky mixture are chock-full of ground beef, ramen noodles and mixed vegetables. —Arlene Lynn, Lincoln, Nebraska

1 pound ground beef
1 can (46 ounces) V8 juice
1 envelope onion soup mix
1 package (3 ounces) beef
  ramen noodles
1 package (16 ounces)
  frozen mixed vegetables

In a large saucepan, cook beef over medium heat until no longer pink; drain. Stir in the V8 juice, soup mix, contents of noodle seasoning packet and mixed vegetables.

Bring to a boil. Reduce heat; simmer, uncovered, for 6 minutes or until vegetables are tender. Return to a boil; stir in noodles. Cook for 3 minutes or until noodles are tender. **Yield:** 8 servings.

Cheesy Beef Buns

These satisfying sandwiches would be great to put together ahead of time and wrap in foil until ready to bake. Warm from the oven, the crispy buns are piled with cheesy slices of roast beef.
—*Marlene Harguth, Maynard, Minnesota*

1 medium onion, chopped
2 tablespoons butter
1 jar (8 ounces) process cheese sauce
1 pound thinly sliced cooked roast beef
6 French *or* Italian sandwich buns, split

In a skillet, saute onion in butter until tender. Stir in cheese sauce until melted. Cook and stir until heated through. Stir in beef until evenly coated.

Spoon onto buns; wrap each in aluminum foil. Bake at 350° for 8-10 minutes or until bread is crispy. **Yield:** 6 servings.

Triple-Decker Salmon Club

You're in for a tasty treat with these deliciously different triple-deckers. Guests love the short-on-time sandwiches. Even those who don't ordinarily like salmon or cottage cheese enjoy them. —*Jane Bone Cape Coral, Florida*

3/4 cup small-curd cottage cheese
1/4 cup dill pickle relish
1 can (6 ounces) salmon, drained, bones and skin removed
1 celery rib, chopped
6 slices bread, toasted
2 lettuce leaves, optional

In a small bowl, combine cottage cheese and pickle relish. In another bowl, combine salmon and celery.

For each sandwich, top one piece of toast with lettuce if desired and half of the cottage cheese mixture. Top with a second piece of toast; spread with half of the salmon mixture. Top with a third piece of toast. Serve immediately. **Yield:** 2 servings.

Applesauce Sandwiches

Cinnamon and sugar spice up these fun sandwiches for breakfast or a snack. Since we have plenty of apple trees, I often use homemade applesauce. But the store-bought kind tastes almost as good.
—Eunice Bralley
Thornville, Ohio

1 cup applesauce
8 slices bread
1/4 cup butter, softened
1 tablespoon sugar
1/4 teaspoon ground cinnamon

Spread the applesauce on four slices of bread; top with remaining bread. Lightly butter the outsides of sandwiches. Toast on a hot griddle for 3-4 minutes on each side or until golden brown. Combine sugar and cinnamon; sprinkle over hot sandwiches. Serve immediately. **Yield:** 4 servings.

|FROM–SCRATCH APPLESAUCE| Quickly make homemade applesauce by combining chunks of apple with a little orange juice, cinnamon and nutmeg in a blender or food processor. Process until mixture reaches the desired texture.

Corny Clam Chowder

Cream gives richness to the canned items that make up this satisfying chowder. I sometimes make it in the slow cooker, so it can simmer while I finish work around the house.
—Karen Johnston
Syracuse, Nebraska

1 can (14-3/4 ounces) cream-style corn
1 can (10-3/4 ounces) condensed cream of potato soup, undiluted
1-1/2 cups half-and-half cream
1 can (6-1/2 ounces) minced clams, drained
6 bacon strips, cooked and crumbled

In a saucepan, combine corn, soup and cream; heat through. Stir in clams; heat through. Garnish with bacon. **Yield:** 4 servings.

Open-Faced Sandwich Supreme

My husband and I first sampled this delicious open-faced sandwich at a restaurant. It seemed so easy, I duplicated it at home. It's also tasty with cheese sauce in place of the hollandaise sauce or asparagus instead of broccoli. *—Phyllis Smith Mariposa, California*

3 cups small broccoli florets
1 envelope hollandaise sauce mix
8 ounces sliced deli turkey
8 ounces sliced deli ham
4 slices sourdough bread, toasted

In a saucepan, cook the broccoli in a small amount of water until tender; drain. Prepare the hollandaise sauce according to package directions. Warm the turkey and ham if desired; layer over the toast. Top with the broccoli and sauce. **Yield:** 4 servings.

Tortellini Soup

This soup is fast to fix, flavorful and good for you. Packaged cheese tortellini meets colorful summer squash, fresh spinach and shredded carrots in every eye-appealing bowl. *—Chris Snyder Boulder, Colorado*

 Uses less fat, sugar or salt. Includes Nutritional Analysis and Diabetic Exchanges.

5 cups chicken broth
3-1/2 cups shredded carrots (about 10 ounces)
1 cup chopped yellow summer squash
3 cups torn fresh spinach
1 package (9 ounces) refrigerated cheese tortellini

In a large saucepan, combine the broth, carrots and squash. Bring to a boil. Reduce heat; simmer, uncovered, for 3 minutes. Stir in spinach and tortellini. Cover and cook for 5 minutes or until the tortellini is heated through. **Yield:** 7 servings.

Nutritional Analysis: One serving (1 cup) equals 160 calories, 3 g fat (2 g saturated fat), 14 mg cholesterol, 806 mg sodium, 24 g carbohydrate, 3 g fiber, 8 g protein. **Diabetic Exchanges:** 2 vegetable, 1 starch.

Creamy Cauliflower Soup

My aunt always made this smooth, rich-tasting soup for me when I came to visit. I could smell it simmering as soon as I arrived. I think of her whenever I have a bowlful.
—*Heather Kasprick*
Keewatin, Ontario

1 medium head cauliflower, broken into florets
2 cans (10-3/4 ounces *each*) condensed cream of chicken soup, undiluted
1 can (10-3/4 ounces) condensed cheddar cheese soup, undiluted
1 can (14-1/2 ounces) chicken broth
2 cups milk

Place cauliflower in a saucepan with 1 in. of water; bring to a boil. Reduce heat; cover and simmer for 5-10 minutes or until crisp-tender.

Meanwhile, in another saucepan, combine soups, broth and milk; heat through. Drain the cauliflower; stir into soup. **Yield:** 9 servings.

Taco Puffs

I got this recipe from a friend years ago and still make these cheesy sandwiches regularly. I serve them for dinner along with a steaming bowl of soup or fresh green salad. Any leftovers taste even better the next day for lunch. A helpful hint: Plain refrigerated biscuits seal together better than buttermilk types. —*Jan Schmid, Hibbing, Minnesota*

1 pound ground beef
1/2 cup chopped onion
1 envelope taco seasoning
2 tubes (16.3 ounces *each*) large refrigerated biscuits
8 ounces cheddar cheese slices *or* 2 cups (8 ounces) shredded cheddar cheese

In a skillet, cook beef and onion over medium heat until beef is no longer pink; drain. Add the taco seasoning and prepare according to package directions. Cool slightly.

Flatten half of the biscuits into 4-in. circles; place in greased 15-in. x 10-in. x 1-in. baking pans. Spoon 1/4 cup meat mixture onto each; top with two cheese slices or 1/4 cup shredded cheese. Flatten the remaining biscuits; place on top and pinch edges to seal tightly. Bake at 400° for 15 minutes or until golden brown. **Yield:** 8 servings.

Hot Dog Sandwiches

These kid-pleasing sandwiches taste just like hot dogs smothered in mustard and relish. Drop the frozen sandwiches in lunch bags before school in the morning. By noon, they'll be thawed and ready to eat.

—*Iola Egle, McCook, Nebraska*

6 hot dogs, minced
1/2 cup dill pickle relish
1/4 cup chili sauce
2 tablespoons prepared mustard
12 slices bread

In a small bowl, combine hot dogs, relish, chili sauce and mustard; mix well. Spread on six slices of bread; top with the remaining bread. Freeze for up to 2 months. Remove sandwiches from the freezer at least 4 hours before serving. **Yield:** 6 servings.

Baked Bean Chili

Who says a good chili has to simmer all day? This zippy chili—with a touch of sweetness from the baked beans—can be made on the spur of the moment. It's an excellent standby when unexpected guests drop in. Served with bread and a salad, it's a hearty dinner everyone raves about.
—*Nancy Wall*
Bakersfield, California

2 pounds ground beef
3 cans (28 ounces *each*) baked beans
1 can (46 ounces) tomato juice
1 can (11-1/2 ounces) V8 juice
1 envelope chili seasoning

In a Dutch oven, cook beef over medium heat until no longer pink; drain. Stir in the remaining ingredients. Bring to a boil. Reduce heat; simmer, uncovered, for 10 minutes. **Yield:** 24 servings.

Zesty Tomato Soup

When some friends stopped by unexpectedly, my husband, Phil, came up with this fast-to-fix soup that tastes home-made. Two easy ingredients give canned soup just the right amount of zip. —*JoAnn Gunio Franklin, North Carolina*

2 cans (10-3/4 ounces *each*) condensed tomato soup, undiluted
2-2/3 cups water
2 teaspoons chili powder
Oyster crackers *or* shredded Monterey Jack cheese, optional

In a saucepan, combine the first three ingredients; heat through. Garnish with crackers or cheese if desired. **Yield:** 4-5 servings.

|SPEEDY SOUP| Create instant soup by combining leftover vegetables with chicken or beef broth in a blender and processing until smooth. For soup in minutes, add chicken or beef broth to leftover rice and stir in some lightly sautéed vegetables. Heat just until warmed through.

Apple Sausage Pitas

This is such a simple recipe, but it's my favorite breakfast for family or company. Filled with sausage and apple slices, the meal-in-hand sandwiches are great to munch on the way to work or school.
—*Michelle Komaroski, Pueblo, Colorado*

1 package (8 ounces) brown-and-serve sausage links, sliced
4 medium tart apples, peeled and thinly sliced
1/4 cup maple syrup
4 pita breads (6 inches), halved

In a skillet, cook sausage and apples until sausage is heated through and apples are tender. Add syrup; heat through. In a microwave, warm pitas on high for 20 seconds. Fill with the sausage mixture. **Yield:** 4 servings.

Wagon Wheel Chili

Youngsters are sure to love the fun shape of the wagon wheel pasta in this zippy chili. It's easy to whip up with canned chili and tomato sauce, so it's great for a hot lunch or quick dinner.
—*Lora Scroggins*
El Dorado, Arkansas

2 cups uncooked wagon wheel *or* spiral pasta
1 can (15 ounces) chili
1 can (8 ounces) tomato sauce
3 tablespoons ketchup
1/2 teaspoon chili powder
Shredded cheddar cheese, optional

Cook pasta according to package directions. Meanwhile, in a large saucepan, combine the chili, tomato sauce, ketchup and chili powder. Mix well; heat through. Drain and rinse pasta; stir into chili. Garnish with cheese if desired. **Yield:** 3-4 servings.

Low-Fat Broccoli Soup

This delicious soup is a great way to eat a nutritious vegetable. It has a wonderful garden-fresh flavor and pretty green color.
—*Kay Fairley, Charleston, Illinois*

 Uses less fat, sugar or salt. Includes Nutritional Analysis and Diabetic Exchanges.

2 cups chopped fresh *or* frozen broccoli
1/2 cup chopped onion
1 can (14-1/2 ounces) reduced-sodium chicken broth
2 tablespoons cornstarch
1 can (12 ounces) fat-free evaporated milk

In a saucepan, combine broccoli, onion and broth; simmer for 10-15 minutes or until vegetables are tender. Puree half of the mixture in a blender; return to the saucepan.

In a small bowl, whisk cornstarch and 3 tablespoons of milk until smooth. Gradually add remaining milk. Stir into the broccoli mixture. Bring to a boil; boil and stir for 2 minutes. **Yield:** 4 servings.

Nutritional Analysis: One 3/4-cup serving equals 112 calories, 157 mg sodium, 5 mg cholesterol, 18 g carbohydrate, 9 g protein, 1 g fat. **Diabetic Exchanges:** 2 vegetable, 1/2 skim milk.

Vegetable Noodle Soup

This creamy soup is great on a cold winter day. I created it when I didn't have all the ingredients for broccoli soup. I like this combo even better.
—Judie Peters, Camden, Indiana

3-1/2 cups milk
1 package (16 ounces) frozen California-blend vegetables
1/2 cup cubed process cheese (Velveeta)
1 envelope chicken noodle soup mix

In a large saucepan, bring milk to a boil. Stir in vegetables and return to a boil. Reduce heat; cover and simmer for 6 minutes.

Stir in cheese and soup mix. Return to a boil. Reduce heat. Simmer, uncovered, for 5-7 minutes or until the noodles are tender and the cheese is melted, stirring occasionally. **Yield:** 5-6 servings.

Bacon-Tomato Bagel Melts

My husband introduced me to this open-faced sandwich shortly after we got married, and it quickly became an all-time favorite. It's good made with plain or onion bagels. Have fun experimenting with various toppings and dressings, too.
—Lindsay Orwig, Grand Terrace, California

2 bagels, split and toasted
8 tomato slices
8 bacon strips, cooked
1 cup (4 ounces) shredded mozzarella cheese
Prepared ranch salad dressing

Place bagel halves cut side up on a baking sheet. Top each with two tomato slices and two bacon strips. Sprinkle with cheese. Broil 5 in. from the heat for 1-2 minutes or until cheese begins to brown. Serve with ranch dressing. **Yield:** 4 sandwiches.

|BACON TIDBITS| If you roll a package of bacon into a tube and secure it with a rubber band before refrigerating, the slices will come apart more easily. Pricking bacon with a fork reduces excess curling and helps it lie flat in the pan.

Cream of Carrot Soup

I came up with this rich yummy soup when I was in a hurry one day and we needed something hot to eat. It's versatile, too. You can substitute most any vegetable with excellent results.

—Ruth Andrewson, Leavenworth, Washington

4 cups chicken broth
4 large carrots, cut into chunks
1/2 cup heavy whipping cream
1 teaspoon sugar

In a saucepan, bring broth and carrots to a boil. Reduce heat; simmer, uncovered, until carrots are tender, about 15 minutes. Cool slightly.

In a blender, cover and process soup in small batches until smooth; return to the pan. Stir in cream and sugar; heat through. **Yield:** 5 servings.

Quick Chili

I've made this mild-tasting and hearty main-dish chili for over 40 years, much to the delight of my family and friends. I can serve up a steaming bowlful in minutes to take the chill out of a cold winter day.

—Jean Ward, Montgomery, Texas

 Uses less fat, sugar or salt. Includes Nutritional Analysis and Diabetic Exchanges.

1 pound ground beef
1 can (10-3/4 ounces) condensed tomato soup, undiluted
1 can (15 ounces) chili beans in gravy, undrained
2 to 3 teaspoons chili powder
1/2 cup water, optional

In a saucepan, cook beef over medium heat until no longer pink; drain. Add soup, beans and chili powder. Reduce heat. Cover and simmer for 20 minutes. Add water if a thinner soup is desired. **Yield:** 4 servings.

Nutritional Analysis: One serving (prepared with lean ground beef and reduced-sodium, reduced-fat tomato soup) equals 344 calories, 341 mg sodium, 108 mg cholesterol, 24 g carbohydrate, 31 g protein, 5 g fat. **Diabetic Exchanges:** 3 meat, 1-1/2 starch.

Italian Beef Hoagies

You'll need just five ingredients to feed a crowd these tender and tangy sandwiches. On weekends, I start the roast the night before, so I can shred it in the morning.
—*Lori Piatt*
Danville, Illinois

1 boneless sirloin tip roast (about 4 pounds), halved
2 envelopes Italian salad dressing mix
2 cups water
1 jar (16 ounces) mild pepper rings, undrained
18 hoagie buns, split

Place roast in a 5-qt. slow cooker. Combine the salad dressing mix and water; pour over roast. Cover and cook on low for 8 hours or until meat is tender.

Remove meat; shred with a fork and return to slow cooker. Add pepper rings; heat through. Spoon 1/2 cup meat mixture onto each bun. **Yield:** 18 servings.

Strawberry Soup

This refreshing chilled soup is a lovely addition to a special brunch or luncheon. With its fruity flavor and thick frothy texture, you could even serve it as a punch! —*Lucia Johnson, Massena, New York*

1 pint fresh strawberries, hulled
1/2 cup white wine *or* apple juice
1/2 cup sugar
2 tablespoons lemon juice
1 teaspoon grated lemon peel

In a blender, combine all ingredients. Cover and process until smooth. Pour into two bowls; cover and refrigerate until thoroughly chilled, about 1-2 hours. **Yield:** 2 servings.

|COLD SOUP CLUE| When making cold soups, remember that chilling food mutes its flavor, so be sure to taste just before serving and adjust the seasoning if necessary. Keep in mind that most cold soups will be thicker than when they were at room temperature.

Spinach Cheese Swirls

My family loves dividing up this super-easy sandwich that's brimming with great spinach and onion flavor. Refrigerated pizza dough shaves minutes off prep time and creates a golden brown crust. The cheesy slices taste terrific warm or cold, so they're great for lunches, picnics or trips.
—*Mary Nichols*
Dover, New Hampshire

1 package (10 ounces) frozen chopped spinach, thawed and drained
2 cups (8 ounces) shredded mozzarella cheese
1 cup finely chopped onion
1 garlic clove, minced
1 tube (10 ounces) refrigerated pizza crust

In a bowl, combine the first four ingredients and mix well. On a greased baking sheet, roll pizza dough into a 14-in. x 10-in. rectangle; seal any holes. Spoon filling over crust to within 1 in. of edge.

Roll up jelly-roll style, starting with a long side; seal the ends and place seam side down. Bake at 400° for 25-27 minutes or until golden brown. Cut into slices to serve. **Yield:** 4 servings.

Chicken Dumpling Soup

Although we were on a tight budget when I was a youngster, we always had good food. This comforting soup with soft dumplings was one of Mom's mainstays. —*Brenda Risser, Willard, Ohio*

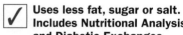 **Uses less fat, sugar or salt. Includes Nutritional Analysis and Diabetic Exchanges.**

2 cans (10-3/4 ounces *each*) condensed cream of chicken soup, undiluted
3-1/3 cups milk, *divided*
1-2/3 cups biscuit/baking mix

In a 3-qt. saucepan, combine soup and 2-2/3 cups of milk. Bring to a boil over medium heat; reduce heat. In a bowl, combine biscuit mix with remaining milk just until blended.

Drop by rounded tablespoons onto simmering soup. Cook, uncovered, for 10 minutes. Cover and simmer 10-12 minutes longer or until dumplings test done (do not lift lid while simmering). Serve immediately. **Yield:** 4 servings.

Nutritional Analysis: One serving (prepared with reduced-fat cream of chicken soup, fat-free milk and reduced-fat biscuit mix) equals 359 calories, 1,276 mg sodium, 16 mg cholesterol, 60 g carbohydrate, 13 g protein, 6 g fat, 1 g fiber. **Diabetic Exchanges:** 3 starch, 1 skim milk, 1 fat.

Meal on a Bun

Looking for a break from the usual peanut butter and jelly sandwich? This easy concoction is sure to be a hit with kids of all ages. I've replaced the jelly with a juicy slice of pineapple and topped it off with cheddar cheese.

—*Lavina Taylor, Moline, Illinois*

4 **hamburger buns, split**
1/2 **cup peanut butter**
1 **can (8 ounces) pineapple slices, drained**
4 **slices cheddar cheese**

Place buns, cut side up, on a baking sheet. Spread with peanut butter. Place a pineapple slice on each bun bottom and a cheese slice on each bun top. Bake at 350° for 5-7 minutes or until cheese is melted. Place cheese-topped buns over pineapple. **Yield:** 4 servings.

Chilled Cantaloupe Soup

A friend in New York shared the recipe for this chilled melon soup that's pleasantly spiced with cinnamon. Most people are skeptical when I describe it, but after one spoonful, they're hooked. It's easy to prepare, pretty to serve and so refreshing.

—*Margaret McNeil, Memphis, Tennessee*

 Uses less fat, sugar or salt. Includes Nutritional Analysis and Diabetic Exchanges.

1 **medium cantaloupe, peeled, seeded and cubed**
2 **cups orange juice, *divided***
1 **tablespoon lime juice**
1/4 **to 1/2 teaspoon ground cinnamon**
Fresh mint, optional

Place cantaloupe and 1/2 cup orange juice in a blender or food processor; cover and process until smooth. Transfer to a large bowl; stir in lime juice, cinnamon and remaining orange juice. Cover and refrigerate for at least 1 hour. Garnish with mint if desired. **Yield:** 6 servings.

Nutritional Analysis: One 3/4-cup serving equals 70 calories, 9 mg sodium, 0 cholesterol, 17 g carbohydrate, 1 g protein, trace fat. **Diabetic Exchange:** 1 fruit.

Spinach Potato Soup

I first made this fresh-tasting soup for a school potluck on St. Patrick's Day. It was a hit, and now I make it throughout the year.
—*Lois McAtee, Oceanside, California*

3 cups milk
1 can (15 ounces) sliced potatoes, drained
1 package (10 ounces) frozen creamed spinach, thawed
1/2 teaspoon dried basil
1/2 to 3/4 teaspoon garlic salt

Combine all ingredients in a saucepan. Bring to a boil. Reduce heat; cover and simmer for 15 minutes. Cool slightly.

Transfer mixture to a blender; cover and process until small pieces of potato remain. Return to the pan and heat through. **Yield:** 4-6 servings.

Dogs in a Sweater

For a new twist on an old favorite, try these skewered hot dogs wrapped with breadstick dough and baked. They're fun to dip in ketchup, mustard or ranch dressing. The dressed-up dog recipe comes kid-tested from the National Hot Dog and Sausage Council.

1 package (11 ounces) refrigerated breadstick dough
8 hot dogs
8 Popsicle sticks
Ketchup, mustard *and/or* ranch dressing

Separate dough; roll each piece into a 15-in. rope. Insert sticks into hot dogs lengthwise. Starting at one end, wrap dough in a spiral around hot dog; pinch ends to seal.

Place 1 in. apart on a baking sheet that has been coated with nonstick cooking spray. Bake at 350° for 18-20 minutes. Serve with the toppings of your choice. **Yield:** 8 servings.

Pizza Grilled Cheese

Combine two all-time lunch favorites into one, and you've got this recipe. My teenage son, Tim, created the sandwich with dipping sauce to satisfy his love for pizza. —*Robin Kettering Newville, Pennsylvania*

1 tablespoon butter, softened
2 slices bread
1 slice provolone *or* mozzarella cheese
6 slices pepperoni
3 tablespoons pizza sauce
Additional pizza sauce, optional

Butter one side of each slice of bread. Place one slice in a skillet, butter side down. Top with the cheese, pepperoni, pizza sauce and second bread slice, butter side up.

Cook over medium heat until golden brown, turning once. Serve sandwich with additional pizza sauce if desired. **Yield:** 1 serving.

|GET A GRIDDLE| If you enjoy grilled sandwiches, you may want to invest in an electric or stove-top griddle, which will allow you to grill four to six sandwiches at a time.

Bacon Bean Sandwiches

My mother-in-law first shared this scrumptious open-faced sandwich with us, and it's now a favorite around our house. The flavors of the bacon, beans, onion and cheese complement each other wonderfully! —*Dorothy Klass, Tabor City, North Carolina*

5 slices bread, lightly toasted
1 can (16 ounces) pork and beans
10 bacon strips, cooked and drained
4 slices onion, separated into rings
5 slices process American cheese

Place toast on an ungreased baking sheet. Spread each slice with 3 tablespoons beans. Top each with two bacon strips, a few onion rings and a cheese slice. Bake at 350° for 15-20 minutes or until cheese is melted and lightly browned. **Yield:** 5 servings.

Fast Fiesta Soup

This spicy soup was served at a very elegant lunch, and the hostess was deluged with requests for the recipe. The colorful combination is a snap to throw together...just open the cans and heat.
—*Patricia White*
Monrovia, California

 Uses less fat, sugar or salt. Includes Nutritional Analysis and Diabetic Exchanges.

2 cans (10 ounces *each*) diced tomatoes and green chilies
1 can (15-1/4 ounces) whole kernel corn, drained
1 can (15 ounces) black beans, rinsed and drained
Shredded cheddar cheese and sour cream, optional

In a saucepan, combine tomatoes, corn and beans; heat through. Garnish servings with cheese and sour cream if desired. **Yield:** 4 servings.

Nutritional Analysis: One serving (prepared with no-salt-added diced tomatoes and without cheese and sour cream) equals 210 calories, 576 mg sodium, 0 cholesterol, 42 g carbohydrate, 10 g protein, 2 g fat, 10 g fiber. **Diabetic Exchanges:** 2-1/2 starch, 1 vegetable.

Tangy Beef Turnovers

My mom's recipe for these flavorful pockets called for dough made from scratch, but I streamlined it by using crescent rolls. My children love them plain or dipped in ketchup.
—*Claudia Bodeker*
Ash Flat, Arkansas

1 pound ground beef
1 medium onion, chopped
1 jar (16 ounces) sauerkraut, rinsed, drained and chopped
1 cup (4 ounces) shredded Swiss cheese
3 tubes (8 ounces *each*) refrigerated crescent rolls

In a skillet, cook beef and onion over medium heat until meat is no longer pink; drain. Add sauerkraut and cheese; mix well. Unroll crescent roll dough and separate into rectangles. Place on greased baking sheets; pinch seams to seal.

Place 1/2 cup beef mixture in the center of each rectangle. Bring corners to the center and pinch to seal. Bake at 375° for 15-18 minutes or until golden brown. **Yield:** 1 dozen.

Chicken Chili

My aunt gave me the recipe for this thick "instant" chili. To save time, I usually cook and cube the chicken the night before or use leftovers. The next day, it's simple to simmer the ingredients on the stovetop. I serve the hearty results with crunchy corn chips or warm bread.
—*Yvonne Morgan*
Grand Rapids, Michigan

2 cans (15 ounces *each*) great northern beans, rinsed and drained
2 jars (16 ounces *each*) picante sauce
4 cups cubed cooked chicken
1 to 2 teaspoons ground cumin
Shredded Monterey Jack cheese

In a saucepan, combine beans, picante sauce, chicken and cumin. Bring to a boil. Reduce heat; cover and simmer for 20 minutes. Sprinkle individual servings with cheese. **Yield:** 6 servings.

Dilly Beef Sandwiches

My younger sister, Jean, shared this recipe, which puts a twist on the traditional barbecue sandwich. As a busy mother of four, Jean never has much time to cook, but she does like to entertain. This crowd-pleaser, made in a convenient slow cooker, is perfect for our large family gatherings.
—*Donna Blankenheim, Madison, Wisconsin*

1 boneless beef chuck roast (3 to 4 pounds)
1 jar (16 ounces) whole dill pickles, undrained
1/2 cup chili sauce
2 garlic cloves, minced
10 to 12 hamburger buns, split

Cut roast in half and place in a slow cooker. Add pickles with juice, chili sauce and garlic. Cover and cook on low for 8-9 hours or until beef is tender.

Discard pickles. Remove roast. When cool enough to handle, shred the meat. Return to the sauce and heat through. Using a slotted spoon, fill each bun with about 1/2 cup meat mixture. **Yield:** 10-12 servings.

Raisin Finger Sandwiches

As a registered nurse and mother of four, I'm very busy. That's why I like these sweet sandwiches. They're simple to assemble but look and taste like you put a lot of effort into them.

—Jeannie Dobbs, Bartlesville, Oklahoma

1 package (8 ounces)
   cream cheese, softened
1/4 cup mayonnaise
1/2 cup chopped pecans
10 slices raisin bread

In a mixing bowl, beat cream cheese and mayonnaise until smooth. Stir in pecans. Spread over five slices of bread; top with remaining bread. Cut each sandwich into three strips. Serve immediately. **Yield:** 5 servings.

Corny Chicken Wraps

My girls like these tortilla roll-ups very much—they'll ask for them practically every week. Tender chicken combines with canned corn and salsa for a fast-to-fix main dish.
—Sue Seymour
Valatie, New York

 Uses less fat, sugar or salt. Includes Nutritional Analysis and Diabetic Exchanges.

2 cups cubed cooked
   chicken breast
1 can (11 ounces) whole
   kernel corn, drained
1 cup salsa
1 cup (4 ounces) shredded
   cheddar cheese
8 flour tortillas (6 inches),
   warmed

In a saucepan or microwave-safe bowl, combine chicken, corn and salsa. Cook until heated through. Sprinkle cheese over tortillas. Place about 1/2 cup chicken mixture down the center of each tortilla; roll up. Secure with toothpicks. **Yield:** 4 servings.

Nutritional Analysis: One serving (prepared with reduced-fat cheese and tortillas) equals 374 calories, 1,088 mg sodium, 61 mg cholesterol, 50 g carbohydrate, 26 g protein, 8 g fat, 3 g fiber. **Diabetic Exchanges:** 3 starch, 2 lean meat, 1 vegetable.

Hot Hoagies

A convenient package of Italian salad dressing mix provides the yummy herb flavor in these broiled sandwiches that I assemble for my family of 10. I use their favorite combination of meats and cheeses, then serve the sandwiches with chips and pickles. They're a hit every time. —Paula Hadley
Forest Hill, Louisiana

3/4 cup butter, softened
1 envelope Italian salad dressing mix
6 hoagie buns, split
12 to 16 ounces sliced luncheon meat (salami, ham *and/or* turkey)
12 thin slices cheese (Swiss, cheddar *and/or* brick)

Combine butter and salad dressing mix; spread 1 table-spoonful inside each bun. On bottom of each bun, layer one slice of meat, two slices of cheese and another slice of meat; replace tops. Spread 1 tablespoon butter mixture over top of each bun.

Place on a baking sheet. Broil 6 in. from the heat for 2-3 minutes or until tops are lightly browned. **Yield:** 6 servings.

Thick 'n' Quick Clam Chowder

You'd never guess that this thick, rich soup is a blend of convenient canned ingredients. My husband and I love it during our busy harvest season...it's so simple to simmer up when time is tight.
—Betty Sitzman, Wray, Colorado

1 can (10-3/4 ounces) condensed cream of celery soup, undiluted
1 can (10-3/4 ounces) condensed cheddar cheese soup, undiluted
1 can (10-3/4 ounces) condensed cream of onion soup, undiluted
3 cups half-and-half cream
2 cans (6-1/2 ounces *each*) chopped clams, drained

In a saucepan, combine the soups and cream; cook over medium heat until heated through. Add clams and heat through (do not boil). **Yield:** 6-8 servings.

Editor's Note: Add chopped clams to soups and chowders at the last minute so they don't lose their texture.

Tomato Corn Chowder

Five common ingredients are all you'll need to prepare this hearty full-flavored chowder. This is a terrific soup, particularly as the cooler fall and winter seasons set in. It's economical as well. —Sue McMichael Redding, California

4 bacon strips, diced
1 large onion, chopped
2 cans (15-1/4 ounces each) whole kernel corn, undrained
2 cans (14-1/2 ounces each) diced tomatoes, undrained
4 medium potatoes, peeled and diced

In a large saucepan, cook bacon over medium heat until crisp. Remove to paper towels. Drain, reserving 1 tablespoon drippings.

In the drippings, saute onion until tender. Add the corn, tomatoes and potatoes. Cook over medium heat for 25-30 minutes or until potatoes are tender. Sprinkle with bacon. **Yield:** 9 servings.

Nutty Marmalade Sandwiches

I make batches of fun-filled sandwiches to freeze for a few weeks' worth of brown-bag lunches. They taste so fresh you would never know they were ever frozen. The marmalade flavor in this hearty combination really shines through. —Iola Egle, McCook, Nebraska

1/2 cup peanut butter
1/4 cup orange marmalade
1/4 cup shredded sharp cheddar cheese
1 to 2 teaspoons lemon juice
6 slices bread

In a small bowl, combine peanut butter, marmalade, cheese and lemon juice; mix well. Spread over three slices of bread; top with remaining bread. Freeze for up to 4 months. Remove from the freezer at least 4 hours before serving. **Yield:** 3 servings.

Five-Can Chili

Who says a thick hearty chili has to simmer all day on the stove? With five canned goods and zero prep time, a warm pot of this zesty specialty is a snap to whip up.

—Jo Mann
Westover, Alabama

1 can (15 ounces) chili with beans
1 can (15 ounces) mixed vegetables, drained
1 can (11 ounces) whole kernel corn, drained
1 can (10-3/4 ounces) condensed tomato soup, undiluted
1 can (10 ounces) diced tomatoes and green chilies

In a saucepan, combine all ingredients; heat through. **Yield:** 6 servings.

|CHILI CHOICES| When making chili, always make a double batch, freezing half for a quick meal another week. Leftover chili is great when spooned over spaghetti, in tacos and burritos, as an omelet filling, as a topping for burgers or hot dogs, or spooned on top of a baked potato and topped with cheese.

Chuck Wagon Burgers

Howdy, pardner! When our son requested a cowboy theme for his birthday party, I planned a Western-style meal including these savory burgers. In the spirit of true chuck wagon fare, I served them on large biscuits rather than buns.

—Sharon Thompson
Oskaloosa, Iowa

2 pounds ground beef
1 envelope onion soup mix
1/2 cup water
1 tube (16.3 ounces) large refrigerated biscuits
1/8 teaspoon seasoned salt

In a bowl, combine the beef, soup mix and water; mix well. Shape into eight 3/4-in.-thick patties. Grill, uncovered, or broil 4 in. from the heat for 5-6 minutes on each side or until meat is no longer pink.

Meanwhile, place biscuits on an ungreased baking sheet; sprinkle with seasoned salt. Bake at 375° for 12-14 minutes or until golden brown. Split; top each biscuit with a hamburger. **Yield:** 8 servings.

Salads & Dressings

Sunshine Salad, p. 133

Cottage Cheese Veggie Salad, p. 137

|DRESSINGS|

Buttermilk Salad Dressing, p. 132

Pimiento Potato Salad

A neighbor shared the recipe for this easy overnight salad. Tender potatoes and crunchy celery get refreshing flavor from a bottle of Italian dressing. It's a delicious change of pace from potato salads made with mayonnaise.
—Dora Ledford
Rockwall, Texas

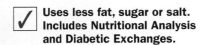 Uses less fat, sugar or salt. Includes Nutritional Analysis and Diabetic Exchanges.

- **2 pounds small red potatoes (about 12), cooked**
- **4 green onions, thinly sliced**
- **3 celery ribs, thinly sliced**
- **1 jar (2 ounces) diced pimientos, drained**
- **1 bottle (8 ounces) Italian salad dressing**

Cut potatoes into 1/4-in. slices. In an ungreased 13-in. x 9-in. x 2-in. dish, layer half of the potatoes, onions, celery and pimientos. Repeat layers. Pour dressing over all. Cover and refrigerate overnight. Stir before serving. **Yield:** 12 servings.

Nutritional Analysis: One 3/4-cup serving (prepared with fat-free salad dressing) equals 65 calories, 202 mg sodium, 0 cholesterol, 13 g carbohydrate, 2 g protein, trace fat. **Diabetic Exchange:** 1 starch.

Buttermilk Salad Dressing

(Pictured on page 131)

This thick creamy mixture has the flavor of ranch dressing and is a breeze to blend together. Use it to top mixed greens or as a dip for raw vegetables.
—Vicki Floden, Story City, Iowa

Uses less fat, sugar or salt. Includes Nutritional Analysis and Diabetic Exchanges.

- **3/4 cup 1% buttermilk**
- **2 cups (16 ounces) 2% cottage cheese**
- **1 envelope ranch salad dressing mix**
- **Salad greens and vegetables of your choice**

In a blender or food processor, combine the buttermilk, cottage cheese and salad dressing mix; cover and process for 20 seconds or until smooth. Pour into a small pitcher or bowl. Cover and refrigerate for 1 hour. Stir before serving with salad. **Yield:** 2-3/4 cups.

Nutritional Analysis: One serving (2 tablespoons dressing) equals 23 calories, 1 g fat (trace saturated fat), 3 mg cholesterol, 177 mg sodium, 2 g carbohydrate, 0 fiber, 3 g protein. **Diabetic Exchange:** 1/2 fat-free milk.

Sunshine Salad

(Pictured on page 130)

I found this recipe years ago and have made it many times since. When I prepare it for an evening meal, I call it "Sunset Salad".
—*Margaret Ulrich, Braidwood, Illinois*

1 can (20 ounces)
pineapple tidbits
1 can (11 ounces)
mandarin oranges
1 package (3.4 ounces)
instant lemon pudding
1 cup quartered
strawberries
1 cup sliced ripe bananas

Drain pineapple and oranges, reserving liquid. In a large bowl, combine pudding mix with reserved fruit juices. Fold in pineapple, oranges and strawberries. Chill for at least 2 hours. Add bananas just before serving. **Yield:** 8-10 servings.

Maple Cream Fruit Topping

Transform fruit salad into a special brunch treat with a dollop of this rich and creamy topping. The topping is also wonderful spooned over sliced melons.
—*Bethel Walters, Willow River, Minnesota*

1 tablespoon all-purpose
flour
3/4 cup maple syrup
1 egg
1 tablespoon butter
1 cup heavy whipping
cream, whipped

In a saucepan, combine flour, syrup and egg until smooth. Add butter. Bring to a boil; boil and stir for 2 minutes or until thickened and bubbly. Cover and refrigerate until completely cooled. Fold in whipped cream. **Yield:** about 2 cups.

Creamy Corn Salad

My daughter-in-law shared this fast five-ingredient recipe. It sounds too easy to be so good. Double the recipe if you're serving several people.
—*June Mullins, Livonia, Missouri*

 Uses less fat, sugar or salt. Includes Nutritional Analysis and Diabetic Exchanges.

1 can (15-1/4 ounces) whole kernel corn, drained
1 medium tomato, seeded and diced
2 tablespoons chopped onion
1/3 cup mayonnaise
1/4 teaspoon dill weed, optional

In a small bowl, combine the corn, tomato, onion, mayonnaise and dill weed if desired; mix well. Cover and refrigerate until serving. **Yield:** 4 servings.

Nutritional Analysis: One 1/2-cup serving (prepared with fat-free mayonnaise) equals 109 calories, 374 mg sodium, 0 cholesterol, 25 g carbohydrate, 3 g protein, 1 g fat. **Diabetic Exchanges:** 1 starch, 1 vegetable.

Orange Buttermilk Salad

I often serve this refreshing yet slightly sweet side dish. It goes great with a variety of main dishes, but I especially like it with ham.
—*Carol Van Sickle*
Versailles, Kentucky

1 can (20 ounces) crushed pineapple, undrained
1 package (6 ounces) orange gelatin
2 cups buttermilk
1 carton (8 ounces) frozen whipped topping, thawed

In a saucepan, bring pineapple to a boil. Remove from the heat; add gelatin and stir to dissolve. Add buttermilk and mix well. Cool to room temperature. Fold in whipped topping. Pour into an 11-in. x 7-in. x 2-in. dish. Refrigerate several hours or overnight. Cut into squares. **Yield:** 12 servings.

Snowball Peaches

Peach halves took on a festive look for a snowman-theme brunch I hosted when I mounded a fruity cream cheese mixture in them. You can put these simple individual salads together very quickly, and they're fun party fare.
—Renae Moncur, Burley, Idaho

2 packages (3 ounces *each*) cream cheese, softened
2 tablespoons apricot preserves
1 cup pineapple tidbits, drained
3 cans (15-1/4 ounces *each*) peach halves, drained
Leaf lettuce
Fresh mint, optional

In a small mixing bowl, beat the cream cheese and preserves until blended. Stir in pineapple. Place peaches cut side up on a lettuce-lined serving platter; fill with cream cheese mixture. Garnish with mint if desired. **Yield:** 15 servings.

|SOFTENING CREAM CHEESE| To quickly soften cream cheese, use the microwave. Simply remove the cream cheese from the foil package and place it on a microwave-safe plate. Microwave on medium power for 20 to 40 seconds, checking it at the minimum amount of time.

Balsamic Salad Dressing

My tomato juice-based dressing offers a nice combination of tangy and tart with only a trace of fat. We like our salad dressing tart, but you may want to add a little more sugar if that suits your family's tastes better.
—Alice Coate, Bryan, Texas

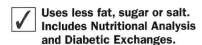 **Uses less fat, sugar or salt. Includes Nutritional Analysis and Diabetic Exchanges.**

3/4 cup tomato juice
1/4 cup balsamic vinegar
1 envelope Italian salad dressing mix
2 teaspoons sugar

In a jar with a tight-fitting lid, combine all ingredients; shake well. Store in the refrigerator. **Yield:** 1 cup.

Nutritional Analysis: One serving (2 tablespoons) equals 18 calories, trace fat (0 saturated fat), 0 cholesterol, 397 mg sodium, 4 g carbohydrate, trace fiber, trace protein. **Diabetic Exchange:** Free food.

Frozen Cherry Salad

Pretty slices of this refreshing salad are dotted with colorful cherries for a festive look. The flavor is pleasant and not overly sweet. Prepared in advance and frozen, it's a treat that fits into many different menus. I serve it throughout the year.

—Gail Sykora
Menomonee Falls, Wisconsin

✓ Uses less fat, sugar or salt. Includes Nutritional Analysis and Diabetic Exchanges.

1 package (8 ounces) cream cheese, softened
1 carton (8 ounces) frozen whipped topping, thawed
1 can (21 ounces) cherry pie filling
2 cans (11 ounces *each*) mandarin oranges, drained
Maraschino cherries and orange wedges, optional

In a mixing bowl, combine the cream cheese and whipped topping. Stir in pie filling. Set aside 1/4 cup oranges for garnish. Fold remaining oranges into cream cheese mixture. Transfer to a 9-in. x 5-in. x 3-in. loaf pan. Cover and freeze overnight.

Remove from the freezer 15 minutes before cutting. Garnish with reserved mandarin oranges, and cherries and oranges if desired. **Yield:** 12 servings.

Nutritional Analysis: One serving (prepared with fat-free cream cheese, reduced-fat whipped topping and reduced-sugar pie filling and without maraschino cherries and oranges) equals 137 calories, 111 mg sodium, 2 mg cholesterol, 24 g carbohydrate, 3 g protein, 3 g fat. **Diabetic Exchanges:** 1 starch, 1/2 fruit, 1/2 fat.

After Thanksgiving Salad

This special salad tastes terrific made with either turkey or chicken. I serve it on a bed of lettuce, as a sandwich or in a croissant for a special occasion. It's a hit with my husband and our three kids.

—Ruthe Holmberg, Louisville, Kentucky

1 hard-cooked egg
4 cups shredded cooked turkey *or* chicken
3/4 cup mayonnaise
1 tablespoon sweet pickle relish
1/2 cup chopped pecans

In a bowl, mash the egg with a fork. Add turkey, mayonnaise and relish. Cover and refrigerate until serving. Stir in pecans just before serving. **Yield:** 4 servings.

Cottage Cheese Veggie Salad

(Pictured on page 131)

Just four ingredients mixed into regular cottage cheese give surprising flavor to this incredibly easy salad. I came up with the idea when I needed a quick side dish for lunch one day. It's light, refreshing and flavorful.
—*Jerraine Barlow, Colorado City, Arizona*

3 cups (24 ounces)
   small-curd cottage
   cheese
1 large ripe avocado,
   peeled, pitted and
   chopped
1 medium tomato, chopped
1/4 cup sliced stuffed olives
2 tablespoons sliced green
   onions

In a serving bowl, combine the first four ingredients. Sprinkle with onions. Serve immediately. **Yield:** 8 servings.

Artichoke Heart Salad

I put together this fast five-ingredient salad after sampling a similar mixture from a salad bar. Bottled Italian dressing gives robust flavor to this simple treatment for canned artichoke hearts. It is a snap to make as a last-minute side dish.
—*Elizabeth Birkenmaier, Gladstone, Missouri*

1 can (14 ounces)
   artichoke hearts,
   quartered and drained
1 can (2-1/4 ounces)
   sliced ripe olives,
   drained, optional
1/3 cup chopped green
   pepper
1/3 cup thinly sliced green
   onions
3/4 cup Italian salad dressing

In a bowl, combine artichokes, olives if desired, green pepper and onions. Add dressing and toss to coat. Cover and refrigerate for at least 30 minutes. Serve with a slotted spoon. **Yield:** 3-4 servings.

Tricolor Pasta Salad

Pretty pasta spirals and convenient frozen veggies are tossed with a light dressing to make this colorful medley. Vegetarians can add protein-rich chickpeas or beans to make it a main dish.

—Lorraine Darocha, Berkshire, Massachusetts

1 package (16 ounces) tricolor spiral pasta
1 package (16 ounces) frozen California-blend vegetables (broccoli, cauliflower and carrots)
1 can (2-1/4 ounces) sliced ripe olives, drained
1 to 1-1/3 cups Italian salad dressing
1/4 to 1/2 teaspoon garlic salt, optional

Cook the pasta according to package directions. Meanwhile, place vegetables in a microwave-safe dish. Cover and microwave at 50% power for 7-8 minutes or until thawed; drain. Drain pasta and rinse in cold water.

In a bowl, combine the pasta, vegetables and olives. Combine salad dressing and garlic salt if desired; pour over salad and toss to coat. Refrigerate until serving. **Yield:** 6-8 servings.

Editor's Note: This recipe was tested in an 850-watt microwave.

French Bean Salad

I jazz up frozen green beans with onion, bacon and bottled salad dressing for a cool dish that's as big on flavor as it is on convenience. I created this recipe after trying a similar salad at a restaurant.

—Penni Barringer
Rosalia, Washington

2 cups frozen French-style green beans, thawed
2 tablespoons chopped onion
3 bacon strips, cooked and crumbled
1/4 cup ranch salad dressing

In a serving bowl, combine the beans, onion and bacon; stir in dressing. Refrigerate until serving. **Yield:** 3 servings.

Watermelon Gelatin Cups

Let these delightful watermelon wannabes add a bit of fun to your next picnic spread. Limes are halved and hollowed to hold pretty pink gelatin while mini chocolate chips serve as seeds in the cute cups. —*Taste of Home Test Kitchen*

  1 package (3 ounces)
    watermelon gelatin
  1 cup boiling water
  1 cup cold water
  4 large limes
1/4 cup miniature chocolate
    chips

In a bowl, dissolve gelatin in boiling water. Stir in cold water. Refrigerate for 1 hour or until slightly thickened.

Meanwhile, slice limes in half lengthwise. With a small scissors or sharp knife, cut the membrane at each end to loosen pulp from shell. Using fingertips, pull membrane and pulp away from shell (discard pulp or save for another use).

Fold the chocolate chips into the gelatin; spoon into lime shells. Refrigerate for 2 hours or until completely set. **Yield:** 8 servings.

Honey Poppy Seed Dressing

This dressing is a light, refreshing way to dress up a plain lettuce salad. We also like it over fresh fruit. —*Michelle Bentley, Niceville, Florida*

1/3 cup vegetable oil
1/4 cup honey
  2 tablespoons cider
    vinegar
  2 teaspoons poppy seeds
1/2 teaspoon salt

In a small bowl or jar with tight-fitting lid, combine all ingredients; mix or shake well. Store in the refrigerator. **Yield:** about 2/3 cup.

Cherry Coke Salad

Since my sister and I grew up in the '50s, I decided to surprise her with a "Fabulous '50s Party" on her birthday. This refreshing salad, which really features cola, was part of the menu. The soda adds to the bright, sparkling taste.
—*Judy Nix*
Toccoa, Georgia

1 can (20 ounces) crushed pineapple
1/2 cup water
2 packages (3 ounces *each*) cherry gelatin
1 can (21 ounces) cherry pie filling
3/4 cup cola

Drain pineapple, reserving juice; set fruit aside. In a saucepan or microwave, bring pineapple juice and water to a boil. Add gelatin; stir until dissolved. Stir in pie filling and cola. Pour into a serving bowl. Refrigerate until slightly thickened. Fold in reserved pineapple. Refrigerate until firm. **Yield:** 10-12 servings.

Fruit Medley

Straight from the pantry comes a super-simple, colorful and pleasant-tasting fruit dish. Pie filling dresses up this combination of canned fruits.
—*Margaret Anders, Helena, Montana*

1 can (21 ounces) peach *or* apricot pie filling
2 cans (15 ounces *each*) fruit cocktail, drained
1 can (20 ounces) pineapple chunks, drained
1 can (15 ounces) mandarin oranges, drained
2 medium firm bananas, sliced

In a large bowl, combine pie filling and canned fruits. Cover and refrigerate. Stir in bananas just before serving. **Yield:** 12-14 servings.

|BANANA HELP| Because refrigeration discolors bananas that have been peeled, always add them to fruit salads and desserts just before serving. You can also toss sliced bananas with lemon or orange juice to keep them from browning.

French Salad Dressing

This simple dressing has served me for many years. Using this basic recipe, I can easily make simple variations, usually with ingredients I have on hand. As a result, I have always made my own salad dressings.

—*Carolyn Ozment, Gaylesville, Alabama*

1/4 cup vegetable oil
2 tablespoons vinegar
3/4 teaspoon salt
1 garlic clove, minced
Dash pepper

In a jar with a tight-fitting lid, combine the oil, vinegar, salt, garlic and pepper; shake well. Store in the refrigerator. **Yield:** about 1/3 cup.

|MAKING HOMEMADE DRESSING| If you plan on serving a vinegar and oil dressing right away, you can combine all of the ingredients in a jar with a tight-fitting lid and shake well. Otherwise, combine all of the ingredients except for the oil in a small bowl. When ready to serve, slowly add oil while mixing vigorously with a wire whisk.

Broccoli Waldorf Salad

This salad is as easy to prepare as it is to eat! A colorful combination of apples, raisins and pecans jazzes up broccoli florets in this summery side dish. Its tangy-sweet flavor makes it a stardout at company picnics and church potlucks.

—*Vicki Roehrick, Chubbuck, Idaho*

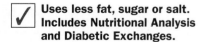 Uses less fat, sugar or salt. Includes Nutritional Analysis and Diabetic Exchanges.

6 cups broccoli florets
1 large red apple, chopped
1/2 cup raisins
1/4 cup chopped pecans
1/2 cup prepared coleslaw dressing

In a large serving bowl, combine the first four ingredients. Drizzle with dressing; toss to coat. Refrigerate leftovers. **Yield:** 10 servings.

   Nutritional Analysis: One 3/4-cup serving (prepared with reduced-fat coleslaw dressing) equals 87 calories, 4 g fat (trace saturated fat), 3 mg cholesterol, 133 mg sodium, 14 g carbohydrate, 2 g fiber, 2 g protein. **Diabetic Exchanges:** 1 vegetable, 1 fruit.

Thousand Island Dressing

It's almost unbelievable that a dressing so easy to fix can be so good. I got the recipe from my daughter, Debbi.
—*Darlis Wilfer, Phelps, Wisconsin*

2 cups mayonnaise
1/4 cup chili sauce
1/4 cup pickle relish

In a bowl, combine all ingredients. Store in the refrigerator. **Yield:** 2-1/2 cups.

Rainbow Gelatin Cubes

These perky gelatin cubes are fun to serve and to eat! I vary the colors to match the occasion—pink and blue for a baby shower, school colors for a graduation party, etc. Kids of all ages snap them up.
—*Deanna Pietrowicz*
Bridgeport, Connecticut

 Uses less fat, sugar or salt. Includes Nutritional Analysis and Diabetic Exchanges.

4 packages (3 ounces *each*) assorted flavored gelatin
6 envelopes unflavored gelatin, *divided*
5-3/4 cups boiling water, *divided*
1 can (14 ounces) sweetened condensed milk
1/4 cup cold water

In a bowl, combine one package flavored gelatin and one envelope unflavored gelatin. Stir in 1 cup boiling water until dissolved. Pour into a 13-in. x 9-in. x 2-in. dish coated with nonstick cooking spray; refrigerate until almost set but not firm, about 20 minutes.

In a bowl, combine the condensed milk and 1 cup boiling water. In another bowl, sprinkle two envelopes unflavored gelatin over cold water; let stand for 1 minute. Stir in 3/4 cup boiling water. Add to the milk mixture. Pour 1-1/4 cups of the creamy gelatin mixture over the first flavored gelatin layer. Refrigerate until set but not firm, about 25 minutes.

Repeat from beginning of recipe twice, alternating flavored gelatin with creamy gelatin layers. Chill each layer until set but not firm before pouring next layer on top. Make final flavored gelatin; spoon over top. Refrigerate for at least 1 hour after completing last layer before cutting into 1-in. squares. **Yield:** about 9 dozen.

Nutritional Analysis: One serving (two cubes, prepared with sugar-free gelatin and fat-free sweetened condensed milk) equals 26 calories, trace fat (0 saturated fat), 0 cholesterol, 27 mg sodium, 4 g carbohydrate, 0 fiber, 2 g protein. **Diabetic Exchange:** 1/2 fruit.

Tomato Avocado Salad

This salad is a family favorite. It's so colorful and very easy to make that I make it year-round, from summer barbecues to the winter holidays.

—*Vicky Rader*
Mullinville, Kansas

2 ripe avocados, peeled and sliced
2 large tomatoes, cut into wedges
1 medium onion, cut into wedges
1 cup Italian salad dressing
Lettuce leaves, optional

In a bowl, combine the avocados, tomatoes and onion; add dressing and stir to coat. Chill for 20-30 minutes. Serve over lettuce if desired. **Yield:** 6-8 servings.

|**TOMATO TIPS**| Buy tomatoes that are firm, well-shaped, richly colored and noticeably fragrant. They should be free from blemishes, heavy for their size and give slightly to palm pressure. Never refrigerate tomatoes—cold temperatures make the flesh pulpy and destroy the flavor. Instead, store them at room temperature away from direct sunlight.

Black Bean Salad

This salad goes wonderfully with chicken and Mexican main dishes and is great when you need something quick to make for a potluck dinner.   —*Peg Kenkel-Thomsen, Iowa City, Iowa*

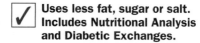 **Uses less fat, sugar or salt. Includes Nutritional Analysis and Diabetic Exchanges.**

2 cans (15 ounces *each*) black beans, rinsed and drained
1-1/2 cups salsa
2 tablespoons minced fresh parsley

Combine all ingredients in a bowl. Chill for 15 minutes. **Yield:** 8 servings.

Nutritional Analysis: One 1/2-cup serving equals 93 calories, 453 mg sodium, 0 cholesterol, 16 g carbohydrate, 6 g protein, 1 g fat. **Diabetic Exchange:** 1 starch.

Mom's Coleslaw

As the name says, this is my mom's recipe. You won't have to fuss with a lot of seasonings to fix this tangy coleslaw. This speedy salad is an old family favorite. We've shared the recipe with many friends over the years.
—*Denise Augostine*
Saxonburg, Pennsylvania

1 small head cabbage, shredded
3 medium carrots, shredded
1 cup mayonnaise
1/3 cup sugar
1/4 cup cider vinegar

In a large bowl, combine cabbage and carrots. In a small bowl, combine the mayonnaise, sugar and vinegar. Pour over cabbage mixture and toss to coat. Serve with a slotted spoon. **Yield:** 10-12 servings.

|SHREDDING CABBAGE| To shred cabbage by hand, cut it into wedges. Place cut side down on a cutting board. With a large sharp knife, cut into thin slices. For the crispest coleslaw, shred the cabbage, then immerse in ice water for an hour. Drain well and blot dry before refrigerating in a plastic bag until ready to use.

Three-Fruit Salad

Nothing could be easier than stirring up this refreshing salad. The tangy honey mustard salad dressing is a wonderful complement to the different fruit flavors.
—*Ruth Andrewson*
Leavenworth, Washington

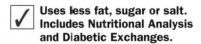 Uses less fat, sugar or salt. Includes Nutritional Analysis and Diabetic Exchanges.

2 medium ripe bananas, sliced
1 cup pineapple chunks
1 cup seedless grapes, halved
3 tablespoons honey mustard salad dressing

In a bowl, combine the fruit. Add dressing and toss to coat. Cover and refrigerate until serving. **Yield:** 4-6 servings.

Nutritional Analysis: One 1/2-cup serving (prepared with fat-free salad dressing) equals 79 calories, 39 mg sodium, 0 cholesterol, 20 g carbohydrate, 1 g protein, trace fat. **Diabetic Exchange:** 1 fruit.

Strawberry Asparagus Salad

This is my family's favorite springtime salad. The dressing is so light and refreshing, and the vivid combination of red berries and green asparagus is a real eye-catcher.
—*Judi Francus*
Morristown, New Jersey

✓ **Uses less fat, sugar or salt. Includes Nutritional Analysis and Diabetic Exchanges.**

1/4 **cup lemon juice**
2 **tablespoons vegetable oil**
2 **tablespoons honey**
2 **cups cut fresh asparagus (1-inch pieces)**
2 **cups sliced fresh strawberries**

In a small bowl, combine lemon juice, oil and honey; mix well. Cook asparagus in a small amount of water until crisp-tender, about 3-4 minutes; drain and cool. Arrange asparagus and strawberries on individual plates; drizzle with dressing. **Yield:** 8 servings.

Nutritional Analysis: One serving equals 68 calories, 1 mg sodium, 0 cholesterol, 9 g carbohydrate, 1 g protein, 4 g fat. **Diabetic Exchanges:** 1 fat, 1/2 fruit.

Olive Lover's Salad

Mom concocted this creative salad with a few simple ingredients. Chopped olives, celery and garlic are drizzled with oil, tossed and chilled for a cool and refreshing side dish that's perfect with any warm meal.
—*Gina Mueller, Converse, Texas*

1 **can (6 ounces) pitted ripe olives, drained and chopped**
1 **jar (5-3/4 ounces) stuffed olives, drained and chopped**
2 **celery ribs, chopped**
2 **garlic cloves, minced**
2 **tablespoons olive oil**

In a bowl, combine olives, celery and garlic. Drizzle with oil; toss to coat. Cover and refrigerate for 4 hours or overnight. **Yield:** 3-1/2 cups.

|ABOUT OLIVES| The olive tree flourished in Spain, Tunisia, Morocco and Mediterranean countries for thousands of years, but it was not until the mid-16th century that there is a record of cuttings being carried to Peru by the Spaniards. In the 1700s, Franciscan monks brought the olive to Mexico and then north to California by way of the missions.

Green Pepper Salad Dressing

If you enjoy the flavor of green peppers, you'll love this salad dressing. Drizzle greens with the thick blend or serve it alongside a veggie tray for a pleasant change of pace.   —Elizabeth Montgomery
Taylorville, Illinois

1 cup mayonnaise
3 tablespoons finely
  chopped green pepper
2 tablespoons finely
  chopped onion
2 tablespoons minced
  fresh parsley
1 tablespoon lemon juice

In a bowl, combine all of the ingredients. Cover and refrigerate until serving. **Yield:** about 1-1/4 cups.

|PEPPER POINTER| Thoroughly wash bell peppers before seeding. Cut peppers in half by slicing vertically from one side of the stem all the way around to the other side of the stem. Break halves apart and the seed core should pop right out. Cut away the membranes, which can be bitter.

Strawberry-Glazed Fruit Salad

I first tasted this delightful salad at a friend's house when she served it with dinner. It tastes so good made with fresh strawberries. After sampling it, no one would ever believe how incredibly easy it is to prepare.
—Jeri Dobrowski
Beach, North Dakota

1 quart fresh strawberries,
  halved
1 can (20 ounces)
  pineapple chunks,
  drained
4 firm bananas, sliced
1 jar *or* pouch (16 ounces)
  strawberry glaze

In a large bowl, gently toss strawberries, pineapple and bananas; fold in the glaze. Chill for at least 1 hour. **Yield:** 6-8 servings.

Editor's Note: Strawberry glaze can often be found in the produce section of most grocery stores.

Lemonade Fruit Dressing

I like to dollop this tart yet rich dressing over an assortment of seasonal fruit. It makes a very colorful and refreshing salad that helps beat the summer heat.

—Emma Magielda
Amsterdam, New York

2 eggs
3/4 cup lemonade concentrate
1/3 cup sugar
1 cup heavy whipping cream, whipped
Assorted fresh fruit

In a heavy saucepan, combine eggs, lemonade concentrate and sugar. Cook and stir over low heat just until mixture comes to a boil. Cool to room temperature, stirring several times. Fold in the whipped cream. Serve over fruit. Refrigerate leftovers. **Yield:** about 3 cups.

Cucumber Shell Salad

Ranch dressing is the mild coating for this pleasant pasta salad chock-full of crunchy cucumber, onion and green peas. Wherever I take it, I'm always asked for the recipe.   —Paula Ishii, Ralston, Nebraska

☑ Uses less fat, sugar or salt. Includes Nutritional Analysis and Diabetic Exchanges.

1 package (16 ounces) medium shell pasta
1 package (16 ounces) frozen peas, thawed
1 medium cucumber, halved and sliced
1 small red onion, chopped
1 cup ranch salad dressing

Cook pasta according to package directions; drain and rinse in cold water. In a large bowl, combine the pasta, peas, cucumber and onion. Add dressing; toss to coat. Cover and chill at least 2 hours before serving. **Yield:** 16 servings.

Nutritional Analysis: One 3/4-cup serving (prepared with fat-free ranch dressing) equals 165 calories, 1 g fat (trace saturated fat), trace cholesterol, 210 mg sodium, 33 g carbohydrate, 3 g fiber, 6 g protein. **Diabetic Exchange:** 2 starch.

Crunchy Coleslaw

This crunchy cabbage salad is so easy to put together that we often have it for spur-of-the-moment picnics or when unexpected company stops by. It gets its nutty flavor from almonds and its crunch from ramen noodles.

—*Julie Vavroch*
Montezuma, Iowa

1/3 cup vegetable oil
1 package (3 ounces) beef-flavored ramen noodles
1/2 teaspoon garlic salt
1 package (16 ounces) shredded coleslaw mix
1 package (5 ounces) sliced almonds

In a small saucepan, heat oil. Stir in contents of noodle seasoning packet and garlic salt; cook for 3-4 minutes or until blended.

Meanwhile, crush the noodles and place in a bowl. Add coleslaw mix and almonds. Drizzle with oil mixture and toss to coat. Serve immediately. **Yield:** 6-8 servings.

Orange Pecan Salad

For a change of pace, replace the pecans with almonds, pistachios or sunflower kernels. Use sweet grapefruit, kiwi, apple slices or grapes in place of the oranges. And orange or plain yogurt with marmalade can be substituted for the peach yogurt. If you'd like to turn the salad into a meal in itself, lend it heartiness with chicken salad or grilled chicken. —*Cheryl Mutch, Edmonton, Alberta*

2 oranges, peeled and sectioned *or* 1 can (11 ounces) mandarin oranges, drained
1 small bunch leaf lettuce, torn
1/4 cup pecan halves, toasted
1/2 cup peach yogurt
3 tablespoons mayonnaise

Toss oranges, lettuce and pecans in a large salad bowl; set aside. Combine yogurt and mayonnaise; pour over salad just before serving. **Yield:** 4 servings.

|WASHING GREENS| Wash greens thoroughly in cool water. Pat them dry with a clean towel or paper towel to remove water. Store in a covered container or plastic bag, and refrigerate at least 1 hour before serving to crisp the greens. Place a piece of paper towel in the bottom of the container or bag to absorb excess moisture.

Walking Salad

This speedy stuffed apple is a great snack for a family hike. In a brown-bag lunch, it's a nice change from the usual peanut butter and jelly sandwich.
—*Mrs. John Crawford, Barnesville, Georgia*

2 tablespoons peanut butter
1 tablespoon raisins
1 teaspoon honey
1 medium apple, cored

In a small bowl, combine peanut butter, raisins and honey. Spoon into center of apple. **Yield:** 1 serving.

Editor's Note: Gala, Golden Delicious and Red Delicious apples are great for eating raw.

Cucumbers With Dressing

It wouldn't be summer if Mom didn't make lots of these creamy cucumbers. Just a few simple ingredients—mayonnaise, sugar, vinegar and salt—dress up slices of this crisp garden vegetable.
—*Michelle Beran, Claflin, Kansas*

1 cup mayonnaise
1/4 cup sugar
1/4 cup vinegar
1/4 teaspoon salt
4 cups sliced cucumbers

In a bowl, combine mayonnaise, sugar, vinegar and salt. Add cucumbers; stir to coat. Cover and refrigerate for 2 hours. **Yield:** 6-8 servings.

Low-Fat Blue Cheese Dressing

You'll never miss the fat in my full-flavored blue cheese dressing. I got the recipe from a chef at a California resort while on vacation a number of years ago.   —*Tracey Baysinger, Salem, Missouri*

 Uses less fat, sugar or salt. Includes Nutritional Analysis and Diabetic Exchanges.

- 1 cup (8 ounces) fat-free cottage cheese
- 1 cup (8 ounces) fat-free plain yogurt
- 2 tablespoons chopped onion
- 1 garlic clove, minced
- 1 tablespoon crumbled blue cheese

In a blender or food processor, combine cottage cheese, yogurt, onion and garlic; cover and process until smooth. Stir in blue cheese. Store, covered, in the refrigerator. **Yield:** 1-3/4 cups.

Nutritional Analysis: One serving (1 tablespoon) equals 11 calories, 34 mg sodium, 1 mg cholesterol, 1 g carbohydrate, 2 g protein, trace fat. **Diabetic Exchange:** Free food.

Cran-Apple Salad

This tart and tasty salad goes so wonderfully with lots of different meals. Folks will think you spent hours on it, but with less than five ingredients, preparation takes only minutes! Crunchy walnuts, celery and apples are a special way to dress up canned cranberry sauce.
    —*Lucille Foster, Grant, Nebraska*

- 1 can (16 ounces) whole-berry cranberry sauce
- 1 medium unpeeled tart apple, diced
- 1 celery rib, thinly sliced
- 1/2 cup chopped walnuts

In a bowl, combine the cranberry sauce, apple and celery. Cover and refrigerate. Stir in walnuts just before serving. **Yield:** 4-6 servings.

Crab and Pea Salad

From picnics to potlucks, this fast-to-fix combination receives rave reviews. I like to garnish it with paprika, sliced hard-cooked eggs, tomatoes and croutons. —*Janine Gillespie* *Milwaukie, Oregon*

1 package (10 ounces) frozen peas, thawed
1 package (8 ounces) imitation crabmeat, flaked
6 to 8 bacon strips, cooked and crumbled
1/2 cup mayonnaise
1/4 teaspoon onion powder

In a bowl, combine peas, crab and bacon. Combine mayonnaise and onion powder; fold into the crab mixture. Cover and refrigerate until serving. **Yield:** 4-6 servings.

|PEA POINTER| For pea salads, simply pour cold water over the frozen peas and let stand about 5 minutes or until the peas are defrosted. Drain well before adding to the salad.

Mallow Fruit Cups

Instead of serving plain fruit cocktail, I toss in a few of my family's favorite ingredients to make this colorful concoction. I created this quick salad when our boys were younger, and it's been around ever since as a good hurry-up fill-in at meals. —*Karen Coffman, Delphi, Indiana*

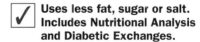 Uses less fat, sugar or salt. Includes Nutritional Analysis and Diabetic Exchanges.

1 can (15 ounces) fruit cocktail, drained
1 medium tart apple, diced
1/2 cup miniature marshmallows
1/2 cup whipped topping

In a bowl, combine all ingredients. Cover and refrigerate until serving. **Yield:** 4-6 servings.

Nutritional Analysis: One 1/2-cup serving (prepared with reduced-fat whipped topping) equals 91 calories, 6 mg sodium, 0 cholesterol, 21 g carbohydrate, trace protein, 1 g fat. **Diabetic Exchange:** 1-1/2 fruit.

Fourth of July Jell-O

With six children, I'm always looking for wholesome quick recipes. This colorful salad can be fixed by school-age children and looks so pretty served in a glass bowl.

—*Mabel Yoder, Bonduel, Wisconsin*

1 package (3 ounces) berry blue gelatin
2 cups boiling water, *divided*
1/2 cup cold water, *divided*
1 package (3 ounces) strawberry gelatin
1 can (15 ounces) pear halves, drained and cubed

In a bowl, dissolve blue gelatin in 1 cup boiling water. Stir in 1/4 cup cold water. Pour into an ungreased 9-in. x 5-in. x 3-in. loaf pan. Refrigerate until firm. Repeat with strawberry gelatin and remaining boiling and cold water.

When gelatin is set, cut into cubes. Just before serving, gently combine gelatin cubes and pears in a large glass bowl or individual dishes. **Yield:** 6-8 servings.

Greens with Herb Vinaigrette

Dijon mustard adds tanginess to the light vinaigrette that coats this salad. For variety, I sometimes add minced garlic or a tablespoon of whipping cream. You can even use flavored vinegars or different types cf oil for a change of pace.

—*Sally Hook, Houston, Texas*

6 to 8 cups torn salad greens
3 tablespoons olive oil
1 tablespoon red wine vinegar
1/2 to 1 teaspoon Dijon mustard
1/2 teaspoon Italian seasoning

Place greens in a salad bowl. Combine remaining ingredients in a jar with tight-fitting lid; shake well. Pour over greens and toss to coat. **Yield:** 6-8 servings.

|TEARING SALAD GREENS| Just before serving, tear—don't cut—the greens into bite-size pieces. Cutting greens with a knife will turn the edges brown with time. Allow greens to stand at room temperature no longer than 15 minutes before serving.

Strawberry Spinach Salad

This is an especially good salad to take to summer potluck dinners. Folks always come back for second helpings of the pretty and refreshing salad. —*Pat Brune, Ridgecrest, California*

3 tablespoons lemon juice
1/4 cup sugar
6 tablespoons vegetable oil
1 package (10 ounces) fresh spinach
2 cups sliced fresh strawberries

Place the lemon juice and sugar in a blender. With blender running, add oil in a slow steady stream; process until slightly thickened.

Just before serving, combine spinach and strawberries in a large salad bowl or individual bowls or plates; drizzle with dressing. **Yield:** 6-8 servings.

Raspberry Congealed Salad

My sisters and I especially enjoyed this cool tangy side dish our mom used to make. Now we make it often ourselves. It looks so lovely on the table. The pineapple and raspberries are a delectable duo, and pecans add a hearty crunch. —*Nancy Duty*
Jacksonville, Florida

1 can (8 ounces) crushed pineapple
1 package (10 ounces) frozen unsweetened raspberries, thawed
1 package (3 ounces) raspberry gelatin
1 cup applesauce
1/4 cup coarsely chopped pecans
Mayonnaise, optional

Drain pineapple and raspberries, reserving juices. Place fruit in a large bowl; set aside. Add enough water to the juice to measure 1 cup. Pour into a saucepan; bring to a boil. Remove from the heat; stir in gelatin until dissolved.

Pour over fruit mixture. Add the applesauce and pecans. Pour into a 1-qt. bowl. Chill until set. Spoon into individual dessert dishes; top with a dollop of mayonnaise if desired. **Yield:** 6 servings.

Strawberry Rhubarb Gelatin

Rhubarb lends a hint of natural tartness to this sweet salad. As a fruity side dish, its vibrant color is sure to add eye-opening appeal to almost any meal. —*Opal Schmidt, Battle Creek, Iowa*

**2 cups diced fresh *or*
    frozen rhubarb
1/2 to 3/4 cup sugar
1/4 cup water
1 package (3 ounces)
    strawberry gelatin
1-1/2 cups whipped topping**

In a saucepan, bring rhubarb, sugar and water to a boil. Reduce heat; simmer, uncovered, for 3-5 minutes or until the rhubarb is softened.

Remove from the heat; stir in gelatin until dissolved. Pour into a bowl. Refrigerate for 20 minutes or until partially set. Fold in whipped topping. Chill until firm. **Yield: 4** servings.

|A "GEL" OF A TIP| If your gelatin mixture sets too fast and you've passed the partially set step, place the bowl of gelatin in a pan of warm water and stir until the gelatin has softened. Chill again until the mixture is the consistency of unbeaten raw egg whites. Then fold in the whipped topping.

Tomato Tossed Salad

I stir chives and thyme into a pleasant dressing to drizzle over this simple salad. It's especially good with sun-ripened tomatoes right out of the garden. —*Edna Hoffman Hebron, Indiana*

**6 cups shredded lettuce
2 medium tomatoes, cut
    into wedges
1/4 cup oil and vinegar salad
    dressing
1 teaspoon snipped chives
1/4 teaspoon dried thyme**

Place lettuce and tomatoes in a salad bowl. Combine salad dressing, chives and thyme; drizzle over salad and toss gently. **Yield:** 4 servings.

Three-Pepper Salad

This salad is a five-ingredient time-saver that serves as an attractive and welcome variation on veggies. After topping the peppers and onion with bottled vinaigrette, I focus on my entree.

—Marilou Robinson, Portland, Oregon

✓ Uses less fat, sugar or salt. Includes Nutritional Analysis and Diabetic Exchanges.

1 *each* medium sweet red, yellow and green pepper, thinly sliced
1 small onion, cut into 1/4-inch wedges
1/3 cup prepared vinaigrette salad dressing

In a bowl, combine the red, yellow and green peppers and onion. Add salad dressing and toss to coat. Refrigerate until serving. **Yield:** 4 servings.

Nutritional Analysis: One 3/4-cup serving (prepared with fat-free Italian salad dressing) equals 58 calories, trace fat (trace saturated fat), 0 cholesterol, 187 mg sodium, 14 g carbohydrate, 2 g fiber, 1 g protein. **Diabetic Exchange:** 2 vegetable.

Simple Caesar Salad

In summer, I'll mix fresh tomato slices and vegetables from our garden in with the salad. I also experiment with different kinds of lettuce than romaine.

—Carolene Esayenko, Calgary, Alberta

6 cups torn romaine
1/2 cup Caesar croutons
2 bacon strips, cooked and crumbled
1/4 cup grated *or* shredded Parmesan cheese
1/3 cup Caesar salad dressing

In a large bowl, combine romaine, croutons, bacon and cheese. Add the salad dressing and toss to coat. **Yield:** 4-6 servings.

Golden Pumpkin Salad

This delicious salad is the result of a bumper crop of pumpkins. I had so many on hand, I started experimenting with different ways of preparing them. The sweet dish I'm sharing here is one we all enjoy.

—Janell Burrell, Cornelia, Georgia

2 cups shredded uncooked fresh pie pumpkin
1 can (8 ounces) crushed pineapple, undrained
1/2 cup raisins
1 tablespoon mayonnaise
1/2 teaspoon sugar
Leaf lettuce, optional

Place pumpkin in a 1-qt. microwave-safe bowl. Cover and microwave on high for 3 minutes; cool. Stir in pineapple, raisins, mayonnaise and sugar. Refrigerate overnight. Serve on lettuce if desired. **Yield:** 4 servings.

Editor's Note: This recipe was tested in an 850-watt microwave.

|TRADING PLACES| Pumpkin can be prepared in almost any way suitable for winter squash. Likewise, winter squash, such as acorn or hubbard, can be substituted for pumpkin in recipes.

Hash Brown Potato Salad

I've used this recipe for over 20 years, and it's still a family favorite. It stirs up and cooks in a jiffy, and it tastes just as good as a German potato salad that you fussed all day to make.

—Joan Hallford, North Richland Hills, Texas

5 bacon strips, diced
6 green onions, sliced
1 package (1 pound) frozen cubed hash brown potatoes
1/4 cup white wine vinegar
1/2 teaspoon celery salt

Place bacon in a 1-1/2-qt. microwave-safe bowl. Cover and microwave on high for 5-6 minutes or until bacon is crisp. Remove with a slotted spoon to paper towels to drain. Add onions to the drippings; cover and microwave on high for 1 minute.

Add the potatoes; cover and cook on high for 10 minutes, stirring several times. Add vinegar, celery salt and bacon; toss. **Yield:** 4 servings.

Editor's Note: This recipe was tested in an 850-watt microwave.

Red-Hot Candy Fluff

A friend at work gave me the recipe for this fluffy pink pineapple salad a few years ago, and I've been preparing it ever since. My two young children really enjoy it, especially when I tell them it has candy in it.

—Shelley Vickrey, Strafford, Missouri

1 can (20 ounces) crushed pineapple, drained
1/4 cup red-hot candies
2 cups miniature marshmallows
1 carton (8 ounces) frozen whipped topping, thawed

In a bowl, combine the pineapple and candies. Cover and refrigerate for 8 hours or overnight. Stir in the marshmallows and whipped topping. Cover and refrigerate until serving. **Yield:** 6-8 servings.

Hawaiian Salad

To add a refreshing spark to any meal, try this tempting salad with tropical flair. A few simple ingredients are easily combined to make a memorable salad. We always empty the bowl. —Lisa Andis Morristown, Indiana

1 can (8 ounces) pineapple tidbits
6 to 8 cups torn salad greens
1 cup (4 ounces) shredded cheddar cheese
1/2 cup mayonnaise
1 tablespoon sugar

Drain pineapple, reserving 1 tablespoon juice. In a large bowl, combine greens, pineapple and cheese. In a small bowl, combine the mayonnaise, sugar and reserved pineapple juice; mix well. Pour over salad; toss to coat. Serve immediately. **Yield:** 6 servings.

Honey Mustard Salad Dressing

From the first time I tasted this salad dressing, it has been a favorite at our house, served almost exclusively. It's quick to prepare, and it's easily made "light" by using fat-free or reduced-fat mayo.
—*Patty Brewer, Kansas City, Missouri*

6 tablespoons mayonnaise
2 tablespoons Dijon mustard
2 tablespoons honey

In a bowl, combine the mayonnaise, mustard and honey; mix well. Store in refrigerator. **Yield:** about 1/2 cup dressing.

Pear Lime Gelatin

Packed with pears, this jolly gelatin salad is a light and refreshing treat for the holidays. My mom knew that fruit served in this fun form would get gobbled right up. She also liked it because the bowl looked like a sparkling jewel on our dinner table.
—*Sandy Jenkins*
Elkhorn, Wisconsin

 Uses less fat, sugar or salt. Includes Nutritional Analysis and Diabetic Exchanges.

1 can (29 ounces) pear halves, undrained
1 package (3 ounces) lime gelatin
1 package (3 ounces) cream cheese, cubed
1 cup whipped topping

Drain pears, reserving juice; set pears aside. Measure the juice; add water if needed to equal 1-1/2 cups. Pour into a saucepan; bring to a boil. Add gelatin; stir until dissolved. Gradually add cream cheese, whisking until smooth. Cover and refrigerate until cool.

Mash reserved pears; fold into gelatin mixture. Fold in whipped topping. Pour into a 6-cup serving bowl. Refrigerate until set. **Yield:** 6 servings.

Nutritional Analysis: One serving (prepared with sugar-free gelatin and reduced-fat cream cheese and whipped topping) equals 172 calories, 3 g fat (2 g saturated fat), 5 mg cholesterol, 398 mg sodium, 21 g carbohydrate, 2 g fiber, 8 g protein. **Diabetic Exchanges:** 2 fruit, 1 fat.

Applesauce Gelatin Squares

I make this attractive soft-set salad during the holidays and garnish it with ranch dressing that's tinted green. Or spoon on a dollop of whipped topping for a light sweet dessert anytime.
—*Judy Ernst*
Montague, Michigan

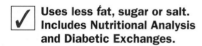 **Uses less fat, sugar or salt. Includes Nutritional Analysis and Diabetic Exchanges.**

4 packages (.3 ounce *each*) sugar-free raspberry gelatin *or* flavor of your choice
4 cups boiling water
2 cups cold water
1 jar (46 ounces) unsweetened applesauce

In a bowl, dissolve gelatin in boiling water. Stir in cold water and applesauce. Pour into a 13-in. x 9-in. x 2-in. dish coated with nonstick cooking spray. Refrigerate for 8 hours or overnight. Cut into squares. **Yield:** 16 servings.

  Nutritional Analysis: One serving equals 42 calories, 48 mg sodium, 0 cholesterol, 10 g carbohydrate, 1 g protein, trace fat. **Diabetic Exchange:** 1/2 fruit.

Zesty Vegetable Salad

This fresh-tasting medley is a terrific way to use your garden bounty. When people rave about it, I'm almost embarrassed to tell them how easy it is to make.   —*Dana Nemecek, Skiatook, Oklahoma*

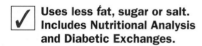 **Uses less fat, sugar or salt. Includes Nutritional Analysis and Diabetic Exchanges.**

10 fresh mushrooms, sliced
 2 medium tomatoes, chopped
 2 medium cucumbers, peeled and chopped
 1 small onion, chopped
 1 bottle (8 ounces) zesty Italian salad dressing

In a bowl, combine mushrooms, tomatoes, cucumbers and onion. Add dressing; toss to coat. Cover and chill at least 2 hours. Serve with a slotted spoon. **Yield:** 12 servings.

  Nutritional Analysis: One 1/2-cup serving (prepared with fat-free salad dressing) equals 29 calories, 137 mg sodium, 0 cholesterol, 5 g carbohydrate, 1 g protein, trace fat. **Diabetic Exchange:** 1 vegetable.

Side Dishes & Condiments

Onion-Roasted Potatoes, p. 162

Green Beans Amandine, p. 167

| CONDIMENTS |

Zucchini Pancakes, p. 163

Onion-Roasted Potatoes

(Pictured on page 160 and on front cover)

Slightly crisp on the outside and tender on the inside, these potatoes are a hit with my family. This side dish is one of my favorites because the soup mix glazes the potatoes so nicely, and it's very simple to prepare. —*Schelby Thompson, Winter Haven, Florida*

> 2 pounds red potatoes, sliced 1/2 inch thick
> 1/3 cup vegetable oil
> 1 envelope dry onion soup mix

Combine all ingredients in a large plastic bag; shake until well coated. Empty bag into an ungreased 13-in. x 9-in. x 2-in. baking pan.

Cover and bake at 350° for 35 minutes, stirring occasionally. Uncover and bake 15 minutes longer or until potatoes are tender. **Yield:** 6-8 servings.

Citrus Carrot Sticks

I frequently serve these julienned carrots that pick up a pleasant tang from orange juice and cumin. I like to tie up the carrots in little bundles with a cut green onion. But they also taste great from a serving bowl. —*Amy Volk Geneva, Illinois*

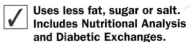

✓ **Uses less fat, sugar or salt. Includes Nutritional Analysis and Diabetic Exchanges.**

> 3 tablespoons orange juice
> 1 teaspoon butter, melted
> 1/2 teaspoon ground cumin
> 1 pound carrots
> 6 cups water

Combine orange juice, butter and cumin; set aside. Cut carrots into 3-in. chunks, then into matchstick strips. In a large saucepan, bring water to a boil. Add carrots; cook for about 2 minutes or until crisp-tender. Drain; place in a serving bowl. Drizzle with orange juice mixture. **Yield:** 6 servings.

Nutritional Analysis: One serving (prepared with margarine) equals 44 calories, 35 mg sodium, 0 cholesterol, 9 g carbohydrate, 1 g protein, 1 g fat. **Diabetic Exchange:** 1-1/2 vegetable.

Corn State Broccoli Bake

Since our state is known for growing corn, I planned a corn theme dinner for our grandson's first visit a number of years ago. A double dose of corn—whole kernel plus cream style—teams up with broccoli in this colorful side dish. —*Nadine Brimeyer*
Denver, Iowa

1 package (8 ounces) Chicken in a Biskit crackers, crushed
1/2 cup butter, melted
1 package (10 ounces) frozen chopped broccoli, thawed
1 can (15-1/4 ounces) whole kernel corn, drained
1 can (14-3/4 ounces) cream-style corn

Combine cracker crumbs and butter; reserve 1/2 cup for topping. In a bowl, combine broccoli, both cans of corn and remaining crumbs.

Transfer to a greased 2-qt. baking dish. Sprinkle with reserved crumb mixture. Bake, uncovered, at 375° for 25-30 minutes or until lightly browned. **Yield:** 6-8 servings.

|A KERNEL ON CORN| Corn was first grown in Mexico and Central America and was a staple of the Native Americans. Today, Americans annually consume about 25 pounds of corn per person. There are more than 200 varieties grown worldwide.

Zucchini Pancakes

(Pictured on page 161)

My Zucchini Pancakes are a delicious change of pace from the more common potato variety. They fry up golden brown, crispy on the outside and tender inside. —*Charlotte Goldberg*
Honey Grove, Pennsylvania

1-1/2 cups shredded zucchini
1 egg, lightly beaten
2 tablespoons biscuit/baking mix
3 tablespoons grated Parmesan cheese
1 tablespoon vegetable oil

In a bowl, combine zucchini, egg, baking mix and cheese. Heat oil in a skillet over medium heat; drop batter by 1/4 cupfuls and flatten. Fry until golden brown; turn and cook the other side. **Yield:** 4 servings.

Never-Fail Egg Noodles

Some 35 years ago, the small church I attended held a chicken and noodle fund-raiser supper. I was put in charge of noodles for 200 people! A dear lady shared this recipe and said it had been tried and tested by countless cooks. These noodles are just plain good eating!

—Kathryn Roach
Greers Ferry, Arkansas

1 egg plus 3 egg yolks
3 tablespoons cold water
1 teaspoon salt
2 cups all-purpose flour
Chopped fresh parsley, optional

In a mixing bowl, beat egg and yolks until light and fluffy. Add water and salt; mix well. Stir in flour. Turn onto a floured surface; knead until smooth. Divide into thirds.

Roll out each portion to 1/8-in. thickness. Cut noodles to desired width (noodles shown in the photo were cut 2 in. x 1/2 in.). Cook immediately in boiling salted water or chicken broth for 7-9 minutes or until tender. Drain; sprinkle with parsley if desired. **Yield:** about 5-1/2 cups.

Editor's Note: Uncooked noodles may be stored in the refrigerator for 2-3 days or frozen for up to 1 month. Unsalted water will reach a boil faster than salted water, so add salt to rapidly boiling water just before adding the pasta.

Blueberry Sauce Supreme

When we get "blue" here at SGB Farms, we're not sad—we're in the middle of our 5-week blueberry harvest, which starts in mid-June! We have 1,500 plants on 1.4 acres. Every day we eat blueberries on our cereal or enjoy them in muffins, pies and desserts. A favorite treat is Blueberry Sauce Supreme, which we love over pancakes and waffles. —Clarence Scrivner, Hartsburg, Missouri

1/2 cup sugar
1/4 cup orange juice
   concentrate
2 tablespoons cornstarch
3 cups fresh or frozen
   blueberries

In a saucepan, combine sugar, orange juice concentrate and cornstarch; stir until smooth. Add blueberries and bring to a boil. Boil for 2 minutes, stirring constantly. **Yield:** 2-1/4 cups.

Sauteed Mushrooms

I frequently fix this speedy side dish for my hungry family. Spiced carrots would be a mouth-watering companion in the pan to the mushrooms.
—*Hope Meece, Fowler, Indiana*

1/4 cup butter
1 pound fresh mushrooms, sliced
1 tablespoon lemon juice
1 tablespoon soy sauce

In a skillet, melt butter. Add mushrooms, lemon juice and soy sauce. Saute for 6-8 minutes or until mushrooms are tender. **Yield:** 4 servings.

|SAUTEING SUGGESTIONS| Sauteing mushrooms brings out and concentrates their flavor. Make sure the pan and butter are hot and don't overcrowd—mushrooms exude a lot of moisture during cooking, and you want to be able to stir them around in the pan. Otherwise, they'll steam rather than saute.

Dilled Zucchini

These super squash couldn't be easier to prepare! Their mild flavor goes well with a variety of main dishes, but I especially like them alongside chicken. The recipe is a great way to put a bumper crop of zucchini to good use.
—*Sundra Lewis
Bogalusa, Louisiana*

 Uses less fat, sugar or salt. Includes Nutritional Analysis and Diabetic Exchanges.

3 medium zucchini, halved lengthwise
1 tablespoon butter, melted
1/4 teaspoon dill weed
Salt and pepper, optional

Place zucchini in a skillet and cover with water; bring to a boil over medium heat. Cook until tender, about 12-14 minutes. Drain; brush with butter. Sprinkle with dill and salt and pepper if desired. **Yield:** 6 servings.

Nutritional Analysis: One serving (prepared with margarine and without salt) equals 28 calories, 25 mg sodium, 0 cholesterol, 2 g carbohydrate, 1 g protein, 2 g fat. **Diabetic Exchanges:** 1/2 vegetable, 1/2 fat.

Easy Pasta Alfredo

Who would believe that five simple ingredients could taste so rich and delicious? This creamy, comforting sauce can be made in a matter of minutes. —*Karin DeCarlo, Milford, Pennsylvania*

1/2 cup butter
1 cup heavy whipping cream
1/8 teaspoon ground nutmeg
1 cup shredded Parmesan cheese
1 package (19 ounces) frozen cheese tortellini

In a saucepan, melt butter over medium-low heat. Add cream and nutmeg; heat through but do not boil. Stir in Parmesan cheese until melted.

Cook tortellini according to package directions; drain. Transfer to a large serving bowl. Add the cheese sauce and toss to coat. Serve immediately. **Yield:** 4 servings.

Mom's Carrot Casserole

Rich and cheesy, this casserole is the very best way to eat carrots. Pretty orange slices peek out from under a bed of buttery cracker crumbs. My mom loves to cook and share recipes. She picked this one up from a dear friend.
—*Gloria Grant, Sterling, Illinois*

2 pounds carrots, sliced
1/2 cup butter, *divided*
6 ounces process cheese (Velveeta), cubed
1/4 teaspoon dill weed
1/2 cup crushed saltines (about 15 crackers)

Place carrots in a saucepan and cover with water; bring to a boil. Reduce heat; cover and simmer until tender, about 10 minutes. Drain; place in a greased 1-1/2-qt. baking dish.

In a small saucepan, melt 1/4 cup butter and cheese, stirring often. Stir in dill. Pour over the carrots. Toss the saltines and remaining butter; sprinkle over carrots. Bake, uncovered, at 350° for 25-30 minutes or until lightly browned and bubbly. **Yield:** 8 servings.

Grilled Peppers and Zucchini

This versatile side dish is so simple and quick that I had to share it. Grilling the colorful veggies in a foil packet means one less dish to wash, but I often stir-fry the mixture on the stovetop instead.

—*Karen Anderson*
Fair Oaks, California

1 medium green pepper, julienned
1 medium sweet red pepper, julienned
2 medium zucchini, julienned
1 tablespoon butter
2 teaspoons soy sauce

Place the vegetables on a double layer of heavy-duty foil (about 18 in. x 15 in.). Dot with butter; drizzle with soy sauce. Fold foil around vegetables and seal tightly. Grill, covered, over medium heat for 10-15 minutes or until vegetables are crisp-tender. **Yield:** 3-4 servings.

Green Beans Amandine

(Pictured on page 161)

It's hard to improve on the taste Mother Nature gives to fresh green beans, but my own mom has for years using this recipe. I have always thought the crunchy almonds were a super addition.

—*Brenda DuFresne, Midland, Michigan*

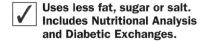 Uses less fat, sugar or salt. Includes Nutritional Analysis and Diabetic Exchanges.

1 pound fresh *or* frozen green beans, cut into 2-inch pieces
1/2 cup water
1/4 cup slivered almonds
2 tablespoons butter
1 teaspoon lemon juice
1/4 teaspoon seasoned salt, optional

In a saucepan, bring beans and water to a boil; reduce heat to medium. Cover and cook for 10-15 minutes or until the beans are crisp-tender; drain and set aside. In a large skillet, cook almonds in butter over low heat. Stir in lemon juice and seasoned salt if desired. Add beans and heat through. **Yield:** 6 servings.

Nutritional Analysis: One 1/2-cup serving (prepared with margarine and without seasoned salt) equals 92 calories, 50 mg sodium, 0 cholesterol, 7 g carbohydrate, 3 g protein, 7 g fat. **Diabetic Exchanges:** 1-1/2 fat, 1 vegetable.

Crumb-Topped Brussels Sprouts

This makes a flavorful side dish sure to dress up any meal. Even folks who normally don't care for brussels sprouts like them prepared this way. The bread crumb and Parmesan cheese coating is a delicious way to top them off. —*Ruth Peterson*
Jenison, Michigan

1-1/2 pounds fresh *or* frozen brussels sprouts
3 tablespoons butter, melted, *divided*
1/4 cup Italian-seasoned dry bread crumbs
2 tablespoons grated Parmesan cheese

Cut an X in the core of each brussels sprout. In a saucepan, cook brussels sprouts in salted water until crisp-tender, about 8-10 minutes; drain. Place in an ungreased shallow 1-1/2-qt. baking dish. Drizzle with 2 tablespoons butter.

Combine bread crumbs, Parmesan cheese and remaining butter; sprinkle over brussels sprouts. Cover and bake at 325° for 10 minutes. Uncover and bake 10 minutes longer. **Yield:** 4-6 servings.

Editor's Note: Brussels sprouts can be cooked, cooled, quartered and made into a cold salad, mixed with diced tomatoes and tossed with a vinaigrette. After cooking and cooling, they can also be cut into 1/4-inch slices and sauteed with scallions, garlic and minced ginger for a wonderful change of pace.

Cherry Sauce for Ham

I often whip up this simple topping to pour over ham at church dinners. It's long been a favored condiment there—and at home, too. The concoction's spicy zing comes from the dab of mustard I pour into the mix.   —*Tess Krumm, Fargo, North Dakota*

1 can (21 ounces) cherry pie filling
1 tablespoon brown sugar
1/2 teaspoon prepared mustard

Combine all the ingredients in a small saucepan; bring to a boil. Reduce heat and simmer for 5-10 minutes. **Yield:** 2 cups.

Sweet-and-Sour Beets

With their lovely jewel tones and tangy glaze, these beets take center stage. They always earn rave reviews!
—*Emily Chaney, Penobscot, Maine*

✓ **Uses less fat, sugar or salt. Includes Nutritional Analysis and Diabetic Exchanges.**

1/2 cup water
1/4 cup vinegar
2 teaspoons cornstarch
4 teaspoons sugar
2 cups sliced cooked beets

In a saucepan, combine water, vinegar and cornstarch; bring to a boil. Cook and stir for 1-2 minutes; remove from the heat. Add sugar and beets; let stand for 1 hour. Heat through just before serving. **Yield:** 4 servings.

Nutritional Analysis: One serving equals 49 calories, 37 mg sodium, 0 cholesterol, 12 g carbohydrate, 1 g protein, trace fat. **Diabetic Exchange:** 2 vegetable.

Chunky Cinnamon Applesauce

As a young girl, I was amazed when Mom transformed fresh apples into this delightful, lovely mixture. I'm not sure if I liked it so much because it was made with candies or because it tasted wonderful.
—*Barbara Hyatt, Folsom, California*

8 medium tart apples,
  peeled and quartered
1 cup water
1 cup sugar
1/4 cup red-hot candies

Place apples and water in a 5-qt. saucepan. Cover and cook over medium-low heat for 20 minutes or until tender. Mash the apples. Add sugar and candies. Cook, uncovered, until sugar and candies are dissolved. Remove from the heat; cool. Refrigerate until serving. **Yield:** 6 cups.

Creamy Italian Noodles

This is an easy recipe for no-fail noodles that are a flavorful accompaniment to most any meat. Rich and creamy, they're special enough for company, too.   —*Linda Hendrix, Moundville, Missouri*

1 package (8 ounces) wide
   egg noodles
1/4 cup butter, softened
1/2 cup heavy whipping
   cream, half-and-half
   cream *or* evaporated milk
1/4 cup grated Parmesan
   cheese
2-1/4 teaspoons Italian salad
   dressing mix

Cook noodles according to package directions; drain and place in a bowl. Toss with butter. Add the remaining ingredients and mix well. Serve immediately. **Yield:** 4-6 servings.

|CRASH COURSE IN CREAM| Cream is categorized according to the amount of milk fat it contains. Heavy whipping cream has a fat content of between 36% and 40%. Half-and-half is a mixture of equal parts milk and cream, and contains from 10% to 18% milk fat. Evaporated milk comes in whole, reduced-fat and fat-free versions, and has had 60% of the water removed.

Cheesy Squash

I'm a retired police officer and now a deputy sheriff who loves to cook. But with my busy schedule, I must rely on speedy side dishes like this one. The squash retains its fresh taste and cooks to a perfect tender-crispness. You can give this cheesy treatment to other fresh veggies, too. It's so quick that I make some variation of it a few times a week. Everyone loves it!   —*Randy Lawrence*
Clinton, Mississippi

1 small zucchini
1 small yellow summer
   squash
Salt and pepper to taste
1 cup (4 ounces) shredded
   mozzarella cheese
1/4 cup grated Parmesan
   cheese

Cut zucchini and yellow squash into 1/4-in. slices. Place in a greased shallow 1-qt. baking dish. Sprinkle with salt and pepper. Top with cheeses. Broil 4 in. from the heat for 7-10 minutes or until squash is crisp-tender and cheese is bubbly. Serve immediately. **Yield:** 2 servings.

Barbecue Butter Beans

Flavorful bacon and a sweet sauce spark the flavor of Barbecue Butter Beans. It takes only minutes to stir together this speedy side dish, making it perfect for potlucks.

—*Linda Hartsell*
Apple Creek, Ohio

2 cans (15 ounces *each*)
  butter beans, rinsed and
  drained
3/4 **cup packed brown sugar**
1/2 **cup ketchup**
1/2 **cup chopped onion**
3 **bacon strips, diced**

In a bowl, combine the beans, brown sugar, ketchup and onion. Transfer to a greased 1-1/2-qt. baking dish. Sprinkle with bacon. Bake, uncovered, at 350° for 1-1/2 hours. **Yield:** 4-6 servings.

Fried Green Tomatoes

My grandmother came up with her own version of fried green tomatoes years ago. Our family loves it. It's a traditional taste of the South that anyone anywhere can enjoy!
—*Melanie Chism*
Coker, Alabama

4 **medium green tomatoes**
1 **teaspoon salt**
1/4 **teaspoon lemon-pepper**
  seasoning
3/4 **cup cornmeal**
1/2 **cup vegetable oil**

Slice tomatoes 1/4 in. thick. Sprinkle both sides with salt and lemon-pepper. Let stand for 20-25 minutes. Coat with cornmeal. In a large skillet, heat oil over medium heat. Fry tomatoes for 3-4 minutes on each side or until tender and golden brown. Drain on paper towels. Serve immediately. **Yield:** 6-8 servings.

|BAKED GREEN TOMATOES| Cut 4 medium green tomatoes into 1/2-inch slices; arrange in a greased baking dish. Season with salt and pepper. Sprinkle 1/2 cup brown sugar and 3/4 cup buttery cracker crumbs over the top; dot with 4 tablespoons butter. Bake at 350° for 25-35 minutes or until tender but still firm.

Cheesy Broccoli Macaroni

You'll need just four ingredients to fix this macaroni and cheese that gets extra flavor from broccoli and bacon. It's a quick and easy dish, and it makes a nice lunch or side dish for supper.
—Dorothy Pritchett
Wills Point, Texas

1 cup frozen chopped broccoli
8 ounces process cheese (Velveeta), cubed
2-1/2 cups cooked elbow macaroni
3 bacon strips, cooked and crumbled

In a large saucepan, cook broccoli according to package directions until crisp-tender; drain. Add the cheese; cook and stir over medium-low heat until cheese is melted. Add macaroni; heat through. Sprinkle with bacon. **Yield:** 4 servings.

|PASTA POINTER| Cook the elbow macaroni for Cheesy Broccoli Macaroni ahead of time. It can be stored in the refrigerator up to 2 days in an airtight container. Warm the pasta by placing it in a colander and rinsing it with hot water. Drain well before adding to the recipe.

Cinnamon Cream Syrup

Looking for a change of pace from maple syrup? Try this special topping. It jazzes up pancakes, waffles or French toast.
—Mrs. Hamilton Myers Jr., Charlottesville, Virginia

1 cup sugar
1/2 cup light corn syrup
1/4 cup water
3/4 teaspoon ground cinnamon
1/2 cup evaporated milk

In a saucepan, combine the sugar, corn syrup, water and cinnamon; bring to a boil over medium heat. Boil for 2 minutes or until thickened. Remove from the heat; cool for 5 minutes. Stir in milk. **Yield:** 1-1/2 cups.

|SWEET SUGGESTION| Before measuring syrupy sweeteners such as honey and corn syrup, lightly coat the measuring cup with vegetable oil. Every drop of the syrup will easily slip out instead of clinging to the sides of the cup. Use clear measuring cups for syrups.

Green Bean Bundles

I like to bake green beans in little bundles secured with strips of bacon. A few minutes under the broiler makes the bacon crispy. This dish gets its tang from Italian dressing, which the beans are baked in.
—*Ame Andrews, Little Rock, Arkansas*

6 cups water
1/2 pound fresh green beans, trimmed
4 to 6 bacon strips
3/4 cup Italian salad dressing

In a saucepan, bring water to a boil. Add beans; cover and cook for 3 minutes. Drain and set aside. Cut bacon in half lengthwise; place on a microwave-safe plate. Microwave on high for 2-1/2 to 3 minutes or until edges curl. Place four or five beans on each bacon strip; wrap bacon around beans and tie in a knot.

Place bundles in an 8-in. square baking dish. Drizzle with salad dressing. Bake, uncovered, at 350° for 10-15 minutes or until beans are crisp-tender. Broil 4 in. from the heat for 2-3 minutes or until bacon is crisp. **Yield:** 4-6 servings.

Seafood Stuffing

For an easy and elegant side dish, I add canned crab and shrimp to boxed stuffing mix. When I served this to my mom as part of her birthday dinner, she said it was the best she had ever tasted...and next time she wanted just the stuffing for her meal!
—*Marcy Thrall, Haddam Neck, Connecticut*

1 package (6 ounces) instant chicken-flavored stuffing mix
1 can (6 ounces) crabmeat, drained and cartilage removed *or* 1 cup imitation crabmeat
1 can (6 ounces) small shrimp, rinsed and drained *or* 1 cup frozen small cooked shrimp
1 teaspoon lemon juice

Prepare stuffing according to package directions. Gently stir in crab, shrimp and lemon juice. Serve immediately. **Yield:** 4-6 servings.

Sweet 'n' Sour Rhubarb Sauce

The beauty of this easy sauce is its natural bright-red color and its versatility. It's so good served over chicken, turkey or pork.
—Sharon Logan, Fort Atkinson, Wisconsin

4 cups diced fresh *or* frozen rhubarb, thawed
2 cups fresh *or* frozen cranberries
1-1/4 cups sugar
1/2 cup orange juice
1/2 cup honey

In a large saucepan, combine all ingredients. Bring to a boil; reduce heat. Simmer, uncovered, for 15-20 minutes or until rhubarb is tender and sauce is thickened. **Yield:** 3-3/4 cups.

Fruited Sweet Potatoes

I dress up convenient canned sweet potatoes and apricot halves with brown sugar and cinnamon. This fast-to-fix side dish is delicious with a ham dinner.
—Nancy Zimmerman
Cape May Court House, New Jersey

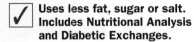

✓ Uses less fat, sugar or salt. Includes Nutritional Analysis and Diabetic Exchanges.

2 cans (15 ounces *each*) cut sweet potatoes
1 can (15-1/4 ounces) apricot halves
3 tablespoons brown sugar
1 tablespoon cornstarch
1/8 teaspoon ground cinnamon

Drain sweet potatoes and apricots, reserving 1/2 cup syrup from each. If desired, cut apricots into fourths. Place potatoes and apricots in a greased 1-1/2-qt. baking dish.

In a saucepan, combine brown sugar, cornstarch, cinnamon and reserved syrup; stir until smooth. Bring to a boil over medium-high heat. Remove from the heat; pour over potatoes and apricots. Bake, uncovered, at 350° for 25 minutes or until bubbly. **Yield:** 6 servings.

Nutritional Analysis: One 1/2-cup serving (prepared with light apricot halves) equals 192 calories, 68 mg sodium, 0 cholesterol, 46 g carbohydrate, 2 g protein, trace fat. **Diabetic Exchanges:** 2 starch, 1 fruit.

Bacon Cheese Fries

These tempting potatoes are one finger food I can make a meal of. Quick to fix, they're a hit with dinner guests. Ranch dressing is a tasty alternative to sour cream. —*Marilyn Dutkus Laguna Beach, California*

1 package (32 ounces) frozen French fried potatoes
1 cup (4 ounces) shredded cheddar cheese
1/2 cup thinly sliced green onions
1/4 cup cooked crumbled bacon
Ranch salad dressing

Cook French fries according to package directions. Place fries on a broiler-proof dish or platter. Sprinkle with cheese, onions and bacon. Broil for 1-2 minutes or until cheese is melted. Serve with ranch dressing. **Yield:** 8-10 servings.

Green Chili Rice

With only five ingredients, this rich and creamy rice casserole mixes up in a snap. I always get requests for the recipe. —*Sandra Hanson, Emery, South Dakota*

1 can (10-3/4 ounces) condensed cream of celery soup, undiluted
1 cup (8 ounces) sour cream
1 can (4 ounces) chopped green chilies
1 cup (4 ounces) shredded cheddar cheese
1-1/2 cups uncooked instant rice

In a bowl, combine the soup, sour cream, chilies and cheese. Stir in rice. Transfer to a greased shallow 1-1/2-qt. baking dish. Bake, uncovered, at 350° for 20 minutes or until rice is tender. **Yield:** 4-6 servings.

Creamy Sweet Corn

I like to use half-and-half cream to dress up both fresh and frozen corn. The simple side dish tastes rich and takes just minutes to simmer together on the stovetop.

—Florence Jacoby
Granite Falls, Minnesota

2 cups fresh *or* frozen corn
1/4 cup half-and-half cream
2 tablespoons butter
1 tablespoon sugar
1/2 teaspoon salt

In a saucepan, combine all ingredients. Bring to a boil over medium heat; reduce heat. Simmer, uncovered, for 6-8 minutes or until heated through. **Yield:** 4 servings.

Light Scalloped Potatoes

Even with lighter ingredients like reduced-sodium chicken bouillon and Parmesan cheese, this is a comforting potato dish.

—Tamie Foley, Pasadena, California

 Uses less fat, sugar or salt. Includes Nutritional Analysis and Diabetic Exchanges.

6 medium potatoes, peeled and thinly sliced
3 cups water
4 reduced-sodium chicken bouillon cubes
1 garlic clove, minced
1/2 cup grated Parmesan cheese
Minced fresh parsley, optional

Place potatoes in a greased 2-qt. baking dish that has been coated with nonstick cooking spray. In a saucepan, heat water, bouillon and garlic until bouillon is dissolved; pour over potatoes. Sprinkle with Parmesan cheese.

Bake, uncovered, at 350° for 1-1/4 to 1-1/2 hours or until tender. Let stand 10 minutes before serving. Sprinkle with parsley if desired. Serve with a slotted spoon. **Yield:** 6 servings.

Nutritional Analysis: One 1/2-cup serving equals 175 calories, 168 mg sodium, 7 mg cholesterol, 32 g carbohydrate, 3 g protein, 3 g fat. **Diabetic Exchanges:** 2 starch, 1/2 fat.

|HOT POTATO HINTS| Store potatoes in a basket, net bag or paper bag in a dry, dark, cool, well-ventilated area for up to 2 weeks; do not refrigerate. Refrigerating potatoes causes them to become overly sweet and to turn dark when cooked.

Crunchy Celery Casserole

I first sampled this tempting treatment for celery when a friend brought it to a 4-H covered dish dinner. We could not believe how good it tastes or how easy it is to prepare in the microwave.
—*Michelle Garretson, Newcomerstown, Ohio*

10 celery ribs, thinly sliced
2 cans (10-3/4 ounces *each*) condensed cream of celery soup, undiluted
1 can (8 ounces) sliced water chestnuts, drained
1 can (2.8 ounces) french-fried onions

In a bowl, combine the celery, soup and water chestnuts. Pour into a greased microwave-safe 8-in. square dish. Cover and microwave on high for 27 minutes or until the celery is tender, stirring every 5 minutes. Sprinkle with onions. Microwave, uncovered, 5 minutes longer. **Yield:** 8 servings.

Editor's Note: This recipe was tested in an 850-watt microwave.

Noodle Rice Pilaf

By adding a few fine egg noodles to a rice pilaf, you can have a deliciously different side dish. Terrific with fish, this dish also goes well with meat or poultry.
—*Kathy Schrecengost, Oswego, New York*

1/4 cup butter
1 cup long grain rice
1/2 cup uncooked fine egg noodles *or* vermicelli
2-3/4 cups chicken broth
2 tablespoons minced fresh parsley

In a saucepan, melt butter. Add the rice and noodles; cook and stir until lightly browned, about 3 minutes. Stir in broth; bring to a boil. Reduce heat; cover and simmer for 20-25 minutes or until broth is absorbed and rice is tender. Stir in parsley. **Yield:** 4 servings.

Tangy Barbecue Sauce

This sweet and tangy basting sauce came from my husband's family. With just four ingredients, it's simple to stir up. A speedy alternative to bottled sauce, it can be brushed on chicken, ribs, pork or even turkey.

—*Jenine Schmidt, Stoughton, Wisconsin*

> 1 cup ketchup
> 2/3 cup packed brown sugar
> 2 teaspoons prepared
>   mustard
> 1/2 teaspoon ground nutmeg

In a bowl, combine all ingredients. Store in the refrigerator. **Yield:** 1-1/3 cups.

|BASTING BASICS| When grilling, brush on thick or sweet sauces during the last 10 to 15 minutes of cooking, basting and turning every few minutes to prevent burning. Use tongs to turn meat instead of a meat fork to avoid piercing and losing juices.

Glazed Carrot Coins

When I pull fresh carrots from the garden, my mouth waters just thinking about how this simple recipe enhances their flavor with brown sugar and a hint of lemon.

—*Pat Habiger, Spearville, Kansas*

> 12 medium carrots, cut
>   into 1-inch pieces
> 1/2 cup packed brown sugar
> 3 tablespoons butter
> 1 tablespoon grated lemon
>   peel
> 1/4 teaspoon vanilla extract

In a saucepan, cook carrots in a small amount of water until crisp-tender; drain. Remove and keep warm. In the same pan, heat brown sugar and butter until bubbly. Stir in lemon peel.

Return carrots to pan; cook and stir over low heat for 10-15 minutes or until glazed. Remove from the heat; stir in vanilla. **Yield:** 6 servings.

Asparagus With Pimientos

This lovely, simple-to-prepare spring dish highlights the asparagus rather than hiding it. The delicate topping of Parmesan cheese and bread crumbs complements the asparagus flavor and looks impressive.

—Adeline Piscitelli
Sayreville, New Jersey

1 **pound fresh asparagus, trimmed**
1/4 **cup dry bread crumbs**
3 **tablespoons butter**
2 **tablespoons grated Parmesan cheese**
2 **tablespoons chopped pimientos**

In a saucepan over medium heat, cook asparagus in boiling salted water until tender, about 8 minutes. Meanwhile, in a skillet, brown bread crumbs in butter. Drain asparagus; place in a serving dish. Sprinkle with crumbs, cheese and pimientos. **Yield:** 4-6 servings.

|ASPARAGUS TIPS| Choose firm, bright-green stalks with tight tips. Avoid limp, dry-looking spears. In general, the thinner the spear, the more tender it will be. If you pick asparagus stalks that are all approximately the same size and thickness, they'll cook more evenly.

Creamy Horseradish Sauce

My favorite way to use this sauce is on cold roast beef sandwiches. But it really complements a variety of foods.

—Florence Palmer, Marshall, Illinois

1 **cup heavy whipping cream**
1 **cup mayonnaise**
1/8 **teaspoon salt**
1/4 **cup prepared horseradish**

In a mixing bowl, whip cream until soft peaks form. Add mayonnaise and salt; blend thoroughly. Fold in horseradish. Store in the refrigerator. **Yield:** 3-1/2 cups.

|ABOUT HORSERADISH| Prepared horseradish is available white (preserved in vinegar) and red (preserved in beet juice). Store it in a tightly covered jar in the refrigerator; it will keep about 4 to 6 weeks. Stored in the freezer, it'll last 6 months. As prepared horseradish ages, it darkens and loses its pungency.

Savory Sprouts

Cream of chicken soup creates the easy sauce that coats these tender sprouts. Seasoned with thyme and sprinkled with sliced almonds, this side dish is special enough for guests.
—Daphne Blandford
Gander, Newfoundland

1 package (16 ounces) frozen brussels sprouts
1 can (10-3/4 ounces) condensed cream of chicken soup, undiluted
3 tablespoons milk
1/4 teaspoon dried thyme
1/4 cup sliced almonds, toasted

Cut an X in the core of each brussels sprout. In a saucepan, cook brussels sprouts according to package directions; drain. Remove sprouts and set aside.

To the saucepan, add soup, milk and thyme; heat through. Return sprouts to pan; stir to coat. Transfer to a serving dish; sprinkle with almonds. **Yield:** 4-6 servings.

Breaded Eggplant Slices

These crisp golden rounds are a fun and different way to serve eggplant. Even folks who aren't fond of eggplant like it fixed this way.
—Phyllis Schmalz, Kansas City, Kansas

 Uses less fat, sugar or salt. Includes Nutritional Analysis and Diabetic Exchanges.

1 medium eggplant (about 1 pound)
1/2 cup dry bread crumbs
1/4 cup grated Parmesan cheese
1 bottle (8 ounces) fat-free Italian salad dressing

Cut eggplant into 1/2-in. slices. In a shallow bowl, combine bread crumbs and Parmesan cheese. Place salad dressing in another bowl. Dip eggplant into salad dressing, then coat with crumb mixture.

Arrange in a single layer on baking sheets coated with nonstick cooking spray. Bake at 450° for 12-15 minutes or until golden brown, turning once. **Yield:** 4 servings.

Nutritional Analysis: One serving equals 153 calories, 3 g fat (2 g saturated fat), 7 mg cholesterol, 975 mg sodium, 25 g carbohydrate, 4 g fiber, 6 g protein. **Diabetic Exchanges:** 2 vegetable, 1 starch.

Stewed Tomato Pasta

I'm the mother of two very active boys, and this flavorful dish is one they'll always eat. Another reason I love it is because I usually have the ingredients on hand. —*Tracey Jones, Chesapeake, Virginia*

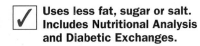

✓ **Uses less fat, sugar or salt. Includes Nutritional Analysis and Diabetic Exchanges.**

2 cans (14-1/2 ounces *each*) **Italian stewed tomatoes, undrained**
1 can (14-1/2 ounces) chicken broth
2 tablespoons vegetable oil
1 teaspoon Italian seasoning
1 package (12 ounces) spiral pasta

In a large saucepan or Dutch oven, combine the tomatoes, broth, oil and Italian seasoning; bring to a boil. Add pasta. Reduce heat; cover and simmer for 16-18 minutes or until pasta is tender, stirring occasionally. **Yield:** 8-10 servings.

Nutritional Analysis: One 3/4-cup serving (prepared with reduced-sodium broth) equals 217 calories, 243 mg sodium, 1 mg cholesterol, 37 g carbohydrate, 6 g protein, 5 g fat. **Diabetic Exchanges:** 2 starch, 1 vegetable, 1 fat.

Maple Apple Topping

I discovered this sweet topping when I had an abundance of apples to use up. It's a great alternative to bottled syrup. My family enjoys the tender apples and crunchy nuts over waffles, but the topping is also wonderful over slices of pound cake or scoops of vanilla ice cream.
—*Ruth Harrow*
Alexandria, New Hampshire

1/2 cup butter
3 large tart apples, peeled and sliced
1-1/2 cups maple syrup
1 teaspoon ground cinnamon
1/2 cup chopped nuts

In a large skillet, melt butter. Add the apples, syrup and cinnamon. Cook and stir over medium-low heat until apples are tender. Stir in nuts. **Yield:** 8 servings.

Peppered Corn

This peppy side dish is always the first to disappear whenever I take it to a potluck dinner. The jalapeno peppers add just the right amount of zip to the corn. —*Kim Garner, Batesville, Arkansas*

1 package (8 ounces) cream cheese, cubed
1/3 cup butter
2 cans (11 ounces *each*) Mexicorn, drained
2 to 4 medium jalapeno peppers, seeded and minced

In a saucepan over low heat, cook and stir the cream cheese and butter until smooth. Stir in corn and jalapenos. Pour into an ungreased 8-in. square baking dish. Bake, uncovered, at 350° for 15-20 minutes or until bubbly. **Yield:** 6-8 servings.

Editor's Note: When cutting or seeding hot peppers, use rubber or plastic gloves to protect your hands. Avoid touching your face.

Easy Berry Relish

This tart, flavorful relish will catch your eye and entice your taste buds. It captures the flavor of the holiday season and adds beautiful color to a meal. Plus, it only has five ingredients. Your guests will be impressed. —*Dorothy Anderson Ottawa, Kansas*

1 package (12 ounces) fresh *or* frozen cranberries
2-1/2 cups sugar
1-2/3 cups ginger ale
1/3 cup lemon juice
1 package (3 ounces) raspberry gelatin

In a saucepan, combine the first four ingredients. Cook over medium heat until the berries pop, about 15 minutes. Remove from the heat; stir in gelatin until dissolved. Pour into serving bowl. Chill overnight. **Yield:** 5 cups.

Golden Potatoes

Golden Potatoes make even canned potatoes taste terrific. I like to serve my fancy-looking side dish to company because it looks like I fussed to make it.
—Carla Cagle
Marceline, Missouri

2 cans (15 ounces *each*) whole white potatoes, drained
1/4 cup butter, melted
1/2 teaspoon seasoned salt
2 to 3 tablespoons grated Parmesan cheese
1 tablespoon minced fresh parsley

Place potatoes in an ungreased 8-in. square baking dish. Pour butter over potatoes. Sprinkle with seasoned salt, cheese and parsley. Bake, uncovered, at 350° for 25 minutes. **Yield:** 4-6 servings.

|A "GRATE" IDEA| Firm cheeses like Parmesan are easier to grate if they're at room temperature. They can be grated ahead of time and refrigerated in a plastic bag until ready to use. If grated cheese sticks together, simply break up the pieces with your fingers.

Creamy Baked Spinach

Cream cheese turns ordinary spinach into a side dish that's pretty enough to serve company. This casserole is a snap to stir up because it relies on convenient frozen chopped spinach.
—Beverly Albrecht, Beatrice, Nebraska

2 packages (10 ounces *each*) frozen chopped spinach
2 packages (3 ounces *each*) cream cheese, softened
4 tablespoons butter, *divided*
1/4 teaspoon salt
1/2 cup seasoned bread crumbs

Cook spinach according to package directions; drain well. Stir in cream cheese, 2 tablespoons butter and salt. Transfer to a greased 1-qt. baking dish.

Melt remaining butter; toss with bread crumbs. Sprinkle over spinach mixture. Bake, uncovered, at 350° for 20 minutes or until lightly browned. **Yield:** 4-6 servings.

Glorified Hash Browns

You'll be surprised at how quick and easy it is to put together this dressed-up potato casserole! When a friend made it for a church supper, I had to have the recipe. It's great for parties, potlucks and family reunions. —*Betty Sitzman*
Wray, Colorado

2 cans (10-3/4 ounces *each*) condensed cream of celery soup, undiluted
2 cartons (8 ounces *each*) spreadable chive and onion cream cheese
1 package (2 pounds) frozen cubed hash brown potatoes
1 cup (4 ounces) shredded cheddar cheese

In a large microwave-safe bowl, combine the soup and cream cheese. Cover and cook on high for 3-4 minutes or until cream cheese is melted, stirring occasionally. Add the potatoes and stir until coated.

Spoon into a greased 13-in. x 9-in. x 2-in. baking dish. Bake, uncovered, at 350° for 35-40 minutes or until the potatoes are tender. Sprinkle with cheddar cheese. Bake 3-5 minutes longer or until the cheese is melted. **Yield:** 10 servings.

Steamed Artichokes with Lemon Sauce

My husband created this smooth, tangy sauce back in the '60s. It complements the steamed artichokes, whether they're served warm or cold. —*Lois Gelzer, Oak Bluffs, Massachusetts*

 Uses less fat, sugar or salt. Includes Nutritional Analysis and Diabetic Exchanges.

6 medium fresh artichokes
1-1/2 cups mayonnaise
4-1/2 teaspoons lemon juice
3/4 teaspoon seasoned salt *or* salt-free seasoning blend
3 drops hot pepper sauce

Place the artichokes upside down in a steamer basket; place the basket in a saucepan over 1 in. of boiling water. Cover and steam for 25-35 minutes or until tender.

In a small bowl, combine the mayonnaise, lemon juice, salt and hot pepper sauce. Cover and refrigerate until serving with the steamed artichokes. **Yield:** 6 servings.

Nutritional Analysis: One serving (prepared with fat-free mayonnaise and salt-free seasoning blend) equals 102 calories, 534 mg sodium, 0 cholesterol, 22 g carbohydrate, 4 g protein, trace fat, 7 g fiber. **Diabetic Exchanges:** 1 starch, 1 vegetable.

Pickled Pumpkin

Cubes of pickled pumpkin make a tasty addition to any meal. We like to have this side dish as part of our Thanksgiving feast. The recipe's a great way to use up any extra pumpkins you might have on hand.
—*Myra Innes, Auburn, Kansas*

2 cups water
1 cup sugar
3-1/2 cups cubed peeled pie
    pumpkin
1/2 cup cider vinegar
1 teaspoon whole cloves

In a saucepan, bring water and sugar to a boil; cook and stir for 5 minutes. Add pumpkin, vinegar and cloves. Reduce heat; simmer, uncovered, for 1 hour and 15 minutes or until pumpkin is tender. Discard cloves. Store in the refrigerator for up to 3 weeks. **Yield:** 4 cups.

|PICK OF THE PATCH| Pumpkin varieties known as pie pumpkins are smaller than the jack-o'-lantern type and make flavorful puree for use in pies and cakes. One pie pumpkin (3 pounds) yields about 2 cups cooked pureed.

Country Baked Beans

After sampling these savory beans at our local John Deere dealer's open house, I asked for the recipe. To my surprise, they had started with canned beans and easily given them a wonderful homemade taste.
—*Jill Steiner, Morris, Minnesota*

4 cans (16 ounces *each*)
    baked beans, drained
1 bottle (12 ounces) chili
    sauce
1 large onion, chopped
1 pound sliced bacon,
    cooked and crumbled
1 cup packed brown sugar

In two ungreased 2-qt. baking dishes, combine all of the ingredients. Stir until blended. Bake, uncovered, at 350° for 45-60 minutes or until heated through. **Yield:** 10-12 servings.

Cheesy Cauliflower

A can of cheese soup gives me a head start on Cheesy Cauliflower. This beautiful side dish takes less than 10 minutes to fix and disappears as soon as I serve it. It's even kid-tested and approved!
—*Edna Shaffer, Beulah, Michigan*

1 medium head cauliflower
(1-1/2 pounds)
1 can (10-3/4 ounces)
condensed cheddar
cheese soup, undiluted
1/8 teaspoon salt
1/4 teaspoon paprika

Break cauliflower into florets or leave whole; place in Dutch oven or large saucepan. Add 1 in. of water. Cover and steam until tender, 7-10 minutes for florets or 15-20 minutes for the whole head.

Meanwhile, heat soup and salt; serve over cauliflower. Sprinkle with paprika. **Yield:** 4-6 servings.

|CAULIFLOWER CLUES| Cook cauliflower only until crisp-tender. Overcooking will turn the texture mushy and the flavor strong. If you do overcook cauliflower, add butter and plenty of freshly ground pepper for a still-delicious dish.

South Liberty Hall Relish

My grandparents originated this recipe that's been treasured in our family for four generations. It's named after a dance hall they ran in rural Iowa. Whenever I bite into a hot dog or hamburger dressed up with this taste bud-tingling relish, I think of them and their delicious country cooking.   —*Melinda Winchell Las Vegas, Nevada*

1 pint dill pickles, drained
1/4 cup chopped onion
2 to 3 tablespoons sugar
1/2 cup yellow mustard

Place the pickles and onion in a food processor; cover and process until finely chopped. Transfer to a bowl; stir in sugar and mustard. Cover and store in the refrigerator for up to 1 week. **Yield:** 2 cups.

Bacon-Wrapped Corn

The incredible flavor of roasted corn combined with bacon and chili powder is sure to please your palate and bring rave reviews at your next backyard barbecue. —*Lori Bramble*
Omaha, Nebraska

8 large ears sweet corn, husks removed
8 bacon strips
2 tablespoons chili powder

Wrap each ear of corn with a bacon strip; place each corn cob on a piece of heavy-duty aluminum foil. Sprinkle with chili powder. Wrap securely, twisting ends to make handles for turning.

Grill, uncovered, over medium-hot heat for 20 minutes or until corn is tender and bacon is cooked, turning once.
Yield: 8 servings.

|CORN COBS| Sweet corn is available with bright yellow or white kernels or a mix of both. Ears should have plump, tender, small kernels in tight rows up to the tip. Kernels should be firm enough to resist slight pressure; a fresh kernel will spurt "milk" if punctured.

Seasoned Potato Wedges

Seasoned Potato Wedges are a tasty accompaniment to hot sandwiches or most any entree. The recipe is easy because you don't peel the potatoes, and you can sprinkle different seasonings on for variety. We also like them with ranch salad dressing and sprinkled with chives. —*Linda Hartsell*
Apple Creek, Ohio

4 medium russet potatoes
2 to 3 tablespoons mayonnaise
1 to 2 teaspoons seasoned salt

Cut the potatoes in half lengthwise; cut each half lengthwise into three wedges. Place in a single layer on a greased baking sheet.

Spread mayonnaise over cut sides of potatoes; sprinkle with seasoned salt. Bake at 350° for 50-60 minutes or until tender. **Yield:** 4 servings.

Creole Rice

I've found a fast and fantastic way to turn leftover rice into a spectacular side dish. I spice it up with Creole seasoning and pepper to give it a boost of flavor, then sprinkle it with paprika for color. Rest assured that no one will figure out the zippy combination is a "second-day dish".
—*Sundra Lewis, Bogalusa, Louisiana*

1/4 cup butter
1 teaspoon Creole seasoning
1/8 teaspoon pepper
2 cups cooked long grain rice

In a saucepan, melt butter; add Creole seasoning and pepper. Cook over medium heat for 3 minutes. Stir in rice. Cover and heat through. **Yield:** 4 servings.

Editor's Note: The following spices may be substituted for the Creole seasoning—1/2 teaspoon *each* paprika and garlic powder, and a pinch *each* cayenne pepper, dried thyme and ground cumin.

Low-Fat Refried Beans

A local Mexican restaurant shared this recipe with me. It's so simple and tasty you'll never go back to canned refried beans.
—*Kitty Shelton, Ketchum, Idaho*

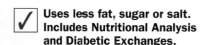 Uses less fat, sugar or salt. Includes Nutritional Analysis and Diabetic Exchanges.

1 package (16 ounces) dried pinto *or* red beans
1 large onion, quartered
3 garlic cloves
1/2 teaspoon ground cumin
3 to 4 drops hot pepper sauce

Place beans in a Dutch oven; add water to cover by 2 in. Bring to a boil; boil for 2 minutes. Remove from the heat; cover and let stand for 1 hour. Drain beans; discard liquid.

Return beans to pan; add water to cover. Add onion and garlic; bring to a boil. Cover and cook over low heat for 2 hours or until beans are very tender, adding water to keep covered if needed. Discard onion and garlic. Mash beans with a potato masher, leaving some beans whole. Stir in cumin and hot pepper sauce. **Yield:** 9 servings.

Nutritional Analysis: One 1/2-cup serving equals 180 calories, 6 mg sodium, 0 cholesterol, 34 g carbohydrate, 11 g protein, 1 g fat. **Diabetic Exchanges:** 2 starch, 1 vegetable.

Crispy Mashed Potato Pancake

Here is a tasty secret for using up leftover mashed potatoes. With just a few basic ingredients, I can fry up this delightful dish in a matter of minutes. —*Mary Schuster, Scottsdale, Arizona*

2 cups cold mashed
  potatoes (prepared with
  milk and butter)
1 egg, lightly beaten
1 teaspoon Italian
  seasoning
1/8 teaspoon garlic powder
1 tablespoon olive oil

Combine the first four ingredients; mix well. In a small skillet, heat oil over medium-high heat. Add potato mixture; press with a spatula to flatten evenly. Cover and cook for 8 minutes or until bottom is crispy. Invert onto a serving plate. **Yield:** 3 servings.

Creamy Vegetable Casserole

Searching for a different way to prepare vegetables? Look no further. I have a fussy eater in my house who absolutely loves this medley. It can be assembled in a snap, leaving time to fix the main course, set the table or just sit back and relax. —*Tami Kratzer*
West Jordan, Utah

1 package (16 ounces)
  frozen broccoli, carrots
  and cauliflower
1 can (10-3/4 ounces)
  condensed cream of
  mushroom soup,
  undiluted
1 carton (8 ounces)
  spreadable garden
  vegetable cream cheese
1/2 to 1 cup seasoned
  croutons

Prepare vegetables according to package directions; drain and place in a large bowl. Stir in soup and cream cheese. Transfer to a greased 1-qt. baking dish. Sprinkle with croutons. Bake, uncovered, at 375° for 25 minutes or until bubbly. **Yield:** 6 servings.

|FROZEN ASSETS| Frozen vegetables such as corn and peas don't require thawing before being added to dishes like soups and casseroles. Such frozen vegetables can also be added to stir-fries, provided they'll be cooked long enough to thaw.

Roasted Tarragon Asparagus

My simple seasoning turns fresh asparagus spears into a special spring side dish that's speedy, too. Oven-roasting the asparagus gives a depth of flavor that is complemented by the tarragon.
—Joyce Speckman, Holt, California

1-1/2 **pounds fresh asparagus, trimmed**
2 **to 3 tablespoons olive oil**
1/2 **teaspoon coarsely ground pepper**
1/8 **teaspoon salt**
1-1/2 **teaspoons minced fresh tarragon** *or* **1/2 teaspoon dried tarragon**

Place asparagus in a shallow baking dish coated with non-stick cooking spray. Drizzle with oil; sprinkle with pepper and salt. Toss to coat.

Bake, uncovered, at 450° for 13-15 minutes or until crisp-tender, turning occasionally. Sprinkle with tarragon. **Yield:** 6 servings.

Broccoli Stir-Fry

Broccoli Stir-Fry is a great way to dress up a nutritious vegetable. As a wife and mother who also works full time, I'm pleased to pass along this easy recipe to other busy cooks. Broccoli stir-fried with lemon pepper makes a mouth-watering side dish.
—Susan Davis
Vernon Hills, Illinois

3 **cups fresh broccoli florets**
1/4 **cup butter**
1-1/2 **teaspoons lemon-pepper seasoning**

In a skillet over medium-high heat, stir-fry broccoli in butter and lemon pepper until crisp-tender, about 2-3 minutes. **Yield:** 4 servings.

Grilled Sweet Potatoes

I love trying new recipes, so my son-in-law suggested we grill sweet potatoes. Served with steak, they're a great change of pace from traditional baked potatoes...and they're pretty, too.
—Lillian Neer
Long Eddy, New York

 Uses less fat, sugar or salt. Includes Nutritional Analysis and Diabetic Exchanges.

2 large sweet potatoes, halved lengthwise
2 tablespoons butter, softened
Garlic salt and pepper to taste
2 teaspoons honey

Cut two pieces of heavy-duty foil (about 18 in. x 12 in.); place a potato half on each. Spread cut side with butter. Sprinkle with garlic salt and pepper. Top each potato with another half. Fold foil over potatoes and seal tightly.

Grill, covered, over medium-hot heat for 30 minutes or until tender, turning once. To serve, fluff potatoes with a fork and drizzle with honey. **Yield:** 4 servings.

Nutritional Analysis: One serving (prepared with margarine and without garlic salt) equals 123 calories, 73 mg sodium, 0 cholesterol, 16 g carbohydrate, 1 g protein, 6 g fat. **Diabetic Exchanges:** 1 starch, 1 fat.

|HOW SWEET IT IS| Sweet potato skins that are darker tend to be sweeter and moister; they are more nutritious if cooked in their skins. Sweet potatoes have a natural affinity for maple syrup and freshly grated nutmeg.

Spicy Mustard Spread

This zippy spread makes taste buds sit up and take notice. It's super on vegetables, hot dogs and hamburgers, in potato salad and more.
—Audrey Thibodeau, Mesa, Arizona

1/4 cup butter, softened
2 tablespoons ground mustard
2 tablespoons vinegar
1/4 teaspoon garlic salt
4 drops hot pepper sauce

In a mixing bowl, combine all ingredients; beat until smooth. Store in the refrigerator. **Yield:** about 1/3 cup.

Carrot Parsnip Stir-Fry

Orange carrot slivers and yellow parsnips make a pretty and different side dish. If parsnips aren't available, you could substitute rutabagas or turnips. Usually, I saute the vegetables until they are crisp-tender. But they're also quite good well-cooked, almost browned.

—Lavonne Hartel
Williston, North Dakota

1-1/2 **pounds parsnips, peeled and julienned**
1/4 **cup butter**
2 **pounds carrots, julienned**
2 **tablespoons dried minced onion**

In a large skillet, saute parsnips in butter for 3-4 minutes. Add carrots and onion; cook and stir until vegetables are tender, about 10-15 minutes. **Yield:** 8 servings.

Acorn Squash Slices

Acorn squash is a favorite with my family. This recipe gets sweet maple flavor from syrup and an appealing nuttiness from pecans. It's easy, too, because you don't have to peel the squash.

—Mrs. Richard Lamb, Williamsburg, Indiana

 Uses less fat, sugar or salt. Includes Nutritional Analysis and Diabetic Exchanges.

2 **medium acorn squash (about 1-1/2 pounds** *each***)**
1/2 **teaspoon salt**
3/4 **cup maple syrup**
2 **tablespoons butter, melted**
1/3 **cup chopped pecans, optional**

Wash squash. Cut in half lengthwise; discard seeds and membrane. Cut each half crosswise into 1/2-in. slices; discard the ends. Place slices in a greased 13-in. x 9-in. x 2-in. baking dish. Sprinkle with salt.

Combine syrup and butter; pour over squash. Sprinkle with pecans if desired. Cover and bake at 350° for 40-45 minutes or until tender. **Yield:** 6 servings.

Nutritional Analysis: One serving of 2 slices (prepared with sugar-free maple-flavored pancake syrup, reduced-fat margarine and pecans) equals 170 calories, 98 mg sodium, 0 cholesterol, 31 g carbohydrate, 2 g protein, 7 g fat. **Diabetic Exchanges:** 1 starch, 1 fruit, 1 fat.

Simple Saucy Potatoes

These rich and creamy potatoes are simple to prepare for potlucks. This saucy side dish always gets rave reviews wherever I take it.
—*Gloria Schroeder, Ottawa Lake, Michigan*

4 cans (15 ounces *each*) sliced white potatoes, drained
2 cans (10-3/4 ounces *each*) condensed cream of celery soup, undiluted
2 cups (16 ounces) sour cream
10 bacon strips, cooked and crumbled
6 green onions, thinly sliced

Place potatoes in a slow cooker. Combine the remaining ingredients; pour over potatoes and mix well. Cover and cook on high for 4-5 hours. **Yield:** 12 servings.

|KITCHEN HELPER| A handy attribute of a slow cooker is that if you can't get home at exactly the time the food should be done, it generally doesn't hurt to leave it cooking on low for an extra hour.

Green Beans With a Twist

Green beans get a makeover with help from fresh mushrooms, ranch salad dressing mix and crumbled bacon. For added convenience, I sometimes use canned mushrooms when fixing this side dish.
—*Nicole Orr, Columbus, Ohio*

1 package (16 ounces) frozen French-style green beans
1 cup sliced fresh mushrooms
2 tablespoons butter
1 envelope ranch salad dressing mix
4 bacon strips, cooked and crumbled

In a skillet, saute the beans and mushrooms in butter. Sprinkle with dressing mix; toss to coat. Just before serving, sprinkle with bacon. **Yield:** 4-6 servings.

Bacon Cabbage Stir-Fry

If you like cabbage, you'll enjoy this stir-fried side dish. It's not only delicious, but fast to fix when you need to get dinner on the table quickly. —*Lori Thompson, New London, Texas*

6 bacon strips, diced
1 small head cabbage, chopped
1 teaspoon garlic powder
3/4 teaspoon salt
1/2 teaspoon ground mustard

In a large skillet, cook bacon over medium heat until crisp. Remove to paper towels; drain, reserving 1 tablespoon drippings. Stir-fry cabbage in drippings for 5 minutes. Add garlic powder, salt, mustard and bacon; cook and stir until heated through. **Yield:** 6 servings.

Roasted Fan-Shaped Potatoes

These wonderful oven-roasted potatoes are very pretty to serve—the partially cut slices spread out in the shape of a fan. Folks at a potluck can easily take as many slices as they want. I especially like these potatoes with ham, roast pork or beef. —*Eunice Stoen, Decorah, Iowa*

12 large baking potatoes
1/2 teaspoon salt
1/2 cup butter, melted, *divided*
6 tablespoons dry bread crumbs
6 tablespoons shredded Parmesan cheese

With a sharp knife, slice the potatoes thinly but not all the way through, leaving slices attached at the bottom. Place the potatoes in a greased shallow baking dish. Sprinkle with salt; brush with 1/4 cup butter. Bake, uncovered, at 425° for 30 minutes.

Brush potatoes with remaining butter and sprinkle with bread crumbs. Bake 20 minutes longer. Sprinkle with Parmesan cheese. Bake 5-10 minutes more or until potatoes are tender and golden brown. **Yield:** 12 servings.

Grilled Cherry Tomatoes

Seasoned with herbs and butter, Grilled Cherry Tomatoes make a colorful and tasty side dish. Just tuck the foil packet beside any meat you happen to be grilling. —*Lucy Meyring*
Walden, Colorado

2 pints cherry tomatoes, halved
2 garlic cloves, minced
1/2 teaspoon dried oregano
3 tablespoons butter

Place tomatoes on a double thickness of heavy-duty foil (about 24 in. x 12 in.). In a skillet, saute garlic and oregano in butter for 2 minutes. Pour over tomatoes. Fold foil around tomatoes and seal tightly.

Grill, covered, over medium heat for 8-10 minutes or until the tomatoes are heated through, turning once. **Yield:** 4-6 servings.

Warm Fruit Compote

Orange marmalade is the secret to the easy sauce I spoon over canned pineapple and fresh grapes. I then sprinkle the combination with coconut and broil it to create a warm, fruity surprise.
—*Doris Heath, Franklin, North Carolina*

 Uses less fat, sugar or salt. Includes Nutritional Analysis and Diabetic Exchanges.

1 can (20 ounces) unsweetened pineapple chunks
2 cups seedless grapes
3 tablespoons orange marmalade
4 teaspoons flaked coconut

Drain pineapple, reserving 2/3 cup juice. Combine the pineapple and grapes in a shallow 1-qt. broiler-proof dish.

In a saucepan, combine marmalade and reserved pineapple juice; cook over medium heat until the marmalade is melted. Pour over fruit. Sprinkle with coconut. Broil 5-6 in. from the heat for 3 minutes or until coconut is toasted. **Yield:** 4 servings.

Nutritional Analysis: One 1-cup serving (prepared with reduced-sugar marmalade) equals 168 calories, 7 mg sodium, 0 cholesterol, 43 g carbohydrate, 1 g protein, 1 g fat. **Diabetic Exchange:** 3 fruit.

Almond Currant Rice

Stirring in the almonds and currants at the last minute is a snap, and my daughter and I love the flavor of this side dish. You can substitute your favorite dried fruits and nuts if you like. —*Felicia Johnson*
Oak Ridge, Louisiana

2 cups uncooked instant rice
2 tablespoons butter
1/4 teaspoon salt
1/4 cup chopped toasted almonds
1/4 cup dried currants

Prepare rice according to package directions, adding butter and salt. Just before serving, stir in almonds and currants. **Yield:** 4 servings.

Pasta with Basil

If you like basil, you'll enjoy the Italian flavor of this speedy side dish. This is one of my husband's favorites. It's super easy to make and tastes wonderful. —*Jaime Hampton, Birmingham, Alabama*

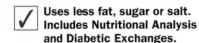 **Uses less fat, sugar or salt. Includes Nutritional Analysis and Diabetic Exchanges.**

2-1/2 cups uncooked small tube pasta
1 small onion, chopped
1 to 3 tablespoons olive oil
2 to 3 tablespoons dried basil
1 cup (4 ounces) shredded mozzarella cheese

Cook pasta according to package directions. Meanwhile, in a skillet, saute onion in oil until tender. Stir in basil; cook and stir for 1 minute.

Drain pasta; add to basil mixture. Remove from the heat; stir in cheese just until it begins to melt. Serve immediately. **Yield:** 4 servings.

Nutritional Analysis: One serving (prepared with 1 tablespoon oil and part-skim mozzarella cheese) equals 332 calories, 135 mg sodium, 16 mg cholesterol, 48 g carbohydrate, 15 g protein, 9 g fat, 2 g fiber. **Diabetic Exchanges:** 3 starch, 1 meat, 1 fat.

Vegetable Rice Skillet

A bag of frozen mixed vegetables conveniently dresses up plain rice in this recipe. It's short on ingredients and preparation time but long on satisfying flavor. —*Ruth Rigoni, Hurley, Wisconsin*

1 can (14-1/2 ounces)
    vegetable broth
2 tablespoons butter
1 package (16 ounces)
    frozen California-blend
    vegetables
1 package (6.2 ounces)
    fast-cooking long grain
    and wild rice mix
3/4 cup shredded cheddar
    cheese

In a large skillet, bring broth and butter to a boil. Stir in the vegetables and rice with seasoning packet. Return to a boil. Reduce heat; cover and simmer for 4-8 minutes or until vegetables and rice are tender. Sprinkle with cheese. **Yield:** 4-6 servings.

Caramelized Onions

These lightly golden onions have a delicate taste that complements green beans, peas and almost any type of meat. Try them over steaks, on burgers, with pork chops and more. —*Melba Lowery Rockwell, North Carolina*

4 large onions, thinly sliced
1/4 cup vegetable oil
3 tablespoons cider
    vinegar
2 tablespoons brown sugar

In a large skillet, saute onions in oil over medium heat until tender, about 15 minutes. Stir in vinegar and brown sugar. Cook 10 minutes longer or until onions are golden. **Yield:** 4-6 servings.

Cranberry Syrup

This flavorful syrup is so appealing over pancakes, your family will think they're in a fancy restaurant. It's very festive-looking to serve at a Christmas brunch. But we like it year-round as a change of pace from maple syrup.
—Teresa Gaetzke, North Freedom, Wisconsin

1 cup sugar
1 cup packed brown sugar
1 cup cranberry juice
1/2 cup light corn syrup

In a saucepan, combine the sugars and cranberry juice; bring to a boil, stirring constantly. Boil for 4 minutes. Add corn syrup; boil and stir 1 minute longer. **Yield:** 2 cups.

Home-Style Mashed Potatoes

Leaving the tender skins on the spuds not only saves time, it sparks the taste and adds color to these hearty mashed potatoes. They're perfect with a pork roast and versatile enough to go well with other entrees.
—Christine Wilson
Sellersville, Pennsylvania

3 pounds red potatoes, quartered
2 teaspoons salt, *divided*
1/4 to 1/2 cup milk
5 tablespoons butter
1/4 teaspoon white pepper

Place potatoes in a large saucepan or Dutch oven; cover with water. Add 1 teaspoon salt. Cover and bring to a boil. Reduce heat; cook for 20-30 minutes or until very tender.

Drain potatoes well and place in a large mixing bowl. Add 1/4 cup milk, butter, pepper and remaining salt. Beat on low speed until potatoes are light and fluffy, adding remaining milk if needed. **Yield:** 8 servings.

Dilly Sweet Peas

A tongue-tingling side dish, Dilly Sweet Peas gets fun flavor from chopped dill pickles and pickle juice balanced with a bit of honey. My daughter and I always go back for seconds.

—*Felicia Johnson*
Oak Ridge, Louisiana

1 package (10 ounces) frozen peas
1/4 cup chopped dill pickles
2 tablespoons butter
1 tablespoon dill pickle juice
1 to 2 teaspoons honey

Prepare peas according to package directions; drain. Add remaining ingredients and toss to coat. **Yield:** 4 servings.

|COOKING PEAS| Be careful not to overcook peas; they should be crisp-tender when done. Overdone peas will lose their bright green color and much of their fresh flavor.

Gingered Squash and Pears

Butternut squash and pears are a delightful duo delicately seasoned with ginger, honey and nutmeg. This is a pretty dish, too.

—*Jane Rossi, Charlotte, North Carolina*

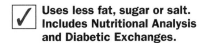 **Uses less fat, sugar or salt. Includes Nutritional Analysis and Diabetic Exchanges.**

1 medium butternut squash, peeled, seeded and cubed (about 6-1/2 cups)
1 medium pear, peeled and cubed
1-1/2 teaspoons grated fresh gingerroot
1 tablespoon honey
1/8 teaspoon ground nutmeg

Place squash in a large skillet; cover with water. Bring to a boil. Reduce heat; cover and simmer for 10 minutes or until tender. Drain. Stir in pear and ginger. Cover and cook for 5-7 minutes or until pear is tender. Stir in honey and heat through. Sprinkle with nutmeg. **Yield:** 8 servings.

Nutritional Analysis: One serving (3/4 cup) equals 72 calories, trace fat (trace saturated fat), 0 cholesterol, 5 mg sodium, 19 g carbohydrate, 4 g fiber, 1 g protein. **Diabetic Exchange:** 1 starch.

Breads & Rolls

Cherry Cream Crescents (p. 203) and Orange Pull-Apart Bread (p. 202)

Teddy Bear Biscuits, p. 204

Banana-Nut Corn Bread, p. 207

Breads & Rolls   201

Cinnamon Nut Twists

These tender treats are good with a hot cup of coffee or a cold glass of milk. The golden twists have a pleasant cinnamon and nut filling and just a hint of sweetness.

—Mary Van Domelen
Appleton, Wisconsin

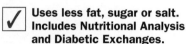 **Uses less fat, sugar or salt. Includes Nutritional Analysis and Diabetic Exchanges.**

2 tubes (8 ounces *each*) refrigerated reduced-fat crescent rolls
2 tablespoons reduced-fat stick margarine
1/4 cup packed brown sugar
1 tablespoon ground cinnamon
1/3 cup finely chopped walnuts

Unroll both tubes of dough; press perforations and seams together to form two rectangles. Spread with margarine. Combine brown sugar and cinnamon; sprinkle over dough. Sprinkle with walnuts.

Fold each rectangle in half, starting from a short side. Cut each into eight strips. Twist each strip; tie into a knot. Place on ungreased baking sheets. Bake at 375° for 10-12 minutes or until golden brown. Serve warm. **Yield:** 16 servings.

Nutritional Analysis: One piece equals 139 calories, 7 g fat (1 g saturated fat), 0 cholesterol, 251 mg sodium, 16 g carbohydrate, trace fiber, 2 g protein. **Diabetic Exchanges:** 1 starch, 1 fat.

Orange Pull-Apart Bread

(Pictured on page 200)

The recipe for this appealing breakfast loaf came from my sister, who's an excellent cook. Brushed with a sweet orange glaze, the bread is so popular I usually double or triple the recipe.

—Kristin Salzman, Fenton, Illinois

1 tube (8 ounces) refrigerated crescent rolls
2 tablespoons butter, softened
2 tablespoons honey
1/2 to 1 teaspoon grated orange peel

Open tube of crescent rolls; do not unroll. Place on a greased baking sheet, forming one long roll. Cut into 12 slices to within 1/8 in. of bottom, being careful not to cut all the way through. Fold down alternating slices from left to right to form a loaf. Bake at 375° for 20-25 minutes or until golden brown. Combine butter, honey and orange peel; brush over the loaf. Serve warm. **Yield:** 6 servings.

Cherry Cream Crescents

(Pictured on page 200)

You'll need refrigerated crescent dough and just four more ingredients to assemble these fruity filled rolls. My family and friends love them. I never have any left over. —*Elouise Bullion*
Kingsville, Texas

1 package (8 ounces) cream cheese, softened
1 cup confectioners' sugar
1 egg, *separated*
2 tubes (8 ounces *each*) refrigerated crescent rolls
1 can (21 ounces) cherry pie filling

In a mixing bowl, beat cream cheese, sugar and egg yolk. Separate dough into 16 triangles; place on lightly greased baking sheets. Spread 1 tablespoon of cream cheese mixture near the edge of the short side of each triangle. Top with 1 tablespoon pie filling.

Fold long point of triangle over filling and tuck under dough. Lightly beat egg white; brush over rolls. Bake at 350° for 15-20 minutes or until golden brown. **Yield:** 16 rolls.

Swiss-Onion Bread Ring

With the ease of prepared bread dough, this tempting cheesy bread has delicious down-home goodness. Its pleasant onion flavor goes great with any entree. You'll find it crisp and golden on the outside, rich and buttery on the inside. —*Judi Messina*
Coeur d'Alene, Idaho

2-1/2 teaspoons poppy seeds, *divided*
2 tubes (11 ounces *each*) refrigerated French bread dough
1 cup (4 ounces) shredded Swiss cheese
3/4 cup sliced green onions
6 tablespoons butter, melted

Sprinkle 1/2 teaspoon poppy seeds in a greased 10-in. fluted tube pan. Cut the dough into forty 1-in. pieces; place half in prepared pan. Sprinkle with half of the cheese and onions.

Top with 1 teaspoon poppy seeds; drizzle with half of the butter. Repeat layers. Bake at 375° for 30-35 minutes or until golden brown. Immediately invert onto a wire rack. Serve warm. **Yield:** 1 loaf.

Teddy Bear Biscuits

(Pictured on page 201)

Children can't resist helping to assemble these cute cinnamony bears before baking. Refrigerated biscuit dough makes them easy, convenient and fun!   —Catherine Berra Bleem, Walsh, Illinois

1 tube (7-1/2 ounces) refrigerated buttermilk biscuits (10 biscuits)
1 egg, beaten
2 tablespoons sugar
1/4 teaspoon ground cinnamon
9 miniature semisweet chocolate chips

For each bear, shape one biscuit into an oval for the body and place on a greased baking sheet. Cut one biscuit into four pieces; shape into balls for arms and legs. Place next to body. Cut one biscuit into two small pieces and one large piece; shape into head and ears and place above body.

Brush with egg. Combine sugar and cinnamon; sprinkle over bears. Bake at 425° for 8-10 minutes (the one remaining biscuit can be baked with the bears). Place chocolate chips on head for eyes and nose while the biscuits are still warm. **Yield:** 3 bears.

Mini Cheddar Loaves

It's hard to believe you need only four ingredients to bake up a batch of these beautiful miniature loaves. Sliced warm from the oven, this golden bread is simple and delicious.
—Melody Rowland
Chattanooga, Tennessee

3-1/2 cups biscuit/baking mix
2-1/2 cups (10 ounces) shredded sharp cheddar cheese
2 eggs
1-1/4 cups milk

In a large bowl, combine biscuit mix and cheese. Beat eggs and milk; stir into cheese mixture just until moistened. Pour into four greased and floured 5-3/4-in. x 3-in. x 2-in. loaf pans.

Bake at 350° for 35-40 minutes or until a toothpick inserted near the center comes out clean. Cool for 10 minutes. Remove from pans; slice and serve warm. **Yield:** 4 mini loaves.

Editor's Note: Bread can also be made in one 9-in. x 5-in. x 3-in. loaf pan. Bake for 50-55 minutes.

Buttered Cornsticks

I need just three ingredients to stir together Buttered Cornsticks. Even with my family's hectic schedule, I like to prepare sit-down dinners during the week. This bread recipe is often on the menu.
—*Fran Shaffer, Coatesville, Pennsylvania*

2-2/3 cups biscuit/baking mix
1 can (8-1/2 ounces) cream-style corn
1/4 cup butter, melted

In a bowl, combine biscuit mix and corn. Stir until a soft dough forms. Knead on a lightly floured surface for 3 minutes. Roll into a 10-in. x 6-in. rectangle. Cut into 3-in. x 1-in. strips. Dip in butter.

Place in an ungreased 15-in. x 10-in. x 1-in. baking pan. Bake at 425° for 12-15 minutes or until golden brown. **Yield:** about 20 breadsticks.

Tex-Mex Biscuits

I love cooking with green chilies because they add so much flavor to ordinary dishes. Once while making a pot of chili, I had some green chilies left over and mixed them into my biscuit dough, creating this recipe. The fresh-from-the-oven treats are a wonderful accompaniment to soup or chili.
—*Angie Trolz, Jackson, Michigan*

2 cups biscuit/baking mix
2/3 cup milk
1 cup (4 ounces) finely shredded cheddar cheese
1 can (4 ounces) chopped green chilies, drained

In a bowl, combine biscuit mix and milk until a soft dough forms. Stir in cheese and chilies. Turn onto a floured surface; knead 10 times.

Roll out to 1/2-in. thickness; cut with a 2-1/2-in. biscuit cutter. Place on an ungreased baking sheet. Bake at 450° for 8-10 minutes or until golden brown. Serve warm. **Yield:** about 1 dozen.

Parmesan Breadsticks

These soft bread sticks are so easy to make and have wonderful homemade flavor. We enjoy them warm from the oven dipped in pizza sauce. *—Marlene Muckenhirn, Delano, Minnesota*

3/4 **cup grated Parmesan cheese**
1-1/2 **teaspoons dried Italian seasoning**
1 **loaf (1 pound) frozen white bread dough, thawed**
1/4 **cup butter, melted**
Warm pizza sauce, optional

Combine cheese and Italian seasoning in a shallow bowl; set aside. Divide dough into 32 sections; roll each into a 5-in. rope. Twist two pieces together. Moisten ends with water and pinch to seal. Dip in butter, then in cheese mixture.

Place on a greased baking sheet. Bake at 400° for 10-14 minutes or until golden brown. Serve with pizza sauce for dipping if desired. **Yield:** 16 servings.

Savory Party Bread

It's impossible to stop nibbling on warm pieces of this cheesy, oniony bread. The sliced loaf fans out for a fun presentation at parties. *—Kay Daly, Raleigh, North Carolina*

1 **unsliced round loaf (1 pound) sourdough bread**
1 **pound Monterey Jack cheese, sliced**
1/2 **cup butter, melted**
1/2 **cup chopped green onions**
2 **to 3 teaspoons poppy seeds**

Cut the bread lengthwise and crosswise without cutting through the bottom crust. Insert cheese between cuts. Combine butter, onions and poppy seeds; drizzle over the bread.

Wrap in foil; place on a baking sheet. Bake at 350° for 15 minutes. Uncover; bake 10 minutes longer or until the cheese is melted. **Yield:** 6-8 servings.

Cinnamon Fruit Biscuits

Because these sweet treats are so easy, I'm almost embarrassed when people ask me for the recipe. They're a snap to make with refrigerated buttermilk biscuits, sugar, cinnamon and strawberry preserves.

—*Ione Burham*
Washington, Iowa

1/2 cup sugar
1/2 teaspoon ground cinnamon
1 tube (12 ounces) refrigerated buttermilk biscuits, separated into 10 biscuits
1/4 cup butter, melted
10 teaspoons strawberry preserves

In a small bowl, combine the sugar and cinnamon. Dip top and sides of biscuits in butter, then in cinnamon-sugar. Place on ungreased baking sheets. With the end of a wooden spoon handle, make a deep indentation in the center of each biscuit; fill with 1 teaspoon preserves.

Bake at 375° for 15-18 minutes or until golden brown. Cool for 15 minutes before serving (preserves will be hot). **Yield:** 10 servings.

Banana-Nut Corn Bread

(Pictured on page 201)

A boxed corn bread mix gets a tasty treatment when dressed up with bananas and chopped walnuts. The moist golden loaves are a great addition to a brunch buffet or bake sale. —*Janice France*
Depauw, Indiana

2 packages (8-1/2 ounces *each*) corn bread/muffin mix
1 cup mashed ripe bananas (about 2 medium)
1 cup chopped walnuts
1 cup milk

In a bowl, combine all ingredients just until blended. Spoon into two greased 8-in. x 4-in. x 2-in. loaf pans. Bake at 350° for 35-40 minutes or until a toothpick inserted near the center comes out clean. Cool for 10 minutes before removing from pans to wire racks to cool completely. **Yield:** 2 loaves.

|GOING BANANAS| Peel and mash overripe bananas in a blender with 1 teaspoon lemon juice per banana. Spoon into an airtight container and freeze for up to 1 month. When you're ready to use the mixture, defrost overnight in the fridge.

Cordon Bleu Stromboli

My recipe has the taste of chicken cordon bleu without all the work. I roll Swiss cheese and deli meats into a swirled sandwich loaf that bakes to a golden brown. My entire gang looks forward to this stromboli.

—Diane Schuelke, Madison, Minnesota

1 loaf (1 pound) frozen bread dough, thawed
2 tablespoons butter, softened
8 ounces thinly sliced deli ham
1/2 cup shredded Swiss cheese
5 ounces thinly sliced deli chicken

On a lightly floured surface, roll dough into a 10-in. x 8-in. rectangle; spread with butter. Top with ham, cheese and chicken. Roll up jelly-roll style, starting with a long side; pinch seam to seal and tuck ends under.

Place seam side down on a greased baking sheet. Cover and let rise for 20 minutes. Bake at 350° for 25-30 minutes or until golden brown. Refrigerate any leftovers. **Yield:** 6 servings.

Bacon Biscuit Wreath

I showed my girl scout troop how to make this pretty golden wreath. The girls (and even some of their parents) enjoyed making and sampling the cheesy party appetizer. It's a snap to prepare with cheese spread and convenient refrigerated biscuits.

—Kathy Kirkland
Denham Springs, Louisiana

1 jar (5 ounces) sharp American cheese spread
3 tablespoons butter-flavored shortening
1 tube (12 ounces) flaky biscuits
4 bacon strips, cooked and crumbled
2 tablespoons minced fresh parsley

In a small saucepan, melt the cheese spread and shortening; stir until blended. Pour into a well-greased 6-cup oven-proof ring mold or 9-in. fluted tube pan. Cut each biscuit into quarters and place over cheese mixture.

Bake at 400° for 12-14 minutes or until golden brown. Immediately invert pan onto a serving platter and remove. Sprinkle with bacon and parsley. Serve warm. **Yield:** 10 servings.

Cheese Biscuits

Cheddar adds a burst of sunny flavor to these flaky biscuits. You can frequently find me in my kitchen making these tender treats.
—Donna Engel
Portsmouth, Rhode Island

2 cups biscuit/baking mix
2/3 cup milk
1/2 cup shredded cheddar cheese
2 tablespoons butter, melted
1/2 teaspoon garlic powder

In a bowl, stir the biscuit mix, milk and cheese just until moistened. Drop by tablespoonfuls onto an ungreased baking sheet. Mix butter and garlic powder; brush over biscuits. Bake at 475° for 8-10 minutes or until golden brown. Serve warm. **Yield:** about 1-1/2 dozen.

Quick Cherry Turnovers

These fruit-filled pastries are my family's favorite at breakfast. You can substitute other fillings for cherry.
—Elleen Oberrueter, *Danbury, Iowa*

1 tube (8 ounces) refrigerated crescent rolls
1 cup cherry pie filling
1/2 cup confectioners' sugar
1 to 2 tablespoons milk

Unroll dough and separate into eight triangles; make four squares by pressing the seams of two triangles together and rolling into shape. Place on an ungreased baking sheet.

Spoon 1/4 cup pie filling in one corner of each square. Fold to make triangles; pinch to seal. Bake at 375° for 10-12 minutes or until golden. Mix sugar and milk; drizzle over turnovers. Serve warm. **Yield:** 4 servings.

Olive Pinwheel Bread

This attractive, well-seasoned loaf is perfect for parties but easy enough to prepare for every day. For extra flavor, stir in chunks of provolone cheese. —*Barbara Manfra*
Saugus, Massachusetts

✓ Uses less fat, sugar or salt. Includes Nutritional Analysis and Diabetic Exchanges.

1 tube (10 ounces) refrigerated pizza crust
1 tablespoon olive oil
1 tablespoon minced fresh rosemary *or* 1 teaspoon dried rosemary, crushed
1/2 cup chopped ripe olives
1 egg yolk, lightly beaten

Unroll pizza dough and place on a lightly floured surface. Brush with oil; sprinkle with rosemary and olives. Roll up jelly-roll style, starting with a short side; pinch seam to seal and tuck ends under.

Place seam side down on a greased baking sheet. Brush with egg yolk. Bake at 350° for 20-25 minutes or until golden brown. Cool before cutting. **Yield:** 1 loaf (10 slices).

Nutritional Analysis: One slice equals 100 calories, 4 g fat (trace saturated fat), 21 mg cholesterol, 248 mg sodium, 14 g carbohydrate, 1 g fiber, 3 g protein. **Diabetic Exchanges:** 1 starch, 1/2 fat.

Tennessee Fry Bread

You'll need only four ingredients to fix this time-easing bread. We like it with scrambled eggs and fried potatoes for breakfast. Or dunk it in soup or serve it with coffee. —*Theresa Sanchez*
Franklin, Tennessee

3 tablespoons butter
1 cup self-rising flour
1/2 cup buttermilk
All-purpose flour

Place butter in a 12-in. ovenproof skillet; place in a 450° oven for 2-3 minutes or until melted. In a bowl, combine flour and buttermilk just until moistened. Turn onto a surface dusted with all-purpose flour; knead 4-5 times.

Pat dough to 1/4-in. thickness. Cut with a 2-1/2-in. biscuit cutter. Place in a single layer in prepared pan; carefully turn to coat. Bake at 450° for 12-13 minutes or until golden brown. **Yield:** 8 servings.

Editor's Note: As a substitute for self-rising flour, place 1-1/2 teaspoons baking powder and 1/2 teaspoon salt in a measuring cup. Add all-purpose flour to measure 1 cup.

Coconut Pecan Rolls

Your family will enjoy the old-fashioned appeal of these nutty rolls. Convenient refrigerated breadsticks are dressed up with a coconut coating that's oh-so-good. —*Theresa Gingery, Blue Springs, Nebraska*

1 tablespoon sugar
1/2 teaspoon ground cinnamon
1 tube (11 ounces) refrigerated breadsticks
2/3 cup coconut pecan frosting
1/3 cup chopped pecans

In a small bowl, combine sugar and cinnamon. Remove breadstick dough from tube (do not unroll); cut into eight slices with a serrated knife. Dip both sides of each slice in cinnamon-sugar.

Place in a greased 9-in. round baking pan. Spread with frosting; sprinkle with pecans. Bake at 350° for 25-30 minutes or until golden brown. Serve warm. **Yield:** 8 rolls.

Pull-Apart Bacon Bread

I stumbled across this recipe while looking for something different to take to a brunch. Boy, am I glad I did! Everyone asked for the recipe and could not believe it called for only five ingredients. It's the perfect item to bake for an informal get-together.
—*Traci Collins, Cheyenne, Wyoming*

12 bacon strips, diced
1 loaf (1 pound) frozen bread dough, thawed
2 tablespoons olive oil, *divided*
1 cup (4 ounces) shredded mozzarella cheese
1 envelope ranch salad dressing mix

In a skillet, cook bacon over medium heat for 5 minutes or until partially cooked; drain on paper towels. Roll out dough to 1/2-in. thickness; brush with 1 tablespoon of oil. Cut into 1-in. pieces; place in a large bowl. Add the bacon, cheese, dressing mix and remaining oil; toss to coat.

Arrange pieces in a 9-in. x 5-in. oval on a greased baking sheet, layering as needed. Cover and let rise in a warm place for 30 minutes or until doubled.

Bake at 350° for 15 minutes. Cover with foil; bake 5-10 minutes longer or until golden brown. **Yield:** 1 loaf.

Cinnamon Monkey Bread

This sweet cinnamon bread looks fancy and has an irresistible rich, buttery glaze when it comes out of the oven and is turned onto a platter. And, of course, it tastes absolutely scrumptious! We enjoy it with big glasses of cold milk.
—Lisa Combs, Greenville, Ohio

4 tubes (7-1/2 ounces each) refrigerated buttermilk biscuits
1/2 cup sugar
2 teaspoons ground cinnamon
1/2 cup butter, melted
1/2 cup packed brown sugar

Cut each biscuit into four pieces; shape into balls. In a small bowl, combine sugar and cinnamon. Roll each ball in cinnamon-sugar. Arrange evenly in a greased 10-in. fluted tube pan. Sprinkle with remaining cinnamon-sugar.

Combine butter and brown sugar; pour over the top. Bake at 350° for 35-40 minutes or until golden brown. Cool for 5 minutes before inverting bread onto a serving platter. **Yield:** 1 loaf.

Candy Bar Croissants

These croissants are a rich, buttery treat that combines convenient refrigerated crescent rolls and chocolate bars.
—Beverly Sterling
Gasport, New York

1 tube (8 ounces) refrigerated crescent rolls
1 tablespoon butter, softened
2 plain milk chocolate candy bars (1.55 ounces each), broken into small pieces
1 egg, beaten
2 tablespoons sliced almonds

Unroll crescent roll dough; separate into triangles. Brush with butter. Arrange candy bar pieces evenly over triangles; roll up from the wide end.

Place point side down on a greased baking sheet; curve ends slightly. Brush with egg and sprinkle with almonds. Bake at 375° for 11-13 minutes or until golden brown. Cool on a wire rack. **Yield:** 8 servings.

Savory Biscuit Bites

These light, golden puffs are super simple to make, and their flavor is oh-so-good. Their small size makes them easy to munch, and they're wonderful warm or cold.
—*Wendy Chilton, Brookeland, Texas*

1/4 cup butter, melted
2 tablespoons grated Parmesan cheese
1 tablespoon dried minced onion
1-1/2 teaspoons dried parsley flakes
1 package (12 ounces) refrigerated biscuits

In a bowl, combine butter, cheese, onion and parsley. Cut biscuits into quarters; roll in butter mixture. Place in a greased 15-in. x 10-in. x 1-in. baking pan; let stand for 25 minutes. Bake at 400° for 8 minutes or until lightly browned. **Yield:** 40 pieces.

Cheesy Corn Muffins

Meat lovers might like having little pieces of chopped ham added to these muffins. Or you could vary the shape and make a loaf of corn bread instead.
—*Joyce Hunsberger, Quakertown, Pennsylvania*

1/4 cup chopped onion
1 tablespoon butter
2 packages (8-1/2 ounces *each*) corn muffin mix
1/2 cup sour cream
1/2 cup shredded cheddar cheese

In a small skillet, saute onion in butter until tender; set aside. Prepare muffin mixes according to package directions; fold in the onion. Fill greased or paper-lined muffin cups two-thirds full. Combine sour cream and cheese; drop by rounded teaspoonfuls onto each muffin.

Bake at 400° for 15-20 minutes or until a toothpick inserted in muffin comes out clean. Cool in pan for 5 minutes before removing to a wire rack. **Yield:** 1 dozen.

Kids' Breadsticks

These cheesy breadsticks are simple to make because they start with convenient hot dog buns. I can whip up a batch in a matter of minutes…and they disappear just as quickly. —*Mary Miller*
Fairfield, California

8 **hot dog buns, split**
6 **tablespoons butter, melted**
1 **cup grated Parmesan cheese**
2 **to 3 tablespoons poppy** *or* **sesame seeds**

Brush the cut sides of buns with butter. Place on ungreased baking sheets. Combine cheese and poppy or sesame seeds; sprinkle over buns. Bake at 450° for 7-9 minutes or until golden brown. **Yield:** 16 breadsticks.

Garlic Bubble Loaf

This lovely golden loaf has great garlic flavor in every bite. People go wild over this bread whenever I serve it. It's a fun change of pace from the more traditional slices of garlic bread. —*Carol Shields*
Summerville, Pennsylvania

1/4 **cup butter, melted**
1 **tablespoon dried parsley flakes**
1 **teaspoon garlic powder**
1/4 **teaspoon garlic salt**
1 **loaf (1 pound) frozen white bread dough, thawed**

In a bowl, combine butter, parsley, garlic powder and garlic salt. Cut dough into 1-in. pieces; dip into butter mixture. Layer in a greased 9-in. x 5-in. x 3-in. loaf pan. Cover and let rise until doubled, about 1 hour. Bake at 350° for 30 minutes or until golden brown. **Yield:** 1 loaf.

Monterey Ranch Bread

This cheesy loaf is a quick-and-easy addition to any meal. Or serve it as an appealing appetizer for a casual get-together.

—Shirley Privratsky
Dickinson, North Dakota

2 cups (8 ounces) shredded Monterey Jack cheese
3/4 cup ranch salad dressing with bacon
1 loaf (1 pound) unsliced French bread
2 tablespoons butter, melted
Minced fresh parsley

In a bowl, combine the cheese and salad dressing; set aside. Cut bread in half lengthwise; brush with butter. Place on baking sheets. Broil 4 in. from the heat until golden brown. Spread with cheese mixture.

Bake at 350° for 10-15 minutes or until cheese is melted. Sprinkle with parsley. Cut into 1-1/2-in. slices. **Yield:** 6-8 servings.

|FROM STALE TO SUPER| Make crostini with second-day French or Italian bread. Cut the bread into 1/4-inch-thick slices, brush one side with olive oil and broil about 30 seconds on each side or until crisp and golden brown. Crostini make great soup or salad accompaniments.

Fiesta Bread

A neighbor gave me this easy recipe more than 25 years ago, when my children were small. You can use your favorite seasoning mix, so it's very versatile.   —Helen Carpenter, Highland Haven, Texas

2 cups biscuit/baking mix
2/3 cup milk
4-1/2 teaspoons chili seasoning mix
2 tablespoons butter, melted

In a bowl, combine the biscuit mix, milk and seasoning mix; mix well. Pat into a greased 8-in. square baking dish; drizzle with butter. Bake at 425° for 15-17 minutes or until a toothpick inserted near the center comes out clean. **Yield:** 9 servings.

Editor's Note: Italian or ranch salad dressing mix, taco seasoning or onion soup mix may be substituted for the chili seasoning mix.

Banana Nut Bread

A yellow cake mix streamlines assembly of this moist golden bread. I searched a long while for a banana bread that was easy to make. This one takes no time at all, and makes two loaves, so one can be frozen to enjoy later.

—*Marie Davis, Pendleton, South Carolina*

1 package (18-1/4 ounces) yellow cake mix
1 egg
1/2 cup milk
1 cup mashed ripe bananas (about 2 medium)
1/2 cup chopped pecans

In a mixing bowl, combine cake mix, egg and milk. Add bananas; beat on medium speed for 2 minutes. Stir in pecans. Pour into two greased 8-in. x 4-in. x 2-in. loaf pans.

Bake at 350° for 40-45 minutes or until a toothpick inserted near the center comes out clean. Cool for 10 minutes before removing from pans to wire racks to cool completely. **Yield:** 2 loaves.

|STORING QUICK BREADS| Quick breads may be wrapped in foil or plastic wrap and stored at room temperature for up to 3 days. For longer storage, place quick breads in heavy-duty resealable plastic bags and freeze for up to 3 months.

Sausage Pinwheels

These savory spirals are very simple to fix but look special on a buffet. Our guests eagerly help themselves—sometimes the eye-catching pinwheels never make it to their plates!

—*Gail Sykora*
Menomonee Falls, Wisconsin

1 tube (8 ounces) refrigerated crescent rolls
1/2 pound uncooked bulk pork sausage
2 tablespoons minced chives

Unroll crescent roll dough on a lightly floured surface; press seams and perforations together. Roll into a 14-in. x 10-in. rectangle. Spread sausage to within 1/2 in. of edges. Sprinkle with chives.

Carefully roll up from a long side; cut into 12 slices. Place 1 in. apart in an ungreased 15-in. x 10-in. x 1-in. baking pan. Bake at 375° for 12-16 minutes or until golden brown. **Yield:** 1 dozen.

Quick Caramel Rolls

Refrigerated crescent rolls and caramel ice cream topping make these yummy, gooey treats a snap to assemble. I used to whip up a huge panful for our kids when they were growing up...now our grandchildren love them, too. They are easy to reheat in the microwave for a speedy snack.

—*Jeannette Westphal, Gettysburg, South Dakota*

1/4 cup butter
1/2 cup chopped pecans
1 cup caramel ice cream topping
2 tubes (8 ounces *each*) refrigerated crescent rolls

Place butter in a 13-in. x 9-in. x 2-in. baking pan; heat in a 375° oven until melted. Sprinkle with pecans. Add ice cream topping and mix well.

Remove dough from tubes (do not unroll); cut each section of dough into six rolls. Arrange rolls in prepared pan with cut side down. Bake at 375° for 20-25 minutes or until golden. Immediately invert onto a serving plate. Serve warm.
Yield: 2 dozen.

Cheese Sticks

When our children were young, I'd pop these scrumptious cheesy snacks in the oven shortly before they'd get home from school. There's no need to thaw them, so they're ready to munch in under 15 minutes.

—*Ruth Peterson, Jenison, Michigan*

1 jar (5 ounces) sharp American cheese spread
1/2 cup butter, softened
1 egg white
1 loaf unsliced bread (1 pound)

In a mixing bowl, beat cheese spread, butter and egg white until fluffy. Cut crust from bread. Slice bread 1 in. thick; cut each slice into 1-in. strips. Spread the cheese mixture on all sides of each strip and place 2 in. apart on greased baking sheets.

Bake at 350° for 12-15 minutes or until lightly browned. Serve warm. Unbaked cheese sticks may be frozen for up to 4 months. Bake as directed (they do not need to be thawed first). **Yield:** 9 servings.

Swiss Onion Crescents

I put a special spin on these golden crescents by filling them with Swiss cheese, green onions and Dijon mustard. They're a snap to prepare because I use refrigerated dough.

—Joy McMillan
The Woodlands, Texas

1 tube (8 ounces) refrigerated crescent rolls
3 tablespoons shredded Swiss cheese, *divided*
2 tablespoons chopped green onion
1-1/2 teaspoons Dijon mustard

Unroll crescent dough and separate into eight triangles. Combine 2 tablespoons cheese, green onion and mustard; spread about 1 teaspoon over each triangle.

Roll up from the short side. Place point side down on an ungreased baking sheet and curve into a crescent shape. Sprinkle with remaining cheese. Bake at 375° for 11-13 minutes or until golden brown. **Yield:** 8 rolls.

Tasty White Bread

It's worth the rising time making this bread just to fill the house with the heavenly aroma as it bakes. But eating a thick slice is even better.
—Angel Olvey, Kokomo, Indiana

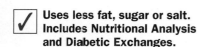 **Uses less fat, sugar or salt. Includes Nutritional Analysis and Diabetic Exchanges.**

1 package (1/4 ounce) active dry yeast
3 teaspoons sugar, *divided*
2-1/4 cups warm water (110° to 115°), *divided*
2 teaspoons salt
6 to 6-1/2 cups all-purpose flour

In a large mixing bowl, dissolve yeast and 1 teaspoon sugar in 1/4 cup water; let stand for 10 minutes. Combine salt, remaining sugar and water; add to yeast mixture. Add 3 cups of flour; beat until smooth. Add enough remaining flour to form a soft dough. Turn onto a floured surface; knead until smooth and elastic, about 6-8 minutes. Place in a greased bowl, turning once to grease top. Cover and let rise in a warm place until doubled, about 1 hour.

Punch dough down; shape into two loaves. Place in two 8-in. x 4-in. x 2-in. loaf pans that have been coated with nonstick cooking spray. Cover and let rise until doubled, about 1 hour. Bake at 350° for 35-40 minutes. Remove from pans and cool on wire racks. **Yield:** 2 loaves (32 slices).

Nutritional Analysis: One slice equals 87 calories, 146 mg sodium, 0 cholesterol, 18 g carbohydrate, 3 g protein, trace fat. **Diabetic Exchange:** 1 starch.

Onion Rye Breadsticks

An envelope of onion soup mix provides the fast flavor you'll find in these rye snacks. They're an easy accompaniment to soup or salad when time's at a premium. The buttery mixture is terrific on multigrain bread, too.
—*Barbara Brown, Kentwood, Michigan*

1/2 **cup butter, softened**
1 **envelope onion soup mix**
14 **slices rye bread**

Combine butter and soup mix; spread over bread. Cut each slice into 3/4-in. strips and place on ungreased baking sheets. Bake at 350° for 5-6 minutes or until butter is melted and breadsticks are crisp. **Yield:** about 7 dozen.

Chive Garlic Bread

A purchased loaf of French bread gets a real boost with a few simple ingredients. Garlic and chives make the savory slices irresistible. Along with lasagna or another Italian meal, we munch them until the last crumbs have vanished! —*Kim Orr*
Louisville, Kentucky

1/4 **cup butter, softened**
1/4 **cup grated Parmesan cheese**
2 **tablespoons snipped chives**
1 **garlic clove, minced**
1 **loaf (1 pound) French bread, cut into 1-inch slices**

In a bowl, combine the butter, Parmesan cheese, chives and garlic. Spread on one side of each slice of bread; wrap in a large piece of heavy-duty foil. Seal the edges. Place on a baking sheet. Bake at 350° for 25-30 minutes or until heated through. **Yield:** 12 servings.

|CUTTING CHIVES| The easiest way to cut fresh chives is to snip them with a scissors. Snip the tops of the entire bunch rather than snipping each chive individually.

Ultimate Cheese Bread

Loaded with mushrooms and cheese, this festive-looking garlic bread is a great party appetizer. Accompanied by soup or a salad, it's hearty enough to serve as a meal.
—*Carolyn Hayes*
Marion, Illinois

1 unsliced loaf French bread (1 pound)
1 package (8 ounces) sliced Swiss cheese
1 jar (4-1/2 ounces) sliced mushrooms, drained, optional
1/2 cup butter, melted
1/8 to 1/4 teaspoon garlic powder

Cut bread diagonally into 1-1/2-in. slices to within 1/2 in. of bottom. Repeat cuts in opposite direction. Cut cheese into 1-in. squares. Place one cheese square and one mushroom if desired into each slit.

Combine butter and garlic powder; spoon over the bread. Place on an ungreased baking sheet. Bake at 350° for 8-10 minutes or until cheese is melted. **Yield:** 10-12 servings.

Sausage Cheese Puffs

People are always surprised when I tell them there are only four ingredients in these tasty bite-size puffs. Cheesy and spicy, the golden morsels are a fun novelty at a breakfast or brunch...and they also make yummy party appetizers!
—*Della Moore, Troy, New York*

1 pound bulk Italian sausage
3 cups biscuit/baking mix
4 cups (16 ounces) shredded cheddar cheese
3/4 cup water

In a skillet, cook and crumble sausage until no longer pink; drain. In a bowl, combine biscuit mix and cheese; stir in sausage. Add water and toss with a fork until moistened.

Shape into 1-1/2-in. balls. Place 2 in. apart on ungreased baking sheets. Bake at 400° for 12-15 minutes or until puffed and golden brown. Cool on wire racks. **Yield:** about 4 dozen.

Editor's Note: Baked puffs may be frozen; reheat at 400° for 7-9 minutes or until heated through (they do not need to be thawed first).

English Muffins With Bacon Butter

For a change from the usual breakfast bread, I toast up a batch of English Muffins with Bacon Butter. The hint of Dijon mustard in this hearty spread really dresses up the English muffins.
—*Edna Hoffman, Hebron, Indiana*

1/2 cup butter, softened
1/2 to 3/4 teaspoon Dijon mustard
4 bacon strips, cooked and crumbled
4 to 6 English muffins, split

In a bowl, combine butter and mustard; stir in bacon. Toast the English muffins; spread with bacon butter. Refrigerate any leftover butter. **Yield:** 4-6 servings.

French Toast Fingers

Bite-size French Toast Fingers are great for a buffet...and kids of all ages love them. Strawberry preserves makes them pretty and taste simply scrumptious. —*Mavis Diment, Marcus, Iowa*

 Uses less fat, sugar or salt. Includes Nutritional Analysis and Diabetic Exchanges.

2 eggs
1/4 cup milk
1/4 teaspoon salt
1/2 cup strawberry preserves
8 slices day-old white bread
Confectioners' sugar, optional

In a small bowl, beat eggs, milk and salt; set aside. Spread preserves on four slices of bread; top with the remaining bread. Trim crusts; cut each sandwich into three strips. Dip both sides in egg mixture. Cook on a lightly greased hot griddle for 2 minutes on each side or until golden brown. Dust with confectioners' sugar if desired. **Yield:** 4 servings.

Nutritional Analysis: One serving of three strips (prepared with egg substitute, fat-free milk and sugar-free preserves and without confectioners' sugar) equals 235 calories, 500 mg sodium, 2 mg cholesterol, 42 g carbohydrate, 10 g protein, 4 g fat. **Diabetic Exchanges:** 2 starch, 1 meat, 1/2 fruit.

Southern Buttermilk Biscuits

The recipe for these four-ingredient biscuits has been handed down for many generations. Served warm with honey or jam, they'll melt in your mouth. —*Fran Thompson, Tarboro, North Carolina*

1/2 cup cold butter
2 cups self-rising flour
3/4 cup buttermilk
Melted butter

In a bowl, cut butter into flour until mixture resembles coarse crumbs. Stir in buttermilk just until moistened. Turn onto a lightly floured surface; knead 3-4 times.

Pat or lightly roll to 3/4-in. thickness. Cut with a floured 2-1/2-in. biscuit cutter. Place on a greased baking sheet. Bake at 425° for 11-13 minutes or until golden brown. Brush tops with butter. Serve warm. **Yield:** 9 biscuits.

Editor's Note: As a substitute for *each* cup of self-rising flour, place 1-1/2 teaspoons baking powder and 1/2 teaspoon salt in a measuring cup. Add all-purpose flour to measure 1 cup.

Pecan Pie Mini Muffins

While these are delicious year-round, you could easily turn them into an edible Christmas gift. They look festive on a decorative tray wrapped in red or green cellophane or tucked into a giveaway cookie plate. And don't forget to include the recipe so your recipient can enjoy this treat over and over again!
—*Pat Schrand, Enterprise, Alabama*

1 cup packed brown sugar
1/2 cup all-purpose flour
1 cup chopped pecans
2/3 cup butter, melted
2 eggs, beaten

In a bowl, combine brown sugar, flour and pecans; set aside. Combine butter and eggs; mix well. Stir into flour mixture. Fill greased and floured miniature muffin cups two-thirds full. Bake at 350° for 22-25 minutes. Remove immediately to cool on wire racks. **Yield:** about 2-1/2 dozen.

Editor's Note: This recipe uses only 1/2 cup flour.

Flaky Garlic Rolls

Flaky Garlic Rolls are a fun and tasty way to dress up handy refrigerator biscuits. Hot from the oven, these rolls are great alongside any meat and also are super with soup or as an evening snack.

—*Peggy Burdick*
Burlington, Michigan

1 tube (6 ounces) refrigerated flaky biscuits
1 to 2 tablespoons butter, melted
1/4 to 1/2 teaspoon garlic salt

Separate each biscuit into three pieces; place on a greased baking sheet. Brush with butter; sprinkle with garlic salt. Bake at 400° for 8-10 minutes or until golden brown. Serve warm. **Yield:** 15 rolls.

|GOT GARLIC?| A member of the lily family, garlic is sold fresh, chopped and packed in jars, or processed into garlic salt and powder. It is used in thousands of dishes in all cuisines and has been used throughout history as a medication.

Upside-Down Orange Puffs

These delicious citrusy morsels are so quick to make with refrigerated biscuits. They're our teenage son's favorite, so I make them often. —*Rosa Griffith, Christiansburg, Virginia*

1/4 cup butter
1/4 cup sugar
2 tablespoons orange juice
1 teaspoon grated orange peel
1 can (7-1/2 ounces) refrigerated buttermilk biscuits

In a saucepan, combine butter, sugar, orange juice and peel. Cook and stir over medium heat until sugar is dissolved. Divide among 10 muffin cups. Make a hole in the center of each biscuit; place over orange mixture. Bake at 450° for 8-10 minutes or until golden brown. Immediately invert onto a wire rack to cool. **Yield:** 10 puffs.

|USE A PEELER| Always thoroughly wash citrus fruit before using their peel for anything. Pare citrus fruit rind with a vegetable peeler rather than a knife to avoid peeling the pith as well. The white pith is bitter and should be avoided.

Cinnamon Flat Rolls

I shared this recipe when 4-H leaders requested an activity for younger members. The kids had a ball rolling out the dough and enjoying the sweet chewy results. What makes these cinnamon rolls unique is you make them on the grill and not in the oven! They're quicker, too. —*Ethel Farnsworth*
Yuma, Arizona

1 package (16 ounces) frozen dinner rolls, thawed
5 tablespoons olive oil
1/2 cup sugar
1 tablespoon ground cinnamon

On a floured surface, roll each dinner roll into a 5-in. circle. Brush with oil. Grill, uncovered, over medium heat for 1 minute on each side or until golden brown (burst any large bubbles with a fork). Combine sugar and cinnamon; sprinkle over rolls. **Yield:** 1 dozen.

Cheese And Sausage Muffins

These small, savory muffins are fun to serve as appetizers or at brunch. With just five ingredients, the tasty bites are easy to whip up to take to a party, the office or a friend.
—*Willa Paget*
Nashville, Tennessee

1 pound bulk hot pork sausage
1 can (10-3/4 ounces) condensed cheddar cheese soup, undiluted
1/2 cup milk
2 to 3 teaspoons rubbed sage
3 cups biscuit/baking mix

In a skillet over medium heat, cook sausage until no longer pink; drain. In a bowl, combine soup, milk, sage and sausage. Stir in the biscuit mix just until moistened.

Fill greased miniature or regular muffin cups two-thirds full. Bake at 400° for 15-20 minutes or until a toothpick inserted near the center comes out clean. **Yield:** 4 dozen mini-muffins or 2 dozen regular muffins.

Grandma's Popovers

Still warm from the oven, popovers are always a fun accompaniment to a homey meal. I was raised on these—my grandmother often made them for our Sunday dinners. The recipe could not be simpler.
—Debbie Terenzini, Lusby, Maryland

1 cup all-purpose flour
1/8 teaspoon salt
3 eggs
1 cup milk

In a bowl, combine flour and salt. Combine eggs and milk; whisk into dry ingredients just until blended. Using two 12-cup muffin tins, grease and flour five alternating cups of one tin and four cups of the second tin; fill two-thirds full with batter. Fill the empty cups two-thirds full with water.

Bake at 450° for 15 minutes. Reduce heat to 350° (do not open oven door). Bake 15 minutes longer or until deep golden brown (do not underbake). **Yield:** 9 popovers.

Quick Garlic Toast

Mom knew how to easily round out a meal with this crisp, cheesy garlic toast. We gobbled it up when she served it alongside of slaw or salad...and used it to soak up gravy from stew, too.
—Teresa Ingebrand, Perham, Minnesota

1/3 cup butter, softened
12 slices bread
1/2 teaspoon garlic salt
3 tablespoons grated
Parmesan cheese

Spread butter on one side of each slice of bread. Cut each slice in half; place plain side down on a baking sheet. Sprinkle with garlic salt and Parmesan cheese. Broil 4 in. from the heat for 1-2 minutes or until lightly browned. **Yield:** 12 slices.

Cookies, Bars & Candies

Mint Sandwich Cookies, p. 229

Marbled Chocolate Bars, p. 228

Chewy Macaroons, p. 230

Cookies, Bars & Candies   227

Brown Sugar Shortbread

These rich buttery cookies have just three ingredients! They're a snap to make for a last-minute gift or when guests will be arriving on short notice. For best results, gradually stir the flour into the dough.

—Shirley Gardiner
Clearwater, Manitoba

1 cup butter, softened
1/2 cup packed brown sugar
2-1/4 cups all-purpose flour

In a mixing bowl, cream butter and sugar. Gradually stir in the flour. Turn onto a lightly floured surface and knead until smooth, about 3 minutes. Pat into a 1/3-in.-thick rectangle measuring 11 in. x 8 in. Cut into 2-in. x 1-in. strips.

Place 1 in. apart on ungreased baking sheets. Prick with a fork. Bake at 300° for 25 minutes or until bottom begins to brown. Cool for 5 minutes; remove to a wire rack to cool completely. **Yield:** 3-1/2 dozen.

Marbled Chocolate Bars

(Pictured on page 227)

These scrumptious chocolate bars with pockets of rich cream cheese are perfect for taking to a potluck. They're quick to assemble, don't need frosting and are easy to transport and serve. Best of all, folks love them!

—Margery Bryan, Royal City, Washington

1 package (18-1/4
ounces) German
chocolate cake mix
1 package (8 ounces)
cream cheese, softened
1/2 cup sugar
3/4 cup milk chocolate
chips, divided

Prepare cake batter according to package directions. Pour into a greased 15-in. x 10-in. x 1-in. baking pan. In a small mixing bowl, beat cream cheese and sugar. Stir in 1/4 cup chocolate chips. Drop by tablespoonfuls over batter. Cut through batter with a knife to swirl the cream cheese mixture. Sprinkle with remaining chocolate chips.

Bake at 350° for 25-30 minutes or until a toothpick inserted near the center comes out clean. Cool on a wire rack. Cut into bars. **Yield:** 3 dozen.

Mint Sandwich Cookies

(Pictured on page 226)

Canned frosting, peppermint extract and chocolate candy coating quickly turn crackers into these wonderful little no-bake cookies. My children and I like to assemble them for parties and holidays. I hope you and your family enjoy them as much as we do. —*Melissa Thompson, Anderson, Ohio*

1 can (16 ounces) vanilla frosting
1/2 teaspoon peppermint extract
3 to 5 drops green food coloring, optional
72 butter-flavored crackers
1 pound dark chocolate candy coating, coarsely chopped

In a bowl, combine the frosting, extract and food coloring if desired. Spread over half of the crackers; top with remaining crackers. Place candy coating in a microwave-safe bowl. Microwave on high for 1-2 minutes or until smooth.

Dip the cookies in coating. Place on waxed paper until chocolate is completely set. Store in an airtight container at room temperature. **Yield:** 3 dozen.

Chocolate Chip Butter Cookies

At the downtown Chicago law firm where I work, we often bring in goodies for special occasions. When co-workers hear I've baked these melt-in-your-mouth cookies, they make a special trip to my floor to sample them. Best of all, these crisp, buttery treats can be made in no time. —*Janis Gruca Mokena, Illinois*

1 cup butter
1/2 teaspoon vanilla extract
2 cups all-purpose flour
1 cup confectioners' sugar
1 cup (6 ounces) miniature semisweet chocolate chips

Melt butter in a microwave or double boiler; stir in vanilla. Cool completely. In a large bowl, combine flour and sugar; stir in butter mixture and chocolate chips (mixture will be crumbly). Shape into 1-in. balls.

Place 2 in. apart on ungreased baking sheets; flatten slightly. Bake at 375° for 12 minutes or until edges begin to brown. Cool on wire racks. **Yield:** about 4 dozen.

Chewy Macaroons

(Pictured on page 227)

My family loves these delicious cookies on special occasions. With only three ingredients, they're a snap to make.
—*Marcia Hostetter, Canton, New York*

5-1/3 cups flaked coconut
1 can (14 ounces) sweetened condensed milk
2 teaspoons vanilla extract

In a bowl, combine all ingredients. Drop 2 in. apart onto greased baking sheets. Bake at 350° for 10-12 minutes or until lightly browned. With a spatula dipped in water, immediately remove to wire racks to cool. **Yield:** 4-1/4 dozen.

Cookie Lollipops

A dip and a drizzle turn crunchy cream-filled sandwich cookies into a deliciously different treat! Kids love Cookie Lollipops because they taste as good as they look. You need just four ingredients and Popsicle sticks, so these fun snacks make great party favors.
—*Jessie Wiggers*
Halstead, Kansas

1 package (10 to 12 ounces) vanilla *or* white chips
2 tablespoons shortening, *divided*
1 package (16 ounces) double-stuffed chocolate cream-filled sandwich cookies
32 wooden Popsicle *or* craft sticks
1 cup (6 ounces) semisweet chocolate chips

In a microwave or double boiler, melt vanilla chips and 1 tablespoon shortening; stir until smooth. Twist apart sandwich cookies. Dip the end of each Popsicle stick into melted chips; place on a cookie half and top with another half. Place cookies on a waxed paper-lined baking sheet; freeze for 15 minutes.

Reheat vanilla chip mixture again if necessary; dip frozen cookies into mixture until completely covered. Return to the baking sheet; freeze 30 minutes longer. Melt the chocolate chips and remaining shortening; stir until smooth. Drizzle over cookies. Store in an airtight container. **Yield:** 32 servings.

S'mores Bars

Glowing campfire coals are not needed to enjoy the traditional taste of s'mores with this recipe. The tasty take-along treat makes a sweet snack any time of day. —*Kristine Brown, Rio Rancho, New Mexico*

8 to 10 whole graham crackers (about 5 inches x 2-1/2 inches)
1 package fudge brownie mix (13-inch x 9-inch pan size)
2 cups miniature marshmallows
1 cup (6 ounces) semisweet chocolate chips
2/3 cup chopped peanuts

Arrange graham crackers in a single layer in a greased 13-in. x 9-in. x 2-in. baking pan. Prepare the brownie batter according to package directions. Spread over crackers. Bake at 350° for 25-30 minutes or until a toothpick inserted near the center comes out clean.

Sprinkle with marshmallows, chocolate chips and peanuts. Bake 5 minutes longer or until marshmallows are slightly puffed and golden brown. Cool on a wire rack before cutting. **Yield:** 2 dozen.

Lemon Crisp Cookies

Lemon Crisp Cookies are a snap to make using a boxed cake mix. The sunny color and lemon flavor are sure to bring smiles. —*Julia Livingston*
Frostproof, Florida

1 package (18-1/4 ounces) lemon cake mix
1 cup crisp rice cereal
1/2 cup butter, melted
1 egg, beaten
1 teaspoon grated lemon peel

In a large bowl, combine all ingredients until well mixed (dough will be crumbly). Shape into 1-in. balls. Place 2 in. apart on ungreased baking sheets. Bake at 350° for 10-12 minutes or until set. Cool for 1 minute; remove from pan to a wire rack to cool completely. **Yield:** about 4 dozen.

Easy Chocolate Drops

Friends and relatives relish these crunchy goodies. I never knew that making candy could be so simple until I tried these!
—*Heather De Cal, Terrace Bay, Ontario*

- **1 cup (6 ounces) semisweet chocolate chips**
- **1 cup (6 ounces) butterscotch chips**
- **1 cup shoestring potato sticks**
- **1 cup salted peanuts**

In a 2-qt. microwave-safe bowl, heat chips on high for 2 minutes or until melted, stirring once. Stir in potato sticks and peanuts. Drop by teaspoonfuls onto waxed paper-lined baking sheets. Chill until set, about 15 minutes. Store in airtight containers. **Yield:** 3-1/2 dozen.

Editor's Note: This recipe was tested using a 700-watt microwave.

Pretzel–Topped Sugar Cookies

It's tough to beat a three-ingredient treat…especially one that's so easy and sweet! I rely on refrigerated cookie dough to make these munchable morsels. I dress up each cookie with a white fudge-covered pretzel and melted white chocolate.
—*Michelle Brenneman, Orrville, Ohio*

- **2 tubes (18 ounces *each*) refrigerated sugar cookie dough**
- **2-1/2 cups vanilla *or* white chips, *divided***
- **1 package (7-1/2 ounces) white fudge-covered pretzels**

Crumble cookie dough into a large bowl; stir in 1-1/2 cups chips. Drop by tablespoonfuls 2 in. apart onto ungreased baking sheets. Bake at 325° for 15-18 minutes or until lightly browned. Immediately press a pretzel into the center of each cookie. Remove to wire racks to cool.

In a microwave, heat remaining chips at 70% power for 1 minute or until melted; stir until smooth. Drizzle over cookies. **Yield:** about 4-1/2 dozen.

Editor's Note: This recipe was tested with Nestle Flipz white fudge-covered pretzels.

Double Chip Bars

Our two children love these sweet, rich dessert bars. They go together so quickly that I can make them even on hectic days.
—*Victoria Lowe*
Lititz, Pennsylvania

1/2 cup butter
1-1/2 cups graham cracker crumbs
1 can (14 ounces) sweetened condensed milk
2 cups (12 ounces) semisweet chocolate chips
1 cup (6 ounces) peanut butter chips

Place butter in a 13-in. x 9-in. x 2-in. baking pan; place in a 350° oven until melted. Remove from the oven. Sprinkle the cracker crumbs evenly over butter. Pour milk evenly over crumbs. Sprinkle with chips; press down firmly.

Bake at 350° for 25-30 minutes or until golden brown. Cool on a wire rack before cutting. **Yield:** 3 dozen.

Anise Hard Candy

I like to wrap pieces of this candy in plastic wrap to share with friends. Slightly sweet, anise has a licorice-like flavor and aroma.
—*Bea Aubry, Dubuque, Iowa*

2 cups sugar
1 cup light corn syrup
1 cup water
2 teaspoons anise extract *or* 1 teaspoon anise oil
6 to 9 drops red food coloring

In a large heavy saucepan, combine sugar, corn syrup and water. Bring to a boil over medium heat, stirring occasionally. Cover and cook for 3 minutes or until sugar is dissolved. Uncover; cook on medium-high heat, without stirring, until a candy thermometer reads 300° (hard-crack stage). Remove from the heat; stir in extract and food coloring (keep face away from mixture as the aroma will be very strong).

Pour into a buttered 13-in. x 9-in. x 2-in. baking pan. When cooled slightly but not hardened, cut into 1-in. squares. Cool completely. Store in an airtight container. **Yield:** about 8-1/2 dozen.

Editor's Note: We recommend that you test your candy thermometer before each use by bringing water to a boil; the thermometer should read 212°. Adjust your recipe temperature up or down based on your test.

Snickers Cookies

Though you wouldn't know by looking, you'll find a sweet surprise inside these cookies. My mother got this recipe from a fellow teacher at her school. It's a great way to dress up refrigerated cookie dough.
—*Kari Pease, Conconully, Washington*

1 tube (18 ounces) refrigerated chocolate chip cookie dough
24 to 30 bite-size Snickers candy bars

Cut dough into 1/4-in.-thick slices. Place a candy bar on each slice and wrap dough around it. Place 2 in. apart on ungreased baking sheets. Bake at 350° for 8-10 minutes or until lightly browned. Cool on wire racks. **Yield:** 2 to 2-1/2 dozen.

Editor's Note: 2 cups of any chocolate chip cookie dough can be substituted for the refrigerated dough. Use 1 tablespoon of dough for each cookie.

Crunchy Dessert Bars

My son-in-law is diabetic and loves these five-ingredient frozen dessert bars. With their nutty crunch from Grape Nuts cereal, we think they taste like the inside of a Snickers candy bar. —*Shirley Reed San Angelo, Texas*

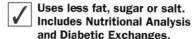 Uses less fat, sugar or salt. Includes Nutritional Analysis and Diabetic Exchanges.

1 pint sugar-free fat-free ice cream, softened
1 cup reduced-fat whipped topping
1/2 cup reduced-fat peanut butter
1 package (1 ounce) instant sugar-free butterscotch pudding mix
1 cup Grape Nuts cereal

In a mixing bowl, combine the first four ingredients; beat until smooth. Stir in cereal. Transfer to a foil-lined 8-in. square pan. Cover and freeze for 3-4 hours or until firm. Use foil to lift out of pan; discard foil. Cut into bars. **Yield:** 2 dozen.

Nutritional Analysis: One bar equals 67 calories, 122 mg sodium, 0 cholesterol, 10 g carbohydrate, 3 g protein, 2 g fat. **Diabetic Exchange:** 1 starch.

Coconut Drops

We enjoy giving friends a gift of festive candy each holiday season. With such limited time, I can rely on this recipe, which is quick and easy to make. —Diane Rathburn, Mt. Pleasant, Michigan

1 package (14 ounces) flaked coconut
6 drops red food coloring
6 drops green food coloring
1 pound white candy coating

Divide coconut between two bowls. Add red food coloring to one bowl and green to the other; toss to coat. In a heavy saucepan over low heat, melt candy coating. Drop by tablespoonfuls onto waxed paper.

While coating is still warm, sprinkle half of each drop with pink coconut and the other half with green; press down gently. Refrigerate until firm. **Yield:** 1-1/4 pounds.

Cookies 'n' Cream Fudge

I invented this confection for a bake sale at our children's school. Boy, was it a hit! The crunchy chunks of sandwich cookie soften a bit as the mixture mellows. It's so sweet that one panful serves a crowd. —Laura Lane, Richmond, Virginia

16 chocolate cream-filled sandwich cookies, broken into chunks, *divided*
1 can (14 ounces) sweetened condensed milk
2 tablespoons butter
2-2/3 cups vanilla *or* white chips
1 teaspoon vanilla extract

Line an 8-in. square baking pan with aluminum foil; coat with nonstick cooking spray. Place half of the broken cookies in the prepared pan.

In a heavy saucepan, combine milk, butter and chips; cook and stir over low heat until chips are melted. Remove from the heat; stir in vanilla. Pour over cookies in pan. Sprinkle with remaining cookies. Cover and refrigerate for at least 1 hour. Cut into squares. **Yield:** 3 dozen.

Cookie Brittle

This recipe originally called for chocolate chips, but my family and friends like it better when I use peanut butter chips. I often make it for unexpected guests.
— *Betty Byrnes Consbruck*
Gainesville, Florida

1 cup butter, softened
1 cup sugar
2 cups all-purpose flour
1-1/4 cups peanut butter chips
1/2 cup coarsely chopped pecans

In a mixing bowl, cream the butter and sugar. Gradually add flour; mix well. Stir in peanut butter chips. Line a 15-in. x 10-in. x 1-in. baking pan with foil; coat with nonstick cooking spray. Gently press dough into the pan; sprinkle with pecans and press into dough.

Bake at 350° for 20-25 minutes or until golden brown. Cool in pan on a wire rack. Invert pan and remove foil. Break brittle into pieces; store in an airtight container. **Yield:** about 4 dozen.

Chocolate Peanut Butter Bars

To complete a meal, I often whip up a pan of Chocolate Peanut Butter Bars. These chewy cereal treats are also the perfect no-fuss contribution to a potluck or bake sale. I've discovered a few minutes in the refrigerator helps the bars' frosting set faster. Of course, the trick is getting them in there before they disappear!
— *Lorri Speer, Centralia, Washington*

1 cup sugar
1 cup light corn syrup
1 cup peanut butter
6 cups crisp rice cereal
2 cups (12 ounces) semisweet chocolate chips, melted

In a large saucepan, combine the sugar, corn syrup and peanut butter. Cook over medium-low heat until the sugar is dissolved. Remove from the heat; add cereal and stir until coated. Spread into a greased 13-in. x 9-in. x 2-in. pan; press lightly. Spread melted chocolate over bars. Chill. **Yield:** 1-1/2 to 2 dozen.

Berries 'n' Cream Brownies

If you like chocolate-covered strawberries, you'll love this sweet treat. It's an ideal ending to summer meals. A fudgy brownie, whipped topping and fresh fruit make this a fuss-free feast for the eyes as well as the taste buds.
—*Anna Lapp*
New Holland, Pennsylvania

1 **package fudge brownie mix (13-inch x 9-inch pan size)**
1 **carton (8 ounces) frozen whipped topping, thawed**
4 **cups quartered fresh strawberries**
1/3 **cup chocolate hard-shell ice cream topping**

Prepare and bake brownies according to package directions, using a greased 13-in. x 9-in. x 2-in. baking pan. Cool completely on a wire rack.

Spread whipped topping over brownies. Arrange strawberries cut side down over top. Drizzle with chocolate topping. Refrigerate for at least 30 minutes before serving. **Yield:** 12-15 servings.

Cookies In a Jiffy

You'll be amazed and delighted at how quickly you can whip up a batch of these homemade cookies. Using a package of yellow cake mix hurries them along. —*Clara Hielkema, Wyoming, Michigan*

1 **package (9 ounces) yellow cake mix**
2/3 **cup quick-cooking oats**
1/2 **cup butter, melted**
1 **egg**
1/2 **cup red and green Holiday M&M's *or* butterscotch chips**

In a mixing bowl, beat the first four ingredients. Stir in the M&M's or chips. Drop by tablespoonfuls 2 in. apart onto ungreased baking sheets. Bake at 375° for 10-12 minutes or until lightly browned. Immediately remove to wire racks to cool. **Yield:** 2 dozen.

Tiger Butter Candy

This candy is big on peanut butter flavor and fun to make. Best of all, it's made in the microwave for added convenience.
—*Pamela Pogue, Mineola, Texas*

1 pound white candy coating, cut into pieces
1/2 cup chunky peanut butter
1/2 cup semisweet chocolate chips
4 teaspoons half-and-half cream

In a microwave-safe bowl, heat coating and peanut butter on medium for 3-4 minutes or until melted; mix well. Pour onto a foil-lined baking sheet coated with nonstick cooking spray; spread into a thin layer.

In another microwave-safe bowl, heat chips and cream on high for about 30 seconds or until chips are soft; stir until smooth. Pour and swirl over peanut butter layer. Freeze for 5 minutes or until set. Break into small pieces. **Yield:** about 1-1/2 pounds.

Editor's Note: This recipe was tested using a 700-watt microwave.

Triple Fudge Brownies

When you're in a hurry to make dessert, here's a "mix of mixes" that's so convenient and quick. The result is a big pan of very rich, fudgy brownies. Friends who ask me for the recipe are amazed that it's so easy. —*Denise Nebel, Wayland, Iowa*

1 package (3.9 ounces) instant chocolate pudding mix
1 package (18-1/4 ounces) chocolate cake mix
2 cups (12 ounces) semisweet chocolate chips
Confectioners' sugar
Vanilla ice cream, optional

Prepare pudding according to package directions. Whisk in cake mix. Stir in chocolate chips. Pour into a greased 15-in. x 10-in. x 1-in. baking pan.

Bake at 350° for 30-35 minutes or until the top springs back when lightly touched. Dust with confectioners' sugar. Serve with ice cream if desired. **Yield:** 4 dozen.

Microwave Truffles

I love to entertain and try new recipes, so I couldn't wait to make these chocolaty confections for the holidays. They're smooth, rich and so pretty topped with pecans. No one will ever guess how easy they are to make. —*Joy Neustel Jamestown, North Dakota*

1/3 cup finely chopped pecans, toasted, *divided*
8 squares (1 ounce *each*) semisweet baking chocolate
1/4 cup butter
1/4 cup heavy whipping cream
1/4 teaspoon almond extract

Place 24 small foil candy cups in miniature muffin cups or on a baking sheet. Spoon 1/2 teaspoon pecans into each; set cups and remaining pecans aside.

In a 2-qt. microwave-safe bowl, combine chocolate and butter. Microwave at 50% power for 1-1/2 to 2 minutes or until melted. Stir in cream and extract. Beat with an electric mixer until slightly thickened, scraping sides of bowl occasionally. Immediately pour into prepared cups. Top with remaining pecans. Refrigerate until set. **Yield:** 2 dozen.

Editor's Note: This recipe was tested using an 850-watt microwave.

Pecan Pie Bars

I'm always on the lookout for recipes that are quick and easy to prepare. A neighbor shared this fast favorite with me. The chewy bars taste just like pecan pie. —*Kimberly Pearce, Amory, Mississippi*

3 eggs
2-1/4 cups packed brown sugar
2 cups self-rising flour
2 cups chopped pecans
1-1/2 teaspoons vanilla extract

In a mixing bowl, beat eggs. Add brown sugar. Stir in flour until smooth. Add the pecans and vanilla (dough will be stiff). Spread in a greased 13-in. x 9-in. x 2-in. baking pan. Bake at 300° for 30-35 minutes or until a toothpick inserted near the center comes out clean. Cool before cutting. **Yield:** 2 dozen.

Editor's Note: As a substitute for *each* cup of self-rising flour, place 1-1/2 teaspoons baking powder and 1/2 teaspoon salt in a measuring cup. Add all-purpose flour to equal 1 cup.

Coated Cookie Drops

It's a good thing these no-bake drops are simple, because I like to serve them throughout the year. Their moist, cake-like center and sweet coating satisfy the chocolate lover in everyone. I'm asked for the recipe time and time again.

—Amanda Reid, Oakville, Iowa

1 package (14 ounces) chocolate cream-filled sandwich cookies
1 package (8 ounces) cream cheese, softened
15 ounces white candy coating
12 ounces chocolate candy coating
Red *and/or* green candy coating, optional

Place the cookies in a blender or food processor; cover and process until finely crushed. In a small mixing bowl, beat cream cheese and crushed cookies until blended. Roll into 3/4-in. balls. Cover and refrigerate for at least 1 hour.

In a small saucepan over low heat, melt white candy coating, stirring until smooth; dip half of the balls to completely coat. Melt chocolate candy coating and dip remaining balls. Place on waxed paper until hardened.

Drizzle white candies with remaining chocolate coating and chocolate candies with remaining white coating. Or melt red or green coating and drizzle over balls. Store in the refrigerator. **Yield:** about 7-1/2 dozen.

S'more Clusters

Our two sons love to help me break up the chocolate and graham crackers for these tasty treats—that way, they can tell their friends they made them! The chocolaty clusters taste just like s'mores, but without the gooey mess.

—Kathy Schmittler, Sterling Heights, Michigan

6 milk chocolate candy bars (1.55 ounces *each*), broken into pieces
1-1/2 teaspoons vegetable oil
2 cups miniature marshmallows
8 whole graham crackers, broken into bite-size pieces

In a large microwave-safe bowl, toss chocolate and oil. Microwave, uncovered, at 50% power for 1-1/2 to 2 minutes or until chocolate is melted, stirring once. Stir in marshmallows and graham crackers. Spoon into paper-lined muffin cups (about 1/3 cup each). Refrigerate for 1 hour or until firm. **Yield:** 1 dozen.

Editor's Note: This recipe was tested in an 850-watt microwave.

Molasses Butterballs

In a hurry to satisfy your sweet tooth? You can whip up a batch of these yummy cookies in just minutes. They're short on ingredients but long on flavor. Better hide them if you want any left—it's hard to eat just one!
—*Zelda Halloran, Dallas, Texas*

1 cup butter, softened
1/4 cup light molasses
2 cups all-purpose flour
1/2 teaspoon salt
2 cups chopped walnuts
Confectioners' sugar, optional

In a mixing bowl, cream butter and molasses. Combine flour and salt; gradually add to creamed mixture. Stir in walnuts. Roll into 1-in. balls. Place 1 in. apart on greased baking sheets.

Bake at 350° for 15 minutes or until set. Remove to wire racks to cool. Roll cooled cookies in confectioners' sugar, if desired. **Yield:** 4-1/2 dozen.

Chocolate-Covered Peanut Butter Bars

My daughter won first place in a contest with this candy, which I make at Christmas. It melts in your mouth! —*Mary Esther Holloway, Bowerston, Ohio*

3 cups sugar
1 cup light corn syrup
1/2 cup water
1 jar (18 ounces) creamy peanut butter, melted
1-1/2 pounds milk chocolate candy coating

In a large heavy saucepan, combine sugar, corn syrup and water. Cook and stir over low heat until sugar is dissolved; bring to a full rolling boil. Boil, stirring constantly, until a candy thermometer reads 290° (soft-crack stage).

Meanwhile, place melted peanut butter in a large greased heat-proof bowl. Pour hot syrup over peanut butter; stir quickly until blended. Pour onto a well-buttered baking sheet; cover with a piece of buttered waxed paper. Roll mixture into a 14-in. x 12-in. rectangle. While warm, cut into 1-1/2-in. x 1-in. bars using a buttered pizza cutter or knife. Cool completely. Melt candy coating; dip bars and place on waxed paper to harden. **Yield:** 6 dozen.

Editor's Note: We recommend that you test your candy thermometer before each use by bringing water to a boil; the thermometer should read 212°. Adjust your recipe temperature up or down based on your test.

Quick Little Devils

Enjoy the classic combination of peanut butter and chocolate in these speedy squares. A short list of ingredients, including devil's food cake mix, yields chocolaty results that are sure to satisfy any sweet tooth.
—Denise Smith, Lusk, Wyoming

1 package (18-1/4
    ounces) devil's food
    cake mix
3/4 cup butter, melted
1/3 cup evaporated milk
1 jar (7 ounces)
    marshmallow creme
3/4 cup peanut butter

In a bowl, combine cake mix, butter and milk; mix well. Spread half the mixture into a greased 13-in. x 9-in. x 2-in. baking pan. Combine the marshmallow creme and peanut butter; carefully spread over cake mixture to within 1 in. of edge. Drop reserved cake mixture by teaspoonfuls over marshmallow mixture.

Bake at 350° for 20-22 minutes or until edges are golden brown. Cool completely. Cut into squares. **Yield:** about 2-1/2 dozen.

Surefire Sugar Cookies

You can invite kids to help make these easy treats. Sometimes I melt white coating instead of chocolate chips because it can be tinted to match the season. And for a short-cut, I purchase sugar cookies from a bakery.
*—Victoria Zmarzley-Hahn
Northampton, Pennsylvania*

1 tube (18 ounces)
    refrigerated sugar
    cookie dough
1-1/2 cups semisweet
    chocolate chips
4-1/2 teaspoons shortening
Colored sprinkles, chopped
    nuts *or* flaked coconut

Slice and bake the sugar cookies according to package directions. Cool on wire racks.

In a microwave-safe bowl, combine the chocolate chips and shortening. Microwave on high for 1-2 minutes or until melted; stir until smooth. Dip each cookie halfway in melted chocolate. Place on waxed paper; immediately sprinkle with colored sprinkles, nuts or coconut. Let stand until chocolate is completely set. **Yield:** 2 dozen.

Pineapple Coconut Snowballs

This is a three-ingredient candy I can whip up quickly. Canned pineapple adds refreshing taste to the frosty-looking sweet treat. —*Marlene Rhodes*
Colorado Springs, Colorado

✓ **Uses less fat, sugar or salt. Includes Nutritional Analysis and Diabetic Exchanges.**

1 package (8 ounces) cream cheese, softened
1 can (8 ounces) crushed pineapple, well drained
2-1/2 cups flaked coconut

In a small mixing bowl, beat cream cheese and pineapple until combined. Cover and refrigerate for 30 minutes. Roll into 1-in. balls; roll in coconut. Refrigerate for 6 hours or overnight. **Yield:** about 2 dozen.

Nutritional Analysis: One snowball (prepared with fat-free cream cheese) equals 67 calories, 5 g fat (5 g saturated fat), 1 mg cholesterol, 55 mg sodium, 4 g carbohydrate, 1 g fiber, 2 g protein. **Diabetic Exchanges:** 1 fat, 1/2 fruit.

Scandinavian Pecan Cookies

We enjoyed these rich, buttery cookies at a bed-and-breakfast in Galena, Illinois, and the hostess was kind enough to share her simple recipe. The pretty nut-topped treats are so special you could give a home-baked batch as a gift.
—*Laurie Knoke, DeKalb, Illinois*

1 cup butter, softened
3/4 cup packed brown sugar
1 egg, *separated*
2 cups all-purpose flour
1/2 cup finely chopped pecans

In a mixing bowl, cream butter, brown sugar and egg yolk. Gradually add flour. Shape into 1-in. balls. In a small bowl, beat egg white. Dip balls in egg white, then roll in pecans.

Place 2 in. apart on ungreased baking sheets; flatten slightly. Bake at 375° for 8-12 minutes or until edges are lightly browned. Cool on wire racks. **Yield:** 4-5 dozen.

Butterscotch Peanut Treats

I use pudding mix to stir up these sweet, crunchy no-bake bites. If you like butterscotch, you will love these delicious treats.
—*Bernice Martinoni, Petaluma, California*

1/2 cup corn syrup
1/3 cup butter, cubed
1 package (3.5 ounces) cook-and-serve butterscotch pudding mix
4 cups cornflakes
1 cup coarsely chopped dry roasted peanuts

In a large heavy saucepan, cook and stir the corn syrup and butter until butter is melted. Stir in pudding mix until blended. Cook and stir until mixture comes to a boil. Cook and stir 1 minute longer.

Remove from the heat. Cool for 1 minute, stirring several times. Stir in the cornflakes and peanuts until evenly coated. Drop by rounded tablespoonfuls onto waxed paper-lined baking sheets; cool. **Yield:** about 2-1/2 dozen.

Peppermint Meringues

These melt-in-your-mouth cookies are super as a Christmas gift or to pass around when guests drop in.
—*Dixie Terry, Marion, Illinois*

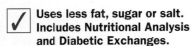 **Uses less fat, sugar or salt. Includes Nutritional Analysis and Diabetic Exchanges.**

2 egg whites
1/8 teaspoon salt
1/8 teaspoon cream of tartar
1/2 cup sugar
2 peppermint candy canes, crushed

In a mixing bowl, beat egg whites until foamy. Sprinkle with salt and cream of tartar; beat until soft peaks form. Gradually add sugar, beating until stiff peaks form, about 7 minutes. Drop by teaspoonfuls onto ungreased foil or paper-lined baking sheets; sprinkle with the crushed candy.

Bake at 225° for 1-1/2 hours. Turn off heat; leave cookies in the oven with the door ajar for at least 1 hour or until cool. Store in an airtight container. **Yield:** 3 dozen.

Nutritional Analysis: One cookie equals 21 calories, 12 mg sodium, 0 cholesterol, 5 g carbohydrate, trace protein, 0 fat. **Diabetic Exchange:** 1/2 fruit.

Graham Cracker Brownies

I enjoy making these brownies for last-minute bake sales and family gatherings alike. My grandmother first baked them nearly 50 years ago, and they're as popular today as they were then! —Cathy Guffey Towanda, Pennsylvania

- **2 cups graham cracker crumbs (about 32 squares)**
- **1 cup (6 ounces) semisweet chocolate chips**
- **1 teaspoon baking powder**
- **Pinch salt**
- **1 can (14 ounces) sweetened condensed milk**

In a bowl, combine all the ingredients. Spread into a greased 8-in. square baking pan. Bake at 350° for 30-35 minutes or until a toothpick inserted near the center comes out clean. Cool on a wire rack. **Yield:** 1-1/2 dozen.

|BAKING BARS & BROWNIES| To easily remove bars and brownies from a pan, line the bottom of the pan with foil, then grease. Add the batter and bake as directed. It's important to evenly spread batter in the pan. If one corner is thinner than another, it will bake faster and be over-baked when the rest of the pan is done.

PB&J Bars

Big and little kids alike will love these four-ingredient bars that offer a cookie crust, a layer of jam and a crunchy peanut butter and granola topping. The delicious treats are also great for picnics or for packing into bag lunches. —Mitzi Sentiff, Alexandria, Virginia

- **1 package (18 ounces) refrigerated sugar cookie dough, *divided***
- **2/3 cup strawberry jam**
- **3/4 cup granola cereal without raisins**
- **3/4 cup peanut butter chips**

Line a 9-in. square baking pan with foil and grease the foil. Press two-thirds of the cookie dough into prepared pan. Spread jam over dough to within 1/4 in. of edges. In a mixing bowl, beat the granola, peanut butter chips and remaining dough until blended. Crumble over jam.

Bake at 375° for 25-30 minutes or until golden brown. Cool on a wire rack. Using foil, lift out of pan. Cut into bars and remove from foil. **Yield:** 9-12 servings.

Christmas Bark Candy

This quick-to-fix candy is sure to please all ages when added to a homemade cookie tray. We show two versions here: vanilla chips with colorful miniature baking bits and milk chocolate chips with broken pretzels. Create your own variations by using different flavored chips and add-ins such as crushed candy canes, dried fruits or crunchy nuts.
—*Taste of Home Test Kitchen*

1 package (10 to 12 ounces) vanilla chips *or* milk chocolate chips
2 teaspoons vegetable oil
1-1/4 to 1-1/2 cups M&M miniature baking bits *or* broken pretzel pieces

In a microwave-safe bowl, heat chips and oil at 70% power for 1 minute; stir. Microwave 10-20 seconds longer or until chips are melted, stirring occasionally. Cool for 5 minutes.

Stir in baking bits or pretzels. Spread onto a waxed paper-lined baking sheet. Chill for 10 minutes. Remove from the refrigerator; break into pieces. Store in an airtight container at room temperature. **Yield:** about 1 pound.

Editor's Note: This recipe was tested in an 850-watt microwave.

Chocolate Chunk Shortbread

Chocolate is a nice addition to shortbread, as this scrumptious recipe proves. The shortbread cookies are delicious served with a cold glass of milk. —*Brenda Mumma, Airdrie, Alberta*

3/4 cup butter, softened
1/2 cup confectioners' sugar
1 cup all-purpose flour
1/2 cup cornstarch
3 squares (1 ounce *each*) semisweet chocolate, coarsely chopped
Additional confectioners' sugar

In a mixing bowl, cream butter and sugar. Gradually add flour and cornstarch. Stir in chocolate. Shape into 1-in. balls. Place 1 in. apart on ungreased baking sheets. Flatten with a glass dipped in confectioners' sugar. Bake at 300° for 30-33 minutes or until edges are lightly brown. Remove to wire racks to cool. **Yield:** about 3-1/2 dozen.

|STORING COOKIES| Allow cookies to cool completely before storing. Store soft cookies and crisp cookies in separate air tight containers. If stored together, the moisture from the soft cookies will soften the crisp cookies, making them lose their crunch. Layer cookies in a container, separating each layer with waxed paper.

Caramel Pecan Bars

These bars are so simple to fix, yet so delicious. You'll want to cut them small because the combination of caramel, chocolate and pecans makes them rich and sweet. —*Rebecca Wyke*
Morganton, North Carolina

1-1/2 cups crushed vanilla wafers (about 50 wafers)
1/4 cup butter, melted
2 cups (12 ounces) semisweet chocolate chips
1 cup chopped pecans
1 jar (12 ounces) caramel ice cream topping

In a bowl, combine the wafer crumbs and butter. Press into a greased 13-in. x 9-in. x 2-in. baking pan. Sprinkle with chocolate chips and pecans.

In a microwave, heat caramel topping on high for 1-2 minutes or until warm. Drizzle over the top. Bake at 350° for 10 minutes or until chips are melted. Cool on a wire rack. **Yield:** 6 dozen.

Buttery Almond Crunch

This delectable candy is crisp but not as hard as peanut brittle. Some people say it reminds them of the toffee center of a well-known candy bar.
—*Mildred Clothier, Oregon, Illinois*

1 tablespoon plus 1/2 cup butter, softened, *divided*
1/2 cup sugar
1 tablespoon light corn syrup
1 cup sliced almonds

Line an 8-in. square pan with foil; butter the foil with 1/2 tablespoon butter. Set aside. Spread the sides of a heavy saucepan with 1/2 tablespoon butter. Add 1/2 cup of butter, sugar and corn syrup. Bring to a boil over medium-high heat, stirring constantly. Cook and stir until mixture is golden brown, about 3 minutes. Stir in almonds.

Quickly pour into prepared pan. Refrigerate until firm. Invert pan and remove foil. Break candy into pieces. **Yield:** 10 ounces.

Peanut Clusters

My husband, Greg, likes to mix up these treats with the kids. With three simple ingredients I usually have on hand, it's easy to make a batch in a matter of minutes. —*Deb Darr, Falls City, Oregon*

4 ounces milk chocolate candy coating
4 ounces white candy coating
1 can (16 ounces) salted peanuts (about 2-1/2 cups)

In a microwave, melt candy coatings, stirring often until blended. Stir in the peanuts until coated. Drop by tablespoonfuls onto a waxed paper-lined baking sheet. Refrigerate until serving. **Yield:** about 3 dozen.

|STORING CANDY| Store homemade candies in tightly covered containers unless otherwise directed. Don't store more than one kind of candy in a single container.

Swedish Butter Cookies

It's impossible to eat just one of these treats. Naturally, they're a favorite with my Swedish husband and children—but anyone with a sweet tooth will appreciate them. My recipe is "well-traveled" among our friends and neighbors. —*Sue Soderlund Elgin, Illinois*

1 cup butter, softened
1 cup sugar
2 teaspoons maple syrup
2 cups all-purpose flour
1 teaspoon baking soda
Confectioners' sugar, optional

In a mixing bowl, cream butter and sugar. Add syrup; mix well. Combine flour and baking soda; gradually add to creamed mixture. Divide dough into eight portions. Roll each portion into a 9-in. log.

Place 3 in. apart on ungreased baking sheets. Bake at 300° for 25 minutes or until lightly browned. Cut into 1-in. slices. Remove to wire racks to cool. Dust with confectioners' sugar if desired. **Yield:** about 6 dozen.

Macaroon Bars

Guests will never recognize the refrigerated crescent roll dough that goes into these almond-flavored bars. You can assemble these chewy coconut treats in no time.
—*Carolyn Kyzer, Alexander, Arkansas*

3-1/4 cups flaked coconut, *divided*
1 can (14 ounces) sweetened condensed milk
1 teaspoon almond extract
1 tube (8 ounces) refrigerated crescent rolls

Sprinkle 1-1/2 cups coconut into a well-greased 13-in. x 9-in. x 2-in. baking pan. Combine milk and extract; drizzle half over the coconut. Unroll crescent dough; arrange in a single layer over coconut. Drizzle with remaining milk mixture; sprinkle with remaining coconut.

Bake at 350° for 30-35 minutes or until golden brown. Cool completely before cutting. Store in the refrigerator. **Yield:** 3 dozen.

Cream Cheese Candies

This four-ingredient recipe was recommended by friends and shared throughout our neighborhood. The rich, simple mints are often seen at wedding receptions and graduation parties, and they make a perfect last-minute addition to holiday candy trays.
—*Katie Koziolek, Hartland, Minnesota*

1 package (3 ounces) cream cheese, softened
1/4 teaspoon peppermint *or* almond extract
3 cups confectioners' sugar
Green and red colored sugar, optional

In a small mixing bowl, combine cream cheese and extract. Beat in 1-1/2 cups confectioners' sugar. Knead in remaining confectioners' sugar until smooth.

Shape into 1/2-in. balls. Roll in colored sugar if desired. Place on ungreased baking sheets and flatten with a fork. Let stand for 1 hour to harden. Store in an airtight container in the refrigerator. **Yield:** 6 dozen.

Almond Bars

This is one of my favorite recipes for last-minute school bake sales. The cake-like snacks are the first items to go...that is, if they're not grabbed by a teacher first. I also include them in Christmas cookie gift baskets.
—*Sandy Kerrison, Lockport, New York*

4 eggs
2 cups sugar
1 cup butter, melted
2 cups all-purpose flour
2-1/2 teaspoons almond extract
Confectioners' sugar, optional

In a mixing bowl, beat the eggs and sugar until lemon-colored. Add the butter, flour and extract; mix well. Spread into a greased 13-in. x 9-in. x 2-in. baking pan.

Bake at 325° for 30-35 minutes or until a toothpick inserted near the center comes out clean. Cool on a wire rack. Sprinkle with confectioners' sugar if desired. **Yield:** 2 dozen.

Cranberry Crispies

At holiday rush time, you can't go wrong with these simple cookies. They're a snap to stir up with a boxed quick bread mix, and they bake up crisp and delicious.
—*LaVern Kraft, Lytton, Iowa*

1 package (15.6 ounces) cranberry quick bread mix
1/2 cup butter, melted
1/2 cup finely chopped walnuts
1 egg
1/2 cup dried cranberries

In a bowl, combine the bread mix, butter, walnuts and egg; mix well. Stir in cranberries. Roll into 1-1/4-in. balls. Place 3 in. apart on ungreased baking sheets. Flatten to 1/8-in. thickness with a glass dipped in sugar. Bake at 350° for 10-12 minutes or until light golden brown. Remove to wire racks to cool. **Yield:** 2-1/2 dozen.

Chocolate Peanut Butter Cookies

It's a snap to make a batch of tasty cookies using this recipe, which calls for a convenient boxed cake mix. My husband and son gobble them up.
—Mary Pulyer
Port St. Lucie, Florida

1 package (18-1/4 ounces) devil's food cake mix
2 eggs
1/3 cup vegetable oil
1 package (10 ounces) peanut butter chips

In a mixing bowl, beat cake mix, eggs and oil (batter will be very stiff). Stir in chips. Roll into 1-in. balls. Place on lightly greased baking sheets; flatten slightly.

Bake at 350° for 10 minutes or until a slight indentation remains when lightly touched. Cool for 2 minutes before removing to a wire rack. **Yield:** 4 dozen.

|SHAPING DOUGH INTO BALLS| Roll the dough between your palms until it forms a ball. A 1-inch ball requires about 2 teaspoons of dough. If the dough is sticky, you can refrigerate it until it is easy to handle, lightly flour your hands or spray your hands with nonstick cooking spray.

Double Chocolate Bars

A friend brought these fudgy bars a few years ago to tempt me with yet another chocolate treat. They are simple to make...and cleanup is a breeze! They're very rich, though, so be sure to cut them into bite-size pieces.
—Nancy Clark, Zeigler, Illinois

1 package (14 ounces) cream-filled chocolate sandwich cookies, crushed
3/4 cup butter, melted
1 can (14 ounces) sweetened condensed milk
2 cups (12 ounces) miniature semisweet chocolate chips, *divided*

Combine cookie crumbs and butter; pat onto the bottom of an ungreased 13-in. x 9-in. x 2-in. baking pan. Combine milk and 1 cup of chips in a microwave-safe bowl. Cover and microwave on high for 1 minute or until chips are melted; stir until smooth. Pour over crust. Sprinkle with remaining chips. Bake at 350° for 10-12 minutes or until chips are melted. Cool. **Yield:** about 4 dozen.

Editor's Note: This recipe was tested in a 700-watt microwave.

Gumdrop Cereal Bars

I was planning to make traditional marshmallow treats but didn't have enough Rice Krispies on hand, so I used Corn Pops instead. I added gumdrops for color, and the result was spectacular.—*Laura Tryssenaar
Listowel, Ontario*

**5 cups Corn Pops cereal
1 cup gumdrops
4 cups miniature
 marshmallows
1/4 cup butter
1 teaspoon vanilla extract**

Place cereal and gumdrops in a large bowl; set aside. In a microwave-safe bowl, heat the marshmallows and butter on high for 2 minutes; stir until melted. Stir in vanilla. Pour over cereal mixture and toss to coat. Spread into a greased 9-in. square pan. Cool on a wire rack. Cut with a buttered knife. **Yield:** 16 bars.

Editor's Note: This recipe was tested in an 850-watt microwave.

Nutty Chocolate Marshmallow Puffs

We like to do things BIG here in Texas, so don't expect a dainty little barely-a-bite truffle from this surprising recipe. Folks are delighted to discover a big fluffy marshmallow inside the chocolate and nut coating.
—*Pat Ball, Abilene, Texas*

**2 cups milk chocolate
 chips
1 can (14 ounces)
 sweetened condensed
 milk
1 jar (7 ounces)
 marshmallow creme
40 large marshmallows
4 cups coarsely chopped
 pecans (about 1 pound)**

In a microwave or heavy saucepan, heat chocolate chips, milk and marshmallow creme just until melted; stir until smooth (mixture will be thick).

With tongs, immediately dip marshmallows, one at a time, in chocolate mixture. Shake off excess chocolate; quickly roll in pecans. Place on waxed paper-lined baking sheets. (Reheat chocolate mixture if necessary for easier coating.) Refrigerate until firm. Store in the refrigerator in an airtight container. **Yield:** 40 candies.

No-Bake Chocolate Cookies

These cookies are my oldest son's favorite. When his children tried them, the cookies became their favorites, too. I like them for two reasons—they're quick and they're chocolate! —*Connie Sackett*
Glennallen, Alaska

1 can (14 ounces) sweetened condensed milk
2 cups (12 ounces) semisweet chocolate chips
3 cups crushed graham crackers (about 48 squares)
1/2 cup chopped walnuts
1 teaspoon vanilla extract
Confectioners' sugar, optional

In a microwave-safe bowl, combine milk and chocolate chips. Microwave, uncovered, on high for 1-2 minutes or until chips are melted; stir until smooth. Stir in cracker crumbs, walnuts and vanilla.

Shape into a 17-in. log; roll in confectioners' sugar if desired. Wrap in plastic wrap. Refrigerate for 1 hour or until firm. Unwrap and cut into 1/4-in. slices. **Yield:** about 5-1/2 dozen.

Editor's Note: This recipe was tested in an 850-watt microwave.

Peanut Butter Snowballs

These creamy treats are a nice change from the typical milk chocolate and peanut butter combination. This recipe is also an easy one for children to help with. I prepare them for a bake sale at my granddaughter's school and put them in gift boxes I share with neighbors at Christmas. —*Wanda Regula*
Birmingham, Michigan

1 cup confectioners' sugar
1/2 cup creamy peanut butter
3 tablespoons butter, softened
1 pound white candy coating

In a mixing bowl, combine sugar, peanut butter and butter; mix well. Shape into 1-in. balls and place on a waxed paper-lined cookie sheet. Chill for 30 minutes or until firm.

Meanwhile, melt the white coating in a double boiler or microwave-safe bowl. Dip balls and place on waxed paper to harden. **Yield:** 2 dozen.

Cranberry Pecan Clusters

I have many candy recipes, and this is one of my favorites. The clusters are quick and easy to make and very festive-looking. They're so pretty on a holiday candy tray.
—*Collette Tubman*
St. Thomas, Ontario

6 squares (1 ounce *each***)**
  white baking chocolate
1 cup dried cranberries
1/4 to 1/2 cup chopped
  pecans

Line a baking sheet with foil; set aside. In a microwave-safe bowl, heat the chocolate, uncovered, at 50% power for about 3 minutes or until melted, stirring once. Stir until smooth. Stir in cranberries and pecans. Drop by teaspoonfuls onto prepared pan. Freeze for 5 minutes, then refrigerate until firm. **Yield:** about 20 pieces.

Editor's Note: This recipe was tested in an 850-watt microwave.

Creamy Caramels

I discovered this recipe in a local newspaper several years ago and have made these soft and buttery caramels ever since. Everyone asks for the recipe once they have a taste. I make them for Christmas, picnics and charity auctions. They are so much better than store-bought caramels.
—*Marcie Wolfe*
Williamsburg, Virginia

1 cup sugar
1 cup dark corn syrup
1 cup butter
1 can (14 ounces)
  sweetened condensed
  milk
1 teaspoon vanilla extract

Line an 8-in. square pan with foil and butter the foil; set aside. Combine sugar, corn syrup and butter in a 3-qt. saucepan. Bring to a boil over medium heat, stirring constantly. Boil slowly for 4 minutes without stirring. Remove from the heat and stir in milk.

Reduce heat to medium-low and cook until candy thermometer reads 238° (soft-ball stage), stirring constantly. Remove from the heat and stir in vanilla. Pour into prepared pan. Cool. Remove from pan and cut into 1-in. squares. Wrap individually in waxed paper; twist ends. **Yield:** 64 pieces.

Editor's Note: We recommend that you test your candy thermometer before each use by bringing water to a boil; the thermometer should read 212°. Adjust your recipe temperature up or down based on your test.

Peanut Butter Cookie Cups

I'm a busy schoolteacher and pastor's wife who always looks for shortcuts. I wouldn't dare show my face at a church dinner or bake sale without these tempting peanut butter treats. They're quick and easy to make and always a hit. —*Kristi Tackett*
Banner, Kentucky

1 package (17-1/2 ounces) peanut butter cookie mix
36 miniature peanut butter cups, unwrapped

Prepare cookie mix according to package directions. Roll the dough into 1-in. balls. Place in greased miniature muffin cups. Press dough evenly onto bottom and up sides of each cup. Bake at 350° for 11-13 minutes or until set.

Immediately place a peanut butter cup in each cup; press down gently. Cool for 10 minutes; carefully remove from pans. **Yield:** 3 dozen.

Editor's Note: 2-1/4 cups peanut butter cookie dough of your choice can be substituted for the mix.

Praline Grahams

Someone brought these crunchy, nutty treats to a meeting I attended, and I wouldn't leave without the recipe. They're super easy to fix, inexpensive and delicious. The recipe makes a lot, so it's a great snack for a crowd. —*Marian Platt*
Sequim, Washington

12 graham crackers (4-3/4 inches x 2-1/2 inches)
1/2 cup butter
1/2 cup packed brown sugar
1/2 cup finely chopped walnuts

Line a 15-in. x 10-in. x 1-in. baking pan with heavy-duty foil. Break the graham crackers at indentations; place in a single layer in pan. In a small saucepan, combine butter and brown sugar. Bring to a rolling boil over medium heat; boil for 2 minutes. Remove from the heat; add nuts. Pour over crackers.

Bake at 350° for 10 minutes or until lightly browned. Let stand for 2-3 minutes. Remove to a wire rack to cool. **Yield:** 4 dozen.

Cakes, Pies & Desserts

Light Berry
Mousse, p. 263

Peppermint Stick Pie, p. 259

Peach Pudding, p. 264 and
Red, White & Blue Refresher, p. 258

Root Beer Float
Cake, p. 260

Cakes, Pies & Desserts   257

Cranberry Shiver

Cool and refreshing, this pretty dessert is delightfully sweet-tart and makes the perfect ending for a bountiful holiday meal. You can make it ahead and keep it in the freezer, so there will be one less thing to do before serving. —*Audrey Thibodeau*
Mesa, Arizona

✓ Uses less fat, sugar or salt. Includes Nutritional Analysis and Diabetic Exchanges.

1 package (12 ounces) fresh *or* frozen cranberries
3 cups water, *divided*
1-3/4 cups sugar
1/4 cup lemon juice
1 teaspoon grated orange peel
Fresh mint, optional

In a saucepan, bring cranberries and 2 cups of water to a boil. Reduce heat; simmer for 5 minutes. Press through a strainer to remove skins; discard skins. To the juice, add sugar, lemon juice, orange peel and remaining water; mix well.

Pour into an 8-in. square pan. Cover and freeze until ice begins to form around the edges of the pan, about 1-1/2 hours; stir. Freeze until mushy, about 30 minutes. Spoon into a freezer container; cover and freeze. Remove from the freezer 20 minutes before serving. Scoop into small dishes; garnish with mint if desired. **Yield:** 10 servings.

Nutritional Analysis: One 1/2-cup serving equals 154 calories, 1 mg sodium, 0 cholesterol, 40 g carbohydrate, trace protein, trace fat. **Diabetic Exchange:** 2-1/2 fruit.

Red, White & Blue Refresher

(Pictured on page 257)

A colorful combination of pineapple sherbet, berries and grape juice makes a refreshing dessert on a hot summer day. —*Carol Gillespie, Chambersburg, Pennsylvania*

1 quart pineapple *or* lemon sherbet
1 cup sliced strawberries
1/2 cup blueberries
1/2 cup white grape juice

Divide the sherbet between four dessert cups or bowls. Top with the berries and grape juice. **Yield:** 4 servings.

Peppermint Stick Pie

(Pictured on page 256)

What's a cook to do when days are filled with holiday preparations and you need to fix a dessert in time for dinner? Try this delicious pie! It's very festive looking, and folks fall for the minty flavor.

—*Mildred Peachey, Wooster, Ohio*

4-1/2 cups crisp rice cereal
1 cup (6 ounces)
　semisweet chocolate
　chips, melted
2 quarts peppermint stick
　ice cream, softened
Chocolate syrup *or* chocolate
　fudge topping
Crushed peppermint candies

Combine cereal and chocolate; mix well. Press into the bottom and up the sides of an ungreased 10-in. pie plate. Freeze for 5 minutes. Spoon ice cream into the crust. Freeze until serving. Garnish with chocolate syrup and peppermint candies. **Yield:** 6-8 servings.

Editor's Note: Pie may be made ahead and frozen. Remove from freezer 15 minutes before serving.

Rhubarb Custard Cake

Rhubarb thrives in my northern garden and is one of the few crops the pesky moose don't bother! Of all the rhubarb desserts I've tried, this pudding cake is my No. 1 choice. It has old-fashioned appeal but is simple to prepare. —*Evelyn Gebhardt Kasilof, Alaska*

1 package (18-1/4
　ounces) yellow cake mix
4 cups chopped fresh *or*
　frozen rhubarb
1 cup sugar
1 cup heavy whipping
　cream
Whipped cream and fresh mint,
　optional

Prepare cake batter according to package directions. Pour into a greased 13-in. x 9-in. x 2-in. baking dish. Sprinkle with rhubarb and sugar. Slowly pour cream over top.

Bake at 350° for 40-45 minutes or until golden brown. Cool for 15 minutes before serving. Garnish with whipped cream and mint if desired. Refrigerate leftovers. **Yield:** 12-15 servings.

Root Beer Float Cake

(Pictured on page 257)

I add root beer to both the cake batter and fluffy frosting of this summery dessert to get that great root beer float taste. Serve this moist cake to a bunch of hungry kids and watch it disappear.

—Kat Thompson, Prineville, Oregon

1 package (18-1/4 ounces) white cake mix
1-3/4 cups cold root beer, *divided*
1/4 cup vegetable oil
2 eggs
1 envelope whipped topping mix

In a mixing bowl, combine dry cake mix, 1-1/4 cups root beer, oil and eggs. Beat on low speed for 2 minutes or stir by hand for 3 minutes. Pour into a greased 13-in. x 9-in. x 2-in. baking pan. Bake at 350° for 30-35 minutes or until a toothpick inserted near the center comes out clean. Cool completely on a wire rack.

In a mixing bowl, combine the whipped topping mix and remaining root beer. Beat until soft peaks form. Frost cake. Store in the refrigerator. **Yield:** 12-16 servings.

Quick Coconut Cream Pie

I've found a way to make coconut cream pie without a lot of fuss and still get terrific flavor. Using a convenient purchased crust, instant pudding and frozen whipped topping, I can enjoy an old-time dessert even when time is short.

—Betty Claycomb
Alverton, Pennsylvania

1 package (5.1 ounces) instant vanilla pudding mix
1-1/2 cups cold milk
1 carton (8 ounces) frozen whipped topping, thawed, *divided*
3/4 to 1 cup flaked coconut, toasted, *divided*
1 pastry shell, baked *or* graham cracker crust (8 *or* 9 inches)

In a mixing bowl, beat pudding and milk on low speed for 2 minutes. Fold in half of the whipped topping and 1/2 to 3/4 cup of coconut. Pour into crust. Spread with remaining whipped topping; sprinkle with remaining coconut. Refrigerate until serving. **Yield:** 6-8 servings.

White Chocolate Tarts

White Chocolate Tarts are scrumptious but really no fuss, because they call for prepared tart shells, instant pudding and whipped topping.
—*Traci Maloney, Toms River, New Jersey*

1 can (14 ounces) sweetened condensed milk
1 cup cold water
1 package (3.4 ounces) instant white chocolate pudding mix
2 cups whipped topping
2 packages (6 count *each*) individual graham cracker tart shells

In a mixing bowl, combine milk, water and pudding mix. Beat on low speed for 2 minutes. Cover and refrigerate for 10 minutes. Fold in whipped topping. Spoon about 1/3 cup into each tart shell. Refrigerate until serving. **Yield:** 12 servings.

Nutty Peach Crisp

A co-worker brought this easy, delicious dessert to work, and I couldn't resist asking for the recipe. A moist bottom layer made with canned peaches and boxed cake mix is covered with a lovely golden topping of coconut and pecans. It tastes wonderful served warm with ice cream.
—*Nancy Carpenter*
Sidney, Montana

1 can (29 ounces) sliced peaches, undrained
1 package (18-1/4 ounces) yellow *or* butter pecan cake mix
1/2 cup butter, melted
1 cup flaked coconut
1 cup chopped pecans

Arrange peaches in an ungreased 13-in. x 9-in. x 2-in. baking dish. Sprinkle dry cake mix over top. Drizzle with butter; sprinkle with coconut and pecans. Bake at 325° for 55-60 minutes or until golden brown. Let stand for 15 minutes. Serve warm or cold. **Yield:** 12-15 servings.

Creamy Lemonade Pie

This luscious lemon pie looks quite elegant for a special dinner, yet it requires little effort. Guests will never suspect they're eating a quick-and-easy dessert. —*Carolyn Griffin, Macon, Georgia*

1 can (5 ounces) evaporated milk
1 package (3.4 ounces) instant lemon pudding mix
2 packages (8 ounces *each*) cream cheese, softened
3/4 cup lemonade concentrate
1 graham cracker crust (9 inches)

In a mixing bowl, combine milk and pudding mix; beat on low speed for 2 minutes (mixture will be thick). In another mixing bowl, beat cream cheese until light and fluffy, about 3 minutes. Gradually beat in lemonade concentrate. Gradually beat in pudding mixture. Pour into crust. Cover and refrigerate for at least 4 hours. **Yield:** 6-8 servings.

Fruit-Topped Almond Cream

Fruit-Topped Almond Cream is a light and refreshing dessert. It's delicious with fresh berries, but it can be made all year using whatever fruit is available. —*Donna Friedrich, Fishkill, New York*

1 package (3.4 ounces) instant French vanilla pudding mix
2-1/2 cups cold milk
1 cup heavy whipping cream
1/2 to 3/4 teaspoon almond extract
3 cups assorted fruit (strawberries, grapes, raspberries, blueberries, mandarin oranges)

In a large mixing bowl, combine pudding mix and milk. Beat on low speed for 2 minutes; set aside. In a small mixing bowl, beat cream and extract until stiff peaks form. Fold into pudding. Spoon into a shallow 2-qt. serving dish. Chill. Top with fruit just before serving. **Yield:** 8 servings.

Coconut Cake Supreme

I make most of my cakes from scratch, but during the holiday rush, this recipe that starts with a mix buys me some time. Most eager eaters don't suspect the shortcut when you dress up the cake with fluffy coconut filling and frosting.

—Betty Claycomb
Alverton, Pennsylvania

1 package (18-1/4 ounces) yellow cake mix
2 cups (16 ounces) sour cream
2 cups sugar
1-1/2 cups flaked coconut
1 carton (8 ounces) frozen whipped topping, thawed
Fresh mint and red gumdrops, optional

Prepare and bake cake according to package directions in two 9-in. round baking pans. Cool in pans for 10 minutes before removing to a wire rack to cool completely.

For filling, combine sour cream and sugar; mix well. Stir in coconut (filling will be soft). Set aside 1 cup of filling for frosting.

To assemble, split each cake into two horizontal layers. Place one layer on a serving platter; cover with a third of the filling. Repeat layers. Fold reserved filling into whipped topping; frost cake. Refrigerate for at least 4 hours. Garnish with mint and gumdrops if desired. **Yield:** 10-12 servings.

Light Berry Mousse

(Pictured on page 256)

Members of my family are diabetic, so I'm always looking for sugar-free recipes. This light, fluffy dessert flavored with fresh strawberries is a refreshing ending to a summer meal. —Peggy Key
Grant, Alabama

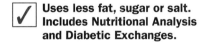 **Uses less fat, sugar or salt. Includes Nutritional Analysis and Diabetic Exchanges.**

3/4 cup boiling water
1 package (.3 ounce) sugar-free strawberry gelatin
1 cup ice cubes
1-1/2 cups sliced fresh strawberries
3/4 cup light whipped topping

In a blender, combine water and gelatin. Cover and process until gelatin is dissolved. Blend in ice cubes until partially melted. Add strawberries; process well. Pour into a bowl; fold in whipped topping. Chill for 2 hours. **Yield:** 4 servings.

Nutritional Analysis: One serving equals 57 calories, 55 mg sodium, 0 cholesterol, 8 g carbohydrate, 2 g protein, 2 g fat. **Diabetic Exchanges:** 1/2 fruit, 1/2 fat.

Peach Pudding

(Pictured on page 257)

This light peach dessert is so fresh it tastes just like summertime. It's a quick way to dress up instant vanilla pudding.
—*Shelby Nicodemus, New Carlisle, Ohio*

1/4 cup peach gelatin powder
1/2 cup hot milk
1-1/2 cups cold milk
1 package (3.4 ounces) instant vanilla pudding mix
Sliced fresh peaches and whipped topping, optional

In a bowl, dissolve gelatin in hot milk; set aside. Meanwhile, in a mixing bowl, beat cold milk and pudding mix on low speed for 2 minutes. Add the gelatin mixture and mix well. Let stand for 5 minutes. Spoon into individual dishes. Garnish with peach slices and whipped topping if desired. **Yield:** 4 servings.

Apple Cream Pie

My four daughters have always shared my love of baking. By their teens, the girls were turning out breads, pies and cakes. This pretty pie is still a family favorite.
—*Eilene Bogar, Minier, Illinois*

4 cups sliced peeled baking apples
1 unbaked pie shell (9 inches)
1 cup sugar
1 cup heavy whipping cream
3 tablespoons all-purpose flour

Place apples in pie shell. Combine sugar, cream and flour; pour over the apples. Bake at 400° for 10 minutes. Reduce heat to 375°; bake for 35-40 minutes or until pie is set in center. Cover crust edges with foil during the last 15 minutes if needed. Cool on a wire rack. Serve, or cover and refrigerate. **Yield:** 6-8 servings.

Easy Cherry Tarts

Refrigerated crescent rolls simplify preparation of these delightful cherry bites. I cut the dough into circles with a small juice glass. —*Frances Poste*
Wall, South Dakota

1 tube (8 ounces) refrigerated crescent rolls
1 package (3 ounces) cream cheese, softened
1/4 cup confectioners' sugar
1 cup canned cherry pie filling
1/4 teaspoon almond extract

Place crescent dough on a lightly floured surface; seal seams and perforations. Cut into 2-in. circles. Place in greased miniature muffin cups. In a small mixing bowl, beat cream cheese and confectioners' sugar until smooth. Place about 1/2 teaspoon in each cup. Combine pie filling and extract; place about 2 teaspoons in each cup.

Bake at 375° for 12-14 minutes or until edges are lightly browned. Remove to wire racks to cool. Refrigerate until serving. **Yield:** 2 dozen.

Raspberry Pudding Parfaits

These parfaits are a fresh, flavorful dessert that have been in my family for ages. They're so easy to prepare, and you can substitute strawberries or blueberries with equally tempting results.—*Fran Shaffer*
Coatesville, Pennsylvania

1-1/2 cups cold milk
1 package (5.1 ounces) instant vanilla pudding mix
1 package (12 ounces) unsweetened frozen raspberries, thawed
Whipped topping, optional

In a mixing bowl, combine milk and pudding mix; beat for 2 minutes or until thickened. Spoon half into four parfait glasses. Top with half of the raspberries. Repeat layers. Garnish with whipped topping if desired. **Yield:** 4 servings.

Cherry Mousse

If you're looking for something to tickle your sweet tooth, consider this cheery mousse. This three-item treat is a cinch to whip up no matter how busy you are. The fluffy dessert is a wonderful way to end a meal. I just know your family will find it as tasty as mine does.
—*Becky Lohmiller*
Monticello, Indiana

1 tablespoon cherry gelatin powder
1 can (14-1/2 ounces) tart cherries, drained
1 carton (8 ounces) frozen whipped topping, thawed

In a bowl, combine gelatin powder and cherries; fold in the whipped topping. Serve immediately. **Yield:** 4 servings.

Black Forest Trifle

When I want a dessert that's fit for a feast, I turn to this trifle. The recipe calls for a convenient brownie mix, so it's simple to make.
—*Peggy Linton*
Cobourg, Ontario

1 package brownie mix (13-inch x 9-inch pan size)
2 packages (2.8 ounces *each*) chocolate mousse mix
1 can (21 ounces) cherry pie filling
1 carton (16 ounces) frozen whipped topping, thawed
4 Skor candy bars, crushed

Prepare and bake brownies according to package directions; cool completely on a wire rack. Prepare mousse according to package directions.

Crumble brownies; sprinkle half into a 4-qt. trifle dish or glass bowl. Top with half of the pie filling, mousse, whipped topping and candy bars. Repeat layers. Cover and refrigerate for 8 hours or overnight. **Yield:** 16 servings.

Raspberry Mallow Pie

Raspberry Mallow Pie is a delightful way to end a meal. It's quick to fix and tastes wonderful either refrigerated or frozen.
—*Judie Anglen*
Riverton, Wyoming

35 large marshmallows
1/2 cup milk
1 package (10 ounces) frozen sweetened raspberries
1 carton (8 ounces) frozen whipped topping, thawed
1 graham cracker crust (9 inches)

In a large microwave-safe bowl, combine marshmallows and milk. Cook on high for 1-2 minutes; stir until smooth. Stir in raspberries. Fold in the whipped topping. Pour into crust. Refrigerate or freeze. **Yield:** 6-8 servings.

Editor's Note: This recipe was tested using a 700-watt microwave.

|**TAKE THE CHILL OFF**| Allow frozen and ice cream desserts to sit at room temperature for 10 minutes before serving. This will make cutting them into slices easier.

Cantaloupe Sherbet

I make this sherbet very early in the day, then we sit outside under the evening Texas sky and enjoy it! It's simply delicious.
—*Rolanda Crawford, Abilene, Texas*

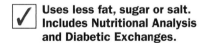 Uses less fat, sugar or salt. Includes Nutritional Analysis and Diabetic Exchanges.

1 medium ripe cantaloupe
1 can (14 ounces) fat-free sweetened condensed skim milk
2 tablespoons honey

Cut cantaloupe in half; discard seeds. Peel and slice cantaloupe; cut into large pieces. Place in a blender container. Add milk and honey; cover and blend until smooth. Pour into a freezer-proof container. Freeze overnight or until firm. **Yield:** 9 servings.

Nutritional Analysis: One 1/2-cup serving equals 158 calories, 52 mg sodium, 3 mg cholesterol, 35 g carbohydrate, 4 g protein, trace fat. **Diabetic Exchanges:** 1-1/2 starch, 1 fruit.

Frozen Mud Pie

Here's one of those "looks like you fussed" desserts that is so easy it's become a standard for me. I love the mocha version, but pure chocolate lovers may prefer using chocolate chip ice cream. The cookie crust is a snap to make.
—Debbie Terenzini, Lusby, Maryland

1-1/2 cups crushed
    cream-filled chocolate
    sandwich cookies
    (about 15)
1-1/2 teaspoons sugar,
    optional
  1/4 cup butter, melted
    2 pints chocolate chip *or*
    coffee ice cream,
    softened
  1/4 cup chocolate syrup,
    divided
Additional cream-filled
    chocolate sandwich cookies,
    optional

In a bowl, combine cookie crumbs and sugar if desired. Stir in butter. Press onto the bottom and up the sides of an ungreased 9-in. pie plate. Refrigerate for 30 minutes.

Spoon 1 pint of ice cream into crust. Drizzle with half of the chocolate syrup; swirl with a knife. Carefully top with remaining ice cream. Drizzle with remaining syrup; swirl with a knife. Cover and freeze until firm.

Remove from the freezer 10-15 minutes before serving. Garnish with whole cookies if desired. **Yield:** 8 servings.

Quick Banana Splits

Quick Banana Splits are a simple but special way to serve ice cream. Made with just five ingredients, there's no need to make a trip to the ice cream stand.　　　　—Doreen Stein, Ignace, Ontario

    2 medium bananas
    1 pint vanilla ice cream
Chocolate syrup *or* ice cream
    topping
Chopped nuts
Maraschino cherries

Slice bananas into four dessert dishes. Top each with 1/2 cup of ice cream. Drizzle with chocolate syrup. Sprinkle with nuts; top with cherries. **Yield:** 4 servings.

Gingered Pear Sorbet

During the hot summer here in Florida, we enjoy this refreshing sorbet. Sometimes I dress up servings with berries, mint leaves or crystallized ginger. —*Donna Cline, Pensacola, Florida*

1 can (29 ounces) pear halves
1/4 cup sugar
2 tablespoons lemon juice
1/8 teaspoon ground ginger
Yellow food coloring, optional

Drain pears, reserving 1 cup syrup (discard remaining syrup or save for another use); set pears aside. In a saucepan, bring the sugar and reserved syrup to a boil. Remove from the heat; cool.

In a blender, process the pears, lemon juice and ginger until smooth. Add cooled syrup and food coloring if desired; cover and process until pureed. Pour into an 11-in. x 7-in. x 2-in. dish. Cover and freeze for 1-1/2 to 2 hours or until partially frozen.

Return mixture to blender; cover and process until smooth. Place in a freezer container; cover and freeze for at least 3 hours. Remove from the freezer 20 minutes before serving. **Yield:** 3 cups.

Blueberry Angel Dessert

Make the most of angel food cake, pie filling and whipped topping by creating this light impressive dessert that doesn't keep you in the kitchen for hours. It's the perfect way to end a summer meal. I frequently get requests for the recipe.
—*Carol Johnson, Tyler, Texas*

1 package (8 ounces) cream cheese, softened
1 cup confectioners' sugar
1 carton (8 ounces) frozen whipped topping, thawed
1 prepared angel food cake (14 ounces), cut into 1-inch cubes
2 cans (21 ounces *each*) blueberry pie filling

In a large mixing bowl, beat the cream cheese and sugar; fold in whipped topping and cake cubes. Spread evenly into an ungreased 13-in. x 9-in. x 2-in. dish; top with pie filling. Cover and refrigerate for at least 2 hours before cutting into squares. **Yield:** 12-15 servings.

Biscuit Apple Cobbler

I like to top off many meals with this comforting cobbler. The sweet treat requires only three ingredients but tastes like you fussed.
—Claudine Moffatt, Manchester, Missouri

1 can (21 ounces) apple
  pie filling
1/2 teaspoon ground
  cinnamon
1 tube (7-1/2 ounces)
  refrigerated flaky
  buttermilk biscuits
Whipped topping and mint,
  optional

Place pie filling in an ungreased 9-in. pie plate. Sprinkle with cinnamon. Separate each biscuit into three layers and arrange over apples.

Bake at 400° for 12-14 minutes or until the biscuits are browned. Garnish with whipped topping and mint if desired. **Yield:** 4-6 servings.

Chocolate Mousse Pie

(Also pictured on back cover)

Sky-high and scrumptious, this fluffy chocolate delight is super to serve to company. You can put the pie together in a wink—and it'll disappear just as fast! For a nice option, mound the filling in a purchased chocolate crumb crust.
—Lois Mulkey, Sublimity, Oregon

1 milk chocolate candy bar
  with almonds (6 ounces)
16 large marshmallows
  or 1-1/2 cups miniature
  marshmallows
1/2 cup milk
2 cups heavy whipping
  cream, whipped
1 pastry shell, baked *or*
  graham cracker *or*
  chocolate crumb crust
  (8 *or* 9 inches)

Place the candy bar, marshmallows and milk in a heavy saucepan; cook over low heat, stirring constantly until chocolate is melted and mixture is smooth. Cool. Fold in whipped cream; pour into crust. Refrigerate for at least 3 hours. **Yield:** 6-8 servings.

Banana Split Shortcake

My shortcut shortcake uses purchased pound or sponge cake instead of from-scratch biscuits. By varying the fruits, it's a treat for any season. Kids enjoy adding their choice of sundae toppings.
—*Christi Gillentine, Tulsa, Oklahoma*

8 slices pound cake (1/2 inch thick) *or* **4 individual round sponge cakes**
2 medium firm bananas, cut into 1/4-inch slices
4 scoops vanilla ice cream
1/4 cup chocolate sauce

Place cake slices on four dessert plates. Top each with bananas and ice cream. Drizzle with chocolate sauce. **Yield:** 4 servings.

Peanut Butter Sundaes

Peanut Butter Sundaes are a peanutty change of pace from the traditional ice cream sundae with chocolate sauce. This delicious recipe proves that even a quick meal doesn't have to go without dessert.   —*Susan Mowery, Newville, Pennsylvania*

1 cup sugar
1/2 cup water
1/2 cup creamy peanut butter
Vanilla ice cream
Salted peanuts, optional

In a saucepan, combine sugar and water. Bring to a boil; boil 1 minute or until sugar is dissolved. Remove from the heat; stir in peanut butter. Place in a blender; blend on high until smooth. Cool slightly; pour over ice cream. Sprinkle with peanuts if desired. Refrigerate any leftovers. **Yield:** 1-1/2 cups sauce.

Fudge Berry Pie

I've made this pie several times and it always gets great reviews. With its refreshing berry flavor and chocolate crust, the no-bake delight is sure to receive thumbs-up approval from your gang, too. —*Sharlene Cullen, Robbinsdale, Minnesota*

2 packages (10 ounces *each*) frozen sweetened raspberries *or* sliced strawberries, thawed and drained
1/4 cup corn syrup
1 carton (12 ounces) frozen whipped topping, thawed, *divided*
1 chocolate crumb crust (9 inches)
1 cup (6 ounces) semisweet chocolate chips

In a blender, process the berries until pureed. Pour into a large bowl. Add the corn syrup; mix well. Fold in 2 cups of whipped topping. Spoon into the crust. Freeze for 2 hours or until firm.

In a saucepan, combine 1 cup of whipped topping and chocolate chips; cook and stir over low heat until smooth. Spread over filling. Cover and freeze for 4 hours or until firm.

Remove from the freezer 30 minutes before serving. Garnish with remaining whipped topping. **Yield:** 6-8 servings.

Apricot Sorbet

I end a summer meal with this refreshing treat. With only three ingredients, it's simple to blend and freeze. —*Ruth Kahan, Brookline, Massachusetts*

1 can (15 ounces) apricot halves, undrained
1 to 2 tablespoons sugar
1 tablespoon lemon juice

Freeze the apricots in a freezer-proof container. Place frozen apricots in a blender or food processor; add sugar and lemon juice. Cover and process until combined. Serve immediately or freeze. **Yield:** 4 servings.

Double Chocolate Torte

If you love chocolate, you won't be able to resist this rich, fudgy torte. I often make it for company because it's easy to prepare yet looks so impressive. For special occasions, I place it on a fancy cake plate and I use a can of whipped topping to decorate it. It looks and tastes awesome! —*Naomi Treadwell Swans Island, Maine*

1 **package fudge brownie mix (13-inch x 9-inch pan size)**
1 **cup (6 ounces) semisweet chocolate chips, melted**
1/2 **cup butter, softened**
2 **cups whipped topping**
1 **teaspoon chocolate sprinkles**

Prepare brownie mix according to package directions for fudge-like brownies. Spread batter in a greased and floured 9-in. round baking pan. Bake at 350° for 38-42 minutes or until center springs back when lightly touched. Cool for 10 minutes. Invert onto a serving plate; cool completely.

In a bowl, stir the chocolate and butter until smooth. Spread over brownie layer; refrigerate for 30 minutes. Just before serving, top with whipped topping. Decorate with sprinkles. **Yield:** 9-12 servings.

Burnt Custard

The recipe for this smooth-as-silk custard came from a local restaurant years ago. With its broiled topping, it looks pretty in individual cups. —*Heidi Main, Anchorage, Alaska*

2 **cups heavy whipping cream**
4 **egg yolks**
1/2 **cup plus 6 teaspoons sugar, *divided***
3 **teaspoons vanilla extract**

In a saucepan, heat cream over medium-low until almost simmering; remove from the heat. In a mixing bowl, beat egg yolks and 1/2 cup sugar until thick and lemon-colored. Gradually beat in cream; add vanilla. Pour into six ungreased 6-oz. custard cups. Place cups in a 13-in. x 9-in. x 2-in. baking pan. Fill pan with boiling water to a depth of 1 in.

Bake at 350° for 45 minutes or until custard center is almost set. Remove cups from pan to a wire rack; cool for 15 minutes. Refrigerate for at least 2 hours or until chilled. Sprinkle with remaining sugar. Broil 4-6 in. from the heat for 2 minutes or until golden brown. Serve immediately. **Yield:** 6 servings.

Cream Cheese Cupcakes

It's hard to believe these cupcakes can taste so delicious, yet be so easy. Frost them if you wish, but my family likes them plain, which is great when I'm having an especially busy day.

—*Nancy Reichert, Thomasville, Georgia*

1 package (3 ounces)
   cream cheese, softened
1 package (18-1/4
   ounces) yellow cake mix
1-1/4 cups water
1/2 cup butter, melted
3 eggs

In a mixing bowl, beat cream cheese until smooth. Add cake mix, water, butter and eggs; mix well. Spoon batter by 1/4 cupfuls into paper-lined muffin cups. Bake at 350° for 25 minutes or until golden brown. Remove to a wire rack to cool completely. **Yield:** 2 dozen.

Tart Cherry Pie

My aunt and I are diabetic. We both enjoy this yummy, fruity pie...and our friends even request this dessert when they come to visit.

—*Bonnie Johnson, DeKalb, Illinois*

✓ **Uses less fat, sugar or salt. Includes Nutritional Analysis and Diabetic Exchanges.**

2 cans (16 ounces *each*)
   pitted tart cherries
1 package (.8 ounce)
   cook-and-serve sugar-
   free vanilla pudding mix
1 package (.3 ounce)
   sugar-free cherry gelatin
Artificial sweetener equivalent
  to 4 teaspoons sugar
1 pastry shell (9 inches),
   baked

Drain cherries, reserving juice; set cherries aside. In a saucepan, combine cherry juice and dry pudding mix. Cook and stir until mixture comes to a boil and is thickened and bubbly. Remove from the heat; stir in gelatin powder and sweetener until dissolved. Stir in the cherries; transfer to pastry shell. Cool completely. Store in the refrigerator. **Yield:** 8 servings.

Nutritional Analysis: One serving equals 176 calories, 293 mg sodium, 0 cholesterol, 24 g carbohydrate, 3 g protein, 8 g fat. **Diabetic Exchanges:** 1 starch, 1/2 fruit, 1/2 fat.

Banana Butterfinger Pudding

As for my dessert, you can substitute other kinds of candy bars to suit your preference. The pudding flavor can be changed as well—perhaps to vanilla or butterscotch.
—LaVerna Mjones
Moorhead, Minnesota

1 cup cold milk
1 package (3.4 ounces) instant banana pudding mix
3 Butterfinger candy bars (2.1 ounces *each*), crushed
1 carton (8 ounces) frozen whipped topping, thawed
3 medium firm bananas, sliced

In a mixing bowl, combine milk and pudding mix until thickened and smooth. Set aside 1/3 cup crushed candy bars for topping. Fold whipped topping, bananas and remaining candy bars into pudding. Spoon into serving dishes; refrigerate until serving. Sprinkle with the reserved candy bars. **Yield:** 4-6 servings.

Gingered Melon

For get-togethers, let guests spoon their melon from a large serving bowl and put on their own topping. Combine the fruit with ice cream or frozen yogurt and ginger ale to make a melon float.
—Patricia Richardson, Verona, Ontario

1/2 medium honeydew, cut into 1-inch cubes
1/4 cup orange juice
1-1/2 teaspoons ground ginger
1/2 to 1 cup whipped cream
1/4 cup fresh *or* frozen unsweetened raspberries

In a bowl, combine the melon, orange juice and ginger; refrigerate for 5-10 minutes. Spoon into tall dessert glasses or bowls. Top with whipped cream and raspberries. **Yield:** 4 servings.

Cakes, Pies & Desserts   275

Lemon Graham Freeze

For a cool and economical treat, try Lemon Graham Freeze. This light, pleasantly tart dessert is convenient since you make it ahead.

—*Barbara Husband, Dorchester, Wisconsin*

1 can (5 ounces) evaporated milk
1/2 cup sugar
2 tablespoons lemon juice
4 drops yellow food coloring, optional
6 whole graham crackers

Place milk in a mixing bowl; add beaters to bowl. Freeze for 25-30 minutes or until soft crystals form around edges of bowl. Beat milk until stiff peaks form. Gradually add sugar, lemon juice and food coloring if desired; mix well.

Place five graham crackers in an ungreased 11-in. x 7-in. x 2-in. dish; pour milk mixture over crackers. Crush remaining graham cracker and sprinkle over top. Cover and freeze until firm. **Yield:** 6 servings.

Frozen Berry Fluff

My family loves this cool, refreshing dessert no matter what flavor pie filling I use, but I must admit raspberry is their favorite.

—*Donetta Brunner*
Savanna, Illinois

2 cans (21 ounces *each*) raspberry *or* strawberry pie filling
1 can (14 ounces) sweetened condensed milk
1 can (8 ounces) crushed pineapple, undrained, optional
1 carton (12 ounces) frozen whipped topping, thawed
Fresh berries, optional

In a bowl, combine pie filling, milk and pineapple if desired. Fold in whipped topping. Spread into an ungreased 13-in. x 9-in. x 2-in. pan. Cover and freeze for 8 hours or overnight.

Remove from the freezer 10-15 minutes before serving. Cut into squares. Garnish each with berries if desired. **Yield:** 12-15 servings.

Swiss Meringue Shells

Folks will know you fussed when you bring out these sweet, cloud-like cups topped with fresh berries (or a tart fruit filling if you like). These meringues from the American Egg Board make an elegant ending to a company dinner.

3 egg whites
1/4 teaspoon cream of tartar
3/4 cup sugar
1/2 teaspoon vanilla extract
Berries of your choice

In a mixing bowl, beat egg whites and cream of tartar until foamy, about 1 minute. Gradually beat in sugar, 1 tablespoon at a time, on high until stiff glossy peaks form and sugar is dissolved. Beat in vanilla.

Cover a baking sheet with parchment paper or greased foil. Spoon meringue into eight mounds on paper. Using the back of the spoon, shape into 3-in. cups. Bake at 225° for 1 to 1-1/2 hours or until set and dry. Turn oven off; leave meringues in oven 1 hour. Cool on wire racks. Store in an airtight container. Fill shells with berries. **Yield:** 8 servings.

Danish Rhubarb Pudding

My grandmother came to the U.S. from Denmark at the age of 16, and she was an excellent cook. A delightful rhubarb pudding that she made often is one of my favorite traditional desserts. It has a sweet, delicious, distinctive flavor and clear, deep color. Since the pudding is soft-set, it could also be used as a sauce over ice cream or pound cake.
—Kay Sundheim, Nashua, Montana

6 cups chopped fresh or
** frozen rhubarb, thawed**
6 cups water
2 cups sugar
1/4 cup cornstarch
3 tablespoons cold water

In a saucepan, bring rhubarb and water to a boil. Reduce heat; simmer, uncovered, for 10-15 minutes or until rhubarb is tender. Drain, reserving liquid; discard pulp. Measure 4 cups liquid; return to the pan.

Add sugar; bring to a boil. Combine cornstarch and cold water until smooth; stir into rhubarb liquid. Cook and stir for 1-2 minutes or until slightly thickened. Pour into individual dishes. Refrigerate for at least 4 hours before serving. **Yield:** 8 servings.

Cherry Cheesecake

When I worked full time and needed a quick dessert to take to a potluck or a friend's home, this pie was always the answer. You can substitute a graham cracker crust or use another type of fruit pie filling for a change of pace. Even the chilling time is flexible if you're in a big hurry.
—*Mary Smith*
Bradenton, Florida

2 packages (one 8 ounces, one 3 ounces) cream cheese, softened
1 cup confectioners' sugar
1 carton (8 ounces) frozen whipped topping, thawed
1 shortbread *or* graham cracker crust (8 *or* 9 inches)
1 can (21 ounces) cherry pie filling

In a mixing bowl, beat the cream cheese and sugar until smooth. Fold in whipped topping; spoon into crust. Top with pie filling. Refrigerate until serving. **Yield:** 6-8 servings.

|CUTTING CHEESECAKE| Cheesecake can be covered and refrigerated for up to 3 days. Use a straight-edge knife to cut cheesecake. Warm the blade in hot water, dry and slice. Clean and rewarm the knife after each cut.

Hot Apple Sundaes

After dinner, everyone usually dashes off, but this ice cream treat makes them linger around the table. It's that good!
—*Delia Gurnow, New Madrid, Missouri*

1 can (21 ounces) apple pie filling
1/4 cup apple juice
1 tablespoon sugar
1/2 teaspoon ground cinnamon
Vanilla ice cream

In a saucepan, combine the first four ingredients. Cook and stir over medium heat until heated through. Serve over ice cream. **Yield:** 2 cups.

Chocolate Cookie Mousse

I have family members who beg me to bring this rich yummy dessert whenever I visit. It calls for just four ingredients, and it's handy to keep in the freezer for a special occasion. —*Carol Mullaney*
Pittsburgh, Pennsylvania

1 package (14 ounces) cream-filled chocolate sandwich cookies, *divided*
2 tablespoons milk
2 cups heavy whipping cream, *divided*
2 cups (12 ounces) semisweet chocolate chips

Crush 16 cookies; sprinkle into an 8-in. square dish. Drizzle with milk. In a microwave-safe bowl, combine 2/3 cup cream and chocolate chips. Microwave, uncovered, on high for 1 minute. Stir; microwave 30-60 seconds or until chips are melted. Stir until smooth; cool to room temperature.

Meanwhile, in a mixing bowl, beat remaining cream until soft peaks form. Fold into chocolate mixture. Spread a third of the chocolate mixture over crushed cookies. Separate eight cookies; place over chocolate mixture. Repeat. Top with remaining chocolate mixture. Garnish with remaining whole cookies.

Cover; freeze for up to 2 months. Thaw in refrigerator for at least 3 hours before serving. **Yield:** 16 servings.

Editor's Note: This recipe was tested in an 850-watt microwave.

Lemon Ice

Pucker up for this sweet-tart treat. The delicious lemon dessert is a perfectly refreshing way to end a summer meal or any meal, for that matter.
—*Concetta Maranto Skenfield, Bakersfield, California*

2 cups sugar
1 cup water
2 cups lemon juice
1 tablespoon grated lemon peel

In a saucepan over low heat, cook and stir sugar and water until sugar is dissolved. Remove from the heat; stir in lemon juice. Pour into a freezer container. Freeze for 4 hours, stirring every 30 minutes, or until mixture becomes slushy. Sprinkle servings with lemon peel. **Yield:** 6 servings.

Kool-Aid Pie

A fun crust of vanilla wafers is easy for kids to make and holds an eye-catching, fluffy filling that's refreshing in summer. Use different flavors of Kool-Aid to vary the pie's taste.
—*Ledia Black*
Pineland, Texas

1 can (12 ounces)
   evaporated milk
36 vanilla wafers
1 cup sugar
1 envelope (.14 ounce)
   unsweetened lemon-lime
   Kool-Aid
Whipped topping, optional

Pour milk into a small metal or glass mixing bowl. Add beaters to the bowl. Cover and chill for at least 2 hours.

Coat a 9-in. pie plate with nonstick cooking spray. Line bottom and sides of plate with wafers. Beat milk until soft peaks form. Add sugar and drink mix; beat until thoroughly mixed. Spoon over wafers; freeze for at least 4 hours. Garnish with whipped topping if desired. **Yield:** 6-8 servings.

Berry Good Ice Cream Sauce

I started cooking in earnest as a bride over 40 years ago. I'm thankful to say I improved in time—though I made something once even the dog refused to eat! Now, my three children are grown and I'm the grandmother of four.
—*Joy Beck*
Cincinnati, Ohio

1-3/4 cups sliced fresh *or*
   frozen rhubarb
2/3 cup pureed fresh *or*
   frozen strawberries
1/4 cup sugar
1/4 cup orange juice
2 cups sliced fresh *or*
   frozen strawberries

In a saucepan, combine the first four ingredients. Cook over medium heat until rhubarb is tender, about 5 minutes. Stir in the sliced strawberries. Store in the refrigerator. **Yield:** 3-1/2 cups.

Watermelon Ice

If you're one of many folks who just can't wait for the county fair, you'll love these snow cones that exhibit plenty of good taste. This sweet, frosty snack is so refreshing on hot summer days. Store it in the freezer, so it's a snap to scoop and serve in snow cone cups. —Darlene Markel, Mt. Hood, Oregon

1/2 cup sugar
1/4 cup watermelon *or* mixed fruit gelatin powder
3/4 cup boiling water
5 cups seeded cubed watermelon

In a bowl, dissolve sugar and gelatin in boiling water; set aside. Place watermelon in a blender; cover and puree. Stir into gelatin mixture. Pour into an ungreased pan. Cover and freeze overnight. Remove from the freezer 1 hour before serving. Spoon into paper cones or serving dishes. **Yield:** 4-6 servings.

Layered Pudding Dessert

High on our list of long-time favorites, this fluffy, fruity refrigerated treat continues to hold its own against new dessert recipes I try. —Pat Habiger
Spearville, Kansas

1 cup crushed vanilla wafers, *divided*
1 package (3 ounces) cook-and-serve vanilla pudding mix
2 medium ripe bananas, *divided*
1 package (3 ounces) strawberry gelatin
1 cup whipped topping

Spread half of the crushed wafers in the bottom of a greased 8-in. square pan. Prepare pudding mix according to package directions; spoon hot pudding over crumbs. Slice one banana; place over pudding. Top with remaining crumbs. Chill for 1 hour.

Meanwhile, prepare gelatin according to package directions; chill for 30 minutes or until partially set. Pour over crumbs. Slice the remaining banana and place over gelatin. Spread whipped topping over all. Chill for 2 hours. **Yield:** 9 servings.

Frozen Banana Pineapple Cups

You can stir together this sweet tangy fruit mixture with just five ingredients, then pop it in the freezer overnight. The frosty results are a refreshing addition to a summer dinner.
—*Alice Miller*
Middlebury, Indiana

3 cups water
2-2/3 cups mashed ripe
    bananas (5 to 6 medium)
1-1/2 cups sugar
1 can (20 ounces) crushed
    pineapple, undrained
1 can (6 ounces) frozen
    orange juice
    concentrate, thawed

In a 2-qt. freezer container, combine all of the ingredients and mix well. Cover and freeze for 5 hours or overnight. Remove from the freezer 15 minutes before serving. **Yield:** 9-12 servings.

Caramel Apple Cupcakes

Bring these extra-special cupcakes to your next bake sale and watch how quickly they disappear—if your family doesn't gobble them up first! Kids will go for the fun appearance and tasty toppings while adults will appreciate the moist spiced cake underneath.
—*Diane Halferty, Corpus Christi, Texas*

1 package (18-1/4
    ounces) spice *or carrot*
    cake mix
2 cups chopped peeled tart
    apples
20 caramels
3 tablespoons milk
1 cup finely chopped
    pecans, toasted

Prepare cake batter according to package directions; fold in apples. Fill 12 greased or paper-lined jumbo muffin cups three-fourths full. Bake at 350° for 20 minutes or until a toothpick comes out clean. Cool for 10 minutes before removing from pans to wire racks to cool completely.

In a saucepan, cook the caramels and milk over low heat until smooth. Spread over cupcakes. Sprinkle with pecans. Insert a wooden stick into the center of each cupcake. **Yield:** 1 dozen.

Sherbet Dessert

This refreshing dessert was served at a baby shower I attended. It was so delicious I asked the hostess to share her secret. I couldn't believe it was made with only three ingredients, and it was low-fat as a bonus.
—*Shirley Colvin*
Tremonton, Utah

✓ **Uses less fat, sugar or salt. Includes Nutritional Analysis and Diabetic Exchanges.**

1/2 gallon orange sherbet *or* **flavor of your choice, softened**
 1 package (10 ounces) frozen sweetened raspberries, thawed
 2 medium ripe bananas, mashed

Place the sherbet in a large bowl; stir in raspberries and bananas. Freeze until firm. **Yield:** 18 servings.

Nutritional Analysis: One 1/2-cup serving equals 150 calories, 40 mg sodium, 4 mg cholesterol, 34 g carbohydrate, 1 g protein, 2 g fat. **Diabetic Exchanges:** 1 starch, 1 fruit, 1/2 fat.

Editor's Note: Rainbow sherbet is not recommended for this recipe.

Cranberry Crumble

My family likes this crumble so much I make it year-round. But I especially like to serve it warm on cool winter evenings.
—*Karen Riordan, Louisville, Kentucky*

1-1/2 cups quick-cooking oats
 1 cup packed brown sugar
 1/2 cup all-purpose flour
 1/3 cup cold butter
 1 can (16 ounces) whole-berry cranberry sauce
Whipped cream *or* **ice cream, optional**

In a bowl, combine oats, brown sugar and flour. Cut in butter until crumbly. Press half into a greased 8-in. square baking dish. Spread the cranberry sauce evenly over crust. Sprinkle with remaining oat mixture.

Bake at 350° for 35-40 minutes or until golden brown and filling is hot. Serve warm with whipped cream or ice cream if desired. **Yield:** 9 servings.

Lime Sherbet

You don't need an ice cream maker to churn out this light, green refresher. The mild lime flavor and frosty consistency make it a perfect treat.
—*Carolyn Hannay, Antioch, Tennessee*

 Uses less fat, sugar or salt. Includes Nutritional Analysis and Diabetic Exchanges.

1 package (3 ounces) lime gelatin
1 cup boiling water
3 cups 1% milk
1/2 cup sugar
1/4 cup lemon juice

In a bowl, dissolve gelatin in boiling water. Add the milk, sugar and lemon juice; stir until sugar is dissolved. Pour into a freezer container; freeze for 4 hours or until frozen.

Remove from the freezer and let stand for 10 minutes or until slightly softened. Beat with a mixer until light and fluffy. Refreeze for at least 1 hour. **Yield:** about 1 quart.

Nutritional Analysis: One serving (1 cup) equals 260 calories, 2 g fat (1 g saturated fat), 11 mg cholesterol, 156 mg sodium, 54 g carbohydrate, trace fiber, 9 g protein. **Diabetic Exchanges:** 2 starch, 1-1/2 fruit.

Cake with Lemon Sauce

This is a family favorite on hot summer nights. Cream cheese, milk and pudding mix are all that's needed for the sunny sauce drizzled over prepared pound cake and topped with a few berries. You could also use sponge cake dessert shells instead.
—*Claire Dion*
Canterbury, Connecticut

1 package (3 ounces) cream cheese, softened
1-3/4 cups cold milk
1 package (3.4 ounces) instant lemon pudding mix
4 slices pound cake *or* **angel food cake**
Fresh raspberries, optional

In a small mixing bowl, beat the cream cheese until smooth. Add milk and pudding mix; beat for 2 minutes or until smooth and thickened. Serve with cake. Garnish with raspberries if desired. **Yield:** 4 servings.

Cookie Ice Cream Sandwiches

Endulge in your love for ice cream by assembling these sandwiches. The tempting treats take advantage of store-bought oatmeal raisin cookies, ice cream and peanut butter. You can roll them in crushed candy bars or nuts for an even fancier look. —*Melissa Stevens, Elk River, Minnesota*

Peanut butter
12 oatmeal raisin cookies
1 pint vanilla ice cream *or* **flavor of your choice**
Miniature chocolate chips

Spread peanut butter over the bottom of six cookies. Top with a scoop of ice cream. Top with another cookie; press down gently. Roll sides of ice cream sandwich in chocolate chips. Wrap in plastic wrap and freeze until serving. **Yield:** 6 servings.

Pineapple Upside-Down Cake

I need just a few easy ingredients to dress up a boxed mix and create this classic cake. It bakes up so moist and pretty, no one will believe it wasn't made from scratch. —*Gloria Poyer*
Hackettstown, New Jersey

6 canned pineapple slices
6 maraschino cherries
1 cup chopped walnuts, *divided*
1 package (18-1/4 ounces) white cake mix

Place pineapple slices in a greased and floured 10-in. tube pan. Place a cherry in the center of each slice. Sprinkle half of the walnuts around the pineapple. Prepare cake mix according to package directions; spoon batter over pineapple layer. Sprinkle with remaining nuts.

Bake at 350° for 40-45 minutes or until a toothpick inserted near the center comes out clean. Cool for 10 minutes before inverting onto a wire rack to cool completely. **Yield:** 10 servings.

Pineapple Ice Cream

I rely on my ice cream maker when whipping up this five-ingredient frozen treat. The creamy concoction has just the right amount of pineapple to keep guests asking for more.   —*Phyllis Schmalz*
Kansas City, Kansas

3 eggs, beaten
2 cups milk
1 cup sugar
1-3/4 cups heavy whipping
    cream
1 can (8 ounces) crushed
    pineapple, undrained

In a saucepan, cook the eggs and milk over medium heat for 8 minutes or until a thermometer reads 160° and mixture coats a metal spoon. Stir in sugar until dissolved. Cool. Stir in the cream and pineapple.

Fill cylinder of ice cream freezer two-thirds full; freeze according to manufacturer's directions. Refrigerate remaining mixture until ready to freeze. Allow ice cream to ripen in refrigerator freezer for 2-4 hours before serving. May be frozen for up to 2 months. **Yield:** 6 servings.

Pistachio Pudding Tarts

For St. Patrick's Day, Christmas or anytime you want a treat that's green, refreshing and delightful, try these tempting tarts.   —*Bettye Linster*
Atlanta, Georgia

1 cup butter, softened
1 package (8 ounces)
    cream cheese, softened
2 cups all-purpose flour
1 package (3.4 ounces)
    instant pistachio pudding
    mix
1-3/4 cups cold milk

In a mixing bowl, combine butter, cream cheese and flour; mix well. Shape into 48 balls (1 in. each); press onto the bottom and up the sides of ungreased miniature muffin cups. Bake at 400° for 12-15 minutes or until lightly browned. Cool for 5 minutes; carefully remove from pans to a wire rack to cool completely.

For filling, combine pudding and milk in a mixing bowl; beat on low speed for 2 minutes. Cover and refrigerate for 5 minutes. Spoon into tart shells; serve immediately. **Yield:** 4 dozen.

Flowerpot Cupcakes

A strip of fruit roll is used to wrap a chocolate cupcake and form a mini flowerpot. Giving color to each pot are easy gumdrop blossoms growing from pretzel stick stems. They're great for a spring or summer birthday party.

—Judi Oudekerk
Buffalo, Minnesota

 1 package (18-1/4 ounces) devil's food cake mix
16 pieces Fruit by the Foot
24 large green gumdrops
48 large assorted gumdrops
48 pretzel sticks

Prepare cake batter according to package directions. Fill greased muffin cups two-thirds full. Bake at 350° for 18-20 minutes or until a toothpick comes out clean. Cool for 5 minutes; remove from pans to wire racks to cool completely.

Cut three 9-in. pieces from each fruit roll piece (save small pieces for another use). With a small pastry brush, lightly brush water on one end of a fruit strip. Wrap around bottom of cupcake; press ends together. Repeat with remaining cupcakes. Lightly brush water on one side of remaining fruit strips; fold in half lengthwise. Brush one end with water; wrap around cupcake top, slightly overlapping bottom fruit strip.

Press each gumdrop into a 1-1/4-in. circle. With scissors, cut each green gumdrop into four leaf shapes; set aside. Cut one end of each remaining gumdrop into a tulip shape. Gently press a pretzel into each tulip-shaped gumdrop. Gently press gumdrop leaves onto pretzels. Press two flowers into the top of each cupcake. **Yield:** 2 dozen.

Five-Minute Blueberry Pie

If you like the taste of fresh blueberries, you'll love this pie. Since it's a breeze to whip up, I make it often, especially in summer.

—Milda Anderson, Osceola, Wisconsin

1/2 cup sugar
 2 tablespoons cornstarch
3/4 cup water
 4 cups fresh *or* frozen blueberries, thawed
 1 graham cracker crust (9 inches)

In a saucepan, combine sugar and cornstarch. Stir in water until smooth. Bring to a boil over medium heat; cook and stir for 2 minutes. Add blueberries. Cook for 3 minutes, stirring occasionally. Pour into crust. Refrigerate until serving. **Yield:** 6-8 servings.

Chocolate Mint Ice Cream

When the weather gets hot, my family enjoys this cool combination of chocolate and mint. It doesn't require an ice cream maker—all that you need is an ordinary freezer. My ice cream's versatile, too. We've used crushed Heath bars, Oreo cookies and miniature chocolate chips in place of the Andes candies.
—*Fran Skaff, Egg Harbor, Wisconsin*

1 can (14 ounces) sweetened condensed milk
1/2 cup chocolate syrup
2 cups heavy whipping cream
1 package (4.67 ounces) mint Andes candies (28 pieces), chopped

In a small bowl, combine the milk and chocolate syrup; set aside. In a mixing bowl, beat cream until stiff peaks form. Fold in chocolate mixture and candies. Transfer to a freezer-proof container; cover and freeze for 5 hours or until firm. Remove from the freezer 10 minutes before serving. **Yield:** 1-1/2 quarts.

Caramel Chocolate Sauce

Chocolate lovers, rejoice! This quick fix takes ice cream toppings to new heights. Melted caramels give the rich fudge-like sauce extra appeal, making it hard to resist a second helping. —*June Smith Byron Center, Michigan*

30 caramels
1 cup (6 ounces) semisweet chocolate chips
1 can (5 ounces) evaporated milk
1/2 cup butter
Ice cream

In a 1-qt. microwave-safe bowl, combine the caramels, chocolate chips, milk and butter. Microwave, uncovered, on high for 2 minutes; stir.

Heat 1-2 minutes longer or until the caramels are almost melted; stir until smooth. Serve warm if desired over ice cream (sauce will thicken upon standing). Refrigerate leftovers. **Yield:** 2 cups.

Editor's Note: This recipe was tested in an 850-watt microwave.

S'more Tarts

I bring a fireside favorite indoors with the taste-tempting treats I fix for movie and game nights. Kids of all ages will quickly gobble up the individual graham cracker tarts filled with a fudgy brownie and golden marshmallows before asking, "Can I have s'more?"
—*Trish Quinn*
Cheyenne, Wyoming

1 package fudge brownie mix (13-inch x 9-inch pan size)
12 individual graham cracker shells
1-1/2 cups miniature marshmallows
1 cup milk chocolate chips

Prepare brownie batter according to package directions. Place graham cracker shells on a baking sheet and fill with brownie batter. Bake at 350° for 20-25 minutes or until a toothpick inserted in the center comes out with moist crumbs.

Immediately sprinkle with marshmallows and chocolate chips. Bake 3-5 minutes longer or until marshmallows are puffed and golden brown. **Yield:** 1 dozen.

Layered Toffee Cake

This is a quick and yummy way to dress up a purchased angel food cake. To keep the plate clean while assembling this pretty layered dessert, cut two half circles of waxed paper to place under the bottom layer and remove them after frosting the cake and sprinkling on the toffee.
—*Pat Squire*
Alexandria, Virginia

2 cups heavy whipping cream
1/2 cup caramel *or* butterscotch ice cream topping
1/2 teaspoon vanilla extract
1 prepared angel food cake (16 ounces)
9 Heath candy bars (1.4 ounces *each*), chopped

In a mixing bowl, beat cream just until it begins to thicken. Gradually add ice cream topping and vanilla, beating until soft peaks form.

Cut cake horizontally into three layers. Place the bottom layer on a serving plate; spread with 1 cup cream mixture and sprinkle with 1/2 cup candy bar. Repeat. Place top layer on cake; frost top and sides with remaining cream mixture and sprinkle with the remaining candy bar. Store in the refrigerator. **Yield:** 12-14 servings.

Praline Parfaits

The recipe for this sweet, nutty ice cream sauce comes from a famous New Orleans restaurant. When we entertain, I top each pretty parfait with whipped cream and a pecan half. —*Cindy Stephenson*
Houston, Texas

1 bottle (16 ounces) dark corn syrup
1/3 cup sugar
1/3 cup water
1 cup chopped pecans
3 to 4 cups vanilla ice cream

In a saucepan, combine the corn syrup, sugar and water; bring to a boil, stirring constantly. Remove from the heat; stir in pecans. Cool completely.

Spoon half of the ice cream into four parfait glasses or dishes. Top each with 2 tablespoons sauce. Repeat layers. Refrigerate leftover sauce. **Yield:** 4 servings (about 2-1/2 cups sauce).

Dipped Strawberries

(Also pictured on front cover)

I dip plump red berries in chocolate and vanilla chips, and they're always a hit. They'll be the delicious red, white and "ooh" center of attention at your place, too.
—*Marlene Wiczek*
Little Falls, Minnesota

1 quart medium fresh strawberries (with stems)
1-2/3 cups vanilla *or* white baking chips
2 tablespoons shortening, *divided*
1 cup (6 ounces) semisweet chocolate chips

Wash strawberries and gently pat until completely dry. In a microwave or double boiler, melt vanilla chips and 1 tablespoon shortening. Dip each strawberry until two-thirds of the berry is coated, allowing the excess to drip off. Place on a waxed paper-lined tray or baking sheet; refrigerate for 30 minutes or until set.

Melt chocolate chips and remaining shortening. Dip each strawberry until one-third is coated. Return to tray; refrigerate for 30 minutes or until set. **Yield:** 2-1/2 to 3 dozen.

Raspberry Cupcake Dessert

A light and fun finish, my cream cake dessert is a hit with kids of all ages. When I'm in a hurry, store-bought cupcakes work fine. And while I prefer homemade whipped cream, purchased whipped topping is an easy option.
—Edith Ruth Muldoon
Baldwin, New York

2 creamed-filled chocolate cupcakes, cut in half
1 to 2 cups heavy whipping cream
3 tablespoons confectioners' sugar
1/2 teaspoon vanilla extract
1 to 1-1/2 cups fresh *or* frozen raspberries, thawed and drained
Additional raspberries, optional

Place one cupcake half each in four dessert dishes. In a mixing bowl, beat cream until soft peaks form. Beat in sugar and vanilla until stiff peaks form. Fold in raspberries. Spoon over cupcakes. Garnish with additional berries if desired. Refrigerate until serving. **Yield:** 4 servings.

Editor's Note: This recipe was prepared with Hostess brand cupcakes.

Caramel Apple Burritos

These are such fun to experiment with. I've made them with different varieties of apples and have substituted applesauce or pie filling. Topped with ice cream, caramel or chocolate sauce, they make a memorable dessert.
—Cindy Reams
Philipsburg, Pennsylvania

3 large tart apples, peeled and sliced
10 caramels
5 flour tortillas (8 inches), warmed

Place apple slices in a saucepan; cover and cook over medium heat for 3-4 minutes or until tender. Reduce heat. Add caramels; cook and stir until caramels are melted. Spoon apple mixture off center on each tortilla; fold sides and ends over filling and roll up. **Yield:** 5 servings.

Pumpkin Ice Cream

This ice cream is as simple as opening a can, stirring and freezing. Plus, if you're like me and looking for a good way of using up your homegrown pumpkins, feel free to substitute fresh-picked for canned.
—Linda Young
Longmont, Colorado

1 cup canned pumpkin
1/4 teaspoon pumpkin pie spice
1 quart vanilla ice cream, softened
Gingersnaps, optional

In a medium bowl, mix the pumpkin and pie spice until well blended. Stir in ice cream. Freeze until serving. Garnish with gingersnaps if desired. **Yield:** 4-6 servings.

Raspberry Pear Delight

Raspberry Pear Delight is a fast-to-fix yet fairly fancy dessert that's a perfect ending to a meal anytime.
—Marion Tipton, Phoenix, Arizona

1 package (10 ounces) frozen sweetened raspberries, thawed
1 can (15 ounces) pear halves, drained
1 pint raspberry sorbet *or* sherbet
Hot fudge ice cream topping
Fresh raspberries, optional

In a blender or food processor, puree raspberries; strain seeds. Pour onto four dessert plates. Top with pears and a scoop of sorbet. Drizzle with hot fudge topping. Garnish with fresh berries if desired. **Yield:** 4 servings.

Candy Bar Pie

I've made this no-bake dessert for many occasions because the recipe is so simple and easy to remember. I freeze the candy bars and use a rolling pin to make crushing them easy.

—*Sharlie Hanson*
Tulsa, Oklahoma

1 package (8 ounces) cream cheese, softened
1 carton (8 ounces) frozen whipped topping, thawed
4 Butterfinger candy bars (2.1 ounces *each*)
1 prepared graham cracker crust (9 inches)

In a small mixing bowl, beat the cream cheese until smooth. Fold in whipped topping. Crush the candy bars; fold 1 cup into cream cheese mixture. Spoon into crust. Sprinkle with remaining candy bar crumbs. Refrigerate for 2-4 hours before slicing. **Yield:** 6-8 servings.

Frosty Cranberry Pie

It's nice to have this light, not-too-sweet pie in the freezer when unexpected guests stop over for coffee. It's so easy to put together, and everyone always asks for the recipe.
—*Mildred Skrha*
Oak Brook, Illinois

1 package (8 ounces) cream cheese, softened
1 cup confectioners' sugar
1 can (16 ounces) whole-berry cranberry sauce
1 carton (8 ounces) frozen whipped topping, thawed
2 pastry shells (9 inches), baked
Additional whipped topping, optional

In a mixing bowl, beat cream cheese and sugar. Stir in cranberry sauce. Fold in whipped topping. Spoon into crusts. Cover and freeze for up to 3 months. Remove from the freezer 10-15 minutes before serving. Garnish with whipped topping if desired. **Yield:** 2 pies (6-8 servings each).

Editor's Note: Shortbread or graham cracker crusts may be substituted for the pastry shells.

Granola Sundaes

My kids like to mix the no-bake granola topping themselves and sprinkle it over ice cream. The versatile granola mix can top off yogurt, fresh fruit and pie filling...or be rolled into a ball for a sweet snack.
—Kim Dunbar, Willow Springs, Illinois

1 cup quick-cooking oats
1/2 cup packed brown sugar
1/4 cup peanut butter
1/4 cup butter, softened
Ice cream

In a bowl, combine oats and brown sugar. Stir in peanut butter and butter until mixture forms coarse crumbs. Sprinkle over ice cream. **Yield:** 2 cups topping.

|ABOUT OATS| Old-fashioned oats and quick-cooking oats can usually be interchanged in recipes. Store oats in an airtight container in a cool, dry place for up to 6 months.

Honey Baked Apples

These tender apples smell so good while they're in the oven—and taste even better. We enjoy the golden raisins inside and the soothing taste of honey. They're a yummy change from the cinnamon and sugar seasoning traditionally used with apples.
—Chere Bell
Colorado Springs, Colorado

2-1/4 cups water
3/4 cup packed brown sugar
3 tablespoons honey
6 large tart apples
1 cup golden raisins

In a saucepan, bring water, brown sugar and honey to a boil. Remove from the heat. Core apples and peel the top third of each. Place in an ungreased 9-in. baking dish.

Fill apples with raisins; sprinkle any remaining raisins into pan. Pour sugar syrup over apples. Bake, uncovered, at 350° for 1 hour or until tender, basting occasionally. **Yield:** 6 servings.

Easy Black Forest Torte

Easy Black Forest Torte couldn't be simpler—all you need is a boxed cake mix, pie filling, miniature marshmallows and whipped topping. I sampled this fancy-looking dessert during a visit with my grandmother. The marshmallows and cherries trade places during baking, and the flavor is excellent.

—Deb Morrison, Skiatook, Oklahoma

4 to 5 cups miniature
    marshmallows
  1 package (18-1/4
    ounces) chocolate cake
    mix
  1 can (21 ounces) cherry
    pie filling
  1 carton (8 ounces) frozen
    whipped topping, thawed

Sprinkle marshmallows in a greased 13-in. x 9-in. x 2-in. baking pan. Prepare cake batter according to package directions; pour over the marshmallows. Spoon pie filling over batter. Bake at 350° for 1 hour or until a toothpick inserted near the center comes out clean. Cool. Frost with whipped topping. Store in the refrigerator. **Yield:** 12-16 servings.

Quick Strawberry Cobbler

Blueberry or cherry pie filling also work great with this easy cobbler. A good friend shared the recipe with me. —Sue Poe, Hayden, Alabama

  2 cans (21 ounces *each*)
    strawberry pie filling *or*
    fruit filling of your choice
1/2 cup butter, softened
  1 package (3 ounces)
    cream cheese, softened
  2 teaspoons vanilla extract
  2 packages (9 ounces
    each) yellow cake mix

Pour pie filling into a greased 13-in. x 9-in. x 2-in. baking dish. Bake at 350° for 5-7 minutes or until heated through.

Meanwhile, in a mixing bowl, cream butter, cream cheese and vanilla. Place cake mixes in another bowl; cut in cream cheese mixture until crumbly. Sprinkle over hot filling. Bake 25-30 minutes longer or until topping is golden brown. **Yield:** 12 servings.

No–Bake Cheesecake Pie

I came up with this creamy white chocolate cheesecake after remembering one evening that I needed to bring a treat to the office the next day. It was a tremendous hit. It's quick to fix yet tastes like you fussed. —*Geneva Mayer, Olney, Illinois*

1 cup vanilla *or* white chips
2 packages (8 ounces *each*) cream cheese, cubed
1 carton (8 ounces) frozen whipped topping, thawed
1 graham cracker crust (9 inches)
1/3 cup English toffee bits *or* almond brickle chips

In a heavy saucepan, melt chips over medium-low heat; stir until smooth. Remove from the heat; stir in cream cheese until smooth. Fold in whipped topping. Pour into the crust.

Cover and refrigerate overnight or until set. Just before serving, sprinkle with toffee bits. **Yield:** 6-8 servings.

Cinnamon Graham Sundaes

For a swift sweet dessert, try four-ingredient Cinnamon Graham Sundaes. Many Mexican restaurants serve ice cream in deep-fried shells. I use cinnamon graham crackers and honey to get a similar taste. You can replace the honey with caramel or chocolate syrup with good results. —*Jennifer Villarreal Texas City, Texas*

20 cinnamon graham cracker squares
1/2 gallon vanilla ice cream
3 tablespoons honey
2 teaspoons ground cinnamon

For each serving, place two graham cracker squares on a plate. Top with ice cream and drizzle with honey. Sprinkle with cinnamon. **Yield:** 10 servings.

Peach-Glazed Cake

After tasting this cake, guests always ask for a second slice and the recipe. Everyone is surprised when they learn this dessert is so easy to make. I often garnish servings with pear slices instead of peaches.

—*Samantha Jones*
Morgantown, West Virginia

1 can (15 ounces) pear halves, drained
1 package (18-1/4 ounces) white cake mix
3 eggs
1 jar (12 ounces) peach preserves, *divided*
Fresh *or* frozen sliced peaches, thawed

In a blender or food processor, cover and process pears until pureed. Transfer to a mixing bowl; add the cake mix and eggs. Beat on medium speed for 2 minutes. Pour into a greased and floured 10-in. fluted tube pan. Bake at 350° for 30-35 minutes or until a toothpick inserted near the center comes out clean. Cool for 10 minutes before removing from pan to a wire rack.

In a microwave-safe bowl, heat 1/2 cup of peach preserves, uncovered, on high for 60-90 seconds or until melted. Slowly brush over warm cake. Cool completely. Slice cake; top with peaches. Melt remaining preserves; drizzle over top. **Yield:** 10-12 servings.

Dessert Waffles

Everyone raves about the contrast between the crunchy waffles and creamy ice cream in this easy dessert.

—*Sheila Watson, Stettler, Alberta*

1/2 cup flaked coconut
1/2 cup packed brown sugar
1/4 cup butter, softened
6 frozen waffles, lightly toasted
6 scoops butter pecan ice cream *or* flavor of your choice

In a small bowl, combine the first three ingredients; mix well. Spread over waffles. Broil for 3-4 minutes or until bubbly. Top with ice cream. **Yield:** 6 servings.

Peach Melba Dessert

My dessert's a no-fuss one. In fact, when we have company, I'll put it together while the after-dinner coffee is perking.
—*Kathryn Awe, International Falls, Minnesota*

4 **individual round sponge cakes** *or* **shortcakes**
4 **canned peach halves in syrup**
4 **scoops vanilla** *or* **peach ice cream**
2 **tablespoons raspberry jam**
1 **tablespoon chopped nuts**

Place cakes on dessert plates. Drain the peaches, reserving 2 tablespoons syrup; spoon 1-1/2 teaspoons syrup over each cake. Place peach halves, hollow side up, on cakes. Put a scoop of ice cream in each peach. Heat jam; drizzle over ice cream. Sprinkle with nuts and serve immediately. **Yield:** 4 servings.

Brownie Caramel Parfaits

I easily transform brownies, ice cream and caramel topping into a tempting treat. Layers of toasted coconut and nuts add nice crunch and make this dessert seem fancy. But it really couldn't be simpler to put together.
—*Chris Schnittka
Charlottesville, Virginia*

1/2 **cup chopped pecans**
1/2 **cup flaked coconut**
1 **package brownie mix (8-inch x 8-inch pan size)**
1 **pint vanilla ice cream**
1 **jar (12-1/4 ounces) caramel ice cream topping**

Place pecans and coconut in an ungreased baking pan. Bake at 350° for 10-12 minutes or until toasted, stirring frequently. Meanwhile, prepare brownies according to package directions. Cool; cut into small squares.

When ready to serve, layer the brownies, ice cream, caramel topping and pecan mixture in parfait or dessert glasses; repeat layers one or two times. **Yield:** 6 servings.

Editor's Note: Any type of nuts, ice cream or topping may be used in these parfaits.

Raspberry Cream Croissants

This heavenly dessert takes only seconds to assemble because it begins with bakery croissants, whipped topping and store-bought jam. A friend and I came up with the recipe. —*Sherry Horton*
Sioux Falls, South Dakota

4 to 6 croissants
1/2 cup seedless raspberry jam
Whipped cream in a can *or* whipped topping
1-1/4 cups fresh *or* frozen unsweetened raspberries, thawed
Confectioners' sugar, optional

Cut the croissants in half horizontally; spread cut halves with jam. Spread whipped cream over bottom halves; top with raspberries. Replace tops. Dust with confectioners' sugar if desired. Serve immediately. **Yield:** 4-6 servings.

Coconut Gingerbread Cake

This unusual dessert came from a little book I bought at a flea market many years ago. The broiled orange-coconut topping really dresses up a boxed gingerbread mix. When I bring it to potlucks and family get-togethers, it never lasts long!
—*Paula Hartlett, Mineola, New York*

1 package (14-1/2 ounces) gingerbread mix
1 large navel orange
1-1/3 cups flaked coconut
1/2 cup packed brown sugar
2 tablespoons orange juice

Prepare and bake cake according to package directions, using a greased 8-in. square baking pan. Meanwhile, grate 1 tablespoon of peel from the orange; set aside. Peel and section the orange, removing white pith; dice the orange. When cake tests done, remove from the oven and cool slightly.

Combine coconut, brown sugar, orange juice, diced orange and reserved peel; spread over warm cake. Broil 4 in. from the heat for 2-3 minutes or until the top is lightly browned. Cool on a wire rack. **Yield:** 9 servings.

Cakes, Pies & Desserts   299

Fancy Fuss-Free Torte

This pretty layered torte relies on convenient frozen pound cake and canned pie filling. It's a snap to assemble. I put toothpicks through the ends to hold the layers in place, then remove them before serving.
—*Joan Causey*
Greenwood, Arkansas

1 loaf (10-3/4 ounces) frozen pound cake, thawed
1 can (21 ounces) cherry pie filling *or flavor of your choice*
1 carton (8 ounces) frozen whipped topping, thawed
1/2 cup chopped pecans

Split cake into three horizontal layers. Place bottom layer on a serving plate; top with half of the pie filling. Repeat layers. Top with third cake layer. Frost top and sides with whipped topping. Sprinkle with pecans. Store in the refrigerator. **Yield:** 8-10 servings.

Yogurt Berry Pies

Yogurt Berry Pies have just two ingredients in the filling, so they're a snap to assemble, yet they look and taste like you fussed. Topped with fresh berries, they're irresistible.
—*Dawn Fagerstrom*
Warren, Minnesota

1 carton (8 ounces) mixed berry yogurt *or flavor of your choice*
2 cups whipped topping
1 package (6 count) individual graham cracker tart shells
Blueberries and raspberries

In a bowl, stir the yogurt and whipped topping until combined. Spoon into tart shells. Cover and freeze for 20 minutes. Top with berries. **Yield:** 6 servings.

Cinnamon Apple Pizza

My son asked me to make something the night before a bake sale. He was pleased with this pizza that I created using on-hand ingredients.

—*Cherron Walker*
Columbus, Ohio

1 tube (12.4 ounces) refrigerated cinnamon roll dough
1 can (21 ounces) apple pie filling
1/4 cup packed brown sugar
1 tablespoon butter, melted

Set cinnamon roll icing aside. Separate dough into individual rolls; roll out each into a 4-in. circle. Arrange on a greased 12-in. pizza pan, overlapping edges. Bake at 400° for 8 minutes.

Spoon the apple pie filling over rolls to within 1/2 in. of edge. Combine the brown sugar and butter; sprinkle over pie filling. Bake 6-8 minutes longer or until the crust is golden brown. Cool. Drizzle with the reserved icing. **Yield:** 10-12 servings.

Spiced Peaches

Canned peaches get special attention from cinnamon and brown sugar. Served warm, these peaches offer down-home comfort. Chilled, they make a refreshing treat with frozen yogurt.

—*Debbie Schrock, Jackson, Mississippi*

 Uses less fat, sugar or salt. Includes Nutritional Analysis and Diabetic Exchanges.

1 can (15 ounces) reduced-sugar peach halves
2 tablespoons brown sugar
1 teaspoon lemon juice
1 teaspoon orange juice
2 cinnamon sticks (3-1/2 inches)

Drain peaches, reserving juice; set the peaches aside. Pour juice into a saucepan; add brown sugar and lemon and orange juices. Bring to a boil over medium heat; add cinnamon sticks. Reduce heat; simmer, uncovered, for 5 minutes. Add peach halves; heat through. Discard cinnamon sticks. Serve warm or cold. **Yield:** 4 servings.

Nutritional Analysis: One serving equals 74 calories, trace fat (0 saturated fat), 0 cholesterol, 7 mg sodium, 19 g carbohydrate, 1 g fiber, 1 g protein. **Diabetic Exchange:** 1 fruit.

Grilled Pineapple

Fresh pineapple adds an elegant touch to a barbecue when grilled, topped with butter and maple syrup and sprinkled with nuts. I cut each pineapple quarter into bite-size pieces before serving.

—Polly Heer, Cabot, Arkansas

1/4 cup maple syrup
3 tablespoons butter, melted
1 fresh pineapple
2 tablespoons chopped macadamia nuts *or* hazelnuts, toasted

Combine syrup and butter; set aside. Quarter the pineapple lengthwise, leaving top attached. Grill, uncovered, over medium heat for 5 minutes. Turn; brush with maple butter. Grill 5-7 minutes longer or until heated through; brush with maple butter and sprinkle with nuts. Serve with remaining maple butter. **Yield:** 4 servings.

Fluffy Mint Dessert

The cool, minty flavor of this fluffy dessert is perfect for Christmas or the hot summer months. Since it has to be made ahead of time, it's a great time-saver on potluck day. I received the recipe from a neighbor a couple years ago. —Carol Mixter Lincoln Park, Michigan

1 package (14 ounces) cream-filled chocolate sandwich cookies, crushed
1/2 cup butter, melted
2 cartons (12 ounces *each*) frozen whipped topping, thawed
2 cups pastel miniature marshmallows
1-1/3 cups small pastel mints (5-1/2 ounces)

Reserve 1/4 cup of crushed cookies for garnish. Combine the remaining cookies with butter; press into an ungreased 13-in. x 9-in. x 2-in. baking dish.

Fold together whipped topping, marshmallows and mints; pour over crust. Garnish with reserved cookies. Cover and refrigerate for 1-2 days before serving. **Yield:** 18-20 servings.

Butterscotch Chocolate Cake

Butterscotch Chocolate Cake is an easy ending to dinner because it can be made ahead and kept in the fridge. A moist chocolate cake is covered with rich butterscotch ice cream topping, spread with whipped topping, then sprinkled with crushed Butterfinger candy bars.
—*Shelley McKinney*
New Castle, Indiana

1 package (18-1/4 ounces) chocolate cake mix
1 jar (17 ounces) butterscotch ice cream topping
1 carton (8 ounces) frozen whipped topping, thawed
3 Butterfinger candy bars (2.1 ounces *each*), coarsely crushed

Prepare and bake cake according to package directions, using a greased 13-in. x 9-in. x 2-in. baking pan. Cool on a wire rack for 30 minutes.

Using the end of a wooden spoon handle, poke 12 holes in warm cake. Pour butterscotch topping over cake; cool completely. Spread with whipped topping; sprinkle with candy bars. Refrigerate for at least 2 hours before serving. **Yield:** 12-16 servings.

Caramel Banana Dessert

This dessert leaves plenty of room for imagination. Chocolate sauce can replace the caramel...you can substitute your favorite nut topping...or you can create a mini sundae by serving the bananas along with scoops of ice cream.
—*Carolene Esayenko*
Calgary, Alberta

4 medium firm bananas, sliced
4 to 6 tablespoons caramel ice cream topping
4 to 6 tablespoons chopped pecans
Whipped topping, optional

Place the bananas in individual serving dishes. Top with caramel topping and pecans. Garnish with whipped topping if desired. **Yield:** 4-6 servings.

Pear Bundt Cake

Five simple ingredients are all I need to fix this lovely light dessert. Tiny bits of pear provide sweetness to the moist slices. —*Veronica Ross*
Columbia Heights, Minnesota

 Uses less fat, sugar or salt. Includes Nutritional Analysis and Diabetic Exchanges.

1 can (15-1/4 ounces) pears in light syrup
1 package (18-1/4 ounces) white cake mix
2 egg whites
1 egg
2 teaspoons confectioners' sugar

Drain pears, reserving the syrup; chop pears. Place pears and syrup in a mixing bowl; add dry cake mix, egg whites and egg. Beat on low speed for 30 seconds. Beat on high for 4 minutes.

Coat a 10-in. fluted tube pan with nonstick cooking spray and dust with flour. Add batter. Bake at 350° for 50-55 minutes or until a toothpick inserted near the center comes out clean. Cool for 10 minutes before removing from pan to a wire rack to cool completely. Dust with confectioners' sugar. **Yield:** 16 servings.

Nutritional Analysis: One slice equals 163 calories, 4 g fat (1 g saturated fat), 13 mg cholesterol, 230 mg sodium, 30 g carbohydrate, 1 g fiber, 2 g protein. **Diabetic Exchanges:** 1 starch, 1 fruit, 1 fat.

Raspberry Sorbet

With an abundant crop of fresh raspberries from the backyard, it's no wonder I rely on this sorbet in the summer months for a no-fuss frozen dessert. This treat is popular whenever I serve it.
—*Karin Bailey, Golden, Colorado*

1/4 cup plus 1-1/2 teaspoons lemon juice
3-3/4 cups unsweetened raspberries
2-1/4 cups confectioners' sugar

In a blender or food processor, combine all ingredients; cover and process until smooth. Pour into six dessert dishes. Cover and freeze for 1 hour or until set. Remove from the freezer 15 minutes before serving. **Yield:** 6 servings.

Eggnog Pudding

For a festive dessert in a hurry, I jazz up instant pudding mix to create Eggnog Pudding. Anyone who likes eggnog loves this creamy concoction—it tastes like the real thing. This recipe is easy to double and serve in a no-fuss graham cracker crust.　　*—Kim Jorgensen, Coulee City, Washington*

✓ **Uses less fat, sugar or salt. Includes Nutritional Analysis and Diabetic Exchanges.**

   2 cups cold milk
   1 package (3.4 ounces) instant vanilla pudding mix
1/2 teaspoon ground nutmeg
1/4 teaspoon rum extract
Additional ground nutmeg, optional

In a bowl, combine the first four ingredients. Beat for 2 minutes. Spoon into individual dishes. Sprinkle with nutmeg if desired. **Yield:** 4 servings.

Nutritional Analysis: One 1/2-cup serving (prepared with sugar-free pudding and fat-free milk) equals 117 calories, 328 mg sodium, trace cholesterol, 23 g carbohydrate, 7 g protein, trace fat. **Diabetic Exchanges:** 1 starch, 1/2 skim milk.

Chocolate Caramel Cupcakes

A few baking staples are all you need to throw together these chewy delights. Boxed cake mix and a can of frosting make them fast, but caramel, walnuts and chocolate chips tucked inside make them memorable. We like them with ice cream.
　　—Bev Spain, Bellville, Ohio

   1 package (18-1/4 ounces) chocolate cake mix
  24 caramels
3/4 cup semisweet chocolate chips
   1 cup chopped walnuts
Chocolate frosting
Additional walnuts, optional

Prepare cake batter according to package directions. Fill 24 greased or paper-lined muffin cups one-third full; set remaining batter aside. Bake at 350° for 7-8 minutes or until top of cupcake appears set.

Gently press a caramel into each cupcake; sprinkle with chocolate chips and walnuts. Top with remaining batter. Bake 15-20 minutes longer or until a toothpick inserted near the center of cake comes out clean. Cool for 5 minutes; remove from pans to wire racks to cool completely. Frost with chocolate frosting. Sprinkle with additional nuts if desired. **Yield:** 2 dozen.

Editor's Note: This recipe was tested with Betty Crocker cake mix.

General Recipe Index

This handy index lists every recipe by food category, major ingredient and/or cooking method, so you can easily locate recipes to suit your needs.

✓ Recipe includes Nutritional Analysis and Diabetic Exchanges

Alphabetical Index

This handy index lists every recipe in alphabetical order so you can easily find your favorite recipes.

✓ Recipe includes Nutritional Analysis and Diabetic Exchanges

CECIL
ESSENTIALS
OF
MEDICINE

EDITORS

THOMAS E. ANDREOLI, M.D.

The Nolan Chair in Internal Medicine
Professor and Chairman
Department of Internal Medicine
University of Arkansas for Medical Sciences
Little Rock;
Chief of Medicine, University Hospital
Little Rock, Arkansas

J. CLAUDE BENNETT, M.D.

Spencer Professor of Medical Science and
Chairman, Department of Medicine
University of Alabama School of Medicine
University of Alabama at Birmingham;
Physician-in-Chief, University of Alabama Hospital
Birmingham, Alabama

CHARLES C.J. CARPENTER, M.D.

Professor of Medicine
Brown University, Providence;
Physician-in-Chief, The Miriam Hospital
Providence, Rhode Island

FRED PLUM, M.D.

Anne Parrish Titzell Professor and Chairman
Department of Neurology
Cornell University Medical College
New York;
Neurologist-in-Chief
The New York Hospital-Cornell Medical Center
New York, New York

LLOYD H. SMITH, Jr., M.D.

Professor of Medicine and Associate Dean
University of California, San Francisco
School of Medicine
San Francisco, California

THIRD EDITION

CECIL
ESSENTIALS
OF
MEDICINE

THOMAS E. ANDREOLI

J. CLAUDE BENNETT

CHARLES C. J. CARPENTER

FRED PLUM

LLOYD H. SMITH, Jr.

W.B. SAUNDERS COMPANY
A Division of Harcourt Brace & Company
Philadelphia, London, Toronto, Montreal, Sydney, Tokyo

W.B. SAUNDERS COMPANY
A Division of Harcourt Brace & Company

The Curtis Center
Independence Square West
Philadelphia, Pennsylvania 19106

Library of Congress Cataloging-in-Publication Data

Cecil essentials of medicine/Thomas E. Andreoli . . . [et al.]. — 3rd ed.
    p.   cm.
    Includes bibliographical references and index.
    ISBN 0-7216-3272-6
    1. Internal medicine.   I. Cecil, Russell L. (Russell La Fayette),
1881–1965.   II. Andreoli, Thomas E.
    [DNLM: 1. Medicine.   WB 100 C3882]
  RC46.C42   1993
  616 — dc20
  DNLM/DLC   92-22928

Cecil Essentials of Medicine

ISBN 0-7216-3272-6

International
Edition:
ISBN 0-7216-4812-6

Printed in the United States of America.

Last digit is the print number: 9   8   7   6   5   4

CONTRIBUTORS

CARDIOVASCULAR DISEASES

WILLIAM M. MILES, M.D.
Associate Professor of Medicine, Indiana University School of Medicine, Indianapolis. Research Associate, Krannert Institute of Cardiology, Indianapolis, Indiana.

DOUGLAS P. ZIPES, M.D.
Professor of Medicine, Indiana University School of Medicine, Indianapolis. Attending Physician, Indiana University Hospital, Wishard Memorial Hospital, and Roudebush Veterans Administration Hospital, Indianapolis, Indiana.

RESPIRATORY DISEASES

DAVID R. DANTZKER, M.D.
Professor of Medicine, Albert Einstein College of Medicine, Bronx, New York. Chairman, Department of Medicine, Long Island Jewish Medical Center, New Hyde Park, New York.

HARLY E. GREENBERG, M.D.
Assistant Professor of Medicine, Albert Einstein College of Medicine, Bronx, New York. Attending Physician, Division of Pulmonary and Critical Care Medicine, Long Island Jewish Medical Center, New Hyde Park, New York.

SEYMOUR I. HUBERFELD, M.D.
Pulmonary Fellow, Long Island Jewish Medical Center, New Hyde Park, New York.

RENAL DISEASE

THOMAS E. ANDREOLI, M.D.
The Nolan Chair in Internal Medicine, Professor and Chairman, Department of Internal Medicine, University of Arkansas for Medical Sciences, Little Rock. Chief of Medicine, University Hospital; Staff Physician, Department of Veterans Affairs Medical Center, Little Rock, Arkansas.

GEORGE V. EVANOFF, M.D.
Assistant Professor of Internal Medicine, University of Arkansas for Medical Sciences, Little Rock. Staff Physician, University Hospital and Department of Veterans Affairs Medical Center, Little Rock, Arkansas.

BEVERLEY L. KETEL, M.D.
Assistant Professor, Department of Surgery, University of Arkansas for Medical Sciences, Little Rock. Staff Physician, University Hospital, Little Rock, Arkansas.

SUDHIR V. SHAH, M.D.

Professor of Internal Medicine and Director, Division of Nephrology, University of Arkansas for Medical Sciences, Little Rock. Chief of Renal Medicine, Department of Veterans Affairs Medical Center, Little Rock, Arkansas.

PATRICK D. WALKER, M.D.

Professor of Pathology, University of Arkansas for Medical Sciences, Little Rock. Staff Physician, University Hospital and Department of Veterans Affairs Medical Center, Little Rock, Arkansas.

GASTROINTESTINAL DISEASE

STEPHEN W. LACEY, M.D.

Assistant Professor of Internal Medicine, Division of Gastroenterology, University of Texas Southwestern Medical Center, Dallas. Staff Physician, Parkland Memorial Medical Center, Dallas, Texas.

JOEL E. RICHTER, M.D.

Professor of Medicine and Director of Clinical Research, Division of Gastroenterology, University of Alabama School of Medicine, University of Alabama at Birmingham, Birmingham, Alabama.

C. MEL WILCOX, M.D.

Assistant Professor of Medicine, Emory University School of Medicine, Atlanta. Chief, Gastroenterology and Endoscopy, Grady Memorial Hospital, Atlanta, Georgia.

DISEASES OF THE LIVER AND BILIARY SYSTEM

NATHAN M. BASS, M.D., Ph.D.

Associate Professor of Medicine, University of California, San Francisco, School of Medicine. Attending Physician, University of California, San Francisco, Hospitals and Clinics, San Francisco, California.

REBECCA W. VAN DYKE, M.D.

Associate Professor at Medicine, University of Michigan Medical School, Ann Arbor. Attending Physician, University of Michigan Hospitals and Clinics, Ann Arbor, Michigan.

HEMATOLOGY

BABETTE B. WEKSLER, M.D.

Professor of Medicine, Department of Medicine, Division of Hematology/Oncology, Cornell University Medical College, New York. Attending Physician, The New York Hospital–Cornell Medical Center, New York, New York.

ONCOLOGY

JEFFREY TEPLER, M.D.

Clinical Assistant Professor, Cornell University Medical College, New York. Assistant Attending Physician, The New York Hospital-Cornell Medical Center, New York, New York.

ANNE MOORE, M.D.

Associate Professor of Clinical Medicine, Cornell University Medical College, New York. Associate Attending Physician, The New York Hospital–Cornell Medical Center, New York, New York.

METABOLIC DISEASES

PETER N. HERBERT, M.D.
Professor of Medicine, Yale University, New Haven. Physician-in-Chief, Hospital of St. Raphael, New Haven, Connecticut.

ENDOCRINE DISEASES

KENNETH R. FEINGOLD, M.D.
Professor of Medicine, University of California, San Francisco, School of Medicine. Chief, Endocrine-Metabolism Clinic, Veterans Administration Medical Center, San Francisco, California.

LAURENCE A. GAVIN, M.D.
Professor of Medicine, University of California, San Francisco, School of Medicine. Attending Physician, University of California, San Francisco, Hospitals and Clinics, San Francisco, California.

MORRIS SCHAMBELAN, M.D.
Professor of Medicine, University of California, San Francisco, School of Medicine. Chief, Division of Endocrinology and Program Director, General Clinical Research Center, San Francisco General Hospital, San Francisco, California.

ELDON SCHRIOCK, M.D.
Assistant Clinical Professor, University of California, San Francisco, School of Medicine. Attending Physician, University of California, San Francisco, Hospitals and Clinics, San Francisco, California.

ANTHONY SEBASTIAN, M.D.
Professor of Medicine, University of California, San Francisco, School of Medicine. Co-Director, General Clinical Research Center, Moffitt-Long Hospital, San Francisco, California.

JEFFREY L. STERN, M.D.
Associate Professor of Obstetrics, Gynecology, and Reproductive Medicine; Director, Division of Gynecologic Oncology, University of California, San Francisco, School of Medicine. Attending Physician, University of California, San Francisco, Hospitals and Clinics, San Francisco, California.

DISEASES OF BONE AND BONE MINERAL METABOLISM

JOEL S. FINKELSTEIN, M.D.
Assistant Professor of Medicine, Harvard Medical School, Boston. Assistant in Medicine, Massachusetts General Hospital, Boston, Massachusetts.

BRUCE HOWARD MITLAK, M.D.
Instructor in Medicine, Harvard Medical School, Boston. Clinical Assistant in Medicine, Massachusetts General Hospital, and Medical Consultant, Massachusetts Eye and Ear Infirmary, Boston, Massachusetts.

DAVID M. SLOVIK, M.D.

Assistant Professor of Medicine, Harvard Medical School, Boston. Director of Endocrinology, Spaulding Rehabilitation Hospital; Clinical Associate, Endocrine Unit, Massachusetts General Hospital, Boston, Massachusetts.

MUSCULOSKELETAL AND CONNECTIVE TISSUE DISEASES

J. CLAUDE BENNETT, M.D.

Spencer Professor of Medical Science and Chairman, Department of Medicine, University of Alabama School of Medicine, University of Alabama at Birmingham. Physician-in-Chief, University of Alabama Hospitals, Birmingham, Alabama.

LARRY W. MORELAND, M.D.

Assistant Professor of Medicine, Division of Clinical Immunology and Rheumatology, University of Alabama School of Medicine, University of Alabama at Birmingham. Attending Physician, University of Alabama Hospitals, Birmingham, Alabama.

INFECTIOUS DISEASES

CHARLES C. J. CARPENTER, M.D.

Professor of Medicine, Brown University, Providence. Physician-in-Chief, The Miriam Hospital, Providence, Rhode Island.

JERROLD J. ELLNER, M.D.

Professor of Medicine, Case Western Reserve University, School of Medicine, Cleveland. Chief, Infectious Diseases, University Hospitals of Cleveland, Cleveland, Ohio.

MICHAEL M. LEDERMAN, M.D.

Associate Professor of Medicine, Case Western Reserve University School of Medicine, Cleveland. Attending Physician, University Hospitals of Cleveland, Cleveland, Ohio.

KENNETH H. MAYER, M.D.

Associate Professor of Medicine and Community Health, Brown University; Director, Brown University AIDS Program, Providence. Chief Infectious Disease Division, Memorial Hospital of Rhode Island, Pawtucket, Rhode Island.

G. RICHARD OLDS, M.D.

Associate Professor of Medicine, Brown University; Director, International Health Institute, Brown University, Providence, Rhode Island. Director, Division of Geographic Medicine, The Miriam Hospital, Providence, Rhode Island.

NEUROLOGIC DISEASES

FRED PLUM, M.D.

Anne Parrish Titzell Professor and Chairman, Department of Neurology, Cornell University Medical College, New York. Neurologist-in-Chief, The New York Hospital–Cornell Medical Center, New York, New York.

JEROME B. POSNER, M.D.

Professor of Neurology, Cornell University Medical College; George C. Cotzias Chair, Memorial Sloan-Kettering Cancer Center, New York. Attending Neurologist, Memorial Sloan-Kettering Cancer Center, New York, New York.

THE AGING PATIENT

DAVID A. LIPSCHITZ, M.D., Ph.D.

Professor of Internal Medicine, Physiology, and Biophysics, University of Arkansas for Medical Sciences, Little Rock. Director, Geriatric Research, Education, and Clinical Center (GRECC), Department of Veterans Affairs Medical Center; Director, Division on Aging, University of Arkansas for Medical Sciences, Little Rock, Arkansas.

DENNIS H. SULLIVAN, M.D.

Assistant Professor of Internal Medicine, University of Arkansas for Medical Sciences, Little Rock. Staff Physician, Geriatric Research, Education, and Clinical Center (GRECC), Department of Veterans Affairs Medical Center, Little Rock, Arkansas.

PREFACE

The Third Edition of CECIL ESSENTIALS OF MEDICINE continues its efforts to provide a readable and concise yet comprehensive textbook that sets forth the "essential" elements required to conduct a biologically effective practice of internal medicine coupled with the compassionate approach that is indispensable to healing. The Third Edition of ESSENTIALS directs its contents to all those who need a thorough account of internal medicine's current knowledge base—physiologic, biochemical, pathophysiologic, clinical, and therapeutic. The text especially directs its contents to the needs of undergraduate medical students and early-stage house officers. Equally, however, practitioners in other specialties and general medicine have found that previous editions of ESSENTIALS provided a succinct account of internal medicine's advances in diagnosis and overall therapy. ESSENTIALS therefore serves as a complementary text to the more encyclopedic CECIL TEXTBOOK OF MEDICINE.

The Third Edition of ESSENTIALS is enlarged in scope, with respect to the first two editions, but retains the convenient size and easy portability of previous editions. This edition of ESSENTIALS contains the original twelve major sections included in the first two editions. Each section has been thoroughly revised, and several have been entirely rewritten, including those on renal diseases, diseases of bone and mineral metabolism, infectious diseases (particularly in the areas dealing with host defense mechanisms and with AIDS), and musculoskeletal and connective tissue diseases. In addition, the table of contents has been expanded to include major text headings of particular significance, such as diseases and diagnostic or therapeutic approaches.

The Third Edition of ESSENTIALS also contains two new features. A specific section has been devoted to the disorders and care of aging persons. There is also an appendix providing normal values for commonly used laboratory determinations described both in conventional units and in Standard International Units, together with the necessary conversion factors relating the two classifications.

Many persons have contributed to this edition of ESSENTIALS. We express our thanks to Mr. Leslie E. Hoeltzel, Manager, Developmental Editors; to Ms. Darlene D. Pedersen, Senior Vice-President and Editorial Director, Book Division; and to Ms. Lorraine Kilmer, Manager of Editorial/Design/Production, all of the W. B. Saunders Company, for their customarily invaluable aid in the design and preparation of the Third Edition of ESSENTIALS. We express our sincere gratitude to Mr. John Dyson, Senior Medical Editor Emeritus of the W. B. Saunders Company, for his aid and guidance in the preparation of the first two editions of ESSENTIALS, as well as in the initial planning for the

Third Edition. We also thank our able secretarial staffs, Ms. Clementine M. Whitman (Little Rock); Ms. Dvora Aksler Konstant (Birmingham); Ms. Barbara S. Ryan (Providence); Ms. Maureen P. O'Connor (New York); and Ms. Judith A. Serrell (San Francisco).

THOMAS E. ANDREOLI
J. CLAUDE BENNETT
CHARLES C. J. CARPENTER
FRED PLUM
LLOYD H. SMITH, JR.

CONTENTS

VII ONCOLOGY

VIII METABOLIC DISEASES

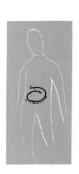

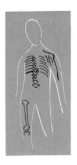

X DISEASES OF BONE AND BONE MINERAL METABOLISM

XI MUSCULOSKELETAL AND CONNECTIVE TISSUE DISEASES

XIV   THE AGING PATIENT

SECTION I

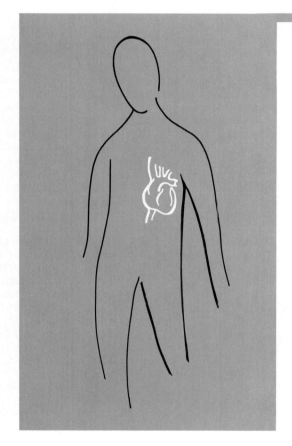

CARDIOVASCULAR DISEASES

1 STRUCTURE AND FUNCTION OF THE NORMAL HEART AND BLOOD VESSELS

GROSS ANATOMY

Two relatively thin-walled upper chambers, the right and left atria, and two thicker-walled lower chambers, the right and left ventricles, compose the heart (Fig. 1–1). The left ventricle has walls thicker than those of the right ventricle because of the considerably higher systemic arterial pressure into which it pumps blood. The interventricular septum separates the two ventricles. The lower and much larger part of the interventricular septum is termed the muscular interventricular septum and is composed of muscle the same thickness as that of the left ventricular free wall. The uppermost portion of the septum, termed the membranous interventricular septum, also forms a portion of the right atrial wall.

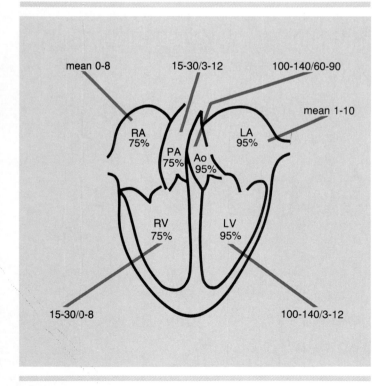

FIGURE 1–1. Orientation of the cardiac chambers and great vessels with normal intracardiac pressures (mm Hg) and O₂ saturations (%).

The tricuspid valve is a three-leaflet structure. The mitral valve has only two leaflets, a large anteromedial and a small posterolateral leaflet. A fibrous ring called the annulus supports each valve and forms a portion of the fibrous structural skeleton of the heart. Chords of fibrous tissue, the chordae tendineae, extend from the ventricular surfaces of both atrioventricular (AV) valves and attach to the papillary muscles. Papillary muscles are bundles of cardiac muscle (myocardium) arising from the interior of the ventricular walls. As the ventricles contract, the papillary muscles also contract, pulling taut the chordae tendineae and preventing the AV valves from prolapsing back into the atria and leaking.

A somewhat different type of valve, the semilunar valve, separates the ventricles from their respective outflow tracts. The pulmonic valve is composed of three fibrous leaflets or cusps that are forced open against the walls of the pulmonary artery during ventricular ejection of blood but fall back into the pulmonary outflow tract during diastole, their free edges coapting to prevent blood from returning into the right ventricle. The aortic valve is a thicker but similar three-cusp structure. The aortic wall behind each aortic valve cusp bulges outward, forming three structures known as sinuses of Valsalva. The two most anterior aortic cusps are known as the left and right coronary cusps because of the origins of the left and right coronary arteries from the respective sinuses of Valsalva, and the remaining posterior cusp is known as the noncoronary cusp.

The pericardium, a double-layered fibrous structure, encloses the heart. The visceral layer is immediately adjacent to the heart and forms part of the epicardium (outer layer) of the heart. The parietal layer is exterior to the heart and is separated from the visceral layer by a thin film of lubricating fluid (10 to 20 ml total) that allows the heart to move freely within the pericardial sac.

Venous blood returning from the body enters the right atrium through the inferior vena cava from below and the superior vena cava from above (Fig. 1–2). Most venous blood returning from the coronary circulation enters the right atrium via the coronary sinus. Blood from these three sources mixes and enters the right ventricle during diastole, when the tricuspid valve is open. The right ventricle subsequently contracts (systole), closing the tricuspid valve to prevent retrograde blood flow, and ejects blood through the pulmonic valve into the pulmonary artery. The pulmonary artery bifurcates into left and right branches that travel to the left and right lungs. The pulmonary artery has thinner walls than the aorta, and pulmonary arterial pressure is normally much less than aortic pressure. The pulmonary artery progressively divides into smaller and smaller arteries, arterioles, and eventually capillaries, where carbon dioxide is exchanged for oxygen via the pulmonary alveoli. The capillaries lead to pulmonary veins that coalesce to form the four larger pulmonary veins entering the left atrium posteriorly. Oxygenated blood from the pulmonary veins passes from the left atrium through the mitral valve to the left ventricle, which ejects blood during systole across the aortic valve into the aorta. The aorta divides into branches that deliver blood to the entire body. The division continues to form smaller arteries, arterioles, and eventually capillaries that deliver oxygen (O_2) and metabolic substrates to the tissues in exchange for carbon dioxide (CO_2) and other waste products. Blood collected from the peripheral capillaries is returned to the right atrium via the venous system.

The right and left coronary arteries course over the epicardial surface of the heart to distribute blood to the myocardium (Fig. 1–3). The left main coronary artery bifurcates within a few centimeters of its origin into two major vessels. The left anterior descending coronary artery proceeds anteriorly in the anterior interventricular groove (between both ventricles) toward the apex of the heart, supplying the anterior free wall of the left ventricle and the anterior two thirds of the septum. The circumflex coronary artery travels posteriorly in the AV groove (between left atrium and ventricle) and usually supplies a portion of the posterolateral surface of the heart. The right coronary artery courses in the right AV groove (between right atrium and ventricle) and distributes several branches to the right ventricle before reaching the left ventricle, where the AV grooves meet the posterior interventricular groove (the "crux" of the heart). In 90 per cent of patients the right coronary artery reaches the crux of the heart and supplies the branches to the AV node and the inferobasal third of the septum (posterior descending artery). This pattern is termed "right dominant distribution" (even though the left coronary artery supplies the majority of the coronary circulation). In approximately 10 per cent of patients, a relatively large circumflex coronary artery reaches the crux of the heart and gives rise to the posterior descending coronary artery and the branch to the AV node. This situation is termed "left dominant," and the diminutive right coronary artery supplies only the right ventricle. Blood is supplied to the sinus node via a branch of the right coronary artery (55 per cent of cases) or the circumflex coronary artery (45 per cent). Most of the venous network of the heart coalesces to form the coronary sinus. A minority of the right ventricular and atrial venous drainage occurs via much smaller

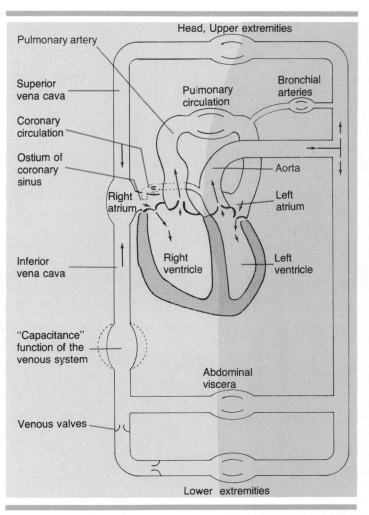

FIGURE 1–2. Schematic representation of the systemic and pulmonary circulatory systems. The venous system contains the greatest amount of blood at any one time and is highly distensible, accommodating a wide range of blood volumes (high capacitance).

anterior cardiac veins and tiny thebesian veins, most of which drain directly into the right atrium.

ELECTRICAL CONDUCTION SYSTEM
(Fig. 1–4)

Cardiac electrical impulses originate in the sinus node, a spindle-shaped structure 10 to 20 mm long located near the junction of the superior vena cava and the right atrium. Even though various specialized tissues have been postulated to conduct the electrical impulse from the sinus node to the AV node, electrical transmission is probably cell to cell via working atrial muscle. The AV node provides the only normal conduction pathway between the atria and the ventricles. It is

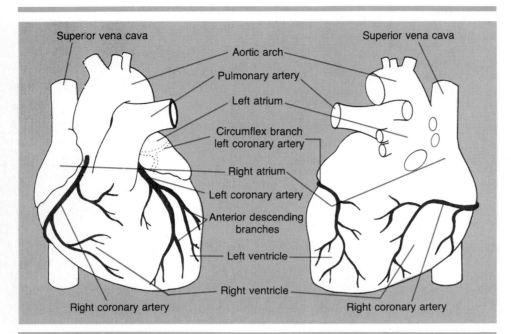

FIGURE 1–3. Major coronary arteries and their branches.

situated just beneath the right atrial endocardium above the insertion of the septal leaflet of the tricuspid valve and anterior to the ostium of the coronary sinus. After conduction delay in the AV node, the electrical impulse travels to the His bundle, which descends posteriorly along the membranous interventricular septum to the top of the muscular septum. The His bundle gives rise to the right and left bundle branches. The right bundle branch is a single group of fibers that travels down the right ventricular side of the muscular interventricular septum. The left bundle branch is a larger, less discrete array of conducting fibers located on the left side of the interventricular septum. The left bundle branch may divide into two somewhat distinct pathways that travel toward the anterolateral (left anterior fascicle) and posteromedial (left posterior fascicle) papillary muscles. The left posterior fascicle is larger and more diffuse than the anterior fascicle and usually has a more reliable vascular supply than either the left anterior fascicle or the right bundle branch. The left and right bundle branches progressively divide into tiny Purkinje fibers that arborize and finally make intimate contact with ventricular muscle tissue.

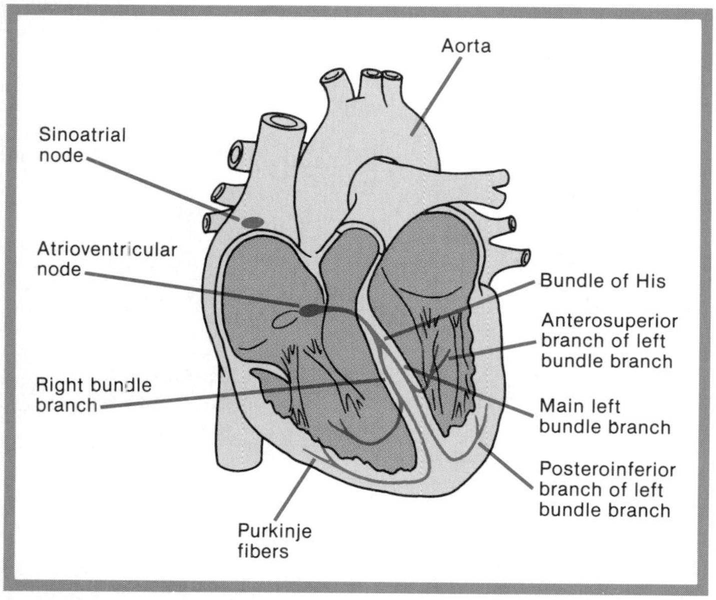

MICROSCOPIC ANATOMY

In general, two functional cell types are present in cardiac tissue: those responsible for electrical impulse generation and transmission and those responsible for mechanical contraction. Nodal cells are thought to be the source of normal impulse formation in the sinus node and are richly innervated with adrenergic and cholinergic nerve fibers. Like the sinus node, the AV node and His bundle regions are innervated with a rich supply of cholinergic and adrenergic fibers. Purkinje cells are large clear cells found in the His bundle, bundle branches, and their arborizations. They have particularly well developed end-to-end connections that may facilitate rapid longitudinal conduction.

Atrial and ventricular myocardial cells, the con-

FIGURE 1–4. Schematic representation of the cardiac conduction system.

tractile cells of the heart, contain numerous cross-banded bundles termed myofibrils that traverse the length of the fiber. Myofibrils are composed of longitudinally repeating sarcomeres (Fig. 1–5). Thick filaments composed of myosin constitute the A band, whereas thin filaments composed primarily of actin extend from the Z line through the I band into the A band, ending at the edges of the central H zone, which is the central area of the A band where thin filaments are absent. Thick and thin filaments overlap in the A band, and interaction between the thick and thin filaments provides the force for contraction of the heart.

The surface membrane of the cell is termed the sarcolemma, and adjacent myocardial cells are connected end to end by a thickened portion of the sarcolemma termed the intercalated disc. Near the Z lines of the sarcolemma are wide invaginations called the T system that traverse the cell. Not continuous with the T system is the sarcoplasmic reticulum that surrounds each myofibril and participates in the excitation of the muscle. When the sarcolemma is depolarized electrically, the impulse conducts through the T system to cause calcium release from the sarcoplasmic reticulum and therefore activates the myofibrils to contract. The thick fibers in the myofibrils are composed of myosin molecules that have the ability to split ATP and interact with the thin actin filaments when activated by calcium. Regulatory proteins, troponin and tropomyosin, inhibit the interaction of actin and myosin unless a calcium-troponin complex is present, which then allows the actin-myosin interaction to proceed. The sarcolemma possesses the ability to control the flux of various ions (especially sodium, potassium, and calcium) into and out of the cell via specific ionic channels located within the membrane. The selective permeability of the membrane establishes ionic gradients and the electrical forces that create and maintain the resting transmembrane potential and generate the action potential (see Chapter 8).

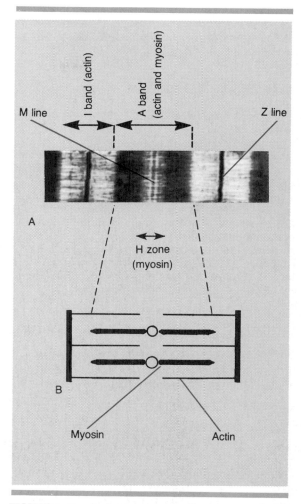

FIGURE 1–5. A, A sarcomere as it appears under the electron microscope. B, Schematic of the location and interaction of actin and myosin (see text).

CARDIAC DEVELOPMENT

Congenital heart disease results from altered embryonic development or failure of the rudimentary portion of a structure ever to be formed. Abnormal development of one structure in turn may hinder the development of another portion of the circulatory system (e.g., abnormal development of the mitral valve may lead to abnormal formation of the left ventricle).

The fetal circulation essentially places the pulmonary and systemic systems in parallel rather than in series as in the adult. Oxygenated blood from the umbilical vein passes into the portal venous system and subsequently into the inferior vena cava and is shunted preferentially across the patent foramen ovale to the left side of the heart to perfuse the coronary arteries, head, and upper trunk. Blood returning from the upper portions of the body arrives at the right atrium via the superior vena cava, and most proceeds through the tricuspid valve to the right ventricle and pulmonary artery. However, only a small proportion of this blood goes into the pulmonary arterial tree; most is shunted via the patent ductus arteriosus to the descending aorta. Note that many congenital lesions that cause intracardiac shunts (e.g., tetralogy of Fallot) or markedly abnormal cardiac outflow (e.g., transposition of the great arteries) would not cause any difficulty during fetal development.

At birth the pulmonary vascular resistance decreases markedly owing to the inflation of the lungs and the increase in O_2 tension to which the pulmonary vessels are exposed. Systemic vascular resistance rises when the umbilical cord is clamped, removing the low-resistance placental circulation. Left atrial pressure rises, which in turn closes the foramen ovale. The increase in arterial Po_2, along with alterations in prostaglandins, causes the ductus arteriosus to close functionally within 10 to 15 hours. Many congenital heart lesions may not become apparent until cyanosis develops after closure of the foramen ovale or ductus arteriosus.

MYOCARDIAL METABOLISM

The heart uses ATP, created by metabolism of carbohydrates or fatty acids, to derive energy for contraction and electrical activity. Energy for electrical activity is minimal compared with that required for contraction. Stored energy reserves are scarce, and the heart must continually have a source of energy in order to function. The principal oxidative substrate for ATP production is fatty acid, but if it is not available, a variety of carbohydrates can be used. Myocardial metabolism is aerobic, and a constant supply of O_2 must be available. The heart, unlike skeletal muscle, is unable to acquire an "O_2 debt" because of its inability to utilize anaerobic metabolism.

CIRCULATORY PHYSIOLOGY

The interaction between myosin and actin, coupled with ATP produced by oxidative phosphorylation, is thought to be the basis for the contraction

TABLE 1–1. FACTORS AFFECTING CARDIAC PERFORMANCE

Preload (left ventricular diastolic volume)	Total blood volume
	Venous tone (sympathetic tone)
	Body position
	Intrathoracic and intrapericardial pressure
	Atrial contraction
	Pumping action of skeletal muscle
Afterload (impedance against which the left ventricle must eject blood)	Peripheral vascular resistance
	Left ventricular volume (preload, wall tension)
	Physical characteristics of the arterial tree (e.g., elasticity of vessels or presence of outflow obstruction)
Contractility (cardiac performance independent of preload or afterload)	Sympathetic nerve impulses ⎫
	Circulating catecholamines ⎪ increased
	Digitalis, calcium, other inotropic agents ⎬ contractility
	Increased heart rate or postextrasystolic augmentation ⎭
	Anoxia, acidosis ⎫
	Pharmacologic depression ⎪ decreased
	Loss of myocardium ⎬ contractility
	Intrinsic depression ⎭
Heart Rate	Autonomic nervous system
	Temperature, metabolic rate

of each myofibril and therefore the contraction of the whole muscle. Each myofibril exhibits a property called contractility (or inotropic state) that represents the ability of the fiber to develop contractile force. The force exhibited by the fiber is influenced not only by its contractile state but also by its initial length, or preload, according to the Starling curve. This concept can be expanded from the single fiber to describe the function of the entire ventricle. Thus, the abscissa, formerly preload or fiber length, becomes left ventricular filling pressure or volume (i.e., the amount of stretch on the myocardial fibers in diastole); and the ordinate, formerly tension, becomes stroke volume or stroke work (i.e., the ability of the heart to generate tension). Note that as diastolic pressure increases, the normal heart is able to increase its stroke volume, up to a point. This relationship is referred to as a ventricular function curve and, given identical states of contractility and afterload (see below), defines the amount of work that a heart is able to perform. Several factors determine left ventricular filling pressure (Table 1–1).

The term afterload describes the "impedance" or resistance against which the heart must contract. Like preload, afterload also can refer either to a single myofibril or to the heart as a whole. The afterload is approximated by the arterial pressure, the major determinant of the impedance to left ventricular contraction. In the intact heart, the afterload determines the amount of blood the heart can pump given a fixed preload and fixed state of contractility; that is, the higher the workload against which the heart must function, the less blood it can eject, and vice versa. Therefore, the ventricular function curve is shifted up and to the left with decreasing afterload and down and to the right with increasing afterload. Shifts in ventricular function with changes in afterload are minimal in normal ventricles but prominent in failing ventricles.

Heart rate is another determinant of cardiac performance. Even though an increased demand for cardiac output increases contractility and stroke volume via sympathetic nervous system activation, the most important response to sympathetic stimulation serving to increase cardiac output is the rise in heart rate (cardiac output = stroke volume × heart rate). A decrease in the cardiac output or blood pressure increases sympathetic and decreases parasympathetic discharge via baroreceptor mechanisms to increase heart rate. Likewise, an elevated blood pressure activates the carotid baroreceptors, augments vagal activity, and slows the heart rate.

Four phases of the cardiac cycle can be identified upon initiation of ventricular myocardial contraction (Fig. 1–6). (1) During "isovolumic contraction," the intramyocardial pressure rises with no ejection of blood or change in ventricular volume. (2) When left ventricular pressure reaches that of the aorta, the aortic valve opens and blood is ejected from the contracting ventricle. (3) As the ventricle relaxes and left ventricular pressure decreases, the aortic valve closes, and "isovolumic relaxation" occurs. (4) Upon sufficient decrease in left ventricular pressure, the mitral valve opens and ventricular filling from the atrium occurs. The ventricle fills most rapidly in early diastole and again in late diastole when the atrium contracts. Loss of atrial contraction (e.g., atrial fibrillation or AV dissociation) can impair ventricular filling, especially into a noncompliant ("stiff") ventricle.

Normal intracardiac pressures are shown in Figure 1–1. Atrial pressure curves are composed of the a wave, which is generated by atrial contraction, and the v wave, which is an early diastolic peak caused by filling of the atrium from the peripheral veins. The x descent follows the a wave, and the y descent follows the v wave. A small deflection, the c wave, occurs after the a wave in early systole and probably represents bulging of the tricuspid valve apparatus into the left atrium during early systole. Ventricular pressures are described by a peak systolic pressure and an end-diastolic pressure, which is the ventricular pressure immediately before the onset of systole. Note that the minimum left ventricular pressure occurs in early diastole. Aortic and pulmonary artery pressures are represented by a peak systolic and a minimum diastolic value.

Cardiac output is a measure of the amount of blood flow in liters per minute. The cardiac index is the cardiac output divided by the body surface area and is normally 2.8 to 4.2 L/min/m². Cardiac output can be measured by either indicator dilution or the Fick technique (see Chapter 3). The pulmonary and systemic vascular resistances are also important parameters of circulatory function. Resistance is defined as the difference in pressure across a capillary bed divided by the flow across that capillary bed, usually the cardiac output: [R = (P₁ − P₂)/flow]. For example, the pulmonary vascular resistance is the difference between the mean pulmonary arterial pressure and mean pulmonary venous pressure, divided by the pulmonary blood flow. Similarly, systemic vascular resistance is the difference between mean arterial pressure and mean right atrial pressure, divided by the systemic cardiac output. Note that an increase in arterial pressure may occur without necessarily causing an increase in vascular resistance. For example, if both pulmonary arterial and venous pressures are elevated to the same degree, pulmonary vascular resistance is unchanged; if pulmonary blood flow and pulmonary arterial pressure increase while pulmonary venous pressure remains the same, resistance is unchanged.

The most widely used parameter for quantitating overall ventricular function is the ejection fraction, defined as the diastolic volume minus the systolic volume (stroke volume), divided by the diastolic volume: [(DV − SV)/DV]. These volumes may be estimated from either invasive (e.g., left ventriculography) or noninvasive (e.g., echocardiography or radionuclide ventriculography) tests. The ejection fraction may be a useful gross evaluation of ventricular function, but there are situations (e.g., when a large left ventricular aneurysm

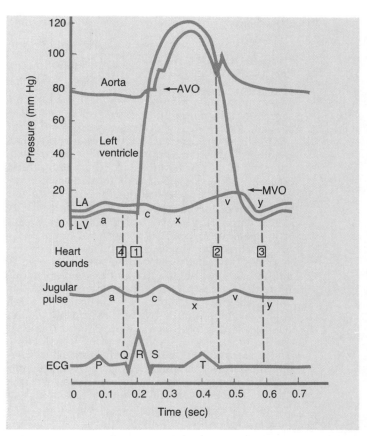

FIGURE 1–6. Simultaneous electrocardiogram (ECG), pressures obtained from the left atrium, left ventricle, and aorta, and the jugular pulse during one cardiac cycle. For simplification, right-sided heart pressures have been omitted. Normal right atrial pressure closely parallels that of the left atrium, and right ventricular and pulmonary artery pressures time closely with their corresponding left-sided heart counterparts, being reduced only in magnitude. The normal mitral and aortic valve closure precedes tricuspid and pulmonic closure, respectively, whereas valve opening reverses this order. The jugular venous pulse lags behind the right atrial pressure.

During the course of one cardiac cycle, note that the electrical events (ECG) initiate and therefore precede the mechanical (pressure) events and that the latter precede the auscultatory events (heart sounds) they themselves produce. Shortly after the P wave, the atria contract to produce the a wave; a fourth heart sound may succeed the latter. The QRS complex initiates ventricular systole, followed shortly by left ventricular contraction and the rapid build-up of left ventricular (LV) pressure. Almost immediately LV pressure exceeds left atrial (LA) pressure to close the mitral valve and produces the first heart sounds. When LV pressure exceeds aortic pressure, the aortic valve opens (AVO), and when aortic pressure is once again greater than LV pressure, the aortic valve closes to produce the second heart sound and terminate ventricular ejection. The decreasing LV pressure drops below LA pressure to open the mitral valve (MVO), and a period of rapid ventricular filling commences. During this time a third heart sound may be heard. The jugular pulse is explained under the discussion of the venous pulse.

is present) in which the ejection fraction can give a misleading impression of overall ventricular function.

PHYSIOLOGY OF THE CORONARY CIRCULATION

Three major determinants of myocardial O_2 consumption are contractility, heart rate, and wall tension. Myocardial wall tension is directly proportional to the pressure within the ventricular chamber and the radius of the ventricular chamber (Laplace relationship). The myocardial mass is a determinant of wall tension and therefore myocardial O_2 consumption; the larger the muscle mass, the more O_2 needed.

The coronary vascular bed is able to autoregulate, enabling myocardial O_2 and substrate delivery to equal the demand. Coronary vascular resistance is normally determined by the arterioles and is influenced by neural and metabolic factors. Both the sympathetic and parasympathetic nervous systems innervate the coronary arteries. Alpha receptor stimulation causes vasoconstriction whereas stimulation of the $beta_2$ receptor as well as the vagus (acetylcholine) causes vasodilation. Metabolic factors regulate regional perfusion. Several mediators, including O_2, CO_2, and metabolites such as adenosine, are important; adenosine is a potent coronary vasodilator formed by tissues in response to decreased coronary perfusion and is a critical mediator in coronary autoregulation. However, when coronary perfusion pressure falls to below 60 to 70 mm Hg, the vessels become maximally dilated and flow depends on perfusion pressure alone because capability for further autoregulation is lost. The normal coronary vascular bed has a capacity to increase its blood flow four- to five-fold during maximal exercise. Hemodynamic factors that affect coronary perfusion include arterial pressure (especially diastolic pressure because coronary flow occurs primarily in diastole), the time spent in diastole, and the intraventricular pressure (which exerts tension on the myocardial walls and diminishes coronary flow).

PHYSIOLOGY OF THE SYSTEMIC CIRCULATION

The aortic wall contains elastic fibers that allow it to expand with the expulsion of blood from the left ventricle, somewhat damping the pulse pressure generated and aiding diastolic flow to the coronary arteries with its recoil. The aorta successively branches into smaller and smaller vessels until arterioles, the major determinants of resistance in the systemic circulation, are reached. The arterioles contain a vascular sphincter that modulates blood flow dependent on regional metabolic needs; for example, acidosis and decreased O_2 tension increase regional perfusion, and vice versa. The capillaries consist of a single endothelial cell layer and allow diffusion of O_2, nutrients, CO_2, and waste products. The capillaries lead into the venous system, where blood is eventually delivered back to the right atrium. The flow of blood returning to the heart is aided by the valves in the venous system, which prevent reverse flow, particularly in the larger veins of the legs. The "milking" action of the muscles of the arms and legs and the pressure changes in the thoracic cavity also help to return blood to the heart. The veins have considerably thinner walls than the arteries and can accommodate a larger blood volume under low pressures (capacitance vessels). Vasoconstriction or vasodilation of the venous system can control the amount of blood returning to the heart. More of the total blood volume is located in the venous than in the arterial portion of the circulation. The lymphatic vessels also contribute to the return of fluid from the periphery. The major terminal vessel of the lymphatic system is the thoracic duct, which usually empties into the left brachiocephalic vein.

PHYSIOLOGY OF THE PULMONARY CIRCULATION

The pulmonary circulation has a rich capillary network similar to that of the systemic circulation. The pulmonary alveoli are adjacent to the capillaries, permitting O_2 to diffuse into and CO_2 out of the capillary blood. O_2 is the major mediator of pulmonary autoregulation. In regions where the partial pressure of O_2 is high, pulmonary vasodilation occurs and blood flow is directed preferentially toward well-oxygenated areas of the lung. When the partial pressure of O_2 is low, pulmonary vasoconstriction occurs, preventing the perfusion of areas of the lung that have relatively poor O_2 availability. These vasodilatory effects of O_2 are opposite to those in the systemic circulation. Acidemia potentiates the pulmonary vasoconstrictive effect of hypoxemia, also opposite to its effect on systemic arterioles.

The lungs receive blood through the bronchial arteries as well as the pulmonary arteries (dual blood supply). The bronchial arteries supply arterial blood to the pulmonary tissue and drain into the bronchial veins, some of which drain into the systemic venous bed. Some bronchial veins drain into the pulmonary veins, creating a small physiologic right-to-left shunt.

Pulmonary vascular resistance is normally onetenth that of systemic vascular resistance and accounts for the small pressure gradient required to propel blood across the pulmonary vascular bed. Because the pulmonary vasculature is very distensible (compliant), a relatively large left-to-right intracardiac shunt may exist with only a minimal rise in pulmonary arterial pressure.

CARDIOVASCULAR RESPONSE TO EXERCISE

The heart responds to exercise principally by adrenergic stimulation and vagal withdrawal, which increase heart rate and contractility, and by peripheral circulatory alterations (Table 1–2). The increase in heart rate usually accounts for the majority of the increase in cardiac output. Increased contractility contributes to the rise in cardiac output by increasing the stroke volume. Vessels supplying exercising muscles dilate, whereas the remaining vascular beds vasoconstrict. Isometric and isotonic exercises affect the cardiovascular system somewhat differently. The predominant response to isometric exercise (e.g., weight lifting) is an increase in peripheral vasoconstriction with a subsequent increase in arterial pressure. In contrast, isotonic exercise (e.g., jogging) reduces systemic vascular resistance primarily in exercising muscles, which improves cardiac output. Those who exercise regularly obtain a cardiac training effect, with a lower resting heart rate and a greater capacity to increase cardiac output during exercise.

CARDIOVASCULAR PHYSIOLOGY DURING PREGNANCY

See Chapter 12.

ELECTROPHYSIOLOGY

See Chapter 8.

TABLE 1–2. PHYSIOLOGIC RESPONSES TO EXERCISE

RESPONSE	MECHANISM
↑Heart rate	↑Sympathetic stimulation
	↓Parasympathetic stimulation
↑Stroke volume	
↑Contractility	↑Sympathetic stimulation
↑Venous return	Sympathetic-mediated venoconstriction
	Pumping action of skeletal muscles
	↓Intrathoracic pressure with deep inspirations
	Arteriolar vasodilation in exercising muscle
↓Afterload	Arteriolar vasodilation in exercising muscle (mediated chiefly by local metabolites)
↑Blood pressure	↑Cardiac output
	Vasoconstriction (sympathetic stimulation) of nonexercising vascular beds
↑O$_2$ extraction	Shift in oxyhemoglobin dissociation curve due to local acidosis

REFERENCES

Berne RM, Levy MN: Cardiovascular Physiology. 6th ed. St. Louis, CV Mosby Co, 1991.
Hurst JW, Anderson RH, Becker AE, Wilcox BR: Atlas of the Heart. New York, McGraw-Hill, 1988.

2 EVALUATION OF THE PATIENT WITH CARDIOVASCULAR DISEASE

HISTORY

The history is the most important tool in the evaluation of a patient (Table 2–1). *Chest pain* is a common presenting symptom of cardiovascular disease and must be characterized carefully. Chest pain may be cardiac (myocardial or pericardial) or noncardiac in etiology (Tables 2–2 and 2–3).

Ischemic myocardial pain is a visceral discomfort caused by insufficient oxygen delivery to an area of the heart. A transient oxygen supply/demand mismatch causes angina pectoris, whereas ischemia followed by myocardial necrosis is termed myocardial infarction. Angina pectoris is typically evoked by emotion, exertion, or a heavy meal, but more severe episodes can occur at rest or awaken the patient from sleep. It generally lasts only a few minutes and diminishes after exertion is stopped. When it is due to fixed coronary obstruction, the same degree of activity tends to reliably reproduce the pain. When it is due to coronary arterial spasm (with or without fixed obstruction) or platelet thrombi, the level of activity that causes pain may vary or it may occur at rest. Nitroglycerin typically relieves anginal pain in about 5 minutes. Pain of a prolonged duration (>30 minutes) suggests either myocardial infarction or noncardiac pain. Respiration does not influence ischemic chest pain. The pain of both angina pectoris and myocardial infarction can be

TABLE 2–1. CARDINAL SYMPTOMS OF CARDIAC DISEASE

Chest pain or discomfort
Symptoms of heart failure
Palpitation
Syncope, presyncope

TABLE 2–2. CARDIOVASCULAR CAUSES OF CHEST PAIN

CONDITION	LOCATION	QUALITY	DURATION	AGGRAVATING OR RELIEVING FACTORS	ASSOCIATED SYMPTOMS OR SIGNS
Angina	Retrosternal region; radiates to or occasionally isolated to neck, jaw, epigastrium, shoulder or arms—left common	Pressure, burning, squeezing, heaviness, indigestion	<10 minutes	Aggravated by exercise, cold weather, or emotional stress, or occurs after meals; relieved by rest or nitroglycerin; atypical (Prinzmetal's) angina may be unrelated to activity and caused by coronary artery spasm	S_4, paradoxical split S_2, or murmur of papillary muscle dysfunction during pain
Rest or unstable angina	Same as angina	Same as angina	>10 minutes	Same as angina, with gradually decreasing tolerance for exertion	Same as angina
Myocardial infarction	Substernal, and may radiate like angina	Heaviness, pressure, burning, constriction	Sudden onset, 30 minutes or longer but variable; usually goes away in hours	Unrelieved	Shortness of breath, sweating, weakness, nausea, vomiting, severe anxiety
Pericarditis	Usually begins over sternum or toward cardiac apex and may radiate to neck and down left upper extremity; often more localized than the pain of myocardial ischemia	Sharp, stabbing, knifelike	Lasts many hours to days	Aggravated by deep breathing, rotating chest, or supine position; relieved by sitting up and leaning forward	Pericardial friction rub, cardiac tamponade, pulsus paradoxus
Dissecting aortic aneurysm	Anterior chest; radiates to thoracic area of back; may be abdominal; pain may move as dissection progresses	Excruciating, tearing, knifelike	Sudden onset, lasts for hours	Unrelated to anything	Lower blood pressure in one arm, absent pulses, paralysis, murmur of aortic insufficiency, pulsus paradoxus, myocardial infarction

atypical in some patients and difficult to diagnose. Many patients describe a chest discomfort or fullness that they do not consider pain. Any patient who has chest discomfort provoked by exertion and relieved by rest or chest discomfort similar to the pain of a previous myocardial infarction should be suspected of ischemic myocardial chest pain.

The pain of pericardial inflammation (Table 2–3) may be difficult to differentiate from ischemic pain in a patient with pericarditis following myocardial infarction.

Patients with mitral valve prolapse sometimes present with a chest pain syndrome that may or may not resemble ischemic myocardial pain. The cause of this chest pain is unclear.

Dyspnea is a subjective sensation of shortness of breath and often is a symptom of cardiac disease, especially in patients with congestive heart failure (Table 2–4). When left ventricular failure occurs, left atrial and subsequently pulmonary venous pressures rise. Pulmonary compliance decreases (stiff lungs) and causes a subjective sensation of air hunger before hypoxia, hypercapnia, or low cardiac output occurs. As congestive heart failure worsens, transudative fluid accumulates in the al-

TABLE 2–3. NONCARDIAC CAUSES OF CHEST PAIN

CONDITION	LOCATION	QUALITY	DURATION	AGGRAVATING OR RELIEVING FACTORS	ASSOCIATED SYMPTOMS OR SIGNS
Pulmonary embolism (chest pain often not present)	Substernal or over region of pulmonary infarction	Pleuritic (with pulmonary infarction) or angina-like	Sudden onset; minutes to <hour	May be aggravated by breathing	Dyspnea, tachypnea, tachycardia; hypotension, signs of acute right heart failure, and pulmonary hypertension with large emboli; rales, pleural rub, hemoptysis with pulmonary infarction
Pulmonary hypertension	Substernal	Pressure; oppressive		Aggravated by effort	Pain usually associated with dyspnea; signs of pulmonary hypertension (Table 5–3)
Pneumonia with pleurisy	Localized over area of consolidation	Pleuritic, well-localized		Painful breathing	Dyspnea, cough, fever, dull to percussion, bronchial breath sounds, rales, occasional pleural rub
Spontaneous pneumothorax	Unilateral	Sharp, well-localized	Sudden onset, lasts many hours	Painful breathing	Dyspnea; hyperresonance and decreased breath and voice sounds over involved lung
Musculoskeletal disorders	Variable	Aching	Short or long duration	Aggravated by movement; history of muscle exertion	Tender to pressure or movement
Herpes zoster	Dermatomal in distribution		Prolonged	None	Rash appears in area of discomfort
Gastrointestinal disorders (e.g., esophageal reflux, peptic ulcer, cholecystitis)	Lower substernal area, epigastric, right or left upper quadrant	Burning, colic-like, aching		Precipitated by recumbency or meals	Nausea, regurgitation, food intolerance, melena, hematemesis, jaundice
Anxiety states	Often localized to a point	Sharp, burning; commonly location of pain moves from place to place	Varies; usually very brief	Situational anger	Sighing respirations, often chest wall tenderness

veoli and hypoxemia results. Because the supine position compared with the upright position augments venous return, patients with congestive heart failure demonstrate orthopnea, that is, shortness of breath in the supine position relieved by sitting up. They also may demonstrate paroxysmal nocturnal dyspnea, that is, awakening with shortness of breath 2 to 3 hours after falling asleep. It usually occurs only once nightly, is relieved by sitting or standing, and is probably related to central redistribution of fluid upon assuming the reclining position.

Occasionally, dyspnea can represent the anginal equivalent, a symptom of acute myocardial ischemia. Dyspnea is also a prominent feature of pulmonary disease, and at times the differentiation between pulmonary and cardiac causes of dyspnea is difficult. For example, patients with pulmonary

TABLE 2–4. SYMPTOMS AND SIGNS OF CARDIAC FAILURE

	SYMPTOMS	SIGNS
Left heart failure	Dyspnea Orthopnea Paroxysmal nocturnal dyspnea	Tachypnea Left ventricular S_3 gallop Left ventricular S_4 gallop (nonspecific) Rales Wheezes (cardiac asthma) Functional mitral regurgitation Pulsus alternans
Right heart failure	Peripheral edema Nocturia Abdominal fullness	Jugular venous distention Peripheral edema Ascites Anasarca Hepatomegaly Splenomegaly Hepatojugular reflux Right ventricular S_3, S_4 gallops Tricuspid regurgitation (holosystolic murmur, pulsatile liver, large jugular v wave) Signs of pulmonary hypertension if present (see Table 5–3)
Either left or right heart failure	Fatigue Weakness Anorexia	Tachycardia Blood pressure often elevated Narrow pulse pressure Sweaty, cool extremities Pleural effusion (usually bilateral or isolated right) Cardiomegaly Cheyne-Stokes (periodic or cyclic) respiration Mental confusion

TABLE 2–5. NEW YORK HEART ASSOCIATION FUNCTIONAL CLASSIFICATION

Class I	No limitation	Ordinary physical activity does not cause symptoms
Class II	Slight limitation	Comfortable at rest Ordinary physical activity causes symptoms
Class III	Marked limitation	Comfortable at rest Less than ordinary activity causes symptoms
Class IV	Inability to carry on any physical activity	Symptoms present at rest

dyspnea can exhibit orthopnea, whereas wheezes may be heard in patients with cardiac dyspnea (e.g., congestive heart failure). Sudden dyspnea is a common presentation of a pulmonary embolus.

Cyanosis is a bluish discoloration of the skin caused by an increased amount of nonoxygenated hemoglobin in the blood. Central cyanosis, often best seen on the oral mucous membranes, is due to right-to-left shunting of blood or impaired pulmonary function. Peripheral cyanosis, best seen in the extremities, may be due to shunting or to local discoloration caused by vasoconstriction (e.g., low cardiac output, peripheral vascular disease, or exposure to cold). Cyanosis is more difficult to see in dark-skinned than in light-skinned individuals. Because cyanosis becomes apparent when 4 grams/dl or more of reduced hemoglobin are present, polycythemia tends to accentuate cyanosis and anemia tends to minimize it.

Syncope has multiple origins, including circulatory (e.g., volume depletion from a variety of causes) and neurologic (e.g., seizures) as well as cardiac (see Chapter 8).

Palpitation refers to an awareness of heart beat, usually either irregular or rapid (see Chapter 8).

Fatigue is a common cardiac symptom but is extremely nonspecific. Patients who have a reduced cardiac output often complain of fatigue that may be exacerbated by drugs (e.g., beta-adrenergic blocking drugs).

Edema is common in patients with congestive heart failure. Edema of the lower extremities (or the sacral area in bedridden patients) often is a symptom of right ventricular failure. Other causes of peripheral edema include the nephrotic syndrome, cirrhosis, and venous insufficiency. Peripheral edema may increase at the end of the day and decrease overnight as the dependent part is elevated and the fluid resorbed. Fluid within the peritoneal cavity is referred to as *ascites* and within the chest cavity as *pleural effusion*. Patients who have severe edema secondary to congestive heart failure may develop ascites, and ascites is especially frequent in patients who have constrictive pericarditis. Noncardiac causes of ascites such as cirrhosis, nephrosis, and peritoneal tumor must be excluded.

Cough and *hemoptysis* may be associated with cardiac disease, but it may be difficult to differentiate cardiac from pulmonary disease on the basis of these two symptoms alone. A cough, often orthostatic in nature, may be the primary complaint in some patients with pulmonary congestion. They tend not to bring up thick purulent sputum as do patients with chronic bronchitis. Hemoptysis occurs in congestive heart failure and is especially common in patients with mitral stenosis. Massive hemoptysis is generally not a cardiac symptom.

Nocturia, secondary to resorption of edema at night, is common in patients with congestive heart failure. Anorexia, abdominal fullness, right upper quadrant tenderness (secondary to hepatomegaly), and weight loss are also symptoms of advanced heart failure. Hoarseness may occasionally result from recurrent laryngeal nerve compression by an aortic aneurysm, dilated pulmonary artery, or large left atrium.

A history of rheumatic fever, prolonged febrile illnesses, sore throats, or any rheumatic complaints as a child should be sought. The patient should be asked about any history of a heart murmur or other cardiac abnormalities noted in a previous examination. Childhood activity levels may be important in evaluating patients suspected of having congenital or rheumatic heart disease. Women should be asked about problems during pregnancy, a state that stresses the cardiovascular system. The presence of risk factors for coronary artery disease (see Chapter 7) should be determined. The New York Heart Association's functional classification of patients with cardiac disease is useful (Table 2–5).

EXAMINATION OF THE NECK VEINS

The purpose of neck vein examination is to estimate the right atrial pressure (central venous pressure) and to evaluate abnormalities in the venous pulse waveform. To estimate central venous pressure, the patient's torso should be at an angle so that the top of the internal jugular pulsation can be visualized. The vertical height of this column from the angle of Louis plus 5 cm (the distance from the angle of Louis to the right atrium at most angles is about 5 cm) approximates the actual venous pressure. Normal venous pressure is between 5 and 9 cm H_2O. Therefore, the normal vertical height of the jugular venous column is less than 3 to 5 cm above the sternal angle. Elevated jugular venous pressure occurs in patients who have right ventricular failure or an abnormality of right ventricular filling (e.g., tricuspid valve abnormality, constrictive pericarditis, or tamponade). The normal jugular venous pressure falls with inspiration and increases with expiration. If the opposite occurs (Kussmaul's sign), constrictive pericarditis or restrictive cardiomyopathy should be suspected.

The jugular venous pulse is composed of two large deflections (the a and v waves) and two negative deflections (the x and y descents) (Fig. 2–1). Even though not usually appreciated on physical examination, a second positive deflection after the a wave, the c wave, is recordable. The a wave results from atrial contraction and is accentuated in patients with right ventricular hypertrophy, tricuspid or pulmonic stenosis, or contraction of the atrium against a closed tricuspid valve as occurs in heart block (cannon a wave). Irregular cannon a waves occur with atrioventricular (AV) dissociation. Regular cannon a waves may occur in a junctional or ventricular rhythm that conducts retrogradely to the atrium or during some supraventricular tachycardias (see Chapter 8). The a wave is absent if atrial fibrillation is present. The c wave is due to transmitted pressure from the closed tricuspid valve thrust upward during right ventricular systole. The v wave is normally smaller than the a wave and is due to blood re-

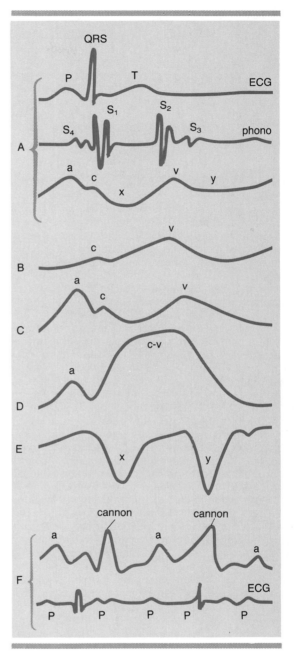

FIGURE 2–1. Normal and abnormal jugular venous pulse tracings. A, Normal jugular pulse tracing with simultaneous electrocardiogram (ECG) and phonocardiogram. B, Loss of a waves in atrial fibrillation. C, Large a waves in tricuspid stenosis. D, Large c-v waves in tricuspid regurgitation. E, Steep x and y descents in constrictive pericarditis. F, Jugular venous pulse tracing and simultaneous ECG during complete heart block demonstrating cannon a waves occurring when the atrium contracts against a closed tricuspid valve during ventricular systole.

turning from the periphery to the right atrium during ventricular systole when the tricuspid valve is closed. The v wave may be the only visible positive deflection in patients with atrial fibrillation. Tricuspid regurgitation results in a large v wave with attenuation of the x descent. The y descent, representing atrial emptying, is decreased in the presence of tricuspid stenosis. Restricted filling of the right side of the heart (e.g., constrictive pericarditis or restrictive cardiomyopathy) produces a venous pulse with distinctive steep x and y descents.

ARTERIAL PRESSURE AND PULSES

Arterial pressure is measured with a sphygmomanometer. Deflation of the arm cuff previously inflated above the systolic arterial pressure results in the sound of blood intermittently entering the artery (Korotkoff sounds) when cuff pressure falls to less than systolic pressure. As the cuff is progressively deflated to the diastolic pressure, the Korotkoff sounds disappear, signifying that blood is flowing within the artery in both systole and diastole. Spurious blood pressure measurements can be obtained if a cuff of incorrect diameter is used; a narrow blood pressure cuff used on an obese arm gives falsely elevated blood pressure readings, and vice versa. In such a patient, blood pressure can be obtained in the forearm with a regular-sized cuff, with the examiner listening over the radial artery. Blood pressure must be measured in the lower extremities when excluding coarctation of the aorta as a cause for upper extremity hypertension. The normal blood pressure in the leg is approximately 10 mm higher than that in the arm.

Arterial pulses can be palpated over the carotid, axillary, brachial, radial, femoral, popliteal, dorsalis pedis, and posterior tibial arteries. The carotid pulses are most closely related to the aortic pressure in both timing and contour and provide the most information concerning cardiac function. Representative carotid pulse contours are shown in Figure 2–2. Note that the normal upstroke is brisk and that the end of ejection is signified by the dicrotic notch, usually not palpable.

Arterial pulses are symmetric bilaterally. Inequalities may be explained by chronic atherosclerosis or more acute processes involving regional circulation, for example, dissection of the aorta, peripheral emboli, or vasculitis (e.g., Takayasu's disease). In supravalvular aortic stenosis, there is streaming of the jet toward the right innominate artery, and the carotid and brachial arterial pulses may be stronger on the right than the left. Strongly palpable pulses in the upper extremities with weakly palpable pulses in the lower extremities may suggest coarctation of the aorta. The amplitude of the carotid pulse increases with anemia, thyrotoxicosis, and aortic insufficiency because of the increased stroke volume and rate of

left ventricular ejection. The carotid pulse amplitude is attenuated (pulsus parvus) in conditions associated with decreased left ventricular stroke volume, for example, myocardial failure, tachycardia, hypovolemia, severe mitral stenosis, and constrictive pericarditis. Severe myocardial failure may result in pulsus alternans, an alternating intensity of the arterial pulse. Pulsus parvus et tardus is a slowly rising, low-amplitude, late-peaking arterial pulse due to severe aortic outflow tract obstruction (Fig. 2–2). In addition, severe aortic stenosis may be associated with a carotid

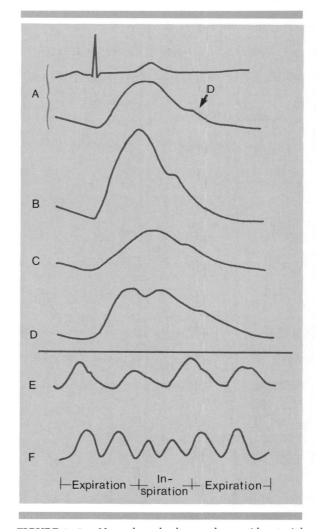

| Expiration | In-spiration | Expiration |

FIGURE 2–2. Normal and abnormal carotid arterial pulse contours. *A*, Normal arterial pulse with simultaneous ECG. The dicrotic wave (D) occurs just after aortic valve closure. *B*, Wide pulse pressure in aortic insufficiency. *C*, Pulsus parvus et tardus (small amplitude with a slow upstroke) associated with aortic stenosis. *D*, Bisferious pulse with two systolic peaks, typical of hypertrophic obstructive cardiomyopathy or aortic insufficiency, especially if concomitant aortic stenosis is present. *E*, Pulsus alternans characteristic of severe left ventricular failure. *F*, Paradoxical pulse (systolic pressure decrease of greater than 10 mm Hg with inspiration), most characteristic of cardiac tamponade.

shudder, coarse palpable carotid arterial vibrations associated with ejection. Pulsus parvus et tardus may not be present in older patients with aortic stenosis and a stiff, noncompliant arterial system or in patients with concomitant aortic insufficiency. Aortic insufficiency is associated with a high-amplitude pulse with a very rapid upstroke, referred to as a Corrigan or water hammer pulse. Severe aortic insufficiency with or without aortic stenosis may be associated with a bisferious pulse, a carotid arterial pressure contour with two palpable systolic peaks. A bisferious pulse is also associated with hypertrophic obstructive cardiomyopathy (Fig. 2–2). In this condition, a rapid initial upstroke of the carotid artery is attenuated in midsystole and followed by a second late systolic peak, indicative of a late systolic attempt by the ventricle to completely expel its blood. Pulsus paradoxus, a greater than normal decrease (>10 mm Hg) in systolic arterial pressure with inspiration, characteristically occurs in pericardial tamponade but may also be present in other conditions such as airway obstruction (acute exacerbation of chronic obstructive pulmonary disease or asthma). The mechanism of pulsus paradoxus is complex and multifactorial. A pulse of irregular intensity may occur in atrial fibrillation or other irregular arrhythmias.

PRECORDIAL EXAMINATION

Before auscultation, the precordium should be inspected and palpated. With good lighting, the point of maximal cardiac impulse may be visible. Cardiac impulses are not normally observed in any other area. The normal apical impulse occurs in early systole and is located within an area of approximately 1 cm^2 in the fourth to fifth left intercostal space near the midclavicular line. Inspection of the precordium should reveal any abnormalities of the bony structures (e.g., pectus excavatum) that may displace the heart to produce unusual findings on physical examination. Precordial palpation should begin with the point of maximal impulse and progress across the precordium, searching for abnormal impulses, palpable sounds, and thrills.

An abnormally prolonged and diffuse left ventricular impulse with increased amplitude is termed a left ventricular heave and is associated with left ventricular hypertrophy. Displacement of the left ventricular impulse downward and to the left indicates left ventricular dilation, common in left ventricular failure or valvular lesions associated with volume overload, such as aortic or mitral regurgitation. A palpable S_4 gallop is associated with pressure overload states, such as aortic stenosis or long-standing hypertension. A double systolic apical impulse is characteristic of obstructive hypertrophic cardiomyopathy. A systolic bulge medial to the point of maximal impulse is sometimes felt after a recent myocardial infarction and probably represents an area of left ventricular asynergy. A left parasternal lift generally indicates

right ventricular dilation and/or hypertrophy and is observed in patients with mitral stenosis or other causes of right ventricular stress. Occasionally, late systolic expansion of the left atrium in patients with severe mitral regurgitation can be palpated in the left parasternal area. Vibrations (thrills) associated with the murmurs of valvular or congenital lesions may be palpable, as, for example, in aortic stenosis or ventricular septal defect. Occasionally, pulmonic closure (P_2) is markedly accentuated and palpable in patients with severe pulmonary hypertension. Systolic retraction of the apical impulse is a characteristic finding in constrictive pericarditis.

CARDIAC AUSCULTATION

Both patient and examiner should be physically comfortable to ensure adequate cardiac auscultation. A good stethoscope has a diaphragm for auscultating relatively high-frequency sounds and a bell for low-frequency sounds. The diaphragm is applied with moderate pressure to the chest, whereas the bell should be applied very lightly, just enough to create a seal. The patient should be auscultated while supine and sitting. Certain sounds (for example, the murmur of aortic insufficiency and the rub of pericarditis) are best heard with the patient sitting upright and leaning forward in end expiration to bring the heart as close to the chest wall as possible. Gallop rhythms are best heard at the apex with the patient supine or in the left lateral decubitus position. The murmur and opening snap of mitral stenosis are best heard with the patient in the left lateral decubitus position, and sometimes leg or arm exercises are needed to make the murmur audible. The click and late systolic murmur of mitral valve prolapse may be accentuated by standing.

There are four major auscultatory zones. The aortic listening area is the second intercostal space just to the right of the sternum, and the pulmonic area is opposite, at the second intercostal space just to the left of the sternum. The tricuspid area is the fourth intercostal space just to the left of the sternum, and the mitral area is at the point of maximal impulse. These areas provide general guidelines to auscultate pathology for each valve, but exceptions exist.

The normal heart sounds consist of a first heart sound (S_1) and a second heart sound (S_2) (see Fig. 1–6). S_1 occurs at the onset of systole and is generated by mitral and tricuspid valve closure. The closure of the aortic (A_2) and pulmonic (P_2) valves at end systole generates S_2. A_2 and P_2 occur almost simultaneously at end expiration. Upon inspiration, venous return increases to the right side of the heart because of decreased intrathoracic pressure and decreases to the left side of the heart because of increased pulmonary vascular capacitance. These changes delay P_2 and slightly advance A_2 so that A_2 and P_2 separate temporally during inspiration, becoming superimposed during expiration. P_2 is normally less intense than A_2 and is best heard at the second intercostal space to the left of the sternum.

An early diastolic gallop rhythm (S_3) is a low-pitched sound heard best with the bell of the stethoscope placed lightly over the point of maximal impulse, especially with the patient in the left lateral decubitus position. It is generated by rapid filling of the left ventricle in early diastole and is a physiologically normal sound in young people into the early 20s. Heard in older age groups, an S_3 signifies left or right ventricular failure. An S_3 must be differentiated from other early diastolic sounds, for example, a widely split S_2, the opening snap of mitral stenosis, a tumor plop from a left atrial myxoma, or the pericardial knock of constrictive pericarditis.

A soft, early-peaking systolic ejection murmur at the second left intercostal space can be a normal finding in some people, especially younger people and patients with high circulatory flow states, such as anemia, thyrotoxicosis, exercise, and pregnancy. It is probably generated by flow across the pulmonic outflow tract. Diastolic murmurs are never physiologic. Systolic and diastolic sounds can sometimes be heard over the cervical venous system (venous hums). These venous hums disappear with a change in position or light pressure over the vein. They are not pathologic but must be differentiated from cardiac murmurs or bruits.

ABNORMAL HEART SOUNDS (Fig. 2-3)

Variation in the intensity of S_1 may have diagnostic importance (Table 2-6). After a short PR interval, the mitral and tricuspid valves are wide open at the onset of systole (louder S_1), whereas after a long PR interval they are already almost closed at the onset of systole (softer S_1). S_1 may vary in intensity in patients with atrial fibrillation or some types of heart block, when the mitral and tricuspid valves are in various stages of closure at the onset of ventricular systole. S_1 is loud in patients who have mitral stenosis and a relatively pliable valve (the mitral valve is wide open at the onset of left ventricular ejection). Splitting of S_1 is rarely of any diagnostic significance.

Abnormalities in S_2 may be related to abnormal intensity or abnormal timing (Tables 2-6 and 2-7). A single S_2 is present in any condition in which the intensity of A_2 or P_2 is markedly attenuated. Persistent splitting of S_2 retaining normal respiratory variation occurs when P_2 is delayed, or occasionally when A_2 is early, as in patients with mitral regurgitation or ventricular septal defect. Fixed splitting of S_2 is characteristic of atrial septal defect or lesions in which the right ventricle is unable to augment its stroke volume, for example, severe pulmonic stenosis. Paradoxical splitting of S_2 (P_2 preceding A_2 during expiration and coincident with A_2 on inspiration) is usually caused by conditions that delay A_2.

The fourth heart sound (S_4 gallop) occurs during late diastolic ventricular filling due to atrial contraction. An S_4 is usually abnormal, but occasionally it may be heard in a healthy adult. Inspiration enhances an S_4 originating from the right ventricle but has little effect on a left ventricular S_4. An S_4 gallop is associated with an elevated left ventricular end-diastolic pressure due to decreased left ventricular compliance, secondary to either left ventricular hypertrophy or ischemia. It is charac-

TABLE 2-6. ABNORMAL INTENSITY OF HEART SOUNDS

	S_1	A_2	P_2
Loud	Short PR interval Mitral stenosis with pliable valve	Systemic hypertension Aortic dilation Coarctation of aorta	Pulmonary hypertension Thin chest wall
Soft	Long PR interval Mitral regurgitation Poor left ventricular function Mitral stenosis with rigid valve Thick chest wall	Calcific aortic stenosis Aortic regurgitation	Valvular or subvalvular pulmonic stenosis
Varying	Atrial fibrillation Heart block		

TABLE 2-7. ABNORMAL SPLITTING OF S_2

SINGLE S_2	WIDELY SPLIT S_2 WITH NORMAL RESPIRATORY VARIATION	FIXED SPLIT S_2	PARADOXICAL SPLITTING OF S_2
Aortic stenosis Pulmonic stenosis Systemic hypertension Coronary artery disease Any condition that can lead to paradoxical splitting of S_2	Right bundle branch block Left ventricular pacing Pulmonic stenosis Pulmonary embolus Idiopathic dilation of the pulmonary artery Mitral regurgitation Ventricular septal defect	Atrial septal defect Severe right ventricular dysfunction	Left bundle branch block Right ventricular pacemaker Angina, myocardial infarction Aortic stenosis Hypertrophic obstructive cardiomyopathy Aortic regurgitation

teristically found in patients with aortic stenosis, hypertrophic cardiomyopathy, acute mitral regurgitation, and myocardial infarction. A right ventricular S_4 is heard in pulmonary hypertension and pulmonic stenosis. An S_4 is not present in atrial fibrillation. A transient S_4 gallop coincident with chest pain may be suggestive of ischemia. The auscultatory rhythm of an S_4 is likened to pronouncing "Tenn' (S_4) - e (S_1) - see (S_2)."

An early diastolic filling sound (S_3 gallop) may be physiologic in older children and young adults (see above), but in adults it occurs with impaired ventricular function of any cause and is the most sensitive and specific physical sign of ventricular dysfunction. It may be heard in chronic aortic or mitral insufficiency, in which it probably also represents some degree of left ventricular dysfunction. Left ventricular gallop sounds are not heard in the presence of significant mitral stenosis. A right ventricular S_3 may be heard at the left lower sternal border or sometimes the epigastrium, and is accentuated with inspiration. The auscultatory cadence of an S_3 is likened to pronouncing "Ken (S_1) - tuck' (S_2) - y (S_3)."

When tachycardia is present and a diastolic gallop cannot be separated into a distinct S_3 and S_4, it often represents the summation of both and is termed a summation gallop. It has a distinct cadence likened to that of a galloping horse.

Normal valves make no sound as they open. However, an abnormal but pliable aortic or pulmonic valve may generate an opening sound called an ejection sound or click (Fig. 2–4, Table 2–8). Ejection sounds are high-pitched and occur early in systole, immediately upon completion of isovolumic contraction. More severe stenosis causes the ejection sound to occur earlier in systole, that is, closer to S_1. The cause of ejection sounds in pulmonary or systemic hypertension is unclear but probably relates to the dilation of the aortic or pulmonary arterial root.

Mid to late systolic clicks, often followed by a late systolic murmur, occur in patients with mitral valve prolapse. The clicks are thought to result from sudden tensing of the mitral valve apparatus as the valve prolapses. The clicks may be single or multiple and may occur at any time during sys-

TABLE 2–8. EJECTION CLICKS

AORTIC	PULMONIC
Noncalcific congenital aortic stenosis	Valvular pulmonic stenosis
Systemic hypertension	Pulmonary arterial hypertension
Dilation of the aorta	Idiopathic dilation of the pulmonary artery
No change with respiration	Increased intensity with *expiration* (opposite to other right-sided events)
Loudest second right intercostal space and apex	Loudest left upper sternal border

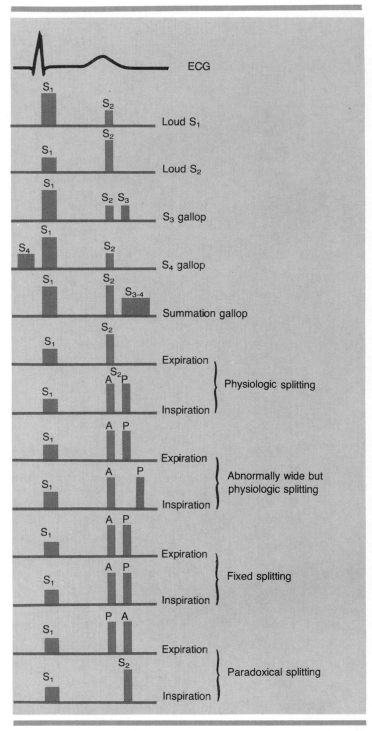

FIGURE 2–3. Abnormal heart sounds can be related to abnormal intensity, abnormal presence of a gallop rhythm, or abnormal splitting of S_2 with respiration.

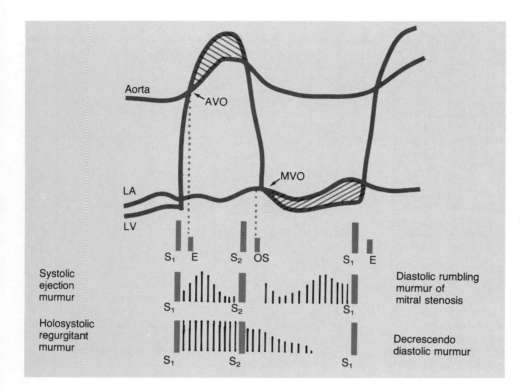

FIGURE 2-4. Abnormal sounds and murmurs associated with valvular dysfunction displayed simultaneously with left atrial (LA), left ventricular (LV), and aortic pressure tracings. AVO = Aortic valve opening; MVO = mitral valve opening; E = ejection click of the aortic valve; OS = opening snap of the mitral valve. The shaded areas represent pressure gradients across the aortic valve during systole or mitral valve during diastole, characteristic of aortic stenosis and mitral stenosis, respectively.

TABLE 2-9. EFFECTS OF PHYSIOLOGIC AND PHARMACOLOGIC MANEUVERS ON AUSCULTATORY EVENTS

MANEUVER	MAJOR PHYSIOLOGIC EFFECTS	USEFUL AUSCULTATORY CHANGES*
Respiration	↑venous return with inspiration	↑right heart murmurs and gallops with inspiration splitting of S_2 (Table 2-7)
Valsalva (initial ↑BP, phase I; followed by ↓BP, phase II)	↓BP, ↓venous return, ↓LV size (phase II)	↑HOCM ↓AS, MR MVP click earlier in systole, murmur prolongs
Standing	↓venous return ↓LV size	↑HOCM ↓AS, MR MVP click earlier in systole, murmur prolongs
Squatting	↑venous return ↑systemic vascular resistance ↑LV size	↑AS, MR, AI ↓HOCM MVP click delayed, murmur shortens
Isometric exercise (e.g., handgrip)	↑arterial pressure ↑cardiac output	↑gallops ↑MR, AI, MS ↓AS, HOCM
Post PVC or prolonged RR interval	↑ventricular filling ↑contractility	↑AS little change in MR
Amyl nitrate	↓arterial pressure ↑cardiac output ↓LV size	MVP click earlier in systole, murmur prolongs ↑HOCM, AS, MS ↓AI, MR, Austin Flint murmur
Phenylephrine	↑arterial pressure ↓cardiac output ↑LV size	↑MR, AI ↓AS, HOCM MVP click delayed, murmur shortens

* ↑ = Increased intensity; ↓ = Decreased intensity
BP = Blood pressure
LV = Left ventricle
HOCM = Hypertrophic obstructive cardiomyopathy
AS = Aortic stenosis

MR = Mitral regurgitation
MVP = Mitral valve prolapse
AI = Aortic insufficiency
MS = Mitral stenosis
PVC = Premature ventricular contraction.

tole, although they are generally later than ejection sounds. The behavior of these clicks and associated murmurs during physiologic maneuvers is summarized in Table 2–9.

The mitral and tricuspid valves also do not normally make an opening sound. However, with mitral or tricuspid stenosis, an early diastolic opening sound is heard if the valve is still pliable (Fig. 2–4). The opening "snap" (OS) of mitral stenosis is earlier in diastole, is of higher pitch than an S_3 gallop, and is located somewhat medial to the point of maximal impulse. More severe stenosis causes the opening snap to occur earlier, that is, closer to S_2; the higher the left atrial pressure, the earlier the valve opens after the onset of isovolumic relaxation. Opening snaps disappear as the stenotic AV valve calcifies and becomes immobile.

A pericardial knock is an early diastolic sound, sometimes difficult to distinguish from an S_3 gallop, heard in patients with constrictive pericarditis. Another abnormal early diastolic heart sound is the tumor "plop" of an atrial myxoma.

ABNORMAL MURMURS

Heart murmurs are vibrations of longer duration than the heart sounds and represent turbulent flow across abnormal valves caused by congenital or acquired cardiac defects (Fig. 2–4). Murmurs are termed diastolic or systolic, and their intensity is graded (Table 2–10). The length of the murmur

TABLE 2–10. GRADING SYSTEM FOR INTENSITY OF MURMURS

Grade 1	Barely audible murmur
Grade 2	Murmur of medium intensity
Grade 3	Loud murmur, no thrill
Grade 4	Loud murmur with thrill
Grade 5	Very loud murmur, stethoscope must be on the chest to hear
Grade 6	Murmur audible with stethoscope off the chest

and its radiation (e.g., to the back, neck, axilla, or listening areas other than that of the valve primarily involved) should be described along with the quality of the murmur (e.g., blowing, harsh, rumbling, musical, or high- or low-pitched).

Systolic murmurs are usually divided into ejection and holosystolic types (Table 2–11). Systolic ejection murmurs are generated by either abnormalities within or increased flow across the aortic or pulmonary outflow tract. The systolic ejection murmur of coarctation of the aorta is late in systole compared with valvular ejection murmurs.

Mitral regurgitation due to the syndrome of mitral valve prolapse may be associated with a late systolic murmur that is often preceded by a systolic click. It may be somewhat atypical for mitral

TABLE 2–11. CLASSIFICATION OF HEART MURMURS

CLASS	DESCRIPTION	CHARACTERISTIC LESIONS
Ejection	Systolic Crescendo-decrescendo Often harsh in quality Begin after S_1; end before S_2	Valvular, supravalvular, and subvalvular aortic stenosis Hypertrophic obstructive cardiomyopathy Pulmonic stenosis Aortic or pulmonary artery dilation Malformed but nonobstructive aortic valve ↑transvalvular flow (e.g., aortic regurgitation, hyperkinetic states, atrial septal defect, physiologic flow murmur)
Holosystolic	Extends throughout systole, up to and sometimes past S_2; relatively uniform intensity	Mitral regurgitation Tricuspid regurgitation Ventricular septal defect
Late systolic	Variable onset and duration, often preceded by a nonejection click	Mitral valve prolapse
Diastolic decrescendo	Begins with A_2 or P_2 Decrescendo with varying duration Often high-pitched, "blowing"	Aortic regurgitation Pulmonic regurgitation

Mid-diastolic	Begins after S_2, often after an opening snap
	Low-pitched "rumble" heard best with bell of stethoscope
	With exercise or left lateral decubitus position
	Loudest in early diastole and upon atrial contraction (presystolic accentuation)
		Mitral stenosis
		Tricuspid stenosis
		↑flow across atrioventricular valves:
		  tricuspid regurgitation
		  mitral regurgitation
		  atrial septal defect
		Atrial myxoma
		Austin Flint murmur

Continuous	Systolic and diastolic components "Machinery murmurs"	Patent ductus arteriosus Coronary AV fistula Ruptured sinus of Valsalva aneurysm into right atrium or ventricle

regurgitation in quality as well as timing and is often best heard more toward the left sternal border than at the traditional mitral listening area.

Early diastolic decrescendo murmurs are heard with aortic and pulmonic regurgitation. Aortic regurgitation can be due to valvular leaks or secondary to dilation of the valve ring (e.g., after aortic dissection). Pulmonic regurgitation also can be valvular or secondary to dilation of the valve ring associated with pulmonary hypertension (Graham Steell murmur).

In addition to mitral and tricuspid stenosis, rumbles across AV valves can be heard in conditions of increased diastolic flow across a nonstenotic valve (e.g., tricuspid regurgitation or atrial septal defect) or nonvalvular obstruction to flow (e.g., atrial myxoma). A diastolic rumbling murmur may be heard in patients with severe chronic aortic insufficiency (Austin Flint murmur; see Chapter 6).

Continuous murmurs or "machinery murmurs" are caused by lesions that generate turbulent flow in both systole and diastole owing to a pressure gradient present throughout the cardiac cycle.

A pericardial friction rub is created when two inflamed layers of pericardium slide over each other. It is a scratchy sound having one to three components. If all three components are present, one occurs during atrial systole, one during ventricular contraction, and one during rapid early diastolic ventricular filling. Pericardial friction rubs are usually best heard along the left sternal border while the patient is leaning forward in held expiration. Frequently only a single systolic component is audible and may be confused with a systolic murmur. A pleuropericardial friction rub involves not only the pericardial but also the pleural surfaces and varies with respiration.

PROSTHETIC VALVE SOUNDS

Metal valves of the ball and cage variety (e.g., Starr-Edwards valves) demonstrate loud, metallic opening and closing sounds that may be audible without a stethoscope. Tilting disk valves (e.g., the Bjork-Shiley valve) demonstrate a closing metallic sound but only a very soft opening sound. Porcine valves may generate no abnormal sounds, but a porcine valve in the mitral position sometimes has an opening snap as well as a soft diastolic rumble. Because there is a persistent gradient across any prosthetic valve, there is a systolic murmur across a prosthetic aortic valve and a soft diastolic rumble over a prosthetic mitral or tricuspid valve.

PHYSIOLOGIC AND PHARMACOLOGIC MANEUVERS

Various physiologic and pharmacologic maneuvers are sometimes useful in augmenting the intensity or delineating the etiology of heart sounds and murmurs (see Table 2-9). Noting the effects of respiration on murmurs is the simplest test. With inspiration right heart filling is increased, and therefore the intensity of most sounds and murmurs generated from the right side of the heart tends to increase. An exception to this rule is when right ventricular failure is present and the right ventricle is unable to increase its output during inspiration.

REFERENCES

Lembo NJ, Dell'Italia LJ, Crawford MH, O'Rourke RA: Bedside diagnosis of systolic murmurs. N Engl J Med 318:1572–1578, 1988.

Perloff JK: Physical Examination of the Heart and Circulation. 2nd ed. Philadelphia, WB Saunders Co, 1990.

Tavel ME: Clinical Phonocardiography and External Pulse Recording. 4th ed. Chicago, Year Book, 1985.

3 SPECIAL TESTS AND PROCEDURES IN THE PATIENT WITH CARDIOVASCULAR DISEASE

CARDIAC RADIOGRAPHY

From routine posteroanterior (PA) and lateral chest radiographs, the size of the heart can be estimated. Cardiomegaly is said to be present radiographically if the diameter of the heart exceeds more than half of the thoracic diameter (cardio-thoracic ratio). Enlarged hearts not meeting this criterion are not uncommon, however. The structures composing the cardiac borders can be seen in Figure 3-1. Dilation of the right atrium causes bulging of the right heart border, whereas dilation of the left atrial appendage straightens or bulges the left heart border between the left ventricle and pulmonary artery. In addition, an enlarged left atrium may cause a double density shadow on the right heart border and may elevate the left mainstem bronchus. Dilation of the posteriorly situated left atrium may be highlighted by barium in the esophagus, used to delineate the posterior cardiac border. Dilation of the right ventricle is seen best on the lateral chest radiograph as an encroachment of the anterior clear space between the heart and the sternum. Left ventricular dilation causes prominence of the lower portion of the left heart border. Enlargement of the central pulmonary arteries can be detected by a bulging of the pulmonary artery segment of the left heart border; enlargement of the aorta can be detected by aortic dilation. On many occasions, the particular chambers responsible for cardiomegaly may not be identifiable on routine PA and lateral chest radiographs.

Fluoroscopy or plain films of the chest may be used to detect calcification in valves, pericardium, or aorta. The chest radiograph can be used to identify prosthetic valves. Cardiac fluoroscopy can determine if a ball valve or tilting disk valve opens and closes properly.

Specific radiographic signs of congenital and valvular lesions are discussed in their respective sections. Evaluation of the pulmonary vasculature from the PA chest radiograph is often useful in the diagnosis of cardiac disease (Table 3–1).

ELECTROCARDIOGRAPHY

It is beyond the scope of this text to provide a comprehensive discussion of electrocardiography; however, some basic principles are reviewed. Impulses are initiated by the sinus node, travel through the atria initiating atrial contraction, and experience conduction delay through the atrioventricular (AV) node. The impulse travels from the AV node through the common bundle of His, down the right and left bundle branches, and through the Purkinje fibers to ventricular myocardium (see Fig. 1–4). The normal electrocardiogram (ECG) is produced by electrical activity of the heart recorded by skin electrodes. The ECG is the

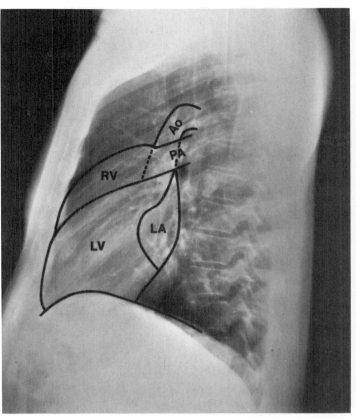

FIGURE 3–1. Schematic illustration of the parts of the heart whose outlines can be identified on a routine chest radiograph. Ao = Aorta; PA = pulmonary artery; RV = right ventricle; LV = left ventricle; LA = left atrium.

sum of all cardiac action potentials of its component cells. The P wave represents atrial depolarization. The PR interval is a measure of the time necessary to travel from the sinus node through the atrium, AV node, and His-Purkinje system up to the point the impulse activates ventricular

TABLE 3–1. EVALUATION OF THE PULMONARY VASCULATURE FROM THE PA CHEST RADIOGRAPH

PHYSIOLOGIC ABNORMALITY	RADIOGRAPHIC FINDINGS	CLINICAL CORRELATES
Decreased pulmonary blood flow	Paucity of vascular shadow throughout the lungs	Right-to-left shunts (e.g., tetralogy of Fallot)
Increased pulmonary blood flow	Generalized increase in pulmonary vascular markings throughout the lung fields	Left-to-right shunts (e.g., atrial septal defect)
Increased pulmonary vascular resistance	Central large pulmonary vessels dilated but peripheral pulmonary markings attenuated	Pulmonary hypertension
Pulmonary venous hypertension	Interstitial edema → indistinct pulmonary vessels, engorged lymphatics → discrete horizontal shadows in the outer lung bases (Kerley B lines); redistribution of pulmonary flow from bases to apices; alveolar infiltrates with "butterfly" distribution, usually bilaterally symmetric	Pulmonary edema

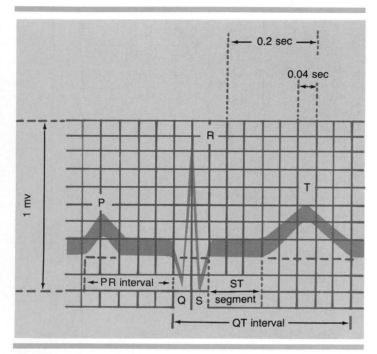

FIGURE 3–2. Normal electrocardiographic (ECG) complex with labeling of waves and intervals.

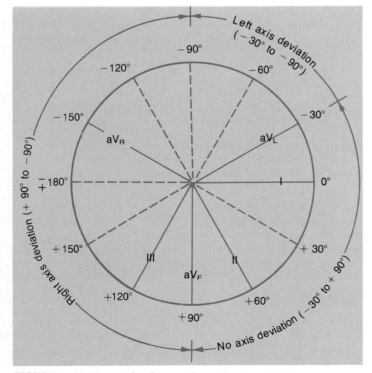

FIGURE 3–3. Hexaxial reference figure for frontal plane axis determination, indicating values for abnormal left and right QRS axis deviation.

myocardial cells. The QRS complex represents the sum of all ventricular muscle cell depolarizations (phase 0 of the cardiac action potential); the ST segment represents the plateau phase (phase 2); and the T wave represents the rapid repolarization (phase 3) of the heart as a whole (see Chapter 8). The ventricular septum is activated from left to right before any other part of the ventricle. Subsequently, the bulk of the ventricular muscle is activated simultaneously, followed lastly by activation of the base of the heart superiorly. Myocardial electrical activity can be represented with a vector, a value with both magnitude and direction, at any time during the cardiac cycle. The mean QRS vector during depolarization is termed the electrical axis and can be identified using the surface ECG.

A diagrammatic representation of an ECG complex is seen in Figure 3–2. The vertical axis represents amplitude in millivolts (10 mm = 1 millivolt). The horizontal scale represents time (5 mm = 0.20 second, 1 mm = 0.04 second). Routine ECG paper speed is 25 mm/sec, and thus one can determine the heart rate by measuring the RR interval in millimeters and dividing that number into 1500, or the RR interval in milliseconds divided into 60,000.

The first relatively low-amplitude and low-frequency deflection of the ECG, the P wave, represents atrial depolarization. The isoelectric portion of the ECG between the P wave and the next rapid deflection (QRS complex) is termed the PR segment. The PR interval is measured between the onset of the P wave and the onset of the QRS complex and is normally between 0.12 and 0.20 second in duration. A PR interval greater than 0.20 second is termed first-degree AV block. The rapid, high-amplitude deflections following the PR segment are termed the QRS complex and represent ventricular depolarization. Atrial repolarization usually is not visible on the ECG because it is a low-amplitude, low-frequency event and occurs simultaneously with ventricular depolarization. An initial negative deflection of the QRS is termed the Q wave; the initial positive deflection is termed the R wave; and if a subsequent negative deflection is present, it is called the S wave. A positive deflection subsequent to the S wave is termed an R' wave. The duration between the onset and the termination of the QRS complex is called the QRS interval and is normally less than 0.10 second. Upper and lower case letters are used to indicate the relative size of QRS deflections; for example, qRs refers to a small Q wave, large R wave, and small S wave. The isoelectric portion of the ECG following the QRS complex is the ST segment, followed by a low-frequency deflection, the T wave, which represents ventricular repolarization. The QT interval is measured from the beginning of the QRS complex to the end of the T wave and represents the time required for ventricular electrical systole. The QT interval is a measure of ventricular muscle refractoriness and varies with heart rate, decreasing as the heart rate increases. The QT interval is usually 0.35 to 0.44

second for heart rates between 60 and 100 beats/min, and one can estimate a corrected QT interval (normally less than 0.46 second in men and 0.47 second in women) by the Bazett formula, $QT_c = QT/\sqrt{RR}$ interval (all values must be expressed in seconds). In some patients, a broad, low-amplitude deflection follows the T wave and is called a U wave. The genesis of the U wave is not clear. The junction between the QRS and the ST segment is the J point.

Figure 3-3 illustrates the Einthoven triangle and the polarity of each of the six limb leads. Electrodes are connected to the left arm, right arm, and left leg (the right leg lead is a ground). Lead I displays the potential difference between the left and right arms (left arm positive); lead II, the potential difference between the right arm and left leg (left leg positive); and lead III, the potential difference between the left arm and left leg (left leg positive). Likewise, the augmented limb leads aV_L, aV_R, and aV_F are positive toward the left arm, right arm, and left leg, respectively. They are unipolar leads; that is, they measure the potential difference between the limb lead and a central point. When these six leads are taken together, they describe a full circle in the frontal plane at 30-degree intervals. Using this "hexaxial" frontal plane lead reference system, the frontal axis of any cardiac vector can be estimated. The most important axis is that of the mean QRS vector, normally between −30 degrees and +90 degrees. Mean QRS axes more superior than −30 degrees are termed left axis deviation, and more rightward than +90 degrees, right axis deviation. The T wave axis is normally within 30 to 45 degrees of the QRS axis. Leads displaying large positive or negative QRS deflections are generally parallel to the mean QRS axis; leads that are isoelectric, or have equal negative and positive deflections, are perpendicular to the QRS axis.

In addition to the six frontal plane leads, there are six standard precordial leads, V_1 through V_6, which are unipolar leads placed across the anterior chest. The precordial leads are considered positive, and a central reference point serves as the negative pole (unipolar lead). Leads V_1 and to some extent V_2 are close to the right ventricle and interventricular septum of the heart; leads V_4, V_5, and V_6 are close to the lateral wall of the left ventricle. Lead V_1 normally has a small R wave and large S wave, the midprecordial leads have equal R and S waves, and leads V_5 and V_6 have a large R wave and small S wave (often preceded by a small Q wave), reflecting the normal left ventricular predominance in the adult. If the right precordial leads (V_1, V_2) have relatively equal R and S waves with no other abnormality, counterclockwise rotation is said to be present; if V_5 and V_6 have relatively equal R and S waves, clockwise rotation is present. These can be normal variants.

A vectorcardiogram is a two-dimensional recording of the vector loop generated by atrial and ventricular depolarization. Vectorcardiograms are infrequently used today.

ABNORMAL ECG PATTERNS

The normal P wave vector is positive in leads I, II, and aV_F and negative in aV_R. Criteria for left and right atrial enlargement are described in Table 3-2.

The ECG can be used to diagnose left ventricular hypertrophy but is relatively insensitive. The hypertrophied ventricle generates increased ECG voltage that may meet any of several voltage criteria to qualify for left ventricular hypertrophy. However, normal young people may have high ECG voltage, and these criteria are not useful for patients under 35 years of age. At least one additional criterion must be present to diagnose left ventricular hypertrophy (Table 3-2).

The ECG findings in right ventricular hypertrophy are summarized in Table 3-2. The degree of right axis deviation correlates somewhat with the degree of right ventricular hypertrophy, as do certain QRS configurations (e.g., a qR complex in V_1 is associated with right ventricular pressure exceeding left ventricular pressure).

Acute pulmonary embolus may be associated with transient and nonspecific ECG changes. These include right atrial abnormality, right axis deviation with clockwise rotation, incomplete or

TABLE 3-2. ECG MANIFESTATIONS OF CHAMBER ENLARGEMENT

Left atrial enlargement
  P wave duration ≥ 0.12 sec
  Notched, slurred P wave in leads I and II (P mitrale)
  Biphasic P waves in V_1 with a wide, deep, negative terminal component
  Mean P wave axis shifted to the left (between +45 and −30 degrees)

Right atrial enlargement
  P wave duration ≤ 0.11 sec
  Tall, peaked P waves of ≥2.5 mm in amplitude in leads II, III, or aV_F (P pulmonale)
  Mean P wave axis shifted to the right (≥ +70 degrees)

Left ventricular enlargement
  Voltage criteria:
    R or S wave in limb lead ≥ 20 mm
    S wave in V_1, V_2, or V_3 ≥ 30 mm
    R wave in V_4, V_5, or V_6 ≥ 30 mm
  Depressed ST segments with inverted T waves in lateral leads ("strain" pattern); more reliable in the absence of digitalis therapy
  Left axis of −30 degrees or more
  QRS duration ≥ 0.09 sec
  Left atrial enlargement
  Time of onset of the intrinsicoid deflection (time from beginning of QRS to peak of R wave) ≥ 0.05 sec in lead V_5 or V_6

Right ventricular enlargement
  Tall R waves over right precordium and deep S waves over left precordium (R:S ratio in lead V_1 > 1.0)
  Normal QRS duration (if no right bundle branch block)
  Right axis deviation
  ST-T "strain" pattern over right precordium
  Late intrinsicoid deflection in lead V_1 or V_2

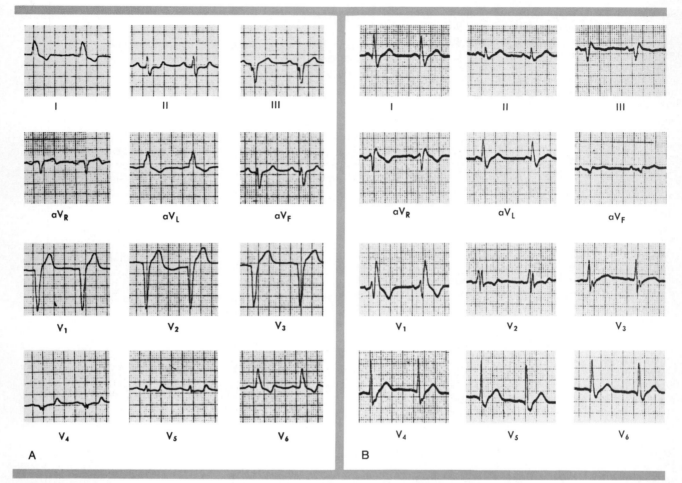

FIGURE 3–4. *A,* Left bundle branch block. *B,* Right bundle branch block. Criteria for bundle branch block are summarized in Table 3–3.

complete right bundle branch block, S waves in leads I, II, and III (S_1 S_2 S_3 pattern), and T wave inversion in the right precordial leads. Atrial arrhythmias are not uncommon.

TABLE 3–3. ECG MANIFESTATIONS OF BUNDLE BRANCH BLOCK

Left bundle branch block
QRS duration $\geq$ 0.12 sec
Broad, slurred, or notched R waves in lateral leads (I, aV_L, V_5–V_6)
QS or rS pattern in anterior precordium
Secondary ST-T wave changes (ST and T wave vectors opposite to terminal QRS vectors)
Late intrinsicoid deflection in leads V_5 and V_6
Right bundle branch block
QRS duration $\geq$ 0.12 sec
Large R' wave in lead V_1 (rsR')
Deep terminal S wave in V_6
Normal septal Q waves
Inverted T waves in lead V_1 (secondary T wave change)
Late intrinsicoid deflection in leads V_1 and V_2

ECG manifestations of chronic obstructive pulmonary disease are due to changes in lung volumes and to right ventricular hypertrophy. Right atrial abnormality, right axis deviation, and clockwise rotation are often present. An S_1 S_2 S_3 pattern may be seen, and QRS voltage may be low. Right ventricular hypertrophy is sometimes present.

The common bundle of His divides into left and right bundle branches. Conduction delay or block in either of these bundle branches results in characteristic ECG patterns (Fig. 3–4, Table 3–3). In each of these, the QRS duration is 0.12 second or more. Left bundle branch block often is an indicator of organic heart disease. During left bundle branch block, initial septal activation is abnormal; therefore, the diagnosis of myocardial infarction, dependent upon Q waves in the first 0.04 second of the QRS, usually cannot be determined. Left ventricular hypertrophy cannot be diagnosed in the presence of left bundle branch block.

Right bundle branch block can be associated with organic heart disease but is sometimes seen in apparently normal hearts. The right ventricle is activated late, and therefore there is a terminal unopposed QRS vector directed rightward and anteriorly. Initial ventricular activation is normal (septal activation occurs normally from the left bundle branch), and thus myocardial infarction can be diagnosed in the presence of right bundle branch block.

The left bundle branch in many hearts appears to divide into two major divisions (fascicles), the left anterior (superior) fascicle and the left posterior (inferior) fascicle. A delay in conduction in either fascicle is termed a hemiblock or fascicular block and changes the sequence of left ventricular depolarization, reflected in a frontal axis shift. Because the left anterior fascicle is smaller and more discrete than the left posterior fascicle, left anterior hemiblock is much more common than left posterior hemiblock; in fact, the presence of left posterior hemiblock is unusual without concomitant right bundle branch block. The ECG criteria for left fascicular blocks are listed in Table 3–4. The term *bifascicular block* refers to a right bundle branch block associated with a left anterior or left posterior fascicular block. If evidence of conduction delay or block exists in all three fascicles, trifascicular block is said to be present (e.g., alternating bundle branch block, left bundle branch block with infra-His first-degree AV block or complete infra-His heart block.)

Pre-excitation syndromes are discussed in Chapter 8.

The ECG is very useful in evaluating patients with ischemic heart disease. Nontransmural ischemia is manifested by downsloping or horizontally depressed (at least 1 mm) ST segments, which is the classic ischemic ST segment response seen with exercise testing. Symmetric T wave inversion with or without ST depression may also indicate ischemia. ST depression and T wave changes, however, are nonspecific and must be correlated with the clinical setting. On the other hand, ST segment elevation is more specific and evokes a fairly narrow differential diagnosis. ST elevation may occur with acute transmural myocardial infarction, ventricular aneurysm after myocardial infarction, pericarditis, variant angina (Prinzmetal's angina, secondary to coronary artery spasm), and as a normal variant (early repolarization). ST elevation caused by acute ischemia is referred to as a "current of injury" (Fig. 3–5).

Infarctions are localized by ECG to different areas of the heart (Table 3–5). Transmural myocardial infarction is usually characterized by the development of Q waves of at least 0.04 second in duration, and by a typical ECG evolution (Table 3–6), the time course of which is extremely variable. Leads reflecting areas of the heart opposite the infarction demonstrate ST depression (reciprocal changes). Persistence of ST elevation past the first few weeks implies the development of a ventricular aneurysm. The presence of Q waves and T wave inversion consistent with a myocardial infarction on a single ECG permits the diagnosis of a myocardial infarction, but of indeterminant age.

TABLE 3–4. ECG MANIFESTATIONS OF FASCICULAR BLOCKS

Left anterior fascicular block
 QRS duration ≤ 0.10 sec
 Left axis deviation (−45 degrees or greater)
 rS pattern in leads II, III, and aV$_F$
 qR pattern in leads I and aV$_L$

Left posterior fascicular block
 QRS duration ≤ 0.10 sec
 Right axis deviation (+90 degrees or greater)
 qR pattern in leads II, III, and aV$_F$
 rS pattern in leads I and aV$_L$
 Exclusion of other causes of right axis deviation (e.g., chronic obstructive pulmonary disease, right ventricular hypertrophy, lateral myocardial infarction)

ECG patterns of subendocardial (also called nontransmural, or non–Q wave) myocardial infarctions include ST depression and T wave inversion that are often nonspecific in themselves. Clinical correlation with cardiac isoenzyme determinations is necessary to verify the infarction.

Abnormal Q waves may be present in the absence of myocardial infarction. These situations include myocarditis, cardiac amyloidosis, neuromuscular disorders such as muscular dystrophy, myocardial replacement by tumor, sarcoidosis, chronic obstructive lung disease, hypertrophic cardiomyopathy, and certain varieties of Wolff-Parkinson-White syndrome.

Many patients have ECGs with nonspecific abnormal ST and T wave changes that preclude a definitive diagnosis. These are interpreted as "nonspecific ST and T wave changes" and must be correlated with the clinical status.

Primary T wave changes are those that occur in the absence of depolarization (QRS) abnormalities, whereas secondary T wave changes are those that result from abnormal QRS depolarization. Thus, secondary T wave changes may be due to bundle branch block or ventricular pre-excitation. Various drugs, electrolyte abnormalities, and ischemia may produce primary T wave changes.

Abnormalities of U waves include either increased amplitude of positive U waves or inverted U waves. Prominent positive U waves may be present normally in patients with bradycardia. They may also occur in hypokalemia and with some drugs, particularly digitalis and antiarrhythmic agents such as amiodarone. Negative U waves occur in left ventricular hypertrophy and ischemia. A large U wave may sometimes be a manifestation of the delayed repolarization (prolonged QT) syndrome (see Chapter 8).

Electrical alternans refers to alternation of QRS voltage and sometimes even P wave and T wave voltage. The most common cause of electrical alternans is a large pericardial effusion.

Metabolic and drug influences on the ECG are enumerated in Figure 3–6. ECG manifestations of pericarditis are discussed in Chapter 9.

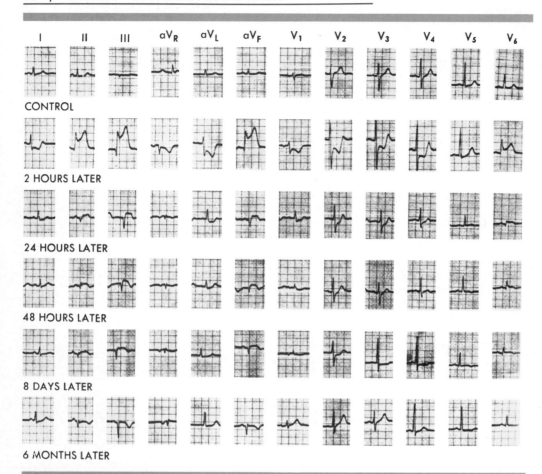

| I | II | III | aV$_R$ | aV$_L$ | aV$_F$ | V$_1$ | V$_2$ | V$_3$ | V$_4$ | V$_5$ | V$_6$ |

CONTROL

2 HOURS LATER

24 HOURS LATER

48 HOURS LATER

8 DAYS LATER

6 MONTHS LATER

FIGURE 3–5. Evolutionary changes in a posteroinferior myocardial infarction. Control tracing is normal. The tracing recorded 2 hours after onset of chest pain demonstrated development of early Q waves, marked ST segment elevation, and hyperacute T waves in leads II, III, and aV$_F$. In addition, a larger R wave, ST segment depression, and negative T waves have developed in leads V$_1$ and V$_2$. These are early changes indicating acute posteroinferior myocardial infarction. The 24-hour tracing demonstrates evolutionary changes. In leads II, III, and aV$_F$ the Q wave is larger, the ST segments have almost returned to baseline, and the T wave has begun to invert. In leads V$_1$ to V$_2$ the duration of the R wave now exceeds 0.04 second, the ST segment is depressed, and the T wave is upright. (In this example, ECG changes of true posterior involvement extend past V$_2$; ordinarily only V$_1$ and V$_2$ may be involved.) Only minor further changes occur through the 8-day tracing. Finally, 6 months later the ECG illustrates large Q waves, isoelectric ST segments, and inverted T waves in leads II, III, and aV$_F$ and large R waves, isoelectric ST segment, and upright T waves in V$_1$ and V$_2$, indicative of an "old" posteroinferior myocardial infarction.

TABLE 3–5. LOCALIZATION OF MYOCARDIAL INFARCTION

AREA OF INFARCTION	ECG CHANGES		LIKELY VESSEL INVOLVED*
Inferior	II, III, aV$_F$		RCA
Anteroseptal	V$_1$–V$_3$	Q waves	LAD
Anterior	V$_3$–V$_4$	ST elevation	LAD
Anterolateral	V$_4$–V$_6$	T wave inversions	CX or LAD
Extensive anterior	V$_1$–V$_6$, I, aV$_L$		large LAD
Lateral	I, aV$_L$		CX
Posterior	V$_1$–V$_2$: tall broad initial R wave, ST depression, tall upright T wave; usually occurs in association with inferior or lateral MI		RCA
Right ventricular	V$_1$ and V$_{4r}$: ST elevation; usually occurs in association with inferior MI		RCA

* This is a generalization, and many variations occur.

RCA = Right coronary artery; LAD = left anterior descending coronary artery; CX = left circumflex coronary artery.

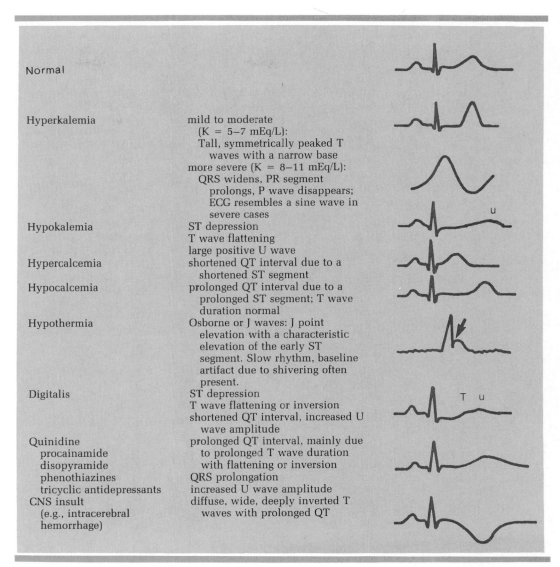

Normal

Hyperkalemia
mild to moderate
(K = 5–7 mEq/L):
Tall, symmetrically peaked T
waves with a narrow base
more severe (K = 8–11 mEq/L):
QRS widens, PR segment
prolongs, P wave disappears;
ECG resembles a sine wave in
severe cases

Hypokalemia
ST depression
T wave flattening
large positive U wave

Hypercalcemia
shortened QT interval due to a
shortened ST segment

Hypocalcemia
prolonged QT interval due to a
prolonged ST segment; T wave
duration normal

Hypothermia
Osborne or J waves: J point
elevation with a characteristic
elevation of the early ST
segment. Slow rhythm, baseline
artifact due to shivering often
present.

Digitalis
ST depression
T wave flattening or inversion
shortened QT interval, increased U
wave amplitude

Quinidine
procainamide
disopyramide
phenothiazines
tricyclic antidepressants
prolonged QT interval, mainly due
to prolonged T wave duration
with flattening or inversion
QRS prolongation
increased U wave amplitude

CNS insult
(e.g., intracerebral
hemorrhage)
diffuse, wide, deeply inverted T
waves with prolonged QT

FIGURE 3–6. Metabolic and drug influences on the ECG.

TABLE 3–6. TYPICAL ECG EVOLUTION OF A TRANSMURAL MYOCARDIAL INFARCTION

ECG ABNORMALITY	ONSET	DISAPPEARANCE
Hyperacute T waves (tall, peaked T waves in leads facing infarction)	Immediately	6–24 hr
ST segment elevation	Immediately	1–6 wk
Q waves > 0.04 sec	Immediately or in several days	Years to never
T wave inversion	6–24 hr	Months to years

LONG-TERM AMBULATORY ECG RECORDING

Ambulatory continuous ECG recording (Holter monitor) or patient-activated ECG event recording is used to detect rhythm disturbances in patients with symptoms suggestive of arrhythmia or to document the efficacy of therapy for arrhythmias. Arrhythmia frequency and complexity can be quantitated and correlated with the patient's symptoms. Arrhythmias that occur infrequently or occur during a patient's normal daily activities can be documented. In addition, long-term ECG recording can document alterations in QRS morphology, ST segment, and T waves and thus may be useful for evaluation of ischemia that produces ECG changes; however, the efficacy of ambulatory ECG recordings for this purpose is controversial.

For continuous ambulatory ECG recording, two ECG leads are usually recorded simultaneously via electrodes attached to the patient's skin. A small box containing the tape recorder is carried for the period of recording, usually 24 hours, and the patient is encouraged to maintain his normal activities and to perform any activity that he feels may precipitate the arrhythmia. The tapes are scanned with a high-speed system with which a technician interacts, and examples are printed on ECG paper for the physician's interpretation.

In a patient whose arrhythmia is infrequent and difficult to document, recording for several days to weeks using a patient-activated recorder (event recorder) at the time of symptoms has replaced the Holter monitor in many situations in which correlation of infrequent symptoms with ECG findings is needed. The simplest type of event recorder can be carried with the patient; upon onset of symptoms it can be held to the chest and the ECG recorded and subsequently transmitted via telephone to a monitoring center. In patients with dizziness or syncope or in those whose symptoms are very fleeting, a continuous closed-loop event recorder is available which is attached to the patient via skin electrodes; upon patient activation the recorder saves several seconds of ECG monitoring prior to the event and several seconds after the event.

STRESS TESTING

Because symptoms of cardiovascular disease may not be evident in the resting state, exercise stress testing is sometimes necessary to demonstrate an abnormality and assess its severity. The most common type of exercise testing consists of walking on a treadmill at increasing speeds and degrees of incline. The test is continued until the patient has reached 90 per cent of the predicted maximal heart rate, has anginal chest pain that is progressive during exercise, has an excessive degree of ischemic ST segment depression or elevation during exercise, or has various arrhythmias (especially ventricular tachycardia or heart block) precipitated by exercise. The test is stopped if there are any signs of circulatory failure (e.g., exhaustion, staggering gait, diminished pulse, or a decrease in systolic blood pressure). In addition to treadmill testing, patients can be stressed with bicycle or arm exercise. Exercise testing results may be enhanced with nuclear (thallium scanning or radionuclide ventriculography) or echocardiographic techniques.

Exercise testing can aid in the differential diagnosis of chest pain. In addition, it can be used to evaluate prognosis and/or functional capacity in patients with known coronary heart disease or following myocardial infarction. In patients with coronary artery disease, an exercise test that is positive (see below) in the first two stages (6 minutes) carries a relatively poor prognosis, and further evaluation to include cardiac catheterization may be considered.

The normal response to exercise is an increase in heart rate and both systolic and diastolic blood pressure. The heart rate times maximal blood pressure may be calculated to estimate the workload obtained (double product).

The normal ECG response to exercise is a normal T wave polarity with either no change in the ST segment or mild depression of the J point with a rapidly upsloping ST segment. Abnormal ECG responses include at least a 1-mm depression of the J point and downsloping or horizontal depression of the ST segment similar to the ECG findings of ischemia. ST elevation is a markedly abnormal response to exercise unless it occurs in an area of old transmural infarction, in which case it may be related to regional wall dysfunction rather than ischemia. It may also occur in patients with significant, usually three-vessel, coronary artery disease or with variant angina. The precipitation of negative U waves with exercise is a positive ischemic response and usually indicates disease of the left anterior descending coronary artery. Arrhythmias occurring with exercise may be due to ischemia. In addition to the reproduction of chest pain and ischemic ECG changes, non-ECG signs may be important; for example, the patient may develop an S_4 or S_3 gallop, a systolic murmur of papillary muscle dysfunction, or pulmonary congestion with exercise. A sustained decrease in blood pressure with exercise is a particularly grave finding indicative of extensive coronary artery disease.

The ECG cannot be considered diagnostically reliable in patients with pre-existing nonspecific ST-T wave abnormalities, left ventricular hypertrophy, left bundle branch block, digoxin administration within the past 10 days, electrolyte abnormalities (e.g., hypokalemia), and labile ST-T changes (abnormal ST-T changes occurring with hyperventilation or position changes). In these patients one should consider nuclear or echocardiographic imaging techniques that can demonstrate regional perfusion or wall motion abnormalities with stress. In patients who cannot exercise because of arthritic, neuromuscular, or peripheral vascular problems, these imaging techniques may be used in conjunction with pharmacologic agents such as dipyridamole or dobutamine, which can mimic the effects of exercise and result in regional perfusion or wall motion defects.

Many physicians perform a limited treadmill test in patients 1 to 2 weeks following myocardial infarction. In this situation, the end point is a heart rate of 70 per cent rather than 90 per cent of predicted maximum, or the production of symptoms. The prognosis of patients after infarction who have early exercise symptoms or ECG changes is poorer than it is in those with good exercise capacity. Patients with the following conditions should not be exercised: unstable angina or acute myocardial infarction; severe aortic stenosis; severe hypertension; congestive heart failure; uncontrolled cardiac arrhythmias; acute myocarditis or pericarditis; any acute, noncardiac systemic illness; and known severe coronary artery disease such as left main coronary artery stenosis.

ECHOCARDIOGRAPHY

It is beyond the scope of this text to describe echocardiography in detail. Abnormal echocardiographic findings in specific disease states are discussed with each disease.

Ultrasound consists of sound frequencies greater than those audible by the human ear which are directed toward the desired structures by a transducer placed on the chest wall. The sound waves

are reflected at the interface of structures with differing acoustic densities and return to the transducer where they are recorded. Changes in tissue planes are generally strong reflectors of ultrasound, whereas body fluids such as blood reflect very little ultrasound. The depth of the structure reflecting the ultrasonic signal back to the transducer can be displayed as a one-dimensional "ice-pick" view against time on a strip chart recorder (M-mode) or can be displayed on an oscilloscope in real time as a two-dimensional cross-sectional "slice" of the heart (two-dimensional echocardiography) (Fig. 3–7). Two-dimensional echocardiography is superior to M-mode for most indications, with the exception of certain situations in which higher resolution and careful timing of motion of certain structures are desired.

Echocardiography can be used to diagnose mitral stenosis with high reliability, and two-dimensional echocardiography can quantitate mitral orifice area in most patients. In addition, concomitant lesions (e.g., aortic insufficiency or tricuspid stenosis) and hemodynamic aberrations (e.g., pulmonary hypertension or right ventricular failure) can be identified in patients with mitral stenosis. Patients with left ventricular outflow obstruction can be evaluated for either aortic valvular, supravalvular, or subvalvular stenosis. Even though quantitation of aortic stenosis is difficult, echocardiography may be useful to exclude signif-

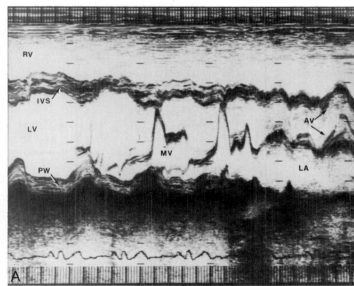

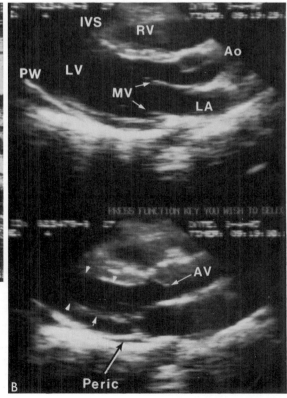

FIGURE 3–7. Portions of normal M-mode (A) and two-dimensional (B) echocardiograms. RV = Right ventricle; LV = left ventricle; MV = mitral valve; IVS = interventricular septum; AV = aortic valve; Ao = aorta; PW = posterior LV wall; Peric = pericardium; LA = left atrium. The four white arrowheads indicate the left ventricular endocardium. (Courtesy of William F. Armstrong, M.D.)

icant aortic stenosis in many patients. Echocardiography is the technique of choice to diagnose mitral valve prolapse, hypertrophic cardiomyopathy, and atrial myxoma. Echocardiography is the most sensitive test for the detection of pericardial effusion, and certain echocardiographic signs are useful clues of hemodynamic compromise (tamponade). Echocardiography may be useful to visualize the vegetations of bacterial endocarditis, but smaller vegetations (<2 mm in diameter) are not usually identified. Even when the vegetations themselves are not seen, echocardiography may detect the structural complications of endocarditis (e.g., flail mitral leaflet), the hemodynamic alterations due to valvular dysfunction (e.g., the elevated left ventricular end-diastolic pressure in patients with acute aortic regurgitation), or the pre-existing valvular abnormality that predisposed the patient to endocarditis. Echocardiography may help detect pulmonic valve stenosis or pulmonary hypertension via abnormal motion of the pulmonic valve. The internal dimensions of the left atrium and left ventricle can be accurately measured, and an estimate of right ventricular and atrial size can be ascertained. The thickness of the septum and the posterior left ventricular wall can be measured accurately. Certain hemodynamic information can be ascertained, such as pulmonary hypertension, decreased flow across the mitral valve, and elevated left ventricular end-diastolic pressure. Conduction abnormalities in left bundle branch block and some cases of the Wolff-Parkinson-White syndrome can be detected. Segmental wall motion abnormalities characteristic of coronary artery disease are detectable. Dilation of the aorta and occasionally an aortic dissection can be noted. The function of prosthetic valves can be evaluated grossly; however, detailed examination of prosthetic valves is often difficult because of their high echogenicity. In patients with congenital heart disease, echocardiography can often establish the diagnosis or complement cardiac catheterization in unraveling complex malformations. Thrombi in the left ventricle and atrium can be detected, but the sensitivity of echocardiography for this purpose is not clear. Mitral regurgitation and aortic regurgitation are often not detectable directly and are inferred indirectly from their effects on wall motion, chamber size, and motion of other valves.

Transesophageal echocardiography is a newer technique whereby images of the heart are obtained by means of a transducer introduced into the esophagus via the oropharynx. Its advantages over transthoracic echocardiography include providing markedly improved image quality and allowing areas of the heart not well seen on transthoracic echocardiography (such as the aorta, left atrial appendage, and structural details of the mitral valve) to be imaged. Transesophageal echocardiography is especially useful for diagnosis of aortic dissection; identification of vegetations in endocarditis, especially if a prosthetic valve is involved; identification of left atrial clots, a source of emboli in young patients with stroke; and identification of the anatomy and pathology of the mitral valve in preoperative, intraoperative, and postoperative assessment of surgical mitral valve repairs.

Contrast echocardiography can be useful in detecting atrial or ventricular intracardiac shunts or tricuspid regurgitation. Contrast agents include agitated saline, indocyanine green dye, and Renografin. Tiny bubbles in agitated solutions are echocardiographically opaque and produce bright echoes. After injection via an antecubital vein, the contrast can be traced through the right atrium and ventricle. The bubbles are absorbed by the pulmonary capillaries and normally do not opacify the left side of the heart. A right-to-left shunt is detected by the appearance of contrast in the left atrium or ventricle. A left-to-right shunt is detected by a negative contrast effect in a right-sided chamber. Tricuspid regurgitation is detected by regurgitation of contrast into the inferior vena cava.

Echocardiography during or immediately following exercise may detect regional wall motion abnormalities not present in the resting state.

Doppler ultrasonography is a newer technique for the noninvasive detection and quantification of valvular lesions and cardiac shunts. It is based on the principle that blood moving toward or away from an ultrasound transducer alters the frequency of the reflected ultrasound waves in proportion to the velocity of the blood flow. In conjunction with two-dimensional echocardiography, the Doppler probe can be aimed to detect forward or regurgitant flow across valves and through any abnormal intracardiac connection. Doppler ultrasonography can help quantitate the severity of aortic or mitral stenosis. The extent of mitral, tricuspid, or aortic regurgitation can be quantitated only roughly. The intracardiac shunts of ventricular septal defect, atrial septal defect, and patent ductus arteriosus can be detected but not adequately quantitated. Right heart and pulmonary arterial pressures can be estimated, and the function of prosthetic valves evaluated. Doppler flow measurements are useful for detecting serial changes in cardiac output but not for accurately measuring absolute cardiac output.

NUCLEAR CARDIOLOGY

Three techniques using radioactive tracers are useful in clinical cardiology: radionuclide angiography, perfusion scintigraphy, and infarct-avid scintigraphy (Table 3–7).

The first-pass study and the equilibrium study are two basic techniques employed in radionuclide angiography. In the first-pass study, a high-speed scintillation camera follows the transit of isotope injected into a peripheral vein through the right heart, pulmonary vasculature, and left heart, much as a radiopaque dye injection is recorded

TABLE 3–7. SELECTED NONINVASIVE CARDIAC LABORATORY TESTS

TEST	REASON FOR TEST	ABNORMAL RESULT	MEANING
Long-term ECG	Palpitations Syncope	Brady- or tachyarrhythmias	Needs correlation with symptoms
Stress testing	Chest pain	ST depression with pain	Ischemia (false-positive and false-negative tests occur)
	Evaluate functional capacity and prognosis in patients with known heart disease	Positive for ischemia within first two stages	High-risk patient, should possibly undergo further evaluation
Radionuclide angiography	LV function	↓Ejection fraction; regional wall motion abnormalities	Abnormal resting ventricular function
	Exercise evaluation of chest pain or ventricular reserve (e.g., aortic regurgitation)	Exercise-induced regional or global wall motion abnormality; inability to ↑ejection fraction with exercise	Ischemia or decreased cardiac reserve
	Intracardiac shunts	Abnormal lung time/activity curve	Left-to-right or right-to-left shunt
Perfusion scintigraphy (exercise)	Chest pain (especially in patients with abnormal baseline ECG); or to evaluate the functional significance of a known coronary lesion	Defect on exercise and reperfusion scans	Myocardial scar
		Defect on exercise scan that reverses on reperfusion scan	Myocardial ischemia
Infarct-avid scintigraphy	Document acute MI, especially if ECG and enzyme evidence are inconclusive	Myocardial uptake of isotope; focal area of uptake is most specific	Acute MI (false-positive scans sometimes occur with older MIs, myocarditis, pericarditis, LV aneurysm, breast lesion, rib fractures, calcified cartilages or valve structures; smaller infarctions can be missed)

LV = Left ventricular; ECG = electrocardiogram; MI = myocardial infarction.

during a cardiac catheterization. The equilibrium method involves labeling the "blood pool" by introducing human serum albumin or red cells labeled with technetium-99. Images are acquired with a camera that times or "gates" acquisition according to the ECG; that is, the cardiac cycle is divided into multiple segments, each of which is counted repeatedly and individually, and the final average is displayed as one cardiac cycle that can be visualized over and over in an endless loop format.

Perfusion scintigraphy, "cold spot scanning," employs a radioactive potassium analogue, thallium-201. Cells must be both perfused and metabolically intact in order to accumulate thallium-201. Therefore, nonperfused or dead myocardium appears as a "cold spot" on the scan. When exercise thallium imaging is performed, the patient is exercised to the usual stress testing end points and a scan is performed immediately after exercise and again 4 hours later, allowing thallium to redistribute into areas of myocardium that are reperfused after recovery from exercise. An area without thallium uptake (cold) on both exercise and reperfusion scans is considered infarcted, scarred, or irreversibly damaged. An area that is cold on the exercise scan but reperfused 4 hours later is considered "ischemic," with a reversible lesion.

In infarct-avid scintigraphy or "hot spot scanning," an isotope (usually technetium-99 stannous pyrophosphate) that accumulates in irreversibly damaged myocardial cells is administered intravenously to detect acute myocardial infarction. Technetium pyrophosphate scans are negative during the first few hours after infarction and usually become positive after about 12 hours. The probability of a positive scan decreases the first week after infarction and is low after 2 weeks. It is most sensitive in patients with transmural myocardial infarctions; however, these infarctions are usually diagnosed with clinical ECG and enzyme determinations, so the usefulness of infarct-avid scintigraphy for questionable small infarcts is unclear.

NEWER TECHNIQUES

Computed tomography (CT scanning) is useful to detect dissecting aortic aneurysms and is probably the most sensitive method for detecting the pericardial thickening associated with constrictive pericarditis. CT scanning may be useful for assessing the patency of saphenous vein grafts used in coronary artery bypass surgery.

Magnetic resonance imaging (MRI) can produce high-resolution tomographic images of the heart without employing ionizing radiation. It also has the potential for generating metabolic information about the heart. Future applications may be non-invasive angiocardiography and possibly characterization of diseased tissue. Positron emission tomography (PET scanning) holds promise for detecting "hibernating" myocardium, that is, muscle that does not contract but is still viable and may be salvagable by interventional techniques.

Digital subtraction angiography is a technique whereby small concentrations of iodinated contrast material introduced in a vascular bed can be detected, analyzed by computer, and displayed as a high-quality angiogram, thus eliminating the need for direct injection of contrast into an artery or cardiac chamber. Venous contrast injections may provide left ventriculograms of good quality. The carotid circulation and coronary bypass grafts may be well visualized by this technique. Venous contrast injection does not usually provide adequate visualization of coronary arteries, but digital subtraction techniques can improve the quality of coronary angiograms obtained by selective coronary catheterization.

CARDIAC CATHETERIZATION

Cardiac catheterization involves introduction of hollow, fluid-filled catheters via the arterial and/or venous system into the heart to measure intracardiac pressures, blood flow, and oxygen saturation, and to inject contrast to perform cardiac angiography. The complexity of the procedure depends on the particular patient and lesion being investigated and ranges from extensive studies in patients with complex congenital and valvular heart disease to straightforward measurement of left heart pressures, ventriculography, and coronary arteriography in patients with coronary artery disease.

Fluid-filled catheters transmit pressure waves obtained in each chamber entered back to a transducer, and pressure waveforms are displayed on an oscilloscope and recorded. Intracavitary pressures are used to judge the performance of the right and left ventricles, and pressure differences across valves (gradient) are used to evaluate valvular stenosis. The pulmonary capillary wedge pressure is measured by wedging the pulmonary arterial catheter as far into the pulmonary arterial tree as possible or inflating a balloon in a distal pulmonary artery, thus blocking out pulmonary arterial pressure and allowing the catheter to record pulmonary capillary or venous pressure. This pressure, given a patent pulmonary venous system, reflects left atrial pressure, which in turn, given a normal mitral valve, reflects the left ventricular diastolic pressure. This measurement is useful not only in the catheterization laboratory but also during bedside right heart (Swan-Ganz) catheterization to estimate the left-sided filling pressures.

The cardiac output may be measured during catheterization by one of two basic techniques. Using the *Fick method*, the oxygen consumption of the patient is measured by collecting the expired air over a known period of time and simultaneously measuring arterial and mixed venous (pulmonary artery) oxygen content. The Fick equation states the following:

$$\text{Cardiac output} = \frac{O_2 \text{ consumption (ml/min)}}{\substack{\text{arterial } O_2 \\ \text{content}} - \substack{\text{mixed venous} \\ O_2 \text{ content (ml/L)}}}$$

Cardiac output is expressed in liters per minute and cardiac index in liters per minute per square meter of body surface. In addition, cardiac output may be measured by an *indicator dilution technique*, using either a dye that is detected by colorimetric methods or temperature (thermodilution) as the indicator. When an indicator is injected into the circulatory system and detected downstream, a curve can be generated. The area under the curve is proportional to the cardiac output.

Intracardiac shunts can be detected by measuring oxygen saturations in various cardiac chambers. For example, an increase in oxygen saturation between the right atrium and right ventricle would occur in a ventricular septal defect in which oxygenated blood is shunted from the left to the right ventricle (oxygen "step-up"). If the cardiac output is known, the shunt can be quantitated. Secondly, indicator dilution methods similar to that used for cardiac output determination may be used to detect shunts. For example, if an indicator is introduced into the right atrium and detected sooner than expected in a systemic artery, a right-to-left shunt is present. In addition, indicator dilution methods can detect valvular regurgitation.

Cardiac catheterization can be used to detect and quantitate the severity of a stenotic valvular lesion. Valves that are regurgitant can be established (but are difficult to quantitate) by cardiac angiography, which involves injecting radiopaque contrast into various chambers of the heart. Upon coronary injection of contrast, atherosclerotic lesions appear as narrowings of the internal caliber of the vessels and are expressed in terms of per cent diameter narrowing, for example, a 70 per cent diminution in the luminal diameter. Lesions producing narrowings of 70 per cent or greater are definitely hemodynamically significant, and lesions of 50 to 70 per cent diameter narrowing are probably hemodynamically significant.

In congenital or acquired valvular defects, cardiac catheterization may be used to establish the diagnosis, assess the hemodynamic severity of the lesion, and exclude unsuspected additional lesions (e.g., concomitant coronary artery disease). A few instances exist in which the value of routine preoperative cardiac catheterization has been questioned. For example, echocardiography is very reliable for diagnosing and quantifying mitral stenosis, and the likelihood of concomitant coronary artery disease in a young patient is small. Therefore, if there is no clinical evidence of significant aortic or tricuspid disease, some physicians would operate on such a patient without catheterization.

In patients suspected of having coronary artery disease, cardiac catheterization is indicated when (1) the cause of the chest pain remains unclear after noninvasive evaluation; (2) angina is refractory to medical management; (3) patients are at high risk for having left main or severe three-vessel stenosis and may have improved survival with revascularization (see Chapter 7); or (4) an acute intervention (i.e., angioplasty or intracoronary thrombolysis) is contemplated in the first 4 to 6 hours after infarction. Cardiac catheterization may be indicated to provoke coronary spasm with ergonovine in a patient suspected of having Prinzmetal's angina. Left heart catheterization with coronary arteriography is a relatively safe procedure, with a mortality of between 0.1 and 0.2 per cent. The risk is higher for patients with significant stenosis of the left main coronary artery.

SPECIAL TECHNIQUES

Biopsies of the left or right ventricular endomyocardium can be obtained at the time of catheterization and are useful for diagnosing myocardial rejection in patients with cardiac transplants and sometimes for diagnosing hypertrophic and congestive cardiomyopathies, especially if amyloid or other infiltrative processes are present.

Percutaneous transluminal coronary angioplasty involves passing balloon catheters into the coronary arteries and across stenotic lesions, where the balloon is inflated. This technique is effective in relieving obstruction in patients who have either single-vessel or multivessel disease. Left main coronary artery stenosis is generally not safe to dilate with angioplasty. Long-term results of this technique are still being evaluated, and restenosis is a major limitation (see Chapter 7).

The infusion of thrombolytic agents (e.g., streptokinase), either intravenously or directly into the coronary system, can reopen an acutely occluded coronary artery in patients suffering an acute transmural myocardial infarction. Complications appear to be low from either intravenous or intracoronary administration, although the risk of serious bleeding from any recent arterial punctures or surgical procedures is high (see Chapter 7).

Bedside right heart catheterization with a balloon flow-directed catheter (Swan-Ganz catheter) can be accomplished in an intensive care unit, and the catheter can remain in place for several hours to several days to guide drug therapy or fluid administration. Serial measurements of pulmonary arterial pressure, pulmonary capillary wedge pressure, right atrial pressure, and cardiac output using the thermodilution technique can be obtained. Swan-Ganz catheterization is useful to help manage patients with cardiogenic, septic, and other forms of shock; during or after surgery in patients with significant cardiac disease; in patients with multiorgan failure in whom the fluid and hemodynamic management is complex; and during serial evaluation of pharmacologic or other interventions in patients with various cardiopulmonary abnormalities. It is useful in the differential diagnosis of cardiac versus noncardiac pulmonary edema and ventricular septal versus papillary muscle rupture in acute myocardial infarction and in patients with hypotension unresponsive to fluid administration. Swan-Ganz catheterization helps in the diagnosis of right heart abnormalities, such as pericardial tamponade or constriction and right ventricular infarction (Table 3–8).

TABLE 3–8. DIFFERENTIAL DIAGNOSIS USING A BEDSIDE BALLOON FLOW-DIRECTED (SWAN-GANZ) CATHETER

DISEASE STATE	THERMODILUTION CARDIAC OUTPUT	PCW PRESSURE	RA PRESSURE	COMMENTS
Cardiogenic shock	↓	↑	nl or ↑	
Septic shock (early)	↑	↓	↓	↓Systemic vascular resistance; myocardial dysfunction can occur late
Volume overload	nl or ↑	↑	↑	
Volume depletion	↓	↓	↓	
Noncardiac pulmonary edema	nl	nl	nl	
Pulmonary heart disease	nl or ↓	nl	↑	↑PA pressure
RV infarction	↓	↓ or nl	↑	
Pericardial tamponade	↓	nl or ↑	↑	Equalization of diastolic RA, RV, PA, and PCW pressure
Papillary muscle rupture	↓	↑	nl or ↑	Large v waves in PCW tracing
Ventricular septal rupture	↑*	↑	nl or ↑	* Artifact due to RA → PA sampling of thermodilution technique. O$_2$ saturation higher in PA than RA; may have large v waves in PCW tracing

PA = Pulmonary artery; PCW = pulmonary capillary wedge; RA = right atrium; RV = right ventricle; nl = normal; ↑ = increased; ↓ = decreased.

REFERENCES

Feigenbaum H: Echocardiography. 4th ed. Philadelphia, Lea & Febiger, 1986.

Fisch C: Electrocardiography of Arrhythmias. Philadelphia, Lea & Febiger, 1990.

Gerson MC: Cardiac Nuclear Medicine. New York, McGraw-Hill, 1987.

Grossman W, Baim DS: Cardiac Catheterization, Angiography and Intervention. 4th ed. Philadelphia, Lea & Febiger, 1991.

Hatle L, Angelsen B: Doppler Ultrasound in Cardiology. 3rd ed. Philadelphia, Lea & Febiger, 1991.

Marriott HJL: Practical Electrocardiography. 8th ed. Baltimore, Williams & Wilkins, 1988.

Popp RL: Echocardiography. N Engl J Med 323:101, 165, 1990.

4 CIRCULATORY FAILURE

Heart failure refers to a state in which the heart cannot provide sufficient cardiac output to satisfy the metabolic needs of the body. It is commonly termed "congestive" heart failure, since symptoms of increased venous pressure (pulmonary congestion with left heart failure and peripheral edema with right heart failure) are often prominent.

Heart failure can result from several underlying diseases, most commonly in industrialized nations from atherosclerotic coronary artery disease with myocardial infarction. Myocarditis, various cardiomyopathies, and valvular and congenital defects may result in heart failure. Mitral and aortic regurgitation, ventricular and atrial septal defects, and patent ductus arteriosus cause volume overload states; aortic and pulmonic stenosis and systemic hypertension cause pressure overload states. Conditions that restrict ventricular filling, such as mitral stenosis, constrictive pericarditis, or restrictive cardiomyopathies, cause heart failure.

Patients with previously compensated heart failure may decompensate as a result of dietary indiscretion (increased sodium intake) or failure to take prescribed medications. Exposure to excess heat or humidity, excess exertion, anemia, pregnancy, hyperthyroidism, or infection may exacerbate heart failure by increasing the metabolic needs of the body. Systemic hypertension, acute myocardial infarction, pulmonary embolus, and endocarditis should be excluded. Recurrence of the primary cause, such as acute rheumatic fever, must be considered. The sudden onset of an arrhythmia, such as atrial fibrillation, may cause decompensation in a previously well-compensated patient.

By adjusting stroke volume and heart rate, the normal heart can increase cardiac output from approximately 5 L/min at rest to as much as 20 L/min during strenuous activity. The stroke volume is dependent upon the inotropic state of the ventricle, the preload (the ventricular filling or end-diastolic pressure), and the afterload (the resistance into which the ventricle empties) (see Chapter 1). The inotropic state or contractility does not limit cardiac output in the normal heart but is the limiting parameter in patients with cardiac muscle dysfunction. In heart failure, the resting cardiac output may be normal, but the ability to increase cardiac output with exercise is abnormal. The autonomic nervous system is important in regulating cardiac function in normal hearts. As heart failure ensues, sympathetic nervous system output increases to help maintain cardiac output via positive chronotropic and inotropic effects (Table 4–1), accounting for some of the clinical features of heart failure (tachycardia, diaphoresis, cool or cyanotic extremities due to peripheral vasoconstriction). However, excessive sympathetic nervous system activity also may be detrimental to cardiac function, most specifically by increasing myocardial oxygen requirements and increasing peripheral vascular resistance (afterload) against which the heart must pump. A downward spiral may occur: increased systemic vascular resistance causes diminished cardiac output, which, in turn, leads to increasing sympathetic tone and even higher peripheral vascular resistance. Therefore, the autonomic nervous system plays an important role in both compensatory and decompensatory responses in congestive heart failure.

Atrial natriuretic factor is a peptide produced by the atria in response to distention. Its plasma levels reflect the severity of heart failure and correlate with mortality. Its physiologic effects of vasodilation and enhanced salt and water excretion may be favorable in heart failure.

In addition to sympathetic augmentation of heart rate and stroke volume, the failing heart may attempt to compensate by either dilating to

TABLE 4–1. COMPENSATORY MECHANISMS IN HEART FAILURE

MECHANISM	FAVORABLE EFFECTS	UNFAVORABLE EFFECTS
↑Sympathetic activity	↑Heart rate ↑Contractility ↑Venoconstriction → ↑venous return (preload)	↑Arteriolar constriction → ↑afterload ↑O$_2$ requirements
Cardiac hypertrophy	↑Working muscle mass	↑Wall tension ↓Coronary flow ↑O$_2$ requirements Abnormal systolic and diastolic properties of hypertrophic muscle
Frank-Starling mechanism	↑Stroke volume for any given amount of venous return	Pulmonary and systemic congestion ↑LV size → ↑wall tension and O$_2$ requirements
Renal salt and water retention	↑Venous return	Pulmonary and systemic congestion ↑Renin-angiotensin → ↑vasoconstriction (afterload)
Increased peripheral O$_2$ extraction	↑O$_2$ delivery per unit of cardiac output	

↑ = Increased; ↓ = decreased; LV = left ventricular.

increase cardiac output via the Starling mechanism or hypertrophying in patients with pressure overload states. Normal and abnormal ventricular function curves are illustrated in Figure 4–1. The curve is shifted downward to the right and has a flattened contour in the patient with decreased cardiac contractility. In both the normal and decreased inotropic states, an increase in the left ventricular end-diastolic volume or pressure (LVEDP) increases cardiac output. The amount of increase in cardiac output for any given rise in

LVEDP is greater in the normal than in the failing heart. In addition, elevation of LVEDP increases pulmonary venous pressures; once the pulmonary capillary wedge pressure exceeds approximately 20 mm Hg, pulmonary edema results. Therefore, augmentation of cardiac output by increasing LVEDP is limited by the relatively flat Starling curve in the failing heart and occurs at the expense of possibly precipitating pulmonary edema. Cardiac dilation increases myocardial oxygen consumption via the increased wall tension.

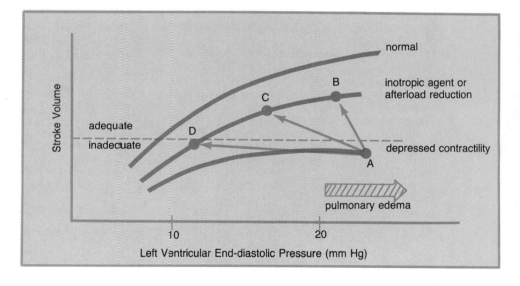

FIGURE 4–1. Normal and abnormal ventricular function curves. When the left ventricular end-diastolic pressure is greater than 20 mm Hg (A), pulmonary edema often occurs. The effect of diuresis or venodilation is to move leftward along the same curve, with a resultant improvement in pulmonary congestion with minimal decrease in cardiac output. The stroke volume is poor at any point along this depressed contractility curve, and thus therapeutic maneuvers that would raise it more toward the normal curve would be necessary to improve cardiac output significantly. Unlike the effect of diuretics, that of digitalis or arterial vasodilator therapy in a patient with heart failure is to move the patient onto another ventricular function curve intermediate between the normal and depressed curves. When the patient's ventricular function moves from A to B by the administration of one of these agents, the left ventricular end-diastolic pressure may also decrease because of improved cardiac function; further administration of diuretics or venodilators may shift the patient further to the left along the same curve from B to C and eliminate the risk of pulmonary edema. A vasodilating agent that has both arteriolar and venous dilating properties (e.g., nitroprusside) would shift this patient directly from A to C. If this agent shifts the patient from A to D because of excessive venodilation or administration of diuretics, the cardiac output may fall too low, even though the left ventricular end-diastolic pressure would be normal (10 mm Hg) for a normal heart. Thus, left ventricular end-diastolic pressures between 15 and 18 mm Hg are usually optimal in the failing heart, to maximize cardiac output but avoid pulmonary edema.

The mechanism of fluid retention and elevation of LVEDP in patients with heart failure is multifactorial. Two important mechanisms involve (1) sympathetic venoconstriction to decrease the capacitance of the venous system and increase venous return to the heart and (2) chronic renal salt and water retention because of decreased perfusion.

Cardiac hypertrophy, which is an increase in the number and size of cardiac cells as a compensatory mechanism, also involves trade-offs: the increased muscle mass increases oxygen consumption. The hypertrophic ventricular muscle is not normal, and its contractility is decreased. The hypertrophied ventricle maintains adequate cardiac output for some time via the increase in muscle mass, the Starling relation, and augmented sympathetic stimulation.

Abnormal systolic function and diastolic (compliance) function are both features of heart failure due to ischemic heart disease and hypertrophic states (Table 4–2). Compliance refers to the pressure required to fill a ventricle to a certain volume. Hypertrophied or ischemic ventricles become "stiff" or relatively noncompliant, requiring a higher LVEDP to achieve diastolic filling adequate to maintain cardiac output. In a patient with congestive heart failure and a relatively noncompliant ventricle, a pulmonary capillary wedge pressure of 15 to 18 mm Hg is usually optimal to maintain adequate left ventricular filling and output but to avoid pulmonary edema.

It is critical to distinguish valvular and congenital causes of congestive heart failure from those due to myocardial damage. In the former, corrective or palliative surgery is often possible. In the latter, however, therapy is imperfect and compensates only partly for the decrease in myocardial function. Patients with myocardial dysfunction unrelated to a correctable lesion have a relatively poor long-term prognosis, with a 50 per cent 1-year mortality in some studies.

Left heart failure refers to decreased function of the left ventricle with resultant low systemic cardiac output and pulmonary vascular congestion. Right heart failure is characterized by the manifestations of elevated right ventricular end-diastolic pressure, jugular venous distention, hepatomegaly, and peripheral edema. Right heart failure may occur in severe lung disease and congenital or acquired defects involving the right-sided chambers or valves. The most common cause of right ventricular failure is chronic left ventricular failure; this probably occurs both because there is a chronic increase in pulmonary pressures in patients with left ventricular failure and because the failing septum is a structure common to both the left and the right ventricles.

Low-output heart failure occurs when myocardial dysfunction prevents normal metabolic requirements from being met. High-output failure refers to the inability of the heart to meet elevated circulatory demands in conditions such as arteriovenous fistula, Paget's disease, anemia, hyperthyroidism, and beriberi.

Backward heart failure and forward heart failure are old terms that refer to the more prominent symptoms in any particular patient. The patient who presents with fatigue and weakness due to decreased cardiac output and azotemia due to decreased renal perfusion would be considered to have predominantly forward failure. On the other hand, the patient who presents with pulmonary or systemic congestive symptoms would be considered to have backward failure.

Acute and chronic forms of heart failure are different clinical entities. A patient has acute heart failure when sudden circulatory decompensation occurs, for example, secondary to an acute myocardial infarction or ruptured chordae tendineae. Chronic compensatory mechanisms do not have time to occur, and the patient may experience acute pulmonary edema. A patient with chronic myocardial dysfunction of the same degree may have adequate compensatory mechanisms to make him or her less symptomatic. Patients with chronic congestive heart failure may develop superimposed acute congestive heart failure if one of the precipitating factors listed above occurs.

The patient's history is important to help establish the diagnosis of congestive heart failure and sometimes to identify its etiology (see Table 2–5). The most common symptoms of left heart failure are respiratory. If heart failure is chronic, dyspnea on exertion occurs before dyspnea at rest, and as the disease progresses, less and less exertion is necessary to provoke dyspnea. Some patients may not complain of shortness of breath but have restricted their activities significantly to avoid it. The patient should be questioned carefully about

TABLE 4–2. COMPARISON OF SYSTOLIC AND DIASTOLIC HEART FAILURE

	PATHOPHYSIOLOGY	EXAMPLES*
Systolic dysfunction	Inability to expel blood due to impaired inotropic state or loss of muscle; decreased forward cardiac output	Dilated cardiomyopathy; loss of muscle contraction due to ischemia
Diastolic dysfunction	Defect in ventricular filling; elevation of ventricular filling pressure → pulmonary or systemic congestion	Hypertrophic cardiomyopathy; infiltrative cardiomyopathy; abnormal ventricular relaxation due to ischemia

* In many clinical states, systolic dysfunction and diastolic dysfunction coexist.

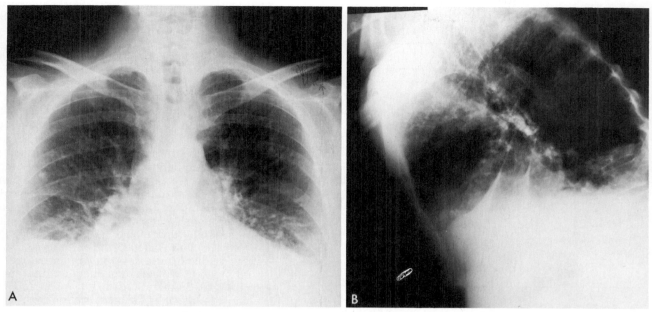

FIGURE 4-2. Posteroanterior chest radiographs showing cardiomegaly (A) and pulmonary vascular congestion typical of pulmonary edema (B).

previous cardiac disease, cardiac medications, and the existence of precipitating factors for congestive heart failure. The physical examination should confirm the physician's suspicion of heart failure (see Table 2-5).

Arterial PO_2—relatively normal in mild heart failure, even though pulmonary stiffness due to interstitial edema may cause a sensation of dyspnea—falls as alveolar edema occurs. In early heart failure, the patient hyperventilates and the PCO_2 decreases; when pulmonary edema becomes severe, carbon dioxide retention occurs. Hepatic congestion may elevate liver enzymes. Increased sympathetic stimulation may slightly increase the white blood cell count. The blood urea nitrogen and, to some extent, the creatinine may be elevated owing to low cardiac output (prerenal azotemia) without necessarily indicating intrinsic renal disease. No electrocardiographic (ECG) changes are specific to heart failure but may reflect underlying cardiac disease (e.g., myocardial infarction, left or right ventricular hypertrophy, or rhythm disturbances).

Radiographic signs of left heart failure depend on its severity and chronicity (Fig. 4-2). Manifestations of pulmonary venous hypertension are discussed in Chapter 2. Cardiomegaly is common in patients with chronic heart failure but is often absent in those with acute forms (e.g., acute severe aortic regurgitation). The radiographic manifestations of pulmonary edema resolve 12 to 24 hours after hemodynamic improvement.

Noninvasive tests may be used to estimate ventricular function. Echocardiography demonstrates segmental or global wall motion abnormalities and provides chamber dimensions. Echocardiography may also suggest the etiology of the congestive heart failure. Radionuclide ventriculography reveals chamber size, regional wall motion abnormalities, and ejection fraction. The left ventricular filling pressure and the cardiac output form the two limbs of the ventricular function curve and may be obtained in unstable patients via Swan-Ganz catheterization.

Since many of the clinical manifestations of cardiac failure involve the lungs, the differentiation between heart failure and pulmonary disease is sometimes difficult. Noncardiac pulmonary edema (adult respiratory distress syndrome, ARDS) must be distinguished from cardiogenic pulmonary edema. A variety of processes can cause ARDS (e.g., infection, shock, neurologic injury, and drug toxicity). ARDS results from leakage of plasma into the alveoli because of leaky capillaries; pulmonary venous (capillary wedge) pressures are normal (see Chapter 19).

Chronic congestive heart failure with peripheral edema must be differentiated from other edematous states, such as the nephrotic syndrome, cirrhosis, and severe peripheral venous disease.

MANAGEMENT OF HEART FAILURE

The ideal treatment of congestive heart failure is to remove or correct the underlying cause, such as replacing a stenotic aortic valve. Next, any factors exacerbating chronic compensated heart failure, such as anemia, should be corrected or elimi-

TABLE 4–3. MANAGEMENT OF CONGESTIVE HEART FAILURE

OBJECTIVE	THERAPY
Reduce cardiac workload	Physical and psychological rest
	Remove exacerbating factors (e.g., infection, anemia, heat, humidity, obesity)
	Vasodilators
	Intra-aortic balloon pump
Improve cardiac performance	Digitalis
	Other positive inotropic agents
	Correct any rhythm abnormality
	Correct underlying defect if possible (e.g., valve malfunction)
Control excess salt and water	Dietary sodium restriction
	Diuretics
	Mechanical fluid removal (e.g., phlebotomy, dialysis)

nated. Finally, medical therapy should be aimed at treating the congestive heart failure itself to improve the pumping function of the heart, reduce its workload, and decrease excessive salt and water retention (Table 4–3).

Activity and Diet

An acute exacerbation of congestive heart failure should be treated with bed rest and adequate oxygenation. Control of excessive salt and water retention can be obtained by salt restriction. The normal American diet contains 10 gm of salt daily. Although the usual patient with heart failure does not require rigid salt restriction, a 4-gm salt diet can be obtained by avoiding salty foods and not adding salt at the table. For patients with more severe heart failure, a 2-gm salt diet can be prescribed that requires food to be cooked and prepared without salt. In particularly refractory cases, diets of 0.5 to 1 gm can be prescribed, but only the most compliant patients adhere to these diets, and diuretic therapy may be used instead of restricting

TABLE 4–4. THE USE OF DIGOXIN

Intravenous Administration	
Initial dose	0.5–1.0 mg
Subsequent dose	0.25 mg q2–4h for total dose ≤ 1.5 mg/24 hr
Onset of action	10–15 min
Peak effect	30 min–4 hr
Elimination half-life ($T_{1/2}$)	36 hr
Oral Administration	
Loading dose (in 24 hr)	1.0–1.5 mg
Maintenance dose (in 24 hr)	0.125–0.5 mg
Gastrointestinal absorption	60–85%
Elimination half-life ($T_{1/2}$)	36 hr
Principal route of elimination	Renal
Therapeutic serum levels	0.7–2.0 ng/ml

salt intake so stringently. Salt substitutes are available that contain potassium chloride instead of sodium chloride. It is unusual to have to restrict water intake except when severe congestive heart failure with dilutional hyponatremia occurs. One of the most common causes of exacerbation of congestive heart failure is failure to adhere to a low-salt diet after hospital discharge.

Digitalis

Digitalis augments cardiac output in patients with myocardial failure by increasing the inotropic state of the heart, possibly by inhibiting the activity of sodium-potassium ATPase. Subsequent accumulation of intracellular sodium enhances sodium-calcium ion exchange, and the resultant increase in intracellular calcium is presumed to be responsible for increased contractile force. In addition to its inotropic effects, digitalis has significant electrophysiologic effects, the most prominent of which at therapeutic doses is an increase in atrioventricular (AV) nodal conduction time and refractoriness. Sinus rate may slow owing to sympathetic withdrawal as heart failure improves.

Digitalis is usually prescribed in the form of digoxin (Table 4–4). The bioavailability of several digoxin preparations appears to differ markedly. Patients with malabsorption syndromes may absorb digoxin poorly, and nonabsorbed substances such as cholestyramine, kaolin and pectin (Kaopectate), nonabsorbable antacids, and neomycin may interfere with digoxin absorption. Excretion of digoxin is proportional to the creatinine clearance, and maintenance doses must be reduced in patients with renal failure. Digoxin has a high degree of protein binding and is not removed from the body by dialysis. Digoxin serum concentrations increase when quinidine or amiodarone is added; therefore, the dose of digoxin should be lowered by approximately half when these drugs are added. Digitalis serum concentrations are only guidelines of either adverse or favorable digitalis effects and should be interpreted in the context of the clinical setting. Digoxin serum concentrations should be determined at least 6 hours after a dose to avoid the peak levels.

The end point of digitalis administration in patients with heart failure is not always clear. Digitalis or any other positive inotropic agent shifts the ventricular function curve (see Fig. 4–1) up and to the left; that is, for any given left ventricular end-diastolic pressure, ventricular function is increased. The improvement in ventricular function increases ventricular emptying, promotes a diuresis, and, in turn, reduces the filling pressures in the failing ventricle. This shifts the ventricular function along the new curve to the left and reduces pulmonary venous congestion. Even though increased contractility increases oxygen consumption, this may be offset by reducing diastolic pressure and volume, leading to decreased wall tension and decreased net oxygen consumption. Digitalis has been used for many years in myocardial failure due to ischemic, hypertensive, valvular, congenital, or pulmonary heart disease and idiopathic dilated cardiomyopathy. Its value as a positive inotropic agent has recently been questioned, but it does appear to have a definite, although relatively weak, inotropic effect. It is not useful in isolated mitral stenosis if normal sinus rhythm and normal right ventricular function are present and is not useful in restrictive states such as pericardial tamponade or constriction. In patients who have dynamic outflow obstruction (obstructive hypertrophic cardiomyopathy), digitalis is contraindicated because the increase in contractility may increase the outflow gradient. A hypertrophied but vigorously functioning ventricle probably does not need digitalis. The need for prophylactic use of digitalis in patients with decreased cardiac reserve about to undergo major surgery is controversial. Use of digitalis in arrhythmias often has a more distinct end point, especially in patients with atrial fibrillation, because the rate of ventricular response reflects the adequacy of digitalization. Digitalis is also useful in many patients with paroxysmal supraventricular tachycardias and atrial flutter.

Digitalis toxicity is one of the most common adverse drug reactions, encountered in 5 to 15 per cent of hospitalized patients receiving digitalis. Elderly individuals are more prone to digitalis toxicity than are younger patients. Manifestations include cardiac arrhythmias of almost any type, commonly ventricular premature complexes and ventricular tachycardia, junctional escape rhythms, nonparoxysmal junctional tachycardia, paroxysmal atrial tachycardia with AV block, and type I (Wenckebach) second-degree AV block. Digitalis toxic rhythms have in common the combination of increased automaticity of ectopic pacemakers and impaired conduction. Noncardiac manifestations include anorexia, nausea, vomiting, disorientation, confusion, and seizures. Visual symptoms are not uncommon and include scotomas, halos, and changes in color perception (yellow-green halo commonly occurs). Massive overdoses of digitalis can cause a refractory hyperkalemia. Despite digitalis plasma levels, the diagnosis of digitalis toxicity requires clinical and ECG correlation. Hypokalemia exacerbates digitalis intoxication.

The treatment of digitalis intoxication depends on the degree of intoxication and specific manifestations. Mild rhythm abnormalities (occasional ectopic beats, first- and second-degree AV block, slow ventricular response to atrial fibrillation) require withdrawal of the drug and ECG monitoring. Symptomatic bradyarrhythmias may respond to atropine or, if more severe, may require temporary pacing. Phenytoin and lidocaine are effective drugs to treat ventricular tachycardia and have little effect on conduction. Correction of a low serum potassium level may suppress ectopic rhythms but must be done cautiously in patients with conduction disturbances, since potassium administration can exacerbate AV block. Direct-current (DC) cardioversion is avoided if possible in digitalis intoxication because it may precipitate re-

fractory ventricular fibrillation or cardiac standstill. If a life-threatening ventricular arrhythmia with hemodynamic collapse occurs, cardioversion must be employed with as low an energy level as possible. Since quinidine increases digoxin levels, it probably should be avoided in digitalis intoxication.

The treatment of digitalis, but more specifically digoxin, intoxication has been simplified since the availability of digoxin immune F_{ab}, antigen-binding fragments specific for digoxin that are capable of removing free digoxin from the serum. The antibody binds molecules of digoxin, making them unavailable for binding at their site of action in the heart and other body tissues. The antibody-antigen complex accumulates in the blood and is excreted by the kidney. Administration of digoxin immune F_{ab} is indicated for potentially life-threatening digoxin intoxication associated with severe ventricular arrhythmias or progressive bradyarrhythmias unresponsive to atropine. The digoxin antibody fragments interfere with digitalis immunoassay measurements, and thus digoxin serum concentrations should be obtained prior to administration. Because digitalis intoxication is associated with a shift of potassium from inside to outside the cell, patients may have hyperkalemia despite a total body deficit of potassium; when digoxin antibody is administered, potassium may shift back inside the cell, with resultant hypokalemia. Therefore, potassium concentration must be monitored carefully over the first several hours of digoxin antibody administration. For adults with digitalis toxicity during chronic therapy, 240 mg of the digoxin antibody administered intravenously over 30 minutes is usually adequate. However, patients who ingested large amounts of digitalis may require larger doses. Improvement in the signs and symptoms of digitalis intoxication occurs within one-half hour of administration of the antibody.

Diuretics (See Chapter 26)

Diuretics are drugs that promote the excretion of sodium and water from the kidney and thus affect predominantly preload. They play a very important role in the treatment of heart failure.

Vasodilators

Vasodilator therapy was introduced initially to treat refractory, severe heart failure, but it is now often used earlier in the treatment of congestive heart failure. Vasodilating agents can be divided into two broad categories: venodilators decrease preload by increasing venous capacitance, and arterial dilators reduce systemic arteriolar resistance and decrease afterload. Many vasodilators dilate both venous and arterial beds (Table 4–5).

The effect of arteriolar vasodilators on the ventricular function curve is demonstrated in Figure

TABLE 4–5. COMMONLY USED VASODILATING AGENTS

AGENT	PREDOMINANT SITE OF ACTION	ROUTE OF ADMINISTRATION	USUAL DOSE	DURATION OF EFFECT	SIDE EFFECTS
Nitroprusside	A, V	IV	Initially 10 μg/min; titrate upward at 5-min intervals to desired hemodynamic effect	Minutes	Hypotension Thiocyanate toxicity (fatigue, nausea, muscle spasms, psychosis, hypothyroidism)
Nitroglycerin	V	IV	Initially 10 μg/min; titrate upward at 5-min intervals to desired hemodynamic effect	Minutes	Postural hypotension, dizziness, syncope, headaches, nausea, ischemica upon abrupt withdrawal
		SL	0.3–0.6 mg	Minutes	
		Topical	1–2 inches of 2% ointment q4–6h; or controlled-release topical patch q24h	Hours	
Isosorbide dinitrate	V	SL	2.5–10 mg q2–3h	Hours	Same as nitroglycerin
		Oral	10–40 mg q3–6h	Hours	
Hydralazine	A	Oral	40–400 mg/day in 2–4 divided doses	Hours	Reflex tachycardia, fluid retention, headache, nausea, lupus erythematosus–like syndrome (usually with doses $\geq$ 200 mg/day)
Prazosin	A, V	Oral	1 mg initially; up to 21 mg/day in 2–3 divided doses; small initial test dose	Hours	Hypotension, especially after first dose; fluid retention, headache, nausea, rash; first dose: impairment of renal function, proteinuria, rash, neutropenia
Captopril	A, V	Oral	6.25–25 mg tid initially; 50–100 mg tid usual dose	Hours	Hypotension, especially after first dose; agranulocytosis; proteinuria; hyperkalemia
Enalapril	A, V	Oral	5.0 mg qid initially; 10–40 mg qid usual dose	Hours	Hypotension, azotemia, hyperkalemia, neutropenia, angioedema
Lisinopril	A, V	Oral	10 mg qd initially; 20–40 mg qd usual dose	Hours	Hypotension, azotemia, angioedema

A = Arterial dilator; V = venous dilator; IV = intravenous; SL = sublingual.

4–1. Changes in afterload have little effect on normally functioning myocardium, since reflexes adapt the heart rate and stroke volume accordingly. However, elevated afterload can detrimentally affect the failing myocardium, markedly decreasing the ability of the heart to eject blood. The lower the resistance to the outflow of blood, the more blood is ejected with each beat. Since the heart is able to pump more blood with each stroke when afterload is decreased, the ventricular function curve is shifted upward and to the left, just as it is with an increase in contractility. The shift in the curve due to decrease in afterload is not associated with the increased demand for oxygen that an increase in contractility requires. As ventricular function moves from the failing curve to the afterload-reduced curve, the improvement in ventricular emptying subsequently also decreases preload and left ventricular dimensions, shifting down on the new curve to the left. This decrease in left ventricular dimension decreases left ventricular wall tension and myocardial oxygen consumption. Since failing myocardium is more sensitive to changes in afterload than is normal myocardium, afterload reduction is particularly effective in patients with poorer myocardial function, whereas therapy to increase contractility depends on the availability of some residual functioning myocardium and is less effective as myocardial function declines.

Pure venodilators, preload-reducing agents, shift ventricular function along the same curve to the left as does diuretic therapy. Thus, preload reduction lowers left ventricular filling pressures; even though it does not directly affect forward cardiac output, the diminished left ventricular size decreases wall tension (one of the determinants of afterload) and oxygen consumption, possibly improving forward cardiac performance somewhat. Since the ventricular function curve for the failing myocardium is relatively flat, decreasing the left ventricular end-diastolic pressure to 15 to 20 mm Hg from higher values does not usually decrease cardiac output significantly.

Note that there are end points beyond which one cannot expect vasodilators to be effective. When agents are administered to reduce preload, the filling pressures must be kept high enough so that cardiac output can be maintained. It is especially important in states associated with decreased ventricular compliance (e.g., acute ischemic heart disease and hypertrophic cardiomyopathy) that ventricular filling pressures be maintained higher than normal (15 to 20 mm Hg, normal being approximately 10 mm Hg). When arterial vasodilators are used to attempt to increase forward output, arterial blood pressure may be a limiting factor. In patients whose blood pressure is high, lowering blood pressure by arterial vasodilators may have a beneficial effect. Patients who have relatively low arterial pressure may still benefit from afterload reduction because blood pressure depends not only upon arteriolar resistance but also upon cardiac output (blood pressure = cardiac output × resistance). Patients may have low normal arterial pressure but still have elevated systemic vascular resistance if the cardiac output is low; therefore, if cardiac output improves as peripheral vascular resistance is decreased by arterial vasodilators, blood pressure may not fall. Once blood pressure falls below acceptable limits (approximately 90 mm Hg systolic) during arteriolar vasodilator therapy, one has reached the limits of such therapy unless the decrease in blood pressure is due to an excessive fall in preload induced either by the afterload decrease or by venodilation from the drug itself. In that case, the hypotension can be corrected by fluid administration or by decreasing preload-reducing agents. At times, afterload reduction therapy may be tolerated only after the addition of an inotropic agent such as dopamine or dobutamine. Because of these limitations, it is often advisable to employ invasive hemodynamic monitoring in patients who are acutely ill and require intravenous vasodilator therapy. Indications for vasodilator therapy in congestive heart failure are listed in Table 4–6. Afterload reduction is particularly useful in aortic or mitral regurgitation (acute or chronic) and ventricular septal defect to decrease the regurgitant volume. Afterload reduction must be used with caution in patients with aortic or mitral stenosis.

Sodium nitroprusside is a commonly used parenteral, short-acting vasodilator that has a direct smooth muscle relaxant effect on both arteriolar and venous systems. Hypotension, the most common adverse effect, is reversed within 10 minutes after discontinuation of the infusion. A metabolite of nitroprusside, thiocyanate, may accumulate after several days of administration, especially in patients with renal insufficiency. Serum levels of thiocyanate should be measured if the infusion is prolonged and should be kept below 6 mg/dl.

Nitroglycerin preparations are primarily venous

TABLE 4–6. INDICATIONS FOR VASODILATOR THERAPY OF HEART FAILURE

PREDOMINANT HEART FAILURE SYMPTOM	CAUSE	VASODILATOR OF CHOICE
Dyspnea	LV filling pressure	Preload reduction (e.g., nitrates)
Fatigue	Cardiac output	Afterload reduction (e.g., hydralazine)
Dyspnea and fatigue	LV filling pressure and cardiac output	Balanced vasodilation (e.g., hydralazine plus nitrates; captopril)

LV = Left ventricular.

dilators with lesser effects on the arterioles. Thus, they relieve pulmonary venous congestion with only a modest increase in cardiac output. An arteriolar dilator such as hydralazine may be combined with nitroglycerin to provide a balanced arteriolar and venous dilation.

Tolerance to the favorable hemodynamic effects of oral vasodilators appears to develop in some patients. The angiotensin-converting enzyme (ACE) inhibitors (captopril, enalapril, and lisinopril) have been reported to be the oral vasodilators to which tolerance is least likely to develop. ACE inhibitors are the only agents that appear to prolong survival in these patients. Thus, the ACE inhibitors have become standard early therapy for congestive heart failure, along with diuretics, either in addition to or instead of digitalis. Increased fluid retention during chronic vasodilator therapy may respond to an increase in diuretic. These drugs must be used with caution in patients with renal insufficiency.

Sympathomimetic Amines

Potent parenteral inotropic agents other than digitalis are sometimes required in severe heart failure, the two most common being dopamine and dobutamine. These are sympathomimetic agents producing less tachycardia and fewer peripheral vascular effects than the older drugs norepinephrine, epinephrine, and isoproterenol. Dopamine stimulates the myocardium directly by activating beta$_1$-adrenergic receptors and indirectly by releasing norepinephrine from sympathetic nerve terminals. Dopamine at low doses (2 μg/kg/min) activates dopaminergic receptors in the renal, mesenteric, coronary, and cerebrovascular beds and causes vasodilation. This is partially responsible for dopamine-induced diuresis in patients with severe congestive heart failure (renal vasodilator plus inotropic effects). With larger doses of dopamine (5 to 10 μg/kg/min), alpha-adrenergic agonism similar to that of norepinephrine causes peripheral vasoconstriction. Thus, with infusion of 2 to 5 μg/kg/min, renal blood flow, cardiac contractility, and cardiac output all increase with little change in the heart rate and possibly a small decrease in peripheral vascular resistance. Higher doses (5 to 10 μg/kg/min) begin to increase arterial pressure, peripheral vascular resistance, and heart rate. In patients with hypotension, the vasoconstrictor effects of doses up to 20 μg/kg/min may be desired. The elevation of heart rate, contractility, and blood pressure associated with dopamine may increase oxygen demand, but if cardiac performance is improved and cardiac size decreases, the net oxygen consumption may not be adversely affected.

Dobutamine increases cardiac contractility but has less effect on the peripheral vasculature than does dopamine. It is useful when the vasoconstrictive effects of higher dopamine doses are to be avoided. Dobutamine does not have the renal vasodilatory effects of dopamine. It is administered intravenously in a dose of 5 to 10 μg/kg/min.

Amrinone is a noncatecholamine, nondigitalis positive inotropic agent with vasodilator activity. It is available for short-term intravenous use in patients with severe congestive heart failure and is usually infused at 5 to 10 mg/kg/min.

Nonpharmacologic Management of Heart Failure

Mechanical support of the failing heart by intra-aortic balloon counterpulsation is sometimes useful. The balloon is inserted either surgically or percutaneously into a femoral artery and advanced to the descending aorta. Timed from the ECG, the balloon is deflated immediately before ventricular ejection to decrease aortic pressure (afterload) during ventricular systole and inflated in early diastole to increase aortic pressure and to maintain coronary perfusion. Thus, the hemodynamic benefits of balloon counterpulsation are greater than those of vasodilatory drugs alone. Balloon counterpulsation is useful in stabilizing patients before an intervention designed to provide long-term benefit (percutaneous transluminal coronary angioplasty [PTCA] or surgical revascularization; surgical correction of acute mitral regurgitation or ventricular septal defect). It may be used prophylactically during cardiac catheterization in severely ill patients, as an aid during or after open heart surgery, during treatment of some life-threatening ventricular arrhythmias, and for relieving angina pectoris in patients in whom medical therapy has been unsuccessful.

The role of surgery in patients with congestive heart failure depends on the etiology; surgically correctable lesions should be identified and corrected if possible. In patients with end-stage myocardial dysfunction, the results with cardiac transplantation have recently improved with the introduction of cyclosporine and other improved immunologic support. In addition, the development of mechanical cardiopulmonary apparatus is promising.

Management of Acute Pulmonary Edema

The general management of acute cardiogenic pulmonary edema is summarized in Table 4–7. Furosemide and morphine constitute standard first-line drug therapy. Digitalis is not necessary acutely unless atrial fibrillation or other supraventricular tachyarrhythmia is contributing to the pulmonary

TABLE 4–7. MANAGEMENT OF ACUTE PULMONARY EDEMA

INTERVENTION	PURPOSE	COMMENT
Sitting position	Decreases venous return and work of breathing; increases lung volumes	
Oxygen	Increases arterial Po_2; pulmonary vasodilation	Humidify oxygen to prevent drying of secretions; mask may make patient feel as though he or she is suffocating
Furosemide, 10–20 mg IV; if no response within 30 min, administer progressively larger doses; usual maximum dose 200 mg, but occasional patient requires more	Decreases pulmonary congestion	Rapid pulmonary vasodilatory effect; diuretic effect onset in 5–10 min, peaks in 30 min
Morphine sulfate, 1–4 mg IV q5–10min as needed	Decreases venous return (venodilator); decreases anxiety	Respiratory depression can be reversed with naloxone
Vasodilators, e.g., sublingual or IV nitroglycerin	Decreases venous return; relieves ischemia	
Aminophylline IV	Dilates bronchioles	Relieves "cardiac asthma"; can exacerbate arrhythmias
Phlebotomy	Decreases intravascular volume	Used only if the above fail
Rotating tourniquets applied to three of the four extremities at a time and inflated above venous but below arterial pressure	Reduces venous return from the extremities	Used only if the above fail
Dialysis	Decreases intravascular volume	Useful in renal patients in whom diuretics have been ineffective

edema. Reversible causes or exacerbating factors of pulmonary edema should be sought (e.g., anemia and arrhythmia).

If initial measures fail to correct pulmonary edema, or if drug administration is limited by the development of hypotension, more aggressive management to include invasive hemodynamic monitoring is usually indicated. Parenteral inotropic and vasodilating agents may be administered. If adequate ventilation cannot be maintained, intubation with mechanical ventilation may be required to maintain oxygenation and decrease the work of breathing. In patients refractory to the above measures in whom a reversible process is present, intra-aortic balloon counterpulsation or a left ventricular assist device may be employed.

SHOCK

Shock is acute severe circulatory failure. Regardless of etiology, shock is associated with marked reduction of blood flow to vital organs, and therefore profound arterial hypotension, impaired mentation, and diminished urinary output usually occur. The common denominator of all four broad categories of shock (Table 4–8) is eventual cellular damage and death. Shock may be divided into three stages. The first is a stage of "compensated hypotension"; that is, the fall in cardiac output or in delivery of cardiac output to the tissues stimulates a variety of compensatory mechanisms that alter myocardial function and peripheral resistance to maintain circulation to vital organs such as the brain and the heart. The clinical symptoms during this stage are minimal. In stage 2, the compensatory mechanisms for dealing with the low delivery of nutrients to the body are overwhelmed, and tissue perfusion is decreased. Early signs of cerebral, renal, and myocardial insufficiency and of excessive sympathetic discharge are present. In stage 3, severe ischemia occurs along with damage to tissues by toxins, antigen-antibody reactions, or complement activation. Especially prone to damage are the capillary endothelia in the kidneys, the liver, and the lungs. Ischemic damage to the gastrointestinal tract allows invasion by bacteria. Renal ischemia may lead to acute renal insufficiency. Damage to capillary endothelia throughout the body allows transudation of fluid and protein into the extracellular space, exacerbating hypotension. The severe acidosis and toxins released into the blood contribute to further myocardial depression.

The etiology of hypoperfusion is evident in cardiogenic and hypovolemic shock. Septic shock is most commonly caused by gram-negative bacterial infections but can occur with infections by other agents. The mechanism of shock appears to be related to the release of an endotoxin (part of the bacterial cell wall) that interacts with substances from the blood and causes increased vascular permeability, intravascular coagulation, depression of myocardial contractility, and other adverse reactions. It is manifest by an abnormality in the dis-

TABLE 4–8. ETIOLOGIES OF SHOCK

CATEGORY OF SHOCK	CAUSES
Cardiogenic or vascular obstructive	Arrhythmias Obstructive outflow (valvular and perivalvular) lesions Atrial myxoma Acute myocardial infarction Severe congestive heart failure Cardiac tamponade Massive pulmonary embolism
Hypovolemic	Hemorrhage Vomiting Diarrhea Dehydration Diabetes (mellitus or insipidus) Addison's disease Burns Peritonitis, pancreatitis
Septic	Gram-negative or other overwhelming infections
Miscellaneous	Anaphylactic Neurogenic Drug overdose Hepatic or renal failure Myxedema

TABLE 4–9. CLINICAL MANIFESTATIONS OF SHOCK

FINDING	SIGNIFICANCE
Hypotension	Blood pressure is normal in early shock (stage 1) because of effective compensatory mechanisms
Tachycardia	Early manifestation
Increased respiratory rate	May represent compensation for metabolic acidosis or pulmonary congestion; may be an early sign
Fever	Septic shock
Cool, pale, moist skin	Sympathetic-mediated vasoconstriction
Warm skin	Septic shock or late shock of any cause when compensatory mechanisms fail
Elevated neck veins	Cardiogenic shock, cardiac tamponade
Collapsed neck veins	Hypovolemic or septic shock
Rales	Pulmonary edema; adult respiratory distress syndrome
Arrhythmias, murmurs, gallops	Suggest cardiac etiology
Abnormal abdominal exam	Source of sepsis, hemorrhage
Blood on rectal exam	Source of hemorrhage
Abnormal neurologic status	Neurogenic shock or manifestation of cerebral hypoperfusion
Oliguria	Sign of renal hypoperfusion
Metabolic acidosis (anion gap)	Early sign of hypoperfusion

TABLE 4–10. MANAGEMENT OF SHOCK

General Measures
Ensure adequate oxygenation
Bladder catheter to monitor urine output
Hemodynamic monitoring to optimize fluid management and cardiac output; indwelling arterial catheter, central venous pressure catheter, and/or Swan-Ganz catheter
Vasopressors as temporizing measures if necessary (e.g., dopamine, norepinephrine)

Specific Types

Cardiogenic	Diuretics
	Inotropic agents
	Vasodilators (if possible)
	Intra-aortic balloon pump
	Correction of underlying lesion (if possible)
Hypovolemic	Fluids/blood products
	Correction of underlying etiology
Septic	Identify source of infection
	Antibiotics
	? Steroids
	Support with fluids (massive edema may develop from leaky capillaries)
Neurogenic	Correct neurologic abnormality (if possible)
Anaphylactic	Epinephrine
	Antihistamines
Addisonian	Fluids
	Mineralocorticoids
	Glucocorticoids
	Correct hypoglycemia

tribution of blood flow to the tissues; that is, arteriovenous shunting of blood occurs and causes decreased delivery of nutrients to tissues despite an increase in cardiac output early in the course of the disease. Increased capillary permeability from the toxic products of infection allows fluid to leak into the interstitium, leaving the intravascular space relatively hypovolemic. Therefore, septic shock often involves the therapeutic paradox of needing to administer large quantities of fluid to a patient who is massively edematous in order to maintain adequate filling pressures. The only definitive therapy for this syndrome is control of the infection, but temporizing therapy includes maintaining intravascular volume via fluid administration, often directed by hemodynamic monitoring. One must remember that myocardial dysfunction may be prominent in stage 3 of septic shock. "Leaky" pulmonary capillaries can cause pulmonary edema without myocardial dysfunction (noncardiogenic pulmonary edema or ARDS) in which left ventricular filling pressures are normal or low (see Chapter 19).

Signs and symptoms of shock are summarized in Table 4–9 and its management in Table 4–10. In-vasive hemodynamic monitoring is often required. Measurement of central venous pressure is sufficient in patients with known hypovolemic shock and good myocardial function; however, in patients with cardiac and lung disease, the central venous pressure may poorly reflect left ventricular filling pressures, and Swan-Ganz catheterization to measure pulmonary arterial and pulmonary capillary wedge pressures should be used in critically ill patients.

HIGH-OUTPUT STATES

If the circulatory system cannot meet a heightened demand for oxygen, high-output cardiac failure is said to occur. In high-output states, the heart must pump abnormally large volumes of blood, and the myocardial failure that ensues is similar to that caused by regurgitant valvular lesions. Disease entities associated with high-output heart failure include severe anemia; hyperthyroidism; systemic arteriovenous fistulas and other left-to-right shunts, such as patent ductus arteriosus; beriberi heart disease (vitamin B_1 deficiency); and Paget's disease. Increased workloads on the normal heart usually do not result in cardiac failure (e.g., pregnancy, hepatic and renal disease, pulmonary disease, and obesity); however, if superimposed on pre-existing heart disease, high-output failure can occur in these conditions.

Symptoms and signs of pulmonary and systemic congestion are similar to those found in patients with low-output congestive heart failure. Because of the increased stroke volume, decreased peripheral vascular resistance, and increased rate of ejection, the pulses are bounding, with a rapid upstroke and a wide pulse pressure. Physical signs of the underlying process should be sought. Treatment must be aimed at the underlying etiologic disorder.

REFERENCES

Braunwald E: ACE inhibitors—a cornerstone of the treatment of heart failure. N Engl J Med 325:351, 1991.
Cohn JN: Current therapy of the failing heart. Circulation 78:1099, 1988.
Consensus Trial Study Group: Effects of enalapril on mortality in severe congestive heart failure: Results of the cooperative north Scandinavian enalapril survival study (consensus). N Engl J Med 316:1429–1435, 1987.
Pouleur H (ed): Diastolic function in heart failure: Clinical approaches to its understanding and treatment. Circulation 81(III):1–158, 1990.
Smith TW: Digitalis: Mechanisms of action and clinical use. N Engl J Med 318:358–365, 1988.
Weber KT (ed): Heart Failure: Current Concepts and Management. Cardiology Clinics, Vol 7. Philadelphia, WB Saunders Co, 1989.

5 CONGENITAL HEART DISEASE

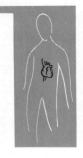

Congenital heart disease refers to cardiac lesions present at birth. Even though these abnormalities exist before birth, they often become clinically evident at the time of delivery, when profound physiologic changes occur in the circulatory system, or months or years after birth. Congenital heart disease (excluding bicuspid aortic valve) occurs in approximately 0.8 per cent of live births and results from both genetic and environmental factors. Congenital heart disease may be familial in some instances, although a distinct pattern of inheritance is usually not recognized. It is more common in children of older mothers. Ventricular septal defect and patent ductus arteriosus are relatively common in premature infants. Environmental factors such as teratogens and maternal rubella are commonly recognized risk factors.

Congenital cardiac defects that are compatible with the fetal circulation (see Chapter 1) may produce symptoms once the child is born. The persistence of normal fetal structures in an infant, such as a patent ductus arteriosus allowing a left-to-right shunt, may be detrimental. However, an abnormal connection may be necessary for an infant to survive in the presence of another congenital anomaly, such as transposition of the great arteries, which must have a connection between the two circuits (e.g., atrial septal defect, patent ductus arteriosus) to allow oxygenation of systemic blood and survival for any period after birth. Those at risk for developing endocarditis should receive prophylactic antibiotics at appropriate times.

Congenital defects can be classified generally into acyanotic and cyanotic groups. The acyanotic congenital defects are those either without a shunt or with left-to-right shunts. Cyanosis occurs in the presence of a right-to-left shunt. In addition, it is important to identify whether malformations arise in the left or the right side of the heart, the site of shunts if present, the status of the pulmonary blood flow (increased, normal, or decreased), and the presence of pulmonary hypertension (Tables 5–1, 5–2, and 5–3).

ACYANOTIC LESIONS

Situs Inversus

Situs inversus involves a mirror image reversal of several organs, including the heart, the liver, and the gastrointestinal tract. These patients have normal longevity unless the disorder is associated with chronic sinusitis and bronchiectasis (Kartagener's syndrome). Situs inversus can be identified by physical examination and chest radiograph (cardiac apex and stomach bubble to the right, liver to the left). If the heart is in the right side of the chest but the abdominal viscera are correctly located, dextroversion of the heart is present and, unlike situs inversus, is often associated with other congenital cardiac anomalies.

Atrial Septal Defect

Atrial septal defects are classified according to their location in the atrial septum. Ostium secundum defects are in the region of the fossa ovalis, ostium primum in the low atrial septum, and sinus venosus in the upper septum near the junction of the vena cava and the right atrium. Ostium primum atrial septal defects are often associated with other endocardial cushion developmental defects, such as a cleft mitral valve or ventricular septal defect. Sinus venosus defects are almost always associated with partial anomalous pulmonary venous return (a pulmonary vein enters the right atrium or vena cava instead of the left atrium, adding to the left-to-right shunt).

In most atrial septal defects, the pressure equilibrates between the left and the right atria, and the degree of left-to-right shunt depends not on a pressure gradient but instead on the relative compliance of the right ventricle and pulmonary arterial system compared with the left ventricle and systemic arterial system. Pulmonary vascular resistance and pulmonary arterial pressure tend to remain low, and thus pulmonary hypertension and right-to-left shunt (Eisenmenger's syndrome) do not commonly occur.

Atrial septal defects may be undetected in children because there are minimal or no symptoms and the ejection murmur across the pulmonic valve is thought to be functional. Survival into adulthood is expected, but longevity is shortened, and death is usually due to cardiac failure. Occasionally, a young adult develops pulmonary hypertension. In addition to findings of congestive heart failure, atrial tachyarrhythmias become more frequent in patients over age 40 and may be the presenting symptom.

Patients with atrial septal defects generally ap-

TABLE 5-1. COMMON CONGENITAL CARDIAC DEFECTS

TYPE	NATURAL HISTORY	PHYSICAL FINDINGS	ECG	RADIOGRAPH	ECHOCARDIOGRAM	THERAPY
Atrial septal defect	Congestive heart failure, atrial tachyarrhythmias in adulthood; occasionally pulmonary hypertension	Ejection murmur across pulmonic valve Hyperdynamic RV Widely and fixed split S_2 Diastolic flow murmur across tricuspid valve	rSr¹ in V_1 (left axis with primum defect)	Large main pulmonary artery; increased pulmonary vascularity	Dilated RV, abnormal septal motion (right ventricular volume overload); direct or contrast visualization of defect	Surgical repair if shunt ratio exceeds 1.5
Ventricular septal defect	Spontaneous closure of small defects occurs; larger defects lead to heart failure or pulmonary hypertension with reversal of shunt (Eisenmenger's syndrome)	Holosystolic left parasternal murmur, ± thrill Diastolic tricuspid flow murmur; occasionally murmur of associated aortic regurgitation Normal or widely split S_2 Findings of pulmonary hypertension if present (Table 5-3)	Biventricular hypertrophy	Increased pulmonary vasculature, large main pulmonary artery, dilation of both ventricles	Dilated hyperdynamic LV (LV volume overload); direct or contrast visualization of defect	Larger defects repaired surgically unless pulmonary hypertension is present
Patent ductus arteriosus	Heart failure in infancy with larger shunts; eventual pulmonary hypertension	Wide aortic pulse pressure Hyperdynamic LV Continuous "machinery" murmur ± thrill Findings of pulmonary hypertension if present; "differential cyanosis" with right-to-left shunting (see text)	LV and/or RV hypertrophy	Increased pulmonary vasculature; large main pulmonary artery; enlarged LA, LV, aorta; occasionally a calcified ductus is visualized	LV volume overload, dilated LV, LA, and aorta	Usually requires surgery; may close spontaneously or with indomethacin in premature infants; recent catheter technique for closure
Pulmonic stenosis	May be asymptomatic for a long period; symptoms of RV failure when decompensation occurs	Large jugular a waves Pulmonic ejection sound RV lift Systolic ejection murmur ± thrill in second left intercostal space Widely split S_2 with soft (or absent) P_2	RA enlargement Right axis QRS deviation RV hypertrophy	Normal pulmonary vascularity, post-stenotic pulmonary arterial dilation Enlarged RV	Differentiates valvular from nonvalvular	Valvulotomy if gradient > 50 mm Hg

TABLE 5–1 **COMMON CONGENITAL CARDIAC DEFECTS** *Continued*

TYPE	NATURAL HISTORY	PHYSICAL FINDINGS	ECG	RADIOGRAPH	ECHOCARDIOGRAM	THERAPY
Congenital aortic stenosis (valvular)	Exertional syncope, angina and heart failure depending on severity	Decreased pulse pressure and carotid pulse LV heave, palpable S_4, systolic ejection murmur ± thrill Aortic ejection click, preserved A_2 (noncalcified valve) with single or paradoxical splitting of S_2 S_4 gallop Concomitant aortic regurgitation common	LV hypertrophy	Prominent LV Poststenotic aortic dilation	Characteristic doming of aortic valve, LV hypertrophy	Aortic valvulotomy or replacement in symptomatic or severe cases
Coarctation of aorta	Most patients live to adulthood but eventually develop heart failure Aorta can dissect or rupture; cerebral hemorrhage occurs	Blood pressure in arms > legs Femoral pulses diminished or late, brisk upper extremity pulses Late systolic or continuous murmur LV lift S_4 gallop Evidence of associated bicuspid aortic valve	LV hypertrophy	Notching of inferior rib surfaces resulting from collateral flow through intercostal arteries Ascending aortic dilation; poststenotic aortic dilation	Occasionally coarctation can be visualized	Surgical repair of all but mild cases
Ebstein's anomaly	Survival into adulthood but longevity decreased due to RV failure Arrhythmias from accessory bypass tracts	Acyanotic or cyanotic (right-to-left shunt due to increased RA pressure) Increased jugular venous pressure S_4 and/or S_3 gallops Systolic murmur of tricuspid regurgitation; large v waves do not occur owing to the large compliant RA	RA enlargement Right bundle branch block PR prolongation Pre-excitation	Enlarged RA Pulmonary vasculature normal or decreased	Abnormal insertion and motion of tricuspid valve	Replace tricuspid valve when RV failure occurs
Tetralogy of Fallot	Usually depends on the degree of pulmonic steno-	Most commonly cyanotic and clubbed but may be acy-	RV hypertrophy	"Boot-shaped" heart due to RV hypertrophy, small	Pulmonic stenosis, ventricular septal defect, RV hypertrophy, overriding	Complete surgical repair is usually treatment of

Table continued on following page

TABLE 5–1 COMMON CONGENITAL CARDIAC DEFECTS *Continued*

TYPE	NATURAL HISTORY	PHYSICAL FINDINGS	ECG	RADIOGRAPH	ECHOCARDIOGRAM	THERAPY
Tetralogy of Fallot (*continued*)	sis: too much leads to right-to-left shunt and cyanosis, too little leads to left-to-right shunt and pulmonary hypertension Pulmonic stenosis tends to gradually increase	anotic; underdeveloped Loud pulmonic ejection murmur along left sternal border, softer with more severe stenosis No murmur across ventricular septal defect (equalization of pressure in LV and RV) Soft P_2 (mild stenosis) or absent P_2 (severe stenosis) Normal jugular venous pressure		LV, and small pulmonary artery	aorta all visualized	choice

ECG = Electrocardiogram; LA = left atrium; LV = left ventricle; RA = right atrium; RV = right ventricle.

TABLE 5–2. CLASSIFICATION OF THE MORE COMMON CYANOTIC CONGENITAL CARDIAC DEFECTS

Increased Pulmonary Blood Flow
  Transposition of the great arteries
  Truncus arteriosus
  Total anomalous pulmonary venous connection
Normal or Decreased Pulmonary Blood Flow
  I. Dominant left ventricle
      Tricuspid atresia
      Ebstein's anomaly of the tricuspid valve
  II. Dominant right ventricle
      a. Normal or low pulmonary arterial pressure
          Tetralogy of Fallot
      b. Elevated pulmonary arterial pressure
          Ventricular septal defect with reversed shunt (Eisenmenger's complex)

TABLE 5–3. PHYSICAL FINDINGS OF PULMONARY HYPERTENSION*

Cyanosis or clubbing from right-to-left shunt via congenital defect or propatent foramen ovale
Large jugular a wave (decreased right ventricular compliance)
Large jugular v wave if tricuspid regurgitation occurs
Left parasternal (right ventricular) lift
Palpable pulmonary arterial pulsations (second left intercostal space)
Pulmonic ejection murmur
Pulmonic ejection click
Loud P_2
Diastolic decrescendo murmur of pulmonic insufficiency (Graham Steell)
Holosystolic murmur of tricuspid regurgitation

* Not all manifestations are present in all patients.

pear normal. However, patients with the Holt-Oram syndrome have upper extremity skeletal abnormalities and a secundum defect, and patients with Down's syndrome have typical features and often a primum defect. The murmur is generated by the increased stroke volume flowing into a dilated pulmonary trunk; a murmur across the atrial septal defect is rare. Echocardiography reveals the dilated right ventricle and abnormal motion of the interventricular septum; these findings are referred to as "right ventricular volume overload" and are also present in pulmonic regurgitation, tricuspid regurgitation, and Ebstein's anomaly. Ostium primum defects and many ostium secundum defects can be visualized directly with two-dimensional echocardiography or indirectly after peripheral venous injection of echocardiographic contrast. However, cardiac catheterization may be required to determine the degree of shunt and evaluate for associated defects. Patients who have uncomplicated atrial septal defects without pulmonary hypertension and shunt ratios exceeding 1.5 should undergo repair electively, preferably during childhood.

Ventricular Septal Defect

Congenital ventricular septal defects are located most commonly in the region of the membranous interventricular septum. As a child grows, there is a tendency for the relative size of the defect to diminish, and sometimes spontaneous closure occurs. The hemodynamic consequences of a ventricular septal defect depend on the size of the defect and on the extent of pulmonary vascular resistance. A small defect causes little problem, a moderate defect causes left-to-right shunting with minimal elevation of pulmonary arterial pressure, and a large defect may result in equalization of systolic pressures in the two ventricles, with the result that the shunt flow depends on the relative resistance in the pulmonary versus the systemic circulation. As pulmonary vascular resistance increases secondary to the increased pulmonary pressure and flow, the left-to-right shunt may gradually decrease and even become right-to-left (Eisenmenger's complex). There is an increased incidence of aortic insufficiency in patients with large ventricular septal defects, in some patients due to primary aortic valve abnormality and in others due to herniation of a valve leaflet through the septal defect.

Echocardiography reveals left ventricular volume overload (hyperdynamic left ventricle). The defect usually cannot be directly visualized but may be indirectly visualized after a peripheral venous injection of echocardiographic contrast.

Patients with small ventricular septal defects should be watched for gradual closure. Larger defects should be corrected surgically unless the pulmonary vascular resistance has become markedly elevated, at which time operative risk is high and results are poor because pulmonary vascular resistance fails to decrease significantly postoperatively.

Patent Ductus Arteriosus

A patent ductus arteriosus is common in premature infants and is more frequently seen in individuals born at high altitudes. In normal infants, the ductus functionally closes several hours after birth, and after 4 to 8 weeks it closes anatomically. The pathophysiology of patent ductus arteriosus depends on the size of the ductus and the degree of pulmonary vascular resistance. After birth, as the pulmonary vascular resistance falls and the ductus fails to close, a left-to-right shunt occurs. When the ductus is small, pulmonary artery pressure is normal and there is little left-to-right shunting. If the defect is bigger, a large shunt results, and aortic pressure is transmitted to the pulmonary arterial tree. Pulmonary hypertension develops with a sizable left-to-right shunt, along with volume overload of the left side of the heart and pressure overload of the right side of the heart. Eventually, as pulmonary vascular resistance reflexly increases, left-to-right flow disappears, and in late stages the patient may develop a right-to-left shunt. The infant may fail to develop normally and, if the shunt is severe, demonstrates congestive heart failure. If right-to-left shunting occurs, "differential" cyanosis may be evident owing to nonoxygenated blood entering the aorta distal to the left subclavian artery via the patent ductus arteriosus, preferentially being shunted to the lower extremities, and resulting in cyanotic toes but pink fingers.

Essentially all patients with persistent left-to-right shunt across a ductus should have surgical interruption; interruption also reduces the risk of bacterial endocarditis. Severely elevated pulmonary vascular resistance (Eisenmenger's syndrome) is not reversible and, if present, contraindicates surgery. The operation usually carries low risk, and cardiopulmonary bypass is not required. In older patients with a calcified ductus, ligation is slightly more risky, although still indicated. Recently, insertion by catheter technique of an umbrella device into the ductus has been successful in occluding the ductus.

Pulmonic Stenosis

Valvular pulmonic stenosis is more common than isolated subvalvular and supravalvular varieties. The murmur is present at birth, but survival into adulthood is common. Dyspnea and fatigue are the most frequent symptoms, but patients may remain asymptomatic for long periods as long as the right ventricle maintains a normal cardiac output via compensatory mechanisms (hypertrophy); if not, right ventricular failure ensues. Valvular pulmonic stenosis can cause hypertrophy of the right ventricular infundibulum, and secondary infundibular (subvalvular) stenosis can occur.

The longer the duration of the systolic murmur and the earlier the systolic ejection click, the higher the degree of stenosis. As the severity of pulmonic stenosis increases, widened splitting of S_2 occurs, with a decrease and eventual disappearance of P_2.

Patients with mild pulmonic stenosis require no treatment other than endocarditis prophylaxis. Those with pulmonic valve gradients exceeding 50 mm Hg should have pulmonary valvulotomy. Balloon dilation techniques via cardiac catheterization are successful in some patients. Pulmonic regurgitation may occur postoperatively but is generally mild and functionally insignificant. Secondary subpulmonic stenosis may require resection, which complicates the procedure significantly.

Aortic Stenosis

Congenitally bicuspid aortic valves occur in up to 2 per cent of the population and constitute the most common congenital cardiac defect manifesting itself in the adult population. Bicuspid valves usually function normally throughout early and mid-life. However, progressive accelerated calcification of the valve can result in significant aortic stenosis during mid-adulthood. Occasionally, bicuspid valves are incompetent, either inherently or secondary to damage from infective endocarditis. A short grade I–II/VI systolic murmur loudest at the second right intercostal space is typical and, if accompanied by an ejection sound or a soft murmur of aortic regurgitation, strongly suggests that the systolic murmur is pathologic. Bicuspid aortic valve is predominantly a disease of males. The identification of a bicuspid valve can be suggested by echocardiography but is sometimes difficult to make.

In contrast to a bicuspid aortic valve, congenital aortic stenosis refers to an inherently stenotic left ventricular outflow tract. Congenital aortic stenosis is usually valvular but may be subvalvular or supravalvular. It is more common in males, with a ratio of approximately 4:1.

An ejection sound is present in valvular but not in nonvalvular aortic stenosis. It is generated by the sudden tensing upon opening of the abnormal aortic valve, implying good valve motion. In adults the abnormal valve gradually calcifies, and the ejection sound may disappear. In general, the longer and louder the murmur and the later its systolic peak, the greater the obstruction. The intensity of the murmur may decrease when the left ventricle fails, but it usually still peaks late in systole if stenosis is severe. An aortic regurgitation murmur may be present in valvular obstruction or, as the aortic cusps become distorted by the subvalvular jet, in subvalvular obstruction.

Cardiac catheterization is necessary to quantitate the degree of aortic stenosis. Aortic valvulotomy may be employed as a temporizing procedure in younger patients with significant aortic stenosis, but prosthetic aortic valves eventually are required in most severe cases.

Subvalvular stenosis is either dynamic (see Hypertrophic Cardiomyopathy in Chapter 9) or fixed. Two forms of fixed subaortic stenosis are the tunnel (fibromuscular) and the localized (fibromembranous) forms. These are unusual in adults. They can be identified with two-dimensional echocardiography. Surgical excision of an obstructing subvalvular membrane can be curative, but correction of a tunnel deformity is difficult. Supravalvular aortic stenosis often occurs in the presence of mental retardation and peculiar facies. The brachial and carotid arterial pressures may be reduced more on the left than on the right. Aortic regurgitation is rare (cf. subvalvular stenosis). The radiograph shows no poststenotic dilatation of the ascending aorta, and the aorta is usually small.

Coarctation of the Aorta

Coarctation refers to a narrowing of the aorta usually located immediately distal to the origin of the left subclavian artery and ligamentum arteriosum. It is associated with a bicuspid aortic valve in approximately 25 per cent of patients and occasionally with a patent ductus arteriosus. Some patients have an associated aneurysm of the circle of Willis that may rupture. Other than coarctation asso-

ciated with Turner's syndrome, males are more commonly affected than females. Most patients live to adulthood, but longevity is significantly decreased. Most patients are asymptomatic when the lesion is diagnosed. Discovery of upper extremity arterial hypertension is usually the initial finding. Patients develop one of four complications: congestive heart failure, rupture of the aorta or dissecting aneurysm, infective endarteritis or endocarditis, or cerebral hemorrhage. Endocarditis is more common on the bicuspid aortic valve than in the region of the coarctation.

Catheterization may be performed to assess the severity of the coarctation and to examine the collaterals. All but mild coarctations warrant surgical repair. In children the optimal age for elective correction is approximately the fifth year. Surgery becomes more difficult in adults.

Miscellaneous Noncyanotic Abnormalities

Congenital coronary arteriovenous (AV) fistulas, low-resistance connections between the arterial and venous circulations without an intervening capillary bed, may steal blood flow away from a portion of the myocardium. Occasionally, a coronary artery may originate from the pulmonary artery and cause myocardial ischemia. A coronary artery may arise from the wrong sinus of Valsalva, most commonly the left circumflex artery arising from the right sinus of Valsalva, and may be subject to compression, especially with exercise. In addition, the odd angle of take-off from the abnormal ostium may limit flow. Congenital aneurysms of a sinus of Valsalva may occasionally rupture into the right atrium or right ventricle, resembling acute aortic regurgitation. Right ventricular dysplasia (Uhl's anomaly) involves a process whereby all or a portion of the right ventricular muscle is replaced with fat and fibrous tissue. It is often associated with ventricular tachycardia.

Ebstein's Anomaly of the Tricuspid Valve

In Ebstein's anomaly, the tricuspid valve leaflets are deformed and displaced into the right ventricular cavity, giving rise to a portion of the right ventricle that is functionally right atrium (atrialized right ventricle). Therefore, the pumping action of the right ventricle is decreased and the tricuspid valve is incompetent. Patients may be acyanotic, but a right-to-left shunt through a patent foramen ovale or an atrial septal defect due to elevated right atrial pressure can cause cyanosis. Ebstein's anomaly is compatible with survival into adulthood, but longevity is decreased. The anomaly is associated with right-sided accessory atrioventricular bypass tracts in approximately 10 per cent of cases (see Chapter 8). Patients can usually be managed medically. A tricuspid valve prosthesis is required when significant right ventricular failure occurs.

Transposition of the Great Vessels

In complete transposition of the great arteries, the aorta and coronary arteries exit from the right ventricle, while the pulmonary artery exits from the left ventricle. The left atrium empties into the left ventricle and the right atrium into the right ventricle. Therefore, the systemic and pulmonary circuits are arranged in parallel instead of in series. For the patient to survive, some means of exchange between the two parallel circuits must exist, for example, an atrial septal defect, a ventricular septal defect, or a patent ductus arteriosus. Transposition usually produces cyanosis and increased pulmonary blood flow. Bidirectional shunting must be present, and the greater the mixing between the two systems, the more likely the patient's survival. Diagnosis can be established by two-dimensional echocardiography. Palliation may be obtained by atrial septostomy via a balloon or surgery. Corrective surgery involves reversing the atrial input by inserting an atrial baffle that redirects the atrial flow to the opposite ventricle (the Mustard procedure) or by transposing the pulmonary artery and aorta.

Total Anomalous Pulmonary Venous Return

In this condition, oxygenated blood returning from the lungs enters the right atrium instead of the left atrium, usually via a confluence of veins connected to the superior or inferior vena cava, the coronary sinus, or the right atrium directly. Blood from the right atrium enters the left atrium and left ventricle via an obligatory atrial septal defect, but because of the low pulmonary compliance most blood enters the right ventricle and pulmonary artery. Therefore, total anomalous pulmonary venous return is a cyanotic anomaly with increased pulmonary blood flow. Signs and symptoms are somewhat similar to those of an atrial septal defect except that cyanosis and signs of pulmonary hypertension may exist. Echocardiography reveals findings similar to those of an atrial septal defect, but the confluence of veins can often be identified. Surgical correction involves an anastomosis of the confluence to the left atrium.

Truncus Arteriosus

In truncus arteriosus, one great artery with one semilunar valve exits the heart, receives blood from both ventricles, and gives rise to the coronary arteries, aorta, and pulmonary artery. Cyanosis and increased pulmonary blood flow are present. Most patients do not survive childhood. Surgical correction can be performed in which the ventricular septal defect is closed, with the left ventricle communicating with the truncus, and the pulmonary arteries are divided from the truncus and connected to the right ventricle by a valved conduit.

Tetralogy of Fallot

Tetralogy of Fallot is the most common cyanotic congenital anomaly in adults. It includes a ventricular septal defect, pulmonic stenosis, an aorta overriding the ventricular septal defect, and right ventricular hypertrophy as a result of the first two defects. The ventricular septal defect is large and nonrestrictive. Right ventricular pressures are systemic. If the pulmonic stenosis is mild to moderate, the patient is acyanotic. If the pulmonic stenosis is severe, right-to-left shunting occurs across the ventricular septal defect and cyanosis results, the most common situation. Typically, the pulmonic stenosis is infundibular, but it can be valvular or located elsewhere in the pulmonary outflow tract.

A large ventricular septal defect with mild pulmonic stenosis results in a left-to-right shunt and physiology similar to that of ventricular septal defect alone, that is, increased pulmonary blood flow and left ventricular volume overload. With severe pulmonic stenosis, right ventricular pressure does not exceed systemic pressure because of the large ventricular septal defect; thus, right-to-left shunting occurs but right ventricular failure usually does not occur. Exercise increases right-to-left shunting and cyanosis by decreasing systemic vascular resistance. Patients typically have intermittent "spells" associated with hyperpnea, cyanosis, and lightheadedness or syncope thought to be due to an increase in right-to-left shunting. Children achieve relief from dyspnea by squatting, a maneuver that increases both systemic vascular resistance and pulmonary blood flow. Infective endocarditis may occur, and there is a high incidence of brain abscess, presumably because the normal filtering mechanisms of the pulmonary vasculature are bypassed.

The natural history of tetralogy of Fallot is a gradual increase in the severity of pulmonic stenosis so that cyanosis increases. Total surgical correction is the treatment of choice and can be performed even in infants; however, the creation of a systemic-to-pulmonary shunt (usually an anastomosis of the subclavian artery to the pulmonary artery, a Blalock-Taussig shunt) is still performed in very young cyanotic infants with complex lesions but adds to the risk of complete repair later. Right bundle branch block occurs after repair, and an increased incidence of ventricular arrhythmias, heart block, and sudden death has been reported years after surgery. Even children with only moderate symptoms should have a complete surgical correction by school age.

Tricuspid Atresia

In tricuspid atresia, no tricuspid valve is present and the right atrium does not connect to the right ventricle. An interatrial connection allows blood to flow to the left side of the heart, and a small ventricular septal defect usually allows some blood flow to the lungs via the rudimentary right ventricle. The patient is usually cyanotic with diminished pulmonary blood flow and has a dominant left ventricle. Transposition of the great arteries is often an associated defect. Systemic arterial–to–pulmonary arterial shunts and enlargement of the atrial septal defect by balloon septostomy are palliative. The insertion of a prosthetic conduit between the right atrium and pulmonary artery with closure of the atrial septal defect (the Fontan procedure) may provide improvement.

General Problems Due to Prolonged Survival

Because of cardiac surgery, more patients with congenital heart disease survive to become adults. Many patients have undergone complete repair of their defects and are asymptomatic. Others, however, may be symptomatic with residual defects or complications from surgery, and some patients may have merely had incomplete correction with palliative surgery. Pregnancy may be complicated in these patients. Infants of patients with cyanotic congenital heart disease tend to be small for their gestational age.

REFERENCES

Adams FH, Emmanouilides GC: Moss' Heart Disease in Infants, Children, and Adolescents. 4th ed. Baltimore, Williams & Wilkins Co, 1989.
Perloff JK: The Clinical Recognition of Congenital Heart Disease. 3rd ed. Philadelphia, WB Saunders Co, 1987.
Perloff JK, Child JS: Congenital Heart Disease in Adults. Philadelphia, WB Saunders Co, 1991.

6 ACQUIRED VALVULAR HEART DISEASE

GENERAL CONSIDERATIONS

When an aortic or pulmonic valve is stenotic, the respective ventricle compensates by undergoing hypertrophy; that is, the mass of myocardium increases with little increase in the size of the ventricular cavity. Hypertrophy increases ventricular oxygen consumption and, because of the elevated intramural pressure, decreases the diastolic flow of blood to the myocardium from the coronary arteries, resulting in an imbalance of myocardial oxygen demand and delivery. Aortic or pulmonic regurgitation places a diastolic volume overload on the respective ventricle and results in dilation with less hypertrophy. This increase in ventricular volume also leads to increased myocardial oxygen consumption via increased wall tension. Mitral or tricuspid regurgitation also places a diastolic volume overload on the ventricle, although not as severe, since the ventricle empties into a lower pressure chamber and systolic pressures are not as high. Mitral regurgitation, therefore, is better tolerated than aortic regurgitation. Mitral stenosis and tricuspid stenosis do not overload the ventricle, but instead the respective atrium dilates, and either pulmonary or systemic venous pressure may increase markedly. Ventricular myocardial dysfunction ultimately occurs in both hypertrophy and dilation. An elevation in venous pressure eventually may develop in any valvular lesion when cardiac decompensation occurs. The S_4 gallop correlates with left ventricular hypertrophy and decreased myocardial compliance, and the S_3 gallop correlates with increased blood volume filling the heart in early diastole and is common in volume overload states, usually with some degree of myocardial dysfunction. As left ventricular failure occurs and pulmonary venous pressures increase, right ventricular failure eventually may ensue.

Echocardiography may obviate cardiac catheterization in certain lesions (e.g., simple, uncomplicated mitral stenosis). However, cardiac catheterization is the standard means to assess the severity or quantitate the degree of most valvular lesions in patients whose clinical status is thought possibly to warrant surgery. Catheterization may be needed to determine the relative severity of multivalvular lesions, to detect significant concomitant lesions, to evaluate the status of the coronary circulation, and to assess left ventricular function.

The decision of whether and when to replace an abnormal valve often is difficult, since the natural history of many valvular lesions is chronic and prolonged. In addition, prosthetic valves carry lifelong risks of endocarditis, emboli, and thrombosis, and the lifespan of many prosthetic valves is unknown. The natural history of each valvular lesion is different; some lesions (e.g., aortic regurgitation) may be associated with irreversible myocardial damage before symptoms occur, whereas other lesions (e.g., mitral stenosis) can await significant progression of symptoms before valve replacement is necessary, since the ventricle is protected by the stenotic valve. In addition, the patient's age, general medical status, and desire to return to previous levels of activity enter into the decision for valve replacement.

MITRAL STENOSIS (Tables 6-1, 6-2, and 6-3)

Mitral stenosis almost always results from rheumatic fever and is rarely congenital. It is the most common lesion caused by rheumatic fever. Two thirds of patients with mitral stenosis are female. The valve leaflets become thickened and the commissures fused, and the chordae tendineae may fuse and shorten. Calcium may be deposited in the valve. This process of valve scarring progresses slowly and may take 10 years or more after the episode of rheumatic fever to become hemodynamically significant. Because of the deformation of the mitral valve, mitral regurgitation also may be present. The left atrium enlarges, but the left ventricle remains normal in size unless mitral regurgitation also occurs. The elevated left atrial pressure determines the extent of pulmonary venous congestion that causes the major symptoms in mitral stenosis of dyspnea, orthopnea, and paroxysmal nocturnal dyspnea. Pulmonary arterial hypertension occurs not only secondary to the elevated pulmonary venous pressure but sometimes also secondary to a reactive increase in the pulmonary vascular resistance. Right ventricular failure and functional tricuspid regurgitation may result. Atrial fibrillation is common. Diastolic filling of the left ventricle is determined not only by the pressure gradient across the stenotic mitral valve but also by the amount of time spent in diastole during which the left ventricle can fill. Therefore, when the patient exercises and develops sinus tachycardia or when atrial fibrillation occurs, the rapid ventricular rate diminishes the percentage of the cardiac cycle spent in diastole, and ventricular filling is limited. A patient's first episode of pulmonary edema often occurs either with exercise or with the onset of atrial fibrillation.

Even though acute rheumatic fever may have occurred in childhood, the age at the onset of cardiac symptoms is usually between 25 and 45 years. There may be a relatively long period, 5 to 8 years, of mild to moderate pulmonary congestive symptoms before severe compromise occurs. Since reduction in cardiac output is a late finding, fatigue and physical wasting are also late manifestations. Occasionally, hemoptysis may occur because of leaking or rupture of pulmonary vessels. The occurrence of intermittent atrial fibrillation as the left atrium dilates may be associated with peripheral emboli. As pulmonary vascular resistance and reactive pulmonary arterial hypertension increase, flow from the right to the left side of the heart is limited, pulmonary venous hypertension stabilizes, and episodes of pulmonary edema may decrease; however, the complaint of fatigue becomes prominent. Findings of right heart failure with hepatomegaly, ascites, and peripheral edema may be present.

The first heart sound is loud because the mitral valve is maximally open at the onset of systole and the left ventricular pressure is rising rapidly when the valve closes because of the high left

TABLE 6-1. ACQUIRED VALVULAR LESIONS: SYMPTOMS AND NATURAL HISTORY

LESION	MAJOR SYMPTOMS	NATURAL HISTORY
Mitral stenosis	Dyspnea, orthopnea, paroxysmal nocturnal dyspnea; later fatigue, wasting, hemoptysis, symptoms of right heart failure Systemic emboli not uncommon Acute decompensation with onset of atrial fibrillation	Onset of symptoms 10+ years after rheumatic fever; slowly progressive
Mitral regurgitation	Pulmonary congestion, fatigue; later right heart failure	Chronic: long asymptomatic phase despite moderately severe regurgitation Acute: if severe, rapid deterioration
Mitral valve prolapse	Chest pain atypical for angina pectoris; palpitations; rarely left heart failure from mitral regurgitation	Usually asymptomatic; endocarditis, rupture of chordae, progressive mitral regurgitation, and sudden death rarely occur
Aortic stenosis	Angina, LV failure; exertional syncope, presyncope	Rapid deterioration once symptoms appear; first manifestation in a rare patient is sudden death
Aortic regurgitation	LV failure Palpitations from arrhythmias or hyperdynamic circulation	Chronic: asymptomatic or minimally symptomatic stage may span years; irreversible myocardial damage may occur in the asymptomatic patient Acute: rapid deterioration
Tricuspid stenosis	Depends on associated mitral valve abnormalities Manifestations of right heart failure	Like mitral stenosis, gradually progressive with onset of symptoms in mid-adulthood
Tricuspid regurgitation	RV failure	Depends on underlying etiology; may improve if associated lesions are corrected

LV = left ventricular; RV = right ventricular.

TABLE 6–2. ACQUIRED VALVULAR LESIONS: PHYSICAL AND LABORATORY EXAMINATION

LESION	PHYSICAL FINDINGS	ECG	RADIOGRAPH	ECHOCARDIOGRAM
Mitral stenosis	Decreased pulse pressure Loud S_1 Opening snap if mitral valve is pliable No S_3 or S_4 Diastolic rumble Concomitant murmur of mitral regurgitation or aortic involvement Late features include pulmonary hypertension and RV failure	Atrial fibrillation common Left atrial abnormality RV hypertrophy when pulmonary hypertension develops	Large LA: double density at right heart border, posterior displacement of esophagus, elevation of left mainstem bronchus, straightening of left heart border due to enlarged left atrial appendage Large pulmonary artery Pulmonary venous congestion	M-mode: thickened mitral leaflets, anterior movement of posterior leaflet during systole, decreased mid-diastolic mitral closure (decreased "E to F slope") Two-dimensional: mitral valve doming, visualization of decreased valve area
Mitral regurgitation	Hyperdynamic LV impulse displaced laterally Left parasternal lift from right ventricle or systolic LA expansion S_3, soft S_1, widely split S_2 (early A_2) S_4 absent in chronic, present in acute form Holosystolic murmur radiating to axilla; murmur may be atypical in acute mitral regurgitation, mitral valve prolapse, papillary muscle dysfunction Later features include pulmonary hypertension and RV failure	Atrial fibrillation less common than in mitral stenosis Left atrial enlargement LV hypertrophy	Enlarged LA and LV; pulmonary venous congestion	Large LV and LA with hypercynamic LV motion (left ventricular volume overload) May reveal underlying cause of mitral regurgitation Doppler: semiquantitation of regurgitant jet
Mitral valve prolapse	One or more systolic clicks, often followed by a late systolic murmur High incidence of bony chest abnormalities: straight back syndrome, pectus excavatum, thoracic scoliosis	Usually normal; occasionally ST depression and T wave inversion inferiorly Ventricular or supraventricular ectopy	Usually normal unless significant mitral regurgitation is present; bony abnormalities	Systolic bowing of anterior or posterior mitral leaflets into LA
Aortic stenosis	Pulsus parvus et tardus (may be absent in older patients or those with aortic insufficiency) Carotid "shudder" (thrill) Systolic ejection murmur in aortic area, usually with thrill, harsh quality, radiates to carotids, peaks late in systole if stenosis is severe Sustained, diffuse, but not displaced LV impulse (LV heave or lift) S_4 gallop, often palpable A_2 decreased, S_2 single or paradoxically split S_3 if LV failure is present Aortic ejection click in noncalcified congenital stenosis	LV hypertrophy Left bundle branch block and intraventricular conduction defects common Rare heart block from calcific involvement of the conduction system	LV predominance without dilation Poststenotic aortic root dilation Calcification in region of aortic valve Cardiomegaly and pulmonary congestion with LV failure	Thick aortic valve leaflets with decreased excursion LV hypertrophy Severity estimated with Doppler techniques
Aortic regurgitation	Chronic: increased pulse pressure (head bobbing), pistol-shot sounds over peripheral arteries, to-and-fro murmur over femoral arteries with light compression by stethoscope (Duroziez's sign), pulsatile blushing of nail beds (Quincke's sign), rapid upstroke with collapsing quality to pulse (water hammer pulse)	LV hypertrophy often with "volume overload" pattern (narrow, deep Q waves in left precordial leads)	LV and aortic dilation	Dilated LV and aorta Left ventricular volume overload Fluttering of anterior mitral valve leaflet Acute: premature diastolic closure of mitral valve Doppler: semiquantitation of regurgitant jet

TABLE 6-2. ACQUIRED VALVULAR LESIONS: PHYSICAL AND LABORATORY EXAMINATION *Continued*

LESION	PHYSICAL FINDINGS	ECG	RADIOGRAPH	ECHOCARDIOGRAM
Aortic regurgitation (continued)	Bifid pulse contour, especially if stenosis is also present Hyperkinetic, displaced apical impulse Diastolic decrescendo murmur; length correlates with severity Systolic flow murmur Systolic and/or diastolic thrill A_2 decreased or absent S_3 in early LV decompensation Austin Flint murmur Acute: apical impulse not displaced; pulse pressure increased much less Diastolic murmur shorter and softer (high LV diastolic pressure) S_1 decreased (because of early mitral valve closure) Severe LV failure			
Tricuspid stenosis	Prominent a wave, attenuated y descent in jugular pulse Jugular venous distention, edema, hepatomegaly Tricuspid opening snap with diastolic rumble loudest in fourth left intercostal space, louder with inspiration	Atrial fibrillation common RA enlargment with RV hypertrophy	Associated valve lesions; large RA	Doming of tricuspid valve; associated lesions
Tricuspid regurgitation	Increased jugular venous pressure with large v waves Hepatomegaly with systolic pulsations Holosystolic murmur along left sternal border ± thrill; increases with inspiration Diastolic flow rumble Right ventricular S_3 (increases with inspiration; loudest along left sternal border) Findings of pulmonary hypertension if tricuspid regurgitation is secondary	RV hypertrophy RA enlargement Atrial fibrillation is common	Enlarged RV and RA; other lesions may be evident	Underlying cause may be identified Contrast echo or Doppler can establish the diagnosis

LA = Left atrium; LV = left ventricle; RA = right atrium; RV = right ventricle.

atrial pressure. More severe mitral stenosis shortens the interval between S_2 and the opening snap (the higher the left atrial pressure, the sooner the valve will open during isovolumic relaxation). A diastolic, low-pitched, rumbling murmur located near the left ventricular apex immediately follows the opening snap, if present. The rumble is loudest in early diastole during rapid ventricular filling and, if sinus rhythm is present, increases again with atrial contraction (presystolic accentuation). In mild mitral stenosis, as well as severe mitral stenosis with low cardiac output, the murmur may be difficult to hear and may be accentuated with the patient in the left lateral decubitus position, especially after exercise. In addition, a markedly enlarged right ventricle may displace the left ventricle posteriorly, making the murmur even harder to hear. Concomitant rheumatic involvement of the aortic valve may generate murmurs of aortic stenosis or regurgitation.

Echocardiography is diagnostic of mitral stenosis. Cross-sectional echocardiography can be used to estimate accurately the valve orifice area in a high percentage of patients, possibly more accurately than the Gorlin formula at cardiac catheterization, since the presence of mitral regurgitation

TABLE 6–3. ACQUIRED VALVULAR LESIONS: MEDICAL AND SURGICAL MANAGEMENT

LESION	MEDICAL MANAGEMENT	SURGICAL MANAGEMENT
Mitral stenosis	Rheumatic fever and endocarditis prophylaxis Diuretics, salt restriction Control of ventricular rate and anticoagulation in atrial fibrillation	*Indication:* Functional Class III despite medical therapy; severe pulmonary hypertension is not a surgical contraindication *Procedure:* Commissurotomy or valve replacement
Mitral regurgitation	Salt restriction, diuretics, digitalis, afterload reduction Endocarditis prophylaxis	*Indication:* Functional Class III despite medical therapy; patients with lesser symptoms and evidence of myocardial dysfunction; acute severe mitral regurgitation *Procedure:* Mitral valve replacement or valvuloplasty
Mitral valve prolapse	Endocarditis prophylaxis Beta blockade for chest pain Beta blockade or other antiarrhythmic agents for arrhythmias	Mitral valve replacement for acute and/or severe mitral regurgitation
Aortic stenosis	Endocarditis prophylaxis Avoid strenuous exercise	*Indication:* Symptoms *Procedure:* Valve replacement
Aortic regurgitation	Endocarditis prophylaxis Salt restriction, diuretics, digitalis, afterload reduction	*Indication:* Controversial; greater than mild symptoms, evidence of early LV dysfunction in asymptomatic patients *Procedure:* Aortic valve replacement
Tricuspid stenosis	Endocarditis and rheumatic fever prophylaxis Depends on associated valvular lesions	*Indication:* Severe tricuspid stenosis, usually concomitant with mitral valve surgery *Procedure:* Tricuspid valve replacement
Tricuspid regurgitation	Endocarditis prophylaxis Treatment of associated lesions Diuretics, salt restriction, digitalis	*Indication:* Severe tricuspid regurgitation, often concomitant with mitral valve surgery *Procedure:* Tricuspid annuloplasty or valve replacement

LV = Left ventricular.

does not affect the valve area determined echocardiographically.

The patient with significant mitral stenosis has an elevated left atrial or pulmonary capillary wedge pressure with a pressure gradient between the left atrium and left ventricle during diastole. The Gorlin formula is used to calculate the valve area according to the following equation:

$$\text{Valve area} = \frac{\text{transvalvular flow}}{\text{constant} \times \sqrt{\text{gradient}}}$$

Because the pressure gradient changes with the square of the flow, small increases in cardiac output are associated with relatively large elevations in left atrial pressure. Less severe cases of mitral stenosis have elevated pulmonary arterial pressures without a gradient between pulmonary arterial and venous pressures (passive pulmonary hypertension), whereas more severe cases have reactive pulmonary hypertension because of an increase in pulmonary vascular resistance. The area of a normal mitral valve is about 4 cm²; severe mitral stenosis occurs when the valve area is less than 1 cm². Left ventricular function is generally normal unless complicating lesions are present.

Control of the ventricular rate using digitalis in patients with atrial fibrillation decreases left atrial pressure. Patients with sinus rhythm who experience exertional dyspnea may benefit from the administration of propranolol to prevent sinus tachycardia. Patients may be managed for many years medically. Systemic embolization despite anticoagulation is an indication for surgery. Since systolic function of the ventricular myocardium is not impaired in uncomplicated mitral stenosis, the inotropic property of digitalis is not beneficial. When the patient experiences functional Class III or IV symptoms despite medical therapy, surgery should be considered. Surgery is not contraindicated by severe pulmonary hypertension, since the increased pulmonary vascular resistance returns toward normal upon correction of the left atrial hypertension (cf. pulmonary hypertension in patients with left-to-right shunts, e.g., ventricular septal defect).

Mitral commissurotomy can be employed in patients with relatively pliable, noncalcified valves without mitral regurgitation. Commissurotomy spares the patient the risks of a prosthetic valve and anticoagulation for several years. A regurgitant valve is likely to become more regurgitant after commissurotomy, and valve replacement is therefore usually performed in patients with concomitant mitral regurgitation, although newer techniques of surgical mitral valvuloplasty in concert with commissurotomy may be applicable in selected patients. The average patient experiences 8 to 12 years of symptomatic relief after commissurotomy, but progression of the disease occurs and usually valve replacement is necessary eventually. In older patients with severe mitral stenosis who are not considered good surgical candidates, mitral valvuloplasty can be attempted in the catheterization laboratory, using a balloon catheter.

MITRAL REGURGITATION

The most common cause of mitral regurgitation is rheumatic fever, and it occurs more often in males. The murmur of mitral regurgitation may appear early after an episode of acute rheumatic fever. Concomitant aortic valve involvement suggests a rheumatic etiology. Mitral regurgitation can also be congenital and in such cases is sometimes associated with other lesions, such as an ostium primum atrial septal defect. Mitral valve prolapse, mitral annular calcification, rupture of chordae tendineae from endocarditis, trauma, or degenerative diseases such as Marfan's syndrome may cause mitral regurgitation. Rupture of a papillary muscle after myocardial infarction results in severe, acute mitral regurgitation, while infarction of a papillary muscle can cause chronic papillary muscle dysfunction. Mitral regurgitation is common in patients with hypertrophic cardiomyopathy. It may occur secondary to left ventricular dilation; this "functional" mitral regurgitation probably occurs not so much from dilation of the mitral annulus as from distortion of the normal alignment of the papillary muscles.

Mitral regurgitation is holosystolic; that is, blood flows from the left ventricle to the low-pressure left atrium from the time the mitral valve closes to its opening after S_2. Left ventricular afterload is reduced. The v wave in the left atrial or pulmonary capillary wedge pressure tracing is often increased. However, large v waves can be seen in entities other than mitral regurgitation; if left atrial compliance is increased, v waves may not be present even in severe mitral regurgitation. Left ventricular diastolic volume increases in chronic mitral regurgitation. Because of the low pressure against which the left ventricle ejects blood (i.e., into the left atrium), the clinical course may extend over many years before decompensation occurs. However, as mitral regurgitation becomes severe and long-standing, left ventricular contractility may be irreversibly impaired. The left ventricular systolic as well as diastolic dimensions subsequently increase. Pulmonary hypertension, like that in mitral stenosis, may occur as a result of both increased pulmonary venous pressure and a reactive increase in pulmonary vascular resistance. In chronic mitral regurgitation, the increased volume of blood entering the left atrium is accommodated by dilation of the left atrium with a modest increase in left atrial pressure. However in acute, severe mitral regurgitation (e.g., that secondary to endocarditis or ruptured chordae tendineae), regurgitant blood enters a relatively small noncompliant left atrium, and left atrial pressure may rise dramatically, with very large v waves.

Doppler echocardiography provides a semiquantitative estimate of the severity of mitral regurgitation. The severity of mitral regurgitation is estimated at catheterization by the amount of contrast regurgitated into the left atrium after injection into the left ventricle. A regurgitant fraction can be calculated, but these calculations can be fraught with error. There may be a pressure gradient across the mitral valve in early diastole in the absence of mitral stenosis because of the large volume of blood flowing across the valve. A normal ejection fraction may mask left ventricular dysfunction despite myocardial depression because of the marked afterload reduction afforded by the mitral regurgitation. Once the valve is replaced, however, the myocardial dysfunction may become evident.

Patients in functional Class III or IV despite medical therapy should be considered for surgery. Patients with lesser symptoms who display early evidence of myocardial dysfunction (e.g., increased systolic left ventricular diameter or decreasing ejection fraction) should be considered for surgery. The mitral valve usually is replaced with a metal or bioprosthetic valve; however, newer surgical valvuloplasty techniques may be possible in many patients, avoiding the complications of prosthetic valves. Acute severe mitral regurgitation generally is not well tolerated and requires emergency valve replacement. Potent afterload reduction, with intravenous nitroprusside, for example, may stabilize the patient until surgery can be performed.

MITRAL VALVE PROLAPSE

Mitral valve prolapse (floppy mitral valve, click murmur syndrome) is common and usually benign, reported to occur in 0.3 to 6 per cent of the population. It derives its clinical significance from its characteristic systolic click and late systolic murmur and the occasional patient who experiences significant mitral regurgitation, chordal rupture, endocarditis, arrhythmias, or sudden death. The severity of mitral regurgitation varies. The mitral valve leaflets are generally redundant, the chordae are elongated, and pathology in more severe cases demonstrates myxomatous degeneration. Mitral regurgitation is occasionally progressive and severe and can occur acutely if a chorda ruptures because of myxomatous degeneration or endocarditis. The cause is unknown, although it is common in Marfan's syndrome and other connective tissue diseases. It has increased incidence in patients with ostium secundum atrial septal defect and hypertrophic cardiomyopathy. It is more common in females than males and occasionally will run in families.

A variety of symptoms have been attributed to mitral valve prolapse, but it is difficult to definitely attribute symptoms to the syndrome, since it is so common. The pathogenesis of the chest pain is not clear but could be related to ischemia or tension on the papillary muscles. Patients may also have a variety of supraventricular or ventricular arrhythmias. Autonomic abnormalities such as orthostatic hypotension have been associated with mitral prolapse.

When the left ventricle contracts, the mitral valve initially closes normally; as ventricular volume decreases, however, the valve leaflets (anterior, posterior, or both) abruptly prolapse into the atrium. This rapid motion generates the midsystolic click, and subsequent mitral regurgitation creates the late systolic murmur. Any maneuver that decreases the volume of the left ventricle causes the mitral valve to prolapse earlier during systole (e.g., the Valsalva maneuver or standing), also causing the click and murmur to occur earlier in systole. The presence of clicks and the length and intensity of the murmur may vary from time to time in the same patient. There are a few patients who have the characteristic click and murmur on auscultation in whom no mitral valve prolapse is identified on echocardiography. Tricuspid valve prolapse is sometimes associated with mitral valve prolapse.

The natural history of this syndrome is variable, and in most cases the syndrome is benign. The risk of sudden death for any individual patient with mitral valve prolapse is very small unless ventricular tachycardia is demonstrated. Ventricular arrhythmias generally are not treated unless symptoms are present or ventricular tachycardia is demonstrated. These arrhythmias have been reported to respond to propranolol, but many cases are difficult to control with either propranolol or other antiarrhythmic agents. Chest pain often is treated effectively with beta-adrenergic blocking agents.

AORTIC STENOSIS

The most common cause of aortic stenosis is a congenitally bicuspid aortic valve (see Chapter 5) that, although usually not obstructive during childhood, gradually thickens, calcifies, and becomes stenotic by approximately the sixth decade of life. Tricuspid aortic valves may also thicken and calcify from wear and tear, causing aortic stenosis in a few patients. Rheumatic fever may cause aortic stenosis but is almost always accompanied by evidence of mitral valve involvement.

Aortic valve obstruction results in elevation of left ventricular systolic pressure, and the resultant left ventricular hypertrophy maintains cardiac output without dilation of the ventricular cavity. Therefore, the stroke volume is normal until the late stages of the disease. Forceful atrial contraction augments filling of the thick, noncompliant ventricle and generates a prominent S_4 gallop that elevates the left ventricular end-diastolic pressure. The mean left ventricular diastolic pressure is nearly normal unless myocardial decompensation occurs. Left ventricular hypertrophy and high intramyocardial wall tension account for the increased oxygen demand and, along with decreased diastolic coronary blood flow, account for the occurrence of angina pectoris even if coronary anatomy is normal. Compensatory mechanisms may be adequate for many years, although outflow obstruction is severe. However, once congestive heart failure, angina, or syncope occurs, the patient experiences a rapid clinical decline. As the myocardium fails, mean left ventricular diastolic pressure increases and symptoms of pulmonary congestion ensue.

Aortic stenosis is three times more common in males than in females. Symptoms occur late, and many patients know of a murmur many years in advance of symptoms. Severe congenital aortic stenosis, however, may present in childhood. In most cases, syncope is due to the inability of the left ventricle to maintain a normal cardiac output with exertion and peripheral vasodilation. Sudden death may be the only symptom of aortic stenosis in a small percentage of patients (3 to 4 per cent). The mechanism of sudden death is not known but is probably similar to that causing syncope or secondary to a ventricular arrhythmia. The onset of symptoms due to aortic stenosis is a grave prognostic sign and an indication for valve replacement.

An ejection murmur may occur across a deformed aortic valve owing to turbulence of flow, without necessarily implying aortic stenosis. The murmur of significant aortic stenosis may diminish in the late stages of the disease when left ventricular failure occurs and flow across the stenotic orifice decreases.

Echocardiography can detect thickening of the aortic valve leaflets with decreased systolic separation. However, because of the multiple echoes generated by the calcified valve, the severity of aortic stenosis often cannot be determined. In the adult the presence of thin, pliable aortic valve leaflets virtually excludes the diagnosis of aortic stenosis. However, in children and young adults the congenitally stenotic aortic valve may appear to move well on M-mode echocardiography, but two-dimensional echocardiography reveals the classic doming of the valve that is diagnostic of congenital aortic stenosis. Identification of a bicuspid valve with echocardiography is difficult. The echocardiographic degree of left ventricular hypertrophy correlates with the severity of aortic stenosis in children but not in adults. Measurement of the aortic valve orifice by two-dimensional echocardiography is possible in a few patients but is not very reliable.

Doppler echocardiography can accurately estimate the pressure gradient across the stenotic aortic valve. If the aortic stenosis is thought to be severe, cardiac catheterization is usually necessary to confirm the severity of stenosis and exclude concomitant coronary artery disease. At cardiac catheterization, the gradient between the left ventricle and aorta is measured simultaneously with the cardiac output, and the valve area is calcu-lated from the Gorlin equation. The pressure gra-dient alone often does not adequately define the severity of aortic stenosis, since the patient with an increased cardiac output may demonstrate an increased gradient across the aortic valve without necessarily having severe aortic stenosis, and a pa-tient with severe aortic stenosis may demonstrate a decrease in the gradient as the ability to main-tain cardiac output decreases. The normal valve area is approximately 2.5 cm², and no gradient is present normally. An aortic valvular area of less than 0.7 cm² defines critical aortic stenosis and is usually associated with a gradient of 50 to 60 mm Hg or more. Right ventricular and pulmonary ar-terial pressures are normal unless left ventricular failure is present.

Aortic stenosis can be complicated by the devel-opment of aortic insufficiency as the valve calci-fies, stiffens, and fails to close properly or by the development of bacterial endocarditis. In younger patients, supravalvular or subvalvular aortic ob-struction should be considered.

To avoid the risk of sudden death, patients with known significant aortic stenosis should not par-ticipate in strenuous physical exercise. The adult patient should undergo catheterization as soon as angina, syncope, or left ventricular failure appears. Surgical mortality is lowest in patients with good left ventricular function. In patients with poor ejection fraction who survive surgery, the ventric-ular function tends to improve considerably once the obstruction is relieved; therefore, poor left ventricular function does not contraindicate aortic valve replacement for aortic stenosis. Aortic valve replacement may be performed in children and young adults who have severe congenital aortic stenosis even in the absence of symptoms in order to lower the risk of sudden death. Operative mor-tality is approximately 3 to 6 per cent, but patients with severe left ventricular dysfunction may have an operative risk as high as 15 per cent. Once symptoms have appeared, survival is improved by surgery. In elderly patients who are poor surgical candidates, a relatively small but often adequate increase in the aortic valve area can be obtained using balloon valvuloplasty at the time of cardiac catheterization.

AORTIC REGURGITATION

Rheumatic fever is the most common cause of aortic regurgitation. Isolated rheumatic aortic valve involvement without mitral valve involve-ment is unusual. Aortic regurgitation from rheu-matic fever may occur with the aortic valvulitis at the time of the acute rheumatic fever or may occur late after the acute attack as the valve be-comes thickened and the leaflets retract. Aortic stenosis and regurgitation often occur together in rheumatic heart disease as well as with bicuspid aortic valves. Aortic regurgitation may result from processes that either involve the valve directly or cause dilation of the aortic root. Aortic regurgita-tion can occur with discrete subvalvular stenosis or ventricular septal defects. Isolated congenital aortic regurgitation is unusual but may occur with a bicuspid aortic valve. Aortic regurgitation may occur after infective endocarditis. The aortic valve leaflets may be affected by rheumatoid arthritis. Conditions that may affect the ascending aorta and cause aortic regurgitation are syphilis, anky-losing spondylitis, Marfan's syndrome, systemic hypertension, aortic dissection, and aortic trauma.

Aortic regurgitation results in a volume over-load of the left ventricle. The ventricle compen-sates by increasing its end-diastolic volume ac-cording to the Frank-Starling mechanism. Left ventricular end-diastolic pressure may not be ele-vated early in the course of the disease as the ventricle dilates and accommodates the increased volume. The amount of blood ejected with each contraction is abnormally increased, consisting of both the blood received from the left atrium and the regurgitant volume. As the ventricular volume increases beyond the capacity of the left ventricle to dilate, however, left ventricular end-diastolic and left atrial pressures may rise. Secondary mi-tral regurgitation may occur owing to the left ven-tricular dilation. The physiology of aortic regurgi-tation is somewhat similar to that of mitral regurgitation, except that the increased cardiac stroke volume is delivered into the high-pressure aorta instead of the low-pressure left atrium, tend-ing to elevate left ventricular pressures instead of unloading the left ventricle. This factor, along with decreased aortic pressure during diastole when the majority of coronary flow occurs, may lead to greater oxygen demand than supply, and angina may occur, even with normal coronary ar-teries. The systolic function of the left ventricle is normal in early chronic aortic regurgitation, but as dilation becomes severe, left ventricular function diminishes. Some patients experience an irrevers-ible decrease in left ventricular function before any symptoms occur. The left ventricular dilation is thought to "overstretch" the myofibrils, leading to less actin-myosin interaction and decreased contractility. The mechanisms of compensation for chronic aortic regurgitation are very efficient, and patients with chronic severe aortic regurgitation may remain asymptomatic for years. However, the pathophysiology of acute, severe aortic regurgita-tion is different because the left ventricle has not had the opportunity to dilate, its compliance is relatively high, and the aortic regurgitation there-fore leads to very high left ventricular end-diastolic pressures. The left atrium and pulmonary vasculature may be protected somewhat, since the elevated left ventricular end-diastolic pressure may cause the mitral valve to close early in dias-tole (mitral preclosure). However, if mitral regur-gitation ensues, the elevated left ventricular dia-stolic pressure is reflected back to the pulmonary vasculature, and acute pulmonary edema may occur. Acute aortic regurgitation is caused most commonly by infective endocarditis, aortic dissection, and trauma. Acute aortic regurgitation results in a lower cardiac output, a narrower aortic pulse pressure, and a smaller left ventricle than does chronic aortic regurgitation. Aortic diastolic pressure decreases in chronic aortic regurgitation because of both the regurgitation of blood into the left ventricle and a compensatory decrease in systemic vascular resistance to maintain forward cardiac flow to the periphery. In acute aortic regurgitation, however, left ventricular diastolic pressure is high, systemic vascular resistance is not low, and aortic diastolic pressure does not fall greatly.

The increased pulse pressure in chronic aortic regurgitation is due to the large stroke volume, causing increased systolic and decreased diastolic pressure. This phenomenon determines many of the characteristic physical findings of aortic insufficiency (see Table 6–2). Aortic regurgitation murmurs are heard best with the patient upright, leaning forward, and in end expiration. The murmur of valvular aortic regurgitation is often loudest at the second left intercostal space, whereas the murmur of aortic regurgitation due to aortic dilation may be loudest in the second right intercostal space. Even if concomitant aortic stenosis is not present, a systolic ejection murmur reflecting a large stroke volume across a deformed valve is usually heard in the aortic area and may be transmitted to the carotid arteries. In severe chronic aortic regurgitation, a diastolic low-pitched rumbling murmur may be heard at the apex (Austin Flint murmur), probably owing to flow across the mitral valve, which closes early because of the regurgitant jet from the aortic insufficiency and also the increased left ventricular diastolic pressure.

Echocardiography shows dilation of the left ventricle and sometimes the aortic root. Wall motion is hyperdynamic if ventricular function is not impaired. Aortic regurgitation is characterized by diastolic fluttering of the anterior mitral valve leaflet caused by the regurgitant aortic jet's striking the open mitral valve during diastole. Acute severe aortic regurgitation with marked elevation of left atrial pressures may result in closure of the mitral valve in diastole before ventricular systole has occurred (mitral preclosure). The cause of the aortic regurgitation may be identified, such as aortic dissection or endocarditis. The presence of concomitant mitral valvular thickening or stenosis implies a rheumatic etiology. Doppler echocardiography can identify the regurgitant aortic jet and give a semiquantitative estimate of the severity of aortic regurgitation.

During cardiac catheterization, supravalvular aortography defines aortic dimensions, and reflux of contrast into the left ventricle grossly quantitates the degree of aortic regurgitation. Left ventriculography is performed to evaluate left ventricular function, and reflux of contrast into the left atrium would reveal mitral regurgitation. Systolic left ventricular and aortic pressures are elevated, and aortic diastolic pressure is low. Left ventricular volume is increased. The left ventricular end-diastolic pressure is normal or only slightly increased until left ventricular failure ensues. Left ventricular dysfunction is demonstrated by decreased cardiac output, decreased ejection fraction, and increased left ventricular end-diastolic pressure. In severe aortic regurgitation, the normally functioning ventricle is hyperdynamic (increased ejection fraction), and even a normal ejection fraction may indicate decreased systolic function. The presence of left ventricular dysfunction markedly increases surgical complications and mortality, and left ventricular function may not be restored after surgery, in contrast to the situation with pure aortic stenosis.

The timing of aortic valve replacement is difficult, since the natural history is prolonged and a long asymptomatic phase occurs. Early replacement of the aortic valve subjects the patient to the immediate surgical risk and the long-term risk created by prosthetic valves. However, if one waits to replace the aortic valve, irreversible left ventricular dysfunction may occur in the absence of symptoms. In these patients with no symptoms, evidence of progressive left ventricular systolic dysfunction may indicate surgery. In patients with severe disease of the aortic root, replacement of a portion of the ascending aorta may be required in addition to the aortic valve replacement.

Patients who develop acute severe aortic regurgitation deteriorate rapidly, and aortic valve replacement must be performed on an emergency basis. Vasodilators such as nitroprusside can acutely reduce afterload and diminish aortic regurgitation to stabilize the patient for a short time until surgery can be performed. Intra-aortic balloon counterpulsation is not effective in the presence of aortic regurgitation.

TRICUSPID STENOSIS

Tricuspid stenosis is usually rheumatic in etiology and does not occur as an isolated lesion. Like mitral stenosis, it is gradually progressive, is more common in women, and usually becomes symptomatic in mid-adulthood. Tricuspid stenosis can occasionally be caused by carcinoid, endomyocardial fibroelastosis, congenital valvular malformations, or right atrial myxoma.

Because it is such a low-pressure system, relatively small gradients across the tricuspid valve (5 mm) may indicate significant tricuspid stenosis. Echocardiographic diagnosis is probably more accurate than catheterization because of the small gradient involved. Tricuspid stenosis can protect the patient with concomitant mitral stenosis from pulmonary congestion.

TRICUSPID REGURGITATION

Tricuspid regurgitation may occur as a result of rheumatic fever, often associated with tricuspid stenosis. Tricuspid regurgitation is most commonly a functional lesion secondary to right ventricular dilation and pulmonary hypertension, and as in patients with mitral regurgitation, the differentiation of functional from organic valvular regurgitation can be difficult. Functional tricuspid regurgitation can occur with forms of congenital heart disease associated with pulmonary hypertension and with severe pulmonary disease. Tricuspid regurgitation can occur with Ebstein's anomaly, carcinoid syndrome, intracardiac tumors, penetrating or nonpenetrating cardiac trauma, and endocarditis. Normal tricuspid valves may be affected by endocarditis, particularly in drug addicts.

Functional tricuspid regurgitation may regress after associated lesions are corrected and pulmonary hypertension resolves. At times, plication of the tricuspid annulus is required to improve functional tricuspid regurgitation. If annuloplasty is unsuccessful or if significant tricuspid stenosis is present, tricuspid valve replacement can be performed.

PULMONIC STENOSIS AND REGURGITATION

Pulmonic stenosis is usually congenital and is discussed in Chapter 5. It can occasionally occur in an acquired form with hypertrophic cardiomyopathy (caused by bulging of the septum into the right ventricular outflow tract) or secondary to pericardial tumor involvement in the area.

Acquired pulmonary regurgitation is usually associated with pulmonary hypertension caused by left heart valvular disease (Graham Steell murmur) or pulmonary disease. The murmur sounds similar to that of aortic insufficiency and is heard best at the second left intercostal space. This murmur is high-pitched, early diastolic, and decrescendo in character. In distinction, isolated congenital pulmonic regurgitation results in a lower-pitched murmur that occurs later in diastole, is heard best at the third to fourth left intercostal space, and resembles more the murmur of tricuspid stenosis.

MULTIVALVULAR DISEASE

Combined valvular lesions are common, especially in rheumatic heart disease. In addition to organic lesions, development of mitral and tricuspid regurgitation or pulmonic regurgitation may occur secondary to the hemodynamic disturbance of other valvular lesions. In general, the manifestations of the more proximal valve lesion are the more prominent. For example, in patients with mitral and aortic valvular lesions of similar severity, mitral valve manifestations may predominate and the degree of aortic stenosis may be underestimated. Failure to correct all significant valvular lesions at the time of surgery may lead to an inadequate clinical result and illustrates the importance of excluding concomitant lesions at the time of catheterization. The surgical risk for double valve replacement is greater than that for single valve replacement.

RHEUMATIC FEVER

Rheumatic fever usually occurs in children 5 to 15 years of age. It is caused by group A beta-hemolytic streptococcal pharyngitis that occurs 1 to 3 weeks prior to the clinical manifestations of rheumatic fever. It is believed that an immune response to the Streptococcus is responsible for the disease. Males and females are equally affected. It is more common in patients of lower socioeconomic level. The incidence of rheumatic fever in the United States has declined in recent years.

Aschoff's nodules in the myocardium are the characteristic pathologic feature of rheumatic fever. The most serious manifestation of rheumatic fever is a pancarditis that may involve the endocardium, myocardium, and pericardium. Usually the mitral valve is involved; less frequently the aortic and even less frequently the tricuspid valves are involved. Pulmonic valve involvement is extremely rare. Valvulitis is recognized by a new insufficiency murmur. Aortic and mitral stenosis murmurs are not heard acutely. Myocarditis may manifest with heart failure. Pericarditis may produce a friction rub, and the PR interval may be prolonged. Because of the difficulty in diagnosing rheumatic fever, guidelines (modified Jones criteria) for establishing the diagnosis were developed. Major manifestations include carditis, polyarthritis, chorea, erythema marginatum, and subcutaneous nodules. Minor manifestations include fever, arthralgia, previous rheumatic fever or rheumatic heart disease, elevated acute phase reactants, and a prolonged PR interval. There should also be laboratory evidence of a preceding streptococcal infection (i.e., positive throat culture or increased antistreptolysin-O [ASO] titer).

Penicillin should be administered to eradicate streptococcal infection. Salicylates are rapidly effective for treating fever and arthritis but probably have no effect on carditis. The usefulness of steroids is unproven. Congestive heart failure is treated traditionally.

The relatively high recurrence rate of rheumatic fever after streptococcal infection continues for at least 5 to 10 years after the initial infection; therefore, rheumatic fever prophylaxis should be discontinued only in adults 5 to 10 years after the acute episode and then only if the risk of the streptococcal infection is low. Adults working with school-age children, those in the military service, those exposed to large numbers of people, and those in the medical or allied health professions should receive prophylaxis indefinitely. Patients with a significant degree of rheumatic heart disease or a history of repeated occurrences should have prophylaxis indefinitely. The recommended regimen for prophylaxis is 1.2 million units of benzathine penicillin monthly. Oral penicillin, erythromycin, or sulfadiazine can be used, but because of noncompliance these agents are somewhat less effective than the parenteral regimen.

TABLE 6-4. PROSTHETIC VALVES

TYPE	EXAMPLES	ADVANTAGES	DISADVANTAGES
Ball and cage	Starr-Edwards	Good durability	Anticoagulation required; more hemolysis than with other types
Tilting disk	Bjork-Shiley St. Jude Medtronic-Hall	Most favorable hemodynamics (i.e., least residual stenosis for any given valve size); good durability	Anticoagulation required; most thrombogenic type
Bioprosthesis	Hancock, Carpentier-Edwards	Anticoagulation usually not required	Early degeneration, especially in younger patients

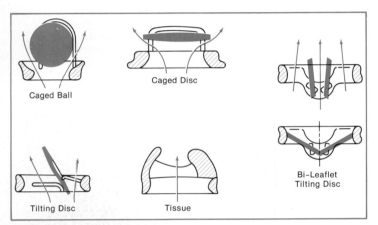

FIGURE 6-1. Designs and flow patterns of major categories of prosthetic heart valves: caged-ball, caged-disc, tilting-disc, bi-leaflet tilting-disc, and bioprosthetic (tissue) valves. While flow in mechanical valves must course along both sides of the occluder, bioprostheses have a central flow pattern. (From Braunwald E [ed]: Heart Disease: A Textbook of Cardiovascular Medicine. 4th ed. Philadelphia, WB Saunders Co, 1992, p 1063. Reprinted with permission from Annals of Biomedical Engineering, Vol 10, FJ Schoen et al, Bioengineering aspects of heart valve replacement, copyright 1982, Pergamon Press, Ltd.; and from Schoen FJ: Pathology of cardiac valve replacement. In Morse D, Steiner RM, Fernandez J [eds]: Guide to Prosthetic Cardiac Valves, p 209. New York, Springer-Verlag, 1985. Copyright Springer-Verlag, Inc., 1985.)

PROSTHETIC VALVES

Prosthetic valves may be either mechanical or bioprosthetic (Fig. 6-1). The two basic designs of mechanical valves are the ball and cage and the tilting disk (like a toilet seat cover). Bioprosthetic valves are made from porcine valve tissue mounted on metal struts (Table 6-4).

All prosthetic valves are somewhat stenotic, and residual gradients over both aortic and mitral valves occur. Any prosthetic valve can develop a perivalvular leak, that is, a leak exterior to the valve sewing ring, resulting in aortic or mitral regurgitation. In addition to hemodynamic effects, the turbulence from a perivalvular leak can cause red cell hemolysis. Even normally functioning prosthetic valves can cause hemolysis in some patients. The mechanical portion of a prosthetic valve may clot or otherwise malfunction. The long-term durability of mechanical valves has been well documented, but the durability of bioprosthetic porcine valves is not established, and many appear to degenerate, especially in younger patients.

All prosthetic valves carry a risk of thromboembolism. Valves in the aortic position are less likely to cause emboli than are valves in the mitral position. Bioprosthetic valves are less likely to cause emboli than are mechanical valves; however, a patient with a high embolic risk (such as one with atrial fibrillation, markedly dilated left atrium, previous history of peripheral emboli, or documented intracardiac thrombus) requires chronic anticoagulation despite the presence of a porcine valve. All patients with prosthetic valves are prone to develop endocarditis, and vigorous endocarditis prophylaxis should be administered prior to dental, gastrointestinal, or genitourinary surgery.

REFERENCES

Boudoulas H, Wooley CF: Mitral Valve Prolapse and the Mitral Valve Prolapse Syndrome. Mount Kisco, NY, Futura Publishing Co, 1988.

Dalen JE, Alpert JS (eds): Valvular Heart Disease. 2nd ed. Boston, Little, Brown and Co, 1987.

Frankl WS, Brest AN (eds): Valvular Heart Disease: Comprehensive Evaluation and Management. Cardiovascular Clinics, Vol 16. Philadelphia, FA Davis, 1986.

Hall RJ, Julian DG: Diseases of the Cardiac Valves. New York, Churchill Livingstone, 1989.

Shulman ST, Amren DP, Bisno AL et al: Prevention of rheumatic fever. Circulation 70:1118A, 1984.

7 CORONARY HEART DISEASE

Coronary artery disease is the leading cause of death in the United States and most of the industrialized Western world. In contrast, it is much less common in Asia, the Near East, Africa, and South and Central America. Inexplicably, death from coronary heart disease has declined in the United States since the late 1960s.

Atherosclerosis

Atherosclerosis is a thickening and hardening of medium-size and larger arteries with narrowing of the arterial lumen by atherosclerotic plaques. Its cause is multifactorial. Preventable risk factors, genetic susceptibility, local arterial and hemodynamic factors, and gender influence the development of atherosclerosis.

The fatty streak, consisting of lipids and lipoid proteins, located in the intima of the vessel with the overlying endothelium intact, is the earliest form of atherosclerosis. This yellow fatty streak seen in childhood is not necessarily a precursor of adult atherosclerosis and occurs in populations in which atherosclerosis is uncommon; it is presumably reversible at this stage. Around age 25, in populations in which atherosclerosis is common, the fibrous plaque begins to develop. It is white and elevated and may compromise the arterial lumen. Reversibility is questionable when fibrous tissue and intimal proliferation are present. In more advanced stages, deposition of fibrin and platelets and necrosis of tissue with growth of new vessels may occur. Cholesterol, calcification, and hemorrhage within the atherosclerotic plaque form complicated plaques. The intimal surface may ulcerate, thrombose, and occlude the vessel. Mechanical, chemical, or immunologic injury that begins with the fatty streak may cause progression of the atherosclerotic lesion. Different arteries appear to have different degrees of susceptibility to atherosclerotic lesions; the coronary arteries are particularly susceptible, mostly within the first 6 cm of origin. Plaques tend to occur at arterial bifurcations, possibly owing to the turbulent flow in these areas.

Atherosclerotic lesions in the coronary arteries may be detected during life by coronary arteriography (Fig. 7–1). When a radiopaque contrast agent is injected into a coronary artery, atherosclerotic plaques appear as narrowings in the column of contrast as it travels down the artery.

Narrowing of vessels is described as a per cent diameter narrowing. Lesions greater than 50 per cent are probably hemodynamically significant, causing approximately 75 per cent narrowing of cross-sectional area, whereas lesions greater than 75 per cent are definitely significant, producing 95 per cent cross-sectional narrowing. The gradation of obstruction at coronary angiography is approximate and often underestimates the actual degree of obstruction. Complete obstruction of a vessel at

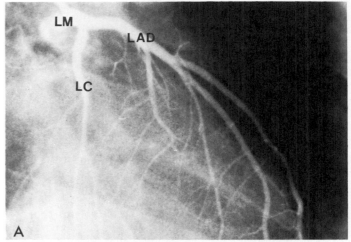

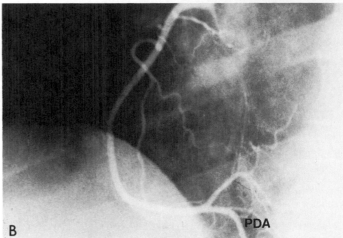

FIGURE 7–1. *A,* Normal left coronary arteriogram in the right anterior oblique projection. LM = Left main coronary artery; LAD = left anterior descending coronary artery; LC = left circumflex coronary artery. *B,* Normal right coronary arteriogram in the left anterior oblique projection. PDA = Posterior descending artery.

63

angiography is usually represented by a stump, the distal portion of the vessel often opacified via collateral circulation.

Risk Factors (Table 7–1)

Several risk factors for the development of coronary artery disease have been identified by epidemiologic studies. The more risk factors present in any individual patient, the greater the likelihood that he or she will develop coronary artery disease. Mortality from coronary artery disease is much higher in men than in women, and women lag behind men in coronary artery disease deaths by approximately 10 years. Coronary disease mortality tends to equalize in men and women at age 50, possibly related to higher risk in women after menopause or the elimination of higher-risk men at an earlier age.

Treatment of even mild hypertension (diastolic pressure of 90 to 104 mm Hg) reduces mortality from both stroke and myocardial infarction, implying not only an association but a causative role for hypertension. Elevations in both systolic and diastolic blood pressure are associated with an increased risk. There is no distinct blood pressure value below which risk suddenly becomes low; that is, over a wide range of blood pressures, the higher the blood pressure, the higher the risk.

The higher the serum cholesterol, the higher the risk of coronary disease, even within the usually accepted "normal" cholesterol values of Americans. The low density lipoprotein (LDL) fraction of total cholesterol is directly associated with the risk of atherosclerosis; the high density lipoprotein (HDL) fraction appears to be inversely related to the incidence of atherosclerosis, and a low HDL value appears to be a stronger risk factor than the total cholesterol value. HDL levels are higher in women than in men at all age levels. They are increased by regular exercise and are reduced in diabetes mellitus. The serum triglyceride level is a weaker risk factor and may not be independent when adjusted for obesity or glucose intolerance. Recent evidence implies that modifications in serum cholesterol may lead to an improvement in risk. Dietary modification to lower serum cholesterol seems prudent both in asymptomatic patients with an elevated or high normal cholesterol (greater than 200 mg/dl) and in patients with known coronary artery disease. Drug treatment to effect reduction in serum cholesterol should probably be reserved for patients with well-defined hypercholesterolemia. (See Chapter 60.)

Nonatherosclerotic Causes of Coronary Artery Obstruction

Although uncommon, several nonatherosclerotic causes of coronary artery obstruction exist. Emboli to coronary arteries can occur in infective endocarditis, from mural thrombi in the left atrium or ventricle, from prosthetic valves, from cardiac myxomas, or associated with cardiopulmonary bypass or coronary arteriography. Trauma to coronary arteries can be associated with both penetrating and nonpenetrating injuries. Various forms of arteritis (syphilis, polyarteritis nodosa, Takayasu's disease, disseminated lupus erythematosus, and rheumatoid arthritis) can affect the coronary arteries. The mucocutaneous lymph node syndrome (Kawasaki's disease) presents as a febrile illness in a child usually below the age of 10. Multiple organ systems can develop vasculitis, but the most significant feature is a vasculitis involving intima, media, and adventitia of the coronary arteries that results in aneurysm and sometimes thrombus formation. Mortality is 1 to 2 per cent secondary to complications from coronary arterial involvement.

Dissection of the aorta involving the coronary arteries or dissection of the coronary arteries themselves may occur in patients with connective tissue abnormalities of the aorta (e.g., Marfan's syndrome). In situ thrombosis may occur in certain rare disorders (e.g., polycythemia vera, thrombocytosis, and disseminated intravascular coagulation). Spasm of the coronary artery (Prinzmetal's angina, discussed further on) is another nonatherosclerotic cause of coronary obstruction.

Nonobstructive Causes of Ischemic Heart Disease

Situations associated with increased left ventricular pressure and wall tension, a decrease in diastolic perfusion pressure, and/or an increase in left ventricular mass (e.g., aortic stenosis) may cause myocardial ischemia by altering the balance of oxygen supply and demand. In addition, conditions in which substrate delivery is decreased (e.g., hypotension, anemia, and carbon monoxide poisoning) may cause myocardial ischemia, especially if pre-existing coronary lesions are present.

A syndrome of myocardial infarction with angiographically normal coronary arteries exists. Approximately 2 per cent of patients with myocardial infarction demonstrate no obstructive lesions on coronary arteriography. These patients tend to be young, have a low incidence of coronary risk factors, and often have no history of angina pectoris

TABLE 7–1. RISK FACTORS FOR CORONARY ARTERY DISEASE

Nonmodifiable risk factors
    Older age
    Male gender
    Family history
Modifiable, independent risk factors
    Hypertension
    Hyperchclesterolemia (LDL)
    Smoking
    Glucose intolerance
Other possible factors (may not be independent of the above)
    Obesity
    Sedentary lifestyle
    Oral contraceptives

prior to infarction. The prognosis for survival after the acute event is usually good. The cause is unknown, but possible etiologies include coronary emboli, coronary artery spasm, coronary artery disease in smaller vessels beyond the resolution of coronary arteriography, and coronary arterial thrombosis with recanalization.

Pathophysiology of Ischemic Heart Disease

The manifestations of ischemic heart disease occur when the oxygen demand to the heart exceeds the oxygen supply. The most common cause of this imbalance is fixed obstruction within a coronary artery. Normally the arterioles regulate the blood flow to any particular area of the heart, and the more proximal epicardial "conductance" vessels, in the absence of a fixed or dynamic obstruction, do not restrict the flow. Once stenosis of 50 per cent or greater occurs in a conductance coronary artery, the vessel is unable to increase its flow sufficiently to maintain perfusion under conditions of increased demand despite the full dilation of the more distal arterioles. In addition to fixed obstruction, transient or "dynamic" obstruction of the conductance vessels may also occur. The caliber of these larger vessels can be altered by factors that are incompletely understood, and spasm of a localized area may decrease blood supply transiently to an area of the heart (variant or Prinzmetal's angina). Coronary artery spasm with or without the coexistent fixed coronary obstructive lesions may cause angina pectoris because of a temporary decrease in oxygen supply rather than any increase in oxygen demand.

Occasionally, oxygen demand can exceed oxygen supply despite normal coronary arteries; the classic example is aortic stenosis, in which the hypertrophied muscle and increased wall tension increase oxygen demand, but increased intramural pressure and decreased aortic pressure decrease diastolic coronary artery flow and oxygen supply.

Ischemia affects the metabolism of cardiac cells, which can alter contractile and electrical functions. The inability to perform oxidative phosphorylation and generate high-energy compounds results in abnormal systolic myocardial contraction and also defects of diastolic compliance (relaxation). Dysfunction can be transient, for example, only after exercise-induced ischemia, or permanent, such as with myocardial infarction. Decreased compliance requires increased pressure to fill the heart to any given end-diastolic volume and accounts for the need to elevate somewhat the left ventricular filling pressure in order to maintain cardiac filling in patients with ischemic heart disease. The loss of cellular integrity allows release of enzymes (serum aspartate aminotransferase, lactate dehydrogenase, and creatine kinase) into the blood that are used clinically to detect the presence of myocardial infarction. Electrical changes occur owing to altered ion transport across the cell membrane. Serious arrhythmias, most frequently ventricular tachycardia and fibrillation, are common.

The time during which ischemia is reversible is clinically important because interventions exist that may restore flow to myocardium distal to an acute occlusion. Reperfusion after complete occlusion of less than 15 to 20 minutes salvages most if not all of the ischemic tissue. However, longer periods of occlusion cause increased amounts of myocardium to remain irreversibly necrotic. After approximately 4 to 6 hours of occlusion, reperfusion salvages very little tissue.

In humans, collateral circulation (small vessels that course from a nonobstructed coronary system to the distal portion of an obstructed system) slowly develops as flow is gradually diminished by fixed coronary obstruction. Collateral flow does provide some perfusion to an ischemic vascular bed, but the adequacy of this perfusion is questionable, especially under periods of increased demand (e.g., exercise). Collateral flow does not develop acutely after sudden obstruction of blood flow.

ANGINA PECTORIS

Angina pectoris is chest discomfort caused by transient myocardial ischemia without necrosis, usually resulting from the inability of atherosclerotic arteries to increase myocardial blood flow under conditions of increased demand. Coronary spasm may occur either alone or in the presence of fixed coronary obstruction and reduces flow without an increase in demand. Angina pectoris is considered stable when there exists a chronic course of predictable exertional chest pain and unstable if a change in chronic angina consisting of increased frequency, duration, or severity occurs. The onset of new angina, angina occurring at rest or with minimal exertion, or angina awakening the patient from sleep is considered unstable. Unstable angina pectoris has also been termed preinfarction angina, crescendo angina, acute coronary insufficiency, and intermediate coronary syndrome and usually requires hospital admission to exclude an acute myocardial infarction (Table 7–2).

The patient's history is crucial in the diagnosis of angina pectoris (see Table 2–2). Even if coronary artery disease is known to exist anatomically —by arteriography, for example—the functional significance of these lesions must be assessed from the patient's history of chest pain. The pattern of precipitation by exertion and disappearance with rest is one of the most characteristic features of angina pectoris. The pain or discomfort is often located in the left precordium or midchest directly under the sternum. It is sometimes not considered pain by the patient but described as pressure, burning, tightness, or fullness; the classic gesture is a clenched fist over the chest. The pain may appear over the period of a few seconds or minutes and disappears gradually in the same manner. It is usually not sharp or knifelike and does not

TABLE 7–2. ANGINA PECTORIS

TYPE OF ANGINA	TYPICAL PATIENT CHARACTERISTICS	PATTERN	COMPLICATIONS	ECG	ANGIOGRAPHY	THERAPY
Stable	Older Male > female Coronary risk factors	Stable, unchanging pattern of aggravation and relief; exertional, lasts <10 min	Usually none	Baseline ECG often demonstrates nonspecific ST-T changes or evidence of old MI but can be normal; ST depression or T wave inversion may occur with pain	Fixed obstructive coronary lesions	Nitrates Beta blockers Calcium blockers
Unstable	Same as above	Markedly increased frequency; prolonged, severe episodes; rest angina, nocturnal angina	Can lead to MI or ischemic arrhythmias	Same as stable angina; ST elevation occasionally occurs with pain	Fixed lesions (although platelet thrombi, release of vasoactive peptides, plaque rupture, and/or coronary spasm can contribute)	Same as above Hospitalization Consider intra-aortic balloon pump, angiography, revascularization
Variant (atypical or Prinzmetal's)	Younger Male ≅ female Lack of coronary risk factors	Typically severe pain at rest, can be provoked with exertion in a few cases; often early morning pattern	Syncope from tachyarrhythmias, heart block during pain; MI on rare occasions	Baseline ECG often normal; typically ST elevation with pain, although ST depression and T wave inversion also occur	Spontaneous or ergonovine-induced spasm in a normal vessel or at a region of a fixed but often nonstenotic lesion	Calcium blockers Nitrates Avoid beta blockers

MI = Myocardial infarction.

occur suddenly at full intensity or leave abruptly. It lasts between one-half minute and approximately 20 minutes. Ischemic pain that lasts longer suggests myocardial necrosis. Typical angina is relieved with nitroglycerin or rest over a period of 30 seconds to several minutes. Immediate relief (within a few seconds), incomplete relief, or relief 20 to 30 minutes after sublingual nitroglycerin is not typical of angina pectoris. The pain may radiate to the neck, jaw, epigastrium, shoulder, and arms, most frequently the left arm. Pain localized to the left inframammary area is less characteristic. Chest wall tenderness is usually not present. Common precipitating factors are brisk walking, climbing stairs, using the hands above the head (e.g., shaving, hair combing), emotional upset, exposure to cold, and a large meal. Redistribution of intravascular volume at night may cause angina decubitus, that is, angina occurring with the supine position. Existence of precipitating causes such as anemia, thyrotoxicosis, infection, aortic stenosis, arrhythmias, and hypertension should be excluded. Weakness, dyspnea, nausea, pallor, and diaphoresis may occur with the pain. Many patients misinterpret the sensation as "gas," and belching is not uncommon.

Findings on physical examination are nonspecific. An S_4 gallop is often present but may be heard only during an episode of acute ischemia (decreased diastolic compliance with ischemia). Likewise, a murmur of papillary muscle dysfunction may occur only with ischemia. When myocardial ischemia is not present at rest, exercise tests may unmask electrocardiographic (ECG) evidence of ischemia (see Stress Testing in Chapter 2). Thallium perfusion scintigraphy, or exercise radionuclide ventriculography increases the sensitivity and specificity of exercise testing, particularly in patients with abnormal baseline ECG because of digitalis, pre-existing nonspecific ST-T wave changes, or left bundle branch block. Exercise echocardiography has become practical with two-dimensional echo techniques and may reveal regional wall motion abnormality during or immediately after exercise. In patients who cannot adequately exercise, dobutamine echocardiography or dipyridamole thallium scanning may be used. In addition to its diagnostic role, the treadmill exercise test is important to assess the functional capacity and prognosis of patients with known coronary artery disease.

If the patient presents with pain of unknown origin, exercise testing may be useful diagnostically, but only after rest and medication have relieved the pain and an acute myocardial infarction has been excluded. Patients with rest pain or particularly severe anginal syndromes should not undergo exercise testing but instead should proceed directly to coronary angiography after stabilization. Patients who present with unstable angina have a higher percentage of left main and severe three-vessel disease than do patients with chronic, stable angina.

The natural history of stable angina pectoris is variable, and several years may pass in some patients without the development of unstable angina or myocardial infarction. The most important factors to judge prognosis are measures of left ventricular function, the number of vessels containing significantly stenotic lesions, and exercise tolerance. Patients with significant left main coronary artery stenoses have a poor prognosis and are considered for surgery on the basis of their anatomy alone.

The indications for coronary angiography are discussed in Chapter 3. For patients in whom the differentiation of coronary artery disease from noncoronary causes of chest pain cannot be made despite a careful history and noninvasive evaluation, coronary arteriography may be the only means to exclude or establish the diagnosis of coronary artery disease. In addition, for patients in whom coronary artery spasm is suspected, the administration of ergonovine at cardiac catheterization may exclude or confirm that diagnosis. When ischemic pain is refractory to medical management, surgery very effectively eliminates pain (Table 7–3). Because specific subgroups of patients may demonstrate increased survival from coronary bypass surgery, some physicians recommend coronary angiography for any patient with known or suspected coronary artery disease in order to exclude left main or certain subsets of three-vessel coronary artery disease. Because this practice subjects many patients to the risk (albeit small) of coronary angiography, most physicians select patients for coronary angiography from subgroups at particularly high risk for having left main or three-vessel coronary artery disease, such as patients with recurrent chest pain after myocardial infarction (especially subendocardial myocardial infarction), patients with poor exercise performance (positive test in first two stages or 6 minutes of exercise), and patients presenting with an unstable pattern of angina pectoris. With the use of these high-risk subgroups as a guide to selecting patients for catheterization, few patients with left main coronary artery stenosis would be missed. Many physicians also catheterize any young patient (below age 40) who presents with significant angina or myocardial infarction and any patient resuscitated from cardiac arrest. The ability of coronary artery bypass surgery to prolong life in many other subgroups of patients with coronary artery disease, particularly those patients who are asymptomatic or have mild degrees of angina, is unproven. In general, the indications listed in Table 7–3 appear to be relevant for coronary angioplasty as well as surgery. The role of prophylactic angioplasty for patients with asymptomatic or mildly symptomatic one- and two-vessel disease is controversial.

Some patients, especially diabetics, may have "silent" ischemia, that is, episodes of ischemia, well-documented by ECG, imaging, or echo techniques, unassociated with chest discomfort. This lack of an anginal "warning system" may result from autonomic nervous system abnormalities and may be dangerous, because severe ischemia can occur without the patient's realizing that he needs to stop his activity. Some patients may manifest symptoms of ischemia as dyspnea rather than chest discomfort (angina-equivalent dyspnea).

TABLE 7–3. INDICATIONS FOR CORONARY REVASCULARIZATION

1. Relief of moderate to severe, significantly disabling stable angina in patients refractory or intolerant to medical management
2. Relief of unstable angina in patients refractory or intolerant to medical management; performed preferably after the patient is stable and pain-free, but can be done on an emergency basis if necessary
3. Improved survival in certain subsets of less symptomatic patients: left main coronary arterial stenosis, three-vessel disease with poor functional capacity or moderate left ventricular dysfunction, multivessel disease with proximal LAD stenosis, or residual ischemia following myocardial infarction

Medical Management of Angina

Angina is treated by decreasing myocardial oxygen demand or increasing oxygen supply. Certain general measures may be helpful. Avoiding situations that may increase oxygen demand (e.g., cold weather, particularly large meals, and excessive exercise) may be effective. Control of hypertension and correction of other exacerbating conditions such as anemia, infection, hypoxia, and thyrotoxicosis are necessary. Cigarette smoking should be stopped. Treatment of congestive heart failure decreases oxygen consumption and improves oxygen delivery. After physical training under supervised programs the patient may be able to perform tasks with a lower heart rate–blood pressure product and less angina. Whether exercise increases collateral circulation and oxygen delivery is controversial.

The most time-honored antianginal medication is nitroglycerin (Table 7–4), a smooth muscle relaxant of both systemic arteries and veins, although it affects veins predominantly. A decrease in venous return to the heart decreases preload, decreases left ventricular volume, and subsequently reduces wall tension and afterload. These hemodynamic effects are also of value in treating congestive heart failure. In addition, nitroglycerin dilates the larger conductance coronary arteries and probably also the collateral vessels, thus directly increasing blood supply to ischemic myocardium. The reduction in ventricular diastolic pressure brought about by nitrates may lower resistance to coronary blood flow within the myocardium during diastole.

Beta-adrenergic receptor blockade (Tables 7–5 and 7–6) slows the resting heart rate, blunts the increase in heart rate with exercise, and decreases myocardial contractility, all of which decrease oxygen consumption. In addition, beta-blocking drugs are useful antihypertensive agents and may reduce cardiac afterload in such patients. Beta-adrenergic receptors can be divided into beta$_1$ and beta$_2$ subgroups. The beta$_1$ receptors mediate the cardiac actions of the sympathetic nervous system, whereas beta$_2$ receptors promote the glycogenoly-

TABLE 7–4. NITRATE PREPARATIONS FOR ANGINA

PREPARATION	INDICATION	ONSET*	DURATION*	USUAL DOSE	SIDE EFFECTS
Sublingual nitroglycerin	Acute anginal episodes; prophylaxis before specific activity	2 min	30 min	0.3–0.6 (usually 0.4) mg; can be repeated at 5-min intervals; if pain unrelieved after three doses patient is usually instructed to seek medical attention	Headache (tolerance may develop in 1–2 wk) Flushing Tachycardia Dizziness Postural hypotension
Topical nitroglycerin 2% nitroglycerin ointment	Angina prophylaxis	15 min	4–6 hr (can be wiped off if side effects occur)	1–2 inches q6h	Same as above Messy; tolerance develops
Sustained-release transdermal		—	24 hr	q24h; dose depends on preparation Patch off overnight may prevent tolerance	Variable drug levels and tolerance to nitrate effects; contact dermatitis
IV nitroglycerin	Unstable, severe angina	Almost immediately	Effects gone 5–10 min after infusion is stopped	Continuous infusion; initially 10 μg/min, titrate upward at 5-min intervals to desired hemodynamic effect	Hypotension
Long-acting sublingual (e.g., isosorbide dinitrate)	Angina prophylaxis	5–10 min	1–3 hr	2.5–10 mg q2–3h	Same as above Ischemia may occur upon abrupt withdrawal
oral		15–20 min	4–6 hr	10–40 mg q6–12h; 8–12 hr/day nitrate-free period may prevent tolerance	

* Varies widely.

TABLE 7–5. SELECTED BETA BLOCKING AGENTS

DRUG	USUAL DOSAGE	BETA$_1$ CARDIO-SELECTIVE	INTRINSIC AGONIST ACTIVITY	HYDRO-PHILIC
Propranolol	Oral: 40–480 mg/day in 2–4 doses (long-acting preparation available) Intravenous: up to 0.10–0.15 mg/kg given as 1-mg increments at 3- to 5-min intervals	−	−	Low
Metoprolol	Oral: 50–100 mg twice a day Intravenous: 5 mg × 3 at 2- to 5-min intervals	+	−	Moderate
Nadolol	Oral: 40–160 mg once a day	−	−	High
Atenolol	Oral: 50–100 mg once a day	+	−	High
Timolol	Oral: 10–20 mg twice a day	−	−	Moderate
Pindolol	Oral: 10–30 mg twice a day	−	+	Moderate
Acebutalol	Oral: 200–800 mg once a day	+	+	Moderate
Labetalol	Oral: 100–400 mg twice a day	(alpha$_1$ selectivity)	−	High
Esmolol	Intravenous: 50–200 μg/kg/min after a loading dose	+	−	Moderate

+ = Present; − = absent.

TABLE 7–6. SIDE EFFECTS OF BETA BLOCKERS

Beta$_2$ blocking effects
  Bronchoconstriction
  Failure to initiate glycogenolysis in insulin-induced hypoglycemia
  Exacerbation of peripheral vascular disease
Other
  Exacerbation of congestive heart failure
  Bradycardia and heart block
  Ischemia upon abrupt withdrawal
  Fatigue, depression, impotence, nightmares

sis induced by catecholamines, vasodilation of peripheral blood vessels, and dilation of pulmonary bronchi. Therefore, beta blockers that have predominantly beta$_1$ rather than beta$_2$ sympathetic antagonism (e.g., atenolol and metoprolol) may be more useful in treating patients with bronchospastic pulmonary disease, chronic obstructive pulmonary disease, diabetes, and peripheral vascular disease. However, selective beta$_1$ blockade is only relative, and at higher doses (e.g., above 100 mg/day of metoprolol) the selectivity may be lost. Hydrophilic beta blockers, such as atenolol and na-dolol, have relatively long half-lives, can be administered once daily, and tend not to penetrate the central nervous system, which may produce fewer neurologic side effects, such as mental depression and sleep disturbances. Thus, side effects attributed to one beta blocker may be eliminated by switching to another. Pindolol has mild intrinsic sympathomimetic activity in addition to its beta receptor-blocking activity; that is, it acts as a beta-receptor agonist as well as antagonist. Theoretically, some of the effects at rest of beta-receptor blockade such as slow heart rate and peripheral vasoconstriction may be less prominent, even though the sympathetic effects of exercise are blocked. Any clinical advantage to beta-receptor blockers with intrinsic sympathomimetic activity is not clear at present.

Calcium ions play critical roles in myocardial contraction, coronary vascular smooth muscle constriction, and the genesis of the cardiac action potential. Slow channel blocking agents are effective antianginal drugs when used either alone or in combination with beta-receptor adrenergic blockers or nitrates (Table 7-7). All the calcium antagonists decrease myocardial contractility and relax coronary and peripheral vascular smooth muscle. Verapamil and diltiazem may decrease the sinus nodal discharge rate and prolong atrioventricular (AV) nodal conduction time. In clinically used doses, nifedipine is a potent vasodilator and exerts little action on myocardial contractility or on the sinus and AV nodes. Therefore, nifedipine decreases afterload via peripheral vasodilation and increases coronary blood flow via coronary vasodilation. The antianginal effect of verapamil may be related to both coronary artery vasodilation and decreased myocardial contractility, thus decreasing oxygen demand. The effects on contractility and sinus rate are minimized owing to reflex sympathetic stimulation in response to the peripheral vasodilation. Verapamil and the other calcium antagonists enhance left ventricular diastolic filling (increase compliance); this is not an effect of simple beta blockade. In general, the effects of diltiazem are intermediate between those of verapamil and nifedipine. Diltiazem has been demonstrated to improve survival when given acutely in patients with non–Q wave myocardial infarctions.

Because the mechanisms of action of nitrates, beta-receptor blockers, and calcium antagonists differ, combination therapy of two or three of these drugs might be effective. Nitrates can cause reflex tachycardia that beta-receptor blockers can prevent. Therefore, in a patient with no contraindication to beta-receptor blockade, the combination of nitrates and a beta-receptor blocker may be beneficial antianginal therapy. In addition, the combination of beta blockers and calcium channel blockers is often useful if unwanted electrophysiologic or inotropic side effects do not become manifest. Patients with particularly severe angina may require one drug from each of the three classes.

A patient experiencing a marked increase in the frequency or severity of angina, the new onset of angina at rest, or nocturnal angina should be admitted to an intensive care unit, placed at bed rest, and sedated if necessary. If not contraindicated, beta blockade should be instituted. Sublingual nitroglycerin and oral and/or cutaneous nitrates should be administered, and if pain recurs, intravenous nitroglycerin can be initiated. Heparin and/or aspirin should be administered to prevent the platelet thrombi associated with unstable an-

TABLE 7–7. CALCIUM ANTAGONISTS

	SINUS AND AV NODAL EFFECTS	NEGATIVE INOTROPIC EFFECTS	CORONARY AND PERIPHERAL VASODILATION	USUAL DOSE	SIDE EFFECTS
Nifedipine	0	0/+	+++	10–20 mg q6–8h (long-acting preparation available)	Hypotension Headache Dizziness Nausea Peripheral edema Reflex tachycardia with worsening of angina
Nicardipine	0	0/+	+++	20–40 mg q8h	Same as nifedipine
Diltiazem	++	+	++	30–60 mg q6–8h (long-acting preparation available)	Left ventricular failure Bradycardia, AV block Hypotension Flushing
Verapamil	+++	++	++	80–120 mg q6–8h (long-acting preparation available)	Left ventricular failure Bradycardia, AV block Nausea Flushing Decreases excretion of digoxin by 30%

0 = None; + = mild effect; ++ = moderate effect; +++ = strong effect.

gina. Nifedipine may be useful in the patient with no hypotension or with congestive heart failure. Verapamil or diltiazem may be useful in the patient with no heart failure. Most patients having unstable angina experience relief of chest pain with this approach, and further evaluation, probably including coronary arteriography, can be undertaken when the patient is stable and pain-free. If angina does not abate with aggressive medical therapy, the patient should be considered for early coronary arteriography and for angioplasty or bypass surgery. An intra-aortic balloon pump may be inserted before cardiac catheterization or surgery to improve diastolic filling of the coronary arteries and to decrease afterload. Many patients experience pain relief once balloon counterpulsation is initiated despite refractoriness to intensive medical antianginal therapy.

Nonmedical Management of Angina Pectoris

Coronary artery bypass surgery and percutaneous transluminal coronary angioplasty (PTCA) are useful in relieving angina unresponsive to medical therapy and, in certain subgroups, in prolonging life. Coronary artery bypass surgery may be combined with aneurysmectomy in patients with refractory cardiac arrhythmias, congestive heart failure, or recurrent emboli due to a large ventricular aneurysm. Coronary artery bypass alone usually does not improve left ventricular function sufficiently to treat patients in whom congestive heart failure is the major manifestation of ischemic heart disease. Intractable, chronic ventricular arrhythmias also are not usually abolished by revascularization alone and require resection of the tachycardia focus.

Coronary artery bypass grafting most commonly involves harvesting saphenous veins from the legs to anastomose from the ascending aorta to the coronary artery at a site distal to the obstruction. The veins are reversed in direction to permit the flow of blood past the venous valves. As many major arterial branches as possible are grafted beyond significant obstructions. Internal mammary grafts demonstrate a superior long-term patency compared with saphenous grafts. Both the left and right internal mammary arteries may be dissected free and anastomosed to a coronary artery distal to its obstruction. The proximal take-off of the internal mammary artery remains intact from the subclavian artery. Internal mammary grafts are most commonly anastomosed to the left anterior descending coronary artery vessels. The distal coronary vessels must be at least 1 to 2 mm in diameter to accept a bypass graft, and the flow distal to the occlusion, determined at the time of coronary arteriography, should be sufficient to maintain flow in the grafts so that thrombosis is unlikely to occur. Left ventricular dysfunction increases the risk of surgery but does not necessarily contraindicate surgery if chest pain is refractory.

Perioperative mortality is approximately 0.7 per cent for those with normal left ventricular function and 1.8 per cent for those with abnormal ventricular function. Surgical mortality in patients with left main coronary artery disease is approximately 2.5 per cent, and if left ventricular function is abnormal, approaches 4 per cent. Surgical mortality increases with age, reaching 2 per cent in patients older than 65 years. The incidence of perioperative myocardial infarction is reported to be 5 to 10 per cent. Chest pain is completely relieved in approximately 65 per cent of patients, and significant improvement in pain occurs in an additional 25 per cent. The remaining patients are either not improved (5 per cent) or worse (5 per cent) after surgery. Approximately 2 to 4 per cent of patients per year have a recurrence of angina, due either to obstruction of the grafts or to progressive atherosclerosis in the native arteries. If angina recurs either early or late after surgery, repeat catheterization may be indicated if surgery or angioplasty is deemed necessary. Repeat operations carry a higher surgical risk and less successfully relieve pain.

Patients with one- or two-vessel coronary artery disease have relatively good survival with medical or surgical therapy as long as their clinical status is stable, and they usually can be followed medically until refractory angina appears. The role of coronary artery bypass grafting in patients with three-vessel coronary artery disease is more controversial, but a recent study suggests that patients with three-vessel coronary artery disease who have either no symptoms or stable angina pectoris have no higher mortality with medicine than with surgery as their initial therapy. These patients, however, represent a select subgroup of relatively stable patients with three-vessel disease; patients with three-vessel disease and poor functional capacity, judged either on the treadmill or by their inability to perform as much daily activity as they would like, may benefit from bypass grafting. In addition, some studies demonstrate improved survival with surgery in patients with three-vessel disease and moderate ventricular dysfunction.

Graft flow rates at the time of surgery can help predict graft closure. The average flow in a technically successful saphenous bypass graft is about 70 ml/min. Grafts in which the flow is less than 45 ml/min frequently occlude. Causes of poor graft flow include grafting to a vessel with a noncritical stenosis proximal to the graft anastomosis, a technically poor anastomosis, and poor distal run-off secondary to distal vessel disease. Graft patency rates at 6 to 12 months are 75 to 87 per cent; because most patients receive more than one graft, 84 to 95 per cent of patients have at least one patent graft. Internal mammary grafts have a much higher patency rate than saphenous grafts, and more than 95 per cent are patent after 1 year. Low-dose aspirin therapy (325 mg qd or qod) may improve saphenous vein graft patency.

PTCA involves passing a balloon catheter into the coronary artery, positioning it across a stenotic lesion, and inflating the balloon with several atmospheres of pressure to dilate the stenosis. This procedure disrupts the intima, splits the atherosclerotic plaque, and often results in a small local dissection with relief of obstruction. Candidates for angioplasty have angina for which surgical revascularization would be recommended and discrete, relatively proximal stenoses in one or more coronary vessels. Studies demonstrate the feasibility of angioplasty on multiple lesions. Patients with left main coronary artery disease are not usually appropriate candidates for coronary angioplasty because a dissection in this vessel would jeopardize the majority of the myocardial blood flow. PTCA is successful (at least 25 to 50 per cent improvement in luminal diameter) in approximately 80 to 90 per cent of cases. In about 3 per cent of cases, coronary occlusion occurs and immediate coronary artery bypass grafting must be undertaken. Restenosis occurs in approximately 25 to 30 per cent of patients who initially have a good result, usually within the first 3 to 6 months. A second angioplasty is successful in many of these patients. The reported mortality from angioplasty ranges from 0.5 to 1 per cent (Table 7–8). Newer techniques such as laser angioplasty, atherectomy catheters capable of scraping or shaving away atherosclerotic plaque, and coronary artery stents that can be left within the coronary lumen after balloon dilation hold promise in certain subgroups of patients; however, none has thus far been shown to reduce the subsequent incidence of restenosis.

Variant Angina

In 1959 Prinzmetal described a syndrome of chest pain unrelated to exertion and associated with ST segment elevation recorded on the ECG (see Table 7–2). The syndrome is often associated with cardiac arrhythmias, including ventricular fibrillation and heart block, and sudden death may occur. These episodes of angina more commonly occur between midnight and 8 a.m. Rarely, acute myocardial infarction results. Prinzmetal's angina appears to be due to spasm in the conductance portion of the coronary arteries, resulting in decreased oxygen delivery to the myocardium. Patients may have concomitant fixed obstructive lesions and therefore also experience angina with exertion. The classic ECG pattern of coronary spasm is localized ST elevation, although ST depression alone or T wave changes may occur. Coronary angiography during Prinzmetal's angina may reveal spasm at the site of a severe coronary atherosclerotic lesion, a mild atherosclerotic lesion, or a normal coronary artery. Patients with no or mild fixed coronary obstruction tend to have a more benign course than those with severe obstructions. The cause of coronary spasm is unknown. Provocative testing with ergonovine, an ergot alkaloid with alpha-adrenergic and serotoninergic effects, is a relatively sensitive and specific test for coronary artery spasm. Vessels prone to spasm appear to be supersensitive to its vasoconstrictive properties. When administered in incre-

mental doses to a total of 0.05 to 0.4 mg intravenously, coronary artery spasm, chest pain, and ST segment elevation are provoked in susceptible individuals. Prolonged spasm with significant ischemia and serious arrhythmias is a potential hazard. Nitroglycerin may be injected directly into the coronary vasculature to quickly reverse the spasm if it is severe. Ergonovine testing generally is safe, especially if performed in the catheterization laboratory, but probably should not be done in patients who have flow-restricting coronary obstructions, and the drug should be administered in extremely low starting doses.

In patients with Prinzmetal's angina beta blockade may be detrimental by allowing unopposed alpha-adrenergic vasoconstriction. Calcium channel blockers are very effective in treating vasospastic angina, and their effects may be additive to that of nitrates, since the mechanism of action is different. Coronary artery bypass surgery or angioplasty is not helpful in patients with vasospasm and normal or nearly normal coronary arteries but may be useful in patients who have fixed significant stenoses.

ACUTE MYOCARDIAL INFARCTION

Pathology and Mechanism

Myocardial infarction refers to irreversible necrosis of myocardium. It usually results from thrombosis where there is pre-existing vessel wall injury or ruptured atherosclerotic plaque in a major coronary artery. Initially ischemia occurs and if severe and prolonged, myocardial infarction follows, the extent of which depends on the severity of the ischemia, the area of muscle supplied by the ob-

TABLE 7–8. COMPARISON OF CORONARY ARTERY BYPASS GRAFTING (CABG) AND PERCUTANEOUS TRANSLUMINAL CORONARY ANGIOPLASTY (PTCA)

PTCA	CABG
Nonsurgical	Major surgery
Useful for proximal, discrete stenosis; multiple vessels increase difficulty and risk; lesions in some vessels (e.g., left anterior descending) are more likely to be successfully dilated than others	Useful for multiple, more distal, and heavily calcified lesions as well as proximal, discrete lesions; procedure of choice for left main coronary artery stenosis
Risk of coronary artery dissection and emergency surgery	Risk of elective surgery
Can be done (although with some risk) in patients who are not surgical candidates	Patient must be a surgical candidate
May be faster in an emergency situation (e.g., acute MI)	Associated defects (aneurysm, valve dysfunction) may be addressed
Long-term results appear favorable, but early restenosis is a major limitation	Long-term results good; graft patency better if internal mammary graft is used

structed coronary artery, the extent of collateral blood flow, and the oxygen demands of the tissue supplied by the artery. Myocardial infarction may be transmural, that is, involving the full thickness of the left ventricular wall, or nontransmural, involving only the subendocardium and adjacent myocardium. The ECG findings of "transmural" versus "subendocardial" infarction do not correlate well with the pathologic extent of infarction. No gross pathologic changes occur in the myocardium until approximately 6 hours after myocardial infarction, and even light microscopic findings until that time are subtle. The myocardium initially appears pale and slightly edematous and over the next few days changes color as exudate and neutrophil infiltration occur. Eight to 10 days after infarction the myocardium in the region of the infarction thins as debris is removed by mononuclear cells, and granulation tissue forms that by 3 to 4 weeks extends through the necrotic tissue. Subsequently, a thin scar develops that becomes firm over a 6-week interval.

Ninety per cent of transmural myocardial infarctions are associated with complete obstruction of a coronary artery, consisting of fresh thrombus superimposed on a critically stenotic lesion. Nontransmural myocardial infarctions frequently occur distal to severely stenotic but still patent arteries, possibly because of spontaneous lysis of a fresh thrombus. Mechanisms by which thrombosis occurs in the region of atherosclerotic plaques may include changes in the atherosclerotic intima promoting thrombosis, hemorrhage into the atherosclerotic plaque, ulceration of the plaque

with activation of clotting factors, platelet thrombi, or coronary spasm at the site of a plaque causing sludging of blood flow and deposition of platelets and fibrin. Reperfusion can be achieved in many cases, using intracoronary or intravenous fibrinolytic agents; however, residual high-grade atherosclerotic lesions are usually present at the site of occlusion after thrombus dissolution.

Clinical Presentation

Signs and symptoms of acute myocardial infarction are summarized in Tables 7–9 and 2–2. The usual patient with myocardial infarction has severe chest pain that lasts until treated. Some patients are discovered to have suffered a myocardial infarction by ECG or noninvasive evaluation of left ventricular function without any clinical history of infarction. In many of these patients, when a very careful history is obtained, an episode can be identified that probably represents the myocardial infarction. However, some people, especially diabetics, have true "silent" myocardial infarctions.

The ECG in acute myocardial infarction is discussed in Chapter 3 (see Tables 3–5 and 3–6 and Fig. 3–5). The diagnosis of subendocardial infarction may be suspected from ECG ST and T wave changes but must be confirmed by enzyme determinations. There are no chest radiographic findings characteristic of myocardial infarction. The white blood cell count rises the first day after a myocardial infarction and returns to normal within a week; it usually peaks between 12,000 and 15,000 cells/mm^3. Acute phase reactants, such as the erythrocyte sedimentation rate, may be elevated. Several cardiac enzymes released into the blood (Fig. 7–2) are used to diagnose myocardial infarction. Creatine kinase (CK) MB (the fraction characteristic of cardiac muscle) is the most sensitive and specific marker of myocardial necrosis, and an MB fraction exceeding 7 to 8 per cent is indicative of myocardial infarction even if the total CK is not greater than normal. Injury to skeletal muscle causes the skeletal muscle fraction (MM) of CK to rise. Other forms of injury to cardiac muscle, such as myocarditis, trauma, and cardiac surgery, may release significant amounts of CK MB fraction. Cardioversion and cardiopulmonary resuscitation (CPR) usually do not elevate the MB fraction. Serum lactate dehydrogenase (LDH) may be fractionated into five isozymes. LDH_1 is principally from the heart, and if LDH_1 exceeds LDH_2, myocardial infarction is likely. LDH is sometimes useful in diagnosing myocardial infarction in a patient who presents several days after the event, when the CK has normalized. Hemolysis can raise LDH_1 activity, but LDH_2 also elevates and exceeds LDH_1. Liver and skeletal muscle contain mainly LDH_4 and LDH_5.

The use of infarct-avid scintigraphy has been discussed in Chapter 3. Echocardiography may demonstrate a segmental wall motion abnormality but cannot distinguish whether it is old or new unless thinning and scarring are present.

TABLE 7–9. SYMPTOMS AND SIGNS OF ACUTE MYOCARDIAL INFARCTION

Symptoms (see Table 2–2)
  Severe, prolonged chest pain, similar in quality to angina pectoris
  Nausea, vomiting
  Diaphoresis
  Shortness of breath
  Weakness
Signs
  Anxiety
  Elevated blood pressure (if shock not present)
  Tachycardia (may have bradycardia with inferior MI)
  Dyskinetic left ventricular impulse
  Small amplitude carotid pulses
  Soft heart sounds
  S_4 gallop
  Fixed or paradoxically split S_2
  Systolic murmur of papillary muscle dysfunction
  Loud systolic murmur with papillary muscle or ventricular septal rupture
  S_3 gallop and/or rales (congestive heart failure)
  Right ventricles S_3 gallop with jugular venous distention (right ventricular infarction)
  Signs of cardiogenic shock if >40% of myocardium is infarcted
  Low-grade fever
  Pericardial friction rub (3rd–4th day, with transmural infarctions)
  Atrial or ventricular tachyarrhythmias, heart block

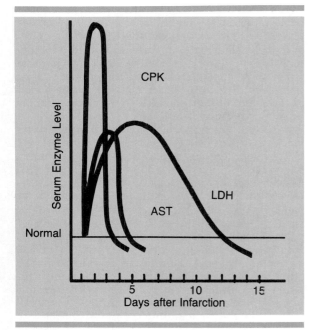

FIGURE 7-2. Typical time course for detection of enzymes released from the myocardium upon necrosis. CPK = Creatine kinase; AST = serum aspartate aminotransferase; LDH = lactic dehydrogenase.

Management of Myocardial Infarction

Because approximately 50 per cent of patients who die of myocardial infarction do so within the first 4 hours after the onset of chest pain, often before they arrive at the hospital, the prehospital management of myocardial infarction is important. Many large cities employ emergency medical technicians who can recognize the symptoms of myocardial infarction, initiate ECG monitoring, and treat ventricular tachyarrhythmias, terminating them with electrical defibrillation if necessary. Airway management, intravenous drug delivery, and CPR may be administered, if needed. Prehospital emergency cardiac care, especially the rapid treatment of life-threatening ventricular arrhythmias, improves both early and late survival from myocardial infarction.

The coronary intensive care unit allows continuous ECG and hemodynamic monitoring, delivery of intensive nursing care, and immediate treatment of arrhythmias or other problems. The advent of the coronary care unit has improved survival of patients with myocardial infarction mainly by reducing mortality from arrhythmias. Death from hemodynamic deterioration has been less preventable and accounts for most of the mortality in coronary care units. Future progress in this area will probably come from thrombolysis of acute coronary obstructions.

Any intervention to limit the size of evolving infarction must be performed within the first 4 to 6 hours of infarction, before cells become irreversibly damaged. The most promising techniques involve early reperfusion by either thrombolysis or coronary angioplasty or both. Most patients (85 to 90 per cent) with acute transmural myocardial infarction have complete obstruction of a coronary artery due to thrombosis in a region of high-grade atherosclerotic narrowing. Streptokinase and urokinase interact with plasminogen to produce plasmin, a proteolytic enzyme that degrades fibrin clots, producing systemic fibrinolytic effects. Tissue plasminogen activator is an enzyme that causes only limited conversion of plasminogen in the absence of fibrin, but when exposed to fibrin in a thrombus converts the entrapped plasminogen to plasmin, initiating local fibrinolysis with limited systemic effects. When a patient presents with ST segment elevation unresponsive to nitroglycerin (to rule out coronary spasm) within 6 hours after the onset of chest pain, streptokinase can be administered intravenously in a dose of 1.5 million units over 30 to 60 minutes. Tissue plasminogen activator dosage is 100 mg intravenously administered over 3 hours (60 mg IV infusion over the first hour, 6 to 10 mg of which is administered as an IV bolus over the first 2 to 3 minutes; 20 mg IV infusion per hour over the second and third hours). Each is followed by heparin for 2 to 5 days and oral calcium blocking agents. Streptokinase and tissue plasminogen activator appear to be equally effective if given early after the onset of symptoms (50 to 80 per cent recanalization of infarct-related vessel). Streptokinase can be given only once to any individual patient because of subsequent immune reactions. Both agents are associated with approximately the same incidence of bleeding complications (e.g., approximately 0.5 per cent incidence of intracranial bleeding) and therefore should not be given to patients having any condition in which bleeding is likely to occur or would be particularly difficult to manage because of its location (Table 7-10). A third substance (anisolylated plasminogen streptokinase activation complex, APSAC) is available and can be adminis-

TABLE 7-10. RELATIVE CONTRAINDICATIONS TO THROMBOLYTIC THERAPY IN ACUTE MYOCARDIAL INFARCTION

Recent (within 10 days) major surgery
Recent puncture of noncompressible vessels
Cerebrovascular disease
Recent gastrointestinal or genitourinary bleeding
Recent trauma
Prolonged cardiopulmonary resuscitation
Hypertension (systolic BP ≥ 180, diastolic BP ≥ 110 mm Hg)
Acute pericarditis
Subacute bacterial endocarditis
High likelihood of left heart thrombus, e.g., mitral stenosis with atrial fibrillation
Hemostatic defects, including those from severe renal or hepatic disease
Pregnancy
Diabetic hemorrhagic retinopathy
Oral anticoagulation
Advanced age

tered as a single bolus injection rather than an intravenous infusion; otherwise it has no advantage over streptokinase as a tissue plasminogen activator. Coronary thrombolysis may be associated with reperfusion arrhythmias that include ventricular tachycardia or fibrillation. ECG evidence of infarction usually still evolves. The time course of cardiac enzyme elevation is accelerated, thought to be evidence of washout of enzymes from the heart by reperfusion. Thus, even if reperfusion does not prevent infarction, it may salvage a portion of the myocardium in jeopardy.

Thrombolysis has been documented to improve left ventricular function and to decrease both early and late mortality after myocardial infarction. It is indicated in patients with suspected Q wave myocardial infarctions presenting within 6 hours of symptom onset in whom contraindications are not present. Although this point is controversial, not all patients seem to require early coronary angiography and angioplasty of the infarct-related lesion after thrombolysis; this may be reserved for patients with recurrent or persistent ischemia. Coronary angioplasty may be indicated within the first 6 hours of acute Q wave myocardial infarction in patients with contraindications to pharmacologic thrombolysis or those with cardiogenic shock refractory to thrombolysis. The role of acute angioplasty in patients who fail to reperfuse with thrombolysis has not been established.

Some general principles in treating patients with uncomplicated myocardial infarction include sedation if necessary; a calm, quiet coronary care unit atmosphere; and control of pain to decrease the patient's anxiety, sympathetic drive, and myocardial oxygen demand. Morphine can be administered intravenously in doses of 2 to 8 mg repeated at intervals of 5 to 15 minutes until pain is relieved or drug side effects (e.g., hypotension, respiratory depression, nausea, vomiting, or vagal side effects such as bradycardia) appear. Small intravenous doses of atropine treat the vagomimetic side effects of morphine, and naloxone, 0.4 mg IV at 5-minute intervals to a maximal dosage of 1.2 mg, reverses respiratory depression if needed. After the acute severe pain is relieved, nitroglycerin can be used cautiously for recurrent angina, and chronic nitrate therapy may be initiated if angina persists. Oxygen can be omitted if the patient is not hypoxemic.

The patient with *uncomplicated* acute myocardial infarction should be confined to bed for the first 24 to 36 hours except for the use of a bedside commode. He should then be allowed to sit up out of bed for short periods of time and can be transferred out of the coronary care unit after 3 days because life-threatening arrhythmias are uncommon after 36 to 48 hours. Ambulation is usually begun on the fourth to fifth day and is increased progressively so that at discharge the patient is able to walk up a flight of stairs. Early mobiliza-

tion increases the patient's psychological wellbeing, prevents deconditioning, and decreases the incidence of thromboembolism. Many patients require stool softeners or laxatives to avoid constipation and straining at stool. Nausea and vomiting either from the infarction or from drugs can be treated with a clear liquid diet. A gentle rectal examination in patients with acute myocardial infarction is not contraindicated.

It is usual practice to fully anticoagulate patients for several days after thrombolysis or angioplasty. "Minidose" heparin (5000 units subcutaneously every 8 to 12 hours) may decrease the incidence of deep vein thrombosis and possibly systemic embolization if full anticoagulation is not used. In patients who have a high risk of embolization, such as those who have a ventricular aneurysm with thrombus, past or present thrombophlebitis, or previous systemic or pulmonary embolism, full systemic anticoagulation may be reasonable in the absence of contraindications. Systemic anticoagulation is contraindicated in patients with postinfarction pericarditis because of the risk of hemorrhage into the pericardium. Minidose heparin is stopped once the patient is ambulating, usually 2 to 3 days prior to hospital discharge. Continuation of systemic anticoagulation depends upon the original indication for therapy. Patients with left ventricular thrombi after myocardial infarction are at high risk of embolization, and this risk may be decreased by prophylactic systemic anticoagulation for about 6 months.

In patients with known or suspected acute myocardial infarction, lidocaine effectively prevents many ventricular tachyarrhythmias. If it is administered appropriately, side effects such as confusion, dizziness, and paresthesias can be minimized. Both the loading and maintenance doses of lidocaine should be decreased in elderly patients, patients with congestive heart failure, and patients with liver disease. The role of lidocaine as routine prophylaxis of ventricular arrhythmias is controversial because the risk of toxicity may outweigh the antiarrhythmic benefit. Suppression of premature ventricular contractions (PVCs) is questionable, because their value (including "R on T" PVCs) as prognostic indicators or precipitators of the onset of more severe arrhythmias has not been proved. If used, prophylactic lidocaine is continued for approximately 48 hours, after which the risk of ventricular tachyarrhythmias is reduced.

Patients with uncomplicated courses are usually discharged from the hospital between 7 and 12 days following infarction. The patient should gradually increase activity but avoid isometric exercise (e.g., lifting weights) and get adequate rest. He should be instructed in the use of sublingual nitroglycerin even if he requires no antianginal therapy on discharge. Many centers have formal rehabilitation programs in which the patient is supervised during activity and his ECG monitored. Exercise testing in patients after acute myocardial infarction helps determine what level of activity can be performed safely at home and is useful in identifying those patients at high risk for recurrent events by finding a positive ST response and/or chest pain within the first two stages of exercise. Some physicians perform a limited treadmill test (the heart rate achieved is only 70 per cent of predicted maximum) just prior to hospital discharge, whereas others prefer a more normal stress test protocol 6 weeks after infarction. Patients who are considered at high risk on the basis of their clinical course and/or treadmill exercise test results may subsequently undergo coronary arteriography.

Large studies with timolol, propranolol, and metoprolol have shown that these agents reduce overall mortality, sudden death, and/or reinfarction if administered to patients after their first infarction. This outcome may be related to anti-ischemic effects, antianginal effects, or some other unknown effect of these drugs. Patients with contraindications to beta-adrenergic receptor blockers, especially heart failure, cannot receive these drugs; unfortunately, these patients are at the highest risk for a recurrent event. In addition, the mortality in the group of patients that can tolerate these drugs is relatively small, and thus even a 50 per cent reduction in sudden death or reinfarction does not represent a large proportion of the total number of patients. Despite these reservations, many physicians believe that it is advisable to administer beta-adrenergic receptor blocking drugs in doses sufficient to blunt the heart rate response to exercise in postinfarction patients who have no contraindication, and the drug should be continued for approximately 2 years. The administration of aspirin (325 mg qd or qod) appears to decrease the incidence of reinfarction (and also possibly the occurrence of a first myocardial infarction).

Early ventricular tachyarrhythmias during acute myocardial infarction (i.e., first 24 to 48 hours) do not warrant chronic antiarrhythmic drug therapy. Patients with chronic complex ventricular ectopy, especially ventricular tachycardia, are at particularly high risk for sudden death in the first 6 months to 1 year after myocardial infarction. However, chronic antiarrhythmic therapy has not been shown to decrease mortality in patients with PVCs or nonsustained ventricular tachycardia after infarction.

In fact, one large multicenter, placebo-controlled study demonstrated that mortality after myocardial infarction in patients with asymptomatic ventricular arrhythmias was greater in those whose arrhythmias were suppressed with encainide or flecainide than in those given placebo. In patients at particularly high risk of sudden cardiac death, studies are in progress to determine whether antiarrhythmic drug therapy or defibrillator implantation may improve survival.

Complications of Myocardial Infarction and Their Management (Table 7–11)

In patients who develop mild congestive heart failure with pulmonary congestion during acute myocardial infarction, administration of a diuretic may be sufficient therapy. Indications for hemody-namic monitoring are listed in Table 7–12. Hemodynamic monitoring allows measurement of left ventricular filling pressures (pulmonary capillary wedge pressure) and cardiac output, and the calculation of systemic vascular resistance. Patients with myocardial infarction may be grouped into subsets based on these measurements (Table 7–13). When the normal cardiac index (approximately 2.5 to 3.6 L/min/m²) is reduced to 1.8 to 2.2 L/min/m², hypoperfusion occurs; shock occurs at levels less than 1.8 L/min/m². The normal pulmonary capillary wedge pressure is 10 to 12 mm Hg, but the optimal wedge pressure in a patient with acute myocardial infarction and a relatively noncompliant ventricle is usually 14 to 18 mm Hg.

Even if pharmacologic therapy or intra-aortic balloon counterpulsation provides temporary improvement, patients with cardiogenic shock due to cardiac muscle destruction have a poor prognosis. However, patients who have cardiogenic shock secondary to surgically correctable mechanical factors—for example, acute mitral regurgitation or acquired ventricular septal defect—have a somewhat more favorable outlook. Myocardial revascularization improves an occasional patient with episodes of profound but reversible myocardial ischemia producing hypotension and shock.

Patients with right ventricular infarction may present with hypotension or shock (due to decreased cardiac output) and signs of right ventricular failure. The lungs are clear if left ventricular failure or pre-existing pulmonary disease is not present. Tricuspid insufficiency may occur. Fluid administration to raise right ventricular filling pressures and augment left ventricular filling reverses the shock and hypotension, even when jugular venous distention and other manifestations of systemic congestion exist. Right ventricular infarction is relatively common in patients with inferior myocardial infarction and is sometimes difficult to differentiate from cardiac tamponade. Most patients with right ventricular infarction do well, and their long-term prognosis depends on the extent of left ventricular infarction.

Approximately 20 per cent of patients extend their myocardial infarction within the first 5 days after infarction. The extension may be associated with recurrent chest pain that is sometimes difficult to distinguish from post–myocardial infarction pericarditis or recurrent angina. Continued angina and extension of myocardial infarction are usually unfavorable signs and may be indications for catheterization.

Many patients upon presentation with an acute myocardial infarction have mild to moderate hypertension because of pain, anxiety, and sometimes mild congestive heart failure. With relief of pain and treatment of heart failure, hypertension usually disappears within a few hours. However, sustained or severe blood pressure elevation should be treated vigorously to decrease myocardial oxygen consumption. Intravenous nitroprus-

TABLE 7–11. COMPLICATIONS OF ACUTE MYOCARDIAL INFARCTION

COMPLICATION	CLINICAL PRESENTATION	PROGNOSIS/NATURAL HISTORY	THERAPY
Congestive heart failure	Symptoms and signs of heart failure (Table 2–4) or cardiogenic shock (Table 4–9)	Severe heart failure carries a poor prognosis unless a surgically correctable condition (e.g., ruptured ventricular septum or papillary muscle) is present	See Table 4–7 See Table 4–10
Right ventricular infarction	Usually accompanies inferior MI; hypotension with clear lungs, distended jugular veins; cardiac output low, left ventricular filling pressure low; ST elevation in leads V_1 and V_{4R}	Depends on extent of left ventricular infarction	Fluid administration
Extension of infarction	Recurrent chest pain after initial stabilization; further ECG changes and enzyme increases	Guarded prognosis	Pain relief Antianginal therapy Consider early catheterization and revascularization
Hypertension	Often related to pain or early heart failure May exacerbate angina	Usually responds to therapy	Pain relief Sedation Treat heart failure Antianginal vasodilators If blood pressure elevation remains significant, may need to use IV nitroprusside
Papillary muscle rupture	Acute onset of congestive heart failure, usually 1–7 days after infarction; loud systolic murmur along left sternal border; echo may show flail mitral valve; Swan-Ganz shows no left-to-right shunt, often large v waves in wedge position	If patient can be stabilized, surgery can be postponed 4–6 wk to allow healing of infarct; if not, early surgery may be life-saving although risky	Afterload reduction Diuretics Digitalis Intra-aortic balloon pump Surgery
Ventricular septal rupture	Same presentation and murmur as above; contrast echo may demonstrate defect; Swan-Ganz shows left-to-right shunt	Same as above	Same as above
Ventricular aneurysm	Often no symptoms, but may be associated with congestive heart failure, arrhythmias, or emboli; persistent ST elevation on ECG; visualized on two-dimensional echo	Does not rupture; prognosis depends on amount of remaining myocardium and complications (heart failure, arrhythmias, emboli)	Anticoagulation if mural thrombus is detected on echo or angiography Antiarrhythmic therapy as needed Treat heart failure Surgery if symptoms persist
Cardiac rupture	Acute onset of cardiogenic shock, usually within first week after infarction; occasional patient walls off the rupture within the pericardial space (pseudoaneurysm) and survives; pseudoaneurysm detectable on echocardiography	Usually rapid death	Emergency surgery if possible
Deep venous thrombosis, pulmonary embolism	Warm, tender edematous extremity; with pulmonary embolus can have dyspnea, tachycardia, hypoxia, pleuritic chest pain, hemoptysis; cardiovascular collapse with massive pulmonary embolus; diagnosis via venogram, lung scan, and/or pulmonary angiogram	Recurrent emboli if therapy is not instituted	Anticoagulation with heparin, then warfarin

TABLE 7–11. COMPLICATIONS OF ACUTE MYOCARDIAL INFARCTION *Continued*

COMPLICATION	CLINICAL PRESENTATION	PROGNOSIS/NATURAL HISTORY	THERAPY
Pericarditis early after MI	Chest pain sharper than that of infarction, usually located to the left of sternum toward the apex, not responsive to nitrates, better when sitting up and leaning forward, occurs within a week after a transmural infarction; causes sinus tachycardia, diffuse ST elevation on ECG	Self-limited	Aspirin Nonsteroidal anti-inflammatory agents Avoid anticoagulation
Postinfarction (Dressler's) syndrome	Occurs 2 wk to 9 mo after MI; pericarditis, pericardial effusion, pleural effusion, pneumonitis, fever; immunologic etiology	Self-limited, but there may be multiple recurrences	Aspirin Nonsteroidal anti-inflammatory agents If above unsuccessful, short course of steroids
Arrhythmias (see also Chapter 8) a. Ventricular tachycardia or fibrillation	Syncope, cardiac arrest; dizziness, palpitations	Immediate prognosis depends on prompt termination; long-term prognosis depends on left ventricular function and chronic recurrences	Cardioversion/defibrillation of sustained arrhythmias Lidocaine or other antiarrhythmic agent
b. Atrial fibrillation/flutter	Increased angina, heart failure, palpitations Associated with pericarditis, pulmonary embolus, and heart failure	Prognosis depends on underlying condition	Digitalis ± quinidine Cardioversion
c. Heart block and conduction disturbances	Dizziness, syncope, increased angina, or heart failure if symptoms occur	Natural history depends on type of block present (see text); long-term prognosis depends on left ventricular function	Indications for pacing in text

side may be employed, and oral agents can be substituted as needed.

Rupture of an entire papillary muscle due to myocardial infarction is usually rapidly fatal owing to massive mitral regurgitation. However, rupture of one head of a papillary muscle may be tolerated for a time, allowing for diagnostic evaluation and surgical correction. Some form of papillary muscle rupture occurs in less than 5 per cent of patients with acute infarction. Papillary muscle dysfunction is more common than rupture and occurs when ischemia interferes with contraction of the papillary muscles and normal coaptation of the mitral valve leaflets. The degree of mitral regurgitation from papillary muscle dysfunction is usually less than that caused by papillary muscle rupture. Acute medical therapy for papillary muscle rupture may require inotropic agents, diuretics, vasodilators, or intra-aortic balloon counterpulsation. If the patient can be stabilized and weaned from balloon counterpulsation, surgical mitral valve replacement may be attempted 4 to 6 weeks after infarction when infarct scar formation is advanced. However, if hemodynamic stabilization cannot be obtained or requires intra-aortic balloon counterpulsation, early mitral valve replacement should be done.

Rupture of the ventricular septum develops in about 1 per cent of myocardial infarctions and results in marked biventricular failure. It may occur with both inferior and anterior infarctions. It is associated with a holosystolic murmur along the left sternal border and is often difficult to differentiate from acute mitral insufficiency. A thrill is more common with ventricular septal defects than with acute mitral regurgitation. Right heart (Swan-Ganz) catheterization may distinguish acute ventricular septal rupture from mitral regurgitation by detecting an oxygen step-up between the right atrium and right ventricle. Increased pulmonary vascularity due to the left-to-right shunt may be seen on chest radiograph. Two-dimensional echo-

TABLE 7–12. INDICATIONS FOR HEMODYNAMIC MONITORING IN ACUTE MYOCARDIAL INFARCTION

Hypotension unresponsive to simple measures such as treatment of bradycardia or fluid administration

Moderate or severe left ventricular failure despite diuretic therapy, especially if blood pressure is unstable

Unexplained features such as persistent sinus tachycardia, cyanosis, hypoxia, or acidosis

Suspicion of ventricular septal defect, rupture of papillary muscle, or cardiac tamponade

TABLE 7–13. HEMODYNAMIC INDICES IN ACUTE MYOCARDIAL INFARCTION

CLINICAL STATE	CARDIAC OUTPUT	PULMONIC CAPILLARY WEDGE	LIKELY CAUSE	THERAPY
No pulmonary congestion, normal systemic perfusion	Normal	Normal	Uncomplicated MI	None
Pulmonary congestion, normal perfusion	Normal	↑	Mild to moderate heart failure	Diuretics, preload reduction
Hypoperfusion but no pulmonary congestion	↓	↓	Volume depletion Right ventricular infarction	Fluids
Hypoperfusion and pulmonary congestion	↓	↑	Severe heart failure, cardiogenic shock	Diuretics, preload and afterload reduction, inotropic agents, intra-aortic balloon pump

cardiography can occasionally visualize the ventricular septal defect, but more often a septal aneurysm is demonstrated, with the ventricular septal defect presumably located in the apex of the aneurysm. Contrast echocardiography may define the defect. Doppler echocardiography can reliably distinguish ventricular septal rupture from acute mitral insufficiency. Surgical mortality is highest within the first month after infarction, but if ventricular failure is severe, surgery must be undertaken early.

A ventricular aneurysm is a localized area of thin, scarred myocardium that protrudes beyond and distorts the ventricular cavity. Ventricular aneurysms may develop within days of myocardial infarction and gradually stretch, thin, and enlarge over weeks to months. The wall motion of an aneurysm on ventriculography may be akinetic or dyskinetic. Large aneurysms may contribute to congestive heart failure by expanding during systole, decreasing the efficiency of blood expulsion. Most patients with ventricular aneurysms are asymptomatic. True ventricular aneurysms do not rupture. Mural thrombi commonly form in the ventricular aneurysms and appear less likely to embolize in patients who are systemically anticoagulated. Ventricular aneurysms often are associated with ventricular tachyarrhythmias originating from the edge of the aneurysm. Patients with ventricular aneurysms usually demonstrate ECG evidence of transmural myocardial infarction, and in many cases there is persistent ST segment elevation in the ECG leads with vectors pointing toward the aneurysm. Occasionally, the aneurysm can distort the cardiac silhouette enough to be visible on chest radiograph, appearing as a localized bulge on the surface of the left ventricle, sometimes with calcium in the wall. Two-dimensional echocardiography reliably delineates ventricular aneurysms. Refractory congestive heart failure or recurrent systemic emboli despite anticoagulation warrant aneurysmectomy. Aneurysmectomy alone is usually insufficient to control recurrent refractory ventricular tachyarrhythmias, which require combined aneurysmectomy and endocardial resection or cryoablation.

Rupture of the ventricular free wall is usually rapidly fatal. Rupture usually occurs within the first 5 days following transmural infarction. The patient's initial course may be uneventful until the abrupt occurrence of cardiogenic shock and rapid progression to death. Rare patients have survived after successful pericardiocentesis and emergency surgical repair. Occasionally, the course is less acute and blood is walled off within the pericardial space, giving rise to a pseudoaneurysm. In contrast to true aneurysms, pseudoaneurysms may rupture and require immediate intervention. The diagnosis of pseudoaneurysm is usually made by echocardiography, showing a narrow-based communication between the ventricular cavity and pseudoaneurysm, whereas the communication between a true aneurysm and the ventricular cavity is wide.

Early ambulation and the use of prophylactic subcutaneous minidose heparin have decreased the risk of venous thrombosis and pulmonary embolism after myocardial infarction. If deep vein thrombophlebitis or pulmonary embolism is documented, intravenous heparin should be administered for at least 7 days and followed by 2 to 6 months of oral warfarin. Patients who have systemic emboli also should be treated with intravenous heparin followed by 2 to 6 months of oral warfarin. Consideration should be given to removal of peripheral emboli by surgical embolectomy.

Pericarditis occurs in 7 to 15 per cent of patients within the first week after acute infarction, most frequently in those with transmural infarction of at least moderate size. If a pericardial friction rub is heard, the diagnosis is confirmed, but many patients do not have audible rubs. It is sometimes difficult to distinguish the pain of pericarditis from that of angina pectoris. Anticoagulation should be avoided in patients with active pericarditis because of the risk of developing hemorrhagic tamponade. Sinus tachycardia occurring with pericarditis must be differentiated from other causes of sinus tachycardia, for example, hemodynamic deterioration.

A small number of patients, probably less than 5 per cent, develop a late postinfarction syndrome

(Dressler's syndrome) consisting of pericarditis, pericardial effusion, pleural effusion, and sometimes fever. The cause is unknown but may be immunologic. Multiple recurrences sometimes occur. If salicylates or nonsteroidal anti-inflammatory agents are not sufficient, short courses of high-dose corticosteroids provide relief.

Arrhythmias in Acute Myocardial Infarction

Arrhythmias occurring in patients with acute myocardial infarction should be treated if they cause hemodynamic compromise, augment myocardial oxygen requirements, or predispose to more malignant arrhythmias such as sustained ventricular tachycardia or fibrillation. Some rhythms not ordinarily deleterious may decrease cardiac output in patients who have stiff, noncompliant ventricles by the loss of AV synchrony. Reversible causes of ventricular ectopy—for example, digitalis excess or metabolic abnormalities—should be considered.

PVCs are very common following acute myocardial infarction. Unless very frequent, they usually cause no problem in themselves but may be forerunners of more serious sustained ventricular tachyarrhythmias. The danger of "R on T" PVCs (a PVC occurring during the T wave of a previous complex) has probably been overestimated in the past and probably does not carry any worse prognosis than any other PVC. Even though PVCs are sometimes considered a warning arrhythmia for the subsequent development of ventricular tachycardia or fibrillation, many episodes of ventricular fibrillation occur without any warning arrhythmia. Approximately half of those patients who develop ventricular fibrillation have no warning PVCs, and half of those with warning PVCs do not develop a sustained ventricular tachyarrhythmia. If ventricular tachycardia is not suppressed by lidocaine, intravenous procainamide can be substituted or added to lidocaine. Intravenous bretylium may also be useful to prevent recurrence of sustained or symptomatic ventricular tachyarrhythmias. High-dose or multiple antiarrhythmic drug therapy in patients with simple ventricular ectopy is not warranted. If sustained ventricular tachycardia occurs, it should be cardioverted immediately if hemodynamic compromise occurs. If it is well tolerated for a short period of time, a limited trial of lidocaine for termination may be tried. The patient with acute infarction should not be allowed to continue having sustained ventricular tachycardia for a prolonged period. Ventricular fibrillation occurs in 2 to 3 per cent of hospitalized patients with acute myocardial infarction and should be promptly defibrillated with 200 to 400 joules.

Ventricular tachycardia and fibrillation during the first 36 to 48 hours of acute myocardial infarction do not carry the same prognosis as when they occur later in the recovery period. These early ventricular arrhythmias appear to be due to acute ischemia and do not necessitate long-term, chronic

antiarrhythmic therapy. On the other hand, ventricular tachycardia and fibrillation occurring more than 48 hours after infarction are probably due to different electrophysiologic mechanisms and may be forerunners of severe, chronic arrhythmias.

Accelerated idioventricular rhythm with rates of 60 to 100 beats/min occurs commonly during the acute infarction period. This arrhythmia probably does not increase the incidence of more rapid ventricular tachyarrhythmias. It usually does not cause hemodynamic deterioration unless cardiovascular compensation is tenuous and depends upon normal atrioventricular synchrony. If the rhythm appears to be affecting hemodynamics adversely or increasing the incidence of ventricular ectopy, it can be treated by lidocaine or in some instances by accelerating the sinus rate slightly with atropine or atrial pacing.

Sinus tachycardia that persists in a patient with acute infarction after relief of pain and anxiety is often due to inability of the ventricle to maintain an adequate stroke volume. It is not only a sign of hemodynamic impairment in some patients but also is detrimental by increasing oxygen demand. Pericarditis, pulmonary embolus, and fever commonly cause sinus tachycardia. The treatment of sinus tachycardia is directed at the underlying cause.

Sinus bradycardia often occurs early after acute inferior myocardial infarction and may be related to ischemia of the sinus node or abnormally elevated vagal tone. If asymptomatic and hemodynamically tolerated, it should not be treated. If it creates symptoms, atropine or temporary pacing may be required.

A rapid ventricular response caused by atrial flutter or fibrillation should be treated vigorously because of the increase in myocardial oxygen consumption. If the ventricular rate cannot be slowed pharmacologically, early electrical cardioversion should be considered. The treatment of atrial tachyarrhythmias is discussed in Chapter 8. Atrial tachyarrhythmias also may be features of pericarditis or pulmonary embolus.

First-degree AV block requires no therapy; if digitalis is thought to be the cause, it should be discontinued. Second-degree AV block of the Mobitz type I (Wenckebach) type (see Chapter 8) is common in patients with inferior myocardial infarction due to increased vagal tone and/or ischemic involvement of the AV node. It is usually temporary and, if asymptomatic, requires no therapy. If hemodynamic compromise occurs, atropine is effective; if sustained improvement does not occur, temporary pacing may be needed. Type I AV block usually does not lead to high-degree AV block; if it does, the ventricular escape is junctional and usually reliable at reasonable rates (40 to 60 per minute). Mobitz type II second-degree AV block is an indication for prophylactic pacing. Type I second-degree AV block is more common with inferior and type II more common with anterior myocardial infarctions.

A prophylactic temporary pacemaker is usually recommended for any patient who has developed complete heart block with an acute myocardial infarction, especially if the infarction is anterior and the site of the heart block likely to be in the His-Purkinje system. Complete AV block should be differentiated from AV dissociation, common in inferior myocardial infarction due to sinus bradycardia with junctional escape or accelerated junctional rhythms (see Chapter 8).

The occurrence of new intraventricular conduction defects (left or right bundle branch block, or right bundle branch block with left anterior or posterior fascicular block) is associated with anterior more often than inferior infarction. The prognosis of these patients, as of those with Mobitz II second-degree heart block, is poor, reflecting the extensive infarction rather than the conduction disturbance itself. Even though temporary pacing in these patients has not been shown definitely to increase survival, it is still reasonable to insert a temporary pacemaker if heart block is deemed likely. Therefore, temporary prophylactic pacing is indicated in patients who develop new bifascicular block. Temporary prophylactic pacing in patients who have a new right bundle branch block and a normal axis or a new left bundle branch block with a normal PR interval is more controversial; the availability of a transcutaneous temporary pacemaker at the bedside may offer an alternative to temporary transvenous pacing. Patients who have pre-existing left or right bundle branch block with or without axis deviation probably do not require prophylactic pacing with acute infarction (see Table 8–6).

REFERENCES

Forrester JS, Diamond G, Chatterjee K, Swan HJC: Medical therapy of acute myocardial infarction by application of hemodynamic subsets. N Engl J Med 295:1356, 1404, 1976.

Grines CL, DeMaria AN: Optimal utilization of thrombolytic therapy for acute myocardial infarction: Concepts and controversies. J Am Coll Cardiol 16:223, 1990.

Gunnar RM (chairman): AHA/ACC Task Force Report. Guidelines for the early management of patients with acute myocardial infarction. J Am Coll Cardiol 16:249, 1990.

Kirklin JW (chairman): AHA/ACC Task Force Report. Guidelines and indications for coronary artery bypass graft surgery. J Am Coll Cardiol 17:543, 1991.

National Cholesterol Education Program Expert Panel: Report of the National Cholesterol Education Program Expert Panel on detection, evaluation, and treatment of high blood cholesterol in adults. Arch Intern Med 148:36–69, 1988.

Parker JO: Drug therapy: Nitrate therapy in stable angina pectoris. N Engl J Med 316:1635–1642, 1987.

Ross R: The pathogenesis of atherosclerosis—an update. N Engl J Med 314:488–500, 1986.

Waller BF: "Crackers, breakers, stretchers, drillers, scrapers, shavers, burners, welders and melters"—the future treatment of atherosclerotic coronary artery disease? A clinical-morphologic assessment. J Am Coll Cardiol 13:969–987, 1989.

8 ARRHYTHMIAS

MECHANISMS OF ARRHYTHMOGENESIS

If a microelectrode is introduced into a single myocardial cell, an action potential (Fig. 8–1) can be recorded by measuring the potential difference between the inside and the outside of the cell (inside negative). The resting membrane potential of a normal Purkinje cell is approximately −90 millivolts (mv) with respect to the outside of the cell. When the membrane potential is depolarized to a certain threshold level, an action potential occurs with a rapid upstroke (phase 0); a return toward zero from the initial overshoot or early rapid repolarization (phase 1); a plateau (phase 2); final rapid repolarization (phase 3); and resting membrane potential and diastolic depolarization (phase 4). The normal resting potential is maintained by the active (i.e., energy-requiring) exclusion of sodium and the accumulation of potassium inside the cell. Phase 0 or rapid depolarization is due chiefly to the opening of the sarcolemmal channels to sodium entrance in atrial and ventricular muscle and cells in the His-Purkinje system. Calcium is important in the maintenance of the action potential plateau of fast sodium channel–dependent cells and in the generation of the action potential upstroke in slow calcium channel–dependent cells such as those of the sinus and atrioventricular (AV) nodes. Phase 3 is mediated chiefly by an outward potassium current, and the

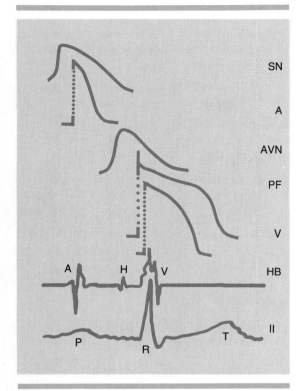

FIGURE 8-1. Action potentials recorded from different tissues in the heart remounted with a His bundle recording and scalar electrocardiogram (ECG) from a patient to illustrate the timing during a single cardiac cycle. SN = Sinus nodal potential; A = atrial muscle potential; AVN = atrioventricular nodal potential; PF = Purkinje fiber potential; V = ventricular muscle potential; HB = His bundle recording; II = lead II. The AH interval measured in the His bundle recording approximates AV nodal conduction time, and the HV interval approximates His-Purkinje system conduction time.

membrane returns to its negative resting potential during electrical diastole.

Automaticity is a property of some cardiac tissues to undergo gradual phase 4 depolarization spontaneously until threshold potential is reached and the cell initiates an action potential that is propagated from one cell to another. Normal automaticity is present in sinus nodal tissue, some atrial and junctional tissues, the bundle branches, and Purkinje fibers. The sinus node discharges more rapidly than the other cells and is the normal pacemaker of the heart. *Conduction* is the propagation of a cardiac impulse and is most closely influenced by the amplitude and upstroke velocity of phase 0 of the action potential. *Refractoriness* is a property of cardiac tissue during which a stimulus occurring soon after a previous action potential fails to elicit another normal action potential; it is most closely related to the duration of phase 3 of the cardiac action potential in most cardiac tissues.

Although the autonomic nervous system may affect atrial and ventricular tissue to a small extent, the most prominent autonomic effects are observed on the sinus and the AV nodes. Sympathetic stimulation increases the rate of automaticity and increases conduction velocity, whereas parasympathetic (vagal) activation does the opposite. Baroreceptors in the carotid sinus, located at the bifurcation of the internal and external carotid arteries, activate the vagus nerve when blood pressure increases and reflexively decrease heart rate and AV nodal conduction velocity.

The genesis of cardiac arrhythmias is divided into disorders of impulse formation, disorders of impulse conduction, and combinations of the two (Table 8-1). One cannot unequivocally determine the mechanism for most clinical arrhythmias, but each arrhythmia may be most consistent with or best explained by a particular electrophysiologic mechanism. Disorders of impulse formation are defined as an inappropriate discharge rate of the normal pacemaker (the sinus node) or abnormal discharge from an ectopic pacemaker that usurps control of the atrial or ventricular rhythm. An appropriate discharge rate of a subsidiary pacemaker that takes control of the cardiac rhythm upon sinus slowing is termed an escape beat or rhythm, whereas an inappropriately rapid discharge rate of an ectopic pacemaker (abnormally increased automaticity) that usurps control of the cardiac rhythm from the normal sinus mechanism is termed a premature complex or, when they occur in a series, an ectopic tachycardia.

Parasystole may be due to abnormal automaticity and refers to an ectopic atrial or ventricular pacemaker that discharges regularly and appears to be protected from the dominant cardiac rhythm by entrance block into the area of abnormal automaticity. Therefore, it may depolarize the myocardium intermittently whenever the myocardium is excitable, but it is not discharged by the dominant

TABLE 8-1. GENESIS OF ARRHYTHMIAS

DISORDERS OF IMPULSE FORMATION	DISORDERS OF IMPULSE CONDUCTION
Atrial tachycardia with or without block	Heart block
Accelerated junctional rhythm	Re-entry:
Nonparoxysmal AV junctional tachycardia	AV nodal re-entrant tachycardia
Accelerated idioventricular rhythm	Reciprocating tachycardia using an accessory pathway (Wolff-Parkinson-White syndrome)
Parasystole	Atrial flutter
	Atrial fibrillation
	Ventricular tachycardia
	Ventricular flutter
	Ventricular fibrillation

EITHER OR BOTH

Atrial, junctional, or ventricular extrasystoles
Flutter and fibrillation
Ventricular tachycardia

AV = Atrioventricular.

rhythm. In addition, the abnormal focus may demonstrate variable degrees of exit block, and thus it may intermittently fail to depolarize the myocardium at a time when it would be expected. Characteristic features of ventricular parasystole are (1) parasystolic premature ventricular complexes (PVCs) that are a multiple of a common integer, (2) coupling of PVCs to preceding normally conducted complexes that is not fixed, as it often is in patients with nonparasystolic PVCs, and (3) periodic fusion complexes between the parasystolic and the normally conducted beat.

Disorders of impulse conduction include conduction delay and block that can result in bradyarrhythmias and provide the basis for re-entry, the most common mechanism responsible for arrhythmia development. Re-entry can occur at any level of the cardiac electrical system, including the sinus node, the atria, the AV node, the His-Purkinje system, and the ventricular myocardium. Normal cardiac tissue has relative homogeneity of

conduction and refractoriness so that an impulse starts at the sinus node, travels through the atrium, the AV node, and the His-Purkinje system, and terminates with organized depolarization of ventricular muscle. Once all tissues are depolarized, the impulse is extinguished because there is no further tissue to activate. However, a re-entrant or reciprocating rhythm can occur within various tissues if certain criteria are met, giving rise to a continuous reactivation of tissue and generating a tachycardia. For re-entry to occur (Fig. 8-2) there must be two functionally dissociated pathways, permitting the impulse to travel in one direction down one pathway but blocking it in the other pathway. Thus, the pathway with longer refractoriness may block a premature impulse traveling antegradely. The first pathway, having shorter refractoriness but slower conduction, conducts the impulse to the distal common pathway with a delay that permits it to travel retrogradely up the second pathway and find the proximal tissue re-excitable. If this circus movement continues, a tachycardia occurs.

Approach to the Patient with Suspected or Confirmed Arrhythmias

History-taking in patients with suspected or confirmed rhythm abnormalities should be aimed at detecting the presence of cardiac or noncardiac disease that may be linked causally to the genesis of a rhythm abnormality. Common symptoms that prompt patients with rhythm disturbances to consult a physician are palpitations, syncope, presyncope, and congestive heart failure. The ability of a patient to sense an irregular, slow, or rapid heart rhythm varies greatly; some patients are completely unaware of a marked arrhythmia, whereas others feel every premature impulse. In addition, some patients may complain of palpitations when they have no detectable rhythm disturbance or merely sinus tachycardia. Dizziness is a common complaint in people with tachy- or bradyarrhythmias but also may be due to nonarrhythmic causes. Syncope refers to complete but transient loss of consciousness and also has a variety of causes (see Table 8-8). Exacerbation of congestive heart failure may occur with arrhythmias. If a patient senses palpitations, the physician should determine whether the patient senses a slow heart beat, a rapid heart beat, a regular or irregular heart beat, its rate, and whether the onset and termination of the palpitations are sudden or gradual.

The physical examination is useful in detecting evidence of underlying cardiac disease. In addition, abnormalities of the pulse may be noted, and clues regarding AV dissociation during an arrhythmia may be detected (e.g., intermittent cannon a waves in the jugular venous pulse or varying intensity of S_1 during a regular tachyarrhythmia).

The resting electrocardiogram (ECG) may reveal the specific arrhythmia responsible for symptoms or give clues regarding a tachyarrhythmia; for ex-

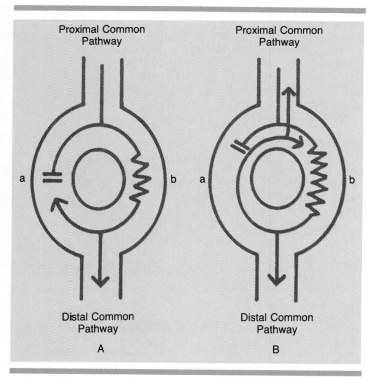

FIGURE 8-2. Mechanism of re-entry. Re-entry requires the presence of two separate pathways that join proximally and distally. Panel A illustrates a premature impulse that blocks antegradely in pathway a (*double bars*) but conducts down pathway b, albeit with a moderate conduction delay (*serpentine arrow*). The impulse attempts to return up pathway a but meets refractory tissue. In Panel B, a more premature impulse blocks earlier in pathway a and experiences more conduction delay in pathway b. This impulse finds pathway a recovered from its previous activation and returns retrogradely to the proximal common pathway. If able to again travel antegradely over pathway b, it would activate the distal common pathway prematurely. If this cycle were to continue, a circus movement or re-entrant tachycardia would result.

ample, short episodes of nonsustained ventricular tachycardia may be recorded in a patient who has presented with syncope or cardiac arrest due to a sustained ventricular tachycardia. In addition, indirect evidence may be obtained from the ECG that may suggest the cause of the arrhythmia; for example, the presence of a delta wave should alert the physician to the possibility that a tachycardia due to Wolff-Parkinson-White syndrome may be present. The ECG may also provide evidence of the cause of the arrhythmia, such as the presence of ischemic heart disease documented by ECG evidence of myocardial infarction.

Twenty-four-hour ambulatory ECG (Holter monitoring) and patient-activated event recorders (given to the patient for weeks at a time) are important tools for evaluating patients with suspected arrhythmias. They permit quantitation of arrhythmia frequency and complexity, correlation with the patient's symptoms, potential diagnosis of an unknown arrhythmia, and evaluation of the effect of antiarrhythmic therapy. They can record arrhythmias while patients are engaged in their normal daily activities; can document alterations in the QRS, ST, and T waves; and may be useful in documenting pacemaker function or malfunction. Certain arrhythmias are common during prolonged ECG monitoring in normal patients and may be of no clinical significance. In many patients symptoms are very infrequent and difficult to detect even with prolonged ECG monitoring. Exercise testing can be used to precipitate arrhythmias in some patients.

Invasive electrophysiologic procedures are useful and involve introducing catheter electrodes into the heart to record electrical activity from the atria, ventricles, and His bundle, and to stimulate the atria or ventricles electrically. Supraventricular or ventricular tachycardias may be induced by programmed electrical stimulation. The test may be used diagnostically to determine whether a particular rhythm disorder exists or to determine the mechanism of a known arrhythmia. The test may also be used therapeutically to terminate a tachycardia, to determine the efficacy of drug or other therapy, or to deliver electrical energy via the catheter to ablate a pathway or focus responsible for a recurrent arrhythmia. Electrophysiologic testing is important in patients with resistant tachyarrhythmias undergoing either surgical resection or ablation of a tachycardia focus or pathway. Patients considered candidates for antitachycardia pacemaker devices or implantable cardioverter-defibrillator devices require electrophysiologic study to confirm the mechanism and origin of the arrhythmia and the efficacy and safety of this mode of therapy. Electrophysiologic study may be helpful in discovering patients with sinus nodal dysfunction or AV block.

Esophageal electrocardiography is sometimes a useful noninvasive technique to diagnose arrhythmias. An electrode introduced approximately 40 cm from the patient's nares into the esophagus can record an atrial electrogram and often can be used to pace the atrium.

Autonomic and pharmacologic manipulations sometimes aid in diagnosing arrhythmias. Most commonly, vagal maneuvers (e.g., carotid sinus massage), edrophonium, or administration of verapamil to slow AV nodal conduction is used. Carotid sinus massage is performed with the patient in the supine position. With the neck hyperextended and the head turned away from the side being tested, light pressure is applied to the carotid impulse at the angle of the jaw. If no change occurs, pressure is more firmly applied with a gentle rotating motion for approximately 5 seconds on one side and then on the other; both sides are not stimulated simultaneously. Prior to carotid sinus massage, the carotid artery should be auscultated; massage should not be performed in patients who have carotid bruits.

Head-up tilt table testing is useful in evaluating patients with suspected neurally mediated syncope. This entity is believed to be due to exaggerated vagal activation in response to a sympathetic stimulus, resulting in vasodilation, hypotension, and relative bradycardia. Head-up passive tilt of 60 to 80 degrees for 15 to 60 minutes can reproduce these signs and symptoms in susceptible individuals, especially if provoked by the administration of intravenous isoproterenol during tilting.

MANAGEMENT OF CARDIAC ARRHYTHMIAS

Before initiating antiarrhythmic therapy, one must determine whether the arrhythmia should be treated. Any arrhythmia that causes symptomatic hypotension or sudden death should be suppressed. However, the situation in which the arrhythmia occurs dictates whether chronic, long-term therapy is necessary. For example, an episode of ventricular fibrillation in a patient at the onset of an acute myocardial infarction does not necessarily require long-term drug therapy because of the low likelihood of recurrence. However, ventricular fibrillation in a patient without an acute myocardial infarction carries a high risk of recurrence. Some patients may have arrhythmias that, while not life-threatening, produce disabling symptoms of dizziness or palpitations and require therapy. Rhythms that are tolerated well in patients with structurally normal hearts (e.g., paroxysms of supraventricular tachycardia) may not be tolerated in patients with diseased hearts (e.g., ischemic heart disease or mitral stenosis) and may require therapy. The decision to treat a patient with an asymptomatic tachyarrhythmia is more difficult. Certain arrhythmias, such as short episodes of asymptomatic nonsustained ventricular tachycardia, are in themselves harmless but may be forerunners of more serious sustained ventricular tachyarrhythmias. The decision to treat is complicated by the side effects, occasionally life-threatening, of antiarrhythmic drugs, such as exacerbation of ventricular arrhythmias in 5 to 15 per cent of cases. Even though patients with premature ventricular complexes and complex nonsustained ventricular ectopy after myocardial infarction are at increased risk of subsequent sudden death, no antiarrhythmic drugs other than beta blockers have been shown to improve survival, and some drugs may make it worse.

Before beginning chronic antiarrhythmic therapy, factors contributing to the occurrence of the arrhythmia should be considered. These include digitalis excess, hypokalemia, hypomagnesemia, hypoxia, thyrotoxicosis, and other severe metabolic derangements. Congestive heart failure, anemia, or infection should be corrected. Smoking, excessive alcohol intake, caffeine- or theophylline-containing beverages or foods, fatigue, emotional upset, and some over-the-counter drugs (e.g., nasal decongestants) may exacerbate arrhythmias.

Drugs

"Therapeutic" serum concentrations of antiarrhythmic drugs are those that usually exert therapeutic effects without adverse effects in most patients. However, dosage and blood concentrations must be adjusted for any particular patient, and the measured serum concentration is of secondary importance if the response to the drug is appropriate and side effects are absent. The therapeutic-to-toxic ratio of most antiarrhythmic drugs is relatively narrow, and knowledge of drug pharmacokinetics is important to avoid toxic peak and subtherapeutic trough concentrations. Most antiarrhythmic drugs can be administered at intervals equal to the elimination half-life of the drug after an initial loading dose. At a constant dosing interval without a loading dose, the time required to reach steady state is a function of the elimination half-life of the drug. Ninety-four per cent of steady-state level is achieved after four half-lives and 99 per cent after seven half-lives. The same

TABLE 8–2. VAUGHN WILLIAMS (MODIFIED) CLASSIFICATION OF ANTIARRHYTHMIC DRUGS

Class I Predominantly reduce the maximum velocity of the upstroke of the action potential (phase 0):
　　　IA: quinidine
　　　　　procainamide
　　　　　disopyramide
　　　IB: lidocaine
　　　　　phenytoin
　　　　　tocainide
　　　　　mexiletine
　　　IC: flecainide
　　　　　propafenone
　　　　　moricizine (?)
Class II Inhibit sympathetic activity: propranolol and other beta blockers
Class III Predominantly prolong action potential duration:
　　　　　amiodarone
　　　　　bretylium
Class IV Block the slow inward current: verapamil and other calcium antagonists

principle applies to the decrease in drug levels after discontinuation of the drug. Therefore, a drug with a longer half-life takes longer to reach steady state and longer to be eliminated than does one with a shorter half-life. Drugs with shorter half-lives are inconvenient to administer orally because of more frequent dosing requirements. Some medications with relatively short half-lives can be given in long-acting forms that release the drug gradually and result in adequate blood concentrations for a longer period of time without a high peak level immediately upon administration of the drug. The pharmacokinetics of drug distribution and elimination are often important; for example, lidocaine blood concentrations may be high after an intravenous bolus but drop very quickly as the drug is redistributed throughout the body. Once this early redistribution phase occurs, blood concentrations fall much less precipitously during the elimination phase, at which time the lidocaine is metabolized by the liver. Therefore, to avoid very high serum concentrations within the first 10 minutes and a subtherapeutic nadir after redistribution has occurred, lidocaine therapy may be initiated in two or more boluses, 5 to 10 minutes apart, instead of as one larger bolus. The organ responsible for elimination of a particular drug, usually the kidneys or liver, must be known, and dosage adjustments must be made in patients with organ dysfunction. The per cent of gastrointestinal absorption of some drugs is important to estimate intravenous versus oral dosages; for example, digoxin is only about 80 per cent absorbed orally, compared with 100 per cent availability of an intravenous dose. Some drugs are metabolized to compounds that also demonstrate antiarrhythmic activity, such as N-acetyl procainamide, which is the active metabolite of procainamide. Drug interactions may necessitate dosage adjustments. For example, quinidine increases digoxin serum concentrations. Changes in pharmacokinetics may occur in some groups of patients, such as decreased lidocaine requirements in elderly patients or those with congestive heart failure. Disparity in drug absorption and metabolism may occur in different patients owing to genetically controlled enzyme systems that allow some patients to metabolize drugs such as procainamide quickly (rapid acetylators). The amount of drug bound to serum proteins affects the activity and metabolism of a drug and also may affect the interpretation of serum drug concentrations, because many assays measure both free and protein-bound drug.

Although in vitro electrophysiologic properties are known for each drug and certain drugs are known to be more useful for one type of arrhythmia than another, much of antiarrhythmic drug therapy is trial and error. Even drugs grouped within the same class (Table 8–2) may vary in their clinical electrophysiologic effects, and when one is unsuccessful in a particular patient, another drug from the same class may be effective. It is important to remember that this classification serves a useful communication purpose but cannot

TABLE 8–3. ANTIARRHYTHMIC DRUGS: DOSAGE AND PHARMACOKINETICS*

DRUG	USUAL DOSE RANGES (mg)				EFFECTIVE SERUM OR PLASMA CONCENTRA-TION (µg/ml)	ELIMINATION HALF-LIFE AFTER ORAL DOSE (hr)	MAJOR ROUTE OF ELIMINATION
	INTRAVENOUS		ORAL				
	Loading	*Maintenance*	*Loading*	*Maintenance*			
Lidocaine	1–3 mg/kg at 20–50 mg/min	1–4 mg/min	—	—	1–5	1–2	Liver
Quinidine	6–10 mg/kg at 0.3–0.5 mg/kg/min	—	600–1000	300–600 q6h	3–6	5–9	Liver
Procainamide	6–13 mg/kg at 0.2–0.5 mg/kg/min	2–6 mg/min	500–1000	2000–6000 qd (q3–4h doses for procaina-mide, q6h doses for sustained-release form)	4–10	3–5	Kidneys
Disopyramide	—	—	300–400	100–400 q6-8h	2–5	8–9	Kidneys
Phenytoin	100 mg q5min for ≤1000 mg	—	1000	100–400 q12–24h	10–20	18–36	Liver
Propranolol	0.25–0.5 mg q5min for ≤0.15–0.20 mg/kg	—	—	10 to 200 q6-8h	—	3–6	Liver
Bretylium	5–10 mg/kg at 1–2 mg/kg/min	0.5–2 mg/min	—	—	0.5–1.5	8–14	Kidneys
Verapamil	10 mg over 1–2 min	0.005 mg/kg/min	—	80–120 q6-8h	0.10–0.15	3–8	Liver
Amiodarone	5–10 mg/kg over 20–30 min; then 1 gm/24 hr	—	800–1600 qd for 1–3 wk	200–400 qd	1–2.5	30–50 days	Liver
Tocainide	—	—	400–600	400–600 q8–12h	4–10	11	Liver
Mexiletine	—	—	400–600	150–300 q6-8h	0.75–2	10–17	Liver
Flecainide	—	—	—	100–200 q12h	0.2–1.0	20	Liver
Propafenone	—	—	600–900	150–300 q8–12h	0.2–3.0	5–8	Liver
Moricizine	—	—	300	200–300 q8h	—	—	—

* Results presented may vary according to doses, disease state, and intravenous or oral administration.

be applied rigidly for several reasons. Not all drugs assigned to a single group exhibit entirely similar actions, and some drugs have properties of more than one class. The classification is based on in vitro electrophysiologic effects on normal Purkinje fibers; drug effects on diseased in vivo tissues may be different, or its mechanism of action may even have nothing to do with its direct electrophysiologic actions. Tables 8–3, 8–4, and 8–5 summarize the currently available antiarrhythmic agents. It is important to remember that a potential adverse effect of any antiarrhythmic agent is arrhythmia exacerbation.

Lidocaine

Lidocaine has minimal effects on automaticity or conduction in vitro unless marked abnormalities are pre-existent. Lidocaine affects fast channel–dependent tissues (atrial and ventricular muscle and His-Purkinje tissue) but usually not slow channel–dependent tissues (sinus and AV nodes). It appears to be particularly potent at altering electrophysiologic parameters in ischemic tissue. Lidocaine rarely causes clinically significant he-

modynamic effects. It is used only parenterally because of extensive first-pass hepatic metabolism upon oral administration. Its metabolism is decreased in elderly patients and those with hepatic disease, heart failure, and shock. Maintenance doses should be reduced by one third to one half

TABLE 8–4. ANTIARRHYTHMIC DRUGS: ELECTROCARDIOGRAPHIC EFFECTS

DRUG	SINUS RATE	PR	QRS	QT
Lidocaine	0	0	0	0
Quinidine	0↑	↓0↑	↑	↑
Procainamide	0	0↑	↑	↑
Disopyramide	0↑	0	↑	↑
Phenytoin	0	0	0	0↓
Propranolol	↓	0↑	0	0↓
Bretylium	0↓	0↑	0	0↑
Verapamil	0↓	↑	0	0
Amiodarone	↓	0↑	0	↑
Tocainide	0↓	0	0	0↓
Mexiletine	0	0	0	0↓
Flecainide	0↓	↑	↑	↑
Propafenone	0↓	↑	↑	0↑
Moricizine	0↓	0↑	0↑	0

TABLE 8–5. ANTIARRHYTHMIC DRUGS: SIDE EFFECTS

DRUG	MAJOR SIDE EFFECTS
Lidocaine	CNS: dizziness, paresthesias, confusion, delirium, stupor, coma, seizures
Quinidine	Hypotension
	GI: nausea, vomiting, diarrhea, anorexia, abdominal pain
	"Cinchonism": tinnitus, hearing loss, visual disturbances, confusion, psychosis
	Rash, fever, anemia, thrombocytopenia
	"Quinidine syncope"
Procainamide	Drug-induced lupus erythematosus
	Nausea, vomiting
	Hypotension
	Giddiness, psychosis
Disopyramide	Anticholinergic: urinary retention, constipation, blurred vision, closed-angle glaucoma
	Congestive heart failure
Phenytoin	CNS: nystagmus, ataxia, drowsiness, stupor
	Nausea, anorexia
	Rash, gingival hypertrophy, megaloblastic anemia, lymph node hyperplasia, peripheral neuropathy, hyperglycemia, hypocalcemia
Propranolol	See Table 7–6
Bretylium	Orthostatic hypotension
	Transient hypertension, tachycardia, and worsening of arrhythmias (initial catecholamine release)
	Nausea, vomiting
Verapamil	See Table 7–7
Tocainide	CNS: dizziness, tremor, paresthesias, ataxia, confusion
	GI: nausea, vomiting
Amiodarone	Agranulocytosis, pulmonary fibrosis, elevation of hepatic enzymes, corneal microdeposits, bluish-gray skin discoloration, hyper- or hypothyroidism, nausea, constipation, anorexia, bradycardia, exacerbation of heart failure; elevates plasma levels of digoxin, quinidine, procainamide; potentiates effects of warfarin
Mexiletine	CNS: dizziness, tremor, paresthesias, ataxia, confusion
	GI: nausea, vomiting
Flecainide	Congestive heart failure, sinus node dysfunction, dizziness, blurred vision, incessant ventricular tachycardia
Propafenone	Dizziness, blurred vision, disturbances in taste
Moricizine	Nausea, dizziness, headache

CNS = Central nervous system; GI = gastrointestinal.

in patients with low cardiac output. Prolonged infusion of lidocaine can reduce its clearance, and dosage may have to be decreased after a day or so. Intramuscular administration has been advocated for use by emergency medical technicians when caring for a patient with an acute myocardial infarction before reaching the hospital, but lidocaine is usually administered intravenously. The ability to achieve rapid effective plasma concentrations and a fairly wide toxic-to-therapeutic ratio with a low incidence of hemodynamic complications make lidocaine a very useful antiarrhythmic drug. It is effective against a variety of ventricular arrhythmias but is generally ineffective against su-

praventricular arrhythmias. The use of lidocaine prophylactically in patients with acute myocardial infarction is controversial (see Chapter 7). Lidocaine is usually the parenteral drug of first choice in patients with ventricular arrhythmias. Even though lidocaine may decrease ventricular response in some patients with Wolff-Parkinson-White syndrome and atrial fibrillation, it usually has no effect on or can even accelerate the ventricular response in patients with rapid ventricular responses.

Quinidine

Quinidine is useful for long-term oral treatment of both atrial and ventricular arrhythmias. Quinidine has little effect on normal automaticity but depresses automaticity from abnormal cells. It prolongs conduction time and refractoriness in most cardiac tissues, and it increases the threshold of excitability in atrial and ventricular tissue. Although the direct effect of quinidine is to prolong conduction time in the AV node, its vagolytic actions may shorten conduction time, and the overall result is a balance between the two effects. Quinidine has alpha-adrenergic blocking effects that may cause significant hypotension, especially if vasodilators are administered concomitantly. If given slowly, quinidine may be administered intravenously. Intramuscular quinidine is incompletely absorbed and may cause tissue necrosis.

Quinidine prolongs the effective refractory period of atrial and ventricular muscle and accessory pathways. It may be effective in treating patients with AV nodal re-entry and tachycardias in Wolff-Parkinson-White syndrome. Quinidine may prevent supraventricular tachycardias not only by its effects on tissue refractoriness but also by preventing the atrial or ventricular premature complexes that may trigger the arrhythmia. Quinidine can terminate existing atrial flutter or fibrillation in about 10 to 20 per cent of patients, especially if the arrhythmia is recent in onset and the atria are of normal size. Because quinidine slows the rate of atrial flutter and also exerts a vagolytic effect on AV nodal conduction, it may increase the ventricular response in patients with atrial flutter. Therefore, the patient should be treated with digitalis, propranolol, or verapamil to control the ventricular rate before administering quinidine. Prior to electrical cardioversion, quinidine may be administered to attempt chemical conversion of atrial fibrillation or atrial flutter and may also help maintain sinus rhythm once it is achieved, either chemically or electrically.

Quinidine may produce syncope in 0.5 to 2 per cent of patients, thought most often to result from a polymorphic ventricular tachyarrhythmia termed torsades de pointes when associated with a long QT interval. Many patients with quinidine syncope have significantly prolonged QT intervals and are also receiving digitalis. Treatment for quinidine syncope entails discontinuation of the drug and avoidance of similar antiarrhythmic agents. Drugs that do not prolong the QT interval, such as lidocaine, tocainide, or phenytoin, may be tried. Phenobarbital or phenytoin and related drugs that induce hepatic enzyme production shorten the duration of quinidine's action by increasing its elimination. Quinidine elevates serum digoxin and digitoxin concentrations.

Procainamide

Electrophysiologic effects of procainamide resemble those of quinidine. Procainamide exerts less intense anticholinergic effects than disopyramide and quinidine. It has a major metabolite, N-acetyl procainamide (NAPA), that exhibits much weaker electrophysiologic effects than does procainamide. In patients with renal failure, NAPA levels increase more than procainamide levels and must be monitored to prevent toxicity. A sustained-release form is available that can be administered every 6 hours instead of every 3 to 4 hours; the total daily dose of both procainamide and the sustained-release form of procainamide should be the same. Procainamide depresses myocardial contractility only in high doses. It may produce peripheral vasodilation, probably via a mild ganglionic blocking action. The clinical indications for procainamide are very similar to those for quinidine. Although the effects of both drugs are similar, an arrhythmia not suppressed by one drug may be suppressed by the other. Conduction disturbances and ventricular tachyarrhythmias similar to those caused by quinidine can occur.

Procainamide does not increase serum digoxin levels. A systemic lupus erythematosus–like syndrome including arthralgia, fever, pleuropericarditis, hepatomegaly, and hemorrhagic pericardial effusion with tamponade has been described. The brain and kidneys are usually spared and hematologic complications are unusual. Sixty to 70 per cent of patients who receive procainamide develop antinuclear antibodies (ANA), but clinical symptoms occur in only 20 to 30 per cent and are reversible when the drug is stopped. A positive ANA titer is not necessarily a reason to stop procainamide therapy.

Disopyramide

Disopyramide has electrophysiologic actions similar to those of quinidine and procainamide but exerts greater anticholinergic effects than either, without antiadrenergic effects. Disopyramide has prominent negative inotropic effects, and patients who have evidence of abnormal ventricular function should receive the drug either not at all or only with extreme caution.

The role of disopyramide in the treatment of atrial and ventricular arrhythmias is similar to that of quinidine. Like quinidine, it can cause a 1:1 conduction during atrial flutter if the patient is not adequately digitalized. Disopyramide does not alter digitalis metabolism.

Phenytoin

Phenytoin is a potent medication to treat central nervous system seizures, but its antiarrhythmic actions are limited. It effectively abolishes abnormal automaticity caused by digitalis toxicity. Sinus nodal automaticity and AV conduction are only minimally affected by phenytoin. Phenytoin's electrophysiologic effects in vitro appear similar to those of lidocaine. It exerts minimal hemodynamic effects. Phenytoin may be successful in treating atrial and ventricular arrhythmias due to digitalis toxicity but is much less effective in treating arrhythmias of other etiologies.

Tocainide

Tocainide is an analogue of lidocaine that undergoes negligible hepatic first-pass metabolism and therefore approaches 100 per cent oral bioavailability. It is effective for ventricular tachyarrhythmias, but its efficacy appears to be less than that of lidocaine. Currently, its use has been curtailed owing to the occasional occurrence of granulocytosis.

Beta Blockers

Propranolol is discussed here as a prototype beta-adrenergic receptor blocker. Differences in the pharmacokinetics, beta-adrenergic receptor selectivity, and antagonist/agonist actions have been discussed in Chapter 7.

Propranolol slows the sinus nodal discharge rate and lengthens AV nodal conduction time (PR interval increases) and refractoriness. These effects may be marked if the heart rate or AV conduction is particularly dependent on sympathetic tone or if sinus or AV nodal dysfunction is present. There is no effect on refractoriness or conduction in the His-Purkinje system at usual doses, and the QRS complex and QT interval do not change. It appears that the beta-blocking activity of propranolol is responsible for its antiarrhythmic effects because a local anesthetic (or quinidine-like) effect of propranolol is present only at doses ten times those causing the beta-blocking effect. Serum concentrations vary from patient to patient, and the appropriate dose is determined by the patient's physiologic response, such as changes in resting heart rate or prevention of an increase in heart rate with exercise. If one beta blocker is ineffective against arrhythmias, the other beta blockers are usually also ineffective.

Propranolol is used most commonly to treat supraventricular tachyarrhythmias. Sinus tachycardia due to thyrotoxicosis, anxiety, and exercise may be slowed by propranolol. Propranolol does not usually terminate atrial flutter or fibrillation but may, by itself or combined with digitalis, control the ventricular response by prolonging AV nodal conduction time or refractoriness. Re-entrant supraventricular tachycardias using the AV node as one limb of the pathway (e.g., AV nodal re-entrant tachycardia and reciprocating tachycardias associated with the Wolff-Parkinson-White syndrome) may be prevented by propranolol alone or combined with other drugs. Propranolol is useful in treating ventricular arrhythmias associated with the prolonged QT syndrome and mitral valve prolapse. It usually does not prevent chronic recurrent ventricular tachycardia in patients with ischemic heart disease if the tachyarrhythmia occurs without acute ischemia. A new short-acting beta blocker, esmolol, has a half-life of only 9 minutes after intravenous infusion and may be useful for the acute termination of supraventricular tachycardias such as AV nodal re-entry.

Bretylium Tosylate

Bretylium tosylate initially releases norepinephrine stores from adrenergic nerve terminals but subsequently prevents further norepinephrine release. This initial catecholamine release may aggravate some arrhythmias and produce transient hypertension. Although the chemical sympathectomy-like state may be antiarrhythmic, other electrophysiologic properties may also contribute to the antiarrhythmic properties of bretylium. Bretylium does not depress myocardial contractility or affect vagal reflexes. After the initial increase in blood pressure, the drug may subsequently cause hypotension, usually orthostatic and controlled if the patient is supine. Bretylium is poorly absorbed orally and is commonly administered intravenously. Bretylium has been reported to induce spontaneous termination of ventricular fibrillation. Bretylium is indicated in patients with life-threatening ventricular arrhythmias that have not responded to lidocaine and possibly to other drugs.

Calcium Antagonists

The calcium antagonists have been discussed in Chapter 7. Verapamil and diltiazem do not affect cells with normal fast response characteristics (atrial and ventricular muscle, His-Purkinje system), but in fast channel–dependent cells rendered abnormal by disease, they may suppress electrical activity. Slow channel–dependent tissue (sinus and AV nodes) exhibits an increase in conduction time and refractoriness after verapamil or diltiazem administration. Therefore, they prolong the AH interval without affecting His-Purkinje conduction or the QRS interval. Sinus rate may decrease, but in intact animals it often does not change significantly because of counteraction by sympathetic reflexes activated by peripheral vasodilation. Verapamil and diltiazem do not affect directly refractoriness of atrial or ventricular muscle or the accessory pathway. Combined therapy with propranolol and verapamil can be attempted in patients with normal cardiac contractility, but the patient should be observed for the development of heart failure and/or symptomatic bradycardias because the compensatory sympathetic response to slow channel blockade is blocked. Calcium infusion or isoproterenol may counteract some of the adverse effects of verapamil until temporary pacing can be initiated.

Intravenous verapamil or diltiazem is effective for terminating sustained paroxysmal supraventricular tachycardias that are not terminated by vagal maneuvers, such as those reciprocating tachycardias employing the AV node or sinoatrial (SA) node in the tachycardia circuit. These drugs can decrease the ventricular response in patients with atrial fibrillation or flutter but convert only a small number of these rhythms to sinus rhythm. Verapamil or diltiazem may be used in patients with congestive heart failure and supraventricular tachycardia if it is thought that termination of the arrhythmia will relieve the heart failure. Verapamil may increase the ventricular response in patients with atrial fibrillation and Wolff-Parkinson-White syndrome, and the drug is relatively contraindicated in that situation. Verapamil is usually not effective in patients with recurrent ventricular tachyarrhythmias and can result in hemodynamic collapse when given intravenously to patients with sustained ventricular tachycardia. A rare patient may have a verapamil-sensitive ventricular tachycardia believed due to triggered activity.

Amiodarone

Amiodarone is an antiarrhythmic agent initially introduced as an antianginal coronary vasodilator. It has a broad spectrum of antiarrhythmic efficacy against supraventricular and ventricular arrhythmias. Even though it prolongs the QT interval, it may suppress arrhythmias in patients with the long QT syndrome. It is effective in AV nodal re-entry, reciprocating tachycardias associated with the Wolff-Parkinson-White syndrome, atrial flutter, and atrial fibrillation, as well as ventricular tachyarrhythmias. Antiarrhythmic efficacy develops after several days of oral administration but may occur earlier with intravenous administration. Amiodarone prolongs action potential duration and refractoriness in all cardiac tissues, slows sinus discharge, and prolongs AV nodal conduction time. Because of a variety of adverse effects, amiodarone should be administered only to patients with highly symptomatic or life-threatening arrhythmias and only if conventional drug therapy has failed.

Mexiletine

Mexiletine is similar to lidocaine in many of its electrophysiologic actions. It is effective for ventricular but not supraventricular tachyarrhythmias and may be useful when combined with type IA antiarrhythmic agents such as quinidine. Adverse effects and efficacy are similar to those of tocainide. Like tocainide, the toxic effects occur at plasma concentrations only slightly higher than therapeutic levels, and therefore effective use of this drug requires careful titration of dosage. A patient's response to intravenous lidocaine may help predict his response to oral mexiletine.

Flecainide

Flecainide profoundly slows conduction in all cardiac fibers but only minimally increases refractoriness. It modestly depresses the cardiac inotropic state and should be used with caution in patients with heart failure. It is useful for ventricular tachyarrhythmias and is especially effective at suppressing PVCs or runs of nonsustained ventricular tachycardia. Therapy should begin in the hospital while the ECG is monitored because of the high incidence of aggravation of existing ventricular arrhythmias or onset of new ventricular arrhythmias (5 to 25 per cent of patients). This proarrhythmic effect is especially prominent in patients who have sustained ventricular tachycardia and poor left ventricular function and receive higher doses of the drug. Dose increases should not be made more frequently than every 4 days. Flecainide has resulted in increased mortality in patients with asymptomatic ventricular arrhythmia following myocardial infarction, apparently a late proarrhythmic effect. Its use for ventricular arrhythmias should therefore be reserved for patients with refractory, sustained, life-threatening ventricular tachyarrhythmias with electrophysiologic study guidance. Flecainide may be very useful in patients with structurally normal hearts and AV nodal re-entry, tachycardias involving accessory pathways, or atrial fibrillation.

Moricizine

Moricizine is a type 1 antiarrhythmic agent that reduces the maximum velocity of the action potential upstroke with potency comparable to that of quinidine, but unlike quinidine, it does not prolong repolarization of atrial or ventricular muscle. It is therefore difficult to subclassify moricizine within class 1. It prolongs both AV nodal and His-Purkinje conduction and has no effect on left ventricular function. It is effective for both ventricular and supraventricular tachyarrhythmias.

Propafenone

Propafenone has electrophysiologic effects similar to those of flecainide but also has mild beta-blocking properties. It must therefore be used with caution in patients with poor left ventricular function, sinus nodal or AV conduction defects, or bronchospastic asthma. Propafenone is effective for ventricular and supraventricular arrhythmias. Its long-term proarrhythmic potential has never been established in a study similar to that described for flecainide.

Adenosine

Adenosine is an endogenous nucleoside available for intravenous administration for termination of paroxysmal supraventricular tachycardias due to AV nodal re-entry or AV re-entry associated with an accessory pathway. It causes marked but transient slowing of AV nodal conduction and sinus nodal discharge. Its half-life is less than 10 seconds, metabolized by erythrocytes and vascular endothelial cells. Therefore, adenosine must be given as a very rapid injection followed by a saline flush. The initial dose is 6 mg, followed, if necessary, in 2 minutes by 12 mg. It is antagonized competitively by methylxanthines such as caffeine and theophylline and potentiated by blockers of nucleoside transport such as dipyridamole. Adenosine terminates more than 95 per cent of AV nodal re-entrant or AV re-entrant tachycardias within 30 seconds of administration. During atrial tachycardias or atrial flutter it often results in transient higher-degree AV block, aiding the differential diagnosis of the tachycardia mechanism. Symptoms of flushing, chest discomfort, and shortness of breath are common but transient.

Direct-Current Cardioversion and Defibrillation

Direct-current (DC) electrical cardioversion or defibrillation is the method of choice for terminating tachyarrhythmias that result in hemodynamic deterioration and those unresponsive to pharmacologic termination. Cardioversion refers to the delivery of a DC shock, usually of relatively low energy, synchronized with the QRS complex of an organized tachyarrhythmia. QRS synchronization is important to avoid delivering a shock during ventricular repolarization (T wave) that may precipitate ventricular fibrillation. Defibrillation refers to an asynchronously delivered, relatively high energy shock to terminate ventricular fibrillation. Most supraventricular and ventricular tachyarrhythmias terminate with DC shock, although rhythms due to abnormally increased automaticity, especially if associated with digitalis intoxication, may not.

Prior to elective cardioversion the procedure should be explained to the patient and a physical examination, including palpation of all pulses, performed. Metabolic parameters (i.e., blood gases, electrolytes) should be normal, and ideally the patient should have fasted for 6 to 8 hours prior to the procedure. Digitalis should be withheld on the morning of cardioversion. Patients receiving digitalis without clinical evidence of toxicity are at very low risk for digitalis-induced complications. A short-acting barbiturate or diazepam can be used for anesthesia. Intravenous access should be available, and resuscitation equipment should be at hand. Paddles should be lubricated with an electrolyte jelly and placed firmly to contact with the chest wall, either one paddle in the left infrascapular region and the other over the upper sternum at the third interspace, or one paddle to the right of the sternum at the first or second interspace and the other in the left midclavicular line at the fourth or fifth interspace. Shocks of 25 to 50 joules terminate most tachyarrhythmias except for atrial fibrillation, which may require 100 to 200 joules, and ventricular fibrillation, which may require 100 to 400 joules. If the first low-energy shock fails to terminate the arrhythmia, the energy should be titrated upward.

Tachycardia that produces complications of hypotension, congestive heart failure, or angina and does not respond promptly to medical management should be terminated electrically. DC shock should be avoided if possible in patients with tachyarrhythmias caused by digitalis toxicity because of the risk of precipitating life-threatening refractory ventricular tachyarrhythmias. The administration of an antiarrhythmic drug prior to electrical termination of the arrhythmia may help maintain sinus rhythm after cardioversion. Many arrhythmias, especially chronic atrial fibrillation, commonly recur, and maintenance of sinus rhythm is sometimes a difficult problem.

Ventricular fibrillation due to an improperly synchronized or at times a properly synchronized shock is a complication of DC cardioversion. Immediate electrical defibrillation is mandatory. Systemic emboli occur, and patients with atrial fibrillation, especially those with a high risk for emboli (e.g., mitral stenosis, atrial fibrillation of recent onset, a history of emboli, a prosthetic mitral valve, enlarged left ventricle or left atrium, or congestive heart failure), may require anticoagulation for 2 weeks before cardioversion to lower the risk of emboli. Anticoagulation should be continued for several weeks after cardioversion. Elevation of myocardial enzyme fractions after cardioversion is not common.

Cardiac Pacemakers

Cardiac pacemakers are devices either implanted permanently or inserted temporarily, consisting of a pulse generator and an electrode that is either placed transvenously into the right ventricle and/or atrium or sutured directly into the epicardium at the time of surgery. Small electrical impulses, generated by the pulse generator and delivered via the electrode catheter, depolarize local cells to threshold potential and cause the entire chamber to depolarize. Pacemakers are widely used for treating bradyarrhythmias but can also be useful for treatment of some tachyarrhythmias. Indicators for temporary and permanent pacing are summarized in Table 8–6.

A pacemaker code has been developed to describe the pacing modalities available in any particular pacemaker. The first letter is the chamber paced (V = ventricle, A = atrium, and D = atrium and ventricle). The second letter is the chamber in which sensing occurs (V = ventricle, A = atrium, D = atrium and ventricle, and O = none). The third letter indicates the mode of response: sensed spontaneous activity inhibiting pacemaker output (I), trigger discharge into the refractory period (T), or trigger ventricular pacing in response to a sensed atrial event as well as inhibition of ventricular pacing during a sensed ventricular event (D). Some examples are illustrated in Table 8–7. An R added as a fourth letter indicates that the pacemaker is rate-responsive; that is, it increases the pacing rate in response to physiologic need. Sensors used to measure physiologic need include activity (vibration), blood temperature, and respiratory rate (thoracic impedance).

The main advantages of dual-chamber pacing modes are the preservation of AV synchrony and the ability to increase ventricular paced rate with an increase in atrial rate. Safeguards are built into the VDD and DDD modes so that the ventricular response cannot exceed a predetermined upper rate, should an atrial tachyarrhythmia occur. A problem unique to dual-chamber pacing modes (DDD or VDD) that trigger ventricular depolarization from sensed atrial activity is pacemaker-mediated tachycardia. During pacemaker-mediated tachycardia, the pacemaker senses a retrograde P wave conducted after a paced ventricular beat or a PVC and triggers a subsequent ventricular depolarization after the programmed AV delay. This paced ventricular complex can again conduct retrogradely to the atrium, creating a sensed P wave that generates another paced ventricular complex. If this continues, a sustained "reciprocating" tachycardia that utilizes the pacemaker as the antegrade limb may occur. Extensive programmability of the newer pacemaker models, particularly that of atrial refractoriness, avoids pacemaker-mediated tachycardia in most cases.

For patients in whom a pacemaker is implanted only for an occasional symptomatic bradycardia or in whom optimal hemodynamic function is of no consequence, a simple VVI pacemaker may be sufficient. However, there are some patients in whom maintenance of physiologic AV synchrony may be advantageous. The normal increase in heart rate with exercise may be preserved either by dual-chamber, atrial-synchronous pacing (e.g., DDD mode), or, if the sinus node is incompetent, by a VVIR or DDDR pacemaker that is able to sense a physiologic event such as activity and increase its discharge rate appropriately. Pacemaker malfunction may be manifested by (1) failure to capture (activate myocardium), (2) abnormal sensing (oversensing or undersensing), or (3) abnormal discharge rate. Malfunction may be intermittent. Many pacemakers alter their discharge rate when the battery approaches depletion.

TABLE 8–6. INDICATIONS FOR TEMPORARY AND PERMANENT PACING

	DEFINITELY INDICATED	PROBABLY INDICATED	PROBABLY NOT INDICATED	DEFINITELY NOT INDICATED
Complete AV block				
Congenital (AV nodal)				
Asymptomatic				X
Symptomatic	T,P			
Acquired (His-Purkinje)				
Asymptomatic		T,P		
Symptomatic	T,P			
Surgical (persistent)				
Asymptomatic	T	P		
Symptomatic	T,P			
Second-degree AV block				
Type I (AV nodal)				
Asymptomatic				X
Symptomatic	T,P			
Type II (His-Purkinje)				
Asymptomatic		T,P		
Symptomatic	T,P			
First-degree AV block				
AV nodal				
Asymptomatic				X
Symptomatic			X	
His-Purkinje				
Asymptomatic				X
Symptomatic			X	
Bundle branch block (BBB)				
Asymptomatic				X
Symptomatic		P†		
Left BBB during right heart catheterization	T			
Acute myocardial infarction				
Newly acquired bifascicular BBB	T			
Pre-existing BBB				X
Newly acquired BBB plus transient complete AV block	T	P		
Second-degree AV block				
Type I (asymptomatic)				X
Type II	T	P		
Complete AV block	T	P		
Atrial fibrillation with slow ventricular response				
Asymptomatic				X
Symptomatic	T,P			
Sick sinus syndrome (bradytachy syndrome)				
Asymptomatic			X	
Symptomatic	T,P			
Hypersensitive carotid sinus syndrome				
Asymptomatic			X	
Symptomatic	T,P			

T = Temporary; P = permanent; X = not indicated; † = no other cause found for symptoms.

Nonpharmacologic Therapy of Tachyarrhythmias

Nonpharmacologic therapy of both supraventricular and ventricular tachyarrhythmias has become commonplace, especially in light of the incomplete efficacy and proarrhythmic potential of drug therapy, as well as the advances in nonpharmacologic techniques. Antitachycardia pacing techniques to terminate supraventricular tachycardias have become less important as catheter ablation techniques for AV nodal re-entrant tachycardia and AV re-entrant tachycardia associated with accessory pathways have improved. Antitachycardia pacing for ventricular tachyarrhythmias has become more important as the technique has been

TABLE 8−7. COMMON PACEMAKERS

PACEMAKER TYPE	CODE	CHAMBER PACED	CHAMBER SENSED	MODE
Ventricular asynchronous	VOO	V	None	Continuous pacing
Ventricular demand	VVI	V	V	Ventricular pacing inhibited by spontaneous QRS
Atrial demand	AAI	A	A	Atrial pacing inhibited by spontaneous P wave
Atrial synchronous, ventricular inhibited	VDD	V	A,V	Ventricular pacing follows a sensed P wave after a preset AV delay; ventricular pacing inhibited by spontaneous QRS; no atrial pacing
AV sequential	DVI	A,V	V	Ventricular pacing follows atrial pacing after a preset AV delay; ventricular and atrial pacing inhibited by spontaneous QRS; no P wave sensing
Optimal sequential	DDD	A,V	A,V	Ventricular pacing follows sensed P waves or atrial pacing after a preset AV delay; ventricular pacing inhibited by spontaneous QRS; atrial pacing inhibited by spontaneous P wave
Rate responsive	VVIR	V	V	Same as VVI or DDD, but pacing rate increases with physiologic demand
	DDDR	A,V	A,V	

incorporated into implantable cardioverter-defibrillators (ICDs). Antitachycardia pacing can terminate many slower monomorphic ventricular tachycardias; the major hazard is acceleration of the ventricular tachycardia to a rapid, hemodynamically unstable rhythm, and therefore immediate defibrillation capability must also be available in the implanted device. If successful, antitachycardia pacing to terminate ventricular tachycardia is more desirable than delivery of a shock.

ICDs have improved survival in patients resuscitated from sudden cardiac death not associated with a myocardial infarction and in patients with hemodynamically unstable drug-resistant ventricular tachycardias. These devices automatically sense a rapid heart rhythm and deliver a 30- to 40-joule discharge to restore sinus rhythm. They can recycle and deliver subsequent shocks if the first shock is unsuccessful. Newer devices also deliver stimuli to treat bradycardias and terminate tachycardias. They are implanted surgically using a sternotomy, thoracotomy, or subcostal approach. Defibrillation patches are sewn to the epicardium, and electrodes for sensing and pacing are inserted either epicardially or endocardially. To avoid thoracotomy, transvenous leads and a subcutaneous patch can be used in approximately 70 per cent of patients. Drug therapy may be required after implantation of an ICD to limit the number of arrhythmia episodes or modify the arrhythmia so that syncope does not result prior to device activation.

Catheter ablation of arrhythmias has assumed major importance. Radiofrequency energy delivered via a catheter provides a safe and effective means of creating small, discrete lesions to ablate either an arrhythmia focus or a pathway associated with an arrhythmia. Catheter ablation should be offered as an early therapy for patients with arrhythmias associated with Wolff-Parkinson-White syndrome and successfully eliminates the tachycardia in more than 95 per cent of patients.

In addition, selective ablation of the slow or fast AV nodal pathway responsible for AV nodal reentrant tachycardia, while preserving anterograde AV nodal conduction, is also possible in more than 95 per cent of patients. Inadvertent complete AV block occurs in approximately 2 per cent. The AV junction can be completely ablated in patients who have refractory atrial fibrillation or other atrial tachyarrhythmias with a rapid ventricular response. This procedure leaves the patient pacemaker-dependent but eliminates the rapid ventricular response. Catheter ablation for ventricular tachycardia is more difficult, but selected patients with monomorphic ventricular tachycardias associated with minimal or no structural heart disease may be good candidates for catheter ablation of ventricular tachycardia. In addition, direct ablation of atrial tachycardia foci or the circuit responsible for atrial flutter may be possible in selected patients.

With the advent of catheter ablation techniques, surgery for patients with Wolff-Parkinson-White syndrome and AV nodal re-entrant tachycardia is performed less often, although it is occasionally used after a failed catheter ablation or in a patient with a concomitant indication for cardiac surgery. Surgical ablation of ventricular tachycardia can be performed in selected patients with sustained ventricular tachycardia unresponsive to medical therapy who have aneurysm formation with otherwise preserved left ventricular function. The operation consists of aneurysmectomy and endocardial resection and/or cryoablation of the tachycardia focus. Surgery eliminates ventricular tachycardia in about 70 per cent of such patients. An additional 20 per cent have ventricular tachycardia suppressed with previously ineffective drug therapy. Surgery for other varieties of ventricular tachycardia can occasionally be performed using direct excision of the focus, for example, the infundibulectomy scar after repairs of tetralogy of Fallot. Operations for prevention of atrial flutter and fibrillation are investigational at present.

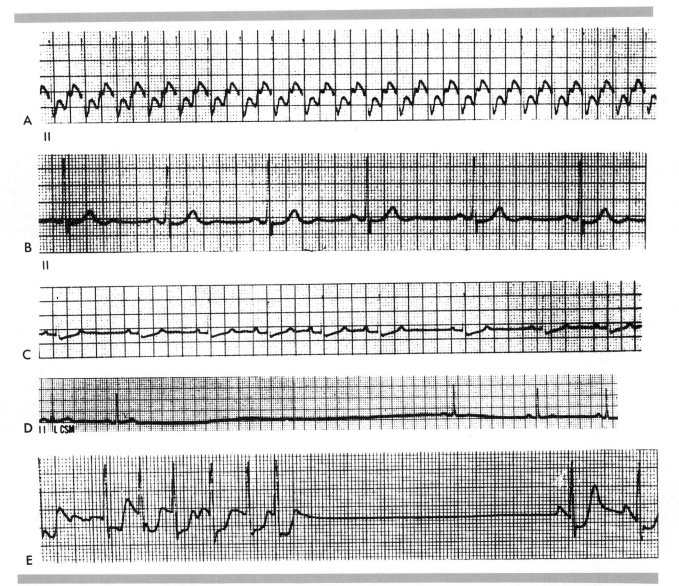

FIGURE 8-3. *A*, Sinus tachycardia (rate, 150 beats/min) in a patient during acute myocardial ischemia; note ST segment depression. *B*, Sinus bradycardia (rate 46 beats/min) in a patient receiving propranolol. *C*, Respiratory sinus arrhythmia. The phasic variation in heart rate corresponds to a respiratory rate of approximately 12/min. *D*, Hypersensitive carotid sinus syndrome. Gentle left carotid sinus massage produced a prolonged period of asystole. *E*, Bradycardia-tachycardia syndrome. A fairly long period of asystole results before restoration of sinus rhythm upon termination of an episode of atrial fibrillation.

SPECIFIC ARRHYTHMIAS

Sinus Nodal Rhythm Disturbances
(Fig. 8–3)

Normal sinus rhythm refers to impulse formation beginning in the sinus node and, in adults, having a rate of between 60 and 100 beats/min. The P wave is upright in leads 1, 2, and aV_F and negative in lead aV_R. The rate of sinus nodal discharge is under autonomic control and increases with sym-

pathetic and decreases with parasympathetic stimulation. *Sinus tachycardia* refers to a tachycardia of sinus origin with a rate exceeding 100 beats/min. Sinus tachycardia occurs with stresses such as fever, hypotension, thyrotoxicosis, anemia, anxiety, exertion, hypovolemia, pulmonary emboli, myocardial ischemia, congestive heart failure, shock, drugs (e.g., atropine, catecholamines, thyroid, alcohol, caffeine), or inflammation. Therapy should be focused on the cause of the tachycardia. If the sinus tachycardia must be treated directly, propranolol may be used. *Sinus bradycardia* refers to sinus node discharge at a rate less than 60 beats/min. The P wave contour is normal, but sinus arrhythmia is often present. Sinus bradycardia frequently occurs in young adults, especially well-trained athletes, and is common at night. Sinus bradycardia can be produced by a variety of conditions, including eye manipulation, increased intracranial pressure, myxedema, hypothermia, sepsis, fibrodegenerative changes, vagal stimulation, and vomiting, and the administration of parasympathomimetic drugs, beta-adrenergic blocking drugs, or amiodarone. It occurs commonly in the acute phase of myocardial infarction, especially inferior myocardial infarction. Treatment of asymptomatic sinus bradycardia is usually not necessary. If cardiac output is low or tachyarrhythmias occur owing to the slow heart rate, atropine or, if necessary, isoproterenol may be effective. There is no drug that effectively and safely increases the heart rate over a long period of time, and therefore electrical pacing is the treatment of choice chronically if symptomatic sinus bradycardia is present.

Sinus arrhythmia refers to phasic variation in the sinus cycle length by greater than 10 per cent. P wave morphology is normal. Respiratory sinus arrhythmia occurs when the PP interval shortens during inspiration as a result of reflex inhibition of vagal tone and lengthens during expiration. Nonrespiratory sinus arrhythmia refers to sinus arrhythmia not associated with the respiratory cycle. Symptoms are unusual and treatment not necessary.

In *sinus pause (sinus arrest)* and *sinoatrial exit block,* a sudden unexpected failure of a P wave occurs. In sinoatrial exit block, the PP interval surrounding the absent P wave is a multiple of the P to P intervals, implying that the sinus impulse was generated but did not propagate through the perinodal tissue to the atrium. If no such cycle relationship can be found, the term sinus pause or sinus arrest is employed. Acute myocardial infarction, degenerative fibrotic changes, digitalis toxicity, or excessive vagal tone can produce sinus arrest or exit block. Therapy involves searching for the underlying cause. Patients are not treated if they are asymptomatic. If they are symptomatic and the arrhythmia is not reversed by correcting the underlying causes, pacing is employed.

Wandering atrial pacemaker involves a transfer of the dominant pacemaker from the sinus node to latent pacemakers in other atrial sites or in the AV junction. The change from one pacemaker focus to another occurs gradually, associated with a change in the RR interval, PR interval, and P wave morphology. Treatment is usually not necessary except if symptoms occur from bradyarrhythmias.

The *hypersensitive carotid sinus syndrome* is characterized by cessation of atrial activity due to sinus arrest or SA exit block with light pressure over the carotid baroreceptors. In addition, AV block may be observed. Adequate junctional or ventricular escape complexes may not occur. Cardioinhibitory carotid sinus hypersensitivity is arbitrarily defined as ventricular asystole exceeding 3 seconds during carotid sinus stimulation. Vasodepressor carotid sinus hypersensitivity is defined as a fall in systolic blood pressure of 30 to 50 mm Hg without cardiac slowing, usually with reproduction of a patient's symptoms. The treatment in symptomatic patients is pacemaker implantation (to include at least a ventricular lead, because the sinus node slowing is usually also associated with AV block). Neither atropine nor pacing prevents the vasodepressor manifestations of carotid sinus hypersensitivity. Severe vasodepressor carotid sinus hypersensitivity occasionally requires denervation of the carotid sinus.

The term *sick sinus syndrome* is applied to a variety of sinus nodal and AV nodal abnormalities that occur alone or in combination. They include (1) persistent spontaneous sinus bradycardia not caused by drugs and inappropriate to the physiologic circumstances, (2) sinus arrest or exit block, (3) combinations of sinus and AV conduction disturbances, and (4) alternation of paroxysms of atrial tachyarrhythmias with periods of slow atrial and ventricular rates (bradycardia/tachycardia syndrome). The sick sinus syndrome may be associated with AV nodal or His-Purkinje conduction disturbances. If symptoms are present from bradyarrhythmias, pacemaker implantation is appropriate. Pacing for the symptomatic bradyarrhythmia combined with drug therapy for the tachyarrhythmia is often needed.

Sinus nodal re-entrant tachycardia accounts for 5 to 10 per cent of paroxysmal supraventricular tachycardias. Its mechanism is presumed to be re-entry within the sinus node and the perinodal tissues, giving rise to a tachycardia, usually with a rate of 130 to 140 beats/min and containing P waves very similar to sinus P waves. AV block may occur without affecting the tachycardia. Vagal activation may slow and then abruptly terminate the tachycardia by its action on sinus nodal tissue. Tachycardia may be induced and terminated at electrophysiologic study with premature atrial stimulation. Treatment with propranolol, verapamil, or digitalis is effective therapy.

Atrial Rhythm Disturbances (Fig. 8-4)

Premature atrial complexes (PACs) are characterized by a premature P wave, usually of differing morphology from the sinus P wave. PACs occurring very early in diastole may be followed by either aberrantly conducted QRS complexes or no QRS complexes (nonconducted PAC). In general, the shorter the interval from the last QRS to the P wave, the longer the PR interval after the PAC. PACs are less likely to be followed by a fully compensatory pause than are PVCs (see discussion further on). PACs are common in normal people but may occur in a variety of situations, such as

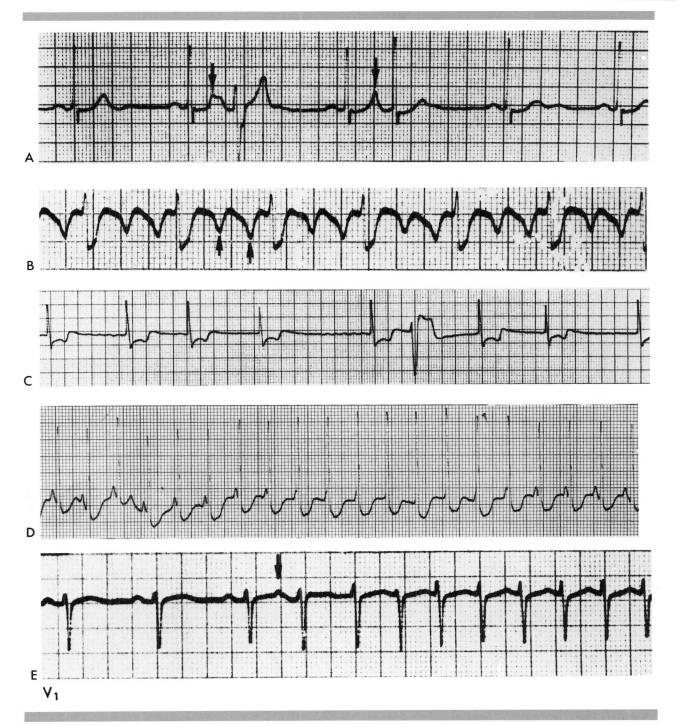

FIGURE 8–4. *A,* Premature atrial systoles with and without aberrancy. The first premature atrial systole *(arrow)* occurs at a shorter PR interval than does the second premature atrial systole *(arrow)* and conducts with a bundle branch block contour. The first premature atrial systole conducts with aberrancy, but the second does not because the first reaches the bundle branch system before complete recovery of repolarization. *B,* Atrial flutter. Flutter waves are indicated by arrows. The conduction ratio is 3:1, that is, three flutter waves to one QRS complex, and is a less common conduction ratio. *C,* Atrial fibrillation. Atrial activity is present as the undulating wavy baseline seen in the midportion of the ECG strip. The premature ventricular complex (PVC) must be differentiated from aberrant supraventricular conduction. *D,* Nonparoxysmal junctional tachycardia with AV dissociation. *E,* Paroxysmal supraventricular tachycardia. Three sinus beats are interrupted by a premature atrial systole *(arrow),* which conducts with PR prolongation and initiates the supraventricular tachycardia. The most common mechanisms of this arrhythmia are AV nodal re-entry and AV re-entry using an accessory pathway as the retrograde limb.

infection, inflammation, myocardial ischemia, psychological stress, tobacco or alcohol use, or caffeine ingestion. PACs can be the forerunner of a sustained supraventricular tachyarrhythmia. They do not require therapy unless they produce symptoms or precipitate tachyarrhythmias.

In *atrial flutter,* the atrial rate is usually 250 to 350 beats/min. Ordinarily, the ventricular rate is half of the atrial rate. If AV block is greater than 2:1 in the absence of drugs, abnormal AV conduction is suggested. In children, patients with preexcitation syndrome, or patients with hyperthyroidism, 1:1 AV conduction can occasionally occur. Drugs such as quinidine, procainamide, or disopyramide may reduce the atrial rate to the range of 200 beats/min, raising the danger of 1:1 AV conduction. The atrial activity appears as regular sawtooth waves without an isoelectric interval between flutter waves. Flutter waves are commonly inverted in leads 2, 3, and aV_F. Ventricular response to atrial flutter may be irregular, generally of a Wenckebach nature, or regular. Chronic atrial flutter is usually associated with underlying heart disease, but paroxysmal atrial flutter may occur in patients without organic heart disease. Toxic and metabolic conditions such as thyrotoxicosis, alcoholism, and pericarditis may be associated with atrial flutter. There are fewer systemic emboli in patients with atrial flutter than in patients with atrial fibrillation, presumably because of the atrial contraction. Carotid sinus massage may decrease the ventricular response but does not terminate the arrhythmia. Cardioversion (less than 50 joules) usually restores sinus rhythm. If atrial fibrillation ensues, a second shock of higher energy may be necessary. Rapid atrial pacing also terminates atrial flutter, although some patients develop atrial fibrillation instead of sinus rhythm; however, atrial fibrillation is usually an easier arrhythmia in which to control the ventricular response.

Intravenous verapamil, beta blockers, or digitalis may slow the ventricular response to atrial flutter, and in a few patients may restore sinus rhythm. Type 1 antiarrhythmic drugs such as quinidine, procainamide, or disopyramide may terminate atrial flutter in some patients and are often useful in preventing recurrences. These drugs should not be administered unless AV nodal block has been previously achieved, because slowing the atrial flutter rate combined with the vagolytic effects of disopyramide or quinidine may lead to 1:1 AV conduction.

Atrial fibrillation is characterized by totally disorganized atrial activation without effective atrial contraction. The ECG shows small, irregular baseline undulations of variable amplitude. The ventricular response is irregularly irregular, usually between 100 and 160 beats/min in the untreated patient with normal AV conduction. It is easier to slow the ventricular response with drugs in patients with atrial fibrillation than in patients with atrial flutter because of the greater number of atrial impulses reaching the AV node and decreasing the overall number of impulses that conduct to the ventricles. Chronic atrial fibrillation is usually associated with underlying heart disease, whereas paroxysmal atrial fibrillation may occur in apparently normal hearts. Atrial fibrillation commonly results from rheumatic heart disease (especially with mitral valve involvement), cardiomyopathy, hypertensive heart disease, pulmonary emboli, pericarditis, coronary heart disease, thyrotoxicosis, or heart failure from any cause. Episodes of atrial fibrillation may cause decompensation of patients with borderline cardiac function, especially those with mitral or aortic stenosis. Patients with chronic atrial fibrillation are at a greatly increased risk of developing systemic emboli, particularly if mitral valve disease is also present. Left atrial diameter tends to be smaller in patients with paroxysmal atrial fibrillation or in patients whose atrial fibrillation is easily terminated with cardioversion. Physical findings in patients with atrial fibrillation include a variation in the intensity of the first heart sound, absence of a waves in the jugular venous pulse, and an irregular ventricular rhythm. A pulse deficit may appear with faster ventricular rates; that is, the auscultated apical rate exceeds the palpable radial rate owing to failure of many of the ventricular contractions to generate a palpable peripheral pulse. Although atrial fibrillation with a very rapid ventricular response can sometimes seem regular, it is always irregular upon careful measurement, and true regularization of the ventricular rhythm in patients with atrial fibrillation should suggest development of sinus rhythm, atrial flutter, junctional rhythm, or ventricular tachycardia (the latter two may be manifestations of digitalis intoxication).

It is important to correct any precipitating causes of atrial fibrillation such as thyrotoxicosis, mitral stenosis, pulmonary emboli, or pericarditis. If the onset of atrial fibrillation is associated with acute hemodynamic decompensation, DC cardioversion should be employed (usually requires 100 to 200 joules). In the absence of decompensation, the patient should be treated with digitalis to maintain a resting apical rate of 60 to 80 beats/min that does not exceed 100 beats/min after mild exercise. At times, the addition of a beta or calcium blocker may be useful in slowing the ventricular rate. Quinidine or other type 1 antiarrhythmic drugs may be useful either to convert atrial fibrillation to sinus rhythm or to maintain sinus rhythm once it is restored with electrical cardioversion. The risks of chronic antiarrhythmic drug therapy must be balanced against the potential benefits of maintaining sinus rhythm. Patients with atrial fibrillation of less than 12 months' duration or without markedly enlarged left atria are more likely to remain in sinus rhythm after cardioversion. Anticoagulation prior to drug or electrical cardioversion is definitely indicated in patients at high risk of emboli (i.e., those with mitral stenosis, previous emboli, a prosthetic mitral valve, or cardiomegaly) and is probably indicated in any patient with atrial fibrillation of greater than 1 week's duration. Anticoagulation therapy should be administered 2 to 3 weeks prior to cardioversion and continued for 2 to 4 weeks afterward. Patients with chronic atrial fibrillation or those with paroxysmal episodes of atrial fibrillation despite drug therapy are at increased risk of embolic stroke, especially if there is underlying heart disease. These patients should receive warfarin (prothrombin time prolongation 1.3 to 1.5 times control) if no contraindications exist, or possibly aspirin therapy. Rapid atrial pacing does not terminate atrial fibrillation.

In *atrial tachycardia with AV block*, the atrial rate is usually 150 to 200 beats/min, and variable degrees of AV conduction are present. This rhythm is often associated with digitalis excess and occurs most commonly in patients with significant organic heart disease, such as coronary heart disease, cor pulmonale, and digitalis intoxication. Isoelectric intervals are present between P waves in contrast to atrial flutter. Carotid sinus massage should be performed with caution in patients suspected of having digitalis toxicity. If the patient is not receiving digitalis, the rhythm may be treated with digitalis to slow the ventricular response, and subsequently quinidine, disopyramide, or procainamide may be added. If atrial tachycardia occurs in a patient receiving digitalis, digitalis toxicity should be suspected. Usually the ventricular response is not rapid, and withholding digitalis is sufficient therapy.

Chaotic or *multifocal atrial tachycardia* is characterized by atrial rates between 100 and 130 beats/min with marked variation in P wave morphology and irregular PP intervals. It occurs commonly in patients with pulmonary disease and in diabetics or older patients who eventually may develop atrial fibrillation. Digitalis is usually not helpful in this arrhythmia, but verapamil may be effective. Therapy is directed toward the underlying disease.

Atrioventricular Junctional Rhythm Disturbances

If suprajunctional pacemakers fail, a *junctional escape rhythm* may emerge at a rate of 35 to 60 beats/min. The junctional escape rhythm is usually fairly regular, but the rate may increase gradually when the escape rhythm first begins (warm-up phenomenon). A junctional rhythm may be associated with retrograde P waves for each QRS complex, or AV dissociation may be present.

Premature junctional complexes arise from the AV junction. A retrograde P wave is usually present but may be prevented by a sinus P wave. They usually do not require therapy.

A regular junctional rhythm with a rate exceeding 60 beats/min (usually between 70 and 130 beats/min) is considered an accelerated junctional rhythm or *nonparoxysmal AV junctional tachycardia*. The gradual onset and termination account for the term nonparoxysmal and may imply that the mechanism of the tachycardia is increased automaticity. Retrograde activation of the atria or AV dissociation may be present. Nonparoxysmal AV junctional tachycardia occurs most commonly in patients with underlying heart disease, such as inferior myocardial infarction, myocarditis, and acute rheumatic fever, or after open heart surgery. The most common cause is digitalis excess. Therapy is directed toward the underlying etiologic factor.

The *paroxysmal supraventricular tachycardias* (PSVTs) are regular tachycardias that occur and terminate suddenly. They are due to a variety of mechanisms, the most common of which are AV nodal re-entry (approximately 60 per cent of cases) and AV re-entry using a concealed accessory bypass tract (approximately 30 per cent of cases). Sinus nodal re-entry, intra-atrial re-entry, and automatic atrial tachycardias account for the remaining PSVTs.

AV nodal re-entry is characterized by narrow QRS complexes (unless functional aberration has occurred), sudden onset and termination, and regular rates, usually between 150 and 250 beats/min. Carotid sinus massage may slow the tachycardia slightly, and if termination occurs, it is abrupt. AV nodal re-entry commonly occurs in patients with no organic heart disease. Symptoms vary according to the rate of the tachycardia and the presence of organic heart disease. In some patients, rest, reassurance, and sedation may abort an attack. Vagal maneuvers including Valsalva, carotid sinus massage, and gagging may terminate the tachycardias and should be repeated after each pharmacologic intervention. Intravenous adenosine, 6 to 12 mg, or verapamil, 5 to 10 mg, terminates AV nodal re-entry in over 95 per cent of cases and is the treatment of choice, should vagal maneuvers fail. If the patient is experiencing hemodynamic compromise, DC cardioversion with low energies is effective. Digoxin, beta blockers, verapamil, and diltiazem are the initial drug choices for chronic therapy, and the type 1 agents are also effective in resistant cases. In patients with drug inefficacy or intolerance, selective catheter ablation of the slow or fast AV nodal pathway should be considered.

PSVT may be caused by re-entry utilizing a retrograde concealed accessory pathway. The presence of the accessory pathway is not evident during sinus rhythm because antegrade conduction is not present, and therefore the ECG manifestations of the Wolff-Parkinson-White syndrome are not evident. However, the mechanism of tachycardia is the same as that in most patients with the Wolff-Parkinson-White syndrome, that is, antegrade conduction over the AV node and retrograde conduction over the accessory pathway. Because it takes a relatively long time for the impulse to travel through the ventricular tissue to the accessory pathway and back to the atrium, the retrograde P wave during this form of tachycardia occurs after completion of the QRS complex, usually in the ST segment or early T wave. In distinction, patients with AV nodal re-entrant tachycardias usually have their retrograde P wave inscribed during or just after the QRS complex, although longer retrograde conduction intervals can occur in AV nodal re-entry. Tachycardia rates tend to be somewhat faster than those in AV nodal re-entry (≥200 per minute), but a great deal of overlap exists. Vagal maneuvers, adenosine, verapamil, and diltiazem are excellent choices for prompt termination. Chronic therapy often involves combinations of drugs that prolong accessory pathway conduction time and refractoriness (e.g., quinidine or flecainide) and drugs slowing AV nodal conduction. Catheter ablation of the accessory pathway is an excellent option.

Pre-excitation Syndromes (Fig. 8–5)

Pre-excitation syndromes occur when ventricular activation occurs earlier than would be expected using the normal AV conduction system. There are several varieties of anomalous AV connections; the most common is the Wolff-Parkinson-White syndrome, in which an accessory AV pathway (the Kent bundle) connects atrium with ventricle, short-circuiting the normal AV conduction system. A portion of the ventricle is activated via conduction over the accessory pathway before the remainder of the ventricle is activated via the normal AV conduction system, and the resultant QRS is a fu-

sion of activation initiated by each of the two (normal and abnormal) AV pathways. Therefore, the PR interval is usually shortened (<0.12 second) and the duration of the QRS is increased (>0.12 second). The initial slurring of the QRS secondary to ventricular pre-excitation is referred to as the delta wave. Although the Wolff-Parkinson-White syndrome has been divided into type A (positive delta wave in V_1 and V_6) and type B (negative delta wave in V_1 and positive delta wave in V_6), this classification system is a gross oversimplification of the many ECG varieties produced by AV connections at different sites and is not very useful clinically. Accessory AV pathways may be located anywhere along the AV ring on either the left or right side or along the septum and are occasionally multiple.

The most common arrhythmia caused by an abnormal AV (Kent) connection is termed *orthodromic* reciprocating tachycardia: the antegrade limb of the re-entrant circuit is the AV node and the retrograde limb is the accessory pathway. *Antidromic* tachycardia utilizes the accessory pathway for the antegrade limb and the AV node as the retrograde limb. In the orthodromic variety, the QRS complexes either are normal or exhibit functional left or right bundle branch block. In the antidromic variety, the QRS complexes are totally pre-excited and consist of a wide, bizarre QRS. Similar pre-excited QRS complexes can occur when an atrial tachyarrhythmia (e.g., atrial fibrillation) results in an extremely rapid ventricular response via the accessory AV connection. Most adults with pre-excitation have normal hearts, although Eb-

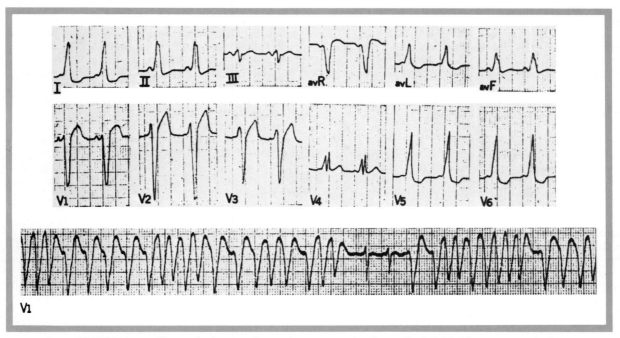

FIGURE 8–5. Pre-excitation syndrome is apparent in the 12-lead ECG (short PR interval, wide QRS, delta wave). During atrial fibrillation the ventricular rate is extremely rapid, at times approaching 350 beats/min. The gross irregularity of the cycle lengths, wide QRS complexes interspersed with normal QRS complexes, and very rapid rate should suggest the diagnosis of atrial fibrillation and an AV bypass tract.

stein's anomaly has an increased incidence of pre-excitation. Sudden death occurs rarely but may be a threat in patients with atrial fibrillation and rapid ventricular responses or in patients with associated congenital anomalies.

Patients who have frequent episodes of tachyarrhythmias and/or in whom the arrhythmias cause significant symptoms should receive therapy. Drugs that prolong refractoriness of the accessory pathway (e.g., quinidine, procainamide, disopyramide, and flecainide) or the AV node (e.g., digitalis, verapamil, and propranolol) may be effective in treating the reciprocating tachycardia; long-term therapy may require one drug from each group. Drugs that prolong accessory pathway refractoriness are effective in slowing the ventricular rate during atrial flutter or atrial fibrillation. Because digitalis has been reported to shorten refractoriness in the accessory pathway and accelerate the ventricular response in some patients with atrial fibrillation, it is advisable not to use digitalis as a single drug in patients with the Wolff-Parkinson-White syndrome. Lidocaine and intravenous verapamil have also been reported to increase the ventricular response during atrial fibrillation in some patients with the Wolff-Parkinson-White syndrome. Termination of an acute episode of orthodromic reciprocating tachycardia may be approached as for AV nodal re-entry, but intravenous verapamil should not be given in patients with atrial fibrillation or flutter. Catheter ablation of accessory pathways is highly effective and safe; it should be considered in any patient with Wolff-Parkinson-White syndrome and symptomatic arrhythmias. Patients with delta waves on their ECG but with no history of tachycardia should generally not be treated.

Ventricular Rhythm Disturbances (Fig. 8–6)

Premature ventricular complexes (PVCs) are premature, bizarrely shaped QRS complexes of prolonged duration differing in contour from the dominant QRS complex. The T wave is large and oriented in the opposite direction from the major QRS deflection. The sinus node and atria are usually not activated prematurely by retrograde conduction from the PVC, and therefore a "compensatory pause" results; that is, the pause after the PVC is sufficiently long that the interval between the two normally conducted QRS complexes flanking the PVC equals two sinus cycle lengths. A PVC that does not produce a pause is termed interpolated. Two successive PVCs are termed a pair or couplet, and three or more successive PVCs are arbitrarily termed ventricular tachycardia. If PVCs have different contours, they are called multifocal, multiform, polymorphic, or pleomorphic. If PVCs are not coupled to the previous QRS, parasystole should be considered; however, many nonparasystolic PVCs do not exhibit fixed coupling. The prevalence of PVCs increases with age. They are often asymptomatic but can give rise to palpitations, or if present in long runs of bigeminy, may produce hypotension, because they are premature and relatively ineffective at ejecting blood. The number of PVCs may increase during infection, ischemia, anesthesia, psychological stress, and excessive use of tobacco, caffeine, or alcohol. In the absence of underlying heart disease, the presence of PVCs probably has no significance regarding longevity or limitation of activity, and antiarrhythmic therapy is not indicated. The presence of PVCs identifies patients at an increased risk of cardiac death if they have coronary artery disease, hypertrophic cardiomyopathy, or mitral valve prolapse; however, treatment of PVCs has not been demonstrated to decrease sudden death. If drug therapy is indicated (usually only in patients with symptoms), lidocaine can be used acutely, and procainamide, quinidine, or disopyramide may be considered for chronic therapy.

Ventricular tachycardia occurs when three or more consecutive PVCs occur with a rate exceeding 100/min. The QRS complexes usually have a prolonged duration and bizarre shape, with ST and T vectors opposite to the major QRS deflection. Atrial activity may be independent of ventricular activity (AV dissociation), or the atrium may be depolarized by the ventricles retrogradely (ventriculoatrial association). QRS contours may be unchanging (uniform) or may vary. The differentiation between sustained and nonsustained ventricular tachycardia is somewhat arbitrary but clinically useful; one guideline is that sustained ventricular tachycardia lasts at least 30 seconds or requires termination prior to 30 seconds because of hemodynamic decompensation.

The ECG distinction between supraventricular tachycardia with abnormal intraventricular conduction and ventricular tachycardia can be difficult. Supraventricular tachycardia may be associated with prolonged QRS complexes when pre-existing bundle branch block is present, functional aberration exists, or conduction over an accessory pathway is present. When fusion or capture QRS complexes occur during a wide-complex tachycardia (that is, early, narrow complexes that are either partially [fusion] or completely [capture] caused by activation from a supraventricular source), the ventricular origin of the tachycardia can be assumed. The identification of AV dissociation, sometimes requiring esophageal or intracardiac recordings to determine atrial activity, is much more characteristic of ventricular than supraventricular tachycardia. However, only about 50 per cent of ventricular tachycardias demonstrate complete AV dissociation. In addition, the following characteristics favor a supraventricular origin: slowing or termination of the tachycardia by increased vagal tone, onset after a premature P wave; RP interval ≤ 100 msec, more atrial impulses than ventricular impulses (e.g., 2:1 AV conduction), initiation of wide complexes after a long/short cycle sequence; and rsR' in V_1. With preceding normal QRS conduction, if left axis deviation or QRS duration of 140 msec or more is

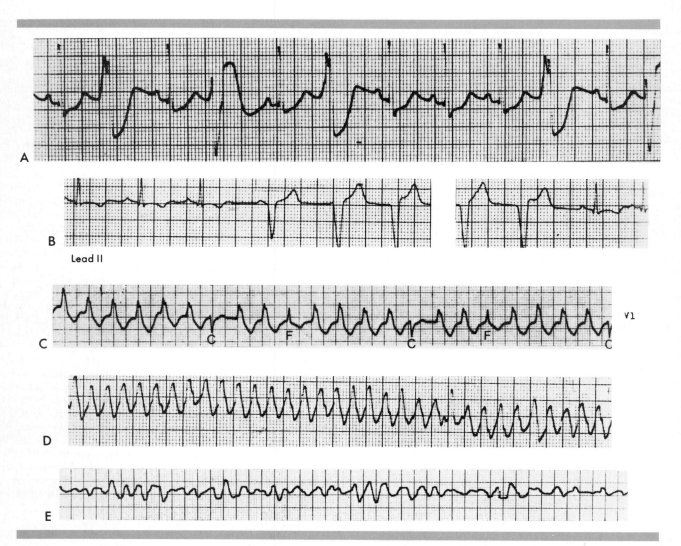

FIGURE 8-6. *A*, Multiform premature ventricular systoles. Each sinus beat is followed by PVCs that have two contours, one predominantly upright and the other predominantly negative. *B*, Accelerated idioventricular rhythm. The sinus rate slows slightly and allows the escape of an idioventricular rhythm. A fusion beat with a short PR interval results. Subsequently the sinus node once again regains control of the ventricular rhythm. *C*, Ventricular tachycardia. A regular wide complex tachycardia is present. Atrial activity is not readily apparent. The complexes marked C and F most likely represent capture and fusion complexes that confirm the ventricular origin of the arrhythmia. *D*, Ventricular flutter. Ventricular depolarization and repolarization appear as a sine wave with regular oscillations. The QRS complex cannot be distinguished from the ST segment or T wave. *E*, Ventricular fibrillation. The baseline is irregular and undulating without any electrical evidence of organized ventricular activity.

present during tachycardia, ventricular tachycardia is likely.

Ventricular tachycardia occurs in patients with ischemic heart disease, congestive and hypertrophic cardiomyopathy, mitral valve prolapse, valvular heart disease, and primary electrical disease (no identifiable structural heart disease). Even short runs of ventricular tachycardia may be important when detected in the late hospital phase of acute myocardial infarction, because the 1-year mortality rate of this group appears to be much greater than for patients without tachycardia.

Deciding when to treat patients with ventricular tachycardia is sometimes difficult. Patients with chronic recurrent sustained ventricular tachycardia and those with symptomatic nonsustained ventricular tachycardia are treated. Treatment of patients with asymptomatic nonsustained ventricular tachycardia is controversial. Acute therapy of ventricular tachycardia is achieved with intravenous lidocaine; if unsuccessful, intravenous procainamide or bretylium may be used. If hypotension, shock, angina, congestive heart failure, or symptoms of cerebral hypoperfusion are present, the rhythm should be terminated promptly with DC cardioversion, beginning with very low energies (10 to 50 joules) synchronized with the QRS. DC cardioversion of digitalis-induced ventricular tachycardia may be hazardous but is sometimes necessary. If ventricular tachycardia is recurrent despite drug therapy, pacing may occasionally be useful for termination. Before chronic drug therapy is instituted, a search for reversible conditions contributing to the arrhythmia should be done; for example, metabolic abnormalities, hypoxia, digitalis excess, and congestive heart failure should be corrected. Effective drugs for chronic therapy include quinidine, procainamide, disopyramide, and mexiletine. Phenytoin is usually not successful unless digitalis toxicity is present, and propranolol is usually unsuccessful unless the ventricular tachycardia is related to ischemia or catecholamine stimulation. Amiodarone is very effective in patients in whom conventional agents have failed. Combinations of drugs are sometimes necessary. Surgery or implantable electrical devices may be considered in patients with ventricular tachycardia refractory to drug therapy.

Accelerated idioventricular rhythm refers to impulse formation originating in the ventricle with a rate of approximately 60 to 110 beats/min. It often competes with the sinus node for control of the heart, and fusion and capture complexes occur commonly. The onset of the arrhythmia is often gradual (nonparoxysmal), and enhanced automaticity is presumed to be the mechanism. Precipitation of more rapid ventricular arrhythmias is not common. The arrhythmia usually occurs in patients with acute myocardial infarction or digitalis toxicity, and suppressive therapy is usually not necessary. If symptoms occur or if more malignant tachyarrhythmias result, therapy as noted above is indicated. Often simply increasing the sinus rate with atropine or atrial pacing suppresses the accelerated idioventricular rhythm.

Ventricular fibrillation generates little or no blood flow and is usually fatal within 3 to 5 minutes unless terminated. Ventricular fibrillation is recognized by the presence of irregular undulations of varying contour and amplitude without distinct QRS complexes, ST segments, or T waves. *Ventricular flutter* appears as a sine wave with regular, large oscillations occurring at a rate of 150 to 300 per minute. Ventricular fibrillation occurs in a variety of situations, including coronary artery disease, antiarrhythmic drug administration, hypoxia, ischemia, atrial fibrillation with rapid ventricular rates in the pre-excitation syndromes, accidental electrical shock, and poorly timed cardioversion. Most patients resuscitated from out-of-hospital cardiac arrest have ventricular fibrillation as their arrhythmia, often without acute myocar-

dial infarction. Treatment is an immediate nonsynchronized DC shock using 200 to 400 joules. If ventricular fibrillation has been present for more than a few minutes, correction of metabolic abnormalities may aid in electrically converting the rhythm, although DC shock should not be delayed to await correction of hypoxia or acidosis. Once ventricular fibrillation has been terminated, medications to prevent recurrence of ventricular fibrillation should be initiated (e.g., lidocaine). Ventricular fibrillation rarely, if ever, terminates on its own and is lethal unless DC shock is applied.

Long QT Syndrome

The term *torsades de pointes* refers to a ventricular tachyarrhythmia characterized by QRS complexes of changing amplitude that appear to twist around the isoelectric line, occurring in the setting of a prolonged QT interval. Episodes of torsades de pointes often terminate spontaneously, but ventricular fibrillation may supervene. The syndrome may be either congenital or acquired. Acquired forms may be caused by any antiarrhythmic drug that prolongs the QT interval (e.g., quinidine, procainamide, or disopyramide) or by psychoactive drugs such as phenothiazines and tricyclic antidepressants. In addition, potassium or magnesium depletion, liquid protein diet, and other metabolic abnormalities may be associated with the long QT syndrome. Acute therapy involves withdrawing the offending drug and correcting metabolic abnormalities. Antiarrhythmic agents that prolong the QT interval may worsen the arrhythmia. Intravenous magnesium, 1 to 2 gm over 5 to 10 minutes, often eliminates the tachycardia. Temporary ventricular or atrial pacing is also effective therapy for suppressing the bursts of polymorphic tachycardia. Isoproterenol has been reported to be effective until pacing is instituted. If a polymorphic ventricular tachycardia resembling torsades de pointes is present but the QT interval is normal, standard antiarrhythmic drugs may be given.

Patients with congenital prolonged QT syndrome who are at increased risk for sudden death include those who have family members who died suddenly at an early age and those who have experienced syncope or torsades de pointes. ECGs should be obtained from all family members when a patient presents with suspected congenital long QT syndrome. Auditory stimuli, psychological stress, and exercise may provoke an arrhythmia in susceptible patients. For patients who have idiopathic long QT syndrome but no syncope, complex ventricular arrhythmias, or family history of sudden cardiac death, no therapy is recommended. In asymptomatic patients with long QT syndrome who have complex ventricular arrhythmias or a family history of premature sudden cardiac death, beta blockers at maximally tolerated doses are recommended. In patients with syncope, beta blockers at maximally tolerated doses, combined with phenytoin or phenobarbital if necessary, are suggested. For patients who continue to have syncope despite drug therapy, left-sided cervicothoracic sympathetic ganglionectomy has been effective, because sympathetic imbalance appears to be important in the pathogenesis of this syndrome.

Heart Block (Fig. 8–7)

Heart block refers to a disturbance of impulse conduction and should be distinguished from interference, a normal phenomenon in which impulse conduction is blocked owing to physiologic refractoriness in the wake of a preceding impulse. Heart block may occur anywhere in the heart but is commonly recognized by ECG in the AV node, His bundle, or bundle branches. In *first-degree AV heart block*, AV conduction time is prolonged (PR interval ≥0.20 second), but all impulses are conducted. *Second-degree heart block* occurs in two forms: *type I second-degree heart block (Wenckebach)* is characterized by a progressive lengthening of the PR interval until a P wave is not conducted. *Type II second-degree AV heart block* denotes occasional or repetitive sudden block of a P wave without prior measurable lengthening of the PR interval. Type II AV block often antedates the development of Stokes-Adams syncope and complete AV block, whereas type I AV block with a normal QRS complex is usually more benign and does not progress to advanced forms of AV conduction disturbances. In the patient with acute myocardial infarction, type I AV block usually accompanies inferior infarction, is transient, and does not require temporary pacing, whereas type II AV block usually accompanies anterior myocardial infarction, may require temporary or permanent pacing, and is associated with a high mortality, mostly due to pump failure. First-degree or type I second-degree AV block can occur in healthy young people, especially well-trained athletes. Any medica-

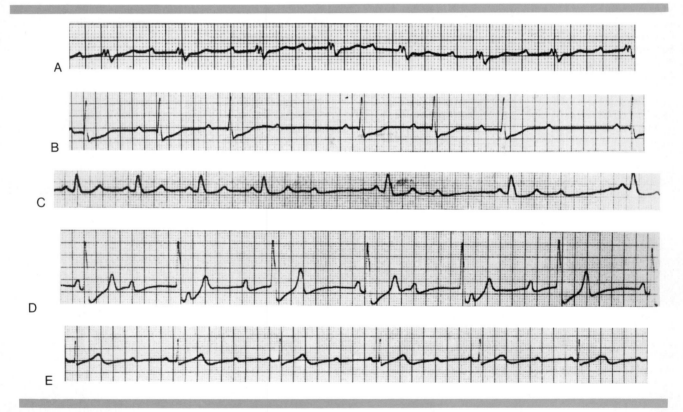

FIGURE 8–7. *A,* First-degree AV block. The PR interval is prolonged. *B,* Second-degree AV block (type I, Wenckebach), characterized by progressive PR prolongation preceding the non-conducted P wave. In the setting of a normal QRS complex, Wenckebach almost always occurs at the level of the AV node. *C,* Second-degree AV block, type II. Left bundle branch block is present in this recording of lead I. Sudden failure of AV conduction results, without antecedent PR prolongation. *D,* Acquired third-degree (complete) AV block. Complete AV dissociation is present owing to complete AV heart block. Atria and ventricles are under control of separate pacemakers, the sinus node and an idioventricular escape rhythm, respectively. *E,* Congenital third-degree (complete) AV block in a young adult at the level of the AV node. The QRS complex is normal.

tion that affects AV nodal conduction (e.g., digitalis, beta blockers, or verapamil) may cause first- or second-degree AV block.

Type I AV block with a normal QRS complex is usually at the level of the AV node proximal to the His bundle. Type II AV block usually occurs in association with a bundle branch block and is localized to the His-Purkinje system. Type I AV block in a patient with a bundle branch block may represent block in either the AV node or the His-Purkinje system. Type II AV block in a patient with a normal QRS complex may be due to intra-His block but is more likely to be type I AV nodal block that exhibits small increments in AV conduction time. Note that 2:1 AV block may represent either AV nodal or His-Purkinje block.

Complete AV block occurs when no atrial activity conducts to the ventricles. The atria and ventricles are controlled by independent pacemakers, and thus complete AV block is one cause of AV dissociation. The ventricular rhythm is usually regular. If the AV block is at the level of the AV node (e.g., congenital AV block), the QRS complexes are normal in morphology and duration, with rates of 40 to 60 per minute, and respond to autonomic influences. If the AV block is in the His-Purkinje system (usually acquired), the escape rhythm originates within the ventricle, has a wide QRS and a slower rate, and is less reliable and under less autonomic influence. Causes of AV block include surgery, electrolyte disturbances, endocarditis, tumor, Chagas' disease, rheumatoid nodules, calcific aortic stenosis, myxedema, polymyositis, infiltrative processes such as amyloid, sarcoid, or scleroderma, drug toxicity, coronary disease, and degenerative processes. In children the most common type of AV block is congenital and is usually asymptomatic; in some, however, symptoms eventually develop, requiring pacemaker implantation. The indications for pacemaker therapy in heart block are summarized in Table 8-6. Atropine (for AV nodal block) and isoproterenol (for heart block at any site) may be used transiently while preparations are made for ventricular pacing. Drugs cannot be relied on to increase the heart rate for more than several hours to a few days without producing significant side effects.

The term *AV dissociation* describes independent depolarization of the atria and ventricles. AV dissociation is not a primary disturbance of rhythm but is a "symptom" of an underlying rhythm disturbance produced by one or a combination of three causes that prevent the normal transmission of impulses from atrium to ventricle:

1. Slowing of the dominant pacemaker of the heart (usually the sinus node), allowing escape of a subsidiary or latent pacemaker. This is AV dissociation by default of the primary pacemaker and is often a normal phenomenon, for example, sinus bradycardia and a junctional escape rhythm.

2. Acceleration of a latent pacemaker that usurps control of the ventricles. This abnormally enhanced discharge rate of a usually slower sub-

sidiary pacemaker is pathologic, for example, junctional or ventricular tachycardia.

3. Block at the AV junction that prevents impulses formed at a normal rate in a dominant pacemaker from reaching the ventricles so that the ventricles beat under the control of a subsidiary pacemaker, for example, complete AV block with a ventricular escape rhythm. It is important to remember that complete AV dissociation is not synonymous with complete AV block.

Syncope (See also Chapter 114)

Syncope refers to sudden transient loss of consciousness, usually due to transient cerebral hypoperfusion. Presyncope is described as a lightheaded spell that, if more prolonged, would cause loss of consciousness. Both may occur in the same patient and have similar etiologies. The causes of syncope are summarized in Table 8-8.

Cardiac syncope is due either to lesions that obstruct outflow of blood from the heart or to arrhythmias. In patients with severe aortic stenosis or other causes of obstructive syncope, when the systemic vascular resistance decreases upon exercise, the heart is unable to augment cardiac output sufficiently to maintain perfusion and syncope results. Both tachyarrhythmias and bradyarrhythmias that result in cerebral hypoperfusion can cause cardiac syncope. The hypersensitive carotid sinus syndrome, described earlier, is a well-recognized cause of syncope.

The history and physical examination are valuable in excluding many causes of syncope (Table 8-8). Even though the ECG may not reveal the actual arrhythmia causing syncope, ECG clues (e.g., the presence of simple or complex ventricular ectopy, evidence of a previous myocardial infarction, or the delta wave of the Wolff-Parkinson-White syndrome) may suggest potential arrhythmic causes. Prolonged ECG recording may be the cornerstone of diagnosis in arrhythmic syncope. On most occasions, more than 24 hours of recording are required to detect the responsible arrhythmia and a patient-activated event recorder is necessary. Exercise testing is also valuable in some patients whose arrhythmias are exercise-induced. Patients with obstructive syncope such as aortic stenosis should not undergo exercise testing. Reproduction of symptoms with upright tilt testing (see above) is valuable in patients with vasovagal syncope. In selected patients invasive electrophysiologic studies may be useful to delineate the etiology of the syncope.

Sudden Cardiac Death

The most commonly used definition of sudden death is unexpected, nontraumatic death occurring within an hour after the onset of symptoms. Sudden cardiac death claims approximately 1200 lives daily in the United States and is the leading

TABLE 8–8. CAUSES OF SYNCOPE

CAUSE	FEATURES
Peripheral Vascular or Circulatory	
Vasovagal syncope (neurally mediated)	Prodrome of pallor, yawning, nausea, diaphoresis; precipitated by stress or pain; occurs when patient is upright, aborted by recumbency; fall in blood pressure without appropriate rise in heart rate
Micturition syncope	Syncope with urination (probably vagal)
Post-tussive syncope	Syncope after paroxysm of coughing
Hypersensitive carotid sinus syndrome	Vasodepressor and/or cardioinhibitory responses with light carotid sinus massage (see text)
Drugs	Orthostasis
	Occurs with antihypertensive drugs, tricyclic antidepressants, phenothiazines
Volume depletion	Orthostasis
	Occurs with hemorrhage, excessive vomiting or diarrhea, Addison's disease
Autonomic dysfunction	Orthostasis
	Occurs in diabetes, alcoholism, Parkinson's disease, deconditioning after a prolonged illness
Central Nervous System	
Cerebrovascular	Transient ischemic attacks and strokes are unusual causes of syncope; associated neurologic abnormalities are usually present
Seizures	Warning aura sometimes present, jerking of extremities, tongue biting, urinary incontinence, postictal confusion
Metabolic	
Hypoglycemia	Confusion, tachycardia, jitteriness prior to syncope; patient may be taking insulin
Cardiac	
Obstructive	Syncope is often exertional; physical findings consistent with aortic stenosis, hypertrophic obstructive cardiomyopathy, cardiac tamponade, atrial myxoma, prosthetic valve malfunction, Eisenmenger's syndrome, tetralogy of Fallot, primary pulmonary hypertension, pulmonic stenosis, massive pulmonary embolism
Arrhythmias	Syncope may be sudden and occurs in any position; episodes of dizziness or palpitations; may be a history of heart disease; brady- or tachyarrhythmias may be responsible—check for hypersensitive carotid sinus

cause of death among men between the ages of 20 and 60. By far the most common cause of sudden death is cardiac, and within that group, the most common cause is ventricular tachyarrhythmias.

Nonarrhythmic causes of sudden death are listed in Table 8–9.

Ventricular tachyarrhythmias, generally related to ischemic heart disease, are the most common

TABLE 8–9. SELECTED CAUSES OF SUDDEN DEATH

Noncardiac
  Central nervous system hemorrhage
  Massive pulmonary embolus
  Drug overdose
  Hypoxia secondary to lung disease
  Aortic dissection or rupture
Cardiac
  Ventricular tachycardia
  Bradyarrhythmias, sick sinus syndrome
  Aortic stenosis
  Tetralogy of Fallot
  Pericardial tamponade
  Cardiac tumors
  Complications of infective endocarditis
  Hypertrophic cardiomyopathy (arrhythmia or obstruction)
  Myocardial ischemia
    Atherosclerosis
    Prinzmetal's angina
    Kawasaki's arteritis

cause of sudden cardiac death. Although 75 per cent of patients resuscitated from ventricular fibrillation have extensive coronary artery disease, only 20 per cent have evidence of acute transmural myocardial infarction. Approximately 75 per cent of patients who experience sudden death have a previous history of cardiac disease; sudden death is the first manifestation of cardiac disease in the remainder. The difference in occurrence of sudden death in patients with (2 per cent at 1 year) and without (22 per cent at 1 year) acute myocardial infarction may be due to different arrhythmia mechanisms. Patients with ventricular fibrillation at the time of an acute myocardial infarction probably do not need long-term antiarrhythmic therapy unless chronic late ventricular tachycardia is documented. The risk of recurrent ventricular fibrillation is higher if there is evidence of left ventricular dysfunction or evidence of previous myocardial infarction. Nonatherosclerotic etiologies of ventricular tachyarrhythmias associated with sudden death are mitral valve prolapse, hypertrophic or other cardiomyopathies, antiarrhythmic drugs, myocarditis, prolonged QT syndrome, and Wolff-Parkinson-White syndrome with rapid antegrade conduction over an accessory pathway.

The identification of patients at high risk for sudden cardiac death can be difficult (Table 8–

10). The occurrence of complex ventricular ectopy, including multiform PVCs, pairs, and ventricular tachycardia in survivors of myocardial infarction, is associated with a two- to threefold increase in subsequent sudden death; however, suppression of ventricular ectopy with antiarrhythmic agents has not been proven to decrease and possibly could increase the incidence of sudden death. The risk of sudden cardiac death and the incidence of complex ectopy are greater in patients with poor left ventricular function.

The signal-averaged ECG is a computerized technique that averages multiple QRS complexes to reduce noise and allow detection of low-amplitude, high-frequency potentials occurring just after the inscription of the QRS complex; these "late potentials" correspond to delayed and fragmented conduction in areas of the ventricle that are responsible for ventricular tachycardia. They are present in 73 to 92 per cent of patients with sustained and inducible ventricular tachycardia after myocardial infarction, 0 to 6 per cent of normal volunteers, and 7 to 15 per cent of patients after myocardial infarction who do not have ventricular tachycardia. Late potentials after myocardial infarction constitute an independent risk factor that detects patients prone to develop ventricular tachycardia and can be combined with other data such as ejection fraction, spontaneous ventricular ectopy, or responses to stress testing to recognize with high sensitivity and specificity patients at risk for ventricular tachycardia or sudden cardiac death. It can also be used to detect patients with nonsustained ventricular tachycardia or syncope who may develop sustained ventricular tachycardia at electrophysiologic study.

The patient who has suffered sudden cardiac arrest in the absence of acute myocardial infarction and the patient with recurrent symptomatic ventricular tachyarrhythmias must be treated with antiarrhythmic therapy. The end point of antiarrhythmic therapy to be used to judge efficacy is often unclear. The mere attainment of "therapeutic" serum levels of an antiarrhythmic agent is not usually sufficient to guard against recurrent ventricular tachyarrhythmias. Prolonged ECG monitoring is noninvasive, simple, and widely available. However, many patients with sudden death demonstrate very little spontaneous ectopy between episodes; therefore, suppression of spontaneous ectopy cannot be used as an end point in these patients. In addition, even in patients with spontaneous ectopy, it is not clear whether an appropriate end point would be elimination of all ventricular tachycardia, all complex ectopy, or all PVCs. Drug evaluation using exercise testing and prolonged ambulatory recording to judge efficacy has been reported to decrease the incidence of recurrent malignant tachyarrhythmias but can be used only in patients with spontaneous high-grade ventricular ectopy between episodes of sustained tachyarrhythmia. Most investigators believe that patients experiencing sudden cardiac arrest in the absence of acute myocardial infarction should undergo serial electrophysiologic testing to guide an-

TABLE 8 – 10. RISK FACTORS FOR SUDDEN CARDIAC DEATH AFTER MYOCARDIAL INFARCTION

1. Decreased left ventricular function (ejection fraction <40%)
2. Residual ischemia
3. Complex ventricular ectopy
4. Late potentials on signal-averaged ECG
5. Evidence of decreased vagal effect (blunted sinus cycle length variability or carotid baroreceptor sensitivity)
6. Induction of sustained monomorphic ventricular tachycardia with programmed ventricular stimulation

tiarrhythmic therapy. The suppression with a drug of ventricular tachycardia inducible by electrical stimulation appears to provide a better indicator of drug success than suppression of spontaneous ectopy and can be used in patients with little or no spontaneous ectopy. If arrhythmias cannot be suppressed or slowed with drug therapy, or if there is no reliable indicator of drug efficacy, then the ICD and cardiac surgery are options. Coronary artery revascularization alone is usually not sufficient to prevent recurrent ventricular tachyarrhythmias.

Antiarrhythmic therapy in patients after myocardial infarction as prophylaxis for malignant cardiac arrhythmias has not been proven effective. Several large multicenter studies have demonstrated a decrease in the incidence of sudden death in patients treated with beta-adrenergic receptor blocking agents after myocardial infarction, and these drugs probably should be considered if no contraindication to their administration exists.

Principles of Cardiopulmonary Resuscitation

Cardiopulmonary resuscitation consists of basic and advanced life support. Upon evaluating a patient with suspected cardiac arrest, one should first quickly establish that the patient is truly unresponsive and not breathing. If a pulse is not present, a precordial thump to the midsternum may be tried. Subsequently, the "ABCs" of basic life support should be observed: Airway, Breathing, and Circulation. The mouth and pharynx should be examined to ensure that no obstruction is present. The tongue should be removed from the posterior pharynx by tilting the head backward and hyperextending the neck. This maneuver can sometimes cause resumption of spontaneous respiration. If no breathing is noted, mouth-to-mouth or mouth-to-nose breathing should be initiated in four quick breaths. Time is often wasted trying to intubate a patient when adequate ventilation could be accomplished immediately via mouth or mask ventilation. One should check to see that the chest rises with each ventilation. If a carotid pulse is not present after the initial ventilations, external cardiac compression over the lower half of the sternum (not over the xiphoid process) should be initiated. The sternum should be depressed 3 to 5 cm, with the patient lying on a hard surface. Compressions should be approximately 80 to 100 per minute, with a ratio of 5 compressions to 1 ventilation if two rescuers are present. A single rescuer must give 15 chest compressions alternating with 2 ventilations.

Advanced life support should be initiated while basic life support continues. Defibrillation should be applied if indicated as soon as possible and *is the single most definitive treatment available for most cardiac arrests.* Oxygen should be administered and an adequate intravenous access should be established. If circulation has not been restored quickly, sodium bicarbonate (1 mEq/kg IV) is given to treat metabolic acidosis and is repeated after 10 minutes; further administration of sodium bicarbonate should be guided by blood gas and pH measurements once effective circulation is restored. Epinephrine (5 to 10 ml of a 1:10,000 solution administered via an intravenous, intracardiac, or endotracheal route every 5 minutes as needed) is useful in treating asystole and also in aiding defibrillation of fine (low-amplitude) ventricular fibrillation. Atropine (boluses of 0.5 mg IV at 5-minute intervals to a total dose of approximately 2 to 4 mg) can be administered for profound bradycardia. Isoproterenol given as a constant infusion (2 to 20 μg/min) and titrated according to response may be used to treat bradyarrhythmias if atropine is ineffective. Emergency cardiac pacing may be attempted for bradyarrhythmias if atropine and isoproterenol are unsuccessful.

Lidocaine, procainamide, or bretylium tosylate can be administered to help terminate ventricular tachyarrhythmias and prevent their recurrence. Intravenous furosemide and/or morphine may be used to relieve pulmonary edema. Calcium chloride (2.5 to 5 ml of a 10 per cent solution repeated, if necessary, in 10 minutes) is given to increase myocardial contractility, especially if electromechanical dissociation is present. Calcium should be used with caution in a patient with known digitalis excess. Calcium chloride precipitates if given in the same intravenous line with sodium bicarbonate.

Electromechanical dissociation refers to the presence of cardiac electrical activity without appropriate mechanical activity. It may be caused by decreased filling of the heart (e.g., hypovolemia, cardiac tamponade, pulmonary embolus) or severe myocardial pump depression that may respond to calcium. Emergency pericardiocentesis may be attempted if cardiac tamponade is suspected.

The widespread application of cardiopulmonary resuscitation via education of the public and extensive emergency care systems in many cities has increased both the number of cardiac arrest victims who reach the hospital and the number who survive to be discharged. Survival critically depends on the time from arrest to the initiation of resuscitation and is best if basic life support can be initiated within 3 to 4 minutes and more definitive therapy (i.e., defibrillation) shortly thereafter.

REFERENCES

Benditt DG, Benson DW (eds): Cardiac Preexcitation Syndrome: Origins, Evaluation, and Treatment. Boston, Martinus Nijhoff, 1986.
Dreifus LS (chairman): ACC/AHA Task Force. Guidelines for implantation of cardiac pacemakers and antiarrhythmia devices. J Am Coll Cardiol 18:1, 1991.
Gallagher JJ, Selle JG, Svenson RH, Fedor JM, Zimmern SH, Sealy WC, Rodicsek FR: Surgical treatment of arrhythmias. Am J Cardiol 61:27A, 1988.
Mason JW: Drug therapy: Amiodarone. N Engl J Med 316:455–466, 1987.
Scheinman MM, Laks MM, DiMarco J, Plumb V: Current role of catheter ablation procedures in patients with cardiac arrhythmias. Circulation 83:2146, 1991.
Standards and guidelines for cardiopulmonary resuscitation (CPR) and emergency cardiac care (ECC). JAMA 255:2905, 1986.
The Cardiac Arrhythmia Suppression Trial (CAST) Investigators: Preliminary report: Effect of encainide and flecainide on mortality in a randomized trial of arrhythmia suppression after myocardial infarction. N Engl J Med 321:406, 1989.
Zipes DP: Cardiac arrhythmias. In Braunwald E (ed): Heart Disease. A Textbook of Cardiovascular Medicine. 4th ed. Philadelphia, WB Saunders Co, 1992.
Zipes DP (ed): An Update on Cardiac Arrhythmias I & II. Progress in Cardiology, 1988.
Zipes DP, Jalife J (eds): Cardiac Electrophysiology: From Cell to Bedside. Philadelphia, WB Saunders Co, 1990.
Zipes DP (chairman): ACC/AHA guidelines for clinical intracardiac electrophysiologic studies. J Am Coll Cardiol 14:1827, 1989.

9 MYOCARDIAL AND PERICARDIAL DISEASE

MYOCARDIAL DISEASE

Myocarditis

Acute myocardial inflammation is termed myocarditis and may be associated with fever, dyspnea, edema, fatigue, palpitations, and pleuropericardial pain. Myocarditis is frequently not clinically apparent and is suspected only on the basis of ST and T wave changes or a transient conduction defect on electrocardiography (ECG) in a patient with a systemic illness. Physical examination may reveal signs of pericarditis or biventricular cardiac failure. Intraventricular or atrioventricular (AV) conduction disturbances or arrhythmias may occur.

Therapy is usually supportive. Congestive heart failure responds to routine management with digitalis, diuresis, and afterload reduction. Significant arrhythmias should be treated with antiarrhythmic agents. Steroids may be of benefit in acute rheumatic carditis but should be avoided in suspected infectious myocarditis. Immunosuppressive therapy may be helpful in selected patients.

Most patients recover completely. An unknown percentage of patients, probably small, develop a chronic process leading to a dilated cardiomyopathy after a varying latency period.

Infectious agents cause myocarditis by three basic mechanisms: (1) invasion of the myocardium; (2) production of a myocardial toxin, as, for example, in diphtheria; and (3) autoimmunity, as in acute rheumatic fever. The infectious agents are multiple, most commonly thought to be viral, especially Coxsackie group B. Primary bacterial myocarditis is a rare but grave complication of bacterial endocarditis, most often caused by streptococci or staphylococci. *Mycoplasma pneumoniae* infections, toxoplasmosis, trichinosis, and rickettsial diseases such as Rocky Mountain spotted fever are associated with myocarditis. Protozoal myocarditis from trypanosomiasis (Chagas' disease) is common in Central and South America, where it is a frequent cause of chronic congestive cardiomyopathy, heart block, and ventricular arrhythmias. Hypersensitivity reactions to various agents and radiation therapy can result in inflammation of the myocardium. A myocarditis associated with the acquired immunodeficiency syndrome has been described.

Cardiomyopathy

Cardiomyopathy, a disease involving the heart muscle itself, is classified into three basic categories (Table 9-1). This classification is not rigid, and some cardiomyopathies may demonstrate characteristics that overlap among the three groups.

Dilated Cardiomyopathy

In dilated cardiomyopathy, ventricular enlargement occurs and systolic dysfunction results in symptoms of congestive heart failure. The cause of dilated cardiomyopathy is often not apparent but appears to be the end result of myocardial damage produced by a variety of toxic, metabolic, and infectious agents (Table 9-2). Clinical symptoms usually develop slowly, and patients may have ventricular dysfunction for some time before symptoms, usually of both left and right ventricular failure, appear. Q waves may be present on the ECG without infarction when extensive left ventricular fibrosis has occurred. Echocardiography is important in excluding other causes of congestive heart failure. A pericardial effusion is sometimes present. Ventriculography shows enlargement of the left ventricle with diffuse wall motion reduction and sometimes left ventricular thrombi. Functional mitral regurgitation may be present, and occasionally it is difficult to distinguish from primary mitral regurgitation. The coronary arteries are normal or incidentally involved. Endomyocardial biopsy may sometimes be useful in diagnosing patients with cardiomyopathy.

Peripartum cardiomyopathy refers to congestive cardiomyopathy occurring in the last month of pregnancy or within 5 months of delivery in the absence of pre-existing heart disease. It occurs most frequently in multiparous blacks and is more common in older women and those with poor nutrition, poor prenatal care, or toxemia. Doxorubicin (Adriamycin) is an effective antitumor drug that commonly produces congestive cardiomyopathy. The risk of toxicity appears to be related to the cumulative dose, increasing as the dose increases but with a relatively abrupt rise in risk after approximately 450 to 550 mg/m². The prognosis after the development of symptoms is extremely poor.

TABLE 9—1. CLASSIFICATION OF CARDIOMYOPATHY

TYPE	CHARACTERISTICS	SYMPTOMS AND SIGNS	LABORATORY DIAGNOSIS
Dilated (congestive)	Cardiac dilation, generalized hypocontractility	LV and RV failure (see Table 2–4)	X-ray: cardiomegaly with pulmonary congestion ECG: sinus tachycardia, nonspecific ST-T changes, arrhythmias, conduction disturbances, Q waves Echo: dilated LV, generalized decreased wall motion, mitral valve motion consistent with low flow Catheterization: dilated hypocontractile ventricle, mitral regurgitation
Hypertrophic	Ventricular hypertrophy, especially the septum, with or without outflow tract obstruction Typically good systolic but poor diastolic (compliance) ventricular function	Dyspnea, angina, presyncope, syncope, palpitations Large jugular a wave, bifid carotid pulse, palpable S_4 gallop, prominent apical impulse, "dynamic" systolic murmur and thrill, mitral regurgitation murmur	X-ray: LV predominance, dilated left atrium ECG: left ventricular hypertrophy, Q waves, nonspecific ST-T waves, ventricular arrhythmias Echo: hypertrophy, usually asymmetric (septum > free wall); systolic anterior motion of mitral valve; midsystolic closure of aortic valve Catheterization: provokable outflow tract gradient, hypertrophy with vigorous systolic function and cavity obliteration, mitral regurgitation
Restrictive	Reduced diastolic compliance impeding ventricular filling, normal systolic function	Dyspnea, exercise intolerance, weakness Elevated jugular venous pressure, edema, hepatomegaly, ascites, S_4 and S_3 gallops, Kussmaul's sign	X-ray: mild cardiomegaly, pulmonary congestion ECG: low voltage, conduction disturbances, Q waves Echo: characteristic myocardial texture in amyloidosis with thickening of all cardiac structures Catheterization: square root sign, M-shaped atrial waveform, elevated left- and right-sided filling pressures

LV = Left ventricular; RV = Right ventricular; ECG = Electrocardiogram.

Hypertrophic Cardiomyopathy

Hypertrophic cardiomyopathy is characterized by myocardial hypertrophy, especially involving the interventricular septum. In many patients a dynamic pressure gradient can be detected in the subvalvular left ventricular outflow tract (hypertrophic obstructive cardiomyopathy or idiopathic hypertrophic subaortic stenosis). This gradient demonstrates wide fluctuations in severity and often is not present at rest, requiring physiologic or pharmacologic maneuvers to be precipitated. Even though much attention has been focused on the systolic gradient, the most characteristic pathophysiologic abnormality in this syndrome is not systolic but rather diastolic dysfunction, characterized by abnormal stiffness of the left ventricle with impaired filling. Therefore, pulmonary venous pressures are elevated, and dyspnea is the most common symptom despite a typically hypercontractile left ventricle. In many patients the disease appears to be transmitted genetically as an autosomal dominant disorder with a high degree of penetrance, but sporadic cases do occur. Hypertrophy can involve predominantly the septum (asymmetric septal hypertrophy) or the septum and free wall equally (concentric left ventricular hypertrophy). Hypertrophied and bizarrely arranged myocardial cells are commonly but not always visualized pathologically, especially in the septum.

Signs and symptoms in hypertrophic cardiomyopathy are summarized in Table 9–1. A large jugular venous "a" wave may be present on physical examination owing to reduced compliance of the right ventricle. The carotid arterial upstroke is brisk and bifid in character, with a rapid initial rise, a midsystolic dip, and a second late systolic rise characteristic of the dynamic outflow tract obstruction (see Fig. 2–2). The systolic outflow murmur typically is harsh, is crescendo-decrescendo, is often heard best between the apex and left sternal border, and radiates to the lower sternum, axilla, and base of the heart but often not into the neck. A murmur of concomitant mitral regurgitation is not uncommon. The systolic outflow murmur is said to be "dynamic" because its intensity varies inversely with the dimensions of the outflow tract. The outflow tract becomes larger with an increase in ventricular diastolic volume, an increase in systolic pressure against which the heart must pump, or a decrease in myocardial inotropic state. The outflow tract narrows with reversal of these factors (Table 9–3).

Left ventricular hypertrophy is common on the ECG, and large Q waves, probably related to abnormal septal depolarization, may simulate septal myocardial infarction. Atrial fibrillation and other tachyarrhythmias are poorly tolerated because of the hemodynamic abnormalities.

Echocardiography is the best technique for visualizing the hypertrophic myocardium and asymmetric septal hypertrophy. It is useful for screening family members of patients with hypertrophic cardiomyopathy. Narrowing of the left ventricular outflow tract by systolic anterior motion of the anterior leaflet of the mitral valve is characteristic of patients with obstructive cardiomyopathy, and the degree of systolic anterior motion appears to correlate with the degree of obstruction. The aortic valve may close partially in midsystole owing to the dynamic outflow obstruction; this finding, in addition to the systolic anterior motion, may be provoked with pharmacologic manipulations (e.g., amyl nitrate, nitroglycerin, or isoproterenol). Mitral valve prolapse is sometimes observed along with evidence of a small left ventricular cavity and poor left ventricular compliance.

At cardiac catheterization, the systolic subvalvular gradient may or may not be present at rest, and provocative maneuvers such as administration of nitroglycerin or amyl nitrate, isoproterenol infusion, and inducing of premature ventricular contractions (PVCs) may provoke a gradient. The left ventricular end-diastolic pressure and a wave are elevated. Angiography demonstrates marked thickening of the ventricular septum and left ventricular free wall, with large papillary muscles distorting the ventricular shape and producing a characteristic hourglass configuration. The left ventricular cavity is usually small and systolic function vigorous, resulting in virtual obliteration of the ventricular cavity with systole. Mitral regurgitation is common.

The clinical course is variable, although symptoms may remain stable over a period of several years. Symptoms are often unrelated to the presence or severity of a gradient. Ventricular arrhythmias are common, and sudden death may occur even in previously asymptomatic individuals. Any protective effect of medical therapy against arrhythmias is unproven, but one study

TABLE 9–2. CAUSES OF DILATED CARDIOMYOPATHY

Idiopathic
Infectious
  Viral
  Parasitic (e.g., Chagas' disease)
Toxins
  Alcohol
  Cobalt
  Doxorubicin
Radiation
Systemic diseases
  Connective tissue diseases (e.g., systemic lupus erythematosus)
  Sarcoidosis
  Hemochromatosis
Metabolic disorders
  Thyrotoxicosis
  Myxedema
  Beriberi
  Starvation
  Glycogen storage diseases
  Mucopolysaccharidoses
Neuromuscular disorders (e.g., certain muscular dystrophies)
Peripartum cardiomyopathy

has suggested that survival is prolonged by amiodarone therapy.

Interventions that decrease ventricular contractility, increase ventricular volume, increase systemic arterial pressure, increase the dimensions of the outflow tract, or increase ventricular compliance decrease symptoms and the converse. Digitalis should not be used unless atrial fibrillation with a rapid ventricular response or left ventricular dilation and dysfunction without a gradient occur. Diuretics should be used with caution, as hypovolemia increases obstruction and symptoms. Beta-adrenergic receptor blockade can prevent the increase in outflow tract gradient that may occur with exercise; its efficacy at preventing sudden death has not been established. It also has antianginal effects. It can be used in large doses (propranolol, ≥ 320 mg/day) if not limited by contraindications, but the overall efficacy of beta blockers

TABLE 9–3. BEHAVIOR OF THE DYNAMIC OUTFLOW MURMUR IN HYPERTROPHIC OBSTRUCTIVE CARDIOMYOPATHY

MANEUVERS	PHYSIOLOGY	INTENSITY OF MURMUR
Valsalva Standing Amyl nitrate	Decrease LV cavity size	↑
Isoproterenol Squatting Phenylephrine Elevation of legs Isometric exercise (handgrip)	Increase contractility Increase LV cavity size	↓

LV = Left ventricular; ↑ = increased; ↓ = decreased.

is disappointing. Calcium channel blockers, such as verapamil, decrease myocardial contractility and probably decrease the outflow gradient. More important, both verapamil and nifedipine appear to improve the diastolic function (i.e., compliance) of the hypertrophic myocardium. Verapamil can exacerbate poor left ventricular contractility if present. Nifedipine has less negative inotropic effect but is a more potent vasodilator, which may be disadvantageous. Combined administration of a beta blocker and calcium antagonist may be effective in some patients. Patients with hypertrophic cardiomyopathy should receive endocarditis prophylaxis, since infection may occur on the aortic or mitral valve or on the endocardium at the site of septal contact of the anterior mitral leaflet. In the patient who is markedly symptomatic owing to an outflow gradient and has not responded to medical management, septal myotomy-myectomy may be performed. This procedure usually relieves obstruction as well as mitral regurgitation.

Restrictive Cardiomyopathy

Restrictive cardiomyopathies are less common than the dilated and hypertrophic varieties. They are caused by a variety of infiltrative processes, including amyloidosis, hemochromatosis, sarcoidosis, endomyocardial fibrosis, Löffler's endocarditis, and Fabry's disease. Restrictive cardiomyopathy is characterized by abnormal diastolic function that impedes ventricular filling. Contractile function is usually relatively normal. Restrictive cardiomyopathy is often difficult to distinguish from constrictive pericarditis, and endomyocardial biopsy may sometimes be necessary to make the distinction. Ventricular pressure recordings reveal a deep nadir in early diastole with a rapid rise to a plateau, termed the "square root" sign. The atrial pressure tracing demonstrates a corresponding prominent y descent with a rapid rise and plateau. The x descent and a wave are also often prominent, resulting in a characteristic M-shaped waveform. The left-sided filling pressures are often higher than the right-sided pressures, in contrast to the equalization of pressures in constrictive pericarditis.

Signs and symptoms are listed in Table 9–1. Kussmaul's sign (an inspiratory increase in central venous pressure) may be present. The apical impulse is usually palpable, in distinction to constrictive pericarditis.

Amyloidosis is characterized by deposition in many tissues of an amorphous, hyalin-like substance and is the most common cause of restrictive cardiomyopathy. In addition, it sometimes may cause systolic dysfunction and symptoms more typical of a dilated cardiomyopathy. Arrhythmias and conduction disturbances are common. The ECG in cardiac amyloidosis is usually abnormal and often demonstrates generalized decreased voltage. Q waves from myocardial infiltration may simulate myocardial infarction. Echocar-

diography reveals increased thickness of all cardiac structures, including the ventricular walls, the atrial septum, and the cardiac valves. A characteristic sparkling texture of the myocardium is typical on echocardiography. Diagnosis is made by biopsy of various tissues; if necessary, endomyocardial left or right ventricular biopsies may be performed. There is no treatment for the cardiac manifestations of amyloidosis, and the disease is slowly progressive. Digoxin must be used with caution because patients are particularly sensitive to its toxic effects. Pacemaker implantation may be necessary in patients who develop AV block. Death from congestive heart failure as well as sudden death, presumably due to arrhythmias, occurs.

PERICARDIAL DISEASE

Acute Pericarditis

Inflammation of the pericardial lining around the heart from a variety of causes (Table 9–4) is termed acute pericarditis. Its typical manifestations include chest pain, a pericardial friction rub, and characteristic ECG changes. Chest pain, often localized substernally or to the left of the sternum, is usually worsened by lying down, coughing, and deep inspiration, and is relieved somewhat by sitting up and leaning forward. There is often adjacent pleural involvement. The pericardial friction rub, diagnostic of pericarditis, is a scratchy, high-pitched sound that has from one to three components corresponding to atrial systole, ventricular systole, and early diastolic ventricular filling. The ventricular systolic component is present most consistently. The rub is often transient; its absence does not exclude the diagnosis of pericarditis, and its presence does not exclude the existence of a large pericardial effusion. The rub often is best heard with the diaphragm of the stethoscope as the patient sits forward at forced end expiration. Single-component friction rubs must be differentiated from systolic cardiac murmurs, the sound of skin rubbing against the diaphragm of the stethoscope, and the crunching sound of mediastinal air.

The ECG may be diagnostic, especially if obtained serially, and reveals ST segment elevation with upright T waves at the onset of chest pain (Fig. 9–1). The ST elevation is characteristic in all leads except aV_R and V_1. The ST segments are often concave upward, in contrast to those of acute myocardial infarction, but this distinction is often difficult or impossible to make. Reciprocal ST segment depression, as is seen in acute myocardial infarction, generally does not occur. Several days later, the ST segments characteristically return to normal, and the T waves begin to flatten. Subsequently, diffuse T wave inversion develops, usually after the ST segments return to normal, in contrast to the typical pattern of myocardial infarction. Weeks to months later, the T waves usually return to normal but may remain abnormal indefinitely. The PR segment may be depressed, reflecting atrial injury. The ECG

TABLE 9-4. CAUSES OF PERICARDITIS

CAUSE	FEATURE	THERAPY
Idiopathic	Specific etiology not identified	Symptomatic: aspirin, nonsteroidal anti-inflammatory agents, short course of steroids if pain persists
	Common; symptoms and natural history resemble those of viral pericarditis	
Viral	Prodromal syndrome resembling a "cold"	Symptomatic
Coxsackie B, echovirus, measles, mumps, influenza, infectious mononucleosis, poliomyelitis, varicella, hepatitis B, cytomegalovirus	Typical pericardial pain, rub, ECG changes	
	Usually self-limited, lasts 1-3 wk	
	Associated myocarditis, recurrent pericarditis, tamponade, and later development of constrictive pericarditis occur infrequently	
Purulent pericarditis	Associated with postoperative infection, endocarditis, hematogenous or contiguous spread	Surgical drainage, antibiotics
Staphylococcus, streptococcus, pneumococcus	High mortality; patients appear acutely ill: fever, chills, sweats, dyspnea; typical pericardial chest pain is unusual	
	If suspected, pericardial fluid must be obtained immediately for examination	
Tuberculosis	Develops slowly; low-grade fever, malaise, anorexia, weight loss, dyspnea; typical pericardial chest pain is unusual	Antituberculosis agents, pericardiectomy for constriction
	X-ray findings of tuberculosis are usually absent; tuberculin skin test is positive if patient is not anergic	
	Constrictive pericarditis is common; pericardium may be calcified on x-ray	
	Diagnostic yield is much higher if pericardial tissue as well as fluid is examined and cultured	
Histoplasmosis	Usually occurs with a self-limited pulmonary infection	Usually not treated with antifungal agents
	Large pericardial effusions with tamponade are common; constriction is uncommon	
	Difficult to culture; serologic tests are usually positive	
	Hilar adenopathy is common on x-ray	
Pericarditis after myocardial infarction (see Chapter 7)	Early form (usually 1-4 days after transmural infarction) is probably due to local irritation and is self-limited	Symptomatic
	Later form (>10 days after infarction, Dressler's syndrome) is probably immunologic in etiology and tends to recur	
Postpericardiectomy syndrome	Similar to Dressler's syndrome; usually occurs 1-4 wk after cardiac surgery	
Cardiac trauma	Penetrating or nonpenetrating trauma	
	Pericarditis can occur early owing to direct pericardial injury or late, analogous to Dressler's syndrome	
Uremia	Large effusions with tamponade are common	May respond to vigorous dialysis, but pericardiectomy is sometimes necessary
Neoplasm	Large effusions with tamponade are common	Needle or surgical drainage, systemic or local chemotherapy
	Most commonly due to metastatic lung and breast carcinoma, leukemia, lymphoma, and melanoma	
	Tumor cells are often detectable in pericardial fluid	
Radiation	Usually doses >4000 rads to the heart	Symptomatic, pericardiectomy if constrictive
	May appear early or several months after radiation; constriction may eventually occur	
Myxedema	Large pericardial effusions without tamponade are characteristic	Thyroid replacement
Connective tissue diseases, hypersensitivity syndromes	For example, systemic lupus erythematosus, rheumatoid arthritis, scleroderma, polyarteritis nodosa, drug reactions (e.g., procainamide)	Anti-inflammatory therapy

ECG = Electrocardiographic.

changes of acute pericarditis must be distinguished from early repolarization. Early repolarization is common in young patients, usually without PR segment depression, more often associated with sinus bradycardia than the sinus tachycardia of acute pericarditis, and without a characteristic evolution as described earlier for pericarditis. Atrial rhythm disturbances during pericarditis are common, especially intermittent atrial fibrillation; AV conduction disturbances and ventricular

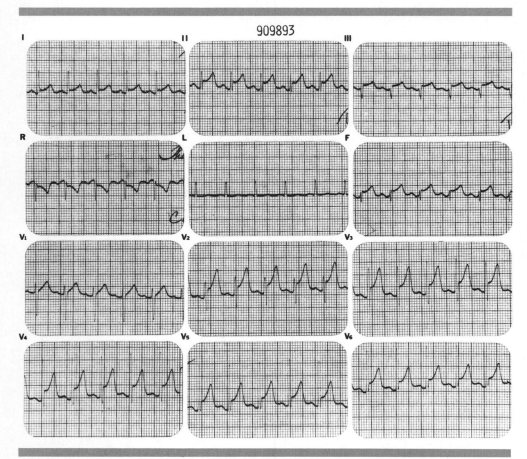

FIGURE 9–1. Typical electrocardiogram in pericarditis, showing diffuse ST elevation.

tachyarrhythmias are unusual and should suggest myocardial infarction. If a large pericardial effusion is present, low QRS voltage and electrical alternans may occur.

The chest radiograph is of little value in the diagnosis of acute pericarditis, but an enlarged cardiac silhouette may be noted if a pericardial effusion is present. Calcification of the pericardium may be detected in patients with long-standing pericarditis, especially that secondary to tuberculosis. The echocardiogram is extremely accurate for detection and quantitation of pericardial fluid and is also useful in evaluating suspected hemodynamic compromise (tamponade).

Nonspecific indicators of inflammation, such as elevated erythrocyte sedimentation rate and leukocytosis, are usually present. Cardiac isoenzymes are ordinarily normal. Other laboratory tests that may exclude specific diagnoses include blood cultures, acute and convalescent viral serologies, fungal serology (e.g., histoplasmosis), antistreptolysin-O (ASO) titer (rheumatic fever), cold agglutinins (mycoplasmal infection), heterophile test (mononucleosis), thyroid function tests (hypothyroidism), blood urea nitrogen (BUN) and creatinine (uremia), and connective tissue disease screens such as antinuclear antibody (ANA), rheumatoid factor, and complement.

Management of the patient with acute pericarditis involves treating its etiology. Patients are usually hospitalized to make sure that myocardial infarction is not present and to watch carefully for the occurrence of cardiac tamponade. Salicylates or nonsteroidal anti-inflammatory agents are often effective in relieving pain. Corticosteroids may be used if necessary, but long-term administration should be avoided. Anticoagulants should not be administered because of the risk of hemopericardium. In rare cases, pericardiectomy may be indicated to relieve recurrent symptoms. Most causes of pericarditis are self-limited, and inflammation abates after 2 to 6 weeks. Recurrent episodes of pericarditis occur in some patients. Rarely, pericarditis eventually results in pericardial constriction or a combination of effusion and constriction (effusive-constrictive pericarditis).

Pericardial Effusion

The hemodynamic effects of fluid in the pericardial cavity depend on the volume and rate of fluid accumulation. Because the pericardium is not compliant, an increase in pericardial effusion that occurs acutely may cause a rapid rise in intrapericardial pressure. If the accumulation of fluid is more gradual, the pericardium may accommodate, and the intrapericardial pressure increase is not as great for any given amount of pericardial fluid. Small increases in the volume of pericardial fluid may have little hemodynamic effect at first, but subsequent small increases may result in a rapid rise in intrapericardial pressure, accounting for the rapid clinical deterioration of patients with stable pericardial effusion.

The patient with pericardial effusion and hemodynamic compromise has dyspnea, tachycardia, distended jugular veins, and a rapid, thready pulse. Rales typical of pulmonary edema are absent. Dullness, increased fremitus, and bronchial breath sounds occurring posteriorly below the angle of the left scapula because of compression of the left lower lung by the pericardium (Ewart's sign) may be present. The precordium often is quiet to auscultation, and the apical impulse frequently is not palpable. Kussmaul's sign, an increase in jugular venous pressure with inspiration, is unusual in pericardial effusion or tamponade. When cardiac tamponade results, pulsus paradoxus, characterized by a decrease in the systolic blood pressure of more than 10 mm Hg with normal inspiration, is frequently present. The paradoxical pulse often can be noted by marked weakening or disappearance of a peripheral pulse during inspiration. Paradoxical pulse is not diagnostic of pericardial tamponade and can occur in chronic lung disease, acute asthma, and severe congestive heart failure.

Any cause of acute pericarditis can lead to pericardial effusion. The ECG may be normal, may demonstrate low voltage, or may reveal ST and T wave changes typical of pericarditis. Electrical alternans, a variation in voltage of P, QRS, and T waves in alternate beats, may occur in patients with large effusions. The chest radiograph may show an enlarged "water bottle" cardiac silhouette, but if the pericardial effusion has developed rapidly, the chest radiograph may show a normal heart size. Definitive diagnosis of pericardial effusion is usually obtained by echocardiography. Cardiac catheterization shows pulsus paradoxus, equalization of diastolic pressures throughout the heart, elevated systemic venous pressure, and normal or reduced cardiac output with reduced stroke volume.

The management of pericardial effusion without tamponade is similar to that of acute pericarditis. Patients with acute significant pericardial effusions should be hospitalized to monitor for impending tamponade. If tamponade occurs, the pericardium should be drained by pericardiocentesis or surgery. Patients with cardiac tamponade and hypotension should receive intravenous volume (and possibly isoproterenol) to optimize cardiac performance until pericardial drainage can be performed. Diuresis is contraindicated.

The pericardial fluid should be examined microscopically for bacteria, cells, glucose, and protein content. An indwelling catheter or drain is sometimes left in place for subsequent drainage of pericardial fluid or chemotherapy instillation.

Constrictive Pericarditis (Table 9–5)

Constrictive pericarditis results from pericardial thickening and fibrosis occurring long after acute episodes of pericarditis. It is less common since the advent of antituberculous therapy but can occur after bacterial, fungal, viral, neoplastic, or uremic pericarditis. The fundamental hemodynamic abnormality is abnormal diastolic filling. Eventually, the underlying myocardial tissue may atrophy, and decreased systolic function may result. Pericardial effusion and constriction may occur together (effusive-constrictive pericarditis), in which case pericardiocentesis may only partially relieve the symptoms. Occasionally, constriction can be localized to only certain chambers of the heart.

Symptoms of dyspnea, peripheral edema, abdominal swelling, and fatigue usually develop gradually. On physical examination, the jugular veins are distended, with a prominent y descent (corresponding to early rapid ventricular filling). Tachycardia, hepatomegaly, ascites, and peripheral edema are common. Splenomegaly may occur. The pulse pressure is usually normal, and pulsus paradoxus is usually not present. Kussmaul's sign may be present. The apical impulse sometimes is not palpable or may retract with systole. An early diastolic apical sound termed a pericardial knock is often present and can be confused with an S_3 gallop.

The ECG findings include low voltage and nonspecific T wave changes. The chest radiograph reveals clear lungs and normal or only slightly increased heart size. Pericardial calcification is most common in tuberculous constriction. Echocardiography sometimes can suggest constrictive pericarditis but is usually not diagnostic. At cardiac catheterization, the right and left ventricular pressures may demonstrate an early diastolic dip with a

TABLE 9–5. FEATURES OF CARDIAC TAMPONADE AND CHRONIC CONSTRICTION

	CARDIAC TAMPONADE	CHRONIC CONSTRICTION
Symptom duration	Hours to days	Months to years
Chest pain	+	−
Friction rub	+	−
Pulsus paradoxus	+	−
Kussmaul's sign	−	+
Pericardial (early diastolic) knock	−	+
Pericardial calcification	−	+
Pericardial effusion	+	−

+ = Usually or often present; − = usually absent.

subsequent rise, the square root sign. The right atrial pressure tracings may show sharp x and y descents, generating a typical M-shaped contour. There is equalization of end-diastolic pressures in all four chambers and the pulmonary artery. Occasionally, these findings become evident only after an infusion of saline (occult constriction).

It is sometimes difficult to distinguish constrictive pericarditis from restrictive cardiomyopathy. Left ventricular ejection fraction is more likely to be decreased in restrictive cardiomyopathy than constrictive pericarditis. Computed tomography is the procedure of choice to demonstrate the thickened pericardium. Endocardial biopsy or even surgical exploration is sometimes necessary.

Constrictive pericarditis is slowly progressive. Patients may be managed conservatively with mild sodium restriction and diuretics; however, the mortality and morbidity of pericardiectomy are less when it is performed early than after progressive calcification and fibrosis have occurred. Therefore, pericardiectomy should probably not be performed in patients with very mild, early disease or in elderly patients with severe disease and a fibrotic, calcified pericardium. Improvement occurs in about 75 per cent of patients who survive the operation but may be delayed for several weeks or months postoperatively. Cardiac function may not normalize after pericardiectomy either because of inability to completely remove the pericardium or because of fibrosis and atrophy of the underlying myocardium.

REFERENCES

Maron BJ, Bonow RO, Cannon RO III, Leon MB, Epstein SE: Hypertrophic cardiomyopathy: Interrelations of clinical manifestations, pathophysiology, and therapy. N Engl J Med 316:780–789, 844–852, 1987.

Spodick DH: The normal and diseased pericardium: Current concepts of pericardial physiology, diagnosis, and treatment. J Am Coll Cardiol 1:240, 1983.

Waller BF, Slack JD, Orr CD, Adlam JH, Bournique MV: "Flaming," "smoldering" and "burned out"; The fireside saga of myocarditis. J Am Coll Cardiol 18:1627, 1991.

Zipes DP, Rowlands DJ (eds): Hypertrophic cardiomyopathy. Prog Cardiol 2(2):3–272, 1989.

Zipes DP, Rowlands DJ (eds): Nonhypertrophic cardiomyopathies. Prog Cardiol 2(1):3–194, 1989.

10 CARDIAC TUMORS AND TRAUMA

CARDIAC TUMORS

Tumors involving the heart may be primary or metastatic; both types are rare. Although a variety of metastatic tumors have been described in the heart, the most common are malignant melanomas, leukemia, and lymphomas. Metastatic tumors are managed by treating the primary malignancy.

Primary cardiac tumors may be benign or malignant. Myxoma is the most common primary tumor of the heart and is usually benign. Almost all malignant cardiac tumors are sarcomas, angiosarcoma and rhabdomyosarcoma being the most frequent. Prior to histologic examination, it is impossible to distinguish benign from malignant tumors, but malignant tumors are more likely to present with evidence of metastases, invasion, or rapid growth. Tumor type may be identified occasionally from tissue at the time of peripheral embolectomy. Malignant primary tumors of the heart have a very poor prognosis. Ventricular tachyarrhythmias may be the presenting symptom in some patients with ventricular tumors.

Myxomas may arise from the endocardial surface of any cardiac chamber, but the majority arise from the left atrium, most commonly in the region of the fossa ovalis. They are usually pedunculated. As a general rule, 10 per cent of cardiac myxomas manifest malignant characteristics and 10 per cent arise in locations other than the left atrium. Occasionally, they can be bilateral and usually present in one of three general ways: (1) progressive interference with mitral valve function that causes decreased exercise tolerance, dyspnea on exertion, and pulmonary edema; syncope or presyncope may occur; (2) stroke or occlusion of a major systemic artery due to an embolus; (3) systemic manifestations that include fever, wasting, arthralgias, malaise, anemia, or Raynaud's phenomenon.

If the left atrial myxoma interferes with mitral valve function, a regurgitant valvular murmur may occur. A murmur resembling that of mitral stenosis may be present owing to obstruction of the valve orifice during diastole. The intensity of the murmur may change with changes in body position. An early diastolic sound termed a "tumor plop" may occur secondary to movement of the tumor toward the left ventricle in early diastole. The erythrocyte sedimentation rate, gamma globulins, and white blood cell count may be elevated. The cause of the systemic manifestations is not clear, but they may result from products secreted by the tumor, necrotic tumor debris, or an immunologic reaction.

Cardiac myxoma is usually diagnosed by echocardiography. Two-dimensional echocardiography shows the tumor location and movement with the cardiac cycle. Cardiac catheterization with angiocardiography usually is not necessary when the diagnosis has been established noninvasively and is associated with risk of tumor embolus.

Cardiac myxomas should be excised surgically once identified. A recurrent or second myxoma occurs following resection in a small number of patients. Atrial myxoma occasionally may behave like a malignant tumor and demonstrate metastases.

NONPENETRATING TRAUMA

Blunt chest trauma is especially common after steering wheel impact from an automobile accident. It may produce myocardial contusion, resulting in myocardial hemorrhage and at times some degree of necrosis. Often there is little or no residual myocardial scar once healing is complete. Large contusions may lead to myocardial scars, cardiac or septal rupture, congestive heart failure, or formation of true or false aneurysms. Necrosis or hemorrhage involving the cardiac conduction system can produce intraventricular or atrioventricular block. Coronary artery laceration, valvular damage, or pericardial tears may occasionally occur after blunt trauma. The chest pain of myocardial contusion is similar to that of myocardial infarction and is often confused with musculoskeletal pain from the chest trauma. The electrocardiogram at the time of injury may show a diffuse injury pattern similar to that of pericarditis. Later, the electrocardiogram may reveal serial development of Q waves similar to that of acute myocardial infarction if significant necrosis has occurred. Bradyarrhythmias and tachyarrhythmias are common. Contractile abnormalities are usually not severe unless concomitant injury to a valve or the septum has occurred. The MB fraction of creatine kinase is elevated. Myocardial contusion is usually treated similarly to myocardial infarction, with initial monitoring and subsequent progressive ambulation. Anticoagulants should not be administered to patients with myocardial contusion. If the patient survives the acute episode, the long-term prognosis is usually good, although late complications such as ventricular arrhythmias occasionally occur.

Rupture of the aorta is a common consequence of blunt trauma. It most commonly occurs just distal to the take-off of the left subclavian artery. The patient may complain of pain in the back or chest similar to that of aortic dissection. The chest radiograph usually reveals widening of the mediastinum. Many patients demonstrate increased arterial pressure in the upper extremities and decreased arterial pressure and pulse pressure in the lower extremities. Signs of decreased renal or spinal cord perfusion may become evident. The diagnosis is usually confirmed by aortography, and the treatment is surgical.

PENETRATING TRAUMA

Penetrating cardiac injuries may be due to external objects such as bullets or knives and also bony fragments resulting from chest injury. Because of its anterior location, the right ventricle is most commonly involved. Iatrogenic causes of cardiac penetrating injury include perforation of the heart during catheterization and cardiac trauma from cardiopulmonary resuscitation.

Penetrating injury to the heart may present as exsanguinating hemorrhage with hemothorax or cardiac tamponade if hemorrhage has been limited to within the pericardial sac. Immediate pericardiocentesis and administration of large volumes of fluids may be performed as preparations are being made for emergency surgery. A "postpericardiotomy" type of pericarditis, infection, arrhythmias, aneurysm formation, and ventricular septal defects are late complications of penetrating cardiac injury. The risk of bacterial endocarditis, infection from a retained foreign body, and foreign body embolus are complications peculiar to penetrating as opposed to nonpenetrating injuries.

REFERENCES

Cheitlin MD: Cardiovascular trauma. Circulation 65:1529, 1982, and 66:244, 1982.

Karrel R, Shaffer MA, Franaszek JB: Emergency diagnosis, resuscitation, and treatment of acute penetrating cardiac trauma. Ann Emerg Med 11:504, 1982.

Murphy MC, Sweeney MS, Putnam JB Jr, Walker WE, Frazier OH, Ott DA, Cooley DA: Surgical treatment of cardiac tumors: A 25-year experience. Ann Thorac Surg 49:612, 1990.

Sutton M, Mercier L, Guiliani E, Lie J: Atrial myxomas. A review of clinical experience in 40 patients. Mayo Clin Proc 55:371, 1980.

11 AORTIC AND PERIPHERAL VASCULAR DISEASE

AORTIC ANEURYSMS (Table 11–1)

Aortic aneurysms, localized areas of increased aortic diameter, may occur in the ascending aorta, aortic arch, descending thoracic aorta, or abdominal aorta, depending on the etiology. For example, aneurysms of the sinuses of Valsalva may occur in Marfan's syndrome or syphilis, as a complication of infective endocarditis, or as a congenital lesion, while aneurysms of the ascending aorta or aortic arch occur in syphilis, aortic dissection, or cystic medial necrosis with or without Marfan's syndrome. Aneurysms of the descending thoracic aorta occur from syphilis, atherosclerosis, or dissection. Aneurysms just distal to the take-off of the left subclavian artery are commonly due to trauma. Abdominal aortic aneurysms are usually atherosclerotic but can be secondary to syphilis or an extension of a dissection from above. Connective tissue diseases such as Takayasu's arteritis can lead to aneurysm formation anywhere in the aorta, most commonly the proximal portion.

Arteriosclerotic aneurysms are characterized in Table 11–1. A prominent abdominal aortic pulsation may be felt in normally thin people and mistakenly diagnosed as an abdominal aortic aneurysm; on the other hand, an abdominal aortic aneurysm may not be palpable in patients who are obese or who have muscular abdominal walls. Aneurysms may rupture into the inferior vena cava, producing an arteriovenous (AV) fistula; into the duodenum with acute massive gastrointestinal hemorrhage; into the retroperitoneal space, manifested by flank or groin hematomas; or into the abdominal cavity, causing abdominal distention. Half of all aneurysms exceeding 6 cm in diameter rupture within 1 year, and surgical resection with prosthetic graft replacement is usually recommended. Aneurysms less than 6 cm also may rupture. In patients with relatively high surgical risk, aneurysms of 4 to 6 cm should be followed closely and surgery undertaken upon signs of expansion or impending rupture.

A dissecting aneurysm (Table 11–1) is caused by a tear of the aortic intima with formation of a false channel within the aortic media. Blood in the false channel may re-enter the true aortic channel via a second intimal tear or rupture through the adventitia into the periaortic tissues. Most dissections arise either in the ascending aorta within several centimeters of the aortic valve or in the descending thoracic aorta just beyond the origin of the left subclavian artery in the region of the ligamentum arteriosum. Patients with proximal dissections tend to be younger and to have a higher incidence of Marfan's syndrome and cystic medial necrosis; distal dissections more commonly involve older patients with hypertension. Surgery generally is indicated in proximal (type I and type II) dissections, whereas medical therapy may be the treatment of choice for uncomplicated distal dissection (type III). Medical therapy must be administered to surgical patients both during the preoperative stabilization period and chronically postoperatively to prevent progression or repeat dissection.

AORTIC ARTERITIS

Aortitis is an inflammatory process of the aortic wall that may be caused by several disease processes. When it involves the origin of various aortic branches (e.g., the innominate artery, the left common carotid artery, and the left subclavian artery), it is termed the "aortic arch syndrome" and is characteristically produced by Takayasu's syndrome but also by syphilis, arteriosclerosis, or dissecting aneurysm. Takayasu's arteritis, or pulseless disease, appears to be most common in Japanese females and is an aortic panarteritis that leads to eventual luminal obliteration from the thickened walls and superimposed thrombus. Localized aneurysm formation may occur. The process may involve the coronary ostia or any of the branches of the aortic arch. Tertiary syphilis causes an aortic arteritis that may lead to an ascending aortic aneurysm, aortic valvulitis with insufficiency, and/or coronary ostial stenosis. It is a late manifestation of syphilis, usually occurring 10 to 30 years after the primary infection. Routine serologic tests may be negative, but the *Treponema pallidum* immobilization or the fluorescent *Treponema* antibody absorption test is almost always positive. The media of the aorta is destroyed from necrosis of smooth muscle and elastic tissue. The intima assumes a wrinkled appearance referred to as "tree barking." Involvement is much more prominent in the aortic root than in the distal aorta, in contrast to atherosclerotic aortic aneurysms. This whole process is often asymptomatic and detected by eggshell calcification of the ascending aorta on chest radiograph.

TABLE 11–1. AORTIC ANEURYSMS

ANEURYSM TYPE	ETIOLOGY	LOCATION	CLINICAL FEATURES	PHYSICAL FINDINGS	LABORATORY FINDINGS	TREATMENT
Arterosclerotic	Arteriosclerosis	Usually abdominal (between renal arteries and aortic bifurcation)	Older males Often asymptomatic until rupture Abdominal fullness or pulsations; back or epigastric pain, worse prior to rupture	Palpable, pulsatile abdominal mass Peripheral emboli Abdominal bruit Associated peripheral vascular disease	Size measured by abdominal ultrasound Angiography less accurate at estimating size but necessary to define surgical anatomy	Rupture or >6 cm diameter: surgery <4 cm diameter: observe
Dissecting	Hypertension Marfan's syndrome Cystic medial necrosis Aortic coarctation Trauma	Type I: proximal ascending aorta to descending aorta Type II: confined to ascending aorta Type III: begins in descending aorta and extends distally	Severe, sudden, tearing chest pain radiating to abdomen and back (occasional patient will have no pain) Aortic branch occlusions causing myocardial infarction, stroke, spinal infarction with paraplegia, renal impairment Aortic root involvement causing acute aortic insufficiency, rupture into pericardium with pericardial friction rub or tamponade	Hypertension Asymmetric pulses Signs of aortic insufficiency, neurologic involvement, or tamponade if present	ECG may show myocardial infarction Wide mediastinum on chest x-ray (not always present) CT scan usually diagnostic Angiography necessary to define surgical anatomy	Surgical indications: Ascending aortic involvement Impairment of vital organs Etiology not hypertensive Hemodynamic impairment Medical therapy may be tried in older patient with distal hypertensive dissection: control hypertension and lessen force of contraction (nitroprusside + beta blocker)

ECG = Electrocardiogram; CT = computed tomography.

MISCELLANEOUS AORTIC DISEASE

Large peripheral arterial emboli may obstruct the abdominal aortic bifurcation, resulting in so-called saddle emboli. These usually originate from the left side of the heart but rarely may originate from the aorta itself in the area of an atherosclerotic lesion. Other, rarer causes are "paradoxical emboli" (from the right side of the heart or venous system in patients with right-to-left shunts), atrial myxomas, or infective endocarditis (very large emboli can occur in acute endocarditis and fungal endocarditis). Obstruction at the aortic bifurcation is characterized by the sudden onset of severe pain in both legs, peripheral neurologic abnormalities, and evidence of decreased perfusion occurring bilaterally. It must be differentiated from acute atherosclerotic aortic thrombosis and dis-

secting aneurysm. The diagnosis is confirmed by angiography. Surgical removal of the clot with subsequent anticoagulation and/or treatment of the underlying cause is necessary.

Infected aortic aneurysms are rare. The most common congenital aortic anomaly is coarctation of the aorta (see Chapter 5). Congenital aortic aneurysms of the sinus of Valsalva may rupture into the right atrium or ventricle, producing a continuous murmur. Sinus of Valsalva aneurysms can occasionally produce coronary occlusion, conduction disturbances, or valvular malfunction.

PERIPHERAL VASCULAR DISEASE
(Table 11–2)

Arteriosclerosis obliterans refers to atherosclerotic narrowing of large and medium-sized arteries,

TABLE 11-2. PERIPHERAL VASCULAR DISEASES

DISEASE	PATHOLOGY	CLINICAL FEATURES	PHYSICAL FINDINGS	LABORATORY FINDINGS	TREATMENT
Arteriosclerosis obliterans	Atherosclerotic narrowing of large and medium-sized arteries of lower extremities; segmental with skip areas; occasionally involves upper extremities (subclavian steal syndrome)	Male > female Common in diabetics Exertional leg pain relieved with rest (claudication); rest pain implies severe compromise Cold, numb legs Buttock claudication and impotence with aorto-iliac obstruction (Leriche's syndrome)	Decreased or absent lower extremity pulses Aortic, iliac, or femoral bruit Limb ischemia: cool, pale, cyanotic; shiny dry skin without hair; nail changes, ulcerations, gangrene	Doppler and arteriography locate obstructions	Intermittent claudication: —exercise (stop when claudication occurs) —stop smoking —avoid peripheral vasoconstricting drugs, e.g., propranolol —meticulous skin and nail care —pentoxifylline Severe claudication or rest ischemia: —percutaneous transluminal angioplasty or surgical bypass; amputation if gangrenous
Thromboangiitis obliterans	Intimal proliferation and thrombi in small to medium-sized vessels with inflammatory infiltrates Segmental involvement of arteries and veins Upper and lower extremity involvement	Male > female Usually occurs before age 30 Etiology not understood but related to smoking Cool extremities Raynaud's phenomenon Distal limb claudication (e.g., instep or hand)	Cool extremities Digital ulcers Migrating thrombophlebitis	Biopsy of artery diagnostic	Stop smoking Sympathectomy to prevent vasospasm Amputation of distal extremities for gangrene
Arterial embolism	Emboli tend to lodge at arterial bifurcations with subsequent thrombus formations (e.g., "saddle embolus" at aortic bifurcation)	Sudden onset of painful extremity (occasionally more gradual)	Cold, pale extremity with absent pulses distal to embolus	Pathologic examination of embolus may reveal etiology Doppler examination helps localize embolus	Heparin Surgical embolectomy for larger vessels Chronic anticoagulation if embolic source cannot be eliminated
Raynaud's phenomenon	Vasospasm of digital vessels precipitated by cold and relieved by heat	Underlying causes: Arterial occlusive diseases Connective tissue diseases Neurologic diseases Ingestion of vasoconstricting drugs Nerve compression syndromes Cryoglobulinemia or cold agglutinins Post frostbite or trench foot Raynaud's disease (female > male)	White, cyanotic digit upon exposure to cold or emotional upset; hyperemic upon resumption of circulation Normal pulses Chronic nail and skin changes (sclerodactyly) in severe cases; small areas of distal gangrene but digital amputation rare		Limitation of cold exposure Stop smoking Vasodilators Regional sympathectomy

usually those supplying the lower extremities (the superficial femoral artery, the aortoiliac area, and the popliteal artery). The symptoms of claudication may remain stable over a very long period. Many of these patients eventually die of other complications. Pentoxifylline, a drug that improves the flow properties of blood, may be useful in relieving symptoms in patients with chronic peripheral arterial disease. The mechanism by which pentoxifylline decreases blood viscosity is unclear but may be related to improving erythrocyte flexibility.

Thromboangiitis obliterans, or Buerger's disease, is an inflammatory process causing obliteration of peripheral arteries and veins. In its later stages, it may be difficult to differentiate from arteriosclerosis obliterans. Patients may do well for long periods, but the need for amputation of distal extremities is common if patients continue to smoke. No medication has been shown to be helpful.

Peripheral arterial emboli usually originate from thrombi in either the left atrium or the left ventricle or, uncommonly, from atheromatous emboli located in atherosclerotic plaques in the aorta. A "paradoxical embolus" refers to an embolus originating from the venous system, passing through a right-to-left intracardiac shunt, and lodging in the systemic arterial tree. Septic emboli may occur with endocarditis and tumor emboli with cardiac myxoma. Acute thrombosis of a vessel is sometimes difficult to distinguish from embolism but should be suspected if no source for emboli is present and if concomitant severe atherosclerotic disease is present.

Raynaud's phenomenon involves bilateral paroxysmal ischemia of fingers or toes, usually precipitated by cold and relieved by heat. The entire hand or foot is usually not affected. Raynaud's phenomenon may be secondary to a variety of underlying diseases; if no underlying disease can be found, the patient is said to have Raynaud's disease.

ENVIRONMENTAL DAMAGE TO THE EXTREMITIES

Both freezing (frostbite) and nonfreezing injuries may damage the extremities. The presence of dampness or peripheral vascular disease enhances the tissue loss for any given temperature reduction or duration of exposure. Tissue damage is probably due to a combination of direct freezing and marked vasoconstriction. Cold produces numbness in tissues that may allow freezing without warning, so that the first indication of frostbite may be a prickling feeling. The affected area initially looks pale or waxy yellow and may be anesthetic. In severe frostbite, edema and bulla formation occur with thawing, and gangrene may result. Frostbite should be treated immediately by rewarming, but excessive warming, massage, and exercise should be avoided. Infection is the greatest danger, and the affected areas must be handled with aseptic technique.

Prolonged immersion of extremities in water leads to a syndrome known as immersion foot or trench foot. Wetness plus cold produces the most serious form of the syndrome. It does not necessarily require freezing temperatures and is due in part to direct and reflex vasoconstriction.

PERIPHERAL ANEURYSMS AND FISTULAS

Occasionally, true or false aneurysms may occur in peripheral vessels. True aneurysms are usually secondary to atherosclerosis; false aneurysms (i.e., a tear in the arterial wall allowing accumulation of blood in the perivascular tissues) may be associated with trauma or rupture of a true aneurysm. True aneurysms of peripheral vessels are located most commonly in the popliteal artery but can occur in the femoral artery, iliac artery, arteries of the upper extremities, and occasionally visceral arteries such as renal or splenic arteries. Aneurysms of the popliteal and femoral arteries are often palpable. Aneurysms may occasionally be infected (mycotic). Symptoms result from arterial occlusion, rupture, distal embolization, or local pressure on adjacent structures such as nerves or veins. Surgery for renal or splenic artery aneurysms is usually recommended in patients who are pregnant (increased incidence of rupture) or whose aneurysm is symptomatic, enlarging, or more than 1.5 to 2.0 cm in diameter. Femoral and popliteal aneurysms should be treated surgically if the patient's condition allows.

Arteriovenous fistulas are acquired or congenital abnormal communications between arteries and veins without an intervening capillary network. Acquired fistulas may be created to facilitate hemodialysis or may occur after trauma such as a gunshot or stab wound. Increased blood flow leads to venous dilation and makes the region of the fistula abnormally warm; the area distal to the fistula may be cool. If the fistula is large, a high cardiac output state may occur and may produce heart failure. Because of the low-resistance pathway, diastolic blood pressure tends to decrease, and systolic blood pressure and pulse pressure increase. A bruit and thrill may be present over the fistula. If the artery serving the fistula is compressed, shunting via the low-resistance circuit is prevented, and a prompt decrease in the pulse rate may occur (Branham's sign). Acquired fistulas are best treated surgically. Congenital AV fistulas are usually multiple, small, and often accompanied by cutaneous birthmarks. Enlargement of the entire involved limb may occur, since the fistulas are present during the period of rapid bone growth. Bruits and pulsatile masses are uncommon, since the fistulas are small and multiple. Treatment is less satisfactory than that of large acquired AV fistulas.

ARTERIAL TRAUMA

Arterial trauma is usually a surgical emergency. It occurs with penetrating or blunt trauma, including fractures and dislocations. Swelling within a compartment of an extremity after blunt trauma can cause both arterial and neurologic damage and responds to decompression of that compartment. Direct arterial injury from trauma requires acute surgical repair. Arterial injury may be iatrogenic from catheterization of brachial or femoral arteries. Loss of local pulse after a catheterization procedure should be approached surgically with early thrombectomy and/or repair, since waiting may necessitate more complicated procedures.

PERIPHERAL VENOUS DISEASE

The most common disorder involving the peripheral veins is venous thrombosis with thrombophlebitis. Thrombophlebitis refers to inflammation of the vein, usually from thrombus but occasionally from trauma or infection. Predisposing factors to thrombophlebitis are venous stasis, local venous injury, and hypercoagulable states. Particular risk factors for thrombophlebitis include oral contraceptives, trauma to or fractures of the extremities, pregnancy, major surgery, prolonged immobilization, heart disease, varicose veins, and myeloproliferative syndromes. Local thrombophlebitis may occur from administration of irritating drugs such as chemotherapeutic agents or from indwelling intravenous catheters, especially if infection has supervened (septic phlebitis). Patients with malignancies appear to be prone to migrating, recurrent thrombophlebitis. Thrombophlebitis can occur with thromboangiitis obliterans or processes causing extrinsic obstruction of venous flow. In some patients, no predisposing factors can be found. Low-dose subcutaneous heparin appears to be effective prophylaxis against deep vein thrombosis in patients with a variety of medical or surgical conditions.

Symptoms and signs of venous thrombosis and thrombophlebitis in the leg vary. The onset may be inapparent until pulmonary embolism occurs. Warmth and edema may be present, and the affected leg may become larger than the other. Tenderness over the deep vein upon palpation or inflation of a blood pressure cuff may be noted. Pain upon dorsiflexion of the foot (Homans' sign) is neither sensitive nor specific. Skin changes such as mottling or cyanosis may be present. A palpable venous "cord" occurs in only about 20 per cent of patients. When thrombophlebitis is superficial, red, tender, indurated areas occur just beneath the skin, often corresponding to the distribution of the superficial veins. The distinction, usually requiring laboratory evaluation, between deep and superficial thrombophlebitis is critical because the former is prone to embolization, whereas the latter is not.

The clinical presentation of iliofemoral thrombosis is characterized by unilateral leg swelling, and the diagnosis usually can be confirmed by Doppler examination. The main differential diagnosis of this syndrome is extrinsic venous obstruction by tumor or adenopathy. Deep venous thrombosis in calf veins is more difficult to diagnose clinically. Doppler studies and impedance plethysmography may be helpful, but a venogram is usually necessary. Venograms are usually reliable diagnostically; however, inadequate opacification of the deep venous system may occur, and areas of previous thrombophlebitis may be difficult to distinguish from new thrombophlebitis. Phlebitis may occur as a complication of venography in a small number of patients.

Management of deep venous thrombosis includes heat, elevation of the extremity, and administration of anti-inflammatory agents. Anticoagulation is required to prevent additional thrombus formation and pulmonary embolism. Heparin should be used for immediate anticoagulation to keep the activated partial thromboplastin time 2 to 2.5 times normal. Heparin is continued for 7 to 10 days. Warfarin should be given for several days before heparin is discontinued, and its effect may be estimated using the prothrombin time. Bed rest is necessary for several days until pain and swelling have improved. Upon ambulation, an elastic support stocking should be worn. The duration of anticoagulation therapy is controversial but is usually between 6 weeks and 6 months. If risk factors for thrombophlebitis cannot be corrected or if thrombophlebitis recurs, chronic anticoagulation may be necessary. In patients with deep vein thrombosis who have contraindications to anticoagulation or in whom pulmonary embolism recurs despite anticoagulation, surgical plication of the inferior vena cava or insertion of an inferior vena caval umbrella is indicated to prevent pulmonary embolism. Fibrinolytic agents such as urokinase or streptokinase may be useful in treating deep venous thrombosis but should be used only in patients with serious iliofemoral thrombophlebitis.

Superficial thrombophlebitis caused by intravenous indwelling catheters is treated by removal of the catheter and warm heat. Because of this potential complication, intravenous lines should not be inserted in the leg. If infection is present, appropriate antibiotics should be given. Anticoagulation is not used unless lower extremity deep venous involvement is present. Heat and elevation should be applied. Ambulation with elastic stockings is possible. Anti-inflammatory drugs may aid in alleviating the symptoms.

Varicose veins (distended, tortuous superficial veins with incompetent valves) can result from thrombophlebitis but may also occur congenitally or in conditions associated with increased venous pressure, such as pregnancy, prolonged standing, and ascites. In most people the edema resolves overnight. Many people complain of aching discomfort from the superficial varicosities, relieved by elastic stockings and leg elevation. Occasionally, stripping or sclerosing of the saphenous veins may be necessary. Chronic deep venous insufficiency is more serious and gives rise to more edema, darkening and induration of the skin, and sometimes indolent skin ulcers (stasis dermatitis). Arterial pulses are normal. The postphlebitic syndrome refers to chronic swelling and skin changes in extremities due to chronic venous insufficiency, often caused by a previous episode of thrombophlebitis.

Swelling of an extremity can also occur from obstruction of the lymphatic outflow (lymphedema). Lymphedema may be idiopathic (primary) or, more commonly, secondary (e.g., that due to lymphangitis, neoplasms, adenopathy, or surgical removal of lymph nodes). Venous distention, stasis

dermatitis, and ulcers are usually not present, but lymphangiography and/or venography may be necessary to differentiate lymphedema from venous obstruction.

REFERENCES

Bergan JJ, Flinn WR, Yao JST: Operative therapy of peripheral vascular disease. Prog Cardiovasc Dis 26:273, 1984.

Gersh BJ, Charanjit SR, Rooke TW, Ballard DJ: Evaluation and management of patients with both peripheral vascular and coronary artery disease. J Am Coll Cardiol 18:203–214, 1991.

12 CARDIAC TRANSPLANTATION; SURGERY IN PATIENTS WITH CARDIOVASCULAR DISEASE; PREGNANCY AND CARDIAC DISEASE

CARDIAC TRANSPLANTATION

Cardiac transplantation was first performed in humans in 1967 but met with a high graft rejection rate. The development of cyclosporine immunosuppression sharply reduced the number of patients with graft rejection, so that now the 1- and 5-year survival rates are about 90 per cent and 80 per cent, respectively.

Candidates are usually less than 55 years old, are free of other illnesses such as diabetes mellitus requiring insulin and coexistent liver or renal disease, and suffer from end-stage heart disease, with a life expectancy of less than 1 year. Most patients have coronary disease, with idiopathic viral or rheumatic cardiomyopathies affecting the rest of the group. Combined heart/lung transplantation may be considered in patients with severe irreversible pulmonary hypertension. Sequential transplantation has been performed in which a patient with severe pulmonary disease but a normal heart receives a heart/lung transplant from one patient and donates his or her heart to another. Donors generally have sustained irreversible cerebral damage from trauma or intracranial hemorrhage.

For orthotopic transplantation, the patient's

heart is removed, leaving the posterior walls of the atria with their venous connections to suture to the donor atria. The great vessels are then anastomosed. Heterotopic heart transplantation involves leaving the recipient's heart in situ and attaching the donor heart in parallel, with anastomoses between the atria, pulmonary arteries, and aortae. Immunosuppression is accomplished with combinations of cyclosporine, azathioprine, prednisone, and antithymocyte globulin. Acute rejection is monitored by histologic analysis of repeated right ventricular endomyocardial biopsies. Accelerated coronary atherosclerosis, possibly due to rejection-induced injury to the coronary arterial intima, is a potential hazard, as is the development of hypertension, renal disease, and infections.

Left ventricular assist devices are means of circulatory support for patients whose hemodynamics cannot be sustained by either pharmacologic therapy or intra-aortic balloon counterpulsation. Left ventricular assist devices consist of a pump with an intake from the left ventricle and output into the ascending thoracic aorta. They are used in patients for temporary support after cardiac surgery if pump-oxygenator dependence develops in spite of conventional measures or refractory cardiogenic shock occurs early after operation, situations in which recovery of left ventricular function is anticipated. In addition, they may be used as "bridges" in patients awaiting availability of a suitable donor heart for cardiac transplantation. Permanent left ventricular assist devices and total artificial hearts are highly investigational.

GENERAL SURGERY IN THE PATIENT WITH HEART DISEASE

Noncardiac surgery is particularly stressful in patients with pre-existing heart disease. The burdens of anesthesia, surgical trauma, wound healing, infection, hemorrhage, and pulmonary insufficiency may overwhelm the diseased heart. The internist is often asked to assess cardiovascular risk in patients undergoing noncardiac surgery and to aid in their preoperative and postoperative management.

General anesthetics reduce myocardial contractility and also have autonomic nervous system effects that may cause either hypotension or hypertension. Regional, spinal, or epidural anesthesia minimizes myocardial depression, but sympathetic blockade and hypotension still may result. In general, there appears to be no difference in risk between general anesthesia and spinal anesthesia in cardiac patients. The anesthesiologist must maintain adequate ventilation, oxygenation, and blood pH throughout the procedure. The electrocardiogram is routinely monitored throughout surgery. If cardiac disease is significant, arterial blood pressure, central venous pressure, and/or pulmonary arterial wedge pressure may need to be monitored throughout the procedure. Cardiac arrhythmias are particularly likely in patients with heart disease and occur most commonly during induction of anesthesia and intubation. Excessive vagal tone can cause bradyarrhythmias and usually responds to adjusting the depth of anesthesia or administering atropine. Antiarrhythmic agents may be administered if needed.

Some patients have life-threatening indications for surgery, and cardiac risk does not affect whether or not the surgery should be performed. In elective surgery, however, the timing of the operation or even whether the operation should be done may depend upon a preoperative estimation of surgical risk. Cardiac risk is strongly associated with the type of surgical procedure. Herniorrhaphy and transurethral resection of the prostate carry relatively low risk, whereas chest, abdominal, and retroperitoneal surgery has a relatively high risk. Emergency surgery is associated with greater risk than nonemergency surgery because there is no time to optimize the patient's cardiac status.

Ischemic heart disease is one of the major determinants of cardiac risk. The incidence of perioperative myocardial infarction is 4 to 8 per cent in patients who have had remote prior infarctions. In addition, the mortality from perioperative myocardial infarction is two to three times greater in patients with previous infarction than in those without previous infarction. The risk of reinfarction is particularly high if surgery is performed early after infarction but levels off if surgery is delayed until 6 months after infarction. The surgical risk in patients with stable angina pectoris is about the same as that in patients with remote myocardial infarction. Patients with unstable angina pectoris should not have elective surgery until the angina is stabilized and, possibly, invasive evaluation of the coronary arteries is done.

Decompensated congestive heart failure is another major operative risk factor and should be treated vigorously prior to noncardiac surgery. Patients with congestive heart failure or atrial tachyarrhythmias should probably receive digitalis prior to surgery.

Patients with symptomatic heart block may need prophylactic pacing prior to surgery. Those with chronic bifascicular block or asymptomatic type I second-degree atrioventricular block probably do not require prophylactic pacemaker placement prior to anesthesia. Patients with frequent or symptomatic atrial or ventricular tachyarrhythmias should be treated prior to surgery.

Patients with valvular heart disease tend to tolerate the operation according to their pre-existing functional status. Patients with critical aortic or mitral stenosis are at particularly high risk. Treatment of heart failure should be optimized preoperatively, and those with severe valvular lesions should be considered for corrective surgery prior to elective noncardiac operation. In patients with valvular disease or prosthetic heart valves, endocarditis prophylaxis should be administered if appropriate. In patients with prosthetic heart valves, anticoagulation can usually be temporarily stopped immediately after the operation and in the early postoperative period to prevent bleeding complications.

Mild to moderate hypertension does not alter surgical risk. Severe hypertension should be controlled prior to surgery, as should heart failure or angina associated with it.

Patients with congenital heart disease are at increased risk according to their functional disability. Patients with cyanotic congenital heart disease and polycythemia have an increased risk of hemorrhage due to coagulation defects and thrombocytopenia, and they may tolerate hypotension and hypoxia poorly. Appropriate endocarditis prophylaxis should be administered. Patients with right-to-left shunts are at risk for paradoxical emboli.

In addition to evaluating and optimizing the patient's cardiac status, the general medical status should also be optimized. Pulmonary function is especially important; cessation of smoking and treatment of chronic bronchitis may improve risk.

HEART DISEASE AND PREGNANCY

Marked changes in normal circulatory physiology occur during pregnancy. The cardiac output rises by the end of the first trimester, peaking at a level (30 to 50 per cent rise) in the twentieth to twenty-fourth week that is maintained until after delivery. Increases in stroke volume, heart rate (10 beats/min), and blood volume (40 to 50 per cent) and decreases in systolic blood pressure and the systemic and pulmonary vascular resistances result. Oxygen consumption and minute ventilation increase. Easy fatigability, decreased exercise tolerance, dyspnea, peripheral edema, a third heart sound, and a midsystolic murmur may be normal in pregnancy. The mechanical pressure of a gravid uterus on the inferior vena cava may decrease venous return and reduce cardiac output. The hemodynamic stresses of pregnancy can exacerbate any pre-existing cardiac abnormality.

Most rheumatic valvular disease in young women involves mitral stenosis. Mitral stenosis is aggravated by the increased cardiac output and heart rate required during pregnancy. The incidence of heart failure increases as pregnancy progresses. These patients have an increased risk of complications from atrial fibrillation, emboli, or endocarditis during pregnancy. Nevertheless, most of these patients can be managed carefully through a relatively uneventful pregnancy. Right ventricular failure may increase the peripheral edema, venous stasis, and risk of pulmonary embolism.

Women with significant mitral or aortic valvular disease who desire children may require surgical correction of the lesion before conception. Cardiac surgical intervention during pregnancy carries an increased risk for both mother and fetus. If a valve is inserted, one should consider a porcine valve so that anticoagulation may be avoided. Warfarin crosses the placenta, but heparin does not. Warfarin may produce fetal developmental abnormalities if administered in the first trimester. The use of heparin versus warfarin during various stages of pregnancy is controversial, but it is clear that warfarin should be replaced by heparin during the last 2 to 3 weeks of pregnancy. Heparin is discontinued and, if necessary, protamine is administered upon the onset of labor. Patients given warfarin should not breast-feed, since it is excreted in breast milk. Patients with prosthetic valves probably should receive peripartum endocarditis prophylaxis.

Survival to reproductive age in patients with congenital heart disease has become more common since the advent of surgical intervention. The risk of pregnancy in patients after surgical correction of congenital heart lesions depends on the completeness of their repair and residual defects such as left ventricular dysfunction or pulmonary hypertension. Patients with uncomplicated cardiac lesions such as ostium secundum atrial septal defects usually tolerate pregnancy without any problem. Patients with uncorrected cyanotic heart disease such as tetralogy of Fallot may have difficulty carrying a pregnancy to term. The infants often have low birth weights. Adverse hemodynamics may result in increased right-to-left shunt and in-creasing maternal cyanosis, magnifying the risk to both mother and child. In patients with severe pulmonary vascular obstruction (e.g., Eisenmenger's syndrome), the fixed resistance allows little circulatory reserve, and fluctuations in systemic vascular resistance, cardiac output, and blood volume are very poorly tolerated, especially during labor and the puerperium. Severe aortic stenosis also limits cardiac reserve, and the risk of exertional syncope may increase during pregnancy. Patients with Marfan's syndrome are at markedly increased risk of aortic dissection during pregnancy. Women with coarctation of the aorta also have an increased risk of aortic dissection during pregnancy. Women with persistent cardiomegaly following peripartum cardiomyopathy are at high risk during subsequent pregnancies.

Maternal and fetal complications and mortality are directly related to functional class, and therapy should be optimized throughout pregnancy. Heart failure should be treated by decreased activity, decreased salt intake, and administration of digitalis and diuretics. If heart failure is refractory to medical therapy, termination of pregnancy should be considered. Patients with heart failure may need to be hospitalized during the final weeks of pregnancy. Serious arrhythmias are managed with conventional therapy. Chest radiographs and cardiac catheterization should be avoided if possible because of the radiation risks to the fetus. Factors that may exacerbate heart failure should be eliminated. Most women with heart disease should undergo a spontaneous term vaginal delivery, although cesarean section may be necessary in selected seriously ill patients.

REFERENCES

Freeman WK, Gibbons RJ, Shub C: Preoperative assessment of cardiac patients undergoing noncardiac surgical procedures. Mayo Clin Proc 64:1105–1117, 1989.

Goldman L: Cardiac risks and complications of noncardiac surgery. Ann Intern Med 98:504, 1983.

Sullivan JM, Ramanathan KB: Current concepts: Management of medical problems in pregnancy—severe cardiac disease. N Engl J Med 313:304–309, 1985.

GENERAL REFERENCES

Braunwald E (ed): Heart Disease. A Textbook of Cardiovascular Medicine. 4th ed. Philadelphia, WB Saunders Co, 1992.

Hurst JW (ed): The Heart: Arteries and Veins. 7th ed. New York, McGraw-Hill Book Co, 1990.

Smith TW (ed): Cardiovascular diseases. In Wyngaarden JB, Smith LH Jr, Bennett JC (eds): Cecil Textbook of Medicine. 19th ed. Philadelphia, WB Saunders Co, 1992.

SECTION II

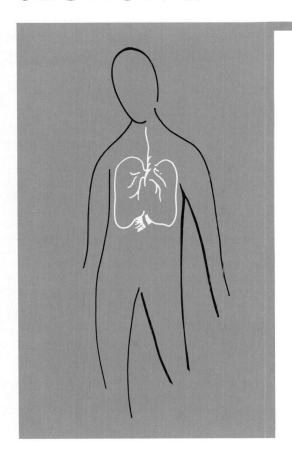

RESPIRATORY DISEASES

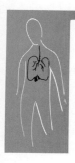

13 APPROACH TO THE PATIENT WITH RESPIRATORY DISEASE

The lungs are the major organs of gas exchange and are affected by a wide variety of acute and chronic diseases. The correct diagnosis of respiratory illness requires careful attention to both the history and the physical examination as well as the use of carefully chosen diagnostic studies.

COMMON PRESENTING COMPLAINTS

Dyspnea, or "shortness of breath," is frequently the first manifestation of respiratory system dysfunction. It may arise from pathology in the lung parenchyma or airways, respiratory muscle or chest wall dysfunction, or arterial blood gas abnormalities. Dyspnea may also be disproportionate to the degree of pulmonary pathology present and may reflect an imbalance between perceived ventilatory demand and output of the respiratory system. Afferent chemoreceptors sensitive to hypercapnia, hypoxemia, and acidosis, pulmonary chest wall and airway irritants, and stretch receptors, as well as anxiety, may contribute to the perception of dyspnea.

In assessing dyspnea, it is critical to ascertain its relationship to activity, body position, and emotional state. Exertional dyspnea is usually cardiac or pulmonary in origin, but this differential diagnosis is challenging and may require special studies. Episodic dyspnea occurring at rest or following exercise suggests bronchospasm, especially if associated wheezing is present. Nocturnal dyspnea may arise from a host of causes, including heart failure, asthma, and esophageal reflux. An occupational history is also critical. A history of dyspnea while the patient is at work or upon returning to work suggests occupational asthma.

Cough, unlike dyspnea, is a complaint almost always directed toward the respiratory system; it is the "watch dog" of the lung. It is provoked by mechanical or chemical stimulation of the airways. The cough is preceded by a deep breath followed by glottic closure. Then active compression causes a rapid rise in intrathoracic pressure until sudden opening of the glottis allows rapid decompression. The high-flow velocity achieved serves to clear the airways of secretions or foreign bodies. Cough has a number of causes, including the presence of secretions, viral infection of the airway epithelium, stimulation of parenchymal receptors by pulmonary edema, and fibrotic lung disease. It may be the sole manifestation of bronchospasm, and up to 45 per cent of patients presenting with chronic cough as the sole complaint have asthma. Chronic cough at night can often be ascribed to the presence of postnasal drip, reflux esophagitis, or aspiration. Recent alteration in the character of a chronic cough may be due to bronchial carcinoma. The cause of chronic isolated cough can usually be elucidated without recourse to invasive measures.

Chest pain is another common presenting complaint and in the context of lung disease suggests involvement of the parietal pleura or mediastinal structures, since the lungs themselves are insensitive to pain. Pleuritic pain is distinctive, being sharp, knifelike, and exacerbated by breathing and coughing. It must be differentiated from pericardial pain, involvement of the intercostal nerves by herpes zoster, and inflammation of the costochondral junctions (Tietze's syndrome). Involvement of the diaphragmatic pleura may manifest as shoulder pain, since the pleura is innervated by the phrenic nerve, which arises from cervical roots.

Blood mixed with the sputum may have its origin from many different sites. Frequently, the origin is outside the lung, such as the nasal passages, or even aspirated blood from the gastrointestinal tract may manifest as hemoptysis. Persistent hemoptysis in the absence of infection strongly suggests the possibility of malignancy. Hemoptysis is difficult to quantify and is frequently underestimated by both physicians and patients. Generally, more than 600 ml over 24 hours is considered "massive" and is a medical emergency, with death resulting more often from asphyxiation than from exsanguination.

Careful review of the remainder of the history is important. Prior episodes of respiratory infections may indicate acquired or congenital abnormalities of pulmonary clearance mechanisms. Similar findings in family members may suggest an inherited disorder such as immotile cilia syndrome. Attention should be paid to occupation, travel, habits (smoking), and hobbies (pets).

PHYSICAL EXAMINATION

The physical examination of the chest remains a cornerstone of the diagnostic process. It is wise to follow a set system to avoid inadvertently neglecting some aspects of the examination (Table 13–1). Unobtrusive observation of the patient as he or she breathes quietly is important. A respiratory rate above 22 breaths/min suggests underlying lung disease. Normally, the rib cage and abdomen move synchronously on respiration, both moving out on inspiration and in on expiration. Movement of the rib cage and abdomen in opposite directions is termed paradoxical breathing. This is observed in the presence of an increased respiratory load, diaphragmatic paralysis, and intercostal muscle paralysis (quadriplegia). Retraction of the intercostal, supraclavicular, and suprasternal spaces reflects the generation of increased negative intrathoracic pressure in the presence of lung disease. Downward pull of the trachea, called tracheal tug, is commonly observed in obstructive lung disease. The distance between the cricoid cartilage and the sternal notch is less than the usual three to four finger breadths in patients with hyperinflation.

Cyanosis is a bluish discoloration of the skin that becomes detectable when the O_2 saturation falls to about 80 to 90 per cent. Accuracy diminishes in the presence of inadequate capillary blood flow or anemia. Finger clubbing is recognized by loss of the angle between the nail and the nail bed. It may be associated with painless swelling of tissues of the terminal phalanx and/or arthralgias of the wrist and ankles (hypertrophic pulmonary osteoarthropathy). Common causes include chronic suppurative diseases, chronic interstitial lung disease, pulmonary malignancy, cyanotic congenital heart disease, endocarditis, and chronic liver and bowel disease, as well as a congenital idiopathic form.

Exaggerated contraction of the sternomastoid muscles while the patient is breathing at rest is an important indicator of respiratory distress. Patients with obstructive lung disease often derive symptomatic benefit from pursed-lip breathing, but the mechanism of this improvement is unknown. A "barrel-shaped" chest wall is seen in emphysema, while deformity of the chest wall may explain a restrictive pattern on pulmonary function testing.

Deviation of the trachea from the midline may reflect a shift in the mediastinum and is helpful in the diagnosis of a pneumothorax (Table 13–2). Vocal fremitus is the palpable vibration associated with transmission of the spoken word to the chest wall. It is increased with consolidation and decreased if fluid or air is present in the pleural space. Its absence helps to differentiate pleural effusion from a dense parenchymal infiltrate seen on radiographs.

Percussion detects the interface between the air-filled lung and solid structures such as pleural fluid, liver, or consolidated lung. Diaphragmatic movement can also be determined, but this is better done fluoroscopically.

During auscultation, the observer needs to compare the two sides of the chest at equidistant points from the midline and, while listening, answer only two questions: (1) What is the character of the breath sounds? (2) Are added sounds present, and if so what is their nature?

Breath sounds are caused by turbulent air flow, with the intensity depending on the flow rate.

TABLE 13–1. SYSTEMATIC APPROACH TO PHYSICAL EXAMINATION OF THE CHEST

I. Inspection
Initial impression—distress, wheeze, malnourishment, etc.
Respiratory rate, depth, and pattern
Asynchronous motion of the rib cage and abdomen
Recession of the intercostal, supraclavicular, or suprasternal spaces
Tracheal tug
Cyanosis
Finger clubbing or nicotine stains
Accessory muscle employment
Pursed-lip breathing
Chest wall shape and deformity

II. Palpation
Tracheal deviation
Chest expansion (globally/locally)
Vocal fremitus
Pleural rub
Lymphadenopathy
Subcutaneous emphysema

III. Percussion
Normal, dull, or increased

IV. Auscultation
Breath sounds—can be only normal, reduced, or bronchial (last associated with increased vocal resonance, whispering pectoriloquy, and egophony)
Added sounds—can be only absent, wheezes, crackles, or pleural rub

They are produced entirely in the trachea and large airways and are transmitted to the chest wall initially by the smaller airways and finally through the lung parenchyma. The passage through the lung filters out the high frequencies and accounts for the differences in normal breath sounds heard at different places. As we move away from the central airways to the periphery of the lung, the filtering effect serves to diminish the inspiratory and almost eliminate the expiratory noise. This is the normal vesicular breath sound. Bronchial breath sounds are essentially unfiltered, and both inspiration and expiration are clearly heard. These are heard normally over the trachea and the central airways in the back.

The breath sounds can be only normal, decreased, or increased. Decreased intensity of the breath sounds is due to either (1) impaired movement of air that normally generates the breath sounds, as in emphysema, diphragmatic paralysis, or bronchial obstruction, or (2) impaired transmission from the lung to the chest wall due to pneumothorax, pleural effusion, or pleural thickening. An increased transmission of the breath sounds is characterized by the finding of bronchial breath sounds (similar to the sound normally heard over the trachea) over the peripheral lung fields. Bronchial breathing is most commonly found with consolidation but also occurs at the interface with a pleural effusion where the lung is compressed. Upon completion of the initial auscultation, the examiner can verify the presence of bronchial breathing by demonstrating the presence of the

TABLE 13 – 2. PHYSICAL FINDINGS IN COMMON PULMONARY DISORDERS

DISORDER	MEDIASTINAL DISPLACEMENT	CHEST WALL MOVEMENT	VOCAL FREMITUS	PERCUSSION NOTE	BREATH SOUNDS	ADDED SOUNDS	VOICE SOUNDS
Pleural effusion	Heart displaced to opposite side	Reduced over affected area	Absent or markedly decreased	Stony dull	Absent over fluid; bronchial at upper border	Absent; pleural rub may be found above effusion	Absent over effusion; increased with egophony at upper border
Consolidation	None	Reduced over affected area	Increased	Dull	Bronchial	Crackles	Increased with egophony and whispering pectoriloquy
Pneumothorax	Tracheal deviation to opposite side if under tension	Decreased over affected area	Absent	Resonant	Absent	Absent	Absent
Atelectasis	Ipsilateral shift	Decreased over affected area	Absent	Dull	Absent or diminished	Absent	Absent
Bronchospasm	None	Decreased symmetrically	Normal or decreased	Normal or decreased	Normal	Wheeze	Normal or decreased
Interstitial fibrosis	None	Decreased symmetrically	Normal or increased	Normal	Normal	Coarse crackles unaffected by cough or posture	Normal

associated features: increased vocal resonance, whispering pectoriloquy (whispered sounds are heard more clearly), and egophony (the phonated e is heard as a).

Added sounds can be of only three types: wheezes, crackles, and pleural sounds. Wheezes are continuous, musical sounds thought to occur as air passes through a narrowed airway, setting up oscillations in the walls. They are more common during expiration, since dynamic compression exaggerates the constriction. Wheezes may be diffuse (asthma or chronic bronchitis) or localized, as in the case of a partially obstructed bronchus (tumor, secretions, or foreign body).

Crackles, formerly called rales or crepitations, are short sequences of discontinuous sounds that may be heard in inspiration or expiration. Very coarse crackles heard over the large airways are thought to result from air moving through secretions. However, most crackles are generated farther out in the lung field as a result of the popping open of small airways that were closed during the previous expiration owing to low lung volumes, alterations in lung compliance, or increases in interstitial pressure. These factors are magnified in the bases, and they are more common there even if the underlying process is diffuse. When fine, a crackle is mimicked by rubbing hair close to the ear between the thumb and finger, whereas the coarse crackle is like the sound of a Velcro fastener opening. The finding of crackles is a nonspecific indicator of pulmonary parenchymal disease, and the crackles of congestive failure cannot be differentiated from those of pulmonary infection or fibrosis.

Pleural sounds may be a rub, like the creaking of leather, found with pleural inflammation, or the mediastinal crunching sound synchronous with systole, found with a pneumomediastinum and likened to the sound created by walking through snow.

The typical physical findings in the major pulmonary disorders are outlined in Table 13–2.

REFERENCE

Bramsen SS (ed): Pulmonary signs and symptoms. Clin Chest Med 8:177–334, 1987.

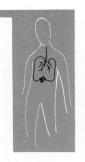

14 ANATOMIC AND PHYSIOLOGIC CONSIDERATIONS

The major function of the lungs is to deliver to the tissues enough oxygen (O_2) to meet their energy demands and to remove the carbon dioxide (CO_2) formed as a by-product of metabolism. This demand varies dramatically, from basal levels of 3 to 4 ml of O_2 or CO_2 $kg^{-1} \cdot min^{-1}$ to as much as 60 ml of O_2 or CO_2 $kg^{-1} \cdot min^{-1}$ at maximum exercise capacity. To accomplish this, sufficient blood and gas must be brought together at a sufficiently large surface area to allow for rapid and adequate gas exchange.

THE AIRWAY

Structure

The inspired air travels through a complex pathway on its way to the alveoli. The nose and pharynx heat, humidify, and filter the air of particulates and water-soluble gases. Air then passes through the larynx, a complex group of muscles and cartilages, which remains patent during inspiration and closes during swallowing and maneuvers that require an increase in intrathoracic pressure, such as defecation and vomiting.

Beyond the larynx is the trachea, a 10- to 12-cm tube supported by U-shaped cartilages and a fibrous posterior membrane. The trachea divides into two mainstem bronchi at the carina. The right mainstem bronchus is a more direct continuation of the trachea; thus, aspirated foreign bodies tend to lodge on the right side. The airways continue to branch, and in the smaller airways the cartilage becomes incomplete and disappears when the airways are 1 to 2 mm in diameter. The first 19 branches, ending at the terminal bronchioles, provide a rapid and enormous expansion of the total airway cross-sectional area, increasing from 2.5 cm² in the trachea to approximately 900 cm² (Fig. 14–1). Beyond this are three genera-

FIGURE 14–1. The subdivision of the airways and their nomenclature. The cross-sectional area increases dramatically as we reach the peripheral, small airways. (Adapted from Weibel ER: Morphometry of the Human Lung. Berlin, Springer, 1963; with permission.)

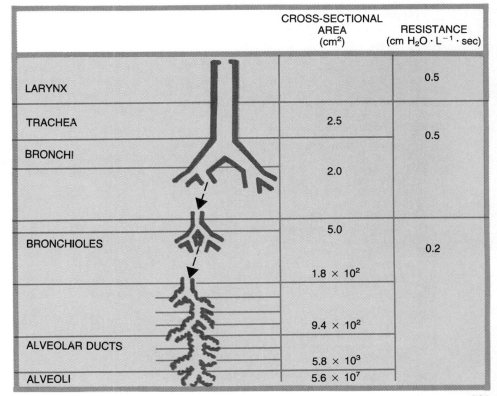

	CROSS-SECTIONAL AREA (cm²)	RESISTANCE (cm H$_2$O · L^{-1} · sec)
LARYNX		0.5
TRACHEA	2.5	0.5
BRONCHI	2.0	
BRONCHIOLES	5.0	0.2
	1.8×10^2	
	9.4×10^2	
ALVEOLAR DUCTS	5.8×10^3	
ALVEOLI	5.6×10^7	

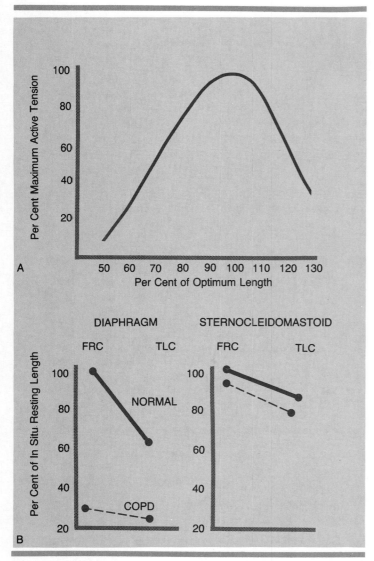

FIGURE 14–2. *A,* The length-tension curve for the diaphragm. At lengths above or below the optimal in situ resting length, the amount of tension generated decreases. *B,* The change in the length of the diaphragm and sternocleidomastoid muscles at functional residual capacity (FRC) and total lung capacity (TLC) in a normal subject and a patient with chronic obstructive lung disease (COPD) and hyperinflation. Increased FRC shortens the resting length of the diaphragm so that contraction during inspiration becomes inefficient. Consequently, rib cage expansion becomes more dependent on accessory muscle contraction. (From Druz WS, Danon J, Fishman HC, et al: Approaches to assessing respiratory muscle function in respiratory disease. Am Rev Respir Dis 119:145, 1979; with permission.)

tions of respiratory bronchioles whose walls are made up of increasing proportions of alveoli. This anatomic arrangement progresses into the alveolar ducts and culminates in the alveolar sacs. At this point, the cross-sectional area of the alveolar capillary membrane has increased to an incredible 50 to 100 m².

The epithelial surface of the alveolar capillary membrane, the site of gas exchange, consists of type I and type II pneumonocytes, the latter thought to be the progenitor of the former. The type II cell is responsible for the production of surfactant and possibly for other metabolic activities within the lung. After a significant injury to the alveolar-capillary membrane, this cell proliferates and is probably responsible for the repair.

VENTILATION

During inspiration, respiratory muscle contraction increases intrathoracic volume, which in turn decreases airway pressure below atmospheric and causes air to enter the lungs. Expiration is passive, as the intrinsic elasticity of the lungs and chest wall returns the volume of the system to its resting position. With increased ventilatory requirements, the expiratory muscles may be enlisted to assist in lung emptying.

The respiratory muscles include the diaphragm, the intercostal and accessory muscles, and the abdominal muscles. The diaphragm is the major muscle of inspiration, and when it contracts, it pushes down against the abdominal contents, causing the thoracic cage to expand by moving the chest wall in a cephalad direction as well as pushing out against the lower ribs. The increase in abdominal pressure causes an outward motion of the abdominal wall, the clinical hallmark of diaphragmatic contraction. The intercostal and accessory muscles, primarily the sternocleidomastoid and the scalene muscles, facilitate inspiration by directly elevating the chest wall. The abdominal muscles increase abdominal pressure and drive the relaxed diaphragm upward during expiration and other situations requiring increases in intrathoracic pressure, such as coughing. As expiration is normally passive, expiratory muscle activity is not necessary unless ventilatory requirements are high or significant airway obstruction is present.

The respiratory muscles, like other skeletal muscles, will, if stressed sufficiently, fatigue. Proper training can induce a small but significant increase in their strength and endurance. The typical relations between resting length and the amount of tension developed also exist. For the respiratory muscles, length can be translated into lung volume, and when length is increased, as in emphysema, inspiratory muscle efficiency is decreased (Fig. 14–2).

To increase intrathoracic volume, the respiratory muscles must overcome elastic and resistive forces. If the lungs of a normal individual were removed from the chest, they would collapse, while the volume of the chest wall would expand to about 80 per cent of the total capacity of the thoracic space. Thus, when combined, the lungs and chest wall pull in opposite directions, with the resting volume of the system, the functional residual capacity (FRC), occurring at the volume at which the outward pull of the chest wall equals

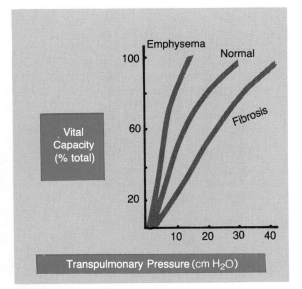

FIGURE 14-3. The compliance curves for normal subjects and patients with emphysema and pulmonary fibrosis. An elevation in the transpulmonary pressure required to achieve a given lung volume increases the work of breathing.

the inward pull of the lungs, which is normally less than 50 per cent of total lung capacity (TLC).

Changes in elasticity are commonly considered in terms of inverse function: compliance equals the change in volume or change in pressure. In normal lungs, near FRC, it takes an average of 1 cm H_2O to inflate the lungs by 200 ml (Fig. 14-3); that is, compliance at this volume is 200 ml/cm H_2O. However, near TLC the lung and chest wall get stiffer, requiring greater inflationary pressure. Compliance decreases with pulmonary fibrosis or pulmonary edema and increases with emphysema. The normal compliance of the chest wall is also 200 ml/cm H_2O, and this may be decreased by skeletal abnormalities such as scoliosis or increased by the loss of respiratory muscle tone in neuromuscular disease.

The second force that must be overcome by the respiratory muscles is airway resistance, defined as the driving pressure divided by air flow, normally 1 to 2 cm H_2O $L^{-1} \cdot sec^{-1}$. It is greatly dependent on the total cross-sectional areas of the airways, and thus, even though the individual peripheral airways are narrow, their contribution to overall airway resistance is small because of the increase in total cross-sectional area (see Fig. 14-1). Many factors influence airway resistance. An increase in lung volume decreases resistance because of the tethering effect of the alveoli on the airways. Other factors that influence airway resistance include bronchial smooth muscle contraction (bronchospasm), intrinsic or extrinsic airway compression, and the dynamic compression of a forced expiration.

The work of breathing is the product of the pressure generated and the change in volume. In normal subjects, this represents a tiny fraction of the overall energy utilized by the body (4 to 5 per cent), even with high ventilatory requirements such as exercise. However, in the presence of lung disease, as the work of breathing increases, the O_2 requirements of the respiratory muscles can become inordinately high, greater than 25 per cent of total-body O_2 consumption. Under these circumstances, the benefit of any increase in gas exchange achieved by increasing ventilation may be offset, or even exceeded, by the increased O_2 consumption and CO_2 production of the respiratory muscles.

Gas entering the lungs is divided into that entering the gas-exchanging regions of the lung, the alveolar volume (VA), and that remaining in the conducting airways, the dead space (VD). At end expiration, VD is filled with gas that has already equilibrated with pulmonary capillary blood, and thus on the subsequent inspiration the amount of fresh gas reaching the alveoli is equal to the tidal volume (VT) minus VD. VD makes up 20 to 40 per cent of a normal VT.

Distribution of VA within the lung depends on the regional pleural pressure. Normally, pleural pressure is most negative at the apex of the lung and becomes less negative as we move toward the lung base. This gradient is caused by a combination of gravity due to the weight of the lung and the different stresses imposed by the shape of the lung and chest wall. As a result of this gradient, the lung bases are better ventilated than the apices.

Control of Ventilation

The precise adjustment in ventilation necessary to meet changing metabolic demands is made by balancing tidal volume and respiratory frequency through the integrative function of the three components of the respiratory control system: respiratory control centers, respiratory sensors, and respiratory effectors (Fig. 14-4).

Respiratory Control Centers

The neurons controlling respiration are located at several levels in the brain stem. The most important network resides in the medulla oblongata, where respiratory rhythm originates. These medullary neurons receive input from the pons, which, while not necessary for rhythmic breathing, appears to fine tune the respiratory pattern. The brain stem centers are responsible for the automatic control of ventilation, but the cerebral cortex can override them during wakefulness to permit speech and other actions requiring voluntary control of ventilation.

Respiratory Sensors

The respiratory sensors consist of the central and peripheral chemoreceptors and the chest wall and

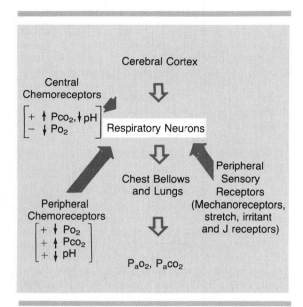

FIGURE 14-4. Schematic representation of the respiratory control system. The respiratory neurons in the brain stem receive information from the chemoreceptors, peripheral sensory receptors, and cerebral cortex. This information is integrated, and the resulting neural output is transmitted to the chest bellows and lungs.

intrapulmonary sensory receptors. The central chemoreceptors, located on the ventral surface of the medulla oblongata, rapidly respond to any increase in CO_2 or hydrogen ion concentration by increasing ventilation (Fig. 14-5A). Under normal circumstances, these receptors are very sensitive, keeping the Pa_{CO_2} constant despite marked variability in CO_2 production. In contrast, hypoxia does not act as a central respiratory stimulant but instead depresses the central chemoreceptors. Conversely, the peripheral chemoreceptors, located in the carotid bodies, are activated mainly by hypoxia and less so by CO_2 and hydrogen ions. They are also sensitive to a fall in blood pressure, which may partly account for hyperventilation seen in shock. Unlike linear response to P_{CO_2}, the ventilatory response to hypoxemia is hyperbolic, and a fall in P_{O_2} causes little increase in ventilation until there is significant hypoxemia (P_{O_2} less than 60 mm Hg) (Fig. 14-5B).

Mechanoreceptors in the chest wall respond to stretch of the intercostal muscles and reflexly modulate the rate and depth of breathing. Tidal volume and respiratory frequency may also be reflexly affected by stimuli arising in (1) airway irritant receptors, which respond to physical or chemical stimulation; (2) pulmonary stretch receptors, which respond to marked increases in lung volume (Hering-Breuer reflex); or (3) J receptors found in the juxtacapillary junctions, which respond to vascular engorgement and congestion.

Signals are transmitted from the respiratory center to the respiratory muscles by (1) the phrenic nerves, which supply the diaphragm; (2) the intercostal nerves, which innervate the intercostal and abdominal muscles; (3) the accessory cranial nerves, which supply the sternomastoid muscles; and (4) the lower cervical nerves, which supply the scalene muscles. In addition, a variety of muscles acting on the soft palate, tongue, and hyoid bone maintain upper airway patency and offset the collapsing effect of the negative pressures generated by the respiratory muscles. During wakefulness, both the upper airway and the chest wall

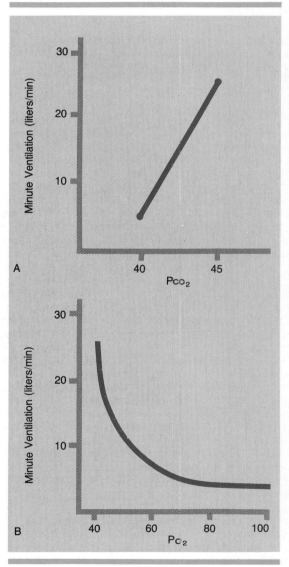

FIGURE 14-5. A rising P_{CO_2} leads to a linear increase in minute ventilation (*A*). The ventilatory response to hypoxemia (*B*) is less sensitive and is clinically relevant only when the P_{O_2} has dropped significantly.

muscles display rhythmic inspiratory activity. During sleep, upper airway muscle activity wanes, whereas diaphragmatic activation changes little.

THE BLOOD VESSELS

Structure

The lung receives its blood supply from two vascular systems—the bronchial and pulmonary circulations. The nutritive blood flow to all but the alveolar structures comes from the bronchial circulation, which originates from the aorta and upper intercostal arteries and receives about 1 per cent of the cardiac output. About one third of the venous effluent of the bronchial circulation drains into the systemic veins and back to the right ventricle. The remainder drains into the pulmonary veins and, along with the contribution from the thebesian veins in the heart, represents a component of the 1 to 2 per cent right-to-left shunt found in normal subjects.

The pulmonary arterial system runs alongside the airways from the hila to the periphery. The arteries down to the level of the subsegmental airways (2-mm diameter) are thin-walled, predominantly elastic vessels. Beyond this, the arteries become muscularized until they reach diameters of 30 μm, at which point the muscular coat disappears. Most of the arterial pressure drop takes place in these small muscular arteries, which are responsible for the active control of blood flow distribution in the lung. The pulmonary arterioles empty into an extensive capillary network and drain into thin-walled pulmonary veins, which eventually join with the arteries and bronchi at the hilum and exit the lung to enter the left atrium.

Perfusion

The pulmonary vascular bed serves as a source of nutritive blood to the alveolar membrane, but its most important role is in pulmonary gas exchange. It delivers the entire systemic venous return to the pulmonary capillary bed, where exchange of O_2 and CO_2 occurs. Although it receives the same blood flow per minute as the systemic circulation, there are differences between the vascular beds. First, since the pulmonary vascular resistance, calculated as (pulmonary arterial pressure/left atrial pressure) cardiac output, is only about one tenth of systemic vascular resistance, the pressure in the pulmonary vascular bed is only one tenth of that in the systemic circulation. Second, all structures within the thorax, including the pulmonary vascular bed, the heart, and the great vessels, are exposed to the surrounding pressures, both pleural and alveolar, which vary during respiration.

The distribution of blood flow within the lung is greatly dependent on the interaction between vascular and alveolar pressure. Alveolar pressure is relatively constant throughout the lung. However, like any column of fluid, pulmonary vascular pressure is lower at the top and greater at the bottom of the lung (Fig. 14–6). At the apex, pulmonary arterial pressure is usually just able to overcome alveolar pressure. However, a fall in arterial pressure or any rise in alveolar pressure (positive pressure breathing) may cause alveolar pressure to exceed arterial pressure, with cessation of flow. This is known as zone 1 conditions. Below this lies zone 2, where the alveolar pressure is less than arterial pressure but greater than venous pressure. Blood flow in zone 2 depends on the difference between arterial pressure and alveolar pressure. Blood flow continues to increase down zone 2 because of rising arterial pressure and eventually reaches a point, zone 3, at which venous pressure finally exceeds alveolar pressure and flow becomes dependent on arterial-venous pressure difference. Blood flow increases progressively down zone 3 because of increasing distention and recruitment of the pulmonary vessels.

Many factors affect the overall pressure-flow relations in the pulmonary circulation. When cardiac output increases in normal upright humans, as during exercise, pulmonary vascular resistance actually falls because of the ability to recruit new vessels and distend the ones already open. This allows large increases in blood flow with lesser increases in pressure, thus preventing the transudation of fluid into the lungs owing to a higher microvascular pressure. Pulmonary vascular resistance is also affected by lung volume. It is low-

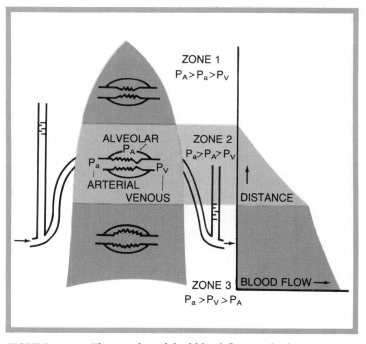

FIGURE 14–6. The zonal model of blood flow in the lung. Because of the interrelationship of vascular and alveolar pressures, the lung base receives the most flow (see text for explanation). (From West JB, Dollery CT, Naimark A: Distribution of blood flow in isolated lung; relation to vascular and alveolar pressures. J Appl Physiol 19:713, 1964; with permission.)

est at FRC and increases at lower lung volumes because there is less distention of the pulmonary arteries, which, like the airways, are tethered by the lung parenchyma. At higher lung volumes, pulmonary vascular resistance also falls owing to compression of capillaries by the distending alveoli.

In addition to these passive influences, a number of factors actively affect pulmonary vascular tone. The most important is alveolar hypoxia, which results in constriction of the perfusing artery by mechanisms as yet unknown. This factor may be useful when alveolar hypoxia is localized, since reduction in perfusion to poorly ventilated alveoli reduces the abnormality of gas exchange, which is otherwise inevitable. During generalized hypoxia, its beneficial nature is not always apparent, as in sojourners at high altitude, in whom it may be a major cause of pulmonary edema. Acidosis causes a vasoconstrictor response of lesser magnitude. Other vasoactive compounds produced in the body, such as prostaglandins and adrenergic substances, may also alter pulmonary vascular tone.

Gas Transfer

CO_2 and O_2 are transported between the environment and the tissues by convection and diffusion (Fig. 14–7). In the blood, O_2 combines with hemoglobin, and the resulting O_2 saturation is determined by the oxyhemoglobin dissociation curve

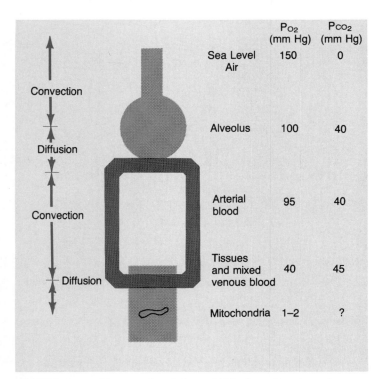

FIGURE 14–7. The transfer of O_2 and CO_2 from the atmosphere to the mitochondria.

(Fig. 14–8A). More than 98 per cent of O_2 in the blood is combined with hemoglobin; the remainder is dissolved in the plasma. Above a Pa_{O_2} of 150 mm Hg, hemoglobin is totally saturated and carries 1.34 ml O_2/gm hemoglobin; further rises in Pa_{O_2} increase only the amount of O_2 dissolved in the plasma at the rate of 0.003 ml O_2/100 ml blood/mm Hg Po_2. CO_2 is carried in the blood in three forms: bicarbonate (90 per cent), dissolved in plasma, or combined with protein, predominantly hemoglobin. The relation between the Pco_2 and the CO_2 content is described by the CO_2 dissociation curve (Fig. 14–8B), which is steeper and more linear than the oxyhemoglobin dissociation curve.

A number of factors influence the relations between Po_2 and Pco_2 and their contents, which can be described as changes in the position of the respective dissociation curves. Increased Pco_2 and temperature and decreased pH shift the oxyhemoglobin dissociation curve to the right, decreasing affinity of hemoglobin for O_2 and expediting its release to the tissues. Converse changes in the above factors have the opposite effect. Increased levels of 2,3-diphosphoglycerate (2,3-DPG), produced during chronic hypoxemia or anemia, also shift the curve to the right, whereas carbon monoxide shifts it to the left and also reduces the O_2 content by competitively binding to hemoglobin. The most important influence on the CO_2 dissociation curve is Po_2; increased Po_2 shifts the curve to the right, thus reducing the affinity of hemoglobin for CO_2 and assisting in the unloading of CO_2 in the lungs.

PULMONARY GAS EXCHANGE

The arterial blood gas values are determined by the composition of alveolar gas and its successful equilibration with the blood in the pulmonary capillaries. In turn, the Po_2 and Pco_2 in the alveoli are determined by the inspired gas tensions, the mixed venous Po_2 and Pco_2, the total ventilation, the blood flow, and, most important, the success with which the lung is able to match ventilation and blood flow. Abnormality of any of these factors leads to hypoxemia and/or hypercapnia.

Hypoventilation. Minute ventilation and the arterial Pco_2 are inversely related. Hypoventilation is defined as a minute ventilation that, for a given metabolic demand, is inadequate to keep the arterial Pco_2 in the normal range. Since ventilation is normally closely coupled to metabolic CO_2 production, hypoventilation usually represents a failure of respiratory control or of the ventilatory pump to respond. Hypoventilation is commonly due to pharmacologic depression of or structural damage to the respiratory center, a neuromuscular disease, or a chest wall abnormality.

The increase in Pco_2 leads to a concomitant fall in the Po_2, as described in the alveolar gas equation

$$PA_{O_2} = (PB - PH_2O)\, FI_{O_2} - \frac{Pa_{CO_2}}{R}$$

where PA_{O_2} is alveolar Po_2, PB is atmospheric

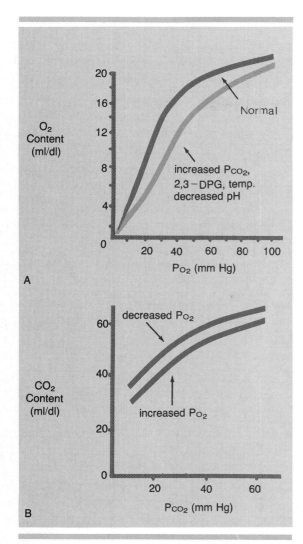

A

B

FIGURE 14–8. *A*, The oxyhemoglobin dissociation curve. The bulk of the O_2 is carried combined with hemoglobin. The various factors that decrease the hemoglobin O_2 affinity are shown. Opposite changes increase hemoglobin O_2 affinity, shifting the curve to the left. *B*, The CO_2 dissociation curve. It is more linear than the oxyhemoglobin curve throughout the physiologic range. Increased Po_2 shifts the curve to the right, which decreases CO_2 content for any given Pco_2 and thus facilitates CO_2 off-loading in the lungs. The shift to the left at a lower Po_2 facilitates CO_2 on-loading at the tissues.

pressure (usually 760 mm Hg), P_{H_2O} is the partial pressure of water vapor (47 mm Hg), Fi_{O_2} is the fractional concentration of inspired O_2, and R is the respiratory exchange ratio (which can be estimated at 0.8). We see that any rise in Pa_{CO_2} leads to a concomitant fall in PA_{O_2} and thus in Pa_{O_2}.

Abnormal Diffusion. Under normal conditions, blood spends about 0.75 second in the pulmonary capillaries. Since it ordinarily takes only about one third of this time for the blood to equilibrate with alveolar gas, there is a wide safety margin before abnormal pathology results in nonequilibration, that is, a diffusion impairment. It has been estimated that the diffusing capacity of the lung must

fall to less than 10 per cent of normal before it affects Pa_{O_2} at rest. Three factors may stress the system sufficiently to interfere with complete equilibration: increased diffusion distance due to a thickening of the alveolar capillary membrane; increased rate of blood flow or a reduction in the number of open capillaries, decreasing the time the blood spends in the process of equilibration; and reduced driving pressure from alveolus to blood, as seen at extreme altitudes. Diffusion impairment almost never plays a role in the hypoxemia of disease unless at least two of the above factors are in force. Even when abnormal diffusion is present, it usually accounts for only a minimal amount of the observed disturbance in gas exchange.

Ventilation-Perfusion Inequality. The proper matching of ventilation and blood flow within the lung is necessary for the adequate uptake of O_2 and elimination of CO_2. While the lung is sometimes regarded as a single gas-exchanging unit, it really contains units that differ in their relative amounts of blood flow and ventilation. In normal persons, the span of ventilation-perfusion ($\dot{V}_A/\dot{Q}$) ratios is very small, varying from about 0.5 to 3.0, with an average of 0.8. As lung disease develops, the range increasingly widens, with some units receiving very little ventilation relative to perfusion, while others are excessively ventilated. If $\dot{V}_A/\dot{Q}$ inequality develops, the arterial Po_2 will fall and the Pco_2 will rise (Fig. 14–9A). In patients with normal respiratory drive and without severe

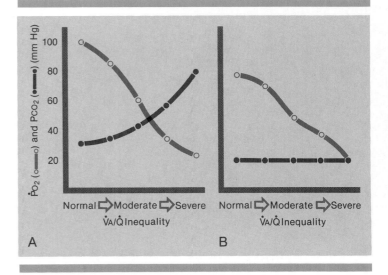

A
B

FIGURE 14–9. *A*, The effect of increasing ventilation-perfusion ($\dot{V}_A/\dot{Q}$) inequality on arterial Po_2 and Pco_2 when cardiac output and minute ventilation are held constant. The change in gas tensions when ventilation is allowed to increase is shown in *B*. Increased ventilation can maintain a normal Pco_2 but can only partially correct the hypoxemia. (Adapted from Dantzker DR: Gas exchange abnormalities. *In* Montenegro H [ed]: Chronic Obstructive Pulmonary Disease. New York, Churchill Livingstone, 1984, pp 141–160; with permission.)

limitation in ventilatory capacity, the increasing P_{CO_2} leads to a progressive increase in ventilation. This increase in ventilation is capable of keeping the P_{CO_2} normal but only minimally attenuates the fall in the P_{O_2} (Fig. 14–9B) because of the different shapes of the oxyhemoglobin and carboxyhemoglobin dissociation curves (see Fig. 14–8). The oxyhemoglobin dissociation curve plateaus at a high P_{O_2}, and thus the increased P_{O_2} in alveoli receiving increased ventilation fails to increase the O_2 content of blood leaving that unit. Since no additional O_2 has been added, it cannot compensate for the poorly ventilated lung units. The carboxyhemoglobin dissociation curve, on the other hand, is linear throughout the physiologic range. Any decrease in P_{CO_2} is accompanied by a fall in CO_2 content, allowing the overventilated alveoli to offset the failure of poorly ventilated lung units to eliminate CO_2. As $\dot{V}_A/\dot{Q}$ inequality worsens with progression of the underlying disease, further increases in ventilation eventually become impossible, and both hypoxemia and hypercapnia result. $\dot{V}_A/\dot{Q}$ inequality is the characteristic abnormality of gas exchange in chronic obstructive and restrictive lung diseases.

Shunt. Intrapulmonary or intracardiac shunt, where blood bypasses ventilated lung units, is a most potent source of hypoxemia, but hypercapnia is not seen (Fig. 14–10). In fact, as the hypoxemia progresses, hypocapnia is usually found owing to the stimulatory effects of the low P_{aO_2} on ventilatory drive. Shunting is the major mechanism of hypoxemia in pulmonary edema, pneumonia, and atelectasis.

NONPULMONARY FACTORS

Abnormalities other than alterations in lung function may influence the P_{aO_2} through their effect on the mixed venous P_{O_2} (P_{vO_2}). The P_{vO_2} is decreased when cardiac output is inappropriately low, when O_2 consumption ($\dot{V}_{O_2}$) is increased (as with exercise or fever), or when the hemoglobin concentration or O_2 saturation is low. For any lung unit, the resultant end-capillary P_{O_2} is influenced by the P_{vO_2}, although the magnitude of this effect on the arterial O_2 content will be greatest in lungs with $\dot{V}_A/\dot{Q}$ inequality or shunt (Fig. 14–11). The importance of this phenomenon is the recognition that a fall in P_{aO_2} in a patient with lung disease may be due to one of these nonpulmonary factors rather than to deterioration in lung function, thus requiring a very different intervention.

TISSUE GAS EXCHANGE

As in the lung, gas exchange in the tissues is accomplished by passive diffusion, which requires, for optimal functioning, that an adequate amount

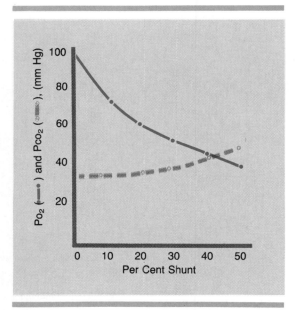

FIGURE 14–10. The effect of increasing shunt on the arterial P_{O_2} and P_{CO_2}. The minute ventilation has been held constant in this example. Under normal circumstances, the hypoxemia would lead to an increased minute ventilation and a fall in the P_{CO_2} as the shunt increases. (From Dantzker DR: Gas exchange abnormalities. *In* Montenegro H [ed]: Chronic Obstructive Pulmonary Disease. New York, Churchill Livingstone, 1984, pp 141–160; with permission.)

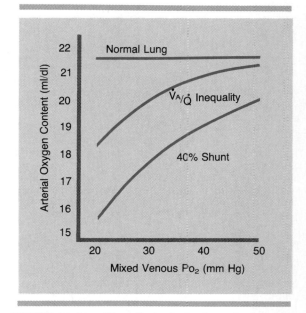

FIGURE 14–11. The effect of altering mixed venous P_{O_2} (P_{vO_2}) on the arterial oxygen content under three assumed conditions: a normal lung, severe ventilation-perfusion ($\dot{V}_A/\dot{Q}$) inequality, and the presence of a 40 per cent shunt. For each situation the patient is breathing 50 per cent O_2 and the P_{vO_2} is altered, keeping all other variables constant. (From Dantzker DR: Gas exchange in the adult respiratory distress syndrome. Clin Chest Med 3:57, 1982; with permission.)

of blood be brought into proximity with the actively metabolizing cells. Unfortunately, much less is known about the factors that control this process than is understood about gas exchange in the lung. It is likely, however, that under pathologic conditions similar pathophysiologic abnormalities are present. A reduction of total O_2 delivery to the tissues (analogous to hypoventilation) leads to a reduction of tissue PO_2 and acidosis. Abnormal diffusion resulting from a shortened residence time of blood in the capillaries or increased distance from the capillary to the cell is likely under conditions of tissue inflammation or abnormal microvascular control. Maldistribution of blood flow with regard to tissue O_2 requirements or even shunting of blood around capillary beds has been postulated in gram-negative sepsis. Confirmation of the role of any of these proposed mechanisms in disease states awaits further technologic advances that will allow measurement of gas exchange at the tissue level.

NONRESPIRATORY FUNCTIONS OF THE LUNG

In addition to its central role in gas exchange, the lung is active in both the metabolism and the degradation of many substances. Surfactant production by the alveolar type II cell is an important metabolic function of the lungs. This phospholipid minimizes surface tension and thus confers stability on the alveoli and small airways, preventing atelectasis and decreasing the work of breathing. The failure of the immature lung to produce sufficient surfactant leads to the respiratory distress syndrome (RDS) of the newborn. The lung is also involved in the biosynthesis of arachidonic acid into products of both the lipoxygenase and cyclooxygenase pathways. Although a myriad of physiologic functions have been ascribed to these agents, a clear relation to pulmonary function is still lacking. In addition, the lung is capable of removing or inactivating a large number of biologically active substances, including serotonin, bradykinin, and prostaglandins. It is also the principal site of the conversion of angiotensin I to angiotensin II.

REFERENCES

Dantzker DR: Cardiopulmonary Critical Care. 2nd ed. Philadelphia, WB Saunders Co, 1991.
Murray JF: The Normal Lung. 2nd ed. Philadelphia, WB Saunders Co, 1986.
Weibel ER: The Pathway for Oxygen. Cambridge, MA, Harvard University Press, 1984.
West JB: Respiratory Physiology—The Essentials. 3rd ed. Baltimore, Williams & Wilkins Co, 1985.

15 DIAGNOSTIC TECHNIQUES AND THEIR INDICATIONS

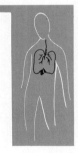

IMAGING PROCEDURES

The standard chest roentgenogram complements the history and physical examination as the starting point for the diagnosis of pulmonary disorders. The chest radiograph may demonstrate a density that only physical examination can distinguish as being either consolidation or loculated fluid. Conversely, the chest radiograph may show dramatic involvement of the lung by tuberculosis, while the physical examination may yield unremarkable findings. Standard views include the posteroanterior (PA) and the left lateral projections; they reduce disproportionate magnification of the heart and anterior mediastinal structures. These films allow visualization of the air-containing lung, vascular markings, heart and mediastinal structures, pleura, lymph nodes, ribs, spine, and soft tissues of the thorax. Correct interpretation requires that the film be taken as close to total lung capacity as possible. A correctly exposed film allows the vertebral bodies to be barely visible behind the heart. A number of specialized views and procedures can be added to the standard PA and lateral films (Table 15–1).

Significant improvement in visualization of chest structures has occurred with the use of computed tomography (CT), which provides excellent visibility of areas previously difficult to see and has 10 times the contrast resolution of conventional radiography. Excellent evaluation of the mediastinum makes it valuable in the work-up of bronchogenic neoplasms. Differentiating pleural from parenchymal densities, a common problem on the routine film, has been improved. CT has virtually replaced the standard tomograms for evaluating the presence of early metastatic spread to the lung parenchyma. Unfortunately, specificity

TABLE 15-1. SPECIALIZED RADIOGRAPHIC TECHNIQUES

STUDY OR VIEW	INDICATION	COMMENT
Oblique	Visualization of hilum and pleural plaques. Contralateral oblique is best view for apical disease.	Better done with CT
Lordotic	Right middle lobe and lingular disease	
Lateral decubitus	Identification of pleural effusions, air-fluid levels, and fungus balls	Both left and right should always be done
Upright-supine	Differentiation of pleural from parenchymal disease in critically ill patients requiring portable radiography	
Inspiratory-expiratory	Obstruction of bronchus or air trapping in enclosed pleural or lung spaces	
Bronchograms	Diagnosis of bronchiectasis	Indicated only in the rare situation when surgery is contemplated; can now be diagnosed by CT
Pulmonary angiogram	Detection of congenital anomalies of the pulmonary vasculature; diagnosis of pulmonary emboli	
Fluoroscopy	Diaphragmatic movement; differentiation between chest wall lesions and lung parenchymal lesions	

CT = Computed tomography.

is low, and 20 to 60 per cent of nodules visualized on the CT scan but not on the radiograph are benign. In addition, CT is useful for detecting calcification in pulmonary nodules. High-resolution CT scanning of the lung parenchyma, possible with newer-generation CT scanners, is more sensitive in detecting interstitial disease than are plain chest radiographs or standard CT scans. While high-resolution CT scanning can yield findings specific for certain interstitial lung diseases, confirmatory clinical and biopsy data remain essential for diagnosis in most cases. Currently, the greatest utility of this technique may be in the evaluation of clinically suspected diffuse interstitial lung disease when specific findings are absent on standard imaging tests.

Ultrasonography is useful in helping to differentiate between solids and fluids in pleural opacities and to localize loculated pleural effusions. The utility of magnetic resonance imaging for most pulmonary diseases remains to be determined.

PULMONARY FUNCTION EVALUATION

Routine studies performed in the pulmonary function laboratory can be grouped into four categories: lung volumes, air flow, diffusing capacity, and maximal pressures.

One problem in interpreting pulmonary function tests is establishment of normative values. Reference studies demonstrate that test results are "normally" distributed. Values ranging within 1.64 standard deviations of the mean encompass 90 per cent of individuals and are considered normal. However, an arbitrary percentage of the mean cannot be used to define normal for all studies, since the width of the normal distribution varies from test to test. In addition, because of the broad range of normal values, patients with results "within normal limits" may still have pulmonary disease if a change is noted upon serial testing.

The lung is conveniently divided into four volumes and three capacities, each capacity consisting of a number of volumes (Fig. 15-1). The components of the vital capacity can be obtained with routine spirometry. The residual volume (RV), however, must be measured indirectly, since it represents air left in the lungs at completion of a full expiration. In fact, we actually measure functional residual capacity (FRC) rather than RV, since the former, that is, the volume at the end of a normal expiration, is a more reproducible point. The expiratory reserve volume (ERV) is then subtracted from FRC to obtain the RV.

Two techniques are commonly used to measure FRC: helium dilution and body plethysmography.

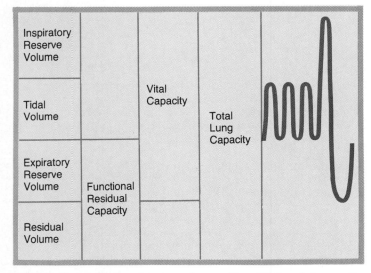

FIGURE 15-1. Lung volumes and capacities. While vital capacity and its subdivision can be measured by spirometry, calculation of residual volume requires measurement of functional residual capacity by body plethysmography, helium dilution technique, or nitrogen washout.

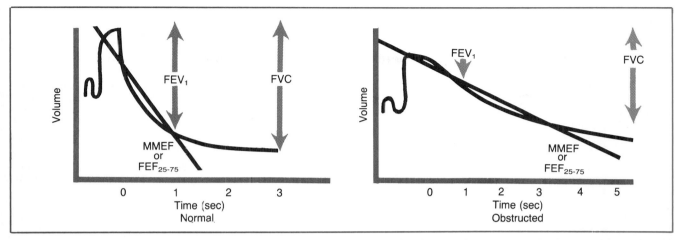

FIGURE 15-2. Spirometry in a normal subject and a patient with obstructive lung disease. FEV$_1$ represents the forced expired volume in 1 second, and FVC represents the forced vital capacity. The slope of the line connecting the points at 25 per cent and 75 per cent of the FVC represents the forced expired flow, FEF$_{25-75}$, or maximum midexpiratory flow (MMEF). The FEF$_{25-75}$ is less reproducible and less specific than the FEV$_1$.

Helium dilution is limited by the ability of the test gas to equilibrate completely with all portions of the lung. In the presence of significant airway obstruction, this will not occur and the FRC will be significantly underestimated. Body plethysmography eliminates this problem and measures the total thoracic gas volume, whether it is located in a bulla or is in direct communication with the airway, and thus provides a truer reflection of the FRC.

The dynamics of air flow can be evaluated during a forced expiratory maneuver by recording the change in volume against time to calculate flow rate or by directly measuring volume and flow (Figs. 15-2 and 15-3). The flow-volume loop is particularly useful in demonstrating the presence of central airway obstruction, which, by affecting primarily the peak inspiratory and expiratory flows, gives a characteristic loop (Fig. 15-3). An estimate of total airway resistance can be determined by body plethysmography.

The measurement of the diffusing capacity for carbon monoxide (DL$_{CO}$) is an indicator of the adequacy of the alveolar-capillary membrane and so is reduced when the latter is decreased, as in pulmonary fibrosis, emphysema, and pulmonary vascular disease. In patients with a restrictive physiologic defect, diffusing capacity helps to differentiate chest bellows (DL$_{CO}$ normal) from parenchymal disease (DL$_{CO}$ decreased). It should be recognized that decreased hemoglobin concentration can reduce measured DL$_{CO}$ in the absence of pul-

FIGURE 15-3. *A,* The maximum expired flow-volume curve in a normal subject. The peak expiratory flow (PEF) and forced expiratory flows at 50 per cent and 75 per cent of the exhaled vital capacity (FEF$_{50}$ and FEF$_{75}$) are indicated. PIF = Peak inspiratory flow. *B,* In obstructive lung disease (OLD), hyperinflation pushes the position of the curve to the left, and there is characteristic scalloping on expiration. In restrictive lung disease (RLD), lung volumes are reduced but flow for any one point in volume is normal. The flow-volume curve displays different patterns with various forms of upper airway obstruction (UAO), with reduction in respiratory flow if the obstruction is outside the thoracic cavity and, additionally, in expiratory flow if the obstruction is due to a fixed deformity.

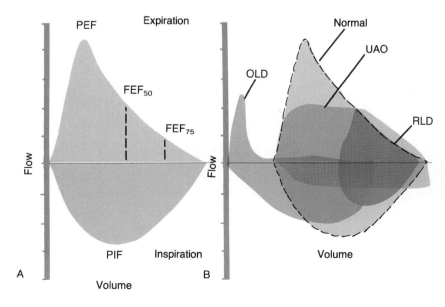

monary parenchymal abnormalities and that correction of the measured DL_{CO} is required when anemia is present.

Measurements of maximal static respiratory pressure are important methods of detecting respiratory muscle dysfunction in patients with neuromuscular disease. Maximal inspiratory pressure is obtained by recording mouth pressure during a maximal inspiratory effort from residual volume, and maximal expiratory pressure is recorded during a maximal expiratory effort at total lung capacity.

Measurement of lung volumes and flow rates after certain challenges such as methacholine, exercise, cold air, or exposure to organic or inorganic substances helps in the diagnosis of bronchospasm. Acute reversibility is determined by the repetition of these challenges after bronchodilator administration. However, failure of flow to improve following a single dose of a bronchodilator does not necessarily indicate irreversible disease and does not exclude the possibility of a clinical response to bronchodilator treatment.

More complex testing is occasionally required to answer specific questions. Exercise studies are valuable in judging the degree of disability as well as in elucidating the cause of dyspnea on exertion. Expired gas, minute ventilation, heart rate, and arterial oxygenation are measured during increased workloads. The degree of limitation and the relative contribution of ventilatory and cardiovascular factors can be assessed. Polysomnography is an essential tool in the diagnosis of sleep apnea (Chapter 21), and measurement of CO_2 sensitivity is used to assess the regulation of breathing.

Clinical Assessment of the Regulation of Ventilation

The respiratory control system activates the ventilatory pump, as well as upper airway pharyngeal dilator muscles, and is a crucial determinant of the arterial blood gases. Primary dysfunction of the ventilatory control system should be suspected when hypercapnia is present in the absence of significant lung or chest bellows disease (Table 15–2). However, control system dysfunction may also result in an inadequate compensatory response for coexisting lung or chest wall disease and may contribute to the development of hyper-

TABLE 15–2. DETECTION OF PRIMARY VENTILATORY CONTROL SYSTEM DYSFUNCTION

Suspect impaired chemosensitivity in the presence of hypercapnia and the following:
1. Disproportionately small reduction in FEV_1
2. Normal alveolar-arterial PO_2 gradient
3. Ability to achieve normocapnia with voluntary hyperventilation
4. Ability to generate a negative inspiratory pressure of at least −30 mm Hg, which eliminates muscle weakness as a cause of hypercapnia

capnia or the exaggeration of hypoxemia in these diseases.

Clinical assessment of ventilatory control focuses on the response to hypercapnia and hypoxia. The rebreathing test is the most common clinical method of assessing CO_2 sensitivity. Normally, minute ventilation increases by an average of 2 L/min/mm Hg CO_2 (range, 1 to 8 $L^{-1} \cdot min^{-1} \cdot mm^{-1}$ Hg CO_2) (see Fig. 14–5A). Blunting of the CO_2 response occurs in idiopathic hypoventilation, obesity-hypoventilation syndrome, narcotic or sedative ingestion, hypothyroidism, metabolic alkalosis, and primary neurologic disorders. The reduced response in patients with chronic obstructive pulmonary disease (COPD) and CO_2 retention is discussed later. Chemosensitivity to hypoxia is technically more difficult to measure, and generally there is a good relationship between reduced chemosensitivity to O_2 and that to CO_2.

Assessing the Efficiency of Pulmonary Gas Exchange

The arterial blood gases are the most valuable indices of pulmonary gas exchange because they are simple to obtain and provide important information to guide patient management. The pH defines the presence and magnitude of acid-base disorders, and the PCO_2 helps to differentiate a metabolic from a respiratory etiology. The PCO_2, in addition, assesses the adequacy of ventilation. The PO_2, measured while the patient is breathing room air, is a sensitive index of lung disease, although it may be influenced by overall ventilation and nonpulmonary factors that alter the mixed venous PO_2 (see Chapter 14). In addition, the arterial PO_2 decreases with age, probably owing to a gradually increasing ventilation-perfusion inequality. Normal values are listed in Table 15–3.

A number of simple relationships can help one use the arterial blood gases to correctly interpret acid-base disorder:

For metabolic acidosis, the expected PCO_2
$$= 1.5 \ (HCO_3) + 8$$

For metabolic alkalosis, the expected PCO_2
$$= 0.7 \ (HCO_3) + 20$$

If the PCO_2 is higher or lower than expected, an additional respiratory acidosis or alkalosis is present.

For primary respiratory abnormalities, the expected change in pH depends on whether or not renal compensation has occurred:

For acute increases or decreases in the arterial PCO_2, there should be a change of 0.008
$$pH \ units/mm \ Hg \ PCO_2$$

TABLE 15–3. NORMAL VALUES FOR ARTERIAL BLOOD GASES

$PO_2 = 104 − 0.27 \times age$
PCO_2: 36–44
pH: 7.35–7.45
Alveolar-arterial O_2 difference $= 2.5 + 0.21 \times age$

For chronic increases or decreases in the arterial P_{CO_2}, the expected change is 0.003 pH units/mm Hg P_{CO_2}

When patients breathe an increased fractional concentration of O_2 (FI_{O_2}), the arterial P_{O_2} may be a less sensitive guide to the degree of underlying lung disease, since the relationship between FI_{O_2} and Pa_{O_2} differs depending on the type of abnormal gas exchange that is present (Fig. 15–4). Measuring arterial blood gases while the patient is breathing room air and while he or she is breathing an FI_{O_2} of 1.0 can help to differentiate between $\dot{V}_A/\dot{Q}$ inequality, with which the Pa_{O_2} will reach above 500 mm Hg, and shunt, with which a much lower Pa_{O_2} will be achieved (see also Fig. 19–3).

A number of indices are derived from the arterial blood gases. The most useful is the alveolar-arterial O_2 difference (A-aD_{O_2}). The ideal PA_{O_2} is calculated from the alveolar gas equation (see Chapter 14). If gas exchange is optimal, then calculated PA_{O_2} should be close to measured Pa_{O_2}. Any factor making gas exchange less efficient will widen the A-aD_{O_2}. In normal persons, this is usually less than 10 mm Hg, increasing to as much as 20 mm Hg in older normal subjects. When hypoxemia is due to hypoventilation, the A-aD_{O_2} remains normal, since the fall in P_{O_2} is due to the rise in P_{CO_2}, and the calculated PA_{O_2} should fall to the same degree as the Pa_{O_2}. Thus, the A-aD_{O_2} is a practical way of differentiating hypoventilation from the other causes of hypoxemia.

Additional indices provide essentially the same information as the alveolar-arterial O_2 gradient: the arterial-alveolar tension ratio and the arterial P_{O_2}/FI_{O_2} ratio. The most complex index is the venous admixture ($\dot{Q}s/\dot{Q}t$), which requires the measurement of mixed venous P_{O_2} in addition to arterial P_{O_2}. This provides an estimate of the true shunt when measured on an FI_{O_2} of 1.0 and the true shunt plus the functional shunt from low $\dot{V}_A/\dot{Q}$ units when measured on room air. A number of nomograms and abbreviated equations do not require the mixed venous P_{O_2}. However, the assumptions inherent in these "shortcuts" make them no more useful than the alveolar-arterial gradient.

A commonly calculated index is the dead space–tidal volume ratio (V_D/V_T). It is measured using the Bohr equation

$$V_D/V_T = \frac{Pa_{CO_2} - P_{E_{CO_2}}}{Pa_{CO_2}}$$

where Pa_{CO_2} and $P_{E_{CO_2}}$ are the arterial and mixed expired P_{CO_2}, respectively. In normal individuals, V_D is 20 to 40 per cent of V_T and consists almost entirely of anatomic dead space (i.e., the conducting airways). Increase of V_D/V_T indicates an additional component of alveolar dead space due to the presence of ventilation-perfusion inequality.

Noninvasive Oximetry

The use of oximeters with lightweight sensors that clip on the ear or fingertip has become common-

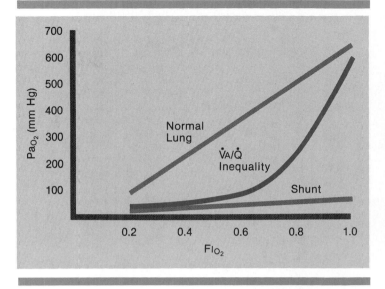

FIGURE 15–4. The relationship between Pa_{O_2} and FI_{O_2} in individuals with normal lungs, ventilation-perfusion ($\dot{V}_A/\dot{Q}$) inequality, and shunt.

place. These devices measure O_2 saturation (Sa_{O_2}) on the basis of the different absorption spectra of oxyhemoglobin and deoxyhemoglobin. User calibration is not required, since the instruments automatically compensate for variations in skin thickness and slight differences in pigmentation and vascular perfusion. Accuracy of the various commercial oximeters differs but is generally about ±4 per cent for Sa_{O_2} levels above 80 per cent; falsely high readings are common below this level. Other factors that may alter accuracy of oximetry readings include elevated carboxyhemoglobin levels, jaundice, deep skin pigmentation, and decreased local perfusion to the ear or fingertip. In addition, oximetry is not a sensitive guide to gas exchange in patients with high baseline Pa_{O_2} values because of the peculiar shape of the O_2 dissociation curve (see Fig. 14–8), whereby large changes in Pa_{O_2} may result in little change in Sa_{O_2}.

Invasive Diagnostic Techniques

Bronchoscopy. This is used to visualize the airways, to sample secretions, and to perform forceps biopsy. The rigid scope remains the instrument of choice when a wide channel is required, such as in massive hemoptysis or removal of large foreign bodies. Otherwise, the flexible scope is preferable because it is easy to maneuver. The latter is invaluable in the evaluation and biopsy of endobronchial lesions or in localizing the site of hemoptysis, since it allows visual access to the segmental airways. In conjunction with fluoroscopy, bronchoscopy can be used in the biopsy of peripheral lung lesions. In the immunocompromised host, bronchoscopy is the standard approach to the diagnosis of fungal or *Pneumocystis* pneumonia. It is also effective in the diagnosis of tuberculosis in a patient not producing sputum. Its indication in the diagnosis of common bacterial infections is less clear, although the development of special protective brushes has reduced the problem of contamination with upper airway flora. In most patients requiring bronchial toilet and drainage, physical therapy is sufficient, but when that fails, especially in patients on mechanical ventilation, bronchoscopy may be effective in re-expanding atelectatic areas.

Although generally a benign procedure, bronchoscopy has a number of complications. Worsening hypoxemia is almost inevitable, and supplemental O_2 should be used in hypoxemic patients. Laryngospasm, bronchospasm, fever, and new pulmonary infiltrates may occur. Significant bleeding and pneumothorax infrequently follow lung biopsy.

Transthoracic Needle Aspiration. Aspiration of lung tissue through a skinny needle inserted percutaneously with CT guidance is most useful with peripheral lesions, with which the bronchoscope has its least success. It provides material for cytologic examination or microbial studies rather than histologic examinations. A larger cutting needle, capable of providing a histologic specimen, may be useful in pleurally based lesions when the cytologic specimen is not helpful. The major complication is pneumothorax, which occurs in 20 to 30 per cent of cases; chest tube drainage is required in only 1 to 15 per cent of cases. Hemoptysis may occur but is rarely of clinical significance.

Thoracentesis and Pleural Biopsy. Pleural fluid examination and interpretation are covered in Chapter 22. Parietal pleural biopsy can be accomplished if sufficient fluid separates the lung from the chest wall. Histologic examination reveals granulomas in greater than 60 per cent of cases of suspected tuberculosis effusion, and when histology is combined with culture of the tissue sample, the yield may be 90 per cent. Biopsy is positive in 39 to 75 per cent of cases of suspected malignancy, which is a lower rate than for cytologic examination of the fluid. Thoracoscopy with biopsy of pleural lesions under direct vision can be performed when the pleural effusion remains undiagnosed after thoracentesis and biopsy.

Transbronchial Needle Aspiration and Mediastinoscopy. During mediastinoscopy, a small tube is passed into the mediastinum through an incision in the sternal notch. Biopsies can be done on lymph nodes in the anterior mediastinum and the right peritracheal region. This procedure is particularly useful for intrathoracic staging of lung carcinoma when CT evaluation reveals lymphadenopathy.

Transbronchial needle biopsy may be a useful technique for sampling mediastinal lymph nodes, especially in the subcarinal and pretracheal regions, and may avoid the need for more invasive procedures, such as mediastinoscopy and mediastinotomy.

Open Lung Biopsy. When the above procedures yield negative findings, an open lung biopsy may be indicated. In the immunocompromised host, as well as in other patients with diffuse interstitial lung disease, open lung biopsy has a greater diagnostic yield than does transbronchial biopsy using a fiberoptic bronchoscope, but still a proportion of patients have nonspecific findings. Despite the critical nature of the patients' illness, the mortality rate in large series of open lung biopsy is less than 0.5 per cent, with a complication rate of 11 per cent.

REFERENCES

Forster RE, DuBois AB, Briscoe WA, Fisher AB: The Lung: Physiologic Basis of Pulmonary Function Tests. Chicago, Year Book Medical Publishers, 1986.

Mahler DA: Pulmonary function testing. Clin Chest Med, Vol 10, No 2, 1989.

Shure D: Diagnostic techniques. Clin Chest Med 3:1–171, 1987.

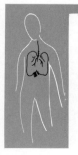

16 OBSTRUCTIVE LUNG DISEASE

The obstructive lung diseases are characterized by reduction of expiratory flow rates and include common disorders such as asthma and chronic obstructive pulmonary disease (COPD) and less common ones such as bronchiectasis and cystic fibrosis. Multiple factors contribute to the development of the airways obstruction in these disorders. Certain of them may be common to more than one entity, occasionally obscuring a clear differentiation between the various illnesses. However, recent studies have provided enough insight into the pathophysiology of obstructive airways disease

TABLE 16−1. OBSTRUCTIVE LUNG DISEASES

DISORDER	MAJOR CLINICAL CRITERIA	DISTINCTIVE LABORATORY FINDINGS
Chronic obstructive lung disease	Chronic progressive dyspnea	Decreased expiratory flow rates, hypoxemia ± hypercapnia
Emphysema	Little or no sputum, cachexia	Hyperinflation, increased lung compliance, and low carbon monoxide diffusing capacity
Chronic bronchitis	Cough and sputum production, history of chronic irritant exposure (mostly smoking, occasionally industrial exposure)	By itself, no significant physiologic impairment
Asthma	Episodic dyspnea; may be associated with allergy to environmental agents	Marked airway hyperreactivity
Bronchiectasis	Large volume of sputum production, clubbing	Chest x-ray findings of dilated bronchi with thickened walls, decreased lung volumes, and decreased expiratory flow
Immotile cilia syndrome	Associated with situs inversus or dextrocardia, sinusitis, and infertility	Abnormal sperm anatomy
Hypogammaglobulinemia		Abnormal decrease in one or more immunoglobulins
Cystic fibrosis	Bronchiectasis associated with gastrointestinal disease, sinusitis, and infertility	Increased sweat Cl and Na, abnormal pancreatic function

to allow a sufficiently clear definition of the various entities to accommodate clinical needs (Table 16−1).

Pathophysiology of Airways Obstruction

Air flow in the lungs is directly proportional to the driving pressure and inversely related to the airway resistance. During most of a forced expiration, the effective driving pressure is the elastic recoil pressure of the lung. Thus, the reduction in elasticity, which is characteristic of emphysema decreases the maximum expiratory flow. An increase in resistance is caused by factors that reduce the cross-sectional area of the airways.

A common cause of increased airway resistance is inflammation. In response to irritants such as cigarette smoke, external pollutants, recurrent infection, or chronic immunologic stimulation, there may be inflammatory goblet cell metaplasia of the bronchiolar epithelium, mucosal edema, narrowing of the airways, and the production of excessive, thick secretions in susceptible patients. If this process is allowed to continue, it often results in the loss of ciliated epithelium, squamous metaplasia, and eventual peribronchial fibrosis.

Another cause of increased airway resistance is bronchoconstriction. The airways are lined by smooth muscle that is innervated by both adrenergic (bronchodilating) and cholinergic (bronchoconstricting) pathways. Cholinergic control is mediated by a vagal reflex, via irritant receptors lying just beneath the mucosa of the large airways, trachea, and upper respiratory tract. Stimulation of these receptors by inhaled irritants or inflammation produces bronchoconstriction. In addition, endogenous mediators such as histamine and prostaglandins may dilate or constrict bronchial smooth muscle directly or reflexly by exciting the irritant receptors. Such mechanisms function to protect the lungs of normal subjects from noxious agents, but hyperreactivity of these pathways exists in patients with obstructive lung disease.

Airways obstruction leads to characteristic changes in lung volumes (Table 16−2), with an increase in residual volume (RV) and functional residual capacity (FRC) and a normal or increased total lung capacity (TLC). The vital capacity (VC) is decreased as the RV takes up more and more of the thoracic gas volume. A number of factors may contribute to the increase in RV and FRC. Decrease in the elastic recoil of the lungs in patients with emphysema moves the FRC closer to the relaxed volume of the chest wall (about two thirds of TLC). The greater tendency of abnormal airways, particularly at the lung base, to collapse during expiration traps air behind the closed airways. The marked resistance to expiratory flow may not permit complete exhalation during the time available for expiration. Finally, certain patients with asthma have persistent activity of the inspiratory muscles during expiration, which actively maintains a high FRC.

There are three major consequences of these changes in lung volume. Because of the nonlinear nature of the pressure-volume relationship of the lung, breathing at high lung volumes along the flat portion of the curve requires a greater pressure for the same change in volume (see Fig. 14−3), further increasing the work of breathing. In addition, the higher the resting lung volume, the shorter the inspiratory muscles are at the beginning of the breath (see Fig. 14−2). This places them at a disadvantaged position on their length-tension curve, diminishing their ability to alter transpulmonary

TABLE 16–2. ABNORMALITIES OF LUNG VOLUME

LUNG VOLUME	PULMONARY DISORDER		
	OBSTRUCTIVE DISEASE	RESTRICTIVE DISEASE	NEUROMUSCULAR DISEASE
Vital capacity	D	D	D
Functional residual capacity	I	D	N
Residual volume	I	D	I
Total lung capacity	N or I	D	D

D = Decreased; I = increased; N = normal.

pressure and predisposing them to fatigue. Hyperinflation, however, has one beneficial effect. Because of the tethering effect of the lung parenchyma on the airways, there is an inverse relationship between lung volume and airways resistance. Thus, hyperinflation is the one strategy immediately available in asthmatics to minimize sudden changes in airway caliber.

Abnormal pulmonary gas exchange is an inevitable consequence of obstructive lung disease. Airways obstruction and the breakdown of alveolar walls produce ventilation-perfusion mismatch that interferes with the efficient transfer of both oxygen (O_2) and carbon dioxide (CO_2). Up to a certain point, patients with obstructive lung disease can increase their minute ventilation sufficiently to prevent the development of hypercapnia despite worsening hypoxemia (see Chapter 14). However, with continued progression of the disease, a point is reached beyond which further increase in ventilation is impractical because of the high energy requirements or the development of muscle fatigue. At some point, it is more efficient, physio-

TABLE 16–3. TYPES OF ASTHMA

CLASSIFICATION	INITIATING FACTORS
Extrinsic	IgE-mediated external allergens
Intrinsic	?
Adult-onset	?
Exercise-induced	Alteration in airway temperature and humidity; mediator release
Aspirin-sensitive (associated with nasal polyps)	Aspirin and other nonsteroidal anti-inflammatory drugs
Allergic bronchopulmonary aspergillosis	Hypersensitivity to *Aspergillus* species (not infection)
Occupational	Metal salts (platinum, chrome, and nickel)
	Antibiotic powder (penicillin, sulfathiazole, tetracycline)
	Toluene diisocyanate (TDI)
	Flour
	Wood dusts
	Cotton dust (byssinosis)
	Animal proteins

logically, to allow the Pa_{CO_2} to rise, eliminating it at a higher concentration but lower minute ventilation and metabolic cost. The onset of hypercapnia is not always clearly related to the degree of mechanical impairment, and it appears that some patients prefer to work harder to maintain normocapnia, whereas others with the same degree of impairment are satisfied to breathe less and allow worse gas exchange (see Chapter 21).

Acute exacerbations of the chronic process brought on by increased bronchospasm, infection, or congestive heart failure may lead to worsening ventilation-perfusion inequality or the development of intrapulmonary shunt and further worsen gas exchange. During sleep, gas exchange is also usually worse owing to a characteristic reduction in minute ventilation. A patient with adequate arterial blood gases during the day may develop significant hypercapnia and arterial desaturation at night.

Asthma

Asthma is characterized by airways obstruction that varies over time and is completely or partially reversible either spontaneously or with treatment. The airways are the site of an inflammatory response consisting of cellular infiltration, epithelial disruption, mucosal edema, and mucous plugging. Airway hyperresponsiveness with an exaggerated bronchospastic response either accompanies the inflammation or occurs as a consequence of the inflammatory process. The stimulus may be immunologic in origin, as in classic extrinsic asthma, in which mast cells, sensitized by IgE antibodies, degranulate and release bronchoactive mediators following exposure to a specific antigen. The cause may also be unclear, as in adult-onset asthma, in which the patients frequently show no evidence of allergy. The recognized categories of asthma are listed in Table 16–3. Clinical differentiation is usually important only in situations in which there are clear-cut, easily identifiable, and avoidable extrinsic factors, such as drugs or industrial substances.

The diagnosis of asthma is based on the presence of episodic dyspnea associated with wheezing. Intermittent cough, probably due to stimulation of the irritant receptors, is commonly seen and may be the sole presenting symptom in some patients. Typically, symptoms are worse at night, following exercise, after going out in the cold, while exposed to irritating gases, and following viral respiratory tract infection. Bacterial infection is a rare cause of asthma exacerbation.

Laboratory studies may be required to determine the presence of specific types of asthma (Table 16–4). The chest radiograph demonstrates hyperinflation in the symptomatic patient, whereas in patients with allergic bronchopulmonary aspergillosis serial films may show infiltrates that change location or features suggestive of central bronchiectasis. Pulmonary function studies show the findings of obstruction, which usually improve significantly following the acute administration of bronchodilators. When airways obstruction is not present on routine spirometry, the diagnosis can often be made by initiating bronchospasm by the inhalation of histamine, methacholine, or cold air.

Acute severe asthma (status asthmaticus) refers to an attack of increased severity that is unresponsive to routine therapy. Although the attack is sometimes prolonged, fatal episodes may occur unexpectedly with overwhelming suddenness. A history of increasing bronchodilator use with little benefit is expected, and clinical signs, such as pulsus paradoxus, use of accessory respiratory muscles, diaphoresis, and orthopnea, are present in severe exacerbations. The degree of physiologic disturbance can best be appreciated by a measure of expiratory flow rates. In the emergency room management of these patients, such indices are helpful in assessing the response to therapy, because they provide immediate quantitative information and can be obtained at frequent intervals without discomfort. Complementary information can be obtained by measurement of arterial blood gases, and this may be the only measurement possible in the critically ill asthmatic. Hypoxemia is usually, but not invariably, present and does not correlate closely with airways obstruction. Pa_{CO_2} is typically reduced early in an attack. With increasing severity, Pa_{O_2} falls and Pa_{CO_2} returns to normal and then rises, accompanied by a mixed respiratory and metabolic acidosis, such that intubation and mechanical ventilation may become necessary. Hypercapnia at presentation is not an indication for intubation, because most patients improve with vigorous treatment, but careful monitoring is essential. In general, arterial blood gas measurements are less sensitive and specific than assessment of airways obstruction in judging the response to therapy.

CHRONIC OBSTRUCTIVE PULMONARY DISEASE (COPD)

Patients with COPD have slowly progressive airways obstruction. The course of the disease is punctuated by periodic exacerbations resulting in an increase in dyspnea and sputum production or, occasionally, the precipitation of acute respiratory failure. These exacerbations are often due to pulmonary infection, the development of heart failure, or poor patient compliance with prescribed therapy. Until recently, an episode of acute respiratory failure was associated with a poor long-term prognosis, but with modern management such an episode does not appear to alter overall prognosis.

COPD generally affects middle-aged and older individuals. Patients usually present with dyspnea and exercise intolerance. Cough and sputum production are other common complaints but may be absent in many patients. Physical examination reveals signs of lung overinflation, prominent use of accessory respiratory muscles, diminished breath sounds, and diffuse wheezing especially during a forced expiration. Patients may vary in their ap-

TABLE 16–4. DIAGNOSTIC STUDIES IN ASTHMA

1. Routine pulmonary function test	Decreased FEV_1; hyperinflation; improvement with bronchodilator
2. Special pulmonary function test	
a. methacholine, histamine, or cold-air challenge	Indicates the presence of nonspecific bronchial hyperreactivity; bronchoconstriction occurs at lower dose in asthma
b. challenge with specific agents: occupational, drugs, etc.	Occasionally performed
c. portable peak flow measurements	Helpful in diagnosis of occupational asthma and outpatient management of brittle asthmatic
3. Chest x-ray	Fleeting infiltrates and central bronchiectasis in ABPA
4. Skin tests	Demonstrate atopy; little value except prick test to *Aspergillus fumigatus* positive in ABPA
5. Blood tests	Eosinophils and IgE usually increased in atopy; levels may be very high in ABPA *Aspergillus* precipitins increased in many but not all patients with ABPA

ABPA = Allergic bronchopulmonary aspergillosis.
FEV_1 = Forced expiratory volume in 1 second.

pearance from thin and even cachectic-looking to edematous and cyanotic. In the past these two extremes of clinical presentation have been associated with specific pathologic entities, emphysema and bronchitis, respectively. However, recent clinicopathologic correlations have not supported this impression. In its early stages, the physical examination may be normal, and the diagnosis will depend on laboratory studies documenting reduced expiratory flow rates.

Pulmonary function studies generally show decreased VC and expiratory flow rates and increased RV, FRC, and TLC. Unlike asthma, COPD is not characterized by marked temporal variability in the degree of airways obstruction. However, as is the case with asthma, bronchospasm is usually present and expiratory flow can often be increased acutely by bronchodilators. The usual improvement in patients with COPD, on the order of 15 to 20 per cent of the prebronchodilator value, is less than that observed in asthma. Arterial blood gases generally evidence hypoxemia of varying severity and, in the advanced stage of the disease, hypercapnia. The degree of hypoxemia may not correlate very well with either the severity of the air flow obstruction or the degree of dyspnea, and some severely limited patients have relatively well preserved blood gases. During sleep, pulmonary gas exchange may further worsen. When the degree of hypoxemia becomes severe (Pa_{O_2} less than

60 mm Hg), hypoxic vasoconstriction with subsequent anatomic remodeling of the pulmonary arteries leads to the development of pulmonary hypertension and subsequent right heart failure (cor pulmonale). It may also result in significant polycythemia.

Three pathophysiologic disorders are recognized as a part of the syndrome of COPD: emphysema, small airways disease, and chronic bronchitis. In any given patient, one or more of these manifestations may predominate.

Emphysema

Emphysema is characterized by two features. Anatomically, it is defined as an abnormal enlargement of the air spaces distal to the terminal bronchioles, accompanied by destructive changes in the alveolar walls. Physiologically, it is characterized by a loss of elastic recoil and thus an increased lung compliance. The degree of airways obstruction in patients with COPD correlates most closely with the severity of emphysema, and patients who have significant functional impairment usually have at least a moderate degree of emphysema.

The pathogenesis of emphysema has yet to be determined with certainty, although most workers favor an imbalance of proteases and antiproteases in the lung, with resultant lung destruction. This theory is based on the discovery of a small number of patients with an inherited deficiency of alpha$_1$-antiprotease, the major antiprotease, who develop emphysema even without other risk factors. Cigarette smoke, the major etiologic factor in the development of emphysema, has been shown to increase the numbers of alveolar macrophages and neutrophils in the lung, enhance protease release, and impair the activity of antiproteases. However, other factors must determine susceptibility to emphysema, because fewer than 10 to 15 per cent of smokers develop clinical evidence of airways obstruction.

The diagnosis of emphysema is usually inferred from the clinical and laboratory findings. Chest roentgenograms demonstrate hyperinflation with depressed diaphragms, increased anteroposterior diameter, and widened retrosternal air space. These findings, however, are seen whenever hyperinflation is present, and more specific features in emphysema include attenuation of the pulmonary vasculature and the presence of hyperlucent areas. The one finding that correlates well with the anatomic presence of emphysema is a reduction in diffusing capacity because of the loss of alveolar capillaries.

Small Airways Disease

The earliest manifestation of COPD appears to be in the peripheral airways. Abnormalities that have been identified include inflammation of the terminal and respiratory bronchioles, fibrosis of the airway walls leading to narrowing, and goblet cell metaplasia. These lesions undoubtedly contribute to airways obstruction, although the correlation is not as close as with the degree of emphysema. Furthermore, only a small proportion of cigarette smokers with these pathologic abnormalities go on to develop symptomatic COPD.

Chronic Bronchitis

Chronic bronchitis is defined as a persistent cough resulting in sputum production for more than 3 months in each year over the previous 3 years. Diagnosis requires exclusion of other conditions associated with cough and sputum production, such as bronchiectasis. As with emphysema, cigarette smoke is the major etiologic factor, although exposure to other pollutants such as dusts may play a role by causing chronic irritation. Cough and sputum production do not appear to have an independent effect on the development of airways obstruction. The airways obstruction seen in the setting of chronic bronchitis is due to associated emphysema, bronchospasm, and obstruction of the peripheral airways. The findings on physical examination, pulmonary function assessment, and radiography depend on the degree of associated airways obstruction.

Bronchiectasis

Bronchiectasis is an abnormal and persistent dilatation of the bronchi due to destructive changes in the elastic and muscular layers of the walls. It may be widespread or localized to a single lung segment. Before the introduction of antibiotics and immunoprophylaxis of common childhood viral illnesses, bronchiectasis was usually a consequence of severe necrotizing lung infection. In underdeveloped countries, it is still most commonly a sequela of gram-negative pneumonia, but in developed nations it is more likely to be associated with other systemic diseases. Inadequately treated patients with allergic bronchopulmonary aspergillosis may develop bronchiectasis due to persistent inflammation. Immunodeficiency states such as hypogammaglobulinemia predispose to frequent respiratory tract infections and the development of bronchiectasis. Interference with the normal clearance mechanisms may also cause chronic inflammation and bronchiectasis. Cystic fibrosis (discussed below) is the most common example of this. An unusual congenital cause of decreased lung clearance and bronchiectasis is the immotile cilia syndrome, which is due to structural abnormalities in the microtubular system. This is often associated with sinusitis, situs inversus or dextrocardia, and infertility.

The diagnosis is made by a history of longstanding chronic cough and the production of large quantities of foul sputum, occasionally blood-tinged, and physical findings of persistent crackles over the affected lung regions. With severe, longstanding disease, clubbing and cor pulmonale are frequent and massive hemoptysis may occasionally occur. The chest radiograph may be normal or may display minor nonspecific features, such as increased markings or linear atelectasis. On occasion, the radiograph is very suggestive of bronchiectasis, demonstrating thickening of the bronchial walls well out to the lung periphery and even cystic lesions. Definitive diagnosis can usually be made using high-resolution computed tomography scanning, and contrast bronchography is rarely indicated. Pulmonary function studies invariably show obstruction and occasionally significant hyperinflation, although restricted lung volumes may be present with severe disease.

Cystic Fibrosis

Cystic fibrosis is a common generalized disorder of exocrine gland function, which impairs clearance of secretions in a variety of organs (Table 16-5). It is associated with abnormal chloride transport in the apical membrane of epithelial cells. This autosomal recessive disorder occurs in about 1 in every 2500 white births. The gene, located on the long arm of chromosome 7, has now been cloned and the cystic fibrosis protein identified. It is thought to be the chloride channel. The pulmonary pathophysiology is similar to that of other causes of bronchiectasis, with tenacious mucus and impaired ciliary function resulting in recurrent infections, chronic inflammation, and bronchial wall destruction.

The disease is usually discovered in childhood and diagnosed by an elevated sweat chloride level (greater than 60 mEq/L). Some patients escape diagnosis until their late teens, and with genetic analysis, increasingly older patients are being recognized. They usually have minimal extrapulmo-

TABLE 16-5. CYSTIC FIBROSIS — ORGAN INVOLVEMENT

I. **Pulmonary**
   Cough and sputum production
   Recurrent pneumonias
   Bronchial hyperreactivity
   Hemoptysis
   Pneumothorax
   Marked digital clubbing
   Cor pulmonale
II. **Upper Respiratory Tract**
   Nasal polyps
   Chronic sinusitis
III. **Gastrointestinal**
   Meconium ileus in the neonate
   Meconium ileus equivalent (childhood, adult)
   Rectal prolapse
   Hernias
   Chronic pancreatic dysfunction causing steatorrhea, malnutrition, and vitamin deficiency
   Acute pancreatitis (rare)
   Diabetes mellitus
   Cirrhosis and portal hypertension
   Salivary gland inflammation
IV. **Genitourinary**
   Sterility in men
   Low fertility rate in women

nary symptoms and only mild respiratory complaints, often labeled asthma or recurrent bronchitis. When it is found in infants, cystic fibrosis usually presents with gastrointestinal symptoms, particularly steatorrhea and bowel obstruction (Table 16-5). However, the pulmonary features eventually pose the biggest problem. Classically, *Staphylococcus aureus* in childhood and the mucoid strain of *Pseudomonas aeruginosa* in later years cause recurrent respiratory infections that are particularly difficult to treat because of chronic colonization of the airways. The course is usually one of gradual but progressive respiratory failure. Recent improvements in antibiotics, nutritional therapy, and supportive care, however, have improved the prognosis such that the median survival has increased from less than 2 years in the 1940s up to more than 20 years today.

Treatment

For the most part, specific therapy aimed at basic pathophysiologic mechanisms of each of the obstructive lung diseases is not yet available. Specific replacement therapy with alpha$_1$-antiprotease is available for patients with emphysema and a homozygous absence of the required gene, but the efficacy of such treatment is not yet known. Thus, the treatment of all forms of obstructive lung disease is symptomatic and directed toward the reduction of abnormal airway tone, the treatment of inflammation, and specific complications such as infection, excessive bronchial secretions, hypoxemia, and cor pulmonale.

Pharmacologic Therapy

Drugs that relax bronchial smooth muscle or decrease bronchial hyperreactivity can be divided into four groups (Table 16-6). The sympathomimetics are the most potent bronchodilators. Subcutaneous epinephrine has a relatively short duration of action, acts on both beta$_1$ and beta$_2$ receptors, and has additional, undesirable alpha effects. The development of noncatecholamine, beta$_2$-specific agents has improved the specificity

TABLE 16-6. PHARMACOLOGIC THERAPY FOR AIRWAYS OBSTRUCTION

Sympathomimetics
   Beta$_2$-specific agents: metaproterenol, terbutaline, albuterol
   Epinephrine
Methylxanthines
   Theophylline
   Aminophylline
Anticholinergics
   Atropine
   Ipratropium bromide
Anti-inflammatory drugs
   Corticosteroids
   Cromolyn sodium

of the sympathomimetic agents for the adrenergic receptor found in airway smooth muscle, but more importantly it has increased the duration of action from 60 to 90 minutes to more than 4 hours and permits oral administration. Aerosol therapy is the preferred route of administration, because the lower total dose reduces side effects. Oral use often leads to muscle twitching, and parenteral administration appears to markedly reduce their apparent beta$_2$ specificity. Tolerance to these agents does not occur, and a failure to respond usually indicates an insufficient dose or ineffective use of the metered-dose device or nebulizer.

Anticholinergic agents were the first clinically available bronchodilators, but their use declined because of concerns about their side effects, specifically the purported inhibition of lower airway secretions, which is no longer considered a problem. As the importance of vagally mediated bronchospasm has been elucidated, these agents have received renewed interest. They are particularly effective in patients with COPD and in selected patients with exacerbations of asthma. A new anticholinergic agent, ipratropium bromide, has been developed; unlike atropine, its systemic absorption is poor, and therefore it has fewer extrapulmonary effects.

Methylxanthines such as theophylline are about 50 per cent as potent as the sympathomimetics. Effectiveness is related to the blood level and is optimal between 8 and 15 μg/ml. Above these concentrations, the incidence of gastrointestinal, cardiac, and neurologic toxicity is unacceptable. The usual adult dose is 10 to 12 mg/kg/day but may vary widely, depending on the presence of factors that alter the metabolism of theophylline (Table 16–7). In patients with COPD it is difficult to demonstrate that the addition of theophylline provides additional bronchodilation to that achieved by optimal doses of beta$_2$-specific sympathomimetics. However, some patients obtain symptomatic improvement that may relate, in part, to the additional small beneficial effects theophylline has on cardiac and respiratory mus-

TABLE 16–7. FACTORS AFFECTING THEOPHYLLINE CLEARANCE

Clearance increased by	Cigarette smoking
	Marijuana smoking
	Charcoal-broiled meat
	Phenobarbital
Clearance decreased	
by 25%	Erythromycin
	Propranolol
	Allopurinol
	Oral contraceptives
by 50%	Cimetidine
	Phenytoin
	Influenza vaccine
	Infection
by 100% or more	Heart failure
	Hepatic cirrhosis

cle function. In asthma, theophylline is indicated mainly to reduce the wide swings in airway smooth muscle tone seen especially in the early morning hours when blood levels of other bronchodilators are low and normal circadian variation causes increased airway tone. In addition, when sympathomimetics are not sufficient, theophylline decreases symptomatic complaints.

Corticosteroids are invaluable to reduce airway inflammation, although they do not work acutely to relieve airways obstruction. Their usage early and in sufficient doses in the treatment of acute asthma or the acute exacerbation of COPD has been shown to lessen the degree of airways obstruction (over 12 to 24 hours), to decrease the total time of hospitalization, and to reduce recurrence. The complications of chronic administration limit their usefulness, although the introduction of potent, inhaled corticosteroids (beclomethasone) has significantly reduced this problem. Inhaled corticosteroids have become first-line therapy for patients with asthma not easily controllable with inhaled sympathomimetics. Suppression of airway hyperresponsiveness often requires larger doses than currently recommended in the United States (e.g., 1600 to 2600 μg instead of 400 to 800 μg of beclomethasone per day). Their role in COPD is less clear.

Inhaled sodium cromolyn prevents bronchospasm in some asthmatics but is not helpful in the management of an acute asthmatic attack. Although stabilization of the mast cell membrane and the prevention of mediator release are the major proposed mechanisms of action, this agent is also effective in forms of asthma without an atopic association, probably because of an anti-inflammatory effect. In asthmatics who are difficult to control, it is a useful drug to try before turning to chronic oral steroid therapy. The drug should be used for 3 to 4 weeks before deciding on its efficacy. It may also be used intranasally to relieve the symptoms of allergic rhinitis.

A suggested scheme for the administration of the bronchodilators is shown in Figure 16–1.

Oxygen

The hypoxemia seen in obstructive lung disease has two major deleterious consequences: decreased O_2 delivery to the tissues and hypoxic pulmonary vasoconstriction with resultant cor pulmonale. O_2 therapy is thus an integral part of the treatment of patients with obstructive lung disease and should be used whenever the arterial saturation falls below 90 per cent. In some patients O_2 may be required only with acute exacerbations, but in those with chronic disease it may be needed during sleep, with exercise, or continuously, depending on when desaturation occurs. Because of the mechanism of the hypoxemia, namely, ventilation-perfusion inequality, the desaturation can be corrected by small increases in the inspired fractional O_2 concentrations, achieved with less than 4 L/min of nasal flow. It has been clearly demonstrated in COPD patients having a resting Pa_{O_2} below 55 mm Hg that long-term O_2 therapy markedly improves survival, and maximal benefit is achieved when it is delivered throughout the 24 hours of the day.

Antibiotics and Vaccines

Some exacerbations of airways obstruction are secondary to acute infections. In patients with obstructive airway diseases, airway colonization with putative bacterial pathogens is common. However, in the absence of systemic signs of infection or a clear-cut change in the quality and quantity of sputum there is no indication for antibiotics. In patients with bronchiectasis or cystic fibrosis, the specific organism responsible, usually S. aureus or Pseudomonas, is easily identifiable. However, in patients with COPD or asthma, a specific agent is not usually isolated. In the first case, the appropriate antibiotic can be chosen, whereas in the latter case it is often more cost-efficient to administer a broad-spectrum antibiotic such as ampicillin, trimethoprim-sulfamethoxazole, or tetracycline. The route of administration, oral or intravenous, depends on the specific agent and the acuteness of the process.

Influenza vaccines directed at specific epidemic strains are effective in reducing morbidity and mortality. Pneumococcal vaccine is effective in preventing infection in young, healthy individuals but has not proved to be similarly effective in patients with chronic lung diseases.

Intermittent Positive Pressure Breathing (IPPB) and Nebulization Therapy

IPPB has been shown to have no specific value in the management of patients with airways obstruction. Thinning of secretions is a controversial topic. Although a normal state of hydration is probably important to maintain normal bronchial secretions, there is no evidence that additional fluids have any effect. Neither is there evidence for the efficacy of nebulized saline, mucolytics, enzymes, detergents, or iodides, and side effects may be significant. Probably the most important measures to improve airway secretions are to control the primary irritants by eliminating smoking, maximizing bronchodilation, and using antibiotics when indicated.

Smoking Cessation

One of the most important factors in the management of patients with COPD is the cessation of cigarette smoking. Susceptible smokers who develop COPD have an increased rate of decline in lung function measured as forced expiratory volume in 1 second (FEV_1) (80 ml/yr) compared with nonsusceptible smokers and nonsmokers (FEV_1, 30 ml/yr) (Fig. 16–2). Following cessation of smoking, the rate of decline in the susceptible smoker is reduced to that in the nonsmoker (30 ml/yr). Drugs that decrease the physical craving for ciga-

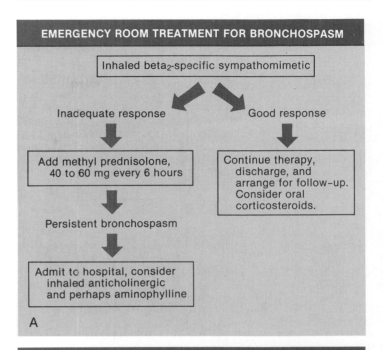

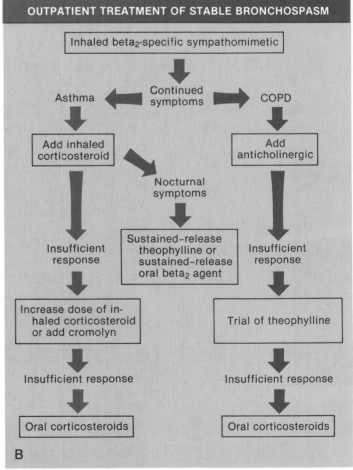

FIGURE 16–1. Scheme for treatment of bronchospasm in the emergency room (A) and in patients with stable disease (B).

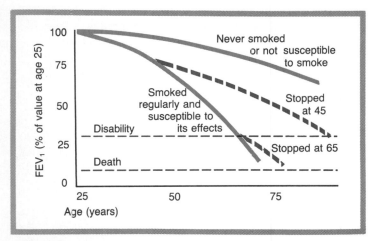

FIGURE 16–2. Pattern of decline in FEV_1, with risk of morbidity and mortality from respiratory disease in a susceptible smoker compared with a normal subject or nonsusceptible smoker. Although cessation of smoking does not replenish the lung function already lost in a susceptible smoker, it decreases the rate of further decline. (Adapted from Fletcher C, Peto R: The natural history of chronic airflow obstruction. Br Med J 1:1645, 1977; with permission.)

rettes, such as clonidine and transdermal nicotine patches, along with behavioral modification, increase the success of cessation attempts.

Physical Therapy and Rehabilitation

Chest physiotherapy (percussion and postural drainage) is employed on the assumption that sputum retention has undesirable consequences. Although this is a reasonable but unproven assumption, and although physiotherapy increases the immediate volume of sputum cleared, there is no evidence that it affects the natural history of any

disease or is better than coughing at clearing secretions. Similarly, breathing training and exercise rehabilitation lack a clear scientific basis. However, patients with pulmonary disease of sufficient severity to prevent normal daily living commonly demonstrate an improved quality of life when enrolled in a properly run rehabilitation program. Finally, nutritional needs in these patients must be addressed. This is important in cystic fibrosis, as supplemental pancreatic enzymes and vitamins are necessary. However, the debilitated patient with emphysema must also be considered for nutritional support, because poor nutrition may render him or her susceptible to respiratory failure through decreased muscle strength.

Lung Transplantation

In selected patients with unresponsive chronic respiratory failure, lung transplantation may be a viable therapeutic option. Single lung transplantation has been successfully performed in patients with end-stage emphysema with reversal of physiologic abnormalities. Patients with cystic fibrosis have also undergone successful transplantations, although they generally require bilateral transplantation because of the risk of infecting a single lung transplant from the remaining native lung.

REFERENCES

Fick RB: Inflammatory disorders of the airway. Clin Chest Med 9:4, 1988.
Guidelines for the diagnosis and management of asthma. US Department of Health and Human Services. Pub #91-3042, 1991.
Snider GL: Emphysema. Clin Chest Med 4:329–499, 1983.
Standards for the diagnosis and care of patients with chronic obstructive pulmonary disease (COPD) and asthma. Am Rev Respir Dis 136:225–244, 1987.

17 DIFFUSE INFILTRATIVE DISEASES OF THE LUNG

A large number of lung diseases are characterized by the replacement or infiltration of normal lung by abnormal tissue (Fig. 17–1). On rare occasions, the insulting agent may be well recognized, as in silicosis. More often, the causative process is unknown and only the response is obvious. The insult may cause injury by direct toxicity, as a result of an inflammatory response, or through an immunologically mediated reaction. Regardless of the mechanism of injury, the influx of inflammatory cells into the lung interstitium, perivascular space, and alveolar space results in the develop-

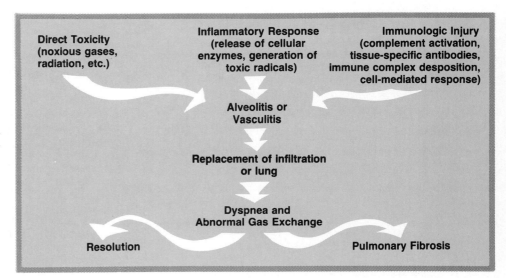

FIGURE 17-1. Pathophysiology and outcome of diffuse infiltrative lung disease.

ment of an alveolitis or vasculitis and, if carried to completion, lung fibrosis.

Clinical Manifestations

The majority of patients present with an insidious onset of dyspnea, exercise limitation, and dry nonproductive cough. Certain historical features may suggest a specific diagnosis as detailed in the discussion of each entity. Examination of the chest characteristically reveals mid to late inspiratory crackles and tachypnea. Physical findings of pulmonary hypertension, cor pulmonale, and cyanosis are usually late manifestations. Evidence of extrathoracic disease is valuable in suggesting a specific diagnosis, such as the skin lesions of sarcoidosis or the arthritis of a collagen vascular disease. The chest radiograph may confirm the presence of diffuse infiltrative disease but is rarely diagnostic on its own.

As fibrosis replaces normal lung structures, there is a decrease in all lung volumes (see Table 16-2), a fall in lung compliance, and a decline in the diffusing capacity. The loss of alveolar space and airway abnormalities produce ventilation-perfusion inequality, but hypoxemia is usually mild until the disease progresses to a significant degree, and hypercapnia is uncommon. However, patients with interstitial fibrosis often demonstrate oxygen desaturation on exercise despite only mild hypoxemia at rest.

A specific diagnosis, when not clear from the presentation, depends on lung biopsy findings. In certain diseases, such as sarcoidosis, sufficient tissue can be obtained using a fiberoptic bronchoscope and a transbronchial biopsy, but this may be insufficient in others, such as idiopathic pulmonary fibrosis, and an open lung biopsy may be required.

SPECIFIC ENTITIES

Diseases with Known Etiologies

Pneumoconioses

Pneumoconioses are lung diseases produced by the inhalation of inorganic dust. These dusts may be fibrous minerals, such as asbestos, or nonfibrous minerals, such as silica or metals. The clinical spectrum varies widely according to the nature of the inhaled substance and the type of response it evokes in the lung. Some substances such as asbestos lead to progressive fibrosis, whereas others such as iron dust produce little or no reaction even when deposited in large amounts. The common inorganic dusts are listed in Table 17-1 and are divided according to their structure and fibrogenic potential.

TABLE 17-1. PNEUMOCONIOSES

SUBSTANCE	FIBRO-GENICITY	OCCUPATION
I. Fibrous minerals		
Asbestos	High	Asbestos mining, shipyard and boiler workers, insulators
Talc	High	Talc mining and milling
Fiber glass	Low	Insulation
II. Nonfibrous minerals		
Silica	High	Mining, sandblasting, etc.
Coal	Low	Mining
III. Metals		
Iron	Low	Mining, refining, and fabricating
Aluminum	Uncertain	Mining, refining, and fabricating
Beryllium	High	Mining and fabricating

TABLE 17-2. ASBESTOS-RELATED RESPIRATORY DISEASE

FORM	COMMENT
Asbestosis	Interstitial fibrosis; long latent period; clubbing; crackles
Pleural thickening	Calcified plaques; intensity proportional to exposure; only significant in that it indicates prior exposure
Benign effusions	Hemorrhagic; asymptomatic; spontaneous remission and recurrence
Pleural mesothelioma	Latent interval 20 to 40 years; not dose-related; probably unrelated to smoking; median survival 12 months
Bronchogenic carcinoma	Fivefold increased risk in exposed nonsmoker and 60- to 90-fold risk in exposed smoker

Among the fibrous minerals, asbestos is the most important health hazard (Table 17-2). The pulmonary fibrosis (asbestosis) is dose-dependent, whereas diseases in the pleural space do not seem to be related to the intensity of exposure. In addition to pulmonary fibrosis and benign pleural disease, there is a fivefold increase in the rate of bronchogenic carcinoma among nonsmoking asbestos workers compared with a nonsmoking control population. Among smoking asbestos workers the risk is 60- to 90-fold. Malignant mesotheliomas of the pleura and peritoneum are also associated with asbestos exposure but bear no apparent relationship to smoking. There is a prolonged latency period between the exposure and the tumors, usually at least 20 years and sometimes as long as 30 to 40 years. Several studies have indicated that the shape, length, and diameter of asbestos fibers are important characteristics in determining carcinogenic potential.

Deposition of coal dust around the first- and second-order respiratory bronchioles causes coal workers' pneumoconiosis, or "black lung." This may be accompanied by minimal inflammation but is insufficiently severe to cause symptoms or measurable physiologic derangement in most workers. Simple pneumoconiosis consisting of a fine, diffuse, reticulonodular pattern seen on chest roentgenogram and the development of a productive cough occur in 5 per cent of coal workers. Physiologic impairment, when present, is slight. In a smaller number of miners, perhaps 0.4 per cent, nodular densities of 1 cm or greater may be visible on chest radiograph, representing dense collagenous nodules (complicated coal workers' pneumoconiosis). Unlike the simple form, this can eventually result in progressive massive fibrosis and restrictive lung disease.

The pulmonary response to a more fibrogenic dust, such as silica, is dramatically magnified. Silica exposure occurs in most mining operations, sandblasting, pottery working, brick making, and foundry work. In most cases, silicosis develops after at least 20 years of exposure, although it can develop in 5 years or less with intense exposure to a high concentration of dust. Roentgenographic gradation of disease ranges from small diffuse nodules with minimal hilar node enlargement to large nodules, predominantly in the upper lobes, which vary from about 1 cm to conglomerate masses occupying most of a lobe (progressive massive fibrosis). Eggshell calcification of the hilar nodes is characteristic. The chest radiographic findings do not correlate well with the symptoms and physiologic impairment in silicosis. The course of the disease may be modified by other factors such as coexisting smoking or superinfection with mycobacterial disease, either *Mycobacterium tuberculosis*, *M. intracellulare*, or *M. kansasii*. The more acute the silicosis, the more likely it will be complicated by tuberculosis.

No specific treatment exists for any pneumoconiosis, and only removal from the offending environment may modify the eventual progression to respiratory failure. A careful and repeated search for mycobacterial disease is mandatory in silicosis, especially with sudden worsening of the condition. Cessation of smoking, aggressive treatment of routine bacterial infections, and the use of oxygen to treat complicating cor pulmonale may improve function and prolong life.

Hypersensitivity Pneumonitis

Hypersensitivity pneumonitis, or extrinsic allergic alveolitis, occurs in individuals who have developed an abnormal sensitivity to some organic agent. Four to 6 hours following exposure in a sensitized subject, there is the onset of cough, dyspnea, fever, and malaise; wheezing is usually absent. Diffuse crackles are heard on auscultation, and the chest radiograph reveals nodular or reticulonodular infiltrates with relative sparing of the apices. In most cases these symptoms gradually resolve but recur on subsequent exposure. The duration of symptoms may gradually increase with repeated exposure and eventually result in the development of pulmonary fibrosis and restrictive lung disease.

A vast array of substances can cause this disorder (Table 17-3), the prototype being farmer's lung, a hypersensitivity to thermophilic *Actinomyces*, a fungus-like organism found in moldy hay. Patients with these disorders have serum precipitins to specific proteins, although the presence of precipitins does not, by itself, define the disease, because 50 per cent of similarly exposed subjects develop precipitins but remain asymptomatic. The disorder is believed to result from both immune complex and cell-mediated immune mechanisms.

The treatment is to remove or avoid the offending agent. Occasionally, in the acute situation corticosteroids are required. The efficacy of corticosteroids in the chronic phase, once fibrosis has set in, however, is less clear, although a trial in symptomatic patients is usually worthwhile.

Other Clearly Extrinsic Causes of Diffuse Infiltrative Lung Disease

External radiation in doses in excess of 5000 rads over a 4- to 6-week period frequently produces radiation pneumonitis within the first 6 months following exposure, and almost always by 13 months after exposure. Many drugs cause diffuse lung disease (Table 17–4). Some cancer chemotherapeutic agents, such as chlorambucil, produce dose-related toxicity, whereas others, like methotrexate, produce hypersensitivity reactions. Both phenomena occur with bleomycin in an acute syndrome; chronic illness is almost inevitable when more than 400 to 500 units are used. Synergism between bleomycin and other causes of lung injury, such as radiation and high concentrations of oxygen, has been suspected. Antibiotics, especially nitrofurantoin and sulfonamides, may cause hypersensitivity lung disease, and a number of sedatives and hypnotics have been implicated in noncardiogenic pulmonary edema, especially with intravenous abuse. Exposure to noxious gases such as chlorine, ammonia, phosgene, ozone, hydrogen sulfide, and nitrogen dioxide can cause severe lung injury. The nature of the injury depends upon the reactivity of the gas, its concentration, and the length of exposure and ranges from tracheobronchitis to adult respiratory distress syndrome.

Diffuse Lung Disease of Unknown Etiology

Collagen Vascular Diseases

Rheumatoid arthritis is associated with five different pulmonary manifestations present in a high percentage of seropositive cases: exudative pleural effusion characterized by a very low glucose concentration; pulmonary nodules varying from a few millimeters to more than 5 cm in diameter; rheumatoid nodules in association with coal workers' pneumoconiosis (Caplan's syndrome); diffuse interstitial fibrosis; and pulmonary vasculitis. With the exception of the nodules and the low glucose in the pleural fluid, patients with systemic lupus erythematosus (SLE) may have many of the same manifestations. Pleuritis and pneumonitis have also been described in Sjögren's syndrome, polymyositis, and dermatomyositis. The lung is commonly involved in scleroderma presenting as pulmonary fibrosis and/or pulmonary hypertension. Last, granulomatous inflammation of the pulmonary parenchyma has been demonstrated in temporal arteritis and polymyalgia rheumatica.

Pulmonary Vasculitis

Pulmonary vasculitis may occur as a part of one of the aforementioned connective tissue disorders or in the course of a systemic granulomatous or hypersensitivity vasculitis.

The granulomatous vasculitides include classic Wegener's granulomatosis, limited Wegener's granulomatosis, and lymphomatoid granulomatosis. Classic Wegener's is a necrotizing vasculitis initially described as involving three organ systems: the lung, the upper respiratory tract, and the kidneys. However, many other organs in the body may be affected. Lung involvement usually takes the form of single or multiple nodular lesions that have a propensity to cavitate. In the limited form of Wegener's granulomatosis, patients have a similar pathology but are free of renal disease. Recently, antineutrophil cytoplasmic antibodies (ANCAs) have been demonstrated in Wegener's granulomatosis and may be useful both diagnostically and in following disease activity. However, ANCAs have been demonstrated in other vasculitides, and their specificity remains controversial. Both Wegener's variants respond well to cyclo-

TABLE 17–3. HYPERSENSITIVITY PNEUMONITIS

ANTIGEN	SOURCE	DISEASE EXAMPLES
Thermophilic bacteria	Moldy hay and other organic material, heated humidifiers	Farmer's lung, bagassosis, humidifier lung
Other bacteria, particularly *Bacillus subtilis*	Water	Detergent worker's and humidifier lung
Fungi	Moldy organic material, water	Maple bark-stripper's lung, suberosis, sequoiosis
Animal protein	Bird droppings, animal dander	Pigeon breeder's lung, rodent handler's disease
Amoeba	Water	Humidifier lung

TABLE 17–4. COMMON DRUG-INDUCED LUNG DISEASES

DRUG	DOSE RELATION	PATHOLOGIC AND CLINICAL APPEARANCE
I. Cancer chemotherapeutic agents		
Bleomycin	Both acute and dose-dependent	Pulmonary fibrosis
Busulfan	Greater than 600 mg	Pulmonary fibrosis
Chlorambucil	Greater than 2 g	Pulmonary fibrosis
Methotrexate	None	Pneumonitis
II. Analgesics and hypnotics		
Aspirin	Serum level greater than 45 mg/dl	Pulmonary edema
Ethchlorvynol, propoxyphene hydrochloride, heroin	Overdose	Pulmonary edema
Opiates and other psychotropic drugs	Chronic intravenous abuse	Pulmonary fibrosis and vasculitis
III. Antibiotics		
Nitrofurantoin	Acute	Hypersensitivity pneumonitis
Sulfonamides	Chronic	Pulmonary fibrosis, Löffler's syndrome

phosphamide in combination with prednisone. Rapid and accurate diagnosis of Wegener's granulomatosis is essential because the disease is often fatal without cyclophosphamide treatment. Lymphomatoid granulomatosis resembles Wegener's but differs in the frequent central nervous system involvement. It is now clear that this disease is really an angiocentric lymphoma and not a true vasculitis. Combination chemotherapy regimens are used, but the prognosis is poor.

In hypersensitivity vasculitis, pulmonary involvement is a less prominent part of a systemic disease. The disorders in which this is most commonly seen are anaphylactoid purpura, essential mixed cryoglobulinemia, and the vasculitis associated with malignancy, infection, or drugs.

Pulmonary Infiltrates with Eosinophilia (PIE)

The combination of pulmonary infiltrates and peripheral eosinophilia occurs in five relatively well characterized disorders. Löffler's syndrome is a benign condition characterized by fleeting pulmonary infiltrates and eosinophilia, probably related to an immune response to some external agent. Chronic eosinophilic pneumonia is a more symptomatic form of PIE. Because of its tendency to involve the periphery of the lung, its roentgenographic appearance is called the inverse of pulmonary edema. Both respond to corticosteroids. PIE in asthma is most commonly due to allergic bronchopulmonary aspergillosis. Tropical eosinophilia consists of symptoms of wheeze, fever, and a diffuse reticulonodular pattern on the radiograph that is thought to result from an infestation with microfilariae of *Wuchereria bancrofti*. Finally, it may be associated with a collagen vascular disease, in which case the underlying disorder determines the overall presentation.

Sarcoidosis

Sarcoidosis is a systemic disease of unknown etiology characterized by noncaseating granulomas found diffusely throughout the body. It occurs most commonly in the third and fourth decades, is slightly more likely in women, and is roughly 10 times more frequent in black people in the United States.

Increasing evidence suggests that T cell activation is an integral factor in the pathogenesis of sarcoidosis, although the stimulus remains unknown. An increased percentage of lymphocytes in bronchoalveolar lavage (BAL) fluid is a marker of alveolitis in sarcoidosis. However, attempts to predict disease progression and need for treatment based on BAL findings have been disappointing. Other immunologic abnormalities include cutaneous anergy with decreased circulating T cells, autoantibodies to T cells, polyclonal gammopathy, and decreased B cell numbers.

Most of the dysfunction associated with sarcoidosis results from the physical presence of the granulomas in the tissues, although systemic signs of inflammation may also be present. Organs commonly involved include the lungs, skin, lymph nodes, liver, spleen, eyes, joints, central nervous system, and muscles (Table 17–5). The presenting symptoms are quite variable, although in the United States 50 per cent of patients present with pulmonary disease, 25 per cent with constitutional symptoms, and 7 per cent with extrapulmonary involvement; the remainder are asymptomatic and are discovered during routine examination. Common respiratory complaints include cough and dyspnea. Erythema nodosum, often seen concomitantly with bilateral hilar adenopathy, indicates acute sarcoidosis and is associated with a good prognosis.

Diagnosis depends on the finding of noncaseating granuloma in the setting of a characteristic clinical picture with typical radiographic findings, in the absence of another specific cause of granulomatous disease, such as tuberculosis, fungal disease, carcinoma, and lymphoma. Histologic confirmation is most commonly obtained by a transbronchial biopsy during bronchoscopy. Conventional chest radiographic staging is as follows: stage 0, normal film; stage 1, bilateral hilar adenopathy; stage 2, adenopathy plus pulmonary infiltrates; and, stage 3, pulmonary infiltrates alone. There is no evidence that staging has any relationship to the natural progression of disease. Rarely, the radiograph may show multiple nodules similar to those seen with metastatic tumor or a pleural effusion. A gallium lung scan may be positive, but this is a nonspecific finding. Other laboratory abnormalities include hypercalcemia and hypercalciuria (up to 20 per cent of patients), which can lead to renal calculi, and anemia. Angiotensin-converting enzyme levels may be elevated, but this is also seen in other diffuse lung disease. Pul-

---

TABLE 17–5. CLINICAL MANIFESTATIONS OF SARCOIDOSIS

Pulmonary
  Asymptomatic with abnormal chest x-ray
  Gradually progressive cough and shortness of breath
  Pulmonary fibrosis with pulmonary insufficiency
  Laryngeal and endobronchial obstruction
Extrapulmonary
  Löfgren's syndrome—fever, arthralgias, bilateral hilar adenopathy, erythema nodosum
  Heerfordt's syndrome (uveoparotid fever)—fever, swelling of parotid gland and uveal tracts, nerve VII palsy
  Skin—lupus pernio or skin plaques
  Central nervous system—cranial nerve palsies, subacute meningitis, diabetes insipidus
  Joints—polyarticular and monoarticular arthritis
  Erythema nodosum
  Punched-out cystic lesions in phalangeal and metacarpal bones
  Peripheral lymphadenopathy and/or splenomegaly
  Heart—paroxysmal arrhythmias, conduction disturbances
  Eye—chorioretinitis, anterior uveitis, keratoconjunctivitis
  Hypercalcemia with nephrocalcinosis or nephrolithiasis
  Granulomatous hepatitis

monary function tests usually reveal a restrictive defect with decreased diffusion capacity and are the most useful studies in assessing response to treatment.

The disorder is usually self-limited with complete resolution of symptoms and chest radiographic changes within 1 to 2 years. A minority have a persistent mild abnormality with some fibrotic changes visible on chest radiography. Approximately 10 per cent develop severe progressive disease with progressive pulmonary fibrosis or significant extrapulmonary involvement.

Corticosteroids are quite effective in ameliorating the acute granulomatous inflammation, but their efficacy in altering the long-term prognosis is unproven. The usual indications for corticosteroid therapy are listed in Table 17-6. Other agents, such as chloroquine, indomethacin, azathioprine, and methotrexate, are occasionally employed, especially for symptomatic skin involvement; satisfactory studies of their efficacy have not been undertaken. Recently, ketoconazole has been demonstrated to be effective in treating hypercalcemia associated with sarcoidosis by inhibiting formation of 1,25-dihydroxycholecalciferol.

Pulmonary Hemorrhagic Disorder

The combination of hemoptysis, anemia, and diffuse pulmonary infiltrates along with the development of glomerulonephritis is known as Goodpasture's syndrome. This is predominantly a disease of young white males. The etiology is unknown, but the presence of anti-glomerular basement membrane antibodies lining both the glomerulus and the alveolus suggests an autoimmune mechanism. Although the lung disease may be intermittent, the kidney disease rapidly progresses to renal failure. On occasion, hemoptysis by itself may be life-threatening. Bilateral nephrectomy results in cessation of the hemoptysis, but present therapy is directed at the presumed immunologic basis for the disease. Plasmapheresis is used to remove the antibodies, immunosuppressive drugs are used to decrease antibody production, and steroids are given empirically to decrease the pulmonary hemorrhage. Untreated patients usually die within 2 years.

Idiopathic pulmonary hemosiderosis can present similarly to Goodpasture's syndrome, although it predominantly affects young girls and does not involve the kidneys. The etiology is unknown, and there are no clear-cut immunologic markers. Despite this, treatment similar to that for Goodpasture's syndrome is usually attempted, although the efficacy in this disease is much less clear and average survival is about 2 to 3 years.

Finally, pulmonary hemorrhage, with or without renal disease, may accompany one of the collagen vascular diseases, particularly SLE and periarteritis nodosa. It may also be seen with systemic vasculitis, in particular, Wegener's granulomatosis; hypersensitivity vasculitis; mixed cryoglobulinemia; and Behçet's syndrome.

TABLE 17-6. INDICATIONS FOR USE OF CORTICOSTEROIDS IN SARCOIDOSIS

Iridocyclitis	Corticosteroid eye drops
	Local subconjunctival depot of cortisone
Posterior uveitis	Oral prednisone
Pulmonary involvement	Steroids rarely recommended for Stage I; usually employed if infiltrate remains static or worsens over 3-month period, or the patient is symptomatic
Upper airway obstruction	Rare indication for intravenous steroids
Lupus pernio	Oral prednisone shrinks the disfiguring lesions
Hypercalcemia	Responds well to corticosteroids
Cardiac involvement	Corticosteroids usually recommended if patient has arrhythmias or conduction disturbances
CNS involvement	Response is best in patients with acute symptoms
Lacrimal/salivary gland involvement	Corticosteroids recommended for disordered function, *not* gland swelling
Bone cysts	Corticosteroids recommended if symptomatic

CNS = Central nervous system.

Miscellaneous

Pulmonary histiocytosis X, or eosinophilic granuloma of the lung, is a relatively benign disease presenting with dyspnea and radiographic evidence of diffuse nodular or reticulonodular infiltrates with relative sparing of the lung bases. It should be suspected in patients in the third and fourth decades presenting with diffusely abnormal chest radiographs. It is easy to confuse with sarcoidosis, although pneumothorax or honeycombing on the chest radiograph and the rarity of hilar adenopathy favor histiocytosis X. Diagnosis is made pathologically, treatment is uncertain, and spontaneous remissions are common.

The lymphocytic infiltrative disorders include lymphocytic interstitial pneumonia and immunoblastic lymphadenopathy, among other specific entities. They differ from other interstitial lung diseases in their common association with dysproteinemia and frequent progression to lymphoid malignancy.

Pulmonary alveolar proteinosis is a rare, idiopathic disease in which the alveoli become filled with a proteinaceous material rich in lipids. Most patients recover spontaneously, but total lung lavage is necessary when diffuse involvement causes severe hypoxemia. These patients are particularly prone to infection with *Nocardia*, and less so to *Aspergillus* and *Cryptococcus*.

Idiopathic Pulmonary Fibrosis

A large number of patients with diffuse interstitial lung disease do not fit into any of the previously mentioned categories. These patients, usually middle-aged with no gender predominance, present with dyspnea and radiographic evidence of interstitial disease. Rarely, the disease progresses very rapidly from respiratory failure to death within 6 months of the onset of symptoms (Hamman-Rich syndrome). When the disease is more slowly progressive, it is termed idiopathic pulmonary fibrosis or cryptogenic fibrosing alveolitis. Open lung biopsy is usually necessary for definitive diagnosis because interstitial fibrosis may accompany many inflammatory processes, and a large tissue specimen, preferably from moderately involved lung regions rather than end-stage fibrotic areas, is necessary to eliminate other disorders.

Bronchiolitis Obliterans with Organizing Pneumonia

Another nonspecific manifestation of pulmonary injury is the proliferation of fibrous and inflammatory tissue in distal bronchioles and the adjacent alveolar regions, termed bronchiolitis obliterans with organizing pneumonia (BOOP). This pattern of injury may result from viral infections and toxic inhalation as well as other unknown factors. The chest radiograph reveals patchy air space opacities, and the clinical history is of continuous nonproductive cough following a flulike illness. The importance of recognizing this disorder and making the diagnosis with open lung biopsy is that most patients demonstrate a significant response to corticosteroids without subsequent progressive pulmonary fibrosis.

Treatment

Although the treatment of these disorders depends on the particular one being discussed, certain general statements can be made. The most rational decisions can be made only if a clear diagnosis has been obtained. If the offending substance is identified, as in the pneumoconioses and hypersensitivity pneumonitis, avoidance is the best solution. When there is an active alveolitis component, corticosteroids may be of benefit. The dose should be high (60 to 100 mg prednisone) initially and then reduced to the lowest possible dose that successfully suppresses the inflammatory response. If there is no objective evidence of improvement, the steroids should be stopped. Immunosuppressive agents are added to effect remission in certain types of vasculitis, such as Wegener's granulomatosis, but are of questionable value in Goodpasture's syndrome and have little efficacy in idiopathic pulmonary fibrosis. Plasmapheresis should be reserved for illnesses in which circulating antibody is known to be the etiologic factor, as in Goodpasture's syndrome. In selected patients with end-stage pulmonary fibrosis, single lung transplantation has been demonstrated to be effective, with significant improvement in pulmonary function and exercise tolerance.

REFERENCES

Cooper JAD: Drug induced pulmonary disease. Clin Chest Med 11(1):1–189, 1990.

Hunningshake GW, Fauci AS: Pulmonary involvement in the collagen vascular diseases, state of the art. Am Rev Respir Dis 119:471–501, 1979.

Morgan WKC, Seaton A: Occupational Lung Disease. 2nd ed. Philadelphia, WB Saunders Co, 1984.

Schwartz MI, King TE: Interstitial Lung Disease. Toronto, BC Decker, 1988.

18 PULMONARY VASCULAR DISEASE

TABLE 18–1. NORMAL ADULT PULMONARY VASCULAR PRESSURES

Pulmonary artery pressure (mm Hg)	Systolic	20
	Diastolic	10
	Mean	15
Pulmonary wedge pressure (mm Hg)	Mean	10
Pulmonary vascular resistance (mm Hg/L/min)		1–2

The pulmonary vascular bed is normally a low-pressure, low-resistance system (Table 18–1). When it is involved in disease, either through obliteration of cross-sectional area or less commonly through an increase in tone, the resulting pulmonary hypertension and redistribution of pulmonary blood flow lead to profound changes in cardiac function and pulmonary gas exchange.

Physiologic Effects of Pulmonary Hypertension

Cardiac Function

The right and left sides of the heart are functionally integrated by their anatomic contiguity. There is continuity between their free walls, they share a common wall (the interventricular septum), and they are covered by the pericardium. When pulmonary vascular resistance is normal, the right ventricle serves as a capacitance chamber, performing only minimal contractile work. It compensates ineffectually for acute rises in pulmonary artery pressure and acutely can only generate a mean pressure of 40 mm Hg. Acute elevations of right ventricular pressure also interfere with left ventricular performance, presumably owing to a shift in the interventricular septum to the left, which decreases left ventricular compliance and impedes left ventricular filling. Chronic elevations of pulmonary artery pressure cause gradual hypertrophy of the right ventricle, which eventually allows it to generate pressures equal to those in the left ventricle.

Pulmonary Function

Abnormalities of pulmonary function in patients with pulmonary vascular disease are usually a consequence of the underlying lung disease rather than an intrinsic effect of the pulmonary vascular disease. An exception is the decreased diffusing capacity due to capillary obliteration. In addition, pulmonary vascular occlusion and obliteration cause shunt and ventilation-perfusion inequality by undefined mechanisms. The resulting hypoxemia is further exaggerated by the associated reduction of cardiac output and low mixed venous PO_2.

Causes of Pulmonary Hypertension

Table 18–2 categorizes the causes of pulmonary hypertension by the underlying pathophysiologic mechanism. In postcapillary pulmonary hypertension, the elevated pulmonary pressures are a reflection of elevated left atrial pressure or rarely of venous obliteration. In hyperkinetic pulmonary hypertension, the disorder is a reflection of the increased flow. Reactive pulmonary hypertension is due predominantly to hypoxic vasoconstriction. The most common etiology is chronic obstructive lung disease, discussed in Chapter 16. This chapter focuses on two disorders that typify primary involvement of the pulmonary vessels—one acute, pulmonary embolism, and one chronic, primary pulmonary hypertension.

PULMONARY EMBOLISM

A great variety of substances may embolize to the pulmonary vascular bed, with the resulting clinical presentation dependent on the composition of the embolic material. Talc granules and cotton fibers injected along with illicit drugs, sickled red blood cells, and blood-borne parasites like schistosomes lead to slowly progressive disease clinically similar to primary pulmonary hypertension. Embolization of fat, air, or amniotic fluid, however, alters alveolar capillary membrane integrity and presents as the adult respiratory distress syndrome (see Chapter 19). The consequences of the most common embolic material, thromboemboli, depend on the amount of clot reaching the lung and the cardiopulmonary status of the patient. They may vary from a persistent tachycardia or mild dyspnea to cardiopulmonary arrest. Thromboemboli directly or indirectly cause 200,000 deaths per year.

Most thromboemboli originate in the iliofemoral deep veins. Less common sources include the vessels below the knee, pelvic veins, upper extremities, and mural thrombi in the right side of the heart. Stasis, intimal injury, and a hypercoagulable state are important factors in the development of thrombosis. The clinical diagnosis of deep venous thrombosis is highly inaccurate, as physical examination is often misleading, and specialized diagnostic techniques should be utilized whenever it is suspected (Table 18–3).

The diagnosis of pulmonary embolism is often missed in sick hospitalized patients, whereas in the healthy outpatient population it is overdiagnosed. Predisposing situations are listed in Table 18–4. Clinical findings suggestive of pulmonary embolism are nonspecific and are often more commonly indicative of other acute cardiopulmonary disorders. Typical symptoms include dyspnea (80 per cent), pleuritic chest pain (70 per cent), and hemoptysis (20 to 30 per cent). Physical findings include tachypnea (invariable), obvious thrombophlebitis (unusual), acute right ventricular strain (right ventricular heave, increased P_2, gallop) in less than 40 per cent of cases, and occasionally rubs, crackles, or wheezing. Patients who present

---

TABLE 18–2. PULMONARY HYPERTENSION

Hyperkinetic Pulmonary Hypertension
  Atrial and ventricular septal defects
  Patent ductus arteriosus
  Peripheral arteriovenous shunts
Postcapillary Pulmonary Hypertension
  Left ventricular failure
  Mitral valve disease
Obliterative or Obstructive Hypertension
  Embolic
  Parenchymal lung disease
  Arteritis
  Pulmonary artery stenosis
  Primary
Reactive Hypertension
  High altitude
  Chronic obstructive lung disease
  Persistent or intermittent hypoventilation
    Neuromuscular disease
    Sleep apnea syndrome

TABLE 18-3. METHODS OF DIAGNOSING DEEP VENOUS THROMBOSIS

METHOD	USEFULNESS
Contrast venography	The "gold standard"; low incidence of poststudy phlebitis
Impedance plethysmography (IPG) and Doppler ultrasonography	Highly specific and sensitive noninvasive techniques for detecting thrombi above the knee; less sensitive for thrombi confined to calf veins; false-positive studies with heart failure, ascites, and prior deep venous thrombosis
Nuclide venography	Functional study; high incidence of false-positive studies

without dyspnea, pleuritic chest pain, or tachypnea are unlikely to have acute pulmonary embolism. A low-grade fever is common, but persistent high fever and marked leukocytosis are unusual in embolic disease and suggest, as a more likely diagnosis, an infectious etiology such as pneumonia or pleurisy.

Abnormal chest radiographic findings are common but nonspecific: atelectasis, infiltrates, pleural effusions, and an elevated diaphragm. Clear-cut hypovascularity is difficult to detect. The chest roentgenogram is most useful in ruling out other causes of dyspnea and chest pain such as pneumothorax and lung abscess. Electrocardiography (ECG) helps to exclude myocardial infarction and pericarditis and may show right ventricular strain, but nonspecific ST and T wave changes are more common, and often sinus tachycardia is the only abnormality, or it may even be normal. Hypoxemia and hypocapnia are typical, but arterial Po_2 is

TABLE 18-4. FACTORS PREDISPOSING TO PULMONARY THROMBOEMBOLI

Medical
  Cancer
  Stroke
  Myocardial infarction
  Congestive heart failure
  Sepsis
  Pregnancy
Surgical
  Orthopedic surgery and lower extremity fractures
  Major surgical procedures (general anesthesia > 30 min)
  Urologic, gynecologic, and neurosurgical procedures
Acquired
  Lupus anticoagulant
  Paroxysmal nocturnal hemoglobinuria
  Nephrotic syndrome
  Polycythemia vera
Inherited
  Antithrombin III, protein S, and protein C deficiency
  Dysfibrinogenemia
  Plasminogen and plasminogen activation disorders

greater than 80 mm Hg in 13 per cent of patients without prior cardiopulmonary disease. The hypoxemia is due to the development of ventilation-perfusion inequality and a low mixed venous Po_2 secondary to reduced cardiac output. In summary, the clinical presentation and routine laboratory studies may suggest diagnosis, but confirmation requires specific investigations.

Absence of activity on the perfusion lung scan, which visualizes the gross distribution of blood flow in the lung, may be due to anatomic blockage of the vessels or to vasoconstriction. A normal perfusion scan excludes pulmonary embolism. A ventilation scan helps to differentiate anatomic from functional blockage of blood flow. Delayed washout of the radioactive gas suggests that airway disease may have caused the decreased perfusion secondary to hypoxic vasoconstriction. A normal ventilation scan with a perfusion scan showing segmental or larger defects is considered a high-probability ventilation-perfusion scan and is highly successful at diagnosing pulmonary embolism. Anything other than normal or high-probability ventilation-perfusion scan is an indeterminate scan and is nondiagnostic and cannot confirm or exclude pulmonary embolism. The designation of low-probability scan should be discouraged because pulmonary emboli have been found in 13 to 46 per cent of patients with indeterminate and low-probability scans.

If the lung scan is indeterminate, the diagnostic work-up must be extended. Two options exist. The simplest approach is to demonstrate the presence of deep venous thrombosis. Unfortunately, in as many as 30 to 40 per cent of patients with acute pulmonary embolism, these studies may be negative because the clot has already embolized. A pulmonary angiogram is then the logical next step, especially in the precarious patient or one who is at high risk if anticoagulated. An alternative approach in patients with stable cardiopulmonary function is repetitive, noninvasive studies of the legs over a 10-day period, to watch for the development of thrombosis. If the studies remain negative, treatment is unnecessary because anticoagulation is directed at preventing the formation of additional thrombi and not at treating the embolism. Definitive diagnosis of pulmonary emboli is vital, as both missed diagnosis and unwarranted anticoagulation result in high morbidity and mortality rates. A diagnostic decision tree is shown in Figure 18-1.

Treatment of deep venous thrombosis and pulmonary embolism consists of anticoagulation with heparin by continuous infusion for 7 to 10 days at a dosage to prolong the partial thromboplastin time (PTT) 1.5 to 2 times the control value. As an alternative, heparin can be given by intermittent boluses or subcutaneous doses adjusted to achieve similar prolongation of the PTT. During heparin therapy, the platelet count should be monitored to prevent the development of thrombocytopenia. The indications for treatment of deep calf vein thrombosis are controversial, but patients with symptomatic occlusion of the calf veins proven by venography should probably be anticoagulated. Oral anticoagulation (warfarin) should be started as soon as a therapeutic PTT is achieved in a dose sufficient to maintain the prothrombin time (PT) at 1.3 to 1.5 times the baseline value. A further prolongation of the PT increases the risk of bleeding without improving the therapeutic outcome. Heparin at a dose adjusted to prolong the PTT to 1.5 times the baseline value can be used as an alternative for long-term maintenance anticoagulation and should always be used in pregnant women, because warfarin may be injurious to the fetus. Long-term anticoagulation should be continued for 3 months in patients whose risk has resolved, or indefinitely if the predisposing condition persists. Patients who have recurrences of thromboembolic disease may also require prolonged therapy. Most emboli completely resolve, and chronic persistent pulmonary hypertension develops in fewer than 2 per cent of patients.

Rarely, additional therapy may be required (Table 18–5), but it should be undertaken only when clear indications are present because of significant added risks. Fibrinolytic drugs (streptokinase, urokinase, or tissue plasminogen activator) are capable of augmenting the dissolution of fresh emboli and have been shown to increase resolution of pulmonary perfusion abnormalities in the first 24 hours when compared with heparin. On the basis of this, it is often recommended that they be used in patients with marked hemodynamic instability following acute pulmonary embolization. They have not, however, been demonstrated to alter overall mortality or morbidity, and because their use is accompanied by a significantly increased incidence of bleeding, routine use is unwarranted.

Vena caval interruption should be considered when the thrombus originates in the lower extremities and there has been proven recurrence after at least 24 hours of heparin therapy. It should also be used when anticoagulation is contraindicated. The preferred technique is the transvenous placement of a Greenfield or "bird's-nest" vena caval filter.

The best way to treat thromboembolic disease is to prevent its occurrence. Appropriate prophylaxis of high-risk patients is safe and efficient. Most can be treated with low-dose subcutaneous heparin, 5000 units every 12 hours. Patients undergoing orthopedic procedures on the lower extremity, especially the hip, may not be protected by this regimen, and present recommendations suggest the use of either heparin adjusted to therapeutic PTT levels or therapeutic doses of warfarin. In patients in whom postoperative bleeding represents an unacceptable risk, as in neurosurgical procedures, intermittent pneumatic compression of the lower extremities is recommended.

PRIMARY PULMONARY HYPERTENSION

Primary pulmonary hypertension can occur at any age but is most common in the third and fourth decades. In children, there is no apparent gender

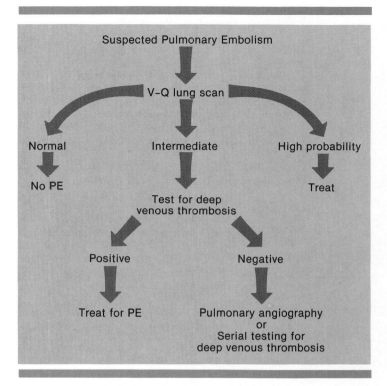

FIGURE 18–1. Diagnostic approach to pulmonary embolism.

predominance, but the female-male ratio is about 2:1 in adults. The etiology is unknown but is possibly related to increased vasoconstrictor substances or in situ thrombosis. Recently, an endothelium-derived vasoconstrictor, endothelin, has been found to be elevated in some of these patients. Abnormal vascular smooth muscle proliferation may also play a contributory role. Occasional clinical associations include chronic portal hypertension, ingestion of an appetite suppressant (aminorex), and a family history.

Patients present with progressive dyspnea and marked exercise limitation. With time, fatigue, chest pain, cor pulmonale, and syncopal episodes on exertion (decreased left ventricular output) develop. Physical examination may be normal or may reveal evidence of pulmonary hypertension.

TABLE 18–5. TREATMENT OF PULMONARY EMBOLI

TREATMENT	INDICATION
Anticoagulation with heparin and warfarin	All patients with pulmonary emboli unless risk of bleeding is unacceptable
Fibrinolytic drugs— streptokinase, urokinase, tissue plasminogen activator	Patients with massive emboli and hemodynamic instability
Vena caval interruption with vena cava filters	When anticoagulants are contraindicated or have failed
Acute embolectomy	Rarely, if ever, useful because of high mortality

The chest radiograph shows an enlarged right ventricle and main pulmonary arteries, with oligemia in the outer lung fields. ECG evidence of right ventricular hypertrophy is invariable when the mean pulmonary artery pressures are chronically elevated above 40 mm Hg. Pulmonary function studies are often normal except for a small reduction in total lung capacity and diffusing capacity. Mild hypoxemia and hypocapnia are almost always found. Diagnosis is made by right heart catheterization and by excluding other causes of pulmonary hypertension. Prognosis is dismal, with only 20 per cent surviving 3 years.

Drug therapy is actively being investigated. Calcium blockers and prostacyclin reduce pulmonary vascular resistance in up to 30 per cent of patients. Chronic anticoagulation is often recommended, because thrombosis in the small pulmonary arteries is thought to contribute to progressive deterioration of right heart function. These therapies should be viewed as a bridge to single lung transplantation, which is the only truly successful approach currently available.

REFERENCES

Dalen JE, Hirsh J: Second ACCP conference on antithrombotic therapy. Chest 95:15, 1989.

Fishman AP: The pulmonary circulation: Normal and abnormal. Philadelphia, University of Pennsylvania Press, 1990.

Moser KM: Venous thromboembolism. Am Rev Respir Dis 141:235, 1990.

The PIOPED Investigators: Value of ventilation/perfusion scan in acute pulmonary embolism. JAMA 263:2753, 1990.

19 THE ADULT RESPIRATORY DISTRESS SYNDROME AND PULMONARY CRITICAL CARE

In 1967 a syndrome of acute respiratory failure characterized by severe hypoxemia, bilateral pulmonary infiltrates, and decreased lung compliance, usually occurring without preceding lung disease, was dubbed the adult respiratory distress syndrome (ARDS). Since that time, it has become increasingly clear that the pulmonary abnormalities are, in most cases, only an obvious manifestation of a more systemic process now called the syndrome of "multiple organ failure" (MOF). The etiology of MOF is unclear and may differ from patient to patient, depending on the initiating stimulus. Diffuse intravascular inflammation resulting in widespread endothelial cell injury, abnormal coagulation, cytokine activation, and abnormal mediator release have all been hypothesized as pathogenic mechanisms. The incidence of ARDS has increased as improvements in intensive care allow more patients to survive the catastrophic illnesses that act as the initiating events, and its mortality rate remains unacceptably high. More than 60 per cent of patients die, and the prognosis becomes increasingly grave as MOF develops.

PATHOPHYSIOLOGY

Fluid movement in the lung is governed by vascular permeability and the balance of the hydrostatic and oncotic pressures across the capillary endothelium as described in the Starling equation (Fig. 19–1). Hydrostatic forces favor fluid filtration, whereas oncotic pressure promotes reabsorption. Normally, filtration forces dominate and fluid continuously moves from the vascular space into the interstitium. Despite this, extravascular water does not accumulate because the lung lymphatics effectively remove the filtered fluid and return it to the circulation. However, the capacity of the lymphatic system is limited, and if the rate of fluid filtration exceeds its functional capabilities, water accumulates. The physiologic abnormalities in the lung of patients with ARDS, regardless of the predisposing event, are associated with a flooding of the interstitium and alveolar spaces with proteinaceous and often hemorrhagic fluid. Initially, it accumulates in the loose interstitial tissues around the airways, pulmonary arteries, and later the alveolar walls (interstitial edema). This causes increased lung stiffness and dyspnea but rarely produces significant abnormalities in the arterial blood gases. If the process continues, the excess fluid accumulates in the alveolar space, with two consequences: alveolar surface forces are altered, leading to a further reduction in compliance and a decreased lung volume, and the flooded alveoli can no longer be ventilated, thus converting their blood supply into intrapulmonary shunt. Shunt is the major cause of the severe hypoxemia characteristic of ARDS (see Chapter 14).

Two alterations of the Starling equation are of clinical importance. Patients with cardiogenic pulmonary edema and fluid overload have an increase in pulmonary capillary hydrostatic pressure. Edema fluid in this setting has a low protein content and is essentially an ultrafiltrate of plasma. In ARDS, the hydrostatic pressure is usually normal and fluid accumulation is due to an alteration in alveolar-capillary membrane permeability, which may result from either endothelial or epithelial cell injury (Fig. 19–2). The etiology of the ARDS is occasionally clear-cut lung injury, as in gastric aspiration or viral pneumonia, but is more commonly elusive and ascribed to complex immunologic or biochemical events similar to those thought to be responsible for MOF. The resulting edema has a high protein content similar to that of plasma. Although it is unusual for alterations in oncotic pressure to be the sole cause of pulmonary edema, the presence of low intravascular oncotic pressure increases the rate of fluid transudation in both low- and high-pressure pulmonary edema. Similarly, any rise in microvascular hydrostatic pressure in the setting of increased capillary permeability dramatically increases the rate of fluid filtration.

CLINICAL PRESENTATION AND DIAGNOSIS

As with any clinically defined syndrome, the diagnosis of ARDS is made by finding the appropriate signs and symptoms (Table 19–1) in the proper clinical setting (Table 19–2) similar to those thought to be responsible for MOF. Some predisposing conditions are more likely than others to result in ARDS. For example, almost 40 per cent of patients with sepsis develop ARDS, and this may increase to more than 80 per cent if other risk factors are also present.

The clinical presentation is relatively uniform regardless of etiology. Initially the signs and symptoms are limited to those of the primary disorder. Within the first 12 to 24 hours, however, early accumulation of lung water causes dyspnea, hyperventilation, and the appearance of a fine diffuse reticular infiltrate on chest radiography. Unless the underlying disease is reversed rapidly, as in some instances of sepsis, the patient quickly progresses to the full-blown syndrome with the development of progressive bilateral pulmonary infiltrates, severe hypoxemia, and a dramatic fall in lung compliance. Most patients manifest respiratory failure within 24 hours of the onset of the predisposing event, and almost 90 per cent of those who eventually develop ARDS do so by 72 hours. Treatment is generally supportive and directed at maintaining an adequate delivery of O_2 to the tissues while minimizing iatrogenic complications. Therapy directed at the predisposing condition, when known, is imperative, because its continued presence prevents resolution of the ARDS.

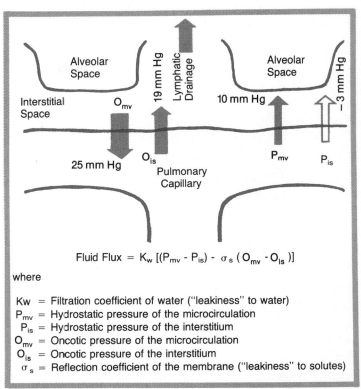

$$\text{Fluid Flux} = K_w \left[(P_{mv} - P_{is}) - \sigma_s (O_{mv} - O_{is}) \right]$$

where

K_w = Filtration coefficient of water ("leakiness" to water)
P_{mv} = Hydrostatic pressure of the microcirculation
P_{is} = Hydrostatic pressure of the interstitium
O_{mv} = Oncotic pressure of the microcirculation
O_{is} = Oncotic pressure of the interstitium
σ_s = Reflection coefficient of the membrane ("leakiness" to solutes)

FIGURE 19–1. Factors affecting fluid filtration in the lung. The filtration is from the pulmonary microcirculation into the interstitium of the lung. Normally, excessive accumulation of fluid is prevented by the capacity of the lymphatics to drain it back into the systemic circulation.

TABLE 19–1. DIAGNOSIS OF ARDS

1. Proper clinical setting (Table 19-2) and the exclusion of left ventricular failure or chronic lung disease
2. Diffuse pulmonary infiltrates on chest radiography
3. $Pa_{O_2} < 50$ mm Hg on $F_{I_{O_2}} > 0.60$
4. Decreased respiratory compliance <50 ml/cm H_2O

TABLE 19–2. CLINICAL CONDITIONS COMMONLY ASSOCIATED WITH ARDS

Sepsis syndrome
Aspiration of gastric contents
Multiple transfusions
Pneumonia in the intensive care unit
Disseminated intravascular coagulation
Multiple bone fractures
Burns
Pulmonary contusion
Pancreatitis
Near-drowning
Caustic gas inhalation

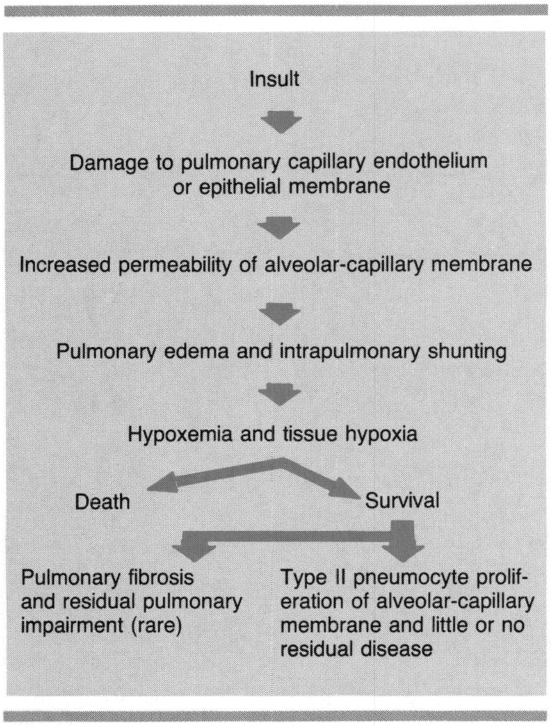

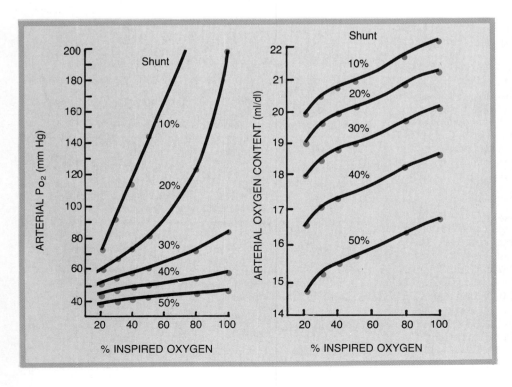

Insult
Damage to pulmonary capillary endothelium or epithelial membrane
Increased permeability of alveolar-capillary membrane
Pulmonary edema and intrapulmonary shunting
Hypoxemia and tissue hypoxia
Death
Survival
Pulmonary fibrosis and residual pulmonary impairment (rare)
Type II pneumocyte proliferation of alveolar-capillary membrane and little or no residual disease

FIGURE 19–2. Pathogenesis and outcome of the adult respiratory distress syndrome (ARDS).

OXYGEN THERAPY AND MECHANICAL VENTILATION

Correction of the severe hypoxemia by increasing the fractional concentration of the inspired O_2 (FI_{O_2}) is useful early in the disease. However, because the hypoxemia is due to shunt, this is less effective than in patients with obstructive or restrictive lung disease in which ventilation-perfusion inequality is the major underlying mechanism. Figure 19–3 plots the relationship between the FI_{O_2} and arterial PO_2 (Pa_{O_2}) and O_2 content for different levels of shunt. Increasing the FI_{O_2} may significantly increase O_2 content and thus the O_2 delivery despite the negligible increase in Pa_{O_2}. Although O_2 content can be increased substantially, a high FI_{O_2} by itself is toxic to the lung, and thus this strategy has distinct limitations. Oxygen toxicity depends on a number of factors, including FI_{O_2}, duration of treatment, and the underlying condition of the lung. The FI_{O_2} likely to induce toxicity in humans is unknown, although it is probable that a continuum rather than a threshold exists. As a general rule, an FI_{O_2} above 0.60 can be tolerated for short periods such as 24 hours, but after 72 hours O_2 toxicity may contribute to further lung damage.

When adequate oxygenation cannot be maintained by O_2 therapy alone, or if hypercapnia develops, mechanical ventilation is essential. The positive pressure generated by the ventilator increases mean airway pressure, which in turn increases lung volume. This results in an increase in

ARTERIAL PO_2 (mm Hg)
200
180
160
140
120
100
80
60
40
Shunt
10%
20%
30%
40%
50%
20 40 60 80 100
% INSPIRED OXYGEN
ARTERIAL OXYGEN CONTENT (ml/dl)
22
21
20
19
18
17
16
15
14
Shunt
10%
20%
30%
40%
50%
20 40 60 80 100
% INSPIRED OXYGEN

FIGURE 19–3. The effect of changing the inspired O_2 concentration on the arterial PO_2 and O_2 content for lungs having shunts of 10 to 50 per cent. When the shunt is small, as may be seen early in the course of ARDS, increasing the inspired oxygen to 40 to 50 per cent effectively increases the Pa_{O_2}. As the shunt increases and approaches 30 to 50 per cent, the levels commonly seen in ARDS, only small increases in arterial PO_2 are achieved even when 100 per cent O_2 is administered. Although PO_2 increases very little *(left panel)*, this occurs at a steep portion of the O_2 dissociation curve so that O_2 saturation increases disproportionately, resulting in a considerable increase in O_2 content *(right panel)*. (From Dantzker D: Gas exchange in the adult respiratory distress syndrome. Clin Chest Med 3:57–67, 1982.)

alveolar size, spreading the fluid that is present over a greater surface area as well as redistributing fluid from the alveolar to interstitial space, allowing gas exchange to take place. Mechanical ventilation also reduces the O_2 demands caused by increased O_2 consumption by the respiratory muscles as patients try to cope with the increased work of breathing caused by stiff lungs.

An oral or nasal endotracheal tube is necessary for mechanical ventilation. Although nasal tubes often seem to be more comfortable to the patient, they usually are smaller in diameter than an oral tube and tend to cause difficulties in suctioning and to increase the work of breathing during the weaning period. In addition, a tube in the nasopharynx may lead to the development of a purulent otitis media, as it interferes with eustachian tube drainage. With proper care, high-compliance cuffed tubes can be left in place for at least 3 to 4 weeks. The major complication from endotracheal tubes is damage to the larynx resulting from tube motion as the patient moves about, a complication that can be minimized by adequate fixation of the tube at the mouth or nose. The decision to proceed to a tracheostomy should not be made on the basis of any arbitrary time limit. Tracheostomy has its own complications, such as tracheal stenosis, which may exceed the morbidity associated with endotracheal tubes. Thus a tracheostomy should be performed only if it is necessary for adequate care or if it is clear that continued mechanical ventilation will be required for a prolonged time.

Mechanical ventilators are classified on the basis of what terminates inspiratory flow. Pressure-cycled ventilators, which terminate flow when a pre-set pressure is reached in the airway, are no longer used for ventilatory support of patients because minute ventilation varies with changes in lung mechanics. Volume-cycled ventilators provide a pre-set volume to the patient over a range of airway pressures. A pressure limit is set to prevent trauma to the lung in the event of a sudden change in pulmonary mechanics when airway pressure increases in an attempt to achieve the required tidal volume. Although the precise volume delivered to the patient may vary somewhat with changes in lung mechanics and compliance of the ventilator circuit, volume-cycled ventilators allow greater control of the patient's ventilation. Time-cycled ventilators set tidal volume by fixing the inspiratory time and flow rate. They accomplish the same goal as volume ventilators but are smaller and more easily manufactured. This is the principle used in many of the new generation of mechanical ventilators.

Mechanical ventilators can be set to operate in a variety of modes (Fig. 19–4). In all modes (except PSV—see below), a certain number of mechanical breaths are delivered per unit time. The difference from mode to mode is how the spontaneous breaths are achieved. In controlled ventilation, all breaths are determined by the machine and thus it should be used only for comatose, anesthetized, or paralyzed patients. In assist-control ventilation

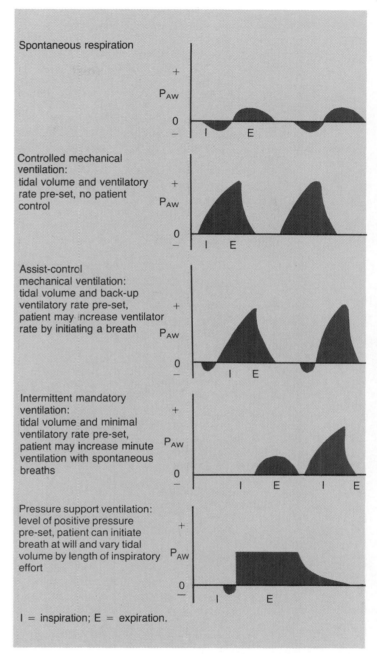

FIGURE 19–4. Changes in airway pressure during spontaneous respiration and various modes of mechanical ventilation.

(ACV), the patient's effort triggers a full mechanical breath. If the patient fails to make an effort, the machine reverts to a previously set back-up rate. In intermittent mandatory ventilation (IMV), the machine delivers a fixed number of breaths and the patient may take additional breaths, according to his ability, from a demand value. Although controversy exists regarding whether ACV or IMV is the more effective, no good comparison has been made, and for most patients it probably makes very little difference as long as sufficient support is provided. A newly introduced mode, pressure support ventilation (PSV), augments a spontaneous breath with a fixed amount of positive pressure, which can be varied depending on the degree of support desired. The role of PSV as a routine ventilatory mode has yet to be determined, but it should be used with caution as a ventilatory technique unless combined with IMV because all breaths are initiated by the patient and tidal volume may vary if lung mechanics change.

The goal of an increased mean airway pressure to increase lung volume is achieved by two strategies regardless of the ventilatory mode: (1) high tidal volume, such as 10 or even 15 ml/kg, rather than the normal 6 ml/kg; (2) positive end-expiratory pressure (PEEP), which prevents the airway pressure from falling back to atmospheric at end expiration. Although these strategies allow inspired gas to enter previously unventilated alveoli, there is no convincing evidence that increasing lung volume alters the primary pathologic process or reverses the transudation of fluid from the blood vessels into the lung. In fact, very high inflation volumes and pressures may further damage the lung. Thus, these ventilatory techniques should be used only to the degree that they may help in achieving an adequate O_2 saturation (90 per cent) at a relatively nontoxic Fi_{O_2} (<0.60). However, improvement in arterial oxygenation by itself is an insufficient guide to ventilatory therapy, as the increase in airway pressure may cause a fall in cardiac output with an overall reduction in O_2 delivery to the tissues. This is a serious problem for tissues unable to increase O_2 extraction, a common problem in the critically ill patient. Pulmonary barotrauma, manifested as subcutaneous emphysema, pneumodiastinum, and pneumothorax, is an additional serious complication.

The mechanism by which high intrathoracic pressure interferes with cardiac output is complex, but a reduction in venous return to the heart is the major problem. With small increases in intrathoracic pressure (5 to 10 cm of PEEP), impairment of cardiac output may be minimal as long as cardiac filling pressures are adequate. With higher levels of PEEP, cardiac output is invariably reduced unless filling pressures are increased above normal. The increase in filling pressure required to maintain cardiac output in the face of large increases in PEEP also elevates pulmonary hydrostatic pressure and thus is likely to increase the accumulation of extravascular lung water. To monitor these important variables, especially in patients with a questionable cardiovascular status or those in whom high levels of PEEP are required, a flow-directed pulmonary artery catheter is often useful. Both pulmonary artery and occlusion pressure (an index of left arterial pressure) can be monitored, as well as cardiac output mea-

sured by thermodilution. In addition to evaluating the adequacy of cardiac filling pressure, the catheter is often required to distinguish between ARDS and congestive heart failure, a distinction that is difficult to make by physical examination alone in many sick patients. The insertion and maintenance of the pulmonary artery catheter must be accomplished with great care to limit the risk of complications, including pneumothorax, myocardial or vascular perforation, bleeding, air embolism, arrhythmias, valve trauma or endocarditis, sepsis, and pulmonary infarction.

Because hypoxemia in ARDS is due to shunting of systemic venous blood through the lung, any alteration in mixed venous P_{O_2} (Pv_{O_2}) proportionally alters the Pa_{O_2} resulting from a given amount of shunt. Increase in the O_2 consumption, decrease in cardiac output, and fall in the hemoglobin concentration may all necessitate increased O_2 extraction by the tissues and thus decrease Pv_{O_2}. Unless this is kept in mind, it is possible that a fall in Pa_{O_2} due to one of these factors may be misinterpreted as a worsening of ARDS and corrective therapy may be aimed in the wrong direction.

Assessing the adequacy of O_2 and ventilatory therapy in these complex conditions remains a major challenge. Clearly, Pa_{O_2} is an inadequate index, because it reflects only one facet of O_2 transport (To_2), which is defined as:

$$To_2 = Cardiac\ output \times arterial\ O_2\ content$$

Thus, To_2 also includes a convection term, cardiac output, and a capacitance term, O_2 content, which, in addition to Pa_{O_2}, includes O_2 saturation and hemoglobin concentration. All components must be adequate to ensure sufficient delivery of O_2 to the tissues. In addition to To_2, tissue oxygenation depends on the distribution of blood flow within various tissues and factors that determine O_2 diffusion into the cells, about which little is known.

There is no single parameter that reflects the adequacy of O_2 delivered to the tissues. The Pv_{O_2} has been suggested, but this represents the weighted means from all the tissues and thus is markedly influenced by the distribution of blood flow and the ability of individual tissue to extract the O_2 that is delivered. For example, in septic shock, because blood flow is redistributed to tissues with a low O_2 extraction, the Pv_{O_2} may actually rise *pari passu* with the development of systemic acidosis. Increased blood lactate levels may be indicative of inadequate tissue To_2, but because lactic acid is rapidly cleared by a well-perfused and functioning liver while its washout is delayed from poorly perfused tissues, the appearance of lactic acidosis is, at best, a late indicator of O_2 deficiency. Elevated lactate levels may also be due to factors other than tissue hypoxia. Even the performance of the end-organs (heart, kidney, and liver) may be insensitive in the early, correctable stage of inadequate O_2 delivery. Techniques that directly or indirectly monitor cell bioenergetics are needed to successfully guide therapy in these critically ill patients.

OTHER THERAPEUTIC MODALITIES

The development of pharmacologic agents to treat or, more important, to prevent ARDS would represent a major advancement. Administration of high-dose corticosteroids is of no value in gram-negative sepsis and has no proven efficacy in ARDS due to other causes. Monoclonal antibodies against endotoxin reduce the mortality of sepsis, presumably by decreasing the risk of MOF. Agents that antagonize or block the response to cytokines are now being tested and may become useful in the future. Prostaglandin inhibitors, such as ibuprofen, affect the course of experimental ARDS but have yet to be shown effective in patients.

Antibiotics are the most important group of agents, because correct treatment of infection may be life-saving whereas the failure to recognize infection ensures the continuation of the pulmonary capillary leak. As far as possible, antibiotics should be selected on the basis of reliable microbial studies, but until the results are known, empirical therapy is not only appropriate but also necessary. Continued bacteremia in the face of appropriate antibiotics raises the possibility of an abscess and should lead to an aggressive diagnostic search, as this is a common cause of persistent ARDS and a fatal outcome. The lungs and the peritoneal cavity are the most common sites of undiagnosed infection.

Appropriate fluid management is important to ensure adequate cardiac output and thus O_2 delivery. Fluid loading to maintain adequate cardiac filling pressures in the face of the high intrathoracic pressures generated during mechanical ventilation must be balanced against the resultant increase in microvascular pressure and its tendency to increase the extravascular lung water accumulation. The controversy over the use of colloid versus crystalloid therapy is moot in the presence of such marked alterations in microvascular permeability. Until more is known concerning the dynamics of fluid movement in this disease, a good rule of thumb is to maintain filling pressures in a range that maintains cardiac output while attempting to minimize pulmonary hydrostatic pressures.

PROGNOSIS

Extracorporeal membrane oxygenation (ECMO) has been successfully used to correct hypoxemia in infants with respiratory distress syndrome of the newborn. Previous attempts to treat patients with ARDS using ECMO were unsuccessful, although modern technology may make some form of extracorporeal gas exchange feasible in the future.

Of those patients who survive the acute event, the prognosis depends primarily on the presence of other underlying disease. For most patients who began with normal lungs, pulmonary function returns slowly toward normal. A small number of patients are left with residual fibrosis, rarely of a severe nature.

REFERENCES

Dantzker R: Cardiopulmonary Critical Care. 2nd ed. Philadelphia, WB Saunders Co, 1991.
Tobin MJ: Respiratory monitoring during mechanical ventilation. Crit Care Clin 6:679–709, 1990.
Wiedemann HP, Matthay MA, Matthay RA: Acute lung injury. Crit Care Clin Vol 2, No 3, 1986.

20 NEOPLASTIC DISEASES OF THE LUNG

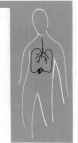

Lung cancer causes more than 120,000 deaths per year in the United States and is the leading cause of cancer deaths in men and women. Carcinoma of the lung is most common in the fifth and sixth decades and is rarely seen before the age of 35.

Cigarette smoking is the most important causative factor, with lung cancer being 10 to 30 times more common among smokers; approximately 4 per cent of those who have smoked for 40 years develop lung cancer. Most studies demonstrate a small but significant risk of lung cancer from environmental smoke exposure. For example, recent investigation of environmental smoke exposure in childhood has demonstrated a doubling of lung cancer risk in later years when exposure is 25 or more smoker-years (number of household smokers times years of exposure). All cell types except bronchoalveolar carcinoma are associated with smoking. Of the other causative agents, asbestos is the most important, especially when combined with cigarette smoking, and up to 14 per cent of smokers with asbestosis develop lung cancer. Other industrial risks include uranium, arsenic, chromium, chloromethyl, methylethers, polycyclic aromatic hydrocarbons, nickel, and possibly beryllium. Lung cancer may rarely develop in pre-existing scars due to old granulomatous disease, diffuse interstitial fibrosis, or scleroderma.

LUNG TUMOR BIOLOGY

The biology of lung carcinoma has received much attention recently, particularly regarding the role of oncogenes and other genetic mechanisms of tumor development. Amplification or mutation of oncogenes may play a role in unregulated cell growth. However, the frequency of oncogene amplification in lung cancer is highly variable, with adenocarcinomas and small cell carcinomas more frequently demonstrating this phenomenon. Although the role of oncogenes in the development or progression of lung cancer is unknown, their expression has been associated with decreased survival. Other genetic factors associated with lung carcinoma may include the variable expression of certain cytochrome P-450 enzymes. This enzymatic activity is inducible by cigarette smoke and may produce carcinogenic metabolites of polycyclic aromatic hydrocarbons present in cigarette smoke. One factor possibly contributing to lung cancer risk may be the genetically regulated activity of these or related enzymes.

PATHOLOGY

Benign tumors, composing 5 per cent of the total, are usually diagnosed on routine chest radiographs, and symptoms, if present, are usually related to bronchial obstruction. The most common central tumor is the bronchial adenoma, which usually appears benign but is potentially malignant and rarely produces features of the carcinoid syndrome. The most common peripheral tumor is the pulmonary hamartoma, which has a characteristic "popcorn" pattern of calcification.

Primary malignant neoplasms in the lung have classically been divided into four cell types, as summarized in Table 20–1. Clinically, though, one speaks of small cell and "non–small cell" lung cancer, as their behavior is so different. Small cell lung cancer has the greatest tendency to metastasize early and is almost always dissemi-

nated on presentation. The non–small cell types spread to a greater or lesser extent in the chest prior to metastasis. In addition, the non–small cell tumors may contain elements of all these cell types, making the distinction between them of little clinical use.

Metastatic spread of neoplasms to the lung is common, involving the parenchyma, endobronchial mucosa, chest wall, pleural space, or mediastinum. Direct extension is the least common mode of spread, occurring with breast, liver, and pancreatic tumors. Hematogenous spread is common with renal, thyroid, and testicular tumors and bone sarcomas and presents with asymptomatic discrete nodules on chest radiography. Lymphangitic spread presents as an infiltrate or diffuse reticulonodular pattern on chest radiography and causes severe dyspnea, usually out of proportion to the radiographic findings. This pattern is typical of spread from adenocarcinoma of the breast, stomach, pancreas, ovary, prostate, and lung.

CLINICAL PRESENTATION

Clinical presentation may be related to tumor location within the chest, metastatic spread, or extrapulmonary paraneoplastic manifestations. Most patients present with weight loss and symptoms related to local involvement, such as cough (75 per cent) that has changed in character, hemoptysis (50 per cent) that is rarely life-threatening, dyspnea (60 per cent), chest pain (40 per cent), and a marked increase in sputum production with bronchoalveolar carcinoma. Pancoast's syndrome refers to apical tumors that involve the brachial plexus and often lead to Horner's syndrome resulting from invasion of the inferior cervical ganglion. Compression and obstruction of the superior vena cava, usually by small cell tumor, cause facial and upper extremity edema, dyspnea, stridor, and symptoms related to increased intracranial pressure. Partial obstruction of a bronchus may lead to unilateral, persistent wheezing, whereas complete obstruction causes postobstructive pneumonia. Recurrent laryngeal nerve involvement, typical of a left hilar mass, causes hoarseness. Phrenic nerve entrapment by a mediastinal mass causes diaphragmatic paralysis. Finally, direct spread of the tumor to the pleural or pericardial space will result in effusions. Bronchogenic carci-

TABLE 20–1. FEATURES OF MALIGNANT NEOPLASMS

CELL TYPE	PATHOLOGICAL FEATURES	COMMON CHEST X-RAY FINDING
Squamous cell carcinoma	Keratin production, intercellular bridges	Central lesion with hilar involvement, cavitation frequent
Adenocarcinoma	Gland formation, mucin production	Peripheral lesion, cavitation may occur
Bronchoalveolar carcinoma	Distinction from adenocarcinoma imprecise	Usually peripheral lesion, pneumonic-like infiltrate, occasionally multifocal
Large cell carcinoma	Probably represents poorly differentiated adenocarcinoma	Usually peripheral lesion, larger than adenocarcinoma with tendency to cavitate
Small cell carcinoma	Involvement by cells twice the size of lymphocytes	Central lesion, hilar mass common, early mediastinal involvement, no cavitation

noma is frequently discovered only after it metastasizes to other organs. The brain, liver, bone, and lymph nodes are common sites, and the evaluation of tumor found in these locations, in a smoker, should include a search for a primary lung neoplasm. In 10 to 50 per cent of patients, bronchogenic carcinoma produces one or more paraneoplastic syndromes. These may manifest as neuromuscular, skeletal, endocrine, hematologic, cutaneous, or cardiovascular abnormalities (Table 20–2).

DIAGNOSIS AND EVALUATION

A careful history and physical examination are crucial in patient evaluation, and availability of a previous chest radiograph is of tremendous value, especially when a solitary pulmonary nodule is present. Routine laboratory studies are rarely helpful in the diagnosis of bronchogenic carcinoma but can be invaluable in evaluating extrathoracic spread of the disease, especially liver function studies and serum calcium and alkaline phosphatase, which screen for bone metastases.

Therapeutic decisions are based on a correct tissue diagnosis. Cytologic examination of expectorated sputum is the easiest and least invasive approach. False-positive results are rare, but false-negative results are relatively common (40 to 50 per cent), especially with peripheral lesions. When cytologic examination of expectorated sputum is negative, bronchoscopy should be the next procedure in patients with central lesions, lung infiltrates, hoarseness, or hemoptysis. Positive yield ranges from 90 per cent for central, endobronchially visible tumors to 50 per cent for peripheral lesions. Small peripheral lung nodules may be approached by percutaneous needle aspiration performed under computed tomographic (CT) guidance, which primarily provides material for cytologic examination. Diagnostic accuracy is greater than 80 per cent for malignant disease but is disturbingly less accurate with benign lesions. Therefore, in a smoker who has a newly diagnosed lung nodule without benign radiographic characteristics and without evidence of metastatic disease and who is a good surgical candidate, proceeding directly to diagnostic and therapeutic thoracotomy is a reasonable approach (see Fig. 20–2).

Once the tumor is diagnosed, the only chance for cure is surgical. Most patients with lung cancer have underlying lung disease as a result of smoking. One must determine whether the tumor is resectable, that is, can be anatomically removed, and whether the patient is operable, meaning capable of withstanding the loss of lung parenchyma. Operability should be investigated first. Patients with hypercapnia generally are not surgical candidates. Hypoxemia, though, may improve if the tumor is causing physiologic obstruction or compression. In the absence of hypercapnia, simple spirometry is used to guide the physiologic assessment (see Fig. 20–1A).

Determination of anatomic resectability is the

TABLE 20–2. COMMON PARANEOPLASTIC SYNDROMES ASSOCIATED WITH BRONCHOGENIC CARCINOMA

SYNDROME	CELL TYPE USUALLY IMPLICATED	MECHANISM
Hypertrophic pulmonary osteoarthropathy	All types except small cell	Unknown
Gynecomastia	Large cell	Chronic gonadotropin production
Syndrome of inappropriate ADH (SIADH) secretion	Usually small cell (may be associated with any cell type)	Inappropriate ADH release
Hypercalcemia	Usually squamous cell	Direct involvement of bone, prostaglandins, osteoclast-activating factor, PTH-like action
Cushing's syndrome	Usually small cell	Ectopic ACTH production
Eaton-Lambert myasthenic syndrome	Usually small cell	Unknown
Other neuromyopathic disorders (see appropriate chapter)	Frequently small cell but reported with most types	Unknown
Thrombophlebitis	All types	Unknown

ADH = Antidiuretic hormone; PTH = parathyroid hormone; ACTH = adrenocorticotropic hormone.

next step (see Fig. 20–1B). Endobronchial lesions within 2 cm of the carina on bronchoscopy are inoperable. Intrathoracic spread to the lungs and to the hilar or mediastinal lymph nodes can often be determined from the plain radiograph, but chest CT is an integral part of presurgical evaluation in patients with potentially resectable tumors. The sensitivity and specificity for detecting mediastinal lymph node metastases on CT depend on lymph node size criteria. Generally, lymph node diameter greater than 1.5 cm detects metastatic spread with sensitivity and specificity approaching 80 per cent. However, when mediastinal adenopathy is demonstrated by CT, nonresectability should be proved by biopsy.

Once intrathoracic spread is excluded, negative findings on the history and physical examination, combined with a normal routine laboratory evaluation, are usually adequate to exclude metastatic spread. Multiple imaging techniques in the absence of symptoms or signs suggesting specific organ involvement are cost-inefficient and are frequently misleading.

SOLITARY PULMONARY NODULE

A solitary pulmonary nodule is defined as a rounded lesion with well-demarcated margins. Be-

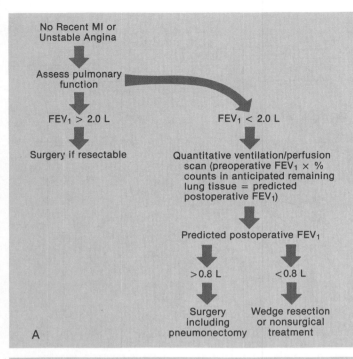

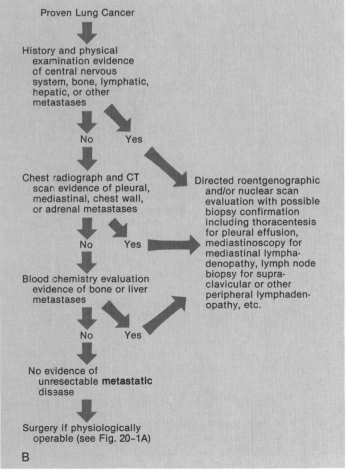

tween 5 and 40 per cent are malignant. Benign lesions are usually smaller (less than 2 cm), have sharp borders and no satellite lesions, and are present in younger people (less than 40 years old). Three characteristics help to distinguish benign from malignant nodules. Nodules with doubling times of less than 10 to 20 or more than 450 days are most likely benign. The presence of calcification with a central, speckled, diffuse, laminar, or "popcorn" pattern, but not eccentric calcification, is also evidence of its benign nature. When calcification is not evident on plain chest radiographs, it may possibly be demonstrated by CT, particularly thin-section CT. On rare occasions, the clinical picture is clearly benign, such as a patient with a previously normal chest radiograph who develops well-documented histoplasmosis that resolves, leaving a single histoplasmoma. A suggested decision tree for the approach to the solitary nodule is shown in Figure 20–2.

TREATMENT AND PROGNOSIS

Surgery is the therapy of choice for patients with non–small cell carcinoma who meet both physiologic and anatomic criteria and have no evidence of extrathoracic spread. Recently, complete surgical resection of localized ipsilateral mediastinal and hilar lymph node metastases has been possible, with encouraging 5-year survival results at some centers. In addition, limited extrapulmonary invasion, particularly peripheral tumors invading the chest wall or minimal involvement of the mediastinal pleura and pericardium, no longer precludes an aggressive surgical approach. Contralateral lymph node involvement, extracapsular lymph node spread, and massive ipsilateral disease remain contraindications for surgery. There has been renewed interest in the surgical treatment of limited small cell carcinoma, but proof of efficacy has not yet been established. There is no evidence that postoperative radiation therapy or chemotherapy improves survival.

For those patients with small cell carcinoma or nonoperable non–small cell tumors, radiation therapy and chemotherapy are the only other modalities. Chemotherapy in various combinations has improved the median survival of patients with small cell carcinoma limited to the thorax from 3 months in untreated patients to 16 to 17 months in those receiving chemotherapy. For non–small cell carcinoma, chemotherapy has not significantly altered the outcome, and because of the significant toxicity involved, it should not be used except in controlled experimental settings.

FIGURE 20–1. Decision regarding operability (*A*) and resectability (*B*) in the presence of proven lung cancer. MI = Myocardial infarction; FEV_1 = forced expiratory volume in 1 second; CT = computed tomography.

Radiation therapy is often used in small cell carcinoma, both to treat the primary lung lesion and as prophylaxis against cerebral metastases. However, there is no evidence that this measure prolongs survival. Radiation therapy is not beneficial in non–small cell carcinoma and is limited to the palliative management of pain, recurrent hemoptysis, effusions, or obstruction of airways or the superior vena cava.

The 5-year survival rate for all patients with bronchogenic carcinoma is 8 to 12 per cent and has improved only slightly over the past few years despite the introduction of multiple new chemotherapeutic agents. Large trials of routine screening of high-risk people with sputum cytology and chest roentgenographs have not improved survival.

REFERENCES

Bunn PA: Lung cancer. Semin Oncol 15:197, 1988.
Filderman AE, Shaw C, Matthay RA: Lung cancer. Invest Radiol 21:80–90, 173–185, 1986.
Iannuzzi MC, Scoggin CH: Small cell lung cancer. Am Rev Respir Dis 134:593–608, 1986.

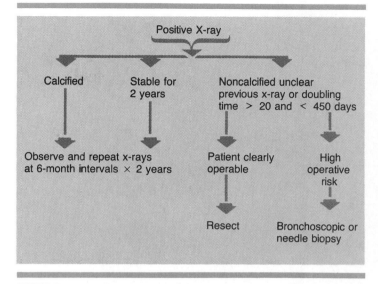

FIGURE 20–2. Decision tree for management of a solitary pulmonary nodule.

21 CONTROL OF BREATHING IN DISEASE STATES

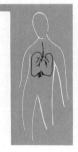

Ventilatory demands reach a nadir during sleep and increase tremendously during vigorous exercise. The respiratory control system preserves homeostasis by maintaining a tight relation between varying demands and output of the ventilatory system. In pulmonary or chest wall disease, this relationship is altered, requiring adjustment of the ventilatory drive to maintain eucapnia and normoxia. Inadequate respiratory drive can result in hypercapnia, while excessive drive may contribute to dyspnea.

A primary abnormality of ventilatory control causing alveolar hypoventilation is rare. When it occurs, it is usually due to brain stem involvement by tumor, ischemia, or inflammatory disease; a primary, idiopathic form has also been described. Patients display decreased chemosensitivity, often with resting hypercapnia and cor pulmonale. Rarely, the impairment of chemosensitivity may be so severe that the patient breathes adequately only when stimulated by wakefulness but hypoventilates or becomes apneic during sleep, when rostral neural influences are removed. More frequently, ventilatory control system abnormalities interact with other disease states, modifying the overall level of ventilation and possibly contributing to the development of dyspnea and hypercapnia. For example, patients with physiologically significant chronic obstructive pulmonary disease (COPD) have a reduced ventilatory response to hypoxia and hypercapnia. This was formerly thought to be due entirely to decreased chemosensitivity of the respiratory centers; however, most of these patients actually display an increased resting respiratory center drive. In hypercapnic patients, this heightened respiratory drive fails to translate into a sufficiently increased minute ventilation to maintain a normal P_{CO_2} owing to the increased work of breathing and marked ventilation-perfusion mismatch. Although some relation exists between the degree of hypercapnia and the severity of airways obstruction, abnormalities of lung mechanics do not fully account for the magnitude of the change (Fig. 21–1). Development

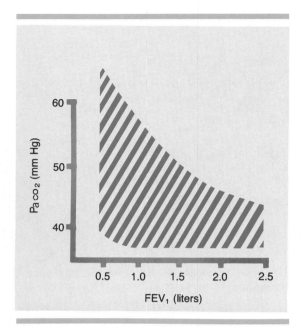

FIGURE 21–1. The increase in Pa_{CO_2} as airway obstruction becomes more severe, as reflected by decreasing FEV_1. Note the large scatter of PCO_2 values for any level of obstruction.

of chronic hypercapnia may, in fact, depend on complex interactions between inherent characteristics of the ventilatory control system, perception of and ability to compensate for increased ventilatory loads (such as elevated airways resistance), and pattern of breathing.

BREATHING PATTERN ABNORMALITIES ASSOCIATED WITH NEUROLOGIC DISEASE

Central neurogenic hyperventilation has been considered a characteristic feature of lower brain stem and upper pontine disease. Rarely, it is an isolated finding, as most patients display associated pulmonary complications that could reflexly stimulate the respiratory center through hypoxia or activation of intrapulmonary sensory receptors. Apneustic breathing consists of sustained inspiratory pauses localizing damage to the midpons, most commonly due to a basilar artery infarct. Biot's or ataxic breathing, a haphazard random distribution of deep and shallow breaths, is caused by disruption of the respiratory rhythm generator in the medulla.

Cheyne-Stokes respiration is characterized by regular cycles of crescendo-decrescendo changes in tidal volume separated by apneic or hypopneic pauses. Many affected patients have evidence of cardiac or neurologic disease. In patients with congestive heart failure, the disturbance arises because of prolongation of the circulation time, which delays transmission of information concerning arterial PO_2 and PCO_2 to the respiratory centers, thus leading to system instability with resulting oscillations in tidal volume. It has no localizing value in patients with neurologic disease but has generally been considered to indicate an ominous prognosis. Although this is sometimes the case, many patients, as well as normal elderly subjects, display subtle evidence of Cheyne-Stokes respiration, particularly during sleep. Fragmentation of sleep, due to recurrent arousals during the hyperpneic phase of the cycle, can occur and may lead to daytime somnolence.

NEUROMUSCULAR DISEASE

Respiratory center function is poorly defined in neuromuscular disease. Decreased ventilatory capacity may result from impaired neural output or poor translation of this neural output into respiratory muscle contraction. Typically, the patients display an increased respiratory rate and inability to take deep breaths, with consequent tendency to atelectasis. Characteristic changes in lung volume result from an inability to adequately inspire above or expire below functional residual capacity (see Table 16–2). Paradoxical motion of the rib cage and abdomen is commonly observed. Hypoventilation may be particularly severe during sleep, especially during rapid eye movement (REM) sleep, when skeletal muscle atonia may further compromise the ventilatory pump. Sleep disruption with resultant daytime somnolence is common and may be a result of nocturnal respiratory abnormalities. Typical causes include inflammatory polyneuropathy, amyotrophic lateral sclerosis, myasthenia gravis, poliomyelitis, and severe kyphoscoliosis. These patients may require long-term mechanical ventilatory support, particularly during sleep.

THE SLEEP APNEA SYNDROME

Sleep apnea is increasingly recognized as a significant cause of morbidity and mortality. More than 1 per cent of the general population is affected, with a dramatic increase in incidence in the elderly. Many patients are obese middle-aged men, although this is not invariable. Typically, conditions that narrow the upper airway, impinging on the oropharyngeal space, such as enlargement of the soft palate, uvula, tonsils, and adenoids, local fat deposition, retrognathia, macroglossia associated with acromegaly and myxedema, and other anatomic abnormalities, predispose to obstructive sleep apnea. Impairment of respiratory drive may interact with these factors, perpetuating the syndrome.

Characteristically, a long history of loud snoring is reported, often combined with restless sleep and early morning headaches. Apneas may occur hundreds of times each night and are usually due to upper airway obstruction with continued respiratory efforts that result in paradoxical motion of the rib cage and abdomen (Fig. 21–2B). Less commonly, central apneas occur, with complete cessation of respiratory effort (Fig. 21–2A). When central apneas occur, they are often terminated by obstructive events as respiratory efforts resume against an occluded airway, resulting in mixed apneas. Repetitive arousals, occurring at the termination of each apnea, produce sleep deprivation and excessive daytime somnolence, which may be mild, causing subtle deterioration in cognitive function, or severe and extremely debilitating.

Transient episodes of hypoxemia result from apneic events. Cardiac arrhythmias may occur during or immediately following an apnea and may rarely lead to sudden death. Recent studies have demonstrated an increased incidence of hypertension and cardiovascular disease in obstructive sleep apnea, further increasing the clinical significance of this syndrome. A small subset of obese patients, denoted as having the pickwickian syndrome, have persistent hypoxia and hypercapnia due to daytime alveolar hypoventilation, which persists even after treatment of the obstructive sleep apnea. This condition may eventually lead to polycythemia and cor pulmonale and may be related to a primary defect of ventilatory control. Polysomnography, including the monitoring of the electroencephalograph (EEG), electro-oculogram, motion of the rib cage and abdomen, and arterial oxygen saturation, is required to make a definitive diagnosis.

The most common mode of therapy is the application of continuous positive airway pressure (CPAP) via a nose mask. This acts as a pneumatic splint and prevents upper airway obstruction. Surgical approaches are designed to increase the caliber of the upper airway and include nasal septoplasty, uvulopalatopharyngoplasty, mandibular advancement, and, in the most severe cases, complete bypass of the upper airway with tracheostomy. Proper selection of patients for surgery requires evaluation of upper airway anatomy as well as assessment of the patient's ability to tolerate surgery. Respiratory stimulants such as medroxyprogesterone are rarely useful. Although weight loss can be helpful in most cases, more rapid and definite treatment is usually required.

REFERENCES

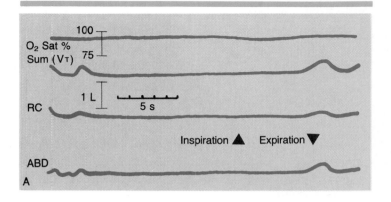

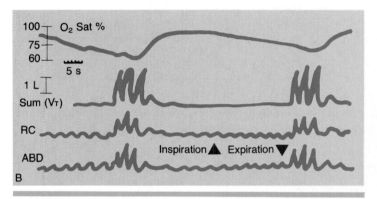

FIGURE 21–2. *A,* Central sleep apnea. There is absence of abdominal (ABD) and rib cage (RC) movement, and their sum (VT), during central apnea associated with a small fall in arterial oxygen saturation (O_2 Sat %) measured by ear oximetry. *B,* Obstructive sleep apnea. This depicts obstructive apnea terminated by deep breaths. Apnea in the midportion of the recording is marked by absence of sum movements (VT) despite respiratory efforts indicated by paradoxical movement of rib cage (RC) (movement downward) and abdominal (ABD) (movement upward) compartments; this apnea is associated with a marked fall in arterial oxygen saturation (O_2 Sat%) measured by ear oximetry. (Modified with permission from Tobin MJ, Cohn MA, Sackner MA: Breathing abnormalities during sleep. Arch Intern Med 143:1221–1228, 1983. Copyright 1983, American Medical Association.)

Kryger MH, Roth T, Dement WC: Principles and Practice of Sleep Medicine. Philadelphia, WB Saunders Co, 1989.

Saunders NA, Sullivan CE: Sleep and Breathing. New York, Marcel Dekker, 1984.

Tobin MJ, Cohn MA, Sackner MA: Breathing abnormalities during sleep. Arch Intern Med 143:1221–1228, 1983.

22 DISORDERS OF THE PLEURAL SPACE, MEDIASTINUM, AND CHEST WALL

PLEURAL DISEASE

The pleural spaces are defined by the visceral pleura of the lungs and the parietal pleura of the rib cage, diaphragm, and mediastinum. The spaces themselves are potential rather than real, since the visceral and parietal pleurae are normally separated by only a thin film of fluid.

The lung's elastic recoil pulls the visceral pleura inward, and the chest wall's recoil pulls the parietal pleura outward. The net pressure in the pleural space at functional residual capacity is below atmospheric pressure. In the pleural space, fluid flows from the parietal surface into the pleural space, with subsequent reabsorption by the capillaries of the visceral pleura (Fig. 22–1). This system is remarkably well balanced and ordinarily prevents the collection of significant amounts of fluid despite the formation and absorption of 5 to 10 L of pleural fluid each day. In addition, fluid and leakage of protein are drained by lymphatics, which can increase their absorptive capacity several-fold.

Fluid accumulates with abnormalities in the hydrostatic and osmotic pressures, increased permeability of the capillaries, or lymphatic dysfunction. Pleural inflammation, either infectious or noninfectious, increases permeability and results in the collection of a high-protein pleural fluid. Alterations in the pulmonary venous pressures, as in heart failure, increase fluid transudation from the parietal capillaries and decrease reabsorption on the visceral side. Decreasing the osmotic pressure (hypoalbuminemia) may also result in more rapid fluid transudation. Finally, lymphatic dysfunction due to anatomic or functional obstruction also facilitates the accumulation of pleural fluid.

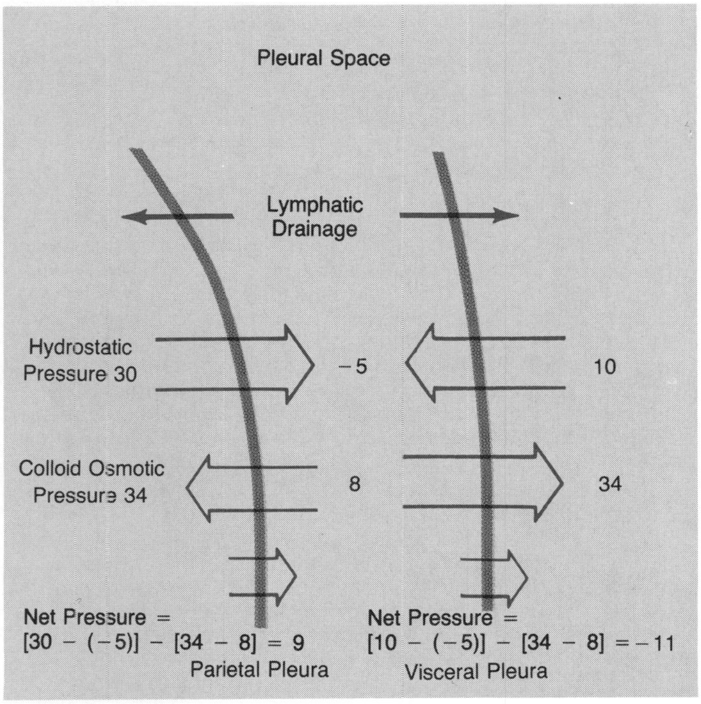

Pleural Effusions

The causes of pleural effusions are best considered in terms of the underlying pathophysiology: transudates due to abnormalities of hydrostatic or osmotic pressure and exudates resulting from increased permeability or trauma (Table 22–1).

Patients usually present with dyspnea or nonspecific discomfort, occasionally accompanied by pleuritic chest pain—a sharp, stabbing pain exacerbated by coughing or breathing. Such pain must be carefully differentiated from pericardial or musculoskeletal pain. Rarely, the effusion is asymptomatic and discovered only on chest radiograph.

Physical examination reveals decreased vocal fremitus, dullness on percussion, and decreased breath sounds over the effusion, with bronchial breathing and egophony at its upper limit. More than 250 ml of fluid can be seen on the upright chest radiograph as blunting of the costophrenic angle. Increasing amounts cause dense opacification of the lung fields with a concave meniscus. In certain situations, the initial radiograph is misleading and further studies are required: (1) a sub-

Pleural Space

Lymphatic Drainage

Hydrostatic Pressure 30   −5   10

Colloid Osmotic Pressure 34   8   34

Net Pressure = [30 − (−5)] − [34 − 8] = 9
Parietal Pleura

Net Pressure = [10 − (−5)] − [34 − 8] = −11
Visceral Pleura

FIGURE 22–1. Factors affecting fluid and solute movement in the pleural space. The blood supply of the parietal pleura is from the intercostal arteries (branches of the systemic circulation), whereas the visceral pleura is predominantly supplied by the pulmonary circulation, a low-pressure system. If the osmotic pressures in the parietal and visceral vessels, which are roughly equal, as well as the changes in intrapleural pressure, are taken into account, fluid flows from the parietal surface into the pleural space and is subsequently reabsorbed by the visceral pleura (indicated pressures are in cm H_2O).

pulmonic effusion presenting as an elevated hemidiaphragm can be confirmed on lateral decubitus radiograph; (2) a hazy diffuse density on the supine film in a seriously ill patient disappears on an upright radiograph; and (3) a loculated effusion, especially with coexisting parenchymal disease, may require ultrasound or computed tomographic (CT) scan for diagnosis.

Thoracentesis is essential in the differential diagnosis. The gross appearance of the fluid is rarely helpful except when frank blood or the milky fluid of a chylous effusion is encountered. The criteria for separation of the fluid into transudate and exudate (Table 22–2) are not rigid, and an effusion due to congestive heart failure may occasionally be exudative, whereas a transudate may occur with malignancy. Pleural fluid glucose concentrations less than 10 to 20 mg/dl are usually diagnostic of rheumatoid arthritis but may be seen in cancer and infection. Pleural fluid amylase is about twice the normal value in effusions due to pancreatitis and esophageal perforation, whereas smaller elevations may be seen with malignancy. The presence of a high rheumatoid factor or lupus erythematosus (LE) cells in the fluid is strong evidence that the effusion is due to rheumatoid arthritis and systemic lupus erythematosus, respectively. Measurement of pleural fluid pH in the diagnosis and management of empyema usually does not add to other, more routine measurements.

Surprisingly few red blood cells are required to impart a red color to the fluid, but a hemothorax should be diagnosed only when the pleural fluid hematocrit is greater than 20 per cent. Bloody fluid should arouse suspicion of malignancy, trauma, or pulmonary embolus, but it may also occur with other disease entities. The number of polymorphonuclear neutrophils is of little or no specific diagnostic value. A high eosinophil count is usually due to air or blood in the pleural space. There is a high probability that an exudate is due to tuberculosis or malignancy if small lymphocytes constitute more than 50 per cent of the white cells. Cytologic examinations for malignant cells are positive in about 60 per cent of patients on first thoracentesis, rising to about 80 per cent if three separate samples are obtained. Gram's stain and routine culture should always be obtained and special stains and cultures added when tuberculosis or fungal disease is suspected.

Transcutaneous needle biopsy of the pleura at the bedside with subsequent histology and culture is positive in more than 90 per cent of tuberculous effusions, whereas fluid culture is positive in only 25 per cent. Although less frequently positive (40 per cent) than cytologic examination, biopsy occasionally makes a diagnosis of malignant effusions when cytology is negative.

Treatment depends on the underlying cause and the degree of physiologic impairment. Specific therapy to control the underlying cause is the only successful approach. Although removal of fluid results in symptomatic improvement, lung volumes

TABLE 22–1. PLEURAL EFFUSIONS

Transudates
  Congestive heart failure
  Hypoalbuminemia—nephrotic syndrome, starvation, cirrhosis
  Abdominal fluid collection—ascites, peritoneal dialysis
Exudates
  Infection
    Empyema
    Bacterial—gram-positive and -negative, *Actinomyces*, *Mycobacterium tuberculosis*
    Viral—Coxsackie virus, *Mycoplasma*
    Fungal—*Nocardia*, *Coccidioides* (rarely)
    Parasitic—*Amoeba*, *Echinococcus*
    Parapneumonic
  Malignancy—bronchogenic cancer, mesothelioma, lymphoma; metastatic cancer—breast, ovary, kidney, pancreas, gastrointestinal tract
  Pulmonary embolism and infarction
  Collagen vascular disease—systemic lupus erythematosus, rheumatoid arthritis
  Intra-abdominal processes—pancreatitis, subphrenic abscess, Meigs' syndrome, post abdominal surgery
  Trauma—hemothorax, chylothorax, ruptured esophagus
  Miscellaneous—myxedema, uremia, asbestosis, lymphedema (yellow nail syndrome), drug sensitivity, Dressler's syndrome

and gas exchange improve very little. Parapneumonic effusions resolve with antibiotic therapy (90 per cent), but empyemas, that is, fluid with positive smear or culture, should be drained by repeated aspirations or tube thoracostomy; otherwise the fluid may spontaneously drain through the chest wall (*empyema necessitans*) or may lead to subpleural lung necrosis with resultant bronchopleural fistula and endobronchial spread of infection. Palliative therapy should be considered for a malignant effusion only if the patient is symptomatic and displays benefit from thoracentesis. Repeated thoracentesis should be avoided, as significant protein loss results and the fluid reaccumulates within 1 to 3 days. Chemical pleurodesis obliterates the pleural space and is helpful in about 80 per cent of malignant effusions.

Pneumothorax

The most common causes of air in the pleural space are listed in Table 22–3. Idiopathic spontaneous pneumothorax typically causes dyspnea,

TABLE 22–2. DIFFERENTIATION OF EXUDATIVE AND TRANSUDATIVE PLEURAL EFFUSION

	EXUDATE	TRANSUDATE
Protein	>3 g/dl	<3 g/dl
Pleural/serum protein	>0.5	<0.5
LDH	>200 IU/L	<200 IU/L
Pleural/serum LDH	>0.6	<0.6

LDH = Lactate dehydrogenase.

TABLE 22-3. CAUSES OF PNEUMOTHORAX

Spontaneous
  Idiopathic
  Emphysema
  Interstitial lung disease
  Eosinophilic granuloma/histiocytosis X
  Cystic fibrosis
  Asthma
  Malignancy
Traumatic
  Penetrating and nonpenetrating chest trauma
  Transbronchoscopic or transthoracic lung biopsy
  Thoracentesis
  Mechanical ventilation
  Esophageal perforation

chest pain, and few abnormalities on physical examination. On chest radiographs, the one-dimensional view grossly underestimates its true volume. Without surgery, 50 per cent of patients develop a recurrence, usually within 2 years. In contrast to the low mortality with idiopathic pneumothorax, that due to underlying lung disease has a 15 per cent mortality rate. Under certain circumstances, particularly in patients on mechanical ventilators, the rent in the pleura forms a one-way valve that permits air to enter but not to escape, causing positive pressure to build up in the chest (tension pneumothorax).

Treatment depends on the amount of air and the underlying status of the patient. Spontaneous pneumothorax in a healthy, asymptomatic patient may require no treatment, whereas treatment is needed for the same size pneumothorax in a patient with cardiopulmonary insufficiency. Treatment is almost always required for pneumothoraces greater than 50 per cent in size or for a pneumothorax of any size in patients on mechanical ventilation or in those with diffuse lung disease. Drainage by tube thoracostomy is successful in most instances. Open thoracotomy with partial pleurectomy and oversewing of apical blebs or abrasion of the pleural surface is required with recurrent episodes.

TABLE 22-4. SYMPTOMS AND SIGNS OF MEDIASTINAL DISEASE

Asymptomatic
Compression or invasion of nearby structures
  Superior vena cava syndrome
  Cough
  Postobstructive pneumonia
  Hoarseness
  Horner's syndrome
Systemic symptoms
  Fever
  Weight loss
  Paraneoplastic syndromes (hypercalcemia, Cushing's syndrome, etc.)

Tumors of the Pleural Space

Mesotheliomas may be localized benign growths curable by surgical resection or aggressive, untreatable malignancies spreading extensively in the pleural space and beyond. Malignant mesotheliomas are almost always associated with asbestos exposure. More commonly, neoplasms of the pleural space are due to adjacent spread (bronchogenic carcinoma) or metastatic disease (carcinoma of the breast, ovary, and kidney and lymphoma). They produce bloody pleural effusions, although chylous effusions resulting from lymphatic obstruction are also seen.

MEDIASTINAL DISEASE

The mediastinum (literally, "middle septum") can be conveniently divided into three compartments based on the lateral chest radiograph. The anterior compartment, which lies between the sternum and the heart shadow, contains the thymus gland, the aortic arch and its branches, lymphatic tissue, and errant thyroid or parathyroid glands. The posterior compartment, lying anterior to the vertebral bodies, contains the esophagus, the descending aorta, the azygous system, the sympathetic chain, the thoracic duct, and lymph nodes. Between lies the middle mediastinum, containing the pericardial sac, the lung hila, and associated lymph nodes. Knowledge of these normal structures is critical in the assessment of mediastinal masses.

Symptoms of mediastinal disease are varied (Table 22-4), although most patients are asymptomatic with a mediastinal mass found on routine radiography. CT is invaluable because it distinguishes vascular from nonvascular lesions and cystic from solid structures and identifies local invasion. Definitive diagnosis often depends on obtaining tissue. Fine-needle cytologic samples are inadequate when lymphoma is in question, as histology is required. Markers for germ cell tumors should also be looked for in both serum and tissue.

Mediastinitis

Acute mediastinitis, formerly a rare but dramatic syndrome, is more often today a "disease of medical progress." It is, to a large extent, a complication of endoscopic procedures of the esophagus and airways. Fever, prostration, and substernal chest pain with tachypnea and tachycardia are noted. Hamman's sign, signifying pneumomediastinum, may be auscultated as a "crunch" in time with cardiac systole. Other signs of mediastinal compression may be seen (Table 22-4). Treatment consists of antibiotics, drainage, and closure of perforated structures. A less dramatic but increasingly important form of mediastinitis is seen after cardiac surgery, either early in the postoperative course or as long as 6 months later. Classic findings are unusual in this form of the disease. As the mediastinum is continuous with the fascial planes of the neck, oropharyngeal infections may rarely spread there. It is a devastating complication that carries a high morbidity and mortality.

Chronic mediastinitis is usually a granulomatous process, most often histoplasmosis and less frequently other fungal infections, tuberculosis, and syphilis. Noninfectious causes include sarcoidosis and, in the past, the use of methysergide. An idiopathic cause should be considered only when specific disorders are ruled out. Treatment other than that specifically directed at the underlying disorder, such as surgery, is usually unsuccessful.

Mediastinal Masses

Mediastinal masses are mostly tumors but also include glandular lesions, vascular abnormalities, and esophageal disease. They are conveniently divided by anatomic location (Fig. 22–2).

CHEST WALL DISEASE

Adequate ventilation depends on efficient movement of the chest wall in response to neural stimulation. Interference with this may result in increased work of breathing, restricted lung volumes, exercise limitation, and gradual progression to respiratory failure. Total lung capacity and vital capacity are decreased, but the residual volume in chest wall disease, unlike that in parenchymal restrictive lung disease, is usually normal or even increased. Hypoventilation is the predominant mechanism of abnormal gas exchange, and thus hypercapnia is found at much higher levels of arterial PO_2 than in parenchymal lung disease.

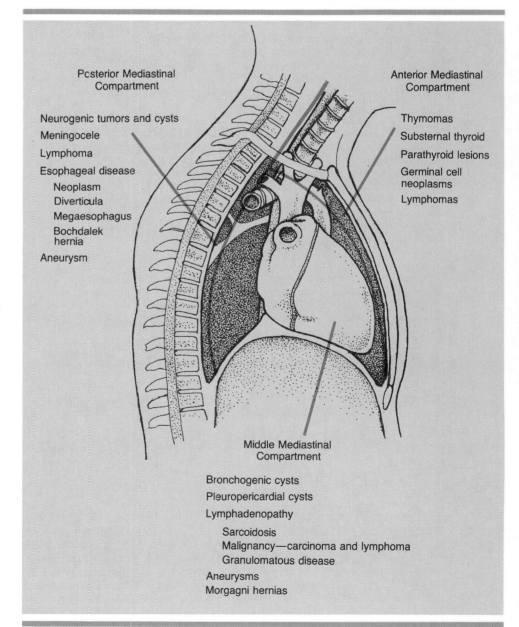

FIGURE 22–2. Masses of the mediastinum indicated by their anatomic location.

Posterior Mediastinal Compartment

Neurogenic tumors and cysts
Meningocele
Lymphoma
Esophageal disease
  Neoplasm
  Diverticula
  Megaesophagus
  Bochdalek hernia
Aneurysm

Anterior Mediastinal Compartment

Thymomas
Substernal thyroid
Parathyroid lesions
Germinal cell neoplasms
Lymphomas

Middle Mediastinal Compartment

Bronchogenic cysts
Pleuropericardial cysts
Lymphadenopathy
  Sarcoidosis
  Malignancy—carcinoma and lymphoma
  Granulomatous disease
Aneurysms
Morgagni hernias

In addition, progressive ventilation-perfusion inequality, resulting from basilar atelectasis, causes gradual widening of the alveolar-arterial gradient. Continued, prolonged hypoxemia eventually causes cor pulmonale.

Kyphoscoliosis. Kyphoscoliosis is usually idiopathic or may be associated with Marfan's syndrome or poliomyelitis. The severity of scoliosis is quantitated by measuring the angle between the upper and lower limbs of the spinal curve. Mild scoliosis (angle >35 degrees) is common (incidence, 1 in 1000); respiratory dysfunction becomes detectable only when the angle is greater than 70 degrees (incidence, 1 in 10,000), and early cardiopulmonary failure is expected when the angle is greater than 120 degrees. Surgical correction of the deformity in adults does not influence the incidence of respiratory complications.

Obesity. Patients have a small expiratory reserve volume (ERV) and thus breathe close to residual volume. This condition leads to decreased ventilation of the lung bases and hypoxemia. This decrease in ventilation is magnified in the supine position, which further reduces the ERV. These abnormalities may be further complicated by disorders of ventilatory control and upper airway obstruction (see Chapter 21).

Diaphragmatic Paralysis. Unilateral diaphragmatic paralysis is usually in and of itself asymptomatic. In fact, most patients have relatively preserved pulmonary function, with about 75 per cent of normal vital capacity. The abnormalities are greater when the patient is supine than when he or she is erect, and recumbent hypoxemia may be noted. Causes include tumor invasion, herpes zoster, and "cold cardioplegia" of cardiac surgery.

Fluoroscopy during a "sniff" maneuver is diagnostic in most cases, showing paradoxical motion of the affected side. Definitive diagnosis is made by nerve conduction studies.

In contrast, bilateral paralysis is rarely subtle; patients are profoundly dyspneic and often cannot sleep while recumbent. Paradoxical inward motion of the abdominal wall during inspiration is the classic physical finding, and the diagnosis can be confirmed by nerve conduction studies. In many cases, it is a manifestation of a generalized myopathy or neuropathy, or it may be idiopathic.

Respiratory Muscle Fatigue. Respiratory muscle dysfunction may arise as a result of excessive demands (increased work of breathing or ventilatory requirements) or decreased energy supplies (malnutrition, metabolic disturbance, decreased oxygen supply). Unfortunately, none of the techniques used to investigate fatigue in experimental settings is satisfactory for the clinical diagnosis of fatigue. In addition, although many disease states affect respiratory muscle function, the importance of respiratory muscle fatigue as a primary determinant of ventilatory failure has not been established.

Treatment

Treatment is directed at correcting reversible abnormalities and minimizing the development of parenchymal lung disease. Respiratory failure develops in some patients, and mechanical ventilation is required. Initially, this is particularly valuable during sleep at night; in many patients, it may be possible to deliver mechanical ventilation via a nose mask, circumventing the need for tracheostomy. Eventually, mechanical ventilation may be required on a continuous basis.

REFERENCES

Heitzman ER: The Mediastinum, Radiologic Correlations with Anatomy and Pathology. St Louis, CV Mosby Co, 1977.
Roussos C, Macklem PT: The Thorax (Parts A and B). New York, Marcel Dekker, 1985.
Sahn SA: The Pleura. Am Rev Respir Dis 138:184, 1988.

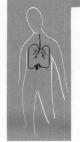

23 INHALATIONAL AND ENVIRONMENTAL INJURY

DROWNING AND NEAR-DROWNING

The human body is naturally buoyant; however, so much as raising a hand out of the water tips the balance to negative buoyancy. This, combined with the natural tendency for people to overestimate their swimming ability, makes drowning an unfortunately common occurrence; it is the most common cause of death in those under 25 years old. The term "drowning" generally refers to episodes resulting in immediate death, whereas the term "near-drowning" applies to all other victims, whether they survive or not.

Once immersed, the normal person can breath-hold for a short time, usually limited by the rising arterial Pco_2. Most drowning victims inhale some water, but in about 10 per cent of cases, laryngeal spasm results in the aspiration of virtually no fluid. This scenario, known as "dry" drowning, results in minimal lung injury, and recovery is rapid if respiration and circulation are restored before permanent neurologic damage occurs.

A great deal of emphasis had, in the past, been placed on the relative importance of freshwater and saltwater drowning in terms of their ensuing complications because of the differential effect on electrolytes and volume status. In fact, most of these are second-order effects and transient at best. The complications of near-drowning fall into two categories. The first is acute lung injury from aspirated fluids. This may be due to effects on surfactant by hypotonic freshwater or the osmolar action of hypertonic seawater. The second category comprises the effects of prolonged anoxia on end-organs such as the brain and kidney. These latter complications, which are far less reversible, often determine the ultimate prognosis.

Treatment of the near-drowning victim is simple: restore ventilation and circulation as soon as possible. No other interventions, such as draining the lungs of aspirated water, should be attempted, as they only waste time and increase mortality. In contrast to other arrest scenarios, prolonged efforts are often worthwhile, perhaps because of the protective effects of bradycardia and shunting of blood to the heart and brain ("diving reflex") as well as the hypothermia that often accompanies near-drowning. Patients have survived as long as 70 minutes of immersion with complete recovery.

Neurologic injury is the most serious and least reversible complication in those successfully resuscitated. It is usually secondary to anoxic damage, with edema resulting in elevated intracranial pressure and decreased cerebral perfusion. Little, if anything, has been shown to help, and it carries a grave prognosis.

A significant percentage of patients who initially appear well after resuscitation may develop adult respiratory distress syndrome (ARDS) as a late complication several hours after the event. Certainly any patient who was unconscious for any length of time should be hospitalized.

DISEASES OF ALTITUDE

Trekking and mountain climbing have become more popular, resulting in an increasing incidence of the complications of high altitude: acute mountain sickness, high-altitude cerebral edema, and high-altitude pulmonary edema.

Both the rate and height of ascent contribute to the degree of illness. Given enough time, climbers can adapt quite well even to heights that would be lethal to the unacclimated. Adaptation occurs at multiple levels, including hyperventilation, polycythemia, increased cardiac output, and changes in the hemoglobin (Hb)-oxygen (O_2) affinity. Failure to allow time for adaptation results in illness.

Acute mountain sickness (AMS) and cerebral edema probably represent a spectrum of the same condition. Clinical manifestations of AMS include headache, nausea, vomiting, and signs of fluid retention, such as facial and hand swelling. Symptoms are often worse after a night's sleep at altitude, and periodic breathing may be noted. Simple rest and mild analgesics can alleviate the symptoms of AMS as the patient acclimates, or the patient may need to descend. Dexamethasone may also be useful as symptomatic treatment. Acetazolamide may be helpful as a prophylactic agent or as therapy.

If the patient does not descend, or worse, if he or she continues to ascend, the full picture of high-altitude cerebral edema may supervene. This syndrome of severe headache, confusion, and ataxia may be fatal and should be treated aggressively with O_2, dexamethasone, and descent as soon as possible.

High-altitude pulmonary edema clinically resembles cardiogenic pulmonary edema, but subjects have a normal wedge pressure. There may be an increase in permeability accounting for the edema fluid. An uneven distribution of hypoxic pulmonary vasoconstriction complicates matters by imposing an elevated pulmonary artery pressure on the microvessels distal to unconstricted arteries.

SMOKE INHALATION INJURY

Three of the mechanisms of noxious gas injury combine in the smoke inhalation syndrome: direct mucosal injury secondary to hot gases, tissue anoxia due to combustion products, and asphyxia as O_2 is consumed by fire.

Thermal injury is most commonly seen in the upper airway, manifesting as upper airway edema and obstruction. This injury may extend to the tracheobronchial tree, particularly if steam heat is the cause, as moist air has a high thermal content and may overwhelm the cooling system in the pharynx. Direct lung injury is rare, but pulmonary edema secondary to inadvertent fluid overload or due to sepsis is not an uncommon late complication.

Incomplete combustion, particularly of industrial compounds, produces a number of both irritant and toxic compounds. Ammonia, acrolein, sulfur dioxide, and others are encountered in today's fires. Cyanide poisoning is increasingly recognized and, in fact, may be an important cause of mortality even in residential fires.

Carbon monoxide (CO) is an odorless, tasteless, and colorless gas that does not produce lung injury but has a dual effect on tissue oxygenation. Its marked affinity for Hb (210 times that of O_2) limits the O_2 carrying capacity of blood. In addition, it shifts the O_2 dissociation curve to the left, which impairs O_2 release to the tissues.

The clinical presentation depends on the predominant form of injury. Facial burns and singed nasal hairs should arouse suspicion of lung injury, although pulmonary involvement occurs in only a small proportion of such patients. Thermal injury may produce upper airway obstruction with stridor, hoarseness, and phonation difficulties, necessitating further evaluation (with possible bronchoscopy) and intubation to maintain a patent airway. Lower airway involvement may be associated with the production of carbonaceous sputum, wheezes, and crackles. The chest radiograph is insensitive in the early stages, although pulmonary infiltrates or edema may subsequently develop. Features associated with CO intoxication include headache, nausea, fatigue, behavioral change, ataxia, and hypoxic damage of the heart or brain. Cherry-red coloration of the lips is usually absent unless the carboxyhemoglobin (COHb) concentration is above 40 per cent. An intoxicated patient displays a normal Pa_{O_2} and *calculated* O_2 saturation, but there is a severe reduction in *measured* O_2 saturation. Despite the severe O_2 desaturation, minute ventilation is not increased in CO intoxication, since the carotid body responds to Pa_{O_2}. Confirmation is made by measurement of blood COHb: less than 2 per cent in healthy subjects, 5 to 10 per cent in cigarette smokers, and 30 to 50 per cent in fire injury victims.

Management includes removing the victim from exposure, checking vital signs, and establishing a patent airway. Administration of supplemental O_2 relieves hypoxemia and enhances the dissociation of CO from Hb, decreasing the half-time for elimination from 300 minutes on room air to 60 minutes, with an $F_{I_{O_2}}$ of 1.0. To achieve an adequate $F_{I_{O_2}}$, intubation and mechanical ventilation may be required. The use of hyperbaric O_2 has been suggested for patients with severe CO intoxication, although its advantage over breathing 100 per cent O_2 is unproved. Bronchospasm usually responds to bronchodilators. Corticosteroids are no longer recommended in the management of smoke inhalation injury. Antibiotics should be prescribed only if there is evidence of infection. In the rare cases in which ARDS supervenes, the management is identical to that described in Chapter 19. Patients surviving the acute clinical course usually recover completely. Long-term complications of tracheal stenosis, bronchiolitis obliterans, or bronchiectasis are rare.

NOXIOUS GASES AND FUMES

Exposure to toxic gases and fumes is an increasing problem in modern industrial society and may cause harm by different mechanisms (Table 23–1). Simple asphyxia occurs by replacement of the O_2 in the air with another nontoxic agent. This requires very high concentrations and usually occurs in an enclosed setting, such as methane exposure in a coal mine. Tissue asphyxia, by contrast, is due to an inability of the body to use available O_2 either secondary to an increase in Hb-O_2 affinity, such as with CO, or by interfering with the cytochrome chain, as in cyanide toxicity.

The most common mechanism of injury is local irritation, the form and extent of which depend on the concentration, solubility, and duration of exposure to the toxic gas. Highly soluble gases, such as *ammonia*, rapidly injure the mucous membranes of the eye and upper airway, causing an intense burning pain in the eyes, nose, and throat, with lacrimation, rhinorrhea, and a sense of suffocation. This, combined with the strong, pungent odor of ammonia, causes the victim to flee from the site of exposure. Lower airway injury is not observed unless the victim is trapped or a massive spill occurs, in which case laryngeal or pulmonary edema may ensue.

In contrast, insoluble gases, such as nitrogen dioxide, are distributed to the peripheral airways and usually cause a diffuse lung injury. Exposure to *nitrogen dioxide* is classically encountered in farmers, as large quantities of this gas are formed by fermentation during the first week after filling a silo. The victim typically presents with cough, dyspnea, bronchospasm, and weakness, with little evidence of ocular or upper airway irritation. After a lag of 1 or more hours, there may be pro-

TABLE 23–1. TOXIC GASES AND FUMES

MECHANISM OF INJURY	AGENT	OCCUPATIONAL EXPOSURE
Simple asphyxia	Carbon dioxide	Mining, foundry work
	Nitrogen	Mining, underwater work
	Methane	Mining
Tissue asphyxia	Carbon monoxide	Mining, petroleum refining, pollution
	Cyanide	Smoke inhalation
Upper airway injury	Ammonia	Fertilizer, refrigeration, cleaning agents
	Hydrogen fluoride	Etching, refining
	Chlorine	Bleaches, swimming pools
Pulmonary edema	Nitrogen dioxide	Farming, fertilizer, silo welding
	Phosgene	Welding, paint removal
Systemic toxicity	Cadmium (renal failure)	Electroplating
	"Metal fume fever"	Welding, galvanizing
	Benzene	Petroleum refining
Allergy	Isocyanates	Plastics, paint
	Platinum	Electroplating, photography
	Formalin	Insulation, textiles, manufacturing

gression to frank pulmonary edema. Following recovery from the acute illness, the patient may develop bronchiolitis obliterans, characterized by progressive dyspnea. Metal fume fever is a systemic response to inhalation of certain metal oxides, such as zinc oxide. Symptoms include fever, myalgias, and malaise. Long-term sequelae are not seen. Exposure to isocyanate, platinum compounds, or formalin vapors may cause asthma, either immediate or delayed in onset; asthma is more fully discussed in Chapter 16.

Management of exposure to a toxic gas is generally supportive in nature. The victim should be removed from the source of exposure and a patent airway with adequate ventilation ensured. Correction of hypoxemia may be possible with supplemental O_2, or intubation and mechanical ventilation may be necessary. The patient should be carefully monitored for a delayed reaction to the agent. Additional measures that may be required include bronchodilators and correction of acid-base disturbance or shock. The role of prophylactic antibiotics or steroids remains undetermined.

REFERENCES

Haponik EF, Summer WR: Respiratory complications in burned patients: Pathogenesis and spectrum of inhalation injury. J Crit Care 2:49–74, 1987.

Loke J: Pathophysiology and Treatment of Inhalation Injuries. New York, Marcel Dekker, 1988.

Morgan WKC, Seaton A: Occupational Lung Diseases. 2nd ed. Philadelphia, WB Saunders Co, 1984.

Schoene RB, Hornbein TF: Respiratory adaptation to high altitude. In Murray JF, Nadel JA (eds): Textbook of Respiratory Medicine. Philadelphia, WB Saunders Co, 1988.

Shaw KN, Briede CA: Submersion injuries: Drowning and near-drowning. Emerg Med Clin North Am 7:355–370, 1989.

SECTION III

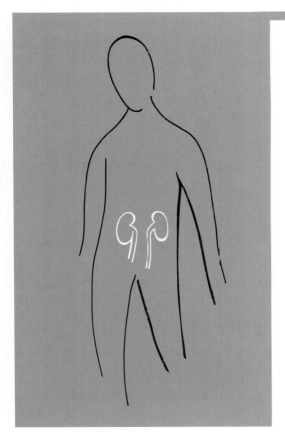

RENAL DISEASE

24 ELEMENTS OF RENAL STRUCTURE AND FUNCTION

ELEMENTS OF RENAL STRUCTURE

The human kidneys are anatomically positioned in the retroperitoneal space at the level of the lower thoracic and upper lumbar vertebrae. Each adult kidney weighs approximately 150 gm and measures about 12 by 6 by 3 cm. A coronal section of the kidney reveals two distinct regions (Fig. 24–1A). The outer region, the cortex, is about 1 cm in thickness. The inner region is the medulla and is made up of several conical structures. The bases of these pyramidal structures are located at the corticomedullary junction, and the apices extend into the hilum of the kidney as the papillae. Each papilla is enclosed by a minor calyx; these calyces collectively communicate with major calyces, forming the renal pelvis. Urine that flows from the papillae is collected in the renal pelvis and passes to the bladder through the ureters.

Blood is delivered to each kidney from a main renal artery branching from the aorta (Fig. 24–1B). The main artery usually divides into two main segmental branches, which are further subdivided into lobar arteries supplying the upper, middle, and lower regions of the kidney. These vessels subdivide further as they enter the renal parenchyma and create interlobar arteries that course toward the renal cortex. These smaller arteries provide perpendicular branches, the arcuate arteries, at the corticomedullary junction. Interlobular arteries arising from the arcuates extend into the cortex. The glomerular capillaries receive blood through afferent arterioles that originate from these terminal interlobular arteries. The glomerular capillary bed is drained by a second muscular vessel, the efferent arteriole. This arteriole leaves the glomerulus and supplies a network of vessels that surround tubular structures in the medulla. This network, the vasa recta, includes capillaries that drain into venules. The venous drainage of the kidney is provided by interlobular, arcuate, lobular, and ultimately renal veins. Each renal vein drains into the inferior vena cava.

Histologically, the kidney is composed of a basic structural unit known as the nephron (Fig. 24–2). Each human kidney contains approximately 1 million nephrons. The nephron is composed of two major components: a filtering element composed of an enclosed capillary network (the glomerulus) and an attached tubule. The tubule contains several distinct anatomic and functional segments.

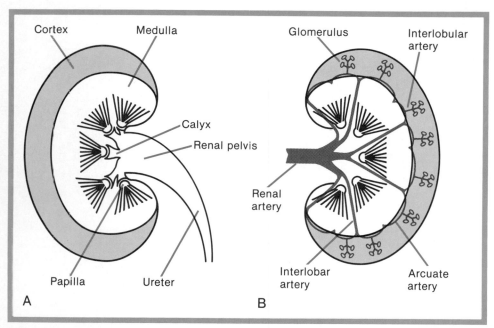

FIGURE 24–1. Basic renal structure. Urinary collecting structures are depicted in A, and the arterial supply is depicted in B.

The Glomerulus

The glomerulus (Fig. 24–3) is a unique network of capillaries suspended between the afferent and efferent arterioles enclosed within an epithelial structure (Bowman's capsule). The capillaries are arranged into lobular structures or tufts. The capillary is made up of the endothelial cell, the basement membrane, and the urinary epithelial cell. The endothelial cells line the capillary lumen and are fenestrated with pores covered by thin diaphragms. The glomerular basement membrane (GBM) is a hydrated gel of glycoproteins containing interwoven collagen fibers. The visceral epithelial cells extend foot processes over the basement membrane. The foot processes are not tightly approximated and allow for formation of a filtration slit covered by a thin membrane.

The barrier created by these three layers allows free entry of water and low molecular weight solutes into the urinary space yet totally excludes the passage of cells and proteins. Clusters of anion-rich macromolecules, both within the GBM and along the surface of epithelial and endothelial cells, further restrict filtration of large serum proteins that carry a net negative charge. The negative charge of the filtration barrier explains why anionic albumin, which has a molecular radius less than the limiting pore size, does not normally enter the urinary space.

The glomerular tufts are suspended within the urinary space of Bowman's capsule on a lattice known as the mesangium. Mesangial cells are enclosed by a matrix of homogeneous fibrillary material containing mucopolysaccharides and glycoprotein. The cells have contractile elements that may contribute to the regulation of hemodynamic properties in the glomerulus. These cells also have phagocytic properties.

The Tubule

The glomerular capsule funnels ultrafiltrate into the renal tubule. The initial portion, the proximal convoluted tubule, is located in the cortex. The proximal straight tubule enters the medulla and delivers fluid to the loop of Henle. The loop forms a hairpin turn in the medulla and returns toward the cortex, forming the distal tubule. The tubule finally is directed again into the medullary tissues as the collecting duct, emptying into the renal pelvis at the ducts of Bellini located at the tips of the renal papillae.

The structural arrangement of the tubule allows the distal tubule to come into close approximation with the vascular pole of the glomerulus. The distal tubular cells in this region are taller and more numerous. This distinct region of the distal tubule is known as the **macula densa** and, together with cells originating from the adjacent afferent arteriole, creates a specialized structure known as the **juxtaglomerular apparatus.** This structure is the site of renin formation and is important in coordinating the function of the glomerulus and tubule.

Very little interstitial connective tissue is normally interspersed among the vessels and ele-

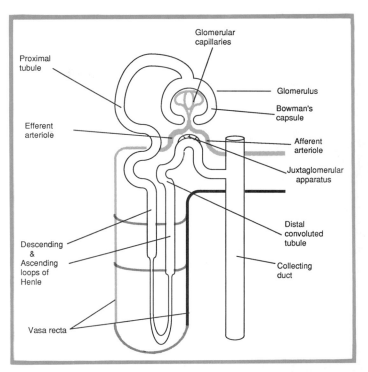

FIGURE 24–2. The nephron with the basic vascular structures. The glomerular capillaries are supplied by the afferent arteriole and drain into the efferent arterioles. Blood then flows through the vasa recta and is returned to the venous circulation.

ments of the nephron. The reticular fibers and cells that are present are more prominent in the medulla. The interstitium contains lymphatics and nerves.

ELEMENTS OF RENAL PHYSIOLOGY

The kidney contributes to body fluid homeostasis by excreting excess solute and water in the urine. This is accomplished by creating an ultrafiltrate of the blood at the glomerulus. This fluid, which is relatively free of cellular elements and proteins, flows through the various tubular segments, which absorb solutes and water. The usual volume of urine thus produced daily (1 to 2 L) is small relative to the normal volume of glomerular filtrate (approximately 180 L). The capacity to excrete excess solute and fluid is therefore quite large and allows maintenance of homeostasis in the setting of excessive intake.

The Glomerulus

Renal plasma flow rate is normally about 600 ml/min and glomerular filtration rate (GFR) is approximately 120 ml/min. These rates are maintained nearly constant over a wide range of mean aortic pressures. This autoregulatory response is accomplished by the activity of effectors on the afferent and efferent arterioles. These effectors in-

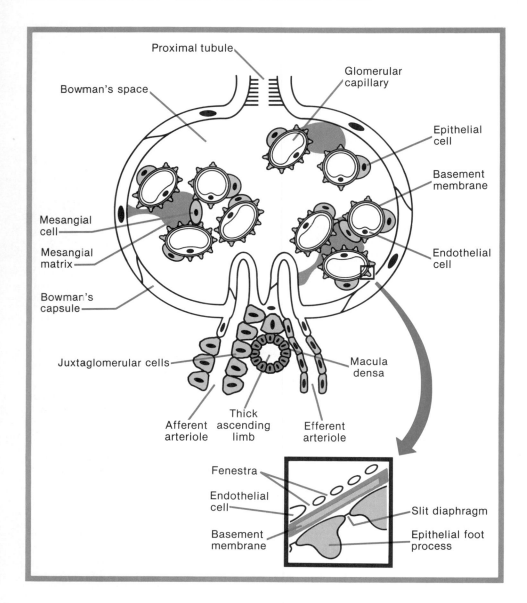

Proximal tubule

Glomerular capillary

Bowman's space

Epithelial cell

Basement membrane

Mesangial cell

Endothelial cell

Mesangial matrix

Bowman's capsule

Juxtaglomerular cells

Macula densa

Afferent arteriole

Thick ascending limb

Efferent arteriole

Fenestra

Endothelial cell

Slit diaphragm

Basement membrane

Epithelial foot process

FIGURE 24–3. The glomerulus. The structures creating the filtration barrier are shown in the inset.

clude angiotensin II, the renal vasodilating prostaglandins PGE_2 and PGI_2, and the contractile response of vascular myoepithelium and the glomerular mesangium.

Glomerular ultrafiltration occurs as a result of an outwardly directed net pressure that moves fluid across the semipermeable capillary wall. The GFR can be expressed as

$$GFR = K_f(\Delta P)$$

where ΔP is the net ultrafiltration pressure. This pressure represents the sum of Starling forces (hydraulic and oncotic pressure gradients) across the capillary wall. The factor K_f expresses both the permeability of the glomerular capillary wall and the surface area of the capillary bed available for ultrafiltration. Changes in the glomerular capillary hydrostatic pressure are regulated by alterations in

the tone of the afferent and/or efferent arterioles. In addition, changes in the permeability or surface area of the glomerular capillary bed affect the GFR.

The Proximal Tubule

The primary function of the proximal tubule is bulk, isosmotic reabsorption of ultrafiltrate. Sodium is the most prevalent compound in the glomerular filtrate, and many of the transport processes in the proximal tubule involve sodium transport (Fig. 24–4).

The majority of sodium reabsorption in the proximal tubule involves active transport mechanisms. Sodium is pumped from the tubular cell across the basolateral membrane by the Na-K-ATPase transporter. This generates an electrochemical gradient for the movement of sodium across the luminal membrane. The absorption of sodium in the proximal tubule is stimulated by angiotensin II and inhibited by atrial natriuretic peptides and parathyroid hormone (PTH). In general, the movement of sodium across the luminal membrane occurs by combined processes involving other solutes. A countertransport mechanism involving hydrogen ions (H+) results in the reclamation of the vast majority of the filtered bicarbonate. The absorption of glucose and amino acids involves cotransport with sodium. Phosphate is substantially reclaimed in this segment by a mechanism coupled to active sodium absorption. Calcium is absorbed in parallel with sodium in the proximal tubule.

Other electrolytes are absorbed in the proximal tubule by mechanisms unrelated to sodium transport. The bulk of filtered potassium is reabsorbed in this segment. A calcium ATPase is involved with active absorption of calcium.

In the straight portion of the proximal tubule, organic acids, including uric acid and drugs such as the penicillins, are secreted. Most pharmacologic diuretics are also secreted at this nephron segment. This secretory process is important for the efficacy of these compounds because their activity is mediated through effects on luminal solute transport mechanisms.

The removal of solutes, principally sodium salts, from the glomerular filtrate creates a slight osmotic gradient for water movement from the proximal tubular lumen to the peritubular space. This slight osmotic gradient is adequate to account for proximal isotonic water absorption because the water permeability is rather high.

Under normal conditions, about two thirds of ultrafiltrate volume is absorbed in the proximal tubule. As long as euvolemia persists, the fractional rate of proximal absorption remains constant when the GFR is varied. This constant relation is known as **glomerulotubular balance** and is modulated by alterations in the effective circulating volume. In empiric terms, this modulation includes, respectively, downsetting and upsetting of glomerulotubular balance in volume-expanded states when filling of the arterial tree is impaired. These alterations occur without changes in the GFR. Thus changes in effective circulating volume, by altering glomerulotubular balance, have a profound effect on the volume of fluid delivered to the loop of Henle.

The Loop of Henle

The loop of Henle begins at the corticomedullary junction as the thin descending limb, continues around a hairpin turn as the thin ascending limb becomes the thick ascending limb in the outer medulla, and ends in the macula densa at the level of the glomerulus from which it originated. Each segment of the loop has different permeabilities to sodium chloride and water, so that about 15 per cent of the volume of the isosmotic ultrafiltrate is absorbed, but about 25 per cent of the

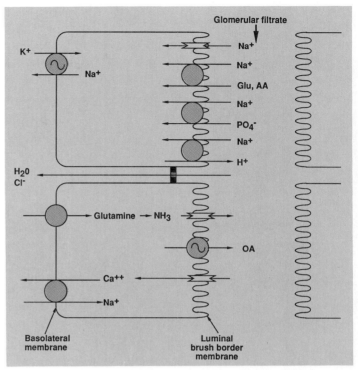

FIGURE 24–4. The major transport processes of the proximal tubular cells. Sodium can be reabsorbed alone; in cotransport with amino acids (AA), glucose (Glu), or anionic compounds such as phosphate; or by antitransport with hydrogen ions. The proximal nephron is also responsible for reabsorption of calcium, secretion of organic acids (OA), and formation of ammonia, which is important for the secretion of hydrogen ions in the distal nephron. Water and chloride absorption occurs primarily through paracellular pathways.

sodium chloride is absorbed. This differential absorption converts the isotonic fluid entering from the proximal tubule into a dilute fluid delivered to the distal tubule (Fig. 24–5).

Passive water absorption in the descending and salt absorption in the ascending thin limbs of the loop occur as a result of the selective permeability of these segments. The thick ascending limb absorbs sodium chloride by an active, energy-dependent process. Specifically, luminal transport involves a furosemide-inhibitable Na+/K+/2 Cl− cotransporter. Because this segment is impermeable to water, the luminal fluid leaving the thick ascending limb is made hypotonic with respect to plasma by active salt absorption, a vital step in urinary dilution. The addition of sodium chloride to the medullary interstitium is the primary step that allows a multiplication process to build and maintain the interstitial hypertonicity necessary to absorb water from thin descending limbs and from collecting ducts during antidiuresis.

The hairpin arrangement and countercurrent flow of the loop minimize the work needed to maintain a papillary osmolality of 1200 mOsm/kg H2O, compared with the 300 mOsm/kg H2O osmolality of the cortex. A similar organization of the

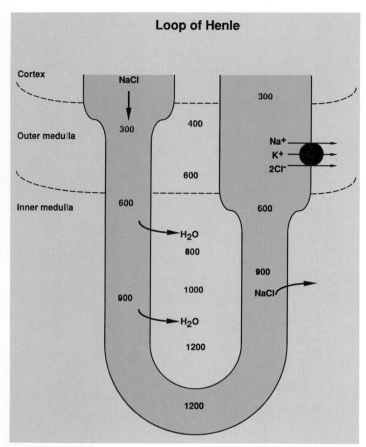

FIGURE 24–5. The loop of Henle is responsible for additional absorption of filtrate. Water is absorbed in the solute-impermeable descending limb. The concentrated medullary interstitium, established by solute transport at the water-impermeable ascending limb, drives water absorption from the descending limb. The hyperosmolar interstitium also provides the driving force for urinary concentration at the collecting duct. The relative osmolarity of the tubular fluid and interstitium is demonstrated by the numerals.

vasa recta allows the sodium chloride absorbed from the loop of Henle and urea absorbed from the papillary collecting duct to be trapped within the interstitium at increasing concentrations. The integrity of these anatomic relationships is essential to the concentrating ability of the kidney.

A major portion of calcium absorption also occurs within the loop of Henle. Calcium absorption in the medullary portion of the thick ascending limb varies with the magnitude of the positive luminal transepithelial voltage that accompanies active salt absorption and is not regulated by PTH. In contrast, PTH stimulates the rate of calcium absorption in the cortical thick ascending limb but sodium absorption is not changed by the hormone.

The Distal Nephron

The distal convoluted tubule is a water-impermeable cortical structure that continues the

dilution of luminal fluid through active sodium chloride absorption. Sodium absorption in the distal nephron occurs primarily by a thiazide diuretic–sensitive, chloride-coupled transport process (Fig. 24–6). The cortical collecting duct can reabsorb sodium by a mineralocorticoid-sensitive process. In states of volume depletion and maximal aldosterone production, the urine can be rendered virtually free of sodium. Because the cortical interstitium remains isotonic to plasma, salt absorption from these segments affects urinary dilution but not urinary concentration.

Potassium secretion begins in the late distal convoluted tubule and continues through the collecting ducts. Virtually all of the filtered potassium is reabsorbed in more proximal nephron segments so that the potassium appearing in the urine is secreted distally. Potassium secretion proceeds by diffusion of the intracellular cation down both concentration and electrical gradients into the tubular lumen. The basolateral Na-K-ATPase establishes the concentration gradient by maintaining a high intracellular potassium concentration. Although some potassium may leak back across the basolateral membrane, two factors favor the movement of potassium into the luminal fluid. First, the concentration of potassium in the luminal fluid is low. Enhanced distal tubular flow thus results in the maintenance of low intraluminal potassium concentrations and stimulates potassium secretion. Second, the electrical potential in the collecting tubules is negative relative to the peritubular fluid owing to the reabsorption of sodium. The electrical gradient favors the movement of potassium from the cell. Increases in the distal delivery of sodium result in further increases in the negative electrical potential of the lumen and further stimulate potassium secretion. Aldosterone stimulates potassium secretion by enhancing the activity of the basolateral Na-K-ATPase transporter and by increasing the permeability of the luminal cell membrane to potassium.

Proton secretion in the distal nephron allows absorption of any bicarbonate present in these segments, thereby completing reclamation of filtered bicarbonate. The major contribution of the distal nephron to acid-base homeostasis, however, is new bicarbonate generation, mediated by proton secretion into tubular fluid by a proton ATPase. The secreted H+ can be either buffered by phosphate or excreted as ammonium ions. The secretory process in the collecting duct generates an intraluminal free H+ concentration 1000 times greater than that of blood. The secretory process allows for the generation within the cell of bicarbonate, which diffuses into the blood to replenish bicarbonate consumed during buffering of nonvolatile acids. The quantity of new bicarbonate added to body fluids is about 1 mEq/kg body weight daily. The factors determining the rate of distal potassium secretion—namely, the luminal delivery of sodium and the presence of aldosterone— also promote secretion of H+ in the distal tubule.

The collecting ducts (cortical, medullary, and papillary) are the primary sites of antidiuretic hormone (ADH) action. They are minimally permeable to water in the absence of ADH and, in that circumstance, can deliver the hypotonic (50 to 100 mOsm/kg H_2O) fluid issuing from the distal convoluted tubule unchanged into the urine. When ADH is present, water passes across the tubule wall readily, and the luminal fluid tonicity approaches that of the interstitium at any level. Maximal urinary concentrating ability thus depends on the availability of ADH plus the degree of the medullary hypertonicity generated from thick ascending limb NaCl absorption and trapping of salt and urea by the countercurrent flow of the loop of Henle and the vasa recta. The intrinsic renal prostaglandin PGE_2 may reduce the ADH-induced increase in collecting duct water permeability and thereby limit maximal urinary concentration.

RENAL HOMEOSTATIC FUNCTIONS

The renal contribution to maintaining fluid and electrolyte homeostasis involves the excretion of metabolic end products as well as any excess solute or water that is ingested. The kidney also contributes to metabolic processes through its role in certain hormonal systems (Table 24–1).

Waste Excretion

The kidney is responsible for elimination of nitrogenous products of protein catabolism. This is accomplished primarily by filtration at the glomerulus. Because homeostatic requirements necessitate the maintenance of low concentrations of these toxic compounds, very large volumes of ultrafiltrate formation are necessary to excrete the absolute quantity of material. The normal daily GFR of 180 L makes possible such mass elimination.

A second mechanism of solute entry into the urine is tubular secretion. Organic acids (such as urate and lactate) and organic bases (such as creatinine) are excreted in this manner. The secretory process is the major route of elimination for substances that are protein-bound. A large number of drugs, including antibiotics and diuretics, are thus excreted by this mechanism.

The kidney contributes to the metabolic degradation of a number of peptide hormones, including most pituitary hormones, glucagon, and insulin. This is accomplished by filtration of these substances at the glomerulus and catabolism by renal tubular cells. Decreased renal catabolism of insulin in diabetics with renal insufficiency may be manifest as a prolongation of the effect of exogenous insulin.

Fluid and Electrolyte Homeostasis

The kidney is responsible, as noted above, for eliminating any excess fluid and solute that are ingested. The most commonly encountered abnormalities in fluid and electrolyte balance are referable to sodium, potassium, water, and acid-base

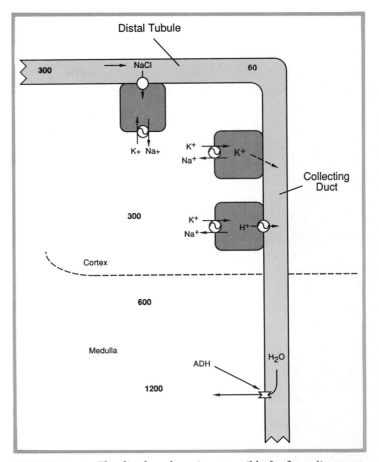

FIGURE 24–6. The distal nephron is responsible for fine adjustment of the final urinary constituents. Solute absorption in the water-impermeable cortical segments results in a dilute urine. Cortical collecting segments provide secretion of potassium and hydrogen ions. The medullary collecting duct is the site of urinary concentration as water is absorbed across a membrane made permeable by antidiuretic hormone (ADH) down a concentration gradient into the hypertonic interstitial compartment.

physiology. The renal contribution to these abnormalities is discussed thoroughly in Chapter 26.

The kidney also plays a major role in the balance of other electrolytes. Calcium reabsorption from the glomerular ultrafiltrate helps to regulate body calcium balance. The bulk of filtered calcium (approximately 60 per cent) is reabsorbed in the proximal tubule in parallel with sodium. Factors that alter fractional proximal tubular reabsorption greatly influence calcium excretion. The separation of calcium from sodium absorption occurs in the cortical thick ascending limb and the distal convoluted tubule, where PTH governs the rate of calcium absorption.

In situations of hypocalcemia, the serum PTH is increased, and the renal conservation of filtered calcium is maximized. Concomitantly, when the serum calcium concentration is elevated, PTH is suppressed and renal tubular calcium absorption

TABLE 24–1. RENAL HOMEOSTATIC FUNCTIONS

FUNCTION	MECHANISM	AFFECTED ELEMENTS
Waste excretion	Glomerular filtration	Urea, creatinine
	Tubular secretion	Urate, lactate, drugs (diuretics)
	Tubular catabolism	Pituitary hormones, insulin
Electrolyte balance	Tubular NaCl absorption	Volume status, osmolar balance
	Tubular K^+ secretion	Potassium concentration
	Tubular H^+ secretion	Acid-base balance
	Tubular water absorption	Osmolar balance
	Tubular calcium transport	Calcium homeostasis
Hormonal regulation	Erythropoietin production	Red blood cell mass
	Vitamin D activation	Calcium homeostasis
	Renin secretion	Blood pressure regulation, K^+/acid-base homeostasis

is diminished. Unfortunately, the symptoms of hypercalcemia often lead to volume depletion, which stimulates sodium conservation by the nephron. Renal tubular calcium absorption may therefore be increased. Extreme hypercalcemia also leads to a decrease in the GFR, further limiting the urinary excretion of calcium.

Magnesium is absorbed in the proximal tubule at a rate less than that of sodium. The majority of magnesium absorption occurs in the loop of Henle. Decreases in fractional proximal tubular absorption (extracellular fluid expansion) and decreases in sodium chloride absorption in the loop of Henle (diuretics) increase the excretion of magnesium. Renal loss of magnesium is a common cause of hypomagnesemia, and hypermagnesemia is almost always the result of a severely diminished GFR.

Renal Hormonal Regulation

The kidney is the major site for producing **erythropoietin.** This hormone is a highly glycosylated protein of 39,000 daltons which has at least two major actions in erythroid-producing tissue. Erythropoietin acts as a differentiating factor to promote transition of the erythrocyte colony-forming unit to the proerythroblast stage and as a growth factor to promote mitosis in the series of cells leading to the reticulocyte. Erythropoietin production increases in states of decreased tissue oxygen delivery. This may occur as a result of chronic hypoxemia, as seen in persons living at high altitudes or in patients with lung disease, or as a result of decreased oxygen-carrying capacity of blood, as is seen in anemic individuals.

The kidney contributes to calcium homeostasis not only by directly regulating excretion but also by affecting hormonal production. **Vitamin D** requires two in vivo hydroxylations to become the potent hormone that regulates intestinal calcium absorption. After hydroxylation in the liver at the 25 position, renal proximal tubular cells add a second hydroxyl ion at the 1 or 24 position of the molecule. This activity may be stimulated by PTH.

As noted above, the juxtaglomerular cells produce and secrete **renin.** This substance promotes the formation of angiotensin II, a potent vasoconstrictor that is a stimulus to aldosterone secretion. Aldosterone stimulates renal sodium absorption and excretion of potassium and hydrogen ions. Thus the renin-angiotensin-aldosterone axis is central to regulating arterial blood pressure, volume homeostasis, potassium balance, and acid-base status.

REFERENCES

DuBose TD Jr (ed): Acidification mechanisms. Semin Nephrol 10:91–180, 1990.

Khraibi AA, Knox FG: Renal hemodynamics and sodium chloride excretion. In Klahr S, Massry SG (eds): Contemporary Nephrology. Vol V. New York, Plenum Publishing Co, 1989, pp 35–79.

Klahr S: Structure and function of the kidneys. In Wyngaarden JB, Smith LH Jr, Bennett JC (eds): Cecil Textbook of Medicine. 19th ed. Philadelphia, WB Saunders Co, 1992, pp 482–492.

Tisher CC, Madsen KM: Anatomy of the kidney. In Brenner BM, Rector FC Jr (eds): The Kidney. 4th ed. Philadelphia, WB Saunders Co, 1991, pp 3–75.

25 APPROACH TO THE PATIENT WITH RENAL DISEASE

This chapter consists of two sections: the approach to patients affected with the more common syndromes involving the kidneys and the urinary tract, and laboratory tests that are useful in assessment of renal function and structure.

THE MAJOR RENAL SYNDROMES

Renal disorders are often nonspecific in their manifestations. However, certain groups of findings may be used to classify some of the more common syndromes and disorders affecting the kidneys and the urinary tract. The division of clinical manifestations into separate clinical syndromes is arbitrary, and overlap exists; however, the classification of the expression of renal injury into common themes serves a useful purpose, namely, consideration of specific clinicopathologic entities (Table 25–1).

The **acute nephritic syndrome** is a clinical syndrome characterized by relatively abrupt onset of renal dysfunction accompanied by hematuria that is glomerular or tubular in origin. The presence of red blood cell (RBC) casts and dysmorphic erythrocytes in the urine sediment, as well as significant degrees of proteinuria, provides highly suggestive evidence that the hematuria is nephronal in origin. For reasons that are not well understood, sodium acquisitiveness in the acute nephritic syndrome is considerably greater than what would be expected solely from the reduction in the glomerular filtration rate (GFR). Plasma albumin is generally normal, so that a significant fraction of the retained sodium remains in the vascular compartment and may result in hypertension, plasma volume dilution, circulatory overload, congestive heart failure, and a suppression of plasma renin activity.

Although acute poststreptococcal glomerulonephritis is the prototype for the acute nephritic syndrome, other infections may also lead to this syndrome. Likewise, this syndrome may be due to other primary glomerular diseases, such as mesangioproliferative glomerulonephritis, and multisystem diseases, such as systemic lupus erythematosus, Henoch-Schönlein syndrome, and essential mixed cryoglobulinemia.

A normal individual excretes less than 150 mg of low molecular weight tubular protein in the urine on a daily basis. The glomerular basement membrane serves as an effective barrier to the passage of high molecular weight proteins such as albumin, and the renal tubules have the capacity

TABLE 25–1. MAJOR RENAL SYNDROMES

SYNDROME	DEFINITION	EXAMPLE
Acute nephritic syndrome	Abrupt onset of renal insufficiency accompanied by hematuria that is glomerular or tubular in origin	Poststreptococcal glomerulonephritis
Nephrotic syndrome:	Increased glomerular permeability manifested by massive proteinuria (>3.5 gm/day/1.73 m²)	
With "bland" urine sediment (pure nephrotic)	Oval fat bodies, coarse granular casts	Minimal change disease
With "active" urine sediment ("mixed" nephrotic/nephritic)	Oval fat bodies, coarse granular casts, RBCs or RBC casts	Membranoproliferative glomerulopathy
Asymptomatic urinary abnormalities	Isolated proteinuria (<2.0 gm/day/1.73 m²) or hematuria (with or without proteinuria)	IgA nephropathy
Tubulointerstitial nephropathy	Renal insufficiency associated with non–nephrotic-range proteinuria and functional tubular defects	Analgesic nephropathy
Acute renal failure	An abrupt decline in renal function sufficient to result in retention of nitrogenous waste (e.g., BUN and creatinine)	Acute tubular necrosis
Rapidly progressive renal failure	Rapid deterioration of renal function over a period of weeks to months	Rapidly progressive glomerulonephritis
Renal calculus syndrome	Renal stones	Calcium stones
Tubular defects	Isolated or multiple tubular transport defects	Renal tubular acidosis

to reabsorb the small amount of protein that is filtered through the glomerulus. Abnormal proteinuria may occur as a transient phenomenon in individuals with febrile illnesses or congestive heart failure or after vigorous exercise. Persistent proteinuria, however, almost always indicates renal disease.

The **nephrotic syndrome** is characterized by increased glomerular permeability manifested by massive proteinuria, usually in excess of 3.5 gm/day/1.73 m² body surface area in the absence of depressed GFR. There is a variable tendency toward edema, hypoalbuminemia, and hyperlipidemia. The urinary protein loss is necessary and sufficient to produce the rest of the abnormalities, so that from a practical point of view, the presence of massive proteinuria is sufficient to define the nephrotic syndrome.

An important step in classifying and therefore determining the type of glomerular involvement present is the urinalysis. On the basis of the urinalysis, a patient with massive proteinuria may be classified as having a pure nephrotic form or a nephritic form. Patients with a pure nephrotic form, in addition to proteinuria, may demonstrate oval fat bodies, coarse granular casts, and occasional cellular elements but lack the "active" sediment characteristic of patients with a nephritic form. The differential diagnosis includes glomerular diseases such as minimal change disease, membranous nephropathy, diabetic nephropathy, and amyloidosis. The nephritic form is characterized by an active sediment that has glomerular hematuria (by virtue of dysmorphic RBCs and/or RBC casts) along with moderate to heavy proteinuria. In nephrotic/nephritic syndromes, membranoproliferative nephritis, systemic lupus erythematosus, and mixed essential cryoglobulinemia would be important diagnostic considerations.

The term **rapidly progressive renal failure** (RPRF) is applied to patients who have a rapid deterioration in renal function over weeks to months. This contrasts with patients with acute renal failure, who have an abrupt decline in renal function, and with patients with chronic renal failure, who have a decline in renal function that is measurable over years. The differential diagnosis of a patient who presents with RPRF is shown in Table 25–2. It should be noted that one of the

TABLE 25–2. CAUSES OF RAPIDLY PROGRESSIVE RENAL FAILURE

Obstructive uropathy
Malignant hypertension
Rapidly progressive glomerulonephritis
Thrombotic thrombocytopenic purpura/hemolytic uremic syndrome
Atheromatous embolic disease
Bilateral renal artery stenosis
Scleroderma
Acute interstitial nephritis

important but uncommon causes of RPRF is an entity called rapidly progressive glomerulonephritis (RPGN), a clinical syndrome of rapid and progressive decline in renal function (usually at least a 50 per cent decline in GFR over 3 months) associated with extensive glomerular crescent formation (usually more than 50 per cent) as the principal histologic finding on renal biopsy. Dysmorphic erythrocytes, RBC casts, and heavy proteinuria are characteristic in RPGN, as in other nephritic syndromes.

Acute renal failure is a syndrome that can be broadly defined as an abrupt decline in renal function sufficient to result in azotemia over days to a few weeks. Acute renal failure can result from a decrease in renal blood flow (prerenal azotemia, underperfusion syndromes [Table 25–3]), intrinsic parenchymal disease (renal azotemia), or obstruction to urine flow (postrenal azotemia). The general approach for evaluating acute renal failure is detailed in Chapter 30.

Tubulointerstitial nephropathy designates a group of clinical disorders that affect the renal tubules and interstitium principally with relative sparing of the glomeruli and renal vasculature. In the majority of cases of interstitial nephropathy, it is possible to classify the disease into acute interstitial nephritis or chronic interstitial nephropathy on the basis of the rate of progression of the azotemia. Chronic tubulointerstitial nephropathy is characterized clinically by renal insufficiency, non–nephrotic-range proteinuria, and tubular damage disproportionately severe relative to the degree of azotemia present. Thus, patients with chronic tubulointerstitial disease often have modest degrees of sodium wasting, hyperkalemia, and a normal anion gap metabolic acidosis even when azotemia is modest (see Chapter 28). Acute interstitial nephritis, often caused by drugs, is characterized by sudden onset of clinical signs of renal dysfunction associated with a prominent inflammatory cell infiltrate within the renal interstitium and is often important in the differential diagnosis of patients with acute renal failure.

CLINICAL ASSESSMENT OF RENAL STRUCTURE AND FUNCTION

Urinalysis

A complete analysis of the urine is a simple, noninvasive, and inexpensive means of detecting renal pathology. A first morning voided urine specimen obtained by a clean catch technique yields the most information. The urine should be examined promptly by both chemical and microscopic means.

Normal urine color ranges from almost colorless to deep yellow, depending on the concentration of a urochrome pigment. Abnormal urine colors may be a sign of disease or may indicate the presence of a pigmented drug or dye. The presence of RBCs or myoglobin often results in red or smoke-colored urine. Cloudiness of the urine may occur when a high concentration of white blood cells is present (pyuria) or when amorphous phosphates precipitate in alkaline urine.

A chemical assessment of the urine is performed with the "dipstick," a plastic strip impregnated with various reagents that detect the presence of protein, occult blood, glucose, and ketones in the urine. These assays are semiquantitative and are graded on the basis of color changes in the various reagent strips. The dipstick method for the detection of urinary protein is very sensitive to albumin but does not detect immunoglobulins or tubular proteins (Tamm-Horsfall mucoprotein). The urine sulfosalicylic acid test is an alternate test that detects all urinary proteins by a process of precipitation. A very concentrated urine may show trace to 1+ protein (10 to 30 mg/dl) in a normal individual. The finding of occult blood in the urine is abnormal and indicates the presence of either intact RBCs or free hemoglobin or myoglobin.

Microscopic examination of the urine sediment is used to detect cellular elements, casts, crystals, and microorganisms (Table 25–4). **Microscopic hematuria** is defined as more than two RBCs per high-power field on a centrifuged urine specimen in the absence of contamination by menstrual blood. **Pyuria** is defined as the presence of more than four white blood cells per high-power field. Epithelial cells are commonly found in the urinary sediment and may derive from any site along the urinary tract from the renal pelvis to the urethra. Renal tubular cells that contain absorbed lipids are termed **oval fat bodies.** Free fat droplets, composed primarily of cholesterol esters, may also be observed in the urine, particularly in association with heavy proteinuria. Both the oval fat bodies and free fat droplets have doubly refractile characteristics under the polarizing microscope and share the characteristic **"Maltese cross"** appearance.

Urinary casts are cylindric structures derived from the intratubular precipitation of mucoprotein and cellular debris. The presence of red or white blood cell casts provides presumptive evidence of inflammatory parenchymal renal disease. RBC casts most frequently indicate the presence of a proliferative glomerular lesion but on occasion may also be seen in patients with acute interstitial nephritis. Renal tubular cell casts (often with dirty brown, coarse granular casts) in a patient with acute renal failure helps to make the diagnosis of acute tubular necrosis. The presence of leukocyte casts in a patient with urinary tract infection indicates a diagnosis of pyelonephritis rather than a lower urinary tract infection.

Crystals of calcium oxalate (envelope-shaped) and uric acid (rhomboid) are often identified in acidic urine, depending on the degree of supersaturation, but in the absence of specific symptoms they are of little clinical significance. The presence of cystine crystals in the urine indicates the rare disease cystinuria. Triple phosphate crystals ("coffin-lid"–shaped) may be identified in alkaline urine. Bacteria in the urine are almost always recognized in a centrifuged specimen but do not nec-

TABLE 25–3. THE UNDERPERFUSION SYNDROMES

CLASS	EXAMPLES
Reduced effective circulating volume	Circulatory collapse Congestive heart failure Cirrhosis with ascites
Occlusive renal artery disease	Renal artery atherosclerosis Fibromuscular hyperplasia
Vasoconstriction of renal microvasculature	Acute transplant rejection Cyclosporine nephrotoxicity Amphotericin B nephrotoxicity

From Andreoli TE: Approach to the patient with renal disease. In Wyngaarden JB, Smith LH Jr, Bennett JC (eds): Cecil Textbook of Medicine. 19th ed. Philadelphia, WB Saunders Co, 1992, p 478.

essarily imply significant bacteriuria. The presence of bacteria in an unspun specimen, however, is significant and provides presumptive evidence for a urinary tract infection.

Renal Function Tests

Determination of the clearance of endogenous creatinine is a more convenient test and provides a reasonable estimate of the GFR. Because 10 per cent of creatinine is excreted by the process of tubular secretion, however, the creatinine clearance overestimates the true GFR, particularly in azotemic patients. The creatinine clearance (C_{cr}) is calculated as $C_{cr} = U_{cr} \times V/P_{cr}$. P_{cr} is the plasma creatinine in milligrams per deciliter, and U_{cr} is the urine excreted over a specific time in-

TABLE 25–4. MICROSCOPIC EXAMINATION OF THE URINE

FINDING	ASSOCIATIONS
Casts	
Red blood cell	Glomerulonephritis, vasculitis
White blood cell	Interstitial nephritis, pyelonephritis
Epithelial cell	Acute tubular necrosis, interstitial nephritis, glomerulonephritis
Granular	Renal parenchymal disease (nonspecific)
Waxy, broad	Advanced renal failure
Hyaline	Normal finding in concentrated urine
Fatty	Heavy proteinuria
Cells	
Red blood cell	Urinary tract infection, urinary tract inflammation
White blood cell	Urinary tract infection, urinary tract inflammation
Eosinophil	Drug-induced interstitial nephritis
(Squamous) epithelial cell	Contaminants
Crystals	
Uric acid	Acid urine, acute uric acid nephropathy, hyperuricosuria
Calcium phosphate	Alkaline urine
Calcium oxalate	Acid urine, hyperoxaluria, ethylene glycol poisoning
Cystine	Cystinuria
Sulfur	Sulfadiazine antibiotics

TABLE 25-5. CALCULATION OF THE CREATININE CLEARANCE

$C_{cr} = U_{cr} \times V/P_{cr}$
C_{cr} = clearance of creatinine (ml/min)
U_{cr} = urine creatinine (mg/dl)
V = volume of urine (ml/min) (for 24-hr volume: divide by 1440)
P_{cr} = plasma creatinine (mg/dl)
Normal range: 95 to 105 ml/min/1.75 m²

terval in milliliters per minute. The creatinine clearance is elevated 30 to 50 per cent over normal values (Table 25–5) in pregnancy. Protein loading is also associated with a transient rise in creatinine clearance.

An approximate assessment of renal function is most easily obtained by the measurement of the concentration of creatinine and urea nitrogen in the serum. Creatinine is a metabolite of creatine, a major muscle constituent. In a given individual, the daily rate of production of creatinine is constant and is determined by the mass of skeletal muscle. Because body creatinine is disposed of almost entirely by glomerular filtration, its steady-state concentration in the serum has been used as a marker of glomerular function. The "normal" range for serum creatinine concentration is 0.5 to 1.5 mg/dl. In any individual, however, a value in this range does not necessarily imply normal renal function. A more accurate assessment of renal function is obtained by determining the creatinine clearance (Table 25–5). However, once the relation between the serum creatinine and the creatinine clearance is established for a given patient, the serum creatinine can be followed as a reliable indicator of renal function.

The blood urea nitrogen (BUN) concentration is often used in conjunction with the serum creati-

TABLE 25-6. CALCULATION OF THE FRACTIONAL EXCRETION OF SODIUM

Fractional excretion of sodium (FE_{Na}) = fraction of sodium filtered at the glomerulus which is ultimately excreted in the urine

$$FE_{Na} = \frac{\text{amount Na}^+ \text{ excreted}}{\text{amount Na}^+ \text{ filtered}} = \frac{U_{Na} \times V}{P_{Na} \times GFR}$$

$$GFR = C_{cr} = \frac{U_{cr} \times V}{P_{cr}}$$

$$FE_{Na} = \frac{U_{Na} \times V}{P_{Na}} \times \frac{1}{U_{cr} \times V/P_{cr}} = \frac{U_{Na} \times P_{cr}}{U_{cr} \times P_{Na}} \times 100$$

C_{cr} = clearance of creatinine (ml/min)

P_{Na} = plasma sodium (mEq/L)

P_{cr} = plasma creatinine (mg/dl)

U_{Na} = urine sodium (mEq/L)

U_{cr} = urine creatinine (mg/dl)

nine concentration as a measure of renal function. Urea is the major end product of protein metabolism, and its production reflects the dietary intake of protein as well as the protein catabolic rate. Urea is excreted by glomerular filtration, but significant amounts of urea are reabsorbed along the renal tubule, particularly in sodium-avid states such as extracellular volume contraction. Consequently, the BUN may vary in relation to the extracellular fluid volume, whereas the serum concentration of creatinine does not. The usual ratio of urea nitrogen to creatinine concentration in the serum is 10:1. This ratio is increased in a number of clinical settings such as volume depletion, catabolic states, increased dietary protein intake, gastrointestinal hemorrhage, drugs such as corticosteroids, and obstructive uropathy.

Renal tubular function is evaluated by tests that examine the ability of the kidney to maintain salt and water balance as well as acid-base homeostasis. Maximal urinary concentrating ability can be assessed by restriction of fluid intake for 18 to 24 hours. In the polyuric patient suspected of a defect in urinary concentrating ability, the administration of 5 units of aqueous vasopressin once the urinary osmolality reaches steady state distinguishes patients with either central or nephrogenic diabetes insipidus. Whereas the patient with central diabetes insipidus has a doubling of the urinary osmolality with aqueous vasopressin, the individual with nephrogenic diabetes insipidus does not respond with further urinary concentration.

The fractional excretion of various solutes in the urine provides useful information about the tubular handling of a solute relative to its GFR. The fractional excretion of sodium, for example, is the fraction of sodium filtered at the glomerulus which is ultimately excreted in the urine (Table 25–6). Determination of the fractional excretion of sodium is most useful in the differential diagnosis of a patient with acute renal insufficiency, as outlined in Chapter 30. Determination of the fractional excretion of calcium, phosphate, uric acid, and amino acids is useful in the evaluation of patients with suspected disorders of renal tubular function and in the evaluation of renal stone disease.

Acidification of the urine is an important tubular function that can be assessed by the measurement of the urine pH. In the presence of systemic acidosis (arterial pH < 7.3), the urine pH should be 5.3 or less. Failure to acidify urine in the presence of systemic acidosis suggests a diagnosis of renal tubular acidosis.

A timed urine collection for the determination of protein excretion is an important study in the evaluation of glomerular and tubular diseases of the kidney. Normal individuals excrete less than 150 mg/24 hr of urinary protein. Patients with various glomerular or tubular diseases typically have increased excretion of protein in the urine. On all timed urine samples for protein, a simultaneous determination of urine creatinine is useful as a means of assuring the accuracy of collection.

The daily excretion of creatinine in the urine is relatively constant and averages 15 to 20 mg/kg in women and 20 to 25 mg/kg in men. If the creatinine excretion deviates significantly from these values, the collection may not be accurate.

Anatomic Imaging of the Urinary Tract
(Table 25-7)

The plain film of the abdomen, or **KUB** (kidney, ureter, bladder), is a simple way of determining renal size and shape. The normal kidney shadow approximates the length of 3.5 vertebral bodies, or about 12 cm. Bilaterally small kidneys in a patient with renal insufficiency imply a chronic, irreversible process, whereas the presence of enlarged kidneys suggests obstructive, inflammatory infiltrative, or cystic disease. Radiopaque renal calculi composed of calcium, magnesium ammonium phosphate (struvite), or cystine are often apparent on a plain film of the abdomen.

Renal ultrasonography is another noninvasive method of obtaining an anatomic image of the kidney and the collecting system. This technique is particularly useful for the detection of renal masses, cysts, and dilatation of portions of the collecting system (hydronephrosis). Renal ultrasonography may serve as the primary imaging procedure for patients with unexplained renal failure, to assess renal size and determine whether a patient has obstructive uropathy. Duplex ultrasonography, in which B-mode ultrasonography has been combined with pulsed Doppler imaging, has emerging applications in suspected diseases of the major renal arteries or veins and in acute failure of the transplanted kidney. Doppler techniques depend on the observation that sound waves emanating or reflecting from objects in motion shift their frequency ("Doppler shift") and that the intensity of the Doppler shift is directly proportional to the velocity of the objects in motion.

The **radioisotopic renal scan** provides important information about renal blood flow and tubular function. The test involves the intravenous administration of radiolabeled compounds that are excreted by the kidney. An external scintillation camera provides an image of the kidneys and calculates the rate of uptake and excretion of the labeled compound. Technetium-99 diethylenetriamine penta-acetic acid (DPTA) is the compound used to assess renal vascular perfusion qualitatively. Impaired renal perfusion, as in unilateral renal artery stenosis or renal infarction, is characterized by asymmetric uptake of technetium. Generalized renal hypoperfusion, as in acute glomerulonephritis or renal transplant rejection, can be recognized as well. An evaluation of renal tubular function may be obtained by the use of sodium iodohippurate [131]I (Hippuran), a compound eliminated by tubular secretion. Impaired Hippuran excretion in association with normal technetium perfusion is commonly observed in acute tubular necrosis or chronic renal disease.

The **intravenous urogram** involves the intravenous administration of iodinated radiographic con-

TABLE 25-7. IMAGING STUDIES OF THE URINARY TRACT: COMPARATIVE ASPECTS

STUDY	INFORMATION	CONSIDERATIONS
KUB	Renal size, opaque calculi	Inexpensive
Ultrasonography	Renal size, cysts, hydronephrosis, renal arterial/venous flow by Doppler	Noninvasive
Renal scan	Renal blood flow, tubular function	Functional study
Intravenous (IV) contrast urogram	Renal size, shape, cysts, tumors, stones, obstruction	Requires IV
Computed contrast tomography (CT)	Renal size, shape, cysts, tumors, stones, obstruction, retroperitoneal space	Requires IV
Retrograde pyelography	Ureteral obstruction	Invasive
Renal arteriography	Renal vasculature, tumors	Invasive
Renal venography	Renal vein thrombosis, renal vein blood sampling	Invasive

trast medium that is excreted through the kidney by glomerular filtration. The contrast medium concentrates in the renal tubules and produces a nephrogram image within the first few minutes after injection. As the medium passes into the collecting system, the calyces, renal pelvis, ureters, and bladder are visualized. The **computed tomography** (CT) scan of the kidney provides more precise information regarding renal masses as well as a definition of the perinephric space and other retroperitoneal structures. The risk of contrast medium–induced nephrotoxicity limits the utility of these studies in certain high-risk patients. CT scanning of the kidney can be performed without intravenous contrast material in selected cases.

Retrograde pyelography is performed by injection of radiocontrast material directly into the ureters at the time of cystoscopy. This technique is useful in the definition of obstructing lesions within the ureter or renal pelvis, particularly in the setting of a nonvisualizing kidney on intravenous pyelography.

Renal arteriography involves the direct injection of radiographic contrast medium into the aorta and renal arteries and is used to assess the renal vasculature. Renal arteriography is particularly useful in the evaluation of patients with suspected renal artery stenosis or thrombosis and in those with a renal mass. Renal arteriography is generally limited to situations in which a strong clinical indication exists and the patient is considered a candidate for surgical intervention. Renal vein catheterization is used to confirm the diagnosis of renal vein thrombosis or to obtain blood samples from the renal vein, particularly when renovascular hypertension is suspected.

Magnetic resonance imaging (MRI) represents a new and emerging diagnostic technology that uses high magnetic fields and radiofrequencies to construct images. The method avoids the use of ionizing radiation and the administration of contrast material. MRI provides images in a tomographic format similar to that of CT. The technique is very sensitive to blood flow and represents an excellent method for evaluation of major vascular structures for patency or tumor involvement.

Renal Biopsy

Most renal biopsies are performed when a glomerular lesion is suspected and less commonly in patients with unexplained acute renal failure. The percutaneous biopsy is the most commonly used technique and is a relatively safe procedure. An open renal biopsy is considered in the patient with a solitary functioning kidney or a bleeding diathesis. Potential complications of a closed renal biopsy include hematuria, renal hematoma, vascular laceration with the development of arteriovenous fistulas, and the inadvertent biopsy of liver, spleen, or bowel.

REFERENCE

Andreoli TE: Approach to the patient with renal disease. *In* Wyngaarden JB, Smith LH, Bennett JC (eds): Cecil Textbook of Medicine. 19th ed. Philadelphia, WB Saunders Co, 1992, pp 477–482.

26 FLUID AND ELECTROLYTE DISORDERS

The concentrations of fluid and electrolytes in the cells and fluid compartments of the body are maintained remarkably constant despite a widely varying intake. This equilibrium is maintained by fluid and solute shifts across the cells of the body following well-defined mechanisms and by the capacity of the kidney to regulate the urinary excretion of water, electrolytes, and solutes in response to the needs of the body.

VOLUME DISORDERS

Water is the most abundant molecular component of living matter and constitutes 60 to 80 per cent of total body weight in humans (Fig. 26–1). The aqueous fraction of the total body mass is determined by the amount of body fat, which varies with age, gender, and nutritional status. Approximately two thirds of the total body water is contained in the intracellular compartment. Potassium is the principal cation of intracellular fluid. The principal anions vary among different cells. The remaining one third of the volume of body water is contained in the extracellular fluid (ECF). Because sodium salts account for almost 90 per cent of the solute in this compartment, the ECF volume can be considered, for practical purposes, to be composed of isotonic saline. One third of the ECF is contained in the vascular space and is critical for stability of cardiovascular function.

The cell membrane represents the barrier between the intracellular and extracellular fluid compartments. Because membranes are relatively permeable to water and low molecular weight solutes, the movement of fluid between these two compartments is determined by the osmotic gradient. The transfer of fluid between vascular and interstitial compartments occurs at the capillary level and is governed by the balance between hydrostatic pressure gradients and plasma oncotic pressure gradients, as related in the Starling equation:

$$J_v = K_f(\Delta P - \Delta \pi)$$

where J_v is the rate of fluid transfer between vascular and interstitial compartments, K_f is the water permeability of the capillary bed, ΔP is the hydrostatic pressure difference between capillary and interstitium, and $\Delta \pi$ is the oncotic pressure difference between capillary and interstitial fluids. The hydrostatic pressure in the interstitial compartment is normally low, and the hydrostatic pressure gradient is thus determined by the pressure gradient from arteriolar to venular ends of a capillary. Likewise, the interstitial fluid oncotic pressure is low because this compartment is relatively protein-poor. The oncotic pressure gradient therefore represents the oncotic pressure of the intravascular fluids, which is determined by the concentration of plasma proteins, particularly albumin.

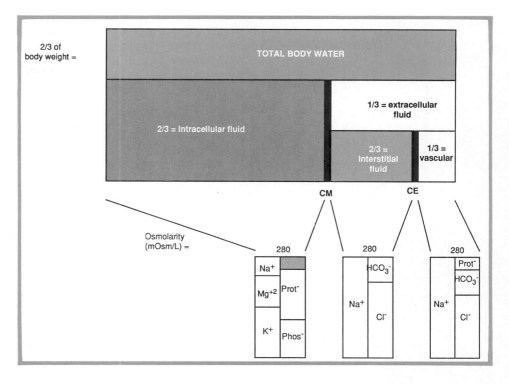

FIGURE 26–1. Composition of body fluid compartments. The compartments are anatomically defined by the cell membrane (CM) and capillary endothelium (CE). The osmolar concentration among compartments is equivalent despite wide variation in cation and anion composition.

Normal Volume Homeostasis

Protection of ECF volume is the most fundamental characteristic of fluid and electrolyte homeostasis. Two cardinal mechanisms protect ECF volume: alterations in systemic hemodynamic variables and alterations in external sodium and water balance. The hemodynamic alterations occur within minutes of a perceived volume reduction and are characterized by tachycardia, increased peripheral resistance due to arterial vasoconstriction, and decreased venous capacitance due to venoconstriction. Alterations in external sodium and water balance lag behind by 12 to 24 hours and are characterized by ingestion as well as by renal excretion of salt and water. Both mechanisms maintain filling of the arterial tree and consequently are activated by external fluid losses, by inability to transfer fluid from the interstitium to the venous system, or by impaired fluid transfer from venous to arterial systems.

The mechanisms responsible for sensing alterations in the effective ECF volume activate a series of effectors that create an **integrated volume response** (Fig. 26–2). Extrarenal baroreceptors in the atria, pulmonary vessels, aortic arch, and carotid bifurcations sense volume changes in the vascular compartment of the ECF. These receptors transmit signals to the central nervous system (CNS), which regulates peripheral sympathetic nerve activity and catecholamine release. This catecholamine response raises blood pressure by increasing arteriolar resistance and heart rate while simultaneously decreasing venous capaci-

tance. Within the kidney this increase in arteriolar resistance results in renal hypoperfusion. Moreover, adrenergic nerve terminals are in direct contact with proximal renal tubular epithelial cells, and direct stimulation of renal sympathetic nerves increases proximal tubular sodium absorption. The stimulation of extrarenal baroreceptors also activates release of antidiuretic hormone (ADH). This hormone is primarily responsible for enhancing renal water conservation but, because of its vasoconstrictive properties, also reduces renal perfusion.

The juxtaglomerular apparatus of the nephron serves as an intrarenal baroreceptor. Sympathetic nerve stimulation, reductions in afferent arteriolar blood pressure, or reductions in the rates of distal tubular sodium delivery enhance renin release by the juxtaglomerular cells. Renal renin release accelerates the formation of angiotensin II, which has three major effects on volume conservation. First, it is a potent pressor agent. Second, angiotensin II is the major stimulus to aldosterone secretion and consequently is a key factor modulating renal sodium conservation. Finally, the angiotensin II formed in the CNS is a potent stimulus to thirst.

Factors produced and released by vascular endothelial cells also play a major role in modulating systemic hemodynamics. The vasoconstricting factors include endothelins I to III, which are potent vasoconstrictor peptides. Endothelins are also released from the posterior pituitary and may play a role in modulating ADH release. The vasoconstrictor agents derived from the cyclo-oxygenase path-

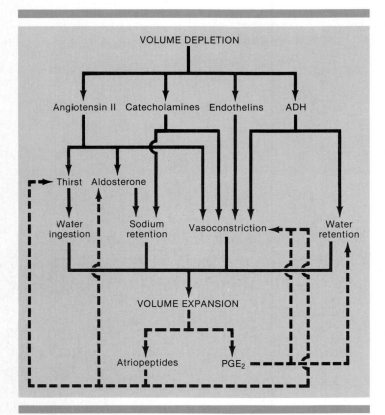

FIGURE 26–2. Volume repletion reaction. Volume depletion leads to activation of mechanisms that stimulate (*solid lines*) fluid intake, mediated through the thirst center, as well as the renal elimination of salt and water. Volume expansion activates counterregulatory mechanisms (*dashed lines*). ADH = Antidiuretic hormone; PGE_2 = prostaglandin E_2.

way in vascular endothelial cells include thromboxane A_2 and prostaglandin H_2.

Counterregulatory factors provide a negative feedback network to the volume depletion reaction and are activated when the ECF volume is expanded. Vascular endothelium produces vasodilators such as nitrous oxide and prostacyclin (PGI_2), although the relative contribution of these factors to the systemic hemodynamic state may be limited. The major effectors in this feedback system include atriopeptin and prostaglandins of the E series.

Prostaglandins of the E series are potent vasodilators. Within the kidney, PGE_2 production is activated by angiotensin II and by response to increased medullary osmolality. The PGE_2 thus produced has two major effects related to volume homeostasis. First, it produces a natriuresis due either to altering renal glomerular hemodynamics or to a direct tubular effect. Second, PGE_2 is a direct antagonist of the renal tubular effects of ADH and thus impairs renal water conservation.

Atriopeptin is a hormone released from cardiac atrial storage granules in response to atrial disten-

tion. Immunoreactive atriopeptin has also been identified within the CNS. Atriopeptin of cardiac origin induces a natriuresis. This diuretic effect is mediated by its vasodilatory properties, resulting in enhanced renal blood flow, by a direct suppression of aldosterone secretion, and perhaps by direct tubular inhibitory activity. Centrally released atriopeptin suppresses pituitary ADH release and angiotensin II–mediated thirst.

Volume Depletion

True hypovolemia occurs when there is a reduction in the total body water, intracellular fluid volume, and effective ECF volume. Volume depletion is established when the rate of salt and water intake is less than the rates of renal and/or extrarenal volume losses (Table 26–1).

Causes of Volume Depletion

Renal fluid losses are due either to defects in the hormonal regulation of the renal mechanisms involved in volume homeostasis or to defects in the intrinsic tubular mechanisms for salt and water absorption. Volume contraction can occur whenever there is a loss of ADH or aldosterone effects on the kidney. Such a defect can occur in the setting of absolute deficiency of the hormone or with tubular unresponsiveness to the actions of the hormone. **Diabetes insipidus** is caused by a

TABLE 26–1. CAUSES OF VOLUME DEPLETION

Renal Fluid Loss
  Hormonal defects
    Antidiuretic hormone
      Central diabetes insipidus
      Nephrogenic diabetes insipidus
    Hypoaldosteronism
      Absolute
        Addison's disease
        Hyporeninemic hypoaldosteronism
      Functional
        Interstitial renal diseases
        Aldosterone inhibitors
  Tubular defect
    Diuretics
    Renal tubular acidosis
    Acute tubular necrosis (diuretic phase)
    Postobstructive diuresis
    Bartter's syndrome
  Osmotic diuresis
Extrarenal Fluid Losses
  Gastrointestinal
    Vomiting
    Mechanical drainage
    Fistulas
    Diarrhea
  Cutaneous
    Sweat
    Burns
  Hemorrhage

Adapted from Andreoli TE: Disorders of fluid volume, electrolyte, and acid-base balance. In Wyngaarden JB, Smith LH Jr, Bennett JC (eds): Cecil Textbook of Medicine. 19th ed. Philadelphia, WB Saunders Co, 1992, p 502.

defect in ADH activity and is characterized by a water diuresis. Deficient secretion of aldosterone is observed in **Addison's disease** or the syndrome of **hyporeninemic hypoaldosteronism.** This latter disorder occurs in patients with a variety of interstitial renal diseases that lead to diminished renin production. The syndrome is characterized by the development of hyperkalemia that, in contrast to normal individuals, fails to stimulate aldosterone secretion, possibly because atriopeptins may inhibit aldosterone production in this disorder. Patients with **interstitial renal diseases** may also exhibit a tubular unresponsiveness to aldosterone. Finally, some diuretics such as spironolactone are **aldosterone antagonists.**

Intrinsic tubular defects can lead to incomplete absorption of sodium. This is most often encountered with the use of pharmacologic **diuretics,** which act by inhibiting tubular sodium absorption. The tubules may lose the ability to function effectively after a variety of ischemic or chemical injuries. This may also occur transiently following relief of urinary tract obstruction. Tubular defects in anion absorption lead to a concomitant urinary sodium loss. This is observed in the **renal tubular acidoses** with bicarbonate loss and in a rare disorder known as **Bartter's syndrome,** which is associated with defective chloride absorption in the thick ascending limb. Finally, an **osmotic diuresis** of nonionic solutes such as glucose or urea can lead to excessive sodium loss.

Extrarenal fluid losses can occur either through the gastrointestinal tract or from cutaneous sources. The intestinal mucosa normally secretes approximately 9 L of fluid daily. Intestinal fluid losses can occur by **vomiting** of gastric contents, **mechanical drainage** of any segment of the intestine or biliary tract, **enterocutaneous fistulas** with loss of fluids through channels on the skin, or **diarrhea.** Excessive **sweating** can lead to volume depletion. Because the skin serves as the barrier between the interstitial compartment and the environment, loss of skin by **burns** or other trauma exposes this compartment to evaporative loss of fluid. Finally, **hemorrhage** from any source results in volume depletion.

Clinical Features of Volume Depletion

The clinical findings in states of true volume contraction are referable to underfilling of the arterial tree and to the renal and hemodynamic responses to this underfilling. Mild volume depletion may be associated with orthostatic dizziness and tachycardia. As the intravascular compartment becomes further depleted, a recumbent tachycardia becomes evident and urine output diminishes. With severe volume depletion, patients may present in a vasoconstricted, hypotensive state with mental obtundation, cool extremities, and negligible urine output.

Volume depletion can occur in the absence of the classic clinical findings. States of volume depletion in patients receiving cardiovascular drugs and excess renal sodium loss due to intrinsic renal disease or diuretics represent examples of clinical circumstances in which an assessment of the state of hydration may be difficult. An appropriate clinical history is always mandatory. If there is doubt about the state of hydration, particularly if the patient appears to be critically ill, measurement of the pulmonary capillary wedge pressure by means of invasive right-sided heart catheterization permits a valid assessment of the intravascular volume status.

The absolute quantity and rate of fluid replacement depend on the severity of volume depletion, which is estimated by the clinical presentation. If fluid repletion is to involve parenteral infusions, it is important to consider the distribution of the infused fluid. This distribution depends upon the permeability of the infused solute across the fluid compartment barriers. Dextrose-containing solutions are distributed to all body fluid compartments. Intravenous administration of 1 L of 5 per cent dextrose, for example, results in expansion of the intravascular compartment by only 150 ml, while 300 ml distribute to the interstitial compartment and 550 ml enter the intracellular space. Solutions containing sodium chloride are distributed throughout the extracellular compartment (approximately two thirds to the interstitium, with one third remaining in the intravascular space). Colloid-containing solutions administered intravenously are generally completely retained within the intravascular compartment but may not be in ascites, nephrotic syndrome, the adult respiratory distress syndrome, or extensive tissue trauma.

Circulatory Compromise Without True Volume Contraction

As noted in the previous section, true volume depletion occurs whenever a negative fluid balance is established. There are, however, disorders in which arterial filling is inadequate in the absence of external fluid losses (Table 26–2). A profound **decline in cardiac output** may result in circulatory collapse because the heart fails to translocate blood adequately from venous to arterial beds. Circulatory collapse occurs when there is a sud-

TABLE 26–2. CIRCULATORY COMPROMISE WITHOUT EXTERNAL FLUID LOSS

Impaired Cardiac Output
  Acute myocardial infarction
  Pericardial tamponade
Increased Vascular Capacitance
  Septic shock
Vascular to Interstitial Fluid Shifts
  Acute pancreatitis
  Bowel infarction
  Rhabdomyolysis

Adapted from Andreoli TE: Disorders of fluid volume, electrolyte, and acid-base balance. In Wyngaarden JB, Smith LH Jr, Bennett JC (eds): Cecil Textbook of Medicine. 19th ed. Philadelphia, WB Saunders Co, 1992, p 504.

den **capacitance increase** in the venous circulation. This occurs most commonly in septic shock. Finally, profound hypotension occurs when there are rapid **fluid shifts** from the intravascular to the interstitial compartments, as in infarction of the intestine, acute pancreatitis, and rhabdomyolysis. Treatment of capacitance increases and fluid shifts involves rapid expansion of the intravascular fluid compartment with saline solutions.

Volume Excess

Volume expansion occurs when salt and water intake exceeds renal and extrarenal losses. The distribution of the excess fluid does not always follow the normal distribution of body fluids. Total body volume may be expanded, for example, while the effective ECF is decreased. Such derangements occur as a result of fluid shifts from the intravascular compartment due to alterations in the Starling forces. Otherwise, fluid excess occurs in the setting of renal underexcretion of salt and water (Table 26–3).

Disorders Associated with Volume Excess

Alterations in the normal Starling forces usually result in a shift of fluid from the intravascular compartment to the interstitium, resulting in edema formation. The effective circulating volume is reduced and stimulates renal sodium and water absorption, further expanding the total body volume. By definition, this group of disorders is characterized by increases in capillary hydrostatic pressure, by decreases in capillary oncotic pressure, or by a combination of these two factors.

TABLE 26–3. DISORDERS OF VOLUME EXCESS

Altered Starling Forces
  Systemic venous pressure elevation
    Right heart failure
    Constrictive pericarditis
  Local venous pressure elevation
    Left heart failure
    Vena cava obstruction
  Reduced oncotic pressure
    Nephrotic syndrome
  Combined disorders
    Cirrhosis
Underexcretion
  Primary renal sodium retention
    Acute glomerulonephritis
  Hormonal excess
    Primary aldosteronism
    Cushing's syndrome
    SIADH

SIADH = Syndrome of inappropriate antidiuretic hormone secretion.
Adapted from Andreoli TE: Disorders of fluid volume, electrolyte, and acid-base balance. *In* Wyngaarden JB, Smith LH Jr, Bennett JC (eds): Cecil Textbook of Medicine. 19th ed. Philadelphia, WB Saunders Co, 1992, p 505.

Increases in the capillary hydrostatic pressure can occur in the systemic venous circulation owing to cardiac disorders in right-sided heart failure or constrictive pericarditis. An increase in the hydrostatic pressure can also be noted as a local elevation in the pulmonary or systemic venous pressure, as in left-sided heart failure, vena caval obstruction, or portal vein obstruction. A reduction in plasma oncotic pressure, and consequently a net increase in the tendency for fluid to translocate from capillaries to interstitium, accounts for edema formation in the nephrotic syndrome. A combination of these factors, represented by hypoalbuminemia and increased portal pressure, may be responsible for ascites formation in hepatic cirrhosis.

Treatment of Volume Excess

The mainstay in treating volume excess is the use of diuretic agents (Table 26–4). The cardinal example of a **proximal tubular diuretic** is acetazolamide, a carbonic anhydrase inhibitor that blocks proximal reabsorption of sodium bicarbonate. Consequently, prolonged use of acetazolamide may lead to hyperchloremic acidosis. Metolazone, a congener of the thiazide class of diuretics, inhibits proximal tubular sodium chloride absorption. Because the major locus for phosphate absorption is in the proximal nephron, profound phosphaturia may accompany use of metolazone. **Loop diuretics,** such as ethacrynic acid and furosemide, inhibit the coupled entry of Na^+, Cl^-, and K^+ across apical plasma membranes in the thick ascending limb of Henle. Given the relatively large contribution of this nephron segment to NaCl absorption, these potent diuretics are often termed high-ceiling diuretics. Thiazide diuretics inhibit NaCl absorption in the **early distal tubule** at the site of urinary dilution. Aldosterone antagonists act at sites in the **late distal tubule.**

OSMOLALITY DISORDERS

Body fluid osmolality, the ratio of solute to water in all fluid compartments, is maintained within a very narrow range. Because water moves freely across most cell membranes, the osmolality of intracellular fluid is dictated by water balance in the ECF. The ECF osmolality can be approximated by calculating the serum osmolality based upon the major solutes in the intravascular compartment:

$$Osmolality = 2[Na^+] + \frac{[glucose]}{18} + \frac{[BUN]}{2.8}$$

where the glucose and blood urea nitrogen (BUN) concentrations are expressed as milligrams per deciliter and the serum sodium concentration is expressed as milliequivalents per liter. In normal circumstances, glucose contributes approximately 5.5 mOsm/kg H_2O to the serum osmolality. When hyperglycemia occurs, the effective ECF osmolality rises because glucose entry into cells is limited.

When azotemia occurs, the effective ECF osmolality does not rise because urea enters cells readily. Osmolar balance depends upon close renal regulation of ECF.

ECF osmolality is regulated by dual pathways in the water repletion reaction (Fig. 26–3). Osmoreceptor cells in the CNS, located in the wall of the third ventricle, sense as little as 1 to 2 per cent change in the osmolality of blood in the internal carotid circulation. Neuronal signals from osmoreceptors stimulate the release of ADH from the posterior pituitary gland and simultaneously stimulate the sensation of thirst. The action of ADH causes water conservation in the kidney by increasing water permeability and water absorption in collecting ducts. Thirst leads to an increase in water intake.

When the ECF volume is reduced by about 10 per cent, water repletion is activated as a means of replenishing ECF volume irrespective of ECF osmolality. In this case, baroreceptors in the venous and arterial circulations stimulate ADH release through neuronal pathways. This nonosmotic stimulation of ADH release occurs independently of osmoreceptor function. Thirst is also stimulated, probably by increased central generation of angiotensin II. The volume stimulus to ADH secretion can override osmotic stimuli, so that significant volume contraction is a cardinal cause of hyponatremia.

Water repletion activates mechanisms that counterregulate water conservation. Atriopeptins of CNS origin participate in the feedback inhibition of ADH release and suppress thirst when body water is in excess. Likewise, oropharyngeal stimulation by water suppresses both ADH release and thirst prior to gastrointestinal absorption of water or a fall in plasma osmolality. Finally, PGE_2, produced in the kidney in response to medullary hypertonicity, inhibits the tubular actions of ADH. The net effect of these processes is a decrease in water ingestion and the excretion of dilute fluid, which passes through the collecting ducts unchanged.

Hypotonic Disorders

A true hypotonic disorder is one in which the ratio of solutes to water in body fluids is reduced, and the serum osmolality and serum sodium are both reduced in parallel. True hypotonic disorders must be distinguished from those entities characterized by a low measured serum sodium with a measured serum osmolality that is either normal or increased.

Extreme hyperlipidemia and hyperproteinemia, for example, may be associated with an apparent low sodium concentration. In some laboratory methods of measuring solute concentration, plasma volume is assumed to represent the water volume of the sample. As macromolecules are added to the plasma, the fraction of water per unit of plasma is decreased. The reported sodium concentration is thus factitiously reduced. Another cause of hyponatremia without hypo-osmolality occurs

TABLE 26–4. CHARACTERISTICS OF COMMONLY USED DIURETICS

SITE OF ACTION/AGENT	PRIMARY EFFECT	SECONDARY EFFECTS
Proximal Tubule		
Acetazolamide	↓Na^+/H^+ exchange	↑K^+, HCO_3^- loss
Metolazone	↓Na^+ absorption	↑K^+, Cl^-, and P loss
Loop of Henle		
Furosemide	↓$Na^+/K^+/2\ Cl^-$	↑K^+ loss, H^+ secretion, Ca^{2+} excretion
Ethacrynic acid	absorption	
Early Distal Tubule		
Thiazides	↓Na^+ absorption	↑K^+ loss, H^+ secretion, ↑Ca^{2+} excretion
Late Distal Tubule		
Aldosterone antagonists (spironolactone)	↓Na^+ absorption	↓K^+ loss, H^+ secretion
Nonaldosterone antagonists (triamterene, amiloride)		

Adapted from Andreoli TE: Disorders of fluid volume, electrolyte, and acid-base balance. In Wyngaarden JB, Smith LH Jr, Bennett JC (eds): Cecil Textbook of Medicine. 19th ed. Philadelphia, WB Saunders Co, 1992, p 506.

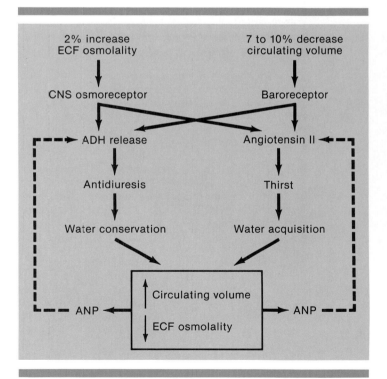

FIGURE 26–3. Water regulatory mechanisms. Alterations in extracellular fluid osmolality or volume stimulate (solid lines) thirst and release of antidiuretic hormone (ADH). The net result is a positive water balance. Counterregulation is provided by the inhibitory effects (dashed lines) of atriopeptins (ANP). ECF = Extracellular fluid; CNS = central nervous system.

TABLE 26–5. HYPONATREMIA DUE TO IMPAIRED RENAL WATER EXCRETION

Reduced Sodium Delivery to the Diluting Segment
 Starvation
 Beer potomania
 Myxedema
Primary Excess of ADH
 SIADH
 Drug-induced ADH production
 Potassium depletion
Mixed Disorders
 Volume contraction
  Addison's disease
  Loop diuretics
 Hypervolemia with decreased effective ECF
  Congestive heart failure
  Constrictive pericarditis
  Cirrhosis

Adapted from Andreoli TE: Disorders of fluid volume, electrolyte, and acid-base balance. In Wyngaarden JB, Smith LH Jr, Bennett JC (eds): Cecil Textbook of Medicine. 19th ed. Philadelphia, WB Saunders Co, 1992, p 509.

when water is redistributed to the vascular compartment. This can occur when relatively impermeable substances, such as glucose or mannitol, are added to the ECF. The ECF osmolality is actually increased and drives the shift of water from the intracellular compartment to dilute the extracellular solutes.

Hypotonic Hyponatremia

True hypotonic hyponatremia occurs only when water intake exceeds excretion. Under normal circumstances, the kidney has the capacity to excrete 10 to 15 L of maximally dilute urine. Dilutional hyponatremia due to **primary polydipsia** therefore necessitates the ingestion of a large volume of water. More commonly, hyponatremia occurs as a result of the inability to dilute urine maximally because of reductions in the rate of salt absorption by the diluting segment, sustained nonosmotic release of ADH, or a combination of these two factors (Table 26–5).

Inadequate salt absorption at the diluting segment can occur when there is a reduction in distal NaCl delivery or when the distal absorptive mechanisms are disrupted. Inadequate delivery occurs when sodium intake is limited. Distal sodium absorption can be disrupted by thiazide diuretics.

Disorders associated with a reduced filling of the arterial circulation may present with hyponatremia. In this instance, there is a nonosmotic release of ADH and enhanced proximal NaCl absorption with diminished distal delivery. These disorders may be associated either with an excess total body volume, as observed with congestive heart failure, constrictive pericarditis, and cirrhosis, or with volume depletion.

The syndrome of inappropriate ADH release (SIADH) is the prototype of primary release of

ADH or ADH-like substances. It occurs most often in association with pathologic processes within the cranium or thorax, or with the administration of certain drugs (Table 26–6). The circulating ADH allows excessive water absorption in the collecting duct with a modest expansion of the ECF volume. With the increase in volume, renal perfusion is increased and the kidney subsequently decreases sodium absorption in an attempt to re-establish euvolemia.

Some patients with hyponatremia associated with inappropriately concentrated urine and natriuresis in the setting of intracranial processes have been demonstrated to have a decreased total body fluid volume. This state of **cerebral salt wasting** may represent a primary release of a central natriuretic factor, which results in volume depletion and a subsequent nonosmotic release of ADH.

Interestingly, estimates of the urine osmolality may not help in distinguishing between patients who are modestly volume-contracted and those who have SIADH. Especially in starvation states, for example, the major problem is the amount of dilute urine formed, rather than a necessarily impaired ability to dilute the urine. Likewise, in SIADH, some 30 per cent of patients have a **reset osmostat,** which means, simply, that they are able to dilute urine, but at serum sodium levels that are appreciably lower than in normal individuals.

Diagnosis and Treatment of Hyponatremic Disorders

Hyponatremic disorders should be considered in any patient experiencing acute mental status changes. The history may indicate excessive water or diminished sodium intake. The physical examination can be most useful in detecting patients with a reduced effective circulating volume despite total volume excess. The most difficult differential diagnosis among hyponatremic disorders involves the distinction between patients who are modestly volume-contracted and those who have SIADH. In both instances, the urine osmolality

TABLE 26–6. CAUSES OF SIADH

Central Nervous System Disorders
 Trauma
 Infection
 Tumors
 Porphyria
Pulmonary Disorders
 Tuberculosis
 Pneumonia
 Positive-pressure ventilation
Neoplasia
 Carcinoma: bronchogenic, pancreatic, ureteral, prostatic, bladder
 Lymphoma and leukemia
 Thymoma and mesothelioma

Adapted from Andreoli TE: Disorders of fluid volume, electrolyte, and acid-base balance. In Wyngaarden JB, Smith LH Jr, Bennett JC (eds): Cecil Textbook of Medicine. 19th ed. Philadelphia, WB Saunders Co, 1992, p 509.

may be inappropriately concentrated relative to the serum osmolality. If the volume depletion is secondary to extrarenal losses, the urine sodium concentration is negligible, whereas it is usually greater than 30 to 35 mEq/L in patients with SIADH.

Treatment of hyponatremic disorders depends on the underlying clinical disease and the volume status of the patient. Sodium and water intake should be restricted in the volume-expanded patient. In patients with decreased ECF volume, treatment should include isotonic sodium chloride. In patients with SIADH, restriction of water intake is the mainstay of therapy, although compliance may be difficult in an uncontrolled setting. In such a case, it is reasonable to "clamp" renal sodium losses with loop diuretics. The sodium intake can then be liberalized, permitting an effective exchange of isotonic intake for hypotonic output. In emergency situations associated with severe hyponatremia and CNS dysfunction, it may be necessary to administer normal saline solutions intravenously while administering furosemide parenterally if the patient is volume-expanded. Because of the risk of inducing pulmonary edema with rapid expansion of the vascular compartment, there is little place in modern therapy for hypertonic saline solutions, except possibly in patients with both symptomatic hyponatremia and circulatory collapse.

The rate at which the sodium concentration is corrected in hyponatremic syndromes is an important consideration and should be determined by the rate at which the hyponatremia has developed. If the serum sodium concentration decreases acutely by more than 12 mEq/L/day, a rapid flux of water into cerebral tissue occurs. The resultant cerebral edema is often accompanied by severe neurologic symptoms, including seizures and coma. The edema may be so severe that it causes transtentorial herniation and death. In acute-onset hyponatremia, a rapid correction of the serum sodium concentration to 120 to 125 mEq/L is indicated. No long-term sequelae appear to follow the rapid correction of hyponatremia to these levels in this setting.

In patients with chronic hyponatremia that has developed during an interval of 48 hours or more, cerebral tissues have accommodated by decreasing the intracellular solute concentration. This reduces the severity of cerebral edema, and the symptoms of chronic hyponatremia are usually more subtle. Initial symptoms may include nausea, anorexia, muscle weakness, and cramps. As the hyponatremia worsens, the patient may become irritable, confused, and hostile. With extreme hyponatremia, gait disturbances, stupor, and seizures may occur.

Delayed neurologic deterioration and demyelinating brain lesions have been reported in chronically hyponatremic patients after rapid correction of the serum sodium concentration. The histologic lesion is central pontine myelinolysis, a condition that is often fatal. Therefore, the serum sodium concentration in such patients should be corrected at a rate of 0.5 mEq/L/hr until it reaches 120 mEq/L. At this point, the patient should be asymptomatic, and the serum sodium level can be gradually returned to normal over several days. Even if severe symptoms are present in the patient with chronic hyponatremia, the sodium concentration should be increased by only 5 to 6 mEq/L in the first few hours.

Hypernatremic Disorders

Hypertonic disorders associated with hypernatremia may occur following the acute administration of **hypertonic solutions,** such as hypertonic sodium bicarbonate during cardiac arrests. In most situations, however, hypernatremia develops as a result of inadequate ingestion of water or the inability of the kidney to conserve water adequately (Table 26–7).

Hypertonicity of the plasma is a powerful stimulus for thirst. Patients unable to sense thirst owing to diseases of the brain or patients physically unable to obtain water may develop hypernatremia. The majority of hypernatremic patients, however, manifest a primary disorder in urinary concentrating ability associated with insufficient administration of free water.

Water can be obligated in the urine in excess of electrolytes in conditions characterized by generation or administration of solutes at rates that exceed the renal capacity for excretion. This type of **osmotic diuresis** can occur in patients with hyperglycemia, following the infusion of mannitol, or in patients excreting excessive amounts of amino acids or urea. Failure to concentrate the urine can take place otherwise only if the collecting tubule is impermeable to water. **Diabetes insipidus** is a disorder in which the collecting tubule does not become water-permeable. There may be a central defect in the release of ADH or a defect in renal responsiveness to the hormone (nephrogenic).

Treatment

An increase in serum osmolality activates thirst mechanisms. If there is a readily accessible supply

TABLE 26–7. CAUSES OF HYPERNATREMIA

Impaired Thirst
  Coma
  Essential hypernatremia
Solute Diuresis
  Glycosuria
  Mannitol
  Urea
Excessive Renal Water Loss
  Central diabetes insipidus
  Nephrogenic diabetes insipidus

Adapted from Andreoli TE: Disorders of fluid volume, electrolyte, and acid-base balance. In Wyngaarden JB, Smith LH Jr, Bennett JC (eds): Cecil Textbook of Medicine. 19th ed. Philadelphia, WB Saunders Co, 1992, p 512.

of water, ingestion of water maintains balance. If water is not accessible or if a lower urinary output is desired, attempts may be made to re-establish a concentrated urine. In patients with central diabetes insipidus, exogenous ADH may be provided. The hormone is not useful in patients with nephrogenic diabetes insipidus. In this condition, a reduction in sodium intake and administration of a thiazide diuretic may induce a degree of volume depletion and an associated increase in the reabsorption of filtrate in the proximal tubule. The decrease in the quantity of filtrate presented to the distal diluting nephron segments results in a decrease in the urine flow rate. This therapeutic strategy may provide symptomatic relief to a patient with nephrogenic diabetes insipidus.

As is the case in hyponatremic patients, the rate of correction of hypernatremia is important. With chronic hypernatremia (i.e., longer than 36 to 48 hours in duration), the brain generates compounds that raise the intracellular osmolality, minimizing cell shrinkage. These osmoles are not dissipated rapidly. Rapid correction of the plasma osmolality, therefore, may lead to a shift of water to the relatively hypertonic intracellular compartment. Tissue swelling, particularly intracranially, may lead to fatal complications. Thus, in chronic hypernatremia, the plasma concentration of sodium should not be reduced by more than 1 mEq/L every 2 hours. If the hypernatremic patient is also volume-depleted, use of isotonic saline solutions is appropriate. If sodium-free glucose solutions are used, glycosuria may hinder correction of the hyperosmolality.

DISTURBANCES IN POTASSIUM BALANCE

The human body contains approximately 3500 mEq of potassium. With a normal concentration of 3.5 to 5.0 mEq/L, the ECF contains approximately 70 mEq of potassium, or only 2 per cent of total-body stores. Although the extracellular potassium fraction is minor, the ratio of extracellular to intracellular potassium establishes the resting membrane potential of cells. Several factors regulate the distribution of potassium between the extracellular and intracellular fluid compartments.

A variety of hormones affect this distribution. Insulin promotes the cellular uptake of potassium. The adrenal hormones, particularly aldosterone, affect the tissue distribution as well as regulate the renal excretion of potassium. The catecholamines, particularly epinephrine, cause movement of potassium into cells. This effect is mediated by beta-adrenergic receptors and is blocked by beta-adrenergic antagonists.

The acid-base status of the patient is another determinant of the serum concentration of potassium. In general, acidosis increases whereas alkalosis decreases the serum concentration of potassium. The association between the acid-base status and the serum concentration of potassium has been presumed to represent an exchange of potassium for hydrogen ions (H^+) in order to maintain electroneutrality. Consequently, in acidotic states, H^+ move down a concentration gradient into the cell in exchange for an outward flux of potassium. The duration of an acidosis, the principal mechanism (respiratory or metabolic), and the associated anions appear to be important variables in determining the magnitude of the potassium flux. The greatest effect on the serum potassium concentration is associated with metabolic acidosis involving mineral acids. The cellular permeability to the anions of the mineral acids is low, so that H^+ move relatively unaccompanied into the cell. By contrast, metabolic acidosis caused by organic acids, such as lactic acid and ketoacids, does not cause hyperkalemia. The anions of these acids are relatively permeable and accompany H^+ into the cell. This diminishes the electrochemical gradient favoring potassium efflux.

Although these mechanisms affect the distribution of potassium between the fluid compartments, other mechanisms are necessary to maintain overall potassium balance. Humans ingest approximately 100 mEq of potassium daily. About 10 per cent of this load is eliminated by the gastrointestinal tract. The remainder is excreted by the kidney. The glomerulus normally filters 700 mEq of potassium daily. There is a net absorption of potassium in the proximal tubule and loop of Henle so that only approximately 10 per cent of the filtered load is delivered to the distal nephron. In states of total-body potassium depletion, the distal nephron can reabsorb potassium. In the absence of potassium depletion, the distal nephron secretes potassium.

The mechanism for distal tubular potassium secretion is described in detail in Chapter 24. The basic mechanism involves movement of intracellular potassium from the principal cell into the tubular lumen down an electrochemical gradient. Factors that enhance this gradient thus promote potassium secretion. These factors include the rate of distal tubular flow, the distal delivery of sodium, the presence of poorly resorbable anions in the tubular fluid, and stimulation by aldosterone.

Hyperkalemia

The major causes of hyperkalemia are outlined in Table 26–8. Vigorous phlebotomy techniques can result in lysis of red blood cells, releasing intracellular potassium into the serum sample. Thrombocytosis and leukocytosis may also be associated with factitious elevations in the serum concentration of potassium. Potassium may diffuse from these excessive cellular elements in vitro. These "pseudohyperkalemic" disorders can be diagnosed rapidly by determining the plasma and serum concentrations of potassium. True hyperkalemia is present if these values differ by 0.2 mEq/L or less.

Pseudohyperkalemia
Vigorous phlebotomy
Thrombocytosis
Leukocytosis
Transcellular Shifts
Acidosis
Cell disruption
Hemolysis
Rhabdomyolysis
Trauma
Hyperkalemic periodic paralysis
Hyperosmolar disorders
Diminished Renal Excretion
Reduced glomerular filtration rate
Decreased secretion
Addison's disease
Hyporeninemic hypoaldosteronism
Aldosterone inhibitors
Primary tubular defects
Sickle cell disease
Systemic lupus erythematosus
Amyloidosis
Postrenal transplant

Adapted from Andreoli TE: Disorders of fluid volume, electrolyte, and acid-base balance. In Wyngaarden JB, Smith LH Jr, Bennett JC (eds): Cecil Textbook of Medicine. 19th ed. Philadelphia, WB Saunders Co, 1992, p 518.

Causes of True Hyperkalemia

The kidney is normally capable of excreting large loads of potassium. True hyperkalemia therefore indicates acute entrance of a large quantity of potassium into the intravascular space or decreased renal capacity for potassium excretion.

Elevations of the serum concentration of potassium can occur whenever there is an **excess flux** of potassium from the intracellular fluid compartment. This can occur from cell lysis with release of intracellular potassium or from a shift out of intact cells. The adaptive capacity of the nephron generally allows adequate excretion of potassium until the glomerular filtration rate diminishes to values lower than 15 to 20 ml/min. Hyperkalemia can result from defects in the **aldosterone-dependent secretory** mechanism in the kidney. This can occur with either a primary or a functional deficiency of the hormone. A primary defect in tubular potassium secretion has been associated with particular systemic diseases.

Clinical Features of Hyperkalemia

The ratio of the intracellular to extracellular potassium concentration is a major determinant of the resting potential of the cell membrane. As the extracellular potassium concentration increases, the cell membrane is partially depolarized, the sodium permeability is diminished, and the ability to generate action potentials is decreased. In muscle tissue, this accounts for muscle weakness and paralysis. In the heart, hyperkalemia is manifest as changes in the electrocardiogram (ECG) (Fig. 26-4).

Treatment of hyperkalemia depends on the urgency of the clinical findings. If cardiac standstill is imminent, the most rapid method of reversing the effects of hyperkalemia is to re-establish the normal membrane potential. Divalent cations, such as calcium, antagonize the membrane effects of hyperkalemia and can provide rapid protection of the cardiac conduction system. This protection, however, is short-lived and must be accompanied by other therapies to decrease the extracellular potassium concentration. Redistribution of potassium into the intracellular compartment by administration of sodium bicarbonate, beta-adrenergic agonists, or insulin rapidly decreases the serum concentration of potassium.

The ultimate goal of the treatment of hyperkalemia is to effect the net removal of potassium from the body. Exchange resins, such as sodium polystyrene sulfonate, can enhance potassium excretion from the gastrointestinal tract. Attempts can be made to enhance renal excretion by improving the distal delivery of sodium utilizing infusions of sodium and the administration of loop diuretics. Finally, dialysis can be used to remove excess ex-

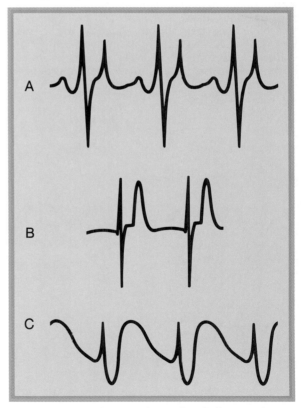

FIGURE 26-4. Electrocardiographic findings in hyperkalemia. The initial variation from the normal complex is tall, peaked T waves (A). This is followed by a decrease in amplitude of the P waves and widening of the QRS complex. The P waves disappear as the PR interval widens (B). The final change is a blending of the QRS complex into the T waves, forming the classic sine wave pattern (C).

tracellular potassium. For long-term chronic management of patients with an aldosterone deficiency or patients with a relative tubular insensitivity to the action of aldosterone, an oral preparation of a mineralocorticoid is available.

Hypokalemia

A schema for assessing a patient with a low serum potassium concentration is outlined in Figure 26–5. Because only 2 per cent of the total body potassium is distributed in the extracellular compartment, serum potassium measurements may not accurately reflect the total-body stores. In fact, hypokalemia can occur in the presence of normal total-body potassium stores. This occurs when potassium is shifted into the intracellular compartment. Acute alkalosis, an unusual familial disorder of periodic paralysis, and injections of vitamin B_{12} or insulin can cause a shift of potassium from extracellular to intracellular compartments.

True potassium deficiency with resultant hypokalemia can be caused by inadequate intake, excessive gastrointestinal losses, or inappropriate renal losses. The colon is capable of secreting potassium, and losses of potassium from the lower gastrointestinal tract due to diarrhea can be massive.

Renal losses of potassium are attributable to abnormalities in the potassium secretory mechanism

of the distal nephron. Excessive mineralocorticoid activity enhances potassium secretion and is generally associated with a metabolic alkalosis. Primary aldosteronism or Cushing's syndrome may be associated with hypokalemia. These disorders of steroid excess are usually accompanied by volume expansion and subsequent hypertension.

Secondary hyperaldosteronism occurs with disorders of volume depletion, which lead to stimulation of the renin-angiotensin system. If the volume losses occur by extrarenal mechanisms, the urinary chloride excretion is diminished. Such "chloride depletion" is observed with excessive gastrointestinal losses by vomiting, gastric suction, or chloride-losing diarrhea. Cystic fibrosis is associated with extrarenal chloride and fluid volume losses. Inadequate chloride content in nutritional formulas can lead to neonatal chloride depletion.

Volume depletion with subsequent renin secretion can also occur as a result of defective renal tubular solute reabsorption. The urinary chloride concentration in this setting is inappropriately increased. This occurs most commonly with the use of diuretics that act primarily to inhibit sodium chloride absorption at the loop of Henle or distal tubule. A rare defect of renal tubular chloride absorption termed Bartter's syndrome is associated with secondary hyperaldosteronism and profound hypokalemia. An increased distal delivery of sodium chloride in Bartter's syndrome further enhances potassium secretion.

The delivery of excessive anionic compounds to the distal nephron increases the luminal negative

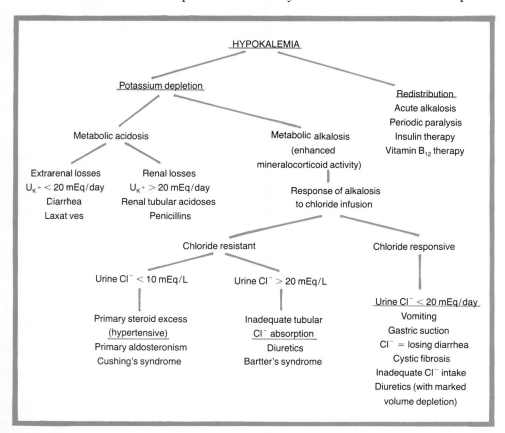

FIGURE 26–5. Pathophysiologic approach to hypokalemia.

potential difference, creating a more favorable electrical gradient for potassium secretion. Administration of penicillins, which are generally prepared as sodium salts, can lead to hypokalemia by this mechanism. In proximal or distal gradient-limited renal tubular acidosis, inadequate buffering of bicarbonate or titratable bases facilitates potassium secretion.

Manifestations and Treatment of Hypokalemia

Because potassium is the most abundant intracellular cation, its deficiency results in a wide variety of defects. A variety of metabolic processes, including protein metabolism, are affected. Carbohydrate metabolism may also be altered. The most prominent cardiovascular abnormality associated with hypokalemia is a change in the ECG. Typically, hypokalemia is associated with flattening of the T waves and the development of U waves. The most urgent abnormality is an association with arrhythmias, particularly in patients receiving digitalis. Rhabdomyolysis has been associated with hypokalemia, particularly in response to muscle exertion as induced by exercise or seizures. Hypokalemia stimulates thirst. Finally, hypokalemia can cause nephrogenic diabetes insipidus.

The treatment of hypokalemia depends on the total-body potassium status. Given the factors that determine transmembrane potassium shifts, it may be difficult to determine the net potassium deficit. An estimate for a 70-kg man based on the serum concentration is a 100 to 200 mEq decrease in total-body potassium when the serum concentration decreases from 4 to 3 mEq/L. Below 3 mEq/L, every 1 mEq/L decrease in the serum concentration of potassium reflects an additional 200 to 400 mEq deficit in total-body potassium. A general guideline is to infuse potassium at rates no greater than 20 mEq/hr. More rapid infusion rates should be undertaken only with monitoring of the ECG.

DISTURBANCES IN ACID-BASE BALANCE

Most metabolic processes occurring in the body result in the production of acids. The largest source of endogenous acid production is from the catabolism of glucose and fatty acids to carbon dioxide and water or effectively carbonic acid. The average daily production of water by this metabolic process is approximately 400 ml, or 22,000 mmol. Thus, the rate of volatile acid production is about 22,000 mEq of H^+ daily. Cellular metabolism of sulfur-containing amino acids, the oxidation of phosphoproteins and phospholipids, nucleoprotein degradation, and the incomplete combustion of carbohydrates and fatty acids also result in the formation of a number of nonvolatile acids. Approximately 1 mEq/kg body weight of H^+ is produced by these processes daily.

The normal concentration of H^- in arterial blood is 40 nEq/L, equating to a pH of 7.40. This con-

centration is maintained relatively constant despite variations in the endogenous and exogenous acid input. An acid load is acutely neutralized by circulating and intracellular buffers. The capacity of these buffering systems is limited, however, and would be quickly depleted by the normal daily endogenous acid production. Mechanisms for excreting acid must therefore be effective in order to maintain acid-base homeostasis.

Volatile acid is effectively eliminated by the lungs. Pulmonary ventilation excretes the carbon dioxide formed by cellular respiration. The primary factors normally regulating alterations in the rate of minute ventilation are subtle changes in cerebrospinal fluid pH or arterial pH. Nonvolatile acid excretion is effected through the kidneys.

Renal Hydrogen Ion Excretion

The kidney contributes to acid-base homeostasis by the reclamation of the 4500 mEq of bicarbonate filtered at the glomerulus daily and by the generation of new bicarbonate that replenishes the body buffer stores. These functions are accomplished by the secretion of H^+ by various nephron segments (Fig. 26–6).

The bulk of this filtered bicarbonate is reabsorbed in the proximal tubule. The rate of proximal bicarbonate reabsorption is increased by ECF volume depletion; by an elevation in the P_{CO_2}, as seen in chronic respiratory acidosis; and by hypokalemia. Conversely, ECF volume expansion or a reduction of the P_{CO_2} lowers the proximal tubular resorptive rate for bicarbonate.

The distal tubule is responsible for reclaiming the remainder of the filtered bicarbonate. This segment must also eliminate H^+ quantitatively equivalent to the nonvolatile acid production. The H^+ excretion is accomplished by secretion into the tubular fluid. The inorganic bases of nonvolatile acid production, such as phosphates, are filtered at the glomerulus and are poorly reabsorbed by the nephron. These "fixed" bases as well as ammonia produced by proximal tubular cells can effectively trap the secreted H^+ in the tubular fluid for elimination in the urine. Aldosterone and the P_{CO_2} affect the distal secretion of H^+.

Assessment of Acid-Base Status

The initial step in evaluating acid-base problems is to obtain an arterial blood gas measurement and the serum electrolyte concentrations (Fig. 26–7). The arterial blood gas measures the pH, P_{O_2}, and P_{CO_2}. The bicarbonate concentration is then calculated using the Henderson-Hasselbalch equation, which relates the pH directly to the bicarbonate concentration and inversely to the P_{CO_2}. Because there is little soluble CO_2 in serum, the total CO_2 obtained with the serum electrolytes is effectively a measure of the serum bicarbonate concentration. This measured value should differ

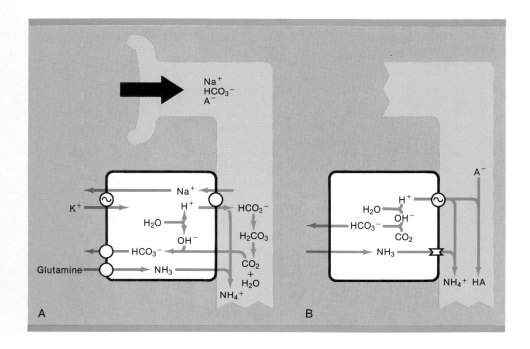

FIGURE 26–6. Renal mechanisms for hydrogen ion secretion. The proximal tubule (A) is responsible for the bulk reabsorption of filtered bicarbonate. The distal nephron hydrogen ion secretion (B) is responsible for reclaiming additional bicarbonate as well as titrating inorganic anions (A⁻).

from that calculated on a concomitant blood gas determination by no more than 2 mEq/L. The validity of the blood gas determination can be estimated further by applying the bicarbonate concentration and the measured P_{CO_2} to the Henderson-Hasselbalch equation:

$$[H^+] = \frac{24 \times P_{CO_2}}{[HCO_3^-]}$$

The normal concentration of H^+ is 40 mEq/L. Within narrow limits, a 0.01 change in the pH is equivalent to a change in the $[H^+]$ of 1 mEq/L. Thus, if the P_{CO_2} measured 50 mm Hg in an arterial blood sample and the serum bicarbonate concentration was 24 mEq/L, the H^+ concentration would be calculated as 50 mEq/L. This 10 mEq/L increase above the normal concentration would estimate a decrease in the arterial blood pH of 0.1, yielding a value of 7.30.

Another important step in assessing acid-base homeostasis is the calculation of the anion gap. Sodium is the most prevalent cation in the ECF compartment. To maintain electroneutrality, anionic compounds, most notably chloride and bicarbonate, must be present in this fluid. The difference between the serum sodium and the sum of the chloride and bicarbonate concentrations is termed the anion gap. This value is normally 12 ± 2 mEq/L and is composed of negatively charged proteins, inorganic anions such as phosphates and sulfates, and organic anions such as lactate.

Any primary defect in the respiratory or metabolic regulation of acid-base homeostasis is normally countered by the alternate regulatory system. For example, when a metabolic acidosis (characterized by a decrease in the pH due to a reduced serum bicarbonate concentration) is present, compensatory hyperventilation occurs in order to reduce the P_{CO_2}, which increases the pH toward normal. There are two important features of compensatory mechanisms. First, the compensation is never complete. Any overcompensation, therefore, indicates combined defects. Second, volatile acid excretion is quantitatively much larger than the capacity for renal bicarbonate regeneration. Respiratory compensation of a primary metabolic defect therefore occurs much more rapidly than renal compensation of a primary respiratory defect. The acuity of the respiratory disorder must be considered when estimating the compensatory response by the kidney.

If the compensation of a primary acid-base defect is inappropriate, a mixed acid-base disorder is considered. Mixed respiratory and metabolic disorders can be discerned by calculating the expected compensatory response. A mixed metabolic disorder can occur when a metabolic acidosis occurs in the setting of a pre-existing metabolic alkalosis. For example, when an organic acid (such as lactic acid) is added to the ECF compartment, the bicarbonate concentration falls as the acid is buffered. The anion gap increases as the organic base is accumulated. Quantitatively, the increase in the anion gap should be equivalent to the decrease in the bicarbonate concentration. Thus, by adding the difference between the calculated and the normal anion gap to the prevailing bicarbonate concentration, an estimate of the "starting" bicarbonate concentration can be made. An abnormally elevated initial bicarbonate indicates an underlying metabolic alkalosis.

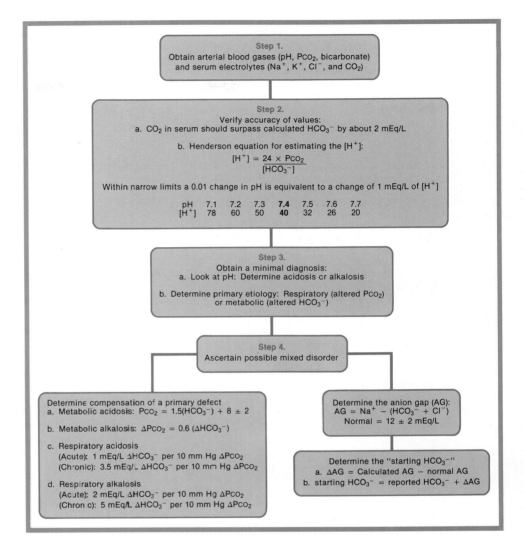

FIGURE 26-7. Scheme for assessing acid-base homeostasis.

Metabolic Acidosis

A metabolic acidosis is characterized by a decrease in the serum bicarbonate concentration. This occurs either by excretion of bicarbonate-containing fluids or by utilization of bicarbonate as a buffer of acids. In the latter instance, the nature of the base pair may affect the electrolyte composition. It is thus convenient to consider the metabolic acidoses by means of the anion gap (Table 26-9).

Normal Anion Gap Acidosis

The metabolic acidoses have a normal anion gap whenever there are abnormally large net bicarbonate losses. This may occur because the kidneys fail to reabsorb or regenerate bicarbonate, because there are extrarenal losses of bicarbonate, or because excessive amounts of substances yielding hydrochloric acid have been administered.

The failure of the kidney to reabsorb bicarbonate occurs in the setting of proximal renal tubular acidosis, carbonic anhydrase inhibitor administration, or hyperparathyroidism. The inability to regenerate adequate quantities of bicarbonate is referable to distal renal tubular defects. This can occur because of a primary tubular defect (distal gradient limited renal tubular acidosis), absolute aldosterone deficiency, or aldosterone insensitivity. Extrarenal bicarbonate losses are most often due to diarrheal disorders or ileal drainage. Finally, hyperchloremic acidosis occurs with the administration of acidifying salts.

The urinary anion gap, defined as

$$\text{Urinary anion gap} = (Na^+ + K^+) - Cl^-$$

is useful in evaluating patients with hyperchloremic acidosis. The test provides an approximate index of urinary NH_4^+ excretion, as measured by a negative urinary anion gap. Thus, in hyperchloremic metabolic acidosis, a normal renal response

TABLE 26–9. CAUSES OF METABOLIC ACIDOSIS

Normal Anion Gap
  Bicarbonate losses
    Extrarenal
      Small bowel drainage
      Diarrhea
    Renal
      Proximal renal tubular acidosis
      Carbonic anhydrase inhibitors
      Primary hyperparathyroidism
  Failure of bicarbonate regeneration
    Distal renal tubular acidosis
    Aldosterone deficiency
      Addison's disease
      Hyporeninemic hypoaldosteronism
    Aldosterone insensitivity
      Interstitial renal disease
      Aldosterone antagonists
  Acidifying salts
    Ammonium chloride
    Lysine or arginine hydrochloride
Wide Anion Gap
  Reduced excretion of acids
    Renal failure
  Overproduction of acids
    Ketoacidosis
      Diabetic
      Alcoholic
      Starvation
    Lactic acidosis
    Toxin ingestion
      Methanol
      Ethylene glycol
      Salicylates

Adapted from Andreoli TE: Disorders of fluid volume, electrolyte, and acid-base balance. In Wyngaarden JB, Smith LH Jr, Bennett JC (eds): Cecil Textbook of Medicine. 19th ed. Philadelphia, WB Saunders Co, 1992, p 523.

would be a negative urinary anion gap, generally in the range of 30 to 50 mEq/L. In such an instance, it is likely that the hyperchloremic acidosis is due to gastrointestinal losses rather than a renal lesion.

The urinary response to oral furosemide loading is another useful test for evaluating tubular acidifying capability. The rationale for the test is that in normal individuals blockade of sodium absorption in diluting segments by furosemide increases sodium delivery to distal nephron segments where potassium and protons are secreted and increases the rate of excretion of these cations. Consequently, the oral administration of 40 to 80 mg of furosemide should be followed by an increase in urinary sodium excretion, an increase in urinary potassium excretion, and a reduction in urinary pH. In some renal tubular acidosis syndromes, proton and/or potassium excretion is impaired (Table 26–10).

Wide Anion Gap Acidosis

A wide anion gap acidosis is observed with the administration of non–chloride-based acids. The elevation of the anion gap occurs when the excretion of the base pair is reduced relative to the rate of acid infusion. This group of acidoses can be considered from the standpoint of the nature of the base.

In general, renal failure is associated with an accumulation of all base pairs. The inorganic compounds (phosphates and sulfates), however, are the major contributors to the increased anion gap. Organic compounds also accumulate with diminished renal function. The rate of organic acid production, however, may increase to levels that surpass the normal renal capacity for excretion of the organic base. Ketoacidosis results from accelerated lipolysis and ketogenesis due to a relative insulin insufficiency. This can occur in the diabetic who has an absolute deficiency in insulin production. Alcoholic ketosis and starvation ketosis result from suppression of endogenous insulin secretion due to inadequate carbohydrate ingestion.

The syndrome of lactic acidosis results from impaired cellular respiration. Lactate is produced from the reduction of pyruvate in muscle, red blood cells, and other tissues as a consequence of anaerobic glycolysis. In situations of diminished oxidative metabolism, excess lactic acid is produced. This anaerobic state also favors the shift of the ketoacids to the reduced form, beta-hydroxybutyrate. The nitroprusside reaction, which is catalyzed by the ketoacids acetoacetate and acetone, is thus nonreactive in the setting of lactic acidosis. Lactic acidosis occurs most commonly in disorders characterized by inadequate oxygen delivery to tissues, such as shock, septicemia, and profound hypoxemia.

Certain toxins may also sufficiently alter mitochondrial function, establishing an effective anaerobic state. Some of these toxins may undergo metabolism into organic acids that can contribute to the generation of a large anion gap acidosis. Methanol is metabolized by alcohol dehydrogenase to formic acid. Ethylene glycol is metabolized to glycolic and oxalic acids. Salicylates are themselves acidic compounds and can cause a wide anion gap acidosis.

Treatment

The treatment of metabolic acidosis depends on the underlying cause, the severity of the manifestations, and the acuity of onset. The rapid administration of parenteral sodium bicarbonate is indicated when the pH is less than 7.1, hemodynamic instability is evident, and the acidosis is due to extrarenal loss of bicarbonate or the kidney is unable to regenerate bicarbonate adequately. This base can be provided as bicarbonate or as salts containing an organic base such as citrate. The metabolism of these organic bases effectively regenerates bicarbonate.

Disorders of renal bicarbonate loss are characterized by an alteration in the proximal tubular threshold for bicarbonate absorption. Administered bicarbonate, therefore, is rapidly excreted. The correction of the acidosis is directed at altering this proximal tubular threshold. Because volume depletion increases proximal tubular bicarbonate reabsorption, diuretics can be administered to induce a state of mild volume depletion and partially correct the pH in proximal renal tubular acidosis.

The treatment of the organic acidoses should be directed at the underlying disorder. If the generation of the organic acid can be interrupted, the organic base pair may be metabolized, effectively yielding bicarbonate regeneration. The acidemia of diabetic ketoacidosis, for example, can be effectively treated by administration of insulin, thereby inhibiting further ketogenesis. As the excessive ketones are eliminated, the serum bicarbonate concentration increases. If bicarbonate is administered in the organic acidoses, the regeneration of additional bicarbonate as the organic base is metabolized may actually result in an overshoot phenomenon yielding a marked alkalosis.

In lactic acidosis, therapy should be directed toward improving tissue perfusion. The response to alkali therapy is not predictable. In experimental lactic acidosis, bicarbonate therapy worsens the disorder by increasing the rate of splanchnic lactate production. Sodium dichloroacetate can prevent or reverse hyperlactatemia by stimulating the activity of pyruvate dehydrogenase, the mitochondrial enzyme that catalyzes the rate-limiting step in the aerobic oxidation of pyruvate and lactate.

Metabolic Alkalosis

The administration of base or the effective removal of H^+ increases the bicarbonate concentration of the ECF. Normally an elevation of the serum bicarbonate concentration is corrected by excretion of the excess bicarbonate. The maintenance of a metabolic alkalosis, therefore, implies a defect in the renal mechanism regulating bicarbonate excretion, namely, the proximal tubular bicarbonate absorption. Elevation of the P_{CO_2}, hypokalemia, or volume depletion increases the proximal tubular bicarbonate absorption and can sustain a metabolic alkalosis.

Causes of Metabolic Alkalosis

The most common cause of metabolic alkalosis is gastric loss of hydrochloric acid by vomiting or mechanical drainage. Excessive delivery of sodium to distal tubular acidifying sites can induce acid

secretion. Diuretic use can therefore generate a metabolic alkalosis. The volume depletion associated with these defects enhances proximal bicarbonate resorption. Volume depletion leads to aldosterone secretion, which stimulates distal tubular H^+ secretion. Potassium secretion is likewise stimulated. The resulting hypokalemia further contributes to sustaining the alkalosis.

The renal compensation for sustained hypercapnia results in an increase in the serum bicarbonate concentration. If the ventilatory rate acutely increases, the P_{CO_2} falls rapidly, but the bicarbonate concentration remains transiently elevated, resulting in a posthypercapnic alkalosis. As noted above, the administration of bicarbonate in a setting of organic acidosis may result in alkalosis when the organic base pair is metabolized.

Manifestations and Treatment

Severe metabolic alkalosis can cause cardiac arrhythmias. Hypoventilation can result from severe alkalosis, particularly in patients with renal insufficiency. The seizure threshold is reduced with alkalosis.

The correction of metabolic alkalosis is directed at re-establishing the normal proximal tubular bicarbonate threshold. This is usually accomplished with volume expansion. Occasionally, the alkalosis does not correct with volume expansion. The urine electrolytes may assist with determining the response to volume administration. A low urinary sodium concentration is usually reliable in determining ECF volume depletion. During the generation or early correction of metabolic alkalosis, however, bicarbonaturia may lead to an obligatory natriuresis. The urine chloride concentration remains low in this instance. An elevated urine chloride concentration is indicative of a chloride (volume)-resistant alkalosis that responds to administration of potassium.

Respiratory Acidosis

Respiratory acidosis occurs with any impairment in the rate of alveolar ventilation. Acute respiratory acidosis occurs with a sudden depression of the medullary respiratory center (narcotic overdose), with paralysis of the respiratory muscles,

TABLE 26–10. CHARACTERISTICS OF DISTAL RENAL TUBULAR ACIDOSIS (RTA) SYNDROMES

CONDITION	URINE pH	SERUM K^+	URINARY ANION GAP	RESPONSE TO FUROSEMIDE		ALDOSTERONE SECRETION
				URINE pH	URINE K^+	
Gradient-limited RTA	>5.5	↓	Positive	Unchanged	↑	Normal
Hyporeninemic hypoaldosteronism	<5.5	↑	Positive	↓	↑	Reduced
Voltage-dependent RTA	>5.5	↑	Positive	Unchanged	Unchanged	Normal

Adapted from Andreoli TE: Disorders of fluid volume, electrolyte, and acid-base balance. In Wyngaarden JB, Smith LH Jr, Bennett JC (eds): Cecil Textbook of Medicine. 19th ed. Philadelphia, WB Saunders Co, 1992, p 523.

and with airway obstruction. Chronic respiratory acidosis generally occurs in individuals with chronic airways disease (emphysema), with extreme kyphoscoliosis, and with extreme obesity (pickwickian syndrome).

The serum bicarbonate concentration is increased, the magnitude of which depends upon the acuity of the respiratory disorder. Acute increases in the PCO_2 result in somnolence, confusion, and ultimately CO_2 narcosis. Asterixis may be present. Because CO_2 is a cerebral vasodilator, the blood vessels in the optic fundi are often dilated, engorged, and tortuous. Frank papilledema may be present in severe hypercapnic states.

The only practical treatment for acute respiratory acidosis involves treatment of the underlying disorder and ventilatory support. In patients with chronic hypercapnia who develop an acute increase in the PCO_2, attention should be directed toward identifying factors that may have aggravated the chronic disorder. Alkalinizing salts should be avoided in patients with chronic respiratory acidosis.

Respiratory Alkalosis

Respiratory alkalosis occurs when hyperventilation reduces the arterial PCO_2 and consequently increases the arterial pH. Acute respiratory alkalosis is most commonly the result of the hyperventilation syndrome. It may also occur in damage of the respiratory centers, in acute salicylism, in fever and septic states, and in association with various pulmonary processes (pneumonia, pulmonary emboli, or congestive heart failure). The disorder may also be produced iatrogenically by injudicious mechanical ventilatory support. Chronic hyperventilation occurs in the acclimatization response to high altitudes (a low ambient oxygen tension), in advanced hepatic insufficiency, and in pregnancy.

Acute hyperventilation is characterized by lightheadedness, paresthesias, circumoral numbness, and tingling of the extremities. Tetany occurs in severe cases. When anxiety provokes hyperventilation, air rebreathing with a paper bag generally terminates the acute attack.

REFERENCES

Andreoli TE: Disorders of fluid volume, electrolyte, and acid-base balance. In Wyngaarden JB, Smith LH Jr, Bennett JC (eds): Cecil Textbook of Medicine. 19th ed. Philadelphia, WB Saunders Co, 1992, pp 499–528.

Gabow PA: Disorders associated with an altered anion gap. Kidney Int 27:472, 1985.

Laragh JH, Atlas SA: Atrial natriuretic hormone: A regulator of blood pressure and volume homeostasis. Kidney Int 34(Suppl 25):S64, 1988.

Stein JH, Kunau RT (eds): Diuretics II: Clinical uses. Semin Nephrol 8:317, 1988.

Thompson CS, Andreoli TE: Hyponatremia and hypernatremia. In Callaham ML (ed): Decision Making in Emergency Medicine. Philadelphia, BC Decker, 1990, pp 172–175.

Zull DN: Disorders of potassium metabolism. Emerg Med Clin North Am 7:771, 1989.

27 GLOMERULAR DISEASES

THE GLOMERULUS

The glomerulus consists of a capillary bed that receives blood from the afferent arteriole and is drained by the efferent arteriole and contains four different cell types: the glomerular (visceral) epithelial cell (podocyte), the endothelial cell, the mesangial cell, and the parietal epithelial cell (Fig. 27–1). The podocyte supports the delicate glomerular basement membrane (GBM) by means of an extensive trabecular network. The mesangium provides a skeletal framework for the entire capillary network and, owing to its contractile capability, can control blood flow along the glomerular capillaries in response to a host of mediators. The endothelial cells line the capillary lumen, and the parietal epithelial cells cover Bowman's capsule.

MECHANISMS OF GLOMERULAR INJURY

Immunologic mechanisms play a major role in glomerular injury and consist primarily of two types (Table 27–1). Occasionally, antibodies to the GBM develop, resulting in a glomerulonephritis (GN) characterized by linear deposition of IgG along the capillary walls. Much more frequently, discrete deposition of granular deposits of immunoglobulins and complement is seen. These immunoglobulins, together with their respective circulating antigens, may be deposited in the GBM. Alternatively, antigens may localize individually to the GBM, and there may occur in situ activation of antigen-antibody complexes. In both instances, the antigen-antibody complex localization in the GBM initiates the cascade of glomerular injury. Such deposits may be seen in the mesangium, along the subendothelial surface of the GBM, or within the outer region of the capillary wall in the subepithelial space.

Other glomerular diseases occur in which immunologic mechanisms are thought to play a role but no deposits are detectable. Minimal change nephrotic syndrome, now thought to be a disorder of the glomerular epithelial cell, may be due to non–complement-fixing anti–glomerular epithelial cell antibodies. Idiopathic crescentic GN (anti-GBM antibodies are absent) is possibly mediated by either mononuclear cell-mediated immune reactions, induction of endothelial leukocyte adhesion molecules (ELAM) on endothelium, or anti-neutrophil cytoplasmic antibody (ANCA)–mediated local neutrophil activation.

Neutrophil infiltration in response to immune complex–complement interaction, ELAM induction, or the presence of ANCA can lead to glomerular injury through the release of proteolytic enzymes and/or reactive oxygen metabolites. Other circulating cells have been suggested to play a role in glomerular injury. Platelets may be important in various forms of glomerular injury and are particularly important in mesangial proliferative lesions. Macrophages in concert with activated lymphocytes are likely important in antibody-independent, cell-mediated glomerular injury. The glomerular cells themselves may be activated to produce oxidants and/or proteases with subsequent damage to either the GBM or the mesangium. Finally, in other disorders such as diabetes or amyloidosis, the glomerular injury may be secondary to metabolic imbalances.

CLINICAL MANIFESTATIONS OF GLOMERULAR DISEASE

The usual initial manifestations of glomerular disease are often nonspecific generalized complaints (hypertension, edema, malaise) or urinary abnormalities (proteinuria, hematuria). Altered glomer-

TABLE 27–1. MEDIATORS OF GLOMERULAR INJURY

Immunologic Mechanisms
  Antigen-antibody complexes
  Anti–basement membrane antibodies
  Antibodies directed against glomerular components
    Anti-glomerular epithelial cell antibodies
  Complement activation
Cell Sensitization (Activation) with Oxidant/Protease Release
  Neutrophils
  Macrophages
  Platelets
  Mesangial cells

ular function, either proteinuria consequent to changes in GBM permeability or decreased glomerular filtration rate (GFR) secondary to abnormal ultrafiltration, characterizes glomerular disease.

The glomerular capillaries provide a filtration barrier that prevents the passage of proteins into the urine on the basis of protein size, shape, and electrical charge. Normally, less than 150 mg of protein is excreted in the urine per day. Nephrotic-range proteinuria (>3.5 gm/day in adults) represents diffuse glomerular injury with loss of the net negative charge on the capillary wall and/or structural defects in the filtration barrier. The first causes selective proteinuria (loss of albumin but not other serum proteins), whereas the presence of structural defects results in loss of all proteins (nonselective proteinuria).

Hematuria, particularly in the form of dysmorphic red blood cells (RBCs) and RBC casts, is the hallmark of the acute nephritic syndrome. The bleeding is due to breaks or gap formation in the glomerular capillaries, with cast formation occurring as the RBCs become embedded in the concentrated tubular fluid. The presence of either RBC casts or dysmorphic RBCs in the urine characterizes bleeding from the glomerulus. Dysmorphic RBCs are best seen using phase contrast microscopy and consist of red cells of varying size, shape, and hemoglobin content.

Renal salt retention is a common feature of glomerular disease and may be expressed as edema, volume overload, congestive heart failure, and hypertension. Although the mechanisms responsible for reduced salt excretion are poorly understood, sodium acquisitiveness is considerably greater than that expected solely from the reduction in GFR. Effective management requires successful sodium restriction, particularly in nephritic patients, in whom diuretics are probably ineffective.

Severe glomerular injury leads to reduced GFR ranging from mild changes with normal serum creatinine to oliguria requiring dialysis. Glomerular injury results in decreased capillary hydrostatic pressure or decreased capillary wall permeability. Morphologic correlates include endothelial cell swelling, endocapillary proliferation with capillary occlusion, sclerosis, and glomerular scarring. In other cases, the overall glomerular architecture remains intact.

APPROACH TO THE PATIENT WITH GLOMERULAR DISEASE

Glomerular diseases have been classified in numerous ways. Here they are organized and discussed as they relate to the four major glomerular syndromes: acute nephritic syndrome, rapidly progressive GN, nephrotic syndrome (with either "bland" or "active" urine sediment), and asymptomatic urinary abnormalities (Table 27–2). The

TABLE 27–2. GLOMERULAR SYNDROMES

Acute nephritic syndrome	Nephronal hematuria (RBC casts and/or dysmorphic RBCs) temporally associated with acute renal failure
Rapidly progressive glomerulonephritis	Nephronal hematuria (RBC casts and/or dysmorphic RBCs) with renal failure developing over weeks to months and diffuse glomerular crescent formation
Nephrotic syndrome	Massive proteinuria (>3.5 gm/day/1.73 m²) with variable edema, hypoalbuminemia, hyperlipidemia, and hyperlipiduria
With "bland" sediment	"Pure" nephrotic syndrome
With "active" sediment	"Mixed" nephrotic/nephritic syndrome
Asymptomatic urinary abnormalities	Isolated proteinuria (usually <2.0 gm/day/1.73 m²) or hematuria (with or without proteinuria)

TABLE 27–3. PATHOLOGIC FEATURES OF GLOMERULAR DISEASE

Focal	Some (but not all) glomeruli contain the lesion
Diffuse (global)	Most glomeruli ($>75\%$) contain the lesion
Segmental	Only a part of the glomerulus is affected by the lesion (most focal lesions are also segmental, e.g., focal segmental glomerulosclerosis)
Proliferation	An increase in cell number due to hyperplasia of one or more of the resident glomerular cells with or without inflammatory cell infiltration
Membrane alterations	Capillary wall thickening due to deposition of immune deposits or alterations in basement membrane
Crescent formation	Epithelial cell proliferation and mononuclear cell infiltration in Bowman's space

diagnosis of glomerular diseases is based on pathologic features related to glomerular alterations. Definitions of some of the more commonly used terms are given in Table 27–3.

ACUTE NEPHRITIC SYNDROME

This syndrome is characterized by the abrupt onset (days) of hematuria with RBC casts or dysmorphic RBCs and proteinuria (usually non-nephrotic range) temporally associated with the development of hypertension and impairment of renal function. The histologic pattern is characterized by cellular proliferation (mesangial, endothelial) and inflammatory cell infiltration (neutrophils, macrophages). Table 27–4 lists the diseases commonly associated with this condition.

Poststreptococcal glomerulonephritis (PSGN) occurs as a postinfectious complication of nephritogenic strains of group A, beta-hemolytic streptococcal infection. Pharyngitis (strep throat) is a common antecedent infection in Northern states, but PSGN occurs in fewer than 5 per cent of those

infected, usually within a 5- to 20-day latent period. Streptococcal pyoderma more commonly occurs in the South and may also lead to PSGN in as many as 50 per cent of infected individuals. PSGN is the hallmark disease for the acute nephritic syndrome and is typically seen in children aged 3 to 12, although it can occur in adults. Both genders are equally affected with PSGN, which occurs more frequently in the summer and autumn in North America. The patient presents with typical acute nephritic syndrome associated with malaise, cola-colored urine, mild hypertension, periorbital edema, and non–nephrotic-range proteinuria.

Laboratory findings include RBCs and RBC casts, white blood cells, and proteinuria on urinalysis, an elevated antistreptolysin O titer (although patients with preceding pyoderma may not demonstrate this rise), a low serum complement (usually returning to normal at 6 to 12 weeks), and azotemia. Histologically, PSGN is a diffuse proliferative (mesangial and endothelial cells) and exudative (neutrophils and monocytes) GN with coarsely granular capillary loop deposits of IgG and C3 and subepithelial electron-dense humplike deposits by electron microscopy (Fig. 27–1).

The differential diagnosis is that of an acute GN with hypocomplementemia and includes other forms of postinfectious GN (e.g., bacterial endocarditis, shunt nephritis), systemic lupus erythematosus (SLE), and membranoproliferative GN. The diagnosis can usually be based on the typical renal presentation following a streptococcal infection, hypocomplementemia, and serologic evidence. Because the diagnosis is most often straightforward, a renal biopsy is indicated only if the disease follows an atypical course.

There is no specific therapy for PSGN, although antibiotics should be administered if cultures are positive for *Streptococcus*. Salt restriction and, in some cases, diuretics and antihypertensive agents may be required to manage sodium retention (manifested by hypertension, edema, congestive heart failure, and other signs). In cases of severe acute renal failure, dialysis is indicated, although most patients still recover renal function spontaneously. Complete recovery occurs in at least 85 to 90 per cent of all patients. However, minor urinary sediment abnormalities may continue for

TABLE 27–4. GLOMERULOPATHIES ASSOCIATED WITH ACUTE NEPHRITIC SYNDROME

Post-streptococcal glomerulonephritis
Nonstreptococcal postinfectious glomerulonephritis
  Staphylococcus, pneumococcus, *Legionella*, syphilis
  Mumps, varicella, hepatitis B, echovirus, Epstein-Barr virus, toxoplasmosis
  Malaria, schistosomiasis, trichinosis
Infective endocarditis
Shunt nephritis
Visceral abscess
Systemic lupus erythematosus
Henoch-Schönlein purpura
Mixed essential cryoglobulinemia

several years in some patients (<2 per cent), but progression to chronic renal failure is exceedingly rare, typically occurring only in older adults who contract the disease. Fewer than 5 per cent of patients have oliguria for more than 7 to 9 days, and the prognosis in these patients is less favorable.

Nonstreptococcal postinfectious glomerulonephritis may occur after bacterial infections (e.g., staphylococcal, pneumococcal), viral infections (e.g., mumps, hepatitis B, varicella, coxsackie, infectious mononucleosis), protozoal infection (e.g., malaria, toxoplasmosis), and a host of others (e.g., schistosomiasis, syphilis). The clinical and histologic manifestations may vary somewhat, depending on the infecting agent. Still, most have features similar to those of PSGN and an equally good prognosis if the underlying infection is eradicated.

Glomerulonephritis associated with infective endocarditis commonly occurs in patients with chronic right-sided cardiac involvement and negative blood cultures. It usually manifests itself as a mild form of the acute nephritic syndrome (hematuria and proteinuria with a mild decrease in renal function). A similar pattern may occur in patients with infected ventriculoatrial shunts **(shunt nephritis).** The histologic and immunofluorescent picture is similar to that of PSGN, although the lesions are usually more focal and segmental. Rarely, crescentic GN develops and is manifested by acute renal failure. Elimination of infection with appropriate antibiotic therapy usually results in a return of renal function to normal.

Glomerulonephritis associated with visceral abscess has been reported most frequently in patients with pulmonary abscesses. However, numerous other sites have also been reported. These patients develop the acute nephritic syndrome with a proliferative GN often showing many crescents. In contrast to PSGN, the complement levels are usually not depressed and immune deposits are usually lacking. Successful antibiotic therapy results in recovery of renal function in only 50 per cent of patients.

Systemic lupus erythematosus, Henoch-Schönlein purpura, and mixed essential cryoglobulinemia may present as an acute GN, but more typically they are associated with other glomerular syndromes and are therefore discussed below.

RAPIDLY PROGRESSIVE GLOMERULONEPHRITIS (RPGN)

RPGN is a syndrome characterized by nephronal hematuria (RBC casts and/or dysmorphic RBCs) with renal failure developing over weeks to months and diffuse glomerular crescent formation on renal biopsy (Fig. 27–1). Classification is complicated by the fact that RPGN can occur with immune deposits (either anti-GBM or immune complex type) or without immune deposits. In addition, it can be an idiopathic primary glomerular disease or can be superimposed on other glomerular diseases, either primary or secondary. The classification scheme used here is based on the

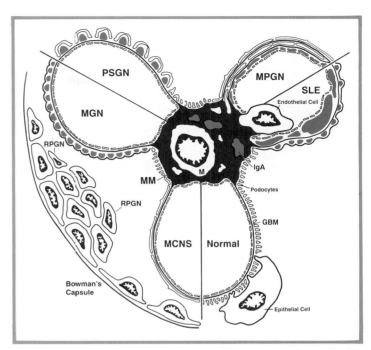

FIGURE 27–1. Schematic drawing of a glomerulus illustrating the normal features as well as several diseases. GBM = Glomerular basement membrane; IgA = IgA deposits in IgA nephropathy; M = mesangial cell; MCNS = minimal change nephrotic syndrome; MGN = membranous glomerulopathy; MM = mesangial matrix; MPGN = membrano-proliferative glomerulopathy; PSGN = post-streptococcal glomerulonephritis; RPGN = rapidly progressive glomerulonephritis; SLE = systemic lupus erythematosus.

immunofluorescence information obtained from renal biopsy (Table 27–5).

Anti-GBM GN, characterized by linear capillary loop staining with IgG and C3 and extensive crescent formation, accounts for 15 to 20 per cent of all cases of RPGN, although overall it accounts for less than 5 per cent of all forms of GN. About two thirds of these patients have Goodpasture's syndrome with associated pulmonary hemorrhage. The remainder have an idiopathic form of anti-GBM GN. Goodpasture's syndrome affects young men six times more frequently than women and usually presents with hemoptysis and dyspnea. Idiopathic anti-GBM GN is seen in older patients (above 50 years) and affects both genders equally. Anti-GBM antibodies are present in serum (detectable using indirect immunofluorescence on normal kidney); serum C3 is normal. Therapy consists of high-dose oral prednisone in concert with plasma exchange. A high index of suspicion resulting in earlier diagnosis and vigorous treatment has increased survival to more than 50 per cent, as opposed to 10 to 15 per cent a decade ago.

Immune complex RPGN is almost always associated with another underlying disease, and the correct diagnosis can usually be made by seeking the other clinical and laboratory features of these conditions. About 40 per cent of all cases of RPGN

TABLE 27–5. TYPES OF RAPIDLY PROGRESSIVE GLOMERULONEPHRITIS (RPGN)

Anti-GBM Antibody–Mediated RPGN (Linear Immunofluorescent Pattern)
  Idiopathic anti-GBM antibody–mediated RPGN
  Goodpasture's syndrome
  Associated with other primary glomerular diseases
    Membranous glomerulopathy
Immune Complex–Mediated RPGN (Granular Immunofluorescent Pattern)
  Idiopathic immune complex–mediated RPGN
  Associated with other primary glomerular diseases
    Membranoproliferative glomerulopathy (type II > type I)
    IgA nephropathy
  Associated with secondary glomerular diseases
    Postinfectious glomerulonephritides
    Systemic lupus erythematosus
    Mixed essential cryoglobulinemia
    Henoch-Schönlein purpura
Non–Immune-Mediated RPGN (Negative Immunofluorescent Pattern)
  Idiopathic pauci-immune RPGN (ANCA-associated)
  Systemic vasculitides

are of this type (granular deposits of immunoglobulins and complement). Prognosis of the underlying condition declines dramatically in the presence of immune complex RPGN, and prompt diagnosis and treatment (as described above) are required if renal function is to be preserved.

Non–immune-mediated RPGN is found in about 40 per cent of patients with crescentic GN and is seen in association with one of the systemic vasculitides such as polyarteritis nodosa or as an idiopathic form that is thought to represent a vasculitis limited to the glomerular capillaries. The idiopathic form is usually found in patients in their sixth or seventh decade, and as many as 25 per cent require dialysis at presentation. Therapy is as described above with the addition of cytotoxic agents in those patients with systemic vasculitis, ANCA, or necrotizing vasculitic lesions. About 25 per cent progress to end-stage renal disease (ESRD), some despite an excellent early response.

NEPHROTIC SYNDROME

The nephrotic syndrome is characterized by the presence of proteinuria, hypoalbuminemia, edema, hyperlipiduria, and hyperlipidemia. However, the finding of proteinuria of greater than 3.5 gm/24 hr/1.73 m^2, so-called nephrotic-range proteinuria, is sufficient for the designation of nephrotic syndrome. Table 27–6 includes the renal lesions commonly associated with the nephrotic syndrome. They are divided into diseases with or without RBC casts ("bland" or "active" urine sediment). Each of these entities may occur as a primary renal lesion or as a secondary component of a systemic disease.

Nephrotic Syndrome with "Bland" Urine Sediment

Minimal Change Nephrotic Syndrome (MCNS). This disorder is also known as nil lesion or lipoid nephrosis; more than 85 to 90 per cent of all children with nephrotic syndrome have this condition. It almost always presents as the sudden onset of the nephrotic syndrome in children aged 2 to 6 years with a male-female ratio of 2:1. In adults, MCNS accounts for only 15 to 20 per cent, with a more equal male-female ratio. As children approach teenage years and early adulthood, the incidence of MCNS as a cause of nephrotic syndrome diminishes, unless an associated hematologic neoplasm is present. An upper respiratory infection precedes the onset of disease in fully one third of the patients, but the relationship between these viral infections and MCNS is not known. There are no etiologic associations known in children with MCNS. Some adults with malignant neoplasms have developed MCNS, most commonly in association with Hodgkin's disease.

Laboratory features include those of the typical nephrotic syndrome with bland urinary sediment, normal renal function (unless there is severe volume contraction), and normal complement levels. Histologically, the light microscopy is normal (hence the term nil lesion) and no immunoglobulins or complement deposition is seen. Electron microscopy reveals effacement (fusion) of the foot processes, which is the result of the proteinuria (Fig. 27–1).

The natural course of MCNS in children includes a spontaneous remission rate in more than 40 to 50 per cent of cases. However, owing to the sensitivity of the proteinuria to steroid therapy, many patients are given a trial of 60 mg/m^2/day in children and 1.5 to 2 mg/kg/day in adults. At 4 weeks (or sooner, if remission occurs), alternate-day therapy with 35 mg/m^2 in children and 0.9 mg/kg in adults is begun and continued for 4

TABLE 27–6. GLOMERULOPATHIES ASSOCIATED WITH NEPHROTIC SYNDROME

Nephrotic-Range Proteinuria with "Bland" Urine Sediment (Pure Nephrotic)
  Primary glomerular disease
    Minimal change nephrotic syndrome (nil lesion, lipoid nephrosis)
    Membranous glomerulopathy
    Focal glomerulosclerosis
  Secondary glomerular disease
    Diabetic nephropathy (Kimmelsteil-Wilson glomerulosclerosis)
    Amyloidosis
Nephrotic-Range Proteinuria with "Active" Urine Sediment ("Mixed," Nephrotic/Nephritic)
  Primary glomerular disease
    Membranoproliferative glomerulopathy, types I, II, III
  Secondary glomerular disease
    Membranoproliferative glomerulopathy
    Systemic lupus erythematosus
    Henoch-Schönlein purpura
    Mixed essential cryoglobulinemia

more weeks, with a tapering regimen given over the next 4 to 6 months. Eighty-five to 90 per cent of all patients with MCNS respond to this protocol (usually by the fourth week in children and the eighth week in adults). Adults older than 40 may require 16 to 20 weeks of steroid therapy before a complete remission occurs. Following development of a complete remission, 40 to 50 per cent remain free of proteinuria or have infrequent relapses. The remainder become "frequent" relapsers (more than twice a year) or steroid-dependent. These patients may benefit from adjunctive therapy with cytotoxic alkylating agents such as chlorambucil (0.15 to 0.2 mg/kg/day) or cyclophosphamide (2.0 mg/kg/day) for 8 to 12 weeks. However, there are significant risks associated with the use of these agents, including gonadal failure and carcinogenesis, particularly with long-term use or in combination with corticosteroids.

About three fourths of individuals are disease-free at 10 years, with a 10-year survival rate of 95 per cent. Patients show an increased risk of infection (particularly pneumococcus and *Haemophilus* infection) and thrombosis of renal and peripheral veins. The development of chronic renal failure due to MCNS is essentially nonexistent. Patients failing to respond to steroids are generally found to have another glomerulopathy, most often focal glomerulosclerosis.

Membranous Glomerulopathy (MGN). MGN is the most common cause of idiopathic nephrotic syndrome in adults, accounting for 25 to 30 per cent of all cases. Its peak incidence is in the fifth decade, and it is unusual in children. Most patients (80 to 85 per cent) present with nephrotic-range proteinuria and other manifestations of the nephrotic syndrome. Although the majority of cases are idiopathic, MGN may develop secondary to a number of conditions (Table 27–7). On occasion, so-called idiopathic MGN may eventually be found to be secondary to an unrecognized underlying illness (e.g., hepatitis B, neoplasia, SLE). Serum complement levels are normal.

The typical feature of MGN by light microscopy is thickening of the GBM with "spike" formation (best seen following silver impregnation) in the absence of cellular proliferation or infiltration (Fig. 27–1). IgG and C3 deposition are seen in a granular pattern along the GBM. Electron micros-

TABLE 27–7. MEMBRANOUS GLOMERULOPATHY

Nephrotic-range proteinuria with "bland" urinary sediment
GBM thickening with "spike" formation, granular deposits of IgG and complement, subepithelial electron-dense deposits
Etiology
  Idiopathic
  Secondary
    Infections: syphilis, hepatitis B
    Neoplasms: carcinoma of the lung, stomach, breast
    Drugs: gold, D-penicillamine, captopril
    Collagen vascular diseases: systemic lupus erythematosus, rheumatoid arthritis, mixed connective tissue disease

TABLE 27–8. FOCAL SEGMENTAL GLOMERULOSCLEROSIS

Nephrotic-range proteinuria with "bland" urinary sediment
Focal, segmental collapse of capillary loops and mesangial sclerosis with hyaline droplets
Etiology
  Idiopathic
  Secondary
    Heroin
    Acquired immunodeficiency syndrome (AIDS)
    Reflux nephropathy

copy demonstrates subepithelial electron-dense deposits.

MGN typically follows a slowly progressive course with intermittent remissions and exacerbations. Spontaneous complete remissions occur in as many as 25 per cent of patients, with another 20 to 25 per cent experiencing a partial remission (proteinuria less than 2 gm but greater than 200 mg/day). These patients may maintain a stable GFR for decades. The remaining 50 per cent progress to end-stage renal failure (ESRF) by 5 to 10 years.

Therapy remains controversial, although an alternate-day steroid regimen (with only minimal side effects) has been suggested to reduce significantly the development of chronic renal failure. Short-term effects on the manifestations of nephrotic syndrome are minimal, but the possible long-term benefits have encouraged many to use this therapeutic protocol. The place of cytotoxic agents in the therapy of MGN is also uncertain. High-dose intravenous methylprednisolone, oral methylprednisolone, and chlorambucil used sequentially over 6 months may increase the likelihood of remission and decrease the incidence of chronic renal failure.

Focal Glomerulosclerosis (FGS). FGS accounts for 10 to 15 per cent of children and 15 to 20 per cent of adults with idiopathic nephrotic syndrome (Table 27–8). Although heavy proteinuria and edema are usually present at onset, some patients have asymptomatic proteinuria and hematuria. Hypertension, azotemia, and microscopic hematuria are commonly found at the time of diagnosis. Serum complement levels are normal.

Light microscopy reveals focal and segmental collapse of capillary loops and mesangial sclerosis sometimes associated with hyalin insudation at the edge of the sclerotic focus. Proliferation or infiltration is absent. Focal mild tubular drop-out with interstitial fibrosis is often present. Patchy deposition of IgM, C3, and occasionally other immunoreactants is seen in the segmental sclerotic foci, but the etiologic significance of these findings is unknown. Electron-dense deposits are typically absent by electron microscopy. Patients with acquired immunodeficiency syndrome (AIDS)–related FGS often show numerous tubuloreticular structures within the endothelial cytoplasm—collections of microtubules that apparently form in response to elevated serum levels of interferon. Such structures are also very common in biopsies of patients with SLE.

Some patients (15 to 20 per cent) respond to steroid therapy with a lasting remission and good long-term renal function. But most (60 to 70 per cent), particularly those with persistent nephrotic syndrome, progress to chronic renal failure (55 per cent by 10 years). The remainder follow a long-term course with relapses and remissions and late onset of renal failure. Recurrence of FGS in transplants occurs in as many as 40 per cent of patients.

Heroin abusers and patients with AIDS may develop the nephrotic syndrome and the histologic lesion of FGS. These patients typically follow a much more rapid downhill course, often with progression to ESRF in less than 1 year.

Diabetic Nephropathy. Diabetes mellitus is associated with a number of serious renal complications (Table 27–9). Glomerular injury is one of the most significant developments in patients with diabetes, and this is discussed below. Diabetic nephropathy eventually develops in as many as 50 per cent of all adult insulin-dependent diabetics, with even greater frequency in juvenile diabetics. It is the single greatest cause of ESRD in the United States. As such, renal insufficiency has become a major limit to survival in diabetics under age 40. Diabetic nephropathy rarely appears until 5 or more years of insulin dependence have passed. The onset of clinically apparent glomerular involvement usually occurs 15 to 20 years after the initial diagnosis of diabetes. Initially, the proteinuria is small and inconstant—so-called microscopic albuminuria—but progresses to constant moderate to severe proteinuria, usually within 2 years. Interestingly, nephrotic levels of proteinuria occur in only 10 to 15 per cent of these patients. Yet, owing to the prevalence of diabetes in the population, diabetic nephropathy is overall the single largest cause of nephrotic syndrome in adults.

TABLE 27–9. RENAL DISEASES ASSOCIATED WITH DIABETES MELLITUS

Diabetic nephropathy
  Capillary basement membrane thickening
  Nodular (Kimmelstiel-Wilson) glomerulosclerosis
  Diffuse glomerulosclerosis
  Capsular drop lesion
  Fibrin cap lesion
Arteriolosclerosis
Urinary tract infection
Acute renal failure
  Papillary necrosis
  Radiocontrast-induced acute renal failure
Hyporeninemic hypoaldosteronism
  Hyperkalemic hyperchloremic renal tubular acidosis

Once proteinuria becomes constant, a rapid decline in GFR begins, with resultant ESRF within 5 years. Although usually not seen in early diabetes, hypertension accompanies the onset of proteinuria in as many as 50 per cent of diabetic patients. Diabetic retinopathy is found in more than 90 per cent of patients with diabetic nephropathy. The reverse association need not hold, because only about one third of all patients with diabetic retinopathy also have clinically significant diabetic nephropathy. A nondiabetic etiology of renal disease is suggested in the absence of retinopathy, diabetes of less than 10 years' duration, and the presence of microhematuria with or without RBC casts.

Kimmelstiel-Wilson nodular glomerulosclerosis, although the classic diabetic glomerular lesion, is found in only 15 to 20 per cent of patients with diabetic nephropathy. It consists of a nodular increase in hyaline material massively expanding the mesangial areas surrounded by dilated and uniformly thickened capillary loops. The nodular foci have a focal and segmental distribution. The more common lesion is that of diffuse glomerulosclerosis, a uniform increase in hyaline material within the mesangial areas associated with capillary loop changes described above. Hyaline arteriolosclerosis involving both the afferent and efferent arterioles, as well as tubulointerstitial atrophy and fibrosis, accompanies both the nodular and the diffuse forms of diabetic glomerulosclerosis. The insudative lesions—capsular drops and fibrin caps—consist of small, eosinophilic droplets on the parietal side of Bowman's capsule or the inner surface of a capillary loop, respectively. The presence of linear deposition of IgG along the capillary walls, as well as focal, segmental deposition of IgM and C3, is nonspecific and is thought to represent passive trapping.

Currently available data strongly support the concept that diabetic nephropathy is a direct result of the metabolic derangements seen in diabetics and that normalization of carbohydrate metabolism would be protective against the development of renal disease. Biochemical alterations of the GBM, including increased disaccharide units in the collagen, decreased sulfation of glycosaminoglycan components of the GBM (especially heparan sulfate), and enhanced synthesis of matrix components all contribute to the renal lesions of diabetic nephropathy. In early diabetics some of these biochemical alterations can lead to hyperfiltration, with the GFR elevated above normal by 20 to 30 per cent. Ultimately, the biochemical abnormalities along with the alterations in hemodynamics cause glomerular injury and sclerosis.

Strict control of blood glucose prevents diabetic microangiopathic lesions in experimental animals, and evidence is accumulating that euglycemia in humans with early diabetes has similar effects. Antihypertensive therapy appears to slow the rate of renal deterioration.

Other Renal Diseases Associated with Diabetes Mellitus. Hyporeninemic hypoaldosteronism develops in diabetics with tubulointerstitial injury and is a major cause of type IV renal tubular acidosis. Hyperkalemia and hyperchloremic metabolic acidosis are the usual presenting features. Renal function is usually somewhat reduced, but hypertension is common. As the patient approaches end stage, the features merge into those of diabetic glomerulosclerosis.

Diabetics are at increased risk to develop papillary necrosis with sloughing of the papillary tips, often bilaterally. Patients may present with acute renal failure, renal colic, hematuria, ureteral obstruction, and the presence of necrotic tissue in the urine. There is usually a concomitant acute pyelonephritis. Intravenous pyelography reveals a classic ring sign of calyceal irregularity. Treatment is directed at the underlying infection and, if present, the ureteral obstruction. Successful therapy results in a return of renal function toward normal, although a concentrating defect may persist.

Classically it has been thought that urinary tract infections are more common in diabetics. However, more recent studies of diabetic patients have provided little evidence for increased risk of urinary tract infections. Still, owing to the risk of more systemic complications in diabetic patients (e.g., diabetic ketoacidosis, papillary necrosis), urinary tract infections should be treated vigorously.

Amyloidosis. Renal involvement is common in all forms of amyloidosis, including the primary form with deposition of AL amyloid protein or the secondary form with protein AA deposition. Primary amyloidosis typically presents in the sixth decade, with more than 85 per cent of the patients 50 years or older at diagnosis. New onset of proteinuria is the usual presentation. This may be accompanied by unexplained splenomegaly, enlarged tongue, cardiac enlargement, and/or malabsorption due to gastrointestinal infiltration. Carpal tunnel syndrome may also be seen. Fanconi's syndrome and paraproteinuria are sometimes discovered during the patient's evaluation. Amyloidosis may also develop in patients with multiple myeloma, chronic infectious diseases (osteomyelitis, tuberculosis), and chronic inflammatory conditions (bronchiectasis).

There is also a hereditary form of amyloidosis termed familial Mediterranean fever. Eosinophilic deposits cause diffuse infiltration of the capillary loops and mesangium and are Congo red–positive and green birefringent under polarized light. Electron microscopy reveals the pathognomonic 8- to 10-nm fibrils arranged in a random pattern.

The usual duration of renal amyloidosis is difficult to determine because proteinuria may be present for years prior to diagnosis. However, the onset of nephrotic syndrome or a fall in GFR signals a rapid progression to chronic renal failure (85 to 90 per cent within 3 years). Therapy has been ineffective except for the use of colchicine to prevent amyloidosis in familial Mediterranean fever. Renal transplantation has been tried in some patients, with a 10 to 15 per cent recurrence rate and graft survival similar to that in GN controls.

Nephrotic Syndrome with "Active" Urine Sediment

Many patients present with pure nephrotic syndrome. However, a variety of glomerular diseases present with a "mixed" pattern of nephrotic/nephritic syndrome, including the various forms of membranoproliferative glomerulopathy as well as some patients with SLE, Henoch-Schönlein purpura, and mixed essential cryoglobulinemia.

Types of Membranoproliferative Glomerulopathy (MPGN). MPGN is a disease of young people, with most of the cases diagnosed in those between the ages of 5 and 30 years. Overall, MPGN accounts for 10 to 15 per cent of all cases of idiopathic nephrotic syndrome. The clinical manifestations are variable, with around 50 per cent presenting with nephrotic syndrome, 25 to 30 per cent with asymptomatic proteinuria, and 15 to 20 per cent with acute nephritic syndrome. Regardless of the major pattern, concurrent hematuria and proteinuria are almost always present. Serum C3 levels are depressed in more than 70 per cent of patients at disease onset. Thus MPGN must be differentiated from other forms of GN showing hypocomplementemia (Table 27–10).

MPGN is characterized overall by thickening of capillary loops and mesangial hypercellularity, often with lobular accentuation. Several subtypes exist. Type I MPGN has subendothelial deposits with mesangial interposition producing capillary loop splitting (Fig. 27–1). Type II (dense deposit disease, DDD) has characteristic broad, very electron-dense deposits widening the GBM. Immunofluorescence examination of both types I and II reveals extensive granular C3 deposition in the capillary loops, usually with absence of immunoglobulins. There are several different morphologic variants with features similar to either type I or II MPGN which have been reported as type III MPGN. The available data are insufficient to determine whether these lesions represent separate entities or are other forms of MPGN.

TABLE 27–10. MEMBRANOPROLIFERATIVE GLOMERULOPATHY

Nephrotic-range proteinuria with "active" urinary sediment

Type I: Mesangial hypercellularity and capillary loop "splitting"

Type II: Mesangial hypercellularity with GBM "dense deposits"

Type III: Morphologic variants
          Type I changes plus subepithelial deposits
          Changes intermediate between type I and type II

Etiology
  Idiopathic
  Secondary
    Hepatitis (acute and chronic active)
    Cirrhosis of the liver
    Partial lipodystrophy

The pathogenesis is unknown, although the association of MPGN with alterations in complement activation suggests a pathogenetic link. The presence of C3 nephritic factor is most likely an associated event rather than a cause of MPGN, and its presence does not appear to alter the prognosis.

MPGN is a slow but progressive disease, with as many as 50 per cent of patients in chronic renal failure at the end of 10 years. Poor prognostic indicators include the presence of nephrotic syndrome or azotemia at the time of diagnosis. Spontaneous remission of proteinuria occasionally occurs but does not usually affect the long-term outcome. The effectiveness of combination steroid and cytotoxic drug therapy is still unestablished, although some studies suggest that alternate-day prednisone therapy has therapeutic benefit. Another protocol using only anticoagulants (dipyridamole and aspirin) has been reported to decrease the rate of decline in GFR in MPGN type I. However, there is currently no consensus on any given therapeutic regimen that is both safe and effective in MPGN.

Type II MPGN recurs in virtually 100 per cent of renal transplants, but recurrence is far less common in type I MPGN (about 25 per cent). However, recurrence does not interfere with long-term graft survival.

Systemic Lupus Erythematosus (SLE) GN. SLE, an acute and chronic inflammatory multisystem process of unknown etiology, is primarily a disease of young women. Diagnosis rests on serologic evidence of antinuclear antibody production in the presence of inflammation of multiple organs. Clinical evidence of renal disease is present in as many as 85 to 90 per cent of lupus patients, varying from minimal changes to the nephritic and/or nephrotic syndrome. Virtually all patients are found to have renal injury if a kidney biopsy is performed. The nephrotic syndrome with a "nephritic" sediment is most common, and 10 to 15 per cent of patients also have azotemia. Serum complement levels are usually low during periods of active renal disease. A small number of patients present with RPGN. Renal function deteriorates over a matter of weeks, and numerous cellular crescents are seen on renal biopsy.

The clinical presentation and the severity of renal disease correlate with the underlying histopathology, best classified using the World Health Organization scheme (Table 27–11). Essentially, these categories can be grouped as proliferative (types II, III, IV) or membranous (type V) glomerulopathies, with greater proliferation (type IV) associated with poorer prognosis. Multiple immunoglobulins and various components of complement are almost invariably present within the glomeruli and may involve all levels of the GBM as well as the mesangium. Overall, the best predictor of progression is probably the presence and amount of subendothelial deposits seen by electron microscopy, which also increase as proliferation increases (Fig. 27–1).

Patients with active, proliferative lesions (types III and IV) benefit from high-dose steroid therapy given for 4 to 6 weeks, with subsequent adjustment based on response (renal parameters, serologic changes, extrarenal manifestations). The addition of a cytotoxic agent may provide better preservation of renal function in patients with moderate to severe proliferation and mild chronic renal changes. Patients with crescents and rapidly progressive renal deterioration should be treated similarly to patients with idiopathic crescentic GN. Protracted SLE can also lead to ESRD.

Patients with SLE tolerate dialysis about as well as patients with non-SLE renal failure. Indeed, for reasons that are not yet understood, SLE patients who are placed on chronic dialysis often note dramatic amelioration of other manifestations of SLE. Renal transplantation is also as well tolerated, with recurrence of SLE GN relatively rare.

Henoch-Schönlein Purpura (HSP). HSP is seen most often in children (boys more than girls) and is characterized by purpuric lesions on the buttocks and legs, episodic abdominal pain, arthralgias, fever, malaise, and proteinuria (often nephrotic range) with hematuria and RBC casts. Serum C3 levels are typically normal, although CH_{50} may be low.

The glomeruli reveal varying degrees of mesangial hypercellularity and crescent formation, with the prognosis declining as the proliferation increases. Uncommonly, exuberant crescent formation occurs associated with a rapid progression to renal failure. IgA and C3 staining of the mesangium is prominent with numerous mesangial electron-dense deposits seen by electron microscopy. Immunofluorescence examination of lesions or of unaffected skin shows IgA and C3 within dermal capillaries.

HSP tends toward a benign, self-limited course of remission and relapse, usually disappearing after a few months to years. More than half of the patients recover completely from their renal in-

TABLE 27–11. WORLD HEALTH ORGANIZATION CLASSIFICATION OF LUPUS NEPHRITIS

CLASS	FREQUENCY	5-YR RENAL SURVIVAL
Type I—Normal kidneys No histologic changes	<5%	~100%
Type II—Mesangial glomerulonephritis Mesangial hypercellularity and immune deposits	15–20%	~85%
Type III—Focal proliferative glomerulo-nephritis Mesangial changes plus proliferation and "activity" in <50% of glomeruli	15–20%	~70%
Type IV—Diffuse proliferative glomerulo-nephritis Type III changes involving >50% of glomeruli	~50%	~25–60%
Type V—Membranous glomerulopathy Subepithelial deposits ~ idiopathic MGN	15–20%	~85%

jury, but about 10 per cent progress to ESRD. Persistent nephrotic syndrome, acute nephritic syndrome at onset, and older age suggest a poor prognosis. Therapy is ineffective against the renal manifestations of HSP, although patients with extensive crescent formation should be managed aggressively. Recurrence is uncommon in renal transplants.

Mixed Essential Cryoglobulinemia (MEC). Mixed essential cryoglobulinemia occurs usually in middle age, affecting women slightly more than men, and presents with purpura, fever, Raynaud's phenomenon, arthralgias, and weakness. Renal manifestations are seen in 40 to 50 per cent of patients and vary from proteinuria and/or hematuria to acute nephritic syndrome. Cold precipitable IgG/IgM complexes with rheumatoid factor activity and sometimes hepatitis B antigen are characteristic and associated with an elevated sedimentation rate and normal C3 levels. The glomeruli show a diffuse proliferative GN with intraluminal hyaline thrombi. IgG, IgM, and C3 are usually present in subendothelial areas and the mesangium.

Patients with renal insufficiency or acute nephritic syndrome usually progress to ESRF. However, the overall survival rate in MEC patients with renal manifestations is about 75 per cent. Plasmapheresis to decrease the circulating cryoprecipitates may improve the prognosis of patients with severe renal MEC.

Sickle Cell Anemia Glomerulopathy. Microscopic hematuria is seen in most sickle cell patients, although dramatic and prolonged bouts of gross hematuria may occur. Bed rest with forced hydration is usually helpful. Renal medullary injury, secondary to vascular occlusion from sickled RBCs in the hypertonic environment of the renal medulla, leads to concentration defects. This ischemic injury to the medullary areas may also lead to papillary necrosis or even cortical infarction in rare cases.

Fewer than 5 per cent of sickle cell patients develop nephrotic-range proteinuria, hematuria, and RBC casts characteristic of sickle cell anemia glomerulopathy. Histologically, mesangial hypercellularity with capillary loop "splitting" produces a typical MPGN pattern. Immunoglobulin and complement deposition are often not present, and serum complement levels are normal. These patients progress quickly to renal failure, and therapeutic intervention has not been shown to be helpful.

ASYMPTOMATIC URINARY ABNORMALITIES

A variety of renal lesions may present as either isolated proteinuria or hematuria, with or without proteinuria (Table 27–12). Isolated proteinuria without hematuria is usually an incidental finding in an asymptomatic patient. They generally excrete less than 2 gm of protein per day with a bland urine sediment and have normal renal function. About 60 per cent of these patients have so-called postural proteinuria, with absence of

TABLE 27–12. ASYMPTOMATIC URINARY ABNORMALITIES

Isolated Proteinuria
  Proteinuria without hematuria
  Postural proteinuria
Isolated Hematuria (with or without Proteinuria)
  IgA nephropathy (Berger's disease)
  Hereditary nephritis
    Alport's syndrome
    Thin basement membrane disease
  Benign recurrent hematuria

proteinuria while lying flat and return of proteinuria upon standing. The long-term outcome of isolated proteinuria (postural or nonpostural) is excellent, with the majority experiencing a steady decline in protein excretion. However, in some patients this condition represents a very early manifestation of a more serious glomerular disease such as MGN, IgA nephropathy, focal glomerulosclerosis, diabetic nephropathy, or amyloidosis. Finally, it should be noted that mild proteinuria may accompany a febrile illness, congestive heart failure, or infectious diseases.

Hematuria with or without proteinuria in an otherwise asymptomatic patient may represent the fortuitous early discovery of another glomerular disease such as SLE, Henoch-Schönlein purpura, postinfectious GN, or idiopathic hypercalciuria in children. However, asymptomatic hematuria is also the primary presenting manifestation of a number of specific glomerular diseases discussed below.

IgA Nephropathy (Berger's Disease). This disease, characterized by mesangial IgA deposits (Fig. 27–1), is the final diagnosis in as many as 50 per cent of patients with asymptomatic hematuria. It has become the most common cause of primary glomerular disease in the United States and Europe. The typical presentation is gross hematuria following a viral illness, with men affected two to three times more frequently than women and whites much more commonly than blacks. Most patients are between the ages of 15 and 35. Microscopic hematuria usually remains after the gross hematuria resolves. Mild proteinuria of less than 1 gm/day is common, but nephrotic-range proteinuria may be seen in as many as 10 per cent of patients. Serum complement is normal.

Light microscopic changes vary from normal glomeruli (grade I), through mesangial hypercellularity (grade II), to a mixed group of abnormalities including segmental sclerosis, crescent formation, tubular atrophy, and interstitial fibrosis (grade III). Mesangial deposits of IgA, even in glomeruli unaffected when judged by light microscopy, are characteristic of this disease (Fig. 27–1); some patients also have IgG and C3 deposition as well.

Progressive renal insufficiency develops in 20 to 30 per cent of patients after 20 years. Some have a more rapid progression, with renal failure in as little as 4 years. Poor prognostic indicators include nephrotic-range proteinuria, hypertension, and the higher-grade renal biopsy changes. No effective therapy is currently available. Mesangial IgA deposits recur frequently in renal transplants, but with minimal long-term effects on function.

Hereditary Nephritis (Alport's Syndrome). This disorder usually presents in childhood with recurrent gross hematuria, with or without vague lower back or abdominal pain. Mild proteinuria is often present, but nephrotic syndrome is rare. Sensorineural deafness is present in about 50 per cent of the patients. Family history may reveal any of a number of different patterns, although most pedigrees show some X linkage. Males are usually more affected than females and often develop renal failure by age 30. Light microscopy reveals nonspecific interstitial foam cells, and immunofluorescence is negative for immunoglobulins and complement. The diagnostic ultrastructural abnormalities include alternating areas of thinned and thickened capillary loops with lamination and splitting of the GBM.

No effective treatment is currently available. It has been demonstrated that the GBM in patients with Alport's syndrome does not react with anti-GBM antibody, implying a lack of certain GBM antigens. Therefore, although Alport's syndrome does not recur in renal transplants, allografts may develop anti-GBM antibody GN owing to the presence of GBM antigens for which the recipient lacks immune "tolerance."

Thin Basement Membrane Disease. This condition affects both genders equally and often occurs in families without an X-linked pattern. The disease presents usually as microscopic hematuria without proteinuria in an otherwise asymptomatic young adult. Light and immunofluorescence examination are normal, whereas ultra-structural examination demonstrates the markedly thinned GBM. Prognosis is excellent, although a few patients with progressive renal failure have been reported.

Benign Recurrent Hematuria. This diagnosis is given to those with asymptomatic hematuria when the other possibilities are excluded. The majority of these patients are young adults found to have microscopic hematuria on routine examination or with gross hematuria associated with a febrile illness, exercise, or immunization. Renal biopsy is normal in most but may show focal or diffuse mesangial proliferation. Immunofluorescence is sometimes negative but may show mesangial deposits of IgM or IgG with C3 or C3 alone. Ultrastructural studies are equally variable, with many reports of normal glomeruli, although electron-dense deposits have been seen in GBM and/or mesangium in some patients. Overall the prognosis is excellent, with as many as 50 per cent in complete remission at 5 years and only a few with declining renal function.

REFERENCES

Balow JE, Austin HA 3d, Tsokos GC, Antonovych TT, Steinberg AD, Klippel JH: NIH Conference. Lupus nephritis. Ann Intern Med 106:79–94, 1987.

Couser WG: Glomerular disorders. In Wyngaarden JB, Smith LH Jr, Bennett JC (eds): Cecil Textbook of Medicine. 19th ed. Philadelphia, WB Saunders Co, 1992, pp 551–568.

Donadio JV, Offord KP: Reassessment of treatment results in membranoproliferative glomerulonephritis, with emphasis on life-table analysis. Am J Kidney Dis 14:445–451, 1989.

Glassock RJ, Adler SG, Ward HJ, Cohen AH: Primary glomerular diseases. In Brenner BM, Rector FC (eds): The Kidney. 4th ed. Philadelphia, WB Saunders Co, 1991, pp 1182–1279.

Glassock RJ, Cohen AH, Adler SG, Ward HJ: Secondary glomerular diseases. In Brenner BM, Rector FC (eds): The Kidney. 4th ed. Philadelphia, WB Saunders Co, 1991, pp 1280–1368.

Ponticelli C, Zucchelli P, Passerini P, et al.: A randomized trial of methylprednisolone and chlorambucil in idiopathic membranous nephropathy. N Engl J Med 320:8–13, 1989.

Shah SV (ed): Mechanisms of glomerular injury. Semin Nephrol 11:253–372, 1991.

28 MAJOR NONGLOMERULAR DISORDERS

This chapter considers five major groups of nonglomerular renal disorders: tubulointerstitial nephropathy, cystic disease of the kidney, obstructive uropathy, urolithiasis, and renal neoplasia.

TUBULOINTERSTITIAL NEPHROPATHY

Tubulointerstitial nephropathy encompasses a group of clinical disorders that affect the renal tubules and interstitium principally, with relative sparing of the glomeruli and renal vasculature. In the majority of cases of interstitial nephropathy, the disease can be placed into one of two categories on the basis of the rate of progression of the azotemia: (1) acute interstitial nephritis (AIN), causing a rapid (days to weeks) decline in renal function and characterized histologically by an acute inflammatory infiltrate, or (2) chronic interstitial nephropathy, causing a slowly progressive (years) azotemia characterized histologically by predominantly interstitial scarring and fibrosis with a variable but less impressive amount of round-cell infiltration.

Acute Interstitial Nephritis

AIN is a clinicopathologic syndrome that is characterized by the sudden onset of clinical signs of renal dysfunction associated with a prominent inflammatory cell infiltrate within the renal interstitium. It is an important cause of acute renal failure (ARF) and may account for as many as 10 to 20 per cent of ARF cases.

Etiology. The most common causes of AIN are listed in Table 28–1. Recently the best-documented cases of AIN have resulted from complication of therapy with a wide variety of drugs, especially antibiotics and nonsteroidal anti-inflammatory drugs. Septicemia of any cause can result in AIN, but certain infectious agents such as leptospirosis, legionnaires' disease, and mononucleosis appear to have a particular predilection for causing AIN.

Acute pyelonephritis is classified on histologic grounds as a form of AIN. The mechanism for the nephritis is direct bacterial invasion of the renal medulla, in contrast to the allergic forms of AIN described above. The clinical manifestations are predominantly those of infection, fever, chills, and flank pain, and only rarely cause ARF.

Severe glomerulonephritis, although sometimes accompanied by an interstitial inflammatory infiltrate, is generally excluded from classifications of AIN. In some patients, such as those with systemic lupus erythematosus (SLE), interstitial inflammation may be out of proportion to the degree of glomerular injury and interstitial nephritis is the predominant finding.

Clinical Features. The major clinical manifestation of AIN is the development of acute renal insufficiency. Many patients develop some combination of fever, skin rash, peripheral eosinophilia, and arthralgias, particularly in the course of AIN due to drugs. The absence of any or all of these features is common and therefore does not preclude the diagnosis of AIN. Hypertension and edema, important features of acute glomerulonephritis, are uncommon in AIN.

AIN is often accompanied by signs of renal inflammation, and urinary abnormalities often provide the first clue to the diagnosis of AIN in a patient with ARF. Hematuria, often macroscopic, is common when AIN is caused by drugs, as are sterile pyuria and leukocyte casts. Eosinophiluria is highly suggestive of AIN but is not often observed. Wright's stain test of the urine is necessary to demonstrate eosinophils. Red blood cell (RBC) casts have been found on rare occasions to be associated with AIN and may make the presentation indistinguishable from that of glomerulonephritis. Mild to moderate proteinuria is present in the majority of patients.

Drug-induced AIN is treated by discontinuing the offending drug. Another appropriate drug can

TABLE 28–1. CAUSES OF ACUTE INTERSTITIAL NEPHRITIS

Drug-related	Antimicrobial drugs
	Penicillins (esp. methicillin)
	Rifampin
	Sulfonamides
	Nonsteroidal anti-inflammatory drugs
	Allopurinol
	Sulfonamide diuretics
Systemic infections	Streptococcal infections
	Cytomegalovirus
	Infectious mononucleosis
	Legionnaires' disease
	Leptospirosis
Primary renal infections	Acute bacterial pyelonephritis
Immune disorders	Acute glomerulonephritis
	Systemic lupus erythematosus
	Transplant rejection
Idiopathic	

be substituted in cases of underlying infection. In the majority of cases, this results in restoration of renal function within several weeks. A short course of high-dose corticosteroids (1 mg/kg/day of prednisone for 1 to 2 weeks) may accelerate recovery, but the added risk in patients with underlying infections must be weighed against possible benefits, especially because the latter have not been established unambiguously.

Chronic Tubulointerstitial Nephropathy

Chronic tubulointerstitial nephropathy is a clinicopathologic entity characterized clinically by slowly progressive renal insufficiency, non–nephrotic-range proteinuria, and functional tubular defects and pathologically by interstitial fibrosis with atrophy and loss of renal tubules. Chronic interstitial nephropathy is an important cause of chronic renal failure and appears to be responsible for 15 to 30 per cent of all end-stage renal disease (ESRD).

Diagnosis and Clinical Features. Chronic tubulointerstitial nephropathy is characterized by tubular defects disproportionately severe relative to the degree of azotemia, as well as the absence of manifestations (RBC casts or the nephrotic syndrome) characteristic of glomerular disease (Table 28–2). Most patients with chronic interstitial nephropathy have little or no clinical evidence of active renal inflammation. The urinalysis may show modest pyuria and minimal hematuria, but in most cases there are no cellular casts.

Certain causes of chronic interstitial nephritis damage principally a specific segment of the nephron and thereby alter only those tubular functions that are normally ascribed to that segment. Conditions such as multiple myeloma or heavy metal toxicity, which affect primarily proximal tubule structures, may present with proximal renal tubular acidosis (RTA), glycosuria, aminoaciduria, and uricosuria. Distal RTA, salt wasting,

TABLE 28–2. CLINICAL FINDINGS SUGGESTING CHRONIC TUBULOINTERSTITIAL DISEASE

1. Hyperchloremic metabolic acidosis (out of proportion to the degree of renal insufficiency)
2. Hyperkalemia (out of proportion to the degree of renal insufficiency)
3. Reduced maximal urinary concentrating ability (polyuria, nocturia)
4. Partial or complete Fanconi's syndrome
   Phosphaturia
   Bicarbonaturia
   Aminoaciduria
   Uricosuria
   Glycosuria
5. Urinalysis
   a. May be normal but may contain cellular elements; absence of RBC casts
   b. Modest proteinuria (<2.0 gm/day); absence of nephrotic-range proteinuria

and hyperkalemia are seen in patients with isolated distal tubular damage, as may occur with chronic obstruction or amyloidosis. Alternatively, patients with analgesic nephropathy, sickle cell disease, or polycystic kidney disease may present with a concentrating defect secondary to medullary involvement.

Specific Causes of Chronic Tubulointerstitial Disease (Table 28–3)

Urinary Tract Obstruction. Urinary tract obstruction is the single most important cause of chronic tubulointerstitial nephropathy and is discussed later in this chapter.

Chronic Pyelonephritis and Reflux Nephropathy. Bacteriuria alone is unlikely to result in chronic renal injury. Urinary tract infection in association with obstruction, or vesicoureteral reflux, however, is associated with a lesion termed "chronic pyelonephritis." The diagnosis is established by radiologic findings that demonstrate deformity of the pelvis and calyces, typically most pronounced in the upper and lower poles. The development of heavy proteinuria is usually due to focal segmental sclerosis seen in association with reflux and is a poor prognostic sign.

Drugs

Analgesic Nephropathy. Excessive consumption of certain analgesic agents such as phenacetin or acetaminophen (phenacetin is largely converted to acetaminophen), usually in combination with aspirin, may result in chronic interstitial nephritis. Analgesic nephropathy occurs more frequently in women (usually middle-aged) who have ingested large quantities (>3 kg) of antipyretic-analgesic mixtures. Emotional stress, neuropsychiatric disturbances, and gastrointestinal disturbances are commonly associated with analgesic nephropathy. Anemia is present in most patients and is frequently more severe than can be attributed to their degree of renal insufficiency, in part because of gastrointestinal blood loss. Sloughing of a necrotic papilla into the urinary tract may be associated with gross hematuria, flank pain (ureteral colic), passage of tissue in the urine, and an abrupt decline in renal function.

A variety of findings on intravenous urography or retrograde pyelography, including calyceal filling defects due to the presence of a sloughed papilla (ring sign), may suggest the diagnosis. Demonstration of papillary necrosis in the absence of other common causes (e.g., diabetes mellitus, urinary tract obstruction, often with infection, or sickle cell disease) should suggest analgesic nephropathy. Patients with analgesic nephropathy are at increased risk for development of transitional cell carcinoma of the urinary tract, particularly of the renal pelvis. The appearance of hematuria should lead to prompt evaluation to exclude a uroepithelial neoplasm. With cessation of analgesic use, renal function generally stabilizes or improves.

TABLE 28–3. CONDITIONS ASSOCIATED WITH CHRONIC TUBULOINTERSTITIAL NEPHROPATHY

I. Urinary tract obstruction
 a. Vesicoureteral reflux
 b. Mechanical
II. Drugs
 a. Analgesics
 b. Nitrosurea
 c. Cisplatin
 d. Cyclosporine
III. Vascular diseases
 a. Nephrosclerosis
 b. Atheroembolic disease
 c. Radiation nephritis
 d. Sickle hemoglobinopathies
 e. Vasculitis
IV. Heavy metals
 a. Lead
 b. Cadmium
V. Metabolic disorders
 a. Hyperuricemia/hyperuricosuria
 b. Hypercalcemia/hypercalciuria
 c. Hyperoxaluria
 d. Potassium depletion
 e. Cystinosis

VI. Hereditary diseases
 a. Medullary cystic disease
 b. Hereditary nephritis
 c. Polycystic kidney disease
VII. Malignancies and granulomatous diseases
 a. Multiple myeloma
 b. Sarcoidosis
 c. Tuberculosis
 d. Wegener's granulomatosis
VIII. Immunologic diseases
 a. Systemic lupus erythematosus
 b. Sjögren's syndrome
 c. Cryoglobulinemia
 d. Goodpasture's syndrome
IX. Endemic diseases
 a. Balkan nephropathy

Cytotoxic and Immunosuppressive Agents. Several agents such as cyclosporine, cisplatin, and nitrosoureas, which are more often associated with ARF, may also sometimes cause chronic tubulointerstitial nephropathy.

Vascular Diseases

Hypertensive Nephrosclerosis. The pathologic hallmark of benign nephrosclerosis is an arteriolopathy that is most pronounced in the interlobular and afferent arterioles. Interstitial and glomerular changes appear to result from the subsequent ischemia. Tubular atrophy and interstitial scarring may precede signs of glomerular injury in arteriolar nephrosclerosis.

Radiation Nephritis. Clinically evident renal injury is uncommon with less than 1000 to 2000 cGy but develops in approximately 50 per cent of patients receiving higher doses. In the early stage of radiation nephritis, tubular necrosis, medial and intimal thickening of the small renal arteries, and damage to the glomerular endothelium are present. Later, glomerulosclerosis, collagenous thickening of the small renal arteries, and interstitial fibrosis are prominent. Evidence for renal damage occurs several months to years after renal irradiation. Manifestations range from mild proteinuria, urinary concentrating defects, and benign hypertension with a reduced glomerular filtration rate (GFR) to malignant hypertension with end-stage renal failure (ESRF).

Heavy Metals

Lead. Although occupational lead exposure has declined over the past several decades, environmental exposure to lead aerosols has markedly in-creased. Lead accumulates in and causes proximal convoluted tubule cell injury, which may result in glycosuria and aminoaciduria and chronic interstitial disease. The presence of hypertension, gout ("saturnine" gout), and renal insufficiency in a patient should suggest the possibility of lead nephropathy. Disodium ethylenediaminetetra-acetic acid (EDTA) administration may be used to test for a lead burden.

Metabolic Abnormalities

Although prolonged hyperuricemia is associated with renal dysfunction, the role of chronic hyperuricemia in producing renal insufficiency is not clear. It has been suggested that the nephropathy seen in association with saturnine gout may actually be secondary to lead exposure, based on greater mobilization of lead following EDTA administration, or to the hypertension that often accompanies primary or secondary hyperuricemia.

Primary hyperoxaluria, enteric hyperoxaluria, and cystinosis, a recessively inherited disease, may result in ESRF from chronic interstitial nephritis. The major renal complication of chronic hypokalemia and hypercalcemia is nephrogenic (vasopressin-resistant) diabetes insipidus, which results in mild polyuria. Chronic hypercalcemia may result in nephrocalcinosis and chronic interstitial nephritis with reduced GFR that may be only slowly and incompletely reversible.

Malignancies

Renal involvement is common in patients with multiple myeloma, with progressive renal insufficiency seen in more than two thirds of patients. The so-called myeloma kidney (cast nephropathy) is characterized by laminated refractile tubular casts (surrounded by inflammatory cells and multinucleated giant cells) and by tubular atrophy and interstitial fibrosis. In those with kappa light chain disease, Fanconi's syndrome may precede the diagnosis of myeloma or the onset of renal insufficiency by many months. In 5 to 15 per cent of cases of myeloma, patients develop nephrotic syndrome as a result of glomerular lesions (amyloidosis). In patients with lymphomas and leukemias, particularly acute lymphoblastic leukemia, neoplastic cells may infiltrate the renal interstitium and cause renal enlargement, but renal function is rarely compromised.

Immune Disorders

A variety of immune disorders may be associated with both acute and chronic interstitial nephritis, including several types of glomerulonephritis, chronic renal transplant rejection, and SLE. Renal involvement in Sjögren's syndrome is usually in the form of chronic interstitial nephritis. The most common functional abnormalities are distal RTA and urinary concentrating defects.

CYSTIC DISEASES OF THE KIDNEY

Renal cyst diseases are characterized by epithelium-lined cavities filled with fluid or semisolid debris within the kidneys. Certain clinical settings suggest specific cystic disorders (Table 28–4). An abdominal mass in a neonate or infant should suggest the possibility of either autosomal dominant (ADPKD) or autosomal recessive polycystic kidney disease (ARPKD). Renal failure in adolescence suggests ARPKD or medullary cystic disease. The finding of a solitary cyst in a 50-year-old person is most compatible with a simple cyst. A history of renal disease in a family raises the possibility of ADPKD, ARPKD, or medullary cystic disease. Recurrent renal stones can occur in ADPKD or medullary sponge kidney. The onset of hematuria in a patient undergoing chronic hemodialysis may possibly indicate acquired cystic disease.

Simple Cysts

Simple renal cysts increase in frequency with age, being present in up to 50 per cent of the population over 50 years of age. Simple cysts are most often asymptomatic and are usually discovered as an incidental finding during imaging studies. Renal ultrasonography together with computed tomography (CT) permits accurate differentiation of benign from malignant lesions in most instances.

Polycystic Kidney Disease

PKDs include ADPKD, usually referred to as adult PKD, and ARPKD, often referred to as infantile or childhood PKD. ARPKD occurs in association with congenital hepatic fibrosis and causes death from renal failure in the first year of life.

Autosomal Dominant Polycystic Kidney Disease

ADPKD is the most common hereditary disease in the United States, affecting 500,000 people. The clinical disorder can be caused by at least two different genes. The most common type, ADPKD1, is carried on chromosome 16. The location of the other gene has not been determined. Complete penetrance of the gene is estimated to occur by 90 years of age.

Clinical manifestations of ADPKD rarely occur before the age of 20 to 25 years. This accounts for the frequent passage of the genetic trait to offspring by asymptomatic yet affected individuals of childbearing age. Patients usually present either for screening because of a family history of the disease or for evaluation of symptoms. Pain and hematuria are the most common clinical manifestations. Nonspecific, dull lumbar pain is a frequent symptom and usually occurs when the kidneys are sufficiently enlarged to be palpable on examination of the abdomen. Sharp, localized pain may result from cyst rupture or infection or from passage of a renal calculus. Microhematuria is frequently the initial sign of PKD; gross hematuria may also occur.

Hypertension, the most common cardiovascular manifestation of ADPKD, occurs in 60 per cent of patients before the onset of renal insufficiency. Nocturia due to a urinary concentrating defect is often present at the time of diagnosis, and most patients show impaired salt conservation on a restricted salt intake. Urinary tract infection and pyelonephritis are common complications. Up to one third of patients with PKD have multiple, asymptomatic hepatic cysts; about 10 per cent of the patients have cerebral aneurysms; and about 25 per cent of all patients have mitral valve prolapse. The natural history of renal functional impairment with ADPKD is variable. The disease progresses to ESRF in about 25 per cent of individuals by age 50 and in almost 50 per cent by age 70.

The diagnosis of PKD is made on the basis of radiographic evidence of multiple cysts distributed throughout the renal parenchyma, in association with renal enlargement, increased cortical thickness, and elongation and splaying of the renal calyces. The demonstration of the characteristic bilateral renal cystic involvement is best accomplished by renal ultrasonography. In adults, CT scan with contrast medium occasionally reveals more cystic involvement than is apparent by ultrasonography. Imaging studies that reveal only a few cysts require differentiation of early ADPKD from multiple simple cysts. The presence of extrarenal involvement, particularly hepatic cysts, lends support to the diagnosis of ADPKD. The information on gene location now permits identification of presymptomatic carriers of ADPKD1 through gene linkage analysis. If there is a need

TABLE 28–4. CHARACTERISTICS OF RENAL CYSTIC DISORDERS

FEATURE	SIMPLE CYSTS	ADPKD	ARPKD	ACKD	MCD	MSK
Inheritance pattern	None	Autosomal dominant	Autosomal recessive	None	Often present, variable pattern	None
Incidence or prevalence	Common, increasing with age	1/200 to 1/1000	Rare	40% in dialysis patients	Rare	Common
Age of onset	Adults	Usually adults	Neonates, children	Older adults	Adolescents, young adults	Adults
Presenting symptoms	Incidental finding, hematuria	Pain, hematuria, infection, family screening	Abdominal mass, renal failure, failure to thrive	Hematuria	Polyuria, polydipsia, enuresis, renal failure, failure to thrive	Incidental, urinary tract infections, hematuria, renal calculi
Hematuria	Occurs	Common	Occurs	Occurs	Rare	Common
Recurrent infections	Rare	Common	Occurs	No	Rare	Common
Renal calculi	No	Common	No	No	No	Common
Hypertension	Rare	Common	Common	Present from underlying disease	Rare	No
Method of diagnosis	Ultrasound	Ultrasound, gene linkage analysis	Ultrasound	CT scan	None reliable	Excretory urogram
Renal size	Normal	Normal to very large	Large initially	Small to normal, occasionally large	Small	Normal

ADPKD = Autosomal dominant polycystic kidney disease; ARPKD = autosomal recessive polycystic kidney disease; ACKD = acquired cystic kidney disease; MCD = medullary cystic disease; MSK = medullary sponge kidney.

From Gabow PA: Cystic diseases of the kidney. In Wyngaarden JB, Smith LH Jr, Bennett JC (eds): Cecil Textbook of Medicine. 19th ed. Philadelphia, WB Saunders Co, 1992, p 609.

for definitive diagnosis, this technique can be used in many families and can predict gene status with 99:1 likelihood. Because gene linkage is expensive, requires the cooperation of other family members, and supplies no anatomic information, it is probably best reserved for patients with nondiagnostic imaging studies.

The treatment for patients with ADPKD is aimed at preventing complications of the disease and preserving renal function. Patients and family members should be educated about the inheritance and manifestations of the disease. Therapy for PKD is directed toward control of hypertension and prevention and early treatment of urinary tract infections. ESRF is managed by either dialysis or transplantation. Bilateral nephrectomy may be required prior to transplantation in patients with inordinately large kidneys or those with a history of frequent or persistent urinary tract infection.

Acquired Cystic Kidney Disease

Acquired cystic kidney disease refers to the development of cysts in a large number of patients with ESRD undergoing dialysis. Occasionally, carcinomas complicate this disorder. Although the diagnosis can be established with ultrasonography, CT scan is the diagnostic method of choice in acquired cystic kidney disease because the kidneys and cysts are often small.

Medullary Cystic Disorders

Medullary cystic disease (nephrophthisis) occurs as a rare, automosomal recessive disease, sometimes accompanied by retinitis pigmentosa. Prolonged enuresis in childhood due to a urinary concentrating defect and anemia are early indications of the renal disease. Neither radiography nor renal biopsy has a high rate of success in demonstrating the small medullary cysts. Medullary cystic disease regularly results in ESRF during adolescence or early adulthood.

Medullary sponge kidney is a more common, benign disorder that is often detected incidentally on abdominal radiographs. Medullary sponge kidney is relatively common and often presents as a result of passage of a renal calculus. It is estimated that about 10 per cent of patients who present with renal stones may have medullary sponge kidney. Nephrocalcinosis occurs in about half the patients and accounts for identification of asymptomatic patients on routine abdominal radiography. The diagnosis is made on intravenous pyelography (IVP) by the characteristic radial pattern ("bouquet of flowers," "paint brush") of contrast-filled medullary cysts. Treatment for urinary tract infection and renal calculus formation is indicated. Renal failure does not occur as part of the basic disease.

URINARY TRACT OBSTRUCTION

Obstruction to urine flow may occur at any point from the renal pelvis to the urethral meatus. The causes of obstruction are manifold but may be classified into the few general groups given in Table 28–5. The age and gender of the patient obviously influence the likelihood of a given pairing of etiology and site. Unilateral ureteral obstruction usually causes no detectable change in urinary flow or total renal function. Azotemia or renal failure occurs only if the drainage of both kidneys is significantly compromised. Total urinary tract obstruction is a significant cause of ESRF.

A change in urinary habits is often the presenting sign of urinary tract obstruction. Complete obstruction is the most common cause of true anuria. However, polyuria, especially nocturia, is not uncommon in partial obstruction and may occur as a consequence of defective urinary concentration.

Renal sonography is the preferred means of diagnosing urinary tract obstruction and depends on identification of hydronephrosis. Dilation of the urinary tract may not be evident within the first 24 hours of obstruction, in which case an IVP showing a prolonged nephrogram phase with delayed filling can provide valuable diagnostic information. A 24- or 48-hour film may show contrast medium concentrated either in dilated calyces or in the renal pelvis. Retrograde examination of the ureters is rarely required to make the diagnosis but may be necessary to define the anatomy of the obstruction before surgical intervention.

Management of urinary tract obstruction is directed toward identification of the site and cause of obstruction and relief of the obstruction, usually through surgical intervention. Elimination of

TABLE 28–5. CAUSES OF URINARY TRACT OBSTRUCTION

Congenital Urinary Tract Malformation
  Pelvic-ureteric junction obstruction
  Meatal stenosis
  Ureterocele
  Posterior urethral valves
Intraluminal Obstruction
  Calculi
  Blood clots
  Sloughed papillary tissue
Extrinsic Compression
  Pelvic tumors
  Prostatic hypertrophy
  Retroperitoneal fibrosis
Acquired Anomalies
  Urethral strictures
  Neurogenic bladder
  Intratubular precipitates

obstruction is at times associated with a postobstructive diuresis, due partially to a solute diuresis from salt and urea retained during obstruction and partially to the renal concentrating defect. In some cases, definitive relief of obstruction is not possible and urinary diversion may be required. This may be as simple as an indwelling urethral catheter or more complex, such as an ileal conduit. In all cases, control of urinary tract infection is of paramount concern. Urinary tract infection in an obstructed kidney constitutes a urologic emergency and requires prompt relief of the obstruction.

UROLITHIASIS

Renal stone formation and its significant morbidity are common, affecting up to 5 per cent of the general population. Calcium, usually calcium oxalate or phosphate, is the most common constituent of renal calculi and is present in some form in almost 90 per cent of all renal stones (Table 28–6). Uric acid, cystine, and magnesium are the other major stone constituents. Up to three fourths of all stones, composed predominantly of calcium oxalate, occur in the syndrome of idiopathic urolithiasis. About 5 per cent of calcium stone formation is attributable to hyperparathyroidism. Some degree of uric acid lithiasis is contributory to about one fifth of all renal calculi.

Urinary stone formation depends on a number of factors. The saturation of urine with a mineral is governed by the amount excreted and the volume of urine in which it is contained. Urine is frequently supersaturated with respect to calcium. Crystallization from solution requires a nidus, or "seed," upon which to grow, and crystal precipitation may be inhibited by certain compounds.

Idiopathic urolithiasis, in which no underlying metabolic or infectious etiology is evident, accounts for the majority of cases of renal stone formation. Hypercalciuria, defined as calcium excretion of more than 4 mg/kg/24 hr without hypercalcemia, occurs in about 80 per cent of these cases. At least two subtypes of hypercalciuria appear to exist: in "renal" hypercalciuria, a deficiency in renal calcium reabsorption appears to drive increased intestinal calcium absorption, whereas "absorptive" hypercalciuria manifests a primary increase in intestinal calcium absorption, necessitating an increase in urinary calcium excretion. In both circumstances, serum calcium, phosphate, and parathyroid hormone levels are normal. Stone formation in idiopathic hypercalciuria depends heavily on the constant supersaturation of urine with calcium.

The cause of stone formation in patients with normal levels of urinary calcium excretion is less certain. However, hyperuricosuria, usually due to excessive purine intake in the form of meat, fish, and poultry, causes calcium stones in about 20 per cent of patients, probably by producing crystals of uric acid or its sodium salt that act as seed nuclei upon which calcium oxalate can deposit.

TABLE 28–6. CHARACTERISTICS OF RENAL CALCULI

CHEMICAL COMPOSITION	PER CENT OF ALL STONES	URINARY MANIFESTATION	RADIOGRAPHIC APPEARANCE
Calcium oxalate/phosphate	75	Hypercalciuria (40–75%) Hyperuricosuria (30–50%) Hyperoxaluria (<5%) Hypocitraturia ($\cong$50%) None ($\cong$5%)	Opaque, round, multiple calculi
Magnesium-ammonium phosphate + (calcium phosphate carbonate)	20	Infection with urease-positive organism	Opaque, staghorn calculus
Uric acid	5	Hyperuricosuria	Radiolucent
Cystine	1–2	Hypercystinuria	Opaque, staghorn ± round calculi

Secondary hypercalciuria, in which the serum calcium concentration may be elevated, occurs in only 5 to 7 per cent of recurrent stone formers. Hyperparathyroidism, distal RTA, sarcoidosis, and hypervitaminosis D account for a large number of these cases.

Although ileal resection or bypass or diseases of the ileum produce hyperoxaluria, intestinal oxaluric states are present in only a small percentage of all patients with renal stones. Primary hyperoxaluria is very rare.

Uric acid is weakly acidic, with a dissociation constant (pK_a) of 5.35. In a urine of that pH, 50 per cent of the uric acid is dissociated into urate and protons. The undissociated acid is very insoluble compared with urate and forms stones, whereas urate forms stones very rarely. Therefore, low urine pH is a critical factor in producing uric acid stones, and such stones rarely form and persist in an alkaline urine. Cystine stones occur only in patients with hereditary defect of amino acid transport by the brush border membranes of the renal proximal tubules involving cystine, arginine, ornithine, and citrulline.

Chronic urinary tract infection with urea-splitting organisms (i.e., *Proteus* species) is associated with struvite (triple phosphate) stones containing ammonium, magnesium, and calcium. Abnormal urine pH is critical to the formation of these stones, because struvite ($MgNH_4PO_4$) contains PO_4^{3-}, which is present only at a high pH, above 8.0; another requirement is that urine $[NH_4^+]$ be high. The kidney itself cannot produce so alkaline a urine that also contains appreciable concentrations of NH_4^+; this combination occurs only when bacteria that possess urease colonize the urinary tract and generate ammonia from urea; the urea hydrolyzes to NH_4^+ and raises the pH above 8.0. At that pH not only does struvite crystallize spontaneously, but calcium carbonate crystals also form and intermingle with the struvite; thus these stones always contain both minerals. These frequently form as "staghorn" calculi, outlining the renal calyces. A vicious circle develops in which urinary tract infection cannot be cleared owing to the presence of the foreign body (calculus) and stone formation continues as long as the urine is infected.

Passage of a renal stone is often the initial manifestation of renal stone disease and presents as ureteral colic—sharp unilateral flank pain that radiates to the groin. Hematuria is characteristically present in the urinalysis, and crystalluria may be obvious. A plain abdominal radiograph demonstrates the densely opaque calcium stones and the faintly opaque, sulfur-containing cystine stones. Only pure uric acid stones are radiolucent. An excretory urogram (IVP) may be required to demonstrate small stones or the site along the urinary tract at which a stone has lodged and in some patients may reveal the presence of medullary sponge kidney.

An important step in the diagnosis of the cause of a kidney stone is to secure the stone for analysis, if at all possible. The analysis should preferably be carried out by a crystallographic technique, which can sometimes reveal the sequence of stone formation from the central nidus to the periphery. The work-up for renal calculus is indicated in Table 28–7. Crystalluria is diagnostically important only in certain specific situations. Cystine crystals, which are flat hexagonal plates, occur only in heterozygous or homozygous cystinuria. Struvite crystals, rectangular prisms that resemble coffin lids, occur only when the urine is infected with urea-splitting bacteria. Although the finding

TABLE 28–7. PATIENT EVALUATION IN UROLITHIASIS

INITIAL	SECONDARY
Blood	Serum parathyroid hormone
Serum calcium	Serum 1,25(OH)$_2$ vitamin D$_3$
Serum uric acid	
Serum phosphate	
Alkaline phosphatase	
Urine	24-hour urine calcium
Urinalysis for crystalluria	24-hour urine uric acid
Urinalysis for pyuria	Urine culture
Radiography	Serial KUBs
Plain film (KUB)	
IVP	

of calcium oxalate, calcium phosphate, or uric acid crystals should arouse suspicions about the probable cause of stones in a patient, any of these crystals can be found in the urine of normal people.

Serial plain abdominal radiographs identify changes in stone size and number, serum calcium determinations identify hypercalcemic disorders associated with stone formation, and urine cultures identify etiologic (urea-splitting) and complicating bacterial involvement. Hypercalciuria and hyperuricosuria are identified by appropriate 24-hour urine collections.

The goal of medical treatment is prevention of recurrent stone formation, whereas that of surgical treatment is removal of existing stones. The initial treatment program, applicable to all patients with renal calculi, consists of a high fluid intake to ensure a minimum urine volume of 2 L/day. At least 3 L of fluid should be drunk each day, dis-

tributed throughout the day. In general, any fluid (with the exception of milk and oxalate-rich tea in certain disorders to be enumerated) may be consumed. In patients with intestinal hyperabsorption of calcium, intake of dairy products and certain calcium-rich foods should be limited. Oxalate intake should be restricted in patients with calcium oxalate stones. An excessive dietary intake of sodium should be discouraged because this may enhance calcium excretion. Urinary tract infection should be vigorously treated.

In cases of idiopathic hypercalciuria, dramatic reductions in urinary calcium excretion and stone formation can be achieved with thiazide diuretics and salt-restricted diet. Thiazide therapy should reduce the 24-hour urinary calcium excretion by almost half. If hyperuricosuria coexists, the addition of allopurinol to reduce the uric acid load is advantageous. Successful treatment of struvite stones may require specific, long-term antibiotic therapy in combination with surgical lithotomy.

Removal of stones may become necessary when nephrolithiasis is complicated by obstruction, in-

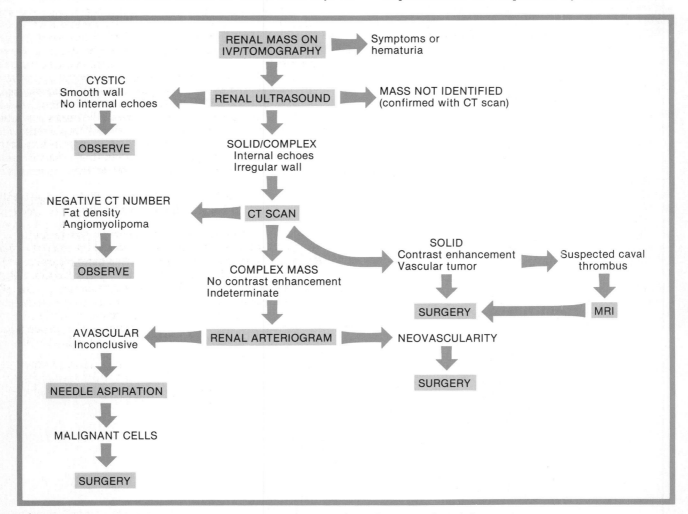

FIGURE 28–1. Scheme for the evaluation of a patient with a renal mass. (Adapted from Williams RD: Tumors of the kidney, ureter, and bladder. In Wyngaarden JB, Smith LH Jr, Bennett JC (eds): Cecil Textbook of Medicine. 19th ed. Philadelphia, WB Saunders Co, 1992, p 615.)

fection, or intractable pain. Certain stones may now be removed less invasively via percutaneous nephroscopy and by extracorporeal shock wave lithotripsy. The latter procedure uses focused, electrically generated shock waves to fragment stones within a human kidney without incision. Single stones of moderate size (≤ 1 cm in diameter) located in the renal pelvis are particularly amenable to this treatment. Not all stones are amenable to shock wave lithotripsy alone (e.g., staghorn calculi and stones in the lower ureter). The criteria for the choice of different methods are undergoing rapid refinement as further experience is gained with new approaches.

RENAL NEOPLASIA

Most renal tumors appear to originate from the tubulointerstitial components of the kidney. Renal cell carcinoma, for instance, is thought to be of proximal tubular origin. The evaluation of a patient for any renal mass may proceed according to the scheme given in Figure 28-1. This plan attempts to differentiate benign cystic lesions from solid masses and to identify malignant characteristics in solid renal masses. Multiple modalities exist for the accurate diagnostic study of renal masses, and because of their sensitivity an increasing number of incidental renal masses are being identified in asymptomatic patients. A systematic algorithmic approach should result in fewer than 10 per cent of renal masses being indeterminate prior to management.

A demonstrated renal mass by IVP with or without nephrotomography requires renal ultrasonography to determine more accurately whether the mass is cystic or solid. About two thirds of renal masses fulfill all ultrasonography criteria for a simple cyst and require no further work-up. When a mass is suspected on IVP but is not confirmed on ultrasonography (15 per cent of cases), renal CT is required, particularly in symptomatic patients.

If the mass on ultrasonography is solid or complex (20 per cent of cases), a renal CT scan (both with and without intravenous injection of iodine contrast) has replaced renal arteriography as the next diagnostic step. CT is as accurate as, and obviates the potential morbidity of, angiography in defining renal masses. In addition, CT can usually give sufficient local staging information to allow definitive surgical management. When contrast enhancement on CT is coupled with areas of a negative CT number (relative tissue density in Hounsfield units) typical of fat, a diagnosis of angiomyolipoma is appropriate and no further work-up is required. In indeterminate cases, arteriography or needle aspiration cytology or both may be needed to define the diagnosis further; however, in these unusual cases, final definition is likely to require surgery.

Benign tumors of the kidney include cortical adenomas and angiomyolipomas (hamartomas). The former are more common in older men and fre-

quently harbor nests of malignant cells. Therefore, adenomas are usually diagnosed after surgical evaluation of a solid renal mass. Angiomyolipomas are highly vascular fatty tumors that mimic renal cell carcinomas in both presentation and angiographic appearance. Significantly, over half of these tumors are seen in patients with tuberous sclerosis. Surgical exploration may be necessary for differentiating angiomyolipoma from renal cell carcinoma in patients without tuberous sclerosis, especially if CT scan results are equivocal.

Renal cell carcinoma, or hypernephroma, is the most frequent malignant renal neoplasm in adults and accounts for about 2 per cent of cancer deaths in both sexes. The term *hypernephroma* originated from the gross appearance of most of these tumors, which, because of their high lipid content, resemble adrenal tissue. The classic clinical presentation of renal cell carcinoma, a triad of hematuria, flank pain, and palpable flank mass, is seen in only about 10 per cent of patients. However, any one of these features is present in well over half of all patients as an initial manifestation of the tumor.

Renal cell carcinoma is notable for the large number of systemic, extrarenal manifestations of the tumor [Table 28-8]. Fever is seen in about one fifth of cases, and an elevated erythrocyte sedimentation rate is seen in half the patients. Anemia is seen in about one third of patients, but polycythemia is a striking finding in some cases. Reversible hepatic dysfunction has been described, as has peripheral neuropathy. Ectopic hormone syndromes associated with renal cell carcinoma include hypercalcemia from osteoclast-stimulating factors and Cushing's syndrome from tumor production of an adrenocorticotropic hormone (ACTH)-like factor. Hypercalcemia in renal cell carcinoma is frequently associated with bone metastasis of the tumor.

TABLE 28-8. MANIFESTATIONS OF RENAL CELL CARCINOMA: APPROXIMATE INCIDENCE AT PRESENTATION

MANIFESTATION	PER CENT OF TOTAL
Local	
Hematuria	60
Abdominal mass	45
Pain	40
"Classic triad"—hematuria/mass/pain	10
Systemic	
Common	
Weight loss	30
Anemia	20
Fever	10
Uncommon	<5 (each)
Erythrocytosis	
Leukemoid reaction	
Varicocele	
Hepatopathy	
Hypercalcemia	
Cushing's syndrome	
Galactorrhea	

The tumors usually have three cell types: clear cells, granular cells, and spindle cells; the last-named cell type and extensive nuclear anaplasia carry a poor prognosis. The tumors are highly vascular, supplied by vessels with thin, amuscular walls. Extension of the tumor into normal renal veins and even into the vena cava is not uncommon. Metastatic spread is chiefly via vascular routes, and the lungs, bone, and liver are most frequently sites of metastasis. The tumors often undergo cystic, internal degeneration, thus mimicking benign renal cysts. Calcification within a renal mass, the result of internal necrosis, is a significant radiographic indicator of malignancy.

Treatment of renal cell carcinoma requires surgical excision of the tumor, usually by radical nephrectomy. A small, localized tumor may be removed by heminephrectomy, or even ex vivo dissection when preservation of renal functional mass is critical. The tumors respond poorly to radiation and chemotherapy. Vena caval angiography may be valuable preoperatively to ascertain the presence of venous tumor thrombus. Survival is related to cellular morphology, local extension, and distant metastases and ranges from about 10 to 50 per cent for a 10-year survival based on these factors.

REFERENCES

Bennett WM, Elzinga LW, Porter GA: Tubulointerstitial disease and toxic nephropathy. In Brenner BM, Rector FC (eds): The Kidney. 4th ed. Philadelphia, WB Saunders Co, 1991, pp 1430–1496.

Gabow PA: Cystic disease of the kidney. In Wyngaarden JB, Smith LH Jr, Bennett JC (eds): Cecil Textbook of Medicine. 19th ed. Philadelphia, WB Saunders Co, 1992, pp 608–612.

McKinney TD: Tubulointerstitial diseases and toxic nephropathies. In Wyngaarden JB, Smith LH Jr, Bennett JC (eds): Cecil Textbook of Medicine. 19th ed. Philadelphia, WB Saunders Co, 1992, pp 568–579.

Pak CYC: Renal calculi. In Wyngaarden JB, Smith LH Jr, Bennett JC (eds): Cecil Textbook of Medicine. 19th ed. Philadelphia, WB Saunders Co, 1992, pp 603–608.

Williams RD: Tumors of the kidney, ureter, and bladder. In Wyngaarden JB, Smith LH Jr, Bennett JC (eds): Cecil Textbook of Medicine. 19th ed. Philadelphia, WB Saunders Co, 1992, pp 614–619.

29 HYPERTENSION AND VASCULAR DISORDERS OF THE KIDNEY

The arterial blood pressure is regulated by a variety of interdependent mechanisms. Inadequately compensated alterations in any of these mechanisms can lead to abnormal elevation of the pressure. The resultant hypertension initially might be quite asymptomatic. Sustained elevations of the arterial pressure, however, can lead to irreversible vascular injury and organ failure. This chapter reviews the pathophysiology and management of hypertension. The complications related to vascular injury are discussed in the context of disorders of the renal vasculature.

ARTERIAL HYPERTENSION

The measurable blood pressure of the general population demonstrates extreme variance. There is a correlation, however, of mortality and morbidity with the level of systolic and diastolic blood pressure. This correlation provides the basis for the arbitrary definition of abnormal blood pressure (Table 29–1). A diagnosis of hypertension is made in an adult over 18 years of age if the average of two or more blood pressure measurements on at least two subsequent visits is 90 mm Hg or higher diastolic or 140 mm Hg systolic. The blood pressure in healthy children and pregnant women is typically lower, so that readings in excess of 120/80 may be considered abnormal. Isolated systolic hypertension (ISH) is described when the systolic blood pressure is greater than 160 mm Hg in asso-

TABLE 29–1. CLASSIFICATION OF HYPERTENSION

RANGE (mm Hg)	CLASSIFICATION
Diastolic	
<85	Normal
85–89	High normal
90–104	Mild hypertension
105–114	Moderate hypertension
>115	Severe hypertension
Systolic (When Diastolic <90)	
<140	Normal
140–159	Borderline systolic hypertension
>160	Isolated systolic hypertension

ciation with a diastolic blood pressure less than 85 mm Hg. ISH is correlated with enhanced morbidity. Hypertension is typically classified as mild, moderate, or severe, depending upon the level of the diastolic blood pressure.

Hypertension occurs in more than 60 million Americans. The prevalence in Caucasians is approximately 15 per cent but is over 25 per cent in the black population. This marked racial difference in the rates of hypertension remains unexplained. The prevalence of hypertension also increases with advancing age. Hypertension is more common in men than in women up to approximately age 50. The rate thereafter is higher in women.

Pathophysiology of Hypertension

Physiologic principles indicate that pressure is a direct function of flow and resistance. The blood pressure, therefore, is related to the cardiac output and the peripheral vascular resistance. The cardiac output depends upon the contractility of the myocardium, the heart rate, and the intravascular blood volume. The regulation of normal blood pressure depends upon several interrelated factors that modulate the output and resistance (Table 29–2).

The autonomic nervous system is responsible for the regulation of abrupt hemodynamic alterations. Baroreceptors located in the carotid sinus can detect minute fluctuations in the arterial blood pressure. The afferent limb of the neural loop relays the message to the brain stem, from which adrenergic outflow directly regulates the myocardial contractility, the heart rate, and the systemic vascular resistance. The efferent limb of the autonomic nervous system also plays a role in the release of catecholamines from the adrenal medulla. The circulating adrenocorticoids act directly on the myocardium and the peripheral vasculature.

The regulation of the blood pressure depends upon other humoral factors, the most important being the renin-angiotensin-aldosterone system. Angiotensin II, a potent vasoconstrictor, is activated by a series of reactions initiated by renin. Angiotensin II stimulates the adrenal gland to synthesize aldosterone, which promotes the absorption of sodium and water by the kidney. The kallikrein-kinin system influences blood pressure by the vasodilatory properties of bradykinin. The kinins also directly and indirectly affect the renal excretion of salt and water. Atriopeptins produced and released from cardiac tissues exert natriuretic activity and contribute to vasodilation. Vascular tissues produce several vasoactive factors, which are detailed in a subsequent section. These factors include prostaglandins, endothelins, and the endothelium-relaxing factor nitric oxide.

Despite the understanding of the mechanisms regulating normal pressure, the primary cause of hypertension is not discernible in most instances. Disorders that lead to excess activity of any of the regulatory factors can lead secondarily to hypertension.

Clinical Assessment of Hypertension

The history and physical examination can be useful in discerning essential from secondary hypertension as well as elucidating the potential end-organ effects of established hypertension. The medical history should include a determination of factors that may predispose to the development of hypertension, including the dietary intake of sodium and caffeine, concomitant medical therapy (particularly oral contraceptives or other estrogen preparations), a positive family history of hypertension, and a stressful lifestyle. A history of weakness, muscle cramps, and polyuria suggests hypokalemia and possible hyperaldosteronism. The presence of headaches, palpitations, or hyperhidrosis suggests catecholamine excess. The end-organ effects of hypertension are usually manifested in the heart, brain, and kidneys, so that the history should include symptoms of coronary artery disease, congestive heart failure, cerebrovascular disease, and uremia.

The physical examination should focus on potential end-organ damage. The optic fundi should be carefully observed for evidence of arteriolar sclerosis. The presence of hemorrhages and exudates (grade III retinopathy) or papilledema (grade IV retinopathy) indicates severe, life-threatening hypertension. Signs of congestive heart failure or peripheral vascular disease should be determined. The abdomen should be auscultated for the presence of a bruit. A careful neurologic examination should be performed to determine possible deficits related to a stroke.

Routine laboratory screening prior to initiating pharmacologic therapy should include serum electrolytes to determine potential metabolic disorders

TABLE 29–2. REGULATORS OF ARTERIAL BLOOD PRESSURE

EFFECTOR	SITE OF PRODUCTION	ACTION
Catecholamines	Adrenal medulla	Alpha vasoconstrict Beta$_1$ increase heart rate and myocardial contractility Beta$_2$ vasodilate, contribute to vasoconstriction by stimulating release of norepinephrine
Humoral Factors		
Angiotensin II	Activation by converting enzyme	Vasoconstrict, stimulate aldosterone secretion
Aldosterone	Adrenal cortex	Enhance renal sodium absorption
Bradykinins	Lung	Vasodilate
Atriopeptins	Heart	Natriuretic, vasodilate
Vascular Factors		
Prostaglandins	Endothelium	PGI$_2$, PGE$_2$ vasodilate, PGH$_2$ vasoconstrict
Endothelins	Endothelium	Vasoconstrict
Nitric oxide	Endothelium	Vasodilate

PGI$_2$ = Prostaglandin I$_2$; PGE$_2$ = prostaglandin E$_2$; PGH$_2$ = prostaglandin H$_2$.

that may be associated with secondary causes of hypertension. The serum creatinine and a urinalysis should be obtained to determine potential renal dysfunction, which could be related as either a cause or an effect of hypertension. The serum glucose, cholesterol, and uric acid levels are helpful in assessing other cardiovascular risk factors and can be used as a baseline for monitoring the effects of antihypertensive therapy. Serial electrocardiograms and echocardiograms may be useful in assessing the effects of hypertension and antihypertensive treatment on the heart.

Extreme elevations of the blood pressure may be observed in asymptomatic patients and are considered to represent accelerated hypertension. When accelerated hypertension is associated with acute cardiovascular sequelae, the patient is considered to be suffering from hypertensive crisis or malignant hypertension. These patients often present with encephalopathy characterized by the rapid onset of confusion, headache, visual disturbances, and seizures. Papilledema occurs as a result of increased intracranial pressure. Death from a cerebrovascular accident frequently occurs if the hypertension is untreated. Renal damage due to necrotizing arteriolitis results in proteinuria, hematuria, and acute renal failure. Acute left ventricular failure or unstable angina may be the presenting feature of malignant hypertension. All of these end-organ sequelae may be reversed by successful treatment of the elevated blood pressure.

Causes of Secondary Hypertension

A small minority of adults with hypertension can be found to have a specific cause. Certain features of the patient may assist in determining those who should undergo evaluation of a potential reversible cause. Patients younger than 30 years have the greatest prevalence of correctable secondary hypertension. Patients with blood pressure that is difficult to manage pharmacologically or with an abrupt increase in the blood pressure after years of adequate control should be considered for evaluation. Certain features of the initial screening history, physical examination, and laboratory evaluation may suggest a specific secondary cause (Table 29–3).

Renovascular Hypertension

An obstruction of the renal vasculature prevents adequate perfusion of the kidney and leads to stimulation of renin production. The subsequent activation of angiotensin induces vasoconstriction and leads to the development of hypertension. Secondary hyperaldosteronism occurs and promotes an increase in renal sodium reabsorption, which aids in sustaining hypertension.

Atherosclerotic lesions account for approximately two thirds of the cases of reversible renovascular hypertension. This disorder is most often observed in older individuals with evidence of extensive atherosclerotic disease. The lesion most often occurs at the aortic ostia. The other major lesion causing renal arterial occlusion is fibromuscular hyperplasia. It typically occurs in young Caucasian women and involves either the renal arteries, generally not at the aortic ostia, or intrarenal segmental branches. Fibromuscular hyperplasia can affect one or both renal arteries. A renal hamartoma can be associated with hypertension. These tumors may grow so large that blood flow is diverted from the remaining tissue, thus activating the renin-angiotensin axis.

Renovascular hypertension should be suspected in any individual with abrupt onset of hypertension, particularly patients who are young or very old. The presence of an upper abdominal bruit that is systolic-diastolic and high pitched and radiates laterally from the midepigastrium is strongly suggestive of functionally significant renal artery stenosis. Hypokalemic metabolic alkalosis may be caused by secondary hyperaldosteronism. Renal dysfunction manifested by an elevated serum creatinine may be present.

Renal ultrasonography may demonstrate asymmetry in renal size if lesions are unilateral. Duplex Doppler studies also provide a noninvasive method of assessing a possible vascular occlusion.

TABLE 29–3. CAUSES OF SECONDARY HYPERTENSION

CAUSE	SYMPTOMS/SIGNS	MANIFESTATIONS	CONFIRMATION
Renovascular	Flank bruit, diffuse atherosclerosis	↓ K⁺, ↑ creatinine	Arteriogram, ↑ renal vein renin
Renal Disease	Edema	Acute or chronic renal failure	↑ Creatinine, BUN
Steroid Excess			
Aldosterone	Weakness, cramps	↓ K⁺, alkalosis	↓ Renin, ↑ aldosterone, CT scan
Dexamethasone suppressible	Hypertension in childhood	↓ K⁺, alkalosis	Hypertension suppressed by dexamethasone
Glucocorticoid	Cushingoid appearance	Hyperglycemia	↑ Cortisol
Pheochromocytoma	Paroxysmal, orthostatic	↑ Urine VMA, catecholamines	CT scan, angiography

BUN = Blood urea nitrogen; VMA = vanillylmandelic acid; ↓ = decrease; ↑ = increase.

The diagnosis of an obstructing lesion is made definitively by angiography.

The functional significance of an obstructing lesion, however, is best determined from measurements of the plasma renin activity (PRA), especially in combination with PRA measurements from both renal veins. Systemic venous PRA may be elevated but is not specific for renal vascular hypertension. In the setting of a unilateral lesion, selective renal vein PRA is elevated on the affected side and suppressed on the contralateral side. A significant increase in the systemic venous PRA or a significant decrease in renal blood flow as demonstrated by nuclear renography after a dose of an angiotensin-converting enzyme (ACE) inhibitor is also suggestive of significant renal vascular occlusion.

Syndromes of Steroid Excess

The autonomous production of aldosterone causes excessive absorption of sodium in the nephron. The resultant increase in the intravascular volume elevates the blood pressure. Renal perfusion is enhanced and renin production is suppressed. The effects of aldosterone on the nephron also lead to excessive renal secretion of potassium and hydrogen ions, resulting in hypokalemia and a metabolic alkalosis.

Excessive aldosterone production is most often described in the setting of a mineralocorticoid-producing adrenal adenoma or bilateral adrenal hyperplasia. Rarely, adrenal carcinoma may also be associated with primary aldosteronism. The diagnosis is made by detecting elevated levels of aldosterone in the plasma or urine in association with a low plasma renin activity coupled with an inability to suppress aldosterone secretion by saline volume expansion or converting-enzyme inhibition. Computed tomography (CT) of the adrenal glands should be performed to determine the presence of an adenoma or bilateral hyperplasia. Use of an iodinated cholesterol scintiscan may be useful in detecting small adenomas. Direct adrenal venous sampling of aldosterone may help differentiate adenoma from bilateral hyperplasia.

Dexamethasone-suppressible hyperaldosteronism is a rare disorder typically presenting as mineralocorticoid-induced hypertension in children. In these patients, an 11β-hydroxylase deficiency impairs renal conversion of cortisol to cortisone. The cortisol occupies renal aldosterone receptors and results in a syndrome resembling aldosterone excess. Dexamethasone ameliorates the disorder by suppressing adrenocorticotropic hormone (ACTH), and hence cortisol synthesis. Glucocorticoid excess (Cushing's syndrome) can lead to findings consistent with hyperaldosteronism owing to the effects of glucocorticoids on aldosterone receptors.

Pheochromocytoma

Pheochromocytoma is a rare tumor of the chromaffin cells of the neural crest. The tumor occurs most often in the adrenal medulla but can be located anywhere along the sympathetic ganglia in the abdomen or chest. The medullary tumors usually produce norepinephrine and epinephrine, whereas the peripheral tumors usually produce only norepinephrine. Hypertension occurs secondary to the increased cardiac output and increased peripheral vascular resistance stimulated by the adrenocorticoids.

The release of the catecholamines from these tumors may be intermittent, so that patients usually describe paroxysms of headaches, flushing, hyperhidrosis, and palpitations in association with hypertension. The diagnosis of pheochromocytoma may be suggested by the demonstration of elevated plasma epinephrine or norepinephrine or elevated urinary excretion of catecholamines or their metabolites, vanillylmandelic acid or metanephrine. The inability to suppress elevated plasma catecholamines by a single dose of clonidine provides additional evidence of the tumor. The localization of the tumor can most often be made by CT of the abdomen (particularly the adrenals) or the chest. The localization by scintigraphy of the guanethidine analogue ^{131}I-metaiodobenzylguanidine (MIBG) may be useful in locating small or extra-adrenal tumors. Selective arteriography or differential venous catecholamine sampling may be required for confirmation of the tumor location.

Treatment of Hypertension

The goal of treating hypertension is to reduce the risk of morbidity and mortality due to the cardiovascular consequences of the disorder. Antihypertensive treatment is indicated in patients with diastolic blood pressures in excess of 95 mm Hg or in patients with diastolic blood pressures of 90 to 94 mm Hg with other risk factors or existing evidence of cardiovascular complications. The treatment of ISH reduces the morbidity and mortality in that population of hypertensive patients.

The initial therapy of hypertension should be directed at nonpharmacologic alterations in the patient's lifestyle. Such therapy should include dietary modifications to reduce sodium, alcohol, and caffeine intake. Weight reduction should be recommended to the obese individual. Exercise should be encouraged and behavior modification should be considered to reduce stressful lifestyles. Occasionally, blood pressure can be reduced adequately by these nonpharmacologic strategies, but more often the patient requires pharmacologic intervention.

The most commonly prescribed antihypertensive agents are described in Table 29–4. The notable advantage of one agent over another is not generally discernible. An individualized approach to therapy, therefore, is more favorable than the traditional stepped-care therapy. This approach should include consideration of the efficacy of the various agents in different populations and the patient's tolerance with regard to side effects and costs of therapy.

Hypertensive emergencies require a more aggressive approach to treatment (Table 29–5). Parenterally administered therapy such as sodium nitroprusside, labetalol, hydralazine, and diazoxide are often indicated to minimize the end-organ damage. Such therapy should be administered in a critical care setting with intensive monitoring of the blood pressure and organ function. Accelerated hypertension without manifestations of acute end-organ dysfunction can be treated with oral agents that acutely lower the blood pressure, such as clonidine or calcium channel blockers.

The treatment of secondary hypertension should obviously be directed at eliminating the primary disorder. The goal of treating renovascular hypertension should be the removal of an obstructing lesion in the renal arterial system by transluminal angioplasty or surgical revascularization. The treatment of choice for patients with a single adrenal adenoma is unilateral adrenalectomy. In patients who are poor surgical candidates or who have bilateral adrenal hyperplasia, pharmacologic therapy with an aldosterone antagonist should be used. Treatment of pheochromocytoma is surgical unless the tumor is metastatic or the patient is inoperable for other reasons. Patients should be prepared for 1 to 2 weeks before surgery with both alpha- and beta-adrenergic blocking agents and volume expansion to avert marked hemodynamic alterations that can occur perioperatively. Alpha blockade must be complete before beta-blocking agents are used. Otherwise, particularly in tumors secreting both epinephrine and norepinephrine, beta blockade without antecedent alpha blockade may result in a hypertensive crisis.

VASCULAR DISORDERS OF THE KIDNEY

The understanding of the normal vascular responses to circulating and physical stresses exerted by blood flow has led to a better understanding of the pathophysiology of many vascular disorders (Fig. 29–1). The renal vasculature exhibits these physiologic responses and demonstrates a wide spectrum of disorders similar to those observed in the vascular tissues throughout the body.

Vascular Biology

Endothelial cells form the inner lining of all vascular tissue and are the elements in direct contact with the blood components. The endothelium plays three major regulatory functions with regard to maintenance of blood flow. First, it is a regulator of vascular tone. Vascular relaxation is me-

TABLE 29–4. COMMONLY PRESCRIBED ORAL ANTIHYPERTENSIVE DRUGS

CLASS	GENERIC	MECHANISM	SIDE EFFECTS	PRECAUTIONS
Diuretics	Thiazide, furosemide	Inhibit tubular NaCl absorption	Hypokalemia, hyperuricemia, hyperglycemia	Furosemide is more useful in chronic renal failure
	Spironolactone	Aldosterone antagonist	Hyperkalemia	Avoid with marked renal failure
Adrenergic Inhibitors				
Central	Clonidine, methyldopa	Decreased CNS sympathetic outflow	Drowsiness, fatigue, dry mouth, sexual dysfunction	Rapid clonidine withdrawal may lead to rebound hypertension
Peripheral	Guanethidine	Vasodilation	Orthostasis, sexual dysfunction	Use with caution in elderly
Beta-	Propranolol	↓ Heart rate and contractility	Bradycardia, fatigue, insomnia	Avoid in obstructive airway disease, CHF, heart block
Alpha$_1$-	Prazosin	Vasodilation	Orthostasis, "first dose" hypotension	Tachyphylaxis to drug effect often noted
Combined alpha-, beta-	Labetalol	↓ Heart rate and contractility, vasodilation	Dizziness, fatigue, headache	Avoid in obstructive airway disease, CHF, heart block
Vasodilators	Hydralazine, minoxidil	Vasodilation	Tachycardia, fluid retention	Positive antinuclear antibody, lupus syndrome with hydralazine, hypertrichosis with minoxidil
Calcium Channel Blockers	Nifedipine, diltiazem, verapamil	Vasodilation	Tachycardia, fluid retention	Useful in patients with concomitant coronary disease
ACE Inhibitors	Captopril	Inhibition of AII production	Rash, neutropenia, cough, hyperkalemia	May cause worsening of renal function with chronic renal disease

diated by endothelium-derived prostacyclin and the endothelium-relaxing factor nitric oxide. The endothelins, potent vasoconstrictors, are peptides produced and released by endothelial cells. Second, the endothelium acts as a regulator of the coagulation cascade. Various circulating stimuli allow the endothelial surface expression of tissue factor that can activate the coagulation cascade. Alternatively, coagulation is inhibited by the production of prostacyclin, which diminishes platelet adherence. The endothelium also metabolizes some factors responsible for clot formation, such as ADP released from platelets. In established thrombi, the endothelium plays a major role in fibrinolysis by forming plasminogen activators. Finally, the endothelium regulates cell growth, which has important implications regarding tissue injury as well as determining normal vascular architecture. The growth of adjacent smooth muscle cells is regulated by platelet-derived growth factor, which is in part produced by endothelial tissue.

Although endothelial cells might be considered regulators, the smooth muscle cells that underlie the endothelium can be considered the effectors of the vascular tissue. These cells constrict in response to the endothelins and dilate in response to relaxing factor. This dilation is mediated through a mechanism that may also be stimulated by atriopeptins. Although the transient architecture of vascular lumen may be mediated by constriction or relaxation of the smooth muscle layer, proliferation of these cells may lead to a chronic alteration in the structure of the vessel. The growth of the smooth muscle cells depends upon local factors derived from the endothelium or platelets. Circulating factors such as angiotensin II and catecholamines are also promoters of vascular smooth muscle cell growth. The smooth muscle cells may

TABLE 29–5. PARENTERAL DRUGS FOR HYPERTENSIVE EMERGENCIES

DRUG	ADVANTAGES	PRECAUTIONS
Vasodilators		
Nitroprusside	Rapid onset, allows effective titration, no sedation	Requires intensive care monitoring, thiocyanate toxicity with prolonged use
Diazoxide	Rapid onset	Large boluses may cause severe hypotension, prolonged effect, sodium retention, reflex tachycardia, angina
Hydralazine	IM preparation	Reflex tachycardia, angina
Nitroglycerin	Dilates coronary vessels	Requires intensive care monitoring; flushing, headache
Enalapril	Longer duration of action	May cause rapid decrease of renal function, hyperkalemia
Adrenergic Inhibitors		
Methyldopa	Gradual decline in blood pressure, safe in pregnancy	Inconsistent effect, sedation
Labetalol	Little reflex tachycardia, prolonged duration	Bronchospasm, bradyarrhythmias; avoid with left ventricular failure

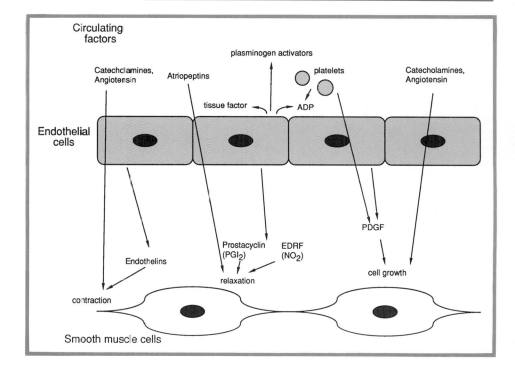

FIGURE 29–1. Principles of vascular biology. Systemic and locally produced factors modulate vascular tone, tissue growth, and platelet activity. EDRF = Endothelium-derived relaxing factor; PDGF = platelet-derived growth factor.

also indirectly affect the vascular architecture by regulating the production of extracellular matrix constituents.

It is evident that vascular tissue contains the capability either to promote or to inhibit the basic processes of vascular tone, intravascular coagulation, and cell growth. Although this complex array may not be active in normal intact vessels, it is essential in the setting of disruption of the vascular architecture. These mechanisms create a balance that allows injured vascular tissue to heal while allowing adequate flow distal to the site of injury. Any imbalance of these systems promotes vascular pathology. These pathologic changes can occur in the major arterial or venous vessels or their branches (Table 29–6).

Renal Arterial Occlusion

Partial obstruction of the renal arterial system by atheromatous plaque or fibromuscular dysplasia leads to renovascular hypertension, as discussed above. Occasionally, complete occlusion of the major renal artery or its main branches occurs. Thrombosis of renal arteries is most often seen in cases of severe blunt abdominal trauma. Thrombosis can also occur rarely after surgical manipulation or during angiographic study of the renal artery and in association with aneurysms of the aorta or main renal arteries. Occlusion of renal arteries may also occur as an embolic phenomenon, often in patients with underlying atherosclerotic vascular disease. The emboli usually originate from the heart during atrial fibrillation or after myocardial infarction. Valvular vegetations of bacterial endocarditis sometimes embolize to and obstruct renal arteries. Simultaneous embo-

lization to other organs may provide evidence of the nature of the occlusive disease in the kidney.

The symptoms of renal artery occlusion reflect tissue ischemia. Sudden renal infarction may cause severe localized flank pain, nausea and vomiting, and oliguria. A sudden onset or exacerbation of hypertension may occur. Laboratory studies often demonstrate a leukocytosis and an elevation of the serum lactate dehydrogenase. Segmental or unilateral renal infarction may be asymptomatic without any evident effect on renal function.

Nuclear renography is useful in the initial evaluation of suspected renal infarction. The absence of blood flow in a dynamic study or defects in activity on static images are strongly suggestive of arterial occlusion. Renal arteriography is necessary to determine the location and extent of the occlusion. Successful revascularization of the main artery or segmental branches usually requires surgical embolectomy or bypass grafting. Thrombolytic agents or transluminal angioplasty followed by anticoagulation may be useful in selected instances. Conservative management may be adequate in most instances of unilateral or segmental occlusion.

Arterioles and Microvasculature

Disorders of the main renal vessels are usually unilateral. The processes that involve the smaller vessels of the kidney, however, are diffuse, involving both kidneys. Most diseases of the renal arterioles are systemic and involve several organ systems. These disorders are usually initiated by vascular injury and advance because of the vascular responses to the injury. Clinically, the arteriolar disorders are usually associated with hypertension due to activation of the renin-angiotensin-aldosterone axis. Renal failure may occur acutely but is usually progressive over a period of weeks to months.

Atheromatous embolization from aortic plaque usually follows manipulation of an atherosclerotic aorta and affects multiple small vessels. There may be evidence of embolization to other tissues, particularly the optic fundi or lower extremities. Pathologic examination of the kidney reveals the presence of cholesterol clefts surrounded by tissue reaction in small to medium-sized renal arteries. There is no treatment for this disorder, and the prognosis is very poor, reflecting the severity of the primary atheromatous disease.

Benign nephrosclerosis is a misnomer used to describe a slow process of intrarenal vascular sclerosis and ischemic change that complicates the course of chronic essential hypertension. Although the intrarenal arteries show signs of sclerotic thickening, the dominant lesion is at the level of the afferent arteriole, where hyaline thickening leads to a homogeneous, eosinophilic appearance of the vessel. The glomeruli have ischemic wrinkling of the basement membranes and become progressively sclerotic, whereas the tubules undergo atrophy and are replaced by fibrotic tissue.

TABLE 29–6. RENAL VASCULAR DISORDERS

VESSEL	DISORDER	MANIFESTATION
Arteries	Thrombosis	Acute renal failure
	Embolization	Hypertension
Arterioles and microvasculature	Atheroembolization	Rapidly progressive renal failure, systemic signs of embolization
	Benign nephrosclerosis	Slowly progressive renal failure
	Malignant hypertension	Acute renal failure, proteinuria
	Scleroderma	Malignant crisis with hypertension and rapidly progressive renal failure
	Thrombotic microangiopathy	Rapidly progressive renal failure, thrombocytopenia, hemolytic anemia
Renal vein	Thrombosis	Acute renal failure, proteinuria, pulmonary embolism

Clinically, there may be mild proteinuria, but the urinary sediment is unremarkable. Radiography shows a progressive decrease in kidney size. The glomerular filtration rate (GFR) slowly diminishes, eventually reaching the stage of symptomatic renal failure. Treatment is directed at control of the blood pressure. Although it is not proven that reduction of blood pressure prevents the development of nephrosclerosis, it is evident that the progression to end-stage renal failure can be abated with adequate antihypertensive therapy.

Malignant nephrosclerosis is a generalized necrotizing arteritis seen in conjunction with accelerated hypertension. The kidneys are generally contracted in size and have petechial hemorrhages on the surface. Fibrinoid necrosis without inflammation in the renal arterioles and sometimes extending into the glomerular tufts is the characteristic lesion. A second prominent lesion is the "onion skin" endothelial proliferation in small arteries produced by concentric layers of collagen and proliferating endothelial cells.

The patient usually presents with extreme elevation of the diastolic blood pressure — in excess of 120 mm Hg. Hypertensive encephalopathy often occurs concomitantly. Proteinuria and hematuria occur in association with acute renal failure. The goal of therapy is to rapidly lower the diastolic blood pressure to about 100 mm Hg, with a more gradual lowering to about 80 mm Hg over the course of a few days. The renal function frequently decreases further during the initial phase of blood pressure control but recovers as the vascular lesions heal and autoregulation of renal blood flow is re-established. If the vascular injury is quite severe, the healing may occur over several weeks or months as normal blood pressure is maintained.

Scleroderma is a progressive connective tissue disease of uncertain etiology. The disease affects the vasculature of several organs, including the kidney. The renal arterioles usually demonstrate intimal proliferation with progressive luminal occlusion. An accelerated process may occur and is associated with the necrotic arteriolar and glomerular changes observed in malignant hypertension. The clinical course of renal involvement reflects the pathologic changes. The initial arteriolar changes may be associated with a normal GFR and urinalysis. The development of proteinuria or mild hypertension often heralds the onset of the accelerated scleroderma renal crisis. This phase is similar to the presentation of malignant hypertension. Therapy is directed at control of the blood pressure. ACE inhibitors initiated at the onset of renal involvement may avert a renal crisis.

The **hemolytic-uremic syndrome** (HUS) and **thrombotic thrombocytopenic purpura** (TTP) are two disorders characterized by thrombotic microangiopathy. The clinical features, pathogenesis, and therapy of these two disorders are similar so that they are often considered one entity with variable presentations. The renal lesion varies in severity and is characterized by fibrin thrombi in the glomerular capillary loops. The arterioles may likewise demonstrate thrombi with fibrinoid necrosis. The disorders are associated with a microangiopathic hemolytic anemia with thrombocytopenia.

HUS is generally observed in children following a nonspecific gastrointestinal or influenzal syndrome. An adult form is observed most often in young women in association with the use of oral contraceptives or in the peripartum period. Some antineoplastic agents have also been associated with HUS. The clinical syndrome in TTP is dominated by neurologic manifestations. The clinical course of renal involvement may be either acute or rapidly progressive renal failure. The rate of spontaneous recovery in children with HUS is high, so that only supportive therapy is necessary. The prognosis in adults is not as good, so additional therapy is indicated. Evidence suggests that plasma exchange in association with fresh plasma and corticosteroids may induce remissions.

Renal Vein Occlusion

Renal vein occlusion is a thrombotic event. The incidence of renal vein thrombosis is high in nephrotic glomerulopathies, especially membranous nephropathy. It may occur in infants who develop severe volume depletion accompanying gastroenteritis or sepsis. The venous occlusion is usually asymptomatic. The thrombus can embolize, however, and the patient may present with an acute pulmonary embolism or infarction. The renal function may decline acutely, particularly in children or adults with the nephrotic syndrome.

Renal ultrasonography may demonstrate a thrombus in the renal vein. Renal venography is usually required for a definitive diagnosis. Anticoagulation is indicated in patients with proven or threatened pulmonary embolism. Fibrinolytic therapy may be considered in patients with acute renal failure or severe flank pain. Renal function generally improves with resolution of the thrombus. Prophylactic anticoagulation is not recommended for the patient with nephrotic syndrome who is at risk for developing thrombosis.

REFERENCES

Bravo EL: Pheochromocytoma: New concepts and future trends. Kidney Int 40:544, 1991.

Calhoun DA, Oparil S: Treatment of hypertensive crisis. N Engl J Med 323:1177, 1990.

The Joint National Committee on Detection, Evaluation, and Treatment of High Blood Pressure: The 1988 Report of the Joint National Committee on Detection, Evaluation, and Treatment of High Blood Pressure. Arch Intern Med 148:1023, 1988.

Vane JR, Angaard EE, Botting RM: Regulatory functions of the vascular endothelium. N Engl J Med 323:27, 1990.

Vaughan ED Jr: Renovascular hypertension. Kidney Int 27:811, 1985.

30 ACUTE RENAL FAILURE

DEFINITION AND ETIOLOGY

Acute renal failure (ARF) is a syndrome that can be broadly defined as an abrupt decrease in renal function sufficient to result in retention of nitrogenous waste (e.g., blood urea nitrogen [BUN] and creatinine) in the body. ARF can result from a decrease of renal blood flow (prerenal azotemia), intrinsic renal parenchymal diseases (renal azotemia), or obstruction to urine flow (postrenal azotemia) (Fig. 30–1).

The most common intrinsic renal disease that leads to ARF is an entity referred to as acute tubular necrosis (ATN), which designates a clinical syndrome in which there is an abrupt and sustained decline in glomerular filtration rate (GFR) occurring within minutes to days in response to an acute ischemic or nephrotoxic insult. Its clinical recognition is largely predicated upon exclusion of prerenal and postrenal causes of sudden azotemia, followed by exclusion of other causes of intrinsic ARF (i.e., glomerulonephritis, acute inter-

stitial nephritis, vasculitis). Said in another way, it is necessary to exclude carefully the other defined renal syndromes before concluding that ATN is present. Although the name acute tubular necrosis is not an entirely valid histologic description of this syndrome, the term is ingrained in clinical medicine and is therefore used in this chapter.

DIFFERENTIAL DIAGNOSIS AND DIAGNOSTIC EVALUATION OF THE PATIENT

Acute Azotemia During Hospitalization

Despite the exhaustive list of conditions that can cause acute azotemia in hospitalized patients, a careful history and physical examination and simple laboratory tests often suffice for diagnosis. In hospitalized adults, prerenal azotemia is the single most common cause of acute azotemia, and ATN is the most common intrinsic renal disease that leads to ARF. Thus, the most important differential diagnosis is between prerenal azotemia (e.g.,

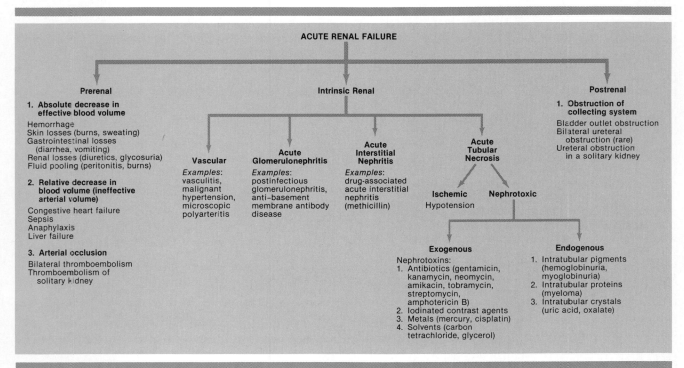

FIGURE 30–1. Causes of acute renal failure.

volume depletion) and ATN (secondary to ischemia or nephrotoxins). In the elderly male patient, bladder outlet obstruction must also be excluded. In addition, depending on the clinical setting, other diagnoses to be considered are acute interstitial nephritis (e.g., secondary to methicillin), atheromatous emboli (prior aortic surgery and/or aortogram), ureteral obstruction (pelvic or colon surgery), or intrarenal obstruction (e.g., acute uric acid nephropathy).

Chart Review, History, and Physical Examination. Determination of the cause of ARF depends on a systematic approach, as depicted in Table 30–1. The difficulty in arriving at a correct diagnosis in a hospitalized patient is not the failure to identify a possible etiology for the ARF; the problem is often just the opposite, that is, there are several possible causes of ARF. Correct diagnosis depends on careful analysis of available data on the clinical course of each patient with ARF and examining the sequence of deterioration in renal function in relation to chronology of the potential etiologies of ARF. Correct diagnosis also requires a knowledge of the natural history of the different causes of ARF. Some of the important data that should be sought from chart review are presented in Table 30–2.

Reduced body weight, postural changes in blood pressure and pulse, and decreased jugular venous pulse all suggest a reduction in extracellular fluid volume. Prerenal azotemia may also develop in states in which extracellular fluids are expanded (e.g., cardiac failure, cirrhosis, nephrotic syndrome) but the "effective" blood volume is decreased. Careful abdominal examination may uncover a distended, tender bladder, indicating lower urinary tract obstruction. In any case in which lower tract obstruction is suspected as a cause of acute azotemia, examination of the prostate and a sterile "in-and-out" diagnostic postvoid bladder catheterization should be performed as a part of the physical examination. The urine volume should be recorded and a specimen saved for studies described below.

Additional findings that may be helpful are the occurrence of fever and rash in some patients with acute interstitial nephritis. A history of a recent aortic catheterization and the finding of livedo reticularis are diagnostic clues for cholesterol or atheromatous emboli.

Differentiating prerenal azotemia from ATN may be difficult, partly because evaluation of volume status in a critically ill patient is not easy and any cause of prerenal azotemia, if severe enough, may lead to ATN. Evaluation of the urine volume and urine sediment and a number of urinary indices are particularly helpful in making the correct diagnosis.

Urine Volume. The urine volume is often less than 400 ml/day in oliguric ATN. Normal urine output does not exclude the diagnosis of ATN because a substantial number of patients with ATN have urine outputs as high as 1.5 to 2.0 L/day. This nonoliguric ATN is frequently associated with nephrotoxic antibiotic-induced ARF. On the

TABLE 30–1. DIAGNOSTIC APPROACH TO ACUTE RENAL FAILURE

1. Record review (see Table 30–2); special attention to evidence for recent reduction in GFR and sequence of deterioration of renal function to determine possible causative factors
2. Physical examination, including evaluation of hemodynamic status
3. Urinalysis, including careful sediment examination
4. Determination of urinary indices
5. Bladder catheterization
6. Fluid-diuretic challenge
7. Radiologic studies, particular procedure being dictated by clinical setting, e.g., ultrasonography to look for obstruction
8. Renal biopsy

GFR = Glomerular filtration rate.

TABLE 30–2. RECORD REVIEW IN A HOSPITALIZED PATIENT WHO DEVELOPS ACUTE RENAL FAILURE

	COMMENTS
1. Prior renal function	Determine whether or not the azotemia is acute
	Patients with prior renal insufficiency are particularly susceptible to ARF, secondary to contrast dyes
2. Presence of infection	Sepsis may cause ARF even in the absence of hypotension
3. Nephrotoxic agents	Aminoglycosides (e.g., gentamicin) are an important cause of ATN in hospitalized patients; typically causes non-oliguric ATN during first 2 wk of therapy
	Methicillin may cause acute interstitial nephritis
	Cytotoxic drugs, e.g., cisplatin, may cause ARF
4. Contrast studies including oral cholecystography, intravenous pyelography, angiography	An important cause of ATN in hospitalized patients; typically causes oliguric ATN within 24–48 hr after study
5. Episodes of hypotension	Suggests prerenal azotemia or ischemic ATN
6. History of blood transfusions	Incompatible blood transfusion is an unusual cause of ATN
7. Review of chart for history of loss or sequestration of extracellular fluid volume, intake-output, and serial weights	Provides important clues to the possibility of prerenal azotemia
8. In surgical patients	Patients who have had cardiac or vascular surgery or with obstructive jaundice are particularly susceptible to ATN
	Methoxyflurane and the related, less toxic enflurane are causes of nonoliguric ATN
9. Amount of blood loss during surgery and whether associated with hypotension	Suggests prerenal azotemia or ischemic ATN

ARF = Acute renal failure; ATN = acute tubular necrosis.

other hand, total anuria (0 urine output) should suggest a diagnosis other than ATN, the most important being obstruction. Widely varying daily urine outputs also suggest obstruction.

Urine Sediment. In prerenal failure a moderate number of hyaline and finely granular casts may be seen, but coarsely granular and cellular casts are infrequent. In ATN, the sediment is usually quite characteristic: "dirty" brown granular casts and renal tubular epithelial cells, free and in casts, are the most striking elements and are present in 70 to 80 per cent of patients with ATN. A "benign" sediment containing few formed elements should alert the physician to the possibility that obstruction is present. In ARF associated with intratubular oxalate (e.g., methoxyflurane anesthesia) or uric acid deposition (associated with acute hyperuricemia after chemotherapy of neoplastic disease), the sediment contains abundant oxalate or uric acid crystals.

The "Urinary Indices." An important series of diagnostic tests relates to an assessment of renal tubular function. The most widely used and convenient tests are measurements of sodium and creatinine simultaneously obtained from plasma and urine serum samples. The rationale for the use of these indices is as follows: the ratio of urine to plasma creatinine (U/P_{cr}) provides an index of the fraction of filtered water excreted. If it is assumed that all of the creatinine filtered at the glomerulus is excreted into the urine and that relatively little is added by secretion (an oversimplification but an acceptable one), any increment in the concentration of creatinine in urine over that in plasma must be due to the removal of water.

In prerenal azotemia, owing to the reduction in the amount of glomerular filtrate entering each nephron and to an added stimulus to salt and water retention, U/P_{cr} typically is considerably greater than it is in ATN, and urinary sodium concentrations characteristically are low (Table 30–3). In contrast, in the ATN variety of ARF, the nephrons excrete a large fraction of their filtered sodium and water, resulting in lower U/P_{cr} and a higher fractional excretion of sodium. Interpretations of these tests, however, must be made in conjunction with other assessments of the patient because there are clinically important exceptions to these generalizations. For example, certain types of ATN, such as radiographic dye–induced renal injury, may present with all the clinical characteristics of ATN but with fractional excretions of sodium less than 1 per cent.

Indications for Other Diagnostic Tests and Renal Biopsy. If the diagnosis of prerenal azotemia or ATN is reasonably certain and the clinical setting does not require the exclusion of other causes of acute azotemia, generally no further diagnostic evaluation is necessary. Further diagnostic evaluation is indicated when (1) the diagnosis is uncertain, especially if the clinical setting suggests other possibilities (e.g., obstruction, vascular accident); (2) clinical findings make the diagnosis of prerenal azotemia or ATN unlikely (e.g., total anuria); and/or (3) the oliguria persists beyond 4 weeks.

Sonography provides a noninvasive method of determining the presence or absence of dilatation of the collecting system. It is, therefore, an important and safe screening test to rule out obstruction. Radionuclide methods are available to assess renal blood flow and excretory (secretory) function. Blood flow studies can easily discriminate between the presence or absence of renal blood flow and the symmetry of flow to the two kidneys but are less accurate in quantitating absolute rates of flow. Renal biopsy is rarely required for ARF occurring in the hospital setting, in contrast to ARF occurring outside the hospital, for which renal biopsy is often indicated.

Evaluation of a Patient Who Presents with Renal Failure

Azotemia first discovered outside the hospital may be either chronic or acute in origin. Useful points in deciding whether the renal failure is acute or chronic are summarized in Table 30–4. The majority of those who present with advanced azotemia have chronic renal failure. Before a detailed evaluation is carried out, priority should be given to identifying complications of renal failure that may be lethal unless treated promptly. Some of these, such as marked fluid overload and pericardial tamponade, may be detected on clinical examination. However, life-threatening complications such as severe hyperkalemia or extreme metabolic acidosis require laboratory evaluation. As mentioned in a previous section, the electrocardiogram (ECG) is valuable in assessing the effects of hyperkalemia on the heart.

Even before the nature of the underlying disease causing azotemia is known, often a decision to initiate dialysis has to be made. Dialysis should be instituted promptly in patients with severe hyperkalemia, acidosis, marked fluid overload, or uremic manifestations. Many uremic manifestations are nonspecific. However, a pericardial rub or neurologic manifestations such as asterixis are indications for prompt dialysis.

TABLE 30–3. URINARY DIAGNOSTIC INDICES

INDEX	PRERENAL AZOTEMIA	ACUTE TUBULAR NECROSIS
Urine sodium U_{Na} (mEq/L)	<20	>40
U_{Cr} (mg/dl)/P_{Cr} (mg/dl)	>40	<20
U_{OSM} (mOSM/kg H_2O)	>500	<350
Renal failure index $RFI = \dfrac{U_{Na}}{U_{Cr}/P_{Cr}}$	<1	>1
Fractional excretion of filtered sodium $FeNa = \dfrac{U_{Na} \times P_{Cr}}{P_{Na} \times U_{Cr}} \times 100$	<1	>1

Laboratory Evaluation. In hospitalized adults in whom prerenal and postrenal azotemia have been excluded, ARF is usually due to ATN. By contrast, in an outpatient setting in which prerenal and postrenal causes have been excluded, ARF is more often due to other renal parenchymal diseases. Examination of the urine for blood and protein and of the urine sediment can give valuable information that often helps to narrow considerably the diagnostic possibilities and to suggest further appropriate laboratory evaluation.

1. Presence of 3+ to 4+ protein, 2+ to 3+ blood, and active sediment with red blood cells (RBCs) and RBC casts is characteristic of proliferative glomerulonephritis. Evaluation of history and physical examination (suggesting, for example, systemic lupus erythematosus), complement levels, antinuclear factor, and kidney biopsy (if the kidney size is normal) generally help to clarify the diagnosis.

2. Presence of only a few RBCs in the urine sediment with a strongly heme-positive urine or a heme-positive supernatant (having removed the RBCs by centrifugation) is most commonly due to myoglobinuria or hemoglobinuria. Patients with rhabdomyolysis have marked increase in the muscle enzymes such as creatinine phosphokinase. The urine sediment in patients with myoglobinuria may show RBCs, pigmented casts, granular casts, and numerous uric acid crystals.

Kidney size gives important clues to whether the renal failure is acute or chronic and to whether obstruction is present. Renal ultrasonography is the initial procedure of choice because it is noninvasive and reliable. Normal-sized kidneys in a patient with advanced azotemia generally suggest that the patient has acute rather than chronic renal failure; however, several important causes of chronic renal failure, including diabetes mellitus, multiple myeloma, and amyloidosis, may be associated with normal-sized kidneys. The renal ultrasound examination is also helpful in (1) making a diagnosis of polycystic kidney disease; (2) determining whether one or two kidneys are present; and (3) localizing the kidney for renal biopsy.

Normal kidney size in a patient who presents with renal failure is often an indication for renal biopsy. Before a renal biopsy is carried out, the blood pressure must be controlled, bleeding and coagulation parameters checked, and the presence of two kidneys confirmed.

CLINICAL PRESENTATION, COMPLICATIONS, AND MANAGEMENT OF ACUTE TUBULAR NECROSIS

ARF results in signs and symptoms that reflect loss of the regulatory, excretory, and endocrine functions of the kidney. The loss of excretory ability of the kidney is expressed by a rise in the plasma concentration of specific substances normally excreted by the kidney. The most widely

TABLE 30–4. USEFUL FEATURES SUGGESTING ACUTE OR CHRONIC RENAL FAILURE

	ACUTE RENAL FAILURE	CHRONIC RENAL FAILURE
Previous history	Normal renal function	Prior history of elevated blood urea nitrogen or creatinine
Kidney size	Normal	Small with exception of multiple myeloma, diabetes, amyloid, polycystic kidney disease
Bone film	No evidence of renal osteodystrophy	May show evidence of renal osteodystrophy
Hemoglobin/hematocrit	Anemia may be present, but a normal hemoglobin level in a patient with advanced azotemia is presumptive evidence of ARF.	Anemia frequently is present.

monitored indices are the concentrations of BUN and creatinine in the serum. In patients without complications, the BUN rises by about 10 to 20 mg/dl/day, and the HCO_3^- falls to a steady-state level of 17 to 18 mEq/L. The serum K^+ need not rise appreciably unless there is a hypercatabolic state, gastrointestinal bleeding, or extensive tissue trauma.

Because ATN is inherently a catabolic disorder, patients with ATN generally lose about ½ pound per day. Further weight loss can be minimized by providing adequate calories (1800 to 2500 kcal) and about 40 gm of protein per day. The use of hyperalimentation with 50 per cent dextrose and essential amino acids has had little effect on minimizing mortality and morbidity in patients with ATN, except in patients who also have significant burns.

Although diuretics do not appear to alter the course of ATN, it is generally easier to manage the polyuric than the oliguric form of ATN. Some clinicians therefore advocate administration of a bolus dose of a loop diuretic once the diagnosis is established. If the diuretic fails to induce a diuretic response, it is discontinued.

Hyperkalemia is a life-threatening complication of ARF and often necessitates urgent intervention. The electromechanical effects of hyperkalemia on the heart are potentiated by hypocalcemia, acidosis, and hyponatremia. Thus, the ECG, which measures the summation of these effects, is a better guide to therapy than a single K^+ determination. The cardiac effects of hyperkalemia are primarily referable to blunting the magnitude of the action potential in response to a depolarizing stimulus. The sequential ECG changes observed in hyperkalemia are peaked T waves, prolongation of the PR interval, widening of the QRS complex, and a sine wave pattern and are mandatory indications for prompt treatment.

Moderate acidosis is generally well tolerated and does not need treatment unless it is used as an adjunct to controlling hyperkalemia or when plasma bicarbonate falls below 15 mEq/L. Hyperkalemia and acidosis not easily controlled by medical therapy are indications for initiating dialysis.

In most patients hypocalcemia is asymptomatic and does not require treatment. Phosphate-binding gels may be used in patients with significant hyperphosphatemia. Anemia regularly develops in patients with ATN and does not require treatment unless symptomatic or contributing to heart failure.

In a well-managed patient (with use of early dialysis), many of the uremic manifestations outlined in Table 30–5 either do not develop or are minimal. However, infection remains the main cause of death despite vigorous dialysis. Thus, meticulous aseptic care of intravenous catheters and wounds and avoidance of the use of indwelling urinary catheters are important in the management of such patients.

The indications for initiating dialysis are severe hyperkalemia and/or acidosis not easily controlled by medical treatment, fluid overload, and a rate of rise of the BUN in excess of 20 mg/dl/24 hr. In the absence of any of the above, most nephrologists advocate dialysis when the BUN reaches about 100 mg/dl because the goal of modern therapy is to avoid the occurrence of uremic symptoms. Indeed, it can be argued that the development of uremic symptoms in patients with ATN indicates that dialysis therapy has been unnecessarily delayed. Finally, it is critical to review carefully the indications for and the doses of all drugs administered to patients with ATN. Monitoring of blood concentrations of drugs is an important adjunct to effective treatment.

Outcome and Prognosis. The oliguric phase of ATN typically lasts for 1 to 2 weeks and is followed by the diuretic phase. It is important to remember that about one fourth to one third of the deaths occur in the diuretic phase. This is not surprising because, with the availability of dialysis, the most important determinant of the outcome is not the uremia per se but rather the underlying disease that causes the ATN.

As noted above, infection continues to be the most important cause of death in patients with ATN. In modern acute care hospitals, the outcome of patients who develop ATN is highly variable. In relatively uncomplicated ATN induced by contrast media in relatively healthy patients, survival rates approach 95 to 100 per cent. In contrast, in immunocompromised patients who develop antibiotic-induced ATN or in burn patients with ATN, mortality rates in excess of 60 per cent are common. In patients who survive the acute episode, the renal function returns essentially to normal, with the only residual findings being a modest reduction in GFR and inability to maximally concentrate and acidify urine.

Prevention. The first principle of good management is prophylaxis. This requires recognition of the clinical settings in which ATN may occur and recognition of patients particularly susceptible to ATN. Correcting fluid deficiencies before surgery and keeping patients particularly at risk adequately hydrated prior to radiocontrast studies are some useful measures. Nephrotoxic drugs should be used only when essential and then only with careful monitoring of the patient. Finally, pretreatment with allopurinol before chemotherapy of massive tumors diminishes uric acid production and helps prevent the tumor lysis syndrome.

Pathogenesis of Acute Tubular Necrosis

Despite the common use of the term acute tubular necrosis, necrosis of the tubules may not be observed and the histologic picture is often nondiagnostic. The vast majority of patients with ATN have, as their initiating event, either a decrease in renal plasma flow or exposure to a nephrotoxic agent. Specific forms of toxic nephropathy are discussed in the following section.

Although an initial decrease in renal blood flow appears to be a requisite for the development of ischemic ATN, blood flow returns nearly to normal within 24 to 48 hours after the initial insult. Despite adequate renal blood flow, tubular dysfunction persists and the GFR remains depressed. Leakage of glomerular ultrafiltrate from the tubular lumen into the renal interstitium across the damaged renal tubular cells, obstruction to flow due to debris or crystals in the lumen of the tubules, and a decrease in the glomerular capillary ultrafiltration coefficient (K_f) have all been proposed to play a pathophysiologic role in sustaining the clinical picture of ATN.

A variety of biochemical changes have been suggested as being responsible for cell injury in ARF. These include mitochondrial dysfunction, ATP depletion, phospholipid degradation, elevation in cytosolic free calcium, decrease in Na^+-K^+-ATPase activity, alterations in substrate metabolism, lysosomal changes, and the production of oxygen free radicals. It is not yet clear which

TABLE 30–5. MAJOR COMPLICATIONS OF ACUTE RENAL FAILURE

Metabolic
  Hyperkalemia
  Hypocalcemia, hyperphosphatemia
  Hypermagnesemia
  Hyperuricemia
Cardiovascular
  Pericarditis
  Arrhythmias
Neurologic
  Asterixis
  Neuromuscular irritability
  Somnolence
  Coma
  Seizures

Hematologic
  Anemia
  Coagulopathies
  Hemorrhagic diathesis
Gastrointestinal
  Nausea
  Vomiting
Infectious
  Pneumonia
  Urinary tract infection
  Wound infection
  Septicemia

changes are causative and which may simply be by-products of advanced cell injury.

SPECIFIC CAUSES OF ACUTE RENAL FAILURE

Exogenous Nephrotoxins

Radiographic Contrast Agents. Radiocontrast-induced ARF is one of the most common causes of nephrotoxic ARF. Nonionic agents do not appear to be any less nephrotoxic than ionic ones. The most important risk factor appears to be underlying renal insufficiency, although dehydration and concomitant exposure to other nephrotoxins are also important. The individuals at highest risk are diabetic patients with serum creatinine greater than 5 mg/dl. In the absence of other risk factors, diabetes per se does not appear to pose a major risk.

Aminoglycosides. The most important manifestation of aminoglycoside (e.g., tobramycin, gentamicin, amikacin) nephrotoxicity is ARF, accounting for 10 to 15 per cent of all cases of this disorder in the United States. Up to 10 per cent of patients receiving aminoglycosides develop some degree of renal dysfunction, even though the blood levels may be maintained in the therapeutic range. ARF is usually mild and nonoliguric and is manifested by a rise in the serum creatinine level after several days of therapy with one of the aminoglycosides. However, oliguria and severe renal failure requiring dialysis may be seen. The prognosis for recovery of renal function after several days is excellent.

The Nonsteroidal Anti-inflammatory Drugs (NSAIDs). Renal toxicity related to NSAIDs has emerged as a very common form of drug-induced nephrotoxicity. NSAIDs are potent inhibitors of prostaglandin synthesis, a property that contributes to their nephrotoxic potential in certain high-risk patients in whom renal vasodilatation depends on prostaglandins. Several distinct patterns of nephrotoxicity have been associated with these agents (Table 30–6). The most frequent pattern of injury related to NSAIDs is a prerenal azotemia, particularly in patients who either are volume-contracted or have a reduced effective circulating volume. Susceptible individuals include those with congestive heart failure, cirrhosis, chronic renal disease, and volume depletion. A hyperchloremic metabolic acidosis, often associated with hyperkalemia, has also been recognized as an effect of the NSAIDs, particularly in individuals with pre-existing chronic interstitial renal disease. Hyporeninemic hypoaldosteronism occurs in these individuals in states of renal prostaglandin inhibition. Hyponatremia is occasionally identified in patients taking NSAIDs and is the result of an impairment in the ability of the kidney to generate a maximally dilute urine when renal prostaglandin production is inhibited. Finally, NSAIDs have been associated with the development of an acute interstitial nephritis, often associated with renal insufficiency and nephrotic-range proteinuria. Discontinuation of the offending agent usually results in a resolution of this disorder.

Cisplatin. Renal injury is a well-recognized and dose-dependent complication of cisplatin use in the management of many carcinomas. Hypomagnesemia due to renal losses of magnesium may be severe and can occur in as many as 50 per cent of patients. Patients should be well hydrated prior to administration of cisplatin, and known nephrotoxins should be avoided whenever possible. The usual lesion is that of ATN, but, with severe damage or recurrent administration of the drug, chronic interstitial disease may ensue.

Ethylene Glycol Toxicity. Ingestion of ethylene glycol, usually in the form of antifreeze, produces a characteristic syndrome of severe high anion gap metabolic acidosis and a large osmolal gap. ARF generally manifests after 48 to 72 hours. Patients exhibit disorientation and agitation initially, progressing to central nervous system depression, stupor, and coma. Cardiovascular collapse is a terminal event.

The Angiotensin-Converting Enzyme (ACE) Inhibitors. ACE inhibitor–associated ARF is thought to be hemodynamic in origin from loss of autoregulation of renal blood flow and GFR and has been typically reported when these drugs are given to patients with bilateral renal artery stenosis or with moderately advanced azotemia. Allergic acute interstitial nephritis similar to that observed with methicillin has also been reported.

Endogenous Nephrotoxins

Rhabdomyolysis. Since the first description of the causative association between rhabdomyolysis and ARF during the crush injuries of World War

TABLE 30–6. SPECTRUM OF RENAL TOXICITY ASSOCIATED WITH NONSTEROIDAL ANTI-INFLAMMATORY DRUGS

TYPE	PATHOPHYSIOLOGY	FEATURES	ASSOCIATED CONDITIONS
Acute renal failure	↓ Renal blood flow	Prerenal azotemia, sodium retention	Congestive heart failure, cirrhosis, volume depletion, renal insufficiency
Hyperchloremic metabolic acidosis	↓ Renin/aldosterone production	$\uparrow K^+$, $\uparrow Cl^-$, $\downarrow CO_2$	Interstitial renal disease
Acute interstitial nephritis	Lymphocytic infiltration of renal interstitium	Acute renal failure, ±heavy proteinuria	Unknown

II, the spectrum of causes of rhabdomyolysis, myoglobinuria, and renal failure has markedly broadened. The most frequent causes are (in order) alcohol abuse, muscle compression, seizures, metabolic derangements, drugs, and infections. Muscle pain and dark brown orthotoluidine-positive urine without RBCs are important diagnostic clues but must be confirmed by elevations of creatine phosphokinase and myoglobin. About one third of patients with rhabdomyolysis develop ARF, frequently associated with hyperkalemia, hyperuricemia, hyperphosphatemia, early hypocalcemia, and a reduced BUN/creatinine ratio because of excessive creatinine release from muscle. Late hypercalcemia is also a typical feature of the disease.

Hyperuricemic Acute Renal Failure. ARF may occur in patients with "high turnover" malignancies (acute lymphoblastic leukemia and poorly differentiated lymphomas) who either spontaneously or more frequently, after cytotoxic therapy, release massive amounts of purine uric acid precursors, leading to uric acid precipitation in the renal tubules. During massive cell lysis, phosphate and potassium are also released in large amounts, resulting in hyperphosphatemia and hyperkalemia. The peak uric acid level is often greater than 20 mg/dl, and a ratio of urinary uric acid–creatinine concentrations greater than 1:1 suggests the diagnosis of acute uric acid nephropathy. Prevention of ARF includes establishing a urinary output of 3 L or more per 24 hours and treatment with allopurinol prior to institution of cytotoxic therapy.

Acute Renal Failure in Pregnancy

Septic abortion may cause renal failure in early pregnancy. In late pregnancy, pre-eclampsia, placenta previa, and abruptio placentae are causative factors. Cortical necrosis is uncommon in nonpregnant individuals but occurs more often in pregnancy, especially in patients more than 30 years of age with third-trimester abruptio placentae. Clinical management of ARF in pregnancy is comparable to that in nonpregnant patients.

REFERENCES

Brezis M, Rosen S, Epstein FH: Acute renal failure. In Brenner BM, Rector FC (eds): The Kidney. 4th ed. Philadelphia, WB Saunders Co, 1991, pp 993–1061.
Grantham JJ: Acute renal failure. In Wyngaarden JB, Smith LH Jr, Bennett JC (eds): Cecil Textbook of Medicine. 19th ed. Philadelphia, WB Saunders Co, 1992, pp 528–533.
Weinberg JM: The cell biology of ischemic renal injury. Kidney Int 39(3):476–500, 1991.

31 CHRONIC RENAL FAILURE

The term *chronic renal failure* (CRF) implies a progressive, irreversible loss of renal function. This progressive failure may be characterized by a stepwise elevation in the serum creatinine concentration as the glomerular filtration decreases. In general, the goals of modern treatment are to institute renal replacement therapy, by either dialysis or transplantation, before patients develop advanced signs of uremia. Thus patients are considered to have reached end-stage renal disease (ESRD) when the glomerular filtration rate (GFR) is below 15 ml/min. At that low level of renal function, the physician can predict with reasonable certainty that, in the absence of replacement therapy, uremia will ensue.

Currently there are approximately 200,000 dialysis and renal transplant patients in the United States, with an annual increase of approximately 10 per cent. The annual incidence of newly diagnosed ESRD is approximately 100 patients per million population. The overall incidence is four times greater in blacks and Hispanics than in Caucasians and is higher with increasing age. The most common causes of ESRD are included in Table 31–1.

TABLE 31–1. CAUSES OF END-STAGE RENAL FAILURE

DISEASE	INCIDENCE (%)
Hypertensive nephrosclerosis	25
Diabetic nephropathy	30
Chronic glomerulonephritis	15
Cystic kidney disease	4
Urologic disorders	6
Other/unknown	20

The kidney has great functional reserve and is able to compensate for a loss of functioning nephrons. In fact, the excretory and homeostatic and, in part, the endocrine functions of the kidney are maintained even when function of the kidney is only 10 to 15 per cent of normal. Further nephron loss usually results in the clinical manifestations of uremia.

The accumulation of endogenous toxins is the factor that usually brings about the clinical presentation of renal dysfunction. This accumulation does not begin, however, until a large fraction of the functioning nephrons is lost. The total GFR following unilateral nephrectomy, for example, remains normal despite the removal of one half of the functioning glomeruli. This occurs because **intact nephrons** that remain increase their individual filtration rates by increasing the rate of blood flow and the hydrostatic pressure in the glomerular capillaries. Eventually, the intact glomeruli reach a point of maximal filtration. Any additional loss of glomerular mass is accompanied by an accumulation of filterable toxins.

The kidney can maintain electrolyte homeostasis in the setting of nephron loss. When single-nephron GFR increases, the quantity of solute filtered and subsequently excreted by each nephron also increases. Even when nephron loss reaches the point at which the total GFR is reduced, the appropriate excretion of most solutes is maintained. For example, an individual with a normal GFR of 100 ml/min filters approximately 20,000 mEq of sodium daily. If that individual ingests 100 mEq of sodium in the diet, the same quantity must be excreted in the urine for the total body sodium balance to be maintained. The urinary sodium excretion would therefore be 100 mEq, or 0.5 per cent of the filtered load. If the GFR is then reduced to 50 ml/min, the filtered sodium is reduced by one half. To excrete the same 100 mEq of sodium, the fractional excretion would require an increase to 1 per cent. This increased fractional excretion of solutes must be mediated by factors that alter the tubular absorption of the filtered solutes. The demands for tubular accommodation are increased with greater reductions in glomerular filtration. In general, renal adjustments in the rates of solute excretion are adequate to accommodate normal rates of intake down to a GFR of 10 to 20 per cent of normal.

The mediators of tubular compensation arise within the kidney or are part of humoral systems that affect both the kidney and other tissues participating in electrolyte homeostasis. Such extrarenal factors are evident when considering calcium and phosphate homeostasis (Fig. 31–1). In the presence of a constant intake of phosphate and progressive loss of nephrons, the following sequence of events occurs. With each decrease in the GFR, the dietary intake of phosphate results in a transient increase in serum phosphate and, as a consequence, a decrease in the serum concentration of ionized calcium. The decrease in ionized

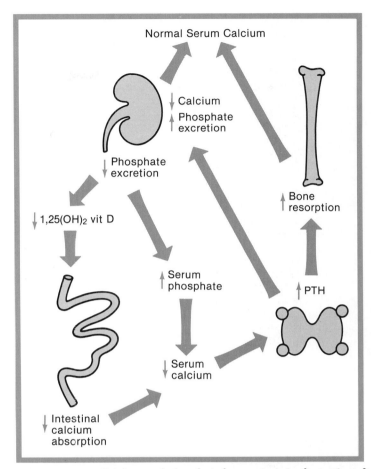

FIGURE 31–1. Calcium and phosphate homeostasis in the setting of renal failure. The decreased excretion of phosphate initiates the cycle directed at normalization of the serum calcium concentration.

calcium causes release of parathyroid hormone (PTH). PTH, in turn, causes an increase in the urinary excretion of phosphate and a reduction in the urinary excretion of calcium. The extraction of calcium from bone is also mediated by PTH. These factors lead to normalization of the serum phosphate and calcium concentrations but come at the expense of progressive elevations of the PTH concentration. Thus, calcium and phosphate homeostasis is maintained by a "trade-off" for secondary hyperparathyroidism and subsequent bone dissolution. The trade-offs for the maintenance of balance of solutes other than phosphate have not been elucidated, but it is likely that the general thesis applies to multiple regulatory functions of the kidney.

FACTORS AFFECTING THE RATE OF NEPHRON LOSS

CRF is associated with a progressive loss of glomeruli over an interval of months to years. As noted above, the aggregate GFR is maintained de-

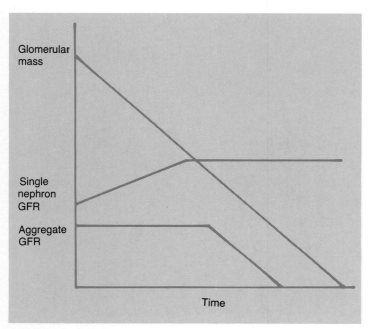

FIGURE 31–2. Renal response to loss of glomerular mass.

spite loss of functioning nephrons. Once a critical nephron mass is reached, however, any subsequent loss is associated with an incremental decline in the GFR (Fig. 31–2). A number of pathogenetic mechanisms have been implicated in the progressive destruction of nephrons.

Continuing Primary Insult

Some systemic diseases that affect the kidney are not responsive to therapeutic modalities. The continued activity of these disorders leads to progressive destruction of the normal renal architecture. Frequently, despite the progressive loss of renal function, it is not possible to identify continued activity of the primary disease or exposure to toxins.

Secondary Renal Insults

There are instances when renal function that is slowly declining or is stabilized at a diminished level acutely deteriorates. This can occur with an alteration in the effective renal perfusion, as observed with congestive heart failure, progression of renal vascular occlusion, or intravascular volume depletion. Nephrotoxic agents administered in the setting of diminished effective circulating volume can acutely affect the chronically diseased kidney. These include radiocontrast agents, non-steroidal anti-inflammatory drugs, angiotensin-converting enzyme inhibitors, urinary tract obstruction, and infections, particularly of the urinary tract.

Effects of Compensatory Mechanisms

The hemodynamic alterations that occur in residual glomeruli have been implicated in causing progressive renal injury. As noted above, loss of glomeruli leads to an increase in filtration of each of the remaining glomeruli. It has been proposed that the hyperfiltration can itself lead to glomerulosclerosis, with a resultant loss of glomerular mass. This could lead to a self-perpetuating loss of nephrons in the absence of a continued primary renal insult. Because ingestion of protein leads to similar intrarenal hemodynamic changes, dietary protein restriction may reduce intraglomerular hydrostatic pressures and slow the rate of nephron loss.

Intrarenal hemodynamic alterations are often associated with systemic arterial hypertension. It is possible that elevation in systemic blood pressure is transmitted into the glomerular circulation. It is known that hypertension does cause a significant acceleration in the rate of decline of renal function regardless of the nature of the primary renal insult. Furthermore, it is known that treatment of elevated arterial blood pressure can slow the progression of renal failure.

As noted above, secondary hyperparathyroidism develops as a trade-off for maintaining phosphate and calcium homeostasis in progressive renal failure. PTH could contribute to injury of renal cells by facilitating deposition of calcium in the renal parenchyma or by translocating calcium into the cells and the mitochondria. This leads to nephron loss and perpetuates the increase in PTH.

Lipid droplets are evident in glomerular sclerotic lesions, suggesting that glomerular deposition of circulating lipids contributes to progressive glomerular injury. Animals with hereditary hyperlipidemia or those fed diets with high lipid content develop glomerular sclerosis. Agents that lower lipid levels can prevent the glomerular injury. The pathogenesis of glomerular sclerosis, therefore, may be analogous to that of systemic atherosclerosis, with hypertension and hyperlipidemia constituting additive risk factors in both processes.

CLINICAL MANIFESTATIONS OF CHRONIC RENAL FAILURE

The complications in patients with renal failure may reflect underlying systemic diseases. Uremia itself, however, should be considered a systemic disorder affecting multiple organ systems. Although kidney failure is associated with an accumulation of potentially toxic substances, no single element can be implicated as the **"uremic toxin."** Much discussion has focused on the possible role of the middle molecules, compounds with a molecular weight of 500 to 2000 daltons. These middle molecules are retained in patients with renal disease, but their exact nature and pathophysiologic role remain to be defined. PTH may be an important factor in the genesis of some of the clinical manifestations of ESRD.

Serum Chemistries

The blood urea nitrogen (BUN) and creatinine concentrations are increased to a variable degree. Because the blood level attained reflects not only the filtration by the kidney but also the rate of generation of these substances, the development of uremic symptoms may not correlate directly with the blood values. In general, however, uremic symptoms, with rare exceptions, are evident when the serum creatinine reaches 8 to 10 mg/dl. Metabolic acidosis is commonly observed, generally with an anion gap of about 10 mEq/L. Hyperkalemia is observed when renal failure is far advanced, when patients are catabolic, or when patients have a coexisting deficiency or tubular insensitivity to aldosterone. The serum concentration of phosphate is increased, as are the concentrations of uric acid and magnesium.

Cardiovascular Disease

One of the most common causes of death in the ESRD patient is cardiovascular disease. The incidence of coronary artery disease is increased in these patients owing in part to the presence of hypertension, glucose intolerance, and abnormalities in lipid metabolism. Renal disease may also result in accelerated atherosclerotic disease and a form of cardiomyopathy. Ingestion of sodium and water in excess of the excretory capacity of the kidney can result in expansion of the extracellular fluid volume. The volume expansion can lead to the clinical manifestations of hypertension, congestive heart failure, and peripheral edema.

Involvement of the pericardium is common in ESRD patients with advanced uremia. Clinical manifestations may include pericarditis with pain, fever, and a pericardial friction rub or pericardial effusion with or without clinically apparent pericarditis. Pericardial tamponade and constrictive pericarditis are less common manifestations but are life threatening. Pericarditis occurs in two distinct clinical situations. In the newly diagnosed uremic patient or in patients who have been inadequately dialyzed, institution of regular dialysis treatments results in resolution of the pericarditis. Pericarditis can also arise in patients who are already established on dialysis and who appear to be well dialyzed. In this circumstance, increasing the number or duration of dialysis treatments does not hasten the resolution of the pericarditis. Cardiac tamponade requires immediate drainage of the pericardial fluid. Constrictive pericarditis requires surgical intervention.

Uremic Osteodystrophy

The changes in PTH and vitamin D metabolism in patients with chronic renal insufficiency have a profound effect on the activity of osteoblasts and osteoclasts. In general, bone dissolution is accelerated and bone formation decreased. These changes are relative to one another such that the clinical and laboratory abnormalities may vary widely. Some patients may manifest only laboratory abnormalities, such as a rise in alkaline phosphatase, whereas others may have severe and disabling bone pain and fractures. The development of bone disease in the uremic patient—uremic osteodystrophy—is universal.

It is convenient to subdivide the metabolic bone disease of the ESRD patients into three subtypes (Table 31–2). Although all are present to a variable degree, one subtype may dominate the clinical picture. **Secondary hyperparathyroidism** is universal in ESRD. The bone manifestation is the development of osteitis fibrosa cystica. In advanced renal disease, there is a failure to convert vitamin D to its active metabolite, 1,25(OH)$_2$ vitamin D, and, as a consequence, **renal rickets** or osteomalacia develops. In addition, recent evidence indicates that the accumulation of **aluminum metabolites** in bone results in a form of vitamin D–resistant rickets. Aluminum accumulation can occur as a result of the inability to excrete the compound, which may be ingested in the form of aluminum hydroxide gels commonly used as dietary phosphate-binding agents. Aluminum is also common in most community water supplies and may be transferred to the patient during hemodialysis treatments. Osteoporosis is common in ESRD patients owing to a variety of factors, including sustained acidosis and poor nutrition.

Neurologic Complications

Central nervous system manifestations of ESRD may range from mild changes in mentation to convulsions, coma, and death. The more severe clinical manifestations occur in patients with advanced uremia and are alleviated by the institution of dialysis. Initial dialysis treatments in ESRD patients should be brief in order to avoid a dialysis disequilibrium syndrome characterized by cerebral edema and convulsions. Usually after a few dialysis treatments, the patient adapts and no longer manifests this dialysis disequilibrium.

TABLE 31–2. CLASSIFICATION OF METABOLIC BONE DISEASE

DISORDER	CONTRIBUTING FACTORS	RADIOGRAPHIC FINDINGS
Osteitis fibrosa cystica	Secondary hyperparathyroidism Skeletal resistance to PTH	Subperiosteal erosions Bone cysts "Ground glass" skull Osteosclerosis ("rugger jersey" spine)
Rickets/osteomalacia	Altered vitamin D metabolism Acidosis Aluminum deposition	Widening of growth plates Looser zones (pseudofractures)
Osteopenia and osteoporosis	Acidosis	Loss of bone mass and fractures

A rare but severe neurologic syndrome may occur in patients maintained on dialysis, called dialysis dementia. This dementing syndrome has an associated movement disorder and a fatal outcome in the majority of patients. The cerebral accumulation of aluminum has been implicated in the genesis of dialysis dementia. Finally, the presence of arteriosclerosis and hypertension makes the ESRD patient vulnerable to the development of cerebrovascular disease.

Involvement of the peripheral nervous system is frequent in advanced renal disease and is manifested by a stocking-and-glove pattern. In some patients, the neuropathy may be quite severe and may preclude successful rehabilitation. The institution of dialysis may stabilize the neuropathy, but only rarely is a severe neuropathy reversed. In some patients, the neuropathy may progress despite seemingly adequate dialysis.

The development of ESRD may also result in dysfunction of the autonomic nervous system. Clinical manifestations may include abnormalities in motility of the gastrointestinal tract with the findings of gastroparesis or diarrhea, labile blood pressure, and intolerance to dialysis. Dialysis generally does not reverse the overt manifestations of the autonomic neuropathy.

Hematopoietic System

Anemia is a nearly universal finding in patients with advanced renal disease. The cause of the anemia is multifactorial. There may be an excess amount of blood loss from the gastrointestinal tract and, in women, the reproductive system. Patients requiring hemodialysis may also chronically lose small amounts of blood in the dialysis equipment. These blood losses in association with inadequate dietary intake may lead to iron deficiency. The poor nutritional status may also cause folate and vitamin B_{12} deficiencies. Red blood cell (RBC) survival is shortened in uremia owing to mechanical factors and changes in RBC membrane composition. The primary cause of anemia, however, is a deficiency of erythropoietin, a glycoprotein normally produced in the kidney in response to hypoxia. It is responsible for normal RBC differentiation from stem cells.

There is usually a normal leukocyte count in patients with ESRD. The chemotactic mechanisms of polymorphonuclear leukocytes, however, are often defective. Production of antibodies and/or the cellular immune response may also be blunted. These defects may be related to abnormalities within the leukocytes or to abnormal circulating factors. The atypical immune responses that result make the ESRD patient relatively immunosuppressed and provide an explanation for the finding that infections are a common cause of death in these patients.

The absolute platelet count is usually normal in patients with advanced renal disease. However, qualitative defects in platelet function occur and lead to a prolongation in the bleeding time. Certain renal disorders may lead to defects in coagulation factors and to a bleeding diathesis.

Gastrointestinal Defects

The initial presenting complaints of uremia usually refer to the gastrointestinal tract. These may be only anorexia or nausea. These symptoms usually improve when dialysis is instituted. Abnormalities in gastrointestinal motility or in the absorptive functions of the gut may also develop.

Gastrointestinal hemorrhage may occur from a variety of pathologic lesions. The most common source of intestinal bleeding is arteriovenous malformations, which can occur at any location along the gastrointestinal tract. The hemodialysis patient is also more likely to develop hepatitis owing to the exposure to blood and blood products. An interesting finding in the uremic patient is low serum transaminase concentrations.

Cutaneous Disorders

Pruritus is a common complaint among patients with uremia. Usually there are no dermatologic findings. There is no identifiable causative factor, although dermal deposition of calcium phosphate and neuronal stimulation by PTH have been implicated. Asymptomatic relief has been reported with more frequent dialysis, parathyroidectomy, dietary phosphate restriction, and exposure to ultraviolet light. Other dermatologic conditions include a yellow discoloration due to deposition of "urochromes," a bronze discoloration due to hemochromatosis, and metastatic calcifications.

Endocrine Dysfunction

Renal disease is associated with low or absent levels of erythropoietin and $1,25(OH)_2$ vitamin D because the kidney is responsible for the production of these two hormones. Gonadotropic hormone production is diminished owing to primary gonadal dysfunction and alterations in the hypothalamic-pituitary axis. This results in amenorrhea and infertility in women and impotence and oligospermia in men.

Several factors regulating carbohydrate metabolism are altered in association with renal failure. Gluconeogenesis and insulin metabolism by renal tubular cells are impaired with diminished renal function. The diabetic patient manifests a tendency to develop hypoglycemia, and the dose of insulin usually requires reduction. Alternatively, uremic patients have defects in the tissue uptake and metabolism of glucose and the number and activity of insulin receptors. In advanced renal disease, the urinary excretion of glucose may be reduced. These factors favor the development of glucose intolerance, which is in fact more common in patients with ESRD.

Infections of the lung occur more commonly in renal disease patients and may be the consequence of poor clearing of secretions and impaired host defense. Calcium may be deposited in the lung parenchyma and may contribute to poor exchange of gases seen in some uremic individuals. Pulmonary congestion secondary to overexpansion of the extracellular fluid volume and congestive heart failure is a common clinical problem. Patients with uremia may also develop pleural effusions not due to other recognizable causes.

CONSERVATIVE MANAGEMENT OF RENAL FAILURE

Uremic symptoms develop as the toxic products of metabolism accumulate. Some manifestations of CRF, however, develop prior to the onset of overt uremic symptoms and often persist even after the initiation of maintenance dialysis. The treatment of these manifestations usually requires intense instruction of the patient and thus a multifaceted approach by various support services.

Regulation of Fluids and Electrolytes

The kidney normally has the capacity to excrete large quantities of solutes and water. This allows for appropriate fluid and electrolyte balance despite marked variations of intake. As noted above, partial nephron loss is countered by adaptive mechanisms in the residual nephrons that allow for preservation of this balance. The limits within which these adaptations in excretion can occur, however, are narrowed as the GFR is progressively diminished. Solute and fluid intake must be restricted as renal failure advances.

The intake of sodium and water must be limited to avoid volume overload. Diuretics may be necessary if patients are unable to restrict the sodium intake adequately. Whereas patients prescribed diuretics are generally susceptible to hypokalemia, patients with renal disease must be cautioned against excessive potassium intake. It may become necessary to prescribe oral potassium-binding resins that allow gastrointestinal elimination of excessive potassium. Bicarbonate or citrate may be used to partially correct systemic acidosis. Antihypertensive agents are indicated if hypertension is evident after control of the intravascular fluid volume. If patients are unable to maintain their volume status by diet and diuretics or if they are persistently hyperkalemic or severely acidotic, dialysis therapy is indicated.

Elimination of Metabolic Products

No single compound can lead to all of the manifestations of uremia. The dietary intake of protein, however, contributes to the genesis of uremic symptoms, presumably because of the metabolic products of protein. Although urea is not a toxic substance alone, the BUN concentration does correlate with systemic manifestations of renal failure. BUN is generally considered to reflect the accumulation of other products of protein catabolism. Restriction of dietary protein intake can lead to symptomatic improvement in the nausea, vomiting, malaise, and encephalopathy of ESRD. Alternatively, uremic patients have a decreased rate of protein anabolism and an increased rate of protein catabolism. Marked restrictions in protein intake therefore can result in protein malnutrition. It is essential that when dietary protein intake is restricted, adequate caloric intake be maintained to minimize the rate of protein catabolism.

The kidney is a major route of elimination of drugs. Some drugs may be filtered at the glomerulus, depending on the size and charge characteristics of the compound as well as the degree to which it is bound to plasma proteins. Drugs that are organic ions can be secreted from the peritubular capillary blood into the tubular lumen by specific transport mechanisms in renal tubular cells. Some drugs that gain access to the tubular fluid by filtration and/or secretion may be reabsorbed into the systemic circulation or may be metabolized by the tubular cells. The alterations in glomerular filtration, tubular secretion, and tubular absorption that occur with renal failure may have a major effect on the elimination of drugs excreted by the kidney.

Renal failure may also be associated with alterations in the binding of drugs by plasma proteins and thus may alter the bioavailability of some compounds. The volume of distribution of certain drugs or the rate of absorption of drugs from the gastrointestinal tract may be altered by uremia. The secondary consequences of renal failure may also alter the metabolic pathways of drugs in other organs. A number of commonly prescribed drugs require alterations in either the amount or the interval of administration in patients with renal dysfunction (Table 31–3). In patients who are dialysis-dependent, the problem is compounded by the effects of drug removal during dialysis.

TABLE 31–3. DRUG DOSAGE IN CHRONIC RENAL FAILURE

MAJOR DOSAGE REDUCTION	MINOR OR NO REDUCTION	AVOID USAGE
Antibiotics		
Aminoglycosides	Erythromycin	Tetracycline
Penicillin G	Nafcillin	Nitrofurantoin
Cephalosporins	Clindamycin	Nalidixic acid
Sulfonamides	Chloramphenicol	
Vancomycin	Isoniazid/rifampin	
	Amphotericin B	
Others		
Digoxin	Antihypertensives	Aspirin
Procainamide	Benzodiazepines	Sulfonylureas
H_2 antagonists	Quinidine	Lithium carbonate
	Lidocaine	Acetazolamide
	Codeine	Spironolactone
	Propoxyphene	Triamterene

Endocrine Disorders

The serum phosphate concentration is intimately related to the development of secondary hyperparathyroidism in patients with renal failure. The dietary intake of phosphate should be limited. A phosphate-free diet is often unpalatable, so that agents that bind phosphate in the gastrointestinal tract, and thus inhibit absorption, may be used. Calcium salts may be used as a dietary phosphate binder. Vitamin D may be administered to enhance gastrointestinal calcium absorption, which suppresses PTH secretion. Vitamin D may also directly suppress the parathyroid gland in the setting of uremia. The administration of calcium salts must be used with caution when the serum phosphate concentration is quite elevated because they can enhance the precipitation of calcium phosphate in soft tissues. Aluminum hydroxide gels can be used as the dietary phosphate binder in that instance. Likewise, the use of these agents must be monitored because they may provide a source of aluminum that can deposit in the bone or contribute to the development of dialysis dementia. If the hyperparathyroidism cannot be controlled by these conservative methods, surgical parathyroidectomy must be considered.

Anemia is a common finding in patients with renal failure. Recombinant erythropoietin is administered routinely to most dialysis patients. This agent stimulates erythropoietic activity and requires adequate substrate for RBC formation. Folate is provided to all dialysis patients because it is removed by dialysis. Iron supplements are administered, but serum iron levels should be monitored to avoid the development of hemochromatosis. If the patients are resistant to the effects of erythropoietin or there are contraindications to its use, androgens may be used to enhance RBC formation. Blood transfusions may become necessary in patients with refractory anemia who are symptomatic. These transfusions should generally be infused slowly or if possible during dialysis to avoid acute intravascular volume overload.

DIALYSIS

The principles underlying the use of dialysis are diffusion and convection (Fig. 31–3). Blood is separated from a dialysis solution by a semipermeable membrane. For hemodialysis, blood is pumped into a dialyzer containing an artificial semipermeable membrane. The dialysis solution bathes the opposite side of the membrane. In peritoneal dialysis, the capillaries of the peritoneal membrane serve as the semipermeable membrane, dialysis solution being instilled into the peritoneal cavity.

The physical separation of blood from the dialysis solution by a semipermeable membrane sets conditions favorable for net transfer of solutes and water from one compartment to the other. If a concentration gradient for a substance is established, passive diffusion of that substance across the membrane can occur. The rate of transfer depends on the concentration gradient of the substance in question and its permeability across the membrane. The removal of substances from the blood can also be accomplished by movement of the substance in solution across the membrane (convection). In hemodialysis, water flow across the membrane is accomplished by imposing a hydrostatic pressure gradient across the membrane. In peritoneal dialysis, water flow is induced by imposing an osmotic gradient across the membrane. The modalities of dialysis employed in clinical practice use principles of both diffusion and convection to achieve optimal removal of solutes and water.

Hemodialysis

Blood delivery in the hemodialysis circuit is maintained by a blood pump that regulates the rate of blood flow. Access to the vascular compartment is achieved in the chronic dialysis patient by the development of an arteriovenous fistula. Synthetic grafting material may be required if the native vessels are inadequate. Unless the patient is at extreme risk for hemorrhage, anticoagulants are administered during hemodialysis. Blood is delivered to one side of the semipermeable membrane and is then returned to the patient. A dialysate solution is pumped across the other side of the membrane in a counterflow direction. The membrane itself is standardized for clearance and the

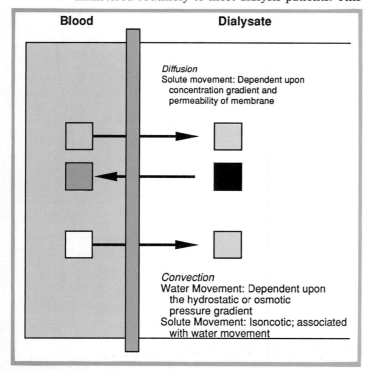

Blood   **Dialysate**

Diffusion
Solute movement: Dependent upon
concentration gradient and
permeability of membrane

Convection
Water Movement: Dependent upon
the hydrostatic or osmotic
pressure gradient
Solute Movement: Isoncotic; associated
with water movement

FIGURE 31–3. Principles of dialysis. Solutes that are permeable to the membrane diffuse down a concentration gradient. Additional solutes may be transferred in association with bulk water flow. Water movement depends upon the prevailing hydrostatic and osmotic pressure gradients across the membrane.

characteristics of water flow relative to the hydrostatic pressure gradient. The rate of blood flow, dialyzer, transmembrane pressure gradient, and duration of dialysis can therefore be selected at each treatment, depending upon the goals for solute clearance and fluid removal.

Hemofiltration involves the movement of large volumes of fluid across extremely porous membranes. As the ultrafiltrate of plasma is removed, it is replaced with physiologic solutions. In effect, an exchange transfusion is used to remove the desired substances. A net fluid removal can be achieved by infusing less volume than that removed. In the acute setting, continuous arteriovenous hemofiltration may be useful. Blood is obtained from an arterial access, circulated into the filtration cartridge, and returned to the venous circulation. The blood flow is driven by the arteriovenous pressure gradient and thus depends upon the hemodynamic status of the patient. Because the treatment is rendered continuously, a large net amount of fluid can be removed over a long interval, providing effective therapy to critically ill, hemodynamically unstable patients.

Clotting and infection of the vascular access are common problems in patients maintained on hemodialysis. In addition, the hemodialysis machine functions as a low-resistance arteriovenous fistula, requiring that cardiac output and/or peripheral vascular resistance increase so as to maintain systemic arterial blood pressure. In patients with significant heart disease or autonomic neuropathy, failure to manifest the appropriate cardiovascular response may result in intolerance to hemodialysis.

Peritoneal Dialysis

Peritoneal dialysis is accomplished by placement of a soft catheter through the abdominal wall into the peritoneal cavity. The external end of the catheter is attached in a closed system to a bag containing dialysis solution. The solution is instilled into the peritoneal cavity, permitted to dwell for varying periods of time, and then drained from the peritoneal cavity. These fill, dwell, and drain cycles may be performed intermittently or continuously, utilizing automated devices.

Peritonitis is the most common complication of peritoneal dialysis and occurs following the inadvertent introduction of bacteria into the peritoneal space through the peritoneal dialysis catheter. Infections may also occur along the intra-abdominal tract of the catheter. Because glucose is the osmotic agent in the dialysate, glycemic control may be difficult in patients with glucose intolerance. The high glucose load may also contribute to the development of hyperlipidemia after prolonged dialysis.

Initiation of Dialysis

Dialysis should be initiated when conservative measures become ineffective. This may be appar-

ent as refractory volume overload, persistent hyperkalemia or acidosis, and uremic symptoms. The implications of maintenance dialysis should be discussed with patients and their families to ascertain a willingness to participate in this chronic therapy. Most patients should be apprised of the various modalities of renal replacement therapy, including renal transplantation.

The selection of the mode of dialysis depends upon several factors, as outlined in Table 31–4. First, certain mechanical factors must be considered. Chronic hemodialysis requires the development and maintenance of an adequate vascular access. Likewise, the abdominal cavity must be capable of receiving an indwelling peritoneal dialysis catheter. The peritoneal cavity must also be relatively free of adhesions and able to contain the large volumes of the fluid instilled during dialysis. The patient's lifestyle should be considered. Hemodialysis is usually performed in a dialysis facility, necessitating a patient's visit for several hours per treatment given two or three times weekly. Hemodialysis can be performed at home but requires a dialysis partner. Peritoneal dialysis is usually performed by the patient at home. This requires some manual dexterity and adequate vision. Peritoneal dialysis patients may also rely upon a dialysis partner or a variety of automated devices to perform some of the required procedures.

TABLE 31–4. CONSIDERATIONS FOR SELECTING HEMODIALYSIS (HD) OR PERITONEAL DIALYSIS (PD)

CLINICAL FACTOR	PREFERRED MODE	COMMENTS
Diabetes	PD	Poor hemodynamic response to rapid volume removal Anticoagulation may worsen retinal hemorrhages
Obesity	HD	Glucose load, hyperlipidemia with PD
Noncompliance	HD	Peritonitis with self-therapy; missing exchanges
Frequent traveler	PD	Freedom from machine
Severe peripheral vascular disease	PD	Avoids vascular access, ischemia
Severe angina	PD	Less cardiovascular stress with less rapid volume removal
Hernia	HD	Exacerbated by intraperitoneal infusions
Back pain	HD	Intra-abdominal fluid may exacerbate pain
Ostomy	HD	Risk of peritonitis
Extensive intra-abdominal adhesions	HD	Poor clearance, difficulty with catheter placement
Large, muscular build	HD	Better nitrogen clearance
Transplant planned	HD	PD requires training interval
Hypoalbuminemia	HD	Protein losses during peritoneal dialysis

Certain medical factors should be considered in choosing the method of dialysis. The rates of fluid removal with the various forms of dialysis must be considered in patients with limited cardiovascular responsiveness. This is particularly important in patients with severely compromised myocardial function and those with a limited vasoconstricting capacity. The effects of anticoagulants administered during hemodialysis should be considered in patients with bleeding complications.

The assessment of the adequacy of dialysis is largely subjective. The fluid and electrolyte status, as well as the RBC count, is evaluated at regular intervals. Dietary and psychosocial issues must be routinely addressed. Recently, models using rates of urea generation and clearance have been proposed as methods of determining the adequacy of maintenance therapy. These methods may allow adjustments in the dialysis and dietary prescriptions in order to provide optimal nitrogen balance.

Death rates in chronic dialysis patients average 10 to 15 per cent annually. The average age of patients who are maintained by dialysis is increasing. Consequently, the severity and nature of coexisting diseases are increasing in the dialysis population. The major causes of mortality and morbidity are infections and cardiovascular events. Patients can be maintained on dialysis while awaiting renal transplantation, and patients who have undergone unsuccessful attempts at renal transplantation can be returned to chronic dialysis.

TABLE 31–5. COMPARISON OF DONOR SOURCES FOR KIDNEY TRANSPLANTATION

ADVANTAGES	DISADVANTAGES
Living Donor	
Better tissue match with less likelihood of rejection	Small potential risk of operation to donor
Smaller doses of drugs for immunosuppression	Requires willing, medically suitable family member
Waiting time for transplant reduced	
Avoid sequelae of chronic dialysis	
Elective surgical procedure	
Better early graft function with shorter hospitalization	
Better short- and long-term success	
Cadaver Donor	
Available to any recipient	Tissue match not as similar
Other organs available for combined transplants (i.e., kidney-pancreas transplant)	Waiting time variable
	Operation must be performed urgently
Vascular conduits available for complex vascular reconstruction	Early graft function may be compromised
	Short- and long-term success not as good as from living donor

TRANSPLANTATION

Of the treatment options for patients with ESRD, renal transplantation most nearly restores normal renal function. Recipients of renal transplants not only do not require time-consuming dialysis treatments but also have no dietary or fluid restrictions. They avoid the complications of long-term uremia, such as renal osteodystrophy, secondary hyperparathyroidism, anemia, peripheral neuropathy, dialysis dementia, loss of fertility in women, and cessation of growth in children. Recipients of renal transplants are generally healthier than their counterparts on dialysis and are much more likely to be employed and to engage in normal daily activities. Five- and 10-year patient survival is better for renal transplant recipients than for patients on dialysis.

Except in cases of transplantation between identical twins, however, successful transplantation requires administration of immunosuppressive drugs to prevent immunologic rejection of the kidney graft. The side effects of long-term immunosuppression outweigh to some extent the advantages of transplantation over dialysis. Development of new, more effective immunosuppressive agents as well as a clearer understanding of the immune system has greatly improved the success and safety of organ transplantation in the past 10 years, and now it is the treatment of choice for many patients with ESRD.

Selection of Patients

Not all patients with ESRD are suitable candidates for transplantation and, for those who are, there is often a long waiting time because of the shortage of donated organs. Transplant candidates can be considered from infancy up to age 65. Kidney transplantation in children, especially infants less than 1 year of age, poses unique hazards and is somewhat less successful than adult renal transplantation. Nevertheless, transplantation is the treatment of choice for children because it offers a chance for normal growth. In patients over 60 years of age, physiologic age becomes the most important consideration. Contraindications to transplantation include chronic infections that cannot be cured, malignancy, the presence of another life-limiting disease that will not be corrected by transplantation, and severe debilitation, which greatly increases the risks of surgery and immunosuppression. The cause of renal failure is rarely a contraindication except in the case of oxalosis.

Certain glomerulonephritides can recur in the renal graft, most notably focal glomerulosclerosis, IgA nephropathy, and membranoproliferative glomerulonephritis type II, but graft loss from recurrent disease is rare, occurring in fewer than 10 per cent of recipients. Systemic metabolic diseases (i.e., diabetes, cystinosis, oxalosis) cause destruction of the renal allograft, but, except for oxalosis, the progression is slow, often allowing good allograft function for more than 10 years.

Renal Donor Selection

Candidates for renal transplantation may receive kidneys from family members or from brain-dead patients whose families have consented to organ donation (so-called cadaver donors). Family members considered for donation are usually human leukocyte antigen (HLA)–identical matches (both chromosomes shared) or single-haplotype matches (one chromosome shared between donor and recipient). Family member donors are usually more closely matched to recipients than are cadaver donors, and consequently graft survival is superior in related donor transplants (Table 31–5). A living donor offers other advantages to the recipient: The delay between onset of renal failure and rehabilitation is shorter, post-transplant renal function is usually immediate, and there are fewer rejection episodes, so that smaller doses of immunosuppressive drugs are required. Family members who wish to be kidney donors are carefully evaluated to ensure that they are in excellent health. The risk to life in a perfectly healthy donor is estimated to be 0.05 per cent. Much evidence suggests that no long-term harm results from life with a single kidney. In the United States, approximately 20 per cent of transplanted kidneys are donated by family members and 80 per cent of kidneys are from cadavers.

Allograft Rejection

Immunologic events depend upon interactions between donor cells expressing foreign histocompatibility antigens and recipients' cells capable of reacting to them. The strength of the immune response depends upon the degree of antigenic disparity between donor and recipient. Histocompatibility testing is the method used to select a kidney from a donor expressing antigens that are most similar to recipient antigens.

Rejection of an organ transplant may be of three types: hyperacute, acute, and chronic. **Hyperacute rejection** is antibody-mediated and occurs within minutes to hours of transplantation. It can be avoided, for the most part, by testing recipient sera for antibody reactivity against donor cells (crossmatch). **Acute rejection** is primarily a lymphocyte-mediated immune response that occurs most commonly 2 to 8 weeks after transplantation. Acute rejection involves lymphocytic infiltration of the graft with concomitant deterioration in function. Acute rejection, if diagnosed early, can be successfully treated with a course of high-dose corticosteroids and/or antilymphocytic monoclonal antibodies. **Chronic rejection** involves both humoral and cell-mediated immunity, is more indolent, and is poorly responsive to antirejection therapy.

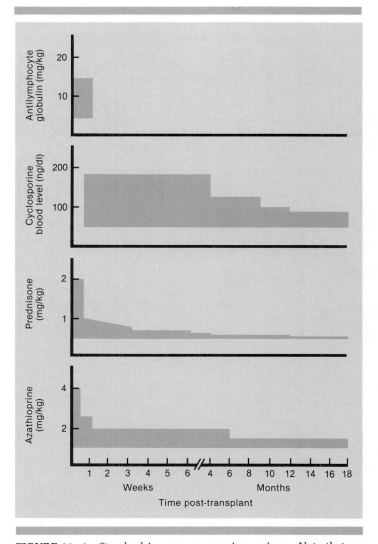

FIGURE 31–4. Standard immunosuppression regimen. Note that cyclosporine levels are measured by HPLC.

Immunosuppression

Successful renal transplantation requires suppression of the immune system to prevent rejection. Potent immunosuppressive medications are available both to prevent and to treat allograft rejection. Prophylactic immunosuppression protocols usually include a combination of three or four medications to optimize immunosuppression and minimize drug effects. Cyclosporine is currently the mainstay of all prophylactic immunosuppressive regimens and is used in combination with antilymphocyte globulin, corticosteroids, and azathioprine. Many centers use an "induction" immunosuppression protocol that includes administration of corticosteroids, azathioprine, and a polyclonal antilymphocyte globulin for the first 1 or 2 weeks after transplantation. "Maintenance" immunosuppression with corticosteroids, azathioprine, and cyclosporine follows induction and serves as long-term preventive immunosuppression. Figure 31–4 provides a typical immunosuppression regimen.

Use of antilymphocyte globulin in the early posttransplant period is thought to protect against early acute rejection and to allow postponement of cyclosporine administration until good graft function is established. With this immunosuppression protocol, 1-year patient survival of 95 per cent and 1-year graft survival of 80 per cent are observed. Approximately 40 per cent of recipients have an acute rejection episode requiring additional immunosuppressive medication. Most commonly, corticosteroids or monoclonal antilymphocytic antibodies are used. Successful reversal of an acute rejection episode varies from 60 to 95 per cent. Second rejection episodes occur in fewer than 15 per cent of recipients.

Cyclosporine

Use of cyclosporine accounts in large part for the dramatic improvement in graft survival observed in the past decade. Cyclosporine selectively inhibits T cells by blocking interleukin-2 release. Its use, however, is complicated by the fact that its toxic-therapeutic ratio is low. Consequently, monitoring of cyclosporine blood levels to achieve therapeutic but nontoxic ranges is necessary.

Nephrotoxicity is the most frequent and troublesome side effect of cyclosporine, occurring to some degree in 75 per cent of patients. Acute cyclosporine nephrotoxicity complicates both cyclosporine dosage adjustment and diagnosis of acute cellular rejection. Hypertension is a second important side effect of cyclosporine and occurs in approximately 40 per cent of patients. Many data suggest that altered renal hemodynamics contribute to cyclosporine-induced hypertension. Calcium channel blockers appear to be very effective in ameliorating the hypertension. Two side effects that concern transplant recipients more than their physicians are hirsutism and gingival hyperplasia. Women, especially, are distressed by the hirsutism. Early studies suggested a markedly increased incidence of lymphomas in patients receiving cyclosporine, but dosage adjustments have reduced the incidence, so that the risk of lymphoma from cyclosporine is currently no higher than that from other immunosuppressive therapy. Although the therapeutic advantage of cyclosporine is undeniable, there is still concern over the nephrotoxicity, hypertension, and cosmetic effects of the drug. A number of new immunosuppressive agents are being investigated that may have more favorable therapeutic-toxic ratios. One such agent, FK506, has received considerable publicity for its purported benefit to liver transplant recipients.

Recipients of organ transplants remain on immunosuppression as long as the graft functions, but the dosage of medication is diminished with time. Long-term consequences of immunosuppressive therapy are increased risk of infections, malignancy (particularly skin cancers), and sequelae of chronic steroid administration.

Outcome

Figure 31–5 shows long-term graft survival for HLA-identical living related transplants and cadaver transplants. In the past 5 years, 1-year cadaver graft survival has improved significantly and long-term cadaver graft survival is likewise expected to improve. Nevertheless, a considerable difference remains in long-term success between living related and cadaver donor transplants. Currently, overall 1-year patient survival is 95 per cent, 1-year graft survival for living related grafts is 91 per cent, and for cadaver grafts it is 81 per cent. Rejection is the most common cause of graft loss in the first year after transplant, but loss in subsequent years is multifactorial, including rejection, infection, death with functioning graft, and recurrent disease.

REFERENCES

Drukker W, Parsons FM, Maher JF: Replacement of Renal Function by Dialysis. 2nd ed. Boston, Martinus Nijhoff Publishers, 1988.

Eschbach JW, Abdulhadi MH, Browne JK, et al: Recombinant human erythropoietin in anemic patients with end stage renal disease: Results of a phase III multicenter clinical trial. Ann Intern Med 111:992, 1989.

Klahr S, Schreiner G, Ichikawa I: The progression of renal disease. N Engl J Med 318:1657, 1988.

Slatopolsky E: Renal osteodystrophy. In Wyngaarden JB, Smith LH Jr, Bennett JC (eds): Cecil Textbook of Medicine. 19th ed. Philadelphia, WB Saunders Co, 1992, pp 1423–1426.

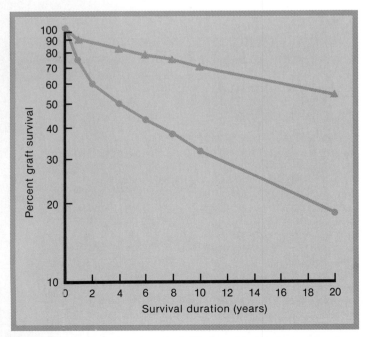

FIGURE 31–5. Long-term survival. Circle = First cadaver; triangle = HLA-identical siblings.

SECTION IV

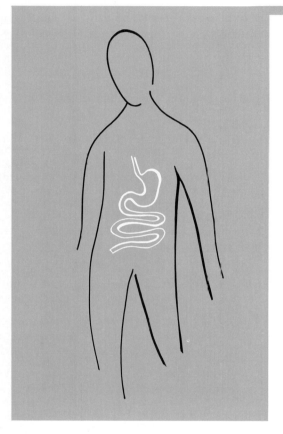

GASTROINTESTINAL DISEASE

Section IV of Cecil Essentials of Medicine, 2nd ed, by Nathan Bass, M.D., Ph.D., Lloyd H. Smith, Jr., M.D., and Rebecca W. Van Dyke, M.D., has been extensively revised and updated by the current authors for this section on Gastrointestinal Disease.

32 THE COMMON CLINICAL MANIFESTATIONS OF GASTROINTESTINAL DISEASE

A. Abdominal Pain

Abdominal pain most commonly heralds gastrointestinal (GI) disease and brings the patient to the attention of the internist or gastroenterologist. The subjective nature of this pain can be confusing but can also be very helpful in establishing a diagnosis. For example, acute appendicitis is frequently not discoverable using the most sophisticated scanning techniques such as computed tomography (CT); in this situation, an accurate diagnosis may be determined only by assessing the location and quality of the pain. In this section, the etiology, characteristics, and patterns of abdominal pain are reviewed and an approach to the problem of acute abdominal pain is discussed.

ORIGIN OF ABDOMINAL PAIN

Sensory information regarding pain travels in sympathetic pathways to spinal sensory neurons. The afferent endings are located in the smooth muscle layers of the hollow organs, in organ capsules, in the peritoneum, and in the walls of intra-abdominal blood vessels. Several of the pain sensations that are familiar to skin injury, such as cutting, tearing, and burning, are absent in the intestines. However, there are three types of sensation that produce pain in the gut: (1) Stretching the wall of a hollow organ or the capsule of a solid organ can produce abdominal pain. This type of stretching usually occurs because of forceful muscle contraction, muscle spasms, distention, or traction. (2) Inflammatory responses associated with the release of mediators such as prostaglandins, histamine, and serotonin or bradykinin may stimulate sensory nerve endings. (3) Ischemia may produce pain owing to the release of tissue metabolites. Spinal sensory neurons may also receive misleading input from peripheral neurons that do not sense pain, leading to the perception of referred pain.

CHARACTERISTICS OF ABDOMINAL PAIN

The position, quality, timing, and pace of abdominal pain are critical to differential diagnosis. Abdominal pain frequently exhibits one of the following three patterns: (1) Visceral pain is usually dull and difficult to localize. Patients may describe it as being in the midline and having a crampy or gnawing quality. (2) Parietal pain is usually severe and is much easier for the patient to localize. Usually this pain is caused by an inflammatory reaction in the parietal peritoneum. (3) Referred pain is any pain remote from the diseased viscus that is generally innervated by the same spinal segment. This pain may be associated with hyperesthesia.

Visceral pain is difficult to localize, although specific patterns may give clues to the part of the GI tract that is involved. Esophageal pain is usually substernal but may localize to a specific region of the chest. Pain in the esophagus may radiate to the left arm or the back and thereby masquerade as cardiac pain. Pain from disease of the stomach, duodenum, or pancreas is generally epigastric and may radiate to the back, especially in disease of the posterior duodenum and pancreas. Pain from the liver, gallbladder, and biliary drainage system may also be epigastric but frequently localizes to the right upper quadrant. Gallbladder or biliary pain may also refer to the scapula, especially on the right. Pain due to abscesses under the diaphragm (subphrenic) or in the liver may be referred to the shoulder. Jejunal and ileal pain is generally periumbilical and tends to be quite vague. The exception is that pain from the terminal ileum may localize to the right lower quadrant, much like appendiceal pain. Colonic pain localizes poorly but is usually felt in the lower half of the abdomen unless the surrounding parietal peritoneum is inflamed. Rectal pain may be felt in the region of the anus but may also be felt over the sacrum posteriorly. Unusual patterns of abdominal pain that may present like angina include esophageal spasm or meat impaction; left upper quadrant discomfort from the transverse colon may produce a similar syndrome. Pain from the transverse or descending colon can also resemble pain from the left side of the back or left hip. Finally, pain from the posterior appendix — either ruptured or unruptured — may produce flank and back pain.

The qualities that patients ascribe to pain and its progression may be very helpful diagnostically. Pain due to esophageal reflux (heartburn) is often described as burning; pain from peptic ulcer disease may also burn but is frequently described as an ache or an annoying sensation relieved with ingestion of food or antacids. Pain that is caused by intestinal obstruction recurs persistently in a severe and crampy (colicky) manner, but between episodes of obstruction these patients usually have no pain. The pain associated with cystic duct obstruction is usually steady rather than colicky despite its name—biliary colic. Pain due to inflammation of the parietal peritoneum is generally steady, may be well localized, and often helps identify the offending organ owing to proximity of the pain to the diseased tissue. Irritation of the peritoneum may be accompanied by percussion tenderness, voluntary guarding, and rigidity of the overlying muscles. Patients with peritoneal irritation generally lie very still because movement intensifies their pain. Ischemic disease of the intestine usually produces severe pain that localizes poorly and is not generally associated with tenderness early on. Pain related to dissection of an abdominal aortic aneurysm is usually abrupt in onset, is severe in nature, and may be described as "ripping" or "tearing."

The character of some types of abdominal pain changes with time. For example, appendicitis may begin with vague abdominal pain that localizes poorly, followed by specific localization of the pain to the right lower quadrant, and subsequently diffuse peritoneal irritation due to rupture of the inflamed appendix ensues. Typical pain patterns are catalogued in Table 32–1.

NAUSEA AND VOMITING

Nausea and vomiting may or may not be associated with abdominal pain. Vomiting is controlled through a center in the medulla and can be provoked by stimulation of either cholinergic neurons from the intestine or dopaminergic neurons in the chemoreceptor trigger zone surrounding the vomiting center. Obstruction and distention of any of the hollow viscera can produce vomiting; this is particularly so with more proximal obstruction. Any disease that irritates or inflames the peritoneum may also induce vomiting. Severe motility disturbances of the stomach, such as in diabetic gastroparesis, frequently produce vomiting. In these intestinal disorders, vagal afferents stimulate the vomiting center, producing nausea and vomiting. Drugs and gastric mucosal irritants may also induce vomiting via this pathway or through the surrounding chemoreceptor trigger zone. Other disorders associated with vomiting include increased intracranial pressure, psychogenic vomiting, hypersecretion of gastric acid (Zollinger-Ellison syndrome), pregnancy, uremia, and early morning emesis of alcoholics.

APPROACH TO THE PATIENT WITH ACUTE ABDOMINAL PAIN

The evaluation and care of patients with severe acute abdominal pain ("acute abdomen") present one of the most difficult challenges in clinical medicine because of the occasional profound dif-

ference in severity between the patient's symptoms and the patient's disease. Some causes of the acute abdomen are emergencies yet may present with minimal findings. In contrast, people with benign self-limited illnesses may present dramatically. The differential diagnosis of the acute abdomen includes the following: acute appendicitis, cholecystitis, pancreatitis, intestinal obstruction, intestinal perforation, intestinal infarction, strangulated viscus, acute diverticulitis, ruptured ectopic pregnancy, and ruptured aortic aneurysm. It is essential to remember that diseases of the lung (pneumonia), kidney (kidney stone), pelvic organs, liver, hematopoietic system (sickle cell crisis), and metabolic disorders (acute porphyria) may also cause acute abdominal pain.

As with most medical problems, a careful, accurate, and detailed history often provides the critical clues to the diagnosis of acute abdominal pain. It should emphasize the onset, quality, and radiation of the pain and the pace of the illness. Symptoms such as fever, nausea, constipation, diarrhea, and bleeding may also give important clues. The medical history may be extremely valuable as well. In particular, prior abdominal surgery or peptic ulcer disease might suggest that the patient has an obstruction due to adhesions or a newly perforated ulcer. During the physical examination, it is important to observe the patient for the immobility associated with diffuse peritonitis or the restlessness associated with intestinal colic. Also, it is essential to rule out pulmonary causes of abdominal pain such as pneumonia, right-sided heart failure, and pulmonary thromboembolism. The abdominal examination must address the following items in particular: (1) the nature, quality, and frequency of bowel sounds; (2) the presence of localized or diffuse tenderness and whether or not it can be elicited by percussion alone; (3) the presence of any masses or hernias; (4) the presence or absence of fluid in the abdomen; (5) the presence or absence of enlargement of the liver and spleen. Examination for peritoneal irritation is best sought by light percussion. Percussion tenderness that refers to a different location in the abdomen has a very high diagnostic value. Aggressive attempts to demonstrate rebound tenderness are contraindicated. Thorough rectal and pelvic examinations are absolutely essential because they provide the best clues to genitourinary, colonic, and appendiceal disease.

Useful laboratory data include hematocrit, white blood cell count and differential, urinalysis, and examination of stool for blood and pus. Serum tests for lipase, amylase, bilirubin, transaminases, and lipids may also be helpful. The diagnosis of acute pancreatitis relies on a combination of clinical and laboratory findings because other diseases such as intestinal ischemia or ruptured ectopic pregnancy can elevate the serum amylase level.

Certain radiographic procedures may be of use as well. These include the chest, upright abdomi-

TABLE 32–1. PAIN PATTERNS OF ABDOMINAL DISEASE

	SUBSTERNAL	EPIGASTRIC					
ONSET	CHRONIC	ACUTE			CHRONIC		
Disease/diagnosis	Reflux esophagitis	Perforated duodenal ulcer	Cholecystitis	Pancreatitis	Duodenal ulcer	Gastric ulcer	Nonulcer dyspepsia
Pain quality	Burning; after meals/at night	Severe; ±history of chronic ulcer pain	Steady/biliary colic	Steady, boring	Gnawing, burning before meals/at night	Gnawing, worsened by food	Same as duodenal ulcer ± bloating
Pain referral	Left arm	±Back	Tip of scapula	Back	±Back	Occasionally to the back	None
Pain progression	Upper chest	Rapid, over entire abdomen	Intensity increases steadily over hours in right upper quadrant	±Peritoneal signs	None	None	None
Associated findings	Water brash in mouth	Guarding; free peritoneal air	Fever, gallstones on sonography, and failure to visualize on ^{99m}Tc-HIDA scan	Nausea and vomiting	Temporary relief with food or antacids	±Relief by antacids	±Relief with food or antacids

nal, and supine abdominal films. These help identify specific gas patterns that have differential diagnostic value and also enhance the search for free intra-abdominal air commonly seen with a perforated viscus. Obstruction or perforation may also be diagnosed by meglumine diatrizoate (Gastrografin), sodium diatrizoate (Hypaque), or barium studies of the small bowel or colon. Additional helpful imaging studies include CT scans, ^{99m}Tc-HIDA (technetium-labeled iminodiacetic acid) scans, ultrasonography, and endoscopic procedures.

All patients with severe abdominal pain deserve adequate pain relief while diagnostic studies are being completed. The outcome, of course, depends on recognizing and treating the underlying disease process. It is frequently important to obtain surgical consultation early because intervention may be required. Occasionally, the final diagnosis must be reached by exploratory laparotomy.

IRRITABLE BOWEL SYNDROME

Irritable bowel syndrome (IBS) is a very common disorder associated with abdominal pain and alternating constipation and diarrhea that has no recognized organic cause. IBS is present in up to 12 per cent of the general population and 50 per cent of referrals to gastroenterologists in the United States. Symptoms of IBS usually begin in young adulthood and last for many years. Women with this disorder are much more likely than men to be seen by physicians. The etiology and pathogenesis of IBS are completely obscure; the syndrome may include some diseases that are not yet characterized. For example, patients with adult-type hypolactasia (lactose intolerance) were previously classified as having IBS. The two major factors that contribute to the pathogenesis of this disease are (1) increased and abnormal colonic motility, particularly segmental contractions stimulated by meals, emotion, mechanical distention, or drugs, and (2) enhanced sensitivity to discomfort produced by normal intestinal gas or pressure in the sigmoid colon.

The abdominal pain of IBS varies greatly in both severity and pattern. The pain may be described as dull in the lower abdomen or sharp in the hypogastrium. It is common for the pain to be meal-related and relieved by passing flatus or stool and quite uncommon for the pain to awaken the patient at night. Almost all patients have disturbed bowel habits—either constipation or diarrhea or both. Bleeding is not a feature of IBS except possibly from irrelevant hemorrhoids. IBS should never be considered an adequate explanation for occult blood in the stool. Certain unpleasant personality characteristics have been attributed to IBS but are

TABLE 32–1. PAIN PATTERNS OF ABDOMINAL DISEASE Continued

PERIUMBILICAL					LOWER QUADRANTS			
ACUTE			CHRONIC		ACUTE		CHRONIC	
Appendicitis	Small bowel obstruction	Intestinal infarction	Inflammatory bowel disease	Intestinal angina	Diverticulitis	Colon obstruction	Dissecting aortic aneurysm	Irritable bowel syndrome
Cramping, steady	Cramping	Severe, aching, diffuse	Cramping, aching, may be in lower quadrants	Colicky, aching, diffuse	Steady, aching, left lower quadrant	Crampy	Sudden, severe, tearing; may be periumbilical	Cramping, steady or intermittent
±Back or groin	Back	None	None	None	Back	Back	Flank, inguinal regions	None
Localization to right lower quadrant	None	If treatment is delayed, peritonitis	None	Pain relief from 1–2 hours	None	None	None	None
Referred percussion tenderness to right lower quadrant	Hyperactive bowel sounds, nausea, and vomiting. Dilated bowel loops on x-ray	Unimpressive clinical presentation, occult blood in stool, absent bowel sounds	Diarrhea, blood and pus in stools, urgency, tenesmus	Weight loss	Palpable inflammatory mass, constipation, fever, leukocytosis	Vomiting, constipation, distention, hyperactive bowel sounds	Shock, abdominal bruit, abdominal mass	Alternating constipation and diarrhea, bloating

more properly associated with the subset of patients who have IBS and seek frequent care from multiple physicians.

Evaluation of patients suspected of having IBS must include a thorough history, physical examination, stool analysis, routine laboratory tests, and probably a proctosigmoidoscopy and barium enema to rule out organic disease of the colon.

Patients with IBS have a need for education and understanding from their physician to cope with their confusing symptoms. Patients who come to the doctor frequently may also need psychological counseling. No drug has been shown to be of great value in IBS, and narcotics must be assiduously avoided. Some patients describe considerable diminution in their symptoms, particularly constipation, with the use of bulk-forming agents such as Metamucil. Anticholinergics may help relieve pain in selected patients. Dietary manipulation has not been shown to be generally helpful.

REFERENCES

Schuster MM: Irritable bowel syndrome. In Sleisenger MH, Fordtran JS (eds): Gastrointestinal Disease. 5th ed. Philadelphia, WB Saunders Co, 1993, pp 917–933.
Silen W (ed): Cope's Early Diagnosis of the Acute Abdomen. 16th ed. Oxford, England, Oxford University Press, 1983.
Wyngaarden JB, Smith LH Jr, Bennett JC (eds): Cecil Textbook of Medicine. 19th ed. Philadelphia, WB Saunders Co, 1992, pp 656–662, 722–723.

B. Gastrointestinal Hemorrhage

DEFINITION

GI bleeding is a common clinical problem, but a small number of lesions account for most GI bleeding episodes. Blood loss ranges from occult bleeding of which the patient is unaware to massive bleeding that anyone would notice. About 80 per cent of acute GI bleeding stops without intervention, but some patients suffer recurrent bleeding that may become a life-threatening emergency.

Management of patients with GI bleeding revolves around three major issues: (1) most important, correction of hypovolemia; (2) cessation of bleeding by the least invasive means; and (3) prevention of recurrent bleeding. Goals 2 and 3 cannot be readily attained until the bleeding source is identified; however, prompt and adequate resuscitation takes priority over all other measures.

PRESENTATION OF GASTROINTESTINAL HEMORRHAGE

Blood loss from the GI tract may be either (1) acute—it is sudden or massive and may present with obvious hypovolemia; or (2) chronic—it is occult and usually the patient is completely unaware of the bleeding.

Acute bleeding may present in one of several ways:

Hematemesis. Vomiting bright red blood or blood that looks like "coffee grounds" is called hematemesis. This clinical finding is extremely valuable because it shows the bleeding to be proximal to the ligament of Treitz.

Melena. Black, tarry, usually foul-smelling stools that are passed after a bleed of more than 500 ml between the pharynx and the right colon are called melena. Melena is usually a sign of bleeding from an upper intestinal tract lesion and may be its only clinical manifestation.

Hematochezia. The passage of bright red or maroon stool is termed hematochezia and is usually due to a GI tract lesion distal to the ligament of Treitz or massive bleeding from a proximal lesion.

The patient with chronic GI blood loss may present with fatigue, dyspnea, syncope, angina, or a positive test for fecal occult blood. Patients with iron deficiency may give a history of melena, although this is unusual. Some patients present with a lesion that has bled chronically, causing them to have iron deficiency anemia and acutely causing hematemesis.

TABLE 32–2. CAUSES OF GI BLEEDING

UPPER GI	UPPER OR LOWER GI	LOWER GI
Duodenal ulcer	Neoplasms	Hemorrhoids
Gastric ulcer	Arterial-enteric fistulas	Anal fissure
Anastomotic ulcer	tulas	Diverticulosis
Esophagitis	Vascular anomalies	Ischemic bowel disease
Gastritis	Angiodysplasia	ease
Mallory-Weiss tear	Arteriovenous malformations	Inflammatory bowel disease
Esophageal varices	Hematologic disease	Meckel's diverticulum
Hematobilia	Elastic tissue diseases	Solitary colonic ulcer
	Pseudoxanthoma elasticum	Intussusception
	Ehlers-Danlos syndrome	
	Vasculitis syndrome	

ETIOLOGY OF GASTROINTESTINAL BLEEDING

It is possible for many lesions in the GI tract to bleed, but most bleeding episodes can be explained by a small number of diagnoses. The distinction between upper and lower GI bleeding is made based on localization proximal or distal to the ligament of Treitz (Table 32–2).

Upper Gastrointestinal Bleeding

More than 90 per cent of cases of upper GI bleeding are caused by peptic ulcer, erosive gastritis, Mallory-Weiss tears, and esophagogastric varices.

Peptic Ulcer. Bleeding may occur from ulceration of the duodenum, stomach (gastric), and regions of surgical anastomoses. Ulcer pain or dyspepsia may be absent, with bleeding being the presenting symptom of the peptic ulcer disease.

Gastritis. Erosive gastritis that leads to bleeding may be caused by ingestion of alcohol or nonsteroidal anti-inflammatory drugs (NSAIDs) such as aspirin and ibuprofen. Gastric erosions are also common in severely ill patients with major trauma or systemic illness, burns, or head injury. Severe forms of erosive gastritis with significant bleeding are also commonly seen in patients with portal hypertension. To prevent gastric bleeding in the severely ill patient, it is essential to keep the gastric pH above 4 using H_2-receptor antagonists. Bleeding episodes are diminished by these therapies, but mortality may not be improved.

Mallory-Weiss Tears. Mallory-Weiss tears occur in the mucosa near the junction of the esophagus and stomach and can present with mild to massive hematemesis. Fifty per cent of these patients give a history of vomiting that precedes emesis of a large amount of blood, but they often have no other history to guide the diagnosis. Definitive diagnosis is made on endoscopy, and the tears are treated with adjunctive H_2-receptor antagonists.

Esophagogastric Varices. Bleeding from esophageal varices is usually massive and occurs without warning. Esophageal varices emerge as a result of portal hypertension that forces the development of collaterals for intestinal venous return. Hepatic cirrhosis due to alcohol consumption is the most common cause of variceal bleeding in the United States, although any cause of portal hypertension, including portal vein thrombosis and schistosomiasis, may produce the same syndrome. Bleeding from esophagogastric varices is complicated in patients with cirrhosis for the following reasons: (1) Patients with varices frequently bleed from other causes such as gastritis or peptic ulceration. (2) Long-term portal hypertension leads to recurrent bleeding in the majority of patients with cirrhotic disease, which leads to the need for decompression of the portal system by portosystemic shunting. This treatment, however, carries considerable morbidity and mortality, especially when performed as an emergency; therefore, sclerosis of esophageal varices has become a more standard therapy. (3) Cirrhosis may also lead to encephalopathy, which frequently worsens during episodes of bleeding. (4) Bleeding may be exacerbated by the liver's inability to make adequate clotting factors and secondary hypersplenism that results in thrombocytopenia. For these reasons, patients with GI bleeding and hepatic cirrhosis are difficult to manage.

Several other lesions of the upper GI tract may lead to bleeding, including carcinoma of the esophagus, carcinoma of the stomach, esophagitis, and catastrophic erosion of synthetic arterial grafts into the upper intestine, in particular the duodenum.

Lower Gastrointestinal Bleeding

Lower GI bleeding is generally caused by lesions of the anorectum and colon.

Non-neoplastic Anorectal Lesions. Small amounts of bright red blood on the surface of the feces and toilet tissue are most commonly caused by hemorrhoids, anal fissures, or fistulas. Inflammation of the rectum (proctitis) from infectious diseases is seen more commonly in male homosexuals and may cause hematochezia.

Neoplastic Lesions of the Colon and Rectum. Carcinoma of the colon and colonic polyps usually present with occult blood loss; however, they may ulcerate and thereby present with acute lower GI bleeding.

Ulcerative, Bacterial, and Ischemic Colitis. Bleeding may accompany inflammatory diarrheas as seen in ulcerative colitis, but it may also occur in infectious diarrheas caused by *Shigella, Campylobacter, Entamoeba histolytica,* and occasionally *Salmonella.* Usually these patients present with diarrhea and have mucus and white blood cells in the stool. Ischemic colitis may also present with bloody diarrhea, particularly in elderly patients.

Colonic Diverticula. Diverticula of the colon, most often the sigmoid colon, are common in the United States. However, most bleeding diverticula are in the more proximal colon and are the most common cause of severe lower GI bleeding. Diverticulitis may produce abdominal pain but usually does not cause bleeding.

Angiodysplastic Lesions. Many patients acquire submucosal malformations of the arteriovenous system called angiodysplasia. These lesions may produce acute bleeding but may also present with occult blood loss, and they are often difficult to visualize by endoscopy or angiography. They tend to develop with aging and long-term renal failure and may be associated with calcific aortic stenosis.

Small Intestinal Lesions. Significant intestinal bleeding is usually not caused by lesions in the small intestine distal to the ligament of Treitz. The one exception is Meckel's diverticulum, which may cause discrete ulceration in or near the diverticulum, producing acute bleeding.

Bleeding Diatheses

Blood dyscrasias (leukemia, thrombocytopenia), disorders of coagulation (disseminated intravascular coagulation), vascular malformations (Osler-Weber-Rendu syndrome), vasculitides (Henoch-Schönlein purpura), and connective tissue disorders (pseudoxanthoma elasticum) may cause GI blood loss from either upper or lower tract lesions.

APPROACH TO THE PATIENT WITH GASTROINTESTINAL HEMORRHAGE

Patients who present with GI bleeding must be approached in a systematic and orderly manner (Fig. 32–1), i.e., (1) initial assessment, (2) resuscitation, (3) definitive diagnosis, and (4) treatment.

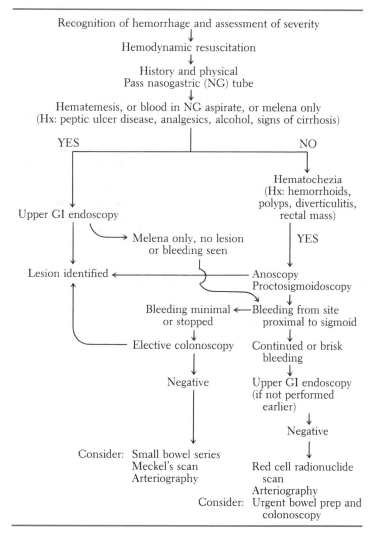

FIGURE 32–1. Diagnostic approach to the patient with gastrointestinal hemorrhage.

The management of GI bleeding must be adapted to the nature and pace of bleeding. Massive, continuous bleeding demands immediate diagnostic and therapeutic intervention, especially when transfusions fail to keep up with the rapid rate of blood loss.

Initial Assessment

If it is suspected that a patient has bled acutely from the GI tract, vital signs are noted and intravenous infusion of crystalloid, such as normal saline, is begun prior to any further investigation. Blood is sent for typing and crossmatching, a complete blood count, prothrombin and partial thromboplastin times, and platelet count. The last three tests identify a bleeding diathesis that may be present in patients with cirrhosis and coagulation difficulties that may worsen with massive transfusion. Serum is sent for routine electrolytes, blood urea nitrogen (BUN), creatinine, and liver enzymes to help evaluate renal and hepatic function. These tests aid in the management of bleeding and may help identify esophageal varices as its source.

The vital signs, including an assessment of orthostatic changes in blood pressure and pulse, determine volume loss. An orthostatic fall in blood pressure greater than 10 mm Hg usually signifies a 20 per cent or greater loss of blood volume. Some patients, however, exhibit only a marked increase in heart rate upon standing without the concomitant fall in blood pressure. When hypotension is present, tachycardia almost always occurs, but heart rate alone is not a reliable indicator. As blood loss worsens to 40 per cent of blood volume, the signs of shock, including pallor, cool limbs, marked tachycardia, and hypotension, are usually apparent. The amount of hematemesis or melena cannot be used to predict the degree of bleeding or risk to the patient. If the bleeding is close to the mouth or anus, the physician may overestimate its importance, and if it is a distance from any orifice, its importance may be underestimated. The hematocrit is completely unreliable for assessing blood loss in its early stages because even massive bleeding does not drop the hematocrit until volume re-expansion has occurred; this equilibration takes place over several hours. Initially low hematocrits are more consistent with chronic than acute blood loss and may be associated with a low mean corpuscular volume.

Resuscitation

The potential for catastrophic complications mandates the placement of patients with acute GI bleeding in an intensive care unit. GI bleeding is generally managed initially by internists, but early surgical consultation is indicated because surgery may be urgently required later. Resuscitation is the primary goal of early management and mandates maintenance of intravascular volume and tissue oxygenation. Nasal oxygen may be a useful adjunct in the elderly patient or those with heart or lung disease. Vital signs, orthostatic blood pressure changes, and urine output are the most valuable clinical indicators, and they may be supplemented with measures of central venous or wedge pressure as needed.

Volume resuscitation is accomplished with crystalloid solutions given through large-bore intravenous lines. Actively bleeding patients may require packed red cells and fresh frozen plasma to replace volume losses. However, fresh frozen plasma is usually used in patients who have a coagulopathy that may be correctable with this therapy; lost red cells are usually replaced with packed red cells rather than whole blood.

The amount of blood given to a patient is determined by an assessment of continued bleeding, the degree of pre-existing anemia, and other conditions that may impair tolerance of blood loss. Massive bleeding may require whole blood administration under pressure. In contrast, a healthy young person with hemodynamic stability who has stopped bleeding from a duodenal ulcer may tolerate a very low hematocrit (20 to 25 per cent) and may be treated with oral iron and no transfusion. The decision to transfuse is therefore based on the presence of hypotension, evidence of decreased tissue perfusion, or ongoing bleeding.

Diagnosis

The first step in the assessment of GI bleeding is to determine whether the bleeding source is upper or lower tract. The history can be extremely helpful in this situation. A description of hematemesis is virtually diagnostic of bleeding proximal to the ligament of Treitz. Recent ingestion of NSAIDs or alcohol may suggest gastritis. A classic history of peptic ulcer pain or a prior or family history of GI bleeding may help; half the patients with Mallory-Weiss tears give a history of vomiting. A change in bowel habits, especially constipation, may suggest colon cancer. In a smoker, abrupt onset of acute abdominal pain with bleeding may suggest ischemic disease of the colon. Patients who have had an abdominal aortic bypass are at risk for development of aortoenteric fistulas.

Physical examination may reveal chronic liver disease and raise the specter of esophageal varices as a bleeding source. Examination of the skin may show telangiectasias that suggest either chronic liver disease or Osler-Weber-Rendu syndrome. The rectal examination is essential to rule out a mass and to detect the presence of melenic stool. The presence of melena suggests bleeding in the upper tract or the right colon.

Placement of a nasogastric tube followed by aspiration of gastric contents is a simple procedure. Gastric aspirates that have no heme-positive material or gross blood make upper GI bleeding proximal to the pylorus much less likely. It is possible to miss active bleeding from duodenal ulcers or from an aortoenteric fistula that is considerably distal to the pylorus. Gastric aspirates should be examined for gross blood, e.g., red, maroon, or coffee grounds–like material. Hemoccult testing is not informative. A negative gastric aspirate does not rule out an upper GI source. The combination of hypovolemia and a protein load from bleeding increases the BUN in many cases.

The choice of additional diagnostic procedures is based on the clinical suspicion of upper versus lower GI tract bleeding, the rate of blood loss, and the possibility of surgery. Although classic barium studies of the upper and lower GI tract are not generally useful, endoscopic examination of the upper tract is frequently diagnostic if the examination is not obscured by blood that remains in the tract. When this condition supervenes, radiolabeled red blood cell scans may be used to grossly localize the region of blood loss. If the bleeding is sufficiently brisk, angiography identifies the site, but if the bleeding is intermittent or only moderate, angiography is generally negative. Most GI bleeding sources are identified by upper or lower endoscopy.

Upper GI endoscopy is the most rapid, safe, and definitive means for diagnosing the site of blood loss in upper tract lesions and is also useful therapeutically. If bleeding has stopped, a double-contrast barium upper GI series detects most malignancies and peptic ulcers but it misses gastritis and Mallory-Weiss tears. Potential malignancies and gastric ulcers require a biopsy, making endoscopy the procedure of choice because of its high sensitivity and specificity for diagnosis, capacity for biopsy, and potential for therapeutic intervention in the bleeding patient.

Lower GI tract bleeding is first evaluated by rectal examination, anoscopy, and proctosigmoidoscopy, which detects lesions in the distal colon, including hemorrhoids, cancer, inflammatory bowel disease, and polyps. Bleeding lesions proximal to the region that can be visualized with the proctosigmoidoscope can be identified after thorough colonic purging. If bleeding is sufficiently brisk, colonoscopy is likely to be futile and angiography more useful. If bleeding has stopped, air-contrast barium enemas may be used but are unable to detect certain bleeding lesions; many lesions demonstrated by air-contrast barium enema require a biopsy. The performance of a barium enema may further complicate colonoscopy during the next 1 to 3 days. If suspected lower GI bleeding has occurred and no diagnosis in the lower tract is forthcoming, an upper GI source must be sought, usually with upper GI endoscopy. Lesions of the small bowel distal to the ligament of Treitz are difficult to detect but are fortunately uncommon. They may be detected with small bowel series, enteroclysis, or, in rare cases, a Meckel scan.

Evaluation of chronic GI blood loss can be undertaken with either an endoscopic or a radiographic approach. The latter includes a barium enema, proctosigmoidoscopy, and an upper GI series. Endoscopic evaluations of chronic GI blood loss usually begin with a full colonoscopy and, if negative, an upper GI endoscopy. If all of these studies are negative, small bowel studies with bar-

ium are performed. Angiography may be used to search for vascular lesions.

Despite the many diagnostic tools available today, the source of bleeding sometimes cannot be determined. In many patients the lesions may be subtle or inaccessible, and some patients have so many lesions that it is impossible to single out the one that is bleeding. Fortunately, few patients are repeatedly hospitalized for bleeding from undiagnosed lesions.

Treatment

About 80 per cent of patients with GI bleeding stop bleeding spontaneously. Management of these patients is focused on prevention of further bleeding and identification of the bleeding source. For example, bleeding due to peptic ulcer disease is treated with antacids, H_2-receptor blockers, or sucralfate. Expectant management is the rule for gastritis, Mallory-Weiss tears, angiodysplasia, and diverticulosis when bleeding has ceased spontaneously. In contrast, malignant lesions and polyps must be removed endoscopically or surgically. If bleeding does not recur in the hospital, long-term management depends on the site and type of lesion as well as the patient's ability to tolerate surgery. For example, a patient with a peptic ulcer that fails to stop bleeding usually requires therapeutic endoscopic intervention and, if that is unsuccessful, surgery.

Several nonsurgical techniques have been developed for management of GI hemorrhage recently, but their role is still debated. These procedures include radiologic techniques such as administering intra-arterial vasopressin and selective embolization of arteries supplying bleeding lesions. Endoscopic treatment of bleeding lesions includes electrocoagulation, thermocoagulation, submucosal injection of epinephrine, and laser photocoagulation.

The treatment of bleeding esophageal varices requires a separate discussion. Patients with these lesions are frequently poor operative candidates because they have poor health status, liver disease, and a bleeding diathesis due to prolonged prothrombin time and/or low platelet counts. These patients frequently rebleed and require considerable in-hospital support. GI bleeding in patients with severe liver disease may provoke hepatic encephalopathy and deterioration in renal function (see Chapter 42). Purging the bowel of blood and treatment with lactulose may help decrease the risk and severity of encephalopathy. Volume replacement is essential in patients with bleeding varices, but overexpansion of blood volume may precipitate rebleeding; infusion of crystalloid tends to worsen edema and ascites in these patients as well. Noninvasive efforts to diminish bleeding include intravenous vasopressin and replacement of clotting factors with fresh frozen plasma and platelets. The use of a Minnesota or

Sengstaken-Blakemore tube to tamponade bleeding varices with a balloon may be required but serves only to temporize. The most accepted treatment of acutely bleeding esophageal varices is endoscopic injection of sclerosant solutions directly into the varices (sclerotherapy). Studies have shown that this procedure arrests bleeding in up to 90 per cent of cases. Emergency decompression of the entire portal system with a portosystemic shunt operation may be the only method available for stopping a massive variceal hemorrhage. Prevention of recurrent bleeding through sclerotherapy or elective shunt surgery is preferred to emergency shunt surgery. The advantages and disadvantages of these procedures are discussed in Chapter 45.

REFERENCES

Cello JP: Gastrointestinal hemorrhage. *In* Wyngaarden JB, Smith LH Jr, Bennett JC (eds): Cecil Textbook of Medicine. 19th ed. Philadelphia, WB Saunders Co, 1992, pp 742–745.
Cello JP, Crass RA, Grendell JH, Trunkey DD: Management of the patient with hemorrhaging esophageal varices. JAMA 256:1480, 1986.
Steer ML, Silen W: Diagnostic procedures in gastrointestinal hemorrhage. N Engl J Med 309:646, 1983.

C. Malabsorption

The purpose of the GI tract is to digest and absorb nutrients and eliminate everything else. These nutrients include macronutrients, such as carbohydrates, proteins, and fat, and micronutrients, including vitamins and trace elements. The GI tract may digest, solubilize, transport, and resynthesize up to 80 gm of fat per day, whereas the terminal ileum needs to absorb only 1 μg of vitamin B_{12} per day. In addition to absorption, the gut circulates water, electrolytes, bile salts, pancreatic juice, and intestinal secretions that are reabsorbed in the small intestine and colon. Food is a complex mixture of nutrients and non-nutrients that must be separated as it passes through the GI tract. The preparation for digestion begins with (1) the controlled release of food that has been fragmented by the stomach into the intestine; (2) the secretion of pancreatic juice, bile, and water into the lumen of the intestine to allow digestion of food into an isotonic mixture of simple molecules; and (3) terminal digestion of peptides and disaccharides by the brush border enzymes of the small intestine enterocyte. All of these steps occur prior to absorption of nutrients.

Nutrients are absorbed at the brush border surface of the enterocytes. The surface area of the enterocytes is expanded by complex folding of the small bowel surface into valvulae conniventes, intestinal villi, and microvilli of the individual enterocyte. The various portions of this surface are exposed to the nutrient mixture during the 1.5 to 2.0 hours required to pass from the stomach to the colon. Colonic absorption focuses primarily on salvage of water and electrolytes. Some molecules may be absorbed throughout the length of the small intestine, and some must be absorbed in a very limited region (e.g., vitamin B_{12} and bile acids in the terminal ileum). The extraordinary complexity of the digestive and absorptive processes lends itself to a large number of disorders that may lead to maldigestion or malabsorption. In this section a general classification of maldigestion and malabsorption disorders and a rational approach to their differential diagnosis are discussed.

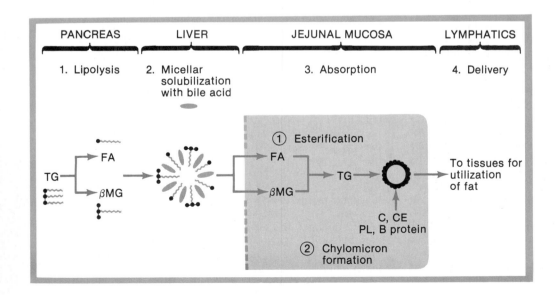

FIGURE 32–2. Schematic of intestinal absorption, showing the participation of pancreas, liver, and intestinal mucosal cells in fat absorption. TG = Triglycerides; FA = fatty acids; βMG = beta-monoglyceride; C = cholesterol; CE = cholesterol esters; PL = phospholipids. (From Wilson FA, Dietschy JM: Gastroenterology 61:911, 1971, © by The American College of Gastroenterology.)

Malabsorption cannot be understood without a thorough understanding of normal absorption. The absorption of only three of the major classes of nutrients (fat, protein, and carbohydrates) is discussed in this section; the absorption of water and electrolytes is discussed in Section D of this chapter because malabsorption of water and electrolytes produces diarrhea. A detailed discussion of the absorption of iron, calcium, and vitamin B_{12} is presented elsewhere.

Digestion and Absorption of Fat (Fig. 32–2). Dietary fat is ingested predominantly in the form of triglycerides with long-chain fatty acids that include saturated (palmitic and stearic) and unsaturated (oleic and linoleic) varieties. It leaves the stomach and enters the duodenum as an emulsion, which prevents absorption. The long-chain fatty acids and peptides in the duodenum stimulate bile flow via cholecystokinin. Lipase secreted by the pancreas and bound to the surface by colipase in the presence of bile salts releases the fatty acids from positions 1 and 3, leaving a 2-monoglyceride. These products of lipolysis are then incorporated into mixed micelles, with the bile salts enhancing their solubility and allowing them to traverse the unstirred water layer that overlies the intestinal epithelium. The fatty acids released from lipolysis and 2-monoglycerides diffuse from the micelles into the cell cytoplasm, where they are, for the most part, resynthesized into triglycerides and packaged into chylomicrons and very low density lipoproteins (VLDL) and exported to the lymphatics. Bile salts remain in the intestinal lumen, are reutilized in new micelles, and are finally reabsorbed in the terminal ileum. More than 95 per cent of ingested neutral fat is efficiently absorbed from the intestine; the fat-soluble vitamins (A, D, E, K) are absorbed in tandem with fat.

Digestion and Absorption of Proteins. Proteins are much simpler to digest and absorb than fat because they are water-soluble. The hydrolysis of proteins to amino acids is initiated in the stomach with pepsin but is accomplished by trypsin, elastase, chymotrypsin, and carboxypeptidase in the proximal small intestine. Hydrolysis of proteins by pancreatic enzymes produces free amino acids, dipeptides, and oligopeptides, which must be terminally degraded to amino acids at the brush border on the surface of the enterocytes. Some amino acids may be absorbed as dipeptides, however. There are several distinct transport systems for amino acids based on their chemical characteristics: (1) the dibasic amino acid system, which may be abnormal in cystinuria; (2) a neutral amino acid system, which is abnormal in Hartnup disease; (3) the imino acid–glycine system; and (4) the dicarboxylic acid system. Amino acids are absorbed in tandem with sodium ions, and this is accomplished almost completely in the jejunum.

Digestion and Absorption of Carbohydrates. The major dietary carbohydrates are starch and the disaccharides sucrose and lactose. Starch is a complex glucose polymer that is degraded to its constituent monosaccharide by salivary pancreatic amylases. In addition, on the brush border there are amylases and limit dextrinases. Oligosaccharides and disaccharides cannot be absorbed at all, so digestion of carbohydrates must be complete to the monosaccharide stage prior to absorption. The terminal digestion of carbohydrates is accomplished by α-dextrinase, sucrase, lactase, maltase, and glucoamylase activities. The constituent monosaccharides, glucose and galactose, are absorbed in conjunction with sodium in a mechanism similar to peptide absorption, and fructose is absorbed by facilitated diffusion.

CLASSIFICATION OF THE MALABSORPTION SYNDROMES (Table 32–3)

Malabsorption can be caused by a multitude of disorders, including genetic defects and diffuse mucosal diseases. This section provides a general understanding of malabsorption; for a detailed understanding of specific diseases, the reader is referred to articles listed at the end of this discussion. It is most helpful to think of maldigestion and malabsorption syndromes in the context of abnormalities of one or more of the normal processes discussed in the previous section.

Inadequate Digestion. Ingested food must be broken down for absorption to take place at the intestinal border. Digestion is accomplished largely by pancreatic enzymes secreted into the intestinal lumen. Of particular importance are lipase and colipase and the proteases, particularly trypsin. Chronic diseases of the pancreas, such as chronic pancreatitis or cystic fibrosis, may lead to malabsorption due to maldigestion. Even Zollinger-Ellison syndrome may cause gastric acid secretion sufficient to lower the luminal pH in the duodenum, thereby impairing lipase activity and causing fat malabsorption as well.

For pancreatic enzymes to digest fat, an adequate concentration of luminal bile salts to solubilize the neutral fats must be present. Inadequate bile salts can be caused by (1) decreased hepatic synthesis and transport, although this is rare; (2) cholestasis such as biliary cirrhosis; (3) deconjugation of bile salts due to bacterial overgrowth; or (4) interference in ileal reabsorption due to cholestyramine given therapeutically or, more commonly, in the setting of ileal disease or surgery. In these circumstances, the liver is unable to deliver enough bile salts to maintain sufficient luminal concentrations to solubilize fats, leading to maldigestion and malabsorption of fat and fat-soluble vitamins.

In addition to disorders of digestion associated with pancreatic enzymes or bile salts, highly specific defects in digestion may occur as well. The digestion and absorption of lactose, the dominant sugar in milk, depends upon an adequate supply

TABLE 32-3. CLASSIFICATION OF THE MALABSORPTION SYNDROMES

Inadequate Digestion
  Pancreatic exocrine deficiency
    primary—e.g., chronic pancreatitis, cystic fibrosis, carcinoma of the pancreas
    secondary—gastrinoma with acid inactivation of pancreatic lipase
  Intraluminal bile salt deficiency
    liver disease—especially biliary cirrhosis
    disease or bypass of the terminal ileum—impaired recycling mechanism
    bacterial overgrowth syndrome—increased deconjugation of bile salts
  Specific abnormalities—disaccharidase deficiencies
Inadequate Absorption
  Inadequate absorptive surface—e.g., short bowel syndrome, bypass fistulas, extensive Crohn's disease
  Specific mucosal cell defects
    genetic—abetalipoproteinemia, Hartnup disease, cystinuria, monosaccharide absorptive defects
    acquired—hypovitaminosis D
  Diffuse disease of the small intestine
    immunologic or allergic injury—celiac disease (gluten-sensitive enteropathy), ? eosinophilic enteritis, ? Crohn's disease
    infections and infestations—Whipple's disease, giardiasis, tropical sprue, bacterial overgrowth syndrome
    infiltrative disorders—lymphoma, mastocytosis, amyloidosis
    fibrosis—systemic sclerosis, radiation enteritis
Lymphatic Obstruction
  Lymphangiectasia
  Whipple's disease
  Lymphoma
Multiple Mechanisms
  Postgastrectomy steatorrhea
  Bacterial overgrowth syndrome
  Disease or bypass of the distal ileum
  Scleroderma, lymphoma, Whipple's disease
  Diabetes mellitus
Drug-Induced Malabsorption
  Neomycin, cholestyramine, antacids, ethanol, chronic ingestion of laxatives, biguanides
Hyperabsorptive "Malabsorption"
  Hemochromatosis, hypervitaminosis D
  Enteric hyperoxaluria

of the enzyme lactase. Failure to absorb ingested lactose leads to flatulence, distention, cramps, and diarrhea. Adult-type lactose intolerance may be inherited, as in African blacks and Asians, or may be secondary to any type of diffuse mucosal injury; these include celiac disease, from which patients may never recover lactase activity, or viral gastroenteritides, which produce temporary or occasionally permanent loss of adequate lactase activity.

Inadequate Absorption. In this condition, food products are fully digested but are not adequately absorbed. This frequently results from inadequate absorptive surface, even though the available surface may be normal. The simplest example is short bowel syndrome due to surgical removal of most of the small intestine. Inadequate absorption most commonly occurs after mesenteric infarction, Crohn's disease, and bypass surgery for morbid obesity.

It is also possible for the absorptive surface to have a normal area but not function normally. This problem occurs frequently within the mucosal cell and may be highly specific owing to a gene defect. Examples of selective absorption defects include cystinuria and Hartnup disease for certain amino acids and abetalipoproteinemia, which leads to fat malabsorption due to defective intracellular synthesis of apolipoproteins. Selective defects can also be acquired, such as reduced calcium absorption in the absence of adequate 1,25-dihydroxycholecalciferol or a drop in lactase production due to gastroenteritis.

More commonly, malabsorption is seen with diffuse disease processes involving the mucosa or submucosa of the small intestine. Several causes of diffuse injury have been identified, although in many cases the mechanisms are complicated or undefined.

IMMUNOLOGIC OR ALLERGIC INJURY. Gluten-sensitive enteropathy and the rare disorder, eosinophilic enteritis, fall into this category.

INFECTIONS AND INFESTATIONS. Whipple's disease is a systemic disorder caused by a bacterium that has recently been identified as an actinomycete, *Tropheryma whippelii*. This disorder is marked by dramatic malabsorption and packing of the small intestinal submucosa with macrophages that stain positively with periodic acid–Schiff (PAS). Patients with this disease may have a complex presentation that includes fever, adenopathy, pigmentation changes, arthralgias, and occasionally severe neurologic manifestations. Whipple's disease is rare but is especially important to diagnose because it is highly treatable. Infestation with *Giardia lamblia* may also cause malabsorption; however, its clinical presentation is dominated by cramps, flatulence, and diarrhea. Bacterial overgrowth syndromes may also produce diffuse mucosal injury.

INFILTRATIVE DISORDERS. The mucosa and/or submucosa may be infiltrated to an extent sufficient to impair absorption. Examples include intestinal lymphoma, amyloidosis, and mastocytosis.

FIBROSIS. The intestinal wall may be thickened in fibrotic diseases such as progressive systemic sclerosis and radiation injury. The cause of malabsorption in these conditions is complex, but it may result in part from a motility disturbance that leads to bacterial overgrowth.

LYMPHATIC OBSTRUCTION. After absorption, long-chain fatty acids are re-esterified into triglycerides and secreted into the lymphatic system in chylomicrons and VLDL. Obstructive lesions of the mesenteric lymphatics may, therefore, impair fat absorption. This may contribute to malabsorption syndromes in diffuse intestinal lymphomas and is also seen in Whipple's disease and congenital lymphangiectasia. In general, lymphangiectasia is more likely to present as a protein-losing enteropathy with secondary hypoalbuminemia.

Multiple Mechanisms. Because the digestive and absorptive processes are complex and interrelated, many disorders may impair multiple processes. For example, subtotal gastrectomy with a Billroth II–type gastroenterostomy may lead to a modest degree of malabsorption. This problem is caused by rapid gastric emptying and intestinal transit, leading to inadequate mixing of pancreatic and biliary secretions from the blind loop of the duodenum. Because the food does not pass through the proximal duodenum, release of secretin and cholecystokinin is decreased and bacterial overgrowth may occur in the afferent blind duodenal loop. Bacterial overgrowth can lead to deconjugation of bile salts and may also injure the intestinal epithelium. All of these events, alone or in concert, may lead to a malabsorptive state. Diabetes mellitus may also cause multiple defects because exocrine deficiency of the pancreas or motility disorders in the small intestine may supervene, producing bacterial overgrowth due to stasis.

Drug-Induced Malabsorption. Drugs that are capable of inducing malabsorption of specific nutrients are well known, and some of them are listed in Table 32–4.

Hyperabsorptive "Malabsorption." Malabsorption is normally thought of as too little absorption, but there are also disorders in which too much nutrient is absorbed. For example, hemochromatosis is a genetic disorder that leads to hyperabsorption of iron, and hypervitaminosis D leads to excessive absorption of calcium. Enteric hyperoxaluria is an acquired disorder in which excessive oxalate is absorbed, resulting in the production of calcium oxalate renal stones.

CLINICAL MANIFESTATIONS OF MALABSORPTION

The clinical presentation of the large number of diseases listed in Table 32–3 is varied. Some of these diseases present with features that seem unrelated to the malabsorption; others present in highly specific ways, such as pernicious anemia with a selective malabsorption of vitamin B_{12} or rickets due to poor absorption of calcium. This brief discussion focuses on the signs and symptoms of malabsorption, particularly the malabsorption of fat.

Early Manifestations. The early manifestations of malabsorption are difficult to detect by patient and physician. A change in bowel habits may occur; the patient may report producing bulky stools with visible oil that can be difficult to flush. More commonly, the patient suffers weight loss, fatigue, depression, and bloating. Nocturia is described by some patients and is believed to be caused by excessive nocturnal reabsorption of intestinal fluids. A high index of suspicion is required to consider the diagnosis in the early stage, but it is important to do so to institute appropriate treatment before more severe symptoms supervene.

Late Manifestations. The major late manifestations of malabsorption are summarized in Table 32–5. They generally relate to nutritional deficiencies that are secondary to the malabsorption.

TABLE 32–4. SOME DRUG-INDUCED ABSORPTIVE DEFECTS

DRUG	SUBSTANCE MALABSORBED
Ethanol	Folates, vitamin B_{12}
Antacids	Phosphate
Phenytoin	Folates
Neomycin	Fatty acids, vitamin B_{12}
Cholestyramine	Bile acids, thyroxine
Tetracycline	Iron

TABLE 32–5. CORRELATION OF DATA IN MALDIGESTION AND MALABSORPTION

CLINICAL FEATURES	LABORATORY FINDINGS	PATHOPHYSIOLOGY
Wasting, edema	↓ Serum albumin	↑ Albumin loss (gut), ↓ protein ingestion, ↓ protein absorption
Weight loss, oily bulky stools	↑ Stool fat excretion, ↓ serum carotene	↓ Ingestion and absorption fat, CHO, protein
Paresthesias, tetany	↓ Serum Ca^{2+}, ↑ alkaline phosphatase, ↓ mineralization bones (x-ray), ↓ serum Mg^{2+}	↓ Absorption Ca^{2+}, vitamin D, Mg^{2+}
Ecchymoses, petechiae, hematuria	↑ Prothrombin time	↓ Absorption vitamin K
Anemia	Macrocytosis, ↓ serum vitamin B_{12}, ↓ absorption vitamin B_{12} and/or folic acid, microcytosis, hypochromia, ↓ serum iron, no iron in marrow	↓ Absorption vitamin B_{12} and/or folic acid, ↓ absorption iron
Glossitis	↓ Serum vitamin B_{12}, folic acid	↓ Absorption B vitamins
Abdominal distention, borborygmi, flatulence, watery stools	↓ Xylose absorption, ↓ disaccharidases in intestinal biopsy, fluid levels, small intestine (x-ray)	↓ Hydrolysis, disaccharides and ↓ absorption, monosaccharides and amino acids

CHO = Carbohydrate.

From Gray GM: Maldigestion and malabsorption: Clinical manifestations and specific diagnosis. *In* Sleisenger MH, Fordtran JS (eds): Gastrointestinal Disease. 3rd ed. Philadelphia, WB Saunders Co, 1983, p 230.

These patients frequently appear wasted owing to diminished muscle mass, but they may have abdominal distention with active bowel sounds. Blood pressure tends to be low, and the patient may exhibit increased skin pigmentation. Abdominal pain is uncommon unless the specific disorder causing the malabsorption causes pain, as in chronic pancreatitis or intestinal lymphoma. At this late stage, clinical diagnosis is much easier, but determining a specific cause of malabsorption may be difficult.

CLINICAL TESTS OF DIGESTION AND ABSORPTION

Many tests are available that aid in the diagnosis of maldigestion and malabsorption. A brief discussion of the more useful tests follows.

Fecal Fat Analysis. Identification of steatorrhea (fat in the stool) is essential in any assessment of maldigestion or malabsorption. The simplest test to detect stool fat is a Sudan III–stained stool smear. This test is qualitatively useful but has no quantitative capacity. The gold standard is to measure quantitatively the total fat in a 3-day stool specimen while the patient is on a diet consisting of 80 to 100 gm of fat per day. Normal fat excretion should be less than 6 gm/day and is usually less than 2.5 gm. Values higher than 6 gm/day clearly indicate steatorrhea (fat malabsorption) but do not help identify the pathogenesis of the steatorrhea.

Tests of Pancreatic Exocrine Function. Some of the tests of pancreatic exocrine function are described in Chapter 38. The bentiromide test determines the split of an orally administered synthetic peptide by pancreatic chymotrypsin. Excretion in 6 hours of less than 50 per cent of a 500-mg dose of bentiromide in the form of urinary arylamines is diagnostic of pancreatic exocrine insufficiency. Pancreatic disease may also be suspected when diffuse calcification is seen in the region of the pancreas on plain abdominal films or a CT scan. A new test that measures stool chymotrypsin is gaining favor.

Xylose Absorption-Excretion Test. The capacity of the mucosa to absorb sugars can be assessed by absorption of D-xylose. D-Xylose is a poorly metabolized 5-carbon sugar that is absorbed well in the intestine, but it is not degraded or concentrated in any tissue and is largely excreted in the urine. The test is performed by having the patient ingest 25 gm of D-xylose and then collecting the urine for 5 hours thereafter. Normal subjects excrete more than 4.5 gm of D-xylose in 5 hours, but this normal value can be reduced somewhat by age, poor renal function, the presence of large amounts of edema or ascites, and bacterial overgrowth. In patients who have bacterial overgrowth, the D-xylose test should return to normal with the use of antibiotics.

Radiographic Studies. Radiographic studies of the stomach and small intestine in malabsorption are nonspecific, although thickening of mucosal folds, modest dilatation of the intestinal lumen, and occasional clumping and segmentation of the barium in a moulage pattern may be observed. On rare occasions, barium studies may provide a definitive diagnosis by identifying a "blind loop," a diverticulum, or an unexpected fistula.

Small Intestinal (Jejunal) Biopsy. Biopsy of the small intestinal mucosa is frequently necessary to identify mucosal defects leading to the malabsorption syndrome. The utility of this procedure is summarized in Table 32–6.

Vitamin B_{12} Absorption (the Schilling Test). Vitamin B_{12} is absorbed in a complex process. It is first conjugated by R-factor proteins in the saliva, which are subsequently degraded in the duodenum under the influence of pancreatic trypsin. After the release of the R-factors, vitamin B_{12} is complexed to intrinsic factor, a protein secreted by the stomach. The vitamin B_{12}–intrinsic factor complex passes through the intestine and is absorbed by a specific receptor in the distal ileum. Defects in pancreatic enzymes required in the degradation of R-proteins, secretion of intrinsic factor, or ileal absorption of vitamin B_{12}–intrinsic factor complexes may lead to vitamin B_{12} deficiency. The Schilling test identifies the source of the malabsorption. Stage 1 of the Schilling test involves ingestion of radiolabeled vitamin B_{12} after a parenteral dose of 1 mg of vitamin B_{12} to prevent hepatic storage, thereby enhancing excretion of the label. Stage 2 of the Schilling test involves administration of vitamin B_{12} plus intrinsic factor. Stage 3 of the Schilling test involves repeating stage 1 after antibiotics are administered. Gastric disease leading to inadequate production of intrinsic factor leads to malabsorption of vitamin B_{12} in all stages of the Schilling test except stage 2, when intrinsic factor is provided. Disease of the pancreas leading to incomplete degradation of R-factors yields to low excretion of vitamin B_{12} in stage 1 because vitamin B_{12} is permanently complexed to the R-factors, but normal absorption in stage 2 because the vitamin B_{12} was already bound to intrinsic factor. Ileal disease leading to vitamin B_{12} malabsorption produces decreased absorption in all three stages of the Schilling test.

TABLE 32–6. UTILITY OF SMALL BOWEL BIOPSY SPECIMENS IN MALABSORPTION

Often Diagnostic

Whipple's disease	Giardiasis
Amyloidosis	Abetalipoproteinemia
Eosinophilic enteritis	Agammaglobulinemia
Lymphangiectasia	Mastocytosis
Primary intestinal lymphoma	

Abnormal But Not Diagnostic

Celiac sprue	Bacterial overgrowth syndrome
Systemic sclerosis	
Radiation enteritis	Tropical sprue
	Crohn's disease

Breath Tests. Several tests detect the presence of compounds produced by intraluminal bacteria by examining the breath. The ^{14}C-xylose test measures $^{14}CO_2$ produced in the breath at 30 and 60 minutes after ingestion of the radioactive sugar; it is elevated in the presence of bacterial overgrowth in the small intestine. A related test detects free hydrogen in the breath after ingestion of any of a variety of sugars. Glucose ingestion should lead to H_2 production via fermentation because it is fully absorbed in the small intestine. In the presence of bacterial overgrowth, breath hydrogen tends to increase early after ingestion. This test can also be used to detect specific carbohydrate maldigestion syndromes such as sucrase or lactase deficiency in which expired H_2 is increased after a 50-gm dose of the sugar. The increase in breath hydrogen occurs in these cases after undigested sugar reaches the colon.

Miscellaneous Tests. Other important but nonspecific tests that may provide clues to the degree and cause of malabsorption include body weight, serum albumin, prothrombin time (indirectly assesses vitamin K), cholesterol, carotene, folic acid, calcium, and magnesium. These tests are used primarily as adjuncts and to assess the severity of malabsorption but do not aid the differential diagnosis.

APPROACH TO THE PATIENT WITH SUSPECTED MALDIGESTION AND/OR MALABSORPTION

Because of the large number of diagnostic tests, a rational algorithm for the use of the various tests is necessary (Fig. 32–3). The best test for fat mal-

absorption is the 72-hour fecal fat analysis; however, this test is difficult to obtain in practice, so it may be necessary to establish steatorrhea with qualitative stool fat examination and serum carotene. If the stool fat is normal, the patient may have selective abnormalities for absorption of a specific carbohydrate. This condition must be suspected if the symptoms are primarily cramps, flatulence, and diarrhea. The most common cause of carbohydrate malabsorption is lactose intolerance; specific tests include oral tolerance tests, but measurement of breath hydrogen is more sensitive and specific. The measurement of an osmotic gap in fecal material suggests an osmotic cause of the diarrhea due to short-chain fatty acids or carbohydrates. The osmotic gap is calculated by the following formula: plasma osmolality -2 $(Na^+ + K^+)$ (fecal sodium plus fecal potassium). Osmotic gap is not calculated by measuring stool osmolality because (1) it increases with time in the specimen container; and (2) true osmolality is equal to serum osmolality because the colon cannot maintain a gradient for the concentration of water.

When fat malabsorption is demonstrated (>6 gm/24 hr or increased qualitative stool fat and decreased serum carotene), a xylose absorption-excretion test should be performed next. A normal xylose test rules out diffuse mucosal disease and suggests that the patient's disorder is digestive, such as pancreatic or bile salt deficiency. Specific tests for pancreatic insufficiency should then be performed. These may include plain abdominal films, bentiromide test, secretin test, or stool chy-

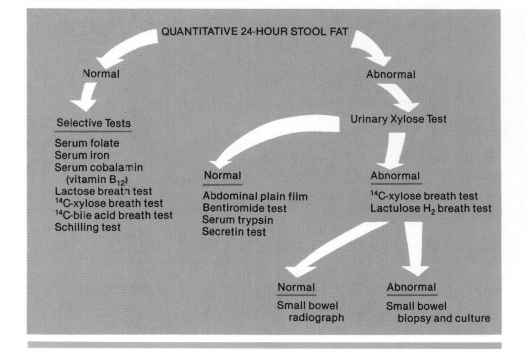

FIGURE 32–3. Approach to the patient with suspected maldigestion or malabsorption. (Adapted from Toskes PP: Malabsorption. *In* Wyngaarden JB, Smith LH Jr [eds]: Cecil Textbook of Medicine. 18th ed. Philadelphia, WB Saunders Co, 1988, p 740.)

QUANTITATIVE 24-HOUR STOOL FAT

Normal

Abnormal

Selective Tests

Serum folate
Serum iron
Serum cobalamin
  (vitamin B$_{12}$)
Lactose breath test
^{14}C-xylose breath test
^{14}C-bile acid breath test
Schilling test

Urinary Xylose Test

Normal

Abnormal

Abdominal plain film
Bentiromide test
Serum trypsin
Secretin test

^{14}C-xylose breath test
Lactulose H$_2$ breath test

Normal

Small bowel
radiograph

Abnormal

Small bowel
biopsy and culture

motrypsin. If the urinary xylose excretion is abnormal, breath hydrogen testing may be used to diagnose bacterial overgrowth using glucose. When no bacterial overgrowth is present, mucosal biopsy should be performed. Small bowel radiographs may also be helpful.

Most cases of malabsorption can be diagnosed through appropriate combinations of the above tests. Occasionally, clinical trials for treatable conditions should be instituted, such as a gluten-free diet for celiac disease, pancreatic enzyme replacement for pancreatic exocrine function, metronidazole for *Giardia lamblia* infection, or broad-spectrum antibiotics for suspected bacterial overgrowth.

TREATMENT OF MALABSORPTION

The treatment of malabsorption is a complex topic that cannot be completely covered here. Various treatments include H_2-receptor antagonists or H^+-K^+-ATPase inhibitors for gastrinoma; the daily use of pancreatic enzymes; antibiotics for bacterial overgrowth or Whipple's disease; a gluten-free diet for celiac sprue; the use of medium-chain fatty acids, which are more easily absorbed; surgical repair of intestinal or biliary obstruction; repair of blind loops or fistulas; and chemotherapy for lymphoma. Replacement therapy for the loss of specific nutrients or vitamins may also be required. In the case of the short bowel syndrome, total parenteral nutrition may be the only feasible treatment option.

DISORDERS ASSOCIATED WITH MALABSORPTION

A large number of conditions may lead to nutrient malabsorption. A sample of these conditions is listed in Table 32–3. In this section, two of these entities, celiac sprue and bacterial overgrowth syndrome, are discussed. Several other specific disorders are discussed elsewhere in this book and appended references.

Celiac Sprue (Gluten-Sensitive Enteropathy, Nontropical Sprue). Celiac sprue is a chronic, familial disorder associated with lifelong sensitivity to dietary gluten. Gluten is a complex of proteins found in wheat and wheat products. In these patients, diffuse mucosal injury results from the ingestion of gluten. The injury produces flattening of the villi, leading to a significant decrease in gut absorptive surface. The crypts are generally hyperplastic, and the lamina propria is infiltrated with lymphocytes.

PATHOGENESIS. The mechanism by which gluten causes injury is not definitively known, but it appears to be immunologic in origin. Celiac sprue is associated with the human leukocyte antigens HLA-B8 and HLA-Dw3, suggesting a linkage on chromosome 6, which supports the immunologic hypothesis. As many as 10 per cent of first-degree relatives of patients with celiac sprue are concordant for the disorder. Another hypothesis suggests that incomplete hydrolysis of gluten peptides leads to toxic intermediates that directly injure the intestinal epithelium. Although the cause is not known, it is clear that the lesion is produced locally because the intestine can fully recover when gluten is removed; the syndrome promptly reappears with reintroduction of gluten. Therefore, the pathogenesis of the malabsorption is a diffuse mucosal abnormality. This loss of functional mucosa may also lead to reduced secretion of cholecystokinin and secretin, which exacerbates the malabsorption by diminishing pancreatic and biliary function.

SIGNS AND SYMPTOMS. The signs and symptoms of celiac sprue are essentially the same as for other malabsorption syndromes. They are often more severe in childhood and diminish in adolescence and adulthood. The GI symptoms may be very mild, but the patient may have severe anemia due to iron deficiency and even a bleeding diathesis due to vitamin K deficiency. Metabolic bone disease due to calcium malabsorption has also been seen.

DIAGNOSIS. Patients with celiac sprue normally have impaired fat absorption, an abnormal xylose test, and an abnormal mucosal pattern on small bowel series. The Schilling test is usually normal, but if the disorder extends to the ileum, it may also be abnormal. Jejunal biopsy is essential to diagnosis, but the diagnosis is proved by response to a gluten-free diet.

TREATMENT AND PROGNOSIS. Treatment requires strict, lifelong adherence to a gluten-free diet. Food starch made from wheat, barley, and oats must be replaced with corn and rice products. The clinical response usually requires a few weeks and may proceed over a period of months. However, reversion to the symptoms can occur within days of reinstitution of a regular diet. The long-term prognosis for this syndrome is excellent, although there may be a slightly higher incidence of non-Hodgkin's lymphoma in adult life.

Bacterial Overgrowth Syndrome. The small intestine normally harbors fewer than 10^4 colony-forming units per milliliter of fluid and is considered relatively sterile as a result of the motility of the intestine, gastric acid, and intestinal immunoglobulins. Overgrowth of bacteria in the small intestine frequently results in malabsorption. This can be due to the loss of normal gut motility in diabetes or to surgically created blind loops, as well as to decreased gastric acid secretion, especially in the elderly.

PATHOGENESIS. The malabsorption seen in bacterial overgrowth syndrome may result from three mechanisms: (1) deconjugation of bile salts leading to impaired micelle formation and fat malabsorption; (2) patchy direct injury to mucosal cells due to bacteria or bacterial products; (3) direct utilization of nutrients by bacteria, best established for vitamin B_{12}.

CONDITIONS ASSOCIATED WITH BACTERIAL OVER-GROWTH. A large number of disorders are associated with bacterial overgrowth. These include gross structural derangements, such as diverticula, fistulas, blind loops, strictures, and obstruction, and also diseases that impair intestinal motility, most commonly diabetes, amyloidosis, progressive systemic sclerosis, and intestinal pseudo-obstruction. Bacterial overgrowth has also been seen in pancreatic insufficiency and hypogammaglobulinemia. Surgical damage to the ileocecal valve leading to reflux of colonic contents may also predispose to small intestinal bacterial overgrowth.

DIAGNOSIS. An approach to the patient with malabsorption is shown in Figure 32–3. When bacterial overgrowth is suspected because of an abnormal D-xylose test, a definitive diagnosis can be obtained by the ^{14}C-xylose, lactulose, or glucose breath hydrogen test. Other approaches include (1) a positive three-stage Schilling test; (2) direct culture of jejunal fluid (usually >10^7 colony-forming units/ml with a mixed culture is required for diagnosis); and (3) a 10- to 14-day therapeutic trial of a broad-spectrum antibiotic.

TREATMENT. Treatment depends upon the cause of the overgrowth syndrome. Surgery may be required for structural abnormalities. More commonly, patients are treated indefinitely with intermittent antibiotics such as metronidazole, trimethoprim-sulfamethoxazole, and tetracycline. Cephalosporins in combination with metronidazole may be required, and in severe cases, total parenteral nutrition is necessary.

REFERENCES

Toskes PP: Malabsorption. In Wyngaarden JB, Smith LH Jr, Bennett JC (eds): Cecil Textbook of Medicine. 19th ed. Philadelphia, WB Saunders Co, 1992, pp 687–698.

Wright TL, Heyworth MF: Maldigestion and malabsorption. In Sleisenger MH, Fordtran JS (eds): Gastrointestinal Disease. 4th ed. Philadelphia, WB Saunders Co, 1989, pp 263–282.

D. Diarrhea

DEFINITION

Diarrhea is defined as an increase in stool weight (>200 gm/day) that may be associated with increased liquidity, stool frequency, perianal discomfort, and urgency, with or without fecal incontinence. This section discusses normal water and solute handling by the intestine and the pathophysiology and evaluation of diarrhea. Other specific clinical entities have already been discussed in Section C and are further discussed in Chapter 36. Infectious causes are covered in Chapter 103.

NORMAL INTESTINAL PHYSIOLOGY

The intestine is normally presented with approximately 10 L/day of fluid, 1.5 to 2 L from ingested food and liquids and the remainder from salivary, gastric, biliary, pancreatic, and small intestinal secretions. The small bowel absorbs all but 1 L of this fluid, with the colon absorbing 90 per cent of the remaining fluid, leading to fecal output of 100 to 150 ml per day.

The mechanisms that control fluid and solute absorption differ in different regions of the gut. A single general principle, however, governs all absorption: solutes are absorbed by specific mechanisms, with water following passively. The energy source for transport of most intestinal solutes is the sodium gradient generated by the Na-K-ATPase pump at the basolateral surface shown in Figure 32–4. The energy provided by this gradient is used to transport protons, sodium chloride, glucose, amino acids, and bile acids across cell membranes. Bicarbonate transport is driven by sodium proton exchange and accounts for the relatively alkaline nature of ileal and colonic contents as well as the fluid immediately adjacent to the enterocytes and under the mucous layer. Jejunal and

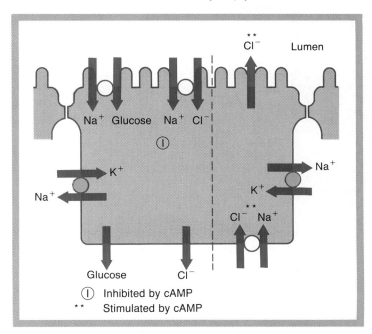

FIGURE 32–4. Schematic representation of electrolyte and glucose transport mechanisms in the small intestine. Absorptive mechanisms (shown on the left) and secretory mechanisms (shown on the right) are driven by Na$^+$-K$^+$-ATPase (shown in closed circles). Cyclic AMP produces a secretory diarrhea by both inhibiting absorption and stimulating secretion of sodium and chloride. Coupled absorption of sodium and glucose is unaffected, and this is the basis for current oral rehydration formulas.

TABLE 32 – 7. CLASSIFICATION OF DIARRHEA*

TYPE	MECHANISM	EXAMPLES	CHARACTERISTICS
1. Secretory	Increased secretion and/or decreased absorption of Na$^+$ and Cl$^-$	Cholera VIP-secreting tumor Bile salt enteropathy Fatty acid–induced diarrhea	Large volume, watery diarrhea No blood or pus No solute gap Little or no response to fasting
2. Osmotic	Nonabsorbable molecules in gut lumen	Lactose intolerance (lactase deficiency) Generalized malabsorption (particularly carbohydrates) Mg^{2+}-containing laxatives	Watery stool, no blood or pus Improves with fasting Stool may contain fat globules or meat fibers and may have an increased solute gap
3. Inflammatory	Destruction of mucosa Impaired absorption Outpouring of blood, mucus	Ulcerative colitis Shigellosis Amebiasis	Small frequent stools with blood and pus Fever
4. Decreased absorptive surface	Impaired reabsorption of electrolytes	Bowel resection Enteric fistula	Variable
5. Motility disorder	Increased motility with decreased time for absorption of electrolytes and/or nutrients	Hyperthyroidism Irritable bowel syndrome	Variable
	Decreased motility with bacterial overgrowth	Scleroderma Diabetic diarrhea	Malabsorption

*Diarrhea is, in many instances, due to a combination of mechanisms. The diarrhea of generalized malabsorption, for example, is attributable to osmotic and secretory diarrhea as well as to decreased absorptive surface.

ileal fluids typically have the following solute concentrations: Na$^+$, 140 mM; K$^+$, 6.0 mM; Cl$^-$, 100 mM; and HCO$_3^-$, 30 mM.

Colonic solute transport is restricted to electrolytes and proceeds by a mechanism different from that of the small bowel. The colon has a specific sodium channel that generates an electrical potential across the colon wall and drives chloride and potassium secretion, leading to the high potassium concentration seen in colonic contents. Organic acids produced by colonic bacteria may react with bicarbonate and produce organic anions and CO$_2$. Thus, colonic fluid has a different concentration profile for the electrolytes outlined above for the small bowel. These include Na$^+$, 40 mM; K$^+$, 90 mM; Cl$^-$, 15 mM; HCO$_3^-$, 30 mM; and organic anions, 85 mM.

The small bowel and the colon are both capable of secreting electrolytes in water. In the small bowel, secretion is historically ascribed to crypt cells and may be due to sodium-coupled entry of chloride anions across the basolateral membrane, followed by secretion of chloride across the luminal cell membrane. Sodium and water are believed to follow the chloride passively owing to electrical and osmotic gradients (Fig. 32–4). Secretion of chloride in the colon may follow a similar mechanism in which chloride uptake across the basolateral membrane is coupled to sodium and potassium entry.

The movement of water across intestinal membranes is passive but prodigious. Water absorption is linked to solute absorption, and therefore the presence of any osmotically active solutes such as magnesium, phosphate, sulfate, or nonabsorbable carbohydrates impairs water absorption or leads to water secretion.

CLASSIFICATION AND PATHOPHYSIOLOGY

Any of the following abnormalities may lead to diarrhea: (1) a decrease in the normal absorption of solutes in water; (2) increased secretion of electrolytes obligating water to the intestinal lumen; (3) the presence of poorly absorbed, osmotically active solutes in the gut lumen; (4) increased intestinal motility; and (5) inflammatory disease producing blood, pus, or mucus (Table 32–7).

Secretory Diarrhea. Secretory diarrhea is usually due to abnormalities in both absorption and secretion of electrolytes; the common causes of the syndrome are outlined in Table 32–8. Secretory diarrhea is normally associated with increased intracellular cyclic adenosine monophosphate (cAMP). The increase in cAMP is caused by

TABLE 32 – 8. SOME CAUSES OF SECRETORY DIARRHEA

Agents That Activate the Adenylate Cyclase – cAMP System
   Cholera toxin
   Escherichia coli heat-labile toxin
   Vasoactive intestinal polypeptide (VIP)
   Prostaglandins
   Salmonella enterotoxin
   ? Dihydroxy bile acids and fatty acids
Agents That Probably Do Not Activate the Adenylate Cyclase – cAMP System
   Escherichia coli heat-stable toxin
   Serotonin
   Enterotoxins of *Clostridium perfringens, Psuedomonas aeruginosa, Klebsiella pneumoniae,* and *Shigella dysenteriae*
   Calcitonin
   Castor oil, phenolphthalein
   Villous atrophy (e.g., celiac sprue)

a chain of events that begins with a signaling molecule. After the signaling molecule has complexed the cell surface receptor, a G-protein is activated in the cell membrane and stimulates adenylate cyclase, producing cAMP. As shown in Figure 32–4, cAMP elevation blocks sodium chloride absorption and stimulates chloride secretion without altering other transport mechanisms. This allows the heat-labile toxin of the cholera bacillus to cause diarrhea by an increasing intracellular cAMP without any damage to the mucosal surface. The signaling pathway through the specific G-proteins is so specific that hydration can be maintained in these patients by administering sodium-glucose solutions because a different pathway is used and it is unaffected.

Secretory diarrhea has other causes, but most of them are poorly understood. Increases in cyclic guanosine monophosphate (cGMP) or intracellular calcium may also lead to secretion. Small bowel disorders that produce atrophic villi, such as celiac sprue, are often associated with electrolyte secretion abnormalities as well. Presumably, this is due to inadequate absorptive surface in the face of normal crypt secretion. Disorders associated with malabsorption in osmotic diarrheas are sometimes associated with secretory components, but the mechanism is not well understood. Nonabsorbed bile acids and fatty acids may stimulate ion secretion in the colon, leading to a non–small-bowel secretory diarrhea.

Secretory diarrhea frequently presents as massive watery diarrhea that continues in spite of fasting. Because the diarrhea is primarily water and electrolytes, fecal osmolality can be entirely accounted for by the measurement of Na^+, K^+, Cl^-,

TABLE 32–9. SOME CAUSES OF OSMOTIC DIARRHEA

Disaccharidase deficiencies
Glucose-galactose or fructose malabsorption
Lactulose, mannitol, sorbitol ("chewing gum diarrhea") ingestion
Magnesium ingestion (antacids, laxatives)
Sulfate, phosphate ingestion (laxatives)
Sodium citrate ingestion
Steatorrhea (pancreatic insufficiency)
Generalized malabsorption
  Small bowel mucosal disease (celiac disease)
  Bacterial overgrowth (bile acid deconjugation, villous atrophy)

and HCO_3^-, with the fecal solute gap [plasma osmolality $-2(Na^+ + K^+)$] near zero.

Osmotic diarrhea is caused by the accumulation or generation of poorly absorbed solutes in the lumen of the intestine. This can occur by three predominant mechanisms: (1) ingestion of poorly absorbed solutes such as lactulose, SO_4^{2-}, PO_4^{3-}, or Mg^{2+}; (2) generalized malabsorption; and (3) failure to absorb a specific dietary component such as lactose. Examples of osmotic diarrhea are listed in Table 32–9.

Osmotic diarrhea is completely preventable by fasting, which eliminates ingestion of the solute responsible for the diarrhea. The colon cannot maintain a water gradient, so the concentration of sodium and potassium falls in the presence of abnormal osmotically active solutes. The measured stool electrolytes $[2(Na^+ + K^+)]$ do not account for

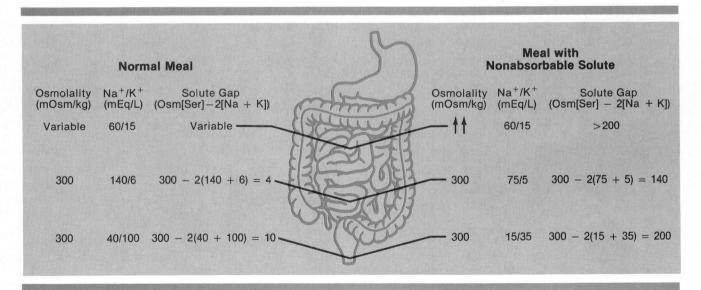

Normal Meal				Meal with Nonabsorbable Solute		
Osmolality (mOsm/kg)	Na⁺/K⁺ (mEq/L)	Solute Gap (Osm[Ser]−2[Na + K])		Osmolality (mOsm/kg)	Na⁺/K⁺ (mEq/L)	Solute Gap (Osm[Ser] − 2[Na + K])
Variable	60/15	Variable			60/15	>200
300	140/6	300 − 2(140 + 6) = 4		300	75/5	300 − 2(75 + 5) = 140
300	40/100	300 − 2(40 + 100) = 10		300	15/35	300 − 2(15 + 35) = 200

FIGURE 32–5. Changes in luminal electrolytes during a normal meal and a meal causing osmotic diarrhea. Each row of data shows a comparison of osmolality, sodium/potassium concentration, and solute gaps at a given level of the intestine for normal meals (*left*) and in meals producing osmotic diarrhea (*right*). Note that the osmolality of luminal contents stabilizes equal to serum in the small intestine. Osmotically active molecules obligate water in the intestine but **do not** elevate the osmolality.

fecal fluid osmolality. Fecal fluid osmolality is assumed to be equal to serum osmolality. In the case of ingestion of poorly absorbed anions such as SO_4^{2-} and PO_4^{3-}, osmotic diarrhea may be present with a normal solute gap because a solute gap is calculated using the cations rather than the anions. Carbohydrate malabsorption leading to osmotic diarrhea often produces acidic stools due to bacterial fermentation of the carbohydrates. The progressive changes in luminal electrolytes during processing of a normal meal and a meal destined to proceed to osmotic diarrhea are depicted in Figure 32–5.

Abnormal Intestinal Motility. At least three types of motility disturbances may result in diarrhea: (1) diminished peristalsis, leading to bacterial overgrowth (see Section C of this chapter); (2) increased small bowel motility, leading to maldigestion and absorption; and (3) rapid colonic emptying, preventing desiccation of the stool associated with increased stool liquidity. Diarrhea due to motility disturbances may be associated with irritable bowel syndrome, postgastrectomy and postvagotomy syndromes, both nephropathic and enteropathic diabetes, progressive systemic sclerosis, and thyrotoxicosis.

EVALUATION OF DIARRHEA

As with all clinical problems, evaluation of diarrhea requires a detailed history and physical examination and prudent selection and interpretation of laboratory tests.

History and Physical Examination. The patient's description, or better, the physician's observation of abnormal stool can be quite informative. Voluminous stools suggest a source in the small bowel or proximal colon, whereas small stools associated with urgency suggest disease of the left colon or rectum. Blood in the stool suggests mucosal damage or inflammation, whereas frothy stools and flatus suggest carbohydrate malabsorption. Stools that are foul-smelling or greasy or have visible oil or fat are uncommon but indicate severe steatorrhea. Obtaining a thorough history of drug exposure with particular attention to over-the-counter drugs is essential and must include antibiotics, antacids, antihypertensives, thyroxine, digitalis, propranolol, quinidine, colchicine, lactulose, ethanol, and especially laxatives. It is essential to determine the pace of the patient's present illness, that is, its duration and its rate of change; prior history of surgery; systemic complaints; history of travel inside or outside the country; family history; and sexual orientation. Acute diarrheas are usually caused by infectious agents or toxins such as staphylococcal food poisoning, whereas chronic diarrheas are usually not infectious.

The physical examination may lead to the diagnosis of diarrhea. Important signs to look for include evidence of weight loss, suggesting malabsorption; systemic signs of rheumatic diseases, such as fever or arthritis; adenopathy that might suggest lymphoma; neuropathy; autonomic neuropathy; orthostatic hypotension (with a pulse rate of 100); or flush, as seen in malignant carcinoid syndrome.

Laboratory Tests

Even when the cause of diarrhea is obvious from the history or physical examination, laboratory tests may be helpful in defining the pathophysiology of a patient's illness. Table 32–10 is a compendium of tests useful in evaluating diarrhea, but of course only a subset should be performed on any given patient. Selecting the most appropriate test is facilitated by grouping the patients into categories:

1. Acute diarrhea is usually associated with toxins, as in food poisoning, infections, drugs, or occasionally fecal impaction. Inflammatory bowel disease and intestinal ischemia are not commonly implicated in acute diarrhea. So-called traveler's diarrhea usually occurs

TABLE 32–10. TESTS THAT MAY BE USEFUL IN THE WORK-UP OF DIARRHEA

Stool
Consistency
Frequency/24 hr
Volume/24 hr
WBCs by Wright's stain
Blood
Sudan stain for fat
Quantitative fat/24 hr
NaOH for phenolphthalein and other laxatives
Cultures for enteric pathogens
Ova and parasites
Clostridium difficile toxin
Osmolality
Na, K, Cl
pH
Reducing substances
Mg, SO_4, PO_4
Proctoscopy
Mucosal appearance
Biopsy
Blood
Electrolytes
Immunoglobulins, albumin
T_3, T_4
Ameba serology
Folate, vitamin B_{12}
Ca, Mg, PO_4
Erythrocyte sedimentation rate
Eosinophil count
Special Assays
Vasoactive intestinal polypeptide (VIP)
Calcitonin
Gastrin
Prostaglandins
Other

Gastric Analysis
X-ray Studies
Upper GI, small bowel, barium enema
Abdominal and pelvic sonogram, CT scan
Abdominal angiogram
Small Bowel Studies
Aspirate (O and P, colony count cultures)
Biopsy
Mucosal disaccharidase assay
D-Xylose absorption test
Schilling test with intrinsic factor
^{14}C-bile acid absorption
Carbohydrate breath tests
Exocrine Pancreatic Function
Upper Endoscopy
Colonoscopy
Urine
5-Hydroxyindoleacetic acid (5-HIAA)
Metanephrines, vanillylmandelic acid (VMA)
NaOH (for phenolphthalein)
Heavy metals, drug screen
Room Search for Drugs
Intestinal Perfusion Studies
Therapeutic Trials

From Fine KD, Krejs GJ, Fordtran JS: Diarrhea. *In* Sleisenger MH, Fordtran JS (eds): Gastrointestinal Disease. 5th ed. Philadelphia, WB Saunders Co, 1993, pp 1043–1072.

within 2 weeks of travel to a tropical or developing area and is a self-limited illness.

2. Chronic diarrhea can be subdivided into multiple categories:
   a. Secretory diarrhea, usually caused by drugs, hormones, bile acids, or fatty acids.
   b. Osmotic diarrhea, generally caused by drugs, laxatives, or malabsorption.
   c. Inflammatory diarrhea due to ischemic colitis, parasitic infection such as that caused by amebae, or inflammatory bowel disease (IBD) (ulcerative colitis, Crohn's disease).
   d. Motility disorders such as irritable bowel syndrome, progressive systemic sclerosis, and the autonomic neuropathy of diabetes.
   e. Disorders of lost absorptive surface, as is seen in postsurgical diarrhea syndromes.

General algorithms for the evaluation of acute and chronic diarrhea are shown in Figures 32–6 and 32–7.

All patients with diarrhea should have their stools examined for consistency, white blood cells by Wright's stain, and blood. Fecal leukocytes in acute diarrheas strongly suggest invasive microorganisms such as *Shigella*, *Entamoeba histolytica*, *Campylobacter*, *Escherichia coli*, and occasionally gonococci or antibiotic-associated colitis. In patients with chronic diarrhea, fecal leukocytes suggest ulcerative colitis, Crohn's disease, or is-

chemia. Toxin-induced secretory diarrheas, malabsorption syndromes, laxative abuse, and giardiasis do not produce fecal leukocytes. The presence of fecal blood indicates inflammation and has a significance similar to pus.

Additional examinations are performed depending on the clinical presentation and progress. When patients suffer prolonged or severe acute diarrhea, stools should be examined for ova and parasites and cultured for bacterial pathogens. Proctoscopy is helpful in these cases primarily when pseudomembranous colitis is present. Blood cultures and white blood count and differential may be helpful in patients with evidence of systemic illness, particularly salmonellosis. Serologic tests for amebiasis can help diagnose this readily treatable disease.

In evaluating chronic diarrhea, the initial selection of tests is designed to answer the following questions: (1) Does the patient exhibit signs of inflammation of the mucosa? If so, imaging studies of the intestine such as endoscopy (upper and lower), barium enema, and possibly enteroclysis, are required with biopsy. (2) Is malabsorption present? In this case, stool fat and the D-xylose absorption test should be performed. (3) Is there evidence of structural, mucosal, or motility distur-

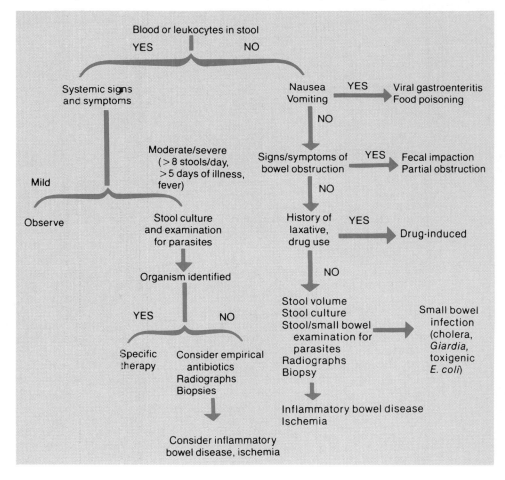

FIGURE 32–6. Evaluation of acute diarrhea.

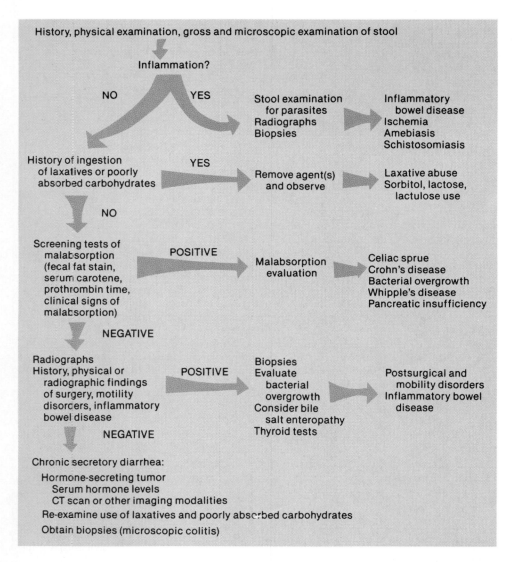

FIGURE 32–7. Evaluation of chronic diarrhea.

bance? Radiographic or endoscopic methods and biopsies should be obtained if appropriate. More specialized tests are then selected on the basis of the observations made on the foregoing examinations.

Stool culture and examination must always be performed prior to purging for endoscopic procedures or radiographic studies because the preparation for the diagnostic studies may interfere with these tests. However, proctosigmoidoscopy can be performed without any special preparation of the bowel. Biopsies of the rectum can be diagnostic of Whipple's disease, schistosomiasis, amyloidosis, and inflammation.

Quantitative fecal fat determination is the most definitive diagnostic procedure for detection of steatorrhea, and if steatorrhea is present, it must be thoroughly evaluated. Interpretation of fecal fat excretion requires knowledge of dietary fat intake, which is generally standardized at 100 gm/day for the duration of the test.

Specialized assays for drug-related hormones such as vasoactive intestinal polypeptide (VIP), prostaglandins, calcitonin, gastrin, and several others are helpful only in the rare patient who has more than 1 L/day of secretory diarrhea and no intrinsic disease or laxative abuse. It is also helpful to alkalinize the patient's stool, watching for the characteristic pink color associated with phenolphthalein (laxative) use.

Therapeutic trials are frequently indicated to diagnose the following: antibiotics for bacterial overgrowth, metronidazole for giardiasis, lactose-free diet for lactose malabsorption, cholestyramine for bile acid malabsorption, and pancreatic enzymes for pancreatic exocrine insufficiency.

Therapy

The ideal therapy should cure the underlying disorder. When this is not possible, drugs may be used to diminish symptoms, such as corticosteroids in the treatment of inflammatory bowel disease or nonspecific treatment for diarrhea such as cholestyramine to bind bile acids. Specific antisecretory drugs are being explored, and, in some patients, the somatostatic analogue has been dramatically effective. The most important aspect of diarrhea therapy is the replacement of fluid and electrolytes, particularly in patients with other diseases, the very young, and the very old. Oral volume replacement is best achieved with sodium glucose solutions because sodium and glucose are easily absorbed together. Opiates such as diphenoxylate, loperamide, and codeine may reduce the frequency and volume of diarrhea stool, probably owing to increased contact time in the colon. Opiates should be avoided in patients with IBD because they may aggravate or precipitate toxic megacolon. Although some diarrheal illnesses, such as shigellosis, are actually prolonged by treatment with opiates, they can be very useful in patients with chronic disabling diarrhea.

Antibiotics are not usually necessary for acute diarrheas because the illness is self-limited and antibiotics frequently do not shorten the duration of the illness. Detailed discussion of the use of antibiotics and antiparasitic agents is included in Chapter 94.

SPECIFIC CLINICAL DISORDERS

Patients with acquired immunodeficiency syndrome (AIDS) and AIDS-related complex (ARC) are susceptible to multiple infections and malignant diseases of the intestine. These are discussed in some detail in Chapters 37, 103, 108, and 109. *Cryptosporidium* infestation has proved to be a very difficult diarrheal illness to manage in AIDS patients. There are no efficacious drugs that eliminate the infestation; management revolves around fluid, electrolytes, and opiates to diminish the diarrheal volume. Patients with AIDS are probably susceptible to multiple other organisms causing diarrhea that have not yet been fully characterized. The management of these is, at this point, similar to that for cryptosporidiosis.

REFERENCES

Fedorak RN, Field M: Antidiarrheal therapy. Dig Dis Sci 32:195, 1987.
Field M, Fordtran JS, Schultz SG (eds): Secretory Diarrhea. Bethesda, MD, American Physiological Society, 1980.
Fine KD, Krejs GJ, Fordtran JS: Diarrhea. *In* Sleisenger MH, Fordtran JS (eds): Gastrointestinal Disease. Pathophysiology, Diagnosis, and Management. 5th ed. Philadelphia, WB Saunders Co, 1993, pp 1043–1072.
Krejs GJ: Diarrhea. *In* Wyngaarden JB, Smith LH Jr, Bennett JC (eds): Cecil Textbook of Medicine. 19th ed. Philadelphia, WB Saunders Co, 1992, pp 680–686.
Wilberts B, Bray D, Lewis J, Laff M, Roberts K, Watson JD (eds): Molecular Biology of the Cell. 2nd ed. Chapter 12, Cell Signaling. New York, Garland Publishing Co, 1989.

33 RADIOGRAPHIC AND ENDOSCOPIC PROCEDURES IN GASTROENTEROLOGY

In the past, barium radiography and fluoroscopy of the luminal gastrointestinal (GI) tract were the only diagnostic methods available for evaluating potential GI lesions. Over the last decade, newer techniques and refinements of older methods have increased our ability to image the GI tract noninvasively. In addition, endoscopic examination of the luminal GI tract and the pancreaticobiliary tree has revolutionized our approach to many disorders. One can actually visualize the GI tract and in some cases direct definitive therapy to identified abnormalities without resorting to surgery.

Radiography and endoscopy can be complementary, with each technique having distinct advantages and disadvantages. This may result in confusion as to the most appropriate diagnostic test in various clinical settings. This chapter briefly reviews the radiographic and endoscopic procedures currently available and their optimal use.

RADIOGRAPHIC PROCEDURES

Table 33–1 summarizes the radiographic and endoscopic procedures in general use.

TABLE 33–1. RADIOGRAPHIC AND ENDOSCOPIC PROCEDURES

PROCEDURE	ADVANTAGES	DISADVANTAGES
Plain film of the abdomen	Identifies gas (intramural, intraperitoneal, as well as luminal) and calcifications	Few specific features
Barium swallow	Shows mass lesions and motility disorders well	Misses many superficial mucosal lesions
Double-contrast barium examination of the upper gastrointestinal tract ("UGI series")	Delineates ulcers and tumors well	Misses some superficial mucosal lesions Misclassifies 9–17% of malignant gastric ulcers
Small bowel series	Simpler to perform Evaluates transit time, caliber, and proximal mucosa and often shows mass lesions	May miss distal or subtle lesions
Enteroclysis (small bowel enema)	Improved definition of mucosa and bowel wall of entire small bowel	Requires oral intubation
Double-contrast barium enema ("pneumocolon")	Shows polyps, tumors, fistulas, diverticula, and other structural changes (e.g., inflammatory bowel disease) well	Uncomfortable for some patients Impossible in those with lax anal sphincter May miss superficial mucosal and rectal lesions Misses angiodysplastic lesions
Oral cholecystography	Outlines most gallstones May delineate tumors or polyps	Will not visualize gallbladder in jaundiced patients and often fails to visualize the inflamed gallbladder
Percutaneous transhepatic cholangiography	Excellent definition of intrahepatic bile ducts Option for therapeutic intervention	Extrahepatic bile ducts may not be well visualized Nondilated ducts may be missed
Angiography	Demonstration of acutely bleeding lesions Definition of vascularity of mass lesions	Invasive Large contrast load Bleeding lesions visualized only if blood loss exceeds 0.5 ml/min Expensive
Ultrasonography	No radiation exposure Real-time examination Best for fluid-filled lesions, gallstones, and bile ducts	Gas obscures examination Bowel poorly visualized

Plain Radiographs and Barium Contrast Studies

Plain radiographs of the abdomen in the supine, upright, and lateral decubitus positions are simple to obtain and relatively inexpensive, but their usefulness is limited. These tests are most valuable for diseases that cause abnormalities in the bowel gas pattern, such as small bowel or colonic obstruction, perforation of a hollow viscus (represented by free intraperitoneal air), and pneumatosis intestinalis. Abnormalities of the bowel wall may also occasionally be identified (e.g., thumbprinting with colonic or small bowel ischemia). Plain abdominal radiographs are also useful in detecting diseases associated with intra-abdominal calcifications such as cholelithiasis, nephrolithiasis, and chronic pancreatitis.

Contrast studies using barium sulfate or water-soluble iodinated agents (Gastrografin [meglumine diatrizoate], Hypaque [sodium diatrizoate]) provide information about the anatomy of the luminal GI tract. Single-contrast studies are performed using a bolus of contrast material and may detect obstruction or large lesions, but they may not detect small mucosal abnormalities. Double-contrast studies, in which barium is administered first followed by a radiolucent substance such as air that results in a thin barium coating of the mucosa, has a much greater sensitivity and may detect tumors, obstructions, and small lesions confined to the mucosa.

In the esophagus, single- and double-contrast barium swallows detect esophageal strictures and masses which produce luminal narrowing, and when severe, proximal dilation. Double-contrast studies may improve the sensitivity for detecting subtle mucosal abnormalities such as reflux esophagitis, esophageal ulcerations, or varices; endoscopy is more sensitive in the detection of these mucosal lesions. The use of fluoroscopy during a barium swallow, particularly when combined with cine or video recordings, demonstrates swallowing disorders in the hypopharynx as well as esophageal motility disorders.

The standard single- or double-contrast examination of the upper GI tract (upper GI series) is commonly used to detect peptic ulcer disease or gastric neoplasms. In addition, motility disorders can be demonstrated by visualizing abnormal or

TABLE 33–1. RADIOGRAPHIC AND ENDOSCOPIC PROCEDURES *Continued*

PROCEDURE	ADVANTAGES	DISADVANTAGES
Computed tomography	Excellent anatomic definition Visualizes bowel wall thickness, mesentery, retroperitoneum, aorta well Density changes may indicate nature of diffuse parenchymal disease	Expensive Radiation exposure Bowel sometimes not well visualized Possible reactions to iodinated intravenous contrast media
MRI of the abdomen	Excellent anatomic definition Identifies patency of vessels Sensitive detection of hepatic tumors No radiation	Expensive Patient must be cooperative No contrast agents available Operator-dependent
Liver-spleen scan	Demonstrates mass lesions (>1–2 cm in size) Increased bone marrow uptake suggests portal hypertension	Limited anatomic definition
^{99m}Tc-HIDA liver scan	Best test for cystic duct obstruction	Will not visualize if bilirubin >6 mg/dl Poor anatomic definition
^{99m}Tc-RBC scan	Approximate localization of intermittently bleeding lesion	Poor anatomic definition
Esophagogastroduodenoscopy	Direct visualization of upper GI tract Identifies virtually all mucosal lesions Permits biopsy, electrocautery	Expensive Invasive May miss motility and compressive lesions
Flexible sigmoidoscopy (to 25 cm)	Direct visualization of rectum, sigmoid, and distal descending colon Permits biopsy and polypectomy Useful for monitoring of inflammatory bowel disease	Invasive Misses lesions in more proximal colon
Colonoscopy	Direct visualization of large bowel Permits biopsy and polypectomy, electrocautery, and laser treatment of bleeding	Expensive Invasive Higher rate of complications than barium enema
Endoscopic retrograde cholangiopancreatography	Only method for visualizing pancreatic ducts permits biopsy of ampullary lesions and sphincterotomy for common duct stones	Requires considerable skill Expensive

decreased gastric emptying. Most gastric ulcerations (benign and malignant) may be identified radiographically; however, it is not always possible to correctly identify an ulcer as benign or malignant based on the radiographic appearance alone. Therefore, endoscopic mucosal biopsy is recommended. In many clinical situations the lesion may simply be followed radiographically until complete healing is documented. The use of the double-contrast technique increases the yield for the detection of erosive gastritis associated with aspirin or nonsteroidal anti-inflammatory drug use, Mallory-Weiss tears at the gastroesophageal junction, or lesions at the anastomosis of prior gastric surgery. As with the esophagus, endoscopy is more sensitive for the detection of shallow mucosal abnormalities. The upper GI series represents a noninvasive, inexpensive, and relatively useful method for the initial evaluation of many upper GI tract complaints.

Radiographic examination of the small bowel is limited by the pooling and dilution of barium. In addition, overlapping loops of bowel segments may obscure pathology. The standard small bowel follow-through examination, in which barium is ingested orally, can evaluate the caliber of the small bowel, provide information about gross mucosal abnormalities, and determine transit time. Small lesions of the more distal small bowel are difficult to detect, whereas large mass lesions, obstruction, and Crohn's disease can usually be demonstrated easily. A more recent technique for evaluating the entire small bowel is the small bowel enema (enteroclysis), in which barium followed by a radiolucent methylcellulose solution is delivered directly into the jejunum through a special tube placed orally. This method of imaging is operator-dependent, time-consuming, and not widely available and involves more radiation than the standard small bowel follow-through, but it is very sensitive in detecting small lesions or a Meckel's diverticulum. The terminal ileum may be identified by enteroclysis or pneumocolon, in which air is introduced into the rectum (introduced rectally) after opacification of the terminal ileum by barium (introduced orally). Radiographic evaluation of the small bowel may be indicated when evaluating malabsorption, inflammatory bowel disease (Crohn's disease), or obstruction. Endoscopic techniques to evaluate the small bowel are currently limited to the distal duodenum and proximal jejunum, although small bowel enteroscopes may soon be widely available.

Single- and double-contrast (air-contrast) radiographs of the colon have long been the standard for colonic evaluation. The double-contrast technique can detect mucosal lesions such as small polyps or early inflammatory bowel disease, which may not be seen with the single-contrast technique. Colonoscopy more reliably identifies these mucosal abnormalities. The clinical problem being investigated (e.g., fecal occult blood loss, inflammatory bowel disease, neoplasm, diarrhea, or obstruction) determines the choice of either double-contrast barium enema or colonoscopy. Importantly, the need for tissue examination may favor initial colonoscopic evaluation. In contrast to barium, water-soluble iodinated compounds are particularly useful when a perforation is suspected (e.g., perforation of a diverticulum or a duodenal ulcer) because these compounds are less toxic to the peritoneum than barium. However, they should not be used in the upper GI tract when aspiration is likely or a fistula to the bronchial tree is present because they are quite toxic to the lungs. Although they demonstrate less mucosal detail, water-soluble contrast agents may be particularly useful when distal colonic obstruction is anticipated (e.g., carcinoma, volvulus). Significant amounts of barium above a colonic obstruction may be problematic if surgery becomes necessary. This is less of a concern with small bowel obstruction due to dilution of the barium.

Ultrasonography and Computed Tomography

Ultrasonography (US) and computed tomography (CT) have revolutionized both the diagnosis and management of many abdominal diseases. US and CT can examine organs such as the pancreas that cannot be directly visualized by barium studies. US and CT are most useful in imaging solid abdominal organs (liver, spleen, pancreas, kidney, retroperitoneal lymph nodes), as well as the gallbladder and bile ducts. Table 33–2 outlines the relative merits of US and CT.

US, which uses high-frequency sound waves rather than x-rays, can examine both solid and fluid-filled structures noninvasively. With the development of real-time images and Doppler techniques, US can now evaluate both dynamic and static abdominal processes. US images, like those of CT, are displayed in cross-section. US has the ability to (1) detect abdominal masses as small as 2 cm in diameter; (2) differentiate fluid-filled cysts from solid masses; (3) identify gallstones more rapidly and with greater sensitivity than can oral cholecystography or CT; (4) evaluate for dilated bile ducts (intra- and extrahepatic); and (5) detect ascites and some vascular abnormalities such as abdominal aortic aneurysms. Air or gas obscures the US beam, so structures under gas-filled loops of bowel may not be visualized reliably.

CT uses multiple x-ray beams and detectors in conjunction with computer analysis to identify and display small differences in tissue density. CT provides a more precise anatomic definition than US, and the imaging quality is not affected by bowel gas. Current scanners obtain very high quality images within seconds. CT is used primarily for the detection and characterization of abdominal mass lesions (tumors, cysts, abscesses) and pancreatic disease. In addition, it may detect biliary dilation, calcified gallstones, and intra-abdominal hemorrhage. CT is also useful in demonstrating increased thickness of the intestinal or colonic wall due to processes such as ischemia, Crohn's disease, appendicitis, and diverticulitis. With this method, mesenteric abnormalities as well as hemochromatosis and fatty liver can be identified. Finally, lesions and parenchymal abnormalities such as rupture or hematoma of the liver, spleen, kidneys, aortoenteric fistulas, and retroperitoneal adenopathy are also well characterized by CT.

Both US and CT also aid in the placement of drainage catheters (e.g., abscess) and direct thin-needle aspiration biopsy of lesions virtually anywhere in the abdomen.

Radionuclide Imaging

The traditional liver-spleen scan, using ^{99m}Tc-sulfur colloid, which undergoes phagocytosis by

TABLE 33–2. COMPARISON OF ULTRASONOGRAPHY AND COMPUTED TOMOGRAPHY

	ULTRASONOGRAPHY	COMPUTED TOMOGRAPHY
Organs best visualized	Kidney Gallbladder Liver and bile ducts Pancreas Spleen Blood vessels	Liver and dilated bile ducts Retroperitoneal lymph nodes Mesentery Gallbladder Aorta Spleen Pancreas Kidney Pelvic organs
Lesions best visualized	Fluid-filled masses/cysts Gallstones Dilated bile ducts Aortic aneurysms Pancreatic tumor Ascites	Tumors/cysts/abscesses Lymphadenopathy Mass lesions Abdominal aortic aneurysm Trauma or parenchymal hematoma of liver, spleen, and kidney Fatty liver
Advantages	Real-time examination Noninvasive Guided needle aspiration	Less dependent upon a skilled operator Guided needle aspiration
Disadvantages	Skilled operator necessary Gas obscures deeper organs	Absence of fat makes examination more difficult Expensive

reticuloendothelial cells, has largely been supplanted by US or CT, although it still remains useful for the evaluation of some benign hepatic neoplasms (see Chapter 44). Recently developed agents, such as ^{99m}Tc-HIDA (technetium-labeled iminodiacetic acid), which are taken up directly by hepatic parenchymal cells and excreted in bile, have improved sensitivity for the diagnosis of acute cholecystitis (see Chapter 45) and biliary atresia in infants. Although common bile duct obstruction may be suggested by these scans, they are generally not useful for other biliary tract disorders because their anatomic definition is poor. There is also a lack of specificity in certain conditions. The affinity of ^{99m}Tc-pertechnetate for gastric mucosa makes this agent useful for the detection of Meckel's diverticula, 85 per cent of which contain ectopic gastric mucosa. Radiolabeled foods are currently used to measure the gastric emptying of both liquids and solids in disorders such as diabetic gastroparesis. ^{111}In-labeled leukocytes injected intravenously may be helpful in localizing intra-abdominal abscesses or detecting the inflammatory activity of Crohn's disease. ^{99m}Tc-sulfur colloid and ^{99m}Tc-labeled red blood cells are commonly used for localizing the site of lower GI bleeding or when small bowel bleeding is suspected.

Visceral Angiography

Angiography is a highly specialized procedure with a small but definite morbidity. To demonstrate the vasculature of an organ, a catheter is inserted into an appropriate artery or vein that is subsequently injected with contrast. At present, angiography is most often employed for the evaluation of acute severe GI bleeding, primarily of the colon or small bowel, that cannot be visualized endoscopically. If a bleeding site is identified, intra-arterial vasopressin may be infused or the vessels may be occluded with embolized material (coils, Gelfoam). Less commonly, angiography can be used to evaluate vascular lesions (e.g., hepatoma, angioma, angiosarcoma) as well as to demonstrate metastatic liver disease not detected by routine imaging studies.

Magnetic Resonance Imaging (MRI)

Cross-sectional images of the body can also be obtained without x-rays by using magnetic field and radiofrequency radiation combined with computer analysis. This imaging study displays organs by their chemical composition rather than x-ray density. In some situations MRI provides better resolution than does CT and may also offer the opportunity to follow in situ chemical reactions. MRI may be particularly useful in the evaluation of intrahepatic tumors. It also visualizes patent blood vessels well and may be useful for assessing patency of grafts, shunts, or veins. It is currently undergoing evaluation for use in detecting many abdominal processes, but it does not yet have a well-established role.

Visualization of the Biliary Tree

Oral cholecystography (OCG) has been used for many years to detect gallbladder stones. OCG involves the oral intake of an iodinated compound that concentrates in the gallbladder; radiographs taken 12 hours after ingestion show filling in the gallbladder. The technique identifies gallstones only in those patients with a functioning gallbladder and a patent cystic duct. In patients with chronic cholecystitis and those with an elevated bilirubin (>2 mg/dl), gallbladder opacification does not occur. US has supplanted OCG for the detection of gallbladder stones, given its greater sensitivity (>95 per cent), lack of radiation, and rapidity. Today, OCG is used to evaluate gallbladder function in patients undergoing extracorporeal gallstone lithotripsy.

Bile ducts are identified only when filled with contrast material. Contrast material may be injected percutaneously through the liver into the biliary tree with a small, 23-gauge needle (percutaneous transhepatic cholangiography [PTC]) or at the level of the ampulla with a small catheter placed endoscopically (endoscopic retrograde cholangiopancreatography [ERCP]). Table 33–3 compares these two procedures; both provide excellent detail of the biliary tree. The choice between PTC and ERCP depends on a number of specific circumstances.

ENDOSCOPIC PROCEDURES

Fiberoptic instruments have rapidly evolved from rigid tools with poor visibility to the present instruments, which are tolerated well by patients, have improved resolution, and are capable of examining the upper and lower GI tract and the pancreaticobiliary tree. Not only can the GI tract be examined diagnostically, but the endoscopist can treat lesions that previously required laparotomy.

An endoscope is a multichanneled tool that permits the passage of air and water and contains one or more channels for aspiration. Through the aspirating channel, one can pass a variety of instruments including cytology brushes, biopsy forceps, injection needles, electrocautery snares, wire baskets, and thermal probes that control hemorrhage.

Endoscopy has important advantages over routine barium contrast studies of the luminal GI tract: (1) greater sensitivity for mucosal lesions (e.g., small peptic ulcer, erosive gastritis, esophagitis); (2) greater specificity in certain circumstances (e.g., a small lesion identified at barium enema could be retained stool rather than a polyp); (3) the ability to perform mucosal biopsies as well as cytology to exclude malignancy; (4) the ability to perform therapy at the time of diagnosis (e.g., injection sclerosis of bleeding esophageal varices).

TABLE 33–3. COMPARISON OF PERCUTANEOUS TRANSHEPATIC CHOLANGIOGRAPHY AND ENDOSCOPIC RETROGRADE CHOLANGIOPANCREATOGRAPHY

	PERCUTANEOUS TRANSHEPATIC CHOLANGIOGRAPHY	ENDOSCOPIC RETROGRADE CHOLANGIOPANCREATOGRAPHY
Lesions best visualized	Intrahepatic ductal lesions Multiple lesions in a single duct system Several punctures may be made to examine ducts in all lobes	Extrahepatic ductal lesions Pancreatic duct Ampulla of Vater
Therapeutic implications	Temporary external drainage of bile Placement of stents through bile duct obstructions Balloon dilatation of biliary stricture	Sphincterotomy for removal of common duct stones Placement of stents Balloon dilatation of strictures Biopsy of ampullary lesions
Success rate		
Dilated ducts	100%	80–90%
Nondilated ducts	60–80%	80–90%
Disadvantages	Experienced operator required May miss additional lesions in left lobe	Experienced operator required May not visualize ducts proximal to a lesion
Complications	Bleeding Biliary infection/sepsis Hemobilia	Pancreatitis Biliary infections/sepsis Bile duct perforation

The primary disadvantages of endoscopy are that it is an invasive procedure with potential for morbidity and mortality, although extremely rare (less than 1 death in 10,000 for upper endoscopy), and its high cost. Further, it cannot detect motility disturbances of the esophagus or small symptomatic rings of the distal esophagus.

The choice of endoscopy versus radiographic imaging depends on the specific question one wishes to answer (e.g., etiology of significant GI bleeding versus vague abdominal pain), the likely diagnosis, the possible need for therapeutic intervention, locally available skill, and cost. In some circumstances, radiographic and endoscopic procedures complement one another.

Esophagogastroduodenoscopy (EGD)

The upper GI tract to the second portion of the duodenum may be evaluated with standard upper endoscopes. EGD is usually performed in the patient with upper GI hemorrhage as well as in suspected upper GI malignancy. Endoscopy has become the diagnostic procedure of choice in most instances of upper GI hemorrhage, especially when the bleeding is brisk and therapeutic intervention is probable. In contrast to severe lower GI hemorrhage, the bleeding lesion in this location can usually be identified at EGD by the experienced endoscopist. In the evaluation of malignancy, endoscopic biopsy supplemented by brush cytology has almost 100 per cent sensitivity, although the accuracy may be reduced for submucosal or infiltrative lesions. Other common indications for EGD include the evaluation of acid-peptic disease when the upper GI series is nondiagnostic or the patient is refractory to standard antiulcer therapy, abdominal pain, esophageal symptoms,

injection of esophageal varices, and removal of foreign bodies.

Endoscopic Retrograde Cholangiopancreatography

Cannulation of the ampulla of Vater in the second portion of the duodenum can be accomplished using a special side-viewing endoscope. This highly technical procedure allows for selective cannulation of either the pancreatic duct or the common bile duct, followed by injection of a radiographic contrast medium that highlights the ductal systems. Standard radiographs can then be taken of the contrast-outlined ducts. The primary indications for ERCP include the diagnosis and treatment of pancreatic cancer and obstructive jaundice, the placement of biliary as well as pancreatic endoprostheses (stent), and sphincterotomy. In obstructive jaundice, ERCP is preferred to PTC when ductal dilation is absent but the possibility of biliary disease remains, if there is associated pancreatic or duodenal pathology, or if a coagulation defect is present. In specialized centers, motility measurements of the sphincter of Oddi, located in the ampulla, are used to diagnose sphincter dysfunction. A detailed comparison of ERCP and PTC is outlined in Table 33–3.

Endoscopic sphincterotomy involves an electrocautery incision into the duodenal papilla with a special catheter. Once the papilla is opened, direct access to the biliary tree is established. This is most useful in patients with common bile duct stones who have previously undergone a cholecystectomy and in those considered a poor surgical risk. Sphincterotomy may also be used for treatment of obstructing ampullary tumors and sphincter of Oddi dysfunction and, in some cases, before insertion of an endoprosthesis. When performed by the experienced endoscopist, sphincterotomy has a morbidity (bleeding, pancreatitis) of 5 to 10 per cent, with a mortality of approximately 0.5 per cent.

Sigmoidoscopy and Colonoscopy

Evaluation of the distal colorectum can be performed with rigid sigmoidoscopy. This is a rapid, inexpensive procedure that is somewhat poorly tolerated by patients. However, this procedure may be useful for the initial evaluation of patients with lower GI bleeding when an anorectal source is suspected (hemorrhoid, fissure, tumor). Sigmoidoscopy, using either the 30- or 60-cm flexible instrument, may be used to evaluate more of the distal colon and rectum with a greater degree of sensitivity. Sigmoidoscopy is commonly used in the evaluation of bloody diarrhea, chronic diarrhea, distal colorectal disease, and occult blood in the stool after a normal barium enema and as a screening tool for colon cancer. Ulcerative colitis may be reliably diagnosed by sigmoidoscopy and mucosal biopsy; Crohn's disease, however, may not involve the distal colon, thus requiring colonoscopy, barium enema, or small bowel follow-through for diagnosis. Colonoscopy allows visualization of the entire colon to the level of the cecum and even into the terminal ileum in most patients. Colonoscopy is commonly performed in the evaluation of suspected colonic neoplasm (e.g., fecal occult blood, iron deficiency anemia), in evaluation of lower GI bleeding, in surveillance for the development of malignancy in ulcerative colitis and polyposis syndromes, and in diagnosis and evaluation of the extent of inflammatory bowel disease. Diagnostic colonoscopy has a perforation rate of 2 to 4 per 1000 and increases with polypectomy to 1 per 100 to 3 per 1000.

Removal of colonic polyps at the time of colonoscopy is an important therapeutic application. In patients with lower GI bleeding, colonoscopy may be used as a therapeutic alternative because the colonoscopist gains the ability to coagulate lesions such as vascular ectasias. In patients with active upper GI bleeding, colonoscopy is a more difficult procedure because the lumen is obscured by blood. In the patient with brisk bleeding, ^{99m}Tc-labeled red cell scanning or angiography may be preferable as the initial diagnostic test.

Laparoscopy

With the widespread use and documented sensitivity of US and CT, laparoscopy is less commonly used to evaluate the peritoneum and liver. At present, it is used primarily to biopsy suspected malignancies of the peritoneum or hepatic surface.

REFERENCES

Federle MP, Goldbert HI: Conventional radiography of the alimentary tract. *In* Sleisenger MH, Fordtran JS (eds): Gastrointestinal Disease: Pathophysiology, Diagnosis, and Management. 3rd ed. Philadelphia, WB Saunders Co, 1983, pp 1634–1667.

Mueller PR, Harbin WP, Ferrucci JT Jr, Wittenberg J, van Jonnenberg E: Fine-needle transhepatic cholangiography: Reflections after 450 cases. AJR 136:85–90, 1981.

Sleisenger MH, Fordtran JS (eds): Gastrointestinal Disease: Pathophysiology, Diagnosis, and Management. 4th ed. Philadelphia, WB Saunders Co, 1989.

Vennes JA: Gastrointestinal endoscopy. *In* Wyngaarden JB, Smith LH Jr, Bennett JC (eds): Cecil Textbook of Medicine. 19th ed. Philadelphia, WB Saunders Co, 1992, pp 630–634.

Wall SW: Diagnostic imaging procedures in gastroenterology. *In* Wyngaarden JB, Smith LH Jr, Bennett JC (eds): Cecil Textbook of Medicine. 19th ed. Philadelphia, WB Saunders Co, 1992, pp 625–629.

34 DISEASES OF THE ESOPHAGUS

Although the esophagus appears to be a simple organ, esophageal diseases are common and range from trivial complaints of heartburn to major clinical problems of aspiration, obstruction, and hemorrhage. This chapter briefly outlines normal esophageal function and describes a group of unique symptoms characteristic of esophageal disorders. The major benign categories of esophageal diseases, gastroesophageal reflux disease, and mo-

tility disorders are discussed, followed by a brief review of other common esophageal diseases. Malignant diseases of the esophagus are discussed in Chapter 37.

NORMAL ESOPHAGEAL PHYSIOLOGY

The esophagus is a hollow tube bordered at each end by high-pressure valves, or sphincters. The esophagus serves a single but very important function: the conveying of solids and liquids from the mouth to the stomach. The upper esophageal sphincter prevents aspiration and swallowing of excessive amounts of air, and the lower esophageal sphincter prevents the movement of gastric contents in the opposite direction (i.e., gastroesophageal reflux). Swallowing is a complex and well-coordinated motor activity that involves many muscle groups and five cranial nerves (V, VII, IX, X, XII). Swallowing can be divided into three stages: the oral stage, which is voluntary, and the pharyngeal and esophageal stages, which are involuntary. The oral stage involves chewing food and forming it into an oral bolus while propelling it by the tongue into the posterior pharynx. In the pharyngeal stage, food is passed from the pharynx across the upper esophageal sphincter into the proximal esophagus. This entire process occurs in about 1 second and involves five important steps: (1) the soft palate is elevated and retracted to prevent nasopharyngeal regurgitation; (2) the vocal cords are closed and the epiglottis swings backward to close the larynx and prevent aspiration; (3) the upper esophageal sphincter relaxes; (4) the larynx is pulled upward, thereby stretching the opening of the esophagus and upper sphincter; and (5) contractions of the pharyngeal muscles provide a driving force to propel food into the esophagus. In the esophageal stage, ingested food is transported from the upper esophageal sphincter to the stomach while the lower esophageal sphincter is relaxed. This is accomplished primarily by an orderly stripping wave initiated by

swallowing and progressing along the esophagus (i.e., primary peristalsis). After passage of the food bolus, the lower esophageal sphincter reestablishes a tonic contraction, thereby preventing regurgitation of gastric contents.

CLINICAL SYMPTOMS OF ESOPHAGEAL DISEASE

Dysphagia is the sensation of food being hindered ("sticking") in its normal passage from the mouth to the stomach. Dysphagia is divided into two distinct syndromes (Fig. 34–1): that due to abnormalities affecting the pharynx and upper esophageal sphincter (oropharyngeal dysphagia) and that due to any of a variety of disorders affecting the esophagus itself (esophageal dysphagia). Oropharyngeal dysphagia is usually described as the inability to initiate the act of swallowing. It is a "transfer" problem of impaired ability to move food from the mouth into the upper esophagus. Esophageal dysphagia results from difficulty in "transporting" food down the esophagus and may be caused by motility disorders or mechanical obstructing lesions. Patients most often report that their food hangs up somewhere behind the sternum. If this symptom is localized to the lower part of the sternum, the lesion is most likely in the distal esophagus, although the patient may also refer the feeling of blockage to the lower part of the neck. To classify the symptom of esophageal dysphagia, three questions are crucial: (1) What type of food causes symptoms? (2) Is the dysphagia intermittent or progressive? and (3) Does the patient have heartburn? An algorithm for approaching patients with dysphagia is shown in Figure 34–1.

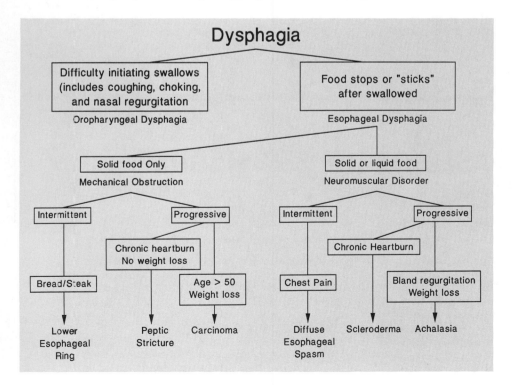

FIGURE 34–1. Algorithm for the differential diagnosis of dysphagia.

Heartburn (pyrosis) is the most common of all esophageal symptoms resulting from the reflux of gastric contents into the stomach. It is usually described as a burning pain that radiates up behind the sternum. It has many synonyms, including "indigestion," "acid regurgitation," "sour stomach," and "bitter belching." Heartburn is predictably aggravated by several factors, including certain foods (high fat, chocolate, or spicy products), bending over or lying down, alcohol (especially red wines), caffeine, smoking, and emotions. Heartburn is usually relieved by the ingestion of antacids, baking soda, or milk, albeit only transiently. Heartburn may be accompanied by regurgitation, or water brash. Regurgitation is a sour or bitter fluid in the mouth which comes from the stomach and often occurs at night or when bending over. Water brash describes the sudden filling of the mouth with clear, slightly salty fluid. This fluid is not regurgitated material but rather secretions from the salivary glands as part of a protective, vagally mediated reflex from the distal esophagus.

Odynophagia, or pain on swallowing, is usually associated with caustic ingestion, pill-induced esophagitis, infectious esophagitis caused by viral or fungal agents, and very rarely severe gastroesophageal reflux disease or obstructing tumors.

Severe substernal chest pain that is often indistinguishable from angina pectoris may be esophageal in origin. Although once commonly thought to be secondary to esophageal motility disorders, such as diffuse esophageal spasm, more recent studies suggest that gastroesophageal reflux is more likely a cause.

GASTROESOPHAGEAL REFLUX DISEASE

Definition. Gastroesophageal reflux disease (GERD) refers to a spectrum of clinical manifestations due to reflux of stomach and duodenal contents into the esophagus. Many otherwise healthy individuals have occasional heartburn or regurgitation. However, this becomes a disease when the symptoms are severe and frequent or associated esophageal mucosal damage occurs.

Etiology and Pathogenesis. The common denominator for gastroesophageal reflux is the creation of a common cavity phenomenon representing equalization of intragastric and esophageal pressures. The lower esophageal sphincter is the major barrier against GERD, with a secondary component from the crural diaphragm during inspiration. Acid refluxing into the esophagus is normally cleared by a two-step process: peristaltic esophageal motor contractions rapidly clear fluid volume from the esophagus, and residual acid is neutralized by swallowed saliva. Patients with symptomatic GERD usually exhibit one or more of the following (Fig. 34–2): decreased or absent tone in the lower esophageal sphincter, inappropriate relaxation of the lower esophageal sphincter unassociated with swallowing, and decreased acid clearance due to impaired peristalsis. Other factors

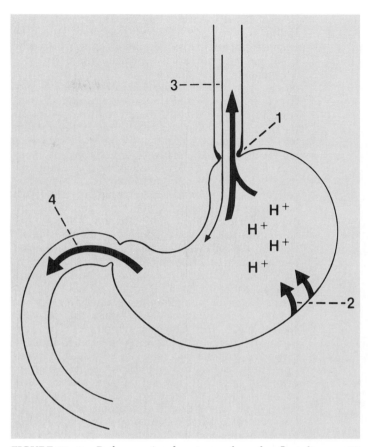

FIGURE 34–2. Pathogenesis of gastroesophageal reflux disease. (1) Impaired lower esophageal sphincter—low pressures or frequent transient lower esophageal sphincter relaxation. (2) Hypersecretion of acid. (3) Decreased acid clearance due to impaired peristalsis or abnormal saliva production. (4) Delayed gastric emptying and/or duodenogastric reflux of bile salts and pancreatic enzymes.

such as abnormal saliva, excessive acid production, delayed gastric emptying, and reflux of bile salts and pancreatic enzymes may be implicated in some patients. Patients with moderate to severe GERD have a sliding hiatal hernia that interferes with normal esophageal clearance by acting as a fluid trap.

Clinical Manifestations. Heartburn, ranging in degree from mild to severe, is the most common symptom of GERD, with associated complaints including dysphagia, odynophagia, regurgitation, water brash, and belching. Dysphagia for solids is usually secondary to a peptic stricture. Other causes may include esophageal inflammation alone, peristaltic dysfunction seen with severe esophagitis, and esophageal cancer arising from a Barrett's esophagus. GERD may present with symptoms not immediately referable to the gastrointestinal (GI) tract, including chest pain, respiratory, and ear, nose, and throat problems. Respiratory complaints include chronic cough, recurrent aspiration, and wheezing. Associated complaints related to the ear, nose, and throat include hoarseness, sore throat, bad breath, and a full sensation in the neck (globus sensation). Bleeding from esophageal erosions and ulcerations may be brisk but most commonly is chronic in nature.

Diagnosis. The diagnosis of GERD is best made on the history and clinical manifestations. Objective tests are useful to quantify the content and severity of disease and to address three questions: (1) Does reflux exist? (2) Is acid reflux responsible for the patient's symptoms? and (3) Has reflux led to esophageal damage? Reflux may be demonstrated during a barium swallow or by radionuclide scintigraphy after placement of ^{99m}Tc-sulfur colloid in the stomach. Esophageal manometry is useful for demonstrating abnormal peristalsis and poor lower esophageal sphincter tone but does not show reflux. The most sensitive and physiologic test for the presence of acid reflux is prolonged esophageal pH monitoring. This is done by placing a pH probe in the distal esophagus and monitoring acid exposure in an ambulatory state in the patient's home or work environment. The presence of reflux does not necessarily mean that it is responsible for the patient's symptoms. The acid perfusion (Bernstein) test may be used to identify atypical symptoms secondary to acid sensitivity. In this study, symptoms should be reproduced by dripping acid, but not saline, via a nasogastric tube into the distal esophagus. More helpful is the correlation of a patient's symptoms with the actual recording of acid reflux episodes during prolonged esophageal pH monitoring. Finally, symptoms due to acid reflux do not always correlate with the extent of damage to the esophageal mucosa. This is important to identify because patients with esophagitis tend to be more difficult to treat and are more likely to develop severe esophageal complications. Esophageal erosions, ulcerations, and strictures can be assessed by barium swallow. To bring out subtle narrowings, it may be necessary to give a solid bolus challenge such as a tablet, marshmallow, or even an aggravating food product. However, the barium swallow misses mild grades of esophagitis; therefore, endoscopy with biopsies is the most sensitive test for reflux-induced mucosal damage. Endoscopic changes range from very shallow linear erosions associated with friability to confluent ulcerations to complete mucosal denudation. Microscopically, basal cell hyperplasia, polymorphonuclear or eosinophilic cell infiltration, or frank ulceration can be seen. A few patients exhibit Barrett's epithelium, columnar epithelium in the esophagus produced by severe chronic reflux and associated with an increased risk of malignant transformation to adenocarcinoma.

Treatment and Prognosis. GERD is a chronic problem that may wax and wane in intensity, and relapses are common. In patients without esophagitis, the therapeutic goal is simply to relieve the acid-related symptoms. In patients with esophagitis, the ultimate goal is to heal or minimize the esophagitis while attempting to prevent further complications. As shown in Table 34–1, lifestyle modifications remain the cornerstone of effective antireflux treatment and may be curative in patients with mild symptoms. Patients with more severe symptoms without esophagitis generally respond to alginic acid, promotility drugs, or H_2-receptor blockers. Promotility drugs, such as bethanechol or metoclopramide, act by increasing lower esophageal sphincter pressure, improving esophageal contractions, and increasing gastric emptying when delayed. H_2-receptor blockers act solely by decreasing acid secretion. Patients with esophagitis generally need an H_2 blocker, usually in a twice-daily dose, to heal their mucosal injury. Patients with intractable symptoms or ulcerative esophagitis may need a proton pump inhibitor (e.g., omeprazole) to control their disease by markedly turning off acid secretion. Chronic therapy is necessary in patients with severe reflux symptoms and those with esophagitis. Surgical management is reserved for those 3 to 5 per cent of patients with objective evidence of reflux who fail to respond to an adequate trial of medical management. Several procedures are available, but all generally consist of returning the hiatal hernia and esophageal gastric junction into the abdomen and restoring lower esophageal sphincter function by wrapping the lower esophagus with a cuff of gastric fundal muscle. These procedures are often successful but cannot be performed in patients with aperistalsis (e.g., scleroderma), who may have severe GERD.

Complications. GERD complications include esophageal (peptic) stricture, esophageal ulcer,

TABLE 34–1. TREATMENT OF GASTROESOPHAGEAL REFLUX DISEASE

Simple (Lifestyle) Measures
Elevation of the head of the bed
Avoidance of food or liquids 2–3 hr before bedtime
Avoidance of fatty or spicy foods
Avoidance of cigarettes, alcohol
Weight loss
Liquid antacid (aluminum hydroxide–magnesium hydroxide) 30 ml 30 min after meals and at bedtime

Persistent Symptoms

Without Esophagitis	*With Esophagitis*
Alginic acid antacids (Gaviscon), 10 ml 30 min after meals and at bedtime	H_2-receptor blockers — regular or double dose depending on severity
Promotility drugs	H_2-receptor blocker and metoclopramide
Bethanechol, 10–15 mg four times a day	Omeprazole, 20 mg every morning
Metoclopramide, 10 mg four times a day	Antireflux surgery
H_2-receptor blockers	
Cimetidine, 400 mg twice a day	
Ranitidine, 150 mg twice a day	
Famotidine, 20 mg twice a day	
Nizatidine, 150 mg twice a day	

Barrett's esophagus, pulmonary aspiration, and upper GI hemorrhage.

MOTILITY DISORDERS OF THE OROPHARYNX AND ESOPHAGUS

Oropharyngeal Disorders

Definition and Pathogenesis. Oropharyngeal motility problems may arise from dysfunction of the upper esophageal sphincter, neurologic disorders (cerebrovascular accidents are most common), skeletal muscle disorders, or local structural lesions (Table 34–2). It is a common problem in the elderly population and frequently associated with poor prognosis owing to a high incidence of aspiration pneumonia.

Clinical Manifestations. Symptoms may occur gradually or have a rapid onset. Patients present with a variety of complaints, including food sticking in the throat, difficulty initiating a swallow, nasal regurgitation, and coughing when swallowing. They also may complain of dysarthria or display nasal speech because of associated muscle weakness.

Diagnosis. The clinical history is often characteristic, and associated neurologic and muscular abnormalities discovered on physical examination may help in making a correct etiologic diagnosis. Rapid-sequence cine-esophagography is required to adequately assess the abnormalities occurring in swallowing over less than a 1-second period. Esophageal manometry and endoscopy have ancillary diagnostic roles.

Treatment and Prognosis. Treatment consists of correcting recognizable reversible causes, including Parkinson's disease, myasthenia gravis, hyper- or hypothyroidism, and polymyositis. Unfortunately, the majority of cases are not amenable to medical or surgical therapy. Some cases may improve or resolve with time. For example, many patients with oropharyngeal dysphagia secondary to cerebrovascular accidents improve over a 3- to 6-month period. Other patients require retraining and use of various swallowing maneuvers

TABLE 34–2. CLINICAL DISORDERS ASSOCIATED WITH OROPHARYNGEAL DYSPHAGIA*

Motility Disorders of the Upper Esophageal Sphincter
  Zenker's diverticulum
  Cricopharyngeal bar
Neurologic Disorders
  Cerebrovascular disease
  Poliomyelitis
  Amyotrophic lateral sclerosis
  Multiple sclerosis
  Brain stem tumors
Skeletal Muscle Disorders
  Polymyositis
  Muscular dystrophies
  Myasthenia gravis
  Metabolic myopathy (thyrotoxicosis, myxedema, steroid myopathy)
Local Structural Lesions
  Neoplasms
  Extrinsic compression (thyromegaly, cervical spur)
  Surgical resection of the oropharynx

*Only a listing of major causes under each subheading.

and techniques to achieve an adequate and safe swallow. This rehabilitation can be managed by a speech and swallowing therapist using cine-esophagography with various types of food products to help plan and evaluate therapy. Rare patients may be helped by a cricopharyngeal myotomy, which cuts the upper esophageal sphincter.

Esophageal Disorders

Definition and Pathogenesis. Motility disorders of the esophageal body may arise from diseases of smooth muscle (e.g., scleroderma) or the intrinsic nervous system (e.g., achalasia, Chagas' disease). In achalasia, degeneration of the ganglion cells in Auerbach's plexus leads to increased tone and impaired relaxation of the lower esophageal sphincter, which is also associated with absent

TABLE 34–3. ESOPHAGEAL MOTOR DISORDERS

	ACHALASIA	SCLERODERMA	DIFFUSE ESOPHAGEAL SPASM
Symptoms	Dysphagia Bolus often passes with time or various maneuvers	Gastroesophageal reflux disease Dysphagia	Substernal chest pain (angina-like) Dysphagia with pain
X-ray appearance	Dilated, fluid-filled esophagus Distal "bird beak" stricture	Aperistaltic esophagus Free reflux Peptic stricture	Simultaneous noncoordinated contractions
Manometric findings			
Lower esophageal sphincter	High resting pressure No or incomplete relaxation with swallow	Low resting pressure	Normal pressure
Body	Low-amplitude, simultaneous contractions after swallow	Low-amplitude peristaltic contractions or no peristalsis	Some peristalsis Diffuse and simultaneous nonperistaltic contractions, occasionally high amplitude

peristalsis. The cause of the other motility disorders, such as diffuse esophageal spasm and its variants, is uncertain.

Clinical Manifestations. The three most common motility disorders are achalasia, scleroderma, and diffuse esophageal spasm, each of which exhibits a unique pattern of symptoms (Table 34–3).

Diagnoses. The clinical history is often very suggestive and cine-esophagography (Fig. 34–3) combined with esophageal manometry (Table 34–3) confirms the diagnosis in most cases. An infiltrating carcinoma of the gastric cardia can mimic achalasia; thus, endoscopy with biopsies is an important part of the evaluation of these patients.

Treatment and Prognosis. Achalasia usually responds to brisk dilatation of the lower esophageal sphincter with a pneumatic bag, a procedure that ruptures some of the sphincter muscle fibers. Surgical myotomy (the Heller procedure) is beneficial for those few patients who do not respond to pneumatic dilatation. Therapy for scleroderma includes aggressive treatment of GERD because more than half of these patients have esophagitis. Patients with diffuse esophageal spasm and its variants may respond to nitroglycerin and anticholinergic agents or calcium channel blocking drugs, although results are often disappointing.

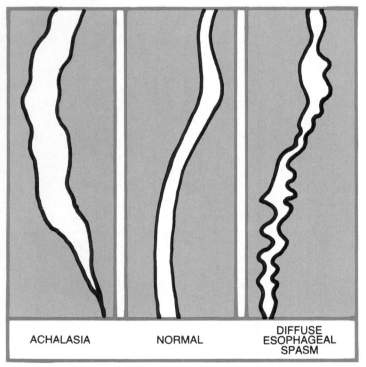

ACHALASIA   NORMAL   DIFFUSE ESOPHAGEAL SPASM

FIGURE 34–3. Radiologic appearance of achalasia *(left)* and diffuse esophageal spasm *(right).* In achalasia the esophageal body is dilated and terminates in a narrowed segment or "bird beak." The appearance of numerous simultaneous contractions is typical of diffuse esophageal spasm. (Courtesy of Dr. EE Templeton and Dr. CA Rohrmann. From Pope CE II: *In* Sleisenger MH, Fordtran JS [eds]: Gastrointestinal Disease. 3rd ed. Philadelphia, WB Saunders Co, 1983.)

Occasionally, these patients, especially if they have severe dysphagia and weight loss, may improve with pneumatic dilatation or a long esophageal myotomy.

OTHER ESOPHAGEAL DISORDERS

Tumors. Carcinoma of the esophagus is discussed in Chapter 37. Benign neoplasms (leiomyoma, lipoma, granular cell tumor, papilloma, esophageal cysts, and fibrovascular polyps) are very rare, representing less than 1 per cent of all esophageal neoplasms. They are usually asymptomatic or present as dysphagia or bleeding.

Rings and Webs. These may occur in the proximal or distal (Schatzki's ring) esophagus. The cause is uncertain but may be congenital or secondary to GERD. The Plummer-Vinson syndrome consists of an upper esophageal web, dysphagia, and iron deficiency anemia, usually in middle-aged women. Many rings and webs are asymptomatic, but dysphagia is the rule if the luminal diameter is less than 13 mm but unlikely if ring diameter is more than 20 mm. Patients complain of intermittent dysphagia for solid foods such as bread and steak. Occasionally, they can present with sudden, total esophageal obstruction caused by a meat impaction—"steak house syndrome." Rings and webs can easily be disrupted mechanically with peroral dilators.

Iatrogenic Esophagitis. Iatrogenic esophageal injury may be caused by ingested pills or caustic material. More than half the cases of pill-induced esophagitis result from tetracycline and its derivatives, particularly doxycycline. Other commonly prescribed medications causing esophageal injury include slow-release potassium chloride, iron sulfate, quinidine, steroids, and nonsteroidal anti-inflammatory agents. A common factor is a history of improper pill ingestion, including taking the pills with too little or no fluids or taking them just prior to bedtime and lying down. Patients usually present with odynophagia and dysphagia. A careful history can make the diagnosis, and endoscopy confirms the mucosal erosions or ulcerations. Symptoms usually resolve with discontinuation of the drug. It is important to educate these people about the proper techniques for ingesting medications. Caustic ingestion of either strong acid or alkali (Drano) agents is generally accidental in children or results from suicide attempts in adults. These agents cause severe esophageal injury, leading to necrosis and eventual stricture formation. Patients with caustic ingestion present with dysphagia, odynophagia, oral pain and burns, and excessive salivation. Steroids and broad-spectrum antibiotics are often used to treat caustic injuries, although their efficacy is uncertain. Severe injuries may produce long strictures that may be difficult to treat even with peroral dilatation.

Trauma. Vomiting may lead to mucosal (Mallory-Weiss) or full-thickness (Boerhaave's syndrome) tears of the lower esophagus. Mallory-Weiss tears usually occur just below the gastroesophageal junction. They frequently occur in the setting of excessive retching as a result of alcohol abuse or viral syndromes. They usually present with hemorrhage and heal spontaneously. Esophageal rupture, either spontaneous or iatrogenic from endoscopic procedures, often occurs just above the gastroesophageal junction and into the mediastinum. The diagnostic test of choice is esophagography performed with water-soluble contrast material—Gastrografin. Treatment usually requires surgical repair of the tear.

Infection. The most common infections causing esophagitis are fungal (*Candida*) and viral (herpes, cytomegalovirus). These usually occur in patients with acquired immunodeficiency syndrome (AIDS) or patients on immunosuppressant therapy. However, these infections also occur in patients with less severe immune defects (diabetic, malnourished elderly, postoperative, and antibiotic- and steroid-treated patients) and occasionally occur in otherwise healthy individuals. Severe odynophagia

and dysphagia are the common symptoms resulting from mucosal inflammation and ulceration. Diagnosis is best made by endoscopic visualization with biopsies and brushings.

REFERENCES

Castell DO, Donner MW: Evaluation of dysphagia: A careful history is crucial. Dysphagia 2:65, 1987.

Hogan WL: Gastroesophageal reflux disease: An update on management. J Clin Gastroenterol 12 (Suppl 2):21, 1990.

Richter JE: Motility disorders of the esophagus. *In* Yamada T (ed): Textbook of Gastroenterology. Philadelphia, JB Lippincott Co, 1991, pp 1083–1122.

Spechler SJ, Goyal RK: Barrett's esophagus. N Engl J Med 315:362, 1986.

35 DISEASES OF THE STOMACH AND DUODENUM

The stomach is a capacious organ between the esophagus and intestines that functions (1) as a reservoir in which food is stored, mixed, and then expelled into the duodenum and (2) as the primary site of acid secretion, which is important in the digestion of food and in protecting the body from ingested toxins and bacteria. This chapter reviews the common medical problems associated with disturbed gastroduodenal physiology. Specifically, acid-peptic diseases, including gastric and duodenal ulcers, Zollinger-Ellison syndrome, and gastritis, and abnormalities of gastric emptying associated with nausea and vomiting are discussed.

NORMAL GASTRIC PHYSIOLOGY

Gastric Emptying. As food enters the proximal stomach, a vagally mediated inhibition of fundic tone (receptive relaxation) permits storage of food without a rise in intragastric pressure. Ingested liquids are dispersed throughout the stomach in rapid fashion and then emptied primarily by low-level tonic contractions that generate a pressure gradient from the proximal stomach to the duodenum. Solids, on the other hand, require the assistance of peristalsis to move from stomach to duodenum. After an initial storage period in the

proximal stomach (approximately 30 minutes), solids are redistributed to the antrum, where they are mixed by segmental contractions. These contractions occur up to three times per minute and originate in a pacemaker situated in the midbody along the greater curvature. The mixed food is pushed toward the pylorus. This valve narrows, expelling into the duodenum only particles of food that have been reduced to a size of 1 mm or less while forcing larger particles backward for further processing. Local mechanisms, including low pH, high osmolarity, fatty acids, and caloric density, control liquid and solid emptying via the vagus nerve and hormones such as secretin, cholecystokinin, gastric inhibitory polypeptide, and glucagon. Nondigestible solids are emptied differently. Particles larger than 1 mm^3 cannot be emptied by contraction waves in the fed state but rather are emptied by the interdigestive migrating motor complex. This pattern occurs in the fasting state every 90 to 120 minutes and consists of a series of contractions beginning in the stomach and sweeping through the small bowel.

Gastric Secretion. Both hydrochloric acid (HCl), secreted by the parietal cells, and pepsinogen, secreted primarily by the chief cells, are found in the gastric mucosa, predominantly in the body and fundus of the stomach. These two agents

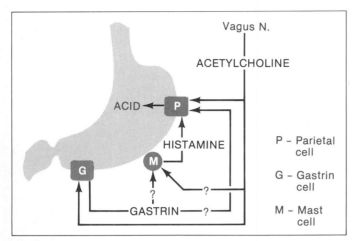

FIGURE 35–1. The parietal cell with three receptors—histamine, gastrin, and acetylcholine. All act to stimulate a K^+-H^+-ATPase (the hydrogen pump at the luminal side of the cell). However, the characteristics of each compound differ enough to suggest that each acts at a different receptor. Histamine causes increases in intracellular adenyl cyclase and cyclic AMP, which in turn activate or increase the amount of the K^+-H^+-ATPase. Cholinergic drugs and gastrin cause influx of Ca^{2+}, which in turn activates the K^+-H^+-ATPase. (From Richardson CT: Peptic ulcer: Pathogenesis. In Wyngaarden JB, Smith LH Jr, Bennett JC: [eds]: Cecil Textbook of Medicine. 19th ed. Philadelphia, WB Saunders Co, 1992, p 653.)

are secreted in parallel; no condition is known in which there is selective secretion of either HCl or pepsinogen. Three endogenous chemicals stimulate the secretion of acid: acetylcholine, gastrin, and histamine (Fig. 35–1). Acetylcholine is released locally from vagal (cholinergic) nerve terminals in the stomach, stimulated by stretch reflexes within the stomach or by the cephalic phase of gastric secretion (the sight, smell, taste, or thought of food). Vagal stimulation also elicits a modest release of gastrin. Gastrin is released from chief cells in the gastric antrum by the presence of food (particularly amino acids) in the gastric lumen, alkalinization of the gastric lumen, and neural release of gastrin-releasing peptide (GRP). The release of gastrin is turned off by low pH levels and the hormone somatostatin. Histamine is found in mast cells in the gastric wall in close proximity to the chief cells. The role and control of local histamine release are unknown, but histamine and its structural analogues are powerful gastric secretagogues when administered systemically; the use of H_2-receptor antagonists markedly inhibits HCl secretion by the stomach. There is also evidence of a nongastrin gut-derived secretagogue stimulated by the products of protein digestion, but its structure has not been defined.

Acid secretion in the resting, unfed stomach does not correlate with serum gastrin concentrations and is primarily related to vagal tone and the presence or absence of the bacterium *Helicobacter pylori*. A high vagal tone may lead to basal hypersecretion whereas *H. pylori* infection can lower

basal acid output. Basal secretion of acid averages about 1.0 to 2.0 mEq/hr in men and less in women, but the normal range varies considerably. In response to a meal, acid secretion is stimulated in three phases: the cephalic phase via primarily the vagus nerve, the gastric phase via the release of gastrin stimulated by amino acids and gastric alkalinization, and the intestinal phase via further release of gastrin and other nongastrin secretagogues by digested food products. Maximally stimulated by a meal or secretagogue (pentagastrin), the acid secretory rate may rise as high as 50 mEq/hr for men and 30 mEq/hr for women. The ratio of basal to maximal acid output (MAO), which is usually much less than 50 per cent, is sometimes determined in the study of patients with suspected abnormal secretory drives.

Secretion of pepsinogen is largely under vagal control. Pepsinogen is converted to pepsin in the gastric lumen by acid. Relatively little digestion takes place in the stomach, but release of peptides and amino acids by pepsin helps trigger the release of other digestive hormones such as gastrin and cholecystokinin. Intrinsic factor, a glycoprotein whose primary role is the facilitation of vitamin B_{12} absorption, is secreted by parietal cells under the same stimulatory conditions as HCl.

Normal Mucosal Defense. The stomach and duodenum have developed several defense mechanisms to protect the mucosa from the acid-pepsin mix of gastric juice (Fig. 35–2). A thin coat of mucus is formed continuously and spreads out protectively over the mucosal cells. This activity diminishes the exposure of these cells to luminal gastric acid. Sodium bicarbonate is secreted from surface epithelial cells of the stomach and duodenum in response to a pH less than 3. Bicarbonate neutralizes the HCl that diffuses back from the lumen. The epithelial cells are constantly being shed and renewed so that damaged cells are promptly replaced. Epithelial cells also migrate to cover denuded areas and in this way contribute to epithelial restitution. Prostaglandins play an important role in protecting gastroduodenal mucosa by stimulating the secretion of mucus and bicarbonate, maintaining blood flow during periods of potential injury, and possibly suppressing acid secretion. Tissue prostaglandins decrease with age and are inhibited by commonly ingested drugs such as nonsteroidal anti-inflammatory agents (NSAIDs).

GASTRITIS

Gastritis can be defined by its gross appearance, histopathology, or clinical presentation, but none of these definitions is perfect. The term *gastritis*, which implies inflammation, is a misnomer because some of the entities considered lack appreciable inflammatory changes, e.g., erosions due to aspirin or NSAIDs. Gastritis may be associated with visible disruption of the gastric mucosa (erosions) or a grossly normal appearing mucosa. It is often blamed for chronic abdominal pain, but the link between symptoms and gastritis is poorly es-

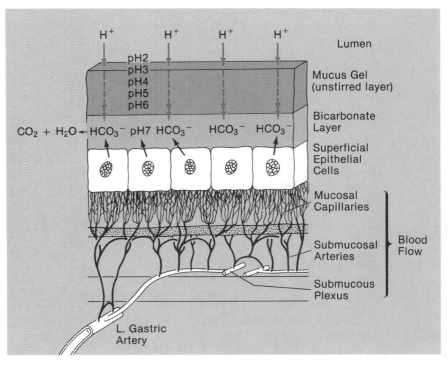

FIGURE 35-2. Model illustrating mechanisms maintaining mucosal integrity. Superficial epithelial cells secrete mucus and bicarbonate that aid in maintaining a pH gradient between lumen and mucosa and protect the underlying epithelial cells from damage by acid and pepsin. Mucosal blood flow is also believed to be a mechanism important in maintaining mucosal integrity. (From Richardson CT: Peptic ulcer: Pathogenesis. In Wyngaarden JB, Smith LH Jr, Bennett JC [eds]: Cecil Textbook of Medicine. 19th ed. Philadelphia, WB Saunders Co, 1992, p 654.)

tablished. For example, NSAIDs produce both gastric damage and symptoms, yet neither is predictive of the other. The diagnosis of gastritis may be suspected if a careful history is taken; however, endoscopy coupled with biopsies is the best way to make the diagnosis.

Erosive or Hemorrhagic Gastric Disease. In these forms of gastritis, infiltration of the lamina propria by inflammatory cells accompanies superficial erosions that may be diffuse or localized. Unlike ulcers, erosions are superficial breaks that do not extend deeper than the mucosa itself and therefore do not cause perforation or severe bleeding. The mechanism of mucosal injury is often unclear and probably multifactorial. Certain drugs, especially aspirin, NSAIDs, and ethanol, cause mucosal injury by suppressing endogenous prostaglandins and producing local damage. Stress-related mucosal disease represents acute erosive injury to the stomach in many severe surgical or medical conditions with bleeding as a complicating factor. The etiology is multifactorial, resulting from a compromise in mucosal blood flow or in other elements of mucosal defense in the presence of back-diffusion of acid. Gastritis can also sometimes be attributed to specific events, such as radiation, ingestion of alkali, and rarely bacterial infection (phlegmonous gastritis). Following surgery, reflux of bile salts and/or pancreatic enzymes may produce acute gastritis.

Many cases of erosive gastritis are probably mild and escape diagnosis. An important complication is bleeding from the superficial erosions. This usually responds to conservative management and removal of the precipitating agents if known. Antac-ids or H_2-receptor antagonists are used as well but have not been shown to affect healing. Severe bleeding, if caused by isolated lesions, may be amenable to endoscopic therapy. Because patients taking NSAIDs and those in intensive care units have such a high incidence of erosive gastritis, prophylactic preventive therapy is very important. Misoprostol (Cytotec), a synthetic prostaglandin, has been shown in doses of either 100 or 200 μg four times daily to markedly reduce the development of NSAID-induced mucosal injury. Stress-related gastritis can generally be decreased or prevented if the gastric pH is maintained above 3.5, a pH level at which pepsin activity is markedly reduced. This can be facilitated by antacid drip or hourly antacids (15 to 30 ml) via nasogastric tube. H_2-receptor antagonists are approved for intravenous use; a slow bolus infusion is effective in increasing gastric pH (cimetidine, 300 mg every 8 hr; ranitidine, 50 mg every 12 hr; famotidine, 20 mg every 12 hr). Continuous infusion may provide smoother control of pH; for example, an infusion of cimetidine (300 mg priming dose, 37.5 mg/hour) produces effective gastric neutralization. Sucralfate in a dose of 1 gm every 4 to 6 hours is also effective in reducing stress-related bleeding.

Nonerosive Gastritis. This form of gastritis involves inflammatory changes in the mucosa that are often grossly normal and lacks, as the name implies, erosive changes. Nonerosive gastritis can be classified by whether the fundus (type A) or antrum (type B) is primarily involved and by whether the inflammation is superficial, deep, or atrophic, with decreased or absent glandular elements and mucosal thinning.

In fundal or type A gastritis, the maximal inflammatory changes occur along the greater curvature in the fundus and body, with minimal or no inflammation in the antrum. Parietal cell antibodies appear in most patients and pernicious anemia may develop, suggesting an immunologic mechanism. Hyposecretion of acid results from fundic gland atrophy. The relative absence of damage to the antrum accounts for the ability of many of these patients to develop marked hypergastrinemia as the feedback inhibition of acid on gastrin release is lost. This type of gastritis may be a normal component of aging, but only a small portion of affected individuals go on to develop pernicious anemia. These patients have an increased risk of gastric carcinoids and adenocarcinoma. No specific therapy exists for fundal gastritis.

In antral or type B gastritis, the predominant inflammatory component is confined to the antrum, and it does not progress to atrophic gastritis; there is also a striking association with both peptic ulcers and *H. pylori*. A gram-negative microaerophilic organism, *H. pylori* may be the most common human infective agent worldwide. It is found primarily in the stomach but may occasionally be found in areas of gastric metaplasia (e.g., duodenal bulb). The organism lives in the gastric crypts, producing a histologic gastritis characterized by a dense neutrophilic infiltration. The mechanism by which the inflammatory response is produced is unknown, but the organism does have the ability to produce a wide variety of virulence factors. In addition to causing gastritis, *H. pylori* can suppress basal acid output and enhance serum gastrin release, especially in response to a meal. *H. pylori* is detected by biopsies with tissue staining, culture, or determination of the presence of urease, which the organism produces in abundance. Although *H. pylori* is clearly associated with antral gastritis, the relationship to symptoms is poor, and no clinical benefit seems to occur from eradication of the organism. *H. pylori* is commonly associated with gastric and duodenal ulcers, and recent studies suggest that it may be an important cofactor in the development of gastric adenocarcinoma.

PEPTIC ULCER DISEASE OF THE STOMACH AND DUODENUM

Epidemiology. The lifetime prevalence of peptic ulcer disease is 5 to 10 per cent, with about equal prevalence in men and women. Duodenal ulcers are more frequent than gastric ulcers. The incidence of ulcer disease increases with age, which may be explained by the increased use of NSAIDs in the elderly and the reduction in tissue prostaglandins with age. Genetic factors seem to be important in some patients with peptic ulcers. There is an increased incidence in first-degree relatives of patients with duodenal ulcers and a positive association with high levels of serum pepsinogen I, which appears to be inherited as a dominant trait and may reflect total chief cell mass. Other factors predisposing to ulcer disease include smoking (possibly due to diminished bicarbonate secretion by the pancreas), ethnic background (African-Americans may develop ulcers at an earlier age), and certain diseases (chronic lung disease, cirrhosis, hyperparathyroidism, chronic renal failure especially after transplantation, polycythemia vera). Regardless of age, the use of NSAIDs increases the incidence of superficial gastric mucosal erosions and gastric ulcers. Duodenal ulcers also occur as a result of NSAID use but to a lesser degree than gastric ulcers. The ulcer risk does not appear to depend upon the type of NSAID used. The evidence that glucocorticoids cause ulcers is controversial. The possible role of psychological factors is unclear, but emotional distress may increase gastric secretion, particularly in the basal state. Although it has been suggested that the overall incidence of ulcer disease is decreasing, this probably does not reflect a true change in the natural history of the disease. However, fewer patients are hospitalized with ulcers today, and perhaps with the ready availability of H_2-receptor antagonists, fewer patients see their physicians for bouts of ulcer pain.

Pathophysiology. Peptic ulcers occur whenever the normal balance between acid-pepsin and mucosal defense factors is disrupted (Fig. 35–3). Although the presence of acid is obligatory for the formation of a peptic ulcer, a large majority of patients have acid secretion well within normal limits. Therefore, the primary event in the formation of an ulcer is disruption of normal mucosal defense factors. Unfortunately, how this occurs remains poorly understood. One theory suggests that the depletion of endogenous prostaglandins leads to ulcer formation. Although this appears to be true for NSAID-induced ulcers, it has been difficult to prove for idiopathic ulcers. The second theory holds that an infection of the gastric mucosa by *H. pylori* predisposes to ulceration, either in the stomach or in areas of inflamed gastric metaplasia in the duodenal bulb. Virtually 100 per cent of patients with duodenal ulcer are infected with *H. pylori*, whereas about 70 to 80 per cent of patients with gastric ulcers are so infected. Gastric ulcers in patients who are not infected with *H. pylori* are usually associated with the use of NSAIDs or the Zollinger-Ellison syndrome. Antibiotic therapy to eradicate *H. pylori* markedly decreases the recurrence rate of duodenal ulcers. On the other hand, *H. pylori* is found in substantial proportions of normal healthy subjects, increasing in prevalence from less than 10 per cent in subjects under 30 years of age to over 60 per cent in subjects over 60 years of age. Thus, most patients with *H. pylori* never develop an ulcer regardless of acid secretory levels, suggesting that other cofactors must be important in the genesis of ulcer disease.

Clinical Manifestations. Although many ulcers may be asymptomatic, especially in the elderly,

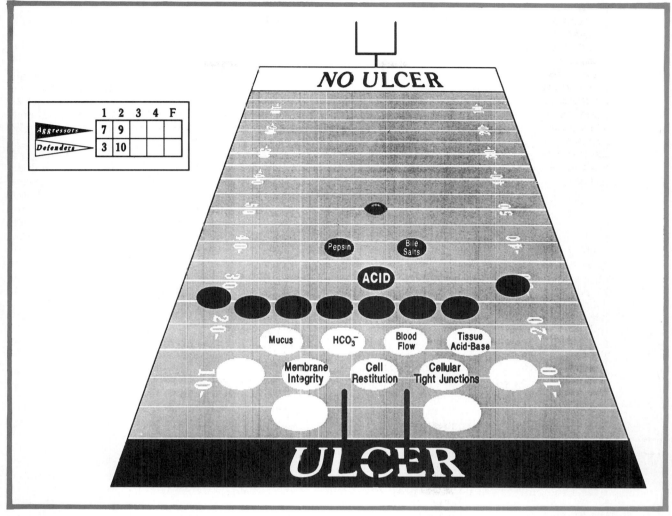

FIGURE 35–3. Schematic diagram of the relationship between aggressive and defensive factors present within gastroduodenal mucosa. Peptic ulcer occurs when aggressive factors, such as acid and pepsin, overwhelm the normal defensive properties inherent to the mucosa. (From Normpleggi DJ, Wolfe MM: Peptic ulcer disease—pathogenesis and treatment. In Zakim D, Dannenberg AJ (eds): Peptic Ulcer Disease and Other Acid-Related Disorders. New York, Academic Research Associates, 1991, p 34.)

the majority of patients with peptic ulcers present with epigastric pain. The pain, frequently described as burning or gnawing, most typically occurs 1 to 3 hours after eating, is relieved with food or antacids, and may awaken the patient from sleep. The cause of the pain is unknown, but the concept of acid bathing an "open wound" and producing pain is overly simplistic. The pain tends to occur in clusters, perhaps over several weeks, with subsequent periods of remission of varying duration. Ulcer pain generally subsides before the complete healing of the ulcer itself. In addition to pain, patients with peptic ulcers tend to have a variety of symptoms that can best be described as "dyspepsia"—bloating, nausea, anorexia, excessive eructations, and epigastric discomfort.

In the absence of complications, the physical examination is rarely helpful in the diagnosis of peptic ulcer disease. Frequently there is a moderate amount of epigastric tenderness, but this finding does not reliably point to the presence of an active ulcer. Physical examination may also give evidence of one of the other diseases associated with an ulcer diathesis.

Complications. Complications are not infrequent in peptic ulcer disease. In fact, it has been estimated that one third of patients with a diagnosis of ulcer have one or more complications in their lifetime. These complications are the main indication for peptic ulcer disease surgery.

Bleeding. Bleeding from peptic ulcer disease is the most common cause of upper gastrointestinal (GI) bleeding. It occurs in more than 20 per cent of ulcer patients, may be the first manifestation of the disease, and carries an overall mortality rate of about 7 per cent. Ulcer bleeding is particularly common in elderly patients and is probably related to their use of NSAIDs, which are not only ulcerogenic but may predispose an ulcer to bleed. Factors associated with a poor outcome from a bleeding ulcer include age (above 60), hemodynamic instability following the bleed, an excessive number of blood transfusions (greater than six units total), the presence of concomitant diseases, and continuation or recurrence of bleeding in hospital. Patients who have bled once from a peptic ulcer have an increased chance of bleeding again (30 to 50 per cent chance).

Ulcers bleed when the crater breaches one wall of a vessel. Large, deep ulcers high on the lesser gastric curve or posterior duodenal bulb are more likely to erode major vessels and result in substantial bleeding. Although bleeding from these large vessels does not cease spontaneously and requires urgent therapy, most ulcers (approximately 85 per cent) do stop bleeding at least temporarily. The treatment of a patient who has bled from a peptic ulcer is determined at the time of diagnostic endoscopy. If the ulcer is actively bleeding, it can be treated with a contact thermal probe (e.g., BICAP or heater probe), injection of a vasoconstrictor agent (e.g., epinephrine), or emergency surgery. No pharmacologic therapy has been shown to be effective in stopping active bleeding. Endoscopic therapy succeeds in more than 90 per cent of cases, but if it is unsuccessful or if bleeding recurs, then surgery should be considered for all patients but those identified as a poor risk. In these latter patients, angiographic embolization of the bleeding vessel may be an effective alternative. If the ulcer is not bleeding, it usually should be left alone. The exception is the presence of an ulcer with a visible vessel. This rebleeds about 50 per cent of the time in hospital and should therefore undergo prophylactic endoscopic therapy. Bleeding ulcers are as likely to heal as nonbleeding ulcers, and follow-up endoscopy is usually not necessary. Maintenance therapy with H_2-receptor antagonists may reduce the potential for rebleeding.

Perforation. A peptic ulcer may erode through the entire wall of the duodenum or stomach. Sometimes this leads to penetration of an adjacent organ such as the pancreas, with resulting pancreatitis and intractable pain. More frequently, especially with anterior duodenal ulcers and lesser curvature gastric ulcers, there is free perforation into the peritoneal cavity. This complication occurs in 5 to 10 per cent of patients with duodenal ulcers and 2 to 5 per cent with gastric ulcers. Factors that predispose to perforation are NSAIDs and perhaps stress. Not infrequently, especially in the elderly, perforation is the first symptom of a peptic ulcer. The presentation is typically that of an acute abdomen, with the sudden onset of severe abdominal pain, peritoneal

signs (abdominal muscle rigidity, rebound tenderness), and hypotension with tachycardia. Free air in the abdominal cavity can usually be demonstrated by an upright radiograph. In most patients with free perforation, emergency surgery is indicated to repair the site and to wash out the peritoneal cavity. Because these patients have a high risk of future problems with ulcer disease, a definitive surgical procedure may be carried out at the same operation. In some poor-risk patients, the perforation is allowed to seal spontaneously while the patient is maintained on nasogastric suction, fluids, antibiotics, and H_2-receptor antagonist therapy.

Obstruction. Today the least common manifestation (5 per cent) of ulcer disease is obstruction leading to symptoms of delayed gastric emptying with nausea, vomiting, epigastric pain, fullness, and early satiety. This complication is most frequent in ulcers involving the pyloric channel. Whereas edema surrounding an acute ulcer may produce transient obstructive symptoms that resolve with ulcer healing, chronic obstruction is the result of repeated bouts of acute ulceration leading to the formation of scar tissue. On physical examination the patient may present with a succussion splash and signs of dehydration. Laboratory studies may show metabolic alkalosis and hypokalemia from intractable vomiting. Obstruction can be readily demonstrated by an upper GI series or a positive saline load test (greater than 400 ml of gastric juice recovered 30 minutes after instilling 750 ml of saline via nasogastric tube into an empty stomach). The specific cause of obstruction can be best demonstrated by endoscopy. An attempt should be made to treat all patients with gastric obstruction initially by medical means—nasogastric tube drainage, repair of fluid and electrolyte deficits, H_2-receptor antagonist therapy, and possibly parenteral nutrition. At least half of the patients so treated, presumably those with edema as the cause, respond to therapy, usually within 7 days. On the other hand, if obstruction persists, resectional surgery with vagotomy or possibly balloon dilatation of the pylorus is required.

Intractable Pain. The pain of a peptic ulcer is rarely intractable if the patient is compliant with a treatment regimen. With the more powerful H_2-receptor antagonists and proton pump inhibitors, most ulcers heal and pain resolves. The persistence of pain with an unhealed ulcer should raise questions about noncompliance with medical therapy, surreptitious use of NSAIDs, or possibly a hypergastrinemia state. A nonhealing ulcer may also represent penetration posteriorly or into an adjacent viscus.

Diagnosis. The definitive diagnosis of a peptic ulcer depends on visualizing the ulcer crater by direct inspection endoscopically (the most sensitive and specific method) or indirectly by radiographic studies (upper GI series). An upper GI series is usually the first screening study performed because it is less expensive than endoscopy. However, if no ulcer is found radiographically and peptic ulcer disease is still strongly suspected, endoscopic examination is indicated because as many of one fifth of ulcers may be missed by an upper GI series. If a gastric ulcer is found radiographically, it is imperative to demonstrate that it is benign rather than malignant. Malignancy should be suspected from the radiograph if (1) the ulcer is located completely within the gastric wall or a mass, (2) there is nodularity of the ulcer mass or the adjacent gastric mucosa, (3) there are no folds radiating to the ulcer margin, or (4) the ulcer is very large. Nevertheless, endoscopy should be performed in all patients with gastric ulcers to obtain brush cytology specimens and a minimum of six to eight pinch biopsies to adequately rule out malignancy.

When the presence of a typical peptic ulcer has been established radiographically or endoscopically, other studies are rarely indicated. In only a few clinical situations is the measurement of serum gastrin or the basal and peak acid output of the stomach indicated (Table 35–1), primarily for the suspicion of a gastrinoma (to be discussed subsequently). In the patient with recurrent or intractable ulcer disease, it may also be important to diagnosis the presence of *H. pylori* infection (see previous section).

Many common diseases may produce epigastric pain simulating peptic ulcer disease. These include functional dyspepsia, gastric cancer, biliary tract disease, pancreatitis, esophagitis, pleurisy, pericarditis, and rarely an inferior myocardial infarction.

Treatment. Most patients with peptic ulcers can be treated successfully by medical methods. Surgery is usually required only for the complications of ulcer disease. In addition to the specific measures to be described, all patients with peptic ulcer disease should discontinue cigarette smoking, drink alcohol only in moderation, and discontinue the use of aspirin and NSAIDs. Although diet was once considered of great importance in the treatment of peptic ulcer, there is no good evidence that changes in diet influence the rate of healing. Patients are best advised simply to avoid foods that lead to dyspeptic symptoms and to limit eating between meals and at bedtime, because eating then further enhances gastric secretion.

Medical Management. The medical treatment of ulcer disease is directed either toward reducing gastric acid or toward reducing mucosal damage from acid-pepsin exposure.

Reduction of Gastric Acid. A number of agents can reduce the rate of secretion of acid by acting at various sites in the normal or hyperstimulated parietal cell (Fig. 35–4). Antimuscarinic drugs (e.g., atropine) reduce fasting and food-stimulated acid secretion but are not frequently used today because of unwanted side effects. H_2-receptor antagonists are the most popular and extensively studied drugs for the treatment of ulcer disease. Four products are commercially available for the acute treatment of duodenal or gastric ulcers. These include cimetidine used in a dose of 300 mg four times a day, 400 mg twice a day, or 800 mg at bedtime; ranitidine, 150 mg twice a day or 300 mg

TABLE 35–1. CLINICAL SITUATIONS IN WHICH MEASUREMENT OF SERUM GASTRIN LEVELS IS INDICATED

Family history of peptic ulcer
Ulcer associated with hypercalcemia or other manifestations of multiple endocrine neoplasia type I
Multiple ulcers
Peptic ulceration of postbulbar duodenum or jejunum
Peptic ulceration associated with diarrhea*
Chronic unexplained diarrhea*
Enlarged gastric folds on upper GI x-ray
Before surgery for "intractable" ulcer
Recurrent ulcer after ulcer surgery

*Not due to antacid ingestion.
Adapted from Schiller LR: Peptic ulcer: Epidemiology, clinical manifestations, and diagnosis. In Wyngaarden JB, Smith LH Jr, Bennett JC (eds): Cecil Textbook of Medicine. 19th ed. Philadelphia, WB Saunders Co, 1992, p 657.

at bedtime; famotidine, 20 mg twice a day or 40 mg at bedtime; and nizatidine, 150 mg twice a day or 300 mg at bedtime. At these doses, all H_2-receptor antagonists are equal, with no clinical advantage of any one over the other three. Maintenance therapy with a half-dose at bedtime also reduces the incidence of recurrent ulcerations. These drugs are remarkably safe but do have some side effects. Most reports cite the effects of cimetidine and ranitidine because these two drugs have been available the longest. The central nervous system side effects (e.g., headache, mental confusion) are rare, reversible, and seen most often in patients with liver and renal failure. Gynecomastia and impotence have been reported with cimetidine because of its antiandrogenic effect. The H_2-receptor antagonists, particularly cimetidine, may also inhibit the metabolism of certain other drugs (e.g., theophylline, warfarin, and phenytoin) by the liver. The substituted benzimidazoles are extremely potent inhibitors of acid secretion because they block the H^+-K^+-ATPase enzyme found at the secretory surface of parietal cells that mediates the

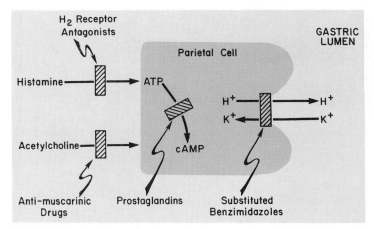

FIGURE 35–4. Sites of action of drugs employed to inhibit acid secretion. (From Peterson WL: Peptic ulcer: Medical therapy. In Wyngaarden JB, Smith LH Jr, Bennett JC [eds]: Cecil Textbook of Medicine. 19th ed. Philadelphia, WB Saunders Co, 1992, p 659.)

final common pathway of hydrogen ion secretion into the gastric lumen. The prototype drug, omeprazole, in doses of 20 mg once daily, produces ulcer healing slightly better than do H_2-receptor antagonists when the latter are given in standard doses. Because of the cost of omeprazole, its major role should be in patients who might require larger than usual doses of H_2-receptor antagonists. The sustained hypochlorhydria produced by omeprazole results in hypergastrinemia, which in rats has led to the development of carcinoid tumors. The hypergastrinemia is reversible, however, and no such drug-related tumors have been documented in humans. Nevertheless, this drug should be used judiciously and at this time for no longer than 8 to 12 weeks continuously.

The concentration of gastric acid can also be neutralized intraluminally with antacids. Large doses of aluminum- and magnesium hydroxide–containing antacids are highly effective in healing gastric and duodenal ulcers and are as effective as H_2-receptor antagonists. However, such large doses often result in bothersome diarrhea. Interestingly, more recent studies from outside the United States suggest that low-dose antacids (e.g., one tablet, 25 mmol neutralizing capacity, four times daily) are as effective as high-dose regimens. At these doses the aluminum- and magnesium hydroxide–containing antacids have comparatively few side effects (constipation for aluminum and mild diarrhea for magnesium). Calcium-containing antacids are no longer in favor because ionized calcium stimulates the secretion of gastrin. Sodium-containing antacids are effective only for brief periods and often add too much sodium to the diet, increasing the danger of edema, hypertension, and metabolic alkalosis.

Improvement of Mucosal Defense. Only one drug is widely used currently in the United States for this purpose, sucralfate. Sucralfate is effective for the acute therapy of duodenal ulcers in doses of 1 gm four times a day or 2 gm twice a day and as a maintenance therapy in a dose of 1 gm twice a day. Results with gastric ulcers are less well studied. Its mechanism of action is unknown, but theories include formation of a viscous shield over the ulcer crater, preventing acid from reaching regenerating tissue; adsorption of pepsin; stimulation of endogenous prostaglandins; destruction of oxygen radicals; and recruitment of epidermal growth factor to the ulcer site. The agent is minimally absorbed and virtually without side effects. Exogenous prostaglandins conceivably could promote ulcer healing either at low doses by mucosal protective effects or at higher doses by inhibiting acid secretion. Unfortunately, lower doses are not effective and high doses are associated with a substantial incidence of diarrhea as well as the potential for abortion. Only misoprostol is commercially available; it is approved in doses of 200 μg four times a day, only for the prevention of NSAID-induced gastric ulcers in patients at high risk of ulcer complications.

More than 80 per cent of duodenal ulcers heal after 6 to 8 weeks of treatment with either H_2-receptor antagonists or sucralfate. If this initial approach is not successful, care should be taken to determine patient compliance and the actual presence of an unhealed ulcer (by endoscopy). These patients should be switched to a proton pump inhibitor, the rationale being that hypersecretion of acid may not have been adequately reduced with standard therapy. Patients should also be carefully questioned about the use of NSAIDs, and one should always consider the Zollinger-Ellison syndrome. Gastric ulcers require special consideration because of the possibility of carcinoma (about 4 per cent of gastric ulcers) and should be carefully followed until healing. Gastric ulcers are usually treated for 8 weeks, at which time assessment of healing is done, preferably with endoscopy or an upper GI series. Biopsies and cytologic specimens are taken any time an unhealed gastric ulcer is noted. If these studies prove negative, gastric ulcers are usually treated longer with the same regimen because these ulcers seem to be larger than duodenal ulcers and therefore take longer to heal. If healing still does not occur, the dose of the H_2-receptor antagonist may be increased or ther-

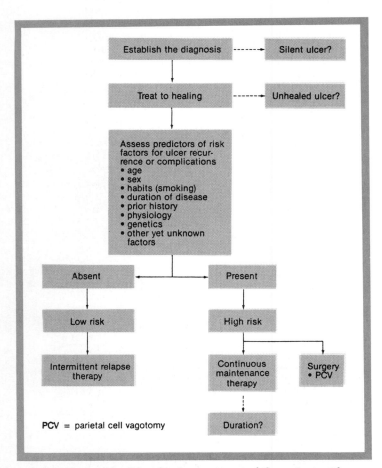

FIGURE 35–5. Algorithm for the treatment of the patient with peptic ulcer disease. (From Van Deventer GM: Approaches to the long-term treatment of duodenal ulcer disease. Am J Med 77(5B):15, 1984.)

apy changed to omeprazole. If intense medical therapy still fails to heal the ulcer, surgery should be considered.

Both gastric and duodenal ulcers have a high recurrence rate after effective medical therapy, with rates being reported as high as 70 to 80 per cent in 1 year. Nevertheless, many patients do not require long-term maintenance therapy. Some with recurrent peptic ulcers can be managed satisfactorily by initiating another 4- to 6-week course of therapy (i.e., "on demand therapy"). If recurrences are frequent (e.g., more than three per year) or the patient falls into a high-risk group (Fig. 35–5), then a long-term management plan should be instituted. Treatment is with H_2-receptor antagonists at half-doses in the evening or, for duodenal ulcers, sucralfate in doses of 1 gm twice daily. Definitive surgical therapy should also be considered; if patient compliance is poor or surgery is not an option, the eradication of *H. pylori* with antibiotics and bismuth compounds may be attempted.

Surgical Management. Today, surgery for peptic ulcer disease is indicated only for complications because failure of healing on medical therapy is rare. The surgical procedures most frequently employed are shown in Figure 35–6. In various combinations, they are devised to decrease acid secretion by reducing the cephalic phase (vagotomy) or the gastric phase (antrectomy) by removing a major source of gastrin. Various drainage procedures are then used to maintain gastric emptying in the postvagotomy state. Increasingly proximal ("superselective") vagotomy rather than truncal vagotomy may be used to reduce acid secretion more selectively without adverse effects on gastric motility and emptying. However, the trade-off has been a higher rate of recurrent ulcer disease (i.e., 10 per cent with proximal gastric vagotomy versus 1 per cent with truncal vagotomy and antrectomy). In patients with intractable, benign gastric ulcers, vagotomy may not be required because acid production is usually normal or low. Antrectomy or subtotal gastrectomy may be the treatment of choice.

Although surgical treatment of peptic ulcer disease is usually successful in relieving symptoms and preventing recurrence, some infrequent complications may be distressing to the patient. The most common of these is the dumping syndrome, which results from disruption of the normal storage function of the stomach. Ingested food is dumped prematurely into the duodenum, leading to nausea, vomiting, weakness, abdominal pain, and diarrhea. These symptoms appear soon after eating. More rarely there are late symptoms (1 to 3 hours after eating), which probably result from reactive hypoglycemia due to rapid and excessive carbohydrate absorption followed by an overshoot of insulin release. Other postsurgery problems include weight loss usually related to early satiety, postvagotomy diarrhea, anemia as a result of iron, vitamin B_{12}, and/or folate deficiency, alkaline reflux gastritis and esophagitis, and the afferent loop syndrome. The latter problem occurs in patients

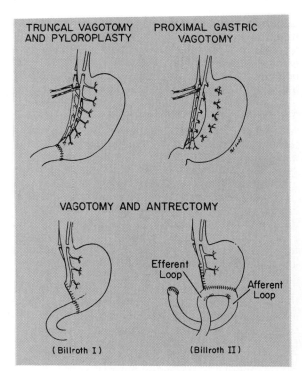

FIGURE 35–6. Model illustrating surgical procedures for peptic ulcer disease. (From Thirlby RC: Peptic ulcer: Surgical therapy. In Wyngaarden JB, Smith LH Jr, Bennett JC [eds]: Cecil Textbook of Medicine. 19th ed. Philadelphia, WB Saunders Co, 1992, p 661.)

who have a Billroth II type of gastroenterostomy. Symptoms occur when pancreatic and biliary secretions collect in a partially obstructed afferent loop, causing distention and pain. Eventually, the fluid bypasses the partial obstruction, rushes into the stomach, and provokes vomiting. This complication may require reconstructive surgery.

THE ZOLLINGER-ELLISON SYNDROME

The Zollinger-Ellison syndrome, caused by a functioning islet cell tumor that secretes gastrin (gastrinoma), accounts for well under 1 per cent of clinically diagnosed peptic ulcers. The possibility of this rare entity should be considered in several circumstances: (1) ulcers located in unusual sites such as the second or third portion of the duodenum or the jejunum; (2) unusually severe peptic ulcer disease that is refractory to treatment or recurrent after surgery; (3) ulcer disease accompanied by diarrhea and sometimes malabsorption (see Chapter 32); and (4) a strong family history of ulcer disease, especially if there is evidence of other endocrine tumors.

Pathogenesis. Single or often multiple gastrinomas secrete excessive amounts of gastrin, which drives acid secretion by the parietal cell. In addition, gastrinomas have a trophic effect on the parietal cells, increasing their number by as much as three to five times. These tumors are generally found in the pancreas or duodenal bulb but rarely can be found outside this area. Although slow growing, most gastrinomas are histologically and biologically malignant, with early metastases regionally and to the liver. In approximately one fourth of patients, the gastrinoma is associated with other endocrine adenomas, most commonly in the pattern known as the multiple endocrine neoplasia type I (MEN I) syndrome, in which adenomas may involve the islet cells, the parathyroid glands, the thyroid, and the pituitary.

Clinical Manifestations. The clinical manifestations are usually those of severe peptic ulcer disease, as noted above. Diarrhea may precede peptic ulcer formation or be a prominent symptom. Approximately 50 per cent of patients have gastroesophageal reflux disease, which can be severe.

Diagnosis. The diagnosis of the Zollinger-Ellison syndrome is usually not difficult. Generally, it depends on the demonstration of an elevated serum gastrin and the presence of increased basal secretion of gastric acid (i.e., BAO greater than 15 mmol/hr or a BAO/MAO ratio of 50 per cent or more). A markedly elevated serum gastrin without hypersecretion is usually the result of hypochlorhydria. Intravenous secretin (1 unit/kg) produces a marked increase in serum gastrin level in most patients with gastrinoma but not in patients with ordinary duodenal ulcers.

Treatment. An attempt should be made to find and remove a resectable tumor, although this can be considered curative in only about one quarter of patients. If surgery is not successful, the patient should be treated with very high doses of H$_2$-receptor antagonists or omeprazole. In this case, omeprazole is advantageous because of its lower price and convenience. Doses of 20 to 120 mg/day are usually required to maintain the BAO at less than 10 mmol/hr. Total gastrectomy may still be required for the rare patient who does not respond or is not compliant with medical therapy.

ABNORMALITIES OF GASTRIC EMPTYING

Abnormal gastric motility can cause rapid or delayed stomach emptying. Rapid emptying is usually secondary to gastric surgery. Delayed stomach emptying is much more common and may be secondary to mechanical obstruction or the inability of the stomach to generate effective propulsive forces (i.e., functional obstruction, or gastroparesis).

Pathogenesis and Clinical Manifestations. Rapid emptying may produce a number of symptoms, including lightheadedness, diaphoresis, palpitations, abdominal pain, and diarrhea. This constellation of symptoms has been referred to as "the dumping syndrome." Potential causes include

the postgastrectomy and postvagotomy states, Zollinger-Ellison syndrome, pancreatic insufficiency, and celiac sprue. Symptoms may be mediated by the release of active agents, such as serotonin, prostaglandins, vasoactive intestinal polypeptides, insulin, opiates, and others. Delayed stomach emptying is much more common and has multiple causes (Table 35–2). Ulcers, strictures, and tumors all decrease the size of the gastric outlet, thereby impeding gastric emptying. Functional causes of gastroparesis interfere with emptying by transiently or permanently disrupting the neural or muscular function of the stomach. Symptoms of delayed gastric emptying include nausea, vomiting, abdominal fullness and bloating, early satiety, anorexia, and weight loss. It is impossible to determine from the presenting symptoms whether delayed emptying is caused by mechanical obstruction or functional gastroparesis.

Diagnosis. The best clues to abnormalities of gastric emptying are a good history and precipitating factors. An audible succussion splash over the abdomen may provide a clue to delayed emptying of the stomach. Patients with rapid gastric emptying and diarrhea may have hyperactive bowel sounds, but these findings are nonspecific. Delayed gastric emptying is suggested by a dilated stomach on an abdominal flat plate film or by obtaining food and a large amount of secretions

TABLE 35–2. CAUSES OF DELAYED GASTRIC EMPTYING

Mechanical Obstruction
  Duodenal or pyloric channel ulcer
  Pyloric stricture
  Tumor of the distal stomach
Functional Obstruction (Gastroparesis)
  Drugs
    Anticholinergics
    Beta-adrenergics
    Opiates
  Electrolyte imbalance
    Hypokalemia
    Hypocalcemia
    Hypomagnesemia
  Metabolic disorders
    Diabetes mellitus
    Hypoparathyroidism
    Hypothyroidism
    Pregnancy
  Vagotomy
  Viral infections
  Neuromuscular disorders
    Myotonic dystrophy
    Diabetes mellitus (autonomic neuropathy)
    Scleroderma
    Polymyositis
    Aberrant gastric pacemaker (i.e., tachygastria)
  Brain stem tumors
  Gastroesophageal reflux
  Psychiatric disorders
    Anorexia nervosa
    Psychogenic vomiting
  Idiopathic

after nasogastric intubation. After the stomach has been decompressed and cleaned out, upper GI endoscopy should be performed to exclude a mechanical cause of obstruction. If this study is negative, a radionuclide scintigraphic study can be done to assess the emptying of a solid meal. If this study is abnormally slow, a diagnosis of gastroparesis is made with confidence. Likewise, rapid emptying would be consistent with a dumping syndrome.

Treatment. Rapid gastric emptying is usually treated with dietary modification and antispasmodic medications. A high-fat, high-fiber diet consumed in six small meals that excludes concentrated carbohydrates and fluids with the meals may be helpful. Antispasmodic agents can delay gastric emptying by means of their anticholinergic effects. Useful agents include propantheline bromide at a dose of 7.5 to 15 mg three to four times a day or dicyclomine at 10 to 40 mg four times a day. Reconstructive surgery aimed at slowing the transit of food through the small intestine using reversed intestinal segment or Roux-en-Y jejunal interpositions is occasionally necessary. Electrolyte abnormalities should be improved and incriminating drugs removed in patients with delayed gastric emptying. Enriched liquids are easier to empty than solids, and multiple small feedings each day are suggested. Prokinetic drugs are used in treating chronic gastroparesis, although the results vary from disease to disease and patient to patient. Most of these drugs promote gastric emptying via cholinergic pathways or the inhibition of dopamine, which slows gastric motility. Available drugs include bethanechol at a dose of 10 to 20 mg four times a day and metoclopramide at a dose of 5 to 20 mg four times a day. Central nervous system side effects (agitation, nervousness, depression) occur in 25 to 30 per cent of patients taking metoclopramide because it crosses the blood-brain barrier. Soon to be available in the United States, cisapride, in a dose of 10 to 20 mg three times a day, is a powerful prokinetic agent that works through the cholinergic nervous system and does not cross the blood-brain barrier. Additionally, the long-used antibiotic erythromycin stimulates motility by interacting with receptors for the hormone motilin and may be a more powerful agent than the three previous drugs. Recent data suggest that erythromycin may be particularly helpful in patients with chronic diabetic gastroparesis.

REFERENCES

Fisher R: Gastroparesis: How can slow gastric emptying be assessed, and how should problems be managed? *In* Barkin JS, Rogers AI (eds): Difficult Decisions in Digestive Diseases. Chicago, Year Book Medical Publishers, 1989, pp 65–73.

Peterson WL: *Helicobacter pylori* and peptic ulcer disease. N Engl J Med 324:1043, 1991.

Richardson CT, Schiller LR, Peterson WL, Thirlby RC, Feldman M: Peptic ulcer. *In* Wyngaarden JB, Smith LH Jr, Bennett JC (eds): Cecil Textbook of Medicine. 19th ed. Philadelphia, WB Saunders Co, 1992, pp 652–667.

Soll AH: Gastritis. *In* Wyngaarden JB, Smith LH Jr, Bennett JC (eds): Cecil Textbook of Medicine. 19th ed. Philadelphia, WB Saunders Co, 1992, pp 648–652.

Soll AH: Duodenal ulcer and drug therapy. *In* Sleisenger MH, Fordtran JS (eds): Gastrointestinal Disease: Pathophysiology, Diagnosis, and Management. 4th ed. Philadelphia, WB Saunders Co, 1989, pp 814–879.

Wolfe MM, Soll AH: The physiology of gastric acid secretion. N Engl J Med 319:1707, 1988.

36 INFLAMMATORY BOWEL DISEASE

Definition

Inflammatory bowel disease (IBD) is the rubric given to ulcerative colitis (UC) and Crohn's disease, which are chronic intestinal diseases characterized by inflammation of unknown etiology. UC and Crohn's disease are discussed together to facilitate their comparison and highlight their differences. IBD is more common in Caucasians than non-Caucasians and in Ashkenazic Jews than in Sephardic Jews and has approximately equal incidence in men and women. The incidence of UC is approximately the same as that of Crohn's disease worldwide. Symptoms frequently begin in early adult life—ages 15 to 30—but may begin in the elderly. A comparison of clinical and pathologic features of Crohn's disease and UC is given in Table 36–1.

TABLE 36 – 1. COMPARISON OF THE PATHOLOGIC AND CLINICAL FEATURES OF ULCERATIVE COLITIS AND CROHN'S DISEASE

FEATURE	ULCERATIVE COLITIS	CROHN'S DISEASE
Pathologic		
Discontinuous involvement	0	+ +
Transmural inflammation	0/+*	+ + +
Deep fissures and fistulas	0	+ +
Confluent linear ulcers	0	+ +
Crypt abscesses	+ + +	+
Focal granulomas	0	+ +
Clinical		
Rectal bleeding	+ + +	+
Malaise, fever	+	+ + +
Abdominal pain	+	+ + +
Abdominal mass	0	+ +
Fistulas	0	+ + +
Endoscopic		
Diffuse, continuous involvement	+ + +	0/+
Friable mucosa	+ + +	0/+
Rectal involvement	+ + +	+
Cobblestoning	0	+ + +
Linear ulcers	0	+ +

*In toxic megacolon.

Etiology and Pathogenesis

Several causes have been proposed, although none has been proved. Genetic factors and immunologic dysregulation are significant in both forms of IBD. Immunologic dysfunction has been found in 20 per cent of families with UC and in 40 per cent of families with Crohn's disease. There is a high concordance rate of IBD in monozygotic twins and a lower concordance rate in dizygotic twins.

Infectious Origin. Several unsupported hypotheses have been put forward to suggest possible etiologic agents. No organism has been consistently isolated or associated with IBD.

Immunologic Origin. The presence of extraintestinal manifestations of IBD, the obvious infiltration of diseased mucosa with lymphocytes, the reports of cytotoxic T cells, and antibodies to colonic epithelial cells all suggest an immunologic basis for mucosal injury in IBD. Many investigations have focused on immune regulatory events, but definitive understanding of the pathogenesis of these diseases is yet to be achieved.

Psychological Origin. Very few gastroenterologists believe that IBD has a psychological origin, but many believe that emotional states can exacerbate symptoms in IBD. Emotional problems may further complicate longer-term management because of the debilitating nature of the disease.

Environmental Factors. Apparently such factors trigger a series of responses that lead to the development of IBD. For example, the incidence of IBD is increasing in regions of Asia that are undergoing technologic development.

Pathology

Examination of tissue in IBD is essential and frequently is required to make the distinction between UC and Crohn's disease.

Ulcerative Colitis. The acute lesions in UC are diffuse, beginning at the anal verge, and superficial, involving only the mucosa and submucosa. The lesions begin in the distal rectum and extend proximally to varying degrees. Patients with pancolitis (total colonic involvement) may have very mild ileitis, but essentially UC involves only the colon. The epithelium in UC is typically infiltrated with neutrophils and exhibits diffuse inflammation; the mucosa is friable owing to diffuse superficial ulceration. Pathologic examination usually shows multiple microabcesses around the crypts. In the presence of severe inflammation, the colon may develop marked distention with thin walls, leading to the syndrome known as "toxic megacolon." Considerable danger of perforation exists in this condition. Chronic UC may lead to hyperplasia of the muscularis mucosae, producing a smooth or shortened colon with the loss of haustral markings. Endoscopic examination of the diseased mucosa in UC frequently reveals pseudopolyps, which are outcroppings of granulation tissue that develop between areas of inflammation. These lesions are called "pseudo" because they have no neoplastic epithelium. With time, the epithelium of the involved colon often develops dysplastic changes and is associated with an increased risk of malignancy. Carcinoma is the only complication of UC likely to produce a stricture or fistula.

Crohn's Disease. Crohn's disease has also been called regional enteritis because of the frequent involvement of the terminal ileum. The typical inflammation in Crohn's disease is quite distinct from that of UC in that it is discontinuous, with uninvolved areas of normal bowel between diseased areas, and transmural, involving all layers of intestinal tissue from the mucosa to the serosa. Furthermore, the rectum is involved in fewer than half the patients with Crohn's disease. Crohn's disease has the capacity to involve any area of the gastrointestinal (GI) tract from the mouth to the anus, with approximately one third involving primarily the colon, one third ileum alone, and one third both ileum and colon. On rare occasions the proximal small bowel, stomach, or mouth may be involved. Because the inflammatory process is transmural, nonadjacent loops of bowel may adhere to each other and develop masses, fistulas, or obstruction. The mucosa may appear relatively normal in Crohn's disease or may develop a cobblestone or ulcerated appearance. Ulcers are occasionally deep and linear, with the long axis of the ulcer parallel to the long axis of the bowel. The inflammatory infiltrate in the thickened bowel wall contains lymphocytes, macrophages, neutrophils, and, in about half of the cases, granulomas. Crohn's disease is frequently complicated by fistula formation and perirectal disease, but epithelial dysplasia is not as common as in UC. There is an increased risk of colon cancer in patients with Crohn's disease, but much less than with UC.

Clinical Manifestations

The clinical manifestations of IBD may be intestinal or extraintestinal.

Intestinal Manifestations. The primary manifestations of acute UC are rectal bleeding, diarrhea, urgency, fever, weight loss, and sometimes abdominal pain. The disease may be quite mild, with only a slight increase in stooling when the disease is limited to the rectum (ulcerative proctitis). In contrast, 10 to 15 per cent of patients with UC present with an acute illness requiring immediate hospitalization to prevent or treat complications such as hypokalemia, toxic megacolon, shock, or colonic perforation. The severity of the diarrhea and extent of inflammatory disease determine whether the patient exhibits additional findings such as leukocytosis, anemia, hypokalemia, fever, weakness, anorexia, tachycardia, or hypotension. The abdomen may be normal on physical examination but may also be distended and tender. Most patients with UC have a remitting-relapsing course, with remissions lasting for weeks, months, or years punctuated by severe exacerbations.

The onset of Crohn's disease is usually more subtle than that of UC, probably because the lesions are not as close to the rectum in Crohn's disease. When the ileum is primarily involved, patients may present with evidence of low-grade intestinal obstruction with colicky pain, with or without diarrhea, and occasionally with a mass in the lower right quadrant. Dramatic rectal bleeding seen in UC is usually not seen in Crohn's disease, although occult blood is common. Because the ileum is in the right lower quadrant and Crohn's disease causes an inflammatory response, patients may present with symptoms mimicking those of acute appendicitis. When Crohn's disease involves the colon, diarrhea is much more common than when it involves only the small bowel. Colonic involvement also predisposes to perirectal fistulas, abcesses, and fissures. Crohn's disease is associated with more frequent extraintestinal manifestations, discussed below. Toxic megacolon as seen in UC is usually not present in Crohn's disease unless there is nearly pancolitis. Perforation of the bowel into the peritoneum is uncommon in Crohn's disease. As one would expect from the pathologic lesions, Crohn's disease is much more likely to produce enterocutaneous, enterourinary, or enterovaginal fistulas and less likely to produce hemorrhage or perforation than is UC. Any part of the intestinal tract may be involved, even the buccal mucosa.

Extraintestinal Manifestations. Both UC and Crohn's disease of the colon have been associated with the extraintestinal manifestations listed in Table 36–2. Nutritional deficiencies occasionally occur but are usually secondary to the anorexia, fever, diarrhea, blood loss, and malabsorption that may be present, especially in Crohn's disease.

TABLE 36–2. EXTRAINTESTINAL MANIFESTATIONS OF INFLAMMATORY BOWEL DISEASE

1. Nutritional abnormalities
   weight loss, hypoalbuminemia, vitamin deficiencies, deficiencies of calcium, zinc, magnesium, phosphate
2. Hematologic abnormalities
   anemia (Fe loss, folate deficiency), leukocytosis, thrombocytosis
3. Skin manifestations
   pyoderma gangrenosum, erythema nodosum
4. Arthritis
   ankylosing spondylitis and sacroiliitis (B27-associated), peripheral large joint involvement
5. Hepatic and biliary abnormalities
   fatty liver, pericholangitis, sclerosing cholangitis, gallstones, carcinoma of the bile ducts
6. Renal abnormalities
   kidney stone diathesis (calcium oxalate, uric acid), obstructive uropathy, fistulas to urinary tract
7. Eye abnormalities
   iritis, conjunctivitis, episcleritis
8. Miscellaneous
   fever, increased thrombophlebitis, osteoporosis, osteomalacia

Modified from Rosenberg IH: Crohn's disease. *In* Wyngaarden JB, Smith LH Jr (eds): Cecil Textbook of Medicine. 18th ed. Philadelphia, WB Saunders Co, 1988, p 745.

IBD is associated with two distinct forms of arthritis, sometimes termed enteropathic arthritis: (1) a nondeforming acute inflammatory arthritis of unknown cause that affects large joints, and (2) a sacroiliitis of the ankylosing spondylitis type in patients who have HLA-B27. The former arthritides parallel the colonic disease, although they may precede the clinical onset of IBD. This process is generally oligoarticular and asymmetric and tends to involve the knees and ankles. The latter arthritides persist and progress even after colectomy for UC, while the former generally resolve with colectomy. The clinical and radiographic findings in the HLA-B27–associated arthritis of IBD are largely indistinguishable from those seen in idiopathic ankylosing spondylitis. Diverse abnormalities of the hepatobiliary system also occur in patients with IBD. Investigators have described the development of fatty liver and mild pericholangitis that may not be detected without noting an increased alkaline phosphatase. A rare but more severe complication called sclerosing cholangitis may supervene. This syndrome is characterized by progressive stricture of intrahepatic and extrahepatic ducts, leading to obstructive jaundice and secondary biliary cirrhosis. Sclerosing cholangitis is seen more commonly in UC than in Crohn's disease, but an increased incidence of cholelithiasis due to inadequate absorption of bile salts by the diseased ileum is seen primarily in Crohn's disease. Primary carcinoma of the bile duct has also been described but is rare. Ocular manifestations of IBD include iritis, uveitis, and episcleritis. Erythema nodosum occurs in approximately 5 per cent of patients and is more common in women. One to 2 per cent of patients with active UC also have pyoderma gangrenosum, a rare indolent, necrotic skin lesion. Patients with IBD may develop renal lesions: (1) kidney stones, especially calcium oxalate stones due to absorptive hyperoxaluria caused by malabsorption of calcium complexed to fatty acids; (2) obstructive uropathy from fibrosis in or near the urinary tract in Crohn's disease; (3) kaliopenic nephropathy; or (4) rarely, amyloidosis. Patients with IBD have an increased risk for thrombophlebitis. Osteoporosis and osteomalacia may complicate the course of IBD as well (see Chapters 75 and 76).

On rare occasions, the extraintestinal manifestations present prior to the bowel disease and occasionally are the most important cause of morbidity. However, most of these symptoms remit with improvement of the colitis or following colectomy except for sclerosing cholangitis, ankylosing spondylitis, and secondary biliary cirrhosis.

Diagnosis

The challenge of the diagnostic process is to determine if a patient with diarrhea, abdominal pain, rectal bleeding, and fever has IBD. In patients who appear to have IBD, it is important to distinguish between UC and Crohn's disease. Other disorders that appear on the differential diagnosis vary with the clinical presentation; they must include bacillary dysentery, amebiasis, ischemic colitis, pseudomembranous colitis, angiodysplasia, dysplasia, colon cancer, collagenous colitis, and microscopic colitis. No laboratory tests distinguish the IBD syndromes from each other or from non-IBD syndromes. The diagnosis depends on (1) direct visualization of the colonic or ileal mucosa with biopsy; (2) radiologic studies that may definitively demonstrate the ileal involvement of Crohn's disease, in which a characteristic appearance distinguishes it from UC; and (3) exclusion of other illnesses that present similarly, including syndromes due to *Yersinia enterocolitica, Entamoeba histolytica, Campylobacter, Chlamydia,* or the toxin of *Clostridium difficile.*

The characteristic endoscopic findings in acute UC are described in the section headed "Pathology." The mucosa is friable and frequently granular, and the lesions are generally diffuse. The lesions bleed easily when rubbed with a cotton swab or bumped with an endoscope. When UC has been established for years, pseudopolyps and deep ulcers may be apparent. In Crohn's disease the mucosa tends to be involved in patches and may exhibit a cobblestone appearance or linear ulcerations.

Radiographic studies are important in the diagnosis and management of IBD. Air-contrast barium enema usually demonstrates the diffuse character of the disease in UC and may even clearly identify pseudopolyps (Fig. 36–1); however, this study may be normal in early disease and is not as sensitive as endoscopy. Late in the disease the "lead-pipe" appearance of the shortened colon with associated loss of haustra may be apparent. Radiographic studies of Crohn's colitis typically show patchy involvement, sparing of the rectum in half of the cases, longitudinal ulcers, and segmental narrowing of the bowel. Barium studies are indispensable in the detection of fistulous communications. The abnormalities of the ileal epithelium may also be diagnosed with barium enema and frequently exhibit the classic "string sign." These entities may

FIGURE 36–1. Double-contrast barium enema in a patient with ulcerative colitis demonstrating (A) pseudopolyps and (B) multiple irregular serrations in the transverse colon representing mucosal ulcerations. (From Sleisenger MH, Fordtran JS [eds]: Gastrointestinal Disease: Pathophysiology, Diagnosis, and Management. 3rd ed. Philadelphia. WB Saunders Co, 1983, pp 1134–1135.)

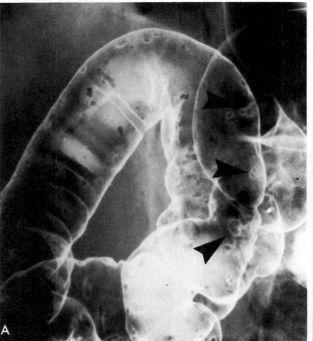

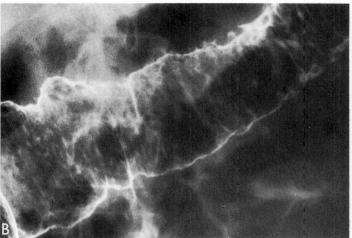

not be easily distinguished early in the course of the disease.

Treatment and Prognosis

The treatment for UC and Crohn's disease is similar because both disorders require long-term treatment using the same or related drugs. In addition, psychological problems, anemia, and other systemic and nutritional difficulties are treated similarly. However, the prognosis is sufficiently different in these illnesses to warrant separate discussions of their management.

Ulcerative Colitis. It is critical to remember during all stages of UC treatment that this disease is completely curable with colectomy. However, most patients prefer to have drug therapy and consider colectomy a last resort or a way of preventing malignancy.

No single drug is curative. Sulfasalazine, related derivatives of pyridine–acetylsalicylic acid, antibacterial compounds, corticosteroids, and symptom-controlling medications such as antispasmodics and sedatives continue to be the drugs of choice. In severe cases, immunosuppressants, such as azathioprine, 6-mercaptopurine, and cyclosporine, are used under very tight control.

Mild to moderate acute colitis often responds to supportive measures supplemented by 3 to 4 gm/day of sulfasalazine alone. Sulfasalazine is hydrolyzed by bacteria in the colon to yield sulfapyridine and 5-aminosalicylate (5-ASA). The latter is considered to be the agent that leads to improvement in the symptoms and the former to allergic reactions. Newer preparations of 5-ASA that utilize different mechanisms for colonic release will be available soon and do not induce the allergies so commonly seen with preparations having the sulfa moiety attached. If treatment with 5-ASA derivatives is insufficient, corticosteroids are usually added. These are given orally in doses ranging from 20 to 60 mg/day initially, then tapered if possible. Patients who exhibit only left-sided involvement may be managed successfully with corticosteroid enemas. When the disease is in remission, patients are normally continued on sulfasalazine or some other 5-ASA derivative indefinitely to minimize recurrence. Severe UC can degenerate into toxic megacolon, discussed under "Complications." This is a medical emergency requiring immediate hospitalization; in addition, electrolytes should be monitored, and blood replacement, high-dose corticosteroids, broad-spectrum antibiotics, and surgical consultation should be initiated. A patient's failure to respond clinically to treatment within 48 hours may indicate the need for colectomy.

In UC, total colectomy with either a permanent ileostomy or an ileoanal pull-through procedure to restore rectal continence is the surgical treatment of choice. This procedure prevents further episodes of IBD because UC does not involve noncolonic tissues. The indications for elective colectomy generally include the following:

1. Failure of medical management. Patients who have had acute exacerbations that fail to respond to therapy ultimately require colectomy. A subset of this group includes patients who respond well, but therapy requires high-dose steroids that have unacceptable long-term side effects.

2. The risk or presence of colonic carcinoma. Patients may develop dysplastic epithelium that is detected by biopsy. When severe dysplastic changes begin to develop, colectomy is indicated.

The mortality from acute exacerbations of UC is low (<1 per cent). More than 90 per cent of patients respond to standard therapy, but recurrence is the rule. The lifespan of patients with UC is not significantly reduced from normal. When patients die of UC, it is usually due to acute complications such as perforated colon, bleeding, sepsis, or late development of carcinoma of the colon.

Crohn's Disease. Medical management of Crohn's disease is quite similar to that of UC; 5-ASA and corticosteroids are the primary pharmacologic agents used. Crohn's disease is usually not acute unless intestinal obstruction is the cause of the presentation, it generally responds slowly, and remissions are frequently incomplete. 5-ASA derivatives are not as effective in Crohn's disease as they are in UC and are usually reserved for patients who have extensive colonic involvement. Some gastroenterologists believe that using parenteral hyperalimentation to "put the bowel to rest" may also assist in the therapy of Crohn's disease.

Surgical treatment of Crohn's disease is not curative and is avoided whenever possible because the disease frequently recurs near the excision and postoperative adhesions can be extensive. Surgery is usually reserved for resection of fistulas, treatment of abscesses, and relief of obstruction. It is critical to remove as little bowel as possible because these patients may require multiple operations and end up with short bowel syndrome.

Patients with Crohn's disease do not enjoy the favorable prognosis seen in UC because their disease does not respond as well to medical management and surgery is not a curative option. However, these patients have a normal lifespan, and when they die of their disease, it is usually due to sepsis rather than bleeding or cancer.

Complications

Complications associated with IBD have been discussed as the extraintestinal and clinical manifestations of these diseases. One must also be concerned about long-term problems such as growth retardation in children, malnutrition, weakness, lassitude, recurrent pain, and depression. These, of course, are complications associated with any chronic debilitating illness; however, two special complications are discussed in more detail.

Toxic Dilatation of the Colon (Toxic Megacolon). This complication is more typically seen in UC than in Crohn's disease and is characterized by an atonic and distended colon with a very thin wall. These patients are frequently toxic, have an explosive onset of illness, and exhibit tachycardia, fever, and leukocytosis. Diarrhea is generally decreased because of a loss of propulsive activity in the colon. Patients frequently have hypokalemia and hypoalbuminemia. Toxic megacolon may occur spontaneously, but it also has occurred after initiation of opiates and anticholinergics and in preparation for colonoscopic or barium enema examinations. The diagnosis is usually suggested by diffuse dilatation of the colon (>6 cm), particularly the transverse colon. There is an impending danger of perforation until the dilatation is reversed, and medical reversal in less than 48 hours is essential or surgery is indicated.

Carcinoma of the Colon. A general discussion of carcinoma of the colon is found in Chapter 37. There is an increased risk of colon carcinoma in IBD, but more so in UC than Crohn's disease. The incidence of carcinoma in UC relates to two variables: (1) pancolitis, that is, the presence of complete colonic involvement with inflammation, and (2) the duration of active colitis. The incidence of cancer begins to increase significantly after 10 years of active disease. The carcinoma typical of UC patients is somewhat different from colon cancer in the general population: (1) its distribution is more even in the colon; (2) it is frequently multifocal; (3) it is typically discovered at a more advanced stage and therefore has a worse prognosis; (4) it is quite difficult to diagnose because the associated symptoms are masked by the underlying disease; and (5) it occurs on a base of very abnormal mucosa. For these reasons, detailed follow-up protocols exist for patients with chronic pancolitis involving repeated colonoscopy and screening biopsies. The biopsies are used to guide the timing of preventive colectomy.

ISCHEMIC COLITIS

In elderly patients ischemic injury to the colon may mimic IBD. Ischemic injury, whether acute or chronic, is usually caused by progressive atherosclerosis. It may also occur from vascular injury due to an aneurysmal dissection, surgery, congestive heart failure, or vasculitis, or from hypercoagulable states. The ischemia occurs most commonly in "watershed areas" between distributions of major vessels and is usually caused by low-perfusion states rather than complete vascular occlusion. Because of extensive collateral supply, the rectum is almost always spared. Presentation may be chronic or acute or any combination of the two.

Acute Ischemic Colitis. This usually presents with sudden local abdominal pain associated with tenderness and rectal bleeding. These symptoms may be accompanied by hypotension, tachycardia, fever, and, in severe cases, peritoneal irritation. Colonoscopy may reveal a normal pericolonic mucosa but more typically shows multiple ulcerations and/or submucosal hemorrhage. Barium enema is somewhat dangerous during the acute period but exhibits classic findings of narrowing and "thumbprinting" subsequently. In the acute phase, ischemic colitis may appear very much like IBD or diverticulitis. The symptoms from acute ischemic episodes involving the colon are generally self-limited and resolve within several weeks. Angiography is rarely needed, and surgery is usually reserved for patients with frank infarction or perforation. After patients recover from the acute episode, they may remain symptom-free for life or they may develop chronic symptoms.

Subacute or Chronic Ischemic Colitis. This is characterized by diarrhea and long periods of mild to moderate abdominal pain that is vague in character and may be accompanied by fear of eating, weight loss, or significant bleeding. Chronic ischemic colitis may resemble IBD clinically as well as endoscopically. Fibrosis frequently develops in the region of ischemic injury, leading to narrowing of the colon and occasionally strictures requiring surgical revision. Revascularization is usually not indicated.

DIVERTICULITIS

Colonic diverticula are saccules of mucosa covered by serosa but do not include the muscular layer. They develop commonly in later life, particularly in Western societies, and occur at the site of arterioles or penetrations of the muscular wall. The formation of diverticula is believed to be caused by any condition that chronically increases local intraluminal pressures, such as low-fiber diets. The majority of diverticula are located in the sigmoid colon and produce no symptoms. They may become clinically important if they bleed or become infected. The vessels in or around diverticula may produce arterial bleeding that must be differentiated from other causes such as angiodysplasia or carcinoma. The differential diagnosis of lower GI bleeding is discussed in Chapter 32B. Inflammatory diverticulitis is a region of localized infection, but may lead to microabscess formation. Occasionally large abscesses involve an adjacent organ. Clinically, acute diverticulitis presents similarly to appendicitis except that symptoms are localized to the left lower quadrant. The left lower quadrant pain is often associated with localized tenderness, leukocytosis, fever, and occasionally a palpable inflammatory mass. Bleeding from the inflamed region is rare. A tender mass is occasionally detectable by rectal examination but is more typically seen on sigmoidoscopy as a narrow lumen and inflamed mucosa. During the acute phase, barium enema should be considered a hazardous procedure. Diverticulitis is managed by withholding solid food and treating with broad-spectrum antibiotics and intravenous fluids. Surgical intervention is usually not required but may be necessary when perforation, fistulas, or large abscesses complicate the presentation. Many physicians recommend diets high in indigestible fiber to promote large-volume daily bowel movements to prevent the development of diverticulosis.

REFERENCES

Jewell DP: Ulcerative colitis. In Sleisenger MH, Fordtran JS (eds): Gastrointestinal Disease: Pathophysiology, Diagnosis, and Management. 5th ed. Philadelphia, WB Saunders Co, 1993, pp 1305–1330.

Danzi JT: Extraintestinal manifestations of idiopathic inflammatory bowel diseases. Arch Intern Med 148:297, 1988.

Kornbluth A, Salomon P, Sachar DB: Crohn's disease. In Sleisenger MH, Fordtran JS (eds): Gastrointestinal Disease: Pathophysiology, Diagnosis, and Management. 5th ed. Philadelphia, WB Saunders Co, 1993, p 1270–1304.

Brandt LJ, Boley SJ: Ischemic and vascular lesions of the bowel. In Sleisenger MH, Fordtran JS (eds): Gastrointestinal Disease: Pathophysiology, Diagnosis, and Management. 5th ed. Philadelphia, WB Saunders Co, 1993, p 1927–1961.

Hanauer SB: Inflammatory bowel disease. In Wyngaarden JB, Smith LH Jr, Bennett JC (eds): Cecil Textbook of Medicine. 19th ed. Philadelphia, WB Saunders Co, 1992, p 699.

Kirsner JB, Shorter RG: Inflammatory Bowel Disease. 3rd ed. Philadelphia, Lea & Febiger, 1988.

37 NEOPLASMS OF THE GASTROINTESTINAL TRACT

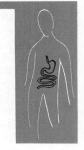

Neoplasms of the gastrointestinal (GI) tract continue to be the most common malignant tumors. The more frequent neoplasms—those of the esophagus, stomach, and colon—are discussed in this chapter. Neoplasms of the pancreas and liver are discussed in Chapters 38 and 44, respectively.

CARCINOMA OF THE ESOPHAGUS

More than 95 per cent of esophageal neoplasms are squamous cell in origin. Adenocarcinomas, which arise from tumors at the gastroesophageal junction, comprise approximately 5 per cent. Benign neoplasms are unusual, with leiomyomas being the most frequent.

Incidence. The incidence of esophageal carcinoma has dropped in the last two decades to approximately 5 per 100,000. Blacks, particularly men, are four to five times more commonly affected than whites, whereas white females have the lowest incidence. Dramatic regional differences exist in the world; in certain areas of China, the incidence exceeds 1 per 1000 people.

Etiology and Pathogenesis. The cause of squamous cell esophageal carcinoma is unknown, although many associations exist. Environmental factors are most commonly implicated, particularly in those areas of the world having the highest incidence. In the United States, tobacco and alcohol abuse are considered primary risk factors not only for esophageal cancer, but for squamous cell tumors of the head and neck as well. Esophageal injury due to lye ingestion, radiation, or long-term stasis (achalasia) also increases the incidence. Adenocarcinoma is strongly identified with Barrett's epithelium, a metaplasia of the distal esophagus in which gastric mucosa and intestinal epithelium appear in association with long-term gastroesophageal reflux. The incidence of esophageal carcinoma is also increased in patients with the rare inherited disorder associated with thickened skin of the palms and soles (tylosis).

Clinical Manifestations. Dysphagia is the most frequent and important symptom of esophageal carcinoma. Initially, patients report difficulty in swallowing solid foods, which progresses to difficulty in swallowing liquids; anorexia and weight loss commonly accompany dysphagia. With complete obstruction, regurgitation and aspiration with secondary pneumonia may result. Pneumonia may also occur with a tracheoesophageal fistula. Less common manifestations are related primarily to the involvement of adjacent structures in the mediastinum and include substernal pain and hoarseness due to impingement on the recurrent laryngeal nerve. GI bleeding is often occult in nature, although it may be massive and fatal when the tumor erodes the aorta. Clubbing of the nails and, rarely, paraneoplastic endocrine abnormalities (hypercalcemia, Cushing's syndrome) have been noted.

Complications. Esophageal cancer tends to be a "silent" malignancy until late in the course owing to the distensibility of the esophagus; therefore, the tumor has to be large before dysphagia results. Local complications are most often related to mediastinal extension or esophageal narrowing. Because the esophagus has no serosal lining, the tumor tends to metastasize early to regional lymph nodes, the liver, and the lungs.

Diagnosis. In patients over age 40 and those with risk factors for esophageal carcinoma, new-onset dysphagia should prompt evaluation for an esophageal tumor. A double-contrast barium study of the esophagus usually shows an abnormality if carcinoma is present. Endoscopy may also be an appropriate initial test to exclude carcinoma and may be required for biopsy of any suspicious lesions. Mucosal biopsy and cytology of an identified esophageal lesion has a high degree of specificity.

Computed tomography (CT) scanning of the chest is often performed in the staging evaluation to exclude involvement of adjacent structures (bronchus, aorta), as well as to detect mediastinal lymphadenopathy or lung or liver metastases. In some centers endoscopic ultrasonography plays a useful role in detecting local extent of the tumor and thus its resectability.

Treatment and Prognosis. Because early warning signs or symptoms may be absent, esophageal cancer is often incurable at the time of diagnosis. Although approximately 10 to 50 per cent of patients undergo surgical resection for its palliative effects, surgical resection may cure the disease in 5 to 10 per cent of cases. However, the operative mortality for curative resection may approach 15 per cent. In the patient who is not an operative candidate, high-dose radiation therapy may provide palliation. Other palliative therapies include placement of a plastic tube (prosthesis) across the obstruction, coagulation of the tumor using either laser or thermal probes, or endoscopic dilation.

TABLE 37–1. ADENOCARCINOMA OF THE STOMACH

FACTOR ASSOCIATED WITH	CLINICAL MANIFESTATIONS
Environment—geographic differences	Anorexia, early satiety, weight loss
Diet—? nitrosamines	Dysphagia, vomiting, weakness
Blood group A	Epigastric distress to severe, boring pain
Atrophic gastritis	Anemia, occult blood in stools
Adenomatous polyps (> 2 cm)	Epigastric mass, signs of metastases
Subtotal resection for benign ulcer disease	Rare—Virchow's node, Blumer's shelf, Trousseau's syndrome, acanthosis nigricans

CARCINOMA OF THE STOMACH

Adenocarcinomas comprise more than 90 per cent of the malignant tumors of the stomach. Other less common neoplasms include lymphomas or metastatic disease (melanoma, breast). Benign neoplasms include leiomyomas and adenomas. This chapter focuses on adenocarcinomas.

Incidence. As recently as the 1940s, gastric carcinoma was the most common neoplasm in the United States. There has been an unexplained decrease in incidence, and now gastric adenocarcinoma is the seventh most common neoplasm. There is marked variation in the incidence of gastric cancer throughout the world, with very high rates reported in Japan, parts of South America, and Eastern Europe. When population groups emigrate from areas of high incidence to those of low incidence, the rate drops very slowly over several generations.

Etiology and Pathogenesis. Environmental factors have long been suggested as a cause of gastric carcinoma because of the regional incidence of the disease as well as the changes that occur in migrating populations. A variety of associations have been described (Table 37–1). Gastric cancer is more common in men, the elderly, blacks as compared with whites, those with a poor socioeconomic status, and those with a positive family history. Gastric mucosal abnormalities (including atrophic gastritis and adenomatous polyps), pernicious anemia (associated with carcinoid tumors), and the postgastrectomy state also appear to be precancerous conditions. A diet high in salt and nitrates is thought to be a potential environmental factor: ingested nitrates may be converted by bacteria in the upper GI tract (increased in patients with hypochlorhydria or achlorhydria—a frequent occurrence in patients with gastric cancer) to nitrites, which are carcinogenic in animal models. Although many of these factors have been associated with gastric cancer, the fall in incidence over the last several decades cannot be explained by any particular factor.

Clinical Manifestations (Table 37–1). The clinical presentation of gastric carcinoma depends on a variety of factors, including the morphologic characteristics of the tumor (infiltrating versus ulcerating), size of the tumor, presence of gastric outlet obstruction, and metastatic versus nonmetastatic disease. Epigastric abdominal pain is a frequent complaint that may mimic peptic ulcer disease or may be more constant and severe in nature, with food exacerbating the pain. Nausea may occur and vomiting is frequent, especially with gastric outlet obstruction. Anorexia and weight loss are also common. Most tumors originate in the distal stomach; proximal lesions may cause obstruction of the distal esophagus, resulting in dysphagia. Acute or chronic blood loss that results in iron deficiency anemia may also occur. Other less frequent symptoms and signs may be related to distant metastases, direct extension in the abdominal cavity, or a paraneoplastic syndrome. Obstructive jaundice, malignant ascites, or a gastrocolic fistula may result from local spread, whereas Trousseau's syndrome (thrombophlebitis), dermatomyositis, and acanthosis nigricans represent paraneoplastic manifestations. Physical examination can reveal a healthy-appearing patient or one with apparent loss of weight. Abdominal examination may document epigastric tenderness or a mass. With metastatic disease, a Virchow node (left supraclavicular), a Blumer shelf (mass in the perirectal pouch), or a Krukenberg tumor (metastases to the ovaries) may also be found on physical examination.

Diagnosis. An upper GI series is often the first examination performed in the evaluation for gastric carcinoma. Using a double-contrast technique with multiple projections increases the sensitivity and more fully evaluates the entire stomach. The radiographic characteristics of the tumor are variable and depend on its morphologic and pathologic characteristics. For example, gastric carcinoma may present as a large polypoid mass, a benign-appearing gastric ulcer (early gastric carcinoma), or abnormal folds with a thickened, nondistensible wall (linitis plastica). Radiographic characteristics that suggest a malignant gastric ulcer include an irregular ulcer base, an ulcer within a mass, and the appearance of convergent folds. However, the true differentiation between a benign and malignant ulcer can be made conclusively only by biopsy.

Upper endoscopic evaluation may also be appropriate as the initial diagnostic test in selected patients because mucosal abnormalities identified using this technique can be biopsied as well as supplemented by brushings for cytology; together they increase the diagnostic specificity to 95 per cent. Gastric ulcers often have to be followed either radiographically or endoscopically until healing is complete to confirm benignancy; however, even malignant ulcers may rarely heal. No serologic cancer markers are useful diagnostically or for detecting recurrence after surgery.

Treatment and Prognosis. Gastric cancer can be cured only by definitive surgical therapy. Unfortunately, fewer than one third of gastric cancers are resectable for cure at presentation. After the diagnosis is established, staging is performed to determine the presence of local spread or distant metastases. This is usually performed by liver chemistry tests, abdominal imaging studies, most commonly CT, and biopsy of any suspected nodes. Occasionally laparoscopy may be performed. If distant metastases are identified, palliative resec-

tion may be performed to prevent obstruction or further bleeding. For a localized tumor, the resection can be limited to the area of the tumor, which limits morbidity. The 5-year survival for most patients is less than 5 per cent. In contrast, the patient with early gastric cancer, in which tumor has not spread to regional lymph nodes, can often be cured with definitive surgical therapy. Radiation therapy for gastric carcinoma is generally unsatisfactory. A variety of chemotherapeutic regimens have been used with only modest success and no cures. Endoscopic therapies offer few palliative options.

CARCINOMA OF THE COLON

Adenocarcinomas comprise more than 95 per cent of all malignant tumors of the large bowel; the following discussion of colonic carcinoma also includes rectal cancer. Other rare colonic neoplasms, such as carcinoid tumor, leiomyomas, and metastatic diseases to the colon, are not discussed here.

Incidence. The colon and rectum are now the third most common site of carcinoma in men and the second in women. Overall, colorectal cancer is the third most common cause of cancer death. Approximately 150,000 new cases are diagnosed annually, which represents 15 per cent of all malignant tumors. Variations in incidence occur throughout the world such that in more developed regions like the United States, Western Europe, Australia, and New Zealand the frequency is much higher than in South America or Africa. People who emigrate tend to acquire the risk characteristic of their new environment.

Etiology and Pathogenesis. The cause of colon cancer is unknown, although a number of associations have been described. Environmental factors, particularly diet, have been commonly implicated, given noted regional variations and changes in incidence with migration. A diet low in fiber but high in animal fat and protein, perhaps that derived from beef, has been most frequently suggested as important and correlates with the diets of persons throughout the world where the incidence is highest. Excess fats and colonic bacteria have been postulated to interact in some way to produce metabolites such as toxic bile acids. In contrast, a diet high in fiber has been associated with a much lower incidence of the disease. Given these associations, the possible protective effects of various dietary factors, including calcium, selenium, and supplemental bran, await further studies.

A number of important risk factors other than dietary are outlined in Table 37–2. Although colon cancer not associated with familial polyposis has been identified in individuals in their second and third decades of life, the incidence clearly increases above the age of 40 and doubles for each succeeding decade. Disorders associated with in-

TABLE 37–2. RISK FACTORS FOR CARCINOMA OF THE COLON

Increasing age
Inflammatory bowel disease
Personal history of colonic cancer or adenoma
Family history of colon cancer
Familial polyposis syndromes (adenomatous polyps)
History of breast or female genital cancer
Peutz-Jeghers syndrome (hamartomas)
Acromegaly

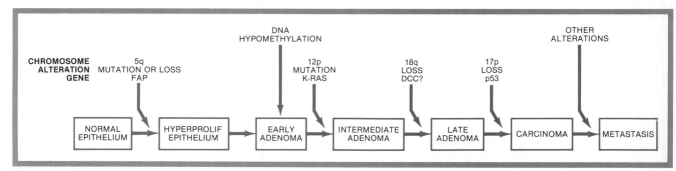

FIGURE 37–1. A genetic model for colorectal tumorigenesis. (Reprinted with permission from Fearon ER, Vogelstein B: A genetic model for colorectal tumorigenesis (review). Cell 61:759–767, 1990. Copyright by Cell Press.)

creased mucosal cell turnover may also lead to an increased risk; inflammatory bowel disease, especially ulcerative colitis (see Chapter 36), and certain familial polyposis syndromes (see below) are examples. A history of previous cancer or adenoma of the colon, colon cancer in one or more first-degree relatives, or the "family cancer syndrome" (multifocal cancers in other organs, especially the female sex organs) increases the risk of colonic carcinoma as well. Thus, hereditary influences may play an important role in some patients. Furthermore, there is evidence that se-

quential activation of several oncogenes may be of key importance in the origin of some colorectal tumors (Fig. 37–1).

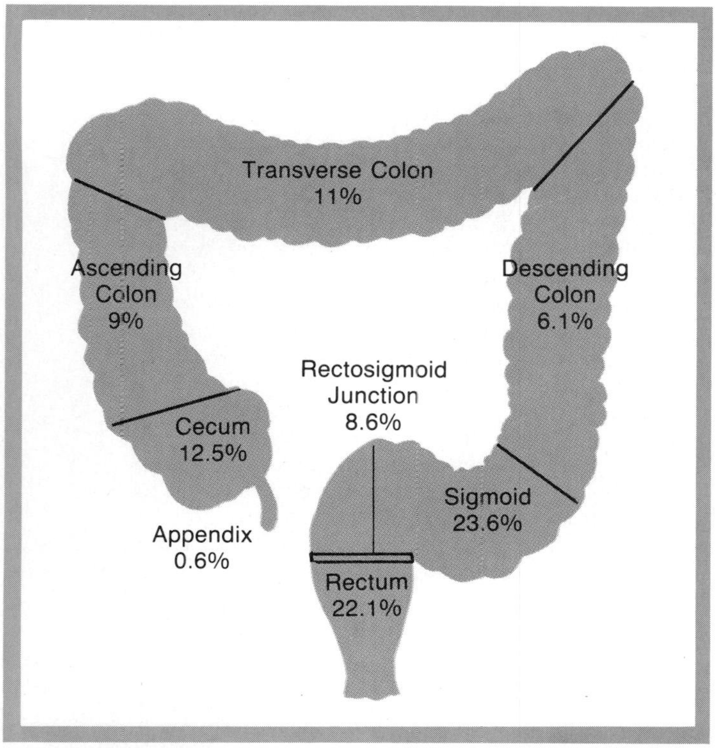

Clinical Manifestations. As with cancer of the esophagus and stomach, colon carcinoma has very few early warning signs. It may be totally asymptomatic and found incidentally during abdominal surgery or at screening sigmoidoscopy. GI blood loss is the most common presenting finding and can be identified as occult blood in the stool, melena, or bright red rectal bleeding, depending on the location of the tumor. Abdominal pain is an uncommon presenting symptom, although it may be a consequence of obstruction (most commonly left-sided tumors) or bowel wall invasion. Alteration of bowel habits is an important but uncommon symptom that usually results from left-sided or distal tumors. Overflow diarrhea may occur when a distal tumor results in severe but incomplete colonic obstruction. Weight loss and anorexia are nonspecific symptoms that may occur in any malignancy, although they usually appear late in the clinical course. Other presenting symptoms and signs include perforation, malignant ascites, and liver metastases with jaundice.

Diagnosis. Carcinoma of the colon should be suspected in any patient over the age of 40 who presents with occult blood in the stool, iron deficiency anemia, overt rectal bleeding, or alteration in bowel habits, especially if associated with abdominal discomfort or any risk factors noted in Table 37–2. Bright red blood from the rectum found on the stool may suggest hemorrhoidal disease, although colon carcinoma must be excluded in the patient over age 40. Initial diagnostic evaluation should begin with digital rectal examination. However, the majority of colorectal tumors cannot be palpated by digital rectal examination, necessitating radiographic or colonoscopic evaluation. Approximately 50 per cent of colorectal tumors can now be identified with the 60-cm flexible sigmoidoscope (Fig. 37–2), although in the elderly tumors tend to be located in the more proximal colon. If a double-contrast barium enema examination is performed, it should be accompanied by a flexible sigmoidoscopic examination because the

FIGURE 37–2. Distribution of large bowel cancer by anatomic segment according to the third national cancer survey (segment unspecified). (Data from Shottenfeld D, Fraumeni J Jr [eds]: Cancer Epidemiology and Prevention. Philadelphia, WB Saunders Co, 1982, pp 703–727.)

barium study tends to be less sensitive in the distal colorectum. Colonoscopy may be the initial diagnostic test used in patients who have a suspicious lesion found on barium enema or in those with persistent symptoms despite a "negative" radiographic examination. Biopsy performed at colonoscopy establishes the diagnosis in almost 100 per cent of cases. Determination of carcinoembryonic antigen (CEA) is not helpful in establishing the diagnosis of colon cancer but is useful in follow-up after surgery to detect recurrence.

The differential diagnosis of colon carcinoma depends on particular clinical symptoms and signs, including diverticulitis, ischemic colitis, colonic vascular ectasias, inflammatory bowel disease, and benign polyps.

Treatment and Prognosis. The only effective therapy is surgical removal of the tumor and the adjacent colon and mesentery. Colonoscopy and abdominal CT are usually performed preoperatively to exclude synchronous colonic neoplasms and to determine the presence of peritoneal, lung, or liver metastases. The type of surgical procedure used depends on the location of the tumor. Hemicolectomy is performed for right- and left-sided lesions, anterior resection with anastomosis to the rectal stump for sigmoid or upper rectal tumors, and a combined abdominal and perineal resection with a permanent colostomy for distal lesions of the rectum. In the patient who has metastatic disease, surgery still provides the best palliation for obstruction, bleeding, or perforation. Radiation therapy is efficacious for rectal cancer and may be done preoperatively or for painful bony metastasis. Chemotherapy with 5-fluorouracil in combination with levamisole improves survival for patients who have Duke's stage C disease at diagnosis. In addition, isolated hepatic metastases may be resected to improve patients' survival.

The results of surgical treatment for carcinoma of the large bowel are excellent, with acceptable morbidity and mortality even in the elderly patient. As with all GI malignancies, the survival for colon carcinoma depends on the stage of tumor at diagnosis, commonly called the Duke's classification: Duke's A lesions (confined to the bowel wall) have a 5-year survival of over 80 per cent; Duke's B (through the bowel wall) have a 5-year survival of 60 to 80 per cent; Duke's C (through the bowel to the serosa) have approximately 50 per cent even when lymph nodes are involved; Duke's D (metastatic disease) have a 5-year survival of 25 per cent or less. After surgery, routine follow-up includes surveillance colonoscopy or barium radiography to exclude missed synchronous polyps, cancers, or recurrent lesions, as well as measurements of CEA.

Screening and Prevention. The complex process of colonic carcinogenesis evolves over many years. Benign adenomatous polyps as well as early localized carcinomas can be cured either by colonoscopic polypectomy (if technically possible) or surgery. Given the link between adenomatous polyps and cancer, there is now considerable interest in screening populations for colonic polyps and carcinomas with annual testing for fecal occult blood and periodic (every 3 to 5 years) proctosigmoidoscopy beginning at age 40 to 50. If occult blood is found in the stool, radiographic or colonoscopic examination of the entire colon should be performed. It is unclear whether this screening strategy is cost-effective or decreases mortality in the general population, although the tumors found as a result of occult blood testing tend to be at an earlier stage. In contrast, individuals at high risk for developing colon carcinoma, such as those having the familial polyposis syndrome, prior adenomatous colonic polyps or cancer, or longstanding ulcerative colitis involving the entire colon, should be screened periodically with examinations of the entire colon.

POLYPS OF THE GASTROINTESTINAL TRACT

A polyp is defined as an overgrowth of tissue, usually of epithelial cells, that arises from the mucosal surface and extends into the lumen of the GI tract. Polyps can be single or multiple, sporadic or familial, pedunculated (on a stalk) or sessile (flat base), neoplastic or non-neoplastic, benign or malignant. Polyps may occur anywhere throughout the GI tract, although those arising in the colon are of greatest importance, given their prevalence and malignant potential. A simplified classification of colonic polyps is given in Table 37–3. Only neoplastic polyps and benign polyps associated with the distinct polyposis syndromes are discussed here.

Incidence. Adenomatous colonic polyps are very common and increase with age, so that a 50-year-old man has a 20 per cent chance of having an adenomatous colonic polyp and a 70-year-old man has a 30 to 40 per cent chance. Patients with one polyp have a higher frequency of synchronous colonic polyps and a greater potential for developing additional polyps over time.

Etiology and Pathogenesis. The cause of colonic polyps, other than that clearly associated with inherited disorders, is unknown. An indirect body of evidence suggests that most colon carcinomas arise from previously benign adenomatous polyps, usually after a period of at least 5 to 10 years. Therefore, the previously identified risk

TABLE 37–3. POLYPS OF THE COLON

Neoplastic Polyps
    Benign adenomatous polyps (tubular, mixed, or villous)
        random occurrences
        familial—familial polyposis of the colon, Gardner's syndrome
          (Fig. 37–3), Turcot's syndrome, family cancer syndrome
    Malignant polyps—carcinomatous changes, in situ or invasive
Non-neoplastic Polyps
    Inflammatory "pseudopolyps"
    Peutz-Jeghers syndrome—hamartomas
    Mucosal polyps with normal epithelium
    Juvenile polyps

factors associated with colonic carcinoma (see Table 37–2) may also pertain to benign adenomatous polyps.

A very small percentage of benign polyps progress to malignancy, and the causative factors for this transition are unknown. Given the malignant potential of colonic polyps, it is advisable to remove any adenomatous polyp when found. The majority of colonic polyps are small (less than 1 cm in diameter), usually asymptomatic, and found incidentally either at autopsy or on radiographic or colonoscopic examination. When the lesions are larger than 2 cm, GI bleeding may occur (usually occult); only very large polyps, which often contain a focus of carcinoma, cause hematochezia. Abdominal pain or alterations in bowel habits are unusual. Very rarely, villous adenomas may produce watery diarrhea containing high concentrations of potassium, which results in symptomatic hypokalemia.

Diagnosis. The accurate diagnosis of a colonic polyp depends on the size of the polyp and is facilitated by the study performed. Single-contrast barium enemas may not reliably demonstrate polyps smaller than 1 cm in diameter, although double-contrast techniques usually identify lesions greater than 5 mm. Colonoscopy identifies most but not all colonic polyps. Regardless of its size, the type of colonic polyp—benign or malignant—can be determined only by mucosal biopsy.

Treatment. Although only a small proportion of adenomatous colonic polyps undergo malignant transformation, all identified adenomas should usually be removed. Although this can be accomplished readily with the colonoscope, large sessile lesions may require surgical resection. Patients with previous adenomatous polyps are at increased risk for subsequent adenomas, and thus follow-up at regular intervals is indicated.

THE FAMILIAL POLYPOSIS SYNDROMES

The familial polyposis syndromes are rare, dominantly inherited disorders in which multiple polyps can be found throughout the GI tract (Table 37–3).

Familial Polyposis of the Colon. In this rare genetic disorder (1 in 8000 births), adenomatous polyps develop progressively throughout the colon so that by the third decade thousands of adenomatous polyps "carpet" the colon. The patient may be asymptomatic unless bleeding or symp-

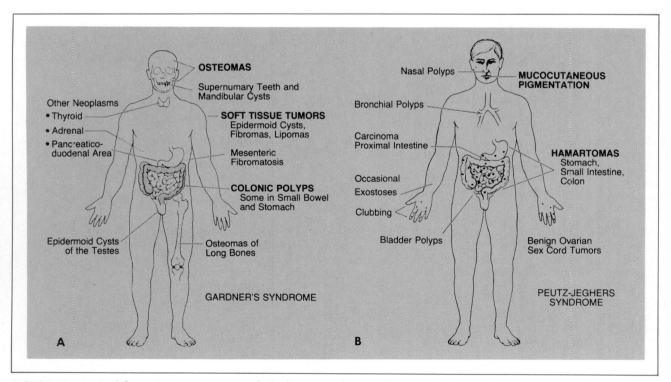

FIGURE 37–3. *A,* Schematic representation of Gardner's syndrome. The triad of colonic polyposis, bone tumors, and soft tissue tumors (heavy print) is the primary feature; other features are indicated in lighter print. *B,* Schematic presentation of the Peutz-Jeghers syndrome. Mucocutaneous pigmentation and benign gastrointestinal polyposis (heavy print) are the primary features of this syndrome. Lighter print shows the secondary features. (From Boland CR, Kim YS: In Sleisenger MH, Fordtran JS [eds]: Gastrointestinal Disease: Pathophysiology, Diagnosis, and Management. 3rd ed. Philadelphia, WB Saunders Co, 1983.)

toms associated with colorectal cancer develop. Colorectal cancer is an inevitable consequence in the natural history of this syndrome, occurring approximately 10 to 15 years after the onset of polyposis. In these patients adenomatous polyps may also occur in the upper GI tract. In the patient with a diagnosis of familial polyposis, elective complete colectomy is required (usually after full growth has been achieved). Given the dominant inheritance pattern, other family members must be screened.

Gardner's Syndrome. In this syndrome resembling familial polyposis coli, extracolonic manifestations of benign soft tissue tumors and osteomas are present (Fig. 37–3). Polyps of the upper GI tract may also occur. As with familial polyposis coli, the colonic polyps have malignant potential and thus total colectomy is indicated.

Peutz-Jeghers Syndrome. In contrast to the polyps found in Gardner's syndrome and familial polyposis coli, these polyps are hamartomas that have no malignant potential themselves but are associated with adenocarcinomas of the small intestine. Characteristic mucocutaneous pigmentation, especially of the buccal mucosa as well as the lips and soles of the feet and dorsum of the hands, is well recognized (see Fig. 37–2). These patients are usually asymptomatic or may present with GI bleeding, abdominal pain, or commonly intussusception with small bowel obstruction requiring urgent surgical intervention.

REFERENCES

Boland CR, Itzkowitz SH, Kim YS: Colonic polyps and the gastrointestinal polyposis syndromes. *In* Sleisenger MH, Fordtran JS (eds): Gastrointestinal Disease: Pathophysiology, Diagnosis, and Management. 4th ed. Philadelphia, WB Saunders Co, 1989, pp 1483–1518.

Boyce HW Jr: Tumors (of the esophagus). *In* Sleisenger MH, Fordtran JS (eds): Gastrointestinal Disease: Pathophysiology, Diagnosis, and Management. 4th Ed. Philadelphia, WB Saunders Co, 1989, pp 619–631.

Bresalier RS, Kim YS: Malignant neoplasms of the large and small intestine. *In* Sleisenger MH, Fordtran JS (eds): Gastrointestinal Disease: Pathophysiology, Diagnosis, and Management. 4th ed. Philadelphia, WB Saunders Co, 1989, pp 1519–1560.

Davis GR: Neoplasms of the stomach. *In* Sleisenger MH, Fordtran JS (eds): Gastrointestinal Disease: Pathophysiology, Diagnosis, and Management. 4th ed. Philadelphia, WB Saunders Co, 1989, pp 745–771.

Levin B: Neoplasms of the large and small intestine. *In* Wyngaarden JB, Smith LH Jr, Bennett JC (eds): Cecil Textbook of Medicine. 19th ed. Philadelphia, WB Saunders Co, 1992, p 713.

Vogelstein B, Fearon ER, Hamilton SR, et al: Genetic alterations during colorectal-tumor development. N Engl J Med 319:525, 1988.

Winawer SJ: Neoplasms of the stomach. *In* Wyngaarden JB, Smith LH Jr, Bennett JC (eds): Cecil Textbook of Medicine. 19th ed. Philadelphia, WB Saunders Co, 1992, p 667.

38 THE PANCREAS

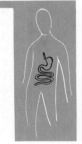

NORMAL STRUCTURE AND FUNCTION

The pancreas is a relatively small (less than 110 gm) but versatile organ containing two specific and seemingly independent components: the endocrine pancreas and the exocrine pancreas. The endocrine pancreas consists of the islets of Langerhans, packets of endocrine cells scattered throughout the pancreas which secrete insulin, glucagon, and other polypeptide hormones. The endocrine pancreas is discussed in other chapters. The cells of the exocrine pancreas cluster into acini that are further grouped into lobules. Acinar cells are drained by ductules that converge into large ducts which terminate in the duct of Wirsung, the main pancreatic duct. Pancreatic juice ultimately drains through the sphincter of Oddi and papilla into the second portion of the duodenum. In addition, the minor accessory duct (duct of Santorini) joins the main pancreatic duct in the head of the gland and runs a separate course through the head of the pancreas, entering the duodenum through the minor ampulla several centimeters cephalad. The minor pancreatic duct remains patent in approximately 70 per cent of people. The head of the pancreas lies within the curvature of the second duodenum, with the body and tail extending retroperitoneally to the hilum of the spleen for a total of 12 to 15 cm (Fig. 38–1). The head of the pancreas is in close anatomic relationship to a number of important structures, including the common bile duct, inferior vena cava, aorta, and origin of the superior mesenteric artery, splenic artery and vein, and right adrenal gland and kidney.

When stimulated, the normal pancreas may secrete a large volume (more than 7 L/day) of a characteristic fluid.

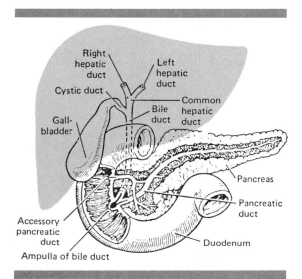

FIGURE 38-1. Connections of the ducts of the gallbladder, liver, and pancreas. (From Bell GH, Emslie-Smith D, Paterson CR: Textbook of Physiology and Biochemistry. 9th ed. Edinburgh, Churchill Livingstone, 1976; with permission.)

Electrolyte Composition. Pancreatic juice is isotonic with extracellular fluid at all rates of secretion. The concentrations of the two principal anions, namely HCO_3^- and chloride, vary reciprocally, totaling about 150 mEq/L. The centroacinar and ductular cells add bicarbonate to the chloride-rich juice from the acini, and at maximal flow rates the concentration of HCO_3^- approaches 130 mEq/L, resulting in an alkaline pancreatic juice. This bicarbonate-rich fluid neutralizes hydrochloric acid entering the second duodenum from the stomach and raises the intraluminal pH to levels at which the pancreatic enzymes become catalytically active (pH > 3.5-4.0).

Protein Content. Pancreatic juice is rich in proteins and is composed primarily of digestive enzymes and proenzymes (inactive until converted into the active form in the small intestine), which are secreted by the acinar cells. Enzymes released in an active form include lipase, amylase, and ribonuclease, whereas the inactive forms include proteases and phospholipase. Inactive enzymes secreted into the duodenum are activated in a cascade fashion: enterokinase converts trypsinogen to trypsin; trypsin then activates all other proenzymes. Colipase (which enhances the activity of lipase) and trypsin inhibitors are also secreted by the pancreas.

Control of Secretion. Pancreatic enzyme secretion is stimulated by a number of factors. Most secretion occurs in the postprandial state in response to one or more stimuli:

1. Hormones—Cholecystokinin (CCK), which stimulates a fluid rich in protein (enzymes), and secretin, which stimulates a bicarbonate-rich fluid, are the two most important stimulators. Both are released from cells of the proximal intestine. CCK may also potentiate the action of secretin.

2. Vagal cholinergic stimulation—Vagal stimulation is in part responsible for basal secretion. Vagal stimulation also enhances enzyme secretion as well as the response to CCK.

3. Feedback inhibition—More recent human studies have documented a feedback loop whereby intraduodenal protease activity (i.e., trypsin) suppresses circulating CCK levels. This may be important in patients with chronic pancreatitis, in whom continued stimulation (due to loss of intraduodenal protease activity) may cause abdominal pain.

Studies of Pancreatic Structure and Function

Until the development of ultrasonography (US) and computed tomography (CT), the pancreas was a relatively "invisible" organ. Now the pancreas can be examined invasively with endoscopic retrograde cholangiopancreatography (ERCP) and noninvasively with US and CT (Fig. 38-2). Pancreatic stones can be removed, pancreatic pseudocysts can be drained, and pancreatic ductal strictures can be stented nonsurgically at the time of ERCP. Percutaneous biopsy as well as drainage of infected cysts can also be accomplished using US and CT. Magnetic resonance imaging (MRI) may be a useful diagnostic tool in the future.

Pancreatic enzymes can be measured in the blood or in the gastrointestinal (GI) fluid. Acute injury to the pancreatic acini results in leakage of the enzyme amylase into the blood, which is measured clinically as an increase in the serum amylase. Approximately two thirds of normal serum amylase (25 to 125 U/L) originates from the salivary glands. In addition to amylase, lipase and trypsinogen are also released into the bloodstream

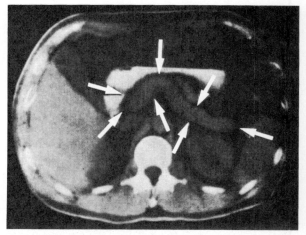

FIGURE 38-2. Normal pancreas demonstrated by computed tomography. (Courtesy of Dr. Eugene P. DiMagno, Mayo Medical School, Rochester, Minnesota.) (Reprinted from Grendell JH: The pancreas. In Smith LH Jr, Thier SO [eds]: Pathophysiology: The Biological Principles of Disease. 2nd ed. Philadelphia, WB Saunders Co, 1985, p 1225.)

with pancreatic injury. Pancreatic secretion can be estimated by aspirating duodenal contents through a tube following stimulation with secretin, secretin-CCK, or a test meal, as summarized in Table 38–1. These tests are cumbersome and are performed only at specialized centers. The bentiromide test, which measures the intestinal hydrolysis of a synthetic peptide by pancreatic chymotrypsin, is described in Chapter 32C on malabsorption. This widely available test is specific but relatively insensitive. These quantitative studies of secretion are performed to determine the presence or absence of pancreatic exocrine insufficiency.

ACUTE PANCREATITIS

Definition. Acute pancreatitis is an inflammatory disorder of the pancreas associated with edema, various amounts of autodigestion, necrosis, and, in some cases, hemorrhage. Clinically, it is defined by a typical symptom complex associated with an elevated serum amylase level. Pathophysiologically, it is a single entity with varying etiologies, degrees of severity, and the potential to progress to chronic pancreatitis.

Etiology and Pathogenesis. The risk factors associated with acute pancreatitis are listed in Table 38–2. In the United States, the two most common causes of the disease are alcoholism and common bile duct stone disease. Acute pancreatitis is thought to result from inappropriate intrapancreatic activation of proteases, which causes autodigestion of the gland (Fig. 38–3). How this occurs and how these diverse causes culminate in a common end-point—namely, pancreatic inflammatory disease—is unknown. Postulated mechanisms of alcohol-induced pancreatitis include physiochemical alterations of protein resulting in plugs that block the small pancreatic ductules and free radical mechanisms. Biliary pancreatitis occurs when a stone passes through the ampulla of Vater, causing an intermittent obstruction. However, the precise mechanisms causing biliary pancreatitis are not fully understood; simply ligating the pancreatic duct or diverting bile through the pancreas does not typically result in pancreatitis. Further episodes may be prevented by removing the risk factors associated with this disorder.

Clinical Manifestations. The cardinal symptom of acute pancreatitis is abdominal pain that is usually constant, moderate to severe although occasionally mild, and located in the epigastrium, frequently radiating to the back. The pain may be relieved by leaning forward. Nausea and vomiting are prominent associated symptoms. On examination, the abdomen is usually tender but without signs of peritoneal irritation. In severe cases, physical findings may include peritoneal signs, ileus, high fever, confusion, and tachycardia with impending hypovolemic shock. Uncommon manifestations resulting from the peripancreatic inflammatory processes include (1) left-sided pleural effusion; (2) discoloration of the flanks (Grey

TABLE 38–1. RANGE OF NORMAL RESPONSES TO SECRETORY TESTS OF THE PANCREAS

Secretin test*
  Volume (ml/80 min): 117–392
  HCO_3^- concentration (mEq/L): 88–137
  HCO_3^- output (mEq/80 min): 16–33
  Amylase output (units/80 min): 439–1921
Secretin + CCK*
  Volume (ml/80 min): 111–503
  HCO_3^- concentration (mEq/L): 88–144
  HCO_3^- output (mEq/80 min): 10–86
  Amylase output (units/80 min): 441–4038
Lundh test
  Mean tryptic activity (IU/L): 61
Bentiromide test
  Excretion of arylamine in urine >57% in 6 hours of that administered in the test dose of the synthetic peptide

*Modified from Dreiling DA, Janowitz HD, Perner CV: Pancreatic Inflammatory Disease. A Physiologic Approach. New York. Hoeber Medical Division, Harper & Row, Publishers. 1964; with permission.

Turner's sign) or around the umbilicus (Cullen's sign) in hemorrhagic pancreatitis; (3) ascites; (4) jaundice from impingement on the common bile duct; and (5) epigastric mass from a pseudocyst. Those resulting from the systemic effects of pancreatic enzymes released into the bloodstream include (1) respiratory distress syndrome; (2) renal failure; and (3) subcutaneous fat necrosis.

Diagnosis. Acute pancreatitis should be considered in any patient having an acute onset of severe continuous epigastric pain, especially when it is associated with any of the known risk factors (Table 38–2). In the patient with moderately severe abdominal pain, the differential diagnosis includes a perforated viscus (especially peptic ulcer disease), acute cholecystitis, acute bowel infarction, and a variety of other causes of the "acute abdomen."

The gold standard for diagnosis is an elevation of the serum amylase. However, the serum amy-

TABLE 38–2. CONDITIONS ASSOCIATED WITH ACUTE PANCREATITIS

* Ethanol abuse
  Cholelithiasis
* Abdominal trauma
  Abdominal surgery
  Hypercalcemia
  Hyperlipidemia
  Drugs—anticonvulsant (valproic acid), antibiotics (sulfonamides, tetracycline), antimetabolite (6-mercaptopurine), diuretics (hydrochlorothiazide, furosemide)
  Viral infections—mumps, coxsackie, hepatitis, others
  Scorpion bite
  Carcinoma of the pancreas
* Pancreas divisum
  Peptic ulcer with posterior penetration
* Hereditary (familial) pancreatitis
  Endoscopic retrograde cholangiopancreatography (ERCP)
  Hypoperfusion (vasculitis)

*Associated with chronic pancreatitis.

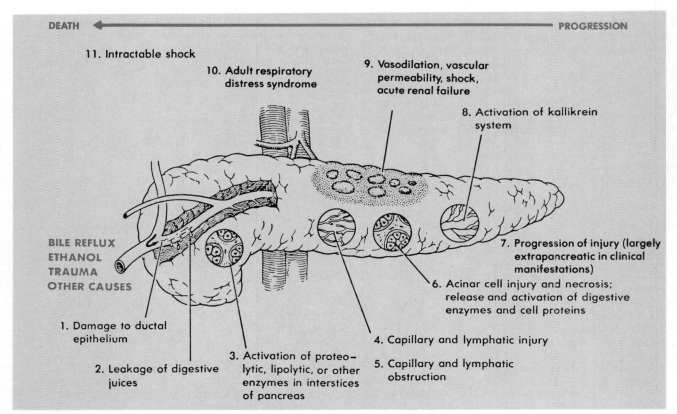

DEATH ←————————————————————————————————————→ PROGRESSION

11. Intractable shock

10. Adult respiratory distress syndrome

9. Vasodilation, vascular permeability, shock, acute renal failure

8. Activation of kallikrein system

BILE REFLUX
ETHANOL
TRAUMA
OTHER CAUSES

7. Progression of injury (largely extrapancreatic in clinical manifestations)

6. Acinar cell injury and necrosis; release and activation of digestive enzymes and cell proteins

1. Damage to ductal epithelium

2. Leakage of digestive juices

3. Activation of proteolytic, lipolytic, or other enzymes in interstices of pancreas

4. Capillary and lymphatic injury

5. Capillary and lymphatic obstruction

FIGURE 38–3. The pathophysiology of acute pancreatitis is not fully understood, but, as the schematic above implies, a cascade of events seems likely, beginning with the release of toxic substances into the parenchyma and ending with shock and death. Damage to the ductal epithelium or acinar cell injury may result from bile reflux, increased intraductal pressure, alcohol, or trauma. (Modified from Grendell JH: The pancreas. *In* Smith LH Jr, Thier SO [eds]: Pathophysiology: The Biological Principles of Disease. 2nd ed. Philadelphia, WB Saunders Co, 1985, p 1228.)

lase may be normal in up to one third of patients having alcoholic pancreatitis and mildly elevated in those having abdominal pain as a consequence of another process (Table 38–3). Therefore, CT studies may be needed to document an enlarged pancreas to confirm the diagnosis. In acute pancreatitis, the serum amylase level usually rises rapidly, as does the serum lipase, and may remain elevated for 3 to 5 days, but its absolute level of elevation does not correlate with severity. The serum lipase may occasionally be elevated even after the serum amylase has returned to normal.

Although urinary clearance of amylase rises with an attack of acute pancreatitis, measurements of this parameter yield little diagnostic information, in contrast to that obtained by measuring the serum lipase alone. In fact, measuring the urinary clearance of amylase is more helpful in the diagnosis of macroamylasemia. Other laboratory abnormalities may include hyperglycemia, hypocalcemia, and leukocytosis. Concomitant elevations of the transaminases, alkaline phosphatase, and bilirubin, which may be both striking and transient, suggest gallstone disease.

Treatment and Prognosis. Because the pathogenesis of pancreatitis is not completely understood, no specific therapy exists that can abort the inflammatory cascade. Treatment remains largely supportive: (1) careful monitoring of volume status because large volumes of fluid may be lost in the retroperitoneum from the "chemical burn"; (2) pain relief, preferably using meperidine; (3) nasogastric suction, which "puts the pancreas at rest"; this is useful primarily in the patient having associated nausea and vomiting or a severe attack; and (4) treatment of complications. Other measures

TABLE 38–3. CAUSES OF HYPERAMYLASEMIA OTHER THAN ACUTE PANCREATITIS

PANCREATIC AMYLASE	NONPANCREATIC AMYLASE
Pancreatic pseudocyst	Salivary adenitis
Gastric, duodenal, small bowel perforation	Diabetic ketoacidosis
Mesenteric infarction	Lactic acidosis
Opiate administration	Renal insufficiency
Following ERCP	Ectopic pregnancy (ruptured)
	Postoperative state

such as empiric antibiotics, H₂-blocker therapy, and glucagon therapy are without proven benefit.

The patient's prognosis may be estimated at the time of admission and at 48 hours by using the Ranson criteria (Table 38–4). A patient having fewer than three criteria on admission has a mortality risk of less than 1 per cent; 40 per cent if five or six signs are positive; and 100 per cent if seven or more signs are positive. *In general, however, the mortality rate of acute pancreatitis is approximately 10 per cent, with approximately 90 per cent recovery within the first 2 weeks.* In the early phases of the disease hemodynamic instability, pulmonary compromise, or renal failure result in death, whereas infection is the most common late complication causing death.

Complications. The local and systemic complications of acute pancreatitis are listed in Table 38–5. A phlegmon is an inflammatory pancreatic mass that usually occurs with a severe attack and subsides spontaneously. A pseudocyst is a liquefied collection of necrotic debris and pancreatic enzymes that is surrounded by either a rim of pancreatic tissue or some adjacent tissues; it contains no true epithelial lining. The spontaneous disappearance of a pseudocyst depends on a number of factors including, most importantly, the size of the cyst and whether it occurred in the setting of acute or chronic pancreatitis. The complications of a pseudocyst include infection, bleeding, and rupture into the peritoneum. A pancreatic abscess is a localized infection of the pancreas that usually occurs late in the course of a severe attack and may result in death unless surgical debridement is performed. Infection of necrotic tissue, termed infected pancreatic necrosis, may also occur early in the course of pancreatitis. Early diagnosis and appropriate management of these infectious complications are important for improving the survival of patients with severe pancreatitis.

CHRONIC PANCREATITIS

Definition. Chronic pancreatitis represents a slowly progressive destruction of the pancreatic acini with varying amounts of inflammation, fibrosis, and dilation and distortion of the pancreatic ducts. Chronic relapsing pancreatitis is defined as superimposed acute attacks that occur in the setting of chronic pancreatitis. Varying degrees of pancreatic destruction and exocrine/endocrine insufficiency result.

Etiology and Pathogenesis. Many of the same conditions listed in Table 38–2 are associated with chronic pancreatitis. In general, biliary tract disease is not associated with chronic pancreatitis. In the United States, the most common cause of chronic pancreatitis is alcoholism in adults and cystic fibrosis in children. In developing countries, protein-calorie malnutrition is the main cause. However, in some cases of chronic pancreatitis the etiology is unknown; the pathophysiologic mechanisms underlying the persistent inflammation and destruction of the gland are poorly understood.

TABLE 38–4. SIGNS USED TO ASSESS SEVERITY OF ACUTE PANCREATITIS

At Time of Admission or Diagnosis
Age > 55 yr
White blood cell count > 16,000/mm³
Blood glucose > 200 mg/dl
LDH > 2× normal
SGOT > 6× normal
During Initial 48 Hours
Decrease in hematocrit > 10%
Serum calcium < 8 mg/dl
Increase in blood urea nitrogen > 5 mg/dl
Arterial Po₂ < 60 mm/Hg
Base deficit > 4 mEq/L
Estimated fluid sequestration > 6000 ml

Modified from Ranson JH, Rifkind KM, Turner JW: Prognostic signs and nonoperative peritoneal lavage in acute pancreatitis. Surg Gynecol Obstet 43:209–219, 1976. By permission of Surgery, Gynecology and Obstetrics.

Clinical Manifestations. The most important symptoms and signs of chronic pancreatitis are listed in Table 38–6. In general, moderate to severe intractable abdominal pain is the most frequent finding, although the pain may be mild or

TABLE 38–5. COMPLICATIONS OF ACUTE PANCREATITIS

LOCAL	SYSTEMIC
Pancreatic	**Cardiovascular**
Phlegmon	Hypotension and shock
Pancreatic fluid collection and pseudocyst complicated by bleeding, infection, rupture, pain, or weight loss	Electrocardiographic changes
	Pericardial effusion and tamponade
Pancreatic abscess and infected necrosis	**Pulmonary**
Nonpancreatic	Hypoxia
Pancreatic ascites or pleural effusion	Atelectasis, pneumonia
	Pleural effusion
Bile duct obstruction	Adult respiratory distress syndrome (ARDS)
Colonic obstruction or stricture	Respiratory failure
	Metabolic
	Hypocalcemia
	Hyperglycemia
	Hypertriglyceridemia
	Metabolic acidosis
	Renal
	Oliguria
	Azotemia
	Acute tubular necrosis
	Renal artery or vein thrombosis
	Hematologic/coagulation
	Vascular thrombosis
	Disseminated intravascular coagulation (DIC)
	Gastrointestinal bleeding
	Other
	Fat necrosis
	Encephalopathy
	Sudden blindness

Adapted from Formark CE, Grendell JH: Complications of pancreatitis. Semin Gastrointest Dis 2:166, 1991; with permission.

TABLE 38–6. SYMPTOMS AND SIGNS OF CHRONIC PANCREATITIS

Abdominal pain	Jaundice
Weight loss	Palpable pseudocyst
Diabetes mellitus	Pancreatic ascites
Steatorrhea	Gastrointestinal bleeding

even absent in some patients or episodic in relapsing pancreatitis. The pain may persist for a number of years before other manifestations such as pancreatic calcifications, diabetes, or malabsorption appear. Rarely, these later signs may be the initial manifestation in the absence of abdominal pain. The pain may be located primarily in the back or may radiate to the back, as in acute pancreatitis. Weight loss may result from anorexia or associated malabsorption (steatorrhea and azotorrhea).

Given the location of the pancreas and its adjacent structures, progressive inflammatory disease may result in encasement of the common bile duct with fibrosis leading to obstructive jaundice. GI bleeding may result from splenic vein thrombosis with formation of gastric varices and subsequent hemorrhage or a pseudoaneurysm of a large artery in the peripancreatic area, leading to massive hemorrhage. Abdominal pain and an associated abdominal mass may be present with a pseudocyst. When there is greater than 90 per cent destruction of the gland, malabsorption and endocrine insufficiency with diabetes mellitus result.

Diagnosis. The diagnosis of chronic pancreatitis is usually considered in the patient with chronic abdominal pain and an associated risk factor for chronic pancreatitis combined with pancreatic calcifications, exocrine insufficiency (malabsorption), and diabetes mellitus. However, the spectrum of presentations is broad; some patients present with diabetes and others are found incidentally to have pancreatic calcification in the absence of any specific symptoms or signs. In the patient with abdominal pain and weight loss, the differential diagnosis includes abdominal malignancies, especially carcinoma of the pancreas, stomach, or colon. Other causes of persistent epigastric abdominal pain include peptic ulcer disease, mesenteric ischemic disease, and even functional abdominal complaints when the pain is mild.

In contrast to acute pancreatitis, chronic pancreatitis does not usually produce an elevated serum amylase level unless associated with a distinct attack. Thus, the diagnosis is often established by the clinical presentation in combination with imaging studies of the pancreas. Imaging studies may demonstrate (1) pancreatic calcification by plain abdominal radiography, US, or CT; (2) dilated pancreatic ducts by US or CT but best

shown by ERCP; and (3) normal pancreatic ductal features by ERCP. In this setting, diagnosis is established only by pancreatic stimulation testing.

Malabsorption can be documented by fecal analysis for fat and its pancreatic origin deduced by the tests described in Chapter 32C. Pancreatic stimulation tests demonstrate reduction in pancreatic juice volume, bicarbonate content, amylase output, and tryptic activity.

Treatment and Prognosis. The treatment of chronic pancreatitis is directed toward prevention of further pancreatic injury, pain relief, and replacement of lost endocrine/exocrine function. Further injury to the pancreas may be prevented if any of the factors in Table 38–2 can be reversed, especially alcohol abuse, although changing this pattern yields inconsistent results. Despite abstinence from alcohol, most cases of acute alcoholic pancreatitis result in chronic pancreatitis. The replacement of lost exocrine function is described in Chapter 32C on malabsorption. Treatment of chronic abdominal pain in the setting of chronic pancreatitis is often frustrating and represents a difficult challenge. General approaches include the following:

1. Analgesics — Attempts should be made to begin with nonaddictive analgesics before narcotics are administered. However, severe pain may require narcotics that carry the potential for addiction.

2. "Putting the pancreas at rest" — Large doses of supplemental pancreatic enzymes may reduce abdominal pain. This has been best established in patients with idiopathic pancreatitis, but it also works occasionally in those with alcoholic chronic pancreatitis. Avoidance of alcohol may prevent further exacerbations of abdominal pain and acute episodes of pancreatitis.

3. Surgical therapy — Intractable pain may require surgical drainage of a presumed obstruction or of an associated pseudocyst, although the long-term results are variable. Partial resection of the gland itself should be based on the location of the ductal changes as assessed by ERCP.

Although the mechanism is unclear, the pain of chronic pancreatitis decreases over time in some patients. When this situation occurs, endocrine and exocrine insufficiencies become the most important management problems.

Complications. The complications associated with chronic pancreatitis are listed in Table 38–7. In contrast to those occurring in acute pancreatitis, these complications are related primarily to destruction of the gland itself and associated peripancreatic diseases rather than to systemic processes.

TABLE 38–7. COMPLICATIONS OF CHRONIC PANCREATITIS

Pseudocyst formation	Splenic vein thrombosis
Pancreatic ascites	Exocrine insufficiency
Common bile duct obstruction	Peptic ulcer
Diabetes mellitus	

Definition. Carcinoma of the pancreas is an almost uniformly fatal malignancy. More than 90 per cent of these tumors are adenocarcinomas arising from the ductal cells. Less common tumors include islet cell tumors, epidermoid tumors, and adenocarcinomas arising from the acinar cells. Carcinoma of the pancreas is now the fourth most common malignant tumor (after tumors of the lung, colon, and breast), accounting for approximately 5 per cent of cancer deaths in the United States.

Etiology and Pathogenesis. The cause of pancreatic carcinoma is unknown. Epidemiologic studies have suggested the following risk factors: advanced age, smoking, diabetes mellitus, some forms of chronic pancreatitis, and certain dietary habits such as increased consumption of animal fat and protein.

Clinical Manifestations. The clinical manifestations tend to be nonspecific and often insidious in nature such that the malignancy has reached an advanced stage by the time of diagnosis. The most common presenting symptoms include epigastric abdominal pain and weight loss. The pain is usually less severe than in acute pancreatitis, is constant, and may radiate to the back. Because the most common location for pancreatic carcinoma is in the head of the gland, obstructive jaundice is a common presenting symptom, often associated with a large palpable gallbladder (Courvoisier's sign). Anorexia, nausea, and vomiting may occur, especially when the tumor obstructs the stomach or duodenum. Emotional disturbances, most commonly depression, have been recognized at the time of diagnosis. Other less common presenting symptoms and signs include migratory thrombophlebitis (Trousseau's sign), acute pancreatitis, diabetes mellitus, paraneoplastic endocrine syndromes (Cushing's syndrome, hypercalcemia), GI bleeding resulting from splenic vein thrombosis or involvement of the stomach, and a palpable ab-

dominal mass. Rarely, with adenocarcinoma, fat necrosis may produce painful subcutaneous nodules or bone pain from intramedullary involvement.

Diagnosis. Pancreatic carcinoma should always be considered in the elderly patient who presents with abdominal pain, weight loss, depression associated with weight loss, the sudden onset of diabetes mellitus or acute pancreatitis without other known risk factors, or obstructive jaundice. If the tumor is located in the head of the gland, laboratory studies may document obstructive jaundice. Tumor markers are rarely helpful, although CA19-9 holds promise.

The diagnosis is often suggested clinically, but either invasive or noninvasive imaging studies are necessary to establish the diagnosis. When an abdominal mass is identified by CT, fine-needle aspiration biopsy may be performed. Figure 38–4 provides an algorithm for using these modalities. The sensitivity of US for the diagnosis of pancreatic carcinoma is less than that of CT (over 80 per cent). ERCP has a sensitivity of over 90 per cent because it reliably detects carcinomas arising from ductal cells. Arteriography is rarely required.

Treatment and Prognosis. The therapy for pancreatic carcinoma is frustrating and disappointing. The tumor is often metastatic at the time of diagnosis, and thus surgical resection for cure is unusual. Surgery is often performed for palliation, especially in the patient with intestinal or gastric outlet obstruction or biliary obstruction. Decompression of the biliary system may provide relief from jaundice, severe pruritus, or cholangitis. ERCP with placement of an endoprosthesis (stent) through the tumor-encased bile duct provides a viable alternative, especially in the older high-risk surgical patient, although persistent tumor growth may later result in symptomatic gastric outlet obstruction. Radiation therapy or chemotherapy may

FIGURE 38–4. Pancreatic cancer diagnosis. (From Cello JP: Carcinoma of the pancreas. In Wyngaarden JB, Smith LH Jr [eds]: Cecil Textbook of Medicine. 18th ed. Philadelphia, WB Saunders Co, 1988, p 783.)

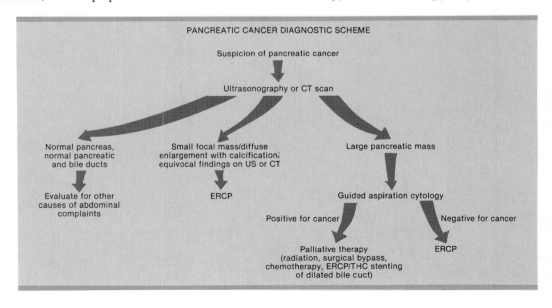

PANCREATIC CANCER DIAGNOSTIC SCHEME

be palliative in some patients but is often ineffective. In those few patients who have the potential for a curative resection, the 5-year survival rate is more than 50 per cent; in general, however, the 5-year survival rate is less than 5 per cent.

Complications. The complications of carcinoma have been discussed as part of the clinical manifestations. The most common site of metastatic disease is the liver.

REFERENCES

Cello JP: Carcinoma of the pancreas. *In* Sleisenger MH, Fordtran JS (eds): Gastrointestinal Disease: Pathophysiology, Diagnosis, and Management. 4th ed. Philadelphia, WB Saunders Co, 1989, pp 1872–1884.

DiMagno EP: Carcinoma of the pancreas. *In* Wyngaarden JM, Smith LH Jr, Bennett JC (eds): Cecil Textbook of Medicine. 19th ed. Philadelphia, WB Saunders Co, 1992, p 727.

Grendell JH, Cello JP: Chronic pancreatitis. *In* Sleisenger MH, Fordtran JS (eds): Gastrointestinal Disease: Pathophysiology, Diagnosis, and Management. 4th ed. Philadelphia, WB Saunders Co, 1989, pp 1842–1872.

Soergel KH: Acute pancreatitis. *In* Sleisenger MH, Fordtran JS (eds): Gastrointestinal Disease: Pathophysiology, Diagnosis, and Management. 4th ed. Philadelphia, WB Saunders Co, 1989, pp 1814–1842.

Steinberg WM: Pancreatitis. *In* Wyngaarden JB, Smith LH Jr, Bennett JC (eds): Cecil Textbook of Medicine, 19th ed. Philadelphia, WB Saunders Co, 1992, p 721.

Van Dyke JA, Stanley RJ, Berland LL: Pancreatic imaging. Ann Intern Med 102:212, 1985.

SECTION V

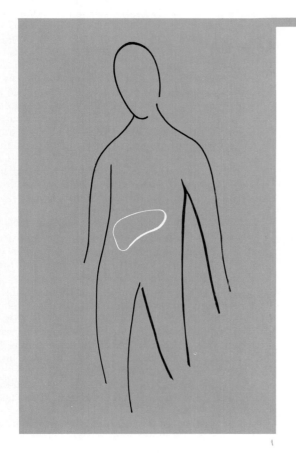

DISEASES OF THE LIVER AND BILIARY SYSTEM

39 LABORATORY TESTS IN LIVER DISEASE

The liver, the largest organ in the body, plays a central role in many essential physiologic processes, including glucose homeostasis, plasma protein synthesis, lipid and lipoprotein synthesis, bile acid synthesis and secretion, and vitamin storage (B_{12}, A, D, E, and K), as well as biotransformation, detoxification, and excretion of a vast array of endogenous and exogenous compounds. The clinical manifestations of liver disease are, likewise, varied and may be quite subtle. Clues to the existence, severity, and etiology of liver disease may be obtained from a careful history and physical examination or by routine laboratory screening tests. Clinical clues to the presence of liver disease are briefly mentioned here and are discussed more fully in other chapters. This chapter focuses on the use of laboratory tests in the evaluation of liver disease.

CLINICAL APPROACH TO LIVER DISEASE

Table 39–1 outlines useful clinical clues to the presence of liver disease that may be elicited from the history and physical examination. Other important information to be obtained includes a history of jaundice or liver disease in family members, recent travel, exposure to individuals or animals with liver or parasitic disease, sexual promiscuity, use of intravenous drugs, and exposure to alcohol, toxins, or drugs.

LABORATORY TESTS OF LIVER FUNCTION AND DISEASE

Unlike tests used to assess function of other organ systems (e.g., arterial blood gas, creatinine clearance), "liver function" tests often do not measure liver function, nor do they accurately reflect etiology or severity of a disease process. Nevertheless, if their limitations are understood, they can be very useful. In general, the tests currently available can be divided into two categories: (1) tests of hepatic function or capacity and (2) screening tests that suggest the presence and/or type of liver disease. Specific diagnostic tests such as serologic tests for hepatitis B infection are covered in other chapters.

TESTS OF HEPATIC FUNCTION

Although the liver performs a great variety of presumably testable functions, it has proved difficult to devise a test that is simple, cheap, reproducible, and noninvasive and that accurately reflects hepatic capacity for all functions. Instead, currently available tests of liver function are indirect, static measurements of serum levels of compounds that are synthesized, metabolized, and/or excreted by the liver. The liver has a large reserve capacity, and therefore "function" tests may remain relatively normal until liver dysfunction is severe. Table 39–2 outlines the most widely available and useful liver function tests. The serum albumin level and prothrombin time both reflect the hepatic capacity for protein synthesis. The prothrombin time responds rapidly to altered hepatic function because the serum half-lives of Factors II and VII are short (hours). In contrast, the serum half-life of albumin is 14 to 20 days, and serum levels fall only with prolonged liver dysfunction.

Serum bile acid levels, particularly when measured 2 hours after a meal, have proved to be the most sensitive test of liver disease, and this is due to the high efficiency with which the liver normally extracts bile acids from portal blood. Small changes in hepatic blood flow, portosystemic shunting, or liver function all result in a substantial elevation of serum bile acid levels, whereas terminal ileal dysfunction (e.g., Crohn's disease) leads to fecal loss of bile acids and decreased serum levels. Although exquisitely sensitive, bile acid levels are nonspecific and fail to reflect accurately overall liver function.

The ^{14}C-aminopyrine breath test was originally developed as a test of liver function. It measures the rate at which the liver metabolizes ^{14}C-labeled aminopyrine to [14]CO_2, which is collected and measured in exhaled breath. This test is performed only in some academic centers.

SCREENING TESTS OF HEPATOBILIARY DISEASE

Screening tests of hepatobiliary disease (Table 39–2) are conveniently divided into two categories: (1) tests of biliary obstruction, and (2) tests of hepatocellular damage, based on the mechanisms responsible for the abnormal test. However, none of the tests is specific for either category, and the pattern and magnitude of abnormalities often provide diagnostic clues to the type of liver disease present.

The *serum bilirubin* level is the result of bilirubin production, bilirubin conjugation, and excretion of bilirubin into bile. Bilirubin's bright orange color made it the first, and the most striking, of liver test indicators. However, the differential diagnosis for hyperbilirubinemia (see Chapter 40) requires consideration of an extensive list of disorders, including hematologic disorders, congenital abnormalities of bilirubin metabolism, and a wide array of liver diseases. Serum bilirubin determination is nonspecific and only moderately sensitive as a test of liver function. Elevation of serum bilirubin, however, should prompt a search for the cause, including potentially treatable biliary obstruction. Serum bilirubin levels may not return promptly to normal after relief of biliary obstruction or improvement in liver disease, because some bilirubin binds covalently to albumin and is removed from the circulation only as albumin is catabolized (half-life, 14 to 20 days).

Serum alkaline phosphatase activity reflects a group of isoenzymes derived from liver, bone, intestine, and placenta. Serum levels are elevated in association with cholestasis, partial or complete bile duct obstruction, and bone regeneration, and also with neoplastic, infiltrative, and granulomatous liver diseases. An isolated elevated alkaline phosphatase level may be the only clue to partial obstruction of the common bile duct, to obstruction of ducts in a single lobe or segment of liver, or to neoplastic or granulomatous disease. Alkaline phosphatase is located on the plasma membrane of hepatocytes. In cholestasis, accompanied by increased serum and tissue levels of bile acids, bits of hepatocyte membrane containing alkaline phosphatase are solubilized into the blood stream. Increased hepatic bile acid levels also stimulate synthesis of alkaline phosphatase, contributing to the elevation of serum levels. 5'-Nucleotidase and gamma glutamyl transpeptidase, other hepatocyte plasma membrane enzymes, are similarly released into the circulation during bile duct obstruction or cholestasis. Patients who present with isolated asymptomatic elevations of liver alkaline phosphatase should be evaluated for the presence of mild cholestatic liver disease, such as primary biliary cirrhosis or partial bile duct obstruction. Many such patients may require endoscopic retrograde cholangiopancreatography.

Aspartate (AST, SGOT) and *alanine (ALT, SGPT) aminotransferases* are intracellular aminotransferring enzymes present in large quantities in liver cells. Following injury or death of liver cells, they are released into the circulation. In general, the serum transaminases are sensitive (albeit nonspecific) tests of liver damage, and the height of the serum transaminase activity reflects the severity of hepatic necrosis, but there are important exceptions. Both enzymes require pyridoxal 5'-phosphate as a cofactor, and the relatively low serum transaminase values seen in patients with severe alcoholic hepatitis (often <300 U/L) may reflect deficiency of this cofactor. Although transaminase levels are increased in a wide array of liver diseases, high levels (>15 times the upper limit of normal) are rare in bile duct obstruction and almost always indicate acute hepatocellular necrosis (e.g., viral or toxic hepatitis). Patients who present with isolated asymptomatic elevations of AST and ALT may have fatty liver (due to obesity or alco-

TABLE 39–1. CLINICAL MANIFESTATIONS OF LIVER DISEASE

SIGN/SYMPTOM	PATHOGENESIS	LIVER DISEASE
Constitutional		
Fatigue, anorexia, malaise, weight loss	Liver failure	Severe acute or chronic hepatitis Cirrhosis
Fever	Hepatic inflammation or infection	Liver abscess Alcoholic hepatitis Viral hepatitis
Fetor hepaticus	Sulfur compounds, produced by intestinal bacteria, not cleared by the liver	Acute or chronic liver failure
Cutaneous		
Spider telangiectasias, palmar erythema	Altered estrogen and androgen metabolism with altered vascular physiology	Cirrhosis
Jaundice	Diminished bilirubin excretion	Biliary obstruction Severe liver disease
Pruritus	Uncertain	Biliary obstruction
Xanthomas and xanthelasma	Increased serum cholesterol	Biliary obstruction/cholestasis
Endocrine		
Gynecomastia, testicular atrophy, diminished libido	Altered estrogen and androgen metabolism	Cirrhosis
Hypoglycemia	Decreased glycogen stores and gluconeogenesis	Acute liver failure Alcohol binge with fasting
Gastrointestinal		
Right upper quadrant abdominal pain	Liver swelling, infection	Acute hepatitis Hepatocellular carcinoma Liver congestion (heart failure) Acute cholecystitis Liver abscess
Abdominal swelling	Ascites	Cirrhosis, portal hypertension
Gastrointestinal bleeding	Esophageal varices	Portal hypertension
Hematologic		
Decreased red cells, white cells, and/or platelets	Hypersplenism	Cirrhosis, portal hypertension
Ecchymoses	Decreased synthesis of clotting factors	Liver failure
Neurologic		
Altered sleep pattern, subtle behavioral changes, somnolence, confusion, ataxia, asterixis, obtundation	Hepatic encephalopathy	Liver failure, portosystemic shunting of blood

hol intake) or hepatocellular disease, such as hemochromatosis or chronic viral hepatitis, and should be screened for treatable diseases. Some patients may require liver biopsy.

TABLE 39–2. CLINICAL TESTS OF HEPATIC FUNCTION

	PROPERTY EXAMINED	SIGNIFICANCE OF ABNORMAL RESULTS		PROPERTY EXAMINED	SIGNIFICANCE OF ABNORMAL RESULTS
Tests of Hepatic Function (Normal values)			**Screening Tests of Hepatobiliary Disease** *Tests of Biliary Obstruction*		
Serum albumin (30–50 gm/L)	Protein synthetic capacity (over days to weeks)	Decreased synthetic capacity Protein malnutrition Increased protein loss (nephrotic syndrome, protein-losing enteropathy) Increased extracellular fluid volume	Serum bilirubin (0.2 — 1.0 mg/dl) (3.4 — 17.1 μmol/L)	Extraction of bilirubin from blood conjugation and excretion into bile	Hemolysis Diffuse liver disease Cholestasis Extrahepatic bile duct obstruction Congenital disorders of bilirubin metabolism
Prothrombin time (10.5 — 13 sec)	Protein synthetic capacity (hours to days)	Decreased synthetic capacity (especially Factors II and VII) Vitamin K deficiency Consumptive coagulopathy	Serum alkaline phosphatase (also 5'-nucleotidase and gamma glutamyl transpeptidase) (56 — 176 U/L)	Increased enzyme synthesis and release	Bile duct obstruction Cholestasis Infiltrative liver disease (neoplasms, granulomas) Bone destruction/remodeling Pregnancy
Serum bilirubin (0.2 — 1.0 mg/dl)	Extraction from blood and excretion into bile	Hemolysis Impaired hepatic function Cholestasis (intrahepatic) Bile duct obstruction	*Tests of Hepatocellular Damage* Aspartate aminotransferase (AST:SCOT) (10 — 30 U/L)	Release of intracellular enzyme	Hepatocellular necrosis Cardiac or skeletal muscle necrosis
Serum bile acids (fasting: 0.7 — 5.6 μM)	Extraction from blood and excretion into bile	Diffuse liver disease Cholestasis Terminal ileal disease Portosystemic shunting of blood	Alanine aminotransferase (ALT:SGPT) (5–30 U/L)	Release of intracellular enzyme	Same as AST: however, more specific for liver cell damage
^{14}C-aminopyrine breath test (5– 19.5% of dose excreted at 2 hr	Drug-metabolizing capacity	Decreased metabolic capacity (diffuse liver disease) Severe portosystemic shunting of blood			

TABLE 39–3. CHARACTERISTIC PATTERNS OF LIVER FUNCTION TESTS

DISORDER	BILIRUBIN	ALKALINE PHOSPHATASE	PROTHROMBIN TIME	AST	ALT
Gilbert's syndrome	↑	nl	nl	nl	nl
Bile duct obstruction (pancreatic carcinoma)	↑↑↑	↑↑↑	↑-↑↑	↑	↑
Acute viral or toxic hepatitis	↑-↑↑↑	↑-↑↑	nl-↑↑↑	↑↑↑	↑↑↑
Cirrhosis	nl-↑	nl-↑	nl-↑↑	nl-↑	nl-↑

nl = Normal; AST = aspartate aminotransferase; ALT = alanine aminotransferase.

Liver function tests usually do not indicate the nature of the underlying liver disease; however, the *pattern* of liver test abnormalities may provide insight in this regard. Table 39–3 outlines the most common patterns of liver test abnormalities.

LIVER BIOPSY

Biopsy and histologic examination of liver tissue are of value in the differential diagnosis of diffuse or localized parenchymal diseases (e.g., cirrhosis, hepatitis, hemochromatosis) or hepatomegaly. Liver biopsy is safe (serious complications <0.5 per cent); however, it is contraindicated in uncooperative patients and those with coagulation abnormalities or thrombocytopenia.

REFERENCES

Stolz A, Kaplowitz N: Biochemical tests for liver disease. *In* Zakim D, Boyer T (eds): Hepatology: A Textbook of Liver Disease. 2nd ed. Philadelphia, WB Saunders Co, 1990, pp 637–667.

Weisiger RA: Laboratory tests in liver disease. *In* Wyngaarden JB, Smith LH Jr, Bennett JC: (eds): Cecil Textbook of Medicine. 19th ed. Philadelphia, WB Saunders Co, 1992, pp 760–763.

40 JAUNDICE

DEFINITION

The term *jaundice* or *icterus* describes the yellow pigmentation of skin, sclerae, and mucous membranes produced by increased serum bilirubin (hyperbilirubinemia). Jaundice, the most colorful and often the earliest sign of a variety of liver and biliary diseases, is a starting point for evaluating many of these disorders. Serum bilirubin normally ranges from 0.5 to 1.0 mg/dl. Jaundice usually becomes clinically evident at levels exceeding 2.5 mg/dl and is most readily detected in the sclerae.

BILIRUBIN METABOLISM

About 4 mg/kg of bilirubin is produced each day, mainly (80 to 85 per cent) derived from the catabolism of the hemoglobin heme group of senescent red blood cells. The heme ring is cleaved in the reticuloendothelial system to form biliverdin, which in turn is oxidized to bilirubin, a water-insoluble tetrapyrrole. A smaller proportion of bilirubin (15 to 20 per cent) is derived from the destruction of maturing erythroid cells in the bone marrow (ineffective erythropoiesis) and from the

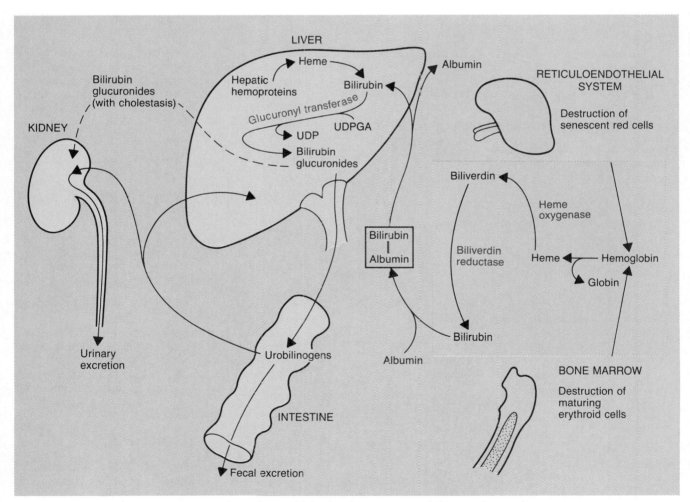

FIGURE 40–1. The pathway of bilirubin formation, metabolism, and excretion.

heme groups of predominantly hepatic hemoproteins such as cytochrome P-450 and cytochrome c (Fig. 40–1).

Bilirubin liberated into the plasma is transported to the liver bound tightly but reversibly to albumin. Three phases of hepatic bilirubin metabolism are recognized: (1) uptake, (2) conjugation, and (3) excretion into the bile, the last step being overall rate-limiting. Uptake is reversible and follows dissociation of bilirubin from albumin. Unconjugated bilirubin is insoluble in water and is virtually incapable of being excreted in bile. This apolar molecule, however, dissolves in lipid-rich environments and readily traverses the blood-brain barrier and placenta.

Bilirubin is rendered water-soluble and hence capable of being excreted in the aqueous bile by its conjugation with a sugar, glucuronic acid. Mono- and diglucuronides of bilirubin are formed in the hepatic endoplasmic reticulum catalyzed by the enzyme uridinediphosphate (UDP)–glucuronyl transferase. If the biliary excretion of conjugated bilirubin is impaired, the pigment from hepatocytes regurgitates into plasma. Conjugated bilirubin is both water-soluble and less tightly bound to albumin than unconjugated pigment, so that it is readily filtered by the glomerulus and appears in the urine when its plasma levels are increased (Fig. 40–1). Unconjugated bilirubin is not excreted in urine. With sustained conjugated hyperbili-

TABLE 40–1. CLASSIFICATION OF JAUNDICE

Predominantly Unconjugated Hyperbilirubinemia
  Overproduction
    Hemolysis (spherocytosis, autoimmune, etc.)
    Ineffective erythropoiesis (e.g., megaloblastic anemias)
  Decreased hepatic uptake
    Gilbert's syndrome
    Drugs (e.g., rifampin, radiographic contrast agents)
    Neonatal jaundice
  Decreased conjugation
    Gilbert's syndrome
    Crigler-Najjar syndrome types I and II
    Neonatal jaundice
    Hepatocellular disease
    Drug inhibition (e.g., chloramphenicol)
Predominantly Conjugated Hyperbilirubinemia
  Impaired hepatic excretion
    Familial disorders (Dubin-Johnson syndrome, Rotor syndrome, benign recurrent cholestasis, cholestasis of pregnancy)
    Hepatocellular disease
    Drug-induced cholestasis
    Primary biliary cirrhosis
    Sepsis
    Postoperative
  Extrahepatic ("mechanical") biliary obstruction
    Gallstones
    Tumors of head of pancreas
    Tumors of bile ducts
    Tumors of ampulla of Vater
    Biliary strictures (post-cholecystectomy, primary sclerosing cholangitis)
    Congenital disorders (biliary atresia)

rubinemia (e.g., obstructive jaundice), a proportion of the conjugated bilirubin becomes covalently bound to albumin and is therefore unavailable for renal or biliary excretion.

Conjugated bilirubin excreted in the bile is not reabsorbed by the intestine but is converted by bacterial action in the gut to colorless tetrapyrroles termed *urobilinogens*. Up to 20 per cent of urobilinogen is reabsorbed and undergoes an enterohepatic circulation, a proportion being excreted in the urine. Thus, both impaired hepatocellular excretion and marked overproduction of bilirubin lead to increased appearance of urobilinogen in the urine.

LABORATORY TESTS FOR BILIRUBIN

The van den Bergh reaction is the most commonly used test for bilirubin in biologic fluids. When carried out in an aqueous medium, the test shows a colored reaction only with water-soluble bilirubin derivatives (called the *direct* van den Bergh fraction). The addition of methanol enables a colored reaction to take place with water-insoluble bilirubin (called the *indirect* van den Bergh fraction). Direct and indirect van den Bergh fractions provide clinically useful estimations of conjugated and unconjugated bilirubin, respectively. However, the correlation between actual levels of conjugated bilirubin and levels estimated by the direct-reacting fraction is poor. Normal plasma actually contains more than 95 per cent unconjugated bilirubin.

Qualitative estimation of bilirubin in urine is carried out with Ictotest tablets or dipsticks, which are positive in cases of conjugated hyperbilirubinemia.

CLINICAL CLASSIFICATION OF JAUNDICE

A logical first step in the study of a jaundiced patient is to determine whether there is an unconjugated or a conjugated hyperbilirubinemia. This question is usually easily resolved by testing the urine for bilirubin. If positive, conjugated hyperbilirubinemia is present, and this is confirmed by finding greater than 50 per cent conjugated bilirubin on serum testing.

Classification of jaundice according to this distinction is shown in Table 40–1. Mechanisms contributing to predominantly unconjugated hyperbilirubinemia include (1) overproduction, (2) decreased hepatic uptake, and (3) decreased conjugation. Conjugated hyperbilirubinemia implies either (1) a defect in hepatocellular excretion of bilirubin or (2) mechanical obstruction to the major extrahepatic bile ducts. Occasionally jaundice may result from a single abnormality in the complex pathway from bilirubin production to its biliary excretion—for example, from hemolysis and from rare conditions, such as Crigler-Najjar syndrome (decreased or absent conjugation) and Dubin-Johnson syndrome (defective hepatocellular excretion of bilirubin). More frequently there are multiple rather than isolated causes of jaundice. For example, the jaundice occurring in patients with hepatocellular disease (i.e., hepatitis, cirrhosis) may result from a combination of diminished red cell survival and impairment of all three stages of hepatocellular bilirubin transport and metabolism.

Unconjugated Hyperbilirubinemia

Overproduction. Hemolysis from a variety of causes may lead to bilirubin production sufficient to exceed the clearing capacity of the liver with subsequent development of jaundice. This *hemolytic jaundice* is characteristically mild; serum bilirubin levels rarely exceed 5 mg/dl. Ineffective erythropoiesis, which may be substantially increased in megaloblastic anemias, may also lead to mild jaundice.

Impaired Hepatic Uptake. Impaired uptake is very rarely encountered as an isolated cause for clinical jaundice, but may play a role in the mild jaundice following administration of certain drugs, such as rifampin (competition for bilirubin uptake) and in Gilbert's syndrome (see below).

Impaired Conjugation. A genetically determined decrease or absence of UDP-glucuronyl transferase is encountered in the Crigler-Najjar syndrome, whereas mild, acquired defects in the enzyme may be produced by drugs (e.g., chloramphenicol).

Neonatal Jaundice. All steps of hepatic bilirubin metabolism are incompletely developed in the neonatal period, while increased production is also present. The major defect is in conjugation, however, leading to unconjugated hyperbilirubinemia between the second and fifth days of life. When increased production of bilirubin occurs in the neonatal period, usually as a result of hemolytic disease secondary to blood group incompatibility, severe unconjugated hyperbilirubinemia may occur, carrying the risk of neurologic damage (kernicterus).

Gilbert's Syndrome. This very common disorder affects up to 7 per cent of the population, with a marked male predominance. It commonly manifests during the second or third decade of life as a mild unconjugated hyperbilirubinemia, exacerbated by fasting, and noted clinically or as an incidental laboratory finding. The mechanism appears to involve increased production, diminished uptake, and defective conjugation of bilirubin to varying proportions in different individuals. Nonspecific gastrointestinal symptoms and fatigue are commonly associated, but this condition is entirely benign. The diagnosis is strongly suggested by unconjugated hyperbilirubinemia with normal hepatic enzymes and the absence of overt hemolysis. Liver biopsy is always normal and is rarely, if ever, indicated to confirm the diagnosis.

Conjugated Hyperbilirubinemia

Determining the cause of unconjugated hyperbilirubinemia rarely poses difficulty. Usually, the major difficulty in evaluating jaundice is encountered in differentiating an intrahepatic defect in excretion from that of obstruction in a patient with predominantly conjugated hyperbilirubinemia. This clinical situation is often described as *cholestatic jaundice,* and the approach to its differential diagnosis is discussed in detail below.

Cholestasis implies that bile formation or flow is impaired. Typically, a patient with cholestatic jaundice has predominantly conjugated hyperbilirubinemia and an elevated alkaline phosphatase, usually to at least three to four times normal. When prolonged, cholestasis may lead to hypercholesterolemia, malabsorption of fat and fat-soluble vitamins, and retention of bile salts, which may lead to pruritus. Biochemical evidence of liver cell damage (elevated transaminases, prolonged prothrombin time uncorrected by administration of vitamin K) may be minimal or marked, depending upon the cause of the cholestasis. All of the features of cholestasis may be present in some patients *without jaundice.*

Impaired Hepatic Excretion. This pathogenetic category of jaundice, also called intrahepatic cholestasis, is applied to all disorders in the transport of conjugated bilirubin from the hepatocyte to the radiologically visible intrahepatic bile ducts. Thus it includes a wide range of conditions from drug-induced cholestasis (impaired canalicular transport) to primary biliary cirrhosis (destruction of the small intrahepatic bile ductules). The following are some important causes of intrahepatic cholestasis.

DRUG-INDUCED CHOLESTASIS. Typical cholestatic jaundice may be produced by phenothiazines, oral contraceptives, and methyltestosterone. Eosinophilia may accompany drug-induced jaundice.

SEPSIS. Systemic sepsis, mainly due to gram-negative organisms, may produce a predominantly conjugated hyperbilirubinemia, usually accompanied by mildly elevated serum alkaline phosphatase levels.

POSTOPERATIVE JAUNDICE. This increasingly recognized syndrome has an incidence of 15 per cent following heart surgery and 1 per cent following elective abdominal surgery. Occurring 1 to 10 days postoperatively and multifactorial in origin, the elevated bilirubin is predominantly of the conjugated variety with increased alkaline phosphatase and minimally abnormal transaminase levels.

HEPATOCELLULAR DISEASE. Hepatocellular disease (i.e., hepatitis and cirrhosis) from a variety of causes (see Chapters 41 and 43) may result in a typical cholestatic jaundice. Evidence of hepatocellular damage and dysfunction is usually prominent and includes marked elevation of transaminases, prolonged prothrombin time, hypoalbuminemia, and clinical features of hepatic dysfunction (see Chapter 42). In hepatocellular disease all three steps of hepatic bilirubin metabolism are impaired. Excretion, the rate-limiting step, is usually the most profoundly disturbed, leading to a predominantly conjugated hyperbilirubinemia. Jaundice may be profound in acute hepatitis (see Chapter 41) without prognostic implications. In contrast, in chronic liver disease, jaundice usually implies severe decompensation of hepatic function with a poor prognosis.

Extrahepatic Biliary Obstruction. Complete or partial obstruction of the extrahepatic bile ducts may result from a variety of causes, including impaction of gallstones, carcinoma of the head of the pancreas, tumors of the bile ducts, bile duct strictures, and chronic pancreatitis with bile duct compression. In complete obstruction, conjugated hyperbilirubinemia is prominent and usually plateaus at 30 to 40 mg/dl in the absence of renal failure, hepatocellular damage, or infection within the bile ducts, all of which may develop during the course of mechanical obstruction. Stools may become clay-colored as a result of the failure of bile to enter the intestine. In partial obstruction, jaundice may be mild or even absent, becoming prominent when infection of the ducts (cholangitis) complicates the obstruction.

APPROACH TO THE DIAGNOSIS OF JAUNDICE

A careful history and physical examination are of paramount importance in obtaining clues to the nature and cause of jaundice. A history of dark-

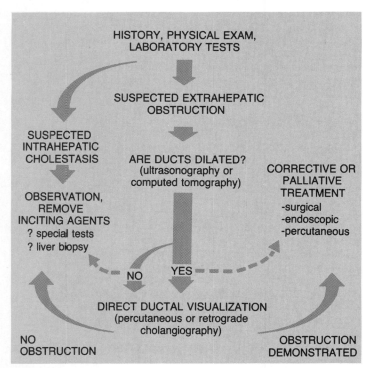

FIGURE 40–2. Approach to the patient with cholestatic jaundice. The algorithm demonstrates the systematic consideration of the available diagnostic options.

ened urine invariably implies conjugated hyperbilirubinemia, whereas pale stools and pruritus suggest a cholestatic process. An inquiry about use of drugs or alcohol, exposure to jaundiced persons (drug or viral hepatitis), recurrent abdominal pain and nausea (gallstones), epigastric pain radiating into the back accompanied by weight loss and a distended gallbladder (carcinoma of the head of the pancreas), and pre-existing liver disease often go far in delineating the probable cause for the jaundice. Routine laboratory tests are helpful in that serum transaminase levels are usually less than 5- to 10-fold elevated in patients with bile duct obstruction, while alkaline phosphatase levels are usually greater than two to three times normal. Conversely, a greater than 10- to 15-fold elevation of serum transaminase levels indicates hepatocellular disease. Serologic tests for hepatitis may be helpful (see Chapter 41), whereas autoantibodies, if strongly positive, may be of diagnostic value, such as the antimitochondrial antibody in primary biliary cirrhosis.

Clinical evaluation and routine laboratory tests serve to identify the cause of jaundice in up to 85 per cent of cases. More sophisticated diagnostic procedures are often needed, however, to determine the cause, especially whether the cholestatic jaundice in a given patient is intrahepatic or due to extrahepatic obstruction.

A diagnostic approach to this question is illustrated in Figure 40–2. If extrahepatic obstruction is suspected, it is necessary to determine first by noninvasive means whether or not the major bile ducts are dilated. In jaundiced patients, dilatation of the ducts is usual when a mechanical obstruction is present but is absent in cases of intrahepatic cholestasis. Either ultrasonography or computed tomographic (CT) scanning may be used to determine the caliber of bile ducts, the former generally preferred because of lesser cost and absence of radiation. Additional definitive clues, such as the presence of stones in the common duct or gallbladder, may be obtained as well. However, both imaging techniques may give rise to false-positive and false-negative results in a small number of patients. Thus, in a patient with cholestatic jaundice, the absence of dilated ducts on ultrasonography should not dissuade the clinician from proceeding to cholangiography if the suspicion of extrahepatic obstruction based on clinical evaluation is high. If dilated ducts are found on noninvasive imaging, direct cholangiography provides the most reliable approach to nonoperative diagnosis of cholestatic jaundice. This may be accomplished by either percutaneous puncture of the intrahepatic biliary tree with a thin needle (percutaneous transhepatic cholangiography) or by means of endoscopic retrograde cholangiography. The percutaneous route is simpler technically, has a success rate of close to 100 per cent in the presence of dilated ducts, and is less expensive. The endoscopic route, although more demanding both technically and in terms of time and cost, is of value in demonstrating duct pathology when the bile ducts are not dilated (in which case the percutaneous route may often fail) or when associated pancreatic disease is suspected. It may also permit direct biopsy of lesions at the ampulla of Vater and sphincterotomy and stone extraction in appropriate instances.

Liver biopsy may be indicated when an intrahepatic cause for cholestasis is strongly suspected on clinical grounds or when extrahepatic obstruction is ruled out by definitive cholangiography. Liver histology itself is often a poor guide to whether cholestasis is intra- or extrahepatic. The decision to perform a biopsy thus rests on the certainty with which extrahepatic obstruction has been excluded in a patient with cholestasis and on the clinical course of the disease. Thus, for example, in a patient with cholestatic jaundice in whom recent ingestion of chlorpromazine is documented and in whom the jaundice is beginning to resolve following cessation of the drug, the best course may be to observe without further investigation.

REFERENCE

Scharschmidt BF: Bilirubin metabolism and hyperbilirubinemia. *In* Wyngaarden JB, Smith LH Jr, Bennett JC (eds): Cecil Textbook of Medicine. 19th ed. Philadelphia, WB Saunders Co, 1992, pp 756–760.

41 | ACUTE AND CHRONIC HEPATITIS

DEFINITION

The term *hepatitis* is applied to a broad category of clinicopathologic conditions that result from the damage produced by viral, toxic, pharmacologic, or immune-mediated attack upon the liver. The common pathologic features of hepatitis are hepatocellular necrosis, which may be focal or extensive, and inflammatory cell infiltration of the liver, which may predominate in the portal areas or extend out into the parenchyma. Clinically, the liver may be enlarged and tender with or without jaundice, and laboratory evidence of hepatocellular damage is invariably found in the form of elevated transaminase levels. Independent of its cause, the clinical course of hepatitis may range from mild or inapparent to a dramatic illness with evidence of severe hepatocellular dysfunction, marked jaundice, impairment of coagulation, and disturbance of neurologic function. Hepatitis is further divided into acute and chronic types on the basis of clinical and pathologic criteria.

Acute hepatitis implies a condition lasting less than 6 months, culminating either in complete resolution of the liver damage with return to normal liver function and structure or in rapid progression of the acute injury toward extensive necrosis and a fatal outcome.

Chronic hepatitis is defined as a sustained inflammatory process in the liver lasting longer than 6 months.

Differentiation of acute from chronic hepatitis on histologic criteria alone may be impossible. Extension of inflammatory cells beyond the limits of the portal tracts surrounding isolated nests of hepatocytes (piecemeal necrosis) and connection of portal and/or central areas of the hepatic lobules by swaths of inflammation, necrosis, and collapse of architecture (bridging necrosis) are seen in liver biopsies taken from patients with severe forms of chronic hepatitis. These features may also be seen, however, in uncomplicated acute hepatitis that will ultimately undergo complete resolution. A purely histologic diagnosis of chronic hepatitis usually requires evidence of progression toward cirrhosis such as significant fibrous scarring and disruption of the hepatic lobular architecture.

ACUTE HEPATITIS

Agents causing acute hepatic injury are listed in Table 41–1. The mechanisms whereby these

TABLE 41–1. CAUSES OF ACUTE HEPATITIS

Viral Hepatitis
  Hepatitis A virus
  Hepatitis B virus
  Hepatitis C virus
  Hepatitis D virus ("delta agent")
  Epstein-Barr virus
  Cytomegalovirus
Alcohol
Toxins
  Amanita phalloides mushroom poisoning
  Carbon tetrachloride
Drugs
  Acetaminophen
  Isoniazid
  Halothane
  Chlorpromazine
  Erythromycin
Other
  Wilson's disease

TABLE 41–2. CHARACTERISTICS OF COMMON CAUSATIVE AGENTS OF ACUTE VIRAL HEPATITIS

	HEPATITIS A	HEPATITIS B	HEPATITIS D	HEPATITIS C	HEPATITIS E
Causative agent	27-nm RNA virus	42-nm DNA virus; core and surface components	36-nm hybrid particle with HBsAg coat	Flavivirus-like RNA agent	27–34 nm nonenveloped RNA virus
Transmission	Fecal-oral; water-, food-borne	Parenteral inoculation or equivalent; direct contact	Similar to HBV	Similar to HBV	Similar to HAV
Incubation period	2–6 wk	4 wk–6 mo	Similar to HBV	5–10 wk	2–9 wk
Period of infectivity	2–3 wk in late incubation and early clinical phase	During HBsAg positivity (occasionally only with anti-HBc positivity)	During HDV RNA or anti-HDV positivity	During anti-HCV positivity	Similar to HCV
Massive hepatic necrosis	Rare	Uncommon	Yes	Uncommon	Yes
Carrier state	No	Yes	Yes	Yes	No
Chronic hepatitis	No	Yes	Yes	Yes	No
Prophylaxis	Hygiene; immune serum globulin	Hygiene; hepatitis B immune globulin; vaccine	Hygiene, HBV vaccine	Hygiene; ? immune serum globulin	Hygiene; sanitation

agents produce hepatic damage include direct toxin-induced necrosis (e.g., acetaminophen, *Amanita phalloides* toxin) and host immune-mediated damage, which probably plays an important, but not well understood, role in viral hepatitis. In the case of frank hepatotoxins such as *Amanita* poisoning, massive hepatic necrosis is the dominant process, and the clinical course is more aptly described as fulminant hepatic failure (see Chapter 42) rather than acute hepatitis. Such a course is less common, but well recognized, with all the causative agents listed in Table 41–1.

Acute Viral Hepatitis

Etiology. Viral hepatitis is caused by five main viruses: hepatitis viruses A, B, C, D, and E (Table 41–2). Cytomegalovirus and Epstein-Barr virus occasionally cause hepatitis. Hepatitis D virus, an incomplete RNA virus, causes hepatitis either simultaneously with the B virus or in individuals already chronically infected with the B virus. The recently characterized C virus accounts for the vast majority of cases of hepatitis previously designated "non-A, non-B." The B virus has been most extensively characterized. The complete B virus (Dane particle) consists of several antigenically distinct components (Fig. 41–1), including a surface coat (hepatitis B surface antigen, HBsAg) and a core of circular DNA, DNA polymerase, hepatitis B core antigen (HBcAg), and hepatitis e antigen (HBeAg). HBsAg may exist in serum either as part of the Dane particle or as free particles and rods. Surface antigen, as well as HBcAg and HBeAg, elicits distinct antibody responses from the host, which are of value in serologic diagnosis and characterization of the state of B virus replication in the liver.

Transmission. Hepatitis A virus (HAV) is excreted in the feces during the incubation period (Fig. 41–2) and is transmitted by the fecal-oral route. It is thus implicated in most instances of water-borne and food-transmitted infection and in epidemics of viral hepatitis. The hepatitis B virus (HBV) is present in virtually all body fluids and excreta of carriers and is transmitted mainly by

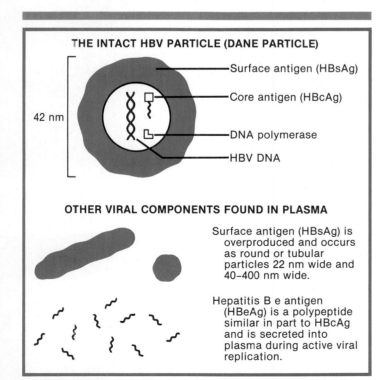

THE INTACT HBV PARTICLE (DANE PARTICLE)

42 nm

Surface antigen (HBsAg)
Core antigen (HBcAg)
DNA polymerase
HBV DNA

OTHER VIRAL COMPONENTS FOUND IN PLASMA

Surface antigen (HBsAg) is overproduced and occurs as round or tubular particles 22 nm wide and 40–400 nm wide.

Hepatitis B e antigen (HBeAg) is a polypeptide similar in part to HBcAg and is secreted into plasma during active viral replication.

FIGURE 41–1. Different types of hepatitis B virus particles in plasma.

parenteral routes. Thus, transmission occurs most commonly via blood and blood products, contaminated needles, and intimate personal contact. Persons at high risk of infection with the B virus therefore include sexual partners of acutely as well as chronically infected individuals, with male homosexuals being at particularly high risk; health professionals, particularly surgeons, dentists, and workers in clinical laboratories and dialysis units; intravenous drug abusers; and infants of infected mothers ("vertical transmission"). Patients with increased exposure to blood or blood products and/or with impaired immunity (e.g., dialysis patients, patients with leukemia or Down's syndrome) are also highly susceptible to B virus infection.

Hepatitis C virus (HCV), similar to HBV, is largely parenterally transmitted. Hepatitis C is currently the main cause of post-transfusion hepatitis. HCV is also a common cause of hepatitis in intravenous drug users and accounts for at least 50 per cent of cases of sporadic, community-acquired hepatitis. In such cases, the mode of transmission of the virus is unclear. The hepatitis E virus is the cause of an epidemic, water-borne hepatitis that has been associated with outbreaks, mainly in Asia.

Clinical and Laboratory Manifestations. Acute viral hepatitis typically begins with a prodromal phase lasting several days and characterized by constitutional and gastrointestinal symptoms including malaise, fatigue, anorexia, nausea, vomiting, myalgia, and headache. A mild fever may be present. Symptoms suggestive of "flu" may be prominent; arthritis and urticaria, attributed to immune complex deposition, may be present, particularly in hepatitis B. Smokers often describe an aversion to cigarettes. Jaundice soon appears with bilirubinuria and a loss of stool color, often accompanied by an improvement in the patient's sense of well-being. Jaundice may be absent (anicteric hepatitis); in such cases—probably the majority of cases of acute viral hepatitis—medical attention is often not sought. The liver is usually tender and enlarged; splenomegaly is found in about one fifth of patients.

Transaminases (alanine transaminase [ALT] and aspartate transaminase [AST]) are released from the acutely damaged hepatocytes and serum transaminase levels rise, often to levels exceeding 20-fold normal. Bilirubinuria and an elevated serum bilirubin are usually found, with mild elevations in serum alkaline phosphatase levels. The white cell count is normal or slightly depressed.

The icteric phase of acute viral hepatitis may last from days to weeks, followed by gradual resolution of symptoms and laboratory values.

Complications

POSTHEPATITIS SYNDROMES. In some patients, prolonged fatigue and malaise may persist for months after return of liver function tests to normal. Reassurance is all that is required, and normal activity is encouraged. Isolated elevation of unconjugated serum bilirubin may persist (an ex-

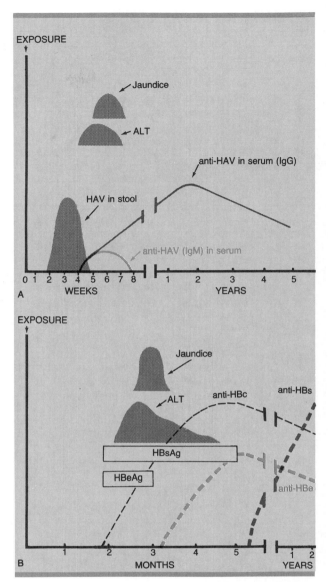

FIGURE 41-2. Sequence of clinical and laboratory findings in (A) a patient with hepatitis A and (B) a patient with hepatitis B.

pression of Gilbert's syndrome; see Chapter 40) and requires no treatment.

CHOLESTATIC HEPATITIS. In some patients, a prolonged, although ultimately self-limited, period of cholestatic jaundice may supervene with marked conjugated hyperbilirubinemia, elevation of alkaline phosphatase, and pruritus. Investigation may be required to differentiate this condition from mechanical obstruction of the biliary tree (see Chapter 45).

FULMINANT HEPATITIS. Massive hepatic necrosis occurs in less than 1 per cent of patients with acute viral hepatitis, leading to a devastating and often fatal condition called fulminant hepatic failure. This is discussed in detail in Chapter 42.

CHRONIC HEPATITIS. This may develop following acute hepatitis B, C, or D. Hepatitis A never progresses to chronicity. Persistence of transaminase elevation beyond 6 months suggests evolution to chronic hepatitis, although a slowly resolving acute hepatitis may occasionally lead to abnormal liver function tests well beyond 6 months with eventual complete resolution. Chronic hepatitis is considered in detail later in this chapter. HBV infection without evidence of any liver damage may persist, resulting in asymptomatic or "healthy" hepatitis B carriers. In Asia and Africa, many such carriers appear to have acquired the virus from infected mothers during infancy.

RARE COMPLICATIONS. Rarely, acute viral hepatitis may be followed by aplastic anemia, whereas cryoglobulinemia, glomerulonephritis, and vasculitis may complicate the course of hepatitis B. Pancreatitis with elevation of serum amylase may also occur.

Serodiagnosis. The ability to detect the presence of viral components in hepatitis B and C and antibodies to components of hepatitis A, B, C, and D has enabled considerable progress to be made in the study of the epidemiology of viral hepatitis. These so-called viral markers can be diagnostic of the cause of acute viral hepatitis (Table 41–3). An etiologic diagnosis is of great importance in planning preventive and public health measures pertinent to the close contacts of infected patients and in evaluating the prognosis. The time course of appearance of these markers in acute hepatitis A and B is shown in Figure 41–2. Epstein-Barr virus and cytomegalovirus hepatitis may also be diagnosed by the appearance of specific antibodies of the IgM class. In acute hepatitis B, HBsAg and HBeAg are present in serum. Both are usually cleared within a period of 3 months, but HBsAg may persist in some uncomplicated cases for 6 months to 1 year. Clearance of HBsAg is followed after a variable "window" period by emergence of anti-HBs, which confers long-term immunity. Anti-HBc and anti-HBe appear in the acute phase of the illness, but neither provides immunity. During the serologic window period, anti-HBc may be the only evidence of hepatitis B infection, and IgM anti-HBc, a marker of active viral replication, is suggestive of recent infection. Hepatitis D infection superimposed on HBV infection may be detected by specific antibody to this agent. Acute hepatitis C is accompanied by a viremia that can be detected using a sensitive polymerase chain reaction assay for the HCV RNA. Antibody to a viral component (C-100-3 antigen) develops after an average of 15 weeks following the clinical onset, and its presence is usually indicative of past or chronic infection.

Management. There is no specific treatment for acute viral hepatitis. Management is largely supportive, including rest in proportion to the severity of symptoms, maintenance of hydration, and adequate dietary intake. Most patients show a preference for a low-fat, high-carbohydrate diet. Vitamin supplementation is of no proven value, although vitamin K administration may be indicated if prolonged cholestasis occurs. Activity is restricted to limit fatigue. Alcohol should be avoided until liver enzymes return to normal. Measures to combat nausea can include small doses of metoclopramide and hydroxyzine. Hospitalization is indicated in patients with severe nausea and vomiting, or with evidence of deteriorating liver function such as hepatic encephalopathy (see Chapter 42) or prolongation of the prothrombin time. In general, hepatitis A may be regarded as noninfectious after

TABLE 41–3. SEROLOGIC MARKERS OF VIRAL HEPATITIS

AGENT	MARKER	DEFINITION	SIGNIFICANCE
Hepatitis A virus (HAV)	Anti-HAV IgM type IgG type	Antibody to HAV	Current or recent infection or convalescence Current or previous infection; confers immunity
Hepatitis B virus (HBV)	HBsAg HBeAg	HBV surface antigen e antigen; a component of the HBV core	Positive in most cases of acute or chronic infection Transiently positive in acute hepatitis B May persist in chronic infection Reflects presence of viral replication and whole Dane particles in serum Reflects high infectivity
	Anti-HBe	Antibody to e antigen	Transiently positive in convalescence May be persistently present in chronic cases Reflects low infectivity
	Anti-HBc (IgM or IgG)	Antibody to HBV core antigen	Positive in all acute and chronic cases Reliable marker of infection, past or current IgM anti-HBc reflects active viral replication Not protective
	Anti-HBs	Antibody to HBV surface antigen	Positive in late convalescence in most acute cases Confers immunity
Hepatitis C virus (HCV)	Anti-HCV	Antibody to C-100-3 polypeptide	Positive on average 15 wk after clinical onset; not protective Persists in chronic infection
Hepatitis D virus (HDV)	Anti-HDV (IgM or IgG)	Antibody to HDV antigen	Acute or chronic infection; not protective

2 to 3 weeks, whereas hepatitis B is potentially infectious to intimate contacts throughout its course, although the risk is very small once HBsAg has cleared. Although hepatitis C may also be transmitted to intimate contacts, the risk of this is considerably less than for hepatitis B.

Prevention. Both feces and blood from patients with hepatitis A contain virus during the prodromal and early icteric phases of the disease. Raw shellfish concentrate the virus from sewage pollution and may serve as vectors of the disease. General hygienic measures should include handwashing by contacts and careful handling, disposal, and sterilization of excreta and contaminated clothing and utensils. Close contacts of patients with hepatitis A should receive immune serum globulin (ISG) as soon as possible. Travelers to endemic areas where sanitation facilities are poor may be protected by prior administration of ISG.

Hepatitis B is rarely transmitted by the fecal-oral route, but it is still prudent to avoid contact with the excreta of patients. Far more important is the meticulous disposal of contaminated needles and other blood-contaminated utensils.

ISG is of very limited value in preventing hepatitis B. However, administration of immune serum globulin enriched in anti-HBs (hyperimmune globulin, hepatitis B immune globulin, HBIG) may afford protection after a needlestick exposure or mucosal exposure (e.g., during pipetting of infectious serum in a clinical laboratory or following eye splash) and is also recommended for sexual contacts of patients with acute hepatitis B. It also appears to be protective to neonates born to mothers who are acutely or chronically infected. The usefulness of HBIG in household contacts is less well established.

An important advance in the field of hepatitis B prevention has been the development of a safe, highly effective vaccine. Available vaccines include the original one manufactured from triple-inactivated HBsAg obtained from the serum of chronic carriers of the B virus, as well as a recombinant vaccine. The vaccine is given in three doses over 6 months and confers immunity in close to 100 per cent of recipients for a period of at least 5 years. Vaccination is currently recommended for high-risk groups and individuals, including health professionals, dialysis patients, hemophiliacs, residents and staff of custodial care institutions, and sexually active homosexual males. It appears also to be of value in combination with HBIG after acute exposure to the virus, such as occurs with accidental needlestick and particularly in infants born to HBsAg-positive mothers.

The advent of widespread screening of donor blood products for anti-HCV is expected to reduce considerably the future incidence of post-transfusion hepatitis.

Alcoholic Fatty Liver and Hepatitis

Alcohol abuse is the most common cause of liver disease in the Western world. Three major pathologic lesions resulting from alcohol abuse are (1) fatty liver, (2) alcoholic hepatitis, and (3) cirrhosis. The first two lesions are potentially reversible, may sometimes be confused clinically with viral hepatitis, and are described in this chapter. Alcoholic cirrhosis is discussed in Chapter 43.

Mechanism of Injury. Alcohol appears to produce liver damage by several mechanisms that are still incompletely understood. Fatty liver may be related to increased nicotinamide-adenine dinucleotide phosphate (NADPH) generated during alcohol metabolism, which promotes fatty acid synthesis and triglyceride formation. Because alcohol also impairs the release of triglyceride in the form of lipoproteins, fat accumulates in hepatocytes. Acetaldehyde produced from oxidation of alcohol may be directly hepatotoxic and is implicated in the production of the more severe hepatic lesions seen in alcoholics. Immune-mediated hepatic damage may also play a role in producing the lesion of alcoholic hepatitis.

Individuals vary considerably in their ability to withstand the effects of alcohol on the liver. Nevertheless, consumption by men in excess of 40 gm of ethanol per day for 10 to 15 years carries a substantial risk of the development of alcoholic liver disease, whereas women appear to have a lower threshold of injury. Malnutrition may potentiate the toxic effects of alcohol on the liver, and genetic factors may contribute to individual susceptibility.

Clinical and Pathologic Features. Alcoholic *fatty liver* may present as an incidentally discovered tender hepatomegaly. Some patients consult a physician because of right upper quadrant pain. Jaundice is very rare. Transaminase levels are usually mildly elevated (less than five times normal). Liver biopsy shows diffuse or centrilobular fat occupying most of the hepatocyte.

Alcoholic hepatitis, a much more severe and prognostically ominous lesion, is characterized by the histologic triad of (1) alcoholic hyalin, an eosinophilic aggregate usually seen near or around the cell nuclei; (2) infiltration of the liver by polymorphonuclear leukocytes; and (3) a network of intralobular connective tissue surrounding hepatocytes and central veins. Patients with this histologic lesion may be asymptomatic or extremely ill with hepatic failure. Anorexia, nausea, vomiting, weight loss, and abdominal pain are common presenting symptoms. Hepatomegaly is present in 80 per cent of patients with alcoholic hepatitis, and splenomegaly is often present. Fever is common, but bacterial infection should always be excluded, because patients with alcoholic liver disease are prone to develop pneumonia as well as infection of the urinary tract and peritoneal cavity. Jaundice is commonly present and may be pronounced with cholestatic features (see Chapter 40). Cutaneous signs of chronic liver disease may be found, including spider angiomas, palmar erythema, and gynecomastia. Parotid enlargement, testicular atrophy, and loss of body hair may be prominent (see Chapter 43). Ascites and encephalopathy may be present and indicate severe disease. The white cell count may be strikingly elevated, whereas transaminase levels are only modestly raised, an important differentiating feature from other forms of acute hepatitis. The AST/ALT ratio frequently exceeds 2, in contrast to viral hepatitis, in which the transaminase levels are usually increased in parallel. A prolonged prothrombin time, hypoalbuminemia, and hyperglobulinemia may be found.

Diagnosis. A history of excessive, prolonged alcohol intake is often difficult to elicit from patients with alcoholic liver disease, whereas others suspected of imbibing to excess are often found to have liver disease from causes other than alcohol, e.g., chronic viral hepatitis. Liver biopsy is extremely helpful in establishing the diagnosis.

Complications and Prognosis. Alcoholic fatty liver reverts to complete histologic normality with cessation of alcohol intake. Alcoholic hepatitis can also revert to normal but more commonly either progresses to cirrhosis, which may already be present at the time of initial presentation, or runs a rapid course to hepatic failure and death. Not infrequently its course is complicated by the development of encephalopathy, ascites, and deteriorating renal function with increasing blood urea nitrogen (BUN) and creatinine levels (hepatorenal syndrome) or gastrointestinal bleeding from varices.

TABLE 41–4. CLASSIFICATION OF DRUG-INDUCED LIVER DISEASE

CATEGORY	EXAMPLES
Predictable hepatotoxins with zonal necrosis	Acetaminophen Carbon tetrachloride
Nonspecific hepatitis	Aspirin Oxacillin
Viral hepatitis–like reactions	Halothane Isoniazid Phenytoin
Cholestasis	
Noninflammatory	Estrogens 17α-substituted steroids
Inflammatory	Chlorpromazine Antithyroid agents
Fatty liver	
Large droplet	Ethanol Corticosteroids
Small droplet	Phenylbutazone Allopurinol
Chronic hepatitis	Methyldopa Nitrofurantoin
Tumors	Estrogens Vinyl chloride
Vascular lesions	6-Thioguanine Anabolic steroids
Fibrosis	Methotrexate
Granulomas	Allopurinol Sulfonamides

Treatment. Treatment of acute alcoholic hepatitis is supportive. Attempts should be made to treat the underlying alcoholism, although this is often unrewarding. A high-calorie diet with vitamin (particularly thiamin) supplementation is instituted and may require administration by nasogastric tube in severely anorectic patients. Protein should be included but may need to be restricted in patients with encephalopathy (see Chapter 43). Treatment with corticosteroids may be of benefit in selected patients.

Drug- and Toxin-Induced Hepatitis

A broad spectrum of hepatic pathology may result from a variety of therapeutic drugs and nontherapeutic toxins (Table 41–4). The pathophysiologic mechanisms whereby this wide variety of hepatic lesions is produced are complex. At one end of the spectrum is a predictable, dose-dependent, direct toxic effect upon hepatocytes leading to frank hepatocellular necrosis. This is typified by the effects of acetaminophen and carbon tetrachloride, both of which produce centrilobular hepatocellular necrosis in virtually all individuals in whom a sufficient quantity is ingested. Other reactions are generally not predictable and usually occur for unknown reasons in susceptible individuals (idiosyncratic drug reaction). In some instances, genetically determined differences in pathways of hepatic drug metabolism may result in metabolites with greater toxic potential. Examples include viral hepatitis-like reactions (halothane, isoniazid), cholestatic hepatitis (chlorpromazine), granulomatous hepatitis (allopurinol), chronic hepatitis (methyldopa), and pure cholestasis without inflammatory cell infiltration or hepatocellular necrosis (estrogens, androgens). Immune-mediated hepatic damage may contribute in some, possibly resulting from the drug or its metabolites acting as a hapten on the surface of hepatocytes. A few important examples of drug-induced hepatitis are discussed here.

Acetaminophen. Acetaminophen is converted by the hepatic cytochrome P-450 drug-metabolizing system to a potentially toxic metabolite that is subsequently rendered harmless through conjugation with glutathione. When massive doses are taken (in excess of 10 to 15 gm), the formation of excess toxic metabolites depletes the available glutathione and produces necrosis. Acetaminophen overdose, commonly taken in a suicide attempt, leads to nausea and vomiting within a few hours. These symptoms subside and are followed in 24 to 48 hours by clinical and laboratory evidence of hepatocellular necrosis (raised transaminase levels) and hepatic dysfunction (prolonged prothrombin time, hepatic encephalopathy). Extensive liver necrosis may lead to fulminant hepatic failure and death. Severe liver damage may be predicted on the basis of blood levels of the drug from 4 to 12 hours after ingestion. Early treatment of patients at high risk with N-acetylcysteine (within 16 hours of the ingestion), which is thought to promote hepatic glutathione synthesis, may be life-saving.

Isoniazid (INH). INH as a single-drug prophylaxis against tuberculosis commonly produces subclinical hepatic injury (20 per cent incidence) as evidenced by raised serum transaminase levels. This appears to be transient and self-limiting in most cases. There is, however, a 1 per cent incidence of overt hepatitis with clinical and pathologic features of viral hepatitis, which progresses to massive, fatal hepatic necrosis in one tenth of affected patients. The incidence of severe hepatic damage increases with age, such that significant elevation of transaminase levels in persons over the age of 35 is an indication for discontinuing the drug.

Halothane. The commonly used anesthetic agent halothane rarely causes a viral hepatitis-like reaction in susceptible individuals within a few days of exposure. Complete recovery is the rule, but massive hepatic necrosis may occur, usually following repeated exposure.

Chlorpromazine. Chlorpromazine produces a cholestatic reaction, often weeks to months after the drug is begun. Fever, anorexia, and a rash may accompany jaundice and pruritus. Eosinophilia is common. Erythromycin may produce a similar picture, but right upper quadrant pain, mimicking acute cholecystitis, is often prominent.

CHRONIC HEPATITIS

An inflammatory process within the liver that fails to resolve after 6 months is called chronic hepatitis.

Etiology. Many of the causes of acute hepatitis can ultimately lead to chronic hepatitis (Table 41–5). Notable exceptions are the hepatitis A and E viruses. Hepatitis B virus is a common cause of chronic hepatitis worldwide, and it is thought that superimposition of hepatitis D virus infection may produce a more severe outcome. Approximately 6 per cent of patients receiving blood transfusions develop hepatitis C, which becomes chronic in 70 per cent of cases. Several drugs may produce a chronic hepatitis, the best recognized being methyldopa. In contrast to acute hepatitis, an etiologic agent is frequently difficult to identify in cases of chronic hepatitis. The pathogenesis of these idiopathic forms of chronic hepatitis is probably autoimmune in some cases, whereas others are likely to have a viral origin.

Pathology and Clinical and Laboratory Manifestations

CHRONIC PERSISTENT HEPATITIS. Chronic persistent hepatitis is defined as a chronic inflammatory process confined to the portal areas without involvement of the periportal region. This is the most common form of chronic hepatitis, particularly following hepatitis B. The prognosis is generally excellent, with nonprogression or resolution being the rule. Patients with this lesion may be asymptomatic or complain of fatigue and/or right

TABLE 41–5. CAUSES OF CHRONIC HEPATITIS

Viral Infections
  Hepatitis B virus
  Hepatitis B virus with superimposed hepatitis D virus
  Hepatitis C
Drugs and Toxins
  Methyldopa
  Amiodarone
  Isoniazid
Idiopathic
  Idiopathic with prominent autoimmune features (lupoid hepatitis)
  Idiopathic with minimal or no autoimmune features
Metabolic Liver Disease
  Wilson's disease
  Alpha$_1$-antitrypsin deficiency

upper quadrant pain. Laboratory abnormalities are usually confined to mildly raised transaminase levels.

CHRONIC LOBULAR HEPATITIS. Chronic lobular hepatitis, an uncommon form of chronic hepatitis, consists of scattered necrosis throughout the hepatic lobule similar to a late-resolving acute viral hepatitis. Most cases are of viral etiology; progression is uncommon.

CHRONIC ACTIVE HEPATITIS. Chronic active hepatitis, the most serious form of chronic hepatitis, may progress to cirrhosis and liver failure. Histologically, the portal areas are expanded with lymphocytes and plasma cells, with spillover into the adjacent lobule (periportal hepatitis, piecemeal necrosis). Bridging necrosis, collapse, and fibrosis, as well as the features of cirrhosis (see Chapter 43), may be present. Twenty per cent of cases are caused by chronic hepatitis B infection; others may follow hepatitis C. Drugs (Table 41–5) may cause an identical picture. Some cases show associated features that suggest autoimmunity ("lupoid hepatitis").

The clinical course ranges from asymptomatic disease to a severe illness with constitutional symptoms, cutaneous signs of chronic liver disease, jaundice, and hepatosplenomegaly. The variety of chronic active hepatitis called *lupoid hepatitis* predominates in young women and is often accompanied by prominent extrahepatic manifestations, including amenorrhea, skin rashes, acne, vasculitis, thyroiditis, and Sjögren's syndrome. In chronic active hepatitis, transaminase levels are elevated over a wide range and are characteristically accompanied by polyclonal hypergammaglobulinemia. Laboratory evidence of liver failure may be present (hyperbilirubinemia, prolonged prothrombin time, hypoalbuminemia). Antibodies to smooth muscle and antinuclear antibodies may be found, particularly in lupoid hepatitis. Wilson's disease may present clinically and histologically as a chronic active hepatitis and should be excluded in patients under the age of 35 (see Chapter 43).

Liver biopsy is of great value in making the diagnosis of chronic active hepatitis, in differentiating it from milder forms of chronic hepatitis, and in assessing the progression of the disease to cirrhosis. Liver biopsy is considered prerequisite to any attempt to treat the disease with immunosuppressive or antiviral agents.

Treatment. In certain selected cases of chronic active hepatitis, corticosteroid therapy may lead to dramatic improvement in clinical, laboratory, and histologic features of the disease as well as to reduced mortality. Azathioprine is also used, but mainly for its steroid-sparing effect. Patients likely to benefit from corticosteroids are those with severe symptoms, a five-fold or greater elevation in transaminase levels, clinical or serologic evidence of autoimmunity, and marked necroinflammatory activity on liver biopsy.

Patients successfully managed with corticosteroids frequently suffer relapse on discontinuation of the drug and may require its reinstitution. In patients with HBsAg-positive chronic active hepatitis, immunosuppression enhances viral replication. In these patients, as well as in patients with chronic hepatitis C, corticosteroids are of no benefit in the course of the liver disease. On the other hand, patients with chronic hepatitis B or C may benefit from treatment with interferon, which re-

duces viral replication and liver damage but rarely eliminates the infectious agents. Patients with drug-induced chronic hepatitis or Wilson's disease also do not respond to corticosteroids.

Liver transplantation is described in Chapter 42.

REFERENCES

Bass NM: Toxic and drug-induced liver disease. *In* Wyngaarden JB, Smith LH Jr, Bennett JC (eds): Cecil Textbook of Medicine. 19th ed. Philadelphia, WB Saunders Co, 1992, pp 771–775.

Dienstag JL (ed): Viral hepatitis. Semin Liver Dis 11(2):73–181, 1991.

Houghton M, Weiner A, Han J, et al: Molecular biology of the hepatitis C viruses: Implications for diagnosis, development and control of viral disease. Hepatology 14:381, 1991.

Ockner RK: Acute viral hepatitis. *In* Wyngaarden JB, Smith LH Jr, Bennett JC (eds): Cecil Textbook of Medicine. 19th ed. Philadelphia, WB Saunders Co, 1992, pp 763–771.

Ockner RK: Chronic hepatitis. *In* Wyngaarden JB, Smith LH Jr, Bennett JC (eds): Cecil Textbook of Medicine. 19th ed. Philadelphia, WB Saunders Co, 1992, pp 775–778.

Zakim D, Boyer TD, Montgomery CM: Alcoholic liver disease. *In* Zakim D, Boyer TD (eds): Hepatology: A Textbook of Liver Disease. 2nd ed. Philadelphia, WB Saunders Co, 1990, pp 821–869.

42 FULMINANT HEPATIC FAILURE

Fulminant hepatic failure is defined as hepatic failure with Stage III or IV encephalopathy (deep somnolence or coma) which develops in less than 8 weeks in a patient *without pre-existing liver disease.* It results from severe widespread hepatic necrosis, commonly due to acute viral infection with B, A, D, or C viruses. It may also result from exposure to hepatotoxins such as acetaminophen, isoniazid, halothane, valproic acid, mushroom toxins (e.g., those of *Amanita phalloides*), or carbon tetrachloride. Reye's syndrome, a disease predominantly of children, and acute fatty liver of pregnancy, both of which are characterized by microvesicular fatty infiltration and little hepatocellular necrosis, often resemble fulminant hepatic failure. In a number of patients with fulminant hepatic failure, no cause is found, although a viral infection is usually presumed to be responsible.

Diagnosis

The diagnosis rests on the combination of hepatic encephalopathy, acute liver disease (elevated serum bilirubin, transaminase levels), and liver failure, the last-named usually indicated by hypoprothrombinemia.

Treatment

Treatment of fulminant hepatic failure remains supportive, as the underlying etiology of liver failure is rarely treatable (see Hepatic Transplantation, below). However, most processes that result in widespread liver cell necrosis and fulminant hepatic failure are transient events, and liver cell regeneration with recovery of liver function often occurs if patients do not succumb to the complications of liver failure in the interim. Meticulous

TABLE 42-1. MANAGEMENT OF FULMINANT HEPATIC FAILURE

COMPLICATION	PATHOGENESIS	MANAGEMENT
Hepatic encephalopathy	Liver failure	Stop protein, cleanse gut, administer lactulose or neomycin
Hypoglycemia	Decreased gluconeogenesis	Monitor blood sugar 10% glucose IV infusion 50% glucose IV if needed
Hemorrhage	Decreased synthesis of clotting factors Stress ulcers	Vitamin K, fresh frozen plasma Prophylactic oral antacids or IV H_2-receptor antagonists to maintain alkaline gastric pH
	Disseminated intravascular coagulopathy	Fresh frozen plasma
Hyponatremia	Impaired free water clearance	Monitor blood electrolytes and fluid balance Free water restriction
Hypokalemia	—	Potassium supplementation
Respiratory alkalosis	Hyperventilation	No therapy required usually
Metabolic acidosis	Lactic acidosis	IV bicarbonate if necessary
Cerebral edema	—	Consider intracranial pressure monitoring and treatment with IV mannitol
Azotemia	Hypovolemia Hepatorenal syndrome Acute tubular necrosis	Identify and correct hypovolemia Dialysis
Infection	Impaired synthesis of complement	Prevent aspiration and catheter-related infection
Hypotension, hypoxia, pulmonary edema	Reduced systemic vascular resistance Pulmonary right-to-left shunts	Pressors, endotracheal intubation and ventilation

supportive treatment in an intensive care unit setting has been shown to improve survival. Patients with fulminant hepatic failure should be cared for in centers with experience with this disease. Numerous complications (Table 42-1) attend fulminant hepatic failure, and careful identification and treatment of each are essential.

Hepatic encephalopathy, the sine qua non of fulminant hepatic failure, is often the first and most dramatic sign of liver failure. The pathogenesis of hepatic encephalopathy, discussed in Chapter 43, remains unclear; however, most clinical observations suggest a role for protein- and gut-derived toxins that are normally taken up and detoxified by the liver. Hepatic encephalopathy that accompanies fulminant hepatic failure differs from that associated with chronic liver disease in two important aspects: (1) it is rarely due to a reversible precipitating factor (see Table 43-6) and often responds to therapy only when liver function improves; and (2) it is frequently associated with two other potentially treatable causes of coma — hypoglycemia and cerebral edema. Therapy for hepatic encephalopathy follows the principles outlined in Chapter 43. Because these patients are severely ill, all protein intake is stopped, intravenous glucose (1000 to 1500 kcal/day) is administered, and lactulose is administered orally, per nasogastric tube, or by enema to cleanse the colon. Intubation is necessary to protect the airway from aspiration and to allow ventilation in patients with advanced encephalopathy.

Hypoglycemia is a common complication of liver failure. All patients should receive 10 per cent glucose IV infusions with frequent monitoring of blood glucose levels. Other metabolic abnormalities commonly occur, including *hyponatremia,* *hypokalemia, respiratory alkalosis,* and *metabolic acidosis.* Thus frequent monitoring of blood electrolytes and pH is indicated.

Gastrointestinal hemorrhage may occur from stress ulcers, particularly in the face of impaired synthesis of clotting factors. All patients should receive vitamin K and prophylactic oral antacids or IV H_2-receptor antagonists to maintain gastric pH above 5. Fresh frozen plasma should be used if clinically significant bleeding occurs, or if major procedures, including intracranial pressure monitoring and central line placement, are performed.

Renal insufficiency is common in patients with liver failure (see Chapter 30). It is essential that hypovolemia be excluded as a cause of azotemia, by measuring central venous pressure if necessary. Patients with either hepatorenal syndrome or acute tubular necrosis who have oliguria or acidosis may require dialysis.

Cerebral edema, the pathogenesis of which is unknown, is a particularly common complication of fulminant hepatic failure. It may result in intracranial herniation and generally portends a fatal outcome. Corticosteroid therapy is not useful; however, the outcome may be improved, at least temporarily, with intracranial pressure monitoring, hyperventilation, IV administration of mannitol, and barbiturate-induced coma in selected patients.

Many other forms of therapy for fulminant hepatic failure have been tried, including corticosteroid administration, exchange transfusion, plasmapheresis, hemodialysis, charcoal hemoperfusion, and extracorporeal perfusion through a human cadaver or pig liver. None has been shown to offer any advantage over conventional supportive therapy, however.

Hepatic Transplantation

Hepatic transplantation (see Chapter 43) has been performed with considerable success in patients with fulminant hepatic failure and is the treatment of choice for patients who appear unlikely to recover spontaneously. Because of the need for urgent transplantation, potential candidates should be transferred to transplant centers before they develop significant complications (such as coma, cerebral edema, hemorrhage, or infection).

Prognosis

Short-term prognosis without liver transplantation is very poor, with the average reported survival being about 20 per cent. Long-term prognosis for those who survive is excellent. Follow-up studies have shown normal liver function and histology in virtually all surviving patients, regardless of the cause of the fulminant hepatic failure. Survival in the range of 80 to 90 per cent can be expected following liver transplantation for fulminant hepatic failure. Transplantation is usually indicated in patients with severe encephalopathy or coagulopathy, or in those whose clinical course is protracted and subacute. The cause is also important in determining prognosis. Patients with fulminant hepatic failure from hepatitis A, acetaminophen overdosage, or microvesicular steatosis are more likely to recover spontaneously; those with idiosyncratic drug-induced liver failure, hepatitis B, or idiopathic fulminant liver failure rarely survive without transplantation.

REFERENCES

Katelaris PH, Jones DB: Fulminant hepatic failure. Med Clin North Am 73:955, 1989.
Scharschmidt BF: Acute and chronic hepatic failure. In Wyngaarden JB, Smith LH Jr, Bennett JC (eds): Cecil Textbook of Medicine. 19th ed. Philadelphia, WB Saunders Co, 1992, pp 796–799.

43 CIRRHOSIS OF THE LIVER AND ITS COMPLICATIONS

DEFINITION

Cirrhosis is the irreversible end result of fibrous scarring and hepatocellular regeneration that constitute the major responses of the liver to a variety of longstanding inflammatory, toxic, metabolic, and congestive insults. In cirrhosis, the normal hepatic lobular architecture is replaced by interconnecting bands of fibrous tissue surrounding nodules derived from foci of regenerating hepatocytes.

Regenerative nodules may be small (<3 mm, micronodular cirrhosis), a typical feature of alcoholic cirrhosis, or large (>3 mm, macronodular cirrhosis). The latter, also termed postnecrotic cirrhosis, is more commonly seen as a sequel to chronic active hepatitis. The pathology of cirrhosis determines its natural history and clinical manifestations. Thus, fibrous scarring and disruption of the hepatic architecture distort the vascular bed, leading to portal hypertension and intrahepatic shunting. Normal hepatocyte function is disturbed by the resulting inadequacy of blood flow and ongoing direct toxic, inflammatory, and/or metabolic damage to the hepatocytes.

ETIOLOGY

Most of the conditions that may lead to cirrhosis (Table 43–1) are rarely encountered. Alcohol abuse and hepatitis C are by far the most common causes of cirrhosis in the Western world, whereas hepatitis B is a major cause in the Third World. Cryptogenic cirrhosis is a diagnosis of exclusion, but many cases are likely to be an end result of chronic hepatitis C infection. Causes of hepatic fibrosis alone (e.g., schistosomiasis, which leads to fibrosis of portal venous radicles and portal hypertension) are not classified as causes of cirrhosis, because the hepatic lobular pattern is well preserved and hepatocellular dysfunction (e.g., disordered protein synthesis) is usually lacking.

CLINICAL AND LABORATORY FEATURES

The presence of cirrhosis may remain undetected until autopsy. Individuals with cirrhosis who experience no symptoms and show little clinical evidence of hepatocellular dysfunction are often said to have *well-compensated* cirrhosis. As evidence of complications develops, particularly signs implying disturbed hepatocellular function, the clinical condition is referred to as *decompensated* cirrhosis. If the disease process leading to cirrhosis primarily affects the hepatocytes, as with excessive alcohol intake (parenchymal liver disease), evidence of failing hepatocellular function may be prominent in the clinical presentation. If the biliary system is primarily affected, as occurs in primary or secondary biliary cirrhosis, the clinical features of cholestasis predominate and hepatic failure is a late event.

It is convenient to divide the main clinical and laboratory features of cirrhosis into four categories (Table 43–2):

1. *Size and consistency of the liver.*
2. *Features attributable to hepatocellular dysfunction.* These result from both intrinsically "sick" hepatocytes and the shunting of portal blood away from hepatocytes with consequent failure to extract toxins and metabolites.
3. *Features attributable to portal hypertension.*
4. *Extrahepatic features related to specific diseases causing cirrhosis.*

Liver size depends upon the underlying pathologic process. In end-stage liver disease due to hepatitis B or C virus infection, the liver is often small, scarred, and shrunken. In alcoholic cirrhosis, fat infiltration may lead to marked enlargement of the liver. Impaired hepatic detoxification of estrogens, as well as disturbed hypothalamic-pituitary function, produces several cutaneous signs (often called "stigmata" of cirrhosis, e.g., spider angiomas, palmar erythema). Marked jaundice in the absence of complete bile duct obstruction is often a grave prognostic sign implying advanced hepatocellular dysfunction. Impaired hepatocellular protein synthesis leads to hypoalbuminemia and hypoprothrombinemia.

SPECIFIC CAUSES OF CIRRHOSIS

Alcohol. Alcoholic cirrhosis may coexist with alcoholic hepatitis. Features of hepatocellular dysfunction are thus often marked and may improve with abstinence. Micronodular cirrhosis is the rule but is not specific for alcoholic cirrhosis. Evidence of malnutrition and vitamin deficiency is frequently found, particularly in the severely alcoholic patient. Anemia of mixed etiology is common, often with macrocytic indices.

Chronic Active Hepatitis. Chronic active hepatitis from any cause may progress to cirrhosis. The liver is typically small with a macronodular pattern. Evidence of continued inflammatory activity is often present, including moderate elevation of transaminase levels and hypergammaglobulinemia. HBsAg is usually persistently positive in cirrhosis due to hepatitis B virus infection, whereas anti-HCV antibody is often present in cirrhosis due to chronic hepatitis C infection.

Primary Biliary Cirrhosis. Almost exclusively a disease affecting women, primary biliary cirrhosis manifests mainly between the ages of 30 and

TABLE 43–1. CAUSES OF CIRRHOSIS

Alcohol
Hepatitis Viruses (B and C)
Drugs
  Methyldopa
  Methotrexate
  Amiodarone
Autoimmune Chronic Active Hepatitis
Biliary Cirrhosis
  Primary biliary cirrhosis
  Secondary biliary cirrhosis
    bile duct strictures
    sclerosing cholangitis
    biliary atresia
    tumors of the bile ducts
    cystic fibrosis
Chronic Hepatic Congestion
  Budd-Chiari syndrome
  Chronic right heart failure
  Constrictive pericarditis
Genetically Determined Metabolic Diseases
  Hemochromatosis
  Wilson's disease
  Alpha$_1$-antitrypsin deficiency
  Galactosemia
Cryptogenic

65 and results from a progressive, probably immune-mediated destruction of the interlobular bile ducts. Cholestatic features predominate with high serum levels of alkaline phosphatase and

TABLE 43–2. CLINICAL AND LABORATORY FEATURES OF CIRRHOSIS

CLINICAL	LABORATORY
Size and Consistency of the Liver	
Hepatomegaly, or small shrunken liver	
Firm to hard consistency	
Hepatocellular Dysfunction	
Jaundice	Hyperbilirubinemia
Spider angiomas	
Palmar erythema	
Gynecomastia	
Loss of body hair	
Testicular atrophy	
Dupuytren's contracture	
Muscle wasting, edema	Hypoalbuminemia, low BUN
Bruising	Prolonged prothrombin time
Signs of hepatic encephalopathy	Elevated blood ammonia
Fetor hepaticus	
Portal Hypertension	
Splenomegaly	Thrombocytopenia, leukopenia
Ascites	
Caput medusa	
Variceal bleeding	
Signs of Specific Diseases	
CREST syndrome	Antimitochondrial antibody (primary biliary cirrhosis)
Kayser-Fleischer rings	Low ceruloplasmin (Wilson's disease)

cholesterol. Pruritus is a major early symptom, followed later in the course of the disease by xanthomas, hyperpigmentation, and bone pain due to osteoporosis or osteomalacia. Commonly associated conditions include Sjögren's syndrome, scleroderma, and the CREST syndrome (calcinosis, Raynaud's syndrome, esophageal dysfunction, sclerodactyly, telangiectasia). Antimitochondrial antibodies are present in high titer, and serum IgM levels are elevated. Liver biopsy may show characteristic destructive lesions of the bile ducts and is of value in confirming the diagnosis. Jaundice is a prominent feature late in the course of the disease.

Hemochromatosis. See Chapter 61.
Wilson's Disease. See Chapter 61.

MAJOR COMPLICATIONS OF CIRRHOSIS

The major sequelae of cirrhosis are:

1. Portal hypertension, with its attendant complications of (a) variceal hemorrhage and (b) splenomegaly and hypersplenism
2. Liver failure
3. Ascites, which may be further complicated by spontaneous bacterial peritonitis
4. The hepatorenal syndrome
5. Portosystemic (hepatic) encephalopathy
6. Hepatocellular carcinoma

The pathophysiologic interrelationships among these complications are shown diagrammatically in Figure 43–1.

Portal Hypertension

The normal liver offers little resistance to portal venous blood flow (about 1 L/min), and portal pressure is normally less than 5 mm Hg above inferior vena caval pressure. The distortion of hepatic architecture in cirrhosis leads to a marked increase in resistance to portal venous flow, which in turn leads to an increase in portal venous pressure.

Although cirrhosis is the most important cause of portal hypertension, any process leading to increased resistance to portal blood flow into (presinusoidal) or through the liver (sinusoidal) or to hepatic venous outflow from the liver (postsinusoidal) results in portal hypertension (Table 43–3). Because the pressure within any vascular system is proportional to both resistance and blood flow, a marked increase in blood flow alone also results in portal hypertension. Although such situations are rare, increased blood flow probably contributes to the portal hypertension that develops in cirrhosis.

Portal hypertension leads to the formation of venous collaterals between the portal and systemic circulations. Collaterals may form at several sites, the most important clinically being those connecting the portal to the azygos vein, which

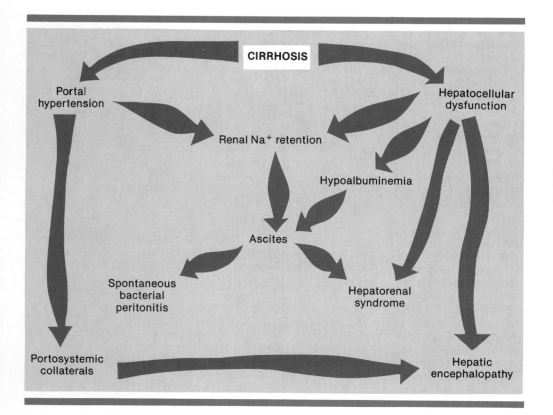

FIGURE 43–1. Interrelationships between the complications of cirrhosis.

TABLE 43-3. CAUSES OF PORTAL HYPERTENSION

I. **Increased Resistance to Flow**
    Presinusoidal
        Portal or splenic vein occlusion (thrombosis, tumor)
        Schistosomiasis
        Congenital hepatic fibrosis
        Sarcoidosis
    Sinusoidal
        Cirrhosis (all causes)
        Alcoholic hepatitis
    Postsinusoidal
        Veno-occlusive disease
        Budd-Chiari syndrome
        Constrictive pericarditis
II. **Increased Portal Blood Flow**
    Splenomegaly not due to liver disease
    Arterioportal fistula

form dilated, tortuous veins (varices) in the submucosa of the gastric fundus and esophagus.

Variceal Hemorrhage. Hemorrhage occurs most frequently from varices in the esophagus and is a common and serious complication of portal hypertension, with a mortality rate of 30 to 60 per cent. Large varices bleed most commonly, and bleeding occurs when high tension in the walls of these vessels leads to rupture. Bleeding may present as hematemesis, hematochezia, melena, or any combination of these (see Chapter 32B). Bleeding may lead to shock, stop spontaneously, or recur. Impaired hepatic synthesis of coagulation factors (hepatocellular dysfunction) and thrombocytopenia (hypersplenism) may further complicate the management of variceal bleeding. The management of variceal bleeding has been discussed in Chapter 32B, and here we emphasize a few important details.

VASOPRESSIN. When given by intravenous infusion, this posterior pituitary hormone causes constriction of splanchnic arterioles and a reduction in portal flow and pressure. Bleeding may be controlled by this measure but recurs in about 50 per cent of patients. The use of vasopressin does not reduce mortality.

BALLOON TAMPONADE. Compression of the varices by inserting a tube with inflatable gastric and esophageal balloons (Sengstaken-Blakemore tube) is an effective, although often temporary, measure. Complications such as aspiration and esophageal rupture may occur, and rebleeding occurs in up to 60 per cent of patients after the tube is removed.

ENDOSCOPIC INJECTION SCLEROTHERAPY. During endoscopy, varices may be injected with sclerosing solutions to arrest acute bleeding. Repeated courses of injection can lead to variceal obliteration, and this approach has been used to prevent recurrent bleeding. However, bleeding frequently recurs prior to complete variceal obliteration, and esophageal strictures are a common complication.

PORTOSYSTEMIC SHUNT SURGERY. Portal decompression may be achieved by a variety of operative procedures aimed at creating a large connection between the high-pressure portal and low-pressure systemic venous systems. Nonselective shunts (e.g., portacaval anastomoses, transjugular intrahepatic portosystemic shunt) decompress the entire portal system. Selective shunts (e.g., the distal splenorenal shunt) decompress the varices only. Survival is not improved by shunt surgery, and hepatic encephalopathy is a major complication. Shunt surgery is usually performed electively to prevent recurrent bleeding in patients with good preservation of liver function. Emergency shunt surgery carries a 50 per cent mortality and is rarely undertaken.

OTHER THERAPEUTIC MEASURES. Long-term treatment with beta-blocking drugs, mainly propranolol, reduces portal pressure and variceal blood flow. Beta blockers have shown promise in the prevention of variceal bleeding.

Splenomegaly. Portal hypertension leads to *congestive splenomegaly*, which is often, but not always, clinically apparent. Thrombocytopenia and, less commonly, leukopenia occur as a result of sequestration of platelets and leukocytes in the enlarged spleen (hypersplenism). Diminished numbers of these formed elements are usually of little clinical significance.

Liver Failure

The cirrhotic liver is often impaired in the synthesis of proteins by hepatocytes (hypoalbuminemia, impaired synthesis of coagulation factors) and in normal hepatic detoxification processes. The latter accounts for the development of signs such as spider angiomas and contributes to the development of hepatic encephalopathy, as well as to poorly understood hemodynamic and hormonal disorders that foster the development of ascites and the hepatorenal syndrome.

Ascites

Ascites is the accumulation of excess fluid in the peritoneal cavity. Although cirrhosis is the most common cause of ascites, it may result from numerous other causes (Table 43-4). Ascites due to cirrhosis is commonly a transudate (protein concentration <3 gm/dl), whereas inflammatory and neoplastic causes usually lead to formation of an exudate (protein >3 gm/dl). Ascites becomes clinically detectable when more than 500 ml has accumulated. Shifting dullness to percussion is the most sensitive clinical sign of ascites, but ultrasonography more readily detects small fluid volumes.

Ascites in cirrhosis is the result of several pathogenetic factors: (1) portal hypertension with increased hepatic and splanchnic lymph production and transudation; (2) impaired renal sodium and water excretion secondary to hyperaldosteronism, increased levels of antidiuretic hormone, and other less well understood factors; and (3) hypoalbuminemia.

TABLE 43-4. CAUSES OF ASCITES

Exudative Ascites
   Tuberculous peritonitis
   Pancreatitis
   Ruptured viscus (including bile peritonitis)
   Tumors (most commonly metastatic to liver and peritoneal lining)
Transudative Ascites
   Cirrhosis
   Chronic hepatic congestion
      Budd-Chiari syndrome
      Constrictive pericarditis
      Right heart failure
   Nephrotic syndrome
   Myxedema
   Meigs' syndrome
Chylous Ascites
   Thoracic duct or abdominal lymphatic trauma
   Mediastinal tumors

Differential diagnosis of ascites: ovarian cyst, pancreatic cyst, mesenteric cyst, urinary tract rupture

Treatment of ascites consists initially of bed rest with restriction of sodium intake. Restricted fluid intake may be necessary if hyponatremia is present. These measures are commonly inadequate, and administration of spironolactone, an aldosterone antagonist, supplemented with a loop diuretic (e.g., furosemide) is often effective. Diuresis should be promoted cautiously, because aggressive diuretic therapy may result in hypokalemia and a depleted plasma volume, leading to hepatic encephalopathy and impaired renal function. A few patients may be extremely refractory to medical measures and may benefit from a surgically implanted plastic shunt between the peritoneal cavity and the superior vena cava (LeVeen shunt). Patients with massive ascites may benefit from repeated abdominal paracentesis of several liters of ascitic fluid, combined with intravenous colloid replacement.

Two important complications occur in patients with cirrhotic ascites: spontaneous bacterial peritonitis and the hepatorenal syndrome.

Spontaneous Bacterial Peritonitis. Infection of ascitic fluid, usually with coliform bacteria, may occur in patients with cirrhosis. Fever, abdominal pain, and tenderness may be present, or the infection may be clinically silent. Hepatic encephalopathy may be precipitated. The diagnosis is strongly suspected if the ascitic fluid polymorphonuclear leukocyte count is greater than 250/mm³, and is confirmed by culture. Vigorous antibiotic treatment is indicated, but mortality from this complication is high.

Hepatorenal Syndrome. Serious liver disease from any cause may be complicated by a form of functional renal failure termed the hepatorenal syndrome. It almost invariably occurs in the presence of severe ascites. Typically, the kidneys are histologically normal, with the capacity of regaining normal function in the event of recovery of liver function. The renal dysfunction is characterized by a declining glomerular filtration rate (GFR), oliguria, low urine sodium (<10 mEq/L), and azotemia, often with a disproportionately high blood urea nitrogen(BUN)/creatinine ratio. The decline in renal function often follows one of three events in a cirrhotic patient with ascites: sepsis, a vigorous attempt to reduce ascites with diuretics, or a large-volume paracentesis.

The hepatorenal syndrome is usually progressive and fatal. It should be diagnosed only after plasma volume depletion (a common cause of reversible, prerenal azotemia in patients with cirrhosis, particularly with diuretic use) and other forms of acute renal injury have been ruled out.

Hepatic Encephalopathy

Hepatic encephalopathy (also called hepatic coma or portosystemic encephalopathy) is a complex neuropsychiatric syndrome that may complicate advanced liver disease and/or extensive portosystemic collateral formation (shunting). Two major forms of hepatic encephalopathy are recognized:

Acute hepatic encephalopathy usually occurs in the setting of fulminant hepatic failure. Cerebral edema plays a more important role in this setting: coma is common and mortality is very high (see Chapter 42).

Chronic hepatic encephalopathy usually occurs with chronic liver disease, commonly manifests as subtle disturbances of neurologic function, and is often reversible.

The pathogenesis of hepatic encephalopathy is thought to involve the inadequate hepatic removal of predominantly nitrogenous compounds or other toxins ingested or formed in the gastrointestinal tract. Inadequate hepatic removal results from impaired hepatocyte function as well as the extensive shunting of splanchnic blood directly into the systemic circulation via portosystemic collaterals. Nitrogenous and other absorbed compounds are thought to gain access to the central nervous system, leading to disturbances in neuronal function. Ammonia, derived from both amino acid deamination and bacterial hydrolysis of nitrogenous compounds in the gut, has been strongly implicated in the pathogenesis of hepatic encephalopathy, but its blood levels correlate poorly with the presence or degree of encephalopathy. Other proposed neurotoxins include gamma-aminobutyric acid, mercaptans, short-chain fatty acids, and benzodiazepine-like compounds. Mercaptans are also thought to produce the characteristic breath odor (fetor hepaticus) of patients with chronic liver failure. Another hypothesis suggests that an imbalance between plasma branched-chain and aromatic amino acids, a common consequence of severe liver disease, leads to decreased synthesis of normal neurotransmitters and to increased formation of "false neurotransmitters" from aromatic amino acids in the central nervous system.

The clinical features of hepatic encephalopathy

include disturbances of higher neurologic function (intellectual and personality disorders, dementia, inability to copy simple diagrams [i.e., constructional apraxia], disturbance of consciousness), disturbances of neuromuscular function (asterixis, hyperreflexia, myoclonus), and rarely, a Parkinson-like syndrome and progressive paraplegia. As with other metabolic encephalopathies (which may show many of the signs of hepatic encephalopathy), asymmetric neurologic findings are unusual but can occur, and brain stem reflexes (e.g., pupillary light, oculovestibular, and oculocephalic responses) are preserved until very late. Hepatic encephalopathy is usually divided into stages according to its severity (Table 43–5). Subtle disorders of psychomotor function may exist in many patients with cirrhosis in whom conventional neurologic examination is normal. Such subclinical encephalopathy (termed stage 0 encephalopathy) is of importance in that it may impair work performance.

The differential diagnosis of hepatic encephalopathy includes hypoglycemia, subdural hematoma, meningitis, and sedative drug overdose, all of which are common in patients, particularly alcoholics, with liver disease.

Treatment. Treatment of hepatic encephalopathy is based on four simple principles:

IDENTIFICATION AND TREATMENT OF PRECIPITATING FACTORS. Table 43–6 lists several important factors that may precipitate or severely aggravate hepatic encephalopathy in patients with severe liver disease. Gastrointestinal bleeding and increased protein intake may provide increased substrate for the bacterial or metabolic formation of nitrogenous compounds that induce encephalopathy. Patients prone to develop hepatic encephalopathy have a markedly increased sensitivity to central nervous system–depressant drugs, and their use should be avoided in these patients.

REDUCTION AND ELIMINATION OF SUBSTRATE FOR THE GENERATION OF NITROGENOUS COMPOUNDS

Dietary protein restriction. Patients in coma should receive no protein, whereas those with mild encephalopathy may benefit from restriction of protein intake to 40 to 60 gm/day. Vegetable protein diets also appear to be less encephalopathogenic.

Bowel cleansing. This is important mainly in patients with encephalopathy precipitated by acute gastrointestinal bleeding or constipation and is achieved by administration of enemas.

REDUCTION OF COLONIC BACTERIA. Neomycin administered orally reduces the number of bacteria that are responsible for production of ammonia and other nitrogenous compounds.

PREVENTION OF AMMONIA DIFFUSION FROM THE BOWEL. This is achieved by administration of lactulose, a nonabsorbable disaccharide, which, when fermented to organic acids by colonic bacteria, leads to a lower stool pH. This lowered pH traps ammonia in the colon as nondiffusible NH_4^+ ions, but other mechanisms such as inhibition of bacterial ammonia production may also be important.

TABLE 43–5. STAGES OF HEPATIC ENCEPHALOPATHY

STAGE	CLINICAL MANIFESTATIONS
I	apathy restlessness reversal of sleep rhythm slowed intellect impaired computational ability impaired handwriting
II	lethargy drowsiness disorientation asterixis
III	stupor (arousable) hyperactive reflexes, extensor plantar responses
IV	coma (response to painful stimuli only)

Stage 0 encephalopathy is used to describe subclinical impairment of intellectual function.

TABLE 43–6. HEPATIC ENCEPHALOPATHY: PRECIPITATING FACTORS

Gastrointestinal bleeding
Increased dietary protein
Constipation
Infection
CNS-depressant drugs (benzodiazepines, opiates)
Deterioration in hepatic function
Hypokalemia ⎤
Azotemia   ⎥ most often induced by diuretics
Alkalosis ⎥
Hypovolemia ⎦

Hepatocellular Carcinoma

Hepatocellular carcinoma and its relationship to cirrhosis are discussed in Chapter 44.

HEPATIC TRANSPLANTATION

Liver transplantation is a highly successful procedure in patients with progressive, advanced, and otherwise untreatable liver disease. Advances in surgical techniques and supportive care, the use of cyclosporine for immunosuppression, and careful selection of patients have all contributed to the recent encouraging results of liver transplantation. Seventy to 80 per cent of patients undergoing liver transplantation survive at least 3 years, usually with good quality of life. The types of liver disease for which transplantation now is most commonly performed include cirrhosis (e.g., primary biliary cirrhosis, chronic active hepatitis, alcoholic liver disease) and sclerosing cholangitis in adults and biliary atresia and metabolic disorders (e.g., alpha₁-antitrypsin deficiency, Wilson's disease) in children. Excellent results have also been obtained in patients with fulminant hepatic failure (see Chapter 42). Transplantation for malignant hepatobiliary disease and hepatitis B virus-related disease has been less successful owing to recurrent disease in the transplanted liver.

The timing of liver transplantation presents a particular challenge because no technology for artificial support, analogous to hemodialysis, is yet available. The survival of ambulatory patients undergoing liver transplantation electively is greater than that of those who are critically ill at the time of the operation. Thus, transplantation is usually considered when deterioration in liver function (e.g., increasing jaundice, encephalopathy, ascites, or variceal bleeding) or declining quality of life becomes evident.

REFERENCES

Boyer TD: Cirrhosis of the liver and its major sequelae. *In* Wyngaarden JB, Smith LH Jr, Bennett JC (eds): Cecil Textbook of Medicine. 19th ed. Philadelphia, WB Saunders Co, 1992, pp 786–796.
Roberts JP: Liver transplantation. *In* Wyngaarden JB, Smith LH Jr, Bennett JC (eds): Cecil Textbook of Medicine. 19th ed. Philadelphia, WB Saunders Co, 1992, pp 799–801.
Scharschmidt BF: Acute and chronic hepatic failure. *In* Wyngaarden JB, Smith LH Jr, Bennett JC (eds): Cecil Textbook of Medicine. 19th ed. Philadelphia, WB Saunders Co, 1992, pp 796–799.
Wilkinson SP, Moore KP, Arroyo V: Pathogenesis of ascites and hepatorenal syndrome. Gut Supplement S-12, September, 1991.

44 HEPATIC NEOPLASMS AND GRANULOMATOUS AND VASCULAR LIVER DISEASE

HEPATIC NEOPLASMS

Hepatic neoplasms can be divided into three groups: (1) benign neoplasms, (2) primary malignant neoplasms, and (3) metastatic malignant neoplasms. The last-named category, that of metastatic tumors, constitutes the bulk of hepatic neoplasms in this country. This chapter briefly reviews all three categories of hepatic neoplasms and concludes with a brief discussion of the diagnostic approach to these lesions.

Benign Neoplasms

The group of benign neoplastic lesions includes hepatocellular adenoma, focal nodular hyperplasia, hemangioma, bile duct adenoma, and other rare tumors of mesenchymal origin (e.g., fibromas, lipomas, leiomyomas). Hemangiomas, the most common hepatic neoplasm, are often readily identified by rapid-sequence computed tomography (CT), dynamic radionuclide scanning with ^{99m}Tc-pertechnetate–labeled red blood cells or T_2-weighted magnetic resonance imaging (MRI). No further evaluation is necessary unless lesions are large and symptomatic. Hepatocellular adenomas occur almost exclusively in women, and strong circumstantial evidence implicates estrogens, especially oral contraceptives, in their development and growth. Adenomas consist of a monotonous array of normal hepatocytes without bile ducts, portal tracts, or Kupffer cells. Although they are not regarded as premalignant lesions, they have a predilection for hemorrhage, tumor infarct, and rupture. Patients usually have signs and symptoms of an abdominal mass or hemorrhage (pain, fever, circulatory collapse). When circulatory collapse occurs, usually emergency surgery with resection of the adenoma is required.

Adenomas usually appear as cold spots on ^{99m}Tc-sulfur colloid scans and as vascular lesions on angiography. Management of asymptomatic lesions is controversial, although elective surgical excision is usually performed. A trial period of observation may be warranted if oral contraceptives can be discontinued, and some adenomas have been noted to regress under this regimen.

Hepatocellular Carcinoma

Hepatocellular carcinoma is rare in the United States (accounting for fewer than 2.5 per cent of all malignancies). In other areas of the world, including sub-Sahara Africa, China, Japan, and Southeast Asia, it is one of the most frequent malignancies and is an important cause of mortality, particularly in middle-aged males. Hepatocellular carcinoma often arises in a cirrhotic liver and is closely associated with chronic hepatitis B or C virus infection. The advent and widespread use of vaccination to prevent infection with hepatitis B virus are expected to reduce markedly the incidence of this disease, the only disease for which effective immunization against a malignancy is currently available. The risk of hepatocellular carcinoma is low in cirrhosis associated with primary biliary cirrhosis and Wilson's disease, intermediate in cirrhosis due to alcohol, and high in hemochromatosis. Other risk factors for development of hepatocellular carcinoma, as well as its clinical manifestations, are listed in Table 44–1. Diagnosis of small, surgically resectable lesions in high-risk areas is possible with intensive screening programs that employ ultrasound examinations and serum α-fetoprotein levels, although the long-term outcome remains unclear. Most patients present with widespread, often multifocal disease, and the median survival from the time of diagnosis is less than 6 months. Chemotherapy, radiation therapy, and hepatic transplantation have yielded disappointing results.

Other primary hepatocellular malignancies include cholangiocarcinoma, angiosarcoma (related to exposure to vinyl choride, arsenic, or Thorotrast), hepatoblastoma, and cystadenocarcinoma.

Tumor Metastases to the Liver

Metastases constitute the bulk of hepatic malignancies in the United States and most commonly derive from tumors of the stomach, pancreas, colon, lung, oropharynx, and bladder and from melanoma. The liver is also a frequent site of involvement by Hodgkin's disease, non-Hodgkin's lymphoma, and malignant histiocytosis.

Diagnostic Approach to Hepatic Neoplasms

Most patients with hepatic neoplasms present with right upper quadrant abdominal pain or a hepatic mass. Hemorrhage, systemic manifestations, and biliary obstruction (from strategically located tumors) may also occur. Visualization of discrete focal lesions and histologic examination of tissue are generally required for diagnosis. Thus evaluation employs one or more imaging procedures followed by percutaneous, laparoscopic, or surgical biopsy of one or more lesions. Radionuclide scanning is a reasonable first step in the work-up, although imaging by CT or ultrasonography may be more sensitive in detecting small lesions and offers the advantage of performing guided percutaneous biopsy or aspiration cytology. MRI may be particularly helpful in this regard. Localization of lesions is generally followed by biopsy; however, additional factors must be considered. Percutaneous biopsies of vascular lesions such as hemangiomas, angiosarcomas, and perhaps hepatocellular adenomas are potentially dangerous, whereas cells obtained by aspiration cytology frequently fail to differentiate hepatocellular adenoma, hepatocellular carcinoma, and normal hepatic tissue. Thus, the choice of procedures depends on the diagnostic and therapeutic options under consideration.

TABLE 44–1. HEPATOCELLULAR CARCINOMA

Incidence
From 1–7 per 100,000 to >100 per 100,000 in high-risk areas

Sex
4:1 to 8:1 male preponderance

Associations
Chronic hepatitis B infection
Chronic hepatitis C infection
Hemochromatosis (with cirrhosis)
Cirrhosis (alcoholic, cryptogenic)
Aflatoxin ingestion
Thorotrast
Alpha$_1$-antitrypsin deficiency
Androgen administration

Common Clinical Presentations
Abdominal pain
Abdominal mass
Weight loss
Deterioration of liver function

Unusual Manifestations
Bloody ascites
Tumor emboli (lung)
Jaundice
Hepatic or portal vein obstruction
Metabolic effects:
Erythrocytosis
Hypercalcemia
Hypercholesterolemia
Hypoglycemia
Gynecomastia
Feminization
Acquired porphyria

Clinical/Laboratory Findings
Hepatic bruit or friction rub
Serum α-fetoprotein level >400 ng/ml

GRANULOMATOUS LIVER DISEASE

Hepatic granulomas are common, being found in 2 to 10 per cent of all liver biopsies, often in association with an elevated serum alkaline phosphatase level. However, they are rarely a specific finding and have been reported in association with a wide variety of infections, systemic illnesses, hepatobiliary disorders, drugs, and toxins, some of which are listed in Table 44–2. Although granulomas are a nonspecific finding, occasionally specific features are seen, such as acid-fast bacilli in tuberculosis, ova in schistosomiasis, larvae in toxocariasis, and birefringent granules in starch, talc, or silicone granulomas. The differential diagnosis of hepatic granulomas is one of the most extensive in medicine, and the work-up requires meticulous attention to details of the history, physical examination, and laboratory tests. Indeed, in 20 per cent or more of patients, no cause for granulomas is found despite extensive investigation. A subset of these patients have a syndrome consisting of fever, hepatomegaly, and hepatic granulomas which responds to administration of corticosteroids, described as "granulomatous hepatitis." These patients may possibly have a variant of sarcoidosis.

Liver biopsy (and culture, particularly of acid-fast bacteria) is of considerable value in the diagnosis of sarcoidosis, miliary tuberculosis, and histoplasmosis, as virtually all patients with these disorders have hepatic granulomas. Characteristic granulomas are seen in many patients with primary biliary cirrhosis, and granulomas may be the first clue to Hodgkin's disease.

TABLE 44–2. DISEASES ASSOCIATED WITH HEPATIC GRANULOMAS

Infections
  Bacterial, spirochetal
    Tuberculosis and atypical
      mycobacterial infections
    Tularemia
    Brucellosis
    Leprosy
    Syphilis
    Whipple's disease
    Listeriosis
  Viral
    Infectious mononucleosis
    Cytomegalovirus infections
  Rickettsial
    Q fever
  Fungal
    Coccidioidomycosis
    Histoplasmosis
    Cryptococcal infections
    Actinomycosis
    Aspergillosis
    Nocardiosis
  Parasitic
    Schistosomiasis
    Clonorchiasis
    Toxocariasis
    Ascariasis
    Toxoplasmosis
    Amebiasis

Hepatobiliary Disorders
  Primary biliary cirrhosis
  Granulomatous hepatitis
  Jejunoileal bypass
Systemic Disorders
  Sarcoidosis
  Wegener's granulomatosis
  Inflammatory bowel disease
  Hodgkin's disease
  Lymphoma
Drugs/Toxins
  Beryllium
  Parenteral foreign material
    (starch, talc, silicone, etc.)
  Phenylbutazone
  Alpha methyldopa
  Procainamide
  Allopurinol
  Phenytoin
  Nitrofurantoin
  Hydralazine

VASCULAR DISEASE OF THE LIVER

Portal vein thrombosis, hepatic vein thrombosis (Budd-Chiari syndrome), and veno-occlusive disease are uncommon disorders of hepatic vasculature; affected patients usually present with portal hypertension with or without associated liver dysfunction.

Portal vein thrombosis may develop after abdominal trauma, umbilical vein infection, sepsis, or pancreatitis or in association with cirrhosis or hypercoagulable states; in most cases, however, and particularly in children, the cause is unknown. The disease produces the manifestations of portal hypertension (see Chapter 43); however, liver histology is usually normal. The diagnosis is established by angiography. Surgical management may be difficult owing to the absence of suitable patent vessels for portal-systemic shunting.

The *Budd-Chiari syndrome* is associated with abdominal trauma, use of oral contraceptives, polycythemia vera, paroxysmal nocturnal hemoglobinuria, other hypercoagulable states, and congenital webs of the vena cava. Illness may be acute or chronic with abdominal pain, hepatomeg-aly, ascites, and portal hypertension as prominent features. The diagnosis is usually suspected when centrilobular necrosis is seen on liver biopsy and is established angiographically by inability to catheterize the hepatic veins. Although elevation of serum bilirubin and transaminase levels may be mild, liver function is often poor and mortality rates of 40 to 90 per cent are reported. Anticoagulants have not proven useful; however, side-to-side portacaval shunts, performed to relieve hepatic congestion, may improve survival, and liver transplantation may be curative.

Veno-occlusive disease, or nonthrombotic occlusion of hepatic venules, is a small vessel variant of the Budd-Chiari syndrome. Veno-occlusive disease develops in humans and animals exposed to native medicinal teas containing pyrrolozidine alkaloids from *Senecio* and *Crotalia* genera of plants. Cases have also been reported in association with the use of certain chemotherapeutic agents and with bone marrow transplantation. The occluded venules can be seen on liver biopsy, and a distinctive abnormal vascular pattern may be seen when contrast is injected into the hepatic vein. Patients with alcoholic liver disease also frequently exhibit some degree of hepatic venule sclerosis or occlusion. No specific treatment is available. Some patients appear to recover spontaneously, whereas others require therapy for the complications of portal hypertension.

LIVER ABSCESS

Pyogenic and amebic liver abscesses are important mass lesions of the liver. Unlike hepatic neoplasms, abscesses often present as a relatively acute febrile illness associated with pain in the right upper quadrant of the abdomen. Lesions can be localized by radionuclide scan, ultrasonography, or CT. The clinical presentation, diagnosis, and treatment of these lesions are discussed in Chapter 102.

REFERENCES

Di Bisceglie AM, Rustgi VK, Hoofnagle JH, et al: Hepatocellular carcinoma. Ann Intern Med 108:390, 1988.
Kew MC: Hepatic tumors. Semin Liver Dis 4:89, 1984.
Margolis S, Homcy C: Systemic manifestations of hepatoma. Medicine 51:381, 1972.
Scharschmidt BF: Hepatic tumors. *In* Wyngaarden JB, Smith LH Jr, Bennett JC (eds): Cecil Textbook of Medicine. 19th ed. Philadelphia, WB Saunders Co, 1992, pp 801–804.
Wright TL: Parasitic, bacterial, fungal, and granulomatous liver disease. *In* Wyngaarden JB, Smith LH Jr, Bennett JC (eds): Cecil Textbook of Medicine. 19th ed. Philadelphia, WB Saunders Co, 1992, pp 778–782.
Zakim D, Boyer T (eds): Hepatology: A Textbook of Liver Disease. 2nd ed. Philadelphia, WB Saunders Co, 1990, pp 572–615, 1098–1114, 1206–1240.

45 DISORDERS OF THE GALLBLADDER AND BILIARY TRACT

The liver produces 500 to 1500 ml of bile per day. The major physiologic role of the biliary tract and gallbladder is to concentrate this material and to conduct it silently and efficiently, in well-timed aliquots, to the intestine. In the intestine, biliary bile acids participate in normal fat digestion whereas cholesterol and a wide variety of other endogenous and exogenous compounds carried in bile are excreted in the feces. Normally unobtrusive, the gallbladder and biliary tree are the source of considerable pain and disability when they become infected or obstructed. This chapter briefly outlines the normal physiology of the biliary system and then focuses on the pathophysiology and clinical consequences of gallstones, the most important biliary tract disorder, closing with a brief discussion of neoplasms and other causes of bile duct obstruction. The reader is referred to Chapter 40 for a detailed discussion of the diagnostic approach to jaundice and biliary obstruction and to Chapter 33 for a review of the various imaging techniques used to study the biliary tract.

NORMAL BILIARY PHYSIOLOGY

Bile, a complex fluid secreted by hepatocytes, passes via the intrahepatic bile ducts into the common bile duct. Tonic contraction of the sphincter of Oddi during fasting diverts about half of hepatic bile into the gallbladder, where it is stored and concentrated. Cholecystokinin, released after food ingestion, causes contraction of the gallbladder and relaxation of the sphincter of Oddi, allowing delivery of a nicely timed bolus of bile, rich in bile acids, into the intestine. Bile acids, detergent molecules possessing both fat-soluble and water-soluble moieties, convey phospholipids and cholesterol from the liver to the intestine, where the latter undergoes fecal excretion. In the intestinal lumen, bile acids solubilize dietary fat and promote its digestion and absorption. Bile acids are, for the most part, efficiently reabsorbed by the small intestinal mucosa, particularly in the terminal ileum, and are recycled to the liver for re-excretion, a process termed *enterohepatic circulation* (Fig. 45–1).

PATHOPHYSIOLOGY OF GALLSTONE FORMATION (CHOLELITHIASIS)

Gallstones, the most common cause of biliary tract disease in the United States, occur in 20 to 35 per

cent of people by the age of 75 and are of two types: 75 per cent consist primarily of cholesterol, whereas 25 per cent, termed pigment stones, are composed of calcium bilirubinate and other calcium salts. Cholesterol, which is insoluble in water, normally is carried in bile solubilized by

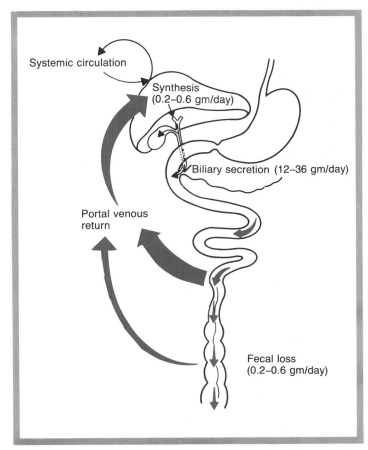

FIGURE 45–1. The enterohepatic circulation of bile salts in humans. The liver secretes 12 to 36 gm of bile salts per day in bile. Ninety-five per cent of these bile salts are reabsorbed, with specific bile salt transporters in the terminal ileum accounting for much of the uptake. Bile salts recycle to the liver via portal blood where they are efficiently extracted by hepatocytes and resecreted into bile. The liver also synthesizes sufficient bile salts to equal daily fecal losses (0.2 to 0.6 gm/day). Because of efficient uptake of bile salts by both intestine and liver, delivery of 12 to 36 gm of bile salts to the intestine daily is achieved by recycling a small pool (3 gm) of bile salts 4 to 12 times per day. (Modified from Carey MC: The enterohepatic circulation. *In* Arias IM, Popper H, Schacter D, et al [eds]: The Liver: Biology and Pathobiology. New York, Raven Press, 1982.)

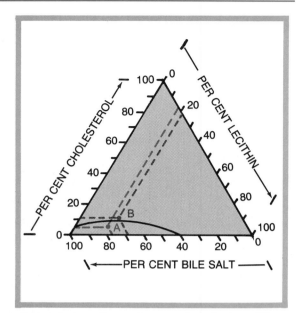

FIGURE 45-2. Phase diagram for plotting different mixtures of bile salt, lecithin, and cholesterol. The curved line represents the boundary of the micellar zone for aqueous solutions containing 4 to 10 per cent solids. Any mixture, such as A, falling within this area contains cholesterol in solution. Any mixture, such as B, falling outside this area has excess cholesterol as a precipitate or supersaturated solution. The points A and B actually depict the average composition of gallbladder bile obtained from normal persons and patients with cholesterol gallstones, respectively.

bile acids and phospholipids. However, in most individuals, many of whom do not develop gallstones, bile contains more cholesterol than can be maintained in stable solution (Fig. 45-2); that is, it is supersaturated with cholesterol. In the supersaturated bile of some individuals, microscopic cholesterol crystals form. The interplay of nucleation (mucus, stasis) and "antinucleating" (apolipoprotein A-I) factors may determine whether cholesterol gallstones form in supersaturated bile. Gradual deposition of additional layers of cholesterol leads to the appearance of macroscopic cholesterol gallstones. The gallbladder is key to gallstone formation; it constitutes an area of bile stasis in which slow crystal growth can occur and it also may provide mucus or other material to act as a nidus to initiate cholesterol crystal formation. Many of the recognized predisposing factors for cholelithiasis can be understood in terms of the pathophysiologic scheme just outlined: (1) biliary cholesterol saturation is increased by estrogens, multiparity, oral contraceptives, obesity, and terminal ileal disease (which decreases the bile acid pool); and (2) bile stasis is increased by bile duct strictures, parenteral hyperalimentation, fasting, and choledochal cysts.

The pathophysiology of pigment stones is less well understood; however, increased production of bilirubin (hemolytic states), increased biliary Ca^{2+} and CO_3^{2-}, cirrhosis, and bacterial deconjugation of bilirubin to a less soluble form are all associated with pigment stone formation.

CLINICAL MANIFESTATIONS OF GALLSTONES

Most individuals with gallstones are asymptomatic. Duct obstruction is the underlying cause of all manifestations of gallstone disease. Obstruction of the cystic duct distends the gallbladder and produces biliary pain, while superimposed infection or inflammation leads to acute cholecystitis. Obstruction of the common duct may produce pain, jaundice, infection (cholangitis), pancreatitis, and/or hepatic damage and biliary cirrhosis. The natural history of gallstone disease is outlined in Figure 45-3.

Asymptomatic Gallstones. Approximately 60 to 80 per cent of patients with gallstones in the United States are asymptomatic, and over a 20-year period it appears that only about 18 per cent of these individuals develop biliary pain and only 3 per cent require a cholecystectomy. Asymptomatic patients should be followed expectantly, with prophylactic cholecystectomy considered in three high-risk groups: (1) diabetics, who have a greater mortality (10 to 15 per cent) from acute cholecystitis; (2) persons with a calcified gallbladder, which is often associated with carcinoma of the gallbladder; and (3) persons with sickle cell anemia, in whom hepatic crises may be difficult to differentiate from acute cholecystitis. Dissolution of cholesterol gallstones by orally administered chenodeoxycholic acid or ursodeoxycholic acid is successful in some selected patients; however, a policy of expectant management followed by cholecystectomy is probably more cost-effective. Alternative methods to eliminate gallstones include (1) dissolution of cholesterol stones by instillation of methyl-tert-butyl ether into the gallbladder and (2) fragmentation of stones by extracorporeal shockwave lithotripsy.

Chronic Cholecystitis and Biliary Pain. The term *chronic cholecystitis* has been used to denote nonacute symptoms due to the presence of gallstones. A better term is *biliary pain*, as only a loose correlation exists between the presence of symptoms and pathologic findings such as inflammation in the gallbladder wall. Gallbladders from symptomatic patients may be grossly normal with mild histologic inflammation or may exhibit shrinking, scarring, and thickening, often as a result of previous attacks of acute cholecystitis. Symptoms arise from contraction of the gallbladder during transient obstruction of the cystic duct by gallstones. Biliary pain usually is a steady, cramplike pain in the epigastrium or right upper quadrant which comes on quickly, reaches a plateau of intensity over a few minutes, and begins to subside gradually over 30 minutes to several hours. Referred pain may be felt at the tip of the scapula or right shoulder. Nausea and vom-

FIGURE 45–3. Natural history of asymptomatic gallstones. The clinical syndromes associated with gallstones are shown here, and the numbers represent the approximate percentage of adults who develop one or more of these symptoms or complications over a 15- to 20-year period. Over this period, approximately 30 per cent of individuals with gallstones undergo surgery. (The risk of developing complications of gallstones varies considerably among series. The figures shown here represent those derived from more recent studies.)

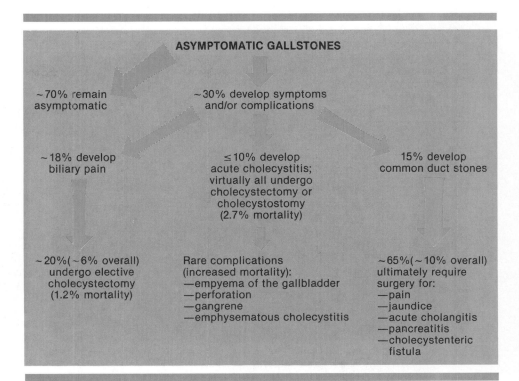

ASYMPTOMATIC GALLSTONES

~70% remain asymptomatic

~30% develop symptoms and/or complications

~18% develop biliary pain

≤10% develop acute cholecystitis; virtually all undergo cholecystectomy or cholecystostomy (2.7% mortality)

15% develop common duct stones

~20%(~6% overall) undergo elective cholecystectomy (1.2% mortality)

Rare complications (increased mortality):
—empyema of the gallbladder
—perforation
—gangrene
—emphysematous cholecystitis

~65%(~10% overall) ultimately require surgery for:
—pain
—jaundice
—acute cholangitis
—pancreatitis
—cholecystenteric fistula

iting may accompany biliary pain, whereas fever, leukocytosis, and a palpable mass (signs of acute cholecystitis) do not. Attacks occur at variable intervals (days to years). Other symptoms such as dyspepsia, fatty food intolerance, flatulence, heartburn, and belching may occur in patients with gallstones; however, they are nonspecific and frequently occur in individuals with normal gallbladders. Gallstones can be best demonstrated by ultrasonography (which demonstrates gallstones in more than 95 per cent of patients). Alternatively, one can use oral cholecystography (which demonstrates stones in two thirds of patients; the gallbladder is not visualized in one third of patients, a finding taken to indicate gallbladder disease). Cholecystectomy, either laparoscopic or conventional, which carries a mortality of less than 0.5 per cent, is the treatment of choice for recurrent biliary pain, and may be accompanied by examination of the common duct for concomitant choledocholithiasis. Surgery relieves symptoms of biliary pain in virtually all patients and prevents development of future complications such as acute cholecystitis, choledocholithiasis, and cholangitis. Alternative approaches to eliminating gallstones, including dissolution and fragmentation, are less commonly employed because gallstones may recur.

Acute Cholecystitis. Acute cholecystitis refers to acute right subcostal pain and tenderness due to obstruction of the cystic duct and subsequent distention, inflammation, and secondary infection of the gallbladder. Acalculous cholecystitis, accounting for 5 per cent of cases, is associated with prolonged fasting, as occurs with trauma, surgery, or parenteral hyperalimentation, and gallbladder bile that is viscous or "sludgelike." Acute cholecystitis usually begins with epigastric or right upper quadrant pain that gradually increases in severity and usually localizes to the area of the gallbladder. Unlike biliary pain, the pain of acute cholecystitis does not subside spontaneously. Anorexia, nausea, vomiting, fever, and right subcostal tenderness are commonly present, as is Murphy's sign (increased subhepatic tenderness and inspiratory arrest during a deep breath). In approximately one third of patients, a tender, enlarged gallbladder may be felt. Mild jaundice occurs in about 20 per cent of patients as a result of concomitant common duct stones or bile duct edema. Complications of acute cholecystitis include emphysematous cholecystitis (bacterial gas present in gallbladder lumen and tissues), empyema of the gallbladder, gangrene, and perforation. Approximately 10 per cent of patients present with or develop one of these complications and require emergency surgery. The onset of severe fever, shaking chills, increased leukocytosis, increased abdominal pain or tenderness, or persistent severe symptoms, alone or in combination, indicates progression of disease and suggests development of one of these complications.

Radionuclide scanning following intravenous administration of ^{99m}Tc-DISIDA is the most accurate test with which to confirm the clinical impression of acute cholecystitis (cystic duct obstruction). If the gallbladder fills with the isotope, acute cholecystitis is unlikely, whereas if the bile duct is visualized but the gallbladder is not, the clinical diagnosis is strongly supported. An ultrasound examination that shows the presence of gallstones (or sludge in acalculous cholecystitis) along with localized tenderness over the gallbladder also provides strong supportive evidence for acute cholecystitis. Oral cholecystograms are of no value in this clinical setting, as they are unreliable in the acutely ill patient.

Patients with acute cholecystitis may improve over 1 to 7 days with conventional expectant management, which includes nasogastric suction, intravenous fluids, and judicious antibiotics and pain medication. Because of the high risk of recurrent acute cholecystitis, most patients need to undergo cholecystectomy, often performed within the first 24 to 48 hours or, less often, 4 to 8 weeks after an acute episode, as either conventional or laparoscopic cholecystectomy (Fig. 45–4).

Emergency surgery is performed on patients with advanced disease and complications, usually associated with infection and sepsis. Cholecystostomy (either operative or percutaneous), rather than cholecystectomy, may be a useful technique in patients in whom there is a high operative risk. Patients who are good operative risks and in whom the diagnosis is certain are scheduled for prompt cholecystectomy within 24 to 48 hours. Antibiotics are used in patients with suppurative complications. Expectant management is reserved for those with uncomplicated disease who are not good operative candidates or those in whom the diagnosis is not clear.

The mortality of acute cholecystitis of 5 to 10 per cent is almost entirely confined to patients over 60 years of age with serious associated diseases and to those with suppurative complications. Complications of acute cholecystitis include infectious complications already listed and gallstone ileus (intestinal obstruction due to erosion of a gallstone through the gallbladder and duodenal walls into the intestinal lumen).

Choledocholithiasis and Acute Cholangitis. In the United States, most gallstones in the common duct come from the gallbladder; this occurs in up to 15 per cent of persons with cholelithiasis. Less commonly, stones may form de novo in the biliary tree. Ductal stones may be asymptomatic (30 to 40 per cent) or may produce biliary colic, jaundice, cholangitis, pancreatitis, or a combination of these. Secondary hepatic effects include biliary cirrhosis and hepatic abscesses.

Intermittent cholangitis, consisting of biliary pain, jaundice, and fever plus chills (Charcot's triad), is the most common manifestation of choledocholithiasis. Biliary infection may be mild or it may be severe, with suppurative cholangitis, sepsis, and shock. Diagnosis is based on a compatible clinical picture and radiologic or endoscopic evidence of ductal stones. Treatment includes hospitalization, treatment of infection, and removal of stones. The latter may be accomplished surgically in patients with an intact gallbladder by cholecystectomy and choledochotomy. In individuals with a previous cholecystectomy or those who are poor surgical candidates, endoscopic sphincterotomy, which opens the sphincter of Oddi and allows passage of gallstones up to 1 cm in size, is the preferred approach. Alternatively, endoscopic sphincterotomy and stone extraction may be combined with laparoscopic cholecystectomy.

The most severe form of cholangitis, suppurative cholangitis, rapidly results in life-threatening sepsis. Initially, patients may have only mild signs of biliary obstruction, yet they require rapid evaluation and treatment, including intravenous fluids and antibiotics and emergency procedures (surgical, endoscopic, or percutaneous) to drain the biliary tree. The high mortality of 50 per cent for this disease reflects the age of the patients generally affected, the speed with which sepsis develops, and the frequent failure to identify the biliary tree as the source of sepsis.

Other Disorders of the Biliary Tree. A number of other processes, all of which may present as biliary obstruction, jaundice, or infection, may involve the biliary tree. The approach to evaluating these entities is outlined in Chapter 33.

Benign biliary strictures usually result from surgical injury and may cause symptoms days to years later. Early diagnosis is important, as strictures that partially obstruct and are clinically asymptomatic may cause secondary biliary cirrhosis. Biliary stricture should be suspected in anyone with a history of right upper quadrant surgery and a persistently elevated serum alkaline phosphatase

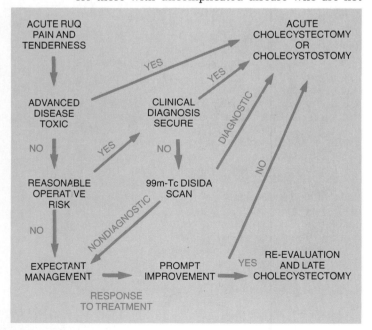

FIGURE 45–4. Scheme for managing patients with right upper quadrant pain and tenderness who are thought to have acute cholecystitis. This scheme is based on a policy of early operation (conventional or laparoscopic) for appropriate patients, and use of cholecystostomy (operative or percutaneous) for patients who are poor operative risks.

level. A similar type of benign stricture is seen in alcoholics in whom the intrapancreatic portion of the common bile duct is compressed by pancreatic fibrosis. Surgical repair or bypass of these lesions is successful in 75 per cent of patients. Balloon catheter dilatation may be useful in selected individuals.

Sclerosing cholangitis is an idiopathic condition of nonmalignant, nonbacterial chronic inflammatory narrowing of the intra- and extrahepatic bile ducts. It most commonly occurs in males, often in association with ulcerative colitis. Patients usually present with pruritus or jaundice, and percutaneous transhepatic cholangiography or endoscopic retrograde cholangiopancreatography shows characteristic changes ("beading") of the bile ducts. Therapy includes attempts at improving biliary drainage, liver transplantation, antibiotics, and support.

Structural abnormalities such as choledochal cysts, Caroli's disease (saccular intrahepatic bile duct dilation), and duodenal diverticuli may also cause bile duct obstruction, often with secondary choledocholithiasis. Hemobilia and intermittent bile duct obstruction by blood clots are caused by hepatic injury, neoplasms, or hepatic artery aneurysms.

Biliary neoplasms are rare but include carcinoma of the gallbladder, scirrhous or papillary adenocarcinoma of the bile ducts, and carcinoma of the ampulla of Vater. The last two neoplasms usually present as unremitting painless jaundice, although necrosis and sloughing of tumor may cause intermittent obstruction and the appearance of occult fecal blood. Carcinoma of the gallbladder often presents as advanced disseminated disease, although symptoms also may resemble those of acute or chronic cholecystitis or bile duct obstruction. Resection of most of these tumors is difficult or impossible and prognosis is poor. For patients with unresectable tumor the goal is palliation, and for those with severe symptoms due to obstruction, percutaneous or endoscopic stenting of the biliary tree may be helpful. Stents should not be used in patients with benign disease because complications due to biliary infection and plugging of the stent invariably occur; rather, definitive surgical repair or bypass is preferred.

Motility disorders of the biliary tree have not been well recognized in the past. With the use of newer endoscopic techniques for measuring biliary pressures and motility, it has become apparent that a small group of patients with biliary-type pain have symptoms due to hypertension, dysmotility, and/or stenosis of the sphincter of Oddi, and in this select group, surgical or endoscopic sphincterotomy is of value.

REFERENCES

Gracie WA, Ransohoff DF: The natural history of silent gallstones. The innocent gallstone is not a myth. N Engl J Med 307:798, 1982.
Malet PF, Soloway RD: Diseases of the gallbladder and bile ducts. In Wyngaarden JB, Smith LH Jr, Bennett JC (eds): Cecil Textbook of Medicine. 19th ed. Philadelphia, WB Saunders Co, 1992, pp 804–816.
Sleisenger MH, Fordtran JS (eds): Gastrointestinal Disease: Pathophysiology, Diagnosis and Management. 4th ed. Philadelphia, WB Saunders Co, 1989.
Thistle JL, Cleary PA, Lachin JM, et al: The natural history of cholelithiasis: The national cooperative gallstone study. Ann Intern Med 101:171, 1984.
Wiesner RH, LaRusso NF: Clinicopathological features of the syndrome of primary sclerosing cholangitis. Gastroenterology 79:200, 1980.
Zakim D, Boyer T (eds): Hepatology: A Textbook of Liver Disease. 2nd ed. Philadelphia, WB Saunders Co, 1990.

SECTION VI

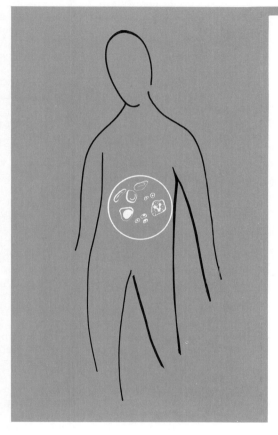

HEMATOLOGY

46 HEMATOPOIESIS

Bone marrow in the adult occupies the vertebrae, sternum, ribs, pelvic bones, and, to a lesser extent, the long bones and skull, and comprises about 1 kg of tissue, producing about 10^{11} cells/day. In the child, hematopoiesis is more prominent in the long bones and skull, whereas in adulthood fatty tissue replaces the hematopoietic marrow in these peripheral areas. In addition, liver and spleen, primary sites of hematopoiesis in the fetus, may regain hematopoietic activity in certain adult diseases, including severe anemias, skeletal marrow failure, myelofibrosis, and hematologic malignancies such as leukemia.

Normal bone marrow consists of about 50 per cent hematopoietic cells and 50 per cent fat, with the hematopoietic cells being arranged in cords around sinusoids; blood vessels are abundant. The space occupied by fat increases during adulthood, although hematopoietic tissue can replace it under appropriate conditions at any age. The hematopoietic cells include a small pluripotential stem cell compartment, consisting of small cells resembling lymphocytes, a large compartment of proliferating cells of committed lineage (the ratio of myeloid to erythroid precursors is normally 3 to 5 : 1), and a large compartment of postmitotic maturing cells of both myeloid and erythroid lineage. Smaller numbers of megakaryocytes, which differentiate into platelets, plasma cells (which produce immunoglobulins), reticulum cells, and lymphocytes are also present. It requires about 1 week for a stem cell to differentiate into mature daughter cells of either erythroid or myeloid type; the marrow additionally contains about 1 week's worth of mature leukocytes and erythrocytes. The circulating half-life of polymorphonuclear leukocytes is about 6 hours, of platelets 8 to 10 days, and of erythrocytes 120 days; thus, the granulocyte pool is released much faster than the erythrocyte pool, which is renewed at a rate of 0.8 per cent per day. Because the ratio in the peripheral blood of granulocytes to erythrocytes to platelets is about 1 : 1000 : 100, approximately equal numbers of these three cell types are released from the bone marrow each day.

Erythropoiesis is under the control of the hormone erythropoietin, released from the kidney under the stimulus of tissue hypoxia. A glycoprotein of molecular weight 46,000, erythropoietin may also be produced in the liver. It stimulates primitive pluripotential or stem cells into erythropoietic differentiation, acting mainly on the CFU-E (colony-forming unit – erythroid) and CFU-B (colony-forming unit – burst) to promote differentiation into proerythroblasts. Recombinant erythropoietin is now approved for use in treatment of anemias of chronic renal failure and of human immunodeficiency virus (HIV) infection, cancer, rheumatoid arthritis, and prematurity. It is also under study for administration to surgical patients perioperatively or to enhance autologous blood donation in preoperative candidates.

The earliest recognizable red cell precursor, the erythroblast, eventually gives rise to eight or more mature erythrocytes. The erythroblast is a large cell with abundant endoplasmic reticulum, which decreases in size as it matures, incorporates transferrin-bound iron via specific membrane receptors, and begins to form hemoglobin. In more mature stages the developing erythroblasts, the basophilic, then polychromatophilic, then orthochromic normoblasts, lose the capacity to divide. Their nuclei become pyknotic and are finally extruded prior to release of the erythrocytes from the bone marrow. Newly released erythrocytes, or reticulocytes, have active mitochondrial function and retain the capacity to form hemoglobin; about 25 per cent of hemoglobin is synthesized after these cells leave the bone marrow, but the mature erythrocyte in the circulation lacks the capacity for protein synthesis and is anucleate. Its energy is supplied by glycolysis.

The earliest recognizable granulocyte precursor is the myeloblast, although developmentally committed stem cells, CFU-C (colony-forming unit – culture), can be identified in tissue culture. Colony stimulating factors (CSF) produced by monocytes and lymphocytes in response to stimuli such as bacterial endotoxin stimulate mitosis in granulocyte precursors. Recombinant G-CSF and GM-CSF (acting respectively on neutrophil precursors and on all leukocytes) are being used to shorten neutropenia in patients who are receiving cancer chemotherapy and in other neutropenic states. Prostaglandin E_2 inhibits granulocyte production. Promyelocytes, the next stage of myeloblast differentiation, are the largest marrow cells except for megakaryocytes. They contain primary lysosomal granules and give rise to neutrophilic, eosinophilic, or basophilic myelocytes, which display the specific granules that identify each myeloid subtype. Myelocytes form the most abundant type of myeloid cell in the marrow and represent the last proliferating cell pool; their descendants, metamyelocytes, bands, and neutrophils (or eosinophils or basophils) are incapable of cell division but show increasing functional activity concomitant with maturation of membrane functions: chemotaxis, phagocytosis, bactericidal action. After extrusion from the bone marrow, granulocytes occupy two geographic pools in free equilibrium: a marginated pool of cells adhering to blood vessel walls and a circulating pool of roughly equal size. Once in the peripheral blood, granulocytes, like erythrocytes, do not normally re-enter the bone marrow. They follow a "one-way traffic" pattern, spending a relatively short time in the peripheral blood (average, 6 hours) and exiting into the tissues.

The megakaryocyte, the only giant, multinucleated cell in the hematopoietic lineage, also derives from the primitive stem cell, and undergoes endomitosis, reaching DNA contents of 32 to 64 n. Specific surface markers characteristic of mature platelets appear at very early stages in megakaryocyte differentiation and persist through maturation. Megakaryocytes tend to stay near marrow sinusoids, where they mature, developing internal membranes that mark off platelet fields. Each megakaryocyte eventually breaks up, releasing some 5000 platelets at the edge of a marrow sinusoid into the blood. Some megakaryocytes circulate and may release their platelets in the lung. Although platelets are anucleate fragments of megakaryocytes, they possess a highly organized structure and glycogen energy stores (and some mitochondria) and circulate for 7 to 10 days. Recombinant GM-CSF and interleukins 3 and 6 are currently under study for stimulatory effects on platelet production.

Marrow lymphocytes are mainly of B cell origin, arising also in spleen and lymph nodes. Primitive T cell precursors arise in the marrow, travel to the thymus, where they undergo further differentiation, and thence to spleen, lymph nodes, or marrow as fully functional mature T cells. Lymphocytes are generally much longer-lived than other marrow cells and may survive for years.

Bone marrow functions include hematopoiesis, the differentiation of antibody-producing plasma cells, and the monitoring of hematopoietic cell quality. Normal bone marrow has an 8- to 10-fold capacity to increase blood cell production in response to humoral signals, which include erythropoietin, CSFs, and prostaglandins. Normal bone marrow function depends upon intact marrow architecture, the availability of key nutrients including iron, folic acid, and vitamin B_{12}, and regulatory hormones such as erythropoietin, the CSFs, and interleukins. The recently discovered stem cell factor (c-kit ligand) also has an important role in regulating the renewable pool of earliest marrow cell precursors.

Two types of injury can induce marrow failure: damage that affects the capacity for stem cells to undergo differentiation (e.g., in aplastic anemia) and damage that alters the marrow microenvironment (e.g., invasion of marrow by infection or tumor).

REFERENCES

Eschbach JW, Kelly MR, Haley NR, Abels RI, Adamson JW: Treatment of anemia of progressive renal failure with recombinant human erythropoietin. N Engl J Med 321:158, 1989.

Robinson BE, Quesenberry PJ: Hematopoietic growth factors: Overview and clinical applications. Parts I, II, and III. Am J Med Sci 300:163; 237; 311, 1990.

Sieff CA: Biology and clinical aspects of the hematopoietic growth factors. Annu Rev Med 41:483, 1990.

47 ANEMIA

Definition

Anemia represents a decrease in red cell mass or hemoglobin content of blood below physiologic need as set by tissue oxygen demand. The conventional limits for normal range of hemoglobin represent the values obtained for 95 per cent of a normal, healthy population, assuming a normal distribution of individuals (Table 47–1). In physiologic terms, different ranges exist for men and women, for infants and growing children, and for different metabolic states. Anemia is an expression of many pathologic conditions and is not itself a disease state but a clinical sign of such disorders. Therefore, analysis of any anemia should follow a tripartite logical pathway: (1) seek mechanisms by which the anemia occurs, such as bleeding, lack of red cell production, or excessive red cell destruc-

TABLE 47–1. NORMAL VALUES FOR HEMOGRAM IN ADULTS

	MALE	FEMALE
Hemoglobin (gm/dl)	13.5–17.5	11.5–15.5
Hematocrit (%)	40–52	36–48
Red cell count ($\times 10^{12}$/L)	4.5–6.5	3.9–5.6
Mean cell hemoglobin (MCH) (pg)		27–34
Mean cell volume (MCV) (fl)		80–95
Mean cell hemoglobin concentration (MCHC) (gm/dl)		30–35
White blood cell count ($\times 10^9$/L)		4–11
Platelet count ($\times 10^9$/L)		150–450
Reticulocyte count (%)		0.5–1.5

tion; (2) identify associated diseases that cause anemia; (3) evaluate morphologically the peripheral blood smear (Fig. 47–1).

Determinants of the normal range for hemoglobin, hematocrit, and red cell count include age, sex, and ambient altitude. Newborn infants have high values, which soon decline with rapid growth in infancy. Prepubertal boys and girls have similar values. At puberty, male sex hormones produce a rise in erythropoiesis so that adult males have hemoglobin levels approximately 2 to 4 gm/dl higher and hematocrits 5 to 7 per cent higher than adult females. The healthy elderly normally suffer no decline in hemoglobin or hematocrit values; however, because of increased incidence of chronic diseases, elderly populations may show slight decreases in these values. Populations living at altitudes over 4000 feet above sea level show increased hematocrits, which appear to represent physiologic adaptation to the desaturation resulting from diminished atmospheric oxygen tension.

Clinical Assessment of Anemia

Signs and symptoms of anemia vary with the rapidity of onset and with underlying disease of the cardiovascular system (Table 47–2). Thus, rapid blood loss, especially if plasma volume decreases rapidly, or brisk hemolysis may result in cardiovascular compensatory reactions, including tachycardia, postural hypotension, vasoconstriction in skin and extremities, dyspnea on exertion, and faintness. Slowly developing anemias, such as those resulting from nutritional deficiency, permit

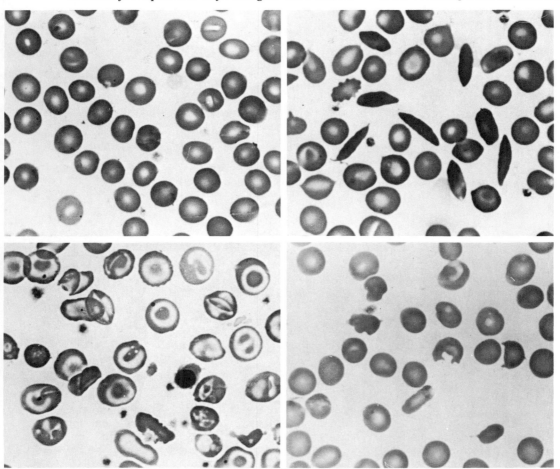

FIGURE 47–1. Photomicrographs of peripheral blood smears. *Upper left,* Spherocytes, round dense cells lacking a central pallor, in a patient with hereditary spherocytes. *Upper right,* Sickle cells, typical of sickle cell anemia. *Lower left,* Target cells, typical of thalassemia. *Lower right,* Schistocytes, typical of microangiopathic hemolytic anemia.

gradual expansion of the plasma volume so that increased cardiac output gradually compensates. The subject may remain asymptomatic, noting only slight exertional dyspnea or, in the case of pre-existing coronary artery disease, increased angina. Pallor of skin and mucous membranes, jaundice, cheilosis (fissuring of the angles of the mouth), a beefy red, smooth tongue, and koilonychia (spoon-shaped nails) are signs that accompany more advanced anemias of different types. The level of anemia at which signs of cardiovascular decompensation occur varies considerably with underlying disease, age, level of activity, and the individual's stoicism. For example, in the sedentary elderly person, a change in mentation can be an important clue to anemia, whereas decreased activity can mask exercise intolerance.

Evaluation of the anemic patient is best served by a systematic evaluation of the clinical and laboratory findings together (Fig. 47–2). First, is the patient truly anemic? Increased plasma volume, fluid overload, or congestive heart failure may produce a dilutional anemia that disappears when fluid balance is restored. Second, is the anemia acquired or inherited? Family history is important, especially in hemolytic anemias, and a positive family history of jaundice, splenomegaly, or gallstones may suggest such a condition. Hemoglobin-

TABLE 47–2. CLINICAL CLUES IN EVALUATION OF ANEMIA

History
1. Family history: anemia, splenomegaly, jaundice, splenectomy
2. Rejection as blood donor
3. Exercise intolerance, syncope, easy fatigue
4. Pallor, jaundice
5. Blood loss or bleeding tendency
6. Malnutrition, malabsorption, alcoholism
7. Chronic disease
8. Transfusion or iron therapy
9. Multiple pregnancy, menorrhagia

Physical Examination
1. Skin and mucous membranes: pallor, jaundice, purpura, smooth or beefy tongue, cheilosis, koilonychia, telangiectasia
2. Adenopathy
3. Hepatomegaly or splenomegaly
4. Tachycardia, cardiomegaly, murmurs
5. Bone tenderness
6. Neuropathy

opathies are frequent in Mediterranean, African, and Far Eastern populations, making ethnic background pertinent. For the immediate problem, a lifelong history versus recent onset is a key differential point. Third, is there evidence for blood

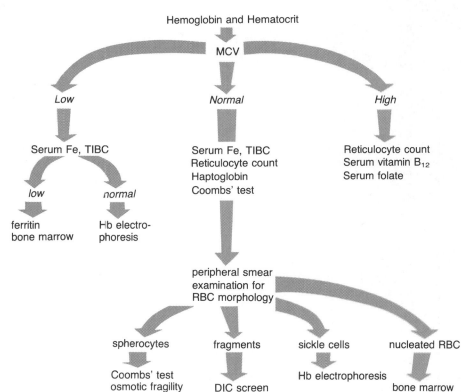

FIGURE 47–2. Laboratory screening for anemia.

loss? The most common reason for anemia is iron loss and iron deficiency. Whereas in growing children and pregnant women iron deficiency may result from dietary lack, the overwhelming cause of iron deficiency in adults is loss of blood from the gastrointestinal (GI) or genitourinary tract. Fourth, is there evidence for nutritional deficiency or malabsorption? In the urban Westerner, folic acid deficiency is a common form of malnutrition, seen especially in pregnant women, growing children who are malnourished, the elderly living alone, and alcoholics. Fifth, is there evidence for hemolysis? Inherited hemolytic anemias are common in certain populations, whereas acquired hemolytic anemia is rare, occurring mainly in settings of autoimmune disease and drug ingestion. Sixth, is there evidence for toxic exposure or drug ingestion that could cause bone marrow depression and anemia? Finally, does the patient have a chronic inflammatory disease, renal insufficiency, or cancer, each of which is associated with secondary mild anemias, the "anemia of chronic disease"?

Laboratory Evaluation of Anemia

Laboratory evaluation of anemia starts with the hemogram, that is, the complete blood count (hemoglobin, hematocrit, white blood cell count, differential, platelet count, and red cell indices) plus the peripheral blood smear. In addition, initial evaluation should include a reticulocyte count, examination of the stool for occult blood, and urinalysis. Automated cell counters directly determine the number and size (volume) of blood cells and measure hemoglobin chemically; the hematocrit is then derived from these values. This complete examination can be carried out on capillary blood from a fingerstick. Automated differential counters report the white cell differential in absolute numbers based on scanning of large populations of leukocytes either on fixed smears or in cell suspensions. Nevertheless, the visual differential performed on stained smears remains an important method and permits evaluation of the morphology of individual leukocytes, erythrocytes, and platelets. Direct examination of the morphology of a stained peripheral blood smear is particularly important in evaluating abnormal cells, as in leukemia. An advantage of automated cell counting is the ability to use the standard deviation of the variable being measured, e.g., red cell volume, to provide information on population heterogeneity, an important factor in certain disease states.

The *red cell indices* give information about the average red cell volume (MCV, mean corpuscular volume) and red cell hemoglobin content (MCH, mean corpuscular hemoglobin) or concentration (MCHC, mean corpuscular hemoglobin concentration). The MCV is the most useful because it permits separation of microcytic anemia (MCV <80 μm^3) from normocytic (MCV 80 to 100 μm^3) and macrocytic anemias (MCV >100 μm^3). These mor-

phologic categories correlate well with several common types of anemia. *Microcytosis* most commonly occurs in iron deficiency, thalassemia trait, and chronic renal insufficiency, whereas normocytosis accompanies acute blood loss. *Macrocytosis* is characteristic of nutritional anemias, including folic acid deficiency and vitamin B_{12} deficiency. Mild macrocytosis (MCV 100 to 110 μm^3) may also be associated with hemolytic anemias with a raised reticulocyte count and with the refractory anemias found in myelodysplastic syndromes. The MCH is generally low in thalassemia trait, thalassemia, and iron deficiency; the MCHC may be high in spherocytic hemolytic anemias.

Inspection of the peripheral blood smear gives information about individual blood cells not readily obtained from the average values reported by the automated blood counters (see Fig. 47–1). For example, the microcytes of iron deficiency are relatively homogeneous, whereas in thalassemia major much more diversity in red cell size and shape occurs. In general, the further red cells diverge from the ideal shape (biconcave disc) and size (8 μm in diameter), the shorter their lifespan in the circulation. The appearance of sickle cells, cells with inclusion bodies, such as Howell-Jolly bodies (nuclear remnants) or basophilic stippling (RNA remnants), parasitized cells (e.g., malaria), microspherocytes, and schistocytes (e.g., microangiopathic anemias, disseminated intravascular coagulation) is rapidly appreciated by inspection of the peripheral blood smear. Similarly, the appearance of individual leukocytes discloses blasts, hypersegmented polymorphonuclear cells, atypical lymphocytes, toxic granulation, and other morphologic abnormalities of disease less accessible to machine recording. Platelet clumping versus true thrombocytopenia and the appearance of very large or small platelets also add clinically relevant information to the numerical counts.

Evaluation of the leukocyte and platelet counts is an integral part of investigating anemia because low counts may signify marrow failure or replacement, and high counts may be associated with leukemia or infection. Suspicion of pancytopenia or of marrow invasion with a pathologic process should lead to a bone marrow examination.

The *reticulocyte count* measures the per cent of newly released erythrocytes in the circulating blood; these are larger than mature red blood cells and contain traces of endoplasmic reticulum, signifying the continuing capacity for hemoglobin synthesis. After 1 to 2 days in the circulation, these methylene blue–stained traces of RNA disappear. Because the normal red cell lifespan is 120 days, the normal reticulocyte count is approximately 1 per cent. Anemia increases the apparent reticulocyte count by decreasing the denominator by which the reticulocyte percentage is calculated (reticulocytes/1000 red blood cells); hence reticulocyte counts should be corrected to a "normal" hematocrit of 45 (corrected reticulocyte count = retic count × patient's hematocrit/45). Further corrections may be needed during severe anemias when reticulocytes circulate for longer than 24 hours. An elevated reticulocyte count (corrected) signifies increased erythropoietic activity, which may represent a normal response to bleeding, replacement of an appropriate hematinic such as iron, folate, or vitamin B_{12}, or a response to hemolysis. A very low reticulocyte count or absence of reticulocytes occurs after transfusion or in aplastic states.

Blood loss from the GI tract is such a common cause of anemia that any initial evaluation of anemia should include testing one to three stool specimens for occult blood. Because bleeding is often intermittent, it is best to obtain several stool specimens on different days. Although blood loss into the urine is less common, it is nevertheless desirable to examine the urine for the presence of red cells or blood as well.

ANEMIAS REPRESENTING BONE MARROW FAILURE

Primary disorders of bone marrow function are rare causes of anemia except as a result of drug or toxin action. These disorders include aplastic anemia, pure red cell aplasia, marrow replacement with fibrotic tissue or tumor (myelophthisis and myelodysplastic syndromes), and certain anemias secondary to cancer.

Aplastic anemia is characterized by a peripheral pancytopenia and markedly decreased hematopoietic activity in the bone marrow without a change in normal marrow architecture or replacement with other cell types. The disorder is considered to be severe when the corrected reticulocyte count is less than 1 per cent, platelets are less than 20,000/mm³, neutrophil count is less than 500/mm³, and marrow cellularity is less than 25 per cent of marrow space. Aplastic anemias, or the tendency toward their development, may be inherited (e.g., Fanconi's anemia) or, more commonly, may develop after a viral infection (e.g., hepatitis) or as a reaction to a drug. Some drugs, such as cytostatic agents used in cancer chemotherapy, regularly cause marrow hypoplasia as part of their cytotoxic action; such aplasia is dose-dependent and usually reversible. The effect of cycle-specific agents such as cytosine arabinoside and methotrexate on more rapidly dividing mature stem cells tends to spare the earlier, pluripotent stem cells, so that marrow recovery occurs after the drug is stopped. Other drugs induce idiosyncratic marrow hypoplasia or aplasia that is unrelated to drug dose and tends to be less reversible. Chloramphenicol, which also induces a dose-related suppression of erythropoiesis, and phenylbutazone are examples of drugs that produce idiosyncratic marrow aplasia in 1 of every 24,000 to 40,000 exposed individuals. An inherited stem cell sensitivity or defect is postulated in such cases because of the findings in family and twin studies. In contrast, aplastic anemia occurring in paroxysmal nocturnal hemoglobinuria probably reflects an acquired genetic defect in membrane attachment of phosphoinositol-linked membrane proteins. A variety of environmental toxins, including solvents such as benzene and insecticides, also can cause a long-lasting marrow aplasia. Radiation exposure of bone marrow also can produce aplastic anemia. Viral infections, particularly hepatitis, Epstein-Barr virus infection, and parvovirus B19, can result in severe aplasia. An increased incidence of acute leukemia is observed in patients who have had aplastic anemia, and preleukemia may present as marrow hypoplasia.

Pure red cell aplasia, producing a severe anemia with absent reticulocytes, but normal leukocyte and platelet counts, is characterized by selective absence of erythroid precursors in the bone marrow. It is associated with immunologic deficiency states, including thymoma.

Two mechanisms have been postulated for aplastic anemia: immunologic suppression of hematopoiesis and damage to marrow stem cells. Suppressor T cells as well as immunoglobulins that inhibit erythropoietin or block differentiation of hematopoietic stem cells in vitro have been demonstrated in some cases. Immunosuppressive therapy has led to remission in certain of these cases, especially in pure red cell aplasia. In other cases, no inhibitory immunologic mechanisms can be demonstrated, and patients respond to bone marrow transplantation, which presumably repopulates the marrow by new stem cells. Recent evidence in model systems links bone marrow failure to defects in bone marrow stem cells or in marrow stromal production of the c-kit ligand, the stem cell growth factor. Early transplantation of normal, human leukocyte antigen (HLA)–matched bone marrow, before the patient becomes alloimmunized to blood cells given as supportive therapy, is the treatment of choice in young patients, especially if the patient has an HLA-compatible donor. For patients in whom transplantation is not possible, androgens have been used in addition to supportive transfusion therapy. Recent studies indicate that treatment with a course of antithymocyte globulin is effective in 40 to 50 per cent of cases. Availability of commercially prepared antithymocyte globulin now makes this treatment a feasible early step in the approach to aplastic anemia, especially in the patient who does not have a bone marrow donor. Trials of bone marrow growth factors, such as erythropoietin and CSF, have not proved effective in correcting aplastic anemia to date but may be of supportive value.

Marrow invasion by infection (e.g., tuberculosis), tumor, or fibrosis can produce hypoplastic anemias characterized by a normocytic red cell, low reticulocyte count, and the presence of nucleated red blood cells on the peripheral smear: *myelophthisic anemia*. Cancer also can produce a hypoplastic, normocytic anemia without direct marrow invasion. Such anemias involve a subnormal response to erythropoietin and represent one type of the anemia of chronic disease.

TABLE 47–3. EVALUATION OF HYPOCHROMIC ANEMIA

A. Iron lack or inability to utilize iron in heme production
  1. Iron deficiency
    a. Blood loss
    b. Dietary lack during high demand (childhood, pregnancy)
    c. Poor absorption of food iron (postgastrectomy, small bowel disease, pica)
  2. Poor iron mobilization from body stores
    a. Chronic inflammatory disease
    b. Malignancy
  3. Sideroblastic anemia; failure of iron incorporation into protoporphyrin
  4. Lead poisoning (similar to No. 3)
B. Defective globin synthesis
  1. Alpha thalassemia
  2. Beta thalassemia

HYPOCHROMIC ANEMIAS

Inadequate or defective hemoglobin synthesis results in poorly hemoglobinized erythrocytes in the peripheral blood, a decreased hemoglobin level, and frequently a small erythrocyte volume (microcytosis). Any lesion in the pathway of heme or of globin synthesis can produce a hypochromic anemia (Table 47–3). By far, the most common cause of hypochromic anemia throughout the world is iron deficiency resulting from blood loss (at any age) or inadequate dietary iron (mainly in children and pregnant women). Other important causes of hypochromic anemia include poor iron utilization, as in the anemia of chronic disease, defective heme or porphyrin synthesis, as in the porphyrias or lead poisoning, or impaired globin synthesis, as in the thalassemic syndromes (see below). In the thalassemias, abnormal globin synthesis results in a secondary impairment of heme production and leads to a hemolytic state; this problem is discussed in the section on hemolytic anemias.

The characteristic findings in iron deficiency anemia reflect exhaustion of body iron stores: absent marrow iron, low plasma iron and ferritin concentrations, a low transferrin saturation (<15 per cent) and high iron-binding capacity, and hypochromic, microcytic erythrocytes on the peripheral smear. The reticulocyte count is reduced.

Normal Iron Metabolism

Iron is the most abundant metal in the human body yet is a trace metal totalling only 3 to 4 gm. Two thirds of total body iron exists as hemoglobin iron in circulating erythrocytes, about one quarter remains in iron stores, and small amounts are found in myoglobin, enzymes, and the plasma (Table 47–4). Body iron is tightly regulated and conserved; the daily absorption from the diet averages 1 to 2 mg, and iron balance is maintained by efficient reutilization of hemoglobin iron from red cells removed from circulation by the reticuloendothelial system or of enzyme iron except for a small amount lost from the body in sweat, shed skin, and intestinal mucosal cells. Elemental iron is extremely toxic and insoluble, and iron within the body is almost entirely bound to protein carriers.

Food iron is absorbed in the ferrous form, after being released from foodstuffs by gastric acid. Heme iron is absorbed directly as hemin (Fe^{3+} heme). The duodenum is the optimal locus of absorption, with less occurring further down the small intestine. An active process transports ferrous iron across the intestinal mucosal cells, governed by the iron content of the cells, with local storage as ferritin if the content is high. The average Western diet contains 10 to 30 mg of iron per day, of which only 5 to 10 per cent is absorbed. In iron deficiency states absorption increases to 20 to 30 per cent. Many common foodstuffs and other materials contain iron-binding substances that interfere with iron absorption. These include phytates in cereals and vegetables, casein in milk, clay, and the drug tetracycline. Clay eating or starch eating (pica) by children or young women, many of whom are already iron-deficient, can produce severe iron deficiency.

Absorbed iron is transported from the intestine to storage in the bone marrow complexed to the plasma protein transferrin, each molecule of which binds two iron molecules. Transferrin-bound iron (Fe^{3+}, reoxidized by ceruloplasmin) is delivered to reticuloendothelial macrophages for storage as ferritin and to developing erythroblasts, where it is released intracellularly for incorporation into protoporphyrin. Because 25 mg of iron are needed daily for new red cell production, and only 1 to 2 mg are absorbed from the diet, most of

TABLE 47–4. IRON DISTRIBUTION AND TURNOVER

	AMOUNT OF IRON IN AVERAGE ADULT			
	MALE (gm)	FEMALE (gm)	PER CENT OF TOTAL	DAILY TURNOVER
Hemoglobin	2.4	1.7	65	20 mg
Ferritin and hemosiderin	1.0	0.3	35	
Myoglobin	0.15	0.12	3.5	
Heme enzymes	0.02	0.015	0.5	
Transferrin-iron	0.004	0.003	0.1	
Total daily requirement	0.001	0.002*		

*Menstruating and pregnant women require two to three times the daily Fe requirement of adult men because of increased blood loss and the iron requirement of the fetus. One ml of blood contains approximately 0.5 mg of iron.

the iron being utilized for erythropoiesis is recycled, derived from effete red cells destroyed by the reticuloendothelial system. The transferrin concentration in plasma (measured as the iron-binding capacity) varies widely diurnally, is decreased in inflammatory diseases or infection, and is increased in iron deficiency.

Iron is delivered to developing erythrocytes by the binding of transferrin to a specific cellular receptor. This step is followed by micropinocytotic internalization of the iron-transferrin complex within acidic vacuoles where the iron is released, and from which the apotransferrin-receptor complex is recycled to the cell surface and the apotransferrin liberated. The iron then enters the mitochondria and is enzymatically incorporated into protoporphyrin to form heme; the heme is bound by globin in the cytoplasm to produce hemoglobin. The level of free heme regulates the uptake of iron by normoblasts and reticulocytes.

Iron is stored as ferritin or hemosiderin. Ferritin consists of a spherical protein shell of apoferritin units surrounding a central core of ferric phosphate; up to 4000 iron molecules may be present per molecule of ferritin. Aggregates of ferritin can be detected in bone marrow smears as ferricyanide-positive granules, having a bright blue-green color. Ferritin circulates at concentrations that generally reflect body iron stores, with a normal range of 12 to 325 ng/ml (mean, 125 ng/ml for men, 55 ng/ml for women). In iron deficiency the serum ferritin is less than 10 ng/ml, and in iron overload the level may be several thousand nanograms per milliliter. Infection tends to reduce the serum ferritin level; liver disease or hepatitis raises the level. *Hemosiderin* is an insoluble, partially dehydrated derivative of ferritin; iron contained in hemosiderin is less accessible for erythropoiesis than is iron in ferritin, which is readily available. Fixed tissue macrophages also serve as a store of ferritin and hemosiderin, derived from phagocytized aged red blood cells. Such iron is rapidly made available after hemorrhage but is poorly available for hemoglobin production during infection, inflammation, and malignancy.

Iron Deficiency

Iron deficiency anemia is a sign of underlying disease, not a disease in itself. The major cause for iron deficiency in adults is blood loss, whereas in growing children and pregnant women dietary iron lack is more common. Malabsorption also can lead to iron deficiency, for example following partial gastrectomy or in adult celiac disease. Rarer associations include esophageal webs (Plummer-Vinson syndrome) and clay or starch pica.

The usual Western diet provides sufficient iron to cover normal losses of adult men, but for menstruating women (who require twice as much iron daily as adult men) dietary iron intake may not be adequate. Women with repeated pregnancies are also at risk of iron lack, because each fetus requires about 400 mg of iron. Gastric acid facilitates iron absorption, since acid is needed to reduce ferric iron in food to the absorbable ferrous form; gastrectomy not only removes the source of acid but by shortening transit time in the intestine may impair duodenal absorption (this is why delayed release forms of iron are less efficacious than simple iron salts).

GI bleeding is the most common cause of iron deficiency in men, and the second after gynecologic bleeding in women. In less developed countries, hookworm infestation is the leading cause of iron deficiency. Both benign and malignant GI lesions may produce iron deficiency, and investigation for possible colon cancer is imperative in adults over the age of 40 with GI blood loss. Peptic ulcer disease, hiatal hernia, bleeding due to aspirin ingestion, diverticulitis, and chronic hemorrhoidal bleeding are other frequent causes of GI blood loss. Hematuria may also produce iron deficiency. Frequent blood donations may deplete iron stores even in males and lead to latent iron deficiency.

Clinical Manifestations. Clinical manifestations may be subtle if the iron deficiency is gradual in onset. The most common symptoms include fatigue, exercise intolerance, irritability, and dizziness, that is, symptoms common to any type of anemia. In severe iron deficiency there may be koilonychia, pallor, and cheilosis. Splenomegaly has been reported in about 10 per cent of patients but is uncommon in American adults.

Laboratory Findings. Laboratory findings range from a normocytic anemia in mild cases to microcytic, hypochromic anemia in severe cases. The blood smear shows an increased central pale area in red blood cells, and increased anisocytosis and poikilocytosis. If bleeding is chronic or active, the platelet count may be increased. The serum iron is depressed early in iron deficiency and the transferrin level or total iron-binding capacity is increased to more than 350 μg/dl, with a transferrin saturation of less than 15 per cent. The plasma ferritin concentration is low, below 10 ng/ml. Free erythrocyte protoporphyrin is elevated. The reticulocyte count is usually normal. The bone marrow characteristically reveals erythroid hyperplasia, with small, poorly hemoglobinized normoblasts. Iron stores are absent.

The sequence of changes in laboratory variables follows a definite pattern as iron deficiency develops. First, iron stores are depleted and serum ferritin falls. The iron-binding capacity increases, plasma iron concentration falls, and transferrin desaturation follows. The hemoglobin decreases. Red cell morphology initially remains normochromic and normocytic while the total red cell count falls. Eventually, microcytic, hypochromic red cells appear (Table 47–5).

Diagnostic Evaluation. Because iron deficiency represents a manifestation of underlying disease, the cause must be sought. The iron deficiency is easily documented by laboratory tests indicating low serum iron, increased transferrin level (or al-

TABLE 47 – 5. STAGES IN DEVELOPMENT OF IRON DEFICIENCY ANEMIA

HEMOGLOBIN (gm/dl)	PERIPHERAL SMEAR*	SERUM Fe (μg/dl)	BONE MARROW	SERUM FERRITIN (ng/ml)
13+ (normal)	nc/nc	50 – 150	Fe 2+	40 – 340 (male) 14 – 150 (female)
10 – 12	nc/nc	↓	Fe absent, erythroid hyperplasia	<12
8 – 10	hypo/nc	↓↓	Fe absent, erythroid hyperplasia	<12
<8	hypo/micro	↓↓	Fe absent, erythroid hyperplasia	<12

*nc/nc = Normochromic, normocytic; hypo/nc = hypochromic, normocytic; hypo/micro = hypochromic, microcytic.

ternatively, a low serum ferritin), and absence of iron stores in the bone marrow. Urinalysis and stool examinations are part of the initial evaluation. In the older patient especially, investigation for a source for GI blood loss requires serial examinations of stool for blood, plus, if indicated, appropriate radiographs and endoscopy. Women should have a careful gynecologic history recorded and a pelvic examination.

Therapy. The goals include treating the cause for the iron loss, correcting the anemia, and replenishing body iron stores. Simple iron salts, ferrous sulfate or ferrous gluconate, are effective treatments. Slow-release preparations or enteric-coated tablets are not recommended because they may bypass upper duodenal absorption, thereby reducing absorption. All iron salts are irritating to the GI tract in a dose-dependent manner and may cause diarrhea, constipation, or epigastric distress. Accordingly, iron salts are best given in divided doses, gradually increasing to a full dose of 200 mg of elemental iron (about three tablets of ferrous sulfate, 325 mg) daily. This dose provides an optimal response. Iron is best absorbed when the stomach is empty, but gastric irritation may be more common. Absorption after meals is sufficient, and the decrease in GI symptoms is offset by better patient compliance. Ascorbic acid taken with the iron enhances absorption by 20 to 30 per cent but adds to expense. Because of the limited extent of iron absorption even in the iron-deficient patient, it is important to continue therapy for 6 to 12 months, by which time anemia is corrected and iron stores are replenished. Patients should be instructed to continue taking their iron tablets for the full period of time.

Subjective improvement in fatigue or lassitude may occur within a few days, well before a detectable hematologic response, which takes about 2 weeks. A mild reticulocytosis can be observed, followed by a slow rise in hemoglobin of about 1 gm per 2 weeks. "Unresponsiveness" to iron therapy is most commonly a sign of poor compliance or continued blood loss. Intercurrent disease, malabsorption, or an ineffective preparation (e.g., sustained-release products) may also impair response.

Parenteral iron therapy should be reserved for patients who cannot tolerate oral iron, have malabsorption, fail to comply, or have a rapid and chronic blood loss. An example of the latter condition is hereditary hemorrhagic telangiectasia (Osler-Weber-Rendu), which in some cases demonstrates a frequency or rate of bleeding exceeding the capacity for oral iron absorption. Iron-dextran complex (Imferon) contains 50 mg iron per milliliter and is the preparation of choice. It can be administered intramuscularly or intravenously. Because of occasional hypersensitivity to the dextran moiety, a test dose of 0.5 ml should be given first and the patient should be observed for anaphylactic reactions. The replacement total dose is calculated from the patient's hemoglobin level:

$$\text{mg Imferon needed} = [15 - \text{Hgb(gm/dl)}] \times \text{body weight (kg)} \times 3$$

The amount is administered in divided doses, 2.5 ml injected into each buttock daily in a Z-track manner, to provide about 250 mg iron daily, or is given intravenously as a single infusion at a rate of up to 1 ml/min.

MEGALOBLASTIC ANEMIAS

Definition. Megaloblastic anemias are anemias in which DNA synthesis is impaired, leading to delayed division of all rapidly proliferating cells—skin, GI tract, mucosae, hematopoietic cells—and cellular gigantism. Because all hematopoietic cell lines proliferate rapidly, megaloblastic anemias usually manifest not only macrocytic anemia but also pancytopenia. Ineffective hematopoiesis results from intramedullary loss of a large proportion of developing cells, related to the asynchrony of DNA synthesis, hence producing a hemolytic state.

Causes. The major causes of megaloblastic anemias are folic acid or vitamin B_{12} deficiency, which may be related to nutritional deficiency, disease of the stomach or small bowel, pregnancy, alcoholism, or drugs that affect DNA synthesis, as in cancer chemotherapy. Rarer inherited defects in DNA synthesis also occur.

Pathophysiology. Pathophysiology of the megaloblastic anemias relates to the interlocking roles of folic acid and vitamin B_{12} in DNA synthesis. Folic acid (in the reduced 5,10-methylene tetrahydrofolate form) is the carrier for one-carbon fragments that are donated to desoxyuridine to form desoxythymidine, the characteristic pyrimidine in DNA. This methylation of desoxyuridine is essential for thymidine synthesis, and subsequent regeneration of 5,10-methylene tetrahydrofolate is necessary for continued delivery of reduced methyl groups to desoxyuridine. Vitamin B_{12} is the cofactor of the reaction that, by accepting a 5-methyl group, regenerates tetrahydrofolate from 5-methyl tetrahydrofolate, a major form of folate in the body that is unable to donate its methyl group to desoxyuridine. In addition, vitamin B_{12} is the coenzyme in the conversion of methylmalonyl coenzyme A (CoA) to succinyl CoA, a reaction necessary for myelin metabolism in the nervous system. Thus, deficiency of vitamin B_{12} leads to neurologic changes as well as megaloblastic anemia, whereas folate deficiency leads only to megaloblastic anemia. In folate deficiency, the inadequate generation of thymidylate leads to increased incorporation of uridylate into developing hematopoietic cell DNA. The incorporated uridylate is then enzymatically excised, leading to fragmentation of the DNA, blocking of DNA synthesis at a normal rate, and impaired cell proliferation. RNA and protein synthesis, however, can proceed normally.

The ineffective hematopoiesis that results from the impaired DNA synthesis in vitamin B_{12} or folate deficiency leads to early intramedullary death of many of these abnormal cells and shortened lifespan of circulating red blood cells. A hemolytic state involving both intramedullary and extramedullary hemolysis results, accompanied by leukopenia and thrombocytopenia.

Clinical and Laboratory Manifestations. Signs and symptoms of megaloblastic anemia are identical for folic acid and vitamin B_{12} deficiency. Thus, a profound and slowly developing macrocytic anemia is observed, with large, oval, well-hemoglobinized red cells, considerable anisocytosis, and frequent nuclear remnants. The reticulocyte count is very low. There is leukopenia with hypersegmentation of polymorphonuclear leukocyte nuclei and thrombocytopenia. The platelets are large. The bilirubin is elevated. The bone marrow is markedly hypercellular with megaloblasts showing "nuclear-cytoplasmic dissociation," that is, normal maturation of the cytoplasm in the face of nuclear immaturity, a finely dispersed chromatin pattern, and large nuclear size. Nuclear condensation is delayed in erythroid cells. The myeloid series also shows megaloblastosis, with giant band forms and hypersegmented polymorphonuclear leukocytes. The number of mitotic figures is increased. Megakaryocytes are large and decreased in number and show decreased budding. The iron stores in the marrow are typically increased (because of the intramedullary hemolysis). Epithelial cells of mucosal surfaces such as the mouth, intestinal tract, stomach, and vagina also show gigantism. The gastric and intestinal mucosae tend to atrophy, leading to further malabsorption of folate.

In vitamin B_{12} deficiency neurologic changes may occur, although their presence correlates poorly with the development of the hematologic

abnormalities: some patients develop severe neurologic manifestations with only mild anemia, and vice versa. Morphologically, the neurologic abnormality initially produces demyelination, first of the large fibers in peripheral nerves, later of the dorsal and lateral columns of the spinal cord, and sometimes in the cerebrum. Irreversible nerve cell damage is a late complication. Earliest symptoms typically include distal paresthesias in the extremities, with a glove-stocking peripheral neuropathy, and impairment of position and vibration sense in combination with increased deep tendon reflexes, according to whether the maximal metabolic lesion affects central or peripheral neural structures. Later a typical spastic ataxia, motor weakness, and paraparesis may occur. Mental changes may also occur with "megaloblastic madness," that is, dementia, in severe cases. In pernicious anemia, in which vitamin B_{12} deficiency is due to gastric atrophy of parietal cells and loss of their product, intrinsic factor, the physiologic vitamin B_{12}–binding protein necessary for ileal absorption of vitamin B_{12}, autoimmune phenomena are common, with vitiligo, early graying of hair, autoantibody formation, and emergence of other autoimmune diseases.

Vitamin Requirements, Absorption, Metabolism, and Action

FOLIC ACID. Folic acid (pteroylglutamic acid) is derived from leafy plants, liver, or yeast and exists as a family of compounds consisting of a pteroyl ring, para-aminobenzoic acid, and one or more glutamates in a gamma glutamyl linkage (Table 47–6). Food folate comprises polyglutamates, whereas medicinal folate is pteroylmonoglutamic acid. The daily requirement for folate is 50 to 200 μg; the body stores of folate (in the liver) of 5 to 20 mg suffice only for weeks to 3 or 4 months. The rate of folate absorption depends upon tissue stores and on the integrity of the intestinal mucosa. Food polyglutamates must be cleaved to the monoglutamate form in the intestinal tract by folate conjugases in the intestinal mucosa before efficient uptake by an active transport mechanism, mainly in the upper portion of the small intestine. Certain drugs, such as phenytoin (Dilantin) and oral contraceptives, or intrinsic small bowel disease or malabsorption syndromes can impair absorption of folate by interfering with conjugase action. Folate is heat-labile and is destroyed by prolonged heating or cooking. Absorbed folate is mainly converted to 5-methyl THF, the main transport and storage form.

Because of the relatively low body stores of folic acid, dietary deficiency is a common cause of folate-related megaloblastic anemia. Thus, a diet devoid of fresh vegetables or limited mainly to alcohol frequently leads to folate deficiency, as in the elderly, who often consume "tea and toast" diets. In alcoholism, several factors combine to produce folate deficiency: poor diet, a toxic effect of alcohol on the intestinal mucosa, and interfer-

TABLE 47-6. COMPARISON OF FOLIC ACID AND VITAMIN B$_{12}$

	FOLIC ACID	VITAMIN B$_{12}$
Source	Leafy vegetables, yeast, liver	Animal products
Dietary intake	500–1000 μg	7–30 μg
Effect of cooking	Destroyed	Unchanged
Minimal daily need	100–200 μg	1–2 μg
Body stores	10–12 mg (4 mo)	2–3 mg (2–4 yr)
Absorption	Active transport, upper small bowel	Carrier-mediated (intrinsic factor), terminal ileum
Physiologic forms	Reduced polyglutamates	Methylcobalamin, adenosylcobalamin
Serum level	3–15 ng/ml	200–900 pg/ml
Function	Transfer one-carbon fragments in thymidine synthesis	Regenerate reduced folate from 5-CH$_3$ THF; succinyl CoA formation in CNS

ence by alcohol with folate utilization in the bone marrow. Increased demands for folate occur during pregnancy, lactation, and rapid growth in childhood. Pregnancy increases the folate requirement 5- to 10-fold. Folate requirements also rise in any chronic hemolytic anemia such as sickle cell anemia, immune hemolytic anemia, or thalassemia, in patients on hemodialysis, and in psoriasis or exfoliative dermatitis. Bacterial overgrowth, as in the blind loop syndrome, more commonly causes vitamin B$_{12}$ deficiency. Folate deficiency may lead to low serum B$_{12}$, whereas in B$_{12}$ deficiency serum folate may be high because of underutilization, although red cell folate may be low.

Folic acid is reduced by the enzyme dihydrofolate reductase to forms capable of carrying one-carbon fragments. Inhibitors of dihydrofolate reductase therefore inhibit DNA synthesis: the first antimetabolite successfully used in leukemia chemotherapy, aminopterin, is an inhibitor of dihydrofolate reductase. Antimalarial drugs such as pyrimethamine also are dihydrofolate reductase inhibitors. Therefore, megaloblastic changes are observed in patients receiving pyrimethamine for malaria, trimethoprim (present in the drug Bactrim) for bacterial infections, or methotrexate. The toxicity induced by such drugs may be counteracted by administration of folinic acid, which bypasses the need for dihydrofolate reductase by supplying the fully reduced folate.

VITAMIN B$_{12}$. Vitamin B$_{12}$ is synthesized in nature only by microorganisms and is obtained by eating animal foods (Table 47-6). This vitamin consists of a group of cobalamins, which contain a porphyrin-like corrin ring similar in structure to heme but with a central cobalt molecule linked to a nucleoside instead of iron. The normal diet contains a large excess of B$_{12}$ (5 to 30 μg) over the daily requirement of 1 μg; only the strictest vegetarian diet is B$_{12}$-deficient. The chief body storage site for vitamin B$_{12}$ is the liver, where 3 to 5 mg are normally present, representing stores sufficient for several years. The much greater body storage of B$_{12}$ compared with folic acid means that in malnutrition or after GI surgery, vitamin B$_{12}$ defi-

ciency develops much more slowly than does folate deficiency. In the stomach, food vitamin B$_{12}$ is released by pepsin from protein complexes at acid pH and binds with R-factors, present in saliva and gastric juice. These complexes stabilize the vitamin during intestinal transit. In the small intestine, pancreatic proteases and an alkaline pH release B$_{12}$ bound to R proteins, and the B$_{12}$ then binds preferentially to intrinsic factor, a glycoprotein produced by gastric parietal cells, to form intrinsic factor–B$_{12}$ complexes. In the distal small ileum, specific mucosal receptors permit attachment of intrinsic factor–B$_{12}$ complexes necessary for absorption of the vitamin (without the intrinsic factor) across the gut wall. R protein–B$_{12}$ complexes are not absorbed. Plasma B$_{12}$ is complexed to several types of transcobalamins (TC) or transport proteins. Only TC II transports B$_{12}$ to hematopoietic and other proliferating cells where the B$_{12}$–TC II complex binds to high-affinity TC II receptors and the vitamin is endocytosed; TC I (from leukocytes) and TC III bind the vitamin avidly and may be important in preventing its loss. The normal plasma level of vitamin B$_{12}$ ranges between 175 and 725 pg/ml. Most of this represents B$_{12}$ bound to TC I. In myeloproliferative diseases, in which granulocyte production is high, serum levels of either TC I or TC III and B$_{12}$ are greatly increased.

An enterohepatic circulation of vitamin B$_{12}$, ensuring recycling of the vitamin, contributes to the low daily requirement. After partial gastrectomy, with loss of antral intrinsic factor production, this recycling mechanism is interrupted and the requirement increases to 5 to 10 μg/day. The result is that clinical B$_{12}$ deficiency arises earlier after gastric surgery than after dietary depletion. B$_{12}$ deficiency is inevitable after total gastrectomy; after partial gastrectomy, owing to the large amount of intrinsic factor normally produced in the gastric antrum, the development of B$_{12}$ deficiency is variable in time of onset and in rate of occurrence, depending upon the extent of surgery.

Different forms of vitamin B$_{12}$ mediate different chemical reactions. Methylcobalamin is key for the regeneration of biologically active folate. Adenosylcobalamin is involved in the isomerization of methylmalonyl CoA to succinyl CoA. Medicinal vitamin B_{12} is cyanocobalamin; the binding of cyanate to the B_{12} molecule may represent a natural detoxification mechanism.

Specific Diagnosis. Diagnosis of megaloblastic anemia is usually made from the blood smear (with an elevated MCV being the earliest sign) and is confirmed by the finding of a megaloblastic bone marrow and low plasma level of folic acid, vitamin B_{12}, or both (Fig. 47–3). Concomitant iron deficiency, however, may mask the MCV changes. Plasma folic acid falls to low levels (less than 3 ng/ml) quickly, within days to weeks of dietary deprivation, whereas red cell folate better reflects total body stores. Vitamin B_{12} levels fall only when body stores are depleted. Both vitamins were formerly measured by bioassays employing vitamin-requiring microorganisms, which thus assessed biologic activity of vitamin; recent development of sensitive radioimmunoassays involving a vitamin B binder has sometimes led to falsely high values for plasma B_{12} because certain assays also measure biologically inactive analogues of B_{12} that bind to R proteins. Assays using intrinsic factor only as the binding protein give true values for plasma B_{12}; the action of the analogues is unknown.

Once a folic acid or vitamin B_{12} deficiency state is verified, the underlying cause must be sought. For folic acid, an accurate dietary history plus an evaluation for possible malabsorption usually uncovers a cause. Vitamin B_{12} deficiency is most commonly seen as a result of pernicious anemia, prior partial gastrectomy, or small bowel disease. Pernicious anemia involves an atrophic gastritis that leads to deficient intrinsic factor secretion, hence vitamin B_{12} malabsorption. The disease is accompanied by numerous autoimmune phenomena (unknown whether primary or secondary), including frequent occurrence of anti–parietal cell and anti–intrinsic factor antibodies. The latter impair the absorption of B_{12}–intrinsic factor complexes in the ileum. Finding anti–intrinsic factor antibodies in the serum is considered diagnostic for pernicious anemia, whereas the presence of anti–parietal cell antibodies is a more common, nonspecific phenomenon found in association with gastric disease in older persons. Impaired absorption of oral vitamin B_{12} occurs in several types of B_{12} deficiency and serves as the basis of the Schilling test, which can be used to distinguish between pernicious anemia, small intestinal bacterial overgrowth, and other malabsorption syndromes. A special advantage of the Schilling test is that it can be carried out after treatment has begun, because it measures absorption of vitamin independent of therapy.

A therapeutic trial can also be undertaken to determine whether a megaloblastic anemia is due to vitamin B_{12} deficiency. Administration of 1 to 5 μg of vitamin B_{12} intramuscularly daily leads to a reticulocytosis within 3 to 4 days, peaking within 10 days. Continuation of the therapy corrects the anemia within a month. Administration of 200 μg of folic acid daily leads to a reticulocytosis in folic acid deficiency but not in vitamin B_{12} deficiency; larger doses of folate induce a reticulocyte response in the vitamin B_{12}–deficient patient, but do not fully correct the megaloblastic anemia and may lead to worsening or induction of the neurologic abnormalities.

The response to specific therapy of megaloblastic anemia is prompt and follows a predictable pattern. Symptoms improve within 48 hours and the bone marrow red cell morphology reverts to normal in 24 to 48 hours. Serum potassium may fall within 48 hours, representing a return of potassium to intracellular sites. Reticulocytosis is ob-

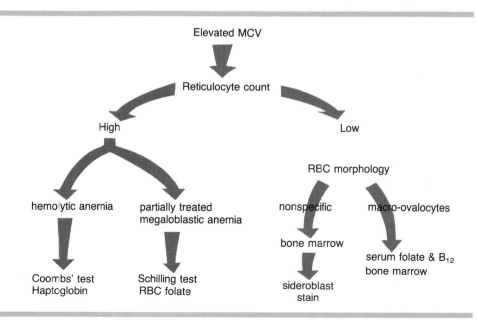

FIGURE 47–3. Evaluation of macrocytosis.

served within 3 to 4 days and may rise to over 25 per cent; leukopenia and thrombocytopenia regress within 10 days. Hypersegmented polys and giant bands (in the marrow) disappear within about a week. The elevated bilirubin and lactate dehydrogenase (LDH), indicating the ineffective erythropoiesis, disappear within 1 to 3 weeks. Anemia is corrected within 1 to 2 months (if iron stores are adequate). Neurologic improvement in corrected vitamin B_{12} deficiency occurs more slowly and may take 6 to 12 months; long-standing neurologic defects, especially long tract dysfunction, may be irreversible.

Less Common Causes of Megaloblastic Anemia. About 5 per cent of megaloblastic anemias are due to inherited disorders of pyrimidine metabolism, such as orotic aciduria, absence of ileal receptors for the intrinsic factor–B_{12} complex (Immerslund's syndrome), or dyspoietic anemias that may represent preleukemia or may be familial. Megaloblastic anemia may also be induced by antimetabolite therapy that interferes with DNA synthesis, as in cancer chemotherapy or with prolonged administration of trimethoprim (Bactrim) in human immunodeficiency virus (HIV) infection.

TABLE 47–7. MECHANISMS OF HEMOLYSIS

Type of Red Cell Defect
1. Intrinsic (usually inherited)
   a. Membrane (e.g., hereditary spherocytosis)
   b. Enzyme (e.g., glucose-6-phosphate dehydrogenase deficiency)
   c. Hemoglobinopathy (e.g., sickle cell disease, Hb C disease)
   d. Globin synthesis (e.g., thalassemia)

In all of the above, the red cell defect leads to membrane or cellular rigidity, splenic sequestration, short red cell lifespan.

2. Extrinsic (usually acquired)
   a. Antibody-induced (e.g., Coombs'-positive hemolytic anemia)
      1. warm antibody
      2. cold antibody
   b. Drug-induced (e.g., penicillin)
   c. Toxin-mediated (e.g., burns, sepsis)
   d. Red cell fragmentation, mechanical hemolysis (e.g., after heart valve surgery)

In all of the above, induced changes in red cell membranes lead to splenic removal, and in some, intravascular hemolysis with hemoglobinemia and hemoglobinuria may occur.

Laboratory Features of Hemolysis
1. Increased red cell breakdown
   a. Increased serum bilirubin (unconjugated)
   b. Increased urine urobilinogen
   c. Decreased serum haptoglobin
2. Increased red cell production
   a. Reticulocytosis and polychromasia
   b. Erythroid hyperplasia in bone marrow
   c. Increased requirement for folic acid (low serum folate)
3. Red cell damage
   a. Morphology: fragments, microspherocytes, spherocytes
   b. Increased osmotic fragility
   c. Short red cell survival
   d. Intraerythrocytic inclusions

HEMOLYTIC ANEMIAS

Definition. Hemolytic anemias result from an increased rate of red cell destruction. Because the bone marrow can increase red cell production eightfold, the rate of red cell destruction may increase considerably without causing anemia (compensated hemolytic state). Normally, red cells survive 120 days in the circulation, gradually losing enzyme activities and becoming denser and less deformable. In hemolytic anemias, the red cell survival ranges from slightly shortened to only a few hours. Hemolytic anemias result from abnormalities of the red cell membrane, enzymes, or hemoglobin, from antibody interactions with the red cell membrane, from toxins or microbial products, or from heat or mechanical trauma. The red cell morphology may be normal or abnormal, reticulocytes are usually increased, nucleated red cells may be present in the peripheral blood, the serum bilirubin and LDH are increased, urine urobilinogen is raised, and red cell survival is short. In chronic hemolytic anemias jaundice and pallor may be present, splenomegaly or hepatomegaly may be observed, gallstones are common, and the bone marrow shows erythroid hyperplasia.

Hemolysis may be intravascular or extravascular, that is, within the reticuloendothelial system (Table 47–7). *Intravascular hemolysis* is relatively rare and occurs with acute transfusion reactions, prosthetic heart valve dysfunction, paroxysmal cold or paroxysmal nocturnal hemoglobinuria (PNH), cold agglutinin disease, heat stroke, and clostridial infections. Hemoglobin released from injured red cells into the plasma is rapidly bound to haptoglobin, hemopexin, or albumin. Haptoglobin-hemoglobin or hemopexin-hemoglobin complexes are promptly cleared from the circulation by the liver, lowering the plasma levels of these proteins. In acute intravascular hemolysis, serum haptoglobin is very low and LDH, released from red cells, is elevated. Methemalbumin (the complex of heme with albumin) circulates for some days. If the binding capacity of these proteins is exceeded, hemoglobinuria occurs. Acute hemoglobinuria is not toxic to the kidney, but the accumulation of red cell stroma in renal vessels can lead to acute renal failure. Chronic hemoglobinuria leads to iron deficiency due to the sloughing of renal tubular cells loaded with hemosiderin derived from reabsorbed heme iron.

Extravascular hemolysis occurs commonly and represents early removal of red cells sequestered by the fixed phagocytes of the spleen and liver. Only a small amount of the hemoglobin removed reaches the plasma, and the heme iron is recycled for further red cell production, so that serum iron levels tend to be high during active hemolysis. Haptoglobin levels also tend to be reduced, but hemoglobinemia is not present. The level of serum LDH is elevated. The level of unconjugated (indirect) bilirubin reflects the net effect of the briskness of hemolysis and the ability of the liver to conjugate bilirubin.

Differential Diagnosis. Differential diagnosis of

hemolytic anemias requires evaluation of whether the process is congenital or acquired, is due to abnormality of the red cell or to an abnormality in the plasma or circulatory system (including red cell antibodies, mechanical trauma, infection), or reflects other underlying disease, and whether it is acute or chronic. Hence, an accurate family history and knowledge of the patient's prior history of jaundice, anemia, splenomegaly, or gallstones are of great importance. Physical findings depend upon the rate and chronicity of hemolysis and range from scleral icterus and pallor in mild cases to splenomegaly and bony changes in severe chronic hemolysis. An important differentiating point is whether antibodies against red cell antigens are present on the red cell surface (direct Coombs' test) or in the plasma (indirect Coombs' test).

Hemolysis due to intracorpuscular abnormalities may be caused by intrinsic defects in the red cell membrane, abnormal hemoglobin (or hemoglobin production), or defective enzymes. The most common inherited hemolytic anemia due to a membrane defect is hereditary spherocytosis, which has an incidence of 1 in 5000 in northern Europeans and less in other population groups. The peripheral blood smear shows a uniform population of spherocytes lacking central pallor. The MCHC is increased. The osmotic fragility of the red cells is increased, and red cell survival is short. Splenomegaly is usually present, bilirubin gallstones commonly develop, and intermittent jaundice is frequent, particularly in conjunction with stress states such as infection or pregnancy. Aplastic crises may occur during infection, as with parvovirus, owing to bone marrow suppression in the face of a short red cell survival.

The pathogenesis of the hemolysis is sequestration of the poorly deformable spherocytes, which require extra expenditure of ATP to maintain membrane flexibility. Several types of cytoskeletal erythrocyte protein defects may cause hereditary spherocytosis, including deficiencies of spectrin, ankyrin, and other structural membrane proteins. In addition, permeability to sodium ion is excessive, requiring increased ATP-dependent cation pump activity to prevent water accumulation by the red cells. Treatment of hereditary spherocytosis includes folic acid administration and splenectomy, which improves red cell survival without altering the red cell defects. Other membrane abnormalities resulting in hemolytic anemia include hereditary elliptocytosis and hereditary stomatocytosis.

The most common red cell enzyme defect is *glucose-6-phosphate dehydrogenase (G6PD) deficiency*, which affects over 100 million individuals worldwide. Other abnormalities in the Embden-Meyerhof enzyme pathway also lead to hemolytic states, but these are extremely rare (pyruvate kinase and hexokinase deficiencies, the next most common, have been reported in only a few hundred cases). Normal red cells depend upon aerobic glycolysis to metabolize 90 per cent of glucose in producing ATP and 2,3-diphosphoglycerate (2,3-DPG). ATP is necessary to preserve membrane flexibility and to support membrane cation pumps, whereas 2,3-DPG influences the binding of oxygen to hemoglobin, to facilitate oxygen unloading in tissues. Ten per cent of glucose is metabolized via the hexose monophosphate shunt, which generates nicotinamide-adenine dinucleotide phosphate (NADPH), the major reducing compound produced by the red cell. NADPH is required for regeneration of reduced glutathione, which prevents hemoglobin denaturation, preserves the integrity of red cell membrane sulfhydryl groups, and detoxifies hydrogen peroxide and oxygen radicals in and on the red cell. Because G6PD is the initial enzyme in the hexose monophosphate shunt pathway, functionally abnormal enzyme or a low level of G6PD leads to increased red cell oxidative damage, particularly during periods of oxidant stress. G6PD deficiency is an X-linked trait that is clinically expressed in male heterozygotes. More than 100 inherited variants of G6PD are recognized; young red cells have higher levels of the enzyme in general than do older cells. The common A(−) variety seen in the black population is less severe than the Mediterranean type, as red cell enzyme levels are about 15 per cent of normal in blacks but less than 5 per cent in the latter group. G6PD deficiency leads to hemolysis in the setting of hepatitis, severe infections, fava bean ingestion, or ingestion of oxidant drugs. Black males with G6PD deficiency and falciparum malaria develop severe intravascular hemolysis (blackwater fever) when treated with antimalarial drugs such as primaquine. G6PD deficiency in persons of Greek or Mediterranean lineage is associated with favism, or hemolysis after ingestion of the fava bean. Acquired G6PD deficiency has been observed in bacterial overgrowth of the bowel and in uremia and myeloproliferative diseases.

ACQUIRED HEMOLYTIC DISORDERS

Red cell lifespan can become shortened in the course of infectious, malignant, cardiovascular, or immunologic diseases. In most of these, hemolysis results from an extracorporeal abnormality such as altered hemodynamics, antibody against red cell antigens, or exposure to toxins. Rarely, the red cells themselves may undergo membrane changes that lead to hemolysis (e.g., in PNH). For convenience, acquired hemolytic anemias are divided into two categories: Coombs'-positive (antibody-mediated) and Coombs'-negative hemolytic anemia.

Antibody-Mediated Hemolytic Anemias

These represent a wide variety of conditions in which antibodies directed against red cell antigens (or neoantigens) coat the red cells and are directly or indirectly responsible for hemolysis. Antibodies that arise after transfusion or sensitization to foreign red cells, as during pregnancy, are called *alloantibodies*. Antibodies that arise without sensitization, representing abnormalities in the subject's own immune regulation, are called *autoantibodies*. The presence of antibody on the red cell surface can alter the behavior of the red cells, making them less deformable and more susceptible to phagocytosis by macrophages in the spleen or liver. Macrophages ingest antibody- or complement-coated portions of the red cell membrane, via Fc or complement receptors. Red cells that have lost part of their plasma membrane reseal but assume a more spherical shape (spherocytosis) owing to decreased surface/volume ratio associated with decreased pliability in the circulation and a shortened lifespan.

Autoimmune hemolytic anemias (AIHA) are characterized by antibodies directed against the patient's own red cell antigens (Table 47–8). In contrast to alloantibodies resulting from transfusion of imperfectly matched red cells, autoantibodies can arise spontaneously, in response to drugs acting as haptens, or in 40 per cent of cases as manifestations of systemic disease. Diseases of disordered immunity, such as collagen vascular diseases, chronic inflammatory bowel disease, chronic lymphocytic leukemia, or lymphomas, manifest an increased incidence of autoimmune hemolytic anemia. Autoantibodies increase in frequency with age, but only a small proportion of red cell autoantibodies actually cause hemolytic anemia. Whether or not hemolysis occurs depends on the density of red cell coating by antibody, the capacity of the antibody to fix complement on the red cell membrane, the thermal amplitude of the antibody, and the tendency for antibody-coated red cells to be phagocytized by splenic macrophages. AIHA fall into two groups, the warm antibody and the cold antibody autoimmune hemolytic anemias.

Warm antibody hemolytic anemias are mediated by IgG antibodies that attach to red cells at body temperature and that may fix complement (Table 47–8). Clinically important antibodies tend to be of the IgG_1 and IgG_3 subclasses. The AIHA may be associated with collagen vascular disease, lymphoma, chronic lymphocytic leukemia, ovarian teratoma, ulcerative colitis, or drug reactions (see below). Almost half the cases with AIHA are idiopathic, although the hemolytic anemia may be the harbinger of a later-appearing systemic disease; such cases may have a very variable course. The clinical picture relates to the rate of hemolysis; thus, the spectrum varies from a mild asymptomatic jaundice with splenomegaly, when the rate of hemolysis is mild and bone marrow production of red cells can compensate for shortened red cell lifespan, to severe anemia with cardiovascular symptoms, when the rate of hemolysis is rapid. A positive direct Coombs (antiglobulin) test using an antiglobulin antiserum detects the coating of the red cell membrane by the autoantibody (Fig. 47–4); if the amount of autoantibody is high, free antibody in the plasma (a positive indirect Coombs test) is also detected. Complement coating on the red cell, usually the biologically inactive cleavage products of the third component of complement, C3b or C3d, may be detected by specific anticomplement antisera or by broad-spectrum Coombs' antisera that incorporate anticomplement as well as antiglobulin antibodies for screening. AIHA may be accompanied by immune thrombocytopenia (Evans' syndrome). As in other hemolytic anemias, the reticulocyte count is elevated, the serum haptoglobin is low, and spherocytes of varied sizes are present on the peripheral blood smear, in contrast to the more uniform spherocytes of hereditary spherocytosis. The bilirubin may be elevated; usually it is mostly unconjugated, but if the total bilirubin exceeds 4 mg/dl, the conjugated fraction may be increased.

Therapy is directed toward decreasing the rate of hemolysis. The first approach is oral corticoste-

TABLE 47–8. AUTOIMMUNE HEMOLYTIC ANEMIAS

	Ab COATING ON RBC	OPTIMAL TEMPERATURE FOR DETECTING Ab
Warm Type		
Idiopathic	IgG or IgG + C	37°C
Secondary	Rarely, IgA or IgM	
Systemic lupus erythematosus		
Other "autoimmune disease"		
Lymphoma		
Chronic lymphocytic leukemia		
Drug-induced		
Cold Type	IgM (in cold only) anti-I or anti-i	4°C
Idiopathic	C3b or C3d	4° or 37°C
Secondary		
Infections		
Mycoplasma pneumoniae		
Infectious mononucleosis		
Lymphoma (diffuse histiocytic lymphoma)		
Paroxysmal cold hemoglobinuria	IgG (anti-P)	4°C — antibody binding
		37°C — complement-mediated lysis

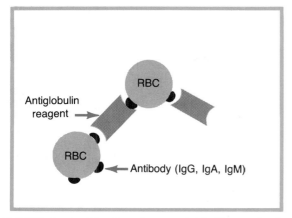

FIGURE 47-4. The Coombs or antiglobulin test. In the Coombs test, an antibody directed against human immunoglobulin is used to detect the presence of antibody on the surface of the red cells by agglutination. Complement coating on the red cells (C3) can similarly be detected by an anticomplement Coombs reagent. Broad-spectrum Coombs' reagents can be prepared which detect either immunoglobulin or complement or both; these are used for screening.

roids, using 1 to 2 mg/kg/day of prednisolone (or equivalent) tapering the dose after the hematocrit returns to normal. Steroid therapy diminishes the binding of antibody to fixed macrophages and thereby limits the rate of red cell destruction. Steroids have a slower and less marked effect on inhibition of autoantibody production. Splenectomy is helpful in steroid-dependent or unresponsive patients. Splenectomy also may remove an important source of antibody production. Immunosuppressive drugs such as azathioprine or cyclophosphamide are reserved for refractory cases. Transfusion is avoided if possible, as the transfused red cells are usually destroyed as quickly as the patient's own cells. Folic acid supplementation is often necessary because the rapid rate of red cell turnover depletes body stores of this vitamin, whereas requirements for folate rise.

Cold antibody autoimmune hemolytic anemia has a complex etiology. Whereas many naturally occurring antibodies react with red cells in the cold, certain IgM autoantibodies with wide thermal amplitude may mediate autoimmune hemolysis (Table 47-8). The term *thermal amplitude* describes the temperature range over which these antibodies attach to red cells. Cold agglutinins causing hemolytic anemia are those with a wide thermal amplitude; that is, the capacity to bind to red cells occurs over a broad range, from 4°C to a few degrees below body temperature, that is, at temperatures that may occur in the nose, ears, or extremities during cold exposure. Polyclonal cold-reacting, IgM autoantibodies may arise transiently during infectious mononucleosis, cytomegalovirus infection, *Mycoplasma* pneumonia, or protozoal infections and can cause significant hemolysis. Such polyclonal cold-reacting antibodies tend to be present transiently for days or weeks and resolve spontaneously following convalescence from the infection. In addition, "idiopathic cold agglu-

tinin syndrome," characterized by monoclonal IgM antibodies, may precede the development of lymphoma or Waldenström's macroglobulinemia or may continue for years in the absence of malignant transformation. Unlike the polyclonal IgM cold antibodies, which appear briefly after infections, the monoclonal cold antibodies can persist for years. They show specificity for the I-i antigen system, glycoprotein precursors of ABO antigens. These IgM antibodies bind directly to red cells in the cold, fixing complement to the red cell surface; at warmer temperatures the antibodies dissociate from the red cells, leaving only activated complement bound to the red cell membrane. The C3b fixed on the red cell surface leads to removal of the coated red cells by macrophages in the spleen; in addition, bound C3 is converted to inactive C3d on the red cell membrane, which interferes with further binding or activation of C3 and limits the rate of hemolysis.

In addition to chronic hemolytic anemia, the patient with cold agglutinin disease may suffer from painful, blue fingers and toes on exposure to cold (acrocyanosis). The mainstay of therapy is to minimize cold exposure. In the rare case of severe hemolysis, plasmapheresis (using warmed equipment) or chemotherapy may be necessary.

Paroxysmal cold hemoglobinuria is a rare form of cold-reactive hemolysis in which a polyclonal IgG directed against the red cell P antigen system binds to red cells in the cold and fixes complement, so that when rewarming occurs, the complement cascade is activated, and brisk intravascular hemolysis follows. This condition is found uncommonly in syphilis or after viral infections. The hemolysis is self-limited, so protection from cold is the most important therapy.

Drug-induced immune hemolytic anemia is a relatively common disorder that can result from three different mechanisms of hemolysis (Fig. 47-5).

1. *Hapten type.* Haptenic drugs bind to red cell membranes, forming neoantigens to which antibodies develop; a Coombs-positive hemolytic process follows, with mainly extravascular destruction of red cells. The drug must be present for hemolysis to occur. Penicillins and cephalosporins are the chief offenders.

2. *Innocent bystander type.* Drugs that bind to plasma proteins elicit antibodies that form circulating immune complexes and activate complement. Red cells as "innocent bystanders" become coated with complement and may undergo intravascular or extravascular hemolysis, depending on the rates of activation and inactivation of complement. Red cells show only complement coating. This represents the hemolytic mechanism for most drugs that produce immune hemolysis, including sulfonamides, phenothiazines, quinine, and isoniazid.

3. *Alpha-methyldopa type.* Upon chronic use of alpha-methyldopa, 15 per cent of patients develop

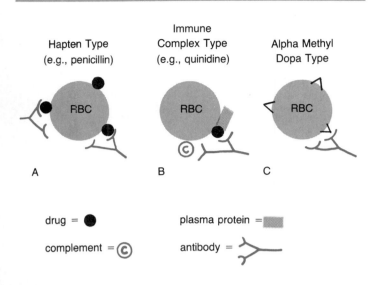

Hapten Type
(e.g., penicillin)

Immune
Complex Type
(e.g., quinidine)

Alpha Methyl
Dopa Type

drug = ●

complement = Ⓒ

plasma protein = ▬

antibody = Ⴤ

FIGURE 47–5. Mechanisms of drug-induced hemolysis. A, The drug binds to the red cell membrane as a hapten. Antibodies to the drug-membrane complex can lyse the red cells, but only in the presence of bound drug. B, The drug binds to a plasma protein or antibody, and the complex attaches to the red cell membrane. Antibodies produce binding of complement, and lysis follows. C, There appears to be a change in the red cell membrane after long-term treatment with the drug, often with Rh specificity. Antibodies that bind to the altered membrane develop, producing a positive Coombs test and, rarely, hemolysis.

a positive direct Coombs test, with IgG present on the red cells; only 1 in 10 has hemolysis. The autoantibodies show Rh specificity, suggesting that the drug may somehow modify this red cell antigen system. The positive Coombs test may persist for months after cessation of the drug. Levodopa and mefenamic acid (an anti-inflammatory drug) may also produce this type of autoimmune phenomenon.

Hypersplenism represents excessive sequestration of blood cells, particularly red cells, by an enlarged or abnormally functioning spleen. Whereas senescent red cells are normally removed by trapping in the tortuous, poorly oxygenated sinusoids of the spleen, an enlarged spleen can randomly remove nonsenescent red cells. Pancytopenia, rather than anemia, may result from hypersplenism, but it appears that platelets and leukocytes are merely sequestered in enlarged spleens rather than being excessively destroyed. Hypersplenism is characterized by the picture of "empty blood and full marrow," which distinguishes this condition from the pancytopenias of marrow failure. It may occur in chronic hemolytic anemias of any cause, chronic infections, chronic leukemias and myeloproliferative diseases, lipid storage diseases, lymphomas, and rheumatoid arthritis (Felty's syndrome).

PNH is an acquired hemolytic disorder associated with increased susceptibility of a red cell subpopulation to complement-mediated damage. It is extremely rare, is considered a stem cell defect, and may be associated with eventual bone marrow aplasia and leukemia. Not only red cells but also granulocytes and platelets are sensitive to the lytic effects of complement and bind increased amounts of C3b compared with normal cells. PNH red cells fail to facilitate inactivation of complement by the plasma C3b inactivator, which may account for their susceptibility to lysis. Clinical manifestations include pancytopenia, intravascular hemolysis, back pain, a tendency to venous thrombosis, and iron deficiency secondary to recurrent hemoglobinuria from intravascular hemolysis. Bone marrow may be hypocellular; the Coombs test is negative. Hemolysis can be demonstrated by placing the patient's red cells in acidified serum (which permits activation of the alternative complement pathway) or in hypotonic medium (sugar-water test). Other markers associated with PNH include a low leukocyte alkaline phosphatase and a low red cell acetylcholinesterase.

Chemical, Toxic, and Parasitic Causes of Hemolytic Anemia

Either inorganic or complex organic toxins, including snake venoms and heavy metals, can cause hemolytic anemia. Arsenic and copper cause hemolysis by binding red cell membrane sulfhydryl groups; copper-induced hemolysis is seen in Wilson's disease and in hemodialyzed patients. Chloramine, generated in urban water supplies purified with chlorine, and alum may cause hemolysis in hemodialysis patients dialyzed against tap water. The lipophilic antifungal drug amphotericin can cause hemolysis, and snake venoms are directly lytic to red cells because of their content of lysolecithinases. Patients with advanced cirrhotic liver disease often develop spur cell anemia, a hemolytic disorder in which red cell membranes absorb excessive cholesterol present in abnormal circulating low density lipoproteins that contain an excess of cholesterol compared with phospholipid. Acanthocytes with irregular "spurs" are typically found in the peripheral blood.

Malaria commonly causes hemolytic anemia. Parasitized red cells become metabolically depleted, change membrane permeability and deformability characteristics, and may develop neoantigens that produce a positive antiglobulin test. The parasitized red cells also are prone to adhere to the vascular endothelium, which may contribute to local thrombosis. Babesiosis and bartonellosis also cause hemolytic anemia via red cell parasitism.

Hemolysis Resulting from Red Cell Trauma

Red cells exposed to excessive mechanical stress intravascularly or during extracorporeal circulation can undergo *fragmentation hemolysis.* Abnormal shear forces arise during passage of red cells through prosthetic heart valves, damaged natural valves, vascular shunts, or strands of fibrin. Chronic intravascular hemolysis due to abnormally functioning heart valves or valve prostheses is relatively uncommon today, when ball valves are less frequently used. Its occurrence usually signals the existence of valve malfunction. Because of higher shear stresses associated with systemic pressures, malfunctioning aortic valves most often cause this type of intravascular hemolysis, but similar syndromes have occurred with mitral valve pathology. In both acute and chronic intravascular hemolysis, the blood smear shows red cell fragments (schistocytes), microspherocytes, and increased polychromasia (indicating reticulocytosis). The plasma haptoglobin is depressed, and the bilirubin and LDH may be elevated. If the process is chronic, hemosiderinuria and consequent iron deficiency may occur, because the hemolysis is intravascular and iron is lost in the urine. Iron therapy is needed to counteract the urinary losses and to correct the anemia. A similar process may occur acutely during extracorporeal circulation as in cardiopulmonary bypass. Red cell fragmentation also occurs after severe burns covering large areas of body surface, or in heat exhaustion. Intravascular hemolysis, without fragmentation of red cells, develops occasionally after prolonged marching or marathon running (march hemoglobinuria).

Microangiopathic hemolytic anemias result when normal red cells are fragmented while traversing intravascular fibrin strands in microvessels partially occluded by thrombi. Acute causes of microangiopathic hemolytic anemia include disseminated intravascular coagulation (DIC), thrombotic thrombocytopenic purpura, hemolytic-uremic syndrome, malignant hypertension, rejection of renal grafts, and mitomycin C toxicity. Certain vascular malformations such as giant hemangiomas (Kasabach-Merritt syndrome), in which sluggish blood flow through abnormally formed vessels triggers localized DIC, produce microangiopathic hemolytic anemia. In each of these settings, localized shearing of red cells within microthrombi results in intravascular hemolysis, usually accompanied by thrombocytopenia because of the concomitant intravascular clotting. In contrast, the schistocytic (fragmentation) hemolytic anemias related to large vessel pathology generally are not accompanied by thrombocytopenia.

Trousseau's syndrome represents chronic DIC in the setting of visceral cancer, with typical schistocytes and thrombocytopenia on the peripheral smear. Coagulation factor levels may be normal or decreased, depending upon the rates of consumption versus compensatory synthesis of clotting factors.

HEMOGLOBINOPATHIES

Hemoglobin, the major protein in the red cell, binds oxygen reversibly and is responsible for the capacity of red cells to transport oxygen to the tissues. Hemoglobin is present as a 5 mM solution in red cells. Each hemoglobin molecule consists of two identical alpha globin chains and two nonalpha chains, which in the adult comprise mainly beta globin, with a small amount of delta globin; in the fetus the main nonalpha polypeptide is gamma globin. Two genes on chromosome 16 code for the alpha chains, whereas the genes for the nonalpha globins are clustered on chromosome 11.

Each polypeptide subunit of hemoglobin holds a single heme group in a hydrophobic pocket. The iron of the heme is bound to the porphyrin ring and is also bound to a histidine residue on the globin chain; its hydrophobic environment protects the Fe^{2+} from being oxidized even in the presence of oxygen. Oxygen is bound to each heme group via the central iron atom. The structure of the tetrameric hemoglobin molecule changes with the binding of oxygen, so that the interactions of the globin chains alter the sequential release of oxygen from the four heme groups, thereby producing the sigmoidal shape of the oxygen dissociation curve. These interactions facilitate the uptake of oxygen in the lungs and its unloading at the tissues, with the steepest part of the curve lying within the ambient oxygen tensions of these two locations. Normal synthesis of alpha and beta chains is balanced, with little excess of either type produced within red cells. Excess globin chains are unstable and tend to precipitate at the red cell membrane (forming Heinz bodies), shortening red cell lifespan.

During transport of red cells from arterial oxygen tension (PO_2, 100 mm Hg) to tissue oxygen tension (PO_2, 40 mm Hg), the saturation of hemoglobin oxygen decreases from 100 to 75 per cent, although the capacity for oxygen delivery is much greater. Oxygen unloading is facilitated by the binding to hemoglobin of the molecule 2,3-diphosphoglyceric acid (2,3-DPG), an intermediate product of glycolysis; acidic pH and the binding of carbon dioxide also assist in the release of oxygen from hemoglobin, as do configurational changes in the hemoglobin molecule itself during oxygen release. Changes in the structure of the globin polypeptide chains, or in the heme itself, can affect the oxygen affinity of hemoglobin.

Mutations in the DNA sequences controlling globin synthesis either can produce structurally abnormal hemoglobins (hemoglobinopathies) or can decrease the rate of hemoglobin synthesis (thalassemias) (Table 47–9). The term *hemoglobinopathy* connotes structurally abnormal hemoglobins with altered function, whereas *thalassemia* refers to mutations resulting in decreased synthesis of one globin type. Because the alpha globin chain contains 141 amino acids and the beta chain 146, and single amino acid substitutions resulting from single mutations produce abnormally functioning molecules, a very large number of mutant forms are possible. Only mutations of certain types, however, lead to functional alterations in

TABLE 47–9. CLINICAL SYNDROMES RELATED TO ABNORMAL HEMOGLOBINS

TYPE OF DEFECT	CLINICAL FEATURES
A. Decreased hemoglobin solubility	
1. Crystalline hemoglobin Hb S, C, D, E	Hemolytic anemia with microvascular occlusion
2. Unstable hemoglobin	Hemolytic anemia
B. Abnormal O₂ transport	
1. Increased O₂ affinity	Polycythemia
2. Decreased O₂ affinity	Normochromic "anemia"
C. Heme oxidation (Hb M)	Cyanosis Methemoglobinemia

hemoglobin resulting in abnormal oxygen carriage or anemia. Examples of these functionally important mutations include surface substitutions that alter hemoglobin solubility (e.g., Hb S), substitutions in internal nonpolar residues resulting in hemoglobin instability (e.g., Hb Koln), substitution for the histidine that binds iron, permitting oxidation of heme iron (e.g., Hb M), or substitution at the alpha-beta contact points, which alters heme-heme interactions and changes oxygen affinity (Hb Kansas or Chesapeake). Mutations causing thalassemic syndromes include deletions, removal of stop codons, and frameshift mutations leading to nonsense sequences; these all tend to alter globin synthesis and to decrease the rate of normal globin production, a process that secondarily regulates heme synthesis and leads to hemolytic anemias. In addition, mutations affecting the normal sequence of expression of the beta cluster genes may result in hereditary persistence of Hb F synthesis after birth.

Anemias Resulting from Abnormalities in Hemoglobin Structure or Function (Fig. 47–6)

Sickle Cell Anemia. A major disease resulting from a mutation to an abnormally functioning hemoglobin is sickle cell disease, in which a single base change in the DNA results in a substitution of valine for glutamic acid at the sixth position in the beta globin chain. The ensuing insolubility of Hb S under deoxygenated conditions results in polymerization of Hb S molecules within the red cells, leading to distortion of shape, membrane changes, cellular dehydration, decreased deformability, and short survival in the circulation. Microvascular occlusion results from the altered behavior of sickled red cells and produces progressive microinfarction of vital organs, painful bony crises, splenic autoinfarction, and renal damage. Patients have a shortened lifespan. The Hb S gene is present in 10 per cent of American blacks and up to 25 per cent of the population in Western Africa. The sickle diseases include sickle cell anemia, sickle cell–beta thalassemia, sickle cell–

hemoglobin C disease, and other complex hemoglobinopathies. In the heterozygote (Hb S trait, Hb SA), protection against falciparum malaria is associated with the hemoglobinopathy. Red cells in the heterozygote state usually have 60 per cent Hb A and 40 per cent Hb S; both types of globins are present in the same cell, but not in the same molecule. Red cells in the homozygous state (Hb SS, sickle cell disease) have over 90 per cent Hb S, with small amounts of Hb F or Hb A₂. The concurrent presence of thalassemia trait or persistence of Hb F tends to ameliorate the clinical course of SS disease, in the first case by decreasing the rate of synthesis of the β^S chain in relation to other globins, and in the second case by introducing a nonaggregating hemoglobin that interferes with Hb S polymerization (Table 47–10).

Clinical manifestations of SS disease begin in infancy, when Hb F levels begin to fall. Major symptoms and signs include painful crises, swelling of the extremities and spleen (in infants and children), bony and pulmonary infarctions, and cerebrovascular accidents. Any organ may be affected. Intrahepatic sickling can produce marked hepatic swelling, dysfunction, and hyperbilirubinemia; intrarenal sickling can cause renal papillary necrosis and hematuria, with loss of renal concentrating ability (usually by age 5); intracutaneous sickling produces necrotic skin ulceration, usually of the ankles and feet; retinal sickling can produce neovascularization and retinal detachment; bony sickling can produce aseptic necrosis and predispose to osteomyelitis. Growth is disturbed, with typical elongated limbs and asthenic habitus. Chronic hemolysis results in a markedly increased incidence of cholelithiasis with multiple bilirubin stones and cholecystitis, a tendency to folic acid deficiency, impaired immunity partially due to loss of spleen tissue and partly related to poor IgM production, and an increased tendency to infections. Cardiomyopathy is common, as is delayed puberty.

Typical laboratory findings in sickle cell anemia include a hemoglobin level ranging from 6 to 8 gm/dl, hematocrit 18 to 24 per cent, and a normal MCV. White blood cells and platelets are normal to increased. The reticulocyte count is chronically elevated, often to more than 20 per cent, and nucleated red blood cells are frequently present. Sickle-shaped, holly-leaf–shaped, or otherwise distorted red cells appear in variable numbers on the peripheral smear and in large numbers in deoxygenated wet preparations (see Fig. 47–6). Hemoglobin electrophoresis shows 90 to 95 per cent Hb S. The serum bilirubin is elevated, with mainly direct-reacting bilirubin; the haptoglobin level is low; and the serum LDH level is elevated. Screening for Hb S is most simply performed with a "sickle cell prep" by mixing the patient's blood with sodium metabisulfite, which deoxygenates the red cells and induces sickling observable with a microscope; commercial tests that demonstrate the insolubility of Hb S (Sickledex) are easier to perform for mass screening, as they do not require a microscope. Screening tests utilizing monoclonal antibodies against the specific hemoglobins are now available for rapid evaluation of small samples of blood. Hemoglobin electrophoresis after positive screening tests is needed to delineate the specific hemoglobinopathy precisely (Table 47–10).

Other sickle cell syndromes representing concomitant SS-thalassemia trait or a mixed hemoglobinopathy (SC, SD) usually have milder clinical courses than does sickle cell anemia (SS). They produce a less severe anemia and may present with splenomegaly rather than an absent spleen. Patients with Hb SC disease, however, can have severe morbidity in pregnancy and a higher rate of ocular complications than patients with SS disease; Hb C, also a β^6 substitution ($\beta^{6glu \rightarrow lys}$), also results in intracellular hemoglobin polymerization, but anemia and vaso-occlusive manifestations are milder in homozygous Hb C disease than in SS disease. In sickle–beta thalassemia trait, the red cells show microcytosis and hypochromia, the percentage of Hb S is less than 80 per cent, with increased Hb F in a heterogeneous distribution, and some Hb A may be present. If hereditary persistence of Hb F is present, the Hb F distribution among the red cells is homogeneous rather than variable, as it is in beta thalassemia trait.

Management of sickle cell anemia is largely symptomatic and supportive. The hemolytic anemia requires folate supplementation. Increased infections reflect the absence of splenic function, deficiency in IgM immunoglobulin response, and abnormalities in lymphocyte function as well as tissue infarction. Aggressive and rapid intervention can be life-saving. Cardiomegaly and cardiomyopathy—especially in older patients—may require careful fluid balance during intravenous therapy. Painful crises are treated with intravenous and oral fluids, correction of acidosis, analgesics, oxygen administration and attention to precipitating causes such as dehydration, fever, and infection. Sickle cell crisis itself does not cause fever, but infection or tissue infarction does. Because of the increased risk of infection and the common development of hyposplenism because of splenic infarction, pneumococcal vaccine should be administered to all sickle cell patients. Transfusion is not useful in treatment of acute sickle cell crises, but chronic transfusion programs (exchange transfusions are preferred to avoid iron overload) have been tried in patients at high risk of recurrent cerebral infarction. Exchange transfusion prior to surgery appears to help prevent initiation of intraoperative and postoperative crises and perhaps to improve healing. Special attention to good oxygenation during surgery and avoidance of hypothermia are imperative to avoid intraoperative sickling and tissue infarction. Transfusions may also be given during the later stages of pregnancy in women with SS disease to counteract placental dysfunction and placental infarction caused by sickling, but this is not a routine practice.

Recently, therapies designed to enhance production of Hb F in patients with SS disease have entered clinical trial; these include administration of

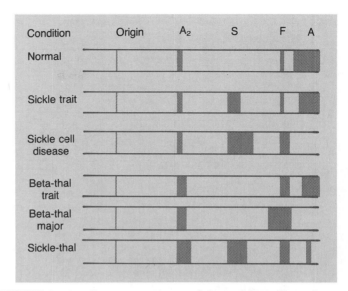

FIGURE 47–6. Common patterns of hemoglobin electrophoresis. Note that in sickle cell anemia, 95 per cent of Hb is S; in sickle trait, 40 per cent is S and 60 per cent is A, but in sickle-thal, 60 to 70 per cent of Hb is A. In beta-thal trait, either Hb A_2 or F (or both) is elevated, whereas in beta-thal major, Hb A is absent and Hb F makes up most of the hemoglobin.

TABLE 47–10. COMPARISON OF SICKLE CELL SYNDROMES

GENOTYPE	CLINICAL CONDITION	Hb A	Hb S	Hb A_2	Hb F	Hb C	OTHER FINDINGS
SA	Sickle cell trait	55–60	40–45	2–3	—	—	Asymptomatic
SS	Sickle cell anemia	0	85–95	2–3	5–15	—	Clinically severe anemia; Hb F is heterogeneous in distribution
S-β^0thal	Sickle cell–beta thalassemia	0	70–80	3–5	10–20	—	Moderately severe anemia Splenomegaly in 50% Smear: hypochromic, microcytic
S-β^+thal	Sickle cell–beta thalassemia	10–20	60–75	3–5	10–20		Hb F distributed heterogeneously
SC	Hb SC disease	0	45–50	—	—	45–50	Moderately severe anemia Splenomegaly; target cells
S-HPFH	Sickle—hereditary persistence of Hb F	0	70–80	1–2	20–30	—	Asymptomatic; Hb F is uniformly distributed

the drugs 5-azacytidine and hydroxyurea, which may derepress the gene for Hb F or initiate differentiation of more primitive stem cells in which this gene is active. Because the presence of Hb F in SS red cells tends to decrease the intracellular polymerization and precipitation of Hb S, leading to less sickling and improved red cell survival, induction of Hb F production is highly desirable. However, because these drugs are cytotoxic (and 5-azacytidine is potentially carcinogenic), such therapy may depress bone marrow function. Adverse long-term effects have not been evaluated. The use of these drugs is considered experimental at present, but hydroxyurea is undergoing multicenter trials. Bone marrow transplantation has been tried abroad in a small number of patients with some success and is now in the early stages of clinical trial in the United States in selected cases of children with severe vasculopathy.

Genetic counseling of heterozygotes for Hb S has not been very successful in decreasing reproductive activity of persons at risk of having children with SS disease. Prenatal diagnosis is now possible using restriction enzyme techniques applied to amniocentesis or chorionic villus samples, taking advantage of several common restriction fragment polymorphisms.

Unstable Hemoglobins. Unstable hemoglobins represent a varied group of disorders, usually autosomal dominant mutants, in which either heme association with globin is defective or the forces holding the globin tetramer together are altered. The result is intracellular precipitation of the denatured hemoglobin as Heinz bodies that bind to the red cell membrane. Such cells are either "pitted" of these inclusions by splenic or hepatic macrophages, resulting in shortened red cell lifespan, or are totally removed in the reticuloendothelial system. Exposure of red cells containing unstable hemoglobin to oxidant stress exacerbates the hemolysis and may cause acute jaundice.

Hemoglobins of Altered Oxygen Affinity. The partial pressure of oxygen at which hemoglobin is half-saturated with oxygen (P_{50}) provides a useful guide to measurement of functional oxygen affinity. The normal P_{50} is about 25 mm Hg. Although more than 80 mutations producing altered oxygen affinity have been found, only a few are of clinical consequence. When hemoglobin is fully oxygenated, it normally assumes the R, or relaxed, state, which manifests a high affinity for oxygen; when it is deoxygenated, it is in the T, or tense, state, having a low oxygen affinity. Mutations that affect hydrogen bonding or hydrophobic interactions at the $\alpha_1\beta_2$ interface of the hemoglobin tetramer change the R-T balance and alter oxygen affinity. Hemoglobins of high oxygen affinity are clinically associated with erythrocytosis, sometimes with thrombotic tendencies; hemoglobins of low oxygen affinity are associated with apparent anemias (actually, low hematocrit values), which actually represent a functional marrow response to the increased tissue oxygen delivery. The latter may be accompanied by an asymptomatic cyanosis.

Methemoglobinemia. Methemoglobinemia represents the oxidation of heme iron, which prevents its capacity to transport oxygen, and may result from enzyme deficiency (e.g., nicotinamide-adenine dinucleotide [NADH]–methemoglobin reductase), abnormal hemoglobins with substitutions in the heme pocket (M hemoglobinopathies), or exposure to oxidant drugs. The clinical manifestation is cyanosis without hypoxemia. The blood is brownish and does not turn red upon shaking with air. The reducing agents methylene blue and ascorbic acid can improve the cyanosis in patients with methemoglobinemia due to enzyme deficiency or oxidant drug exposure, but not in patients with M hemoglobinopathies. The drugs that induce methemoglobinemia in normal individuals include nitrites (especially toxic to infants), primaquine, dapsone, aniline dyes, and sulfanilamide.

Thalassemias

As mentioned above, hemolytic anemia in the thalassemias results from mutations that affect globin synthesis (Table 47–11). The hemoglobin that is produced is less than normal in amount but is structurally normal. A decreased synthetic rate of one type of globin chain results in ineffective erythropoiesis, with markedly enhanced intramedullary loss of developing red cells. Several mechanisms are involved: a primary decrease in synthesis of the involved globin chain; the accumulation and precipitation of the other type of globin chain, which is produced in relative excess; and secondarily depressed heme synthesis. The red cells are hypochromic and markedly microcytic and have a shortened circulating lifespan. Because of the complexity of abnormalities in hemoglobin synthesis, thalassemic states can vary clinically from "silent" carrier (e.g., heterozygotes for alpha thalassemia) to severely anemic thalassemia major (homozygotes for beta thalassemia) to death in utero from hydrops fetalis (homozygotes for alpha thalassemia). The incidence of beta thalassemia is greatest in persons of Mediterranean and African origin and that of alpha thalassemia in persons of Far Eastern origin; the trait is present in 3 to 5 per cent of such populations. In the United States as many as 20 per cent of blacks and persons of Mediterranean origin carry thalassemia trait.

Beta thalassemia syndromes include thalassemia trait (heterozygous beta thalassemia), thalassemia intermedia, and thalassemia major (Cooley's anemia). The genetic alterations that produce these syndromes are many. Mutations of the beta globin gene that depress synthesis of beta globin include the following: deletions, nonsense mutation, or frame shifts that prevent any messenger RNA (mRNA) production (β^0), and mutations affecting promoter or splice sites, which permit reduced levels of mRNA and hence some hemoglobin synthesis (β^+). The clinical features of thalassemia trait are a mild anemia that is markedly microcytic in relation to the hemoglobin level and is

TABLE 47–11. COMPARISON OF THE THALASSEMIA SYNDROMES

GENETIC ABNORMALITY	PER CENT Hb A	PER CENT Hb A$_2$	PER CENT Hb F	OTHER	CLINICAL SYNDROME
Normal ($\alpha_2 \beta_2$)	90–98	2–3	2–3		None
Beta Thalassemias					
Thalassemia major					
β thal^0 β thal^0	0	2–5	95	—	Severe anemia, abnormal growth, iron overload, needs transfusion
β thal$^+$ β thal$^+$	Very low	2–5	20–80	—	
Thalassemia intermedia (varied genetic globin abnormalities)	Overlaps with thalassemia major				Severe hypo/micro anemia with Hb 7–9 gm/dl, hepatosplenomegaly, bone changes, iron overload, less need for transfusion
Thalassemia minor					
β β thal^0 or β β thal$^+$	90–95	5–7	2–10		Hypo/micro blood smear, mild to no anemia
Alpha Thalassemias					
Homozygous alpha thalassemia $- - / - -$	—	—	—	Hb H (β_4) Hb Barts (γ_4)	Hydrops fetalis, stillborn
Hemoglobin H disease $- - / - \alpha$	60–70	2–5	2–5	Hb H 30–40	Hypo/micro anemia, Hb 7–10 gm/dl, Heinz bodies
Alpha thalassemia trait $- \alpha / - \alpha$ $\alpha \alpha / - -$	90–98	2–3	2–3		Hypo/micro smear, no anemia
Silent carrier $- \alpha / \alpha \alpha$	90–98	2–3	2–3		Normal

sometimes accompanied by splenomegaly. The MCV is frequently in the 60s, with a hemoglobin level of 10 to 12 gm/dl and marked anisocytosis on the peripheral smear. Serum iron and transferrin levels are normal. Hemoglobin electrophoresis (see Fig. 47–5) reveals elevation of Hb A$_2$ to 3 to 5 per cent, and Hb F to 2 to 3 per cent. Morbidity is not associated with thalassemia trait, and iron therapy should not be given.

In contrast to this asymptomatic picture, the homozygous *thalassemia major* is a lethal, severe hemolytic anemia characterized by growth abnormalities, dysfunction of almost all organ systems, and iron overload. Because both beta genes are abnormal, very little to no beta chain synthesis occurs, and the excess of insoluble alpha globin chains in the red cells leads to intracellular precipitation that affects both erythropoiesis and red cell lifespan. The resulting ineffective erythropoiesis causes extreme expansion of marrow space into long bones, skull, and facial bones, as well as the development of extramedullary hematopoiesis in liver, spleen, and around the spinal vertebrae. Growth abnormalities and cortical bone fragility ensue, with an increased rate of fractures. Growth retardation and delay of puberty are universal. The peripheral smear shows severe microcytosis and anisocytosis, many nucleated red blood cells, and hypochromia. The hemoglobin level in the untransfused patient is 3 to 6 gm/dl. Hb A is very low to absent, and the major hemoglobin is Hb F, with a variably increased amount of Hb A$_2$. Early death by age 2 to 3 years was common before transfusion therapy was instituted. With regular

transfusion, the hemoglobin level can be maintained at 8 to 10 gm/dl and many of the growth and bony abnormalities decreased.

An absolute increase in iron absorption as a physiologic response to the anemia, plus severe iron overload from transfusion therapy, has led to a different set of complications, that of tissue fibrosis from iron deposition. This abnormality results in cardiomyopathy, diabetes mellitus, and adrenal, parathyroid, and thyroid hypofunction. Affected children also show increased susceptibility to infection and functional hyposplenism; splenectomy is usually performed in late childhood to lessen the transfusion requirements and adds to the risk of sepsis. Iron chelation therapy with subcutaneous desferrioxamine, now begun in early childhood, appears to decrease the devastating consequences of iron overload if chronically maintained; use of carefully phenotyped frozen blood can decrease alloimmunization and prevent transfusion refractoriness. With the most modern of these supportive therapies, the lifespan of patients with thalassemia major has been extended from early childhood to the 20s. Newer approaches, still highly experimental, include bone marrow transfusion and agents that increase Hb F production, such as 5-azacytidine and hydroxyurea (see above). Prenatal diagnosis by restriction enzyme polymorphism techniques is currently more useful in alpha than in beta thalassemia, but direct measurement in fetal blood of depressed beta globin synthesis can be made.

Thalassemia intermedia is genetically variable and frequently appears to represent double heterozygosity for two different thalassemic mutations. Affected persons can maintain an untransfused hemoglobin level of 8 to 10 gm/dl. They have more normal growth and sexual maturation, suffer fewer clinical complications than patients with thalassemia major, and frequently live into mid-adulthood. Iron overload, however, may occur, as can the tendency to infections, bony fragility, and organ dysfunction, but with a slower time course.

Alpha thalassemia syndromes depend upon the combination of mutations in the four alpha gene loci. In order of increasing severity they are alpha-thal$_2$ trait, alpha-thal$_1$ trait, Hb H disease, and hydrops fetalis. The first condition is asymptomatic without anemia, except that the MCV and MCH are decreased, whereas the second condition results in a mild microcytic anemia. Hb H disease presents a mild, variable degree of hemolytic anemia characterized by red cell inclusions, which result from precipitation of the unstable β_4 hemoglobin. Hydrops fetalis, the absence of all alpha globin production, consistently leads to death in

utero or to stillbirth. The amount of Hb Bart's (γ_4) present in the blood of an infant with alpha thalassemia corresponds directly to the number of thalassemic alpha gene loci. The occurrence of alpha thalassemia trait together with another hemoglobinopathy such as Hb SS tends to ameliorate the latter disease, probably by decreasing the intracellular concentration of the abnormal hemoglobin. There is a high incidence of alpha thalassemia trait in American blacks, and this factor ameliorates the clinical severity of sickle cell disease in this population. Silent carrier states for both alpha and beta thalassemia genes are common and can be detected only by family studies.

REFERENCES

Bunn HF, Forget BG: Hemoglobin: Molecular, Genetic and Clinical Aspects. Philadelphia, WB Saunders Co, 1986.

Hoffman R, Benz EJ Jr, Shattil SJ, Furie B, Cohen HJ (eds): Hematology: Basic Principles and Practice. New York, Churchill Livingstone, 1991.

Rosse WF: Clinical Immunohematology: Basic Concepts and Clinical Applications. Boston, Blackwell Scientific Publications, 1990.

48 THERAPY WITH BLOOD PRODUCTS

Human blood is an invaluable resource in the supportive therapy of patients with hemorrhage, severe anemias, and coagulation deficits and those undergoing surgery, yet blood can be dangerous if improperly used. Modern blood banking has been made possible by the science of immunohematology and by the development of special methods for the maintenance and preservation of blood ex vivo. Each unit of 450 ml of blood is mixed with 63 ml of an anticoagulant solution containing citrate to prevent clotting, as well as dextrose, phosphate, and adenine to prolong red cell viability. The shelf life is usually 35 days, but addition of nutrient solutions can extend storage time to 42 days. Transfusion of whole blood is rarely necessary and currently constitutes approximately 5 per cent of all red cell transfusions. It is physiologically and economically more reasonable to separate each unit of fresh blood into components that can be used to treat several different recipients (Table 48–1). These components include red blood cells, platelets, and granulocytes, and plasma and its protein constituents, including albumin, Factor

VIII:antihemophilic factor (AHF), other coagulation factors, protein C, antithrombin III, and gamma globulin.

Red blood cells can be transfused as packed red cells (most of plasma removed); leukocyte-poor (buffy coat–poor) red cells, from which about 80 per cent of the leukocytes have been removed; or frozen-thawed red cells (from which about 90 per cent of leukocytes have been removed). Each unit of red cells transfused should raise the hematocrit by 3 to 4 per cent or the hemoglobin concentration by 1 gm/dl if there is no red cell destruction or sequestration. Platelets are separated from red cells by differential centrifugation and are administered as concentrates of 4 to 10 units suspended in a small volume of plasma. *Platelet transfusion* is indicated as therapy for severely thrombocytopenic patients who are bleeding or as prophylaxis for patients with aplastic anemia or with leukemia during myelosuppressive chemotherapy. A rise in platelet count can be expected for 1 to 3 days following transfusion, unless the patient has fever, which shortens the survival of transfused platelets, or immune thrombocytopenia, which destroys transfused platelets as fast as autologous ones. Patients who require repeated platelet transfusion may become allosensitized and refractory to random donor platelets and require human leukocyte antigen (HLA)–matched platelets. *Granulocytes* can be separated from whole blood by leukapheresis and administered to neutropenic patients or given as buffy coat preparations; both preparations contain considerable lymphocyte and platelet admixture. Because the effect of granulocyte transfusions is transitory (the half-life is about 6 hours), such therapy is usually reserved for treating life-threatening neutropenia. Moreover, bone marrow stimulatory growth factors such as G-CSF or GM-CSF (see below) can now be used to stimulate leukocyte production and to enhance function, further limiting usefulness of granulocyte transfusion. Fresh frozen plasma supplies several of the labile coagulation factors. Fibrinogen, fibronectin, von Willebrand factor, and Factor VIII:AHF can be concentrated in cryoprecipitate prepared from individual units of plasma. At the present time the only approved form of fibrinogen for replacement therapy is cryoprecipitate. Other plasma protein components, such as albumin, gamma globulins, antithrombin III, and protein C as well as Factor IX, prepared from pooled plasma, can also be administered for specific indications. Heat-treated preparations of Factor VIII:AHF and Factor IX complex that are free of the danger of viral transmission are also available.

BLOOD COMPATIBILITY TESTING

More than 300 different antigenic determinants have been identified on human red blood cells, the most important being the ABO system (Table 48–2). Almost all human red cells belong to one of the four major blood groups—A, B, AB, or O. Subjects of one type, for example, A, who bear the A antigen on their red cells, carry in their plasma natural IgM antibodies to the B antigen. Plasma from type AB individuals contains no such natural antibodies, whereas serum from type O carries both anti-A and anti-B. These antibodies are easily demonstrable in saline solution. The ABO types are inherited as autosomal codominant traits. ABO compatibility is essential for blood transfusion. In contrast to the natural IgM antibodies, acquired

antibodies against ABO antigens, produced by alloimmunization following transfusion, pregnancy, or exposure to heterologous antigens, usually microbial, are IgG in type.

A second clinically important blood antigen group is Rh, which consists of at least three linked loci—Cc, D, and Ee. IgG antibodies can develop to the Rh antigens after sensitization by prior transfusion or pregnancy. These antibodies are more difficult to detect than the natural ABO isoagglutinins and usually require testing in the presence of protein-containing medium rather than saline. The most clinically important locus in the Rh system is D; the absence of D is called Rh negative. Transfusion of Rh+ (D+) blood to a sensitized Rh− person rarely provokes acute hemolysis. Occasionally, it can produce delayed intravascular hemolysis. Moreover, an Rh+ fetus carried by a sensitized

TABLE 48–1. BLOOD COMPONENT THERAPY

COMPONENT	INDICATION FOR USE
Whole blood	Massive hemorrhage, exchange transfusion
Packed red cells	Standard unit for transfusion
Leukocyte-poor or washed red cells	Reduce incidence of febrile and allergic reactions
Frozen red cells	Useful in multitransfused patient to decrease sensitization to HLA and leukocyte antigens
Fresh frozen plasma	Replaces coagulation factors
Plasma protein fraction	Plasma expansion (hepatitis-free)
Cryoprecipitate	Replaces Factor VIII and fibrinogen
Platelet concentrates	Raise platelet count in nonimmune thrombocytopenia
Granulocyte concentrates	May be of *transient* use in infected, granulocytopenic patient; rarely used
Lyophilized Factor VIII concentrate	Treatment of choice in hemophilia A
Lyophilized prothrombin complex concentrate	Treatment of choice in hemophilia B; emergency correction of oral anticoagulant effect
"FEIBA"	Bypasses acquired inhibitors to clotting factors
Protein C	Prevention of thrombosis in factor deficiency
Antithrombin III	Replacement in deficiency or following surgery

TABLE 48–2. ABO BLOOD GROUP SYSTEM

PHENOTYPE	GENOTYPES	RED BLOOD CELL ANTIGENS		NATURAL ANTIBODIES	FREQUENCY*
		A	B		
O (universal donor)	OO	−	−	Anti-A, anti-B	45%
A	AA or AO	+	−	Anti-B	40%
B	BB or BO	−	+	Anti-A	9%
AB (universal recipient)	AB	+	+	None	3%

*For Caucasian population.

Rh— mother can develop erythroblastosis fetalis. In the past, maternal sensitization in such cases occurred at the time of delivery of the first child. This problem has been prevented in about 80 per cent of potential cases by treating Rh— mothers immediately after delivery, amniocentesis, or abortion with Rh immune globulin (RhoGAM) to block Rh immunization of the mother. In Rh— mothers who incur transplacental antibodies during pregnancy (best documented by the Kleihauer-Betke test), Rh immune globulin should be administered if the patient is anti-D negative. Intrauterine transfusion of the fetus can also be carried out in those Rh— mothers who become sensitized.

Antibodies to Kell (K), Duffy (Fy), and Kidd (Jk) antigens occur after sensitization by allogeneic red cells and may cause hemolytic transfusion reactions. Overall, A, B, and D are the most immunogenic red cell antigens. Rh antibodies other than anti-D represent approximately 50 per cent and anti-K, anti-Fy^{a}r, and anti-Jk^a 45 per cent of alloantibodies detected by transfusion services. Antibodies to many other antigens, such as the MN system, Lewis, P, or Ii, occur commonly but generally are inactive at body temperature and do not usually cause clinical problems (Table 48–3).

Compatibility testing for red cell transfusion consists of several sequential steps. First, the potential recipient's own red cells are typed. Then an antibody screen is performed, that is, testing the potential recipient's serum against a panel of red cells selected to include the most frequent antigens that cause clinical reactions. Third, crossmatching is carried out, that is, testing the recipient's serum with samples of the red cells from units intended for transfusion. Under emergency circumstances, packed type O red cells can be given to a recipient of any ABO type. Rh+ cells can, in an emergency, be transfused to an Rh— recipient if the latter's serum contains no anti-D; the likelihood of sensitizing the recipient is 70 per cent. In the presence of sudden hemorrhage, plasma expanders such as albumin can be used until crossmatched blood becomes available.

TABLE 48–3. MAIN BLOOD GROUP SYSTEMS

NAME	FREQUENCY OF ANTIBODIES	CAUSE OF HEMOLYTIC REACTIONS
ABO	Very common	Yes
Rhesus	Common	Yes
Kell	Occasional	Yes
Duffy	Occasional	Yes
Kidd	Occasional	Yes
Lutheran	Rare	Yes
Lewis	Rare	No
P	Rare	Rare
MNS	Rare	No
Ii	Rare	Yes

HAZARDS OF BLOOD TRANSFUSION

The hazards of administering blood products include transfusion reactions, circulatory overload, transmission of disease, iron overload, coagulation disturbances, and graft-versus-host disease (Table 48–4).

Transfusion reactions include acute hemolytic reactions, anaphylaxis, and febrile reactions. Most commonly, acute hemolytic reactions result from mislabeling of blood samples intended for typing and crossmatching or from mistakenly administering to one patient a unit of blood intended for another. Most such errors are made on the hospital floor or clinic. Less commonly, transfusion reactions may result from errors made in the blood bank procedures. Hemolytic reactions may also occur when blood has been properly typed and crossmatched by standard techniques but unusual alloimmunization has escaped detection.

Because *acute hemolytic transfusion reactions* may lead to anaphylaxis and renal failure or death, rapid and orderly response to such catastrophes is essential. Acute hemolytic transfusion reactions usually present with the sudden onset of back pain, hypotension, sweating, fever, and chills. The blood transfusion must first be discontinued, a tube of blood drawn from the patient for inspection and for evaluation at the blood bank, and intravenous fluids immediately started. Urine output and vital signs must be monitored, and diuretics or mannitol administered in an effort to maintain a brisk urine flow. A hematocrit tube of freshly drawn blood from the patient should be immediately centrifuged and the plasma inspected for the presence of hemoglobin; pink plasma confirms an intravascular hemolytic transfusion reaction. Hemoglobinuria also should be sought but may be delayed in time of appearance. If oliguria or anuria occurs, dialysis is warranted. In all cases, fluid and electrolyte balance requires careful monitoring, especially to guard against hyperkalemia.

Hemolytic transfusion reactions may be not only immediate but also delayed in onset, whereas ABO incompatibility can activate the complement cascade and therefore produce acute reactions with intravascular hemolysis. Rh or Kell antibodies do not activate complement at a rapid rate and tend not to produce acute hemolysis. Instead, they cause a shortened red cell lifespan and produce extravascular hemolysis. Patients receiving incompatible blood while under anesthesia also may fail to exhibit such reactions, and postoperative oliguria, hemoglobinuria, or renal failure may be the first sign that a prior hemolytic transfusion reaction has occurred. Delayed hemolysis is common in the repeatedly transfused patient owing to anamnestic increases in initially undetectable antibody after prior sensitization, and takes place 5 to 10 days after the transfusion. Such delayed transfusion reactions produce a rapid fall in hematocrit accompanied by jaundice or a rise in bilirubin. A previously negative alloantibody screen often becomes positive at this time.

TABLE 48–4. EVALUATION OF TRANSFUSION REACTIONS

TYPE OF REACTION	CLINICAL SIGNS	MANAGEMENT OF PROBLEM
Major hemolytic acute (incompatibility)	Shock, back pain, flushing, fever, intravascular hemolysis	1. Stop transfusion. Return blood to blood bank with fresh sample of patient's blood. 2. Hydrate IV; support blood pressure, maintain high urine flow. 3. Check for hemoglobinemia and hemoglobinuria.
Febrile	Fever, urticaria (usually due to sensitization to WBC antibodies)	Pretreat with hydrocortisone, diphenhydramine hydrochloride (Benadryl), or both. Use buffy coat-poor RBC.
Allergic	Fever, urticaria, anaphylactoid reaction (often due to sensitivity to donor plasma proteins)	Use Benadryl, hydrocortisone. Use washed RBC or frozen RBC.
Delayed hemolytic	Anemia, jaundice 7–10 days after transfusion	Repeat type and crossmatch to identify anamnestic antibody production. Transfuse with appropriately matched RBC if needed.

IV = Intravenous; WBC = white blood cell; RBC = red blood cell.

Febrile reactions (0.5 per cent of all transfusions) or urticaria (1 to 3 per cent) are much more common than hemolytic transfusion reactions. They usually represent alloimmunization to leukocyte antigens, which may be acquired during pregnancy (20 per cent of women) or prior multiple transfusion (70 to 90 per cent of multitransfused recipients). They range in severity from simple fever, to urticaria plus fever and chills, to vomiting and hypotension. These symptoms can usually be prevented by administering leukocyte-poor blood or by pretreatment of the patient with chlorpheniramine and hydrocortisone. If these measures do not suffice, then frozen-thawed, washed red cells should be substituted. Anaphylactoid reactions (3 to 5 per cent of transfusion recipients develop urticaria) may also be caused by recipient antibody to IgA, especially in transfusion recipients who are IgA-deficient. IgA-deficient patients should receive washed red cells and should avoid plasma-containing preparations.

Circulatory overload, especially with whole blood transfusion, may occur in patients with cardiopulmonary dysfunction or congestive heart failure and can be avoided by using packed red cells or other concentrated components. In patients with congestive heart failure who need red cells, exchange transfusion consisting of removal of a unit of the patient's own blood before administering one to two units of packed red cells may avoid circulatory overload.

Disease Transmission Associated with Transfusion

Transmission of disease by transfused blood components rarely involves bacterial infection, because modern blood banking practices utilize closed blood collecting systems that guard effectively against bacterial contamination. Parasitic diseases such as malaria and babesiosis may be so transmitted.

Hepatitis transmission, however, remains a serious hazard of blood transfusion, despite the reduction in transmission of hepatitis B. Thanks to the development of sensitive methods of detecting hepatitis B antigen (HB Ag) positivity, hepatitis B now represents only 10 per cent of all posttransfusion hepatitis. Hepatitis C, formerly called non-A, non-B hepatitis, and delta agent account for the balance of cases. Up to 4 per cent of patients receiving blood products develop hepatitis, the highest risk being in recipients of non–heat-treated commercial coagulation factor concentrates. Patients receiving red cells, platelets, or plasma also incur considerable risk. Transfusion can also transmit cytomegalovirus infection, particularly to patients undergoing organ grafts who have activated lymphocytes in which this virus multiplies. Syphilis can also be transmitted by transfusion, but this is now rare.

Acquired immunodeficiency syndrome (AIDS) has developed in a small percentage of persons receiving transfusion of red cells, platelets, or commercial coagulation factor concentrates. By the end of 1991, about 4000 persons in the United States with no risk factors other than transfusion had developed AIDS out of some 180,000 total reported cases of AIDS. The risk of human immunodeficiency virus (HIV) infection by transfusion is low overall, calculated at 1 in 10^6 transfusions. Hemophiliacs who receive coagulation factor concentrates have been at highest risk among transfusion recipients because of exposures to pooled blood products prepared from thousands of donors. AIDS has also been reported in infants following neonatal exchange transfusion, although the majority of pediatric cases (approximately 3000 by the end of 1990) were associated with maternal transmission from HIV-positive mothers. Elimination of high-risk individuals from blood donor pools has reduced this risk further, as has more sensitive screening for anti–HTLV-III (human T cell lymphotropic virus III) antibodies in prospective blood donors. Screening for HTLV-I, a retrovirus that causes adult T cell leukemia/lymphoma, and for HIV-2, which causes AIDS, is also undertaken.

Graft-versus-host disease, representing engraftment of donor lymphocytes in the recipient, can be observed after transfusion of blood products to immunocompromised recipients, such as patients with congenital T cell defects or those being prepared for bone marrow transplantation. Irradiation of the blood products prior to transfusion prevents this complication.

Bone marrow transplantation is discussed in Chapter 50.

Problems Associated with Massive Transfusions

A bleeding tendency may occur in patients receiving multiple units of blood over a short time period. This is due in part to dilutional thrombocytopenia, because blood stored longer than 24 hours contains few viable platelets. Conditions requiring massive transfusion support are often accompanied by disseminated intravascular coagulation, adding the problems of consumption of platelets and coagulation factors. In such cases, it may be necessary to replace platelets, coagulation factors (using fresh frozen plasma), or fibrinogen (as cryoprecipitate) in addition to red cells. Furthermore, administration of large amounts of citrated blood may temporarily depress the serum calcium level and require calcium supplementation.

ALTERNATIVES TO HOMOLOGOUS BLOOD TRANSFUSION

Autologous Blood Donation

Autologous blood donation has become more common for transfusion support in elective surgery, especially for orthopedic and cardiac procedures. Donating blood for one's own use, of course, eliminates risks of alloimmunization and disease transmission. Combined with administration of iron, and perhaps of erythropoietin, to stimulate red cell production during the several weeks of donation prior to surgery, this practice can be applied to a large proportion of candidates for elective surgery. Similarly, directed donations of blood by rel-

atives and associates has also been encouraged in an attempt to improve safety of the blood supply, although the cost is high. Perioperative blood salvage with reinfusion of red cells is also utilized to reduce the need for homologous transfusion.

Use of Hematopoietic Growth Factors

Use of erythropoietin in renal dialysis patients to stimulate erythropoiesis and correct the anemia of renal failure has resulted in the well-being of patients and reduced transfusion requirements. Erythropoietin can also replace transfusion support by correcting anemia in some patients with other anemias of chronic disease, including rheumatoid arthritis and AIDS, and can be administered perioperatively to correct blood loss anemia more quickly.

More than 14 different growth factors that stimulate hematopoiesis have been identified. Granulocyte colony-stimulating factor (G-CSF) has been shown to stimulate blood granulocyte counts by shortening marrow maturation time and inducing earlier release of the marrow neutrophil reserve. Administration of G-CSF shortens the neutropenic period associated with cancer chemotherapy and bone marrow transplantation and may permit cancer patients to tolerate more intensive chemotherapy. Chronic neutropenias such as cyclic neutropenia or congenital neutropenia may also be effectively corrected long term. Granulocyte-monocyte colony-stimulating factor (GM-CSF) appears to recruit early marrow precursors into myeloid differentiation and to increase the metabolic activities of neutrophils and monocytes. Thus GM-CSF can be used to shorten leukopenia after chemotherapy or bone marrow transplantation. Because of its effects on monocytes, GM-CSF may exacerbate viremia in HIV-positive patients, so G-CSF is preferred in the latter group. Clinical application of interleukin-3 (IL3), which stimulates myeloid precursors in the bone marrow, together with GM-CSF or G-CSF is under study. In addition, the combination of IL3 and GM-CSF may stimulate megakaryocyte proliferation and is being investigated for use in thrombocytopenias.

REFERENCES

Menitove JE: The decreasing risk of transfusion-associated AIDS (editorial). N Engl J Med 321:966, 1989.

Mollison PL: Blood Transfusion in Clinical Medicine. 7th ed. New York, Blackwell Scientific Publications, 1987.

Petz LD, Swisher SN: Clinical Practice of Blood Transfusion. 2nd ed. New York, Churchill Livingstone, 1988.

Surgenor DM, Wallace EL, Hao SH, Chapman RH: Collection and transfusion of blood in the United States, 1982–1988. N Engl J Med 322:1646, 1990.

49 LEUKOCYTE DISORDERS

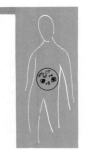

The main function of leukocytes is to maintain host defenses against disease, especially infection. Mononuclear phagocytes (monocytes and tissue macrophages) and granulocytes accomplish this by ingestion and killing of microorganisms, digestion of tissue debris, and release of inflammatory cytokines and mediators. Lymphocytes participate in the activation and effector functions of the immune system, and macrophage/monocytes play essential roles in the responses of lymphocytes.

NEUTROPHIL STRUCTURE AND FUNCTION

Polymorphonuclear leukocytes make up the largest percentage of circulating leukocytes (50 to 70 per cent). Originating in the bone marrow from pluripotential stem cells induced to differentiate by colony-stimulating factors (CSFs), they are nondividing, terminally differentiated cells that are motile, phagocytize a variety of microorganisms and inert particles, and release enzymes from cytoplasmic granules both into phagocytic vacuoles, and, under many circumstances, into the extracellular milieu. The three phases of microbial attack by neutrophils include chemotaxis, the directed movement along a concentration gradient of attractant substance toward a target organism; phagocytosis, the engulfment of the microbe in a membrane-lined phagocytic vacuole; and microbial killing, a chemical attack on the ingested microorganisms via the release of granule contents into the phagocytic vacuoles (bactericidal proteins, myeloperoxidase, cathepsins) plus the formation of oxygen free radicals such as superoxide and hydroxyl ion.

Chemotaxis involves the margination of circulating neutrophils along the endothelial lining of postcapillary venules, their penetration through the vascular wall via intercellular junctions, and their directed migration toward the extravascular source of the infection. The initial *adhesion* of neutrophils to the vascular endothelium is mediated by surface glycoproteins on the neutrophils (CD11/CD18 family), which bind to adhesion molecules expressed on activated endothelium (ICAM-1, ELAM-1). The migration of the neutrophils takes place along a chemical gradient of an attracting substance, which may be N-methylated bacterial peptides, complement fragments (C5a), or leukotriene B_4. Leukocyte proteases are responsible for the production of complement-derived che-

motaxins, whereas lipoxygenases mediate production of arachidonic acid-derived leukotrienes and hydroxyacids. These latter substances also have chemotactic and leukocyte-activating functions. Chemotactic substances binding to tissue sites may also serve to localize neutrophil accumulation.

Recognition of microorganisms or other particulate substances is required for subsequent ingestion by phagocytes. Opsonins, or proteins that coat microorganisms and promote their avid uptake by neutrophils, include the complement fragment C3b, the large plasma protein fibronectin, and immunoglobulins. These substances adhere to the surface of microorganisms and promote binding to C3b and Fc receptors on the neutrophil plasma membrane. *Phagocytosis*, the localized invagination of the leukocyte surface membrane to form a vacuole or vesicle, follows, with internalization and then fusion of the phagocytic vacuoles with intracellular enzyme-containing granules.

Microbicidal activity of neutrophils combines two interacting functions: degranulation and activation of the respiratory burst. Neutrophils possess a double set of cytoplasmic granules. The primary or azurophilic granules contain lysozyme, acid hydrolases, neutral proteases including cathepsin G and elastase, myeloperoxidase, and basic proteins. Specific granules contain lysozyme, transcobalamin III, apolactoferrin, collagenase, and the C5-cleaving protease. These enzymes aid in the digestion of the bacterial cell wall, dissolve connective tissue, degrade cellular debris, or bind specific substances useful to bacterial metabolism such as iron.

The same stimuli that activate phagocytosis and granule release also initiate the respiratory burst by activating a plasma membrane-bound oxidase that catalyzes one-electron reduction of oxygen to superoxide (O_2^-) in the presence of the electron acceptor nicotinamide-adenine dinucleotide phosphate (NADPH). Interaction of O_2^- with H_2O yields hydroxyl radical $OH \cdot$, which is directly bactericidal. In addition, H_2O_2 and Cl^- in the presence of myeloperoxidase form the microbicidal hypochlorite ion OCl^-. These reactions are essential for the killing of catalase-positive microorganisms.

Granulocytes have a short lifespan in the circulation (half-life about 6 hours) and undergo one-way traffic from the bone marrow through the blood into the tissues, where they may live for a few days. In the blood, about 50 per cent of granulocytes normally are marginated along vascular endothelium, remaining in dynamic equilibrium with the circulating neutrophil pool. Epinephrine, stress, or certain steroids shift more granulocytes to the circulating pool.

Neutrophil dysfunction includes congenital or acquired defects in adhesion, chemotaxis, or microbial killing capacity. An example of the latter is chronic granulomatous disease, a group of disorders in which superoxide is not properly synthesized. In adults, such defects are usually acquired either transiently, as after hemodialysis or cardiopulmonary bypass, owing to interactions of circulating neutrophils with foreign surfaces, or in association with disease. In myelodysplasias and leukemias, neutrophil function may be abnormal. Drugs like corticosteroids and alcohol can also depress normal neutrophil function.

MONOCYTE STRUCTURE AND FUNCTION

Monocytes represent a second type of circulating and fixed (tissue macrophage) phagocyte of even greater functional versatility than neutrophils. They constitute a much smaller fraction of the leukocytes, about 10 per cent, and are longer-lived. The circulating monocytes display slower chemotaxis than do neutrophils, appear later at sites of inflammation, and participate in the killing of intracellular microorganisms, both bacterial and parasitic. When monocytes are exposed to lipopolysaccharide or gamma-interferon, they become "activated" and display increased motility, metabolic activity, size, and microbicidal potency. Like neutrophils, monocytes express increased surface CD11/CD18 glycoproteins upon activation. The three basic functions of mononuclear phagocytes are secretion, ingestion, and interaction with lymphocytes. Monocytes synthesize more than 50 different protein mediators and enzymes, release interleukins that affect lymphocyte function and cause fever, present antigen to T cells for immune responses, and have very active arachidonic acid metabolism resulting in production of prostaglandins (PGE_2, which regulates bone marrow and immunologic cell proliferation), leukotrienes, and thromboxane. Activated monocytes, by producing tissue factor, also potentiate blood coagulation. In addition to complement and immunoglobulins, fibronectin also serves as an opsonin for mononuclear phagocytes. The process of pinocytosis permits macrophages to ingest and process large volumes of fluid, including plasma. Activated monocytes are also tumoricidal, producing both active oxygen and active nitrogen metabolites.

A series of reciprocal interactions between monocytes and lymphocytes is necessary for normal immune function. Monocytes and macrophages activate T cells by presenting antigen; special subpopulations of monocytes subserve this function, especially dendritic and Langerhans (skin) cells. Dendritic cells are a recently identified minor population of monocytic cells with long surface processes that appear to be the antigen-presenting cells of the blood, whereas Langerhans cells have a similar function in the skin. Lymphokines secreted by activated T cells cause accumulation and activation of monocytes. One such lymphokine, interleukin-2, is the T cell growth factor that permits expansion of T cell populations in immune responses. In addition, macrophages stimulate proliferation and differentiation of B lymphocytes via secretion of interleukin-1. PGE_2 secreted by monocytes and macrophages, in contrast, downregulates lymphocytic responses.

NEUTROPENIA

The normal white blood cell count varies between 5,000 and 10,000/μl, with 50 to 70 per cent neutrophils. The normal lower limit for neutrophil concentration is approximately 2000/μl for Caucasians and 1500/μl for blacks, the difference resulting from different sizes of marginated pools. Normal bone marrow contains a postmitotic compartment of mature neutrophils sufficient for 7 to 10 days, although under stress, neutrophil transit time in the marrow from early differentiation to the appearance of mature forms in the blood can be as short as 5 days (Fig. 49–1).

Neutropenia can result from depressed production of leukocytes, increased peripheral destruction, increased pooling in the spleen, or an increased rate of loss into tissues (Tables 49–1 and 49–2). The most common cause of neutropenia is marrow depression caused by drugs or radiation. Idiosyncratic drug reactions may result in sudden marrow suppression (e.g., chlorpromazine) or neutrophil destruction (e.g., amidopyrine); removal of the drug usually results in recovery. The latter situation often involves an antineutrophil antibody or an innocent bystander mechanism, in which drug-antibody complexes attach to the neutrophil surface (e.g., cephalosporins).

In *agranulocytosis*, the bone marrow appears normal except for the absence of granulocyte precursors; profound neutropenia is observed in the blood smear, and sore throat and fever are common symptoms. Drugs causing this syndrome include antithyroid drugs, phenylbutazone, chlorpromazine, and sulfonamides.

Neutropenia also is frequent in collagen vascular diseases such as systemic lupus erythematosus, and accompanies hypersplenism, as in Felty's syndrome. It is also seen in vitamin B_{12} or folic acid deficiency, acute leukemia, and viral infections including human immunodeficiency virus (HIV) infection, infectious mononucleosis, and viral hepatitis and in alcoholism. Many types of congenital neutropenias and benign familial neutropenias have been described. A rare form is *cyclic neutropenia*, which is familial or sporadic and is characterized by periodic falls in the neutrophil count to

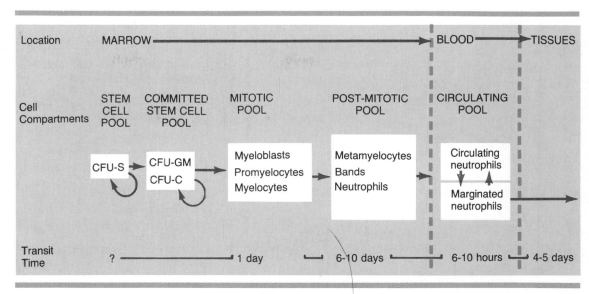

FIGURE 49–1. Neutrophil granulocyte maturation and kinetics.

near zero; granulocyte precursors are absent from the marrow at such times. Marrow production spontaneously resumes to restore granulocyte counts to normal levels; then the entire cycle repeats. A defective stem cell is postulated and other blood cells may also cycle, but less dramatically. Fever and sepsis may occur during the granulocyte nadirs. A temporary neutropenia or "pseudoneutropenia" can be found early in hemodialysis, when complement activation on the dialyzer membrane induces neutrophil aggregation and temporary sequestration in the lungs.

Evaluation of neutropenia involves a search for underlying disease, examination of the bone marrow, testing for antibodies directed against leukocytes, and elimination of drugs. An absolute neutrophil count of less than 1000/μl is considered life-threatening. Meticulous oral and anal hygiene, stool softener therapy, and immediate evaluation of fever or any sign of infection are required throughout the duration of neutropenia. Rapid initiation of broad-spectrum antibiotics for fever or infection is needed, with attention to the danger of superinfection. Transfusion of neutrophil concentrates has not proved to be of benefit in recent controlled trials, probably because of a combination of dysfunction of neutrophils that occurs during preparation of the cells for transfusion and the brief half-life of neutrophils in the circulation (approximately 6 hours) following their infusion. Instead, current therapy favors administration of G-CSF or GM-CSF (see Chapter 48) to stimulate endogenous production of neutrophils in the bone marrow. Such treatment can shorten periods of neutropenia and enhance granulocyte function in many clinical settings ranging from cyclic neutropenia to chemotherapy-induced neutropenia.

TABLE 49–1. ACQUIRED ABNORMALITIES OF NEUTROPHIL FUNCTION

1. Adhesiveness
   Increased: Bacteremia, hemodialysis (early)
   Decreased: Corticosteroids, epinephrine (demargination), aspirin, alcohol
2. Phagocytosis
   Decreased: Diabetes mellitus, acute infections
   Myeloproliferative syndromes
   Leukemia
3. Chemotaxis
   Increased: Bacterial infection
   Decreased: Diabetes mellitus, uremia, cirrhosis
   Severe burns
   Hodgkin's disease, leprosy, sarcoid
   Neonates
   Myeloproliferative syndromes

TABLE 49–2. CAUSES OF NEUTROPENIA

Benign familial
Drug-induced
   Anti-inflammatory drugs
   Antibacterial drugs (chloramphenicol, cotrimoxazole)
   Anticonvulsants
   Antithyroid drugs
   Phenothiazines
Cyclic
Disease-related
   Viral infection
   Bacterial sepsis
   Anaphylaxis
   Autoimmune
   Felty's syndrome
   Systemic lupus erythematosus
   Bone marrow failure
   Hypersplenism
   Vitamin B_{12} and folic acid deficiency
   Leukemia

TABLE 49–3. CAUSES OF NEUTROPHIL LEUKOCYTOSIS

Bacterial infections (pyogenic)
Inflammation; tissue necrosis
Acute hemolysis or hemorrhage
Corticosteroid therapy
Lithium therapy
Myeloproliferative disease
Metastatic cancer
Familial

TABLE 49–4. DISEASES ASSOCIATED WITH EOSINOPHILIA

Helminth infections
Allergic syndromes
Hypersensitivity drug reactions
Myeloproliferative diseases
Pulmonary fungal infections
Connective tissue disorders
Graft-versus-host disease
Inflammatory bowel disease
Loeffler's syndrome
Tryptophan ingestion

NEUTROPHIL LEUKOCYTOSIS

Neutrophil leukocytosis, or a persistent increase in circulating neutrophil levels above 7500/μl, is frequently observed in bacterial infection, inflammatory diseases, and hemorrhage and in association with malignancy or myeloproliferative disease (Table 49–3). There are also familial leukocytoses, which are benign. Transient leukocytosis can be induced by stress or severe exercise. A leukemoid reaction can usually be distinguished from the high white cell count of myeloproliferative disease or leukemia by the maturity of the leukocytes, an orderly "left shift" or appearance of band forms and a few metamyelocytes, and an elevated leukocyte alkaline phosphatase.

EOSINOPHILIA

An increased eosinophil count in the peripheral blood usually reflects parasitic infection (especially with helminths), allergic reactions, or other underlying disorders such as collagen vascular disease. Tissue eosinophilia may exist without high blood eosinophil counts. Eosinophils participate in many immune processes by secreting lipid mediators, eliciting release of mediators from mast cells, and interacting with lymphocytes. (Table 49–4).

REFERENCES

Antman KS, Griffin JD, Elias A, Socinski MA, Ryan L, Cannistra SA, Oette D, Whitley M, Frei E 3d, Schnipper LE: Effect of recombinant human granulocyte-macrophage colony stimulating factor on chemotherapy-induced myelosuppression. N Engl J Med 319:593, 1988.

Metcalf D: The molecular control of cell division, differentiation, committment and maturation in hematopoietic cells. Nature 339:27, 1989.

50 HEMATOLOGIC MALIGNANCIES

The hematologic malignancies include diseases that arise in bone marrow and lymph nodes. The primary bone marrow disorders are the *leukemias*, the *"immunoproliferative diseases"* such as multiple myeloma, and the *myeloproliferative syndromes* such as polycythemia vera and myelofibrosis with myeloid metaplasia. Evidence suggests that all of these diseases arise from single cell mutations that develop into malignant clones having a growth advantage over normal cells in the marrow. The evidence has arisen from different avenues. In B cell lymphoproliferative disorders, the malignant lymphocyte expresses a clonal rearrangement of an immunoglobulin gene. In chronic lymphocytic leukemia, the malignant lymphocytes all express an identical surface immunoglobulin of a single light chain type, and in multiple myeloma the malignant plasma cells express the identical cytoplasmic and secreted immunoglobulin. In chronic myelogenous leukemia, all the cells of the myeloid series as well as the erythroid precursors, the megakaryocytes, and the B lymphocytes bear the same marker chromosome, the Philadelphia (Ph[1]) chromosome. Further evidence for the clonal nature of the hematologic malignancies has come from the study of females

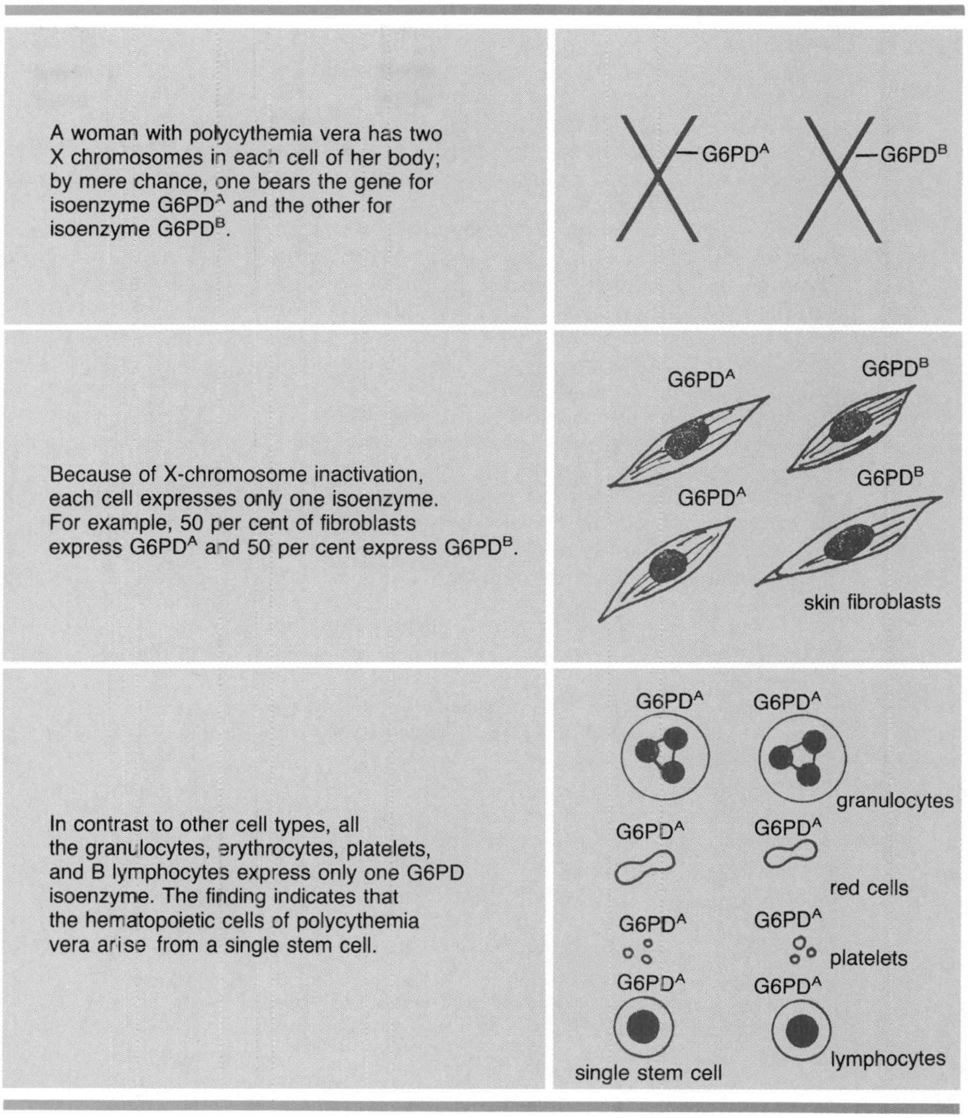

FIGURE 50-1. Polycythemia vera represents a clonal expansion of an abnormal pluripotent stem cell: Analysis using G6PD expression as a marker of clonality.

Panel text within figure:

A woman with polycythemia vera has two X chromosomes in each cell of her body; by mere chance, one bears the gene for isoenzyme G6PD^A and the other for isoenzyme G6PD^B.

Because of X-chromosome inactivation, each cell expresses only one isoenzyme. For example, 50 per cent of fibroblasts express G6PD^A and 50 per cent express G6PD^B.

In contrast to other cell types, all the granulocytes, erythrocytes, platelets, and B lymphocytes express only one G6PD isoenzyme. The finding indicates that the hematopoietic cells of polycythemia vera arise from a single stem cell.

who are heterozygous for the X-linked enzyme, glucose-6-phosphate dehydrogenase (G6PD). Because only one X chromosome is active in any single cell (inactivation of a maternal or paternal X chromosome occurring at random), half of all the somatic cells of a female heterozygote carry the gene for one G6PD type (e.g., G6PD^A) and the other half carry the gene for the other type (e.g., G6PD^B). Figure 50-1 demonstrates a study of G6PD expression in the cells of such a woman who developed polycythemia vera. Whereas the skin fibroblasts express either one or the other G6PD isoenzyme, the malignant cells express only one isoenzyme. This finding indicates that the malignant cells arise from a single cell that has expanded into a malignant clone.

THE MYELOPROLIFERATIVE DISORDERS

Four diseases are commonly grouped together as the myeloproliferative disorders: polycythemia vera, myelofibrosis with myeloid metaplasia, essential thrombocythemia, and chronic myelogenous leukemia. All represent clinical conditions that result from uncontrolled expansion of all bone marrow elements. The increased production of erythroid, myeloid, and megakaryocytic lines results from a malignant transformation of a pluripotent stem cell. The malignant cell may be a primitive stem cell capable of pluripotential differentiation or a more committed precursor cell that generates a single lineage, be it myeloid or erythroid. The increased marrow fibrosis often present in these diseases represents a reaction of normal fibroblasts to growth stimuli provided by the neoplastic cells. Present evidence suggests that the fibroblast growth factor is produced by the bone marrow megakaryocytes that are increased in the myeloproliferative disorders. Chronic myelogenous leukemia is discussed separately.

The myeloproliferative disorder *polycythemia vera* is a neoplastic disease of a bone marrow stem cell which affects primarily the erythroid line. Hyperplasia of all bone marrow elements is characteristic, but the increase in erythroid precursors with an elevated red cell mass is the most prominent feature. The increased red blood cell production is autonomous; that is, there is no secondary stimulus such as hypoxia or elevated erythropoietin levels driving red cell production. The typical clinical presentation is that of a patient with an elevated hematocrit. The physician must approach all patients with elevated hematocrits in a systematic way (Table 50–1) to decide first whether the high hematocrit actually represents an increased red cell mass and, if so, whether the increased red cell mass is secondary to a stimulus external to the bone marrow or represents true polycythemia, polycythemia vera.

A hematocrit above 54 per cent for men or 50 per cent for women should lead the physician to question whether the patient has polycythemia. The hematocrit or per cent packed red cell volume reflects the ratio of red cells to plasma. Thus, the hematocrit may be elevated either if there is truly an excess of red cells or if there is decreased plasma volume, as in dehydration. The best available direct measurement of red cell mass is the ^{51}Cr-labeled red cell mass. This test distinguishes between absolute polycythemia, in which the red cell mass is truly expanded, and "relative" polycythemia, in which the red cell mass is normal but the plasma volume is contracted.

Relative polycythemia (also called spurious, stress, or Gaisbock's polycythemia) is a chronic condition that typically affects obese, hypertensive, tense men who present with hematocrit values between 55 and 60 per cent. The red cell mass is normal; the plasma volume is contracted for unknown reasons. The pathophysiology of relative polycythemia is not well understood. Because the red cell mass is normal, aggressive phlebotomy is not indicated.

As noted, an elevated red cell mass (men > 36 ml/kg; women > 32 ml/kg) defines *absolute polycythemia*. Absolute polycythemia may be primary, as in the autonomous increase in red cell production that occurs in polycythemia vera, or it may be secondary to a physiologic mechanism driving red cell production to a higher than normal level. The most common cause for secondary polycythemia is decreased tissue oxygen delivery, usually due to decreased arterial oxygen saturation, as, for example, in chronic obstructive pulmonary disease. In this setting, the tissue hypoxia

causes an increase in renal erythropoietin production. The erythropoietin in turn stimulates the bone marrow erythroid precursors and increases the number of red cells produced in order to increase tissue oxygen delivery. The increase in red cell mass may be beneficial to the hypoxic tissue, but the associated increase in total blood viscosity and the marked increase in total blood volume may be clinically detrimental. For example, patients with cyanotic congenital heart disease with a hematocrit of 75 per cent require repeated phlebotomy to decrease the total blood volume and whole blood viscosity. The consequences of the marked hyperviscosity that accompanies a hematocrit greater than 60 per cent include decreased cerebral blood flow, decreased cardiac output, and a tendency to thrombosis.

The approach to the patient with absolute polycythemia should follow a logical pathway to determine whether the patient has secondary or primary polycythemia, polycythemia vera. The history and physical examination may provide the answer. A wheezing, cyanotic, barrel-chested man with severe chronic obstructive pulmonary disease can be distinguished quickly from the plethoric patient with splenomegaly who most likely has typical polycythemia vera. Simple laboratory data complete the analysis in the majority of patients. White blood count and platelet count are elevated in most patients with polycythemia vera; they are normal in most patients with secondary polycythemia. A low arterial oxygen saturation indicates that the polycythemia is a compensatory mechanism for hypoxemia. Thus, the history, physical examination, and screening laboratory data should distinguish between primary and secondary polycythemia. Sometimes, however, the cause of the secondary polycythemia may not be obvious and requires further testing for rare causes; these include abnormal hemoglobins with increased oxygen affinity, erythropoietin-secreting renal cysts, cerebellar hemangioblastoma, and hepatocellular carcinoma (Table 50–1).

In polycythemia vera, normal control of bone marrow cell production is lost. Although the erythroid line is primarily affected, resulting in an elevated red cell mass, increased granulocyte and platelet production are frequently found as well. Polycythemia vera shares some clinical features with the other myeloproliferative disorders: myelofibrosis with myeloid metaplasia, essential thrombocythemia, and chronic myelogenous leukemia. In all these diseases, there is abnormal (although variable) expansion of all the bone marrow elements: the myeloid precursors, the megakaryocytes, the erythroid precursors, and the fibroblasts of the bone marrow.

The cause of polycythemia vera is not known. The disorder occurs sporadically in both sexes, with a mean age of presentation of about 60 years. Some affected patients are asymptomatic, whereas others can suffer symptoms due to hypervolemia, hyperviscosity, or platelet dysfunction.

The combination of intravascular hyperviscosity due to a high red cell mass and a high platelet

TABLE 50-1. EVALUATION OF THE PATIENT WITH AN ELEVATED HEMATOCRIT

1. History

    Family history? Social history (e.g., smoking)?

2. Physical examination

    Splenomegaly? Cardiac or pulmonary disease?

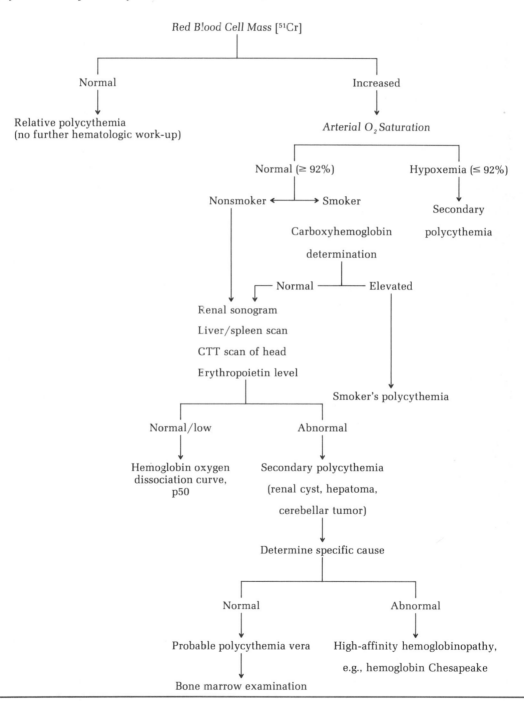

TABLE 50-2. CLINICAL MANIFESTATIONS OF POLYCYTHEMIA VERA

Hyperviscosity and/or **hypervolemia** may lead to:
1. Decreased cerebral blood flow with:
   a. Tinnitus
   b. Lightheadedness
   c. Stroke (rarely)
2. Congestive heart failure
3. Thrombosis

Platelet dysfunction may lead to:
1. Thrombosis due to:
   a. Thrombocytosis
   b. Intrinsically abnormal platelets
      (e.g., prolonged bleeding time, absent aggregation to epinephrine, abnormal prostaglandin metabolism, increased Fc receptor expression)
2. Hemorrhage:
   a. Upper gastrointestinal bleeding may occur.
   b. Aspirin aggravates bleeding tendency.
3. Microvascular thrombosis may produce painful toes and fingers.

Increased cell turnover can lead to:
1. Gout (due to hyperuricemia)
2. Itching (due to increased histamine production from basophils)

count with functionally abnormal platelets puts patients with polycythemia vera at high risk for stroke, myocardial infarction, and venous thromboembolism.

The metabolic consequences of increased cell turnover also can cause symptoms such as gout or itching (Table 50-2).

The diagnosis of polycythemia vera may be readily apparent or may require extensive laboratory testing to exclude secondary polycythemia (see Table 50-1). Clinical criteria diagnostically useful for the disease are outlined in Table 50-3. If a full evaluation does not convince the physician that a patient has polycythemia vera, two other laboratory tests may be helpful when available: a serum erythropoietin level (which should be zero in polycythemia vera) and an assay of bone marrow erythroid colony growth (which should demonstrate growth of erythroid colonies independent of added erythropoietin in polycythemia vera).

Polycythemia vera, appropriately treated, is

TABLE 50-3. CRITERIA FOR THE DIAGNOSIS OF POLYCYTHEMIA VERA

A1—Elevated red cell mass
    Male: >36 ml/kg
    Female: >32 ml/kg
A2—Normal arterial O_2
    saturation ($>92\%$)
A3—Splenomegaly

B1—Thrombocytosis: Platelet count $>400,000/\mu l$
B2—Leukocytosis: White cell count $>12,000/\mu l$
B3—Elevated leukocyte alkaline phosphatase (LAP): >100
B4—Elevated serum vitamin B_{12}: >900 pg/ml (due to elevated transcobalamin)

Diagnosis requires:
A1 + A2 + A3 or
A1 + A2 and any two from B category

compatible with many years of active life. The treatment involves two steps: lowering the hematocrit by phlebotomy and, if necessary, decreasing bone marrow red cell and platelet production by chemotherapy or radioactive phosphorus. Initially, phlebotomy serves to lower the hematocrit, which optimally should be brought to 45 per cent or less. With repeated phlebotomies, bone marrow iron stores (which may be low at the time of diagnosis in polycythemia vera) are further depleted, and red cell production is retarded. In response to repeated phlebotomy, however, platelet production may be increased by as yet incompletely understood mechanisms. If the platelets increase to more than $10^6/\mu l$, the risk of thrombosis or hemorrhage increases. Accordingly, treatment with chemotherapy or radioactive phosphorus may be indicated in this setting. Use of antiplatelet drugs such as aspirin has not proved beneficial in preventing thrombosis in patients with polycythemia vera and may promote hemorrhage. In patients over age 50 the risk of thrombosis is high enough, however, to warrant myelosuppressive therapy with hydroxyurea to control platelet counts.

With appropriate therapy, the median survival for patients with polycythemia vera is at least 10 years. Thrombosis is a major cause of death. Acute leukemia occurs in a small percentage. This tendency to malignant transformation is increased if the patient receives an alkylating agent or radioactive phosphorus for treatment. The current choice of chemotherapy in polycythemia vera is the antimetabolite hydroxyurea, which so far has not been associated with an increased incidence of acute leukemia. Late in the course of polycythemia vera, the "spent" phase may occur. This is marked by increasing bone marrow fibrosis with decreased red cell production and, commonly, the development of anemia and marked splenomegaly. At this stage of the disease, the patient's clinical picture resembles that of myelofibrosis with myeloid metaplasia.

Myelofibrosis with myeloid metaplasia (MMM) (agnogenic myeloid metaplasia) is a myeloproliferative disorder in which, as in the other myeloproliferative disorders, there is expansion of all bone marrow elements due to malignant transformation of a pluripotent stem cell. Bone marrow fibrosis is a reaction to this event and may progress to cause almost complete obliteration of normal marrow space. Extramedullary hematopoiesis in the liver and spleen is a cardinal feature of the disease. The extramedullary hematopoiesis due either to reactivation of a fetal site of hematopoiesis or to new migration of bone marrow stem cells may produce marked hepatosplenomegaly.

The clinical presentation of MMM may be subtle, consisting merely of the presence of nucleated red blood cells detected in a peripheral blood smear, a hallmark of extramedullary hematopoiesis. Anemia with teardrop forms and nucleated red cells on peripheral smear, leukocytosis with a shift to the left, and splenomegaly provide additional suggestive features. The diagnosis is strengthened by bone marrow aspiration (usually a

TABLE 50–4. DIFFERENTIAL DIAGNOSIS OF AN ELEVATED WHITE BLOOD COUNT

	MYELOFIBROSIS WITH MYELOID METAPLASIA	CHRONIC MYELOGENOUS LEUKEMIA	LEUKEMOID REACTION
WBC	Usually >100,000/μl with early myeloid forms	May be >100,000/μl with early myeloid forms	Rarely >100,000/μl; promyelocytes or blasts are rare
RBC morphology	Nucleated RBC and teardrop cells	Occasional nucleated RBC	Usually normal
Leukocyte alkaline phosphatase (LAP score)	Normal or high	Low (<20)	High
Bone marrow	Usually "dry tap" with fibrosis	Panhypercellular	Myeloid hyperplasia
Philadelphia chromosome	Absent	Present (about 90% of cases)	Absent

WBC = White blood cell; RBC = red blood cell.

"dry tap") and confirmed by biopsy showing fibrosis and sometimes osteosclerosis. The differential diagnosis of MMM includes a leukemoid reaction or chronic myelogenous leukemia as outlined in Table 50–4.

The course of MMM is one of slowly progressive splenomegaly, hepatomegaly, and anemia with thrombocytopenia. Sixty per cent of cases occur between ages 50 and 70. The spleen may become so massive that the patient can barely eat or sit comfortably. Portal hypertension due to increased splenic blood flow may become a major clinical problem late in the course of the disease. Unfortunately, no treatment alters the natural history of MMM. Supportive care includes treatment with folic acid and iron supplementation when indicated, but most patients eventually require transfusion to counteract anemia. Androgens may decrease the transfusion requirement, at least temporarily. Splenectomy is used cautiously for those selected patients in whom the enlarged organ produces unbearable pressure symptoms, pain, or poor nutrition. The procedure carries a substantial morbidity and mortality. Furthermore, following splenectomy, the liver may enlarge rapidly. Patients may live 5 or even 10 years after the diagnosis of MMM is made, but most suffer serious morbidity during this time.

Essential thrombocythemia is a myeloproliferative disorder characterized by platelet counts consistently elevated over 1 million/μl. The differential diagnosis between essential thrombocythemia and benign reactive thrombocytosis is outlined in Table 50–5 and is mainly a diagnosis of exclusion of the other myeloproliferative syndromes. In primary thrombocythemia there is no anemia; iron is present in the bone marrow, whereas fibrosis and the Philadelphia (Ph[1]) chromosome are not. The major presenting symptom of this disease is hemorrhage, although thrombotic events also may occur. Many patients, particularly young women, remain totally asymptomatic. The optimal therapy is not known. Because the natural history may include a long lifespan, aggressive therapy with alkylating agents usually is not indicated. Occasionally, a patient presents with very painful or even gangrenous fingers and toes due to microvascular thrombosis. Such patients respond well to antiplatelet drugs (e.g., aspirin) and/or to decreasing the platelet count with a cytotoxic drug such as hydroxyurea. Acute management with plateletpheresis is rarely indicated.

THE LEUKEMIAS

Leukemia is a condition in which the bone marrow is replaced by a malignant clone of lym-

TABLE 50–5. DIFFERENTIAL DIAGNOSIS OF AN ELEVATED PLATELET COUNT

	ESSENTIAL THROMBOCYTHEMIA	BENIGN REACTIVE THROMBOCYTOSIS
Platelet number	>1 × 10⁶/μl; may have bizarre morphology	Usually >4 × 10⁵ to 1 × 10⁶/μl; may have large platelets
Platelet function	Prolonged bleeding time may be present; absent aggregation response to epinephrine	Normal
Spleen	Usually palpable	Normal
Course	Platelets remain elevated without treatment	Platelets return to normal after inciting event is past (e.g., splenectomy, gastrointestinal bleeding, infection)
Complications	Hemorrhages more common than thrombosis; both may occur Erythromelalgia	Rare

phocytic or granulocytic cells. The course of the disease may be chronic or explosive; if left untreated, all leukemias are fatal. Lymphomas, by contrast, are tumors arising from cells of the lymphatic system. The bone marrow may be involved by lymphoma cells, but this is rarely the primary site of a lymphoma.

Chronic Myelogenous Leukemia

Chronic myelogenous leukemia (CML) is often classified as a myeloproliferative disease as well as a leukemia, because it shares the major feature of the myeloproliferative diseases: uncontrolled expansion of all marrow elements. All marrow cell lines in CML express a marker chromosome, the Ph[1] chromosome, pointing to a mutation in a pluripotent stem cell as the initiating event. The Ph[1] chromosome represents a reciprocal translocation of part of the long arm of chromosome 22 to chromosome 9. This translocation juxtaposes the oncogene c-*abl* with bcr, a breakpoint cluster region, to form a fusion gene bcr:*abl*, whose product is a tyrosine kinase (P210) that promotes granulocyte proliferation.

Although CML is usually a disease of adults, it sometimes affects children as well. The average age at onset is between 40 and 50 years. The disorder is not familial, and most patients have no history of excess exposure to carcinogenic chemicals or increased radioactivity. Nonetheless, the incidence of CML did increase markedly 7 years after the atomic bomb explosion in Japan in 1945.

The typical patient with CML has few initial symptoms, and the disease may be discovered on routine blood count. Leukocytosis with early myeloid precursors in the peripheral blood and splenomegaly are almost always present at the time of diagnosis. Thrombocytosis is also common. The bone marrow shows myeloid hyperplasia with a left shift and often increased numbers of megakaryocytes and increased reticulin or fibrosis. Table 50–4 outlines the differential diagnosis between CML, MMM, and a leukemoid reaction. Initially, affected patients are managed easily with periodic oral chemotherapy (alkylating agents or hydroxyurea) to normalize the blood count and reduce splenomegaly. This chronic phase of CML lasts 3 to 5 years. Adverse prognostic features include older age, hepatosplenomegaly, marked thrombocytosis or thrombocytopenia, marked leukocytosis and basophilia, and progression of clonal abnormalities. Subsequently, the course of the disease accelerates. The white count and spleen size become more difficult to control. Anemia and, eventually, thrombocytopenia develop, and fever and increasing weakness may appear. Eventually, white cell maturation ceases, so that the peripheral blood contains increasing numbers of promyelocytes and myeloblasts. This is termed the "blast phase," and it heralds death within 3 to 6 months.

The events that transform CML from the chronic to the blast phase are not understood. Hyperdiploidy or other chromosome abnormalities in addition to the Ph[1] chromosome often develop. In approximately 20 per cent of blast crises, the blast cells bear markers of lymphoid cell origin such as the enzyme terminal deoxynucleotidyl transferase (Tdt). This finding is important in therapeutic management, because drugs that are effective in lymphoid malignancies (e.g., vincristine and prednisone) may be useful in a lymphoid type (Tdt-positive) of blast crisis. Overall, however, the treatment of blast crisis is unsatisfactory, and any remissions are short.

Recombinant human alpha-interferon in the chronic phase of CML may induce hematologic remission and suppress the Ph[1] chromosome. At present, allogeneic bone marrow transplantation in highly selected patients with CML offers the only chance of producing long-term disease-free survival (and possibly cure).

Chronic Lymphocytic Leukemia

Chronic lymphocytic leukemia (CLL) was described by Dr. William Dameshek as an "accumulative disease of immunologically incompetent lymphocytes," a concise definition that describes the majority of patients. CLL is a disease of older persons, and fewer than 10 per cent of patients are under 50 years old. Men develop CLL twice as often as women and, as in all forms of leukemia, the disorder is more common in whites than blacks.

The diagnosis of CLL is based on an absolute and sustained lymphocytosis in the peripheral blood of no less than 15,000 cells/μl. The bone marrow is hypercellular, and more than 40 per cent of the cells are lymphocytes. The lymphocytes in the peripheral blood and marrow are of the small, well-differentiated type. Slowly enlarging lymph nodes and gradual enlargement of the liver and spleen due to the accumulation of neoplastic lymphocytes may occur early or late in the course of the disease. The immunologic incompetence of the expanding lymphocyte population expresses itself in hypogammaglobulinemia with predisposition to infections and in the emergence of such autoimmune phenomena as the production of antibodies against host red blood cells, causing Coombs'-positive hemolytic anemia. Table 50–6 outlines the immune disorders in CLL.

Lymphocytes in CLL usually consist of a clonal proliferation of B lymphocytes characterized by a single clonal rearrangement of an immunoglobulin gene (Fig. 50–2). The malignant cells all display immunoglobulin molecules on their plasma membranes bearing the same idiotype and the same single light chain type. The most common surface immunoglobulins represented are IgM and IgD, suggesting blocked maturation of the malignant clone. The finding of two heavy chain classes does not preclude the concept of monoclonality, as the IgD and IgM have the same idiotype specificity and presumably reflect an early, frozen stage of differentiation of normal B lymphocytes. CLL lymphocytes also express the Ia antigen, the receptor for C3, and the receptor for the Fc portion of immunoglobulin but have impaired B cell responses to mitogens. T cell function is also abnormal in B cell CLL.

About 1 per cent of patients with CLL demonstrate predominantly T lymphocytes in their peripheral blood. These lymphocytes form rosettes with sheep red blood cells and do not bear surface immunoglobulin. The T cell form of CLL appears to carry a poorer prognosis than the B cell type. Skin involvement is seen frequently in these patients, and standard forms of therapy for CLL are less effective.

The etiology of CLL is unknown. Despite occasional familial clusterings of CLL, no firm genetic basis for the disease has been found, nor does exposure to radiation or other potentially mutagenic agents such as alkylating agents appear to predispose. Chromosome abnormalities (particularly involving chromosomes 12 and 14) have been described in about half of patients with CLL. To date, no convincing data support a viral etiology.

A major contribution to understanding the natural history of CLL is the clinical staging system devised by Rai et al, which identifies prognosis according to the state of illness at the time of first diagnosis (Table 50–7). The stages of the disease reflect the concept of the "accumulative" nature

TABLE 50–6. IMMUNE DISORDERS IN CLL

Autoantibody Production
  Autoimmune hemolytic anemia
    Coombs' test positive in 20 to 30% of patients with CLL
    Hemolysis rare
    Usually responds to corticosteroids
  Autoimmune thrombocytopenic purpura
    Thrombocytopenia also possibly due to bone marrow replacement by CLL or to splenic sequestration
    Usually responds to corticosteroids
Disorders of Immunoglobulin Synthesis
  Monoclonal gammopathy
    Monoclonal spike present in 10% of patients with CLL—IgG or IgM
    Usually not of clinical importance
  Hypogammaglobulinemia
    Present in majority of cases, particularly stages III and IV
    Results in increased susceptibility to bacterial infection

of CLL. Stage 0 is lymphocytosis alone. Stages I and II reflect the development of increasing tumor mass (nodes, liver, or spleen), whereas the anemia and thrombocytopenia of stages III and IV indicate bone marrow replacement interfering with normal hematopoiesis, and splenomegaly causing decreased red blood cell and platelet survival. Most patients are in stage 0, I, or II at the time of diagnosis.

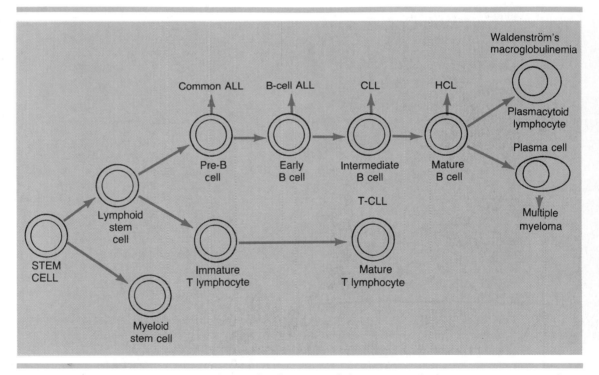

FIGURE 50–2. Lymphocyte development and the stages at which maturation arrest results in various immunologic subtypes of lymphoid leukemia or in an "immunoproliferative" malignancy. B cell = Bursa or bone marrow–derived lymphocyte; T cell = thymus-derived lymphocyte; ALL = acute lymphoblastic leukemia; CLL = chronic lymphocytic leukemia; HCL = hairy cell leukemia. (Adapted from Markowitz MJ, Mouradian J, Moore A: Acute and chronic lymphocytic leukemia. *In* Molander DW [ed]: Disease of the Lymphatic System. New York, Springer-Verlag, 1984; with permission.)

TABLE 50 – 7. CRITERIA FOR CLINICAL STAGING OF CLL (RAI)

Stage 0: Lymphocytosis alone
 >15,000/μl in peripheral blood
 >40% marrow lymphocytosis
Stage I: Lymphocytosis and enlarged nodes
Stage II: Lymphocytosis and splenomegaly, hepatomegaly, or both
Stage III: Lymphocytosis and anemia: hemoglobin <11 gm/dl
Stage IV: Lymphocytosis and thrombocytopenia: platelets <100,000/μl

Although palliative treatment exists, there is no cure for CLL. Treatment is generally withheld in the asymptomatic stage. When symptoms such as enlarging lymph nodes, splenomegaly, progressive anemia, and/or thrombocytopenia occur, alkylating agents (e.g., chlorambucil) and prednisone prove beneficial. Radiation therapy to the spleen or to areas of bulky adenopathy may be useful. Patients presenting in stages III and IV should be treated promptly because of poor survival in these groups (median survival, 2 years). Administration of intravenous gamma globulin may help decrease incidence of severe infection.

Unlike CML, there is no predictable blast phase in CLL. However, the disease sometimes can transform into a clinically more malignant lymphocytic neoplasm called diffuse histiocytic lymphoma ("Richter's syndrome"). Prolymphocytic leukemia, a more aggressive form of CLL, may also arise in a patient with CLL.

Hairy Cell Leukemia

Hairy cell leukemia (HCL) (also called leukemic reticuloendotheliosis) is a neoplastic disorder characterized by "hairy cells" in the peripheral smear and bone marrow. Hairy cells look like lymphocytes with fine cytoplasmic projections. Unlike typical B cells, they are capable of phagocytosis. The cells stain positive for tartrate-resistant acid phosphatase (TRAP) and are positive for the low-affinity interleukin-2 receptor (CD2S+).

HCL is a rare form of leukemia, constituting 1 to 2 per cent of all leukemias, is more common in men than women, and usually presents as a slowly developing pancytopenia with splenomegaly. Splenectomy may be useful if the spleen enlarges painfully or severe cytopenia develops. Chemotherapy has not helped most patients with hairy cell leukemia. Most patients with HCL, however, respond to alpha-interferon, 2'-deoxycoformycin (Pentostatin), or 2-chloroadenosine with a complete hematologic remission. Granulocyte colony-stimulating factor (G-CSF) administration may also correct the leukopenia. The median survival for patients with hairy cell leukemia is 3 to 5 years; some patients live many years after diagnosis with little treatment.

Acute Leukemias

In acute leukemias immature hematopoietic cells proliferate without differentiation into normal mature blood cells. The proliferating cells, whether myeloblasts or lymphoblasts, do not allow the normal bone marrow production of erythrocytes, granulocytes, and platelets to take place. This results in the major clinical complications of the disease: anemia, susceptibility to infection, and bleeding. The immature leukemic cells also infiltrate tissues, leading to organ dysfunction.

In most cases of acute leukemia, one finds no recognizable predisposing condition or event. In a few circumstances, however, an association with a possible leukemogenic agent (or agents) has been identified. Known agents associated with the development of acute leukemia include radiation, viruses, genetic predisposition, and chemicals (Table 50–8). How these agents interact with normal marrow stem cells so as to produce a malignant clone that lacks the ability to differentiate is not known.

Acute leukemias are divided into two broad categories: *acute lymphoblastic leukemia* (ALL) and *acute myeloblastic leukemia* (AML). ALL is primarily a disease of children, AML primarily of adults. Approximately 20 per cent of adult leukemias, however, are of the lymphoblastic type. Because the natural history and the treatment of these two types of leukemia differ, it is important to distinguish between them. The major distinction lies in bone marrow morphology; histochemical stains, surface and cytoplasmic markers, cytogenetics, and oncogene expression are also useful (Table 50–9). Chromosome changes in acute leukemia reveal some correlation with cell type. For example, the chromosome rearrangement t(15;17) is found in acute promyelocytic leukemia. There is a subgroup of patients with atypical ALL whose cells demonstrate the Ph[1] chromosome.

Because of heterogeneity within the two broad categories of acute leukemia, a French, American,

TABLE 50 – 8. EXAMPLES OF AGENTS ASSOCIATED WITH THE DEVELOPMENT OF ACUTE LEUKEMIA

AGENT	EXAMPLE
Ionizing radiation	Incidence of leukemia was increased in persons exposed to atomic bombings in Japan, 1945.
Viruses	A T cell leukemia that clusters in Southern Japan, the Caribbean, and Africa and is associated with a human type C retrovirus (human T cell lymphotropic virus, HTLV-I)
Genetic predisposition	An identical twin of a young child with acute leukemia has a 20% chance of developing the disease.
	Autosomal recessive disorders with chromosomal instability (Fanconi's anemia, Bloom's syndrome, ataxia-telangectasia)
Chemicals	Alkylating agents: chlorambucil, a treatment for polycythemia vera, leads to increased development of acute leukemia.
	Benzene

TABLE 50-9. LABORATORY AIDS TO DISTINGUISH BETWEEN AML AND ALL

	AML	ALL
1. Morphology of leukemic blasts	Granules in cytoplasm; Auer rods* may be present	Agranular, basophilic cytoplasm
	Multiple nucleoli	Regular, folded nucleus with one prominent nucleolus
	FAB (see Table 50-10) subclassification M_1–M_7	FAB subclassification, L_1–L_3
2. Histochemistry	Myeloperoxidase-positive	Myeloperoxidase-negative; PAS-positive
3. Cytoplasmic markers	—	Terminal deoxynucleotidyl transferase (Tdt)–positive
4. Surface markers (% of cases)	—	B cell markers (5%)
		T cell markers (15–20%): CD 2, 3, or 5
		CALLA† (50–65%): CD 10
5. Cytogenetic and oncogenetic abnormalities	M_3: t (15,17) Abnormal retinoic acid receptor gene	L3: t (8,14) abnormal c-*myc*
	M_5: t (9,11)	Some ALL: Ph¹ bcr:*abl* fusion gene

*Auer rods are a linear coalescence of cytoplasmic granules that stain pink with Wright's stain.
†CALLA = Common acute lymphoblastic leukemia antigen.

and British (FAB) group developed a subdividing classification that has proved useful in studying the course and therapy of the acute leukemias (Table 50-10). Among the myeloblastic leukemias the morphologic subtypes possess relatively distinctive clinical correlation. For example, acute promyelocytic leukemia (M_3) is associated with disseminated intravascular coagulation (DIC); the prominent cytoplasmic granules in the promyelocytes release enzymes that stimulate the coagulation cascade and promote intravascular coagulation. Acute monocytic leukemia (M_5) is associated with skin and gum infiltration with leukemic cells. Among lymphoblastic leukemias, the L_1 subtype is found predominantly in children and the L_2 subtype is found primarily in adults. The L_3 subtype is uncommon and carries a poor prognosis.

The diagnosis of acute leukemia is rarely difficult. The patient is usually acutely ill and presents with symptoms that indicate abnormal bone marrow function: infection due to granulocytopenia, bleeding due to thrombocytopenia, and/or anemia due to lack of erythroid maturation. Bone pain due to the expanded leukemic marrow may be present. In ALL, lymphadenopathy and splenomegaly are common. The total white blood count usually is elevated, sometimes above 100,000/μl, but can be normal or even low (<3000/μl). A small percentage of patients present with pancytopenia (aleukemic leukemia), which must be distinguished from aplastic anemia. The blood smear is almost always abnormal, showing predominantly blast cells with only a few normal mature leukocytes present. The hemoglobin and platelet count are almost always depressed, although their absolute values depend on the rapidity of onset of the leukemic process. The blood uric acid is usually elevated owing to the increased white cell turnover; clinical gout is rare, but renal damage due

to the hyperuricemia may occur. A bone marrow aspirate and biopsy make the diagnosis. The marrow is almost always hypercellular or "packed" with sheets of monotonous undifferentiated cells that replace the normal marrow elements.

The diagnosis of acute leukemia represents a medical emergency. The initial hours or days after diagnosis should be spent stabilizing the patient and preparing him for treatment. If the white blood cell count is greater than 100,000/μl, the patient is at high risk for cerebral hemorrhage caused by leukostasis, that is, obstruction of and damage to blood vessels plugged with rigid blasts. In this setting, immediate steps should be taken to reduce the white count by initiating chemotherapy, if possible, or performing leukapheresis. Allopurinol, a xanthine oxidase inhibitor, is given concurrently to decrease the hyperuricemia that results when treatment begins to destroy leukocytes. Antibiotics may be needed to treat infections, which can be life-threatening when patients have few or no mature granulocytes. Transfusion

TABLE 50-10. FRENCH-AMERICAN-BRITISH (FAB) CLASSIFICATION OF ACUTE LEUKEMIA

Acute Myelocytic Leukemia
M_1—Acute myelocytic leukemia without differentiation
M_2—Acute myelocytic leukemia with differentiation (predominantly myeloblasts and promyelocytes)
M_3—Acute promyelocytic leukemia
M_4—Acute myelomonocytic leukemia
M_5—Acute monocytic leukemia
M_6—Erythroleukemia
M_7—Megakaryotic leukemia
Acute Lymphocytic Leukemia
L_1—Predominantly "small" cells (twice the size of normal lymphocyte), homogeneous population; childhood variant
L_2—Larger than L_1, more heterogenous population; adult variant
L_3—"Burkitt-like" large cells, vacuolated abundant cytoplasm

TABLE 50–11. A TYPICAL PROGRAM FOR TREATMENT OF ACUTE LYMPHOBLASTIC LEUKEMIA

PHASE	PURPOSE	TREATMENT
Induction of complete remission	To eradicate all detectable leukemia cells	Vincristine, prednisone, daunorubicin, L-asparaginase
Central nervous system prophylaxis	To treat a potential "sanctuary" of leukemia	Intrathecal methotrexate (? cranial radiation therapy)
Intensification or consolidation during remission	To decrease further the leukemic burden	Chemotherapy similar to induction
Maintenance of remission	Continual suppression of the leukemic clone	Methotrexate, 6-mercaptopurine, vincristine, and prednisone
Relapse	To reinduce remission	Reinduction followed by bone marrow transplantation in remission

with red cells to maintain adequate blood hemoglobin levels and/or platelets to prevent hemorrhage are usually required. Acute leukemia is one of the most dreaded diagnoses that a patient can receive. The initial management must include enough time spent with the patient and his family to reassure them and to explain the treatment and support programs.

The specific treatment of acute leukemia consists primarily of chemotherapy; radiation therapy sometimes may be used as an adjunct. The total leukemic cell burden is estimated to be from 10^{11} to 10^{12} cells at clinical presentation. Chemotherapeutic drugs follow first-order kinetics. This means that the drugs kill a constant percentage of cells (e.g., 99 per cent) with each administration. A clinically complete remission with disappearance of all detectable leukemia in the blood and bone marrow may mean a reduction in tumor burden from 10^{12} to 10^9 cells. A similar amount of treatment is needed to reduce the number of cells from 10^9 to 10^7. Thus, the eradication of the last leukemia cell by chemotherapy becomes almost an impossible task.

Chemotherapeutic drugs are administered with the goal of stopping leukemic cell proliferation. The drugs are targeted against different phases of the cell cycle, with specific programs designed to follow the kinetics of the cell cycle. An example of a treatment program for ALL is outlined in Table 50–11. Similar programs are used to treat AML, cytosine arabinoside and daunorubicin being the agents of choice.

Cure of acute leukemia with rigorous chemotherapy programs and meticulous supportive care is sometimes possible, although the encouraging results achieved in children with ALL (i.e., more than 60 per cent alive in complete remission and probably cured at 5 years) have not been reproduced in adults. About 30 per cent of adults with ALL may obtain a long-term remission. The percentage is considerably smaller in AML, with only 10 to 20 per cent surviving 5 years in remission, although 60 to 80 per cent of patients achieve a first remission averaging 1 year in duration. Differentiation treatment is now possible in acute promyelocytic leukemia (M_3) using all-trans retinoic acid. In greater than 80 per cent of patients

this therapy induces remission by causing maturation of the leukemic cells. Consolidation of the therapy with customary chemotherapeutic antileukemic drugs is currently necessary following the initial remission to maintain the remission state.

Bone marrow transplantation from a related HLA-matched donor is being investigated as a treatment for patients with acute leukemia. Patients under age 30 who achieve an initial complete remission with chemotherapy can be considered possible candidates for this procedure if they have a suitable donor. The complications of bone marrow transplantation are substantial, however, and include acute and/or chronic graft-versus-host disease, interstitial pneumonias, and the infections and hemorrhagic complications expected during an initial period of bone marrow aplasia. Late recurrence of the leukemia is still a major concern and is believed to represent inadequate eradication of the leukemic clone by the initial cytotoxic treatment. Since in one case, however, post-transplant recurrence in a male patient involved a female's donor cells, it appears possible that the recipient passed a transmittable agent to the new cell line.

Other innovative approaches to the cure of acute leukemias include the use of monoclonal antibodies directed to leukemia-associated cell surface antigen in order to purge residual leukemic cells present in the bone marrow. The technology of this approach is progressing rapidly and has been incorporated into treatment programs in which autologous bone marrow transplantation during remission is combined with purging of leukemia residual cells by monoclonal antibody treatment.

MYELODYSPLASTIC SYNDROMES

In contrast to the explosive nature of acute leukemia, the myelodysplastic syndromes are characterized by the slow development of an anemia refractory to standard therapy. Affected patients are usually elderly; however, in recent years an increasing number of younger patients have developed myelodysplastic syndromes following prior treatment with radiation therapy, combination chemotherapy, or both, for another neoplasm such as Hodgkin's disease or ovarian carcinoma. Typically, the patient presents with the insidious onset of increasing fatigability and decreasing exercise tolerance; often the patient ascribes the symptoms to "growing old." Physical examination may reveal pallor, and laboratory examination shows an anemia that may be profound. The anemia is typically macrocytic, with a mean corpuscular volume (MCV) of 100 to 110 μ^3; the peripheral smear may show a dimorphic erythrocyte population, and the patients may also have leukopenia with or without thrombocytopenia. The bone marrow is hypercellular, with increased iron stores and morphologically abnormal erythroid precursors (dyserythropoiesis) as well as an increased percentage of early myeloid cells. This syndrome has been called "refractory anemia" or "preleukemia" in the past. Because the initial presentation and the course are variable, the condition is now referred to as the myelodysplastic syndrome and further defined according to a classification proposed by the FAB cooperative group mentioned above. Table 50–12 outlines the major clinical features and relative incidence of the five types of myelodysplastic syndromes. For refractory anemia (with or without ringed sideroblasts), the median survival time is approximately 3 to 4 years. The other three categories (refractory anemia with excess blasts, chronic myelomonocytic leukemia, and refractory anemia in transformation) carry a survival of 1 to 2 years or less. The risk of developing acute leukemia increases with the number of blasts in the bone marrow at presentation; thus, about 20 to 30 per cent of patients with refractory anemia (type 1 or 2) develop acute leukemia, but more than 60 per cent of patients with refractory anemia with excess blasts in transformation develop acute leukemia.

Treatment of the myelodysplastic syndrome is primarily directed toward improving the anemia. Blood transfusions are a mainstay of treatment. A few patients with refractory anemia with ringed sideroblasts respond to large doses of vitamin B_6. Chemotherapy has been used when increased numbers of blasts appear in the bone marrow. The role for chemotherapy, either in conventional doses or in low doses, is still being studied.

THE LYMPHOMAS

The lymphomas are a group of malignant neoplasms that arise in lymph nodes or extranodal lymphoid tissue. They are a heterogeneous group of malignancies from both a pathologic and a clinical viewpoint. The two major subgroups are Hodgkin's disease and non-Hodgkin's lymphoma. In both these subgroups, the most common clinical presentation is that of a patient who notices an enlarged lymph node. Before the physician considers a biopsy of the enlarged node, he must obtain a thorough history and perform a physical examination and selected laboratory tests to evaluate possible causes of the swollen lymph node. Cervical lymphadenopathy most commonly is associated with infections such as streptococcal pharyngitis, infectious mononucleosis, and toxoplasmosis. Axillary lymphadenopathy, particularly if it is unilateral, should direct the physician to perform a careful breast examination for possible cancer. Inguinal adenopathy may reflect skin infections of the legs or infection of the genitalia or anus such as syphilis. Scrofula, or tuberculous lymphadenitis, may present as asymptomatic isolated lymphadenopathy. Table 50–13 outlines various common causes of lymphadenopathy. HIV infection is now an important cause of lymphadenopathy. If the cause of the enlarged lymph node(s) is not obvious after consideration of the above, the physician should consider lymph node biopsy for diagnosis.

Hodgkin's Disease

This is primarily a disease of young adults but also appears in children and the elderly. The patient usually presents with asymptomatic lymphadenopathy; for example, on routine pre-employment chest radiography the radiologist finds mediastinal lymphadenopathy. Some patients with Hodgkin's disease have symptoms of fever, night sweats, or loss of weight; the factor or factors responsible for the production of these symptoms are not known.

Hodgkin's disease is classified by pathologic subtype, by clinical stage, and by the presence or

TABLE 50–12. CLASSIFICATION OF THE MYELODYSPLASTIC SYNDROMES

DIAGNOSIS (RELATIVE INCIDENCE)	PATIENT CHARACTERISTICS	PERIPHERAL BLOOD	BONE MARROW
Refractory anemia (56%)	Elderly patient; anemia	May have abnormal red cell morphology	<5% blasts
Refractory anemia with ringed sideroblasts (21%)	Elderly; anemia	May have dimorphic picture (microcytic/hypochromic and macrocytic)	Hypercellular; iron stain shows iron in a ring around red cell nuclei.
Refractory anemia with excess blasts (10%)	May have pancytopenia	<5% blasts	5–20% blasts
Chronic myelomonocytic leukemia (11%)	Similar to above	Absolute monocytosis <5% blasts	5–20% blasts
Refractory anemia in transformation (1%)	Any age; symptoms of brief duration	>5% blasts	20–30% blasts

TABLE 50-13. COMMON CAUSES OF LYMPHADENOPATHY

Infection
Bacterial: Localized infection with regional adenopathy (e.g., streptococcal pharyngitis, foot ulcer with inguinal adenopathy)
Viral: Infectious mononucleosis, cytomegalovirus, cat scratch fever
Retroviral: HIV, HTLV-1
Parasitic: Toxoplasmosis
Spirochetal: Syphilis
Mycobacterial: Tuberculosis, *Mycobacterium avium* (in immunosuppressed patients)
Fungal: Actinomycosis, cryptococcosis (in immunosuppressed patients)
Drug Reaction
Serum sickness
Phenytoin (may cause "pseudolymphoma")
Malignancy
Solid tumors—metastatic patterns:
Cervical adenopathy: head and neck cancer
Supraclavicular adenopathy: gastrointestinal tumors
Axillary adenopathy: breast cancer
Inguinal adenopathy: carcinoma of the anus
Lymphoma
Miscellaneous
Sarcoidosis

TABLE 50-14. HODGKIN'S DISEASE: PATHOLOGIC TYPES

SUBGROUP	RELATIVE FREQUENCY
Lymphocyte predominance	5–15%
Nodular sclerosis	40–75%
Mixed cellularity	20–40%
Lymphocyte depletion	5–15%

TABLE 50-15. MODIFIED ANN ARBOR STAGING CLASSIFICATION FOR HODGKIN'S DISEASE

Stage I: Involvement of a single lymph node region (I) or a single extralymphatic site (I_E)
Stage II: Involvement of two or more lymph node regions on the same side of the diaphragm (II) or a solitary extralymphatic site and one or more lymph node areas on the same side of the diaphragm (II_E)
Stage III: Involvement of lymph node regions on both sides of the diaphragm (III), accompanied by spleen involvement (III_S), or solitary involvement of an extralymphatic organ or site (III_E) or both (III_{SE}). III_1 = upper abdomen; III_2 = lower abdomen
Stage IV: Diffuse involvement of extralymphatic sites with or without lymph node enlargement
In addition to above, presence or absence of constitutional symptoms (specifically, fever, night sweats, loss of 10% body weight) is designated by B (presence) or A (absence).

absence of symptoms. The four pathologic subtypes are nodular sclerosis, lymphocyte predominance, mixed cellularity, and lymphocyte depletion (Table 50-14). In all four subtypes the finding of Reed-Sternberg cells assures the pathologist that the diagnosis of Hodgkin's disease is correct. The typical Reed-Sternberg cell is a large cell with two prominent nuclei. Each nucleus contains a prominent nucleolus surrounded by a "halo." This pattern gives the cell the appearance of "owl's eyes." Pathologists have puzzled over the cell of origin of the Reed-Sternberg cell since it was first described around 1900. It has features of lymphocytes and of reticulum cells and most frequently appears to be of T cell origin.

Nodular sclerosis is the most common pathologic subtype of Hodgkin's disease. Broad bands of fibrosis disrupt the lymph node architecture. "Lacunar" cells and scattered Reed-Sternberg cells are characteristic. This subtype of Hodgkin's disease typically presents as an asymptomatic mediastinal mass in a young woman. Hodgkin's disease of the *mixed cellularity* subtype demonstrates a pathologic picture of a heterogeneous cellular background with lymphocytes, eosinophils, and plasma cells; the Reed-Sternberg cell is present. Young and middle-aged men rather than women are more likely to have this subtype. *Lymphocyte-predominant* Hodgkin's disease is an uncommon subtype. An asymptomatic young man presenting with an enlarged high cervical node would be a typical patient. The prognosis for this subtype is generally excellent. *Lymphocyte-depleted* Hodgkin's disease is also uncommon. An older patient with fever, night sweats, or weight loss would be most likely to have this subtype, and the prognosis is generally poor.

Cure of the patient with Hodgkin's disease is the goal of treatment. Treatment is planned once the extent of disease or the stage is known. The definition of stages I, II, III, and IV is outlined in Table 50-15. Figure 50-3 shows examples of the various stages. The presence or absence of systemic symptoms is also part of the staging criteria. The staging process is rigorous, and a basic outline of tests that should be done to establish the stage is shown in Table 50-16. Hodgkin's disease tends to follow a logical anatomic progression of node involvement. For example, a patient with cervical adenopathy may have supraclavicular or mediastinal adenopathy but in the absence of supraclavicular or mediastinal adenopathy is unlikely to have pelvic adenopathy or liver involvement. This principle is important when considering how far to pursue a staging evaluation. For example, the patient with a high cervical node and no other adenopathy by computed transaxial tomography scan is very unlikely to have abdominal disease. An exploratory laparotomy with liver biopsy, multiple node biopsies, and splenectomy may be necessary to establish an accurate stage for a patient. A laparotomy should be considered in two situations: first, if the findings at laparotomy will alter the treatment plan; and, second, if abdominal or pelvic radiation therapy is being considered for a young woman of child-bearing age, the laparotomy would include transposing the ovaries out of the radiation field. If a patient has clinical stage IIIB or stage IV Hodgkin's disease, the treatment is chemotherapy; laparotomy is not necessary because the findings will not change this recommendation. If a patient has a mediastinal mass and cervical node involvement

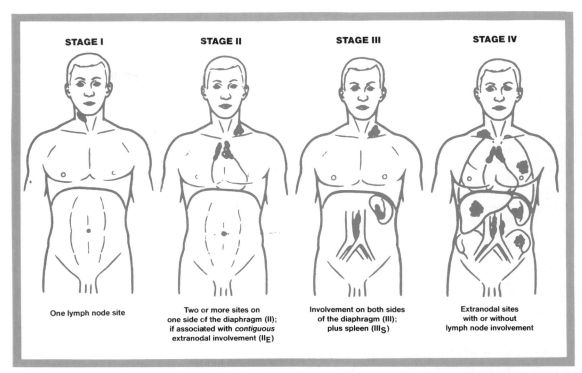

FIGURE 50-3. Malignant lymphoma: Examples of stages I through IV. (Reprinted from Tindle BH: Teaching monograph: Malignant lymphomas. Am J Pathol 116:115, 1984; with permission.)

but a lymphangiogram suggests pelvic node involvement, a laparotomy may be necessary to establish whether the patient has stage IIA or stage IIIA disease. Both these stages can be treated with radiation therapy, but the ports would differ according to the findings at laparotomy.

The treatment of Hodgkin's disease is radiation therapy, chemotherapy, and, in certain cases, both therapies. Radiation therapy is the recommended treatment for patients with stages I and IIA. Some patients with stage II or IIIA will have such massive adenopathy that chemotherapy may be used initially to shrink the bulk of the disease before curative radiation therapy. Patients with stage IIB are a controversial group; because of a high relapse rate after radiation therapy alone, combined modality (i.e., radiation therapy and chemotherapy) may be recommended. Patients with stage IIIB or IV are considered to have widespread disease that cannot be cured by radiation therapy; curative chemotherapy is used in these patients.

Radiation therapy is delivered in tumoricidal doses to areas of known disease and to adjacent areas. For example, a patient with stage I Hodgkin's disease in a cervical node receives a "mantle" port designed to treat cervical, supraclavicular, axillary, mediastinal, and hilar lymph nodes. A patient with inguinal node involvement receives an "inverted Y" to encompass the para-aortic, iliac, and inguinal nodes. The immediate side effects of radiation depend on the field irradiated

and include sore throat, dysphagia, nausea, and diarrhea. Delayed effects include radiation pneumonitis and hypothyroidism if the thyroid has been included in the field. Ovarian function will be suppressed unless the ovaries are surgically moved out of the radiation field prior to treatment.

A major advance in Hodgkin's disease has been the development of combination chemotherapy that can cure the majority of patients with stages IIIB and IV. The original program was the "MOPP" program (nitrogen-mustard, vincristine [oncovin], procarbazine, and prednisone). It is still one of the best programs for advanced-stage Hodgkin's disease. The immediate side effects include nausea, vomiting, and bone marrow suppression. The delayed side effects include sterility and the potential for the late development of leukemia. The risk of leukemia or other secondary neoplasms in-

TABLE 50-16. STAGING EVALUATION FOR A PATIENT WITH LYMPHOMA

1. Complete history and physical examination
2. Complete blood count, differential, platelet count, urinalysis
3. Screening blood chemistries
4. Chest x-ray, CT scan of chest, abdomen, and pelvis
5. Bone marrow aspirate and biopsy
6. Consider lymphangiogram, gallium scan
7. Staging laparotomy if therapy will be changed by documentation of subdiaphragmatic disease

creases if the patient is over 40 and also receives radiation therapy. Alternative treatment regimens such as ABVD (Adriamycin, bleomycin, vincristine, and dacarbazine) have equal efficacy as MOPP with less long-term toxicity and are non–cross-resistant.

The long-term prognosis for patients with Hodgkin's disease is related to stage at diagnosis. Patients with stages IA and IIA disease have a 5-year survival of over 90 per cent. Most patients with stage IIIA have a 5-year survival of over 80 per cent. B symptoms decrease the survival figures at each stage. Stage IIIB and stage IV patients can expect a 5-year survival of over 50 per cent. The 5-year survival rates can translate to cure rates in most instances.

The risk of infection is a major problem in Hodgkin's disease. Immunologic abnormalities, particularly reflecting T cell dysfunction, can be detected even before patients receive any treatment, a finding that explains the frequent occurrence of herpes zoster in Hodgkin's disease. These patients also are susceptible to fungal infections such as cryptococcosis. Bacterial infections, particularly pneumococcal and meningococcal, especially affect patients who have undergone laparotomy and splenectomy.

Non-Hodgkin's Lymphomas

These are a heterogeneous group of neoplasms that arise from a monoclonal proliferation of a malignant cell of lymphoid origin, either T cell or B cell. As in Hodgkin's disease, the cause of lymphoma is not known. Viruses, radiation, immunosuppression (e.g., renal transplantation, AIDS), and certain genetic conditions have all been implicated. Burkitt's lymphoma, a rare monoclonal B cell neoplasm, has provided some clues about the pathogenesis of lymphoma. In Africa, there is a "lymphoma belt" in which the development of Burkitt's lymphoma mirrors the endemic area for malaria. This distribution, along with the finding of Epstein-Barr virus in the majority of cases of African Burkitt's lymphoma, suggests a viral pathogenesis. Chromosomal translocations in Burkitt's lymphoma involve chromosomes 8 and 14 and less commonly 2 and 22. These chromosomes carry the genes for the immunoglobulin heavy chains and light chains and their translocations produce immunoglobulin rearrangements. The translocations also occur at the chromosome site where a cellular oncogene (c-myc) is found. The relationship of the translocation at the site of a cellular oncogene and monoclonal proliferation of this malignant neoplasm is not yet understood.

Non-Hodgkin's lymphomas are classified by pathologic subtype and clinical stage. The pathologic subtype depends on the overall pattern of nodal architecture and on the morphology of the predominant cell in the neoplastic node. The malignant cells may replace the node in a diffuse pattern obliterating the germinal centers or follicles completely. This pattern defines a "diffuse" lymphoma. Alternatively, the malignant cells may form a pattern of nodules or follicles that defines the lymphoma as a nodular or follicular lymphoma. The predominant cell type further classifies the lymphoma. The major lymphoma cell types are the small, well-differentiated lymphocyte; the slightly larger, poorly differentiated lymphocyte with a cleaved nucleus; and the large lymphoid cell with characteristics of a histiocyte or lymphoblast. Two major lymphoma classification systems use these criteria, nodal architecture, and cell type to define the subtypes of lymphoma. Table 50–17 shows the International Formulation classification of lymphoma next to the classification of Rappaport. Both these systems have received wide acceptance because of their clarity and clinical applicability. These classifications are morphologic and do not depend on immunologic subtyping of the malignant cells. If lymph node biopsies are further subjected to studies of cell origin using surface immunoglobulin markers for B cells, erythrocyte rosettes for T cells, monoclonal antibodies for B and T cells, or gene rearrangements, most of the lymphomas are of B cell origin. Particularly aggressive B cell lymphomas, refractory to therapy, occur in patients with acquired immunodeficiency syndromes. Some lymphomas are of T cell origin; in rare lymphomas, the cell of origin cannot be determined (Table 50–18).

Clinical staging of non-Hodgkin's lymphoma is defined by the same criteria as those for Hodgkin's disease (see Table 50–15). Two aspects of the staging process are different from those for Hodgkin's disease. First, the non-Hodgkin's lymphomas are more likely than Hodgkin's lymphomas to present in an extranodal site (Fig. 50–4). Second, the pro-

TABLE 50–17. CLASSIFICATION OF THE NON-HODGKIN'S LYMPHOMAS

INTERNATIONAL WORKING FORMULATION	RAPPAPORT CLASSIFICATION
I. Low-grade lymphoma	
a. Small lymphocytic cell	Diffuse lymphocytic, well-differentiated
b. Follicular, mixed cleaved cell	Nodular lymphocytic, poorly differentiated
c. Follicular, mixed small cleaved and large cell	Nodular mixed lymphocytic-histiocytic
II. Intermediate-grade lymphoma	
d. Follicular, large cell	Nodular histiocytic
e. Diffuse, small cleaved cell	Diffuse lymphocytic, poorly differentiated
f. Diffuse, mixed small cleaved cell	Diffuse mixed lymphocytic-histiocytic
g. Diffuse large cell	Diffuse histiocytic
III. High-grade lymphoma	
h. Large cell immunoblastic	Diffuse histiocytic
i. Lymphoblastic cell	Diffuse undifferentiated
j. Small noncleaved cell (Burkitt and non-Burkitt)	

gression of the non-Hodgkin's lymphomas does not follow the orderly anatomic progression described above for Hodgkin's disease. Non-Hodgkin's lymphoma is much more likely to be disseminated at the time of diagnosis. True stage I or stage II non-Hodgkin's lymphomas are rare. The treatment and prognosis of the patient with non-Hodgkin's lymphoma depend on the clinical stage and the pathologic classification. Patients with stage I or stage II disease may be treated with radiation therapy alone. The overall cure rate for these patients is less than 50 per cent. This suggests that there may be a role for adjuvant chemotherapy in the treatment of some of these patients. Patients with stage III or IV disease are treated primarily with chemotherapy. Curability in this group depends on the pathologic subtype. Paradoxically, some patients with "high-grade" or "high-intermediate grade" lymphomas in whom the natural history would lead to survival of less than 1 or 2 years are now curable with aggressive combination chemotherapy programs incorporating drugs such as cyclophosphamide, doxorubicin (Adriamycin), vincristine, prednisone, and bleomycin. Autologous bone marrow transplantation combined with aggressive chemotherapy can be curative even in older patients with lymphoma. Patients with low-grade lymphomas are rarely curable by chemotherapy unless the disease is truly local (<30 per cent of cases). The natural history of these lymphomas tends to be an indolent one, with median survivals of 5 years and sometimes longer. Treatment offers palliation but may not alter survival. Thus,

TABLE 50–18. IMMUNOLOGIC CLASSIFICATION OF THE NON-HODGKIN'S LYMPHOMAS

B cell neoplasms	Low-grade lymphomas Intermediate-grade lymphomas (most) High-grade lymphomas (most)
T cell neoplasms	
Thymic T cell	Lymphoblastic lymphoma (an aggressive lymphoma, particularly of young men, associated with mediastinal mass and central nervous system involvement)
Mature T cell	Peripheral T cell lymphoma HTVL-I–associated lymphoma (a virus-related lymphoma, clustered in South Japan, the Caribbean, and Africa) Mycosis fungoides (a "helper" T cell lymphoma of the skin, associated with circulating lymphoma cells, "Sézary cells")

observation alone, less aggressive chemotherapy, and palliative radiation therapy may be used in the management of the patient with an indolent lymphoma (Fig. 50–5).

Non-Hodgkin's lymphomas, particularly at extranodal sites including the central nervous system and gastrointestinal tract, are common in human immunodeficiency virus (HIV)–infected patients. They are usually B cell lymphomas of high-grade malignancy or immunoblastic lymphoma, respond poorly to therapy, and progress rapidly, with short median survival times even in

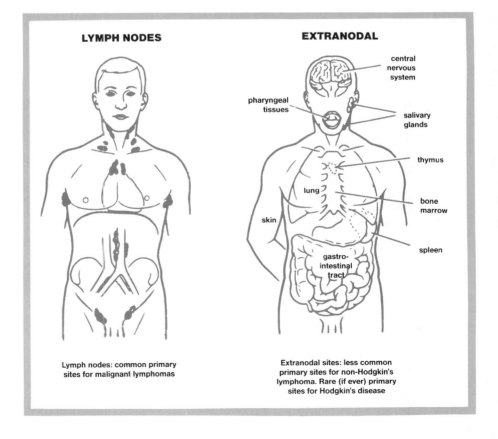

FIGURE 50–4. Malignant lymphomas: Examples of nodal and extranodal sites. (Reprinted from Tindle BH: Teaching monograph: Malignant lymphomas. Am J Pathol 116:115, 1984; with permission.)

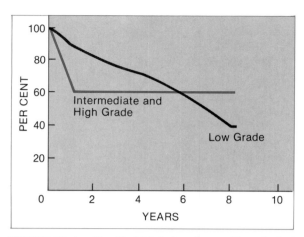

FIGURE 50–5. Non-Hodgkin's lymphoma: Hypothetical actuarial survival according to classification, based on 1985 data. (From Portlock CS: Non-Hodgkin's lymphomas. *In* Wyngaarden JB, Smith LH Jr, Bennett JC [eds]: Cecil Textbook of Medicine. 19th ed. Philadelphia, WB Saunders Co, 1992, p 955.)

therapy-responsive cases. Underlying immunosuppression and bone marrow depression make treatment difficult to administer without excessive toxicity.

PLASMA CELL DISORDERS

The plasma cell disorders include a group of B cell neoplasms that arise from a clone of immunoglobulin-secreting cells and produce a monoclonal immunoglobulin (or part of an immunoglobulin). If the monoclonal immunoglobulin (Ig) is of the IgM class, the disease is Waldenström's macroglobulinemia and the malignant cells are plasmacytoid lymphocytes. If the monoclonal immunoglobulin is of the IgG, IgA, IgD, or rarely the IgE class, the disease is multiple myeloma and the malignant cells are plasma cells. Normal plasma cells represent the most specialized cells in the B cell lineage. Figure 50–2 illustrates one scheme of maturation proceeding from a pluripotent stem cell to an early B cell to a well-differentiated plasma cell, indicating the malignant diseases that can arise from neoplastic proliferation at each stage of B cell maturation.

Plasma cells normally secrete immunoglobulins and are responsible for maintaining humoral immunity. The basic structure of all immunoglobulins is the same and includes two heavy ("H") polypeptide chains and two light ("L") polypeptide chains, bound together by disulfide bonds. Both H chains and L chains have "constant" regions of amino acid sequence and "variable" regions that allow for antibody specificity. The five subclasses of immunoglobulin—immunoglobulin gamma (IgG), mu (IgM), alpha (IgA), delta (IgD), and epsilon (IgE)—are determined by the constant region

of their H chains. Light chains are of two types: kappa and lambda. Each antibody molecule has two identical H chains and two identical L chains; hybrid molecules are not synthesized. Protein electrophoresis provides the first step in detecting a monoclonal immunoglobulin in serum. Analysis of the protein "spike" (peak) by agar gel immunoelectrophoresis or immunofixation using specific antibodies (e.g., anti-human IgG, anti-kappa) further defines the exact type of monoclonal immunoglobulin.

Monoclonal immunoglobulin elevations can be found in conditions other than multiple myeloma or Waldenström's macroglobulinemia. Approximately 10 per cent of patients with CLL have monoclonal IgG or IgM peaks (M proteins) in their serum. In addition, an M protein on serum electrophoresis may be found in patients with no detectable associated disease. The peak is usually not large (i.e., <2 gm/dl) and is accompanied by no other clinical or laboratory evidence of multiple myeloma or Waldenström's macroglobulinemia. This finding, formerly called "benign monoclonal gammopathy" and now designated MGUS (monoclonal gammopathy of unknown significance), increases in frequency with age above 60 years. Approximately 10 per cent of these patients later develop a true immunoproliferative disorder.

Multiple Myeloma

This is a malignant disease of plasma cells that is characterized by the presence of monoclonal immunoglobulin or light chains in the serum and urine and bone destruction. The typical patient is over 50 and presents with back pain, mild anemia, and an elevated sedimentation rate. Initial bone radiography may demonstrate only osteoporosis, although widespread lytic lesions are typical. Less frequently the patient has hypercalcemia and renal disease ("light chain nephropathy") at the time of diagnosis. Serum immunoelectrophoresis generally demonstrates a monoclonal elevation of one immunoglobulin (e.g., IgG^k), with reciprocal depression of the other classes of immunoglobulins (e.g., IgA and IgM). Free kappa or lambda light chains (Bence Jones protein) may be excreted in excess in the urine and are usually detected by a 24-hour urine immunoelectrophoresis. About 20 per cent of patients with multiple myeloma do not have a serum M protein but have free light chains detectable in urine and serum ("light chain disease"); about 1 per cent of patients with multiple myeloma have neither monoclonal nor free light chains detectable. These patients with "nonsecretory" myeloma can be shown to have a malignant clonal proliferation of plasma cells by immunofluorescent staining of the bone marrow. The plasma cells are shown to stain with either the anti-kappa or anti-lambda antiserum, but not with both reagents.

Bone marrow aspiration is important for the diagnosis of myeloma, although the nonhomogeneous distribution of tumor in the marrow means that myeloma cannot be ruled out by normal findings. Plasma cells usually make up less than 5 per cent of bone marrow cells; greater than 10 to 20 per cent plasma cells are required to make a bone marrow diagnosis of multiple myeloma. Some of the plasma cells may have bizarre morphology with binucleated and multinucleated plasma cells, or they may be normal in appearance. The clinical manifestations of multiple myeloma center on the systemic effects of the monoclonal protein (the paraprotein) and the concomitant humoral immunodeficiency state, as well as the effects of the bone and bone marrow invasion by malignant cells. Table 50–19 outlines the common clinical syndromes associated with multiple myeloma. Despite high levels of paraprotein, syndromes of hyperviscosity are rare in myeloma.

The prognosis of multiple myeloma is a reflection of the tumor cell burden. A poor prognosis is associated with a high tumor cell burden, as reflected by anemia, decreased renal function, hypercalcemia, extensive bony involvement, and large monoclonal protein peaks. A patient without any of these poor prognostic criteria may have a median survival of 5 years; a patient in the poor prognosis category is likely to have a median survival of less than 2 years. The development of a staging system that correlates clinical criteria with the "measured" myeloma cell mass has been useful for predicting prognosis and selecting therapy.

The treatment of a patient with multiple myeloma requires meticulous attention to supportive care as well as expertise in the administration of chemotherapy. Cautious exercise and ambulation are important to retard bone resorption. Bone lesions may require local radiation therapy to prevent a pathologic fracture. Adequate hydration and avoidance of intravenous dye injection (e.g., for intravenous pyelography) helps to prevent renal failure. Administration of pneumococcal vaccine and early detection and treatment of infections are important in these susceptible patients. Administration of intravenous gamma globulin to correct the profound hypogammaglobulinemia may help decrease the incidence of severe infections, but this therapy is costly.

The current chemotherapy of multiple myeloma centers on the use of cell cycle–nonspecific cytotoxic drugs (alkylating agents, nitrosoureas, and anthracycline antibiotics) and corticosteroids. Improvement in symptoms ensues in the majority of patients. Clinical remission is associated with a decrease of less than 1 log of tumor cells (e.g., 10^{12} to 10^{11}). Eradication of all tumor cells and cure of multiple myeloma are not attainable with available therapy, but bone marrow transplantation combined with intensive chemotherapy has been successful in a small number of cases, especially in young patients with myeloma.

Waldenström's Macroglobulinemia

This is a clonal disease of IgM-secreting plasmacytoid lymphocytes. It is a chronic disorder that usually affects older people. The patient commonly

TABLE 50–19. COMMON CLINICAL MANIFESTATIONS OF MULTIPLE MYELOMA

Bone Involvement
Malignant plasma cells may secrete cytokines that activate osteoblasts, leading to:
   a. osteoporosis, pathologic fracture, and bone pain
   b. hypercalcemia
Anemia
Decreased red cell production due to tumor inhibition of erythropoiesis and marrow invasion by plasma cells
Renal Disease
Calcium nephropathy
Light chain nephropathy
Uric acid nephropathy
Amyloidosis (may develop in about 15% of patients)
Elevated Sedimentation Rate
The paraprotein causes red cell rouleaux.
Infection
Normal immunoglobulin production is suppressed.
There is poor response to immunization.
Pneumococcal disease is particularly prevalent.
Bleeding Diathesis
Platelet function impaired by M protein
Thrombocytopenia
Vascular fragility (amyloidosis)
Hyperviscosity
Caused by M protein (IgA, IgG_3, high levels of IgG_1)

presents with anemia and symptoms due to the physical properties of the elevated monoclonal IgM. IgM is a large molecule and remains primarily in the intravascular space. If the IgM level is elevated, plasma viscosity may be high. Nosebleeds, retinal hemorrhages, mental confusion, and congestive heart failure are clinical presentations of the hyperviscosity syndrome. Some IgM molecules precipitate in the cold. The patient with this type of IgM may manifest the clinical picture of cryoglobulinemia. Blue (cyanotic) fingers, toes, nose, and earlobes on exposure to cold are a typical presentation. Foot and leg ulcers may develop, and vascular occlusion with gangrene may ensue. Leukocytoclastic vasculitis is seen on biopsy of these skin lesions. Some monoclonal IgM molecules may have activity directed against red cells, particularly the "I" antigen (see Hemolytic Anemias in Chapter 47). This type of IgM, a cold agglutinin, agglutinates red cells at temperatures below 37°C (e.g., in the extremities). These patients present with Raynaud's phenomenon and a hemolytic anemia. Keeping patients with cryoglobulinemia or the cold agglutinin syndrome warm is a primary part of their treatment. Peripheral neuropathy is a rare presentation of Waldenström's macroglobulinemia. A few patients have been described in whom the IgM monoclonal protein had antimyelin activity. Splenomegaly and lymphadenopathy may develop during the course of Waldenström's macroglobulinemia but are rarely a major cause of disability. Bone pain and hypercalcemia rarely occur.

The treatment of Waldenström's macroglobulinemia is directed to relief of symptoms. If the symptoms are primarily due to the elevated IgM (e.g., hyperviscosity syndrome), plasmapheresis is a useful tool and may be combined with chemotherapy. If the IgM is a cold agglutinin or a cryoglobulin, the plasmapheresis must be done in a warm environment. Chemotherapy (e.g., alkylating agents) may be useful to decrease the lymphadenopathy and splenomegaly but does not alter the natural history of the disease. The median survival is about 3 years, although some patients may live 10 or more years with indolent disease.

Rarer Plasma Cell Dyscrasias

Rarely, a patient may present with *heavy chain disease,* a disorder that has some characteristics of myeloma or Waldenström's macroglobulinemia but behaves clinically more like lymphoma. Analysis of the serum reveals only the heavy chain of IgG, IgA, or IgM. Gamma chain disease is associated with lymphadenopathy and edema of the soft palate. Alpha chain disease ("Mediterranean lymphoma") is characterized by intestinal infiltration by lymphoma; mu chain disease is associated with chronic lymphocytic leukemia.

Plasma cell leukemia may either be primary or appear secondary to multiple myeloma. It responds poorly to therapy. *Osteosclerotic myeloma,* or POEMS syndrome, is characterized by polyneu-

ropathy, organomegaly, endocrinopathy, an M protein, and skin changes and primarily produces a chronic demyelinating myelopathy with osteosclerosis. *Primary amyloidosis* represents pathologic tissue deposition of monoclonal light chains (variable portions) resulting in abnormal cardiac, hepatic, gastrointestinal, neurologic, or renal function, depending on the sites of deposition of the light chains as insoluble, Congo red–birefringent fibrils. Congestive heart failure, hemorrhage, nephrotic syndrome, and peripheral neuropathy are common complications. Treatment is supportive.

REFERENCES

Champlin R, Gale RP: Acute lymphoblastic leukemia: Recent advances in biology and therapy. Blood 73:2051, 1989.

Foon KA, Rai KR, Gale RP: Chronic lymphocytic leukemia: New insights into biology and therapy. Ann Intern Med 113:525, 1990.

Longo DL, Glatstein E, Duffey PL, et al: Radiation therapy versus combination chemotherapy in the treatment of early-stage Hodgkin's disease: Seven year results of a prospective randomized trial. J Clin Oncol 9:906, 1991.

Schiffer CA, Lee EJ: Approaches to the therapy of relapsed acute myeloid leukemia. Oncology 3:23, 1989.

Warrell RP, Frankel SR, Miller WH, et al: Differentiation therapy of acute promyelocytic leukemia with tretinoin (all-trans retinoic acid). N Engl J Med 324:1385, 1991.

Williams SF, Golomb HM (eds): Non-Hodgkin's lymphoma. Semin Oncol 17:1, 1990.

51 HEMOSTASIS

The arrest of bleeding after blood vessel injury involves a complex interaction between three responding systems: the blood vessel wall, the platelets, and the plasma coagulation proteins. This interaction results in normal *hemostasis,* but if pathologically exaggerated produces *thrombosis.* Although hemostasis is initiated within a few seconds after blood vessel injury, it is not completed for minutes to about an hour.

Primary hemostasis involves constriction of the injured vessel, exposure of subendothelial collagen, and the adhesion and aggregation of blood platelets on the damaged surface to form a *primary hemostatic plug* that is completed within 3 to 7 minutes. This process also involves participation of von Willebrand factor (Factor VIII: von Willebrand Factor [VWF]), which mediates platelet adhesion and the release from platelets of

vasoactive materials that augment aggregation. Clinical assessment of primary hemostasis is made with the bleeding time, which is a sensitive index of the adequacy of platelet function.

Secondary hemostasis represents the formation of a *fibrin clot* at the site of the initiating primary hemostatic plug. The surface of activated platelets catalyzes the formation of thrombin by its efficient assembly of coagulation factors involved in the prothrombinase complex in the presence of membrane phospholipid and calcium released upon platelet activation. At the same time, tissue factor, a protein-phospholipid complex, becomes exposed in the injured tissue and initiates clotting by binding to and activating Factor VII, leading to thrombin formation. Such localized thrombin activation in turn has several crucial effects: (1) Thrombin catalyzes fibrinogen conversion to fibrin, the fibrous protein that consolidates the platelet plug and entraps erythrocytes to provide bulk for the permanent clot. (2) Thrombin stimulates further platelet activation, prothrombin conversion, platelet release, and thromboxane production. (3) Thrombin activates coagulation Factor XIII, fibrin-stabilizing factor, which covalently cross-links and stabilizes the fibrin clot. Measurement of secondary hemostasis is made with the whole blood clotting time, which averages 8 to 10 minutes. Further details about coagulation are found in Chapter 52.

The *third stage of coagulation* is clot retraction, a process in which the loose meshwork of platelet aggregates, fibrin strands, and trapped red cells is formed into a firm clot. This process involves the contraction within individual platelets of the smooth muscle protein thrombosthenin, which compresses the clot. This stage may be evaluated in vitro and takes about 1 hour.

Finally, fibrinolysis is initiated and dissolves the clot.

Evaluation of a Bleeding Tendency

A clinically important bleeding tendency may result from defects in the blood vessels, the platelets, or the coagulation proteins. The defects may be qualitative or quantitative. Inherited hemorrhagic disorders tend to result from single defects, whereas acquired disorders result from single or multiple deficiencies. Evaluation of a patient for a bleeding tendency is needed in three settings: (1) screening prior to surgery, (2) when prior episodes of spontaneous or traumatic bleeding are reported, and (3) during active bleeding unresponsive to simple measures (Table 51–1).

The personal and family history is essential in evaluation of a bleeding tendency. A positive family history of bleeding in males suggests one of the hemophilias, which make up 95 per cent of congenital coagulation deficiencies. Spontaneous bleeding or bruising or easy bruising and bleeding after minor trauma are important, especially if bruises are large or raised (hematomas). Excessive bleeding after prior surgery or dental extraction, events that stress the hemostatic process, may indicate a bleeding tendency in persons without a spontaneous bleeding history. A history of menorrhagia or peripartum hemorrhage in a woman can also signify an underlying bleeding diathesis.

If bleeding has occurred, its timing, location, and clinical setting provide key clues to the type of defect. In platelet disorders, bleeding tends to be immediate and transient and involves mucous membranes or skin (e.g., epistaxes or bruising). In contrast, delayed bleeding after trauma or surgery, or bleeding into joints or muscles, is typical of coagulation disorders. Systemic diseases such as liver disease, hematologic malignancy, or uremia impair hemostasis. Drug ingestion is the single most common cause of acquired hemostatic defects; a careful drug history should include direct questioning about ingestion of aspirin, nonsteroidal anti-inflammatory drugs (NSAIDs), antibiotics, anticoagulants, and alcohol. All of these substances can cause bleeding or exacerbate an underlying bleeding disorder, as can profound nutritional impairment. A normal past history with recent bleeding symptoms suggests an acquired condition such as drug effect, circulating anticoagulant, or hemostatic defect secondary to a systemic disease. Some specific bleeding disorders to be considered from the patient's history are listed in Table 51–2.

Pertinent aspects of the physical examination include examination of the skin, mucous membranes, and retina for petechiae, ecchymoses, or

TABLE 51–2. CLINICAL CLUES TO BLEEDING DISORDERS

CLINICAL SIGN	DISORDER
Lifelong history of easy bruising or bleeding	Congenital coagulopathy (factor deficiency) Von Willebrand's disease
Family history of bleeding in males only	Hemophilia A or B
Family history of bleeding in both sexes	Factor XI deficiency Von Willebrand's disease
Excessive bleeding at surgery	Mild coagulation factor deficiency Von Willebrand's disease Thrombocytopenia
Acquired bruising tendency	Aspirin or other drug ingestion Thrombocytopenia
Delayed bleeding after trauma or surgery	Factor XIII deficiency
Bleeding after dental extraction	If negative, a bleeding disorder is unlikely
Bruising or bleeding starting during another illness	Drug ingestion Thrombocytopenia Acquired anticoagulant

TABLE 51–1. DIFFERENTIAL DIAGNOSIS OF BLEEDING DISORDERS

	COAGULATION DEFECT	PLATELET DEFECT	VASCULAR DEFECT
Family history	Usually positive	Rarely positive	Usually negative
Sex predominance	Males	Often females	Mainly females
Type of bleeding	"Deep" joint, muscle, and visceral; spontaneous and post-traumatic	Skin, mucous membranes	Purpuric or gastrointestinal
Time sequence	Delayed after trauma followed by prolonged oozing	Immediate, brief	Ecchymoses after trauma
Response to local pressure	Ineffective	Effective	Effective

hematomas and examination of the abdomen for hepatosplenomegaly. Petechiae, pinpoint hemorrhages from microvessels in the skin, are associated with platelet disorders or thrombocytopenia. Because pressure can exacerbate petechial bleeding, these lesions are commonly found on the legs or in other areas of increased hydrostatic pressure (e.g., on the buttocks in a bedridden patient). Purpura (confluent petechiae) is also common in thrombocytopenia. Ecchymoses, especially if spontaneous or raised (hematomas), and hemarthroses suggest defects in plasma coagulation factors as in hemophilia. Hepatomegaly suggests liver disease, and splenomegaly is associated with thrombocytopenia or with hematologic malignancy.

Laboratory Evaluation of Hemostasis

Basic screening for hemostatic integrity can be accomplished with a prothrombin time, partial thromboplastin time, platelet count, and bleeding time (Table 51–3). If all results from these tests are normal, a serious bleeding diathesis is unlikely. The most important screening tests of hemostasis after the blood count are the prothrombin time and activated partial thromboplastin time (see Table 51–3). If the platelet count is normal, the bleeding time is generally normal in plasma coagulation disorders except for von Willebrand's disease, in which the deficient factor affects platelet function, and therefore primary hemostasis is also impaired. The prothrombin time measures activity of Factors II, VII, IX, and X; the activated partial thromboplastin time measures Factors XII, XI, IX, VIII, and X. Both tests measure Factors V and II and fibrinogen. A history of delayed bleeding or rebleeding suggests Factor XIII deficiency, which requires specific testing of the stability of the fibrin clot (e.g., in 8M urea) for detection. Any abnormalities indicate that further investigation for particular defects should be made. Levels of individual coagulation factors, the presence of circulating anticoagulants, the nature of thrombocy-

topenia, abnormal platelet function, and signs of intravascular consumption of procoagulants can all be assessed.

PLATELET DISORDERS

Normal platelet function and a platelet count greater than $100,000/\mu l$ in the peripheral blood are needed for normal primary hemostasis (Fig. 51–1). The platelet count represents the net balance between platelet production rate and the rate of loss or peripheral destruction of platelets. Because the bone marrow has the capacity to increase platelet production 8- to 10-fold, and platelets survive 8 to 10 days in the circulation, the platelet count can be maintained under most circumstances, even if loss or destruction is increased. Young platelets are more metabolically active and more hemostatically effective than older ones. Platelet adhesion, procoagulant activity, and aggregation and release of vasoactive substances must also be normal for hemostatic effectiveness. Impairment of one or several of these functions leads to a bleeding tendency characterized by mucosal and skin bleeding, purpura, and prolonged oozing of blood after trauma or surgery.

Thrombocytopenia

Platelet counts below $100,000/\mu l$ portend an increased bleeding risk, which correlates roughly with the depression of the platelet count. Counts above $50,000/\mu l$ are rarely associated with spontaneous bleeding, whereas counts below $20,000/\mu l$ are frequently associated with spontaneous bleeding, especially if the patient is febrile or anemic. Bleeding is observed more often in a thrombocytopenic patient with a rapidly falling platelet count than in a patient with a low, stable count. The mechanisms for severe thrombocytopenia include (1) decreased or ineffective platelet production, (2) increased peripheral destruction, (3) splenic sequestration, and (4) intravascular dilution (Table 51–4).

Decreased platelet production occurs with systemic infection, nutritional defects (folate or vita-

TABLE 51–3. SCREENING TESTS FOR BLEEDING DISORDERS

TEST	MECHANISM TESTED	NORMAL	WHERE ABNORMAL
Prothrombin time (PT)	Extrinsic and common pathways	<12 sec	Defect in vitamin K–dependent factors, liver disease, DIC, oral anticoagulants
Activated partial thromboplastin time (APTT)	Intrinsic and common pathways	25–40 sec	Hemophilia, von Willebrand's disease, heparin therapy, DIC; deficient XII, IX, IX circulating anticoagulant
Thrombin time (TT)	Fibrinogen-fibrin conversion	10–15 sec	Third-stage anticoagulant; fibrin split products, DIC; severe hypofibrinogenemia
Bleeding time (BT)	Primary hemostasis, platelet function	3–7 min	Platelet dysfunction, von Willebrand's disease, thrombocytopenia

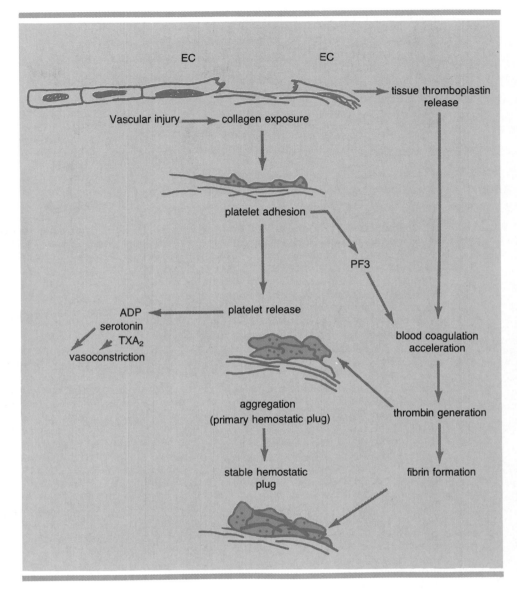

FIGURE 51–1. Hemostasis and platelet interactions with coagulation. Upon vascular injury, collagen fibrils underlying the endothelial cells (EC) are exposed when the endothelium is damaged. Adhesion of single platelets that flatten out and expose PF3 (procoagulant phospholipid) follows, then platelet release and primary aggregation to form a platelet plug. Release of ADP, serotonin, and thromboxane A_2 (TXA_2) induces vasoconstriction, while the PF3 accelerates blood coagulation, the formation of thrombin, and the generation of fibrin. Fibrin strands stabilize the hemostatic plug. Thrombin also promotes platelet aggregation and vasoconstriction.

min B_{12}), radiation, chemotherapy, or marrow replacement by fibrosis or tumor. Transient decreases in platelet production are common in viral infections and are the rule after radiation therapy to bone or after most types of cancer chemotherapy. Bone marrow megakaryocytes may appear decreased or immature. Numerous drugs can inhibit megakaryocytopoiesis, including alcohol, anticonvulsants, and thiazides. Marrow hypoplasia as in aplastic anemia, Fanconi's syndrome, or Wiskott-Aldrich syndrome also results in thrombocytopenia.

Increased platelet destruction is a common cause of thrombocytopenia and may be induced by commonly used drugs, including heparin, digitalis, quinidine, thiazides, imipramine, phenothiazines, sulfonamides, antibiotics (penicillins and cephalo-

TABLE 51–4. CAUSES OF THROMBOCYTOPENIA

Failure of platelet production	
Selective megakaryocyte depression	Drugs, viral infections
	Aplastic anemia, hematologic malignancy
General bone marrow failure	Myelophthisis
	Megaloblastic anemia
	Radiation
Increased platelet destruction	Drug-induced
	ITP
	Heparin
	DIC, TTP
Abnormal distribution	Hypersplenism
Dilutional	Massive transfusion of bank blood
	Extracorporeal circulation

ITP = Idiopathic thrombocytopenic purpura; TTP = thrombotic thrombocytopenic purpura; DIC = disseminated intravascular coagulation.

sporins), and gold salts. These agents usually produce thrombocytopenia by an immune mechanism in which a drug-antibody or drug–plasma protein complex adsorbs passively to the platelet surface ("innocent bystander") via the platelet Fc receptor, coating the platelets and resulting in their rapid removal from the circulation by the spleen. Other drugs may directly adsorb to the platelet surface, resulting in neoantigens that provoke antiplatelet antibody formation. Stopping all drugs, if possible, and substituting drugs of different chemical structure if discontinuation is not possible is the first step in the evaluation and treatment of drug-induced immune thrombocytopenia. Unfortunately, direct tests of drug involvement are difficult to perform and often are insensitive, so that clinical assessment after drug discontinuation or switching is the main instrument for detecting drug-related thrombocytopenias.

Idiopathic (or autoimmune) thrombocytopenic purpura (ITP) represents immune thrombocytopenic purpura occurring without toxic or drug exposure. A polyclonal antiplatelet antibody has been demonstrated by transfer experiments. Platelet-associated IgG (and complement) may be elevated, large platelets circulate in the blood, and megakaryocytes are increased in the bone marrow. The spleen is not enlarged. The platelet survival is short. Acute ITP is mainly a disease of childhood, having a sudden onset following acute viral infection and resolving spontaneously in 70 per cent of affected children within a few weeks. In adults, chronic ITP is more common, has an insidious onset, and affects women more often than men. Fewer than 10 per cent of cases resolve spontaneously. In some cases an autoimmune hemolytic anemia is also present (Evans' syndrome). Adult ITP occurs alone or in association with diseases of disturbed immunity such as systemic lupus erythematosus, lymphoproliferative disorders, or acquired immunodeficiency syndrome (AIDS). ITP can herald such diseases, appearing even years in advance of the full-blown disease. Pregnant women with ITP can deliver thrombocytopenic infants, as the antiplatelet antibody is usually an IgG_1 or IgG_3 and thus crosses the placenta. The infant's platelet count does not correlate with the mother's count, so that a mother with ITP by history and a normal platelet count can deliver a thrombocytopenic infant. ITP is common in patients who are human immunodeficiency virus (HIV)–positive and in those who have AIDS. Because of increased risk of infection in these immunosuppressed patients, steroid therapy is used with caution in mild cases or avoided. Intravenous gamma globulin or anti-D may be useful therapy.

Diagnosis of ITP is by exclusion. It is made in a patient with thrombocytopenia, increased megakaryocytes in the bone marrow, and increased platelet-associated IgG in the absence of drug exposure or toxic exposure. Aside from thrombocytopenia marked by large platelets, the blood count is otherwise normal. Platelet function may be entirely normal or may show diminished aggregation responses. Platelet survival is shortened, sometimes to hours compared with the normal survival of 8 to 10 days. Direct measurement of platelet survival can be made with ^{51}Cr- or ^{112}In-labeled autologous platelets. This test, however, is not routinely performed because of expense and technical difficulty.

Treatment of both drug-induced thrombocytopenia and ITP is similar. Any suspected drug is stopped, and essential drugs are switched to substitutes of different chemical composition. All aspirin-like drugs are avoided. If the thrombocytopenia is severe, with purpura on the mucous membranes or retina, corticosteroids (1 to 2 mg/kg/day prednisolone) are given. Platelet transfusion should be avoided except for treatment of intracerebral bleeding because of the extremely short survival of transfused platelets. Plasmapheresis is generally not effective because of the IgG nature of most of the antiplatelet antibodies, which are inefficiently removed by this technique. In acute ITP of childhood or drug-induced thrombocytopenia, steroids can be tapered within a few weeks as platelet counts rise. In chronic ITP steroids should be administered for 2 to 3 months before tapering the dose or moving to alternative therapy, in order to achieve the maximum number of remissions and responses. In 70 per cent of patients the platelet count rises toward normal within that period. Once a normal platelet count has been reached, the steroid dosage should be slowly tapered to avoid precipitating a relapse. The probable actions of steroids include inhibition of splenic reticuloendothelial phagocytic activity, decreased immune complex binding to platelets, decreased capillary fragility, and decreased immunoglobulin synthesis. When steroids are tapered following an initial increase in platelet count to the normal range, thrombocytopenia recurs in as many as 80 per cent of initially responding adult patients. Reinstitution of steroids may restore the platelet count, but many patients may require splenectomy for permanent remission. After splenectomy, 60 to 80 per cent of patients with ITP maintain an adequate platelet count, whereas the remainder require further therapy with steroids (at a lower dose) or with immunosuppressive drugs such as vincristine, cyclophosphamide, or azathioprine. For short-term therapy intravenous high-dose gamma globulin can transiently raise the platelet count in patients with refractory ITP (e.g., in preparation for emergency surgery), but adults do not respond as well to repeated high-dose IgG therapy. Children with chronic ITP who are refractory to other therapy have been successfully managed with repeated infusion of high-dose intravenous IgG. Anabolic steroids such as danazol have also been reported to raise platelet counts in refractory ITP.

Other Causes of Immune Thrombocytopenia. Antibody-mediated thrombocytopenia is seen in lymphoproliferative malignancies, systemic lupus erythematosus, HIV infection, infectious mononucleosis, cytomegalovirus infection, and, occasionally, solid tumors. *Post-transfusion purpura* is a rare syndrome that follows the administration of PL^{A1}-positive blood to patients who lack this common platelet antigen and who have developed anti-PL^{A1} antibodies after previous transfusion or pregnancy. An explosive thrombocytopenia develops 5 to 8 days after transfusion (anamnestic response) and may require plasmapheresis and exchange transfusion with PL^{A1}-negative blood. The thrombocytopenia may persist a few weeks but is self-limited. Other platelet antigen systems are occasionally involved. *Neonatal purpura* may be seen in infants of PL^{A1}-negative mothers or mothers with ITP. In *systemic anaphylactic reactions* thrombocytopenia may result from sequestration of platelets coated with circulating antigen-antibody complexes. Thrombocytopenia may also result from platelet coating with anti-i cold antibodies that arise following viral infections such as rubella or infectious mononucleosis.

Platelet Consumption Syndromes. These include disseminated intravascular coagulation (DIC), thrombotic thrombocytopenic purpura, and the hemolytic-uremic syndrome or can result from platelet damage during extracorporeal circulation. Intravascular activation of the coagulation mechanism is associated with sepsis, shock, exposure to toxins, malignant hypertension, pre-eclampsia, or malignancies and may present with either hemorrhage or thrombosis (see below). Thrombin-induced platelet aggregation or vascular damage that initiates platelet activation can cause thrombocytopenia. Vascular malformations such as cavernous hemangiomas (Kasabach-Merritt syndrome) sometimes produce localized DIC and platelet trapping, resulting in chronic thrombocytopenia.

Thrombotic thrombocytopenic purpura (TTP, Moschcowitz's disease) is an acute, relapsing disease affecting the microcirculation. There is a pentad of signs and symptoms, including thrombocytopenia, microangiopathic hemolytic anemia, neurologic abnormalities, renal dysfunction, and fever. Two thirds of affected persons are young women. There is often a history of preceding viral infection. The characteristic lesions are hyaline thrombi, consisting of platelet aggregates and fibrin, plugging small arterioles and capillaries. Endothelial proliferation may be seen, but vasculitis is not present. The blood smear shows schistocytes, increased reticulocytes, and normoblasts, reflecting the microangiopathic and hemolytic nature of the characteristic anemia; thrombocytopenia is usually severe, the serum lactic dehydrogenase and bilirubin are elevated, and the Coombs test is negative. Early in the disease DIC is absent, but it appears as renal failure ensues. Abnormal forms of von Willebrand factor have been observed (released by injured endothelium), and some patients possess a plasma factor that promotes platelet activation. TTP is frequently fatal. Treatment by splenectomy, steroids, or platelet-inhibitory drugs such as aspirin and dipyridamole has had variable results. Exchange transfusion, plasmapheresis, and plasma infusion have more recently been used with greater success and represent the current approach of choice.

Hemolytic-uremic syndrome, usually seen in children, involves a Coombs-negative microangiopathic hemolytic anemia, thrombocytopenia, diarrhea, and acute renal failure. Unlike TTP, this disorder does not affect the brain to produce neurologic signs. DIC may be present. The major pathologic lesion consists of hyaline thrombi in the renal microcirculation, probably representing a form of immune complex disease. Renal dialysis is the mainstay of therapy. The role of plasmapheresis has not been defined.

Extracorporeal Circulation. Extracorporeal circulation frequently produces thrombocytopenia as the result of platelet activation, with subsequent adherence of platelets to the surface of the membrane oxygenator, dialyzer membrane, or other extracorporeal device. Platelet dysfunction induced by such contact may contribute to postoperative hemorrhage, over and above the contribution of thrombocytopenia.

Thrombocytopenia Produced by Platelet Sequestration. Normally the spleen contains about one third of the circulating pool of platelets. Increased splenic sequestration occurs with splenomegaly; very large spleens may sequester up to 90 per cent of the circulating platelets, resulting in a moderate thrombocytopenia of 50,000 to 100,000/mm.^{3} Platelet lifespan, however, is not shortened in hypersplenism, and severe hemorrhage is unusual.

Dilutional thrombocytopenia can follow massive transfusion of whole blood or plasma and lasts for several days. Platelet transfusions may be needed if the patient's residual platelets are dysfunctional or if bone marrow function is depressed and there is threatened or actual hemorrhage; the condition is transient in patients with normal marrow function.

Thrombocytosis

Elevation of the platelet count above 500,000/μl may be physiologic, secondary to bleeding, trauma, or infection, or can result from a primary bone marrow disease (thrombocythemia or other myeloproliferative disease). Transitory thrombocytosis follows stress or exercise and represents mobilization of platelets from the spleen or lung under the influence of epinephrine (Table 51–5).

Secondary, or reactive, *thrombocytosis* results from increased platelet production in response to hemorrhage, hemolysis, infection (such as tuber-

TABLE 51–5. CAUSES OF THROMBOCYTOSIS

Acute stress (release of splenic pool)
Secondary to inflammatory disease or infection: tuberculosis, rheumatoid arthritis, chronic inflammatory bowel disease, malignancy
Postsplenectomy
Myeloproliferative disease (primary thrombocytosis)

culosis), inflammatory disease, or malignancy. The platelets are normal in function and the platelet count may reach $10^6/\mu l$. A similar secondary thrombocytosis follows splenectomy and lasts for several weeks. In general, secondary thrombocytosis does not lead to hemorrhagic or thrombotic complications. Therapy to lower the platelet count or inhibit platelet function is not necessary. Treatment of the underlying disease usually results in a return of the platelet count to normal levels.

Primary thrombocytosis, or essential thrombocythemia, represents increased platelet production independent of normal regulatory control, except that the platelet count can increase further after hemorrhage. Platelet counts may exceed 1 to 2 × $10^6/\mu l$. The platelets are large and bizarre in appearance, may appear in clumps on the blood smear, and are dysfunctional. The number of epinephrine receptors is decreased, and platelet aggregation responses to epinephrine are abnormal. The clinical picture of essential thrombocythemia is discussed in Chapter 50.

Qualitative Platelet Disorders

Inherited defects in platelet function are rare and produce mucosal bleeding when severe. Acquired defects in platelet function are common and are chiefly associated with drug ingestion—particularly of aspirin—or with underlying hematologic disease. They become clinically important if accompanied by another hemostatic defect, such as thrombocytopenia, or during therapy with anticoagulants. Acquired platelet function defects may also cause excessive bleeding at surgery. Evaluation of platelet disorders requires specialized testing (Table 51–6).

Congenital platelet disorders include *thrombasthenia* (Glanzmann's syndrome), characterized by a prolonged bleeding time, absent platelet aggregation despite normal platelet adhesion to collagen, and episodes of mucosal bleeding. The disorder is transmitted by an autosomal recessive gene. Thrombasthenic platelets lack two surface glycoproteins (IIb and IIIa) necessary for fibrinogen binding to the platelet membrane and for platelet aggregation. Bleeding may be life-threatening. The only therapy is transfusion of normal platelets. *Platelet release defects* resulting in impaired platelet aggregation constitute several syndromes. First, a mild bleeding tendency results from an "aspirin-like" defect in which all platelet structures are normal, but normal activation does not take place when platelets are exposed to the usual agonists. The causes of this syndrome include defective phospholipase activation or a deficiency in enzymes of the prostaglandin pathway, such as cyclooxygenase or thromboxane synthase. Several types of *storage pool deficiency* present with impaired platelet release reactions, associated with poor platelet aggregation, a long bleeding time, and mucosal bleeding. The storage pool deficiencies are varied: they involve defects in platelet granule storage of ADP or serotonin or abnormalities in platelet granule structure. In the *Hermansky-Pudlak syndrome*, platelet granule abnormalities are associated with albinism. An acquired storage pool defect occurs after exposure of blood to extracorporeal circulation and, rarely, in myeloproliferative disease. Because ADP release is necessary for normal platelet function, defective storage or release results in a hemorrhagic tendency. Bleeding episodes in affected patients are usually limited to trauma, surgery, or childbirth. Aspirin and nonsteroidal aspirin-like drugs should be avoided. As in thrombasthenia, platelet transfusion provides the only therapy.

Platelet adhesion is abnormal in two inherited bleeding disorders: von Willebrand's disease and the Bernard-Soulier syndrome. *Von Willebrand's disease* is a common bleeding disorder that affects both sexes and is transmitted as an autosomal recessive trait. In this condition, platelets are normal in structure and number but fail to adhere to the vascular subendothelium because of the lack of a

TABLE 51–6. LABORATORY EVALUATION OF PLATELET DISORDERS: COMPLETE BLOOD COUNT (CBC), PLATELET COUNT, AND PERIPHERAL SMEAR EXAMINATION

Low Platelet Count

1. Bone marrow examination	Increased megas:	ITP, immune purpura
	Decreased megas:	Drug, aplasia, infection
2. Screen for DIC		Sepsis, malignancy
3. Platelet-associated IgG		
4. Serum folate and vitamin B_{12}		

Normal Platelet Count

1. Bleeding time	if prolonged:	Thrombasthenia, uremia, drug ingestion (aspirin)
2. Platelet aggregation	if depressed:	Aspirin, other drugs, uremia, DIC
3. Platelet agglutination with ristocetin	if depressed:	von Willebrand's disease
4. Factor VIII: AHF and Factor VIII: VWF	if depressed:	von Willebrand's disease
5. Platelet procoagulant activity	if decreased:	Thrombocytopathy, uremia

High Platelet Count

1. Bone marrow examination		Myeloproliferative disease, malignancy
2. Platelet aggregation	if absent to epi:	Myeloproliferative disease
3. Peripheral smear	if normal-sized platelets:	Secondary thrombocytosis
	if giant platelets:	Primary thrombocytosis is likely

AHF = Antihemophilic factor; VWF = von Willebrand's factor.

plasma factor essential for platelet interaction with collagen in the vessel wall, the von Willebrand factor (VWF). The clinical manifestations include mucosal bleeding, menorrhagia, and bruising. Both laboratory and clinical abnormalities are corrected by administration of exogenous VWF. Further discussion of von Willebrand's disease follows the discussion of hemophilia A.

In *Bernard-Soulier syndrome,* a very rare autosomal recessive disease, giant platelets are observed on the blood smear, the bleeding time is prolonged, and mucosal hemorrhage is common. A platelet membrane glycoprotein (Ib) that mediates VWF binding is absent. Plasma VWF is normal, but VWF cannot correct defective platelet adhesion in the absence of the platelet receptor. Treatment is limited to platelet transfusion.

The gray platelet syndrome consists of a lack of platelet alpha granules containing VWF, fibronectin, and thrombospondin, the proteins necessary for normal platelet adhesion and aggregation. Their deficiency leads to a mild bleeding tendency, correctable by platelet transfusion.

Thrombocytopathy or impaired expression of platelet procoagulant activity, that is, the acceleration of thrombin formation by the surface of activated platelets, produces a mild bleeding tendency mainly following trauma or surgery.

Acquired Disorders of Platelet Function

Aspirin and other NSAIDs inhibit platelet cyclooxygenase, the key enzyme in transformation of platelet arachidonic acid to products that induce platelet aggregation, the cyclic endoperoxides and thromboxane A_2. These substances mediate the normal platelet release reaction initiated by platelet agonists such as ADP, epinephrine, or collagen. After contact with aspirin or similar drugs, platelets exhibit impaired aggregation and release, the bleeding time is moderately prolonged, and the number of microaggregates of platelets detectable in the blood is diminished. The duration of these platelet effects of the NSAIDs varies widely. Only aspirin, by virtue of covalent acetylation of cyclooxygenase at its active site, has a prolonged effect on platelet function (because platelets do not synthesize enzymes as they circulate, one dose of aspirin inhibits platelet function for up to a week); other NSAIDs have antiplatelet effects lasting less than 24 hours. Thrombin-induced platelet activation is unaffected by aspirin or similar drugs, accounting for the limited hemorrhagic tendency produced by these agents. However, when a second defect of hemostasis exists, such as hemophilia, thrombocytopenia, or anticoagulant therapy, ingestion of aspirin may lead to serious bleeding.

Acquired defects in platelet function can accompany several types of systemic diseases. *Uremia* produces a hemorrhagic tendency with epistaxes, ecchymosis, and gastrointestinal bleeding related to platelet dysfunction and often to thrombocytopenia. Platelet aggregation and platelet procoagulant activity are both abnormal and the bleeding time is prolonged. Accumulation of toxic metabolites in the plasma may be partly responsible for these dysfunctions, as may be an inadequate synthesis of thromboxane. Hemodialysis tends to improve platelet function. Infusion of cryoprecipitate or des-amino des-arginine vasopressin (DDAVP) or administration of estrogens has been reported to correct the hemostatic abnormalities. *Paraproteinemias* such as *multiple myeloma* can induce bleeding by coating the platelet surface with monoclonal immunoglobulin, which prevents platelet-platelet interaction, and by interfering with fibrin polymerization. In *leukemias* and *myeloproliferative syndromes,* defects in platelet function are common. In DIC, the presence of fibrin split products in the circulating blood also can impair platelet function (Table 51–6).

Laboratory findings distinguish *vascular purpuras* from purpuras directly involving the components of the hemostatic mechanism. The typical findings in vascular purpura include an abnormal tourniquet test (positive Rumpel-Leede test), indicating increased capillary fragility, and prolonged bleeding time in the presence of a normal platelet count, normal platelet function, and normal coagulation screen. Congenital vascular purpura is found in inherited diseases of connective tissue. Acquired vascular purpura can occur in paraproteinemias, scurvy, Cushing's disease, or corticosteroid treatment, in association with other drugs, or in old age. In children, *Henoch-Schönlein purpura* is an allergic-type vasculitis manifested by abdominal pain, hematuria and glomerulonephritis, hemorrhagic urticaria, and arthralgias.

Bleeding in *hereditary hemorrhagic telangiectasia* (Osler-Weber-Rendu disease) results from fragile, easily bleeding mucosal telangiectases. This disorder is inherited as an autosomal dominant trait in which the vascular abnormalities continue to form throughout life, becoming more prominent after puberty. All mucosal surfaces may be involved, with bleeding commonly originating from the nose and from the respiratory, gastrointestinal, and genitourinary tracts. Pulmonary arteriovenous fistulas are common (15 per cent). Telangiectases may or may not be present on the skin. The mainstays of treatment are cauterization of accessible lesions, vigorous iron replacement therapy to correct continual blood loss, and efforts at maintaining local hemostasis.

REFERENCES

Colman RW, Hirsh J, Marder VJ, et al (eds): Hemostasis and Thrombosis: Basic Principles and Clinical Practice. 2nd ed. Philadelphia, JB Lippincott Co, 1987.

Comp PC, Esmon CT: Regulatory mechanisms in hemostasis: Natural anticoagulants. *In* Hoffman R, Benz EJ Jr, Shattil SJ, Furie B, Cohen HJ (eds): Hematology: Basic Principles and Practice. New York, Churchill Livingstone, 1991, pp 1243–1251.

Furie B, Furie BC: The molecular basis of blood coagulation. Cell 53:505, 1988.

52 COAGULATION DISORDERS

THE BLOOD CLOTTING MECHANISM

Blood clotting involves the generation of a powerful serine protease, thrombin, which cleaves the soluble plasma protein fibrinogen so that an insoluble meshwork of fibrin strands develops, enmeshing red cells and platelets to form a stable clot (Table 52–1). This process is triggered by injury to the blood vessels and involves the rapid, highly controlled interaction of more than 20 different proteins to amplify initial activation of a few molecules to an appropriately sized, fully developed clot (see Fig. 51–1). Both the injured vessel wall and platelet aggregates provide specialized surfaces that localize and catalyze the coagulation reactions.

Blood coagulation proteins circulate as inactive zymogens in amounts far greater than are required for blood clotting. Two activation pathways are recognized: an intrinsic pathway, initiated by activation of plasma contact factors, and an extrinsic pathway, initiated by exposure of blood to tissue factor, a lipoprotein activity released from injured tissues (Fig. 52–1). These pathways converge in

the activation of Factor X at the platelet surface. Most of the blood coagulation proteins are serine proteases that show a high degree of homology (Factors II, VII, IX, and X); others are cofactors without enzyme activity (Factors V and VIII).

The liver is the site of synthesis for most of the coagulation proteins. Factors II, VII, IX, and X and proteins C and S require vitamin K for their synthesis. In the absence of vitamin K, abnormal molecules lacking the gamma-carboxyglutamate binding sites for Ca^{2+} binding are produced. These abnormal molecules do not function in clotting. Fibrinogen, Factor V, and the protease inhibitors are also produced in the liver, and their levels may be depressed in liver disease. Vitamin K is not required for their synthesis or function. Factor VIII is probably synthesized in the liver, but the precise location of its production is not known. Von Willebrand factor and tissue plasminogen activator are produced in the vascular endothelium. While von Willebrand factor and Factor VIII circulate together as a macromolecular complex, they are produced in different sites, are regulated by different genes, and are completely different in structure and function.

The *intrinsic pathway of coagulation* begins by activation of Factor XII upon the altered or injured vascular surface or another negatively charged surface such as glass. Cofactors or promoters of Factor XII activation include prekallikrein, high molecular weight kininogen (HMWK), and Factor XI. A surface-localized complex is formed which optimally activates Factor XII. Factor XIIa then converts complex-bound Factor XI to its active form, XIa, and prekallikrein to its active form, kallikrein, which then cleaves HMWK to form bradykinin. In turn, Factor XIa activates Factor IX but may also activate Factor VII (in the extrinsic coagulation pathway) as well as cleaving plasminogen to form plasmin, thus initiating fibrinolysis as well as coagulation.

Factor XIa requires calcium ions (Ca^{2+}) to activate Factor IX, which binds to Factor VIII (antihemophilic factor, AHF). In the presence of Ca^{2+} and phospholipid, Factor IXa activates Factor X to Xa. This activation usually takes place at the plasma membrane of stimulated platelets but also may occur on the vascular endothelium.

In the *extrinsic pathway*, the release of tissue factor from injured tissues directly activates Factor VII, which then activates Factor X to Xa in the presence of Ca^{2+}. In addition, the complex tissue

TABLE 52–1. BLOOD COAGULATION FACTORS

GROUP	HALF-LIFE (hr)	COMMENTS
Contact Factors		
XII (Hageman)	50	Deficiency does not produce bleeding tendency
XI	60	
Prekallikrein		Does not require Ca^{2+} to act
High molecular weight kininogen		Does not require Vitamin K
		Stable, well preserved in plasma
Prothrombin Group		
II (prothrombin)	72	All vitamin K–dependent
VII	3–5	Requires Ca^{2+} for activity
IX (Christmas factor)	24	Not consumed in serum (except prothrombin)
X	40	
Protein C		Stable
Protein S		
Fibrinogen Group		
I (fibrinogen)	72–96	All interact with thrombin
V	15–30	Activity is lost on clotting
VIII	3–6	Increase in inflammation, pregnancy, birth control pill
XIII	>100	
		V, VIII unstable in stored plasma

factor–Factor VIII–Ca²⁺ can activate Factor IX. Tissue factor is present in activated endothelium and monocytes as well as in brain, vascular adventitia, skin, and mucosa.

Assembly of the plasma prothrombinase complex on the surface of activated platelets in the presence of Factor V, another cofactor, enhances the efficiency of prothrombin (Factor II) activation to thrombin on the platelet surface. Thrombin cleaves fibrinogen, a large, asymmetric, soluble protein (MW 340,000) consisting of three pairs of polypeptide chains: Aα, Bβ, and γ. Thrombin first removes small peptides from the Aα chain of fibrinogen to form Fibrin I, which polymerizes end to end; further thrombin cleavage of small peptides from the Bβ chain leads to formation of Fibrin II molecules, which polymerize side to side and are then cross-linked via the plasma glutaminase (Factor XIII) to form an insoluble fibrin clot.

Thrombin has multiple critical actions during coagulation, in addition to the cleavage of fibrinogen to fibrin. It activates platelets, exposing their procoagulant activity (e.g., binding sites for the prothrombinase complex) and inducing the release of platelet-aggregating substances such as thromboxane, Ca²⁺, ADP, von Willebrand factor, fibronectin, and thrombospondin. Thrombin cleaves Factors VIII and Va, augmenting clotting, and Factor XIII, promoting fibrin stabilization. Thrombin acts on the endothelium by binding to the surface protein thrombomodulin to activate protein C, a potent inactivator of Factors Va and VIIIa, that stimulates fibrinolysis. Thrombin also causes endothelial cell contraction. Conversely, endothelium can bind and inactivate thrombin, and in some cases can generate the vasodilatory substance prostacyclin in response to thrombin. Thus, thrombin activation contributes to the limitation as well as the initiation of clotting.

The final stage of the coagulation process is fibrinolysis, or clot resolution (Fig. 52–2). Fibrinolysis is initiated during clotting by the action of thrombin. When complexed to thrombomodulin in the endothelium, thrombin activates protein C and initiates release of plasminogen activators from the blood vessel wall. Protein C, together with its cofactor protein S, inactivates Factors Va and VIIIa. Plasminogen, a circulating proenzyme, is cleaved to the active protease, plasmin, by plasminogen activators. Plasmin then digests fibrin. The activity of tissue plasminogen activators is enhanced by their binding to fibrin, so that plasmin generation is localized to the clot. In addition, the plasma protease inhibitors α_1-antitrypsin, α_2-plasmin inhibitor, and α_2-macroglobulin rapidly inactivate any circulating serine proteases including thrombin and plasmin. Antithrombin III binds all the serine protease procoagulant proteins (Factor Xa as well as thrombin); its activity is enhanced by heparin or heparin-like substances. Complexes of antithrombin III and protease are rapidly cleared by the liver and the reticuloendothelial system.

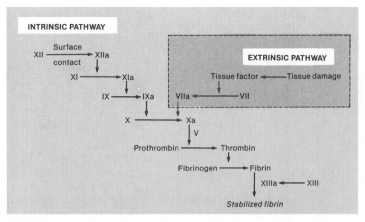

FIGURE 52–1. Simplified pathways of blood coagulation. (The "a" denotes the activated form of the circulating inactive zymogen.)

INHERITED DISORDERS OF BLOOD COAGULATION

Hemophilia A

Classic hemophilia is the most common severe, inherited coagulation disorder. The gene for Factor VIII has recently been cloned and sequenced. It is an unusually large gene occupying 0.1 per cent of the length of the X chromosome. In 70 per cent of cases of hemophilia A, a positive family history of affected males is obtained; the gene appears to have a high rate of spontaneous mutation, accounting for the remaining 30 per cent of cases. Because of the random inactivation of one X chromosome in females, the carrier mother of a hemophiliac has a 50 per cent (on the average) level of Factor VIII. Identification of the carrier state can frequently be made. Prenatal diagnosis can now be carried out in pregnancies at risk, and development of restriction polymorphism techniques for identifying hemophilic fetuses is now possible since the Factor VIII gene has been cloned. Laboratory results in hemophilia A show a normal PT, markedly prolonged APTT corrected by mixing with normal plasma, and a normal bleeding time. Specific assay for Factor VIII shows a deficient level of functional activity. Hemophilia A can rep-

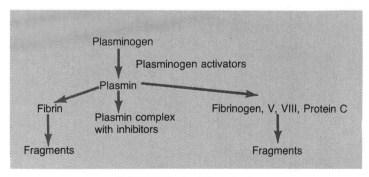

FIGURE 52–2. Fibrinolysis.

resent either a quantitative deficiency or a dysfunctional molecule, so that both functional and immunologic assays need to be combined. About half of affected patients have severe hemophilia with Factor VIII activity less than 1 per cent of normal; they have spontaneous and trauma-induced hemorrhage from infancy. Levels above 5 per cent are associated with a mild clinical course except with trauma or surgery, when supportive therapy is necessary. As the hemophilic child becomes physically active, bleeding into muscles and joints is common, and painful deformities follow. Bleeding is frequently spontaneous or may be related to stress or other illness. Any organ can be affected, and pressure on vital structures from deep hemorrhages can be life-threatening.

Replacement therapy with concentrates of Factor VIII to raise the plasma Factor VIII to hemostatic levels has become a mainstay of treatment. In home therapy programs, the hemophilic patient or his parent administers Factor VIII concentrate according to a preset schedule based on bleeding severity. This approach prevents delay in treatment following onset of bleeding and can reduce morbidity, cost of therapy, and emotional stress. Reconstructive joint surgery and dental care can also be undertaken with such replacement coverage. A high incidence of hepatitis, however, has previously accompanied extensive use of commercial Factor VIII concentrates prepared from pools of thousands of units of donor plasma. Moreover, transmission of acquired immunodeficiency syndrome (AIDS) to hemophilic patients receiving replacement therapy with Factor VIII concentrates (presumably carrying human immunodeficiency virus [HIV]) became common in the early 1980s. Improved testing for HIV in donor blood and the availability of heat-inactivated and recombinant Factor VIII preparations have now greatly reduced or eliminated this danger.

Factor VIII has a short half-life (8 to 12 hours); infusion schedules are calculated according to the patient's plasma volume (40 ml/kg), the severity of the bleeding episode, and the percentage of normal Factor VIII level desired to control each type of bleeding. About 15 to 20 per cent of patients develop inhibitors to transfused Factor VIII and have accelerated destruction and decreased efficacy of the replacement therapy. Such inhibitory activity must also be taken into account when calculating Factor VIII replacement needs.

For milder hemophiliacs or during episodes of less severe hemorrhage, cryoprecipitate may suffice. Epsilon-aminocaproic acid, a potent inhibitor of fibrinolysis, diminishes bleeding after dental procedures. In addition to replacement of Factor VIII, local therapy such as joint immobilization and ice packs is helpful. For relief of pain, hemophiliacs should avoid aspirin and nonsteroidal anti-inflammatory drugs, which impair platelet function and worsen bleeding. Acetaminophen, codeine, or choline-magnesium salicylate should be used, as these analgesics do not affect platelets and thus preserve primary hemostasis.

The long-term complications of hemophilia A include (1) hemorrhage, (2) progressive arthropathy, (3) development of inhibitor to Factor VIII, (4) hepatitis, (5) hypertension, and (6) AIDS. Although in recent years the lifespan of hemophiliacs has markedly increased and morbidity lessened, hemorrhage still remains the major cause of death.

Von Willebrand's Disease (VWD)

This is one of the most common inherited bleeding disorders. It affects both sexes and is transmitted as an autosomal codominant or recessive trait. A double defect is observed in this disorder: abnormal platelet adhesion (producing a prolonged bleeding time) in combination with low Factor VIII procoagulant activity. Normal platelet adhesion to vascular subendothelium requires the presence of the plasma glycoprotein, von Willebrand factor (VWF). VWF circulates in the form of high molecular weight multimers (MW $> 2 \times 10^6$) complexed with antihemophilic factor (Factor VIII:AHF), which is stabilized thereby. In VWD the level of VWF is decreased, absent, or present in a functionally abnormal form. The level of antihemophilic factor may be mildly to severely depressed in VWD. This finding is reflected in the prolonged APTT (partial thromboplastin time) in addition to the prolonged bleeding time (Table 52–2).

The clinical manifestations of VWD vary widely in the same patient at different times, in different affected members of the same family, and in different families. Mucosal bleeding, ecchymoses, epistaxis, gastrointestinal bleeding, and menorrhagia are common symptoms; severely affected persons may also have hemarthroses and behave like hemophiliacs, with the added complication of defective primary hemostasis. There are numerous subtypes of von Willebrand's disease. In 75 per cent of patients the bleeding time and APTT are prolonged, with an absolute decrease in the levels of both VWF and Factor VIII:AHF as measured by functional and immunologic tests (type I). Platelet agglutination to ristocetin is impaired but is restored by VWF or normal plasma. Other platelet aggregation responses are normal. All sizes of VWF multimers in plasma are decreased. Infusion of normal plasma (or hemophilic plasma) to type I VWD patients results in a prolonged rise in VWF levels that is greater and longer-lasting than would be expected from the amount of VWF infused or its half-life. Several variant types of VWD occur in which VWF is only slightly depressed by immunoassay despite a long bleeding time (type IIA) or in which increased agglutination of platelets by ristocetin is observed and the large multimeric forms of plasma VWF are absent (type IIB).

Treatment of von Willebrand's disease relies upon cryoprecipitate infusion for severe bleeding episodes and desmopressin for milder disease. The prolonged bleeding time and hemorrhagic diathesis are corrected by transfusion of normal plasma or cryoprecipitate (which is rich in VWF). In mild

TABLE 52–2. COMPARISON OF HEMOPHILIA A, HEMOPHILIA B, AND VON WILLEBRAND'S DISEASE

	HEMOPHILIA A	HEMOPHILIA B	VON WILLEBRAND'S DISEASE
Inheritance	X-linked	X-linked	Autosomal dominant or recessive
Factor deficiency	VIII (coagulant) (= VIII:AHF)	IX	von Willebrand's factor and VIII:AHF
Bleeding sites	Muscle, joints, surgical	Muscle, joints, surgical	Mucous membranes, skin, surgical
Prothrombin time (PT)	Normal	Normal	Normal
Partial thromboplastin time (APTT)	Prolonged	Prolonged	Prolonged or normal
Bleeding time	Normal	Normal	Prolonged
Factor VIII coagulant activity	Low	Normal	Low
Factor VIII antigen (VIII:VWF)	Normal	Normal	Low
Factor IX	Normal	Low	Normal
Platelet aggregation	Normal	Normal	Normal
Ristocetin-induced platelet agglutination	Normal	Normal	Impaired

VWD, infusion of desmopressin (DDAVP, desamino, des-arginine vasopressin) can raise VWF levels and correct the bleeding tendency. Desmopressin can be used before dental or other surgery in many cases. However, in type IIB VWD, desmopressin is contraindicated because it can induce thrombocytopenia. Most commercial Factor VIII concentrates contain low levels of VWF and are not effective therapy in VWD. In women with severe VWD, menorrhagia can be managed by hormonal suppression. The bleeding tendency may improve during pregnancy when the levels of VWF and antihemophilic factor rise. Aspirin and similar drugs should be completely avoided by patients with VWD.

INHERITED DISORDERS OF OTHER COAGULATION FACTORS

Contact Factor Defects

Contact factor defects are rare disorders that produce prolongation of the APTT or clotting time without any clinical bleeding tendency, except for Factor XI deficiency. *Factor XII (Hageman factor) deficiency* is suspected when the clotting time or APTT is prolonged in an asymptomatic patient. This diagnosis is confirmed by mixing experiments, in which the patient's plasma is mixed with plasma from patients with known specific factor deficiencies to determine the type of defect (e.g., in Factor XII deficiency there is no correction of APTT upon mixing with known Factor XII deficient plasma, but the APTT becomes normal after mixing 1:1 with known Factor XI–deficient plasma). *Prekallikrein deficiency (Fletcher trait)* and *high molecular weight kininogen deficiency (Fitzgerald trait)* are also asymptomatic, rare conditions. A bleeding tendency, however, does exist in persons with *Factor XI (PTA) deficiency* when they undergo trauma, dental extraction, or surgery. This autosomal recessive trait is most common in persons of Jewish or Japanese origin. The APTT is prolonged, and the prothrombin time (PT)

is normal. The bleeding tendency does not correlate well with the calculated deficiency of Factor XI, and some patients with low values have no bleeding problems. The half-life of Factor XI is about 3 days, so that treatment of bleeding or prophylaxis for surgery consists of daily infusion of fresh frozen plasma.

Defects in Vitamin K–Dependent Coagulation Factors

Defects of the vitamin K–dependent coagulation factors cause severe bleeding tendencies. The only common example is *Factor IX deficiency (hemophilia B, or Christmas disease)*, an X-linked recessive trait that is clinically similar to hemophilia A, producing muscle, joint, gastrointestinal, and central nervous system bleeding. A quantitative severe deficiency of Factor IX is the usual finding, but some families possess a functionally abnormal Factor IX molecule present in the blood in normal levels when measured by antigenic assay. Diagnosis of hemophilia B is suspected when a normal PT but prolonged APTT is observed and the APTT is corrected by normal serum but not by barium-adsorbed plasma ($BaSO_4$ adsorbs the vitamin K–dependent factors from plasma). The diagnosis is confirmed by specific factor assay. Fresh frozen plasma or prothrombin complex concentrates containing Factor IX correct the deficiency and are used to treat bleeding. The plasma half-life of 20 hours permits twice-daily infusion. Factor IX concentrates are contaminated with activated coagulation factors. The latter can cause thromboembolism, so that use of prothrombin complex concentrates should be reserved for severe hemorrhage. Specific antibodies to transfused Factor IX develop in 10 to 15 per cent of patients and may complicate management, similar to the situation with acquired Factor VIII inhibitors in hemophilia A.

Factor VII deficiency is a rare autosomal recessive defect, leading to a lifelong history of bleeding in homozygotes: mucous membrane and gastrointestinal bleeding, epistaxes, hemarthroses, and menorrhagia are observed. Individual patients show varied manifestations of bleeding over time. The PT is prolonged with a normal APTT. Treatment is with plasma or prothrombin complex concentrates; the half-life of Factor VII is short (2 to 6 hours), requiring frequent administration.

Factor X deficiency is another rare autosomal recessive trait that produces bleeding. Two types exist, a quantitative decrease in the factor and a dysfunctional molecule. Epistaxis, gastrointestinal bleeding, and occasionally joint or muscle hemorrhage result. Postpartum bleeding and menorrhagia may be severe in affected women. Both the PT and the APTT are prolonged; a specific factor assay establishes the diagnosis. Treatment is with fresh frozen plasma.

Afibrinogenemia or *congenital dysfibrinogenemia* represents a variety of disorders in which the plasma fibrinogen level is very low or abnormal fibrinogens are produced. The latter may lead to either hemorrhage or thrombosis. Both the PT and the APTT are abnormal in these disorders. More than 80 different types of dysfibrinogenemia have been described, varying widely in clinical effects. Current replacement therapy consists of cryoprecipitate, which is rich in fibrinogen, because formerly available fibrinogen concentrates carried a very high risk of transmitting hepatitis. The half-life of fibrinogen is 4 days, so that infusion to reach a normal plasma level of 150 mg/dl can be readily achieved.

Factor XIII deficiency is a rare, autosomal recessive trait in which only the homozygote shows a bleeding tendency, manifested by delayed bleeding after trauma and impaired wound healing. Affected persons usually have less than 1 per cent of the normal Factor XIII level; heterozygotes are asymptomatic. Absence of the fibrin-stabilizing factor also impairs cross-linking of fibronectin, the cell surface protein, and fibrin, which may contribute to poor wound healing. Because the initial formation of fibrin is unimpaired, PT, APTT, and thrombin time are normal. Dissolution of the patient's fibrin clot in 8M urea indicates a Factor XIII level of less than 1 per cent. Treatment is with fresh frozen plasma or cryoprecipitate to reach a Factor XIII level of 10 per cent. The prolonged half-life of the factor (21 days) makes infrequent replacement infusions (every 3 weeks) effective.

ACQUIRED DISORDERS OF BLOOD COAGULATION

Acquired coagulation abnormalities can result from several causes, including deficient production or increased consumption of clotting factors, production of functionally abnormal molecules, selective inhibition of factors by acquired anticoagulants, and selective inhibition or adsorption of factors, resulting in functional deficiency. The first three mechanisms are common complications of systemic disease; the last two are rare. For example, the adsorption of Factor X by vascular amyloid, producing a severe bleeding diathesis, has been reported in only a few cases.

Acquired Vitamin K Deficiency

Because vitamin K is not stored in the body but is obtained from green vegetables in the diet and is a fat-soluble vitamin, a deficiency of vitamin K occurs in malabsorption or bile-salt deficiency, when dietary intake is poor, and when the gastrointestinal tract is sterilized by antibiotic therapy. Common clinical states producing vitamin K deficiency include the following: (1) in newborn infants, especially premature infants, liver immaturity and lack of synthesis of vitamin K by intestinal bacteria until the gut is colonized; (2) malabsorption, including biliary tract disease; (3) prolonged parenteral feeding in combination with antibiotic therapy, especially bowel sterilization; and (4) ingestion of oral anticoagulants. Vitamin K absorption depends upon fat absorption, and any condition impairing that process (e.g., celiac disease, oral neomycin, cholestyramine, biliary obstruction, regional enteritis) can result in vitamin K deficiency. Mucosal or gastrointestinal bleeding may develop. Oral administration of vitamin K_1 (2 to 10 mg/day) can correct the vitamin deficiency, and 10 to 25 mg IM can correct an overt bleeding tendency.

Coumarin anticoagulants competitively inhibit the effects of vitamin K on gamma carboxylation of the vitamin K–dependent coagulation proteins and thus produce anticoagulation, which is monitored by the PT. The therapeutic goal is to maintain a PT 1.3 to 1.5 times greater than a normal control, achieved by administering 2.5 to 10 mg of warfarin (Coumadin) once daily. Because many drugs affect the action of coumarins, either directly enhancing or depressing their effect or altering their metabolic disposition, it is essential to monitor coumarin effects carefully during treatment with multiple drugs. Coumarin drugs possess a narrow toxic/therapeutic ratio. Administration of vitamin K can reverse the effects of warfarin (Coumadin) anticoagulation within hours, and administration of fresh frozen plasma (or prothrombin concentrates) reverses anticoagulant effects even more rapidly. In emergency circumstances, such as with brain hemorrhage, severe gastrointestinal bleeding, or need for immediate surgery, anticoagulation can be reversed within minutes by Factor IX concentrates or prothrombin complex.

Liver Disease

In addition to the vitamin K–dependent coagulation factors, the liver synthesizes Factor V, fibrinogen, plasminogen, and Factors XII and XI. Patients with advanced liver disease commonly suffer bleeding tendencies. If these mainly involve deficiencies of vitamin K–dependent clotting factors, they are corrected by administering parenteral vitamin K. Bleeding in severe liver disease also results from dysfibrinogenemias, localized disseminated intravascular coagulation (DIC), lack of Factor V, increased fibrinolysis, and thrombocytopenia. Treatment of these deficiencies employs fresh frozen plasma.

Renal Disease

Uremia is associated with mucous membrane, gastrointestinal, and skin bleeding. The cause of the bleeding tendency is complex. Thrombocytopenia may be present as part of depressed bone marrow function or may arise secondary to immunosuppressive drugs. Platelet dysfunction is typical and represents thrombocytopathy (impaired platelet procoagulant activity) with depressed platelet adhesion and aggregation, producing a prolonged bleeding time. Conjugated estrogens may correct the bleeding time in patients with renal disease. In the nephrotic syndrome, urinary loss of plasma proteins may result in Factor IX deficiency. In patients undergoing hemodialysis, inaccurate reversal of heparinization at completion of dialysis may also contribute to uremic bleeding.

Disseminated Intravascular Coagulation

DIC represents the consumption of coagulation factors resulting from intravascular activation of the coagulation process with secondary activation of fibrinolysis. Depending upon the rates of these two processes, the compensatory synthesis of procoagulants, and the nature of the underlying disease, DIC may cause either thrombosis or hemorrhage. DIC is always secondary to another disease process and often resolves when the primary disease is controlled. Intravascular coagulation is initiated by release of procoagulant substances into the blood (amniotic fluid embolism, snakebite, abruptio placentae, malignancy, crush injury), by contact of blood with an abnormal surface (infections, burns, extracorporeal circulation, grafts), or by generation of procoagulants in the blood (promyelocytic leukemia, hemolytic transfusion reactions). The formation of microthrombi within the circulation secondarily activates fibrinolysis, as does the presence of injured endothelium. Circulating plasmin may further deplete Factors V and VIII and cleave fibrinogen. The degradation products of both fibrinogen and fibrin (formed by thrombin or plasmin action) act as circulating anticoagulants, delay fibrin polymerization, and impair platelet function.

Common clinical settings for DIC (Table 52–3) include sepsis, obstetric emergencies, burns, and liver disease. Chronic DIC is characteristic of Trousseau's syndrome, widespread visceral malignancy presenting as migrating superficial thrombophlebitis.

The diagnosis of DIC depends upon a pattern of laboratory test results (Table 52–4). No single test is diagnostic. In acute DIC the typical laboratory results include thrombocytopenia, a prolonged PT and PTT, decreased fibrinogen level,

TABLE 52–3. CLINICAL SETTINGS FOR DISSEMINATED INTRAVASCULAR COAGULATION (DIC)

ACUTE	CHRONIC
1. Sepsis	1. Visceral malignancy
2. Obstetric emergencies Abruptio placentae Amniotic fluid embolism	2. Large arteriovenous malformations
3. Burns	3. Toxemia
4. Heat stroke	4. Retained dead fetus
5. Shock	5. Malignant hypertension
6. Snakebite	6. Severe liver cirrhosis
7. Promyelocytic leukemia	
8. Hemolytic transfusion reactions	

decreased Factors V and VIII, and increased fibrin split products and D-dimers. The thrombin time is also elevated because of the anticoagulant action of the fibrin split products. A microangiopathic hemolytic anemia may be present, resulting from shear damage to red cells passing intravascular fibrin strands. In chronic DIC, compensatory increases in synthesis of coagulation factors may produce normal levels of fibrinogen, Factors V and VIII, platelets, and the PT and PTT may be normal or even decreased. However, fibrin split products are usually elevated. Microangiopathic hemolytic anemia is more likely to be present in chronic DIC. Localized DIC may occur in the liver in severe cirrhotic liver disease and in the kidney during malignant hypertension. DIC must be distinguished from the microangiopathic thrombocytopenias such as thrombotic thrombocytopenic purpura (TTP) and hemolytic-uremic syndrome (HUS) (see under Platelet Disorders in Chapter 51).

Therapy for DIC should be aimed at the underlying disease, for example, by treating sepsis in the infected patient or by emptying the uterus in the case of abruptio placentae. If the symptoms of bleeding or thrombosis are mild, no specific therapy is needed. If DIC produces significant bleeding, replacement of depleted clotting factors using fresh frozen plasma, cryoprecipitate, and platelets may be necessary. If thrombosis is the clinical problem, heparinization may be required (provided that the patient does not have central nervous system bleeding, is not hypertensive, and has not undergone surgery within the past few days). Replacement of fibrinogen and of antithrombin III (as plasma) may also be required. Heparin is gen-

TABLE 52–4. SCREENING LABORATORY TESTS FOR DIC

1. Prolonged prothrombin time
2. Prolonged partial thromboplastin time
3. Low fibrinogen
4. Thrombocytopenia
5. Presence of fibrin degradation products
6. Depressed Factors V and VIII
7. Elevated D-dimers

erally reserved for cases that fail to respond to other measures. Special situations in which heparin is used include meningococcemia, acute promyelocytic leukemia, and Trousseau's syndrome. Oral anticoagulation cannot be substituted for heparin in the treatment of DIC.

Acquired Circulating Anticoagulants

Antibodies to procoagulants occur in hemophiliacs receiving replacement therapy (see above) as well as in states of disturbed immunity such as systemic lupus erythematosus, lymphoproliferative diseases, the postpartum period, and old age. Acquired inhibitors to Factor VIII:AHF can produce severe hemorrhagic disease. Several cases of inhibitors of von Willebrand's factor causing an acquired von Willebrand's disease have been reported in patients with lymphoma. Very rarely, a heparin-like anticoagulant molecule can circulate, producing a bleeding tendency.

In contrast to the above, the "lupus anticoagulant," which is the most common cause of a prolonged APTT in asymptomatic individuals, is rarely associated with a bleeding tendency unless combined with another hemostatic defect, such as thrombocytopenia. Only about half of "lupus anticoagulants" occur in patients with systemic lupus erythematosus. These antibodies are directed against membrane phospholipids or against the phosphodiester bond structure, which is a common chemical moiety in many diverse compounds, including DNA, membrane phospholipids, and organic sugars. This circulating anticoagulant is associated with a tendency to thrombosis rather than hemorrhage. Antibodies to cardiolipin, in association with the lupus anticoagulant or alone, may also be associated with acute arterial or venous thrombosis in young adults who have no other predisposing factor. Some of these autoantibodies may alter normal endothelial functions to predispose toward thrombosis. Oral anticoagulation on a chronic basis is the treatment of choice in patients with these autoantibodies once a definite thrombotic episode has appeared.

DISORDERS OF BLOOD COAGULATION: THE PATIENT WHO CLOTS

Many clinical situations can disrupt the hemostatic balance and lead to excess clotting, thromboembolic disease. To pinpoint the reason for a prothrombotic or hypercoagulable state and to plan for appropriate therapy, one must consider the physiologic pathways of thrombus formation and dissolution (see Chapter 51).

The history of the acute thrombotic event is critical for correct diagnosis and treatment. Is there an obvious systemic or local predisposing reason for a thrombosis? An increased tendency toward thrombosis accompanies surgery, many inflammatory disorders, malignancy, pregnancy, and vascular disorders and occurs following stasis. Inherited thrombotic tendencies, which are much rarer, are being increasingly recognized and include disorders of the protein C–protein S system, deficiencies of antithrombin III (AT III), dysfibrinogenemias, and disorders of the fibrinolytic system (Table 52–5).

Whereas the blood coagulation pathways involve a series of enzymatic activations of serine protease zymogens, downregulation of blood clotting is influenced by several natural anticoagulant mechanisms, including AT III, the protein C–protein S system, and fibrinolysis. In addition, normal vascular endothelium promotes the activation of these anticoagulant mechanisms by acting as a source of (1) heparin-like substances that enhance AT III activation, (2) thrombomodulin, a cofactor in protein C activation, and (3) tissue plasminogen activators that initiate fibrinolysis.

Primary hypercoagulable states involve defects in the above three systems, in fibrinogen structure, or in abnormalities of endothelial function. The reader should recall that partial deficiencies of the natural anticoagulant systems (i.e., about 50 per cent of normal levels) are associated with excess thrombosis, in contrast to the severe deficiencies of procoagulants (i.e., less than 10 per cent of normal values and often less than 1 per cent) which are necessary to precipitate bleeding disorders.

Evaluation of hypercoagulable risk involves checking family history of thromboembolism, eliciting other systemic predisposing diseases or conditions that favor localized vascular stasis, such as prolonged immobilization, pregnancy, or malignancy, and evaluating possible laboratory abnormalities, such as thrombocytosis, elevated blood or plasma viscosity, and elevated plasma levels of coagulation factors or fibrin degradation products. The latter, as well as measurement of AT III, protein C, or protein S levels, should be tested judiciously and only when suspicion is high, because such abnormalities are uncommon compared with factors such as stasis or localized injury.

TABLE 52–5. UNDERLYING CONSIDERATIONS IN THE PATIENT WHO CLOTS

Acquired Conditions
Prolonged immobilization
Obesity
Medications (e.g., oral anticoagulants)
DIC (e.g., underlying malignancy, sepsis)
Myeloproliferative syndrome (e.g., polycythemia vera)
Circulating anticoagulant (e.g., "lupus anticoagulant")
Inherited Conditions
Protein C deficiency
Protein S deficiency
Antithrombin III deficiency
Dysfibrinogenemia
Homocystinuria

AT III is a broadly acting inhibitor of serine proteases which blocks not only the potent coagulation enzyme, thrombin, but also other procoagulant proteins such as Factor X. AT III greatly potentiates the anticoagulant effect of heparin, which it binds. Heterozygous deficiency of AT III (levels 25 to 60 per cent of normal) is associated with venous thrombosis developing in young adults under the age of 40. Apparent resistance to heparin may be a clinical clue to this disorder, because AT III is necessary for full heparin efficacy. Inherited AT III deficiency varies clinically even within a single family; both functional and immunologic tests may be needed to diagnose the condition, as immunologically reactive but functionally abnormal protein variants occur. Acquired deficiency of AT III can occur in liver disease, nephrotic syndrome (due to urinary loss of the factor), during thrombosis, accompanying DIC, or during cancer chemotherapy with L-asparaginase. AT III concentrates can be used to correct this deficiency.

Protein C and Protein S Deficiencies

Both protein C and protein S are vitamin K–dependent proteins that are central to the natural anticoagulant pathway involving activated protein C. This pathway not only inhibits blood coagulation but also stimulates fibrinolysis. In the presence of thrombomodulin on the endothelial surface, thrombin forms a complex in which its procoagulant activity is neutralized and its ability to activate protein C is enhanced. Activated protein C, with protein S as a cofactor, then inactivates Factors V and VIII, thereby blocking generation of more thrombin. Activated protein C also stimulates fibrinolysis, in part by neutralizing a major inhibitor of tissue plasminogen activator.

Familial venous thromboembolism can occur in patients with inherited deficiencies of either protein C or protein S. Heterozygotes with a partial protein C deficiency (autosomal dominant form) may present with thromboembolism as adolescents or young adults. In its autosomal recessive form, however, heterozygotes remain asymptomatic, but homozygous deficiency causes neonatal purpura fulminans, which is rapidly fatal without replacement plasma therapy combined with anticoagulants.

Protein S deficiency also leads to venous thromboembolism in heterozygotes. Here, the plasma level of free protein S is key, because the protein circulates partially bound to a plasma factor, C4b-binding protein, and the bound complex is biologically inactive. During pregnancy both increased plasma binding of protein S and decreased total protein S levels occur; these changes may contribute to the thrombotic tendency observed during pregnancy.

Treatment for protein C or protein S deficiency consists of the chronic use of oral anticoagulants. Because protein C has a short half-life, its level drops quickly after initiation of oral coumarin-type anticoagulants, the result leading to a coumarin-induced skin necrosis (actually a thrombotic necrosis). For this reason, initial therapy for protein C deficiency should include heparinization during the first few days.

Antithrombotic Therapy

Four main types of therapy are used to prevent or treat thrombosis: antiplatelet agents, heparin, vitamin K antagonists, and thrombolytic agents. Each type of agent interferes with clotting at a different site in the coagulation pathway (Table 52–6).

In general, antiplatelet agents are used as prophylaxis against arterial thrombosis, because platelets are more important in initiating arterial than venous thrombi. Anticoagulants are used for

TABLE 52–6. ANTICOAGULANT DRUGS

AGENTS	MECHANISM OF ACTION	LENGTH OF EFFECT	LABORATORY MEASUREMENT	ANTIDOTE
Aspirin	Irreversibly inhibits platelet cyclo-oxygenase	7 days	Bleeding time may be prolonged	Platelet transfusion
Heparin	Accelerates antithrombin III activity to inhibit thrombin generation	2–4 hr	Partial thromboplastin (maintain at 1.5 to 2 times control)	Protamine sulfate
Vitamin K antagonists (e.g., warfarin)	Interfere with hepatic synthesis of Factors II, VII, IX, and X and proteins C and S	~48 hr	Prothrombin time (PT) (maintain at 1.5 to 2 times control)	Vitamin K (reverses PT in 12–36 hr) Fresh frozen plasma (reverses PT immediately for 4–6 hr) Factor II, VII, IX, or X concentrate (reverses PT immediately for 4–6 hr)
Thrombolytic agents: streptokinase (SK), urokinase (UK), tissue plasminogen activator (TPA)	Accelerate fibrinolysis	Minutes	SK, UK: thrombin time (should be 2 times control) TPA: no systemic effect	Fresh frozen plasma

both prevention and treatment of arterial and venous thrombosis. Heparin, which prevents the generation of thrombin as well as antagonizes thrombin's action, has an immediate anticoagulant effect; however, it must be administered parenterally. The coumarin anticoagulants prevent the synthesis of active coagulation factors and therefore have a slow onset of anticoagulant effect over several days. They are given orally; once the dose is established for an individual patient, they can provide a steady level of anticoagulation. The most recently developed category of antithrombotic drugs, the fibrinolytic agents, include activators of fibrinolysis (tissue plasminogen activator [TPA]) and fibrinolytic enzymes (streptokinase, urokinase) that directly activate plasmin. The fibrinolytic drugs are used to lyse freshly formed arterial and venous thrombi; fibrinolytic agents are not efficacious in dissolving thrombi that have been present for more than a few hours.

The major risk of antithrombotic therapy is bleeding, observed especially in patients who are predisposed to bleed easily because of a preexisting defect in the coagulation pathway, such as may be caused by alcoholism, uremia, thrombocytopenia, or the ingestion of aspirin. In general, the simultaneous use of two different types of these drugs (e.g., aspirin and warfarin) should be avoided because of increased bleeding risk. Many drugs interact with antithrombotic agents, and physicians should be aware of all other medications being taken by patients on anticoagulants, because they may either increase the sensitivity to the anticoagulant or decrease efficacy (e.g., phenobarbital stimulates metabolism of warfarin).

Indications for Antithrombotic Therapy

Venous Thromboembolism. Although this is a major clinical problem, prophylaxis is not universally applied because of varying risk and the cost of accurate predictive tests. Low-dose subcutaneous heparin is frequently used as prophylaxis against thromboembolism in surgical patients but is ineffective in those at highest risk, for example, after hip fracture. Warfarin reduces mortality from pulmonary embolism and can be given more safely to immobilized or post-surgical patients in low-dose or stepwise regimens. Once a venous thrombosis has developed, however, full-dose heparinization followed by full-dose warfarin therapy is necessary to prevent clot progression and/or pulmonary embolism. Treatment of pulmonary embolism with thrombolytic agents is promising. Aspirin offers little value in treating venous thromboembolism and may promote bleeding risks if combined with anticoagulation.

Arterial Thrombosis. Intravenous thrombolytic therapy may act rapidly to re-establish the patency of thrombosed peripheral arteries if administered within a few hours after acute thrombosis. Similarly, thrombolysis is recognized as an important treatment of acute coronary artery thrombosis (see below). Such treatment should be followed by heparin and then oral anticoagulants to prevent further clot promulgation or recurrence, similar to the regimen used in follow-up treatment after surgical embolectomy.

The use of anticoagulants versus aspirin in the management of patients with transient ischemic attacks or threatened or acute stroke is discussed in Chapter 116.

Cardiovascular Disease. Currently recommended prophylaxis against acute myocardial infarction includes aspirin on a daily basis for men; no unequivocal advantage for women has been clearly established. Aspirin also appears to be beneficial in patients with crescendo angina to decrease the incidence of myocardial infarction or sudden death. In patients with a fresh coronary thrombosis, intravenous fibrinolytic therapy (e.g., TPA, streptokinase, or urokinase) can permit rapid reperfusion of the thrombosed coronary artery if the fibrinolytic agent is administered within a few hours of the onset of symptoms. Such treatment is immediately followed by anticoagulation, but optimal long-term therapy to prevent restenosis has not been established. Aspirin is not effective in this setting. Streptokinase and TPA have similar efficacy for acute recanalization. At the clinical doses needed, both of these agents cause significant fibrinogenolysis, despite the theoretically greater fibrin specificity of TPA. The systemic loss of fibrinogen and platelet dysfunction caused by the fibrinolytic agents engender a hemorrhagic tendency. Bleeding complications, including cerebrovascular bleeding, are usually at a low level, depend upon the dose of the fibrinolytic agent as well as other therapies, and represent lysis of hemostatic plugs as well as the thrombosis being treated. Much effort is being devoted to the development of more fibrin-specific fibrinolytic drugs in order to diminish the hemorrhagic side effects of this therapy.

Following a myocardial infarction, acute anticoagulation is often given during the early period of patient immobility to prevent venous thromboembolism; "miniheparin" is a common regimen. However, chronic full anticoagulation following a myocardial infarction is no longer recommended (see Chapter 7).

REFERENCES

Marder VJ, Sherry S: Thrombolytic therapy: Current status. N Engl J Med 318:1512, 1585, 1988.
Prevention of venous thrombosis and pulmonary embolism. JAMA 256:744, 1986.

SECTION VII

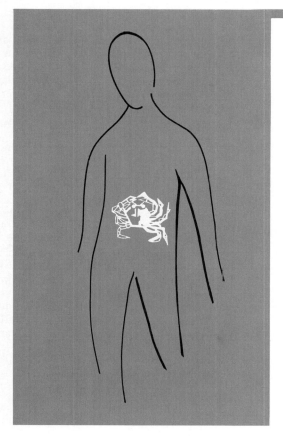

ONCOLOGY

53 GENERAL CONSIDERATIONS

In the United States, cancer accounts for more than 450,000 deaths annually, a toll second only to that from cardiovascular diseases. Current statistics suggest that approximately 30 per cent of Americans develop cancer in their lifetime, of whom two thirds will die as a result of their disease. The leading sites of cancer are the prostate gland and lung in males, the breast and lung in females, and the colorectal region in both sexes (Fig. 53–1). During the past 25 years, cancers of the skin, breast, pancreas, bladder, and testes have increased in incidence, while gastric and invasive cervical cancers have declined. Recently, lung cancer in men has declined in association with a decrease in smoking, but the drop is more than compensated for by an increase in women. Striking geographic differences exist in specific cancer rates. In Japan, for example, gastric and hepatocellular carcinomas are common, while breast and colon carcinomas are relatively rare. Presumably, the differences reflect environmental factors, as Japanese immigrants to the United States display American cancer rates within just one or two generations of residence.

ETIOLOGY

Oncogenes

The last decade has focused attention on the genes that control cell proliferation as the targets for mutations leading to the disruption in normal cell growth that results in cancer. Some of these gene mutations may be inherited through the germ line and explain the high incidence of cancer in some families. Others may be acquired through exposure to environmental carcinogens, viruses, or other agents. The occurrence of cancer in an individual is the end result of more than one mutation in normal cellular DNA, and a number of distinct changes in the cellular genome are necessary for full expression of a cancer cell.

Two elements of the human genome have received the most attention in research involving human DNA and cancer: the oncogenes and the tumor suppressor genes. Proto-oncogenes (or cellular oncogenes) are normal constituents of all cells and are critically important in regulating normal cell growth and differentiation. Proto-oncogenes are highly conserved in vertebrate evolution and are prime candidates for a substrate upon which the multitude of carcinogenic stimuli may play. Oncogenes are tumor-promoting segments of DNA that are activated or potentiated by a perturbation of the proto-oncogenes. The tumor suppressor genes are recessive genes that also act to control normal cell proliferation. An imbalance between the activation of oncogenes and the inactivation of tumor suppressor genes is important in carcinogenesis.

More than 20 proto-oncogenes have been identified. Their products are proteins located in the

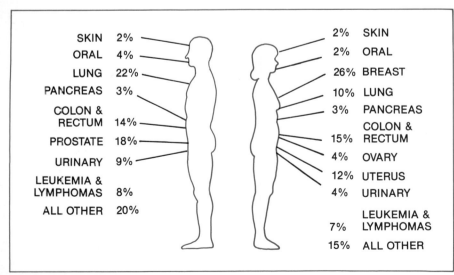

FIGURE 53–1. Estimated cancer incidence by site and sex, excluding nonmelanoma skin cancer and carcinoma in situ. The estimates of the incidence of cancer are based on data from the National Cancer Institute's Surveillance, Epidemiology and End Results (SEER) Program (1983–1987).

nucleus, cytoplasm, and plasma membrane of cells. Some of the functions of these proteins are known (Table 53–1). Many are tyrosine kinases and some are growth factors (e.g., platelet-derived growth factor and epidermal growth factor). One example of activation of a proto-oncogene is the Philadelphia chromosome (Ph[1]), consisting of reciprocal translocation between chromosomes 9 and 22 in chronic myelogenous leukemia (CML). Ph[1] (Fig. 53–2) exists in the hematopoietic cells of nearly all patients with CML. The c-*abl* proto-oncogene is localized to chromosome 9 near the breakpoint and is invariably translocated to chromosome 22, with the breakpoint on 22 occurring in a tightly restricted region called the "breakpoint cluster region (bcr)." The resulting bcr:c-*abl* fusion gene encodes a chimeric fusion protein, p210 (i.e., molecular weight of 210 Kd). Unlike the native c-*abl* gene product, p145, the fusion protein, p210, undergoes autophosphorylation of its tyrosine residues and possesses potent tyrosine kinase activity that may be fundamental to the pathogenesis of CML. The recent demonstration that a disease resembling CML develops in mice in which the blood stem cells had been transfected with a bcr:c-*abl* fusion gene confirms the importance of the chromosomal translocation in the pathogenesis of this disease.

Although cellular oncogenes promote cell growth, normal cells also possess recessive tumor suppressor genes that constrain cell growth. Tumor suppressor genes were first described for the rare childhood tumor, retinoblastoma. This tumor is associated with the inactivation of both functional copies of the RB gene on chromosome 13. Another syndrome associated with loss of the tumor suppressor genes is familial polyposis, a disorder predisposing to colon cancer. The precise

TABLE 53–1. PROTO-ONCOGENE FAMILIES

FAMILY	CARDINAL PROPERTIES	EXAMPLES
Tyrosine-specific protein kinase	Protein phosphorylation with specificity for tyrosine. Most kinases localize to the cell surface, and some members are bona fide receptors.	c-erbB (EGF-receptor; erythroleukemia) c-fms (CSF-1 receptor; sarcoma) c-abl (CML) c-src (sarcoma)
Serine-threonine	Protein phosphorylation with specificity for serine or threonine. Proteins are homologous to tyrosine kinase. Proteins localize to the cytosol.	c-mos (sarcoma) c-raf
Receptor for thyroid hormone	Homology to steroid receptors	c-erbA
GTP-binding proteins	Bind guanine nucleotides and hydrolyze GTP. Are analogous to G proteins that modulate receptor signals, including transducin, Gi, Gs, and Go.	c-Ha-ras (sarcoma) ci-Ki-ras
Growth factor	Beta chain of platelet-derived growth factor	ci-sis (sarcoma)
Nuclear proteins	Generally short half-life and rapid inducibility, DNA binding or transcription factors	c-myc (carcinomas; leukemia; sarcoma) c-fos (osteosarcoma) p53 (colon cancer)

EGF = Epidermal growth factor; CSF = colony-stimulating factor; CML = chronic myelogenous leukemia.
Adapted from Nienhuis AW, Sherr CJ: Oncogenes in hematopoietic neoplasms. *In* HEMATOLOGY—1987. The Educational Program of the American Society of Hematology.

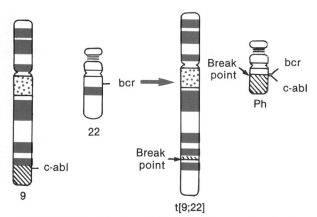

FIGURE 53–2. Reciprocal translocation resulting in the formation of the Ph[1] chromosome pathognomonic of CML. The c-*abl* proto-oncogene on chromosome 9 is translocated to the breakpoint cluster region (bcr) on chromosome 22. A new bcr:abl fusion gene is created on the Ph[1] chromosome which encodes a fusion protein, p210, likely to be important in the pathogenesis of CML. (Adapted from Champlin RE, Golde DW: Chronic myelogenous leukemia: Recent advances. Blood 65:1039, 1985; with permission.)

nature of the tumor suppressor gene products is not known.

Proto-oncogenes and tumor suppressor gene sites in cellular DNA are prime targets for various carcinogens. It is unlikely that any one carcinogen acts on a single site to produce cancer; most cancers result from a sequence of events that disturb the cellular balance between promotion and inhibition of growth.

The cells of several human malignancies, including bladder cancer and acute myelogenous leukemia, contain *ras* oncogenes that result from point mutations in normal *ras* genes. *Ras* genes normally encode GTP-binding proteins (Table 53–1); the mutated *ras* proteins contain single amino acid substitutions and are capable of neoplastic transformation.

TABLE 53–2. SOME HEREDITARY NEOPLASMS AND PRENEOPLASTIC SYNDROMES

	INHERITANCE*	CLINICAL FEATURES
Hereditary Neoplasms		
Retinoblastoma	AD	Susceptibility to other cancers, particularly osteosarcoma; deletion in long arm of chromosome 13 in some cases
Multiple endocrine neoplasia I	AD	Adrenal, pancreatic, pituitary, parathyroid tumors; carcinoid tumors
Multiple endocrine neoplasia II	AD	Medullary thyroid carcinoma, pheochromocytoma; parathyroid tumors and neurofibromas in some
Polyposis coli	AD	Multiple adenomatous polyps; adenocarcinoma of large bowel
Dysplastic nevus syndrome	AD	Hereditary melanomas derived from nevi
Hereditary Preneoplastic Syndromes		
Neurofibromatosis	AD	Multiple neurofibromas; café au lait spots; some develop neurofibrosarcomas, gliomas, acoustic neuromas, leukemias
Xeroderma pigmentosum	AR	Skin cancers; defective repair of DNA damaged by UV light
Bloom's syndrome; Fanconi's anemia	AR	Acute leukemia; other malignancies; associated with chromosomal instability
X-linked lymphoproliferative syndrome	XR	Immunoblastic sarcoma; B cell lymphoma; associated with abnormal immune response to EBV

*AD = Autosomal dominant; AR = autosomal recessive; XR = X-linked recessive; UV = ultraviolet; EBV = Epstein-Barr virus.

Adapted from Fraumeni JF Jr: Epidemiology of cancer. In Wyngaarden JB, Smith LH Jr (eds): Cecil Textbook of Medicine. 18th ed. Philadelphia, WB Saunders Co, 1988, pp 1095–1096.

Amplification of proto-oncogene sequences has been detected in some tumors, such as N-myc in neuroblastoma and neu in breast cancer. In these cancers proto-oncogene amplification is associated with a poor prognosis, suggesting that its enhanced expression may be critically related to disease progression.

Environmental Carcinogens

Tobacco is the major environmental carcinogen, contributing to 25 per cent of all cancer deaths. Tobacco exposure strongly potentiates the carcinogenic effect of other agents, most notably asbestos and alcohol; it leads not only to cancer of the lung but also of the head, neck, esophagus, and bladder, among others. This synergistic effect exemplifies how environmental carcinogens cause cancer. Lung cancer, for example, is thought to result from a multistage process characterized by several exposures, some acting as initiators (true carcinogens) and others as promoters (cocarcinogens). The actual induction of carcinogenesis by a chemical carcinogen may involve covalent modification of host DNA, dose dependence, and the existence of a lag period between exposure and malignant transformation.

Occupational exposure to chemical carcinogens (e.g., asbestos, vinyl chloride) accounts for about 5 per cent of all cancers. In certain occupations, as in furniture makers with a high exposure to wood dusts, nasal sinus cancers are an occupational hazard. Other important known carcinogens include smokeless tobacco, which is increasingly popular among young adults in the southwestern United States and is associated with oropharyngeal carcinoma.

Medications form another major category of chemical carcinogens. For example, alkylating agents used to treat lymphoma, multiple myeloma, and ovarian cancer may induce acute myelogenous leukemia. Maternal ingestion of prenatal diethylstilbestrol leads to the later development of adenocarcinomas of the vagina and cervix in some daughters exposed in utero.

Immunosuppression either by medication, as in patients with renal transplants, or by the acquired immunodeficiency syndrome (AIDS)–causing HTLV-III (human T cell lymphotropic virus III) virus predisposes to certain cancers, particularly high-grade lymphomas. Other viruses have been linked to human cancer. The HTLV-I retrovirus is commonly found in patients with adult T cell leukemia/lymphoma. Also, the association of the papillomavirus (type 16) with cervical cancer and the hepatitis B virus with hepatoma is well established.

Evidence derived from animal and epidemiologic studies as well as from limited clinical trials suggests that diet plays an important causative and protective role in carcinogenesis. However, data regarding the carcinogenicity of specific dietary factors are largely inconclusive. Possible associations include high dietary fat intake with colon and breast cancer and aflatoxin with liver cancer. Protective roles have been postulated for micronutrients and trace metals such as selenium, carotene, vitamins E and C, and calcium.

Hormones are important in the development of certain cancers. Breast and uterine cancers are associated with high levels of estrogen, both endogenous and exogenous. Prostate cancer is sensitive to male hormones. Androgen ablation, either by orchiectomy or by medication, is the treatment of choice.

Radiation-induced carcinogenesis has been observed in atomic bomb survivors, patients receiving therapeutic irradiation for Hodgkin's disease and phosphorus-32 for polycythemia vera, children exposed to x-rays prenatally, and patients irradiated in the distant past for nonmalignant conditions such as thymus enlargement. Radiation exerts its carcinogenic effects in a dose-dependent manner and spares no organ, although bone marrow, breast, and thyroid are the most radiation sensitive. The time lag varies: radiation-induced leukemia first appears at 2 to 5 years and peaks at 6 to 8 years, whereas solid tumors develop after a latency period of at least 5 to 10 years. Experts estimate that natural background irradiation (i.e., cosmic rays, radium, and other radionucleotides in the earth's crust) causes fewer than 2 per cent of all cancers. Exposure to ultraviolet irradiation, however, is the major risk factor for the development of melanoma and nonmelanoma skin cancers.

Genetic Susceptibility

More than 200 single gene disorders have been linked to the development of neoplasms. Certain genes create a greater than 90 per cent risk of developing cancer (hereditary retinoblastoma, familial polyposis coli). Table 53–2 lists some hereditary neoplasms and preneoplastic syndromes. Most cancers demonstrate a minor familial component (twofold to threefold excess risk), exceptions being early and multifocal breast and colon cancers, in which familial risks increase to 20 to 30 times that of the general population. Appropriate management of hereditary cancers includes avoidance of environmental carcinogens (e.g., ultraviolet light in the dysplastic nevus syndrome), prophylactic treatment (e.g., colectomy in polyposis coli), early detection (e.g., thyrocalcitonin determinations in multiple endocrine neoplasia), and genetic counseling (e.g., retinoblastoma).

SCREENING FOR EARLY CANCER DETECTION

Periodic, thorough physical examinations as well as analyses of simple blood tests (i.e., a complete blood count and routine chemistries) and urine are critical for the early detection of malignancy. Rectal, breast, and testicular examinations are the most effective means of diagnosing early cancers of the prostate and rectum, breast, and testes, respectively. A microcytic anemia in a nonmenstruating patient should alert one to the possibility of an occult gastrointestinal malignancy. Similarly, microscopic hematuria in an asymptomatic patient should prompt a search for a bladder or kidney cancer.

More complex screening procedures must take into account cost-benefit ratios. Costs include not only the dollar cost to society, but the risk of the procedure to the individual. Costs can be reduced by using epidemiologically derived data to restrict screening to (1) individuals at highest risk of developing cancer and (2) cancers whose early detection and treatment lead to significantly increased survival.

The American Cancer Society recommends screening as detailed in Table 53–3. Only one of the recommendations results from controlled, randomized, prospective clinical trials: mammography in women over the age of 40 years. The basis for the remaining recommendations is less firm. The recommendations do not include chest radiographs and sputum cytologies even in populations at high risk for developing lung cancer, as several studies demonstrate that this approach fails to detect lung cancers at a resectable stage.

Tumor Markers

Routine radiographs rarely detect tumor masses of less than 1 cm³, a size that reflects approximately 1 billion tumor cells. This has prompted a search for tumor-specific products—tumor markers—in

TABLE 53–3. AMERICAN CANCER SOCIETY RECOMMENDATIONS FOR SCREENING OF ASYMPTOMATIC INDIVIDUALS

TEST	SEX	AGE	FREQUENCY
Sigmoidoscopy	M & F	Over 50	Every 3–5 yr after 2 negative exams 1 yr apart
Stool guaiac test	M & F	Over 50	Every year
Digital rectal exam	M & F	Over 40	Every year
PAP test	F	All women who have reached age 18 or	Every year[1]
Pelvic exam		have been sexually active	
Endometrial biopsy	F	High-risk[2] or menopausal on estrogen therapy	Every year
Breast self-exam	F	Over 20	Every month
Breast physical exam	F	20–40	Every 3 yr
		Over 40	Every year
Mammography	F	35–39	One baseline study
		40–49	Every 1–2 yr
		Over 50	Every year
Health counseling	M & F	Over 20	Every 3 yr
Cancer check-up[3]	M & F	Over 40	Every year

[1] After three or more consecutive satisfactory normal annual exams, PAP test may be done less frequently at the discretion of the physician.
[2] History of infertility, obesity, failure of ovulation, abnormal uterine bleeding, or estrogen therapy.
[3] To include examination for cancers of the thyroid, testicles, prostate, ovaries, lymph nodes, oral region, and skin.

TABLE 53–4. TUMOR MARKERS USEFUL IN FOLLOWING KNOWN MALIGNANCIES

TUMOR MARKER	POSITIVE IN SOME	FALSE-POSITIVES IN
Carcinoembryonic antigen (CEA)	Gastrointestinal (GI), lung, breast cancers	Smokers, cirrhotics Inflammatory bowel disease Rectal polyps Pancreatitis
Alpha-fetoprotein (αFP)	Hepatocellular, gastric, pancreatic, colon, and lung cancers Nonseminomatous germ cell cancers	Pregnancy Alcoholic and viral hepatitis Cirrhosis
Human chorionic gonadotropin (beta subunit of hCG)	Trophoblastic tumors Germ cell neoplasms Adenocarcinomas of ovary Pancreatic, gastric, and hepatocellular cancers	Pregnancy (the alpha subunit cross-reacts with luteinizing hormone)
Prostate-specific antigen	Prostatic cancer (especially if bony metastases are present), myeloma, bony metastases from nonprostatic cancers	Benign prostatic hypertrophy, osteoporosis, hyperthyroidism, hyperparathyroidism
CA 125 (ovarian tumor marker)	80% of ovarian cancer 20% of nongynecologic cancers	1% healthy control, 5% benign diseases
Beta$_2$-microglobulin	Multiple myeloma	

Note that none of these tumor markers is specific enough to be useful in screening programs, except possibly prostate-specific antigen.

body fluids. A number of available tumor markers are useful as indices of response to treatment and early disease recurrence (Table 53–4). However, lack of sensitivity and specificity precludes their use as screening tests for asymptomatic populations.

SYSTEMIC EFFECTS OF CANCER

Most symptoms caused by cancer are due to the physical presence of the tumor. Common examples are headache caused by brain metastases from lung cancer, backache from prostatic metas-

TABLE 53–5. HEMATOLOGIC MANIFESTATIONS OF MALIGNANCY

MANIFESTATION	ASSOCIATED TUMORS	CONTRIBUTING FACTORS
Anemia	About 50% of all advanced malignancies	Chronic disease; extrinsic blood loss; bone marrow invasion by tumor or suppression by therapy; autoimmune hemolytic anemia; disseminated intravascular coagulation (DIC); microangiopathic hemolytic anemia; erosion of the tumor into a blood vessel; splenic sequestration
Thrombocytopenia	Lymphoma, chronic lymphocytic leukemia (CLL), carcinoma	Immune thrombocytopenia
Erythrocytosis	Hepatoma, hypernephroma, cerebellar hemangioblastoma	Inappropriate production of erythropoietin
Leukemoid reaction	Carcinomas of lung, pancreas, stomach; hepatoma; lymphomas	Tumor necrosis; tumor elaboration of colony stimulating factors; marrow invasion by metastases
Eosinophilia	Lymphomas, especially Hodgkin's disease; melanoma; brain tumors	Tumor elaboration of eosinophilopoietin
Thrombocytosis	Carcinoma; lymphoma	
Bleeding diatheses	Myeloma; Waldenström's macroglobulinemia Myeloproliferative diseases	Platelet dysfunction; abnormal fibrin polymerization Platelet dysfunction

Hypercoagulability
  Migratory thrombophlebitis (Trousseau's syndrome)
  Disseminated intravascular coagulation
  Nonbacterial thrombotic endocarditis
	Mucin-secreting adenocarcinoma of GI tract; carcinomas of lung, breast, ovary, prostate	Tumor cell expression of tissue factor; mucin activation of Factor X; prothrombinase-promoting tumor cell activity

tases to the spine, and jaundice caused by biliary tract obstruction from a pancreatic cancer. Cancer also can cause indirect effects on the host. Some of these effects are common, generalized, and poorly understood (e.g., anorexia). Some less common effects such as cerebellar degeneration are known as paraneoplastic syndromes and are due to tumor-related mediators, some of which are now well defined.

Anorexia and Cachexia

Complex factors act to produce tumor cachexia. They include anorexia due to aberrations in taste and smell, depression, and malaise; gastrointestinal dysfunction due to obstruction and the deleterious effects of chemotherapy, radiation, and surgery; and increased catabolism due to fever, tumor-induced alterations in protein and energy metabolism, and loss of protein into third spaces (e.g., ascites). Patients receiving effective oncologic therapy have higher response rates if they concomitantly receive nutritional support.

Hematologic Manifestations

Malignancy can cause prominent abnormalities in coagulation and all hematopoietic cell lines (Table 53–5). Most can be reversed only by successfully treating the underlying malignancy.

Endocrine Manifestations

Some tumors develop a remarkable capacity to express one or another of the body's natural hormones (Table 53–6). Such hormone production is usually independent of normal regulatory mechanisms.

Neurologic Manifestations

Metastases to the brain, epidural space, and meninges constitute the major cause of neurologic dysfunction in cancer patients. Neurologic symptoms may also result from metabolic abnormalities, opportunistic infections of the central nervous system, and vascular disease due to hemorrhage (intraparenchymal, subdural, and subarachnoid) and infarction (thrombotic and embolic).

Tables 119–2 and 119–3 list some of the remote effects of cancer on the central nervous system; these can be the presenting signs of occult malignancy.

Cutaneous Manifestations

The skin is a common site of metastatic cancer. In addition, paraneoplastic skin lesions include a variety of erythemas (e.g., necrolytic migratory erythema), pigmented lesions (e.g., acanthosis nigricans), and miscellaneous lesions (e.g., dermatomyositis). They can occur before, concomitant with, or after the diagnosis of malignancy. Their association with malignancy may be specific (e.g., necrolytic migratory erythema and glucagonoma) or generalized (e.g., dermatomyositis).

TABLE 53–6. ECTOPIC HORMONES PRODUCED BY MALIGNANCY

HORMONE	MANIFESTATIONS	ASSOCIATED TUMORS
ACTH	Cushing's syndrome (psychosis, hyperglycemia, generalized weakness)	Lung (especially oat cell); thymus; pancreas, medullary thyroid, pheochromocytoma
HHM factor	Hypercalcemia	Carcinomas of lung (especially epidermoid and large cell), kidney, head and neck, and ovary
Somatomedins (also called NSLIA)	Hypoglycemia	Mesenchymal tumors (especially mesothelioma), hepatoma, adrenal carcinomas, GI tumors
ADH	Hyponatremia, hyperosmolar urine, high urinary sodium concentration	Small cell carcinoma of lung
hCG	Gynecomastia in men; oligomenorrhea in premenopausal women	Germ cell tumors, lung cancer

HHM = Humoral hypercalcemia of malignancy (a parathyroid hormone–like peptide); NSLIA = nonsuppressible insulin-like activity; ADH = antidiuretic hormone; hCG = human chorionic gonadotropin.

Renal Manifestations

Etiologies of renal dysfunction in malignancy include direct tumor or amyloid infiltration, urinary tract obstruction, electrolyte imbalances (e.g., hypercalcemia, hyperuricemia) and the toxicities of chemotherapy. Glomerular lesions associated with the nephrotic syndrome constitute the primary paraneoplastic manifestation. In Hodgkin's disease, the malignancy most commonly associated with the nephrotic syndrome, the predominant renal lesion is lipoid nephrosis. In contrast, membranous glomerulonephritis is the most frequent glomerular lesion observed in patients with carcinoma.

REFERENCES

Bishop JM: Oncogenes and clinical cancer. In Weinberg RA (ed): Oncogenes and the Molecular Origins of Cancer. New York, Cold Spring Harbor Press, 1989, pp 327–358.

Blot WJ: The epidemiology of cancer. In Wyngaarden JB, Smith LH Jr, Bennett JC (eds): Cecil Textbook of Medicine. 19th ed. Philadelphia, WB Saunders Co, 1992, pp 1027–1032.

Devita VT, Hellman S, Rosenberg SA (eds): Cancer: Principles and Practice of Oncology. 3rd Ed. Philadelphia, JB Lippincott Co, 1989.

Sager R: Tumor suppressor genes: The puzzle and the promise. Science 246:1406, 1989.

54 PRINCIPLES OF CANCER THERAPY

Advances in the fields of surgery, radiation therapy, and medical oncology have made many cancers curable or amenable to palliation. This chapter outlines the basic principles governing the use of these modalities. Therapy of specific tumors is discussed in chapters related to diseases of the affected organ.

Forming a Treatment Plan

The first step in the evaluation of a patient diagnosed as having cancer is a thorough review of the diagnostic biopsy material with an experienced pathologist. Accurate classification of tumors and valuable prognostic information may be obtained by careful analysis of the following: morphology, histochemical stains, cell surface immune markers, hormone receptors, karyotype, oncogene expression, and electron microscopic appearance. Certain malignancies such as lymphomas, leukemias, and lung cancers require accurate subclassification, because prognosis and treatment are different and distinct for the various subtypes.

Determination of the stage of the cancer at diagnosis is essential. Most cancers are staged according to the TNM system, which incorporates information about the size of the primary tumor (T), involvement of regional lymph nodes (N), and the presence or absence of metastases (M). Staging of lymphomas and hematologic malignancies is discussed in Chapter 50. This requires knowledge of the usual pattern of metastasis for the neoplasm in question. Staging procedures, particularly if invasive or costly, should be carried out only if the derived information will alter the therapeutic approach or significantly change the prognosis. Low-yield procedures, such as bone scans in asymptomatic patients with localized breast cancer, should be avoided.

The biologic aggressiveness and curability of the tumor must be assessed. Patients with indolent malignancies such as early-stage chronic lymphocytic leukemia and systemic low-grade lymphomas are not curable with available chemotherapy and often can be safely followed without therapy for several years. In contrast, those with biologically aggressive high-grade lymphomas are eminently curable with combination chemotherapy and should generally be treated even in the absence of symptoms.

Patients with curable malignancies (e.g., Hodgkin's disease) should receive an optimal therapeutic regimen that is not compromised in any way, as the potential toxicities of treatment are generally justified. Even when curative therapy is available, however, patients with serious underlying medical conditions may not be suitable candidates.

In patients with incurable cancers, one often can achieve a significant prolongation of survival. In these instances, the physician must consider the probability of extending meaningful survival as well as the impact of the therapeutic program on the quality of the patient's remaining life. Ultimately, effective palliation of symptoms and improvement of the functional status and quality of life of the incurable cancer patient represent the physician's twin objectives. Effective palliation requires close observation for the development and treatment of the complications of malignancy, such as bony metastases, metabolic disturbances, visceral obstruction, persistent pain, and emotional distress.

PRINCIPLES OF ONCOLOGIC SURGERY

Definitive surgical resection with attainment of tumor-free margins is the treatment of choice for the majority of localized solid tumors. However, because many malignant tumors have already micrometastasized at the time of diagnosis, surgery is increasingly being integrated with other modalities to achieve local as well as distant disease control and to minimize the magnitude and morbidity of operative procedures. For example, conservative surgery, local radiation therapy, and adjuvant chemotherapy are widely applied to the treatment of localized breast cancer as well as to childhood rhabdomyosarcoma. In rare circumstances, such as with solitary lung metastases in sarcoma patients and solitary hepatic metastases in colorectal cancer patients, resection of isolated metastases may be curative. Although not itself curative, cytoreductive or debulking surgery plays a role in the treatment of some cancers (e.g., ovarian), presumably by increasing the growth fraction of the remaining cells, thereby rendering them more susceptible to the effects of chemotherapy.

Regional lymph node dissection, as in axillary lymph node sampling for breast cancer, provides prognostic information about the likelihood of distant tumor recurrence and serves as a guide to the administration of adjuvant therapy.

Surgical intervention also can offer palliation of symptoms resulting from complications of cancer such as intestinal or biliary obstruction, hemorrhage (e.g., from gastric carcinoma), perforation (e.g., in the setting of chemotherapy for gastrointestinal lymphoma), and compression of vital structures (e.g., spinal cord compression). Reconstructive and plastic surgery also figures prominently in the rehabilitation of treated cancer patients. Examples include breast reconstruction after mastectomy and lysis of radiation-induced contractures.

PRINCIPLES OF RADIATION THERAPY

Radiation exerts its biologic effect by ejecting electrons from target molecules, a process called ionization. Ionizing radiation may interact with DNA directly or indirectly, the latter by generating free radicals. The biologic end point is loss of cellular reproductive capacity.

Radiation therapy is delivered in the form of electromagnetic waves such as x-rays or gamma rays or as streams of particles such as electrons. High-energy (megavoltage) beams in the form of gamma rays generated by radioactive isotopes (e.g., cobalt-60) or x-rays generated by linear accelerators are ideal for the treatment of visceral tumors, as they penetrate to great depths before reaching full intensity and thereby spare toxicity to skin. Electron beam irradiation is most useful in the treatment of superficial tumors, as energy is deposited at the skin and quickly dissipates, sparing toxicity to deeper tissues.

Fractionation

Radiation therapy is generally administered in fractions of 1.8 to 2.5 Gy (180 to 250 rads)/day, 5 days a week. Fractionation improves the therapeutic index (the margin of safety between therapeutic and toxic doses), presumably because sublethal radiation injury is repaired more effectively in normal tissues than in tumors. Weekend treatment breaks allow the patient to recover from acute toxicities and the tumor to regress and reoxygenate. Such improved oxygenation renders the tumor more susceptible to subsequent radiation therapy, because hypoxic cells at the center of poorly vascularized neoplasms are two to three times more resistant to radiation than their well-oxygenated counterparts.

Clinical Considerations

The goal of radiation therapy is to deliver a tumoricidal dose while sparing normal tissues. The probability of both achieving tumor control and producing toxicity in normal tissue increases with dose in a sigmoid-curve relationship (Fig. 54–1). Greater separation of these curves results in an improved therapeutic index. The tumoricidal dose depends on the inherent radiation sensitivity of the neoplasm as well as its volume. The tumorici-

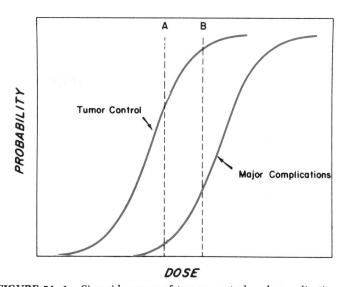

FIGURE 54–1. Sigmoid curves of tumor control and complications. *A,* Dose for tumor control with minimal complications. *B,* Maximum tumor dose with significant complications. (From Hellman S: Principles of radiation therapy. *In* Devita VT, Hellman S, Rosenberg SA [eds]: Cancer: Principles and Practice of Oncology. 3rd ed. Philadelphia, JB Lippincott Co, 1989, p 1021; with permission.)

dal dose for lymphomas, for example, is 40 to 50 Gy (4000 to 4500 rads), whereas that for most solid tumors ranges from 50 Gy for microscopic disease to 70 Gy for 4-cm tumors. The normal tissue tolerance to radiation also varies considerably (Table 54–1). Cell renewal tissues requiring rapid, continued proliferation for their function—skin, bone marrow, and gastrointestinal mucosa—are most vulnerable to acute toxicities (e.g., stomatitis, diarrhea, cytopenias). Late toxicities such as fibrosis, necrosis, and nonhealing ulcerations are determined by the total radiation dose and fraction size rather than by the proliferative potential of the affected tissue.

Radiation therapy is preferable to surgery in the management of localized tumors such as laryngeal

TABLE 54–1. NORMAL TISSUE TOLERANCE TO RADIATION THERAPY*

ORGAN	TOXICITIES	DOSE LIMIT† (Gy)
Bone marrow	Aplasia, pancytopenia	2.5
Liver	Acute and chronic hepatitis	25.0
Stomach, intestine	Ulceration, diarrhea, hemorrhage	45.0
Brain	Infarction, necrosis	60.0
Spinal cord	Infarction, necrosis	45.0
Heart	Pericarditis, pancarditis, coronary artery disease	45.0
Lung	Pneumonitis, fibrosis	15.0
Kidney	Nephrosclerosis	20.0
Skin	Dermatitis, sclerosis	55.0

*Assuming 2 Gy/fraction, 5 fractions/wk.
†Dose for 5% injury in 5 yr; 1 Gy = 100 rads.

carcinomas or certain deep-lying malignant brain tumors whose resection would be associated with significant functional impairment or mutilation. Tumors curable by radiation include Hodgkin's and non-Hodgkin's lymphomas, seminomas, and localized carcinomas of the larynx, cervix, and prostate.

Radiation therapy is frequently administered in an "adjuvant" setting with surgery, chemotherapy, or both. Postoperative adjuvant radiation therapy may eradicate residual foci of microscopic tumor and decrease the likelihood of local recurrence. It may also permit a more conservative surgical approach, such as is attained by employing lumpectomy and radiation therapy rather than mastectomy for localized breast cancers. The addition of adjuvant chemotherapy in such a setting may further increase the likelihood of cure by eradicating occult distant micrometastases. Examples of this principle include the administration of adjuvant radiation therapy and chemotherapy after resection of localized breast and rectal carcinomas. Adjuvant radiation therapy to sanctuary sites, such

as the central nervous system and testes, which are not accessible to systemic chemotherapy, increases the likelihood of cure in malignancies such as acute lymphocytic leukemia and small cell lung cancer.

Chemotherapy and radiation therapy are combined in the primary treatment of a number of malignancies, including bulky Hodgkin's lymphoma, limited-stage small cell lung cancer, and anal carcinoma. In another dimension, chemoradiation therapy is administered in supralethal doses as a preparative regimen for bone marrow transplantation (discussed below).

Radiation therapy can be a potent palliative modality, as is illustrated in the treatment of painful bony metastases. It is also employed as the primary therapy for many oncologic emergencies, including the superior vena cava syndrome, spinal cord compression, and brain metastases.

PRINCIPLES OF CHEMOTHERAPY

Many cancers have established metastatic clones by the time they become clinically detectable. Systemic chemotherapy and hormonal therapy play a major role in the management of the 60 per cent of cancer patients who are not curable by regional modalities. The advent of effective combination chemotherapy has produced cures in a number of advanced malignancies (Table 54–2) and meaningful remissions in many others (Table 54–3).

Tumor Kinetics

Exponentially growing tumors double approximately 30 times before becoming clinically detectable (as a 10^9 cell or 1-cm mass). Each tumor has a characteristic doubling time ranging from 2 to 5 days for Burkitt's lymphoma to over 100 days for adenocarcinomas of the lung and breast. Tumor kinetics are best described by the Gompertz growth curve (Fig. 54–2)—over a short time, tumor growth appears exponential; with time, a progressively greater percentage of the cell population enters a nonproliferative pool by virtue of cell death, differentiation, and entry into the G_0 or resting phase of the cell cycle. Eventually, a plateau is reached, where the rate of new cell production equals that of cell death. The exponential increase in the proportion of nonproliferating cells decreases the susceptibility of large tumors to antineoplastic agents, which are most active against rapidly dividing cells. This principle provides the rationale for "debulking" tumors (by surgery or irradiation) so as to recruit residual G_0 cells into an active proliferative state with an enhanced susceptibility to chemotherapy.

Most chemotherapeutic agents exploit kinetic differences between normal and malignant cells by acting preferentially on dividing cells. Such "cell cycle–specific" agents (e.g., cyclophosphamide, methotrexate, cytosine arabinoside) achieve a kill rate of certain lymphoproliferative tumor

TABLE 54–2. ADULT TUMORS CURABLE WITH CHEMOTHERAPY

TUMOR	LONG-TERM DISEASE-FREE SURVIVAL (%)
Choriocarcinoma	90
Burkitt's lymphoma (Stage I)	90
Testicular carcinoma	90
Diffuse large cell non-Hodgkin's lymphoma	50–60
Hodgkin's disease	60
Acute lymphocytic leukemia	35–45
Acute myelogenous leukemia	20
Ovarian carcinoma	10–20
Small cell lung carcinoma	10

TABLE 54–3. ADULT TUMORS RESPONSIVE TO CHEMOTHERAPY

TUMOR	PARTIAL OR COMPLETE RESPONSE (%)
Chronic lymphocytic leukemia	75
Chronic myeloproliferative disorders	80
Hairy cell leukemia	75
Multiple myeloma	75
Low- and intermediate-grade non-Hodgkin's lymphoma	80
Mycosis fungoides	75
Breast carcinoma	65
Bladder carcinoma	40–50
Gastric carcinoma	35
Head and neck carcinoma	65
Ovarian carcinoma	75
Prostate carcinoma	75
Islet cell tumors	50

cells that is several thousandfold greater than that of bone marrow stem cells that are partially in a resting phase. This results in rapidly reversible cytopenias but permanent tumor eradication.

Mechanisms of Action of Antineoplastic Drugs

All chemotherapeutic agents act by interfering with cell division (Fig. 54–3). Antimetabolites, acting as fraudulent analogues of vital physiologic substrates, inhibit the synthesis of DNA or their nucleotide building blocks. Examples include methotrexate, a folic acid analogue; cytosine arabinoside, a pyrimidine analogue; and 6-mercaptopurine, a purine analogue. Alkylating agents such as cyclophosphamide chemically interact with DNA. They contain highly reactive alkyl groups that cause DNA breaks and cross-link complementary DNA strands that prevent replication. Cisplatin, a heavy metal compound, achieves its cytotoxicity by a similar mechanism. Many of the antitumor antibiotics, such as the anthracyclines, daunomycin and doxorubicin, intercalate themselves between strands of the DNA double helix and thereby inhibit DNA, RNA, and ultimately protein synthesis. The vinca alkaloids, vincristine and vinblastine, are plant products that arrest cells in the metaphase of mitosis by binding to tubulin and thereby inhibit microtubular function. The enzyme L-asparaginase depletes cells of the nonessential amino acid asparagine. Most human tissues have the capacity to synthesize asparagine by the action of L-asparigine synthetase. Some tumor cells, particularly those of T cell lineage, lack this enzyme. As a result, depletion of circulating pools of asparagine by L-asparaginase results in inhibition of protein synthesis and ultimately cytotoxicity.

Toxicity

Safe administration of antineoplastic drugs, with their narrow therapeutic indices, requires knowledge of their routes of metabolism and elimination. Dose modification in the setting of renal or hepatic dysfunction minimizes toxicity. Major dose modifications of the anthracyclines and vinca

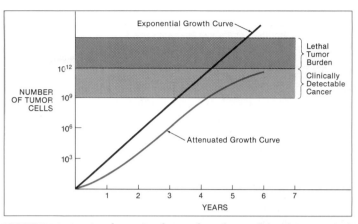

FIGURE 54–2. A schematic plot to describe models of exponential and gompertzian growth curves. (From Chabner BA: Introduction to oncology. *In* Wyngaarden JB, Smith LH Jr, Bennett JC [eds]: Cecil Textbook of Medicine. 19th ed. Philadelphia, WB Saunders Co, 1992, p 1021.)

alkaloids are required when hepatic dysfunction exists and of cisplatin, methotrexate, streptozocin, bleomycin, and hydroxyurea when azotemia is present. The toxic manifestations of chemotherapy are legion and spare no organ. The patterns of toxicity of some commonly used drugs are outlined in Table 54–4.

Dose Intensity

Most antineoplastic agents produce a steep dose-response curve. Dose intensity and dose rate (drug delivered per unit time) are powerful determinants of response to therapy and overall survival. The strong correlation between the dose and cure rates of chemosensitive malignancies such as Hodgkin's disease justifies the enhanced toxicity of aggressive treatment in these settings.

Resistance to Chemotherapy

The major cause of treatment failure is drug resistance. Although most neoplasms arise from a

TABLE 54–4. MAJOR TOXICITIES OF COMMONLY USED CANCER CHEMOTHERAPEUTIC AGENTS

SHORT-TERM EFFECT	EXAMPLES	LONG-TERM EFFECT	EXAMPLES
Nausea, vomiting	Cisplatin, doxorubicin	Leukemia	Alkylating agents
Alopecia	Doxorubicin	Cardiomyopathy	Doxorubicin
Myelosuppression	Alkylating agents	Pulmonary fibrosis	Bleomycin
	Cyclophosphamate	Hemolytic-uremic syndrome	Mitomycin
	Methotrexate	Peripheral neuropathy	Vincristine, cisplatin
	Etoposide	Premature menopause, sterility	Alkylating agents
Hypersensitivity	Bleomycin, L-asparaginase		
Tissue necrosis	Doxorubicin, vincristine		
Stomatitis	Methotrexate		
Renal failure	Cisplatin		
Hemorrhagic cystitis	Cyclophosphamide		
Ileus	Vincristine		

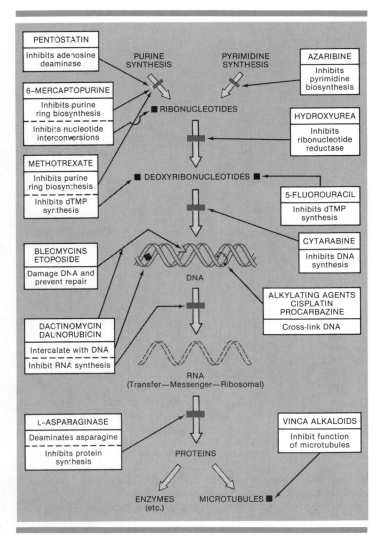

PENTOSTATIN			AZARIBINE
Inhibits adenosine deaminase			Inhibits pyrimidine biosynthesis

PURINE SYNTHESIS   PYRIMIDINE SYNTHESIS

RIBONUCLEOTIDES

6-MERCAPTOPURINE
Inhibits purine ring biosynthesis
Inhibits nucleotide interconversions

HYDROXYUREA
Inhibits ribonucleotide reductase

DEOXYRIBONUCLEOTIDES

METHOTREXATE
Inhibits purine ring biosynthesis
Inhibits dTMP synthesis

5-FLUOROURACIL
Inhibits dTMP synthesis

DNA

BLEOMYCINS ETOPOSIDE
Damage DNA and prevent repair

CYTARABINE
Inhibits DNA synthesis

DACTINOMYCIN DAUNORUBICIN
Intercalate with DNA
Inhibit RNA synthesis

ALKYLATING AGENTS CISPLATIN PROCARBAZINE
Cross-link DNA

RNA
(Transfer—Messenger—Ribosomal)

L-ASPARAGINASE
Deaminates asparagine
Inhibits protein synthesis

VINCA ALKALOIDS
Inhibit function of microtubules

PROTEINS

ENZYMES   MICROTUBULES
(etc.)

FIGURE 54–3. Mechanisms and sites of action of antineoplastic agents. (Modified from Calabresi P, Chabner BA: Chemotherapy of neoplastic disease. In Gilman AG, Rall TW, Nies AS, Taylor P [eds]: The Pharmacologic Basis of Therapeutics. 8th ed. New York, Pergamon Press, 1990, p 1208; with permission of McGraw-Hill.)

single clone, random mutations lead to marked cellular heterogeneity with regard to radiation sensitivity and susceptibility to cytotoxic drugs. The probability of drug resistance within a tumor is proportional to the size of the neoplasm and the rate at which the drug-resistant gene mutates (Goldie-Coldman hypothesis). This principle explains the greater curability of small cancers with a low likelihood of drug resistance and the relative refractoriness of widely metastatic cancers that are likely to contain cells resistant to several drugs. Many solid tumors have long doubling times because of a high rate of cell loss; by the time they become clinically detectable (approximately 30 doublings), they have undergone nu-

merous divisions and mutational events. This biologic characteristic may account for their relative resistance to chemotherapy compared with rapidly dividing lymphoproliferative malignancies such as high-grade lymphomas. The practice of giving adjuvant chemotherapy shortly after tumor resection when the systemic tumor burden is low derives from this principle. Such an approach may bring a cure to patients with malignancies that have a propensity to recur, such as breast and rectal carcinomas and osteogenic and soft tissue sarcomas.

Chemotherapy selectively eradicates sensitive tumor clones and permits the overgrowth of resistant cell populations. Mechanisms of drug resistance include impaired drug uptake or activation, enhanced drug inactivation, increased expression of the target enzyme by gene amplification, and altered target proteins. Some tumor cells develop pleiotropic (multidrug) resistance to several classes of drugs which are structurally and functionally distinct (vinca alkaloids, anthracyclines, dacarbazine). Such multidrug-resistant cells contain amplified gene sequences that encode a 170-kd protein, P-glycoprotein, involved in drug efflux. Overexpression of this protein results in decreased intracellular drug accumulation and clinical resistance.

Combination Chemotherapy

The cure of advanced malignancies, when possible, has been achieved primarily with combination chemotherapy. The rationale for combination regimens stems from the fact that antineoplastic agents have diverse mechanisms of action. Hence, tumor cells resistant to one drug may still be sensitive to another. The most effective regimens consist of drugs that are individually effective against the neoplasm and have nonoverlapping toxicities, thereby permitting administration of full dosage of all drugs (e.g., mustard, Oncovin [vincristine], procarbazine, prednisone [MOPP] for Hodgkin's disease). Proper scheduling of combination regimens is integral to their efficacy. The administration of nonmyelosuppressive drugs, such as bleomycin or methotrexate, with leucovorin rescue between cycles of myelotoxic drugs, such as the alkylating agents or anthracyclines, allows the bone marrow to recover despite continued treatment. Treatment breaks of 2 to 3 weeks between cycles also permit recovery of sensitive normal tissues, such as gastrointestinal mucosa and bone marrow. Newer approaches include instituting alternating cycles of equally effective non–cross-resistant combinations and the early introduction of all effective drugs in an effort to prevent the emergence of resistance.

As mentioned above, combination chemotherapy has been successfully integrated with radiation therapy in the treatment of certain cancers such as bulky Hodgkin's disease. A regimen of high-dose chemotherapy and total body irradiation followed by reconstitution with allogeneic or autologous bone marrow has been administered with varying degrees of success to patients with acute and chronic leukemias, refractory lymphomas, and a number of chemoradiation-sensitive solid tumors, including small cell lung, breast, ovarian, and testicular cancers. Allogeneic human leukocyte antigen (HLA)–matched bone marrow transplantation has become the treatment of choice for younger patients with chronic myelogenous leukemia in chronic phase, acute lymphocytic leukemia in second remission, and acute myelogenous leukemia in relapse. Bone marrow transplantation as a treatment of refractory lymphomas and solid tumors is promising but remains experimental in view of its extreme toxicities, which include interstitial pneumonitis, graft-versus-host disease, opportunistic infections, and hepatic veno-occlusive disease.

HORMONAL THERAPY

A number of cancers, most notably breast and prostate, respond to manipulations of their hormonal milieu. Manipulation involves alteration in steroid hormone levels or their activity. Steroid hormones enter the cell and bind to cytoplasmic receptors. The hormone-receptor complex is translocated to the nucleus, where it influences the transcription of messenger RNA for growth-inhibitory or -stimulatory proteins.

Steroid antagonists, such as the antiestrogen tamoxifen used in the treatment of breast cancer, compete with endogenous hormones for binding to receptor sites. Hormone antagonist-receptor complexes fail to initiate transcription changes induced by the native hormone. Estrogen and progesterone receptor levels in breast cancer tissue correlate well with hormonal dependence and predict responsiveness to hormonal therapy.

Aminoglutethimide inhibits adrenal steroidogenesis by blocking the enzymatic conversion of cholesterol to pregnenolone as well as the aromatization in peripheral tissues of androgens to estrone, a major source of estrogen in postmenopausal women. This agent has almost entirely replaced surgical adrenalectomy in the treatment of breast cancer.

Estrogens such as diethylstilbestrol and analogues of luteinizing hormone–releasing hormone, which are potent inhibitors of testosterone production, help to palliate prostate cancer.

Glucocorticoids are used extensively in the treatment of lymphomas, lymphocytic leukemias, multiple myeloma, and breast cancer.

BIOLOGIC RESPONSE MODIFIERS

Human beings possess cellular and humoral antitumor capacity. Three classes of cytotoxic lymphocytes exist—lymphokine-activated killer (LAK) cells, natural killer cells, and natural cytotoxic cells. Biologic substances such as interferons and interleukins potentiate the antitumor effects of lymphocytes. The reinfusion of LAK cells that are derived from patients with renal cell carcinoma and malignant melanoma and then expanded in vitro with exogenous interleukin-2 (IL-2) has produced significant regressions of these chemoresistant tumors. Broad application of this technique has been limited by its serious toxicities, which include a capillary leak syndrome, hypotension, and marked fluid retention.

Naturally occurring products of lymphocytes (lymphokines), such as interferons, are antiproliferative and immunomodulatory and are endowed with direct antitumor activity. Alpha-interferon has been successfully used to treat hairy cell leukemia, chronic myelogenous leukemia, and low-grade non-Hodgkin's lymphomas. More modest responses have been observed with solid tumors such as renal cell carcinoma and Kaposi's sarcoma.

Monoclonal antibodies against specific tumor antigens have been utilized in purging autologous bone marrow from patients with B cell lymphoma and acute lymphocytic leukemia. Similarly, T cell antibodies have been used to purge allogeneic marrow of T lymphocytes in order to prevent graft-versus-host disease. The use of monoclonal antibodies against the idiotype of the immunoglobulin on the surface of B cell lymphomas and leukemias has also been attempted but has met with limited success owing to the emergence of mutations within the idiotype.

REFERENCES

Chabner BA, Collins JM: Cancer Chemotherapy: Principles and Practice. Philadelphia, JB Lippincott Co, 1990.

Drugs of choice for cancer chemotherapy. Med Lett 33:21–28, 1991.

Salmon SE: Principles of cancer therapy. In Wyngaarden JB, Smith LH Jr, Bennett JC (eds): Cecil Textbook of Medicine. 19th ed. Philadelphia, WB Saunders Co, 1992, pp 1049–1067.

55 ONCOLOGIC EMERGENCIES

The natural history of malignancies leads to several types of medical emergencies. Many gastrointestinal and genitourinary tumors present with acute obstruction or hemorrhage. Bone marrow infiltrated by tumor or suppressed by chemotherapy can lead to life-threatening infection. Tumor erosion into a blood vessel and tumor- or treatment-induced thrombocytopenia can precipitate life-threatening hemorrhage. Other types of oncologic emergencies include those summarized in Table 55–1, a few of which are discussed in detail below.

HYPERCALCEMIA

Hypercalcemia occurs in 10 to 20 per cent of cancer patients. It is seen in association with solid tumors in the presence (e.g., breast cancer) or absence (e.g., renal cell and squamous cell lung cancers) of bone metastases as well as with hematologic malignancies (e.g., myeloma and adult T cell lymphoma). Tumor cells in bone can directly stimulate bone resorption or induce bone resorption by secreting cytokines (interleukin-1, tumor necrosis factors) or prostaglandin E_2. Tumor-derived parathyroid hormone–like peptides and growth factors appear to be important humoral mediators of cancer-associated hypercalcemia.

Common presenting symptoms include an altered mental status (ranging from apathy to coma), generalized muscle weakness, nausea and vomiting, abdominal pain, polyuria (resulting from a reversible renal tubular defect in urine concentrating ability), and polydipsia. Clinical findings associated with hypercalcemia include an altered mental status, dehydration, renal insufficiency, hyporeflexia, pancreatitis, peptic ulcer, hypertension, cardiac arrhythmias, prolonged PR interval, shortened QT interval, and widening of the T wave on electrocardiogram (ECG).

Although definitive treatment of hypercalcemia requires tumor control, interim therapy should be aimed at enhancing calcium excretion and diminishing calcium resorption from bone.

Repleting intravascular volume is of primary importance in the management of hypercalcemia. This enhances the glomerular filtration rate and increases the clearance rates of sodium and calcium. Once the patient is euvolemic, a diuretic such as furosemide, which diminishes renal tubular reabsorption of sodium and calcium and promotes calciuresis, may be administered. During this time, fluid and electrolyte balance must be carefully monitored and congestive heart failure vigorously treated. Such therapy usually lowers serum calcium by 2 to 4 mg/dl within 24 hours.

Glucocorticoids are most useful in the treatment of hypercalcemia associated with hematologic malignancies and breast cancer, as they are effective antineoplastic agents in these diseases. Steroids also act by decreasing intestinal absorption and increasing renal excretion of calcium, as well as by blocking activation of osteoclasts by osteoclast-activating factors and reducing prostaglandin synthesis. Calcium levels decline only after several days of steroid therapy.

Refractory hypercalcemia may be treated with the antitumor antibiotic mithramycin, which directly inhibits bone resorption. Its effects are usually detectable within 24 to 48 hours and can last for a week or more. The adverse effects of mithramycin (including bone marrow suppression, postural hypotension, and hepatocellular and renal damage) limit its usefulness as a first-line agent.

Calcitonin, a polypeptide hormone secreted by thyroid parafollicular cells, is moderately effective in treating malignancy-associated hypercalcemia. Its hypocalcemic effect is due to inhibition of bone resorption and is manifest within hours of administration. Concomitant administration of steroids may prolong its hypocalcemic effect.

Diphosphonates, synthetic analogues of pyrophosphate, inhibit osteoclastic bone resorption and are effective in treating malignancy-associated hypercalcemia.

Oral phosphates can be used for chronic maintenance of normocalcemia, but their use should be limited to patients with normal renal function who are not hyperphosphatemic.

SPINAL CORD COMPRESSION

Extradural spinal cord compression (SCC) is found at autopsy in as many as 5 per cent of patients with cancer. Vertebral or occasionally paravertebral metastases from carcinomas of the lung, breast, and prostate, as well as lymphoma and myeloma, account for most cases.

Back pain, with or without a radicular component, is the presenting symptom in nearly all patients with SCC; the pain is frequently worse when the patient is supine. Later signs and symp-

TABLE 55-1. SOME ONCOLOGIC EMERGENCIES

TYPE OF EMERGENCY	MOST COMMON MANIFESTATIONS	MOST COMMON ETIOLOGIES
Hemodynamic		
Superior vena cava syndrome	Superficial thoracic vein collaterals Neck vein distention Facial edema Tachypnea	Bronchogenic carcinoma Lymphoma
Pericardial tamponade	Congestive heart failure (CHF)–like symptoms Kussmaul's sign Pulsus paradoxus Distant heart sounds	Lung carcinoma Breast carcinoma Lymphoma
Hyperviscosity syndrome	Confusion, coma Stroke Hypervolemia Retinopathy	Waldenström's macroglobulinemia Myeloma
Thrombosis	Trousseau's syndrome (migratory thrombophlebitis) Nonbacterial thrombotic endocarditis (NBTE) Disseminated intravascular coagulation (DIC)	Mucinous adenocarcinomas Myeloproliferative disorders Prostatic carcinoma Acute promyelocytic leukemia
Neurologic		
Increased intracranial pressure	Mental status changes Seizures Signs of herniation	Brain metastases Primary brain tumors Carcinomatous or lymphomatous meningitis
Spinal cord compression	Pain (usually radicular) Weakness Autonomic dysfunction Sensory abnormalities	Carcinoma of lung, breast, prostate Lymphoma Myeloma
Metabolic		
Hypercalcemia	Anorexia, nausea, and vomiting Abdominal pain Apathy, coma Muscle weakness Polyuria, azotemia Cardiac conduction abnormalities	Carcinoma of breast, lung, kidney, head, and neck Myeloma
"Tumor lysis syndrome"	Acute renal failure	Undifferentiated lymphomas (particularly Burkitt's and lymphoblastic lymphomas) Acute lymphoblastic leukemia Anaplastic small cell carcinoma
Hypoglycemia	Confusion, loss of consciousness	Insulinoma Mesenchymal tumors Hepatoma
Hyponatremia	Confusion, coma Seizures Anorexia	SIADH (usually small cell carcinoma)

toms include weakness, sensory loss, autonomic dysfunction, and ataxia.

Unless diagnosed and treated early, SCC leads to irreversible neurologic deficits, making prompt diagnosis and initiation of appropriate treatment a crucial matter. A high index of suspicion must be employed in any older patient presenting with back pain of recent onset, especially if there is a history of malignancy. Once SCC enters into the differential diagnosis of neurologic symptoms, diagnostic and therapeutic measures must be undertaken immediately. Interim medical management includes the use of high-dose steroid therapy in an attempt to decrease pressure on the cord.

Although plain films are likely to demonstrate extensive vertebral involvement or destruction by tumor, magnetic resonance imaging (MRI) or myelography is required to diagnose SCC, to demonstrate the number of lesions, and to define the upper and lower margins of the blockage to free flow of spinal fluid. If myelography is performed, spinal fluid should be obtained for cell count and chemical and cytologic analysis. In the rare case that myelography is contraindicated and MRI is unavailable, computed tomography (CT) scanning with contrast enhancement can be helpful.

Available treatment approaches are listed in Table 115-10. They include radiation therapy and surgical decompression with or without postoperative radiation. Surgery causes more morbidity and mortality and is usually reserved for (1) cases in which there has not been a previous diagnosis of malignancy and there is no more accessible site for biopsy, (2) lesions known to be radiation resistant, and (3) tumors involving areas already treated with radiation. In certain instances, chemotherapy can be used as adjunct therapy but is not recommended as the primary mode of treatment.

In general, neurologic prognosis (sphincter control and independence of ambulation) depends on the degree of impairment when treatment is initiated and on the radiation sensitivity of the primary tumor.

INCREASED INTRACRANIAL PRESSURE

Patients with mass lesions or diffuse infiltrative processes such as lymphomatous or carcinomatous meningitis may present with signs and symptoms of increased intracranial pressure (ICP).

Early signs of increased ICP include headache, seizures, lethargy, confusion, and papilledema. Additional signs and symptoms of neurologic dysfunction reflect the anatomic site of metastasis. The CT or MRI scan has become the safest and most reliable diagnostic test and should be promptly obtained in all patients with suspected mass lesions in the brain. Prompt recognition of the cause of increased ICP and rapid institution of medical therapy (prior to definitive diagnosis and treatment of the precipitating cancer) are essential for preservation of cerebral function.

While definitive diagnostic and therapeutic measures are being planned and executed, medical therapy including pharmacologic doses of intravenous steroids, diuretics, and fluid restriction can temporarily decrease ICP (Table 55–2). Anticonvulsant therapy is not routinely administered except to patients presenting with seizures. Patients with elevated ICP, carcinomatous meningitis, and melanoma have seizures more frequently and should be considered for prophylactic anticonvulsant therapy.

Care must be taken to exclude nonmalignant intracranial masses, particularly in patients without a previous diagnosis of malignancy or widely disseminated cancer. For example, there is an increased incidence of benign meningioma in women with breast cancer. Similarly, brain abscesses occur more commonly in the immunocompromised cancer patient. Radiation-induced brain necrosis may be difficult to differentiate from recurrent tumor. Surgical intervention is indicated in these instances of uncertain diagnosis.

Once a diagnosis of brain metastasis is established, radiation therapy should be instituted promptly. Fifty to 75 per cent of patients so treated demonstrate neurologic improvement, although in many, tumors eventually recur.

SUPERIOR VENA CAVA SYNDROME

The onset of a superior vena cava (SVC) syndrome creates a subacute or acute medical emergency whose diagnosis and treatment usually require the multidisciplinary efforts of the medical oncologist, surgeon, and radiation therapist. The SVC is the major venous channel for blood return from the head, neck and upper extremities, and thorax. A thin-walled vessel enclosed in a relatively unyielding compartment, its low intravascular pressures make it particularly vulnerable to extrinsic compression by an adjacent mass.

Common presenting symptoms include distended thoracic and neck veins, facial edema, tachypnea, cyanosis, upper extremity edema, Horner's syndrome, and vocal cord paralysis. Chest radiography almost invariably shows a mass — usually in the right superior mediastinum. Lung carcinoma and lymphoma cause most cases of the SCV syndrome; fewer than 5 per cent result from benign causes such as thyroid goiter, pericardial constriction, idiopathic sclerosing mediastinitis, and thrombosis of the SVC.

Sputum cytology, bronchoscopy, mediastinoscopy, or lymph node biopsy usually yields a tissue diagnosis, although a diagnostic thoracotomy may be required.

Radiation therapy is generally the therapeutic modality of choice, although chemotherapy may be equally efficacious in patients with small cell lung carcinoma. The vast majority of patients have prompt palliation of symptoms. Failure to respond usually signifies thrombotic obstruction of the SVC. Supportive medical therapy with steroids, diuretics, anticoagulation, and (in the case of SVC thrombosis) fibrinolytic therapy may help to ameliorate symptoms.

TABLE 55–2. MANAGEMENT OF INCREASED INTRACRANIAL PRESSURE FROM BRAIN TUMORS

Stable Patient
1. Dexamethasone (or equivalent corticosteroid), 4 mg qid po; double q48h as necessary to control symptoms

Unstable Patient (Cerebral Herniation)
1. Dexamethasone, 100 mg IV stat; continue at 24 mg qid
2. Mannitol, 0.5–1 gm/kg IV stat; repeat as necessary
3. Intubate; control ventilation to keep Pa_{CO_2} at 25–30 mm Hg

REFERENCES

Kaufman D, Rosen N, Young RC: Medical emergencies in patients with solid tumors. In Parillo JE, Masur H (eds): The Critically Ill Immunosuppressed Patient—Diagnosis and Management. Rockville, MD, Aspen Publishers, 1987, pp 481–498.

SECTION VIII

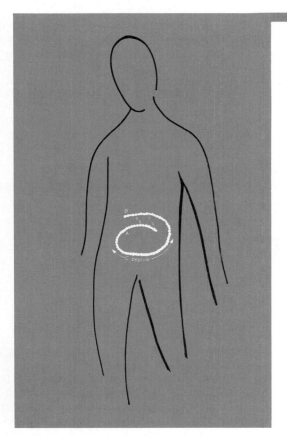

METABOLIC DISEASES

56 INTRODUCTION

A disorder is classified as a disease of metabolism when the fundamental pathogenic mechanism includes one of numerous chemical transformations that occur within living organisms. Such chemical reactions are divided into two large categories. Anabolic reactions are usually energy-requiring and generally result in the synthesis of molecules larger than those of the initial reactants. Catabolic reactions are energy-yielding processes that cause degradation of larger molecules into smaller products. Many diseases of metabolism involve specific enzyme defects that alter anabolic or catabolic processes. Defects that can be attributed to an un-

derlying genetic abnormality are termed inborn errors of metabolism. Other metabolic diseases are acquired rather than hereditary.

The diseases discussed in this section are chiefly those whose manifestations are multisystemic or in which biochemical and genetic factors dominate the clinical presentation. A complete discussion of all known inborn errors of metabolism falls beyond the scope of this text. Many inborn errors are life-limiting, leading to death in infancy or early childhood. This section focuses upon the more common hereditary or acquired metabolic diseases encountered in adults.

57 EATING DISORDERS

OBESITY

Clinicians most frequently use body weight or preferably the body mass index (BMI) (weight [kg]/height [m]²) to judge if a patient is "overweight." Very muscular individuals may be moderately overweight and not obese. Others with small frames and low muscle mass may be obese without fulfilling criteria for overweight. Nevertheless, most seriously overweight patients are also obese. An obesity classification scheme based on BMI is presented in Table 57–1.

Pathogenesis. Obesity and overweight are

largely genetically determined and are strongly conditioned by available palatable food and sedentariness. A child of two obese parents has about an 80 per cent chance of becoming obese, whereas the risk is only 15 per cent for the offspring of two parents of normal weight. Moreover, a correlation between parental and child BMI is found across a broad spectrum of values, suggesting both polygenic inheritance of obesity and several contributing metabolic mechanisms. The precise causative mechanisms remain unknown.

Fat accounts for 25 to 40 per cent of the weight of middle-aged men and women (Table 57–2). Body fat cells vary from 10 to 200 μ in diameter or about 8000-fold in total volume. Their numbers may vary between 2×10^{10} and 16×10^{10}. Fat cell size generally increases (hypertrophy) with increasing adiposity until the body fat content is about 30 kg. There is little increase in size as more body fat accumulates. Fat cell number, in contrast, increases in a linear fashion (hyperplasia) as total body fat increases from 10 to 90 kg.

A remarkable feature of adiposity is its constancy. Small increases in adiposity occur regularly with age (Table 57–2), but these are slight

TABLE 57–1. OBESITY CLASSIFICATION BASED ON BODY MASS INDEX (BMI)*

CLASSIFICATION	BMI
Underweight	<20
Normal	20–25
Overweight	25–30
Obese	30–40
Severely obese	>40

*In kilograms per square meter.

relative to the differences in adiposity among individuals. The extent of adiposity is therefore carefully and unconsciously regulated. Intentional overfeeding to increase weight is very difficult for experimental subjects and is followed by spontaneous caloric restriction until body weight returns to baseline.

How then does obesity occur? Fat people do not generally eat more than lean people, and many eat less. Because mass and energy are conserved, it is clear that at some time in life the obese individual consumed more calories than he or she expended. This temporary imbalance between energy intake and expenditure could be due to several factors (Table 57-3) involving the central nervous system or the adipocyte itself. Reduced sympathetic activity manifested by lower plasma norepinephrine and epinephrine levels, reduced fat mobilization, or low thermogenesis could reduce energy mobilization and expenditure. Enhanced parasympathetic activity, typical of ventromedial hypothalamic lesions, may augment food consumption. And, at least in theory, the brain may be insensitive to normal neural or humoral satiety signals.

Fat cells with enhanced lipoprotein lipase activity may have a competitive advantage in assimilating lipoprotein triglycerides. This occurs in the syndrome of multiple symmetric lipomatosis. The adipocyte itself may also resist lipolytic stimuli from nerves or circulating catecholamines. Gluteal fat in both men and women, for example, has a lower lipolytic response to alpha-adrenergic stimulation than does abdominal fat. Some fat depots may resist mobilization even when the rest of the body is starving, as in women with steatopygia who have massive accumulation of gluteal and femoral fat. Abdominal fat in men appears to have more alpha$_2$-adrenergic receptor function (antilipolytic) than abdominal fat in women, leading to more "beer bellies" in men. The fat cell may also fail to provide the brain with neural (afferent) or humoral (e.g., adipsin) signals indicating that peripheral fat stores are replete. Finally, when adipocytes of some individuals reach nearly maximal size, they may trigger differentiation and replication of preadipocytes and thus perpetuate growth of adipose mass.

Irrespective of the basic mechanism, at least transient reductions in energy expenditure seem to be important in the pathogenesis of most obesities. Babies with low total energy expenditure are likely to gain more weight in the first year of life, and low energy expenditure is a risk factor for weight gain even in adulthood. Paradoxically, the very weight gain that causes obesity can lead to a normalization of energy expenditure. Caloric restriction to achieve weight loss, in contrast, is associated with reductions in energy expenditure to levels far below those in naturally lean individuals.

The Anatomy of Obesity

It has been puzzling that obesity is associated with risk factors for vascular disease, but in prospective

TABLE 57-2. VARIATION OF FAT AND LEAN BODY MASS (LBM) WITH AGE

| | MEN | | WOMEN | |
| | (% Body Weight) | | | |
AGE	LBM	Fat	LBM	Fat
25	81	19	68	32
45	74	26	58	42
65	65	35	51	49

TABLE 57-3. POSSIBLE CAUSES OF OBESITY

Neurologic	Reduced sympathetic activity
	Increased parasympathetic activity
	Insensitivity to satiety signals
Adipocyte	Increased lipoprotein lipase activity
	Diminished fatty acid mobilization
	Reduced feedback to central nervous system
	Excessive cell replication
Other	Hyperinsulinemia

studies obesity is poorly predictive of vascular disease. Regional patterns of body fat distribution may partially explain this inconsistency. It appears that the form of obesity that characteristically occurs in men, called android or abdominal obesity, is closely associated with metabolic complications such as hypertension, insulin resistance, hyperuricemia, and dyslipoproteinemia. The typical female or gynecoid obesity, with fat deposited in hips and gluteal and femoral regions, has much less metabolic significance. The waist to hip circumference ratio has been used to distinguish these forms of obesity. In men a ratio above 1.0 and in women above 0.8 suggests the undesirable male obesity pattern. Thus, it is better to be shaped like a pear than like an apple. The BMI range associated with the lowest mortality is 20 to 25 kg/m^2.

Medical Consequences of Obesity

Clinically Severe Obesity. Subjects weighing 45 kg or 100 lbs (~60 per cent) more than desirable are designated severely obese. This corresponds to a weight of 240 lb in a woman 63 inches tall or 260 lb in a man of 68 inches. Cardiorespiratory problems present the greatest risk (Table 57-4). Chronic hypoventilation is common and leads to hypercapnia, pulmonary hypertension, and right heart failure. Left ventricular dysfunction also occurs and may be related to both hypertension and hypervolemia. Severe episodic hypoxia can cause arrhythmias, and sudden death is 10 times more common in the severely obese. Most devastating, however, are the psychosocial consequences of the disorder. Self-esteem and body image are impaired, immobility greatly limits

TABLE 57 – 4. MEDICAL COMPLICATIONS OF SEVERE OBESITY

Sudden death
Obstructive sleep apnea
Pickwickian syndrome: daytime hypoventilation, somnolence, polycythemia, and cor pulmonale
Congestive heart failure
Nephrotic syndrome/renal vein thrombosis
Immobility limiting daily activities

work and recreational activities, and humiliation is a daily experience when body size is too large for conventional scales, furniture, vehicles, and clothes.

Moderate Obesity. A weight more than 20 per cent above ideal poses increased risk of early mortality. Subjects more than 30 per cent overweight have about a 50 per cent greater mortality rate than those of average weight. Such naked statistics, however, can be deceiving. Overweight young adults (<45 years), for example, appear at risk from complications of moderate obesity, whereas obesity is less of a risk factor in older people. Restated, obesity does not appear to be a major risk factor in the age range where mortality is greatest. Moreover, there has been a slight increase in obesity prevalence in the United States in the past two decades, whereas total mortality rates have fallen by 20 to 30 per cent.

Some disorders are clearly related to obesity. Hypertension is more frequent in obese people than in those of normal weight. This may be due to sympathetic hyperactivity or to hyperinsulinemia, but neither mechanism is clearly established. Type II diabetes mellitus can be unmasked and aggravated by excess weight, and this may be the most important medical complication of moderate obesity. The cause appears to be insulin resistance, but many obese individuals never develop hyperglycemia. Obesity is often associated with high triglyceride and low high density lipoprotein (HDL) concentrations, particularly when mild glucose intolerance is also present. Finally, obesity clearly increases the risk of cholelithiasis and endometrial carcinoma.

Treatment of Obesity

Clinically Severe Obesity. Severe caloric restriction (200 to 800 kcal/day), with or without anorectic drugs, should be tried first. A greater than 90 per cent failure rate is the rule. Subjects more than 100 lb overweight who have failed medical treatment may be candidates for surgery (gastroplasty or gastric bypass) to reduce stomach size. Patients in general lose 40 to 50 per cent of excess weight within a year of gastric surgery, but some consume calorically dense liquids and regain weight. The long-term safety and efficacy of this surgery are not certain. The once common intestinal bypass surgery for morbid obesity has been abandoned because of unacceptable long-term complications.

Moderate Obesity. Low-calorie diets remain the most widely advocated treatment for obesity. The recommendation to count calories and eat less of everything has intuitive appeal but little success. Behavior modification techniques focusing on stimulus control, the obese eating style, group and spouse support, reinforcement procedures, and exercise are far more effective. More popular, but less successful, are innumerable eating plans based on marked diet imbalance (e.g., rice diet, ice cream diet, Fit-for-Life diet). These are only transiently helpful because a diet very low in either fat or carbohydrate rapidly becomes monotonous and unpalatable. Diets very low in carbohydrate are also ketogenic and inhibit appetite. Most dramatic in effect, but potentially hazardous, are the very low calorie diets that approximate a supplemented fast, rely on withdrawal of most conventional foods, and entail purchase and consumption of an expensive diet supplement. No diet calling for 800 or fewer calories should be undertaken without medical supervision. More than 50 deaths, some from documented ventricular tachycardia and fibrillation, occurred with the early "liquid protein," very low calorie diets.

No program consisting of caloric restriction alone has been generally successful beyond 12 to 18 months despite the enormous commercial success of diet books and systems.

Anorectic drugs are potentially addicting, often unsafe, and only marginally effective. Patients with any history of drug abuse should avoid any of the amphetamines. These agents may be useful in the short term when incorporated in a program that includes diet counseling, behavior modification, and close medical supervision.

When the pathophysiology of obesity is better defined, then more specific and effective measures should emerge.

ANOREXIA NERVOSA AND BULIMIA NERVOSA

These two psychiatric disorders are characterized by a distorted body image and abnormal eating patterns. Neither has a distinctive pathognomonic feature; the two disorders share some common features, and they may overlap (Table 57–5). Bulimia nervosa is not associated with cachexia, whereas this is the most prominent aspect of anorexia nervosa. The primary treatment of both disorders is psychiatric, although they may manifest important medical complications.

Anorexia Nervosa

Prevalence. The overall prevalence of anorexia nervosa is not known but has apparently increased over the past decade. In amenorrhea clinics, between 5 and 15 per cent of patients may be affected, and in a London study the prevalence among girls 16 to 18 years old was about 1 per cent. The disorder affects girls at least 10 times as often as boys, with typical onset in adolescence but occurrence as late as the menopause.

Pathogenesis and Clinical Features. Some individuals can recall life situations or events that triggered their preoccupation with thinness. The usual pubertal weight increase may be critical in most girls. The restriction of food intake is initially voluntary, and a compulsion to lose weight may lead to self-induced vomiting, abuse of purgatives and diuretics, and exhausting exercise. Patients view their own body dimensions as excessive, but their view of other people is not abnormal.

In typical cases, the diagnosis of anorexia nervosa presents little difficulty. In atypical cases (e.g., males, older women), individuals warrant careful evaluation for hyperthyroidism, malignancy, and malabsorption. Amenorrhea occurs early in the disorder. Weight loss, as in young female endurance athletes, is probably the cause of the amenorrhea. Hypothalamic dysfunction with markedly low gonadotropin secretion appears to be the responsible mechanism. Other signs of hypothalamic dysfunction include abnormal thermoregulation in hot and cold environments and sometimes frank hypothermia, loss of the cyclic pattern of adrenocorticotropin (ACTH) secretion, reduced vasopressin secretion with mild diabetes insipidus, delayed thyroid-stimulating hormone (TSH) response after thyrotropin-releasing hormone (TRH), and abnormal growth hormone response to glucose or apomorphine infusion.

Physical examination reveals little subcutaneous fat, with gaunt facies, atrophic breasts and buttocks, and often excessive growth of lanugo hair on neck and extremities. Hypotension may occur in association with hypovolemia (secondary to starvation and diabetes insipidus) and bradycardia (secondary to low triiodothyronine [T_3] levels due to reduced conversion of thyroxine [T_4]). Psychiatric evaluation may reveal a major depressive disorder in up to 50 per cent of patients. Otherwise, patients are often well behaved, perfectionistic, competitive, and achieving.

Treatment and Prognosis. There are no strict guidelines for treatment of anorexia nervosa. Patients should be evaluated by a psychologist or psychiatrist familiar with treatment of this disorder. Occasional patients may be successfully managed as outpatients. Most benefit more from psychiatric hospitalization and supervised diets of 3000 to 5000 kcal/day. Acutely ill and cachectic patients may require short-term parenteral nutrition with careful avoidance of water intoxication and hyperkalemia. More than one hospitalization of 20 to 50 days is required in half the patients.

Hypothalamic and endocrine problems generally resolve when 85 per cent of normal body weight is restored. Amenorrhea may persist for several more months, but menses usually return without specific intervention.

Anorexia nervosa causes death in at least 5 per cent of patients because of the starvation-dehydration-hypokalemia syndrome or deliberate

TABLE 57–5. DIAGNOSTIC CRITERIA FOR ANOREXIA NERVOSA AND BULIMIA NERVOSA

Anorexia Nervosa
Intense fear of obesity undiminished with weight loss
Disturbed body image
Loss of 25% original body weight; if <18 yr, 25% less than original + projected weight gain
No identifiable illness accounting for weight loss
Refusal to maintain normal body weight

Bulimia Nervosa
Recurrent binge eating and at least three of following criteria:
Ingestion of high-calorie, easily ingested food during a binge
Termination of binge by abdominal pain, sleep, social interruption, or self-induced vomiting
Repeated weight loss attempts using severe diet restriction, induced vomiting, or cathartics or diuretics
Weight fluctuations >4.5 kg due to binges and fasts

suicide. The illness may also be lifelong and appears less likely to remit when present for more than 10 years. Overall, 40 to 60 per cent of individuals make a good physical and psychosocial recovery.

Bulimia Nervosa

Prevalence. Bulimia nervosa may affect as many as 1 to 3 per cent of female adolescents and young adults in North America. As in the case of anorexia nervosa, the prevalence in boys is only 10 per cent of that in girls.

Pathogenesis and Clinical Features. Patients with bulimia often have a family history of major affective disorder (depression or manic-depression). The increase in weight and adiposity at puberty is probably the stimulus for bulimia, just as for anorexia nervosa. The hallmark of bulimia is not induced vomiting but binge eating; bulimia is synonymous with paroxysmal hyperphagia. Binges leave the patient embarrassed, guilty, and focused again on maintaining weight below an arbitrary level. This end is achieved by prolonged fasting, self-induced vomiting, nonprescription anorectics, and use of substances like diuretics and laxatives. In marked contrast to patients with anorexia nervosa, bulimics generally feel out of control and often welcome help.

Because bulimics are not wasted, physical findings may be subtle or absent. Calluses or scratches on the dorsum of the hand may result from abrasion by teeth during induced gagging. Puffy cheeks from parotid or other salivary gland enlargement are present in up to 50 per cent of patients, and serum salivary amylase levels may be elevated. Erosions occur on the lingual, palatal, and posterior occlusal surfaces of the teeth from acid-induced enamel dissolution and decalcification.

Frequent binge eating and vomiting may cause gastric or esophageal perforation or bleeding, pneumomediastinum, or subcutaneous emphysema. Heavy use of ipecac to induce vomiting may cause myopathic weakness and electrocardiographic abnormalities from emetine toxicity. Loss of gastric fluids can result in metabolic alkalosis with elevated carbon dioxide and hypochloremia. Diuretic abuse can produce both hypokalemia and hyponatremia. Menstrual irregularities are common, but amenorrhea is rare.

Treatment and Prognosis. Bulimics, in general, do not need psychiatric hospitalization. Depression and very abnormal beliefs about body weight and shape are typically present and underlie attitudes toward eating and weight control. Outpatient psychotherapy stresses self-monitoring and acquisition of a normal eating pattern, because fear of being out of control is intense. Issues of diet pills, laxatives, and diuretics must be directly addressed. Anticonvulsants and antidepressants have been successfully employed by some therapists, although such agents are not necessary in the majority of patients. The natural history of bulimia nervosa is poorly defined, and it is not certain how often current therapeutic approaches result in cures as opposed to short-term remissions.

REFERENCES

Epstein LH, Valoski A, Wing RR, McCurley J: Ten year follow-up of behavioral, family-based treatment for obese children. JAMA 264:2519–2523, 1990.

Herzog DB, Copeland PM: Eating disorders. N Engl J Med 313:295–303, 1985.

Mitchell JE, Seim HC, Colon E, Pomeroy C: Medical complications and medical management of bulimia. Ann Intern Med 107:71–77, 1987.

Stunkard AJ, Stellar E (eds): Eating and Its Disorders. New York, Raven Press, 1984.

58 PRINCIPLES OF ALIMENTATION AND HYPERALIMENTATION

PRINCIPLES OF NUTRITION AND NUTRITIONAL ASSESSMENT

Good nutrition is a prerequisite not only for optimal resistance to illness but also for optimal response to medical and surgical therapy. The recognition and treatment of malnutrition that accompanies illness play an important role in optimizing patient care. Energy needs vary with body size, age, sex, activity, and the presence or absence of disease. The use of recommended dietary allowances (RDAs) that have been established for most essential nutrients may not apply to sick or traumatized patients or to those with metabolic disorders. Increasingly, methods of nutritional assessment that have been used to assess the severity of malnutrition among populations in developing countries are being applied to hospitalized patients. New modes of delivering nutrients to sick patients by both the enteral and parenteral routes may improve morbidity and mortality by eliminating the role of malnutrition in the natural history of many diseases.

Protein, carbohydrate, and fat are the basic nutrients that provide energy in health and disease. Protein and carbohydrate supply about 4 kcal of energy per gram and fat 9 kcal per gram. Basal energy expenditure (BEE) is estimated from the oxygen consumed under resting conditions in healthy, nonobese subjects and usually approximates 25 kcal/kg/day. A number of calories are required in addition to the BEE depending on daily activity: 400 to 800 kcal for sedentary activity, 800 to 1200 kcal for light activity, 1200 to 1800 kcal for moderate activity, and up to 4500 kcal for strenuous exercise. Fasting and malnutrition reduce energy expenditure; however, the stress of illness increases caloric requirements. For example, in catabolic patients, an additional 50 to 100 per cent of the BEE may be required to prevent further tissue breakdown. In febrile patients, a 13 per cent increase in calories is required for each 1°C of fever.

Although carbohydrates are the main source of energy for most people in the world, there is no fixed requirement for this food group in the diet. Protein is needed to maintain body structure and function. The quality of dietary protein varies depending on the digestibility of the protein and its amino acid composition. High-quality proteins are easily absorbed and contain adequate amounts and proportions of the nine essential amino acids. The recommended allowance for dietary protein in healthy adults is 0.8 gm/kg/day. Catabolic patients may require 1.2 to 1.6 gm/kg/day. Dietary fat is a concentrated source of calories and a source of lipid-soluble vitamins. Essential fatty acids (i.e., linoleic acid, linolenic acid) are needed for membrane structure and integrity and serve as precursors for important eicosanoids. With the exception of neurons and erythrocytes, all body cells can utilize fatty acids as a direct source of energy. In addition to providing nutrients to match energy needs, the judicious diet must supply adequate amounts of water, essential minerals, and vitamins.

Nutritional assessment of hospitalized patients most often focuses on the recognition and treatment of the malnutrition that accompanies many illnesses. Protein-calorie malnutrition occurs whenever inadequate protein and/or calories are ingested to meet an individual's nutritional requirements (Table 58–1). The diagnosis of malnutrition is based on the dietary history, physical examination, anthropometric measurements, and laboratory studies. Dietary evaluation should include an assessment of the intake of major food groups and should focus on a history of recent weight loss, alterations in appetite, and symptoms of gastrointestinal disorders, including problems with chewing or swallowing, diarrhea, constipation, nausea, vomiting, and early satiety. The social history is an important facet of the dietary evaluation because social isolation, old age, poverty, and depression increase the risk of malnutrition.

The most obvious physical manifestation of chronic malnutrition is loss of body weight. Most individuals can tolerate a loss of up to 10 per cent of body weight without significant consequences; however, losses greater than 40 per cent below ideal weight are almost always fatal. Temporal muscle wasting, edema, and depigmentation of hair are other signs of malnutrition that can be confirmed by anthropometric and laboratory measurements. "Ideal" body weights for each inch of height have been derived from life insurance actuarial data. Other commonly employed anthropometric parameters include measurements of triceps skinfold thickness (an estimate of body fat reserves) and midarm muscle area (an estimate of lean body or skeletal muscle mass). Direct measurement of mineral or vitamin concentrations in body fluids may identify specific nutrient deficiencies; more often, measurements of various serum proteins (e.g., hemoglobin, albumin, transferrin) are used in assessing a patient's overall nutritional status, recognizing that certain laboratory abnormalities that could reflect malnutrition may have a non-nutritional cause (e.g., hypoalbuminemia, anemia). Serum albumin values more than 20 per cent below the lower limit of the normal range generally are regarded as substandard and corroborate a diagnosis of malnutrition in the proper clinical setting. In malnourished patients, the number of circulating lymphocytes diminishes, and delayed hypersensitivity to common skin antigens is impaired. A lymphocyte count of fewer than 1200/μl is substandard.

TABLE 58–1. CAUSES OF PROTEIN-CALORIE MALNUTRITION IN HOSPITALIZED PATIENTS

Decreased Oral Intake

Anorexia	Gastrointestinal disease
Nausea	Poor dentition
Dysphagia	

Increased Nutrient Losses

Malabsorption	Fistula drainage
Diarrhea	Protein-losing enteropathy
Bleeding	Nephrotic syndrome

Increased Nutrient Requirements

Fever	Trauma
Infection	Burns
Neoplasms	Surgery

PRINCIPLES OF NUTRITIONAL SUPPORT

Nutritional support of the hospitalized patient has become a complex system using alternate routes of metabolic support (enteral, peripheral venous, central venous) and multiple types of solutions. Decisions about the mode of nutritional support may be guided by the algorithm shown in Figure 58–1. The algorithm begins with a nutritional assessment based on the dietary history, physical examination, laboratory studies, and anthropometric measurements. If the diet is meeting requirements, no further therapy is needed. If the diet is inadequate, the decision to provide nutritional support is guided by the degree of nutritional depletion as assessed by body weight and by the anticipated duration of nutritional depletion. If body weight has declined by less than 5 per cent and the anticipated duration of inadequate nutrition is less than 7 days, nutritional supplements may not be necessary. If the degree of depletion is moderate (5 to 10 per cent) or severe (greater than 10 per cent) and the anticipated duration of illness is more than 7 days, intensive therapy may be needed. Whether forced enteral feeding or parenteral nutrition is chosen depends on the availability and adequacy of the gastrointestinal tract.

Enteral nutritional therapy encompasses the use of nutritional supplements to provide part or all of daily requirements and the use of special diets that either restrict a particular element of the diet (e.g., fat, lactose) or add a nutrient (e.g., fiber, calcium, potassium) that may be required in larger amounts than are available in conventional diets. If requirements are not great and appetite is good, table foods can be recommended as protein and calorie supplements. Chronically ill patients with anorexia, those with chronic inflammatory disorders who have increased requirements, and those who are marginally nourished and preparing for surgery are candidates for oral supplementation with one of a variety of commercial products that are high in caloric density. Forced enteral feeding (via nasogastric tube or gastrostomy tube) typically is used for those patients who have moderate to severe anorexia, those who cannot maintain a ca-

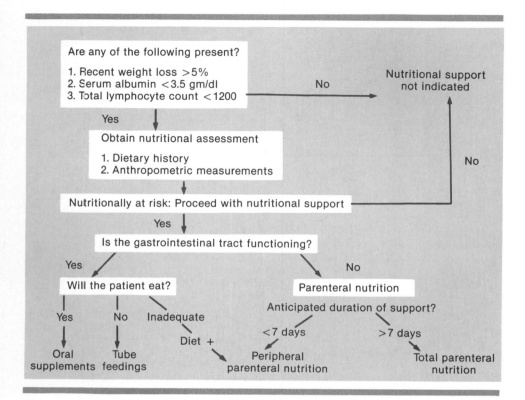

Are any of the following present?

1. Recent weight loss >5%
2. Serum albumin <3.5 gm/dl
3. Total lymphocyte count <1200

No → Nutritional support not indicated

Yes ↓

Obtain nutritional assessment

1. Dietary history
2. Anthropometric measurements

↓

Nutritionally at risk: Proceed with nutritional support → No

Yes ↓

Is the gastrointestinal tract functioning?

Yes ↙   No ↘

Will the patient eat?   Parenteral nutrition

Yes / No / Inadequate   Anticipated duration of support?

Oral supplements / Tube feedings / Diet +   <7 days / >7 days

Peripheral parenteral nutrition   Total parenteral nutrition

FIGURE 58–1. An algorithm for selecting nutritional therapy.

loric intake commensurate with their needs, or those with swallowing disorders. Nasoduodenal tubes are preferred in patients at high risk for aspiration. Feeding via a percutaneous gastrostomy tube is now used when the anticipated time for enteral supplementation is long (greater than 6 weeks) and the patient cannot swallow.

Parenteral nutrition provides protein and calories to partially meet, totally meet, or exceed daily nutritional requirements. Total parenteral nutrition (TPN) is indicated for two groups of patients: (1) those selected for nutritional support in whom the gastrointestinal tract is not usable for forced enteral feedings and (2) those in whom a nothing-by-mouth regimen (i.e., "bowel rest") is deemed beneficial for a primary gastrointestinal disease. TPN solutions must provide a source of protein (amino acids) and energy. A combination of dextrose, amino acids, and water provides the base solution to which vitamins and minerals can be added. The amino acid contents of standard commercial solutions are based largely on normal plasma amino acid concentrations; special formulas with an increased proportion of essential amino acids often are used in patients with renal failure to minimize the generation of urea. The monohydrate form of dextrose used in most commercial solutions provides 3.4 kcal/gm and can be used alone to achieve both positive energy balance and positive nitrogen balance as long as adequate amino acids are supplied. However, lipid emul-

sions of soybean or safflower oil are often added to provide up to 70 per cent of the daily caloric requirement, because they contain a concentrated source of calories, reduce the volume of fluid needed, and reduce the likelihood of hyperglycemia.

Parenteral solutions that provide all energy and protein requirements are hypertonic and must be administered through a central vein. Lesser concentrations of dextrose and amino acids (with a final osmolarity less than 600 mOsm/L) can be administered through a peripheral vein and often are employed as supplements to an inadequate enteral regimen. Isotonic lipid emulsions are regularly used as an energy source in peripheral vein parenteral nutrition because they reduce the osmolarity of the solution, thereby reducing the risk of thrombophlebitis.

REFERENCES

Frisancho AR: New standards of weight and body composition by frame size and height for assessment of nutritional status of adults and the elderly. Am J Clin Nutr 40:808, 1984.

Kaminski MV Jr (ed): Hyperalimentation: A Guide for Clinicians. New York, Marcel Dekker, 1985.

Siberman H, Eisenberg D: Parenteral and Enteral Nutrition for the Hospitalized Patient. East Norwalk, CT, Appleton-Century-Crofts, 1982.

59 HYPERURICEMIA AND GOUT

The term *gout* refers to a group of disorders characterized by a derangement in purine metabolism manifested by hyperuricemia, crystalline deposits of monosodium urate monohydrate in tissues (tophi), and recurrent episodes of acute arthritis. Hyperuricemia and gout may be classified as primary or secondary (Table 59–1). *Primary gout* results from inborn errors in the metabolism of purines or inherited defects in the renal tubular secretion of urate. *Secondary gout* occurs in disorders characterized by increased catabolism of nucleic acids or by acquired defects in the renal excretion of urate.

Pathogenesis

The biochemical hallmark of gout is an elevated level of serum urate, a metabolic end product formed by the oxidation of both exogenous and endogenous purine bases. The concentration of uric acid in body fluids reflects the balance between rates of production and elimination. Approximately one third of uric acid produced on a daily basis (100 to 300 mg in the adult) is excreted in the gastrointestinal tract, where it is destroyed by bacteria. The remaining two thirds (300 to 600 mg) is excreted in the urine. Hyperuricemia may result from increased production of uric acid, decreased renal excretion, or some combination of these factors.

The risk of developing gout increases with the degree of hyperuricemia; however, the pathogenesis of gout is related more closely to the *solubility* of urate in various body fluids than to its absolute concentration. The solubility of urate is influenced by temperature and pH. At 37°C and pH 7.40, the solubility of urate is 6.4 to 6.8 mg/dl. But solubility is considerably less at the lower temperatures of peripheral joints. A urate concentration of 7.0 mg/dl usually constitutes the physicochemical upper limit of normal beyond which supersaturation occurs and crystal formation increases. Virtually all patients with gout have serum urate levels above 7.0 mg/dl. Occasional patients exhibit lower levels during an acute attack, but hyperuricemia can almost always be demonstrated during quiescent periods.

Overproduction of uric acid, detected clinically by the urinary excretion of more than 600 mg of uric acid per day, accounts for fewer than 10 per cent of all cases of gout. Increased production of uric acid occurs as the result of an inherited en-zyme defect, as the secondary consequence of a disorder in which nucleic acid turnover is increased, or as an idiopathic phenomenon probably representing as yet undetected enzyme defects.

Uric acid is overproduced whenever there is increased turnover of nucleic acids due to rapid division or lysis of cells. Myeloproliferative and lymphoproliferative diseases, hemolytic anemias, and various hemoglobinopathies are the most common disorders in which this occurs. Hyperuricemia is a prominent feature of the "tumor lysis syndrome" that may follow treatment of patients with lymphoma, myeloproliferative disorders, or carcinomatosis.

Underexcretion of uric acid accounts for more than 90 per cent of all cases of gout. Impaired excretion may result from (1) reduced glomerular filtration of uric acid, (2) enhanced renal tubular reabsorption, (3) reduced tubular secretion, or (4) a combination of defects in filtration and tubular handling. In most instances of primary renal gout the defect remains undefined.

A number of factors can secondarily reduce renal urate excretion and cause gout. In patients with acute or chronic renal failure, reductions in glomerular filtration rate lead to a decrease in the filtered load of uric acid. Although renal disease is a frequent cause of hyperuricemia, clinical gout

TABLE 59–1. CLASSIFICATION OF HYPERURICEMIA AND GOUT

Primary (Presumably Genetic)
I. Metabolic (overproduction)
  A. Idiopathic (10% of primary gout)
  B. Associated with specific enzyme defects (<1% of primary gout)
    1. PP-ribose-P synthetase overactivity
    2. Partial deficiency of hypoxanthine-guanine phosphoribosyl transferase
    3. "Complete" deficiency of hypoxanthine-guanine phosphoribosyl transferase
II. Renal (idiopathic underexcretion—90% of primary gout)

Secondary (Acquired)
I. Metabolic
  A. Increased nucleic acid turnover (e.g., chronic hemolysis, lymphoproliferative or myeloproliferative disorders)
  B. Glucose-6-phosphatase deficiency (i.e., type I glycogen storage disease)
II. Renal
  A. Acute or chronic renal failure
  B. Volume depletion
  C. Altered tubular handling by drugs or endogenous metabolic products

TABLE 59–2. SOME DRUGS THAT AFFECT SERUM URIC ACID CONCENTRATION

Drugs That Increase Serum Uric Acid
Thiazides
"Loop" diuretics (furosemide, ethacrynic acid)
Small doses of salicylate (<2 gm/day)
Acetazolamide
Pyrazinamide
Ethambutol
Drugs That Decrease Serum Uric Acid
Increased renal excretion
Probenecid
Sulfinpyrazone
Phenylbutazone, oxyphenylbutazone
Large doses of salicylate (4–6 gm/day)
Decreased production
Allpurinol

seldom ensues, perhaps because uremia blunts the inflammatory response to urate crystals. Because renal tubular reabsorption of urate is linked to sodium reabsorption, hyperuricemia frequently accompanies disorders characterized by renal sodium avidity. Extracellular volume depletion of any cause (e.g., hemorrhage, gastrointestinal losses, adrenal insufficiency, diabetes insipidus) leads to decreased filtration and enhanced renal tubular reabsorption of uric acid. In clinical practice, diuretic therapy is probably the most common cause of secondary hyperuricemia and gout mediated by volume depletion. A number of other drugs can cause hyperuricemia by directly altering renal tubular handling of uric acid (Table 59–2). Some of these (e.g., thiazides, "loop" diuretics) are organic acids that may occupy uric acid secretory sites along the proximal nephron, thus impairing tubular secretion of urate. Competitive inhibition of uric acid secretion by *endogenous* organic acids accounts for hyperuricemia in patients with lactic acidosis and ketoacidosis.

Clinical Features

Gout is chiefly a disorder of adult males; only about 5 per cent of cases occur in women. The natural history encompasses four distinct clinical syndromes: (1) asymptomatic hyperuricemia, (2) acute gouty arthritis, (3) chronic tophaceous gout, and (4) nephrolithiasis. In most patients, these syndromes arise in roughly chronologic order; however, nephrolithiasis may precede the development of arthritis in approximately 20 per cent of cases. Clinical gout is uncommon before the third decade of life; its peak age of onset in men is about 45 years, usually after 20 to 30 years of sustained hyperuricemia. *Asymptomatic hyperuricemia* refers to elevation of serum urate prior to the development of arthritic symptoms, tophi, or nephrolithiasis.

Acute Gouty Arthritis. The primary manifestation of gout is a painful arthritis, usually involving the lower extremities. Ninety per cent of initial attacks are monoarticular, and at least half involve the first metatarsophalangeal joint (podagra). Other initial sites of involvement, in order of frequency, include the ankles, heels, knees, wrists, fingers, and elbows. Acute gouty arthritis may be precipitated by events such as trauma, surgery, alcohol ingestion, or systemic infection. Although the course of an untreated attack varies, initial episodes are usually self-limited. More than 50 per cent of patients, however, experience recurrent arthritis within 1 year of the first attack. Later attacks tend to be more prolonged and severe and more commonly involve multiple joints.

A presumptive diagnosis of gout can be made if the patient is hyperuricemic and has the classic clinical features described above. Unfortunately, a substantial minority of patients with acute gout exhibit *normal* uric acid levels. A dramatic response to colchicine is highly suggestive but not pathognomonic of acute gout. When the diagnosis is in doubt, acute gouty arthritis can be confirmed by demonstration of negatively birefringent, needle-shaped urate crystals within the white blood cells of synovial fluid examined under a polarizing lens. Synovial fluid analysis otherwise exhibits nonspecific signs of acute inflammation. The leukocyte count ranges from 1000 to more than $70,000/\mu l$, with a predominance of polymorphonuclear cells. Concentrations of glucose and uric acid in synovial fluid are usually similar to those in serum.

Chronic Tophaceous Gout. In untreated patients, tophaceous deposits of monosodium urate ultimately appear in cartilage, tendons, bursae, soft tissues, and synovial membranes at a rate that parallels the degree and duration of hyperuricemia. Common sites include the external ear and pressure points such as the Achilles tendons and olecranon bursae. Gouty tophi may spontaneously ulcerate and extrude a pasty material consisting of pure urate. Although tophi themselves are painless, their presence in and around joints ultimately can limit joint mobility.

Nephrolithiasis. Two distinct renal syndromes are associated with hyperuricemia. (1) *Acute urate nephropathy* results from the precipitation of urate within renal tubules and occurs almost exclusively in patients with myeloproliferative or lymphoproliferative disorders with severe hyperuricemia (serum uric acid >25 mg/dl), especially following chemotherapy. Intratubular obstruction with uric acid may cause profound reductions of glomerular filtration rate and severe azotemia. (2) *Uric acid urolithiasis* occurs in approximately 20 per cent of patients with a history of gouty arthritis. Increased urinary excretion of uric acid is the main factor favoring the formation of uric acid stones. Both gouty and nongouty uric acid stone formers also exhibit inappropriate urine acidity that favors the precipitation of uric acid. Gouty subjects also have an increased incidence of calcium oxalate stones, perhaps because uric acid crystals serve as a nidus for calcium stone formation.

More than 90 per cent of patients with chronic

tophaceous gout exhibit interstitial urate deposits. There is, however, no clear-cut evidence that chronic gout directly causes renal insufficiency. The observation that renal disease is a common cause of death in patients with gouty arthritis may be explained by the frequent occurrence of hyperuricemia in patients with hypertension and diabetes mellitus. In some patients, especially younger adults, the concurrence of hyperuricemia and renal dysfunction may reflect underlying lead nephropathy.

Treatment

Management of Asymptomatic Hyperuricemia. Controversy surrounds the management of asymptomatic hyperuricemia. Because only 10 to 20 per cent of patients with asymptomatic hyperuricemia develop arthritis, treatment should be withheld unless the patient (1) has a strong family history of gout or uric acid nephrolithiasis, (2) is excreting greater than 1100 mg/day of uric acid, or (3) has a serum uric acid level greater than 11 mg/dl.

Treatment of Acute Gouty Arthritis. Acute gout is treated with one of three types of antiinflammatory agents: colchicine, nonsteroidal antiinflammatory drugs (NSAIDs), or corticosteroids. Colchicine is the only therapeutic agent with specific diagnostic value in acute gout. An initial oral dose of 0.6 to 1.2 mg should be administered as soon as the diagnosis is suspected. The initial dose should be followed by 0.6 mg every hour until (1) symptoms of arthritis abate, (2) nausea, vomiting, or diarrhea develops, or (3) a maximum dose of 6 mg has been administered. When this regimen is initiated within 12 hours of the onset of symptoms, colchicine is effective in more than 90 per cent of cases; however, gastrointestinal side effects preclude administration of optimal doses in a number of patients. Intravenous colchicine is advantageous when a rapid response is desired or when gastrointestinal side effects prohibit oral administration of the drug. Occasionally, intravenous colchicine is effective when the oral preparation is not. The initial intravenous dose of colchicine is 2 mg (injected over 2 to 5 minutes), followed by 0.5 mg every 6 hours until a daily satisfactory response is achieved. The total daily dose of intravenous colchicine should not exceed 4 mg.

NSAIDs, including indomethacin, phenylbutazone, naproxen, fenoprofen, and ibuprofen, are also effective in the treatment of acute gouty arthritis. In general, these agents should initially be administered at nearly maximal doses, with gradual tapering as symptoms subside. For example, indomethacin may be given as an oral dose of 75 mg, followed by 50 mg every 8 hours for three doses, and then 25 mg every 8 hours for three doses.

Corticosteroids should be reserved for patients in whom full doses of colchicine or NSAIDs are either contraindicated or ineffective. Intraarticular injections of steroids (e.g., 5 to 10 mg of triamcinolone) are effective in treating acute gout limited to a single joint. Alternatively, 40 to 80 mg/day of prednisone for 3 to 4 days may be effective, but rebound attacks of gout are common. Uricosuric agents and allopurinol are of no value in the treatment of acute gouty arthritis. Once an attack subsides, administration of small daily doses of colchicine (0.6 to 1.2 mg/day) is effective in preventing further attacks.

Prevention or Reversal of Urate Deposition and Nephrolithiasis. Antihyperuricemic drugs should be administered to patients with recurrent gouty arthritis, nephrolithiasis, or tophi. The goal is to maintain the serum urate level below 7.0 mg/dl. Reductions to these levels can be achieved by drugs that increase the renal excretion of uric acid or decrease uric acid production. Although a number of drugs exhibit uricosuric properties (Table 59–2), only probenecid and sulfinpyrazone are widely employed specifically as antihyperuricemic agents. Uricosuric therapy is accompanied by a transient increase in uric acid excretion, which returns to pretreatment levels a few days later as the total body urate pool is depleted. To avoid overt nephrolithiasis during this transient hyperuricosuric phase, the uricosuric agents should be started at low doses and gradually increased. For example, probenecid is started in doses of 250 mg twice daily and increased over a period of several weeks to the dose necessary to achieve effective reversal of hyperuricemia. Sulfinpyrazone is begun at 50 mg twice daily and increased to maintenance levels of 300 to 400 mg/day in divided doses. In addition, maintaining an ample urine flow with adequate hydration reduces the likelihood of stone formation. Probenecid and sulfinpyrazone are ineffective in patients with impaired renal function (glomerular filtration rate <30 ml/min).

Hyperuricemia may also be controlled by allopurinol, a drug that decreases uric acid production by inhibiting xanthine oxidase, the enzyme that catalyzes the conversion of hypoxanthine to xanthine and xanthine to uric acid. In most patients, 300 mg/day is effective, but the half-life of allopurinol is increased in patients with renal insufficiency so that a smaller dose (100 to 200 mg) may be sufficient. Although uncommon, adverse effects with allopurinol are more severe than with uricosuric drugs and include fever, dermatitis, elevation of hepatic enzymes, diarrhea, and occasional vasculitis. *Initiation of antihyperuricemic therapy with any agent may precipitate acute gouty arthritis, because acute gout may occur whenever there is a rapid change in the serum urate concentration.* It is prudent to begin prophylactic therapy with colchicine just prior to the initiation of antihyperuricemic drugs.

Acute urate nephropathy can be prevented by administration of allopurinol to patients with neoplastic disorders prior to administration of chemotherapy. For prophylaxis during treatment of lymphoproliferative or myeloproliferative disorders, treatment with 600 to 900 mg/day is advisable during the first few days of therapy; thereafter the dose is tapered to 300 mg/day, so long as the serum urate remains less than 7.0 mg/dl. A generous intake of fluids should be maintained to ensure a high rate of urine flow. Urinary alkalinization also helps to prevent intrarenal precipitation of uric acid. The pKa of uric acid is 5.75. In urine at pH 5.0, only 15 per cent of uric acid exists in soluble, ionized form. The solubility increases more than 10-fold at pH 7.0 and more than 100-fold at pH 8.0. Administration of sodium bicarbonate and/or the carbonic anhydrase inhibitor acetazolamide should be considered in patients at high risk for developing acute urate nephropathy.

OTHER DISORDERS OF PURINE METABOLISM

Xanthinuria is a rare genetic disorder, probably inherited as an autosomal recessive trait, that results from deficiency of the enzyme xanthine oxidase. Affected patients exhibit hypouricemia, increased urinary excretion of hypoxanthine and xanthine, and sometimes xanthine kidney stones. They are otherwise asymptomatic.

Immune dysfunction may be associated with certain enzyme deficiencies in the purine pathway. Patients with deficiency of adenosine deaminase, which normally catalyzes the deamination of adenosine to inosine, have severe combined immunodeficiency (i.e., severe dysfunction of cell-mediated immunity with milder abnormalities of humoral immunity). Deficiency of purine nucleoside phosphorylase, which catalyzes the conversion of inosine to hypoxanthine and guanosine to guanine, has also been associated with an inherited immunodeficiency syndrome.

REFERENCES

Berger L, Yu TF: Renal function in gout. IV. An analysis of 624 gouty subjects including long-term follow-up studies. Am J Med 59:605, 1975.
Wyngaarden JB: Gout. In Wyngaarden JB, Smith LH Jr, Bennett JC (eds): Cecil Textbook of Medicine. 19th ed. Philadelphia, WB Saunders Co, 1992, pp 1107–1114.

60 DISORDERS OF LIPID METABOLISM

PLASMA LIPOPROTEIN PHYSIOLOGY

The major properties of the plasma lipoproteins are summarized in Table 60–1. Normal men and women daily consume 80 to 120 gm of fat (triglyceride, TG). Dietary fat is hydrolyzed by pancreatic lipase, absorbed by the intestinal mucosal cells, and secreted into the mesenteric lymphatics as chylomicrons (Fig. 60–1). One hundred grams of dietary fat mixed in an adult plasma volume of 25 dl can theoretically increase plasma TG by 4000 mg/dl! The liver also transforms unneeded plasma free fatty acids and calories from any source into TG and daily secretes an additional 10 to 30 gm of very low density lipoprotein (VLDL) TG into the plasma. This potentially further increases TG by 1000 mg/dl. Both chylomicrons and VLDL acquire a 9000 MW peptide called apolipoprotein C-II (apo C-II) from plasma high density lipoproteins (HDL). Apo C-II is a critical cofactor for lipoprotein lipase, which is located on the capillary endothelium of muscle and adipose tissue. After hydrolysis of chylomicron and VLDL TG, excess phospholipid, cholesterol, and apoproteins transfer to HDL and increase HDL mass. The remnants remaining after hydrolysis of chylomicron TG are cleared very rapidly by the liver and do not normally accumulate in plasma. This process is mediated by apolipoprotein E (apo E) on the chylomicron surface and the B,E receptor on the hepatocyte cell membrane.

TABLE 60–1. PROPERTIES OF LIPOPROTEINS

LIPOPROTEIN CLASS	ORIGIN	MAJOR APOPROTEIN GROUPS	MAJOR CORE LIPID
Chylomicrons	Intestine	B-48, C, E	Dietary triglycerides
VLDL	Liver	B-100, C, E	Hepatic triglycerides
LDL	VLDL catabolism	B-100	Cholesteryl esters
Lp(a)	Liver	B-100, (a)	Cholesteryl esters
HDL	Liver, intestine	A, C	Cholesteryl esters

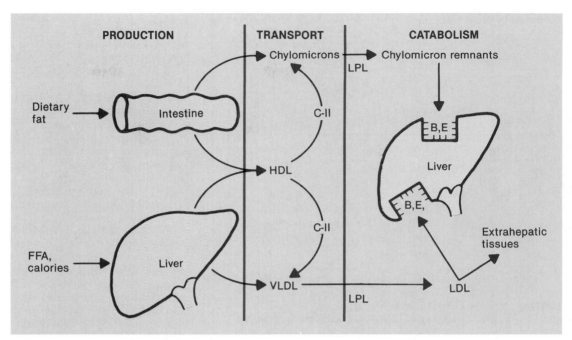

FIGURE 60–1. Normal metabolism of plasma lipoproteins. See text for details. FFA = Free fatty acids; HDL = high density lipoproteins: VLDL = very low density lipoproteins; LDL = low density lipoproteins; B,E = membrane receptor for lipoproteins containing apo B and apo E.

Some VLDL remnants (10 to 30 per cent) are also cleared directly by the liver, but the majority are converted to intermediate density lipoproteins (IDL). IDL are normally short-lived and by the action of lipases are converted to the final VLDL catabolic product, low density lipoproteins (LDL) (Fig. 60–1). In contrast to VLDL, which survive about 20 minutes in plasma, LDL circulate for 3 to 5 days. Although LDL normally account for 70 per cent of the total plasma cholesterol, they are basically metabolic garbage. Most LDL clearance from plasma takes place when apo B on the LDL surface binds to the B,E receptor on membranes of many tissues, particularly the liver.

Lp (a) lipoproteins are secreted by the liver, constitute 10 per cent or less of the total plasma lipoprotein mass, possess regions homologous to plasminogen, and are associated with vascular disease risk. Genetic heterogeneity produces 100-fold concentration differences among individuals, and levels are little affected by diet, habits, and most lipid-lowering drugs.

HDL are secreted into plasma by both intestine and liver. It is thought that HDL readily accept cholesterol from cells and other lipoproteins. This cholesterol initially is absorbed onto the HDL surface, where it is substrate for the plasma enzyme lecithin:cholesterol acyltransferase (LCAT). LCAT transfers a fatty acid from phosphatidyl choline to the 3-hydroxyl group of cholesterol. This produces cholesteryl esters that move from the hydrophilic HDL surface into the hydrophobic HDL core. The HDL surface is then free to accept more choles-

terol from cells or other lipoproteins. The cholesteryl esters in the HDL core can be removed and transferred by a plasma protein and are the major source of cholesteryl esters contained in VLDL, microns, and LDL.

At least 10 well-characterized apolipoproteins are located on lipoprotein surfaces. These stabilize the lipoprotein micelle, are recognized by cell membrane receptors, and serve as enzyme cofactors. Their major lipoprotein associations are listed in Table 60–1. The usefulness of quantifying these apolipoproteins in clinical practice is uncertain.

EVALUATION OF SERUM LIPOPROTEIN CONCENTRATIONS

Cholesterol levels should be measured in children who have a parent with hyperlipidemia or coronary heart disease before age 55 years. Routine screening of other children is not recommended. Every adult should have a total serum cholesterol and HDL-cholesterol determined during his or her third decade. A total cholesterol value less than 200 mg/dl at any time of day does not require retesting for 5 years. A level greater than 200 mg/dl should lead to measurement of total cholesterol, TG, and HDL-cholesterol after a 14-hour fast. Similar testing is indicated in adults who have first-degree relatives with vascular disease or lipid disorders. An HDL-cholesterol level below 35 mg/dl in men and below 45 mg/dl in women signifies clearly increased risk. If TG levels are over 500

TABLE 60–2. APPROACH TO ELEVATED LDL-CHOLESTEROL LEVELS BASED ON CORONARY RISK STATUS*

LDLc LEVEL	TREATMENT
<130 mg/dl	None
130–160 mg/dl	Diet
160–190 mg/dl	Diet; consider drugs if two CHD risk factors present
>190 mg/dl	Diet and consider drugs if diet fails

*CHD risk factors include male sex, peripheral vascular disease, diabetes mellitus, hypertension, cigarette smoking, >30% overweight, low HDL (<35 mg/dl), and family history of CHD before 55 years.

mg/dl, then specific treatment of hypertriglyceridemia should be undertaken. The highest total cholesterols commonly encountered (600 to 2000 mg/dl) are usually due to increases in chylomicrons and VLDL. Elevated cholesterols, therefore, cannot be interpreted without knowledge of TG levels.

If TG levels are less than 400 mg/dl, then the LDL-cholesterol (LDL_c) is calculated as follows:

$$LDL_c = Total\ C - (HDL_c + VLDL_c)$$
$$= Total\ C - (HDL_c + TG/5)$$

A therapeutic strategy based on LDL is indicated in Table 60–2.

Elevated HDL levels are thought to confer protection against coronary heart disease (CHD) and do not require treatment. Low HDL levels justify aggressive modification of other factors, including even mild LDL elevations (>130 mg/dl).

ELEVATED CHYLOMICRONS, VLDL, AND IDL

Disorders Manifest in Childhood. The occurrence of eruptive xanthomas, lipemia retinalis, hepatosplenomegaly, and abdominal pain in an infant or small child suggests a primary defect in clearance of chylomicrons and VLDL. This may be due to a deficiency of lipoprotein lipase (assayed in plasma after heparin injection) or of apo C-II, the cofactor for lipoprotein lipase. These abnormalities have a prevalence less than one or two in a million.

Disorders Manifest in Adulthood. Chylomicrons and VLDL are both catabolized by lipoprotein lipase, and the enzyme is saturable. The enzyme prefers chylomicrons, so VLDL usually accumulate first until TG levels exceed 500 mg/dl. At higher levels, both VLDL and chylomicrons contribute to the hypertriglyceridemia. Testing to resolve the independent contribution of these two lipoproteins is rarely indicated, and tests for lipoprotein lipase and apo C-II should be reserved for cases arising in childhood. Most hypertriglyceridemia in adults appears to be due to VLDL overproduction, although defective catabolism is responsible in a subset of patients.

Moderate to severe hypertriglyceridemia is relatively common in men and women older than 30 years. The disorder is usually genetic and is commonly associated with hypertension, hyperuricemia, and abnormal glucose tolerance. Hypertriglyceridemia may be aggravated by obesity, even moderate alcohol consumption, exogenous estrogens, and drugs such as diuretics and beta-adrenoreceptor blockers. Common secondary causes of hypertriglyceridemia are renal disease with proteinuria, both hyper- and hypothyroidism, exogenous and endogenous glucocorticoids, and type II diabetes mellitus. A very severe form of hypertriglyceridemia (2000 to 6000 mg/dl) can occur in patients with chronic insulin deficiency and very mild acidosis. This abnormality is completely corrected by insulin administration. The hypertriglyceridemia occurring in acute diabetic ketoacidosis is usually milder [250 to 800 mg/dl] and also responds to insulin.

The importance of hypertriglyceridemia in vascular disease risk is controversial. A National Institutes of Health (NIH) consensus conference concluded that TG levels under 250 mg/dl were normal, those 250 to 500 mg/dl were borderline, and only higher values were considered abnormal. Nevertheless, TG levels in the upper normal range (120 to 250 mg/dl) are very prevalent in CHD populations, and within this range the inverse relationship between TG and HDL-cholesterol is strongest. The association of hypertriglyceridemia with diabetes mellitus, obesity, and hypertension has further confounded efforts to define its independent role in vascular disease.

Dysbetalipoproteinemia. This disease is characterized by the accumulation of chylomicron remnants and IDL in plasma. It is caused by homozygosity for a species of apo E (E_2) which does not bind normally to the B,E receptor (Fig. 60–1). This leads to defective hepatic clearance of chylomicron remnants and ineffective catabolism of IDL to LDL.

Apo E_2 differs from normal apo E_3 and apo E_4 because of a point mutation causing a cysteine-for-arginine substitution. Homozygosity for apo E_2 occurs in 1 to 2 per cent of the population, but less than one in a thousand develops hyperlipidemia. Dysbetalipoproteinemia occurs only if the E_2 homozygote also has an additional disorder such as hypothyroidism or familial hypertriglyceridemia. This abnormality is suspected in individuals who have elevated levels of both cholesterol and TG. Diagnosis requires demonstration of the apo E_2 homozygosity (not generally available) or unusual cholesterol enrichment of the VLDL. If the ratio of cholesterol to TG in VLDL isolated by ultracentrifugation is higher than 0.40, then dysbetalipoproteinemia is likely. This form of hyperlipoproteinemia causes palmar and tuboeruptive xanthomas as well as coronary and peripheral vascular disease. The condition is worth identifying because it is exquisitely sensitive to weight reduction, cholesterol-lowering diets, and drugs such as clofibrate, gemfibrozil, lovastatin, and fenofibrate.

Familial Combined Hyperlipoproteinemia This term has been used to describe families with a mixture of lipoprotein abnormalities that appear to segregate as an autosomal dominant trait. Affected members may have high VLDL levels, high LDL levels, or elevations of both VLDL and LDL. The basic abnormality is probably VLDL overproduction. Subjects who do not effectively catabolize VLDL show only hypertriglyceridemia. Those who are very efficient in VLDL catabolism manifest only increased cholesterol and LDL levels. Others show combined elevations of TG (VLDL) and cholesterol (LDL). Family screening is required for a confident diagnosis, but the label is often loosely used to describe anyone with both VLDL and LDL elevations. The abnormality occurs frequently in patients with CHD, and affected patients often require diet and several lipid-lowering drugs to achieve normal lipid concentrations. This is one of the most difficult treatment problems.

TREATMENT OF HYPERTRIGLYCERIDEMIA

General Principles. The treatment of the hyperlipoproteinemias requires a systematic approach (Table 60-3). In general, the abnormality should be documented twice before treatment is undertaken. About half of affected individuals are sensitive to diet (>10 per cent reduction in lipids), and the extent of sensitivity should be defined by administering a very strict diet for 2 to 3 weeks (Table 60-4). Patients are retested once or preferably twice on this diet, and the results provide a point of reference for all future diet and drug interventions. If diet reduces lipids to target values —at or below the general population means— then it may be liberalized to give greater menu variety. Skinned, defatted fowl may substitute for some fish entrees and lean red meat may be consumed once each week. If target values are not achieved, then drug treatment is considered (Table 60-5). Compliance is best when patients chart their lipid levels, have ready access to test results, and have follow-up testing every 3 to 4 months. Assessment of drug effects takes no more than 1 to 2 months, and in general the efficacy of individual agents should be established before combinations are prescribed.

Diet. Reduced fat consumption is the only treatment for patients with deficiencies of lipoprotein lipase or apo C-II. The daily fat intake is limited to 25 gm by restricting all fat-enriched foods, including those made from vegetable oils. Adults with more common forms of severe hypertriglyceridemia and levels over 1000 mg/dl should also follow a low-fat diet to reduce TG levels to less than 500 mg/dl. Subjects with milder TG elevations benefit from a diet that is close to a fish-vegetarian diet (see Table 60-4). This very strict diet typically lowers cholesterol levels by 15 to 20 per cent and TG levels by 30 to 40 per cent in hypertriglyceridemics. A second major objective of diet is to reduce body fat content. Most hypertriglyceridemics show marked improvement while

TABLE 60-3. TREATMENT OF HYPERLIPOPROTEINEMIA

1. Document abnormality twice after a 14-hr fast while on typical American diet. Provisionally classify as cholesterol or triglyceride problem. Test total cholesterol, TG, HDL_C.
2. Evaluate potential for control with diet modification—fish-vegetarian diet for 3 wk; retest after 2 and 3 wk.
3. Return to conventional lipid-lowering diet (30% fat with equal proportions of polyunsaturated, monounsaturated, and saturated fats) for 4 wk; retest.
4. If target values are not achieved, add lipid-lowering medicine or food supplements. Retest 4 wk after each change in regimen.

Maintenance

5. Patient keeps lipid record on flow sheet and has rapid access to test results.
6. Minimum follow-up test frequency is every 4 mo.

TABLE 60-4. FISH-VEGETARIAN DIET

Permissible Foods/Beverages	Foods to Be Omitted
Fish (including clams, oysters, lobster, shrimp, and scallops)	Meat (including fowl)
Bread	Baked goods (including desserts and "chips")
Pasta (with vegetable oil, tomato, or clam sauce if desired)	Dairy products (including eggs, butter, and cheese)
Potato	**Restaurants**
Rice	None
Vegetables (all)	**Fast Foods**
Fruits (except avocado) and fruit juices	None
Vegetable oils, margarine, and mayonnaise	
Peanut butter	
Nuts (except for coconut and macadamia)	
Cereal (except granola-type "natural" cereals)	
Low-fat crackers (Matzo, Ry Krisp, Stoned Wheat Thins)	
Angel food cake (plain)	
Skimmed (not 1%) milk	
Coffee, tea, soda	
Alcohol	
Nondairy creams	
Coffee-Rich	
Poly-Rich	
Poly-Perx	

TABLE 60-5. DRUGS FOR HYPERLIPOPROTEINEMIA

CHOLESTEROL PROBLEMS	TRIGLYCERIDE PROBLEMS
Resins (cholestyramine, colestipol)	Fibrates (clofibrate, gemfibrozil, fenofibrate, etc.)
Niacin (regular or timed-release)	Niacin
Lovastatin, pravastatin	Fish oils
Combinations	Combinations
Others (probucol, fibrates)	

actively losing weight, and a significant proportion are cured after weight reduction. Finally, alcohol should be restricted to one or two servings a week, and this alone may correct the problem. If TG levels of 300 mg/dl or less are not sustained by diet, then exercise programs or drugs are appropriate in many patients.

Exercise. TG levels are reduced after even a single exercise session, and exercise has been shown to augment lipoprotein lipase activity. The efficacy of regular aerobic exercise in mild to moderate hypertriglyceridemia has been repeatedly demonstrated, and exercise has great potential in promoting weight loss. The program goal should be 45 minutes of submaximal exercise on 5 days each week. The type of aerobics, duration, and intensity should be explicitly defined by the physician to promote compliance.

Drugs. The fibrate class of drugs (Table 60–5) enhances lipoprotein lipase activity and may have dramatic effects in severe hypertriglyceridemics requiring drug treatment. Fibrates are most effective in patients with dysbetalipoproteinemia and in others with high VLDL levels reflected by high total cholesterol levels (500 to 1000 mg/dl) as well as high triglyceride levels (1000 to 10,000 mg/dl). When hypertriglyceridemia is due primarily to chylomicronemia and the cholesterol is only modestly elevated (250 to 500 mg/dl), the fibrates are less effective than dietary fat restriction. Use of niacin in moderate hypertriglyceridemia (500 to 1000 mg/dl) can be gratifying but requires considerable patience by both physician and patient. The starting dose is 100 mg three times daily after meals, with very slow dose escalation to 1.5 to 4.5 gm/day. The user should be thoroughly familiar with niacin's side effects and their significance and control. Fish oils reduce hepatic VLDL production and are a popular but still experimental treatment for hypertriglyceridemia. The minimum effective dose is 12 to 16 gm/day (e.g., 4 gm with each meal and at bedtime), and TG levels are usually reduced by 40 per cent in moderately severe hypertriglyceridemia (500 to 1500 mg/dl).

Fibrates and fish oils can increase LDL levels while lowering VLDL and chylomicrons. Occasionally, LDL levels are raised above 160 mg/dl (see Table 60–2), and this undesirable effect must be weighed against the potential gain.

ELEVATED LDL

Polygenic Hypercholesterolemia. An individual's total cholesterol level is, on average, intermediate between that of his parents. About 60 to 70 per cent of a patient's cholesterol or LDL level is, therefore, genetically determined, with the remaining contribution from age, sex, diet, and other factors. The nature of these genetic effects is not defined. Subjects in the upper range of the normal distribution have an increased CHD risk, and the upper 50 per cent contribute about 80 per cent of CHD cases. Those in the highest 25 per cent are generally considered targets for diet or even drug intervention.

Familial Monogenic Hypercholesterolemia. About 1 in 500 North Americans has a monogenic disorder producing an abnormality of the B,E receptor (Fig. 60–1). Affected individuals exhibit roughly half the normal number of receptors when their fibroblasts are grown in tissue culture. As a consequence, they generally have total cholesterol levels around 370 mg/dl and more than twice the average concentration of LDL. Increased LDL is manifest in the first year of life and is associated with early corneal arcus, xanthomas of the Achilles tendon and extensor tendons of the hands, and a risk of CHD that is about 25 times that in unaffected relatives. Heterozygous men have a 50 per cent chance of myocardial infarction by 50 years of age, and the comparable risk in women is 10 to 20 per cent. Homozygotes or those heterozygotic for two abnormal alleles (compound heterozygotes) have cholesterol levels of 650 to 1000 mg/dl and severe xanthomatosis and typically die of cardiovascular disease before age 30.

TREATMENT OF HYPERCHOLESTEROLEMIA

General Principles. These are the same as defined for hypertriglyceridemia and as outlined in Table 60–3.

Diet. Limitation of dietary saturated fat is central to both cholesterol- and TG-lowering diets. Carbohydrates are often substituted for the saturated fats, but high-carbohydrate diets may increase TG and reduce HDL. Monounsaturated fats may prove better substitutes for saturated fat. Reduction of dietary cholesterol has a small additional LDL-lowering effect. In practice, the optimal diet approaches the fish-vegetarian diet used to establish diet sensitivity (see Table 60–4). The average hypercholesterolemic lowers total cholesterol by 12 per cent (range, 0 to 40 per cent) on this diet. When diet responders show secondary failure, the usual cause is noncompliance. This can be identified by asking patients to complete a 7-day diet diary and reviewing the record with them. Subjects who travel extensively and eat frequently in restaurants have greatest trouble with diet prescriptions.

Exercise. Although trained endurance athletes have LDL levels about 10 per cent lower than those of controls, endurance training is generally not effective in reducing LDL concentrations. As noted above, exercise effects in hypertriglyceridemics are much more substantial.

Drugs. Several considerations govern choice of drugs for hypercholesterolemics not controlled by diet. The drugs are usually prescribed for years to decades, and most are moderately expensive. The risk-benefit profile must be carefully assessed because any significant morbid or mortal effects can offset the modest potential gains. Annoying side effects limit compliance with some agents, and no drug has been shown to prolong life in populations at CHD risk.

The resins (Table 60–5) are safe and effective and are the only agents appropriate for children. The starting dose is 2 scoops or unit dose packets before supper; this dose is enough in many mild hypercholesterolemics; and more than 6 unit doses a day is rarely worth the cost and inconvenience. A large bowl of wheat or corn bran cereal can prevent constipation during resin use, but some patients still feel bloated. Resins are contraindicated in the hypertriglyceridemias, and TG levels should be reduced to under 300 mg/dl before resins are used in mixed or combined hyperlipidemics.

Niacin is useful in patients with LDL elevations, and the same precautions apply that were noted for niacin use in hypertriglyceridemia. The drug can cause fatty liver and cirrhosis, and the long-term safety is not established. Lovastatin and pravastatin are among the first of a series of drugs that competitively inhibit hydroxymethyl glutaryl coenzyme A (HMG-CoA) reductase, the rate-limiting enzyme in cholesterol biosynthesis. This inhibition induces an increase in hepatic B,E receptors, and LDL typically are lowered by 30 per cent. Reductase inhibitors are appropriate for hypercholesterolemics of any age who have established CHD and for other adults with moderately severe hypercholesterolemia (LDL > 190 mg/dl). These drugs are expensive but well tolerated, and compliance is excellent. Use in combination with niacin, fibrates, or cyclosporine may cause myositis and even rhabdomyolysis.

The fibrates are not approved for simple hypercholesterolemia. They typically lower LDL levels by only 8 to 10 per cent but may produce dramatic results in some patients. Many patients, particularly those who have heterozygotic familial hypercholesterolemia, require two or three drugs to achieve adequate control. Resins plus niacin plus lovastatin or resins plus fibrates have been widely used. Resins plus fish oils are also effective in mixed hyperlipidemics. Familial monogenic hypercholesterolemia homozygotes are poorly responsive to diet and drugs and are considered candidates for liver transplantation.

LIPIDS AND VASCULAR DISEASE

Intervention studies in the last decade have shown that cholesterol reduction using diet, drugs, or surgery reduces the risk of development or progression of CHD. In general, a 1 per cent fall in LDL-cholesterol has been associated with roughly a 2 per cent reduction in disease end points. Arteriographic studies have shown small but convincing regressions of arterial lesions. Thus, few experts doubt the wisdom of treating lipid disorders in men and women known to have coronary or peripheral vascular disease.

There is still considerable debate about the cost-effectiveness of screening the general population for lipid disorders and treating individuals found to have cholesterol elevations. The reference ranges established by the National Cholesterol Education Program would lead to 27 per cent of adult Americans being classified as having "high cholesterol" and another 30 per cent as having "borderline high" values. Indeed, almost half of all postmenopausal women have total and LDL_c levels over 240 mg/dl and 160 mg/dl, respectively. It has been estimated that about 100,000 people must be treated annually to prevent 70 heart disease deaths. Moreover, no intervention study to date has shown a favorable influence on all-cause mortality.

Nevertheless, general agreement exists that eating less saturated fat and cholesterol and adopting diet and exercise habits to reduce obesity will benefit the health of most people. Preliminary data suggest a significant fall in American cholesterol levels in the past decade, and vascular disease rates have been falling for almost three decades. These public health effects will probably have a much greater impact than medical intervention approaches.

REFERENCES

Brown MS, Goldstein JL: Drugs used in the treatment of hyperlipoproteinemias. In Gilman AG, Rall TW, Nies AS, Taylor P (eds): The Pharmacological Basis of Therapeutics. 8th ed. New York, Pergamon Press, 1991.

Part 7, Chapters 44–51. In Scriver CR, Beaudet AL, Sly WS, Valle D (eds): The Metabolic Basis of Inherited Disease. 6th ed. New York, McGraw-Hill Information Services Co, 1989.

Report of the National Cholesterol Education Program Expert Panel on Detection, Evaluation, and Treatment of High Blood Cholesterol in Adults. Arch Intern Med 148:36–69. 1988.

Rossow JE, Lewis B, Rifkind BM: The value of lowering cholesterol after myocardial infarction. N Engl J Med 323:1112–1119, 1990.

61 DISORDERS OF METALS AND METALLOPROTEINS

WILSON'S DISEASE (HEPATOLENTICULAR DEGENERATION)

Wilson's disease is a rare autosomal recessive disorder characterized by a defect in hepatic excretion of copper. Toxic levels accumulate in the liver, basal ganglia of the brain, and other tissues. The serum concentration of the copper-containing protein ceruloplasmin is low in 95 per cent of patients with Wilson's disease.

Pathogenesis. The primary genetic defect accounting for impaired biliary copper excretion in Wilson's disease is unknown. It is thought that hepatocytes of patients with this disorder contain an abnormal protein with an increased affinity for copper. Affected livers lack the ability to excrete copper that has been cleaved from circulating ceruloplasmin. This may cause a secondary deficiency of ceruloplasmin, because excess copper inhibits the formation of ceruloplasmin from apoceruloplasmin. The capacity of hepatocytes to store copper is eventually overwhelmed, resulting in release of the metal into blood and accumulation at extrahepatic sites. In the brain, copper is deposited in the pericapillary areas and astrocytes of the basal ganglia and frontal lobe, leading eventually to atrophy of those structures, with cystic changes in the putamen.

Clinical Features. The age of onset and initial signs and symptoms of Wilson's disease are quite variable; clinical manifestations of copper excess are rare before the age of 6 years. Approximately one third of patients present with symptoms of liver disease that may mimic acute viral hepatitis or cirrhosis with portal hypertension. More frequently, patients first present with extrahepatic manifestations of copper excess.

The early neurologic signs of Wilson's disease include intellectual deterioration, tremor, loss of coordination of fine movements, an unsteady gait, and a slightly dystonic facies in which the upper lip is drawn tightly over the teeth. Dysarthria, muscle rigidity or contractures, and drooling are late features. Seizures are rare and sensory abnormalities absent. The neurologic symptom complex includes personality changes and unstable behavior. The neurologic manifestations begin usually between ages 11 and 25, occasionally as late as 40 years.

The intellectual deterioration, especially in adolescents, may be an isolated finding, not accompanied by movement disorders or other signs of Wilson's disease. Wilson's disease must therefore be considered in the differential diagnosis of any individuals under the age of 30 with unexplained decrease in intellectual ability (e.g., the high school student with an unexplained fall in academic achievement). This is a critical issue, because early treatment can arrest and sometimes reverse the intellectual impairment.

Other clinical features of Wilson's disease include Kayser-Fleischer corneal rings caused by copper deposition at the margins of the cornea. The rings, which may require slit-lamp detection, are uniformly present in patients with neurologic symptoms but may be absent in patients with isolated hepatic involvement. Like other heavy metals, copper may be nephrotoxic; renal deposition of copper is usually manifested by tubular dysfunction, including glycosuria, phosphaturia, aminoaciduria, renal tubular acidosis, or the complete Fanconi syndrome. Acute or chronic hemolytic anemia in Wilson's disease has been attributed to the release of copper from overloaded tissues, but the exact mechanisms have not been elucidated. As with intellectual dysfunction, the hemolytic anemia may precede the development of the more characteristic clinical manifestations of Wilson's disease.

The diagnosis of Wilson's disease is supported in suspected cases by (1) detection of Kayser-Fleischer rings, (2) a serum concentration of ceruloplasmin less than 20 mg/dl, (3) a concentration of copper in a liver biopsy sample greater than 250 μg/gm of dry weight, or (4) urinary excretion of more than 100 μg/day of copper. Although none of these criteria are sufficiently sensitive or specific to make an unequivocal diagnosis of Wilson's disease, they serve to corroborate the diagnosis in patients with appropriate clinical signs and symptoms. Although the level of direct-reacting (non–ceruloplasmin-bound) copper in the serum is typically elevated, total levels are not consistently altered, so that measurement of serum copper levels serves little purpose in the diagnosis of this disorder.

Treatment. D-Penicillamine is the drug of choice. Daily doses of 1 to 2 gm increase urinary copper excretion more than fivefold over pretreatment levels and can prevent virtually every maanifestation of Wilson's disease, provided that treatment is begun before major neurologic impairment has occurred.

An increase in the quantity of storage iron in the body is called *hemosiderosis*. The term *hemochromatosis* refers to an increase in total body iron stores with iron deposition in parenchymal tissues that ultimately leads to functional impairment of the most severely affected organs. Acquired hemochromatosis results from exogenous iron overload due to excessive dietary iron ingestion or repeated blood transfusions. This section focuses on familial hemochromatosis, a genetically determined iron storage disorder that is linked to the human leukocyte antigen (HLA) locus and is clinically manifest in roughly 1 in 5000 Caucasians in the United States. The clinical and pathologic features of acquired and familial hemochromatosis can be identical.

Etiology, Genetics, and Pathogenesis. Normally, the total body iron content of 3 to 4 gm is maintained by a balance between intestinal absorption and fecal excretion of iron. The amounts of iron absorbed and excreted daily are small, being approximately 1.0 mg in men and 1.5 mg in menstruating women. In familial hemochromatosis, intestinal iron absorption is inappropriately large, usually amounting to more than 3 mg/day. The progressive accumulation of iron produces an early elevation of plasma iron and an increased saturation of circulating transferrin. In advanced disease, total body iron content may exceed 20 gm.

The tendency to absorb iron excessively is inherited as an autosomal recessive trait. This is the most common recessive trait in the Caucasian population of the United States, occurring in 1 in 10 individuals. Homozygotes have large iron stores and may manifest the disease. Fortunately, only a minority of the homozygotes develop clinical manifestations of the disease. Heterozygotes exhibit minor derangements in iron metabolism but may rarely develop clinical manifestations when an added factor such as alcohol consumption or increased oral iron intake enhances the accumulation of iron in excess of their usual stores. Hemochromatosis is observed 5 to 10 times more commonly in men than in women, presumably because menstrual blood losses protect against iron overload. The gene for hemochromatosis is located on the short arm of chromosome 6 and is linked to the HLA locus. Among families that include at least one affected homozygote, additional homozygotes as well as heterozygote carriers often can be identified by HLA testing using the principles of genetic linkage. Siblings with both HLA haplotypes identical to that of the affected patient carry the linked hemochromatosis allele, are at high risk of developing iron overload, or may already be affected. Siblings who share only one HLA haplotype are heterozygotes.

Excess iron is deposited predominantly in parenchymal cells of the liver, heart, pancreas, and other endocrine organs. In early stages of the disease, deposits of iron in these organs consist of ferritin and hemosiderin stored within lysosomes.

Tissue injury results from disruption of lysosomes and lipid peroxidation of subcellular organelles by iron. Varying degrees of fibrosis occur in affected organs. Cirrhosis of the liver is almost invariably present in symptomatic cases. Iron deposition in the liver is initially limited to lysosomes in the pericanalicular cytoplasm of hepatocytes. As the disease progresses, iron is also deposited in bile duct epithelium and in Kupffer cells. In the advanced stage, an irregular multilobular cirrhosis develops, with a paucity of inflammatory cells and prominent bile duct proliferation.

Clinical Features. Signs and symptoms of hemochromatosis usually develop between the ages of 40 and 60. The early clinical manifestations are subtle and are often not attributed to hemochromatosis. Constitutional symptoms include lassitude and weakness, but the most prominent symptoms relate to iron deposition in specific organs. The liver is usually the first organ to be affected. Although firm hepatomegaly is present in more than 95 per cent of cases at the time of diagnosis, liver function tests may remain normal during early stages of the disease. The spleen is enlarged in almost half of recognized cases, but other clinical manifestations of portal hypertension occur less commonly than in other forms of cirrhosis. Hepatocellular carcinoma develops as a sequel to cirrhosis in about 35 per cent of cases. Each of these diseases—hepatocellular carcinoma and cirrhosis—accounts for about 25 per cent of deaths in treated patients.

About 90 per cent of patients exhibit excessive skin pigmentation, developing a characteristic metallic gray appearance from increased deposition of melanin and hemosiderin in the basal layer of the epidermis. Pigmentation is usually greatest on the face, neck, genitalia, and extensor surfaces of the extremities.

Insulin-dependent diabetes mellitus develops in approximately 80 per cent of cases from iron deposition in pancreatic islet cells. Vascular complications of diabetes, such as retinopathy, peripheral neuropathy, and nephropathy, may develop in long-term survivors.

Cardiac manifestations include congestive heart failure, a variety of ventricular and supraventricular arrhythmias, and conduction disturbances including heart block. Cardiac involvement is the presenting manifestation in about 15 per cent of cases. Congestive heart failure in hemochromatosis may be resistant to digitalis therapy. Cardiomyopathy accounts for about one third of deaths.

Loss of libido, sexual impotence, and testicular atrophy are present in more than 50 per cent of clinically recognized cases. Although hypogonadism may result in part from chronic liver disease, the symptoms more often are due to deficient production of trophic hormones by the anterior pituitary gland. Adrenal insufficiency and hypothyroidism rarely have been described.

About 25 per cent of patients develop acute at-

TABLE 61-1. IRON INDICES IN NORMAL SUBJECTS AND IN PATIENTS WITH SYMPTOMATIC HEMOCHROMATOSIS

INDEX	NORMAL SUBJECTS	PATIENTS WITH HEMOCHROMATOSIS
Plasma iron (μg/dl)	50-150	180-300
Total iron binding capacity (μg/dl)	250-375	200-300
Per cent transferrin saturation	20-40	80-100
Serum ferritin (ng/ml)	10-200	900-6000
Urinary iron after 0.5 gm desferrioxamine	0-2	9-23
Liver iron (μg/100 mg dry weight)	30-140	600-1800

tacks of synovitis due to synovial deposition of calcium pyrophosphate (i.e., chondrocalcinosis). In late stages, a progressive polyarthritis involving the hands, wrists, knees, and hips may develop. Radiographic findings include cystic changes in subchondral bone, loss of articular cartilage, and diffuse demineralization. The pathophysiologic link between the rheumatologic manifestations of hemochromatosis and the underlying disturbance in iron metabolism is unknown.

Hemochromatosis should be suggested by the above clinical features and confirmed by laboratory tests (Table 61-1). Measurements of the plasma iron concentration and the plasma iron-binding capacity provide the best screening tests. Plasma iron is usually greater than 200 μg/dl; total iron-binding capacity is normal or slightly decreased, but the transferrin saturation is greatly elevated, usually between 80 and 100 per cent. Other available measures of excessive parenchymal iron stores include the serum ferritin concentration and urinary iron excretion following administration of the chelating agent desferrioxamine. Because all of the above tests are limited in their sensitivity and specificity, the definitive test for hemochromatosis is liver biopsy; parenchymal hemosiderin deposits can be demonstrated histochemically and the actual content of iron can be estimated biochemically. Magnetic resonance imaging can also be used to estimate liver iron content, and may prove to be a useful alternative to liver biopsy.

Treatment and Prognosis. Treatment consists of removing excess body iron and supportive treatment of complications such as diabetes mellitus and heart failure. Body iron is best removed by phlebotomy. Because 500 ml of blood contains 200 to 250 mg of iron, 2 to 3 years of weekly phlebotomies may be required to remove 20 gm of iron and to restore normal plasma iron concentrations. Once plasma iron levels return to normal, less frequent phlebotomies are continued to maintain a plasma concentration less than 150 μg/dl, or a ferritin level less than 300 ng/ml.

Phlebotomy is more effective and less expensive than administration of chelating agents, but the latter may be useful when anemia precludes frequent venisections. Daily intramuscular injection or overnight subcutaneous infusion of 0.5 to 1.0 gm of desferrioxamine removes 10 to 20 mg of iron per day—one tenth or less of the latter amount mobilized by weekly phlebotomy.

Without treatment, hemochromatosis offers an average life expectancy of 4.5 years following development of clinical symptoms. Life expectancy is extended to more than 15 years by removal of excessive iron stores. Therapy improves carbohydrate intolerance in almost half the cases, but established cirrhosis is irreversible.

Early detection and treatment prevent the clinical manifestations of hemochromatosis. If adequate treatment is initiated *before* the development of cirrhosis, a nearly normal life expectancy can be anticipated. Blood relatives of affected patients should undergo HLA testing. Siblings who share all HLA determinants with the index case are homozygotes and should have measurements of iron indices. Testing of siblings should be initiated at puberty for males and after the age of 20 for females. HLA-identical male sibs found to have normal iron stores should be restudied every 2 to 3 years, females less frequently.

PORPHYRIA

The porphyrias are a group of heterogeneous disorders resulting from inherited or acquired disturbances in heme biosynthesis. Porphyrins are pigments that serve as intermediates in this synthetic pathway. Heme, the ferrous iron complex of protoporphyrin IX, serves as a prosthetic group for a number of hemoproteins, including hemoglobin and mitochondrial cytochromes. Each of the porphyrias results from a deficiency of a specific enzyme in the heme biosynthetic pathway and is characterized by a unique pattern of overproduction and accumulation of porphyrin intermediates (Table 61-2). The porphyrias are usually categorized into two main groups, erythropoietic and hepatic, according to the major site at which the metabolic error is expressed.

Pathogenesis. Porphyrins are "side-products" of intermediates in the heme biosynthetic pathway, schematically outlined in Figure 61-1. The precursors glycine and succinyl coenzyme A are converted to aminolevulinic acid (ALA) in a reaction catalyzed by ALA synthetase. This reaction is the rate-limiting step in heme biosynthesis, subject to feedback regulation by heme, the end product of the pathway. Two moles of ALA combine to form porphobilinogen. Only protoporphyrin is utilized in heme synthesis. The other porphyrins (i.e., uroporphyrin, coproporphyrin) have no physiologic function and must be excreted; their fluorescent properties account for the diagnostic appearance of the urine in some patients.

Clinical Features. Congenital *erythropoietic porphyria* is a very rare disorder manifested by massive overproduction of uroporphyrinogen III

TABLE 61–2. CLASSIFICATION AND CHARACTERISTICS OF THE PORPHYRIAS: HEME PRECURSORS PRESENT IN ABNORMAL AMOUNTS

TYPE	URINE	PLASMA	ENZYME DEFECT
Erythropoietic			
Congenital erythropoietic porphyria	URO ∫ COPRO	URO	UROgen III cosynthetase
Erythrohepatic			
Protoporphyria	—	PROTO	Ferrochelatase
Hepatic			
Acute intermittent porphyria	ALA < PBG ∫ URO	ALA, PBG	PBG deaminase
Hereditary coproporphyria	ALA < PBG < URO < COPRO	COPRO	COPROgen oxidase
Variegate porphyria	ALA < PBG < URO < COPRO	COPRO, PROTO	PROTOgen oxidase
Porphyria cutanea tarda	URO ∫ COPRO	URO	UROgen decarboxylase

ALA = δ-Aminolevulinic acid; PBG = porphobilinogen; URO = uroporphyrin; COPRO = coproporphyrin; PROTO = protoporphyrin.

and secondary accumulation of uroporphyrin and coproporphyrin, suggesting a defect in the activity of uroporphyrinogen III cosynthetase. Fewer than 100 cases have been described. Patients exhibit hemolytic anemia and severe photosensitivity, with mutilating bullous lesions on light-exposed skin. Treatment relies on avoidance of sunlight.

Protoporphyria results from partial deficiency of ferrochelatase, the final enzyme in heme biosynthesis that catalyzes the conversion of protoporphyrin to heme. The disease is characterized by excess protoporphyrin IX in erythrocytes, plasma, and feces. Cutaneous photosensitivity is the major clinical manifestation. About 10 per cent of patients develop protoporphyrin-containing gallstones, and some develop mild liver disease. Treatment includes avoidance of sunlight and administration of beta-carotene, which blocks light- and porphyrin-induced cutaneous injury.

The three variants of *hepatic porphyria* can be considered together because their clinical manifestations and treatments are similar. Acute intermit-

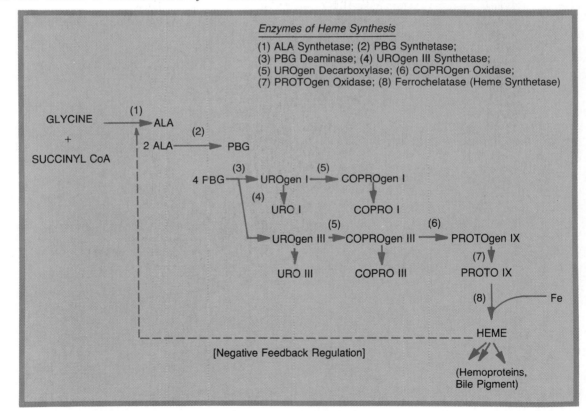

FIGURE 61–1. Pathway of heme biosynthesis. ALA = δ-Aminolevulinic acid; URO = uroporphyrin; COPRO = coproporphyrin; PROTO = protoporphyrin; PBG = porphobilinogen. (Adapted from Bissell DM: Porphyria. In Wyngaarden JB, Smith LH Jr [eds]: Cecil Textbook of Medicine. 18th ed. Philadelphia, WB Saunders Co, 1988, p 1183.)

TABLE 61–3. DRUGS THAT MAY PRECIPITATE ACUTE ATTACKS IN HEPATIC PORPHYRIA

Barbiturates	Estrogens
Ethanol	Ergot preparations
Chlordiazepoxide	Methyldopa
Imipramine	Chloroquine
Meprobamate	Griseofulvin
Glutethimide	
Chlorpropamide	

tent porphyria results from partial deficiency of porphobilinogen deaminase, leading to accumulation and excess urinary excretion of porphobilinogen and ALA. Hereditary coproporphyria is characterized by excess excretion of ALA, porphobilinogen, uroporphyrin, and coproporphyrin due to partial deficiency of coproporphyrinogen oxidase. Partial deficiency of protoporphyrinogen oxidase underlies variegate porphyria and leads to excess excretion of the entire series of heme precursors.

Clinical manifestations are protean, and the physician must consider acute hepatic porphyria in the differential diagnosis of a wide variety of symptoms, ranging from acute abdominal pain to delirium tremens. Focal or generalized seizures or severe motor polyneuropathies may be the presenting features. Intense abdominal pain during the first 24 to 48 hours of an attack may suggest acute cholecystitis, appendicitis, or other surgical diagnoses and may provoke unnecessary surgery. Psychiatric disturbances include personality changes and acute delirious reactions, with signs and symptoms resembling delirium tremens. Attacks may be precipitated by a variety of drugs (Table 61–3), especially those such as barbiturates that increase the demand for heme synthesis by induction of cytochrome P-450. Attacks are rare prior to puberty and are more common in women than in men, suggesting that endogenous hormones may play a role. Infection and fasting may also precipitate attacks. Because urinary porphobilinogen is increased in each of these porphyrias, the diagnosis is suspected by qualitative detection of porphobilinogen with the Watson-Schwartz test. Quantification of urinary and fecal porphyrins identifies the specific variant of porphyria. Treatment includes elimination of possible precipitating drugs, administration of carbohydrate to reverse fasting, analgesia, and supportive management of seizures, delirium, and other neurologic complications. Hematin, a commercial preparation of ferriprotoporphyrin IX, has been administered to patients with prolonged attacks that do not respond to conservative therapy, but its efficacy remains unproven.

Porphyria cutanea tarda is another variant of porphyria. The condition results from partial deficiency of uroporphyrinogen decarboxylase, leading to increased urinary excretion of uroporphyrin and modest increments of urinary coproporphyrin. Mechanical fragility and photosensitivity of the skin are the primary clinical manifestations. Most affected patients give a history of ethanol abuse and/or chronic liver disease. The liver abnormalities are nonspecific but include increase in stainable iron and fluorescence resulting from the high content of uroporphyrin. Treatment includes avoidance of alcohol and phlebotomy to remove hepatic iron when clinically overt liver disease is present. Beta-carotene offers little or no protection against light-induced injury in this disorder.

REFERENCES

Bissell DM: Heme metabolism and the porphyrias. In Wright R, Alberti KGMM, Karran S, Millward-Sadler GH (eds): Liver and Biliary Disease. 2nd ed. London, WB Saunders Co, 1986.

Cartwright GE: Diagnosis of treatable Wilson's disease. N Engl J Med 298:1347, 1978.

Fairbanks VF, Baldus WP: Hemochromatosis: The neglected diagnosis. Mayo Clin Proc 61:296, 1986.

Stein JA, Tschudy DP: Acute intermittent porphyria. A clinical and biochemical study of 46 patients. Medicine 49:1, 1970.

Strickland T, Len ML: Wilson's disease: Clinical and laboratory manifestations in 40 patients. Medicine 54:113, 1975.

62 DISORDERS OF AMINO ACID METABOLISM

Defects in the membrane transport or catabolism of amino acids account for more than 70 inherited or acquired "aminoacidopathies." Each of these disorders is rare, but collectively they occur in approximately 1 in 1000 live births. This section describes selected disorders that illustrate the problems posed by aminoacidopathies.

HYPERAMINOACIDURIA (MEMBRANE TRANSPORT DEFECTS)

Although most of the body's 20 amino acids are contained within various polypeptides and proteins, a small but critical pool of *free* amino acids circulates in extracellular fluid. Most amino acids are freely filtered by renal glomeruli, but more than 95 per cent of the filtered load is actively and specifically reabsorbed in the proximal renal tubule via receptors that recognize and transport individual amino acids or groups of structurally related ones. Aminoaciduria results from either an acquired or a hereditary disturbance of cellular metabolism or when the transport of amino acids is impaired by (1) saturation of the receptor sites, (2) competition for the receptor sites by other substrates, or (3) a defect in the function or structural integrity of the receptor. Defects in membrane transport may affect a single amino acid, a group of structurally related amino acids, or all amino acids (Table 62–1).

Cystinuria, the most common inborn error of amino acid transport, results from an inherited defect in the membrane receptor for the dibasic amino acids lysine, arginine, and ornithine, as well as cystine. The disorder is inherited as an autosomal recessive trait. Cystine is the least soluble of all amino acids, and its excessive excretion in urine predisposes to the formation of calculi. Normally, the maximum solubility of cystine in urine is about 300 mg/L. Affected homozygotes regularly excrete 600 to 1800 mg of cystine per day.

Signs and symptoms of cystinuria are those of urolithiasis: renal colic, hematuria, obstructive uropathy, and secondary infection, usually beginning during the second or third decade of life. Recurrent episodes of urolithiasis and infection can lead to progressive renal insufficiency.

The diagnosis of cystinuria requires either demonstration of the characteristic aminoaciduria by chromatography or electrophoresis or the detection of cystine in a urinary tract calculus. As many as 50 per cent of stones excreted by cystinuric patients, however, have a mixed composition. Urinary cystine crystals have a characteristic hexagonal shape; their discovery in the urine of a patient with signs and symptoms of urolithiasis is often the first clue to the diagnosis of cystinuria.

Treatment of cystinuria consists of efforts to reduce the urinary concentration of cystine. Vigorous hydration, with fluid ingestion of 4 to 8 L/day, is the most important aspect of medical management. Because the solubility of cystine increases sharply as urine pH rises above 7.5, urinary alkalinization may be effective in preventing stone formation; however, vigorous administration of sodium bicarbonate and/or acetazolamide is required to maintain a persistently alkaline urine. Administration of D-penicillamine in doses of 1 to 3 gm/day effectively lowers the urinary concentration of free cystine, prevents new stone formation, and promotes the dissolution of existing calculi. The drug undergoes sulfhydryl-disulfide exchange with cystine to form a mixed penicillamine-cysteine disulfide that is 50 times more soluble than cystine. D-Penicillamine, however, has a number of serious side effects (e.g., exfoliative dermatitis, heavy proteinuria, bone marrow depression) and should be reserved for patients who fail to respond to more conservative measures.

TABLE 62–1. CLASSIFICATION OF MAJOR HYPERAMINOACIDURIAS

	TRAIT	SUBSTANCE(S) AFFECTED
Substrate-specific	Histidinuria	Histidine
	Hypercystinuria	Cystine
Group-specific	Cystinuria	Lysine, ornithine, arginine, cystine
	Hartnup disease	Neutral amino acids
	Iminoglycinuria	Proline, glycine, hydroxyproline
	Dicarboxylic aminoaciduria	Glutamic acid, aspartic acid
	Hyperdibasic aminoaciduria	Lysine, ornithine, arginine
Generalized	Idiopathic Fanconi's syndrome	Generalized effect on all amino acids, solutes, and water
	Acquired Fanconi's syndrome	Generalized effect on all amino acids, solutes, and water

TABLE 62–2. SOME DISORDERS ASSOCIATED WITH ACQUIRED FANCONI'S SYNDROME

Systemic or Hereditary Diseases
Multiple myeloma	Wilson's disease
Amyloidosis	Hereditary fructose intolerance
Sjögren's syndrome	Galactosemia
Cystinosis	

Heavy Metal Poisonings
Mercury	Uranium
Lead	Strontium
Cadmium	

Drugs
6-Mercaptopurine

Generalized aminoaciduria reflects a generalized defect in the renal tubular reabsorption of all filtered amino acids and is characteristic of patients with Fanconi's syndrome. The renal loss of amino acids in Fanconi's syndrome is usually outweighed by other disturbances of proximal tubular function, including glycosuria, phosphaturia, bicarbonaturia, and uric aciduria. Presenting manifestations of this disorder may include hypophosphatemic rickets in children, osteomalacia in adults, proximal renal tubular acidosis, or hypouricemia. Fanconi's syndrome may be acquired or associated with an inherited enzymatic disorder (e.g., hereditary fructose intolerance). In addition, a primary hereditary disorder (idiopathic Fanconi's syndrome) has been identified. The common causes of acquired Fanconi's syndrome are listed in Table 62–2.

AMINO ACID STORAGE DISEASES

Cystinosis is a rare idiopathic disorder characterized by the accumulation of cystine crystals in various tissues, including the cornea, bone marrow, lymph nodes, and kidneys. Three clinical forms exist: (1) *infantile cystinosis*, characterized by the Fanconi syndrome and progressive renal failure, occurs during the first decade of life; (2) in *juvenile cystinosis*, renal failure does not occur until the second decade; (3) *adult cystinosis* is a relatively benign disorder in which cystine accumulation is usually limited to the cornea, resulting in photophobia or mild irritation of the eyes. Adult cystinosis requires no treatment. Treatment of nephropathic cystinosis consists of supportive management of progressive renal failure; D-penicillamine is ineffective. Renal transplantation has been performed successfully in patients with cystinosis and end-stage renal failure, but reaccumulation of cystine can occur in the transplanted allograft after many years.

Alcaptonuria, a rare disorder of tyrosine catabolism resulting from hereditary deficiency of homogentisic acid oxidase, is associated with the excretion of large amounts of homogentisic acid in the urine and the accumulation of oxidized homogen-

tisic acid in connective tissues. *Ochronosis*, a bluish-gray pigmentation, occurs when homogentisic acid and its oxidized polymers bind to collagen. The earliest clinical manifestations of alcaptonuria include slight pigmentation of the sclerae and external ears during the second and third decades. The urine tends to darken on standing, a finding that frequently goes unnoticed. Most patients develop degenerative joint disease by the fourth or fifth decade, ankylosis of the lumbar spine being a common late finding. The diagnosis is suggested by the triad of degenerative arthritis, ochronotic pigmentation, and the detection of urine that blackens on standing and is confirmed by measurement of urinary homogentisic acid. There is no known specific treatment.

OTHER DISORDERS OF AMINO ACID METABOLISM MEDIATED BY ENZYMATIC DEFECTS

Phenylketonuria is an autosomal recessive disorder resulting from impaired conversion of the essential amino acid phenylalanine to tyrosine due to deficient activity of the enzyme phenylalanine dehydroxylase. This disorder is manifested by accumulation of phenylalanine and its minor metabolites and by severe mental retardation. Infants with phenylketonuria are usually normal at birth, but signs of mental and psychomotor retardation, hyperactivity, tremors, or seizures usually develop within the first year of life. Early recognition of this disorder is imperative, because its devastating consequences can be prevented completely if dietary restriction of phenylalanine is instituted within the first 30 days of life. Most newborns in the United States are screened for this disorder by determinations of blood phenylalanine concentrations using a bacterial inhibition assay. Quantitative chromatographic assays are employed for definitive diagnosis in infants with abnormal screening results. Treatment of phenylketonuria consists of a diet in which the bulk of protein is replaced by an amino acid mixture low in phenylalanine. Although scrupulous adherence to such a dietary regimen is of critical importance during the early months of life, it is probably wise to continue dietary therapy at least through the first decade of life. Phenylalanine ingestion must also be monitored carefully in the pregnant woman with phenylketonuria to prevent central nervous system damage in the fetus.

The term *homocystinuria* refers to a group of biochemically and clinically distinct disorders characterized by accumulation of the sulfur-containing amino acid, homocystine, in blood and urine. Homocystine is the disulfide oxidation product formed by two molecules of homocysteine. Accumulation of homocystine results in impaired collagen formation, a phenomenon that accounts for many of the clinical manifestations of this disorder. The most common variant of homocystinuria is due to deficiency of cystathionine β-

synthase, resulting in a failure of homocysteine to react with serine to form cystathionine. Deficiency of this enzyme is inherited as an autosomal recessive trait. Patients with homocystinuria and cystathionine β-synthase deficiency exhibit dislocated optic lenses, lax ligaments, and sparse, fine hair. They may resemble patients with Marfan's syndrome. Mental retardation occurs in approximately 50 per cent of cases. Thromboembolic disease is the major cause of morbidity and mortality and may be initiated by damage to vascular endothelium.

REFERENCES

Scriver CR: Hyperaminoaciduria (with a classification of the inborn and developmental errors of amino acid metabolism). In Wyngaarden JB, Smith LH Jr, Bennett JC (eds): Cecil Textbook of Medicine. 19th ed. Philadelphia, WB Saunders Co, 1992, pp 1094–1100.

Wellner D, Meister A: A survey of inborn errors of amino acid metabolism and transport in man. Annu Rev Biochem 50:911, 1981.

63 DISORDERS OF CARBOHYDRATE METABOLISM

GALACTOSEMIA

Two inherited enzyme deficiencies impair the metabolic conversion of galactose to glucose and cause accumulation of galactose in the body, or galactosemia. *Classic galactosemia* results from deficient activity of the enzyme galactose-1-phosphate uradyl transferase; a less common form of galactosemia results from *galactokinase deficiency*. Accumulation of galactose in the ocular lens produces excessive hydration, precipitation of lens protein, and formation of cataracts. Classic galactosemia also features liver disease, mental retardation, and failure to thrive, untreated infants surviving only a few days to weeks. Further details regarding the clinical features of these neonatal disorders can be found in pediatric textbooks.

THE GLYCOGEN STORAGE DISEASES

Glycogen is present in virtually all animal cells and constitutes the principal storage form of carbohydrate. In contrast to starch, the storage form of carbohydrate in plants, glycogen has a highly branched structure that enhances its solubility. A variety of inherited enzyme defects adversely affect the synthesis and degradation of glycogen. In general, such defects produce either an elevated tissue concentration of glycogen or an abnormality in the structure of the carbohydrate. As specific enzyme defects were recognized, the glycogen storage diseases were numbered or assigned eponyms. The diseases are grouped as either hepatic or muscular disorders, according to the major site affected by the metabolic error. The enzyme deficiencies, clinical manifestations, and laboratory findings of the glycogen storage diseases are shown in Table 63–1. Hepatic variants are largely disorders of children and frequently cause death

early in life. Clinical features of the muscle glycogen storage diseases are discussed elsewhere in this text.

PRIMARY HYPEROXALURIA

Primary hyperoxaluria results from either of two rare autosomal recessive genetic disorders, each of which results in excessive synthesis and urinary excretion of oxalic acid. The two variants of this disorder can be distinguished by characteristic excretion of oxalate metabolites in the urine. *Type I primary hyperoxaluria* results from a defect in the enzyme alanine:glyoxalate aminotransferase with resultant increased urinary concentrations of oxalate and glycolate. In *type II hyperoxaluria*, there is a defect in the enzyme D-glyceric dehydrogenase, resulting in increased urinary excretion of oxalate and L-glycerate. Each of these disorders is characterized by recurrent calcium oxalate nephrolithiasis and/or nephrocalcinosis during childhood, resulting in renal failure and death in patients not supported by dialysis. Once renal failure supervenes, the diagnosis may be difficult to establish because urinary excretion of oxalate metabolites declines as the glomerular filtration rate falls. Calcium oxalate deposition also occurs in other tissues, including the liver, spleen, testes, and bone marrow. Deposition of calcium oxalate in the walls of blood vessels may result in severe peripheral vascular insufficiency. Milder forms of primary hyperoxaluria have been described in adults with calcium oxalate kidney stones. The vast majority of patients with calcium oxalate nephrolithiasis have normal oxalate metabolism.

There is no specific treatment for primary hyperoxaluria. Phosphate or magnesium supplementation and forced diuresis have been variably successful in decreasing urinary stone formation.

TABLE 63–1. THE GLYCOGEN STORAGE DISEASES

NUMERIC TYPE	EPONYM	ENZYME DEFICIENCY	CLINICAL MANIFESTATIONS	LABORATORY FINDINGS	DIAGNOSIS
Hepatic Forms					
I	Von Gierke's	Glucose-6-phosphatase	Massive hepatomegaly, short stature, failure to thrive, severe hypoglycemia, retinal lesions	↑ Lactate, pyruvate, triglycerides, cholesterol, uric acid	↓ Enzyme activity or ↑ glycogen on liver biopsy
III	Cori's	Debrancher	Similar to type I, but less severe; myopathy in adults	Normal lactate and uric acid, cholesterol, triglycerides	Enzyme assay on liver, muscle, WBCs, or RBCs
IV	Anderson's	Brancher	Cirrhosis, hepatosplenomegaly, ascites, early death from liver failure	↑ Transaminase, normal glucose tolerance	Normal liver glycogen
VI	Hers'	Liver phosphorylase	Mild hepatomegaly, mild hypoglycemia	Minimal	Enzyme assay on liver, ↑ liver glycogen
VIII	None	Phosphorylase β-kinase	Marked hepatomegaly, X-linked disorder	Minimal	Enzyme assay on liver or WBCs
Muscle Forms					
II	Pompe's	α-1,4-glucosidase (acid maltase)	Massive cardiomegaly, hypotonia, early death from cardiorespiratory failure; milder form in adults	↑ CPK	Enzyme assay on WBCs
V	McArdle's	Muscle phosphorylase	Exercise-induced muscle pain and cramps, rhabdomyolysis	↑ CPK with episodes; no blood lactate with exercise	↑ Glycogen and ↓ enzyme activity on muscle biopsy

CPK = Creatine phosphokinase; WBCs = white blood cells; RBCs = red blood cells.

High doses of pyridoxine (200 to 400 mg/day) may reduce oxalate excretion in type I hyperoxaluria. More physiologic doses of pyridoxine (2 to 10 mg) may be effective in some patients. Patients with end-stage renal disease can be maintained on chronic dialysis. Successful renal transplantation has been hampered by rapid deposition of calcium oxalate in the transplanted kidney; however, intensive daily hemodialysis in the early post-transplant period may reduce plasma oxalate to sufficiently low levels to minimize renal oxalate deposition.

REFERENCES

Howell RR; The glycogen storage diseases. In Wyngaarden JB, Smith LH Jr, Bennett JC (eds): Cecil Textbook of Medicine. 19th ed. Philadelphia, WB Saunders Co, 1992, pp 1078–1080.

Segal S: Disorders of galactose in metabolism. In Stanbury JB, Wyngaarden JB, Frederickson DS, et al (eds): The Metabolic Basis of Inherited Disease. 5th ed. New York, McGraw-Hill Book Co, 1982.

Yendt ER, Cohanim M: Response to a physiological dose of pyridoxine in type I primary oxaluria. New Engl J Med 312:953, 1985.

64 INHERITED DISORDERS OF CONNECTIVE TISSUE

The genetically transmitted disorders discussed in this chapter are characterized by histologically or ultramicroscopically demonstrable structural changes in the integumentary system. They are neither inflammatory nor immunologic in origin and must be distinguished from acquired immunologic diseases such as systemic lupus erythematosus, scleroderma, rheumatoid arthritis, and polymyositis, which have been improperly termed connective tissue diseases.

The mucopolysaccharidoses are a group of disorders resulting from deficiencies of specific lysosomal enzymes involved in the degradation of the glycosaminoglycans, including chondroitin sulfate, dermatan sulfate, heparan sulfate, and keratan sulfate. Clinical manifestations derive from the accumulation of partially degraded glycosaminoglycans in connective tissues, heart, bony skeleton, and central nervous system. Features common to most of the mucopolysaccharidoses include onset in childhood, coarse facial features, corneal clouding, hepatosplenomegaly, joint stiffness, and a tendency to develop inguinal and umbilical hernias. Changes in the body skeleton, collectively referred to as dysostosis multiplex, include short stature, impaired growth of long bones, short, stubby hands, and a variety of cranial abnormalities. Enzyme deficiencies and clinical manifestations of the more common mucopolysaccharidoses are summarized in Table 64–1.

MARFAN'S SYNDROME

Marfan's syndrome is generally inherited in an autosomal dominant pattern, although about 20 per cent of patients appear to be new mutants. The biochemical defect is not clear. The disorder affects the eyes, causing myopia, lens dislocation, and retinal detachment. Skeletal abnormalities are easily recognized because of tall stature, an arm span that measures greater than the height, kyphoscoliosis, and pectus excavatum or pigeon breast deformities.

In the past, patients with Marfan's syndrome typically died at age 30 to 40 years of aortic dissection or rupture. Currently, aortic root dimensions are monitored, and prophylactic grafts, including a prosthetic valve, are considered when aortic root size reaches 6.0 cm. It is less clear whether treatment with beta-adrenoreceptor blockers retards aortic dilatation.

Other disorders sharing features of Marfan's syndrome are homocystinuria (lens dislocation) and the mitral valve prolapse syndrome (thoracic skeletal abnormalities). Neither of these is associated with aortic dilatation.

EHLERS-DANLOS SYNDROME

The Ehlers-Danlos syndrome, a group of inherited defects in collagen biosynthesis, causes hyperextensible skin and joints, easy bruisability, friability of tissues, and poor wound healing. Ten variants of Ehlers-Danlos syndrome have been distinguished on the basis of clinical manifestations. Biochemical defects have been defined for several variants. Ehlers-Danlos syndrome type I is the prototype with the most severe clinical manifestations. The skin is unusually soft, velvety, and hyperextensible, having a rubber-like quality allowing it to be stretched away from the underlying structures, promptly returning to its original position upon release. With aging, the skin may sag and become redundant, particularly over the elbows. Extreme fragility affects the skin, so that minor trauma may produce gaping wounds. Minor injuries may also produce large hematomas that may organize into tumor-like calcified masses. Hyperextensibility of the joints allows affected pa-

TABLE 64–1. THE MUCOPOLYSACCHARIDOSES (MPS)

ABBREVIATION	EPONYM	ENZYME DEFICIENCY	MAJOR STORAGE PRODUCT	INHERITANCE	CLINICAL FEATURES
MPS-IH	Hurler's	α-L-Iduronidase	DS + HS	AR	Corneal clouding, dysostosis multiplex, progressive mental retardation, heart disease, death by age 10
MPS-IS	Scheie's	α-L-Iduronidase	DS + HS	AR	Corneal clouding, joint stiffness, claw hands, aortic valve disease, normal intelligence, long survival
MPS-II	Hunter's	Iduronate sulfatase	HS − DS	X-linked	Clear corneas; if severe, similar to MPS-IH, death by age 15; if mild, survival to 30s to 60s
MPS-III	Sanfilippo's	Four enzymes, types A to D	HS	AR	Variable but often severe dementia; mild skeletal changes
MPS-IV	Morquio's	Galactose-6-sulfatase or β-galactosidase	KS + CS	AR	Short trunk dwarfism, odontoid hypoplasia, and cervical myelopathy
MPS-VI	Maroteaux-Lamy	N-Acetyl-galactosamine-4-sulfatase (arylsulfatase B)	DS	AR	Like MPS-IH with normal intelligence; aortic valve disease; may be severe or mild
MPS-VII	Sly's	β-Glucuronidase	HS, DS, CS	AR	Like MPS-IH but mild mental retardation; coarse granulocyte inclusions; variable severity

DS = Dermatan sulfate; HS = heparan sulfate; KS = keratan sulfate; CS = chondroitin sulfate; AR = autosomal recessive.

tients to perform unusual contortions. Chronic or recurrent joint dislocations are common, particularly affecting the hips, knees, shoulders, and temporomandibular joints. Many patients suffer inguinal, hiatal, and umbilical hernias as well as gastrointestinal or genitourinary diverticula. Ophthalmologic changes include blue sclerae, myopia, microcorneas, dislocated lenses, retinal detachment, and the appearance of widely spaced eyes. Cardiac manifestations are generally mild and include mitral valve prolapse. Spontaneous rupture of large arteries, the colon, and the gravid uterus occurs most commonly in Ehlers-Danlos syndrome type IV. Weakness of blood vessel walls or abnormal interaction of platelets with collagen often leads to a hemorrhagic diathesis.

The diagnosis of Ehlers-Danlos syndrome is usually suggested by the combination of hyperextensible skin and hypermobile joints. Additional clinical features and a family history of similar manifestations help in establishing the genetic type. Loose joints may also occur in Marfan's syndrome, several of the chondrocystrophies, and osteogenesis imperfecta. No specific treatment is available. Protection of the skin and joints from trauma is important, and surgery should be undertaken with extreme caution. Pregnancy carries a great risk.

REFERENCES

Byers PH: Disorders of collagen biosynthesis and structure. In Scriver CR, Beaudet AL, Sly WS, Valle D (eds): The Metabolic Basis of Inherited Disease. 6th ed. New York, McGraw-Hill, 1989.

McKusick VA: Heritable Disorders of Connective Tissue. 4th ed. St Louis, CV Mosby Co, 1972.

Newfeld EF, Muenger J: The mucopolysaccharidoses. In Scriver CR, Beaudet AL, Sly WS, Valle D (eds): The Metabolic Basis of Inherited Disease. 6th ed. New York, McGraw-Hill, 1989.

SECTION IX

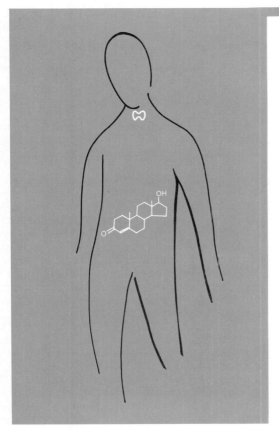

ENDOCRINE DISEASES

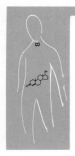

65 HYPOTHALAMIC-PITUITARY AXIS

The pituitary gland is a complex endocrine organ located in a bony fossa, the sella turcica, at the base of the brain. It consists of two distinct portions: the anterior pituitary (adenohypophysis) or glandular portion, derived from Rathke's pouch, and the posterior pituitary (neurohypophysis), which is an anatomic extension of the hypothalamus, derived from the diencephalon. Hormonal secretion by both portions of the pituitary gland is under the control of the central nervous system: the posterior lobe by a direct neurosecretory pathway from the anterior hypothalamus and the anterior lobe by a neuroendocrine system in which peptide and monoamine products of cells of the ventral hypothalamus are transported to the anterior pituitary via the hypothalamic-hypophyseal portal system. Owing to its unique location and intimate relationship with the central nervous system, the pituitary gland or, more appropriately, the hypothalamic-pituitary axis, is often referred to as the master gland of the endocrine system.

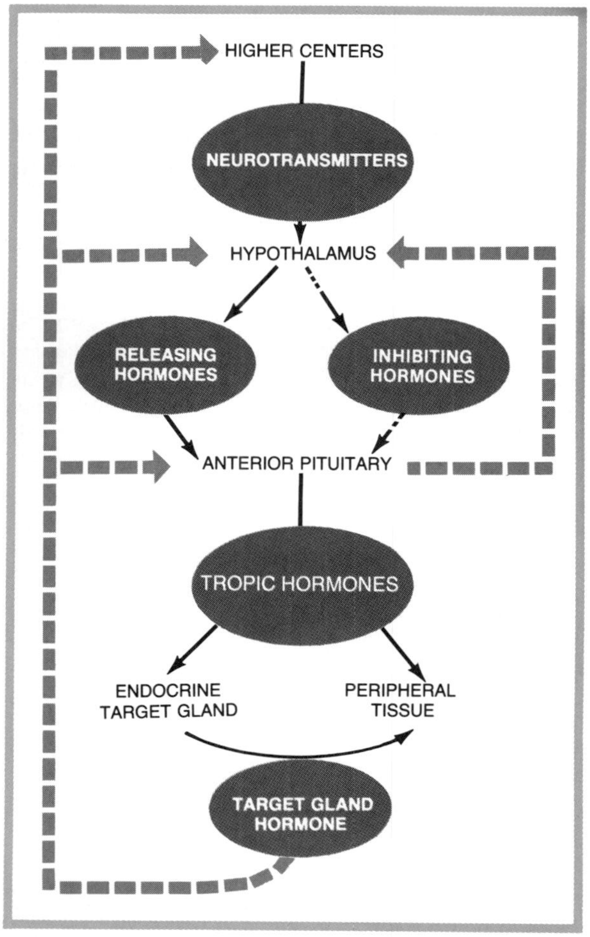

HYPOTHALAMIC HORMONES

Hypothalamic peptides stimulate the secretion of the anterior pituitary hormones. As an exception, dopamine, a monoamine, provides tonic inhibition of prolactin secretion. Releasing hormones for thyrotropin (thyrotropin-releasing hormone, or TRH), gonadotropin (GnRH), corticotropin (CRH), and growth hormone (GRH), and an inhibitory hormone for growth hormone secretion (somatostatin, or SRIF) have been sequenced and synthesized. In addition to their roles in the regulation of anterior pituitary function, several of these peptides and amines are found elsewhere in the brain and even outside the central nervous system, particularly in the gut, where they may have neurotransmitter and other regulatory functions.

Hypothalamic hormones are secreted under neural regulation involving a variety of neurotransmitters (e.g., biogenic amines such as catecholamines and serotonin) (Fig. 65–1). Their secretion is also regulated by a blood-borne (closed-loop) feedback system involving the secretory products of pituitary and endocrine target cell origin. The hypothalamic hormones enter the hypophyseal portal system in complex mixtures, but the selectivity of their effects is ensured by the presence of highly specific receptors on the various subtypes of endocrine cells in the anterior pituitary gland.

ANTERIOR PITUITARY HORMONES

The anterior pituitary gland contains several cell types, each of which is capable of synthesizing, storing, and releasing specific hormonal products. Six major and distinct secretory products have been recognized, which can be further subdivided into three classes of hormones: somatomammotropins, corticotropin and related peptides, and glycoproteins. The pituitary hormones and the hypothalamic factors that stimulate or suppress their secretion are shown in Figure 65–2.

FIGURE 65–1. Neural regulation and feedback control of the hypothalamic-pituitary axis. Solid lines indicate positive regulation, and broken lines indicate negative regulation.

The *somatomammotropins* include growth hormone and prolactin as well as a placental secretory product known as chorionic somatomammotropin. These structurally similar hormones have primarily lactogenic and growth-promoting effects. The somatomammotropins differ from the other hormonal products of the anterior pituitary in that they do not have a single classic endocrine target organ through which their effects are mediated. Many actions of growth hormone are mediated by a peptide—somatomedin-C, or insulin-like growth factor I (IGF-I)—that is synthesized in the liver and other tissues. Prolactin acts directly on the breast to promote synthesis of constituents of breast milk, but it is not responsible for breast development or milk release. The release of breast milk is regulated by oxytocin, a peptide that is released from the posterior pituitary.

Corticotropin (ACTH) is a 39 amino acid peptide that is part of a larger precursor molecule, proopiomelanocortin, which is the actual secretory product of the corticotrope. The larger molecule contains a number of biologically active peptides, including β-lipotropin, β-endorphin, melanocyte-stimulating hormone (MSH), and a large N-terminal fragment containing peptides that have natriuretic properties of uncertain physiologic significance. The mechanism controlling the differential release of these various fragments is unclear. ACTH stimulates secretion of glucocorticoid and, to a lesser extent, mineralocorticoid hormones by the adrenal cortex. ACTH also has extra-adrenal effects, such as stimulation of lipolysis in adipose tissue.

The *pituitary glycoprotein hormones*—thyroid-stimulating hormone (TSH), follicle-stimulating hormone (FSH), and luteinizing hormone (LH)—contain an alpha and a beta subunit. The alpha units are identical, whereas the beta units differ and thereby confer the specificity of the biologic effects of each of these substances. A gonadotropin of chorionic origin, similar in structure to the glycoproteins of pituitary origin, also possesses an identical alpha subunit. The glycoprotein hormones exert their biologic effects via the secretory products of their respective target organs: TSH modulates secretion of thyroxine and triiodothyronine by the thyroid gland; FSH and LH in women regulate ovulation and secretion of the steroid products of the ovary, whereas in men these gonadotropins regulate development of the seminiferous tubules and production of testosterone by the Leydig cells.

Tests of Anterior Pituitary Function

Radioimmunoassays for all of the major secretory products of the anterior pituitary gland are currently available in most clinical laboratories. When measurements of these hormones are used in conjunction with the appropriate physiologic maneuvers and pharmacologic probes, a precise characterization of states of anterior pituitary hypofunction and hyperfunction is generally possible.

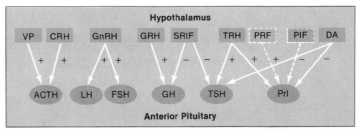

FIGURE 65–2. Interrelationships between hypothalamic and pituitary hormones. Interrupted lines indicate "factors" the structure of which is not yet known. VP = Vasopressin; CRH = corticotropin-releasing hormone; GnRH = gonadotropin-releasing hormone; GRH = growth hormone–releasing hormone; SRIF = somatotropin release–inhibiting factor; TRH = thyrotropin-releasing hormone; PRF = prolactin-releasing factor; PIF = prolactin-inhibiting factor; DA = dopamine. (From Frohman LA: Neuroendocrine regulation and its disorders. *In* Wyngaarden JB, Smith LH Jr, Bennett JC [eds]: Cecil Textbook of Medicine. 19th ed. Philadelphia, WB Saunders Co, 1992, pp 1215–1224.)

Corticotropin (ACTH)

Levels of plasma ACTH may be undetectable in normal individuals when obtained under basal conditions. Demonstration of ACTH deficiency therefore requires the use of a stimulatory maneuver such as induction of hypoglycemia with insulin (0.1 U/kg intravenously) or of hypocortisolism with the 11β-hydroxylase inhibitor metyrapone (750 mg orally every 6 hours for four doses). If ACTH assays are not available, ACTH reserve can be evaluated indirectly by measuring the response of plasma cortisol to the former and of 11-deoxycortisol to the latter stimulus; this approach presupposes that adrenal function is intact. The use of CRH to determine ACTH secretory reserve may soon be available for general use. When used in conjunction with indirect stimuli such as insulin hypoglycemia, CRH testing may detect patients with hypothalamic lesions causing ACTH deficiency (e.g., a positive CRH test but a negative response to hypoglycemia).

In states of suspected ACTH excess, suppression tests using exogenous glucocorticoid hormones such as dexamethasone are generally employed (see Chapter 67). Administration of CRH may also prove to be of value in this setting, particularly in distinguishing pituitary from ectopic sources of ACTH.

Thyroid-Stimulating Hormone

In patients with hypothyroidism and normal or undetectable levels of TSH, the distinction between hypothalamic and pituitary abnormalities can be made using TRH. In this procedure, TSH levels are obtained before and 15 to 30 minutes after administering 500 μg of TRH intravenously. Normally, TSH levels will increase to values of up to 15 μU/ml in response to this stimulus. Patients with pituitary hypothyroidism have a flat response, whereas TSH levels increase in those with hypothalamic hypothyroidism, although the response may be delayed. A flat TSH response to TRH may also be found in hyperthyroidism, acromegaly, renal insufficiency, and depression and during steroid therapy.

Gonadotropins

Administering 100 μg of GnRH intravenously can frequently distinguish between pituitary and hypothalamic etiologies of gonadotropin deficiency. Normally, the response of LH is greater than that of FSH, averaging three to five times the control value. Repeated injections may be required to elicit normal responses in some patients with hypothalamic disorders. In children, the pattern of response also differs, depending on the age of the patient and, in particular, the stage of pubertal development. The estrogen antagonist clomiphene can stimulate LH and FSH secretion in patients with hypothalamic hypogonadism and may be used as a therapeutic as well as diagnostic agent in this setting.

Prolactin

Prolactin secretory reserve can be evaluated by administration of dopamine antagonists such as metoclopramide. For evaluation of hyperprolactinemia, tests of suppressibility with L-dopa or water loading are employed. However, the failure of these latter procedures to distinguish readily between prolactin-secreting adenomas and other causes of hyperprolactinemia has reduced their usefulness.

Growth Hormone

Growth hormone secretory reserve can be evaluated by its response to insulin-induced hypoglycemia (0.1 U of insulin per kilogram, given intravenously), to GRH (1 μg/kg intravenously), during a 30-minute infusion of arginine (0.5 gm/kg), or by its response to L-dopa (0.5 gm orally). Autonomy of growth hormone secretion can be evaluated by oral glucose loading, a maneuver that normally suppresses growth hormone secretion.

ANTERIOR PITUITARY HYPOFUNCTION: HYPOPITUITARISM (Table 65–1)

Etiology

Hypopituitarism, an endocrine deficiency state characterized by diminished or absent secretion of the hormones of the anterior pituitary gland, results either from a primary disorder of the secretory cells of the anterior pituitary gland or as a secondary consequence of reduced stimulation by the releasing hormones of the hypothalamus. When the deficiency of anterior pituitary hormones is generalized, the condition is referred to as panhypopituitarism.

Hypopituitarism can be caused by destruction of the pituitary by tumors or granulomas or by hem-

orrhagic necrosis of a hypertrophied pituitary gland in pregnancy as a complication of postpartum hemorrhage and shock (Sheehan's syndrome). Secondary hypopituitarism can result from lesions of the hypothalamus per se, from destruction of the pituitary stalk, or from a deficiency of one or more of the specific hypothalamic-releasing hormones that regulate secretion of the anterior pituitary gland. Isolated growth hormone deficiency in children is a typical example of a secondary form of anterior pituitary deficiency presumed to be due to a selective deficiency of GRH.

Clinical Features

The clinical manifestations of hypopituitarism depend upon the rapidity with which the hormonal deficiencies occur, the specific hormones that are deficient, the sex of the patient, and the age at the time of onset of the disease. Often pituitary insufficiency occurs insidiously, and the complaints are vague and nonspecific. Much less commonly, the onset of hypopituitarism occurs with dramatic suddenness in association with acute infarction of a pituitary tumor, a condition referred to as pituitary apoplexy.

In prepubertal children, the deficiencies of growth hormone and gonadotropins result in short stature and delayed puberty. In adults, growth hormone deficiency has been thought to be of little clinical consequence. Growth hormone replacement may affect the relative amounts of lean tissue and fat in such individuals, however. Deficiency of ACTH results in findings similar to those of primary adrenocortical insufficiency (Addison's disease), including weakness, malaise, nausea, vomiting, and eventual collapse (see Chapter 67). These manifestations of glucocorticoid deficiency, however, are generally of lesser severity than in primary adrenal insufficiency. In contrast to Addison's disease, hyperpigmentation is absent and severe sodium depletion is rare, since aldosterone secretion is maintained at normal or nearly nor-

TABLE 65–1. CAUSES OF HYPOPITUITARISM

Neoplasms
  1. Pituitary tumors
  2. Hypothalamic tumors, e.g., craniopharyngioma
  3. Metastatic tumors, lymphoma, etc.
Infections or Granulomas
  1. Tuberculosis
  2. Sarcoidosis
  3. Meningitis
  4. Syphilis
Vascular
  1. Postpartum necrosis (Sheehan's syndrome)
  2. Hemorrhagic infarction of a pituitary tumor
  3. Aneurysm of the carotid artery
Infiltrative
  1. Hemochromatosis
  2. Histiocytosis X
Physical Injury
  1. Head trauma
  2. Surgery
  3. Radiation therapy
Isolated or Combined Hypothalamic Releasing Hormone Deficiencies

mal levels. Hyponatremia can occur, however, as a consequence of impaired water excretion secondary to cortisol deficiency. Deficiency of TSH results in many of the typical findings of thyroid hormone deficiency, but the severity is generally less than that seen in primary hypothyroidism, and true myxedema is rare. Gonadotropin deficiency results in amenorrhea and atrophy of the breasts in women, testicular atrophy in men, and diminished libido and the absence of pubic and axillary hair in both sexes. Additional findings include a waxy character and color of the skin and a fine wrinkling in the periorbital area that suggests premature aging. Hypothermia, hypotension, and hypoglycemia may also occur.

Diagnosis

Once suspected, the diagnosis of hypopituitarism can usually be established without difficulty, although care must be taken to distinguish the multiple deficiencies of target organ hormone production due to pituitary insufficiency from those due to primary polyglandular deficiency states resulting from autoimmune processes (e.g., Schmidt's syndrome). Demonstration of deficiency of the major target organ products (cortisol, thyroxine, testosterone, estrogen), together with an absence of compensatory increases in levels of the trophic hormones of pituitary origin (ACTH, TSH, FSH, LH), establishes that the abnormality resides in the hypothalamic-pituitary axis.

In patients with hypopituitarism, the finding of increased levels of prolactin, which is normally under tonic inhibition by the hypothalamus, suggests that the lesion is in the hypothalamus or pituitary stalk. The distinction between primary pituitary abnormalities and secondary deficiencies due to impaired hypothalamic function can also be made using the specific hypothalamic-releasing hormones as outlined above.

Treatment

Treatment of patients with panhypopituitarism consists of replacement of the specific hormone deficiencies with glucocorticoid, thyroxine, and the appropriate gonadal steroid. Growth hormone replacement is indicated in children who have not reached adult stature. Growth hormone and prolactin deficiencies in adults require no specific therapy. Restoration of fertility is theoretically possible with a combination of human menopausal gonadotropin and chorionic gonadotropin and by GnRH therapy in cases in which the lesion is in the hypothalamus or pituitary stalk.

Special precautions are required when initiating hormonal replacement therapy in patients with panhypopituitarism. Administration of thyroxine in patients who have concomitant ACTH deficiency can result in an increase in the metabolic clearance rate of glucocorticoid hormones and the sudden precipitation of an addisonian crisis. Accordingly, such patients should always receive glucocorticoid therapy at the same time or preceding the onset of thyroid hormone replacement. Initiation of therapy with glucocorticoid hormones

and thyroxine can unmask coexisting diabetes insipidus by improving free water clearance in patients with combined anterior and posterior pituitary insufficiency. Such patients may require concomitant treatment with antidiuretic hormone, as discussed in a subsequent section.

SYNDROMES OF ANTERIOR PITUITARY HYPERFUNCTION: THE PITUITARY ADENOMA

Adenomas of the pituitary gland may be nonfunctioning, or they may secrete any of the trophic hormones normally produced by the gland. Hypersecretion of prolactin, growth hormone, or ACTH occurs commonly, resulting in the syndromes of amenorrhea-galactorrhea, acromegaly, and Cushing's syndrome, respectively. Hypersecretion of TSH or of gonadotropins from a pituitary adenoma is rare. Whether or not hyperfunction of the anterior pituitary represents a primary disorder or is secondary to increased stimulation by hypothalamic releasing factors has not been resolved. Even the demonstration of a microadenoma and reversal of the clinical abnormalities with removal of the neoplasm does not exclude the latter possibility, since long-term follow-up is necessary to ensure that the disease will not recur. In the following sections, we discuss the management of pituitary tumors in general as well as the pathogenesis, clinical features, and management of the specific syndromes produced by excess secretion of prolactin and growth hormone. For a discussion of Cushing's syndrome, the reader is referred to Chapter 67.

Pituitary Neoplasms: General Considerations

Pituitary neoplasms are usually benign and slow-growing and may remain undetected for many years. Neurologic symptoms, principally headache and visual disturbances, may be the first manifestations, or the patient may present with findings consistent with pituitary insufficiency or with excessive secretion of any of the anterior pituitary hormones. Not infrequently, the presence of a pituitary neoplasm may be discovered in an asymptomatic patient in whom a skull radiograph is obtained for unrelated reasons.

Because of the close proximity of the optic nerves and optic chiasm, visual field defects are often the principal neurologic findings when a pituitary tumor extends beyond the confines of the sella turcica. Typically, this is manifested as bitemporal hemianopsia, often beginning in the upper quadrants of the visual field. Extraocular nerve palsies can also occur when the tumor enlarges laterally into the cavernous sinus. Headache, due in some cases to increased intracranial pressure secondary to obstruction of outflow of cerebrospinal fluid from the third ventricle, may also be a prominent complaint with large tumors. Headache is also common with smaller tumors owing to stretching of the diaphragma sellae and overlying dura.

Decisions regarding the management of pituitary tumors should be made in collaboration with a neurosurgeon. The optimal approach usually depends upon the size, location, and whether or not the tumor is endocrinologically active. Large tumors that impinge on extrasellar structures usually require surgical management whether or not they are secretory. Smaller tumors that are actively secreting anterior pituitary hormones, such as prolactinomas, as well as large tumors that are surgically incurable, can often be managed medically with bromocriptine (see below).

An enlarged sella turcica does not of itself indicate the presence of a pituitary tumor. Many patients with an enlarged sella, particularly obese women, have the so-called empty sella syndrome, in which the pituitary gland is displaced by cerebrospinal fluid that enters the sella via a defect in the diaphragm above the sella. These patients rarely have clinically significant endocrinologic abnormalities. Distinction from pituitary tumor is usually possible with magnetic resonance imaging (MRI) or high-resolution computed tomography (CT) scans.

Hyperprolactinemia: Galactorrhea-Amenorrhea Syndrome

Etiology (Table 65–2)

Prolactin is under chronic inhibitory control by a hypothalamic factor (presumably dopamine). Any pharmacologic agent or lesion of the hypothalamus or pituitary stalk that interferes with do-

TABLE 65–2. CAUSES OF HYPERPROLACTINEMIA

Physiologic
1. Pregnancy and lactation
2. Breast stimulation
3. Estrogen therapy
4. Stress
5. Newborn

Hypothalamic-Pituitary Lesions
1. Prolactinoma
2. Stalk section
3. Hypothalamic disorders—craniopharyngioma, granulomas
4. Empty sella syndrome

Metabolic Disorders
1. Hypothyroidism
2. Renal failure

Chest Wall Injury

Drugs
1. Phenothiazines, haloperidol
2. Alpha-methyldopa
3. Reserpine
4. Metoclopramide
5. Opiates

pamine secretion or its action can result in hyperprolactinemia. In view of the wide clinical use of pharmacologic agents that interfere with dopaminergic action, such as the phenothiazines, it is not surprising that the majority of patients with hyperprolactinemia do not harbor a pituitary adenoma. Once the use of such an agent can be excluded, however, and mechanical or neurogenic factors eliminated, the frequency with which a pituitary microadenoma is found is quite high. The most common pituitary tumor, chromophobe adenoma, once thought to be nonfunctioning and endocrinologically silent, is frequently a prolactin-secreting adenoma (prolactinoma).

Clinical Manifestations

The clinical manifestations of hyperprolactinemia depend upon the hormone level, the sex of the patient, and individual sensitivity to the lactogenic and mammotropic effects of the hormone. In women, hyperprolactinemia results in the so-called galactorrhea-amenorrhea syndrome. Persistent lactation, unprovoked by breast stimulation, and amenorrhea are the classic features. The syndrome may appear following pregnancy or may be unrelated to pregnancy. In men, galactorrhea can occur, but impotence and loss of libido are more frequent complaints.

Diagnosis

The diagnosis of hyperprolactinemia should be considered in patients with any of the previously described clinical manifestations, that is, galactorrhea, secondary amenorrhea, and impotence. Serum prolactin determinations are required to establish a diagnosis of hyperprolactinemia. If levels are markedly elevated (>150 ng/ml; normal, <20), the presence of a prolactin-secreting adenoma is highly likely. With lower levels, a greater degree of overlap with non-neoplastic causes of hyperprolactinemia occurs. Some overlap may occur with physiologically elevated levels in response to stress. Prolactin levels may also vary widely as a consequence of intermittent secretory bursts in patients with tumors. For these reasons, multiple levels should be obtained to establish the presence of pathologic hyperprolactinemia. Galactorrhea can occur with persistently normal serum prolactin levels, presumably as a consequence of increased sensitivity to the hormone.

Treatment

For tumors located in the sella, or with minimal suprasellar extension, many centers now prefer an initial trial of medical therapy. Administration of bromocriptine, a dopamine agonist, at doses of 10 to 15 mg daily usually results in cessation of lactation, resumption of menses and fertility, and restoration of libido and potency. Bromocriptine may also result in regression of the tumor per se, although surgical therapy is probably indicated in patients with tumors large enough to produce neurologic symptoms. The surgical procedure of choice is trans-sphenoidal microsurgery. This procedure preserves the surrounding normal pituitary tissue and rarely results in hypopituitarism. Pituitary irradiation, using either conventional sources or heavy particle beams, is also frequently successful, but the incidence of hypopituitarism is greater than in patients treated with transsphenoidal hypophysectomy. This may be a very important consideration in women in the child-bearing years or in children who have not yet achieved adult height.

Gigantism and Acromegaly

Clinical Manifestations (Table 65–3)

The manifestations of excess growth hormone production are critically dependent on the age of the patient at the time that the abnormality first occurs. If growth hormone is present in excess before the epiphyses close, the increase in linear skeletal growth results in gigantism. After closure of the epiphyses, growth hormone excess results in acromegaly, a disorder characterized by physical changes in the bones and soft tissues as well as metabolic abnormalities reflecting the physiologic actions of this polypeptide.

The typical physical changes of acromegaly result from enlargement of the skeleton and soft tissues and thickening of the skin (Fig. 65–3). Enlargement of the acral parts (fingers and toes), coarsening and enlargement of the facial features, prognathism, frontal bossing, enlargement of the

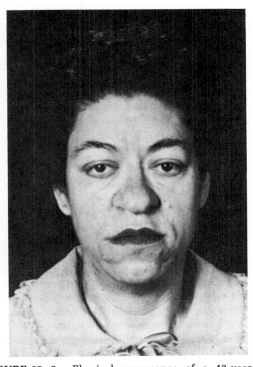

FIGURE 65–3. Physical appearance of a 43-year-old woman with acromegaly of 15 years' duration. Note the coarsening and enlargement of the facial features, prognathism, and thickening of skin folds. (From Frohman LA: In Felig P, Baxter JD, Broadus AE, et al [eds]: Endocrinology and Metabolism, 2nd ed, p 302. Copyright © 1987 by McGraw-Hill, Inc. Used by permission of McGraw-Hill Book Company.)

TABLE 65–3. CLINICAL MANIFESTATIONS OF ACROMEGALY IN 100 PATIENTS

Manifestations of GH Excess	
Acral enlargement	100*
Soft tissue overgrowth	100
Hyperhidrosis	88
Lethargy or fatigue	87
Weight gain	73
Paresthesias	70
Joint pain	69
Photophobia	46
Papillomas	45
Hypertrichosis	33
Goiter	32
Acanthosis nigricans	29
Hypertension	24
Cardiomegaly	16
Renal calculi	11
Disturbance of Other Endocrine Functions	
Hyperinsulinemia	70
Glucose intolerance	50
Irregular or absent menses	60
Decreased libido or impotence	46
Hypothyroidism	13
Galactorrhea	13
Gynecomastia	8
Hypoadrenalism	4
Local Manifestations	
Enlarged sella	90
Headache	65
Visual deficit	20

*Percentage of patients in whom these features were present.
From Findling JW, Tyrrell JB: Anterior pituitary and somatomedins: I. Anterior pituitary. In Greenspan FS, Forsham PH (eds): Basic and Clinical Endocrinology. Los Altos, CA, Lange Medical Publishers, 1983, p 77.

tongue, and deepening of the voice are characteristic findings. Since these changes may occur insidiously, comparison of pictures of the patient taken serially over the years is often very helpful in recognizing their appearance. An increase in shoe size, hat size, or ring size may be noted by the patient. Additional complaints include headache, weakness, increased perspiration, paresthesias, and bilateral carpal tunnel syndrome. Enlargement of the viscera, hypertension, and congestive heart failure can also occur.

In addition to the physical changes that result from excess growth hormone secretion, a variety of metabolic abnormalities may also occur. Impaired glucose tolerance is present in more than half the cases, but frank diabetes mellitus is not evident unless pancreatic insulin secretion is incapable of responding to the counterregulatory effect of growth hormone. An increase in glomerular filtration rate and in renal tubular reabsorption of phosphate may also be observed, the latter causing the typical finding of hyperphosphatemia.

Diagnosis

In fully developed acromegaly, the physical findings are so characteristic as to provide an unmistakable diagnosis. Confirmation of this diagnosis as well as determination of whether or not the disease is in an active phase requires measurement of growth hormone. Levels of growth hormone obtained under basal conditions generally exceed the upper limit of normal (5 ng/ml) and typically cannot be suppressed by a physiologic maneuver such as administration of glucose. A paradoxical increase in growth hormone levels in response to administration of glucose occurs in some patients with acromegaly, whereas administration of L-dopa, which normally stimulates secretion of growth hormone, usually reduces the levels in acromegaly. Both TRH and GnRH, which normally have no effect on growth hormone, may cause a paradoxical rise in growth hormone levels in patients with acromegaly. Measurement of plasma concentrations of IGF-I may also be useful, inasmuch as plasma levels of this mediator of growth hormone action fluctuate less than those of growth hormone and are thought to reflect more accurately the state of disease activity.

Treatment

Treatment of acromegaly depends partially on the size of the tumor, particularly whether or not the mass extends beyond the sella and whether or not the optic nerves are involved. Surgical results are often not as gratifying as with other pituitary neoplasms, presumably because the secretory cells are more widely dispersed and therefore are not entirely removed with the microsurgical technique. External radiation using either standard cobalt or proton beams generally results in a slow decrease in elevated growth hormone levels and eventually arrests the progress of the disease, but at the cost of a high incidence of hypopituitarism. A somatostatin analogue has been effective in reducing growth hormone levels in some patients with acromegaly and in decreasing tumor size in a few. Bromocriptine has been far less effective in the treatment of acromegaly than in the treatment of the amenorrhea-galactorrhea syndrome.

DISORDERS OF THE POSTERIOR PITUITARY

The posterior lobe of the pituitary gland (neurohypophysis) is an anatomic extension of the hypothalamus, containing the axons and axon terminals of neurons whose nuclei originate in the supraoptic and paraventricular areas of the hypothalamus. Two peptide hormones, arginine vasopressin and oxytocin, and their carrier proteins, the neurophysins, are synthesized in the cell bodies of these neurons. These peptides and their carrier proteins travel down the axons to the nerve terminals from which they are released in response to a variety of physiologic stimuli.

Oxytocin causes release of breast milk and may promote uterine contractions during labor. There is no known function for this peptide hormone in men. Arginine vasopressin (also known as antidi-

uretic hormone [ADH]) is the principal hormonal factor regulating water metabolism. Deficiency of ADH or impaired action in its major target organ, the kidney, results in a polyuric state known as diabetes insipidus. Excessive and physiologically inappropriate secretion of ADH results in hyponatremia (the syndrome of inappropriate ADH secretion, SIADH). Arginine vasopressin, as the name implies, also has pressor activity, the physiologic relevance of which is unknown.

Physiologic Regulation of Antidiuretic Hormone Secretion

Variations in the secretion of ADH by the posterior pituitary occur primarily in response to changes in body osmolality. Normally, osmolality averages approximately 285 mOsm/kg body water. An increase in body osmolality as small as 1 per cent (3 mOsm/kg), such as occurs after 10 to 12 hours of water deprivation, normally increases ADH secretion (Fig. 65–4). Conversely, reduction in osmolality following administration of an oral water load causes dilution of body fluids and a prompt suppression of ADH secretion. The concomitant stimulation and suppression of the hypothalamic thirst center in response to hypertonicity and hypotonicity, respectively, provides a parallel physiologic mechanism for regulating body osmolality.

In addition to osmotic regulation, several nonos-

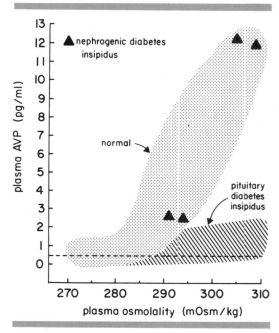

FIGURE 65–4. The relations between plasma arginine vasopressin (AVP) concentrations and plasma osmolality. Patients with nephrogenic diabetes insipidus (*triangles*) respond normally to increases in plasma osmolality. (From Reeves WB, Andreoli TE: Nephrogenic diabetes insipidus. *In* Scriver CR, Baudet AL, Sly WS, et al [eds]: The Metabolic Basis of Inherited Disease. 6th ed. Copyright © 1989 by McGraw-Hill, Inc. Used by permission of McGraw-Hill Book Company.)

motic factors can influence ADH secretion. Most notable among these is the state of the so-called effective extracellular fluid (ECF) volume, perceived by high-pressure baroreceptors in the aorta and by low-pressure volume receptors in the left atrium. Hypotension or decreased effective ECF volume or both result in stimulation of ADH secretion via adrenergically mediated signals to the hypothalamus. Other nonosmotic stimuli include stress, hypoxemia, and certain drugs (e.g., morphine and nicotine). Although minute-by-minute regulation of ADH secretion is probably through its osmotic control mechanism, nonosmotic factors will predominate in situations in which there is diversion of the two stimuli (e.g., hypovolemia in a hypotonic individual).

ADH acts primarily on the distal nephron to induce an increase in osmotic water permeability of the collecting tubule and collecting duct. Permeability to urea is also increased in response to ADH. The hormone acts through a cyclic AMP–dependent mechanism that is initiated by binding to a receptor on the basolateral surface of the target cell. This process is modulated by a number of factors, including calcium, prostaglandins, adrenal corticosteroids, and a variety of adrenergic agents.

Diabetes Insipidus

Etiology

In diabetes insipidus the urinary concentrating mechanism is impaired either as a consequence of a failure to secrete adequate amounts of vasopressin (central diabetes insipidus) or as a consequence of failure of the distal tubule and collecting duct to respond normally to the hormone (nephrogenic diabetes insipidus). Central diabetes insipidus is usually caused by head trauma, surgical hypophysectomy, granulomatous diseases, histiocytosis X, or primary or metastatic neoplasms, or it can follow anoxic brain damage or meningoencephalitis. In at least one third of patients, no pathologic cause is evident. Diabetes insipidus after surgery or head trauma may occur transiently, may be followed by a transient period of hyponatremia due to inappropriate release of ADH from the damaged pituitary tissue, and may then resolve completely or progress to a permanent ADH-deficient state. Rarely, central diabetes insipidus is familial, presumably owing to hypoplasia of the secretory cells in the hypothalamus. Nephrogenic diabetes insipidus can occur as an inherited disorder, predominantly affecting males, or can be an acquired condition resulting from a variety of renal diseases, electrolyte disorders (hypokalemia, hypercalcemia), or drug therapies (e.g., lithium).

Diagnosis

In both central and nephrogenic diabetes insipidus, the principal findings are polyuria and polydipsia with urinary volumes generally in excess of 3 L/day and occasionally, depending upon the concomitant water intake, exceeding 5 to 10 L/day. The diagnosis is suspected in patients who excrete large quantities of a dilute urine in which the specific gravity is less than 1.010 or the osmolality is less than 300 mOsm/kg. The major diagnostic challenge is to distinguish diabetes insipidus of either type from compulsive water drinking (psychogenic polydipsia), in which maximal urinary concentrating ability may be impaired as a consequence of "washout" of the normally hypertonic medulla by continuous excretion of a dilute urine. Demonstration of frank hypertonicity (serum osmolality > 295 mOsm/kg) excludes primary polydipsia, but usually a protocol employing water deprivation (overnight dehydration) followed by administration of aqueous vasopressin (Pitressin) is required to distinguish among these three polyuric states. In this procedure, water is withheld until the osmolality of hourly voided urine samples reaches a plateau. In patients with primary polydipsia, urine osmolality is generally much greater than plasma osmolality and increases minimally in response to the subsequent subcutaneous administration of 5 U of aqueous vasopressin. In patients with severe central diabetes insipidus, urine osmolality is usually much less than plasma osmolality and increases by at least 50 per cent in response to vasopressin. Those with nephrogenic diabetes insipidus are distinguished by the failure of a low urine osmolality to respond normally to vasopressin. Occasionally, patients with partial defects in ADH secretion require further investigation using hypertonic saline infusion or more elaborate water deprivation tests.

Treatment

Treatment of central diabetes insipidus depends to a large extent on the severity of the hormone deficiency. In patients in whom the deficiency is only partial, chlorpropamide potentiates the effect of ADH on the renal tubule. However, hypoglycemia may result, particularly if the dose of chlorpropamide exceeds 250 mg/day. Patients with more complete hormone deficiency require ADH replacement therapy using a synthetic analogue, 1-desamino-8-D-arginine vasopressin (DDAVP). Devoid of significant pressor activity, DDAVP can be conveniently administered by nasal insufflation in doses of 5 to 10 μg every 12 to 24 hours or intramuscularly if necessary. No specific treatment is available for patients with nephrogenic diabetes insipidus, but reduction of solute load by salt restriction and administration of thiazide diuretics will reduce the polyuria.

The Syndrome of Inappropriate Antidiuretic Hormone Secretion (SIADH)

Autonomous secretion of ADH, either from an ectopic neoplasm or as a consequence of central nervous system or pulmonary disease, results in hypotonic volume expansion, renal sodium wasting, and hyponatremia. This syndrome is discussed in greater detail in Chapter 26.

REFERENCES

Andreoli TE: The posterior pituitary. *In* Wyngaarden JB, Smith LH Jr, Bennett JC (eds): Cecil Textbook of Medicine. 19th ed. Philadelphia, WB Saunders Co, 1992, pp 1239–1246.

Cook DM: Pituitary tumors: Diagnosis and therapy. Cancer 33:215, 1983.

Frohman LA: The anterior pituitary. *In* Wyngaarden JB, Smith LH Jr, Bennett JC (eds): Cecil Textbook of Medicine. 19th ed. Philadelphia, WB Saunders Co, 1992, pp 1224–1238.

Lufkin EG, Kao PC, O'Fallon WM, et al: Combined testing of anterior pituitary gland with insulin, thyrotropin-releasing hormone, and luteinizing hormone-releasing hormone. Am J Med 75:471, 1983.

Reeves WB, Andreoli TE: The posterior pituitary and water metabolism. *In* Foster DW, Wilson JD (eds): Williams Textbook of Endocrinology. 8th ed. Philadelphia, WB Saunders Co, 1991, pp 311–356.

Wollesen F, Andersen T, Karle A: Size reduction of extrasellar pituitary tumors during bromocriptine treatment: Quantitation of effect on different types of tumors. Ann Intern Med 96:281, 1982.

66 THE THYROID

Dysfunction of the thyroid gland causes some of the most common endocrine disorders seen by the physician. Thyrotoxicosis (hyperthyroidism) is a consequence of excess thyroid hormone; a deficiency of thyroid hormone causes hypothyroidism (myxedema). Thyroid dysfunction is frequently manifested clinically by a swelling (enlargement) of the gland, a condition referred to as goiter formation.

The thyroid gland arises embryologically from the thyroid diverticulum, an outgrowth of a median endothermal thickening of the pharynx. The lateral components combine to develop the easily palpable, butterfly-shaped mature thyroid gland (20 gm). The lateral lobes (2 cm × 3 cm), partially hidden by the sternocleidomastoid muscles, are connected by the isthmus, which sits just below the cricoid cartilage. A pyramidal lobe is present in about 30 per cent of cases; it extends upward from the isthmus lateral to the trachea. The gland consists of spherical follicles (acini) lined by epithelial tissue and filled with colloid. This substance consists of thyroglobulin, the storage form of thyroxine (T_4), 3,5,3′-triiodothyronine (T_3), and the precursors monoiodothyronine (MIT) and diiodothyronine (DIT). Other functioning cells of neural crest origin located in the parafollicular area of the thyroid (C cells) secrete calcitonin.

THYROID PHYSIOLOGY

Iodide, a substrate for thyroid hormone synthesis, also plays an autoregulatory role in the metabolism of the thyroid gland. The normal gland contains approximately 10,000 μg of iodine, which is predominantly organically bound. The minimal daily requirement of iodide is only about 200 μg (renal loss replacement). Iodide deficiency is a rare occurrence in the iodide-replete Western world but remains the most common cause of goiter (endemic goiter) in the world. Many patients with endemic goiter are mentally deficient owing to hypothyroidism dating from birth (cretinism) or suffer from retarded musculoskeletal development resulting from thyroid hormone deficiency during childhood.

The thyroid gland concentrates iodide through a unique trapping mechanism and maintains a cell-to-plasma iodide ratio of about 50:1. Trapped iodide is rapidly oxidized by peroxidase to iodine and subsequently undergoes organification by iodinating tyrosine residues on thyroglobulin to form MIT and DIT. Coupling of these compounds results in the formation of T_3 and T_4. The secretory process is initiated by pinocytosis of thyroglobulin from the follicular lumen followed by the release of T_4 and T_3 from their storage form by proteolysis induced by lysosomal enzymes. The active hormones T_4 and T_3 are then secreted into the circulation. The thyroid gland is the only source for T_4, whereas it contributes only about 20 per cent of the T_3 produced daily.

A number of chemicals interfere with thyroid gland metabolism. These effects have been exploited for therapeutic purposes in the case of propylthiouracil (PTU) and methimazole. Both drugs effectively block thyroid hormone synthesis and are utilized clinically in the treatment of hyperthyroidism. Agents that are preferentially trapped by the thyroid (iodide, pertechnetate) are used diagnostically for gland imaging. Pharmacologic amounts of iodide also inhibit thyroid gland synthesis and release of hormones. This inhibitory effect is generally of short duration in normal people, but if sustained it can lead to hypothyroidism and compensatory goiter formation. Lithium has a similar effect to that of iodide. Its extensive use in manic-depressive illness has led to a significant problem with hypothyroidism in this group of patients.

Thyroid hormones circulate in two forms, protein-bound and free. Thyroxine-binding globulin (TBG), the principal carrier, binds about 70 per cent of the thyroid hormones under normal conditions. Other carrier proteins, transthyretin and albumin, play a lesser role. A small but very important quantity of T_4 (0.03 per cent) and T_3 (0.3 per cent) is free and remains in rapid equilibrium with the protein-bound fraction. The metabolic state of the patient correlates with the free component rather than the total (bound) thyroid hormone level. Alterations in serum TBG concentration are common and account for the majority of changes in serum total T_4 not attributable to hyperthyroidism or hypothyroidism (Table 66–1). These changes in serum total T_4 levels are not accompanied by changes in the free T_4 concentration. Thus a measurement of free T_4 or an index of free T_4 is obligatory under these conditions in order to interpret accurately the significance of a change in the total hormone value.

The thyroid gland is the only endogenous source of T_4. Although the thyroid also secretes T_3, 80 per cent of the daily T_3 produced is derived from extrathyroidal T_4 deiodination. Since T_3 is biologically the most active thyroid hormone, this process is regarded as an activation step. In addition, T_4 can be deiodinated to 3,5',3'-triiodothyronine (reverse T_3, rT_3). This pathway inactivates T_4, as rT_3 is calorigenically inactive. These balanced pathways for T_4 deiodination are frequently disturbed during acute illness (Fig. 66–1). This results in an impairment in T_3 neogenesis (low T_3 syndrome) and increased levels of serum rT_3. Despite these alterations, such patients are currently considered euthyroid, and T_3 replacement is not indicated. Should the low T_3 state persist, however, such patients may become hypothyroid.

The integrated control of thyroid hormone metabolism is regulated by the hypothalamic-

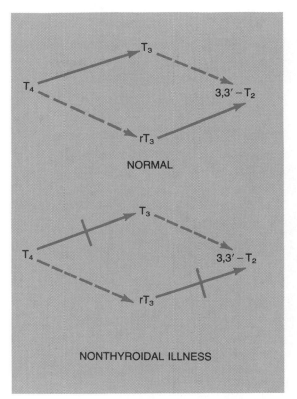

FIGURE 66–1. Sequential deiodination of thyroxine (T_4) to 3,3'-diiodothyronine (3,3'-T_2) via 3,5,3'-triiodothyronine (T_3) and 3,3',5'-triiodothyronine (reverse-T_3, rT_3), in the normal subject and in a patient with nonthyroidal illness. The solid arrows reflect outer-ring deiodination. The dashed arrows reflect inner-ring deiodination. The changes in serum T_3 and rT_3 associated with nonthyroidal illness are consequent to the indicated lesions in deiodination.

pituitary-thyroid axis (Fig. 66–2). Thyrotropin-releasing hormone (TRH) secreted by the hypothalamus controls the synthesis and secretion of pituitary thyroid-stimulating hormone (TSH). The set point for the pituitary TSH response to TRH is regulated by the feedback inhibitory effect of the thyroid hormones. TSH stimulates all aspects of the synthesis and secretion of thyroid hormone.

The metabolic effects of thyroid hormone are mediated through a variety of mechanisms. Thyroid hormones regulate protein synthesis by binding to specific nuclear receptors. They enhance mitochondrial oxidation and regulate the activity of membrane-bound enzymes. Normal brain maturation during fetal and infant development depends on adequate quantities of thyroid hormone. Irreversible mental retardation develops in the absence of thyroid hormone (cretinism). During childhood, deficiency of thyroid hormone results in delay of somatic growth and development. In the geriatric population, reversible dementia consequent to hypothyroidism is not an uncommon problem.

TABLE 66–1. ALTERATIONS IN THYROXINE-BINDING GLOBULIN (TBG) CONCENTRATION

TBG Increased (Total $T_4\uparrow$, $FT_4\rightarrow$)
  Newborn
  Pregnancy (estrogen effect)
  Acute hepatitis
  Acute intermittent porphyria
  Genetic TBG excess
  Oral contraceptives (estrogens)
  Heroin and/or methadone abuse
  Clofibrate or 5-fluorouracil use
TBG Decreased (Total $T_4\downarrow$, $FT_4\rightarrow$)
  Cirrhosis
  Nephrotic syndrome
  Severe nonthyroidal illness
  Genetic TBG deficiency
  Anabolic steroids (androgens)
  Glucocorticoids

T_4 = Serum thyroxine level; FT_4 = serum level of free (unbound) thyroxine.

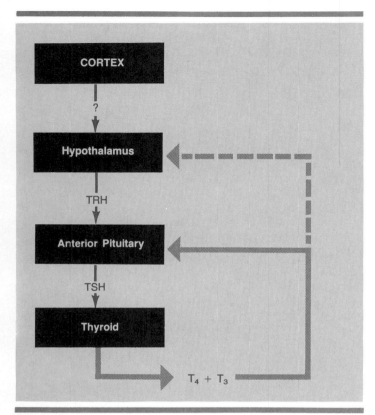

FIGURE 66-2. The normal hypothalamic-pituitary-thyroid axis. Both T_4 and T_3 feed back negatively on the pituitary and inhibit the secretion of thyroid-stimulating hormone (TSH). A similar process may regulate the hypothalamic secretion of thyrotropin-releasing hormone (TRH).

THYROID FUNCTION TESTS

Serum Thyroid Hormone Concentration. No one test can specifically determine thyroid status. Thus a variety of tests have been developed. These must be interpreted in an integrated fashion, keeping the patient's clinical presentation clearly in mind. Measurement of serum total T_4 (5 to 11 μg/dl) and free T_4 concentration (1.5 to 3.5 ng/dl) (or the free T_4 index) is the best current initial screening for the determination of thyroid dysfunction. Since the serum total T_4 can be altered by changes in carrier-protein concentration as well as by changes in thyroid function, its value must be assessed in conjunction with a measurement of serum free T_4 or an indirect index of free T_4. Direct measurement of serum free T_4 is preferable. Many centers, however, continue to use indirect methods and derive a "free T_4 index" (0.5 to 1.5 units) from a combination of serum total T_4 and a thyroid hormone binding ratio (THBR). The latter procedure allows an estimation of changes in serum TBG. The patient's serum, a trace amount of radioiodine-labeled T_3, and a solid matrix (resin, charcoal, talc, or antibody) are coincu-

bated. The matrix-bound T_3 is measured and expressed as a percentage of the residual serum protein-bound counts (25 to 35 per cent). Values correlate inversely with the concentration of unsaturated TBG. Generally, a parallel increase or decrease in both total T_4 and THBR indicates hyperthyroidism or hypothyroidism, whereas opposite changes suggest alterations in TBG binding. The derivation of the free T_4 index from the total T_4 and THBR generally gives a normal value in the setting of alterations in TBG. The free T_4 index or absolute free T_4 concentration is high or low in the hyperthyroid or hypothyroid subject, respectively. Occasionally, free T_4 values may be misleadingly low in patients with severe nonthyroidal illness, "euthyroid sick syndrome." Serial analysis of thyroid function tests generally resolves this dilemma.

Measurement of total and free T_3 values is clinically useful only when T_3 thyrotoxicosis is suspected. In this setting, T_4 values are normal and the hyperthyroidism will be missed in the absence of a T_3 measurement. Measurement of serum rT_3 has limited value as a routine clinical test.

A measurement of serum TSH is the single best test to detect primary thyroid failure, since the value is invariably elevated in primary hypothyroidism owing to loss of the inhibitory feedback effect of thyroid hormone. The new TSH immunometric assays (TSH-IMA) can differentiate between a normal TSH level (0.5–5.0 μU/ml) and the undetectable value (<0.005 μU/ml) found in clinically obvious hyperthyroidism. These assays, especially the very sensitive third-generation class of TSH-IMA, may eliminate the need for confirmatory TRH testing in patients with suspected hyperthyroidism. These improved assays may be used as a screening test for thyroid hyperfunction in the ambulatory patient. Considerable overlap in serum TSH values exists between milder hyperthyroidism and the moderate degrees of TSH suppression (TSH ≤0.1 μU/ml) associated with nonthyroidal illness. TSH-IMA should not be used, therefore, as the initial screening test in the hospitalized patient.

The TSH response to TRH remains a very useful test in the latter situation. The normal TSH response ranges between a serum level of 15 and 30 μU/ml at 20 minutes after administration of 500 μg of intravenous TRH. An incremental TSH rise of 5 μU above baseline in response to TRH is consistent with a normal axis. In hyperthyroidism the TSH response is flat. The mildly hypothyroid patient with a borderline high serum TSH value has an exaggerated response to TRH.

Thyroid Radioiodide Uptake (RAIU) Test. The accumulation of tracer iodide (^{123}I, ^{131}I) in the thyroid can be quantitated at standard intervals (6 to 24 hours) to assess thyroid activity. Owing to the enrichment of Western diets with iodide, this procedure is of no value in the differentiation between a normal and a hypoactive gland. In addition, the uptake value may be normal in many hyperthyroid patients (approximately 30 per cent), especially with multinodular goiter and with T_3

thyrotoxicosis. Consequently, a normal RAIU test does not exclude hyperthyroidism. In patients with thyrotoxicosis associated with thyroiditis, low (<3 per cent) uptake values are usually found, in contrast to normal or high values in Graves' disease. A low uptake value is also a feature of thyrotoxicosis consequent to excess thyroid hormone medication.

Immunologic Tests. Autoimmune thyroid disease (Hashimoto's thyroiditis and Graves' disease) is associated with positive tests for antibodies to specific thyroid antigens (antimicrosomal, antithyroperoxidase, and antithyroglobulin), which are useful in the detection of these autoimmune disorders. A biologic assay for thyroid-stimulating immunoglobulin (TSI), a specific marker for Graves' disease, has helped in both the diagnosis and the management of this common disorder. A reduction in TSI level during therapy with antithyroid drugs is a good indicator that a remission has been induced and that therapy can be modified or withdrawn.

Scintiscan. The RAIU test provides useful information on the anatomy of the thyroid. A scan at 6 hours demonstrates a homogeneous distribution of ^{123}I in the normal gland, whereas ^{123}I activity is heterogeneous in Hashimoto's thyroiditis and multinodular goiter. Furthermore, this procedure differentiates a functioning (benign) from a nonfunctioning (possible carcinoma) thyroid nodule. Functioning nodules demonstrate normal (warm) to increased (hot) ^{123}I activity, whereas nonfunctioning nodules fail to concentrate ^{123}I (cold).

Sonography. Ultrasound imaging decisively differentiates whether a nonfunctioning nodule on ^{123}I scan (cold nodule) is cystic or solid. In addition, this noninvasive procedure is very helpful in the serial sizing of the thyroid nodule and provides an objective basis for the evaluation of T_4 suppressive therapy.

Needle Biopsy. Fine-needle aspiration biopsy with cytologic analysis of the tissue has now become the best test in the evaluation of a thyroid nodule. The specificity and sensitivity of this procedure are now so reliable that most centers use needle biopsy as the first step in the evaluation of a thyroid nodule, even before scintiscanning.

THYROTOXICOSIS (HYPERTHYROIDISM)

Thyrotoxicosis, a common clinical condition consequent to excess thyroid hormone, can be caused by a number of different disorders; these should be differentiated in the individual patient for proper management (Table 66–2). Graves' disease is the most common cause of thyrotoxicosis. Toxic nodular goiter is most prevalent in the elderly. Transient thyrotoxicosis is frequently associated with thyroiditis. In addition, exposure to iodide (contrast studies) and iodine-containing drugs (e.g., amiodarone) has become a relatively common cause of thyrotoxicosis. The other conditions listed are relatively rare.

TABLE 66–2. CAUSES OF THYROTOXICOSIS

Graves' disease
Toxic multinodular goiter
Toxic adenoma
Thyroiditis
Iodide-induced hyperthyroidism
Factitious thyrotoxicosis
Thyrotoxicosis due to excess TSH
Toxic thyroid carcinoma
Toxic struma ovarii

TSH = Thyroid-stimulating hormone.

Graves' Disease

This complex autoimmune disorder consists of toxic goiter, ophthalmopathy, and rarely (<1 per cent) dermopathy, which may occur together or separately. The abnormal immunoglobulin or immunoglobulins (TSH receptor antibodies—TRAb) responsible for the hyperthyroidism can now be measured by bioassay. TSIs are antibodies to the normal thyroid gland TSH receptor site. They have powerful agonist action and consequently induce hyperthyroidism. The initiating factors in the development of TRAb and the role of TRAb in the development of the ophthalmopathy or dermopathy have not been elucidated.

Clinical Features

The clinical presentation of the thyrotoxic patient is extremely variable (Table 66–3). The actual features relate to the age at onset, the duration of the condition, and the degree of hormone excess. The patient most frequently presents with a history of nervousness, heat intolerance, sweating, palpitations, tremor, and weight loss. In addition, a change in collar size (goiter formation) and eye discomfort (Graves' ophthalmopathy) may be noted.

More prolonged disease is associated with features of chronic catabolism. Skeletal muscle wasting, especially of the limb girdles, induces a proximal myopathy. Patients may experience difficulty in climbing stairs or getting up from the sitting position. Although dyspnea in the absence of car-

TABLE 66–3. CLINICAL FEATURES OF THYROTOXICOSIS

SYMPTOMS	SIGNS
Nervousness	Thyroid enlargement
Heat intolerance (sweating)	Eyestare and lid lag
Palpitations	Proptosis and ophthalmoplegia*
Tremulousness	Warm, smooth skin
Weight loss (with good appetite)	Pretibial myxedema*
Muscle weakness	Fine tremor
Emotional lability	Brisk reflexes
Hyperdefecation	Onycholysis
	Tachycardia or atrial fibrillation

*Graves' disease only.

diac failure is common, more severe disease can be manifested by a severe cardiomyopathy and congestive failure, especially in the elderly.

The mental and emotional changes include anxiety, irritability, poor concentration, restlessness, and emotional lability. In addition, insomnia and forgetfulness may be disturbing features.

Physical Findings (Table 66–3)

The majority of young patients with hyperthyroidism have an enlarged thyroid (goiter). Diffuse symmetric enlargement of the thyroid is characteristic of Graves' disease, whereas asymmetric changes occur in toxic nodular goiter. A bruit over the thyroid indicates extreme vascularity and is generally found only in Graves' disease. In addition, the finding of a palpable pyramidal lobe in a hyperthyroid patient is suggestive of Graves' disease.

The eye changes may be due to excess thyroid hormone or to the ophthalmopathy of Graves' disease. Enhanced sympathetic tone resulting from excess thyroid hormone causes the characteristic widening of the palpebral fissure (stare) and failure of the upper lid to closely follow globe movement (lag). Proptosis (exophthalmos), forward protrusion of the globe due to retro-orbital deposition of fat, mucopolysaccharides, and lymphocytes, is the cardinal feature of Graves' ophthalmopathy. In addition, extraocular muscle weakness may limit eye movement and result in diplopia.

Smooth, shiny, silky, warm skin is frequently noted in hyperthyroidism. Thinning and loss of hair may be particularly worrisome for women. Hyperpigmentation over extensor surfaces and clubbing (thyroid acropachy) are rare features. Onycholysis, separation of the distal portion of the nail from the nail bed (Plummer's nails), fine tremor of the outstretched hands, and brisk reflexes are commonly noted. Pretibial myxedema may occasionally be seen in Graves' disease.

A spectrum of cardiovascular abnormalities may be detected on physical examination. Sinus tachycardia with a wide pulse pressure may progress to atrial fibrillation and congestive heart failure. Systolic flow murmurs and a forceful apical pulse are common features.

Diagnosis

A typical case of Graves' disease is easily diagnosed. In many instances, however, the typical eye features are minimal, goiter may be moderate (especially in the elderly), and systemic features may be few. Thus, the condition may remain unrecognized for years. In the majority of cases, serum total and free T_4 levels are high. If these values are normal, a serum total T_3 must be performed, as T_3 toxicosis occurs in 5 to 10 per cent of cases. If all other tests are equivocal, the TSH response to TRH should be flat if the patient is indeed hyperthyroid. Measurement of basal TSH by TSH-IMA has now replaced the need for a TRH test in most ambulatory patients and indeed may now be the initial test of choice.

The recognition of hyperthyroidism in the elderly is frequently delayed owing to the insidious nature of the disease. These patients have been classically described as "apathetic" owing to the paucity of features of sympathetic overactivity. The dominant features may be reflected in other systems, such as the cardiovascular system. Patients present with atrial fibrillation and congestive heart failure. In the absence of ophthalmopathy and goiter, the hyperthyroid state is generally missed. All elderly patients presenting with new-onset cardiovascular disorders should be screened for hyperthyroidism. It must be remembered, however, that patients with nonthyroidal systemic disorders may have a transient rise in serum total and free T_4 values as a by-product of their disease and require close monitoring with serial thyroid function tests to elucidate their thyroid status. In this setting the TSH-IMA test may be misleading, as moderate suppression (TSH ≤ 0.1 μU/ml) may be found in both the sick patient with nonthyroidal illness and the individual suffering from mild hyperthyroidism. In the latter case, the TSH response to TRH will be flat, and this confirms the hyperthyroid state.

Anxiety neurosis may be difficult to differentiate clinically from hyperthyroidism. These patients may present with tremor, tachycardia, irritability, and fatigue. Typical anxiety neurosis is generally associated with depression; weight loss accompanied by anorexia; cold, moist hands; and a normal resting (sleeping) pulse. If the clinical suspicion for hyperthyroidism remains, a baseline screening test with total and free T_4 should clarify the diagnosis. Some patients with psychiatric disorders (10 per cent) have a transient elevation in serum total and free T_4 levels, so that serial analyses may be needed or further detailed testing may be indicated to exclude hyperthyroidism.

Graves' ophthalmopathy may occur in a euthyroid or even a hypothyroid patient. Other diseases of the orbit or retro-orbital space must be considered as a cause of exophthalmos. Orbital pseudotumor may display similar extraocular muscle swelling on computed tomography (CT) scan or sonogram. When the ophthalmopathy is bilateral and the TRH test and TSI analysis are positive, the diagnosis of Graves' disease can generally be made. Other features of the disease eventually become evident in most cases.

Hyperthyroidism in the absence of goiter suggests factitious thyrotoxicosis or thyroiditis (or very rarely struma ovarii). In both conditions the RAIU test is suppressed. Serum thyroglobulin is high in those with thyroiditis but reduced in subjects taking exogenous thyroid hormone.

Therapy

Graves' disease is a self-limiting disease; 30 per cent of patients go into spontaneous remission within 1 to 2 years. Antithyroid drugs can be used for the temporary control of symptoms, or the gland can be ablated with ^{131}I or surgery. The choice of therapy is usually dictated by the patient's age, the size of the gland, and the severity of the disease.

Drugs. The thionamides PTU and methimazole (Tapazole) control the features of hyperthyroidism in almost all cases. These drugs inhibit the synthesis of thyroid hormone and restore a euthyroid state in 4 to 8 weeks. The initial dose recommended is 150 to 300 mg every 8 hours for PTU or 10 to 15 mg every 12 hours for methimazole. Once achieved, euthyroidism can generally be maintained by smaller doses of PTU (50 to 100 mg twice daily) or methimazole (5 to 10 mg once daily). Antithyroid drugs are preferred for children, young adults, and the pregnant patient. They are also used in the adult and elderly patient to induce euthyroidism prior to definitive therapy with ^{131}I or surgery. Antithyroid drugs induce a permanent remission in about 30 per cent of patients with Graves' disease, usually within 3 to 6 months of therapy. A reduction in TSI during therapy generally indicates that a remission has occurred and consequently is a good guide for the discontinuation of therapy.

Transient dermatitis, the most common side effect of antithyroid drugs, is not dose-related and generally disappears despite continued therapy. Urticaria and pruritus may also occur. Dose-related leukopenia, myalgia, arthralgia, and elevated serum alkaline phosphatase levels may occur in patients during therapy with PTU. Generally, these abnormalities can be controlled by dose adjustment. The most serious side effect (agranulocytosis) is not dose-related. A routine blood count is of no value as a predictor, since this complication occurs acutely. Thus patients should be advised to watch for fever and sore throats and to report such developments immediately to their physician. Fortunately, the majority of patients recover from agranulocytosis once the drug is stopped.

Sympathetic overactivity can be controlled with beta-adrenergic blockade. Such therapy with propranolol (40 mg every 6 hours) is indicated for severe agitation, tremor, sweating, and tachycardia. Beta blockers should not be used in the patient with severe thyrotoxic heart disease.

Radioactive iodine therapy with ^{131}I is the preferred form of therapy for the majority of patients with Graves' disease. An appropriate dose (7 to 12 mCi of ^{131}I) induces euthyroidism in most patients. This form of therapy is inexpensive and easy to administer. Since the gonadal exposure is extremely low (less than a diagnostic radiograph), genetic effects are unlikely. Thus ^{131}I can be used in all adult patients. ^{131}I is contraindicated during pregnancy; a pregnancy test should therefore be performed prior to therapy, or the dose should be given during the first half of the menstrual cycle. Long-term hypothyroidism (70 per cent at 10 years) is the major disadvantage of ^{131}I therapy. In addition, dose-related hypothyroidism occurs acutely after therapy (in 6 months) in a number of subjects. These complications are currently unavoidable, since lower doses may fail to induce euthyroidism.

Surgery. Surgical ablation is still preferred for children who cannot be controlled with antithyroid drugs and possibly for young adults with extremely large glands. The procedure, subtotal thyroidectomy, should be performed only by an experienced surgeon. In the proper hands, it is very effective therapy associated with minimal morbidity. Recurrent laryngeal nerve damage with vocal cord paralysis, permanent hypoparathyroidism, and hypothyroidism may be significant postoperative problems. Long-term hypothyroidism (40 per cent at 10 years) occurs despite the best of surgery, and immediate postoperative hypothyroidism may occur in 5 to 10 per cent of patients. Furthermore, recurrent hyperthyroidism also occurs in about 5 to 10 per cent of cases and should always be treated with ^{131}I therapy, since reoperation is more frequently accompanied by major complications.

Hyperthyroidism During Pregnancy

Graves' disease is responsible for the majority of cases of thyrotoxicosis associated with pregnancy. It should always be treated with antithyroid drugs. Surgery is rarely indicated, and ^{131}I therapy should never be used. The dose of antithyroid drug used should be the minimum needed to restore euthyroidism. These drugs freely cross the placenta; thus hypothyroidism and goiter can be induced in the fetus with an inappropriately high dosage. In general, PTU is the drug of choice in the pregnant patient needing thionamide therapy, since aplasia cutis has been described in fetuses following methimazole therapy. The maternal thyroid status should be monitored with free T_4 determinations, since the total T_4 concentration is normally elevated during pregnancy because of the estrogen-induced high serum TBG level. The physician caring for the newborn infant of a mother with Graves' disease should carefully monitor for neonatal Graves' disease. Passive transfer of TSI occurs and may produce transient neonatal hyperthyroidism. The cord blood TSI level may predict the infant at risk.

Toxic Nodular Goiter

This common cause of hyperthyroidism in the elderly generally occurs in patients with a long history of nodular goiter, but only a few patients with nodular goiter develop hyperthyroidism. It is not clear why these few nodular goiters progress to the toxic state and become autonomous in function. These patients generally present with symptoms and signs referable to the cerebrovascular, cardiovascular, musculoskeletal, or gastrointestinal system. Their hyperthyroidism is frequently masked by the nonthyroidal manifestations, so that the true diagnosis is often delayed.

Elderly patients with nodular goiter should be screened for thyroid dysfunction whenever they present with features of a new illness. The majority of these hyperthyroid patients have an unequivocal increase in serum total and free T_4 values. Since 10 to 15 per cent may have normal T_4 values but a high serum T_3 concentration (T_3 toxicosis), the latter measurement should always be included when hyperthyroidism is clinically suspected in the elderly patient.

The majority of these patients can be treated with ^{131}I, but the effective dose generally ranges from 15 to 30 mCi. Hypothyroidism follows less frequently than in Graves' disease. It is preferable to induce a euthyroid state with antithyroid drugs prior to definitive therapy to avoid aggravation of the thyrotoxicosis. Surgery may be indicated in individuals with very large goiters (>100 gm) and in those patients who have pressure complications from goiter.

Thyroiditis

Transient thyrotoxicosis may be a feature of subacute granulomatous and lymphocytic thyroiditis. Subacute granulomatous thyroiditis is viral in origin, whereas lymphocytic thyroiditis probably results from autoimmune injury. The thyrotoxicosis associated with subacute granulomatous thyroiditis is generally mild, and symptomatic therapy is rarely needed. However, patients with subacute lymphocytic thyroiditis may need therapy for more prolonged and severe thyrotoxicosis. The latter condition is estimated to cause 15 to 20 per cent of thyrotoxicosis in adults and is also a common cause of postpartum thyroiditis. Both forms of thyroiditis are characterized by low RAIU test values. It is important to differentiate thyroiditis from Graves' disease, since therapy with ^{131}I or surgery is not indicated and antithyroid drugs (PTU or methimazole) are not effective. These patients are treated symptomatically with beta blockers (propranolol) until remission occurs.

Hyperthyroxinemia of Acute Illness

Both serum total and free T_4 values may be elevated transiently during acute systemic (nonthyroidal) illness, especially in the elderly. This situation does not represent true hyperthyroidism. Serum T_3 concentrations are usually normal or low, and the TSH response to TRH is usually normal or slightly blunted. Hyperthyroidism can generally be excluded by demonstrating that the T_4 values return to normal during the recovery from the acute disorder. A similar phenomenon can be associated with acute psychiatric illness. It is important not to confuse these features of nonthyroidal illness with the diagnosis of true hyperthyroidism.

Familial Dysalbuminemic Hyperthyroxinemia (FDH)

This autosomal dominant condition may be a relatively common and misleading cause of an elevated total T_4 and free T_4 index. Subjects with this disorder possess an abnormal albumin that has a high affinity for T_4, resulting in a high serum total T_4. Furthermore, the free T_4 index, when derived from the T_3 uptake method, is also high because the abnormal albumin does not have a high affinity for T_3. Thus, an incorrect diagnosis of hyperthyroidism may be made. The serum free T_4 concentration and the total T_3 level are normal in these subjects. Thus, in the absence of clinical features of thyrotoxicosis, a high free T_4 index should suggest FDH as a differential possibility.

Thyrotoxic Crisis

This medical emergency is due to stress-induced exaggeration of the features of thyrotoxicosis. Additional clinical features include mental disorientation, fever, disproportionate tachycardia, and jaundice. Patients may rapidly deteriorate with shock and coma. The mortality of thyrotoxic crisis (thyroid storm) remains high. The diagnosis is made clinically, as time generally does not permit the laboratory confirmation of hyperthyroidism. Treatment should be initiated on the basis of clinical suspicion.

Supportive measures are as important as specific therapy. Hyperpyrexia is controlled with a cooling blanket and acetaminophen (aspirin is contraindicated), and the hypotension is reversed by volume expansion and vasopressor agents. During the extreme catabolic phase, adequate attention to nutritional support is mandatory. Other therapy includes glucocorticoids (hydrocortisone, 100 mg tid), to cover the severe stress and purported relative adrenal insufficiency. Specific therapy includes propylthiouracil (200 mg q4h), propranolol (40 mg q6h), and iodide (500 mg bid). Iodide is given as a specific blocker of thyroid hormone secretion. It is preferable to give PTU before iodide or at the same time. Cardiac decompensation should be treated with conventional doses of digoxin and diuretics. If cardiac failure is the dominant component of the crisis, beta blockade may be contraindicated. This combined therapeutic approach should provide an effective amelioration of the thyrotoxic crisis within a few days.

HYPOTHYROIDISM

Deficiency of thyroid hormone may occur as a primary thyroid defect or more rarely may be due to pituitary or hypothalamic disease (secondary hypothyroidism). Primary thyroid failure is a common disorder (prevalence, 0.8 per cent) whose clinical features range from mild hypothyroidism to severe myxedema. The latter condition develops in the setting of prolonged severe hypothyroidism and is due to the deposition of mucopoly-saccharides in the skin and other tissues.

Two acquired and possibly related autoimmune disorders, atrophic (idiopathic) and Hashimoto's thyroiditis, are responsible for most cases of hypothyroidism (Table 66–4). Iatrogenic hypothyroidism consequent to definitive therapy (^{131}I or surgery) for hyperthyroidism constitutes a second major group. More recently, drugs (iodide, lithium, and amiodarone) have become increasingly common causes of hypothyroidism in the hospital setting. The congenital causes are rare and generally present in childhood. Secondary causes induce hypothyroidism infrequently (approximately 1 per cent).

Clinical Features (Table 66–5)

The spectrum of clinical presentation depends on the degree, severity, and age at onset of the hypothyroidism. Cretinism, irreversible mental and motor retardation, presents within 6 months after delivery in the hypothyroid infant. Mass screening at birth should help to eliminate this correctable metabolic deficiency, since prompt replacement therapy with thyroid hormone can prevent or minimize this serious condition. Congenital hypothyroidism occurs in 1 in 5000 newborns. The development of hypothyroidism in childhood is associated with growth retardation and delayed puberty. Bone age is delayed relative to chronologic age. In the adult, the insidious nature of hypothyroidism may result in its being undetected for years. Symptoms are nonspecific, and in the absence of goiter the primary thyroid defect is frequently overlooked. Fatigue, lethargy, tiredness, cold intolerance, myalgias, and arthralgias are generally the earliest symptoms. The skin is dry and scaly, and hair loss is frequent. Facial puffiness and periorbital edema are characteristic features. The voice becomes hoarse and rough. In older subjects, mental changes, confusion, paranoia, depression, and dementia are often attributed to aging per se. Nerve entrapment syndromes are common, such as deafness and hand paresthesia (median nerve distribution) due to the carpal tunnel syndrome.

In severe hypothyroidism (myxedema), the above features are exaggerated and characteristic clinical features develop. Extensive scaling of the skin leads to exfoliation, and diffuse subcutaneous infiltration with mucopolysaccharides gives the skin a thickened or doughy feeling. The edematous change is characteristically nonpitting, except when hypoproteinemia develops. Deposition of carotene gives the skin a yellow-orange appearance. Sinus bradycardia may progress to variable degrees of heart block. This, in conjunction with myocardial dilatation, may lead to decompensation and congestive heart failure. More commonly, the heart appears enlarged owing to pericardial effusion. Pleural effusions and ascites may also be prominent.

Deep tendon reflexes show the characteristic delayed relaxation phase (hung-up reflexes). Slow mentation progressing to confusion, disorientation,

TABLE 66–4. CAUSES OF HYPOTHYROIDISM

Primary
Autoimmune	Hashimoto's thyroiditis
	Idiopathic myxedema
Iatrogenic	[131]I therapy for hyperthyroidism
	Subtotal thyroidectomy
Drug-induced	Iodide deficiency or excess
	Lithium, amiodarone
	Antithyroid drugs
Congenital	Synthetic enzyme defect
	Thyroid dysgenesis or agenesis

Secondary
Hypothalamic dysfunction	Therapeutic irradiation
	Granulomatous disease
	Neoplasms
Pituitary dysfunction	Therapeutic irradiation
	Pituitary surgery
	Idiopathic hypopituitarism
	Neoplasms
	Postpartum pituitary necrosis

and coma is not uncommon. Rarely, marked cerebellar ataxia occurs.

Myxedema Coma. This severe form of myxedema is frequently fatal. Decompensation is often precipitated by stress, such as infection, alcohol (drugs), or cold exposure. Severe respiratory failure (CO_2 narcosis), hypothermia, and sluggish cerebral perfusion all contribute to the development of coma. The diagnosis is based on the clinical presentation. Therapy must be instituted before the clinical suspicions are substantiated by laboratory tests, since delay may lead to a fatal outcome in this medical emergency.

Laboratory Findings

Primary thyroid failure can be definitely diagnosed with the demonstration of low serum total T_4 and free T_4 values combined with a high serum TSH level. Measurement of serum T_3 is of no value in the diagnosis of hypothyroidism. Occasionally, when the serum TSH value is borderline, the exaggerated TSH response to TRH will substantiate the diagnosis of primary hypothyroidism. Secondary hypothyroidism is associated with an

TABLE 66–5. CLINICAL FEATURES OF HYPOTHYROIDISM

SYMPTOMS	SIGNS
Weakness	Dry, coarse, cold skin
Lethargy, fatigue	Periorbital and peripheral edema
Memory impairment	Coarse, thin hair
Dementia	Pallor of skin
Cold intolerance	Thick tongue
Weight gain (anorexia)	Slow speech
Constipation	Decreased reflexes
Loss of hair	Hypertension
Hoarseness	Bradycardia
Deafness	Pleural, pericardial effusions
Dyspnea	Ascites
Myalgia, arthralgia	Vitiligo
Paresthesias	
Precordial pain	
Menstrual irregularity (menorrhagia)	

inappropriately low serum TSH level. The finding of other features of pituitary or hypothalamic disease generally confirms the diagnosis.

In addition to the definitive diagnostic tests noted above, hypothyroidism is associated with other abnormal laboratory tests. Muscle enzymes, especially creatine phosphokinase (CPK), are frequently elevated. In fact, CPK isoenzyme analysis may show a modest increase in MB bands (cardiac). This finding, in conjunction with myalgias and arthralgias, especially of the anterior chest wall, should not be mistaken for myocardial infarction. Hyponatremia, consequent to a relative excess of antidiuretic hormone (ADH) and impaired free water clearance, may be difficult to differentiate from the syndrome of inappropriate ADH secretion (SIADH). Hypercholesterolemia is also an associated finding.

Anemia in hypothyroidism is generally normochromic normocytic but may be macrocytic (vitamin B_{12} deficiency due to pernicious anemia) or microcytic because of poor nutrition or blood loss in women (menorrhagia). The combination of Hashimoto's disease, pernicious anemia, and type I diabetes mellitus is called Schmidt's syndrome.

The electrocardiogram classically demonstrates bradycardia and low voltage. In addition, variable degrees of heart block may be found, and nonspecific ST/T changes can occur. Blood gas analyses show moderate to severe hypoxia and hypercapnia consequent to hypoventilation.

Differential Diagnosis

A clinical awareness of the wide spectrum of presentation and a high index of suspicion for hypothyroidism will generally detect most cases. A number of clinical states may mimic hypothyroidism, such as nephrotic syndrome and cirrhosis, including an associated reduction in serum TBG and consequent low serum total T_4 value. However, the serum free T_4 is generally normal. The diagnosis of hypothyroidism during acute illness is complicated by the finding of a low serum total T_4 and free T_4 index in many (10 to 20 per cent) of these patients. Serum T_3 is also low, and serum TSH is generally within the normal range. The serum TSH response to TRH is either normal or blunted. These patients do not have primary thyroid failure but appear to have a stress-related form of secondary hypothyroidism. They are currently considered euthyroid ("euthyroid sick syndrome"), and T_4 replacement therapy is not warranted. In the majority of these patients, the serum free T_4 concentration is normal and serum rT_3 is elevated. Furthermore, should clinically relevant primary hypothyroidism be present, the serum TSH will be unequivocally elevated (> 20 μU/ml) despite their acute illness.

Treatment

Hypothyroidism should be treated with a synthetic preparation of L-thyroxine. In young,

healthy individuals with hypothyroidism of recent onset and without cardiac disease, thyroxine replacement may be initiated at full dosage. Elderly subjects with heart disease or a history of pre-existing heart troubles should be slowly corrected to euthyroidism by incremental dose adjustments over several months to reduce the risk of cardiac complications. The average full replacement dose of L-thyroxine in the healthy adult ranges between 75 and 100 μg daily. In the elderly patient, thyroxine therapy should begin at 25 to 50 μg daily, with an incremental dose of 25 μg every 2 to 4 weeks. The therapeutic response should be monitored clinically and with serial serum T_4 and TSH analyses.

In a patient with myxedema coma, a large dose of thyroxine (300 to 500 μg) is given parenterally as a bolus and is followed by 100 μg daily over the succeeding 5 days. Even elderly subjects with cardiac disorders tolerate these doses under this condition. The underlying stressful, precipitating event (e.g., infection) must obviously be corrected. Furthermore, standard supportive therapy for the comatose patient must be promptly introduced. This is especially important with respect to respiratory support. Many of these patients need mechanical ventilatory assistance, which may persist for some period after improvement in mental status. In addition, because of the associated relative adrenal insufficiency, these patients are treated with glucocorticoids. With proper therapy, patients with myxedema coma should improve clinically within 24 to 36 hours. If this does not occur, the clinical diagnosis may not have been correct or the underlying aggravating medical illness may have persisted or advanced. The expected mortality from myxedema coma with adequate therapy remains around 25 per cent.

GOITER

This most common thyroid abnormality means basically an enlargement of the thyroid gland. Patients suffering from goiter are predominantly euthyroid (simple goiter) but may be hyperthyroid (toxic goiter) or hypothyroid. In areas where iodine deficiency is still prevalent, goiter formation is said to be endemic. The development of euthyroid simple colloid goiter, termed *sporadic goiter*, in an iodide-replete location is predominantly due to congenital defects in thyroid hormone synthesis. Dietary goitrogens, such as the thiocarbamides found in cabbage, turnips, and soybeans, may also induce sporadic goiter. Thyroid enlargement may be symmetric and diffuse (simple goiter, Graves' disease, Hashimoto's thyroiditis) or may be asymmetric and nodular (nodular goiter, Hashimoto's thyroiditis).

Goiter formation is generally a TSH-mediated compensatory enlargement of the thyroid gland that ensures sufficient synthesis and secretion of thyroid hormone and prevents hypothyroidism. In addition, goiter formation may be consequent to an autoimmune process, as in Hashimoto's thyroiditis and Graves' disease.

Pain is unusual with a goiter, except in the course of subacute thyroiditis or consequent to cystic or hemorrhagic degeneration. Most frequently, patients with nontoxic goiter present because of the neck swelling or features of obstruction. A large goiter can cause dysphagia, respiratory distress, or hoarseness. The last symptom generally indicates recurrent laryngeal nerve invasion and most likely thyroid cancer rather than a benign simple goiter. Enlargement of the thyroid as the cause of neck swelling can be readily confirmed by either radioiodine scan or sonogram. In addition, the functional activity of the goiter can be determined from the radioiodine scan.

Most simple nontoxic goiters can be treated with continuous T_4 suppression of TSH, which should prevent further enlargement and eventually induce regression. It is important to determine that the gland is suppressible, since hyperthyroidism may develop from exogenous hormone therapy if the gland is autonomous. Autonomous function is frequent in patients with nontoxic multinodular goiter and patients with euthyroid Graves' disease. Thus, a careful monitoring of the serum T_4 response to T_4 suppression is mandatory. If the serum T_4 level increases inappropriately during standard suppression therapy (75 to 150 μg L-thyroxine daily), the gland is probably autonomous and the dose should be reduced accordingly.

A diffusely enlarged gland should regress in 6 to 12 months, but long-standing multinodular goiter may take several years to respond. Therapy may be continued indefinitely or terminated when appropriate. Permanent loss of TSH secretion never occurs, even after years of T_4 suppression. Recovery takes place within 6 to 8 weeks following the withdrawal of therapy. Goiters that fail to suppress, that are associated with pressure features, or that are large enough to be cosmetically embarrassing should be surgically removed.

THE SOLITARY THYROID NODULE

Thyroid nodules occur in approximately 5 per cent of the population. A nodule is a focal area of gland enlargement. It can be caused by a number of factors, but solitary nodules are predominantly adenomatous and benign (Table 66–6). Since a small percentage are carcinomatous, a practical clinical approach must be pursued to detect these patients. A number of factors from the clinical history, examination, and specific evaluations are helpful in the differentiation of benign from malignant lesions (Table 66–7). These relate to the patient's age and sex and whether the nodule is single or part of a multinodular gland. A young man presenting with a single dominant nodule associated with hoarseness and lymph node enlargement has a high possibility of malignancy. Any individual who presents with a nodule and a past history of head-neck irradiation should be referred for thyroidectomy, as these lesions are frequently malignant (~30 per cent).

THE THYROID / 479

TABLE 66–6. PATHOGENESIS OF THYROID NODULES

LESIONS*	PREVALENCE (%)
Benign thyroid nodule	40
Multinodular goiter	20
Cyst	12
Thyroiditis	10
Follicular adenoma	12
Carcinoma	6

*Data are representative of findings on fine-needle aspiration followed by surgical excision in indicated cases.

The traditional approach is to perform a RAIU study initially to determine the functional status of the nodule. Scanning with ^{123}I demonstrates no accumulation ("cold nodule"), equal isotope trapping ("warm nodule"), or greater accumulation ("hot nodule") when compared with the rest of the gland. Warm and hot nodules are overwhelmingly benign (99.8 per cent). Cold nodules are also predominantly benign (90 per cent). Patients with hot nodules may be hyperthyroid (toxic adenoma). These can be treated effectively with ^{131}I therapy or surgery. Generally, however, they are not currently hyperthyroid, but they should be followed carefully, since approximately 30 per cent will eventually become hyperthyroid.

Most solitary nodules are "cold" (80 per cent). A definitive pathologic diagnosis can be made in most of these subjects (80 per cent) by cytologic examination of a tissue specimen obtained by fine-needle aspiration biopsy (FNA). In fact, most centers perform FNA as the initial procedure. Benign lesions (75 per cent), such as benign thyroid nodules, multinodular goiter, and thyroiditis, can be identified by the *expert* cytologist. In addition, malignant lesions (5 per cent), such as papillary, anaplastic, and medullary carcinoma, can be specifically diagnosed. Follicular neoplasms (20 per cent), however, cannot be identified as benign or malignant by this technique and require examina-

TABLE 66–7. HIGH RISK FACTORS FOR CANCER IN A THYROID NODULE

History	Childhood therapeutic irradiations (low dose, <500 rads) of head or neck
	Hoarseness
	Rapid growth
	Pain
Clinical features	Children, young adults, men
	Solitary, firm, dominant nodule
	Associated lymphadenopathy
	Vocal cord paralysis
	Distant metastasis
Serum factors	Elevated serum calcitonin
Scanning techniques	
Pattern on [123]I	"Cold" nodule
Echo scan	Solid lesion
Thyroxine therapy	No regression

tion of tissue specimens obtained by surgical excision. Despite the lack of sensitivity in the analysis of the follicular neoplasm, FNA has proved to be a powerful diagnostic procedure in the evaluation of the thyroid nodule. The ability to make a definitive diagnosis through the application of this safe and simple technique has markedly reduced the need for diagnostic thyroid surgery. The therapy for a malignant nodule is considered in the section on thyroid carcinoma. Benign lesions are treated with T_4 suppression therapy. Regression of the nodule may occur during a 6-month course. Generally, long-standing nodules remain stable and do not progress. If the nodule increases in size, it should be re-evaluated and the appropriate therapy instituted.

THYROID CARCINOMA

Thyroid cancer is a relatively rare disorder. Furthermore, most varieties of thyroid cancer are of low-grade malignancy. Papillary or follicular carcinomas constitute about 90 per cent of all thyroid cancers. Anaplastic and medullary carcinomas account for the remainder.

Papillary carcinoma generally presents as a thyroid nodule that may be associated with local invasion and lymph node spread. The size of the initial lesion (>4.0 cm) and the presence of lymph node involvement adversely influence the recurrence rate and long-term prognosis. Follicular carcinoma is more aggressive and frequently presents with metastases, especially to the lung, bone, or brain. The size of the initial lesion does not influence prognosis. In many cases, the small thyroid primary lesion is overlooked and is diagnosed in retrospect following examination of the metastatic tissue. Both of these cancers have a low recurrence rate and a relatively good prognosis.

Primary therapy entails total thyroidectomy with nodal dissection, followed in most cases (6 weeks postoperatively) by ^{131}I ablative therapy for any remnant tissue. Lobectomy and isthmectomy with no radiation are adequate for small (<2.5 cm), noninvasive papillary lesions. Both surgical and radioactive ablative therapies are followed with T_4 suppression of TSH. Measurement of serum thyroglobulin has no pretherapeutic diagnostic value. It is, however, an excellent way to determine the effect of treatment and to monitor for recurrence.

Anaplastic carcinoma predominantly affects older individuals (>50 years). It is very aggressive and rapidly induces pain and symptoms related to local pressure (dysphagia, hoarseness). Death generally occurs within 12 months, but surgically resectable disease may have a better prognosis, with a 5-year survival of approximately 30 per cent.

Medullary carcinoma, which develops in the parafollicular cells (C cells), may be sporadic or familial (autosomal dominant). When familial, it is frequently a component of a multiple endocrine neoplasia syndrome (MEN type II). This tumor produces calcitonin; measurement of basal serum calcitonin can substantiate its presence. Provocative testing with calcium or pentagastrin (calcitonin response) may detect early C cell hyperplasia in subjects at risk (MEN type II families). Surgical excision of the primary lesion in the absence of nodal involvement produces an excellent prognosis (90 per cent survival at 10 years). In contrast, patients with nodal disease have only a 40 per cent survival at 10 years.

One of the most important factors in the evaluation of a patient with suspected thyroid cancer is a history of low-dose irradiation (<500 rads) to the head or neck area during childhood. Such individuals are at high risk for thyroid cancer. Careful investigation of such patients will detect follicular or papillary carcinoma in about 30 per cent of cases. It is now recommended that these patients have a thyroid (clinical) examination at 2-year intervals. In the absence of palpable disease, laboratory evaluation is not warranted. Patients with a palpable dominant nodule who have been irradiated should receive total thyroidectomy, with removal of nodes if there is metastatic disease. If invasive carcinoma is present, postoperative remnant ablation with ^{131}I should be carried out at 6 weeks. Suppressive therapy with T_4 will be necessary for life.

THYROIDITIS

In subacute granulomatous (de Quervain's) thyroiditis, a common disorder, the thyroid gland is painful and tender, and symptoms may be preceded by or associated with fever. Clinical hyperthyroidism may occur during the early phase (5 per cent), followed by transient hypothyroidism and then eventual recovery. The elevated serum total and free T_4 values are associated with a depressed RAIU test value. Antithyroid antibodies are rarely detected. The erythrocyte sedimentation rate is characteristically high.

Therapy is symptomatic; the symptoms of thyroid pain and tenderness generally respond to aspirin. However, a small percentage of patients may need a short course of prednisone (20 mg bid) for relief. Symptomatic hyperthyroidism should be treated with propranolol (40 mg tid). Since both the hyperthyroid and the hypothyroid phases are self-limiting (total disease course is 8 to 12 weeks), reassurance of the patient is generally all that is needed.

Subacute lymphocytic thyroiditis (silent thyroiditis) is currently considered an autoimmune disorder that is responsible for 20 to 30 per cent of all cases of thyrotoxicosis, with a high prevalence during the postpartum period. This condition is discussed in the section on hyperthyroidism. Chronic lymphocytic thyroiditis (Hashimoto's disease) is probably the most common cause of goiter in the Western world. High titers of antithyroid antibodies are present in 90 per cent of cases. It is frequently complicated by hypothyroidism and is discussed in that section. Acute suppurative thyroiditis, an unusual disorder, generally follows bacteremia rather than being a primary infection.

REFERENCES

Chopra IJ, Hershman JM, Pardridge WM, Nicoloff JT: Thyroid function in nonthyroidal illness. Ann Intern Med 98:946, 1983.

Gavin LA: The diagnostic dilemmas of hyperthyroxine-mia and hypothyroxinemia. Adv Intern Med 33:185, 1988.

Larsen PR: The thyroid. In Wyngaarden JB, Smith LH Jr, Bennett JC: (eds): Cecil Textbook of Medicine. 19th ed. Philadelphia, WB Saunders Co, 1992, pp 1248–1271.

Nicoloff JT, Spencer CA: The use and misuse of the sensitive thyrotropin assays. J Clin Endocrinol Metab 71:553, 1990.

Van Herle AJ, Rich P, Ljung BM, et al: The thyroid nodule. Ann Intern Med 96:221, 1982.

67 ADRENAL GLAND

The adrenal glands, paired structures located retroperitoneally at the upper pole of each kidney, include two distinct endocrine organs: an outer cortex that secretes steroid hormones and an inner medulla that, as part of the sympathetic nervous system, secretes catecholamines (epinephrine and norepinephrine). The cortex consists of three zones: the outer zona glomerulosa, which secretes a potent mineralocorticoid hormone, and the inner zonae fasciculata and reticularis, which secrete glucocorticoids, androgens, and minute quantities of estrogens. Each of these steroid hormones as well as the catecholamines causes striking effects when produced in excess. In contrast, only glucocorticoid and mineralocorticoid hormones, which are secreted exclusively by the adrenal gland, are physiologically important products. The gonadal production of androgens in men and estrogens in women and the secretion of norepinephrine by sympathetic ganglia are quantitatively more important sources of these hormones and neurotransmitters.

MAJOR HORMONES OF THE ADRENAL GLAND

Cortisol is the major glucocorticoid secreted by the adrenal cortex. Glucocorticoids are involved in multiple biologic processes, affecting carbohydrate, protein, lipid, and water metabolism. Cortisol secretion is under the control of adrenocorticotropin (ACTH), which in turn is regulated by the secretion of corticotropin-releasing hormone (CRH) (Fig. 67–1A). Secretion of ACTH and cortisol is pulsatile, manifests a diurnal circadian rhythm, and is under negative feedback control. Stress in a vari-ety of forms can override the diurnal rhythm as well as the negative feedback relationship of the system.

Aldosterone, the principal mineralocorticoid hormone, is secreted by the adrenal cortex largely under the control of the renin-angiotensin system (Fig. 67–2). Renin is released from the juxtaglomerular cells of the kidney in response to a reduction in renal perfusion pressure, a decrease in effective circulating volume, or sympathetic stimulation. Renin enzymatically cleaves the hepatic renin substrate (angiotensinogen) to liberate a decapeptide, angiotensin I. Removal of the carboxy terminal dipeptide by an endothelial converting enzyme produces the octapeptide angiotensin II. Angiotensin II stimulates the zona glomerulosa of the adrenal gland directly to increase aldosterone secretion. Aldosterone increases transepithelial transport of sodium by the kidney, and the resultant sodium retention tends to ameliorate the initial stimulus for renin secretion. Increases in plasma K^+ concentration normally increase aldosterone secretion, whereas hypokalemia suppresses it. Inasmuch as aldosterone promotes K^+ secretion by the kidney, this provides a second feedback mechanism regulating aldosterone secretion. When stimulation by the renin-angiotensin system is reduced during periods of recumbency, plasma aldosterone concentration correlates with the pulsatile release of cortisol, implying that ACTH also plays a role in the physiologic regulation of aldosterone secretion.

The clinical disorders of the adrenal glands discussed in this chapter result in some of the most striking syndromes in clinical medicine and, not infrequently, are considered in the differential diagnosis of many disorders. When suspected, the

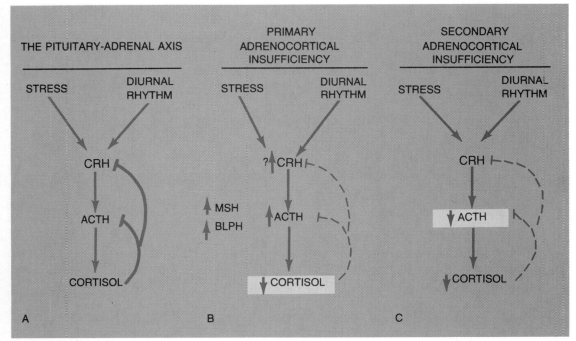

FIGURE 67–1. The hypothalamic-pituitary-adrenal axis. Secretion of corticotropin-releasing hormone (CRH) normally regulates secretion of adrenocorticotropic hormone (ACTH), which in turn controls cortisol production (*A*). The system is subject to negative feedback control: reduced levels of cortisol result in diminished feedback regulation (*dashed lines*) and marked increases in ACTH levels, as in primary adrenocortical insufficiency. Levels of melanocyte-stimulating hormone (MSH) and lipotropin (BLPH) also increase, resulting in hyperpigmentation (*B*). Hypothalamic-pituitary disorders that diminish ACTH secretion result in secondary adrenocortical insufficiency (*C*).

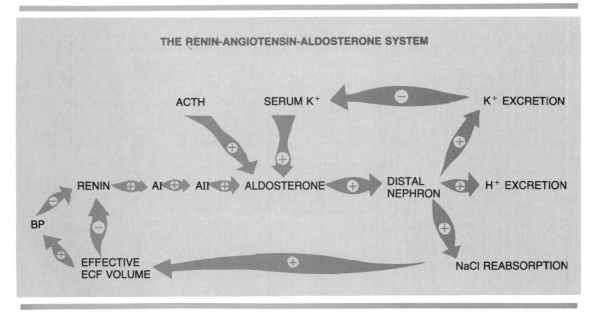

FIGURE 67–2. The renin-angiotensin-aldosterone system. Aldosterone secretion is principally regulated by the renin-angiotensin system. Potassium (K^+) and ACTH also stimulate aldosterone secretion, whereas sodium and dopamine (not shown) may inhibit it. Negative feedback control occurs by virtue of mineralocorticoid-induced kaliuresis and sodium retention, which reduce levels of K^+ and angiotensin II (AII), respectively. $\oplus$ = Increases; $\ominus$ = decreases.

diagnosis can be established using biochemical measurements that are readily available in clinical laboratories, and in most instances the response to appropriate therapy is dramatic and rewarding.

SYNDROMES OF ADRENOCORTICAL HYPOFUNCTION (Table 67–1)

Hypofunction of the adrenal cortex occurs either from primary adrenal disorders or from disordered extra-adrenal regulation of adrenal steroid biosynthesis and secretion. Clinical manifestations vary depending upon the relative dysfunction of mineralocorticoid, glucocorticoid, or androgen/estrogen secretion. Table 67–1 lists the most common disorders.

Generalized Adrenocortical Insufficiency

Pathophysiology

Generalized adrenocortical insufficiency (Addison's disease) occurs when adrenocortical tissue injury, bilateral adrenalectomy, or inherited disorders of steroid biosynthesis reduce secretion rates of both mineralocorticoid and glucocorticoid hormones below physiologic needs. If untreated, such panhypoadrenocorticoidism is often fatal.

Cortisol deficiency results in anorexia, weight loss, weakness, apathy, hypotension, and inability to withstand "stress" (Table 67–2). Because cortisol normally inhibits ACTH secretion, levels of ACTH are characteristically elevated (see Fig. 67–1B). Increased levels of ACTH or related proopiomelanocortin–derived peptides (lipotropin, melanocortin) cause hyperpigmentation. Mineralocorticoid deficiency results in impaired renal Na^+ conservation and impaired K^+ and hydrogen ion secretion. If sodium chloride intake is sufficiently large, extracellular fluid volume and plasma K^+ and bicarbonate levels can be maintained at nearly normal levels. If sodium chloride intake is low, however, or if extrarenal losses of Na^+ occur, impaired Na^+ conservation results in marked Na^+ deficits, hyponatremia, hyperkalemia, acidosis, hypovolemia, and increased plasma renin levels. Glucocorticoid deficiency may exacerbate hypovolemia by redistributing fluid between vascular and extravascular compartments and may exacerbate hyponatremia by impairing renal solute-free water excretion.

A variety of pathologic processes can result in generalized adrenocortical insufficiency: tuberculosis, histoplasmosis and other fungal diseases, metastatic carcinoma, amyloidosis, and bilateral adrenal hemorrhage. At present, Addison's disease appears to occur most frequently as a component of an autoimmune process that results in selective atrophy of the adrenal cortex ("idiopathic" adrenal insufficiency), usually sparing the adrenal medulla. Patients so affected often manifest evidence of other autoimmune injury affecting the thyroid, islet cells, gonads, or other tissues. Adrenal insufficiency can also occur in patients with acquired immunodeficiency syndrome (AIDS), presumably as a consequence of adrenal involvement by opportunistic infections.

Combined glucocorticoid and mineralocorticoid deficiency also occurs in several inherited disorders characterized by diffuse bilateral enlargement of the adrenal cortex and collectively termed "congenital adrenal hyperplasia." In these disorders, abnormalities of specific biosynthetic enzymes lead to reduced secretion of adrenal steroids and, secondarily through release of feedback inhibition, to increased circulating levels of adrenotropic hormones (ACTH and/or angiotensin). The latter hormones induce adrenal hyperplasia in an attempt to increase the rate of secretion of the steroids by the defective gland.

TABLE 67–1. SYNDROMES OF ADRENOCORTICAL HYPOFUNCTION

I. Primary Adrenal Disorders
  A. Combined Mineralocorticoid and Glucocorticoid Deficiency
    1. Acquired adrenal injury (Addison's disease)—over 90% due to autoimmune injury
    2. Bilateral adrenalectomy
    3. Adrenal enzyme deficiency states
  B. Aldosterone Deficiency Without Glucocorticoid Deficiency
    1. Corticosterone methyloxidase deficiency
    2. Isolated zona glomerulosa defect
    3. Critically ill patients
    4. Heparin therapy
    5. Converting enzyme inhibitors

II. Secondary Adrenal Disorders
  A. Secondary Adrenal Insufficiency
    1. Panhypopituitarism
    2. Selective deficiency of ACTH
    3. Exogenous glucocorticoids
  B. Hyporeninemic Hypoaldosteronism
    1. Injury to the juxtaglomerular apparatus
    2. Autonomic neuropathy
    3. Extracellular volume expansion
    4. Impaired conversion of prorenin to active renin
    5. Impaired renal prostaglandin production caused by nonsteroidal anti-inflammatory drugs

ACTH = Adrenocorticotropin.

TABLE 67–2. CLINICAL FEATURES OF CHRONIC PRIMARY ADRENOCORTICAL INSUFFICIENCY

SIGNS AND SYMPTOMS	PER CENT
Weakness and fatigue	100
Weight loss	100
Anorexia	100
Hyperpigmentation	92
Hypotension	88
Gastrointestinal symptoms	56
Salt craving	19
Postural symptoms	12

Adapted from Baxter JD, Tyrrell JB: The adrenal cortex. In Felig P, Baxter JD, Broadus AH, et al (eds): Endocrinology and Metabolism, 2nd ed, p 587. Copyright © 1987 by McGraw-Hill, Inc. Used by permission of McGraw-Hill Book Company.

In the most common form of congenital adrenal hyperplasia, that resulting from defective 21-hydroxylation, secretion of all glucocorticoid and mineralocorticoid hormones (21-hydroxylated steroids) is subnormal, whereas secretion of progesterone and 17-hydroxyprogesterone (the normal substrates for 21-hydroxylation) is increased. Manifestations of combined glucocorticoid and mineralocorticoid deficiency are common but not invariable. Increased levels of 17-hydroxyprogesterone result in overproduction of androgens, causing virilization (female pseudohermaphroditism, male precocious puberty), differing greatly in severity among patients. Increased circulating levels of 17-hydroxyprogesterone and progesterone contribute to clinical hypomineralocorticoidism inasmuch as those steroids are mineralocorticoid receptor antagonists that inhibit the renal action of aldosterone.

Diagnosis and Treatment (Fig. 67–3)

The diagnosis of generalized adrenocortical insufficiency is confirmed by the finding of subnormal plasma levels of cortisol and aldosterone in association with increased levels of ACTH and

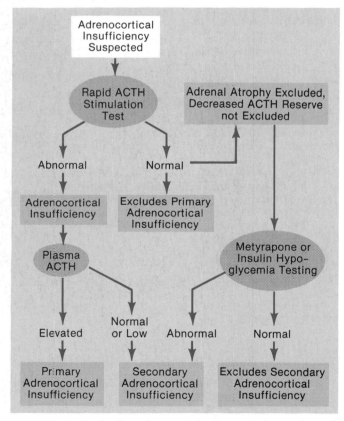

FIGURE 67–3. Evaluation of suspected primary and secondary adrenocortical insufficiency. Boxes enclose clinical decisions, and ovals enclose diagnostic tests. (From Baxter JD, Tyrrell JB: The adrenal cortex. In Felig P, Baxter JD, Broadus AE, et al [eds]: Endocrinology and Metabolism, 2nd ed, p 593. Copyright © 1987 by McGraw-Hill, Inc. Used by permission of McGraw-Hill Book Company.)

renin. Because plasma ACTH assays are not always available and special precautions are required for handling plasma samples, the primary nature of the adrenal disorder is frequently demonstrated by measurement of cortisol levels following either acute or chronic stimulation by exogenous ACTH. A subnormal cortisol response suggests a primary adrenal abnormality. Aldosterone levels also fail to increase normally in such patients. Prolonged administration of ACTH may be required in certain circumstances to distinguish primary from secondary syndromes of adrenocortical deficiency.

Generalized adrenocortical insufficiency often manifests as a medical emergency; therapy should never be withheld pending laboratory results that establish the diagnosis. When the diagnosis of adrenal insufficiency is suspected in a critically ill patient, it is prudent to obtain plasma samples in which cortisol, aldosterone, ACTH, and renin activity can be measured subsequently. Intravenous administration of ¹⁻²⁴ACTH (Cortrosyn, 25 U) given as a bolus, followed by a second plasma sample 1 hour later, is an additional useful step in diagnosis. If delay of therapy for even 1 hour is deemed inadvisable, glucocorticoid therapy can be initiated with dexamethasone, a potent synthetic glucocorticoid that does not interfere with the subsequent measurement of plasma cortisol. In adrenal crisis, glucocorticoids should be administered in doses that reflect the levels normally secreted by the adrenal cortex under maximal stress, usually 200 to 300 mg of hydrocortisone per day or its equivalent. The manifestations of associated mineralocorticoid deficiency are best treated in such circumstances with parenteral fluids and salt replacement rather than with mineralocorticoid hormones.

Lifelong treatment with hydrocortisone (usually 20 to 30 mg/day) or another glucocorticoid is required. Doses should be increased at times of stress (e.g., surgery, severe medical illnesses). Because aldosterone secretion is reduced, mineralocorticoid replacement may be needed. The need for mineralocorticoid replacement therapy is best assessed by clinical indices (orthostatic hypotension, hyperkalemia, hyponatremia). Plasma renin activity provides a sensitive index of extracellular volume but is not a practical or necessary guide to treatment. The usual therapeutic mineralocorticoid is the orally effective steroid fludrocortisone.

Administration of fludrocortisone in adrenal insufficiency requires special attention. With fixed exogenous administration, circulating mineralocorticoid levels cannot vary inversely with potentially large variations in dietary salt intake, as can endogenous aldosterone in normal subjects. If dietary salt increases, abnormal renal sodium and chloride retention and K⁺ secretion can result in hypervolemia, hypertension, cardiac decompensation, and hypokalemia, because mineralocorticoid levels are inappropriately high. If dietary salt decreases, or extrarenal (sweating, diarrhea) salt losses occur, hypovolemia and hyperkalemia may supervene, because mineralocorticoid levels are inappropriately low. Thus, patients must be carefully monitored. Some patients can be maintained on a high salt intake without a mineralocorticoid.

Aldosterone Deficiency Without Glucocorticoid Deficiency

Aldosterone deficiency in the absence of glucocorticoid deficiency is most commonly the result of deficient secretion of renin, so-called hyporeninemic hypoaldosteronism (see below). Rarely, isolated deficiency of aldosterone may result from a primary abnormality of the adrenal cortex, either as a consequence of an inherited deficiency of the enzyme responsible for the final step of aldosterone biosynthesis (corticosterone methyloxidase) or as a manifestation of rare acquired disorders that selectively impair zona glomerulosa function. In primary isolated aldosterone deficiency, plasma renin activity is increased (Fig. 67–4).

Acquired lesions that selectively destroy the zona glomerulosa include a chronic autoimmune process in which antibodies are directed only against cells of the zona glomerulosa, or as the initial phase of a pathologic process that eventually leads to generalized adrenocortical insufficiency. Mineralocorticoid replacement is given as in other primary adrenal disorders. Hypoaldosteronism that occurs in critically ill patients or in those on heparin therapy rarely results in clinically significant electrolyte disorders, and thus mineralocorticoid therapy may not be indicated. Administration of converting enzyme inhibitors may cause significant hyperkalemia, particularly in patients with underlying renal insufficiency. In such patients, hyperreninemic hypoaldosteronism is present as a consequence of reduced angiotensin II levels and does not imply the presence of a primary adrenal abnormality. Mineralocorticoid therapy corrects the electrolyte abnormalities, but the usual approach is to discontinue the agent.

Secondary Adrenal Insufficiency

In secondary adrenal insufficiency, glucocorticoid deficiency results from inadequate stimulation of the adrenal cortex by ACTH. Causes include destructive lesions in the hypothalamic-pituitary axis, isolated defects of ACTH secretion, and prolonged suppression of the pituitary-adrenal axis by exogenous glucocorticoids. Clinically significant mineralocorticoid deficiency is rare in those cases because aldosterone secretion is not regulated primarily by ACTH.

The clinical findings are similar to those of primary glucocorticoid deficiency, with several important differences. Hyperpigmentation is absent because plasma levels of ACTH and related pro-opiomelanocortin–derived peptides are not increased (see Fig. 67–1C). Because mineralocorticoid levels are normal, hyperkalemia and metabolic acidosis also do not occur, but hyponatremia can occur as a consequence of the impaired water excretion that accompanies glucocorticoid deficiency. In primary pituitary diseases, the clini-

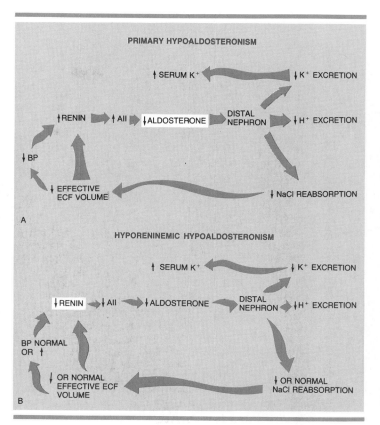

FIGURE 67–4. Perturbations of the renin-angiotensin-aldosterone system in primary hypoaldosteronism (A) and in hyporeninemic hypoaldosteronism (B). Hypoaldosteronism in primary adrenal disorders can occur as an isolated defect or as a component of generalized adrenocortical deficiency. In the latter, ACTH levels are also increased as a consequence of cortisol deficiency (see Fig. 67–1B).

cal manifestations may also be complicated by hypothyroidism and hypogonadism (see Chapter 65).

Prior administration of glucocorticoids is a common cause of secondary adrenocortical insufficiency. Suppression of the hypothalamic-pituitary axis by glucocorticoids occurs rapidly, to a degree that depends upon the duration and dose of the therapy. The use of alternate-day therapy with glucocorticoids, when feasible, reduces the frequency and severity of this complication. Three potential problems occur when glucocorticoids are withdrawn: (1) exacerbation of the underlying inflammatory disease being treated; (2) clinical manifestations suggesting adrenal insufficiency, despite glucocorticoid levels still in the normal range; and (3) true adrenal insufficiency that occurs when the doses of glucocorticoid are reduced below maintenance levels. Recovery of adrenal function may take up to a year; resumption of normal ACTH secretion must occur first. Recovery is hastened if the patient can tolerate total withdrawal of glucocorticoid therapy, but glucocorticoids should be given without hesitation in the event of intercurrent medical or surgical illness.

Hyporeninemic Hypoaldosteronism

Pathophysiology

Mineralocorticoid deficiency occurs in numerous renal and extrarenal disorders that cause diminished renal secretion of renin. Under ordinary physiologic conditions, the product of renin's action, angiotensin II, provides the major tonic stimulatory effect on aldosterone secretion. With diminished renin secretion, hypoangiotensinemia leads to a clinically significant state of mineralocorticoid deficiency: hyporeninemic hypoaldosteronism. Diabetes mellitus and chronic renal tubulointerstitial diseases are the most common underlying disorders.

Mineralocorticoid deficiency manifests usually as hyperkalemia and commonly as hyperchloremic metabolic acidosis. Sodium depletion and renal sodium wasting are not invariably present. In some patients, total body sodium and extracellular fluid volume are supernormal, suggesting that deficient renin secretion is a functional consequence of reduced renal clearance of sodium chloride.

The pathogenesis of the hyporeninemia is probably multifactorial. Renin secretory impairment may result from renal injury (e.g., sclerosis of the juxtaglomerular apparatus) and from functional impairment of renin secretion. Functional impairment occurs in patients with autonomic insufficiency and during treatment with beta blockers and nonsteroidal anti-inflammatory agents (NSAIDs). Angiotensin-converting enzyme (ACE) inhibitors can produce aldosterone deficiency by inhibiting the production of angiotensin II. Clinically significant mineralocorticoid deficiency does not usually occur, however, unless associated renal insufficiency is present.

Treatment

Patients with this syndrome are usually asymptomatic. Nevertheless, marked hyperkalemia can cause life-threatening arrhythmias, and protracted metabolic acidosis can adversely affect bone mineralization and other cellular functions. Administration of fludrocortisone in doses from 100 to 300 μg/day generally results in a prompt increase in renal potassium and hydrogen ion excretion and amelioration of hyperkalemia and metabolic acidosis. Patients with renal insufficiency may be more resistant to the renal effect of mineralocorticoids.

Fludrocortisone treatment, however, is not always effective and safe, particularly in patients who are hypertensive and have pretreatment increases in extracellular volume and body sodium. By increasing renal reabsorption of sodium chloride, fludrocortisone can exacerbate hypertension and other deleterious consequences of extracellular fluid volume expansion. Furosemide, in doses of 40 to 120 mg daily, increases potassium and net acid excretion and ameliorates the hyperkalemia and metabolic acidosis in such patients. With severe hypoaldosteronism, the beneficial effect of furosemide is attenuated, so that pretreatment with small doses of fludrocortisone increases its effectiveness. Combined therapy with fludrocortisone and furosemide offers the advantages of mutual potentiation of kaliuretic and acid-excretory effects and countervailing natriuretic and chloruretic effects. The combination reduces hyperkalemia and acidosis and, concomitantly, through adjustment of relative doses, allows control of body content of sodium chloride.

SYNDROMES OF ADRENOCORTICAL HYPERFUNCTION (Table 67–3)

The major clinical manifestations of adrenocortical hyperfunction vary depending upon the predominant steroid produced in excess. Hypersecretion of glucocorticoid hormone results in Cushing's syndrome, a metabolic disorder affecting carbohydrate, protein, and lipid metabolism. Hypersecretion of aldosterone and related mineralocorticoid hormones results in a disturbance of electrolyte and blood pressure homeostasis.

Cushing's Syndrome

Pathophysiology

Cushing's syndrome, the consequence of chronic exposure to excessive amounts of glucocorticoid hormone, occurs as a consequence of increased endogenous production of cortisol (Fig. 67–5) or, more commonly, as the result of prolonged exposure to glucocorticoids administered exogenously in superphysiologic doses. Of the endogenous causes, the most common in adults is bilateral adrenal hyperplasia due to excessive pituitary secretion of ACTH, a condition referred to as Cushing's disease (Fig. 67–5A). Bilateral adrenal hyperplasia can also result from ectopic production of ACTH by a variety of neoplasms (Fig. 67–5B). Primary adrenal tumors, either adenomas or carcinomas, account for the remaining cases (Fig. 67–5C).

In Cushing's disease, the hypersecretion of ACTH by the pituitary gland is due to the presence of an adenoma in approximately 90 per cent of cases. These are frequently small (microadenomas) and basophilic. Whether such an adenoma arises spontaneously or as a secondary consequence of excessive secretion of CRH has not been resolved. This disorder is much more common in women (female-male ratio, 5:1), typically occurs during the childbearing years, and, as a consequence of an insidious onset, may go undetected for many years.

In patients with bilateral adrenal hyperplasia due to ectopic ACTH secretion, the level of cortisol may be several times higher than in Cushing's disease, yet the clinical manifestations are often less striking. This difference is presumably due to the more rapid progression of the disease, as a consequence of the underlying neoplasm. In addition to marked increases in cortisol production, such patients may have greatly increased levels of deoxycorticosterone (DOC), a potent mineralocorticoid that can result in severe hypertension and hypokalemic metabolic alkalosis. Small cell carcinoma of the lung, bronchial carcinoid, and medullary carcinoma of the thyroid are among the neoplasms reported to secrete ACTH ectopically. Ectopic ACTH syndrome occurs more frequently in men, and the age of onset is typically later than in Cushing's disease.

The primary adrenal neoplasms that result in Cushing's syndrome may also be associated with severe hypokalemic metabolic alkalosis and hypertension as a consequence of marked increases in mineralocorticoid hormone secretion. Such tumors may also manifest with findings reflecting predominant secretion of androgens or estrogens, causing virilization and feminization in women and men, respectively. Adrenal carcinomas are the most frequent cause of Cushing's syndrome in children.

Clinical Manifestations

The clinical manifestations of Cushing's disease are very diverse (Table 67–4). Regardless of the etiology, hypercortisolism results in obesity, carbohydrate intolerance, muscle wasting, and osteoporosis. Obesity is centripetal, manifested typically by a "buffalo hump," increased supraclavicular fat pads, and moon facies. Easy bruisability and abdominal striae may be noted. Mild hypertension is common. Depression occurs often, and, rarely, patients may be frankly psychotic. An increase in adrenal androgen production can result in hirsutism, acne, and menstrual disorders in women. Men may complain of impotence and loss of libido.

TABLE 67–3. SYNDROMES OF ADRENOCORTICAL HYPERFUNCTION

I. **Syndromes of Glucocorticoid Excess (Cushing's Syndrome)**
  A. Secondary to Increased ACTH Stimulation
    1. Hypothalamic-pituitary abnormality (Cushing's disease)
    2. Ectopic ACTH secretion
  B. Primary Adrenal Abnormality
    1. Adenoma
    2. Carcinoma
  C. Exogenous Glucocorticoid Therapy
II. **Syndromes of Mineralocorticoid Excess**
  A. Primary Aldosteronism
    1. Aldosterone-producing adenoma
    2. Bilateral adrenal hyperplasia (idiopathic hyperaldosteronism)
    3. Adrenal carcinoma
  B. Adrenal Enzyme Defects
    1. 11β-Hydroxylase deficiency
    2. 17α-Hydroxylase deficiency
  C. 11β-Hydroxysteroid Dehydrogenase Deficient Activity
    1. Inherited
    2. Acquired—licorice, carbenoxolone
  D. Secondary Aldosteronism
    1. Nonhypertensive disorders
    2. Hypertensive disorders

Diagnosis (Fig. 67–6)

The diagnostic approach in patients who are suspected of having Cushing's syndrome consists of two phases. In the first, the presence of hypercortisolism is established to separate patients with Cushing's syndrome from those who may have certain clinical features that suggest the diagnosis but in whom glucocorticoid excess is not present. Once hypercortisolism is established, the challenge is to differentiate among the causes discussed above.

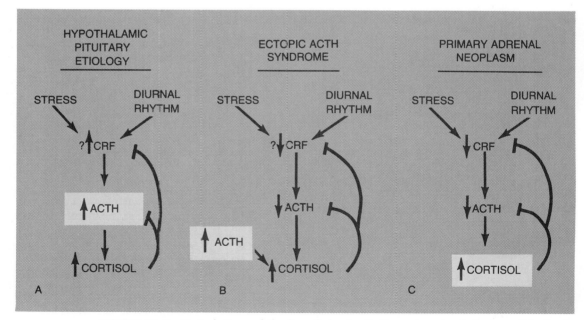

FIGURE 67–5. Perturbations of the hypothalamic-pituitary-adrenal axis that result in Cushing's syndrome.

TABLE 67–4. COMMON CLINICAL FEATURES OF CUSHING'S SYNDROME

FEATURE	INCIDENCE (%)
Obesity	94
Facial plethora	84
Hirsutism	82
Menstrual disorders	76
Hypertension	72
Muscular weakness	58
Back pain	58
Striae	52
Acne	40
Psychological symptoms	40
Bruising	36

Modified from Plotz CM, et al: Am J Med 13:597, 1952; and Ross EJ, et al: Q J Med 35:149, 1966; by permission of Oxford University Press.

Does the patient have Cushing's syndrome? Although surreptitious administration of glucocorticoids may occur rarely, one is generally able to exclude an exogenous cause of Cushing's syndrome by the medical history. Endogenous Cushing's syndrome is relatively uncommon. Since many of these abnormalities (e.g., obesity, hirsutism, hypertension, acne) occur in patients without Cushing's syndrome, a reliable means of differentiating among such individuals is necessary.

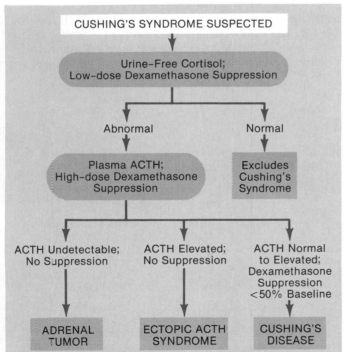

FIGURE 67–6. Evaluation of Cushing's syndrome. Boxes enclose clinical decisions, and ovals enclose diagnostic tests. See the text for details and the potential for false-positive and false-negative results. (From Baxter JD, Tyrrell JB: The adrenal cortex. *In* Felig P, Baxter JD, Broadus AE, et al [eds]: Endocrinology and Metabolism, 2nd ed, p 609. Copyright © 1987 by McGraw-Hill, Inc. Used by permission of McGraw-Hill Book Company.)

Endogenous Cushing's syndrome is characterized by varying degrees of autonomous production of cortisol, resulting in an overall net increase in steroid production. Because cortisol secretion is normally pulsatile, only distinctly elevated random measurements of plasma cortisol help in establishing the diagnosis. A more reliable index of the integrated plasma concentration can be obtained by measurement of the 24-hour urinary excretion of cortisol. Measurement of a urinary metabolite of cortisol (such as 17-hydroxycorticoids) can also be done, but values often overlap normal levels, limiting the usefulness of this procedure.

One of the most reliable means of detecting Cushing's syndrome is the overnight dexamethasone suppression test. Dexamethasone, 1 mg, is administered orally between 11:00 p.m. and midnight, and the plasma cortisol is obtained at approximately 8:00 a.m. the following morning. A value of plasma cortisol of less than 5 μg/dl excludes the diagnosis of Cushing's syndrome. False-negative results are unusual. False-positive results can occur in patients with depression or other stressful situations and with ingestion of drugs such as phenytoin and estrogens. In patients in whom this screening test suggests the diagnosis of Cushing's syndrome, confirmation should be sought by other means, such as measurement of urinary free cortisol.

If Cushing's syndrome is present, what is its cause? Once the diagnosis of Cushing's syndrome is established, additional procedures are required to identify the underlying etiology (see Table 67–3). The high-dose dexamethasone suppression test should distinguish between patients with Cushing's disease and those with ectopic ACTH secretion or a primary adrenal neoplasm. In this test, dexamethasone, 2 mg every 6 hours, is administered orally for 2 consecutive days or as a single "overnight" dose of 8 mg. Suppressibility of endogenous cortisol production is evaluated either by a plasma cortisol measurement at the end of this period or by measurement of urinary free cortisol or 17-hydroxycorticoid excretion on the second day of dexamethasone administration. Patients with Cushing's disease, in whom cortisol production is not entirely autonomous, usually manifest a 50 per cent or greater suppression of cortisol levels in response to these large doses of dexamethasone. In contrast, cortisol production in patients with adrenal neoplasms or ectopic ACTH syndrome is usually more autonomous, so that little or no change in the cortisol level occurs during this procedure. Some patients with ectopic tumors, however, particularly those with a bronchial carcinoid or an adenoma, undergo at least partial suppression and may appear therefore to have Cushing's disease. Also, some patients with Cushing's disease do not adequately suppress with dexamethasone. Despite these relatively uncommon exceptions, the high-dose dexamethasone suppression test remains one of the most reliable means of distinguishing among the causes of Cushing's syndrome.

Measurement of the plasma ACTH level, when

available, is also helpful in differentiating among subtypes of Cushing's syndrome. Plasma ACTH levels are normal to only modestly increased in patients with Cushing's disease, are usually markedly elevated in those with ectopic ACTH secretion, and are generally undetectable in patients with primary adrenal neoplasms. Additional procedures that can help to localize the primary abnormality and to confirm the etiologic diagnosis include magnetic resonance imaging (MRI) and high-resolution contrast-enhanced computed tomography (CT) scans of the pituitary, CT scans of the adrenal, and measurement of ACTH levels in venous samples obtained simultaneously from both inferior petrosal sinuses, particularly following the administration of CRH.

Treatment

Treatment of Cushing's syndrome depends on its cause. Pituitary microsurgery employing the transsphenoidal approach is now the treatment of choice for patients with suspected pituitary adenomas. In experienced hands, an adenoma may be localized in 90 per cent of patients and removed with a low morbidity. This approach has the advantage of preserving the surrounding pituitary tissue, so that hypopituitarism is a rare complication. Pituitary irradiation using either conventional sources or heavy particle beams is also successful in many cases, but the incidence of hypopituitarism is higher than with transsphenoidal hypophysectomy. This may be an important consideration in women in the childbearing years or in children who have not yet achieved adult height. Bilateral adrenalectomy, once commonly performed, is associated with a high incidence of subsequent enlargement of the pituitary neoplasm and hyperpigmentation (Nelson's syndrome) and should be reserved for patients who do not respond to the other approaches. Treatment of patients with primary adrenal neoplasms generally consists of surgical removal of the affected adrenal gland. Even those with carcinoma, in whom cure is rare, should have the tumor removed in an effort to control the hyper-

cortisolism. Surgery is also recommended in patients with ectopic ACTH syndrome due to well-localized ACTH-secreting tumors. In those with benign ACTH-secreting tumors, such as bronchial carcinoid, pheochromocytoma, or thymoma, such an operation is frequently curative. In patients with ectopic malignancies that are already metastatic, as well as in those who have inoperable adrenal carcinoma, medical inhibition of adrenal cortisol secretion by drugs such as mitotane, aminoglutethimide, ketoconazole, and metyrapone may be helpful.

Primary Aldosteronism

Pathophysiology

Hypersecretion of aldosterone can occur as a primary adrenal disorder or in response to increased stimulation by the renin-angiotensin system. Primary aldosteronism is an adrenal disorder characterized by autonomous production of mineralocorticoid hormone (Fig. 67–7). Secondary aldosteronism results from the overstimulation of an otherwise normal adrenal gland by the renin-angiotensin system. The latter disorders are pathophysiologically and clinically distinct from primary aldosteronism and are considered in a separate section.

Primary overproduction of aldosterone results in increased sodium reabsorption in the distal nephron. As a consequence, the extracellular fluid volume is expanded until approximately 1.5 to 2.5 kg of excess fluid has been retained. At this point, proximal tubular sodium reabsorption becomes markedly reduced. The resultant increased delivery of sodium to the distal tubule overwhelms the increased capacity for distal sodium reabsorption, so that a new steady state of sodium balance is achieved. This phenomenon is referred to as "mineralocorticoid escape." Further expansion of extracellular fluid volume does not occur despite continued hypersecretion of mineralocorticoid

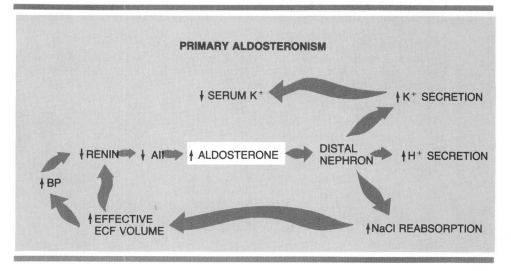

FIGURE 67–7. Perturbations of the renin-angiotensin-aldosterone system in primary aldosteronism. By tending to suppress aldosterone secretion, hypokalemia mitigates hyperaldosteronemia.

hormone. Affected subjects actually excrete an administered sodium load more rapidly than do normal persons. Two of the cardinal findings of the syndrome of primary aldosteronism, hypertension and suppressed plasma renin activity, probably result from this expansion of extracellular fluid volume.

The mineralocorticoid hormone–enhanced sodium reabsorption in the distal tubule and collecting duct results in increased secretion of potassium and hydrogen ion in these portions of the nephron. Even when the renal escape mechanism allows a new steady state of sodium balance to develop, mineralocorticoid-dependent potassium secretion and hydrogen ion secretion continue. The increased delivery of sodium to the distal nephron may actually augment the potassium secretion.

In the syndrome of primary aldosteronism, autonomous overproduction of aldosterone by the adrenal gland can be due to a benign adenoma, a carcinoma, or diffuse bilateral nodular hyperplasia, with adenomas accounting for 75 to 85 per cent of cases. Less than 1 per cent are due to a functioning carcinoma, and the remaining 15 to 25 per cent result from bilateral hyperplasia. The extremely rare cases of so-called glucocorticoid-remediable hyperaldosteronism are believed to result from excessive stimulation of the adrenal cortex by ACTH. The patterns of mineralocorticoid secretion and the degree of autonomy from the renin-angiotensin system vary among the different entities.

Clinical Manifestations

The major clinical manifestations of primary aldosteronism are hypertension and hypokalemia. In addition, hypernatremia and metabolic alkalosis are characteristically found. A dilute urine may be present because hypokalemia impairs the renal concentrating mechanism. The severity of the presenting symptoms depends on the degree of potassium depletion. Mildly hypokalemic patients complain of muscle weakness, polyuria (especially nocturia), polydipsia, and paresthesias. Patients with more severe hypokalemia experience intermittent paralysis of the legs and arms or even tetany. Patients with marked hypokalemia sometimes experience autonomic dysfunction, with orthostatic hypotension occurring without reflex tachycardia.

Diagnosis and Treatment

Recognition of primary aldosteronism, usually during evaluation of hypertension, is important because it is a potentially curable form of hypertension. Less than 1 per cent of unselected hypertensive patients have this disorder, which is found in women more often than in men by a 2:1 margin. The patients are usually between 30 and 50 years of age.

Hyperaldosteronism can be documented by showing an increased secretion rate, an increased excretion rate, or an elevated plasma concentration of the hormone. Single measurements of plasma aldosterone concentration may be misleading because even patients with markedly increased secretion rates show diurnal variations in plasma levels that can obscure recognition of hyperaldosteronism. Aldosterone production is best assessed by measuring its 24-hour urinary excretion or that of its 18-glucuronide metabolite. The urine should be collected while the patient consumes a typical sodium intake (120 to 180 mEq/day).

Demonstration of suppressed and nonstimulable plasma renin activity in a patient with elevated plasma or urinary aldosterone levels establishes the diagnosis of primary aldosteronism. Autonomy of aldosterone production can be confirmed by demonstrating failure of suppression of the hormone levels by maneuvers that normally suppress the renin-angiotensin-aldosterone system, such as administration of mineralocorticoid hormones (fludrocortisone) or intravenous infusion of normal saline.

The principal reason for attempting to differentiate between aldosterone-producing adenoma and bilateral hyperplasia is to select the most appropriate therapy. Unilateral adrenalectomy cures approximately 70 per cent of cases due to an adenoma, whereas even bilateral adrenalectomy does not ameliorate the hypertension in most cases of hyperplasia. Several biochemical determinations have been proposed to differentiate adenoma from hyperplasia. Patients with an adenoma generally have lower plasma renin activity values and plasma potassium concentrations with higher basal plasma aldosterone and 18-hydroxycorticosterone concentrations than do patients with hyperplasia. Plasma aldosterone levels in patients with adenoma fail to increase with upright posture, in contrast to a twofold to threefold increase in those with hyperplasia. Specific techniques for localizing an adenoma (iodocholesterol scan, CT scan, MRI, and adrenal venous catheterization) also aid in differentiating those with tumor from those with bilateral hyperplasia.

Adrenal Enzyme Defects

Genetically transmitted deficiencies of the enzymes required for adrenal steroid biosynthesis lead to distinct clinical syndromes of disturbed mineralocorticoid production. In two such enzyme deficiency states, 11β- and 17α-hydroxylase deficiency, impaired cortisol production results in increased ACTH secretion and secondary increased production of DOC, which produces a typical syndrome of mineralocorticoid excess. In 11β-hydroxylase deficiency, conversion of DOC to corticosterone and its derivatives is impaired; thus corticosterone, 18-hydroxycorticosterone, and/or aldosterone may be deficient. In 17α-hydroxylase deficiency, conversion of DOC to its derivatives is not enzymatically blocked. Despite the intact enzymatic pathway to aldosterone, aldosterone production is generally subnormal, presumably as a consequence of the reduced plasma renin activity and the hypokalemia that occur because of the hypermineralocorticoid state.

These two syndromes can be readily distinguished clinically by their different effects on sexual development. In the 17α-hydroxylase deficiency syndrome, biosynthesis of adrenal and gonadal androgen and estrogen is impaired, inhibiting normal sexual maturation. Genotypic female patients fail to undergo menarche or to develop secondary sex characteristics. Genotypic male patients become pseudohermaphrodites as a consequence of androgen deficiency in utero. In the 11β-hydroxylase deficiency syndrome, the enzymatic steps required for the synthesis of adrenal sex steroids are unimpaired. The increased ACTH level stimulates increased production of adrenal androgen, frequently causing virilism. In both syndromes, glucocorticoid hormone replacement therapy inhibits both ACTH secretion and the resultant excess mineralocorticoid production and therefore ameliorates the hypermineralocorticoid state. In treated patients with the 11β-hydroxylase deficiency syndrome, androgen production diminishes and signs of virilization tend to disappear.

Secondary Aldosteronism (Table 67–3)

Aldosterone is secreted as a physiologic response to reduced effective arterial blood volume owing to activation of the renin-angiotensin system. The resultant increase in plasma aldosterone concentration stimulates renal tubular reabsorption of Na^+ and Cl^- and thereby tends to restore normal "effective" blood volume. When hypovolemia is of extrarenal origin (vomiting, diarrhea, and hemorrhage) and renal tubular reabsorption of Na^+ and Cl^- is not specifically impaired, the Na^+-retaining effect of hypermineralocorticoidism is manifested by reduced urinary excretion rates of Na^+ that persist until effective arterial blood volume is restored. Provision of adequate amounts of dietary salt may normalize the effective arterial blood volume. The Na^+-retaining effect of hypermineralocorticoidism does not reduce excretion rates of Na^+ when hypovolemia is caused predominantly by impaired renal tubular reabsorption of Na^+ and Cl^- (e.g., diuretic administration, Bartter's syndrome, and some types of renal tubular acidosis). When the reduction in effective arterial blood volume is due to congestive heart failure, cirrhosis, or the nephrotic syndrome, provision of dietary salt leads to progressive expansion of extracellular fluid volume and edema without restoration of effective blood volume.

Hyperaldosteronism secondary to activation of the renin-angiotensin system also occurs in patients with accelerated hypertension, renovascular or segmental renal lesions, and, rarely, renin-secreting neoplasms. Activation of the renin-angiotensin-aldosterone system in the absence of hypovolemia results in hypertension.

The exact contribution of excess mineralocorticoid production to the pathophysiology observed in states of secondary hyperaldosteronism is not always clear. Hypertension persists despite adrenalectomy in patients with a renin-secreting tumor and in animals with experimental renovascular hypertension. Reduction of Na^+ excretion and edema formation can occur in patients with cardiac, renal, or hepatic disease without increased aldosterone secretion. Potassium wasting persists despite sustained correction of secondary hyperaldosteronism in some patients with type 1 renal tubular acidosis and in some patients with Bartter's syndrome. In these disorders, it seems likely that the secondary aldosteronism serves to amplify the consequences of the primary defect causing renal potassium wasting.

ADRENAL MEDULLARY HYPERFUNCTION

The adrenal medulla synthesizes and releases biologically active amines derived from the amino acid tyrosine. Norepinephrine, the major product of this biosynthetic pathway, is also synthesized in the central nervous system and sympathetic postganglionic neurons, whereas epinephrine originates nearly entirely from the adrenal gland. A third catecholamine, dopamine, which acts as a neurotransmitter in the central nervous system, has a less clearly defined role as a circulating hormone, although dopamine may normally inhibit aldosterone secretion.

Catecholamines have a variety of potent hemodynamic and metabolic effects, depending upon their relative abilities to serve as agonists for the alpha- and beta-adrenergic receptors. Epinephrine acts chiefly on beta receptors, having a positive chronotropic and inotropic effect on the heart and producing vasodilatation in most vascular beds. Epinephrine also increases plasma glucose concentration by inhibiting insulin secretion and stimulating glycogenolysis in the liver. Epinephrine is released from the medulla in response to a variety of stresses, including hypoglycemia. Norepinephrine has predominant alpha-agonist effects, causing vasoconstriction with relatively little metabolic action. Inasmuch as norepinephrine is secreted widely throughout the sympathetic nervous system, the contribution by the adrenal medulla is relatively small. Bilateral adrenalectomy results in little, if any, measurable change in the levels of norepinephrine, although epinephrine levels are markedly reduced. Thus, adrenal medullary hypofunction has little or no physiologic impact, whereas hypersecretion of catecholamines produces a dramatic clinical syndrome, namely, pheochromocytoma.

Pheochromocytoma

Pathophysiology

Pheochromocytoma, an uncommon but important tumor of chromaffin cells, occurs most commonly (90 per cent) in the adrenal gland but can be found in any sympathetic ganglion, particularly those in the mediastinum or abdomen. Bilateral adrenal pheochromocytomas or multiple tumors may be present in 5 to 10 per cent of cases. Affected patients may also have medullary carcinoma of the thyroid and other manifestations of the multiple endocrine neoplasia syndrome, type 2 (Sipple's syndrome).

Clinical Manifestations

The clinical manifestations of pheochromocytoma depend upon the predominant catecholamine secreted. Since most tumors secrete principally norepinephrine, hypertension, usually sustained, is the most common finding. Superimposed are paroxysms in which a sudden release of catecholamines results in exacerbation of hypertension, accompanied by palpitation, headache, pallor, sweating, flushing, and anxiety. Such attacks can be provoked by ingestion of tyramine-containing foods, particularly in patients taking monoamine oxidase inhibitors. Occasionally, patients with pheochromocytoma may not exhibit hypertension at all and in fact may become hypotensive during paroxysms. Such patients usually have epinephrine-secreting tumors or tumors whose principal product is dopamine. Orthostatic hypotension is common in patients with pheochromocytoma, even in those who have sustained hypertension while supine.

TABLE 67–5. DIAGNOSIS OF PHEOCHROMOCYTOMA

Clinical Suspicion
1. Paroxysmal symptoms (especially headache, palpitations, and diaphoresis)
2. Intermittent or unusually labile hypertension or hypertension refractory to therapy
3. Incidental adrenal mass (rarely a pheochromocytoma in the absence of one or more of the above)
4. Family history of pheochromocytoma, MEN 2, or MEN 3

Biochemical Confirmation
1. Plasma norepinephrine and epinephrine (± dopamine)
   Patient sampled in the basal state (and supine position) and, if possible, during a paroxysm
   Radioenzymatic or HPLC method
   Note blood pressure, heart rate, and any symptoms
2. Urinary catecholamines or metanephrines (or VMA)
   If plasma values are normal or equivocal but clinical suspicion is high, repeated plasma measurements are an alternative
   Can be used as the initial test

Anatomic Localization
1. Computed tomography
   Of the abdomen, including the adrenals, initially; of the pelvis and thorax if the abdomen is negative
   Indicated in the absence of biochemical evidence only if clinical suspicion is very high (e.g., positive family history)
2. Magnetic resonance imaging
3. Iodobenzylguanidine scan

MEN = Multiple endocrine neoplasia; HPLC = high-pressure liquid chromatography; VMA = vanillylmandelic acid.
From Cryer PE: The adrenal medullae. In Wyngaarden JB, Smith LH Jr, Bennett JC (eds): Cecil Textbook of Medicine. 19th ed. Philadelphia, WB Saunders Co, 1992, p 1392.

Diagnosis and Treatment

The diagnosis of pheochromocytoma is based on clinical suspicion, biochemical confirmation, and anatomic localization (Table 67–5). Pheochromocytomas, particularly those arising from the adrenal medulla, are usually several centimeters in diameter by the time symptoms develop and can be readily visualized on abdominal CT or MRI scans. In the absence of an obvious adrenal tumor, localization of the tumor in the sympathetic ganglia may be difficult. Catheterization of the inferior vena cava with sampling of multiple sites for catecholamine measurements may help to localize the tumor preoperatively. An isotope scan technique utilizing ^{131}I-metaiodobenzylguanidine can often localize small neoplasms effectively. The possibility of multiple pheochromocytomas should be considered, particularly in patients with family histories of other endocrine neoplasms.

Pheochromocytomas should be surgically removed if possible. Preoperative adrenergic blockade has markedly improved the once formidable surgical morbidity and mortality. In patients with norepinephrine-secreting lesions, alpha blockade should be effected first, using phenoxybenzamine, dibenzyline, or prazosin in sufficient doses and for a sufficient period to prevent episodes of hypertension and to allow expansion of the effective extracellular fluid volume. Beta-adrenergic blockade may also be useful, particularly in those who develop tachycardia while using alpha blockers. Careful preoperative planning by an experienced anesthesiologist, an endocrinologist, and a surgeon usually ensures a good outcome.

In patients with inoperable tumors or with metastatic pheochromocytoma, pharmacologic therapy may be continued on a chronic basis. In addition, alpha-methyltyrosine may be of some benefit in reducing catecholamine secretion by the neoplastic tissue.

REFERENCES

Crapo L: Cushing's syndrome: A review of diagnostic tests. Metabolism 28:955, 1979.

Cryer PE: The adrenal medullae. In Wyngaarden JB, Smith LH Jr, Bennett JC (eds): Cecil Textbook of Medicine. 19th ed. Philadelphia, WB Saunders Co, 1992, pp 1390–1394.

Kannan CR: Diseases of the adrenal cortex. DM 34:603, 1988.

Mampalam TJ, Tyrrell JB, Wilson CB: Transsphenoidal microsurgery for Cushing disease. A report of 216 cases. Ann Intern Med 109:487, 1988.

Oldfield EH, Doppman JL, Nieman LK, et al: Petrosal sinus sampling with and without corticotropin-releasing hormone for the differential diagnosis of Cushing's syndrome. N Engl J Med 325:897, 1991.

Sebastian A, Schambelan M: Renal hyperkalemia. Semin Nephrol 7:223, 1987.

Tyrrell JB, Baxter JD: Disorders of the adrenal cortex. In Wyngaarden JB, Smith LH Jr, Bennett JC (eds): Cecil Textbook of Medicine. 19th ed. Philadelphia, WB Saunders Co, 1988, pp 1271–1291.

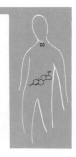

68 FEMALE ENDOCRINOLOGY

Each adult ovary (approximately 4 cm × 3 cm × 1 cm) is attached to the lateral pelvic wall and to the uterus by the ovarian ligament. The follicle in its different stages of maturation is the critical structural and functional component of the ovary. Both steroidogenesis and gametogenesis depend on the follicle complex. The primary components of the follicle are the oocyte, granulosa cells, and interstitial cells (theca cells).

SEXUAL DEVELOPMENT AND DIFFERENTIATION

Normal sexual development and differentiation depend on a full complex of sex and autosomal chromosomes. The genital ridge develops at approximately 3 weeks' gestation. Subsequently, germ cells migrate to the genital ridge from the yolk sac. Undifferentiated reproductive tracts consisting of both müllerian and wolffian ducts are present by 6 weeks' gestation. Differentiation of the female reproductive tract proceeds in the absence of müllerian-inhibiting factor and androgens from the testes. Appropriate female genitalia develop consequent to the lack of androgen secretion.

Normal ovarian function requires the integrated action of the hypothalamic-pituitary-ovarian axis (Fig. 68–1). Follicular growth, steroid hormone production (secretion), ovulation, and atresia are gonadotropin-dependent (follicle-stimulating hormone, FSH; luteinizing hormone, LH). Subsequent to synthesis (Fig. 68–2) and secretion, ovarian sex steroid hormones (estrogens, androgens, and progestins) mediate their effects locally on the ovary and the genital tract (uterus, cervix, and vagina) and systemically to coordinate functions of the hypothalamic-pituitary complex. Measurement of serum estradiol, progesterone, FSH, and LH levels with specific radioimmunoassays provides accurate information on the integrity of the hypothalamic-pituitary-ovarian axis in health and disease. In addition, the biologic activity of the sex steroids on target organs can be reliably evaluated. Estrogens increase the quantity and elasticity ("spinnbarkeit") of the cervical mucus as well as the tendency of the electrolytes to crystallize in a "ferning" pattern. Progesterone inhibits these

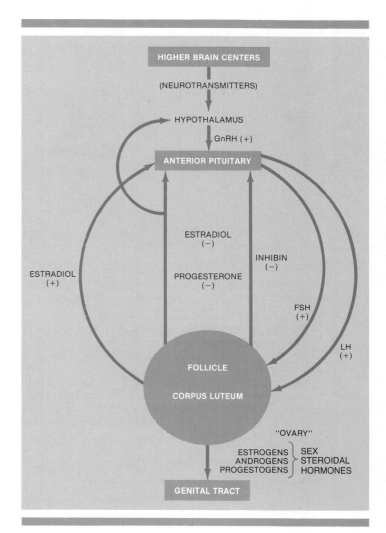

FIGURE 68–1. Hypothalamic-pituitary-ovarian axis. Gonadotropin-releasing hormone (GnRH) stimulates the pituitary gland to synthesize and secrete the gonadotropins FSH (follicle-stimulating hormone) and LH (luteinizing hormone). These hormones stimulate sequential ovarian follicle development and differentiation. The sex steroid hormones secreted by the ovary regulate genital tract changes and modulate hypothalamic GnRH secretion. In addition, inhibin secreted by the follicle specifically inhibits the release of FSH. (Modified from Cecil Essentials of Medicine. 2nd ed. Philadelphia, WB Saunders Co, 1990, p 479.)

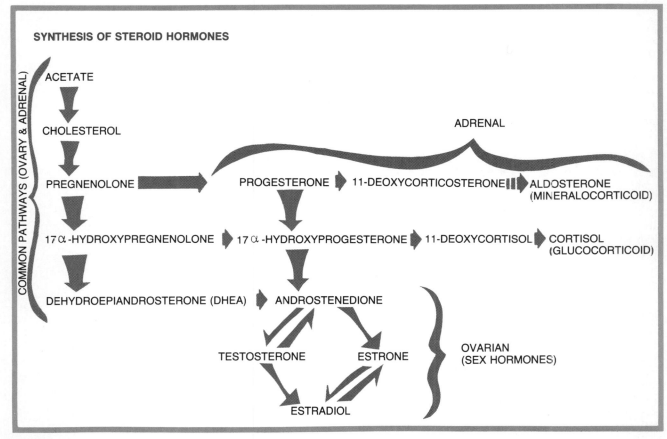

SYNTHESIS OF STEROID HORMONES

FIGURE 68–2. Synthetic pathways for steroid hormone production by the ovary and adrenal gland.

changes in mucus. In addition, the endometrium undergoes characteristic changes during the menstrual cycle. The follicular phase is associated with proliferation of the endometrial glands under the influence of estrogen. During the luteal phase, progesterone induces the glands to become secretory. Endometrial biopsies are used to date the stage of the cycle and to assess the tissue response to gonadal steroids.

Abnormal Sexual Differentiation

Chromosomal

Turner's syndrome, the most common disorder of gonadal differentiation in the female, results from a 45XO chromosomal abnormality. It has an incidence of 1 in 3000 newborn females. These patients have nonfunctioning streak gonads (gonadal dysgenesis) and unambiguous female external genitalia and internal ducts and may exhibit many or all of the following abnormalities: sexual infantilism, short stature, musculoskeletal abnormalities (webbed neck, low hairline, shield chest, cubitus valgus, short digits), hypertension, coarctation of the aorta, renal disorders, and deafness. Patients with a mosaic karyotype present fewer stigmata, and gonadal function may be normal.

The short stature can be treated with anabolic steroids and growth hormone when the patient is between 10 and 14 years old. Feminization can be induced with estrogen replacement.

Enzymatic

Female pseudohermaphrodites have a normal 46XX karyotype and internal sexual organs but masculinized external genitalia (male phenotype) due to excess androgens. The extent of the virilization and the degree of ambiguity in genital development depend on the timing and severity of the androgen exposure. Female pseudohermaphroditism is most commonly caused by *congenital adrenal hyperplasia* (CAH), which has a wide spectrum of clinical presentations due to the variable involvement of specific enzymes necessary for cortisol synthesis by the adrenal cortex (Fig. 68–2). This syndrome complex is inherited in an autosomal recessive manner and expresses itself only in the homozygous offspring. It has a prevalence of 1 per 60,000 births. The cortisol deficiency results in increased adrenocorticotropin (ACTH) secretion and consequent adrenal hyperplasia. The most frequent lesion involves a deficiency of 21-hydroxylase. The hyperplastic glands secrete androgens in excess, which masculinize the female fetus. Furthermore, the decreased production of aldosterone and excess secretion of 17-hydroxyprogesterone cause salt wasting. In the 11-hydroxylase form, masculinization also occurs, but salt retention and hypertension develop because of the excess production of 11-deoxycorticosterone. CAH can be successfully treated with a glucocorticoid (hydrocortisone); this is supplemented with a mineralocorticoid (fludrocortisone) in the salt-wasting form of the syndrome. Surgical correction of the external genitalia, if necessary, should be performed before the age of 3 years.

PUBERTY

The adolescent or pubescent phase of development provides the individual with reproductive capacity. In the female, somatic growth accelerates, the breasts develop (thelarche), pubic hair appears (pubarche), and finally the menarche occurs. This process generally begins in girls between 8 and 14 years of age, with full development over a 3-year period. The order of appearance of pubertal features varies greatly.

The age of onset of puberty is variable and influenced by genetic factors, socioeconomic conditions, and general health. Prepubertal girls have low serum levels of gonadotropins and sex steroid hormones. During the progression of puberty, the characteristic inhibitory effect of estrogens on gonadotropin (FSH, LH) secretion declines, and in the case of LH a positive feedback process develops (see Fig. 68–1). An early feature of the pubescent girl is the nocturnal pulsatile secretion of LH. Enhanced LH activity stimulates the ovary to secrete increasing amounts of estrogens, and secondary sex characteristics subsequently develop.

Precocious Puberty

Isosexual precocious puberty is defined as the premature (<8 years) development of adult genitalia consistent with the chromosomal sex of the child. In girls the majority of cases (80 per cent) are idiopathic, with both gonadotropins (FSH and LH) and sex steroid hormones (estradiol and progesterone) in the normal adult range. Isosexual precocious puberty also occurs in the McCune-Albright syndrome (polyostotic fibrous dysplasia). High gonadotropin levels suggest an intracranial lesion or a tumor secreting human chorionic gonadotropin (hCG). Hypothyroidism can also be associated with precocious puberty due to increased secretion of gonadotropins. Precocious puberty associated with low levels of gonadotropins suggests an ovarian or adrenal tumor. Adrenal tumors generally secrete large amounts of steroids that can be detected as urinary 17-ketosteroids and the tumors can be detected by computed tomography (CT) scan of the abdomen. Ovarian tumors can usually be detected on physical examination or ultrasonography of the pelvis.

In heterosexual precocious puberty, pubertal changes that are consistent with the opposite sex of the child take place. This situation occurs most frequently in CAH or is due to androgen-secreting tumors of the adrenal cortex or ovary. High serum levels of 17-hydroxyprogesterone are typically found in congenital adrenal hyperplasia.

Treatment. Gonadal and adrenocortical tumors should be removed surgically. Intracranial tumors may be treated surgically, by radiation, and/or by chemotherapy. The progression of idiopathic precocious puberty can be delayed by medical intervention. This measure avoids psychosocial problems in the young child and may prevent premature closure of the epiphyses with resulting permanent short stature. Depomedroxyprogesterone acetate (200 to 300 mg given intramuscularly, weekly) stops breast development and menstruation. However, adult short stature may remain a problem. Agonists of gonadotropin-releasing hormone (GnRH) also effectively stop the progression of precocious puberty without causing short stature and are the treatment of choice. Patients with CAH must receive replacement therapy with a glucocorticoid preparation.

Incomplete Sexual Precocity

Isolated premature breast development (thelarche) and pubic hair growth (pubarche or adrenarche) are benign conditions that rarely warrant specific therapy. Bone age may be slightly advanced in association with either of these forms of incomplete precocious puberty.

Delayed Puberty

Girls who have not displayed breast growth by age 14 years are considered to have delayed onset of puberty, but most eventually undergo puberty spontaneously. Understandably, these delays create psychological problems and parental anxiety. Thus, reassurance can be provided only once other lesions have been excluded. Delayed puberty is also associated with excessive exercise (endurance training), nutritional disorders such as anorexia nervosa, chronic systemic illnesses (especially those involving the gastrointestinal tract), and hypothyroidism. Rarely, delayed puberty is due to hypogonadotropic hypogonadism (hypothalamic-pituitary disorders) or to primary gonadal failure (gonadal dysgenesis), in the latter case with increased levels of gonadotropins. If indicated, secondary sex characteristics can be induced with estrogens (e.g., ethinylestradiol, 20 μg given orally, daily) over a 6-month period. Spontaneous progression of puberty frequently develops during or subsequent to therapy.

MENSTRUAL CYCLE

The onset of menarche (initiation of regular menstrual cycles) indicates the near-completion of normal sexual development. Menarche occurs at a mean age of 12.6 years, with a standard deviation of 1.2 years. The current age range of menarche in the United States is 9 to 16 years. Early (<9 years) and delayed (>16 years) menarche warrants evaluation.

The menstrual cycle is conveniently divided into three phases—the follicular, the ovulatory, and the luteal phases (Fig. 68–3). Menstruation conventionally marks the beginning of a new cycle. Plasma FSH increases at the completion of the luteal phase of the previous cycle and initiates maturation of the follicle. During this phase, the developing follicle secretes increasing amounts of estradiol, reaching a peak secretion about 12 hours before the LH ovulatory surge. This sudden increase in estradiol triggers the LH/FSH spike through a positive feedback process on the anterior hypothalamus. The midcycle surge in gonadotropins induces ovulation. Following ovulation, the ruptured follicle is transformed into the corpus luteum. Serum estradiol decreases and serum progesterone increases rapidly during the early part of the luteal phase. Subsequently, the developing corpus luteum secretes increasing amounts of progesterone and estradiol, with peak serum levels at about 7 days after ovulation. The corpus luteum then regresses, with a consequent decrease in serum hormone levels. At day 28 of the cycle, serum estradiol and progesterone levels are at their nadir, menstruation occurs, and a new cycle begins.

Dysmenorrhea

Dysmenorrhea (pain just prior to and during menstruation) affects about half of all women. Primary dysmenorrhea is due to prostaglandin-induced uterine contractions. Systemic features may include headache, nausea, diarrhea, and emotional disturbances. Endometriosis is the most common cause of secondary dysmenorrhea. Inhibitors of prostaglandin synthesis generally relieve primary dysmenorrhea. If it persists or remains severe, the addition of an oral contraceptive is generally effective. Laparoscopy is currently the only reliable method of diagnosing endometriosis and, with the use of lasers, can be used to treat most patients. Continuous suppression with an oral contraceptive

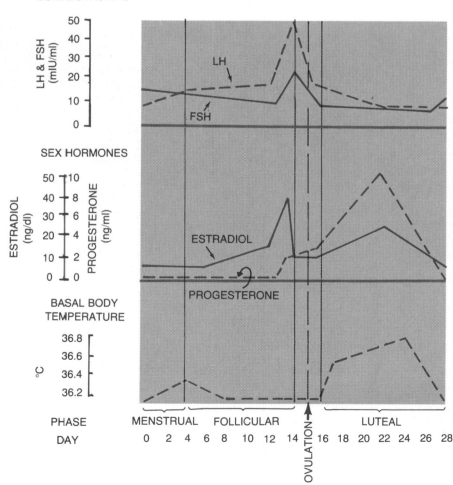

FIGURE 68–3. Normal menstrual cycle. The sequential changes that occur in serum gonadotropins (LH and FSH), estradiol, and progesterone during the various phases of the cycle are outlined. Day 0 correlates to the first day of menstruation. A typical basal body temperature chart is also depicted.

agent, GnRH agonist, or danazol for 6 months should give relief. Subsequent to a course of therapy, an oral contraceptive agent should be prescribed until fertility is desired.

The Premenstrual Syndrome

This common clinical entity, which affects about 70 per cent of women, may produce any or all of the following symptoms before menses—bloating and weight gain, emotional lability, headaches (migraine), breast congestion, acne, and arthralgias. For most women, these symptoms are merely a nuisance; about 20 per cent of patients, however, may experience problems from the time of ovulation to menstruation that are severe enough to interrupt normal daily activities.

The cause of the premenstrual syndrome is not understood. Water retention and possibly deficiency of dopamine or endorphin in the central nervous system have been postulated as pathogenetic factors. Affected patients should be advised to maintain a healthy diet and to exercise regularly. Women with symptoms of severe fluid retention may benefit from diuretic therapy during the second half of the menstrual cycle. Therapeutic modalities can be divided into two groups: (1) inhibition of ovulation with oral contraceptives, progestins, or GnRH agonists and (2) medications that affect mood.

AMENORRHEA

Absence of menses for 3 months or longer defines amenorrhea. Failure of menarche to occur during adolescent development is primary amenorrhea, whereas the discontinuation of menses after the onset of menarche is secondary amenorrhea. Physiologic amenorrhea occurs during pregnancy and after menopause. Approximately 5 per cent of women experience nonphysiologic amenorrhea, a sign of any of several disorders involving different organ systems. Although traditionally the evaluation of amenorrhea is approached by focusing on the primary and secondary presentations, it is important to note the overlap in the etiologies (Tables 68–1 and 68–2).

Primary Amenorrhea

Primary amenorrhea always calls for a detailed history and physical examination. It may occur in association with normal, decreased, or increased sex steroid hormone production (see Table 68–1). Women with normal secondary sex characteristics may have an abnormality of the outflow tract (vaginal aplasia or imperforate hymen) and retain the menstrual effluent. This situation may lead to endometriosis and cyclic abdominal pain but absent menstruation.

Male pseudohermaphroditism (genetic males) is a common cause of primary amenorrhea. These patients develop as phenotypic females because of deficient testosterone synthesis or various androgen-resistant syndromes.

TABLE 68–1. CAUSES OF PRIMARY AMENORRHEA

1. Normal Sex Hormone Production
   a. Müllerian dysgenesis
   b. Amenorrhea traumatica
2. Decreased Sex Hormone Production
   a. Male pseudohermaphroditism due to an absolute or relative deficiency of testosterone
   b. Gonadal dysgenesis (Turner's syndrome)
   c. Hypothalamic-pituitary disease
      Familial hypogonadotropic hypogonadism (Kallmann's syndrome)
      Pituitary and parapituitary tumors
      Anorexia nervosa
   d. Systemic diseases
3. Increased Sex Hormone Production
   a. Congenital adrenal hyperplasia
   b. Polycystic ovarian disease (Stein-Leventhal syndrome)
   c. Androgen-secreting ovarian and adrenal tumors

A spectrum of sexual immaturity may occur consequent to hypofunction of the hypothalamic-pituitary complex (hypogonadotropic hypogonadism). Secondary sex characteristics do not develop, and menses do not occur. Kallmann's syndrome is a familial disorder characterized by anosmia or hyposmia, various midline defects (harelip, cleft palate), and sexual immaturity due to low gonadotropin levels. Acquired forms of hypogonadotropic hypogonadism may result from pituitary tumors, craniopharyngiomas, and other parapituitary lesions. Psychogenic and stressful systemic disorders may also interfere with hypothalamic-pituitary function and delay sexual maturation and menarche.

The most common cause of primary amenorrhea without secondary sex characteristics is gonadal dysgenesis (Turner's syndrome). This syndrome,

TABLE 68–2. CAUSES OF SECONDARY AMENORRHEA

1. Normal Sex Hormone Production
   a. Amenorrhea traumatica
      Postinfectious
      Postoperative
2. Decreased Sex Hormone Production
   a. Primary ovarian failure (high serum gonadotropins)
      Post surgery, irradiation, chemotherapy, or toxins
      Autoimmune premature ovarian failure
      Gonadal dysgenesis
   b. Secondary ovarian failure (low serum gonadotropins)
      Hypothalamic-pituitary dysfunction
      Post surgery, irradiation, infection, infarction
      Pituitary tumor with normal prolactin
      Empty sella syndrome
      Pituitary tumor with hyperprolactinemia
      Postpartum or postpill amenorrhea
      Psychogenic
      Anorexia nervosa
      Endocrine disorders—thyroid, adrenal, diabetes
      Systemic disorders
3. Increased Sex Hormone Production
   a. Polycystic ovarian disease
   b. Androgen-secreting ovarian or adrenal tumor

characterized by streak gonads, elevated serum gonadotropin levels, short stature, and various other abnormalities, was described above.

CAH may cause primary amenorrhea if not detected and treated. Mild forms with minimal genital ambiguity are often not detected until puberty. These patients are usually of short stature because of androgen-induced premature closure of the epiphyses. Primary amenorrhea can rarely be associated with polycystic ovaries or with androgen-secreting tumors.

Secondary Amenorrhea

Secondary amenorrhea is not a disease entity but a signal that function has been compromised at some level in the hypothalamic-pituitary-ovarian-uterine axis. Absence of menses for 3 to 6 months in a previously normally menstruating woman establishes the diagnosis of secondary amenorrhea. The most common cause of secondary amenorrhea is pregnancy. Thus, such a patient should be considered pregnant until proved otherwise with a sensitive pregnancy test.

Secondary amenorrhea also occurs in association with normal, decreased, or increased sex steroid hormone production (Table 68–2). Amenorrhea associated with normal cyclic changes in the secretion of ovarian steroid hormones is a frequent finding in women with a damaged endometrium. This damage may occur consequent to repeated uterine curettage following delivery or abortion or following infection (e.g., tuberculosis). Surgical or medical correction of these lesions generally leads to a resumption of menses.

Primary ovarian failure may develop after abdominal irradiation, chemotherapy, or surgery. However, premature ovarian failure probably occurs most commonly secondary to autoimmune injury. Serum gonadotropin levels are high. Destructive lesions of the hypothalamus and pituitary, such as those caused by surgery, irradiation, chemotherapy, infection, infarction, or tumor, may result in secondary ovarian failure. Pituitary tumors secreting prolactin account for about 30 per cent of patients with secondary amenorrhea. Most of these lesions can be detected by magnetic resonance imaging (MRI) scans. These patients have high serum prolactin levels and low serum levels of gonadotropins. Many cases of secondary amenorrhea are due to hypothalamic-pituitary dysfunction resulting from severe emotional stress or systemic disease. Thus, amenorrhea may occur in association with anorexia nervosa, intensive exercise, endocrine disease (thyroid or adrenal disorders, diabetes), and medications (phenothiazines, metoclopramide). Ovarian tumors may produce excess sex steroids (androgens), which suppress gonadotropins and cause amenorrhea. Polycystic ovary syndrome (chronic hyperandrogenic anovulation) frequently causes secondary amenorrhea. An elevated LH/FSH ratio, increased production of androgens, and insulin resistance are characteristic of this disorder. The etiology of polycystic ovaries is not known in most cases. These patients commonly present with amenorrhea (anovulation), hirsutism, and obesity.

Diagnosis and Treatment

In a patient with amenorrhea, the physician should first exclude pregnancy, pituitary tumor, and premature menopause. Pregnancy can be easily detected by measuring the serum level of the beta subunit of hCG. A normal serum FSH level rules out premature menopause. Pituitary microadenoma can generally be detected by MRI scanning of the sella turcica. A positive finding in conjunction with high serum prolactin and low gonadotropin levels documents the presence of a pituitary tumor (see Chapter 65). Additional studies should focus on specific disorders of the central nervous system, thyroid, adrenal, pancreas (diabetes), ovary, uterus, and vagina.

In the absence of clinically detectable disease, very valuable information concerning the cause of amenorrhea can be obtained by proceeding through the following diagnostic steps. In most cases, the need for expensive laboratory tests can be avoided.

A normal estrogen effect (sex steroid hormone production) can generally be deduced from a healthy vaginal mucosa and copious amounts of clear cervical mucus. A progesterone withdrawal (medroxyprogesterone acetate, 10 mg daily for 5 days) screening test can be performed to test the integrity of the reproductive axis. Menstrual bleeding following this short course of progesterone indicates that the axis is functional and that the amenorrhea is most likely due to anovulation. If bleeding does not occur, a course of conjugated estrogens (Premarin, 1.25 mg daily for 21 days) should be administered, followed by the progesterone withdrawal test. Failure to bleed after this regimen indicates target organ (endometrium) or outflow tract failure. The patient should be referred to a gynecologist for further investigations. A positive withdrawal test should be followed by measurement of gonadotropin and prolactin levels. High gonadotropin levels are consistent with primary ovarian disease, whereas low values indicate hypothalamic-pituitary dysfunction or failure. Individuals with high levels should have a karyotype done to detect Turner's syndrome (XO) or male pseudohermaphroditism (female phenotype).

The approach to therapy for each specific cause of amenorrhea should be dictated by the lesion and the patient's wishes. If no clearly detectable lesion is evident, reassurance and follow-up are appropriate. A desire for regular menstrual cycles can be fulfilled by medication with a cyclic estrogen-progesterone preparation.

Amenorrhea associated with hyperprolactinemia can be treated surgically or medically (bromocriptine given orally, 2 to 5 mg bid). This therapy restores regular cycles and fertility in the majority of patients. Premature ovarian failure should usually be treated with estrogen replacement (e.g.,

Premarin, 0.625 to 1.25 mg/day, and medroxyprogesterone acetate [Provera], 10 mg/day, 12 days per month).

ABNORMAL UTERINE BLEEDING

The causes of abnormal uterine bleeding during the reproductive years include complications from the use of oral contraceptives, pregnancy (threatened, incomplete, or missed abortion), coagulation disorders, uterine polyps, leiomyomas, and tumors of the cervix and vagina. A history of diethylstilbestrol (DES) exposure would place the patient at a low but increased risk for adenocarcinoma of the vagina or cervix. Abnormal bleeding may also be a feature of trauma, endocrinopathies (diabetes mellitus, thyroid disorders, and adrenal disease), or other systemic diseases.

Dysfunctional uterine bleeding (DUB), defined as abnormal uterine bleeding that cannot be attributed to an organic lesion, is the most common cause (75 per cent) of abnormal uterine bleeding. The majority of these cases are associated with anovulation and occur at each end of the reproductive years, as postmenarcheal adolescent bleeding secondary to hypothalamic immaturity or as premenopausal bleeding consequent to imminent ovarian failure. Most cases of anovulatory bleeding are examples of estrogen withdrawal or estrogen breakthrough bleeding. Unopposed estrogen induces a progressive endometrial hyperplasia. In the absence of growth-limiting progesterone and natural periodic menstruation, the endometrium achieves an abnormal height without the necessary structural support. This fragile tissue intermittently undergoes spontaneous necrosis, and bleeding results. The classic presentation is one of a pale, frightened teenager who has bled excessively for weeks or an older woman with prolonged bleeding who is concerned about the development of a possible neoplasm. It is important to exclude the organic causes listed above before attributing abnormal uterine bleeding to DUB.

Therapy attempts to control the acute bleeding and to prevent recurrent bleeding. Acute hemostasis can be accomplished rapidly (<24 hours) with a high dose of a progesterone-estrogen combination birth control pill. Therapy is administered as one pill four times a day for 7 days. These patients must be warned that a heavy flow associated with severe cramping will probably occur 2 to 4 days after stopping therapy. This initial withdrawal bleeding should be followed with three cycles of therapy using a low-dose combined contraceptive pill. The 3 months of therapy will restore the endometrium to its normal height. Each patient should subsequently be followed closely to document normal ovulatory cycles.

HIRSUTISM

Excessive growth of body hair in women is called hirsutism. An abnormal pattern of body hair

TABLE 68-3. HIRSUTISM

1. Ovarian Causes
   a. Idiopathic hirsutism
   b. Polycystic ovarian disease
   c. Ovarian tumors secreting excess androgens
2. Adrenal Disorders
   a. Congenital adrenal hyperplasia
   b. Virilizing adrenal tumors
3. Medications
   a. Minoxidil, phenytoin, diazoxide
   b. Androgens, glucocorticoids

growth, such as terminal hair on the abdomen, shoulders, back, and face, may be a sign of disease. In the majority of patients, however, no underlying disease can be found. Hirsutism is predominantly an androgen-dependent process, except when associated with specific drugs (phenytoin, steroids, minoxidil), malnutrition (anorexia nervosa), or rare genetic disorders. Because androgens in women are secreted only by the ovaries or adrenal glands, a disorder of one or the other must be the source of any excess androgens (Table 68-3). Thus, excessive secretion of testosterone or of its immediate precursors androstenedione and dehydroepiandrosterone, which are subsequently converted to testosterone in peripheral tissues, can cause abnormal terminal hair growth.

Clinical hirsutism may be associated with acne, temporal balding, increased muscle strength, altered libido, and, in virilized patients, clitoral enlargement and deepening of the voice. There may be general defeminization, with amenorrhea, decrease in breast size, and an alteration in the female body habitus. However, the two most common causes of hirsutism, idiopathic hirsutism (normal serum androgen levels) and polycystic ovarian disease, are rarely associated with virilization or deepening of the voice. The hair growth is generally first noted in the peripubertal period and tends to stabilize after progressing for a few years. Adrenal and ovarian tumors generally manifest in adults. Overt virilization occurs with most of the androgen-secreting ovarian tumors but rarely consequent to the weak androgens secreted by adrenal tumors. CAH, usually clinically apparent at birth or during childhood, is characterized by rapid growth, heterosexual precocious puberty in girls, and occasionally hypertension. However, it may not become apparent until later life in a small percentage of patients.

The cause of most cases of hirsutism can be determined by measuring serum total testosterone, dehydroepiandrosterone sulfate (DHEA sulfate), and 17-OH progesterone (17-OHP). Increased levels of plasma testosterone (values in excess of 200 ng/dl) are rarely associated with idiopathic hirsutism or polycystic ovarian syndrome but are frequently present in patients with ovarian tumors. Adrenal lesions (CAH) are accompanied by high 17-OHP plasma levels. Ovarian and adrenal tumors are treated surgically. CAH is suppressed with glucocorticoid replacement. Hirsutism associated with idiopathic hirsutism and polycystic ovarian disease is generally stable and rarely progresses to virilization. Thus, the abnormal hair growth is primarily a cosmetic and psychological problem. Suppressive therapy is appropriate, with oral contraceptives, glucocorticoids, or antiandrogens (spironolactone). Combination therapy with oral contraceptives and spironolactone can be very successful, providing contraception while controlling dysfunctional uterine bleeding, hirsutism, and acne.

GALACTORRHEA

Nonpuerperal lactation (galactorrhea) is of benign significance in about 30 per cent of patients. This type of galactorrhea is termed idiopathic and is associated with regular menses. If associated with amenorrhea, however, galactorrhea often indicates the presence of a serious condition, such as a pituitary tumor (30 per cent). Table 68–4 outlines the relative frequency of disorders causing galactorrhea. The measurement of basal serum prolactin is very helpful in the evaluation of a patient with galactorrhea. The serum prolactin level is normal in the majority (85 per cent) of patients with idiopathic galactorrhea associated with continued menstruation. A normal prolactin level generally indicates a benign disorder. Hyperprolactinemia is present in most (70 per cent) patients having galactorrhea associated with amenorrhea. This is the most common presentation of a prolactin-secreting pituitary tumor in women. A patient presenting with a serum prolactin level greater than 300 ng/ml invariably has a prolactinoma. Hyperprolactinemia of lesser magnitude (<300 ng/ml) may be associated with a prolactinoma or, more frequently, with one of a spectrum of other causes (Table 68–4). Galactorrhea in this latter group may be idiopathic (with amenorrhea), postpartum, or postpill or may be associated with endocrine disease (hypothyroidism, acromegaly, Cushing's syndrome) or drug therapy (phenothiazines, benzodiazepines, alpha-methyldopa, or metoclopra-

mide). Rarely, galactorrhea may be due to the empty sella syndrome or hypothalamic disease. The suspected presence of a pituitary tumor can generally be documented by an MRI scan of the sella.

Treatment of galactorrhea depends upon the primary disorder. Hypothyroidism, acromegaly, and Cushing's syndrome can be effectively corrected. Offending drugs should be stopped. Hyperprolactinemia due to a pituitary microadenoma (<10 mm) or idiopathic hyperprolactinemia can be successfully treated with bromocriptine, a dopamine agonist. Macroadenomas also respond successfully to bromocriptine therapy. The high rate of persistent and recurrent hyperprolactinemia after surgery has made bromocriptine the first choice for therapy in both small and large tumors.

INFERTILITY

Infertility can be defined as the involuntary inability to conceive. Sterility is the total inability to reproduce. The problem may or may not be correctable for each particular couple. About 10 per cent of couples seek medical evaluation for infertility. In approximately 40 per cent of cases, infertility is attributable to the man. This may be due to decreased production of spermatozoa, ductal obstruction, or inability to deliver sperm to the vagina. Female infertility can be secondary to fallopian tube pathology, endometriosis, amenorrhea (anovulation), cervical or uterine disorders, systemic disorders, and immunologic disorders. Infertility remains idiopathic in about 10 per cent of couples. Assessment involves a detailed history and physical examination of both subjects. Separate interviews may reveal significant information. Evaluation includes (1) semen analysis; (2) documentation of ovulation by basal body temperature records, timed serum progesterone determination, or endometrial biopsy; and (3) hysterosalpingography. Basal levels of prolactin and thyroid hormones should be measured. If all the tests are normal, laparoscopy with tubal dye instillation should be performed, as endometriosis or tubal disease is common (30 to 50 per cent). Treatment is determined by the findings on the infertility evaluation.

MENOPAUSE

The menopause represents the cessation of ovarian function. The mean age of spontaneous menopause is currently 50 years, although generally a transitional phase of ovarian failure takes place over 6 to 18 months during the perimenopausal period. Pituitary gonadotropins are secreted excessively as progressive ovarian (follicular) failure reduces estrogen secretion. Measurement of serum FSH is the single best test to detect ovarian failure (FSH > 50 mIU/ml). FSH values higher than 20 mIU/ml can be present for a few years prior to the last menses. This perimenopausal period is

TABLE 68–4. GALACTORRHEA

CAUSES	FREQUENCY
Idiopathic with menses	32%
Idiopathic with amenorrhea	9%
Pituitary tumor	18%
Postpartum or postabortion	8%
Postpill or pill-related	10%
Drugs (phenothiazines, etc.)	8%
Hypothyroidism	4%
Empty sella syndrome	2%
Miscellaneous	9%
	100%

associated with a marked decrease in fertility. The majority (85 per cent) of women experience some feature of estrogen deficiency at menopause. Breasts atrophy, thermoregulatory dysfunction begins (hot flushes, sweats), the vaginal epithelium thins, vaginal and cervical secretions decline (dyspareunia may be experienced), the endometrium atrophies, and osteoporotic changes in bone accelerate (see Chapter 76).

Estrogen replacement usually controls hot flushes. The generally effective dose of conjugated estrogens (Premarin) ranges from 0.625 to 1.25 mg/day. These preparations can be administered daily. This approach, when combined with a progestin (Provera, 10 mg orally daily, for 12 to 14 days per month), eliminates the increased risk of uterine cancer associated with estrogen-only therapy. Local estrogen creams may be used to treat vaginal atrophy and the frequently associated dyspareunia. Vaginally administered estrogens are readily absorbed into the systemic circulation. Long-term estrogen use at low doses retards the accelerated bone loss associated with menopause and prevents the related fractures (see Chapter 76). Estrogen therapy decreases the risk of cardio-

vascular disease. Preventing cardiovascular disease may become the primary indication for estrogen replacement therapy.

Estrogen use is contraindicated in patients with a history of undiagnosed abnormal uterine bleeding, uterine cancer, or breast cancer. The presence of significant diffuse liver disease or benign or malignant liver tumors also prohibits the use of estrogens. Estrogen therapy does not cause hypertension in postmenopausal women. Whether estrogen increases the risk of breast cancer remains unproved and controversial.

REFERENCES

Rebar RW: The ovaries. *In* Wyngaarden JB, Smith LH Jr, Bennett JC (eds): Cecil Textbook of Medicine. 19th ed. Philadelphia, WB Saunders Co, 1992, pp 1355–1375.

Speroff L, Glass RH, Kase NG: Clinical Gynecologic Endocrinology and Infertility. 4th ed. Baltimore, The Williams and Wilkins Co, 1989.

Yen SSC, Jaffe RB (eds): Reproductive Endocrinology. Philadelphia, WB Saunders Co, 1991.

69 CANCER OF THE BREAST, CERVIX, UTERUS, AND OVARY

CANCER OF THE BREAST

Cancer of the breast is the most common malignancy in women in the United States. Approximately 175,000 women developed breast cancer in 1992, and more than 45,000 died of it. The lifetime risk of developing breast cancer is a staggering 11 per cent, or one in nine women. Although two thirds of cases occur after the menopause, 15 per cent occur in women before the age of 40.

Etiology

The etiology of carcinoma of the breast is not known, but a number of risk factors are associated with it (Table 69–1).

Histologic Types

The most prevalent histologic types of breast cancer are infiltrating ductal carcinoma (50 per cent), infiltrating lobular carcinoma (5 to 10 per cent), and intraepithelial ductal carcinoma. The remainder represent various combinations of infiltrating ductal, mucinous, papillary, and lobular carcinomas. Ductal carcinoma is usually unilat-

eral, while lobular carcinoma tends to be bilateral. Most breast cancers are adenocarcinomas, but occasionally medullary carcinoma (6 per cent), mucinous, tubular, or squamous cell carcinoma, sarcomas, and Paget's disease occur.

Screening

Usually women detect their own breast cancers; all adult women should therefore be taught the importance and technique of self-examination of the breast. A breast examination should also be performed every year by a physician. Mammography, an effective routine screening test, is recommended as a baseline in all women age 40. It should be obtained every 1 to 2 years from age 40 to 49 and annually for women over age 50. When a family history of breast cancer or other increased risk factors are present, yearly mammograms should be performed after age 35.

The smallest palpable mass is approximately 1 cm. Routine mammography can detect cancers less than 0.5 cm. The survival rate is significantly improved in women in whom cancer is detected by mammography, as opposed to palpation. The risk of frequent breast radiographs does not out-

TABLE 69–1. RISK FACTORS FOR CANCER OF THE BREAST

Increased Risk Factors
  Increasing age
  Familial history of breast carcinoma
  First- and second-degree relatives with breast cancer (including relatives on the father's side), especially premenopausal cancer
  Premalignant breast lesions (multiple papillomatosis, atypical hyperplasia)
  Previous carcinoma in one breast, especially premenopausal
  Early menstruation (<12 yr)
  Late menopause (>52 yr)
  Nulliparity
  Radiation therapy to the chest
  Family history of carcinoma of the ovary, uterus, or colon
  Obesity (postmenopausal women)
  Resident of North America or Europe
Lower Risk Factors
  Term pregnancy under age 18
  Early menopause
  Castration before age 37
  Asians residing in Asia

weigh the potential benefits of screening, as the radiation dose is approximately one tenth of that used 20 years ago.

Clinical Presentation

The most common presentation of breast cancer is that of a painless, palpable breast mass in a postmenopausal woman. The more common signs and symptoms are listed in Table 69–2.

Diagnosis

It is often difficult to distinguish benign breast masses, such as fibroadenomas, lipomas, inflammatory masses, and cysts, from malignant ones, especially in premenopausal women. Definitive diagnosis requires histologic examination. A fine-needle aspiration (5 per cent false-negative rate), a percutaneous needle biopsy, or an excisional or incisional biopsy is required for diagnosis. Mammography is helpful in examining the remainder of the breast, as well as the opposite breast, but is not universally diagnostic; 10 per cent of cancers may not be detected with this technique. A biopsy should be done on a suspicious mass, even if the

TABLE 69–2. SYMPTOMS AND SIGNS OF BREAST CANCER

Early Disease
  Palpable lump (75%)
  Breast pain
  Nipple discharge, retraction, or ulceration
  Skin dimpling, edema, or erythema
  Mass in the axilla
  Scaling of the nipple
Advanced Disease
  Fixation of the mass to the chest wall
  Edema of the arm
  Ulceration
  Distant metastases to the lung, bone, liver, and brain
  Weight loss (tumor cachexia)
  Hypercalcemia

mammogram is negative. A mammogram may also be used to guide a biopsy when a mass is not palpable. An ultrasound study may detect and diagnose breast cysts and cancer. A chest radiograph is performed to assess the lungs, ribs, and spine for metastases. A bone scan is performed to rule out bone metastases; however, this is usually not necessary with small cancers. An abdominal computed tomography (CT) scan and liver function tests are also obtained to detect liver metastases. Occasionally, a serum carcinoembryonic antigen (CEA) level and/or a CA-15-3 level may be elevated. The presence or absence of estrogen and progesterone receptors in breast tumors should be determined, as this may provide useful information concerning prognosis and subsequent hormone therapy.

Staging and Treatment

The treatment of cancer of the breast is extremely complex and has changed rapidly over the years. Therapy is based on the histologic type, size, and location of the tumor, age of the woman, menopausal status, presence or absence of hormone receptors, preference of the patient, and experience of the physician (Table 69–3). Adjuvant chemotherapy and/or hormone therapy is usually recommended for women with positive axillary nodes. Postmenopausal women with metastatic disease who are hormone receptor–positive are treated with various combinations or sequences of tamoxifen, progestin, and, occasionally, oophorectomy, adrenalectomy, and androgens. For those who are estrogen receptor–negative or who no longer respond to hormonal manipulation, combination chemotherapy is commonly given. Premenopausal women with positive axillary lymph nodes are also treated with adjuvant combination therapy. A number of different chemotherapeutic agents are used in varying dosages and combinations, including cyclophosphamide, doxorubicin, methotrexate, and 5-fluorouracil. Experimental high-dose chemotherapy with granulocyte colony-stimulating factor (G-CSF) or granulocyte-macrophage colony-stimulating factor (GM-CSF) or with bone marrow transplantation is currently being studied.

CARCINOMA OF THE CERVIX

Carcinoma of the cervix accounts for 2.5 per cent of all malignancies of women in the United States. Approximately 15,500 cases are diagnosed each year. In addition, many more women have preinvasive cervical carcinoma, known as cervical intraepithelial neoplasia. Since the advent of cervical and vaginal cytology in the early 1940s, the incidence and mortality from invasive carcinoma of the cervix have been decreasing.

Etiology and Risk Factors

Intraepithelial neoplasia and invasive carcinoma of the cervix are venereal in origin. A genital human papillomavirus (HPV) is either the cause of or a strong cofactor in the development of warts, intraepithelial neoplasia, or invasive carcinoma. Approximately 90 to 95 per cent of squamous cell carcinomas of the cervix contain HPV DNA. Although more than 60 types of HPV infect humans, some are more commonly associated with lower genital tract neoplasia. Types 6 and 11 are believed to have a more benign behavior, while types 16, 18, 31, and 33 result in higher-grade intraepithelial neoplasia and carcinomas. HPV is also thought to be responsible for adenocarcinoma of the cervix, as well as intraepithelial and invasive squamous cell carcinoma of the vagina and the vulva. Other risk factors are listed in Table 69–4.

Classification

Ninety per cent of all cervical carcinomas are squamous cell. Approximately 5 to 9 per cent are adenocarcinomas, of which the majority are of endocervical cell type. Small cell carcinoma and sarcomas may occur but are rare.

Clinical Presentation

Almost all cases of intraepithelial neoplasia and many cases of early invasive cervical cancer are asymptomatic and are detected by a Papanicolaou (Pap) smear. Abnormal vaginal bleeding, vaginal discharge, bleeding after intercourse, and pelvic pain may result from an invasive malignancy. Advanced disease due to local extension or metastases is associated with severe chronic pelvic, low back, or leg pain; leg edema; a chronic cough; or weight loss.

Diagnosis

All women with an abnormal Pap smear or a suspicious cervical lesion should undergo a colposcopy-directed biopsy of the cervix. A cervical conization is required when colposcopy is unable to determine whether or not the lesion is intraepithelial. A careful pelvic and rectal examination to detect local extension is important for clinical staging. Liver function tests, a serum creatinine level, a serum squamous cell carcinoma antigen level, and a CEA level may also be useful. Squamous cell carcinoma antigen is elevated in 50 per cent of women with invasive squamous cell caracinoma of the cervix, while CEA is elevated in approximately 10 to 20 per cent. A chest radiograph and a magnetic resonance imaging (MRI) scan of the pelvis and abdomen are usually obtained. Cystoscopy and sigmoidoscopy are important in women with advanced disease.

Staging, Treatment, and Prognosis

These data are presented in Table 69–5.

Follow-up

A Pap smear and a careful physical examination should be done every 3 months for the first 2 years, and then every 6 months from years 3 to 5. Routine radiographic studies are not warranted in the absence of symptoms. Elevated levels of CEA or squamous cell carcinoma antigen can be fol-

TABLE 69–3. STAGING, TREATMENT, AND PROGNOSIS OF BREAST CANCER

Stage 0 (in situ carcinoma): 5-yr survival, over 95%
  a. Intraductal carcinoma in situ:
    Wide local excision, excisional biopsy with radiation therapy, or total mastectomy (with or without axillary node dissection)
  b. Lobular carcinoma in situ (commonly occurs bilaterally):
    No further treatment, unilateral or bilateral total mastectomy with or without low axillary lymph node dissection, or "lumpectomy" with radiation therapy

Stage I: Primary tumor less than 2 cm, negative axillary lymph nodes, and no distant metastases; 5-yr survival, 85%
  "Lumpectomy" or quadrantectomy, or modified radical or total mastectomy with axillary lymph node dissection

Stage IIA: Primary tumor less than 2 cm and positive axillary nodes, or primary lesion between 2 and 5 cm in diameter with negative nodes; 5-yr survival, 75%

Stage IIB: Tumor between 2 and 5 cm in diameter with positive nodes or a tumor greater than 5 cm with negative nodes; 5-yr survival, 65%
  Modified radical mastectomy and axillary node dissection, or "lumpectomy" with axillary node dissection and postoperative radiation therapy

Stage IIIA: Primary tumor greater than 5 cm with ipsilateral axillary node involvement or fixed lymph nodes; 5-yr survival, 50%
  Surgery, radiation, chemotherapy, hormone therapy in varying sequences

Stage IIIB: Internal mammary lymph nodes are involved; tumor extends to the chest wall and ulcerates the skin; 5-yr survival, 41%
  Surgery, radiation, chemotherapy, hormone therapy in varying sequences

Stage IV: Distant metastases; 5-yr survival, 10%
  Surgery, radiation, chemotherapy, hormone therapy in varying sequences

lowed serially in women with these laboratory abnormalities.

Symptoms of recurrent cervical cancer include vaginal bleeding or discharge; pelvic, back, or leg pain; leg edema; chronic cough; and weight loss. Central pelvic recurrences can be treated with radiation therapy if not given previously, or with pelvic exenteration if indicated. Distant metastases are treated with combination chemotherapy.

CANCER OF THE UTERUS

Endometrial carcinoma is the fourth most common cancer of women, accounting for 13 per cent

TABLE 69–4. RISK FACTORS FOR CARCINOMA OF THE CERVIX

Immunosuppression
History of genital warts
History of genital herpes
Multiple sexual partners
Partner with penile warts, dysplasia, or cancer
Low socioeconomic status
Early age at first intercourse
Cigarette smoking
Multiple pregnancies

TABLE 69–5. STAGING, THERAPY, AND PROGNOSIS FOR CARCINOMA OF THE CERVIX

Stage 0
  a. Squamous cell carcinoma in situ: 5-yr survival, 100%
     Cryotherapy, laser vaporization, loop electrocautery, cone biopsy, or hysterectomy
  b. Adenocarcinoma in situ: 5-yr survival rate, 100%
     Conization for diagnosis (may be curative); hysterectomy

Stage IA1: Cancer involves the cervix with only minimal microscopic invasion; 5-yr survival, 100%
  Cone biopsy; hysterectomy

Stage IA2: Cervical stromal invasion less than 5 mm and less than 7 mm wide; 5-yr survival, 100%
  Depth of invasion less than 3 mm and no vascular space involvement—cone biopsy, abdominal hysterectomy; invasion greater than 3 mm or vascular space involvement is treated like Stage IB cancer

Stage IB: Cancer greater than Stage IA2 confined to the cervix; 5-yr survival, 80–90%
  Radical abdominal hysterectomy with bilateral pelvic lymphadenectomy, or whole-pelvis external beam radiation therapy and intracavitary cesium

Stage IIA: Carcinoma extends into the vagina, but not the lower third; 5-yr survival rate, 75–80%
  Radical abdominal hysterectomy or bilateral pelvic lymphadenectomy, or whole-pelvis external beam radiation therapy and intracavitary cesium

Stage IIB: Parametrial involvement but not to the pelvic side wall; 5-yr survival rate, 66–80%
  Whole-pelvis external beam radiation therapy followed by two intracavitary cesium insertions

Stage IIIA: Disease involving the lower third of the vagina; 5-yr survival rate, 50–60%
  Whole-pelvis external beam radiation therapy followed by two intracavitary cesium insertions

Stage IIIB: Extension to the pelvic side walls or obstruction of one or both ureters or a nonfunctioning kidney; 5-yr survival rate, 30–40%
  Whole-pelvis external beam radiation therapy followed by two intracavitary cesium insertions or interstitial iridium radiation

Stage IVA: Carcinoma involves the bladder or rectal mucosa; 5-yr survival rate, 20–30%
  Whole-pelvis external radiation therapy followed by two intracavitary cesium insertions or interstitial iridium radiation, or pelvic exenteration

Stage IVB: Distant metastases
  Palliation with radiation therapy to relieve symptoms and/or combination chemotherapy, including various doses and combinations of cisplatin, etoposide, bleomycin, mitomycin-C, 5-fluorouracil, carboplatin, and ifosfamide

of all malignancies. Approximately 34,000 cases of endometrial carcinoma are diagnosed each year in the United States. The incidence of this tumor has decreased each year since 1975, however, and the death rate has declined since 1950. Since this cancer is usually diagnosed at an early stage, the cure rate is excellent, with an overall 5-year survival of 83 per cent.

Risk Factors

Uterine cancer and its precursor, endometrial hyperplasia, occur most commonly in postmenopausal women. Women who undergo menopause after the age of 52 are 2.5 times more likely to develop uterine cancer. Obesity greater than 50 pounds over ideal body weight increases the risk 10-fold, and previous pelvic radiation therapy (usually for cervical carcinoma) increases the risk 8-fold. Women who are on unopposed estrogen replacement therapy have a 7-fold increased risk of developing uterine cancer. On the other hand, oral contraception that includes progestins decreases the risk of developing endometrial cancer. Women who do not ovulate, secondary to polycystic ovaries, or who have not had children have a slightly increased risk, as do women with hypertension or diabetes.

Classification

Adenocarcinoma accounts for 70 per cent of all endometrial carcinomas. Adenoacanthoma (adenocarcinomas associated with benign squamous metaplasia) accounts for approximately 15 per cent of cases. Adenosquamous carcinoma, papillary adenocarcinoma, and uterine sarcoma also occur.

Clinical Presentation

More than 90 per cent of women who have uterine cancer have a history of abnormal uterine bleeding. Postmenopausal bleeding, even if only staining or spotting, should be evaluated promptly. Advanced cases are associated with pelvic, back, and leg pain; increased frequency of urination; and weight loss. Advanced endometrial carcinoma can also manifest with symptoms similar to those of ovarian carcinoma, as it may spread within the abdominal cavity. Approximately 5 per cent of women with cancer of the uterus are asymptomatic.

Diagnosis

A careful pelvic and abdominal evaluation, as well as an examination of groin and supraclavicular nodes, should be performed. All women with abnormal uterine bleeding should undergo an office endometrial biopsy or a dilation and curettage. A Pap smear is only occasionally diagnostic. A significant number of women with endometrial adenocarcinoma have an elevated serum CA-125.

Staging

Cancer of the uterus is surgically staged. Between 70 and 80 per cent of all endometrial cancers are stage I. The grade of the malignancy (well-differentiated, moderately differentiated, and poorly differentiated) is also part of the staging system (Table 69–6).

Treatment

Standard therapy for uterine cancer is an abdominal hysterectomy, bilateral salpingo-oophorectomy, cytologic examination of the peritoneal fluid, and selective pelvic and aortic lymph node sampling. Most gynecologic oncologists measure estrogen and progesterone receptors from the tumor to guide subsequent hormone therapy if the tumor should recur. Postoperative pelvic radiation therapy is usually given to those with an increased risk of recurrent disease, such as a higher-grade lesion or a deeply invasive cancer. Progestational agents, such as megestrol acetate, or combination chemotherapy is given to women with advanced disease. Active drugs include cisplatin, carboplatin, doxorubicin, cyclophosphamide, mitoxantrone, and ifosfamide.

Follow-up and Recurrent Disease

A careful pelvic examination and Pap smear should be performed every 3 months for the first 2 years after treatment. Other diagnostic studies should be performed only in the presence of signs or symptoms. Recurrences confined to the central pelvis are managed with a pelvic exenteration, with reported 5-year survival rates of 40 to 50 per cent. Recurrent cancer of the uterus outside the central pelvis is usually treated with hormone therapy or combination chemotherapy.

OVARIAN CARCINOMA

Carcinoma of the ovary is the eighth most common malignancy in women. Approximately 1 in every 70 women develops cancer of the ovary and 1 in 100 dies of it. Approximately 21,000 cases of ovarian cancer are diagnosed in the United States each year, resulting in approximately 12,500 deaths.

Risk Factors

The incidence of epithelial carcinoma of the ovary is increased slightly in nulliparous women and in those who have a late menopause, a history of pelvic radiation therapy, or a high-fat diet. Women who live in industrialized countries are at higher risk, whereas the use of oral contraceptives appears to decrease the risk of developing ovarian cancer. In some families there is a hereditary predisposition.

Histologic Classification

Eighty-five per cent of malignant ovarian tumors are epithelial in origin; in decreasing frequency, these are serous, mucinous, endometrioid, clear cell, and undifferentiated carcinoma. Clear cell carcinoma and undifferentiated carcinoma have poorer prognoses than do the other epithelial cell types. Epithelial cancers are also graded—well-differentiated, intermediately differentiated, or poorly differentiated tumors. Approximately 40 per cent are tumors of low malignant potential or borderline tumors; these grow extremely slowly with an excellent prognosis. Approximately 10 per cent of the cancers are germ cell tumors and occur in premenopausal women. Approximately 5 per cent of cancers arise from the gonadal stroma.

Clinical Presentation

Unfortunately, two thirds of all women with ovarian carcinoma have advanced disease at the time of diagnosis. The diagnosis is frequently delayed because early symptoms tend to be nonspecific—vague abdominal pain or fullness, indigestion, bloating, early satiety, or altered bowel habits. Advanced carcinoma often manifests with ascites or intestinal obstruction. Occasionally, women with early-stage disease are asymptomatic and are found to have an adnexal or pelvic mass on a routine physical examination. Gonadal stromal tumors can secrete estrogen or testosterone, which may result in abnormal uterine bleeding, precocious puberty, or virilization. Ovarian carcinoma may also be associated with a variety of other medical manifestations, including neuropathy, hypercalcemia, hyperglycemia, Cushing's syndrome, or thyrotoxicosis.

Screening, Diagnosis, and Staging

The utility of an abdominal or vaginal ultrasound examination and measurement of the serum CA-125 level for routine screening is currently being studied, especially for those women at increased risk of developing ovarian carcinoma. A palpable ovary in a postmenopausal woman may suggest ovarian cancer, since normal ovaries often cannot be palpated. The pelvis, abdomen, chest, and peripheral lymph nodes should be carefully examined. Preoperative studies should include measurement of the serum CA-125, liver function tests, a chest radiograph, abdominal CT scan or MRI, and, if symptoms warrant, an upper gastrointestinal series, barium enema, or sigmoidoscopy. Cancer of the ovary is surgically staged (Table 69–7).

Therapy

The mainstay of therapy is surgical resection, including a total abdominal hysterectomy, bilat-

TABLE 69–6. STAGING OF UTERINE CANCER

	STAGE	5-YR SURVIVAL (%)
Stage IA	Cancer confined to the endometrium	95
Stage IB	Tumor invades the myometrium, but less than 50%	80
Stage IC	Tumor invades the uterine wall by more than half its thickness	70
Stage IIA	Endocervical gland involvement	65
Stage IIB	The cancer involves the cervical stroma	60
Stage IIIA	Involvement of the surface of the uterus and/or fallopian tubes and/or positive peritoneal cytology	Up to 30
Stage IIIB	Vaginal metastasis	30
Stage IIIC	Metastasis to the pelvic and/or periaortic lymph nodes	30
Stage IVA	The tumor involves the bladder or rectal mucosa	10
Stage IVB	Distant metastases, intra-abdominal spread, or groin node metastases	5

TABLE 69 – 7. STAGING OF OVARIAN CANCER

Stage IA	Cancer is confined to the ovary; there is no ascites or tumor on the ovarian surface, and the capsule is unruptured
Stage IB	Cancer is confined to both ovaries; there is no ascites or tumor on the ovarian surface, and the capsule is unruptured
Stage IC	The cancer is either stage IA or IB, and there is tumor on the ovarian surface, the capsule has ruptured, there is ascites, or the peritoneal cytology is positive; 5-yr survival rate, 60–100%
Stage IIA	Cancer extends to the uterus and/or fallopian tubes
Stage IIB	Cancer extends to the other pelvic organs
Stage IIC	The cancer is either stage IIA or IIB, and there is tumor on the surface of one or both ovaries, the tumor has ruptured, there is ascites, or the peritoneal cytology is positive; 5-yr survival rate, 50–60%
Stage IIIA	The tumor is grossly limited to the pelvis with microscopic cancer on the abdominal tumor implants; the pelvic and periaortic nodes are histologically negative
Stage IIIB	The tumor involves one or both ovaries, and there are tumor implants on the abdominal peritoneal surfaces less than 2 cm in diameter; the pelvic and periaortic lymph nodes are negative
Stage IIIC	The tumor involves one or both ovaries, and there are tumor implants on the abdominal peritoneal surfaces greater than 2 cm in diameter, or there are positive pelvic, periaortic or groin lymph nodes; 5-yr survival rate, 20–40%
Stage IV	There are metastases to the liver or lung parenchyma, or there is a pleural effusion with cytologically positive fluid; 5-yr survival rate, 10%

eral salpingo-oophorectomy, omentectomy, and selective pelvic and periaortic lymph node sampling. Unilateral salpingo-oophorectomy may suffice in premenopausal women with either a low-grade malignancy or a germ cell tumor. For women with advanced disease, aggressive surgical debulking is performed in an attempt to remove as much diseased tissue as possible. Combination multiagent chemotherapy is given postoperatively. Drugs active in ovarian carcinoma include cisplatin, carboplatin, cyclophosphamide, doxorubicin, etoposide, ifosfamide, hexamethylmelamine, melphalan, and 5-fluorouracil (5-FU). Open-field whole-abdomen radiation therapy or intra-abdominal radioactive phosphorus (^{32}P) may be used in early-stage disease or in women with minimal residual disease after surgery. Intraperitoneal chemotherapy is sometimes effective in carcinoma of the ovary.

REFERENCES

Harris JR, Lippman ME, Veronesi U, Willett W: Medical progress: Breast cancer. N Engl J Med 327:319, 390, 473, 1992.

Holloway RW, To A, Moradi M, Boots L, Watson N, Shingleton HM: Monitoring the course of cervical carcinoma with the serum squamous cell carcinoma serum radioimmunoassay. Obstet Gynecol 74:944, 1989.

Jones HW III: Ovarian carcinoma. In Wyngaarden JB, Smith LH Jr, Bennett JC (eds): Cecil Textbook of Medicine. 19th ed. Philadelphia, WB Saunders Co, 1992, pp 1395–1397.

Lewis BJ: Breast carcinoma. In Wyngaarden JB, Smith LH Jr, Bennett JC (eds): Cecil Textbook of Medicine. 19th ed. Philadelphia, WB Saunders Co, 1992, pp 1381–1386.

Lippman ME, Lichter AS, Danforth DN Jr (eds): Diagnosis and Management of Breast Cancer. Philadelphia, WB Saunders Co, 1988.

Van Nagell JR Jr, Higgins RV, Donaldson ES, Gallion HH, Powell DE, Pavlik EJ, Woods CH, Thompson EA: Transvaginal sonography as a screening method for ovarian cancer. A report of the first 1,000 cases screened. Cancer 65:573, 1990.

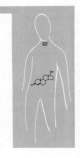

70 TESTICULAR AND BREAST DISORDERS IN MALES

Hypogonadism can refer to either (1) the failure of the testes to produce adequate testosterone, resulting in the signs and symptoms of androgen deficiency, or (2) impaired spermatogenesis, resulting in infertility. Impaired spermatogenesis and infertility may be present with normal testosterone production, but testosterone production is necessary for normal spermatogenesis. Normal adult males produce approximately 7 mg of testosterone per day, and normal serum plasma concentrations are 3 to 10 ng/ml. Testosterone production is dependent on an intact hypothalamus, pituitary gland, and Leydig cells in the testis (Fig. 70–1). Spermatogenesis requires both intact pituitary and Leydig cell function. The 5α-reduced derivative of testosterone, 5α-dihydrotestosterone, is an active form of the hormone and is responsible for inducing growth and differentiation of the male secondary sex structures.

The causes of hypogonadism can be divided into two major categories (Table 70–1):

1. *Primary hypogonadism* is due to testicular disorders and is associated with elevated serum gonadotropin levels as a result of a diminished negative feedback.

2. *Secondary hypogonadism* results from hypothalamic pituitary disease and is associated with low or low-normal serum gonadotropin levels. In primary hypogonadism when testosterone levels are low, serum luteinizing hormone (LH) levels are increased, and when spermatogenesis is impaired, serum follicle-stimulating hormone (FSH) levels are elevated.

ANDROGEN DEFICIENCY

The signs and symptoms of androgen deficiency depend upon the age of onset and the severity of the deficiency. If androgen deficiency occurs prior to puberty, the usual changes associated with puberty do not occur and the patient will develop the features of eunuchoidism (Table 70–2). Disproportionate growth of long bones occurs owing to the delay in epiphyseal closure. If testosterone secretion fails after sexual maturity, the signs of androgen deficiency are much less overt (Table 70–2). The most common symptoms and signs are a reduction in prostate size, decreased rate of growth of beard and body hair, the appearance of fine wrinkles around the eyes, decreased semen volume, decreased libido, and impotence. Occasionally, libido and potency persist despite androgen deficiency.

When androgen deficiency is suspected, serum testosterone levels should be measured. If the serum testosterone concentration is low, serum LH and FSH levels should be determined next. Elevated LH and FSH concentrations indicate primary hypogonadism, whereas low or normal LH and FSH levels are most consistent with secondary hypogonadism.

Androgen deficiency, regardless of etiology, is treated by administering testosterone. Testosterone may be given orally, sublingually, buccally, or intramuscularly via injections. In general, androgen replacement is most effective when long-acting testosterone preparations are administered intramuscularly. Undesirable effects of androgen replacement include edema secondary to sodium retention, erythremia, acne, gynecomastia, and premature closure of the epiphyses (if given dur-

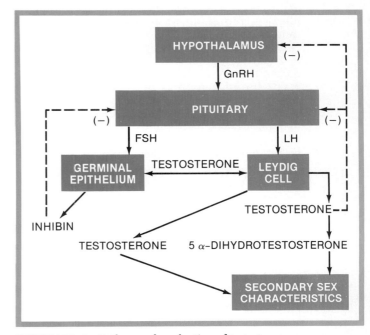

FIGURE 70–1. Pathway of production of testosterone.

TABLE 70–1. CLASSIFICATION OF THE CAUSES OF ABNORMALITIES IN TESTICULAR FUNCTION

	ANDROGEN DEFICIENCY AND INFERTILITY	INFERTILITY ONLY
Primary Hypogonadism		
1. Developmental and genetic disorders	Klinefelter's syndrome Noonan's syndrome	Sertoli cell only syndrome Kartagener's syndrome Cryptorchidism
2. Structural defects	Anorchia	Varicocele
3. Acquired defects	Viral or bacterial orchitis Trauma Radiation Polyendocrine autoimmune failure Granulomatous disease Drugs—spironolactone, alcohol, marijuana, ketoconazole Ischemia (torsion)	Radiation Drugs—alkylating agents and antimetabolites
4. Associated with systemic disease	Liver disease Renal disease Sickle cell disease	Myotonic dystrophy Paraplegia Febrile illness
Secondary Hypogonadism	Panhypopituitarism Hyperprolactinemia Kallmann's syndrome Malnutrition Cushing's syndrome Hemochromatosis Massive obesity	Isolated FSH deficiency Congenital adrenal hyperplasia Exogenous sex steroid use
Other	Androgen resistance	Absence or obstruction of the vas deferens (cystic fibrosis)

FSH = Follicle-stimulating hormone.

ing or before puberty). Testosterone therapy has also been reported to cause obstructive sleep apnea. Methyltestosterone and other oral androgens occasionally cause intrahepatic cholestatic jaundice. The most serious complication of oral androgens is hepatoma or peliosis hepatis (blood-filled cysts in the liver). Androgen therapy is contraindicated in patients with prostatic carcinoma and on occasion can precipitate urinary retention secondary to prostatic hypertrophy. Exogenous androgen therapy will not restore fertility.

The use of androgens by male athletes in the belief that performance will be improved is widespread. Currently there is no objective evidence that androgens enhance athletic performance even when given in very high doses. Excessive doses of testosterone do increase lean body mass and de-crease body fat, reflecting its powerful anabolic action. Impaired spermatogenesis and hepatotoxicity (including hepatoma) have been described in athletes abusing androgenic steroids. In women, androgens do have a positive effect on nitrogen retention, but there are distressing virilizing side effects. Because of the potential of toxicity, the use of androgens has been barred by most athletic organizations.

INFERTILITY

About 15 per cent of married couples have fertility problems, and in 30 to 40 per cent of these cases the male is the major cause of the infertility. The initial diagnostic procedure in evaluating a male for the many possible causes of infertility is a semen analysis. The test is considered abnormal if (1) the total sperm count is less than 60 million, (2) fewer than 60 per cent of the sperm are actively motile, or (3) more than 60 per cent of the sperm have an abnormal morphology. There is considerable variability in the sperm count for a given individual, so several counts over a period of time should be done if the count is borderline. Abnormalities in semen do not preclude fertility; many men with low sperm counts have fathered children. Fertility in the male is dependent on his female partner's fertility; that is, a male with a relatively low sperm count may father a child with a partner of relatively high fertility.

TABLE 70–2. CLINICAL FEATURES OF EUNUCHOIDISM AND HYPOGONADISM

Eunuchoidism
Increased height and an arm span more than 2 inches greater than height
Lack of adult hair distribution
High-pitched voice
Small penis, testes, and scrotum
Decreased muscle mass

Hypogonadism Beginning After Puberty
Decreased prostate size
Diminished rate of growth of beard and body hair
Fine wrinkles around eyes
Decreased potency and libido

If the semen analysis is abnormal, serum testosterone and FSH levels should be measured next. If a patient has azoospermia with a normal testosterone and FSH level, an obstructive disorder is a likely diagnostic possibility. Normal testosterone levels and elevated FSH concentrations indicate a primary testicular disorder of spermatogenesis as the basis for the infertility.

PRIMARY HYPOGONADISM

Klinefelter's Syndrome. Klinefelter's syndrome and its variants are important causes of male infertility and occur in approximately 1 in 500 newborn males. This syndrome is characterized by more than one X chromosome, most commonly a 47XXY karyotype, but occasionally 48XXYY, 48XXXY, or 49XXXXY karyotype has been described.

The classic features of this disorder are small, firm testes (usually less than 2 cm in length), azoospermia, gynecomastia, decreased signs of androgenicity, and elevated gonadotropin levels. Patients with this disorder are often tall, but the span-to-height ratio is frequently less than 1, suggesting that the increased height is not simply due to eunuchoidism. In some patients a mild degree of mental retardation is present, and poor social adaptation is not uncommon. Chronic pulmonary disease and varicose veins have been described as being more common in patients with Klinefelter's syndrome.

The manifestations of Klinefelter's syndrome may vary and may be minimal in some patients. Sex chromosome mosaicism, in which at least two populations of cells have different chromosomal complexes (e.g., XY in one cell type and XXY in another), perhaps accounts for this remarkable variability in severity. In fact, fertility has been documented in rare individuals with this disorder.

Serum testosterone levels in patients with Klinefelter's syndrome vary from very low to low-normal. FSH levels are invariably elevated, but LH levels may be within the normal range, especially in those individuals with adequate testosterone levels. Buccal smears frequently detect the condensed X chromosome (Barr bodies), but karyotyping of various cell types is the most definitive diagnostic procedure.

The treatment of this disorder is by testosterone replacement if there is evidence of androgen deficiency.

Myotonic Muscular Dystrophy. This syndrome is characterized by muscle wasting, myotonia, frontal baldness, cataracts, diabetes, and testicular atrophy, which occurs in the third to fourth decade. Androgen deficiency and gynecomastia occur in only a small percentage of these patients.

Sertoli Cell Only Syndrome (Germ Cell Aplasia). This syndrome is characterized by fully developed secondary sex characteristics and azoospermia. FSH levels are increased, and testosterone and LH levels are within the normal range. Testicular biopsy reveals seminiferous tubules that do not contain germinal cells and are lined only with Sertoli cells.

Kartagener's Syndrome. This genetic syndrome includes situs inversus, chronic sinusitis, bronchiectasis, and infertility secondary to nonmotile sperm. The immotility of the sperm and the respiratory difficulties are due to the absence of the protein dynein, a constituent of both the tail of the sperm and the cilia of the respiratory tract mucosa.

Anorchia. Absence of both testes in a phenotypically normal male is very rare. It is important to distinguish bilateral abdominal cryptorchidism from anorchia because of the increased incidence of malignancy in cryptorchidism. Low testosterone levels that fail to rise following human chorionic gonadotropin (hCG) stimulation suggest anorchia, but the final diagnosis depends on surgical exploration. Unilateral anorchia is more common and may result from developmental disturbances or following surgical procedures such as orchiopexy or herniorrhaphy.

Acquired Hypogonadism. Numerous chemical and physical factors can affect gonadal function and result in either transient or permanent dysfunction. Germ cells are sensitive to ischemia, and testicular torsion, if not rapidly corrected, can irreversibly damage the testes. In adults, mumps is complicated by orchitis in 15 to 25 per cent of patients, and the affected testes may sustain permanent damage. Mumps orchitis is usually unilateral and typically does not affect testosterone production. Other viruses and bacterial infections can also cause orchitis and result in hypogonadism. Many chemicals and drugs are directly toxic to spermatogenesis or affect the androgen-estrogen ratio and thus may result in oligospermia or azoospermia. Many of the alkylating agents and antimetabolites that are commonly used in cancer chemotherapy adversely affect spermatogenesis. Ionizing radiation primarily inhibits spermatogenesis. Testicular failure occurs rarely as part of the polyendocrine failure syndrome secondary to an autoimmune process. Finally, systemic disorders such as hepatic or renal failure can result in hypogonadism.

SECONDARY HYPOGONADISM

Secondary hypogonadism, due to the decreased secretion of gonadotropins by the pituitary gland, may result from any disorder that adversely affects pituitary or hypothalamic function (see Table 70–1). Gonadotropins may be decreased as an isolated deficiency or in association with deficiency of other pituitary hormones. A functional and reversible suppression of gonadotropin secretion occurs in malnutrition and in disorders that cause hyperprolactinemia. High serum concentrations of either androgens or estrogens can also inhibit gonadotropin secretion. The hypogonadism that occurs in patients with liver disease, for example, is partially due to increased levels of estrogen. Exogenous sex steroid intake by athletes also leads to infertility.

Kallmann's syndrome, a familial disorder characterized by hypogonadotropic hypogonadism, occurs in association with anosmia or hyposmia. The hypogonadism is due to an abnormality in the secretion of gonadotropin-releasing factor by the hypothalamus.

Fertility can occasionally be restored in individuals with secondary hypogonadism by treatment with menotropins (Pergonal) (FSH activity) and hCG (LH activity).

CRYPTORCHIDISM

Cryptorchidism refers to a testis that has never descended into the scrotum. Unilateral cryptorchidism is approximately four times as common as bilateral cryptorchidism. Undescended testes are found at birth in 3 to 4 per cent of male infants, but by 1 year of age only 0.5 per cent have an undescended testis. In adult males, approximately 0.2 to 0.4 per cent have either unilateral or bilateral cryptorchidism.

It is important to distinguish an undescended testis from the more common retractile testes of childhood. Repeated examinations in a warm room with the patient standing, squatting, recum-

TABLE 70–3. CLASSIFICATION OF THE CAUSES OF IMPOTENCE

Psychogenic
Endocrine
  Hypogonadism
  Hyperprolactinemia
Chronic Illness
  Cirrhosis
  Uremia
  Malignancy
  Cardiac disease
Neurologic
  Spinal cord lesions
  Diabetes mellitus
  Tabes dorsalis
  Polyneuropathies
  Parasympathetic nerve damage following surgical procedure such as prostatectomy, aortic bypass, or rectosigmoid operation
  Temporal lobe disorders
Vascular Disease
Drugs
  Antihypertensives—clonidine, methyldopa, propranolol, reserpine, spironolactone, thiazides
  Antihistamines—cimetidine, diphenhydramine
  Antidepressants—doxepin, amitriptyline
  Antipsychotics—chlorpromazine, haloperidol
  Tranquilizers—diazepam, barbiturates, chlordiazepoxide
  Anticholinergics
  Addicting drugs—alcohol, heroin, methadone
Penile Disease
  Priapism
  Peyronie's disease

bent, and performing a Valsalva maneuver are necessary. Careful questioning to determine if the testis has ever been in the scrotum is mandatory. Absence of the testis in the scrotum historically and on repeated physical examination suggests that the testis is truly undescended. Ultrasonography or computed tomography (CT) scans may successfully locate nonpalpable testes.

Adult men with bilateral cryptorchidism are sterile. However, the age at which these testes become infertile is uncertain. Abnormalities in testicular histology have been noted in those as young as 6 years of age, but the significance of these changes is uncertain. After puberty, the undescended testis shows degenerative changes that eventually progress to atrophy. Even when cryptorchid testes are placed in the scrotum, degenerative changes occur in approximately 50 per cent, suggesting that intrinsic abnormalities of the organ account for the failure of normal descent. Even when unilateral cryptorchidism is corrected, many patients have abnormal spermatogenesis, suggesting that the testicular abnormality is bilateral. Thus in many cases the degenerative changes are due to a testicular abnormality that orchiopexy will not correct. The incidence of malignancy in an undescended testis is 30 to 50 times greater than in the normal testis.

Cryptorchidism is treated by orchiopexy, although some clinicians first administer hCG followed by orchiopexy if the testis does not descend. The age at which therapy should be initiated is uncertain, but it certainly should be prior to the onset of puberty. Many experts recommend treatment when the child is between 5 and 7 years of age.

IMPOTENCE

Impotence is a common problem that can occur secondary to a wide variety of causes (Table 70–3). Although impotence that is psychogenic in origin is not uncommon, a specific etiology can frequently be identified. Patients with psychogenic impotence have morning erections and/or erections that are associated with rapid eye movement (REM) sleep, whereas in patients with physiologic impotence, erections at these times are either impaired or absent. The measurement of nocturnal penile tumescence by a variety of different procedures can therefore be helpful in the evaluation of impotent men. A very careful drug history is also indicated in all patients. The physical examination should search thoroughly for the signs of peripheral vascular disease or neuropathies. The measurement of penile blood flow using Doppler techniques may successfully demonstrate penile arterial insufficiency in some patients. On occasion, hyperprolactinemia may be the cause of impotence, and potency may be restored by lowering the prolactin level. If a specific cause of impotence cannot be identified and corrected, a number of potential nonspecific therapies are available. Intracavernosal self-injections of papaverine and/or phentolamine can induce erections and are very effective and well tolerated in selected patients. Vacuum constriction devices can create erections by pulling blood into the penis by generating negative pressure; the erections are then maintained by a constriction band to prevent decongestion. Penile prostheses can also be implanted to correct impotence.

GYNECOMASTIA

Gynecomastia, enlargement of the male breast, may occur unilaterally or bilaterally. Gynecomastia is very commonly observed during the newborn period and puberty and in senescence. For example, approximately 50 per cent of normal boys at puberty and 40 per cent of elderly men have been noted to have gynecomastia. If significant gynecomastia develops between late puberty and male senescence, one should search carefully for an underlying disorder that can account for the breast enlargement (Table 70–4).

Estrogens stimulate and androgens inhibit breast development; therefore, disorders that alter the usual ratio of estrogens to androgens can result in gynecomastia. Increased estrogen production secondary to adrenal carcinoma, testicular tumors, and some types of congenital adrenal hyperplasia will lead to breast development. Similarly, the increased conversion of androgens to estrogens that occurs in liver disease, thyrotoxicosis, obesity, and refeeding after starvation also results in gynecomastia. Conversely, the decreased production of androgens in primary or secondary testicular failure or insensitivity to the cellular effects of testosterone can also result in breast enlargement. Finally, gynecomastia occurs in association with the use of a wide variety of drugs. Estrogen treatment will lead to gynecomastia; androgen administration may also on occasion result in breast development because of the biotransformation of androgens to estrogens. Some drugs, such as hCG, increase endogenous estrogen production, and other drugs such as digitalis or marijuana have an estrogen-like effect. In addition, drugs can block testosterone synthesis (chemotherapeutic agents, high doses of spironolactone) or interfere with the action of testosterone (cyproterone, low doses of spironolactone), resulting in gynecomastia.

It is essential to be sure that "true" gynecomastia is present. The most frequent error is to confuse the fatty breast of the obese patient, which lacks the glandular elements, with gynecomastia. The diagnosis of gynecomastia is based on the palpation of subareolar glandular tissue. Particular attention should be paid to the testes, as either small testes or a testicular mass suggests the likely mechanism for the gynecomastia. In addition, a careful search for signs of liver disease, thyrotoxicosis, other evidence of feminization, and galactorrhea is indicated. Finally, in all patients with gynecomastia, a complete drug history (including illicit drugs) is essential.

Many laboratory studies can be useful in the evaluation of gynecomastia when judiciously se-

TABLE 70–4. CLASSIFICATION OF THE CAUSES OF GYNECOMASTIA

Physiologic—Newborn, Puberty, Senescence
Pathologic
  Increased Estrogen Secretion
    Adrenal carcinoma
    Testicular tumors
    hCG-secreting tumors (lung, liver, etc.)
    Congenital adrenal hyperplasia
    Hermaphroditism
  Increased Conversion of Androgens to Estrogens
    Liver disease
    Adrenal disease
    Nutritional (refeeding after starvation)
    Thyrotoxicosis
  Decreased Androgen Secretion
    Primary hypogonadism
    Secondary hypogonadism
  Androgen Resistance
    Testicular feminization
    Reifenstein's syndrome
Drugs
  Hormones—estrogens, androgens, hCG
  Antihypertensives—reserpine, methyldopa, spironolactone
  Psychotropics—phenothiazine, butyrophenone, marijuana, methadone, heroin, tricyclic antidepressants, diazepam
  Cardiac—digitalis
  Gastrointestinal—cimetidine, metoclopramide
  Cytotoxic—cyclophosphamide, vincristine, mitotane
  Miscellaneous—penicillamine, ketoconazole

hCG = Human chorionic gonadotropin.

lected on the basis of history and physical examination. In the pubertal boy, for example, laboratory studies are not usually indicated. Liver function tests, serum estrogen, testosterone, LH and hCG concentrations, and adrenal androgen levels are sometimes useful in the evaluation of patients with gynecomastia.

Regression or significant improvement in gynecomastia occurs in a substantial number of patients. Gynecomastia usually improves after stopping an offending drug or after correcting a hormonal deficiency or excess. Pubertal gynecomastia spontaneously regresses and drug therapy is not indicated. Long-standing cases of gynecomastia or large breasts will rarely regress entirely after the causal disorder has been corrected. In these instances, cosmetic mastectomy may be very helpful. The risk of breast cancer in men is proportional to the amount of breast tissue present and therefore is increased in patients with substantial gynecomastia.

TUMORS OF THE TESTIS

Tumors of the testis are uncommon (6 per 100,000 males annually), and the peak age of incidence is 20 to 35 years. The most significant risk factor for developing testicular cancer is cryptorchidism. In unilateral cryptorchidism, both the undescended and the normally descended testis have an increased risk of malignancy. Whether orchiopexy reduces the risk of cancer is unresolved.

The vast majority of testicular tumors are malignant (95 per cent) and are derived from germ cells. Germ cell cancers may be subdivided into two groups: seminomas and nonseminomas (embryonal cell carcinoma, choriocarcinoma, and teratoma). The presence of any nonseminomatous element indicates that the tumor should be classified as a nonseminoma.

Patients with germ cell tumors usually present with a painless testicular mass. Pain or a sudden increase in tumor size is usually due to bleeding into the tumor. Other symptoms include back or abdominal pain secondary to retroperitoneal lymphadenopathy, supraclavicular lymphadenopathy, shortness of breath due to pulmonary metastases, gynecomastia, and ureteral obstruction.

Nonseminomatous tumors may secrete biologic markers: alpha-fetoprotein by embryonal cell cancers and hCG by choriocarcinomas or embryonal cell cancers. Increased hCG levels may lead to gynecomastia. Pure seminomas never produce alpha-fetoprotein and only rarely secrete hCG. Both alpha-fetoprotein and hCG levels are useful in monitoring the response to therapy, and increasing levels can be an early indicator of tumor recurrence.

Seminomas usually metastasize via the lymphatics, resulting in retroperitoneal, mediastinal, and supraclavicular lymph node invasion. Seminomas are very sensitive to radiation, and therefore the combination of surgical orchiectomy and radiation therapy has resulted in cure rates of 80 to 95 per cent. Nonseminomatous cancers, which metastasize by both the lymphatic and the hematogenous routes, are radiation-resistant. Multiple drug chemotherapy has resulted in long-term remissions in approximately 40 percent of patients.

Non–germ cell tumors are rare (5 per cent of testicular tumors) and usually benign (90 per cent). They are composed of Leydig and Sertoli cells, which may secrete estrogens or androgens and thereby result in feminization or virilization. Gynecomastia is present in 30 per cent of patients with non–germ cell tumors. In children, non–germ cell tumors may result in precocious puberty.

CARCINOMA OF THE PROSTATE

Prostate cancer is the second most common tumor of men and the third most common cause of cancer deaths. It is rare prior to age 50, but the incidence steadily increases with advancing age.

Prostate cancer may be detected in asymptomatic patients on routine prostate examination, with lesions ranging from small nodules to large masses. Occasionally, the presence of an elevated prostate-specific antigen (PSA) level on routine blood screening can lead to the diagnosis of prostate cancer. Unfortunately, patients with prostate cancer not infrequently present with symptoms caused by widespread disease. Urinary tract obstruction and bone pain and/or fractures due to bony metastases secondary to local spread are common examples. It has not yet been established whether screening for prostate cancer by routinely measuring serum PSA levels and/or using transrectal ultrasonography is warranted.

The diagnosis of prostate cancer is made by biopsy of the prostatic lesion. The treatment of prostate cancer depends on the stage of the tumor. Transrectal ultrasonography and magnetic resonance imaging (MRI) of the prostate are useful in assessing the local extent of the tumor. Elevated levels of serum acid phosphatase indicate metastatic disease. Bone scans detect osseous metastases with high sensitivity. A staging pelvic lymphadenectomy is useful for determining the extent of pelvic lymph node metastases prior to radical prostatectomy. The use of these tests allows for accurate staging and facilitates planning of treatment (Fig. 70–2).

Stage A prostatic carcinomas are those tumors that are discovered incidentally on the histologic examination of tissue removed during surgery for benign prostatic hypertrophy. If these tumors are well differentiated (A1), most patients do well, and

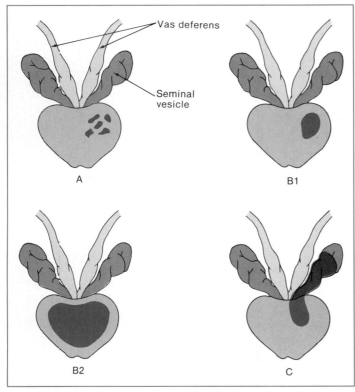

FIGURE 70–2. Whitmore staging classification of prostatic carcinoma. A = Microscopic disease in a clinically benign gland. B1 = Nodule involving less than one posterior lobe. B2 = Nodule involving one entire lobe or both posterior lobes. C = Extension beyond the peripheral capsule of the prostate. D (not pictured) = Metastatic disease. (From Brendler CB: Diseases of the prostate. *In* Wyngaarden JB, Smith LH, Bennett JC [eds]: Cecil Textbook of Medicine. 19th ed. Philadelphia, WB Saunders Co, 1992, p 1354.)

further treatment, other than close observation, is not indicated. Because a small percentage (10 to 20 per cent) of untreated patients with A1 disease develop metastatic disease, it may be advisable to treat healthy men under age 65 aggressively.

Stage A2 tumors are incidentally discovered but are histologically poorly differentiated. Stage B tumors are palpable on rectal examination and confined within the boundaries of the prostate. Patients with stage A2 or B disease are treated with either radical prostatectomy or radiation therapy. Radical prostatectomy in patients with localized tumors results in the cure of the disease, but urinary incontinence and impotence are potential serious complications. Stage C tumors extend beyond the boundaries of the prostate but are confined within the pelvis. Radiation therapy is the treatment of choice.

Stage D tumors are metastatic; hormone therapy is the chief treatment. Hormone ablation can be achieved by castration or by administration of estrogens, which lower the plasma testosterone to levels achieved with castration. Alternatively, androgen ablation can also be accomplished by the administration of luteinizing hormone–releasing hormone (LHRH) analogues (leuprolide acetate) that inhibit testosterone secretion. These ana-

logues can be used either alone or in combination with antiandrogens (e.g., flutamide) that block androgen action on prostatic tissue. Hormone therapy is usually initiated when stage D patients become symptomatic, since early therapy has not been shown to extend life. Chemotherapy for prostatic carcinoma has rarely been successful.

The clinical course of prostate cancer varies greatly. Not infrequently, patients with prostate cancer die as a result of other medical conditions rather than from prostate cancer per se.

REFERENCES

Gittes RF: Medical progress: Carcinoma of the prostate. N Engl J Med 324:236, 1991.
Krane RJ, Goldstein I, Saenz de Tejada I: Impotence. N Engl J Med 321:1648, 1989.
Matsumoto AM: The testis and male sexual function. In Wyngaarden JB, Smith LH Jr, Bennett JC (eds): Cecil Textbook of Medicine. 19th ed. Philadelphia, WB Saunders Co, 1992, pp 1333–1350.
Swerdloff RJ: Infertility in the male. Ann Intern Med 103:906, 1985.

71 DIABETES MELLITUS

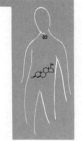

Diabetes mellitus is a very common disorder, with an estimated prevalence between 2 and 4 per cent in the United States. The complications of diabetes account for more than 25 per cent of all new cases of end-stage renal failure and more than 50 per cent of all lower extremity amputations. Diabetes is also the leading cause of blindness, with approximately 5000 new cases per year. In addition, diabetic patients account for 10 per cent of all acute care hospital days.

DIAGNOSIS

A patient is considered to have diabetes mellitus if any of the three criteria shown in Table 71–1 are met. Nearly all patients who are diabetic according to oral glucose tolerance test criteria also have fasting plasma glucose levels greater than 140 mg/dl. Routine screening of patients with glucose tolerance tests is therefore not usually indicated. An oral glucose tolerance test may be indicated in individuals with normal fasting blood glucose

levels if there is a strong suspicion of diabetes, such as the presence of complications possibly secondary to diabetes, an extensive family history

TABLE 71–1. CRITERIA FOR THE DIAGNOSIS OF DIABETES IN NONPREGNANT ADULTS

Any one of the following is considered diagnostic of diabetes:
A. Presence of the classic symptoms of diabetes, such as polyuria, polydipsia, ketonuria, and rapid weight loss, together with gross and unequivocal elevation of plasma glucose levels.
B. Elevated fasting glucose concentration on more than one occasion, venous plasma glucose > 140 mg/dl (7.8 mmol/L).
C. Fasting glucose concentration less than that which is diagnostic of diabetes (B), but sustained elevation of glucose concentration during the oral glucose tolerance test (OGTT)* on more than one occasion. Both the 2-hr sample and some other sample taken between the administration of the oral 75-gm glucose dose and the 2-hr sample must meet the following criteria, venous plasma glucose > 200 mg/dl (11.1 mmol/L).

*OGTT should be performed in the morning after at least 3 days of unrestricted diet (>150 gm carbohydrate) and physical activity. The subject should have fasted at least 10 hr and should remain seated throughout the study.
Adapted with permission from National Diabetes Data Group, Diabetes 28:1049, 1979. Copyright © 1979 by American Diabetes Association.

TABLE 71–2. CLASSIFICATION OF DIABETES

Type I—Insulin-Dependent Diabetes
Type II—Non–Insulin-Dependent Diabetes
Secondary Diabetes
   Pancreatic disease
   Hemochromatosis
   Hormonal
   Drug-induced
   Insulin receptor abnormalities
   Specific genetic syndromes
   Gestational diabetes
Genetic defects of the insulin receptor (rare)

of diabetes, or certain genetic syndromes. In general, the diagnosis of diabetes mellitus should rarely be made in the absence of fasting hyperglycemia.

"Impaired glucose tolerance" exists if the fasting plasma glucose level is less than 140 mg/dl and, during glucose tolerance testing, the 30-, 60-, or 90-minute plasma glucose level exceeds 200 mg/dl, with a 2-hour value between 140 and 200 mg/dl. Most individuals with impaired glucose tolerance do not progress to diabetes, and the specific microvascular complications associated with diabetes occur infrequently. The clinical significance of impaired glucose tolerance is therefore unclear.

CLASSIFICATION OF DIABETES (Tables 71–2 and 71–3)

Type I Insulin-Dependent Diabetes Mellitus (IDDM)

Type I diabetes is characterized by little or no endogenous insulin secretion. Because of the marked hypoinsulinemia, patients with this disorder usually present with the acute complications of diabetes mellitus, such as polyuria, polydipsia, polyphagia, and ketoacidosis. To prevent ketoacidosis and death, these patients require exogenous insulin replacement. After the onset of diabetes,

patients occasionally enter a "honeymoon phase" that may last several weeks or months, during which time endogenous insulin secretion is restored and glucose metabolism may approach normal. Unfortunately, the disease invariably relapses and lifelong insulin therapy is required.

The peak age of onset of IDDM is between 11 and 13 years, coinciding with the onset of puberty, but type I diabetes can begin at any age, including in the elderly. Patients with this disorder usually are of normal weight or thin. Specific human leukocyte antigen (HLA) phenotypes (DR3, DR4) occur at a much greater frequency in patients with IDDM than in the general population. There is less than a 50 per cent concordance rate for diabetes in identical twins with IDDM (i.e., fewer than 50 per cent of identical twins both have diabetes), suggesting the importance of both genetic and environmental factors.

The etiology of IDDM is unknown. A leading hypothesis is that a viral illness or another, yet unspecified initiating event may damage the beta cells of the pancreas, followed by a slow autoimmune destruction of the remaining beta cells in susceptible individuals. Anti–islet cell and anti-insulin antibodies may be detected in individuals several years prior to the onset of diabetes, followed by a slow deterioration in glucose tolerance, which finally results in the abrupt onset of clinical diabetes. Soon after the onset of the disease, antibodies against the islet cells of the pancreas are present in as many as 90 per cent of type I diabetic patients, but they diminish in frequency to 5 to 10 per cent after 20 years. This autoimmune hypothesis also accounts for the increased risk of developing diabetes in individuals with certain HLA genes, because the genes that control the immune response are located on the sixth chromosome close to the HLA loci.

On the basis of the presumed autoimmune origin of IDDM, studies are being carried out on the acute treatment of these patients with immunosuppressive agents. Some initial success in preventing permanent diabetes has been reported, but at the cost of continued immunosuppression. Whether this aggressive early treatment of IDDM is warranted has not been established.

Type II Non–Insulin-Dependent Diabetes Mellitus (NIDDM)

Type II diabetes is much more common than IDDM (approximately 10 cases of type II diabetes for every case of type I) and usually has its onset after age 40. Between 50 and 90 per cent of patients with NIDDM are overweight. Abdominal obesity is more closely associated with NIDDM than is excess adipose tissue localized to the hips and thighs. Some patients are asymptomatic, and an elevated plasma glucose level is noted on routine laboratory study. In other patients, polyuria, polydipsia, weakness, fatigue, or weight loss brings the patient to the attention of the physician. More rarely, patients with NIDDM first seek medical care because of the complications of long-standing diabetes.

TABLE 71–3. COMPARISON OF TYPE I AND TYPE II DIABETES

	TYPE I	TYPE II
Synonym	IDDM	NIDDM
	Juvenile onset	Adult onset
Age of onset	Usually <30	Usually >40
Ketosis	Common	Uncommon
Body weight	Nonobese	Obese (50–90%)
Endogenous insulin secretion	Severe deficiency	Moderate deficiency
Insulin resistance	Occasional	Almost always
HLA association	DR3, DR4	None
Identical twins	<50% concordant	Almost 100% concordant
Islet cell antibodies	Frequent	Absent
Association with other autoimmune disease	Frequent	No
Treatment with insulin	Always necessary	Usually not required

HLA = Human leukocyte antigen.

Plasma insulin levels are relatively decreased in patients with NIDDM but are not as severely reduced as in type I diabetics. In some individuals, plasma insulin levels may be within the normal range or even elevated. Patients with NIDDM almost always secrete decreased amounts of insulin, however, following oral glucose challenge. Because insulin deficiency is not marked, ketoacidosis rarely occurs in NIDDM unless a stressful event, such as a myocardial infarction or infection, is superimposed.

In addition to the abnormalities of insulin secretion, patients with NIDDM are also resistant to the action of insulin. This insulin resistance is due both to a decrease in insulin binding to its plasma membrane receptor and to postreceptor defects in insulin action. Thus, both a decrease in insulin secretion and impaired insulin action contribute to the hyperglycemia observed in NIDDM (Fig. 71–1). At this time, the relative importance of these abnormalities in producing the impaired glucose metabolism is unclear.

Identical twins are almost 100 per cent concordant for NIDDM, suggesting a very strong genetic component to this disorder.

Although this classification is convenient and useful, some patients are difficult to place in a specific category. In addition, patients will, on occasion, progress from a type II form of diabetes to a type I. It is likely that within each category there are multiple subtypes that have not yet been recognized and defined.

Secondary Diabetes

Diabetes secondary to an identifiable condition is comparatively rare. For example, destruction of the pancreas secondary to pancreatitis or of beta cells by excessive iron (hemochromatosis) will impair insulin secretion and result in diabetes. In certain endocrine disorders, such as Cushing's syndrome, acromegaly, pheochromocytoma, and glucagonoma, the increased secretion of hormones that counteract the effect of insulin can also result in hyperglycemia. By a variety of mechanisms, a number of commonly used drugs, such as diuretics, corticosteroids, propranolol, phenytoin, and adrenergic agents, also cause or exacerbate diabetes.

Acanthosis nigricans may be associated with severe insulin resistance, resulting in diabetes by two distinct mechanisms:

1. *Type A.* The insulin resistance is due to a marked decrease in the number of cellular insulin receptors. These patients are usually young females with hirsutism and polycystic ovaries.

2. *Type B.* The insulin resistance is due to autoantibodies against the insulin receptor as part of a more generalized autoimmune process manifested by proteinuria, leukopenia, and antinuclear antibodies.

Genetic Defects of the Insulin Receptor

In several families, diabetes and hyperinsulinemia have been associated with specific abnormali-

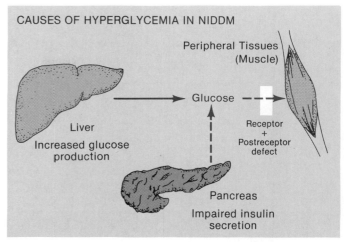

FIGURE 71–1. Summary of the metabolic abnormalities in non-insulin-dependent diabetes mellitus (NIDDM) that contribute to hyperglycemia. Increased hepatic glucose production, impaired insulin secretion, and insulin resistance due to receptor and postreceptor defects all combine to generate the hyperglycemic state. (From Olefsky JM: Diabetes mellitus. *In* Wyngaarden JB, Smith LH Jr, Bennett JC [eds]: Cecil Textbook of Medicine. 19th ed. Philadelphia, WB Saunders Co, 1992, p 1295.)

ties of the insulin receptor on cell membranes. It seems unlikely, however, that this type of genetic defect accounts for more than a very small proportion of patients with glucose intolerance or clinical diabetes.

GENETICS

Diabetes has a strong familial tendency. Genetic factors are clearly important in the development of both type I and type II diabetes, but the mode of inheritance of both disorders is unknown. The direct transmission of clinical diabetes from a single parent with the disorder to offspring is relatively low: only 2 to 5 per cent for IDDM and 10 to 15 per cent for NIDDM. If a nonidentical sibling has either IDDM or NIDDM, the chance of an individual's having diabetes is only approximately 10 per cent. However, in IDDM, if the siblings are identical for HLA phenotypes, the chances of being concordant for diabetes are greatly increased, whereas if all HLA phenotypes are different, the chances of concordance are greatly reduced. Recognizing these low rates of transmission from parent to sibling and the low incidence of concordance between siblings is important in counseling and reassuring patients.

ACUTE SYMPTOMS OF DIABETES

Hyperglycemia can result in a wide variety of symptoms (Table 71–4). When plasma glucose concentration exceeds the renal threshold for glu-

TABLE 71-4. SYMPTOMS OF HYPERGLYCEMIA

TABLE 71-4. SYMPTOMS OF HYPERGLYCEMIA

Polyuria	Fatigue
Polydipsia	*Candida* infections
Polyphagia	Blurred vision
Weight loss	Vulvovaginitis

cose reabsorption (approximately 180 mg/dl), glycosuria occurs and results in an osmotic diuresis. The resulting symptoms of nocturia and polyuria are directly attributed to this osmotic diuresis. The osmotic diuresis tends to lead to dehydration and hyperosmolality, which stimulate thirst and polydipsia. Each gram of urinary glucose represents approximately 4.5 kcal. A poorly controlled diabetic who spills 100 gm of glucose per day in the urine, for example, loses 450 kcal/day, enough to result in weight loss and stimulation of food intake (polyphagia). Thus, the polyuria, polyphagia, polydipsia, and weight loss, which are the cardinal signs of poorly controlled diabetics, are all attributable to increased urinary loss of glucose.

In addition to the above symptoms, transient visual blurring secondary to osmotic swelling of the lens is a common complaint of a poorly controlled diabetic and should not be confused with diabetic retinopathy. *Candida* vaginitis, thrush, or balanitis is occasionally observed and frequently does not respond to appropriate antibiotics until the plasma glucose concentration is lowered and the urine becomes glucose-free. Finally, generalized fatigue is a common complaint in diabetic patients with persistent hyperglycemia.

THERAPY

General Principles

The initial goal of treatment in all diabetic patients is the elimination of the symptoms that occur secondary to hyperglycemia. A second goal of therapy is the prevention of the long-term complications of diabetes. At this time, there is no *definitive* evidence that a reduction in blood glucose levels will prevent the long-term complications of diabetes. Nevertheless, currently there is substantial clinical and experimental evidence that elevated blood glucose levels may be detrimental. It seems worthwhile, therefore, to attempt to normalize blood glucose levels in diabetic patients. Hypoglycemia is a serious and potentially fatal complication of therapy, and therefore the physician must balance the possible benefits of "tight" glucose control with the risks of inducing hypoglycemia.

Factors that predispose to serious hypoglycemia, such as end-stage liver or kidney disease, adrenal or pituitary insufficiency, autonomic insufficiency, ethanol abuse, and psychiatric disturbances, are strong contraindications to "tight" control.

In patients with cerebrovascular disease or coronary artery disease, the potential complications of hypoglycemia are more severe and therefore aggressive therapy should also not be undertaken lightly. The goal of "tight" metabolic control is to prevent complications; if a patient already has severe diabetic complications, there is little evidence to suggest that aggressive therapy will be beneficial. The complications of diabetes usually take 10 to 20 years to develop; and therefore, in a patient whose life expectancy is greatly reduced owing to other medical disorders, "tight" control is not usually indicated. Success in normalizing blood glucose levels requires a patient who is willing and able to undertake the responsibility of extensive self-care.

In a patient who is capable of undertaking the responsibilities of extensive self-care and who has no contraindications to aggressive metabolic control, an attempt should be made to control blood glucose in the range of a fasting plasma glucose concentration between 100 and 140 mg/dl and a 2-hour postprandial plasma glucose level between 100 and 200 mg/dl.

Treatment of Type I Diabetes

By definition, type I diabetics require insulin therapy. Nevertheless, dietary treatment is also an important part of the management of IDDM.

Diet

Dietary therapy for type I diabetics attempts to maintain consistency in the timing and caloric content of meals and to furnish a diet that will diminish the risks of vascular disease. In patients treated with intermediate- or long-acting insulin, the timing of meals must be coordinated with the action of insulin. If meals are delayed or missed or are substantially smaller than usual, the chances of hypoglycemia are increased. Conversely, meals much larger than usual can result in hyperglycemia. Consistency in the timing and caloric content of meals allows an insulin regimen to be tailored to suit the particular patient's lifestyle. If consistency in meal patterns is impossible, the goal of good control will not be achievable using intermediate- or long-acting insulins alone, but may require additional rapid-acting insulin prior to and proportional to the meal.

To diminish the risk of vascular disease, all diabetic patients should be placed on a diet low in saturated fat and cholesterol. This can be accomplished by increasing the quantity of complex carbohydrates and by using a "diabetic" diet of between 25 and 30 per cent lipid, 50 and 60 per cent carbohydrate, and 10 and 20 per cent protein. Diets containing this percentage of carbohydrate are no longer believed to be detrimental to diabetic control. Alternatively, the quantity of monounsaturated fat in the diet can be increased.

The role of dietary fiber in the diabetic diet is unresolved. Large quantities of dietary fiber tend to slow the rate of carbohydrate absorption and lower serum lipid levels. Patients should be encouraged, therefore, to incorporate foods with a high fiber content into their diets.

The effect of simple sugars and complex carbohydrates on blood glucose levels is currently being reevaluated. Simple sugars ingested with meals do not, as previously thought, adversely affect blood glucose levels. All complex carbohydrates cannot be grouped together, because the glycemic response to different starches varies greatly. When incorporated into meals, various complex carbohydrates may also have significantly different effects on blood glucose levels. As a result, definitive recommendations regarding simple and complex carbohydrates must await further data.

Insulin

The various insulins currently in use differ in their time course of action, degree of purity, and source (Table 71-5). The time of the peak effect of insulin and the duration of action of insulin may vary a great deal from patient to patient. Even in a particular patient, the absorption of subcutaneous insulin can vary from site to site and from day to day. For example, exercise of an extremity injected with insulin can increase the speed of insulin absorption and contribute to exercise-induced hypoglycemia. Most insulin-dependent patients require between 20 and 60 units of insulin per day. A requirement of greater than 200 units of insulin per day indicates insulin resistance, which can be due to a variety of factors, including circulating antibodies that bind insulin. Insulin resistance secondary to antibodies, allergic reactions to insulin, and lipodystrophy should be treated with either highly purified pork insulin or human insulin.

Rather than using rigid recipes, it is far better to tailor the insulin regimen for each patient. The degree of glycemic control desired, the time of insulin action, the timing and size of meals, and the preferences of the individual patient are all factors that determine the appropriate insulin regimen.

As one approach, patients of normal weight who have IDDM can be started on a single morning dose of intermediate-acting insulin (approximately 20 to 25 units 30 to 45 minutes before breakfast), with close monitoring of their plasma glucose levels. If glucose values are uniformly elevated, the morning insulin dose can be slowly increased (approximately 5 units every other day) until glucose levels are lowered. In the occasional patient in whom plasma glucose levels measured at 7 a.m., 11 a.m., 4 p.m., and 9 p.m. are all within an acceptable range, this single daily dose of intermediate-acting insulin suffices. More commonly, glucose levels are decreased only for a particular portion of the day and more complex insulin regimens are required. If glucose levels are high early in the day but are in an acceptable range later in the day (late-acting insulin), a short-acting insulin should be added in the morning. Conversely, if control is reasonable early in the day but glucose levels are not acceptable later in the day (early-acting insulin), a second injection of intermediate-acting insulin is indicated in the af-

TABLE 71-5. INSULIN PREPARATIONS

TYPE	PROTEIN ADDITIVE	PEAK ACTION (hr)	DURATION OF ACTION (hr)
Rapid			
Regular	None	2-4	6-8
Semilente	None	2-6	10-12
Intermediate			
NPH	Protamine	6-12	18-24
Lente	None	6-12	18-24
Long-acting			
Protamine zinc	Protamine	14-24	36
Ultralente	None	18-24	36

NPH = Neutral protamine Hagedorn.

ternoon. Further refinements in the insulin regimen can be carried out on the basis of additional glucose measurements.

The type, dose, and timing of the insulin given should be based on the patient's response and not on a preconceived ideal. Furthermore, an insulin regimen established for a particular patient is not fixed and will in all likelihood need adjustments with time. Changes in physical activity, growth status, or meal content and the use of other drugs or the advent of intercurrent illnesses or stresses will require adjustments in the insulin regimen. The physician and patient must constantly monitor the diabetic control and be prepared to make changes as indicated.

Intensive insulin treatment programs are sometimes used. The administration of regular insulin delivered via an insulin pump in carefully selected patients has resulted in excellent control. In this regimen, continuous regular insulin is given subcutaneously at a basal rate, supplemented by an additional bolus of regular insulin prior to meals. Another intensive treatment regimen involves the use of very long-acting ultralente insulin (basal insulin delivery) and injections of regular insulin prior to each meal. This regimen can also result in the normalization of blood glucose levels. Success with either of these regimens requires a highly motivated and educated patient who is dedicated to the achievement of excellent control. Ultimately, implantable insulin pumps coupled with a glucose sensor (closed-loop system) may be developed, which would allow tight glycemic control without the associated problems of hypoglycemia. Alternatively, it may become possible to transplant functioning islet cells. Currently, pancreatic transplants, usually carried out in conjunction with renal transplants, can normalize glycemic control. The shortage of available organs and the necessity for continued immunosuppressive therapy limit the wider application of this form of therapy.

Complications of Insulin Therapy. The major complication of insulin therapy is hypoglycemia. The symptoms and signs of hypoglycemia are listed in Table 72–1. Occasional mild episodes of hypoglycemia, especially if due to an identifiable cause such as increased exercise or delaying a meal, are not indications for changing the insulin regimen. However, frequent mild hypoglycemic reactions or a severe reaction is unacceptable and requires an alteration in insulin treatment. The ability of some diabetics to recover from hypoglycemia is seriously impaired. In normal individuals, the secretion of glucagon is chiefly responsible for the recovery from hypoglycemia. In the absence of glucagon, the secretion of epinephrine can result in a relatively normal recovery. In some diabetics, especially those with long-standing diabetes and autonomic insufficiency, the release of these two counterregulatory hormones is impaired, and recovery from hypoglycemia is absent or sluggish.

Hypoglycemia occasionally results in rebound hyperglycemia, perhaps because of excessive secretion of counterregulatory hormones (the Somogyi phenomenon). Characteristically, unrecognized nocturnal hypoglycemia may result in morning hyperglycemia. If the insulin dose is increased, the frequency of hypoglycemia is increased, resulting in a paradoxical worsening of the morning hyperglycemia. The appropriate therapy is to decrease the insulin dose. The Somogyi phenomenon should be considered in a poorly controlled diabetic.

A variety of local and systemic allergic reactions occur occasionally with insulin administration, but the frequency of these reactions has decreased with the use of purified insulins. Similarly, lipoatrophy at the injection site is only rarely observed with purified insulin. Lipohypertrophy secondary to the lipogenic effects of insulin occasionally occurs, but it can be prevented by rotating injection sites.

Treatment of Type II Diabetes

In patients with NIDDM, diet therapy is of greatest importance. If diet does not satisfactorily control blood glucose levels, the use of oral hypoglycemic agents or insulin is indicated. The choice of an oral hypoglycemic drug or insulin depends on many factors, including the degree of hyperglycemia, the social and economic situation, the relative risks and dangers of hypoglycemia, and the personal preferences of the patient and physician.

Diet

The majority of type II patients are obese; the main goal of diet therapy is therefore weight loss. A diet restricted in calories usually results in a marked amelioration of the patient's hyperglycemia. This effect on blood glucose levels can occur even before significant weight loss is achieved. In some cases, a reduction in caloric intake results in a normalization of fasting plasma glucose concentrations.

A wide variety of different diets have been ad-

vocated for weight loss. The success rate of long-term weight loss is very poor both in the general population and in patients with NIDDM. It is crucial that the physician stress to the patient the important relationship between food intake and diabetic control. Occasionally, a short hospitalization with strict dietary supervision will convince the patient that caloric restriction can greatly improve his or her metabolic control. Exercise often benefits patients who are attempting to lose weight and should therefore be strongly encouraged, unless a contraindication, such as severe coronary artery disease, exists. In thin type II patients, calories should not be restricted. The diet of patients with NIDDM should be limited in saturated fat and cholesterol.

Oral Hypoglycemic Drugs

A substantial number of patients with type II diabetes do not attain successful metabolic control with dietary therapy alone. In these patients, the use of an oral hypoglycemic agent in conjunction with diet is the next therapeutic step. Several different oral hypoglycemic agents are available in this country (Table 71–6). The main difference between these sulfonylureas is their duration of action and the mode by which they are metabolized and excreted. Although they exhibit a wide range of potency, no specific sulfonylurea, including the "second-generation" drugs, has been shown to be any more effective in lowering blood glucose levels. The sulfonylureas lower blood glucose levels by enhancing insulin secretion by the beta cells of the pancreas and/or by increasing the sensitivity of tissues to the metabolic effects of insulin.

The major complication of oral hypoglycemic drug therapy is hypoglycemia, most frequently observed with long-acting agents such as chlorpropamide. Elderly patients, those who abuse ethanol, and those with either renal or hepatic disease are most likely to become hypoglycemic. Some diabetics, especially those receiving chlorpropamide, develop a disulfiram (Antabuse)–like intolerance to alcohol, with flushing. Idiosyncratic reactions may occur, with gastrointestinal symptoms, diffuse skin rashes, cholestatic jaundice, agranulocytosis, and aplastic anemia, but these adverse reactions are very rare. Chlorpropamide potentiates the secretion and/or the action of antidiuretic hormone (ADH) and therefore can result in water retention and hyponatremia, especially in patients with congestive heart failure or cirrhosis.

Insulin

Some patients with NIDDM require insulin therapy. Acceptable metabolic control may not be achievable with oral hypoglycemic agents (primary failure), or a patient who initially responded to oral agents may, with time, no longer achieve adequate control (secondary failure). In addition, in some type II diabetic patients who are thin and have had very high blood glucose levels, it may be preferable to treat initially with insulin because these patients, in general, do not do well with

TABLE 71–6. ORAL HYPOGLYCEMIC DRUGS

GENERIC NAME	BRAND NAME	DAILY DOSE (mg)	DOSES/DAY	DURATION OF EFFECT (hr)
Tolbutamide	Orinase	500–3000	2–3	6–12
Chlorpropamide	Diabinese	100–500	1	60
Acetohexamide	Dymelor	250–1500	1–2	12–14
Tolazamide	Tolinase	100–1000	1–2	10–18
Glyburide	Micronase Diabeta	2.5–20	1–2	10–30
Glipizide	Glucotrol	5–40	1–2	18–30

other treatments. In fact, some such patients may really have type I diabetes, as evidenced by the presence of islet cell or insulin antibodies prior to their having received insulin therapy.

The use of insulin in type II diabetes is similar to that described in type I patients above, except that because of the presence of insulin resistance, higher doses of insulin are frequently required. In addition, because of some residual endogenous insulin secretion, NIDDM patients are more likely to be well controlled on simpler regimens, such as a single daily dose of an intermediate insulin, than are patients with IDDM.

Monitoring Diabetic Control

Traditionally, diabetic control has been monitored by measuring urine glucose concentration at various times throughout the day. The concentration of glucose in the urine depends on the renal threshold for glucose excretion (quite variable in the diabetic patient), the renal blood flow, and the urine volume. As a result, the correlation between urine glucose values and blood glucose measurements has generally been poor. In addition, because the renal threshold for plasma glucose is approximately 180 mg/dl, urinary glucose measurements are negative when the plasma glucose is less than 180 mg/dl, and therefore one cannot determine the degree of control in the glucose range that is most important.

Home blood glucose monitoring, employing a variety of different techniques, is the method of choice for monitoring diabetic control. Patients are instructed to measure their blood glucose levels at various times throughout the day as a basis for therapy. The accurate and routine measurement of home blood glucose levels is an essential ingredient in any intensive treatment regimen.

The measurement of glycosylated hemoglobin is very useful in assessing the degree of control over the preceding several months. Nonenzymatically glycosylated hemoglobin is proportional to and therefore reflects average blood glucose experienced by the red blood cell during its lifespan. In normal persons, approximately 5 to 8 per cent of the hemoglobin is glycosylated, whereas in diabetics, as much as 20 per cent is in the glycosylated form. With tight control, the percentage of hemoglobin that is glycosylated will decrease and approach that in normal subjects. Glycosylated hemoglobin measurements, while useful in giving an overall picture of metabolic control, are not helpful in making specific adjustments in insulin therapy.

Finally, quantitative measurement of glucose in 24-hour urine samples has been used to assess diabetic control. The excretion of less than 10 gm of glucose per day is indicative of excellent control.

ACUTE COMPLICATIONS

Diabetic Ketoacidosis

Pathophysiology. Diabetic ketoacidosis is characterized by hyperglycemia, acidosis (pH < 7.2, $HCO_3^- < 15$ mEq/L), and elevated plasma ketone concentrations. The hyperglycemia is secondary to insulin deficiency, which leads to both an increase in hepatic glucose production and a decrease in peripheral glucose utilization. Hyperglycemia produces an osmotic diuresis that can result in volume depletion and urinary loss of electrolytes.

Plasma ketone levels rise because of their overproduction by the liver. In the insulin-deficient state, especially if there is an increased secretion of catecholamines, excessive amounts of free fatty acids are released from the adipose tissue and transported to the liver. In the liver, free fatty acids can either be reesterified or enter the mitochondria and be oxidized to ketones. In patients with hypoinsulinemia and hyperglucagonemia, fatty acids preferentially enter the mitochondria at an accelerated rate, resulting in an increased production of ketones. Thus, ketosis requires both an increased delivery of free fatty acids to the liver and a liver that is primed to transport them into the mitochondria. Low plasma insulin levels, in conjunction with elevations in glucagon and other hormones, can result in both of these conditions and thus account for the ketosis. The accompanying acidosis results from the accumulation of β-hydroxybutyrate and acetoacetate and is associated with low serum bicarbonate levels and an anion gap.

Clinical and Laboratory Presentation. Patients with diabetic ketoacidosis usually present after several days of polyuria and polydipsia with associated progressive nausea, vomiting, anorexia, and occasionally abdominal pain. The abdominal pain can sometimes mimic an acute abdominal condition. Diabetic ketoacidosis occurs in both young and old diabetic patients and may be the presenting manifestation of the disease. Infections, trauma, cardiovascular events, emotional stress, and omission of insulin are common precipitating causes, but in some cases there is no obvious etiology for the diabetic ketoacidosis. In all patients with diabetic ketoacidosis, a careful search for the precipitating factor is required.

Patients with diabetic ketoacidosis typically exhibit tachypnea, dehydration, acetone halitosis (a fruity odor on the breath), and an altered mental status ranging from disorientation to coma. The alteration in mental status correlates directly with elevations in the serum osmolality. Kussmaul's respirations are usually present when the acidosis is severe.

The clinical diagnosis of diabetic ketoacidosis should be confirmed by demonstrating elevations in blood glucose levels, ketones in the blood or urine, and acidosis. The blood glucose levels can be quite variable, ranging from values in the normal range to greater than 1000 mg/dl. Blood and urine ketones are usually measured semiquantitatively by using Keto-Diastix or Acetest tablets. Both of these methods detect primarily acetoacetate (the nitroprusside reaction). In ketoacidosis, β-hydroxybutyrate levels are higher than the acetoacetate levels, and thus the actual degree of ketosis is not accurately measured by the nitroprusside reaction. In patients with concomitant lactic acidosis or ethanol intake, β-hydroxybutyrate levels are much higher than acetoacetate levels, and the routine tests for ketosis can be falsely low. In addition, during the course of treatment of diabetic ketoacidosis, β-hydroxybutyrate may be converted to acetoacetate, giving the false impression that the diabetic ketoacidosis is worsening.

Treatment. In the treatment of diabetic ketoacidosis, the clinical status must be frequently and carefully assessed. A complete flow sheet, including fluids, electrolytes, and insulin administered, as well as laboratory data, is mandatory in monitoring therapy.

Many insulin regimens have been successfully used in the treatment of diabetic ketoacidosis, varying from continuous intravenous insulin to intermittent boluses of intramuscular or subcutaneous insulin. In the majority of patients, 5 to 10 units of regular insulin per hour given by a continuous intravenous infusion or by intermittent intramuscular or subcutaneous injections are adequate to correct the metabolic disturbance. In patients who are hypotensive, intravenous administration of the insulin is desirable because the absorption of the insulin may be impaired by poor tissue perfusion. Regardless of the route of administration and dosage, it is important to follow closely the decline in blood glucose levels. If the blood glucose concentrations are not decreasing, one should increase the insulin dosage and strongly consider employing the intravenous route.

Patients with diabetic ketoacidosis are virtually always dehydrated and hypovolemic. The average fluid deficit in adults is approximately 6 L. Rapid volume expansion is usually required; this is best begun by administering normal saline at a rate of 1 L/hr. In patients with cardiovascular or renal disease, slower rates of administration may be necessary. After the delivery of 2 L of normal saline, if there are no signs of orthostatic hypotension, the rate of fluid administration can be decreased and the solution switched to half-normal saline. The remainder of the fluid deficit should be replaced over the next 12 to 24 hours.

On initial evaluation, many patients with diabetic ketoacidosis are hyperkalemic because of acidosis, dehydration, and hypoinsulinemia, but total body potassium stores are usually depleted. With correction of the acidosis and dehydration and the administration of insulin, plasma potassium concentrations will decrease. To prevent hypokalemia, it is very important to administer potassium in the intravenous fluids (20 to 40 mEq KCl per liter) as soon as urine flow is established and renal function is adequate. This is even more important if the patient presents with normal or low levels of serum potassium.

Phosphate depletion also occurs in diabetic ketoacidosis, but its replacement has not been shown to have a beneficial clinical effect. Therefore, the routine administration of phosphate is not indicated unless an additional disorder that also depletes body phosphate stores is present. Bicarbonate replacement also should not routinely be administered to patients with diabetic ketoacidosis unless the patient is severely acidotic (pH < 6.9). Excessive bicarbonate therapy can lead to harmful rebound acidosis in the central nervous system.

Once the plasma glucose level is in the range of 250 mg/dl, glucose should be included in the intravenous fluids to prevent hypoglycemia. Insulin administration should not be discontinued when the glucose falls because this will result in the recurrence of diabetic ketoacidosis. When the acidosis has cleared, the dehydration has been corrected, and the patient is eating, it is possible to return to the usual diabetic treatment schedules.

The major complications of the treatment of diabetic ketoacidosis are (1) hypoglycemia, (2) hypokalemia, and (3) cerebral edema. Both the hypoglycemia and the hypokalemia can be prevented by careful management. Cerebral edema is very rare, is usually observed in children, and may occur because of the too rapid correction of the metabolic disturbance.

Nonketotic Hyperosmolar Syndrome

This disorder occurs primarily in type II diabetics who present with dehydration, hypovolemia, and cerebral symptoms ranging from confusion to coma. Blood glucose levels are markedly elevated (600 to 2000 mg/dl), but ketosis and acidosis are usually not present. The absence of significant ketosis may be secondary to residual insulin secretion sufficient to suppress lipolysis. The symptoms of poorly controlled diabetes have frequently been present for several days to weeks prior to presentation, and the acute decompensation is often secondary to an inability to consume adequate quantities of water, which may be precipitated by infection, stroke, myocardial infarction, an abdominal disorder, and so on. In the absence of sufficient water replacement, the hyperglycemia-induced osmotic diuresis results in dehydration, hypovolemia, impaired renal function, and decreased renal glucose excretion, which further increases plasma glucose levels. The decreased renal function associated with aging, especially in the diabetic, makes these patients more susceptible to develop the syndrome.

As in diabetic ketoacidosis, the alterations in mental status are believed to be secondary to the high serum osmolality. Stupor and coma occur only when the effective serum osmolality is greater than 340 mOsm/L [effective serum osmolality = $2(Na + K) + glucose/18$]. If the effective serum osmolality is not in this range, another cause for the change in mental status should be sought.

Therapy for the hyperosmolar syndrome is very similar to that for diabetic ketoacidosis, with the administration of insulin, fluids, and potassium being the chief priorities. Patients with the hyperosmolar syndrome have a substantial mortality that is usually secondary to concomitant medical disorders such as myocardial infarction, stroke, infection, and pulmonary emboli.

CHRONIC COMPLICATIONS (Table 71–7)

The chronic complications of diabetes can be divided into three main categories:

1. *Microvascular disease*, which is specific for diabetes, involves small blood vessels, and is clinically manifested by eye and kidney disease.

TABLE 71–7. CHRONIC COMPLICATIONS OF DIABETES

Microvascular Disease
  Retinopathy
  Nephropathy
Macrovascular Disease
  Coronary artery disease
  Cerebrovascular disease
  Peripheral vascular disease
Neuropathic
  Peripheral symmetric polyneuropathy
  Mononeuropathies
  Autonomic neuropathies
  Diabetic amyotrophy
Foot Ulcers
Dermopathies
Infections
  Gingival
  Dermal
  Vulvovaginal

2. *Macrovascular disease*, which involves the large blood vessels and is clinically manifested by coronary, cerebral, and peripheral vascular disease. The macrovascular disease is similar to that observed in nondiabetics but with a greater tendency to affect the extremities, especially the legs and feet.

3. *Neuropathy*, which can affect motor, sensory, cranial, and autonomic nerves. The diabetic is also particularly susceptible to develop foot ulcers as well as certain skin lesions, especially of the legs, known as necrobiosis lipoidica diabeticorum, and diabetic dermopathy.

Diabetic Microangiopathy

Eye

Diabetic retinopathy can be classified as *nonproliferative retinopathy* (background) or *proliferative retinopathy*. Nonproliferative retinopathy is characterized by microaneurysms, hard waxy exudates, cotton-wool or soft exudates, and retinal hemorrhages. Nonproliferative retinopathy is very common, and its frequency increases with the duration of diabetes. By 10 years, approximately 50 per cent, and by 20 years, approximately 90 per cent of diabetics have nonproliferative retinopathy. Nonproliferative retinopathy usually does not impair vision and, in many diabetics, remains relatively stable. All diabetic patients (IDDM and NIDDM) with disease existing longer than 5 years should be examined annually by an ophthalmologist.

In a small percentage of diabetics, nonproliferative retinopathy progresses to proliferative retinopathy. Proliferative retinopathy is characterized by neovascularization (new vessel formation), which can result in vitreous hemorrhages and traction retinal detachments that lead to severe vision loss or blindness. The incidence of proliferative retinopathy increases with the duration of diabetes. Approximately 25 per cent of type I diabetics develop proliferative retinopathy after 20 years of disease. Laser photocoagulation, the main treatment of proliferative retinopathy, can greatly decrease the incidence of vision loss.

Macular edema, which is due to the accumulation of intraretinal fluid secondary to breakdown of the blood-brain barrier, can result in a marked impairment of central vision. Macular edema is a common cause of vision loss in elderly diabetics. Laser therapy is also beneficial in the treatment of this type of diabetic eye disease.

Other nonmicroangiopathic disorders, such as cataracts and glaucoma, occur more frequently in patients with diabetes and can adversely affect visual acuity. Fluctuations in levels of glycemia can affect visual adaptation of the lens and lead to blurred vision. Refraction studies should therefore be delayed until glycemia has been stabilized for at least several weeks.

Kidney Disease

Diabetic nephropathy usually occurs between 15 and 20 years after the onset of diabetes in approximately 50 per cent of insulin-dependent diabetics. In non–insulin-dependent diabetics, nephropathy occurs more rarely. The clinical manifestations and treatment of diabetic nephropathy are discussed in detail in Chapter 27.

The diagnosis of diabetic nephropathy is usually obvious; renal biopsy is rarely required. An active urinary sediment, the absence of retinopathy, or an atypical clinical course is an indication for renal biopsy. Contrast studies, such as intravenous pyelography, should not be routinely conducted without clear indications, since rapid deterioration of renal function has been observed in azotemic diabetic patients following such studies. When a contrast study is necessary, diabetic patients should be well hydrated prior to the procedure.

In any diabetic with renal failure, it is important to consider other factors that could be contributing to the renal dysfunction. The possibility of a neurogenic bladder secondary to diabetic neuropathy, urinary tract infections, uncontrolled hypertension, or renal papillary necrosis needs to be considered. Renal failure, regardless of etiology, tends to decrease the daily insulin requirement; therefore, the treatment regimen may need to be adjusted.

Macrovascular Disease

Arteriosclerosis is a common problem in diabetics and occurs more extensively and earlier than in the general population. The etiology of the accelerated atherosclerosis in diabetics is unknown, but the causes are probably multifactorial. Because of the high risk of atherosclerosis, the usual risk factors for vascular disease must be aggressively treated. Diabetic patients should be strongly encouraged to stop smoking, and hypertension, if present, should be carefully treated. Elevated plasma lipid levels are frequently observed in diabetic patients, and efforts should be made to reduce them. Plasma lipid levels will frequently improve with control of the hyperglycemia. In countries such as Japan, with a low incidence of atherosclerosis, the incidence of vascular disease in diabetic patients is much lower than in the United States, suggesting that the amelioration of other risk factors is very beneficial.

Atherosclerotic vascular disease in diabetic patients affects the coronary, cerebral, and peripheral vessels, and the manifestations of vascular disease are similar to those observed in nondiabetics. Silent myocardial ischemia may be more common in diabetic patients because of associated neuropathy. There is a tendency for the vascular disease to be more diffuse in diabetics, making vascular reconstructive surgery more difficult. Nevertheless, the indications for vascular surgery and the success of vascular surgery are not significantly different from those in the nondiabetic population.

Neuropathy

Diabetic neuropathy is a common disabling complication of diabetes, resulting in a great deal of morbidity and a reduced quality of life. Diabetic neuropathy may be classified into four main categories.

Symmetric Distal Polyneuropathy

This form of neuropathy is the most common and usually presents with a loss of sensation in a "stocking-glove" distribution that is most commonly observed bilaterally in the distal lower extremities but can also affect the upper extremities. The decreased sensory perception may result in neuropathic foot ulcers or Charcot's joints. Rarely, proprioception can be so severely diminished that patients have difficulty walking in the dark. Frequently, in addition to the lack of sensation, there is associated numbness, tingling, a "pins-and-needles" sensation, burning, cramping, or shooting pains. The pain and discomfort that occur in association with diabetic neuropathy can be very disabling and are often worse at night. In most instances, the pain spontaneously disappears in 6 months to 1 year. The pain associated with neuropathy has been treated with variable success with phenytoin, carbamazepine, or a combination of amitriptyline and fluphenazine. Topical applications of capsaicin cream may be beneficial. In addition to sensory nerve dysfunction, symmetric motor nerve abnormalities can occur and are often manifested by bilateral wasting of the interosseous muscles of the hand. This polyneuropathy and the autonomic neuropathies described below are thought to be secondary to the metabolic abnormalities of diabetes.

Autonomic Neuropathy

Diabetic autonomic neuropathy has a wide variety of clinical manifestations affecting a number of different organs. Most patients with significant autonomic neuropathies also have symmetric distal polyneuropathies.

Impotence is a common manifestation of autonomic neuropathy but, of course, is often due to other causes, such as vascular insufficiency, psychological factors, or endocrinologic dysfunction. A neurogenic bladder with associated urinary retention and urinary tract infections is another very troublesome complication. Orthostatic hypotension occurs secondary to autonomic neuropathies and can be disabling if severe. The entire gastrointestinal tract can be affected by autonomic nerve dysfunction, resulting in dysphagia, gastroparesis, intermittent diarrhea, especially with postprandial and nocturnal discharge, constipation, and anal incontinence. Gastroparesis can result in poor diabetic control because of the erratic food absorption. Abnormal sweating, manifested by anhidrosis or hyperhidrosis, is also sometimes observed.

Whereas the polyneuropathies usually appear late in the course of established diabetes, mononeuropathies often occur in mild diabetes or prior to the diagnosis of diabetes. Diabetic mononeuropathies can involve cranial nerves III, IV, or VI, resulting in extraocular muscle paralysis with diplopia. The most common syndrome is a cranial nerve III palsy with sparing of the pupillary reflex, which distinguishes this condition from compressive neuropathies of the oculomotor nerve, such as that caused by a carotid aneurysm. The onset is usually abrupt, and pain around the eye frequently occurs. Findings are occasionally bilateral, and more than one cranial nerve can be involved. Spontaneous recovery generally occurs in 3 to 12 months, but recurrences are not uncommon.

Peripheral nerve mononeuropathies usually occur at sites of external pressure and can result in wrist or foot drop. Mononeuropathies can also affect sensory nerves and result in painful dysesthesias and hypesthesias localized to the anatomic distribution of the nerve. Similar to the mononeuropathies affecting the cranial nerves, these neuropathies frequently remit spontaneously in several weeks to months. These mononeuropathies are thought to be due to a vascular insult.

Diabetic Amyotrophy

Diabetic amyotrophy is a type of neuropathy that occurs mainly in elderly men and most commonly presents with unilateral atrophy and weakness of the large muscle groups of the upper leg and pelvic girdle. Pain localized to the involved muscle groups may be present, and the patellar reflex may be lost. The neuropathy on occasion can be bilateral and/or affect the upper extremity. In addition to the neuropathy, marked weight loss and depression are frequently observed. In the majority of cases, recovery occurs spontaneously in 6 to 12 months.

Foot Ulcers

Foot ulcers can occur in diabetic patients secondary to large vessel atherosclerosis, microangiopa-thy, neuropathy, or a combination of these factors. Ulcers secondary to large vessel disease characteristically occur on the tips of the toes, whereas those secondary to neuropathy occur in areas of weight bearing and pressure (plantar surface).

The best therapy for diabetic foot ulcers is prevention. Patients with diabetes should be instructed to examine their feet daily for calluses, blisters, or inflammation, and their feet should be kept clean and dry. In addition, the shoes of a diabetic should be properly fitted, and patients should be instructed to wear new shoes for short periods until well broken-in. Walking barefoot is dangerous and should be strongly discouraged. Meticulous foot care can decrease the incidence of ulcers and gangrene and prevent amputations. If an ulcer occurs, treatment includes bed rest, elevation of the foot, and debridement. If there is evidence of infection, cultures, including anaerobic cultures, should be obtained. Initial antibiotic therapy needs to be effective against gram-positive, gram-negative, and anaerobic bacteria, with further therapy guided by the culture results.

REFERENCES

Brownlee M, Cerami A, Vlassara H: Advanced glycosylation end products in tissue and the biochemical basis of diabetic complications. N Engl J Med 318:1315, 1988.

Feingold KR: Hypoglycemia: A pitfall of insulin therapy. West J Med 139:688, 1983.

Foster DW, McGarry JD: The metabolic derangements and treatment of diabetic ketoacidosis. N Engl J Med 309:159, 1983.

National Diabetes Data Group: Classification and diagnosis of diabetes mellitus and other categories of glucose intolerance. Diabetes 28:1039, 1979.

Nutall FQ: Diet and the diabetic patient. Diabetes Care 6:197, 1983.

Olefsky JM: Diabetes mellitus. In Wyngaarden JB, Smith LH Jr, Bennett JC (eds): Cecil Textbook of Medicine. 19th ed. Philadelphia, WB Saunders Co, 1992, pp 1291–1310.

72 HYPOGLYCEMIA

The diagnosis of hypoglycemia is based on the presence of the triad of a low plasma glucose concentration, symptoms consistent with hypoglycemia, and the improvement of these symptoms following an increase in plasma glucose levels. Hypoglycemia has often arbitrarily been defined as a plasma glucose level less than 50 mg/dl, but plasma glucose levels below 50 mg/dl may occur in normal subjects, especially during intense exercise or oral glucose tolerance tests. For this reason, oral glucose tolerance tests are not an appropriate procedure for the diagnosis of hypoglycemia. Furthermore, in a significant percentage of healthy, young women (but rarely in men), a 24-hour fast also results in a plasma glucose level below 50 mg/dl. Therefore, in men a *fasting* plasma glucose less than 45 to 50 mg/dl is highly suspicious of significant hypoglycemia, whereas in women the fasting plasma glucose may be below 45 mg/dl after a prolonged fast.

Plasma glucose levels should be interpreted in relation to a patient's symptoms. During a 5-hour oral glucose tolerance test, at least 10 per cent of normal individuals have plasma glucose levels less than 50 mg/dl, but few are symptomatic. Conversely, many patients have symptoms resembling those observed with hypoglycemia, even though the plasma glucose level is not below the "normal" range. In addition, it is important to demonstrate that the symptoms, presumed to be secondary to hypoglycemia, improve or disappear soon after increases in plasma glucose following carbohydrate ingestion. Therefore, *the triad of a low plasma glucose level, symptoms consistent with hypoglycemia, and the improvement of these symptoms following an increase of plasma glucose concentration is necessary to confirm the diagnosis of hypoglycemia (Whipple's triad).*

CLINICAL MANIFESTATIONS

The symptoms of hypoglycemia result from catecholamine release, from impaired central nervous system function, or both (Table 72–1). The degree of hypoglycemia that produces symptoms and the clinical manifestations produced are quite variable from individual to individual and from time to time. In a particular individual, the symptoms induced by hypoglycemia tend to be reproducible. The adrenergic symptoms may predominate when plasma glucose concentrations fall rapidly, whereas the cerebral manifestations of hypoglycemia may appear without the adrenergic warning when the decrease in plasma glucose levels occurs slowly or when hypoglycemia is a chronic problem. The symptoms and signs of hypoglycemia usually are rapidly reversible with treatment, but permanent brain damage can result from prolonged severe hypoglycemia.

CAUSES OF HYPOGLYCEMIA (Table 72–2)

The classification of the causes of hypoglycemia is based on whether symptoms occur in the fasting state or following food intake (postprandial). An approach to the evaluation of patients suspected of having hypoglycemia is shown in Figure 72–1.

Fasting Hypoglycemia

Insulinoma

Insulinomas are relatively rare tumors that occur most commonly between the ages of 40 and 70 years. Approximately 60 per cent of patients with an insulinoma are women. Between 5 and 10 per cent of insulinomas are malignant; in 10 per cent of cases, multiple benign tumors are present. In patients with the multiple endocrine neoplasia type I (MEN I) syndrome, insulinomas occur at an earlier age and multiple benign tumors are very

TABLE 72–1. SYMPTOMS AND SIGNS OF HYPOGLYCEMIA

Secondary to Catecholamine Release (Adrenergic)

Sweating	Tremor
Shakiness	Hunger
Anxiety	Faintness
Palpitations	Tachycardia
Weakness	

Secondary to Central Nervous System Dysfunction
(Neuroglucopenic)

Confusion	Diplopia
Irritability	Inappropriate affect
Headaches	Motor incoordination
Abnormal behavior	Convulsions
Weakness	Coma

Nocturnal Hypoglycemia (Usually due to excessive insulin therapy)

Morning headaches	Difficulty in waking
Lassitude	Psychological changes
Night sweats	Restlessness during sleep
Nightmares	Loud respirations

(Symptoms do not usually awaken the patient.)

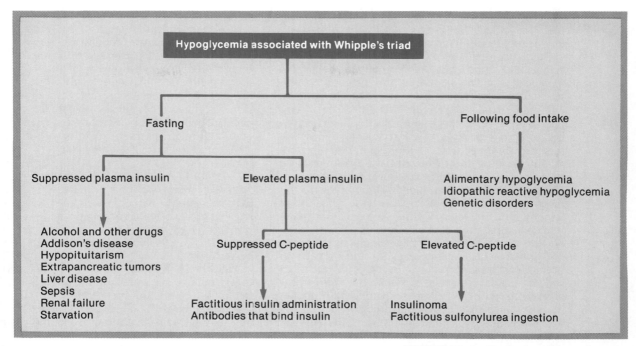

FIGURE 72-1. Evaluation of hypoglycemia.

common. In these individuals, a family history of other endocrine tumors is usually present.

The symptoms of hypoglycemia may be present for many years prior to the diagnosis of an insulinoma because the symptoms of chronic hypoglycemia are nonspecific and not initially attributed to hypoglycemia. Often the patients are thought to have a psychiatric or neurologic disorder prior to the correct diagnosis. Patients sometimes increase their food consumption to prevent symptoms, and therefore weight gain is occasionally observed.

The diagnosis of an insulinoma is based on the demonstration of a low plasma glucose level in the presence of an inappropriately high plasma insulin concentration. The most reliable test is a prolonged *supervised fast*. In normal individuals, fasting results in a decline in both plasma glucose and insulin levels. In the majority of patients with an insulinoma, hypoglycemia occurs within 24 hours, but in a small number of patients a fast lasting 72 hours with or without exercise is required to induce hypoglycemia. Plasma for insulin measurements should be obtained at the time the patient is hypoglycemic. In patients with an insulinoma, plasma insulin levels are inappropriately elevated. During the fast, a patient suspected of harboring an insulinoma must be closely observed for symptoms of hypoglycemia, and if symptoms occur, the plasma glucose must be rapidly determined and the fast terminated if the patient is hypoglycemic. In addition, it is important to measure plasma glucose levels every 4 to 6 hours because patients with hypoglycemia may at times be asymptomatic.

In addition to determining plasma insulin levels,

it is also helpful to measure plasma C-peptide concentrations during the fast to eliminate the possibility of self-administration of insulin as the cause of the hypoglycemia. In individuals who surreptitiously administer insulin, plasma C-peptide levels are very low; in patients with an insulinoma, plasma C-peptide levels are elevated in parallel with insulin, reflecting its rate of secretion.

In the past, many provocative maneuvers, such as the use of glucagon, tolbutamide, leucine, or calcium, were employed to diagnose insulinomas.

TABLE 72-2. CAUSES OF HYPOGLYCEMIA

Fasting
 Insulinoma
 Extrapancreatic tumors
 Hormonal deficiency—glucocorticoids, growth hormone, and epinephrine
 Chronic renal failure
 Extensive hepatic dysfunction
 Starvation
 Sepsis
 Drugs—insulin, oral hypoglycemic agents, ethanol, salicylates, propranolol, pentamidine, disopyramide, and quinine when used to treat malaria
 Disorders of childhood—glycogen storage diseases
 Immune disease with antibodies that bind insulin
 Antibodies that bind to insulin receptor
Postprandial
 Alimentary hypoglycemia
 Idiopathic reactive hypoglycemia
 Genetic disorders—galactosemia, fructose intolerance
Artifactual
 Leukemia
 Polycythemia

Currently, because of the high frequency of false-positive and false-negative results, these tests are only rarely used for this purpose.

Once the diagnosis of an insulinoma is firmly established, additional studies may be helpful in localizing the tumor within the pancreas. Computed tomography (CT) scans, ultrasonography, and pancreatic angiography have all been employed to localize the tumor. During angiography, the tumors appear as vascular masses. Nevertheless, in some patients with insulinomas, radiographic studies do not localize the insulinoma. In some centers, percutaneous transhepatic portal venography with selective blood sampling for insulin measurement may be useful in the localization of insulinomas. However, failure to localize an insulinoma should not obviate surgery, since experienced surgeons are usually successful in localizing the tumor intraoperatively. Serum levels of human chorionic gonadotropin (hCG) or one of its subunits are elevated in approximately two thirds of patients with a malignant insulinoma, but not in individuals with benign insulinomas.

The treatment of an insulinoma is the surgical removal of the tumor, which will usually restore normal glycemia. In approximately 5 to 10 per cent of individuals, hypoglycemia persists following surgery, owing to metastatic insulinomas, islet cell hypertrophy, or a tumor that could not be located during surgery. These patients will require medical therapy to prevent hypoglycemic episodes. Initial treatment should include frequent high carbohydrate feedings. If this is not successful, diazoxide, a drug that inhibits insulin secretion, can be administered. Other drugs that are occasionally beneficial in the medical treatment of insulinomas include phenytoin, propranolol, and verapamil. Streptozotocin, with or without 5-fluorouracil, may be useful in the treatment of malignant insulinomas that cannot be completely removed surgically.

Extrapancreatic Tumors

Hypoglycemia also occurs secondary to a wide variety of neoplasms. Mesenchymal tumors or sarcomas located in the retroperitoneal spaces of the chest and abdomen are the tumors most commonly implicated and are usually very large and easily detectable. Hypoglycemia has also been described in association with hematologic malignancies, hepatomas, and adrenocortical, gastrointestinal, and pancreatic carcinomas.

The mechanism by which tumors cause hypoglycemia is unresolved and probably varies depending upon tumor type. Plasma insulin levels are low during hypoglycemia, indicating that ectopic insulin production by the tumor is not the cause of the hypoglycemia. In some instances, elevated levels of insulin-like growth factor II (IGF II) have been found, and it is possible that the production by the tumor of this hormone could account for the hypoglycemia. Other possible mechanisms for tumor-induced hypoglycemia include increased utilization of glucose by the tumor when there is a very large tumor burden; metastatic destruction of the liver, adrenals, or pituitary glands; the production of substances that inhibit hepatic glucose production; and generalized cachexia. Total or partial surgical removal of the tumor is the ideal treatment and usually results in the amelioration of the hypoglycemia. However, most of the tumors associated with hypoglycemia cannot be resected; therefore, management must be directed toward increasing plasma glucose levels through frequent feedings, glucose infusions, and prednisone therapy.

Hepatic, Renal, and Endocrine Disease

Hypoglycemia secondary to liver disease, other than that due to hepatomas, is rare and is usually associated with massive hepatic necrosis. For hypoglycemia to occur as a result of liver disease, approximately 80 to 90 per cent of the liver must be dysfunctional, and therefore the hypoglycemia is frequently a premorbid event. Hypoglycemia that occurs in the setting of cirrhosis is most commonly due to ethanol ingestion.

In patients with Addison's disease, hypoglycemia may occur with fasting. Adequate cortisol replacement prevents the hypoglycemia. Hypopituitarism, regardless of etiology, may also result in hypoglycemia because of low cortisol levels and impaired growth hormone production. Cortisol replacement prevents symptomatic hypoglycemia in adults, but in children hypoglycemia can still occur despite apparently adequate cortisol replacement.

Occasional patients with chronic renal failure develop hypoglycemia; this complication is observed most commonly in cachectic individuals.

Drug-Induced Hypoglycemia

Insulin. Insulin-induced hypoglycemia is a frequent occurrence in insulin-requiring diabetics. Most of these hypoglycemic reactions are mild and rapidly relieved by food ingestion. However, severe hypoglycemia requiring admission to the hospital is not infrequent. Moreover, death due to hypoglycemia occurs in approximately 2 to 7 per cent of insulin-dependent diabetics.

On rare occasions, a nondiabetic surreptitiously takes insulin and induces hypoglycemia. Most of these individuals are women who have been associated with the health professions. The presence of insulin antibodies in the plasma of a nondiabetic patient being evaluated for hypoglycemia is very suggestive of surreptitious insulin usage. The presence of antibodies to insulin results in an artifactual elevation in plasma insulin levels when assayed in most radioimmunoassays. In addition, as discussed earlier, the presence of hypoglycemia, high insulin levels, and a low C-peptide level suggests exogenous insulin administration as the cause of hypoglycemia.

Oral Hypoglycemic Drugs. Hypoglycemia in diabetics on oral hypoglycemic drugs is much less common than in insulin-treated diabetic patients.

Long-acting oral hypoglycemic agents such as chlorpropamide are more frequently associated with hypoglycemia than are short-acting agents such as tolbutamide. Severe hypoglycemia secondary to oral hypoglycemic agents occurs most commonly in elderly patients or in those who abuse ethanol or have renal or hepatic disease.

The surreptitious use of oral hypoglycemic agents can induce hypoglycemia in nondiabetics. In these cases, the insulin and C-peptide measurements are identical to those seen in patients with insulinomas. When oral agents are suspected as the cause of hypoglycemia in nondiabetics, either blood or urine should be assayed for the presence of these drugs.

Ethanol Ingestion. The syndrome of ethanol-induced hypoglycemia is most prevalent in chronically malnourished alcoholic males and occurs because ethanol inhibits hepatic gluconeogenesis. Nonalcoholics are also susceptible to ethanol-induced fasting hypoglycemia, which can occur with moderate ethanol intake in individuals who have missed one or two meals. Diabetics using insulin or oral hypoglycemics are particularly at risk for ethanol-induced hypoglycemia.

Postprandial Hypoglycemia (Reactive Hypoglycemia)

True postprandial hypoglycemia is most commonly observed in patients who have undergone gastric surgery (alimentary hypoglycemia). The presumed mechanism is rapid gastric emptying with brisk glucose absorption and secretion of gastrointestinal hormones leading to excessive insulin release. Glucose is metabolized rapidly, but the insulin levels remain high, resulting in hypoglycemia approximately 1 to 2 hours postprandially. Very rarely, alimentary hypoglycemia is present in patients who have not undergone gastric surgery. The elimination of simple sugars, especially beverages, from the diet and the institution of frequent small feedings usually result in an improvement of symptoms.

Diabetes mellitus, in its earliest phases, is frequently listed as a cause of reactive hypoglycemia, but this is not well documented. Symptomatic hypoglycemia as a premonitory symptom of diabetes occurs very rarely, if at all.

Idiopathic postprandial hypoglycemia is a rare syndrome whose mechanism is unknown. Much more common are patients with "nonhypoglycemia," who have a wide variety of nonspecific symptoms that occur 2 to 5 hours after a meal. The lay press and misinformed physicians have often attributed these nonspecific symptoms to hypoglycemia. In some of these patients, oral glucose tolerance tests are performed, and as in normal individuals without symptoms, occasionally low blood glucose levels are observed. Because of the high frequency in normal individuals of plasma glucose concentrations below 50 mg/dl during oral glucose tolerance tests, this procedure is not very helpful in attempting to diagnose postprandial hypoglycemia. It is far better to measure plasma glucose levels after meals that are similar to those that caused the symptoms in the individual under study. After these more typical test meals, hypoglycemia is not consistently observed in the majority of patients. Rarely, one observes a patient in whom both symptoms and low plasma glucose levels occur simultaneously and consistently after a test meal. In these individuals, idiopathic postprandial hypoglycemia is a reasonable diagnosis, and they should be treated with frequent small meals that are low in carbohydrate and high in protein. Much more commonly, the symptoms attributed to hypoglycemia occur after the test meal but the plasma glucose levels are within the normal range. The explanation for these patients' symptoms may be related to adrenergic stimulation, but the symptoms should not be attributed to hypoglycemia.

TREATMENT OF SEVERE HYPOGLYCEMIA

In every unconscious patient, hypoglycemia should be considered and blood should be obtained for a glucose determination prior to treatment. The initial treatment of a confused or comatose patient is to infuse a bolus of 50 ml of 50 per cent glucose intravenously, after a sample for measuring glucose levels has been obtained. The bolus of glucose should be followed by the continuous infusion of 10 per cent glucose at a rate sufficient to keep the plasma glucose level greater than 100 mg/dl. When the patient is capable of eating, a diet with a minimum of 300 gm/day of carbohydrates should be supplied. In many situations, especially following administration of long-acting insulin or oral hypoglycemic drugs, the hypoglycemia will last for an extended time. It is very important to continue treatment and close observation for an extended period to prevent a relapse.

REFERENCES

Gastineau CF: Is reactive hypoglycemia a clinical entity? Mayo Clin Proc 58:545, 1983.

Merimee TJ: Spontaneous hypoglycemia in man. Adv Intern Med 22:301, 1977.

Nelson RL: Hypoglycemia: Fact or fiction. Mayo Clin Proc 60:844, 1985.

Service FJ: Hypoglycemic disorders. In Wyngaarden JB, Smith LH Jr, Bennett JC (eds): Cecil Textbook of Medicine. 19th ed. Philadelphia, WB Saunders Co, 1992, pp 1310–1317.

Service FJ, McMahon MM, O'Brien PC, Ballard DJ: Incidence, recurrence and survival of insulinoma. A sixty-year study. Mayo Clin Proc 66:711, 1991.

SECTION X

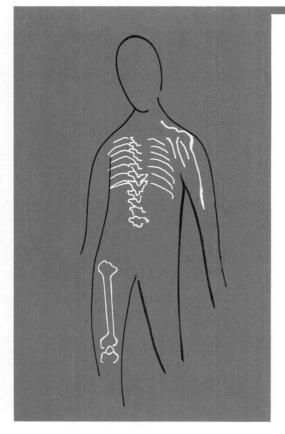

DISEASES OF BONE AND BONE MINERAL METABOLISM

Section X of Cecil Essentials of Medicine, 2nd ed, by Lloyd H. Smith, Jr., M.D., has been extensively revised and updated by the current authors for the section on Diseases of Bone and Bone Mineral Metabolism.

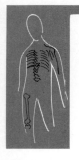

73 NORMAL PHYSIOLOGY OF BONE AND BONE MINERALS

BONE STRUCTURE AND METABOLISM

Bone is one of the largest organs in the body; although it may appear static, it remains a living, metabolically active tissue throughout life. It is superbly designed to carry out several vital functions, including (1) providing support for the body; (2) protecting the hematopoietic system and the structures within the cranium, pelvis, and thorax; (3) allowing for movement by providing levers, articulations, and points of attachment for muscles; and (4) serving as a reservoir for essential ions such as calcium, phosphorus, magnesium, and sodium.

Types of Bone

The skeleton is composed of two types of bone. Cortical bone, sometimes called compact bone, is arranged as circumferential lamellae in the subperiosteal and endosteal layers and as concentric lamellae around a central vascular supply (referred to as osteons or haversian systems) between these two surfaces (Fig. 73–1). Cortical bone constitutes about 80 per cent of the adult skeleton and predominates in the shafts of the long bones. Trabecular bone, sometimes called spongy or cancellous bone, is arranged in microscopically parallel lamellae. It forms a more open pattern than cortical bone and predominates in the vertebral bodies, ribs, pelvis, and ends of the long bones. In general, cortical bone serves the mechanical and protective functions of the skeleton, whereas trabecular bone serves most of the metabolic functions.

Composition of Bone

Cellular Components

Bone is composed of cellular and noncellular components. The three specialized cells necessary for the metabolic activities of bone are the osteoblast, osteoclast, and osteocyte. Osteoblasts are derived from local mesenchymal stem cells and synthesize the uncalcified bone matrix, or osteoid. The primary component of the matrix is type I collagen, a triple helix of two $\alpha1$ [$\alpha1(I)$] and one $\alpha2$ [$\alpha2(I)$] chains. Osteoblasts also synthesize other, less abundant collagens and noncollagenous proteins; two of them—alkaline phosphatase and osteocalcin—are clinically useful markers of osteoblast activity. Osteoblasts also appear to influence the local availability of calcium and/or phosphate necessary for mineralization. Osteoblasts have both parathyroid hormone and estrogen receptors, and both hormones stimulate their activity. Insulin-like growth factor–1 and transforming growth factor–β also stimulate osteoblast activity.

Osteoclasts are multinucleated giant cells that are probably derived from mononuclear phagocytic cells of hematopoietic origin. By creating a localized acidic environment under the ruffled border of the cell, osteoclasts resorb the bone mineral and provide an ideal environment for proteolytic enzymes to degrade the bone matrix. Although parathyroid hormone (PTH) stimulates osteoclast activity in vivo, osteoclasts appear to lack PTH receptors. Thus, stimulation of osteoclasts by PTH appears to be indirect, probably via release of an unidentified paracrine factor from osteoblasts. Osteoclasts do, however, have calcitonin receptors. Osteoclast activity is also stimulated by interleukin-1, prostaglandin E_2, and tumor necrosis factor.

Osteocytes are osteoblasts that have become embedded within the structure of bone and are relatively quiescent. They communicate with each other and with surface osteoblasts through canaliculi and may play a role in mobilizing bone minerals.

Noncellular Components

The noncellular components of bone are the organic matrix and the inorganic matrix. By weight, the organic matrix constitutes about 30 to 35 per cent of bone mass and the inorganic matrix about 60 to 65 per cent of bone mass, with the remainder made up of the cellular components. Type I collagen composes 90 per cent of the organic matrix of bone. Other proteins in bone include small amounts of other collagens and noncollagenous proteins, the most abundant of which are osteonectin, osteocalcin, osteopontin, fibronectin, thrombospondin, bone sialoprotein, proteoglycans, and serum proteins. The inorganic matrix of bone is largely composed of hydroxyapatite, a mineral with the formula $Ca_{10}(PO_4)_6(OH)_2$. Its crystals are laid down on the collagen fibrils and in the glycoproteins and proteoglycans (i.e., ground substance) between collagen fibrils. The remaining inorganic components of bone are other calcium phosphates and trace minerals.

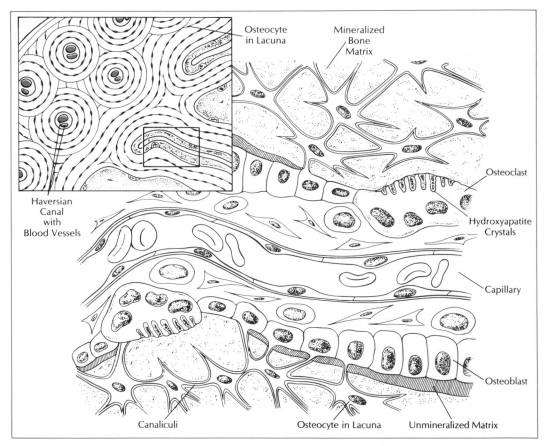

FIGURE 73–1. The most active bone remodeling occurs around the haversian canals, through which capillaries run. Osteoclasts and osteoblasts in all stages of development are found in greatest density in these areas. Larger-scale inset drawing depicts the syncytium-like layer of osteoblasts, connected with lacunar osteocytes via canaliculi, across which substances are exchanged between the modified bone interstitial fluid and the systemic extracellular fluid (ECF). (Reprinted with permission from Levine MM, Kleeman CR: Hypercalcemia: Pathophysiology and treatment. Hospital Practice Volume 22, issue 7, page 95. Illustration by Robert Margulies.)

CALCIUM METABOLISM

Total body calcium in normal adults is about 1 to 2 kg. Ninety-nine per cent of total body calcium is in the skeleton, 1 per cent is in the extracellular fluid, and 0.1 per cent is in the cytosol. Calcium has two important physiologic roles. In bone, calcium salts are essential for maintaining the structural integrity of the skeleton. In the extracellular fluid and the cytosol, calcium is essential for a variety of cellular processes. Calcium also acts as an intracellular second messenger for many hormones, paracrine factors, and neurotransmitters. Because of these various and important functions, the level of ionized calcium in extracellular fluid is carefully maintained.

Extracellular Calcium

Calcium circulates in the plasma in three forms (Fig. 73–2): (1) ionized calcium (approximately 50 per cent), (2) protein-bound calcium (approximately 40 per cent), and (3) calcium that is complexed, mainly to bicarbonate, citrate, and phosphate (about 10 per cent). The free or ionized fraction of blood calcium is physiologically the most important. Albumin accounts for most of the protein binding of calcium; globulins account for the remainder. Acidosis decreases binding of calcium to albumin, thereby increasing ionized calcium, whereas alkalosis produces the converse situation. Changes in the concentration of albumin in the blood affect the measurement of the total blood calcium. One frequently used formula for estimating the total blood calcium concentration when blood protein concentrations are altered is

Corrected total calcium concentration (mg/dl) =
measured total calcium concentration (mg/dl)
+ 0.8 × [4 − measured albumin concentration
(gm/dl)]

Because this formula is only a rough approxima-

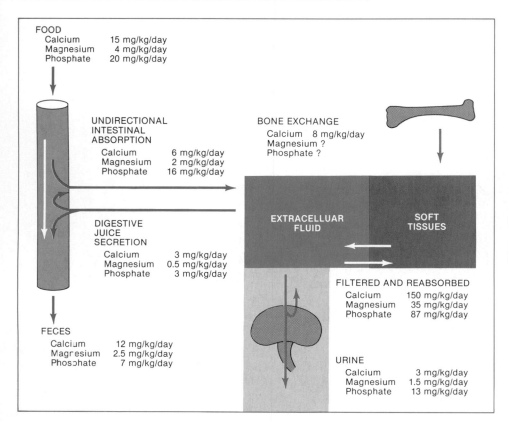

FIGURE 73–2. Typical mineral fluxes in adults. (Modified from Aurbach GD, Marx SJ, Spiegel AM: Parathyroid hormone, calcitonin, and the calciferols, In Wilson JD, Foster DW [eds]: Williams Textbook of Endocrinology. 7th ed. Philadelphia, WB Saunders Co, 1985, p 1144.)

tion, direct measurement of ionized calcium is especially useful in critically ill patients, in those with significant acid-base disturbances, and in hypoalbuminemic states.

Intracellular Calcium

The normal cytosolic calcium concentration is about 1/10,000 of extracellular levels. This low concentration is maintained by a system of active transport pumps in the plasma membrane, the inner membrane of the mitochondria, the sarcoplasmic reticulum, and the endoplasmic reticulum.

Calcium Balance

The level of ionized calcium in the extracellular fluid is homeostatically maintained by an effective balance of bone formation, bone destruction, calcium absorption, and calcium excretion. The principal sites of this regulation are in bone, kidney, and the gastrointestinal tract and are controlled by PTH, 1,25-(OH)$_2$D, and other factors.

Calcium Absorption

The normal dietary intake of healthy adults varies greatly. The average diet of an adult in the United States contains approximately 400 to 1000 mg of calcium, mostly derived from dairy products. The amount of calcium absorbed also varies greatly and is on the order of 25 to 70 per cent of the ingested calcium. On average, adults require daily calcium intakes greater than 400 mg to balance obligate losses in urine, feces, and sweat. When dietary calcium intake exceeds 1000 mg/day, net intestinal calcium absorption tends to increase less steeply in relation to dietary intake than at low intakes. Calcium absorption occurs principally in the duodenum and the jejunum by an active process against an electrochemical gradient. The principal determinant of intestinal absorption of calcium is 1,25-(OH)$_2$D. Calcium absorption is also influenced by dietary intake (at low calcium intakes fractional calcium absorption is greater than at high calcium intakes), age (calcium absorption declines with advancing age), and underlying medical conditions such as intestinal malabsorption and absorptive idiopathic hypercalciuria.

Calcium Excretion

Calcium is lost in urine, feces, and, to a minor extent, sweat. Fecal calcium excretion consists of both the fraction of the ingested calcium that was not absorbed and the calcium secreted into the gastrointestinal tract in biliary, pancreatic, and gastric juices. The calcium from these intestinal fluids that is not reabsorbed is known as the "endogenous fecal calcium" and accounts for approximately 60 to 150 mg/day of fecal calcium.

The other major route of calcium excretion is the kidneys. Approximately 7 to 10 gm of calcium are filtered by the glomerulus each day, 98 per cent of which is normally reabsorbed. The principal sites of renal calcium reabsorption are the proximal tubule and the loop of Henle. The amount of calcium excreted in the urine of normal individuals varies widely, usually ranging from 50 to 300 mg/day but occasionally being as much as 400 mg/day. Reabsorption of renal tubular calcium is enhanced by PTH, phosphate, metabolic alkalosis, thiazide diuretics, and increased reabsorption of sodium. Renal calcium clearance is enhanced by metabolic acidosis, hypermagnesemia, loop diuretics, saline diuresis, high dietary protein intake, ethanol, severe phosphate depletion, and deficiencies of PTH.

PHOSPHORUS METABOLISM

Phosphate is necessary for a variety of structural and metabolic functions. In the adult, phosphorus constitutes about 10 to 13 gm/kg of body weight, of which 80 to 85 per cent is in the skeleton and 10 per cent is intracellular. In the skeleton, phosphorus is mainly in the form of hydroxyapatite crystals, which are essential for the structural strength of bone. Extracellular phosphorus exists largely as inorganic phosphate ions. Intracellular phosphate is primarily bound or in the form of organic phosphate esters.

Normal Plasma Phosphorus

Normal plasma inorganic phosphate concentration is 0.8 to 1.4 mmol/L (2.5 to 4.5 mg/dl). This is conventionally expressed as elemental phosphorus because the amount of phosphorus in its different forms ($H_2PO_4^-$ and HPO_4^{2-}) varies with pH. In contrast to calcium, phosphorus is 85 per cent free and 15 per cent protein-bound. Of the non-protein-bound component, some is complexed to sodium, calcium, and magnesium. The intra- and extracellular concentrations of phosphorus are less closely regulated than those of calcium or magnesium and may vary by 30 to 50 per cent during the course of the day. Plasma phosphorus levels are influenced by age (higher in children and postmenopausal women), diet (levels decrease after carbohydrate ingestion), pH, and a number of hormones, such as PTH, 1,25-$(OH)_2D$, insulin, and growth hormone.

Absorption of Dietary Phosphate

The average diet in the United States contains approximately 600 to 1600 mg of phosphorus per day, 60 to 80 per cent of which is absorbed by passive transport related to the luminal phosphorus concentration and by active transport stimulated by 1,25-$(OH)_2D$. Phosphorus absorption is directly proportional to dietary phosphorus intake.

Deficiency in dietary phosphate or an abnormality of absorption is rarely a cause of phosphorus deficiency except in alcoholics or individuals taking large amounts of antacids containing aluminum hydroxide, which binds phosphate and prevent its absorption.

Excretion of Phosphate

Most plasma phosphate is filtered by the glomerulus, after which 80 to 90 per cent is actively reabsorbed, largely in the proximal tubule. In normal adults, urinary phosphate excretion is directly related to dietary phosphate intake. Proximal tubular reabsorption of phosphate is increased by phosphate depletion, hypoparathyroidism, volume contraction, growth hormone, and hypocalcemia. Urinary phosphate excretion is increased by PTH, PTH-related protein, phosphate loading, volume expansion, hypercalcemia, systemic acidosis, hypokalemia, hypomagnesemia, glucocorticoids, calcitonin, carbonic anhydrase inhibitors, thiazides, and furosemide.

Hypophosphatemia

Causes of hypophosphatemia are listed in Table 73–1. Hypophosphatemia does not necessarily indicate a depletion of total body inorganic phosphate because only 1 per cent of total body phosphate is in the extracellular fluid compartment.

TABLE 73–1. CAUSES OF HYPOPHOSPHATEMIA

Increased Urinary Losses
  Hyperparathyroidism
  Humoral hypercalcemia of malignancy
  Oncogenic osteomalacia
  Extracellular fluid volume expansion
  Diabetes mellitus
  Acquired renal tubular defects (hypokalemia, hypomagnesemia)
  X-linked vitamin D–resistant rickets
  Alcohol abuse
  Renal tubular acidosis
  Hypothyroidism
  Drugs: diuretics, glucocorticoids, calcitonin, bicarbonate
Decreased Intestinal Absorption
  Vitamin D deficiency
  Malabsorption syndromes
  Antacid abuse
  Starvation
  Alcohol abuse
Shifts into Cells
  Carbohydrate administration
  Acute alkalosis
  Nutritional recovery syndrome
  Acute gout
  Salicylate poisoning
  Gram-negative bacteremia
  Posthypothermia

Adapted from Favus MJ (ed): Primer on the Metabolic Bone Diseases and Disorders of Mineral Metabolism. Kelseyville, CA, American Society for Bone and Mineral Research, 1990; with permission.

TABLE 73–2. CONSEQUENCES OF SEVERE HYPOPHOSPHATEMIA

Acute
  Hematologic
    Red cell dysfunction and hemolysis
    Leukocyte dysfunction
    Platelet dysfunction
  Muscle
    Weakness
    Rhabdomyolysis
    Myocardial dysfunction
  Kidney
    Increased 25-OH-D 1α-hydroxylase activity
    Increased calcium, bicarbonate, and magnesium excretion
    Metabolic acidosis
  Reduced formation of 2,3-DPG with impaired tissue oxygen delivery
  Central nervous system dysfunction
Chronic
  Osteomalacia or rickets

Revised from Smith LH Jr: Phosphorus deficiency and hypophosphatemia. In Wyngaarden JB, Smith LH Jr, Bennett JC (eds): Cecil Textbook of Medicine. 19th ed. Philadelphia, WB Saunders Co, 1992, p 1137.

Conversely, serious phosphate depletion can exist with normal serum inorganic phosphate levels. The pathogenesis and differential diagnosis of hypophosphatemia are discussed in Chapter 75.

Symptoms of hypophosphatemia usually do not occur until serum inorganic phosphate levels fall below 1 mg/dl. The acute effects are listed in Table 73–2. Phosphate depletion is associated with a reduction in erythrocytic 2,3-diphosphoglycerate (2,3-DPG). Because this molecule normally stimulates the dissociation of oxygen from hemoglobin, phosphorus depletion can impair tissue oxygen delivery. In severe phosphate deficiency (serum level < 1.0 mg/dl), erythrocyte membrane integrity may be compromised by a lack of ATP, with resultant hemolytic anemia. Dysfunction of leukocytes and platelets as a result of hypophosphatemia may occasionally occur. In muscle, phosphate depletion may be associated with myalgias and weakness and can lead to rhabdomyolysis. Phosphate depletion has multiple effects on renal function, including increasing excretion of urinary calcium, bicarbonate, and magnesium, and increasing synthesis of 1,25-$(OH)_2D$. Central nervous system function may be impaired, with symptoms varying from irritability, fatigue, and weakness to encephalopathy and coma. The consequences of long-term phosphate depletion include osteomalacia and rickets (see Chapter 75).

The metabolic abnormalities associated with phosphate depletion are rapidly reversible by correcting the underlying disorder or using phosphate therapy, although correcting the structural changes in bone requires months or years of replacement therapy. Milk is an excellent source of phosphorus, containing about 1000 mg/L. Alterna-

tively, sodium and/or potassium phosphate tablets (which contain 250 mg of inorganic phosphate) can be given in amounts of up to 3 gm/day in divided doses. Diarrhea is a common side effect of oral phosphate therapy. In rare circumstances, such as with neurologic disturbances, hemolysis, or rhabdomyolysis, intravenous phosphate administration may be indicated.

Hyperphosphatemia

Causes of hyperphosphatemia are listed in Table 73–3. Common causes of hyperphosphatemia include renal insufficiency (acute or chronic), hypoparathyroidism, acromegaly, rhabdomyolysis, acute tumor lysis, hemolytic anemia, vitamin D intoxication, and sodium etidronate administration. As noted, serum inorganic phosphate is normally elevated in growing children compared with the normal adult range. In chronic renal insufficiency, normal serum inorganic phosphate levels are maintained by decreased renal phosphate reabsorption until the glomerular filtration rate falls below 20 to 25 ml/min. The most important acute effects of hyperphosphatemia are hypocalcemia and tetany (see Chapter 74). Hyperphosphatemia lowers serum calcium levels acutely by complexing with calcium and chronically by inhibiting the activity of renal 1α-hydroxylase, thereby diminishing synthesis of 1,25-$(OH)_2D$. This aggravates hypocalcemia both by impairing intestinal calcium absorption and by inducing a state of skeletal resistance to the action of PTH. Acute or chronic hyperphosphatemia can cause metastatic calcifications, particularly in patients with normal or elevated serum calcium levels. Treatment of hyperphosphatemia generally requires restricting dietary phosphorus plus administering phosphate

TABLE 73–3. CAUSES OF HYPERPHOSPHATEMIA

Decreased Renal Phosphate Excretion
  Renal failure (acute or chronic)
  Hypoparathyroidism
  Pseudohypoparathyroidism
  Acromegaly
  Etidronate
  Tumoral calcinosis

Increased Phosphate Entry into Extracellular Fluid
  Excess phosphate administration (IV, oral, or rectal)
  Transcellular shifts
    Rhabdomyolysis
    Acute tumor lysis
    Hemolytic anemia
    Acidosis
    Catabolic states
    Infections
    Hyperthermia
    Fulminant hepatitis
  Vitamin D intoxication

Adapted from Favus MJ (ed): Primer on Metabolic Bone Diseases and Disorders of Mineral Metabolism. Kelseyville, CA, American Society for Bone and Mineral Research, 1990; with permission.

binders such as aluminum hydroxide or calcium carbonate. Because of the risk of aluminum toxicity with long-term aluminum therapy, calcium salts have become the first-line therapy for chronic hyperphosphatemia in renal failure.

MAGNESIUM METABOLISM

In the adult, magnesium constitutes about 0.35 gm/kg of body weight. Slightly more than half of total body magnesium is in bone, and most of the remainder is localized in the intracellular compartment. Magnesium is the second most abundant intracellular cation, after potassium, and the most abundant intracellular divalent cation. Approximately 60 per cent of intracellular magnesium is contained in the mitochondria and only about 5 to 10 per cent is free in the cytosol. It plays an important structural role in bone crystals and is a cofactor in many vital enzymatic reactions.

Normal adults require about 0.15 to 0.18 mmol/kg/day of magnesium to maintain a positive balance. The average diet contains about 7 to 30 mmol (168 to 720 mg) of magnesium per day, derived mainly from meats and green vegetables. About 40 per cent of ingested magnesium is absorbed in the intestine; the amount varies directly with dietary intake. Magnesium metabolism bears some relationship to that of calcium: (1) these cations compete for renal tubular reabsorption and may compete for intestinal absorption; (2) magnesium and calcium are physiologic antagonists in the central nervous system; (3) magnesium is necessary for the release of PTH and for the action of the hormone on its target tissues.

Magnesium balance is usually assessed by its serum concentration, although this does not parallel its tissue concentration. In the plasma, magnesium circulates at a concentration of 0.75 to 1.05 mmol/L (1.8 to 2.5 mg/dl), of which approximately 30 per cent is protein-bound and the remainder is ionized. The extent of body stores of magnesium can be assessed more sensitively by measuring basal urinary magnesium excretion or the percentage of an intravenous load of magnesium that is excreted in the urine (the Thoren test). Retention of more than 25 to 50 per cent is presumed to reflect depleted stores.

The kidney is the main site of magnesium excretion, with less than 2 per cent of endogenous magnesium appearing in the feces. About 2 to 10 per cent of the filtered load of magnesium is normally excreted in the urine; the remainder is reabsorbed primarily in the thick limb of the ascending loop of Henle. Urinary magnesium excretion increases with the inhibition of proximal tubular reabsorption by osmotic diuretics or with extracellular fluid volume expansion. Some drugs, notably furosemide and cisplatin, inhibit magnesium reabsorption in the loop of Henle. PTH and aldosterone both decrease renal magnesium reabsorption. When dietary magnesium is restricted, urinary losses can fall to less than 1 mEq/day.

Hypomagnesemia

Magnesium deficiency usually occurs in association with more generalized nutritional and metabolic abnormalities. It can be due to decreased absorption, increased renal or intestinal losses, or redistribution of magnesium. The most common causes of hypomagnesemia are listed in Table 73–4. Clinically, magnesium deficiency is most often encountered in alcoholics (poor dietary intake, vomiting, diminished absorption, and/or increased renal excretion), diabetics, patients with malabsorption, and during prolonged intravenous fluid therapy. Significant depletion of magnesium may result in any or all of the abnormalities listed in Table 73–5, many of which are nonspecific. The most common clinical presentations of hypomagnesemia are caused by associated hypocalcemia (due to interference with the secretion and action of PTH) and hypokalemia (due to an inability of the kidney to preserve potassium). Other clinical manifestations of hypomagnesemia include neuromuscular hyperexcitability and electrocardiographic abnormalities such as prolongation of the PR and QT intervals and arrhythmias.

Treatment of magnesium deficiency is rarely an emergency. A common regimen is the administration of 2 gm of $MgSO_4$ (16 mEq Mg) as a 50 per cent solution every 8 hours intramuscularly. Be-

TABLE 73–4. CAUSES OF HYPOMAGNESEMIA

Decreased Absorption
  Poor dietary intake
  Malabsorption syndromes
  Extensive bowel resection
  Ethanol effect on absorption
Increased Gastrointestinal Losses
  Acute and chronic diarrhea
  Intestinal and biliary fistulas
  Vomiting or nasogastric suction
Increased Renal Losses
  Chronic intravenous fluid therapy
  Chronic renal disease (tubular, glomerular, interstitial)
  Osmotic diuresis
  Diabetes mellitus
  Hypercalcemia
  Phosphate depletion
  Metabolic acidosis
  Primary aldosteronism
  Drugs
    Diuretics (furosemide, ethacrynic acid)
    Aminoglycosides
    Cisplatin
    Cyclosporine
    Amphotericin B
    Ethanol
Internal Redistribution
  Acute pancreatitis
  "Hungry bone syndrome"

Revised from Smith LH Jr: Disorders of magnesium metabolism. In Wyngaarden JB, Smith LH Jr, Bennett JC (eds): Cecil Textbook of Medicine. 19th ed. Philadelphia, WB Saunders Co, 1992, p 1139.

TABLE 73-5. CONSEQUENCES OF MAGNESIUM DEFICIENCY

Neuromuscular
    Lethargy, weakness, fatigue, decreased mentation
    Neuromuscular irritability (partly due to associated hypocalcemia)
Gastrointestinal
    Anorexia, nausea, vomiting
    Paralytic ileus
Cardiovascular
    Prolongation of PR and QT intervals
    Tachyarrhythmias
    Increased sensitivity to digitalis
Metabolic
    Hypocalcemia (due to decreased PTH secretion and action)
    Hypokalemia (due to renal potassium wasting)

Revised from Smith LH Jr: Disorders of magnesium metabolism. *In* Wyngaarden JB, Smith LH Jr, Bennett JC (eds): Cecil Textbook of Medicine. 19th ed. Philadelphia, WB Saunders Co, 1992, p 1139.

cause the injections can be painful, an alternative is to administer 48 mEq/day (preferably as $MgCl_2$ to prevent binding of calcium by sulfate) by continuous intravenous infusion. Either regimen usually produces a normal or slightly elevated serum magnesium level. However, because a normal serum level frequently does not indicate repletion of total body magnesium stores, therapy should be continued for several days, during which time associated abnormalities such as hypocalcemia and hypokalemia should correct themselves. In pa-

tients with chronic magnesium loss, magnesium oxide can be given orally in a dose of 300 mg of elemental magnesium per day in divided doses. The most common side effect of oral replacement therapy is diarrhea. Caution should be exercised when administering magnesium to patients with renal insufficiency in order to prevent hypermagnesemia.

Hypermagnesemia

Hypermagnesemia is seldom an important clinical problem. It almost always occurs in the setting of renal insufficiency. In such patients, excessive use of magnesium-containing antacids, magnesium-containing cathartics, or parenteral magnesium may produce hypermagnesemia. Magnesium is a standard form of therapy for pre-eclampsia and may cause intoxication in both the mother and the neonate. Modest elevations of serum magnesium levels are seen in familial hypocalciuric hypercalcemia, lithium ingestion, and volume depletion.

Neuromuscular symptoms are the most common presenting problem of hypermagnesemia. Somnolence may be seen at concentrations of 3 mEq/L; the deep tendon reflexes generally disappear at serum concentrations of 4 to 7 mEq/L; and respiratory depression and apnea occur at higher concentrations. Moderate hypermagnesemia may result in hypotension. At concentrations above 5 mEq/L, electrocardiographic abnormalities such as prolonged PR and QT intervals and increased QRS duration may occur and at extremely high levels — above 15 mEq/L — patients may experience complete heart block or cardiac arrest. In most circumstances, the only treatment needed is to discontinue magnesium administration. In patients with renal failure, dialysis against a low magnesium bath lowers magnesium levels. In emergencies, intravenous calcium can be given in a dose of 100 to 200 mg over 5 to 10 minutes to antagonize the toxic effects of magnesium.

VITAMIN D

In terms of its availability, metabolism, and mechanism of action, vitamin D is more properly a steroid hormone than a vitamin. Although there is a dietary necessity for vitamins, no dietary source of vitamin D is needed when there is sufficient exposure to sunlight. Like other steroid hormones, it undergoes several chemical transformations to synthesize the biologically active form. The close regulation of renal 1,25-(OH)$_2$ vitamin D synthesis is typical of hormones. Finally, like other steroid hormones, it exerts its biologic effects by binding to specific, high-affinity receptors in target tissues.

Synthesis of Vitamin D (Fig. 73-3)

The active form of vitamin D is synthesized in three sequential steps in the skin, liver, and kidneys. In the skin, ultraviolet light converts 7-dehydrocholesterol to previtamin D$_3$, which is then slowly converted nonenzymatically to vita-

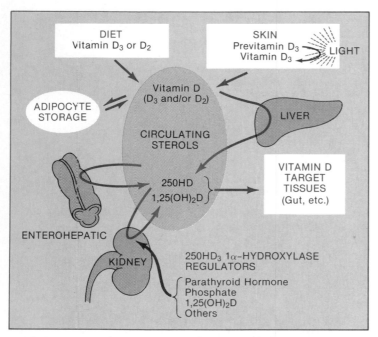

FIGURE 73-3. The vitamin D endocrine system. Vitamin D$_2$ (from diet) and vitamin D$_3$ (from diet or from conversion of 7-dihydrocholesterol in skin) are progressively hydroxylated in liver and kidney to produce 1,25-(OH)$_2$D (calcitriol). (From Marx SJ: Mineral and bone homeostasis. *In* Wyngaarden JB, Smith LH Jr, Bennett JC [eds]: Cecil Textbook of Medicine. 19th ed. Philadelphia, WB Saunders Co, 1992, p 1402.)

min D_3 (cholecalciferol). Vitamin D_3, bound to a specific vitamin D–binding protein (DBP), is then transported to the liver, where it is enzymatically hydroxylated to 25-hydroxyvitamin D (calcifidiol or 25-OH-D). This activation step, catalyzed by a cytochrome P-450 mixed-function oxidase in hepatocytes, is not under tight homeostatic regulation. Although 25-OH-D is only weakly biologically active, its circulating level furnishes a good index of the bioavailability of vitamin D because it has a long serum half-life (2 weeks). Its precursor, vitamin D, has a very short serum half-life owing to rapid metabolism. Then, 25-OH-D, bound to DBP, is transported to the kidney and other organs, where it is either hydroxylated at the 1 position to produce 1,25-dihydroxycholecalciferol [calcitriol or 1,25-$(OH)_2$D], the most biologically active form of vitamin D, or in other positions to produce a variety of other steroids. Renal 1α-hydroxylation is under tight metabolic control and is increased by PTH, hypophosphatemia, hypocalcemia, growth hormone, insulin, estrogens, prolactin, and low levels of 1,25-$(OH)_2$D. Conversely, renal synthesis of 1,25-$(OH)_2$D is diminished by hypercalcemia, hyperphosphatemia, high levels of 1,25-$(OH)_2$D, low levels of PTH, severe renal disease, and in many elderly people.

Absorption of Vitamin D

When vitamin D is ingested, the dermal step in activation is bypassed. The dietary source is either vitamin D_2 (ergocalciferol) formed from irradiation of ergosterol (a plant sterol) or vitamin D_3. Ergocalciferol differs from cholecalciferol in the structure of its side chain but is equal in potency, undergoes the same biotransformations, and is measured by the same commonly employed competitive protein-binding assays.

Although the minimal dietary requirement for vitamin D is difficult to establish, the suggested daily intake for adults in the United States is 10 μg (400 International Units) of vitamin D_2 or vitamin D_3. Because it is a fat-soluble vitamin, chronic malabsorption of fat without adequate exposure to ultraviolet light can lead to hypovitaminosis D.

Molecular Mechanism of Action of 1,25-$(OH)_2$D

When 1,25-$(OH)_2$D encounters a target cell, it binds to a specific, high-affinity receptor in either the cytoplasm or the nucleus. The DNA-binding domain of the hormone-receptor complex then interacts with the hormone-responsive element in the genome of the target cell, producing either up- or downregulation of the gene in question. This interaction results in either increased or decreased synthesis of the protein for which that messenger RNA codes.

Function of Vitamin D

Vitamin D acts with PTH to maintain the level of ionized calcium in extracellular fluid and to en-

hance calcification of osteoid by actions on the intestine, on bone, and, to a lesser extent, on the kidney. Vitamin D, largely as 1,25-$(OH)_2$D, enhances the intestinal absorption of calcium through complex mechanisms, including the synthesis of a cytosolic calcium-binding protein. It also enhances phosphate absorption. By virtue of its effect on the absorption of calcium and phosphate, it enhances the mineralization potential of extracellular fluid. Vitamin D as 1,25-$(OH)_2$D also has a direct effect on bone: it increases bone resorption. In vivo, vitamin D metabolites are also necessary for normal bone formation. Vitamin D may enhance renal tubular reabsorption of calcium, although such a direct effect is difficult to separate from its interactions with PTH and phosphate. Recent data suggest that vitamin D may play an important role in cellular differentiation and proliferation, such as the differentiation of hematopoietic cells of the monocyte-macrophage line into osteoclasts, and may have an important role in immune function.

Diagnosis of Vitamin D Deficiency

The diagnosis of vitamin D deficiency is often difficult. It is generally indicated by a low serum level of 25-OH-D. In many patients with low levels of 25-OH-D, serum 1,25-$(OH)_2$D levels are normal or increased, particularly if serum PTH levels are high. Other findings that often support the diagnosis of vitamin D deficiency include mild hypocalcemia, hypophosphatemia, secondary hyperparathyroidism, and low levels of urinary calcium excretion. Deficiency of 1,25-$(OH)_2$D secretion is seen most often in patients with severe renal disease but also occurs in patients with hypoparathyroidism or with inherited or acquired defects in 1α hydroxylation of 25-OH-D (see Chapter 75).

Hypervitaminosis D

Hypervitaminosis D occurs from the excessive ingestion of vitamin D or one of its active metabolites or from the abnormal conversion of 25-OH-D to 1,25-$(OH)_2$D at sites not subject to normal metabolic regulation. The former usually occurs during therapy of hypocalcemia, osteomalacia, or osteoporosis. The latter occurs in granulomatous diseases such as sarcoidosis and tuberculosis, and in certain T cell lymphomas in which the 1α-hydroxylase is pathologically expressed in the abnormal tissue. Clinically, hypervitaminosis D presents with hypercalcemia and/or metastatic calcification. The hypercalcemia is due not only to vitamin D's effect on calcium absorption but also to its osteolytic effects as it persists even on a low-calcium diet. For any level of hypercalcemia, patients with vitamin D intoxication are more likely to have metastatic calcification than are patients with hyperparathyroidism or humoral hypercalcemia of malignancy because serum inorganic phosphate levels are higher. Vitamin D intoxication caused by ingesting ergocalciferol can persist for several weeks after discontinuing therapy, whereas the effects of intoxication with calcitriol generally subside in several days. Treatment of vitamin D intoxication involves discontinuing vitamin D and, in some patients, the usual acute treatment of hypercalcemia (see Chapter 74) or the use of corticosteroids.

Hypovitaminosis D

The clinical picture of hypovitaminosis D is that of hypocalcemia (see Chapter 74), osteomalacia (see Chapter 75), or rickets (see Chapter 75).

CALCITONIN

Calcitonin is a 32-amino acid peptide that is secreted by the parafollicular C cells of the thyroid gland. Its secretion is regulated acutely by the serum calcium concentration (when the blood calcium level rises, calcitonin secretion increases) and chronically by gender and, perhaps, age (women tend to have lower calcitonin levels than men, and some studies report a progressive decline in calcitonin levels with age). The main biologic effect of calcitonin is to inhibit osteoclastic bone resorption, and when bone turnover is sufficiently high calcitonin treatment produces hypocalcemia and hypophosphatemia. Calciuria, phosphaturia, and analgesia occur at supraphysiologic concentrations.

Hypocalcitoninemia

Patients with calcitonin deficiency do not have any recognized abnormalities. Patients who have undergone a total thyroidectomy do not require calcitonin replacement and do not have a greater incidence of osteoporosis.

Hypercalcitoninemia

Elevated serum calcitonin concentrations are seen in individuals with medullary carcinoma of the thyroid gland, a malignancy of the calcitonin-producing C cells. Despite high calcitonin levels, these patients do not have any associated bone disease or metabolic disorders of calcium or inorganic phosphate. Early stages of the disease may be detected by measuring the calcitonin response to intravenous calcium or pentagastrin administration. Patients with sporadic medullary thyroid carcinoma usually present with a thyroid nodule. Some patients have a secretory diarrhea. Familial medullary thyroid carcinoma occurs as part of multiple endocrine neoplasia types IIA (Sipple's syndrome) and IIB, both of which are inherited in an autosomal dominant fashion. Hypercalcitoninemia may also be seen in patients with small cell lung cancer, carcinoid tumors, islet cell tumors, renal failure, and hypercalciuria.

REFERENCES

Austin L, Heath H III: Calcitonin: Physiology and pathophysiology. N Engl J Med 304:269, 1981.

Avioli LV, Haddad JG: The vitamin D family revisited. N Engl J Med 311:47, 1984.

Bringhurst FR: Calcium and phosphate distribution, turnover, and metabolic actions. In DeGroot LJ (ed): Endocrinology. Philadelphia, WB Saunders Co, 1989, pp 805–843.

Favus MJ (ed): Primer on the Metabolic Bone Diseases and Disorders of Mineral Metabolism. Kelseyville, CA, American Society for Bone and Mineral Research, 1990.

Knochel JP: The clinical status of hypophosphatemia: An update. N Engl J Med 313:447, 1985.

Neer RM: Calcium and inorganic phosphate homeostasis. In DeGroot LJ (ed): Endocrinology. Philadelphia, WB Saunders Co, 1989, pp 927–953.

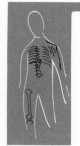

74 THE PARATHYROID GLANDS, HYPERCALCEMIA, AND HYPOCALCEMIA

NORMAL PHYSIOLOGY

The four parathyroid glands are found in close association with the thyroid gland. Occasionally, one of the glands may be in an aberrant location, usually in the superior mediastinum. Each normal gland weighs approximately 25 mg.

Secretion of Parathyroid Hormone

Parathyroid hormone (PTH) is an 84 amino acid single-chain polypeptide with a molecular weight of 9500. PTH is initially a larger precursor molecule, pre-pro-PTH, consisting of 115 amino acids. This precursor is rapidly converted within the glands to an intermediate form of 90 amino acids, termed pro-PTH, which is subsequently converted to the 84 amino acid hormone. The biologic activity of PTH resides in the first 30 residues. After release into the circulation, the intact hormone is cleaved, primarily in the liver and kidney, to smaller biologically inactive midregion and carboxy-terminal fragments. Biologically active amino-terminal fragments do not seem to circulate.

PTH secretion is controlled primarily by the serum ionized calcium level: when the level falls, PTH secretion is stimulated; when it rises above the normal set point, the secretion of PTH is suppressed. With prolonged hypocalcemia, the parathyroid glands can become markedly hyperplastic.

Actions of Parathyroid Hormone (Fig. 74–1)

The main function of PTH is to defend against hypocalcemia. PTH acts by binding to specific receptors on the cell membrane. Signal transduction occurs by activation of membrane-bound adenylate cyclase with the subsequent intracellular release of cyclic AMP or by increasing inositol phosphate metabolism with release of intracellular calcium. The major actions of PTH are the following:

1. Stimulation of bone resorption by osteoclasts, thereby releasing calcium and phosphate into the extracellular fluid. How PTH works on bone is not well understood. PTH receptors have not been demonstrated on osteoclasts so that, at the present time, the bone-resorbing effect of PTH appears to be indirect. In contrast, osteoblasts do contain PTH receptors. In response to PTH, osteoblasts release a factor (or factors) that stimulates osteoclastic bone resorption. The action of PTH on bone is partially impaired with deficiencies of calcitriol or intracellular magnesium.

2. Stimulation of renal tubular reabsorption of calcium (and magnesium).

3. Inhibition of the renal tubular reabsorption of phosphate and bicarbonate, enhancing their loss in urine. This action helps to eliminate the phosphate released from bone, which might otherwise tend to reduce ionized calcium levels. A mild metabolic acidosis due to the bicarbonate loss occurs with PTH excess.

4. Stimulation of synthesis of the active form of vitamin D, calcitriol, from 25-OH-D by activating the specific 1α-hydroxylase in the kidney. By virtue of its effect on calcitriol synthesis, PTH indirectly enhances the intestinal absorption of calcium.

Measurement of Parathyroid Hormone

The circulating level of PTH can be measured directly by radioimmunoassay. In the past, the antibodies used to measure PTH were multivalent and heterogeneous, recognizing fragments of the PTH molecule that were often biologically inert. This problem was particularly noteworthy in patients with renal failure because the biologically inert

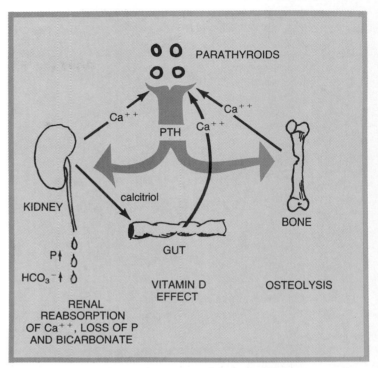

FIGURE 74–1. Actions of parathyroid hormone (PTH) in calcium homeostasis.

C-terminal fragments of PTH are normally cleared by the kidney. Recently, the development of double-antibody assays (immunoradiometric assays; IRMA) has allowed measurement of intact, biologically active PTH, thereby helping more clearly to differentiate between hypercalcemic disorders that are PTH-mediated and those that are not.

HYPERCALCEMIA

Hypercalcemia is a common clinical disorder that may develop in the setting of an obvious serious underlying illness or may often be detected by routine laboratory testing in patients without any obvious illness. Overall, primary hyperparathyroidism is the most common cause of hypercalcemia in the adult population, although malignancy remains the most common cause of hypercalcemia among hospitalized patients.

Clinical Manifestations. The clinical manifestations of hypercalcemia are summarized in Table 74–1. In general, the severity of the symptoms tends to parallel the level of ionized calcium in extracellular fluid, but wide variations can occur. The severity of the symptoms may also depend on the rate at which serum calcium levels rise. Nausea, vomiting, and polyuria, which can produce dehydration and thus decrease renal calcium clearance, can worsen hypercalcemia.

Differential Diagnosis. Causes of hypercalcemia are listed in Table 74–2. More than 90 per

TABLE 74-1. SIGNS AND SYMPTOMS OF PRIMARY HYPERPARATHYROIDISM

Related to Hypercalcemia
Central nervous system
  Lethargy
  Drowsiness
  Depression
  Impaired ability to concentrate
  Confusion
  Stupor
  Coma
Neuromuscular
  Proximal muscle weakness
  Hyporeflexia
Gastrointestinal
  Nausea
  Vomiting
  Anorexia
  Constipation

Gastrointestinal (*cont.*)
  Peptic ulcer disease (?)
  Pancreatitis
Renal
  Polyuria
  Polydipsia
  Decreased concentrating ability
  Impaired renal function
  Nephrocalcinosis
  Nephrolithiasis
Cardiovascular
  Hypertension
  Short QT interval
  Bradycardia
  Increased sensitivity to digitalis

Related to Hypercalciuria
Nephrolithiasis

Related to PTH Effect on Bone and Joints
Arthralgias
Bone pain
Bone cysts
Gout
Pseudogout

cent of patients with hypercalcemia have either primary hyperparathyroidism or a malignancy. With the use of modern immunoradiometric assays, the distinction between these two disorders can almost always be made on the basis of the serum PTH level, which is elevated or inappropriately normal in patients with primary hyperparathyroidism and suppressed in patients with hypercalcemia associated with malignancy.

TABLE 74-2. DIFFERENTIAL DIAGNOSIS OF HYPERCALCEMIA

Primary hyperparathyroidism
Malignant disease
  Osteolytic metastases (e.g., breast cancer, multiple myeloma)
  Humoral hypercalcemia of malignancy (e.g., lung, head and neck, esophagus, renal cell, ovary)
  Hematologic malignancies (e.g., multiple myeloma, lymphoma, leukemia)
  Production of 1,25-$(OH)_2D$ (lymphoma)
Sarcoidosis, tuberculosis, and other granulomatous diseases
Thyrotoxicosis
Drug-induced
  Vitamin D intoxication
  Vitamin A intoxication
  Thiazide diuretics
  Lithium
  Tamoxifen
Immobilization (in setting of high bone turnover)
Milk-alkali syndrome
Familial hypocalciuric hypercalcemia (FHH)
Adrenal insufficiency
Acute and chronic renal failure
Pheochromocytoma

Primary Hyperparathyroidism

In primary hyperparathyroidism, PTH is secreted inappropriately despite an elevation in the ionized calcium level in the extracellular fluid. Although PTH secretion is partially autonomous, negative feedback regulation can be demonstrated (although with an altered set point) because PTH can be partially suppressed by calcium. The peak incidence of primary hyperparathyroidism occurs in the third to fifth decade, and it is more common in women than in men. The annual incidence of primary hyperparathyroidism is estimated to be 1 in every 1000 men over age 60 and 2 in every 1000 women over age 60. Many patients are identified by multiphasic screening while still asymptomatic.

Etiology. Enlargement of a single parathyroid gland (parathyroid adenoma) is seen in approximately 85 per cent of cases. Recent studies have demonstrated that many parathyroid adenomas result from the clonal expansion of a single cell. Most of the remaining 15 per cent of patients have hyperplasia of all four glands, although the enlargement is often asymmetric, so that some glands may look grossly like adenomas, whereas others appear indistinguishable from normal parathyroid glands. In some patients, hyperparathyroidism occurs as part of a familial disorder without other endocrinologic abnormalities. In others, it occurs as part of multiple endocrine neoplasia type I (Wermer's syndrome)—hyperparathyroidism, pancreatic islet cell tumors, and pituitary tumors, or multiple endocrine neoplasia type II (Sipple's syndrome)—hyperparathyroidism, medullary carcinoma of the thyroid, and pheochromocytoma. Most patients with familial hyperparathyroidism have parathyroid hyperplasia, and the disorder is inherited in an autosomal dominant fashion. Carcinoma of the parathyroids occurs rarely in patients with primary hyperparathyroidism. Parathyroid carcinoma tends to grow slowly and to spread locally, although it occasionally metastasizes to liver, lungs, or bone. Long-term survival is common. Although serum calcium and PTH levels are usually higher in parathyroid carcinoma than in other patients with primary hyperparathyroidism, it may be clinically indistinguishable from other forms of primary hyperparathyroidism and difficult to diagnose at the time of initial surgery.

Symptoms and Signs. With the widespread use of multiphasic chemistry screening, most patients with primary hyperparathyroidism today are asymptomatic at presentation or present with vague symptoms, such as fatigue, weakness, arthralgias, mental disturbances, polyuria, constipation, and nausea (see Table 74-1). Although symptoms are usually mild, they may worsen with intercurrent illnesses, leading to severe alterations in mental status. On rare occasions, patients may present with life-threatening hypercalcemia and severe symptoms—so-called acute primary hyperparathyroidism, or parathyroid crisis. Approximately 10 to 15 per cent of patients with primary hyperparathyroidism today develop kidney stones, usually composed of calcium oxalate or calcium phosphate, in contrast to a prevalence of 60 to 70 per cent before the advent of routine chemistry screening. Other complications of hyperparathyroidism include pancreatitis, chondrocalcinosis, calcific periarthritis, and perhaps peptic ulcer disease.

Laboratory and Radiologic Manifestations. In primary hyperparathyroidism serum calcium levels are continuously or intermittently elevated, and serum phosphorus levels tend to be low. Occasionally, the total serum calcium is in the upper normal range, but with an elevated ionized calcium level. The serum calcium level may also be normal in the setting of concomitant vitamin D deficiency. In these patients, frank hypercalcemia develops when correcting the vitamin D deficiency. Serum alkaline phosphatase is usually normal but may be elevated, especially in patients with osteitis fibrosa cystica. Urinary calcium levels may be normal or elevated. Elevated urinary calcium levels help distinguish patients with primary hyperparathyroidism from those with familial hypocalciuric hypercalcemia (see below). A mild hyperchloremic acidosis is often present. Serum PTH levels are frankly elevated in most patients, but a few patients have PTH levels in the "normal" range, although inappropriately high for the level of serum calcium. Serum $1,25\text{-}(OH)_2D$ levels may be elevated owing to the stimulatory effect of PTH on renal 1α-hydroxylase activity.

Most patients with primary hyperparathyroidism show no radiographic evidence of bone disease. The classic radiographic finding of osteitis fibrosa cystica is uncommon today. The most common radiographic finding in patients with primary hyperparathyroidism is osteopenia. Occasionally, radiographs may show subperiosteal bone resorption of the distal phalanges (Fig. 74–2); resorption of the distal end of the clavicle, or a "salt-and-pepper" appearance of the skull. Bone densitometry measurements often indicate a disproportionate loss of cortical bone. Radiographic or ultrasound examination of the kidneys may show renal stones or diffuse deposition of calcium in the renal parenchyma (nephrocalcinosis).

Evaluation and Diagnosis. The diagnosis of primary hyperparathyroidism is based on finding hypercalcemia with an elevated or inappropriately normal PTH level. With the newer immunoradiometric assays that have high specificity for intact PTH, distinguishing primary hyperparathyroidism from non–PTH-mediated causes of hypercalcemia is rarely a problem (Fig. 74–3), although a 24-hour urine collection should be made to rule out familial hypocalciuric hypercalcemia (see below). Most of the other causes of hypercalcemia listed in Table 74–2 can be readily identified by other clinical manifestations or by laboratory studies.

The diagnosis of hyperparathyroidism can be strengthened if radiologic evidence of subperiosteal bone resorption is present. Parathyroid ultrasonography is usually reserved to assist the surgeon prior to neck exploration once the diagnosis

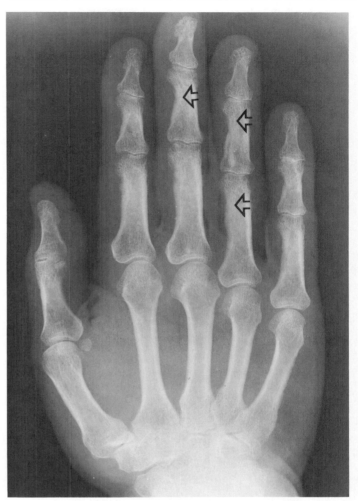

FIGURE 74–2. Subperiosteal bone resorption in the phalanges of a patient with primary hyperparathyroidism.

of primary hyperparathyroidism has been established biochemically. Many masses identified by ultrasound examination of the neck turn out to be thyroid nodules, lymph nodes, or asymmetric parathyroid hyperplasia. A nodule felt in the neck is more likely to be a thyroid nodule than a parathyroid adenoma.

Indications for Treatment. The treatment of choice for symptomatic patients with primary hyperparathyroidism is surgical removal of the abnormal gland or glands. Recently, a panel of experts from a National Institutes of Health (NIH) Consensus Conference suggested the following guidelines, which are somewhat arbitrary, for surgical treatment of patients with asymptomatic primary hyperparathyroidism:

1. A markedly elevated serum calcium level (i.e., 1.0 to 1.6 mg/dl above the upper limit of normal).

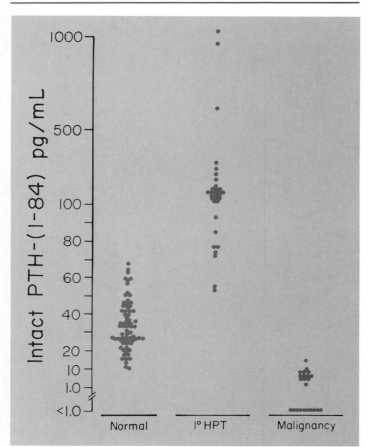

FIGURE 74–3. Intact PTH 1-84 levels measured by immunoradiometric assay in sera from 72 normal individuals, 37 patients with surgically proven hyperparathyroidism, and 24 patients with hypercalcemia associated with malignancy. (From Nussbaum SR, et al: Highly sensitive two-site immunoradiometric assay of parathyrin, and its clinical utility in evaluating patients with hypercalcemia. Clin Chem 33:1364, 1987; with permission.)

2. A history of prior life-threatening hypercalcemia.

3. Kidney stone (or stones) detected by abdominal radiography.

4. Creatinine clearance reduced by more than 30 per cent compared with age-matched normal subjects.

5. Marked hypercalciuria (>400 mg/24 hr).

6. Substantially reduced bone density, particularly if more than 2 standard deviations (SD) below age- and gender-matched controls.

7. Patients in whom medical surveillance is neither desirable nor suitable:
   a. Patient requests surgery.
   b. Consistent follow-up is deemed unlikely.
   c. Coexistent illness complicates medical management.
   d. Patient is ≤50 years old.

Among those in whom medical surveillance is recommended, the NIH Consensus Panel recommended that patients be seen at least two times each year until the stability of the preceding parameters has been established. At each visit the patient should be questioned carefully about potential symptoms of hypercalcemia, and blood pressure, serum calcium, and creatinine clearance should be measured. Abdominal radiographs, a 24-hour urinary calcium determination, and a bone density measurement of the proximal radius should be performed annually. Adequate hydration should be encouraged. Thiazide diuretics should be avoided because they may worsen hypercalcemia. Dietary intake of calcium should be moderate because severe restriction could further stimulate PTH secretion. Oral phosphate administration may be beneficial if hypophosphatemia is present but requires close attention to avoid hyperphosphatemia. In postmenopausal women, estrogen replacement therapy may lower serum calcium levels, although at the expense of a compensatory rise in PTH secretion.

Hypercalcemia of Malignancy

Hypercalcemia of malignancy occurs in 10 to 20 per cent of cancer patients during the course of their illness. Hypercalcemia usually occurs late in the course of malignancy, and survival is often limited to weeks or months after it appears, although some patients may survive for considerably longer periods of time. Malignancy is rarely the cause of unexplained hypercalcemia. Hypercalcemia is most frequently seen in patients with squamous carcinomas of the lung or head and neck, breast cancer, renal cell cancer, and hematologic malignancies such as multiple myeloma or lymphoma. In patients with T cell lymphomas associated with the human T cell lymphotrophic virus type I (HTLV-I), the incidence of hypercalcemia approaches 100 per cent.

Localized Bone Destruction

In patients with malignancies, hypercalcemia can be caused either by localized bone destruction by osteolytic metastases or by release of humoral factors that stimulate osteoclastic bone resorption, increase renal calcium reabsorption, and/or increase intestinal calcium absorption. Extensive localized bone destruction is often an important cause of hypercalcemia in patients with multiple myeloma, breast cancer, or lymphomas. In these patients, tumor metastases may release bone-resorbing cytokines directly into the skeleton or may stimulate host mononuclear cells to elaborate mediators, which stimulate nearby osteoclasts to resorb bone. Recently, it has been found that the cytokine lymphotoxin, a member of the same family of immune cell products as tumor necrosis factor (TNF) and interleukin-1 (IL1), is the major bone-resorbing factor produced by cultured human myeloma cells. Breast cancer cells can produce prostaglandin E_2, whereas lymphocytes in lymphomas can elaborate IL-1α and β and TNF, all of which are potent stimulators of osteoclastic bone resorption. However, even in patients with these malignancies, humoral mechanisms may contribute to hypercalcemia, as evidenced by the diffuse osteoporosis often seen in patients with multiple myeloma, the occurrence of hypercalcemia in some patients with breast cancer in the absence of detectable skeletal metastases, and the enhanced intestinal absorption of calcium in patients with lymphomas that produce 1,25-(OH)$_2$D.

Parathyroid Hormone – Related Protein

In many patients with malignancy-associated hypercalcemia, the primary mechanism for hypercalcemia is increased osteoclastic bone resorption caused by production of a PTH-like protein (PTHrP). This syndrome is frequently referred to as humoral hypercalcemia of malignancy (HHM). HHM is most common in patients with squamous cell carcinomas of the lung, esophagus, or head and neck, but it is also seen in patients with renal, bladder, ovarian, breast, and other carcinomas. PTHrP is a 141 amino acid protein in which 9 of the first 13 amino acids are identical to PTH. Like PTH, the full biologic activity of PTHrP on mineral ion homeostasis resides in its first 34 amino acids. PTH and PTHrP bind to the same receptors on bone and kidney, and both peptides increase bone resorption, renal calcium reabsorption, urinary phosphate excretion, and nephrogenous cyclic AMP excretion. Although PTHrP stimulates 1,25-(OH)$_2$D production in some experimental systems, 1,25-(OH)$_2$D levels are typically normal in patients with HHM. As noted above, immunoassays for PTH do not detect PTHrP, although assays are now available to assess PTHrP levels directly. PTHrP has been identified in many normal tissues, including keratinocytes, breast, nerve cells, and placenta, and thus it may have a normal physiologic role that has not yet been discovered.

Other Causes of Hypercalcemia

Familial hypocalciuric hypercalcemia (FHH, or familial benign hypercalcemia) is a rare genetic disorder transmitted as an autosomal dominant trait. It is characterized by modest hypercalcemia and relative hypocalciuria. Patients are usually asymptomatic and are detected as a result of screening after a family member has been identified or in the evaluation of those initially thought to have asymptomatic primary hyperparathyroidism. Hypercalcemia has been detected in family members as early as the first months of life. Immunoactive PTH levels are usually normal but may be mildly elevated, occasionally causing confusion with primary hyperparathyroidism. Serum magnesium levels are higher in FHH than in primary hyperparathyroidism, usually high normal or frankly elevated. Because parathyroid surgery fails to cure the hypercalcemia unless a total parathyroidectomy is performed, surgery is usually contraindicated in FHH. To screen for this disorder, urinary

calcium excretion should be determined in patients with asymptomatic hypercalcemia, and serum calcium levels should be measured in their relatives. The diagnosis should be suspected in hypercalcemic patients with normal or elevated PTH levels who present at a young age, have a family history of hypercalcemia or FHH, have hypermagnesemia, and/or have a urinary calcium excretion of less than 100 mg/24 hr despite a normal creatinine clearance.

Hypercalcemia due to vitamin D intoxication can be caused by excessive ingestion of vitamin D or endogenous overproduction of 1,25-(OH)$_2$D. The latter occurs in some patients with granulomatous diseases or hematologic malignancies due to extrarenal 25-OH-D 1α-hydroxylase activity. Hypercalcemia sometimes develops in patients who ingest large doses of calcium and are receiving thiazide diuretics (which decrease urinary calcium excretion). As a result of high bone turnover, hypercalcemia occasionally occurs in patients with hyperthyroidism. Immobilization regularly leads to accelerated bone turnover and can produce hypercalcemia in patients whose underlying rate of bone turnover is high, as is seen in young people, patients with primary or secondary hyperparathyroidism, and individuals with Paget's disease (see Chapter 77). Other uncommon causes of hypercalcemia include adrenal insufficiency, pheochromocytoma, the milk-alkali syndrome, vitamin A intoxication, and the use of thiazide diuretics, particularly in patients who have some degree of underlying parathyroid autonomy.

Treatment of Hypercalcemia

Whenever possible, the treatment of hypercalcemia should be directed toward reversing the underlying pathogenic abnormality. For example, severe or symptomatic primary hyperparathyroidism is usually treated by surgery. Successful treatment of malignancy may reverse or diminish its associated hypercalcemia, at least temporarily. The slight hypercalcemia found with hyperthyroidism or with adrenal insufficiency is readily reversible by treating the underlying disorder.

In patients who have severe hypercalcemia (≥ 13 to 14 mg/dl) or who are symptomatic, medical treatment is indicated. The following approaches, presented briefly, are available and may be used in sequence or concurrently, if indicated by the severity of the hypercalcemia.

1. *Hydration.* Dehydration frequently accompanies severe hypercalcemia. Restoring intravascular volume may significantly reduce hypercalcemia. Intravenous isotonic saline is the fluid of choice because renal calcium excretion is directly linked to sodium excretion. Caution must be exercised in administering large volumes of saline, particularly in elderly individuals and those with cardiac or renal disease.

2. *Furosemide* (or ethacrynic acid). Loop diuretics facilitate sodium and calcium excretion. However, they should not be administered until intravascular volume has been restored with saline administration. Otherwise, further dehydration and worsening hypercalcemia may ensue. Because patients given these diuretics also lose potassium and magnesium, their serum levels must be monitored closely during intensive treatment and the losses replaced. Thiazide diuretics should be avoided because they decrease renal calcium excretion and may worsen hypercalcemia.

3. *Glucocorticoids.* High doses of glucocorticoids (prednisone, 50 to 100 mg/day, or the equivalent of another agent) may lower serum calcium levels, especially in patients with sarcoidosis, vitamin D intoxication, multiple myeloma, or other hematologic malignancies.

4. *Calcitonin.* Calcitonin inhibits osteoclastic bone resorption and increases urinary calcium excretion. When administered subcutaneously or intramuscularly in a dose of 2 to 4 IU/kg every 6 to 12 hours, it decreases the release of calcium from bone. However, tachyphylaxis may develop in several days with a rebound in serum calcium levels.

5. *Mithramycin.* Mithramycin diminishes osteoclastic activity when given intravenously. The usual dose is 15 to 25 μg/kg body weight by slow infusion over 2 to 4 hours. Its utility is often limited by kidney, liver, or bone marrow toxicity. Responsiveness may diminish after several courses of therapy.

6. *Phosphate.* Phosphate must be given with great care when treating severe hypercalcemia because of the danger of metastatic calcification. In the presence of hypophosphatemia and good renal function, oral phosphate can be given in amounts sufficient to return the serum inorganic phosphate level to normal. Diarrhea is a common side effect of therapy. Phosphate should rarely, if ever, be given intravenously now that equally potent but safer alternatives are available.

7. *Bisphosphonates.* Bisphosphonates are structural analogues of pyrophosphate that inhibit osteoclast-mediated bone resorption. Two bisphosphonates are available for the treatment of hypercalcemia in the United States: ethane hydroxy 1,1-diphosphonic acid (etidronate disodium, EHDP, Didronel) and aminohydroxypropylidene bisphosphonate (pamidronate APD, Aredis). EHDP is administered as a daily intravenous infusion for 3 days at a dose of 7.5 mg/kg/day. APD is administered at a dose of 60 to 90 mg intravenously over 24 hours. Fever is a common side effect during APD infusion. Serum calcium levels may remain in the normal range for weeks to months after bisphosphonate therapy.

8. *Gallium nitrate.* In selected patients, gallium nitrate can be used to treat hypercalcemia due to malignancy. The usual dose is 200 mg/m² of body surface daily for 5 consecutive days.

9. *Dialysis.* On rare occasions, such as in patients with acute hypercalcemia and renal insufficiency, dialysis may be required for the treatment of hypercalcemia.

HYPOCALCEMIA

Hypocalcemia is an abnormal reduction in serum ionized calcium concentration. A reduction in the total serum calcium concentration, as may occur in patients with hypoalbuminemia, does not necessarily reflect a reduction in ionized calcium (see Chapter 73).

Etiology and Pathogenesis

Causes of hypocalcemia are summarized in Table 74–3. Hypocalcemia is usually due to a deficiency in the production, secretion, or action of PTH or 1,25-$(OH)_2$D. Hypocalcemia is occasionally due to hyperphosphatemia or malabsorption of calcium.

Hypoparathyroidism

The causes of hypoparathyroidism range from surgical removal of the parathyroid glands to resistance to the action of PTH at the tissue level. In hypoparathyroidism, there is reduced mobilization of calcium from bone, reduced renal reabsorption of calcium, reduced renal clearance of inorganic phosphate, and decreased intestinal calcium absorption due to reduced synthesis of 1,25-$(OH)_2$D. The results are hypocalcemia and hyperphosphatemia. Hypoparathyroidism can result from autoimmune destruction of the parathyroid glands, either as a sporadic disorder or as part of an inherited syndrome associated with other hormone deficiencies, including adrenal insufficiency, gonadal failure, and diabetes mellitus (multiple endocrine deficiency with mucocutaneous candidiasis, MEDAC syndrome). Hypoparathyroidism after neck surgery may reflect removal of the parathyroid glands or disruption of their blood supply. Transient hypocalcemia frequently occurs after surgical removal of solitary parathyroid adenomas because of rapid movement of calcium and phosphate into bones (e.g., "hungry bones syndrome"). Hypomagnesemia induces a functional state of hypoparathyroidism caused by a combination of impaired PTH secretion and end-organ resistance to the effects of PTH. The causes of hypomagnesemia are listed in Table 73–4. Less common causes of hypoparathyroidism include granulomatous or malignant infiltration of the parathyroid glands, iron overload of the parathyroid glands, the DiGeorge syndrome (congenital abnormality representing absence of the embryologic formation of the parathyroid glands and the thymus with severe immunodeficiency), and neck irradiation.

Pseudohypoparathyroidism

In contrast to patients with hypoparathyroidism in whom PTH levels are inappropriately low for the degree of hypocalcemia, PTH levels are elevated in patients with pseudohypoparathyroidism (PHP) due to end-organ resistance to PTH action. Recent studies have demonstrated that PHP represents a group of disorders that share resistance to PTH action but have variable biochemical abnormalities, end-organ responses to exogenous PTH, and molecular defects in PTH action. Patients with PHP type Ia have a deficient response in urinary cyclic AMP following administration of PTH. These patients also have a more generalized abnormality impairing production of cyclic AMP in other tissues and often have a group of somatic abnormalities referred to as Albright hereditary osteodystrophy (AHO) (short stature, round face, subcutaneous ossifications, short metacarpals and metatarsals, obesity, and basal ganglia calcifications). The molecular defect in patients with PHP Ia is reduced activity of the alpha stimulatory subunit of the guanine nucleotide–binding protein that couples PTH to adenyl cyclase ($G_s\alpha$). Some subjects exhibit the somatic abnormalities of AHO and variable $G_s\alpha$ activity but have a normal serum calcium level and a normal response of urinary cyclic AMP to exogenous PTH. This variant is called pseudopseudohypoparathyroidism (pseudo PHP). Pseudo PHP is genetically related to PHP and may represent a mild variant of PHP type Ia. Patients with PHP type Ib have normal $G_s\alpha$ activity and biochemical abnormalities similar to PHP Ia, but lack the AHO phenotype. A defect in the PTH receptor may be the cause. Patients with PHP type II have a reduced phosphaturic increase to exogenous PTH despite a normal response in urinary cyclic AMP excretion, suggesting a defect in the ability of cyclic AMP to initiate the metabolic events typical of PTH action. There does not appear to be a genetic basis for PHP type II.

Vitamin D Deficiency and Resistance

Hypocalcemia can also result from vitamin D deficiency, abnormalities in vitamin D metabolism, or resistance to the actions of vitamin D. In these patients, hypocalcemia is usually accompanied by normal or low levels of serum inorganic phosphate and elevated serum PTH concentrations. The causes of vitamin D deficiency and resistance are discussed in Chapter 75.

Chronic Renal Failure

Chronic renal failure is the most common cause of hypocalcemia. The hypocalcemia is due to several factors, including hyperphosphatemia, reduced 1,25-$(OH)_2D$ production, and impaired sensitivity of the skeleton to PTH action. Patients develop secondary hyperparathyroidism and parathyroid gland hyperplasia. With long-standing secondary hyperparathyroidism, autonomous parathyroid function and hypercalcemia can occur (e.g., "tertiary hyperparathyroidism").

Other Causes

Other causes of hypocalcemia include hyperphosphatemia, for example, from administering paren-

TABLE 74–3. CAUSES OF HYPOCALCEMIA

Hypoparathyroidism
  Idiopathic
  Postsurgical
  Hypomagnesemia
  Post–neck irradiation
  Infiltrative; e.g., hemochromatosis, granulomatous diseases
  DiGeorge's syndrome
  MEDAC syndrome
Parathyroid hormone resistance
  Pseudohypoparathyroidism
  Hypomagnesemia
Vitamin D deficiency
  Decreased dietary intake
  Lack of sunlight exposure
  Intestinal malabsorption
  Postgastrectomy
  Anticonvulsant therapy
  Vitamin D–dependent rickets type I
Vitamin D resistance
  Vitamin D–dependent rickets type II
Chronic renal failure
Hyperphosphatemia
  Renal failure
  Tumor lysis
  Rhabdomyolysis
  Excessive phosphate administration
Hungry bones syndromes
Osteoblastic metastases (e.g., prostate)
Acute pancreatitis
Multiple citrated blood transfusions
Gram-negative sepsis

MEDAC = Multiple endocrine deficiency with mucocutaneous candidiasis.

teral phosphate, rhabdomyolysis, malignant hyperthermia, or acute tumor lysis; acute pancreatitis, possibly due to chelation of calcium by free fatty acids; osteoblastic metastases, as in prostate cancer; citrate administration in people receiving multiple blood transfusions; administering EDTA (ethylenediaminetetra-acetic acid) in people receiving large doses of certain iodinated radiographic contrast media; gram-negative sepsis; and medications that inhibit bone resorption, such as bisphosphonates, calcitonin, and mithramycin.

Signs and Symptoms (Table 74–4)

Hypocalcemia is often asymptomatic. Symptoms depend on the level of blood calcium, the duration of hypocalcemia, and the rate at which hypocalcemia develops. The most frequent symptoms of hypocalcemia are caused by neuromuscular irritability, including paresthesias of the hands and feet and circumoral region, and muscle cramps. Severe hypocalcemia can produce bronchospasm, laryngeal stridor, diplopia, blepharospasm, and seizures. Other central nervous system manifestations include electroencephalographic abnormalities, increased intracranial pressure with papilledema, myelopathy, and extrapyramidal disturbances from calcification of the basal ganglia. Cardiac manifestations of hypocalcemia include prolonga-

TABLE 74-4. SIGNS AND SYMPTOMS OF HYPOCALCEMIA

Neuromuscular Irritability
Paresthesias — circumoral, fingers, and toes
Carpal pedal spasm — positive Chvostek's and Trousseau's signs
Laryngospasm
Bronchospasm
Blepharospasm
Tetany
Central Nervous System
Seizures
Electroencephalographic abnormalities
Increased intracranial pressure with papilledema
Extrapyramidal disturbances
Cardiovascular
Prolonged QT interval
Heart block
Congestive heart failure
Other
Abnormalities of teeth, fingernails, skin, and hair
Lenticular cataracts

tion of the QT interval and, rarely, congestive heart failure. Physical examination may reveal a positive Chvostek sign (twitching of the facial muscles following tapping of the facial nerve) and a positive Trousseau sign (carpal spasm following inflation of the blood pressure cuff for 2 minutes above the systolic blood pressure). Cataracts, basal ganglia signs, and abnormalities of the teeth, hair, skin, and fingernails are occasionally seen.

Laboratory and Radiologic Manifestations

Hypocalcemia due to hypoparathyroidism is characterized by hyperphosphatemia and serum PTH levels that are either undetectable or inappropriately low for the levels of serum calcium. In PHP, PTH levels are high owing to end-organ resistance to PTH. The diagnosis of PHP may require determining urinary cyclic AMP and phosphaturic responses to exogenous PTH infusion (the Ellsworth-Howard test). In hypocalcemia caused by malabsorption or deficiency of vitamin D, serum inorganic phosphate levels are generally low or normal, and serum PTH levels are increased. A notable exception is chronic renal failure, which is characterized by secondary hyperparathyroidism and hyperphosphatemia. In patients with hereditary PHP, calcifications in the basal ganglia as well as short fourth and fifth metacarpals and metatarsals can be seen on radiography.

Treatment

The mainstays of therapy for hypocalcemia are calcium and vitamin D. Patients with acute symp-

tomatic hypocalcemia may require intravenous calcium salt solutions. In such situations, one ampule of 10 per cent calcium gluconate, which contains approximately 90 mg of elemental calcium, can be infused over 5 to 10 minutes. Less acute administration of intravenous calcium gluconate can be achieved by mixing calcium gluconate with dextrose and infusing 500 to 1000 mg of calcium over 24 hours and closely monitoring blood calcium levels. If hypomagnesemia is present, it should be corrected (see Chapter 73).

The management of chronic hypocalcemia depends on its underlying cause. Most patients require a combination of oral calcium and one of several vitamin D preparations. In mild vitamin D deficiency, a multivitamin containing 400 IU of vitamin D and 800 to 1200 mg of oral calcium may be sufficient. Patients with hypoparathyroidism typically require high doses of vitamin D (e.g., vitamin D_2, 25,000 to 100,000 IU/day or 1,25-$(OH)_2D$, 0.25 to 2.0 μg/day) plus oral calcium in amounts sufficient to maintain serum calcium levels in the low-normal range. Compared with vitamin D_2, 1,25-$(OH)_2D$ has the advantages of more rapid onset of action and short half-life but is considerably more expensive. If patients are hyperphosphatemic, administering aluminum-containing antacids may be necessary. Hypercalciuria due largely to the absence of PTH-induced renal calcium reabsorption can be controlled by thiazide diuretics, which may also help maintain normocalcemia. In patients with chronic renal failure, hyperphosphatemia should be controlled with oral calcium supplements alone, if possible, to avoid metabolic bone disease from aluminum toxicity.

REFERENCES

Bilizikian JP: Etiologies and therapy of hypercalcemia. Endocrinol Metab Clin North Am 18:389–413, 1989.

Broadus AE, Mangin M, Ikeda K, Insogna KL, Weir EC, Burtis WJ, Stewart AF: Humoral hypercalcemia of malignancy: Identification of a novel parathyroid hormone–like peptide. N Engl J Med 319:556–563, 1988.

Juan D: Hypocalcemia.: Differential diagnosis and mechanisms. Arch Intern Med 139:1166, 1979.

Levine MA, Aurbach GD: Pseudohypoparathyroidism. In DeGroot LJ (ed): Endocrinology. Philadelphia, WB Saunders Co, 1989, pp 1065–1079.

Parfitt AM: Surgical, idiopathic, and other varieties of parathyroid hormone–deficient hypoparathyroidism. In DeGroot LJ (ed): Endocrinology. Philadelphia, WB Saunders Co, 1989, pp 1049–1064.

Potts JT Jr (ed): Proceedings of the NIH Consensus Development Conference on Diagnosis and Management of Asymptomatic Primary Hyperparathyroidism. J Bone Miner Res 6(Suppl 2), 1991.

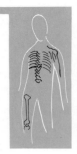

75 OSTEOMALACIA AND RICKETS

Osteomalacia and rickets are disorders of calcification. Osteomalacia is a failure to mineralize the newly formed organic matrix (osteoid) normally. In rickets, a disease of children, there is also an abnormality in the zone of provisional calcification related to endochondral skeletal growth at the open epiphyses.

Pathogenesis

In forming new bone, the osteoblasts lay down osteoid in an appositional fashion. Bone mineralization, a complex process in which calcium-phosphate bone salts are deposited in the osteoid, begins soon thereafter. Optimal mineralization requires (1) an adequate supply of calcium and phosphate ions from the extracellular fluid, (2) an appropriate pH (approximately 7.6), (3) bone matrix that is normal in composition and rate of synthesis, and (4) control of inhibitors of mineralization. Several metabolites of vitamin D may also play important roles in the process of mineralizing normal bone. Defects in any of these steps can lead to osteomalacia.

Specific Causes

The conditions in which osteomalacia and rickets are most frequently found are listed in Table 75–1. The major categories of diseases that produce osteomalacia or rickets are vitamin D deficiency (due to decreased intake, impaired absorption, impaired activation, increased catabolism, or peripheral resistance to its action), phosphate depletion, systemic acidoses, and inhibitors of mineralization. The major entities associated with osteomalacia are discussed briefly.

Vitamin D Deficiency

Decreased Formation of Vitamin D or Metabolites. As can be seen in Figure 73–3, formation of 1,25-(OH)$_2$D requires an adequate source of precursors, in the form of either vitamin D$_3$ from ultraviolet light or diet or vitamin D$_2$ from the diet. These precursors must then be converted to 25-OH-D in the liver and then to 1,25-(OH)$_2$D in the kidney in order to produce the biologically active metabolite. Disorders that interfere with any of these processes can lead to vitamin D deficiency and osteomalacia. In elderly people who get little exposure to sun and eat diets deficient in

milk, eggs, and fish liver oils, osteomalacia is relatively common. It also occurs in patients with vitamin D malabsorption, particularly if there is inadequate exposure to sunlight. Patients with end-stage liver disease may have impaired 25-hydroxylase activity. Similarly, patients with chronic renal failure frequently have impaired activity of the renal 25-OH-D 1 α-hydroxylase. Patients with vitamin D–dependent rickets type I (VDDR-I) have a congenital defect in the activity of the renal 25-OH-D 1 α-hydroxylase. These children generally present with hypocalcemia, normal or high levels of 25-OH-D, low levels of 1,25-(OH)$_2$D, and elevated levels of parathyroid hormone (PTH) (Table 75–2) and can be treated effectively with physiologic replacement doses of 1,25-(OH)$_2$D.

TABLE 75–1. CAUSES OF OSTEOMALACIA AND/OR RICKETS

A. Vitamin D deficiency
  1. Decreased formation of vitamin D or metabolites
    Dietary lack, too little sunshine, malabsorption (post gastrectomy, sprue, Crohn's disease, intestinal bypass or resection, pancreatic insufficiency), cirrhosis, renal insufficiency, nephrosis, hypoparathyroidism, VDDR-I, X-linked VDRR
  2. Decreased action of 1,25-(OH)$_2$D VDDR-II
  3. Increased metabolism or excretion of vitamin D
    Isoniazid, rifampin, anticonvulsants, nephrotic syndrome, CAPD
B. Chronic phosphate depletion
  1. Alcohol abuse
  2. Vitamin D deficiency (see above), especially with secondary hyperparathyroidism
  3. Aluminum hydroxide overdosage
  4. Selective renal tubular leaks
  5. Fanconi's syndrome
  6. X-linked VDRR and adult-onset VDRR
  7. Oncogenic osteomalacia
C. Systemic acidosis
  1. Distal renal tubular acidosis
  2. Proximal renal tubular acidosis
  3. Ureterosigmoidostomy
  4. Fanconi's syndrome
D. Calcium malabsorption and chronic hypocalcemia
E. Inhibitors of mineralization
  1. Sodium fluoride
  2. Disodium etidronate
  3. Aluminum
F. Miscellaneous
  1. Hypophosphatasia

VDDR-I = Vitamin D–dependent rickets type I; VDDR-II = vitamin D–dependent rickets type II; VDRR = vitamin D–resistant rickets; CAPD = chronic ambulatory peritoneal dialysis.

547

TABLE 75–2. TYPICAL LABORATORY FINDINGS IN RICKETS

	Ca^{2+}	PO_4	25-OH-D	1,25-$(OH)_2$D	iPTH
VDDR-I	D	D	N or I	D	I
VDDR-II	D	D	N or I	I	I
VDRR	N	D	N	N or D	N

D = Decreased; N = normal; I = increased; iPTH = immunoreactive PTH.

Decreased Action of 1,25-(OH)₂D. Hereditary resistance to 1,25-(OH)₂D, often called vitamin D–dependent rickets type II (VDDR-II), is a rare disorder caused by a variety of defects in the vitamin D receptor. These defects include (1) a failure of 1,25-(OH)₂D to bind to its receptor due either to a gene deletion or a mutation in the receptor's hormone-binding domain, (2) a decrease in the number of hormone-binding sites with normal binding affinity, (3) a defect in hormone-binding affinity, (4) a defect in the localization of the hormone-receptor complex to the nucleus, and (5) decreased binding by the hormone-receptor complex to DNA due to mutations in the DNA-binding domain of the vitamin D receptor. Biochemical abnormalities are similar to those of patients with VDDR-I except that serum concentrations of 1,25-(OH)₂D are markedly elevated (Table 75–2).

Increased Metabolism or Excretion of Vitamin D. Vitamin D metabolism can be accelerated by drugs, notably isoniazid and rifampin and possibly anticonvulsants. Renal excretion of vitamin D is increased in patients with nephrotic syndrome and in chronic ambulatory peritoneal dialysis.

Chronic Phosphate Depletion

The causes of hypophosphatemia are summarized in Table 75–1. Hypophosphatemia can be produced by a dietary deficiency of the element, excessive losses in the urine or stool, or shifts into cells. Whatever the cause, hypophosphatemia may reduce the mineralization potential of bone salts below the critical level for normal deposition in the osteoid. Because phosphorus is present in most foods, it is difficult to create a selective phosphorus deficiency by dietary means alone. Alcohol abuse is the most common cause of severe hypophosphatemia, probably due to poor food intake, vomiting, antacid use, and marked phosphaturia. Hypophosphatemia often accompanies vitamin D deficiency, particularly when secondary hyperparathyroidism is present, owing to both decreased intestinal absorption and increased urinary excretion of phosphate. Hypophosphatemia can also be caused by ingestion of large amounts of nonabsorbable antacids, selective defects in renal tubular phosphate reabsorption, and generalized renal tubular disorders (Fanconi's syndrome) in which increased urinary calcium excretion, abnormal vitamin D metabolism, and systemic acidosis may also contribute to the mineralization defect. Pa-

tients with X-linked vitamin D–resistant rickets (VDRR) have severe renal phosphate wasting and an abnormality in renal 25-OH-D 1-α-hydroxylase activity. They present as children with severe hypophosphatemia, normal serum calcium concentrations, normal 25-OH-D levels, low-normal 1,25-(OH)₂D levels, lower limb deformities, and impaired growth (Table 75–2). Similar biochemical abnormalities have been reported in patients with a variety of mesenchymal tumors, so-called oncogenic osteomalacia. In these individuals, removing the neoplasm normalizes the biochemical abnormalities and cures the bone disease.

Pure Calcium Malabsorption

Malabsorption of calcium, independent from alterations in vitamin D metabolism, may be the primary or a contributing factor in the development of osteomalacia in patients who have undergone partial gastrectomy, intestinal resection, or bypass or who have generalized intestinal diseases such as regional enteritis or sprue. In these patients, serum calcium levels are usually normal or slightly low, serum inorganic phosphate levels are low, 25-OH-D and 1,25-(OH)₂D levels are normal, and serum immunoreactive PTH (iPTH) concentrations are increased.

Systemic Acidosis

The occurrence of osteomalacia and/or rickets in patients with systemic acidosis has several causes. Acidosis increases resorption of bone mineral to buffer retained hydrogen ions. A decrease in systemic pH may inhibit mineralization by lowering the pH below the critical level needed for normal mineralization at calcification sites. Finally, acidosis may alter the response to vitamin D. Conditions that produce chronic acidosis and are associated with rickets and/or osteomalacia include proximal and distal renal tubular acidosis, ureterosigmoidostomy, and Fanconi's syndrome.

Inhibitors of Mineralization

Using aluminum-containing antacids or dialysis fluid high in aluminum in patients with chronic renal failure may inhibit mineralization, as may sodium fluoride and etidronate disodium (EHDP).

Miscellaneous

In patients with hypophosphatasia, serum levels of alkaline phosphatase are low. Inheritance in the infantile form is autosomal recessive, whereas the adult form is autosomal dominant with variable penetrance. Because alkaline phosphatase is a pyrophosphatase, high levels of inorganic pyrophosphate may inhibit normal bone mineralization. Alternatively, low serum alkaline phosphatase levels may indicate a generalized defect in osteoblast function. The disease varies from severe, deforming rickets in children to mild osteomalacia in adults.

Clinical Manifestations

The clinical features of rickets are mainly related to skeletal pain and deformity, fracture of the abnormal bone, slippage of epiphyses, and disturbances in growth. The child is usually listless, weak, and hypotonic, particularly when vitamin D deficiency is also present. Dental eruption is delayed and enamel defects are common. The epiphyses are enlarged, as are the costochondral junctions, the latter producing the classic "rachitic rosary." Depending on the underlying cause, the child may have symptoms of hypocalcemia. If treated appropriately before the age of 4, the skeletal deformities are usually reversible.

In adults, osteomalacia is often difficult to diagnose on clinical grounds alone. Diffuse skeletal pain, often prominent around the hips, and proximal muscle weakness are the most common complaints. Physical examination may reveal a waddling gait, muscle weakness, bone tenderness, and hypotonia with preservation of brisk reflexes.

Laboratory and Radiographic Features

The laboratory findings depend on the specific cause of the mineralization defect. The most typical findings are slight hypocalcemia, somewhat more profound hypophosphatemia, an elevated serum alkaline phosphatase, low-normal urinary calcium excretion, and an elevated level of iPTH. Serum levels of 25-OH-D are often depressed. Serum 1,25-$(OH)_2$D levels are often elevated, despite low 25-OH-D levels, in patients with secondary hyperparathyroidism but may occasionally be depressed, particularly in patients with renal disease. Osteomalacia can exist in the absence of any of these findings, however. A comparison of the typical laboratory features of osteomalacia, primary hyperparathyroidism, and osteoporosis is given in Table 75–3.

The radiographic findings in osteomalacia are usually nonspecific and show only diffuse osteopenia. Trabeculae are poorly defined, the corticomedullary junction is blurred, and the cortices are thinned. The only specific radiographic manifestation is the pseudofracture, or Looser's zone. Classically, pseudofractures are bilateral and symmetric and oriented perpendicular to the surface of the bone (Fig. 75–1). They are most common on the concave surface of the proximal femur, femoral neck, pubic and ischial rami, pelvis, ribs, and axillary margins of the scapula. In some patients, particularly those with renal tubular phosphate leaks, the radiologic density of bone may be increased.

In rickets, the most characteristic alterations occur at the epiphyseal growth plate, which is widened. Enlargement of the growth plate leads to flaring, cupping, and fraying of the metaphyses (Fig. 75–2). Bowing of long bones, scoliosis, a bell-shaped thorax, basilar invagination of the skull, and acetabular protrusion all may occur in rachitic bones.

TABLE 75–3. TYPICAL LABORATORY FINDINGS IN SERUM IN METABOLIC BONE DISEASE

	Ca^{2+}	PO_4	ALKALINE PHOSPHATASE	iPTH
Osteomalacia	N or D	D	I	I
Primary hyperparathyroidism	I	D	I	I
Osteoporosis	N	N	N	N

N = Normal; D = decreased; I = increased; iPTH = immunoreactive PTH.

Diagnosis

In osteomalacia and rickets, mineralization of osteoid (and of cartilage in rickets) does not keep pace with formation of osteoid. The diagnosis of rickets is usually apparent on clinical and radiographic grounds, whereas the diagnosis of osteomalacia is best established by iliac crest bone biopsy after double tetracycline labeling. In pa-

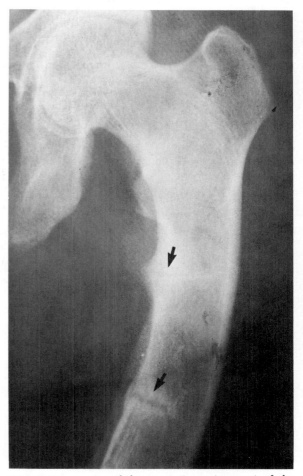

FIGURE 75–1. Pseudofractures (Looser's zones) of the medial aspect of the femur of a patient with osteomalacia. (Courtesy of Dr. Daniel Rosenthal.)

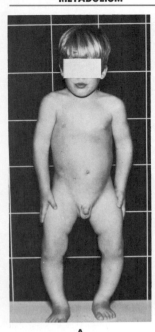
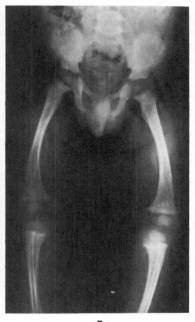

A   B

FIGURE 75-2. The clinical (A) and radiographic (B) appearance of a young boy with X-linked hypophosphatemic rickets. Note the striking bowing of the legs, apparent in both femora and tibiae, with flaring of the ends of these bones at the knee. (Courtesy of Dr. Sara B. Arnaud. From Bikle DB: Osteomalacia and rickets. *In* Wyngaarden JB, Smith LH Jr, Bennett JB [eds]: Cecil Textbook of Medicine. 19th ed. Philadelphia, WB Saunders Co, 1992, p 1408.)

tients with osteomalacia, osteoid seams are wider than normal and cover a greater extent of bone surface, and the rate of bone formation is depressed. A mean osteoid seam width greater than

15 μm and a mineralization lag time greater than 100 days are generally considered appropriate kinetic criteria to diagnose osteomalacia; however, some experts also require an absolute increase in the total osteoid volume and an increased number of osteoid lamellae.

Treatment

Because of the diverse causes of osteomalacia and rickets, it is difficult to generalize treatment. Most patients require calcium and vitamin D therapy, and some require large supplements of phosphate. In patients with vitamin D deficiency, administering vitamin D produces a rapid increase in levels of serum inorganic phosphate. Normalization of serum calcium levels is often delayed, as is the fall in levels of alkaline phosphatase and iPTH. In patients with severe hypophosphatemia, as in VDRR, oral phosphate therapy is associated with a rapid rise in serum inorganic phosphate levels, which is often accompanied by a slight fall in serum calcium levels, reduced excretion of urinary calcium, and a transient increase in serum iPTH levels. Combined therapy with vitamin D and phosphate accelerates healing of the bone disease and allows the use of lower doses of oral phosphate supplements in patients with VDRR.

REFERENCES

Favus MJ (ed): Primer on the Metabolic Bone Diseases and Disorders of Mineral Metabolism. Kelseyville, CA, American Society for Bone and Mineral Research, 1990.

Goldring SR, Krane SM: Disorders of calcification: Osteomalacia and rickets. *In* DeGroot LJ (ed): Endocrinology. Philadelphia, WB Saunders Co, 1989, pp 1165–1187.

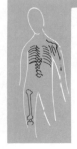

76 OSTEOPOROSIS

Osteoporosis, the most common type of metabolic bone disease, is characterized by a parallel reduction in bone mineral and bone matrix so that bone is decreased in amount but is of normal composition. Osteoporosis is a major public health problem, affecting 20 million Americans and leading to approximately 1.3 million fractures in the United States each year. Thirty per cent of all postmenopausal white women eventually sustain osteoporotic fractures, and by extreme old age, one third of all women have had an osteoporotic hip fracture. In the United States, the annual cost of health care and lost productivity due to osteoporosis exceeds $10 billion.

Etiology and Pathogenesis

At any point in time, bone density depends on both the peak bone density achieved during development and the subsequent adult bone loss (Fig. 76–1). Thus, osteopenia, which can be defined as a bone density value below the lower limit of normal for young adults of the same gender and race, can result either from deficient pubertal bone accretion, accelerated adult bone loss, or both.

Determinants of Peak Bone Density. Bone density increases dramatically during puberty in response to increases in secretion of sex steroids and eventually reaches values in young adults that are nearly double those of children. Other factors that influence peak bone density include gender, genetics, race, timing of puberty, and both dietary calcium intake and physical activity during adolescence. For example, bone density is lower in daughters of women with osteoporosis than in those without osteoporosis, which demonstrates the role of genetics in determining peak bone mass. Because blacks have higher peak bone density than whites, they develop osteoporotic fractures less often. Recent data indicate that men with histories of constitutionally delayed puberty have decreased peak bone density, a finding that may be important in the pathogenesis of osteoporosis in men.

Physiologic Causes of Adult Bone Loss. After peak bone density is achieved, bone density declines throughout life. Although the time when bone loss begins is not firmly established, considerable evidence suggests that it starts before menopause in women and in the third to fifth decade in men. However, it is clear that when gonadal steroid secretion declines at menopause, the rate of bone loss is accelerated several fold in women. This period of rapid bone loss lasts for roughly 5 years. A subset of these patients, in whom osteoporosis is more severe than expected for their age, are said to have type I or "postmenopausal" osteoporosis (Fig. 76–2). Because it is more metabolically active, trabecular bone is affected to a greater degree than cortical bone in type I osteoporosis. A woman can easily lose 15 to 20 per cent of her trabecular bone mass during the first several years of menopause, a loss that can be prevented by estrogen replacement therapy. Clinically, type I osteoporosis often presents with vertebral fractures. Why estrogen deficiency leads to bone loss is still not established. It has been suggested that estrogen deficiency increases the skeleton's sensitivity to the resorptive effects of parathyroid hormone (PTH). In this model, small increases in serum calcium suppress PTH secretion, thereby decreasing renal $1,25\text{-}(OH)_2D$ formation and limiting intestinal calcium absorption (Fig. 76–2). The recent discovery of estrogen receptors on osteoblasts suggests that estrogens may directly affect bone formation. Finally, it is possible that estrogen deficiency alters the actions of cytokines in bone which mediate the effects of estrogen on bone formation and resorption.

Once the period of rapid postmenopausal bone loss ends, bone loss continues at a more gradual rate throughout life. This type of bone loss, which occurs in both women and men, has been termed

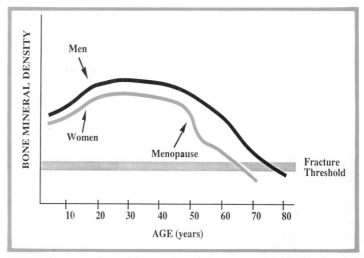

FIGURE 76–1. Cortical bone mineral density versus age in men and women. Women have lower peak bone mineral density than men and experience a period of rapid bone loss at the time of the menopause, thus reaching the fracture threshold (the level of bone density at which the risk of developing osteoporotic fractures begins to increase) earlier than men.

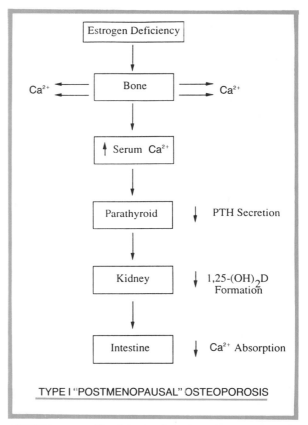

FIGURE 76–2. Physiologic alterations in women with type I ("postmenopausal") osteoporosis.

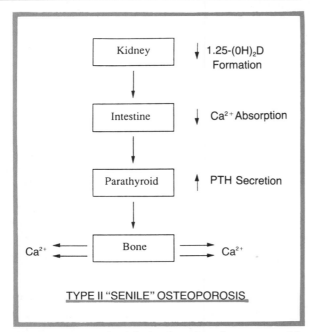

FIGURE 76–3. Physiologic alterations in women with type II ("senile") osteoporosis.

type II or "senile" osteoporosis (Fig. 76–3). Because type II osteoporosis leads to a more balanced loss of cortical and trabecular bone, fractures of the hip, pelvis, wrist, and vertebral bodies all occur commonly. Factors that may be important in the pathogenesis of type II osteoporosis include (1) a primary defect in the ability of the kidney to make 1,25-$(OH)_2D$, leading to diminished calcium absorption and mild secondary hyperthyroidism; and (2) a decrease in osteoblastic bone formation with aging.

Secondary Causes of Adult Bone Loss. Many of the secondary disorders that can lead to osteoporosis are shown in Table 76–1. These conditions should be considered when evaluating patients with osteoporosis and include endogenous and exogenous glucocorticoid excess, hypogonadism, hyperthyroidism, hyperparathyroidism, gastrointestinal diseases, bone marrow disorders, immobilization, connective tissue diseases, rheumatoid arthritis, and a number of drugs.

Clinical Manifestations

Osteoporosis is usually asymptomatic unless it results in a fracture—usually a vertebral compression fracture or a fracture of the wrist, hip, ribs, pelvis, or humerus. Vertebral compression fractures often occur with minimal stress, such as with sneezing, bending, or lifting a light object. Back pain usually begins acutely and is sometimes associated with pain radiating laterally and anteriorly. With multiple vertebral fractures, usually

with anterior wedging, patients lose height and develop the characteristic dorsal kyphosis and cervical lordosis sometimes known as the "dowager's hump." Vertebral compression fractures often occur without symptoms. Hip fractures generally are associated with falls, occurring either as a result of modest trauma or, in many instances, prior to the fall. Secondary complications of hip fractures carry a mortality rate of 15 per cent in elderly patients and lead to severe disability and the need for long-term care in many of the survivors.

Diagnosis

The diagnosis of osteoporosis can be established either by documenting a typical osteoporotic fracture or by directly measuring bone mineral density. Several techniques are available for measuring bone mineral density in the axial and

TABLE 76–1. SECONDARY CAUSES OF OSTEOPOROSIS

Endocrine diseases
  Female hypogonadism
    Hyperprolactinemia
    Hypothalamic amenorrhea
    Anorexia nervosa
    Premature and primary ovarian failure
  Male hypogonadism
    Idiopathic hypogonadotropic hypogonadism
    Hyperprolactinemia
    Klinefelter's syndrome
    Primary gonadal failure
    Delayed puberty
  Hyperthyroidism
  Hyperparathyroidism
  Hypercortisolism
Gastrointestinal diseases
  Subtotal gastrectomy
  Malabsorption syndromes
  Chronic obstructive jaundice
  Primary biliary cirrhosis and other cirrhoses
  Alactasia
Bone marrow disorders
  Multiple myeloma
  Lymphoma
  Leukemia
  Hemolytic anemias
  Systemic mastocytosis
  Disseminated carcinoma
Connective tissue diseases
  Osteogenesis imperfecta
  Ehlers-Danlos syndrome
  Marfan's syndrome
  Homocystinuria
Drugs
  Alcohol
  Heparin
  Glucocorticoids
  Thyroxine
  Anticonvulsants
  GnRH agonists
  Cyclosporine
  Chemotherapy
Miscellaneous causes
  Immobilization
  Rheumatoid arthritis

appendicular skeleton (Table 76-2). Large prospective studies have demonstrated that bone density measurements of the distal and proximal radius, os calcis, proximal femur, or spine can predict the development of all of the major types of osteoporotic fractures, including hip fractures. Of the available techniques, quantitative computed tomography (QCT) is the most sensitive for diagnosing osteoporosis because it exclusively measures trabecular bone in the center of the vertebral body. However, because the radiation dose is high and the reproducibility of measurements is relatively poor, it is not an ideal technique when repeat measurements aimed at detecting small changes in bone density are needed. Single-photon absorptiometry (SPA) has excellent precision, but its utility is limited by the fact that it can be used only to measure bone density in the appendicular skeleton and not in the spine, where osteoporosis occurs first. Dual-photon absorptiometry (DPA), the first technique available for measuring bone density in the spine and the hip, is outdated. For most patients, dual-energy x-ray absorptiometry (DEXA) is currently the method of choice for measuring bone density. Because DEXA scans of the spine in the anteroposterior projection include both the vertebral body (which is predominantly trabecular bone) and the posterior spinal elements (which contain a significant portion of cortical bone), DEXA is not as sensitive as QCT for detecting early trabecular bone loss. However, its far greater precision, miniscule radiation dose, faster scan time, and lower cost make it preferable to QCT in most situations. Lateral DEXA scans, which allow measurements of the vertebral bodies without the posterior spinal elements, are now becoming widely available and may approach QCT in their diagnostic sensitivity for detecting trabecular osteopenia.

In patients with an established diagnosis of oste-

oporosis, secondary causes of osteoporosis should be excluded by history, physical examination, and several laboratory tests. Levels of serum calcium, inorganic phosphate, and alkaline phosphatase are usually normal in patients with osteoporosis, although the last may rise slightly after a recent fracture. Other routine chemistries can help exclude renal or hepatic diseases, and a complete blood count may help uncover a hematologic or myeloproliferative disorder. Because multiple myeloma can mimic involutional osteoporosis, it should be carefully considered in all patients, particularly when the degree of osteoporosis exceeds that expected for the patient's age and gender. A serum PTH level should be measured to exclude primary or secondary hyperparathyroidism, and a 25-OH-D level should be checked to help screen for vitamin D deficiency. The serum thyroid-stimulating hormone level should be checked when thyroid disease is suspected and the serum testosterone level should be measured in all men with unexplained osteoporosis. The clinical utility of measuring biochemical markers of bone formation (e.g., serum osteocalcin, heat-labile alkaline phosphatase, or procollagen-1 extension peptide) and bone resorption (e.g., urine hydroxyproline, urine pyridinoline, or urine deoxypyridinoline) has not yet been established. However, these indices may help guide therapy in the future by classifying patients as having high- or low-turnover osteoporosis.

Radiographic Findings

A characteristic radiograph of osteoporosis of the spine is shown in Figure 76-4. With the loss of trabecular bone, the end plates of the vertebral

TABLE 76-2. TECHNIQUES FOR MEASURING BONE MINERAL DENSITY*

SITES MEASURED	PRECISION (%)	ACCURACY (%)	SCAN TIME (min)	RADIATION DOSE (mrems)
Quantitative computed tomography (QCT) Lumbar spine	2-10	5-20	10-15	100-1000
Single-photon absorptiometry (SPA) Proximal radius Distal radius Calcaneus	1-3	4-6	3-5	10-20
Dual-photon absorptiometry (DPA) Lumbar spine AP Lumbar spine lateral Proximal femur Total body	2-6	4-10	20-45	10-15
Dual-energy x-ray absorptiometry (DEXA) Lumbar spine AP Lumbar spine lateral Proximal radius Distal radius Proximal femur Total body	1-2	3-5	2-8	1-3

*For SPA, numbers refer to measurements of the proximal radius. For DPA and DEXA, numbers refer to AP measurements of the lumbar spine.

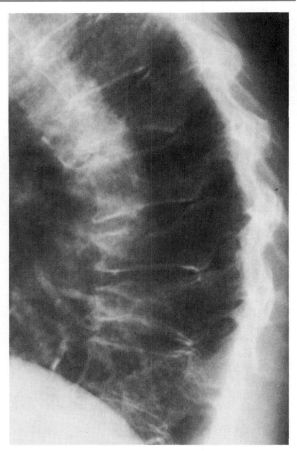

FIGURE 76-4. Radiograph showing radiolucency, compression fractures, and kyphosis in the spine of a patient with osteoporosis.

bodies become prominent. The washed-out radiolucent vertebral bodies tend to show fine vertical striations due to the preferential loss of horizontal trabeculae. The intervertebral discs expand into concavities within the vertebral bodies and may rupture into the body (Schmorl's nodules). There may be loss of height with compression fractures producing anterior wedging.

Treatment

The treatment of osteoporosis depends on its cause and the stage of the illness. If a secondary cause of osteoporosis is present, specific treatment should be aimed at correcting the underlying disorder. During the acute phase of a vertebral compression, attention is directed toward relieving pain with analgesics, muscle relaxants, heat, massage, and/or rest. Most patients with discomfort related to osteoporotic fractures or deformity benefit from a well-designed program of physical therapy. Both weight-bearing (e.g., jogging or weight-lifting) and non–weight-bearing (e.g., swimming) exercises appear to have beneficial effects on bone mass.

For most patients, exercises to strengthen the abdominal and back muscles are appropriate. Pharmacologic therapy is aimed at preventing further bone loss to decrease the likelihood of future fracture.

Calcium. Both dietary calcium intake and intestinal calcium absorption decrease with aging. Many postmenopausal women consume less than 400 mg/day of calcium, far below the U.S. recommended dietary allowance (RDA) of 800 to 1000 mg. Recent studies have demonstrated that calcium supplementation slows the rate of bone loss from the forearm without affecting the rate of bone loss from the spine in women who are within the first 5 years of menopause. In women who are in the later stages of menopause, calcium supplementation appears to retard bone loss from the forearm, spine, and hip. Although the doses of calcium have varied in different studies, most experts recommend that postmenopausal women consume between 1000 and 1500 mg of calcium per day, either in their diet or from supplements, in the absence of estrogen replacement.

Vitamin D. Many elderly people have low vitamin D intakes and insufficient exposure to sunlight, leading to vitamin D deficiency. The ability to convert 25-OH-D to 1,25-(OH)$_2$D in the kidney is also impaired in many elderly people. Clinical trials using pharmacologic doses of 1,25-(OH)$_2$D as a therapy for osteoporosis have produced conflicting results. However, it is widely recommended that all elderly patients take physiologic doses of vitamin D (i.e., 400 units/day) to prevent vitamin D deficiency, particularly during the winter months when exposure to ultraviolet radiation may be limited and the rate of bone loss accelerated.

Estrogens. Both oral and transdermal modes of estrogen replacement therapy prevent bone loss in estrogen-deficient women, regardless of when therapy is begun. However, because bone loss is most rapid in the first years of menopause, the benefits of estrogen therapy are greater if started before a substantial amount of bone loss has occurred. Case-control studies have suggested that estrogen therapy reduces the risk of forearm, vertebral, and hip fractures in postmenopausal women. The minimally effective doses of estrogen to prevent bone loss are 0.625 mg/day of oral conjugated estrogens or its equivalent, or 50 μg/day of transdermal estrogen. When given without concomitant progestin administration, estrogen replacement therapy increases the risk of endometrial carcinoma. Thus, in women whose uterus is intact, estrogen replacement therapy should be combined with a progestin, administered either as a small daily dose or cyclically for 10 to 14 days each month, to eliminate the increased risk of endometrial carcinoma associated with unopposed estrogens.

Calcitonin. In short-term studies, calcitonin therapy has prevented bone loss in both early and late menopausal women. Currently, calcitonin is available in the United States only for administration by subcutaneous injection, and the effective dose may vary from 50 IU every other day to 100 IU per day. Side effects such as nausea, flushing, and polyuria sometimes occur, particularly at the onset of therapy. These symptoms can be minimized by starting with a low dose, increasing it gradually, and administering the medication at bedtime. Alternative forms of administration, notably a nasal spray, are currently under active investigation and appear promising.

Bisphosphonates. Recent reports have shown that etidronate disodium, one of several bisphosphonates, increases spinal bone density and may decrease the rate of fractures in elderly postmenopausal women when given cyclically for 2 to 3 years. If long-term data confirm early reports and if they are equally effective in the early stages of menopause, bisphosphonates could become a particularly useful therapy for osteoporosis.

Sodium Fluoride. Although sodium fluoride therapy increases spinal bone density, randomized, controlled data indicate that fractures in the appendicular skeleton are more common in fluoride-treated patients. Thus, the use of sodium fluoride to treat osteoporosis is currently experimental.

REFERENCES

Johnston CC, Slemenda CW, Melton LJ III: Clinical use of bone densitometry. N Engl J Med 324:1105–1109, 1991.

Melton LJ III, Eddy DM, Johnston CC: Screening for osteoporosis. Ann Intern Med 112:517–528, 1990.

Raisz LG: Local and systemic factors in the pathogenesis of osteoporosis. N Engl J Med 318:818, 1988.

Riggs BL: Osteoporosis. *In* DeGroot LJ (ed): Endocrinology. Philadelphia, WB Saunders Co, 1989, pp 1188–1207.

Riggs BL, Melton LJ III: Involutional osteoporosis. N Engl J Med 314:1676–1686, 1986.

77 PAGET'S DISEASE OF BONE

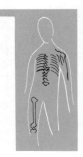

Paget's disease is a chronic disorder of bone that may be focal or may involve many sites throughout the skeleton; it is characterized by increased osteoclastic activity, usually coupled with osteoblastic activity. The disease is often asymptomatic and may be identified after finding an elevated serum alkaline phosphatase level or as an incidental abnormality on radiographs. However, it may result in pain, gross deformity, fracture, or neurologic compression syndromes. After osteoporosis, Paget's disease is the second most prevalent bone disease; it affects more than 3 per cent of adults over age 40 in the United States. Its prevalence varies with geographic location: it is high in the United States, Great Britain, France, Germany, and Australia and low in Scandinavia, the Middle East, and Asia.

Etiology

The cause of Paget's disease is currently unknown. Twenty to 30 per cent of affected patients have a family history of the disorder, and there is an increased frequency of human leukocyte antigen (HLA)–DQW1 antigen in pagetic subjects. Inclusion bodies that resemble paramyxoviruses are seen in pagetic osteoclasts. Immunohistochemical staining has identified the presence of measles and respiratory syncytial virus antigens in pagetic osteoclasts, and in situ hybridization has identified the presence of measles and canine distemper virus sequences. These observations suggest that a viral infection may also be important in the pathogenesis of Paget's disease, possibly in genetically susceptible hosts, although none of these viruses has been cultured and detection by polymerase chain reaction gene amplification has yielded conflicting results.

Pathology and Pathophysiology

The initiating event in Paget's disease is an increase in bone resorption. Osteoclasts are more numerous and contain many more nuclei than normal. In response to the increase in bone resorption, osteoblastic activity is increased; the resulting bone is abnormal in composition, thickened, and structurally weak. In the earliest phases of the disease, increased osteoclastic bone resorption dominates. This phase is followed by activity that combines increased resorption and new bone formation. Eventually, in some patients, bone turnover slows, leaving sclerotic "burned out" pagetic bone.

Clinical Picture (Table 77–1)

Most patients with Paget's disease are asymptomatic. The disease is localized and may affect one, two, or more bones in noncontiguous areas. Patients may present with a painless deformity of the skull or other involved bones. Physical examination may reveal increased warmth and erythema over the pagetic bone and skeletal deformities, particularly enlargement of the skull and bowing of the legs. Back pain, headache, and pain in the pelvis, femur, and tibia are common symptoms because these areas are most frequently affected. Arthritis is often found in joints near areas of the bone affected by Paget's disease, particularly when subchondral bone or normal bone-joint geometry is compromised. Sudden onset of pain may result from a complete transverse fracture. More common are small fissure fractures along the convex surfaces of bowed long bones, which may or may not produce symptoms. Hearing may be impaired owing to bony involvement of the ossicles or auditory canal or compression of cranial nerves. Spinal cord or nerve root compression that leads to radicular pain and muscle weakness may result from expanded pagetic bone. Other cranial nerve palsies occur less often. A softening of the base of the skull may produce flattening (platybasia) with the development of basilar invagination and may lead to neurologic compression syndromes. Fatigue is common in severe cases.

TABLE 77–1. CLINICAL MANIFESTATIONS OF PAGET'S DISEASE

Musculoskeletal pain
Degenerative arthritis in joints near affected areas
Headache
Skeletal deformity
Pathologic fractures
Enlarged skull
Erythema and warmth over pagetic bones
Hearing loss
Platybasia with or without basilar invagination
Neurologic compression syndromes
Angioid streaks in retina
Increased cardiac output — rarely congestive heart failure
Bone tumors
   Osteogenic sarcoma
   Fibrosarcoma
   Chondrosarcoma
   Reparative granuloma
   Giant cell tumor
Laboratory abnormalities
   Increased serum alkaline phosphatase
   Increased urinary hydroxyproline
   Hypercalciuria and hypercalcemia during immobilization
   Hyperuricemia
   Characteristic radiographs
   Increased uptake on bone scan

Associated Conditions

Secondary arthritis is a common and often debilitating complication of periarticular Paget's disease. Hyperuricemia, gout, and primary hyperparathyroidism occur with increased frequency in affected patients. The most serious complication of Paget's disease is sarcomatous degeneration, which occurs most commonly in the setting of severe polyostotic disease and may be heralded by a sudden increase in pain, a soft tissue mass, or pathologic fracture. The majority of tumors are osteogenic sarcomas, although fibrosarcomas and chondrosarcomas are also seen. Benign giant cell tumors, most often in the skull, are occasionally observed. Rarely, in severe cases, increased cardiac output to the involved bone may result in high-output congestive heart failure.

Laboratory Assessment

Urinary hydroxyproline excretion, which reflects collagen degradation, is usually increased and reflects increased osteoclastic activity. Serum alkaline phosphatase, which reflects osteoblastic activity, is also increased owing to the coupled increase in bone formation. Newer markers of bone turnover, notably urinary excretion of 3-hydroxypyridinium residues and serum levels of procollagen-1 extension peptide, may prove to be more sensitive indicators of bone resorption and formation, respectively.

Bone scans are the most efficient means of surveying pagetic sites. Plain films of the involved areas provide more detailed information. Radiographs obtained early in the course of the disease demonstrate osteolysis that may be seen as an advancing "blade of grass" in the long bones (Fig. 77–1B) or as osteoporosis circumscripta in the skull or pelvis (Fig. 77–1A). Later, in the mixed phase of the disease, enlarged or expanded bones with cortical thickening, coarsening of trabecular markings, and both lytic and sclerotic areas are seen on radiographs (Fig. 77–1C). In the late stages of the disease, when bone turnover is quiescent, sclerotic bone is predominant (Fig. 77–1D).

Bone biopsy is rarely needed to diagnose Paget's disease and should be avoided in weight-bearing bones. When done, biopsies show that older lamellar bone is replaced by woven, randomly oriented bone. The distinction between cortical and trabecular bone is obscured. The result of the disordered bone turnover is the so-called mosaic pattern of woven bone plus irregular sections of lamellar bone linked in a disorganized way by numerous cement lines.

Treatment

The two major goals of therapy are to relieve symptoms and prevent complications. Most people with Paget's disease are asymptomatic or have minimal symptoms that can be managed with salicylates or nonsteroidal anti-inflammatory medications. Treatment with antiresorptive agents is often recommended when pain does not respond to such therapy or when bone deformity, hearing loss, neurologic impairment, or high-output congestive heart failure is present. Some experts also recommend treatment in asymptomatic individuals if the Paget's disease involves a weight-bearing bone or the skull or is near major joints, particularly if biochemical indices of bone turnover are markedly elevated. Treatment may be indicated during periods of immobilization to prevent accelerated bone loss, hypercalciuria, and hypercalcemia due to increased bone turnover.

The available treatments (calcitonin, bisphosphonates, and plicamycin) are directed toward reducing osteoclastic activity and thereby suppressing bone turnover. Salmon and human calcitonin are currently available only for parenteral use in the United States, although a nasal spray is being evaluated. Because salmon calcitonin inhibits osteoclastic activity with fewer side effects than the human hormone, it is the preferred treatment except in patients in whom neutralizing antibodies develop and cause escape from the treatment. In addition to decreasing bone turnover, calcitonin has a significant analgesic effect in some patients. The usual dosage is 50 to 100 units daily or on alternate days by subcutaneous injection. Side effects include nausea and flushing and usually resolve with continued use. The incidence of side effects can be minimized by increasing the dose gradually and administering the medication at bedtime. Calcitonin therapy can also decrease the

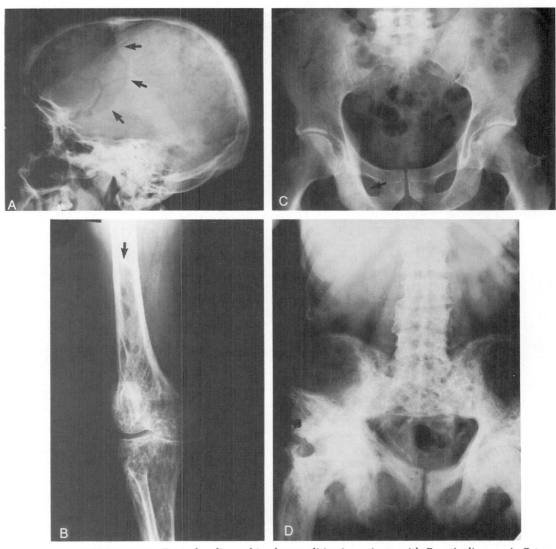

FIGURE 77–1. Typical radiographic abnormalities in patients with Paget's disease. *A*, Osteoporosis circumscripta of the skull. *B*, Lytic lesions in the femur with the characteristic "blade of grass" or "flamelike" lesion. *C*, Blastic involvement of the right ischial ramus of the pelvis with thickening of the medial cortex. *D*, Mixed lytic and blastic disease involving entire pelvis along with L4 and L5 and both femoral heads. (Courtesy of Dr. Daniel Rosenthal.)

blood flow to pagetic bone prior to surgical intervention.

Etidronate disodium (EHDP) was the first bisphosphonate available for treatment of Paget's disease in the United States. Because EHDP can induce a mineralization defect when given in high doses or for prolonged periods, the recommended regimen is 5 mg/kg/day orally for 6 months, followed by a 6-month period of no treatment. Resistance may develop after multiple courses of treatment. Side effects are uncommon but may include gastrointestinal symptoms, pruritus, and dizziness. EHDP should probably be avoided in patients with extensive lytic disease in weight-bearing bones. Because newer diphosphonates such as aminohydroxypropylidene bisphosphonate (APD) do not produce mineralization defects and appear to be more potent in suppressing disease activity, they may supersede EHDP as agents for treating Paget's disease in the future.

Plicamycin is generally reserved for patients with severe Paget's disease refractory to other therapies or with neural compression, in which rapid responses are needed. Serum calcium and inorganic phosphate levels often fall with plicamycin therapy. The use of plicamycin in these patients may be replaced by intravenous APD in the future.

REFERENCES

Singer FR, Wallach S (eds): Paget's Disease of Bone. Clinical Assessment, Present and Future Therapy. New York, Elsevier, 1991.

Siris ES: Paget's disease of bone. In Favus MJ (ed): Primer on the Metabolic Bone Diseases and Disorders of Mineral Metabolism. Kelseyville, CA, American Society for Bone and Mineral Research, 1990. pp 253–259.

SECTION XI

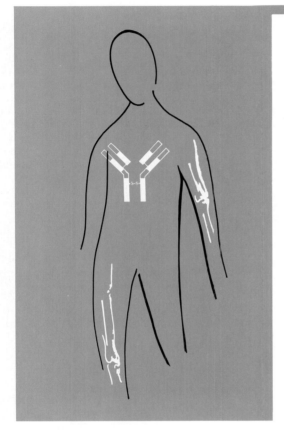

MUSCULOSKELETAL AND CONNECTIVE TISSUE DISEASES

Section XI of Cecil Essentials of Medicine, 2nd ed, by George Ho, Jr., M.D., and Gary M. Kammer, M.D., has been extensively revised and updated by the current authors for this section on Musculoskeletal and Connective Tissue Diseases.

78 APPROACH TO THE PATIENT WITH MUSCULOSKELETAL DISEASE

Rheumatology involves the study of diseases affecting joints and periarticular structures. One in six visits to a health professional is for a musculoskeletal complaint; the majority of patient visits to physicians are for nonarticular problems and common musculoskeletal diseases such as osteoarthritis (OA) and rheumatoid arthritis (RA). However, many of the musculoskeletal diseases present major diagnostic and therapeutic challenges. Despite rapid advances in immunology, radiology, and other technologies, *a complete medical history and careful physical examination are the most important steps in the evaluation of the patient with musculoskeletal complaints.* Many musculoskeletal symptoms present with prominent findings that extend to other organ systems. Therefore, the clinician must evaluate the whole patient even when symptoms appear to be localized. After the complete evaluation, the clinician should be able to classify a patient's problem in order to direct laboratory and radiographic studies to aid in confirming the clinical diagnosis. On the basis of the initial comprehensive evaluation, the clinician should be able to answer the following questions:

1. Is the condition limited to the musculoskeletal system or is it a systemic process?
2. Is the process articular or nonarticular?
3. Is the process monoarticular or polyarticular?
4. Is the process acute or chronic?
5. Is the condition inflammatory or noninflammatory?
6. Is the arthritis axial, peripheral, or both?
7. Is the process symmetric or asymmetric?
8. Is the pain intermittent or persistent?
9. Is there evidence of muscle or neurologic dysfunction?
10. Is there a family history of a similar process?

Musculoskeletal diseases can be divided into several distinct categories based on pathology (Table 78–1). Identification of the predominant pathophysiologic process (Fig. 78–1) may suggest different therapeutic decisions.

A critical decision in the initial evaluation of a patient with musculoskeletal complaints is whether the problem requires immediate evaluation and treatment. For most musculoskeletal complaints, the decision to investigate or treat can wait until the chronicity and severity of the complaints can be fully elucidated. Some clinical situations, however, mandate immediate investigation and treatment:

1. Febrile patient.
2. Single or a few joints involved with acute pain; an acute infectious or crystal arthritis must be excluded or treated immediately.
3. Signs and symptoms suggestive of renal, cardiac, or pulmonary compromise.
4. Symptoms associated with trauma; fracture or internal derangement of joint.
5. Neurologic compromise; bowel or bladder

TABLE 78–1. CATEGORIES OF MUSCULOSKELETAL DISEASES

PATHOLOGY OR PROCESS	DISEASE EXAMPLE	DIAGNOSTIC TEST(S)
Infection	Septic arthritis, osteomyelitis	Gram's stain and culture of synovial fluid or tissue
Crystal-induced	Gout, pseudogout	Synovial fluid examination for crystals
Autoimmune	Rheumatoid arthritis, systemic lupus erythematosus	Clinical and radiographic evaluation, serologies (rheumatoid factors, antinuclear antibody)
Degenerative	Osteoarthritis	Clinical and radiographic evaluation
Enthesopathy	Ankylosing spondylitis, Reiter's syndrome	Clinical and radiographic evaluation
Vasculitis	Polyarteritis nodosa	Clinical evaluation, biopsy and/or arteriogram
Nonarticular, focal	Bursitis, carpal tunnel syndrome	Clinical evaluation, nerve conduction velocities
Nonarticular, diffuse	Fibromyalgia syndrome	Clinical evaluation
Muscle inflammation	Polymyositis/dermatomyositis	Clinical evaluation, serum muscle enzymes, muscle biopsy
Fibrosis	Scleroderma	Clinical evaluation

dysfunction; cervical or lumbar cord nerve root compression.

6. Vasculitic process that may result in loss of limb or irreversible organ damage.

A comprehensive physical examination is necessary in the evaluation of connective tissue disorders, even in a patient with localized symptoms. Many apparent local musculoskeletal complaints have their origin distant from the region of pain. A musculoskeletal examination should include evaluation of specific joints for warmth, swelling, tenderness, crepitus, range of motion (active and passive), and deformity. The evaluation of muscle function requires a simultaneous evaluation of the nervous system in addition to determining the bulk, tone, tenderness, and strength of appropriate muscle groups. Pain and dysfunction in the area of a joint are not necessarily articular in origin; attention should also be directed to the periarticular region. Enthesopathy, bursitis, and tendinitis (Fig. 78–1) are all causes of periarticular pain. The cervical, thoracic, and lumbar spine and sacroiliac joints should be tested for mobility.

LABORATORY TESTS

Laboratory tests in patients with musculoskeletal diseases most often provide data to confirm the clinical diagnosis obtained by the detailed history and comprehensive physical examination. The majority of patients presenting with musculoskeletal problems do not require numerous laboratory tests. However, diagnosis of complicated or subtle clinical problems may require more extensive testing to assist in diagnosis and to determine therapeutic options.

Synovial Fluid Analysis

Analysis of the synovial fluid is the most useful test in the practice of rheumatology. It should be performed as part of the diagnostic evaluation in any patient with joint disease. Synovial fluid analysis provides the physician with valuable information about processes occurring inside the joint. Many textbooks offer a long list of tests to perform on synovial fluid; however, just a few tests may provide the evidence to establish a specific diagnosis (most commonly gout and infection) (Table 78–2). Gross examination of the fluid plus a leukocyte count may narrow the diagnostic possibilities to diseases causing noninflammatory versus inflammatory joint effusions (Table 78–3). These

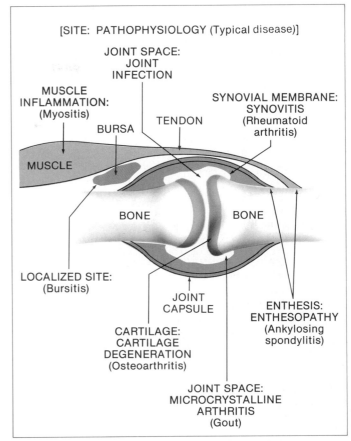

FIGURE 78–1. Location of musculoskeletal disease processes. (From Fries JF: Approach to the patient with musculoskeletal disease. *In* Wyngaarden JB, Smith LH Jr, Bennett JC [eds]: Cecil Textbook of Medicine. 19th ed. Philadelphia, WB Saunders Co, 1992, p 1488.)

categories are based on the total synovial fluid white cell count; however, in practice this system is not definitive because disease categories may overlap. For example, a "noninflammatory" synovial fluid does not exclude septic or crystal arthritis.

A macroscopic and microscopic inspection of the fluid may alert the physician to specific diagnoses. The presence of blood in the fluid should suggest a number of disorders (Table 78–4). Lipid droplets may be noted in traumatic arthritis, various inflammatory effusions, and pancreatic fat necrosis. Crystals such as monosodium urate, calcium pyrophosphate dihydrate, oxalate, and cholesterol can be detected in synovial fluid using a polarized light microscope. Special stains on synovial fluid may be helpful in diagnosing Whipple's disease (periodic acid–Schiff stain), hemochromatosis, or pigmented villonodular synovitis (Prussian blue stain for iron), amyloidosis (Congo red stain), and systemic lupus erythematosus (SLE) (Wright's stain for LE cells).

TABLE 78–2. STANDARD TESTS TO PERFORM ON SYNOVIAL FLUID

Volume and gross appearance
Wet preparation
White cell concentration and differential
Polarized light microscopy
Gram's stain and culture (when clinically indicated)

TABLE 78–3. CLASSIFICATION OF SYNOVIAL EFFUSIONS BY SYNOVIAL WHITE CELL COUNT

GROUP	DIAGNOSIS (Examples)	APPEARANCE	SYNOVIAL FLUID (White Cell Count per mm³)*	POLYMORPHONUCLEAR CELLS
Normal		Clear, pale yellow	0–200	<10%
Noninflammatory	Osteoarthritis Trauma	Clear to slightly turbid	50–2000 (600)	<30%
Mildly inflammatory	Systemic lupus erythematosus	Clear to slightly turbid	0–9000 (3000)	<20%
Severely inflammatory (noninfectious)	Gout	Turbid	100–160,000 (21,000)	~70%
	Pseudogout	Turbid	50–75,000 (14,000)	~70%
	Rheumatoid arthritis	Turbid	250–80,000 (19,000)	~70%
Severely inflammatory (infectious)	Bacterial infections	Very turbid	150–250,000 (80,000)	~90%
	Tuberculosis	Turbid	2500–100,000 (20,000)	~60%

*Mean values in parentheses.

TABLE 78–4. DIFFERENTIAL DIAGNOSIS OF HEMARTHROSIS

Hemophilia
Trauma with or without fracture
Pigmented villonodular synovitis
Synovioma, other tumors
Hemangioma
Charcot joint or other severe joint destruction
Von Willebrand's disease
Anticoagulant therapy
Myeloproliferative disease with thrombocytosis
Thrombocytopenia
Scurvy
Ruptured aneurysm
Arteriovenous fistula
Idiopathic

From Schumacher HR: Synovial fluid analysis and synovial biopsy. In Kelley WN, Harris ED Jr, Ruddy S, Sledge CB (eds): Textbook of Rheumatology. 3rd ed. Philadelphia, WB Saunders Co, 1989, p 638.

TABLE 78–5. COMMON SEROLOGIC TESTS USED IN MUSCULOSKELETAL DISEASES

TEST	DISEASE ASSOCIATION
Rheumatoid factor	RA, several other diseases
Antinuclear antibody	SLE, scleroderma, RA, myositis, other diseases
Anti-Sm	SLE
Anti-dsDNA	SLE
Antihistone H_1, H_3–H_4	SLE
Antihistone H_{2A}, H_{2B}	More common in drug-induced SLE
Anti-RNP	MCTD (high titers), SLE
Anti-SSB	Sjögren's syndrome, SLE
Anti-SSA	Sjögren's syndrome, SLE, neonatal lupus
Anticentromere	More common in limited scleroderma
Antitopoisomerase I (Scl-70)	More common in diffuse scleroderma
Antineutrophil cytoplasmic antibody (ANCA)	Wegener's granulomatosis, less common in other vasculitides
Anticardiolipin	SLE, antiphospholipid antibody syndrome
Lupus anticoagulant	SLE, antiphospholipid antibody syndrome
Anti-Jo-1	Dermatomyositis/polymyositis with interstitial lung disease

RA = Rheumatoid arthritis; SLE = systemic lupus erythematosus; MCTD = mixed connective tissue disorders.

Immunologic Testing

Autoantibodies are antibodies directed against tissue self-antigens, including immunoglobulins and cell surfaces and nuclear, cytoplasmic, and circulating molecules. Common serologic tests used to detect autoantibodies in the evaluation of musculoskeletal diseases are listed in Table 78–5. These tests should not be used as "screening" tests for patients with musculoskeletal complaints, because most of these autoantibodies are found in several different connective tissue diseases. For example, serum rheumatoid factors can be demonstrated in a variety of other acute and chronic inflammatory conditions (Table 78–6) as well as in healthy persons. The same lack of specificity of disease associations applies to antinuclear antibodies. However, a few of these serologic tests do appear to be disease-specific: anti-dsDNA and anti-Sm are seen only in patients with SLE; anti-RNP in high titers is only found in mixed connective tissue disease but is found in low titers in other diseases; and anti-neutrophil cytoplasmic antibody (ANCA) is fairly specific for Wegener's granulomatosis.

Serum protein electrophoresis is used routinely to characterize and quantitate serum immunoglobulins. Hypergammaglobulinemia may be seen in several of the autoimmune diseases and vasculitis. Monoclonal immunoglobulin spikes may be indicative of multiple myeloma. A seronegative (for rheumatoid factor) inflammatory arthritis that clinically resembles RA is occasionally seen in persons with hypogammaglobulinemia. Elevated levels of circulating immune complexes occur in many autoimmune diseases as well as in infections and malignancies. Measurement of circulating immune complexes may be useful in following the disease activity of SLE and various systemic vasculitides.

Measurement of total hemolytic complement (CH_{50}) and individual complement components, especially C3 and C4, are often helpful in the diagnosis and management of SLE and vasculitis. The CH_{50} depends on intact and functional classic and alternative pathways, resulting in effective target lysis (Fig. 78–2). CH_{50} measures the ability of serum to lyse antibody-coated erythrocytes and reflects the activity of all complement components. Decreased CH_{50} levels suggest either depletion of complement proteins by an immune-mediated process or inherited deficiency of an individual protein. Low levels of C3 and C4 are usually seen when a decreased CH_{50} is secondary to an immune mechanism. An extremely low CH_{50} in the presence of relatively normal values of C3 and C4 suggests a genetic complement deficiency, with C2 deficiency being most common. Deficiencies of C1, C4, and C2 are associated with SLE, glomerulonephritis, and nonspecific vasculitis. The acquired deficiency of C1 inhibitor is associated with SLE and lymphoid malignancies.

TABLE 78–6. DISEASES COMMONLY ASSOCIATED WITH RHEUMATOID FACTOR

Rheumatic diseases: rheumatoid arthritis, systemic lupus erythematosus, scleroderma, mixed connective tissue disease, Sjögren's syndrome

Acute viral infections: mononucleosis, hepatitis, influenza, and many others; after vaccination (may yield falsely elevated titers of antiviral antibodies)

Parasitic infections: trypanosomiasis, kala-azar, malaria, schistosomiasis, filariasis, etc.

Chronic inflammatory diseases: tuberculosis, leprosy, yaws, syphilis, brucellosis, subacute bacterial endocarditis, salmonellosis

Neoplasms: after irradiation or chemotherapy

Other hyperglobulinemic states: hypergammaglobulinemic purpura, cryoglobulinemia, chronic liver disease, sarcoid, other chronic pulmonary diseases

From Schumacher HR: Synovial fluid analysis and synovial biopsy. *In* Kelley WN, Harris ED Jr, Ruddy S, Sledge CB [eds]: Textbook of Rheumatology. 3rd ed. Philadelphia, WB Saunders Co, 1989, p 200.

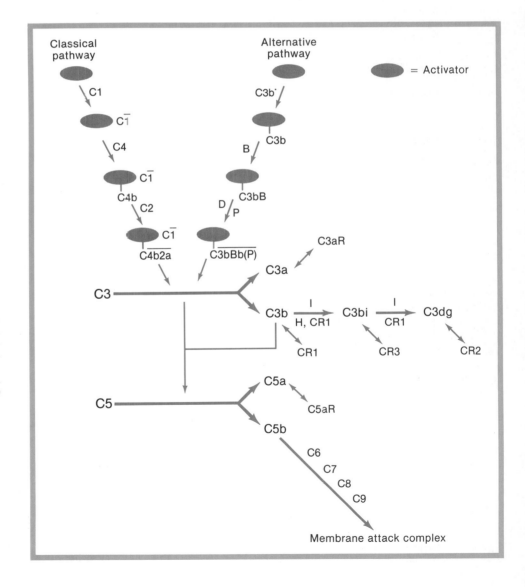

FIGURE 78–2. Complement activation. Formation of the C3 and C5 convertases in the two pathways of complement activation and the major biologically active fragments generated from C3 and C5 are shown. Bidirectional arrows indicate interactions with major receptors. C3b* indicates metastable C3b; overbars indicate enzymatically active proteins or protein complexes; CR refers to complement receptor. (From Volanakis JE: Molecular genetics of complement and autoimmune diseases. *In* Talal N [ed]: Molecular Autoimmunity. San Diego, Academic Press, 1991, p 84; with permission.)

Acute Phase Reactants

The most clinically useful measures of acute phase response are the erythrocyte sedimentation rate (ESR) and C-reactive protein (CRP). Because the ESR is inexpensive and quick and easy to do, it is more commonly used to detect inflammation than is CRP, even though the latter may be more accurate. Although it is a sensitive indicator of inflammation, the ESR lacks specificity, but is particularly useful in following the treatment of patients with polymyalgia rheumatica and temporal arteritis.

Other Laboratory Tests

A complete blood count and urinalysis are routinely done in patients with signs and symptoms of a systemic illness. In a small percentage of patients with nonspecific joint complaints, more extensive laboratory testing may be required. In such cases, a chemistry profile, serum iron and ferritin, and thyroid function tests may provide useful clues for certain systemic diseases. Renal and liver function should also be evaluated to monitor for potential toxicity from commonly used medications such as nonsteroidal anti-inflammatory drugs.

RADIOLOGIC EVALUATION

Radiographs are a vital investigative tool in rheumatology and provide information about the distribution of joint involvement as well as specific diagnoses. Radiographs of the hands and feet may reveal certain "target" joints and changes that are characteristic of specific diseases (e.g., gout — first metatarsophalangeal [MTP] joint erosions; rheumatoid arthritis — fourth and fifth MTP joint erosions). A single anteroposterior view of the pelvis and a lateral view of the lumbar spine and sacroiliac joints are sufficient to evaluate most disorders of the lumbosacral spine and sacroiliac joints. Radiographic changes that show joint space loss with osteophyte formation are diagnostic of OA. Chrondocalcinosis and other soft tissue calcifications can be easily demonstrated using plain x-ray films. Chrondrocalcinosis is detected primarily in the menisci of knees, triangular fibrous cartilage of the wrist, symphisis pubis, acetabular and glenoid labra, and intervertebral discs.

Ultrasonography in rheumatology is used primarily to detect synovial cysts, chiefly in the popliteal area (Baker's cyst). Computed tomography and magnetic resonance imaging (MRI) are useful in evaluating the spine and sacroiliac joints and in detecting disc herniations. In addition, they are useful in diagnosing other disorders such as avascular necrosis and osteomyelitis. MRI can also detect damage to the menisci and ligaments of the knee. Bone and joint scans are useful in the diagnosis or exclusion of several musculoskeletal disorders, including osteomyelitis, septic arthritis, avascular necrosis, reflex sympathetic dystrophy, stress fractures, and bone tumors.

REFERENCES

Fries JF: Approach to the patient with musculoskeletal disease. *In* Wyngaarden JB, Smith LH Jr, Bennett JC (eds): Cecil Textbook of Medicine. 19th ed. Philadelphia, WB Saunders Co, 1992, pp 417–424.
Schumacher HR: Synovial fluid analysis and synovial biopsy. *In* Kelley WN, Harris ED Jr, Ruddy S, Sledge CB (eds): Textbook of Rheumatology. 3rd ed. Philadelphia, WB Saunders Co, 1989, pp 637–648.

79 RHEUMATOID ARTHRITIS

Rheumatoid arthritis (RA) is a chronic inflammatory disease that can affect various organs but predominantly involves the synovial tissues of the diarthrodial joints. It occurs worldwide in all ethnic groups, but with significant variations in the prevalence rates among populations. The major histocompatibility complex (MHC)–determined human leukocyte antigen (HLA)–DR4 is significantly increased in patients with RA. The molecular biology suggests that with HLA-DR4 and its related molecules, Dw14 and Dw15, predisposition to RA depends on the binding site for antigen presentation. This information indicates that an unknown antigen initiates the rheumatoid process. Hence, the infectious origin of RA has been continually hypothesized and has ranged from various

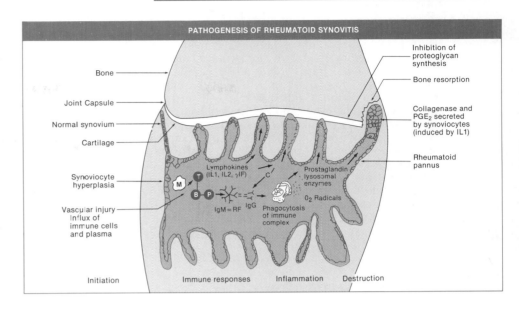

FIGURE 79–1. Events involved in the pathogenesis of rheumatoid synovitis progress from left to right. M = Macrophage; T = T lymphocyte; B = B lymphocyte; P = plasma cell; IL1 = interleukin-1; IL2 = interleukin-2; γIF = gamma-interferon; RF = rheumatoid factor; PGE$_2$ = prostaglandin E$_2$; IgM = immunoglobulin M; IgG = immunoglobulin G; C = complement. (From Arnett FC: Rheumatoid arthritis. In Wyngaarden JB, Smith LH Jr, Bennett JC [eds]: Cecil Textbook of Medicine. 19th ed. Philadelphia, WB Saunders Co, 1992, p 1509.)

bacteria, including streptococci, mycoplasma, clostridia, and diphtheroids, to a variety of viral infections including parvovirus, Epstein-Barr virus (EBV), and retroviruses. To date, no conclusive evidence has been presented for any of these as precipitating events.

PATHOGENESIS

A hallmark of the pathology of rheumatoid synovitis is membrane proliferation and ultimate erosion of articular cartilage and subchondral bone (Fig. 79–1). Although the precise initiating event

TABLE 79–1. STAGES OF RHEUMATOID ARTHRITIS

STAGE	PATHOLOGIC PROCESS	SYMPTOMS	PHYSICAL SIGNS	RADIOGRAPHIC CHANGES*
1	Presentation of antigen to T cells	Probably none	—	—
2	T-cell proliferation B-cell proliferation Angiogenesis in synovial membrane	Malaise, mild joint stiffness and swelling	Swelling of small joints of hands or wrists, or pain in hands, wrists, knees, and feet	None
3	Accumulation of neutrophils in synovial fluid Synovial-cell proliferation without polarization or invasion of cartilage	Joint pain and swelling, morning stiffness, malaise and weakness	Warm, swollen joints, excess synovial fluid, soft-tissue proliferation within joints, pain and limitation of motion, rheumatoid nodules	Soft-tissue swelling
4	Polarization of synovitis into a centripetally invasive pannus Activation of chondrocytes Initiation of enzyme (proteinase) degradation of cartilage	Same as stage 3	Same as stage 3, but more pronounced swelling	MRI reveals proliferative pannus; radiographic evidence of periarticular osteopenia
5	Erosion of subchondral bone Invasion of cartilage by pannus Chondrocyte proliferation Stretched ligaments around joints	Same as stage 3, plus loss of function and early deformity (e.g., ulnar deviation at metacarpophalangeal joint)	Same as stage 3, plus instability of joints, flexion contractures, decreased range of motion, extraarticular complications	Early erosions and narrowing of joint spaces

*MRI denotes magnetic resonance imaging.
Reprinted, by permission, from the New England Journal of Medicine, Vol 322, pp. 1277–1289, 1990.

is unknown, it does seem to involve some specific antigenic stimulation of susceptible T lymphocytes bearing the appropriate MHC molecules. This results in both T and B cell proliferation, stimulation of blood vessel proliferation in the synovial membrane, accumulation of inflammatory cells including polymorphonuclear leukocytes, synovial cell proliferation, and development of a rapidly growing and invasive pannus. The last-named grows almost like a benign tumor, to invade cartilage, activate chondrocytes, and release digestive enzymes that degrade cartilage and bone, finally resulting in destructive erosions associated with inflammatory processes surrounding tendons.

TABLE 79–2. CLASSIFICATION CRITERIA FOR RHEUMATOID ARTHRITIS*

1. Morning stiffness (≥ 1 hr)
2. Swelling (soft tissue) of three or more joints
3. Swelling (soft tissue) of hand joints (PIP, MCP, or wrist)
4. Symmetric swelling (soft tissue)
5. Subcutaneous nodules
6. Serum rheumatoid factor
7. Erosions and/or periarticular osteopenia, in hand or wrist joints, seen on radiograph

*Criteria 1 to 4 must have been continuous for 6 weeks or longer and must be observed by a physician. A diagnosis of rheumatoid arthritis requires that four of the seven criteria be fulfilled.

PIP = Proximal interphalangeal; MCP = metacarpophalangeal.

From Arnett FC: Rheumatoid arthritis. *In* Wyngaarden JB, Smith LH Jr, Bennett JC (eds): Cecil Textbook of Medicine. 19th ed. Philadelphia, WB Saunders Co, 1992, p 1508.

TABLE 79–3. EXTRA-ARTICULAR ORGAN SYSTEM INVOLVEMENT IN RHEUMATOID ARTHRITIS

ORGAN SYSTEM	EXTRA-ARTICULAR MANIFESTATIONS
Skin	Cutaneous vasculitis
	Rheumatoid nodules
Eye	Episcleritis
	Scleritis
	Scleromalacia perforans
	Corneal ulcers/perforation
	Uveitis
	Retinitis
	Glaucoma
	Cataract
Lung	Pleuritis
	Diffuse interstitial fibrosis
	Vasculitis
	Rheumatoid nodules
	Caplan's syndrome
	Pulmonary hypertension
Heart and blood vessels	Pericarditis
	Myocarditis
	Coronary arteritis
	Valvular insufficiency
	Conduction defects
	Vasculitis
	Felty's syndrome
Nervous system	Mononeuritis multiplex
	Distal sensory neuropathy

CLINICAL MANIFESTATIONS

The articular manifestations of RA are best understood from knowledge of the sequential events that take place in the pathogenetic process (Table 79–1). As indicated, the inflammatory process may be under way for some time before swelling, tissue reaction, and joint destruction are seen. Appreciation of this sequence of events is important in considering therapeutic approaches.

RA affects about 1.5 per cent of most populations, but frequencies as high as 5 per cent have been reported in some Native American tribes. The disease afflicts women in the childbearing years three times more frequently than men. In older age groups, there is a trend toward more equal involvement of men and women.

RA is an idiopathic, symmetric synovitis affecting similar joints bilaterally. The criteria for classification of RA are presented in Table 79–2. Occasionally, the disease presents as a monoarthritis or asymmetric oligoarthritis but eventually assumes a symmetric distribution. Very early in its course, the predominant symptoms may be vague: variable aching, polyarthralgias, and fatigability with little, if any, evidence of synovitis (see Table 79–1). During this early phase the diagnosis may be unclear, and alternative possibilities, such as fibrositis and polymyalgia rheumatica, are considered. A second, commonly observed onset is frank synovitis in an otherwise healthy individual. The synovitis most commonly affects the metatarsophalangeal (MTP) joints of the feet and the metacarpophalangeal (MCP) and proximal interphalangeal (PIP) joints of the hands, although other joints can be simultaneously involved. A third but uncommon mode of presentation is a rapidly progressive and debilitating polyarticular synovitis. Rarely one may observe the onset of extraarticular disease before clinical evidence of synovitis (Table 79–3). Although these patterns of onset may not be associated with the early presence of IgM rheumatoid factors, the aggressive/destructive form of RA is often characterized by high titers of these immunoglobulins.

The clinical course of RA is highly variable and can be (1) sporadic, punctuated by intervals of disease inactivity; (2) insidious, with relentless progression of synovitis and periodic, debilitating flares; and (3) aggressive and "malignant," with no period of relative remission. The last is characterized by severe polyarticular synovitis, rheumatoid nodules, weight loss, very high titers of rheumatoid factor, and hypocomplementemia. Extraarticular organ involvement (Table 79–3) is common.

The small joints of the hands and feet are the most common diarthrodial articulations affected. Initially, the synovitis of the PIP joints results in fusiform swelling associated with warmth, erythema, pain, and limitation of motion. MCP joints develop soft tissue swelling, squeeze tenderness, and limitations of motion due to synovitis.

Chronic synovitis of joints and tendon sheaths often leads to permanent deformities. In the feet

FIGURE 79-2. Hand deformities characteristic of chronic rheumatoid arthritis. *A*, Subluxation of metacarpophalangeal joints with ulnar deviation of digits. *B*, Hyperextension ("swan neck") deformities of proximal interphalangeal joints. (From Arnett FC: Rheumatoid arthritis. *In* Wyngaarden JB, Smith LH Jr, Bennett JC [eds]: Cecil Textbook of Medicine. 19th ed. Philadelphia, WB Saunders Co, 1992, p 1511.)

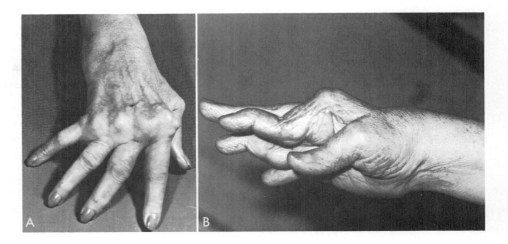

one commonly sees subluxation of the heads of the MTPs and foreshortening of the extensor tendons, giving rise to "hammer toe" or "cock-up" deformities. A similar process in the hands results in volar subluxation of the MCP joints and ulnar deviation of the fingers. An exaggerated inflammatory response of an extensor tendon can result in a spontaneous, often asymptomatic rupture. Hyperextension of a PIP joint and flexion of the distal interphalangeal (DIP) joint produces a swanneck deformity (Fig. 79-2). The boutonniere deformity is a fixed flexion contracture of a PIP joint and extension of a DIP joint.

The joints of the wrists are frequently affected in RA. There is variable tenosynovitis of the dorsa of the wrists and, ultimately, interosseous muscle atrophy and diminished movement due to articular destruction and/or bony ankylosis. Volar synovitis can lead to a compression neuropathy termed *carpal tunnel syndrome* (see Chapter 115).

Chronic synovitis of the elbows, shoulders, hips, knees, and/or ankles creates special secondary disorders. Destruction of the elbow articulations can lead to flexion contracture, loss of supination and pronation, and/or subluxation. When the shoulder is involved, limitation of shoulder mobility, dislocation, and spontaneous tears of the rotator cuff resulting in chronic pain can occur. A result of long-term synovitis of the knee is hypertrophy of the gastrocnemius-semimembranous bursa (Baker's cyst) of the popliteal fossa. Dissection of the cyst distally into the leg and rupture can mimic acute thrombophlebitis.

Involvement of the cervical spine by RA tends to be a late occurrence in more advanced disease. Inflammation of the supporting ligaments of C1–C2 eventually produces laxity, sometimes giving rise to atlantoaxial subluxation. Spinal cord compression can result from anterior dislocation of C1 or from vertical subluxation of the odontoid process of C2 into the foramen magnum.

TREATMENT

The objectives of treatment for RA are (1) pain relief, (2) reduction or suppression of inflammation, (3) avoidance or early recognition of side effects, (4) preservation or restoration of function, and (5) maintenance of lifestyle.

Therapy of RA requires a multifaceted approach. The importance of an ongoing educational program cannot be overstated. The patient's education should emphasize the benefits of a balanced daily program of rest and exercise. Physical and occupational therapy instruction in the appropriate exercises, along with the judicious application of splinting, can prevent and treat deformities, enhance muscle tone and strength, and preserve or improve function.

The pharmacologic therapy of RA often necessitates a combination of agents. Treatment is usually initiated with either aspirin or another nonsteroidal anti-inflammatory drug (NSAID). The use of aspirin should result in a therapeutic serum salicylate level (20 to 30 mg/dl).

Owing to the potential side effects of acetylated salicylates, such as gastrointestinal hemorrhage secondary to peptic ulcer or gastritis or a bleeding diathesis resulting from aspirin-induced inhibition of platelet aggregation, the use of a nonacetylated derivative (e.g., choline magnesium salicylate) should be considered. Similarly, the use of NSAIDs requires monitoring for gastrointestinal blood loss. Antimalarials, notably hydroxychloroquine, are also active in early or mild cases. The major toxicity of the antimalarials is their potential to deposit on the cornea, to produce macular pigmentation, or to result in field defects. Although emphasis has been placed upon these potential adverse reactions, the occurrence of visual impairment due to hydroxychloroquine is rare and can be prevented by routine ophthalmologic examinations. If the desired therapeutic response is not obtained within 6 months, the agent is discontinued.

Gold salts are regarded as remitting agents. Although the precise mode (or modes) of action in RA is unknown, these agents appear to alter macrophage function. Two intramuscular forms of the agent are currently available—gold thioglucose and gold sodium thiomalate—and are generally given in doses of 25 to 50 mg/wk. In general, the agents are more efficacious when begun early in the course of seropositive disease. In the absence of significant side effects, the response to therapy should be evaluated after a total of about 1 gm has been given. If there has been improvement, therapy is usually maintained, with an increasing time interval between injections. Because multiple potential adverse reactions to gold salts are possible, these agents should be carefully monitored at regular intervals for hematologic, dermatologic, and renal side effects.

Penicillamine has been found useful in the treatment of RA and can sometimes induce remission. However, like gold, its effects are slow in expression, and it can have significant toxicity on the bone marrow and kidneys. Penicillamine has been observed to induce other autoimmune diseases such as myasthenia gravis, Goodpasture's syndrome, and lupus erythematosus. Immunosuppressive agents such as azathioprine, cyclophosphamide, chlorambucil, and methotrexate have been used and found effective, particularly in severe RA. At the present time, relatively low doses of oral methotrexate have been found to be very effective and relatively free of toxicity. The oral dose generally begins at 7.5 mg one time per week. Toxic effects of methotrexate target the liver and may produce cirrhosis; it may also cause bone marrow suppression and pneumonitis with pulmonary fibrosis. As with any of these drugs, frequent monitoring at regular intervals is advised.

Corticosteroids are routinely used in both the acute and chronic management of RA. Although the agents are clearly beneficial in the therapy of an acute flare, their long-term use is not warranted because steroids neither cure nor alter the natural course of the disease. Although the prolonged use of corticosteroids, even in small or "maintenance" doses, is fraught with numerous unwanted complications (cataracts, osteopenia, myopathy, and accelerated atherosclerosis), 5 to 10 mg every other day may be required in some patients in conjunction with other agents. Corticosteroids may be necessary in the immediate therapy of rapidly progressive RA complicated by anorexia, weight loss, fever, and other extra-articular complications. Intra-articular corticosteroids are useful following arthrocentesis to quell synovitis, reduce pain, and improve function.

REFERENCES

Arnett FC: Rheumatoid arthritis. In Wyngaarden JB, Smith LH Jr, Bennett JC (eds): Cecil Textbook of Medicine. 19th ed. Philadelphia, WB Saunders Co, 1992, pp 1508–1515.

Fassbender HG: Normal and pathological synovial tissue with emphasis on rheumatoid arthritis. In Cohen AS, Bennett JC (eds): Rheumatology and Immunology. 2nd ed. Orlando, FL, Grune & Stratton, 1986.

Harris ED: Rheumatoid arthritis; pathophysiology and implication for therapy. N Engl J Med 322:1277, 1990.

80 SYSTEMIC LUPUS ERYTHEMATOSUS

Systemic lupus erythematosus (SLE) is a disorder characterized by inflammation in several organ systems and the production of autoantibodies that participate in immunologically mediated tissue injury. No one clinical abnormality or one single test definitively establishes the diagnosis. Therefore, criteria developed for epidemiologic and research purposes can be used to identify patients with SLE and differentiate them from patients with other disorders (Table 80–1). Although these criteria may be helpful diagnostically, they are not foolproof. It is possible for a patient to fail to fulfill the criteria and still have SLE; it is also possible to fulfill these criteria but not have SLE. The clinical spectrum of SLE ranges from the mildest forms of skin rash to fulminant life-threatening internal organ involvement. Common causes of death include renal failure, hemorrhage, infection, pulmonary disease, and vasculitis. The 10-year survival rate is approximately 85 per cent.

SLE can occur at any age, with the peak incidence of onset between ages 13 and 40 years. SLE is 10 times more common in women and appears to be more common in certain racial groups, particularly blacks and possibly Chinese and other Asian populations.

ETIOPATHOGENESIS

Essentially every aspect of the immune system has been reported to be abnormal in patients with SLE. Therefore, it is unclear which defects are fundamental to the pathogenesis of SLE. Immune hyperactivity is illustrated by the production of numerous autoantibodies that may result from the interplay of genetic, environmental, and hormonal factors (Fig. 80–1). What triggers this immune overactivity is not fully understood. However, various environmental agents such as drugs or ultraviolet light can trigger the disease. In some persons, the inherited predisposition to SLE may be very important. If a family member has SLE, the likelihood of developing SLE increases approximately 30 per cent for identical twins and 5 per cent for other first-degree relatives. Several complement deficiencies, the most common being C2 deficiency, have also been associated with SLE.

SLE is classified as an immune complex disorder; it is a disease mediated primarily by antibodies. This process has been well demonstrated in renal disease associated with SLE but has not been as well defined in other organ systems. Antibodies—antinuclear (ANA) and anti-double stranded DNA (anti-dsDNA)—react with antigens in the circulation or the glomerulus, resulting in complement fixation followed by release of chemotactic factors and release of mediators of inflammation from leukocytes. Continued deposition of antibody and induction of inflammation may ultimately lead to irreversible renal damage. Similar processes may occur in other organs or with other cells; autoantibodies may be produced against erythrocytes, platelets, and lymphocytes.

Three histologic lesions are most characteristic of SLE: "onion-skin lesions," found in arteries of the spleen, that consist of concentric layers of fibrosis surrounding the vessel; Libman-Sacks verrucous endocarditis, vegetations on heart valves; and hematoxylin bodies, globular masses of bluish, dense, homogeneous material seen on hematoxylin and eosin stain. The hematoxylin bodies, which can be found in all organs, are identical to the inclusion bodies of LE cells and probably represent the interaction of antibodies to nucleoprotein.

Specific Subsets of Lupus

SLE is a disease of extreme variability in clinical presentation and course. Certain subtypes of SLE deserve special mention (Table 80–2). Discoid lupus erythematosus (DLE) is a subset of SLE be-

*The classification is based on 11 criteria. For the purpose of identifying patients in clinical studies, a person shall be said to have systemic lupus erythematosus if any 4 or more of the 11 criteria are present, serially or simultaneously, during any interval of observation.

From Steinberg AD: Systemic lupus erythematosus. In Wyngaarden JB, Smith LH Jr, Bennett JC (eds): Cecil Textbook of Medicine. 19th ed. Philadelphia, WB Saunders Co, 1992, p 1522.

TABLE 80–1. CRITERIA FOR CLASSIFICATION OF SLE*

CRITERIA	DEFINITION
1. Malar rash	Fixed erythema, flat or raised, over the malar eminences, tending to spare the nasolabial folds
2. Discoid rash	Erythematous raised patches with adherent keratotic scaling and follicular plugging; atrophic scarring may occur in older lesions.
3. Photosensitivity	Skin rash as a result of unusual reaction to sunlight, by patient history or physician observation
4. Oral ulcers	Oral or nasopharyngeal ulceration, usually painless, observed by a physician
5. Arthritis	Nonerosive arthritis involving two or more peripheral joints, characterized by tenderness, swelling, or effusion
6. Serositis	a. Pleuritis—convincing history of pleuritic pain or rub heard by a physician or evidence of pleural effusion OR b. Pericarditis—documented by electrocardiogram or rub or evidence of pericardial effusion
7. Renal disorder	a. Persistent proteinuria greater than 0.5 gm/day or greater than 3+ if quantitation not performed OR b. Cellular casts—may be red cell, hemoglobin, granular, tubular, or mixed
8. Neurologic disorder	a. Seizures—in the absence of offending drugs or known metabolic derangements, e.g., uremia, ketoacidosis, or electrolyte imbalance OR b. Psychosis—in the absence of offending drugs or known metabolic derangements, e.g., uremia, ketoacidosis, or electrolyte imbalance
9. Hematologic disorder	a. Hemolytic anemia—with reticulocytosis OR b. Leukopenia—less than 4000/mm³ total on two or more occasions OR c. Lymphopenia—less than 1500/mm³ on two or more occasions OR d. Thrombocytopenia—less than 100,000/mm³ in the absence of offending drugs
10. Immunologic disorder	a. Positive LE cell preparation OR b. Anti-DNA—antibody to native DNA in abnormal titer OR c. Anti-Sm—presence of antibody to Sm nuclear antigen OR d. False-positive serologic test for syphilis known to be positive for at least 6 months and confirmed by Treponema pallidum immobilization or fluorescent treponemal antibody absorption test
11. Antinuclear antibody	An abnormal titer of ANA by immunofluorescence or an equivalent assay at any point in time and in the absence of drugs known to be associated with drug-induced lupus syndrome

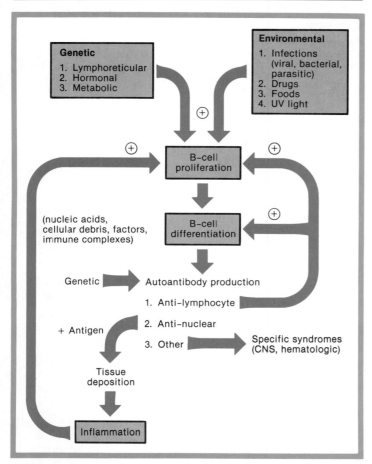

FIGURE 80–1. Initiation and perpetuation of systemic lupus erythematosus. (Modified from Steinberg AD: Systemic lupus erythematosus. *In* Wyngaarden JB, Smith LH Jr, Bennett JC [eds]: Cecil Textbook of Medicine. 19th ed. Philadelphia, WB Saunders Co, 1992, p 1523.)

cause 90 per cent of patients with DLE have disease limited to the skin. Ten per cent of patients with idiopathic SLE have discoid skin lesions at the start of their illness, and 25 per cent may develop these lesions during the course of their illness. The characteristic lesions are erythematous scaly plaques with follicular plugging. Central scarring often results in permanent depigmentation.

Subacute cutaneous lupus erythematosus (SCLE) usually occurs in patients who are negative for ANA and positive for the anti-Ro(SS-A) antibodies. About 10 per cent of patients with SLE have this

TABLE 80–2. SUBSETS OF LUPUS

Idiopathic
    Systemic
    Discoid
    Subacute cutaneous (ANA-negative)
    Late-onset
    Neonatal
Drug-induced

type of skin lesion. These lesions are annular, symmetric, superficial, and nonscarring. Patients with SLE-associated complement deficiencies often present with this type of skin lesion. These patients are often markedly photosensitive.

Late-onset SLE, defined as presentation after age 50, accounts for approximately 15 per cent of all cases. There is a higher incidence of interstitial lung disease, but much less neuropsychiatric or renal involvement in the late-onset form. Diagnosing SLE in the older group may be difficult owing to a greater prevalence of autoantibodies in the aging population, a greater exposure of drugs causing the serologic hallmark of SLE, and a higher prevalence of other rheumatic diseases such as Sjögren's syndrome that may present with the same features observed with SLE.

Neonatal lupus, a rare syndrome, appears to be a complication of maternal antibodies to Ro(SS-A) and/or La(SS-B) transferred through the placenta. Shortly after birth, infants develop typical discoid lesions with exposure to ultraviolet light. However, very few of these infants develop SLE later in life. Some infants develop other transient complications such as thrombocytopenia, hemolytic anemia, and, rarely, congenital heart block, which may be fatal. Patients with SLE who have a child with neonatal lupus have a 25 per cent likelihood of having another child with neonatal lupus in a subsequent pregnancy.

Several drugs have been reported to induce features of SLE, but only hydralazine, procainamide, chlorpromazine, methyldopa, and isoniazid are considered to have a definite association. The clinical features of drug-induced lupus are similar to those of idiopathic SLE except for the uncommon involvement of the renal and central nervous systems. In addition, the symptoms are usually mild and reversible when the drug is stopped. However, the ANA can remain positive for months or years. A strong association exists between high doses of procainamide, hydralazine, and isoniazid and slow acetylation of these drugs.

CLINICAL FEATURES

The "typical" presentation of SLE occurs in only a few patients. More commonly, patients initially present with one or two symptoms such as fatigue and arthritis and later may develop additional features of SLE (Table 80–3). Patients vary in organ system involvement and in severity of disease with regard to a given organ system. Also, SLE is characterized by periods of exacerbation followed by remission or inactive disease. Most patients have constitutional symptoms such as fatigue, fever, and weight loss at the time of diagnosis. Fatigue, although difficult to evaluate, may be the first sign of an exacerbation of disease.

Arthralgias or arthritis occur in 90 per cent of patients with SLE. The joint manifestations are usually more transient than in patients with rheumatoid arthritis (RA). The arthritis is typically symmetric and involves small joints of hands, wrists, and feet. Deformities similar to those in RA develop in 10 to 15 per cent of patients; however, bony erosions characteristic of RA do not occur. In addition, rheumatoid nodules (7 per cent) and rheumatoid factors (15 to 20 per cent) can be detected in SLE patients. Infectious arthritis and avascular necrosis of bone are two additional causes of joint pain that should be considered in SLE patients.

Abnormalities of the skin, hair, or mucous membranes are the second most common manifestations of SLE, occurring in 85 per cent of patients. Many different types of skin manifestations may appear in SLE. The classic malar butterfly rash, a nonpapular erythematous rash covering both cheeks and the bridge of the nose, with sparing of the nasolabial folds, may occur in the absence of skin exposure but may worsen with sun exposure. The second most common erythematous rash seen in SLE patients is a maculopapular rash that may be located anywhere on the body. Systemic flares of disease are often preceded by exacerbations of skin lesions. In addition to the discoid and SCLE lesions discussed above, other skin manifestations include urticaria, bullae, livedo reticularis, panniculitis (lupus profundus), alopecia, and vasculitic lesions. One fifth of patients have vasculitic skin lesions that are manifested as livedo reticularis, tender nodules, purpuric leg ulcers, or splinter hemorrhages. Mucosal ulcers, often painless, occur on the hard and soft palate. Raynaud's phenomenon may be severe enough to result in digital gangrene.

Conjunctivitis, episcleritis, or keratoconjunctivitis occurs in approximately 20 per cent of patients. Retinal vasculitis is uncommon but may lead to blindness. Cytoid bodies, white exudates adjacent to retinal blood vessels, are associated with active disease of the central nervous system.

Abdominal pain, often a diagnostic problem, may be a manifestation of serositis, mesenteric arteritis, or pancreatitis or may be secondary to visceral perforation (drug-induced peptic ulceration or secondary to vasculitis). Hepatosplenomegaly is noted in about 30 per cent of patients.

Pleuritic chest pain with or without pleural effusions occurs commonly. The presence of pulmonary emboli should be excluded because thrombophlebitis occurs in about 10 per cent of SLE patients. Acute parenchymal lung involvement may present as acute pneumonitis with or without pulmonary hemorrhage. However, the diagnosis of lupus pneumonitis should be made only after a rigorous search for an infectious cause. "Shrinking" lung syndrome, an uncommon entity, results from a myopathy of the diaphragm and usually causes progressive loss of lung volume.

Clinically significant renal involvement occurs in about 50 per cent of patients with SLE, but fortunately only a minority have renal involvement that results in irreversible organ failure. Proteinuria is the most common clinical sign of lupus nephritis; hypertension, hematuria, and red blood cell casts are other clues to active renal disease. The degree of active disease and scarring are fac-

TABLE 80–3. COMMON CLINICAL ABNORMALITIES IN PATIENTS WITH SLE

ABNORMALITY	APPROXIMATE FREQUENCY (%)*
Constitutional	
Fatigue	90
Fever	80
Weight loss, anorexia	60
Musculoskeletal	
Arthritis, arthralgia	90
Myalgia, myositis	30
Skin and mucous membranes	
Butterfly rash	60
Alopecia	50
Photosensitivity	50
Raynaud's phenomenon	30
Mucosal ulcers	30
Discoid lupus	20
Urticaria	10
Edema or bullae	10
Eye (conjunctivitis/episcleritis/sicca syndrome)	20
Gastrointestinal	30
Serosal (pleurisy, pericarditis, peritonitis)	50
Lymphoreticular	
Lymphadenopathy	50
Splenomegaly	30
Hepatomegaly	30
Hypertension	30
Bacterial infections	40
Pneumonitis (all)	30
"Lupus"	10
Renal (all)	50
Severe	20
Central nervous system	
Personality disorders	50
Seizures	20
Psychoses	20
Stroke or long tract signs	10
Migraine headaches	10
Cardiac	
Myocarditis	30
Murmurs and valvular disease	30
Coronary artery disease	20
Hematologic	
Anemia (all)	70
Hemolytic	10
Purpura (all)	50
Thrombocytopenia	10
Peripheral neuropathy	10

*Frequencies are compiled from a number of series and are rounded off to the nearest 10 per cent. There was some variation from series to series depending upon patient population, non-SLE therapy, and therapy for SLE. Some abnormalities are more common in younger patients than in older patients (e.g., splenomegaly and lymphadenopathy) and vice versa (e.g., muscle disease and sicca syndrome).

From Steinberg AD: Systemic lupus erythematosus. In Wyngaarden JB, Smith LH Jr, Bennett JC (eds): Cecil Textbook of Medicine. 19th ed. Philadelphia, WB Saunders Co, 1992, p 1526.

tors that significantly affect the patient's prognosis; therefore, a renal biopsy is often done to help guide therapy by determining the activity and chronicity of disease.

Neuropsychiatric manifestations of SLE are frequent and encompass the entire range of neurologic diseases. Depression and psychosis are frequent. Central nervous system involvement may also be manifested by organic brain disease, such as impairment of orientation, memory, or cognition. Abnormal cerebrospinal fluid findings during active neuropsychiatric disease include an elevated protein in about 50 per cent of patients. Nonsteroidal anti-inflammatory drug (NSAID)–induced aseptic meningitis has been reported in several SLE patients. The clinical usefulness of antineuronal or ribosomal P antibodies as an indicator of active disease is unproven.

Pericarditis, the most common cardiac manifestation, occurs in up to 30 per cent of patients; it rarely progresses to tamponade or constrictive pericarditis. LE cells are found frequently in pericardial fluid. Myocarditis, often associated with pericarditis, manifests clinically as tachycardia, ST-T wave changes, congestive heart failure, and cardiomegaly. Severe valvular lesions, primarily of the mitral and aortic valves, may occur. Verrucous endocarditis is present at autopsy in nearly all patients; subacute and acute bacterial endocarditis has occurred on valves affected by lupus endocarditis. Myocardial infarctions may result from coronary arteritis, thrombosis, or premature atherosclerosis secondary to chronic corticosteroid use.

One or more hematologic abnormalities are

TABLE 80–4. AUTOANTIBODIES FOUND IN PATIENTS WITH SLE

SPECIFICITY OF ANTIBODY	COMMENT
Nuclear	Present in about 90% of SLE patients, also found in several other disorders
Double-stranded DNA	Restricted to SLE; occurs in 50% of patients
Histones H1, H3–H4	SLE
Histones H2A–H2B	More common in drug-induced SLE
Sm	Restricted to SLE; found in 25%–60% of patients
Nuclear ribonucleoprotein	Highest titers in mixed connective tissue disease; also found in SLE
SS-A (Ro)	Sjögren's syndrome, SLE (30%–40%)
SS-B (La)	Sjögren's syndrome, SLE (15%)
Cell membrane determinants	Common in SLE
Red cells	May occur with or without hemolysis
White cells	Granulocytes, T cells, B cells
Platelets	Common with or without thrombocytopenia
Others	
Clotting factors	SLE and other diseases
Phospholipids (cardiolipin) (lupus anticoagulant)	SLE, others, without other diseases
Neuronal	Active CNS lupus
Ribosomal P protein	Active CNS lupus

CNS = Central nervous system.
Modified from Steinberg AD: Systemic lupus erythematosus. *In* Wyngaarden JB, Smith LH Jr, Bennett JC (eds): Cecil Textbook of Medicine. 19th ed. Philadelphia, WB Saunders Co, 1992, p 1524.

present in nearly all SLE patients with active disease; these include normochromic, normocytic anemia, hemolytic anemia (sometimes Coombs'-positive), leukopenia (usually lymphopenia), and thrombocytopenia. Antibodies to several clotting factors have been noted in SLE patients; the most common is the lupus anticoagulant, which is found in up to 25 per cent of patients and is usually recognized by a prolonged partial thromboplastin time. However, it is associated with thrombotic disease and not with bleeding. Arterial and venous thrombosis, placental infarction, and thrombocytopenia are all more common in patients with the lupus anticoagulant. Inhibitors that specifically inactivate clotting factors (II, VIII, IX, and XII) are associated with major bleeding episodes. False-positive tests for syphilis have been noted in up to 25 per cent of patients, and there is a strong association between the presence of the circulating lupus anticoagulant and false-positive tests for syphilis.

The use of oral contraceptives containing estrogen derivatives has often been associated with an exacerbation of SLE; thus, they should be avoided in these patients. Current data suggest that SLE patients in remission are not likely to have exacerbations during pregnancy; however, women with active SLE, especially those with renal disease, have an increased frequency of exacerbation of their disease as well as missed abortions, stillbirths, and premature labor and delivery. Preeclampsia is a frequent complication of pregnancy that may be difficult to distinguish from a flare of nephritis in a patient with SLE.

LABORATORY EVALUATION

The serologic hallmark of SLE is the production of high-titer autoantibodies directed against a variety of nuclear components (ANAs) (Table 80–4). The ANA is useful as a screening test, but many patients with other autoimmune diseases and even unrelated diseases may also have positive tests. Serum antibodies to dsDNA and Sm are detected almost exclusively in patients with SLE.

Anemia is usually present in patients with active disease. Leukopenia is present in half the patients. Leukocytosis may occur but should not be attributed to SLE until there has been a careful search for an infection. Hypergammaglobulinemia and reduced hemolytic complement levels (CH_{50}) are common, especially in active disease.

Proteinuria, casts, and white blood cells are found in the urine of patients with active kidney disease. Pleural effusions are usually exudative. LE cells may be seen in the pleural and pericardial fluid.

TREATMENT

SLE is a disease without a known cure, so treatment is based on relief of symptoms, suppression of inflammation, and prevention of future pathology. The risk-benefit ratio of potentially toxic drugs must be tailored to the individual patient. The organ system (or systems) involved and the severity of disease dictate specific therapy. A patient with skin rash and/or joint symptoms requires different management than a patient with proteinuria, red blood cell casts in urine, and low serum complement levels.

Patients need to be educated about the disease, the treatments, and the generally good prognosis of SLE. Many of the more serious problems do not affect most patients. Ultraviolet light should be limited or avoided. Estrogens may worsen disease and thus should be avoided. Hypertension should be treated aggressively. Renal disease demands special therapeutic decisions; renal biopsies are done to determine appropriate therapy and prognosis. A biopsy demonstrating active proliferative lesions provides the rationale for use of cytotoxic drugs, whereas histology consistent with membranous nephropathy may lead the clinician to use only corticosteroids.

Specific pharmacologic intervention includes the use of NSAIDs, corticosteroids, antimalarials, and cytotoxic agents. NSAIDs are used to treat arthralgias, mild arthritis, pleurisy, pericarditis, myalgias, and headaches. The potential side effects of NSAIDs include gastrointestinal symptoms, altered renal function, and, rarely, aseptic meningitis. Corticosteroids are frequently given, but the indications for their use are imprecise. The primary objective of corticosteroid therapy is to control the inflammatory response to prevent end-organ damage. High doses (>60 mg/day) may be necessary for brief periods, and attempts should be made to taper to every-other-day dosing as quickly as possible because the side effects with steroids given every other day are much less severe than with daily therapy. The long-term toxicities of cortico-steroids must continually be weighed against the benefits of continued therapy.

Antimalarials are often used for dermatologic and musculoskeletal manifestations. Retinal toxicity is the major side effect of these drugs, and patients should be seen by an ophthalmologist before starting treatment and every 6 months while receiving therapy. Azathioprine may be useful for patients with moderate renal disease or intractable skin disease or arthritis. Daily oral cyclophosphamide or monthly pulse intravenous cyclophosphamide combined with corticosteroids is commonly used to treat proliferative types of nephritis. Current data suggest that renal function can be preserved for long periods with cyclophosphamide therapy.

REFERENCES

Schur PH: Clinical features of SLE. In Kelley WN, Harris ED Jr, Ruddy S, Sledge CB (eds): Textbook of Rheumatology. 3rd ed. Philadelphia, WB Saunders Co, 1989, pp 1101–1124.

Steinberg AD: Systemic lupus erythematosus. In Wyngaarden JB, Smith LH Jr, Bennett JC (eds): Cecil Textbook of Medicine. 19th ed. Philadelphia, WB Saunders Co, 1992, pp 1522–1530.

Tan EM: Systemic lupus erythematosus: Immunologic aspects. In McCarty DJ (ed): Arthritis and Allied Conditions. 11th ed. Philadelphia, Lea & Febiger, 1989, pp 1049–1054.

Woods VL Jr, Zvaifler NJ: Pathogenesis of systemic lupus erythematosus. In Kelley WN, Harris ED Jr, Ruddy S, Sledge CB (eds): Textbook of Rheumatology. 3rd ed. Philadelphia, WB Saunders Co, 1989, pp 1077–1100.

81 SJÖGREN'S SYNDROME

Sjogren's syndrome (SS) is a chronic inflammatory disorder of probable autoimmune nature characterized by infiltration and destruction of the exocrine glands, particularly the salivary and lacrimal glands, by lymphocytes and plasma cells. The spectrum of the disease includes the primary form referred to as the sicca complex, and the secondary form, which is commonly associated with rheumatoid arthritis, systemic lupus erythematosus (SLE), or, less commonly, other connective tissue disorders and lymphoproliferation, which may be benign or malignant.

CLINICAL FEATURES

Signs and symptoms of SS may be subtle and therefore require a thoughtful history and careful physical examination. Lymphocytic infiltration of the lacrimal and salivary glands results in the sicca complex. Dryness of the eyes and accumulation of thick, ropy secretions along the inner canthus occur because of the decreased and altered tear production, giving the sensations of a "film" across the field of vision and of grittiness or the presence of a foreign body. With time, variable conjunctival injection, reduced visual acuity, and photosensitivity develop. Prolonged desiccation leads to the development of erosions and sloughing of the corneal epithelium (filamentary keratitis), as demonstrated by rose bengal staining and slit-lamp examination. Drying of the mouth, xerostomia, is frequent but variable in severity. Patients may describe difficulty in eating dry foods as being like trying to eat crackers without water. Dental caries are accelerated owing to a decrease in the volume of saliva and the relative loss of its antibacterial factors.

Other mucosal surfaces can also be affected by the same inflammatory response. Epistaxis, hoarseness, bronchitis, or pneumonia can result if the respiratory tract is involved. Inspissation of secretions in eustachian tubes leads to obstruction, chronic otitis media, and conduction deafness. Mucosal gland involvement of the gastrointestinal tract can be associated with dysphagia, reduced gastric acid output, constipation, and pancreatic insufficiency. Vaginal dryness can result in dyspareunia.

Extraglandular features can complicate the course of SS but occur more frequently in patients having primary rather than secondary SS. Renal tubular acidosis results from infiltrative interstitial nephropathy. Both peripheral and cranial neuropathies have been attributed to vasculitis of the vasa nervorum. Other associated neuromuscular disorders include myopathy, polymyositis, and cranial vasculitis. Dyspnea may be the presenting symptom of underlying diffuse interstitial pneumonitis due to lymphocytic infiltration. An obstructive ventilatory defect has been attributed to lymphocytic infiltration around small airways. Nonthrombocytopenic purpura of the dependent regions is associated with a polyclonal hypergammaglobulinemia. Raynaud's phenomenon occurs in about 20 per cent of patients. Several other chronic disorders have been reported in association with SS (Table 81–1).

TABLE 81–1. DISORDERS ASSOCIATED WITH SJÖGREN'S SYNDROME

Rheumatoid arthritis
Systemic lupus erythematosus
Progressive systemic sclerosis
Overlap syndrome
Polymyositis/dermatomyositis
Graft-versus-host disease
Malignant lymphoma
Chronic Hashimoto's thyroiditis
Chronic active hepatitis
Biliary cirrhosis
Graves' disease
Premature ovarian failure
Celiac disease
Dermatitis herpetiformis
Myasthenia gravis
Pemphigus
Lipodystrophy

Malignant or pseudomalignant lymphoproliferation may be a prominent part of the illness, especially in primary SS. Most of these lymphomas derive from B cell lineage and may develop into monoclonal gammopathies. These include Waldenström's macroglobulinemia, light chain myeloma, and occasionally IgG and IgA monoclonal gammopathies. Clinically, one may expect an increased risk of malignancy in patients who have a persistent or greatly increased parotid swelling, splenomegaly, or generalized lymphadenopathy. An elevated serum β-microglobulin level may offer a clue to this clinical subset of SS disease.

DIAGNOSIS

The diagnosis of SS is based upon the results of Schirmer's filter paper test (wetting of less than 5 mm in 5 min in an unanesthetized eye), ophthalmologic examination, and minor salivary gland biopsy. The demonstration of superficial corneal erosions by rose bengal staining and filamentory keratitis by slit-lamp examination indicates more advanced keratoconjunctivitis sicca.

Biopsy of the minor salivary glands of the lower lip in SS demonstrates lymphocytic infiltration of the acinar glands and progressive destruction of glandular tissue. The diagnosis of SS requires the presence of two of the following three criteria: (1) a focus score of more than one in the labial salivary gland biopsy (each aggregate of 50 or more lymphocytes equals a focus; the number of foci per 4 mm² of tissue represents the focus score); (2) keratoconjunctivitis sicca; (3) an associated connective tissue or lymphoproliferative disorder.

Autoantibodies are common in SS (see Table 78–5). Multiple organ-specific antibodies can be noted, including those directed against gastric parietal, thyroid microsomal, thyroglobulin, mitochondrial, smooth muscle, and salivary duct antigens. Antibodies to a nuclear protein antigen, SS-B (also termed La), occurs in approximately 50 to 70 per cent of patients with primary SS and to a lesser extent in patients with SLE. Antibodies to a related antigen SS-A (also termed Ro) are somewhat less specific for SS, may occur in SLE, and are more frequently associated with vasculitis. The B cell hyper-reactivity in patients with SS gives rise to hyperglobulinemia and sometimes circulating immune complexes and may be associated with rheumatoid factor activity. Complement is only infrequently low.

TREATMENT

The treatment of SS is directed at the alleviation of symptoms and the complications of xerophthalmia and xerostomia. Xerophthalmia can be treated with artificial tears or surgical punctal occlusion. The common complication, staphylococcal blepharitis, should be treated immediately with topical or, if necessary, systemic antibiotics. Xerostomia is managed by maintaining oral hydration and the liberal use of sialogogues. Bronchopulmonary infections require both supportive regimens and antibiotics. Dyspareunia is treatable with commercial water-soluble vaginal lubricants. Corticosteroids or immunosuppressive agents should be used only in patients with severe functional disability such as that seen in renal or pulmonary involvement.

REFERENCES

Moutsopoulos HM, Youinou P: New developments in Sjögren's syndrome. Curr Opin Rheumatol 3:815–822, 1991.
Talal N: Sjögren's syndrome. In Rose N, Mackay I (eds): The Autoimmune Diseases. New York, Academic Press, 1985, pp 145–159.

82 POLYMYOSITIS AND OTHER IDIOPATHIC INFLAMMATORY MYOPATHIES

The group of idiopathic inflammatory myopathies (IIM) includes polymyositis (PM) and dermatomyositis (DM) as well as myositis associated with other connective tissue diseases (CTD), myositis associated with cancer (CAM), and inclusion-body myositis (IBM) (Table 82–1). They are all generally characterized by progressive symmetric muscle weakness usually associated with elevated serum levels of muscle enzymes, a muscle biopsy showing mononuclear cell inflammation, and characteristic patterns of electromyographic abnormalities. From a clinical perspective, IIM may be viewed as three rather discrete groupings: (1) polymyositis, (2) dermatomyositis, and (3) inclusion-body myositis.

On biopsy of these groups, one sees prominent histologic evidence of necrosis and regeneration of muscle fibers. Capillary obliteration and endothelial damage are common. Inflammatory infiltrates in DM are predominantly perivascular or in the septa around, rather than within, fascicles of muscle. In PM and IBM, endomysial inflammation is generally seen, and lymphocytes and macrophages surround or invade individual muscle fibers. In DM, the intramuscular blood vessels also show endothelial hyperplasia, fibrin thrombi, and obliteration of capillaries. IBM is characterized by basophilic granular inclusions around the edge of vacuoles, termed "rimmed" vacuoles, and eosinophilic cytoplasmic inclusions. Electron microscopic studies of biopsies are often required to make the diagnosis because paraffin processing can distort the basophilic granule and rimmed vacuole pattern.

CLINICAL COURSE

IIM has an incidence of approximately 1 per 100,000. Both children and adults can be afflicted with DM (females more than males); PM occurs primarily in adults, generally past the second decade of life; IBM (males more than females) tends to occur past the fifth decade of life.

The common presenting manifestation of all of the IIMs is symmetric muscle weakness that develops over weeks to months. Difficulties in climbing stairs, getting up from a chair, and lifting objects are common initial symptoms. Involvement of ocular muscles and facial muscles is extremely rare, except in very advanced cases, and generally fine-motor movements of the hands are preserved. Respiratory muscles also are preserved until very late in the disease. Myalgia and muscle tenderness can be predominant manifestations in some patients, particularly in DM.

DM is distinct by virtue of its accompanying characteristic rash. The so-called heliotrope rash occurs typically on the upper eyelids and generally with edema. Gottron's sign is characterized by erythema of the knuckles of the fingers and often presents as a raised, somewhat scaly eruption. An erythematous rash may also recur on other body surfaces, including knees, elbows, the V-region of the neck and upper chest, and across the back and shoulders. DM in children is notable for its more frequent extramuscular manifestations, generally due to a systemic vasculitis that can involve al-

TABLE 82–1. CLASSIFICATION OF IDIOPATHIC INFLAMMATORY MYOPATHIES (IIM)

DESCRIPTION	GROUP DESIGNATION
Primary idiopathic polymyositis	PM
Primary idiopathic dermatomyositis	DM
Autoimmune connective tissue diseases with myositis	CTM
Myositis associated with malignancy	CAM
Inclusion-body myositis	IBM

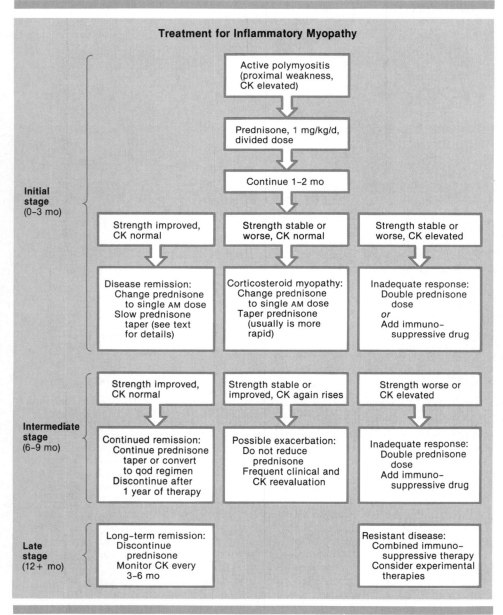

FIGURE 82-1. Treatment algorithm for inflammatory myopathy. CK = creatine kinase; qod = every other day. (Modified from Oddis CV: Therapy for myositis. Curr Opin Rheumatol 3: 921, 1991; with permission.)

most any organ system. PM has no distinguishing clinical manifestations, and the diagnosis is generally made by exclusion of other muscular and neuromuscular diseases.

IBM may not be suspected early in the course but generally comes to mind when the patient is observed to respond poorly to therapy. Clinically, there is a greater likelihood of involvement of distal muscles of the fingers and feet. These patients may lose their patellar reflex early because of weakness of the quadriceps muscle and may even give the early impression of a neurologic disease.

As in PM, IBM can also be found in association with a diversity of autoimmune connective tissue

diseases such as systemic lupus erythematosus (SLE) and scleroderma. The association of IIM with other diseases such as scleroderma, SLE, and rheumatoid arthritis constitutes what has been referred to as an overlap syndrome. When this is seen, arthralgias, myalgias, and Raynaud's phenomenon may be quite prominent.

The occurrence of malignancy in the setting of IIM is relatively uncommon (less than 10 per cent, but may be higher in older age groups). Carcinomas of the breast, lung, ovaries, colon, endometrium, prostate, and stomach are the leading tumors that have been reported in association with IIM. In approximately three fourths of CAM

TABLE 82-2. DIAGNOSTIC CRITERIA FOR INFLAMMATORY MYOPATHIES

| CRITERION | POLYMYOSITIS | | DERMATOMYOSITIS | | INCLUSION-BODY MYOSITIS |
	DEFINITE	PROBABLE*	DEFINITE	MILD OR EARLY	DEFINITE
Muscle strength	Myopathic muscle weakness†	Myopathic muscle weakness†	Myopathic muscle weakness†	Seemingly normal strength‡	Myopathic muscle weakness with early involvement of distal muscles†
Electromyographic findings	Myopathic	Myopathic	Myopathic	Myopathic or nonspecific	Myopathic with mixed potentials
Muscle enzymes	Elevated (up to 50-fold)	Elevated (up to 50-fold)	Elevated (up to 50-fold) or normal	Elevated (up to 10-fold) or normal	Elevated (up to 10-fold) or normal
Muscle-biopsy findings	Diagnostic for this type of inflammatory myopathy	Nonspecific myopathy without signs of primary inflammation	Diagnostic	Nonspecific or diagnostic	Diagnostic
Rash or calcinosis	Absent	Absent	Present	Present	Absent

*An adequate trial of prednisone or other immunosuppressive drugs is warranted in probable cases. If, in retrospect, the disease is unresponsive to therapy, another muscle biopsy should be considered to exclude other diseases or possible evolution to inclusion-body myositis.

†Myopathic muscle weakness, affecting proximal muscles more than distal ones and sparing eye and facial muscles, is characterized by a subacute onset (weeks to months) and rapid progression in patients who have no family history of neuromuscular disease, no endocrinopathy, no exposure to myotoxic drugs or toxins, and no biochemical muscle disease (excluded on the basis of muscle-biopsy findings).

‡Although strength is seemingly normal, patients often have new onset of easy fatigue, myalgia, and reduced endurance. Careful muscle testing may reveal mild muscle weakness.

Reprinted, by permission, from the New England Journal of Medicine, Vol 325, p 1487, 1991.

patients, the myositis precedes the diagnosis of malignancy by 12 to 24 months. It would, therefore, be appropriate to search for malignancy in patients over 50, that is, those with greater risk for associated cancer.

The clinical course in these diseases is generally prolonged, with remissions and exacerbations, but can involve fatal complications, including cardiac arrhythmias, probably due to involvement of myocardial muscle, and the development of restrictive lung disease, which may occur in as many as 20 per cent of cases.

DIAGNOSTIC AND LABORATORY FINDINGS

The clinical picture of positive electromyographic findings, elevated muscle enzymes, and distinctive muscle biopsy are the tools necessary for the diagnosis of IIM and its various subgroups (Table 82-2).

Recent work has been directed at examining possible subsets of IIM based on a variety of serologic measurements. These include the myositis-specific antibodies, anti-aminoacyl-tRNA synthetases, anti-signal recognition particle (anti-SRP), as well as other markers, including human leukocyte antigen (HLA)-DRw52 and DRw53. The clinical relevance of these subsets, as well as their etiologic significance, remains to be determined.

TREATMENT

Treatment of PM or DM generally involves corticosteroids with supportive physical therapy; if indicated, immunosuppressive agents may be added (Fig. 82-1). It is important to recognize that IBM generally does not respond to corticosteroid therapy. One must also be aware of the entity of corticosteroid myopathy when treating with high-dose corticosteroids for a long period of time. In that case, reducing the corticosteroid dose may become the appropriate therapy.

The long-term prognosis in the PM and DM groups is extremely good with corticosteroid and immunosuppressive therapy, with 15-year survivals of 85 to 90 per cent.

REFERENCES

Dalakas MC: Polymyositis, dermatomyositis and inclusion-body myositis. N Engl J Med 325:1487, 1991.
Love LA, Leff RL, Fraser DD, Targoff IN, Dalakas MC, Plotz PH, Miller FW: A new approach to the classification of idiopathic inflammatory myopathy: Myositis-specific autoantibodies define useful homogeneous patient groups. Medicine 70:360, 1991.
Oddis CV: Therapy for myositis. Curr Opin Rheumatol 3:919, 1991.
Sigurgeirsson B, Lindelöf B, Edhag O, Allander E: Risk of cancer in patients with dermatomyositis or polymyositis. N Engl J Med 326:363, 1992.

83 SCLERODERMA (SYSTEMIC SCLEROSIS)

Scleroderma (literally "hard skin") has various presentations and, depending on the extent of visceral involvement, varied outcomes. Scleroderma may be classified according to the degree and extent of skin thickening (Table 83–1). Systemic sclerosis (SSc) is seen most commonly in adults, whereas the localized forms of scleroderma (morphea) are seen most often in children. Persons with limited SSc, formerly called CREST syndrome (C = calcinosis, R = Raynaud's phenomenon, E = esophageal disease, S = sclerodactyly, T = telangiectasias), may not develop internal organ involvement for several years. In contrast, persons with rapidly progressive, widespread skin thickening (diffuse SSc) that affects the proximal extremities and trunk are at greater risk for developing early, serious visceral involvement. SSc is

TABLE 83–1. CLASSIFICATION OF SCLERODERMA

Localized Scleroderma
  Morphea
    Plaquelike, guttate
    Generalized
  Linear scleroderma (includes *en coup de sabre*), with or without melorheostosis
Systemic Scleroderma (SSc)
  Diffuse SSc
  Limited SSc (formerly called CREST syndrome)
  Systemic Scleroderma sine scleroderma
  Overlap with other connective tissue diseases
Chemically Induced Scleroderma–like Skin Conditions
  Vinyl chloride disease
  Pentazocine
  Bleomycin
  Toxic oil syndrome
  Trichloroethylene
  5-Hydroxytryptophan and carbidopa
  Breast augmentation mammoplasty (paraffin, silicone)
Diseases with Skin Changes Mimicking Scleroderma
  Eosinophilic fasciitis
  Eosinophilic myalgia syndrome
  Chronic graft-versus-host disease
  Carcinoid syndrome
  Acromegaly
  Diabetic cheiroarthropathy (syndrome of limited joint mobility)
  Scleroderma adultorum of Buschke
  Scleromyxedema (papular mucinosis)
  Lichen sclerosis et atrophicus
  Werner's syndrome
  Porphyria
  Acrodermatitis chronica atrophicans
  Amyloidosis (primary and myeloma-associated)
  Progeria

three to four times more common in women than in men.

The clinical hallmarks of SSc are tight skin and Raynaud's phenomenon. SSc is a generalized disorder of small arteries and the connective tissue characterized by vascular obliteration and fibrosis in skin and internal organs, including the gastrointestinal tract, lungs, heart, and kidneys. The mechanisms of excessive fibrosis are unknown.

Localized Scleroderma

Localized scleroderma affects primarily children and young adults; this heterogeneous group of conditions does not have the typical visceral and serologic manifestations seen with SSc. Morphea starts with areas of erythema or violaceous discoloration of the skin, which evolve to sclerotic and waxy or ivory-colored lesions. The plaques may increase in size to several centimeters in diameter and often are surrounded by a violaceous border of inflammation. Lesions may become widespread and confluent, a condition called generalized morphea. Most often, the lesions soften spontaneously over months to years. With the linear form, sclerotic lesions appear as linear streaks or bands, most commonly on the extremities and less frequently on the forehead, trunk, or frontoparietal scalp. When the frontoparietal area is involved, it is termed *en coup de sabre* and may result in disfiguring facial asymmetry with hemiatrophy.

Limited Systemic Sclerosis (CREST Variant)

The usual age of onset of limited SSc is in the third to fourth decade. The patient may have a history of Raynaud's phenomenon for several years and subsequently presents with skin edema or tightening of hands, face, and feet. Patients with limited SSc have a much lower frequency of serious internal organ involvement (renal, pulmonary); however, pulmonary hypertension and esophageal disease are not uncommon in limited SSc (Table 83–2).

Diffuse Systemic Sclerosis

Although diffuse SSc is less common than limited SSc, it has a worse prognosis owing to more frequent renal and pulmonary involvement (Table 83–2). Abrupt onset of swollen hands, face, and feet associated with Raynaud's phenomenon may occur. These changes may evolve over several weeks or months to include more proximal areas of the extremities as well as the thorax and abdomen. These patients should be followed closely for visceral involvement, especially hypertension and renal involvement.

Scleroderma sine Scleroderma

Scleroderma sine scleroderma is an uncommon condition in which there are characteristic internal organ manifestations, vascular and serologic abnormalities, but no clinically detectable skin changes.

CLINICAL FEATURES

Raynaud's phenomenon and tight skin are the hallmarks of SSc. There are no specific diagnostic tests, so the diagnosis is made on clinical grounds. Fibrosis and vascular obliteration in the skin, gastrointestinal tract, lungs, heart, and kidneys determine the extent and severity of the clinical manifestations.

Virtually all patients with SSc have Raynaud's phenomenon, which is defined as episodic *pallor* of digits following cold exposure or stress associated with *cyanosis*, followed by *erythema*, tingling, and pain. Raynaud's phenomenon is attributable to both vasospasm and structural disease of the blood vessels. Raynaud's phenomenon primarily affects the hands and feet and less commonly the ears, nose, and tongue. The duration of the triphasic color change can vary from minutes to hours. Severe Raynaud's phenomenon can exhibit a predominant phase of cyanosis and can result in digital pitting scars, frank gangrene, and/or autoamputation of the fingers or toes.

The appearance of the skin is the most distinctive diagnostic feature of SSc; the diagnosis can be made by examining the texture and location of hidebound skin. By definition, patients with diffuse SSc have taut skin in the more proximal parts of extremities, in addition to the thorax and abdomen. However, the skin tightening of SSc begins on the fingers and hands in nearly all cases; therefore, making the distinction between limited and diffuse SSc may be difficult early in the illness. The initial phase of skin involvement is characterized by painless pitting edema followed by gradual loss of edema, leaving thick, indurated, tight skin. At later stages of disease, atrophy (thinning) may develop, leading to laxity of the superficial dermis; the clinical observation of improving skin change in late SSc may reflect this atrophic phase. Atrophy is noted primarily over joints at sites of flexion contractures such as the elbow and proximal interphalangeal joints; these areas are prone to the development of ulcerations. Areas of hypo- and hyperpigmentation are common. Other skin changes include subcutaneous calcifications and telangiectasias of the fingers, face, lips, and forearms.

Involvement of the gastrointestinal tract is the third most common manifestation of SSc, following only skin changes and Raynaud's phenomenon. Esophageal hypomotility can be documented in more than 90 per cent of patients having either diffuse or limited SSc. With the loss of lower esophageal sphincter function, reflux of gastric contents occurs, resulting in peptic esophagitis. Substernal burning pain or "heartburn," primarily at night, is a common early symptom. Dysphagia, especially for solid food with food "sticking" in the substernal region, is also common, especially with the development of esophageal strictures. The hypomotility and strictures can be detected with barium contrast and esophageal motility studies. Severe complications such as esophageal stricture and ulcerations can be prevented by early management. Therefore, the esophagus of all patients suspected of having SSc should be examined using manometry for evidence of hypomotility.

Similar changes occur in the small intestine, resulting in reduced motility, and may cause intermittent diarrhea, bloating and cramping, malabsorption, and weight loss. Bacterial overgrowth occurs in areas of intestinal stasis and is often responsive to broad-spectrum antibiotics such as tetracycline. Although colon involvement is

TABLE 83-2. COMPARISON OF CLINICAL FEATURES OF LIMITED VERSUS DIFFUSE SYSTEMIC SCLEROSIS

	LIMITED (% PATIENTS)	DIFFUSE (% PATIENTS)
Demographic		
Age (<40 at onset)	50	35
Gender (female)	85	75
Duration of symptoms (years before first diagnosis)	8.5	3.0
Organ System Involvement		
Skin	95	100
Telangiectasis	80	30
Calcinosis	45	5
Raynaud's phenomenon	95	85
Arthralgias or arthritis	60	80
Joint contractures	5	65
Tendon friction rubs	45	85
Myositis	10	20
Esophageal hypomotility	75	75
Pulmonary fibrosis	35	35
Pulmonary hypertension	10	<1
Congestive heart failure	1	10
"Scleroderma renal crisis"	1	15
Laboratory Data		
Antinuclear antigen-positive	50	55
Anticentromere antibody-positive	50	<5
Anti-Scl-70 antibody-positive	15	40
Cumulative survival (10 years after first diagnosis)	75	55

From DJ McCarty: Arthritis and Allied Conditions. 11th ed. Philadelphia, Lea & Febiger, 1989. Reprinted with permission.

common, it is an infrequent cause of clinical symptoms, but constipation, obstipation, and pseudoobstruction may occur. Pathognomonic radiographic findings on barium contrast studies include wide-mouth diverticula of the large bowel (due to atrophy of the muscularis); these may be sites of bleeding or abscess. Primary biliary cirrhosis is well described in patients with SSc, primarily those with long-standing limited SSc.

"Scleroderma renal crisis," the abrupt onset of accelerated hypertension, oliguria, and microangiopathic hemolysis, once accounted for the majority of deaths in SSc. At present, however, with the early diagnosis and treatment of hypertension with inhibitors of angiotensin-converting enzymes, renal failure in SSc is less common. Clinically, "scleroderma renal crisis" is usually observed in an individual with diffuse SSc whose disease is relatively early and at a stage of rapid progression of skin involvement.

The leading cause of mortality in SSc is pulmonary disease. Interstitial lung disease with fibrosis, pulmonary hypertension, pleurisy, and pleural effusions are the pulmonary manifestations of SSc. Patients with diffuse SSc are at a higher risk of developing interstitial fibrotic disease, whereas patients with limited SSc are at a higher risk of developing pulmonary hypertension. Physical findings include fine inspiratory crackles and an audible splitting of S_2 on deep inspiration. Chest radiography is not a sensitive screening test to detect pulmonary abnormalities in early SSc. In long-standing disease, increased interstitial markings, enlarged pulmonary arteries, or pleural effusions may be demonstrated. The single-breath diffusion capacity is the most sensitive pulmonary screening test for SSc pulmonary disease. Reductions in vital capacity or restrictive lung disease can also be detected with pulmonary function testing.

Cardiac involvement in SSc can be manifested clinically as a cardiomyopathy, pericarditis, pericardial effusion, or arrhythmias. Although more than 90 per cent of patients with diffuse SSc have some form of cardiac involvement, clinical evidence of myocardial involvement is uncommon (<10 per cent). Physical findings include ventricular gallops, tachycardia, signs of congestive heart failure, and occasional pericardial friction rubs. Echocardiography reveals evidence of pericardial thickening and effusion in 50 per cent of patients, but pericarditis and tamponade are infrequent clinically. The cardiomyopathy is a result of intermittent myocardial ischemia and necrosis with resultant fibrosis. Fibrosis of the conducting pathways can lead to arrhythmias and conduction disturbances.

Musculoskeletal manifestations of SSc include arthralgias, arthritis, and myopathy. Morning stiffness and generalized arthralgias are common. Clinically significant synovitis is uncommon. An erosive arthropathy indistinguishable from rheumatoid arthritis can be seen. Muscle weakness

(proximal or distal) may be secondary to disuse atrophy. Two other forms of myopathy may occur in SSc: a bland, nonprogressive myopathy, characterized by proximal weakness, mild elevation of serum creatine kinase, and noninflammatory replacement of muscle tissue; and, less frequently, an inflammatory myositis indistinguishable from polymyositis.

Less common clinical abnormalities in patients with SSc include unilateral or bilateral trigeminal neuralgia, impotence, keratoconjunctivitis sicca, and xerostomia. Hashimoto's thyroiditis and fibrous replacement of thyroid tissue have been observed and are commonly associated with clinical evidence of hypothyroidism.

Antinuclear antibodies are common in SSc. The anticentromere antibody (ACA) is most commonly seen in limited SSc, whereas antibodies to topoisomerase I (Scl-70) are fairly specific for diffuse SSc. However, ACA and anti–Scl-70 are detected in the serum of less than 50 per cent of all patients with SSc. The clinical and biologic relevance of the ACA and anti–Scl-70 remains to be elucidated; they may be of prognostic value in patients with early signs and symptoms of SSc.

DIFFERENTIAL DIAGNOSIS

Raynaud's Phenomenon

The prevalence of Raynaud's phenomenon is estimated to be 5 to 10 per cent in nonsmokers and up to 22 per cent in premenopausal females. The initial evaluation of a person presenting with Raynaud's phenomenon should include a comprehensive history and physical examination (Table 83–3). A careful history that elicits the patient's drug exposure and occupational history is essential. Patients with idiopathic Raynaud's phenomenon should be monitored yearly because surveillance of such persons may permit early recognition of potentially treatable diseases.

Scleroderma-like Skin Changes

As listed in Table 83–1, there are several conditions in which thick or hidebound skin may occur. Raynaud's phenomenon is usually absent in these disorders. *Eosinophilic fasciitis* is a syndrome that typically manifests as swelling and tightness of the skin of the trunk and proximal extremities. This is followed by progressive induration of the skin and subcutaneous tissue. The skin is typically shiny with a coarse orange-peel appearance. Onset frequently follows periods of physical exertion and trauma, particularly in males. Although reported to occur in children and the elderly, it is more frequent in young adults. Skin of the hands and feet is spared. Deep skin and subcutaneous biopsy confirm inflammatory changes. Peripheral eosinophilia is present, but eosinophils may or may not be present in the skin lesions. Most patients improve spontaneously or with corticosteroids. Eosinophilic fasciitis has been associated with aplastic anemia and myeloproliferative syndromes.

More recently, a syndrome called *eosinophilic myalgia syndrome* (EMS) has been documented in persons who have ingested L-tryptophan. The putative cause is a contaminant in the preparation of L-tryptophan–containing products. The early phase of EMS is characterized by an acute onset of intense myalgia, skin rashes, dyspnea, fever, and weight loss. Later clinical manifestations include skin induration, myopathy, and a diffuse peripheral neuropathy. The most characteristic laboratory abnormality in EMS is profound eosinophilia. Although treatment with corticosteroids results in prompt amelioration of symptoms, the optimal management and natural history of EMS are not yet known.

Scleroderma-like skin changes occur commonly in patients with diabetes mellitus (see Chapter 89).

TREATMENT

Educating the patient regarding measures to prevent exacerbations of Raynaud's phenomenon may be the most important aspect of treatment. Such measures include avoiding cold exposure and wearing protective clothes, especially gloves. Pharmacologic agents used to treat Raynaud's phenomenon include calcium channel blockers, such as verapamil, diltiazem, and nifedipine. When digital gangrene occurs, stellate ganglion blockade, epidural blocks, or surgical sympathectomy may prevent autoamputation.

No single drug or combination of drugs has been shown to halt the progression of cutaneous or visceral manifestations of SSc. D-Penicillamine, an agent that interferes with the intermolecular cross-linking of mature collagen and also acts as an immunomodulating agent, has been advocated on the basis of retrospective studies that showed minimal skin softening and improved pulmonary function in some patients with SSc. Despite its widespread use, this potentially toxic drug has not been shown to alter the natural history of SSc. A major breakthrough in treating hypertension and preventing renal failure has been the use of angiotension-converting enzyme inhibitors. Dialysis and renal transplantation have offered an increased lifespan for those who do develop renal failure. Glucocorticoids are indicated for treatment of inflammatory myositis and pericarditis. Gastrointestinal reflux is successfully treated by raising

TABLE 83–3. DIFFERENTIAL DIAGNOSIS OF RAYNAUD'S PHENOMENON

Idiopathic Raynaud's Phenomenon (Raynaud's Disease)
Connective Tissue Diseases
  Systemic sclerosis (95%)
  Mixed connective tissue disease (80%)
  Systemic lupus erythematosus (30%)
  Polymyositis/dermatomyositis (20%)
  Rheumatoid arthritis (10%)
  Vasculitis
  Thromboangiitis obliterans and Takayasu's arteritis
Occupational
  Vibration and physical trauma (e.g., jackhammer operator)
  Cold injury (frostbite)
Chemical Exposure
  Vinyl chloride (plastics industry)
  Mining exposure (coal, silicates, gold, heavy metals)
  Organic solvents (trichlorethylene)
Environmental and Drug-Associated
  Toxic oil syndrome
  Arsenic
  Bleomycin
  Vinblastine
  Cisplatin
  Ergotamine
  Beta blockers
  5-Hydroxytryptophan and carbidopa
Intravascular Causes
  Intravascular coagulation
  Cold agglutinin disease
  Cryoglobulinemia
  Cryofibrinogenemia
  Paraproteinemia and hyperviscosity syndromes
  Polycythemia
Structural
  Thoracic outlet syndrome
  Crutch pressure
  Atherosclerosis

the head of the bed and using histamine$_2$ (H$_2$) blockers. Dilatation may be required for esophageal strictures.

REFERENCES

Medsger TA: Systemic sclerosis (scleroderma), localized scleroderma, eosinophilic fasciitis, and calcinosis. *In* McCarty DJ (ed): Arthritis and Allied Conditions. 11th ed. Philadelphia, Lea & Febiger, 1989, pp 1118–1165.

Seibold JR: Scleroderma. *In* Kelley WN, Harris ED Jr, Ruddy S, Sledge CB (eds): Textbook of Rheumatology. 3rd ed. Philadelphia, WB Saunders Co, 1989, pp 1215–1244.

84 MIXED CONNECTIVE TISSUE DISEASE, OVERLAP SYNDROME, AND ANTIPHOSPHOLIPID ANTIBODY SYNDROME

MIXED CONNECTIVE TISSUE DISEASE AND OVERLAP SYNDROME

As many as 25 per cent of all patients with features suggestive of a connective tissue disease do not fit into a definite diagnostic category such as systemic lupus erythematosus (SLE), rheumatoid arthritis (RA), scleroderma, or polymyositis. As a result, there has been confusion about the appropriate way to classify these patients' diseases. Three terms used to describe such patients have been *early undifferentiated connective tissue disease* (EUCTD), *mixed connective tissue disease* (MCTD), and *overlap syndrome*.

When a patient has features suggestive of connective tissue disease but not definitively diagnostic of any one disorder, it is best to label the patient as having EUCTD. Most patients with EUCTD have Raynaud's phenomenon; many of them develop definite scleroderma, a few develop SLE, and some remain undifferentiated.

TABLE 84–1. GUIDELINES FOR DIAGNOSING MCTD

General
 Clinical features of a diffuse connective tissue disorder
Serologic
 1. Positive ANA, speckled pattern, titer >1:1000
 2. Antibodies to U1 RNP
 3. Absence of antibodies to dsDNA, histones, Sm, Scl-70, and other specificities
 4. Commonly: Hypergammaglobulinemia and positive rheumatoid factor
Clinical
 1. Sequential evolution of overlap features over course of *several years*, including Raynaud's phenomenon, serositis, gastrointestinal dysmotility, myositis, arthritis, sclerodactyly, skin rashes, and an abnormal DL_{CO} on pulmonary function tests
 2. Absence of truncal scleroderma, severe renal disease, and severe CNS involvement
 3. A nailfold capillary pattern identical to that seen in PSS (dropout and dilated vessels)

ANA = Antinuclear antibodies; RNP = ribonucleoprotein; dsDNA = double-stranded DNA; CNS = central nervous system; PSS = progressive systemic sclerosis.
 From Bennett RM: Mixed connective tissue disease and other overlap syndromes. *In* Kelley WN, Harris ED Jr, Ruddy S, Sledge CB (eds): Textbook of Rheumatology. 3rd ed. Philadelphia, WB Saunders Co, 1989, p 1150.

The terms *MCTD* and *overlap syndrome* have often been used interchangeably; however, specific serologic criteria should be applied to make the diagnosis of MCTD. The designation of overlap syndrome is appropriate when a patient exhibits features of more than one established diagnosis. An example would be a patient with rheumatoid factor–positive, nodular, erosive arthritis who has RA and who subsequently develops high-titer antinuclear antibodies, oral ulcers, malar rash, and antibodies to native DNA. An additional diagnosis of SLE could then be made. It would be appropriate to label this patient as having an overlap syndrome. The designation of overlap syndrome should be reserved for patients who over time have exhibited distinct features of one or more established connective tissue diseases, such as RA and SLE. Myositis is a frequent component of SLE, scleroderma, and RA, as well as of polymyositis/dermatomyositis; therefore, the finding of myositis in a patient with scleroderma, RA, or SLE does not justify a diagnosis of overlap syndrome.

The diagnosis of MCTD is generally reserved for patients with evidence of an overlap syndrome who also have very high titers of antibodies to a ribonucleoprotein (RNP) (Table 84–1). The presenting features of MCTD do not differentiate it from other diffuse connective tissue diseases such as SLE, scleroderma, or polymyositis. Antibodies to RNP constitute the only constant feature in patients with MCTD. An equally important feature in MCTD is the absence of antibodies to double-stranded DNA, Sm antigen, and histones. Many patients (35 to 40 per cent) who fulfill the criteria for a diagnosis of SLE (see Table 80–1) may also have low titers of serum antibodies to RNP, and most do not have myositis or sclerodactyly. Patients with high titers of anti-RNP experience a relatively favorable prognosis and a low frequency of renal disease.

The pattern of organ system involvement is a useful guide to therapy in patients with MCTD or overlap syndrome. For example, treatment of erosive arthritis should be the same as that for RA. Patients with scleroderma-like features are least likely to improve. Although the prognosis of patients with MCTD is favorable, serious and sometimes fatal complications such as pulmonary hypertension do occur.

ANTIPHOSPHOLIPID ANTIBODY SYNDROME

Antiphospholipid antibodies, those responsible for the in vitro lupus anticoagulant test and those directed against negatively charged phospholipids (e.g., cardiolipin), are associated with a variety of clinical manifestations (Table 84–2). Approximately one third of patients with SLE have antiphospholipid antibodies or a lupus anticoagulant.

The specific serologic feature of this syndrome is the production of antibodies that cross-react with cardiolipin and other negatively charged phospholipids. The most useful tests for detecting antiphospholipid antibodies are the lupus anticoagulant and the anticardiolipin antibody tests. Only a minority of patients with antiphospholipid antibodies develop thrombosis, fetal loss, or thrombocytopenia. Approximately 30 per cent of patients with the lupus anticoagulant develop thrombosis. Thrombosis and fetal loss occur more frequently in persons with moderate to high titers of IgG anticardiolipin antibodies. To fulfill the minimum criteria for this syndrome, patients must have both a positive antiphospholipid test and a related clinical complication.

The lupus anticoagulant test relies on the ability of some antiphospholipid antibodies to inhibit in vitro clot formation. Antiphospholipid syndrome patients are often first identified by their prolonged partial thromboplastin time or prothrombin time not corrected by the addition of normal plasma. The most sensitive test for antiphospholipid antibodies is the anticardiolipin antibody test. Antiphospholipid antibodies are paradoxically associated with thrombosis rather than hemorrhage. Treatment for the antiphospholipid antibody syn-

TABLE 84–2. CLINICAL MANIFESTATIONS OF THE ANTIPHOSPHOLIPID ANTIBODY SYNDROME

Common
Venous thrombosis
Arterial thrombosis
  Stroke
  Extremity gangrene
  Visceral infarction
Recurrent fetal loss
Thrombocytopenia
Livedo reticularis
Uncommon
Coombs'-positive hemolysis
Valvular heart disease
Chorea
Nonstroke ischemia syndrome
Transverse myelopathy

drome has not been clearly defined. Aspirin, corticosteroids, and heparin have been used to prevent fetal loss, but their efficacy has yet to be determined. Patients with thrombotic events should be treated with anticoagulants. However, because thrombosis occurs only in a minority of patients with antiphospholipid antibodies, prophylactic treatment is not justified in patients who have these antibodies but no history of thrombosis.

REFERENCES

Bennett RM: Mixed connective tissue disease and other overlap syndromes. In Kelley WN, Harris ED Jr, Ruddy S, Sledge CB (eds): Textbook of Rheumatology. 3rd ed. Philadelphia, WB Saunders Co, 1989, pp 1147–1165.
Harris EN, Hughes GRV: Antiphospholipid antibodies. In McCarty D (ed): Arthritis and Allied Conditions. 11th ed. Philadelphia, Lea & Febiger, 1985, pp 1068–1079.
Sharp GC, Singsen BH: Mixed connective tissue disease. In McCarty D (ed): Arthritis and Allied Conditions. 11th ed. Philadelphia, Lea & Febiger, 1985, pp 1080–1091.

85 VASCULITIDES

The vasculitides represent a heterogeneous group of syndromes. They are characterized by inflammation of the blood vessel wall and may involve vessels of any size and in any location. The syndrome may be exclusively an arteritis, exclusively a venulitis, or a combination of the two. The location of the inflammatory process, that is, arteries, or arterioles, postcapillary venules, or veins, determines the diffuse symptoms that may occur in each of these syndromes. Some vasculopathies involve only skin and surface areas, whereas others involve deep tissues, are systemic, and can be rapidly fatal.

CLASSIFICATION

Historically, the vasculitides are classified by the pathologist and reflect the size of the artery involved. However, because extensive overlaps occur with this method, a system of categorization by clinical syndrome has recently grown in popularity among clinicians. Table 85–1 presents a useful classification that combines some of the earlier histopathologic descriptions as well as the more modern understanding of the clinical settings in which these various syndromes occur.

IMMUNOPATHOGENESIS

A precise definition of the immunopathogenic process in the vasculitides remains incomplete. In many of these syndromes, antigen-antibody complexes and complement can be identified and are associated with the endothelial layer of the blood vessel wall. These complexes may be either deposited from the circulation or formed in situ.

Definition of the broad spectrum of possible antigens has also proved elusive, although in lupus complexes of DNA and its antibody and in rheumatoid vasculitis, rheumatoid factors can be found. Similarly, in some cases of polyarteritis nodosa, hepatitis B virus, together with its antibody

TABLE 85–1. THE CLINICAL SPECTRUM OF VASCULITIS

1. Polyarteritis nodosa group
   Classic polyarteritis nodosa
   Allergic angiitis and granulomatosis (Churg-Strauss disease)
   Overlap syndrome
2. Hypersensitivity vasculitis
   Henoch-Schönlein purpura
   Serum sickness and serum sickness–like reactions
   Vasculitis associated with infectious diseases
   Vasculitis associated with neoplasms
   Vasculitis associated with connective tissue diseases
   Vasculitis associated with other underlying diseases
   Congenital deficiencies of the complement system
   Erythema elevatum diutinum
3. Wegener's granulomatosis
4. Giant cell arteritides
   Cranial or temporal arteritis
   Takayasu's arteritis
5. Other vasculitis syndromes
   Angiocentric immunoproliferative lesions
   Mucocutaneous lymph node syndrome (Kawasaki's disease)
   Behçet's disease
   Vasculitis isolated to the central nervous system
   Thromboangiitis obliterans (Buerger's disease)
   Miscellaneous vasculitides

From Wolff SM: The vasculitic syndromes. In Wyngaarden JB, Smith LH Jr, Bennett JC (eds): Cecil Textbook of Medicine. 19th ed. Philadelphia, WB Saunders Co, 1992, p 1537.

and complement, may be observed. However, it is also clear that antigen-antibody complexes do not account for the entire syndrome. For example, in Wegener's granulomatosis, granulomas consist of T cells and macrophages; presumably, they form at least some part of the pathogenic process above and beyond what is usually seen in a typical immune complex–mediated vasculitis.

HYPERSENSITIVITY ANGIITIS

Hypersensitivity angiitis is the most common form of vasculitis and is usually localized to the small vessels of the skin. The characteristic histopathologic picture is a leukocytoclastic venulitis. Leukocytoclasis refers to nuclear debris derived from infiltrating neutrophils. Red blood cell extravasation, thrombosis of the vessel lumen, and fibrinoid necrosis can also be seen. A variety of cutaneous lesions are associated with this form of vasculitis, but usually they appear first on the lower extremities as erythematous macules that evolve into a relatively specific physical sign, palpable purpura.

Diagnosis of cutaneous vasculitis is usually made by biopsy. Laboratory findings are variable: erythrocyte sedimentation rate (ESR) can be either normal or elevated; complement can be normal or depressed; and immune complexes can be detected, usually in low concentrations.

Certain hypersensitivity vasculitides are seen as discrete clinical syndromes. Henoch-Schönlein purpura is characterized by fever, abdominal pain, nonthrombocytopenic purpura, arthralgia, and renal disease. The classic triad of purpura, arthritis, and abdominal pain occurs in about 80 per cent of patients. Children and young adults are most commonly affected, but the disorder can afflict persons of any age. Although the disease is of limited duration (usually 6 to 16 weeks), 5 to 10 per cent of patients can develop a relapsing renal disease characterized by glomerulonephritis. Involvement of the wall of the gastrointestinal tract can result in colicky abdominal pain, intestinal bleeding, obstruction, infarction, intussusception, or perforation. Immunoglobulin and complement can be demonstrated in involved blood vessels. In Henoch-Schönlein purpura serum IgA levels can be elevated; complement levels are usually normal, but IgA deposits can be demonstrated in the vessel wall.

Another syndrome of hypersensitivity vasculitis is essential mixed cryoglobulinemia, which is characterized by arthralgia, purpura, weakness, and cryoglobulinemia. There are recurrent bouts of palpable purpura of the lower extremities, hepatosplenomegaly, lymphadenopathy, and polyarthralgias. Renal failure can result from a diffuse proliferative glomerulonephritis. Cryoglobulins containing IgG and IgM, sometimes with rheumatoid factor activity, can be detected. This syndrome may also coexist with other autoimmune disease. Bacterial infections (i.e., streptococcal), serum sickness, chronic active hepatitis, ulcerative colitis, Sjögren's syndrome, retroperitoneal fibrosis, and Goodpasture's syndrome may be seen in association with the histopathologic picture of hypersensitivity vasculitis.

Treatment of hypersensitivity angiitis includes management of the associated entities (e.g., drug reactions, bacterial infections). Fortunately, this form of vasculitis is usually self-limited, but occasionally patients require nonsteroidal anti-inflammatory agents, corticosteroids, or immunosuppressive agents.

POLYARTERITIS NODOSA

Polyarteritis nodosa involves primarily the medium and small muscular arteries. It can occur in any age group but has a peak incidence in the fifth and sixth decades of life. The male-female ratio is approximately 2.5:1. Early signs and symptoms are fever, weight loss, abdominal pain, and musculoskeletal pain (Table 85–2).

Renal. The kidneys are the most commonly involved organ system. Inflammation of the arcuate arteries as well as other medium-sized vessels can result in segmental aneurysmal dilatations. A rapidly progressive, necrotizing glomerulonephritis can lead to the sudden onset of severe hypertension, nephrotic syndrome, and renal failure. Spontaneous rupture of aneurysms can result in retroperitoneal hemorrhage or a perinephric hematoma.

Cardiovascular. Coronary arteritis can produce angina pectoris or myocardial infarction. Pericarditis is common but is often diagnosed only post mortem. Approximately 70 per cent of patients eventually have cardiac involvement.

Gastrointestinal. Polyarteritis nodosa also involves the gastrointestinal tract, causing abdominal pain, intestinal bleeding, obstruction, or perforation. Rupture of mesenteric aneurysms can lead to intraperitoneal hemorrhage, hypovolemic shock, and death.

TABLE 85–2. PRESENTING COMPLAINTS IN PATIENTS WITH CLASSIC POLYARTERITIS NODOSA

PRESENTING COMPLAINT	PER CENT OF PATIENTS
Malaise/weakness	13
Abdominal pain	12
Leg pain	12
Neurologic signs/symptoms	10
Fever	8
Cough	8
Myalgias	5
Peripheral neuropathy	5
Headache	5
Arthritis/arthralgia	4
Skin involvement	4
Painful arms	4
Painful feet	4

From Cupps T, Fauci A: The Vasculitides. Philadelphia, WB Saunders Co, 1981, p 30.

Neurologic. Disorders of the peripheral nervous system are attributable to arteritis of the vasa nervorum. The peripheral neuropathies include mononeuritis multiplex, which is characterized by paresthesia, pain, weakness, and sensory loss. Involving several or many individual nerves at the same time, the neuropathy is asymmetric and has both a sensory and a motor distribution.

Vasculitis of the central nervous system (CNS) in polyarteritis nodosa is estimated to occur in 20 to 40 per cent of cases. Encephalopathy secondary to severe hypertension and/or primary neuronal dysfunction produces a global cognitive disorder. Vasculitis affecting different anatomic structures of the CNS can lead to seizures and hemorrhagic or ischemic events.

Cutaneous. Polyarteritis nodosa affects the integument in some form in 25 per cent of patients. An uncommon but quite characteristic sign is cutaneous and subcutaneous nodules. These nodules, which measure 0.5 to 1.0 cm, are usually movable and are often transient. Livedo reticularis, peripheral gangrene, and polymorphic lesions with purpura and urticaria also occur.

Diagnosis

The laboratory findings of polyarteritis nodosa often reflect the presence of a severe systemic inflammation. The ESR, serum immunoglobulin levels, C-reactive protein, white blood cell count, and platelet count are all frequently elevated. Anemia is frequently observed and can be due to blood loss or renal failure. Microscopic hematuria, cylindruria, and proteinuria result from glomerulonephritis. Hypocomplementemia may be present, but antinuclear antibodies and rheumatoid factor are absent. As many as 30 per cent of patients exhibit hepatitis B surface antigenemia. The cerebrospinal fluid is normal unless a subarachnoid hemorrhage has occurred.

Biopsy provides the definitive diagnosis. Any affected organ, such as the skin, muscle, testis, sural nerve, liver, or kidney is an appropriate biopsy site. Angiography of the renal, hepatic, and mesenteric arteries is often performed to seek evidence of aneurysmal formation or other signs of vasculitis. When CNS vasculitis is suspected, angiography is necessary because neither the magnetic resonance nor computer tomography scan provides sufficient evidence to confirm the diagnosis.

Treatment

Effective treatment requires a combination of a corticosteroid and immunosuppressive agents. The current recommended initial therapy is prednisone, 1 to 2 mg/kg/day, and cyclophosphamide, 2 mg/kg/day. These drugs are tapered gradually as the clinical response allows but may be required to maintain remission.

ALLERGIC GRANULOMATOUS VASCULITIS OF CHURG AND STRAUSS

The Churg-Strauss syndrome belongs to the polyarteritis nodosa group and is characterized by hypereosinophilia, allergic rhinitis and/or asthma, and evidence of systemic vasculitis.

This syndrome tends to evolve over many years, during which the predominant clinical findings appear to have an allergic basis. Rhinitis usually precedes the onset of extrinsic asthma. Hypereosinophilia and eosinophilic tissue infiltration occur, and with time a systemic necrotizing vasculitis develops. Hypereosinophilia and asthma are

TABLE 85–3. PRESENTING SIGNS AND SYMPTOMS IN WEGENER'S GRANULOMATOSIS

SIGN OR SYMPTOM	PER CENT
Pulmonary infiltrates	71
Sinusitis	67
Joint (arthralgia or arthritis)	44
Fever	34
Otitis	25
Cough	34
Rhinitis or nasal symptoms	22
Hemoptysis	18
Ocular inflammation (conjunctivitis, uveitis, episcleritis, and scleritis)	16
Weight loss	16
Skin rash	13
Epistaxis	11
Renal failure	11
Chest discomfort	8
Anorexia or malaise	8
Proptosis	7
Shortness of breath or dyspnea	7
Oral ulcers	6
Hearing loss	6
Pleuritis or effusion	6
Headache	6

Reproduced with permission from Fauci AS, Haynes BF, Katz P, et al: Wegener's granulomatosis: Prospective clinical and therapeutic experience with 85 patients for 21 years. Ann Intern Med 1983;98:76–85.

TABLE 85–4. ORGAN SYSTEM INVOLVEMENT IN WEGENER'S GRANULOMATOSIS

ORGAN SYSTEM	PER CENT
Lung	94
Paranasal sinuses	91
Kidney	85
Joints	67
Nose or nasopharynx	64
Ear	61
Eye	58
Skin	45
Nervous system	22
Heart	12

Reproduced with permission from Fauci AS, Haynes BF, Katz P, et al.: Wegener's granulomatosis: Prospective clinical and therapeutic experience with 85 patients for 21 years. Ann Intern Med 1983;98:76–85.

essential criteria for the diagnosis of the Churg-Strauss syndrome.

Vasculitis of the Churg-Strauss syndrome is similar to polyarteritis nodosa and Wegener's granulomatosis in that it involves medium and smaller blood vessels. However, its unique histology distinguishes it from Wegener's disease, and its predominance of respiratory tract allergic-like symptoms and hypereosinophilia distinguishes it from the usual polyarteritis nodosa.

The treatment of Churg-Strauss syndrome is similar to that of the other systemic necrotizing vasculitides. It generally responds readily to high-dose corticosteroids (i.e., prednisone, 60 mg/day), but addition of cyclophosphamide may be required.

WEGENER'S GRANULOMATOSIS

Wegener's granulomatosis is a systemic necrotizing vasculitis characterized by (1) necrotizing granulomatous vasculitis of the upper and lower respiratory tract and (2) a focal necrotizing glomerulonephritis and vasculitis of other organ systems. The disease has a male-female ratio of 3:2. Although the peak incidence occurs in the fourth and fifth decades, with an average age of 40, the age range varies between 15 and 75 years.

The majority of individuals in whom the diagnosis of Wegener's granulomatosis is eventually made present with symptoms of upper respiratory tract disease (Table 85–3), including nasal ulcers, rhinorrhea, and sinus pain. Ocular inflammation also develops in more than half of all patients (Table 85–4) and includes conjunctivitis, episcleritis, scleromalacia, corneal ulcers, and retinal artery thrombosis.

The lungs become involved in the majority of patients. Although variable, the radiographic findings of solitary or multiple infiltrates or nodules and multilocular, irregular cavities can be seen. Biopsy of the lung usually provides documentation of the necrotizing granulomatous process.

The pathologic lesions are a focal or diffuse proliferative glomerulonephritis and interstitial nephritis. The glomerulonephritis often produces a urinary sediment with proteinuria, hematuria, and cylindruria. Nodular skin lesions and purpuric papules can be seen. Active synovitis is rare, but about one half of patients complain of joint pains.

Diagnosis

Laboratory studies usually reveal an elevated ESR; a normochromic, normocytic anemia; and a polyclonal hypergammaglobulinemia. Further, the serum of many patients with Wegener's granulomatosis contains antibodies to a cytoplasmic antigen from polymorphonuclear leukocytes; however, this antibody is not entirely specific and may be present to a lesser extent in other forms of vasculitis. Definitive diagnosis is made on the basis of the biopsy. Occasionally it may be necessary to distinguish between Wegener's granulomatosis and midline granuloma. The latter consists of destructive granuloma involving the nose, paranasal sinuses, and palate, but vasculitis is not a prominent feature and does not appear to be part of the underlying process.

Treatment

The current therapy for Wegener's granulomatosis utilizes corticosteroid and cytotoxic agents. Critically ill patients should be treated with intravenous cyclophosphamide until the course of the disease is stabilized and may then be switched to oral therapy. Treatment with corticosteroids alone is insufficient to control disease activity and induce remission.

POLYMYALGIA RHEUMATICA AND GIANT CELL ARTERITIS

Polymyalgia rheumatica (PMR) and giant cell arteritis are closely related entities, and many believe that they represent the spectrum of a single disease. PMR is characterized by aching and myalgia of the shoulder and pelvic girdle musculature, neck, and proximal extremities. Onset is in the sixth decade or later, and it is about twice as frequent in women as in men. The yearly incidence is approximately 54 per 100,000 population.

Symptoms of aching, stiffness after rest, and myalgia often begin precipitously, although the disease may progress relatively slowly over time. Polyarthralgias or a true synovitis can be present. Other commonly observed constitutional features include fever, weight loss, malaise, and anorexia.

The physical examination reveals tender muscles but no weakness or atrophy. Synovitis of the knees with or without small effusions occurs, but synovitis of the small joints of the hands and feet is rare (Table 85–5).

There are no specific laboratory tests to identify

TABLE 85–5. POLYMYALGIA RHEUMATICA: DIAGNOSTIC CRITERIA

> 50 yr of age
Aching and morning stiffness in at least two of the following areas:
  Neck
  Shoulder girdle
  Pelvic girdle
Erythrocyte sedimentation rate (ESR) >40 mm in 1 hr
Duration of symptoms for 1 mo
No other disease present

From Hunder G: Polymyalgia rheumatica and giant cell arteritis. *In* Wyngaarden JB, Smith LH Jr, Bennett JC (eds): Cecil Textbook of Medicine. 19th ed. Philadelphia, WB Saunders Co, 1992, p 1545.

PMR, but nearly all patients have an elevated Westergren sedimentation rate. The absence of rheumatoid factor differentiates PMR from rheumatoid arthritis. The differential diagnosis includes infections, neoplasia (i.e., plasma cell dyscrasia), fibromyalgia, and painful myopathies. Giant cell arteritis can present or be associated with PMR in 20 to 40 per cent of patients (Table 85–6).

Giant cell arteritis (temporal arteritis) usually affects individuals over the age of 50, with an approximate annual incidence of 12 per 100,000 individuals. The onset of giant cell arteritis may be precipitous or insidious. When the disorder coexists with PMR, proximal extremity aching, stiffness, fatigue, and headache are common presenting symptoms. Other constitutional symptoms include recurrent and unexplained fevers, anorexia, weight loss, and malaise (Table 85–7). In addition, confusion, depressive reactions, psychosis, and, rarely, dementia can occur.

The symptoms of headache, vision changes, and scalp tenderness are the result of arteritis. Jaw claudication, a symptom in one third to one half

TABLE 85–6. DIFFERENTIAL FEATURES IN POLYMYALGIA RHEUMATICA AND SIMILAR DISORDERS

	POLYMYALGIA RHEUMATICA	GIANT CELL ARTERITIS	RHEUMATOID ARTHRITIS	DERMATOMYOSITIS	FIBROMYALGIA
Morning stiffness >30 min	+	±	+*	±	Variable
Headache and/or scalp tenderness	0	+	0	0	Variable
Pain with active joint movement	+	0	+*	0	Inconstant
Tender joints	±	0	+*	0	Tender spots
Swollen joints	±	±	+	0	0
Muscle weakness	±†	0	+*	+	0
Normochromic anemia	+	+	+	0	0
Elevated ESR	+	+	+	±	0
Elevated serum creatine kinase	0	0	0	+	0
Serum rheumatoid factor	0	0	70%	0	0
Distinct electromyographic abnormality	0	0	0	+	0
Response to nonsteroidal antiinflammatory drug (NSAID)	±	0	+	0	0

0 = Absent; + =present; ± =present in minority of cases.
* = Associated with affected joints.
† = Pain inhibits movement. Disuse atrophy may occur.
From Hunder G: Polymyalgia rheumatica and giant cell arteritis. *In* Wyngaarden JB, Smith LH Jr, Bennett JC (eds): Cecil Textbook of Medicine. 19th ed. Philadelphia, WB Saunders Co, 1992, p 1545.

TABLE 85-7. GIANT CELL ARTERITIS: CLINICAL FINDINGS IN 94 PATIENTS

CLINICAL MANIFESTATION	FREQUENCY (%)
Headache	77
Abnormal temporal artery	53
Jaw claudication	51
Scalp tenderness	47
Constitutional symptoms	48
Polymyalgia rheumatica	34
Fever	27
Respiratory symptoms	23
Facial pain	14
Diplopia/blurred vision	12
Transient vision loss	5
Blindness (partial or complete)	13
Hemoglobin <11.0 gm/dl	24
Erythrocyte sedimentation rate >40 mm/hr	97

After Machado EBV, Michet CJ, Ballard DJ, et al: Trends in incidence and clinical presentation of temporal arteritis in Olmsted County, Minnesota, 1950–1985. Arthritis Rheum 31:745–749, 1988. Reprinted from Arthritis and Rheumatism Journal, copyright 1988. Used by permission of the American College of Rheumatology.

of patients, is a consequence of impaired blood flow in the temporal or maxillary arteries.

The visual alterations of giant cell arteritis include transient blurring, ptosis, diplopia, and transient, permanent partial, or complete blindness. These symptoms are the result of arteritis affecting the posterior ciliary or ophthalmic vessels or, less commonly, the central retinal artery. Although blindness is usually preceded by other visual changes for weeks or months, it can occur precipitously without warning.

Headache and scalp tenderness, very common early symptoms, are due to arteritis of the temporal or occipital vessels. The new onset of an ill-defined headache of variable severity in an older person should raise the suspicion of giant cell arteritis.

Diagnosis

There are no specific laboratory abnormalities in giant cell arteritis, but evidence of inflammation may be seen. Leukocytosis of less than 20,000/

mm³ and a thrombocytosis of less than 1,000,000/mm³, elevated fibrinogen, alpha₂-globulin, IgG, and total hemolytic complement are frequently observed. The elevated ESR remains a sine qua non for the diagnosis of giant cell arteritis, just as it does for PMR.

When the diagnosis is suspected, biopsy of a clinically involved or symptomatic portion of the temporal artery should be obtained. If the temporal artery appears clinically uninvolved, biopsy of a segment several centimeters in length should be taken to obtain sufficient tissue to identify the commonly observed "skip" lesions of temporal arteritis. History of claudication of an extremity and the presence on examination of a bruit implicate large vessel arteritis, which should be confirmed by angiography.

Treatment

The treatment of choice is corticosteroids. The usual initial daily dosage is the equivalent of prednisone, 60 mg. If there is a moderate to high likelihood of giant cell arteritis, corticosteroid therapy should be instituted immediately, prior to biopsy, to avert the dreaded potential for blindness. The characteristic histologic findings are present if biopsy is performed within 1 week of initiation of corticosteroid therapy. The response to therapy is monitored clinically by resolution of symptoms as well as by a decrease in the ESR. Upon remission and return of the ESR to normal levels, the corticosteroid dose can be tapered as the ESR is periodically monitored.

REFERENCES

Cupps T, Fauci A: The Vasculitides. Philadelphia, WB Saunders Co, 1981.

Haynes BF, Allen NB, Fauci AS: Diagnostic and therapeutic approach to the patient with vasculitis. Med Clin North Am 70:355, 1986.

Hoffman GS, Kerr GS, Leavitt RY, Hallahan CW, Lebovics RS, Travis WD, Rottem M, Fauci AS: Wegener's granulomatosis: An analysis of 158 patients. Ann Intern Med 116:488, 1992.

Hunder G: Polymyalgia rheumatica and giant cell arteritis. In Wyngaarden JB, Smith LH Jr, Bennett JC (eds): Cecil Textbook of Medicine. 19th ed. Philadelphia, WB Saunders Co, 1992, p 1544.

86 THE SPONDYLOARTHROPATHIES

The spondyloarthropathies are a group of inter-related disorders that share certain epidemiologic, pathogenetic, clinical, and pathologic features. They characteristically have involvement of the sacroiliac joints, as well as peripheral inflammatory arthritis, and by definition are not seropositive for rheumatoid factor. They have a tendency to a familial aggregation of cases and demonstrate inflammation of the ligamentous insertion into bone (esthesis). There is extensive overlap among the several diseases that compose this group (Fig. 86–1).

ANKYLOSING SPONDYLITIS

Ankylosing spondylitis (AS) is the prototype of the spondyloarthropathies. It is characterized by enthesopathy, sacroiliitis, and spondylitis; inflammatory ocular diseases; an asymmetric oligoarthritis predominantly of the large joints of the lower limbs; and an association with human leukocyte antigen (HLA)–B27. The European Spondyloarthropathy Study Group (ESSG) has recently defined criteria for the inclusive diagnosis of all spondyloarthropathies (Fig. 86–2).

Prevalence

The prevalence of AS is about 0.2 per cent of the general population.

Clinical Features

AS usually presents during young adulthood with vague symptoms of mid and low back stiffness and pain. Complaints are radiation of the pain into the buttocks and prominent stiffness in the back after rest. Thoracic cage pain also occurs in AS and can have a pleuritic quality. Dactylitis, Achilles tendinitis, plantar fasciitis, and iliac crest tenderness occur as a result of inflammation at the entheses. The proximal synovial joints, including the shoulders, hips, and knees, are more often involved than the smaller distal joints. Acute anterior uveitis occurs in approximately one quarter of patients with AS and appears as pain, redness, and photophobia that is usually episodic and may be unilateral or bilateral. Examination of the patient with early AS can demonstrate reduced spinal mobility, partial or complete loss of the physiologic lumbar

lordosis, and increased thoracic kyphosis. Later findings include restriction of chest wall expansion during deep inspiration (<2.5 cm), gradual development of a stooped posture, fixation of the spine, and a shuffling gait.

Radiologic Features

The long-standing pathologic changes produce characteristic radiographic features in AS. Inflammation of the sacroiliac joints leads to gradual destruction of cartilage and subchondral erosions, giving the radiographic appearance of "pseudo-widening." An osteoblastic response of the af-

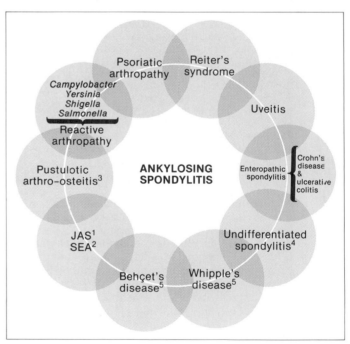

FIGURE 86–1. Individual conditions that overlap to form the spondyloarthritides. (1) Juvenile ankylosing spondylitis. (2) Seronegative enthesopathic arthropathy syndrome. (3) Considered by Japanese to be part of spondyloarthropathy spectrum (rare in United States and Europe). (4) Undifferentiated spondylitis (i.e., subset of patients who have spondyloarthropathic features but who fail to meet criteria for ankylosing spondylitis, Reiter's syndrome, or other condition, e.g., dactylitis, uveitis, plus unilateral sacroiliitis). (5) Not universally accepted as members of the spondyloarthropathy group. (From Calin A: The spondyloarthropathies. In Wyngaarden JB, Smith LH Jr, Bennett JC [eds]: Cecil Textbook of Medicine. 19th ed. Philadelphia, WB Saunders Co, 1992, p 1516.)

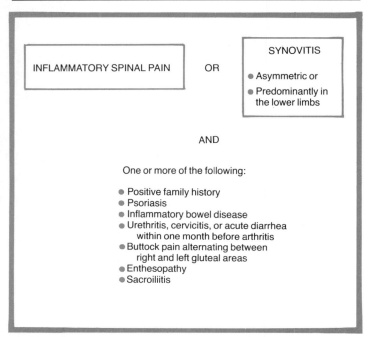

INFLAMMATORY SPINAL PAIN   OR

SYNOVITIS

● Asymmetric or
● Predominantly in the lower limbs

AND

One or more of the following:

● Positive family history
● Psoriasis
● Inflammatory bowel disease
● Urethritis, cervicitis, or acute diarrhea within one month before arthritis
● Buttock pain alternating between right and left gluteal areas
● Enthesopathy
● Sacroiliitis

FIGURE 86–2. European Spondylarthropathy Study Group (ESSG) criteria for the classification of spondyloarthropathy. (Modified from Dougados M, et al: The European Spondylarthropathy Study Group: Preliminary criteria for the classification of spondylarthropathy. Arthritis Rheum 34:1218, 1991. Reprinted from Arthritis and Rheumatism Journal, copyright 1991. Used by permission of the American College of Rheumatology.)

fected bone then results in sclerosis of the joint margins. Subsequent fusion of the joint results from the ingrowth of osteoid tissue, calcification, and bony bridging of the joint margins.

Osteitis of subchondral vertebral bone results in the radiographic picture of squaring of the bodies, which can be the earliest radiographic change of AS. Healing of the cartilage and bone inflammation are associated with fibrosis, calcification, new bone formation with replacement of the annulus fibrosus, and development of syndesmophytes that bridge the margins of adjacent vertebral bodies. The gradual ossification of the annulus fibrosus, formation of syndesmophytes, and ossification of the perispinal ligaments give the radiographic appearance of the "bamboo" spine. Extra-articular involvements in AS and the other spondyloarthropathies are compared in Table 86–1.

Treatment

The management of AS is predicated upon a vigorous approach to physical therapy and the judicious use of certain nonsteroidal anti-inflammatory drugs (NSAIDs). Although NSAIDs do not alter the course of AS, by providing analgesia they promote function. The long-term objective of the exercise regimen is to halt the insidious development of disabling axial immobility and to preserve maximal motion and function.

REITER'S SYNDROME

Reiter's syndrome is characterized by arthritis, urethritis, conjunctivitis, and mucocutaneous lesions. The disease most commonly affects young males (male-female ratio approximates 10–15:1) during the third and fourth decades.

Epidemiology and Immunogenetics

The onset of Reiter's syndrome often occurs following venereal infections or dysentery. The venereal relationship appears more frequently in the United States. Chlamydia can be cultured from the urethras of untreated patients in 33 to 47 per cent of cases. Moreover, antichlamydial antibodies can eventually be detected in about one half of patients, and chlamydial antigens have been found in inflamed synovial tissue. The postdysenteric form of Reiter's syndrome, which is found more frequently in Africa, Europe, and the Far and Middle East, usually results from a gastrointestinal infection with *Shigella flexneri* but may also follow enteric infections with *Salmonella* spp., *Yersinia enterocolitica*, or *Campylobacter jejuni*. Joint fluids of Reiter's syndrome patients yield no bacterial growth, and therefore the syndrome has been regarded as a reactive arthritis. In fact, many patients have only arthritis without the full-blown Reiter's syndrome and are classified (see Fig. 86–1 and Table 86–1) as having reactive arthritis. However, the pathogenic pathways are considered to be similar.

HLA-B27 is found by serotyping in 80 per cent of white and 35 per cent of black patients. Although the precise significance of the B27 allotype remains uncertain, this cellular surface antigen may predispose individuals with certain bacterial infections (i.e., *Shigella*, *Salmonella*, *Y. enterocolitica*) to the eventual development of a reactive arthritis, including Reiter's syndrome.

Clinical Features

Characteristically, Reiter's syndrome develops 1 to 4 weeks following venereal exposure or diarrhea. Urethritis manifested by burning and frequency is often the earliest symptom. An erosion of the glans penis around the meatus—circinate balanitis—may be found in association with the urethritis. A profuse and watery diarrhea can precede the onset of urethritis in Reiter's syndrome. Following an epidemic of *Shigella* dysentery, approximately 2 of every 1000 affected persons can be expected to develop Reiter's syndrome.

The conjunctivitis of Reiter's syndrome is mild and is characterized by an evanescent irritation with burning usually lasting a few days, or, less commonly, as long as several weeks. The process is ordinarily self-limiting. In contrast, the development of an acute uveitis can be complicated by pain and potential vision loss. Mucocutaneous lesions are commonly observed during Reiter's syndrome. Lesions can be identified on the buccal mucosa, tongue, palate, and pharyngeal mucosa as

TABLE 86–1. COMPARISON OF SERONEGATIVE SPONDYLARTHROPATHIES

	ANKYLOSING SPONDYLITIS	REITER'S SYNDROME	PSORIATIC ARTHROPATHY	ENTEROPATHIC SPONDYLITIS	JUVENILE ARTHROPATHY (JAS* SUBSET)	REACTIVE ARTHROPATHY
Gender	Male ≥ female	Male ≥ female	Female ≥ male	Female = male	Male > female	Male = female
Age at onset	20	Any age	Any age	Any age	<16	Any age
Uveitis	++	++	+	+	+	+
Conjunctivitis	−	+	−	−	−	+
Peripheral joints	Lower > upper: often	Lower usually	Upper > lower	Lower > upper	Lower > upper	Lower > upper
Gender differences	Yes	No	No	No	No	No
Sacroiliitis	Always	Often	Often	Often	Often	Often
HLA-B27	95%	80%	20% (50% with sacroiliitis)	50%	90%	80%
Enthesopathy	+	+	+	+	+	+
Aortic regurgitation	+	+	?+	?	?	+
Familial aggregation	+	+	+	+	+	+
Risk for HLA-B27–positive individual	±20%	20%	?	?	?	20%
Onset	Gradual	Sudden	Variable	Gradual	Variable	Sudden
Urethritis	−	+	−	−	−	+/−
Skin involvement	−	+	++	+	−	−
Mucous membrane involvement	−	+	−	+	−	+
Symmetry (spinal)	+	−	−	+	+	−
Self-limiting	−	+/−	+/−	+/−	+/−	+/−
Remission, relapses	−	+/−	+/−	−	+/−	+/−

*JAS = Juvenile ankylosing spondylitis.
Modified from Calin A: The spondyloarthropathies. In Wyngaarden JB, Smith LH Jr, Bennett JC (eds): Cecil Textbook of Medicine. 19th ed. Philadelphia, WB Saunders Co, 1992, p 1517.

painless vesicles, elevated erythematous papules, or superficial ulcers. Keratoderma blennorrhagicum, which occurs in 20 per cent of patients and is found most often on the plantar surfaces of the feet, has the appearance of a brown or yellow cone-shaped papule. Coalescence of the papules leads to desquamating lesions.

The arthritis of Reiter's syndrome often presents precipitously and frequently affects the knees and ankles. The distribution of the arthritis is asymmetric and can be monoarticular and pauciarticular. A particularly notable feature of Reiter's syndrome is the enthesopathy. Although enthesopathic signs are present in other forms of spondyloarthritides, these symptoms are present so often, especially during the early phase of the disorder, as to suggest the diagnosis of Reiter's syndrome.

The onset of Reiter's syndrome can be abrupt, occurring over several days or more gradually over several weeks. Patients can appear quite toxic and exhibit high fevers, weight loss, malaise, and debilitation. Although the recognition of Reiter's syndrome presenting in this manner can be difficult, the presence of urethritis and diarrhea, especially if a history of enthesopathy can be elicited, should suggest the diagnosis. Although the course of Reiter's syndrome is variable, nearly two thirds of patients experience only acute self-limited disease.

Laboratory Findings

During active disease a normocytic, normochromic anemia, leukocytosis (<30,000/mm³), and elevation of the erythrocyte sedimentation rate are often observed. Urinalysis can show microscopic hematuria and pyuria, but cultures are sterile.

Radiographic Findings

Radiographic changes are notably absent early in the disease course. Juxta-articular osteoporosis can be observed around affected peripheral joints. Periostitis of the os calcis is common. The sacroiliitis associated with Reiter's syndrome tends to be asymmetric but becomes symmetric late in the disease. The spondylitis is notable radiographically for nonmarginal syndesmophytes bridging the vertebrae.

Treatment

The management of Reiter's syndrome requires both supportive and preventive measures. Careful ophthalmologic examinations should be performed because failure to diagnose and effectively manage iridocyclitis can lead to significant visual loss. A regimen of bed rest, physical therapy, and NSAIDs is often very effective in the symptomatic management of the arthritis. The local injection of corticosteroids into regions of tendinitis temporarily ameliorates the pain. Low-dose oral methotrexate has been found to be effective in more resistant cases.

PSORIATIC ARTHRITIS

Arthropathy occurs in approximately 20 per cent of individuals with psoriasis, most particularly in those with involvement of the nails. Psoriasis itself is associated with HLA-B13, HLA-Bw17, and HLA-Cw6. HLA-Bw38, HLA-DR4, and HLA-DR7 appear to be genetic markers associated with peripheral arthropathy. The major histocompatibility complex (MHC) marker, HLA-B27, occurs in about 20 per cent of individuals with arthropathy but in 50 per cent of those who have psoriatic spondylitis. Psoriatic arthropathy can take several forms, and it is often difficult to separate from Reiter's syndrome, rheumatoid arthritis, and other inflammatory joint diseases. There are at least five clinical subsets:

1. *Asymmetric oligoarthropathy.* This is characterized by asymmetric involvement of both large and small joints, and the appearance of sausage-shaped digits is common. There appears to be little relationship between the joint and skin activity in this group. This form of arthropathy may appear before any evidence of skin disease.

2. *Symmetric polyarthropathy resembling rheumatoid arthritis.* This pattern is rare, but when it occurs is indistinguishable from that seen in rheumatoid disease and may, in fact, represent coincidental occurrence of the two diseases.

3. *Arthritis mutilans.* This is a severe destructive arthropathy resulting in mutilation of the joints and telescoping of digits to produce the so-called opera-glass hand.

4. *Psoriatic spondylitis.* Approximately 20 per cent of patients with psoriasis and arthritis have radiographic sacroiliitis. There is a male predominance of 3.5:1.

5. *Psoriatic nail disease and distal interphalangeal joint involvement.* This form is found in association with depressions of the nail, nail splitting, and subungual hyperkeratosis. The direct relationship between destructive lesions on the nail and in the distal interphalangeal joints is striking, but what role this proximity plays in pathogenesis is unclear.

Radiographic Findings

The radiographic features of the peripheral joints include soft tissue swelling, demineralization, loss of cartilage space, erosions, bony ankylosis, subluxation, and subchondral cysts. Several radiographic findings are classically observed in arthritis mutilans. These findings include "whittling," "pencil-in-cup," "la main en lorgnette" (opera-glass hand), and "doigt en lorgnette" (telescope finger).

Treatment

Aspirin and NSAIDs can be used for short-term treatment to give anti-inflammatory action and to reduce synovitis and control pain. Short-term treatment with corticosteroids may be used if the patient fails to respond to the conservative approach.

In the presence of more severe disease with attendant erosive arthritis, a remitting agent should be used. Gold salts, 6-mercaptopurine, and methotrexate have been used with some success. The use of remitting agents may be complicated by dermatoses, bone marrow toxicity, and hepatotoxicity. Care must be taken to follow the clinical course at regular intervals and to obtain appropriate laboratory studies to exclude toxicity.

ARTHRITIS ASSOCIATED WITH INFLAMMATORY BOWEL DISEASE

Inflammatory bowel disease is an idiopathic chronic inflammatory process involving the gastrointestinal tract. Both ulcerative colitis and regional enteritis (Crohn's disease) can be associated with an inflammatory arthritis. Two distant types are observed in these disorders: a peripheral arthritis and ankylosing spondylitis. These entities are discussed in Chapter 36.

REFERENCES

Calin A: The spondyloarthropathies. *In* Wyngaarden JB, Smith LH Jr, Bennett JC (eds): Cecil Textbook of Medicine. 19th ed. Philadelphia, WB Saunders Co, 1992, pp 1515–1520.

Dougados M, van der Linden S, Juhlin R, Huitfeldt B, Amor B, Calin A, Cats A, Dijkman B, Olivieri I, Pasero G, Veys E, Zielder H: The European Spondyloarthropathy Study Group: Preliminary criteria for the classification of spondyloarthropathy. Arthritis Rheum 34:1218, 1991.

Fox R, Calin A, Gerber RC, Gibson D: The chronicity of symptoms and disability in Reiter's syndrome: An analysis of 181 consecutive patients. Ann Intern Med 91:190–193, 1979.

Kammer GM, Soter NA, Gibson DJ, Schur PH: Psoriatic arthritis: A clinical, immunologic and HLA study of 100 patients. Semin Arthritis Rheum 9:75–97, 1979.

87 OSTEOARTHRITIS

Osteoarthritis (OA), or degenerative joint disease, is the most common musculoskeletal disease. Well over 60 million Americans have pain and limitation of motion as a result of OA. It is characterized as a slowly progressive loss of articular cartilage as well as formation of new bone at the joint surfaces. It is not a single entity but rather the end result of several mechanical and biologic factors that trigger the processes resulting in cartilage destruction (Fig. 87-1).

CLASSIFICATION

Because OA is a "final common pathway" for a variety of conditions, classification is difficult. Table 87-1 represents the latest classification of OA. OA is classified as (1) *primary* (idiopathic), which is the type often referred to as "aging" and is unrelated to known systemic or local diseases; it also includes certain hereditary and erosive subsets; (2) *secondary*, in which a clearly identifiable underlying cause, such as an inflammatory, metabolic, endocrine, developmental, traumatic, or heritable connective tissue disease, can be identified. These classification criteria are not designed for diagnosis; their primary purpose is to develop standardized reporting and investigation in various subsets of OA.

ETIOPATHOGENESIS

The prevalence of OA increases with age; of all risk factors for primary OA, age is the strongest. At age 60, more than 60 per cent of the population have some degree of cartilage abnormality in many of their joints. Almost 100,000 total hip replacements and about as many knee procedures are performed annually in the United States; most of these are for OA. Certain genetic factors play a role; OA of the distal interphalangeal joints of the hands has an incidence in women 10 times greater than in men. Repetitive trauma causes stiffness of subchondral bone, resulting in increased wear of overlying cartilage. Obesity, with its added mechanical stress, is associated with OA of the knee. Certain occupational or sports-related stress is associated with OA: the lumbar spine is affected in coal miners, the shoulders in bus drivers, for example.

There is a role for mechanical, biochemical, inflammatory, and immunologic factors in the path-

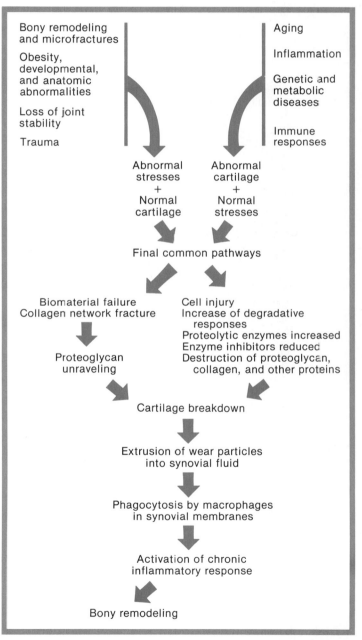

FIGURE 87-1. Etiopathogenic factors in osteoarthritis. (Modified from DJ McCarty: Arthritis and Allied Conditions. 11th ed. Philadelphia, Lea & Febiger, 1989. Reprinted with permission.)

TABLE 87–1. CLASSIFICATION OF OSTEOARTHRITIS

Idiopathic (primary)
  Localized
  Generalized—includes three or more areas
  Mineral deposition diseases
Secondary
  Post-traumatic
  Congenital or developmental
  Disturbed local tissue structure by primary disease, e.g., ischemic
    necrosis, tophaceous gout, rheumatoid arthritis
  Miscellaneous additional diseases
    Endocrine
    Metabolic
    Neuropathic arthropathies
    Mechanical

Modified from Howell DS: Osteoarthritis (degenerative joint disease). In Wyngaarden JB, Smith LH Jr, Bennett JC (eds): Cecil Textbook of Medicine. 19th ed. Philadelphia. WB Saunders Co, 1992, p 1555.

ologic changes of OA (Fig. 87–1). A working hypothesis of the pathogenesis of OA is that the insult (or insults) leads to release of proteolytic and collagenolytic enzymes from chondrocytes, which then degrade collagen and proteoglycans; this is followed by reparative processes with increased bone formation. The role of calcium pyrophosphate dihydrate (CPPD) crystal deposition in the development of OA is not clear. Approximately half of the knees treated surgically in patients over age 65 have evidence of meniscal chondrocalcinosis. Many endocrine and metabolic disorders such as acromegaly, hyperparathyroidism, Wilson's disease, ochronosis, hemochromatosis, and hypothyroidism are associated with secondary OA (Table 87–1), and their association may be a result of the increased frequency of chondrocalcinosis in these disorders. Repeated shedding of these crystals may result in an inflammatory process with release of proteolytic enzymes from neutrophils with resultant cartilage damage.

Gross pathologic changes in OA include cartilage fibrillation, fissuring, and erosions, which lead to completely bare areas of bone. Spur formation (osteophytes) seen predominantly at joint margins represents the proliferative response. *Osteophytes* are a cardinal feature of OA. Other pathologic changes include sclerosis and thickening of subchondral bone in addition to juxtaarticular bone cyst formation. In more advanced disease, synovitis is common; this may result from crystal-induced synovitis (CPPD or calcium apatite) or from synovial clearance of cartilage breakdown products.

CLINICAL FEATURES

OA is generally suspected on the basis of history and physical examination (Table 87–2). Despite a multiplicity of possible causes and pathogenetic mechanisms, the clinical presentation of the disease is often remarkably stereotypic, which may explain why many clinicians consider OA to be a single distinct entity.

The most commonly affected joints are the hips, knees, spine, and small joints of the hands (first carpometacarpals, proximal and distal interphalangeals) and feet (metatarsophalangeals). The wrist, elbow, shoulder, and ankle are usually spared unless there is evidence of trauma or congenital abnormality. OA of the first metatarsophalangeal joints of the feet and distal interphalangeal joints of the hand is most often encountered in women and occurs with high frequency in families. Cervical and lumbar spine OA is common in elderly persons.

Signs and symptoms are usually local, confined to one or a few joints. There are no systemic symptoms. The most common symptom is progressive *pain*; the pain initially is intermittent and mild but becomes constant and more disabling. The pain almost always is partially relieved by rest and exacerbated by movement, especially weight-bearing movement. The pain may be referred; OA of the hip may localize to the medial side of the knee. There may be "stiffness" of the joint after a period of inactivity. With severe disease there may be gradual limitation of motion of the affected joints and nocturnal pain.

Another common complaint includes *crepitus*, or "cracking" of the affected joint. This may be painless but often is associated with pain and is more pronounced in the patellofemoral joint. As the OA progresses, a noticeable *deformity* may develop; this most often is manifested as one knee larger than the other or an enlargement of a finger joint. Joint enlargement can be a result of increased bone, increased amounts of synovial fluid, and synovitis. Other deformities include a lateral (varus) or medial (valgus) bowing of a knee. When OA of the hip or knee has progressed to a severe

TABLE 87–2. CLINICAL FEATURES OF PRIMARY OSTEOARTHRITIS

Symptoms
  Pain: Progressive pain (months to years), exacerbated by movement
    and weight bearing, relieved partially with rest;
    may be referred or radicular
  Limitation of motion: Flexion contracture
  Crepitus
  Deformity: Bony enlargement, bowing of knee, limp
Signs
  Limitation of motion: Flexion contracture
  Crepitus
  Joint enlargement: Heberden's and Bouchard's nodes
  Joint effusion
  Deformity: Varus, valgus, etc.
Radiographs
  Marginal osteophytes
  Subchondral sclerosis
  Subchondral cysts
  Joint space narrowing
Laboratory
  Synovial fluid—noninflammatory (white cell count <1500/mm^3)

stage, there may be a noticeable limp or an antalgic gait related to the pain associated with weight bearing. Acute inflammatory flares may be precipitated by crystal-induced synovitis in response to shedding of CPPD crystals.

Symptoms of OA in the cervical spine depend upon the neural segment involved; pain often radiates into the supraclavicular and upper trapezius regions and distal upper extremities. A myelopathy may result from overgrowth of bone in the cervical or lumbar spine; neurogenic claudication is an important symptom in lumbar spinal stenosis.

Large synovial effusions are uncommon. *Osteophytes* (spurs) account for most of the enlargement of joints; in the distal interphalangeal joint they are referred to as Heberden's nodes and if associated with the proximal interphalangeal joints, Bouchard's nodes.

Limitation of motion is the most frequent finding on examination. Early on this may not be present, but it gradually worsens and becomes severe with progressive disease. With advanced disease there often is a *joint contracture*. The degree and nature of the contracture depend on the joint involved. Varus or valgus deformities are often seen in more advanced stages of knee OA. These deformities are due to cartilage loss of the medial and lateral compartments, respectively.

Characteristic radiographic findings of primary OA are summarized in Table 87-2. These radiographic findings confirm the pathologic findings—loss of cartilage (narrowed joint space) with new bone formation (osteophytes and sclerosis). Conditions associated with secondary OA usually have radiographic findings that are more indicative of the underlying pathology, such as Paget's disease, rheumatoid arthritis, and hyperparathyroidism.

Routine laboratory studies are generally unremarkable in OA and are of little diagnostic help. The synovial fluid is generally clear and noninflammatory. Leukocyte counts in synovial fluid are generally in the range of 150 to 1500/mm³. CPPD crystals may be seen in many OA joint effusions.

DIFFERENTIAL DIAGNOSIS

Primary OA of a hip or knee can usually be diagnosed rather easily and is not often confused with other types of arthritis. Other diagnoses that should be entertained in someone with suspected OA of the hip include pigmented villonodular synovitis and osteonecrosis. Internal joint derangements, chronic infections, and osteochondritis are among several less common entities that should be considered in the differential diagnosis of someone with knee OA. An erosive inflammatory OA that involves primarily the distal or proximal interphalangeal joints of the hands may be mistaken for rheumatoid arthritis, Reiter's syndrome, or psoriatic arthritis.

TREATMENT

Therapeutic options need to be individualized to fit the severity of the disease. The multidisciplinary components of a treatment program for the patient with OA include education, drugs, physical measures, and surgery. Although no cures are available for OA, much can be done to alleviate pain, maintain mobility, and minimize disability. Early disease with no evidence of joint contracture or instability can often be treated with intermittent analgesics, appropriate joint protection and rest, and if needed, weight reduction. Appliances such as canes and other physical therapy means such as exercise programs are beneficial in joint protection.

Pharmacologic agents commonly used to provide analgesia include acetaminophen, aspirin, and nonsteroidal anti-inflammatory drugs (NSAIDs). Gastrointestinal side effects such as peptic ulceration are common with the use of NSAIDs, and they should be used cautiously, especially in persons over age 60. Oral or parenteral corticosteroids are contraindicated in the treatment of OA. However, intra-articular injections with corticosteroids may be beneficial when used for acute flares.

Hip and knee arthroplasties (replacements) produce significant symptomatic relief and improved range of motion. Surgical procedures are reserved for patients with more severe disease, with persistent pain and impaired function. Arthroscopy with debridement of the joint and removal of free cartilage fragments may prevent joint locking and rapid wear of the joint surfaces. Spinal surgery is indicated when there is evidence of spinal cord impingement (neurologic deficits, altered bowel or bladder function) or intractable pain unresponsive to medical management.

REFERENCES

Hough AJ Jr, Sokoloff L: Pathology of osteoarthritis. In McCarty DJ (ed): Arthritis and Allied Conditions. 11th ed. Philadelphia, Lea & Febiger, 1989, pp 1571–1594.

Howell DS: Osteoarthritis (degenerative joint disease). In Wyngaarden JB, Smith LH Jr, Bennett JC (eds): Cecil Textbook of Medicine. 19th ed. Philadelphia, WB Saunders Co, 1992, pp 1554–1557.

Mankin HJ: Clinical features of osteoarthritis. In Kelley WN, Harris ED Jr, Ruddy S, Sledge CB (eds): Textbook of Rheumatology. 3rd ed. Philadelphia, WB Saunders Co, 1989, pp 1480–1500.

Moskowitz RW: Clinical and laboratory findings in osteoarthritis. In McCarty DJ (ed): Arthritis and Allied Conditions. 11th ed. Philadelphia, Lea & Febiger, 1989, pp 1605–1630.

88 THE CRYSTAL-INDUCED ARTHROPATHIES

CHONDROCALCINOSIS AND ASSOCIATED DISORDERS

Several different forms of crystals are known to induce various patterns of arthritis. The most extensively studied is gout (see Chapter 59), in which urate crystals are associated with acute synovial inflammation. Calcium in various crystalline configurations, including pyrophosphate, oxalate, and apatite, can deposit in articular cartilage, synovium, and periarticular tissues. Chondrocalcinosis results from the deposition of calcium pyrophosphate dihydrate (CPPD) crystals in cartilage (Fig. 88–1). The resulting clinical disorder, pseudogout, generally begins as a monoarticular or pauciarticular arthritis, but may become polyarticular. Most often it is idiopathic, but it can be associated with aging and certain metabolic disorders (Table 88–1). It affects about 5 per cent of the adult population and may exceed 25 per cent in the over-80 population. The acute attacks resemble gout clinically, but as time passes it may be confused with rheumatoid arthritis, neurotrophic arthritis, or osteoarthritis.

Pseudogout is an acute inflammatory arthritis that results from phagocytosis of IgG-coated CPPD crystals by synovial fluid neutrophils and the sub-

TABLE 88–1. METABOLIC DISORDERS ASSOCIATED WITH CPPD DEPOSITION

Diabetes mellitus
Gout
Hemochromatosis
Hyperparathyroidism
Hypomagnesemia
Hypophosphatasia
Myxedematous hypothyroidism
Ochronosis
Wilson's disease

sequent release of inflammatory mediators. Initially monoarticular, the attacks soon become oligoarticular or polyarticular. Frequently, acute attacks are self-limiting, lasting for 1 to several days, as in gout. However, more severe attacks involving both the peripheral and axial joints can more slowly resolve over weeks. The large joints of the lower extremities are the more likely targets, with the knee joint being involved in more than one half of all cases of pseudogout. The presence of chondrocalcinosis can be identified radiographically by the characteristic punctate or linear radiodensities in hyaline articular cartilage and in the menisci in the knee. Other areas frequently exhibiting these findings include the wrists and pelvis.

The diagnosis of pseudogout should not depend upon the radiographic findings alone because chondrocalcinosis is observed in only 75 per cent of cases of pseudogout. Arthrocentesis is a necessary diagnostic procedure because acute infectious arthritis and gout can clinically resemble pseudogout. The synovial fluid exhibits a leukocytosis with a predominance of neutrophils and has a low viscosity (see Table 78–3). CPPD crystals are rhomboid in shape and produce weakly positive birefringence under compensated polarizing microscopy. The typical crystals are seen in the synovial fluid but can also be observed within neutrophils. It should also be noted that monosodium urate and CPPD crystals can coexist within the same joint.

Chronic CPPD crystal disease can exhibit a symmetric polyarticular distribution and can clinically mimic rheumatoid arthritis. Patients describe prolonged morning stiffness, fatigability, and malaise, and the course can extend over many months. Although flexion contractures may be

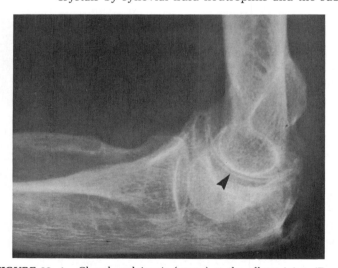

FIGURE 88–1. Chondrocalcinosis (*arrow*) at the elbow joint. (From Schumacher HR Jr: Crystal deposition arthropathies. *In* Wyngaarden JB, Smith LH Jr, Bennett JC [eds]: Cecil Textbook of Medicine. 19th ed. Philadelphia, WB Saunders Co, 1992, p 1552.)

seen and the sedimentation rate may be elevated, radiographs show secondary osteoarthritic changes of affected joints; and the synovial fluid contains CPPD crystals and shows none of the inflammatory markers of rheumatoid arthritis.

About half of all cases of CPPD crystal disease develop signs of osteoarthritis (pseudo-osteoarthritis) involving the knees, wrists, metacarpophalangeal joints, hips, shoulders, elbows, and ankles. As expected, CPPD crystals are found in synovial fluid even when radiographs do not demonstrate the punctate or linear calcification of the cartilage. In contrast, asymptomatic persons can inadvertently be found to have CPPD crystal deposits on radiographs.

Clinically symptomatic CPPD disease responds to rest, joint protection, and use of a nonsteroidal anti-inflammatory drug (NSAID). Colchicine is efficacious in acute attacks of pseudogout as well as in gout. The instillation of a corticosteroid preparation may hasten resolution of the inflammatory process but should not be started until arthrocentesis and crystal identification have established the diagnosis. Maintenance therapy with a NSAID is usually satisfactory.

Calcium oxalate deposition is usually seen in patients with renal failure who are on chronic dialysis. Examination of the synovial fluid shows the characteristic bipyramidal crystals. These crystals may also be seen in synovial tissue biopsies of involved joints. It should be noted that vitamin C can potentiate oxalate deposition.

The third calcium crystal–induced rheumatic syndrome is associated with apatite crystals. The spectrum of clinical manifestations ranges from calcific tendinitis to frank arthritis that is typically episodic and monoarticular. Apatite crystals seem to play a causative role in "Milwaukee shoulder," an inflammatory and extremely destructive arthritis that can be associated with rotator cuff tears.

The differentiation of apatite-induced inflammation from acute septic arthritis, gout, or pseudogout is made by synovial fluid examination. Apatite crystals are nonbirefringent globules, and definitive identification can be made only by electron probe elemental analysis or x-ray diffraction. Acute arthritis or periarthritis is treated with NSAIDs. Apatite deposits can be found in soft tissue in chronic renal disease owing to phosphate retention and can be seen in association with repeated depot corticosteroid injection and in scleroderma.

REFERENCES

Gibilisco PA, Schumacher HR, Hollander JL, Soper KA: Synovial fluid crystals in osteoarthritis. Arthritis Rheum 28:511, 1985.

McCarty DJ: Diagnostic mimicry in arthritis—patterns of joint involvement associated with calcium pyrophosphate dihydrate crystal deposits. Bull Rheum Dis 25:804, 1974–1975.

Schumacher HR, Smolyo AP, Tse RL, Maurer K: Arthritis associated with apatite crystals. Ann Intern Med 87:411, 1977.

89 MISCELLANEOUS FORMS OF ARTHRITIS

Many of the disorders discussed in this chapter have prominent systemic features; however, their musculoskeletal manifestations often provide clues to their initial and perhaps earlier diagnosis.

MUSCULOSKELETAL SYNDROMES ASSOCIATED WITH MALIGNANCY

Musculoskeletal manifestations are not prominent features of most malignancies. However, several syndromes may present with features suggestive of gout, rheumatoid arthritis (RA), and other connective tissue diseases. In addition, several musculoskeletal diseases are associated with increased frequencies of malignancy (Table 89–1).

Hypertrophic Osteoarthropathy. Hypertrophic osteoarthropathy is defined as a syndrome of (1) chronic proliferative periostitis of long bones, (2) clubbing of fingers and toes, and (3) synovitis. Although the underlying disease is usually readily apparent, occasionally clinical manifestations may precede symptoms of the associated disease by several months. If associated with a malignancy, the onset may be explosive, with exquisite tenderness resembling acute gout. A bone scan may be abnormal before there is other radiologic evidence of periostitis.

TABLE 89–1. MALIGNANCY AND MUSCULOSKELETAL DISEASES

Hypertrophic osteoarthropathy
Carcinomatous polyarthritis
Arthritis of metastatic disease
Leukemia
Lymphoma
Vasculitis
Reflex sympathetic dystrophy
Polymyositis
Panniculitis
Scleroderma
Sjögren's syndrome
Rheumatoid arthritis
Paget's disease

Hypertrophic osteoarthropathy is often associated with lung carcinoma, most frequently with adenocarcinomas and squamous cell carcinomas; it is rarely seen with small cell carcinoma. It occurs in 5 to 10 per cent of all intrathoracic malignancies, especially those involving the pleura or the periphery of the lung.

Carcinomatous Polyarthritis. Carcinomatous polyarthritis is an inflammatory polyarthritis of unknown pathogenesis that clinically may resemble RA. Eighty per cent of women with this syndrome have breast carcinoma. Prostate and bladder carcinomas are also common.

Metastatic Disease. The arthritis associated with metastatic disease is most commonly monoarticular, usually involving the knee or hip. Breast and lung carcinomas are the most common neoplasms.

Leukemia. Arthritis or arthralgias occur in approximately 12 per cent of adults with chronic leukemia, 13 per cent of adults with acute leukemia, and up to 60 per cent of children with acute lymphoblastic leukemia. Articular symptoms are the result of leukemic infiltrates of the synovium, periosteum, or periarticular bone or of secondary gout or hemarthrosis. In children, acute lymphocytic leukemia may produce fevers as well as arthritis, thereby mimicking Still's disease or acute rheumatic fever.

Lymphoma. Skeletal involvement has been found at autopsy in as many as 50 per cent of patients with Hodgkin's disease; however, these lesions are usually asymptomatic.

Vasculitis. Necrotizing vasculitis has been reported with lymphomas, leukemias, sarcomas, and multiple myeloma. Polyarteritis nodosa has been described in patients with Hodgkin's disease and with hairy cell leukemia.

Reflex Sympathetic Dystrophy. Reflex sympathetic dystrophy has been reported in patients with metastatic ovarian carcinoma and lung and brain tumors. Palmar fasciitis and arthritis have been described in association with ovarian carcinoma and cancer of the prostate.

Polymyositis. Neoplasms are reported in 5 to 10 per cent of all patients with polymyositis or dermatomyositis. In most patients evidence of myositis precedes discovery of the malignancy by less than 2 years; however, 30 per cent have a malignancy diagnosed prior to the development of myositis. The most common malignancies are breast and lung cancer (see Chapter 82).

Panniculitis. Pancreatic panniculitis is a triad consisting of subcutaneous fat necrosis, arthralgia or arthritis, and a pancreatic abnormality such as pancreatitis or pancreatic cancer. The arthropathy, which is secondary to periarticular fat necrosis, may be monoarticular or polyarticular.

Scleroderma. A few scleroderma patients with lung involvement have been found at autopsy to have not only pulmonary fibrosis but also alveolar cell carcinoma.

Sjögren's Syndrome. The incidence of lymphoma is increased 44-fold in Sjögren's syndrome. Pseudomalignant or malignant lymphoproliferation may be present initially or may develop later in the illness.

Rheumatoid Arthritis. The incidence of lymphoma and myeloma is increased in RA. Rheumatoid nodules in the lung may mimic neoplastic disease.

Paget's Disease. Osteosarcoma occurs in less than 1 per cent of patients with Paget's disease of bone; other less common neoplasms include giant cell tumors and non-neoplastic granulomas.

ARTHROPATHIES ASSOCIATED WITH ENDOCRINE DISEASES

The endocrine diseases are associated with a wide spectrum of musculoskeletal syndromes (Table 89–2). Therefore, endocrine disorders should be included in the differential diagnosis of many musculoskeletal conditions.

Diabetes Mellitus. Carpal tunnel syndrome is present in about 5 per cent of diabetic patients. Charcot's arthropathy occurs most commonly in the ankle-foot area, but the knee is also frequently involved. This must be differentiated from osteomyelitis, which is also common in the feet of patients with diabetes mellitus. Calcific peritendinitis and bursitis of the shoulder leading to adhesive capsulitis and reflex sympathetic dystrophy have also been associated with diabetes.

Scleroderma diabeticorum, or scleroderma adultorum of Buschke, is a syndrome characterized by thick, hidebound skin over the posterior neck and upper back. Diabetic cheiroarthropathy, or syndrome of limited joint mobility, is a sclerosing cutaneous disorder that occurs in one third of patients with type I diabetes mellitus and less frequently in type II diabetics.

Hypothyroidism. Musculoskeletal symptoms are most likely to occur in patients with fully developed myxedema, and most respond to hormone replacement. Unlike in RA, the joint fluid is highly viscous and the white blood cell count is usually less than 1000 cells/mm³. Muscle weakness, usually proximal, may be profound. Elevated serum creatine kinase levels occur in about 90 per cent of cases. Although chondrocalcinosis is found in a large percentage of patients with myxedema, pseudogout is uncommon in untreated patients, but attacks may develop after patients are started on thyroid replacement.

Hyperthyroidism. Patients with hyperthyroidism can also present with proximal muscle weakness. Serum muscle enzyme levels are usually not elevated. Hyperthyroidism, either endogenous or exogenous, results in increased bone turnover and remodeling, the net result being osteoporosis.

Thyroid acropachy, an unusual but very distinctive syndrome, occurs in less than 1 per cent of patients with fully developed Graves' disease. Patients can be euthyroid at the time of its recognition, and it has been reported to appear as long as 28 years after successful treatment of the hyperthyroidism. The syndrome is characterized by an insidious onset of diffuse, often painless swelling of the extremities. Radiographically a periosteal reaction involves the diaphyses of the metacarpals, metatarsals, and proximal phalanges.

Hyperparathyroidism. Arthralgias and inflammatory arthritis with erosions are the most common musculoskeletal manifestations of hyperparathyroidism. Chondrocalcinosis, most often asymptomatic, or acute calcium pyrophosphate dihydrate (CPPD) crystal arthritis has been reported in 18 to 40 per cent of cases.

Hypoparathyroidism. Patients with hypoparathyroidism can have hypocalcemic muscular cramps and carpopedal spasm. Soft tissue calcifications produce symptoms because of their localization in muscles or tendons.

Acromegaly. Musculoskeletal manifestations of acromegaly include myopathy, back pain, carpal tunnel syndrome, and peripheral arthropathy. At least half of the patients with acromegaly complain of nonradiating lumbosacral back pain. Radiographically, the intervertebral disc spaces are increased and large anterior osteophytes with ligamentous calcification are seen. Acromegaly is also associated with an accelerated premature osteoarthritis of the hips and knees.

Cushing's Syndrome. A proximal myopathy without elevation of serum muscle enzyme occurs in some patients with Cushing's syndrome. Generalized osteoporosis resulting in fractures is characteristic of both excessive endogenous and exogenous steroids.

ADDITIONAL MISCELLANEOUS DISORDERS

A few additional disorders that are not common should be included in the differential diagnosis of many patients with musculoskeletal complaints (Table 89–3).

Pigmented Villonodular Synovitis. This uncommon benign disorder of young adults usually affects the entire synovium of a single joint. The pathology consists of lipid- and hemosiderin-laden cells and multinucleated giant cells with exuberant proliferation of synovial lining cells and the formation of villi and lobulated masses that fuse

TABLE 89–2. MUSCULOSKELETAL MANIFESTATIONS OF ENDOCRINE DISEASE

ENDOCRINE DISEASE	MUSCULOSKELETAL MANIFESTATION
Diabetes mellitus	Carpal tunnel syndrome
	Charcot's arthropathy
	Adhesive capsulitis
	Syndrome of limited joint mobility (cheiroarthropathy)
	Scleroderma adultorum of Buschke
Hypothyroidism	Proximal myopathy
	Arthralgias
	Joint effusions
	Carpal tunnel syndrome
	Chondrocalcinosis
Hyperthyroidism	Myopathy
	Osteoporosis
	Thyroid acropachy
Hyperparathyroidism	Myopathy
	Arthralgias
	Erosive arthritis
	Chondrocalcinosis
Hypoparathyroidism	Muscle cramps
	Soft tissue calcifications
	Spondyloarthropathy
Acromegaly	Carpal tunnel syndrome
	Myopathy
	Raynaud's phenomenon
	Back pain
	Premature osteoarthritis
Cushing's syndrome	Myopathy
	Osteoporosis
	Avascular necrosis

TABLE 89–3. ADDITIONAL MISCELLANEOUS FORMS OF ARTHRITIS

DISORDER	DISTINCTIVE FEATURES
Pigmented villonodular synovitis	Monoarticular indolent arthritis, dark brown synovial fluid
Multicentric reticulohistiocytosis	Reddish-purple skin nodules, symmetric destructive polyarthritis
Charcot's arthropathy	Diabetes mellitus, syphilis, syringomyelia
Hemarthrosis	Hemophilia, other bleeding disorders, trauma, scurvy, pigmented villonodular synovitis
Sarcoidosis	Acute arthritis, erythema nodosum, bilateral hilar adenopathy
Amyloidosis	Green birefringence with Congo red staining of affected tissues
Primary biliary cirrhosis	Antimitochondrial antibodies
Familial Mediterranean fever	Triad of recurrent fever, serositis, and arthritis
Whipple's disease	PAS-positive macrophages in bowel or synovial tissue
Sickle cell disease	Acute arthritis, osteomyelitis, avascular necrosis, dactylitis

PAS = Periodic acid–Schiff.

into nodules. The knee is the joint most commonly involved. Treatment is total synovectomy.

Multicentric Reticulohistiocytosis. Multicentric reticulohistiocytosis, a rare systemic disease, is characterized by infiltration of multinucleated giant cells and histiocyte-like cells into various tissues. Destructive polyarthritis and skin lesions are the most common clinical features. Confluence of nodules over the face and malar areas can give the appearance of leonine facies. Mucosal surfaces are involved in about 50 per cent of cases.

The symmetric polyarthritis affects most commonly the interphalangeal joints of the fingers and may clinically resemble RA. Progressive destruction of articular cartilage and underlying bone results in arthritis mutilans in 30 to 45 per cent of cases.

Charcot's Arthropathy. Charcot's arthropathy, or neuropathic joint disease, is a progressive degenerative arthritis most commonly seen in patients with diabetes mellitus. Other diseases associated with Charcot's arthropathy are syphilis and syringomyelia. The knee and hip joints are most often affected in patients with tabetic neuropathic joint disease. In syringomyelia, upper limb involvement is typical. Neuropathic joint disease in diabetes mellitus is more likely to involve the joints of the feet.

Hemarthrosis. Trauma and hemophilia (see Chapter 51) are the most common causes of hemarthrosis (see Chapter 78). The presence of fat globules floating on the surface of bloody synovial fluid usually indicates a fracture.

Sarcoidosis. Sarcoidosis (see Chapter 17) is a multisystem disorder that may involve any organ but has a predilection for lung tissue and thoracic lymph nodes. Acute arthritis of the ankles or knees is the most common musculoskeletal manifestation (15 per cent); this may occur early or late in the disease. Erythema nodosum often coexists with acute arthritis; when accompanied by bilateral hilar adenopathy, this triad is called *Löfgren's syndrome*.

Amyloidosis. Amyloidosis is characterized by the accumulation of extracellular fibrous protein (amyloid) in connective tissues. Carpal tunnel syndrome may result from the local deposition of amyloid around the median nerve. Amyloid may infiltrate the synovium and periarticular tissues, resulting in an arthritis that clinically resembles RA. The joints most frequently involved are the shoulders, wrists, knees, and fingers. Subcutaneous nodules are present in 70 per cent of cases. Most patients with amyloid arthropathy eventually develop multiple myeloma. The diagnosis is established by the demonstration of the typical birefringent tissue deposits seen with Congo red staining.

Primary Biliary Cirrhosis. Primary biliary cirrhosis (see Chapter 43), a disease primarily of middle-aged women, is a rare, chronic, immunologically mediated progressive liver disease. Serum autoantibodies, elevated levels of immunoglobulins, and circulating immune complexes are typically observed in this disorder. Musculoskeletal manifestations include polyarthritis with erosive bone lesions, hypertrophic osteoarthropathy, avascular necrosis, osteomalacia, and osteoporosis.

Familial Mediterranean Fever. The major clinical features of familial Mediterranean fever are serositis, fever, and arthritis. Arthritis, most commonly an acute intermittent monoarthritis of a large joint of the lower extremities, occurs in 70 per cent of patients. Daily oral colchicine decreases the frequency and severity of the febrile attacks and arthritis.

Whipple's Disease. Arthritis or arthralgias occur in 65 to 90 per cent of patients with Whipple's disease. Fever, diarrhea, and weight loss are other prominent features. Arthritis is intermittent in 60 per cent of patients with acute attacks lasting from days to weeks. Chronic arthritis lasting for several years can occur, although joint destruction is rare. Characteristic periodic acid-Schiff (PAS)–positive macrophages with rod-shaped bacilli may be identified in the small bowel or synovial tissue. Antibiotics, especially penicillin or tetracycline, are effective in treating the joint symptoms.

Sickle Cell Disease. Sickle cell crisis is frequently associated with intense periarticular pain and arthritis. The arthritis is secondary to occlusion of small vessels caused by local sickling. Subchondral and interosseous hemorrhages contribute to the destruction of articular cartilage. The knees and elbows are the joints most commonly involved. Avascular necrosis, most commonly of the femoral head, occurs in both SC and SS disease. Sickle cell dactylitis, or hand-foot syndrome, is a condition in young children of transient swelling and tenderness of the hands and feet secondary to periostitis.

REFERENCES

Caldwell DS: Musculoskeletal syndromes associated with malignancy. *In* Kelley WN, Harris ED Jr, Ruddy S, Sledge CB (eds): Textbook of Rheumatology. 3rd ed. Philadelphia, WB Saunders Co, 1989, pp 1674–1689.

McGuire JL: Arthropathies associated with endocrine disorders. *In* Kelley WN, Harris ED Jr, Ruddy S, Sledge CB (eds): Textbook of Rheumatology. 3rd ed. Philadelphia, WB Saunders Co, 1989, pp 1648–1665.

90 NONARTICULAR RHEUMATISM

The term *nonarticular rheumatism* describes a group of common disorders that primarily affect soft tissues or periarticular structures such as bursae, tendons, and fasciae. Many manifest as acute localized pain (bursitis) or chronic diffuse pain (fibromyalgia syndrome).

PAINFUL SHOULDER

Shoulder pain affects approximately 20 per cent of the adult population at some point in their lives and is a common reason for visiting a physician. It is the most common musculoskeletal complaint in individuals over age 40. As illustrated by the numerous causes of shoulder pain (Table 90–1), the clinician needs to understand the anatomy of the shoulder and to recognize that shoulder pain can be referred from several other locations. Pain may be referred from the cervical region (spondylosis), the intrathoracic region (Pancoast's tumor or myocardial infarction), or the intra-abdominal region (gallbladder disease). Most shoulder problems can be diagnosed by performing a detailed history and physical examination.

TABLE 90–1. DIFFERENTIAL DIAGNOSIS OF THE PAINFUL SHOULDER

Periarticular
  Bursitis (subdeltoid)
  Calcific tendinitis
  Rotator cuff rupture
  Bicipital tendinitis
  Acromioclavicular arthritis
  Fibromyalgia
  Impingement syndrome
  Amyloid arthropathy
  Polymyalgia rheumatica
Glenohumeral
  Adhesive capsulitis
  Osteoarthritis
  Milwaukee shoulder
  Dislocation/subluxation
  Infection
  Neoplasia
  Inflammatory arthritis
  Osteoarthritis
  Osteonecrosis
Referred
  Cervical nerve root compression
  Brachial neuritis
  Reflex sympathetic dystrophy
  Thoracic outlet syndrome
  Gallbladder disease
  Subphrenic abscess
  Myocardial infarction

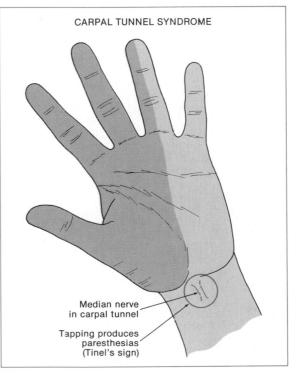

FIGURE 90–1. Distribution of pain and/or paresthesias (*shaded area*) when the median nerve is compressed by swelling in the wrist (carpal tunnel). (From Arnett FC: Rheumatoid arthritis. In Wyngaarden JB, Smith LH Jr, Bennett JC [eds]: Cecil Textbook of Medicine. 19th ed. Philadelphia, WB Saunders Co, 1992, p 1511.)

Caption within figure: CARPAL TUNNEL SYNDROME — Median nerve in carpal tunnel — Tapping produces paresthesias (Tinel's sign)

BURSITIS

Bursae are synovium-lined, fluid-filled sacs located between tendons, muscles, and bone (Fig. 78–1). Bursitis has many causes, but overuse or strain is commonly implicated; gout and infection may also cause acute bursitis. Commonly involved bursae include the subdeltoid, olecranon, trochanteric, iliopsoas, ischial, anserine, prepatellar, Achilles, and calcaneal.

CARPAL TUNNEL SYNDROME

Carpal tunnel syndrome, the entrapment neuropathy of the median nerve, is the most common of entrapment neuropathies. It is characterized by episodes of burning pain or tingling in the hands which often occur at night and are relieved by

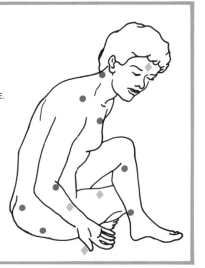

8 PAIRED TENDON POINTS (●)

1. INSERTION OF NUCHAL MUSCLES INTO OCCIPUT.
2. UPPER TRAPEZIUS (MID PORTION).
3. PECTORALIS MUSCLE-JUST LATERAL TO SECOND COSTO-CHONDRAL JUNCTION.
4. 2 CM BELOW LATERAL EPICONDYLE.
5. UPPER GLUTEAL AREA.
6. 2 CM POSTERIOR TO GREATER TROCHANTER.
7. MEDIAL KNEE IN AREA OF ANSERINE BURSA.
8. GASTROCNEMIUS-ACHILLES TENDON JUNCTION.

4 CONTROL POINTS (◆)

1. MIDDLE OF FOREHEAD.
2. VOLAR ASPECT OF MID-FOREARM.
3. THUMB NAIL.
4. MUSCLES OF ANTERIOR THIGH.

FIGURE 90–2. The tender point locations in fibromyalgia are remarkably constant from patient to patient. Multiple locations have been described; the eight paired tender points shown represent frequently occurring points in wide distribution. Most patients with fibromyalgia usually have seven or more tender points. Control points are not unduly tender; their examination should be interspersed with the tender points. (Modified from DJ McCarty: Arthritis and Allied Conditions. 11th ed. Philadelphia, Lea & Febiger, 1985. Reprinted with permission.)

TABLE 90–2. THE ACR 1990 CRITERIA FOR THE CLASSIFICATION OF FIBROMYALGIA

1. History of widespread pain
   Definition: Pain is considered widespread when all of the following are present: pain in the left side of the body, pain in the right side of the body, pain above the waist, and pain below the waist. In addition, axial skeletal pain (cervical spine or anterior chest or thoracic spine or low back) must be present. In this definition, shoulder and buttock pain is considered as pain for each involved side. "Low back" pain is considered lower segment pain.
2. Pain in 11 of 18 tender point sites on digital palpation
   Definition: Pain on digital palpation must be present in at least 11 of the following 18 tender point sites:
   Occiput: bilateral, at the suboccipital muscle insertions
   Low cervical: bilateral, at the anterior aspects of the intertransverse spaces at C5–C7
   Trapezius: bilateral, at midpoint of the upper border
   Supraspinatus: bilateral, at origins, above the scapular spine near the medial border
   Second rib: bilateral, at the second costochondral junctions, just lateral to the junctions on upper surfaces
   Lateral epicondyle: bilateral, 2 cm distal to the epicondyles
   Gluteal: bilateral, in upper outer quadrants of buttocks in anterior fold of muscle
   Greater trochanter: bilateral, posterior to the trochanteric prominence
   Knee: bilateral, at the medial fat pad proximal to the joint line
Digital palpation should be done with an approximate force of 4 kg. For a tender point to be considered "positive," the subject must state that the palpation was painful. "Tender" does not mean "painful."

From Wolfe F, Smythe HA, Yunus MB, et al: The American College of Rheumatology, 1990, criteria for the classification of fibromyalgia. Arthritis Rheum 33:160–172, 1990. Modified from Arthritis and Rheumatism Journal, copyright 1990. Used by permission of the American College of Rheumatology.

shaking the hand. Patients often complain of numbness that affects the three radial fingers and thumb (Fig. 90–1). Weakness and atrophy of the muscles of the thenar eminence may occur. Several disorders are associated with carpal tunnel syndrome, such as rheumatoid arthritis, gout, and amyloidosis, but often no obvious cause can be found.

FIBROMYALGIA SYNDROME

Fibromyalgia syndrome, also referred to as fibrositis, is a syndrome characterized by chronic diffuse pain with characteristic tender points (Fig. 90–2) and disturbed sleep. It occurs predominantly (80 to 90 per cent) in women of childbearing age; its prevalence in the general population may be as high as 5 per cent. The major complaints are diffuse musculoskeletal pain, stiffness, and fatigue. A sleep disturbance, although usually not a presenting complaint, is a common feature. Patients awaken feeling tired; this has been linked to a disturbance of stage 4 (non–rapid eye movement [non-REM]) sleep. The only abnormal finding on examination is the presence of numerous tender points; these are sought by firm palpation with the thumb.

Common associations with fibromyalgia syndrome are mitral valve prolapse and irritable bowel syndrome. Fibromyalgia syndrome has many of the same clinical characteristics as the chronic fatigue syndrome. Chronic fatigue syndrome, myofascial pain syndrome, and fibromyalgia syndrome probably belong to a spectrum of syndromes with overlapping features. However, the exact relationships of these three common clinical conditions have yet to be determined. The American College of Rheumatology has published diagnostic criteria for fibromyalgia (Table 90–2). The diagnosis of fibromyalgia syndrome is a clinical diagnosis that is made after other numerous causes of diffuse aching and fatigue are excluded.

Education of the patient should emphasize the benign, nondeforming nature of this syndrome and its lack of progression to total disability. Treatments should encourage patients to improve their level of physical fitness, minimize stress, and adopt sound sleeping habits. Medications that help achieve restorative sleep include amitriptyline and cyclobenzaprine at bedtime. Other tricyclic antidepressants can be used but have not been studied in controlled trials. Narcotics and corticosteroids are contraindicated.

REFERENCES

Bennett RM: Fibrositis. In McCarty D (ed): Arthritis and Allied Conditions. 11th ed. Philadelphia, Lea & Febiger, 1985, pp 541–553.
Thornhill TS: Shoulder pain. In McCarty D (ed): Arthritis and Allied Conditions. 11th ed. Philadelphia, Lea & Febiger, 1985, pp 491–507.
Wolfe F, Smythe HA, Yunus MB, et al: The American College of Rheumatology, 1990, criteria for the classification of fibromyalgia. Arthritis Rheum 33:160–172, 1990.

SECTION XII

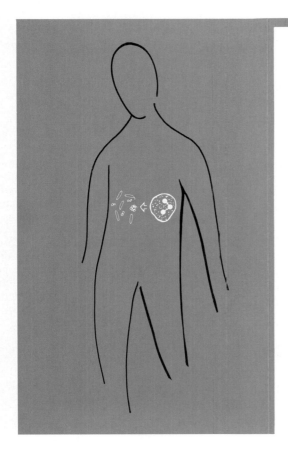

INFECTIOUS DISEASES

91 ORGANISMS THAT INFECT HUMANS

Of diseases afflicting humans, the great majority of those that are curable and preventable are caused by infectious agents. The infectious diseases that capture the attention of physicians and the public periodically shift—for example, from syphilis to tuberculosis to AIDS—but the challenges of dealing with these processes endure. To the student, an understanding of infectious diseases offers insights into medicine as a whole. Osler's adage (with updating) remains relevant. "He (or she) who knows syphilis (AIDS), knows medicine."

VIRUSES

Viruses produce a wide variety of clinical illnesses. A virus consists of either DNA or RNA (rarely, both) wrapped within a protein nucleocapsid. The nucleocapsid may be covered by an envelope composed of glycoproteins and lipids. Viral genes can code for only a limited number of proteins, and viruses possess no metabolic machinery. They are entirely dependent upon host cells for protein synthesis and replication and are therefore obligate intracellular parasites. Some viruses are dependent upon other viruses to produce active infection. Such is the case with the delta agent, which produces disease only in the presence of hepatitis B infection. All must attach to "receptors" on the host cell and achieve entry into the cell through host-derived mechanisms, including receptor-mediated endocytosis, fusion, and pinocytosis. Once within the cells, the virus uncoats, allowing its nucleic acid to utilize host cellular machinery to reproduce (productive infection) or to integrate into the host cell (latent infection). Some viruses, such as influenza virus, cause disease by lysis of infected cells. Others, such as hepatitis B virus, do not directly cause cell destruction but may involve the host immune responses in the pathogenesis of disease. Still others, such as the human T lymphotropic virus type I and II, promote neoplastic transformation of infected cells.

Viruses have developed several mechanisms of evading host defense mechanisms. By multiplying within host cells, viruses can avoid cytotoxic antibodies and other extracellular host defenses. Some viruses can spread to uninfected cells by intercellular bridges. Some viruses, especially the herpes group, are capable of persisting without multiplication in a metabolically inactive form within host cells for prolonged periods (latency). The influenza virus is capable of extensive gene rearrangements, resulting in significant changes in surface antigen structure. This allows new strains to evade host antibody responses directed at earlier strains.

Some viruses, as they exit the host cell during productive infection, may carry antigens of host cell origin, thus providing another mechanism for evading host defenses.

CHLAMYDIAE

Chlamydiae are also obligate intracellular parasites, but, unlike viruses, they always contain both DNA and RNA, divide by binary fission (rather than multiplying by assembly), can synthesize proteins, and contain ribosomes. They are unable to synthesize ATP and thus depend on energy from the host cell to survive. The three chlamydial species known to cause disease in humans are *Chlamydia trachomatis, Chlamydia psittaci*, and the TWAR agent. *C. trachomatis* causes trachoma, the major cause of blindness in the developing world, and a variety of sexually transmitted genitourinary disorders, including urethritis, salpingitis, and lymphogranuloma venereum. *C. psittaci*, cause of a common infectious disease of birds, can produce a serious systemic illness, with prominent pulmonary manifestations, in humans. The TWAR agent is a recently described cause of pneumonia. Chlamydiae are susceptible to tetracycline and erythromycin.

RICKETTSIAE

Rickettsiae are also small bacterial organisms that, like chlamydiae, are obligate intracellular parasites. Rickettsiae are primarily animal pathogens that generally produce disease in humans through the bite of an insect vector, such as a tick, flea, louse, or mite. The organisms specifically infect vascular endothelial cells. With the exception of Q fever, rash due to vasculitis is a prominent manifestation of these often disabling febrile illnesses. These organisms are susceptible to tetracyclines and chloramphenicol.

MYCOPLASMAS

Mycoplasmas are the smallest free-living organisms. In contrast to viruses, chlamydiae, and rickettsiae, mycoplasmas can grow on cell-free media and produce disease without intracellular penetration. Like other bacteria, these organisms have a membrane, but, unlike other bacteria, they have no cell walls. Thus, antibiotics that are active against bacterial cell walls have no effect on mycoplasmas. Four major species of mycoplasmas cause disease in humans. *Mycoplasma pneumoniae* is an agent of pharyngitis and pneumonia, whereas *Mycoplasma hominis* and *Ureaplasma urealyticum* are agents of genitourinary disease. *Mycoplasma fermentans* is a possible cause of disseminated disease in normal humans and may also be an opportunistic pathogen in persons with acquired immunodeficiency syndrome (AIDS). Mycoplasmas are sensitive to erythromycin or tetracycline or both.

BACTERIA

Bacteria are a tremendously varied group of organisms that are generally capable of cell-free growth, although some produce disease as intracellular parasites. There are numerous ways of classifying bacteria, including morphology, ability to retain certain dyes, growth in different physical conditions, ability to metabolize various substrates, and antibiotic sensitivities. Although combinations of these methods are used to identify bacteria in clinical bacteriology laboratories, relatedness for taxonomic purposes is established by DNA homology.

Spirochetes

Spirochetes are slender, motile, spiral-shaped organisms that are not readily seen under the microscope unless stained with silver or viewed under darkfield illumination. Many of these organisms cannot yet be cultured on artificial media or in cell culture. Four genera of spirochetes cause disease in humans. *Treponema* species include the pathogens of syphilis and the nonvenereal endemic syphilis-like illnesses of yaws, pinta, and bejel. The illnesses caused by these organisms are chronic and characterized by prolonged latency in the host. Penicillin is active against *Treponema*. *Leptospira* species are the causative agents of leptospirosis, an acute or subacute febrile illness occasionally resulting in aseptic meningitis, jaundice, and (rarely) renal insufficiency. *Borrelia* species are arthropod-borne spirochetes that are the causative agents of Lyme disease (see Chapter 95) and relapsing fever. During afebrile periods in relapsing fever, these organisms reside within host cells and emerge with modified cell surface antigens. These modifications may permit the bacterium to evade host immune responses and produce relapsing fever and recurrent bacteremia. *Spirillum minor* is one of the causative agents of rat-bite fever.

Anaerobic Bacteria

Anaerobes are organisms that cannot grow in atmospheric oxygen tensions. Some are killed by very low oxygen concentrations, whereas others are relatively aerotolerant. As a general rule, anaerobes that are pathogens for humans are not as sensitive to oxygen as nonpathogens. Anaerobic bacteria are primarily commensals. They inhabit the skin, gut, and mucosal surfaces of all healthy individuals. In fact, the presence of anaerobes may inhibit colonization of the gut by virulent, potentially pathogenic bacteria. Anaerobic infections generally occur in two circumstances:

1. Contamination of otherwise sterile sites with anaerobe-laden contents. Examples include (a) aspiration of oral anaerobes into the bronchial tree, producing anaerobic necrotizing pneumonia; (b) peritonitis and intra-abdominal abscesses following bowel perforation; (c) fasciitis and osteomyelitis following odontogenic infections or oral surgery; (d) some instances of pelvic inflammatory disease.

2. Infections of tissue with lowered redox potential as the result of a compromised vascular supply. Examples include (a) foot infections in diabetic patients, in whom vascular disease may produce poor tissue oxygenation; and (b) infections of pressure sores, in which fecal anaerobic flora gain access to tissue whose vascular supply is compromised by pressure.

The pathogenesis of anaerobic infections, that is, soilage by a complex flora, generally results in polymicrobial infections. Thus, the demonstration of one anaerobe in an infected site generally implies the presence of others. Often, facultative organisms (organisms capable of anaerobic and aerobic growths) coexist with anaerobes. Certain anaerobes, such as *Clostridium*, produce toxins that cause well-defined illnesses such as food poisoning, tetanus, and botulism. Other toxins may play a role in the soft tissue infections—cellulitis, fasciitis, and myonecrosis—occasionally produced by *Clostridium* species. *Bacteroides fragilis*, the most numerous bacterial pathogen in the normal human colon, has a polysaccharide capsule that inhibits phagocytosis and promotes abscess formation. Clues to the presence of anaerobic infection include (1) a foul odor (the diagnosis of anaerobic pneumonia can, on occasion, be made from across the room); (2) the presence of gas, which may be seen radiographically or manifested by crepitus on examination (however, not all gas-forming infections are anaerobic); and (3) the presence of mixed gram-positive and gram-negative flora on a Gram stain of purulent exudate, especially when there is little or no growth on plates cultured aerobically. Most pathogenic anaerobes are sensitive to penicillin. Exceptions are strains of *Bacteroides fragilis* (usually sensitive to metronidazole, clindamycin, or ampicillin/sulbactam) and *Clostridium difficile*, which is almost always sensitive to metronidazole and vancomycin. Strains of *Fusobacterium* may also be relatively resistant to penicillin. As a general rule, infections caused by anaerobes originating from sites above the diaphragm are more often penicillin-sensitive, whereas infections below the diaphragm are often caused by penicillin-resistant organisms, notably *Bacteroides fragilis.*

Gram-Negative Bacteria

The cell walls of these bacteria, which appear pink on a properly prepared Gram stain, contain lipopolysaccharide, a potent inducer of fever and mediators associated with septic shock, such as tumor necrosis factor (TNF). These organisms cause a wide variety of illnesses. Gram-negative bacteria are the most common cause of cystitis and pyelonephritis. *Haemophilus* species organisms are common pathogens of the respiratory tract causing otitis media, sinusitis, tracheobronchitis, and pneumonia. Lower respiratory tract infections due to these organisms are particularly common in adults with chronic obstructive pulmonary disease. *Haemophilus* is also an important cause of meningitis, particularly in children. Excepting *Haemophilus* species, gram-negative bacteria are uncommon causes of community-acquired pneumonia but common causes of nosocomial pneumonia.

Except for the peculiar risk of *Pseudomonas* infection in intravenous drug users, gram-negative organisms are rare causes of endocarditis on natural heart valves but are occasional pathogens on prosthetic valves. The Enterobacteriaceae include *Escherichia coli, Klebsiella, Enterobacter, Serratia, Salmonella, Shigella,* and *Proteus.* These are large gram-negative rods. Except for the occasional presence of a clear space surrounding some *Klebsiella* (representing a large capsule), these organisms are not readily distinguished from each other on Gram stain. The Enterobacteriaceae can be thought of as gut-related or genitourinary pathogens. *Salmonella,* a relatively common cause of enteritis, may occasionally infect atherosclerotic plaques or aneurysms. *Shigella* is an agent of bacterial dysentery. *Proteus* species, which split urea, are the agents associated with staghorn calculi of the ureters and urinary collecting system.

Gram-negative cocci that cause disease in humans include *Neisseria* and *Moraxella* species. These kidney bean–shaped diplococci are not distinguishable from one another on Gram stain. *N. meningitidis* is an important cause of meningitis, and *N. gonorrhoeae* causes gonorrhea. *Moraxella catarrhalis,* part of the normal oral flora, is a recently recognized cause of lower respiratory tract infection.

Gram-Positive Bacteria

Although these organisms (which appear deep purple on Gram stain) lack endotoxin, infections with gram-positive bacteria also produce fever and cannot be reliably distinguished, on clinical grounds, from infections caused by gram-negative bacteria.

Gram-Positive Rods

Infections due to gram-positive rods are relatively uncommon outside certain specific settings. Diphtheria is rare, but other corynebacteria produce infections in the immunocompromised host and on prosthetic valves and shunts. Because corynebacteria are regular skin colonizers, they often contaminate blood cultures; in the appropriate setting, however, they must be considered potential pathogens. *Listeria monocytogenes* resembles *Corynebacterium* on initial isolation and is an important cause of meningitis and bacteremia in the immunocompromised patient. *Bacillus cereus* is a recognized cause of food poisoning. Serious infections due to this and other *Bacillus* species occur among intravenous drug users. *Clostridium* species are gram-positive rods. Infections due to clostridia are discussed under anaerobes (see above).

Gram-Positive Cocci

Staphylococcus aureus is a common pathogen that produces a wide spectrum of disease in humans. Staphylococci can infect any organ system. They are common causes of bacteremia and sepsis. The organism often colonizes the anterior nares, particularly among insulin-treated diabetics, hemodialysis patients, and intravenous drug users; these populations also have a greater frequency of infections due to this organism. Hospital workers colonized with *Staphylococcus aureus* have also been responsible for hospital epidemics of staphylococcal disease.

Generally protected by an antiphagocytic polysaccharide capsule, staphylococci also possess catalase, which inactivates hydrogen peroxide—a mediator of bacterial killing by neutrophils. Staphylococci tend to form abscesses; the low pH within an abscess cavity also limits the effectiveness of host defense cells. Staphylococci elaborate several toxins that mediate certain manifestations of disease. A staphylococcal enterotoxin is responsible for staphylococcal food poisoning. Staphylococcal toxins also mediate the scalded skin syndrome and the multisystem manifestations of toxic shock syndrome. Most staphylococci are penicillinase-producing, and some are resistant to penicillinase-resistant penicillin analogues as well. Vancomycin is active against almost all strains. Some staphylococci are "tolerant" to cell wall–active antibiotics such as penicillins or vancomycin; such organisms are inhibited but not killed by these agents. The clinical significance of tolerance is not certain. Other staphylococci are distinguished from *Staphylococcus aureus* primarily by their inability to produce coagulase. Some of these coagulase-negative staphylococci produce urinary tract infection (*Staphylococcus saprophyticus*). Another, *Staphylococcus epidermidis,* is part of the normal skin flora and an important cause of infection on foreign bodies such as prosthetic heart valves, ventriculoatrial shunts, and intravascular catheters. Like *Corynebacterium, Staphylococcus epidermidis* may be a contaminant of blood cultures but in the appropriate setting should be considered a potential pathogen. *Staphylococcus saprophyticus* is sensitive to a variety of antibiotics used in the treatment of urinary tract infection; *Staphylococcus epidermidis* is often resistant to most antimicrobials but is usually sensitive to vancomycin.

Streptococci are classified into groups according to the presence of serologically defined carbohydrate capsules (Lancefield typing). Group A streptococci produce skin infections and pharyngitis. These organisms also are associated with the immunologically mediated poststreptococcal disorders—glomerulonephritis and acute rheumatic fever. Group D streptococci include enterococci, which are unique among the streptococci in their uniform resistance to penicillin. Streptococci can be classified according to the pattern of hemolysis on blood agar—alpha for incomplete hemolysis (producing a green discoloration on the agar), beta for complete hemolysis, and gamma for nonhemolytic strains. Most Lancefield group strains are beta-hemolytic. An important alpha-hemolytic strain is *Streptococcus pneumoniae* (pneumococcus), the most common cause of bacterial pneumonia and an important cause of meningitis and otitis media. A heterogeneous group of streptococci, often improperly referred to as viridans streptococci (these organisms show alpha- or gamma-hemolysis) includes several species of streptococci that are common oral or gut flora and are important agents of bacterial endocarditis, abscesses, and odontogenic infections.

Mycobacteria

Mycobacteria are a group of rod-shaped bacilli that stain weakly gram-positive. These organisms are rich in lipid content and are recognized in tissue specimens by their ability to retain dye after washing with acid-alcohol (acid-fast). These bacteria are generally slow-growing (some require up to 6 weeks to demonstrate growth on solid media) obligate aerobes. They generally produce chronic disease and manage to survive for years as intracellular parasites of mononuclear phagocytes. Some escape intracellular killing mechanisms by blocking phagosome/lysosome fusion or by disrupting the phagosome. Almost all provoke cell-mediated immune responses in the host, and clinical disease expression may be related in large part to the nature of the host immune response. Tuberculosis is caused by *Mycobacterium tuberculosis*. Other mycobacteria—nontuberculous mycobacteria—can produce diseases resembling tuberculosis. Certain rapid-growing mycobacteria cause infections following surgery or implantations of prostheses, and *Mycobacterium avium-intracellulare* is an important cause of disseminated infection among patients with AIDS. This organism is frequently resistant to drugs usually used in the treatment of tuberculosis. Multidrug treatment regimens can provide symptomatic relief and decrease the bacterial load in blood, but they rarely eradicate the infection. Leprosy is a mycobacterial disease of skin and peripheral nerves caused by the noncultivatable *M. leprae*.

Actinomycetales

Nocardia and *Actinomyces* are weakly gram-positive filamentous bacteria. *Nocardia* is acid-fast and aerobic; *Actinomyces* is anaerobic and not acid-fast. *Actinomyces* inhabits the mouth, gut, and vagina and produces cervicofacial osteomyelitis and abscess, pneumonia with empyema, and intra-abdominal and pelvic abscess, the last often associated with intrauterine contraceptive devices. *Nocardia* most commonly produces pneumonia and brain abscess. Approximately half of patients with *Nocardia* infection have underlying impairments in cell-mediated immunity. Infections with either of these organisms require long-term treatment. *Actinomyces* is relatively sensitive to most antibiotics; penicillin is the treatment of choice. *Nocardia* infections are best treated with high doses of sulfonamides.

FUNGI

Fungi are larger than bacteria. Unlike bacteria, they have rigid cell walls that contain chitin as well as polysaccharides. They grow and proliferate by budding, by elongation of hyphal forms, and/or by spore formation. Excepting *Candida* and related species, fungi rarely are visible on Gram-stained preparations but can be stained with Gomori's methenamine silver stain. They also are resistant to potassium hydroxide and can often be visualized on wet mounts of scrapings or secretions to which several drops of 10 per cent solution of potassium hydroxide has been added. Fungi are resistant to antibiotics used in the treatment of bacterial infections and must be treated with drugs active against their unusual cell wall. Most fungi can exist in a yeast form—round to ovoid cells that may reproduce by budding—and a mold form—a complex of tubular structures (hyphae) that grow by branching or extension.

Candida species are oval yeasts that often colonize the mouth, gastrointestinal tract, and vagina of healthy individuals. They may produce disease by overgrowth and/or invasion. *Candida* stomatitis (thrush) often occurs in individuals who are receiving antibiotic or corticosteroid therapy or who have impairments of cell-mediated immunity. Vulvovaginitis due to *Candida* may occur in these same settings but is also seen among women with diabetes mellitus or with no apparent predisposing factors. *Candida* can also colonize and infect the urinary tract, particularly in the presence of an indwelling urinary catheter. Occasionally, *Candida* species may gain entry into the blood stream and produce sepsis. This may occur in the setting of neutropenia after chemotherapy, where the portal of entry is the gastrointestinal tract, or in individuals receiving intravenous feedings, in whom the catheter is the source of the infection. Mucosal candidiasis can be treated with topical (clotrimazole) or systemic (fluconazole) imidazole drugs; systemic candidiasis is generally treated with amphotericin B.

Histoplasma capsulatum is a fungus, endemic to the Ohio and Mississippi River valleys, which produces a mild febrile syndrome in most individuals and a self-limited pneumonia in some. Occasionally, patients develop potentially fatal disseminated disease. Some individuals with chronic pulmonary disease may develop chronic pneumonia due to this yeast. Systemic or progressive disease is treated with amphotericin B; ketoconazole may also be effective in some cases.

Coccidioides immitis is endemic in the southwestern United States and, like *Histoplasma capsulatum*, produces a self-limited respiratory infection or pneumonia in most infected individuals. Immunocompromised individuals are at greatest risk for fatal systemic dissemination. Amphotericin B is used for progressive or extrapulmonary disease.

Cryptococcus neoformans is a yeast with a large polysaccharide capsule. It produces a self-limited or chronic pneumonia, but the most common clinical manifestation of infection with this fungus is a chronic meningitis. Although patients with impairment in cell-mediated immunity are at risk for cryptococcal meningitis, some patients with this syndrome have no identifiable immunodeficiency. Treatment is with amphotericin B combined with flucytosine. Long-term oral fluconazole therapy is effective in preventing relapse in persons with AIDS.

Blastomyces dermatitidis is a yeast also endemic in the Ohio and Mississippi River basins. Acute self-limited pulmonary infection is followed rarely by disseminated disease. Skin disease is most common, but bones and the genitourinary tract may be involved as well. Amphotericin B is used for treating systemic disease.

Aspergillus is a mold that produces several different clinical illnesses in humans. Acute bronchopulmonary aspergillosis is an IgE-mediated hypersensitivity to *Aspergillus* colonization of the respiratory tract. This condition produces wheezing and fleeting pulmonary infiltrates in patients with asthma. Occasionally, *Aspergillus* will colonize a pre-existent pulmonary cavity and produce a mycetoma or fungus ball. Hemoptysis is the most serious complication of such infection. Invasive pulmonary aspergillosis rarely is a chronic illness of marginally compromised hosts, but more often it is a cause of acute, life-threatening pneumonia in patients with neutropenia or in recipients of organ transplants. Amphotericin B is the drug of choice for invasive aspergillosis.

The zygomycetes (Mucorales) are molds with ribbon-shaped hyphae that produce disease in patients with poorly controlled diabetes mellitus or hematologic malignancy and among recipients of organ transplantation. Invasive disease of the palate and nasal sinuses, which may extend intracranially, is the most common presentation, but pneumonia may be seen as well. These infections are generally treated with surgical excision plus amphotericin B.

PROTOZOANS

The protozoal pathogens listed in Table 91–1 are all transmitted within the United States. Infections caused by these organisms are diagnosed as indicated in Table 91–1 and are discussed in the relevant disease-oriented chapters.

HELMINTHS

Diseases due to helminths are among the most prevalent diseases in the developing world but are

TABLE 91–1. SOME PROTOZOAN DISEASES OF HUMANS

PROTOZOAN	CLINICAL ILLNESS	TRANSMISSION	DIAGNOSIS
Plasmodium	Malaria: fever, hemolysis	Mosquito, transfusion	Peripheral blood smear
Babesia microti	Fever, hemolysis	Tick, transfusion	Peripheral blood smear
Trichomonas vaginalis	Vaginitis	Sexual contact	Vaginal smear
Toxoplasma gondii†	Fever, lymph node enlargement; encephalitis, brain abscess in compromised host	Raw meat, cat feces	Serologies, tissue biopsy
Pneumocystis carinii†	Pneumonia in immunocompromised host	?Airborne*	Lung biopsy, bronchial lavage
Entamoeba histolytica	Colitis, hepatic abscess	Fecal-oral	Stool smear, serologies
Giardia lamblia	Diarrhea, malabsorption	Fecal-oral	Stool smear, small bowel aspirate
Cryptosporidium†	Diarrhea	?Fecal-oral	Sugar flotation, acid-fast stain of stool, biopsy
Isospora belli†	Diarrhea, malaborption	?Fecal-oral	Acid-fast stain of stool
Microsporidium†	Diarrhea, malabsorption, dissemination	?Fecal-oral	Small bowel biopsy Electron microscopy

* *Primary* infection is presumably airborne, but clinical disease usually results from multiplication of resident microorganisms in an immunocompromised host. Respiratory isolation is not indicated.

† Important opportunistic pathogens in persons with AIDS (see Chapter 108).

uncommon causes of illness in North America. In contrast to the pathogens discussed above, helminths are multicellular parasites. Helminth diseases acquired in the United States include ascariasis (maldigestion, obstruction), hookworm (intestinal blood loss), enterobiasis (pinworm, anal pruritus), and strongyloidiasis (gastroenteritis, dissemination in the immunocompromised host). It is important to recognize the risk of other helminthic diseases in travelers returning from endemic regions (see Chapter 110).

REFERENCE

Gardner P, Provine HT: Manual of Acute Bacterial Infections. Boston, Little, Brown & Co, 1975.

92 HOST DEFENSES AGAINST INFECTION

Infectious agents and hosts are engaged in a complex struggle that has evolved over eons. The pathogenic and evasive mechanisms of microbes are countered by multiple and overlapping host immune and nonspecific defense mechanisms. In some cases, the pathogen "wins," with destruction of the host; in others, the host immune response prevails, with eradication of the parasite. Often there is a standoff characterized by latent infection; pathogens capable of a latent phase have the capacity to reactivate as the host ages or as its immune response deteriorates because of superimposed diseases.

A few general statements are germane regarding the roles of the components of the host defense network in the response to infectious diseases. The skin and mucosal surfaces represent the primary interface with the external world and its microbial flora. At these sites, anatomic barriers, the nonspecific inflammatory response, secretory IgA, products of effector cells, and the normal microbial flora defend against the development of invasive disease. Neutrophils are the critical effector cells in defense against infection with organisms constituting the normal microbial flora, such as Enterobacteriaceae, *Staphylococcus aureus*, *Candida*, and *Aspergillus*. Once local barriers are breached, the specific immune response, often acting in concert with nonspecific effector mechanisms, is required to control the infection.

The elements of the host response that are critical in combating many of the more common infectious agents are known; in fact, awareness of infections that occur in the immunocompromised host (Chapter 109), as well as research in experimental models, provides the basis for this understanding. Antibody, which is the product of the interactions of B cells, antigen, and T helper cells, is critical for defense against encapsulated pathogenic bacteria such as *Streptococcus pneumoniae*. The cellular immune response—specifically, T cell–dependent macrophage activation—is the critical effector arm against organisms capable of evading destruction by the effector cell and replicating intracellularly. An example of such an organism is *Mycobacterium tuberculosis*. Antiviral immunity is more difficult to characterize and varies with the agent in question. Neutralizing antibody is sufficient to disturb the life cycle of viruses with an important extracellular phase (such as rubella). Protective mechanisms operant against viruses with a latent intracellular phase in the host, such as herpes simplex virus, are chiefly provided by T cells. In this case, cytotoxic T cells often must destroy the infected host cells to expose the virus to neutralizing factors in the external milieu (antibody, complement).

This chapter is organized as follows. First, local barriers to infection are discussed. Then, the interaction of the components of the immune system is presented, followed by discussion of nonspecific effector mechanisms. Finally, host defenses against representative infectious agents are discussed. As noted, infections in immunocompromised hosts will be dealt with in Chapter 109.

LOCAL BARRIERS TO INFECTION

Both nonspecific and specific host defense mechanisms contribute to the prevention of infectious diseases. The integument, mucous membranes, and epithelial surfaces provide a vital mechanical barrier to infection. The indigenous flora of these surfaces, particularly the anaerobic bacteria, prevent colonization with virulent organisms by competing for nutrients and receptor sites on host cells and by producing factors, termed bacteriocins, that are toxic to other bacteria. The local milieu, chiefly the pH and redox potential, provides an additional barrier to colonization and infection with certain pathogenic organisms. Gastric acid reduces bacterial counts by 10- to 10,000-fold. The normal flow of mucus and other secretions helps to eliminate microorganisms from mucosal surfaces. The mucociliary blanket, for example, transports organisms away from the lungs. In addition, locally produced and active antimicrobial substances prevent infection. Lactoperoxidase, lysozyme, and lactoferrin in salivary and vaginal secretions and milk have microbicidal activity. Secretory IgA has a particularly important role in this respect, opsonizing organisms and thereby blocking their ability to adhere to epithelial surfaces and colonize the mucosa.

COMPONENTS OF THE IMMUNE SYSTEM

The principal cells of the immune system are bone marrow–derived (B) and thymus-dependent (T) lymphocytes and mononuclear phagocytes. They are organized as a recirculating pool of lymphocytes and monocytes, bone marrow cells, and organized lymphoid tissue (lymph nodes, spleen, Peyer's patches, and the thymus).

The primary function of the immune system is to destroy foreign organisms and clear foreign antigens without damaging host tissues. Immunity also is important in maintaining certain infectious agents in a latent stage and may play a role in destroying virally infected cells or cells that have undergone malignant transformation. The immune response is characterized by three features—immunologic memory, specificity, and systemic action. The functional organization of the immune response can be considered in six sequential steps: encounter, recognition, activation of lymphocytes, deployment, discrimination, and regulation.

Encounter

Microbes and soluble antigens encounter antigen-presenting cells (APCs) in the tissues and are ingested and catabolized. Monocytes, macrophages, dendritic cells, and Langerhans cells are examples of APCs. The physical form of the antigen and the

site of exposure or breaching of tissue determine which type of APC is relevant. Particulates are more readily ingested by active phagocytes such as macrophages; dendritic cells may be critical to the handling of soluble protein antigens. The gastrointestinal and respiratory tracts, important sites for interface of the immune system with the environment, possess well-differentiated APCs in submucosal areas. Some microbes elicit a neutrophilic inflammatory response and are phagocytosed and degraded by neutrophils, thereby bypassing traditional APCs and eliciting inflammation but little detectable immune response. Nonetheless, acute infection almost invariably produces an antibody response and memory for the same, presumably as the result of the processing of soluble microbial products. The disposition of soluble antigen is determined by the likelihood of uptake by APCs; an aggregated form of antigen or antigen bound by specific antibody in immune complexes favors uptake by APCs. Following ingestion by APCs, the foreign antigen is degraded in acidic vesicles and reprocessed to the surface of the cell, where, in close approximation, or bound, to determinants encoded by the class II major histocompatibility complex (MHC), it is accessible to lymphocytes. APCs also produce cytokines such as interleukins (e.g., IL1 and IL6), which amplify immune induction.

Recognition

The immune system has the capability of responding to an almost infinite number of antigens. It appears that B cells and T cells utilize similar mechanisms to generate and express the diversity required for such a broad range of specific antigenic responses.

Five classes of antibodies (isotypes) are recognized (Table 92–1). An IgG1 antibody (Fig. 92–1) consists of two light (kappa or lambda) and two heavy chains. Each antibody has constant regions, which are identical in structure to all antibodies of that class, and distinctive antigen recognition sites whose structures are quite variable. An IgG1 molecule has two such antigen-combining sites. The antigen-combining sites of antibody molecules recognize the three-dimensional structure of an

TABLE 92–1. PROPERTIES OF HUMAN IMMUNOGLOBULINS

	IgG	IgA	IgM	IgD	IgE
H chain class	γ	α	μ	δ	ϵ
Molecular weight (approximate)	160,000	170,000	900,000	180,000	190,000
Complement fixation + (classic)	+	0	++	0	0
Serum concentration (approximate mg/dl)	1,500	150–350	100–150	2	2
Serum half-life (days)	23	6	5	3	2.5
Major functions	Recall response; opsonization; transplacental immunity	Secretory immunity	Primary response; complement fixation	?	Allergy; parasite immunity

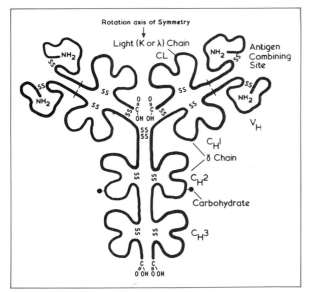

FIGURE 92-1. Schematic diagram of a molecule of human IgG, showing the two light (κ or λ) chains and two heavy (γ) chains held together by disulfide bonds. The constant regions of the light (CL) and heavy (C_H1, C_H2, and C_H3) chains and the variable region of the heavy chain (V_H) are indicated. Loops in the peptide chain formed by intrachain disulfide bonds (C_H1 and so forth) constitute separate functional domains. (Reprinted, by permission, from the New England Journal of Medicine, Vol 316, p 1320, 1987.)

antigen and bind to an antigen in a lock-and-key manner, through multiple weak, noncovalent interactions. The variable regions consist of the approximately 110 N-terminal amino acids of each chain. There are three short, hypervariable regions in each of the light and the heavy chains. The six hypervariable regions form the combining site.

The generation of antibody diversity is understood at the molecular level. The variable portion of the heavy chain is encoded by three different genes—V, D, and J; there are 500 to 1000 different V genes, 10 D genes, and 4 J genes. The variable portions of the light chains are encoded by V and J genes; there are 200 possible V genes and 6 J genes. During the differentiation of B cells, somatic translocations randomly select the V, D, and J heavy chain genes and the V and J light chain genes that will be transcribed in that cell. The diversity achieved by these means is enormous. Somatic mutations in B cells allow the possibility of improving the fit between antibody and antigen; repeated or sustained exposure to antigen selects B cells capable of producing antibody with the highest binding affinity. These circulate as memory cells.

T lymphocytes can be divided into two subpopulations based on the polypeptide chains constituting the antigen receptor. The $\alpha\beta$ T cells, constituting the larger population (~95 per cent), possess a receptor comprising a heterodimer of α and β polypeptide chains (Fig. 92–2). The variable portion of the $\alpha\beta$ T cell receptor is composed of the

approximately 100 N-terminal amino acids. The generation of diversity is by translocation of V, D, and J genes, as is the case for B lymphocytes. The T cell receptor is directed at the foreign antigen associated with MHC determinants. $\alpha\beta$ T cells can be divided by their surface expression of glycoproteins into CD4 and CD8 subpopulations. CD4 and CD8 cells also differ in their genetic restriction and function. Class I MHC products are recognized by CD8 suppressor/cytotoxic T cells, and Class II by CD4 helper T cells. The T cell receptor recognizes linear peptides of 5 to 20 amino acids in length. The second subpopulation of T lymphocytes, $\gamma\delta$ T cells, constitutes approximately 5 per cent of circulating and lymphoid T cells; their T cell receptor contains a heterodimer of γ and δ chains. Activation of $\gamma\delta$ T cells does not require recognition of either the Class I or the Class II MHC on APCs.

Activation of Lymphocytes

The initial physical apposition of T cells and APCs is stabilized by interactions of so-called accessory molecules on T cells with their respective ligands on APCs. Accessory molecules usually are members of the immunoglobulin or the integrin gene family. For example, leukocyte functional antigen (LFA)–1 on the T cell binds to intercellular adhesion molecule (ICAM)–1 on the APCs, and CD2 on the T cell binds with LFA-3 on APCs. These reciprocal interactions facilitate the initial cell contact and are reinforced during the process of activation. CD4 helper T cells are activated when the T cell receptors are occupied and effectively cross-linked by the antigen–class II MHC complex on the surface of an APC (Fig. 92–3). Activation of the T cell is promoted by IL1 and IL6 released as a consequence of the cellular interactions. The

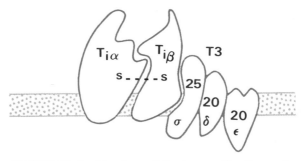

FIGURE 92-2. Structure of the human T cell receptor and its subunits. This diagram shows subunit composition of the human T cell receptor. The Tiα and Tiβ subunits are held together by S-S bonds and are anchored in the cell membrane with their transmembrane segments. The T_1 protein of the T cell receptor is most closely associated with the 25-kd γ chain of the T3 molecule. The T3 complex includes two additional subunits (δ and ϵ), with molecular weights of 20,000. (Reprinted, by permission, from the New England Journal of Medicine, Vol 316, p 1320, 1987.)

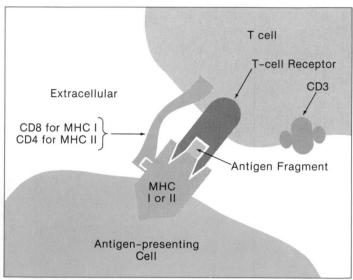

FIGURE 92-3. The molecular events in antigen presentation. Shown are the interactions between the various molecules, including the MHC, the T cell receptor, the CD8 or CD4 molecules, and the CD3 complex. [From Bennett JC: Introduction to diseases of the immune system. *In* Wyngaarden JB, Smith LH Jr, Bennett JC [eds]: Cecil Textbook of Medicine. 19th ed. Philadelphia, WB Saunders Co, 1992, p 1440.]

helper T cell enlarges, secretes a variety of lymphokines, and divides to form a clone. The antigen molecule may also form a bridge between T cells and B cells, permitting the targeted delivery of B cell growth and differentiation factors from T cell to B cell. The B cell, which is activated by a combination of signals provided by binding of antigen and by T cells, enlarges, divides, and differentiates

into an antibody-producing cell. T cell products also promote an isotype switch from IgM to production of IgG, IgA, or IgE.

The initial exposure of humans to microbial antigens leads to the proliferation of B cells recognizing the antigen and differentiation into antibody-forming plasma cells. T cell help is required for responses to most antigens, although bacterial polysaccharides may directly elicit antibody production. Following the first exposure to an antigen, IgM is the main antibody class or isotype produced. An isotype switch then occurs such that IgG predominates. On any re-exposure to the antigen, production of IgG antibody is accelerated, and antibody is produced in high titer and with high avidity for the antigen. Secretory IgA is found in tears, saliva, and bronchial, nasal, vaginal, prostatic, and intestinal secretions. Its primary role is to prevent organisms and antigens from attaching to and breaching mucosal barriers.

IgM accounts for 10 per cent of normal immunoglobulins and is the antibody isotype most efficient at complement fixation. Both IgM and IgG can neutralize the infectivity of viruses and lyse bacteria through complement fixation. Mononuclear phagocytes, neutrophils, and some lymphocytes possess surface receptors for the Fc fragment of IgG and/or the third component of complement. Therefore, IgG antibody or complement can bind to and opsonize bacteria, facilitating their phagocytosis (Fig. 92-4), and IgG antibody can arm host effector cells for preferential destruction of selected targets by the process of antibody-dependent cell-mediated cytotoxicity (ADCC).

APC and CD4 cells acting in concert are required for activation of CD8 cells for cytotoxic and suppressor cell activity. The activated CD4 cell also secretes a number of factors important in hematopoiesis, mobilization of bone marrow precur-

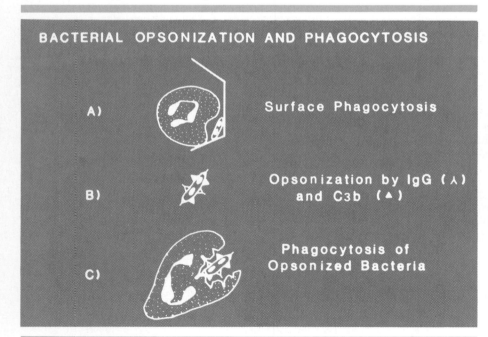

FIGURE 92-4. Ingestion of pneumococci by the neutrophil. In the absence of opsonins, the slippery pneumococcus must be forced against an alveolar surface to be ingested, the inefficient process of surface phagocytosis. Bacteria are opsonized by C3b and IgG, which interact with receptors on the neutrophil, thereby facilitating phagocytosis.

sor cells, chemotaxis of mononuclear and other cells to areas of inflammation, and expression of the cellular immune response.

In experimental studies, helper T lymphocytes can be divided into two subpopulations. The Th1 subset secretes IL2, interferon-gamma, and lymphotoxin and is most effective at stimulating cellular immune responses. For example, interferon-gamma activates macrophages to destroy certain facultative intracellular pathogens. By contrast, Th2 cells secrete IL4, IL5, and IL6 and are more effective in promoting antibody secretion by B cells. Further distinctions concerning the heterogeneity of CD4 cells in humans are not nearly so clear.

Special consideration is warranted concerning cytotoxic mechanisms that destroy parasitized host cells. Certain viruses usurp the machinery of cells that they infect and replicate intracellularly, where they are inaccessible to antibody and complement. The only effective host response requires destruction of the parasitized host cell. This usually is accomplished by class I MHC–restricted CD8 cells that target on virally encoded proteins expressed on the host cell surface. Antibody to the viral products can also bind to the host cell surface, rendering it susceptible to destruction by Fc receptor–bearing effector cells in the process of ADCC. Class II MHC–restricted cytotoxicity mediated by CD4 lymphocytes can be called into play when host cells are heavily parasitized with certain organisms such as mycobacteria, or after ingestion and presentation of viral or other microbial products by APCs. The relative roles of class II as opposed to class I MHC–restricted cytotoxicity and ADCC in the destruction of parasitized host cells vary with the infectious agent. Once the host cell is destroyed, however, the microbe is susceptible to antibody, complement, or the attack of other phagocytes and T lymphocytes.

Deployment

The mobility of lymphocytes is central to the memory and systemic function of the immune response. Some progeny of activated B and T cells return to the resting stage, leaving the peripheral lymphoid tissue to traffic as memory cells in the recirculating pool. These lymphocytes perfuse the tissues of the body and can re-enter the lymph nodes. Reinfection or re-exposure to an antigen at any site can lead to activation of memory lymphocytes.

The events thus far discussed are required for activation of antigen-specific lymphocytes. Neither antibody nor activated lymphocytes are capable of directly destroying pathogenic organisms. Rather, they act in concert with antigen-nonspecific components of the immune response, including phagocytes and the complement and other molecular systems, to destroy pathogenic microbes. For example, one of the key cytokines produced by activated CD4 cells is interferon-gamma; this interferon activates mononuclear phagocytes and thus renders them capable of killing intracellular parasites and tumors.

Discrimination

Tolerance of self-antigens prevents autoimmune disease. Several mechanisms contribute to tolerance. Early in ontogeny, exposure to antigen leads to refractoriness to that antigen. This process has been termed "clonal anergy." Suppressor T cells are activated when soluble antigen is injected intravenously without adjuvant; this resembles exposure to most self-antigens. Moreover, self-antigens are not presented to reactive CD4 cells in combination with class II MHC determinants, so that immune induction fails to occur. The breakdown of tolerance and autoimmune disease may result from a combination of factors: tissue damage exposing new antigens to the immune system and genetic factors that regulate the response to self-antigens and determine end-organ susceptibility to damage.

Cross-reactivity exists between bacterial and mammalian cellular products. For example, the heat shock protein (HSP)60 of mycobacteria has polypeptide spans with close homology to human HSP60. In fact, synovial fluid T cells from patients with rheumatoid arthritis are reactive with these bacterial peptides. For individuals expressing an autoimmune diathesis, whether on a genetic or some other basis, bacterial infection may trigger autoimmune tissue damage.

Regulation

The immune response must be appropriate to the challenging event; too little may permit unchecked infection, whereas too great a response may damage tissue. Regulatory mechanisms amplify or mute an immune response and may be specific or nonspecific.

Antigen itself regulates the immune response. As antigen is cleared, a process enhanced by specific antibody, only lymphocytes bearing the highest-affinity receptors are activated. Once antigen is cleared entirely, the immune response diminishes, although memory cells continue to provide surveillance for re-exposure to the antigen. Antibody has an additional role in immunoregulation, since immune complexes may directly modulate the response of specific lymphocytes. Antibody may also be directed at the antigen-combining site of antibody itself. Production of "anti-idiotypic antibodies" is stimulated by the immune response and may suppress further production of the relevant antibody.

Activation of the immune response also induces cellular regulatory mechanisms. For example, the activated CD4 cell is an important stimulus for induction of suppression by CD8 cells and mononuclear phagocytes. Cytokines that may mediate suppression of CD4 cell responses include IL4, IL10, transforming growth factor β, and the IL1 receptor antagonist.

NONSPECIFIC EFFECTOR MECHANISMS

Complement. Complement activity results from the sequential interaction of a large number (25 are recognized) of plasma and cell membrane interactive proteins. The classic complement pathway is activated by antibody-coated targets or antigen-antibody complexes. The alternative pathway is activated by bacterial polysaccharides. Complement binds to bacteria, facilitating their attachment by C3b receptors on phagocytes, thus constituting the heat-labile opsonic system (Fig. 92–4); it directly damages certain bacteria and viruses, and it induces inflammation through chemotactically active fragments. The classic complement pathway is the major effector mechanism for antibody-mediated immune responses. It is the Fc receptor of antigen-activated antibody molecules that binds and activates C1. The alternative pathway is activated in the absence of antibody by constituents of the microbial surface, including polysaccharides, and generates C3 convertase, which catalyzes proteolysis of C3. Both the classic and the alternative pathways converge and result in the formation of the membrane attack complex involving C5 to C9. This complex forms pores in the membrane of microbes, subjecting them to osmotic lysis.

The complement system has several other notable biologic functions. C3b or iC3b deposited on the surface of microbes binds to complement receptors (CR1, CR3, and CR4) on neutrophils and macrophages, promoting phagocytosis. C5a is a chemotaxin for neutrophils and activates oxidative burst activity. C5a and C3a also stimulate histamine release from mast cells, thus promoting inflammation. Finally, C3b promotes clearance of immune complexes by linking them to CR1 on the erythrocyte surface.

Neutrophils. Neutrophils respond rapidly to chemotaxins and are the primary effector cells of the acute inflammatory response. They are activated by cytokines, including interferon-gamma and tumor necrosis factor (TNF); this activation enhances neutrophil adhesion to vascular endothelium near the sites of infection, the first step in local accumulation. The cytokines also activate oxidative metabolism. Neutrophils ingest antibody and complement-opsonized bacteria and destroy so-called "extracellular" bacteria by exposing them to toxic oxygen metabolites in the presence of myeloperoxidase and halide. Neutrophils also possess potent antibacterial peptides termed defensins.

Mononuclear Phagocytes. Macrophages differ from other phagocytic cells in that they have immunoregulatory and secretory properties in addition to their role as effector cells of cell-mediated immunity. Macrophages ingest and kill extracellular bacteria directly and in antibody-dependent reactions. Facultative intracellular pathogens have evolved a variety of means for escaping intracellular destruction. These include disruption and escape from the phagosome, as well as blockage of phagosome-lysosome fusion. It is the process of activation of macrophages by T cells and their products that overcomes the evasive mechanisms to destroy the organism. The macrophage activation factor (MAF) varies according to the microbe in question. For many, including *Toxoplasma gondii* as an example, it is interferon-gamma. Recent data suggest that TNF may have a critical role in activating the killing of *Mycobacterium tuberculosis*.

Natural Killer (NK) Cells. NK cells are large lymphocytes with cytoplasmic granules, sometimes referred to as large granular lymphocytes. They lack specific antigen receptors but possess the ability to kill certain tumor cells or normal cells infected by virus. NK cells are neither T nor B cells, although they express the CD2 molecule and a low-affinity receptor for the Fc portion of IgG (CD16). They can acquire additional "specificity" by virtue of FcR-dependent attachment to IgG antibody–coated targets, thereby serving as an effector cell of ADCC. They produce and respond to cytokines, which modulate their functions. The mediators of target lysis include porins and other granule contents.

γδ T Cells. γδ T cells have excited interest as a potential intermediary between nonspecific inflammatory and specific immune effector cells. They constitute approximately 5 per cent of T cells in circulation and in lymphoid organs. γδ T cells are not class I or class II MHC–restricted and appear to target to broadly cross-reactive HSPs. They may function, therefore, in the initial or innate response to microbes, and possibly in the pathogenesis of autoimmune diseases. γδ T cells express cytokines and possess cytotoxic function. Their relative role in infection and immunity awaits definition.

Integration of the various host defense mechanisms is apparent as one examines resistance to specific representative infectious agents.

RESISTANCE TO EXTRACELLULAR BACTERIA

Encapsulated Organisms

Streptococcus pneumoniae. The type-specific polysaccharide capsule is a major virulence factor because of its antiphagocytic properties. Antibody to the polysaccharide is itself capable of preventing pneumococcal disease, as reflected by experimental studies and the efficacy of pneumococcal polysaccharide vaccines.

In the absence of immunity, pneumococci reaching the alveoli are not effectively contained by the host. Their phagocytosis by neutrophils is inefficient, since organisms must be trapped against a surface to be ingested ("surface phagocytosis"—Fig. 92–4). The pneumococcus does, however, elicit a neutrophilic inflammatory response. The organism activates complement by the alternative pathway and interactions of C-reactive protein in serum with pneumococcal C-polysaccharide. Activated complement fragments (C3a, C5a, C567) and bacterial oligopeptides are chemotactic for neutrophils. Opsonic complement fragments (C3b) coating pneumococci favor their attachment to neutrophils but are less effective in promoting phagocytosis and killing than is specific antibody. Clinical observations also directly support the primal role of antibody in immunity. It is the development of specific antibody on days 5 to 9 of untreated pneumococcal pneumonia that produces a clinical "crisis," with dramatic resolution of symptoms. Opsonization of S. pneumoniae by type-specific antipolysaccharide antibody promotes ingestion and oxidative burst activity, with destruction of the organism.

Neisseria meningitidis. Capsular polysaccharide also represents an important virulence factor for meningococci. In addition, pathogenic Neisseria species produce an IgA protease that dissociates the Fc fragment from the Fab portion of secretory and serum IgA, thus interfering with effector properties of the antibody molecule. Antibody-dependent complement-mediated bacterial killing is the critical host defense against meningococci. In illustration of this principle, the age-specific incidence of meningococcal meningitis during the first 12 years of life is inversely proportional to the age-related frequency of serum bactericidal antibody directed against capsular and cell wall bacterial antigens. Therefore, the presence of bactericidal antibody is associated with protection against the meningococcus. In epidemic situations, 40 per cent of individuals who become colonized with the epidemic strain but lack bactericidal antibodies develop disease. Protective serum antibody is elicited by colonization with (1) nonencapsulated and encapsulated strains of meningococci of low virulence, which elicit antibodies cross-reactive with virulent strains, and (2) *Escherichia coli* and *Bacillus* species with cross-reacting capsular polysaccharides. The lack of bactericidal activity in the serum of adolescents and adults manifesting susceptibility to N. meningitidis may be due to blocking IgA antibody. Susceptibility of patients lacking C6, C7, or C8 to meningococcal infection provides important evidence that the dominant protective mechanism against this organism involves complement-mediated bacteriolysis. Evaluation of individuals developing meningococcal disease in a nonepidemic setting sometimes reveals underlying abnormalities of the complement system.

Exotoxin-Producing Organisms

Clostridium tetani. All disease manifestations produced by this organism can be ascribed to the tetanus toxin, tetanospasmin. Antibody to toxin is protective. Survival from tetanus does not, however, lead to immunity to subsequent infection, because the toxin is sufficiently potent to cause disease at subimmunogenic concentrations.

RESISTANCE TO OBLIGATE INTRACELLULAR PARASITES: VIRUSES

Host antiviral defense is characterized by overlap and redundancy, which allow a rapid and effective response to most viral agents. The key element of the response varies with the virus, the site, and the timing. Initially, infection is limited at the local site by type I interferons, which increase the resistance of neighboring cells to spread of the infection. Complement directly neutralizes some enveloped viruses. NK cells destroy infected cells, a process enhanced by the interferons. As specific antibody is produced, IgA neutralizes the virus at mucosal surfaces; IgG neutralizes virus that has spread systemically to extracellular sites and allows uptake and destruction by FcR-bearing effector cells through antibody-dependent cellular cytotoxicity (ADCC). Later effector cells, cytotoxic T lymphocytes (CTLs), are expanded and activated to lyse host cells expressing viral antigens in the context of MHC products. CTLs disrupt parasitized cells, exposing viruses to extracellular neutralization and clearance mechanisms.

The host thus directs several defenses against viral infection. The same humoral and cellular mechanisms that destroy bacteria serve to clear extracellular viruses. The host immune response also is effective against intracellular replicative stages of viruses and may destroy infected host cells that express viral antigens on their surfaces. Clinical and experimental observations indicate the respective roles of humoral and cellular immunity in resistance against certain viruses. In Hodgkin's disease and in T lymphocyte–deficient experimental models, selective defects in cellular immunity lead to reactivation of certain latent Herpesviridae: herpes simplex, varicella-zoster, and cytomegalovirus. The prominent role for cellular immunity against these agents is biologically advantageous because virions spread intercellularly via desmosomes or intercellular bridges; viruses thereby avoid exposure to the antibody-rich extracellular milieu. Destruction of virus-infected cells by specific cytotoxic T cells becomes an essential first step in host defense by allowing extracellular mechanisms to mop up free viral particles.

In contrast, antibody- and complement-dependent mechanisms assume major importance against viruses that themselves lyse host cells and spread by extracellular means; for these agents, passive transfer of antibody confers protection. Nevertheless, the absence of greatly increased susceptibility of hypogammaglobulinemic patients to measles and influenza implies the continued contribution of cellular immunity in protection against these agents and indicates important overlap in antiviral host effector mechanisms.

The major antiviral defenses include humoral mechanisms, cellular immunity, and interferons.

Humoral Defenses

Complement-Independent Neutralization. Specific IgG, IgM, and IgA neutralize infectivity of viruses. The respective antibodies first combine with proteins of the virus coat. Resultant conformational changes may prevent adsorption of viruses to cells and cellular penetration; sometimes, antibody coating of extracellular virus interferes with subsequent intracellular events, such as uncoating. Alternatively, antibody may physically aggregate viral particles.

IgA is the key defender against viral infections that begin on or are confined to respiratory epithelium. For infections such as polio, measles, and rubella, which begin on a mucosal surface and then disseminate hematogenously, local IgA antibody prevents infection, whereas serum IgG antibody prevents disease.

Complement-Facilitated Neutralization. Complement neutralizes some enveloped viruses by direct or antibody-dependent steric changes or aggregation. Infected host cells expressing surface virus antigens also are susceptible to lysis by mechanisms involving the alternate complement pathway and further enhanced by antibody.

Opsonization of extracellular viruses by complement and IgG antibody facilitates phagocytosis by neutrophils and macrophages. This process destroys some viruses (enteroviruses) but aids cellular penetration and replication of others (arboviruses).

Enzyme Inhibition. Antibody may interfere with release of progeny influenza virus by blocking viral neuraminidase. Replication is thereby limited, although the virion is not neutralized.

Cellular Immunity

Cellular Cytotoxicity. These defenses are of chief relevance for viruses that spread by intercellular means.

Cytotoxic T Lymphocytes (CTL). These cells appear early in viral infection and are specific for viral antigens expressed on the surface of parasitized cells. Most are CD8 cells that effect class I MHC–restricted killing. Class II MHC–restricted killing by CD4 cells is also important in the immune response to certain viruses. CD4 cells also promote differentiation and activation of CD8 and CTLs.

Antibody-Dependent Cellular Cytotoxicity (ADCC). Virus-infected cells that display surface viral antigens are opsonized by IgG antibodies and lysed by ADCC. The effector cells are lymphocytes (killer cells), macrophages, and neutrophils; all bear surface Fc receptors.

Natural Killer (NK) Cells. NK cells spontaneously lyse virally infected cells; this effector mechanism is activated by interferon-gamma and interleukin-2.

Interferons

The antiviral action of interferons provides a major host defense against viruses. Interferons are a family of proteins produced by lymphocytes, fibroblasts, epithelial cells, and macrophages early in the course of viral infection, before specific antibody develops. Exposure of cells to interferon induces their synthesis of proteins that, in turn, selectively inhibit the production of viral proteins. The immunoregulatory effects of interferon-gamma may also contribute indirectly to antiviral immunity by activating effector cells.

Type I interferons consist of two serologically distinct families of proteins. Interferon-gamma is produced by mononuclear phagocytes and interferon-beta by fibroblasts; other cells can also secrete these factors in response to viral infection. Viral infection induces type I interferon, which protects uninfected neighboring cells by inducing synthesis of enzymes such as 2′, 5′-oligoadenylate synthetase that interfere with replication of viral RNA or DNA. Type I interferons have two other functions that promote viral defense: they promote the lytic potential of NK cells, and they increase target expression of class I MHC molecules, thus increasing target susceptibility to lysis by CTLs. Interferon-gamma is a type II interferon, with prominent immunoregulatory activity, produced by activated T lymphocytes.

RESISTANCE TO FACULTATIVE INTRACELLULAR PARASITES: *MYCOBACTERIUM TUBERCULOSIS*

Activation of host phagocytes provides the critical defense mechanism against *M. tuberculosis*. Primary infection progresses locally in the nonhypersensitive host, since ingested organisms persist and multiply within mononuclear phagocytes. The bacteria escape intracellular digestion by virtue of constituents (sulfatides, suramin, poly-D-glutamic acid) that inhibit phagolysosomal fusion. Antibody-coated mycobacteria do not evade phagolysosomal fusion but nonetheless resist degradation, probably because of shielding provided by their rich lipid content. The development of cellular immunity leads to T lymphocyte–dependent macrophage activation and to the killing of the intracellular tubercle bacillus organism. The lesions of primary tuberculosis regress. However, latent foci persist, and delayed reactivation remains a threat throughout the lifetime of the host.

REFERENCES

Abbas AK, Lichtman AH, Pober JS: Cellular and Molecular Immunology. Philadelphia, WB Saunders Co, 1991.

Nossal GJV: Current concepts: Immunology. The basic components of the immune system. N Engl J Med 316:1320, 1987.

Pizzo PA: The compromised host. In Wyngaarden JB, Smith LH Jr, Bennett JC (eds): Cecil Textbook of Medicine. 19th ed. Philadelphia, WB Saunders Co, 1992, pp 1573–1584.

93 LABORATORY DIAGNOSIS OF INFECTIOUS DISEASES

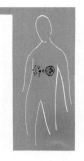

Five basic laboratory techniques can be used in the diagnosis of infectious diseases: (1) direct visualization of the organism; (2) detection of microbial antigen; (3) a search for "clues" produced by the host immune response to specific microorganisms; (4) detection of specific microbial nucleotide sequences; and (5) isolation of the organism in culture. Each technique has its use and each its pitfalls. The laboratory can usually provide the clinician with prompt, accurate and, if used judiciously, inexpensive diagnosis.

DIAGNOSIS BY DIRECT VISUALIZATION OF THE ORGANISM

In many infectious diseases, pathogenic organisms can be directly visualized by microscopic examination of readily available tissue fluids, such as sputum, urine, pus, and pleural, peritoneal, or cerebrospinal fluid. With the use of Gram or acid-fast stains, bacteria, mycobacteria, and *Candida* can be readily identified. An India ink preparation can often identify *Cryptococcus*, and potassium hydroxide (KOH) preparations can occasionally identify other fungal pathogens.

Preparation of Specimens for Staining

Sputum and pus are often thick, and thinning is necessary to obtain a helpful preparation. A drop of sputum or pus is placed on a clean glass slide, and another slide is pressed on top of the specimen and pulled away. This step can be repeated as often as necessary (using a clean slide each time) until the specimen has been thinned sufficiently to allow newsprint to be read through it. Unless grossly purulent, fluids such as cerebrospinal fluid (CSF) must be centrifuged to concentrate the organisms and the pellet used for staining. If no organisms are seen upon examining unspun CSF, the pellet must then be examined. To prevent the specimen from washing away during the staining procedure, a drop of CSF may be mixed with a drop of fresh serum or other sterile protein source. The specimen is allowed to air dry and is then gently fixed by being passed quickly through a flame.

Gram Stain

1. Flood the slide with crystal violet—15 seconds.
2. Rinse with water.
3. Flood with Gram iodine—15 seconds.

4. Rinse with water.
5. Decolorize with 95 per cent ethyl alcohol. This step is critical. Rinse with alcohol until blue stain just disappears from the rinse.
6. Immediately rinse with water.
7. Flood with safranin—15 seconds.
8. Rinse with water.
9. Air dry.
10. Examine using oil immersion lens.

Proper decolorization is crucial. A good Gram stain should show neutrophil nuclei as deep pink in all but the most dense regions, where they may have a touch of blue. Interpretation of the staining of organisms should be based on inspection of the areas in which transition of the coloration of neutrophil nuclei is present, that is, where some nuclei show minimal blue or purple staining. This will avoid areas that are overdecolorized or underdecolorized.

Acid-Fast Stain

The Kinyoun stain for acid-fast bacilli should be examined for at least 10 minutes using oil immersion lens. Mycobacteria will appear pink, often beaded, and slightly curved. Other bacteria will not retain pink dye. (Exceptions: *Nocardia* and the Pittsburgh agent [*Legionella micdadei*] may also appear acid-fast.) Experience is necessary to distinguish acid-fast bacilli that may be slightly refractile from debris and other artifacts that may be highly refractile. Microbiology laboratories may be able to stain clinical samples for mycobacteria using the auramine-rhodamine technique. Mycobacteria fluoresce when stained in this way. This feature permits rapid screening of many microscopic fields. A positive auramine-rhodamine stain should be confirmed by a Kinyoun acid-fast stain.

India Ink Preparation. A drop of centrifuged CSF is placed on a microscope slide next to a drop of artist's India ink. A coverslip is placed over the drops, and the area of mixing of CSF and India ink is examined at 100× magnification. Cryptococci are identified by their large capsules, which exclude the India ink (Fig. 93–1). The entire slide should be examined.

KOH Preparation. A drop of sputum, a skin scraping, or a smear of vaginal or oral exudate is placed on a slide together with 1 drop of 5 to 40 per cent KOH. A coverslip is placed on the specimen, and the slide is heated for 2 to 5 seconds above a flame. The condenser of the microscope is lowered, and the specimen is examined at 100×

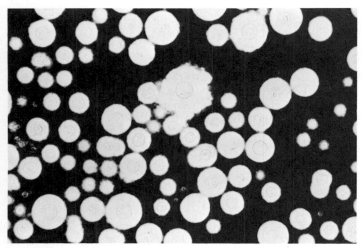

FIGURE 93–1. India ink preparation of cerebrospinal fluid revealing encapsulated cryptococci. Note the large capsules surrounding the smaller organisms.

magnification when searching for elastin fibers (whose presence in sputum suggests a necrotizing pneumonia) or 400× when looking for fungal forms. The KOH will partially dissolve host cells and bacteria, sparing fungi and elastin fibers.

Tzanck's Preparation. A vesicle suspected of harboring herpesvirus (zoster or simplex) is unroofed with a scalpel, and the base is gently scraped. The scrapings are placed on a glass slide, air-dried, and stained with Wright's stain, Giemsa's stain, or a rapid stain such as methylene blue. The slide is then examined at low (100×) power for the presence of multinucleated giant cells; their characteristic appearance is then confirmed at high (400×) power. Demonstration of giant cells is diagnostic for herpesvirus infection.

TABLE 93–1. DISEASES OFTEN DIAGNOSED BY DETECTION OF MICROBIAL ANTIGENS

Disease	Assay	Agent Detected
Meningitis	Latex agglutination	*Streptococcus pneumoniae, Haemophilus influenzae, Neisseria meningitidis, Cryptococcus*
Respiratory tract infection	Immunofluorescence	*Bordetella pertussis,* legionnaires' disease, influenza virus, respiratory syncytial virus, adenovirus
Genitourinary tract infection	Enzyme immunoassay	*Chlamydia* species, herpes simplex virus 1 and 2.
Hepatitis	Radioimmunoassay	Hepatitis B surface antigen
Human immunodeficiency virus (HIV) infection	Enzyme immunoassay	HIV p24 core antigen

These simple bedside techniques provide rapid and inexpensive diagnosis of many infectious diseases. There are other techniques that directly visualize pathogens, but they require more sophisticated techniques. Silver staining using the Gomori methenamine technique can identify most fungi and *Pneumocystis carinii*. Experienced pathologists also can identify *Pneumocystis carinii* on Giemsa-stained specimens of induced sputum. Immunofluorescence techniques using antibodies directed against the organisms rapidly identify pathogens such as *Legionella pneumophila* and *Bordetella pertussis*. Immunofluorescence also can be used to identify cells infected with influenza virus, respiratory syncytial virus, and adenovirus in respiratory secretions. Darkfield microscopy can identify *Treponema pallidum,* and electron microscopy can often detect viral particles in infected cells.

DIAGNOSIS BY DETECTION OF MICROBIAL ANTIGENS

Certain pathogens can be detected by examination of specimens for microbial antigens (Table 93–1). These studies can be performed rapidly — often within 1 hour. The diagnosis of meningitis due to *Pneumococcus, Haemophilus,* some strains of *Meningococcus,* and *Cryptococcus* can be made rapidly by detection of specific polysaccharide antigen in the CSF using latex agglutination. Although these diagnoses can often be more rapidly made by Gram stain or India ink preparation, antigen detection is especially helpful when attempts at direct visualization of the pathogen are not diagnostic (e.g., in the patient with partially treated bacterial meningitis). The demonstration of hepatitis B surface antigen in blood establishes the presence of infection by this virus.

DIAGNOSIS BY EXAMINATION OF HOST IMMUNE OR INFLAMMATORY RESPONSES

Histopathologic examination of biopsied or excised tissue often reveals patterns of the host inflammatory response that can narrow down diagnostic possibilities. As a general rule, a polymorphonuclear leukocytic infiltrate is compatible with acute infection and suggests a bacterial process. A lymphocytic infiltrate is compatible with a more chronic process and is seen in viral, mycobacterial, fungal, and other nonbacterial infections. Eosinophilia is often seen in helminthic infestations. Granuloma formation suggests mycobacterial and certain fungal infections. Some diseases such as syphilis (obliterative endarteritis), cat-scratch disease (mixed granulomatous, suppurative, and lymphoid hyperplastic changes), and lymphogranuloma venereum (stellate abscesses) have fairly characteristic histologic features. Several viral infections produce characteristic changes in host cells; these may be detected by cytologic examination. Skin or respiratory infection due to herpesviruses, or pneumonia due to cytomegalovirus or measles virus, for example, can be diagnosed with reasonable accuracy by cytologic examination. Similarly, examination of cells and chemistries in infected fluids such as CSF will provide clues to the etiology of the infection. Bacterial infections generally provoke a polymorphonuclear leukocytosis with elevated protein and depressed glucose concentrations. Viral infections most often provoke a lymphocytic pleocytosis; protein elevations are less marked, and glucose levels are usually but not always normal.

Host cell–mediated immune responses can be used to help make certain diagnoses. A positive skin test for delayed-type hypersensitivity to mycobacterial or fungal antigens indicates active or previous infection with these agents. A negative skin test may be seen despite active infection in individuals with depression of cell-mediated immunity (anergy). Therefore, control skin tests using commonly encountered antigens (e.g., Candida, mumps, Trichophyton) must also be applied to ascertain if the patient can mount a delayed-type hypersensitivity response. Occasionally, the response to disease-related antigens is depressed selectively.

Host humoral responses may be used to diagnose certain infections, particularly those due to organisms whose cultivation is difficult or expensive to perform or hazardous to laboratory personnel (Table 93–2). In general, two sera are obtained at intervals of at least 2 weeks. A fourfold or greater rise (or fall) in antibody titer generally suggests a recent infection. Antibodies of the IgM class also suggest recent infection.

DIAGNOSIS BY DETECTION OF MICROBIAL NUCLEOTIDE SEQUENCES

Most techniques for detection of microbial antigens cannot reliably detect fewer than 1 million molecules in clinical samples. Recent techniques are capable of detecting as few as three to five molecules in clinical samples. These techniques utilize a heat-stable DNA polymerase to amplify microbial DNA or RNA sequences to levels that are readily detectable. This technique, gene amplification using the polymerase chain reaction

TABLE 93–2. DISEASES OFTEN DIAGNOSED BY MEASUREMENT OF HOST HUMORAL RESPONSES (ANTIBODY LEVELS)

Many viral infections
Mycoplasmal pneumonia
Rickettsial infections
Chlamydial infections
Lyme disease
Syphilis
Leptospirosis
Rheumatic fever
Legionnaires' disease
Tularemia
Brucellosis
Histoplasmosis
Coccidioidomycosis
Amebiasis

(PCR), has been used successfully to diagnose infection with the human immunodeficiency virus, *Treponema pallidum*, and a variety of other pathogens. It is anticipated that numerous infectious diseases will soon be diagnosed with great sensitivity, using this technique. The exquisite sensitivity of this technique may, however, yield false-positive results unless performed with great care.

DIAGNOSIS BY ISOLATION OF THE ORGANISM IN CULTURE

Isolation of a single microbe from an infected site is generally considered evidence that the infection is due to this organism. Information obtained from the culture must, however, be interpreted according to the clinical setting. For example, cultures obtained from ordinarily contaminated sites (e.g., vagina, pharynx) may be overgrown with nonpathogenic commensals, and fastidious organisms such as *Neisseria gonorrhoeae* will be difficult to recognize unless cultured on medium that selects for their growth. Similarly, cultures of expectorated "sputum" may also be uninterpretable if heavily contaminated with saliva. The culture of an organism from an infected but ordinarily sterile site is reasonable evidence for infection due to that organism. On the other hand, the failure to culture an organism may simply result from inadequate culture conditions (e.g., "sterile" pus from brain abscess cultured only on aerobic media. Most brain abscesses are caused by anaerobic bacteria that do not grow under the aerobic conditions most commonly utilized.) Thus, when submitting samples for culture, the physician must alert the laboratory to likely pathogens.

Gram stains of specimens submitted for culture are often invaluable aids to the interpretation of culture results. A Gram stain of "sputum" will readily detect contamination by saliva if squamous epithelial cells are seen. On the other hand, a Gram stain revealing bacteria despite negative cultures suggests infection by fastidious organisms. The presence of an organism in high density and within neutrophils also suggests that the corresponding bacterial isolate is causing disease rather than colonizing the patient or contaminating the specimen. Gram stain of the initial clinical specimen may also help determine the relative importance of different isolates when cultures reveal mixed flora.

Viral Isolation. Since all viral pathogens that can be cultured require eukaryotic cells in which to grow, virus isolation is expensive and often laborious. Throat washings, rectal swabs, or cultures of infected sites should be transported immediately to the laboratory or, if this is not possible, placed in virus transport medium—usually an isotonic salt solution containing antibiotics and protein—and refrigerated overnight until they can be cultured in the laboratory. Notifying the laboratory of the suspected pathogens allows selection of the best cell lines for culture. The clinician must be aware of the viruses that the hospital's laboratory can isolate. As the antiviral armamentarium expands, cultivation of viruses will become more routine. A fourfold rise in titer of antibody to the isolated virus suggests that it is causing disease rather than simply colonizing the area sampled.

Isolation of Rickettsia, Chlamydia, and Mycoplasma. Rickettsiae are cultivated primarily in reference laboratories. Diagnosis of rickettsial illness is generally made on clinical grounds and confirmed serologically. Chlamydiae can be propagated in cell cultures used in most hospital virology laboratories. Mycoplasmas will grow on selective media; the prolonged period of incubation required results in little advantage over serologic diagnosis.

Bacterial Isolation. Isolation of common bacterial pathogens is achieved readily by most hospital laboratories. Specimens should be carried promptly to the laboratory. In instances in which likely isolates may be fastidious (e.g., bacterial meningitis) and laboratories are closed, the specimen should be placed directly onto the culture medium, with careful attention to sterile technique. The specimen is placed onto the culture plate. A loop is sterilized in a flame until it is red, then allowed to cool. The specimen is then streaked on bacteriologic medium. This practice allows separation of different bacterial colonies and rough quantitation of bacterial growth.

Isolation of anaerobic bacteria is often critically important for clinical diagnosis. When anaerobes are suspected, the specimen, if pus or liquid, can be drawn into a syringe, the air expelled, and the syringe capped before transport to the laboratory. Otherwise, specimens must be taken immediately to the laboratory or placed in an anaerobic transport medium appropriate for survival of pathogens. Alternatively, the specimen may be placed in a vial containing thioglycolate broth. This practice will permit anaerobic growth but will not allow quantification of growth. Because of contamination by oral anaerobes, sputum should not be cultured anaerobically unless the sample was obtained by transtracheal or percutaneous lung aspiration.

Isolation of Fungi and Mycobacteria. Specimens for fungal and mycobacterial culture must be processed and cultured by the microbiology laboratory. Although some fungi and rapid-growing mycobacteria grow readily on standard agars used for routine isolation of bacteria, others, such as *Mycobacterium tuberculosis* and *Histoplasma capsulatum*, must be cultured on special media for as long as several weeks.

REFERENCES

Finegold SM, Martin WJ, Scott EG (eds): Bailey & Scott's Diagnostic Microbiology. St Louis, The CV Mosby Co, 1978.

Menegus MA, Douglas RG: Viruses, rickettsia, chlamydia and mycoplasmas. *In* Mandell GL, Douglas RG, Bennett JE (eds): Principles and Practice of Infectious Diseases. 3rd ed. New York, Churchill Livingstone, 1990, p 193.

Washington JA: Bacteria, fungi and parasites. *In* Mandell GL, Douglas RG, Bennett JE (eds): Principles and Practice of Infectious Diseases. 3rd ed. New York, Churchill Livingstone, 1990, p 160.

94 ANTIMICROBIAL THERAPY

The advent of antimicrobial therapy has been the most dramatic advance in medical practice in this century. Antimicrobials are agents that interfere with microbial metabolism, resulting in inhibition of growth or death of bacteria, viruses, fungi, protozoa, or helminths. Some, like penicillin, are natural products of other microbes. Others, such as sulfa drugs, are chemical agents synthesized in the laboratory. Still others are semisynthetic—chemical modifications of naturally occurring substances that result in enhanced activity (e.g., nafcillin) and/or diminished toxicity.

The most effective antimicrobials are characterized by their relatively selective activity against microbes. Some, such as penicillins and amphotericin B, interfere with the synthesis of microbial cell walls that are absent in human cells. Others, such as trimethoprim and sulfa drugs, inhibit obligate microbial synthesis of essential nucleic acid intermediates, pathways not required by human cells. Still others, such as acyclovir, an antiviral agent, are relatively inactive until metabolized by pathogen-derived enzymes. Nonetheless, these agents, although relatively selective in activity against microbes, have variable degrees of toxicity for human cells. Thus, monitoring for toxicity during antimicrobial therapy is important.

In the selection of an antimicrobial agent for a patient, the following factors must be considered.

THE PATHOGEN

If the pathogen has been clearly identified by culture or histopathologic techniques (Chapter 93), a drug with a narrow spectrum of activity (i.e., highly selective for the particular pathogen) is usually the most reasonable choice. If the pathogen responsible for the patient's illness has not been identified, then the physician must choose a drug or combination of drugs active against the most likely pathogens in the specific setting. In either instance, the physician must be guided by patterns of antimicrobial resistance common in the community and in the specific hospital. Some pathogens (e.g., pneumococcus, group A streptococcus) are almost always sensitive to narrow-spectrum antimicrobials such as penicillin. Other pathogens such as staphylococci are variably resistant to penicillins but almost always susceptible to vancomycin. Resistance patterns, particularly among hospital-acquired bacteria, may vary widely and are important in devising antimicrobial strategies. Broad-spectrum antimicrobial coverage for all febrile patients ("shotgunning") must not be substituted for carefully evaluating the clinical problem and pinpointing therapy directed toward the most likely pathogen or pathogens. Widespread use of broad-spectrum antimicrobials almost invariably leads to emergence of resistant strains. On the other hand, the more sick a patient appears and the less certain the physician is of the responsible pathogen, the more important initial empiric broad-spectrum coverage becomes. Initial empiric treatment is also frequently indicated in the immunocompromised febrile patient (e.g., the patient with severe neutropenia secondary to chemotherapy). Once the pathogen is isolated and its antimicrobial sensitivities are known, empiric therapy must be scaled down to a definitive regimen with narrow and optimal activity against the specific microorganism.

SITE OF INFECTION

The location of the infection is also important in determining the selection and dosage of an antimicrobial. Deep-seated infections and bacteremic infections generally require higher doses of antimicrobials than, for example, superficial infections of the skin, upper respiratory tract, or lower urinary tract. Penetration of various antimicrobials into sites such as meninges, eye, and prostate is quite variable. Thus, treatment of infections at these sites involves selection of an antimicrobial agent that penetrates these tissues in concentrations sufficient to inhibit or kill the pathogen. The meninges are relatively resistant to penetration by most antimicrobials; inflammation renders the meninges somewhat more permeable. Therefore, high doses of antibiotics are the rule when treating meningitis. Bacterial infections of certain sites such as the heart valves or meninges must be treated with antibiotics that kill the microbe (bactericidal) as opposed to simply inhibiting its growth (bacteriostatic). This is so because local host defenses at these sites are inadequate to rid the host of infecting organisms. Infections involving foreign bodies are often difficult to eradicate without removing the foreign material.

Antimicrobials alone are often insufficient in the treatment of large abscesses. Although many drugs achieve reasonable concentrations in abscess walls, the low pH antagonizes the activity of some drugs (e.g., aminoglycosides), and some drugs bind to and are inactivated by white blood cells or their products. The large number of organisms, their depressed metabolism in this unfavorable milieu, and the frequent polymicrobial nature of certain abscesses increase the likelihood that some organisms present may be resistant to antimicrobial therapy. Most extracranial abscesses should be drained whenever anatomically possible.

CHARACTERISTICS OF THE ANTIMICROBIAL

The physician must know the pharmacokinetics of the drug (i.e., its absorption, its penetration into various sites, its metabolism and excretion) and its toxicity, as well as its spectrum of antimicrobial activity, before selecting it for use (Table 94–1).

Distribution and Excretion. Lipid-soluble drugs, such as chloramphenicol and rifampin, penetrate most membranes, including the meninges, more readily than do more ionized compounds, such as the aminoglycosides. The physician must be certain that the drug concentration achievable at the site of infection is sufficient to inhibit or kill the pathogen. Understanding a drug's distribution, rate and site of metabolism, and route of excretion is essential in selecting the appropriate drug and dose. Drugs excreted unchanged in the urine may be particularly good for the treatment of lower urinary tract infection or for the treatment of systemic infection in the presence of renal insufficiency. Some antimicrobials are metabolized in the liver and must be adjusted appropriately in the presence of hepatic insufficiency.

Activity of the Drug. The physician must understand both the spectrum of activity of the drug against microbial isolates and the mechanism of activity of the agent and whether it is bactericidal or bacteriostatic in achievable concentrations. As a general rule, cell wall–active drugs are likely to be bactericidal. Bactericidal drugs are necessary for treatment of infections sequestered from an effective host inflammatory response such as meningitis and endocarditis. With the exception of aminoglycosides and certain azalide and macrolide antibiotics, agents inhibiting protein synthesis at ribosomal sites are generally bacteriostatic.

TABLE 94–1. CHARACTERISTICS OF COMMONLY USED ANTIMICROBIAL AGENTS

DRUG CLASS	SITE OF ACTION	CNS PENETRATION	EXCRETION	USES/ACTIVITY
Antibacterials				
Beta-lactams				
Penicillins	Cell wall	+/−	Renal	Streptococci, *Neisseria*, oral anaerobes
Beta-lactamase resistant penicillins, e.g., nafcillin	Cell wall	+/−	Renal and/or hepatic	Methicillin-sensitive staphylococci
Amino penicillins, e.g., ampicillin	Cell wall	+/−	Renal	Gram-positive organisms, not staphylococci, some gram-negative organisms
Extended-spectrum penicillins, e.g., mezlocillin	Cell wall	+/−	Renal	Broad-spectrum gram-positive organisms; gram-negative organisms, including *Pseudomonas*, not *Staphylococcus*
Beta-lactamase inhibitors, e.g., clavulanic acid	Inactivates beta-lactamase	−	Renal/metabolic	Used with ampicillin or ticarcillin, expands activity to include anaerobes, many gram-negative organisms, and methicillin-sensitive staphylococci
Cephalosporins*	Cell wall			
First-generation, e.g., cefazolin		−	Renal	Broad-spectrum
Second-generation, e.g., cefuroxime		+/−	Renal	Some with anaerobic activity, e.g., cefoxitin
Third-generation, e.g., ceftriaxone		+	Renal or hepatic	Some active against *Pseudomonas*, e.g., ceftazidime
Monobactams				
Aztreonam	Cell wall	+/−	Renal	Aerobic gram-negative bacilli
Carbapenems				
Imipenem/cilastatin	Cell wall	+/−	Renal	Very broad-spectrum, some enterococci, and methicillin-sensitive staphylococci
Vancomycin	Cell wall	+/−	Renal	Coagulase-positive and -negative staphylococci, other gram-positive bacteria
Sulfonamides/trimethoprim	Inhibit nucleic acid synthesis	+	Renal	Gram-negative bacilli, *Salmonella*, *Pneumocystis carinii*, *Nocardia*
Quinolones	DNA gyrase	+/−	Some hepatic metabolism	Very broad-spectrum, not including streptococci or anaerobes
Metronidazole	DNA disruption	+	Hepatic metabolism	Anaerobes, *Clostridium difficile*, amebas, *Trichomonas*
Rifampin	Transcription	+	Hepatic metabolism/renal	*M. tuberculosis*; meningococcal and *Haemophilus influenzae* prophylaxis
Aminoglycosides	Ribosome	−	Renal	Gram-negative bacilli, no activity in anaerobic conditions
Chloramphenicol	Ribosome	+	Hepatic metabolism/renal	Broad-spectrum; especially useful for *Salmonella*, anaerobes, *Rickettsia*
Clindamycin	Ribosome	−	Hepatic metabolism/renal	Anaerobes; gram-positive cocci
Tetracyclines	Ribosome	+/−	Renal/hepatic metabolism	Broad-spectrum; especially useful for spirochetes, *Rickettsia*
Macrolides/Azalides				
Erythromycin	Ribosome	−	Hepatic	Gram-positive cocci, legionella, mycoplasma
Azithromycin Clarithromycin	Ribosome	+	Hepatic	High intracellular levels have enhanced activity against mycobacteria, *Toxoplasma*
Antifungals				
Polyenes				
Amphotericin B	Binds membrane ergosterol	+/−	?	Most fungi
Nystatin	Binds membrane ergosterol	−	Fecal	Mucosal candidiasis
Flucytosine	Blocks DNA synthesis	−	Renal	Candidiasis; *Cryptococcus* with amphotericin B
Imidazoles	Block membrane biosynthesis			

TABLE 94-1. CHARACTERISTICS OF COMMONLY USED ANTIMICROBIAL AGENTS *Continued*

DRUG CLASS	SITE OF ACTION	CNS PENETRATION	EXCRETION	USES/ACTIVITY
Ketoconazole		−	Hepatic	Mucosal candidiasis, pulmonary histoplasmosis (nonmeningeal)
Fluconazole		+	Renal	Candidiasis, cryptococcosis, coccidioidomycosis
Antivirals				
Acyclovir	DNA polymerase	+	Renal	Herpes simplex, including encephalitis; herpes zoster in immunosuppressed hosts
Ganciclovir	DNA polymerase	+	Renal	Cytomegalovirus, herpesviruses
Foscarnet	DNA polymerase	+	Renal	Cytomegalovirus, herpesviruses, ?HIV
Amantadine/Rimantadine	?Uncoating	+	Renal	Influenza A treatment and prophylaxis
Vidarabine	DNA polymerase	+	Renal	Neonatal herpes simplex
Zidovudine (AZT)	Reverse transcriptase	+	Hepatic glucuronidation/renal	HIV
Didanosine (ddI)	Reverse transcriptase	+	Renal	HIV
Zalcitabine (ddC)	Reverse transcriptase	?	Renal	HIV
Ribavirin		+	Hepatic/renal	RSV, ?influenza, ?hemorrhagic fever, ?Lassa fever

*As a rule, first-generation cephalosporins have better activity against gram-positive cocci and minimal CNS penetration. Second-generation cephalosporins have somewhat better activity against gram-negative bacteria and may penetrate the CNS. Third-generation cephalosporins have the broadest activity against gram-negative bacteria and generally penetrate the CNS, but they are relatively less active against gram-positive cocci.

CNS = Central nervous system; HIV = human immunodeficiency virus; RSV = respiratory syncytial virus.

Toxicity of the Drug. The physician must have a thorough understanding of the contraindications of the drug, as well as the major toxicities of the drug and their general frequency. This will help in evaluating the risks of treatment and also will assist in advising the patient about the drug's effects and in anticipating possible adverse reactions. History of drug hypersensitivity must be sought before prescribing any antimicrobials. The presence or absence of previous reactions to penicillin should be documented for every patient. Patients with a history suggestive of immediate hypersensitivity to penicillin, such as hives, wheezing, hypotension, laryngospasm, or angioedema at any site, must be considered at risk for anaphylaxis. These patients should not receive penicillins or related drugs (cephalosporins) if adequate alternatives are available. The major and minor determinants of penicillin allergy (breakdown products that bind to serum proteins to form haptens) can be used to detect most persons at risk for serious immediate hypersensitivity. If skin test reactivity to these determinants is present and there are no reasonable alternatives to therapy with a penicillin or related compound, these patients may be desensitized to penicillin using a graduated protocol of intracutaneous penicillin administration. Desensitization should be done only in consultation with an experienced allergist. Patients with a history of an uncomplicated morbilliform or delayed rash after penicillin therapy are not likely to be at risk for immediate hypersensitivity and may be treated with cephalosporins, for which the risk of cross-hypersensitivity to penicillins is likely to be in the range of 5 per cent. Patients with immediate hypersensitivity reactions to penicillin are also at risk for anaphylactic reactions to cephalosporins and imipenem. Evidence to date suggests that cross-hypersensitivity to aztreonam is less common.

ROUTE OF ADMINISTRATION

Oral administration of antimicrobials can often avoid the morbidity and expense associated with parenteral (intravenous or intramuscular) administration. Although some antimicrobials (e.g., amoxicillin and the fluoroquinolones) are very well absorbed after oral administration, most patients hospitalized with severe infections should, at least initially, be treated with intravenous antibiotics. Gut absorption of antimicrobials can be unpredictable, and the intravenous route often permits administration of greater amounts of drug than can be tolerated orally. Intramuscular administration of some antimicrobials can result in excellent drug absorption but should be avoided in the presence of hypotension (erratic absorption) and coagulation disorders (hematomas). Repeated intramuscular injections are uncomfortable and also can result in the formation of sterile abscesses (e.g., pentamidine).

Duration of Therapy. Antimicrobial therapy should be initiated as part of a treatment plan of defined duration. In some settings, the duration of optimal antimicrobial therapy is established (e.g., 10 days but not 7 days of oral penicillin will prevent rheumatic fever after streptococcal pharyngitis); in many others, the duration of treatment is empiric and sometimes can be based on the clinical and bacteriologic course. Blood stream infections without endocarditis or other focal infections can generally be treated for 10 to 14 days. Pneumococcal pneumonia can be effectively treated in 7 to 10 days. The duration of therapy for endocarditis is largely dictated by the characteristics of the culpable microorganism but generally is at least 4 weeks.

Combinations. Combinations of antimicrobials are indicated in serious infection when they provide more effective activity against a pathogen than any single agent. In some instances, combinations of drugs are used to prevent the emergence of resistance (e.g., infections due to *Mycobacterium tuberculosis*). In others, combinations are used because they provide synergistic action against the pathogen (e.g., penicillin, a cell wall activity antibiotic, facilitates uptake of aminoglycosides by enterococci). In still other instances, drug combinations are used in empiric therapies to cover a wide spectrum of potential pathogens when the causative agent is unidentified or when infection is likely to be due to a mixture of organisms (e.g., fecal soilage of the peritoneum). Use of more than one drug increases the likelihood of toxicity, increases costs, and often increases the risk of superinfection.

MONITORING OF ANTIMICROBIAL THERAPY

The physician (and patient) should be alert to potential toxicities and should be prepared to halt the drug in the event of serious toxicity. For some antimicrobials, such as aminoglycosides, the ratio of effective to toxic drug levels is low. Thus, serum levels of the drug must be monitored to ensure appropriate dosing. For some infections (e.g., infective endocarditis due to relatively resistant organisms), monitoring of antimicrobial activity in serum shortly after (peak) and just before (trough) drug administration may help guide antimicrobial choices and usage. Although these techniques are not well standardized, clinicians often adjust drugs and doses to maintain serum bactericidal titers of at least 1:8 in treating certain forms of endocarditis (e.g., enterococcal) in which the antimicrobial resistance pattern of the microorganism may be quite variable.

REFERENCES

Lupski JR: Molecular mechanisms for transposition of drug resistance genes and other movable genetic elements. Rev Infect Dis 9:357, 1987.

Peterson PK, Verhoef J (eds): The Antimicrobial Agents Annual. Vol 3. Amsterdam, Elsevier, 1988.

Young LS: Antimicrobial therapy. In Wyngaarden JB, Smith LH Jr, Bennett JC (eds): Cecil Textbook of Medicine. 19th ed. Philadelphia, WB Saunders Co, 1992, pp 1596–1608.

95 FEVER AND FEBRILE SYNDROMES

REGULATION OF BODY TEMPERATURE

Although "normal" body temperature ranges vary considerably, oral temperature readings in excess of 37.8°C (100.2°F) are generally abnormal. In healthy humans, core body temperature is maintained within a narrow range, so that for each individual, daily temperature variations greater than 1 to 1.5°C are distinctly unusual. This homeostasis is controlled by hypothalamic nuclei that establish "set points" for body temperature. Homeostasis is effected by a complex balance between heat-generating and heat-conserving mechanisms that raise body temperature, on the one hand, and mechanisms that dissipate heat and lower body temperature, on the other (Table 95–1). Heat is regularly generated as a by-product of obligate energy utilization (e.g., cellular metabolism, myocardial contraction, breathing). When an

increase in body temperature is needed, shivering —nondirected muscular contraction—generates large amounts of heat. Peripheral vessels constrict

TABLE 95–1. MECHANISMS OF HEAT REGULATION

To Raise Body Temperature
Heat generation
Obligate heat production
Muscular work
Shivering
Heat conservation
Vasoconstriction
Heat preference
To Lower Body Temperature
Heat loss
Obligate heat loss
Vasodilatation
Sweating
Cold preference

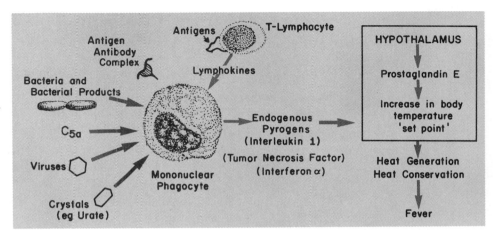

FIGURE 95–1. Pathogenesis of fever.

to diminish heat lost to the environment. At the same time, the person feels cold; this heat preference promotes heat-conserving behavior, such as wrapping up in a blanket.

Obligate heat loss to the environment occurs through the skin and by evaporation of water through sweat and respiration. When the body must cool down, heat loss is promoted. Vasodilation flushes the skin capillaries, temporarily raising skin temperature but ultimately lowering core body temperature by increasing heat loss through the skin to the cooler environment. Sweating promotes rapid heat loss via evaporation, and at the same time, the subject feels warm and sheds blankets to promote heat loss.

FEVER AND HYPERTHERMIA

Fever is an elevated body temperature that is mediated by an increase in the hypothalamic heat-regulating set point. Thus, although fever may be precipitated by exogenous substances such as bacterial products, the increase in body temperature is achieved through physiologic mechanisms. In contrast, hyperthermia is an increase in body temperature that overrides or bypasses the normal homeostatic mechanisms. As a general rule, body temperatures in excess of 41°C are rarely physiologically mediated and suggest hyperthermia. Hyperthermia may be seen after vigorous exercise, in patients with heat stroke, as a heritable reaction to anesthetics (malignant hyperthermia), as a response to phenothiazines (neuroleptic malignant syndrome), and occasionally in patients with central nervous system disorders such as paraplegia (see also Chapter 113). Some patients with severe dermatoses are also unable to dissipate heat and therefore experience hyperthermia.

Fever usually is a physiologic response to infection or inflammation. Monocytes or tissue macrophages are activated by various stimuli to liberate various cytokines with pyrogenic activity (Fig. 95–1). Interleukin-1 (IL1) is also an essential cofactor in initiation of the immune response. Another pyrogenic cytokine, tumor necrosis factor (TNFα), or cachectin, activates lipoprotein lipase and also may play a role in immune cytolysis. Another cytokine, TNFβ, or lymphotoxin, has similar properties. A fourth, interferon-alpha, has antiviral activity (see Chapter 92). Interleukin-6 (IL6), a cytokine that potentiates B cell immunoglobulin synthesis, also has pyrogenic activity. Endogenous pyrogens activate the anterior preoptic nuclei of the hypothalamus to raise the set point for body temperature by the mechanisms shown in Table 95–1. A list of classes of disorders that can cause fever is shown in Table 95–2. Infection by all types of microorganisms can be associated with fever. Tissue injury with resultant inflammation, as is seen in myocardial or pulmonary infarction or after trauma, can produce fever. Certain malignancies such as lymphoma, renal carcinoma, and hepatic carcinoma are also associated with fever; in some instances, this is related to liberation of endogenous pyrogen by monocytes in the inflammatory response surrounding the tumor, and in other cases, the malignant cell may release an endogenous pyrogen. Many immunologically mediated disorders, such as connective tissue diseases, serum sickness, and some drug reactions, are characterized by fever. In most cases of drug-induced fevers, the mechanisms of fever are unknown. Virtually any disorder associated with an inflammatory response (e.g., gouty arthritis) can be associated with fever. Certain endocrine disorders such as thyrotoxicosis, adrenal insufficiency, and pheochromocytoma also can produce fever.

The association of fever with infections or inflammatory disorders raises the question of

TABLE 95–2. CAUSES OF FEVER

Infection
Tissue injury—infarction, trauma
Malignancy
Drugs
Immune-mediated disorders
Other inflammatory disorders
Endocrine disorders

whether fever is beneficial to the host. For example, IL1 (an endogenous pyrogen) is critical for initiation of the immune response, certain in vitro immune responses are marginally enhanced by elevated temperatures, and some organisms prefer cooler temperatures. It is not certain, however, that fever is helpful to humans in any infectious disease with the possible exception of neurosyphilis. Fever is deleterious in certain situations. Among individuals with underlying brain disease, and even in the healthy elderly, fever can produce disorientation and confusion. In young children, fever can result in seizures. Fever should be controlled if the patient is particularly uncomfortable or whenever it poses a specific risk to the patient. Fever in children with a history of febrile seizures and in patients with severe congestive heart failure or recent myocardial infarction should be treated with antipyretics, such as salicylates or acetaminophen. Acetaminophen is preferred for children because of the association of salicylates with Reye's syndrome.

Heat stroke almost always results from prolonged exposure to high environmental temperature and humidity, usually associated, in otherwise healthy individuals, with strenuous exercise. It is characterized by a body temperature greater than 40.6°C and is associated with altered sensorium or coma and with cessation of sweating. Rapid cooling is critical to the patients' survival. Covering the patient with cold (11°C), wet compresses until core temperature reaches 39°C is the most effective initial therapeutic approach and should be followed by intravenous infusions of fluids appropriate to correct the antecedent fluid and electrolyte losses.

Fever Patterns. The normal diurnal variation in body temperature results in a peak temperature in the late afternoon or early evening. This variation often persists when patients have fever. In certain instances, fever patterns may be helpful in suggesting the cause of fever. Rigors—true shaking chills—often herald a bacterial infection, although they may occur in cases of viral infection, as well as in drug or transfusion reactions. Hectic fevers, characterized by wide swings in temperature, may indicate the presence of an abscess. Patients with malaria may have a relapsing fever with episodes of shaking chills and high fever, separated by 1 to 3 days of normal body temperature and relative well-being. Patients with tuberculosis may be relatively comfortable and unaware of a markedly elevated body temperature. Patients with uremia or diabetic ketoacidosis generally have a lowered body temperature, and "normal" temperature readings in these settings may indicate infection. Similarly, elderly patients with infection often fail to mount a febrile response and may present instead with loss of appetite, confusion, or even hypotension without fever. The administration of anti-inflammatory drugs (aspirin, nonsteroidal anti-inflammatory drugs [NSAIDs], corticosteroids) also blunts or ablates the febrile response.

ACUTE FEBRILE SYNDROMES

Fever is one of the most common complaints that bring patients to a physician. The challenge is in discerning the few individuals who require specific therapy from among the many with self-limited benign illness. The approach is simplified by considering patients in three groups: (1) fever without localizing symptoms and signs, (2) fever and rash, and (3) fever and lymphadenopathy. This chapter deals only with fever caused by microbial agents. Clearly autoimmune, neoplastic, and other disease processes may cause fever as well (Table 95–2).

Fever Only

Most patients with fever as their sole complaint defervesce spontaneously or present with localizing clinical or laboratory findings within 2 to 3 weeks of onset of illness (Table 95–3). Beyond 3 weeks, the patient can be considered to have a fever of unexplained or unknown origin (FUO), a designation with its own circumscribed group of management considerations, as discussed below.

Viral Infections

In young, healthy individuals, acute febrile illnesses generally represent viral infections. The causative agent is rarely established, largely because establishing the precise diagnosis seldom has major therapeutic implications. Rhinovirus, parainfluenza, or adenovirus infections usually, but not invariably, are associated with symptoms of coryza or upper respiratory tract infection (rhinorrhea, sore throat, cough, hoarseness). Enterovirus and ECHO (enteric cytopathogenic human orphan) virus infections occur predominantly in summer, usually in an epidemic setting. Undifferentiated febrile syndromes account for the majority of enteroviral infections, but the etiology is more likely to be established definitively when a macular rash, aseptic meningitis, or a characteristic syndrome such as herpangina (vesicular pharyngitis due to coxsackievirus A) or acute pleurodynia (fever, chest wall pain, and tenderness due to coxsackievirus B) is present. Serologic surveys also indicate that many arthropod-borne viruses (California encephalitis virus; eastern, western, and Venezuelan equine encephalitis; St. Louis encephalitis) usually produce mild, self-limited febrile illnesses. Influenza causes myalgias, arthralgias, and headache in addition to fever; it most often occurs in an epidemic pattern during the winter months. It is unusual, however, for fever to persist beyond 5 days in uncomplicated influenza.

The mononucleosis syndromes caused by Epstein-Barr virus, cytomegalovirus, and (rarely) *Toxoplasma gondii* may present in a typhoidal manner—that is, with fever but little or no

TABLE 95–3. INFECTIONS PRESENTING AS FEVER WITHOUT LOCALIZING SIGNS OR SYMPTOMS

INFECTIOUS AGENT	EPIDEMIOLOGY/ EXPOSURE HISTORY	DISTINCTIVE CLINICAL AND LABORATORY FINDINGS	DIAGNOSIS
Viral			
Rhinovirus, adenovirus, parainfluenza	None (adenovirus in epidemics)	Often URI symptoms	Throat and rectal cultures, serologies
Enterovirus, ECHO virus	Summer, epidemic	Occasionally, aseptic meningitis, rash, pleurodynia, herpangina	Throat and rectal cultures, serologies
Influenza	Winter, epidemic	Headache, myalgias, arthralgias	Throat cultures, serologies
EBV, CMV	(See text)		
Colorado tick fever	Southwest, Northwest, tick exposure	Biphasic illness, leukopenia	Blood, CSF cultures, erythrocyte-associated viral antigen (indirect immunofluorescence)
Bacterial			
Staphylococcus aureus	IV drug users, patients with intravenous plastic cannulas, hemodialysis, dermatitis	Must exclude endocarditis	Blood cultures
Listeria monocytogenes	Depressed cell-mediated immunity	One half have meningitis	Blood, CSF cultures
Salmonella typhi, S. paratyphi	Food or water contaminated by carrier or patient	Headache, myalgias, diarrhea or constipation, transient rose spots	Early blood, bone marrow cultures; late stool culture
Streptococci	Valvular heart disease	Low-grade fever, fatigue, anemia	Blood cultures
Post Animal Exposure			
Coxiella burnetii (Q fever)	Infected livestock	Retrobulbar headache, occasionally pneumonitis, hepatitis, culture-negative endocarditis	Serologies
Leptospira interrogans	Water contaminated by urine from dogs, cats, rodents, small mammals	Headache, myalgias, conjunctival suffusion Biphasic illness Aseptic meningitis	Serologies
Brucella sp.	Exposure to cattle or contaminated dairy products	Occasionally epididymitis	Blood cultures, serologies
Granulomatous Infection			
Mycobacterium tuberculosis	Exposure to patient with tuberculosis, known positive tuberculin skin test	Back pain suggests vertebral infection; sterile pyuria or hematuria suggests renal infection	Liver, bone marrow histology, cultures
Histoplasma capsulatum	Mississippi and Ohio River valleys	Pneumonitis, oropharyngeal lesions	Serologies; histology and cultures on liver, bone marrow, oral lesions

ECHO = Enteric cytopathogenic human orphan; URI = upper respiratory infection; EBV = Epstein-Barr virus; CMV = cytomegalovirus; CSF = cerebrospinal fluid; IV = intravenous.

lymphadenopathy. Diagnosis and management are discussed below under "Generalized Lymphadenopathy," the more typical presentation of these processes.

Colorado tick fever is a disease caused by arbovirus and transmitted by tick bite. Viremia is prolonged, lasting about 4 weeks. The illness is biphasic—2 to 3 days of fever followed by a similar period of remission, then a second febrile episode. Some patients have rash, pericarditis, or aseptic meningitis.

The above syndromes are self-limited and untreatable. The impetus for establishing a specific diagnosis, therefore, is small. The differentiation between viral and other causes of febrile illnesses is, on the other hand, of critical importance. Viral cultures of throat and rectum and virus-specific antibodies in acute and convalescent serum samples may allow retrospective diagnosis of viral etiology. Usually, however, the fever is gone long before results of serologies become available.

Bacterial Infections

Bacterial disease may cause septicemia, which dominates the clinical presentation (see Chapter 96). *Staphylococcus aureus* frequently causes sepsis, sometimes without an obvious primary site of infection. Fever may be the predominant clinical manifestation of the illness. S. aureus sepsis should be considered in patients undergoing intravenous therapy with a plastic cannula, hemodialysis patients, intravenous drug users, and patients with severe chronic dermatoses. In the patient with S. aureus bacteremia, the question of whether intravascular infection exists is key in determining the length of therapy. The following are more typical of endocarditis: community-acquired infection, long duration of symptoms, absence of removable focus of infection (e.g., intravenous cannula, soft tissue abscess), metastatic sites of infection (e.g., septic pulmonary emboli, arthritis, meningitis), and new heart murmur. Listeria monocytogenes septicemia is seen predominantly in patients with depressed cell-mediated immunity. One half of patients with Listeria sepsis have meningitis. Occasionally, a relatively indolent clinical syndrome belies the bacterial etiology of S. aureus and L. monocytogenes bacteremia.

Enteric fevers also may present in a subacute fashion despite the presence of bacteremia. The major species producing this syndrome are Salmonella typhi, which has a human reservoir, and S. paratyphi A, B, and C. The paratyphoid strains also have their major reservoir in humans but produce less severe disease than S. typhi. S. typhi is acquired by ingestion of food or water contaminated with fecal material from a chronic carrier or a patient with typhoid fever. A large number of bacteria (10^6 to 10^8) must be ingested to cause disease in the normal host. Major host risk factors are achlorhydria, malnutrition, malignancy (particularly lymphomas and leukemias), sickle cell anemia, and other defects in cellular and humoral immunity. Major protective mechanisms are gastric acidity and fatty acid products of bacteria composing the normal gut flora. Salmonella typhi penetrates the gut wall and enters the lymphoid follicles (Peyer's patches), where it multiplies within mononuclear phagocytes and produces local ulceration. Primary bacteremia occurs with spread to the reticuloendothelial system (liver, spleen, and bone marrow). After further multiplication at those sites, a secondary bacteremia occurs and can localize to lesions such as tumors, aneurysms, and bone infarcts. Infection of the gallbladder, particularly in the presence of gallstones, leads to the chronic carrier state. Approximately 2 weeks after exposure, patients develop prolonged fever with chills, headache, and myalgias. Diarrhea or constipation may be present but usually does not dominate the clinical picture. Crops of rose spots (2- to 4-mm erythematous maculopapular lesions) appear on the upper abdomen but are evanescent. Untreated, typhoid fever usually resolves in about 1 month. However, complication rates are high owing to bowel perforation, metastatic infection, and general debility of patients. Salmonella typhi may be isolated from blood or stool to confirm the diagnosis. Culture of the bone marrow often is positive early in the course of disease. Typhoid fever should be treated with chloramphenicol, 50 mg/kg/day given intravenously or orally, for 2 weeks. Chloramphenicol-resistant strains of S. typhi have appeared in Mexico, India, and Vietnam and should be treated with ampicillin, 100 mg/kg/day given intravenously or orally, or trimethoprim, 320 to 640 mg/day, with sulfamethoxazole, 1600 to 3200 mg/day. Ampicillin becomes the drug of choice in endocarditis or infected aneurysms (because of its bactericidal activity) and in patients with sickle cell anemia, in whom the dose-related bone marrow suppression by chloramphenicol is unacceptable.

Localized bacterial infection can be clinically occult and present as an undifferentiated febrile syndrome. Intra-abdominal abscess, vertebral osteomyelitis due to S. aureus or Pseudomonas aeruginosa, streptococcal pharyngitis, urinary tract infection, infective endocarditis, and early pneumonia may all cause fever with surprisingly few clinical clues to the location of the infection. Therefore, urinalysis, throat and blood cultures, and chest radiography should be performed in the febrile patient presenting with features suggestive of a bacterial infection.

Febrile Syndromes Associated with Animal Exposure

Q fever, brucellosis, and leptospirosis are diseases associated with exposure to fluids from infected animals and may have similar clinical presentations.

Q Fever. Q fever is an underrecognized cause of acute febrile illness. Coxiella burnetii, the causative agent, produces mild infection in livestock. Humans are infected by inhalation of aerosolized particles or by contact with placental and amniotic fluids from infected animals. The source of animal exposure may go unnoticed. For example, in an outbreak of Q fever at the University of Colorado Medical School, 70 per cent of infected individuals lacked direct exposure to infected sheep.

Q fever characteristically begins explosively with severe, often retrobulbar headache, high fever, chills, and myalgias. Pneumonitis and hepatitis may occur but are seldom severe. Diagnosis usually is based on a fourfold rise in titer of complement-fixing antibodies. Untreated, Q fever lasts 2 to 14 days. C. burnetii is sensitive to tetracycline, which should be used in its treatment (2 gm/day orally for 14 days). Q fever may cause endocarditis, apparently as a form of reactivation of infection. The occurrence of hepatomegaly and thrombocytopenia in a patient with apparently culture-negative endocarditis may be a clue to this diagnosis.

Leptospirosis. Humans are infected with Leptospira interrogans by exposure to urine from infected dogs, cats, wild mammals, and rodents. Exposure on the farm, in the slaughterhouse, on camping trips, or during swims in contaminated water is frequent. After an incubation period of about 1 week, patients develop chills, high fever, headache, and myalgias. The illness often pursues a biphasic course. During the second phase of illness, fever is less prominent, but headache and myalgias are excruciating, and nausea, vomiting, and abdominal pain become prominent complaints. Aseptic meningitis is the most important manifestation of the second or immune phase of the illness. Suffusion of the bulbar conjunctivae, with visible corkscrew vessels surrounding the limbus, is a useful early sign, suggesting the diagnosis of leptospirosis. Lymphadenopathy, hepatomegaly, and splenomegaly may occur. Leptospirosis also may pursue a more severe clinical course characterized by renal and hepatic dysfunction and hemorrhagic diathesis. Although darkfield examination will reveal leptospires in body fluids, most laboratories do not have the expertise to identify the organisms. The diagnosis is made, rather, by a fourfold rise in indirect hemagglutination antibody titer. Antibiotic treatment shortens the duration of fever and may reduce complications. However, to be effective, antibiotics must be initiated presumptively, before serologic confirmation. Penicillin G, 2.4 to 3.6 million units/day, or tetracycline, 2.0 gm/day given orally, is effective therapy.

Brucellosis. *Brucella* species infect the genitourinary tract of cattle (*Brucella abortus*), pigs (*B. suis*), and goats (*B. mellitensis*). Humans are exposed occupationally or by ingestion of unpasteurized dairy products. Acute disease is characterized by chills, fever, headache, arthralgias, and sometimes lymphadenopathy, hepatomegaly, and splenomegaly. During the associated bacteremia, any organ may be seeded. Epididymo-orchitis is one of the more characteristic findings. With or without antibiotic treatment of the acute infection, brucellosis may relapse or enter a chronic phase. *Brucella* species can be isolated from blood or other normally sterile fluids. However, the laboratory should be alerted to the suspicion of this infection, since the organism requires special conditions for growth. Otherwise, diagnosis must be made serologically. Treatment consists of tetracycline, 2 gm/day given orally for 21 days, and streptomycin, 1.0 gm/day administered intramuscularly for 14 days. Trimethoprim, 480 mg/day, with sulfamethoxazole, 2400 mg/day given orally, is an acceptable alternative regimen.

Granulomatous Infection

Tuberculosis. Extrapulmonary and miliary tuberculosis may present as febrile syndromes. In disseminated tuberculosis, initial chest radiographs may be normal, and tuberculin skin tests often are nonreactive. Protracted fevers of uncertain origin should always suggest this possibility. Liver biopsy and bone marrow biopsy should be performed and have a high yield in miliary disease. Genitourinary and vertebral tuberculosis may present as unexplained fever. However, careful history, urinalysis, intravenous pyelography, and radiographs of the spine should reveal the site of tissue involvement. Extrapulmonary tuberculosis should be treated with isoniazid, 300 mg orally,

rifampin, 600 mg orally, ethambutol, 15 mg/kg/day, and pyrazinamide, 15–30 mg/kg (maximum, 2 gm/day), given orally, for the first 2 months. Thereafter, isoniazid and rifampin are continued for 7 months, and longer in cases of skeletal tuberculosis. The ethambutol can be discontinued once the organism is shown to be sensitive to isoniazid. Corticosteroids may be a useful adjunctive measure in the patient with severe systemic toxicity; steroids should be tapered as soon as the patient shows symptomatic improvement.

Histoplasmosis. Most individuals living in endemic areas in the Mississippi and Ohio River valleys have a subclinical, self-limited febrile illness as a manifestation of acute pulmonary histoplasmosis. Although patients may complain of chest pain or cough, physical examination of the chest usually is unremarkable despite radiographic findings of infiltrates and mediastinal and hilar adenopathy. Therefore, in the absence of chest radiographs, the lower respiratory tract component of the illness is easily overlooked. A complement fixation titer of at least 1:32 or a fourfold rise in titer is suggestive of the diagnosis of acute histoplasmosis. Although spontaneous resolution of symptoms is the norm, unusually prolonged illness (more than 2 to 3 weeks) may require antifungal treatment with amphotericin B or ketoconazole.

Progressive disseminated histoplasmosis may occur as a consequence of reactivation of latent infection in immunosuppressed individuals or may reflect an uncontained or poorly contained primary infection. The febrile illness in such patients is protracted, and the differential diagnosis is that of FUO. Oropharyngeal nodules and ulcerative lesions are commonly found in disseminated histoplasmosis. Biopsy of such lesions permits rapid diagnosis. Serologies are less helpful in disseminated histoplasmosis, as they are positive in only one third of cases; cultures and methenamine silver stains of bone marrow biopsy specimens, however, should establish the diagnosis. Disseminated histoplasmosis is treated with amphotericin B, 0.5 to 0.6 mg/kg/day administered intravenously for a total dose of 2 to 3 gm. Ketoconazole, 400 mg/day for 6 to 12 months, appears to be an effective alternative for patients who are unable to tolerate amphotericin B.

Other. Malaria produces febrile paroxysms that in some cases occur every 48 to 72 hours. The diagnosis should be suspected in travelers who have returned from endemic areas, intravenous drug users, and recipients of blood transfusions. *Plasmodium falciparum* causes a high level of parasitemia and is associated with a high mortality rate unless recognized and treated promptly. Daily fevers may be seen early in the course of this form of malaria. Although *P. vivax* and *P. malariae* may cause relapse long after primary infection, owing to latent extraerythrocytic infection, the course is milder. Demonstration of parasites in blood smears establishes the diagnosis of malaria.

Many, if not most, infectious diseases may present with fever as an early finding, with subclinical or eventual clinical involvement of specific organ systems. Examples include cryptococcosis, coccidioidomycosis, psittacosis, *Legionella* species and *Mycoplasma pneumoniae* infections. Pulmonary involvement by these infectious agents tends to produce few signs on physical examination; chest radiographs often reveal more prominent abnormalities than are suspected clinically.

Fever and Rash

Some of the febrile syndromes already discussed may occasionally be associated with a skin rash (Table 95–4). This section, however, considers diseases in which rash is a prominent feature of the presentation.

Bacterial Diseases

Petechial lesions, purpura, and ecthyma gangrenosum are lesions associated with bacteremia (see Chapter 96). Disseminated gonococcemia causes sparse vesiculopustular, hemorrhagic, or necrotic lesions on an erythematous base, typically on the

TABLE 95–4. DIFFERENTIAL DIAGNOSIS OF INFECTIOUS AGENTS PRODUCING FEVER AND RASH

Maculopapular Erythematous
  Enterovirus
  EBV, CMV, *Toxoplasma gondii*
  HIV
  Colorado tick fever virus
  Salmonella typhi
  Leptospira interrogans
  Measles virus
  Rubella virus
  Hepatitis B virus
  Treponema pallidum
Vesicular
  Varicella-zoster
  Herpes simplex virus
  Coxsackie A virus
Cutaneous Petechiae
  Neisseria gonorrhoeae
  Neisseria meningitidis
  Rickettsia rickettsii (RMSF)
  Rickettsia typhi (murine typhus)
  Viridans streptococci (endocarditis)
Diffuse Erythroderma
  Streptococcus sp. (scarlet fever)
  Staphylococcus aureus (toxic shock syndrome)
Distinctive Rash
  Ecthyma gangrenosum — *Pseudomonas aeruginosa*
  Erythema chronicum migrans — Lyme disease
Mucous Membrane Lesions
  Vesicular pharyngitis — Coxsackie A virus
  Palatal petechiae — rubella, EBV, scarlet fever (group A streptococci)
  Erythema — toxic shock syndrome (*Staphylococcus aureus*)
  Oral ulcer-nodular lesion — *Histoplasma capsulatum*
  Koplik's spots — measles virus

HIV = Human immunodeficiency virus; RMSF = Rocky Mountain spotted fever.

extremities, particularly their dorsal surfaces (see Chapter 107). Meningococcemia is also an important cause of fever and a petechial skin rash that may be sparse.

Bacterial toxins produce characteristic clinical syndromes. Pharyngitis or other infections with an erythrogenic toxin-producing *Streptococcus* may lead to scarlet fever. Diffuse erythema begins on the upper chest and spreads rapidly, although sparing palms and soles. Small red petechial lesions are found on the palate, and the skin has a sandpaper texture caused by occlusion of the sweat glands. The tongue at first shows a yellowish coating and then becomes beefy red. The rash of scarlet fever heals with desquamation. *Corynebacterium hemolyticum* also produces pharyngitis and skin rash.

Toxic shock syndrome (TSS) was first recognized as a distinct entity in 1978 and became epidemic in 1980 and 1981, probably because of the marketing of hyperabsorbable tampons. *Staphylococcus aureus* strains producing toxic shock syndrome toxin (TSST-1) or other closely related exotoxins cause the syndrome. TSST-1 is a potent stimulus of IL1 production by mononuclear phagocytes and enhances the effects of endotoxin; these properties may be important in the pathogenesis of this syndrome. Most cases have occurred in 15- to 25-year-old females using tampons. Other settings include prolonged use of contraceptive diaphragms, vaginal or cesarean deliveries, and nasal surgery. TSS in males usually is caused by superficial staphylococcal infections and abscesses. Patients with TSS develop the abrupt onset of high fever (temperature >40°C), hypotension, nausea and vomiting, severe watery diarrhea and myalgias, followed in severe cases by confusion and oliguria. Characteristically, diffuse erythroderma (a sunburn-like rash) with erythematous mucosal surfaces is apparent. Later, intense scaling and desquamation of skin, particularly of the palms and soles, occurs. Laboratory abnormalities include elevated liver and muscle enzymes levels, thrombocytopenia, and hypocalcemia. Diagnosis is based on the clinical findings and requires specific exclusion of Rocky Mountain spotted fever, meningococcemia, leptospirosis, and measles. Management of the patient consists of restoring an adequate circulatory blood volume by administration of intravenous fluids, removal of tampons if present, and treatment of the staphylococcal infection with nafcillin, 12 gm/day intravenously. Vancomycin is the alternative therapy for nafcillin-resistant staphylococci. Patients must be advised against using tampons in the future, as TSS often recurs within 4 months of the initial episode if tampon use continues.

A streptococcal toxic shock–like syndrome associated with scarlet fever toxin A has recently been documented as a complication of group A streptococcal soft tissue infections. Major manifestations include cellulitis and/or fasciitis with septicemia, shock, acute respiratory distress syndrome, renal failure, hypocalcemia, and thrombocytopenia. Treatment consists of high-dose penicillin and supportive measures. The mortality remains high (greater than 30 per cent) with optimal current therapy.

Viral Infections (Table 95–5)

The rashes associated with viral infections may be so typical as to establish unequivocally the cause of the febrile syndrome. Varicella-zoster requires special consideration because of the availability of an effective antiviral drug, acyclovir. In the normal host, neither chickenpox nor herpes zoster confined within specific dermatomes requires treatment with antiviral agents. Ophthalmic zoster demands antiviral treatment, since it is associated with potentially severe complications, including orbital compression syndromes and intracranial extension. Acyclovir is also effective in decreasing the severity of chickenpox in immunocompromised children and in limiting the extradermatomal spread of zoster in immunocompromised adults.

Rickettsial Diseases

In the United States, three rickettsial diseases are endemic: Rocky Mountain spotted fever (RMSF), Q fever, and murine typhus. Rash is not a characteristic of Q fever. RMSF is a misnomer, as most cases occur in the southeastern United States. The causative organism, *Rickettsia ricketts-ii*, is transmitted from dogs (or small wild animals) to ticks to humans. Infection occurs primarily during warmer months, periods of greatest tick activity. About two thirds of patients cite a history of tick exposure. After 2 to 14 days, there is the fulminant onset of severe frontal headache, chills, fever, myalgias, conjunctivitis, and, in one fourth, cough and shortness of breath. At this point, the diagnosis may be particularly obscure. Rash characteristically begins on the third to fifth day of illness as 1- to 4-mm erythematous macules on hands, wrists, feet, and ankles. Palms and soles may be involved. The rash spreads to the trunk and may become petechial. Intravascular coagulopathy develops in some severely ill patients. Diagnosis and institution of appropriate therapy should be based on the clinical findings. The specific complement fixation test shows a rise in titers and allows retrospective confirmation of the diagnosis. Treatment is with chloramphenicol, 50 mg/kg given orally or parenterally, or tetracycline, 25 to 50 mg/kg/day administered orally for 7 days.

Lyme Disease

Lyme disease is a common, multisystem spirochetal infection caused by *Borrelia burgdorferi* and transmitted by the tick *Ixodes dammini*. Initial case reports were clustered in several major foci (the Northeast, Wisconsin and Minnesota, California, and Oregon), but it is now clear that this infection is distributed broadly throughout North America and Western Europe. Three days to 3 weeks after the tick bite, of which most individuals are unaware, patients develop a febrile illness, usually associated with headache, stiff neck,

TABLE 95–5. FEVER AND RASH IN VIRAL INFECTION

Coxsackie/ECHO virus	Maculopapular "rubelliform": 1–3 mm, faint pink, begins on face, spreading to chest and extremities "Herpetiform": vesicular stomatitis with peripheral exanthem (papules and clear vesicles on an erythematous base), including palms and soles (hand, foot, and mouth disease)	Summertime, no itching or lymphadenopathy; multiple cases in household, or community-wide epidemic; mostly diseases of children
Measles	Erythematous, maculopapular rash begins on upper face and spreads down to involve extremities, including palms and soles; Koplik's spots are bluishgray specks on a red base found on buccal mucosa near second molars; atypical measles occurs in individuals who received killed vaccine, then are exposed to measles; the rash begins peripherally and is urticarial, vesicular, or hemorrhagic	Incubation period, 10–14 days; first, severe upper respiratory symptoms, coryza, cough, conjunctivitis; then Koplik's spots, then rash
Rubella	Maculopapular rash beginning on face and moving downward; petechiae on soft palate	Incubation, 12–35 days; adenopathy: posterior auricular, posterior cervical, and suboccipital
Varicella	Generalized vesicular eruption; lesions in different stages from erythematous macules to vesicles to crusted; spread from trunk centrifugally Zoster—see text	Incubation, 14–15 days; late winter, early spring
Herpes simplex virus	Oral primary: small vesicles on pharynx, oral mucosa, which ulcerate; painful and tender. Recurrent: vermillion border, one or few lesions. Genital: see Chapter 107.	Incubation, 2–12 days
Hepatitis B	Prodrome in one fifth; erythematous maculopapular rash, urticaria	Arthralgias, arthritis; abnormal liver function tests; hepatitis B antigenemia
EBV	Erythematous, maculopapular rash on trunk and proximal extremities; occasionally urticarial or hemorrhagic	Transiently occurs in 5–10% of patients during first week of illness
HIV	Maculopapular truncal rash may occur as early manifestation of infection	Associated fever, sore throat, and lymph node enlargement may persist for 2 or more wk

myalgias, arthralgias, and erythema chronicum migrans (ECM). ECM begins as a red macule or papule at the site of the tick bite; the surrounding bright red patch expands to a diameter of up to 15 cm. Partial central clearing often is seen. The centers of lesions may become indurated, vesicular, or necrotic. Several red rings may be found within the outer border. Smaller secondary lesions may appear within several days. Lesions are warm but nontender. Enlargement of regional lymph nodes is common. The skin rash usually fades in about 1 month.

Several weeks after the onset of symptoms, important neurologic manifestations occur in more than 15 per cent of patients. Most characteristic is meningoencephalitis with cranial nerve involvement and peripheral radiculoneuropathy. Bell's palsy may occur as an isolated phenomenon; when associated with fever, this finding is strongly suggestive of Lyme disease. The cerebrospinal fluid (CSF) at this time shows about 100 lymphocytes per milliliter. Heart involvement also may become manifest as atrioventricular block, myopericarditis, or cardiomegaly.

Joint involvement eventually occurs in 60 per cent of patients. Early in the course, arthralgias and myalgias may be quite severe. Months later, arthritis often develops, with marked swelling and little pain in one or two large joints, typically the knee. Episodes of arthritis may recur for months or years; in about 10 per cent of patients, the arthritis becomes chronic, and erosion of cartilage and bone occurs. Diagnosis is suspected on clinical grounds and confirmed by demonstration of IgM antibody to the spirochete, which peaks by the third to sixth week. Total serum IgM is increased, as are IgM-containing immune complexes and cryoglobulins. The level of IgM is reflective of disease activity and predictive of neurologic, cardiac, and joint involvement. Serologic studies are, however, not precise. Antibody titers may be negative in early disease, and early antibiotic therapy may blunt the antibody response. Synovial fluid contains an average of 25,000 cells per milliliter, most of them neutrophils.

Treatment of the early manifestations of Lyme disease with doxycycline, 100 mg twice daily for 14 to 21 days, usually prevents late complications. Meningitis, cardiac involvement, or arthritis should be treated with aqueous penicillin G, 20 million units, or intravenous ceftriaxone, 4 gm/day for 14 to 21 days. Repeated courses may be necessary if relapses occur.

TABLE 95–6. INFECTIOUS DISEASES ASSOCIATED WITH GENERALIZED LYMPHADENOPATHY BUT WITH OTHER DOMINANT FEATURES

Viral—measles, rubella, hepatitis B
Bacterial—scarlet fever, brucellosis, leptospirosis, tuberculosis, syphilis, Lyme disease

Fever and Lymphadenopathy

Many infectious diseases are associated with some degree of lymphadenopathy (Table 95–6). However, in some, lymphadenopathy is a major manifestation of the disease. These can be further divided according to whether lymphadenopathy is generalized or regional.

Generalized Lymphadenopathy

The mononucleosis syndromes are important causes of fever and generalized lymphadenopathy.

Mononucleosis Syndromes

Epstein-Barr Virus (EBV). Approximately 90 per cent of American adults have serologic evidence of EBV infection; most infections are subclinical and occur before the age of 5 years or midway through adolescence.

Clinically manifest infectious mononucleosis usually develops late in adolescence after intimate contact with asymptomatic oropharyngeal shedders of EBV. Patients develop sore throat, fever, and generalized lymphadenopathy and sometimes experience headache and myalgias. Five to 10 per cent of patients have a transient rash that may be macular, petechial, or urticarial. Palatal petechiae often are present, as is pharyngitis, which may be exudative. Cervical lymphadenopathy, particularly involving the posterior lymphatic chains, is prominent, although some involvement elsewhere is common. The spleen is minimally enlarged in about 50 per cent of patients. Although rare, autoimmune hemolytic anemia, thrombocytopenia, encephalitis or aseptic meningitis, Guillain-Barré syndrome, hepatitis, or splenic rupture may dominate the clinical presentation. Three fourths of patients present with an absolute lymphocytosis. At least one third of their lymphocytes are atypical in appearance: large, with vacuolated basophilic cytoplasm, rolled edges often deformed by contact with other cells, and lobulated, eccentric nuclei. Immunologic studies indicate that some circulating B cells are infected with EBV and that the cells involved in the lymphocytosis are mainly cytotoxic T cells capable of damaging EBV-containing lymphocytes. Atypical lymphocytes are not restricted to infectious mononucleosis but may be seen in other viral illnesses.

B cell infection with EBV is a stimulus to production of polyclonal antibodies. Antibodies to foreign red cells (heterophile) can be helpful in the diagnosis. Rapid diagnostic tests, such as the Monospot test, have, however, largely replaced the need for heterophile determination. The Monospot test is sensitive and specific; false-positive results occur rarely in patients with lymphoma or hepatitis. Some patients with EBV infection show delayed development of heterophile antibodies. Recourse to determination of antibodies to EBV is necessary only in atypical, heterophile-negative cases. The presence of IgM antibody to viral capsid antigen is diagnostic of acute infectious mononucleosis. The appearance of antibody to EBV nuclear antigen also is indicative of EBV infection.

Infectious mononucleosis pursues a surprisingly benign course even in patients with neurologic involvement. The fever resolves after 1 to 2 weeks, although residual fatigue may be protracted. Occasional patients have a persistent or recurrent syndrome with fever, headaches, pharyngitis, lymphadenopathy, arthralgias, and serologic evidence of chronic active EBV infection. Patients should be managed symptomatically. Acetaminophen may be useful for sore throat. Antibiotics, particularly ampicillin, should be avoided. The use of ampicillin causes a skin rash in almost all patients with EBV infection. Corticosteroids are indicated in the rare individual with serious hematologic involvement (i.e., thrombocytopenia, hemolytic anemia).

Acute bacterial superinfections of the pharynx and peritonsillar abscesses should be considered when the course is unusually septic.

The differential diagnosis of heterophile-negative mononucleosis is shown in Table 95–7.

Cytomegalovirus (CMV). Serologic surveys indicate that most adults have been infected with CMV. The ages of peak incidence of CMV infection are in the perinatal period (transmission by breast milk) and during the second to fourth decade. CMV shares with the other Herpesviridae the propensity to reactivate, particularly in immunosuppressed patients.

Two modes of transmission of CMV are particularly important in the development of lymphadenopathy in otherwise healthy adults. CMV can be transmitted sexually. Semen is an excellent source for viral isolation. The frequency of antibody to CMV and active viral excretion is particularly high in male homosexuals. Blood transfusions carry a risk of approximately 3 per cent per unit of blood for transmitting CMV infection. This risk becomes substantial in the setting of open heart surgery or multiple transfusions for other indications.

Primary infection with CMV causes about 50 per cent of cases of heterophile-negative mononucleosis. The distinction between CMV and EBV may be impossible on clinical grounds alone. However, CMV tends to involve older patients (mean age, 29) and produce milder disease, that is, it may be typhoidal in its presentation, that is, fever with little or no adenopathy. The infrequent but serious forms of neurologic and hematologic involvement that occur in EBV infection also can occur with CMV. In addition, pneumonitis and hepatitis (which may be granulomatous) may be found. Isolation of CMV from urine or semen and

demonstration of conversion of serologies (indirect fluorescent antibody test or complement fixation) from negative to positive are useful in establishing etiology. However, in groups such as male homosexuals, in whom asymptomatic excretion of CMV is found frequently, viral isolation alone is inadequate for determining the etiology of lymphadenopathy. CMV mononucleosis is a self-limited disease that does not require or respond to specific therapy. CMV infection in the immunocompromised host may be life-threatening; in this setting, it often responds to long-term therapy with ganciclovir.

Acute Acquired Toxoplasmosis. *Toxoplasma gondii* is acquired by ingesting oocysts contaminating meat and other foods or by exposure to cat feces. In certain geographic areas, such as France, 90 per cent of individuals have serologic evidence of *Toxoplasma* infection. In the United States, the figure is close to 50 per cent by age 50. Ten to 20 per cent of infections in normal adult hosts are symptomatic. Presentation may take the form of a mononucleosis-like syndrome, although maculopapular skin rash, abdominal pain due to mesenteric and retroperitoneal lymphadenopathy, and chorioretinitis also may occur. Striking lymph node enlargement and involvement of unusual chains (occipital, lumbar) may necessitate lymph node biopsy to exclude lymphoma. Overall, however, toxoplasmosis accounts for less than 1 per cent of mononucleosis-like illnesses. Histologically, focal distention of sinuses with mononuclear phagocytes, histiocytes blurring the margins of germinal centers, and reactive follicular hyperplasia indicate *Toxoplasma* infection. Acute acquired toxoplasmosis is suggested by conversion of the indirect fluorescent antibody test from negative to positive or a fourfold increase in titer. Usually the titer is greater than 1:1000 and is associated with increased specific IgM antibody. Acute acquired toxoplasmosis generally is self-limited in the immunologically intact host and does not require specific therapy. Significant involvement of the eye is an indication for treatment with pyrimethamine plus sulfadiazine.

Granulomatous Disease. Disseminated tuberculosis, histoplasmosis, and sarcoidosis may be associated with generalized lymphadenopathy, although involvement of certain lymph node chains can predominate. Lymph node biopsy shows granulomas or nonspecific hyperplasia.

Persistent Generalized Lymphadenopathy (PGL) Patients infected by the human immunodeficiency virus (HIV) (see Chapter 108) may develop lymph node enlargement in at least two extrainguinal sites, persisting for at least 3 months, thereby fulfilling the standard diagnostic criteria for PGL. Additional symptoms such as fever, night sweats, fatigue, diarrhea, and weight loss may develop as the severity of immunodeficiency increases. Among individuals belonging to groups at increased risk for acquired immunodeficiency syn-

TABLE 95–7. DIFFERENTIAL DIAGNOSIS OF HETEROPHILE-NEGATIVE MONONUCLEOSIS

EBV mononucleosis (particularly in children)
CMV
Acute toxoplasmosis
Streptococcal pharyngitis
Hepatitis B
Acute HIV infection

drome (AIDS), the presence of generalized lymphadenopathy also could represent Kaposi's sarcoma, CMV infection, toxoplasmosis, tuberculosis, cryptococcosis, B cell lymphoma, or syphilis. Lymph node biopsy in a patient with HIV-related PGL is rarely necessary. A serum VDRL should be performed to exclude secondary syphilis. A tuberculin skin test should also be performed.

Regional Lymphadenopathy

Pyogenic Infection. *Staphylococcus aureus* and group A streptococcal infections produce acute suppurative lymphadenitis. The most frequently affected lymph nodes are submandibular, cervical, inguinal, and axillary, in that order. Involved nodes are large (>3 cm), tender, and firm or fluctuant. Pyoderma, pharyngitis, or periodontal infection may be present and the presumed primary site of infection. Patients are febrile and have a leukocytosis. Fluctuant nodes should be aspirated. Otherwise, antibiotic therapy should be directed toward the most common pathogens. Penicillin G therapy is appropriate if pharyngeal or periodontal origin implicates a streptococcal or mixed anaerobic infection. Skin involvement suggests possible staphylococcal infection and is an indication for nafcillin (or dicloxacillin) therapy. The dosage and route of administration of the drug should be determined by the severity of the infection.

Tuberculosis. Scrofula, or tuberculous cervical adenitis, presents in a subacute to chronic fashion. Fever, if present, is low-grade. A large mass of matted lymph nodes is palpable in the neck. If *Mycobacterium tuberculosis* is the causative organism, other sites of active infection usually are present. The most common causative agent in children in the United States is *M. scrofulaceum*. Infection with this and other drug-resistant nontuberculous mycobacteria usually requires surgical excision.

Cat-Scratch Disease. Chronic regional lymphadenopathy following exposure to cats or cat scratch should suggest the diagnosis. Histopathologic studies indicate a gram-negative bacterial origin of this syndrome. About 1 week after contact with the cat, a local papule or pustule may develop. One week later, regional adenopathy appears. Lymph nodes may be tender (sometimes exquisitely so) or just enlarged (1 to 7 cm). Fever is low-grade if present at all. Lymph node enlargement usually persists for several months. Lymph node biopsy shows necrotic granulomas with giant cells and stellate abscesses surrounded by epithelial cells. Pleomorphic gram-negative bacilli ("cat-scratch bacilli") can be identified by the Warthin-Starry silver stain in lymph node biopsies during the first 4 weeks of illness. The diagnosis can usually be established on clinical grounds. The course usually is self-limited and benign in immunocompetent individuals but may be life-threatening in

persons with severe immunodeficiency. The best approach to treatment of cat-scratch disease in the immunocompromised patient is not known; apparent responses to erythromycin, doxycycline, or antimycobacterial drugs have been described in small numbers of patients.

Ulceroglandular Fever. Tularemia is the classic cause of ulceroglandular fever. The syndrome is acquired by contact with tissues or fluids from an infected rabbit or the bite of an infected tick. Patients have chills, fever, an ulcerated skin lesion at the site of inoculation, and painful regional adenopathy. When infection is acquired by contact with rabbits, the skin lesion usually is on the fingers or hand, and lymph node involvement is epitrochlear or axillary. In tick-borne transmission, the ulcer is on the lower extremities, perianal region, or trunk, and the adenopathy is inguinal or femoral. Most cases are diagnosed serologically, as Gram-stained preparations usually are negative, and culture of the causative organism, *Francisella tularensis*, is hazardous. A fourfold rise in agglutination titer is diagnostic. Patients should be treated presumptively with streptomycin, 15 to 20 mg/kg/day for 7 to 10 days.

Oculoglandular Fever. Conjunctivitis with preauricular lymphadenopathy can occur in tularemia, cat-scratch disease, sporotrichosis, lymphogranuloma venereum infection, listeriosis, and epidemic keratoconjunctivitis due to adenovirus.

Inguinal Lymphadenopathy. Inguinal lymphadenopathy associated with sexually transmitted diseases (see Chapter 107) may be bilateral or unilateral. In primary syphilis, enlarged nodes are discrete, firm, and nontender. Early lymphogranuloma venereum causes tender lymphadenopathy with later matting of involved nodes, and sometimes fixation to overlying skin, which assumes a purplish hue. The lymphadenopathy of chancroid is very painful and composed of fused lymph nodes. Tender inguinal lymphadenopathy also occurs in primary genital herpes simplex virus infection.

Plague. Bubonic plague usually presents as fever, headache, and a large mat of inguinal or axillary lymph nodes, which go on to suppurate and drain spontaneously. Plague is an important consideration in the acutely ill patient with possible exposure to fleas and rodents in the southwestern United States. If plague is suspected, blood cultures and aspirates of the buboes should be obtained, and tetracycline, 30 to 50 mg/kg/day, plus streptomycin, 30 mg/kg/day, instituted. Gram-stained preparations of the aspirate reveal gram-negative rods in two thirds of cases. A fluorescent antibody test allows rapid specific diagnosis and is available through the Centers for Disease Control.

FEVER OF UNDETERMINED ORIGIN (FUO)

Fever of undetermined origin is the term applied to febrile illnesses with temperatures exceeding

101°F that are of at least 3 weeks' duration and remain undiagnosed after 1 week in hospital. The evaluation of an FUO remains among the most challenging problems facing the physician. The majority of illnesses that cause FUO are treatable, making pursuit of the diagnosis particularly rewarding. There is no substitute for a meticulous history and physical examination. These should be repeated frequently during the patient's hospital course, as frequent questioning of the patient may jar an important historical clue from the patient and important physical findings may develop while the patient is in the hospital. These clues may direct the next series of diagnostic studies. Patients with unexplained fevers should be evaluated for their risk of HIV infection and should be offered HIV testing if at risk or if ancillary clinical or laboratory findings (e.g., thrush, generalized lymph node enlargement, lymphocytopenia) are suggestive of HIV infection. Directed biopsies of lesions should be stained and cultured for pathogenic microbes. In many instances, however, localizing clues are not present or fail to yield rewarding information. In these cases, bone marrow biopsy can reveal granulomatous or neoplastic disease, even in the absence of clinical evidence of bone marrow involvement. Similarly, liver biopsy may also reveal the etiology of an FUO, but seldom in the absence of any clinical or laboratory evidence of liver disease. Exploratory laparotomy is generally not helpful unless signs, symptoms, or laboratory data point to abdominal pathology. Recent refinements in computed tomography may assist in determining the need for laparotomy in

TABLE 95-8. FEVER OF UNDETERMINED ORIGIN*

> **Infections**
>   Intra-abdominal abscesses
>   Subphrenic
>   Splenic
>   Diverticular
>   Liver and biliary tract
>   Pelvic
>   Mycobacterial
>   Cytomegalovirus
>   Infection of the urinary tract
>   Sinusitis
>   Osteomyelitis
>   Catheter infections
>   Other infections
> **Neoplastic diseases**
>   Hematologic neoplasms
>   Non-Hodgkin's lymphoma
>   Leukemia
>   Hodgkin's disease
>   Other
>   Solid tumors
> **Collagen diseases**
> **Granulomatous diseases**
> **Miscellaneous**
> **Factitious fever**
> **Undiagnosed**

*Adapted from Larson EB, Featherstone HJ, Petersdorf RG Fever of undetermined origin: Diagnosis and follow-up of 105 cases, 1970–1980. Medicine 61:269–292, 1982. ©1982, The Williams & Wilkins Company, Baltimore.

cases of FUO. If tuberculosis remains a reasonable possibility after careful work-up fails to establish a diagnosis, an empiric trial of antituberculous therapy may be initiated while awaiting results of bone marrow, liver, and urine cultures.

Table 95-8 indicates the final diagnosis in a study of over 100 cases of FUO observed in the decade 1970 to 1980. This table simply emphasizes the range of diagnostic possibilities to be considered. Numbers in each category are not presented, as regional and temporal variations in the frequency of specific diagnoses are great. Infectious diseases were the cause of about one third of these cases; another third were due to neoplasms; the remainder were due to connective tissue disorders, granulomatous diseases, and other illnesses.

Causes of FUO

Infections

Abscesses account for as many as one third of infectious causes of FUO. Most of these abscesses are intra-abdominal or pelvic, as abscesses elsewhere (e.g., lung, brain, or superficial abscesses) are readily identifiable radiographically or as a result of the signs or symptoms they produce.

Intra-abdominal abscesses generally occur as a complication of surgery or leakage of visceral contents, as might be seen with perforation of a colonic diverticulum. Surprisingly, large abdominal abscesses may be present with few localizing symptoms. Abscesses of the liver (see Chapter 102) occur as a consequence of inflammatory disease of the biliary tract or of the bowel; in the latter instance, bacteria reach the liver via portal blood flow. Occasionally, blunt trauma predisposes to abscesses of the liver or spleen. Hepatic, splenic, or subdiaphragmatic abscesses are generally readily detected by ultrasonography or computed tomography (CT) scan. Diagnosis of intra-abdominal abscess may, however, be challenging, since even large abscesses in the pericolonic spaces may be difficult to distinguish from fluid-filled loops of bowel on CT scan. Gallium scanning, ultrasonography, or barium enemas may assist if the diagnosis is suspected and CT scans are not definitive.

Endovascular infections (infective endocarditis, mycotic aneurysms, infected atherosclerotic plaques) are uncommon causes of FUO, since blood cultures are generally positive unless the patient has received antibiotics within the preceding 2 weeks. Infections of intravascular catheter sites generally are also associated with bacteremia unless the infection is limited to the insertion site. Diagnosis of endovascular infection is more difficult to make when blood cultures are negative and infection is due to slow-growing or fastidious organisms, such as *Brucella* species, *Coxiella burnetii* (Q fever), or *Haemophilus* species. It is especially difficult among patients who have been treated with antimicrobials. If endocarditis is suspected, blood cultures should be repeated for at least 1 week after antimicrobials are discontinued, the bacteriology laboratory should be alerted to the possibility of infection due to a fastidious organism, and evidence of valvular vegetations should be sought by two-dimensional echocardiography. A transesophageal echocardiogram may be helpful if the two-dimensional study is equivocal. Occasionally, the suspicion of valvular infection is strong enough to warrant empiric antibiotic treatment of a presumed culture-negative endocarditis.

Although most patients with osteomyelitis have pain at the site of infection, localizing symptoms are occasionally absent and patients present only with fever. Technetium pyrophosphate bone scans and gallium scans demonstrate uptake at sites of osteomyelitis, but positive scans are not always specific for infection.

Mycobacterial infections, generally due to M. tuberculosis, are important causes of FUO. Patients with impaired cell-mediated immunity are at particular risk for disseminated tuberculosis, and occult infection with this organism is seen with particular frequency among patients with renal failure who are undergoing hemodialysis. Fever may be the only sign of this infection. Both among immunocompromised patients and previously well persons with disseminated tuberculosis, purified protein derivative (PPD) skin tests are often negative. In some patients, careful review of chest radiographs reveals apical calcifications or upper lobe scars suggestive of remote tuberculous infection. A diffuse, often subtle, radiographic pattern of "millet seed" densities, best appreciated on the lateral chest views, is highly suggestive of disseminated tuberculosis. In this setting, transbronchial or open lung biopsy will establish the diagnosis. Similar radiographic patterns may be seen in sarcoidosis, disseminated fungal infection (e.g., histoplasmosis), and some malignancies. Bone marrow or liver biopsy often reveals granulomas, and cultures of these sites are positive in 50 to 90 per cent of disseminated tuberculosis.

Viral infections such as those caused by CMV or EBV can produce prolonged fevers. Both infections may be seen in young, healthy adults. Recipients of blood are at risk for acute post-transfusion CMV infection. Recipients of organ transplantation and other immunosuppressed patients may experience reactivation of latent CMV infection producing fever, leukopenia, and pulmonary and hepatic disease. Lymph nodes are often enlarged in EBV infection, and peripheral blood smear usually reveals a lymphocytosis with increased numbers of atypical lymphocytes. Occasionally, the atypical lymphocytosis is delayed several weeks after the onset of fever. A positive Monospot test may clarify the diagnosis. Unexplained fever may be a complication of infection with HIV; most such fevers are attributable to complicating opportunistic pathogens (see Chapter 108).

Simple lower urinary tract infections are readily diagnosed by symptoms and urinalysis. Compli-

cated infections such as perirenal or prostatic abscess may be occult and present as FUO. Generally there is a history of antecedent urinary tract infection or disorder of the urinary tract. In prostatic abscess the prostate is usually tender on rectal examination. In suspected cases of perirenal and prostatic abscess, the urinalysis should be repeated if it is initially normal, as abnormalities of the sediment may be intermittent. Ultrasonography or CT scan will detect most of these lesions.

Although most patients with sinusitis have localizing symptoms, infections of the paranasal sinuses may occasionally present with fever only, particularly among hospitalized patients who have had nasotracheal and/or nasogastric intubation. Sinus films reveal fluid in the sinuses. Infection of the sphenoid sinus may be difficult to detect unless special views or CT scans are obtained.

Neoplastic Diseases

Neoplasms account for approximately one third of cases of FUO. Some tumors particularly those of hematologic origin and hypernephromas, release endogenous pyrogens. In others the mechanism of fever is less clear but may result from pyrogen release by infiltrating or surrounding inflammatory cells. Lymphomas can present as FUO; usually there is enlargement of lymph nodes or spleen. Some lymphomas present with intra-abdominal disease only. CT scan may be helpful in detecting these tumors. Leukemia also may present as FUO, sometimes with a normal peripheral blood smear. Bone marrow examination reveals an increased number of blast forms. Hypernephroma, atrial myxoma, primary hepatocellular carcinoma, and tumor metastatic to the liver also may present as FUO. Liver function abnormalities (predominantly alkaline phosphatase) are common in all these tumors except atrial myxoma. Myxoma can be suspected in the presence of heart murmur and multisystem embolization (mimicking endocarditis) and is readily diagnosed by echocardiogram. Radiographic studies of the abdomen and retroperitoneum (CT scan or ultrasonography) generally detect the other tumors. Colon carcinoma also must be considered in the differential diagnosis, since as many as a third or more of patients with this diagnosis may present with low-grade fever, and in some this is the only sign of disease.

Other Causes of FUO

Collagen vascular diseases account for approximately 10 per cent of cases of FUO. Systemic lupus erythematosus is readily diagnosed serologically and thus accounts for a small proportion of cases of FUO. Vasculitis remains an important cause of FUO and should be suspected in febrile patients with "embolization/infarctions" or with "multisystem disease." Giant cell arteritis should be considered in older patients with FUO, particularly in the presence of polymyalgia rheumatica symptoms (see Chapter 85). Juvenile rheumatoid arthritis, or Still's disease, can present as FUO with joint symptoms. An evanescent rash, sore throat, and leukocytosis occur in this disorder, which is diagnosed on the basis of clinical criteria in the absence of other potential causes of fever.

Granulomatous diseases without a defined etiology have been associated with FUO. Sarcoidosis is a multisystem granulomatous disorder often involving the lungs, skin, and lymph nodes. The majority of patients are anergic to skin test antigens. Diagnosis is based upon the demonstration of discrete, noncaseating granulomas on biopsy of bone marrow, liver, lung, or other tissues. Granulomatous hepatitis can present with prolonged fevers, occasionally lasting for years. Serum alkaline phosphatase levels are generally elevated; liver biopsy reveals granulomas, and no underlying etiology can be demonstrated.

A number of miscellaneous disorders make up the remainder of FUO cases, including Crohn's disease, familial Mediterranean fever, and hypertriglyceridemia. Drug-related fevers and recurrent pulmonary emboli always demand consideration in the differential diagnosis. A significant minority of FUOs (approximately 10 per cent) remain undiagnosed after careful evaluation. The majority of these patients have experienced an undefinable but self-limited illness, with fewer than 10 per cent of these patients developing an underlying serious disorder after several years' follow-up.

Factitious or Self-Induced Fever. Patients with factitious or self-induced illness present unique ethical and therapeutic problems. Once the possibility of factitious or self-induced illness is considered, the doctor-patient relationship is changed. Typically, the physician can rely on the good faith of the patient's history. In the case of factitious or self-induced illness, the physician must assume a more detached role to establish the diagnosis. Patients with factitious fever are typically young, often female. Many have been or are employed in health-related professions. Usually articulate and well-educated, these patients are adept at manipulating their family, friends, and physicians. In these instances, a consultant new to the patient may provide a detached and helpful perspective on the problem.

Clues to factitious fever include the absence of a toxic appearance despite high temperature readings, lack of an appropriate rise in pulse rate with fever, and absence of the physiologic diurnal variation in temperature. Suspected factitious readings can be evaluated by immediately repeating the reading with the nurse or physician in attendance. Use of electronic thermometers allows rapid and accurate recording of a patient's temperature (see also Chapter 112).

Self-injection of pyrogen-containing substances, usually bacteria-laden culture medium, urine, or feces, can produce bacteremia and high fever; usually these bacteremic episodes are polymicrobial and intermittent, often suggesting a diagnosis of intra-abdominal abscess. However, patients with self-induced bacteremia may appear remarkably well between episodes of fever, in contrast to most patients with abscesses. The occurrence of polymicrobial bacteremia in an otherwise healthy person should suggest the possibility of self-induced infection. Illicit ingestion of medications known by the patient to produce fever can also present a very difficult diagnostic problem. Clues to the presence of self-induced illness are subtle. The patients are often emotionally immature; some exaggerate their importance and fabricate unrelated aspects of their history. Some are surprisingly stoic about the apparent seriousness of their illness and the procedures employed to diagnose or treat them. In some instances, interview of family members can elicit clues to the possibility of factitious or self-induced illness. Confirming the diagnosis is crucial and, in many instances, requires search of the patient's hospital room. Although most will deny their role in inducing or feigning illness, the diagnosis must be explained, and psychiatric care is essential. These complicated patients are at risk for inducing life-threatening disease; some respond to psychiatric counseling.

REFERENCES

Aduan RP, Fauci AS, Dale DC, et al: Factitious fever and self-induced infection. A report of 32 cases and review of the literature. Ann Intern Med 90:230–242, 1979.

Dinarello CA, Cannon JG, Wolff S: New concepts of the pathogenesis of fever. Rev Infect Dis 10:168–169, 1988.

Larson EB, Featherstone HJ, Petersdorf RG: Fever of undetermined origin: Diagnosis and follow-up of 105 cases, 1970–1980. Medicine 61:269–292, 1982.

96 BACTEREMIA AND SEPTICEMIA

The clinical syndromes of septicemia and septic shock are due to local or circulating microbial products. These syndromes may occur without demonstrable bacteremia (Table 96–1). In fact, bacteremia is documented in only half the cases of septic shock. About 40 per cent of documented episodes of gram-negative bacillary bacteremia are, however, accompanied by shock (a blood pressure less than 80 mm Hg systolic, unresponsive to volume replacement).

TABLE 96–1. SEPTICEMIA WITH NEGATIVE BLOOD CULTURES

Prior administration of antibiotics
Severe local infection (often intra-abdominal, mixtures of aerobic and anaerobic bacteria)
Fastidious, slow-growing organisms in blood
Toxemia—toxic shock syndrome
Rarely, severe infections due to organisms not routinely cultured (e.g., mycobacteria, fungi, viruses, rickettsiae, mycoplasma)

TABLE 96–2. RISK FACTORS FOR SEPSIS

Underlying Disease or Condition
  Immunodeficiency—hypogammaglobulinemic states, neutropenia
  Immunosuppression—corticosteroid and cytotoxic drug treatment, e.g., renal allograft recipients
  Leukemia and lymphoma
  Advanced solid tumors
  Metabolic diseases—uremia, chronic liver disease, diabetes mellitus
  Neurologic diseases—paraplegia
  Intravenous drug use
  Severe burns, trauma
Invasive Medical Devices/Instrumentation
  Indwelling urinary catheter
  Plastic intravenous cannula
  Monitoring devices (arterial line, Swan-Ganz catheter)
  Genitourinary instrumentation
Therapeutic Procedures
  Hemodialysis
  Genitourinary or abdominal surgery
  Splenectomy
Community-Acquired Infections
  Pneumonia
  Pyelonephritis
  Meningitis
  Obstruction, gastrointestinal or genitourinary
  Perforation of viscera
Hospital-Acquired Infections
  Urinary tract
  Biliary tract
  Pneumonia
  Wound infection

The presence of bacteria in the blood indicates that the rate of entrance of organisms from a local infection into the circulation exceeds the capacity of the clearance mechanisms of the reticuloendothelial system and the capillary beds. The bacteremia may be low-grade, intermittent, and of little consequence. As the intensity of the local infection increases, however, high-grade bacteremia itself causes symptoms and signs, justifying the designation septicemia. In pneumococcal bacteremia, for example, mortality increases only when more than 1000 colony-forming units of pneumococci are present per milliliter of blood. Quantitative blood cultures rarely are performed, however, so that the intensity and significance of bacteremia must be judged on clinical grounds.

EPIDEMIOLOGY

Septicemia due to gram-negative enteric organisms is the most serious infectious disease of medical progress. Only 100 cases of gram-negative bacteremia were reported before 1920. Bacteremias among the Enterobacteriaceae were virtually restricted to *Escherichia coli* and *Salmonella* species. Antibiotic usage has been associated with a dramatic increase in occurrence of gram-negative rod bacteremia; a broadening of the spectrum of causative agents to include *Klebsiella, Pseudomonas, Serratia, Enterobacter,* and *Proteus*; and an increase in the fraction of bacteremic episodes resulting from hospital-acquired infections. Other factors that contribute to the upsurge in frequency of gram-negative sepsis are use of invasive monitoring devices and indwelling catheters, extensive surgical procedures, and the growing number of immunosuppressed patients. Patient groups at particular risk of sepsis are shown in Table 96–2. Overall, an estimated 100,000 to 300,000 cases of gram-negative bacteremia occur in the United States each year.

Gram-negative septicemia may occur without a recognized tissue site of origin; however, more commonly it is secondary to infection in the urinary tract, lungs, peritoneal cavity, biliary tract, soft tissue, or wounds.

Gram-positive bacteremia, particularly that caused by *Staphylococcus aureus*, also has become an increasing problem owing to the nonsterile use of intravenous drugs and the therapeutic placement of chronic venous access sites.

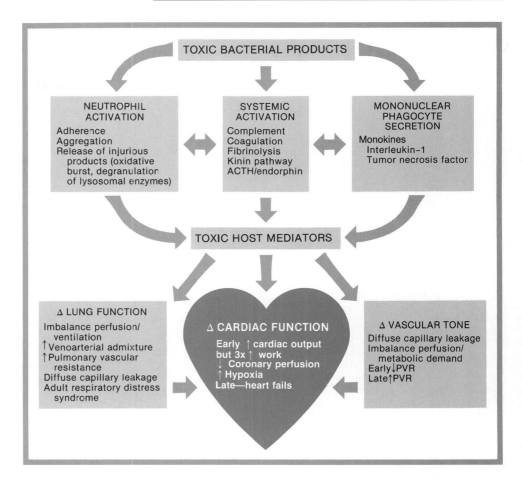

FIGURE 96–1. Pathogenesis and pathophysiology of septic shock. ACTH = Adrenocorticotropin; PVR = peripheral vascular resistance.

PATHOGENESIS

Toxic bacterial products account for the cardiovascular and ventilatory derangements characterizing septic shock, as depicted in Figure 96–1. The main toxic product in gram-negative organisms is endotoxin; in gram-positive organisms, the peptidoglycan/teichoic acid complex; and, in yeast, polysaccharide substances. In some cases, initiation of antibiotic treatment may be associated with massive release of toxic microbial products, precipitating septic shock. This may explain the effectiveness of antibodies against endotoxin, as discussed below. The released microbial products are responsible for intravascular activation of the complement, clotting, and fibrinolytic pathways and may directly activate neutrophils. Bacterial products induce release of interleukin-1 (IL1) and cachectin/tumor necrosis factor (TNF) by mononuclear phagocytes. IL1, TNF, and possibly other cytokines are key mediators of the clinical syndrome of septicemia. IL1 and TNF both cause fever and appear to act synergistically in the pathogenesis of shock. IL1, in addition, promotes release of neutrophils from the bone marrow, and both IL1 and TNF induce hepatic synthesis of acute phase reactants associated with inflammation (haptoglobin, C-reactive protein). Recent laboratory studies support a dominant role for TNF in the pathogenesis of septic shock.

CLINICAL FINDINGS

The history and physical examination usually indicate the site of origin of the bacteremia. The findings attributable to septic shock depend on whether the patient is evaluated early or late. Shaking chills, often accompanied by nausea, vomiting, and diarrhea, mark the early toxic state characteristic of "warm shock." Patients appear hot, dry, flushed, and animated. Hyperventilation, confusion, apprehension or lethargy, and obtundation are apparent. In "cold shock." patients are cold, clammy, hypotensive, and lethargic. At this stage, findings of end-organ dysfunction due to hypoperfusion may predominate. These include a bleeding diathesis, jaundice, cyanosis, congestive heart failure, oliguria, and acidosis.

Skin lesions, when present, are particularly helpful, since they not only suggest sepsis but also may provide a clue to the specific etiology. Ecthyma gangrenosum is a round or oval lesion 1 to

15 cm in diameter, with a central vesicle that evolves into a necrotic ulcer, set on an erythematous, indurated base. The typical lesion is caused by *Pseudomonas* species septicemia in neutropenic hosts and results from direct infection of blood vessel walls by bacteria. Other Enterobacteriaceae, particularly *Aeromonas* and *Serratia* species, cause similar lesions on occasion. *Candida tropicalis* may cause hyperpigmented macular lesions in the neutropenic patient. Vesiculobullous and petechial skin lesions, cellulitis, and diffuse erythema also may appear in the septic patient. A sunburn-like rash also is characteristic of the toxic shock syndrome (see Chapter 95). Biopsy and aspiration of skin lesions sometimes allow rapid etiologic diagnosis (see Chapter 93). For example, smears of material expressed from purpuric lesions have a high diagnostic yield (>80 per cent) in meningococcemia.

LABORATORY FINDINGS

The white blood cell count is increased or decreased, with an increased proportion of circulating immature neutrophils (band forms). Vacuolization of circulating neutrophils is a useful finding, since it suggests bacterial infection with a high probability of bacteremia. Such changes as toxic granulations and Döhle bodies (pale intracytoplasmic inclusions), on the other hand, merely are indicative of neutrophil immaturity. The platelet count may be decreased in sepsis, the prothrombin and partial thromboplastin times are prolonged, and the bilirubin and blood urea nitrogen are increased. Sometimes laboratory abnormalities relating to specific end-organ damage are so striking that misdiagnosis or faulty localization of the site of infection may result. An example is the disseminated intravascular coagulation of sepsis that may be suggestive of a primary hematologic disease. Jaundice may develop as the result of hepatic damage.

Bacteriologic diagnosis is, of course, essential. Gram-stained preparations should be prepared from urine, sputum, and pus (see Chapter 93). The Gram stain not only allows rapid diagnosis but also may indicate organisms that are not easily cultured (e.g., fastidious, slow-growing bacteria in-

TABLE 96–3. FACTORS AFFECTING SELECTION OF ANTIBIOTICS IN THE PATIENT WITH PRESUMED SEPSIS

Community or hospital acquisition of infection
Underlying disease of the host, particularly the presence of neutropenia
Likely source of bacteremia
Organisms suspected on clinical grounds
Results of previous cultures from the patient
Meningitis present
Prevailing sensitivities of bacteria in the hospital, particularly patterns of aminoglycoside resistance and prevalence of methicillin-resistant staphylococci

cluding anaerobes). The Gram and Wright stains of a buffy coat smear also may be extremely helpful, as intracellular organisms, particularly gram-positive cocci and meningococci, are present in more than one third of cases of sustained bacteremia. Three sets of blood cultures should be obtained, each from a different venipuncture site.

Most patients with fever and confusion should have a lumbar puncture. If meningitis is present, the selection of antibiotics must ensure good penetration into cerebrospinal fluid.

TREATMENT AND OUTCOME

The mortality of bacteremic shock remains in the range of 20 to 60 per cent, depending upon the clinical population, despite rapid institution of what should be effective antibiotics. In large part, the adverse outcome reflects a lethal bacterial load at the time of diagnosis and/or a serious underlying disease.

Management of the infection dictates removal of such potential infective foci as intravenous catheters, surgical drainage of accessible abscesses, and administration of appropriate antibiotics. The possibility of infected intravenous catheters or intravenous infusates should be considered at the first suggestion of sepsis. Stabilization and survival may depend on interrupting the vicious circle that culminates in septic shock. If the setting suggests toxic shock syndrome (e.g., a menstruating woman with a rash and a tampon in place), the foreign body should be removed and any local focus of staphylococcal infection incised and drained.

Appropriate antibiotics should be administered immediately. The selection of antibiotics depends on a number of factors indicated in Table 96–3. Two antibiotics with overlapping activities clearly are necessary to treat *Pseudomonas* species infection in neutropenic patients and probably in patients with severe burns. In general, the administration of synergistic combinations of antibiotics also appears to be associated with improved outcome in patients with severe underlying disease. An additional rationale for two-drug regimens stems from problems incurred by the use of aminoglycosides in most patients with sepsis. Treatment with a second effective agent is particularly important while aminoglycoside pharmacokinetics are being assessed and dosage schedules optimized in the individual patient. In addition, aminoglycosides are ineffective when the pH is low, as may occur in pulmonary infection. Initial antibiotic regimens suggested for patients with sepsis are presented in Table 96–4. If blood cultures are negative at 48 hours and there is no evidence of serious local infection, consideration should be given to stopping the antibiotics. If toxic shock syndrome is suspected, the patient should be treated with an antistaphylococcal drug, despite negative blood culture.

Hemodynamic stabilization of the patient with septic shock requires assessment of cardiac function. This usually necessitates monitoring with a central venous or a Swan-Ganz catheter. In the warm stage of shock, peripheral vascular resistance and left ventricular end-diastolic pressure (LVEDP) are decreased; isotonic intravenous fluids are needed, sometimes in large amounts. Pressors may be necessary as well. Dopamine is the inotropic agent of choice, since it increases cerebral, coronary, renal, and mesenteric perfusion when used at low doses. Some patients require intubation and mechanical ventilation, including positive end-expiratory pressure, to maintain acceptable oxygenation. In the cold state of shock, congestive heart failure with increased LVEDP limits the use of fluids.

Controlled studies do not support the use of corticosteroids in septic shock. A promising new approach to the management of septic shock is to detoxify bacterial products. Although still of uncertain value, administration of an IgM monoclonal antibody directed against the lipid A core of endotoxin appears to improve survival from gram-negative bacteremia and from gram-negative bacteremia with shock. The commercial availability of this and similar products will have an immediate impact on the management of patients with presumed sepsis. The use of monoclonal antibodies directed against bacterial toxins or host proteins mediating sepsis (IL1 and TNF) and corresponding receptor antagonists ultimately may revolutionize management.

The optimal use of preventive measures would have the greatest impact on the morbidity and mortality of septic shock. The pneumococcal polysaccharide vaccine, for example, is effective and available but tremendously underutilized. Antibiotics should be used only when indicated and then in narrow spectrum and for appropriately short intervals. Intravenous catheters and indwelling urinary catheters should be used only when unavoidable; when necessary, they should be inserted, changed at regular intervals, and maintained by experienced personnel, preferably organized in special teams. The duration of endotracheal intubation and mechanical ventilation should be kept to a minimum.

TABLE 96–4. ANTIBIOTIC REGIMENS FOR THE SEPTIC PATIENT

CLINICAL SETTING	LIKELY BACTERIA	ANTIBIOTICS
Uncertain source	Enterobacteriaceae Staphylococcus	Gentamicin* or tobramycin +third-generation cephalosporin +vancomycin*
Abdominal or pelvic source likely	Enterobacteriaceae Enterococcus Bacteroides fragilis	Gentamicin or tobramycin +ampicillin +metronidazole
Neutropenic patient	Pseudomonas species Enterobacteriaceae Staphylococcus species	Tobramycin +mezlocillin +vancomycin*

*Selection of an aminoglycoside and an antistaphylococcal drug depends on patterns of bacterial sensitivity in the individual hospital.

REFERENCES

Sheagren JN: Shock syndromes related to sepsis. In Wyngaarden JB, Smith LH Jr, Bennett JC (eds): Cecil Textbook of Medicine. 19th ed. Philadelphia, WB Saunders Co, 1992, pp 1584–1588.

Tracey KJ, Beutler B, Lowry SF, et al: Shock and tissue injury induced by recombinant human cachectin. Science 234:470, 1986.

Young LS, Martin WJ, Meyer RD, et al: Gram-negative rod bacteremia: Microbiologic, immunologic and therapeutic considerations. Ann Intern Med 86:456, 1977.

Ziegler EJ, Fisher CJ, Sprung CL, et al: Treatment of Gram-negative bacteremia and septic shock with HA-1A human monoclonal antibody against endotoxin. N Engl J Med 324:429, 1991.

97 INFECTIONS OF THE NERVOUS SYSTEM

Infections of the central nervous system (CNS) range from fulminating, readily diagnosed septic processes to indolent illnesses requiring exhaustive searches to identify their presence and define their cause. Neurologic outcome and survival depend largely on the extent of CNS damage present before effective treatment begins. Accordingly, it is essential that the physician move quickly to achieve a specific diagnosis and institute appropriate therapy. The initial evaluation must, however, take into account both the urgency of beginning antibiotic treatment in bacterial meningitis and the potential hazard of performing a lumbar puncture in the presence of focal neurologic infection or mass lesions.

Patients with CNS infection present with some combination of fever, headache, altered mental status, depressed sensorium, seizures, focal neurologic signs, and stiff neck. The history and physical examination, results of lumbar puncture (Table 97–1), and neuroradiographic procedures provide the mainstays of diagnosis. The order in which the last two procedures are performed is critical. A subacute history, evolving over 7 days to 2 months, of unilateral headache with focal neurologic signs and/or seizures implies a mass lesion that may or may not be infectious. A brain-imaging procedure should be performed first; lumbar puncture is potentially dangerous, as it may precipitate cerebral herniation, even in the absence of overt papilledema. By contrast, patients admitted with fulminating symptoms of fever, headache, lethargy, confusion, and stiff neck should have an immediate lumbar puncture and, if this test proves abnormal, antibiotics should be instituted for presumed bacterial meningitis. If the distinction between focal and diffuse CNS infection is unclear or not adequately evaluable, as in the comatose patient, cultures of blood, throat, and nasopharynx should be obtained, antibiotic therapy started, and an emergency scanning procedure performed. If the last is unavailable, lumbar puncture should be delayed pending evidence that no danger of herniation exists. Inevitably, this approach means that some patients will receive parenteral antibiotics several hours before a lumbar puncture is performed. In acute bacterial meningitis, 50 per cent of cerebrospinal fluid (CSF) cultures will be negative by 4 to 12 hours after institution of antibiotics; negative CSF cultures are even more likely if the causative organism is a sensitive pneumococcus. Should the CNS infection actually represent acute bacterial meningitis, however, the characteristics of the CSF still would suggest the diagnosis, since neutrophilic pleocytosis and hypoglycorrhachia (low CSF sugar) usually persist for at least 12 to 24 hours after antibiotics are instituted. Furthermore, Gram-stained preparation (or assay for microbial antigen in the CSF by latex agglutination) should indicate the causative organism even after antibiotics have rendered the CSF culture-negative. Blood and nasopharyngeal cultures obtained before therapy also are likely to be positive in view of the high frequency of isolation of causative organisms from these sites. The approach of treating suspected CNS infections promptly ("shoot first, tap later") is often life-saving and does not significantly compromise management. This approach to the use of scanning procedures is germane only for adults with community-acquired CNS infection. In children, technically adequate computed tomography (CT) scans require heavy sedation; therefore, scanning procedures must be reserved for more stringent indications.

Armed with the clinical presentation and the results of the lumbar puncture and CT scan, the clinician must decide on a probable cause and develop a plan for initial management and definitive evaluation. The task is simplified by addressing the following issues:

1. Is the host normal? The spectrum of CNS diseases and their causes shifts dramatically in the immunocompromised host (see Table 97–2). The possibility of human immunodeficiency virus (HIV) infection must be determined expeditiously by serologies. Primary HIV infection may cause CNS signs and symptoms prior to seroconversion, requiring additional testing if the suspicion is sufficiently high (see Chapter 108).

2. Are there relevant exposures? Exposure to persons with syphilis, tuberculosis, or HIV may be associated with acquisition of same. Ticks may transmit Lyme disease or spotted fever, and mosquitoes, arboviral encephalitis. Exposure to livestock or unpasteurized dairy products suggests brucellosis. Residence in the Ohio and Mississippi River valleys increases the risk of histoplasmosis and blastomycosis; coccidioidomycosis is endemic to semiarid regions of the Southwest. Travel and particularly residence in developing countries may suggest cysticercosis, echinococcal cyst disease, and cerebral malaria.

3. Does the patient have meningitis, encephalitis, or meningoencephalitis? Is the disease acute, subacute, or chronic? These distinctions narrow the differential diagnosis considerably and form the basis for organization of the sections that follow. The meningitis syndrome consists of fever, headache, and stiff neck. Confusion and a depressed level of consciousness may occur as part of the metabolic encephalopathy in patients with acute bacterial meningitis. Seizures are rare and may indicate complicating processes such as cortical vein thrombosis. In contrast, encephalitis characteristically causes confusion, bizarre behavior, depressed levels of consciousness, focal signs and seizures (grand mal or focal). A presentation sug-

TABLE 97–1. TYPICAL CSF FINDINGS IN CNS INFECTION

INFECTION	CELLS	NEUTROPHILS	GLUCOSE	PROTEIN
Bacterial meningitis	500–10,000/μl	>90%	<40 mg/dl	>150 mg/dl
Aseptic meningitis	10–500/μl	Early >50%; late <20%	Normal	<100 mg/dl
Herpes simplex virus encephalitis	0–1000/μl	<50%	Normal	<100 mg/dl
Tuberculosis meningitis	50–500/μl	Early >50%; late <50%	<30 mg/dl	>150 mg/dl
Syphilitic meningitis	50–500/μl	<10%	<40 mg/dl	<100 mg/dl

gestive of encephalitis raises a variety of issues quite different from those surrounding a patient with bacterial meningitis.

MENINGITIS

Definition. Meningitis is an inflammation of the leptomeninges caused by infectious or noninfectious processes. The most common types of infectious meningitis are bacterial, viral, tuberculous, and fungal. The most common noninfectious causes are subarachnoid hemorrhage, cancer, and sarcoidosis. Infectious meningitis is considered in three categories: acute bacterial meningitis, aseptic meningitis, and subacute to chronic meningitis.

Acute Bacterial Meningitis

Epidemiology. Three fourths of cases of acute bacterial meningitis occur before the age of 15 years. *Neisseria meningitidis* causes sporadic disease or epidemics in closed populations. Most cases occur in winter and spring and involve children less than 5 years of age. *Haemophilus influenzae* meningitis is even more selectively a disease of childhood, most cases developing by the age of 10 years. Infections are sporadic, although secondary cases may occur in close contacts. In contrast, pneumococcal meningitis is a disease seen in all age groups. Extensive clinical series of adults hospitalized 20 years ago showed a relative frequency of 68 per cent pneumococcal, 18 per cent meningococcal, and 10 per cent *H. influenzae* meningitis. At University Hospitals of Cleveland in the period from 1972 to 1981, the relative frequencies were 40 per cent, 30 per cent, and 20 per cent, respectively, in keeping with the general experience that serious *H. influenzae* infections are increasingly common in adults.

Close contact with a patient with meningococcal or *H. influenzae* disease is particularly important in the development of secondary cases of meningitis and other severe disease manifestations (sepsis, epiglottitis) as well. For example, the risk of meningococcal disease is 500 to 800 times greater in a close contact of a patient with meningococcal meningitis than in a noncontact. Asymptomatic pharyngeal carriers of *Haemophilus influenzae* also can spread infection to their contacts.

Pathogenesis and Pathophysiology. The bacteria that cause most community-acquired meningitis transiently colonize the oropharynx and nasopharynx of healthy individuals. Meningitis may occur in nonimmune hosts following bacteremia from an upper respiratory site (meningococcus or *Haemophilus influenzae*) or pneumonia and by direct spread from contiguous foci of infection (nasal sinuses, mastoids).

The pathogenesis of acute bacterial meningitis is best understood for meningococcal disease. The carrier state occurs when meningococci adhere to pharyngeal epithelial cells via specialized filamentous structures termed pili. The production of IgA

TABLE 97–2. MENINGITIS AND MENINGOENCEPHALITIS IN THE IMMUNOCOMPROMISED HOST

ABNORMALITY	INFECTIOUS AGENT
Complement deficiencies (C6–C8)	*Neisseria meningitidis*
Splenectomy and/or antibody defect	*Streptococcus pneumoniae* *Haemophilus influenzae* Enterovirus *Neisseria meningitidis*
Sickle cell disease	*Streptococcus pneumoniae* *Haemophilus influenzae*
Impaired cellular immunity	*Listeria monocytogenes* *Cryptococcus neoformans* *Toxoplasma gondii* *Histoplasma capsulatum* *Coccidioides immitis* *Mycobacterium tuberculosis* *Treponema pallidum* J C virus Cytomegalovirus

protease by pathogenic *Neisseria* species favors adherence by inactivating IgA, a major host barrier to colonization. Organisms enter and pass through epithelial cells to subepithelial tissues, where they multiply in the nonimmune individual and produce bacteremia. The localization of organisms to the CSF is not well understood but presumably depends on invasive properties of the capsular polysaccharide, which permit penetration of the blood-brain barrier. Immunity is conferred by bactericidal antibody and presumably is acquired by earlier colonization of the pharynx with nonpathogenic meningococci and cross-reacting bacteria. The presence of blocking IgA antibody may increase susceptibility transiently in some individuals.

Table 97–2 summarizes host factors conferring a particular risk of meningitis. Bacterial meningitis remains confined to the leptomeninges and does not spread to adjacent parenchymal tissue. Focal and global neurologic deficits develop because of involvement of blood vessels coursing in the meninges and through the subarachnoid space; in addition, cranial nerves and cerebral tissue can be affected by the attendant inflammation, edema, and scarring as well as by the development of obstructive hydrocephalus.

Gram-negative enteric meningitis occurs mainly in severely debilitated persons or individuals whose meninges have been breached or damaged by head trauma, a neurosurgical procedure, or a parameningeal infection.

Clinical Presentation. Patients with bacterial meningitis may present with fever, headache, lethargy, confusion, irritability, and stiff neck. There are three principal modes of onset. About 25 per cent of cases begin abruptly with fulminant illness; mortality is high in this setting. More often, meningeal symptoms progress over 1 to 7 days. Finally, meningitis may superimpose itself on 1 to 3 weeks of an upper respiratory–type illness; diagnosis is most difficult in this group. Occasionally, no more than a single additional neurologic symptom or sign hints at disease more serious than a routine upper respiratory infection. Stiff neck is absent in about one fifth of all patients with meningitis, notably in the very young, the old, and the comatose. A petechial or purpuric rash is found in one half of patients with meningococcemia; although not pathognomonic, palpable purpura is very suggestive of *N. meningitidis* infection. About 20 per cent of patients with acute bacterial meningitis have seizures, and a similar fraction have focal neurologic findings.

Laboratory Diagnosis. The CSF in acute bacterial meningitis usually contains 1000 to 10,000 cells per microliter, mostly neutrophils (Table 97–1). Glucose content falls below 40 mg/dl, and the protein level rises above 150 mg/dl in most patients. The Gram-stained preparation of CSF is positive in 80 to 88 per cent of cases. However, certain cautionary notes are appropriate. Cell counts can be lower (occasionally zero) early in the course of meningococcal and pneumococcal meningitis. Also, predominantly mononuclear cell pleocytosis may occur in patients who have received antibiotics before the lumbar puncture (Table 97–3). A similar mononuclear pleocytosis may be seen in *Listeria monocytogenes* meningitis, tuberculous meningitis, and acute syphilitic meningitis. Gram-stained preparations of CSF may be negative or misinterpreted when meningitis is caused by *H. influenzae*, *N. meningitidis*, or *L. monocytogenes*; the presence of gram-negative diplococci and coccobacilli may be difficult to appreciate, particularly when the background consists of amorphous pink material. In addition, bacteria tend to be pleomorphic in CSF and may assume atypical forms. In the case of *Listeria*, CSF colony counts are low ($10^3/\mu l$). If interpretation of the Gram-stained CSF is not clear-cut, broad-spectrum antibiotics should be instituted while the results of cultures are being awaited. If the initial Gram-stained preparation does not contain organisms, examining the stained sediment prepared by concentrating up to 5 ml of CSF with a cytocentrifuge may reveal the causative organism.

Cultures of CSF, blood, fluid expressed from purpuric lesions, and nasopharyngeal swabs have a high yield. The last mentioned is particularly

TABLE 97–3. PRESENTATIONS OF BACTERIAL MENINGITIS WITHOUT POLYMORPHONUCLEAR NEUTROPHIL PREDOMINANCE

Antecedent antimicrobial therapy
Listeria monocytogenes meningitis
Tuberculous meningitis
Syphilitic meningitis

drugs do not achieve substantial levels in nasopharyngeal secretions.

Recognition of meningitis may be difficult following head trauma or neurosurgery, since the symptoms, signs, and laboratory findings of infection can be difficult to separate from those of trauma. A low CSF glucose level usually indicates infection. The causative organism, characteristically an enteric rod, may already have been cultured from an extraneural site, such as a wound or urine. The known antibiotic sensitivities of such isolates, therefore, may provide a valuable guide to the initial treatment of meningitis.

All patients with meningitis caused by *Streptococcus pneumoniae*, *H. influenzae*, and unusual agents or mixed infections should have radiographs of nasal sinuses and mastoids to exclude a parameningeal focus of infection.

Differential Diagnosis. Classic acute bacterial meningitis resembles few other diseases. Ruptured brain abscess should be considered, particularly if the CSF white blood cell count is unusually high and focal neurologic signs are present. Parameningeal foci of infection usually cause fever, headache, and local signs. CSF characteristically shows neutrophilic pleocytosis and moderately increased protein, but CSF glucose is usually normal. In patients with bacterial meningitis who have already been given antibiotic treatment, the CSF may be sterile, but neutrophils commonly are present in CSF and the glucose level is depressed. Early in the evolution of viral or tuberculous meningitis, the pleocytosis may be predominantly neutrophilic. Serial examinations, however, will show a progressive shift to a mononuclear cell predominance. Acute viral meningoencephalitis may be difficult to distinguish clinically from bacterial meningitis; the evolution of CSF findings and the clinical course usually decide the matter.

Treatment and Outcome. Bacterial meningitis requires the prompt institution of appropriate antibiotics. If the Gram-stained smear of CSF indicates pneumococcal or meningococcal disease, penicillin G should be administered intravenously in a dose of 25,000 units/kg every 2 hours (up to 24 million units/day). The alternative drug for patients with severe penicillin allergy is chloramphenicol, 25 mg/kg given intravenously every 6 hours. Suspected cases of *H. influenzae* meningitis should be treated with cefotaxime, 2 gm given intravenously every 4 hours, or ceftriaxone, 2 gm given intravenously every 12 hours. In a case of suspected community-acquired meningitis, if the Gram-stained preparation of CSF is negative, but clinical and laboratory findings suggest bacterial meningitis, penicillin and cefotaxime therapy should be started. Third-generation cephalosporins are the indicated choice for treating sensitive gram-negative enteric organisms causing meningitis. Agents such as ceftazidime, 2 gm given intravenously every 12 hours, may be effective against *Pseudomonas aeruginosa*. If the organism is resistant to cephalosporins, the patient should be treated with a combination of intraventricular plus parenteral aminoglycoside and a beta-lactam antibiotic selected on the basis of the sensitivity of the isolate (e.g., mezlocillin or piperacillin). The placement of an intraventricular reservoir facilitates treatment of such patients. Regardless of the results of sensitivity testing, chloramphenicol is not an adequate drug for treatment of gram-negative bacillary meningitis; its use has been associated with unacceptably high mortality rates.

The management of bacterial meningitis extends beyond the patient. Contacts must be protected, as they are at substantial risk of developing meningococcal meningitis or serious *H. influenzae* disease. At the time one first suspects bacterial meningitis, respiratory isolation procedures should be initiated. One should begin antibiotic prophylaxis of contacts when the clinical course or Gram-stained preparation of CSF suggests meningococcal or *H. influenzae* meningitis. The recommended drug for household and other intimate contacts of patients with meningococcal meningitis is rifampin, 10 mg/kg (up to 600 mg) twice daily for 2 days. The goal of prophylaxis of contacts of *H. influenzae* type B meningitis is to protect children less than 4 years of age. Since the organism may be passed from patient to asymptomatic adults to at-risk child, rifampin, 20 mg/kg (up to 600 mg) daily for 4 days, should be given to all members of the household and day care center of the index case who have contact with children less than 4 years old. Despite parenteral antibiotic therapy, patients with *N. meningitidis* or *H. influenzae* meningitis may have persistent nasopharyngeal carriage and should receive rifampin treatment before discharge from the hospital.

Although hospital contacts of patients with meningococcal meningitis are at low risk of acquiring the carrier state and disease, occasional secondary cases do occur. Thus personnel in close contact with the patient's respiratory secretions should receive prophylactic antibiotics. All persons receiving rifampin prophylaxis should be warned that their urine and tears will turn orange and that oral contraceptives will be inactivated temporarily by the antiestrogen effects of the drug.

About 30 per cent of adults with bacterial meningitis die of the infection. Of the survivors, deafness (6 to 10 per cent) and other serious neurologic sequelae (1 to 18 per cent) are common. The prognosis in individual cases depends largely on the level of consciousness and extent of CNS damage at the time of the first treatment. Misdiagnosis (>50 per cent of patients) and attendant delays in starting antibiotics are factors in morbidity that the physician must try to offset. Patients with fulminant meningitis should be treated with antibiotics within 30 minutes of reaching medical care. Even after antibiotic therapy and presumed cure, bacterial meningitis may recur. The pattern of recurrence usually suggests a parameningeal infective focus or dural defect (Table 97–4).

The most common types of bacterial meningitis can be prevented by vaccinating susceptible individuals. Effective polysaccharide vaccines are available for some strains of *N. meningitidis* and *S. pneumoniae* and for *H. influenzae* type B.

TABLE 97–4. 3 R's OF CNS INFECTION

R	DETERIORATION	POSSIBILITIES
Recrudescence	During Rx, same bacteria	Wrong Rx
Relapse	3–14 days after stopping treatment, same bacteria	Parameningeal focus
Recurrence	Delayed, same or other bacteria	Congenital or acquired dural defects

Aseptic Meningitis

Leptomeningitis associated with negative Gram stains of CSF and negative cultures for bacteria has been designated aseptic meningitis, a somewhat unfortunate designation that implies a benign illness that resolves spontaneously. It is important, however, to assume a high level of vigilance in this group of patients, as they may have a potentially treatable but progressive illness.

Epidemiology. Viral infections are the most frequent cause of aseptic meningitis. Of those cases in which a specific causal agent can be established, 97 per cent are due to enteroviruses (particularly Coxsackie virus B and enteric cytopathogenic human orphan [ECHO] virus), mumps, lymphocytic choriomeningitis virus (LCM), herpes simplex virus (HSV), and leptospirosis. Viral meningitis is a disease mainly of children and young adults (70 per cent of patients are less than 20 years of age). Seasonal variation reflects the predominance of enteroviral infection, so that most cases occur in summer or early fall. Mumps usually occurs in winter and LCM in fall or winter.

Pathogenesis and Pathophysiology. Localization to the meninges occurs during systemic viremia. The basis for the meningotropism of those viruses that cause aseptic meningitis is not understood. Herpes simplex virus type 2 may cause meningitis during the course of primary genital herpes.

Clinical Presentation. The syndrome of aseptic meningitis of viral origin begins with the acute onset of headache, fever, and meningismus associated with CSF pleocytosis. The headache often is described as the worst ever experienced and is exacerbated by sitting, standing, or coughing. In typical cases, the course is benign. The development of changes in sensorium, seizures, or focal neurologic signs shifts the diagnosis to encephalitis or meningoencephalitis. Additional clinical features may suggest a particular infectious agent. Patients with mumps may have or may develop parotitis or orchitis and usually give a history of appropriate contact. LCM infection often follows exposure to mice, guinea pigs, or hamsters and causes severe myalgias; an infectious mononucleosis–like illness can ensue, with rash and orchitis. Leptospirosis often follows exposure to rats or mice or swimming in water contaminated by their urine; aseptic meningitis occurs in the second phase of the illness. Aseptic meningitis also can be seen in persons with HIV infection, either as a manifestation of primary infection by the virus or as a later complication. The pleocytosis generally is modest, the protein level is only slightly elevated, and the glucose concentration is normal or slightly depressed. HIV serology may be negative with early infection and should therefore be repeated if suspicion is high (see Chapter 108).

Laboratory Diagnosis. In viral meningitis, the CSF shows a pleocytosis of 10 to 2000 white blood cells per microliter. Two thirds of patients have mainly neutrophils in the initial CSF specimen. However, serial lumbar punctures reveal a rapid shift (within 6 to 8 hours) in the CSF differential count toward a mononuclear cell predominance. CSF protein is normal in one third of cases and almost always less than 100 mg/dl. The CSF glucose level characteristically is normal, although minimal depression occurs in mumps (30 per cent of cases), in LCM (60 per cent), and less frequently in ECHO virus and HSV meningitis. Serial lumbar punctures show a 95 per cent reduction in cell count by 2 weeks. Stool cultures have the highest yield for viral isolation (40 to 50 per cent); CSF and throat cultures are positive in about 15 per cent of cases. Serologies also may indicate a specific causative agent; a fourfold rise in antibody titer is helpful in confirming the significance of a virus isolated from the throat or stool.

Differential Diagnosis. Partially treated bacterial meningitis and a parameningeal focus of infection may be particularly difficult to distinguish from aseptic meningitis. Serial lumbar punctures may be helpful in establishing the former and x-ray films of paranasal sinuses and mastoids the latter. Also in the differential diagnosis are infectious agents that are not cultured on routine bacterial media and are considered to be causes of subacute meningitis (see below). Infective endocarditis may cause aseptic meningitis and is an important diagnostic consideration in the appropriate setting (see Chapter 100).

Treatment and Course. Viral meningitis is generally benign and self-limited. HSV meningitis associated with primary genital herpes occasionally causes sufficient symptoms to warrant treatment with acyclovir.

Subacute and Chronic Meningitis

Certain infectious and noninfectious diseases can present as a subacute or chronic meningitis. Chronic meningitis refers to a clinical syndrome of at least 4 weeks' duration and will be discussed in Chapter 120. More germane to the differential diagnosis of aseptic meningitis is a neurologic disease that develops over a course of several days to weeks, clinically takes the form of meningitis or meningoencephalitis, and is associated with a predominantly mononuclear pleocytosis in the CSF.

The infectious causes of this syndrome may present as a subacute to chronic meningitis (Table 97–5).

At the outset it is important to consider the possible role of HIV as directly causing this syndrome or predisposing to specific opportunistic infections, such as cryptococcosis or toxoplasmosis, which frequently present as subacute meningitis. The patient in a high-risk category for the acquired immunodeficiency syndrome (AIDS) requires special consideration in this regard (see Chapter 108).

Tuberculous meningitis results from the rupture of a parameningeal focus into the subarachnoid space. The presentation is generally one of semiacute or subacute meningitis, with a neurologic syndrome being present for less than 2 weeks in over half of patients. Headache, fever, meningismus, and altered mental status are characteristic, with papilledema, cranial nerve palsies (II, III, IV, VI, or VII), and extensor plantar reflexes each occurring in about one fourth of cases. The initial CSF sample may show predominance of neutrophils, but the differential shifts to mononuclear cells within the next 7 to 10 days. Acid-fast bacilli are identified in the CSF of 10 to 20 per cent of patients; the intermediate-strength tuberculin skin test is positive in 65 per cent. Since delay in institution of treatment is associated with increased mortality, therapy is initiated before confirmation of the diagnosis in most cases. The clinical suspicion of tuberculosis is heightened by a history of remote tuberculosis in one half of patients; concurrent pulmonary disease occurs in about one third, so that the diagnosis may be supported by smears or culture of pulmonary secretions. Appropriate therapy consists of isoniazid, rifampin, ethambutol, and pyrazinamide. "Vasculitis" related to entrapment of cerebral vessels in inflammatory exudate may lead to stroke syndromes. This has been offered as a rationale for the use of corticosteroids as adjunctive therapy. Although evidence of their advantage remains unproved, some authorities believe that corticosteroids should be given, in tapering doses, for 4 weeks when the diagnosis of tuberculosis is established, particularly if cranial palsies appear or stupor or coma supervenes.

Cryptococcal meningitis is the most common fungal meningitis and can occur in apparently normal as well as immunocompromised hosts. The presentation is of insidious onset followed by weeks to months of progressive meningoencephalitis, sometimes clinically indistinguishable from the course of tuberculosis. Certain associations are useful in this differential diagnosis. The presence of immunosuppression suggests cryptococcosis, whereas chronic debilitating disease, miliary infiltrates on chest radiograph, or the syndrome of inappropriate antidiuretic hormone suggests tuberculosis. An India ink preparation of CSF reveals encapsulated yeast in 50 per cent of cases. More than 90 per cent have cryptococcal polysaccharide antigen in CSF or serum. Fungal cultures of urine, stool, sputum, and blood should be obtained; they may be positive in the absence of clinically apparent extraneural disease. Treatment of cryptococcal meningitis requires amphotericin B. Addition of flucytosine allows use of less amphotericin B. Fluconazole is also effective but causes less rapid sterilization of the CSF.

Coccidioides immitis is a major cause of granulomatous meningitis in semiarid areas of the southwestern United States; *Histoplasma capsulatum* may cause a similar syndrome in endemic areas (Ohio and Mississippi River valleys).

Neurosyphilis reflects the fact that the spirochete causing syphilis invades the CNS in most instances of systemic infection. The organism then may either be cleared by host defenses or persist to produce a more chronic infection expressed symptomatically only years later. The most common form of neurosyphilis is asymptomatic; patients harbor in the CSF a few white cells and have a positive serologic test for syphilis. Symptomatic neurosyphilis can appear as acute or subacute meningitis (meningitic form) resembling that of other bacterial infections and usually occurring during the stage of secondary syphilis when there are cutaneous changes as well. Hydrocephalus and cranial nerve (VII and VIII) abnormalities may develop. CSF and serum serologies usually are strongly positive, and the disease is responsive to penicillin.

Vascular syphilis begins 2 to 10 years after the primary lesion. The disorder is characterized by both meningeal inflammation and a vasculitis of small arterial vessels, the latter leading to arterial occlusion. Clinically, the disorder produces few signs of meningitis but results in monofocal or multifocal cerebral or spinal infarction. The disorder may be mistaken for an autoimmune vasculitis or even arteriosclerotic cerebrovascular disease. The early and prominent spinal cord signs should lead one to expect syphilis, whereas the findings in the CSF of pleocytosis, elevated gamma globulin, and a positive serologic test for syphilis establish the diagnosis. Patients respond to antibiotic therapy, although recovery from focal abnormalities may be incomplete. Syphilis is more difficult to diagnose and may have an accelerated course in the HIV-infected individual. Meningovascular syphilis may develop within months of primary infection, despite treatment with intramuscular benzathine penicillin (see Chapter 107).

General paresis, once a common cause of admission to mental institutions, is now rare. The disorder results from syphilitic invasion of the parenchyma of the brain and begins clinically 10 to 20 years after the primary infection. Paresis is characterized by progressive dementia, sometimes with manic symptoms and megalomania and often with coarse tremors affecting facial muscles and tongue. The diagnostic clue is the presence of Argyll Robertson pupils (p. 778). The CSF is always abnormal. The diagnosis is made by serologic tests. Early treatment with antibiotics usually leads to improvement but not complete recovery.

Tabes dorsalis is a chronic infective process of the dorsal roots that appears 10 to 20 years after primary syphilitic infection. The disorder is characterized by lightning-like pains and a progressive

TABLE 97–5. SUBACUTE TO CHRONIC MENINGITIS

CAUSATIVE AGENT	ASSOCIATION
Human immunodeficiency virus (HIV)	Direct involvement or opportunistic infection
Mycobacterium tuberculosis	May have extraneural tuberculosis
Cryptococcus neoformans	Compromised host
Coccidioides immitis	Southwestern United States
Histoplasma capsulatum	Ohio and Mississippi River valleys
Treponema pallidum	Acute syphilitic meningitis, secondary meningovascular syphilis
Lyme disease	Tick bite, rash, seasonal occurrence

sensory neuropathy affecting predominantly large fibers supplying the lower extremities. There is profound loss of vibration and position sense as well as areflexia. Autonomic fibers are also affected, causing postural hypotension, trophic ulcers of the feet, and traumatic arthropathy of joints. Argyll Robertson pupils are usually present. CSF serologic tests are usually positive. The disorder responds only partially to treatment with antibiotics.

Rare complications of syphilis include *progressive optic atrophy*, *gumma* (a mass lesion in the brain), *congenital neurosyphilis*, and syphilitic infection of the *auditory and vestibular system*. Descriptions can be found in appropriate texts.

Lyme disease, a tick-borne spirochetosis (Chapter 95), is associated in 15 per cent of clinically affected individuals with meningitis, encephalitis, or cranial or radicular neuropathies. Characteristically, the neurologic disease begins several weeks after the typical skin rash, erythema chronicum migrans. Furthermore, the skin rash may have been so mild as to go unnoticed and usually has faded by the time neurologic manifestations appear. The diagnosis should be suspected when a patient develops subacute or chronic meningitis during late summer or early fall, with CSF changes consisting of a modest mononuclear pleocytosis, protein values below 100 mg/dl, and normal glucose levels. The diagnosis is established serologically. Patients with early Lyme disease usually respond to oral doxycycline. Patients with later, or disseminated, Lyme disease respond less predictably to prolonged (14 to 21 days) courses of intravenous ceftriaxone.

Several noninfectious diseases may manifest as a subacute or chronic meningitis. Typical of this group is a CSF containing 10 to 100 lymphocytes, elevated protein levels, and a mild to severely lowered glucose content. Meningeal carcinomatosis represents diffuse involvement of the leptomeninges by metastatic adenocarcinoma, lymphoma, or melanoma. Cytologic analysis often identifies malignant cells. Sarcoidosis may cause a basilar meningitis and asymmetric cranial nerve involvement, as well as a low-grade pleocytosis, sometimes associated with borderline low CSF glucose levels. Granulomatous angiitis and Behçet's disease also belong in this category.

Approach to Diagnosis. Diagnosing the specific cause of subacute or chronic meningitis may be quite difficult. In patients with tuberculous or fungal meningitis, cultures may not become positive for 4 to 6 weeks or longer; moreover, meningitis caused by some fungi (e.g., *Histoplasma capsulatum*) is often associated with negative cultures of the CSF.

Because of the uncertainties involved in establishing the diagnosis of infectious cases, and even the question of whether a particular patient has an infectious or noninfectious disease, an organized approach must be taken. In addition to routine laboratory tests (on multiple samples of CSF), including India ink and cultures for bacteria, mycobacteria, and fungi, the patient with chronic meningitis of unknown cause should have the following: VDRL and cryptococcal antigens (and, when appropriate, antibody to *Borrelia burgdorferi*) determined on blood and CSF; fluorescent treponemal antibody (FTA)–absorbed, antinuclear antibody, and antibody to HIV and *Histoplasma capsulatum* (and, where appropriate, *Coccidioides immitis*) on serum; and cytologies (×3) on CSF. A tuberculin skin test (intermediate strength, 5 TU) should be done, along with anergy skin testing (mumps, *Candida*, tetanus). If the CSF findings are consistent with tuberculous meningitis, tuberculostearic acid should be determined on the CSF (by arrangement with the Centers for Disease Control [CDC]).

The appropriate management is decided by the patient's clinical status and the results of these tests. If the CSF pleocytosis consists of more than 50 to 100 cells per microliter, then an infectious disease is likely. Empiric therapy for tuberculous meningitis is appropriate. If the tuberculin skin test is negative, however, fungal meningitis becomes more likely. Repeated cytologic and microbiologic studies of the CSF may reveal the diagnosis. If the pleocytosis is low-grade, fewer than 50 to 100 cells per microliter, a noninfectious cause becomes more likely; the condition even may be self-limited, the so-called chronic benign lymphocytic meningitis. The approach to such patients must be individualized. Only rarely is brain or meningeal biopsy necessary or helpful. If all CSF studies are nondiagnostic and the patient's clinical condition is stable, a period of careful observation is almost always preferable to an invasive diagnostic procedure.

ENCEPHALITIS

Definition. Acute viral and other infectious causes of encephalitis usually produce fever, headache, and stiff neck, and, in addition to confusion, alterations in consciousness, focal neurologic signs, and seizures.

Epidemiology. A large number of viral and nonviral agents can cause encephalitis (Table 97–6). Seasonal occurrence may help to limit the differential diagnosis. Arthropod-borne viruses peak in the summer (California encephalitis [La Crosse virus] and western equine encephalitis in August, St. Louis encephalitis slightly later). The tick-borne infections (Rocky Mountain spotted fever) occur in early summer, enterovirus infections in later summer and fall, and mumps in the winter and spring. Geographic distribution is also helpful. Eastern equine encephalitis is confined to the coastal states. Serologic surveys indicate that infections by encephalitis viruses are most often subclinical. It is not clear why so few among the many infected subjects develop encephalitis.

HSV is the most frequent and devastating cause of sporadic, severe focal encephalitis; overall it is implicated in 10 per cent of all cases of encephalitis in North America. There is no age, sex, seasonal, or geographic preference.

Pathogenesis. Viruses reach the CNS by the blood stream or peripheral nerves. HSV presumably reaches the brain by cell-to-cell spread along recurrent branches of the trigeminal nerve, which innervate the meninges of the anterior and middle fossae. Although this would explain the characteristic localization of necrotic lesions to the inferomedial portions of the temporal and frontal lobes, it is not clear why such spread is so rare, one case of HSV encephalitis occurring per million in the population per annum.

Clinical Features. The course of HSV encephalitis is considered here in detail because of the importance of establishing the diagnosis of this treatable entity. Patients affected by HSV commonly describe a prodrome of 1 to 7 days of upper respiratory tract symptoms followed by the sudden onset of headache and fever. The headache and fever may be associated with acute loss of recent memory, behavioral abnormalities, delirium, difficulty with speech, and seizures, often focal. Disorders of the sensorium are not, however, always apparent at the time of presentation and are *not* essential for the working diagnosis of this eminently treatable, but potentially lethal, infection of the CNS.

Laboratory Diagnosis. In HSV encephalitis, the CSF can contain 0 to 1000 white blood cells per microliter, predominantly lymphocytes. Protein is moderately high (median, 80 mg/dl). CSF glucose is reduced in only 5 per cent of individuals within 3 days of onset but becomes abnormal in additional patients later in the course. In about 5 per cent, the CSF is normal. Other laboratory findings at onset are of little help, although focal abnormalities may be present in the electroencephalogram and develop in CT or magnetic resonance imaging (MRI) brain scan by the third day in most patients. Acyclovir offers such high likelihood of therapeutic benefit in HSV encephalitis, with so little risk in this highly fatal and neurologically damaging disease, that brain biopsy should not be performed unless an alternative, treatable diagnosis seems very likely. A low CSF glucose level should increase suspicion that a granulomatous infection is present (tuberculosis, cryptococcosis). If the initial CSF shows a low glucose level, roughly one third of individuals will have an alternative treatable infection. If CSF studies and brain imaging remain inconclusive in such circumstances, biopsy may be appropriate.

Viral cultures of stool, throat, buffy coat, CSF, and brain biopsy specimens and indirect immunofluorescence or immunoperoxidase staining of tissues may provide a specific diagnosis, but both viral isolation and serologic evidence of a rise in antibody titer usually come too late to guide initial treatment. In the case of HSV encephalitis, serologies are particularly helpful in the 30 per cent of individuals with a primary infection. Also, CSF titers of antibody to HSV, which reflect intrathecal production of antibody, may show a diagnostic fourfold rise.

Differential Diagnosis. Acute (demyelinating) encephalomyelitis, infective endocarditis producing brain embolization, meningoencephalitis caused by *Cryptococcus neoformans*, *Mycobacterium tuberculosis*, or the La Crosse virus, acute bacterial abscess, acute thrombotic thrombocytopenic purpura, cerebral venous thrombosis, vascular disease, and primary and metastatic tumors may all simulate HSV encephalitis.

Treatment and Outcome. The course of viral encephalitis depends on the etiologic agent. Untreated HSV encephalitis has a high mortality (70 per cent), and survival is associated with severe neurologic residua. Acyclovir therapy improves survival and greatly lessens morbidity in patients if initiated early, before deterioration to coma. Prognosis is particularly favorable in patients less than 30 years old.

Rabies

Rabies encephalitis is always fatal, requiring one to place major attention on prevention. Currently, zero to six cases of rabies occur each year in the United States, and approximately 20,000 people receive postexposure prophylaxis.

The incubation period for rabies is generally 20 to 90 days, during which the rabies virus replicates locally and then migrates along nerves to the spinal cord and brain. Rabies begins with fever, headache, fatigue, and pain or paresthesias at the site of inoculation; confusion, seizures, paralysis, and stiff neck follow. Periods of violent agitation are characteristic of rabies encephalitis. Attempts at drinking produce laryngospasm, gagging, and apprehension. Paralysis, coma, and death supervene. When rabies is suspected, protective isolation procedures should be instituted to avoid additional exposure of the hospital staff to saliva and other infected secretions. Confirmation of the diagnosis is possible by assaying rabies-neutralizing antibody or isolating virus from saliva, CSF,

TABLE 97–6. INFECTIOUS AGENTS CAUSING ENCEPHALITIS AND MENINGOENCEPHALITIS

VIRAL	NONVIRAL
Herpes simplex	*Rickettsia rickettsii*
Epstein-Barr	*Rickettsia typhi*
Varicella-zoster	*Mycoplasma pneumoniae*
Cytomegalovirus	*Leptospira* species
Mumps	*Brucella* species
Measles	*Mycobacterium tuberculosis*
La Crosse virus	*Histoplasma capsulatum*
St. Louis encephalitis	*Cryptococcus neoformans*
Eastern equine encephalitis	*Naegleria* species
Western equine encephalitis	*Acanthamoeba* species
Coxsackie	*Toxoplasma gondii*
ECHO	*Trypanosoma* species
Rabies	*Plasmodium falciparum*
HIV	*Borrelia burgdorferi*

and urine sediment. Immunofluorescent rabies antibody staining of a skin biopsy taken from the posterior neck is a rapid means of establishing the diagnosis.

Indications for prophylaxis are based on the following principles. (1) The patient must have been exposed. Nonbite exposure is possible if mucous membranes or open wounds are contaminated with animal saliva; exposure to bat urine in heavily contaminated caves has been followed by rabies. (2) Small rodents (rats, mice, chipmunks, squirrels) and rabbits rarely are infected with rabies and have not been associated with human disease. Consultation with local or state health authorities is essential, since certain areas of the United States are considered rabies-free. In other areas, if rabies is present in wild animals, dogs and cats have the potential to transmit rabies. Domestic dogs and cats should be quarantined for 10 days after biting someone; if no signs of illness develop, there is no risk of transmission by their earlier bite. Other animals should be destroyed and their brains examined for rabies virus by direct fluorescent antibody testing. If the biting animal escapes, postexposure prophylaxis is usually indicated. Bites of bat, skunk, and racoon require treatment unless the animal is caught. Unusual behavior of animals and truly unprovoked attacks (as opposed to those incurred during handling or feeding) increase the likelihood of rabies.

Currently, postexposure management consists of (1) thorough wound cleansing; (2) human rabies immune globulin, 20 IU/kg, one half infiltrated locally in the area of the bite and one half intramuscularly; and (3) human diploid cell rabies vaccine, 1.0 ml given intramuscularly five times during a 1-month period. Individuals at high risk of exposure to rabies should be vaccinated. Veterinarians, laboratory workers, and those who frequent caves belong in this category.

SPECTRUM OF TUBERCULOUS, FUNGAL, AND PARASITIC INFECTIONS

The approach to this point in the chapter has been syndromic. Now the spectrum of tuberculous, fungal, and parasitic infections of the CNS is briefly considered. Many, but not all, of these infections are increasing in incidence as the direct result of the increasing prevalence of HIV infection in the population (see Chapter 108).

Tuberculosis

CNS tuberculosis can occur in several forms, sometimes without evidence of active infection elsewhere in the body. The most common form is *tuberculous meningitis*. This disorder is characterized by the subacute onset of headache, stiff neck, and fever. After a few days, affected patients become confused and disoriented. They often develop abnormalities of cranial nerve function, particularly hearing loss due to marked inflammation at the base of the brain. Most patients, if untreated, lapse into coma and die within 3 to 4 weeks of onset. An accompanying arteritis may produce focal signs, including hemiplegia, during the course of the disorder. Tuberculous meningitis must be distinguished from other causes of acute and subacute meningeal infection, a process that often is not easy even after examination of the CSF. The pressure and cell count are elevated with up to a few hundred cells, a mixture of leukocytes and lymphocytes. The protein level is elevated, usually above 100 mg/dl and often to very high levels, and the glucose concentration is depressed. Smears for acid-fast bacilli are positive in only about 10 to 20 per cent of samples. Tuberculosis organisms grow on culture, but only after several weeks. Recently, accurate CSF markers for the rapid diagnosis of the disease have been reported and are available through the Centers for Disease Control in the United States. Pending complete availability and accuracy of such measures, patients with subacutely developing meningitis suspected of having tuberculosis should be treated with antituberculous agents prior to definitive diagnosis. Large samples of CSF should be sent for culture, and a careful search should be made for tuberculosis elsewhere in the body. Seventy-five per cent of such patients have a positive tuberculin skin test, and a careful search may yield evidence of systemic tuberculosis.

Tuberculomas of the brain produce symptoms and signs either of the mass lesion or of meningitis, the tuberculomas being found incidentally. One or multiple lesions are identified on CT scan, but the scan itself does not distinguish tuberculomas from brain tumor or other brain abscesses. In the absence of evidence of meningeal or systemic tuberculosis, biopsy is necessary for diagnosis. Patients with tuberculomas, like those with tuberculous meningitis, respond to antituberculous therapy, but brain lesions may remain visible in the CT scan long after the patient has improved clinically; the clinical course, not the scan, predicts the outcome.

Less common manifestations of CNS tuberculosis include *chronic arachnoiditis* characterized by a low-grade inflammatory response in the CSF and progressive pain with signs of either cauda equina or spinal cord dysfunction. The diagnosis of arachnoiditis is suggested by a myelogram showing evidence of fibrosis and compartmentalization instead of the usually smooth subarachnoid lining. The disorder responds poorly to treatment. *Tuberculous myelopathy* probably results from direct invasion of the organism from the subarachnoid space. Patients present with a subacutely developing myelopathy characterized by sensory loss either in the legs or in all four extremities, depending on the site of the spinal cord invasion. Many patients have additional signs of meningitis, including fever, headache, and stiff neck. The CSF usually contains cells and tuberculous organisms. The myelogram may show evidence of arachnoiditis and frequently demonstrates an enlarged spinal cord or complete block to the passage of contrast material in the thoracic or cervical region.

Fungal and Parasitic Infections

Fungal and parasitic infections of the CNS are less common than viral and bacterial infections and often affect immunosuppressed patients. Table 97–7 lists the more common of these infections. Like bacterial infections, fungal and parasitic infections may cause either meningitis or parenchymal abscesses. The meningitides, when they occur, manifest with clinical symptoms that, while similar, are usually less severe and abrupt than those of acute bacterial meningitis. The common fungal causes of meningitis include especially cryptococcosis, coccidioidomycosis, and histoplasmosis. *Cryptococcal meningitis* is a sporadic infection that affects both immunosuppressed patients (50 per cent) and non-immunosuppressed patients. The disorder is characterized by headache and sometimes fever and stiff neck. The clinical symptoms may evolve for periods as long as weeks or months; diagnosis can be made only by identifying the organism or its antigen in the CSF. *Histoplasma* and coccidioidomycosis meningitides occur in endemic areas and

TABLE 97–7. SOME FUNGAL AND PARASITIC CAUSES OF CNS INFECTIONS

FUNGAL INFECTION	HELMINTHIC INFECTION	PROTOZOAN INFECTION
Cryptococcosis	Trichinosis	Toxoplasmosis
Coccidioidomycosis	Cysticercosis	Amebiasis
Aspergillosis	Echinococcosis	Malaria
Mucormycosis	Schistosomiasis	Chagas' disease
Actinomycosis	Angiostrongyliasis	Trypanosomiasis (African)
Histoplasmosis	Ascariasis	
Blastomycosis		
Candidiasis		

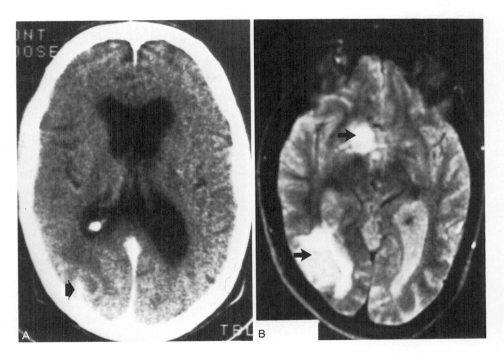

FIGURE 97–1. *Toxoplasma* abscesses in a patient with acquired immunodeficiency syndrome (AIDS). *A,* Computed tomography (CT) scan shows a contrast-enhanced mass *(arrow). B,* Magnetic resonance image (MRI) reveals multiple masses *(arrows)* not seen on CT scan, leading physicians to suspect abscesses rather than tumor.

often affect nonimmunosuppressed individuals. The diagnosis is suggested by a history of residence in the appropriate geographic area and is confirmed by CSF and serologic evaluation. Antifungal treatment, particularly in the nonimmunosuppressed patient, is usually effective.

Parasitic infections of the nervous system usually produce focal abscesses rather than diffuse meningitis. The most common to affect the nonimmunosuppressed host is cysticercosis, a disorder caused by the larval form of the *Taenia solium* tapeworm and contracted by ingesting food or water contaminated with parasite eggs. The disorder is common in the underdeveloped world and parts of the United States having a large Hispanic population. The brain may be invaded in as many as 60 per cent of infected persons. Invasion of the brain leads to formation of either single or multiple cysts, which often lie in the parenchyma but sometimes reside in the ventricles or subarachnoid space. Seizures and increased intracranial pressure are the most common clinical symptoms. CT scanning identifies small intracranial calcifications and hypodense cysts. Serum indirect hemagglutination tests are usually positive and confirm the diagnosis. Where cysts obstruct the ventricular system to cause symptoms, shunting procedures may be necessary. The anthelmintic praziquantel is effective therapy.

Toxoplasmosis of the brain, when it occurs in the adult, is a manifestation of immunosuppression. Patients with abnormal cellular immunity may develop single or multiple abscesses, which appear usually as ring-enhancing lesions on CT scan (Fig. 97–1). The diagnosis and treatment of

toxoplasmosis of the brain are discussed in Chapter 108.

REFERENCES

Bacterial Meningitis

Spagnuolo PJ, Ellner JJ, Lerner PI, McHenry MC, Flatauer F, Rosenberg P, Rosenthal MS: *Hemophilus influenzae* meningitis: The spectrum of disease in adults. Medicine 61:74, 1982.
Swartz MN: Bacterial meningitis. *In* Wyngaarden JB, Smith LH Jr, Bennett JC (eds): Cecil Textbook of Medicine. 19th ed. Philadelphia, WB Saunders Co, 1992, pp 1655–1671.
Tunkel AR, Wispelwey B, Schald WM: Bacterial meningitis: Recent advances in pathophysiology and treatment. Ann Intern Med 112:610, 1990.

Aseptic Meningitis

Lepow ML, Carver DH, Wright HT, et al: A clinical, laboratory and epidemiologic investigation of aseptic meningitis during the 4-year period 1955–1958. N Engl J Med 266:1181, 1962.

Encephalitis

Johnson R: Viral Infections of the Nervous System. New York, Raven Press, 1982.
Nahmias AJ, Whitley RJ, Visintine AN, Takei Y, Alford CA Jr: HSV encephalitis; Laboratory evaluations and their diagnostic significance. J Infect Dis 145:829, 1982.
Price RW: Herpesvirus infections of the nervous system. *In* Wyngaarden JB, Smith LH Jr, Bennett JC (eds): Cecil Textbook of Medicine. 18th ed. Philadelphia, WB Saunders Co, 1992, pp 2182–2183.
Sawyer J, Ellner JJ, Ransahoff DF: To biopsy or not to biopsy in suspected herpes simplex encephalitis. Med Decis Making 8:95, 1988.

98 INFECTIONS OF THE HEAD AND NECK

INFECTIONS OF THE EAR

Otitis externa is an infection of the external auditory canal. The process may begin as a folliculitis or pustule within the canal. Staphylococci, streptococci, and other skin flora are the most common pathogens. Some cases of otitis externa have been associated with swimming in hot tubs. This infection (swimmer's ear) is usually due to *Pseudomonas aeruginosa*.

Patients with otitis externa complain of ear pain that is often quite severe, and they may also complain of itching. Examination reveals an inflamed external canal; the tympanic membrane may be uninvolved. (Patients with otitis media, in contrast, will not have involvement of the external canal unless the tympanic membrane is perforated.) Otitis externa with cellulitis can be treated with systemic antibiotics such as dicloxacillin or erythromycin and local heat. In the absence of cellulitis, irrigation and administration of topical antibiotics such as neomycin and polymyxin are sufficient. Patients with diabetes mellitus are at risk for an invasive external otitis (malignant otitis) due to *P. aeruginosa*. In malignant otitis externa, pain is a presenting complaint, and infection rapidly invades the bones of the skull and may result in cranial nerve palsies, invasion of the brain, and death. Treatment must include debridement of as much necrotic tissue as is feasible and at least 4 to 6 weeks of treatment with an aminoglycoside plus a penicillin derivative active against *Pseudomonas* (e.g., ticarcillin). Ceftazidime and imipenem may also be especially effective for this infection.

Otitis media is an infection of the middle ear seen primarily among preschool children but occasionally in adults as well. Infection caused by upper respiratory tract pathogens is promoted by obstruction to drainage through edematous, congested eustachian tubes. *Streptococcus pneumoniae*, *Haemophilus influenzae*, and *Moraxella catarrhalis* are the most common pathogens, and viral infection with serous otitis may predispose to acute otitis media. Fever, ear pain, diminished hearing, vertigo, or tinnitus may be seen. In young children, however, localizing symptoms may not be appreciated. The tympanic membrane may appear inflamed, but to diagnose otitis media with certainty, either fluid must be seen behind the membrane or diminished mobility of the membrane must be demonstrated by tympanometry or after air insufflation into the external canal.

Treatment with amoxicillin–clavulanic acid, trimethoprim-sulfamethoxazole, or cefaclor is generally effective; addition of decongestants is of no proven value. Complications of otitis media are uncommon but include infection of the mastoid air cells (mastoiditis), bacterial meningitis, brain abscess, and subdural empyema.

INFECTIONS OF THE NOSE AND SINUSES

Rhinitis is a common manifestation of numerous respiratory virus infections. It is characterized by mucopurulent or watery nasal discharge that may be profuse. When rhinitis is due to respiratory virus infection, pharyngitis, conjunctival suffusion, and fever may be associated. Rhinitis can also be caused by hypersensitivity responses to airborne allergens. Patients with allergic rhinitis often have a transverse skin crease on the bridge of the nose a few millimeters from the tip. The demonstration of eosinophils in a wet preparation of nasal secretions readily distinguishes allergic rhinitis from rhinitis of infectious origin. (Eosinophils can be identified in wet preparations by the presence of large refractile cytoplasmic granules.) Occasionally, following head trauma or neurosurgery, cerebrospinal fluid (CSF) may leak through the nose. "CSF rhinorrhea" places patients at risk for bacterial meningitis. CSF is readily distinguished from nasal secretions by its low protein and relatively high glucose concentrations.

Sinusitis is an infection of the air-filled paranasal sinuses that may complicate viral upper respiratory infections. Allergic rhinitis and structural abnormalities of the nose that interfere with sinus drainage also predispose to sinusitis. Acute sinusitis is primarily caused by upper respiratory tract bacterial pathogens, *Streptococcus pneumoniae* and *Haemophilus influenzae*, and less often by anaerobes and staphylococci.

Sinusitis may be difficult to distinguish from a viral upper respiratory illness that in many instances precedes sinus infection. Patients may complain of headache, "stuffiness," and purulent nasal discharge. Headache may be exacerbated by bending over. There may be tenderness over the involved sinus, and pus may be seen in the turbinates of the nose. Failure of a sinus to light up on transillumination may suggest the diagnosis; sinus radiographs revealing opacification, mucosal thickening, or air-fluid levels establish the diagnosis of sinusitis. Most patients with sinusitis can be treated with a 10-day course of ampicillin, amoxicillin, or trimethoprim-sulfamethoxazole, along with nasal decongestants. Patients who appear toxic or otherwise are severely ill should undergo sinus puncture for drainage, Gram stain, and culture. Sinusitis may be complicated by bacterial meningitis, brain abscess, or subdural empyema. Therefore, patients with sinusitis and neurologic abnormalities must be evaluated carefully for these complications by computed tomography (CT) scan if a space-occupying lesion is suspected or by CSF examination if meningitis is suspected (see Chapter 97).

Rhinocerebral mucormycosis is an invasive infection arising from the nose or sinuses caused by fungi of the order Mucorales. This infection can result in progressive bony destruction and invasion of the brain. Rhinocerebral mucormycosis is seen primarily among poorly controlled diabetics with ketoacidosis, recipients of organ transplants, and patients with hematologic malignancy. Black necrotic lesions of the palate or nasal mucosa are characteristic. Most patients have a depressed sensorium at presentation. Vascular thrombosis and cranial nerve palsies are common. Diagnosis is made by demonstration of the broad, ribbon-shaped, nonseptate hyphae on histologic examination of a scraping or biopsy specimen. Differential diagnosis includes infection due to *Pseudomonas aeruginosa* or to other fungi such as *Aspergillus* species, and cavernous sinus thrombosis. Rhinocerebral mucormycosis is a surgical emergency. Treatment involves correction of the underlying process if possible, broad surgical debridement, and administration of amphotericin B.

INFECTIONS OF THE MOUTH AND PHARYNX

Stomatitis

Stomatitis, or inflammation of the mouth, can be caused by a wide variety of processes. Patients with stomatitis may complain of diffuse or localized pain in the mouth, difficulty in swallowing, and difficulty in managing oral secretions. Various nutritional deficiencies (vitamins B_{12} and C, folic acid, and niacin) can also produce stomatitis and soreness of the mouth.

Thrush is an infection of the oral mucosa by *Candida* species. Thrush may be seen among infants and also in patients receiving broad-spectrum antibiotics or corticosteroids (systemic or inhaled), among patients with leukopenia (e.g., acute leukemia), and among patients with impairments in cell-mediated immunity (e.g., acquired immunodeficiency syndrome [AIDS]). In its milder form, thrush is manifested by an asymptomatic white, "cheesy" exudate on the buccal mucosa and pharynx, which, when scraped, leaves a raw, bleeding surface. In more severe cases, there may be pain and also erythema surrounding the exudate. The diagnosis is suggested by the characteristic appearance of the lesions and is confirmed by microscopic examination of a KOH preparation of the exudate, which reveals yeast and the pseudo-

TABLE 98-1. ORAL VESICLES AND ULCERS

Aphthous stomatitis	Systemic lupus erythematosus
Primary herpes simplex infection	Reiter's syndrome
Vincent's stomatitis	Crohn's disease
Syphilis	Erythema multiforme
Coxsackie virus A (herpangina)	Pemphigus
Fungi (histoplasmosis)	Pemphigoid
Behçet's syndrome	

hyphae characteristic of *Candida*. Thrush related to administration of antibiotics and corticosteroids should resolve after the drugs are withdrawn. Otherwise, thrush can be managed with clotrimazole troches. Refractory thrush or *Candida* involving the esophagus should be treated with ketoconazole or fluconazole.

Oral Ulcers and Vesicles (Table 98-1)

Aphthous Stomatitis. Aphthae are discrete, shallow, painful ulcers on erythematous bases; they may be single or multiple and are usually present on the labial or buccal mucosa. Attacks of aphthous stomatitis may be recurrent and quite debilitating. Symptoms may last for several days to 2 weeks. The cause of these ulcerations is unknown, and treatment is symptomatic with saline mouth wash or topical anesthetics. Giant aphthous ulcers may occur in persons with AIDS; they may respond to topical or systemic steriods.

Herpes Simplex Virus Infection. Although most recurrences of oral herpes simplex infections occur on or near the vermillion border of the lips, the primary attack usually involves the mouth and pharynx. Generalized symptoms of fever, headache, and malaise often precede the appearance of oral lesions by as much as 24 to 48 hours. The involved regions are swollen and erythematous. Small vesicles soon appear; these rupture, leaving shallow, discrete ulcers that may coalesce. The diagnosis can be made by scraping the base of an ulcer. Wright's or Giemsa's stain of this material may reveal the intranuclear inclusions and multinucleated giant cells characteristic of herpes simplex infection. Viral cultures are more sensitive but more expensive. Diagnosis may also be established by immunoassay for viral antigen in the scraping. Treatment of primary infection with acyclovir will decrease the duration of symptoms but has no effect on the frequency of recurrence.

Vincent's Stomatitis. This is an ulcerative infection of the gingival mucosa due to anaerobic fusobacteria and spirochetes. Breath is often foul, and the ulcerations are covered with a purulent, dirty-appearing, gray exudate. Gram stain of the exudate reveals the characteristic gram-negative fusobacteria and spirochetes. Treatment with penicillin is curative. Untreated, the infection may extend to the peritonsillar space (quinsy) and even involve vascular structures in the lateral neck (see below).

Syphilis. Syphilis may produce a painless primary chancre in the mouth or a painful mucous patch that is a manifestation of secondary disease. The diagnosis should be considered in the sexually active patient with a large (>1 cm) oral ulceration and should be confirmed serologically, since darkfield examination may be confounded by the presence of nonsyphilitic oral spirochetes.

Herpangina. This is a childhood disease that causes tiny, discrete ulcerations of the soft palate and is due to infection with Coxsackie virus A.

Fungal Disease. Occasionally, an oral ulcer or nodule may be a manifestation of disseminated infection due to histoplasmosis. These ulcers are generally mildly or minimally symptomatic and are overshadowed by the constitutional symptoms of disseminated fungal illness.

Systemic Illnesses Causing Ulcerative or Vesicular Lesions of the Mouth. Recurrent aphthous oral ulcerations may be part of Behçet's syndrome. Oral ulcerations have been associated with connective tissue diseases, such as systemic lupus erythematosus and Reiter's syndrome, and with Crohn's disease. Although isolated oral bullae and ulcerations may be seen in patients with erythema multiforme, pemphigus, and pemphigoid, almost all patients have an associated skin rash. The "iris" or "target" lesion of erythema multiforme is diagnostic. Otherwise, biopsy will establish the diagnosis. Corticosteroids may be life-saving for pemphigus. Corticosteroids are also used in the treatment of erythema multiforme majorum (Stevens-Johnson syndrome), although proof of their efficacy is not available.

Approach to the Patient with "Sore Throat"

This section discusses the clinical approach to patients with sore throat and also discusses several less common but serious illnesses that can manifest as a "sore throat." When evaluating a patient with a sore throat, it is first important to distinguish between the relatively common and benign sore throat syndromes (viral or streptococcal pharyngitis) and the less common but more dangerous causes of sore throat. Patients with viral or streptococcal pharyngitis often give a history of exposure to individuals with upper respiratory tract infections. Symptoms of cough, rhinitis, and hoarseness (indicating involvement of the larynx) suggest a viral upper respiratory tract infection, although it is important to remember that hoarse-

TABLE 98 – 2. SEVEN DANGER SIGNS IN PATIENTS WITH "SORE THROAT"

1. Persistence of symptoms longer than 1 week without improvement
2. Respiratory difficulty, particularly stridor
3. Difficulty in handling secretions
4. Difficulty in swallowing
5. Severe pain in the absence of erythema
6. A palpable mass
7. Blood, even in small amounts, in the pharynx or ear

ness may also be seen with more serious infections, such as epiglottitis.

Examination of the Throat. Two points regarding examination of the throat need emphasis. The first is that complete examination of the oral cavity is important. Not only will a thorough examination give clues to the cause of the complaint, but it may also provide early diagnosis of an asymptomatic malignancy at a time when cure is feasible. The second point is that the normal tonsils and mucosal rim of the anterior fauces are generally a deeper red than the rest of the pharynx in healthy subjects. This should not be mistaken for inflammation. Patients with pharyngitis often have a red, inflamed posterior pharynx. The tonsils are often enlarged and red and may be covered with a punctate or diffuse white exudate. Lymph nodes of the anterior neck are often enlarged.

If any of the seven *danger signs* listed in Table 98 – 2 is present, the clinician must suspect an illness other than viral or streptococcal pharyngitis. Symptoms persisting longer than 1 week are rarely due to streptococci or viruses and should prompt consideration of other processes (see "Persistent or Penicillin-Unresponsive Pharyngitis," below). Respiratory difficulty, particularly stridor, difficulty in handling oral secretions, or difficulty in swallowing should suggest the possibility of epiglottitis or soft tissue space infection. Severe pain in the absence of erythema of the pharynx may be seen with some of the "extrarespiratory" causes of sore throat, as well as in some cases of epiglottitis or retropharyngeal abscess. A *palpable mass* in the pharynx or neck suggests a soft tissue space infection, and *blood in the ear or pharynx* may be an early indication of a lateral pharyngeal space abscess eroding into the carotid artery.

A good history and careful examination will distinguish between the common and benign causes of a sore throat, and the unusual but often more serious causes.

Pharyngitis

A list of agents that have been associated with pharyngitis is presented in Table 98 – 3. Almost half of all cases are due to respiratory viruses or group A streptococci. Most of the remainder of the cases are without defined etiology. Most cases occur during the winter months. In practice, once a diagnosis of pharyngitis is established clinically, it is most important to distinguish between group A streptococcal infections, which should be treated with penicillin, and viral infections, which should be treated symptomatically (e.g., salicylates, saline gargles). Since clinical criteria do not reliably distinguish streptococcal from nonstreptococcal pharyngitis, all patients with pharyngitis should have a throat swab cultured for streptococci. Recently, test kits that rapidly detect group A streptococcal antigen on throat swabs, with high levels of accuracy, have become available. These tests may be substituted for culture and provide more rapid diagnosis of group A streptococcal infection.

Pharyngitis and Respiratory Virus Infections.

Many patients with common colds due to rhinovirus or coronavirus or with influenza have an associated pharyngitis. Other cold symptoms—rhinorrhea, conjunctival suffusion, and cough—suggest a cold virus; fevers and myalgias suggest influenza. Symptoms generally resolve in a few days without treatment.

Infectious mononucleosis due to Epstein-Barr virus is often associated with pharyngitis. Patients often also complain of malaise and fever. On examination, the pharynx may be inflamed and the tonsils hypertrophied and covered by a white exudate. Cervical lymph node enlargement is often prominent, and generalized lymph node enlargement and splenomegaly are common. Examination of a peripheral blood smear reveals atypical lymphocytes, and the presence of heterophile antibodies (e.g., Monospot test) or a rise in antibodies to Epstein-Barr virus viral capsid antigen will confirm the diagnosis.

Streptococcal Pharyngitis. Streptococcal pharyngitis may produce mild or severe symptoms. The pharynx is generally inflamed, and exudative tonsillitis is common but not universal. Fever may be present, and cervical lymph nodes may be enlarged and tender. Clinical distinction between streptococcal and nonstreptococcal pharyngitis is inaccurate, and patients with pharyngitis should therefore have a swab of the posterior pharynx cultured on sheep blood agar plates or tested for streptococcal antigen. The growth of group A beta-hemolytic streptococci or detection of group A streptococcal antigen is an indication for treatment with penicillin (or erythromycin if the patient is penicillin-allergic). Antibiotics may shorten the duration of symptoms due to this infection but are given primarily to decrease the frequency of rheumatic fever, which may follow untreated streptococcal pharyngitis.

Corynebacterial Disease. Diphtheria, caused by *Corynebacterium diphtheriae*, is a rare disease in the United States, with only three cases reported to the Centers for Disease Control (CDC) in 1980. The grey pseudomembrane bleeds when removed and rarely may cause death via airway obstruction. Most morbidity and mortality in diphtheria are related to the elaboration of a toxin with neurologic and cardiac effects. Treatment consists of antitoxin plus erythromycin. A self-limited pharyngitis, often associated with a diffuse scarlatiniform rash, may be caused by *Corynebacterium hemolyticum*. This infection can be treated with penicillin or erythromycin.

Epiglottitis

Epiglottitis, usually an aggressive disease of young children, occurs in adults as well. Early recognition of this entity is critical, because delay in diagnosis or treatment frequently results in death, which may occur abruptly, within hours after the onset of symptoms. This diagnosis must be considered in any patient with a sore throat and any of the following key symptoms or signs: (1) difficulty in swallowing; (2) copious oral secre-

TABLE 98–3. CAUSES OF PHARYNGITIS

Viral	**Bacterial** (continued)
Respiratory viruses*	Vincent's fusopirochetes
Herpes simplex	*Corynebacterium diphtheriae*
Epstein-Barr virus	*Corynebacterium hemolyticum*
Coxsackie virus A (herpangina)	*Neisseria gonorrhoeae*
Mycoplasma pneumoniae	**Fungal**
Bacterial	*Candida* species (thrush)
Group A streptococcus*	

*Most frequent identifiable causes of pharyngitis.

tions; (3) severe pain in the absence of pharyngeal erythema (the pharynx of patients with epiglottitis may be normal or inflamed); and (4) respiratory difficulty, particularly stridor.

Patients with epiglottitis often display a characteristic posture; they lean forward to prevent the swollen epiglottis from completely obstructing the airway and resist any attempt at placement in the supine position. The diagnosis can be confirmed by lateral radiographs of the neck or by indirect laryngoscopy with visualization of the swollen erythematous epiglottis. This examination should be performed with the patient in the sitting position to minimize the risk of laryngeal spasm. Furthermore, the physician must be prepared to perform emergency tracheostomy should spasm occur. Therapy has two major objectives: protecting the airway and providing appropriate antimicrobial coverage. Prophylactic endotracheal intubation or tracheotomy is often indicated if respiratory distress increases under observation. As the most likely pathogen is *Haemophilus influenzae*, which may be beta-lactamase–producing, good antibiotic choices are a second- or third-generation cephalosporin or trimethoprim-sulfamethoxazole. Corticosteroids may relieve some inflammatory edema; however, their role in this disease remains unproven. Patients with respiratory difficulty should have their airway protected by endotracheal intubation or tracheostomy. Patients without respiratory complaints may be monitored continuously in an intensive care setting and intubated at the first sign of respiratory difficulty. Young children who are close contacts of patients with invasive disease due to *H. influenzae* are themselves at particular risk of serious infection. Children less than 4 years of age who are close contacts of the index patient and all family members in a household with children less than 4 years of age should receive prophylaxis with rifampin (20 mg/kg given orally, up to 600 mg twice daily for four doses).

Soft Tissue Space Infections

Quinsy. Quinsy is a unilateral peritonsillar abscess or phlegmon that is an unusual complication of tonsillitis. The patient has pain and difficulty in swallowing and often trouble in handling oral secretions. Trismus (inability to open the mouth due to muscle spasm) may be present. Examination reveals swelling of the peritonsillar tissues and lateral displacement of the uvula. Digital examination may reveal a mass. In the phlegmon stage, penicillin therapy may be adequate; abscess can be identified by CT scan and requires surgical drainage (Table 98–4). Untreated, quinsy may result in glottic edema and respiratory compromise or lateral pharyngeal space abscess.

Septic Jugular Vein Thrombophlebitis. An uncommon complication of bacterial pharyngitis or quinsy is septic jugular vein thrombophlebitis (syndrome of postanginal sepsis). Several days following a "sore throat," the patient (generally a teenager or young adult) will note increasing pain and tenderness in the neck. Often there is swelling at the angle of the jaw. The patient will experience high fevers; bacteremia, usually with *Fusobacterium* species; and often septic pulmonary emboli. Treatment is intravenous penicillin, 10 million units/day, plus metronidazole, 500 mg every 6 hours. Patients with persistent fevers may require surgical excision of the jugular vein.

Lateral Pharyngeal Space Abscess. This rare infection is associated with serious morbidity because of its proximity to vascular structures. Extension to the jugular vein may result in thrombophlebitis with septic pulmonary emboli and bacteremia (syndrome of "postanginal sepsis"), discussed above. Erosion of the carotid artery may also complicate this infection, with resultant exsanguination. This may be preceded by small amounts of blood in the ear or pharynx. This infection is generally associated with tenderness and a mass at the angle of the jaw. Prompt surgical intervention may be life-saving.

Retropharyngeal Space Abscess. This complication of tonsillitis is rare in adults, since by adulthood the lymph nodes that give rise to this infection are generally atrophied. Most cases in adults are secondary to trauma (e.g., endoscopic) or to extension of a cervical osteomyelitis. The patient often has difficulty in swallowing and may complain of dyspnea, particularly when sitting upright. Diagnosis may be suspected by the presence of a posterior pharyngeal mass and confirmed by lateral neck films.

Ludwig's Angina. This cellulitis/phlegmon of the floor of the mouth generally is secondary to an odontogenic infection. The tongue is pushed upward, and there is often firm induration of the submandibular space and neck. Laryngeal edema and respiratory compromise may also occur and necessitate protection of the airway. Penicillin is the antibiotic of choice; some patients may require a broad guillotine incision across the submandibular space to provide decompression and adequate drainage, although incision may be unnecessary if the airway can be protected.

Extrarespiratory Causes of Sore Throat

Several extrarespiratory causes of sore throat should be kept in mind. The older patient who complains of soreness in his throat when he climbs stairs or when he is upset may be suffering from angina pectoris with an unusual radiation. The hypertensive patient who presents with an abrupt onset of a "tearing pain" in his or her throat may have a dissecting aortic aneurysm. In these patients, swallowing is generally unaffected. Patients with DeQuervain's subacute thyroiditis may present with fever and pain in the neck radiating to the ears. In patients with thyroiditis, the thyroid is generally tender and the sedimentation rate is increased. Patients with vitamin deficiencies may complain of soreness in the mouth and throat (see Table 98–1). Examination may reveal a red "beefy" tongue with flattened papillae, resulting in a smooth appearance.

Persistent or Penicillin-Unresponsive Pharyngitis

Most cases of viral or streptococcal pharyngitis are self-limited, and symptoms generally resolve within 3 to 4 days. Persistent sore throat should prompt consideration of the following possibilities.

Soft Tissue Abscess or Phlegmon. Rarely, tonsillitis extends to the soft tissues of the pharynx, producing a potentially life-threatening infection (see above).

Pharyngeal Gonorrhea. Although most cases of pharyngeal gonorrhea are asymptomatic, mild pharyngitis may be seen occasionally. This infection will not respond to doses of penicillin used for pharyngitis; moreover, the gonococcus is relatively resistant to phenoxymethyl penicillin (PenV). The gonococcus will not likely be identified on routine culture medium; isolation generally requires culture of a fresh throat swab on a selective medium such as Thayer-Martin (see Chapter 107).

Infectious Mononucleosis. One virus that can produce a more protracted exudative pharyngitis is the Epstein-Barr virus, causative agent of infectious mononucleosis. Adenopathy, splenomegaly, generalized malaise, and rash may accompany this illness. Peripheral blood smear usually reveals numerous atypical lymphocytes. The patient should be advised to abstain from contact sports, as traumatic rupture of the enlarged spleen may be fatal.

Acute Lymphoblastic Leukemia. Persistent exudative tonsillitis may be a presentation of acute lymphoblastic leukemia (ALL). Diagnosis can be

TABLE 98–4. INDICATIONS FOR SURGICAL DRAINAGE: PARAPHARYNGEAL SOFT TISSUE SPACE INFECTIONS

INFECTION	INDICATIONS FOR SURGERY
Quinsy	Abscess or respiratory compromise
Lateral pharyngeal space abscess	Abscess
Jugular vein septic thrombophlebitis	Febrile after 5–6 days of medical therapy
Retropharyngeal abscess	Abscess or respiratory compromise
Ludwig's angina	Abscess or respiratory compromise

suspected by examination of the peripheral blood smear; however, some experience may be required to distinguish between the blasts of ALL and the atypical lymphocytes of infectious mononucleosis.

Other Leukopenic States. Stomatitis or pharyngitis may be the presenting complaint of patients with *aplastic anemia* or *agranulocytosis*. As some of these cases are drug-induced (e.g., propylthiouracil, phenytoin), a complete medication history on initial presentation may suggest this possibility. Prompt discontinuation of the offending drug may be life-saving.

Although sore throat is a common complaint of patients with relatively benign illness, rarely it is the presenting complaint of a patient with a serious or life-threatening disease. Any of the key signs or symptoms shown in Table 98–2 should

alert the clinician to the possibility of an extraordinary process.

REFERENCES

Evans FO, Sydnor JB, Moore WE, et al: Sinusitis of the maxillary antrum. N Engl J Med 293:735, 1975.

Krause RM: Streptococcal diseases. *In* Wyngaarden JB, Smith LH Jr, Bennett JC (eds): Cecil Textbook of Medicine. 19th ed. Philadelphia, WB Saunders Co, 1992, pp 1625–1632.

Mayo Smith MF, Hirsch PJ, Wodzinski SF, Schiffman FJ: Acute epiglottitis in adults: An eight year experience in the State of Rhode Island. N Engl J Med 314:1133, 1986.

99 INFECTIONS OF THE LOWER RESPIRATORY TRACT

Pneumonia currently accounts for about 10 per cent of admissions to adult medical services in North America and is one of the leading causes of death during the productive years of life. Although pneumonia ranks sixth among the causes of death in the United States today, it is first among the potentially lethal illnesses that are readily reversible by the alert physician. Every physician must therefore be adept at the *rapid* diagnosis and management of the patient with pneumonia. Viruses, chlamydiae, rickettsiae, mycoplasmas, bacteria, protozoans, and parasites can all produce serious infection of the lower respiratory tract. Careful history and physical examination can provide clues to the likely cause of infection. The clinical spectra of pneumonias caused by different pathogens overlap considerably, however. Microscopic examination of respiratory secretions provides a rapid and essential step in the differential diagnosis of pneumonia.

PATHOGENESIS OF PNEUMONIA

Microbes can enter the lung to produce infection by hematogenous spread, by spread from a contiguous focus of infection, by inhalation of aerosolized particles, or, most commonly, by aspiration of oropharyngeal secretions. In the last instance, the organisms colonizing the oropharynx will determine the flora of the aspirated secretions and presumably the nature of the resultant pneumonia. Some organisms, like *Streptococcus pneumoniae*, may transiently colonize the oropharynx in healthy individuals. Others, such as gram-negative

bacilli, are more prevalent in the upper respiratory tract of debilitated and hospitalized patients. Aspiration of normal oropharyngeal flora may lead to necrotizing pneumonia caused by mixtures of oral anaerobic bacteria.

Inoculum size (the number of bacteria aspirated) may be an important factor in the development of pneumonia. Studies using radioisotopes have demonstrated that up to 45 per cent of healthy men aspirate some oropharyngeal contents during sleep. In most instances, the bacteria aspirated are relatively avirulent, and back-up defenses, including cough and mucociliary clearance, are adequate to prevent the development of pneumonia. Individuals with structural disease of the oropharynx or patients with impaired cough reflexes due to drugs, alcohol, or neuromuscular disease are at particular risk for the development of pneumonia due to aspiration. The specialized ciliated cells of the bronchial mucosa are covered by a layer of mucus that traps foreign particles, which are propelled upward by rhythmic beating of the cilia to a point where a cough can expel the particles. Impaired mucociliary transport, as may be seen in persons with chronic obstructive pulmonary disease, may predispose to bacterial infection. Denuding of the respiratory epithelium by infection with the influenza virus may be one mechanism whereby influenza predisposes to bacterial pneumonia.

Infection by *Mycobacterium tuberculosis* is usually acquired through inhalation of aerosolized contaminated droplet nuclei. A primary infection is established in the parenchyma of the lungs and

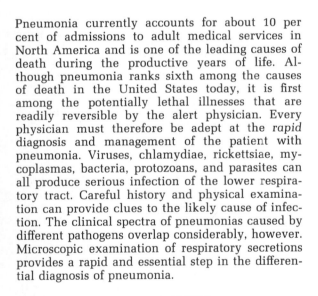

TABLE 99–1. IMPORTANT PATHOGENS CAUSING PNEUMONIA

Young, healthy adult	*Streptococcus pneumoniae, Mycoplasma pneumoniae,* virus
Elderly	*Streptococcus pneumoniae,* influenza virus, *Mycobacterium tuberculosis*
Debilitated	*Streptococcus pneumoniae,* influenza virus, oral flora, *Mycobacterium tuberculosis,* gram-negative bacilli
Hospitalized	Oral flora, *Staphylococcus aureus,* gram-negative bacilli, *Legionella* sp.

TABLE 99–2. SPECIFIC DISORDERS AND ASSOCIATED PNEUMONIAS

Seizures	Aspiration (mixed anaerobes)
Alcoholism	Aspiration, *Streptococcus pneumoniae,* gram-negative bacilli
Diabetes mellitus	Gram-negative bacilli, *Mycobacterium tuberculosis*
Sickle cell disease	*Streptococcus pneumoniae, Mycoplasma pneumoniae*
Chronic lung disease	*Streptococcus pneumoniae, Haemophilus influenzae, Moraxella catarrhalis,* gram-negative bacilli, *Legionella pneumophila*
Chronic renal failure	*Streptococcus pneumoniae, M. tuberculosis, Legionella pneumophila*

TABLE 99–3. EXPOSURES ASSOCIATED WITH PNEUMONIA

Cattle, goats, sheep	Q fever, brucellosis
Rabbits	Tularemia
Birds	Psittacosis, histoplasmosis*
Southwestern United States	Coccidioidomycosis
Mississippi and Ohio River valleys	Histoplasmosis, blastomycosis
Southeast Asia	Tuberculosis, melioidosis, paragonimiasis

*Exposure to bird and bat droppings.

in the draining lymph nodes, which may result in a progressive primary infection, but in most instances it resolves after producing a mild respiratory illness. The organism remains alive, sequestered within host macrophages, and contained by host cell-mediated defenses. Reactivation of infection may never occur or may occur without apparent precipitating events or at times when host cell-mediated immune responses are impaired. Examples of these impairments include starvation, intercurrent viral infections, administration of corticosteroids or cytotoxic drugs, and illnesses associated with immunosuppression such as Hodgkin's disease and human immunodeficiency virus (HIV) infection.

EPIDEMIOLOGY

Common pathogens of community-acquired and nosocomial pneumonia are shown in Table 99–1. As a general rule, the pneumococcus is an important pathogen in all age groups, and influenza and tuberculosis become more frequent with increasing age. Although *Mycoplasma* occasionally produces pneumonia in the elderly, it is primarily a pathogen of the young. Certain systemic disorders appear to be associated with pneumonias due to particular organisms (Table 99–2). The exposure history may be helpful in suggesting specific causative agents (Table 99–3). Pneumonias associated with bone marrow suppression and malignant disorders are discussed in Chapter 109.

DIAGNOSTIC APPROACH TO THE PATIENT

A critical historical point in the differential diagnosis of pneumonia is the duration of symptoms. Pneumonia due to the pneumococcus, *Mycoplasma,* or virus is usually an acute illness. Symptoms are measured in hours to a few days, although there may occasionally be a longer viral prodrome before bacterial superinfection. In contrast, symptoms of pneumonia lasting 10 days or more are rarely due to the common bacterial pathogens and should raise suspicion of mycobacterial, fungal, or anaerobic pneumonia (anaerobes can produce acute or chronic infection) or the presence of an anatomic defect such as an endobronchial mass.

Occupational exposure and travel history often provide clues to the etiology of some less common pneumonias (Table 99–3). Although these pneumonias are uncommon, they should be considered in the appropriate setting because, if improperly treated, some may be fatal.

A history of rhinitis or pharyngitis suggests respiratory virus or *Mycoplasma* pneumonia. Diarrhea has been associated with *Legionella* species pneumonia in some, but not all, outbreaks. A persistent hacking, nonproductive cough characterizes some *Mycoplasma* infections; symptoms of grippe—malaise and myalgias—are common in influenza and may also be seen with *Mycoplasma* pneumonia. A true rigor is very suggestive of a bacterial (often pneumococcal) pneumonia. Whereas small pleural effusions may be seen in nonbacterial pneumonias, severe pleuritic pain in a patient with pneumonia is suggestive of bacterial infection. Night sweats are seen in chronic pneumonias and suggest tuberculous or fungal disease.

Most patients with pneumonia have cough, fever, tachypnea, and tachycardia. Fever without a concomitant rise in pulse rate may be seen in legionellosis, *Mycoplasma* infections, and other "nonbacterial" pneumonias. Patients with pulmonary tuberculosis often maintain high fevers in relative comfort when compared with patients with acute bacterial pneumonia. Respirations may be shallow in the presence of pleurisy. Increasing tachypnea, cyanosis, and the use of accessory muscles for respiration indicate serious illness. Foul breath suggests anaerobic infection. Mental confusion in a patient with pneumonia should immediately raise the suspicion of meningeal involvement, which occurs most commonly in patients with pneumococcal pneumonia. Confusion may, however, be the most prominent clinical feature of pneumonia in elderly patients, in the absence of associated meningitis. Nonetheless, patients with pneumonia who are confused must be evaluated by examination of cerebrospinal fluid.

Physical evidence of consolidation—dullness to percussion, bronchial breath sounds, rales, increased fremitus, and whispered pectoriloquy—suggest bacterial pneumonia. Early in the course of pneumonia, however, the physical examination may be normal.

RADIOGRAPHIC PATTERNS IN PATIENTS WITH PNEUMONIA

Clinical-radiographic dissociation is seen often in patients with *Mycoplasma pneumoniae* or viral pneumonia. Chest radiographs of patients with *Mycoplasma* infection often suggest a more serious infection than does the appearance of the patient or the physical examination. The converse is true in patients with *Pneumocystis carinii* infection, who may appear quite ill despite normal or nearly normal chest radiographs. This may also be true early in the course of acute bacterial pneumonias, when pleuritic chest pain, cough, purulent sputum, and inspiratory rales may precede specific radiographic findings by many hours. A "negative" radiograph can never "rule out" the possibility of acute bacterial pneumonia when the patient's symptoms and signs point to this diagnosis. A lobar consolidation suggests a bacterial pneumonia; however, patients with chronic lung disease often fail to manifest clinical or radiographic evidence of consolidation during the course of bacterial pneumonia. Interstitial infiltrates suggest a nonbacterial process but may also be seen in early staphylococcal pneumonia. Enlarged hilar lymph nodes suggest a concomitant lung tumor but may also be seen in primary tuberculous, viral, or fungal pneumonias. Large pleural effusions should suggest streptococcal pneumonia or tuberculosis. Pneumatoceles are seen in patients after respirator-mediated barotrauma but occur frequently in the evolution of staphylococcal pneumonia, particularly among children. The presence of cavitation identifies the pneumonia as necrotizing. This finding virtually excludes viruses and *Mycoplasma* and makes pneumococcal infection unlikely (Table 99–4).

OTHER LABORATORY FINDINGS

In patients with bacterial pneumonia, the white blood cell (WBC) count is often (but not invariably) elevated. Among patients with pneumococcal infection, WBC counts of 20,000 to 30,000/μl or more may be seen. A left shift with immature forms is common. Patients with nonbacterial pneumonias tend to have lower WBC counts. Modest elevations of serum bilirubin (conjugated) may be seen in many bacterial infections but are particularly common in patients with pneumococcal pneumonia.

TABLE 99–4. NECROTIZING PNEUMONIAS

COMMON	RARE	? NEVER
Tuberculosis	*Streptococcus pneumoniae*	*Mycoplasma pneumoniae*
Staphylococcus	*Legionella*	Virus
Gram-negative bacilli	*Pneumocystis carinii*	
Anaerobes		
Fungi		

DIAGNOSIS AND MANAGEMENT OF THE PATIENT WITH PNEUMONIA

When the patient presents with abrupt onset of shaking chills, followed by cough, pleuritic chest pain, fever, rusty or yellow sputum, and shortness of breath, and the physical examination reveals tachypnea and even minimal signs of alveolar inflammation (e.g., harsh breath sounds at one lung base), the presumptive diagnosis of bacterial pneumonia should be made, sputum should be examined, and appropriate therapy should be begun regardless of radiographic findings. The radiographic abnormalities may lag for several hours after the clinical onset of pneumonia.

Examination of Respiratory Secretions

Examination of respiratory secretions is essential for accurate diagnosis and proper treatment of pneumonia. When the history and physical examination suggest pneumonia, a specimen of sputum must be Gram-stained and examined immediately. The adequacy of the specimen can be ascertained by (1) the absence of squamous epithelial cells and (2) the presence of polymorphonuclear leukocytes (10 to 15 per high-power field). The presence of alveolar macrophages and bronchial epithelial cells confirms the lower respiratory tract source of the specimen. A specimen with many (more than five per high-power field) squamous epithelial cells is of no value for either culture or Gram stain, since it is contaminated with upper respiratory tract secretions.

In some cases, the patient cannot produce an adequate sputum sample, despite vigorous attempts at sputum induction using an aerosolized solution of 3 per cent hypertonic saline. The sicker the patient and the greater the likelihood of a penicillin-resistant pathogen, the more important it is to get an adequate sample of sputum for examination and culture. This can often be achieved by nasotracheal aspiration, which is done by placing the patient supine, hyperextending the neck, and passing a well-lubricated, clear, flexible plastic catheter from the nose to the posterior pharynx. During inspiration, the tube is then passed swiftly past the glottis into the trachea, suction is applied, and secretions are collected in a Lugen trap. The vigorous coughing stimulated by this procedure often produces an additional excellent expectorated specimen.

If nasotracheal aspiration still fails to provide a good specimen for analysis, transtracheal aspiration should be considered *only* if the physician is experienced in this technique and bronchoscopy is not available. (*Note:* Expectorated sputum and sputum obtained through nasotracheal aspiration cannot be cultured anaerobically because of universal contamination with oral flora.)

The Gram-stained specimen should be examined using an oil immersion lens. The presence of a predominant organism, particularly if found within WBCs, suggests that this is the pathogen. In cases of aspiration of mouth flora, a mixture of oral streptococci, gram-positive rods, and gram-negative organisms is found. In some cases, there may be inflammatory cells and no organisms seen on Gram stain. This finding suggests a number of possibilities, many of which are nonbacterial pneumonias (Table 99–5). Unless the diagnosis of acute bacterial pneumonia is clear, an acid-fast stain or fluorescent auramine-rhodamine stain of sputum for mycobacteria should be performed. If legionellosis is suspected, immunofluorescence stains for *Legionella* can be used, although the yield on expectorated sputum is low. The demonstration of elastin fibers in a potassium hydroxide (KOH) preparation of sputum establishes a diagnosis of necrotizing pneumonia (see Table 99–4). Importantly, this test can be positive in the absence of radiographic evidence of cavitation. Blood cultures should be obtained and may be positive in approximately 20 to 30 per cent of patients with bacterial pneumonia.

Results of sputum cultures must be interpreted with caution, since pathogens causing pneumonia may fail to grow and sputum isolates may not be the pathogens responsible for infection. Careful screening of sputum specimens using Gram stain (see above) will increase the accuracy of culture results. A tuberculin skin test and control skin tests such as mumps, *Candida,* and *Trichophyton* should be applied in all cases of pneumonia of uncertain etiology. If the tuberculin is negative

but tuberculosis remains a diagnostic possibility, the tuberculin test should be repeated in 2 weeks.

SPECIFIC PATHOGENIC ORGANISMS

Viral Agents. Viral infection is usually limited to the upper respiratory tract, and only a small proportion of infected patients develop pneumonia. In children, viruses are the most common cause of pneumonia, and respiratory syncytial virus is the most frequent organism. In adults, viruses are estimated to account for fewer than 10 per cent of pneumonias, and the influenza virus is the most common organism. Patients at increased risk of influenzal pneumonia include the aged; patients with chronic disease of the heart, lung, or kidney; and women in the last trimester of pregnancy. Cytomegalovirus has developed prominence as a cause of pneumonia in immunosuppressed patients, particularly in the acquired immunodeficiency syndrome (AIDS) and the post-transplantation state, in which it has a mortality rate of about 50 per cent. When varicella occurs in adults, some 10 to 20 per cent develop pneumonia, which commonly leaves a pattern of diffuse punctate calcification on chest radiograph. Measles is occasionally complicated by pneumonia. Viral pneumonias typically occur in community epidemics and usually develop 1 to 2 days after the onset of "flu-like" symptoms. Major features include a dry cough, dyspnea, generalized discomfort, unremarkable physical examination, and an interstitial pattern on the chest radiograph. Influenza-induced necrosis of respiratory epithelial cells predisposes to bacterial colonization. This may result in superimposed bacterial pneumonia, most often caused by *Streptococcus pneumoniae* or *Staphylococcus aureus.* A presumptive diagnosis may be made on the basis of the clinical presentation and the epidemiologic setting. Gram stain of sputum reveals inflammatory cells and rare bacteria. When available, detection of viral antigens in sputum can confirm the diagnosis rapidly. Viral isolation or serology also can establish the diagnosis but not in time to guide management decisions.

Streptococcus pneumoniae. The pneumococcus

TABLE 99–5. SPUTUM GRAM STAIN REVEALING INFLAMMATORY CELLS AND NO ORGANISMS

POSSIBILITIES	CLINICAL SETTING	CONFIRMATION OF DIAGNOSIS	TREATMENT
Prior antibiotic treatment			
Viral pneumonia	Winter months—influenza, may be mild or life-threatening	Serologies, virus culture, antigen detection	Amantadine for influenza A, ribavirin for respiratory syncytial virus
Mycoplasma pneumoniae	Hacking, nonproductive cough	Cold agglutinins, serologies	Erythromycin, tetracycline
Legionella pneumophila infection	Chronic lung disease—hospital-acquired, summer predominance	DFA* of sputum, bronchial brush biopsy, or pleural fluid, culture, serologies	Erythromycin
Chlamydia psittaci infection	Exposure to birds, e.g., parrots, turkeys	Serologies	Tetracycline
Chlamydia pneumoniae	Hacking cough, sinusitis	Serologies	Tetracycline
Q fever	Exposure to cattle, South Africa	Serologies	Tetracycline or chloramphenicol

*Direct immunofluorescence assay.

is still the most common bacterial cause of pneumonia in the community. The organism colonizes the oropharynx in up to 25 per cent of healthy adults. An increased predisposition to pneumococcal pneumonia is observed in persons with sickle cell disease, prior splenectomy, chronic lung disease, hematologic malignancy, alcoholism, HIV infection, and renal failure. Clinical features include fever, rigors, chills, cough, respiratory distress, signs of pulmonary consolidation, confusion, and herpes labialis. By the second or third day of illness, the chest radiograph typically shows lobar consolidation with air bronchograms, but a patchy bronchopneumonic pattern may also be found. Abscess or cavitation rarely occurs. Sterile pleural effusions occur in up to 25 per cent of cases and empyema in 1 per cent. Typically, a leukocytosis of 15,000 to 30,000 cells/μl with neutrophilia is found, but leukopenia may be observed with fulminant infection and among alcoholics and persons with HIV infection. Demonstration of gram-positive diplococci on Gram stain of sputum is helpful in the rapid diagnosis of pneumonia but may fail to demonstrate organisms in some cases of pneumococcal pneumonia. Positive blood cultures are found in 20 to 25 per cent of patients. Penicillin G remains the treatment of choice, although rarely resistant forms have emerged, sensitive to vancomycin.

Staphylococcus aureus. This accounts for 2 to 5 per cent of community-acquired pneumonia, 11 per cent of hospital-acquired pneumonia, and up to 26 per cent of pneumonia following a viral infection. Persistent nasal colonization is observed in 15 to 30 per cent of adults, and 90 per cent of adults display intermittent colonization. Presentation is similar to that of pneumococcal pneumonia, but contrasting features include the development of parenchymal necrosis and abscess formation in up to 25 per cent and empyema in 10 per cent. A hematogenous source of infection, such as septic thrombophlebitis, infective endocarditis, or an infected intravascular device, should be suspected in cases of staphylococcal pneumonia, particularly if the chest radiograph reveals multiple or expanding nodular or wedge-shaped infiltrates. Early in staphylococcal pneumonia of hematogenous origin, sputum is rarely available. Blood cultures are usually positive, and associated skin lesions occur in 20 to 40 per cent. When sputum is available, Gram stain reveals grapelike clusters of gram-positive cocci. S. aureus is recovered very easily from mixed culture samples, so that its absence in a purulent specimen usually excludes it as a cause of the pneumonia. Treatment requires a penicillinase-resistant agent, such as nafcillin or vancomycin. In hospital-acquired infections or in communities with endemic methicillin-resistant Staphylococcus aureus, vancomycin should be used until sensitivity studies indicate that the isolate is sensitive to semisynthetic penicillins.

Streptococcus pyogenes. This is now a rare cause of pneumonia, probably accounting for less than 1 per cent of all cases. Carriage rate in the pharynx, about 3 per cent in adults, is less than with the other gram-positive cocci. Presentation is similar to that observed with Streptococcus pneumoniae and Staphylococcus aureus, except that empyema, often massive, is found in 30 to 40 per cent of cases. Gram stain reveals gram-positive cocci in pairs or chains. Penicillin G is the treatment of choice.

Haemophilus influenzae. This organism is a gram-negative coccobacillus often present in the upper respiratory tract, particularly among patients with chronic obstructive pulmonary disease. Its isolation from sputum in these patients is to be expected. Confirmation of its role in the pathogenesis of pneumonia depends on isolating the organism in the blood, pleural fluid, or lung tissue. Nevertheless, many cases of pneumonia due to this organism will not be confirmed using these rigid criteria, and in a patient with pneumonia the demonstration of gram-negative coccobacilli on Gram stain of sputum should prompt institution of treatment with ampicillin plus a beta-lactamase inhibitor, a second- or third-generation cephalosporin, or trimethoprim-sulfamethoxazole, since 20 per cent of these organisms may show resistance because of beta-lactamase production.

Gram-Negative Bacilli. These have emerged as pathogens of major importance with the introduction of potent antibiotics and the proliferation of intensive care units. They are frequently encountered in patients with debilitating diseases, such as chronic alcoholism, cystic fibrosis, neutropenia, diabetes mellitus, malignancy, and chronic diseases of the lungs, heart, or kidney. They are ubiquitous throughout the hospital, contaminating equipment and instruments, and are the major source of nosocomial pneumonia.

Specific organisms are associated with certain situations; for example, Klebsiella pneumoniae is particularly common in chronic alcoholics, Escherichia coli pneumonia is associated with bacteremias arising from the intestinal or urinary tract, and Pseudomonas aeruginosa is almost universal in cystic fibrosis. Precise etiologic diagnosis is confounded by the frequency with which these organisms colonize the upper airways in predisposed patients. Treatment in this situation generally includes the use of a penicillinase-resistant penicillin or a cephalosporin and an aminoglycoside.

Mycoplasma pneumoniae. Not only is this a common cause of pneumonia in young adults, but it also produces a wide range of extrapulmonary features that may be the only findings. Fewer than 10 per cent of infected patients develop symptoms of lower respiratory tract infection. Respiratory findings resemble those of viral pneumonia. Hacking, nonproductive cough is characteristic. Nonpulmonary features include myalgias, arthralgias, skin lesions (rashes, erythema nodosum and multiforme, Stevens-Johnson syndrome), and neurologic complications (meningitis, encephalitis, transverse myelitis, cranial nerve or peripheral neuritis). The occurrence of acute, multifocal neurologic abnormalities may be helpful in distinguishing *Mycoplasma* pneumonia from that caused by *Chlamydia* or *Legionella*. The neurologic abnormalities characteristically resolve completely as the acute illness subsides.

Cold agglutinins can be demonstrated at the bedside by observing red blood cell clumping on the walls of a glass tube containing anticoagulated blood incubated on ice for at least 10 minutes; they are also occasionally positive in other respiratory infections. A specific complement fixation test allows confirmation of the diagnosis. Tetracycline or erythromycin decreases the duration of symptoms and hastens radiographic resolution but does not eradicate the organism from the respiratory tract.

Legionella Species. These are fastidious gram-negative bacilli that were responsible for respiratory infections long before the well-publicized outbreak of legionnaires' disease in 1976, which led to the recognition of this distinct disease entity and to the identification of the responsible bacillus. (The high mortality rate from this outbreak of a hitherto unrecognized disease among participants in a legionnaires' convention destroyed the reputation of one of Philadelphia's finest hotels.) These organisms are distributed widely in water, and outbreaks have been related to their presence in water towers, condensers, potable water, and even hospital shower heads. Infection may occur sporadically or in outbreaks. Although healthy subjects are affected, there is an increased risk in patients with chronic diseases of the heart, lungs, or kidneys; malignancy; and impairment of cell-mediated immunity. After an incubation period of 2 to 10 days, the illness usually begins gradually with a dry cough, respiratory distress, fever, rigors, malaise, weakness, headache, confusion, and gastrointestinal disturbance. The chest radiograph shows alveolar shadowing that may have a lobar or patchy distribution, with or without pleural effusions. The diagnosis is suggested clinically by the combination of a rapidly progressive pneumonia, dry cough, and multiorgan involvement. Gram stain of sputum shows neutrophils and no organisms.

Diagnosis can be made by three methods. (1) Indirect fluorescent antibody testing of serum is positive in 75 per cent of patients, but up to 8 weeks are required for seroconversion. (2) Direct fluorescent antibody testing of respiratory secretions is the most rapid method of establishing the diagnosis and has a specificity of 95 per cent. Sensitivity of this method is greater in specimens obtained from bronchoscopy or transtracheal aspirate than expectorated sputum. (3) The organism can be cultured on charcoal yeast extract medium, but up to 10 days are required for growth.

Erythromycin is the treatment of choice. Prompt treatment results in fourfold to fivefold reduction in mortality. Patients usually respond within 12 to 48 hours, and it is very unusual for fever, leukocytosis, and confusion to persist beyond 4 days of therapy. In severe cases, rifampin may be added. Ciprofloxacin may also be effective, but clinical experience is limited to date.

Tuberculosis. Approximately 25,000 new cases of tuberculosis occur in the United States each year, with a worldwide incidence of 7 to 10 million. These figures will increase because tuberculosis is the major communicable complication of AIDS. In North America, a disproportionately high number of cases occur among the foreign-born, the racial and ethnic minorities, and the poor. *Mycobacterium tuberculosis* is transmitted by the respiratory route from an infected patient with cavitary pulmonary tuberculosis to a susceptible host not previously infected with the organism. Primary infection usually is manifested only by development of a positive tuberculin skin test. Occasionally, the patient develops sufficient symptoms of fever and nonproductive cough to visit a physician, and a chest radiograph is taken; patchy or lobular infiltrates are noted in the anterior segment of the upper lobes or in the middle or lower lobes, often with associated hilar adenopathy. Pleurisy with effusion is a less common manifestation of primary tuberculosis. Primary infection usually is self-limited, but hematogenous dissemination seeds multiple organs, and latent foci are established and become the nidus for delayed reactivation. Overall, 5 to 15 per cent of infected individuals develop disease. Factors associated with progression to clinical disease are age (the periods of greatest biologic vulnerability to tuberculosis being infancy, childhood, adolescence, and old age); underlying diseases that depress the cellular immune response (see Chapter 109); diabetes mellitus, gastrectomy, silicosis, and sarcoidosis; and the interval since primary infection, with disease progression most likely in the first few years after infection.

Early progression of infection to disease is known as progressive primary tuberculosis and may manifest as miliary tuberculosis, sometimes with meningitis, or as pulmonary disease of the apical and posterior segments of the upper lobes or lower lobe disease.

Most commonly, tuberculosis represents delayed reactivation. Factors influencing reactivation are not well understood. Symptoms begin insidiously with night sweats or chills and fatigue; fever is noted by fewer than 50 per cent of patients, and hemoptysis by fewer than 25 per cent. Physical examination may be unremarkable or may show dullness and rales in the upper lung fields, occasionally with amphoric breath sounds. The chest radiograph may show cavitary disease with infiltrates in the posterior segment of the upper lobes or apical segments of the lower lobes.

Extrapulmonary tuberculosis also reflects reactivation of latent foci and accounts for approximately 15 per cent of cases. Miliary tuberculosis is discussed in Chapter 95, meningeal tuberculosis in Chapter 97, and tuberculosis of bones and joints in Chapter 104.

Because of the growing proportion of elderly individuals in our society and the growing prevalence of HIV infection, "atypical" presentations of tuberculosis are increasingly common. The elderly and patients with diabetes mellitus are more likely to have lower lobe tuberculosis. In HIV-infected patients, involvement of the lower lobes is frequent, extrapulmonary tuberculosis is almost as common as pulmonary involvement, and tuberculin skin tests are likely to be negative. The index of suspicion must be high in these settings.

Before starting antituberculosis drug treatment, two or three sputum samples should be obtained for cultures; bronchoscopy and bronchial washing are indicated only if sputum smears are negative for acid-fast bacilli. It is important to obtain baseline evaluation of liver function for individuals who are to receive potentially hepatotoxic drugs (isoniazid, rifampin, pyrazinamide); color vision, visual fields, and acuity when ethambutol will be used; and audiometry for patients who are to receive streptomycin.

The main principle of chemotherapy for tuberculosis is to avoid resistance by treating with at least two drugs to which the organism is likely to be sensitive. Pulmonary tuberculosis assumed to be caused by sensitive organisms should be treated with daily isoniazid (5 mg/kg up to 300 mg), rifampin (10 mg/kg up to 600 mg), and pyrazinamide, 15 to 30 mg/kg/day for 2 months, followed by isoniazid and rifampin for 4 more months. Additional or alternative drugs are necessary if the patient has life-threatening disease as assurance against unsuspected drug resistance, or when the likelihood of resistance is deemed high (Asians, Hispanics, individuals acquiring infection in an area with high levels of resistance, or persons exposed to a patient known to harbor drug-resistant bacilli). In such instances, ethambutol (15 to 25 mg/kg) or streptomycin (15 mg/kg intramuscular) should be added to the regimen until drug sensitivities are known. At that point, the regimen can be tailored to include at least two drugs to which the organism is sensitive. One of these drugs must be bactericidal. Close monitoring during treatment is mandatory to maximize compliance and minimize side effects.

Contact tracing is critical, as recent infection or additional cases of tuberculosis are likely in some household contacts. Preventive therapy with isoniazid is discussed below.

TREATMENT AND OUTCOME

Bacterial Pneumonia

As soon as the causative organism is identified on Gram stain, antibiotics must be administered without delay. If the pathogen is readily identified, the antibiotic choices are straightforward (Table 99–6). Patients with *Mycoplasma* and viral pneumonia can generally be treated on an ambulatory basis. An occasional young patient with no underlying disease can also be managed at home, provided that the patient is reliably attended by friends or family and has ready access to a physi-

cian or hospital. Otherwise, patients with bacterial pneumonia should be hospitalized.

Supplemental oxygen should be provided if the patient is tachypneic or hypoxemic. Patients at risk for the development of respiratory insufficiency should be monitored in a critical care setting. Patients who are not capable of adequately coughing up respiratory secretions should have frequent clapping and drainage; meticulous attention must be paid to suctioning of oral secretions. Patients with suspected pulmonary tuberculosis should be isolated from other patients.

Patients treated for pneumococcal pneumonia should begin to improve within 48 hours after institution of antibiotics; patients with pneumonia caused by gram-negative bacilli, staphylococci, and oral anaerobes may remain ill for longer periods after initiation of treatment. Several possibilities should be considered among patients who fail to improve or who deteriorate while on treatment.

Endobronchial Obstruction. Physical examination may fail to reveal sounds of consolidation, and radiographs may show evidence of lobar collapse. Bronchoscopy can establish the diagnosis.

Undrained Empyema. Radiographs may not always distinguish between fluid and consolidation; ultrasonography and computed tomographic (CT) scans can identify the fluid and provide direction for its drainage.

Purulent Pericarditis. This should be suspected in a very ill patient with pneumonia involving a lobe adjacent to the pericardium. Chest pain and electrocardiographic evidence of pericar-

TABLE 99–6. INITIAL ANTIBIOTICS FOR TREATMENT OF PNEUMONIA

PATHOGEN	TREATMENT
Streptococcus pneumoniae	Penicillin G, 1.2 million units/day*
Mycoplasma pneumoniae	Erythromycin, 500 mg po qid
Haemophilus influenzae†	Trimethoprim-sulfamethoxazole, 80 mg/400 mg q6h, or cefuroxime, 1 gm q8h IV
Staphylococcus aureus	Nafcillin, 3 gm IV q6h, or vancomycin, 1 gm IV g12h
Legionella pneumophila	Erythromycin, 750 mg q6h
Mixed oral flora (anaerobes)	Ampicillin/sulbactam, 500 mg q8h day‡
Gram-negative rods	Aminoglycoside (e.g., gentamicin, 1.7 mg/kg IV q8h) plus third-generation cephalosporin (e.g., ceftazidime, 6 gm/day)§
Tuberculosis	Isoniazid, 300 mg/day, plus rifampin, 600 mg/day, and pyrazinamide, 1500 mg/day

*Erythromycin, 500 mg q6h for penicillin-allergic patients.
†Beta-lactamase–producing *H. influenzae* has caused disease in adults. If patient is very ill, avoid ampicillin and use instead trimethoprim-sulfamethoxazole or a third-generation cephalosporin.
‡Clindamycin, 600 mg q6h, if patient fails to respond to penicillin.
§Add beta-lactam antibiotic active against *Pseudomonas aeruginosa* (e.g., ceftazidime, 2 gm q8h) if *Pseudomonas* is a possibility. Antibiotics can be adjusted when sensitivity data are available.

ditis are usually absent. Distended neck veins and pericardial friction rubs are present in a minority of cases. Echocardiography or chest ultrasonography reveals fluid in the pericardium. If purulent pericarditis is suspected, emergency pericardiocentesis can be life-saving (see Chapter 9).

Incorrect Diagnosis or Treatment. In cases in which clinical response is poor, the patient's hospital course and admission sputum stains should be reviewed by a clinician with expertise in the diagnosis and treatment of pneumonia. Pulmonary embolism with infarction, a treatable disease, can prove fatal if misdiagnosed as bacterial pneumonia. Misinterpretation of sputum Gram-stained preparations—either failure to recognize an important pathogen or a treatment decision based upon examination of an inadequate specimen—is an avoidable pitfall of medical practice. Bronchoscopy should be considered both to obtain better specimens for diagnosis and to exclude underlying endobronchial obstruction.

TABLE 99–7. PREVENTION OF PNEUMONIA: CANDIDATES FOR PNEUMOCOCCAL AND INFLUENZA VACCINES

	PNEUMOCOCCAL VACCINE (ONE TIME ONLY)	INFLUENZA VACCINE (YEARLY)
Patients ≥ 65 years	Yes	Yes
Chronic lung or heart disease	Yes	Yes
Sickle cell disease	Yes	Consider
Asplenic patients	Yes	No
Hodgkin's disease	Yes	Consider
Multiple myeloma	Yes	Consider
Cirrhosis	Yes	Consider
Chronic alcoholism	Yes	Consider
Chronic renal failure	Yes	Consider
Cerebrospinal fluid leaks	Yes	No
Residents of chronic care facilities	Consider	Yes
Diabetes mellitus	Yes	Yes
HIV infection	Yes	Consider

TABLE 99–8. INDICATIONS FOR PROPHYLAXIS WITH ISONIAZID (INH)

Documented new skin test conversion to tuberculin over past 2 yr
Tuberculin-positive contacts of patients with active tuberculosis (TB)
Tuberculin-negative contacts of patients with active TB*
Tuberculin-positive persons with HIV infection
Positive tuberculin skin test of unknown duration in patients under 35 years of age
Patients with radiographic evidence of inactive TB who have never received an adequate course of antituberculosis drugs
Consider INH prophylaxis for patients with positive tuberculin skin tests and:
    gastrectomy, diabetes mellitus, organ transplantation, silicosis, and prolonged (>1 mo) administration of corticosteroids or immunosuppressive drugs

*These individuals should have repeat skin tests 3 mo after INH is begun. If the repeat test is negative, INH may be discontinued.

The Patient with Pleural Effusion and Fever

The approach to such patients is quite straightforward; the fluid must be examined. If a bacterium other than *Streptococcus pneumoniae* is seen on Gram stain of pleural fluid or grown in culture, chest tube drainage is required. A pleural effusion infected with the pneumococcus can often be treated with simple needle aspiration and antibiotics. Among patients with pneumonia, even fluids that do not reveal organisms on Gram stain but that have a pH of less than 7.00 and/or a glucose concentration below 40 mg/dl may require chest tube drainage for satisfactory resolution.

Pleurisy caused by *Mycobacterium tuberculosis* is often an acute illness. In most cases, a pneumonia is not present or readily appreciated. Inflammatory cells—polymorphonuclear leukocytes, mononuclear leukocytes, or both—are present in the pleural fluid. Mesothelial cells are usually sparse (<0.5 per cent of the total cell count). Pleural fluid glucose levels are often low but may be normal. Mycobacteria are rarely seen on stains of pleural fluid. As many as one third of patients do not have positive tuberculin skin tests. Other causes of pleural effusion in this setting may be pulmonary infarction (fewer than half of patients produce a hemorrhagic exudate), malignancy (most do not have fever), and connective tissue diseases such as systemic lupus erythematosus and rheumatoid arthritis. If the cause of the effusion is not evident, a biopsy of the pleura is needed.

PREVENTION

Pneumococcal pneumonia may be preventable by immunizing patients at high risk with polyvalent pneumococcal polysaccharide vaccine. The current polyvalent vaccine is 60 to 80 per cent effective in individuals with normal immune responses. Booster immunizations should not be given because of the possibility of serious reactions. Yearly immunization with influenza vaccine is also advised for many of these patients; by decreasing the attack rate of influenza, immunization also decreases morbidity and mortality due to secondary bacterial pneumonia (Table 99–7).

Patients without active tuberculosis but with skin test reactivity to tuberculosis are at risk for reactivating their infection. The development of active tuberculosis can be prevented in most instances by treatment for 6 to 12 months with isoniazid, 300 mg/day. Indications for prophylaxis are shown in Table 99–8.

REFERENCES

Duma RJ: Pneumococcal pneumonia. *In* Wyngaarden JB, Smith LH Jr, Bennett JC (eds): Cecil Textbook of Medicine. 19th ed. Philadelphia, WB Saunders Co, 1992, pp 1608–1615.
Karnad A, Alvarez S, Berk SL: Pneumonia caused by gram-negative bacilli. Am J Med 79 (Suppl 1A):61, 1985.
Wolinsky E: Tuberculosis. *In* Wyngaarden JB, Smith LH Jr, Bennett JC (eds): Cecil Textbook of Medicine. 19th ed. Philadelphia, WB Saunders Co, 1992, pp 1733–1742.

100 INFECTIONS OF THE HEART AND VESSELS

INFECTIVE ENDOCARDITIS (IE)

Infective endocarditis ranges from an indolent illness with few systemic manifestations, readily responsive to antibiotic therapy, to a fulminant septicemic disease with malignant destruction of the heart valves and life-threatening systemic embolization. The varied features of endocarditis relate in large measure to the different infecting organisms. Viridans streptococci are the prototype of bacteria that originate in the oral flora, infect previously abnormal heart valves, and may cause minimal symptomatology despite progressive valvular damage. *Staphylococcus aureus*, in contrast, can invade previously normal valves and destroy them rapidly.

Epidemiology

The average age of patients with endocarditis has increased in the antibiotic era to the current mean of 54 years. This change can be attributed to the decreasing prevalence of rheumatic heart disease, the increasing prevalence of underlying degenerative heart disease, and the increasing frequency of procedures and practices predisposing older patients to bacteremia (genitourinary procedures, intravenous catheters, hemodialysis shunts). Rheumatic heart disease remains a predisposing factor in 20 to 30 per cent of patients with IE. About 15 per cent of patients have congenital heart disease (exclusive of mitral valve prolapse). The propensity to develop endocarditis varies with the congenital lesion. For example, infection of a bicuspid aortic valve accounts for one fifth of cases of IE occurring over the age of 60; a secundum atrial septal defect, however, rarely becomes infected. Mitral valve prolapse is the predisposing condition in more than one third of cases of endocarditis restricted to the mitral valve. Intravenous drug users have a unique propensity to develop IE of the tricuspid valve, although infection of the mitral or aortic valve also is common.

Pathogenesis

Endocarditis ensues when bacteria entering the blood stream from an oral or other source lodge on heart valves that may already bear platelet-fibrin thrombi. The frequency of bacteremia is quite high after dental extraction (18 to 85 per cent) or peridontal surgery (32 to 88 per cent) but also is significant following everyday activities such as tooth brushing (0 to 26 per cent) and chewing candy (17 to 51 per cent). The production of extracellular dextran by some strains of *Streptococcus* is responsible for their adherence to dental enamel and also is a factor in the entrapment of circulating organisms on damaged valves and platelet-fibrin thrombi. The localization of infection is partly determined by the production of turbulent flow. The mitral valve is the most frequent site of infection. Vegetations usually are found on the valve surface facing the lower pressure chamber (e.g., atrial surface of the mitral valve), a relative haven for deposition of bacteria from the swift blood stream. Occasionally, "jet lesions" develop in which the regurgitant stream strikes the heart wall or the chordae tendineae. Once infection begins, bacteria proliferate freely within the interstices of the enlarging vegetation; in this relatively avascular site, they are protected from serum bactericidal factors and leukocytes.

The infection may cause rupture of the valve tissue itself or of its chordal structures, leading to either gradual or acute valvular regurgitation. Some virulent bacteria (e.g., *Staphylococcus aureus*) or fungal vegetations may become large enough to obstruct the valve orifice or create a large embolus. Aneurysms of the sinus of Valsalva may occur and can rupture into the pericardial space. The conducting system may be affected by valve ring or myocardial abscesses. The infection may invade the interventricular septum, causing intramyocardial abscesses or septal rupture that can also damage the conduction system of the heart. Systemic septic embolization may occur with left-sided endocarditis, and septic pulmonary emboli with right-sided endocarditis.

Clinical Features

Some cases of streptococcal endocarditis become clinically manifest within 2 weeks of initiating events, such as dental extraction. Diagnosis usually is delayed an additional 4 to 5 weeks or more, however, because of the paucity of symptoms. If the causative organism is slow-growing and produces an indolent syndrome, symptoms may be extremely protracted (6 months or longer) before definitive diagnosis. The symptoms and signs of IE relate to systemic infection, emboli (bland or septic), metastatic infective foci, congestive heart failure, or immune complex–associated lesions. The most common complaints in patients with IE are fever, chills, weakness, shortness of breath, drenching night sweats, loss of appetite, and weight loss. Musculoskeletal symptoms develop in nearly one half of patients and may dominate the presentation. Proximal arthralgias are typical and are frequently accompanied by oligoarticular arthritis of the lower extremities. Fever is present in 90 per cent of patients. Fever is more often absent in elderly or debilitated patients or in the setting of underlying congestive heart failure, renal dysfunction, or previous antibiotic treatment. Heart murmurs are frequent (85 per cent); changing murmurs (5 to 10 per cent) and new cardiac murmurs (5 per cent) are unusual but highly suggestive of the diagnosis of IE. With endocarditis involving the aortic or the mitral valve, congestive heart failure occurs in two thirds of patients and may begin precipitously, for example, with perforation of a valve or rupture of chordae tendineae. At least one of the peripheral manifestations of endocarditis occurs in one half of patients (Table 100–1). Splenomegaly (25 to 60 per cent) is more likely when symptoms have been prolonged. Clubbing occurs in 10 to 15 per cent of patients.

The clinical syndrome of IE differs in users of intravenous drugs. Tricuspid valve infection is most common. Patients most often present with fever and chills but may present with pleuritic chest pain caused by septic pulmonary emboli. Round, cavitating infiltrates may be found on the chest radiograph. The infective foci are initially centered in blood vessels; only after they erode into the bronchial system does cough develop, productive of bloody or purulent sputum.

Serious systemic emboli may cause dramatic findings, at times masking the systemic nature of IE. Embolism to the splenic artery may lead to left upper quadrant pain, sometimes radiating to the left shoulder, a friction rub, and/or left pleural effusion. Renal, coronary, and mesenteric arteries are frequent alternative sites of clinically important emboli. Central nervous system (CNS) embolization is one of the most serious complications of IE, since it may produce irreversible and disabling neurologic deficits.

Overall, neurologic manifestations occur in one third of patients with IE. The diagnosis is easily missed when CNS signs and symptoms are the presenting features of IE, as occurs in approximately 10 per cent of cases. Patients with IE may complain of headache or may develop seizures. The pathophysiologic explanation for these symptoms is not always apparent. In addition, stroke due to vascular occlusion by an embolus, toxic encephalopathy, which may mimic psychosis, and meningoencephalitis also occur. The aseptic meningitis or meningoencephalitis seen in such patients is not readily distinguished from viral and other etiologies of a similar syndrome.

Clinical syndromes caused by CNS emboli may be more distinctive. The consequences of embolization depend on the site of lodging and the bacterial pathogen. Organisms such as viridans streptococci initially produce a syndrome entirely attributable to the vascular occlusion; however, damage to the blood vessel can result in formation of a mycotic aneurysm that may leak or burst at a later date. Resolution of aneurysms may occur after antimicrobial therapy. In many patients, however, surgical clipping is necessary to prevent recurrent hemorrhage. Single aneurysms in accessible areas should be considered for prompt surgical clipping. Staphylococcus aureus, in contrast, produces progressive infection extending from the site of embolization; brain abscess and purulent meningitis are common sequelae.

The kidney can be the site of abscess formation, multiple infarcts, or immune complex glomerulonephritis. When renal dysfunction develops during antibiotic therapy, drug toxicity is an additional possibility.

Laboratory Findings

Nonspecific laboratory abnormalities occur in IE and reflect chronic infection. These include anemia, reticulocytopenia, increased erythrocyte sedimentation rate, hypergammaglobulinemia, and circulating immune complexes and rheumatoid factor. The presence of rheumatoid factor may be a helpful clue to diagnosis in patients with culture-negative endocarditis. Urinalysis frequently shows

TABLE 100–1. PERIPHERAL MANIFESTATIONS OF INFECTIVE ENDOCARDITIS (IE)

PHYSICAL FINDING (frequency)	PATHOGENESIS	MOST COMMON ORGANISMS
Petechiae (20–40%) (red, nonblanching lesions in crops on conjunctivae, buccal mucosa, palate, extremities)	Vasculitis or emboli	Streptococcus, Staphylococcus
Splinter hemorrhages (15%) (linear, red-brown streaks most suggestive of IE when proximal in nail beds)	Vasculitis or emboli	Staphylococcus, Streptococcus
Osler's nodes (10–25%) (2- to 5-mm painful nodules on pads of fingers or toes)	Vasculitis	Streptococcus
Janeway's lesions (<10%) (macular, red or hemorrhagic, painless patches on palms or soles)	Emboli	Staphylococcus
Roth's spots (<5%) (oval, pale retinal lesions surrounded by hemorrhage)	Vasculitis	Streptococcus

proteinuria (50 to 60 per cent) and microscopic hematuria (30 to 50 per cent). The presence of red blood cell casts is indicative of immune complex–mediated glomerulonephritis.

The bacteremia of IE is continuous and low-grade (often 1 to 100 bacteria per milliliter in subacute cases). Three sets of blood cultures should be obtained in the first 24 hours of hospitalization. Two or three additional blood cultures are important if the patient has received antibiotic therapy in the preceding 1 to 2 weeks and if initial blood cultures are negative at 48 to 72 hours. Ten to 20 per cent of patients with the clinical diagnosis of IE have negative blood cultures, usually because of previous antibiotic therapy.

Echocardiography is a useful technique for identifying vegetations in endocarditis. The finding of vegetations is helpful diagnostically and also indicates an increased risk of valvular destruction with congestive heart failure, systemic embolization, and death. Echocardiographic findings may be misleading, however, and the absence of vegetations on the echocardiogram does not exclude the diagnosis of IE. Transesophageal echocardiography provides improved resolution of bacterial vegetations and valve ring abscesses and may be helpful in difficult determinations concerning the need for surgery. Magnetic resonance imaging (MRI) of the heart similarly may demonstrate myocardial, septal, or valve ring abscesses.

Differential Diagnosis

The diagnosis of IE usually is firmly established on the basis of the clinical findings and the results of blood cultures. In some instances, the distinction between IE and nonendocarditis bacteremia may be difficult. Since the bacteremia is usually continuous in IE and intermittent in other bacteremias, the fraction of blood cultures that are positive may be helpful. In streptococcal infection, the speciation of the blood culture isolate may provide circumstantial evidence for or against infection of the heart valves (Table 100–2). The identity of the causative organism may be helpful for other bacteria as well; the ratio of IE to non-IE bacteremias is approximately 1:1 for *Staphylococcus aureus*, 1:7 for group B streptococci, and 1:200 for *Escherichia coli*. *Streptococcus bovis* bacteremia and endocarditis are often (>50 per cent) associated with

TABLE 100–2. RELATIVE FREQUENCY OF IE AND NON-IE BACTEREMIAS FOR VARIOUS STREPTOCOCCI

SPECIES	IE/NON-IE
Streptococcus mutans	14:1
Streptococcus bovis	6:1
Streptococcus faecalis	1:1
Group B streptococci	1:7
Group A streptococci	1:32

Modified from Parker MT, Ball LC: Streptococci and aerococci associated with systemic infection in man. J Med Microbiol 9:275, 1976.

colonic carcinomas and polyps, so that isolation of this organism warrants thorough evaluation of the lower gastrointestinal tract.

The initial presentation of IE can be misleading: the young adult may present with a stroke, pneumonia, or meningitis; the elderly patient may present with confusion or simply with fatigue or malaise without fever. The index of suspicion of IE, therefore, must be high, and blood cultures should be obtained in these varied settings, particularly if antibiotic use is contemplated.

Major problems in diagnosis arise if antibiotics have been administered before blood is cultured or if blood cultures are negative. Attempts to culture slow-growing organisms, including those with particular nutritional requirements, should be planned by discussion with a clinical microbiologist. The differential diagnosis of culture-negative endocarditis includes acute rheumatic fever, multiple pulmonary emboli, atrial myxoma, and nonbacterial thrombotic endocarditis (NBTE). NBTE (sometimes called marantic endocarditis) occurs in patients with severe wasting, whether due to malignancy or other conditions. Also, patients with systemic lupus erythematosus may develop sterile valvular vegetations, termed Libman-Sacks lesions, on the undersurfaces of the valve leaflets. These diagnoses should be considered and excluded, if possible, before beginning therapy for presumed culture-negative IE.

Management and Outcome

The outcome of endocarditis is determined by the extent of valvular destruction, the size and friability of vegetations, and the choice of antibiotics. These factors, in turn, are influenced by the nature of the causative organism and delays in diagnosis. The goal of antibiotics is to halt further valvular damage and to cure the infection. Surgery may be necessary for hemodynamic stabilization, prevention of embolization, or control of drug-resistant infection.

Antibiotics should be selected on the basis of the clinical setting (Table 100–3) and started as soon as blood cultures are obtained if the diagnosis of IE appears highly likely and the course is suggestive of active valvular destruction or systemic embolization. The antibiotics can be adjusted later on the basis of culture and sensitivity data.

Antibiotics

Several general considerations are important in choosing a regimen of antibiotics. A number of different regimens have been advocated for the treatment of IE due to each of the causative organisms. Since few have been subjected to valid comparative trials, the selection of drugs, dosages, and duration is somewhat empiric. Similarly, although sophisticated laboratory tests such as serum bactericidal activity are used to monitor

TABLE 100–3. SYNDROMES SUGGESTING SPECIFIC BACTERIA CAUSING INFECTIVE ENDOCARDITIS

Indolent Course
Viridans streptococci
Streptococcus bovis
Streptococcus faecalis
Fastidious gram-negative rods
Aggressive Course
Staphylococcus aureus
Streptococcus pneumoniae
Streptococcus pyogenes
Neisseria gonorrhoeae
Drug Users
Staphylococcus aureus
Pseudomonas aeruginosa
Streptococcus faecalis
Candida sp.
Bacillus sp.
Frequent Major Emboli
Haemophilus sp.
Bacteroides sp.
Candida sp.

and adjust drug regimens, they have not been standardized or validated adequately.

Most viridans streptococci and nonenterococcal group D streptococci, such as *Streptococcus bovis*, are exquisitely sensitive to penicillin. The penicillin concentration inhibiting growth of such organisms is less than 0.1 μg/ml, and they are killed by similar concentrations of penicillin. A variety of antibiotic regimens have been advocated to treat this form of IE, and several appear to be equally effective. Aqueous penicillin G, 12 million units/day given intravenously for 4 weeks, is curative in almost all patients. In the stable patient at low risk of complications, some or most of the antibiotic course can be administered on an outpatient basis.

Treatment of enterococcal endocarditis and IE caused by other penicillin-resistant streptococci is much less satisfactory because of frequent relapses and high mortality. The recommended regimen is intravenous aqueous penicillin G, 20 million units/day, plus intravenous gentamicin or tobramycin, 3 mg/kg/day. This relatively low dose of aminoglycoside is associated with less nephrotoxicity. Tobramycin is the preferred aminoglycoside because of its slightly lower risk of nephrotoxicity, unless sensitivity testing reveals greater potency of gentamicin. The aminoglycoside dose should be adjusted according to measured serum levels and the bactericidal activity of serum. Streptomycin, 0.5 gm administered intramuscularly every 12 hours, can be substituted as the aminoglycoside if the organism is sensitive; however, streptomycin is associated with irreversible vestibular and auditory toxicity in some patients.

Although the value of serum bactericidal determinations has not been firmly established, most experts rely on them as a general guide to the adequacy of antibiotic regimens for enterococcal

endocarditis. A drug regimen is considered adequate for treatment of IE if trough serum bactericidal activity is present at dilutions of 1:8 or greater. In view of the high frequency of relapses, regimens to treat enterococcal infection should be continued for 4 to 6 weeks. Culture-negative endocarditis should be treated similarly.

Staphylococcus aureus endocarditis should be treated with intravenous nafcillin, 12 gm/day. Infection with a methicillin-resistant species of *Staphylococcus* necessitates the use of vancomycin. The addition of an aminoglycoside hastens clearance of bacteremia and is indicated in the patient with a fulminant septic presentation and in the initial treatment of left-sided endocarditis. Once sepsis is controlled, the aminoglycoside should be discontinued. Minimal bactericidal concentrations of antibiotic should be determined. If the bactericidal concentration is more than 32 times the bacteriostatic concentration, the organism can be considered drug-tolerant. Patients with IE caused by tolerant staphylococci may have a more complicated clinical course. If the organism fulfills the criteria for tolerance, determination of serum bactericidal activity is appropriate; if this proves inadequate (i.e., bactericidal activity <1:8 dilution of serum), and the patient shows signs of persistent infection, addition of a drug (aminoglycoside or rifampin) or substitution of vancomycin for nafcillin should be considered. The duration of antibiotic therapy for staphylococcal endocarditis of the mitral or aortic valve is a minimum of 6 weeks.

In the patient with streptococcal or staphylococcal IE and a history of serious penicillin allergy, vancomycin can be substituted for penicillin. Outcome generally is comparable, although auditory or renal toxicity may occur with vancomycin.

Pseudomonas endocarditis is a particular problem in intravenous drug users. Therapy should be initiated with tobramycin, 8 mg/kg/day given intravenously, and mezlocillin, 4 gm given intravenously every 8 hours. The unusually high doses of aminoglycosides have improved the outcome of medical therapy of *Pseudomonas* infection of the tricuspid valve with surprisingly few side effects such as nephrotoxicity. Left-sided *Pseudomonas aeruginosa* infections, however, generally require surgery for cure. Although third-generation cephalosporins have attractive in vitro efficacy against *Pseudomonas* species, in vivo development of resistance and clinical failure have limited their usefulness, especially as single agents, in this setting. Some young adults have rapid clearance of aminoglycosides, so it is particularly critical to evaluate pharmacokinetics and adjust dosages as appropriate when these agents are employed.

Fungal endocarditis is refractory to antibiotics and requires surgery for management. Amphotericin B generally is administered to such patients but is not in itself curative.

Surgery

The indications for early surgery in IE need to be individualized and forged by discussions with the cardiac surgeon. Refractory infection is a clear indication for surgery; as noted, the requirement for surgery is predictable in IE caused by certain organisms. Persistence of bacteremia for longer than 7 to 10 days, despite the administration of appropriate antibiotics, frequently reflects paravalvular extension of infection with development of valve ring abscess or myocardial abscesses. Medical cure is not possible in this setting. Intravenous drug users are more likely to have IE due to organisms refractory to medical therapy (*Candida, Pseudomonas*). Refractory tricuspid endocarditis may be amenable to valve debridement or excision without immediate placement of a prosthetic valve. Valvulectomy may, however, be associated with the eventual onset of right-sided congestive heart failure.

Protracted fever is not unusual in patients undergoing treatment of endocarditis and should not automatically be equated with refractory infection. In fact, 10 per cent of patients remain febrile for more than 2 weeks and persistent fever is not an independent indication for surgery, particularly when tricuspid endocarditis is complicated by multiple septic pulmonary emboli with necrotizing pneumonia. Delayed defervescence also is common, despite appropriate antimicrobial therapy, with endocarditis due to *Staphylococcus aureus* and enteric bacteria.

Congestive heart failure refractory to medical therapy is the most frequent indication for early cardiac surgery. The extent of valvular dysfunction may be difficult to gauge clinically, particularly in patients with acute aortic regurgitation (AR); in the absence of compensatory ventricular dilatation, classic physical signs associated with AR, such as wide pulse pressure, may not be present. Echocardiography, fluoroscopy, and cardiac catheterization may be necessary to evaluate the extent of aortic regurgitation in some instances. However, when congestive heart failure develops in the patient with *Staphylococcus aureus* IE, aortic valvular destruction usually is extensive, necessitating early surgery. Delaying surgery to prolong the course of antibiotic therapy is never appropriate if the patient is hemodynamically unstable or fulfills other criteria for surgical intervention. Prosthetic valve endocarditis seldom occurs after cardiac valve replacement for IE, and its incidence is not influenced by duration of preoperative antibiotics.

Recurrent major systemic embolization is another indication for surgery. If valvular function is preserved, vegetations sometimes can be removed without valve replacement. Septal abscess, although often difficult to recognize clinically, and aneurysms of the sinus of Valsalva are absolute indications for surgery.

PROSTHETIC VALVE ENDOCARDITIS (PVE)

PVE complicates approximately 3 per cent of cardiac valve replacements. Two separate clinical syndromes have been identified. Early PVE occurs within 60 days of surgery and most often is caused by *Staphylococcus epidermidis*, gram-negative enteric bacilli, *Staphylococcus aureus*, or diphtheroids. The prosthesis may be contaminated at the time of surgery or seeded by bacteremia from extracardiac sites (intravenous cannula, indwelling urinary bladder catheter, wound infection, pneumonia). In addition to forming vegetations, which may be quite bulky and cause obstruction, particularly of mitral valve prostheses, circumferential spread of infection often causes dehiscence and paravalvular leak at the site of an aortic prosthesis. The combination of intravenous vancomycin, 2 gm/day, and intravenous tobramycin, 3 to 5 mg/kg/day, plus oral rifampin, 600 mg/day, is indicated to treat *Staphylococcus epidermidis* infection. Other infections should be treated with synergistic combinations of antibiotics based on in vitro sensitivity testing. Surgery is mandatory in the presence of moderate to severe congestive heart failure. The mortality of early PVE is approximately 75 per cent.

Late PVE usually is caused by viridans streptococcal bacteremia from an oral site that seeds a re-endothelialized valve surface. Treatment with intravenous aqueous penicillin G, 20 million units/day, plus intravenous tobramycin, 3 to 5 mg/kg/day, is appropriate. The prognosis for cure with antibiotic therapy alone is better in patients infected with penicillin-sensitive streptococci. Moderate to severe congestive heart failure is the main indication for surgery. The mortality of late PVE is approximately 40 per cent.

PROPHYLAXIS OF INFECTIVE ENDOCARDITIS

Patients with prosthetic heart valves or mitral or aortic valvular heart disease are at relatively high risk of developing IE. Mitral valve prolapse associated with a systolic murmur is another significant risk factor. Neither the value of antibiotic prophylaxis nor the optimal regimens have been definitively established. Recommended regimens are presented in Table 100–4.

Administration of antibiotics has become an accepted practice for patients undergoing open heart surgery, including valve replacement. Intravenous cefazolin, 2.0 gm at induction of anesthesia, repeated 8 and 16 hours later, or intravenous vancomycin, 1.0 gm at induction and 0.5 gm 8 and 16 hours later, is an appropriate regimen. Cardiac diagnostic procedures (catheterization), pacemaker placement, and coronary artery bypass do not pose sufficient risk to warrant the use of prophylactic antibiotics for IE or prosthetic valve endocarditis.

Devices that are associated with high rates of infection and bacteremia (intravenous cannulas, indwelling urinary bladder catheters) should be avoided in hospitalized patients at risk for IE if at all possible; established local infections should be treated promptly and vigorously.

TABLE 100-4. PROPHYLAXIS OF INFECTIVE ENDOCARDITIS

INDICATIONS	REGIMEN*
Aortic or mitral valve disease in patients undergoing dental procedure with bleeding gums	**Oral**
As above for penicillin-allergic patient or when chronic penicillin prophylaxis has been used to prevent rheumatic fever	1. Amoxicillin, 3.0 gm orally 1 hr before and 1.5 gm 6 hr after procedure
	2. Erythromycin, 1.0 gm orally 1 hr before and 0.5 gm orally 6 hr after procedure
Patient with prosthetic heart valve undergoing dental, gastrointestinal, or genitourinary procedure. Patient with aortic or mitral valve disease undergoing gastrointestinal surgery or genitourinary instrumentation or surgery	**Parenteral**
	1. Ampicillin, 2.0 gm IM or IV, plus gentamicin, 1.5 mg/kg IM or IV, 30 min before procedure
	Repeat parenteral antibodies 8 hours after procedure
Penicillin-allergic patient with prosthetic heart valve undergoing dental procedure	
Penicillin-allergic patient with aortic or mitral valve disease undergoing gastrointestinal surgery or genitourinary instrumentation or surgery.	2. Vancomycin, 1.0 gm IV over a 1-hr period beginning 1 hr before procedure
Penicillin-allergic patient with prosthetic valve undergoing gastrointestinal or genitourinary procedure	3. Vancomycin, 1.0 gm IV, plus gentamicin, 1.5 mg/kg IV, beginning 1 hr before procedure

*These are empiric suggestions. Additional doses of antibiotic may be given if there is risk of prolonged bacteremia.
IM = Intramuscular; IV = intravenous.

BACTERIAL ENDARTERITIS AND SUPPURATIVE PHLEBITIS

Bacterial endarteritis usually develops by one of three mechanisms: (1) Arteries, particularly those with intimal abnormalities, may become infected as a consequence of transient bacteremia. (2) During the course of IE, septic emboli to vasa vasorum may lead to mycotic aneurysms. (3) Blood vessels also may be infected by direct extension from contiguous foci and trauma.

A septic presentation is characteristic of endarteritis due to organisms such as *Staphylococcus aureus*. Besides sepsis, the major problem caused by endarteritis is hemorrhage. About 3 to 4 per cent of patients with IE develop intracranial my-

cotic aneurysms. Mycotic aneurysms in IE typically are situated peripherally and in the distribution of the middle cerebral artery. Focal seizures, focal signs, or aseptic meningitis may herald catastrophic rupture of such aneurysms. These premonitory findings, therefore, indicate the need for evaluation with arteriography; neurosurgical intervention should be contemplated if accessible lesions are demonstrated. Other forms of bacterial endarteritis also require combined medical and surgical management; antibiotic selection should be based on the results of in vitro sensitivity testing.

Suppurative thrombophlebitis usually is a complication of the use of intravenous plastic cannulas. Burn patients, especially those with lower extremity catheterization, are at particular risk. Typically, intravenous cannulas have been left in place 5 days or more. Symptoms may be delayed until several days after removal of the catheter and reflect septicemia, septic pulmonary emboli, or metastatic abscess formation. Local findings at the site of infection are present in only one third of burn patients with this complication. Therefore, surgical exploration is imperative when the diagnosis of suppurative phlebitis is first suspected. Involved segments of vein must be excised. Antibiotics should be selected to ensure coverage of the most common pathogens, *Staphylococcus aureus* (nafcillin, 12 gm/day IV) and Enterobacteriaceae (gentamicin, 5 mg/kg/day IV). When infection of an intravenous cannula is suspected, the catheter should be removed and 2-inch segments rolled across a blood agar plate. The growth of more than 15 colonies suggests infection. The infusate also should be cultured.

Suppurative phlebitis is preventable. Steel "scalp vein" needles are associated with 40-fold less risk of infection than are plastic cannulas and should be used preferentially for intravenous therapy. When plastic peripheral intravenous cannulas are necessary, they should be inserted aseptically and replaced at least every 48 hours.

REFERENCES

Durack DT: Infective endocarditis. *In* Wyngaarden JB, Smith LH Jr, Bennett JC (eds): Cecil Textbook of Medicine. 19th ed. Philadelphia, WB Saunders Co, 1992, pp 1638–1647.

Lederman MM, Sprague L, Wallis RS, Ellner JJ: Duration of fever during infective endocarditis. Medicine 71:52, 1992.

Reller LB: The serum bactericidal test. Rev Infect Dis 8:803, 1986.

101 SKIN AND SOFT TISSUE INFECTIONS

Normal skin is remarkably resistant to infection. Most common infections of the skin are initiated by breaks in the epithelium. Hematogenous seeding of the skin by pathogens is less frequent.

Some superficial infections, such as folliculitis and furuncles, may be treated with local measures. Other superficial infections (e.g., impetigo and cellulitis) require systemic antibiotics. Deeper soft tissue infections, such as fasciitis and myonecrosis, require surgical debridement. As a general rule, infections of the face and hand should be treated particularly aggressively because of the risks of intracranial spread in the former and the potential loss of function due to closed-space infection in the latter.

SUPERFICIAL INFECTIONS OF THE SKIN

Circumscribed Infections of the Skin

Vesicles, pustules, nodules, and ulcerations are the lesions in this category (Table 101–1).

Folliculitis is a superficial infection of hair follicles. The lesions are crops of red papules or pustules; careful examination using a hand lens reveals hair in the center of most papules. Staphylococci, yeast, and, occasionally, *Pseudomonas* species are the responsible pathogens. Local treatment with cleansing and hot compresses is usually sufficient. The skin lesions of disseminated candidiasis seen in neutropenic patients may resemble folliculitis. In this setting, skin biopsy readily distinguishes these two processes; in disseminated disease, yeast are found within blood vessels and not simply surrounding the hair follicle.

Furuncles and *carbuncles* are subcutaneous abscesses due to *Staphylococcus aureus*. The lesions are red, tender nodules that may have a surrounding cellulitis and occur most prominently on the face and back of the neck. They often drain spontaneously. Furuncles may be treated with local compresses. If fluctuant, the larger carbuncles require incision and drainage. Antistaphylococcal antibiotics should be given if the patient has systemic symptoms, such as fever or malaise, if there is accompanying cellulitis, or if the lesions are on the head.

Impetigo is a superficial infection of the skin due to group A streptococci, although occasionally *Staphylococcus aureus* may also be found in the lesions. Impetigo is seen primarily among children, who initially develop a vesicle on the skin surface; this rapidly becomes pustular and breaks down, leaving the characteristic dry golden crust. This infection is highly contagious—usually spread by the child's hands to other sites on the child's body or to other children. Gram stain reveals gram-positive cocci in chains (streptococci); occasionally, clusters of staphylococci are also seen. Certain strains of streptococci causing impetigo have been associated with the later development of post-streptococcal glomerulonephritis. The differential diagnosis of impetigo includes herpes simplex infection and varicella. These viral lesions may become pustular; Gram stain of an unruptured viral vesicle or pustule should not, however, contain bacteria. A Tzanck preparation (see Chapter 93) can establish the diagnosis of herpes simplex or varicella if the differential diagnosis is uncertain. Penicillin is the treatment of choice for impetigo, since staphylococci represent secondary infection and will disappear when the streptococci are eradicated. Antibiotics do not appear to affect the development of poststreptococcal glomerulonephritis but will prevent the spread of infection to others.

TABLE 101–1. CIRCUMSCRIBED CUTANEOUS INFECTIONS

DESCRIPTION	PREDOMINANT ORGANISM
Folliculitis	*Staphylococcus aureus*
Furuncles, carbuncles	*Staphylococcus aureus*
Impetigo	Group A streptococci
Ecthyma gangrenosum	Gram-negative bacilli (systemic infection)

VESICULAR OR VESICULOPUSTULAR LESIONS OF THE SKIN
Impetigo
Folliculitis
Herpes simplex virus infection
Varicella-zoster virus infection
Rickettsialpox

ULCERATIVE LESIONS OF THE SKIN
Pressure sores
Stasis ulcerations
Diabetic ulcerations
Sickle cell ulcers
Mycobacterial infection
Fungal infection
Ecthyma gangrenosum

Ecthyma gangrenosum is a cutaneous manifestation of disseminated gram-negative rod infection, usually due to *Pseudomonas aeruginosa* in neutropenic patients. The initial lesion is a vesicle or papule with an erythematous halo. Although generally small (<2 cm), the initial lesion may exceed 20 cm in diameter. In a short time, the vesicle ulcerates, leaving a necrotic ulcer with surrounding erythema or a violaceous rim. Gram stain of an aspirate may reveal gram-negative rods; cultures of the aspirate are generally positive. Biopsy of the lesion shows venous thrombosis, often with bacteria demonstrable within the blood vessel walls. Since these lesions are manifestations of gram-negative rod bacteremia, treatment should be instituted immediately with an aminoglycoside plus a third-generation cephalosporin with good activity against *Pseudomonas aeruginosa* (e.g., ceftazidime) until the results of culture and sensitivity studies are known (see also Chapter 96).

Herpes Simplex Virus. Oral infections due to this virus are discussed in Chapter 98, and genital infection in Chapter 107. On occasion, infection with this virus occurs on extraoral or extragenital sites, usually on the hands. This is most often the case in health care workers but also may result from sexual contact or from autoinoculation. The virus may produce a painful erythema, usually at the junction of the nail bed and skin (whitlow). This progresses to a vesiculopustular lesion. At both stages of infection, herpetic whitlow can resemble a bacterial infection—paronychia. When more than one digit is involved, herpes is much more likely. It is important to distinguish between herpetic and bacterial infections, since incision and drainage of a herpetic whitlow are contraindicated. Puncture of the purulent center of a paronychia and Gram stain of the exudate allow prompt and accurate diagnosis. In the case of herpetic whitlow, bacteria are not present unless the lesion has already drained and become superinfected. In the case of a bacterial paronychia, bacteria are readily seen. Recurrences of herpetic whitlow may be seen but are generally less severe than the primary infection. Treatment with oral acyclovir may shorten the duration of symptoms.

Varicella-Zoster Virus (see also Chapter 95). Primary infection with varicella-zoster virus (chickenpox) is thought to occur via the respiratory route but may also occur through contact with infected skin lesions. Viremia results in crops of papules that progress to vesicles, then pustules followed by crusting. The lesions are most prominent on the trunk. This is almost always a disease of childhood. Systemic symptoms may precede development of the characteristic rash by 1 or 2 days but are mild except in the case of an immunocompromised patient or primary infection in the adult. In the immunocompromised, chickenpox can produce a fatal systemic illness. In otherwise healthy adults, chickenpox can be a serious illness with life-threatening pneumonia. Clinical diagnosis is based on the characteristic appearance of the rash. Impetigo and folliculitis are readily distinguished clinically or by Gram stain or Tzanck's preparation of the pustule contents. Disseminated herpes simplex virus infection is seen only in the immunocompromised host or in patients with eczema. Viral culture or viral antigen detection will distinguish herpes simplex from herpes zoster in these settings. Most patients with rickettsialpox, which is confused with chickenpox rarely, also have an ulcer or eschar that precedes the generalized rash by 3 to 7 days and represents the bite of the infected mouse mite, which transmits the disease.

Immunocompromised children exposed to varicella should receive prophylaxis with zoster immune globulin. Immunocompromised persons and seriously ill elderly patients with varicella should be treated with acyclovir.

After primary infection, the varicella-zoster virus persists in a latent state within sensory neurons of the dorsal root ganglia. The infection may reactivate, producing the syndrome of zoster (shingles). Pain in the distribution of the affected nerve root precedes the rash by a few days. Depending upon the dermatome, the pain may mimic pleurisy, myocardial infarction, or gallbladder disease. A clue to the presence of early zoster infection is the finding of dysesthesia—an unpleasant sensation when the involved dermatome is gently stroked by the examiner's hand. The appearance of papules and vesicles in a dermatomal distribution confirms the diagnosis. Herpes zoster infections of certain dermatomes merit special attention. The Ramsay Hunt syndrome can be caused by infection involving the geniculate ganglia and presents with painful eruption of the ear canal and tympanic membrane, often associated with an ipsilateral seventh cranial nerve (facial nerve) palsy. Infection involving the second branch of the fifth cranial nerve (trigeminal nerve) often produces lesions of the cornea. This infection should be treated promptly with systemic acyclovir to prevent loss of visual acuity. A clue to possible ophthalmic involvement is the presence of vesicles on the tip of the nose (see also Chapter 114).

In most instances, dermatomal zoster is a disease of the otherwise healthy adult. However, immunocompromised patients (e.g., persons with HIV infection) are at greater risk for reactivation of this virus. Patients with zoster should receive a careful history and physical evaluation; in the absence of specific suggestive findings, these patients do not require an exhaustive evaluation for a malignancy or immunodeficiency.

In older, nonimmunocompromised patients, postherpetic neuralgia (severe, prolonged burning pain, with occasional lightning-like stabs in the involved dermatomes) may persist for 1 to 2 years and become disabling. A brief course of corticosteroids (60 mg of prednisone, rapidly tapered over 10 days) during the acute episode of zoster decreases the incidence of, but does not consistently prevent, postherpetic neuralgia. The constant burning pain may be relieved by tricyclic antidepressants. When this fails, an anesthetic approach, with either subcutaneous local injection or sympathetic blockage, is sometimes helpful.

Cutaneous Mycobacterial and Fungal Diseases. Mycobacteria and fungi can produce cutaneous infection, manifesting generally as papules, nodules, ulcers, crusting lesions, or lesions with a combination of these features. *Mycobacterium marinum*, for example, can produce inflammatory nodules that ascend via lymphatic channels of the arm among individuals who keep or are exposed to fish; similar lesions due to *Sporothrix schenckii* may be seen among gardeners. *Blastomyces dermatitidis* and *Coccidioides immitis* are other fungi that produce skin nodules or ulcerations.

As a general rule, a biopsy should be done on a chronic inflammatory nodule, crusted lesion, or nonhealing ulceration that is not readily attributable to pressure, vascular insufficiency, or venous stasis. Mycobacteria and fungi should be carefully sought, using acid-fast and silver stains and appropriate cultures.

Ulcerative Lesions of the Skin. A common factor in the pathogenesis of many skin ulcers is the presence of vascular insufficiency. Microbial infection of these lesions is secondary but often extends into soft tissue and bone.

Pressure sores occur at weight-bearing sites among individuals incapable of moving. Patients with strokes, quadriplegia, or paraplegia or patients in coma who remain supine rapidly develop skin necrosis at the sacrum, spine, and heels, since pressures at these weight-bearing sites can exceed local perfusion pressure. Patients kept immobile on their sides will ulcerate over the greater trochanter of the femur. As the skin sloughs, bacteria colonize the necrotic tissues; abetted by further pressure-induced necrosis, the infection extends to deeper structures. Infected pressure sores are common causes of fever and occasional causes of bacteremia in debilitated patients. Not infrequently, a necrotic membrane hides a deep infection. The physician should probe the extent of a pressure sore with a sterile glove; potential sites of deeper infection should be probed with a sterile needle. Necrotic material must be debrided, and the ulceration may be treated with topical antiseptics and relief of pressure. Systemic antibiotics are indicated when bacteremia, osteomyelitis, or significant cellulitis is present. Anaerobes and gram-negative rods are the most frequent isolates. Skin grafting can be used to repair extensive ulceration in patients who can eventually be mobilized. Prevention of pressure sores by frequent turning and by inspection of pressure sites among immobilized patients is far more effective than treatment. The use of specialized beds that distribute pressure more evenly may be of particular value among these patients.

Stasis Ulceration. Patients with lower extremity edema are at risk for skin breakdown and formation of stasis ulcers. These may become secondarily infected; but unless cellulitis is present, systemic antibiotics are not necessary, and treatment is aimed at reducing the edema.

Diabetic Ulcers. Patients with diabetes mellitus often develop foot ulcers. Peripheral neuropathy may result in the distribution of stress to sites on the foot not suited to weight bearing and may also result in failure to sense foreign objects stepped on or caught within the shoe. The resulting ulceration heals poorly. This may be related to vascular disease, poor metabolic control, or both. Secondary infection with anaerobes and gram-negative bacilli progresses rapidly to involve bone and soft tissue. Prevention of these events requires meticulous foot care, avoidance of walking barefoot, the use of properly fitting shoes, and checking the inside of the shoe before use. Once an ulcer develops, the physician should evaluate the patient promptly. Bed rest and topical antiseptics are always indicated. Systemic antibiotics active against anaerobes and gram-negative bacilli should be employed for all but the most superficial and clean wounds. In most instances, this treatment requires admission to the hospital. Aggressive management is indicated, since, if the ulcer is left untreated or improperly treated, the proximate bones and soft tissues of the entire foot may become involved. Once this involvement occurs, eradication of infection without amputation may be difficult.

More Diffuse Lesions of Skin (Table 101–2)

Erysipelas. Erysipelas is an infection of the superficial layers of the skin; it is almost always caused by group A streptococci. This infection, seen primarily among children and the elderly, most commonly occurs on the face. Erysipelas is a bright red to violaceous raised lesion with sharply demarcated edges. This sharp demarcation distinguishes erysipelas from the deeper tissue infection — cellulitis — the margins of which are not raised and merge more smoothly with uninvolved areas of skin. Fever is generally present, and bacteremia is uncommon; rarely, the pathogen can be isolated by aspiration or biopsy of the leading edge of the erythema (clysis culture). Penicillin, 2 to 6 million units/day, is curative, but defervescence is gradual.

Cellulitis. Cellulitis is an infection of the deeper layers of the skin. Cellulitis has a particular predilection for the lower extremities, where

TABLE 101–2. DIFFUSE CUTANEOUS AND SUBCUTANEOUS BACTERIAL INFECTIONS

DESCRIPTION	PREDOMINANT ORGANISMS
Erysipelas	Group A streptococci
Cellulitis	Group A streptococci, *Staphylococcus aureus*, *Haemophilus influenzae*, *Clostridium perfringens*, other anaerobic organisms, gram-negative bacilli
Fasciitis	Group A streptococci, *Clostridium perfringens*, other anaerobic organisms, Enterobacteriaceae
Myonecrosis	*Clostridium perfringens*, other anaerobic organisms

venous stasis predisposes to infection. Cellulitis predisposes to recurrent infection, perhaps by impairing lymphatic drainage. A breakdown in normal skin barriers almost always precedes this infection. Lacerations, small abscesses, or even tiny fissures between the toes due to minor fungal infection antedate the onset of pain, swelling, and fever. Although shaking chills often occur, bacteremia is infrequently documented. Linear streaks of erythema and tenderness indicate lymphatic spread. Regional lymph node enlargement and tenderness are common. Patches of erythema and tenderness may occur a few centimeters proximal to the edge of infection; this is probably due to spread through subcutaneous lymphatics. Cellulitis of the calf is often difficult to distinguish from thrombophlebitis. Rupture of a Baker cyst or inflammatory arthritis may also mimic cellulitis. Pain within the joint on passive motion suggests arthritis, but after a Baker cyst rupture, examination of the joint may be relatively benign. Lymph node enlargement and lymphatic streaking virtually confirm the diagnosis of cellulitis. Most cases of lower extremity cellulitis are due to group A beta-hemolytic streptococci, but on occasion *Staphylococcus aureus* is responsible. Gram-negative bacilli often cause cellulitis in neutropenic and other immunosuppressed patients. Cellulitis of the face or upper extremities, particularly among children, may be due to *Haemophilus influenzae*. Among patients with diabetes mellitus, streptococci and staphylococci are the predominant pathogens of cellulitis. However, if the cellulitis is associated with an infected ulceration of the skin, there is a good chance that anaerobic bacteria and gram-negative rods are also involved.

As in the case of erysipelas, cultures of blood and clysis cultures of the leading edge of infection rarely yield the pathogen. Almost all patients with cellulitis should be hospitalized and treated with a semisynthetic penicillin active against staphylococci and streptococci, such as nafcillin, 6 to 12 gm/day. If *Haemophilus* is suspected, a third-generation cephalosporin or trimethoprim-sulfamethoxazole is effective. Diabetics with foot ulcers

complicated by cellulitis should be treated with agents active against anaerobes and enteric gram-negative rods (e.g., ampicillin/sulbactam). Radiologic studies should be performed on patients with ulcers to determine if osteomyelitis is present (see Chapter 104). Prevention of cellulitis can be achieved by institution of measures aimed at reducing venous stasis and edema. Patients with recurrent cellulitis may benefit from eradication of fungal infection of toes or interdigital regions if present. Repeated attacks of cellulitis may be prevented by monthly 1-week courses of an oral antibiotic such as erythromycin.

Soft Tissue Gas. Crepitus on palpation of the skin indicates the presence of gas in the soft tissues. Although this often reflects anaerobic bacterial metabolism, subcutaneous gas can also be found after respirator-induced barotrauma or after application of hydrogen peroxide to open wounds.

In the setting of soft tissue infection, crepitus suggests the presence of gas-forming anaerobes. Roentgenograms will occasionally demonstrate gas before crepitus is appreciated (Fig. 101–1). The presence of gas requires emergency surgical incision to determine the extent of necrosis and requirements for debridement. Involvement of the muscle establishes the diagnosis of myonecrosis (see below) and mandates extensive debridement. Despite the often extensive crepitus seen in clostridial cellulitis, exploration reveals the muscles to be uninvolved, and proper treatment is limited to debridement of necrotic tissue, open drainage, and antibiotics, usually penicillin G, 10 to 20 million units/day, and metronidazole, 500 mg every 6 hours. Thus, the principles of treatment for anaerobic soft tissue infections are (1) removal of necrotic tissue, (2) drainage, and (3) appropriate antibiotics. These apply to superficial anaerobic infections (clostridial cellulitis), deeper anaerobic infections (anaerobic fasciitis—see below), and deepest infections (anaerobic myonecrosis—see below).

DEEPER INFECTIONS OF THE SKIN AND SOFT TISSUE

Fasciitis. This is a deep infection of the subcutaneous tissues that generally occurs following trauma, sometimes minor, or surgery. Most cases are caused by beta-hemolytic streptococci with or without staphylococci; some, especially among diabetics, are due to mixtures of anaerobic organisms and gram-negative bacilli. Because fasciitis involves subcutaneous tissues, the skin may appear normal or may have a red or dusky hue. The clue to this diagnosis is the presence of subcutaneous swelling. In some instances, crepitus is present. The patient appears more toxic than one would expect from judging only the superficial appearance of the skin. Radiographs may reveal gas within tissues; its absence does not exclude the diagnosis. Men with diabetes mellitus, urethral trauma, or obstruction may develop an aggressive fasciitis of the perineum called Fournier's gan-

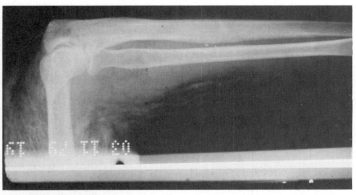

FIGURE 101–1. Radiograph in a case of clostridial myonecrosis showing gas within tissues. (Courtesy of Dr. J. W. Tomford.)

grene. Perineal pain and swelling may antedate the characteristic discoloration of the scrotum and perineum. Prompt debridement of all necrotic tissue is critical to the cure of these infections. Once the diagnosis is suspected, the patient must be taken to the operating room, where incision and exploration will determine if fasciitis is present. Gram stain of necrotic material will guide antibiotic choice.

Infections of Muscle

Pyomyositis. Pyomyositis is a deep infection of muscle usually caused by *Staphylococcus aureus* and occasionally by group A beta-hemolytic streptococci or enteric bacilli. Most cases occur in warm or tropical regions, and most occur among children. Nonpenetrating trauma may antedate the onset of symptoms, suggesting that infection of a minor hematoma during incidental bacteremia may be causative. Patients present with fever and tender swelling of the muscle; the skin is uninvolved or minimally involved. In older patients, myositis may mimic phlebitis. Diagnosis can be readily made, if suspected, by needle aspiration or ultrasonography. Drainage and appropriate antibiotics are usually curative.

Clostridial Myonecrosis (Gas Gangrene). This anaerobic infection generally occurs following a contaminated injury to muscle. Within a day or two of injury, the involved extremity becomes painful and begins to swell. The patient becomes toxic-appearing, often delirious. The skin may appear uninvolved at first but eventually may develop a bronzed-blue discoloration. Crepitus may be present but is not as prominent as in patients with clostridial cellulitis (a more benign lesion). Rarely, clostridial myonecrosis occurs spontaneously in the absence of trauma; most of these patients have an underlying malignancy, usually involving the bowel. Regardless of etiology, this illness progresses rapidly, producing extensive necrosis of muscle. Hypotension, hemolytic anemia caused by bacterial lecithinase, and renal failure can complicate this illness. Gram stain of the thin and watery wound exudate reveals large grampositive rods and very few inflammatory cells. Emergency surgery with wide debridement is essential if the patient is to survive. Large doses of penicillin (10 to 20 million units/day) may prevent further spread of the bacilli. Chloramphenicol may be used in patients with hypersensitivity to penicillin. Hyperbaric oxygen therapy is of uncertain value.

REFERENCES

Finegold DS: The diagnosis and treatment of gangrenous and crepitant cellulitis. In Remington JS, Swartz MN: Current Clinical Topics in Infectious Diseases. Vol 2. New York, McGraw-Hill Book Co, 1981.

Gorbach SL: Diseases caused by non–spore forming anaerobic bacteria. In Wyngaarden JB, Smith LH Jr, Bennett JC (eds): Cecil Textbook of Medicine. 19th ed. Philadelphia, WB Saunders Co, 1992, pp 1685–1689.

Swartz MN: Skin and soft tissue infections. In Mandell GL, Douglas RG, Bennett JE (eds): Principles and Practice of Infectious Diseases. 3rd ed. New York, Churchill Livingstone, pp 796–824.

102 INTRA-ABDOMINAL ABSCESS AND PERITONITIS

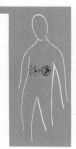

INTRA-ABDOMINAL ABSCESS

There are two general categories of intra-abdominal abscess. The first is an infection of a solid intra-abdominal viscus, generally arising as a consequence of hematogenous or enteral spread. The second includes extravisceral abscesses, which are localized collections of pus within the peritoneal or retroperitoneal space. These abscesses usually follow peritonitis or contamination by rupture or leakage from the bowel. Most patients with intra-abdominal abscess are febrile. The fever may be recurrent and may be associated with rigors, suggesting intermittent bacteremia. Nausea, vomiting, and paralytic ileus are common with extravisceral abscesses. Clues to the presence of intra-abdominal abscess may be subtle and may include extravisceral gas or air-fluid levels on plain radiographs. The availability of computed tomography (CT) has simplified both the diagnosis and the management of these potentially life-threatening infections.

With the exception of amebic abscess of the liver, antibiotic therapy alone is rarely curative. Failure of the antibiotic to penetrate the abscess cavities, inactivation of antibiotics within the abscess by bacterial enzymes, low pH, and low redox potential all contribute to the failure of medical management. Drainage is essential; antibiotics are important primarily to prevent bacteremia and seeding of other organs.

ABSCESSES OF SOLID ORGANS

Hepatic Abscess

Pyogenic liver abscess is a disease that occurs predominantly among individuals with other underlying disorders, most commonly biliary tract disease. Obstruction to biliary drainage allows infected bile to produce ascending infection of the liver. Inflammatory diseases of the bowel, such as appendicitis and diverticulitis, may also lead to hepatic abscess via spread of infection through portal veins (Table 102–1).

Clinical findings in patients with pyogenic hepatic abscess are often nonspecific. Most are febrile, but only about half have abdominal pain and tenderness. Two thirds have palpable hepatomegaly, but less than one in four is clinically jaundiced.

The chest roentgenogram may reveal an elevated right hemidiaphragm and atelectasis or effusion at the right lung base. The diagnosis is best achieved by contrast-enhanced CT of the abdomen or ultrasonography of the right upper quadrant. Pyogenic abscesses may be single or multiple; multiple abscesses often arise from a biliary source of infection.

Anaerobic bacilli, microaerophilic streptococci, and gram-negative bacilli are the predominant microorganisms in pyogenic liver abscess. Occasionally, *Staphylococcus aureus* causes hepatic abscesses during the course of bacteremic seeding of multiple organs. Positive blood cultures are obtained from about half the patients with pyogenic liver abscess.

Clinical laboratory studies generally show a moderate elevation of the alkaline phosphatase level, which is disproportionate to the modest elevation in bilirubin level that occurs in roughly half the patients. (In contrast, patients with the nonspecific jaundice that occasionally accompanies bacterial infection at other sites generally have elevated bilirubin levels—as much as 5 to 10 mg/dl or more—and only slightly elevated alkaline phosphatase levels.)

Hepatic abscess due to *Entamoeba histolytica* is rare in North America, though it should be suspected in a patient with fever and right upper quadrant pain who has traveled to or emigrated from the developing world. Amebic abscesses are generally single and are usually located in the right lobe of the liver. Only a minority of patients with amebic liver abscess have concurrent intestinal amebiasis. Antibody titers against *E. histolytica* are almost always positive in patients with parasitic liver abscess.

The Fitz-Hugh–Curtis syndrome, or gonococcal periphepatitis, may share some clinical manifestations suggestive of hepatic abscess and should be suspected in young, sexually active women with fever and right upper quadrant tenderness. Tumors involving the liver may produce fever and a clinical and radiologic picture that may mimic

TABLE 102–1. INTRA-ABDOMINAL ABSCESSES

SITE	PREDISPOSING FACTORS	LIKELY PATHOGENS	DIAGNOSIS	EMPIRIC TREATMENT*
Solid Organs				
Hepatic	Trauma, GI or biliary sepsis	Gram-negative bacilli, anaerobes, streptococci, amebae	CT	Ampicillin/sulbactam, drainage; metronidazole for amebic abscess
Splenic	Trauma, hemoglobinopathy, endocarditis	Staphylococci, streptococci, gram-negative bacilli	CT	Ampicillin/sulbactam or vancomycin/tobramycin, splenectomy
Pancreatic	Pancreatitis, pseudocyst	Gram-negative bacilli, streptococci	CT	Ampicillin/sulbactam or clindamycin/tobramycin, drainage
Extravisceral				
Subphrenic	Abdominal surgery, peritonitis	Gram-negative bacilli, streptococci, anaerobes	CT	Ampicillin/sulbactam or clindamycin/tobramycin, drainage
Pelvic	Abdominal surgery, peritonitis, pelvic or GI inflammatory disease	Gram-negative bacilli, streptococci, anaerobes	CT	Ampicillin/sulbactam or clindamycin/tobramycin, drainage
Perinephrenic	Renal infection/obstruction, hematogenous	Gram-negative bacilli, staphylococci	CT	Ampicillin/sulbactam or vancomycin/tobramycin, drainage
Psoas	Vertebral osteomyelitis, hematogenous	Staphylococci, gram-negative bacilli, mycobacteria	CT	Ampicillin/sulbactam or vancomycin/tobramycin, drainage

*Ampicillin/sulbactam, 2 gm/1 gm given intravenously (IV) q8h; vancomycin, 1 gm IV q12h; tobramycin, 1.7 mg/kg IV q8h; clindamycin, 600 mg IV q8h.
CT = Computed tomography; GI = gastrointestinal.

hepatic abscess. This is complicated by the occasional concurrence of malignancy and hepatic abscess.

If pyogenic abscess is suspected, needle aspiration is indicated. With the guidance of ultrasonography or CT, a percutaneous catheter can be inserted into the abscess cavity for both diagnostic and therapeutic purposes. The pus should be Gram-stained and cultured aerobically and anaerobically. Unless the Gram stain indicates otherwise, initial therapy for pyogenic liver abscess should include drugs active against enteric aerobic and anaerobic bacteria (Table 102–1). Antibiotics should be continued for at least 4 to 6 weeks. Duration of therapy may be guided by serial CT scans. Surgery is required to relieve biliary tract obstruction and to drain abscesses that do not respond to percutaneous drainage and antibiotics. Patients with pyogenic liver abscess should be evaluated for a primary intra-abdominal source of infection.

If epidemiologic features strongly suggest an amebic abscess, metronidazole is the drug of choice. Needle aspiration is necessary only to exclude pyogenic infection or, if the abscess is large or close to other viscera, to prevent rupture. In the case of amebic abscess, the anchovy paste material obtained by needle drainage is not pus but necrotic liver tissue. Large numbers of white cells suggest pyogenic abscess or bacterial superinfection. Trophozoites of *Entamoeba histolytica* are infrequently seen on aspiration of abscesses but are often seen on biopsy of the abscess capsule.

Splenic Abscess

Splenic abscesses are generally the result of hematogenous seeding of the spleen. In the preantibiotic era, splenic infarction and abscess were common complications of infective endocarditis. Now the most common predisposing factors are trauma and (in children) sickle cell disease. Patients with splenic abscess most often present with left upper quadrant abdominal pain, which may be pleuritic. The left hemidiaphragm may be elevated, and there may be an associated pleural rub or effusion. The diagnostic approach, most likely etiologic agents, and initial antimicrobial therapy are outlined in Table 102–1. Splenectomy is usually the definitive treatment, but CT-guided percutaneous drainage of large, solitary abscesses may also be successful in selected cases.

Pancreatic Abscess

Pancreatic abscess is an uncommon complication of pancreatitis. The symptoms of pancreatic abscess, fever, nausea, vomiting, and abdominal pain radiating to the back resemble those of pancreatitis. Thus, abscess should be suspected in cases of persistent recurrent fever following pancreatitis. The inflamed organ becomes colonized and infected with microbes inhabiting the upper gastrointestinal tract. Enterobacteriaceae, anaerobes, and streptococci (including the pneumococcus) are likely pathogens. The diagnosis may be made by CT scanning; however, radiographic definition of the pancreatic bed is often difficult. Initial antibiotic therapy (Table 102–1) should be followed by surgical drainage of the abscess as soon as the patient is stable. The mortality exceeds 30 per cent even with optimal management.

EXTRAVISCERAL ABSCESSES

Extravisceral abscesses most often arise following peritonitis, after intra-abdominal surgery, as a consequence of rupture of the bowel, or after extension of infection of a viscus, such as diverticulitis or appendicitis. Abscesses may occur in the subphrenic, pelvic, or retroperitoneal spaces. Fever, nausea, vomiting, and paralytic ileus are common. Although fever is almost always present, localizing symptoms may be very subtle, making the diagnosis difficult. Predisposing factors, most likely etiologic pathogens, and appropriate initial antimicrobial therapy are outlined in Table 102–1.

When an abscess is suspected, CT or ultrasound scans should be obtained. CT can identify abscesses in the retroperitoneal and abdominal spaces and guide percutaneous drainage. Ultrasonography may be more helpful in the identification of pelvic fluid collections. Drainage of an abscess either by radiologic guidance or by surgery in conjunction with antibiotics is the mainstay of treatment.

PERITONITIS

Peritonitis may occur "spontaneously" (primary peritonitis) or as a consequence of trauma, surgery, or peritoneal soilage by bowel contents (secondary peritonitis). Peritonitis also may be caused by chemical irritation. Patients with peritonitis generally complain of diffuse abdominal pain. They may have nausea and vomiting; some have diarrhea, others paralytic ileus. Patients are usually febrile and uncomfortable and prefer to lie quietly in the supine position. Physical examination may reveal diffuse tenderness, diminished bowel sounds, and evidence of peritoneal inflammation, including rebound tenderness and involuntary guarding. In patients with underlying ascites, the signs and symptoms of peritonitis may be more subtle, with fever as the only manifestation of infection.

Primary Peritonitis

Primary or spontaneous peritonitis occurs principally among persons with ascites associated with chronic liver disease or the nephrotic syndrome. Bacteria may infect ascitic fluid via bacteremic spread, transmural migration through the bowel, or through the fallopian tubes. In cirrhotic pa-

TABLE 102–2. CAUSES, DIAGNOSIS, AND TREATMENT OF PERITONITIS

SITE	PREDISPOSING FACTORS	CAUSATIVE AGENT	CLUES TO DIAGNOSIS	EMPIRIC TREATMENT*
Primary Spontaneous	Cirrhosis, nephrotic syndrome	Gram-negative bacilli, streptococci	>300 neutrophils per milliliter of ascites	Ampicillin/sulbactam or clindamycin/tobramycin
Secondary Postoperative	Hemorrhage, visceral rupture	Gram-negative bacilli, streptococci, staphylococci, anaerobes	Postoperative fever, pain, prolonged ileus	Ampicillin/sulbactam or metronidazole/tobramycin
Chemical	Abdominal surgery	Bile, starch, talc	Postoperative fever, pain	Biliary drainage when indicated
Visceral rupture	Perforating ulcer, ruptured appendix, bowel infarction	Gram-negative bacilli, anaerobes, streptococci	Polymicrobial Gram stain or culture	Ampicillin/sulbactam or metronidazole/tobramycin
Peritoneal dialysis	—	Staphylococci, gram-negative bacilli	Pain, fever, neutrophilic pleocytosis	Vancomycin/tobramycin; consider catheter removal
Periodic peritonitis	Familial	—	Recurrent, familial	Colchicine prophylaxis, 0.6 mg 2–3 times daily
Tuberculous	Infection of fallopian tubes or ileum	*Mycobacterium tuberculosis*	Lymphocytic pleocytosis, high protein level (>3 gm/dl) in ascitic fluid	Isoniazid, rifampin, pyrazinamide

*Ampicillin/sulbactam, 2 gm/1 gm IV q8h; vancomycin, 1 gm IV q12h; tobramycin, 1.7 mg/kg IV q8h; clindamycin, 600 mg IV q8h; isoniazid, 300 mg qd; ethambutol, 800 mg qd; pyrazinamide, 1.5 gm qd.

tients, clearance of portal bacteremia by hepatic reticuloendothelial cells may be impaired by intrahepatic portosystemic shunting. Not surprisingly, therefore, gram-negative rods, especially *Escherichia coli*, are the predominant pathogens in spontaneous bacterial peritonitis; enteric streptococci are isolated in approximately one third of cases. Staphylococci, *Streptococcus pneumoniae*, or anaerobic bacilli are isolated in fewer than 10 per cent of cases (Table 102–2).

In patients with underlying ascites, the presenting symptoms may be nonspecific abdominal pain, nausea, vomiting, diarrhea, or altered mental status. Thus, febrile patients with ascites should undergo paracentesis unless there is another certain explanation for fever. A white blood cell count in the fluid that exceeds 300 to 500/μl is suggestive of infection. Gram stain may reveal the responsible pathogen. Antibiotic penetration into the peritoneum is excellent, and medical therapy is the treatment of choice (Table 102–2). If Gram stain or culture reveals a mixed flora with anaerobes, secondary peritonitis due to leakage of bowel contents should be suspected.

Secondary Peritonitis

Secondary peritonitis may follow penetrating abdominal trauma or surgery or may result from contamination of the peritoneum with bowel contents. This syndrome may be heralded by the sudden presentation of visceral rupture (e.g., perforated duodenal ulcer or appendix) or visceral infarction. In the postoperative setting, secondary

peritonitis should be suspected in the patient whose abdominal discomfort and fever do not resolve, or even worsen, after the first few postoperative days. If peritonitis is secondary to the leakage of bowel contents, immediate surgical intervention is mandatory. Despite the use of appropriate antibiotics (Table 102–2) and intensive support systems, the mortality of generalized peritonitis approaches 50 per cent.

Tuberculous Peritonitis

Tuberculous peritonitis may occur as a result of hematogenous or local extension of tuberculous infection into the peritoneal cavity. Fever, abdominal pain, and weight loss are common. In patients with underlying ascites, a lymphocytic pleocytosis in the peritoneal fluid should suggest the diagnosis. Laparoscopy, with biopsy of the granulomatous peritoneal nodules, is the most effective approach to diagnosis. Antituberculous therapy is generally curative (Table 102–2).

REFERENCES

Walker AP, Condon RE: Peritonitis and intraabdominal abscesses. *In* Schwartz SI (ed): Principles of Surgery. 5th ed. New York, McGraw-Hill Book Co, 1989, pp 1459–1490.

Wilcox CM, Dismukes WE: Spontaneous bacterial peritonitis, a review of pathogenesis, diagnosis and treatment. Medicine 66:447–456, 1987.

Wright TL: Parasitic, bacterial, fungal and granulomatous liver disease. *In* Wyngaarden JB, Smith LH Jr, Bennett JC (eds): Cecil Textbook of Medicine. 19th ed. Philadelphia, WB Saunders Co, 1992, pp 778–782.

103 ACUTE INFECTIOUS DIARRHEA

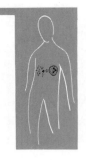

Acute diarrheal illnesses caused by bacterial, viral, or protozoal pathogens vary from mild bowel dysfunction to fulminant, life-threatening diseases. With the best techniques available, a specific causative agent can be identified in 70 to 80 per cent of cases (Table 103–1).

PATHOGENESIS AND PATHOPHYSIOLOGY: GENERAL CONCEPTS

All pathogens and/or microbial toxins that produce acute diarrhea must be ingested. Normally, the low pH of the stomach, the rapid transit time of the small bowel, and antibody produced by cells in the lamina propria of the small bowel are adequate to keep the jejunum and proximal ileum relatively free of microorganisms (although not sterile). Furthermore, the ileocecal valve inhibits proximal migration of the huge numbers of bacteria that reside in the large bowel.

Pathogenic microorganisms are able to pass through the hostile environment of the stomach if (1) they are acid-resistant (e.g., *Shigella*), (2) they are ingested in huge numbers that allow for a few survivors (e.g., *Vibrio cholerae* or *Escherichia coli*), or (3) they are ingested with food and therefore partially protected in the neutralized environment. People with decreased gastric acidity, either natural or surgically induced, are at increased risk to develop acute diarrheal disease.

Once in the small bowel, the organisms either must colonize (e.g., *V. cholerae*, *E. coli*) and/or invade (e.g., rotavirus, Norwalk agent) the local mucosa or must pass through into the terminal ileum (*Salmonella*) or colon (*Shigella*) to colonize and invade the mucosa in those sites. Active peristalsis of the small bowel is an effective deterrent to the successful colonization of most organisms. The organisms (e.g., *V. cholerae*, *E. coli*) that are able to colonize this area have developed special colonization factors such as fimbria (hairlike projections from the cell wall) or lectins (special proteins that attach to specific carbohydrate-binding sites) that allow them to adhere tightly to the mucosal cell surface.

Organisms that do not have special colonization properties pass into the terminal ileum and colon, where they compete with the established flora. The normal fecal flora produce substances that serve to prevent most newly introduced bacterial species from proliferating. (*Bacteroides*, for example, produces fatty acids; certain other enteric bacteria produce specific colicins). The ability of the colonic enteropathogens to invade intestinal mucosa allows these microorganisms (e.g., *Shigella*) to multiply preferentially.

Diarrheas Caused by Enterotoxigenic Pathogens

In enterotoxin-induced or secretory diarrheas, the patient seldom has fever or other major systemic symptoms, and there is little or no inflammatory response. The diarrhea is watery, often voluminous, with a low protein concentration and an electrolyte content, isosmotic with plasma, that reflects its source. Rapid loss of this diarrheal fluid results in predictable saline depletion, base-deficit acidosis, and potassium deficiency. The amount and rate of fluid loss determine the severity of the illness. Certain of the secretory diarrheas, such as those caused by *V. cholerae* or *E. coli* enterotoxins, can result in massive intestinal fluid losses, exceeding 1 L/hr in adults.

Characteristically, large numbers of bacteria (10^5 to 10^8) must be ingested with grossly contaminated food or water (although a small inoculum may produce disease in individuals with achlorhydria). The enterotoxin-producing bacteria then colonize, but do not invade, the small bowel mucosal cells. After multiplying to large numbers (10^8 to 10^9 organisms per milliliter of fluid), the bacteria produce enterotoxins that bind to mucosal cells, causing hypersecretion of isotonic fluid at a rate

TABLE 103–1. MAJOR ETIOLOGIC AGENTS IN ACUTE DIARRHEAL ILLNESSES

INVASIVE/ DESTRUCTIVE PATHOGENS	NONINVASIVE PATHOGENS	BACTERIAL TOXINS (FOOD POISONING)
Shigella	*Escherichia coli*	*Staphylococcus aureus*
Salmonella	*Vibrio cholerae*	*Clostridium perfringens*
Campylobacter jejuni	*Giardia lamblia*	*Bacillus cereus*
Vibrio parahaemolyticus	*Isospora belli*	
Yersinia enterocolitica	*Cryptosporidium parvum*	
Clostridium difficile		
Rotavirus		
Other viruses		
Entamoeba histolytica		

that overwhelms the reabsorptive capacity of the colon. The *V. cholerae* enterotoxin rapidly binds to monosialogangliosides of the gut mucosa and causes sustained stimulation of cell-bound adenylate cyclase. This results, via both an increased secretion and a decreased absorption of electrolytes, in net secretion of large quantities of isotonic fluid into the gut lumen. The disease runs its course in 2 to 7 days, during which time continued fluid and electrolyte repletion is of critical importance. *E. coli* produces two other major types of bacterial enterotoxins. The labile toxin (LT) of *E. coli* is similar in structure and nearly identical in mode of action to cholera enterotoxin. The *E. coli* heat-stable toxins (ST) are much smaller than LT and act via a different biochemical pathway (stimulation of cellular guanylate cyclase) but also stimulate secretion of isotonic fluid into the gut lumen.

Three conditions provide well-recognized exceptions to the above schema of enterotoxigenic diarrheas. In each of these exceptions, the culpable enterotoxin exerts its effect by some means other than stimulation of one of the known secretory mechanisms of the small bowel mucosa, and the resulting fluid losses are seldom voluminous.

1. Enterotoxins may be ingested directly in food, as with staphylococcal and *Bacillus cereus* food poisoning. These organisms grow to high concentration in the food rather than the small intestine and often cannot be recovered from the stool. Distinctive features of staphylococcal food poisoning include a short incubation period (2 to 6 hours), high attack rates (up to 75 per cent of the population at risk), and prominent vomiting (probably due to the direct effect of absorbed toxin on the central nervous system). *Bacillus cereus* produces two distinct enterotoxins, one of which is similar to the *E. coli* LT and the other to the staphylococcal enterotoxin; therefore, two different clinical syndromes may be produced, one indistinguishable from staphylococcal food poisoning and the other similar to the diarrhea caused by enterotoxigenic *E. coli* (ETEC). The former syndrome is usually associated with ingestion of contaminated rice.

2. *Clostridium perfringens*, usually contracted by eating contaminated meat or poultry, produces an enterotoxin in the small bowel. Like staphylococcal food poisoning, the illness caused by *C. perfringens* enterotoxin has a short incubation period, has a high attack rate, and generally causes a relatively brief diarrhea (< 36 hours) with a small volume of liquid lost. However, unlike staphylococcal enterotoxin, *C. perfringens* enterotoxin damages gut mucosa.

3. *Clostridium difficile*, unlike the previously described organisms, colonizes the large bowel. This organism produces enterotoxins that cause severe mucosal damage, yielding colonic lesions that may be indistinguishable from those caused by *Shigella*. *C. difficile* diarrhea is usually associated with or follows antibiotic usage. Diagnosis is reliably made by assaying stool for toxins. Inflammatory cells may be present on methylene blue–stained stool samples.

Diarrheas Caused by Invasive Pathogens

Diarrheas caused by mucosal invasion by microorganisms are often accompanied by fever and other systemic symptoms, including headache and myalgias. Cramping abdominal pain may be prominent, and small amounts of stool are passed at frequent intervals, often associated with tenesmus. These microorganisms often induce a marked inflammatory response, so that the stool contains pus cells, large amounts of protein, and often gross blood. Significant dehydration rarely results from this kind of diarrhea, since the diarrheal fluid volume is small relative to that caused by the secretory enterotoxins, seldom exceeding 750 ml/day in adults. Although certain clinical features are statistically more frequent in invasive diarrheas caused by specific enteropathogens (e.g., more severe myalgias with shigellosis, higher temperature spikes with salmonellosis), epidemiologic characteristics are more helpful than signs or symptoms in determining the etiologic agent in invasive diarrheal illnesses (Table 103–2).

Acute shigellosis occurs when susceptible individuals ingest fecally contaminated water or food. Shigellosis can occur after ingestion of only 10 to 100 microorganisms. Largely for this reason, direct person-to-person transmission (e.g., in day care centers) is more common with shigellosis than with other bacterial enteric infections. The organism multiplies in the small intestine, during which time a watery, noninflammatory diarrhea may occur. Later, the organisms invade the colonic epithelium, causing the characteristic bloody stool. Unlike *Salmonella*, *Shigella* rarely causes bacteremia. The disease usually resolves spontaneously after 3 to 6 days, but the clinical course can be shortened by antimicrobials (Table 103–2).

Acute salmonellosis usually results from ingestion of contaminated meat, dairy, or poultry products. In the industrialized world, *Salmonella* is often transmitted via commercially prepared dried, processed foodstuffs. Unlike *Shigella*, *Salmonella* is remarkably resistant to dessication. The nontyphoidal salmonellae invade primarily the distal ileum. The organism typically causes a short-lived (2 to 3 days) illness characterized by fever, nausea, vomiting, and diarrhea. (This is in marked contrast to the 3- to 4-week febrile illness, usually not associated with diarrhea, that is caused by *Salmonella typhi*.)

Campylobacter jejuni may be responsible for up to 10 per cent of acute diarrheal illnesses worldwide. This organism may invade both the small intestine, most commonly the terminal ileum, and the colon, which may account for the broad spectrum of symptoms, ranging from an acute shigella-type syndrome to a milder, but more protracted, diarrheal illness.

In addition to *Shigella*, *Salmonella*, and *Campy-*

TABLE 103-2. EPIDEMIOLOGIC CHARACTERISTICS OF COMMON INVASIVE ENTERIC PATHOGENS

MICROORGANISMS	EPIDEMIOLOGIC FEATURES	ANTIBIOTICS
Shigella	Outbreaks in child care centers or custodial institutions; person-to-person transmission	Yes
Salmonella enteritidis	Zoonosis; survives dessication in processed dairy, poultry, and meat products	Rarely
Campylobacter jejuni	Zoonosis; worldwide distribution; transmitted in dairy products	Maybe
Yersinia enterocolitica	Zoonosis; occasionally transmitted in dairy products	Maybe
Vibrio parahaemolyticus	Coastal salt waters; transmitted by inadequately cooked shrimp and shellfish	No
Clostridium difficile	Almost always follows antimicrobial therapy	Yes
Rotavirus	Outbreaks among children; worldwide distribution; unusual and mild in adults	No
Norwalk virus	Microepidemic pattern; no specific age predilection	No
Entamoeba histolytica	Person-to-person transmission; very rare in United States, Canada, and Western Europe	Yes

lobacter, three other organisms—*Yersinia enterocolitica, Vibrio parahaemolyticus,* and *enteroinvasive E. coli* (EIEC—distinct from ETEC)—also cause tissue invasion and acute diarrheal illnesses that may be clinically indistinguishable from those caused by the more commonly recognized invasive bacterial enteropathogens (Table 103-2). Another distinct *E. coli* strain, enterohemorrhagic *E. coli,* produces bloody diarrhea without evidence of mucosal inflammation (i.e., grossly bloody stool with few or no leukocytes).

Viruses must grow in host cells; by definition, therefore, both the rotavirus and the Norwalk agent produce invasive diarrheal disease. Both these organisms damage the villous epithelial cells, with the degree of injury ranging from modest distortion of epithelial cells to sloughing of villi. Presumably, both the rotavirus and the Norwalk agent cause diarrhea by interfering with the absorption of normal intestinal secretions. Affected patients may have low-grade fever and mild to moderate cramping abdominal pain. The stool is usually watery, and its contents resemble those of a noninvasive process, with few inflammatory cells, probably because of lack of damage to the colon.

Although few protozoa cause acute diarrheal illness, *Giardia lamblia* is an important pathogen. In North America, Rocky Mountain water sources are frequent origins of microepidemics. As is the case in shigellosis, ingestion of only a few organisms is required to establish infection. The organisms multiply in the small bowel, attach to and occasionally invade the mucosa, but do not cause gross damage to the mucosal cells. Clinical manifestations span the spectrum from an acute, febrile diarrheal illness to chronic diarrhea with associated malabsorption and weight loss. Diagnosis may be made by identification of the organism in either the stool or the duodenal mucus or by small bowel biopsy. *Entamoeba histolytica* may cause intestinal syndromes ranging from mild diarrhea to fulminant amebic colitis with multiple bloody stools, fever, and severe abdominal pain. Although *E. histolytica* has a worldwide distribution, it is an uncommon cause of diarrhea in the United States. Two other protozoa, *Cryptosporidium parvum* and *Isospora belli,* occasionally cause self-limited acute

diarrheal illness in normal individuals and may cause voluminous, life-threatening diarrheal disease in patients with acquired immunodeficiency syndrome (AIDS). Stool examination is critical to distinguish between the cysts of *Giardia, Entamoeba, Isospora,* and *Cryptosporidium.*

Although most diarrheogenic pathogens produce either invasive (cytopathic) or enterotoxic (secretory) diarrhea, both processes contribute to the illness in some situations. Certain strains of *Shigella,* nontyphoidal *Salmonella, Y. enterocolitica,* and *C. jejuni* both invade and possess the capacity to produce enterotoxins in vitro. Such enterotoxins may play a contributory role in the acute disease process. The invasive capacity of these organisms is, however, of paramount importance in their ability to produce disease.

GENERAL EPIDEMIOLOGIC CONSIDERATIONS

In developing countries, where sanitation is generally inadequate, young children (up to 2 years of age) contract multiple episodes of diarrhea (often four to eight per year), a process that engenders intestinal immunity to the majority of enteropathogens in their immediate environment. Most of these diarrheal episodes are mild, but some are life-threatening. In these areas, ETEC and rotavirus together cause the large majority of diarrheal illnesses. *Shigella* infections are far less common during this period.

In the industrialized world, infants and small children have fewer episodes of diarrhea, and the most common etiologic agent is the rotavirus. Most episodes are mild. ETEC and *Shigella* infections infrequently occur except in a few defined population groups (e.g., individuals in custodial institutions). On the other hand, throughout the world, clinically significant diarrhea in adults is relatively unusual except in specific defined epidemics or common-source outbreaks due to contaminated food or water. The same etiologic agents are largely responsible for the acute diarrheas of both adults and children. This is made apparent by immunologically inexperienced adults from the developed world who visit developing countries. Such tourists have an extremely high incidence of diarrheal disease (traveler's diarrhea), and the organisms responsible are the same ones as those causing most childhood diarrhea in the country visited.

Gender preference is an important epidemiologic consideration in the patient with acute diarrheal disease, as certain pathogens responsible for acute diarrheal illnesses among sexually active gay males (see Chapter 107) differ from those that most commonly occur in the general population.

DIAGNOSIS

In managing acute diarrheal illnesses, determining the specific etiologic agent is much less important than promptly repleting lost electrolytes. All pathogens that cause serious diarrheal disease produce similar electrolyte losses. The fluid losses represent the chief cause of serious morbidity and mortality. Determination of the specific cause is less important, since antimicrobial therapy has proven value in only a minority of cases (Table 103–2). Discerning the epidemiology of the illness is often more helpful than laboratory techniques in identifying cases in which antimicrobial therapy is likely to be helpful. Figure 103–1 provides a useful schematic approach to diagnosis and management.

The examination of a methylene blue–stained stool preparation for erythrocytes and pus cells may be helpful in distinguishing between acute diarrheal illnesses caused by invasive pathogens and those caused by noninvasive pathogens. This is easily accomplished by adding one drop of methylene blue dye to one drop of liquid stool or mucus, allowing the preparation to air dry, and examining under the high dry microscope lens. Few, if any, leukocytes or red cells are seen in the stools of patients with diarrhea caused by noninvasive organisms (e.g., ETEC). Variable numbers of leukocytes and red cells are present in diarrheas secondary to invasive bacteria (e.g., *Shigella*) or cytopathic toxins (*C. difficile* toxin).

The precise diagnosis of any diarrheal illness lasting longer than 4 to 5 days is important, as specific antimicrobial therapy may be helpful, as with giardiasis. Furthermore, among patients with negative stool examinations and cultures, endoscopy may yield a diagnosis of a noninfectious disease (e.g., ulcerative colitis or Crohn's disease).

MANAGEMENT: GENERAL PRINCIPLES OF ELECTROLYTE REPLETION THERAPY

Intravenous Fluids

All acute diarrheal diseases respond to a similar fluid repletion regimen. Voluminous infectious diarrhea in adults consistently produces the same pattern of fecal electrolyte loss. The electrolyte characteristics differ somewhat in diarrhea in young children in that the mean sodium and chloride concentrations are 15 to 20 mEq/L less than those in adults. Sodium and chloride concentrations in stool may be even less with diarrheal diseases of viral etiology, in which massive fluid loss seldom occurs.

The fluid losses of massive diarrhea can rapidly be corrected by infusing fluids intravenously that approximate those that have been lost. Lactated Ringer's solution is readily available and provides uniformly good results. With patients who are hypotensive, the intravenous fluids should initially be infused rapidly, at a rate of up to 100 ml/min, until a strong radial pulse is restored. The rate can then be slowed until skin turgor has returned to normal. Subsequent maintenance fluid administration can be guided by the patient's clinical appearance, including the vital signs, the appearance of neck veins, and skin turgor. Clinical evaluation *alone* provides an adequate guide to fluid replacement in most acute diarrheal illnesses. If intravenous fluids are administered in adequate quantities throughout the diarrheal illness, virtually every patient with diarrhea caused by toxigenic bacteria should be restored to health. Complications (e.g., acute renal failure secondary to hypotension) are exceedingly rare if these principles are followed.

Oral Fluids

In most patients with acute diarrheal illness, fluid repletion can also be achieved via the oral route, using isotonic glucose-containing electrolyte solutions. Oral therapy is based on the fact that glucose facilitates sodium absorption by the small bowel and that glucose-facilitated sodium absorption remains intact during enterotoxigenic diarrheal illnesses. A uniformly effective solution can be prepared by the addition of 20 gm of glucose, 3.5 gm of sodium chloride, 2.5 gm of sodium bicarbonate, and 1.5 gm of potassium chloride to a liter of drinking water (Table 103–3). Such fluids should be administered initially in large quantities, 250 ml every 15 minutes in adults, until clinical observations indicate that fluid balance has been restored. Thereafter, one administers fluids in quantities sufficient to maintain normal balance; if stool output is measured, roughly 1.5 L of glucose-electrolyte solution should be given orally for each liter of stool. The oral fluid regimen does *not* decrease the volume of fluid lost via the intestinal tract but rather facilitates absorption of adequate fluid to counterbalance the toxin-induced fluid secretion.

TABLE 103–3. ORAL REHYDRATION FLUID

CONSTITUENTS (gm/L)	ELECTROLYTE CONTENT (mmol/L)
NaCl — 3.5 gm	Na — 90
NaHCO$_3$ — 2.5 gm	Cl — 80
KCl — 1.5 gm	K — 20
Glucose — 20 gm	HCO$_3$ — 30
	glucose — 110

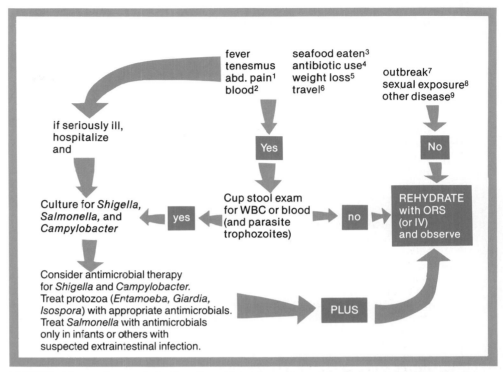

FIGURE 103–1. Approach to the diagnosis and management of acute infectious diarrhea. WBC = White blood cell; IV = intravenous; ORS = oral rehydration solution.

1. If unexplained abdominal pain and fever suggest an appendicitis-like syndrome, culture for *Yersinia enterocolitica*.
2. Bloody diarrhea, in the absence of fecal leukocytes, suggests enterohemorrhagic *Escherichia coli* or amebiasis (where leukocytes are destroyed by the parasite).
3. Ingestion of inadequately cooked seafood prompts consideration of *Vibrio* infections or Norwalk-like viruses.
4. Associated antibiotics should be stopped and *Clostridium difficile* considered.
5. Persistence (>10 days) with weight loss prompts consideration of giardiasis or cryptosporidiosis.
6. Travel to tropical areas increases the chance of enterotoxic *E. coli* (ETEC) as well as viral, protozoal (*Giardia, Entamoeba, Cryptosporidium*), and, if fecal leukocytes are present, invasive bacterial pathogens.
7. Outbreaks should prompt consideration of *Staphylococcus aureus, Bacillus cereus, Clostridium perfringens,* ETEC, *Vibrio, Salmonella, Campylobacter,* or *Shigella* infection.
8. Sigmoidoscopy in symptomatic homosexual males should distinguish proctitis in the distal 15 cm (caused by herpesvirus, gonococcal, chlamydial, or syphilitic infection) from colitis (*Campylobacter, Shigella,* or *C. difficile* infections).
9. Immunocompromised hosts should have a wide range of viral (e.g., cytomegalovirus [CMV], herpes simplex virus [HSV], rotavirus), bacterial (e.g., *Salmonella, Mycobacterium avium-intracellulare*), and protozoal (e.g., *Cryptosporidium, Entamoeba,* and *Giardia*) agents considered. (Adapted from Guerrant RL, Shields DS, Thorson SM, et al: Evaluation and diagnosis of acute infectious diarrhea. Am J Med 78:91–98, 1985; with permission.)

Since a similar pattern of fluid loss occurs in diarrheal illnesses caused by other intestinal pathogens, patients with fluid depletion caused by invasive microbial agents (e.g., rotavirus, *Salmonella*) also respond well to oral glucose-electrolyte therapy. Although the pathogenesis of diarrheal disease caused by the rotavirus is quite different from that caused by enterotoxigenic bacteria, patients with rotavirus illness consistently respond well to oral glucose-electrolyte replacement.

Antimicrobial Therapy

Most acute infectious diarrheas do not require antibiotic therapy (see Table 103–2). Of the noninvasive bacterial diarrheas, only in cholera do antibiotics dramatically decrease the volume of diarrhea. Oral tetracycline, 40 mg/kg in four divided doses daily for 48 hours, is the drug of choice.

Of the invasive bacterial diarrheas, short-term antimicrobial treatment significantly decreases the duration and severity of shigellosis. In North America, trimethoprim-sulfamethoxazole, twice daily for 5 days, is the drug of choice. Because of the increasing frequency of plasmid-mediated antimicrobial resistance, sensitivity testing is necessary to determine the appropriate antibiotic in many other areas of the world.

Antimicrobial therapy *may* be helpful in decreasing the duration and severity of enteritis caused by *Yersinia* and *Campylobacter*. Oral erythromycin appears to be the drug of choice for *Campylobacter jejuni*, and trimethoprim-sulfamethoxazole is the preferred treatment for *Yersinia enterocolitica*. Antimicrobials are of no known value in *V. parahaemolyticus* infections. In uncomplicated nontyphoidal *Salmonella* enteritis, antibiotics may prolong the fecal shedding of salmonellae.

Antimicrobial therapy is, paradoxically, indicated for treatment of antibiotic-associated diarrhea (AAC). AAC develops in 1 to 15 per cent of patients who receive broad-spectrum antimicrobials and is caused by cytotoxins produced by *Clostridium difficile*, which proliferate in the colonic mucosa when the normal flora is disturbed. Although generally characterized by mild diarrhea, AAC may result in a potentially lethal pseudomembranous colitis. In all cases, the responsible antibiotic should be stopped. In moderate to severe cases (fever, mucosal ulceration, and/or pseudomembranes), vancomycin (250 mg q6h orally for 7 days) or metronidazole (500 mg q8h for 7 days) should be initiated on the basis of strong clinical suspicion, before the diagnosis is confirmed by stool assay for *C. difficile* toxins.

Antimicrobials decrease the duration and severity of giardiasis. In adults, metronidazole, given 750 mg every 8 hours for 3 days, and quinacrine, 300 mg/day for 7 days, appear to be equally effective in adults. Acute intestinal amebiasis demands antimicrobial therapy. Metronidazole, 750 mg every 8 hours for 5 days, is the drug of choice in adults. The duration of diarrhea caused by *Isospora belli* is significantly shortened by administration of trimethoprim-sulfamethoxazole twice daily for 5 days.

Antimicrobial Prophylaxis

Prophylactic antimicrobials are effective in preventing traveler's diarrhea, a generally self-limited illness caused most often by ETEC. Doxycycline, trimethoprim-sulfamethoxazole, and norfloxacin are each effective when taken once daily for up to 3 weeks. However, because of the rapid response of most patients to early treatment with any of these three agents, the advantages of prophylactic drugs are, in most instances, outweighed by their potential risks (adverse reactions).

Symptomatic Therapy

Adjuvant symptomatic therapy is not essential but may provide modest symptomatic relief in acute infectious diarrheas associated with cramping abdominal pain. Bismuth subsalicylate, 0.6 gm every 6 hours, may ameliorate symptoms of traveler's diarrhea. Agents that decrease intestinal motility (e.g., codeine, diphenoxylate, loperamide) also relieve the cramping abdominal pain associated with many acute diarrheal illnesses but are potentially hazardous because they may enhance severity of illness in shigellosis, the prototype of invasive bacterial diarrheas.

REFERENCES

Greenough WB: Cholera. *In* Wyngaarden JB, Smith LH Jr, Bennett JC (eds): Cecil Textbook of Medicine. 19th ed. Philadelphia, WB Saunders Co, 1992, pp 1699–1701.

Guerrant RE: Enteric *Escherichia coli* infections. *In* Wyngaarden JB, Smith LH Jr, Bennett JC (eds): Cecil Textbook of Medicine. 19th ed. Philadelphia, WB Saunders Co, 1992, pp 1701–1705.

Guerrant RL, Shields DS, Thorson SM, Schorling JB, Gröschel DH: Evaluation and diagnosis of acute infectious diarrhea. Am J Med 78:91–98, 1985.

Stevens DP: Giardiasis: Host-pathogen biology. Rev Infect Dis 4:851–856, 1982.

104 INFECTIONS INVOLVING BONES AND JOINTS

ARTHRITIS

In adults, almost all cases of infectious arthritis of natural joints occur via hematogenous seeding of the joint. Rarely, intra-articular trauma results in septic arthritis. Bacteria, viruses, mycobacteria, and fungi can all produce an arthritis by infection of the joint. In addition, certain viruses such as hepatitis B virus can produce a polyarthritis via immune complex deposition. Immune mechanisms may also underlie arthritis syndromes seen in Lyme disease and after diarrhea due to *Salmonella*, *Shigella*, and *Yersinia* infections; the majority of individuals with postdysentery arthritis syndrome share the human leukocyte antigen HLA-B27 (see Chapter 86).

Underlying joint disease, particularly rheumatoid arthritis, predisposes to septic arthritis. Many patients with septic arthritis give a history of joint trauma antedating symptoms of infection. Conceivably, disruption of capillaries during an unrecognized and transient bacteremia allows bacteria to spill into hemorrhagic and traumatized synovium or joint fluid, resulting in the initiation of infection.

Microbiology of Acute Infectious Arthritis
(Table 104–1)

Staphylococcus aureus is the most common cause of septic arthritis. Patients with underlying joint disease and intravenous drug users are at particular risk for infection with this organism. *Pseudomonas aeruginosa* is another important cause of septic arthritis among intravenous drug users.

Other gram-negative bacilli are infrequent causes of septic arthritis and are seen primarily among elderly debilitated patients with chronic arthritis. In adults under 30, *Neisseria gonorrhoeae* is the most likely pathogen. Isolates causing disseminated gonococcal infection (DGI) with arthritis are generally resistant to killing by normal serum.

Clinical Presentation

Symptoms of septic arthritis are generally present for only a few days before the patient seeks medical attention. Fever is usual; shaking chills may occur. The knee is the most commonly affected joint and is generally painful and swollen. Fluid can be demonstrated in most infected joints, and limitation of motion is marked. In some cases, however, particularly among patients with underlying rheumatoid arthritis who are receiving corticosteroids, physical findings indicating infection may be subtle. In these individuals, who are at particular risk for septic arthritis, superimposed infection may be difficult to distinguish from a flare-up of underlying disease. Symmetric symptoms in multiple joints are more indicative of a rheumatoid flare-up. Approximately 10 per cent of cases of septic arthritis, however, involve more than one joint.

Differential Diagnosis of Acute Monoarticular or Oligoarticular Arthritis

Crystal deposition (uric acid—gout; calcium pyrophosphate—pseudogout), rheumatoid arthritis, systemic lupus erythematosus, and degenerative joint disease can also produce an acute monoarticular arthritis. Radiographs may show evidence of osteoarthritis, gouty tophi, or the linear densities of chondrocalcinosis, which are characteristic of pseudogout. All red, warm, tender joints must be aspirated. The synovial fluid should be cultured anaerobically and aerobically. A Gram-stained preparation should be examined; a wet mount of fluid should be examined, using a polarized microscope to look for crystals. Synovial fluid

TABLE 104–1. INFECTIOUS ARTHRITIS—ACUTE

	ETIOLOGIC AGENT	CHARACTERISTICS
Bacterial	*Staphylococcus aureus*	Most common overall; usually monoarticular, large joint involvement
	Neisseria gonorrhoeae	Most common in young, sexually active adults; commonly polyarticular in onset; often associated with skin lesions
	Pseudomonas aeruginosa	Largely restricted to intravenous drug users; often involves sternoclavicular joint
Viral	Hepatitis B, rubella, mumps	Usually polyarticular, with minimal joint effusions, normal peripheral white blood cell count

leukocyte counts and chemistries are of limited value in the differential diagnosis of a suspected septic joint. As a general rule, however, synovial fluid white blood cell (WBC) counts in excess of $100,000/\mu l$ suggest either infection or crystal-induced disease (see Table 78–3). Blood cultures should be obtained in all cases of suspected septic arthritis.

Treatment of Acute Infectious Arthritis

The two major modalities for treatment of acute septic arthritis are drainage and antibiotics. During the first needle aspiration of a septic joint, one should remove as much fluid as possible. Initial antibiotic choice should be based upon the clinical presentation and the results of Gram stain. Staphylococcal infection can be treated with penicillinase-resistant penicillin or vancomycin. Gonococcal infections should be treated with ceftriaxone, 1 gm every 24 hours for 10 days. Arthritis due to gram-negative rods should be treated with an aminoglycoside plus another drug active against gram-negative bacilli, such as a cephalosporin. In intravenous drug users, the second drug should be active against *Pseudomonas*; therefore, an extended-spectrum penicillin, such as mezlocillin, or a third-generation cephalosporin, such as ceftazidime, is indicated. Arthritis due to *Staphylococcus aureus* or gram-negative bacilli should be treated with antibiotics for 4 to 6 weeks. Otherwise, 2 to 3 weeks of antibiotics are sufficient to eradicate infection.

Septic joints (with the notable exception of joints infected with the gonococcus) generally reaccumulate fluid after treatment is initiated. These reaccumulations must be removed by repeated needle aspirations as often as necessary. Indications for open surgical drainage of the joint include failure of the synovial fluid WBC count to fall after 5 days of antibiotic treatment and repeated needle aspirations, and the presence of loculated fluid within the joint. Septic arthritis of the hip is generally drained surgically because of the difficulty and potential hazard of repeated needle aspirations of this joint. Early surgical drainage also should be considered for joint infections due to gram-negative rods and to *Staphylococcus aureus*. Osteomyelitis is an uncommon complication of untreated or inadequately treated septic arthritis. In instances in which the diagnosis and treatment have been delayed, radiographs of the involved joint should be obtained at the beginning and termination of treatment.

Polyarticular Arthritis

Arthritis involving multiple joints is infrequently attributable to direct microbial invasion. In many instances, a polyarticular arthritis represents an immunologically mediated process. *Acute rheumatic fever*, a delayed immune-mediated response to group A streptococcal infection, may manifest with a migratory, asymmetric arthritis of the knees, ankles, elbows, and wrists. Heart involvement, subcutaneous nodules, or erythema marginatum is present in a minority of cases. Most patients have serologic evidence of recent streptococcal infection. Antistreptolysin-O, anti-DNase, and antihyaluronidase antibodies are usually present. The importance of making this diagnosis lies primarily in the requirement for long-term prophylaxis against streptococcal infection and the clinical response of this process to salicylates.

Viral infections such as *hepatitis B, rubella,* and *mumps* may be associated with polyarthritis. In mumps, the arthritis results from direct infection of articular tissue; with rubella and hepatitis B, the joint inflammation is a secondary result of the host immune response to the virus. These processes are self-limited. Serum sickness, polyarticular gout, sarcoidosis, rheumatoid arthritis, and other connective tissue disorders must be considered in the differential diagnosis. Since 10 per cent of cases of septic arthritis involve more than one joint, all acutely inflamed joints containing fluid should be tapped to exclude bacterial infection.

DGI (see Chapter 107) may manifest with fever, tenosynovitis, or arthritis involving several joints and a characteristic rash. The rash may be petechial but usually consists of a few to a few dozen pustules on an erythematous base. Cultures of the joint fluid are usually negative at this stage, but blood cultures are often positive; Gram stain of a pustule may reveal the pathogen. Ceftriaxone, 1 gm/day for 10 days, is curative.

Chronic Arthritis (Table 104–2)

Mycobacteria and fungi may produce an indolent, slowly progressive arthritis, usually involving only one joint or contiguous joints, such as those of the wrist and hand. Fever may be low-grade or absent. Cultures of joint fluid may be negative. Some patients with tuberculous arthritis have no evidence of active disease in the lungs. As a general rule, patients with inflammatory chronic monoar-

TABLE 104–2. CAUSES OF INFECTIOUS ARTHRITIS — CHRONIC

Tuberculosis
Nontuberculous mycobacteria
Fungi
Lyme disease (oligoarticular)

ticular arthritis should have a synovial biopsy for culture and histology. Granulomas indicate the likelihood of fungal or mycobacterial infection. Cultures should confirm the diagnosis.

Fungal arthritis is treated with amphotericin B. Mycobacterial arthritis must be treated for 18 months with at least two drugs active against the isolate. Since some mycobacterial isolates causing joint disease are nontuberculous, extensive susceptibility testing may be needed to guide antimicrobial therapy.

A spirochete is the pathogen responsible for Lyme disease. Several months to 2 years after the bite of the ixodid tick and the characteristic rash of erythema chronicum migrans, some patients develop an intermittent arthritis involving one or more joints—usually including the knees. This chronic arthritis may result in joint destruction, but fever is unusual. Treatment with intravenous ceftriaxone, 2 gm/day for 14 to 21 days, will halt the progression of disease in the majority of cases (see Chapter 95).

SEPTIC BURSITIS

Septic bursitis is almost always due to *Staphylococcus aureus* and involves either the olecranon or the prepatellar bursa. In most instances, there is a history of antecedent infection or irritation of the skin overlying the bursa. On examination, the skin over the bursa is red and often peeling. The bursa has a doughy consistency and may reveal fluid on careful examination. Needle aspiration and antistaphylococcal antibiotics are generally curative. Occasionally, long courses of antibiotics (>4 weeks) may be required for cure.

OSTEOMYELITIS

Infections of the bone occur either as a result of hematogenous spread or via extension of local infection.

Hematogenous Osteomyelitis (Table 104–3)

This infection occurs most commonly in the long bones or vertebral bodies. The peak age distributions are in childhood and old age. Individuals predisposed to hematogenous osteomyelitis include intravenous drug users, who are at risk for infections with *Staphylococcus aureus* and *Pseudomonas aeruginosa*, and patients with hemoglobinopathy, in whom nontyphoidal salmonellae often infect infarcted regions of bone. Recently, *Staphylococcus epidermidis* has emerged as an important nosocomial pathogen among patients with infected intravenous catheters. Like patients with septic arthritis, patients with hematogenous osteomyelitis often give a history of trauma antedating symptoms of infection, suggesting that transient, unrecognized bacteremia might result in infection of traumatized tissue.

Patients with acute hematogenous osteomyelitis generally present with acute onset of pain, tenderness, and fever; there may also be soft tissue swelling over the affected bone. In most instances, physical examination distinguishes acute osteomyelitis from septic arthritis, since range of joint motion is preserved in osteomyelitis. In the first 2 weeks of illness, roentgenograms may be negative or show only soft tissue swelling; technetium scans or gallium scans are almost always positive, but technetium scans may also be positive in the setting of increased vascularity or increased bone formation of any etiology. After 2 weeks of infection, radiographs generally show some abnormality, and untreated osteomyelitis may produce areas of periosteal elevation or erosion followed by increased bone formation (sclerosis). The erythrocyte sedimentation rate is generally elevated, as is the WBC count.

A patient with back pain and fever must be considered to have a serious infection until proven otherwise. Spasm of the paravertebral muscles is common in patients with vertebral osteomyelitis, but nonspecific. Point tenderness over bone suggests the presence of local infection. A good history should be obtained and a careful neurologic examination performed. Abnormalities of bowel or bladder or of strength or sensation in the lower extremities suggest the possibility of spinal cord involvement via spinal epidural abscess with or without osteomyelitis. Acute spinal epidural abscess is a *surgical emergency*. The challenge is to make the diagnosis before neurologic signs appear (see Chapter 120). Demonstration of an epidural abscess mandates prompt surgical decompression to avoid disastrous neurologic sequelae. Magnetic resonance imaging (MRI) provides excellent definition of epidural or paravertebral abscess and is the diagnostic procedure of choice when available. As an alternative, emergency myelogram can confirm the diagnosis.

Although most cases of hematogenous osteomyelitis have an acute presentation, some cases, particularly those involving the vertebral bodies among intravenous drug users, may have an indolent course. These patients may have an illness of more than 1 year's duration characterized by pain and low-grade fever. Radiographs are abnormal but may reveal only collapse of a vertebral body. This most often occurs in infections due to *Pseudomonas aeruginosa*, but *Candida* species and *Staphylococcus aureus* may also occasionally present in this manner.

Blood cultures are positive in about half of acute cases of osteomyelitis. Patients with acute osteomyelitis should have a needle biopsy and culture of the involved bone unless blood culture results are known beforehand. Antibiotic treatment should be continued for 4 to 6 weeks, using agents active against the pathogen.

TABLE 104-3. FACTORS PREDISPOSING TO HEMATOGENOUS OSTEOMYELITIS

SETTING	LIKELY PATHOGENS
Intravenous drug use	*Staphylococcus aureus*
	Pseudomonas aeruginosa
Intravenous catheters	*Staphylococcus aureus*
	Staphylococcus epidermidis

Osteomyelitis Secondary to Extension of Local Infection

Local infection predisposes to osteomyelitis in several major settings (Table 104-4). The first is after penetrating trauma or surgery where local infection gains access to traumatized bone. In postsurgical infections, staphylococci and gram-negative bacilli predominate. Generally, there is evidence of wound infection with erythema, swelling, increased postoperative tenderness, and drainage. A traumatic incident often associated with osteomyelitis is a bite—either human or animal. Human bites, if deep enough, may result in osteomyelitis due to anaerobic mouth flora. Cat bites notoriously result in the development of osteomyelitis because the thin, sharp, long cat's teeth often penetrate the periosteum. *Pasteurella multocida* is a frequent pathogen in this setting. A 4- to 6-week course of penicillin G, 10 million units/day, is indicated.

The intimate relationship of the teeth and periodontal tissues to the bones of the maxilla and mandible may predispose to osteomyelitis following local infection. Debridement of necrotic tissue and penicillin constitute the treatment of choice, since penicillin-sensitive anaerobes are the usual agents of these infections.

The third setting in which local infection predisposes to osteomyelitis is that of an infected sore or ulcer. Pressure sores of the sacrum or femoral region may erode into contiguous bone and produce an osteomyelitis (see Chapter 101) due to a mixed flora containing anaerobic organisms. Patients with diabetes mellitus often develop ulcerations of their toes and feet, with eventual development of osteomyelitis. Anaerobes, streptococci, staphylococci, and gram-negative bacilli are often involved in these infections (see Chapter 101).

TABLE 104-4. OSTEOMYELITIS SECONDARY TO CONTIGUOUS SPREAD

SETTING	LIKELY MICROORGANISMS
Surgery, trauma	*Staphylococcus aureus*, aerobic gram-negative bacilli
Cat or dog bites	*Pasteurella multocida*
Human bites	Penicillin-sensitive anaerobes
Periodontal infections	Penicillin-sensitive anaerobes
Cutaneous ulcers	Mixed aerobic and anaerobic organisms

Treatment involves debridement (often amputation in the case of diabetics) and antibiotics active against the pathogens involved.

Chronic Osteomyelitis

Untreated or inadequately treated osteomyelitis results in avascular necrosis of bone and the formation of islands of nonvascularized and infected bone called sequestra. Patients with chronic osteomyelitis may tolerate their infection reasonably well, with intermittent episodes of disease activity manifested by increased local pain and the development of drainage of infected material through a sinus tract. Some patients have tolerated chronic osteomyelitis for decades. A normochromic normocytic anemia of chronic disease is common in this setting, and occasionally amyloidosis and rarely osteogenic sarcoma complicate this disorder.

Staphylococcus aureus is responsible for the great majority of cases of chronic osteomyelitis; the major exception is among patients with sickle cell anemia, in whom nontyphoidal salmonellae may cause chronic infection of the long bones.

Cultures of sinus tract drainage do not reliably reflect the pathogens involved in the infection. Diagnosis and cure are best effected by surgical debridement of necrotic material followed by long-term administration of antibiotics active against the organism found in the surgical specimens.

Mycobacteria, especially *Mycobacterium tuberculosis*, can produce a chronic osteomyelitis. The anterior portions of vertebral bodies are the most common sites of infection. Hematogenous dissemination and lymphatic spread are the most likely routes of infection. Paravertebral abscess (often termed "cold abscess" because of lack of signs of acute inflammation) may complicate this infection. Diagnosis is usually confirmed by histologic examination and culture of biopsy material. Treatment with antituberculous drugs is usually curative.

REFERENCES

Goldenberg DL, Reed JI: Bacterial arthritis. N Engl J Med 312:764–770, 1985.
Waldvogel FA: Osteomyelitis. In Wyngaarden JB, Smith LH Jr, Bennett JC (eds): Cecil Textbook of Medicine. 19th ed. Philadelphia, WB Saunders Co, 1992, pp 1672–1674.

105 INFECTIONS OF THE URINARY TRACT

The urethra, bladder, kidneys, and prostate are all susceptible to infection. Most urinary tract infections (UTIs) cause local symptoms, yet clinical manifestations do not always pinpoint the site of infection. In addition, the criteria used by different clinical laboratories to confirm infection of the urinary tract are also variable. This chapter will attempt to simplify the clinical and laboratory approach to diagnosis and treatment of UTIs. Infections associated with indwelling urinary catheters are discussed in Chapter 106.

URETHRITIS

Urethritis is predominantly an infection of sexually active individuals, usually observed in males. The symptoms are pain and burning of the urethra during urination, and there is generally some discharge at the urethral meatus. Urethritis may be gonococcal in origin. However, nongonococcal urethritis (NGU) is now more frequent in

North America. NGU may be due to *Chlamydia trachomatis* or *Ureaplasma urealyticum* and less commonly to *Trichomonas vaginalis* or *Herpesvirus hominis*. Diagnosis and management of urethritis are considered in Chapter 107.

CYSTITIS AND PYELONEPHRITIS

Epidemiology. Bacterial infection of the bladder (cystitis) and kidney (pyelonephritis) is more frequent in females, and the incidence of infection increases with age. Factors that predispose to UTI include instrumentation (e.g., catheterization, cytoscopy), pregnancy, and possibly diabetes mellitus.

Pathogenesis. Although some infections of the kidney may arise as the result of hematogenous dissemination, most UTIs "ascend" via a portal of entry in the urethra. Most pathogens responsible for community-acquired UTIs are part of the subject's normal bowel flora. *Escherichia coli* is the most common isolate, and in the female, colonization of the vaginal and periurethral mucosa may antedate infection of the urinary tract. The longer and protected male urethra may account for the lower incidence of UTI in men. Motile bacteria may swim "upstream," and reflux of urine from the bladder into the ureters may predispose to the development of kidney infection. Congenital anomalies or obstruction of urine flow at any level also predispose to infection.

Clinical Features. Suprapubic pain, discomfort, or burning sensation on urination and frequency of urination are common symptoms of infection of the urinary tract. Back or flank pain or the occurrence of fever suggests that infection is not limited to the bladder (cystitis) but involves the kidney (pyelonephritis) or prostate as well. However, clinical presentation often fails to distinguish between simple cystitis and pyelonephritis. Approximately one half of infections that appear clinically to involve the bladder can be shown only by instrumentation and other specialized techniques to actually affect the kidneys. Elderly or debilitated patients with infection of the urinary tract may have no symptoms referable to the urinary tract and may present only with fever, altered mental status, or hypotension.

Laboratory Diagnosis of Urinary Tract Infection. Analysis of a midstream urine sample obtained from patients with infection of the bladder or kidney should reveal white blood cells (WBCs) and may also have red cells and slightly increased amounts of protein. The presence of an increased number (see below) of WBCs (pyuria) in a midstream urine sample indicates the likelihood of a UTI. However, since most laboratories count WBCs by examining the sediment of a centrifuged urine sample, and since the urinary WBC count may vary according to the degree of urine concentration, quantitation of pyuria is imprecise. As a general rule, more than 5 to 10 WBCs per high-power field on a centrifuged specimen of urine is abnormal. Resuspending a sedimented urine should be done gently, using a Pasteur pipette; in this way casts are not disrupted. The presence of WBC casts in an infected urine sample indicates the presence of pyelonephritis. Bacteria may be seen in sedimented urine and can be readily identified using Gram stain.

At present, most clinical laboratories consider bacterial growth of greater than 10^5 colony-forming units/ml to be indicative of infection. Recent studies indicate that smaller numbers of bacteria can produce lower UTIs (see below). A hazard in interpreting results of urine culture is that if the sample is allowed to stand at room temperature for a few hours before planting on culture plates, bacteria can multiply. This results in spuriously high bacterial counts. For this reason, urine for culture should not be obtained from a catheter bag. Specimens that are not plated immediately should be refrigerated. Biochemical tests to detect bacteriuria are not reliable.

Treatment and Outcome. Patients with cystitis may be treated with a 7-day course of antibiotics such as sulfisoxazole, ampicillin, or trimethoprim-sulfamethoxazole. Recent studies suggest that most patients with cystitis are cured by a single high dose of antibiotic (e.g., 3 gm of amoxicillin or 2 gm of sulfisoxazole). Culture and sensitivity confirm the diagnosis and ascertain if the antibiotic is active against the pathogen. Because of the difficulty in clinical distinction between cystitis and upper tract disease, some patients treated for cystitis with a single dose of an antibiotic may relapse because of unrecognized upper tract disease.

Occasionally, urine cultures obtained from a patient with symptoms of UTI and pyuria are reported as exhibiting "no growth" or "insignificant growth." This situation has been labeled the "urethral syndrome." Low numbers of bacteria (as few as 100/ml of urine) may produce such infections of the urinary tract. In other instances, the urethral syndrome may be caused by *Chlamydia* or *Ureaplasma*, which will not grow on routine culture media. Thus, if a patient with the urethral syndrome has responded to antibiotics, the course should be completed; otherwise, if symptoms and pyuria persist, the patient should receive a 7- to 10-day course of tetracycline, which is active against *Chlamydia* and *Ureaplasma*. Other considerations for patients with lower urinary tract symptoms and no or "insignificant" growth on cultures of urine include vaginitis, herpes simplex infection, and gonococcal infection. (*Neisseria gonorrhoeae* will not grow on routine media used for urine culture.) Thus, a pelvic examination and culture for gonococci may be indicated in this setting if the patient is sexually active. Men with urethral discomfort and discharge should be evaluated for urethritis (see Chapter 107). Men with suprapubic pain, frequency, and urgency should be evaluated for cystitis, as discussed above.

The presence of fever suggests that infection involves more than just the bladder. Young, otherwise healthy, febrile patients with UTI may be treated on an ambulatory basis with trimethoprim-sulfamethoxazole for 2 weeks, provided that (1) they do not appear toxic, (2) they have friends or family at home, (3) they have good provisions for follow-up, and (4) they have no potentially complicating features, such as diabetes mellitus, history of renal stones, history of obstructive disease of the urinary tract, or sickle cell disease. Gram stain of urine in patients hospitalized for pyelonephritis will guide initial therapy. Gram-negative rod infection may be treated initially with an aminoglycoside plus ampicillin or a cephalosporin. The aminoglycoside should be promptly discontinued if antibiotic sensitivity studies indicate that it is not essential. The finding of gram-positive cocci in chains suggests that enterococci are the pathogens. This infection should be treated, at least initially, with ampicillin plus an aminoglycoside. Gram-positive cocci in clusters may indicate staphylococci. *Staphylococcus saprophyticus* is a likely agent in otherwise healthy women and is sensitive to most antibiotics used in the treatment of UTI. In the older patient, *Staphylococcus aureus* should be considered, and this infection may be treated with a penicillinase-resistant penicillin, such as nafcillin. Gram-positive cocci in the urine may represent a case of endocarditis with septic embolization to the kidney.

Therapy should be simplified when reports of antimicrobial susceptibility are available. Repeat urine culture after 2 days of effective treatment should show sterilization or a marked decrease in the urinary bacterial count. If the patient fails to demonstrate some clinical improvement after 2 to 3 days of treatment or if the patient presents with the clinical picture of sepsis or has been febrile for more than 1 week, a complicating feature should be suspected. Intranephric or perinephric abscess or obstruction due to a stone or an enlarged prostate may underlie this presentation. Plain films of the abdomen may occasionally reveal a radiopaque stone, but ultrasonography is a good first diagnostic procedure in this setting. This will generally detect obstruction and collections of pus and may also detect stones greater than 3 mm in diameter. Obstruction must be relieved and abscesses drained to result in cure. Computed tomographic (CT)–guided percutaneous drainage is the procedure of choice whenever possible.

All patients with UTI should have repeat urine cultures 1 to 2 weeks after treatment is completed, to check for relapse. If relapse occurs, the patient may have pyelonephritis, prostatitis, or neuropathic or structural disease of the urinary tract. If a 6-week course of antibiotics active against the bacterial isolate is not effective in eradicating infection, the possibility of structural abnormalities or prostatic infection should be investigated. Urologic evaluation should be performed for all males with UTI (excepting urethritis) because of the high frequency of correctable anatomic lesions in this population.

Some women have frequent episodes of UTI due to different bacterial isolates. In some instances, these reinfections are related to sexual activity. Prompt voiding and a single dose of an active antibiotic such as cephalexin just after sexual contact can decrease reinfection rate in these women. In other women, in whom no precipitating factor can be found and infections are frequent, prophylaxis with one half of a tablet of trimethoprim-sulfamethoxazole nightly has been effective.

On occasion, urine cultures reveal bacterial growth in the absence of symptoms. If the sample has been obtained properly and repeat culture reveals the same organism, this is termed *asymptomatic bacteriuria*. This condition is generally observed in elderly or middle-aged individuals and, in the absence of structural disease of the urinary tract or diabetes mellitus, may not require treatment. Asymptomatic bacteriuria occurring during pregnancy should be treated because of the high risk of pyelonephritis in this setting.

The occurrence of pyuria in the absence of bacterial growth on culture of urine ($<10^2$ colonies/ml) may be termed *sterile pyuria*. If this occurs in the patient with lower urinary tract symptoms, chlamydial or gonoccocal infection, vaginitis, or herpes simplex infection should be considered. In the absence of lower urinary tract symptoms, sterile pyuria may be seen among patients with interstitial nephritis of numerous causes or with tuberculosis of the urinary tract. Patients with renal tuberculosis often have nocturia and polyuria. More than half of male patients also have involvement of the genital tract, most commonly the epididymis. Diagnosis can be made by biopsy of genital masses, when present, and by three morning cultures of urine for mycobacteria.

PROSTATITIS

Although prostatic fluid has antibacterial properties, the prostate can become infected, usually by direct invasion through the urethra. Symptoms of UTI, back or perineal pain, and fever are common. Some patients experience pain with ejaculation. Rectal examination usually reveals a tender prostate. Patients with acute prostatitis generally have an abnormal urinary sediment and pathogenic bacteria (usually gram-negative enteric rods) in cultures of urine.

Acute prostatitis may be due to the gonococcus but is most often due to gram-negative bacilli. Treatment is directed against the pathogen observed on Gram stain of urine and is generally effective. Chronic prostatitis should be suspected in males with recurrent UTI. The urine sediment may be relatively benign in patients with chronic prostatitis. In this instance, comparison of the first part of the urine sample, midstream urine, excretions expressed by massage of the prostate, and postmassage urine should reveal bacterial counts more than 10-fold greater in the prostatic secretions and postmassage urine samples than in first-void and midstream samples. Treatment of chronic prostatitis is hampered by poor penetration of the prostate by most antimicrobials. Long-term (4 to 12 weeks) treatment with trimethoprim-sulfamethoxazole has cured approximately one third of patients and prevented symptomatic relapse in another third. Ciprofloxacin also appears to be effective in this setting.

REFERENCES

Andriole VT: Urinary tract infections and pyelonephritis. *In* Wyngaarden JB, Smith LH Jr, Bennett JC (eds): Cecil Textbook of Medicine. 19th ed. Philadelphia, WB Saunders Co, 1992, pp 593–598.
Komaroff AL: Acute dysuria in women. N Engl J Med 310:368–374, 1984.

106 NOSOCOMIAL INFECTIONS

A nosocomial or hospital-acquired infection is an infection, not present on admission to the hospital, that first appears 72 hours or more after hospitalization. A patient admitted to a hospital in the United States has an approximately 5 to 10 per cent chance of developing a nosocomial infection. These infections result in significant morbidity and mortality (approximately 1 per cent of these infections are fatal, and an additional 4 per cent contribute to death) and greatly increased medical costs (more than 1 billion dollars per year).

Numerous factors are associated with a greater risk of acquiring a nosocomial infection. These include factors that are not avoidable by optimal medical practice, such as age and severity of underlying illness. Contributing factors that can be minimized by thoughtful management of the patient include prolonged duration of hospitalization, the inappropriate use of broad-spectrum antibiotics, the use of indwelling catheters, and the failure of health care personnel to wash their hands.

APPROACH TO THE HOSPITALIZED PATIENT WITH SUSPECTED NOSOCOMIAL INFECTION

The first clue to the presence of a nosocomial infection is often a rise in temperature. The only sign of infection, particularly in the elderly or demented patient, may be a change in mental status (Table 106–1). Some patients with serious infection do not initially develop fever but instead become tachypneic or confused for no apparent reason. Analysis of arterial blood gases may reveal at first a respiratory alkalosis, followed by a metabolic acidosis due to increased levels of lactate. Arterial oxygen content may be normal or depressed.

When evaluating a hospitalized patient for a new fever (Table 106–2) or suspected nosocomial infection, the physician should first assess the stability of the patient. Hypotension, tachypnea, or new obtundation mandates rapid evaluation and treatment. The patient's problem list must be reviewed; the physician must ascertain if the patient was recently subjected to a potentially hazardous intervention (e.g., genitourinary tract instrumentation or administration of blood products). If the patient can cooperate, the physician should elicit a history directed at possible causes of the fever. Often the patient has a specific complaint that helps identify the source of the fever. The skin must be examined carefully. Maculopapular

TABLE 106–1. SIGNS OF INFECTION IN THE HOSPITALIZED PATIENT

Fever
Change in mental status
Tachypnea
Hypotension
Oliguria
Leukocytosis

rashes often accompany drug fevers; ecthyma gangrenosum can be a sign of gram-negative sepsis (see Chapter 96). Surgical wounds should be examined for the presence of infection. Among debilitated patients, pressure sores located near the sacrum or over the greater trochanters may become infected and produce fever. Abscesses at these sites may be covered by a necrotic membrane, so that exploration with a gloved finger or sterile needle may be required to demonstrate a focus of pus. Patients receiving multiple intramuscular injections may develop fever as a result of the development of sterile abscesses at the injection sites. Headache or sinus tenderness may be present in patients with sinusitis—this may be a problem among patients after nasogastric or nasotracheal intubation. Nuchal rigidity may be a sign of nosocomial meningitis, although it may be absent in some cases, particularly following neurosurgery or head trauma. Furthermore, generalized rigidity is often seen in elderly demented patients without central nervous system infection. The physician should examine the nose and oropharynx and attempt to elicit symptoms of viral upper respiratory tract infections. These do occur in hospitals. A pleural friction rub may indicate a recent pulmonary thromboembolism as a cause of fever; rales or other evidence of consolidation may indicate a nosocomial pneumonia; basilar rales and even egophony and bronchial breath sounds may also be due to atelectasis in debilitated patients. A new S_4 gallop or pericardial friction rub may be

TABLE 106–2. COMMON CAUSES OF FEVER IN THE HOSPITALIZED PATIENT

Pneumonia
Catheter-related infection
Surgical wound infection
Urinary tract infection
Drugs
Pulmonary emboli
Infected pressure sores

the only clinical manifestation of a myocardial infarction.

The abdomen may also be a source of fever in the hospitalized patient. The patient with antibiotic-induced colitis generally has fever, diarrhea, and abdominal pain. Patients with indwelling urinary catheters are at particular risk of infection. These patients should have a careful examination of the prostate—looking for abscess or tenderness—and of the urine—looking for white blood cells and bacteria.

The extremities must be examined carefully, particularly the sites of current and old intravenous catheter placements, for evidence of phlebitis. If no other source of fever is found and an intravenous catheter has been in place, it should be replaced and a segment of the catheter should be rolled on an agar plate for culture.

Deep vein thrombophlebitis and pulmonary thromboemboli are life-threatening complications of hospitalization whose only clinical manifestations may be fever. The lower extremities should be examined and measured carefully. An asymmetry in leg or calf circumference, which may not be obvious without a measurement, may be an important clue to an underlying thrombosis. A crystal-induced arthritis is another potential source of fever in a hospitalized patient. Gout and pseudogout may be precipitated by acute infections.

The patient's medication list should be reviewed for drugs likely to produce fever. In this regard antimicrobial agents (particularly penicillins, sulfa drugs, and cephalosporins) are among the most common causes of drug-induced fevers. A drug fever can occur at any time but usually occurs during the second week of drug administration. A review of the peripheral blood smear can give important clues to the cause of the fever. Eosinophilia may suggest drug reaction and lymphocytosis a viral process. A left shift and vacuolization within neutrophils suggest a bacterial infection. Unless the etiology of the fever is apparent, cultures of blood and urine and a chest radiograph should be obtained.

NOSOCOMIAL PNEUMONIA

Although some hospital-acquired pneumonias occur as a result of bacteremic spread, the vast majority occur via aspiration of oropharyngeal contents. The oropharynx of the patient admitted to the hospital rapidly becomes colonized with aerobic gram-negative bacilli and often staphylococci. The administration of broad-spectrum antibiotics, severe underlying illness, respiratory intubation, and prolonged duration of hospitalization predispose to colonization.

Sedation, loss of consciousness, and other factors that depress the gag and cough reflexes place the colonized patient at greater risk for aspiration and the development of nosocomial pneumonia. The development of a new pulmonary infiltrate in a hospitalized patient may represent pneumonia, atelectasis, aspiration of gastric contents, drug reaction, or pulmonary infarction. If pneumonia is suspected, prompt definition of the pathogen and appropriate treatment are critical, since nosocomial pneumonia carries a 20 to 50 per cent mortality. If the patient cannot produce good-quality sputum, nasotracheal or transtracheal aspiration should be performed (see Chapter 99). Antibiotic therapy is guided by the results of Gram stain of the sputum or of the tracheal aspirate. Gram-negative rods are the predominant pathogens in this setting; these infections should be treated with an aminoglycoside plus an extended-spectrum penicillin or cephalosporin until results of culture and sensitivity testing are known. In certain hospitals, nosocomial pneumonia due to *Legionella* species is frequent, and erythromycin should be included in the initial treatment regimen. Patients with nosocomial pneumonia should also receive respiratory therapy consisting of clapping, postural drainage, and promotion of coughing to assist in bringing up secretions.

The patient in the intensive care unit with an endotracheal tube in place is at particular risk for nosocomial pneumonia. This patient has an ineffective gag reflex and often a depressed cough as well. He or she is therefore entirely dependent upon suctioning by the staff to clear secretions from the airways. The airways of these patients become rapidly colonized with bacteria. Epidemics of nosocomial pneumonia have sometimes been associated with contamination of tubing and machinery used for ventilation or respiratory therapy, but more often infection is due to transmission of pathogens on the hands of medical personnel. Large-volume nebulizers, when contaminated, are also capable of delivering droplets containing bacteria to the lower respiratory tract. Patients whose airways are simply colonized but whose lower respiratory tracts are not infected should not be treated with antibiotics, despite positive sputum cultures. Premature treatment of colonization results in replacement of the initial colonists by more resistant organisms, whereas delay in treatment of nosocomial pneumonia can result in death from overwhelming infection. The physician must therefore be able to distinguish accurately between colonization and infection. The development of new fever, leukocytosis, pulmonary infiltrate, and/or deterioration of respiratory status as ascertained by blood gas determinations indicates infection (pneumonia) rather than colonization. A Gram stain of sputum should be performed to identify the predominant organism (or organisms). The appearance of elastin fibers in potassium hydroxide preparations of sputum is a very specific indicator of bacterial infection in this setting (see Chapter 93). The appearance of these fibers may actually precede the development of infiltrates on chest radiograph. This test, however, detects less than one half of nosocomial pneumonias in the intensive care unit.

Nosocomial pneumonias are best prevented by (1) avoiding excessive sedation; (2) providing frequent suctioning and respiratory therapy—drainage and clapping—to patients who have difficulty managing secretions; (3) avoiding the use of large-volume reservoir nebulizers; (4) avoiding the injudicious use of broad-spectrum and/or high-dose antibiotic therapy; (5) frequent handwashing by medical and nursing personnel; (6) weaning the patient from mechanical respiratory support as soon as possible.

INTRAVASCULAR CATHETER-RELATED INFECTIONS

Infections related to intravascular catheters may occur via bacteremic seeding or through infusion of contaminated material, but the vast majority of these infections occur via bacterial invasion at the site of catheter insertion.

Intravenous catheters may produce a sterile phlebitis. Certain drugs such as tetracycline or erythromycin, when administered intravenously, are particularly likely to produce phlebitis. Bacteria migrating through the catheter insertion site may colonize the catheter and then produce a septic phlebitis or bacteremia without evidence of local infection. Factors associated with a greater risk of intravenous catheter-related infection are shown in Table 106-3. *Staphylococcus epidermidis* and *Staphylococcus aureus* are the predominant pathogens in this setting, followed by the enteric gram-negative rods. A peripheral catheter (and all readily removable foreign bodies) should be replaced if bacteremia occurs and no other primary site of infection is found. *The catheter should also be removed if fever without an obvious source occurs or if local phlebitis develops.* The value of culturing a peripheral catheter tip is uncertain unless semiquantitative techniques are used (i.e., rolling the catheter across an agar plate). During the evaluation of a hospital-acquired fever, an inflamed vein should be examined carefully, and after the catheter is removed, the inflamed portion of the vein should be compressed in an attempt to express pus through the catheter entry site. If pus can be expressed or the patient remains febrile or bacteremic while on appropriate antibiotics, the vein should be surgically explored and excised if septic phlebitis is found.

Central venous catheters remain in place longer than peripheral catheters and are therefore associated with a greater overall infection rate. This is particularly true if total parenteral nutrition is provided by this route. Patients receiving parenteral nutrition are at particular risk for systemic infection with *Candida* species and gram-negative bacilli as well as with staphylococci. Pus at the catheter insertion site or positive blood cultures without another source are indications for catheter removal. In an attempt to decrease percutaneous spread of bacteria to intravascular sites, most centers are now placing long Silastic catheters into the subclavian vein after subcutaneous tunneling.

TABLE 106-3. FACTORS ASSOCIATED WITH GREATER RISKS OF INTRAVENOUS CATHETER-RELATED INFECTION

Duration of catheterization > 72 hr
Plastic catheter > steel needle
Lower extremities and groin > upper extremity
Cutdown > percutaneous insertion
Emergency > elective insertion
Breakdown in skin integrity, e.g., burns
Inserted by physician > intravenous therapy teams

These catheters may be kept in place for prolonged periods, with a lower infection risk. As a general rule, persistent bacteremia while the patient is taking appropriate antibiotics, recurrent bacteremia, and fungemia with *Candida* or related yeasts are indications for catheter removal.

PRESSURE SORES

See Chapter 101.

NOSOCOMIAL URINARY TRACT INFECTION

Placement of an indwelling catheter into the urethra of a hospitalized patient facilitates access of pathogens to an ordinarily sterile site. Factors that predispose to infection are shown in Table 106-4. The most common pathogens are enteric gram-negative rods; however, among immunocompromised patients and patients receiving broad-spectrum antibiotics, *Candida* species are also important causes of infection. Prophylactic antibiotics, irrigation, urinary acidification, and use of antiseptics are of no value in prevention of infection in this setting. Nosocomial urinary tract infections can be best prevented by adherence to the following guidelines:

1. Catheterize only when necessary. (Monitoring of intake and output and urinary incontinence are generally not appropriate indications for catheterization.)

2. Remember that repeated straight ("in-and-out") catheterizations are less likely to produce infection than indwelling catheters. Many patients with dysfunctional bladders (e.g., those with multiple sclerosis) have used this technique for years without developing significant urinary tract infections. Thrice-daily straight catheterization, using sterile technique, is vastly preferable to a chronic indwelling catheter.

TABLE 106-4. FACTORS PREDISPOSING TO NOSOCOMIAL URINARY TRACT INFECTION

Indwelling catheters
Duration of catheterization
Open drainage (versus closed-bag drainage)
Interruption of closed drainage system
Use of broad-spectrum antibiotics (*Candida*)

3. If an indwelling catheter is unavoidable, observe the following guidelines:
   a. Remove the catheter as soon as possible.
   b. Emphasize handwashing.
   c. Maintain a closed and unobstructed drainage system. (Urine specimens for culture and analysis may be obtained by inserting a 22-gauge needle aseptically through the distal end of the catheter wall.) Do not disconnect the catheter from the drainage bag.
   d. Secure the catheter in place.
   e. Keep the catheter bag below the level of the bladder.
   f. Irrigate the catheter only if it is obstructed.

Asymptomatic bacterial colonization of the catheterized bladder need not be treated. If the patient has fever or local symptoms, antibiotic treatment is indicated. *Candida* infection of the bladder often resolves once broad-spectrum antibiotics are discontinued. If *Candida* infection persists, the catheter may be changed; if infection still persists, twice-daily irrigation of the bladder with amphotericin B can eradicate the organism.

The best way to prevent catheter-related infections of the urinary tract is to avoid catheterization unless absolutely necessary.

REFERENCES

Kunin CM: Detection, Prevention and Management of Urinary Tract Infections. 4th ed. Philadelphia, Lea & Febiger, 1986.

Salata RA, Lederman MM, Shlaes DM, et al: Diagnosis of nosocomial pneumonia in intubated, intensive-care unit patients. Am Rev Resp Dis 135:426–432, 1987.

Schaffner W: Prevention and treatment of hospital-acquired infections. In Wyngaarden JB, Smith LH Jr, Bennett JC (eds): Cecil Textbook of Medicine. 19th ed. Philadelphia, WB Saunders Co, 1992, pp 1589–1594.

107 SEXUALLY TRANSMITTED DISEASES

Changes in sexual attitudes and practices have contributed to a resurgence of all venereal infections. Gonorrhea, for example, has tripled in incidence in the United States since 1963; approximately 3 million cases now occur each year. The number of new cases of syphilis has increased each year since 1986. The incidence of syphilis began to decrease in homosexual males in the same period, in association with safer sex practices. The increase in cases is predominantly due to heterosexual spread and may relate, in part, to the widespread use of crack cocaine.

At the outset, two common errors in approaching the patient with sexually transmitted disease (STD) should be avoided. The first is to fail to consider that an individual is at risk for STD. All sexually active persons are at risk, not just because of their own sexual behavior, but that of their sexual partners as well. Failure to consider risk factors often results in mistakes in diagnosis, inappropriate treatment, poor follow-up of infected sexual contacts, and, ultimately, recurrent or persistent infection. For example, a common error on the part of the physician is the treatment of females for "urethral syndrome" caused by the gonococcus as a presumed urinary tract infection. A second problem with STDs is the failure to recognize and diagnose coinfection. For example, *Chlamydia trachomatis* coinfection is present in 30 to 50 per cent of females with gonococcal cervicitis, and 20 per cent of females with gonococcal cervicitis are coinfected with *Trichomonas vaginalis*. The most serious coinfection is with the human immunodeficiency virus (HIV).

STDs can be considered in broad groups according to whether major initial manifestations are (1) genital sores; (2) urethritis, cervicitis, and pelvic inflammatory disease; or (3) vaginitis. All patients with any STD should be strongly encouraged to undergo screening for HIV infection. HIV infection is discussed in Chapter 108.

GENITAL SORES

Six infectious agents cause most genital lesions (Table 107–1). The appearance of the lesions, natural history, and laboratory findings allow a clear-cut distinction among the possible causes in most instances. The two most common and significant infections in North America are herpes simplex virus infection and syphilis.

TABLE 107–1. DIFFERENTIATION OF DISEASES CAUSING GENITAL SORES

DISEASE	PRIMARY LESION	ADENOPATHY	SYSTEMIC FEATURES	DIAGNOSIS/Rx
Herpes genitalis, primary 5%–10% sexually active adults, due to HSV-2	Incubation 2–7 days; multiple painful vesicles on erythematous base; persist 7–14 days	Tender, soft adenopathy	Fever	Tzanck's smear positive; tissue culture isolation, HSV-2 antigen, fourfold rise in antibodies to HSV-2; Rx: acyclovir
Recurrent	Grouped vesicles on erythematous base, painful; last 3–10 days	None	None	Tzanck's, HSV-2 antigen, tissue culture positive; titers not helpful; Rx: acyclovir
Syphilis, 90,000 cases in U.S. per year, caused by *Treponema pallidum*	Incubation 10–90 days (m. 21); chancre: papule that ulcerates; painless, border raised, firm, ulcer indurated, base smooth; usually single; may be genital or almost anywhere; persists 3–6 wk, leaving thin, atrophic scar	1 wk after chancre appears; bilateral or unilateral; firm, discrete, moveable, no overlying skin changes, painless nonsuppurative; may persist for months	Later stages	Cannot be cultured; positive darkfield; VDRL positive, 77%; FTA–ABS positive, 86% (see Table 107–2)
Chancroid, 2000 cases in U.S. per year caused by *Haemophilus ducreyi*	Incubation 3–5 days; vesicle or papule to pustule to ulcer; soft, not indurated; very painful	1 wk after primary in 50%; painful, unilateral (two thirds) suppurative	None	Organism in Gram stains of pus; can be cultured (75%) but direct yields highest from lymph node; Rx: erythromycin, 2 gm/day, or trimethoprim-sulfamethoxazole, 160/800 mg bid × 10–14 days
Lymphogranuloma venereum, 600–1000 cases per year in U.S. due to *Chlamydia trachomatis*	Incubation 5–21 days; painless papule, vesicle, ulcer, evanescent (2–3 days), noted in only 10%–40%	5–21 days post primary, one third bilateral, tender, matted iliac/femoral "groove sign"; multiple abscesses; coalescent, caseating, suppurative, sinus tracts; thick yellow pus; fistulas; strictures; genital ulcerations	Fever, arthritis, pericarditis, proctitis, meningoencephalitis, keratoconjunctivitis, preauricular adenopathy, edema of eyelids, erythema nodosum	LGV CF positive 85%–90% (1–3 wk); must have high titer (>1:16), as cross-reacts with other *Chlamydia*; also positive STS, rheumatoid factor, cryoglobulins; Rx: tetracycline, 2 gm/day × 2–4 wk
Granuloma inguinale, 50 cases in U.S. per year caused by *Calymmatobacterium granulomatis*	Incubation 9–50 days; at least one painless papule that gradually ulcerates; ulcers are large (1–4 cm), irregular, nontender, with thickened, rolled margins and beefy red tissue at base; older portions of ulcer show depigmented scarring, while advancing edge contains new papules	No true adenopathy; in one fifth, subcutaneous spread via lymphatics leads to indurated swelling or abscesses of groin—"pseudobuboes"	Metastatic infection of bones, joints, liver	Scraping or deep curetting at actively extending border—Wright's or Giemsa's stain reveals short, plump, bipolar staining "Donovan's bodies" in macrophage vacuoles; Rx: tetracycline, 2 gm/day × 10 days or trimethoprim-sulfamethoxazole
Condyloma acuminatum (genital warts), frequent, due to human papillomavirus (HPV)	Characteristic large, soft, fleshy, cauliflower-like excrescences around vulva, glans, urethral orifice, anus, perineum	None	None per se; association with cervical dysplasia/neoplasia	Chief importance is distinction from syphilis and chancroid; Rx: topical podophyllin ± cryosurgery, laser resection

HSV = Herpes simplex virus; VDRL = Venereal Disease Research Laboratory; FTA–ABS = fluorescent treponemal antibody absorption; CF = complement fixation; STS = serologic test for syphilis.

Herpes Simplex Virus (HSV) Infection

Genital herpes infection has reached epidemic proportions, causing a corresponding increase in public awareness and concern. Genital herpes differs from the other sexually transmitted disease in its tendency for spontaneous recurrence. Its importance stems from the morbidity, both physical and psychic, of the recurrent genital lesions, and the danger of transmission of a fulminant, often fatal, disease to newborn infants.

Epidemiology

HSV has a worldwide distribution. Humans are the only known reservoir of infection, which is spread by direct contact with infected secretions. Of the two types of HSV, HSV-2 is the more frequent cause of genital infection. The major risk of infection is in the 14- to 29-year-old cohort and varies with sexual activity. The prevalence of HSV-2 serum antibody is 3 per cent in nuns and 70 per cent in prostitutes.

After exposure, HSV replicates within epithelial cells and lyses them, producing a thin-walled vesicle. Multinucleated cells are formed with characteristic intranuclear inclusions. Regional lymph nodes become enlarged and tender. HSV also migrates along sensory neurons to sensory ganglia, where it assumes a latent state. Inside the sacral ganglia, HSV DNA can be demonstrated, but the virus does not replicate and is inactive metabolically. Just how viral reactivation occurs is uncertain. During reactivation, the virus appears to migrate back to skin along sensory nerves.

Clinical Presentation

Primary genital lesions develop 2 to 7 days after contact with infected secretions. In males, painful vesicles appear on the glans or penile shaft; in females, they occur on the vulva, perineum, buttocks, cervix, or vagina. A vaginal discharge frequently is present, usually accompanied by inguinal adenopathy, fever, and malaise. Sacroradiculomyelitis or aseptic meningitis can complicate the primary infection. Perianal and anal HSV infections are common, particularly in male homosexuals; tenesmus and rectal discharge often are the main complaints.

The precipitating events associated with genital relapse of HSV infection are poorly understood. In individual cases, stress or menstruation may be implicated. Overall, genital recurrences develop in about 60 per cent of HSV-infected patients. Clinically apparent recurrences are more frequent in males with HSV-2 infection. The frequency of asymptomatic cervical recurrence in women is not known. Many patients describe a characteristic prodrome of tingling or burning for 18 to 36 hours before the appearance of lesions. Recurrent HSV genital lesions are fewer in number, are usually stereotyped in location, are often restricted to the genital region, heal more quickly, and are associated with few systemic complaints.

Laboratory Diagnosis

The appearance of the characteristic vesicles is strongly suggestive of HSV infection. However, diagnosis should be confirmed by a Tzanck smear (see Chapter 93), Pap smear, immunofluorescent assay for viral antigen, or viral isolation. Serologies for HSV may be useful in the diagnosis of primary infection.

Treatment

Acyclovir, topical or oral, shortens the course of primary genital HSV infection. Intravenous or oral administration is recommended for severe cases with fever, systemic symptoms, and extensive local disease. Antiviral agents do not, however, prevent the latent stage of virus and cannot prevent recurrent infections. Prophylactic oral acyclovir decreases the frequency of symptomatic recurrences by 60 to 80 per cent when used over a 4- to 6-year period, but asymptomatic viral shedding may occur despite prophylaxis. Oral acyclovir also hastens recovery from severe recurrent episodes. Cervical shedding of HSV from active lesions late in pregnancy, near the time of parturition, is an indication for cesarean section. The risk to the neonates exposed to asymptomatic shedding of HSV during parturition is uncertain.

Syphilis

Syphilis is of unique importance among the venereal diseases because early lesions heal without specific therapy; however, serious systemic sequelae pose a major risk to the patient, and transplacental infections to the offspring occur.

Epidemiology

Primary syphilis occurs mostly in sexually active 15- to 30-year olds, and the incidence of primary syphilis has increased sharply in North America during the past decade. Approximately 50 per cent of the sexual contacts of a patient with primary syphilis become infected. The long incubation period of syphilis becomes a key factor in designing strategies for contact tracing and management. Unless successful follow-up seems certain, contacts of proven cases must be treated with penicillin. Unfortunately, the most rapid increase in syphilis has occurred in groups of individuals at increased risk of HIV infection. This poses a serious problem, since the mucosal lesions of primary syphilis facilitate transmission of HIV infection (see Chapter 108).

Pathogenesis

Treponema pallidum penetrates intact mucous membranes or abraded skin, reaches the blood stream via the lymphatics, and disseminates. The incubation period for the primary lesion depends on inoculum size, with a range of 3 to 90 days.

Natural History and Clinical Presentation

Primary syphilis is considered in Table 107–1.
Secondary syphilis develops 6 to 8 weeks after the chancre, if it has not been treated. Skin,

mucous membranes, and lymph nodes are involved. Skin lesions may be macular, papular, papulosquamous, pustular, follicular, or nodular. Most commonly, they are generalized, symmetric, and of like size, and they appear as discrete, erythematous, macular lesions of the thorax or as red-brown hyperpigmented macules on the palms and soles. In moist intertriginous areas, large, pale, flat-topped papules coalesce to form highly infectious plaques or condylomata lata; darkfield microscopy reveals that they are teeming with spirochetes. Mucous patches are painless, dull erythematous patches or grayish-white erosions. They, too, are infectious and darkfield-positive. Systemic manifestations of secondary syphilis include malaise, anorexia, weight loss, fever, sore throat, arthralgias, and generalized, nontender, discrete adenopathy. Specific organ involvement also may develop: gastritis (superficial, erosive), hepatitis, nephritis or nephrosis (immune complex–mediated, remits spontaneously or with treatment of syphilis), and symptomatic or asymptomatic meningitis. One fourth of patients have relapses of the mucocutaneous syndrome within 2 years of onset. Thereafter, infected patients become asymptomatic and noninfectious except via blood transfusions or transplacental spread.

Late syphilis develops after 1 to 10 years in 15 per cent of untreated patients. The skin gumma is a superficial nodule or deep granulomatous lesion that may develop punched-out ulcers. Superficial gummas respond dramatically to therapy. Gummas also may involve bone, liver, and the cardiovascular or central nervous system. Deep-seated gummas may have serious pathophysiologic consequences; treatment of the infection often does not reverse organ dysfunction.

Gradually progressive cardiovascular syphilis begins within 10 years in more than 10 per cent of untreated patients, most frequently men. Patients develop aortitis with medial necrosis secondary to an obliterative endarteritis of the vasa vasorum. There may be asymptomatic linear calcifications of the ascending aorta or (in decreasing frequency) aortic regurgitation, aortic aneurysms (saccular or fusiform, most commonly thoracic), or obstruction of coronary ostia.

Central nervous system (CNS) syphilis develops in 8 per cent of untreated patients 5 to 35 years following primary infection and includes meningovascular syphilis, tabes dorsalis, and general paresis (see Chapter 120). Although general paresis and tabes are classified as separate neurologic syndromes, many patients show elements of both. Late CNS syphilis also may be asymptomatic despite cerebrospinal fluid (CSF) abnormalities indicating active inflammation. The natural history of syphilis may be dramatically altered by coinfection with HIV. Patients with dual infections may more rapidly develop signs and symptoms of secondary syphilis, sometimes even before healing of the primary chancre (see Chapter 108).

Diagnosis and Treatment

The clinical diagnosis of syphilis must be con-

TABLE 107–2. SEROLOGIES IN SYPHILIS

	VDRL	FTA–ABS
Technique	Standard nontreponemal test; antibody to cardiolipin-lecithin	Standard treponemal test; antibody to Nichol's strain of *Treponema pallidum* after absorption on nontreponemal spirochetes
Indications	Screening and assessing response to therapy; should be quantified by diluting serum	Confirmation of specificity of positive VDRL; remains reactive longer than VDRL; useful for late syphilis, particularly neurosyphilis
Per Cent Positive in Syphilis		
Primary	77%	86%
Secondary	98%	100%
Early latent	95%	99%
Late latent and late	73%	96%
False-Positives	Weakly reactive VDRL is common (ca. 30% of normals); positive VDRL should be repeated and, if confirmed, FTA–ABS performed; relative frequency of false-positives determined by prevalence of syphilis in the population	Borderline positive is frequent (80%) in pregnancy; should be repeated

firmed by darkfield examination and/or serologies. Spirochetes are seen in darkfield preparations of chancres or moist lesions of secondary syphilis. Saprophytic treponemes confuse darkfield diagnosis of oral lesions. Serologic diagnosis is considered in Table 107–2. The differential diagnosis of primary syphilis consists of herpes simplex and three conditions that are relatively rare in the United States: chancroid, lymphogranuloma venereum, and granuloma inguinale. The characteristics of these diseases are presented in Table 107–1.

The presence of neurosyphilis requires modifying the standard antibiotic treatment of syphilis. For this reason, a lumbar puncture should be performed in all patients with latent syphilis (positive VDRL [Venereal Disease Research Laboratory] at least 1 year after primary syphilis) or syphilis of unknown duration. An elevated CSF white blood cell count, elevated protein, and positive VDRL test on diluted samples of CSF establish the diagnosis of neurosyphilis. A patient with persistent positive blood VDRL and a positive CSF VDRL should be considered to have neurosyphilis and treated accordingly. Because the VDRL may be negative in late syphilis, the presence of a positive serum fluorescent treponemal antibody absorption (FTA-ABS) test in a patient with a neurologic syn-

TABLE 107-3. TREATMENT FOR SYPHILIS IN THE NORMAL HOST

CLINICAL CATEGORY	REGIMEN OF CHOICE	HISTORY OF PENICILLIN ALLERGY
Primary Secondary Early latent Healthy contact*	Benzathine penicillin, 2.4 MU IM	Tetracycline or erythromycin, 2 gm/day × 15 days
Late latent or late	Benzathine penicillin, 2.4 MU IM q week × 3	No regimen adequately evaluated; ? tetracycline or erythromycin, 2 gm/day × 30 days
Neurosyphilis	Aqueous penicillin G, 20 MU IV qd × 10 days	Same as for late latent or late

*Contact of patient with active skin or mucous membrane lesions.
MU = Million units; IM = intramuscular.

drome consistent with syphilis is a sufficient indication for treatment. A small proportion (2 to 3 per cent) of patients with neurosyphilis may undergo abrupt deterioration following treatment with penicillin; this Jarisch-Herxheimer reaction, thought to represent a systemic response to penicillin-induced lysis of spirochetes, may be ameliorated by concomitant treatment with corticosteroids. After treatment of neurosyphilis, lumbar puncture should be repeated at 6-month intervals for 3 years to ensure adequacy of treatment, as reflected by normalization of CSF and progressive decline in CSF VDRL titer. Retreatment may be necessary if CSF abnormalities persist or recur. Treatment protocols are shown in Table 107-3.

Syphilis serologies must be followed after treatment. With the recommended treatment schedules, 1 to 5 per cent of patients with primary syphilis will develop recurrence (? relapse, ? reinfection). In adequately treated primary syphilis, the VDRL should become negative by 2 years after therapy (usually by 6 to 12 months). The FTA-ABS, however, often remains positive for life. Seventy-five per cent of adequately treated patients with secondary syphilis will have a negative serum VDRL by 2 years. If the VDRL does not become negative or achieve a low fixed titer, lumbar puncture should be performed to evaluate the possibility of asymptomatic neurosyphilis, and the patient should be retreated with penicillin. Two to 10 per cent of patients with CNS syphilis will relapse following treatment. However, it is rare for asymptomatic patients to develop symptomatic disease after penicillin therapy; the only major exception is the HIV-infected patient, in whom meningovascular syphilis can develop within months of the standard treatment for primary syphilis. Every patient who is treated for syphilis should be seronegative or "serofast" with a low fixed titer before termination of follow-up. If not, therapy should be repeated.

Because of the documented progression to neurosyphilis in some HIV-infected individuals who have received treatment for primary syphilis, the following approach is suggested. All patients with syphilis should be tested for HIV infection. All HIV-infected individuals should be tested for syphilis. If dual infection is likely or documented, a lumbar puncture is indicated regardless of the stage or activity of the syphilis. Any CSF abnormality warrants a 10- to 14-day course of intravenous penicillin to treat neurosyphilis. If the CSF is unremarkable, 3 weekly doses of benzathine penicillin plus a 10-day course of amoxicillin may be appropriate. In any event, careful clinical and laboratory follow-up is essential.

URETHRITIS, CERVICITIS, AND PELVIC INFLAMMATORY DISEASE (PID)

These syndromes can be considered broadly as gonococcal and nongonococcal in etiology.

Gonorrhea

Neisseria gonorrhoeae is second only to *Chlamydia trachomatis* as a cause of sexually transmitted diseases in the United States, and the incidence of gonorrhea has risen sharply in the past decade. An estimated 2 million cases now occur annually in the United States.

Epidemiology

The incidence of gonorrhea reached a plateau in the United States between 1975 and 1980, possibly reflective of a decrease in the size of the at-risk cohort. Reinfection is common, and it is not unusual for one sexually active patient to have 20 or more discrete infections. Particular risk factors are urban habitat, low socioeconomic status, unmarried status, and large numbers of unprotected sexual contacts. Fifty per cent of females having intercourse with a male with gonococcal urethritis will develop symptomatic infection. The risk for males is 20 per cent after a single sexual contact with an infected female. Orogenital contact and anal intercourse also transmit infection. Asymptomatic infection of males is an important factor in transmission. Forty per cent of male contacts of symptomatic women have asymptomatic urethritis. If untreated, about one quarter develop symptomatic infection within 7 days; a like number spontaneously become culture-negative within this period. The rest remain culture-positive and asymptomatic but capable of transmitting infection for periods of up to 6 months.

Pathogenesis

Neisseria gonorrhoeae is a gram-negative, kidney bean–shaped diplococcus. Specialized projections from the organism, pili, aid in attachment to mucosal surfaces, contribute to resistance to killing by neutrophils, and constitute an important virulence factor. Production of an IgA protease by the organism contributes to pathogenicity. In females, several factors alter susceptibility to infection. Group B blood type increases susceptibility, while diverse factors such as vaginal colonization with normal flora, IgA content of vaginal secretions, and high progesterone levels may be protective. Spread from the cervix to the upper genital tract is associated with menstruation because changes in the pH and biochemical constituents of cervical mucus lead to increased shedding of gonococci; cervical dilatation, reflux of menses, and binding of the gonococcus to spermatozoa may be additional factors in ascending genital infection and dissemination. Intrauterine contraceptive devices increase the risk of endometrial spread of infection twofold to ninefold (oral contraceptives are associated with a twofold decrease).

Clinical Presentation

In males who develop symptomatic urethritis, disturbing symptoms of spontaneous purulent discharge and severe dysuria usually develop 2 to 7 days after sexual contact. Prompt treatment usually follows, so that more extensive genital involvement is uncommon.

In females, cervicitis is the most frequent manifestation and results in a copious yellow vaginal discharge. Overall, 20 per cent of females with gonococcal cervicitis develop PID, usually beginning at a time close to the onset of menstruation. PID is manifest as endometritis (abnormal menses, midline abdominal pain), salpingitis (bilateral lower abdominal pain and tenderness), or pelvic peritonitis. Salpingitis can cause tubal occlusion and sterility. Gonococcal perihepatitis (Fitz-Hugh–Curtis syndrome) also may complicate pelvic inflammatory disease and present as right upper quadrant pain.

Females also may develop urethritis with dysuria and frequency. In certain populations of sexually active women, one fourth of women complaining of urinary tract symptoms and 60 per cent of those with symptoms but no bacteriuria have urethral cultures positive for N. gonorrhoeae.

Anorectal gonorrhea occurs in homosexual males and heterosexual females who practice receptive anal intercourse. In males, the resultant rectal pain, tenesmus, mucopurulent discharge, and bleeding may represent the only site of infection. Anorectal infection may be recognized only by cultures of asymptomatic contacts of patients with gonorrhea. In females, asymptomatic anorectal involvement is a frequent complication of symptomatic genitourinary disease even in the absence of anal intercourse (44 per cent); isolated anorectal infection (4 per cent) as well as acute or chronic proctitis (2 to 5 per cent) is rare. Treatment failures are frequent in anorectal gonorrhea (7 to 35 per cent).

Because of the frequency of asymptomatic infection in each of the potential sites, patients with symptoms suggestive of gonococcal infection should have cultures from the urethra, anus, pharynx, and (when applicable) cervix.

Pharyngeal gonorrhea occurs in homosexual males or heterosexual females following fellatio and less frequently in heterosexual males. Symptoms of pharyngitis occurring in this setting may be due to associated trauma or to gonococcal pharyngitis. Pharyngeal gonorrhea rarely is the sole site of gonococcal infection (5 to 8 per cent). Infection of the pharynx is important, however, as a source of dissemination, particularly in males.

Extragenital dissemination occurs in approximately 1 per cent of males and 3 per cent of females with gonorrhea. Strains of N. gonorrhoeae causing dissemination differ from other gonococci in several respects. They are more penicillin-sensitive and resist the normal bactericidal activity of antibody and complement. The latter finding may be due to their binding of a naturally occurring blocking antibody. Dissemination of gonococcal infection may take the form of the "arthritis-dermatitis syndrome," with 3 to 20 papular, petechial, pustular, necrotic, or hemorrhagic skin lesions, usually found on the extensor surfaces of the distal extremities. An associated finding is an asymmetric polytenosynovitis, with or without arthritis, which predominantly involves wrists, fingers, knees, and ankles. Joint fluid cultures usually are negative in the arthritis-dermatitis syndrome, leading to speculation that circulating immune complexes, demonstrable in most patients, are important in its pathogenesis. Synovial biopsies may yield positive cultures. Biopsy of skin lesions reveals gonococcal antigens (by immunofluorescent antibody staining) in two thirds of cases. Blood cultures are positive in 50 per cent. Septic arthritis is another manifestation of dissemination; N. gonorrhoeae is the most frequent cause of septic arthritis in 16- to 50-year-olds. Sometimes the history indicates an antecedent syndrome suggestive of bacteremia. The joint fluid cultures usually are positive (particularly when the leukocyte count in joint fluid exceeds $80,000/\mu l$), and blood cultures are usually negative. Gonococcemia rarely may lead to endocarditis, meningitis, myopericarditis, or toxic hepatitis.

Laboratory Diagnosis and Management

Gram stain of the urethral discharge will determine the cause of urethritis in most males with gonorrhea, typical intracellular diplococci being diagnostic (Fig. 107–1). The finding of only extracellular gram-negative diplococci is equivocal. The absence of gonococci on a smear of urethral discharge from a male virtually excludes the diagnosis. Diagnosis by Gram staining of cervical exudates is relatively specific but insensitive (<60 per cent). Modified Thayer-Martin medium contains antibiotics that inhibit the growth of other organisms and increase the yield of gonococci from samples likely to be contaminated; it is not necessary for culture of normally sterile fluids, such as joint fluid, blood, and CSF. Specimens from these sites should be cultured on chocolate agar. The addition of 3 per cent trimethoprim to Thayer-

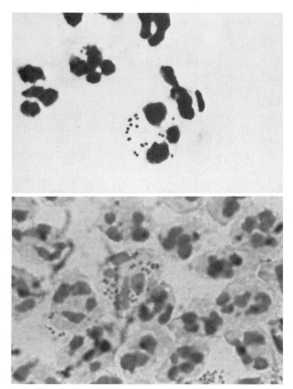

FIGURE 107–1. Gram stain of urethral discharge showing typical intracellular diplococci associated with neutrophils.

Martin medium inhibits fecal *Proteus* and is useful for anorectal cultures. Other important considerations for the isolation of gonococci include the use of synthetic swabs (unsaturated fatty acids in cotton may be inhibitory), the introduction of a very thin calcium alginate swab or a loop 2 cm into the male urethra, and the avoidance of vaginal douching (12 hr), urination (2 hr), and vaginal speculum lubricants before culture. In all suspected cases of gonorrhea, the urethra, anus, and pharynx should be cultured. In females, 20 per cent of cases in which initial cervical cultures were negative yield *N. gonorrhoeae* when cultures are repeated.

Gonococcal resistance to penicillin is increasing worldwide. The current recommendation for the treatment of uncomplicated gonorrhea is ceftriaxone, 250 mg given intramuscularly once. This should be followed by a course of tetracycline (2 gm/day orally for 7 days) to treat concurrent chlamydial infection. Spectinomycin, 2.0 gm given intramuscularly as a single injection, is an effective alternative except in pharyngeal infections. Spectinomycin does not, however, treat concomitant chlamydial infections. PID should be treated with cefoxitin, 2 gm given intramuscularly, followed by doxycycline, 100 mg twice daily administered orally for 10 days. Seriously ill females with PID should be hospitalized. If they appear toxic, the initial antibiotic regimens should be broad-spectrum. Evaluation by ultrasonography for the presence of a pelvic abscess or peritonitis usually is warranted in this setting. Surgery may be indicated to drain a tubo-ovarian or pelvic abscess.

Disseminated gonococcal infection should be treated with ceftriaxone, 1 gm every 24 hours for 10 days. Cephalosporins should not be used, however, if the history suggests an IgE-mediated allergy to penicillin (anaphylactoid reaction, angioedema, urticaria). In such a case, ciprofloxacin, 500 mg twice daily for 7 days, is an effective alternative.

A VDRL should be obtained in all patients with gonorrhea. If negative, no further follow-up is necessary, since ceftriaxone in the dosage used is effective in treating incubating syphilis. This is not true of therapy with all alternative drugs; if they are used, the VDRL should be repeated after 4 weeks. Anal cultures should be part of the routine follow-up of females, since persistent anorectal carriage may be the source of relapse. Postgonococcal urethritis occurs in 30 to 50 per cent of males 2 to 3 weeks after penicillin therapy, if it is not followed by tetracycline. It usually is caused by *C. trachomatis* or *U. urealyticum*.

Nongonococcal Urethritis, Cervicitis, and PID

The diagnosis of nongonococcal urethritis (NGU) requires the exclusion of gonorrhea, since considerable overlap exists in the clinical syndromes.

Epidemiology

At least as many cases of urethritis are nongonococcal as gonococcal. Typically, NGU predominates in higher socioeconomic groups. *Chlamydia trachomatis* causes 30 to 50 per cent of NGU and can be isolated from 0 to 11 per cent of asymptomatic, sexually active males. *C. trachomatis* also can be isolated from 20 per cent of males with gonorrhea and presumably represents a concurrent infection. Some cases of *Chlamydia*-negative NGU are due to *Ureaplasma urealyticum* or *Trichomonas vaginalis*.

Clinical Syndromes

NGU is less contagious than gonococcal infection. The incubation period is 7 to 14 days. Characteristically, patients complain of urethral discharge, itching, and dysuria. Importantly, the discharge is not spontaneous but becomes apparent after "milking" the urethra in the morning. The mucopurulent discharge consists of thin, cloudy fluid with purulent specks; these charac-

TABLE 107–4. ORGANISMS CAUSING PROCTOCOLITIS IN MALE HOMOSEXUALS

Neisseria gonorrhoeae	*Campylobacter* species
Chlamydia trachomatis	*Entamoeba histolytica*
Herpesvirus hominis	*Giardia lamblia*
Treponema pallidum	*Cryptosporidium parvum*
Shigella species	*Strongyloides stercoralis*
Salmonella species	

TABLE 107–5. VAGINITIS

DISEASE	EPIDEMIOLOGY/ PATHOGENESIS	CLINICAL FINDINGS	LABORATORY DIAGNOSIS	TREATMENT
Candidiasis	Yeast are part of normal flora; overgrowth favored by broad-spectrum antibiotics, high estrogen levels (pregnancy, before menses, oral contraceptives), diabetes mellitus, may be early clue to HIV infection	Itching, little or no urethral discharge, occasional dysuria; labia pale or erythematous with satellite lesions; vaginal discharge thick, adherent, with white curds; balanitis in 10% of male contacts	Vaginal pH = 4.5 (normal), negative whiff test, yeast seen on wet mount in 50%, culture positive	Miconazole, butoconazole, or clotrimazole cream or suppositories for 3–7 days
Trichomonas vaginalis infection	STD; incubation 5–28 days; symptoms begin or exacerbate with menses	Discharge, soreness, irritation, mild dysuria, dyspareunia; copious loose discharge, one fifth yellow/green, one third bubbly	Elevated pH; wet mount shows large numbers of WBCs, trichomonads; positive whiff test (10% KOH causes fishy odor)	Metronidazole, 2 gm as single dose; treat sexual contacts
Nonspecific	Synergistic infection, *Gardnerella vaginalis* and anaerobes (*Mobiluncus* sp.)	Vaginal odor, mild discharge, little inflammation; grayish, thin, homogeneous discharge with small bubbles	Elevated pH; positive whiff test. Wet prep contains clue cells (vaginal epithelial cells with intracellular coccobacilli), few WBCs	Metronidazole, 500 mg bid × 7 days; do not treat contacts unless recurrent vaginitis

STD = Sexually transmitted disease; WBCs = white blood cells.

teristics do not always allow clear distinction from gonococcal disease. *Trichomonas vaginalis* causes a typically scanty discharge.

C. trachomatis also is a common cause of epididymitis in males under 35 years of age and can produce proctitis in men and women who practice receptive anal intercourse.

Chlamydial infections are also more common than gonococcal infections in females but frequently escape detection. Two thirds of women with mucopurulent cervicitis have chlamydial infection. Similarly, many females with the acute onset of dysuria, frequency, and pyuria, but sterile bladder urine, have *C. trachomatis* infection. *C. trachomatis* is at least as common a cause of salpingitis as is the gonococcus.

Laboratory Diagnosis

Ordinarily, the distinction between gonococcal and nongonococcal infections relies mainly on Gram-stained preparations of exudate and cultures. In a male with urethritis and typical gram-negative diplococci associated with neutrophils, the diagnosis of gonococcal urethritis is clear-cut and the culture is unnecessary. Coincident NGU cannot be excluded, however. Whenever interpretation of the Gram stain is not straightforward in males, and in all females, culture on Thayer-Martin medium is appropriate. Techniques for isolation and detection of chlamydiae are widely available and should be used routinely in evaluating genital infections.

Treatment

The patient and all sexual contacts should be treated with a 7-day course of tetracycline, 500 mg 4 times a day; or doxycycline, 100 mg twice a day,

given orally. Recurrence may occur and requires longer periods (2 to 3 weeks) of treatment.

Proctocolitis in Homosexual Males

Male homosexuals who practice receptive anal intercourse may present with proctitis/proctocolitis causing anorectal pain, mucoid or bloody discharge, tenesmus, diarrhea, or abdominal pain. Sigmoidoscopy should be performed with culture and Gram stain of the discharge. Potential causative organisms are shown in Table 107–4. The diarrheal syndromes are considered in Chapter 103. Ten per cent of patients harbor two or more pathogens. Proctitis also may occur in male homosexuals without a definable pathogen (42 per cent). Diarrhea in the patient infected with HIV has an entirely different set of implications, as will be discussed in Chapter 108.

Vaginitis

Table 107–5 considers salient features in the diagnosis and management of patients with vaginitis.

REFERENCES

Holmes KK, Mardh P-A, Sparling PF, Weisner PJ (eds): Sexually Transmitted Diseases. 3rd ed. New York, McGraw-Hill Book Co, 1990.

Sparling PF: Sexually transmitted diseases. In Wyngaarden JB, Smith LH Jr, Bennett JC (eds): Cecil Textbook of Medicine. 19th ed. Philadelphia, WB Saunders Co, 1992, pp 1751–1770.

Stamm WE, Guinan ME, Johnson C, Starcher T, Holmes KK, McCormack WM: Effect of treatment regimens for *Neisseria gonorrhoeae* on simultaneous infection with *Chlamydia trachomatis*. N Engl J Med 310:545, 1984.

108 HIV INFECTION AND THE ACQUIRED IMMUNODEFICIENCY SYNDROME

The acquired immunodeficiency syndrome (AIDS) is the most severe expression of a spectrum of related disorders due to infection by the human immunodeficiency virus (HIV-1). Since the initial reports of otherwise unexplained *Pneumocystis carinii* pneumonia and Kaposi's sarcoma in sexually active homosexual males in New York and California, epidemiologic, virologic, and clinical investigations have clearly established that the AIDS pandemic is attributable to sexual and parenteral transmission of HIV-1. By 1993 more than 12 million persons had been infected worldwide, and the World Health Organization estimates that this number will increase to 40 to 80 million by the year 2000.

EPIDEMIOLOGY

AIDS was first recognized in 1981 as a distinct clinical syndrome in which previously healthy men experienced serious infections with unusual

TABLE 108–1. OPPORTUNISTIC INFECTIONS INDICATIVE OF A DEFECT IN CELLULAR IMMUNE FUNCTION ASSOCIATED WITH ACQUIRED IMMUNODEFICIENCY SYNDROME (AIDS)

Protozoan Infection
  Pneumocystis carinii pneumonia
  Disseminated toxoplasmosis, or *Toxoplasma* encephalitis, excluding congenital infection
  Chronic *Cryptosporidium* enteritis (>1 mo)
  Chronic *Isospora belli* enteritis (>1 mo)
Fungal Infection
  Candida esophagitis
  Cryptococcal meningitis or disseminated infection
  Disseminated histoplasmosis*
  Disseminated coccidioidomycosis*
Bacterial Infection
  Disseminated *Mycobacterium avium-intracellulare* or *Mycobacterium kansasii*
  Extrapulmonary *Mycobacterium tuberculosis*
  Recurrent *Salmonella* septicemia*
Noncongenital Viral Infection
  Chronic (>1 mo) mucocutaneous herpes simplex or bronchial or esophageal herpes simplex
  Histologically evident cytomegalovirus infection of any organ except liver, spleen, or lymph nodes
  Progressive multifocal leukoencephalopathy secondary to JC virus
Helminthic Infection
  Strongyloidiasis (disseminated beyond the gastrointestinal tract)

*Requires laboratory evidence of human immunodeficiency virus (HIV) infection.

opportunistic pathogens, most commonly *Pneumocystis carinii*, formerly seen only among patients with severe cellular immunodeficiency. Laboratory studies confirmed profound cell-mediated immunodeficiency in these previously healthy individuals, leading to the name of acquired immunodeficiency syndrome.

In the male homosexual population, receptive anal intercourse with multiple sexual partners was associated with highest risk for infection. As epidemiologists at the Centers for Disease Control (CDC) received increasing reports of similar opportunistic infections in injecting drug users, men with hemophilia, and their female sexual partners, it became clear that this syndrome was caused by an agent transmissible via sexual contact or through parenteral contact with blood or blood products. Since HIV-1 was identified in 1983–84 as the causative agent for AIDS, clinical recognition of a wide spectrum of HIV disease, ranging from asymptomatic infection to severe immunocompromise with life-threatening opportunistic infections and/or neoplasms, has emerged.

The CDC criteria for the diagnosis of AIDS, as modified in 1987, included a large number of opportunistic infections and/or neoplasms indicative of a deficit in cellular immunity (Tables 108–1 and 108–2). The occurrence of any one of these conditions in an individual with no other cause of immunosuppression constituted the diagnosis of AIDS. By the end of 1991, the CDC estimated that there were more than 1 million persons infected with HIV in the United States, with more than 200,000 having already developed serious illnesses meeting CDC criteria for AIDS. In January 1993, the CDC broadened the HIV case definition to include all persons with severely depressed levels of cell-mediated immunity as indicated by T helper lymphocyte counts of less than 200/mm³. By the mid-1990s, approximately one-half million HIV-infected persons in the United States will have met the CDC surveillance criteria for the diagnosis of AIDS (Fig. 108–1).

Once HIV was identified as the causative agent of AIDS, retrospective studies of stored serum specimens revealed that HIV had been present in parts of Central and East Africa for at least two decades prior to the recognition of the clinical syndrome of AIDS. During the 1980s, the epidemic spread widely, to become a major worldwide pandemic. Seroprevalence studies indicate that HIV infection continues to spread rapidly throughout all continents. Exceptionally rapid transmission occurred from 1986 through 1993 in several areas of South Asia, particularly in Western India and in Thailand. By the end of 1992, almost every nation of the world had reported cases of AIDS.

Although AIDS was initially recognized among sexually active homosexual males and intravenous drug users in the United States, heterosexual contact has been the dominant mode of HIV transmission throughout most of the world, accounting for more than 90 per cent of infections. The virus is present in both semen and cervicovaginal secretions and can be transmitted both from man to woman and from woman to man during vaginal intercourse. The concurrent presence of other sexually transmissible diseases (STDs), especially those associated with genital ulcerations, is strongly associated with greater risk of acquisition of HIV-1 infection.

Free- and cell-associated virus is present in the blood of infected patients. Thus, prior to the implementation of a blood screening test in late 1985, infection via transfusion of contaminated blood or blood products (e.g., clotting Factors VIII and IX for hemophiliacs) accounted for approximately 3 per cent of AIDS cases in the United

TABLE 108–2. OTHER CONDITIONS FULFILLING CRITERIA FOR AIDS

CONDITION	COMMENTS
Neoplasm	
Kaposi's sarcoma (in a person <60 yr old)	Most commonly present in homosexual males in U.S.; uncommon elsewhere and among other risk groups
High-grade, B cell non-Hodgkin's lymphoma* (e.g., Burkitt's lymphoma)	
Undifferentiated non-Hodgkin's lymphoma*	
Immunoblastic sarcoma*	
Primary brain lymphoma*	Limited to brain; hard to diagnose; may be multicentric
Systemic Illness	
HIV wasting syndrome*	Unintentional loss of >10% of body weight
Neurologic Impairment	
HIV encephalopathy*	Variety of symptoms, dementia most common (see text)

*Requires laboratory evidence of HIV infection.

States. Currently, all blood products in North America are screened for evidence of HIV infection prior to administration. Factor VIII and Factor IX concentrates are also now heat-treated to inactivate HIV. The risk of transfusion-acquired HIV infection in North America and Western Europe is now extremely small, but finite. Persons recently infected with HIV-1 may still donate blood in the weeks before they have developed detectable HIV antibodies, resulting in false-negative screening tests; these instances are extremely rare.

Because of the long latency between HIV infection and AIDS-associated clinical illnesses, the epidemic of AIDS lags behind the spread of the virus into new populations. Gay and bisexual men accounted for approximately three quarters of the cases of AIDS through 1985; by 1990 this group accounted for fewer than 60 per cent of AIDS cases in the United States. Through 1985, fewer than 1 per cent of the cases of AIDS in the United States were acquired through heterosexual contact; by the mid-1990s, this mode of acquisition will explain more than 10 per cent of the cases of AIDS and a considerably higher proportion of persons with HIV infection. Through 1985, fewer than 4 per cent of AIDS cases in the United States occurred in women. Women constitute the group in which the incidence of HIV infection is now increasing most rapidly in the United States; 12 per cent of new AIDS cases in 1991 occurred in women. In some cities, women accounted for over one third of new cases.

The sharing of needles for injectable drug use transmits the virus efficiently and continues to be a major mode of spread of HIV infection in North America and Western Europe. Because of the concentration of injecting drug users in impoverished

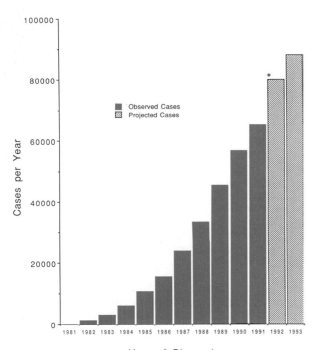

FIGURE 108–1. Observed and projected annual incidence of AIDS in the United States from 1981 through 1993. Current estimates indicate a continued annual increase in the incidence of AIDS through the mid-1990s. * Because of new criteria established by the Centers for Disease Control (CDC), the incidence of AIDS in the United States in 1993 may exceed these projections by 30 to 50 per cent. This will reflect a broader definition of AIDS rather than a change in the course of the epidemic.

inner city areas, in which minority populations are relatively high, a disproportionate number of women infected by HIV are black or Latino.

Introduction of HIV into the intravenous drug-using heterosexual population also has accounted for a rapid rise in the occurrence of neonatal HIV infection. HIV can be transmitted from infected mother to child, either during pregnancy or, more commonly, during childbirth. Approximately 20 per cent of infants born to HIV-infected mothers are themselves infected. Seroprevalence surveys at prenatal clinics in several large cities in the United States have indicated that up to 3 per cent of women are HIV-infected. Of particular concern, more than half of these women were not aware that they were at high risk of HIV infection.

HIV infection also has occurred after occupational parenteral exposures of health care workers to the blood of HIV-infected patients. With a needlestick injury introducing blood of a HIV-infected patient, the risk of infection is approximately 0.3 per cent. The acquisition of HIV by five patients of an HIV-infected dentist has raised the possibility that infected health care workers who perform invasive procedures may also have the potential to transmit HIV to patients. This risk, if present, is extremely small; not 1 of several thousand systematically evaluated patients of HIV-infected surgeons have acquired HIV infection in this manner.

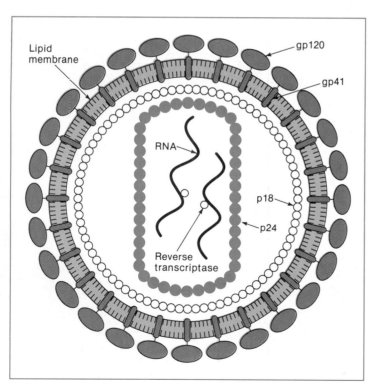

FIGURE 108–2. Structure of HIV. (Adapted from "The AIDS virus," copyright © 1987 by Scientific American, Inc., George V. Kelvin, all rights reserved.)

A second human immunodeficiency virus (HIV-2) was identified in West Africa in the mid-1980s. Although HIV-2 has been associated with AIDS-like syndromes, the majority of known HIV-2–seropositive persons are asymptomatic. Whether HIV-2 is a less virulent strain, or HIV-2–seropositive persons have been more recently exposed to an equally virulent virus, is not yet known. Although HIV-2 shares many biologic and genetic characteristics with HIV-1, each of the two viruses also has regulatory and structural genes that are unique. HIV-2 is more closely related to the simian immunodeficiency virus (SIV). The rare HIV-2 infections in the United States to date have been of West African origin. Throughout this chapter, the term HIV refers to the HIV-1 virus.

PATHOPHYSIOLOGY

HIV is a member of the lentivirus family of retroviruses, which includes the agents of visna, equine infectious anemia, and the closely related SIV. The core of HIV contains two single-stranded copies of the viral RNA genome, together with a virus-encoded enzyme, reverse transcriptase (Fig. 108–2). Surrounding the core (p24) and matrix (p18) proteins is a lipid bilayer derived from the host cell, through which protrude the transmembrane gp41 and surface gp120 envelope glycoproteins.

The HIV-1 envelope glycoprotein has a high affinity for the CD4 molecule found on the surface of T helper lymphocytes and cells of the monocyte-macrophage lineage. After binding to CD4, the viral and cellular membranes fuse, and the viral nucleoprotein complex enters the cytoplasm. The RNA viral genome undergoes transcription by a virally encoded reverse transcriptase. The double-stranded viral DNA gains entry into the nucleus, where integration of the double-stranded DNA provirus into the host chromosome is catalyzed by another retroviral enzyme, integrase (Fig. 108–3). Within the host genome, the provirus may remain in a latent state without appreciable transcription of RNA or synthesis of viral protein. As such, the infected cell is essentially undetectable by host defense mechanisms.

When a T lymphocyte containing integrated provirus is activated (e.g., by recognition of antigenic peptides), nuclear factors such as NF-kB act on sequences of the HIV promoter region to cause increased expression of viral messenger RNA (mRNA). Virus-encoded regulatory proteins *tat* and *rev* facilitate mRNA expression and cytoplasmic transport, respectively. Core proteins, viral enzymes, and envelope proteins are encoded by the *gag*, *pol*, and *env* genes of HIV, respectively. Viral proteins are cleaved by both virus-encoded and host cell–derived proteases, and the envelope protein is glycosylated by host glycosylases. Viral particles are assembled, each containing two copies of unspliced mRNA within the core as the viral genome, and virions then are released from the cell by budding. Productive viral replication is lytic to infected T cells, but the mechanisms of lysis are not well understood. Macrophages and dendritic cells also are infected by HIV, but these cells do not appear to be lysed by the virus. Infected macrophages may play a major role in the spread of HIV infection to other tissues, particularly the central nervous system (CNS).

Immunodeficiency in HIV Infection. During HIV infection, there is a gradual, but apparently inexorable, decline in the numbers of circulating lymphocytes, particularly but not exclusively the CD4+ T helper cell subset, associated with a profound functional abnormality of the remaining circulating lymphocyte populations. The relatively low frequency of HIV-infected T lymphocytes (between 1 in 100,000 and 1 in 10) in HIV-infected persons suggests that mechanisms in addition to virus-induced cell lysis may contribute to the pathogenesis of lymphocyte depletion in HIV infection and that a large proportion of HIV-infected cells reside in solid tissues, such as lymph nodes. Some of these potential mechanisms are presented in Table 108–3.

In association with the progressive decrease in circulating CD4+ T helper lymphocytes, there also is profound functional immune impairment. Anergy—the failure to demonstrate delayed hypersensitivity to recall antigens—may develop early in HIV infection and occurs in virtually all AIDS patients. T lymphocyte proliferation in response to antigenic stimuli is dramatically impaired, as is production of several lymphokines, such as interleukin-2, and interferon-gamma. T cell cytotoxic responses are diminished, and natural killer cell activity against virus-infected cells and tumor cells is impaired, despite the presence of normal numbers of these cells. B lymphocyte function also is crippled. Despite a polyclonal or oligoclonal hypergammaglobulinemia, B cell function is diminished, as measured by the ability to synthesize antibody in response to new antigenic stimulation. These functional immune impairments may be the result of a decrease in both the number and the function of CD4+ T cells. The specific mechanisms of the broad impairment of immune function in the HIV-infected individual have not yet been fully clarified.

Inadequacy of Host Defense Mechanisms. A remarkable aspect of HIV infection is the ability of the infection to persist and progress despite the development of host immune responses to the virus. Brisk humoral responses to viral proteins are readily demonstrable on Western blot analysis in almost all infected persons. Neutralizing antibodies are found frequently, but generally in rela-

TABLE 108–3. POTENTIAL CAUSES OF CD4 CELL DEPLETION

1. Direct lytic consequences of HIV infection
2. Syncytia formation
3. Innocent bystander destruction of cells with absorbed gp120
4. HIV infection of stem cells
5. Autoimmune destruction

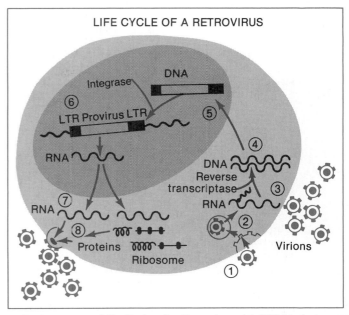

FIGURE 108–3. Life Cycle of a Retrovirus. (1) HIV binds to a specific CD4 receptor of a human lymphocyte. (2) Virus fuses to cell membrane and nucleoprotein complex gains entry to cytoplasm. (3) Viral RNA is transcribed to double-stranded viral DNA. (4) Viral DNA is transported to the nucleus and (5) catalyzed by the retroviral enzyme integrase, the DNA provirus is integrated into the cellular genome. (6) Viral DNA is transcribed to produce genomic RNA and viral messenger RNA (7), which is translated into new viral protein and assembled at the cell membrane to complete the viral life cycle by budding (8).

tively low titer when compared with the responses to other viral infections. Cell-mediated immune responses to several HIV-derived proteins occur among HIV-infected persons; the importance of these responses in regulating the progression of infection is unknown.

There are several possible explanations for the apparent inability of host responses to control HIV infection. The presence of a latent phase in the viral replication cycle allows virus to persist in the cellular genome in a latent state, in which it may escape host defenses (Fig. 108–3). An integrated latent virus that does not synthesize proteins is not recognizable either by humoral or by cellular immune responses. The CD4 binding domain of the HIV envelope, which is a natural target of neutralizing antibody and is relatively conserved, is apparently recessed and relatively inaccessible. Nearby regions that may also elicit neutralizing antibody are not conserved and vary among different isolates. In this regard, HIV has tremendous potential for genetic alteration. In fact, significant genetic diversity may be found among different viral isolates obtained from the same patient. Inconsistencies in retroviral reverse transcription probably result in the high degree of genetic variability. One can easily envision how a selective pressure—for example, the development of antibodies against a nonconserved region of the envelope—can result in the emergence of viral mutants with altered envelope sequences resistant to neutralizing activity of a specific antibody. The consequent genetic variability may prove to be one of the chief obstacles to the development of an effective vaccine.

DIAGNOSIS AND TESTING FOR HIV INFECTION

Since HIV transmission is preventable and effective therapy for HIV infection exists, it is important that persons at risk for HIV infection undergo serologic testing. Testing should not be confined only to individuals at highest risk (e.g., injecting drug users) but should be encouraged in persons with even lower risk. This includes persons with a history of any STD or of unprotected intercourse with an individual who might be HIV-infected. In addition, all recipients of blood, blood products, or organ transplants between 1978 and 1985 should be screened for infection. Testing must be provided in an environment of confidentiality consistent with relevant state laws. Pretest and post-test counseling is essential to ensure that persons appreciate the importance and consequences of the test results, and are offered appropriate help. Regardless of the outcome of the test, all patients should be counseled regarding safer sexual practices. Injecting drug users should be advised not to share needles and instructed to disinfect needles and syringes with a 1:10 dilution of household bleach. HIV-infected persons must be encouraged to notify their sexual partners and persons with whom they have shared needles. This is often difficult; regional health authorities may be of great assistance in confidential notification of persons at risk.

Diagnosis of HIV infection is established by detection of serum antibody to HIV by enzyme-linked immunosorbent assay (ELISA) and confirmed by Western blot. These techniques are very sensitive in detecting HIV antibody, but individuals who are recently infected may be antibody-negative. For recently exposed individuals whose initial ELISA test is negative, retesting at 6 weeks, 3 months, 6 months, and 12 months may be indicated. False-positive ELISA tests are rare; when they occur, they are more frequent among patients with autoimmune disorders and among multiparous women. Western blot reactivity with at least two different HIV gene products is a necessary confirmatory test. Other Western blot reaction patterns are classified as indeterminate. In a person at risk for HIV exposure, an indeterminate Western blot may represent an early seroconversion; in such cases, ELISA and Western blot testing should be repeated after 2 to 3 months.

Infants born to HIV-infected mothers have a 25 to 30 per cent risk of acquiring HIV infection, but all such babies have circulating maternal anti-HIV antibodies until they are at least 6 months of age. Early diagnosis of HIV infection in this and other settings may utilize viral cultures, gene amplification by polymerase chain reaction (PCR), detection of neonatal IgA antibody, or detection of specific viral proteins, such as p24. At present, these tests are both expensive and not widely available.

SEQUENTIAL CLINICAL MANIFESTATIONS OF HIV INFECTION

Acute Retroviral Syndrome. Acute symptomatic illness may follow initial infection with HIV-1. Thirty to 70 per cent of HIV-infected persons experience a mononucleosis-like syndrome from 2 to 12 weeks after exposure to HIV-1 (Fig. 108–4). Acute symptoms of fever, sore throat, lymphadenopathy, arthralgias, and headache usually predominate and last 3 days to 3 weeks. A maculopapular rash is common and usually affects the trunk or face. Neurologic involvement, documented by isolation of HIV from CSF, may occur during the acute retroviral syndrome. Acute, self-limited aseptic meningitis is the most common neurologic manifestation, although meningoencephalitis, peripheral neuropathy, myelopathy, and Guillain-Barré syndrome have all occurred during the acute retroviral illness.

During the acute infection, HIV antibody is usually not detectable, but HIV infection can be demonstrated by direct cultivation of HIV from blood, by HIV gene amplification by PCR, or by detection of specific viral components, such as the p24 antigen in serum. Following primary HIV infection, within 6 weeks to 6 months, specific antibodies develop that are directed against the three main gene products of HIV: *gag* (p55, p24, p15), *pol* (p34, p68), and *env* (gp160, gp120, gp41).

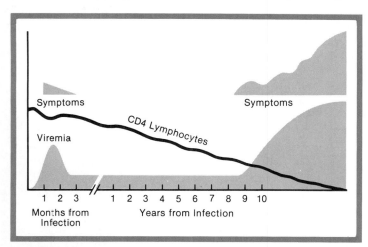

FIGURE 108–4. Natural history of HIV-1 infection in the adult. Note the long asymptomatic period, the erratic but inexorable decline in CD4 lymphocyte count, and the uncertain progression of symptoms once severe immunodepression has occurred. (Modified from Shaw GM: Biology of human immunodeficiency viruses. In Wyngaarden JB, Smith LH Jr, Bennett JC [eds]: Cecil Textbook of Medicine. 19th ed. Philadelphia, WB Saunders Company, 1992, p 1916.)

Asymptomatic Phase. HIV infection results in a slow, often erratic, but usually inexorable progression to severe immunodeficiency, marked by a progressive depletion of CD4 helper lymphocytes. Approximately 50 per cent of adults develop AIDS within 10 years after HIV infection (Fig. 108–4); an additional 30 per cent have symptoms related to immunodeficiency, and only 20 per cent are entirely asymptomatic 10 years after infection. Progression of disease varies greatly among individuals and is also related to age at time of infection. Adolescents with HIV progress to AIDS at a slower rate than adults, with fewer than 30 per cent developing AIDS within 10 years after HIV infection. Although there are no definitive data relating the mode of HIV transmission to the rapidity of development of AIDS, some persons infected by blood transfusions may develop severe immunodeficiency at a more rapid rate, perhaps because of the relatively large intravenous inoculum of HIV. In individual patients, evidence of active viral replication, (e.g., elevated p24 antigen in serum) is associated with more rapid fall in CD4 count and concomitant disease progression.

The majority of HIV-infected individuals, most of whom are unaware of their infection, are asymptomatic, with CD4 counts in the normal range (>500/mm³) or between 200 and 500/mm³. Major life-threatening opportunistic infections seldom occur until the CD4 count is less than 200/mm³. During the longest phase of the illness, when CD4 counts are greater than 200/mm³, "dysregulation" of the immune system is commonly manifested by increased polyclonal production of antibody (as measured by elevated levels of gamma globulins). Despite the abundance of antibody, a fourfold to sixfold increase in the incidence of bacterial pneumonias caused by the common encapsulated pulmonary pathogens *Streptococcus pneumoniae* and *Haemophilus influenzae* occurs during this time.

Generalized lymphadenopathy occurs in up to one third of asymptomatic HIV-infected persons, may persist for years, and is not associated with the rate of progression of immunodeficiency or with development of lymphoma. During the early years of HIV infection, autoimmune-like illness—in particular, immune thrombocytopenia and arthritis—are common. Mucocutaneous manifestations of immune dysfunction are frequent, especially recurrent oral or genital infections with herpes simplex virus (HSV) (which are responsive to therapy but may recur frequently), polydermatomal varicella-zoster infection, and oral hairy leukoplakia. These manifestations may occur relatively early in the course of HIV infection but generally become more frequent and severe as immune function deteriorates. In women, recurrent vaginal candidiasis is most often the first symptom. Infection by *Mycobacterium tuberculosis* (which may be pulmonary, extrapulmonary, or disseminated) most often occurs with CD4 counts over 200/mm³.

Symptomatic Phase: Severe Immunosuppression. When the CD4 count drops below 200/

TABLE 108–4. PREDICTIVE VALUE OF CD4 LYMPHOCYTE COUNTS FOR CERTAIN HIV-ASSOCIATED INFECTIONS AND NEOPLASMS IN NORTH AMERICA

CD4 COUNT CELLS/mm³*	OPPORTUNISTIC INFECTION OR NEOPLASM	FREQUENCY (%)†
>500	Recurrent *Candida* vaginitis	20–40 (F)
	Cervical dysplasia/neoplasia	5–40 (F)
	Herpes zoster, polydermatomal	5–10
	Bacterial pneumonia	10–15
200–500	*Mycobacterium tuberculosis* infection, pulmonary and extrapulmonary	1–40
	Oral hairy leukoplakia	40–70
	Candida pharyngitis (thrush)	40–70
	Kaposi's sarcoma, mucocutaneous	15–40 (M)
100–200	*Pneumocystis carinii* pneumonia	45–70
	Herpes simplex, chronic, ulcerative	10–20
	Histoplasma capsulatum infection, disseminated	0–25
	Kaposi's sarcoma, visceral	3–8 (M)
	Progressive multifocal leukoencephalopathy	2–3
	Lymphoma, non-Hodgkin's	2–5
<100	*Cryptosporidium* enteritis	2–10
	Mycobacterium avium-intracellulare, disseminated	25–40
	Toxoplasma gondii encephalitis	3–15
	Cryptococcus neoformans encephalitis	3–10
	Candida albicans esophagitis	15–20
	Cytomegalovirus, (CMV), focal and/or disseminated	25–40
	Lymphoma, central nervous system (CNS)	1–3

*Table indicates CD4 count at which specific infections or neoplasms generally begin to appear. Each infection my recur at any subsequent time in the course of infection.

† Even within the U.S., great regional differences in the incidence of specific opportunistic infections are apparent. For example, disseminated histoplasmosis is common in the Mississippi River drainage area, but very rare in individuals who have lived exclusively on the East or West Coast.

F = Exclusively in women; M = almost exclusively in men.

mm³, individuals are at high risk of developing multiple opportunistic infections (Table 108–4). For example, in the absence of antiretroviral therapy and specific prophylaxis, 60 per cent of HIV-infected North American men develop *Pneumocystis carinii* pneumonia. Disseminated and CNS fungal infections with *Cryptococcus neoformans*, *Histoplasma capsulatum*, or *Coccidioides immitis* may occur. (The incidence of each infection varies, depending on geographic locale.) Protozoal infections with *Toxoplasma gondii* or with *Cryptosporidium parvum* or *Isospora belli* may cause encephalitis or enteritis, respectively.

CD4 counts under 100/mm³ indicate profound immunosuppression and are associated with a high mortality within the subsequent 12 to 18 months. In particular, cytomegalovirus (CMV) infection of the retina or the gastrointestinal (GI) tract, disseminated *Mycobacterium avium-intracellulare* (MAI) infection, and lymphoma occur frequently and usually respond only transiently to the best available therapy.

TABLE 108–5. GENDER-RELATED MANIFESTATIONS OF HIV INFECTION IN WOMEN

1. Recurrent vaginal candidiasis
2. Extensive chronic perineal ulcers, secondary to HSV-2
3. Cervical dysplasia/neoplasia

Gender-Specific Clinical Manifestations in Women. At least three gender-specific manifestations are relevant to the management of HIV infection in women (Table 108–5).

1. The earliest clinical manifestation of HIV infection in women is most often the new onset, or frequent recurrence, of *Candida* vaginitis in the absence of known predisposing factors (e.g., broad-spectrum antimicrobial therapy). Since recurrent *Candida* vaginitis often develops at a time of only modest immunodeficiency (e.g., CD4 lymphocyte counts above 300/mm³), it should serve as a trigger to discuss HIV testing and thus lead to earlier diagnosis in otherwise asymptomatic women.

2. Chronic, painful perianal or perineal ulcers, caused by HSV-2, appear to be more frequent in women than in men. Although occurring at a time of more advanced immunodeficiency than *Candida* vaginitis, this lesion should always prompt HIV testing, as well as specific antiviral therapy (see Chapter 107).

3. A major life-threatening consequence of HIV infection in women is the frequent development of cervical dysplasia/neoplasia, which may result from synergy between HIV and the human papillomavirus (HPV). HIV-infected women who have had multiple sexual partners show a 5- to 10-fold increase in the prevalence of high-grade squamous intracellular lesions (SIL) on cervicovaginal examination. The increased prevalence of SIL is especially prominent in adolescents and young adults with HIV infection. Women with HIV infection should therefore obtain Papanicolaou (Pap) smears at 6-month intervals. Conversely, any woman with high-grade SIL on the Pap smear should be encouraged to undergo testing for HIV infection.

TABLE 108–6. AMBULATORY MANAGEMENT OF EARLY HIV DISEASE

Monitoring
  Complete baseline history and physical exam; directed interval interview and exam approximately every 6 mo
Laboratory Evaluation
  Baseline complete blood count and absolute CD4 cell count with repetition every 3–6 mo
  Baseline purified protein derivative (PPD) and anergy panel
  Baseline anticardiolipin (RPR) test, liver function tests, *Toxoplasma* antibody titer, and chest x-ray
Health Care Maintenance
  Assessment for ongoing counseling needs and referral for significant psychiatric or social problems
  Pneumococcal vaccine
  Yearly influenza vaccine (value uncertain)

MANAGEMENT OF HIV INFECTION

Since patients are asymptomatic during most of the course of HIV infection (Fig. 108–4), and even seriously immunocompromised individuals often function as productive citizens between bouts of opportunistic infections, a major emphasis on the ambulatory management of persons with HIV infection is of critical importance.

Initial Ambulatory Evaluation. Once an individual is found to be HIV-positive, the physician should discuss, in an unhurried manner, the manifestations of HIV infection and the use of immunologic studies (e.g., CD4 lymphocyte count) to guide therapy and, perhaps most important, should emphasize the fact that most patients, even without antiviral therapy, survive for 8 to 12 years after acquiring HIV infection and are asymptomatic during most of that time. The physician should also stress that the asymptomatic period can be extended by currently available antiviral drugs and prophylaxis against opportunistic infections, and that promising new drugs are in the developmental stage.

A complete history of STDs and HIV risk behavior is vital. Prevention of further transmission through unprotected sexual behaviors and sharing of intravenous needles must be discussed not only at the first visit but also periodically thereafter.

Initial evaluation should include both an HIV-oriented review of symptoms and a complete physical examination (Table 108–6). In particular, the skin must be examined for HIV-associated rashes and Kaposi's sarcoma. Examination of the oral cavity may reveal thrush, HSV-1 lesions, gingivitis, hairy leukoplakia, or aphthous ulcers. Lymphadenopathy, hepatomegaly, splenomegaly, or genital lesions should all be carefully noted. Neurologic examination for both peripheral neuropathy and decreased global cognition deserves close attention. Pelvic examination with Pap smear is especially important.

HIV-infected individuals who are purified protein derivative (PPD)–positive are at very high risk of active tuberculosis and require antituberculosis therapy. Therefore, PPD testing, in conjunction with a baseline chest radiograph, is mandatory. Skin testing should be performed as early in the course of HIV infection as possible, in association with determining cutaneous reactivity to other antigens, usually mumps, *Candida*, and tetanus toxoid. An induration of 5 mm or more should be considered positive. Any patient with a positive PPD should be evaluated for the presence of active disease; if none is present, the patient should receive at least 1 year of prophylaxis with isoniazid. If active tuberculosis infection is identified, multidrug therapy should be initiated, as described in Chapter 99. Serologic testing for *Toxoplasma gondii* infection may be important in the event that a person subsequently develops an intracerebral lesion (see below). Because of the increased prevalence of syphilis in persons with HIV infection, serologic testing for syphilis should be done at the first visit and treated aggressively if

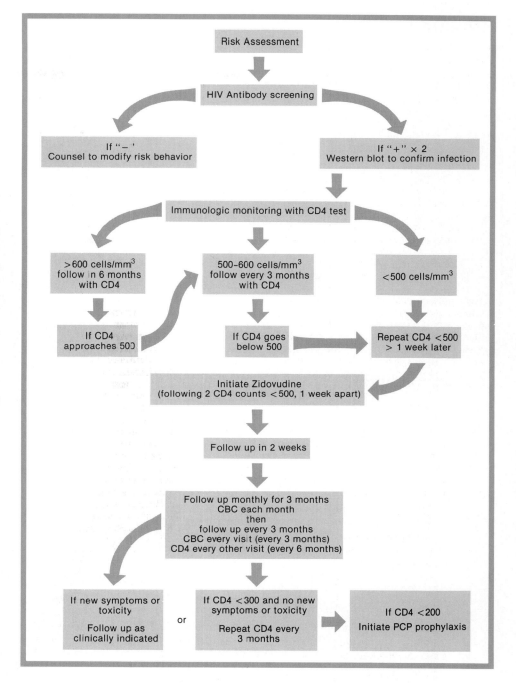

FIGURE 108–5. General guidelines for the use of zidovudine (ZDV) in the management of HIV disease. An expert panel participated in a 1990 State-of-the-Art Conference on AZT Therapy for Early HIV Infection. The panel recommended use of low doses (500 mg) of zidovudine for HIV-infected individuals with CD4 cell counts less than 500/mm³ and published a series of recommendations derived from its deliberations. The above algorithm is based upon the panel's recommendations for management of HIV-infected patients. (Data from State-of-the-Art Conference on Azidothymidine Therapy for Early HIV Infection. Am J Med 89:335–344, 1990.)

positive (see Chapter 107). Vaccination against pneumococcus is more effective the higher the CD4 count, and therefore should be offered as soon as possible after the diagnosis of HIV infection is established.

Since the most important currently available guide to the degree of immunodeficiency and to appropriate therapy is the CD4 lymphocyte count, this should be obtained at the first visit and repeated at the intervals suggested in Figure 108–5. The patient should understand that the CD4 lymphocyte count is only a rough guide to the degree

of immunodeficiency, that modest fluctuations in the CD4 count are generally not indicative of a change in clinical course, and, finally, that many persons function well with very low (<50/mm³) CD4 counts.

Antiretroviral Therapy

Elucidation of the mechanisms of HIV replication has identified a variety of potential sites at which retroviral replication can be limited or blocked

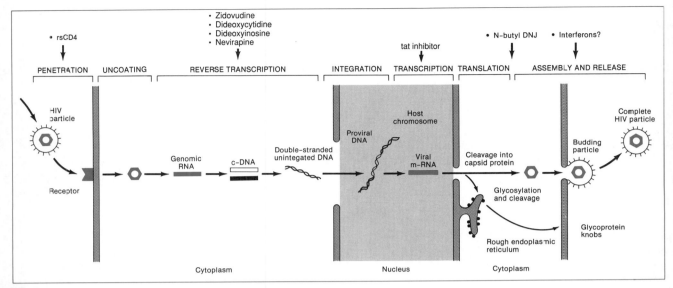

FIGURE 108-6. The life cycle of HIV. The target sites for antiretroviral agents are listed. (Modified from Johnson VA, Hirsch MS: *In* Volberding P, Jacobson M (eds): AIDS Clinical Review 1990. New York, Marcel Dekker, 1990, p 238. Reprinted by courtesy of Marcel Dekker, Inc.)

(Fig. 108–6). To date, three nucleoside analogues that inhibit HIV reverse transcriptase, zidovudine (AZT), didanosine (ddI), and zalcitabine (ddc) have been approved by the Food and Drug Administration (FDA) for treatment of HIV infection. Ongoing research is evaluating the effectiveness of other approaches to disrupting the HIV life cycle.

Patients with CD4 counts less than 500/mm³ are candidates for antiretroviral therapy (see Fig. 108–5). Among patients without symptoms and CD4 counts between 200 and 500/mm³, treatment with zidovudine provides significant clinical benefits, outlined in Table 108–7. Among persons with CD4 cells less than 500/mm³, zidovudine results in a decrease in AIDS-associated morbidity for periods of 18 to 36 months. In addition, individuals receiving zidovudine have demonstrated weight gain, improved performance status, and often improved cognitive and neurologic function.

Zidovudine is usually administered in a dosage of 100 mg 5 times per day, or 200 mg every 8 hours orally. Patients receiving zidovudine occasionally show early intolerance to the drug (nausea or headache). These symptoms generally resolve after a few weeks. Bone marrow toxicity, particularly anemia or dose-limiting granulocytopenia, also may occur. Persons with HIV infection

who develop anemia should be evaluated for other possible treatable causes. In the absence of other treatable causes, HIV-associated anemias may be responsive to the administration of recombinant erythropoietin if the serum erythropoietin level is not greatly elevated.

For patients who cannot tolerate zidovudine, didanosine is also active against HIV. Toxicities include pancreatitis (unusual but life-threatening) and peripheral neuropathy, both of which mandate discontinuation of ddI.

Zalcitabine (ddc) shares neurologic toxicity with didanosine. It may be helpful when administered in combination with zidovudine in patients with CD4 counts less than 300/mm³.

Among patients receiving long-term zidovudine and/or didanosine therapy, HIV isolates resistant to the in vitro activities of these agents may develop. The clinical significance of resistant isolates is not certain; drug resistance may be associated with heightened viral proliferation and acceleration of disease. Current experimental protocols are comparing combination and sequential antiretroviral strategies with single-agent therapy.

MANAGEMENT OF SPECIFIC CLINICAL MANIFESTATIONS OF IMMUNODEFICIENCY: A PROBLEM-ORIENTED APPROACH

The opportunistic infections that occur in persons with HIV infection vary considerably in time of onset (see Table 108–4). For example, some women may begin having recurrent *Candida* vaginitis with CD4 lymphocyte counts of 600/mm³ and may have no other opportunistic infections

TABLE 108–7. CLINICAL BENEFITS OF ZIDOVUDINE THERAPY IN EARLY HIV DISEASE (CD4 COUNTS OF 200–500/mm³)

1. Decreases frequency and severity of opportunistic infections
2. Delays progression to symptomatic disease
3. Weight gain
4. Improves performance status

until they develop *Pneumocystis carinii* pneumonia at a CD4 lymphocyte of 100/mm³. By the same token, occasional patients may remain entirely asymptomatic until the CD4 count is below 50/mm³, at which time they may develop a life-threatening opportunistic infection, such as *Toxoplasma gondii* encephalitis. In general, life-threatening opportunistic infections do not occur with CD4 counts greater than 200/mm³; most opportunistic infections that occur when CD4 counts are less than 100/mm³ are potentially life-threatening (see Table 108–4). Although the onset of certain opportunistic infections, such as thrush, are sometimes regarded as harbingers of rapidly advancing illness, this is not necessarily the case. Some patients may have a severe opportunistic infection, such as *Pneumocystis carinii* pneumonia, and following successful therapy, enjoy a relatively normal life for a period of 2 or more years before developing another serious opportunistic infection.

In general, opportunistic infections that occur with CD4 counts greater than 200/mm³ respond to routine therapy for the specific infection (e.g., penicillin for pneumococcal pneumonia, standard multidrug therapy for pulmonary tuberculosis), whereas opportunistic infections occurring with CD4 counts less than 200/mm³ require chronic suppressive therapy following subsidence of acute infection (e.g., *Pneumocystis carinii* pneumonia, *Cryptococcus neoformans* meningitis).

An important principle in the management of opportunistic infections is the recognition that the great majority do respond to appropriate antimicrobial therapy, and many patients have many months or years of productive life after the successful treatment of life-threatening opportunistic infections.

Constitutional Symptoms

Constitutional symptoms may be the initial manifestation of severe immunodeficiency. Patients may develop unexplained fever, night sweats, anorexia, weight loss, or diarrhea. These symptoms may last for weeks to months before the development of identifiable opportunistic infections. These constitutional symptoms may represent the earliest manifestations of specific opportunistic infections or may be due to HIV disease itself. The constitutional symptoms may be accompanied by generalized lymphadenopathy or by the presence of mucocutaneous disease caused by *Candida albicans*, herpes zoster virus, or HSV.

Mucocutaneous Diseases

Disorders of the skin and mucosa are among the most common and earliest clinical manifestations of HIV disease.

Oral Disease. *Candida* stomatitis, or thrush, may be the earliest recognized opportunistic infection. Thrush may be precipitated by a course of broad-spectrum antibiotics. Early thrush may be entirely asymptomatic, but as infection becomes more extensive, it may cause severe pain and discomfort upon eating. The cheesy white exudate on the mucous membranes can easily be scraped off. The underlying mucosa may be normal or inflamed and red. A saline or potassium hydroxide preparation reveals the budding yeast or pseudohyphae typical of *Candida* species.

Oral hairy leukoplakia is a lichenified, plaque-like lesion, most commonly seen on the lateral surfaces of the tongue (less commonly on the buccal mucosa). It may be a very early manifestation of immunodeficiency. Hairy leukoplakia is painless and may remit and relapse spontaneously.

Patients may develop painful ulcers in the mouth. They may be caused by HSV infection but also may represent aphthous lesions of uncertain etiology.

Kaposi's sarcoma, a malignant proliferative disorder seen most often in HIV-infected homosexual men, has a predilection for the oral cavity and skin. Oral lesions may be purple, red, or blue and may be raised or flat. Usually painless, these lesions cause symptoms when they enlarge and/or ulcerate.

Esophageal Disease. Dysphagia and substernal burning are common and usually indicate candidal esophagitis, particularly when associated with oral thrush. Ulcerative disease of the esophagus may also be caused by HSV, CMV, or giant aphthae (Table 108–8). Esophagoscopy with biopsy should be performed in patients whose symptoms do not rapidly respond (within 3 to 5 days) to antifungal therapy.

Genital Disease. Recurrent genital ulcers are most often due to HSV. A Tzanck preparation reveals multinucleated giant cells, and culture or specific immunofluorescence of ulcer scrapings confirms the diagnosis; biopsy is seldom indicated. Primary syphilis also occurs with increased frequency (see Chapter 107). Chancroid is still unusual in North America.

Vaginal and Cervical Disease. *Candida* species, generally not sexually transmitted, can cause an irritating vulvovaginitis in women with HIV infection as well as among healthy HIV-seronegative women. New onset or increased frequency of episodes of *Candida* vaginitis appears to be the most

TABLE 108–8. HIV-ASSOCIATED ESOPHAGITIS

CONDITION	CHARACTERISTICS	TREATMENT
Candida infection	Thrush usual, esophageal plaques	Ketoconazole, 200 mg/day; fluconazole, 200 mg/day
CMV infection	Giant shallow esophageal ulcers on endoscopy	Ganciclovir, 5 mg/kg bid
Herpes simplex	Deep ulceration on endoscopy	Acyclovir, 200–800 mg 5× day
Aphthae	Giant ulcers on endoscopy; no virus on biopsy	Prednisone, 40–60 mg/day

common early manifestation of HIV infection in women. A cheesy white exudate can be examined under light microscopy for budding yeast or pseudohyphae.

Infection with HPV is associated not only with rapid proliferation of genital warts but also with a greater risk of cervical dysplasia and carcinoma in HIV-infected women. Thus there is need for pelvic examinations and Pap smears at 6-month intervals in HIV-infected women.

Cutaneous Disease. HIV-infected patients may experience a variety of dermatologic ailments; many of these are readily treatable (Table 108–9). HIV-infected persons have higher than normal frequency of cutaneous and systemic reactions to a variety of medications, particularly sulfa-containing drugs. Severe seborrheic dermatitis, often manifest as a scaly eruption between the eyebrows and the nasolabial fold, often occurs. Psoriasis, a scaling eruption usually most prominent on the elbows, also occurs with greater than expected frequency among HIV-infected persons.

Herpes zoster, the appearance of crops of vesicular lesions on an erythematous base in a dermatomal or polydermatomal distribution, is often preceded by unexplained pain in the involved dermatome (or dermatomes). *Molluscum contagiosum*—umbilicated pearly papules due to poxvirus infection—may occur in crops on the face, neck, and abdomen of HIV-infected persons. Facial and genital warts due to HPV infection also occur with increased frequency. Generalized pruritus may be a drug reaction but also may be due to dry skin or to "pruritic papules"—a syndrome of undefined etiology that is frequent in this population.

Cutaneous lesions of Kaposi's sarcoma may be flat or raised; may be red, brown, or blue in color; and may resemble insect bites, nevi, or cutaneous ecchymoses. On examination, Kaposi's sarcoma lesions often have a firm texture when rolled between the fingers, whereas many benign lesions like ecchymoses are not distinguishable from normal skin by this maneuver.

Treatment. Many of the minor mucocutaneous problems can be readily treated, but recurrence is frequent. Thrush and candidal vaginitis usually respond initially to topical therapy but may require longer-term oral therapy to prevent frequent relapses. Esophageal candidiasis invariably necessitates treatment with a systemic agent, utilizing one of the imidazoles (e.g., fluconazole, 200 mg every day).

Recurrent or chronic ulcerative perioral or perianal herpes simplex usually responds rapidly to treatment with oral acyclovir (200 mg administered orally 5 times per day), but chronic acyclovir therapy may be required to prevent frequent relapses. Acyclovir-resistant strains of HSV may develop with chronic suppressive therapy, necessitating treatment with intravenous foscarnet. Although the effectiveness of antiviral therapy of uncomplicated multidermatomal herpes zoster in persons with HIV infection is uncertain, many clinicians prescribe acyclovir in this setting (800 mg given orally 5 times per day).

Aphthous ulcers are difficult to treat. Giant ulcers and esophageal ulcers may respond to systemic corticosteroids. It is important to obtain cultures to be sure that these ulcers are not viral (e.g., HSV, CMV) in origin before initiating corticosteroid therapy. Documentation of CMV in an esophageal ulcer is an indication for intravenous ganciclovir or foscarnet therapy for 2 to 3 weeks, or until resolution is confirmed endoscopically.

Seborrheic dermatitis often responds to hydro-

TABLE 108–9. DERMATOLOGIC CONDITIONS COMMON IN HIV INFECTION

CONDITION	DESCRIPTION	TREATMENT
Herpes simplex	Clear or crusted vesicles with an erythematous base; ulceration common when chronic; location: oral or genital mucous membranes, face, and hands	Acyclovir, 200 mg 5× day
Herpes zoster (shingles)	Cluster of vesicles in a dermatomal distribution; may involve adjacent dermatomes or may disseminate	Acyclovir, 800 mg 5× day; if disseminated or involvement of ophthalmic branch of trigeminal nerve, IV acyclovir 10 mg/kg q8h
Staphylococcal folliculitis	Erythematous pustules on face, trunk, and groin, often pruritic	Dicloxacillin, 500 mg qid, or erythromycin, 500 mg qid
Bacillary angiomatosis	Friable vascular papules or subcutaneous nodules on skin; may involve liver, spleen, and lymph nodes	Erythromycin, 500 mg qid
Molluscum contagiosum	Chronic, flesh-colored papules, often unbilicated, on face or anogenital area	Cryotherapy and curettage
Seborrheic dermatitis	White scaling or erythematous patches on scalp, eyebrows, face, trunk, axilla, and groin	Hydrocortisone cream, 2.5%, and ketoconazole cream
Psoriasis	Scaling, marginated patches on elbows, knees, and lumbosacral areas	Triamcinolone acetonide cream, 0.1%
Candidal rash	Urticarial scaling or erythematous patches on face, trunk, axilla, and groin	Hydrocortisone, 1% cream, and ketoconazole or clotrimazole cream
Candida infection (thrush)	White or erythematous patches on mucous membranes of mouth	Clotrimazole troches, 5× day; refractory cases: ketoconazole, 200 mg, or fluconazole, 100 mg qd

cortisone cream. Warts due to HPV, as well as lesions of molluscum contagiosum, may be treated with cryotherapy.

Nervous System Diseases

Nervous system complications ultimately occur in the majority of HIV-infected persons and range from mild cognitive disturbances or peripheral neuropathy to severe dementia or life-threatening opportunistic infections. The physician must be alert to the development of early signs of treatable neurologic complications of HIV disease. As is often the case with other lentiviruses, HIV enters microglial cells of the CNS early in the course of HIV infection. This process may be associated with neuronal cell loss, vacuolization, and occasional lymphocytic infiltration. The mechanism whereby HIV infection itself results in neurologic disease is not understood, but direct neuronal destruction and effects of viral proteins on neuronal cell function are two of the postulated mechanisms of nervous system disease in AIDS.

Cognitive Dysfunction. Intellectual impairment rarely occurs early in the course of HIV infection, but among persons with far-advanced immunodeficiency (CD4 cells <100/mm³), cognitive impairment is common. AIDS dementia complex (ADC) often begins insidiously and progresses over months to years, although occasionally the disorder may be acute in onset (Table 108–10). ADC is characterized by poor concentration, diminished memory, slowing of thought processes, motor dysfunction, and occasionally behavioral abnormalities characterized by social withdrawal and apathy. The symptoms of clinical depression overlap with many of the characteristics of early ADC and must be considered carefully in differential diagnosis and therapy. A few patients become agitated, confused, or overtly psychotic. Motor abnormalities may include a mild gait ataxia. As ADC progresses, patients may become more demented and/or may develop focal neurologic complications, characterized by spastic weakness of the lower extremities and incontinence, secondary to vacuolar myelopathy.

ADC must be distinguished from opportunistic complications of HIV infection. Computed tomographic (CT) scan of the head in ADC reveals only evidence of atrophy with enlarged sulci and ventricles. Examination of cerebrospinal fluid (CSF) is most often normal but may show mild elevations of protein and a few lymphocytes. High-dose zidovudine (200 mg every 4 hours) therapy may lead to functional improvement in persons with ADC.

A large variety of neurologic problems may complicate the later stages of HIV infection. A neuroanatomic classification of these manifestations is presented in Table 108–11, and certain of the more frequent and/or treatable problems are discussed below.

Focal Lesions of the CNS. A variety of opportunistic complications of HIV infection produce focal lesions of the CNS. Patients with focal neurologic signs, seizures of new onset, or the recent onset of rapidly progressive cognitive impairment should undergo CT scanning with contrast or magnetic resonance imaging (MRI) of the brain.

Toxoplasmosis, CNS lymphoma, and progressive multifocal leukoencephalopathy are the most common causes of CNS focal lesions in this setting (Table 108–12).

Toxoplasmosis of the CNS may occur in up to one third of HIV-infected patients who have serologic evidence of prior *Toxoplasma gondii* infection but is rare in individuals who have no antibodies to *Toxoplasma*. Fewer than 30 per cent of young adults born in the continental United States have antibodies to *T. gondii*, but more than 80 per cent of young adults in Puerto Rico have evidence of antecedent infection. Thus, the importance of toxoplasmosis as an opportunistic infection varies

TABLE 108–10. MAJOR CLINICAL MANIFESTATIONS OF AIDS DEMENTIA COMPLEX

Cognition	Inattention, reduced concentration, forgetfulness, impaired memory	Global dementia
Motor performance	Slowed movements, clumsiness, ataxia	Paraplegia
Behavior	Apathy, altered personality, agitation	Mutism

TABLE 108–11. NEUROANATOMIC CLASSIFICATION OF THE COMMON COMPLICATIONS OF HIV-1 INFECTION

Meningitis and Headache
  Cryptococcal meningitis
  Aseptic meningitis (HIV-1)
  Tuberculous meningitis (*Mycobacterium tuberculosis*)
  Syphilitic meningitis
Diffuse Brain Diseases
  With preservation of consciousness
    AIDS dementia complex
  With concomitant depression of arousal
    Toxoplasma encephalitis
    Cytomegalovirus encephalitis
Focal Brain Diseases
  Subacute
    Cerebral toxoplasmosis
    Primary CNS lymphoma
    Progressive multifocal leukoencephalopathy
    Tuberculous brain abscess (*M. tuberculosis*)
    Cryptococcoma
Myelopathies
  Subacute/chronic, progressive
    Vacuolar myelopathy
  Subacute with polyradiculopathy
    Cytomegalovirus myelopathy
Peripheral Neuropathies
  Predominantly sensory polyneuropathy
  Toxic neuropathies (dideoxycytidine, dideoxyinosine)
  Autonomic neuropathy
  Cytomegalovirus polyradiculopathy
Myopathies
  Polymyositis
  Noninflammatory myopathy
  Zidovudine myopathy

TABLE 108–12. **COMPARATIVE CLINICAL AND RADIOLOGIC FEATURES OF CEREBRAL TOXOPLASMOSIS, PRIMARY CNS LYMPHOMA, AND PROGRESSIVE MULTIFOCAL LEUKOENCEPHALOPATHY**

CONDITION	CLINICAL ONSET			NEURORADIOLOGIC FEATURES		
	TEMPORAL PROFILE	LEVEL OF ALERTNESS	FEVER	NUMBER OF LESIONS	TYPE OF LESIONS	LOCATION OF LESIONS
Cerebral toxoplasmosis	Days	Reduced	Common	Multiple	Spherical, ring-enhancing	Basal ganglia, cortex
Primary CNS lymphoma	Days to weeks	Variable	Absent	One or few	Irregular, weakly enhancing	Periventricular
Progressive multifocal leukoencephalopathy	Weeks	Variable	Absent	Multiple	Nonenhancing	White matter

according to region. Patients with CNS toxoplasmosis often present with progressive headache and focal neurologic abnormalities; they are usually febrile. CT scan usually demonstrates single or multiple ring-enhancing lesions after the administration of contrast dye but may show only focal edema. Management of symptomatic, ring-enhancing brain lesions in persons with AIDS includes initiation of empiric therapy with pyrimethamine, sulfadiazine, and folinic acid. Brain biopsy should be reserved for patients with atypical presentations, those with no serum antibodies to *T. gondii*, or those whose lesions do not respond after 10 to 14 days of antiprotozoal treatment. Because cyst forms of toxoplasmosis are not eradicated with current therapy, patients must remain on chronic suppressive therapy.

Primary CNS lymphoma complicates HIV infections in up to 2 per cent of cases. On CT or MRI scan, lesions are characteristically located in the periventricular space, are often single but may be "oligofocal," and usually enhance weakly with contrast (Table 108–12). Irradiation will usually provide brief remission, but most persons with CNS lymphoma survive less than 6 months after diagnosis.

Progressive multifocal leukoencephalopathy (PML) is a demyelinating disease due to a papovavirus. PML may cause progressive dementia, visual impairment, and hemiparesis. CT or MRI scans reveal multiple lesions predominantly involving white matter. These lesions only rarely enhance after injection of contrast and thereby are often distinguishable from other common mass lesions of the CNS in AIDS patients. There is no effective treatment for PML.

CNS Diseases Without Prominent Focal Signs. Evaluation of the HIV-infected patient who presents with fever and headache is complicated by the often subtle manifestations of CNS mass lesions in these patients. Patients with bacterial meningitis (see Chapter 97) are managed as are noncompromised patients. Meningeal diseases in most HIV-infected patients, however, fall into the broad categories of aseptic meningitis, chronic meningitis, and meningoencephalitis.

Aseptic Meningitis. Patients with aseptic meningitis complain most often of headache; the sensorium is generally intact, and the neurologic examination is normal (see Chapter 97). HIV infection can itself cause aseptic meningitis at any time during the course of HIV disease. Acute retroviral syndrome must be considered in the differential diagnosis; HIV antibody testing may be negative, and persons at risk should be offered follow-up serologic testing 2 to 3 months after the onset of symptoms if the first serology study is negative.

In the management of the HIV-infected person with aseptic meningitis, particular consideration must be given to the potentially treatable causes of this syndrome (see Chapter 97). Syphilitic meningitis may be particularly difficult to diagnose and treat in HIV-infected patients (see Chapters 97 and 107), as CSF serologies for syphilis may occasionally be negative. If the serum Venereal Disease Research Laboratory (VDRL) or fluorescent treponemal antibody (FTA) test is positive or there is a history of inadequately treated syphilis in the past, the physician may elect to treat for CNS syphilis (see Chapter 107). HIV-infected patients with cryptococcal meningitis may have only a mild CSF pleocytosis, and glucose and protein levels may resemble the pattern seen in aseptic meningitis. The absence of cryptococcal antigen in serum or CSF makes the diagnosis of cryptococcal infection remote (see Chapter 97).

Chronic Meningitis. Patients with chronic meningitis present with a history of headache, fevers, difficulty in concentrating, and/or changes in sensorium. CSF examination reveals a low glucose concentration, an elevated protein level, and a mild to modest lymphocytic pleocytosis. Cryptococcal meningitis is the most common etiology for this presentation. Either amphotericin B or fluconazole is effective in rapidly sterilizing the CSF, but fluconazole is preferred for the necessary maintenance therapy.

Tuberculous meningitis is an increasingly important cause of chronic meningitis in the HIV-infected patient. Antituberculosis therapy should be initiated in the setting of chronic meningitis if the cryptococcal antigen test is negative (see Chapter 97).

Coccidioidomycosis and histoplasmosis must be considered as possible causes of chronic meningitis in patients residing in, or with a travel history to, endemic regions (desert Southwest and Ohio and Mississippi River drainage areas, respectively) (see Chapter 97).

Meningoencephalitis. Patients with meningo-encephalitis present with alterations in sensorium varying from mild lethargy to coma. Patients are febrile, and neurologic examination often reveals evidence of diffuse CNS involvement. CT or MRI scanning reveals only nonspecific abnormalities, and electroencephalography often shows diffuse disease of the brain.

CMV encephalitis is difficult to diagnose. Patients may present with confusion, cranial nerve abnormalities, or long tract signs. CSF findings, as well as MRI and CT scanning, do not provide specific diagnostic information. Many patients have CMV disease elsewhere, often retinitis. The diagnosis can be definitively established only by biopsy, but this is of little benefit, as no treatment has proved effective for CMV encephalitis.

Meningoencephalitis due to HSV is rare in HIV infection but should be considered with an illness of acute onset that is characterized by fever, headache, and alteration in sensorium (see Chapter 97).

Pulmonary Diseases

Pulmonary manifestations of HIV infection are common; they range from nonspecific interstitial pneumonitis to life-threatening bacterial or opportunistic pneumonias (Table 108–13). Pneumonia is the most common serious infectious complication of HIV infection.

Patients have a substantially greater frequency of bacterial pneumonia; this is generally caused by encapsulated bacteria, including *Streptococcus pneumoniae* and *Haemophilus influenzae*. Impaired generation of specific antibody to these organisms most likely underlies this risk, which begins with modest degrees of immunodeficiency (CD4 counts of 200 to 500/mm^3). The intracellular bacterium *Legionella pneumophila* also causes pneumonia with increased frequency. The onset of bacterial pneumonia is usually abrupt; patients may have rigors and cough productive of purulent sputum. Physical examination and chest radiographs often reveal evidence of consolidation. The response to prompt initiation of therapy is usually good. Initial therapy is guided by the results of Gram stain of sputum (see Chapter 99).

Pneumocystis carinii pneumonia (PCP) is the most common life-threatening infection in North American persons with AIDS; more than half the initial AIDS-defining infections are due to PCP. In developing countries, where tuberculosis and other opportunistic infections are more prevalent, PCP is less common. Patients with PCP frequently complain of nonproductive cough, fever, and shortness of breath with exertion; a productive cough suggests another process. Patients with PCP often experience an end-inspiratory substernal "catch" or pain sensation that is unusual with other illnesses. In contrast to the acute onset of PCP in other immunocompromised patients, AIDS patients with PCP may have pulmonary symptoms for weeks before presentation. Arterial hypoxemia is almost constant; the chest radiograph generally reveals a subtle interstitial pattern but may be entirely normal. The patient is usually more sick than the radiograph would suggest. The presence of pleural effusions is suggestive of a process other than PCP.

If PCP is suspected, the patient should be started on therapy immediately; treatment for several days does not interfere with the ability to make a specific diagnosis. Confirmation of a diagnosis of PCP is essential, since treatment is often complicated by drug reactions. In addition, delay in establishing a correct diagnosis of another condition may be lethal. The diagnosis may be made by examination of induced sputum. If this fails, bronchoalveolar lavage, with silver staining or immunofluorescence of specimens, is adequate to diagnose PCP in more than 95 per cent of patients.

Treatment with high doses of intravenous trimethoprim-sulfamethoxazole (5 mg/kg of trimethoprim and 25 mg/kg of sulfamethoxazole every 6 hours) for 3 weeks is effective therapy; this drug combination, however, frequently produces side effects (rash, fever and granulocytopenia are most common) that limit its effectiveness. Intravenous pentamidine (4 mg/kg/day) is comparably effective but has more serious side effects; azotemia and pancreatitis presenting with

TABLE 108–13. PULMONARY DISEASE ASSOCIATED WITH HIV INFECTION

CONDITION	CHARACTERISTIC	CHEST X-RAY	DIAGNOSIS	TREATMENT
Pneumocystis carinii pneumonia	Subacute onset, dry cough, dyspnea	Interstitial infiltrate	Sputum or bronchoalveolar lavage for organism by stain	Trimethoprim-sulfamethoxazole, pentamidine
Bacterial (pneumococcus, *Haemophilus* most common)	Acute productive cough, fever, chest pain	Lobar or localized infiltrate	Sputum Gram stain and culture	Penicillin or cefuroxime
Mycobacterial (*Mycobacterium tuberculosis* or *M. kansasii*)	Chronic cough, weight loss, fever	Localized infiltrate, lymphadenopathy	Sputum acid-fast stain and mycobacterial culture	Isoniazid, rifampin, pyrazinamide
Kaposi's sarcoma	Asymptomatic or mild cough	Pulmonary nodules, pleural effusion	Open lung biopsy	Chemotherapy

hypoglycemia may occur and persist for days after the drug is stopped. The use of aerosolized pentamidine (600 mg/day) is often effective for milder cases of PCP and has few systemic toxicities. Patients with advanced PCP and arterial hypoxemia ($Po_2 \leq 75$ mm on breathing room air) benefit from administration of corticosteroids (40 mg of prednisone twice daily), utilizing a rapid taper over a period of 2 to 3 weeks.

On occasion, bronchoscopically obtained specimens yield CMV or MAI. Interpretation of these findings may be difficult in the setting of severe immunodeficiency. Evidence of active CMV retinitis or invasive disease elsewhere, or histologic demonstration of intracellular CMV inclusions obtained from bronchoalveolar lavage, indicates treatment with ganciclovir or foscarnet. MAI is an unusual cause of clinical pneumonia in AIDS.

Some AIDS patients (most often children) with interstitial pneumonitis may have no pathogen identified on transbronchial biopsy.

Mycobacterium tuberculosis infection occurs with greatly increased frequency in regions having a high prevalence of tuberculosis. Clinical signs of infection due to *M. tuberculosis* may precede the diagnosis of AIDS at a time when immunodeficiency is relatively mild (Table 108–4). Chest radiographs in HIV-infected patients may demonstrate features of primary tuberculosis, including hilar adenopathy, lower or middle lobe infiltrates, miliary pattern, or pleural effusions, as well as classic patterns of reactivation. Extrapulmonary *M. tuberculosis* infection occurs with greatly increased frequency in persons with HIV infection. Blood cultures often yield *M. tuberculosis* in the severely immunocompromised patient.

Both pulmonary and extrapulmonary forms of tuberculosis generally respond promptly to standard antituberculosis therapy, although several outbreaks of multidrug-resistant *M. tuberculosis* have occurred in people with HIV infection, associated with very high case fatality rates. Treatment therefore should begin with at least three antituberculosis drugs (see Chapter 99). Because HIV-infected patients are at risk for relapse once initial therapy is completed, long-term monitoring for reactivation is critical. Since nosocomial transmission of multidrug resistant *M. tuberculosis* has occurred in hospitals and in ambulatory care centers, physicians must take adequate precautions to prevent spread of drug-resistant tuberculosis, especially in the health care setting.

The disseminated fungal infections histoplasmosis and coccidioidomycosis occur with much greater frequency in persons with HIV infection. Either infection may present with nodular infiltrates or a miliary pattern on chest radiograph. Histoplasmosis usually involves bone marrow and often the GI tract, as well as skin. Bone marrow biopsy often demonstrates the organism. The standard treatment of disseminated mycoses in AIDS patients is high-dose amphotericin; oral flucona-

zole is, however, well tolerated and may prove to be equally effective. Since relapse is common, oral antifungal therapy should be continued following resolution of signs and symptoms.

Nodular pulmonary disease or isolated pleural effusions in AIDS patients may represent involvement with AIDS-associated malignancies such as Kaposi's sarcoma. Since hilar or mediastinal lymphadenopathy is seldom a part of the generalized, HIV-associated lymphadenopathy syndrome, enlargement of these nodes usually represents either an opportunistic infection or a neoplasm.

Prevention of Pulmonary Infections. Some of the serious pulmonary complications of HIV infection are preventable. Since less immunocompromised patients may have better antibody responses, immunization against *Streptococcus pneumoniae* and *Haemophilus influenzae* should be performed as early in the course of HIV disease as practical.

Among persons with a CD4 cell count lower than $200/mm^3$, prophylaxis, using trimethoprim-sulfamethoxazole (1 double-strength tablet daily), dapsone (50 mg/day), or aerosolized pentamidine (300 mg/month), is effective in preventing PCP. Among patients who have already experienced an episode of PCP, trimethoprim-sulfamethoxazole is substantially more effective than aerosolized pentamidine.

All HIV-infected patients should undergo routine skin testing with PPD. All patients with positive PPD skin tests should be evaluated for the presence of active disease; if none is present, they should receive 1 year of prophylaxis with isoniazid and pyridoxine (see Chapter 99).

Gastrointestinal Diseases

GI disease manifesting as dysphagia, diarrhea, or colitis is common. These processes often contribute to inadequate nutrition, compounding the anorexia and weight loss associated with advanced HIV disease. Dysphagia is discussed above.

Nausea and Vomiting. Nausea and vomiting are frequent. Often these symptoms are related to medications; these must be reviewed and the likely offending drug (or drugs) withheld as a therapeutic trial. If symptoms of nausea and vomiting remain undefined and do not respond to empiric therapy with histamine$_2$ (H$_2$) antagonists and an antiemetic, endoscopy may be performed. Biopsy may reveal a lymphoma, Kaposi's sarcoma, or viral gastritis, as well as conditions not directly attributable to HIV disease. Liver function tests may identify a hepatocellular basis for these symptoms, since many patients with HIV disease are also at risk for hepatitis B or C.

Abnormalities of liver function tests are common in HIV disease and often are nonspecific. Marked elevations in serum alkaline phosphatase levels may reflect infiltrative disease of the liver (e.g., MAI or CMV infection) and also can be seen in patients with acalculous cholecystitis, cryptosporidiosis, or AIDS-associated sclerosing cholangitis.

TABLE 108-14. INFECTIOUS DIARRHEA IN ADVANCED HIV INFECTION

CONDITION	CHARACTERISTIC	DIAGNOSIS	TREATMENT
Frequent			
Cytomegalovirus	Small bowel movements with blood or mucus (colitis)	Colonoscopy and biopsy	Ganciclovir, 5 mg/kg bid
Cryptosporidium	Varies from increased frequency to large-volume diarrhea	Acid-fast stain of stool	None consistently effective
Mycobacterium avium-intra-cellulare	Abdominal pain, fever, retroperitoneal lymphadenopathy	Blood culture or endoscopy with biopsy	Multidrug regimen, including clarithromycin
Less Frequent			
Salmonella or Campylobacter	Blood or mucus in bowel movements (colitis)	Stool culture	Norfloxacin (check sensitivities)
Isospora belli	Watery diarrhea	Acid-fast stain of stool	Trimethoprim-sulfamethoxazole
Clostridium difficile	Abdominal pain, fever common	Clostridium difficile toxin in stool or endoscopy	Metronidazole or vancomycin po

Diarrhea. Diarrhea occurs, at least intermittently, in more than 50 per cent of persons with AIDS and may be due to a variety of bacterial or opportunistic pathogens (Table 108-14). In many cases, no clear etiology is found, and the diarrhea is attributed to HIV enteropathy.

As in other patients with persistent diarrhea, profuse, watery diarrhea suggests a secretory diarrhea, and bloody diarrhea with mucus is most consistent with colitis (Chapter 103). Stool specimens should be sent for bacterial culture. *Salmonella, Campylobacter,* and *Yersinia* species are common in HIV-infected persons; although patients may respond to antibiotic treatment, bacteremia is common and recurrences are frequent. Similarly, AIDS patients may experience recurrent episodes of diarrhea associated with the isolation of *Clostridium difficile* toxin from stool. Whether this reflects the frequent use of broad-spectrum antibiotics or is attributable to some other factor in HIV disease is unknown.

A fresh stool specimen also should be studied for ova and parasites and should be examined using a modified acid-fast stain for *Cryptosporidium parvum* and *Isospora belli*. *Cryptosporidium* species and *Isospora belli* are the most common enteric protozoal infections in AIDS patients throughout the world. Although cryptosporidiosis may be self-limited, massive diarrhea (up to 20 L/day) may occur. Clinical responses to oral paromomycin, a poorly absorbed aminoglycoside, are often transient and incomplete. Isosporiasis frequently responds to oral trimethoprim-sulfamethoxazole, but relapse is frequent. Chronic therapy may be necessary.

If diagnostic studies are nonrevealing and diarrhea persists, patients should undergo endoscopy (see Chapter 33). Biopsy of the duodenum or small bowel may reveal histologic evidence of cryptosporidiosis, MAI infection, or CMV infection. Nonspecific inflammation and villous atrophy are present in patients with HIV enteropathy. Electron microscopy or special stains of small bowel biopsy specimens or stool may reveal evidence of micro-sporidan infection. Biopsy of the colon may show histologic abnormalities indicative of herpes simplex proctitis, CMV colitis, or MAI infection.

For patients with refractory diarrhea, a variety of nonspecific approaches may improve the quality of life. Patients with chronic diarrhea often have an acquired mucosal disaccharidase deficiency; a trial of a lactose-free diet may provide symptomatic improvement. Agents that alter motility (e.g., loperamide hydrochloride [Imodium]) or secretion (octreotide) may provide symptomatic relief for some patients. Parenteral hyperalimentation may improve both the quality and the duration of life in patients with refractory AIDS-related diarrheal diseases.

Unexplained Fever

Persistent fever without localizing signs may be part of HIV seroconversion illness. However, most, if not all, persistent fevers late in the course of HIV infection reflect an underlying definable process.

Mycobacterium avium-intracellulare (MAI) infection may manifest with nonspecific findings, including persistent fever, anorexia, weight loss, abdominal pain, and/or diarrhea in patients with CD4 counts below 80/mm³. This organism may cause extensive disease, involving bone marrow, liver, spleen, and GI tract. Rapid diagnosis may often be made by histologic examination of bone marrow specimens, although blood cultures will also eventually yield the organism. Unlike *M. tuberculosis*, MAI rarely causes pulmonary disease or meningitis, and aerosolization does not place immunocompetent persons at risk. MAI is resistant to conventional antituberculosis chemotherapy and is treated with combinations of agents that generally include rifampin or rifabutin, clofazimine, ethambutol, and ciprofloxacin, with or without amikacin. Although complete eradication of infection may be impossible, combinations of these drugs have resulted in resolution of fevers and weight gain in patients with disseminated MAI infection. Clinical studies suggest that the newer azalide antibiotics, azithromycin and clarithromycin, may improve and simplify treatment of MAI infection.

Unexplained fever also may be due to disseminated infection by CMV. The hemorrhagic exudates that characterize CMV retinitis support the diagnosis. In the absence of retinal or visceral disease, isolation of CMV from the blood is not a definite indication for treatment.

Aggressive non-Hodgkin's lymphoma may present in AIDS patients with unexplained fever. A rapidly enlarging spleen or asymmetric lymph node enlargement may suggest the diagnosis. The lymphomas often have a visceral or intra-abdominal presentation. CT-guided biopsy of enlarged intra-abdominal nodes may provide the diagnosis.

Weight Loss and Anorexia

Cachexia is a prominent feature of advanced HIV disease. In some instances, cachexia is due to an intercurrent infectious process. In many instances, however, no opportunistic process is identified and the cachexia is attributed to progressive HIV disease. Heightened production of tumor necrosis factor/cachectin may be responsible for the fevers, cachexia, and hypertriglyceridemia in AIDS.

If orthostatic hypotension associated with hyperkalemia is identified, an adrenocorticotropin (ACTH) stimulation test should investigate the possibility of adrenal insufficiency, most often secondary to CMV infection.

Many patients with AIDS-associated cachexia gain weight and achieve a sense of well-being after initiation of antiretroviral therapy (zidovudine or didanosine). Some also gain weight after administration of the appetite-stimulating progestational drug megesterol.

AIDS-Associated Malignancies

Kaposi's sarcoma was recognized early in the epidemic as a manifestation of AIDS. In the United States, epidemic Kaposi's sarcoma occurs primarily among homosexual and bisexual men. Among HIV-infected homosexuals, the frequency of Kaposi's sarcoma has fallen from 40 per cent at the outset of the epidemic to less than 20 per cent in 1990. These data, together with observation of Kaposi's sarcoma in occasional HIV-seronegative homosexual men, suggest that this tumor may result from infection with an unidentified sexually transmissible pathogen and that tumor growth is promoted by HIV-associated immunodeficiency. Neither HIV nor any other infectious pathogen has been reproducibly identified within the tumor cells.

Kaposi's sarcoma is primarily a tumor of the skin and mucosal surfaces that can involve the GI tract, lungs, and lymph nodes. Symptomatic or rapidly progressive disease should be treated. Systemic chemotherapy can provide remissions in most patients with disseminated disease or symptomatic visceral disease. Some patients with modest immune impairment may respond to treatment with interferon-alpha.

Non-Hodgkin's B cell lymphomas may also complicate HIV infection. Most AIDS-associated lymphomas are of small noncleaved or immunoblastic histology. Extranodal presentation of these tumors is the rule, with a high frequency of GI or intracranial presentation. Patients usually, but not always, present with these malignancies late in the course of HIV disease. Chemotherapy for systemic disease or radiation therapy for CNS disease can provide brief clinical responses, but few patients survive more than 6 months after diagnosis.

Other Complications of HIV Infection

Cardiac. Whereas subclinical cardiac abnormalities are very common in HIV-infected persons, a small proportion of HIV-infected patients develop clinically important congestive cardiomyopathy. This usually occurs in the presence of severe immunodeficiency.

Renal. Renal insufficiency in AIDS patients may be a consequence of nephrotoxic drug administration, acute tubular necrosis following hypotension, or HIV-associated nephropathy (HIVAN). HIVAN occurs most often among injecting drug users; certain histologic features may distinguish HIVAN from renal failure associated with intravenous heroin use. Focal and segmental glomerulosclerosis is present in HIVAN, and the disease usually manifests with progressively severe proteinuria, nephrotic syndrome, and progressive renal insufficiency. Most patients develop end-stage renal disease within several months. Renal biopsy may be helpful in excluding other potentially treatable causes of renal failure.

Rheumatologic. Musculoskeletal complaints are common. The relationship of circulating autoantibodies to the rheumatologic manifestations is unknown. Muscle weakness may reflect generalized debilitation, or, if localized, myelopathy-neuropathy (see Table 108–11). When weakness is proximal or is associated with myalgias and tenderness, myopathy should be suspected. The myopathy may be HIV-associated or may rarely represent toxicity of zidovudine. Muscle biopsy may distinguish between these two processes, with inflammation most prominent in AIDS-associated myopathy and mitochondrial abnormalities in AZT-related myopathy. Arthralgias are frequent, and both a Reiter-like syndrome and Sjögren-like syndrome occur with increased frequency in HIV infection.

PREVENTION OF HIV INFECTION

The development of an effective vaccine is the target of active research. Early trials of potential vaccines are currently under way.

Behavioral change is the only currently available method to prevent transmission of HIV. In several communities of persons at increased risk for HIV infection (e.g., homosexually active men in the United States and Western Europe), adoption of safer sexual practices has been associated with a decrease in the rates of newly acquired HIV infection. Sustaining these behavioral changes over long periods may, however, be difficult, and thus behavioral reinforcement is important. Moreover, negative attitudes regarding condom use enhance the continuing risk of HIV transmission. Counseling regarding risk behavior, particularly unprotected sexual intercourse without condoms and sharing of needles, must be part of routine visits in the health care setting.

Infection control procedures that are routinely recommended to protect health care workers involve the use of universal blood and body fluid precautions. Meticulous attention to the utilization and disposal of sharp instruments is most important, since most nosocomial acquisition of HIV infection has occurred through accidental needlestick. In particular, needles should never be recapped. Health care workers who have experienced accidental parenteral HIV exposure have an overall 0.3 per cent risk of HIV seroconversion;

most exposures that result in HIV transmission involve accidental deep injection. Exposed health care workers are often offered zidovudine chemoprophylaxis, although data confirming that zidovudine will prevent HIV infection are not available.

REFERENCES

Carpenter CCJ, Mayer KH, Stein MD, et al: Human immunodeficiency virus infection in North American women: Experience with 200 cases and a review of the literature. Medicine 70:307–325, 1991.

Mann J: AIDS—the second decade: A global perspective. J Infect Dis 165:245–250, 1992.

Saag MS, et al: HIV and associated disorders. In Wyngaarden JB, Smith LH, Bennett JC (eds): Cecil Textbook of Medicine. 19th ed. Philadelphia, WB Saunders Co, 1992, pp 1908–1970.

Stein DS, Korvick JA, Vermund SH: CD4+ lymphocyte enumeration for prediction of clinical course of human immunodeficiency virus disease. J Infect Dis 165:352–363, 1992.

109 INFECTIONS IN THE IMMUNOCOMPROMISED HOST

Immunosuppression is an increasingly common by-product of diseases and modern approaches to their treatment. The immunocompromised host suffers from increased susceptibility to opportunistic infection, defined as infection caused by organisms of low virulence that compose normal mucosal and skin flora or by pathogenic microbial agents usually maintained in a latent state.

Immunocompromise is not an all-or-none phenomenon. The extent of immunosuppression varies with the underlying cause and must exceed a threshold to predispose to opportunistic infections. Importantly, the type of immunosuppression predicts the spectrum of agents likely to cause infections. Accordingly, opportunistic infections can best be considered in categories that reflect the nature of immunocompromise.

DISORDERS OF CELL-MEDIATED IMMUNITY

Cell-mediated immunity is the major host defense against facultative and some obligate intracellular parasites, as discussed in Chapter 92. A partial list of diseases and situations that produce impaired cell-mediated immunity is presented in Table 109–1. However, only certain of these result in increased susceptibility to infection with intracellular parasites. Foremost among acquired immunodeficiencies are human immunodeficiency virus (HIV) infection (see Chapter 108), Hodgkin's disease and other lymphomas, hairy-cell leukemia, and advanced solid tumors. Severe malnutrition, as well as treatment with high-dose corticosteroids, cytotoxic drugs, or radiotherapy, can produce a similar predilection to infections. Congenital immunodeficiencies are associated with severe infections early in childhood and will not be considered here. Patients

TABLE 109–1. CONDITIONS CAUSING IMPAIRED CELL-MEDIATED IMMUNITY

Infectious diseases—measles, chickenpox, typhoid fever, tuberculosis, leprosy, histoplasmosis, human immunodeficiency virus (HIV) infection

Vaccinations—measles, mumps, rubella

Malignancies—Hodgkin's disease, lymphomas, advanced solid tumors

Drugs—corticosteroids, cytotoxic drugs

Miscellaneous—congenital immunodeficiency states, sarcoidosis, uremia, diabetes mellitus, malnutrition, old age

TABLE 109-2. INFECTIONS IN PATIENTS WITH IMPAIRED CELL-MEDIATED IMMUNITY

Viruses—varicella-zoster, herpes simplex, cytomegalovirus, JC virus
Fungi—pathogenic: *Histoplasma, Coccidioides;* saprophytic: *Cryptococcus, Candida;* less commonly, *Aspergillus, Zygomycetes*
Bacteria—*Listeria monocytogenes, Nocardia, Mycobacterium tuberculosis, Legionella pneumophila,* nontuberculous mycobacteria
Protozoa—*Pneumocystis carinii, Toxoplasma gondii, Cryptosporidium* species
Helminths—*Strongyloides stercoralis*

with impaired cell-mediated immunity are especially susceptible to the organisms shown in Table 109-2. The relative frequency of occurrence varies with the underlying disease (e.g., *Mycobacterium avium* is frequent in HIV infection, *Listeria* is not); geographic area (*Mycobacterium tuberculosis* is more frequent in developing countries); and the extent of immunosuppression (*M. tuberculosis* is an early and *M. avium* a late complication of HIV infection).

Thus, with depression of cell-mediated immunity, organisms ordinarily constituting the normal flora such as *Candida* species act as virulent opportunistic pathogens capable of causing aggressive infections. Latent viruses, fungi, mycobacteria, and protozoa reactivate to cause locally progressive and/or disseminated disease. Often the signs, symptoms, and laboratory abnormalities suggesting the diagnosis are subtle and nonspecific.

The association between defective cell-mediated immunity and disease produced by the infectious agents listed in Table 109-2 is clear-cut. Sometimes, treatment of the underlying disease causing immunodeficiency or progression of this disease produces a more severe and generalized compromised state, which predisposes to infection by additional microorganisms. For example, during chemotherapy for lymphoma, bacterial infections predominate. Disease progression also results in local factors favoring bacterial infections such as mucosal breakdown and tumor masses obstructing bronchi, ureters, or biliary tract. The result is a marked increase in severe bacterial infection and septicemia late in the course of many diseases associated with impaired cell-mediated immunity.

DISORDERS OF HUMORAL IMMUNITY

The acquired disorders of antibody production associated with increased frequency of infection in adults are common variable immunodeficiency, chronic lymphocytic leukemia, lymphosarcoma, and multiple myeloma. The paraproteinemic states belong in this category because of secondary decreases in levels of functioning antibody. Therapy with cytotoxic drugs may produce similar immunocompromise.

Infections due to the pneumococcus, *Haemophilus influenzae*, streptococci, and staphylococci predominate early in the course of the humoral immu-

nodeficiency. As the underlying disease itself progresses, infections due to gram-negative bacilli become more frequent. Treatment of the underlying condition with corticosteroids and cytotoxic drugs causes additional defects in cell-mediated immunity, providing susceptibility to infections with the group of pathogens presented in Table 109-2.

In sickle cell anemia, heat-labile opsonic activity is abnormal. Complement depletion by erythrocyte stroma causes impairment of opsonization of pneumococci and *Salmonella* species, leading to frequent infections with these organisms. Impaired reticuloendothelial system function due to erythrophagocytosis and functional asplenia also may predispose patients with sickle cell disease to serious bacterial infections. The predisposition to infection is age-related; once children with sickle cell disease develop antibodies to pneumococcal capsular polysaccharide, they lose their thousandfold increased susceptibility to severe pneumococcal infection.

Splenectomy results in a loss of mechanisms for the clearing of opsonized organisms. Over a period of years, the liver compensates in regard to this filtration function. The splenic tissue also represents a major source of production of antibody as well as other opsonic factors, such as tuftsin, which opsonizes staphylococci. Splenectomy therefore predisposes to fulminant infections caused by encapsulated bacteria. The risk of infection is greater soon after splenectomy, and when the spleen is removed for indications other than trauma.

IMPAIRED NEUTROPHIL FUNCTION

Many inherited and acquired diseases impair neutrophil function. The defect may be extrinsic or intrinsic to the neutrophil. Impaired chemotaxis is a significant factor predisposing patients with inherited C3 and C5 deficiencies to frequent bacterial infections (see Chapter 92). Corticosteroid therapy also interferes with chemotaxis. Whereas circulating neutrophil counts may be normal or increased in patients treated with corticosteroids, these cells are dysfunctional, since they do not localize normally to the site of infection. Defective cell-mediated immunity also contributes to the spectrum of infections associated with corticosteroid therapy.

Intrinsic defects in neutrophils are rare but provide insights into the microbicidal mechanisms of these cells. Neutrophils from patients with chronic granulomatous disease (CGD) cannot develop an oxidative burst. Catalase-negative organisms produce sufficient hydrogen peroxide to facilitate their own killing by CGD neutrophils through the myeloperoxidase pathway. Catalase-producing organisms such as staphylococci, *Serratia, Nocardia,* and *Aspergillus* scavenge the hydrogen peroxide that they produce; these infectious agents, therefore, cannot be killed by CGD neutrophils and produce serious, deep-seated infections.

The most severe intrinsic neutrophil defects occur in the Chédiak-Higashi syndrome. Patients have giant granules in their leukocytes and defective microtubule assembly. The result is impaired chemotaxis, abnormal phagolysosomal fusion, delayed bacterial killing, and recurrent infections. Diagnosis of this rare syndrome is aided by phenotypic abnormalities: partial albinism, depigmentation of the iris, peripheral neuropathies, and nystagmus.

NEUTROPENIA

As the neutrophil count falls below $500/\mu l$, an exponential increase occurs in the frequency and severity of infections. Most reliable data derive from patients with acute leukemia. For example, in one study, neutrophil counts of 100 to $500/\mu l$ were associated with infections during 35 per cent of hospitalized days, whereas at counts below $100/\mu l$ infections increased to 55 per cent of days. However, granulocytopenia of other causes, when sustained, may result in a comparable risk of infection. In patients with chronic and cyclic neutropenias, the susceptibility to infection varies inversely with the monocyte count; the mononuclear phagocytes provide some of the antibacterial capacity of the missing neutrophils. Following chemotherapy of acute leukemia, neutropenia usually is sustained and associated with damage to mucosal barriers to infection. Patients become susceptible to organisms that are ubiquitous in the environment and ordinarily compose the normal flora (Table 109–3).

DIAGNOSTIC PROBLEMS IN THE COMPROMISED HOST

Pulmonary Infiltrates

The immunocompromised patient with pulmonary infiltrates presents a particularly vexing diagnostic problem. The pulmonary infiltrates could represent infection, extension of underlying tumor, complication of chemotherapy, or some combination of these. Specific diagnosis is necessary. Unfortunately, noninvasive serodiagnostic tests rarely are helpful in this setting, yet concomitant thrombocytopenia too often increases the risk of lung biopsy.

The clinical setting and radiographic appearance of the pulmonary infiltrate influence the probable yield of lung biopsy and the decision about whether to proceed. For example, in patients with leukemia, parenchymal infiltrates occurring before or within 3 days of initiating chemotherapy usually are bacterial, as are focal infiltrates developing later in the course. Major efforts should be directed at obtaining adequate sputum samples for Gram stain and culture (see Chapter 99); the evolution of the pneumonitis during antibiotic therapy becomes a useful factor in deciding whether to proceed with lung biopsy.

In contrast, diffuse infiltrates occurring *after* treatment of leukemia are more suggestive of opportunistic infection. *Pneumocystis carinii* is an important treatable cause of diffuse infiltrates and occurs most often after treatment of acute lymphocytic leukemia or in patients with an acquired deficiency of cell-mediated immunity (see also Chapter 108). In

TABLE 109–3. INFECTIOUS AGENTS THAT FREQUENTLY CAUSE INFECTIONS IN NEUTROPENIC PATIENTS

Bacteria—*Pseudomonas, Klebsiella, Serratia, Escherichia coli, Staphylococcus aureus, Staphylococcus epidermidis, Corynebacterium* group JK
Fungi—*Candida, Aspergillus, Zygomycetes*
Viruses—Cytomegalovirus, *Herpesvirus hominis*
Protozoa—*Pneumocystis carinii*

these settings, the diagnosis should be established by examination of induced sputum, by bronchoalveolar lavage, or, less commonly, by transbronchial biopsy. If these diagnostic approaches are not helpful, empiric therapy with trimethoprim-sulfamethoxazole may be initiated.

The indications and timing of lung biopsy, when needed, must be individualized. Delay in proceeding with biopsy, to a point at which the patient is severely hypoxic, reduces the chances of affecting the outcome with therapy, even if the biopsy shows a potentially treatable disease.

Once the decision has been made to perform a biopsy, the next question is which procedure to use. Fiberoptic transbronchial biopsy has provided a good diagnostic yield, particularly in the evaluation of diffuse pulmonary lesions. This technique should not be performed in the thrombocytopenic patient. It is imperative that the tissue obtained be processed and examined quickly. Open lung biopsy has an additional yield of 50 to 75 per cent in the patient with a nondiagnostic transbronchial biopsy and should be performed without delay if the tempo of progression of the patient's illness mandates immediate diagnosis. Open lung biopsy can generally be performed in thrombocytopenic patients if prophylactic transfusions can achieve an increment in the platelet count and diminish the bleeding time.

Early treatment of most pulmonary infections in immunocompromised hosts, even aspergillosis (Fig. 109–1), is associated with an initially favorable outcome. The long-term result, however, is dependent on the natural history of the underlying disease process.

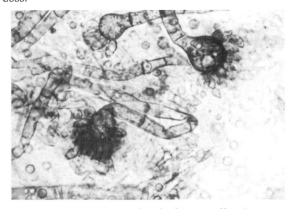

FIGURE 109–1. Fruiting head of *Aspergillus fumigatus* on lung biopsy. Aspergillosis usually causes an expanding perihilar pulmonary infiltrate. Prompt institution of amphotericin B therapy may lead to a good clinical response.

Disseminated Mycoses

Disseminated mycoses represent another major diagnostic problem in the immunocompromised host. Fungal infections are found post mortem in more than one half of patients with leukemia and lymphoma; usually, the nature of the infection has not been established ante mortem. Culture of a saprophytic organism such as *Candida* from superficial sites does not establish pathogenicity. Even in patients with widespread infection, however, detectable fungemia is a late event.

How, then, can the diagnosis of fungal infection be established early, at a time when the infection is potentially curable? It is important to search for superficial lesions accessible to scraping, aspiration, or biopsy (Fig. 109–2). Dissemination of *Candida tropicalis* frequently causes hyperpigmented macular or pustular skin lesions that show the organism within blood vessel walls on biopsy. Cryptococcal polysaccharide antigen may be present in the serum or cerebrospinal fluid of the patient with disseminated cryptococcosis. Serodiagnosis for other fungi has, in general, been disappointing. The presence of "bulls'-eye" lesions on computed tomography (CT) scan of the liver and spleen suggests hepatosplenic candidiasis.

In the absence of adequate diagnostic procedures, empiric use of antifungal drugs is often indicated in the immunocompromised host when there is appropriate clinical suspicion of disseminated mycoses (e.g., in the neutropenic patient with fever for more than 7 days despite broad-spectrum antibiotic therapy).

PREVENTION AND TREATMENT OF INFECTIONS IN THE NEUTROPENIC PATIENT

Prevention

Acute bacterial infections and septicemia arising from organisms composing the gut flora occur frequently in granulocytopenic patients and may have fever as their sole manifestation. Prophylactic nonabsorbable antibiotics and protective isolation have generally failed to prevent such infection. Trimethoprim-sulfamethoxazole, given prophylactically, may decrease the number of infections and bacteremic episodes in some neutropenic patients, in addition to preventing the development of *Pneumocystis carinii* pneumonia. However, its bone marrow toxicity and selection of resistant organisms make it unsuitable for widespread use as a prophylactic agent in neutropenic patients. Quinolones, such as ciprofloxacin, may be at least as effective in preventing bacterial infections and are less toxic; quinolones lack activity, however, against *Pneumocystis carinii*. Prophylactic administration of imidazoles to prevent systemic fungal infections is of uncertain value in this setting.

Prophylactic granulocyte transfusions decrease

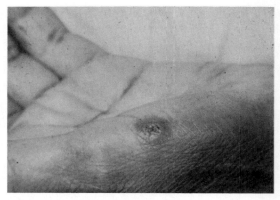

FIGURE 109–2. Skin lesion in a 76-year-old woman treated with corticosteroids and cytotoxic drugs for chronic lymphocytic leukemia and presenting with nodular pulmonary infiltrates and lymphocytic meningitis. Fluid expressed from the lesion contained encapsulated yeast seen on India ink preparation and yielded *Cryptococcus neoformans* on culture.

the occurrence of bacterial sepsis in patients with acute myelogenous leukemia but are costly and do not affect overall remission rate and duration of survival.

Treatment

Empiric antibiotic therapy is indicated in febrile granulocytopenic patients, since up to two thirds have an underlying infection. Selection of two drugs with activity against *Pseudomonas aeruginosa*, such as tobramycin and mezlocillin, is essential. This two-drug regimen also provides adequate initial antibiotic coverage of staphylococcal infections, although clinical experience favors the use of other drugs (e.g., vancomycin) for their definitive therapy. Despite the early empiric use of antibiotics, the outcome of bacterial infections is poor unless the initial neutrophil count exceeds 500/μl, the count rises during treatment, or the pathogen is a gram-positive organism.

The appropriate duration of antimicrobial therapy of febrile neutropenic patients is uncertain. Many physicians continue antibiotics until neutropenia resolves. The empiric addition of amphotericin B therapy is indicated in the neutropenic patient who remains febrile for at least 1 week despite broad-spectrum antibiotics. In this setting, it often is best to continue broad-spectrum antibiotics for the duration of the neutropenia unless the cause of the fever can be clearly defined.

REFERENCES

Pizzo PA, Young LS: Limitations of current antimicrobial therapy in the immunosuppressed host: Looking at both sides of the coin. Am J Med 76:78, 1984.

Pizzo PA: The compromised host. *In* Wyngaarden JB, Smith LH Jr, Bennett JC (eds): Cecil Textbook of Medicine. 19th ed. Philadelphia, WB Saunders Co, 1992, pp 1573–1584.

110 INFECTIOUS DISEASES OF TRAVELERS; PROTOZOAL AND HELMINTHIC INFECTIONS

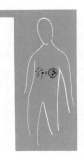

This chapter reviews the medical preparation of patients for overseas travel, some common clinical symptoms that may develop on return, and the diagnosis and treatment of common parasitic diseases endemic in the United States and abroad.

PREPARATION OF TRAVELERS

More than 10 million Americans travel to Third World countries each year. They often encounter health risks with which they and their doctors are unfamiliar. The Centers for Disease Control (CDC) publishes a book, *Health Information for International Travel*, which can be obtained from the United States Government Printing Office in Washington, DC (Telephone: 202-783-3238). This book provides general guidelines for travelers. Specific recommendations must be adjusted to specific locations within a country, as well as to the duration and type of travel anticipated.

The immunizations that are required by law and those that are medically indicated are generally separate issues; both must be addressed prior to departure. Most departments of health, travel agents, and foreign embassies concentrate on the legal requirements and neglect the relevant medical issues. Both legal requirements and health recommendations may change suddenly; thus, current information should always be obtained from well-informed travelers' clinics (available in a number of university-affiliated hospitals), from local health departments, or from the CDC. The American Committee on Clinical Tropical Medicine and Health (617-527-4003) maintains a list of qualified facilities in the United States and Canada.

In general, destinations within the United States, Japan, Canada, Western Europe, Australia, and New Zealand require no specific health precautions. In contrast, a 6-week backpacking trip through East Africa could demand six or seven different vaccinations given over 6 to 8 weeks, several prescription medications, and extensive education to prepare the novice traveler properly.

Immunizations

In general, only yellow fever and cholera vaccinations are required by law for international travel. On occasion, however, both polio and meningococcal meningitis vaccinations have been required during outbreak situations. Although not generally considered "travel" immunizations, many Americans have allowed routine diphtheria-tetanus immunizations to lapse or may not have been fully immunized against measles and polio in their youth. Finally, other immunizations are often strongly recommended, depending on the type and duration of travel.

Yellow Fever. This live attenuated virus vaccine is highly effective and recommended for travel to areas in South America and Africa where yellow fever is endemic. It is required by law for travel out of an area endemic for yellow fever and into many other developing countries. These requirements are published in the *Health Information for International Travel* book. Vaccination lasts for 10 years but must be given at a designated vaccination center (check with state health department).

Cholera. This vaccine is of very limited effectiveness, and cholera is not a common disease of tourists. Cholera has recently returned to South and Central America, where it has become a major concern to travelers. The vaccine available at present is not very effective and is therefore not currently recommended for travel into endemic areas. Health education on likely sources of transmission (e.g., food, water) is emphasized and is more effective in preventing disease than the current vaccine. Despite active discouragement by both the CDC and the World Health Organization (WHO), cholera vaccination is still a legal requirement for travel between some specific Third World countries. These requirements may change frequently; thus, up-to-date information is vital. Because of the uncertainty of international travel (e.g., unexpected transit into a neighboring country) and the uncertainty of obtaining sterile, disposable needles overseas, cholera vaccine is often given to protect primarily against unwanted needlesticks rather than the disease itself. Although this biological can be given by any physician, vaccination must be accompanied by an official stamp (check with local health department) to be legally valid.

Measles and Mumps. Up to 20 per cent of college freshman have no serologic evidence of prior measles or mumps infection or immunization and must be presumed to be susceptible. Individuals born after 1956 for measles, and 1970 for mumps, with no physician-documented record of immunization, are at greatest risk. In addition, a single immunization with measles vaccine at 15 months of age may permit breakthrough infection as a young adult. As a result, a second measles vaccine is now recommended for international travel for individuals who have never experienced the clinical illness. The same considerations apply to mumps, but this is not yet an official recommendation. All live virus vaccines should be given at least 2 weeks before gamma globulin administration.

Diphtheria-Tetanus. A booster within the past 5 years is recommended. This eliminates the need for a tetanus booster if the traveler sustains an injury overseas. This recommendation is made primarily because of the uncertainty of obtaining sterile, disposable needles in many overseas locations.

Polio. Most young adults have been immunized with at least 4 doses of trivalent oral polio vaccine (OPV); an additional booster dose is recommended for international travel. Many adults (>18 years of age) cannot remember, however, whether they received all serotypes of OPV; such individuals should be given inactivated polio vaccine (IPV). IPV should be boosted every 5 years for international travel.

Gamma Globulin. Most travelers from industrialized nations are susceptible to hepatitis A, which is the most common serious infectious disease contracted abroad. Published attack rates vary from 1 in 150 to 1 in 500 for a routine 2-week trip to most developing countries. Immune serum globulin (ISG) is effective in reducing the risk of hepatitis A in travelers without pre-existing antibody to the virus. For adults, 2 ml is given intramuscularly for trips of less than 2 months' duration, while 5 ml is of benefit for up to 4 to 6 months. ISG should not be given with, or prior to, immunizations with live attenuated virus vaccines. There is no evidence that ISG presently prepared in the United States can transmit any infectious disease or that ISG can passively transfer human immunodeficiency virus (HIV) antibody.

Meningococcal Meningitis. Vaccinations with the quadrivalent polysaccharide vaccine (A, C, Y, + W135) is recommended for travel to South Asia and for certain parts of sub-Saharan Africa (meningitis belt). As a result of several recent outbreaks resulting from religious pilgrimages to Saudi Arabia, this vaccine is also now currently recommended for travel to the Middle East and East Africa.

Typhoid. Adequate vaccination with the injectable vaccine takes time (2 injections 1 month apart for those without prior immunizations) and is associated with significant side effects (frequently a sore arm and a flu-like reaction), but it does provide partial protection. A new oral vaccine (4 enteric-coated capsules given over 7 days) is equally efficacious and has fewer side effects. Typhoid vaccination is always indicated for travelers with achlorhydria, immunosuppression, or sickle cell anemia and for those taking broad-spectrum antibiotics. Travelers to Mexico, South Asia, and sub-Saharan Africa for prolonged travel (>3 weeks) are at greatest risk of acquiring disease. Booster shots are given every 3 years with injectable typhoid vaccine; the oral vaccine lasts for 5 years.

Other Vaccines. Some travelers, including missionaries, physicians, and anthropologists, need special consideration. These individuals live for prolonged periods in developing countries or are at special risk for contracting certain highly contagious diseases. Consideration should be given to immunization with hepatitis B, Japanese B encephalitis, plague, rabies, and bacille Calmette-Guérin (BCG) vaccines. In general, such consultations should be referred to a qualified travelers' clinic.

Malaria Prophylaxis

Malaria prophylaxis is a major problem for international travelers because of the high prevalence of drug resistance by the malaria parasite. The need for, as well as the type of, prophylaxis is dependent upon the exact itinerary within a given country, since transmission risk is quite regional. For example, malaria transmission does not occur in most urban centers in Southeast Asia (e.g., Bangkok), but highly drug-resistant strains of *Plasmodium falciparum* may be encountered in the countryside. Recommended chemoprophylactic regimens have changed frequently within the past few years. Detailed information on malaria risk is contained in the annual *Health Information for International Travel* but must be updated frequently. In general, travelers to areas where chloroquine-sensitive *P. falciparum* strains are exclusively found (Central America, the Caribbean, North Africa, and the Middle East) should take chloroquine phosphate (300 mg base or 500 mg salt) weekly starting 2 weeks before, during, and for 6 weeks after leaving areas in which malaria is endemic. Travelers to areas where chloroquine-resistant *P. falciparum* is common should take mefloquine (Larium), 250 mg a week starting a week before travel, during travel, and for 4 weeks after. These areas currently include Southeast Asia, sub-Saharan Africa, South America, and South Asia. Mefloquine is contraindicated in individuals on certain cardiac medications or in those with a history of seizures or psychotic disorders. Alternative regimens include weekly chloroquine with back-up treatment for presumptive breakthrough malaria with 3 tablets of pyrimethamine-sulfadoxine (Fansidar). Daily doxycycline (100 mg) is another reasonable alternative. No antimalarial regimen is completely effective in Burma, rural Thailand, or some parts of East Africa, where mefloquine resistance is a growing problem. Because of these facts, more emphasis should be given to the use of netting, screens, and insect repellants as well as to the prompt diagnosis and treatment of any febrile episodes (temperature > 102°F [39°C]) overseas.

Traveler's Diarrhea

All travelers to developing countries should be informed about how to stay healthy. Between 20 and 50 per cent of individuals traveling to foreign countries will develop diarrhea during or shortly after their trip. The risk is highest when traveling to Latin

America, Africa, the Middle East, and South Asia. The average duration of an episode of traveler's diarrhea is 3 to 6 days. About 10 per cent of episodes last longer than 1 week. The diarrhea may be accompanied by abdominal cramping, nausea, headache, low-grade fever, vomiting, or bloating. Fewer than 5 per cent of persons will have fever greater than 101°F (38°C), bloody stools, or both. Travelers with these symptoms may not have simple traveler's diarrhea and should see a physician at once. Traveler's diarrhea is most frequently caused by toxigenic *Escherichia coli*.

Both mild and serious diarrheal illness (including cholera) can be avoided through care with food and water. All water should be presumed to be unsafe. The most common mistakes made by travelers are the use of ice, brushing teeth using tap water, or failure to check the seal on bottled water. Hot tea, coffee, carbonated beverages, beer, and wine are generally safe. Salads are often contaminated by protozoal cysts and, along with street vendor foods, are the most dangerous foods encountered by most travelers. Food should be well cooked, including meat, seafood, and vegetables. Milk is often unpasteurized; therefore, dairy products should be avoided.

Bismuth subsalicylate (Pepto-Bismol) can be used as a prophylactic measure (2 tablespoons 4 times a day) or used to treat acute bouts of diarrhea (1 oz every 30 minutes for 8 doses). Diphenoxylate (Lomotil) and loperamide (Imodium) may give some symptomatic relief of diarrhea but should be avoided if the diarrhea is severe, fever exists, or blood is present in the stool. Trimethoprim-sulfamethoxazole (Bactrim), doxycycline (Vibramycin), or one of the newer quinolones with or without concomitant use of loperamide can be taken orally for 3 to 5 days to treat episodes of diarrhea. These regimens dramatically reduce the duration of symptoms and are effective against a wide variety of bacterial pathogens, including most *Shigella* and *Salmonella* species. Prophylactic antibiotics are not generally recommended except for very short trips because of the emergence of resistant strains and the development of photosensitivity or other reactions to prophylactic medications.

General Health Information

Other potentially dangerous activities overseas include petting dogs and cats (rabies), swimming in fresh water (schistosomiasis), walking barefoot (hookworm or strongyloidiasis), and insect bites. In addition to malaria, many diseases, including dengue, sleeping sickness, and yellow fever, are transmitted by biting insects.

Special Problems

Children. In general, the same recommendations apply to children as adults, although the doses may change. A special problem is created by children 6 months to 1 year of age who have not yet received the measles, mumps, rubella (MMR) vaccine. These children risk significant mortality (5 to 15 per cent) if they develop measles, yet the vaccine is not 100 per cent effective when given to children under 1 year of age. If travel cannot be postponed, MMR should be given prior to travel but repeated at 18 months. Gamma globulin administered several weeks after the MMR may also provide some protection. Oral typhoid vaccine is not currently recommended for children less than 6. Careful consideration of toxicity and benefit is therefore needed in recommending the injectable vaccine.

Malaria prophylaxis is a particular problem in children because of the bitter taste of chloroquine. The dose is adjusted by weight (5 mg/kg base) and often can be mixed with honey (in children > 1 year of age) or chocolate syrup. Tetracyclines, often used in malaria chemoprophylaxis or for treatment of traveler's diarrhea, are contraindicated in young children. Mefloquine is not currently recommended for children weighing less than 30 lb (a reduced dose is used for older children). Oral rehydration therapy for diarrhea should be discussed with all parents of small children. Insect repellents containing high concentrations of DEET should not be used in small children, since their ingestion (e.g., hands in mouth) can cause seizures.

Infants. In general, small, breast-feeding infants (> 6 months of age) are partially protected by passive maternal antibodies and have a constant source of safe food (breast milk). Exceptions are infants of nonimmunized mothers who may be highly susceptible to diseases such as measles. Infants less than 2 weeks of age should not travel by air. Finally, if infants are fed powdered formula or given water, great care must be taken to sterilize the water by vigorously boiling for 10 minutes. Avoidance of insects in this age group is very important, since antimalarials are difficult to give to small infants and the consequences of acute malaria are severe.

Pregnant Women. Most vaccines are contraindicated in pregnant women and greatly complicate pretravel preparations. Chloroquine probably can be used safely. Travel to areas of chloroquine-resistant malaria is of great risk and should be strongly discouraged. No drug regimen to prevent or treat chloroquine-resistant malaria is safe in pregnancy, and malaria in a pregnant women is a medical emergency for both the mother and her fetus.

Acquired Immunodeficiency Syndrome (AIDS). Travelers and host countries are increasingly concerned about AIDS. Many countries, including the United States, now bar entry to AIDS patients. Several countries require human immunodeficiency virus (HIV) serologic testing for all travelers applying for more than a 3-month visa, which requires official documentation well in advance of travel. Patients with HIV infection need special preparation prior to travel to developing countries because of their increased susceptibility to certain illnesses (e.g., pneumococcal infection and tuberculosis) and a different cost-benefit ratio for vaccines and prophylactic drugs.

Most international travelers are concerned about the risk of acquiring AIDS while abroad. AIDS is acquired by the same high-risk activities associated with transmission in the United States (Chapter 108). Most legitimate concerns center on untested blood or nonsterile needles, which might be used in an emergency. Obviously, risk is greatest in any country that does not routinely use sterile disposable needles or routinely screen all blood prior to transfusion. In general, a few hospitals in almost all countries frequented by tourists now have sterile needles and screen their blood supply. Information in this regard is often available through United States embassies.

THE RETURNING TRAVELER

With the exception of skin testing for tuberculosis, asymptomatic returning travelers generally do not need screening tests. The clinical problems that most often arise in travelers soon after return are fever and diarrhea, while eosinophilia lasting weeks to months after return is the most common cause for later referral. Of the three, fever is most important, since delay in the diagnosis of *P. falciparum* malaria can be fatal. Fever should always prompt consideration of malaria until proved otherwise in travelers returning from countries where malaria is endemic, even if they are still taking prophylactic drugs. It is important to speciate the malaria with a thin and thick blood film, since this affects therapy. Chloroquine-sensitive *P. falciparum* is treated with 1 gm of chloroquine given orally, followed by 500 mg at 6, 24, and 48 hours. For *P. vivax* and *P. ovale* (also generally chloroquine-sensitive), this regimen is followed by primaquine daily for 14 days to eradicate hepatic forms. Resistant *P. falciparum* is treated with quinine sulfate, 650 mg given orally every 8 hours for 3 days, and tetracycline, 250 mg given orally every 6 hours for 10 days. Some patients may require longer treatments with quinine. All patients with suspected resistant infection should be hospitalized. In smear-negative cases in which clinical suspicion remains high, repeated smears every 8 to 12 hours should be obtained. If fever is not due to malaria, then tuberculosis, typhoid fever, hepatitis, and amebic liver abscess should be considered.

Traveler's diarrhea unresponsive to empiric antibiotics and persistent until the traveler returns home often represents giardiasis (treatment outlined below). Three stool specimens for ova and parasites, one stool examination for red blood cells and white blood cells, and a stool culture are usually warranted. Unfortunately, *Giardia lamblia* may be missed in up to one third of cases even after this work-up. If clinical suspicion is high, an empiric course of quinacrine (100 mg po tid × 10 days) is usually justified. Antibiotic-resistant bacteria, amebiasis, temporary lactose intolerance, and bacterial overgrowth should also be considered.

Eosinophilia in a returning traveler is less common and usually manifests weeks or months after travel. It is usually caused by any one of a variety of helminth infections. A stool specimen for ova and parasites is indicated but may be negative during the tissue-migrating phase of many intestinal worms or in tissue nematode infections, such as filariasis or onchocerciasis. Management of the more common parasitic infections encountered in travelers is included in the next section. Finally, it should be remembered that some diseases acquired abroad can take several years to manifest symptoms. When presenting with an unknown illness, all travelers should be advised to remind their doctor of past international travel.

PROTOZOAL AND HELMINTHIC INFECTIONS

Protozoal Infections in the United States
(Table 110–1)

Protozoal infections in the United States occur more frequently in selected patient populations and may be particularly severe in immunocompromised hosts. For example, giardiasis and amebiasis are common causes of diarrhea in homosexual men. Babesiosis is very severe in asplenic individuals, and *Toxoplasma* encephalitis primarily affects patients with AIDS. A few of these infections are discussed below.

Amebiasis and Giardiasis. Giardiasis is a common cause of persistent, nonbloody diarrhea in returning travelers. Although *Giardia lamblia* is prevalent throughout much of the developing world, travelers from St. Petersburg, Russia, have had consistently high attack rates, sometimes exceeding 50 per cent for large tour groups. Institutionalized patients and children in day care centers often have persistent problems with *Giardia* because of reinfection. Homosexual males also have a high prevalence of infection because of specific sexual practices. The diagnosis is generally made by identification of ova and/or trophozoites on stool examination (at least three stool specimens should be examined). The drug of choice for adults is quinacrine, 100 mg 3 times a day for 10 days, or metronidazole, 500 to 750 mg three times a day for 7 days.

Like *Giardia*, *Entamoeba histolytica* is transmitted via the fecal-oral route; the vast majority of infected individuals are asymptomatic. In contrast to *Giardia*, invasive extraintestinal illness can occur, and thus it is important to treat even asymptomatic individuals. When *Entamoeba histolytica* causes acute illness, it is generally manifested by bloody diarrhea. As with giardiasis, homosexual males have a high prevalence of cyst carriage. In the United States, amebic dysentery is occasionally misdiagnosed as ulcerative colitis or Crohn's disease. Stool examination for ova and parasites is generally diagnostic, but sigmoidoscopy may be required with either a touch preparation of the punctate ulcers or a biopsy. Serology is useful to rule out this diagnosis in patients considered to have inflammatory bowel disease. This is particularly true in individuals from industrialized countries, since the background serologic positivity is quite low in this population. Extraintestinal amebiasis generally presents as hepatic liver abscess (see Chapter 102). Diagnosis of these cases is supported by serology, since individuals may be stool-negative for the parasite at this point in the illness.

Protozoal Infections Common in Travelers and Immigrants (Table 110–1)

Malaria. Management of this parasitic infection is discussed above under "The Returning Traveler."

Leishmaniasis. Cutaneous and mucocutaneous leishmaniasis should be considered in any traveler returning from the Middle East who has a persistent skin or mucus membrane lesion. Diagnosis is made by tissue biopsy. Visceral leishmaniasis should be suspected in immigrants with fever and splenomegaly. Diagnosis is made by bone marrow biopsy and culture. Cutaneous leishmaniasis is generally self-limited. Other types are treated with Pentostam, 20 mg/kg/day for up to 20 days.

African Trypanosomiasis. In Africa, this protozoal infection causes sleeping sickness. Although only rarely imported into developed countries, it should be suspected in systemically ill patients from Africa. Many patients will remember a painful chancre at the site of an insect bite. Patients may have relapsing fever, adenopathy, headache, and a rash, particularly with the West African form. The East African form is more acute and, if unsuspected, may rapidly lead to coma and death. Diagnosis is made by direct examination of the blood, lymph aspirate, or cerebrospinal fluid. Treatment is not uniformly effective, demands the use of antimicrobials with considerable toxicity (e.g., suramin, pentamidine), and should be supervised by an expert in the field.

Chagas' Disease (American Trypanosomiasis). Trypanosoma cruzi is the most common cause of heart failure in South America, particularly Brazil. Transmission is through contact with feces from infected reduvid bugs (kissing bugs). Most cases are asymptomatic for decades and then manifest with cardiomegaly, megaesophagus, or megacolon. Diagnosis of acute disease is made by direct examination of the blood. Early diagnosis is critical, as patients may respond to nitrofuran or nitroimidazole derivatives. Unfortunately, unless inflammation is present at the site of inoculation (often the conjunctiva), individuals are usually asymptomatic at the acute stage. Chronic cases are suspected on the basis of serology, but background seropositivity is high in many endemic countries. Treatment of chronic Chagas' disease is largely supportive.

Helminthic Infections Common in the United States (Table 110–2)

Pinworms. Enterobiasis is common in the United States, particularly among children. Perianal pruritis is the major clinical presentation. Infection is maintained by fecal-oral contamination. Diagno-

TABLE 110–1. PROTOZOAL INFECTIONS

PROTOZOAN	SETTING	VECTORS	DIAGNOSIS	SPECIAL CONSIDERATIONS	TREATMENT
ENDEMIC IN U.S.					
Babesia microti	New England	Ixodid ticks, transfusions	Thick or thin blood smear	Severe disease in asplenic persons	Quinine and clindamycin
Giardia lamblia	Mountain states	Humans, ? small mammals	Microscopic exam or stool or duodenal fluid exam	Common in homosexual men, travelers, children in day care	Quinacrine or metronidazole
Toxoplasma gondii	Ubiquitous	Domestic cats, raw meat	Clinical; serologic confirmation	Pregnant women, immunosuppressed host (AIDS)	Pyrimethamine and sulfadiazine
Entamoeba histolytica	Southwest	Human	Microscopic exam of stool or "touch prep" from ulcer	Common in homosexual men, travelers, institutionalized persons	Metronidazole
Cryptosporidium sp.	Ubiquitous	Human	Acid-fast stain of stool	Severe in immunosuppressed hosts (AIDS)	None
Trichomonas vaginalis	Ubiquitous	Human	"Wet prep" of genital secretions	Common cause of vaginitis	Metronidazole
PRIMARILY SEEN IN TRAVELERS AND IMMIGRANTS					
Plasmodium sp.	Africa, Asia, South America	Anopheles mosquito	Thick or thin blood smear	Consider in returning travelers with fever	Dependent upon regional resistance pattern (see text)
Leishmania donovani	Middle East	Sandfly	Tissue biopsy	Consider in immigrants with fever and splenomegaly	Pentostam
Trypanosoma sp.	Africa, South America	Reduvid bugs, transfusion	Direct exam of blood or CSF	Very rare in travelers	Supportive

CSF = Cerebrospinal fluid; AIDS = acquired immunodeficiency syndrome.

sis is made by the application of cellophane tape to the anus and subsequent direct examination for ova. Treatment is with mebendazole, 100 mg given once. It is advisable to treat all family members, and repeated doses may be necessary.

Other Intestinal Nematodes. *Ascaris* (giant roundworm), *Ancylostoma duodenale* and *Necator americanus* (hookworm), and *Trichuris* (whipworms) are still endemic in the United States, particularly in the South. These infections are extremely common in immigrants and are ubiquitous in the developing world. Most individuals are asymptomatic. Ascariasis and hookworm may cause transient pulmonary infiltrates with eosinophilia during the tissue migratory phase of infection. Heavy *Ascaris* infection may cause intestinal, biliary, or pancreatic obstruction, but generally the patient is alerted to infection by the passage of a 6- to 8-inch-long dead adult worm. Hookworm infection can be associated with iron deficiency, whereas whipworm infection on occasion can cause rectal prolapse. Diagnosis is made on the basis of stool examination for ova and parasites. Each of these worms can be eradicated with appropriate antihelminthic therapy.

Helminth Infections Common in Travelers and Immigrants (Table 110–2)

Strongyloidosis. *S. stercoralis* is a common cause of eosinophilia in immigrants, particularly those from Southeast Asia. Infection can persist for years; many men who served in the Pacific theater during World War II still harbor active infections. Although usually asymptomatic, infection can cause diarrhea, abdominal pain, and malabsorption. This helminth can cause life-threatening disseminated infection in individuals immunosuppressed by cancer chemotherapy or steroids. Diagnosis may be made by stool examination, but this is not a very sensitive technique. Treatment with thiabendazole twice daily for 2 days is curative in more than 90 per cent of immunocompetent hosts.

Schistosomiasis. *Schistosoma mansoni* (Africa, South America, and the Caribbean), *Schistosoma japonicum* (Philippines, China, and Indonesia), and *Schistosoma mekongi* (Cambodia, Laos, and Viet Nam) are the most common causes of hepatosplenic enlargement in the world. Chronic infection can lead to an unusual form of periportal hepatic fibrosis, obstruction of portal blood flow, and bleeding esophageal varices. Unsuspected cases in the United States are often misdiagnosed as hepatitis B or alcohol-induced liver disease. A clue to the correct diagnosis is that the liver is enlarged, in contrast to the small, shrunken liver of alcoholic cirrhosis. *Schistosoma japonicum* can also cause seizures, which result from aberrant central nervous system migration of adult worms. *S. haematobium* (Africa) commonly causes hematuria and leads to urinary obstruction. Squamous cell carcinoma of the bladder is also a consequence of chronic infection. Diagnosis is made by examination of stool or urine for ova and parasites.

Lymphatic Filariasis. *Wuchereria bancrofti* and *Brugia malayi* cause elephantiasis throughout the tropics. Patients may present with acute lymphadenitis or asymptomatic eosinophilia. Occasional patients have pulmonary symptoms, infiltrates, and marked eosinophilia (tropical pulmonary eosinophilia). The diagnosis is made by finding microfilariae in blood specimens obtained at midnight. Treatment currently consists of a 3-week course of diethylcarbamazine (DEC), but this does not kill the adult worms.

Loa Loa. Eyeworm is endemic in West and Central Africa. Patients present with transient pruritic subcutaneous swellings. Eosinophilia is universal. In the United States, cases are often misdiagnosed for years as chronic urticaria. In rare patients, the adult worm can be visualized as it crosses the anterior chamber of the eye, giving this worm its common name. Diagnosis is generally suspected on clinical grounds and is confirmed by biopsy.

River Blindness. Infection with *Onchocerca volvulus* occurs in West and Central Africa as well as South and Central America. Although the most severe manifestations occur in the eye, the most common clinical presentation in the United States is recurrent pruritic dermatitis. The diagnosis can be made by direct examination of skin snips for microfilariae; a specific serologic test is also available. Ivermectin is the treatment of choice.

TABLE 110–2. HELMINTHIC INFECTIONS

HELMINTH	SETTING	VECTORS	DIAGNOSIS	TREATMENT
ENDEMIC IN U.S.				
Pinworm (enterobiasis)	Ubiquitous	Human	Direct exam for ova	Mebendazole, albendazole
Ascaris lumbricoides	Southeast	Human	Stool exam for ova	Mebendazole, albendazole
Trichuris trichiura	Southeast	Human	Stool exam for ova	Mebendazole, albendazole
Hookworm	Southeast	Human	Stool exam for ova	Mebendazole, albendazole
COMMON IN TRAVELERS AND IMMIGRANTS				
Strongyloides stercoralis	Developing world	Human	Stool exam for ova	Thiabendazole
Schistosoma sp.	Developing world	Snails	Stool exam for ova	Praziquantel
Wuchereria sp.	Asia	Mosquitos	Nocturnal blood exam	Diethylcarbamazine
Onchocerca volvulus	Africa, South and Central America	Blackfly	Biopsy	Ivermectin
Loa loa	Africa	Mosquitos	Blood exam, clinical setting	Diethylcarbamazine

Clonorchiasis. The Chinese liver fluke, *Clonorchis sinensis*, is important to diagnose in Asian immigrants. Symptoms may be confused with those of biliary tract disease. If untreated, infection can lead to cholangiocarcinoma. Praziquantel is curative.

Cysticercosis. The invasive larval form of pork tapeworm is the most common cause of seizures throughout the world, as well as in young adults in Los Angeles, chiefly immigrants from Mexico. Typically, patients present with new onset of seizures or severe headache. A single ring-enhancing lesion is the characteristic finding on computed tomographic (CT) scan. The diagnosis may be confirmed by an immunoblot assay using peripheral blood. Praziquantel is curative but may precipitate focal cerebral edema and seizures by killing other cysticercariae within the cerebrospinal fluid. In general, an expert should be consulted prior to treatment.

Intestinal Tapeworms. Three intestinal tapeworms commonly infect humans: *Taenia saginata* from raw beef, *Taenia solium* from raw pork, and *Diphyllobothrium latum* from raw fish. Most individuals are asymptomatic, but *T. solium* can cause invasive disease (cysticercosis) if ova of the adult worm are ingested by humans. *D. latum* is associated with vitamin B_{12} deficiency. All three are treated with niclosamide.

Hydatid Disease. This disease commonly manifests as a cystic liver mass in emigrants from sheep-raising parts of the world. Diagnosis is important, since rupture of the cyst can lead to dissemination.

Diagnosis is often suspected owing to the appearance of the cyst (calcified wall and dependent hydatid "sand") on abdominal CT scan. Serology can be helpful but is occasionally negative if the cyst has not leaked. Currently, primary therapy is the surgical removal of the cyst without spillage of its contents.

REFERENCES

Centers for Disease Control: Health Information for International Travel. U.S. Public Health Service, Department of Health and Human Services. Washington, DC, Government Printing Office. Updated on a weekly basis with the blue summary sheet.

General Recommendations on Immunizations. Guidelines from the Immunization Practices Advisory Committee. Ann Intern Med 111:133–142, 1989.

Jong EC (ed): The Travel and Tropical Medicine Manual. Philadelphia, WB Saunders Co, 1987.

Steffan R, Rickenbach M, Wilhelms U, et al: Health problems after travel to developing countries. J Infect Dis 156:84–91, 1987.

Warren KS, Mahmoud AAF (eds): Tropical and Geographical Medicine. 2nd ed. New York, McGraw-Hill Book Co, 1990.

Wilson ME, VonReyn F, Fineberg HV: Infections in HIV infected travelers: Risk and prevention. Ann Intern Med 114:482–492, 1991.

SECTION XIII

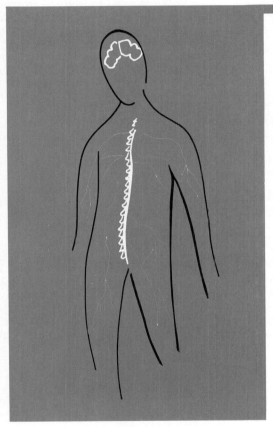

NEUROLOGIC DISEASES

111 EVALUATION OF THE PATIENT

Disorders of the nervous system cover a wide spectrum of etiologies. In the broadest sense, all symptoms of disease are neurologic, because the ability of the patient to recognize that he is ill requires (1) that sensory pathways carry information from the diseased organ to the brain and (2) that the brain interpret that information as a symptom of something wrong. Furthermore, the brain can extract from its memory symptoms identical to those it receives from the body's peripheral organs and sometimes interprets these cryptic inner perceptions as indicating bodily dysfunction (Table 111-1). For example, both emotionally generated anxiety and a catecholamine-secreting pheochromocytoma can cause headache, shortness of breath, and feelings of panic. It takes a perceptive physician both to distinguish the correct etiology and to guide the patient accordingly.

Diagnosing disorders of the nervous system places

TABLE 111-1. COMMON COMPLAINTS IN NEUROLOGIC PRACTICE

| | EXAMPLES | |
COMPLAINTS	STRUCTURAL	PHYSIOLOGIC OR PSYCHOPHYSIOLOGIC
Headache	Brain tumor	Migraine or tension
Backache	Herniated disc	Myofascial pain syndromes
Dizziness	Meniere's disease	Hyperventilation attacks, perceptual imbalance
Weakness and/or fatigue	Myasthenia gravis	"Neurasthenia"
Memory loss	Alzheimer's dementia	Depression, preoccupation
Episodic alterations of consciousness	Seizures, syncope	Anxiety, hyperventilation

TABLE 111-2. CRUCIAL STEPS IN NEUROLOGIC DIAGNOSIS

Does the patient have a nervous system disorder?
  Do psychological mechanisms play a role in the genesis of symptoms?
Where in the nervous system is the disorder?
  Central or peripheral, brain or spinal cord, left or right, single or multiple
What are the mechanisms (pathophysiology)?
  Structural or physiologic, vascular, neoplastic, inflammatory, etc.
What is the cause (etiology)?
  Specific tests

special requirements upon clinical skills. Systemic or psychiatric illnesses often produce symptoms that mimic those of nervous system disease (e.g., somewhat similar headaches may be caused by brain tumor, giant cell arteritis, and involutional depression). To minimize error the physician must systematically approach patients with potentially neurologic complaints and answer four fundamental questions, as outlined in Table 111-2.

The Neurologic History

The neurologic history in most respects is similar to the general medical history. Many neurologic diseases, however, are not accompanied by either abnormal physical or laboratory findings, so that the neurologic history often supplies a greater proportion of the diagnostically relevant information than does a medical history. Furthermore, because neurologic abnormalities affect such important functions as thinking, moving, and feeling, most patients will perceive that something is awry even before physical signs appear. Physical findings not previously recognized by the patient or his family are likely to be irrelevant or even misleading. By contrast, recent symptoms, such as mild weakness or alterations of sensation, often reflect disease even if the process is still too subtle to be detected by meticulous neurologic examinations. Because neurologic symptoms are so keenly sensed, a careful history often allows the examiner to localize the disease anatomically and to understand its pathophysiology even before he or she begins the physical examination.

Certain guidelines aid in taking complete and accurate histories:

Require Precision. Do not accept jargon or diagnoses from the patient. For example, a patient who complains of dizziness may mean vertigo (a vestibular symptom), lightheadedness (potentially caused by cardiovascular disease), syncope, ataxia, diplopia, or psychogenic dissociation—all of which have very different implications.

Both Listen and Ask. Elicit the history in the patient's own words and, whenever possible, without interruption. However, the physician must ask direct questions to encourage relevance, achieve precision, and place each symptom in its correct context. If the information is not volunteered, ask about the temporal profile of the complaint: was the onset abrupt or gradual? Is it static, progressive, waxing and waning, or improving? Inquire into the intensity and frequency of the symptoms and the events and the factors that precipitate or relieve them, and determine how the symptoms affect the patient's daily life.

Form Hypotheses. Do not be a passive recipient of the patient's story. Most patients supply excessive information, much not diagnostically pertinent. One must sift and distill the information in order to focus on what is relevant and weed out the irrelevant. Concurrently, one must form anatomic and/or pathophysiologic hypotheses about the nature of the symptoms and gradually refine them into etiologic terms as the history develops.

Hypotheses should favor illnesses that are *probable* (i.e., common diseases are more likely than rare diseases), *serious* (e.g., brain tumors should be excluded before diagnosing tension headache), *treatable* (e.g., combined systems disease and spinal cord meningioma should be ruled out before making a diagnosis of multiple sclerosis), and *novel* (some patients do have rare diseases, and these should not be forgotten).

Always Cover the Main Points of a Complete History. However justified the chief complaint appears to be, ensure that other physical or psychological disabilities are not playing a role. In particular, inquire about the patient's mood (e.g., is he/she depressed or suicidal?), his or her usual daily activities and whether the illness interferes with them, sexual function, and his/her own view of the illness and what effects it produces. Always ask about alcohol and drug intake, both prescription and recreational.

End by Summarizing. Summarize for the patient the history, asking if the summary is correct and if anything has been missed. Such a summary tends to reassure patients and offers a chance to supply information and to correct misunderstandings.

Obtain Further History from the Family and Friends. If the history appears incomplete, and particularly if part of the illness involves changes in mental state or consciousness, the family, friends, and colleagues should be asked to corroborate the story and to supply missing elements.

Gear the Neurologic Examination to Hypotheses Generated by the History. The hypotheses generated during the course of the history determine which of the nonroutine neurologic maneuvers the physician will carry out during the examination.

The Neurologic Examination

A screening neurologic examination, as outlined in Table 111–3, takes only a few minutes. More time may be required to evaluate areas that the history suggests may be disordered. The *level of arousal* must be noted: is the patient awake and alert, drowsy and lethargic, responsive only when externally stimulated (stuporous), or behaviorally unarousable, even to vigorous external stimulation (comatose)? The *mental state* can be examined during the history. Persons who give articulate and comprehensive histories with accurate attention to detail and dating of complaints almost always possess normal cognitive functions. Nevertheless, it is

TABLE 111–3. IMPORTANT ELEMENTS OF THE NEUROLOGIC EXAMINATION

Level of arousal
Mental status
   Orientation, mood, language, memory, intellect, thought
Station and gait
Cranial nerves
Motor system
   Strength, tone, muscle bulk, adventitious movements
Sensory system
   Pin, temperature, vibration, proprioception, object identification
Reflexes
   Deep tendon
   Abdominals
   Plantar
   Anal wink
Autonomic system
   Blood pressure
   Sphincter
Vascular system
   Carotid pulse and bruits; distal arteries

best to check (1) orientation, particularly for place and date, (2) short-term memory (the most vulnerable memory function) by asking the patient to repeat three unrelated words 5 minutes after he/she has heard them, and (3) capacity to abstract, by interpreting proverbs and by recognizing similarities and differences (boy-dwarf, apple-pear). Because anxiety can interfere with cognitive functions, one must be patient and reassuring. A formal quantitative screening examination such as the "mini mental status" examination (see Table 112–18) is useful for appraising and following a patient suspected of suffering cognitive dysfunction.

Observe the patient's *stance and walk.* A patient who can turn briskly, walk on heels and toes, do a deep-knee bend, and tandem walk has no substantial disability of motor or coordinative functions of the lower extremities.

Examine the *cranial nerves:* test visual acuity and visual fields in all patients and scrutinize the optic fundi for abnormalities of the blood vessels, retina, or optic disc. Quickly test pupillary activity, ocular movements, corneal reflexes, jaw movement, facial movement, hearing, swallowing, speaking, and breathing. Postural tests of labyrinthine function need not be administered in the absence of a history of dizziness or vertigo.

Assess *upper extremity* form, strength, and proprioception by having the patient extend the arms forward in a supinated position and spread the fingers. If, with the patient's eyes closed, neither arm drifts and there are no tremors or adventitious movements of the fingers, and if the patient can accurately touch his (or her) index finger in rapid succession to his (or her) nose and the examiner's outstretched finger, it is likely that, in the absence of complaints, no neurologic abnormalities affect the upper extremities. If complaints of weakness or sensory loss exist, test the affected areas individually.

Any significant sensory loss of the extremities will almost certainly have been described by the sentient patient during the history and demands careful sensory testing of each dermatome and peripheral

---

TABLE 111–4. CONSIDERATIONS FOR PERFORMING A LUMBAR PUNCTURE (LP)

Indications for Test

Absolute (before brain imaging)
  Suspicion of acute CNS infection unaccompanied by primary neurologic signs and symptoms
  Before anticoagulant therapy for cerebrovascular disease (if no image available)
Relative (following brain imaging)
  Increased intracranial pressure suspected, CT or MR normal
  Suspicion of cryptic nervous system disease
  Intrathecal therapy for meningeal leukemia or fungal meningitis
  Symptomatic treatment of severe headache from subarachnoid hemorrhage or pseudotumor cerebri

Contraindications to Test

Absolute
  Tissue infection in region of puncture site
Relative
  Spinal cord or brain tumor known or probable
  Bleeding tendency (anticoagulant or thrombocytopenia)
  Increased intracranial pressure due to mass lesions

Diagnostic Evaluation of CSF

Sediment
  Cell count and differential; cytologic examination for neoplastic cells; stains for bacteria and fungi; culture for organisms
Supernatant Fluid (essential)
  Protein concentration; polymerase chain reaction (PCR) for tuberculosis, spirochetal disease; protein electrophoresis (gamma globulin, oligoclonal bands); glucose concentration; serologic tests for syphilis; when indicated: viral antibodies and cultures; spectrophotometric test for bilirubin, oxyhemoglobin, or methemoglobin

Complications of Test

Common: headache, backache
Rare: transtentorial or foramen magnum herniation; worsening of spinal tumor symptoms; spinal epidural hematoma (in patients with bleeding tendency); herniated or infected disc; reaction to anesthetic agent; meningitis (contaminated needle)

TABLE 111–5. TISSUE ANALYSIS FOR NEUROLOGIC DIAGNOSIS

TISSUE	INDICATION(S)	COMMENT
Muscle	Weakness suggesting myopathy (helps distinguish specific myopathies from neuropathy)	Histochemical and enzyme analyses require special laboratory processing
Peripheral nerve (usually sural)	Polyneuropathy (helps distinguish demyelination from axonal neuropathy)	Should be performed only at specialized centers; has low diagnostic yield
Brain	Tumors (for specific diagnosis) Occasionally for puzzling infections, vasculitides, some dementias	Not indicated for viral encephalitis unless antiviral therapy fails

nerve in the area of complaint. Screen *deep tendon reflexes* by testing at biceps, triceps, brachioradialis, knees, and ankles. Test the plantar responses, recalling that equivocal Babinski signs usually are not abnormal. *Autonomic activity* and *sphincter functions* are usually estimated from the history. Careful assessment of sphincter tone, voluntary sphincter contraction, the anal wink reflex, and perianal sensation are essential if complaints of urinary-fecal incontinence or recent impotence exist. Always test for postural hypotension when evaluating autonomic impairment or dizziness. The carotid arteries, the aorta, and peripheral pulses should be palpated and auscultated for evidence of vascular disease.

Do not be misled by equivocal neurologic signs. In office practice, many anxious patients hyperdiscriminate and interpret mild changes in pin prick or vibratory perception as important. When persons complain of sensory disturbance, ask them to map its distribution before examining them.

DIAGNOSTIC TESTS: SCOPE AND LIMITATIONS

Technology has remarkably increased the accuracy of neurologic diagnosis but, if overused, needlessly raises the cost of medical care. Before ordering, the judicious physician must consider the precise advantages conferred by each positive or negative test.

Tissue Analysis

Lumbar Puncture (LP). Performed with proper indications, this safe and simple technique indirectly assesses biochemical abnormalities in the extracellular fluid of the central nervous system (CNS). Because headache and backache can follow an LP, the procedure should be reserved for specific indications (Table 111–4). The test is mandatory and usually diagnostic for leptomeningeal infection or cancer. The test also establishes the diagnosis (in the presence of a normal computed tomographic [CT] scan) of pseudotumor cerebri (p. 859) or idiopathic intracranial hypotension (p. 860). The total protein concentration gives nonspecific information about the presence of nervous system disease and assists in the diagnosis of polyneuropathies. Protein electrophoresis may assist in the diagnosis of multiple sclerosis, paraprotein abnormalities, and other inflammatory diseases of the nervous system. Patients should not receive anticoagulants for a presumed stroke unless an LP or a brain image has ruled out intracranial hemorrhage. LP should not be performed in patients with suspected intracranial mass lesions until after a brain scan has been obtained and diagnostic uncertainty remains. The tests in Table 111–4 are most commonly ordered. Small needles and technically smooth punctures are the best ways to reduce the risk of post-LP headache.

Tissue Biopsy. Diagnostic biopsies of muscle, less often of peripheral nerve or brain, should be used sparingly, but when indicated sometimes can give data achievable in no other way (Table 111–5).

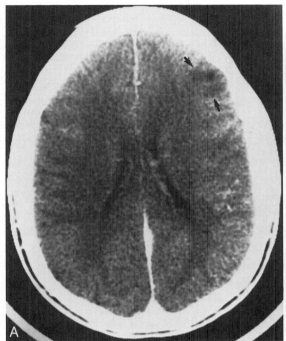
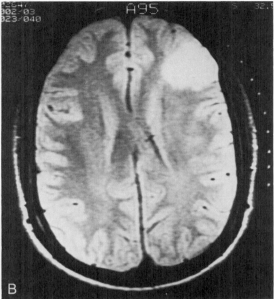

FIGURE 111-1. Comparison of imaging techniques in a patient suffering from a low-grade glioma of the left frontal lobe. The computed tomography (CT) scan (*A*) was taken after an injection of double the standard dose of contrast material. It shows only a vague area of hypodensity in the frontal lobe (*arrows*). Magnetic resonance (MR) scan (*B*) taken at the same level within a few days of the CT scan reveals a large area of hyperdensity caused by the altered proton density of the low-grade tumor. A biopsy revealed a low-grade glioma. The patient had suffered a single generalized convulsion and had no other neurologic signs or symptoms.

Imaging Techniques (Fig. 111-1)

Modern techniques of imaging (magnetic resonance [MR] and CT) identify most structural diseases of the brain and spinal cord. A negative test often reassures the patient (and his physician) that no serious structural disease is present. However, the tests are expensive, seldom diagnose metabolic or inflammatory disorders, and should not substitute for clinical judgment.

MR is available in many centers and its technical advantages make it superior to CT scanning as the imaging technique of the future (Table 111-6). MR is unaffected by bone and usually does not require the injection of contrast material. The technique gives excellent tissue delineation and modern machines possess a 2-mm resolution. Furthermore, images can be procured in any plane, whereas CT images are limited to horizontal and coronal planes. MR also has better resolution than CT and frequently reveals lesions, including tumors, arteriovenous anomalies, and areas of demyelination, that CT scanning fails to detect. No irradiation is involved.

Myelography. MR has largely replaced plain radiographs and myelograms in diagnosing problems involving the spine and spinal cord. Occasionally, to obtain finer definition of spinal root lesions, for example, myelography is performed in conjunction with CT scanning. Water-soluble contrast material is run up and down the spinal canal and visualized fluoroscopically, after which CT images are obtained. The test is particularly valuable for identifying herniated discs as well as compression of the spinal cord, cauda equina, or nerve roots.

Angiography. The blood vessels of the brain and spinal cord can be visualized either by injection of contrast material directly into an artery or by the injection of a larger amount of contrast material intravenously, with the images enhanced by computerized subtraction techniques. These approaches generally are reserved for specialized radiologic centers. New computer programs are likely to enable MR to replace arteriography for many diagnostic indications.

TABLE 111-6. MR VERSUS CT IN NEUROLOGIC DIAGNOSIS

Advantages of MR
    No bone artifact on images
    Gadolinium contrast agent safer than iodine
    Resolution (1-2 mm) and tissue discrimination generally better
    Parasagittal planes of section available
Disadvantages of MR
    Contraindicated with cardiac pacemakers; metal intracranial clips
    Difficult for critically ill patients
    Engenders claustrophobia

TABLE 111–7. NONINVASIVE ELECTRICAL STUDIES OF THE NERVOUS SYSTEM

TEST	SOME INDICATIONS	COMMENT
Electroencephalogram (EEG)	Any brain dysfunction, especially epilepsy	Sensitive but not specific; inexpensive
Visual evoked potentials (VER)	Tests integrity of optic nerve and cerebral visual pathway	Sensitive for asymptomatic optic neuritis, e.g., from multiple sclerosis
Brain stem auditory evoked potentials (BAER)	Tests integrity of auditory pathways	Sensitive for acoustic nerve tumors and brain stem disease
Somatosensory evoked potentials (SEP)	Tests integrity of central sensory pathways	Sensitive for spinal cord and lower brain stem disease
Nerve conduction velocity (see Table 111–8)	Tests rate of conduction in peripheral nerve	Distinguishes demyelination from axonal disease; sometimes establishes site of nerve compression
Neuromuscular transmission studies	Myasthenia gravis, Lambert-Eaton syndrome, botulism	Noninvasive but unpleasant
Electromyogram (EMG)	Identifies denervated areas of muscle, detects reduced muscle action, identifies myopathic changes	Helps identify lower motor neuron disorders, nerve root compression, etc.; helps distinguish neurogenic from myopathic disorders

Electrodiagnostic Studies (Table 111–7)

Electrodiagnostic tests can be extremely useful in the differential diagnosis of neurologic disease, but they do not substitute for a clinical formulation derived from a careful history and neurologic examination. The tests are expensive, some are uncomfortable, and, all too often, the results mislead the physician who places more faith in a laboratory report than in his or her clinical judgment. Electrodiagnostic tests should be ordered to answer specific questions concerning the history and examination in a given patient. They should be interpreted only in light of that patient's history and neurologic findings.

Electroencephalography (EEG). EEG records the electrical activity of the cerebral cortex (Fig. 111–2). It is particularly helpful in the differential diagnosis of seizures, especially if an attack occurs spontaneously or can be evoked during the recording process. It also helps differentiate seizures from metabolic encephalopathy, and it aids in distinguishing between organic and psychogenic causes of unresponsiveness. The absence of EEG activity, properly recorded, supports the diagnosis of brain death.

Nerve Conduction Studies (Table 111–8). Percutaneous electrical stimulation of a peripheral nerve generates an action potential. For motor nerves, electrodes are placed over a muscle to record the evoked muscle action potential. One stimulates the nerve innervating that muscle at various points along its length and determines the conduction velocity from the time required to travel from each site of stimulation to the onset of the evoked muscle response. For sensory nerves, one stimulates cutaneous nerve branches distally and places recording electrodes over the nerve at various proximal sites. These peripheral nerve and muscle electrophysiologic studies assist in determining whether disease involves nerve, muscle, or

TABLE 111–8. TYPICAL ELECTROPHYSIOLOGIC FEATURES OF NEUROPATHIES AND MYOPATHIES

	NERVE CONDUCTION VELOCITY	F-RESPONSE	H-REFLEX	ELECTROMYOGRAPHY
Inflammatory myopathy or dystrophy	Normal	Normal	Normal	Fibrillations; positive sharp waves; small motor units
Metabolic myopathy	Normal	Normal	Normal	Small motor units
Axonal neuropathy	Normal	Normal	Normal	Fibrillations; positive sharp waves; fasciculations; large motor units with distal predominance
Demyelinating neuropathy	Slowed diffusely	Delayed or absent diffusely	Delayed or absent	Normal motor units
Radiculopathy	Normal	Delayed or absent in damaged root	Delayed or absent if S1 is involved	Fibrillations; positive sharp waves; fasciculations; large motor units if chronic
Motoneuron disease	Normal	Normal	Normal	Fibrillations; positive sharp waves; fasciculations; large motor units diffusely

From Victor JD: Neurologic diagnostic procedures. In Wyngaarden JB, Smith LH Jr, Bennett JC (eds): Cecil Textbook of Medicine. 19th ed. Philadelphia, WB Saunders Co, 1992, p 2038.

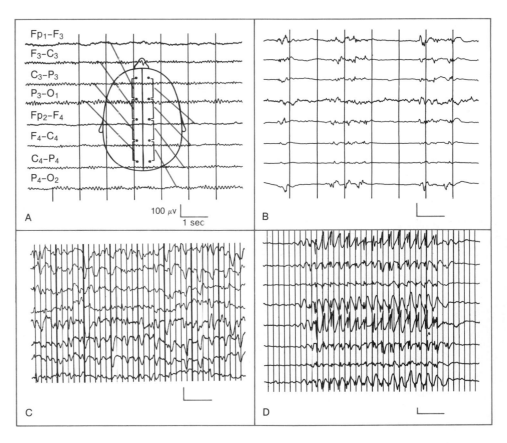

FIGURE 111-2. Normal and abnormal electroencephalograms (EEGs). *A,* The EEG of a normal alert adult. *B,* Burst-suppression, a pattern seen in severe cerebral dysfunction. *C,* Triphasic slow waves, seen in metabolic encephalopathies. *D,* A brief spike-and-wave seizure. In each record, the top four tracings are from parasagittal left-sided bipolar electrode placements (Fp_1–F_3, F_3–C_3, C_3–P_3, P_3–O_1); the lower four tracings are from the corresponding right-sided placements (Fp_2–F_4, F_4–C_4, C_4–P_4, P_4–O_2). The scale represents 1 sec and 100 μV. Note the reduced vertical scale in *D.* (From Victor JD: Neurologic diagnostic procedures. *In* Wyngaarden JB, Smith LH Jr, Bennett JC [eds]: Cecil Textbook of Medicine. 19th ed. Philadelphia, WB Saunders Co, 1992, p 2036.)

both and in determining the distribution of the abnormality. They facilitate the differentiation of demyelinating neuropathy from axonal neuropathy, neuropathy from radiculopathy, and primary muscle disease from disease of the motor unit. Demyelinating neuropathies affect mainly large fibers and slow the conduction velocity. When disease damages axons in addition to myelin, there is a decrease in the number of axons that can be electrically activated, resulting in a diminution in the size of the compound action potential.

Electromyography (EMG) (Tables 111–7 and 111–8). EMG is performed by inserting a needle electrode into a muscle to record the structure's electrical activity. Normal muscle is silent at rest, but denervated or diseased muscle membranes become spontaneously excitable, generating *fibrillation potentials* of small amplitude. When the nerve or motor neuron is diseased, entire motor units may become spontaneously active. The resulting *fasciculations* are often visible and can be detected by the electrode. Furthermore, when damaged axons cease to innervate muscle fibers, the remaining axons gradually sprout collaterals that reinnervate the denervated fibers; as a result, during voluntary contraction the few remaining muscle units show a decrease in their number and an increase in the size of their electrical potentials. When the patient voluntarily contracts the muscle being examined, action potentials appear and with full voluntary contrac-

tion cannot be distinguished one from the other (interference pattern). With neurogenic weakness, the interference pattern is reduced or disappears because of the paucity of voluntary action potentials. By contrast, in primary disease of muscle, the size of motor units decreases as muscle fibers degenerate because each nerve now innervates fewer fibers. During voluntary contraction the number of activated units remains normal, but their amplitude declines; the interference pattern remains normal. In primary myopathies, the distribution of abnormality helps in characterizing the myopathy itself. Table 111–8 provides guides to the usefulness and pertinent changes in electrophysiologic tests in various neuromuscular disorders. The EMG must be interpreted in light of the clinical findings, because occasional fibrillation potentials may be found in normals. Also, myopathies and neuropathies sometimes produce confusingly similar changes.

Neuromuscular Transmission Studies. Diseases of the neuromuscular junction (p. 815) are characterized by normal nerve conduction velocity and usually a normal EMG. Repetitive electrical activation of the neuromuscular junction, however, produces either an abnormal diminution (myasthenia gravis) or an abnormal facilitation (Lambert-Eaton pseudomyasthenia, botulism) of the successively evoked muscle action potential.

Evoked Potentials. External stimuli evoke changes in electrical activity of the brain. Using a signal-averaging technique, scalp recordings can often identify these stimuli. Clinically useful tests include visual evoked potentials (VEPs), brain stem auditory evoked potentials (BAEPs), and somatosensory evoked potentials (SEPs). VEPs can identify abnormalities of central response time in one or both eyes even when visual acuity is normal. They are particularly useful for identifying unsuspected optic nerve and brain abnormalities in patients with clinical signs of brain stem and spinal cord disease (e.g., multiple sclerosis). BAEPs, elicited by brief clicks presented to one ear, identify abnormalities of the acoustic nerve and its brain stem pathways. Abnormalities are associated with lesions in the cerebellopontine angle and the brain stem. This test is particularly useful in identifying hearing abnormalities in infants. SEPs are used to identify compressive, demyelinating, or metabolic disturbances affecting central sensory pathways, particularly in the spinal cord. A new technique of magnetically stimulating the brain and recording evoked motor potentials in the extremities may have clinical value in the future.

Positron Emission Tomography (PET). PET is an isotopic CT method for imaging focal cerebral blood flow and metabolism. Although resolution is poorer than with MR scan, the technique's ability to measure metabolic rate (e.g., glucose) helps differentiate low-grade from high-grade brain tumors and helps distinguish radiation damage from recurrent brain tumors in treated patients.

Thermography. Thermography is a method of measuring temperature of the extremities. The concept is that differences in temperature result from dysfunction of autonomic nerves to the extremities and can identify root and peripheral nerve disease. The test has poor sensitivity and specificity and is inferior to electrodiagnostic techniques.

REFERENCES

Adams RD, Victor M: Principles of Neurology. 4th ed. New York, McGraw-Hill Book Co, 1989.

Bradley WG, Daroff RB, Fenichel GM, Marsden CD: Neurology in Clinical Practice. 2 vols. Boston, Butterworth-Heinemann, 1989.

DeYoung RN, Haerer AF: Case taking and the neurological examination. In Joynt RJ (ed): Clinical Neurology, Vol 1. Rev ed. Philadelphia, JB Lippincott Co, 1991.

Landau WM: Strategy, tactics and accuracy in neurological evaluation. Ann Neurol 27:86, 1990.

Mayo Clinic and Mayo Foundation: Clinical Examinations in Neurology. 6th ed. Philadelphia, WB Saunders Co, 1991.

Rowland LP (ed): Merritt's Textbook of Neurology. 8th ed. Philadelphia, Lea & Febiger, 1989.

112 DISORDERS OF CONSCIOUSNESS AND HIGHER BRAIN FUNCTION

The human conscious state expresses the interaction of two major neurologic functions: one, the level of arousal, and the other, the mental content and expressed behavior of the awakened state. Arousal, i.e., the recurrent cycling of wakefulness from sleep, expresses a normal, phylogenetically primitive activity regulated by nuclear structures contained within the reticular core of the brain stem that extends from the level of the rostral pons forward to the ventromedian hypothalamus. Mental content and learned behavior, by contrast, express the workings of much more complicated brain mechanisms that require arousal for their expression and represent the functional product of many millions of interacting nerve and supporting cells located in the gray matter of the cerebral hemispheres, with their directly related subcortical nuclei.

This chapter discusses changes in consciousness from several aspects. It first addresses problems related to normal sleep and the frequent but seldom incapacitating disorders that affect that state. The chapter then discusses a variety of pathologic alterations of the conscious state that pose more serious threats to the brain and the integrity of the individual.

A. Sleep and Its Disorders

Sleep represents a rhythmically recurring, active physiologic state regulated by brain stem autonomic mechanisms. Both the pattern and the necessary amount of sleep vary widely from person to person.

Some healthy persons sleep as little as 4 to 5 hours per day, whereas others seem unable to function with less than 9 or 10 hours. Moderate exercise reduces the latent period required to fall asleep and generally increases the depth and somewhat the length of sleep as well. Anxiety, preoccupation, depression, drugs such as caffeine, and somatic conditions such as fever, pain, and cardiopulmonary disease all contribute to subjective difficulties in sleeping. Distressing insomnia or hyposomnia can have several aspects. Older persons generally sleep with less satisfaction than do younger ones. Some insomniacs complain of an increased latent period before sleep occurs, whereas others report middle-of-the-night or early-morning awakenings. Although subjectively distressing, such common variations produce little or no physiologic harm. Scientific observations of patients with hyposomnia find that periods of sleep almost always are longer than the subject believes; what the subject remembers is the awakenings. Severe insomnia, e.g., a reduction of total sleep to 3 to 4 hours or less per day, whatever the cause, does appear to reduce mental efficiency.

Insomnia of recent origin is best handled by reassurance, with efforts directed toward correcting underlying medical or psychological problems and, if necessary, the parsimonious prescribing of mild sedatives. Such cautious approaches may fail to please all patients, but the realities are that most chronic insomnia is extremely difficult to treat effectively because almost all soporifics sooner or later induce tolerance. Acute insomnia due to intercurrent illness, acute physical or emotional pain, jet lag, and the like is best treated in otherwise healthy persons with small doses (e.g., 0.125 mg or less) of the short-acting benzodiazepine triazolam at bedtime. Milder agents such as benadryl, chloral hydrate, or flurazepam may be preferable for elderly patients or those with fever or systemic illness. Tricyclic antidepressants, with the entire dose taken at bedtime, help in the management of the insomnia of depression. Alcohol, although widely employed, is a poor choice of sedative; it shortens the sleep latency interval but tends to shorten the duration of sleep and to produce unpleasant hangovers. Tolerance often occurs, resulting in patients' taking increasing doses to achieve effect.

Hypersomnia of recent onset can reflect overwhelming fatigue or psychological depression. In all other instances one should regard it as possibly reflecting serious neurologic disease. Chronic or recurrent hypersomnia is a symptom most often of narcolepsy or of one of the sleep apnea syndromes described on page 170.

Narcolepsy is a chronic disorder of unknown cause characterized by recurrent brief episodes of uncontrollable drowsiness. The disorder usually starts in the late teens or early 20s, accompanied by one or more of the following experiences: (1) sleep attacks consisting of sudden, uncontrollable, and inappropriately timed episodes of rapid eye movement sleep that interrupt normally scheduled wakefulness; (2) cataplexy, a phenomenon of abrupt muscular hypotonia precipitated by surprise or emotion; (3) hypnagogic hallucinations, intense dreamlike experiences accompanying the twilight zone between sleep and wakefulness; (4) sleep paralysis, an overwhelming sense that one cannot move, occurring during the moments of awakening from sleep. All these features may be experienced to some degree by normal persons, but in narcolepsy the symptoms intensify to the point of disrupting social and vocational occupations or producing dangerous situations such as drowsy driving. The predisposition to narcolepsy appears to be inherited as an autosomal dominant trait, with most narcoleptics possessing the human leukocyte antigen HLA-DR2. The clinical expression varies considerably, and its underlying cause is unknown. Medications are of limited value, although therapy with methylphenidate helps some sufferers. In intractable cases, symptomatic treatment with monoamine oxidase inhibitors or other amphetamine congeners occasionally brings relief.

The *Klein-Levin syndrome* is a rare disease of adolescent boys and young men marked by episodic periods of hypersomnia and hyperphagia lasting days to weeks. The condition usually subsides in adulthood.

Sleep disturbances that can occur in otherwise normal persons include enuresis (bedwetting), night terrors, nightmares, sleep walking, and sleep talking. All of these conditions affect more children than adults. Efforts to establish consistent psychiatric correlations have been unsuccessful. Although tension, anxiety, or other psychological problems may accentuate the tendencies, they are probably not the cause. Imipramine, 25 to 50 mg at bedtime, helps some cases of enuresis. Several of the other disorders improve with the taking of short-acting benzodiazepines at bedtime. Most of the conditions subside during late adolescence or adulthood. The potentially serious sleep apnea syndromes are discussed on page 170.

REFERENCE

Kales A: Sleep and its disorders. *In* Wyngaarden JB, Smith LH Jr, Bennett JC (eds): Cecil Textbook of Medicine. 19th ed. Philadelphia, WB Saunders Co, 1992, pp 2063–2067.

B. Pathologic Alterations of Consciousness

This topic includes abnormalities of arousal or of the cognitive content of the aroused state, or the two combined. Abnormal arousal states discussed first in this chapter, fall into two large categories — sustained and brief. Table 112–1 defines the most common, sustained alterations of consciousness encountered in the medical setting. States of brief loss of consciousness are listed later in Table 112–12.

TABLE 112–1. CONSCIOUSNESS AND ITS ALTERATIONS: DEFINITIONS

Consciousness. The awake state of awareness of self and environment, judged externally by evidence of the individual's capacity to express learned and anticipatory behavior.

Coma. An eyes-closed state of unarousable behavior in which patients lack any recognizable evidence of learned responses to internal or external stimulation.

Stupor. A state of psychological unresponsiveness that can be interrupted only by vigorous and sustained external stimulation.

Hypersomnia. Sleep behavior that consistently exceeds the subject's norm by 25 to 30% or more. Most pathologic hypersomnia is accompanied by a degree of delirium or reduced intellectual capacity.

Delirium. An acute or subacute state characterized by a transient, confused reduction in the clarity of awareness of the environment. Symptoms include poor memory, at least partial disorientation, misperceptions, poor judgment, and delusions. Prolonged confusional states may be difficult to distinguish from the early stages of chronic dementia. Agitated or severe forms of delirium can accompany toxic or infectious illnesses. Affected patients become boisterous and restless; many suffer hallucinations, usually of a visual nature. A dreamlike state characterized by a loss of self-recognition can occur, as can reversals of sleep-wake cycles, accompanied by episodic insomnia or hypersomnia.

Vegetative state. A condition of severe brain damage in which sleep-wake cycles remain or recover but all cognitive activity, including self-awareness, is lost. Relatively normal autonomic thermal control, chewing, swallowing, breathing, and circulatory regulation remain. Behavioral responses consist of no more than primitive motor reflexes or instinctive emotional patterns of agitation or crying.

Locked-in state. An uncommon condition in which severe damage to central or peripheral motor pathways prevents all communication. Sufficient oculomotor activity may be spared to permit coded signaling in response to questions or inner needs. Affected patients retain self-aware consciousness but cannot express it because of paralysis of communication. Either bilateral interruption of the corticospinal tracts in the brain stem or severe motor polyneuropathy can cause the condition. Comparable but less prolonged experiences affect conscious patients who are intubated for life-support ventilation.

Brain death. The permanent loss of all essential brain functions, despite the continued activity of artificially supported heart, lungs, and other viscera. Brain death has been accepted as representing death of the person in most of the United States as well as Western Europe. Table 112–2 provides diagnostic criteria.

SUSTAINED IMPAIRMENTS OF CONSCIOUSNESS

Sustained impairments of consciousness are defined as lasting for a matter of hours to indefinitely. Primary, sustained disturbances of arousal include stupor and coma. Organically caused, acutely occurring, sustained but reversible abnormalities of the content of consciousness are termed *delirium* or *metabolic encephalopathy*; impaired arousal and attention accompany most instances of the latter as well. Sustained disturbances of consciousness are caused by either (1) pathologic interruptions of the upper brain stem arousal mechanisms or (2) global-diffuse organic impairments of cerebral regions regulating mental and behavioral function or both in combination. Restricted, focal psychological impairments such as aphasia, selective perceptual loss, or specific learning deficits are described in a later part

of the chapter, as are the permanent declines in cognitive function called dementia.

Mechanisms of Coma and Approach to Diagnosis

Mechanisms

Disorders that can damage the brain so extensively or strategically as to interrupt consciousness fall into three general categories (Table 112–3): (1) supratentorial mass lesions such as neoplasms or hemorrhages that either (a) directly invade or destroy the posterior ventromedial diencephalon or (b) enlarge so as to compress these basal diencephalic areas or herniate them through the tentorial notch; (2) structural subtentorial lesions that bilaterally damage or destroy the midbrain–upper pontine activating-arousal systems; (3) diffuse metabolic or multifocal structural abnormalities that simultaneously or in close succession cause widespread, severe cerebral hemispheric dysfunction. These latter conditions can depress arousal mechanisms either directly or by abruptly removing their normal feedback stimulation from the cerebral cortex. Many of these diffuse or multifocal conditions have chemical rather than structural causes. Such nonstructural illnesses may produce no abnormalities on brain imaging and often create an intellectual challenge in diagnosis and management.

Approach to the Unconscious Patient

Once the history is obtained, physical and laboratory tests provide crucial clues. An evaluation of motor and neuro-ophthalmologic signs plus an appraisal of the breathing pattern often yields the most useful clinical information in reaching a provisional diagnosis. Brain imaging abets clinical localization and reveals most mass or destructive lesions. Systematic studies of blood, urine, cerebrospinal fluid (CSF), and other tissues offer specific indications of the causes of many of the metabolic encephalopathies. The following paragraphs amplify these principles.

Supratentorial Mass Lesions (Fig. 112–1). The most frequent supratentorial causes of acutely or subacutely altered consciousness consist of expanding hemispheric masses that squeeze the surrounding cerebrum, shifting it either downward to displace the diencephalon against the midbrain or down and laterally to compress the temporal lobe against the thalamus and midbrain.

According to their anatomic locations in the cerebrum, most supratentorial masses cause signs of focal cerebral dysfunction before they produce discernible changes in consciousness (Table 112–4). The initial clinical signs may be behavioral-psychological or can consist of sensorimotor abnormalities on the opposite side of the body. As such cerebral masses grow in size, they compress against the thalamus and hypothalamus, causing reduced arousal and bilateral abnormal motor signs. Brain stem–controlled pupillary reflexes, conjugate eye movements, and oculovestibular responses remain largely or completely spared in early supratentorial coma. Unless the progressive diencephalic compression is halted, however, the process proceeds to transtentorial herniation, described below.

Primary destructive or invasive lesions of the posterior paramedian thalamus are a well-established but proportionately unusual supratentorial cause of stupor and coma. The area can be selectively damaged by stroke secondary to rostral basilar artery occlusion; by neoplasms, particularly primary lymphomas; by granulomas such as those of sarcoid, or by acute encephalitis. With any of these conditions the chief clinical manifestation usually consists of gradually or acutely progressing hypersomnia, sometimes with nearly unarousable sleep lasting most of the 24-hour day. Specific diagnosis depends on other signs of thalamic or brain stem dysfunction plus information gained from imaging studies and, less often, CSF analysis.

Herniation Syndromes. Transtentorial herniation can occur in either a downward or an upward direction. Downward herniation can take two forms (Table 112–5). *Central compression-herniation* compresses and eventually displaces the midline diencephalon caudally toward and through the tentorial notch against the midbrain. As this occurs, the level of arousal declines, bilateral upper motor neuron signs tend to replace early focal cerebral changes, and signs of hypothalamic dysfunction ensue, including small, light-reactive, equal pupils. Evidence of brain stem dysfunction (e.g., eye movement changes) appears as the midbrain becomes severely compressed by the downward shift. *Uncal (lateral) herniation* results when a lesion occupying the temporal fossa expands and pushes the uncus over the edge of the ipsilateral tentorium so as to compress the third nerve and midbrain (see Fig. 119–1). Reduced consciousness and bilateral motor signs appear relatively late, the earliest evidence of serious trouble usually being incipient parasympathetic paralysis of the pupil. Either form of herniation, however, warns of impending upper brain stem compression and calls for quick and effective action to prevent irreversible neurologic damage.

Subtentorial Lesions. In order for subtentorial lesions to cause coma, they necessarily must damage or depress the function of the posterior hypothalamus plus the activating systems located in the tegmentum of the upper pons and midbrain. Because the reticular formation surrounds or lies adjacent to oculomotor pathways and upper brain stem cranial nerve nuclei, signs of damage to these latter structures always accompany the onset of stupor or coma caused by subtentorial lesions. Furthermore, subtentorial lesions causing coma almost always have a structural nature that MR images identify. Table 112–3 lists their most common causes and Table 112–6 gives their characteristic signs and symptoms.

Metabolic, Diffuse, and Multifocal Disorders Producing Altered Consciousness. Table 112–3 lists major examples. They tend to affect the brain diffusely, and they characteristically produce symptoms and signs of both widespread cerebral and concurrent brain stem dysfunction. Depending on the particular illness, its severity, and its rate of appear-

TABLE 112–2. CRITERIA FOR DIAGNOSIS OF BRAIN DEATH

1. Nature and duration of coma are known.
   a. Known structural disease or irreversible systemic metabolic cause.
   b. No chance of drug intoxication or hypothermia below 32°C; no paralyzing or sedative drugs recently given for treatment.
   c. Six-hour observation of no brain function is sufficient in cases of known structural cause when no drug or alcohol is involved in cause or treatment; otherwise, 12 to 24 hr plus a negative drug screen is required.
2. Absence of cerebral and brain stem function
   a. No behavioral or reflex response to noxious stimuli above foramen magnum level
   b. Fixed pupils
   c. No oculovestibular responses to 50-ml ice water calorics
   d. Apneic off ventilator with oxygenation for 10 min
   e. Systemic circulation may be intact.
   f. Purely spinal reflexes may be retained.
3. Supplementary (optional) criteria* (any one acceptable)
   a. EEG isoelectric for 30 min at maximal gain
   b. Auditory evoked responses reflect absent function in vital brain stem structures.
   c. No circulation present on cerebral blood flow examination

*May be useful if medicolegal issues are in question or when taking organs for transplantation, especially within 6 hours of the time that diagnosis is first reached.

ance, symptoms in metabolic-multifocal encephalopathy can include either changes in cognitive capacities or a reduction in arousal. Acute, self-induced drug overdose, or sudden, severe hypoglycemia, for example, can precipitate acute coma with few prodromal symptoms. By contrast, mild drug intoxication or a moderate reduction in blood sugar is more likely to be reflected by more sustained confused or bizarre behavior. If the history is lacking or indefinite, an important clue to diagnosis

TABLE 112–3. COMMON CAUSES OF STUPOR AND COMA

I. Supratentorial lesions
   A. Compressing or herniating diencephalon against the upper brain stem (common): cerebral hemorrhage, large cerebral infarction, subdural hematoma, epidural hematoma, brain tumor, brain abscess (rare)
   B. Directly invading or destroying the posterior ventromedial diencephalon (less common): neoplasms, infarcts, encephalitis
II. Subtentorial lesions (compressing or damaging the midbrain–upper pontine reticular formation): pontine or cerebellar hemorrhage, midbrain–upper pontine infarction, tumor, cerebellar abscess, acute demyelination
III. Metabolic and diffuse lesions
   A. Exogenous psychoactive drugs or poisons
   B. Anoxia or ischemia
   C. Mixed encephalopathies: pathologic aging, postoperative state, systemic infection, therapeutic drugs in various combinations
   D. Hepatic, renal, pulmonary, pancreatic insufficiency
   E. Hypoglycemia
   F. Infections: meningitis, encephalitis
   G. Multifocal small structural lesions, e.g., metastases, emboli, thrombi
   H. Concussion and postictal states
   I. Ionic and electrolyte disorders
   J. Nutritional deficiency
IV. Psychogenic unresponsiveness

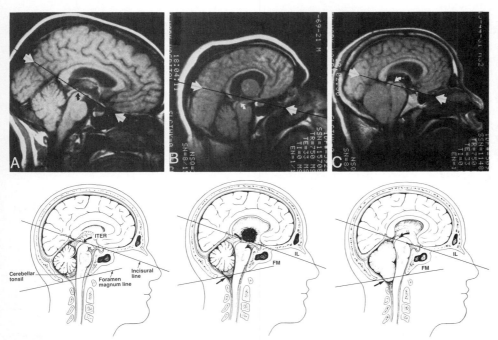

FIGURE 112–1. Midsagittal diagrams and magnetic resonance (MR) images of a normal adult brain compared with downward and upward transtentorial herniation as well as foramen magnum herniation. *A*, Normal 45-year-old male brain. The incisural line (IL) defines the plane of the tentorial opening, which extends from the junction between the vein of Galen and the cerebral venous straight sinus posteriorly to the anterior clinoid process. The iter, i.e., the rostral opening of the aqueduct of Sylvius *(black curved arrow),* lies on or within 2 mm of the IL. The cerebellar tonsils remain well above the foramen magnum (FM). *B*, Downward transtentorial herniation due to a chronic colloid cyst lying in the third ventricle of a 52-year-old man (dark round shadow on diagram). The curved white arrow on the MR scan points to the aqueduct, posterior thalamus, and mesencephalon, which are displaced 8 mm caudally of the IL. The cerebellar tonsils are visible at the level of the foramen magnum. *C*, Upward tentorial plus foramen magnum herniation has occurred secondary to a cerebellar lymphoma in a 32-year-old man with HIV-I infection. The cerebellum is enlarged. The iter *(black curved arrow)* and the rostral mesencephalon have herniated 6 mm above the IL, and the brain stem is flattened against the base of the skull. The cerebellar tonsils have herniated into the foramen magnum. (From Plum F: Sustained impairments of consciousness. *In* Wyngaarden JB, Smith LH Jr, Bennett JC [eds]: Cecil Textbook of Medicine. 19th ed. Philadelphia, WB Saunders Co, 1992, p 2050.)

in all the recoverable metabolic encephalopathies is that except for poisoning with drugs that contain anticholinergic agents, almost no reversible examples paralyze the pupillary light reflex. Also, except for sedative drug poisonings, most metabolic comas fail to block reflex oculovestibular responses.

SIGNS AND SYMPTOMS. Table 112–7 lists the most common signs and symptoms. Characteristic in the early stages is an acute or subacute delirium accompanied by restlessness and reduced alertness. Mental status examination (see Table 112–18) shows impaired recall, poor concentration, and often disorientation. Confabulation, obtundation, and stupor follow in varying degrees and combinations. Fluctuations in behavior are common; some patients may alternate widely between stupor and agitation. Symptoms of delirium tend to be accentuated by nightfall and unfamiliar surroundings.

Characteristic motor changes include tremor, asterixis, and multifocal myoclonus (defined on page 792). The tremor of delirium tends to be coarse, irregular, rapid at 8 to 10 Hz, and intensified by movement. Bilateral asterixis or multifocal myoclonus arising acutely or subacutely and accompanying a recent impairment of consciousness is pathognomonic of metabolic encephalopathy. Seizures, hyperactive stretch reflexes, and even focal signs sometimes accompany several of the metabolic encephalopathies (e.g., drug withdrawal, global cerebral anoxia, hypoglycemia, hyperosmolar coma, fulminating hepatic encephalopathy). Such focal signs usually are transient and always are accompanied by other neurologic changes that reflect diffuse or multifocal brain disease.

Pupillary light reflexes usually are preserved in metabolic coma. Exceptions include the following: poisoning with hyoscine, strong narcotics, or glutethimide; deliberate or accidental contact with mydriatics; and irreversible anoxia-asphyxia. Except in cases of severe sedative overdose, spontaneous conjugate eye movements or conjugate oculovestibular reflexes are preserved until the terminal phases of most metabolic comas.

Breathing alterations are common: vigorous hyperpnea (Kussmaul breathing) accompanies the metabolic acidosis of diabetes, uremia, lactacidosis, and organic alcohol ingestion, whereas less prominent overbreathing reflects the alkaloses of hepatic disease, septic shock, and early salicylism. Hypoventilation is prominent in CO_2 encephalopathy, whether due to pulmonary disease or medullary respiratory depression such as drugs or hypoglycemia may cause.

Psychogenic Unresponsiveness

This can accompany several disorders, including the catatonia of schizophrenia or severe depression as well as hysteria or malingering. Often, the clinical picture may superficially resemble metabolic coma. Certain signs differentiate, however (Table 112–8). Careful examination reveals a normal general physical and somatic neurologic condition. Psychogenically unresponsive patients may resist answers during attempts to appraise mental status, but, unless they are hysterical or malingering, they do not give wrong ones. Those with closed eyes resist passive opening of the lids, and when the lids are passively raised, they shut abruptly when released; neither is true in organic coma. Pupils are briskly reactive unless mydriatics have been self-instilled, ice water calorics give normal responses, and the electroencephalogram (EEG) is normal. One must always remember, however, that much hysteria arises in the setting of organic disease, presumably due to excess anxiety.

Diagnosis of Coma and Emergency Management

A careful history discloses most causes of coma. When that is unavailable or misleading (some families, for example, hide evidence of drug ingestion) one proceeds as in Table 112–9. Once ventilation and the circulation are protected, brain images usually indicate whether or not a surgically treatable condition exists. If not, some of the clues given in Table 112–10 may suggest which tests to do first. Except when acute meningitis is suspected, lumbar puncture is best withheld until an MR or CT scan excludes an acute intracranial mass, including cerebral hemorrhage. EEG is helpful only when serial seizures (status epilepticus) due to petit mal or partial complex seizures (p. 843) produce a severe confusional state.

Most cases of coma of unknown cause that begins rapidly or abruptly in previously healthy persons result from self-induced drug poisoning, and patients lacking definite alternate diagnoses must be managed for this possibility until another cause is definitively established. Among older persons, especially those with chronic illness or receiving multiple medications, other puzzling metabolic encephalopathies also are common. These especially occur in the hospital setting where confusion, obtundation, or delirium due to a mixture of adverse causes

TABLE 112–4. CHARACTERISTICS OF SUPRATENTORIAL LESIONS LEADING TO COMA

Initiating symptoms usually cerebral-focal: aphasia; focal seizures; contralateral hemiparesis, sensory changes, or neglect; frontal lobe behavioral changes; headache.
Dysfunction moves rostral to caudal: e.g., focal motor → bilateral motor → altered level of arousal.
Abnormal signs usually confined to a single or adjacent anatomic level (not diffuse).
Brain stem functions spared unless herniation develops.

TABLE 112–5. SIGNS OF CENTRAL AND UNCAL HERNIATION

	CENTRAL	UNCAL
Arousal	Declines early	Declines late
Pupils	Small, equal, reactive	Ipsilateral dilation
Oculocephalics	Full, conjugate	Unilateral third nerve palsy
Motor	Decerebrate early	Decerebrate late
Breathing	Sighs, yawns, periodic (Cheyne-Stokes)	Central hyperventilation, late

TABLE 112–6. CHARACTERISTICS OF SUBTENTORIAL LESIONS CAUSING COMA

Onset of coma often sudden
Symptoms of brain stem dysfunction may precede coma.
Localizing brain stem signs always present
  Caloric responses disconjugate or absent
  Pupil(s) abnormal: pinpoint (pons), fixed (midbrain), irregular and/or unequal (midbrain-pontine)
  Often "bizarre" signs: ocular bobbing, ataxic breathing, etc.
  Often signs of cerebellar or bilateral motor dysfunction

TABLE 112–7. CHARACTERISTICS OF METABOLIC ENCEPHALOPATHY

Confusion, lethargy, delirium often precede or replace coma.
Motor signs, if present, are usually symmetric.
Bilateral asterixis, myoclonus appear.
Pupillary reactions usually preserved; tonic calorics are often present.
Sensory abnormalities are usually absent.
Moderate hypothermia is common.
Abnormal signs reflect incomplete brain dysfunction simultaneously affecting multiple anatomic levels.

TABLE 112–8. SIGNS OF PSYCHOGENIC PSEUDOCOMA

Lids close actively and often resist examiner's attempt to open them.
Breathing: eupnea or acute hyperventilation
Pupils responsive or dilated (self-administered cycloplegics)
Oculocephalic responses unpredictable; calorics produce quick nystagmus.
Motor responses unpredictable and often asymmetric or bizarre
No pathologic reflexes. EEG normal awake

can complicate the course of many acute medical or surgical illnesses. Standard blood chemistries plus a search for offending medications frequently reveal the cause of such conditions. Table 112–11 outlines the major emergency steps that protect the patient acutely in almost all of the major conditions producing sustained loss of consciousness.

TABLE 112–9. KEY TO CLINICAL DIAGNOSIS OF COMA

Pursue history diligently and provide immediate life-support (see Table 112–11).
How do signs of dysfunction evolve?
    Rostral-caudal? (Supratentorial)
    Focal brain stem from onset? (Subtentorial)
    Multifocal diffuse? (Metabolic-diffuse)
    Do they represent nonphysiologic abnormalities? (Psychogenic)
Obtain emergency brain scan.
Move to specific tests or treatment.

TABLE 112–10. HELPFUL CLUES IN EARLY DIAGNOSIS OF COMA

Fever	Meningitis, encephalitis, postictal state, acute bacterial endocarditis, scopolamine poisoning
Hypothermia	Myxedema, hypoglycemia, drug poisoning, brain stem infarct
Signs of trauma	Cerebral contusion; extradural, subdural, or parenchymal hematoma
Severe hypertension	Cerebral or subarachnoid hemorrhage; hypertensive encephalopathy
Hypotension	Occult (usually gastrointestinal) bleeding, septic shock, hypovolemia, poor cardiac output, depressant drug poisoning
	Tachycardia > 180/min, bradycardia < 40/min: poor cardiac output
Arrhythmias	Tricyclic antidepressant overdose, myocardial infarction
Hyperventilation	Diabetic ketosis; uremia; organic alcohol poisoning; lactic acidosis, hepatic coma; salicylate poisoning
Hypoventilation	Pulmonary insufficiency, depressant drug or opiate poisoning, low brain stem infarct or hemorrhage
Petechiae	Meningococcemia; thrombocytopenic and nonthrombocytopenic purpura; bacterial endocarditis
Pink skin	Carbon monoxide poisoning
Stiff neck	Acute meningitis, subarachnoid hemorrhage

TABLE 112–11. EMERGENCY MANAGEMENT OF COMA

1. Assure airway and oxygenation.
2. Maintain adequate systemic circulation.
3. Give thiamine, 50 to 100 mg intravenously.
4. Give glucose after first obtaining blood for analysis.
5. Stop generalized seizures.
6. Restore blood acid-base and osmolar balance but do not change serum sodium by more than 15 mOsm/day.
7. Treat infection specifically.
8. Ameliorate extreme body temperature (>41° or <35°C).
9. Consider naloxone.
10. Control agitation-tremulousness with lorazepam or haloperidol.

BRIEF AND EPISODIC ALTERATIONS OF CONSCIOUSNESS

Table 112–12 lists disorders that produce recurrent, short-lived, relatively stereotyped alterations in perceptions, psychological feeling states, somatic functions, or global consciousness. Although each of these conditions produces fairly characteristic symptoms and signs, only hypoglycemia, seizure disorders, or certain forms of syncope (e.g., with cardiac arrhythmia) are associated with diagnostic laboratory findings and then only during the episodes. Accordingly, the cause of most episodes of brief loss of consciousness must be inferred from retrospective evidence. In such instances, the patient's age, the medical history, and, especially, an accurate recounting of symptoms or reports of direct observers provide the greatest help in diagnosis.

Syncope describes brief loss of consciousness due to a global reduction in cerebral blood flow. The disorder almost always is due to an abrupt or semiabrupt loss of cardiac output, most frequently secondary to acutely impaired right heart output (cardiac rhythm maintained) or severe left heart output (asystole or severe arrhythmia) (see Table 8–8).

Syncope due to reduced right heart filling usually results from pooling of blood in capacitance veins of the lower extremities or trunk. Most often, this comes from the triggering of vasodepressor reflex mechanisms. Orthostatic hypotension secondary to depleted blood volume, hypotensive drugs, and neurologic disease, as well as mechanical increases in pulmonary resistance such as those that may accompany severe coughing or acute pulmonary infarction, are less frequent mechanisms. Cardiac tamponade interferes with both right and left heart filling and output.

Vasodepressor syncope (simple fainting) exceeds in frequency all other causes of acute brief unconsciousness combined. Simple fainting tends to be a recurrent problem in some individuals; a few give a family history of the disorder. No associated neurologic or cardiac abnormality can be found in most cases. Attacks are engendered by emotional crises, acute painful visceral stimuli, hyperventilation after micturition, recent ascent to high altitude, and, in susceptible persons, various combinations of alcohol, hunger, and drugs. Often, one can identify no precipitating cause. Attacks begin in some persons with a brief prodrome of anxiety, giddiness, diaphoresis, and nausea before collapse. Others precipitously sink to the floor as heart rate and blood pressure fall and cardiac output declines. Except with prolonged asystole, syncope always occurs in the erect or sitting position, never when supine. Patients are pale and sweaty and may have one or two generalized clonic twitches as a result of a profound faint (convulsive syncope). Incontinence is unusual, but vomiting, micturition, and diarrhea commonly follow the attack. In young persons with a negative physical examination and characteristic history, physiologic or structural disease almost never is present and laboratory studies need not be extensive. Tilt-table test results are not reliable in pre-

Brief Loss of Consciousness
Syncope (Tables 9–9 and 118–7)
Hypoglycemia (Chapter 72)
Seizures (Chapter 118)
Recurrent Psychological Disturbances
Hyperventilation attacks
Panic attacks
Fugue states (p. 755)
Episodic Neurologic Dysfunction Without Impaired Arousal
Transient global amnesia (p. 748)
Cerebral transient ischemic attacks (p. 825)
Drop spells
Migraine (p. 768)

dicting future recurrences. Hysteria and drug-alcohol intoxication are the chief resemblers. Table 118–7 outlines the differences from minor seizures. Simple fainting can affect persons older than 50 years, but a first episode in that age group deserves careful evaluation to rule out serious cardiac disorders. Cerebral transient ischemic attacks rarely simulate syncope. Occasionally, vasodepressor syncope accompanies attacks of severe migraine in adolescents and young adults.

Syncope resolves too quickly to treat except posturally by placing the subject supine and elevating the lower extremities; there are no effective preventive measures except when severe cardiac disorders are found and corrected. Avoiding offending foods as well as eliminating bouts of alcohol ingestion without accompanying food helps when the history incriminates such associations.

Other causes of briefly altered unconsciousness are uncommon or discussed elsewhere (Table 112–12). Hyperventilation attacks more closely resemble the syndrome of panic than syncope. Affected patients may complain of feeling unreal, floating, or dizzy, but they do not lose contact with the environment. Perioral paresthesias, a sense of suffocating dyspnea, and carpopedal spasm are diagnostic. Treatment consists of attempting to provide the sufferer with insight and emphasizing the benign nature of the condition. Propranolol, up to 40 mg three times daily, or amitriptyline in doses up to 50 mg daily, may reduce the frequency of panic attacks. Propranolol is especially helpful in warding off stage fright.

REFERENCES

Kapoor WN: Evaluation and outcome of patients with syncope. Medicine 69:160–175, 1990.
Manolis AS, Linzer M, Salem D, Estes NAM: Syncope: Current diagnostic evaluation and management. Ann Intern Med 112:850–863, 1990.
Plum F: Coma and related global disturbances of the human conscious state. In Jones EG, Peters A (eds): Cerebral Cortex. Vol 9: Altered Cortical States. New York, Plenum, 1991.
Plum F, Posner JB: Diagnosis of Stupor and Coma. 3rd ed rev. Philadelphia, FA Davis Co, 1982.

C. Focal Disturbances of Higher Brain Function

REGIONAL SYNDROMES

The human cerebral cortex contains the final receiving areas for somatic and special sensory information, as well as the primary motor cortex — the "executive director" of all voluntary movement (Fig. 112–2). Lying between the main sensorimotor regions are large areas of association cortex that convert sensation into perception and integrate instinctive and acquired memory and emotion into language and actions. Damage to particular regions of association cortex often produces specifically recognizable psychological symptoms. This principle especially applies to functions such as language and spatial orientation that are strongly lateralized in one hemisphere or the other.

Frontal lobe injury may produce one or more of the syndromes indicated in Table 112–13. The frontal lobes are large structures, however, and the nature and degree of symptoms depend on the specific locus and size of the damage, as well as on how rapidly it enlarges. Relatively small abnormalities involving the posterior frontal areas of either hemisphere can cause seizures, motor deficits, or, on the dominant side, aphasia. By contrast, only large or bilateral anterior frontal lobe disturbances are likely to cause clinically detectable behavioral abnormalities.

Small lesions of the *parietal lobe* that lie outside the immediate postcentral gyrus often produce no symptoms. Large injuries such as those that may ac-

TABLE 112–13. SYNDROMES OF FRONTAL LOBE DAMAGE

Contralateral upper motor neuron spastic weakness, more distal than proximal
Contralateral seizures: focal hand, face, foot (rare); adversive body or eyes
Aphasia (dominant hemisphere)
Impaired conceptualization and planning
Acquired "sociopathy"

TABLE 112–14. SYNDROMES OF PARIETAL LOBE DAMAGE

Postcentral cortex: Homunculus-patterned contralateral impairment of somesthetic abstraction: stereoanesthesia-astereognosis
Inferior parietal lobe
Dominant: Aphasia, apraxia, acalculia, right-left disorientation
Nondominant: Spatial disorientation; perceptual neglect, especially contralaterally; inappropriate affect, sometimes delirium

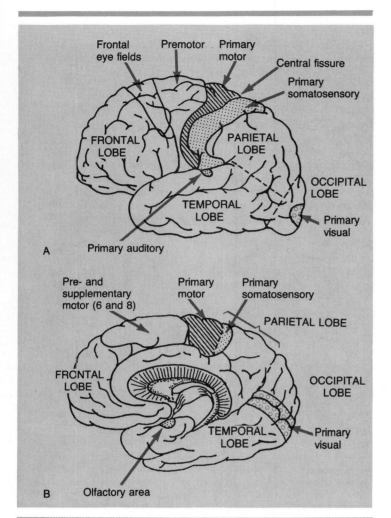

FIGURE 112–2. Major anatomic and functional areas of the cerebral hemispheres. *A*, Lateral surface. *B*, Medial surface.

company stroke or malignant neoplasms produce abnormalities of the kind briefly summarized in Table 112–14.

Temporal lobe injuries are likely to interfere with language function (see below) or to cause partial complex seizures (see Chapter 118).

LANGUAGE AND APHASIA

The critical areas for language processing consist of Wernicke's area, which extends posteriorly along the superior temporal gyrus from the primary auditory cortex; the adjacent posterolateral temporal cortex and inferior parietal lobe cortex; and the inferior, posterolateral part of the frontal lobe cortex, called Broca's area (Fig. 112–3).

Language function is strongly lateralized, arising entirely or predominantly from the left hemisphere in roughly 95 per cent of the population. Dominance for handedness is less exclusive: about 15 per cent of persons are left-handed or ambidextrous, but only a third of left-handers possess a right hemisphere that is dominant for language. Most left-handers tend to have some language function in both hemispheres, so that they seldom become completely and permanently aphasic, even after an injury or surgical removal of either hemisphere.

Aphasia or *dysphasia* consists of a loss or impairment of language function as a result of damage to or dysfunction in the specific language areas of the dominant hemisphere (Table 112–15). *Dysarthria*, by contrast, consists of a disturbance in the articulation of speech.

Broca's aphasia is characterized by severe disturbances in expressing either spontaneous or commanded speech and writing. Comprehension is relatively better but incompletely preserved, with things spoken being better understood than things read. Many patients with Broca's aphasia also have an associated right hemiparesis or hemiplegia, the result of a concurrent vascular lesion affecting the internal capsule.

Wernicke's aphasia consists of an incapacity to recognize the nature or meaning of symbolic sensory stimuli, including language, or to connect learned words with either inner thoughts or stored memories. Affected patients cannot recognize spoken, written, or symbolized language or gestures. Nevertheless, they articulate a fluent nonsense with a natural, meaningless rhythm. Insight is minimal and prognosis is poor.

Many aphasic patients show mixtures of the above categories. As a rule, however, expressive defects correlate with frontal lobe injury, whereas receptive and word-finding deficits are associated with temporoparietal abnormalities. *Conduction aphasia* is characterized by a fluent, Wernicke-like

TABLE 112–15. PRINCIPAL APHASIA TYPES

	LOCUS OF LESION	SPEECH	COMPREHENSION	ASSOCIATED SIGNS
Broca's area	Inferior posterior frontal lobe	Halting; reduced; non-fluent	Good	Often right hemiparesis; self-aware; frustrated
Wernicke's area	Superior-lateral posterior temporal lobe	Abundant, fluent, semantic nonsense	Poor to absent	Often none
Conduction	Supramarginal gyrus; primary auditory cortex or insular region	Fluent but some expressive defects	Poor to absent	Often none
Global	Large frontotemporal lesions	Dense, expressive, non-fluent language loss. Brief expletives may remain.	Poor	Usually right hemiparesis or hemiplegia

pattern coupled with the ability of the patient to repeat after the examiner phrases and often long sentences. The responsible lesions must lie near but not within the primary speech areas.

Global aphasia describes the combined severe loss of all major aspects of language function due to frontotemporal damage in the dominant hemisphere.

Mutism, the inability to speak or make sounds, can occur with acute left pre–Broca area lesions, bilateral frontal lobe damage, the locked-in state (see Table 112–1), or hysteria. All but the last produce associated signs of organic brain disease.

Anarthria consists of the inability to speak because of abnormal innervation or mechanical disease of the vocal apparatus. Most affected patients can make sounds, however. Causes include severe bulbar or pseudobulbar palsy.

Apraxia refers to a disturbance of the ability or an inability to perform learned motor acts despite the retention of sufficient sensory and language function to understand the command and enough crude motor capacity to carry it out (praxis). The condition most commonly accompanies deep lesions of one or both parietal lobes.

Agnosia is the inability to recognize a complex sensory stimulus or body part despite the preservation of elemental perceptions and language. The phenomenon accompanies certain large parieto-occipital-posterior temporal lobe lesions. It most often is caused by a large stroke or one of the degenerative dementias.

MEMORY

Disturbances of memory include defects in past memory, called *retrograde amnesia*, and the inability to form new memories from ongoing events, called *anterograde amnesia*.

Patterns of Memory Failure. Memory can be divided into immediate, intermediate, and remote epochs. *Immediate memory* consists of holding in the mind material just heard or read with no necessary intervening storage process. *Intermediate memory* covers the time span beginning within a few seconds past and extending backward for 24 to 48 hours or more. *Long-term memory* extends beyond that epoch, but this too has its gradations; many childhood memories tend to be well recalled even as recent ones begin to fade. Illustrating this principle, adults suffering from diseases that impair or destroy recent and anterograde memory often score normally on parts of IQ tests which include definitions of words and functions learned before the age of 14 years.

Memory Mechanisms. The brain possesses substantial *instinctive memory*, reflected in many aspects of automatic human behavior and motor skills. *Learned memories* are generated from perceptions of the external world and inner thoughts and have at least three distinct components: perception-registration, storage, and retrieval. Storage of both perceived events and motor skills is distributed widely in the brain, especially in the parietal-

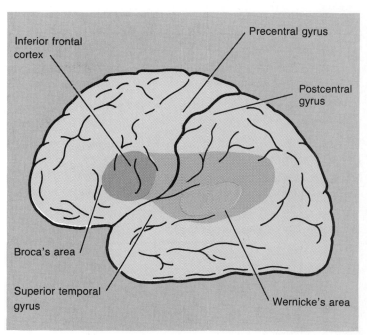

FIGURE 112–3. Primary language areas in the dominant cerebral hemisphere. Damage to Broca's area or Wernicke's area produces characteristic language abnormalities (see Table 112–15). Injury to the surrounding stippled areas causes less classic language impairments, including conduction aphasia.

temporal areas for perceptual-verbal memories or prefrontal regions for motor skills. The agnosias described above reflect damage to such distributed areas. Memory formation and retrieval of perceptions, by contrast, appear to require the integrity of the hippocampal areas of the temporal lobe and thalamus. The considerable redundancy of memory-processing functions means that clinically severe memory impairment usually requires extensive unilateral or bilateral injury. Illustrating this, bilateral damage or surgical removal of the hippocampus results in profound and usually permanent deficits in intermediate memory affecting especially the verbal-visual-spatial spheres. Similarly, bilateral damage to several paramedian areas of the thalamus and probably the mammillary bodies results in a profound multidimensional memory disturbance, the most severe form of which produces a Korsakoff syndrome (see below).

Event memories relate in incompletely understood ways to cholinergic and other autonomic projections that link the subcortical basal forebrain with the hippocampus and areas of the association cortex. Degeneration of these projections is a prominent accompaniment of the dementia of Alzheimer's and certain other dementias.

Clinical Memory Disorders. Many middle-aged and elderly persons experience an increasing, relatively isolated difficulty in recalling proper names and recent events of minor importance. This "benign forgetfulness" bears no consistent relationship to the progressive dementias and is best treated with

TABLE 112–16. ORGANIC AND PSYCHOGENIC AMNESIA COMPARED

	ORGANIC	PSYCHOGENIC
Time frame	Recent worse than remote	Unpredictable mixture of recent and remote, often for circumscribed events
Pattern	Anterograde amnesia as bad as retrograde	No anterograde amnesia except in total fugues ("who am I?")
	Emotionally important events recalled better	Such events often "forgotten"
Self-recognition	Intact except with severe delirium or seizures	May be denied
Behavior	Questions about illness asked repeatedly	Often no questions asked

prompt and vigorous reassurance.

More serious amnesias accompany or follow severe thiamine deficiency (e.g., Korsakoff's syndrome), the organic dementias discussed in the next section, severe head trauma, brain anoxia or ischemia, encephalitis, and, less frequently, intracranial mass lesions.

Korsakoff's syndrome is a profound recent memory loss, usually accompanied by lack of insight, disorientation to time and place, and confabulation. Nutritional Korsakoff's syndrome most frequently affects alcoholics but also can result from prolonged vitamin-free infusions such as those given to treat postoperative states, severe burns, or hyperemesis gravidarum. Global cerebral anoxia-ischemia, status epilepticus, and subarachnoid hemorrhage can selectively and bilaterally damage vulnerable neurons in the hippocampus and medial diencephalon, producing similar results.

Even modest head trauma temporarily interrupts memory-mediating neural connections. Concussive injuries frequently produce an initially severe retrograde and lesser anterograde amnesia; usually the memory loss disappears with time. A less fortunate prognosis accompanies prolonged post-traumatic coma. When this lasts more than 2 to 3 weeks, most adults never fully recover from memory impairment.

Herpes simplex encephalitis has a predilection to produce necrotic-inflammatory lesions in the limbic system lying along the medial surfaces of the temporal lobes. It characteristically leaves severe amnesia in its wake.

Transient global amnesia (TGA) is a condition marked by periods lasting from several minutes to as long as 12 hours or so of abruptly beginning, acute alert confusion. A severe but isolated deficit in retrograde memory accompanies the beginning of the attack and gradually disappears as it wears off. Affected persons can identify themselves but are severely disoriented for time and place and distressed about the experience. Most TGA attacks affect middle-aged or elderly persons and reflect temporary vascular insufficiency affecting the hippocampal memory areas or their thalamic connections. Temporal lobe seizures or hysterical fugue states represent the principal conditions to be distinguished from this disorder. Most attacks neither leave residual limitations nor carry a strong risk of recurrence.

Psychogenic memory impairment can affect either recent or remote recall, usually in clinically recognizable patterns. Table 112–16 lists the principal features. In general, with organic disturbances in memory, emotionally reinforced material is recalled better than neutral events. Also, with organic memory loss, disorientation is worst for time, less for place and persons, and never for self; remote events are recalled better than recent ones, and cues often improve recall. By contrast, psychogenic amnesia tends to be greatest for emotionally important events, may delete from the patient's memory well-defined blocks of past events while leaving intact the recall of preceding or following material, and may affect remote memories equally with recent ones.

Treatment. A high percentage of patients with acute post-traumatic amnesia recover spontaneously. Patients with other forms of organic amnesia do less well unless the memory loss was caused by an excess use of medication or a temporary systemic disorder such as hepatic, renal, or pulmonary insufficiency. Neither medications nor diets have proved useful in treatment.

REFERENCES

Damasio AR: Diagnosis of regional cerebral dysfunction; Disturbances of memory and language. *In* Wyngaarden JB, Smith LH Jr, Bennett JC (eds): Cecil Textbook of Medicine. 19th ed. Philadelphia, WB Saunders Co, 1992, pp 2067–2075.
Mesulam MM: Principles of Behavioral Neurology. Philadelphia, FA Davis Co, 1985.

D. Dementia

GENERAL CONSIDERATIONS

Dementia describes a sustained or permanent, multidimensional decline of intellectual function that interferes seriously with the individual's social or economic adjustment. Table 112–17 lists causes of dementia and their approximate frequency. Several, such as Huntington's disease, Creutzfeldt-Jakob disease, and acquired immunodeficiency syndrome (AIDS), are discussed elsewhere in this book.

Static dementia follows acute brain injury and, once a few days or weeks have elapsed, remains either fixed or improves only modestly. Severe head injury, global brain ischemia from cardiac arrest, large intracranial neoplasms or hemorrhages with their surgical removal, or infections such as severe encephalitis or meningitis are typical causes. *Progressive dementias* may begin either suddenly or insidiously but, by definition, worsen with the passage of time, often ending in total incapacity or death.

Early Clinical Manifestations. Acute, static dementia seldom provides a problem in diagnosis. Most often the issue becomes not whether a mental decline has occurred but to what degree and how the patient can restructure his world to his new, possibly permanent limitations.

Early diagnosis in the progressive dementias may be difficult because both families and patients may attribute cognitive deterioration to ordinary personality variations. Initial symptoms involve deterioration in mood, personality, recent memory, judgment, and the capacity to form abstractions. Families or work associates usually detect a change before the patient does, and persons who live by intellectual efforts display their limitations earlier than do those with routine or manual jobs. Some patients become so apathetic as to seem depressed; in others great anxiety, increased irritability, or paranoia can disrupt a once pleasant personality. Others suffer from a secondary depression. Loss of recent memory is universal. Appointments are missed, plans forgotten, and stories of recent events become narrated repeatedly with little insight. Eventually, orientation fails, first for days, then years, then months, and finally for place. Interest lags. Debts may be accumulated silently, property unwisely sold, accounts lost, and meals cooked twice over or served half-done. Mental capacities can fluctuate without apparent relationship to external events. In Alzheimer's disease and some of the other progressive primary dementias, social amenities tend to be retained until late in the course. By contrast, incontinence, vulgarity, soup on the shirt, and a disheveled appearance characterize the mental deterioration that accompanies frontal lobe disease, intracranial mass lesions, or chronic drug-alcohol abuse.

Diagnosis. All patients with symptoms of subacute or chronic brain disease should receive a brief evaluation of mental function such as represented by the Mini Mental Status (Table 112–18). For further quantitation, the Wechsler Adult Intelligence Scale (WAIS) provides useful information but requires the assistance of a trained psychologist. In mild to moderate dementia the verbal score of the WAIS provides an index of early life learning capacity, whereas the performance part reflects current mental abilities. A discrepancy of more than 15 points between the two reflects acquired brain dysfunction.

In addition to a pertinent history and physical examination, baseline initial evaluation for all demented patients should include a complete blood count (CBC), standard chemistry screen, Venereal Disease Research Laboratory (VDRL) test, serum free thyroxine (T_4) index, and thyroid-stimulating hormone (TSH) level, as well as a brain scan by computed tomography (CT) or magnetic resonance (MR). A few causes of dementia are potentially

TABLE 112–17. MAJOR CAUSES OF PROGRESSIVE DEMENTIA

1. Senile dementia, Alzheimer type	50%
2. Multi-infarct (arteriosclerotic)	10%
3. Combination of 1 and 2	15%
4. Communicating hydrocephalus	
5. Alcoholic or post-traumatic	
6. Huntington's disease (p. 794)	15%
7. Intracranial mass lesions	
8. Uncommon or mixed with above:	10%

Chronic drug use; Creutzfeldt-Jakob (p. 865); metabolic (thyroid, liver, nutritional); degenerative (spinocerebellar, amyotrophic lateral sclerosis, parkinsonism, multiple sclerosis, Pick's, Wilson's, epilepsy); AIDS dementia (p. 713); static post-anoxic dementia

TABLE 112–18. MINI MENTAL STATUS EXAMINATION*

TEST	SCORE
What is the year, season, date, day, month?	5
Where are you: state, county, town, place, floor?	5
Name three objects: State slowly and have patient repeat (repeat until patient learns all three).	3
Do reverse serial 7's (five steps) or spell "WORLD" backwards.	5
Ask for three unrelated objects above.	3
Name from inspection a pencil, a watch.	2
Have patient repeat "No if's, and's, or but's."	1
Follow a three-stage command (1 pt each). (Take a paper in your hand, fold it, and put it on the floor.)	3
Read and obey the command "Close your eyes."	1
Write a simple sentence.	1
Copy intersecting pentagons.	1

*Out of a possible total score of 30, most patients with true dementia score below 15, whereas those with uncomplicated depression score above 25. Mixed or transient cognitive impairments produce scores that fall between normals and those with irreversible dementia.

treatable, including those listed in Table 112–19. Most of these are at least suspected at the time of the patient's initial evaluation. Special tests for the others need be applied only when specific clinical indications exist.

Pseudodementia is a term applied to reversible states in which chronic drug intoxication, depressive illness, or psychogenic fugue states seemingly impair memory (see Table 112–23) or cognition (see Table 112–16). Aging persons are especially suscep-

TABLE 112–19. POTENTIALLY TREATABLE DEMENTIAS

Chronic medication; drug or alcohol exposure
Intracranial mass lesions
Communicating hydrocephalus
Deficiency of vitamin B_1, B_6, or B_{12}
Chronic hepatic encephalopathy
Wilson's disease
Syphilis
Granulomatous meningitis

tible to the first two. Among drugs, the barbiturates, benzodiazepines, butyrophenones, tricyclic antidepressants, monoamine oxidase (MAO) inhibitors, anticholinergics, corticosteroids, and digitalis are frequently responsible.

THE MOST FREQUENT DEMENTIAS
(Table 112–20)

Alzheimer's Presenile and Senile Dementia (ASD). This devastating, increasingly frequent disorder occasionally affects persons younger than 50 years but is uncommon up to age 65. Subsequently, the prevalence increases to more than 20 per cent of those who live beyond age 80 years. The cause of ASD is unknown, but recent attention has focused on a possible hereditary factor associated with a gene abnormality on chromosome 21. Pathologically, the condition includes amyloid plaques and intraneuronal tangles prominently scattered through the hippocampus, amygdala, and association areas of the cerebral hemispheres. Neuronal loss affects the same areas as well as the cholinergic nuclei in the basal forebrain. Brain images usually show only moderate cerebral atrophy. A major current hypothesis regards an abnormality in the large precursor protein of amyloid plaques as important in causing the disease. Clinically, ASD usually begins insidiously with memory impairment, personality alterations, and affective shallowness giving way at varying rates to severe amnesia for past events and for spatial relationships. Language errors later develop. Social amenities are preserved until late in the disease. Focal neurologic abnormalities or convulsions are not a feature. Specific diagnostic laboratory markers are lacking. The duration of ASD varies widely between extremes of 3 to 20 years, with patients declining slowly toward a terminal near-vegetative state. Death comes from pneumonia or intercurrent illness. Alzheimer variants have been described in association with parkinsonism and motor neuron disease. No effective treatment has been established, but haloperidol in small amounts often is useful in calming excessive agitation.

Multi-infarct Dementia. This occurs as a result of successive large and small strokes, affecting the cerebral hemispheres and their deep subcortical nuclei. Hypertension, diabetes mellitus, or hyperlipidemia most often underlies the vascular changes. The usual clinical picture is of successive, cumulative episodes of focal neurologic worsening, resulting in a disheveled appearance, accompanied commonly by aphasia, focal neurologic deficits, and CT or MR scans that show multiple lucencies reflecting past infarctions. Occasionally, successive small strokes in hypertensive patients result in a less obviously episodic decline but a progressive amnesia.

Progressive Hydrocephalic Dementia. The condition is caused by chronic interference with CSF absorption pathways over the surface of the hemispheres. Ultimate causes include acutely or remotely occurring inflammatory or neoplastic meningitis, subarachnoid hemorrhage, and traumatic head injury; in many instances the initiating mechanism escapes detection. Principal diagnostic features include age greater than 55 years; moderate, diffuse cognitive decline; fatigue on exercise; and a broad-based, moderately spastic ataxic gait, usually accompanied by extensor plantar responses. Brain images show abnormal cerebral ventricular dilatation accompanied by reduced vertical sulcus markings, usually coupled with evidence of periventricular edema (Fig. 112–4). Some patients improve following surgical ventricular shunting.

TABLE 112–20. CHARACTERISTICS OF THE MOST COMMON DEMENTIAS

TYPE	INCIDENCE AND RISKS	MAJOR FEATURES	LABORATORY FINDINGS
Alzheimer's dementia (AD)	5–10% < 80 yr; >20% > 80 yr. Rarely autosomal dominant; 25% have affected relatives	Neat appearance; social amenities preserved until late; event and spatial memory loss produce disorientation. Patients have little insight; many display nocturnal restlessness-agitation. Sensorimotor abnormalities are absent.	None relevant. Brain images are normal or show mild atrophy.
Multi-infarct dementia	>60 yr. Hypertension, smoking, diabetes, and hyperlipidemia increase the risk.	Successive strokes, large and small. Rarely, gradually progressive. Upper motor neuron abnormalities common on examination.	MR shows multiple strokes or diffuse, T2-weighted "bright spots" in hemispheric white matter.
Hydrocephalic dementia	60 yr. Can follow head trauma (accidents, boxing, surgery, meningeal infection or bleeding). Often no antecedents are identified.	Mild to moderate slowness of thinking, global dementia; broad-based, stiff, shuffling gait; incontinence. Mild bilateral upper motor neuron dysfunction, legs > arms.	CT or MR shows dilated cerebral ventricles, effaced hemispheric sulci. CSF pressure normal in most.
Parkinson's disease (PD)	Dementia coexists in 20–50% over age 65.	Cognitive loss accompanies advanced PD, often with associated depression. Clinically resembles AD.	None relevant

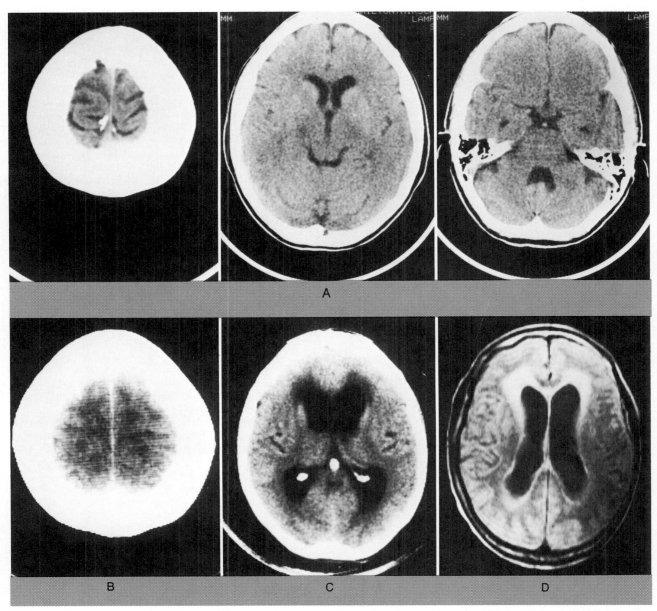

FIGURE 112-4. Communicating hydrocephalus. A 61-year-old woman 7 years following uncomplicated removal of carcinoma of the lung developed symptoms of headache and depression of
mood in the setting of her husband's catastrophic stroke. Neurologic examination and computed
tomographic (CT) evaluation (A) were considered unremarkable, although in retrospect the fourth
ventricle was slightly dilated. Over the next 4 months she became increasingly withdrawn, occasionally incontinent, and finally disoriented. She developed a broad-based ataxic gait, and CT
scan showed (B) absence of markings at the vertical sulcus with (C) ventricular dilatation. Magnetic resonance imaging (MRI) confirmed the ventricular enlargement (D) and showed periventricular increased signals typical of edema. Spinal fluid contained increased protein, hypoglycorrhachia (glucose 25 mg/dl), and malignant cells. Cerebrospinal fluid (CSF) pressure was 180 mm in
the lateral recumbent position. Her alertness and gait temporarily improved following spinal
drainage.

REFERENCES

Friedland RP, et al: Alzheimer disease: Clinical and biological heterogeneity. Ann Intern Med 109:298, 1988.
Katzman R, Rowe JW: Principles of Geriatric Neurology.
Philadelphia, FA Davis Co, 1992.
Yanker BA, Mesulam M-M: β-Amyloid and the pathogenesis of Alzheimer's disease. N Engl J Med 325:1849–1857,
1991.

E. Disorders of Mood and Behavior

Table 112–21 lists the most common types of mood and behavior disorders. This text treats these disorders only briefly, devoting attention to conditions that may enter the differential diagnosis of common medical problems. It is likely that future discovery will bring greater knowledge of the mechanisms of psychiatric disorders and a clearer understanding of the interface between so-called organic and psychogenic illnesses. In the meantime, however, one must sift out for most patients with chronic medical problems the relative degrees of both psychological and physical distress and give due weight to each in devising treatment. The Diagnostic and Statistical Manual of Mental Disorders III — Revised (DSM III-R) of the American Psychiatric Association (1987) provides objective diagnostic criteria for psychiatric disorders which, if rigorously applied, will help to minimize diagnostic errors.

SCHIZOPHRENIC DISORDERS

The term schizophrenia describes a group of symptomatic psychologic disorders, possibly of different origins, that are characterized by disturbances of mind and personality, including hallucinations, delusions, and altered behavior toward others. The common thread consists of a disturbance in the form and content of thought and a deterioration in psychosocial functioning, which often causes downward social mobility. The disorder, which affects about 1 per cent of the population, sometimes can be mimicked by structural or physiologic-pharmacologic diseases involving the brain's limbic system, and the diagnosis requires that such structural disease be absent. The symptoms of schizophrenia usually begin during adolescence or early adulthood. Thought blocking and a lack of emotional warmth are frequent early symptoms. Many patients suffer from auditory hallucinations in which they either hear their own thoughts aloud or hear voices derogating their behavior. Others experience delusions that their actions or thoughts are controlled by outside forces and that they are commanded to carry out unwanted acts. Schizophrenic persons often appear vague, unresponsive, and unemotional, with awkward, slowed thinking and ideas poorly related to one another. The affect is often flat or inappropriate. Some schizophrenic patients show facial grimaces or tics that can resemble chorea or other extrapyramidal disorders. Occasional patients become immobile (catatonia), resembling the apathy and indifference of frontal lobe disturbances.

The cause or causes of schizophrenia are unknown, although recent studies employing brain imaging techniques describe abnormalities in the structure and function of the left temporal lobe. Along the same lines, studies of identical twins have shown a strong genetic basis for the disorder. Early claims for a chromosomal locus for the disease have not been confirmed.

Diagnosis rests on recognizing the distinctive symptoms and ruling out other potential causes for the emotional and personality disorders. Schizophrenic patients, if their cooperation can be assured, are oriented and show no abnormality of cognitive functions. Sometimes it is difficult to distinguish schizophrenia from an affective psychosis (see below). The distinction is important because treatment differs and prognosis is considerably better in the affective psychoses.

The treatment of schizophrenia requires considerable expertise. Neuroleptic drugs including phenothiazine, butyrophenones, and thioxanthenes are the mainstay and have been in large measure responsible for allowing most schizophrenic patients to be treated outside mental institutions. However, difficulties in patient compliance and side effects make pharmacotherapy best left to experts. Long-term use of phenothiazines predisposes more than 10 per cent of patients to *tardive dyskinesias* in the form of either continuous orolingual facial movements or, less commonly, dystonic movements of the trunk or extremities. Because tardive dyskinesia may persist even when neuroleptics are discontinued, one should attempt to control psychotic symptoms with the smallest possible dose. With early, appropriate treatment, the condition remits in about one third to one half of schizophrenic patients, and another 30 per cent are able to live in the community.

AFFECTIVE DISORDERS

This category includes a group of disorders characterized by an excessive disturbance of mood, either elation or depression. The major patterns include recurrent episodes of either manic or depressive behavior or both (bipolar disorders), with attacks recurring repeatedly but usually clearing after weeks or months with or without treatment. The patho-

TABLE 112–21. PSYCHOGENIC DISORDERS OF MOOD AND BEHAVIOR

Major psychoses
  Schizophrenic disorders
  Affective disorders
Major neuroses
  Anxiety disorders
  Somatoform disorders
  Dissociative disorders
  Factitious disorders
  Not attributable to a mental disorder, e.g., malingering

genesis is unknown, although monozygotic twin studies suggest a major genetic component. Between episodes most patients behave relatively normally.

Depression. The most common affective disorder is depression (Table 112–22). Depression is a feeling of sadness and misery, usually accompanied by lowered self-esteem and ranging from feelings of inadequacy and incompetence to a full-blown delusion that the patient is evil and responsible for many of the world's ills. The delusions (usually of a bizarre nature) distinguish "psychotic" from situational depressions (i.e., excessive sadness related to a true environmental event). Both groups of patients, however, suffer from physical symptoms as well as depression of mood.

The diagnosis of depression may be difficult, but it is important. At first contact, depressed patients with severe psychomotor retardation may be considered mistakenly to suffer from an organic dementia. Features listed in Table 112–23 help to distinguish between these conditions. The second challenge lies in distinguishing severe depression from physical illness. Depression, no matter what its underlying cause, can be treated, but if untreated may lead to prolonged illness, lengthy and unnecessary medical testing, and even suicide. Many patients complaining of somatic symptoms have lost weight and may look so ill that the physician searches for a disease such as cancer without considering depression as the primary process. Early morning awakening, loss of appetite, and, particularly, recent-onset headache unaccompanied by structural disease should suggest depression; direct questioning about mood is essential. Patients should be asked if they feel blue or hopeless. If so, one should ask them gently and supportively if they have considered suicide as an option. An affirmative answer greatly strengthens the diagnosis and suggests a need for psychiatric consultation.

An additional diagnostic task is to identify depression in the setting of established physical illness or environmental stress. Such reactions can too easily be regarded as appropriate to the situation. However, profound depression even in terminally ill patients is not the rule but its presence adds great misery. The physician should consider it an added illness meriting specific treatment.

Finally, one also must distinguish structural disease of the brain from psychogenic apathetic depression. Patients with large frontal lobe brain tumors, some with hydrocephalus or subdural hematomas, and many with myxedema can appear to be withdrawn and depressed. Generally, however, one finds other clinical signs of neurologic dysfunction with structural disease of the brain. In doubtful instances obtaining a brain scan or appropriate laboratory test provides accurate differentiation.

Most depression, whatever the cause, responds to appropriate treatment with antidepressant drugs. The tricyclic antidepressant drugs such as amitriptyline, given in appropriate doses, often relieve symptoms promptly. These drugs should be started in low doses and gradually increased. This gradual approach is particularly important in the elderly, to avoid excessive sedation and sometimes hallucina-

TABLE 112–22. COMMON MANIFESTATIONS OF DEPRESSION

Feelings of sadness and low self-esteem
Delusions of self-evil, often bizarre
Insomnia (most) or hypersomnia
Relative anorexia, weight loss, apathy
Ill-founded aches and pains, especially headache and backache
Complaints of mental loss despite normal cognitive tests

TABLE 112–23. FEATURES DISTINGUISHING DEPRESSION FROM DEMENTIA

	DEPRESSION	DEMENTIA
Duration of symptoms	Weeks to months	Months to years
Insight	Hypochondriacal	Often minimal
Prominent personalities and events	Recalled	Forgotten
Speech	Sparse to mute	Mute to excessive
Vegetative signs: insomnia, constipation, anorexia	Prominent	Minimal
Nocturnal behavior	Better	Worse
Sensorimotor changes	Absent	Often present
Brain images or EEG	Normal	Often abnormal

tions. If the drug is given as a single dose at night, it promotes sleep, frequently relieving almost immediately one of the most disturbing symptoms in the depressed patient. The full psychological benefit usually takes 2 to 4 weeks. Other antidepressant drugs include monoamine oxidase inhibitors, tetracyclic antidepressants, trazodone, and fluoxetine, the latter two drugs being unrelated to the others. The *Physicians' Desk Reference* should be consulted for dosage. Benzodiazepines are *not* useful. Furthermore, they may exacerbate an unrecognized depression. If antidepressant drug therapy fails, electroshock therapy is often efficacious, particularly in patients with psychotic depression.

Mania. Manic signs and symptoms are the antithesis of depression, that is, elation, grandiosity, and constant restless activity. Alternating episodes of manic "highs" with depressive "lows" are termed *bipolar disease*, which is more common than recurrent, isolated manic attacks. In the earliest stages of mania, patients actually may become more productive. As the disease progresses, however, they deteriorate. Manic persons are easily distracted, show flight of ideas, and become so grandiose and implausible as to be recognized easily as "crazy." Patients with intense mania may go for days without sleep and yet deny fatigue. The mood can suddenly change to anger and violence with little or no provocation.

The diagnosis of mania is usually easy because of the typical symptoms. Sometimes thyrotoxicosis, structural disease of the limbic system, or corticosteroid drug intoxication can mimic mania. Alternately, it may be difficult to distinguish a manic episode from schizophrenic agitation, but the extreme self-confidence that accompanies mania or a history of bipolar swings usually confirms the diagnosis.

TABLE 112-24. THE PRIMARY ANXIETY DISORDERS

Phobic disorders
    Agoraphobia with panic attacks
    Agoraphobia without panic attacks
    Social phobia
    Simple phobia
Anxiety states
    Panic disorder
    Generalized anxiety disorder
    Obsessive-compulsive disorder
Post-traumatic stress disorder
    Acute
    Chronic or delayed
Atypical anxiety disorder

Modified with permission from Brown JT, Mulrow CD, Stoudemire CA: The anxiety disorders. Ann Intern Med, 1984, Vol 100, pp 558–564.

The treatment of mania is difficult, in part because patients feel well and see no need for medicine. Phenothiazines or butyrophenones often control agitated behavior. Lithium is the mainstay. The drug is given in a dose of 900 to 2400 mg/day, with careful monitoring of plasma lithium levels to keep the concentration below 2 mEq/L. Excessive lithium levels lead to confusion, disorientation, tremor, anorexia, and, sometimes, seizures with permanent neurologic damage. Maintenance lithium in patients with a history of manic psychosis or bipolar disease often prevents further episodes.

Anxiety Disorders (Table 112–24). Abnormal anxiety is an unpleasant mood of tension and apprehension related to fear but not focused on an immediately stressful situation or object of danger. Anxiety is generally accompanied by autonomic symptoms including tachycardia, perspiration, dry mouth, and sometimes hyperventilation. In predisposed individuals, perception of the autonomic changes, particularly palpitations (tachycardia) and lightheadedness (hyperventilation), increases the anxiety, thereby intensifying the autonomic symptoms.

The cause of the primary anxiety disorders is unknown. The condition is common, with a prevalence rate of about 1 per cent and a higher incidence in women. Genetic as well as behavioral-develop-

TABLE 112-25. DIAGNOSTIC CRITERIA FOR PANIC DISORDER

I. An average of one or more panic attacks weekly
II. Attacks manifested by discrete periods of apprehension or fear, plus at least four of the following symptoms: dyspnea; palpitations; chest pain or discomfort; choking or smothering sensations; dizziness, vertigo, or unsteady feelings; feelings of unreality; paresthesias (tingling in hands or feet); hot and cold flashes; sweating; faintness; trembling or shaking; fear of dying, "going crazy," or doing something uncontrolled.
III. Major depression, somatization disorder, or schizophrenia ruled out

Modified with permission from American Psychiatric Association: Diagnostic and Statistical Manual of Mental Disorders, Third Edition, Revised, Washington, DC, American Psychiatric Association, 1987.

mental factors undoubtedly play a role. Anxiety disorders have a higher concordance in monozygotic than in dizygotic twins, generally run in families, and are often associated with alcoholism. A disproportionate number of patients have mitral valve prolapse.

Clinically, anxiety states include (1) *phobias*, which can vary from simple phobic fears of particular objects, to agoraphobia, fear of being either alone or in public places, (2) panic attacks marked by fear, apprehension, and feelings of impending doom without underlying cause (Table 112–25), and (3) a generalized and constant feeling of fear and apprehension.

The diagnosis usually is easy: no organic disease produces such a litany of sensory experiences. Having such patients hyperventilate often reproduces their symptoms and distinguishes the disorder from a primary cardiac or neurologic abnormality. Only rarely can structural disease be responsible for attacks of autonomic dysfunction that appear to have their origin in panic. Some temporal lobe seizures produce an aura of intense fear or anxiety associated with abnormalities of pulse and respiration, in early stages indistinguishable from panic attacks. Such seizures, however, culminate in a recognizable psychomotor attack or a generalized convulsion. Sudden changes in cardiovascular function, such as arrhythmias or acute hypertension (as from a pheochromocytoma), can mimic panic or anxiety attacks. The strongest clinical clue to such organically generated episodes is their recent onset.

Behavioral therapy and pharmacologic agents are reported to ameliorate recurrent panic attacks. Behavior modification in which the patient is desensitized by exposure to the fear-producing object has been useful in the treatment of phobias. Useful drugs for generalized anxiety disorders and panic attacks include monoamine oxidase inhibitors, tricyclic antidepressants, and modest doses of anxiolytic agents such as the benzodiazepines. Beta blockers such as propranolol sometimes help patients with major autonomic symptoms, especially those who have mitral valve prolapse as well.

Somatoform, Dissociative, and Factitious Disorders. The essential features consist of physical symptoms unexplained by either demonstrable organic findings or known physiologic mechanisms, accompanied by evidence of severe psychologic instability. These disorders putatively differ from factitious disorders or malingering in that the symptoms are believed not to be under conscious control. Somatoform disorders are often grouped together under the rubrics of "hysteria" or conversion reaction.

Somatoform disorders can produce almost any of the symptoms of physical illness (Table 112–26). Most conversion symptoms involve the nervous system and consist of abnormalities of consciousness or gait, paralysis, sensory loss, blindness, hearing loss, speech loss, or seizures. (Many patients with "pseudoseizures" also have true epilepsy.) Non-neurologic somatic complaints such as nausea, multiple aches and pains, excessive fatigue, and weakness are common conversion symptoms that often lead to excessively repeated medical studies until their nonsomatic origins are realized.

Conversion symptoms occur in a variety of forms, some more elaborate than others. Most often, they arise in patients with severe repressed or expressed anxiety who displace their inner symptoms onto a fixed idea of disease located in a specific organ or member. Less often, such symptoms are superimposed on those of an actual organic disease, presumably as an attention-getting device or an unconscious displacement of vaguely sensed ill health onto a less emotionally threatening sensory or motor infirmity.

A third variety, called *Munchausen's syndrome*, involves persons who actively simulate organic disease, either by symptoms alone or by self-medication or self-mutilation in order to deceive medical personnel. Many such persons either have been health care workers or have had close association with health professionals. Typical examples are individuals who induce "idiopathic" hypokalemia by ingesting surreptitiously obtained diuretics or nondiabetics who self-inject insulin to simulate disease-produced hypoglycemia. Some memorize the details of medical textbooks in order to present a credible story of a severe disease such as acute intermittent porphyria. Others have been known to ingest anticoagulants in an effort to imitate a cryptic blood dyscrasia. Munchausen's syndrome is a serious disease with a high incidence of self-invited invasive medical procedures and operations. Women predominate in its incidence. Characteristically, as the cause of their symptoms begins to be recognized, they travel from hospital to hospital until the nature of their illness becomes apparent to all. Most refuse psychiatric assistance and continue to insist that their medical complaints have an organic origin. Many eventually commit suicide.

Malingering, that is, conscious simulation of nonexistent sensations or motor loss, is more common in men, especially when the illness is work-related or influences retirement benefits. The diagnosis can be difficult to prove but should be suspected when signs and symptoms are physiologically absurd and good evidence of potential secondary gain of either a psychological or financial nature can be identified.

Dissociative disorders consist of sudden, temporary alterations in self-aware consciousness not caused by structural or physiologic disease of the nervous system. Such disturbances include the following:

1. *Factitious amnesia*, for either a circumscribed event or all past life events, neither associated with recent memory impairment as tested by routine instruments (see also Table 112–17).

2. *Fugue states*, episodes in which individuals disappear from their ordinary location, travel elsewhere, and assume a new identity, denying knowledge of their previous existence.

3. *Multiple personalities*, conditions in which individuals claim several exclusively different inner selves, each one freed, when another is acting, of responsibility for the knowledge or acts of the absent self-persona.

4. *Depersonalization disorders*, in which persons

TABLE 112–26. DIAGNOSTIC CRITERIA FOR SOMATIFORM DISORDER

A. Sustained symptoms beginning before age 30
B. Complaints of at least 14 of the following for women and 12 for men:
Sickly much of his or her life
Pseudoneurologic symptoms: difficulty swallowing, loss of voice, deafness, diplopia, blurred vision, blindness, fainting or loss of consciousness, memory loss, seizures or convulsions, trouble walking, paralysis or muscle weakness, urinary retention, or difficulty urinating
Gastrointestinal symptoms: abdominal pain, nausea, vomiting, bloating, intolerance of several foods, diarrhea
Female reproductive symptoms: excessively painful menstruation, menstrual irregularity, excessive bleeding, severe vomiting throughout pregnancy
Psychosexual symptoms for the major part of the individual's life
Pain in back, joints, extremities, genital area on urination
Shortness of breath, palpitations, chest pain, dizziness

Modified with permission from American Psychiatric Association: Diagnostic and Statistical Manual of Mental Disorders, Third Edition, Revised, Washington, DC, American Psychiatric Association, 1987.

suffer a change in their self-perception so that they lose or alter their sense of reality. Fleeting feelings of depersonalization are fairly widespread among normal individuals, especially children and adolescents. Similar experiences lasting for seconds or a few minutes in duration occur with temporal lobe epilepsy. Long periods of depersonalization almost always reflect psychological rather than physiologic abnormalities of the brain.

Diagnosis of the above disorders often is far from easy and depends heavily on the physician's experience and level of suspicion. Whether the symptoms follow a neurologic, systemic, or psychiatric pattern, the key to their understanding lies in the fact that they are inexplicable on a physiologic basis.

All of these conditions are difficult to treat. Physical, particularly neurologic, symptoms in their early stages can often be relieved by a matter-of-fact approach in which the physician reassures the patient that he is going to get well but avoids initiating a long discussion of the symptom's pathogenesis. Firmness and support often restore strength to a hemiplegic hysteric and sight to a blind one. At the same time, psychological support should be given to relieve anxiety and to ameliorate the environmental stresses that produced the symptoms in the first place. Many such patients, however, are intractable to treatment. This is especially true of those with Munchausen's syndrome, dissociative states, and malingering.

REFERENCES

Marsden CD: Hysteria—A neurologist's view. Psychol Med 16:277–288, 1986.
Tucker GJ: Psychiatric disorders in medical practice. In Wyngaarden JB, Smith LH Jr, Bennett JC (eds): Cecil Textbook of Medicine. 19th ed. Philadelphia, WB Saunders Co, 1992, pp 2079–2090.

F. Drug and Alcohol Abuse

Drug abuse is a huge medical-social problem world wide. Almost any drug as well as many household substances, including some common plants, can produce toxic changes if ingested in large amounts. Most abused drugs, as well as those taken for suicidal purposes, exert their primary effects on the brain. Drugs, including alcohol, that affect higher brain function generally possess in varying combinations and severity the addiction-promoting potentials of *psychological dependence* leading to craving, *tolerance-habituation* leading to the ingestion of increasing amounts of drugs to achieve a constant effect, and *physical dependence* leading to neurogenic *withdrawal phenomena* unless the drug is taken continuously. Individual susceptibility to these changes varies widely and is influenced by both environmental and inherited qualities. Whatever these contributions may be, however, the physician's level of suspicion and his or her courage in facing the patient with the evidence provide the critical key to obtaining proper treatment.

THERAPEUTIC DRUG OVERDOSE

This condition is frequent, especially among the elderly, whose susceptibility is enhanced both by poor memories for what they have taken and their involutionally weakened neurologic and metabolic reserves. The chief offenders are listed in Table 112–27. Several of these agents, such as digitalis and corticosteroids, can cause confusion and hallucinations in "standard" therapeutic doses, especially in patients over age 70.

RECREATIONAL-SEDATIVE DRUG ABUSE AND POISONING (Table 112–28)

Marijuana

This widely used, predominantly inhaled agent depends primarily on metabolites of delta-9-tetrahydrocannabinol for its pharmacologic action. Autonomic effects include conjunctival congestion, tachycardia, flushing, orthostatic hypotension, dry mouth, and sometimes vomiting. Psychic reactions depend considerably on the user and the setting in which the drug is inhaled. Users report perceptual enhancement, euphoria, a sense of timelessness, infectious joviality, and drowsiness. Coordination and reaction time are impaired. Mild tolerance and physical dependence usually develop, but most persons suffer only moderately adverse effects. Physiologic effects include respiratory tract irritation, tachycardia, decreased sperm formation, and, possibly, reduced fertility. Enduring psychic changes are uncertain. Acutely, depression, panic, paranoia, and toxic psychosis have been reported. Some chronic heavy users become unable to undertake goal-directed efforts, but whether the traits precede or follow cannabis use is uncertain.

Central Nervous System (CNS) Depressants

Those most frequently abused include benzodiazepines, short-acting barbiturates, and other sedatives, especially methaqualone (Quaalude) and methyprylon (Noludar). The agents are mostly ingested orally and are widely used to counteract insomnia and anxiety. Most self-medicators develop mild habituation. Severe addiction can develop among secret sedative users, much as it does among closet alcoholics. Street use of all the CNS depressants is usually combined with marijuana, alcohol, or cocaine.

Withdrawal symptoms commonly follow the removal of any of these drugs after heavy usage, usually beginning 2 to 6 days after cessation. Symptoms consist of heightened insomnia, anxiety, and apprehension, together with tremulousness and mild autonomic changes. Withdrawal from chronic heavy barbiturate use is particularly distressing and causes symptoms and signs similar to those of the alcohol abstinence syndrome (p. 760). Treatment is similar to that of alcohol withdrawal syndromes and consists of reintroducing the drug, then tapering it gradually to avoid symptoms. Overprescribing by physicians commonly underlies addiction to these drugs. Barbiturates probably should be avoided except for the treatment of epilepsy. All CNS depressant drugs tend to intensify pre-existing feelings of psychological depression, contraindicating their use for treating such symptoms.

Cocaine

This powerfully addicting agent is predominantly insufflated but also can be taken by mouth, vein, or absorption through mucous membranes. Its use has increasingly spread among adolescents and young adults, especially in the free-based form termed "crack." Mortality climbs apace. Physiologic effects include local anesthesia, fever, tachycardia, hypertension, pupillary dilatation, peripheral vasoconstriction, tachypnea, and anorexia. Psychologically, users report feelings of increased energy, alertness, and psychic power, often coupled with irritability

TABLE 112–27. THERAPEUTIC DRUGS POTENTIALLY CAUSING CONFUSION OR DELIRIUM

Digitalis	Yellowed vision; paranoid complex hallucinations
Sedatives, Anxiolytics, Antidepressants, Antipsychotics	Dull confusion, occasionally agitation, withdrawal, irritability, and insomnia. Some have anticholinergic effects
Corticosteroids, salicylates, levodopa, theophylline, cimetidine, amantadine, etc.	Occasionally confusion, hallucination, or organic psychosis

TABLE 112-28. COMMON DRUG POISONINGS AFFECTING BEHAVIOR

DRUG	SIGNS AND SYMPTOMS		DIAGNOSTIC TEST	TREATMENT: INTENSIVE CARE PLUS
	MILD	SEVERE		
Opiates Heroin Morphine Meperidine (Demerol) Methadone Hydromorphone Oxycodone Levorphanol	"Nodding" drowsiness, small pupils, urinary retention, slow and shallow breathing; skin scars and subcutaneous abscesses; duration 4–6 hr; with methadone, duration to 24 hr	Coma, pinpoint pupils, low irregular breathing or apnea, hypotension, hypothermia, pulmonary edema	Response to naloxone Urine	Naloxone, 0.4 mg IV; repeat at 15-min intervals if responds and gradually increase intervals; repeat in 3 hr if necessary; if no response by second dose, suspect another cause; find and treat infection.
Depressants Alcohol Benzodiazepines (Librium, Valium, Tranxene, Ativan, Dalmane, etc.) Barbiturates Methaqualone (Quaalude, Sopor, Mandrax) Ethchlorvynol (Placidyl)	Confusion, rousable drowsiness, delirium, ataxia, nystagmus, dysarthria, analgesia to stimuli Hallucinations, agitation, motor hyperactivity, myoclonus, tonic spasms Often taken with another sedative or alcohol if poisoning is attempted	Stupor to coma, pupils reactive, usually constricted, rarely fixed, oculovestibular response absent, motor tonus usually flaccid, respiration and blood pressure depressed; hypothermia. With methaqualone: coma, occasional convulsions, tachycardia, cardiac failure, bleeding tendency	Blood, urine, breath Blood Blood Blood Blood	Intubate, ventilate, lavage; drainage position; antimicrobials; keep mean blood pressure above 90 mm Hg and urine output above 300 ml/hr; avoid analeptics; hemodialyze for severe phenobarbital poisoning; otherwise, diuresis of little help.
Stimulants Amphetamines Methylphenidate	Hyperactive, aggressive, sometimes paranoid, repetitive behavior; dilated pupils, tremor, hyperactive reflexes; hyperthermia, tachycardia, arrhythmia Acute torsion dystonia	Agitated, assaultive, paranoid; occasionally convulsions; hyperthermia; circulatory collapse	Blood	Chlorpromazine
Cocaine	Similar to but less prominent than above; less paranoid, often euphoric	Twitching, irregular breathing, tachycardia, arrhythmia, occasionally convulsions	Blood, urine	Diazepam, plus symptomatic
Psychedelics: LSD, psilocybin, phencyclidine (PCP, angel dust)	Confused, perceptual distortions, distractable, withdrawn or eruptive, leading to accidents or violence; dilated pupils; restless, hyperreflexic; less often, hypertension or tachycardia	Panic		Reassure; diazepam satisfactory; avoid phenothiazines
Scopolamine-atropine (knockout drops, Transderm delirium)	Agitated or confused, visual hallucinations, dilated pupils, flushed and dry skin	Florid delirium, hallucinations, amnesia, fever, tachyarrhythmia, dilated pupils, urinary retention		Reassure; sedate lightly, avoid phenothiazines; if severe, do not leave alone.
Antidepressants Tricyclics (Toframil, Elavil, Desipramine, etc.)	Restlessness, drowsiness, tachycardia, ataxia, sweating	Agitation, vomiting, hyperpyrexia, sweating, muscle dystonia,	Blood	Symptomatic; gastric lavage. If severe, anticonvulsants and

Table continued on following page

TABLE 112–28.   COMMON DRUG POISONINGS AFFECTING BEHAVIOR *Continued*

DRUG	SIGNS AND SYMPTOMS		DIAGNOSTIC TEST	TREATMENT: INTENSIVE CARE PLUS
	MILD	SEVERE		
Antidepressants (*continued*)				
Tricyclics (Toframil, Elavil, Desipramine, etc.)		convulsions, ta-chyarrhythmia, QT prolongation		antiarrhythmics
Neuroleptics (phenothiazines, butyrophenones, etc.)	Acute dystonia, som-nolence, hypotension	Coma, convulsions (rare), arrhythmias, hypotension	Blood	Anticholinergics; di-phenhydramine; gas-tric lavage
Lithium	Mild lethargy	Intention tremor, dis-tracted lethargy, muteness, coma, multifocal seizures, slow or fluctuating course	Blood	Hydrate if mild; hemo-dialyze for delirium, coma, or convulsions.
Acid-forming Intoxicants				
Methanol (formic); ethylene glycol (ox-alic and hippuric); other organic alco-hols	Inebriation with hy-perpnea	All produce progres-sive hyperventila-tion, drunkenness, stupor, eventually convulsions and death. Early blind-ness with methanol	Blood: increasing anion-gap acidosis	Inhibit hepatic alcohol dehydrogenase by giving alcohol until acidosis is con-trolled; treat acidosis vigorously.
Salicylate				
Aspirin	Tinnitus, dyspnea	Older persons: confu-sion or toxic delir-ium leading to stu-por, convulsions, coma	Blood salicylate >55 mg/dl	Alkaline diuresis

Adapted from Plum F: Sustained impairments of consciousness. *In* Wyngaarden JB, Smith LH Jr, Bennett JC (eds): Cecil Textbook of Medicine. 19th ed. Philadelphia, WB Saunders Co, 1992, pp 2055–2056.

and some anxiety. Reportedly, intravenous use or the smoking of crack induces an intense, euphoric "rush" followed by a craving to repeat the experi-ence. Complications include social dissolution asso-ciated with craving, ulceration of the nasal septum, intracranial stroke-causing angiitis, occasionally convulsions and, with high doses, coma and death. Amphetamine abuse can cause somewhat similar experiences and complications. Treatment of co-caine abuse consists of withdrawal in a protective environment plus giving benzodiazepines or pheno-thiazines to control severe agitation. Psychological dependence is strong, leading to repetitive or con-tinuous use, with a "crash" of debilitated disorgani-zation and deep sleep at the end. Postwithdrawal craving reportedly is intense and protracted, leading to frequent recidivism even after weeks or months of abstinence.

Opiates

Heroin, morphine, methadone, and meperidine are the chief offenders, in that order. Two principal medical problems arise with their acute use: acci-dental or intentional overdose and the development of complications resulting from idiosyncratic reac-tions, infections, and immunologic abnormalities.

Efforts by amateur chemists to produce psychedelic congeners have sometimes generated molecular variants with disastrous results, as exemplified by a recent miniepidemic of chemically induced severe parkinsonism.

Acute overdose with opiates produces stupor or coma, pupillary miosis, and slow, irregular, shallow breathing. Body temperature and blood pressure fall, seizures can occur, and some patients develop acute pulmonary edema. Treatment of acute over-dose consists of immediately giving naloxone, a powerful opiate antagonist, intravenously or, if no veins can be found, intramuscularly. If no immedi-ate response occurs, the injection should be re-peated. Because the effects of naloxone wear off within 2 to 3 hours and the depressant effects of the opiates can last much longer, the antagonist should be repeated at 2- to 3-hour intervals until all evi-dence of a response disappears. Stuporous or hypo-ventilating patients who do not respond immedi-ately should be treated according to the general program for care of the patient in coma (see Table 112–11).

Chronic opiate addicts can develop severe with-drawal symptoms consisting of yawning, anxiety, restlessness, rhinorrhea, lacrimation, and influenzal symptoms within minutes after receiving naloxone. The symptoms can be reduced by clonidine or ameliorated by small doses of narcotics. Naloxone should be confined to overdose situations and not employed in a nonemergency setting either as a diagnostic measure or to induce withdrawal.

Complications of illicit narcotic use include arrhythmias, pulmonary edema, and convulsions due to adulterants. Opiate users suffer a high incidence of bacteriologic infections of skin, veins, blood, heart, and lung. Many develop viral hepatitis and AIDS (see Chapter 109). Serious neurologic complications consist of neuropathy, myelopathy, optic neuritis, and myriad infections, including tetanus and brain abscess.

Tricyclic Antidepressants

These agents possess potentially serious cardiovascular effects, oral doses of more than 2 gm often being lethal. Because behavioral changes can take some hours to develop and blood levels may not be easily available, patients reporting acute self-overdose should have an immediate electrocardiogram (ECG). The presence of a widened QRS to greater than 100 msec indicates serious toxicity and a need for intensive supervision and cardiac monitoring. A more common presentation consists of a state of stupor or coma, combined with anticholinergic signs reminiscent of atropine poisoning and the presence of cardiac arrhythmias on the ECG. Treatment in alert patients consists of ipecac-induced vomiting and in stuporous ones of gastric lavage followed by activated charcoal instillation. Convulsions and arrhythmias are treated by appropriate standard measures. Otherwise, management follows that outlined in Table 112–11. Most tricyclics have half-lives of many days, so that monitoring and intensive treatment can be required for as long as a week in severe cases.

Salicylate Poisoning

Salicylate intoxication can occur in older adults as an accident of overzealous attempts to relieve pain and in adolescents and young adults owing to intentional overdose. Salicylates in high doses uncouple oxidative phosphorylation, and aspirin itself adds acid radicals. The resulting acid-base disturbance in adults is almost diagnostic: tissue glycolysis produces intracellular lactacidosis, which produces an acid urine and stimulates the brain stem respiratory centers. The result is a mixed respiratory alkalosis–metabolic acidosis with an elevated blood pH, a low $PaCO_2$, and low serum bicarbonate. Early symptoms include tinnitus, deafness, disequilibrium, drowsiness, and a moderate delirium. With blood levels greater than 60 mg/dl, stupor, coma, and potentially fatal convulsions can ensue. Treatment consists of gastric lavage and giving generous bicarbonate solutions, using alkaline diuresis as an end point.

Phencyclidine (PCP)

PCP is currently the most widely abused of the psychedelic-hallucinogenic group of drugs that include, among numerous others, LSD, amphetamines, and scopolamine. Users describe various experiences, most prevalent of which is a state of altered perception in which dreams and heightened reality become indistinguishable. Excess inhalation or ingestion of PCP can induce ataxia, confusion, aggressive violence, prolonged psychotic states, coma, or convulsions. Treatment is symptomatic, but the "bad trip" may be shortened by acidifying the urine with ammonium chloride and applying continuous gastric suction to accelerate excretion of the drug.

Nonethyl Alcohols

Most cases of poisoning from these agents occur in alcoholics or drug abusers unaware of the toxic nature of the substance. Methanol and ethylene glycol both produce potentially fatal metabolic acidosis through their metabolic products. The hepatic enzyme alcohol dehydrogenase acts on both substrates to produce acid products. Inhibiting alcohol dehydrogenase by giving 4-methylpyrazol or 5 to 10 gm of ethyl alcohol per hour by mouth or vein effectively halts this highly toxic step and is the treatment of choice. Severe poisoning requires that ethanol blood levels of 100 to 150 mg/dl be maintained for at least 48 to 72 hours while stabilizing blood acid-base levels with the bicarbonate buffer. Ethylene glycol may cause subsequent renal damage from oxylate and hippurate crystalluria.

ALCOHOL ABUSE AND ITS COMPLICATIONS

Ethyl alcohol is the oldest and still most widely taken psychotropic drug. Used by more than half of all Americans and abused by 1 in 20, the agent creates a huge medical and sociologic problem.

Pharmacology

Ethanol is usually ingested as a fraction of some vehicle of distinctive taste such as beer (5 per cent), wine (12 per cent), or various stronger agents containing 20 to 50 per cent alcohol (40 to 100 proof). Ethanol enters the blood within minutes from the stomach and intestine and quickly penetrates all aqueous body compartments, including the brain and alveolar air. Ethanol is excreted through the lungs by physical diffusion and detoxified by hepatic dehydrogenase at a rate that approximates 8 ml/hour, clearing about 15 mg/dl/hour from the blood.

Blood levels of alcohol correlate directly with clinical signs and symptoms, chronic alcoholics showing great tolerance compared with novices (Table 112–29). In less than near-fatal amounts, aside from producing vasodilatation and gastric irritation, alcohol exerts almost all its ill affects on the central nervous system, acting entirely as a depressant. The earlier euphoriant-excitatory stage reflects a removal of higher inhibitory effects from limbic system restraints, and larger doses increasingly depress first forebrain and then brain stem functions. Death from acute intoxication usually re-

TABLE 112–29. BLOOD-ALCOHOL LEVELS AND SYMPTOMS

LEVEL (mg/dl)	SPORADIC DRINKERS	CHRONIC DRINKERS
50 (party level)	Congenial euphoria	No observable effect
75	Gregarious or garrulous	Often no effect
100	Incoordinated. Legally intoxicated	Minimal signs
125–150	Unrestrained behavior Episodic dyscontrol	Pleasurable euphoria or beginning incoordination
200–250	Alertness lost → lethargic	Effort required to maintain emotional and motor control
300–350	Stupor or coma	Drowsy and slow
>500	Some die	Coma

sults from central respiratory depression followed by circulatory failure.

Clinical Features

Acute Intoxication. The behavioral effects of acute intoxication vary with the user, ranging among social drinkers from pleasant conviviality to angry argumentativeness. A small number of younger male drinkers develop pathologically severe, aggressive, violent behavior ("dyscontrol") for which they later claim no memory. The syndrome has potentially dangerous consequences, and its diagnosis calls for total abstinence and immediate psychiatric referral. *Alcoholic blackouts,* periods of amnesia lasting for several hours or more during or at the end of a heavy drinking bout, are a sign of serious intoxication bordering on anesthesia. When recurrent, they signify impending or already existing alcoholic addiction.

Treatment of acute alcoholic attacks depends upon the degree of intoxication and the associated blood levels. Mild drunkenness requires no treatment. More severe intoxication producing heavy drowsiness or stupor deserves attention, especially if one does not know whether or not additional drugs have been ingested. The level of CNS depression can increase rapidly as alcohol is absorbed, and stuporous drunks need close attention to vital functions. Alcoholic deep stupor or coma requires hospital monitoring until symptoms subside. Patients with associated severe trauma or fever need especially close evaluation for potentially masked neurologic injury, blood loss, or infection.

Withdrawal Syndromes. Headache, giddiness, difficulty in concentrating, nausea, and mild tremulousness characterize the well-known *hangover.* Classic but unproved remedies or preventives include forcing nonalcoholic fluids while still intoxicated, avoiding the ingestion of agents such as red wines or brandies, and taking antacids. When hangover appears, another alcoholic drink aborts most of the symptoms but represents an early step toward the development of chronic alcoholism.

The serious withdrawal states of chronic alcoholism consist of prominent tremulousness, rum fits, and delirium tremens (DTs). They usually are preceded by years of problem drinking and usually are precipitated by continuous alcoholic ingestion lasting many days or weeks.

Tremulousness, insomnia, and agitation, although much more common, symptomatically blend into DTs, discussed below. Each reflects a state of central adrenergic hyperexcitation that emerges as alcohol's inhibitory influence dissipates. *Withdrawal convulsions* (rum fits) consist of single or short runs of generalized seizures, usually with no focal features. Their necessary stimulus consists of no more than a falling blood alcohol level and, in contrast to the more delayed appearance of DTs, they can occur during the course of a prolonged spree within hours of the last drink. About one third are followed by the DTs if abstinence continues. Treatment is symptomatic, using diazepam to stop the seizures and dampen the often associated tremulousness. Interictal laboratory tests, including CT scans and EEGs, show no specific abnormality, but if focal seizures occur a brain scan should be done to rule out a localized lesion such as subdural hematoma. Prophylactic anticonvulsants confer no protection.

Delirium tremens (DTs) represents the most serious and occasionally fatal withdrawal complication of alcohol, usually appearing only after a decade or more of fairly continuous, heavy drinking. The course is worsened when complicated by systemic infection, hepatic insufficiency, or head trauma. A somewhat similar although less florid condition affects patients withdrawing from chronic heavy barbiturate use, and the treatment described below applies equally well to that syndrome. Either alcoholic or *barbiturate withdrawal* DTs can arise unexpectedly in patients abruptly withdrawn from these drugs as a result of being admitted to the hospital for conditions such as trauma or emergency surgery.

Characteristically, DTs most often emerge only 3 to 5 days after complete alcohol or drug withdrawal. First symptoms consist of severe tremulousness, disorientation, visual hallucinations, and agitation. Signs of beta-adrenergic autonomic hyperactivity are prominent, including fear, sweating, tachycardia, hypertension, tachypnea, and incontinence. Many affected patients are malnourished and display associated signs of hepatic insufficiency, gastritis, dehydration, infection, polyneuropathy, myopathy, or Wernicke's syndrome (see below). Treatment consists of sedation with a drug cross-tolerant for alcohol, the benzodiazepine diazepam being most useful (Table 112–30). Huge amounts may be required: authorities report that as much as 215 mg may be necessary to control agitation initially, and some patients may need as much as 1200 mg given intravenously during the first 60 hours in order to remain calm.

Chronic Alcoholism. This condition is widespread and requires the physician's constant vigilance to detect it sufficiently early to modify its course. Psychological dependence, closet drinking, increasing social lapses, more than an occasional mild hangover, and, among spouses, an increasing number of nights out with the boys (or girls) are danger signals. Blackouts, absenteeism, drunken driving, occupational downgrading, or any medical complications including poorly explained, repeated physical injury imply serious trouble.

Even to get a potential alcoholic to consider that he or she has a psychological-medical problem can be a thankless and often unsuccessful task. Nevertheless, the doctor must try. Success usually requires sustained and effective psychotherapy by an experienced therapist plus participation in a reinforcement group, such as Alcoholics Anonymous. Several industries and large universities recently have established such groups, reporting successes as high as 70 per cent or more once persons come to realize that their jobs are on the line and their employer is genuinely interested. Disulfiram (Antabuse) produces conditioned avoidance to alcohol by introducing a violently adverse reaction to its ingestion. Its use is best supervised by experienced therapists.

Complications of Alcohol Abuse

Drunkenness contributes to a large fraction of deaths and severe injuries from traffic accidents, trauma, murder, suicide, and the inadvertent overdose of other drugs. Chronic complications can affect many body organs (Table 112–31). Some of these may be due to a direct, but tenuously established, toxic effect. Nutritional deprivation, however, causes the majority. Alcohol contains 7 calories per gram, but most of its vehicles include negligible amounts of vitamins, trace metals, or other nutrients, including protein. Alcoholics, supplying their immediate energy needs by carbohydrates, can wear the mask of nutritional good health for years while their brains, nerves, livers, and hearts degenerate to a degree that, sooner or later, becomes irreversible.

TOXIC AND DEFICIENCY NEUROLOGIC DISORDERS RELATED TO ALCOHOLISM AND NUTRITIONAL DEPRIVATION
(Table 112–32)

In addition to chronic alcoholism, severe nutritional insufficiencies can accompany any debilitating, energy-consuming illnesses, such as metastatic cancer, disseminated infection, thyrotoxicosis, advanced connective tissue disease, impaired intestinal absorption, and chronic behavioral disorders. Nutritional insufficiency with these illnesses only occasionally is confined to a single vitamin or nutrient fraction, although thiamine lack is perhaps most prevalent. Signs that suggest nutritional failure include apathetic listlessness, darkening of the skin, a sore red tongue, fissuring at the corners of the mouth, burning feet, progressive unexplained weight loss, and unexplained anemia. This section focuses on the most common neurologic complications, all of which, in the United States occur more with alcoholism than any other single disorder.

Chronic severe alcoholics suffer an increased incidence of middle-life–onset *optic neuropathy*, a

TABLE 112–30. TREATMENT OF SEVERE TREMULOUSNESS OR DELIRIUM TREMENS

1. Attempt control by reassurance and observation.
2. Treat systemic problems promptly.
3. Give thiamine first; continuously supply and balance electrolytes and other vitamins.
4. Treat uncontrollable agitation: Control with diazepam, 10 mg IV given slowly followed by 5–10 mg IV slowly every 5 minutes, to induce calmness. Once calm, maintain with diazepam, 5–10 mg IV or more every 1–4 hours.

TABLE 112–31. MAJOR NON-NEUROLOGIC COMPLICATIONS OF ALCOHOLISM

Heart
Cardiomyopathy
Arrhythmia
Hyperlipidemia
Gastrointestinal
Gastritis
Hepatitis-cirrhosis
Pancreatitis
Head, neck, and esophageal cancer
Malabsorption
Blood
Iron or folate deficiency
Anemia
Thrombocytopenia
Prothrombin deficiency

Endocrine
Male sexual impairment
Increased fetal risk
Immune System
Increased susceptibility to infection and impaired healing
Electrolyte Disturbances
Hypocalcemia
Hypomagnesemia
Hypophosphatemia
Acute water intoxication
Alcoholic hyperosmolality
Alcoholic ketosis

condition marked by reduced visual acuity, central or paracentral scotomas, and normal optic fundi. Dietary and vitamin therapies sometimes bring improvement. Advanced problem drinkers in as early as the fourth decade of life also can develop CT-imaged *cerebral atrophy* and signs of early dementia. Abstinence sometimes reverses the severity of these changes.

Alcoholic-nutritional peripheral neuropathy usually occurs only in company with advanced, mixed nutritional deprivation and usually improves only with total replacement and weight gain. The disorder produces axonal degeneration affecting predominantly the small pain- and temperature-mediating fibers in the distal lower extremities. Because the larger, touch-mediating peripheral fibers determine sensory nerve conduction velocities, that function can remain normal in the early stages of the neuropathy. Distal motor loss occurs relatively early. Spontaneous, often burning, pain and autonomic neuropathy commonly affect ad-

TABLE 112–32. MAJOR NEUROLOGIC COMPLICATIONS OF SEVERE ALCOHOLISM

Amblyopia and optic atrophy
Progressive cerebral degeneration and dementia
Peripheral neuropathy
Myopathy
Wernicke-Korsakoff disease
Parenchymatous cerebellar degeneration

vanced cases. Deep tendon reflexes disappear in a distal-to-proximal pattern. Recovery, often incomplete, requires months or years of renourishment.

Alcoholic myopathy is confined to chronic, severe alcoholics and can have either an acute or a chronic onset. The acute form consists of sudden transient rhabdomyolysis, often following a cluster of rum fits or possibly other trauma. It includes muscle pain, tenderness, cramping, weakness, and an elevated serum creatine kinase. Severe cases can develop myoglobinuria with associated renal complications. Chronic myopathy, a less blatant and distinctive disorder, consists of diffuse proximal muscle wasting and weakness disproportional to any existing neuritic impairment. It improves gradually with nutritional replacement.

Wernicke-Korsakoff disease reflects the acute and chronic CNS effects of severe, sustained thiamine depletion in the face of a continued caloric intake. In the United States, severe alcoholism most often causes the disorder, but other impoverished diets, including those associated with nonsupplemented hospital glucose infusions, hemodialysis, various food faddisms, and hyperemesis gravidarum, can lead to the same condition. The pathologic process affects the brain to produce axonal demyelination, neuronal loss, glial proliferation, endothelial thickening, and petechial pericapillary hemorrhages. The oculomotor, vestibular, and medullary autonomic nuclei as well as the brain stem reticular formation suffer the greatest damage. At higher levels the mammillary bodies, the mediodorsal thalamic nuclei, and scattered cortical regions including the hippocampus suffer most.

The clinical manifestations of Wernicke's disease reflect the major neuropathologic alterations. Acutely such patients are confused, often drowsy or semistuporous, ataxic, and dysarthric. Partial or complete external ophthalmoplegia and nystagmus are cardinal features. Further examination often discloses tachycardia, orthostatic hypotension, hypothermia, and a diffuse analgesia. The pupils seldom are affected, but almost any motor cranial nerve can be partially paralyzed. Most patients have at least mild signs of peripheral neuropathy. Treatment consists of giving thiamine, 50 mg parenterally, upon suspicion of the diagnosis, followed by replenishment of blood volume and electrolytes. Glucose administration should not precede thiamine treatment, as its metabolic processing can precipitate acute worsening. Evidence of severe anemia, hepatic insufficiency, or infection should be corrected and the patient watched closely for evidence of impending seizures or DTs. General good nourishment and efforts to halt the destructive slide of chronic alcoholism necessarily follow.

Wernicke's disease is readily diagnosed clinically, provided that one has enough history to suspect thiamine deficiency. The eye signs provide a critical clue: only acute idiopathic polyneuropathy, myasthenia gravis, botulism, and intoxication with phenytoin are likely to cause a similarly acute symmetric or asymmetric bilateral external ophthalmoplegia with preserved arousal. Of these, only Wernicke's disease and, rarely, phenytoin intoxication produce mental changes. The response to thiamine injection is usually diagnostic: the ophthalmoplegia usually begins to improve within a matter of hours to a day or so, a response produced with no other disorder.

Korsakoff's amnestic syndrome usually emerges as the acute confusional delirium of Wernicke's disease subsides. Affected patients show a profound, relatively isolated loss of recent memory for events. This, coupled with a placid lack of insight, often leads to total disorientation mixed with absurd conversations or answers to questions (confabulation). Arousal, language functions, and remote memories are spared. Korsakoff's arises only after either several preceding attacks of Wernicke's encephalopathy or an unusually severe one. Treatment is as for Wernicke's. About half the patients treated for the first time improve to the point of regaining independence.

Acute cerebellar degeneration occurs most often in alcoholics as a complication of an acute superimposed, severe binge. The disease reflects acute neuronal degeneration in the anterior and superior cerebellar vermis, leading to a gradually or suddenly appearing broad-based, stiff-legged ataxia unaccompanied by incoordination in the upper extremities or nystagmus. Many patients have an associated nutritional peripheral neuropathy, treatment of which sometimes lessens their functional difficulties.

Central pontine myelinolysis (CPM) occurs as a complication of severe hyponatremia or its treatment, usually following the correction of serum sodium levels at or below 110 mEq/L. Such severe hyponatremia can be a complication of prolonged alcoholism but more often arises in association with severe systemic illness. The disorder consists of the development of a symmetric zone of demyelination affecting the basis pontis of the brain stem, leading to lethargy or stupor, a quiet confused delirium, and more or less severe quadriparesis. Best evidence suggests that the disorder most often follows the overly rapid correction of severe hyponatremia. Most authorities recommend raising the serum sodium by no more than about 0.5 mEq/hr. Most examples of CPM become visible on MR or CT brain images within a week or so after onset. Many patients treated symptomatically recover in a matter of weeks.

REFERENCES

Dafy MA, Williams C, Caruso EH, et al: Physicians' Desk Reference. Montvale, NJ, Medical Economics Co, 1992.

Dreisbach RH, Robertson WO: Handbook of Poisoning. 12th ed. Norwalk, CT, Appleton and Lange, 1987.

O'Brien CP: Drug abuse and dependence. In Wyngaarden JB, Smith LH Jr, Bennett JC (eds): Cecil Textbook of Medicine. 19th ed. Philadelphia, WB Saunders Co, 1992, pp 47–55.

113 DISORDERS OF AUTONOMIC FUNCTION

The autonomic nervous system contains three major components. One links the brain to the pituitary gland via the hypothalamus to regulate the peripherally located endocrine organs (see Chapter 65). The second diffusely projects to higher brain centers cholinergic, noradrenergic, and serotoninergic pathways that originate, respectively, in ventral basal forebrain nuclei, the pontine locus ceruleus, and the raphe nuclei of the midbrain and pons. These ascending systems modulate arousal as well as cognitive and emotional expression. The third component consists of descending and peripheral autonomic sympathetic and parasympathetic pathways that originate in the hypothalamus and other brain stem centers and connect with the viscera and the extremities so as to regulate internal homeostasis. This chapter describes some of the more common examples of disorders affecting the last-mentioned components.

HYPOTHALAMUS (HT)

Direct damage to the HT can impair normal arousal mechanisms, interfere with trophic regulation of the pituitary gland, blunt learning, memory, and emotion, and disrupt mechanisms that regulate body temperature, visceral functions, water balance, and feeding behavior. Table 113–1 lists the principal disorders that result.

Disturbances of Temperature Regulation. Sustained relative *hypothermia* or *poikilothermia*, with body temperatures varying with the environment and falling below 35°C, can follow destructive lesions of the posterior hypothalamus or adjacent midbrain. Hypothermia also accompanies several metabolic comas as well as depressant drug poisoning. In addition, impaired autonomic responses to dehydration and ambient cooling frequently affect alcoholics and elderly persons, increasing their susceptibility to cold exposure and intensifying fluid loss and hypothermia. Small epidemics of exposure-induced hypothermia have been reported among residents of insufficiently heated nursing homes. Body temperatures below 33 to 34°C usually induce severe apathy or stupor, a reduction in amplitude of vital signs, and a palpably cold skin. Treatment of core temperatures between 31° and 35°C consists of gradual rewarming by blankets in a warmed environment. Heating blankets set at 38°C, tub immersions at 40° to 42°C, or warmed peritoneal dialysis can be employed for persons with colder core temperatures. Fluids and auxiliary treatment are guided by specific cardiac or infectious complications.

Paroxysmal hypothermia is an uncommon disorder, probably representing a form of diencephalic epilepsy; body temperature episodically drops to 32°C or less, associated with reduced alertness, mental slowness or confusion, and, usually, cardiorespiratory irregularities. Some affected patients respond to antiepileptic therapy.

Hyperthermia accompanies several disorders, including hypothalamic damage as well as heat exhaustion, heat stroke, and malignant hyperthermia. *Neurogenic hyperthermia* occurs as an acute phenomenon in association with several disorders affecting the hypothalamic region. Fever can rise to potentially fatal levels of 42°C or higher. If standard

TABLE 113–1. PRINCIPAL NONENDOCRINE DISORDERS OF AUTONOMIC REGULATION

Central (mainly hypothalamic)
  Emotional disorders
    Panic: intermittent, otherwise unexplained cardiac arrhythmia
  Thermoregulatory disorders
    Hyperthermia (rare)
      Acute trauma, local diencephalic region surgery, encephalitis, heat stroke, malignant hyperthermia, malignant neuroleptic syndrome
    Hypothermia–poikilothermia
      Episodic hypothermia (primary, developmental), destructive HT damage, metabolic (sedative drugs, hypoglycemia), senility or nutritional impairment plus exposure
  Water balance
    ADH dysregulation: SIADH (p. 764); "essential hypernatremia" (i.e., disconnection between HT osmoreceptor and ADH regulation), episodic hyperdipsia with hyponatremia (some is behavioral, some centrally induced)
  Feeding behavior
    Hyperphagia-obesity (medial HT)
    Anorexia-inanition (rare, lateral HT)
  Arousal-sleep disorders
Peripheral-central autonomic insufficiencies or dysregulation
  Idiopathic autonomic insufficiency (Shy-Drager syndrome)
  Visceral organ dysregulation: cardiovascular, gastrointestinal, genitourinary
  Tetanus (autonomic components)
  Inherited dysautonomia (e.g, Riley-Day)
Peripheral autonomic disorders
  Polyneuropathy: generalized inflammatory-demyelinating, selective acute autonomic neuropathy, diabetes, syphilis (tabes), acute intermittent porphyria, amyloidosis, leprosy, geriatric
  Reflex sympathetic dystrophies

HT = Hypothalamus, ADH = antidiuretic hormone; SIADH = syndrome of inappropriate antidiuretic hormone.

antipyretic measures fail, adding small doses of opiates sometimes ameliorates the elevated temperature. Other measures are discussed under heat stroke (below). Subacute or chronic fever almost never results from primary hypothalamic disorders.

Heat exhaustion and heat stroke (Table 113–2) result from combinations of high environmental temperature, increased generation of body heat, and decreased bodily adaptive functions. Muscular heat cramps commonly follow exhausting exercise in hot weather. They respond quickly to fluid and salt ingestion. More extensive heat exhaustion and heat stroke represent more serious problems. *Heat exhaustion* results from continued heat generation in the presence of a gradual net loss of water or salt and water. Muscle cramps progress to impairment of cardiovascular mechanisms manifested by feelings of giddiness, dizziness, and syncope. With more protracted and severe exposures, fever and delirium follow. Sweating continues until the late stages. Treatment consists of cool spongings or tubs plus generous salt and water replacement.

Heat stroke, a potentially fatal disorder, characteristically affects its victims during the summer's first severe heat wave or upon the sudden movement of vigorously active young persons from a cool to a hot climate, such as occurs with troops during war. As with heat exhaustion, risk factors include a lack of acclimatization, old age and infirmity, alcoholic excess and, especially, the ingestion of anticholinergic or antipsychotic drugs. The disorder results when high ambient temperatures and humidity combine to generate heat and prevent its loss while, at the same time, age, neurologic disease, or drugs impair central autonomic mechanisms. Clinical signs include hyperpyrexia greater than 41°C; hot, dry skin; and increasing prostration, confusion, stupor and, finally, coma accompanied by signs of

TABLE 113–2. HEAT EXHAUSTION AND HEAT STROKE COMPARED

	HEAT EXHAUSTION	HEAT STROKE
Time of occurrence	Any hot weather	First sustained heat wave
Principally affected	Elderly hypodipsics, young heavy laborers, strenuous athletes, etc.	Elderly; infirm; obese; alcoholics; psychotics
Principal pathogenesis	Salt or water loss	Failure of heat loss
Contributing factors	Prolonged exercise	Antiperspirants; anticholinergics, phenothiazines, diuretics, neuroleptics; old age; dehydration
Body temperature	37–38.5°C	39–43°C
Sweating	Usually present	Absent
Treatment	Fluids and adjusted electrolytes	Prompt body cooling (ice water immersion)

TABLE 113–3. CHIEF DRUG GROUPS ASSOCIATED WITH THE NEUROLEPTIC MALIGNANT SYNDROME

Phenothiazines	Sudden discontinuation of anti-Parkinson drugs
Butyrophenones	
Thioxanthines	Dopamine-depleting agents
Other antipsychotic agents	

brain stem dysfunction. Associated abnormalities can include tachycardia, ST and T wave abnormalities on the electrocardiogram (ECG), hypotension, consumption coagulopathy, signs of dehydration, potassium and sodium depletion, and hepatic damage. Treatment is aimed at bringing core temperature below 39°C in an ice tub bath and meeting systemic problems, including high-output heart failure, as they arise. Mortality and permanent neurologic disability relate directly to the duration of hyperthermia and the prompt effectiveness of its treatment.

Malignant hyperthermia is a rare disorder that results from a genetically determined, autosomal dominant point mutation in the ryanodine receptor of skeletal muscle. The error leads to excessive calcium release from muscle sarcoplasm during anesthetic induction. Immediately following a preoperative administration of succinylcholine followed by an inhalation anesthetic, diffuse, severe skeletal muscle contraction takes place, producing generalized rigidity, increased heat production, and potentially fatal fevers of 39 to 42°C or greater. Treatment consists of quick interruption of anesthesia and surgery, with vigorous measures taken to counteract fever and systemic lactacidosis. Blood relatives of those who show the disorder should be pretested for potential susceptibility before receiving general anesthesia. The *neuroleptic malignant syndrome,* a less frequent idiosyncratic response, follows a similar clinical pattern, with hyperthermia, muscle rigidity, autonomic instability, and reduced consciousness following administration of one or more of the drugs cited in Table 113–3. The pathogenesis is poorly understood. Treatment consists of neuroleptic withdrawal and cooling measures. Dantrolene and, less often, procainamide have been reported to counter the muscle rigidity in some but not all examples of both hyperthermic syndromes.

Disorders of Water Balance.

1. Hypoplasia or direct damage to the supraoptic or paraventricular nuclei or their major connections to the posterior pituitary gland leads to antidiuretic hormone (ADH) deficiency and the disorder *diabetes insipidus* (p. 468).

2. Neurogenic imbalance or biologically erroneous signals from peripheral receptors or their CNS connections can lead to *inappropriately increased ADH* secretion, producing excessive hemodilution and hyponatremia (p. 200).

3. HT-engendered failure of thirst associated with reduced ADH secretion causes the rare condition of *essential hypernatremia,* in which appetite for water is lacking despite pathologically elevated serum sodium levels.

Generalized systemic *autonomic insufficiency* (pandysautonomia) can occur on either a central or a peripheral basis. Diffuse, moderate sympathetic-parasympathetic dysfunction accompanies occasional cases of parkinsonism and several of the late-life cerebellar degenerations. *Shy-Drager disease* is an uncommon midlife, slowly progressive, degenerative disorder that affects central and, to a lesser degree, peripheral autonomic pathways, accompanied by variable abnormalities in cerebellar, extrapyramidal and, occasionally, corticospinal motor systems. Cardinal symptoms and signs include male impotence, anhidrosis, orthostatic hypotension, absent autonomic cardiovascular reflexes, impaired pupillary control, gastrointestinal hypomotility, urinary retention or incontinence, hoarseness, and signs of parkinsonism or cerebellar dysfunction. Patients develop refractory bradycardia, orthostatic hypotension, and symptoms of lightheadedness or syncope when assuming the erect or even the sitting position. Treatment is symptomatic and consists of counteracting the hypotension with elastic stockings, increasing fluid intake, and giving mineralocorticoids to assist in blood volume expansion. Central-peripheral autonomic dysfunction of a more benign but protracted type is responsible for a variety of psychosomatically engendered functional abnormalities involving the heart, gastrointestinal tract, and urogenital system.

Autonomic abnormalities including severe hypotension also can accompany a number of peripheral neuropathies as noted in Table 113–1. Moderate autonomic dysfunction consisting of persistent tachycardia, impaired volume reflexes, and mild orthostatic insufficiency accompanies most examples of acute inflammatory neuropathy. Pandysautonomia or peripheral autonomic insufficiency contributes importantly to the major symptoms of idiopathic orthostatic hypotension. Similarly, tachycardia, neurogenic ECG changes, fluctuating hypertension, and abnormal sweating patterns mark the course of acute tetanus, porphyria, and inherited amyloidosis.

Autonomic dysfunction commonly develops among the elderly as a result of gradual degeneration of central-peripheral adaptation pathways plus an increasing susceptibility to the autonomic side effects of commonly used medications. Reflex and spontaneous sweating declines and impairs adaptation to extremes of environmental temperature in the elderly. Baroceptors, vasculotonic reflex controls, gastrointestinal reflexes, and urogenital controls gradually deteriorate as well. As a result, postural hypotension, reduced exercise tolerance, abnormal bradycardia, dyspepsia and constipation, male impotence, and urinary incontinence frequently plague life's later years. A host of cardiotropic, antidepressant, and psychotropic drugs can intensify these susceptibilities. Treatment of these common geriatric problems requires both patience and resourcefulness. Anecdotal evidence suggests that continued exercise and close attention to diet and blood volume may ameliorate many of these difficulties; it may be, however, that only the still healthy are capable of such self-regulation. Otherwise one treats symptomatically, minimizing both prescription and other drug use, checking on the autonomic effects of necessary medications, and treating bowel and bladder problems with the mildest possible remedies that may help. The references that follow discuss these problems in greater detail.

REFERENCES

Loewy AD, Spyer KM: Central Regulation of Autonomic Functions. New York, Oxford Press, 1990.

McLeod JG, Tuck RR: Disorders of the autonomic nervous system. Part 1: Pathophysiology and clinical features. Ann Neurol 21:419, 1987; Part 2. Investigation and treatment. Ann Neurol 21:519, 1987.

Plum F, van Uitert R: Non-endocrine diseases and disorders of the hypothalamus. Res Publ Assoc Res Nerv Ment Dis 15:415, 1977.

Saper C: Autonomic disorders and their management. *In* Wyngaarden JB, Smith LH Jr, Bennett JC (eds): Cecil Textbook of Medicine. 19th ed. Philadelphia, WB Saunders Co, 1992, pp 2091–2098.

Williams ME, Pannill FC: Urinary incontinence in the elderly. Physiology, pathophysiology, diagnosis and treatment. Ann Intern Med 97:895, 1982.

114 DISORDERS OF SENSORY FUNCTION

A. Pain and Painful Syndromes

PAIN AS A SIGNAL OF DAMAGE

Pain (Table 114–1) is the most common symptom for which patients seek medical assistance, and chronic pain the most vexing problem that physicians face. Pain has two aspects: the first is an emotionally neutral perception of a stimulus that is usually sufficiently strong to produce tissue damage; the second is an affective response to the perception of that stimulus. Pain implies damage to the organism, either physical or psychological, and chronic pain, if untreated, itself damages the organism.

DIAGNOSIS OF PAINFUL DISORDERS

Pain can be either acute or chronic; pain of more than 3 months' duration is usually considered chronic. Several clinical features differentiate acute from chronic pain. Patients suffering from *severe* acute pain usually give a clear description of its location, character, and timing. Signs of autonomic nervous system hyperactivity with tachycardia, hypertension, diaphoresis, mydriasis, and pallor are often present. Acute pain usually responds well to analgesic agents, and psychological factors often play only a minor role in pathogenesis. By contrast, patients suffering from chronic pain describe less precisely the localization, character, and timing of the pain, and, because the autonomic nervous system adapts, signs of autonomic hyperactivity disappear. Furthermore, chronic pain usually responds less well to analgesic agents, and psychological colorings are usually more pertinent than with acute pain. All of these factors may lead the physician to believe that the patient exaggerates his complaints. Because there are no reliable objective tests to as-

TABLE 114–1. ASPECTS OF PAIN

Definition: An unpleasant sensory and emotional experience associated with either actual or potential tissue damage, or described in terms of such damage (International Association for Study of Pain)

Temporal Characteristics	Pathogenesis
Acute (less than 3 months)	Structural
Chronic (more than 3 months)	Psychophysiologic
Physiology	Delusional
Somatic	
Visceral	
Neuropathic	

sess chronic pain, the physician is advised to accept the patient's report, taking into consideration age, cultural background, environment, and psychological factors known to alter reaction to pain.

Chronic pain can be divided into three somewhat overlapping categories in decreasing order of frequency:

1. Chronic pain associated with *structural disease,* such as occurs with rheumatoid arthritis, metastatic cancer, or sickle cell anemia, may be characterized by episodes of pain alternating with pain-free intervals or by unremitting pain waxing and waning in severity. Psychological factors may play an important role in exacerbating or relieving pain, but treatment of the pain by analgesics or correcting the underlying disease is usually most helpful.

2. *Psychophysiologic disorders.* Structural disease, such as a herniated disc or torn ligaments, may once have been present, but whether or not structural disease was ever present, psychological factors may have engendered chronic physiologic alterations, such as muscle spasm, which produce pain long after the underlying deficit has healed. Such patients tend to respond poorly to analgesic drugs, but often respond well to combination therapy directed at the end-organ (i.e., injection of trigger points in muscles) and at correcting or at least discussing disturbing psychological factors.

3. *Somatic delusions.* Pain caused by neither structural nor physiologic disorders occurs in patients with profound psychiatric disturbances such as psychotic depression or schizophrenia. The history of the pain is so vague and bizarre and its distribution so unanatomic as to suggest the diagnosis. These patients respond *only* to psychiatric therapy. History, examinations, laboratory studies, and management must be pursued with these principles in mind.

Pain associated with either structural or psychophysiologic disorders can arise from somatic, visceral, or neural structures. *Somatic pain* results from activation of peripheral receptors and somatic efferent nerves, without injury to the nerves themselves. The pain can be either sharp or dull but is typically well-localized and intermittent. *Visceral pain* results from activation of visceral nociceptive receptors and visceral efferent nerves and is characterized as a deep aching, cramping sensation, often referred to cutaneous sites. *Neuropathic pain* results from injury to peripheral receptors, nerves, or central nervous system. It is typically burning and dysesthetic and often occurs in an area of sensory loss (e.g., postherpetic neuralgia). The autonomic nervous system plays a significant modulatory role in all three types of pain, most prominently in visceral and deafferentation pain. Somatic and visceral pain are readily managed with a wide variety of nonopioid and opioid analgesics, anesthetic blocks, and neurosurgical approaches. In contrast, neuropathic pain may respond poorly to nonopioid and opioid analgesics and to anesthetic and neurosurgical procedures.

Referred pain is perceived at a site remote from the source of the noxious disturbance. It is evoked by disease of deep structures that are usually innervated by the same dermatome. Referred pain may be associated with cutaneous hyperalgesia and even relieved by procaine injection into the area of referral. When pain is referred to the same dermatome or myotome that includes the diseased structure (e.g., pain down the medial aspect of the arm [T1-T2] produced by myocardial infarction or angina pectoris, or diaphragmatic irritation causing shoulder pain [C4]), it is often helpful in diagnosis. However, pain is sometimes referred at a great distance from the primary site to segments not similarly innervated, in which case the mechanism is perplexing (e.g., anginal pain referred to the jaw, gallbladder pain felt in the chest or shoulder). Various theories have been suggested to account for referred pain. Such theories as division of the same nerve into deep (visceral) and superficial branches, release of chemical mediators in the nervous system, and convergence of cutaneous and visceral nerves into common synaptic pools at the spinal cord all might explain the dermatomal referral of pain but fail to explain pain at remote sites.

HEADACHE AND OTHER HEAD PAIN

Head pain can result from distortion, stretching, inflammation, or destruction of pain-sensitive nerve endings as a result of either intra- or extracranial disease in the distribution of any of the cranial and upper cervical nerves. Most head pain, however, arises from extracerebral structures and carries a benign prognosis. Table 114–2 classifies the common causes of headache.

Because headache is so common and so rarely due to structural disease, excessive application of expensive and highly technical laboratory procedures to its diagnosis and management substantially increases unnecessary medical costs. Nevertheless, in some instances a timely brain image by CT or MR scan or a lumbar puncture can give life-saving information about an otherwise undiagnosable problem. The following principles may help to manage the individual patient:

1. A complete history, with special attention to the location and character of the pain; associated symptoms (e.g., nausea, paresthesias); precipitating, exacerbating, and relieving factors; and previous history of headache can usually establish the diag-

TABLE 114–2. PATHOPHYSIOLOGIC CLASSIFICATION OF HEADACHE

Vascular Headache
  Migraine headache
    Classic migraine
    Common migraine
    Complicated migraine
    Variant migraine
  Cluster headache
    Episodic cluster
    "Chronic" cluster
    Chronic paroxysmal hemicrania
  Miscellaneous vascular headache
    Carotodynia
    Hypertension
    Orgasmic, exertional, and cough headache
    Hangover
    Toxins and drugs
    Occlusive vascular disease
Cranial Neuralgias
Tension-Type Headache
  Common tension headache

Depressive equivalent
Conversion reaction
Temporomandibular joint dysfunction
Atypical facial pain
Traction-Inflammation Headache
  Cranial arteritis
  Increased or decreased intracranial pressure
  Extracranial structural lesions
  Pituitary tumors
Extracranial Structural Lesions
  Paranasal sinusitis and tumors
  Dental infections
  Otitis
  Ocular lesions
  Pituitary tumors
  Cervical osteoarthritis

From Posner JB: Headache and other head pain. *In* Wyngaarden JB, Smith LH Jr, Bennett JC (eds): Cecil Textbook of Medicine. 19th ed. Philadelphia, WB Saunders Co, 1992, p 2118.

nosis. The physical and laboratory examinations are rarely helpful unless the history suggests structural disease. (For example, headaches of recent origin have a consistently focal distribution, follow trauma, or begin after the age of 30 years.) The vast majority of patients complaining of headache suffer from either vascular headache of the migraine type or tension-type headaches (Table 114–3).

2. Electroencephalographs (EEGs) and skull ra-

TABLE 114–3. DIFFERENTIAL DIAGNOSIS OF MIGRAINE AND TENSION HEADACHE

	MIGRAINE	TENSION
Intensity	Moderate to severe	Mild to moderate
Duration	4–48 hr	Minutes to weeks
Location	Unilateral (parietotemporal)	Bilateral (variable
Precipitating factors	Food, alcohol, menstruation, bright lights, exercise	Fatigue, anxiety
Age	Children, adolescents, and young adults	Any
Sex	Females more than males	Either
Associated symptoms	Nausea, vomiting, photophobia, phonophobia, malaise	Tight, tender muscles
Treatment	Dark room, sleep; analgesics; sumatriptan; ergot; prophylactic drugs available	Analgesics and/or antidepressants
Diurnal pattern	Morning, often interrupts sleep	Anytime, usually afternoon or evening, rarely interrupts sleep

diographs are almost never useful in the diagnosis of headache. When an imaging test is required, computed tomographic (CT) or magnetic resonance (MR) scans should be performed.

3. Diagnostic lumbar puncture should be performed with any acute headache that (a) is accompanied by fever or (b) is explosive or the most severe headache ever suffered (a history typical of acute subarachnoid hemorrhage). Lumbar puncture should, if possible, be deferred until after CT scanning with other forms of acute headache, especially if stiff neck but no fever is present. (This combination may indicate partial herniation of cerebellar tonsils into the foramen magnum secondary to an intracranial mass lesion.)

Migraine and Other Vascular Headaches
(Tables 114–2, 114–3)

The term *vascular headache* applies to a group of clinical syndromes of unknown etiology in which the final step in pathogenesis of the pain appears to be dilatation or irritation of one or more branches of the carotid artery (particularly the superficial temporal artery), leading to stimulation of nerve endings supplying that artery. The pain threshold of these nerve endings is lowered by release of neurotransmitters or other substances from nerve endings in the vessel wall.

A recent study suggests that 11 million Americans suffer from migraine headaches with moderate to severe disability. Other vascular headache syndromes are less common, but each has distinctive clinical findings. Most acute vascular headaches last only several hours and are best treated by rest in a quiet, dark room accompanied by a mild analgesic agent such as aspirin, if the patient is not too nauseated to take it. Occasionally more potent analgesics such as codeine or Demerol may be required, but such drugs should generally be avoided, in part because they add to the nausea frequently accompanying vascular headaches and in part because of their potential for abuse. Patients with prolonged or severe migraines usually respond to vasoconstrictive agents such as ergotamine given orally, rectally, or subcutaneously. If the headaches recur frequently

TABLE 114–4. CHARACTERISTICS OF CLUSTER HEADACHE

1. Severe unilateral orbital, supraorbital, and/or temporal pain lasting 15 to 180 minutes, often at the same time each day
2. Headache associated with at least one of the following signs on the side of pain:
   a. Conjunctival injection
   b. Lacrimation
   c. Nasal congestion
   d. Rhinorrhea
   e. Forehead and facial sweating
   f. Miosis
   g. Ptosis
   h. Eyelid edema
3. Frequency of attacks: from 1 every other day to 8 per day
4. Occur in cluster of 3 to 6 weeks; rarely are the headaches chronic.

TABLE 114–5. CLASSIFICATION OF TENSION-TYPE HEADACHES

Common tension headache
Depressive equivalent
Conversion reaction
Post-traumatic headache
Temporomandibular joint dysfunction
Atypical facial pain

(twice a week or more), prophylactic agents such as beta-adrenergic blockers (e.g., propranolol), methysergide, calcium channel blockers, or sometimes tricyclic antidepressants (e.g., amitriptyline) may provide effective prophylaxis. A new agent, sumatriptan, is a selective agonist of 5-hydroxytryptamine receptors and will soon be available in the United States. The drug is effective in treating acute migraine and cluster headaches.

Migraine is characterized by recurrent headaches, often severe, frequently beginning unilaterally, and usually associated with malaise, nausea and/or vomiting, and photophobia (Table 114–2). The disorder often begins in childhood, affects women more often than men, and runs in families. The disorder may be preceded by an aura (classic migraine) or may not (common migraine).

In *classic migraine* (about 15 to 20 per cent of migraine patients), brief (up to 30 minutes) neurologic dysfunction precedes or, less often, accompanies headache. The neurologic symptoms are usually visual, consisting of bright flashing lights (scintillation or fortification scotomas) beginning in the center of a homonymous visual half-field and radiating outward toward the periphery over 10 to 30 minutes. Other neurologic disturbances can include unilateral paresthesias of the hand and perioral area, aphasia, hemiparesis, and hemisensory defects. Neurologic symptoms usually disappear before the headache begins. If the neurologic symptoms are unilateral, the headache almost always affects the other side. *Migraine equivalent* (e.g., recurrent attacks of neurologic dysfunction that mimic the migraine alone but do not culminate in headache) may be confused with transient ischemic attacks or focal seizures. If the neurologic dysfunction continues into or outlasts the duration of the headache, the disorder is called *complicated migraine*. In rare instances, a neurologic disorder may be permanent, the vasoconstriction having resulted in cerebral infarction.

Cluster headaches are short-lived attacks of extremely severe, unilateral head pain that occur in clusters, often occurring several times daily and lasting several weeks, only to disappear for months or years before recurring. The diagnosis is established by the characteristic history (Table 114–4). Because the headaches frequently recur at known times, the ingestion of ergotamine tartrate prophylactically an hour or two before the expected headache may abort the headache. Sumatriptan as well as the serotonin inhibitor methysergide also is often successful in preventing cluster headaches.

Tension-Type Headache (Table 114–5)

So-called tension-type headaches are characterized by a steady, nonpulsatile, unilateral or bilateral aching pain, usually beginning in the occipital region but often involving frontal or temporal regions as well. Their pathogenesis is unknown, but they are frequently accompanied by tender posterior cervical, temporalis, and masseter muscles. Unique among headaches, the pain may be constantly present for days, weeks, or months. Tension-type headaches are more frequent in women, in individuals who are tense and anxious, and in those whose work or posture requires sustained contraction of posterior cervical, frontal, or temporal muscles. There is much overlap between the symptoms of common migraine and tension-type headaches, and many patients suffer from both. Similar headaches are often associated with depression or other severe psychological abnormalities.

Tension headache variants include the so-called temporomandibular joint (TMJ) syndrome with unilateral or bilateral head pain, usually in the temporal region and in the jaw, often radiating into the ear. *Post-traumatic headaches* are dull, generalized, aching head pains that follow head injury. The disorder can blend into *depressive headache*, a chronic generalized headache, usually vaguely described, sometimes associated with giddiness and unsteadiness, that occurs as a frequent and sometimes predominant manifestation of depression.

Atypical facial pain or atypical facial neuralgia is a term used to describe a syndrome characterized by steady aching face pain, usually unilateral, localized to the lower part of the orbit, maxillary area, and sometimes the jaw. The pain begins without a known precipitating episode and may last for hours or indefinitely. It may spread to involve the head or neck, and the muscles of the jaw and neck often become tender. Sometimes autonomic symptoms including sweating, flushing, rhinorrhea, and pallor are present. The disorder almost exclusively affects tense, anxious, and often chronically depressed women, often in early middle age. The importance of diagnosis lies in minimizing expensive laboratory tests and avoiding addicting drugs or mutilating surgical or dental procedures.

Headache from Intracranial Disorders

Most of the intracranial disorders that cause headache (Table 114–6) are discussed under their respective headings.

In *acute and subacute meningitis* the headache is usually generalized, throbbing, and very severe. It may be rapid or gradual in onset, and by the time it is fully developed is associated with nuchal rigidity. The diagnosis is established by lumbar puncture. In *subarachnoid hemorrhage* (p. 835), the initial sudden headache is caused by an abrupt alteration of intracranial pressure. This immediate pain is succeeded by a chronic persistent headache, often accompanied by gradually increasing nuchal rigidity that results from a chemical meningitis caused by the blood.

Intracranial hypotension, usually from loss of spinal fluid from lumbar puncture or a dural tear, decreases the buoyancy of the brain so that the organ descends when the upright position is assumed, ex-

TABLE 114–6. HEADACHE FROM INTRACRANIAL DISORDERS

Increased Intracranial Pressure
  Benign intracranial hypertension
  High-pressure hydrocephalus
Increased Venous Pressure
  Septic or aseptic intracranial thrombophlebitis
  Extracranial venous occlusion
Decreased Intracranial Pressure
  Cerebrospinal fluid leakage
  Post-lumbar puncture headache
Infection
  Meningitis
  Encephalitis
  Subdural abscess
  Emphyema
Vascular Disorders
  Subarachnoid hemorrhage
  Intracranial hematoma
Tumors
  Brain
  Pituitary

erting traction on structures at its apex and compression on structures at its base. (In rare instances, the small bridging veins that enter the sagittal sinus may rupture and cause subdural hematomas.) *Intracranial hypertension* causes headaches when vascular and neural structures over the apex or at the base of the brain are compressed by tumor or edematous brain. The most common cause of headache related to intracranial hypertension is brain tumor. The characteristics of brain tumor headache are discussed on page 853. Another cause of increased intracranial pressure headache is pseudotumor cerebri (benign intracranial hypertension).

Headache caused by *pituitary tumors* is the result of compression and distortion of pain-sensitive structures at the base of the skull, particularly the diaphragma sellae. Pain is generally referred to the frontal or temporal regions bilaterally and may on occasion be referred to the vertex or occipital regions. Acute headache occurring with known pituitary lesions (pituitary apoplexy) usually results from infarction of or hemorrhage into the tumor. Sudden expansion of the tumor may compromise the overlying optic chiasm, leading to visual loss, or invade the laterally lying cavernous sinus, producing ocular palsies. Pituitary apoplexy should be treated surgically by emergency drainage of the hemorrhagic or infarcted material.

Extracranial Structural Headache (Table 114–7)

Nasal and Sinus Headache. Sinus headache, like headache caused by "eye strain," is uncommon. Most so-called sinus headache is in reality migraine or tension-type headache. True sinus headache results from acute inflammation of the paranasal sinuses, which produces pain localized over the involved sinus and is associated with the stigmata of acute infection. Sinus radiographs and a physical examination are diagnostic.

TABLE 114–7. HEADACHE FROM EXTRACRANIAL STRUCTURAL LESIONS

Paranasal sinusitis and tumors
Dental infections
Otitis
Ocular lesions
Cervical osteoarthritis
Cranial arteritis

Dental Pain. Noxious stimuli in a tooth usually evoke local toothache, but severe dental pain can be extremely difficult to localize because pain may spread to other teeth or distant tissues that may exhibit surface hyperalgesia, tenderness, and vasomotor reactions, such as tender eyeballs, reddening of the conjunctivae, and tenderness of the auricular and temporal tissues. Patiently tapping each tooth for tenderness, using a blunt object or rod, often gives a localizing clue.

Aural Pain. Pain in the vicinity of the ear can be caused by disease of the teeth, tonsils, larynx and nasopharynx, TMJ, or cervical spine and its soft tissues. Pain in the ear can be associated with vascular headaches, atypical facial pain, and herpes zoster of the fifth and seventh cranial nerves as well as, rarely, the glossopharyngeal nerve. True glossopharyngeal neuralgia causes severe pain radiating from the tonsil into the ear. Primary ear disease is relatively infrequent — but important — as a source of headache, because it almost always indicates inflammation or destructive disease.

Eye Pain and Headache. Errors of refraction (hypermetropia, astigmatism, anomalies of accommodation), ocular muscle imbalance (strabismus), glaucoma, and iritis are universally described as causing headache. For most, the headache is mild in degree and usually starts around and over the eyes and subsequently radiates to the occiput and back of the head. The pain of glaucoma or iritis begins in the eye, can become severe, and then later extends to include a periorbital distribution.

Cervical Osteoarthritis. Any of the pain-sensitive structures of the upper neck (see p. 771) can cause pain that radiates toward or is referred to the cranium. The pain is usually precipitated or exacerbated by active or passive movement of the neck

TABLE 114–8. MISCELLANEOUS CAUSES OF HEADACHE

Headache Associated with Substances or Their Withdrawal
  Ergotamine abuse and withdrawal
  Analgesic abuse and withdrawal
  Alcohol abuse and withdrawal (hangover)
  Caffeine withdrawal
  Nitrates/nitrites (hot dog headache)
  Monosodium glutamate (Chinese restaurant syndrome)
  Carbon monoxide
Headache Associated with Systemic Infection or Fever
Headache Associated with Metabolic Abnormality
  Hypoxia and ischemia
  Dialysis

and is relieved by resting the neck with a cervical collar or bedrest. At times the pain is chronic and difficult to differentiate from tension-type headache. Lidocaine block of the C2-C3 zygapophyseal joint may help establish the diagnosis by identifying the source of pain.

Cranial Neuralgias

The term *cranial neuralgias* refers to several distinctive, extremely severe, paroxysmal head pains that appear to result from sudden episodic, intrinsic, and excessive discharges from the involved nerve. The best known is trigeminal neuralgia. Similar but much rarer disorders than trigeminal or glossopharyngeal neuralgia have been reported to involve the greater occipital nerve and the nervus intermedius portion of the facial nerve. The clinical features and treatment of these rare disorders are similar to those of trigeminal neuralgia.

Trigeminal Neuralgia. Trigeminal neuralgia is characterized by sudden, lightning-like paroxysms of pain in the distribution of one or more divisions of the trigeminal nerve. Most trigeminal neuralgia is probably caused by compression of the trigeminal nerve by tortuous arteries of the posterior fossa. Occasionally the syndrome can result from a gasserian ganglion tumor, multiple sclerosis, or a brain stem infarct.

The history is diagnostic. The pain occurs as brief, lightning-like stabs, frequently precipitated by touching a trigger zone around the lips or the buccal cavity. At times, talking, eating, or brushing the teeth serves as a trigger. The pains rarely last longer than seconds, and each burst is followed by a refractory period of several seconds to a minute in which no further pain can be precipitated. The pain is limited to the distribution of the trigeminal nerve, usually involving the second or third division or both. Spontaneous remissions are common. Between paroxysms of pain, the patient is asymptomatic. The pain rarely occurs at night. Ordinarily, the neurologic examination is entirely normal. Sensory changes in the distribution of the trigeminal nerve should prompt a careful search for structural disease such as tumor.

Carbamazepine is the initial treatment of choice for trigeminal neuralgia; phenytoin and baclofen are also sometimes effective. The drugs are not analgesics and are effective only for specific kinds of pain such as trigeminal neuralgia, glossopharyngeal neuralgia, and the lightning pains of tabes dorsalis. If medical treatment fails, surgery, either radiofrequency lesions of the gasserian ganglion (to block sensory conduction) or posterior fossa craniotomy (to relieve the trigeminal nerve of compression by vascular structures), is indicated.

Glossopharyngeal Neuralgia. Glossopharyngeal neuralgia is characterized by pain similar to that of trigeminal neuralgia but in the distribution of the glossopharyngeal and vagus nerves. Occasionally patients suffer cardiac slowing or brief arrest (syncope) during attacks of pain as a result of the intense afferent discharge over the glossopharyngeal nerve. Carbamazepine is often effective, but, if drugs fail, glossopharyngeal nerve roots are sectioned in the posterior fossa. Symptomatic glossopharyngeal neuralgia is occasionally the presenting complaint in a patient with a tonsillar tumor, and careful examination of the pharynx and tonsillar fossa for mass lesions must be carried out.

Miscellaneous, less frequent causes of headache are listed in Table 114–8.

REFERENCES

Bonica JJ (ed): The Management of Pain. 2nd ed. Philadelphia, Lea & Febiger, 1990.

Diamond S (ed): Headache. Med Clin North Am 75:521–791, 1991.

Mathew NT (ed): Headache. Neurol Clin 8:781–977, 1990.

Stewart WF, Lipton RB, Ceentano DD, Reed ML: Prevalence of migraine headache in the United States. JAMA 267:64–69, 1992.

NECK AND BACK PAIN

Neck and/or back pain is one of man's most common afflictions. About 80 per cent of individuals suffer significant low back pain at least once, and the annual incidence is 5 per cent. Next to alcoholism, back pain is the leading cause of time lost from work. Most neck and back pain, although incapacitating, is transient and neither life-threatening nor associated with obvious pathologic abnormalities. The symptoms are usually more severe than found on physical examination or imaging studies. Because the pathophysiology of most such pain is poorly understood, the physician often encounters patients in whom he can neither make a certain diagnosis nor prescribe rational therapy. Fortunately, most patients suffering from back pain recover within a few weeks regardless of the treatment. Only 4 per cent of patients suffering from back pain are disabled longer than 6 months.

Pain in the neck or back may arise from one or more of several pain-sensitive structures (Table 114–9). Table 114–10 lists some common causes of neck or back pain. Most acute neck or back pain is probably caused by muscle strain and spasm due to unaccustomed exercise or stretching, is transient, and is not life-threatening (see also myofascial pain, below). Patients suffering from such pain usually recover within a few weeks no matter what the treatment, but a few suffer chronic disability. Most chronic neck or back pain is either myofascial in origin or associated with vertebral arthritis and/or intervertebral disc disease, the former causing pain by compression of small nerve twigs supplying the facet joints and the periosteum of the vertebral bodies, the latter causing pain by compression of the nerve root. More rarely, tumors and inflammatory or degenerative arthritic lesions of the spine may be responsible.

In patients with acute neck or back pain, particularly when the precipitating cause (such as unaccustomed exercise) cannot be identified, heat and rest suffice without further diagnostic work-up. In patients with persistent or recurrent pain, meticulous diagnostic evaluation and vigorous therapy

TABLE 114–9. PAIN-SENSITIVE STRUCTURES IN AND AROUND THE SPINE

SENSITIVE	INSENSITIVE
Ligaments	Ligaments
Anterior and posterior longitudinal ligaments	Intraspinous and ligamentum flavum
Facets	Vertebral body
Articular cartilage	Intervertebral disc
Capsule	
Nerve roots	
Paraspinal muscles	

TABLE 114–10. COMMON CAUSES OF NECK AND/OR BACK PAIN

Trauma
  Muscle strain or spasm
  Subluxed facet joints
  Compression fractures (osteoporosis)
Psychophysiologic
  Muscle tension and spasm
  Fibromyalgia
Degenerative Disorders
  Herniated disc
  Spondylosis
    Spinal stenosis
  Osteoarthritis
Neoplasm
  Extradural (usually malignant)
  Intradural extramedullary (usually benign)
  Intramedullary (either benign or malignant)
Inflammation
  Arthritis
  Osteomyelitis of vertebral body
  Disc infection

often prevent or reverse serious or potentially lethal neurologic damage.

The diagnostic evaluation begins with a history. Most benign back or neck pain is of acute or subacute onset and frequently follows by minutes to hours some unaccustomed physical activity, particularly lifting or bending. Other patients awaken feeling stiff and sore the morning after unusual exercise. Sometimes low back pain begins acutely, frequently on arising in the morning, without any obvious precipitating event. Most neck pain begins as a stiff neck, often on awakening in the morning, without a previous history of unusual activity. Many patients' neck or back pains occur episodically over many years. Most benign neck or back pain is dull or aching in quality, exacerbated by movement, and relieved by rest. The majority of patients are comfortable when recumbent and immobile or at least are able to find one position that relieves the pain. Pain that is present when the patient is immobile and that cannot be relieved by postural manipulation should lead the physician to search for a serious disorder. Likewise, pain that radiates in a clear dermatomal distribution is probably a result of nerve root compression, especially if there are paresthesias or loss of sensation. Radiating pain in a nondermatomal distribution often accompanies neck and back muscle spasms; it usually does not portend serious neurogenic disease.

A careful physical and neurologic examination may reveal an obvious cause for the pain. Systemic disease such as cancer, urinary tract infection, pelvic disease, or abdominal aneurysm may be a cause of back pain because a lesion impinges on the vertebral body or paravertebral structures. Evidence for neurologic disease such as weakness, sensory loss, or reflex abnormalities suggests spinal cord or nerve root dysfunction. Such evidence of neurologic disability requires a careful laboratory examination, including plain radiographs, MR scan of vertebral and paravertebral structures, and, if clinically indicated, myelography. Specific findings resulting from intervertebral disc disease are found on page 807 and those from spinal tumor and congenital anomalies on page 799.

In the absence of a clear abnormality on physical examination, conservative treatment of back pain with immobility, heat, analgesics, and sometimes physical therapy ameliorates symptoms in a short period of time without the necessity of substantial laboratory evaluation. Even in the absence of neurologic signs, however, if pain persists after conservative treatment, radiographic and laboratory evaluation become mandatory.

MYOFASCIAL PAIN

A major part of head, back, and neck pain arises from skeletal muscle, particularly from the paravertebral muscles. Unaccustomed exercise causes soreness and tenderness in the involved muscles but is rarely a source of patient complaint. Prolonged tonic contraction of skeletal muscles, however, has a pathogenesis that originates in psychological tension, resentment, and anxiety and may produce pain whose cause is not immediately apparent to the patient. Examples are chest pain from contraction of the pectoralis majors, posterior thoracic or lumbar pain from paraspinous muscle contraction, and abdominal pain from rectus muscle contraction. The pain is initially localized over the area of muscle contraction but may spread widely in a distribution characteristic for the muscles involved. The affected muscles are usually tender to palpation, and one often finds a particularly tender area somewhere in the muscle, called a trigger zone, which, when palpated, reproduces the distribution of the spontaneous pain. One common variant of myofascial pain is the fibrositis/fibromyalgia syndrome, a disorder of middle-aged women characterized by generalized musculoskeletal pain, morning stiffness, disturbed sleep and fatigue (nonrestorative sleep), and at times vague complaints of digital swelling or paresthesias. Symptoms sometimes are so general that they overlap those of somatoform disorders (p. 754). Headache and "irritable bowel" symptoms are common, and most patients are concurrently anxious and/or depressed. Tender points can be

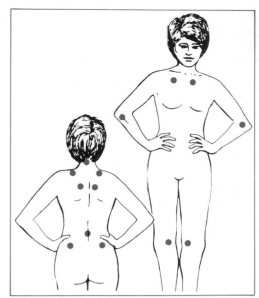

FIGURE 114–1. Tender point map: 14 sites of local tenderness. The unilateral sites are at the intertransverse and/or interspinous ligaments of C4 to C6 and the interspinous ligament at L4 to L5 and the bilateral sites at the upper borders of the trapezius, the supraspinatus origins at the medial border of the scapula, the upper outer quadrants of the buttocks, the second costochondral junctions, the lateral epicondyles, and the medial fat pads of the knees. (From Wolfe F: The clinical syndrome of fibrositis. In The fibrositis-fibromyalgia syndrome. Am J Med 81 (Suppl 3A): 1986; with permission.)

found on examination in most or all of the 14 sites illustrated in Figure 114–1. It is likely that other myofascial and referred pain syndromes are fragments of the fibromyalgia syndrome.

The pathophysiology of myofascial pain is poorly understood, and the treatment is often difficult and frustrating. In some patients mild analgesic drugs (aspirin), heat, and massage yield temporary or long-term relief. In other patients, massage or even injection of trigger points with local anesthetics gives relief. Biofeedback with the patient trying consciously to relax contracted muscles recorded by surface electromyography (EMG) has been reported to be useful. Antidepressants are modestly effective and produce at least a short-term remission in about 20 per cent of patients. For most patients, a combination of the above physical methods with investigation and treatment of the underlying psychological disorder is necessary if long-term relief is to be achieved.

SYMPATHETICALLY MAINTAINED PAIN

This term applies to severe pain, usually burning in quality and associated with autonomic changes including swelling, vasomotor instability, and abnormalities of sweating. The pain syndrome usually follows an injury, often minor, to an extremity. If the injury has involved a peripheral nerve, particularly the sciatic or median nerve, the syndrome is called *causalgia.* If the injury does not involve a peripheral nerve, if there has been no trauma, or if the syndrome follows a visceral illness (e.g., myocardial infarction), the term applied is *reflex sympathetic dystrophy.* (Older and outmoded terms include post-traumatic painful osteoporosis, Sudek's atrophy, post-traumatic spreading neuralgia, minor causalgia, and shoulder-hand syndrome.) The exact pathophysiology of the disorder is unknown, but, as the name implies, abnormal activity of the sympathetic nervous system plays an important role in both the pain and the autonomic symptoms.

Severe pain, usually of a burning quality, is the first symptom after the injury. The pain is continuous, worsened by emotional stress, and sometimes associated with such severe hyperpathia that moving or touching the limb is intolerable. At first the pain is localized to the site of injury or the distribution of the nerve injured, but with time it often spreads to involve the entire extremity. Along with the pain there develop vasomotor changes, first vasodilation (warm and dry skin) and later vasoconstriction (edema, cyanosis, and cool skin). Other autonomic abnormalities include either hyper- or hypohidrosis, atrophy of the skin and subcutaneous tissues, and osteoporosis. The entire symptom complex is rarely present in any one patient, and one sign or symptom usually predominates. Untreated, the disorder leads eventually to muscle atrophy, fixation of joints, and a useless extremity. The mechanism of the pain and sympathetic changes is poorly understood.

Treatment is sometimes effective, particularly if begun early. Repeated local anesthetic infiltration of the painful site with lidocaine sometimes leads to relief. If local measures fail, most patients are relieved by sympathetic ganglion block, which, if repeated, may give permanent relief. A short course of corticosteroids has been reported to be effective. Analgesic drugs usually offer little relief.

REFERENCES

Bonica JJ (ed): The Management of Pain. 2nd ed. Philadelphia, Lea & Febiger, 1990.

Borenstein DG, Wiesel SW: Low Back Pain: Medical Diagnosis and Comprehensive Management. Philadelphia, WB Saunders Co, 1989.

Cailliet R: Neck and Arm Pain. 3rd ed. Philadelphia, FA Davis Co, 1991.

B. The Special Sensory System

EXAMINATION OF THE PATIENT

Special (i.e., nonsomatic) sensation is subserved by several of the cranial nerves and their central extensions. In most instances, even the most subtle abnormality of special sensory function is immediately apparent to the patient. Such disorders, which include visual loss, hearing loss, dizziness, and abnormalities of smell or taste perception, are a frequent cause for physician consultation. It follows that, with a few exceptions, unless the patient reports symptoms, meticulous physical evaluation of this system is likely to be unrewarding. However, a brief screening examination, even in asymptomatic patients, may yield some important findings of which the patient is unaware.

Odor perception (olfactory nerve) is best tested by having the patient, with eyes closed, obstruct the naris on one side and sniff with the other. The patient is alternately presented with nothing and an odoriferous object (e.g., coffee, toothpaste, soap, perfume) and asked both to identify if an odor is present and its nature. Many normal persons can detect but not identify odors. Unilateral anosmia in the absence of nasal obstruction may be unrecognized by the patient and should lead to further neurologic work-up. Most bilateral anosmia is due to nasal disease. If malingering (as in litigation) is suspected, try a pungent substance such as ammonia, because this stimulates trigeminal nerve endings and the patient should perceive it even with total olfactory loss.

Visual acuity should be tested in each eye with the patient wearing his glasses and, if necessary, by the addition of a pinhole held against the lens. Corrected vision in either eye of less than 20/40 suggests a cataract or a retinal or a neurologic disorder, and further work-up is indicated. Most patients are immediately aware of unilateral central visual loss but some patients may fail to notice such amaurosis, particularly in the nondominant eye, until they inadvertently close the other one. Color sensation in each eye should be tested. Acquired diminution of color vision strongly suggests a lesion of the optic nerve; even when visual acuity is normal the patient may note that colors appear "washed out" in the involved eye. *Visual fields* in all four visual quadrants should be tested, comparing the patient's field with the examiner's. Many patients, particularly with cerebral lesions, may be unaware of a visual field defect although the astute patient may report that he bumps into things or has had an automobile accident on the "blind side." The field should be tested first with unilaterally and then bilaterally presented objects. In particular, bitemporal defects should be sought, as they may be unrecognized by the patient and be the only sign of a pituitary tumor. Normal visual fields with unilateral testing but an abnormal field (in particular a left field defect), when tested bilaterally (extinction), suggests a central defect. Suspicious findings on bedside confrontation or a positive history warrant formal perimetry, which should be performed by a specialist.

The *pupils* should be inspected in both dim and bright light (significant anisocoria may be present in only one). Pupillary inequalities of 1 mm or less are rarely significant (15 per cent of normal individuals have some anisocoria). At the same time as pupillary size is evaluated, the size of the palpebral fissure should also be noted. Ptosis with a small pupil suggests a Horner syndrome; ptosis with a large pupil, a partial third nerve palsy. Pupillary reactions should be tested using a bright light in a relatively dim room. The reaction should be brisk and symmetric. The bright light is moved quickly from one eye to the other. If there is dilatation of one pupil as the light is moved to it from the other side, one should suspect an abnormality of the optic nerve in that eye. The accommodative pupillary response can be tested by asking the patient first to look into the distance and then at the examiner's finger held a foot from his nose. The pupils should constrict symmetrically and rapidly.

Eye movements are examined first by asking a patient to voluntarily move his eyes laterally and up and down and then to track a flashlight in the same directions. Failure of voluntary movement with normal following movements suggests a supranuclear brain disorder (e.g., a progressive supranuclear palsy). Failure of conjugate movement, either voluntarily or on tracking, also suggests a supranuclear disorder. Disconjugate movements suggest a brain stem or peripheral disorder. One should inquire about double vision and look for nystagmus both on forward and on eccentric gaze. Diplopia identified at extremes of gaze but not complained of by the patient is probably not pathologic. Unsustained nystagmus on extremes of gaze is usually physiologic. Sustained nystagmus unassociated with vertigo is probably due to a central lesion.

Patients with ocular paralyses complain either of blurred vision ("like a ghost on a television set") or frank diplopia. The former may follow the latter as progressive weakening of the ocular muscle causes increasing divergence of the eyes. Horizontal diplopia implies either lateral rectus (abducens nerve) or medial rectus (oculomotor nerve) dysfunction. Vertical or oblique diplopia must involve other muscles. The patient should be closely questioned about the onset of the diplopia (progressive worsening after onset suggests compressive lesions; sudden onset, vascular lesions). Inquire about diurnal pattern (most diplopia worsens with fatigue but diplopia absent in the morning and present later in the day suggests myasthenia gravis) and about relationship to other neurologic symptoms. In a patient complaining of diplopia, one should try to determine by examination the position in which the diplopia is most marked. This defines the ocular muscle (or muscles) involved. Deviations of ocular muscles too subtle to be seen by the examiner may be perceived as diplopia to the patient. Red glass testing should be left to the expert, because in the hands of a nonspecialist it is often more misleading than helpful. Intermittent diplopia suggests myas-

thenia gravis, and one should attempt to fatigue the muscles by sustained repetitive action to produce the abnormality. All patients complaining of diplopia in whom an immediate cause is not apparent should have a Tensilon test (see p. 816). Frank abnormalities of ocular movements on examination without diplopia suggest a slowly developing, longstanding lesion such as ocular myopathy with compensation on the part of the patient suppressing the experience of diplopia. Monocular diplopia is usually caused by disease of lens or retina and only rarely by psychogenic or cerebral disease.

Hearing should be tested by having the patient listen to a softly ticking watch or by rubbing one's fingers a few inches from the ear. The examiner can use his own hearing as a standard. If hearing is diminished, the Weber test (see p. 779) should be carried out. Lateralization to the poorly hearing side suggests conductive loss. Lateralization to the normally hearing side suggests a sensorineural abnormality. More thorough evaluation of hearing requires audiometry.

Dizziness. This exceedingly common symptom is only sometimes due to abnormality of the vestibular system (vertigo) (Table 114–11). The physician's first task with a dizzy patient is to distinguish vertigo from other symptoms and then, if the patient is suffering from vertigo, to assign a cause (Table 114–12). Because in most patients dizziness is an episodic and not a continuous symptom, a patient usually has neither symptoms nor signs when examined by the physician. Thus, the physician must try to evoke the symptom or sign in order to determine its cause. The heart and blood pressure examination deserve special attention, because orthostatic hypotension or cardiac arrhythmias may lead to syncope. Cerebellar or peripheral nerve dysfunction may cause ataxia. The visual and ocular motor system should be examined for diplopia or other visual distortions. Provocative tests may be used to simulate the patient's dizziness:

Hyperventilation lowers the PCO_2 and decreases cerebral blood flow, causing a "lightheaded" sensation. Ask the patient to hyperventilate maximally for 3 minutes. If the procedure exactly mimics the patient's symptoms, it suggests that anxiety and hyperventilation may be playing an important role. In addition, during the course of hyperventilation the patient may suffer dry mouth, chest tightness, and paresthesias, which he may then recognize are part

TABLE 114–11. DIFFERENTIAL DIAGNOSIS OF DIZZINESS

Vertigo
    Physiologic
    Pathologic
Lightheadedness or syncope
Ataxia
    Cerebellar dysfunction
    Proprioceptive loss
Diplopia or other visual abnormalities
Anxiety
Hyperventilation
Dissociative episodes
Partial complex seizures

of his spontaneous attacks, thus helping in the diagnosis. Tandem walking (heel to toe) with eyes open or closed intensifies ataxia and simulates the sensation of dysequilibrium. The Bárány rotation maneuver (rotating the patient about a vertical axis 10 times over 20 seconds), caloric tests (see below), and positional tests (see below) simulate the symptoms of vestibular vertigo.

Examine the patient carefully for nystagmus. The patient should fix upon a light successively requiring horizontal and vertical gaze in both the erect and supine positions. Nystagmus and vertigo can sometimes be precipitated by rapid movements of the head (Nylen-Bárány test). The examiner tilts the seated patient so that the head is hanging 45 degrees below horizontal, with first one ear and then the other dependent. He observes for nystagmus and vertigo. In some patients rapid head turning (once from center to side or vice versa or from supine to erect) suffices to bring out positional nystagmus and vertigo. A latency of 15 seconds or so characteristically separates the abrupt head movement from the appearance of the nystagmus.

SMELL AND TASTE

Smell. Table 114–12 lists common causes of anosmia. Most acquired disturbances of smell result from transient or sustained diseases of the nasal mucous membranes that obstruct access to or dry out or deaden the receptor areas. Such disorders seldom are complete and they commonly respond to local treatment. No satisfactory treatment has been found for neurogenic anosmias. Affected patients must be warned explicitly to avoid gas heating and to install smoke alarms to compensate for the life-threatening hazards of the defect. *Dysosmia* is a distortion of olfactory perception (normal odors perceived as a foul smell) that may occur without prior anosmia or during the recovery phase from anosmia. The cause most often lies in paranasal infections or, sometimes, in psychiatric illness. Hallucinations of smell, usually of a foul quality, occur with epileptogenic lesions affecting the region of the amygdala and are termed uncinate fits.

Taste. Much of what is perceived as taste derives indirectly from olfaction, which should be checked in any patient complaining of taste loss. Disorders that directly cause taste abnormalities are listed in Table 114–12. Epileptic discharges occasionally cause gustatory hallucinations. Psychologically depressed or paranoid patients often complain of a foul taste, but taste perception is usually normal.

DISORDERS OF VISION AND OCULAR MOVEMENT

Vision

Introduction and Definitions

A knowledge of the anatomy of visual pathways is important in clinical diagnosis, because lesions damaging or interrupting the visual sensory system can usually be discretely localized by history and visual field examination (Fig. 114–2). Partial or complete visual loss in one eye, sparing the other, implies damage to the retina or optic nerve anterior to the chiasm, whereas a visual field abnormality affecting both eyes originates at the chiasm or posterior; the more congruent the visual fields, the more posterior lies the lesion. *Scotomas* are areas of relative or complete visual loss. *Central scotomas* severely decrease vision because the macular fibers are damaged, whereas scotomas away from the macula may hardly be noticed by the patient. Visual field abnormalities impairing half or nearly half of the field are termed hemianoptic. A *homonymous hemianopia* implies a postchiasmal lesion; a *bitemporal hemianopia* a chiasmal lesion; and an *altitudinal hemianopia*, whether unilateral or bilateral, vascular damage to retinal structures. Smaller defects involving only a quarter of the visual field are called *quadrantanopia*. Homonymous *superior quadrantanopia* implies temporal lobe damage, whereas homonymous *inferior quadrantanopia* implies parietal lobe damage. *Scintillating scotomas* refer to hallucinations of flashing lights. Such abnormalities imply an abnormal discharge of the visual system anywhere along its course. The disorder is common in migraine and also in seizures originating from the occipital lobe.

Diseases Causing Visual Impairment

Corneal, lenticular, or vitreous diseases large enough to produce visual symptoms can usually be detected by funduscopic inspection. *Glaucoma* with high intraocular pressure causes either slow or rapid visual loss associated with ring or annular scotomas and a deeply cupped optic disc. Visual loss may be preceded by halos seen around illuminated lights and pain in the affected eye. Diagnosis can be made only by tonometry. *Retinal detachment* gives rise to unilateral distortion of visual images that

TABLE 114–12. COMMON CAUSES OF LOSS OF TASTE AND SMELL

	TASTE	SMELL
Local	Radiation therapy	Allergic rhinitis, sinusitis, nasal polyposis, bronchial asthma
Systemic	Cancer, renal failure, hepatic failure, nutritional deficiency (B_{12}, zinc), Cushing's syndrome, hypothyroidism, diabetes, mellitus, infection (influenza), drugs (antirheumatic and antiproliferative)	Renal failure, hepatic failure, nutritional deficiency (B_{12}), Cushing's syndrome, hypothyroidism, diabetes mellitus, infection (viral hepatitis, influenza), drugs (nasal sprays, antibiotics)
Neurologic	Bell's palsy, familial dysautonomia, multiple sclerosis	Head trauma, multiple sclerosis, Parkinson's disease, frontal brain tumor

From Baloh RW: Smell and taste. In Wyngaarden JB, Smith LH Jr, Bennett JC (eds): Cecil Textbook of Medicine. 19th ed. Philadelphia, WB Saunders Co, 1992, p 2098.

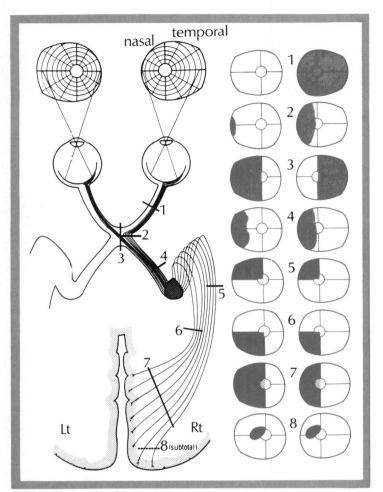

FIGURE 114–2. Visual fields that accompany damage to the visual pathways. 1. Optic nerve: unilateral amaurosis. 2. Lateral optic chiasm: grossly incongruous, incomplete (contralateral) homonymous hemianopia. 3. Central optic chiasm: bitemporal hemianopia. 4. Optic tract: incongruous, incomplete homonymous hemianopia. 5. Temporal (Meyer's) loop of optic radiation: congruous partial or complete (contralateral) homonymous superior quadrantanopia. 6. Parietal (superior) projection of the optic radiation: Congruous partial or complete homonymous inferior quadrantanopia. 7. Complete parieto-occipital interruption of optic radiation. Complete congruous homonymous hemianopia with psychophysical shift of foveal point often sparing central vision, giving "macular sparing." 8. Incomplete damage to visual cortex: congruous homonymous scotomas, usually encroaching at least acutely on central vision. (From Baloh RW: Neuro-ophthalmology. *In* Wyngaarden JB, Smith LH Jr, Bennett JC [eds]: Cecil Textbook of Medicine. 19th ed. Philadelphia, WB Saunders Co, 1992, p 2100.)

may be mistaken for monocular scintillating scotomas. Detachment can usually be identified by irregularities seen in the retina on funduscopic examination.

Unilateral Visual Loss. Serious visual loss from optic nerve lesions affects either one eye or both eyes asymmetrically, leading to nonhomonymous visual defects; the pupillary light reflex is diminished to the same degree as is vision. Most acute or subacute optic nerve disease is due to demyelinat-

ing disease (optic neuritis), vascular disorders (retinal or optic nerve ischemia from arterial embolism or occlusion), or neoplastic lesions. The history is important: If the visual loss is abrupt, whether transient or permanent, the cause is usually vascular. A slower onset over hours or days suggests demyelination; progressive visual loss over weeks or months implies a compressive lesion (e.g., tumor). If the disorder is at the nerve head, it produces papillitis, but if more posteriorly the same disease process can cause a central scotoma or even blindness with no visible change in the optic nerve. *Demyelinating optic neuritis* is usually unilateral. It may be a symptom of multiple sclerosis, but many patients with optic neuritis recover and do not develop other neurologic dysfunction. Demyelinating lesions of the optic nerve appear to have a particular predilection for the myelinated fibers that supply the macula, thus leading to central scotomas. Visual acuity is severely impaired, but the peripheral vision may remain intact. *Ischemic optic neuropathy* may be a symptom of *cranial arteritis* or more often occurs in late middle-aged, usually hypertensive individuals as a result of arterial embolism. Blinded patients with giant cell (cranial) arteritis are usually elderly and suffer from headache, malaise, fever, and an elevated sedimentation rate. Emergency treatment with corticosteroids may prevent blindness in the other eye. In patients with ischemic optic neuropathy, the second eye also tends to become involved, but there is no treatment to prevent it. Tumors can usually be identified by either funduscopic examination, brain imaging, or both. Acute and *transient monocular blindness* is usually a result of embolization of the central retinal artery or one of its branches. The emboli may originate from an atherosclerotic plaque in the carotid or ophthalmic artery or from thrombotic material in the left heart or on cardiac valves such as may complicate rheumatic heart disease and mitral valve prolapse.

Bilateral Visual Loss. Gradually developing bilateral retinal or optic nerve disease occurs with heredodegenerative conditions, vascular diseases such as diabetes, idiopathic (senile) macular degeneration, or diseases such as retinitis pigmentosa. These conditions can be diagnosed by funduscopic or sometimes slit lamp examination. Acute *transient bilateral blindness* (bilateral visual obscuration) is usually a symptom of increased intracranial pressure; it is almost always associated with severe papilledema and can occur with either brain tumors or pseudotumor cerebri (p. 859).

Acute or subacute bilateral optic neuritis may reflect a demyelinating process, but most examples are due to toxic-nutritional problems or inherited optic atrophy rather than multiple sclerosis. Most chiasmal lesions in the adult result from tumors compressing that structure; the most common are pituitary adenomas, but also include craniopharyngiomas, meningiomas, and large aneurysms of the carotid artery. In small children, optic gliomas are a major cause of chiasmal visual loss. Lesions of the optic tract producing incongruous homonymous field defects are usually caused by infarcts or less commonly tumors. Disorders posterior to the optic tract produce congruent field defects that usually involve macular fibers. When the lesion is occipital, sparing the occipital pole (which often has a bilateral supply from both the middle and the posterior cerebral artery), macular fibers may be spared. The phenomenon cannot be detected at bedside but can be identified by careful visual field testing. Most postchiasmal visual loss is caused by vascular disease or tumor.

Bilateral damage to the visual radiation or occipital cortex produces *cortical blindness.* Such blindness is characterized by a normal funduscopic examination, normal pupillary light reflexes, and often unawareness of the blindness on the part of the patient. Most transient cortical blindness is a symptom of basilar artery insufficiency, hypertensive encephalopathy, or more rarely of migraine. The disorder may also occur in the postictal state after a generalized seizure. The reason for the vulnerability of the cerebral cortex to these diffuse cerebral disorders is not clear. Cortical blindness, because of the preservation of pupillary reflexes, may at first be confused with a conversion reaction (hysteria). If there is any question, however, visual evoked responses establish the diagnosis.

Any complaint of visual loss, particularly unilateral and transient, is an emergency. Lesions that involve one eye can often soon involve the second, and transient or incomplete lesions can become permanent or complete. Many disorders of the visual system are caused by vascular disease, inflammation, or tumors and are thus potentially treatable. Accordingly, a rapid and meticulous examination is necessary first to localize the site of the lesion by funduscopic and visual field examination and then to identify its pathogenesis (usually by a CT or MR scan). These steps may lead to appropriate treatment that preserves vision. Examples of sight-saving procedures include reduction of pressure in acute glaucoma, the early use of corticosteroids for the treatment of cranial arteritis, anticoagulation for crescendo carotid or basilar insufficiency, and prompt surgical decompression for the treatment of tumors.

Pupils

The size of the pupil is determined by the balance between discharges of the sympathetic and parasympathetic (oculomotor nerve) fibers (Fig. 114–3). The pupillary light reaction is determined on the afferent side by visual sensory fibers originating in the retina and traveling through the optic nerve, chiasm, and tract to the midbrain and on the efferent side by parasympathetic fibers that arise in the oculomotor nucleus of the midbrain (Table 114–13).

When *sympathetic fibers* are damaged, the pupil narrows (the light reaction is still normal) and the palpebral fissure becomes smaller as the upper lid descends and the lower lid elevates (Horner's syndrome). The eye, however, does not close as it does with oculomotor nerve lesions. Sweat fibers may be involved as well, leading to anhidrosis on the entire half of the body if the damage is central, on the ipsilateral face and neck if the damage is between the spinal cord and the superior cervical ganglion, or on the medial side of the forehead only if the damage is above the superior cervical ganglion.

Horner's syndrome may be caused by vascular damage to the hypothalamus or brain stem, but lesions in those loci produce other neurologic signs

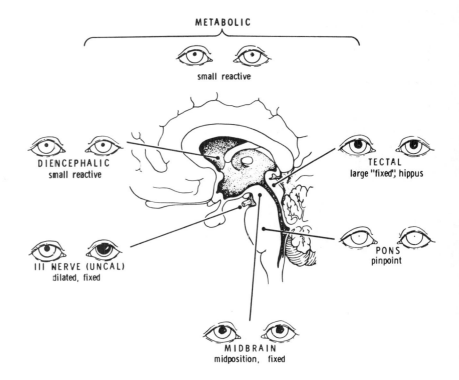

METABOLIC

small reactive

DIENCEPHALIC
small reactive

TECTAL
large "fixed", hippus

III NERVE (UNCAL)
dilated, fixed

PONS
pinpoint

MIDBRAIN
midposition, fixed

FIGURE 114–3. Pupillary responses in comatose patients. The schematic shows abnormalities resulting from damage to various points along the central pupillary pathways. In patients with metabolic encephalopathy, pupils are small and reactive, as are pupils resulting from diencephalic damage such as occurs with early herniation. Lesions of the upper brain stem usually produce unilaterally or bilaterally large or mid-position fixed pupils, whereas pontine lesions result in pinpoint pupils. (From Plum F, Posner JB: Diagnosis of Stupor and Coma. 3rd ed. Philadelphia, FA Davis Co, 1980; with permission.)

TABLE 114-13. COMMON CAUSES OF PUPILLARY ABNORMALITIES

SIZE		REACTION TO LIGHT
SMALL PUPILS	**LARGE PUPILS**	
Argyll Robertson pupil	Holmes-Adie pupil	Nonreactive
Pontine hemorrhage	Post-traumatic iridoplegia	
Opiates	Mydriatic drops	
Pilocarpine drops	Glutethimide overdose	
	Cerebral death	
	Atropine or scopolamine poisoning	
	Amphetamine or cocaine poisoning	
Old age	Childhood	Reactive
Horner's syndrome	Anxiety	
	Physiologic anisocoria	

Modified from Patton J: Neurological Differential Diagnosis. New York, Springer-Verlag, 1983.

that locate the disorder. An isolated Horner's syndrome may be the first sign of a lung cancer of the superior sulcus or may occur with tumors or other diseases involving the carotid artery. In some instances the cause of the disorder is not found. Horner's syndrome is valuable as a localizing diagnostic sign but in and of itself does not require treatment in that it impairs neither vision nor ocular motor function.

Parasympathetic disorders occur unilaterally with any lesion of the oculomotor nerve, particularly those that compress the nerve, such as tumors or aneurysms. Cerebral herniation leads to pupillary dilatation if it affects the third nerve or to bilaterally midpositioned and fixed pupils if it affects the midbrain.

The pupils are not always equal in size. Essential anisocoria (lifelong difference in the sizes of the pupils with a normal light reaction) occurs in about 15 per cent of normal people. Tonic (Adie's) pupil is a somewhat larger than normal pupil that constricts little or not at all to light and shrinks slowly on accommodation. It constricts more than normal when dilute pilocarpine is instilled, suggesting that the pupil is parasympathetically denervated (denervation hypersensitivity). The disorder may be unilateral or bilateral and when symptomatic is characterized by a long delay in focusing when the patient attempts to move from far to near vision. There may be pain or a dazzling sensation when affected patients exit from a dark to a light room. In some persons the disorder is associated with absent deep tendon reflexes (Adie's syndrome), but neither the pupillary nor the reflex disorder causes serious disability.

Argyll Robertson pupils are small (1 to 2 mm), unequal, irregular, and fixed to light. They constrict briskly on accommodation. Their principal causes are neurosyphilis and diabetic and certain other autonomic neuropathies. Unexplained unilaterally or

bilaterally dilated pupils with visual blurring can result from accidental or intentional instillation of mydriatics such as scopolamine or atropine. Such an abnormality is typified by failure of the pupil to constrict promptly with 1 per cent pilocarpine.

Damage to visual fibers (the afferent arc of the pupillary light reflex) leads to the "paradoxical pupillary response," in which the direct reaction to light is impaired (because the afferent information is not carried to the oculomotor nerve), but the consensual reaction to light directed in the other eye is normal because the efferent information reaches both oculomotor nerves. The response is best seen when a bright light is rapidly moved from a normal to a visually impaired eye; the consensually constricted pupil in the impaired eye then dilates.

Ocular Movement

Definitions

Abnormal disjunctive eye movements can result from disturbances at several levels of the neuraxis. These include abnormalities in the action of individual muscles (ocular myopathies), the myoneural junction (myasthenia gravis), the oculomotor nerve, the three paired nuclei in the brain stem, or the internuclear medial longitudinal fasciculus that yokes the eyes in parallel movement. The term *strabismus* refers to an involuntary deviation of the eyes from normal physiologic position. Nonparalytic strabismus is due to an intrinsic imbalance of the ocular muscle tone and is usually congenital. Paralytic strabismus results from defects in ocular muscle innervation and thus implies a neuromuscular disorder. A congenital strabismus may be compensated during life only to become manifest with aging, fatigue, or systemic disease. With strabismus, the patient often suppresses vision in one eye in order to prevent diplopia. If this occurs in early infancy, the suppressed eye develops permanent reduction of vision (amblyopia ex anopsia). This does not occur if strabismus develops later in life.

Defects in ocular movement resulting from faulty action of the eye muscles or their peripheral innervation (such as the third, fourth, and sixth cranial nerves) are called ocular paralyses. Abnormalities of conjugate gaze are called gaze paralyses and result from disease of central structures.

Ocular Paralyses

The *abducens* (sixth cranial) nerve subserves the lateral rectus muscle. Selective involvement of the abducens nerve anywhere along its pathway, in or outside the brain stem, leads to isolated weakness of abduction of the affected eye. If the nucleus itself is involved, there is also a gaze paresis to the ipsilateral side as a result of damage to supranuclear structures in the same area. The *trochlear* (fourth cranial) nerve subserves the superior oblique muscle, which intorts the eye and moves it down when it is medially deviated. All other muscles, including the pupilloconstrictor and the levator of the upper lid, are controlled by the *oculomotor* (third cranial) nerve. Abnormalities of the cranial nerves in the brain stem are almost always associated with other neurologic signs and are usually caused by vascular disturbances, tumors, or demyelinating disease. The peripheral nerves may be involved individually or together by lesions lying anywhere from their site of exit in the brain stem to where they enter the muscle. The nerves are most widely separated in the posterior fossa and run closest to each other in the cavernous sinus and superior orbital fissure. Accordingly, compressive lesions in the cavernous sinus usually cause multiple unilateral ocular palsies, whereas those in the posterior fossa may cause single (sometimes bilateral) nerve dysfunction. Intrinsic lesions of the third nerve (e.g., diabetic vasculopathy) often spare the pupil, whereas compressive lesions (tumors and aneurysms) involve the pupil early. Table 114–14 lists the major causes of acute ophthalmoplegia.

Conjugate Paralysis

Conjugate movement of the eyes is regulated by supranuclear pathways that descend from the forebrain to reach the medial longitudinal fasciculus in the brain stem. Unilateral hemispheral disease resulting from hemorrhage, infarct, or tumor acutely paralyzes conjugate gaze to the contralateral side and often causes deviation of the eyes to the ipsilateral side. Sometimes, particularly in deep-lying hemispheral hemorrhages involving the thalamus, the eyes deviate in the opposite direction. The eye deviation can usually be overcome by vestibular stimulation (p. 782) and is generally transient. Lesions of brain stem pathways cause more permanent conjugate paralysis to the ipsilateral side, with the eyes at rest deviating slightly to the contralateral side. This abnormality usually cannot be overcome by vestibular stimulation.

Lesions of the medial longitudinal fasciculus (MLF), which connects the third and sixth nerves in the brain stem, lead to *internuclear ophthalmoplegia*, in which the eyes at rest may either be parallel or show a mild skew deviation but move disjunctively on lateral gaze. (Skew deviation results from any of a number of lesions involving the brain stem and has little localizing value.) A characteristic of internuclear ophthalmoplegia is that during lateral gaze toward the side of the MLF lesion, the ipsilateral eye abducts and shows nystagmus (see below), whereas the contralateral, adducting eye partially or completely fails to move nasally because of the failure of ascending impulses to reach the opposite third nerve nucleus. Internuclear ophthalmoplegia may be caused by an infarct from small vessel disease (e.g., systemic lupus erythematosus) or by demyelinating disease. Bilateral internuclear ophthalmoplegia is almost always a result of multiple sclerosis.

HEARING AND ITS IMPAIRMENTS

Symptoms of Auditory Dysfunction

Only two symptoms result from disease of the auditory system: The first is hearing impairment, sometimes associated with pitch distortion (diplacusis) as well as a decrease in the intensity of sound,

TABLE 114–14. MAJOR CAUSES OF ACUTE (< 48 HR) OPHTHALMOPLEGIA

CONDITION	DIAGNOSTIC FEATURES
Bilateral	
Botulism	Contaminated food, high-altitude cooking, pupils involved
Myasthenia gravis	Fluctuating degree of paralysis; responds to edrophonium chloride IV
Wernicke's encephalopathy	Nutritional deficiency; responds to thiamine IV
Acute cranial polyneuropathy	Antecedent respiratory infection; elevated CSF protein
Brain stem stroke	Other brain stem signs
Unilateral	
Carotid-posterior	Third cranial nerve, pupil involved communicating aneurysm
Diabetic-idiopathic	Third or sixth cranial nerve, pupil spared
Myasthenia gravis	As above
Brain stem stroke	As above

and the second is tinnitus, a sound heard in the ear or head not arising from the external environment. Hearing loss is termed conductive (external and middle ear), sensorineural (cochlea and auditory nerve), or central (brain stem and cerebral hemispheres). The approach to the patient complaining of hearing loss is illustrated in Figure 114–4.

Conductive hearing loss is characterized by equal loss of hearing at all frequencies and by well-preserved speech discrimination once the threshold for hearing is exceeded. The ear often feels full, as if "blocked." Bone conduction exceeds air conduction and, if unilateral, the Weber test (tuning fork in the center of the head) is referred to the deaf ear. With *sensorineural hearing loss*, one typically hears better for low- than for high-frequency tones, and it may be difficult to hear speech that is mixed with background noise; small increases in the intensity of sound may cause discomfort (recruitment). Air conduction exceeds bone conduction and the Weber test refers to the hearing ear. With hearing loss resulting from cochlear disease (usually due to selective destruction of hair cells), diplacusis and recruitment are common. *Central hearing loss* is uncommon and usually characterized by loss of speech more than of pure tone perception. Substantial central hearing loss requires bilateral lesions of such areas as inferior colliculus, medial geniculate bodies, or temporal lobe. When the primary receiving areas (Heschl's gyrus) are destroyed, hearing is diminished or absent even for pure tone. If association areas in the superior temporal gyrus are damaged, a patient may hear the sounds but be unable to comprehend their meaning.

Causes of Hearing Loss

Conductive hearing loss arises from abnormalities of the external or middle ear and can raise hearing threshold no more than 60 dB, because bone conduction is intact. Otoscopic examination may reveal obstruction in the external auditory meatus (the

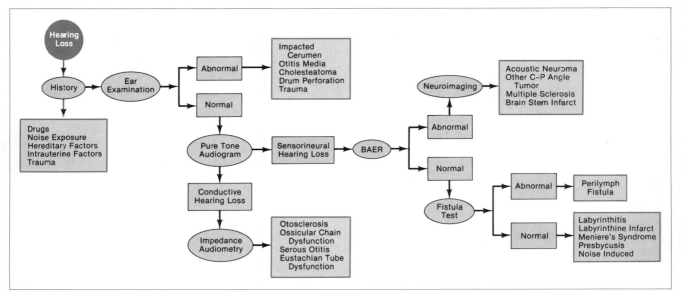

FIGURE 114-4. Evaluation of deafness (unilateral and bilateral). (From Baloh RW: Hearing and equilibrium. *In* Wyngaarden JB, Smith LH Jr, Bennett JC [eds]: Cecil Textbook of Medicine. 19th ed. Philadelphia, WB Saunders Co, 1992, p 2107.)

most common cause of conductive hearing loss) which impairs sound wave transmission to the tympanum. This benign condition is most often caused by *impacted cerumen,* but it occasionally results from canal infection or similar causes. A *fluid-filled middle ear,* a result of middle ear infection (otitis media), reduces movement of the ossicles against the oval window. If the otoscopic examination is negative, *otosclerosis,* a process in which the annular ligament that attaches the stapes to the oval window overgrows and calcifies, is a likely diagnosis. Chronic tinnitus sometimes marks the early stages of this process, which reduces ossicular transmission via the window to the cochlear basement membrane.

Sensorineural hearing loss from genetically determined deafness may be present at birth or develop in adulthood. The diagnosis of *hereditary deafness* rests on the finding of a positive family history.

Acute unilateral deafness usually has a cochlear basis. Bacterial or viral infections of the labyrinth, head trauma with fracture or hemorrhage into the cochlea, or vascular occlusion of a terminal branch of the anterior inferior cerebellar artery can damage the cochlea and its hair cells. An acute, idiopathic, often reversible, unilateral hearing loss strikes young adults and is presumed to reflect either a viral infection or a vascular disorder of the cochlea. Sudden unilateral hearing loss, often associated with vertigo and tinnitus, can result from a perilymphatic fistula. Such fistulas may be congenital, follow stapes surgery, or result from severe or mild trauma to the inner ear.

Drugs fairly often cause sudden bilateral hearing impairment. Salicylates, furosemide, and ethacrynic acid can cause intense tinnitus and transient deafness when taken in high doses. Aminoglycoside an-

tibiotics can destroy cochlear hair cells in direct relation to the height of their serum concentrations, thereby causing permanent hearing loss. Some anticancer chemotherapeutic agents, particularly cisplatin, cause severe ototoxicity by a similar mechanism. Subacute, relapsing cochlear deafness occurs with *Meniere's syndrome,* a condition associated with fluctuating hearing loss and tinnitus, recurrent episodes of abrupt and often severe vertigo, and a sensation of fullness or pressure in the ear. Recurrent endolymphatic hypertension (hydrops) is believed to cause the episodes. Pathologically, the endolymphatic sac is dilated and contains atrophic hair cells. The resulting deafness is subtle and reversible in the early stages but subsequently becomes permanent. What hearing remains is characterized by *diplacusis* (a different pitch heard in the affected ear) and loudness recruitment (quiet sounds are not heard but loud sounds are heard as loud as or louder than in the good ear). The disorder is usually unilateral. When bilateral (<20 per cent of cases), it begins in one ear before the other.

Gradually progressive hearing loss with age (*presbycusis*) reflects deterioration in the cochlear receptor system with degeneration of the hair cells, especially at the base. As a result, higher tones are lost early, a change similar to that which follows the recurrent trauma of noise-induced hearing loss from exposure to loud military or industrial noises or loud blaring modern music. Unilateral hearing loss that begins and progresses insidiously is characteristic of a benign neoplasm of the cerebellopontine angle (e.g., acoustic neurinoma); a high-resolution CT or MR scan usually establishes that diagnosis.

Treatment of Hearing Loss. The best treatment is prevention. Early detection of noise- or drug-induced hearing loss and removal of the offending agent often preserves hearing. Otosclerosis can often be corrected by surgery; closure of a perilymph fistula may improve hearing. Hearing aids are helpful in patients with conductive hearing loss, and sometimes newer hearing aids help patients with cochlear or other sensorineural abnormalities.

Tinnitus

Tinnitus is the term applied generally to extraneous noises heard in one or both ears. Figure 114–5 illustrates the approach to the patient with tinnitus and lists most of the causes of tinnitus. Tinnitus is either *objective*, i.e., the patient hears a real sound, one that can usually be heard by the examiner with a stethoscope, or *subjective*, i.e., the sound arises from an abnormal discharge of the auditory system and cannot be heard by the observer. Most objective tinnitus has a benign cause, but the finding may also be an early sign of increased intracranial pressure. Such tinnitus, which can be obliterated by pressure over the jugular vein, probably arises from turbulent flow in compressed venous structures at the base of the brain. The symptom is also relieved transiently by decreasing the intracranial pressure, e.g., by lumbar puncture.

Subjective tinnitus can arise from anywhere in the auditory system. A faint, moderately high-pitched metallic ring can be observed by almost everyone if they concentrate their attention on auditory events in a quiet room. Sustained, louder tinnitus accompanied by audiometric evidence of deafness occurs in association with either conductive or sensorineu-

ral disease. The phenomenon can be a manifestation of salicylate, quinine, or quinidine toxicity. Tinnitus observed with otosclerosis tends to have a roaring or hissing quality, while that associated with Meniere's syndrome often produces sounds that vary widely in intensity with time and quality, sometimes including roarings or clangings. Tinnitus with other cochlear or auditory nerve lesions tends to be higher-pitched and ringing in quality. Clanging or tonally fluctuating tinnitus or formed auditory hallucinations can be manifestations of temporal lobe seizures.

Treatment. If the underlying disorder causing objective tinnitus can be corrected, tinnitus may disappear. Most tinnitus is chronic, of no pathologic importance, and can be overcome by the physician's reassurance and the patient's withdrawing attention from the symptom. Otherwise, masking noises placed into the ear sometimes make patients more comfortable and better able to function.

DIZZINESS AND VERTIGO

Symptoms of Vestibular Dysfunction

The vestibular system, consisting of the bilateral semicircular canals and otolithic apparatus of the inner ear as well as their central connections, is a finely tuned discharging system. Any imbalance in

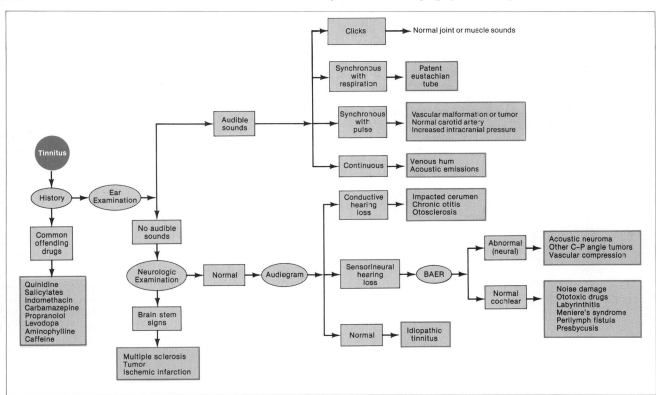

FIGURE 114–5. Evaluation of tinnitus. (Modified from Baloh RW: Hearing and equilibrium. *In* Wyngaarden JW, Smith LH Jr, Bennett JC [eds]: Cecil Textbook of Medicine. 19th ed. Philadelphia, WB Saunders Co, 1992, p 2108.)

input-output between the paired vestibular end organs or their primary receiving areas in the vestibular nuclei that is not caused by a true movement of the head or body produces a mismatch between vestibular stimulation and that going to other sense organs (especially the eyes and proprioceptive organs). This mismatch leads to an illusory sensation of movement in space, called vertigo. Vertigo is the only direct symptom of a vestibular abnormality, but because the vestibular system influences other neural systems, vertigo may be accompanied by autonomic symptoms (nausea, vomiting, diaphoresis), motor symptoms (ataxia, past pointing, falling), or ocular symptoms (oscillopsia—a visual sensation that the environment is moving). The clinical sign of a vestibular abnormality is *nystagmus*, a rhythmic to-and-fro movement of the eyes. Patients suffering from vertigo and nystagmus have an abnormality, either physiologic or pathologic, of the labyrinthine-vestibular system. As indicated on page 783, many patients are unable to distinguish vertigo from lightheadedness or other dizziness, and the physician must first determine whether the patient is truly vertiginous (see Table 114–12).

Nystagmus reflects an imbalance in the complex neural network that involves the visual pathways, the labyrinthine proprioceptive influences from neck muscles, the vestibular and cerebellar nuclei, the reticular formation of the pontine brain stem, and the oculomotor nuclei. It can be of two types: *Jerk nystagmus* consists of a slow phase away from the visual object followed by a quick saccade back toward the target. The quick eye movement describes the direction of jerk nystagmus. Benign jerk nystagmus, at the extremes of lateral gaze, is a common finding without pathologic significance. It is more common with fatigue or poor lighting. When bidirectional gaze-evoked nystagmus is prominent or involves vertical as well as horizontal movements to an equal degree, excessive sedative or anticonvulsant drug ingestion is most often the cause. Sustained gaze-evoked nystagmus with combined horizontal and torsional components inhibited by fixation suggests a peripheral lesion, whereas vertical nystagmus, particularly that which is not inhibited by fixation, suggests a central lesion. With rebound nystagmus there is nystagmus on lateral gaze that either disappears or reverses direction as the gaze position is held and then rebounds in the opposite direction when eyes are returned to the primary position. It is believed to be the only kind of nystagmus that specifically implicates cerebellar disease. *Pendular nystagmus* is nystagmus that is usually slow and coarse and equal in rate in both directions. It is usually congenital in origin or develops after birth as a result of severe visual impairment but can occasionally be a symptom of cerebellar or brain stem disease.

Several unusual forms of nystagmus have neurologic localizing qualities: *Dissociated nystagmus*, i.e., unequal in the two eyes, implies a brain stem lesion. *Periodic alternating nystagmus* consists of a horizontal jerk nystagmus that changes its direction periodically. It has been associated with a variety of posterior fossa abnormalities, especially those involving the region of the craniocervical junction. *Downbeat nystagmus* produces downward jerks with the eyes in the primary gaze position; it often reflects a craniocervical abnormality such as the Arnold-Chiari malformation but can occur with parenchymal lesions such as multiple sclerosis. Some subjects have the capacity to induce *voluntary nystagmus*, which is extremely rapid, occurs in short bursts of 10 to 15 seconds or so, is present on the extremes of gaze, and may be unequal in the two eyes.

Other abnormalities of conjugate eye movements include *ocular bobbing*, consisting of fast conjugate downward eye jerks followed by a slow return to the primary gaze position. The phenomenon accompanies severe displacement or destruction of the pons or, much less often, metabolic central nervous system (CNS) depression. *Ocular myoclonus* consists of continuous, rhythmic, pendular oscillations, most often vertical, with a rate of two to five beats per second. Often it accompanies palatal myoclonus and has a similar pathogenesis. Square wave jerks (defined by electronystagmography) and *ocular flutter* consist of brief, intermittent, horizontal oscillations arising from the primary gaze position. The abnormalities blend into *opsoclonus*, a pattern of rapid, chaotic, conjugate, repetitive saccadic eye movements ("dancing eyes"). Both of these disorders reflect cerebellar or brain stem dysfunction and also can emerge as a remote effect of systemic neoplasm, especially neuroblastoma in children. *Ocular dysmetria* consists of saccadic overshoots or undershoots of conjugate eye movement during rapid saccadic shifts of visual fixation. The phenomenon reflects cerebellar dysfunction.

Laboratory Tests of Vestibular Function

Bedside *caloric tests* induce vertigo. With the patient lying supine and the head elevated approximately 30 degrees, water 7°C above or below body temperature is douched against the tympanic membrane. In the normal situation, cold water produces nystagmus away from the side of stimulation (because of inhibition of the horizontal semicircular canal) and warm water nystagmus to the side of stimulation (because of stimulation of the semicircular canal). An astute patient suffering from labyrinthine vertigo can often tell which stimulation reproduces the symptoms, thus assisting in the localization of the lesion. Absence of the caloric response on one side suggests ipsilateral labyrinthine failure. Because most peripheral nystagmus is partially inhibited by the visual fixation of the open eyes, accurate quantitative evaluation requires electrical recording of the eye movement with the eyes closed. *Electronystagmography* can be performed in the resting position, with the head rotated into various positions to provoke nystagmus, and before, during, and after caloric stimulation. Electronystagmography is often helpful in identifying the pathology of the vestibular system and localizing it when identified.

Causes of Vertigo

Vertigo can be either physiologic or pathologic. *Physiologic vertigo* occurs when there is a mismatch among the vestibular, visual, and somatosensory systems induced by an external stimulus. Common examples of physiologic vertigo include motion sickness, height vertigo (the sensation that occurs when one looks down from a great height), and visual vertigo (the sensation sometimes felt when one views a motion picture of a roller coaster or other violent movement). In almost all instances, the diagnosis is clear from the history. One exception may be head extension vertigo, a sensation of vertigo or postural imbalance induced with the head maximally extended while standing; the sensation abruptly stops when the head is flexed to a neutral position. The symptoms may mistakenly be attributed to vertebral artery insufficiency. Head extension vertigo does not occur when the head is extended in the lying position and appears rarely when sitting. If physiologic vertigo becomes a clinical problem, it is best treated by supplying sensory cues that help to match the various sensory systems. Thus, *motion sickness*, which is often exacerbated by sitting in a closed space or reading, giving the visual system the miscue that the environment is stationary, may be relieved by looking out at the environment and watching it move. *Height vertigo* caused by a mismatch between sensation of normal body sway and lack of its visual detection can often be relieved by the patient either sitting or visually fixing a nearby stationary object.

Pathologic vertigo usually arises from an abnormality of the vestibular system but less commonly can be produced by visual or somatic sensory disorders. Vestibular vertigo can be caused by disease of either the peripheral or central vestibular apparatus (Table 114–15). In general, peripheral vertigo is more intense, more likely to be associated with hearing loss and tinnitus, and often leads to nausea and vomiting. Nystagmus associated with peripheral vertigo is frequently inhibited by visual fixa-

tion. Central vertigo is generally less severe, more sustained, and often associated with other signs of CNS disease. The nystagmus of central vertigo is not inhibited by visual fixation and frequently is disproportionately prominent to the degree of vertigo. Figure 114–6 illustrates the diagnostic approach to the vertiginous patient.

Benign positional vertigo is an extremely common disorder of middle and old age which accounts for the symptoms of at least 25 per cent of such patients with vertigo. Typically, the patient first experiences severe whirling vertigo when turning over, first lying down in bed at night, or arising in the morning. Less commonly, the patient may experience similar symptoms when he turns suddenly while standing or walking. Usually the symptoms are greatest when the patient lies on his side with the affected ear undermost. The vertigo is delayed for several seconds following the motion, sudden in

TABLE 114–15. CAUSES OF VESTIBULAR VERTIGO

PERIPHERAL CAUSES	CENTRAL CAUSES
Peripheral vestibulopathy*	Brain stem ischemia
Labyrinthitis and/or vestibular neuronitis	Cerebellopontine angle tumors
Acute and recurrent peripheral vestibulopathy	Demyelinating disease
"Benign" positional vertigo*	Cranial neuropathy
Meniere's syndrome*	Seizure disorders (rare)
Vestibulotoxic drugs	Heredofamilial disorders
Focal labryrinthine-third cranial nerve disease	Spinocerebellar degeneration
Trauma	Friedreich's ataxia
Cancer	Olivopontocerebellar atrophy, etc.
Infection	Other central caues
Otosclerosis	Brain stem tumors
Perilymph fistula	Cerebellar degenerations
	Paraneoplastic syndromes

*Common causes of acute severe vertigo.

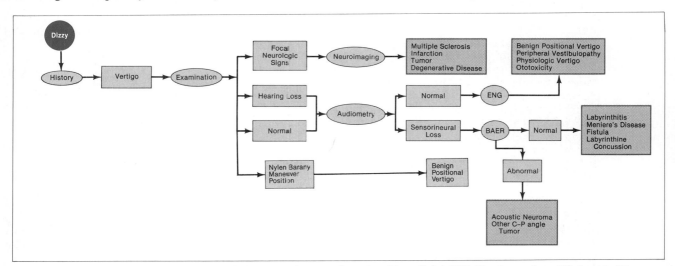

FIGURE 114–6. Evaluation of vertigo. (From Baloh RW: Hearing and equilibrium. *In* Wyngaarden JW, Smith LH Jr, Bennett JC [eds]: Cecil Textbook of Medicine. 19th ed. Philadelphia, WB Saunders Co, 1992, p 2111.)

onset, very severe, and may be accompanied by nausea or vomiting. The patient usually reports that the vertigo ceases when he moves out of the position that causes it, but in fact if he remains in that position, it rarely lasts more than a minute. The pathophysiology of the disorder is not established. Some investigators have postulated that debris from otoliths may enter the posterior canal to artificially stimulate it in the dependent position. The diagnosis is made by the characteristic history. The symptoms and nystagmus sometimes can be reproduced by seating patients erect on an examining table, then quickly moving them to the supine position. The illness usually lasts several weeks and then resolves, but may recur. If the patient has the classic history and physical findings, no further evaluation is necessary. If the history or findings are atypical, the condition must be distinguished from other causes of vertigo and nystagmus, such as tumor or infarct of the posterior fossa. Typical benign positional vertigo is rarely associated with such conditions. The treatment for most patients is simple reassurance. Because the vertigo can be fatigued, many patients find that repetitively reproducing the sudden head movement 10 to 20 times each morning and evening prevents recurrences.

Peripheral Vestibulopathy. This disorder, also called acute labyrinthitis or vestibular neuronitis, may occur as a single bout or may recur repeatedly over months or years. The vertigo is acute, and sometimes so severe that the patient is unable to sit or stand without vomiting and ataxia. He or she prefers to lie absolutely still in bed with the involved ear uppermost. Attacks sometimes follow a respiratory infection. Nystagmus is invariably present, usually horizontal or rotatory, and directed away from the involved labyrinth. The severe symptoms usually improve substantially within 48 to 72 hours, allowing the patient to be up and about. However, many patients report that for weeks or months following the episode sudden movements of the head produce mild vertigo or nausea. Although the disorder is called *acute labyrinthitis,* suggesting a viral infection of the labyrinth, EMG evoked potential studies suggest that in many patients there are accompanying eighth nerve or brain stem abnormalities, leading some to refer to the disorder as *vestibular neuronitis.* Labyrinthine fistulas have been reported to produce episodic vertigo. Fistula testing by a skilled otolaryngologist should establish that diagnosis. There has been a recent suggestion that some vertigo results from compression of the vestibular nerve by blood vessels of the posterior fossa in a manner analogous to trigeminal neuralgia (p. 770). *Other peripheral causes of vertigo* include Meniere's syndrome (p. 780) and the taking of vestibulotoxic drugs, most of which are also ototoxic (p. 780). Vertigo may be an additional symptom in patients suffering from *sudden hearing loss.* The pathogenesis of the disorder is unknown but may be vascular in some, viral infections in others. Bacterial infection of the labyrinth or occasionally otitis media causes vertigo. Degenerative and genetic abnormalities of the labyrinthine system can cause vertigo. *Cervical vertigo* is the term given to the feelings of dysequilibrium associated with head movement described by some patients with cervical osteoarthritis or spondylosis. The disorder probably is caused by unbalanced input from cervical muscles to the vestibular apparatus. Acute neck strain may be occasionally associated with vertigo. Local anesthetics injected into one side of the neck can produce vertigo and ataxia by a similar lack of balanced input. There is no nystagmus in these disorders.

Central Vertigo

Central causes of vertigo, less common than peripheral causes, are characterized by less severe vertigo than that resulting from peripheral lesions, no hearing loss or tinnitus, and concomitant neurologic signs of brain stem or cerebellar dysfunction.

Cerebrovascular Disease. If ischemia, infarction, or hemorrhage affects the brain stem or cerebellum, vertigo accompanied by nausea and vomiting is a relatively common symptom. Occipital headache as well as nystagmus and other neurologic signs suggesting brain stem or cerebellar dysfunction usually accompany vertigo. Rarely, vertigo (nonpositional) is the sole symptom of *transient ischemic attacks* of the brain stem, but most patients suffering such attacks, if carefully questioned, report headache, diplopia, facial or body numbness, and ataxia as well.

Cerebellopontine Angle Tumors. Most tumors growing in the cerebellopontine angle (e.g., acoustic neuroma, meningioma) grow slowly, allowing the vestibular system to accommodate. Thus they usually produce vague sensations of dysequilibrium rather than acute vertigo. Frequently such neoplasms produce complaints of tinnitus, hearing loss, and a sensation that the person is being pulled or pushed when he walks. Occasionally episodic vertigo or positional vertigo heralds the presence of a cerebellopontine angle tumor. Virtually all affected patients have retrocochlear hearing loss and decreased or absent caloric responses on the involved side. CT or MR scans through the temporal bone and posterior fossa usually reveal the tumor.

Demyelinating Disease. Acute vertigo may be the first symptom of *multiple sclerosis,* although only a small percentage of young patients with acute vertigo eventually develop multiple sclerosis. Vertigo may also be a symptom of *parainfectious encephalomyelitis* or, rarely, *parainfectious cranial polyneuritis* of the Guillain-Barré type. In this instance, the accompanying neurologic signs establish the diagnosis.

Cranial Neuropathy. A variety of acute or subacute illnesses affecting the eighth cranial nerve can produce vertigo as an early or sole symptom, the most common being *herpes zoster.* The *Ramsay Hunt syndrome (geniculate ganglion herpes)* is characterized by vertigo and hearing loss, variably associated with facial paralysis and sometimes pain in the ear. The typical lesions of herpes zoster, which may follow the appearance of neurologic signs, are found in the external auditory canal and sometimes over the palate. Whether herpes zoster is ever responsible for vertigo in the absence of the full-blown syndrome is not certain. *Granulomatous meningitis* or *leptomeningeal metastases* and cerebral or systemic *vasculitis* may involve the eighth nerve, producing vertigo as an early symptom. In these disorders, cerebrospinal fluid (CSF) analysis usually suggests the diagnosis.

Seizure Disorders. Patients suffering from temporal lobe epilepsy occasionally suffer vertigo as the aura. Vertigo in the absence of other neurologic signs or symptoms, however, is never caused by epilepsy or other diseases of the cerebral hemispheres.

Other Central Causes. Many structural lesions of the brain stem or cerebellum, particularly if rapid in onset, may cause vertigo. In a few instances, vertigo may initiate the symptoms of *paraneoplastic brain stem or cerebellar degeneration.* As with *brain stem tumors, cerebellar degenerative diseases* and other structural disease of the brain stem and posterior fossa, there are usually other neurologic symptoms, almost always including signs of brain stem or cerebellar dysfunction in addition to the vertigo and nystagmus.

Treatment

The best treatment of symptomatic vertigo is to cure the underlying disease. In many instances, however, that is not possible and one must resort to symptomatic treatment only. In acute vertigo, such as occurs with labyrinthitis, most patients insist on being at bedrest. Vestibulosedative drugs such as meclizine or diazepam may be helpful. Prochlorperazine suppositories can be used to circumvent vomiting. Vestibulosuppressive drugs such as meclizine also sometimes help more chronic vertiginous disorders. Scopolamine, 0.4 to 0.8 mg, together with methylphenidate, 5 mg orally, may give relief of vertigo, particularly motion sickness. Recently, transdermal scopolamine paste-on units placed behind the ear have been reported to be effective in preventing motion sickness for up to 72 hours. These, like all scopolamine products, may produce anticholinergic side effects. If head or neck movement precipitates vertigo, a cervical collar sometimes relieves the symptoms.

REFERENCES

Baloh RW, Honrubia V: Clinical Neurophysiology of the Vestibular System. 2nd ed. Philadelphia, FA Davis Co, 1990.

Brandt T: Vertigo: Its Multisensory Syndromes. London, Springer-Verlag, 1991.

Glaser JS: Neuro-ophthalmology. 2nd ed. Hagerstown, MD, Harper & Row, 1990.

Leigh RH, Zee DS: The Neurology of Eye Movement. 2nd ed. Philadelphia, FA Davis Co, 1991.

C. Disorders of Somatic Sensation

EVALUATION OF THE PATIENT

Because sensory fibers are so intimately associated with fibers subserving other neurologic functions in almost their entire anatomic pathway, isolated disorders of somatic sensation are uncommon. Thus, most abnormalities of somatic sensation are discussed along with their accompanying motor abnormalities (e.g., peripheral nerve disorders) or under the various causative diseases (e.g., neoplasms or vascular disease of the brain or spinal cord). Only a few purely sensory disorders are discussed here.

Somatosensory disorders may diminish, increase, or distort sensation depending on the pattern and intensity of the damage to sensory pathways: Diminution of function is readily recognized by the patient as "numbness." Hyperfunction of a disordered sensory system is perceived as tingling (paresthesia) that presents spontaneously or when the disturbed area is stimulated. Dysesthesias are unpleasant or painful sensations produced by stimuli that are ordinarily painless (allodynia).

Mild sensory abnormalities, readily perceived by the patient, often cannot be confirmed on examination. In this situation the patient should be asked to describe the abnormality as precisely as possible and to map its distribution. Such careful mapping allows the physician to determine whether the sensory abnormality is in the distribution of a single nerve (e.g., meralgia paresthetica), many nerves (sensory peripheral neuropathy), a nerve root, or a portion of the CNS. The physician should attempt to document sensory complaints by careful sensory testing.

Deep tendon reflexes disappear early in patients with large fiber sensory abnormalities, because dysfunction of the large fiber afferent arc impairs simultaneous firing of the monosynaptic stretch reflex. The clinical implication is that patients with normal deep tendon reflexes (in particular the ankle reflexes) are not suffering a substantial large fiber sensory neuropathy.

SPECIFIC DISORDERS OF SENSATION

Isolated disorders of somatic sensation occur in two settings. The first is when a focal structural disorder strikes a portion of the nervous system that is restricted to subserving sensation. Examples are entrapment neuropathies of pure sensory nerves (e.g., lateral cutaneous nerve of the thigh), compression of the sensory portion of a nerve root in a herniated disc, a small syrinx damaging only spinothalamic fibers crossing in the anterior commissure of the spinal cord, and small infarcts or tumors restricted

TABLE 114–16. PREDOMINANTLY OR EXCLUSIVELY SENSORY POLYNEUROPATHY

Metabolic	Toxins
Diabetes	Arsenic
Uremia	Acrylamide
Paraproteinemia	Thallium
Amyloidosis	Trichlorethylene (face)
Drugs	**Miscellaneous**
Pyridoxine	Parainfectious
Cisplatin	Paraneoplastic
Thalidomide	Rheumatoid arthritis
Isoniazid	

to the sensory thalamus, or, less often, the somatosensory cortex. The second instance is when a genetic, metabolic, or degenerative disorder affects sensory fibers as a system, sparing intermixed motor fibers (Table 114–16).

The most common pure sensory mononeuropathy is *meralgia paresthetica*, an entrapment neuropathy resulting from compression of the lateral cutaneous nerve of the thigh which passes under the inguinal ligament. Numbness or burning sensations occur over the lateral thigh; sometimes prolonged standing or walking provokes the symptoms. Weight reduction may help, but in many cases the condition subsides spontaneously. A similar syndrome can affect the dorsal aspect of the thumb when a tight watchband compresses a cutaneous branch of the radial nerve. Carpal tunnel and thoracic outlet syndromes may be purely sensory in the beginning; they cause serious disability only if motor fibers are involved as well.

Compression of sensory nerve roots or sensory pathways in the spinal cord, such as occurs with herniated discs or cervical or lumbar spondylosis, is discussed on page 807. Herpes zoster may cause sensory loss (and pain) in the distribution of the affected nerve root.

Polyneuropathies (p. 811) may begin with sensory loss or, less often, remain purely sensory. *Acute inflammatory sensory neuropathy*, or neuronopathy, is the rare sensory counterpart of the motor polyradiculopathy of the Guillain-Barré syndrome. Unlike with the Guillain-Barré syndrome, the prognosis for recovery is poor, patients usually being left with substantial disability resulting from the sensory loss. A clinical picture similar to that of inflammatory sensory neuropathy is sometimes encountered as a "remote effect" of cancer on the nervous system or as a manifestation of Sjögren's syndrome.

Hereditary sensory neuropathies are rare inherited disorders of sensory fibers. Type I is a dominantly inherited radicular neuropathy that affects pain and temperature sensation more than touch and proprioception. It may lead to perforating ulcers of the feet. The disorder is slowly progressive, and the diagnosis is made by the family history. Types II and III are recessive disorders that begin in childhood. Type III (dysautonomic or Riley-Day) is also associated with autonomic dysfunction. Familial amyloid disease similarly causes maximal damage to pain and autonomic fibers.

REFERENCES

Lindblom U, Ochoa JL: Somatosensory function and dysfunction. *In* Asbury AK, McKhann GM, McDonald WI (eds): Diseases of the Nervous System. 2nd ed. Philadelphia, WB Saunders Co, 1992, pp 213–228.

Ropper AH, Wijdicks EFM, Truax BT: Guillain-Barré Syndrome. Philadelphia, FA Davis Co, 1990.

Schaumburg HH, Berger AR, Thomas PK: Disorders of Peripheral Nerves. Philadelphia, FA Davis Co, 1991.

115 DISORDERS OF THE MOTOR SYSTEM

A. Introduction

The normal human voluntary motor system originates in the premotor areas of the frontal lobe cortex and sends its messages caudally via the corticospinal tract after the basal ganglia and cerebellum have added their postural, reinforcing, and coordinating influences (Fig. 115–1A). Additional descending influences from the red nuclei, vestibular nuclei, and brain stem reticular formation converge with descending corticospinal pathways on bulbo-spinal motor neurons to activate integrated, functionally automatic motor programs. At every level, from muscle, nerve, spinal segment, brain stem, cerebellum, basal ganglia, and cortex, afferent feedback impulses guide the efferently directed action so as to assure its healthy success.

Disease potentially can affect selectively every level of the motor system from muscle to brain. Table 115–1 briefly lists most common anatomic locations of diseases affecting the motor system. Later sections of this chapter discuss most of them in greater detail. The first step in recognizing any of these categories lies in evaluating symptoms and signs, giving specific attention to deciding whether the origin of the complaints lies in the peripheral (muscles, nerves, roots) or the central nervous system (CNS). Once the latter decision is reached, it becomes easier to ferret out exactly which level or which component of motor control is most likely to be the offender. Because many diseases of the human motor system are unaccompanied by specific neurodiagnostic laboratory abnormalities, the carefulness of the clinical examination and the examiner's ingenuity often provide the most reliable guide to the nature of the patient's illness. Laboratory tests for examining neuromuscular disease are described in Chapter 111.

SIGNS AND SYMPTOMS OF MOTOR DYSFUNCTION

Generalized Weakness and Fatigue

Fatigue refers to a perception of intellectual or physical exhaustion that may follow or even precede concerted mental and/or physical effort. Normal degrees of activity-related fatigue require little more than a common-sense appraisal. Pronounced fatigue after the act can have either an organic or a psychological pathogenesis. Localized muscular fatigability most often reflects a regional disorder or deconditioning of the nerves or muscles; when accompanied by detectable, exercise-induced local reductions in muscle strength, the symptom is characteristic of myasthenia gravis. Chronic, generalized fatigability can accompany a number of specifically diagnosable systemic illnesses, such as chronic liver disease or chronic well-characterized immune disorders. Neurologic disorders that characteristically produce fatigue include myasthenia gravis, progressive muscular dystrophy, motor neuron disease, Parkinson's disease, stroke, and severe trauma. All of these conditions produce other clinical abnormalities that identify their specific cause. More difficult to understand and classify are states of long-lasting, generalized weakness coupled with feelings of pre-effort fatigue for which no objectively verifiable cause can be found. Variously called over the years neurasthenia, effort syndrome, and, at

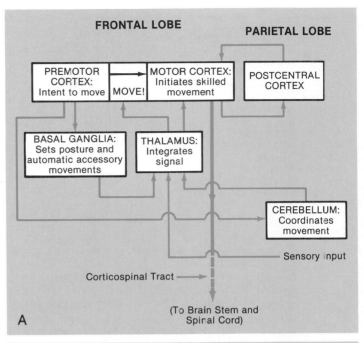

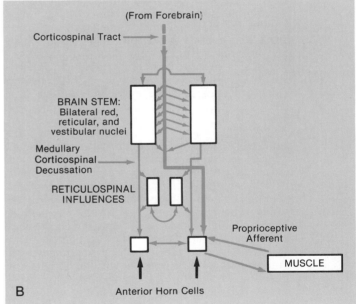

FIGURE 115-1. *A,* The principal cerebral-cerebellar influences involved in initiating learned motor activities. The frontal lobe sends initiating and, subsequently, continuous signals of "intent to move" to the basal ganglia and cerebellum as much as 0.4 second or more before the actual movement occurs. The basal ganglia programs postural and automatic accessory movements appropriate to the intended act while the cerebellar return coordinates the movement's smooth flow. Both structures forward their modified messages to the thalamus. That structure integrates the several motor signals with sensory input and transmits the processed message back to premotor and motor cortices, which flash it downward via the corticospinal tract to innervate motor neurons and thereby skeletal muscle. Throughout the process, continuous feedback activity at every level from a fronto-parietal-frontal loop as well as from more peripheral receptors constantly monitors the act and influences its satisfactory execution. *B,* Brain stem and spinal accessory motor nuclei, as diagrammed, receive cerebral motor and proprioceptive activity, integrate it, and pass additional messages to the anterior horn cells bilaterally. The combined result enables the limbs and body to execute even the simplest coordinated learned act as dictated by the cerebral motor cortical areas. Within these indispensable, automatically acting areas also lies the genesis of abnormal posture, motor tone, tremor, and incoordination that mark motor diseases. In association with lesions of the specific corticospinal pathway, varying influences of these brain stem spinal accessory nuclei explain the different forms of spasticity and postural abnormalities that may accompany the syndrome of upper motor neuron dysfunction.

TABLE 115–1. PRINCIPAL DISORDERS OF THE MOTOR SYSTEM FROM DISTAL TO PROXIMAL

Muscular
  Dystrophies, metabolic myopathies, myositis
Myoneural junction
  Myasthenia, Lambert-Eaton syndrome, botulism
Peripheral nerve disorders
  Polyneuropathy
  Mono- or focal neuropathy
Radiculopathies and lower motor neuron diseases
Spinal cord diseases
Cerebellar ataxias
Movement, "extrapyramidal" disorders
Corticospinal diseases (disorders of the upper motor neuron)

present, chronic fatigue syndrome, the condition is widespread.

Chronic fatigue syndrome affects two principal categories of patients. One is represented by a small fraction of persons who, by all past records, were healthy and energetic until struck by an ill-defined, generalized, flu-like illness. Following the latter, prostrating, isolated fatigue limits their normal physical and mental activity for periods lasting many weeks or months or indefinitely. Some examples of this putatively self-limited disorder have erupted in mini-epidemics among primary caregivers. Many efforts have been made to establish an infectious nature for the condition. Only one, however, which suggested a chronic immunologic reaction to human herpes virus type 6, has provided strong evidence that the epidemic disorder may have an organic cause. Far more common than epidemic chronic fatigue are sporadic cases. Indeed, chronic fatigue is the seventh most common complaint presented to primary care physicians. In addition to feeling chronically tired, with or without undertaking physical activity, many such patients typically complain of multiple somatic symptoms including abdominal pain, bizarre pain patterns affecting other body parts, menstrual complaints, sleep disorders, headaches, vague myalgias, and postexercise fatigue. Many of the complaints resemble those found in the equally poorly understood disorder *fibromyalgia* (see Chapter 90). Others are consistent with patterns seen in somatoform disorders (p. 754). In keeping with science news reports, which recurrently report new organic causes for the syndrome, most affected patients believe strongly or unshakably that they suffer from a chronic virus infection or other externally generated disorder. Careful psychiatric and past history evaluation, however, characteristically discloses chronic somatoform illness long preceding the putatively recent onset of fatigue. Fully three quarters of chronic fatigue patients fulfill criteria for having at least one psychiatric disorder in their lifetime, and several studies have found evidence for major depressive episodes, in as many as 50 per cent, past or present. A consistent feature in all studies that have closely examined the matter has been that patients with chronic fatigue syndrome sturdily avoid expressing psychiatric symptoms unless specifically asked and even then tend to disassociate their somatic complaints from their mood disorder.

Although it is possible that chronic fatigue syndrome has multiple somatic and psychosomatic causes, one should not ignore the latter because several studies report that antidepressives coupled with cognitive behavioral group therapy can bring relief to as many as half such patients. The experience is that repeated efforts to find organic causes for the symptoms not only fail to improve symptoms but also block other, psychologically based efforts at treatment. Among other steps, in addition to strong psychological counseling efforts, chronically fatigued patients should be urged to undertake full physical and mental activity.

Weakness refers to an impaired capacity to carry out a voluntary motor act due to a loss of muscular power. The term *paresis* is synonymous. *Paralysis* designates more complete loss of motor function. Most weakness or paralysis results from disease or dysfunction of the central or peripheral nervous system or the muscles. Never the less, muscle guarding and immobility that surround injured or inflamed areas of the trunk or extremities sometimes cause the false appearance of weakness when motion accentuates the pain. The qualities of hysterical weakness are described below.

The history is of major importance in recognizing the nature and significance of weakness. Most persons promptly recognize a recently developing or rapidly progressing muscle motor loss but tend to ignore insidiously developing, painless weakness until it produces substantial functional disability (e.g., inability to climb stairs). Families or physicians may sometimes detect such gradually evolving limitations (e.g., limping or dragging a leg) before the patient does. Conversely, although most patients with motor system disorders complain of "weakness," an occasional patient may use the term *numbness* to indicate why objects drop from the weak hand. In other instances, patients use the term *weakness* to mean fatigability, asthenia, or even incoordination. Patients should be pressed to be specific about the terms they use and, if they are truly weak, to describe which motor acts are limited. In the legs, for example, proximal muscle weakness is usually characterized by difficulty getting out of low chairs, arising from the toilet seat, or climbing stairs, whereas distal motor weakness is characterized by tripping because of failure to dorsiflex the foot while walking on irregular ground or when climbing stairs or curbs. Shoulder girdle weakness is characterized by difficulty using a hair dryer or lifting heavy objects to a high shelf, whereas distal weakness is noted in manipulative tasks such as turning keys, opening door knobs, or unscrewing jar tops.

Patterns of Neurologic and Muscular Weakness. Corticospinal tract dysfunction-weakness can be divided into respective patterns of upper motor neuron and lower motor neuron disability (Table 115–2). *Upper motor neuron lesions* arising at the cerebral level typically produce regional weakness predominating in the hand and arm, the lower face, or the foot and leg, in that order of frequency. A hemiparesis (face, arm, and leg) can originate from the cerebrum, as can face-hand-arm weakness. Face-leg weakness, sparing the arm, implies two anatomically distinct lesions, whereas arm-leg weakness sparing the face can originate anywhere along the corticospinal pathway between the internal capsule and the upper cervical cord. Upper motor neuron weakness typically affects skilled movement, with paresis being more marked distally than proximally in the limbs. Various components of spasticity emerge, including increased muscular resistance to passive stretch with lengthening and shortening reactions, increased deep tendon reflexes, abnormal postural responses to stimulation, including decorticate, decerebrate, and spinal flexor responses, and the classic Babinski sign. Upper motor neuron lesions seldom severely paralyze the face and never completely so. As a result, the brow and orbicularis oculi, like other bodily midline muscle groups, are relatively spared. Atrophy of the limbs, if it occurs at all, is mild and due to disuse. The electromyogram (EMG) usually shows no abnormality beyond a reduction or loss of voluntary contraction activity.

Disease of the lower motor neuron, including the anterior horn cells, the motor nerve root, or the motor nerve, causes a classic syndrome (Table 115–2). Weakness is focally distributed according to areas of denervation, so that a major clue to anatomic diagnosis lies in distinguishing among the respective paralytic patterns produced by damage to spinal cord, ventral motor root, plexus, or peripheral nerve. Characteristic sensory defects accompany many of these causes. With severe denervation-weakness, muscle atrophy begins within days. Motor resistance is subnormal, deep tendon reflexes diminish or disappear, and with proximally originating denervation, fasciculations may, in time, become visible through the skin. Electric signs of denervation, including first fibrillation and later fasciculation, begin within 3 to 4 weeks of injury.

Among *basal ganglia diseases,* asthenia is prominent in parkinsonism and chorea. Some patients in the early stages of parkinsonism complain of a hemiparetic weakness that can misleadingly suggest corticospinal tract dysfunction. Most persons with Parkinson's disease, however, suffer only mild to moderate weakness but report disproportionately prominent difficulty in initiating and continuing movements, "as if starting through molasses." Their limbs show rigidity rather than spasticity, their deep tendon reflexes are at most only moderately increased, and they lack Babinski signs or other evidence of pathologic reflex spasticity.

Cerebellar diseases, especially those of the hemisphere and dentate nuclei, cause ipsilateral asthenia and weakness. Ataxia and incoordination, however, are more prominent. Muscle resistance to passive stretch is, if anything, reduced, but deep tendon reflexes may be moderately hyperactive, and impaired cerebellar regulation of the stretch reflex can cause pendular swinging of the knee jerk. Pathologic reflexes and muscle atrophy are lacking.

Nerve-muscle junctional disease is of two kinds. The more frequent, myasthenia gravis (MG), consists of an autoimmune blockage of the acetylcho-

TABLE 115–2. CLINICAL SIGNS OF UPPER AND LOWER MOTOR NEURON LESIONS

	UPPER	LOWER
Paralysis	Mostly distal, distributed in major body part	Proximal or distal, distributed by nerve root or anterior horn cell anatomy
Atrophy	Minimal, late, disuse	Prominent, early, neurotropic
Fasciculations	Absent	Often present
Spasticity	Present	Absent
Deep tendon reflexes	Increased	Decreased or absent
Babinski reflex	Present	Absent

line receptor in the muscle. The other, the Lambert-Eaton myasthenic syndrome, involves immunologic blockage of presynaptic calcium channels, reducing release of neurotransmitter from the nerve terminals. Weakness in MG affects most often the oculomotor, bulbar, and proximal limb muscles, which rapidly fatigue with quick successive action. Weakness in the Lambert-Eaton syndrome, by contrast, affects mainly the distal limbs, is maximal with first effort, and lessens with repeated tries. Atrophy occurs in neither disorder except when severe chronic MG induces muscle disuse. Muscle tone is normal, deep tendon reflexes are usually preserved or reduced, and sensation is unaffected. EMG changes are diagnostic.

Myopathies, diseases intrinsic to muscle, produce insidiously beginning weakness that symmetrically affects anatomic groups characteristic of the particular variant of degenerative (dystrophy), metabolic (e.g., thyrotoxic), or inflammatory (myositis) diseases. Weakness occasionally remains constant (congenital myopathy) but usually progresses either slowly (dystrophy), rapidly (metabolic or inflammatory myopathy), or episodically (periodic paralysis). Resistance to passive stretch is normal, but the muscles may be tender (myositis), show myotonia (congenital myotonia, myotonic dystrophy), be abnormally soft (thyrotoxicosis), look abnormally large (pseudohypertrophy), or feel unduly firm (connective tissue infiltration). Deep tendon reflexes are preserved until late except in hypokalemic myopathy. Serum enzymes often are abnormal in muscular dystrophy, and EMGs in many instances are characteristic. Sensation remains intact.

Major Abnormal Movements

Table 115–3 lists the major conditions causing nonparoxysmal, focal, or generalized abnormal gross skeletal muscle movements. Several of the focal movements can be confused with epileptic attacks (see Chapter 118). Categories overlap, especially those of dystonia, chorea, athetosis, and dyskinesia.

Myotonia comprises a prolonged (seconds) involuntary contraction of a group of adjacent muscle fibers following a self-limited, voluntary effort or an

TABLE 115–3. MAJOR MOVEMENT DISORDERS

Tremor	Dystonia (Table 115–7)
Parkinson's	Athetosis (congenital)
Cerebellar	Dyskinesia
Familial—senile	Hemifacial spasm
Chorea	Levodopa-associated
Huntington's	Tardive
Sydenham's	Myoclonus
Lupus- or pregnancy-related	Tics
Ballism	

abrupt local percussion as with a reflex hammer. A genetically caused abnormality of the postsynaptic muscle membrane produces self-repetitive muscle membrane depolarizations and afterdischarges that lead to sustained fiber shortening.

Cramps are a sudden, painful, abrupt shortening of muscles. Motor units during cramps fire at about 300 per second, much faster than the most vigorous voluntary contraction. The high rate of discharge causes a sustained, strong muscular contraction and secondarily induces pain. Both aspects can be relieved by stretching the affected muscle or by massage. Central mechanisms may also be involved, because certain conditions are associated with a propensity to cramps: denervation (especially amyotrophic lateral sclerosis), pregnancy, and electrolyte disorders (especially water intoxication and hyponatremia). Cramps attributed to hypo-osmolarity are seen in some patients treated by maintenance hemodialysis. They respond to treatment with hypertonic solutions of glucose or sodium.

Cramps occur commonly in otherwise normal individuals, and some people with or without a family history of cramps are more susceptible than others for unknown reasons. Cramps that occur only at night or after sustained exercise can sometimes be prevented by quinine sulfate, 0.3 gm taken orally. Others can occur frequently during the day, occasionally so often that the individual is effectively crippled. Phenytoin, 0.3 to 0.6 gm daily, may be helpful in these patients, but some are resistant to this as well as to other drugs that may be tried, including diazepam, carbamazepine, and diphenhydramine. Patients with benign fasciculations (lacking weakness, wasting, or other signs of motor neuron disease) seem especially prone to frequent cramps.

Tetany is a special form of cramp, identified by its predilection for flexor muscles of the hand and fingers, its association with laryngospasm, and its relationship to hypocalcemia. Tetany can be painful. It differs from other cramps electromyographically because of a characteristic rhythmic grouping of discharging potentials. Hyperventilation-induced tetany is sometimes overlooked as a cause of cramps or laryngospasm.

Muscle fibrillation is continuously recurrent, spontaneous contractions of single muscle fibers due usually to denervation but sometimes to dystrophic degeneration of single fiber membranes. In either event, the phenomenon reflects hypersensitivity of the muscle membrane and contractile system to circulating or locally diffusing acetylcholine (ACh). *Fasciculations* represent spontaneous, synchronous, recurrent depolarization-contraction of the fibers of a single motor unit or of a group of partially denervated motor units that have been reinnervated by fibers that have sprouted from adjacent, still-conducting motor axons. The pathogenesis reflects denervation hypersensitivity to ACh of the damaged motor axon. Fasciculations of larger motor units and grouped motor units are visible through the skin. Fibrillations and fasciculations produce characteristic EMG changes (p. 737).

Myokymia has been used to describe a variety of apparently different disorders characterized by cramps in association with continuous spontaneous twitching of muscle. The EMGs in some cases show prolonged trains of spontaneous potentials, whereas in others grouping of potentials is found. Some patients have difficulty in relaxing grip, a phenomenon called neuromyotonia, because, unlike myotonia, the muscular activity is abolished by neuromuscular blocking agents, indicating a neural rather than a muscular origin. Hyperhidrosis is prominent in some patients and is secondary to the increased muscular activity.

In patients with severe myokymia, continuous shortening of muscle leads to abnormal postures and abnormally increased resistance to passive movement. Such abnormalities are often due to central neurologic disorders and are thought to result from poorly understood genetically related autoimmune disorders. Some affected patients suffer fluctuating rigidity of axial and limb muscles and continuous EMG activity despite authentic attempts to relax. The resulting disorder has been labeled *stiff-man syndrome*. Ordinary cramps may be superimposed upon the persistent stiffness. Phenytoin, carbamazepine, or diazepam in therapeutic doses may bring dramatic relief. The condition may have several causes; in several cases antibodies have been demonstrated against central gamma-aminobutyric acid (GABA) receptors.

Tremor exists in three major forms (Table 115–4). *Essential tremor* or *benign familial tremor* is an accentuation of a physiologic, 8- to 12-Hz rhythmic oscillation that can affect the distal arms, the head, or, less often, the vocal apparatus. Coarse in its pattern but absent at complete rest, the tremor begins with the maintenance of posture and is accentuated by voluntary, intentional movement, sometimes to an incapacitating degree. The abnormality depends on cerebellar mechanisms as well as basal ganglia dysfunction and can be blocked by lesions placed in the ventrolateral nucleus of the thalamus. Essential tremor varies widely in intensity and can appear at any age but becomes more common and prominent in elderly life (*senile tremor*). Accompanied by neither rigidity, akinesia, ataxia, nor weakness, its predisposition is transmitted as an autosomal dominant trait. Alcohol in small amounts and, less often, anxiolytic agents suppress the movement. The beta blocker propranolol reduces the intensity of the tremor in about 25 per cent of affected persons. Primidone and baclofen are useful for some patients.

Resting or *parkinsonian tremor*, a 4- to 7-Hz oscillation, reflects the alternating contractions of agonist-antagonist muscles, most often of the distal extremities, especially the hand ("pill rolling"). Less frequently the lower facial muscles, the tongue, or the lower extremities are involved. The tremor worsens with anxiety or fatigue and tends to quiet down or briefly disappear with relaxation or periods of intense manual concentration. As with all abnormal movements of basal ganglia origin, parkinsonian tremor disappears during sleep. Its genesis is believed to reflect excess cholinergic activity in the striatum, leading to an abnormally high GABA output from the putamen to the pallidum. The tremor can be abolished by lesions of the thalamic ventrolateral nucleus and is improved by antiparkinsonian drugs, as discussed below.

Intention (cerebellar) tremor can take any of three patterns. One relates to damage of the vermis and anterior lobe and results in an oscillating, rhythmic ataxia of the trunk and lower limbs during attempts to walk (titubation). A second, associated with lesions of the afferent spinocerebellar input, produces a more irregular high-steppage shaking ataxia of the lower extremities, which can blend into titubation. The third, resulting from damage to the dentate outflow pathway of the superior peduncle, produces the classic hand or foot intention tremor, consisting of an irregular, coarse 3- to 6-Hz distal oscillation that increases in amplitude and irregularity as the voluntarily moving extremity approaches its object. In all instances, cerebellar tremor reflects a disruption in the balance between afferent impulses to the roof nuclei of the cerebellum and the immediately following inhibitory loop that normally feeds back on these roof nuclei from the Purkinje cells. Cerebellar intention tremor so far has resisted efforts at pharmacologic control.

Asterixis is an irregular, flaplike tremor, distributed more distally than proximally, that involves the extremities, less often the tongue, with a frequency varying from less than 1 to as high as 3 Hz. It is most often observed to accompany the metabolic encephalopathies and usually is accompanied by an accentuated physiologic tremor. Its mechanism reflects a brief loss of muscle contraction in muscles controlling extension of the involved member, followed by a rapid myoclonic-like flexor movement during recovery.

Chorea describes involuntary, nonrhythmic, irregularly distributed, coarse, quick twitching movements affecting the face, tongue, and proximal and distal extremities. Slower athetoid twistings sometimes intersperse themselves concurrently. Mild cases may resemble little more than anxiety-provoked fidgets, whereas the appearance of severe forms blends into generalized dystonia. Efforts at sustained muscular contraction accentuate the disorder, which possesses features of both basal ganglia and cerebellar dysfunction. Pharmacologically, the phenomenon most closely resembles the effects of central dopamine hyperactivity. *Ballism* consists of irregular, abrupt, repetitive, wide-amplitude flinging movements of the limbs initiated predominantly

TABLE 115-4. CHARACTERISTICS OF COMMON TREMORS

	ASSOCIATED DISORDER	POSITION	FREQUENCY, CHARACTER
Essential	Normal or anxiety-accentuated	Sustained posture	8–12 Hz Oscillating, distal extremities
Familial	Autosomal pattern of inheritance; linked to essential tremor	Sustained posture Intention	8–12 Hz Oscillating head-neck, distal extremities
Parkinson's	Basal ganglia disease Wilson's disease	Resting or postural Not intention	4–7 Hz Reciprocally alternating Tongue, facial muscles, distal extremities
Cerebellar	Vermis, anterior cerebellar	Action-intention tremor. Rhythmic regular titubation of trunk lower extremities	Coarse, 3–6 Hz Oscillating
	Spinobulbar cerebellar input	Distal lower extremity	Coarse, somewhat irregular ataxia
	Neocerebellar dentate outflow	Distal upper extremity	Often irregular. Increases as target is approached
Asterixis	Metabolic encephalopathy, particularly hepatic	Outstretched tongue or, more often, hands. Flaplike appearance	Coarse 1–3 Hz Rapid twitches with variable intervals between

by proximal girdle muscles. Less prominent distal choreiform movements often accompany the condition, which involves body parts opposite to an infarcted or, rarely, otherwise damaged subthalamic nucleus. Usually unilateral in distribution (hemiballismus), the condition is ameliorated by haloperidol or reserpine. Ordinarily it subsides spontaneously within a few weeks after onset.

Dystonia can accompany several basal ganglia disorders and is the major sign of a primary movement disorder of late childhood, adolescence, or adult life (see Table 115-3). The abnormality is characterized by bizarre twisting or turning motions, most but not all of which affect more distal body parts. The distinctive feature of the movements is that they involve the simultaneous tonic co-contraction of agonist and antagonist muscle groups. Brief dystonia usually lasts for a second or more, a rate somewhat faster than in *athetosis*, a slow, proximally distributed twisting observed most commonly in children who have suffered perinatal or infantile basal ganglia-thalamic damage. Most dystonic movements also tend to recur in longer spasms, sometimes lasting minutes to hours at a time. Dystonia can be generalized or restricted, inherited or acquired. It can arise as a distinct, idiopathic disorder or as an accompaniment to several basal ganglia diseases, including Huntington's chorea and Wilson's disease. The pathophysiology and pharmacologic basis of dystonic movements are poorly understood. Several phenothiazine derivatives, however, can induce acute dystonia as an idiosyncratic response in susceptible hosts. Structural lesions involving the basal ganglia–thalamic motor pathways sometimes cause a contralateral hemidystonia. The anticholinergic, antihistamine drug diphenhydramine hydrochloride blocks drug-induced dystonia but not the naturally occurring form.

Motor tics are sudden, quick, irregular, stereotyped movements of variable complexity that repetitively involve similar but not identical groups of muscles. They can come on at any age, most often in adolescence or young adulthood, and most frequently involve the face, eyes, or mouth but seldom the extremities. Some mild forms represent psychologically generated habit patterns. More severe examples, often combined with bizarre barkings or the shouting of scatologic and other obscenities, comprise *Gilles de la Tourette's syndrome.*

Myoclonus consists of sudden, abrupt contractions of single muscles or restricted groups of muscles, most frequently affecting the limbs, less often the trunk. The phenomenon has many causes and can arise from abnormally excitable gray matter at any level of the nervous system. Single generalized myoclonic jerks occur normally as startle responses or when drifting off to sleep. Myoclonic seizures generated from the cerebrum usually occur in distal muscles, whereas myoclonus generated in the lower brain stem or spinal gray matter usually has a proximal distribution that affects the pectoral girdle, trunk, or pelvic girdle. Myoclonic jerks accompany

several forms of epilepsy (see page 844). They also occur in a multifocal pattern in association with several metabolic encephalopathies, especially those associated with uremia or penicillin intoxication. They can follow severe cerebral anoxia or slow virus infection (Creutzfeldt-Jakob disease).

Palatal myoclonus relates more to a form of continuous tremor than to true myoclonus. The condition consists of rhythmic, regular, 2- to 3-Hz contractions of the soft palate and, less commonly, the adjacent pharynx. It arises in association with infarction or degeneration of the pathway that links together the dentate, red nucleus, and inferior olive. Unlike tremor of basal ganglia or cerebellar origin, palatal myoclonus persists during sleep. The serotonin precursor 5-hydroxytryptamine sometimes ameliorates the contractions, which have been attributed to denervation hypersensitivity of olivary neurons.

Hemifacial spasm can affect the motor distribution of either facial nerve, producing rapidly recurring, painless, nonstereotyped fragmentary twitching of any of the facial muscles. The condition persists into sleep and has been attributed to ephaptic cross-conduction of fibers within the facial nerve secondary to damage caused by long-standing intracranial compression from an overlying branch of the basilar artery. Surgical decompression sometimes relieves the condition, which is disfiguring but neither painful nor dangerous.

REFERENCES

Buchwald D, Cheney PR, Peterson DL, et al: A chronic illness characterized by fatigue, neurologic and immunologic disorders and active human herpes virus type 6 infection. Ann Intern Med 116:103–113, 1992.

Lane TJ, Manu P, Mathews DA: Depression and somatization in the chronic fatigue syndrome. Am J Med 91:335–344, 1991.

B. Movement Disorders

The term *movement disorders* refers to a group of neurologic conditions generated by abnormalities that arise in the brain and affect resting skeletal muscles in a nonparoxysmal manner so as to produce gross, functionally inappropriate activity in the face, limbs, or trunk. All appear only during the waking state and all are believed to represent dysfunction or damage related primarily to or confined to the basal ganglia and its subcortical connections in the thalamus. Included anatomically are the symmetrically placed deep cerebral nuclei of the caudate nucleus and putamen (together known as the striatum), the globus pallidus or pallidum, the subthalamic nucleus, and the substantia nigra of the midbrain (Fig. 115–2). The functions of the basal ganglia are best deduced from their diseases. The ganglia especially influence the control of trunk and proximal appendicular movement by feeding information forward to the frontal cortex before that re-

gion sends its final signals to the craniospinal motor neurons via the corticospinal tract. In fact, secondary interruption of the corticospinal pathway ameliorates or interrupts pre-existing signs of basal ganglia dysfunction. This observation has led to diseases of the basal ganglia being termed "extrapyramidal disorders." The basal ganglia also exert a major influence on the planning of movement and in establishing the postural "set" or "platform" upon which corticospinal influences superimpose learned motor activity.

The basal ganglia contain a distinct neurotransmitter anatomy. Corticostriatal and thalamostriatal afferents are both excitatory in their action, probably employing glutamate as a transmitter (Fig. 115–2). The well-known nigrostriatal input employs dopamine. Dopaminergic synapses probably exist on all neuronal types within the striatum, although the functionally most important receptors appear to lie on the axon terminals of incoming corticostriate fibers. The striatum also contains many cholinergic interneurons believed functionally to oppose the dopaminergic input. This latter action may help to explain why anticholinergic drugs sometimes improve the symptoms of parkinsonism. The major outputs of the basal ganglia to all of their known projection areas predominantly employ the inhibitory transmitter GABA. A number of neuropeptides have been identified in the nuclei, but their functional significance remains unknown.

PARKINSONISM

Parkinsonism is a syndrome consisting, in variable combinations, of slowness in the initiation and execution of movement (bradykinesia), increased muscle tonus (rigidity), tremor, and impaired postural reflexes. The underlying pathogenesis is primarily a defect in the dopaminergic pathway that connects the substantia nigra to the striatum. In idiopathic or postencephalitic parkinsonism, the deficiency results from degeneration of the pigmented dopamine-secreting neurons in the substantia nigra, whereas most drug-induced parkinsonism reflects a blocking of dopamine receptors in striatal neurons. Several rare diseases that cause degeneration of striatal receptor neurons also produce clinical parkinsonism but fail to improve with the use of levodopa or its congeners. Similar therapeutic limitations apply to the parkinsonian manifestations that sometimes accompany advanced vascular diseases, neoplasms, and certain degenerative disorders, such as progressive supranuclear palsy, the Shy-Drager form of generalized idiopathic autonomic insufficiency, and some of the progressive cerebellar degenerations. In most of these conditions treatment with dopamine agonists confers few, if any, benefits.

Parkinson's Disease

This idiopathic disorder of adults has its highest incidence in men over 40 years. The cause is unknown. Epidemiologic studies have traced some cohorts to long-preceding influenza epidemics, and a few others have been poisoned by the illegally synthesized opiate MPTP. The occurrence of the latter effect hints that other exogenous agents may also contribute to the cause. Most patients, however, relate no hint of a specific cause or a family predisposition. The early motor deficits can be traced to incipient degeneration of nigral dopamine-transmitting cells. Later, refractory motor, autonomic, and mental abnormalities develop in many cases, implying degeneration of striatal receptor mechanisms plus, sometimes, degeneration of the locus ceruleus and the basal nucleus of Meynert.

Symptoms and Signs (Table 115–5). Most cases of idiopathic parkinsonism begin with either weakness, tremor, or both. Early in the disease, most patients describe motor slowness, stiffness, or easy fatigability in a single limb or hemiparetic distribution. The typical 4- to 7-Hz resting tremor affects approximately 70 per cent but may not exist at all in some patients, especially those affected by prominent rigidity.

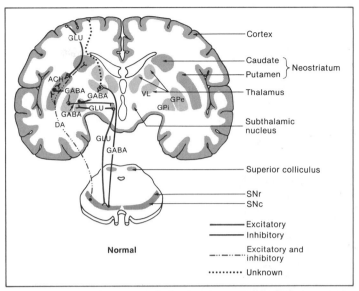

FIGURE 115–2. Anatomy of the basal ganglia and their connections. ACH = Acetylcholine; GABA = γ-aminobutyric acid; GLU = glutamate; GP = globus pallidum (e = external, i = internal); DA = dopamine; SN = substantia nigra (c = compacta, r = reticulata); VL = ventrolateral. (From Jancovic J: The extrapyramidal disorders. *In* Wyngaarden JB, Smith LH Jr, Bennett JC [eds]: Cecil Textbook of Medicine. 19th ed. Philadelphia, WB Saunders Co, 1992, p. 2129.)

Patients with parkinsonism often have a diagnostically typical appearance. The body stoops stiffly forward, bent at the knees, hips, and neck, with arms held close to the sides and flexed at the elbows. Steps are small or shuffling, turns are taken slowly, and patients with advanced cases tend uncontrollably to accelerate their gait (festination) or to suffer from retropulsion. The outstretched, often trembling hands are extended at the wrist and thumb and flexed at the metacarpophalangeal joints (pill rolling posture). The face becomes masklike, unblinking, and often greasy. Speech becomes slurred, monotonous, and sometimes barely understandable. Handwriting becomes cramped and small in size. Deep tendon reflexes can be of average, slightly increased, or decreased amplitude. Percussion of the eyebrow brings out Myerson's sign, the failure of the blink reflex to adapt to repeated gentle taps. Other abnormal motor reflexes are absent early, but Babinski signs sometimes emerge as a late change, reflecting the development of corticospinal tract dysfunction. The limbs of most patients display a nonspastic, steadily increasing resistance to movement, often interrupted by an 8-Hz tremor, conferring the classic "cogwheel" rigidity. Behavioral dis-

TABLE 115–5. MAJOR FEATURES OF PARKINSON'S DISEASE

Mental:	Slowed thinking, mild dementia, depression, insomnia, drug effects (usually late changes)
Autonomic:	Sexual difficulties, sweats, seborrhea, constipation, fatigue
Postural:	Stooped, bent stance; festination, shuffling gait
Motor:	Asthenia, tremor, hypokinesia, rigidity

orders are common. Many if not most patients become depressed in the early stages, and as many as half develop dementia by 7 or more years after onset.

Postencephalitic parkinsonism was particularly a problem in the 1930s and 1940s following the worldwide epidemic of lethargic encephalitis that occurred during the years 1918 to 1926. Persons involved with that illness, in addition to the above-mentioned classic signs and symptoms, also suffered a variety of acute behavioral disorders, as well as autonomic abnormalities, oculogyric crises, and various dystonias, choreiform movements, and tics. The illness has now largely disappeared.

Drug-induced parkinsonism can follow the taking of several antipsychotic agents given chronically in high doses. Chief present offenders are the pheno-thiazines and butyrophenones, both of which pharmacologically block dopamine receptors in the striatum and may interfere with the dopamine output of nigral cells as well. Other toxic syndromes in addition to typical parkinsonism can occur with these agents, including a diffuse motor restlessness; acute dystonic reactions that dissipate with anticho-linergic, antihistamine, or diazepam therapy; and oculogyric crises, which reflect an oculomotor dystonia. Drug-induced parkinsonism may somewhat benefit from anticholinergic agents but fails to subside with levodopa. The late complication of tardive dyskinesia is discussed below.

Treatment. Three major lines of treatment offer help to victims of Parkinson's disease (Table 115–6). First, the physician must understand and respond to the fear that the disease engenders, the high incidence of depression it causes, and the mild to moderate intellectual decline that accompanies many cases. Second, a consistent plan for pharmacotherapy must be developed. Third, surgical procedures occasionally are applied to patients with refractory cases. These are largely experimental, and their consideration lies outside the scope of this book.

Most authorities in the United States currently try to defer treatment with dopaminergic drugs as long as possible in an effort to delay proportionately the late, toxic stages of levodopa therapy. Accordingly, selegiline, the antioxidant drug that prevents MPTP-induced parkinsonism in animals is initiated, usu-

ally at 5 mg twice a day. On theoretical grounds, many authorities recommend concurrent administration of vitamin E capsules. After an interval to allow any undesirable side effects of selegiline to develop (they are uncommon), a trial of amantadine, 100 mg twice a day, may be given. Unless clinically beneficial effects appear within 1 month, the latter drug should be discontinued and replaced by the anticholinergic trihexyphenidyl, in small doses of 2 mg three times a day. The dose can be advanced slowly according to tolerance and symptom relief. Ultimately, these agents become insufficient to control symptoms of parkinsonism and either levodopa-carbidopa or pergolide (a dopamine agonist) must be used to attempt symptom control. When this stage is reached, it is wise to seek consultative assistance in further management, as several options exist to maximize long-term benefits.

Given over a long period of time or in high doses, both levodopa and the anticholinergic drugs can produce limiting side effects. Full benefits of levodopa seldom last more than 5 to 7 years, and large doses or long usage eventually produces uncontrollable abnormal movements of the trunk and extremities, termed dyskinesias. Furthermore, with time, the dose acts more briefly and is followed by intermittent, unpredictable periods of immobility (the "off" effect). Anticholinergic drugs are prone to cause dry mouth, visual blurring, and, occasionally, urinary retention in almost any subject; nightmares or daytime delirium can be a distressing consequence in the elderly.

Many patients become depressed during the course of Parkinson's disease, some suicidally so. Tricyclic or other antidepressant medications may ameliorate these symptoms.

Progressive Supranuclear Palsy

This is an uncommon disorder of middle-aged or older persons marked by insidiously developing and progressive degenerative changes in the basal ganglia, basal nuclei, and cerebellum. Clinical features include a Parkinson-like rigidity and loss of postural reflexes combined with rigidity of the body and a postural dystonia marked by extension of the head. A progressive external ophthalmoplegia, consisting of paralysis first of voluntary conjugate vertical gaze and later of lateral gaze, is diagnostic. Full-range tonic abnormal oculocephalic reflex responses during arousal emerge concurrently and are easily elicited by bedside examination. A moderate dementia usually accompanies the motor changes. Dopamine agonist drugs occasionally bring symptomatic improvement.

Huntington's Disease

Huntington's disease is an uncommon inherited disorder transmitted as an autosomal dominant trait with complete penetrance. Recent research has succeeded in bracketing the Huntington gene, on the short arm of chromosome 4. It seems likely that specific genetic identification soon will be available to facilitate the identification of those at risk for trials of therapy and for appropriate genetic counseling.

Huntington's disease affects striatal neurons, es-

TABLE 115–6. TREATMENT OF PARKINSON'S DISEASE (PD)

General measures: Maintain full physical and social activities.

Emotional: Outline cognitive and emotional encouragements and reassurances. If necessary, provide tricyclic antidepressants.

Pharmacologic: Start with selegiline. Test effects of amantadine and anticholinergics; continue if tolerated *and* helpful. Start levodopa-carbidopa if signs of PD remain prominent. If or when levodopa side effects develop, try slow-release preparations or dopa agonists.

Surgical: Last resort, still experimental and for experts only: Stereotaxic thalamotomy or pallidotomy Transplants of dopamine-generating fetal cells

pecially the small GABA-transmitting cells and scattered nerve cells in the frontal lobe cortex, claustrum, subthalamus, and cerebellar Purkinje and dentate systems. Gliosis is prominent. Neurochemically, GABA, acetylcholine, and angiotensin II decline in the striatum, with less severe reductions affecting substance P, cholecystokinin, and enkephalin. Somatostatin-containing neurons are selectively preserved.

The principal clinical changes include dyskinesia, altered behavior, and dementia. The age of onset averages 40 years, with most cases beginning between ages 30 and 50. Early motor symptoms often include dystonic posturing and rigidity, but these changes give way to prominent choreiform activity in most affected adults. Signs of corticospinal tract dysfunction or sensory changes are lacking. Eccentricity, inappropriateness, a loss of social amenities, excess irritability, and sexual hyperactivity can mark the early stages. Occasionally, a schizophreniform illness precedes the motor abnormality by several years. Depression is common and suicide occurs frequently, partially explained because the progressing dementia often fails to blunt insight.

Diagnosis comes from recognizing the characteristic progressive generalized choreiform activity accompanied by behavioral or personality changes, especially in a person with a tell-tale family history. Spontaneous mutations are uncommon, but some affected persons inevitably lack knowledge of their true antecedents. Computed tomography (CT) or magnetic resonance (MR) scans in fully developed cases show cerebral atrophy, especially of the caudate and putamen, to a degree that is almost specific to the disease. Symptomatic treatment is aimed at minimizing the distressing movements, reserpine or baclofen being the most useful agents. Psychological symptoms may require major antipsychotic drugs for their control. Until the specific gene is identified, genetic counseling remains largely based on statistical probabilities. The principal disorders to be considered in differential diagnosis are as follows: *Gilles de la Tourette's syndrome* (p. 792) most often is transmitted in an autosomal dominant pattern, but such patients have an earlier onset, show motor tics rather than chorea, and lack the behavioral-mental changes. *Senile chorea* is a rare disorder beginning in persons older than 60 years. The abnormal movements usually are less prominent than in Huntington's, and there is no comparable degree of dementia. *Hemiballismus* is a disorder of older persons described on page 791. A reversible adult chorea also can develop in association with lupus erythematosus or thyrotoxicosis. It has an abrupt onset and gradually disappears within weeks or months.

Sydenham's Chorea

This now uncommon, self-limited disorder usually lasts 2 to 6 months and is related to rheumatic fever. It occurs most often in children under the age of 15 years but can sometimes affect pregnant women or those with systemic lupus erythematosus. Choreiform activity in Sydenham's chorea takes a fidgety, fragmented form, sometimes difficult to separate from habit tics. The children are clumsy and often dysarthric and walk unsteadily. An inability to sustain tonic movement, such as steadily protruding the tongue or sustaining an uninterrupted grasp of the examiner's fingers, is common to all the choreas.

Treatment is symptomatic. Recurrent attacks occur in as many as one third of affected children.

DYSTONIA

Dystonia can appear either as part of a primary basal ganglia disease or as a symptom secondary to a number of other conditions affecting those structures (Table 115–7). The chronic dystonias include a group of uncommon disorders of inherited or sporadic origin. The specific cause and pathophysiology are unknown for any of these conditions, and no neuropathologic changes have been found consistently in the brain. An imbalance of neurotransmitter function in the basal ganglia has been postulated, but specific neurochemical candidates remain elusive, inasmuch as both dopamine excess and presumed dopamine receptor blockade can induce acute transient dystonic movement.

Severe generalized dystonia, sometimes called *dystonia musculorum deformans,* begins predominantly in young children and adolescents, most often beginning with an equinovarus posturing of the foot or a tonically flexed hand, then spreading to involve the neck, face, and trunk in nearly continu-

TABLE 115–7. THE MAJOR DYSTONIAS

PRIMARY DYSTONIA

CONDITIONS	INHERITANCE	AGE OF ONSET
Generalized dystonia	Autosomal recessive Autosomal dominant Sporadic	Childhood Adolescence or adulthood
Focal dystonia Foot-leg or hand-arm	Inherited or sporadic	Mostly adulthood, occasionally late
Blepharospasm	Sporadic	Late adulthood
Facial mandibular (Meige's syndrome)	Sporadic	Late adulthood
Spasmodic dysphonia	Sporadic	Adulthood
Spasmodic torticollis	Mostly sporadic, occasionally autosomal recessive	Middle adulthood
Occupational dystonia Writer's cramp Musician's cramp	Sporadic	Early-middle adulthood

SECONDARY DYSTONIA

CHRONIC	ACUTE
Wilson's disease	Head trauma
Huntington's disease	Phenothiazines
Postencephalitic	Butyrophenones
Severe cerebral anoxia-ischemia	Levodopa
Manganese poisoning	

ous, recurrent, intense, involuntary, asymmetric contractions. The movements, which characteristically lead into prolonged spasms, eventually produce bizarre contortions with severe musculotendinous contractures. Ensuing bone deformities can produce scoliosis, chest deformities, and a foreshortening of natural height. Lesser degrees of the illness can arise during adulthood and tend to produce restricted impairments of the lower or upper extremities.

Spasmodic torticollis is the most common of the focal dystonias. It affects predominantly the muscles of the neck and shoulders, which bilaterally and simultaneously contract to produce recurrent unilateral head turning or head extension. Elevations of the shoulder and, often, platysmal contractions may accompany the movements of the head and neck. In mild cases the movement can be restrained by the subject's placing gentle antagonistic pressure against the chin. More severe examples can spread to produce spastic dysphonia and hand-arm dystonia. Discussion of other forms of focal dystonia can be found in the references.

Treatment of the dystonias is unsatisfactory. High doses of the anticholinergic drug trihexyphenidyl somewhat relieve a few patients. The use of carbamazepine or diazepam occasionally has been reported favorably in others. Stereotaxic surgical attacks on the thalamus benefit some children with severe generalized dystonia but carry a high risk of complications and must be regarded as desperation measures. Recently, investigators have reported success with judiciously repeated fractional injection of botulinum toxin into the periocular muscles of patients with incapacitating blepharospasm.

DYSKINESIA

The dopamine-induced dyskinesia of chronic treated parkinsonism has been described above.

Tardive dyskinesia follows the taking and, often, withdrawal of antidopaminergic antipsychotic drugs and consists of abnormal, semirhythmic involuntary movements affecting the mouth (lingual-oral-buccal), trunk, or extremities. Once it appears, the condition almost always remains permanently. A few cases are known to have appeared within no more than a few days of phenothiazine medication. Much more often, the complication follows prolonged drug use. Its appearance can be delayed until weeks, months, or even years after the drugs were taken. The facial movements most often consist of chewing, tongue darting, and grimacing. Other forms include repeated flexion and extension of the trunk, piano playing-like successive contraction of the fingers and toes, and repetitive steppings of the feet while standing erect. Supersensitivity of the dopamine receptors of the basal ganglia is believed to be the cause. Reserpine or, in the presence of continued psychosis, a higher dose of antidopaminergic antipsychotics sometimes bring partial relief. Tardive dyskinesia is a disfiguring, seriously disturbing, and frequent complication. The potential for producing it should discourage the use of phenothiazine drugs for any but serious medical-psychiatric problems. *Meige's syndrome,* a dystonia involving the jaw and lower face, somewhat resembles tardive dyskinesia but produces slower, more twisting movements. There is no necessary history of antipsychotic medication. Baclofen or valproate has been reported to improve selective cases.

REFERENCES

Cedarbaum JM: Pharmacokinetic and pharmacodynamic considerations in management of motor response fluctuations in Parkinson's disease. Neurol Clin 8:31, 1990.

Jankovic J: The Extrapyramidal disorders. *In* Wyngaarden JB, Smith LH Jr, Bennett JC (eds): Cecil Textbook of Medicine. 19th ed. Philadelphia, WB Saunders Co, 1992, pp 2128–2139.

Marsden CD, Fahn S (eds): Movement Disorders. 3rd ed. London, Butterworths Scientific, 1991.

C. The Major Cerebellar Ataxias

SIGNS AND MECHANISMS OF CEREBELLAR DYSFUNCTION

Disorders of the cerebellum or its principal connections produce characteristic symptoms and signs, including *asthenia* or easy fatigability; *ataxia* of gait; *dysmetria,* an inability to control the range of movement, producing under- or over-shoot; *dysdiadokokinesia,* the impairment of rapidly alternating movements; *decomposition of movement,* the inability to synergize motion around two or more joints; *postural (sustention)* or *intention tremor; dysarthria;* and, possibly, *nystagmus* with the fast component toward the side of the cerebellar lesion.

Ataxias linked to the cerebellum and its major afferent and efferent connections fall into three major groups (Table 115–8). These include (1) diseases affecting predominantly the afferent spinocerebellar and associated spinal pathways; (2) diseases or disorders involving the cerebellum proper and its immediate outflow tracts; and (3) diseases in which cerebellar involvement comprises only part of a widespread degeneration of CNS structures. Clinically, the signs and symptoms of the three categories sometimes overlap, but distinction usually is possible. Mass lesions or demyelinating disorders affecting the cerebellar system usually can be identified by MR or CT imaging. The following paragraphs describe the principal degenerative disorders affecting the system.

Spinocerebellar disease produces a wide-based,

lurching sensory ataxia due to involvement of ascending proprioceptives and spinocerebellar pathways. At their worst, patients stagger from side to side, stepping with high, irregularly placed feet that often pound the floor. Large afferent fibers carrying position and vibratory sense from the lower extremities degenerate, leading to rombergism and an accompanying loss of deep tendon reflexes. Sometimes, involvement of descending corticospinal pathways results in pathologic reflexes, whereas direct cerebellar involvement can impair oculomotor control as well as upper extremity coordination.

Within the cerebellum itself, damage or degeneration of the posterior midline *floccular nodular area* produces a narrow-based ataxia with a tendency to fall backwards plus nystagmus on lateral and, sometimes, downward gaze. Dysfunction of the more anterior midline *vermis and anterior lobe* is more common and accompanies especially deep midline cerebellar tumors and alcohol-nutritional or paraneoplastic degeneration. A broad-based, stiff-legged ataxia often is accompanied in severe cases by an oscillating, rhythmic sustention tremor of the trunk and lower extremities (titubation). Deep tendon reflexes tend to be accentuated, but nystagmus is uncommon unless the disease concurrently affects the vestibular nuclei.

Lateral hemispheric lesions characteristically produce subtle signs consisting of mild ipsilateral incoordination and perhaps hypotonia. If they directly involve the cerebellar roof nuclei or outflow pathways, they cause in the upper extremities the classic signs of cerebellar incoordination and tremor as described in the first paragraph of this section. Lesions that expand the cerebellum to compress the adjacent brain stem or infiltrate it produce the additional symptoms and signs of headache, nausea, vomiting, cranial nerve abnormalities, or long tract dysfunction.

PRIMARY CEREBELLAR DEGENERATIONS

This category includes a heterogeneous group of largely genetically caused *system degenerations* in which neuroaxonal death variously affects afferent pathways to the cerebellum, the cerebellum itself, and, often, trans-synaptically connected CNS structures. Although one can identify more or less distinct syndromes of spinocerebellar and primary cerebellar degeneration, different diseases may overlap considerably in their neuropathology; and phenotypes can differ clinically in single kindreds. These considerations suggest molecular linkages among these disorders and several other degenerative CNS diseases. Related conditions include peroneal muscular atrophy, other degenerative neuropathies, hereditary spastic paraplegia, motor neuron disease, atypical forms of parkinsonism, and the Shy-Drager form of progressive autonomic insufficiency. Most of the CNS system degenerations are uncommon, and in only a few is the specific cause known. The following section describes the most frequent types; the references contain more extensive discussions as well as descriptions of the rarer entities.

TABLE 115-8. PRINCIPAL DISEASES OF THE CEREBELLUM AND ITS CONNECTIONS

I. **Primarily Spinocerebellar**
  A. Inherited spinocerebellar ataxias (childhood or adolescent onset, chronic course, few positive sensory symptoms)
    1. Molecular genetic defect uncertain: Friedreich's ataxia and its variants; Roussy-Lévy
    2. Genetic defect known: phytanic acid α-hydroxylase deficiency (Refsum); abetalipoproteinemia (Bassen-Kornzweig); others
  B. Acquired spinal sensory ataxia (acute, subacute, or insidious onset): polyneuropathy; sensory polyradiculopathy (tabes dorsalis); vitamin B_{12} deficiency; spinal cord damage (e.g., multiple sclerosis, neoplasm)

II. **Primarily Cerebellar**
  A. Inherited degenerative (course progressive): restricted olivopontocerebellar atrophy (young to mid-adulthood); ataxia-telangiectasia (childhood onset)
  B. Developmental abnormalities (onset of signs varies, progressive): basilar impression; Arnold-Chiari malformation
  C. Nutritional-immunologic (mostly adult onset, acute or subacute course)
    1. Acute, parainfectious cerebellar ataxia of children
    2. Alcoholic-nutritional cerebellar degeneration
    3. Paraneoplastic cerebellar–brain stem degeneration
  D. Structural cerebellar lesions (acute or subacute course): trauma, neoplasms, hemorrhage, anoxia-ischemia, etc.
  E. Intoxication (acute or subacute or chronic): alcohol; sedatives; anxiolytics; phenytoin; anticancer agents

III. **Cerebellar-Plus Disorders**
  A. Inherited or sporadic system degenerations (mid-adulthood onset, gradual progression)
    1. Olivopontocerebellar atrophy plus, variably, spasticity, parkinsonism, sensory changes, optic atrophy, retinitis pigmentosa, ophthalmoplegia, dementia
    2. Shy-Drager syndrome
    3. Generalized mitochondrial dysfunction with ataxia, ophthalmoplegia, myopathy
  B. Acquired disseminated disorders affecting cerebellar and other systems (e.g., disseminated cancer, abscess)

Friedreich's Ataxia

Friedreich's ataxia, the prototypic spinocerebellar degeneration, affects children and young adults. The disease can be transmitted in autosomal dominant or autosomal recessive patterns, but sporadic cases are common. Neuronal loss involves the dorsal root ganglia and the spinal cells of origin of the spinocerebellar tracts, with degeneration beginning caudally and progressing rostrally. Axonal loss and demyelination affect the spinal nerves, the dorsal column, and the spinocerebellar tracts as well as the descending corticospinal tract. Some cases show cell loss in the cerebellum and occasionally in brain stem nuclei as well.

The molecular cause of the spinocerebellar degenerations can vary from patient to patient despite considerable overlap in clinical presentations. Examples of such clinically similar disorders are listed in section I.A.2 of Table 115-8.

Friedreich's ataxia typically begins insidiously, usually before age 10 years, and progresses steadily. Most patients become unable to walk unassisted during their third decade. Position and vibratory sense are lost initially in the lower extremities, and this plus the corticospinal defect leads to an increasing sensorimotor staggering ataxia. Concurrently, one finds atrophic, hypotonic lower limbs with areflexia and extensor plantar responses. By their late teens or 20s, most patients develop dysarthria and many have nystagmus. Orthopedic changes include a characteristic pes cavus deformity (which can affect some family members as the sole mark of the abnormal trait) as well as a mild to moderate scoliosis and, sometimes, a high arched palate. Low intelligence affects some victims from the start, while a few appear to decline mentally as the disorder progresses. Associated, less common, abnormalities include optic atrophy, retinal degeneration, deafness, and anterior horn cell degeneration. Many victims develop cardiac enlargement and most show conduction defects on the electrocardiogram (ECG). Some develop heart failure; few survive beyond 40 years. Diagnosis usually is apparent from the patient's appearance and physical findings. Among laboratory tests, none is specific except in the specific deficiency syndromes, most of which appear sufficiently distinctive clinically to prompt appropriate biochemical study. Visual evoked potentials are abnormally slow in most cases of either spinocerebellar or primary cerebellar ataxia, and somatosensory evoked potentials tend to be particularly slowed in Friedreich's ataxia but not in olivopontocerebellar atrophy. The spinal fluid is normal.

Roussy-Lévy ataxia closely resembles Friedreich's ataxia except that the condition runs a much slower course, often with little progression into adulthood. Position and vibration sensations are spared, and extensor plantar responses fail to develop. Other family members may show evidence of the more common peroneal muscular atrophy or hereditary spastic paraplegia.

The Olivopontocerebellar Degenerations (OPCD)

This category includes a group of uncommon, progressive degenerative disorders of middle to late adult life producing cerebellar dysfunction with or without signs of degeneration in other motor-sensory systems, including spinal cord, cerebellar outflow pathways, basal ganglia, autonomic nervous system, optic nerves, and even cerebral cortex. The illnesses occur in both sporadic and hereditary patterns.

Pathologically, the most frequent denominator to the OPCD group includes degeneration of the inferior olive and the pontine-cerebellar relay nuclei, with degeneration and demyelination of their respective climbing axons into the cerebellum. Trans-synaptic death occurs in the target cells of the cerebellar cortex. Less consistent abnormalities affect neurons and their axons in the more remote neurologic structures mentioned above. Degeneration of the basal ganglia and central autonomic neurons usually is prominent in the Shy-Drager variant.

OPCD can affect either sex, most often between the ages of 40 and 60 years. Progression is relatively rapid, and most patients become totally dependent within 6 years of onset. Initial symptoms and signs include a relatively wide-based ataxia accompanied by incoordination of the upper extremities and dysarthria. Dysmetria usually remains worse in the lower than the upper extremities. The limbs become hypotonic, and deep tendon reflexes are preserved except when an associated spinal degeneration occurs. Most patients develop nystagmus. Among those with basal ganglia involvement, parkinsonian signs emerge during the moderately advanced stages of the illness. Babinski signs and other manifestations of corticospinal tract dysfunction occur late if at all. Some patients develop palatal myoclonus. A functional dementia accompanies the late stages of approximately one third of cases.

No specific test is diagnostic of OPCD. Brain stem auditory evoked potentials are abnormal in a majority. Differential diagnosis requires ruling out the conditions listed in sections II and III of Table 115–8. MR imaging usually discloses cerebellar and pontine atrophy and rules out other structural lesions. Nutritional disease and possible drug intoxication can be identified by the history. Paraneoplastic syndromes are discussed in Chapter 119.

The cause being unknown, only symptomatic treatment can be offered.

Ataxia-Telangiectasia

This disorder affects spinal cord, cerebellum, and basal ganglia functions. The illness begins in early childhood, inherited as an autosomal recessive trait. Progressive ataxia of gait, incoordinated upper extremities, facial and appendicular choreoathetosis, and opsoclonus are characteristic. Most children become wheelchair-bound and begin to show mental retardation by the second decade. Prominent telangiectases stud the conjunctivae, the ears, the nose, and the cheek areas. The disease includes thymic hypoplasia with a severe deficiency of IgA. Patients suffer a high incidence of endocrine abnormalities, respiratory infections, chromosomal aberrations, and neoplasms; most die before age 20 years.

REFERENCE

Harding AE: Cerebellar and spinocerebellar disorders. *In* Bradley WG, Daroff RB, Fenichel GM, Marsden CD (eds): Neurology in Clinical Practice. Boston, Butterworth-Heinemann, 1991, pp 1603–1624.

D. Disorders of the Spine and Spinal Cord and Neurocutaneous Syndromes

The spinal cord connects the body below the head with the brain. It carries sensory fibers from the periphery to the brain and motor instructions, including those that control autonomic function (e.g., bladder and bowel), from the brain to the periphery. Fibers subserving different sensory modalities (e.g., pain, temperature, vibration, position) are sorted into different pathways in the spinal cord. Moreover, the different modalities cross to the contralateral side at different levels. Descending motor fibers that lie contralateral to their target nuclei in the brain become ipsilateral in the spinal cord. As a result, dissociated sensory and motor abnormalities (Table 115–9) mark syndromes of the spinal cord and help the examiner to identify the site of the lesion in both the cephalocaudal direction (e.g., arm weakness implies a cervical cord lesion, paraplegia a thoracic or lumbar lesion) and also in the transverse plane (Table 115–9). Such localization may also suggest a diagnosis. For example, Brown-Séquard syndrome is a common presenting finding in radiation myelopathy, whereas a central cord or anterior commissure lesion suggests trauma or syringomyelia.

SPINAL CORD NEOPLASMS

Neoplastic growths that cause nerve root or spinal cord disorders can begin in the paravertebral, extradural, intradural, or intramedullary compartments. Most neoplasms that cause spinal cord compression are extradural and metastatic. Most extradural neoplasms originate in the vertebral body and compress spinal roots or cord without invading them. Most intradural neoplasms also cause symptoms by compressing spinal roots or cord without invading, but unlike extradural neoplasms, the majority are benign and slow growing. Intramedullary neoplasms cause symptoms by both invading and compressing spinal structures; the tumors may be either benign or malignant.

Paravertebral Tumors. Neoplastic lesions that begin in or metastasize to the extraspinal paravertebral space often cause serious and perplexing neurologic problems. The tumor may extend longitudinally within the paravertebral space, progressively compressing nerve roots as it grows. At times, the tumor may grow through an intervertebral foramen and compress not only the nerve root but also the spinal cord. Rarely, spinal cord symptoms may be caused by ischemia from compression of radicular arteries that supply the spinal cord. If the tumor lies lateral to the immediate paravertebral space, it may compress the brachial, lumbar, or sacral plexus, causing symptoms similar to root compression but

with a different pattern of sensory and motor loss. The symptoms of extravertebral tumors begin insidiously with severe, unrelenting pain, often with a burning quality. The pain is localized just lateral to the spine and radiates, bandlike, in the distribution of the involved dermatome (or dermatomes). If the lesion involves abdominal or thoracic roots, objective motor and sensory changes often are minimal, but autonomic changes may be prominent or the only neurologic sign. *Hyperhidrosis* occurring in a band coinciding with the site of the pain strongly suggests the diagnosis. When the tumor involves cervical or lumbar roots, the pain may be soon followed by numbness in the fingertips or toes, with accompanying weakness and reflex diminution, depending on the roots involved. Autonomic changes, including anhidrosis or hyperhidrosis, can affect the

TABLE 115–9. CLINICAL SIGNS OF SPINAL CORD LESIONS

ANATOMIC SITE	NEUROLOGIC FINDINGS	PATHOLOGIC EXAMPLE(S)
Transverse myelopathy	Paraplegia or quadriplegia with sensory and autonomic loss	Trauma Cord compression by tumor
Brown-Séquard syndrome (hemicord section)	Ipsilateral spastic hemiparesis or leg-only paresis with position and vibration loss; and contralateral pin and temperature sensation loss	Radiation myelopathy
Posterolateral column syndrome	Spastic paraparesis with position and vibration loss but preserved pin and temperature sensation	AIDS myelopathy Multiple sclerosis
Anterior cord syndrome	Spastic quadriparesis or paraparesis with pin and temperature sensation loss but preserved position and vibration sensation	Anterior spinal artery occlusion
Central cord syndrome (cervical)	Flaccid weakness of arms with normal legs ± pin and temperature sensation loss	Trauma (hematomyelia)
Anterior commissure syndrome	Bilateral loss of pin and temperature sensation with or without flaccid weakness; sometimes sacral segments spared	Syringomyelia

arm or leg, whereas Horner's syndrome and/or diaphragmatic paralysis often accompany cervical or upper thoracic paravertebral tumors. The diagnosis of paravertebral tumors is best established by MR scan at the level suggested by the clinical findings. The MR scan also can determine whether the lesion has grown through the intervertebral foramen or has eroded vertebral bodies.

The differential diagnosis of paravertebral tumor includes several disorders that can cause paravertebral pain with or without compression of nerve roots. *Psychophysiologic muscle tension* syndromes often cause paravertebral low back or neck pain. In some instances, there may be radiation of the pain, but usually in a nondermatomal distribution. On examination, there is often marked tenderness of muscle, which sometimes can be relieved by injecting the trigger point with saline solution or a local anesthetic. Temporary improvement of pain after such injections does not imply that structural disease is absent, because trigger points can equally well be a reaction to spinal or nerve root disease. In muscle tension syndrome, autonomic, sensory, or motor changes are not present. Disease of the kidneys and other viscera lying in the retroperitoneal space may cause pain similar to that of paravertebral tumors, but the pain usually does not radiate and is not associated with autonomic, motor, or sensory changes. Percussion of the involved viscera reproduces the pain that is usually described as a dull ache rather than a neurogenic burning pain. Entrapment neuropathies occasionally mimic the symptoms of paravertebral tumor. Chronic *postthoracotomy pain* probably results from entrapment of nerve roots at the time of operation, perhaps with neuroma formation. The pain characteristically appears shortly after surgery and may be unremitting for many years. Motor, sensory, or autonomic changes are rare. Such pain sometimes can be relieved by paravertebral anesthetic blocks.

The management of paravertebral masses depends on the diagnosis. In patients known to have cancer, particularly lymphomas or carcinomas of the breast or lung, the tumor can be assumed to be metastatic and should be treated with radiation therapy and, if available, chemotherapy. If the patient has no known primary lesion, resection may be attempted, both to establish a diagnosis and to decompress the nerve roots. Once biopsy establishes diagnosis, further therapy such as radiation or chemotherapy can be chosen.

Extradural Tumors. Extradural neoplasms can compress spinal roots and cord in one of two ways. Either they arise in vertebrae surrounding the spinal cord and grow into the epidural space, or they arise in the paravertebral space and grow through the intervertebral foramen so as to compress the cord without involving either vertebral or paravertebral structures. Most extradural neoplasms are metastatic from carcinomas of the breast, lung, prostate, or kidney or from malignant melanoma. Some extradural neoplasms arise de novo in the vertebral bodies (e.g., chordoma, osteogenic sarcoma, myeloma, chondrosarcoma). A minority of extradural neoplasms are benign (e.g., chordoma, osteoma, osteoid osteoma, angioma). Pain, the first symptom, may precede other symptoms of spinal cord compression by weeks or months, depending on the rate of growth of the tumor. Rarely, extradural neoplasms may be painless, with the first symptoms being those of spinal cord dysfunction. The first spinal cord symptoms other than pain usually consist of corticospinal tract dysfunction with weakness, spasticity, and hyperreflexia, followed by paresthesias with loss of vibration and position sense. Unless the lesion compresses the conus medullaris or the cauda equina, bladder and bowel dysfunctions are late signs. As with other causes of spinal cord compression, extradural neoplasms cause symptoms first distally and later proximally. Thus, even thoracic and cervical neoplasms generally cause weakness and numbness in the legs before trunk and upper extremity muscles are involved. The diagnosis of extradural spinal cord compression must be suspected by the history of pain followed by signs and symptoms of spinal cord dysfunction and confirmed by imaging studies. In about 85 per cent of patients suffering from extradural spinal cord compression, plain radiographs reveal bone lesions at the site of compression. In the few remaining patients, radionuclide bone scan or CT or MR scan may demonstrate a bone lesion. The diagnosis of extradural spinal cord compression and its localization can be made by either MR scan or myelography. The differential diagnosis of extradural neoplasms includes inflammatory disease of bone and epidural abscess (e.g., vertebral tuberculosis, bacterial osteomyelitis), acute or subacute epidural hematomas, herniated intervertebral discs, spondylosis, and, very rarely, extreme extramedullary hematopoiesis (in patients with severe and chronic anemias) or epidural lipomatosis (in patients on chronic steroid therapy). Often a definitive diagnosis can be made only by biopsy of the lesion, either during the course of a decompressive operation or by percutaneous needle biopsy of the involved vertebral body.

The treatment of extradural neoplasms depends on the cause. Most neoplasms that cause extradural spinal cord compression are malignant and progress rapidly. Once spinal cord symptoms begin, paraplegia may develop in a matter of days. Complete paraplegia is usually irreversible, whereas patients with only moderate spinal cord dysfunction often recover. Thus, the early diagnosis and vigorous emergency treatment of extradural spinal cord compression is mandatory (Table 115–10). The treatment includes corticosteroids (dexamethasone, 16 to 100 mg daily) to decrease spinal cord edema. In patients not known to be suffering from a primary cancer, metastatic disease remains the most common cause of extradural spinal cord compression, but a definitive diagnosis can be made only by biopsy. Such patients should begin corticosteroid therapy followed by surgery with removal of as much tumor as possible for both diagnostic and therapeutic purposes. When a primary cancer already has been diagnosed, treatment consists of radiation therapy and chemotherapy (if an effective agent is available). In patients in whom radiation therapy and chemotherapy are ineffective, resection of the vertebral body involved by tumor may delay the development of paraplegia. Benign extradural tumors require surgery and usually can be completely removed.

Intradural Extramedullary Tumors. Most intradural tumors are benign. Meningiomas and neurofibromas are the two most common types. Teratomas, arachnoid cysts, and lipomas are less common causes. Meningiomas occur especially in middle-aged and elderly women, predominantly in the thoracic spinal cord. Another common site is the foramen magnum. Meningiomas grow slowly. Pain is the first symptom in most patients, but in about 25 per cent the growth is painless, the first symptoms being those indicating gradually developing spinal cord compression. Because meningiomas are often located on the posterior aspect of the cord, paresthesias and sensory changes beginning distally in the lower extremities are a frequent early symptom and are often mistaken for peripheral neuropathy. As

the disease progresses, however, the development of corticospinal tract signs indicates the spinal origin of the symptoms. Even when spinal cord signs and symptoms are obvious, the occasional lack of pain may lead one to suspect a degenerative or demyelinating disease such as multiple sclerosis rather than a neoplasm. In patients with meningiomas, the lumbar puncture reveals an elevated cerebrospinal fluid (CSF) protein content well above that found in degenerative or demyelinating diseases. MR with contrast enhancement usually establishes the diagnosis. The treatment of spinal cord compression from meningiomas is surgical removal. Because the tumor grows so slowly and the cord has an opportunity to adapt to compression, even patients with severe neurologic disability often recover fully.

The second most common cause of intradural spinal cord compression is neurofibroma. Because these tumors usually arise from the dorsal root, radicular pain is often the first symptom, preceding signs of spinal cord compression by months or years.

TABLE 115–10. MANAGEMENT OF METASTATIC SPINAL CORD COMPRESSION

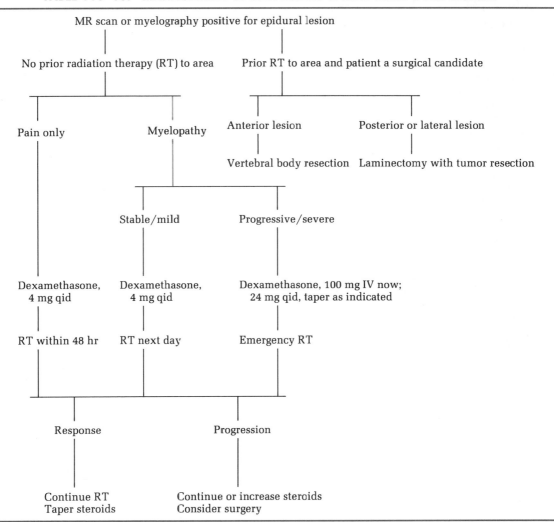

When spinal cord compression develops, it progresses slowly. Some patients with spinal neurofibromas suffer from neurofibromatosis (see p. 804). That diagnosis may be suspected either by a positive family history or by the cutaneous stigmata of the disorder. As neurofibromas grow through the intervertebral foramen, they enlarge it, a finding appreciated by an appropriately positioned radiograph. The CSF protein is almost always elevated. The diagnosis is established by MR scan. Surgical extirpation of the lesion usually leads to recovery.

Occasionally, metastatic tumors involving the leptomeninges produce intradural but extramedullary mass lesions. Pain is almost always a prominent early symptom, and spinal cord compression develops more rapidly than it does with the more benign intradural tumors. In addition, malignant cells are usually found on CSF examination. The glucose concentration may be low and the protein concentration elevated. The treatment of intradural malignant neoplasms is radiation therapy and chemotherapy because complete surgical extirpation is almost always impossible.

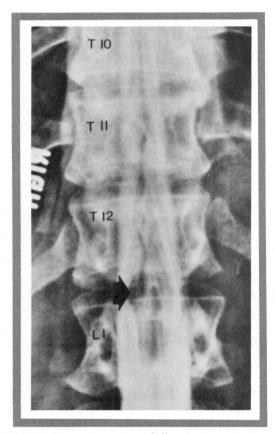

FIGURE 115–3. An intramedullary metastasis. A man with oat cell carcinoma of lung, in remission, complained of progressive weakness of the lower extremities and loss of bladder, bowel, and sexual function. A metrizamide myelogram revealed an area of enlargement at the conus medullaris (*arrow*), indicating a hematogenous metastasis to the spinal cord.

Intramedullary Tumors. The most common intramedullary spinal tumors are astrocytomas (usually benign) and ependymomas. Other tumors that occasionally cause intramedullary spinal lesions are hemangioblastomas, lipomas, and metastases (Fig. 115–3). Pain is an early symptom of most intramedullary tumors, and signs of spinal cord dysfunction progress rapidly or slowly, depending on the growth characteristics of the tumor. Intramedullary tumors are often associated with syringomyelia, the syrinx sometimes lying at a distance from the primary tumor and producing its own symptoms of spinal dysfunction (p. 804). The diagnosis is established by MR. In some patients with long-standing benign intramedullary lesions, plain radiographs of the spine may show widening of the spinal canal and erosion of the pedicles. The differential diagnosis of intramedullary tumors includes intramedullary abscesses and syringomyelia without tumor. A definitive diagnosis is established by biopsy. Successful surgical removal of intramedullary tumors is possible, particularly with ependymomas and hemangioblastomas but sometimes with gliomas as well. A highly skilled and experienced surgeon, however, is necessary for tumors to be removed without producing increased neurologic symptoms. If the tumor cannot be totally excised, postoperative radiation may delay recurrence.

VASCULAR DISORDERS OF THE SPINAL CANAL

Extradural, intradural, and intramedullary vascular disorders all can cause spinal cord compression. The most common and serious extradural vascular disease is *spinal epidural hematoma.* Hemorrhage into the spinal epidural space may occur spontaneously or be associated with trauma, a bleeding diathesis, or a vascular malformation. The condition occurs particularly among patients being treated with anticoagulants. It may occasionally follow lumbar puncture, particularly in patients with bleeding abnormalities or those receiving anticoagulants. The hemorrhage usually arises from the epidural venous plexus and tends to collect over the dorsum of the spinal cord, covering several segments. The clinical picture is characterized by the sudden or rapid onset of severe localized back pain and spinal cord dysfunction, often leading to complete paraplegia in several hours. If the patient has a known bleeding disorder, the clinical diagnosis is easily established. In patients without known bleeding or clotting disorders, the differential diagnosis includes acute epidural abscess and acute transverse myelopathy. Although occasionally patients recover spontaneously from paraparesis related to epidural spinal cord compression, most require emergency surgical evacuation to save spinal cord function. The more rapidly the paralysis develops and the longer the delay in decompression, the less likely is recovery.

Spinal arteriovenous malformations may cause symptoms by hemorrhage (Fig. 115–4), compression, or ischemia. Spinal subarachnoid hemorrhage is characterized by the sudden onset of back pain, often with a radicular component, with or without the development of signs of spinal cord compression. A lumbar puncture reveals evidence of subarachnoid hemorrhage with red cells, xanthochromic spinal fluid, and usually an elevated protein concentration. In the absence of spinal cord signs, the differential diagnosis includes spontaneous intracranial subarachnoid hemorrhage. The diagnosis of spinal subarachnoid hemorrhage often can be suspected clinically because symptoms begin with back pain rather than with headache as in intracranial hemorrhage.

Vascular malformations within the substance of the spinal cord may give rise to intramedullary hemorrhage (hematomyelia) as well as subarachnoid hemorrhage. The sudden development of partial or complete transverse myelopathy is the most common onset. If there is bleeding into the subarachnoid space, pain in the neck and back and other signs of meningeal irritation occur.

Spinal arteriovenous malformations may also gradually compress the spinal cord or give rise to hemodynamic changes that result in spinal ischemia. In such cases, patients present with slowly progressive, sometimes episodically worsening symptoms of spinal cord dysfunction. Transient exacerbation of symptoms may occur in association with menstrual periods or pregnancy.

Complete or partial recovery of function can follow episodes of spinal cord ischemia or even small hemorrhages. The unchanging localization of the attacks and the prominence of pain help differentiate symptoms caused by arteriovenous malformations from other recurrent neurologic disorders such as multiple sclerosis. Rarely, a bruit may be heard by auscultation of the spine or back over the site of the malformation. MR usually identifies an arteriovenous malformation. Advances in microsurgery have increased considerably the chances for satisfactory removal or obliteration of spinal vascular malformations. Embolization of the malformation or ligation of feeding arteries has been performed when the lesion cannot be removed surgically.

INHERITED AND DEVELOPMENTAL SPINAL STRUCTURAL DISORDERS

Congenital anomalies of the spine are common and are often encountered on radiographs of patients suffering from neck or low back pain. Some congenital anomalies such as spina bifida occulta are so common as to be considered variants of normal and are probably never responsible in and of themselves for low back pain. Other congenital anomalies that are usually asymptomatic but are potential causes of neck or back pain include *facet tropism* (misalignment of the facets on the two sides of the corresponding vertebral body; several authorities believe that this increases rotational stress on the facet joints and may cause back pain); *transitional vertebrae* (e.g., sacralization of a lumbar vertebra or lumbarization of a sacral vertebra) altering spinal mechanics, resulting in instability and stress, and sometimes producing back pain; and *spondylolisthe-*

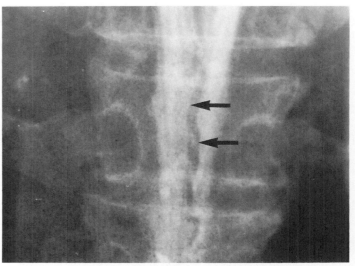

FIGURE 115–4. Spinal arteriovenous malformation. A metrizamide myelogram demonstrates a tangle of abnormal vessels (*arrows*) on the surface of the cord.

sis (forward slipping of one vertebral body onto another, caused by a defect between the articular facets).

A third group of congenital anomalies of the spine consists of those that are likely to cause not only neck or back pain but also neurologic disability. These include basilar impression, which is often associated with Arnold-Chiari malformation (see next section). Severe spinal scoliosis or kyphosis, congenital stenosis of the lumbar or cervical spinal canal, anterior and lateral spinal meningoceles, and diastematomyelia are other causes of back pain and neurologic disability. *Diastematomyelia* is a bony abnormality that divides the spinal canal, leading to duplication of the spinal cord. It is usually associated with spina bifida. Sometimes the bony septum can be identified on plain radiographs. Patients who become symptomatic in adulthood almost always have some cutaneous abnormality, especially hypertrichosis over the sacral area. The disorder may be associated with other congenital abnormalities of the CNS as well.

Abnormalities of the Craniocervical Junction

Basilar impression consists of invagination of the odontoid process into the foramen magnum. Occasionally the condition arises from occipital bone softening due to Paget's disease, fibrous dysplasia, or cancer. Much more often basilar impression occurs as a congenital defect, often associated with anomalies of the foramen magnum, the Arnold-Chiari malformation, or syringomyelia. Symptoms of congenital basilar impression often first appear in the third or fourth decade of life and reflect the presence of either vertebral artery compression-ischemia or direct medullopontine compression-displacement. Occipital headache, vertigo, nystagmus, dysarthria, dysphagia, ataxia, abnormalities of cen-

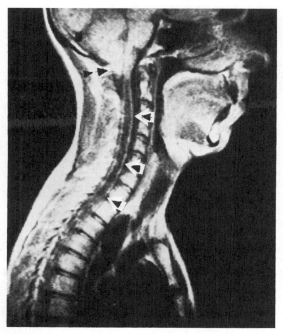

FIGURE 115–5. Midsagittal MR image of Arnold-Chiari malformation *(small black arrows)* and syringomyelia *(three white-black arrows)* in a 33-year-old man. Note the cerebellar tonsils extending below the posterior rim of the foramen magnum *(dark structure immediately above the black arrow).* The syrinx extends from the medulla well into the thoracic cord.

tral respiratory control, and long tract signs begin insidiously and progress gradually. Many patients develop a secondary obstructive hydrocephalus. Diagnosis is suggested by the clinical findings plus an abnormally short neck on inspection. MR reveals not only the protrusion of the odontoid process above the foramen magnum but also whether the Arnold-Chiari malformation is present (Fig. 115–5).

The *Arnold-Chiari malformation* is a developmental displacement of the cerebellar tonsils through the foramen magnum, with (type II) or without (type I) elongation of the medulla and lower end of the fourth ventricle into the cervical canal. Symptoms can resemble those described for basilar impression, can be entirely due to obstructive hydrocephalus, or can reflect a progressive cerebellar ataxia. Rarely, intermittent headache and/or syncope may be the only symptom(s). MR imaging is diagnostic (Fig. 115–5). Treatment of either basilar impression or the Arnold-Chiari malformation causing progressive neurologic deficits consists of surgical decompression or, when appropriate, ventricular shunting to relieve hydrocephalus.

Syringomyelia refers to a cavity within the central spinal cord, arising most often at the cervical level (Fig. 115–5). Syringomyelia can arise either as a congenital abnormality or in association with intramedullary spinal neoplasms. In the congenital form, the lesions often extend into the medulla (sy-

ringobulbia) or can penetrate caudally into the thoracic and lumbosacral regions.

Pathologically, the syringomyelic cavity usually is associated anatomically with the central spinal canal; some communicate directly with the floor of the fourth ventricle. As life advances, the syrinx progressively replaces the centrally located gray matter of the posterior and anterior horns of the spinal cord and also interrupts the decussating spinothalamic pain-carrying fibers in the anterior commissure. Often, syringomyelia is associated with other congenital malformations, including the Arnold-Chiari malformation (Fig. 115–5), fusion of the cervical vertebrae, or malformations at the lumbosacral region, including spina bifida and associated meningomyelocele.

Clinical manifestations of congenital syringomyelia most often begin in the second or third decade, frequently affecting the hands or upper trunk with a typically dissociated impairment of pain and temperature sensation coupled with preservation of the senses of touch, vibration, and joint position. Progressive muscular atrophy usually develops in the involved segments, especially in the upper extremities, and commonly leads to kyphoscoliosis. The analgesia results in painless ulcers, burns, and traumatic arthropathy. As a rule, areflexia marks the upper extremities, whereas upper motor neuron signs eventually develop in the legs, accompanied in those members by reduced vibratory and position sensations. In most affected patients the disease process progresses slowly but relentlessly.

In patients with syringobulbia, dissociated impairment of pain and temperature develops over the face, along with nystagmus, pharyngeal and vocal cord paralysis, and lingual atrophy.

Clinical diagnosis is usually not difficult once considered. Leprosy, other rare and acquired peripheral neuropathies, and intramedullary destructive or neoplastic lesions of the spinal cord and brain stem are the only insidiously developing conditions that cause widespread dissociated loss of pain and temperature sensation. Leprosy can be dismissed if the subject has not been raised in an endemic area, and neither it nor other peripheral neuropathies produce signs of spinal cord dysfunction. The important consideration is whether or not an associated spinal neoplasm exists. MR imaging definitively outlines most syrinxes and neoplasms if present. Treatment generally is unsatisfactory unless a tumor is found and can be removed. Surgical drainage has been claimed to halt the disease process in some patients.

NEUROCUTANEOUS SYNDROMES

Neurocutaneous syndromes, or phakomatoses, are congenital disorders characterized by abnormal growth of ectodermal tissues, leading to distinctive skin lesions and nervous system malformations and/or tumors. More than 20 syndromes have been described; neurofibromatosis is the most common.

Neurofibromatosis is a common disorder (1 in 3000 births) inherited as an autosomal dominant trait with a high spontaneous mutation rate (40 to 60 per cent of cases are clinically sporadic). There are two forms of the disorder. One (von Recklinghausen's neurofibromatosis, or neurofibromatosis 1) relates to a gene abnormality on chromosome 17. It is characterized by the occurrence of pigmented skin lesions (café au lait spots), multiple tumors of spinal or cranial nerves (neurofibromas composed of proliferating fibroblasts or neurilemmal sheath cells), skin tumors, and the frequently intracranial meningiomas. There is an increased association with pheochromocytomas, cystic lung disease, renal vascular lesions causing hypertension, fibrous dysplasia of bone, and medullary thyroid carcinoma, as well as other tumors of endocrine glands. The tumors can overlap in the region of the brachial or sacral plexus to produce large plexiform neuromas that can evolve into malignant sarcomas. Intracranial astrocytomas and glioblastomas occur with a greater than normal frequency. Stenosis of the aqueduct with noncommunicating hydrocephalus is sometimes observed.

The presence of multiple cutaneous neurofibromas accompanied by nonraised café au lait spots represents the clinical hallmark. The pigmented skin lesions occur most commonly over the trunk and in the axilla. If greater than 1.5 cm in diameter and more than six in number, they indicate the presence of the disease. Nerve involvement can be solitary or multiple and diffuse. Multiple cranial nerves can be affected, resulting in facial weakness, numbness, deafness, and optic nerve atrophy. Local confluent tumors with associated fibrosis result in elephantiasis neuromatosa, as well as gross asymmetric hypertrophy of body parts. Neurofibromas arising from nerve roots can invade the intervertebral foramina to compress the spinal cord or brain stem. A preliminary report suggests that ketotifen, a mast cell stabilizer, may slow tumor growth.

The second form (neurofibromatosis 2), characterized by bilateral acoustic neuromas, is less common. Cutaneous manifestations may be absent, but meningiomas and spinal neurofibromas occur with increased frequency. The disorder is related to specific loss of alleles on chromosome 22.

Tuberous sclerosis is a neurocutaneous disorder inherited as an autosomal dominant trait. Its triad of findings, all present by late childhood, include facial nevi (adenoma sebaceum), epilepsy, and mental retardation. The importance of the disorder for adult medicine is that subtle cases occasionally produce problems in the differential diagnosis of early or late adolescent epilepsy, and funduscopic examination can disclose nodules or phakomas of the retina that look neoplastic but in fact are stable and similar in structure to the adenoma sebaceum. Some patients develop intracranial or optic gliomas. Rhabdomyomas of the heart as well as renal tumors and neoplasms of the endocrine organs can be observed.

Sturge-Weber disease produces a port wine–colored capillary hemangioma on the face accompanied by a similar vascular malformation of the underlying meninges and cerebral cortex. The cause is unknown. Diagnosis is made by observing the disfiguring stain involving the sensory dermatomal distribution of the first, second, or third portions of the trigeminal nerve. General or focal motor seizures may occur with or without associated mental retardation and require antiepileptic medication. The disfiguring stain deserves cosmetic repair if possible.

Von Hippel–Lindau disease is inherited in a simple autosomal dominant pattern and is characterized by hemangioblastomas of the cerebellar hemispheres with associated angiomas of the retina and cystic changes in the kidney and pancreas. Recent evidence maps the abnormal gene to chromosome 3 in the region associated with renal carcinoma. Hemangioblastomas can sometimes also be found in brain or spinal cord. An association with pheochromocytomas, polycythemia, and several forms of cancer has been noted.

REFERENCES

Byrne TN, Waxman SG: Spinal cord compression. Philadelphia, FA Davis Co, 1990.

Callen JP, Meckler RJ (eds): Neurocutaneous disorders. Neurol Clin 5(3):August 1987.

Wolsey RM, Young RR (eds): Disorders of the spinal cord. Neurol Clin 9(3):August 1991.

E. Peripheral Nerve and Motor Neuron Disorders

PERIPHERAL NERVES

General Considerations

Diseases of the peripheral nervous system may affect one (or more) of three structures: (1) the cell body (neuronopathy), (2) the axon (axonopathy), or (3) the Schwann cells and/or their metabolic product, the myelin sheath (demyelinating neuropathy). Any of these processes may be focal, leading to mononeuropathy (involvement of a single nerve) or multiple mononeuropathy (involvement of several different single nerves), or diffuse, causing polyneuropathy (a diffuse, predominantly symmetric, and often distal involvement of the nerves of the extremities) (Table 115–11). The distal nature of most polyneuropathies reflects the fact that the longest nerves are the most metabolically active. Although each of the anatomic and pathologic disorders listed in Table 115–11 can have distinctive clinical symptoms, there is considerable overlap. Furthermore, individual etiologic agents, such as diabetes or cancer, may cause more than one type of neuropa-

TABLE 115-11. ANATOMIC AND PATHOLOGIC CLASSIFICATION OF PERIPHERAL NEUROPATHIES

LESION	CLINICAL EXAMPLE(S)
Focal	
Mononeuropathy or radiculopathy	Median nerve compression (carpal tunnel syndrome)
	Herniated disc
Multiple monoradiculopathies or radiculopathies	Periarteritis nodosa; diabetes
	Lumbar spondylosis
Diffuse (Polyneuropathies)	
Axonopathies	Nutritional deficiency (Table 115-14); toxic exposure; diabetes; uremia; rare subacute motor neuropathies
Myelinopathy	Guillain-Barré syndrome
Neuronopathies	
Sensory	Paraneoplastic sensory neuronopathy
Motor	Amyotrophic lateral sclerosis, etc.
Autonomic	Shy-Drager syndrome

thy. Accordingly, in the pages that follow, the peripheral neuropathies are discussed first pathophysiologically and then etiologically. The same pathophysiologic and etiologic considerations apply to nerve roots that are the proximal extension of peripheral nerves and can be affected by focal (single or multiple monoradiculopathy) or diffuse (polyradiculopathy) processes. This discussion also covers focal nerve root lesions.

In *demyelinating neuropathy,* segments of myelin degenerate, usually from immunologic or infectious causes. Clinically, demyelinating neuropathy is characterized by functional failure of large myelinated fibers, leading to decreased light touch, position, and vibration sensation, as well as to weakness and reduction or absence of deep tendon reflexes. A relative sparing of lightly myelinated or unmyelinated fibers partially preserves temperature and pain sensation, although these modalities become involved if the disorder is severe. The onset of demyelinating neuropathy may be rapid, and with Schwann cell proliferation and remyelination, recovery may be equally rapid. Because the myelin sheath can be involved anywhere throughout its peripheral course, the disease, although usually symmetric, sometimes affects both proximal and distal fibers to a similar degree. Cranial nerves are often involved, as well as peripheral nerves. The CSF protein is elevated in diffuse demyelinating neuropathies because of damage to spinal roots. Electrical studies of demyelinated nerves reveal that conduction velocity is slowed, often to 20 or 25 per cent of normal values, and the amplitude of the action potential is small because it is dispersed over a longer duration.

Axonal neuropathy is characterized by degeneration of the distal ends of long axons, with secondary loss and degeneration of the myelin sheath. The disorder usually causes an equal loss of all sensory modalities, although in some instances small axons carrying pain and temperature suffer a loss dispro-

portionate to larger axons. The first symptoms are usually sensory, with paresthesias or sensory loss of the tips of the fingers and toes. Only later, as the sensory loss spreads more proximally, does motor involvement occur in a typical "stocking and glove" distribution. Unlike demyelinating neuropathy, recovery is usually slow because of the slow rate of regeneration of the damaged axons. Spinal roots usually are not involved and the CSF protein remains normal. Electrically, axonal neuropathies are characterized by normal or only slightly (10 to 15 per cent) slowed conduction velocity and by small sensory action potentials.

Neuronopathies affect either sensory or motor nerves, or both. Neuronopathies cause either acute or gradual onset of sensory and/or motor loss with little or no recovery.

FOCAL RADICULOPATHY AND NEUROPATHY

The agents that cause focal neuropathy usually differ from those causing polyneuropathy, although some diseases, such as diabetes and hypothyroidism, can cause either mononeuropathy or polyneuropathy. Most focal neuropathies result from vascular disease, compression, or trauma. Clinically, the mononeuropathies are characterized by sensory and/or motor loss (usually both) in the anatomic distribution of all or part of a nerve root, nerve plexus, or peripheral nerve. One can determine the site of the injury clinically by observing the anatomic distribution of dysfunction (e.g., an injury to the radial nerve at the humerus causes weakness of the brachioradialis muscle and extensors of the wrist and fingers, but spares the triceps muscle because radial nerve fibers in the triceps depart from the nerve more proximally in the upper arm).

Trauma and Compression

Most mononeuritides and monoradiculopathies are caused by trauma and result either from compression, transection, or stretching of nerve or from chronic entrapment by various anatomic structures. Perhaps the most common disabling disorder is entrapment of a cervical or lumbar nerve root by a herniated intervertebral disc as the root passes through the intervertebral foramen. Mild injury to a nerve may leave the nerve structurally intact but cause a conduction block first by ischemia and subsequently by demyelination. Acute ischemic lesions recover rapidly when pressure is released; if demyelination ensues, the nerve recovers more slowly. A more severe injury interrupts the axons but leaves the connective tissue sheaths intact. Such lesions are common in closed crush injuries. Depending on the degree of damage, recovery may be partial or complete, but it proceeds slowly. The most severe injury is transection of both axons and connective tissue sheaths, such as occurs with severe stretch injuries or penetrating wounds. Because of the interruption of the sheath, recovery does not occur unless the nerve is surgically repaired, and even then the prognosis is poor.

Any portion of the peripheral nervous system can be damaged by trauma. In wartime, penetrating wounds of peripheral nerves and nerve plexuses are major causes of disability. In peacetime, traumatic peripheral nerve lesions usually result from closed crush or traction injuries. The brachial plexus is a major site of stretch injuries, commonly resulting from motorcycle accidents or compression injury when the arm is hyperabducted, as under anesthesia. The former injuries are usually permanent, the latter transient. Other acute compression injuries that sometimes follow general anesthesia for surgery or are self-induced by alcohol or sedatives include radial nerve palsy from compression of the nerve in the radial groove of the humerus (Saturday night palsy), peroneal nerve palsy from compression between the surface and the head of the fibula (crossed-leg palsies), ulnar palsy (often from compression by an intravenous board in the ulnar groove at the elbow), and sciatic palsies from compression of the buttocks or ill-placed injections into that site.

Chronic Compression Radiculopathies and Myelopathies

Herniated Intervertebral Disc. When disc material herniates into the vertebral canal, generally lateral to the posterior longitudinal ligament, it compresses spinal roots as they enter the intervertebral foramen. Occasionally, the disc herniates more centrally, compressing either the spinal cord in the cervical or thoracic area or the cauda equina in the lumbar area. The specific signs and symptoms of herniated discs depend in part on whether the predominant compression is spinal cord or nerve root, and in part on the level at which the neural structures are compressed (Table 115–12). Thoracic disc herniations are rare, but when they occur they usually compress the spinal cord as well as the emerging root.

The most common symptom of herniated disc is pain. Local pain is felt as a dull aching in the neck or back, with an associated stiffness of those structures, frequently occurring episodically in response to minor trauma (or no discernible trauma at all) months or years prior to the development of radicular pain. Muscle spasm often splints the neck or back. Radicular pain may occasionally be the first sign of disc disease but is far more likely to follow repetitive bouts of local pain. Both local and radicular pain have the characteristics of being exacerbated by activity and relieved by rest.

Raising the intraspinal pressure, as by coughing, sneezing, or straining, increases the pain sharply. Directly stretching the compressed root also aggravates the pain. In the upper extremities, extending the arm and laterally flexing the neck away from the extended arm often reproduces radicular pain. In the lower extremities, raising the extended leg with the patient in the recumbent position frequently reproduces the pain of an L5 or S1 radiculopathy and, if the pain is felt on the opposite side as well (crossed straight leg raising), the sign suggests herniated disc disease.

If an intervertebral disc herniates medially, rather than laterally, the lesion then mimics a spinal tumor except that with disc disease there may be little or no pain. The diagnosis of herniated disc is deduced from the characteristic clinical symptoms and findings. Both CT and especially MR are effective in identifying most disc disease (Fig. 115–6) and in most cases are sufficient for preoperative localization of the site of herniation.

No consensus exists about the preferred management of herniated discs. Most physicians believe that the first step is bed rest. Surgery is indicated when (1) bed rest fails, and the patient is incapacitated by severe, intractable pain; (2) a centrally placed lumbar disc compresses the cauda equina, producing urinary dysfunction; or (3) there is motor weakness caused by compression of the spinal cord. Some believe that peripheral motor weakness caused by root compression is also an indication for immediate surgery.

Disc dissolution by the injection of the enzyme chymopapain directly into the lumbar disc space is

TABLE 115–12. SIGNS AND SYMPTOMS OF HERNIATED DISC

Site of disc herniation	C4-C5	C5-C6	C6-C7	L3-L4	L4-L5	L5-S1
Involved root	C5	C6	C7	L4	L5	S1
Pain	Medial scapula, lateral border of arm	Lateral forearm, thumb and index finger	Posterior arm, lateral hand, mid-forearm, and medial scapula	Down to medial malleolus	Back of thigh, lateral calf, dorsum of foot	Back of thigh, back of calf, lateral foot
Sensory loss	Lateral border of upper arm	Lateral forearm, including thumb	Mid-forearm and middle finger	Medial leg to malleolus	Dorsum of foot	Behind lateral
Reflex loss	Biceps	Supinator	Triceps	Knee jerk	None	Ankle jerk
Motor deficit	Deltoid, supraspinatus, infraspinatus, rhomboids	Biceps, brachioradialis, brachialis (pronators and supinators of forearm)	Latissimus dorsi, pectoralis major, triceps, wrist flexors	Inversion of foot	Dorsiflexion of toes and foot (latter L4 also)	Plantar flexion and eversion of foot

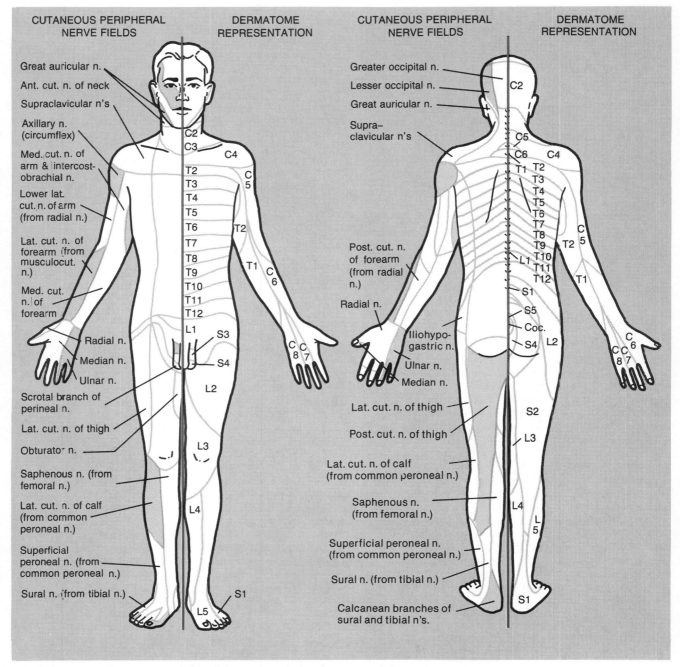

FIGURE 115–6. The cutaneous fields of the major peripheral nerves and dermatomes seen on the anterior (A) and posterior (B) surfaces of the body. (Redrawn from Haymaker W, Woodhall B: Peripheral Nerve Injuries. Philadelphia, WB Saunders Co, 1953.)

less widely used than formerly because of the complications of spinal damage and anaphylactic shock. A new technique in which disc material is suctioned out through a percutaneous catheter is currently under clinical trial.

Spondylosis. Spondylosis is a term applied to chronic degenerative disease of intervertebral discs associated with reactive changes in the adjacent vertebral bodies. Spondylotic changes in the neck

and low back increase with age and are almost invariably present in the elderly. Most spondylosis causes no symptoms, except when the reactive tissue compresses a nerve root or the spinal cord. When this occurs, the signs and symptoms resemble those of a herniated disc, but the onset is less abrupt and the treatment often more difficult. In both the cervical and lumbar areas, spondylosis is more likely to produce spinal cord or cauda equina symptoms if the sagittal diameter of the spinal canal is further impinged upon by osteophytes. The signs and symptoms of *cervical spondylosis* result from compression either of the spinal cord or its emerging roots and are thus similar to those of a herniated disc (Table 115–12). Most patients suffer either radiculopathy or myelopathy (see p. 800) but not both. The classic picture of cervical spondylotic *myelopathy* is one of little or no pain but slowly developing weakness, atrophy, and fasciculations in the upper extremities, particularly the small muscles of the hand, or an insidiously developing spastic paraparesis with decreased proprioception in the legs. At first the findings may suggest a diagnosis of amyotrophic lateral sclerosis (see p. 813). However, in cervical spondylosis there are sensory changes, particularly vibration loss in the lower extremities, and in amyotrophic lateral sclerosis there are fasciculations arising in areas different from motor roots compressed at the cervical level (e.g., the tongue). The differential diagnosis also includes other compressive lesions of root and spinal cord.

When neurologic signs suggest that cervical spondylosis is causing a myelopathy, MR imaging is the examination of choice, often making more invasive myelography unnecessary (Fig. 115–7).

Many physicians prefer, once having established the diagnosis, to begin conservative treatment with a period of bed rest accompanied by cervical traction and stabilization of the neck with a soft collar. If the patient develops progressive neurologic signs,

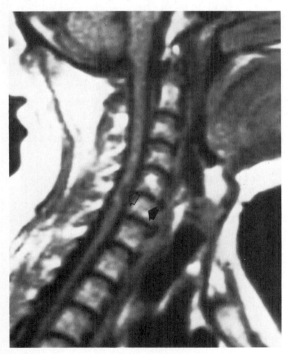

FIGURE 115–7. Cervical disc herniation causing myelopathy. MR image from a middle-aged patient with a 1-year history of numbness in the right arm and progressive spastic weakness of both legs. There was no pain. Although MR does not image bone, the bone marrow in the vertebral bodies is clearly visible *(closed arrow)*. The herniated disc impinging on the cervical cord between C5 and C6 can be easily seen *(open arrow)*.

especially weakness and atrophy or spasticity, surgical therapy is indicated.

The considerations described above under cervical spondylosis also apply to *lumbar spondylosis.* The symptoms of lumbar spondylosis are similar to those of herniated disc, often occurring at multiple levels. One outstanding difference is the frequent presence of "pseudoclaudication" from cauda equina compression in patients with spinal stenosis from either spondylosis or congenital narrowing. Typically, symptoms and signs are evoked or accentuated by walking and include pain, paresthesias, and weakness in the lower extremities. All of the symptoms may disappear when the patient ceases walking, even though he remains in the standing position. At times, however, the symptoms may be exacerbated by prolonged standing and relieved only by sitting or lying down. Pseudoclaudication of the cauda equina may be distinguished from intermittent vascular claudication in several ways. In vascular disease, the pulses in the lower extremities are usually absent or become absent as the patient begins to exercise. With vascular disease, the symptoms are usually reproducible and stereotypic; i.e., the patient can predict the exact distance he can walk at a given speed before symptoms develop. Symptoms of cauda equina pseudoclaudication are less stereotypic, so that on some days patients can walk much longer distances than on others. The reason for this variability is not known. In patients with pseudoclaudication, the neurologic examination may be normal when the patient is at rest, but abnormal signs, particularly absence of deep tendon reflexes, may appear as the patient exercises. In patients with pseudoclaudication the lumbar canal is narrowed on either lateral radiograph, CT, or MR scan, and there is a substantial block to the passage of myelographic dye. With severe lumbar stenosis, conservative treatment usually fails and decompressive laminectomy is the treatment of choice.

Chronic Compression Neuropathies

In order to reach their peripheral targets, many nerves must pass through narrow channels where they can become chronically compressed in fibro-osseous tunnels, angulated and stretched over arthritic joints or bony structures, or recurrently compressed by repeated trauma. Table 115–13 lists the major compression neuropathies. The most common are discussed below.

Carpal Tunnel Syndrome. The median nerve is compressed at the wrist as it passes deep to the flexor retinaculum. The usual symptoms include numbness, tingling, and burning sensations in one or both palms and in the fingers supplied by the median nerve, including the thumb, index, middle, and lateral half of the ring finger. Some patients complain that all fingers become numb, but if tested this is usually found not to be the case. Pain and paresthesias are most prominent at night and often interrupt sleep. The pain is prominent at the wrist but may radiate to the forearm or at times to the

TABLE 115–13. COMMON SITES OF NERVE ENTRAPMENT

Median nerve
   Carpal tunnel—wrist
   Pronator muscle—elbow
Ulnar nerve
   Elbow
   Wrist
Radial nerve—humeral groove
Brachial plexus—thoracic outlet
Sciatic nerve—buttock (sciatic notch)
Peroneal nerve—behind knee
Lateral femoral cutaneous nerve—inguinal ligament
Cervical and lumbar root—intervertebral canal

shoulder. Both pain and paresthesias are relieved by shaking the hands. In some patients, symptoms may persist for years without objective signs of median nerve damage. In others, sensory loss may appear over the tips of the fingers and/or weakness can develop in the median nerve–innervated thumb muscles in association with atrophy of the lateral aspect of the thenar eminence.

The carpal tunnel syndrome occurs mostly in middle-aged and obese women. It may affect those who use the wrists and hands occupationally, as in gardening, house painting, meat wrapping, or typing. Other predisposing causes include pregnancy, myxedema, acromegaly, rheumatoid arthritis, and primary amyloidosis.

The diagnosis is based on clinical symptoms, the finding of Tinel's sign (paresthesias in the fingers with a light tap over the nerve at the wrist), and the demonstration of a conduction block at the wrist by motor nerve velocity studies. The most effective treatment is section of the transverse carpal ligament, decompressing the nerve.

Ulnar Palsy. The ulnar nerve may be entrapped at the elbow (cubital tunnel) or at the wrist. Injury may also occur years after a "malunited" supracondylar fracture of the humerus with bony overgrowth (*tardive ulnar palsy*). Contrary to the findings in the carpal tunnel syndrome, muscle weakness and atrophy characteristically predominate over sensory symptoms and signs. Patients notice atrophy of the first dorsal interosseous muscle and difficulty performing fine manipulations of the fingers. There may be numbness of the small finger, the contiguous half of the ring finger, and the ulnar border of the hand.

Cervical Rib and Thoracic Outlet Syndrome. The brachial plexus as it passes through the thoracic outlet can be compressed by a cervical rib or by normal bone, muscles, and fibrous tissue. The compression usually occurs when the arm is abducted and may involve the subclavian artery as well as the plexus. Symptoms include paresthesias of ulnar fingers and rarely weakness and wasting of the small hand muscles. The sensory abnormalities usually respond to avoiding the abducted position. Surgical removal of the first rib and fibrous band sometimes is performed as treatment, but its indica-

tions and effects are controversial.

Immune Focal Neuropathies

A few acute focal neuropathies are believed to have an immune cause. The most common is *acute brachial neuritis*, characterized by the acute onset of severe pain, usually in the distribution of the axillary nerve (over the lateral shoulder) but at times extending into the entire arm. It generally subsides after a few days to a week. Usually coincident with the subsidence of the pain, weakness of the proximal arm becomes apparent. The serratus anterior is the most commonly paralyzed muscle, but other muscles of the shoulder girdle, including the deltoid and muscles of the upper arm, may be paralyzed as well. Rarely, most of the arm and even the ipsilateral diaphragm are paralyzed. Sensory loss is usually restricted to the distribution of the axillary nerve. Weakness may last weeks to months and be accompanied by severe atrophy of the shoulder girdle. Total recovery occurs in most patients within several months to 2 or 3 years. The disorder has been reported to follow upper respiratory infection or an immunization, but often there is no antecedent illness. Considerably less common is a similar disorder affecting the *lumbosacral plexus*, causing pain and weakness of a lower extremity. As with acute brachial neuritis, although the pain may be severe and the weakness profound, recovery usually occurs. Differential diagnosis from acute disc herniation is made readily by identifying the distribution, which involves incomplete dysfunction of multiple nerve roots rather than a single root.

Infectious Focal Neuropathies

Cranial nerves and nerves of the cauda equina may be damaged by acute bacterial meningitis, subacute meningitis (e.g., tuberculosis), or less commonly, chronic meningitis (e.g., fungal meningitis). Common infections of the peripheral nervous system include herpes zoster, leprosy, Lyme disease, and acquired immunodeficiency syndrome (AIDS).

Vascular Neuropathies

Several diseases that affect small or medium-sized vessels may lead to ischemia or infarction of isolated peripheral nerves. The most common disorder is a mononeuropathy that complicates diabetes. Mononeuropathy or multiple mononeuropathies commonly arise as early complications or first symptoms of periarteritis nodosa. Less commonly, rheumatoid arthritis, systemic lupus erythematosus, hypersensitivity angiitis, Sjögren's syndrome, or Wegener's granulomatosis may cause a similar peripheral neuropathy. Vascular neuropathies are characterized by the acute onset of motor and sensory loss in the distribution of one or more single peripheral nerves. With the passage of time, other nerves become involved. Depending on the intensity of the vasculitis, the neurologic deficit may resolve after weeks or months, only to affect another nerve at a distant place. Severe cases can involve so many nerves that the condition resembles a polyneuropathy rather than a mononeuritis multiplex. Usually a careful history distinguishes the focal onset of the latter.

Several disorders cause acute or chronic dysfunction of one or more cranial nerves. *Acute cranial nerve mononeuropathies* include optic neuropathy, described on p. 776. Ocular motor mononeuropathies (i.e., sudden dysfunction of cranial nerves III, IV, or VI) usually have a vascular basis. An example is *diabetic ophthalmoplegia*, which generally occurs in mildly affected diabetics, sometimes before the diagnosis of diabetes is made. It is characterized by painful onset of single cranial nerve paralysis (most commonly the oculomotor, sparing the pupil). The pain resolves in a few days and the paralysis subsides over a few months. Similar disorders affecting nondiabetics are called acute ocular neuropathy, which likewise has a benign prognosis. The differential diagnosis includes compression lesions (i.e., tumor or aneurysm) and inflammatory lesions (meningitis). *Acute facial palsy* is usually of unknown cause and has a benign prognosis (Bell's palsy). The disorder may follow a banal infection or exposure to a draft and usually begins with mild pain behind the ear followed, within several hours, by paralysis of the muscles supplied by the facial nerve. Unilateral loss of taste is common (chorda tympani). Recovery usually begins within 2 months, and within 9 months to 1 year 80 per cent of patients report virtually normal function. The pathogenesis of the disorder is believed to be an infectious-inflammatory swelling of the facial nerve in the facial canal of the middle ear, leading to an acute compression neuropathy. Differential diagnosis includes herpes zoster as well as tumors and basal meningitis (e.g., Lyme disease, sarcoid). In herpes, the vesicles may be found only in the auditory canal behind the ear.

The most important aspect of management is to protect the cornea. Patients with acute, severe facial paralysis cannot close the eye, and the cornea should be protected with a lens when out of doors and the eye should probably be patched at night. Although the evidence of efficacy is weak, many physicians who encounter a patient with Bell's palsy during the first 48 to 72 hours of paralysis treat the disorder with a short course of corticosteroids (60 mg of prednisone for 1 week, with gradual tapering over the next week) when not otherwise contraindicated. *Acoustic* or *vestibular nerve neuropathies* are believed to result from either vascular or inflammatory (viral) disorders and are discussed on page 784. Acute neuropathy of other cranial nerves occurs rarely. The cause and pathogenesis are usually unexplained and recovery is common.

Multiple cranial nerve neuropathies are uncommon except as they complicate tumors at the base of the skull (e.g., nasopharyngeal carcinoma), leptomeningeal metastases, or meningitis (e.g., tuberculosis, sarcoid, Lyme disease). Idiopathic multiple cranial neuropathies typically begin with pain in the eye or face; paralysis develops acutely, often responds to treatment with corticosteroids, and may be recurrent. The most common and well-defined syndrome is the Tolosa-Hunt syndrome, characterized by unilateral paralysis of muscles supplied by oculomotor, trochlear, and abducent nerves, sometimes accompanied by sensory loss in the first division of the trigeminal nerve. The disorder is thought to result from granulomatous inflammation of the superior orbital fissure or cavernous sinus. Similar syndromes can involve lower cranial nerves or a combination of oculomotor and lower cranial nerves. When the disorder is painless and symmetric it may represent a restricted form or initial manifestation of the Guillain-Barré syndrome.

Chronic cranial mononeuropathies can affect the same nerves as their acute counterparts. In addition, a slowly developing sensory *trigeminal neuropathy* may occur unilaterally or bilaterally. The disorder can complicate the course of several collagen vascular diseases (e.g., Sjögren's syndrome) or be idiopathic. *Trigeminal neuralgia* (see p. 770) and *hemifacial spasm* are disorders believed to result from compression of the cranial nerve by tortuous arteries in the posterior fossa.

POLYNEUROPATHY

Inflammatory/Immune Polyneuropathies

Several acute and chronic polyneuropathies are associated with inflammatory infiltrates in the peripheral nerves and roots. The mechanism of neurologic dysfunction is usually demyelination, believed to be on an immune basis. Most of these disorders are rare, the exception being the Guillain-Barré syndrome (GBS, or acute postinfectious polyneuropathy). An acute disorder, GBS has a peak incidence in middle age but can affect all ages and races and both sexes. The disorder is characterized by a rapidly progressive, predominantly motor neuropathy that may paralyze all voluntary muscles, including those supplied by the cranial nerves and those controlling respiration. Sensory changes are usually milder than motor abnormalities and may include no more than tingling paresthesias in the hands and feet. Rarely, sensory loss may be profound and more significant than motor weakness. Pain is common, as is some degree of autonomic dysfunction. Many patients suffer from hypertension or cardiac arrhythmias, the latter being the usual cause of death in the 5 per cent of patients who die. Bilateral facial paralysis is also common and helps distinguish the GBS from other polyneuropathies.

Characteristically, a previously healthy person who has suffered a mild respiratory infection in the past 2 or 3 weeks (other predisposing factors include *Campylobacter jejuni* infection, surgical procedures, and Hodgkin's disease) notes the painless onset of mild weakness in the lower extremities, often accompanied by tingling paresthesias in toes and fingers. Although the patient is aware of weakness, particularly when walking or climbing stairs, the examiner at this early stage may be unable to discern any abnormality save for diminished deep tendon reflexes. Over a matter of a few days in untreated cases, the weakness becomes more profound and often ascends from the lower extremities to the upper extremities and finally to the face (Landry's ascending paralysis). Deep tendon reflexes disappear, and the patient may complain of proprioceptive loss in arms and legs. It may become difficult for him or her to swallow and breathe. Examination now reveals symmetric motor weakness of both proximal and distal muscles of all extremities. The CSF protein concentration, which is normal during the first several days, rises often above 100 mg/dl, usually without an accompanying pleocytosis. In most instances the weakness progresses for several days to a couple of weeks and then stabilizes. After a period of stability, recovery begins and in 85 per cent of patients it is complete over several weeks to months. Some patients require respiratory support and careful monitoring of cardiovascular function during the acute stages. Thus hospitalization is necessary until recovery is well under way. In a small minority of patients, neural function recovers only partially or not at all, and a few patients with persistently high CSF proteins develop headaches and papilledema as a late complication of the illness. The pathogenesis of the latter is believed to be the plugging of arachnoid villi by the persistently elevated protein.

An unusual variant of GBS is characterized by ataxia, oculomotor paralysis, and reflex absence. Other less common neuropathies that are probably GBS variants include a *chronic inflammatory demyelinating neuropathy*, which may be progressive or relapsing and, unlike classic GBS, responds favorably to corticosteroid therapy, and acute neuropathies that predominantly involve either sensory or autonomic fibers.

There are two aspects to the treatment of the disorder. Plasmapheresis, particularly when applied early in the course of the illness, halts its progression and shortens its duration, often in a dramatic manner. Recent evidence suggests that intravenous immune globulin may be equally or even more effective than plasmapheresis. Supportive care, including respiratory support and careful monitoring

TABLE 115–14. METABOLIC AND NUTRITIONAL DISEASES OF PERIPHERAL NERVES

Endocrine
  Diabetes (polyneuropathy)
  Hypothyroidism
  Acromegaly (usually entrapment neuropathies)
Nutritional
  Vitamin deficiency
    Thiamine (beriberi; Wernicke's disease)
    Pyridoxine (isoniazid toxicity)
    Vitamin B_{12} (pernicious anemia, gastrectomy)
  Multiple factors (alcohol)
  Malnutrition (Vitamins B_6 and E)
Renal (uremia)
Hepatic
  Porphyria
  Chronic liver failure

of cardiovascular function, prevents the major complications that lead to death.

Other immune polyneuropathies not related to GBS are those associated with multiple myeloma, particularly of the osteoblastic variety, and benign monoclonal gammopathies. The neuropathy in these instances slowly progresses and has a sensorimotor distribution with no distinct systemic signs other than the alterations of serum proteins. The pathogenesis is thought to be immune in that the gamma globulin produced in excess by the primary disorder deposits on the nerves to react with a myelin-associated glycoprotein and cause demyelination. In the case of multiple myeloma, treatment of the primary disease sometimes leads to amelioration of the neuropathy.

Metabolic Neuropathies

Several metabolic or nutritional diseases are associated with polyneuropathy (Table 115–14). Diabetic neuropathy can take several forms (see Chapter 71).

These subacute or chronic sensorimotor neuropathies have few individually characteristic signs, and the diagnosis is usually suggested by identifying the underlying systemic disease; e.g., most patients with the peripheral neuropathy of acute intermittent porphyria have mental changes and/or abdominal pain preceding the onset of the neuropathy. Likewise the characteristic slow reflexes of hypothyroidism are usually present in addition to the sensorimotor polyneuropathy. In any patient suffering from a chronic progressive sensorimotor polyneuropathy, a careful search for metabolic disorders is essential to establish the diagnosis.

Toxic Neuropathies

Table 115–15 lists some of the toxins known or believed to cause polyneuropathies. In general, polyneuropathies produced by toxins are sensorimotor in pattern, although a few, such as those caused by acrylamide and pyridoxine toxicity, produce predominantly sensory changes. In every instance of obscure polyneuropathy, a careful occupational history and search for intoxicants, either knowingly or unknowingly ingested, is warranted.

Hereditary Neuropathies

Hereditary neuropathies are slowly progressive inherited disorders in which the pathogenesis is not clearly defined. Hereditary disorders may produce sensorimotor neuropathies, relatively pure sensory neuronopathies, or autonomic neuropathies (Table 115–16). In addition to the obvious hereditary disorders of peripheral nerves and sensory and autonomic neurons, several motor neuropathies have a genetic basis and others are of unknown cause. These are considered in the next section on motor neuron diseases.

Critical Illness Polyneuropathy

A significant number of patients with sepsis and multiorgan failure, who are intubated and admitted to intensive care units, develop weakness, hyporeflexia, and electrophysiologic signs of motor and sensory axonal dysfunction. Most patients who develop such "critical illness" or "intensive care unit" polyneuropathy have been critically ill for 2 weeks to 1 month. The disorder is often first suspected when the patient cannot be weaned from a respirator. Most patients who survive the underlying illness recover over several months. The exact pathogenesis of the axonal neuropathy is not known.

THE MOTOR NEURON DISEASES

The term *motor neuron disease* refers to a group of chronic neurologic disorders affecting the anterior horn cells of the spinal cord and lower brain stem plus, in many instances, the large motor neurons of the cerebral cortex that give rise to the corticospinal tract. Sensory changes and cerebellar dysfunction are absent. Some apply the term *amyotrophic lateral sclerosis* to all of the motor neuron diseases of unknown cause beginning in adulthood. Others use the term *motor neuron disease* to apply to the general condition and subclassify the variations (Table 115–17). If both upper and lower motor neuron abnormalities are found, the disorder is called *amyotrophic lateral sclerosis* (ALS). *Progressive bulbar palsy* causes relatively rapidly advancing upper and lower motor neuron involvement of the muscles of the jaw, pharynx, and tongue. When there are no signs of upper motor neuron disease and only slowly progressive muscle wasting and weakness, the disorder is termed *progressive muscular atrophy* (PMA). The rarest form begins as bilateral upper motor neuron disease affecting the extremities (*progressive lateral sclerosis*), the bulbar muscles (*pseudobulbar palsy*), or both.

Motor neuron disease may first affect bulbar muscles, one or both of the extremities on one side of the body, the lower or upper extremities symmetrically, or all four limbs simultaneously. The disorder's incidence increases with advancing age and progresses over 2 to 7 years until death. (An acute reversible motor neuron disease has been reported to affect children and young adults in rural China. A subacute developing but reversible motor neuron disease, difficult to distinguish from ALS, also has been reported in a few patients in the United States.) The bulbar form has the shortest course, PMA the longest (often more than 10 years), and ALS intermediate. The disease usually is sporadic, but familial groupings have occurred, indicating either a genetic predisposition or common exposure to an unknown causative agent. ALS was once the common cause of death among the indigenous population of the Mariana Islands. This disorder, which is now decreasing dramatically in incidence, has been related by some investigators to ingestion of a neurotoxin contained in the false sago plant, which was used in food and traditional medicine. Other endemic areas have been identified in Japan and New Guinea, but in these areas the nature of possible causative agents is less clear. Familial cases tend to affect younger persons and to progress more rapidly than do sporadic ones. The cause of the motor

TABLE 115–15. SOME CAUSES OF TOXIC NEUROPATHIES

PHARMACEUTICAL AGENTS	OTHER AGENTS
Chloramphenicol	Acrylamide (truncal ataxia)
Dapsone*	Arsenic (sensory, brown skin, Mees' lines)
Dichloroacetate	
Disulfiram	Carbon disulfide
Ethionamide	Cyanide
Hydralazine	Dichlorophenoxyacetic acid
Isoniazid†	Biologic toxin in diphtheritic neuropathy
Lithium	
Metronidazole-misonidazole	Ethylene oxide
Nitrofurantoin*	n-Hexane
Nitrous oxide	Lead (wrist drop, abdominal colic)
Nucleosides (ddC, ddI)	Methyl bromide
Platinum (*cis*-platinum)†	Organophosphates (cholinergic symptoms, delayed onset of neuropathy)
Pyridoxine†	
Sodium cyanate	
Suramin	Thallium (pain, alopecia, Mees' lines)
Taxol	Trichloroethylene (facial numbness)
Vincristine	

* Predominantly motor.
† Predominantly sensory.
Modified from Schaumburg HH: Toxic neuropathies. *In* Wyngaarden JB, Smith LH Jr, Bennett JC (eds): Cecil Textbook of Medicine. 19th ed. Philadelphia, WB Saunders Co, 1992, pp 2246–2247.

neuron degeneration is unknown. Autoimmune disorders and/or viral infections are suspected. Paraproteins and antiganglioside antibodies are found in the serum of some patients. IgG has been found at autopsy in the motor neurons of a few others.

The typical patient with ALS develops progressive weakness distally more than proximally, especially affecting the small muscles of the hand. Early atrophy and fasciculations are prominent. Some patients may have muscle cramps, but sensory symptoms are rare. The deep tendon reflexes are usually preserved in the early phase of the disease, at least in the upper extremities. Signs of upper motor neuron involvement may develop at any time but almost always appear by the time muscle involvement has lasted a year. Characteristically bladder and bowel functions remain unaffected. ALS spares the extraocular muscles but in the late stages can interfere with supranuclear oculomotor control. Some patients show signs of emotional lability. Intellectual functions deteriorate in approximately 5 per cent. The CSF is normal. Electrodiagnostic testing is help-

TABLE 115–16. HEREDITARY NEUROPATHIES

Lipid Disorders
 Metachromatic leukodystrophy (sulfatide metabolism)
 Bassen-Kornzweig (beta-lipoprotein deficiencies)
 Refsum's disease (phytanic acid metabolism)
Others
 Hereditary sensorimotor neuropathy types I and II (Charcot-Marie-Tooth)
 Hereditary sensorimotor neuropathy type III (Déjérine-Sottas)
 Familial amyloid polyneuropathies

TABLE 115–17. MOTOR NEURON DISEASES

Motor Neuron Disease (Amyotrophic Lateral Sclerosis) includes:
Progressive muscular atrophy
Progressive bulbar palsy
Amyotrophic lateral sclerosis
   Sporadic forms
   Familial forms
   Western Pacific (Guam and Japan)
Spinal Muscular Atrophies
   Werdnig-Hoffmann disease
   Wohlfart-Kugelberg-Welander disease
   Facioscapulohumeral form
Motor Neuron Disease Associated with Other Disease of the Central Nervous System
   Mental disorder
   Extrapyramidal disorders
   Spinal disease including the hereditary spinocerebellar ataxias
Miscellaneous Diseases
   Viral poliomyelitides
   Metabolic, including hypoglycemia
   Toxicity—heavy metals, organophosphorus compounds
   Ischemic myelopathy, including radiation damage
   Trauma, including electrical injury
   Paraneoplastic

ful (see Chapter 111). The motor nerve conduction velocities remain normal even in the presence of severe atrophy, a finding that separates this disorder from the peripheral motor neuropathies, in which conduction velocities are reduced.

In its classic form, ALS, with painless weakness and atrophy of the hands, fasciculations in the en-

TABLE 115–18. DIFFERENTIAL DIAGNOSIS OF AMYOTROPHIC LATERAL SCLEROSIS (ALS)

DISEASE	DISTINGUISHING FEATURES
Benign fasciculations	No weakness, atrophy, or EMG abnormality
Motor neuron diseases	
*Lead or mercury toxicity	Increased lead or mercury levels
Benign focal amyotrophy	Onset in youth, strictly focal, no upper motor neuron signs
Postpolio progressive muscular atrophy	Slow course, no upper motor neuron signs
Subacute motor neuronopathy in lymphoma	Plateau in few months, later improvement
*ALS in lung cancer or B cell dyscrasia	Improves on treatment of tumor
Hereditary spinal muscular atrophy	Symmetric, slow course, no upper motor neuron signs
*Thyrotoxic myopathy with fasciculations	Myopathic EMG
*Compressive myelopathy due to cervical spondylosis or extramedullary tumor	Sensory symptoms, no lower motor neuron signs in legs, cord compression on MR or myelography
*Immune-mediated multifocal motor neuropathy	Multifocal nerve conduction block, very high antiganglioside antibody titers

* Treatable conditions.
From Layzer RB: Hereditary and acquired intrinsic motor neuron diseases. In Wyngaarden JB, Smith LH Jr, Bennett JC (eds): Cecil Textbook of Medicine. 19th ed. Philadelphia, WB Saunders Co, 1992, p 2142.

tire upper extremities, and spasticity and reflex hyperactivity of the legs with extensor plantar responses, seldom is mistaken for a cervical spinal cord tumor or other myelopathy. Less completely developed stages of the illness, however, sometimes are more difficult to differentiate on clinical grounds alone (Table 115–18).

Progressive bulbar palsy must be distinguished from myasthenia gravis and myopathies, in particular polymyositis. Upper motor neuron signs such as a hyperactive jaw jerk and emotional lability and spastic speech establish the presence of motor neuron disease. Marked atrophy and fasciculations of the tongue likewise establish that diagnosis. If these findings are absent, an edrophonium test (see p. 816) and EMG of bulbar muscles may be necessary to make the distinction. Early in its course, if motor neuron disease affects only a few contiguous muscles, it must be distinguished from nerve root plexus disease or intramedullary neoplasms or syrinxes. Along with the absence of sensory changes, the finding of widespread electromyographic abnormalities, when clinical abnormalities are localized, usually establishes the diagnosis of motor neuron disease.

Childhood Motor Neuron Diseases

Werdnig-Hoffmann disease produces progressive destruction of spinal anterior motor neurons in infancy and early childhood. The disease is transmitted as an autosomal recessive trait. The lower motor neuron involvement leads to paralysis of muscles innervated by motor cranial nuclei and the anterior horn cells of the spinal cord. Infants and young children may present with this syndrome at birth or in the first few months of life with diffuse flaccidity, muscular atrophy, muscle fasciculations, and reduced to absent myotatic reflexes with associated respiratory and swallowing difficulties. There is no effective treatment.

Wohlfart-Kugelberg-Welander disease is a form of progressive muscular atrophy that begins during late childhood, adolescence, or early adulthood with symptoms that include *proximal* muscle atrophy, weakness, and fasciculations. It progresses slowly and is usually compatible with a lifespan into the third or fourth decade. Typical examples have been described in families in which other children have Werdnig-Hoffmann disease. Thus, varying penetrance of a single genetic mutation inherited in an autosomal recessive manner may produce either an aggressive form of early childhood motor neuron disease (Werdnig-Hoffmann disease) or a more benign form of motor neuron disease in later childhood and early adulthood (Wohlfart-Kugelberg-Welander disease). The onset in the first and second decade of life of proximal weakness and atrophy with fasciculations but a very slow progression without evidence of upper motor neuron involvement distinguishes the disorder from ALS. If fasciculations are not prominent, EMG findings (denervation with the insertional irritability of polymyositis) and the results of muscle biopsy distinguish the neurogenic disease from acquired or inherited myopathies. The cause of the disorder is unknown. Specific therapy is not available.

Other Anterior Horn Cell Diseases

Monomyelic (benign focal) amyotrophy is an uncommon disorder in which lower motor neurons supplying one extremity (usually an arm) are affected. The disease usually begins in the second or third decade and progresses over a period of 2 to 4 years and then stops. The patient is left with a variable degree of weakness in the involved extremity, but the disease does not generalize and is usually not disabling. *Poliomyelitis* is an acute, viral inflammatory disease affecting anterior horn cells that was a major cause of paralysis in the United States before the development of an effective polio vaccine. A similar but much less severe weakness can occasionally be caused by other neurotropic viruses. The *post-polio syndrome* is characterized by muscle weakness developing years after recovery from acute paralytic poliomyelitis. The disorder appears to be a "wear and tear" problem, resulting in increasing dysfunction of overburdened surviving motor neurons, causing a slow but not life-threatening disintegration of the terminals of individual nerve axons.

REFERENCES

Dawson DM, Hallet M, Millender LH (eds): Entrapment Neuropathies. 2nd ed. Boston, Little, Brown and Co, 1990.

DeJong JMBV (co-ed): Hereditary neuropathies and spinocerebellar atrophies. In Vinken PJ, Bruyn GW, Klawans HL (eds): Handbook of Clinical Neurology. New York, Elsevier, 1991.

Dyck PJ, Thomas PK, Lambert EH, Bunger R (eds): Peripheral Neuropathy. 3rd ed. Philadelphia, WB Saunders Co, 1991.

Schaumburg HH, Berger AR, Thomas PK (eds): Disorders of Peripheral Nerves. 2nd ed. Philadelphia, FA Davis Co, 1992.

F. Disorders of Myoneural Junction

Three kinds of abnormalities can cause myoneural junction dysfunction or disease:

1. Impaired postjunction receptor mechanisms cause myasthenia gravis.
2. Deficiency of acetylcholine release characterizes the Lambert-Eaton myasthenic syndrome as well as the toxicity of botulism and the adverse effect of certain chemical poisons.
3. Depolarizing or nonpolarizing blockage of the action of acetylcholine at the muscle receptor mechanism can be caused by several drugs and poisons, the most notorious being curare.

Neuromuscular junction disorders are characterized by weakness and often by fatigability of muscle, so that repetitive use of the muscle often leads to increased weakness. In some, but not all, of the diseases, cranial and respiratory muscles are peculiarly susceptible. Drugs may cause or exacerbate pre-existing neuromuscular junction disorders. They are particularly likely to cause postoperative respiratory depression. The major disorders are listed in Table 115–19.

MYASTHENIA GRAVIS

Myasthenia gravis is an autoimmune disease caused by circulating antibodies that damage acetylcholine receptors lying within the postsynaptic muscle membrane. The disorder may occur in isolation or be associated with other autoimmune disorders, such as systemic lupus erythematosus and hyperthyroidism. The disorder is usually associated with an abnormality of the thymus gland, either hyperplasia (65 per cent) or a thymoma (10 to 15 per cent).

It is accompanied by accumulation of lymphocytes in muscle and other organs, an increased frequency of nonspecific antibodies against nuclear antigens, and the presence of antithyroid antibodies. That a circulating substance plays a major role in production of the weakness is proved by two facts: (1) Transplacental passage of a substance occurs, so that infants born to myasthenic women suffer transient myasthenia-type bulbar weakness. Symptoms subside as the antibody supplied to the infant by the mother disappears, usually within a week to a

TABLE 115–19. DISORDERS OF NEUROMUSCULAR TRANSMISSION

Autoimmune
  Myasthenia gravis
  Lambert-Eaton myasthenic syndrome
Toxic
  Botulism
  Tick paralysis
  Drug-induced
  Pesticide poisoning
Congenital
  Familial infantile myasthenia*
  End-plate acetycholinesterase deficiency*
  Slow-channel syndrome†
  End-plate AChR deficiency*
  High-conductance fast-channel syndrome*
  Paucity of synaptic vesicles and reduced quantal release‡
  Putative abnormality of ACh-AChR interaction‡

* Autosomal recessive inheritance.
† Autosomal or X-linked recessive inheritance.
‡ Autosomal-recessive inheritance suspected.
Modified from Engel AG: Disorders of Neuromuscular transmission. In Wyngaarden JB, Smith LH Jr, Bennett JC (eds): Cecil Textbook of Medicine. 19th ed. Philadelphia, WB Saunders Co, 1992, p 2265.

month. (2) Plasmapheresis relieves symptoms in patients with the disease.

Myasthenia gravis may begin at any time in life, including in the newborn, but there are two major peaks of onset, one in young adulthood, when the incidence is about three times more common in women than men, and another in older persons, with men and women about equally affected. There are occasional familial cases, but most are sporadic.

Clinically, the disease is characterized by weakness and fatigability. Weakness usually begins in the extraocular muscles, with ptosis and diplopia. The symptoms may be localized to the ocular muscles or generalized, mild or severe (Table 115–20). Symptoms tend to become more prominent toward the end of the day, following fatiguing activity, or with continuous use of extraocular muscles, such as in driving or reading. Closing the eyes or relaxing the muscles for a few minutes makes the symptoms disappear. Other bulbar muscles may also be affected, with difficulty in swallowing, chewing, or speaking, becoming more noticeable after sustained activity of the involved muscles or when the patient is otherwise fatigued. If limb muscles are involved, weakness is more often proximal than distal. Respiratory weakness alone or in combination with swallowing paralysis is the most feared complication of myasthenia gravis. Because all symptoms of the disorder may be exacerbated by fatigue or infection, a patient who is otherwise not severely affected may suddenly develop acute breathing failure during a respiratory infection.

The diagnosis is suggested by the history and can usually be confirmed on physical examination, by observing weakness that develops in extraocular or other muscles as repetitive activity continues. The physician asks the patient to look fixedly at an object on the ceiling. After 30 or 40 seconds, the lids begin to droop and the eyes may diverge. Similarly, repetitive contraction of arm muscles may cause weakness of those muscles or may cause ptosis. In a symptomatic patient, an intravenous injection of *edrophonium chloride* (Tensilon), an anticholinesterase agent, leads to rapid amelioration of clinical symptoms and improved or normal muscle function for a few minutes, until the effects of the drug wear off. When positive, in a fully symptomatic patient, the results are so dramatic that they establish the diagnosis. False-positive results can occur with increased muscular effort by the patient during the test and can sometimes be identified by a similar positive response to a placebo. Occasionally, when the muscles are very weak, they may be refractory to edrophonium, giving rise to false-negative results. Additional confirmatory evidence is provided by EMG response to nerve stimulation. With repetitive stimulation of the nerve, there is a rapid decline in the muscle action potential, the electrical counterpart of muscle fatigability. More recently, single fiber EMG, which measures the interval between discharges of different fibers within the same motor unit, has been found to show excessive variation called jitter in patients with myasthenia gravis. Eighty to 90 per cent of patients with myasthenia gravis harbor antibodies against the acetylcholine receptor. Such antibodies can be identified in at least half the patients with ocular myasthenia and in more than 80 per cent of patients with generalized myasthenia. Virtually no false-positive tests becloud the diagnosis although patients in remission from myasthenia may continue to have elevated levels of antibodies.

In a typical patient the diagnosis is not difficult to make once considered. However, the disorder must be distinguished from neurasthenia, a subjective feeling of weakness and fatigability caused by psychological disorders, as well as from other myopathies and neuropathies. Careful attention to the effects of pharmacologic agents and studies of the electrical activity of muscle almost always establishes the diagnosis.

The treatment of myasthenia has three components: (1) One can increase the effectiveness of acetylcholine released at the myoneural junction by preventing its breakdown. The anticholinesterase drugs neostigmine and pyridostigmine rapidly ameliorate most myasthenic symptoms. Drugs are given in sufficient doses and with sufficient frequency to keep muscle function as close as possible to normal. An average dose of pyridostigmine is 60 to 120 mg every 4 to 5 hours. Dosage is begun low and gradually adjusted upward to achieve maximal function. Unfortunately, excessive treatment itself can cause weakness because cholinesterase inhibitors may produce a depolarizing block at the neuromuscular junction. In addition, the augmented release of acetylcholine may cause distressing abdominal cramping. Because the autonomic acetylcholine receptors are muscarinic, they can be blocked by atropine-like agents (e.g., atropine, 0.4 to 0.6 mg orally bid or tid) without affecting the nicotinic neuromuscular receptors. (2) One can remove the circulating antibody that produces the symptoms. Plasmapheresis has proved to be a safe, beneficial, but short-lasting treatment for most patients with myasthenia. Patients who are severely weak may improve within minutes of completion of plasmapheresis and may be free of symptoms for days to weeks. In some patients who are refractory to other treatments, plasmapheresis given once a week to once every 2 weeks allows the patient to maintain relatively normal function. (3) One can suppress production of the antibody. That the thymus gland has a causal role in myasthenia gravis has been known for a long time.

TABLE 115–20. CLASSIFICATION OF MYASTHENIA GRAVIS

I. Ocular myasthenia
IIA. Mild generalized myasthenia with slow progression; no crisis; drug-responsive
IIB. Moderate generalized myasthenia; severe skeletal and bulbar involvement, but no crisis; drug response less satisfactory
III. Acute fulminating myasthenia; rapid progression of severe symptoms with respiratory crisis and poor drug response; high incidence of thymoma; high mortality
IV. Late severe myasthenia; same as III, but takes 2 years to progress from Classes I or II; crisis; high mortality

Thymectomy is a well-established treatment that improves about 85 per cent of patients. All patients with generalized myasthenia should be considered for thymectomy, although that option may not be chosen in severely ill elderly patients. Another method of suppressing production of the antibody is to use immunosuppressive drugs, either corticosteroids or azathioprine. Corticosteroids in high doses often produce an exacerbation of myasthenia symptoms, rarely even culminating in respiratory paralysis. The risk of exacerbation is minimized by starting the drug slowly and, in any event, after a few days or a week patients begin to improve. Many patients with myasthenia can be well-controlled on doses (20 to 50 mg) of prednisone every other day. Steroids, in addition to their effect in suppressing acetylcholine receptor antibody concentration, also have direct effects on neuromuscular transmission. Azathioprine is the other drug currently used to suppress antibody formation. Most investigators believe that doses of 150 to 200 mg/day can be helpful in the treatment of myasthenia.

Patients with myasthenia are prone to develop sudden worsening of symptoms, particularly associated with respiratory infections. These patients are best treated in intensive care units with respiratory support and without the use of anticholinesterase drugs. Plasmapheresis may be useful in hastening resolution of such *myasthenic crises.*

THE LAMBERT-EATON MYASTHENIC SYNDROME

The *Lambert-Eaton or myasthenic syndrome* is an uncommon autoimmune disorder of neuromuscular transmission that in many respects is the electrical opposite of myasthenia gravis. Repetitive stimulation of the nerve leads to a facilitation of the muscle action potential rather than a diminution. In about two thirds of instances, the myasthenic syndrome is a paraneoplastic phenomenon associated with small cell lung cancer; in the remaining one third the disorder occurs without an underlying illness. Patients complain of proximal weakness of limb muscles, particularly in the lower extremities, and increased fatigability. They also complain of paresthesias in the thighs, a dry mouth and, in men, impotence. Examination reveals proximal weakness, but strength may increase as the patient attempts to sustain the contraction (the clinical counterpart of the electrical facilitation) and hypoactive or absent deep tendon reflexes, particularly at the knees and ankles. Mild ptosis is common, but other cranial nerve abnormalities are not. The diagnosis is confirmed by the electrical response. The presence of the Lambert-Eaton syndrome should prompt a careful search for lung cancer because the neuromuscular symptoms may precede other evidence of the cancer by months to years. The disorder results from impaired release of acetylcholine when autoantibodies react with voltage-dependent calcium channels to block these functions. As in myasthenia gravis, plasmapheresis often relieves the symptoms.

OTHER JUNCTIONAL DISORDERS

The *slow channel syndrome* is an autosomal dominant disorder caused by slow closure of the acetylcholine receptor ion channel. It may present in adult life with weakness, fatigability, and atrophy of cervical, shoulder girdle, and forearm muscles. Other muscles, including those innervated by cranial nerves, may be involved as well. The EMG declines as in myasthenia gravis; the disorder responds poorly to anticholinesterases.

Botulism is caused by the exotoxin of *Clostridium botulinum* and occurs following the ingestion of contaminated, improperly canned food. The toxin interferes with adequate release of acetylcholine at the neuromuscular junction. Symptoms usually begin within a few days of ingestion with blurring of vision, diplopia, and difficulty in swallowing and chewing. Gastrointestinal symptoms may precede the neurologic symptoms, and the weakness spreads rapidly to cause paralysis of cranial and respiratory muscles and lesser paralysis of arms and legs. Autonomic fibers, particularly the pupilloconstrictor fibers, are affected early in the disorder, and there is loss of visual accommodation. If electrical neuromuscular transmission studies are performed early, the findings may resemble the myasthenic syndrome. The disease may produce death from respiratory paralysis unless artificial respiration is started promptly. The history, its explosive onset and progression, and its normal spinal fluid protein distinguish botulism from the ophthalmoplegic form of the Guillain-Barré syndrome, which it can resemble closely. If the patient's physiologic functions, particularly respiration, are supported, full recovery usually occurs.

Tick paralysis is a disorder caused by a tick neurotoxin that blocks transmission at the neuromuscular junction. Most cases of tick paralysis occur in children, particularly girls, in whom the tick embeds in the skin near the hairline and goes unnoticed. After 5 or 6 days of embedding, paresthesias and progressive weakness develop, which may progress to flaccid paralysis of cranial and respiratory muscles and the extremities, resembling botulism or the Guillain-Barré syndrome. CSF protein is normal and the paralysis subsides promptly following removal of the embedded tick.

Aminoglycoside antibiotics rarely interfere with neuromuscular transmission. The most common manifestation is postoperative apnea without other evidence of paralysis, particularly in patients who have renal failure, leading to high antimicrobial drug levels. Some patients may have a flaccid quadriplegia that responds to administration of calcium and quinidine. Other drugs that can cause or exacerbate myasthenic syndromes include tetracycline, antiarrhythmic agents (procainamide, quinidine), β-adrenergic blockers (propranolol, timolol), phenothiazines, lithium, trimethaphan, methoxyflurane, and magnesium given parenterally or in cathartics.

Pesticides containing long-acting anticholinesterases cause weakness from acetylcholine receptor desensitization and may also cause delirium. Atropine and pralidoxime reverse the symptoms.

Several rare congenital or hereditary disorders of function of the neuromuscular junction can cause weakness in infants and newborns.

REFERENCE

Engel AG, Banker B (eds): Myology. New York, McGraw-Hill Book Co, 1986.

G. Disorders of Skeletal Muscle

Muscle, the largest organ in the body, can be directly affected by several diseases primary to the structure itself or by the secondary effects of a number of systemic diseases. Furthermore, because weakness is so easily recognized by the patient, the muscular dysfunction can lead to early consultation with the physician even when the primary disease is elsewhere. Most myopathies are characterized by muscle weakness (usually of proximal but sometimes distal muscles) and atrophy (sometimes pseudohypertrophy). Myopathies can usually be distinguished from neuropathies by clinical examination, serum enzyme measurement, and EMG (Table 115–21). To distinguish among the myopathies often requires a muscle biopsy, which may have to be studied biochemically and by electron microscopy. Recent genetic discoveries promise to allow genetic identification of carriers and prenatal diagnosis of most muscular dystrophies.

Table 115–22 classifies the myopathies. This text places its emphasis on disorders that are common or that have characteristic clinical findings.

MUSCULAR DYSTROPHIES

Muscular dystrophies (Table 115–23) are inherited myopathies characterized by progressive weakness, usually beginning early in life. The genetics are well established for most of the dystrophies. The gene product has been identified in Duchenne dystrophy.

Duchenne dystrophy is an X-linked recessive disorder of boys (rarely girls) characterized by painless weakness that is maximal in the pelvic girdle and thighs, less prominent about the shoulders, and least prominent in the distal extremities. The abnormal gene positioned on band Xp21 fails to produce *dystrophin*, a 400-kDa protein whose absence allows calcium and complement components to enter and destroy muscle fibers. The disorder reveals itself with abnormal and increasing clumsiness when the child begins to walk (beyond 18 months). Affected boys run awkwardly and rise from the floor by placing hands on knees and using the hands to walk up the thighs (Gowers' sign). With time the calf muscles appear abnormally enlarged (pseudohypertrophy). Gradually the weakness becomes more severe, and adolescents are usually wheelchair-bound. Death occurs in early adulthood, usually from pneumonia. The diagnosis can be made early in life before symptoms appear by an elevated serum creatine kinase. The mutation rate is high, and in about two thirds of individuals, no other family member is affected. Efforts are under way to transplant dystrophin-producing fibroblasts into affected muscles in patients with Duchenne dystrophy. Results thus far are inconclusive. The disorder must be distinguished from two similar dystrophies: *Becker's dystrophy* reflects the presence of an abnormality in dystrophin rather than its absence. The disease also is X-linked but has its onset later in childhood or adolescence and has a slower or more variable tempo (some patients functioning well into adult life). *Emery-Dreifuss dystrophy* also begins later and is more benign than Duchenne dystrophy; pseudohypertrophy is lacking

TABLE 115–21. CLINICAL CLUES DIFFERENTIATING MUSCLE FROM NERVE DISEASE

	MYOPATHY	NEUROPATHY-NEURONOPATHY
Distribution	Mainly proximal and symmetric	Distal if symmetric; nerve or root distributon if mono- or multifocal
Atrophy	Late and mild	Early and prominent
Onset	Usually gradual	Often rapid
Fasciculations	Absent	Sometimes present
Reflexes	Lost late	Lost early
Tenderness	Diffuse in myositis	Focal in nerve or root disease
Cramps	Rare	Common
Sensory loss	Absent	Often present
Muscle enzymes	Usually elevated	Usually not or slightly elevated

From Engel AG: General approach to muscle diseases. *In* Wyngaarden JB, Smith LH Jr, Bennett JC (eds): Cecil Textbook of Medicine. 19th ed. Philadelphia, WB Saunders Co, 1992, p 2252.

TABLE 115–22. MYOPATHIES

Muscular dystrophy (see Table 115–23)
Myotonias (see Table 115–24)
Inflammatory myopathies
   Infections (e.g., toxoplasmosis, trichinosis, viral)
   Immune processes: polymyositis dermatomyositis, inclusion body myositis, sarcoidosis, polymyalgia rheumatica, eosinophilic syndromes (see Ch. 82)
Endocrine myopathies (see Section IX)
   Hyperthyroidism and hypothyroidism
   Hyperparathyroidism
   Hyperadrenalism (glucocorticoids)
   Hyperpituitarism
Periodic paralysis (see Table 115–25)
Metabolic myopathies
   Glycogen storage diseases
   Lipid storage diseases
   Mitochondrial diseases
Congenital muscle disorders
Drugs and toxins

and serum enzymes are normal or only slightly increased. This form is also characterized by cardiac arrhythmias that can lead to sudden death.

Limb-girdle dystrophies are a group of disorders affecting muscles of the pelvic and shoulder girdle, usually beginning late in childhood or adolescence, affecting girls as often as boys, and progressing at extremely variable rates. Pseudohypertrophy is not common. Muscle biopsy and EMG may be necessary to distinguish this disorder from a similar-appearing, also proximal neurogenic disorder—the Wohlfart-Kugelberg-Welander syndrome.

Facioscapulohumeral dystrophy is characterized by prominent weakness in the perioral muscles of the face and eventually weakness of eye closure. Latissimus dorsi degeneration leads to scapular winging, and the sternal head of the pectoral muscle is affected more than the clavicular. The shoulder and pelvic girdle muscles are affected as well. Weakness of the trunk muscles may cause severe scoliosis. The disorder is transmitted as an autosomal dominant trait with variable but usually extremely slow progression.

Ocular muscular dystrophy is a slowly progressive disorder characterized by ptosis and progressive external ocular paralysis. The pupils are spared, and both eyes are usually affected symmetrically, so that diplopia is not common. Other muscles of the head, neck, and limbs may be affected, but this varies from family to family. Because each oculomotor nerve fiber supplies only a few muscle fibers, it is exceedingly difficult to distinguish neuropathies from myopathies by either EMG or histologic examination of the eye muscles. As a result, the clinical distinction between ocular myopathies and neuropathies rests on findings in other skeletal muscles. In some disorders producing ocular myopathy, the skeletal muscles of the neck or limbs contain abnormally large mitochondria in increased numbers, producing a characteristic "ragged red fiber" appearance on trichrome stains.

Distal myopathy, unlike most muscular dystrophies, affects distal leg and hand muscles first. It is rare and can be identified only by characteristic signs of myopathy on EMG and muscle biopsy. *Scapuloperoneal dystrophy*, with its distal weakness in the legs, resembles neurogenic peroneal atrophy, but there is no sensory loss and proximal weakness often affects the shoulder girdle. The disorder is transmitted as an autosomal dominant trait with relatively slow progression.

Treatment

There is no treatment for any of the inherited muscular dystrophies. Physical therapy along with splints and braces may keep many patients walking who would otherwise be confined to a wheelchair. Corticosteroids have been reported to slow the progression of Duchenne dystrophy.

OTHER INHERITED MYOPATHIES

Several rare congenital or inherited biochemical defects cause muscle weakness, which is usually life-

TABLE 115–23. MUSCULAR DYSTROPHIES

X-linked Recessive Dystrophies
  Duchenne dystrophy
  Becker dystrophy
  Emery-Dreifuss dystrophy with joint contractures and atrial paralysis
Autosomal Recessive Dystrophies
  Autosomal recessive childhood (limb-girdle) muscular dystrophy
  Scapulohumeral (limb-girdle) muscular dystrophy
  Autosomal-recessive distal muscular dystrophies
  Congenital muscular dystrophies
Autosomal Dominant Dystrophies
  Facioscapulohumeral dystrophy
  Autosomal dominant scapuloperoneal dystrophy
  Dominantly inherited adult-onset limb-girdle dystrophy
  Oculopharyngeal dystrophy
  Autosomal dominant distal dystrophy

Modified from Engel AG: Muscular dystrophies. *In* Wyngaarden JB, Smith LH Jr, Bennett JC (eds): Cecil Textbook of Medicine. 19th ed. Philadelphia, WB Saunders Co, 1992, p 2253.

long. Among these are congenital myopathies, glycogen storage diseases, lipid storage diseases, and mitochondrial myopathies.

Congenital myopathies are a group of disorders characterized by mild weakness that generally persists unchanged throughout life. The cause is not known: a few are familial and many are sporadic. The disorders are present at birth, and their chief importance lies in distinguishing them from the more severe progressive muscular dystrophies and neonatal anterior horn cell disorders. A number of glycogen storage diseases cause muscle symptoms. *McArdle's disease*, type 5 glycogen storage disease, results from an absence of muscle phosphorylase, so that patients are unable to break down glycogen during anaerobic exercise. They are usually asymptomatic until early adolescence or early adulthood, when they develop painful muscle cramps (actually contractures) after exercise. Myoglobinuria and renal failure may ensue, and patients may eventually become weak. A similar deficit results from phosphofructokinase deficiency. The diagnosis of both is established by the failure of venous lactate to rise during ischemic exercise. Biochemical study of biopsied muscle defines the exact enzyme deficiency. *Lipid storage* and *mitochondrial myopathies* usually become symptomatic in childhood and can be responsible for neurologic symptoms in addition to muscle weakness. The references provide sources that discuss these conditions more extensively.

MYOTONIAS

Table 115–24 classifies muscle diseases associated with myotonia. Myotonia results from an abnormality of the muscle membrane leading to delayed relaxation. The diagnosis is easily made clinically by asking a patient to grip one's fingers and then quickly let go. There is also a characteristic EMG displaying repetitive action potentials that may wax or wane over many seconds when the needle is in-

TABLE 115-24. MYOTONIAS

Myotonic muscular dystrophy
Myotonia congenita
    Autosomal dominant
    Autosomal recessive
Paramyotonia congenita
Hyperkalemic periodic paralysis
Chondrodystrophic myotonia
Acquired myotonia

serted or after the patient attempts to relax from a voluntary contraction. The most common myotonic abnormality is *myotonic dystrophy,* occurring once in 7500 births, an autosomal dominant disorder characterized by progressive, primarily distal muscle weakness, myotonia, cranial muscle weakness, and endocrine abnormalities. The gene lies on chromosome 19 with linkage to the gene encoding complement C3. The disorder may begin early in life or be delayed into adulthood. Affected persons have facial weakness with ptosis, difficulty puckering the lips, and dysarthria. In addition, wasting involves the temporalis and masseter muscles, which, when combined with the ptosis, gives the face a characteristic appearance. Selective weakness and wasting affect the sternocleidomastoid muscles, giving the neck a long and thin appearance (swan neck).

Extremity muscles are affected distally. The myotonia occurs primarily in the hands and usually is the first symptom. It becomes less severe as weakness develops and may not be easy to identify clinically in the late stages. In addition to the muscle symptoms, almost all patients eventually develop cataracts, and men experience early frontal baldness and testicular atrophy. Conduction defects in the heart may lead to cardiac arrhythmias, and cardiac myopathy may cause congestive heart failure. The disease runs a long course and does not generally cause disability until well into adulthood. The clinical and EMG features are characteristic. There is no effective treatment.

Myotonia congenita is rarer and occurs in both autosomal dominant and recessive forms. The disease begins early in life and is characterized by diffuse myotonia, which makes the patient stiff when he begins to exercise but loosens as activity continues. Affected persons move clumsily and have a stiff and wooden appearance. Cold generally makes their symptoms worse. The disorder is annoying more than disabling. Drugs such as phenytoin and quinine, which affect neuromuscular transmission, may relieve the symptoms.

Paramyotonia congenita is a rare disorder of autosomal dominant inheritance that differs clinically only slightly from myotonia congenita but relates to the periodic paralyses, with a genetic defect at the skeletal muscle sodium channel. Facial muscles and muscles of the forearm and hand are predominantly involved; the myotonia shows extreme sensitivity to cold, and indeed may be present only when the patient is exposed to cold. Similar myotonias sometimes occur in hyperkalemic paralysis, and paramyotonia may simply be a manifestation of the more common periodic paralysis. In addition to the congenital disorders, myotonia can be acquired after exposure to a number of toxins, including cholesterol antagonists and the herbicide 2,4-D.

DRUG, NUTRITIONAL, AND TOXIC MYOPATHIES

With the exception of corticosteroids, drug-induced myopathy is rare. *Steroid myopathy* complicates the course of almost every patient treated for more than a few weeks with pharmacologic doses of corticosteroids and can even occur after a long period of doses that are considered close to replacement. Patients receiving every-other-day steroid therapy seem to have less myopathy. Muscle enzymes and EMG are usually normal. Other drugs that can cause myopathy include vincristine, chloroquine, bretylium, emetine, ipecac, carbenoxolone, guanethidine, epsilon-aminocaproic acid, penicillamine, colchicine, amiodarone, lovastatin, isoretinoic acid, cocaine, zidovudine, and clofibrate. Thiazide diuretics, the repeated use of laxatives, or the ingestion of other drugs that cause potassium loss may lead to chronic hypokalemia and a proximal myopathy that may be acute at onset, with elevated serum enzymes and even necrosis on muscle biopsy. For severe weakness to occur, the serum potassium concentration must fall below 2 mEq/L.

Nutritional deprivation of vitamin E or selenium ingestion causes a myopathy in animals, but these are not clinical problems in humans. However, chronic alcoholism can lead to severe proximal muscle weakness.

PERIODIC PARALYSES

Periodic paralyses are disorders characterized by recurrent attacks of flaccid weakness, often associated with an abnormally high or low serum potassium concentration, although rarely is the potassium level sufficiently abnormal to produce weakness in an otherwise normal individual (Table 115–25). Many of the cases are familial, usually inherited in a pattern consistent with an autosomal dominant trait. The specific defect relates to a genetic error on chromosome 17 that affects the skeletal muscle sodium channel. Periodic paralysis has two major forms: hypokalemic and hyperkalemic. The former is characterized by sudden attacks of flaccid weakness, usually beginning in late childhood or adolescence and frequently occurring at night after a large carbohydrate meal. The attacks may totally paralyze the extremities and trunk, sparing the respiratory, bulbar, and cranial muscles, and may last a day or more before spontaneously resolving. During the course of the attack, the serum potassium is usually low (e.g., 2.5 to 3 mEq/L), and the patient may respond to oral or intravenous potassium. Repeated attacks can lead to permanent weakness. Muscle biopsy shows vacuoles within muscle fibers. The hyperkalemic variety generally begins in early childhood with attacks that occur more frequently than the hypokalemic variety, are usually milder, and generally last only minutes to hours rather than days. Typically, the hyperkalemic attack begins while the patient is resting after vigorous exercise. Hyperkalemic attacks may begin with paresthesias in the extremities, but no sensory changes are found on examination. Lid lag and Chvostek's sign may be present along with prominent myalgias. During attacks, the serum potassium usually rises to between 5 and 7 mEq/L, and some patients develop myotonia, often limited to percussion myotonia of the tongue. Although the serum potassium levels and the clinical symptoms separate typical examples of the hypo- and hyperkalemic disorders, the conditions overlap, and many patients suffer periodic paralyses without alteration of the serum potassium.

The diagnosis of periodic paralysis is made by the typical history and confirmed by finding an abnormal serum potassium level during an acute attack. If an acute attack is not observed, one may be precipitated (in the hypokalemic form by glucose and insulin or in the hyperkalemic form by potassium), but this should be done only in a hospital setting where one is prepared to deal with complications. Thyroid function should be assessed in all patients suffering hypokalemic periodic paralysis; diuretic ingestion should be suspected if the serum potassium is below 2.5 mEq/L.

MYOGLOBINURIA

Myoglobinuria results when major injuries to muscles lead to *rhabdomyolysis* and release of myoglobin into the serum and urine, giving the urine a brown-rust color. Myoglobinuria either can occur as a hereditary disease or can complicate a variety of sporadic muscle injuries. Crush injury, such as occurs in accidents, is a common cause, as is pressure injury to muscles, resulting from a patient's lying immobile after poisoning from sedatives or carbon monoxide. Prolonged unconsciousness in the snow likewise can lead to myoglobinuria, as can arterial occlusion by tourniquet or embolism. Snake bites and binge alcohol ingestion also can cause myoglobinuria, as can malignant hyperthermia. Even normal people may develop some degree of myoglobinuria after vigorous exercise. Strenuous exercise among army recruits, during ritual hazing,

TABLE 115-25. PERIODIC PARALYSIS

Primary
  Hypokalemic
  Hyperkalemic (including those with cardiac arrhythmias)
  Normokalemic
Secondary
  Hypokalemic
    Thyrotoxic
    Potassium-losing states
      Urinary potassium wastage
        Hyperaldosteronism
        Licorice intoxication
        Various renal diseases
        Thiazide diuretics
    Gastrointestinal potassium wastage
  Hyperkalemic
    Renal failure
    Adrenal failure
    Drug-induced: triamterene, spironolactone
    Self-induced: geophagia
    Iatrogenic: potassium supplements

or in marathon runners leads to myoglobinuria in a small percentage of individuals. In addition to the discoloration of the urine, the clinical syndrome is characterized by muscle aches and swelling as well as some weakness. Symptoms may persist for several days, even though the pigment in the urine rarely lasts more than 4 hours. The muscles most affected are those most vigorously exercised or crushed, but cranial musculature and respiratory muscles are almost never affected. The major potential problem is kidney injury due to myoglobin plugging the renal tubules. The disorder should be considered as a possible cause of acute renal failure of uncertain etiology. Myoglobin can be identified spectrophotometrically in the urine.

REFERENCES

Engel AG, Franzini-Armstrong, C (eds): Myology. 2nd ed. New York, McGraw-Hill Book Co, 1993.
Layzer RB: Neuromuscular Manifestations of Systemic Disease. Philadelphia, FA Davis Co, 1985.
Walton J (ed): Disorders of Voluntary Muscle. 5th ed. New York, Churchill-Livingstone, 1988.

116

CEREBROVASCULAR DISEASE

Cerebrovascular diseases include disorders of the arterial or venous circulatory systems or their contents that produce or threaten to produce injury to the central nervous system (CNS). The general term *stroke* describes the functional neurologic injury. The cause of stroke can be either *anoxic-ischemic,* the result of vasogenic failure to supply sufficient oxygen and substrate to the tissue, or *hemorrhagic,* the result of abnormal leakage of blood into or around CNS structures. *Arteriovenous malformations* of the brain or spinal cord can produce neuro-logic abnormalities by bleeding, producing ischemic damage, or acting as space-occupying lesions.

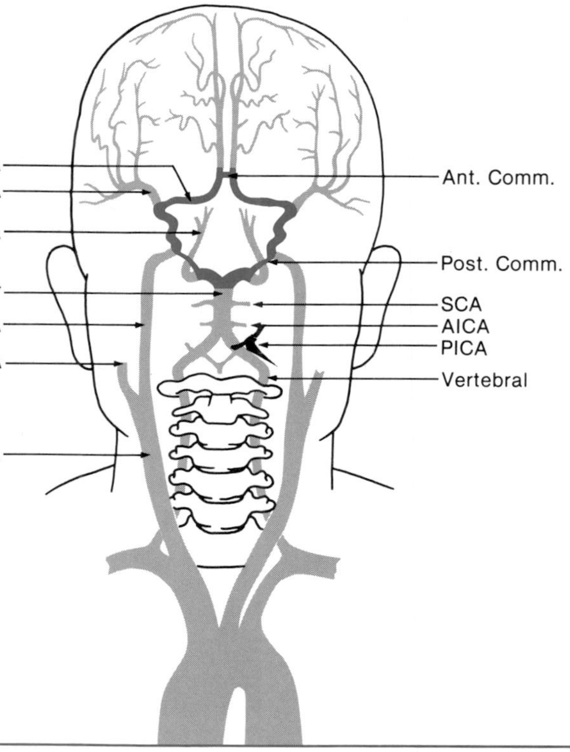

Anatomy and Pathophysiology of the Cerebral Circulation

Anatomy. The cerebral arterial circulation derives from four major extracerebral (neck) arteries, the paired internal carotids (ICA) and the vertebrals (VA) (Fig. 116–1). Acute, complete occlusion of these extracranial arteries can result at any age from atherosclerosis, embolization, inflammation, intrinsic arterial disease, or trauma. Age and the effectiveness of the intracranial arterial anastomotic pattern determine whether ischemic brain damage ensues.

Inside the skull the two VAs fuse to form the basilar artery (BA) at the pontine-medullary junction. The BA, in turn, divides at its apex into the two posterior cerebral arteries (PCA). The posterior inferior cerebellar artery (PICA) arises from the VA. The anterior inferior cerebellar (AICA) and superior cerebellar arteries (SCA) emerge from the BA. Together the VA, BA, and PCA and their tributaries sometimes are designated the brain's *posterior intracranial circulation,* supplying the entire brain stem, most of the diencephalon, and the posteromedial aspects of the cerebral hemispheres. Each ICA gives off an ophthalmic artery, which, in turn, gives off the retinal artery. Soon after it enters the skull, the ICA divides into an ipsilateral anterior (ACA) and middle cerebral artery (MCA) and posterior communicating artery. The ACAs supply the medial surfaces of the hemispheres as far back as the parietal lobe. The MCAs irrigate the hemispheres' lateral surfaces as well as the basal ganglia and the central core of hemispheric white matter of each side. The ICAs, together with their daughter ACAs, MCAs, and collective drainage vessels, often are grouped together as the *anterior intracranial circulation.*

The *circle of Willis* provides in most persons a potentially effective intracranial anastomotic pathway to compensate for sudden focal reductions in blood flow at the base of the brain. Congenital asymmetry of the vertebral arteries and narrowing or absence of its anterior or posterior communicating segments are relatively common findings that reduce the circle's anastomotic effectiveness. Beyond the circle, the major intracranial arterial beds anastomose over the surface of the brain through tiny interconnecting pial arterioles, most of which are too small to compensate for major arterial occlusions. Penetrat-

FIGURE 116–1. Coronal view of the extracranial and intracranial arterial supply to brain. Vessels forming the circle of Willis are highlighted. ACA = Anterior cerebral artery; MCA = middle cerebral artery; PCA = posterior cerebral artery; ICA = internal carotid artery; ECA = external carotid artery; CCA = common carotid artery; Ant. Comm. = anterior communicating artery; Post. Comm. = posterior communicating artery; SCA = superior cerebellar artery; AICA = anterior inferior cerebellar artery; PICA = posterior inferior cerebellar artery. (Modified from Lord R: Surgery of Occlusive Cerebrovascular Disease. St. Louis, CV Mosby Co, 1986; with permission.)

ing arteries, descending from the pial surface into the deep white matter or subcortical nuclei, enjoy little anastomotic protection.

Physiology. Cerebral arteries contain less muscle, no elastic tissue, and less adventitia than systemic arteries. The reduced musculature especially affects the junctions where major branches diverge from the large arteries at the base of the brain, creating vulnerable points from which most intracranial aneurysms arise.

The *blood-brain barrier* insulates the brain and its extracellular fluid, including the cerebrospinal fluid (CSF), from many of the body's blood-borne chemical perturbations, including circulating drugs, immunogenic antigens, and electrolyte changes. The anatomic barrier lies in the intracranial endothelium, where tight intercellular junctions weld the entire inner surface into a continuous membranous sheet. As a result, only nonpolar materials that either have a small molecular size, are lipid soluble, or are transported across the membrane by specific carrier systems or pumps penetrate the endothelium with any rapidity. Transient breaches of the barrier occur under a variety of circumstances but have little ill effect on brain function. Sustained, partial barrier alteration occurs in areas of cerebral neoplasms, inflammation, or necrosis and contributes to the formation of edema associated with such conditions. Severe damage to barrier transport mechanisms contributes to brain infarction during ischemia.

Autoregulation is the intrinsic functional capacity of the brain's resistance arterioles to adjust their degree of constriction according to the metabolic requirements of the tissue and the systemic blood pressure. Normally, the arterioles automatically and locally dilate in response to increases in local brain functional activity, and constrict as functional requirements decline. Similarly, they dilate as systemic blood pressure falls and intrinsically constrict as it rises. Although the two responses are independently regulated, they synergize to fulfill the brain's metabolic need. The normal limits of cerebral autoregulation to pressure extend between approximately 60 and 160 mm Hg of systemic mean pressure. Impaired autoregulation to pressure changes can contribute to brain injury in several circumstances, including brain trauma, acute mass lesions, and large strokes. At such times widespread abnormal vasodilatation allows the intracranial pressure (ICP) to rise, sometimes to levels that approach the arterial blood pressure. Impaired arterial autoregulation also can accompany severe hypertension (mean BP greater than 160 torr), in which case intense elevations of systemic blood pressure can produce vascular and brain tissue injury.

Epidemiology and Risk Factors

Stroke takes a worldwide toll, affecting especially persons 55 years and older. Although the incidence has declined somewhat in recent years, only heart disease and cancer exceed stroke as causes of death and disability in developed countries.

Table 116–1 lists the major immediate causes of stroke. In addition, a number of systemic conditions

TABLE 116–1. CAUSES OF ACUTE CEREBRAL ISCHEMIA

Mainly Focal
  Arterial disease, thrombotic or embolic
  Cardiac emboli
  Functional arterial spasm or constriction
    a. Migraine
    b. Subarachnoid hemorrhage
    c. Acute bacterial meningitis
  Intracranial venous sinus or venous thrombosis
Mainly Global
  Absolute or functional (ventricular fibrillation) asystole >8 sec in duration
  Severe decline in cardiac output
    Shock; bradycardia $<30–40$/min; cardiac tamponade; severe heart failure
  Three- or four-vessel stenosis of cervical arteries plus TIA
  Profound anemia, Hct usually <20
  Profound hypoxemia: $Pa_{O_2} <35–40$ mm Hg
  Carbon monoxide poisoning
  Prolonged status epilepticus
  Disseminated intravascular coagulation
  Fat embolization

and social habits predispose to the arterial and hematologic changes that cause stroke (Table 116–2). *Hypertension* adversely affects the heart and induces progressive narrowing of the cerebral arterioles; it creates the greatest risk factor. The increasingly successful treatment of hypertension and reduction in smoking habits deserve the greatest credit for the decline in stroke incidence. Population studies show an especially strong association among dietary salt intake, hypertension, and cerebral hemorrhage.

Alcoholic excess increases stroke risk, with several studies reporting an increase of severe strokes immediately following bouts of heavy intoxication. Modest alcohol ingestion on the order of one to two glasses of wine per day may actually reduce stroke risk. Combined progesterone/estrogen *oral contraceptives*, especially if combined with smoking, triple the risk of stroke among women of childbearing age.

ISCHEMIC STROKE

Etiology and Mechanisms

Focal ischemic stroke is caused by either embolic or thrombotic occlusion of a major artery in the neck or head. *Global ischemic stroke* results in total failure of blood supply, e.g., following cardiac arrest or, rarely, from severe impairments of the oxygen supply alone to the brain.

TABLE 116–2. MAJOR RISK FACTORS IN STROKE

Hypertension—systolic, diastolic, or both
Smoking
Atrial fibrillation
Myocardial infarction
Hyperlipidemia
Diabetes
Congestive heart failure
Acute alcohol abuse

Vascular Factors. These can be either primarily thrombotic or embolic, as listed in Table 116–3. In either case, the critical event is reduction of blood flow to the brain.

Hematogenous Factors. Table 116–3 lists the major causes. Except for anesthetic or industrial ac-

TABLE 116–3. VASCULAR AND HEMATOLOGIC FACTORS CONTRIBUTING TO STROKE

Mural Abnormalities
A. Extracranial-intracranial atherosclerosis
 1. Thrombotic narrowing or occlusion of cervical vessels
 2. Ulcerated aortocervical plaques generating platelet-fibrin or cholesterol emboli
 3. Thrombotic occlusion of intracranial vessels
B. Inflammatory-immunologic vascular occlusions
 1. Extracranial only — cranial arteritis
 2. Extracranial and intracranial
  a. Generalized polyarteritis
  b. Septic emboli (bacterial endocarditis)
 3. Intracranial only
  a. Bacterial or granulomatous arteritis
  b. Amphetamine — cocaine-like drugs
  c. Idiopathic
C. Invasion or compression of arterial or venous vascular walls by trauma, neoplasms, etc.

Embolic Disorders
A. Artery to artery: platelet or cholesterol emboli from aortocervical atherosclerotic plaques
B. Cardiogenic
 1. Mural (post myocardial infarction)
 2. Atrial
 3. Valvular
  a. Septic (endocarditis)
  b. Nonseptic (rheumatic, atherosclerotic, mitral prolapse, nonbacterial endocarditis)
 4. Neoplastic — arterial myxoma, etc.
C. Latent atrial septal defect with right to left emboli from deep vein thrombosis
D. Hematologic abnormalities
 1. Hematocrit >55
 2. WBC >500,000
 3. Thrombocytosis >600,000
 4. Platelet hyperaggregability
E. Hemoglobinopathies and autoimmunopathies
 1. Sickle cell disease
 2. Paraproteinemia
 3. Lupus anticoagulant
 4. Cardiolipin antibody

TABLE 116–4. FINDINGS SUGGESTING CARDIAC-EMBOLIC ORIGIN FOR FOCAL STROKE

Persons <45 yr with no evident systemic risk factors but mitral prolapse
Known heart disease: Rheumatic aortic or mitral valve; atrial fibrillation; recent anterior wall infarction; murmur plus unexplained fever (Subacult bacterial endocarditis [SBE]); chronic cardiomyopathy; mitral annular calcification
Multiple cerebral arteries involved
Emboli in other organs
Hemorrhagic infarct
Demonstrated internal carotid artery narrowing >70%
Changing cardiac murmurs: SBE or nonbacterial thrombotic endocarditis (NBTE)

cidents that result in severe reductions in inhaled oxygen, or carbon monoxide poisoning, which blocks oxyhemoglobin formation, uncomplicated hypoxemia and anemia are uncommon causes of ischemic stroke, inasmuch as arterial oxygen supplies must be reduced to about 40 per cent of normal before cerebral insufficiency develops; this level of anoxemia is likely to produce cardiac as well as cerebral difficulties. In the absence of severe hypotension, acute hemorrhage, or anatomic abnormalities in the cervicocranial circulation, isolated hemoglobin levels greater than 7 to 8 gm/dl or Pa_{O_2} values greater than 40 to 45 mm Hg seldom can be incriminated as primary causes of stroke. Indeed, because of blood flow adjustments, even lower hemoglobin values may cause no symptoms, even in chronically anemic persons.

Among the coagulopathies causing stroke, physiologic platelet aggregation deserves specific attention. Vascular changes producing partial or complete ischemia in the brain stimulate an immediate increase in platelet aggregation in the abnormal areas. Similarly, ulcerated arteriosclerotic plaques attract fibrin-platelet aggregations to their surface as part of the healing process. The ensuing detritus provides a potential source for the extension of a thrombosis or the formation of artery-to-artery emboli.

Blood Flow and Tissue Factors. The brain and spinal cord metabolize at the highest basal rate of any large organ, consuming approximately 20 per cent of the body's resting oxygen requirement. The brain contains practically no reserves of oxygen and only tiny stores of glucose, its normal substrate. As a result, any severe reduction of blood supply threatens the organ's vitality. In most instances, cerebral autoregulation and increased tissue oxygen extraction can support normal or nearly normal brain function despite blood flow reductions down to about 40 per cent of normal. Below this threshold only a small additional decline causes membrane failure and death of brain cells. Partial or complete vascular occlusion (focal ischemia) and profound hypotension (global ischemia) represent the most common causes of such catastrophes. Any significant degree of anemia, hypoxemia, or hypercoagulability accentuates the hazards.

How long severe anoxia or ischemia must last to cause irreversible brain damage is uncertain. Humans faint by about the eighth second of asystole, but much evidence suggests that some brain tissues can recover from severe partial ischemia lasting as long as an hour or more.

Heart and systemic vascular diseases are the most important associated factors causing clinical stroke (Table 116–4). Most focal stroke results from emboli lodging in the intracranial arteries, with about 40 per cent coming from the heart, and the remainder from artery-to-artery emboli, most of which are presumed to originate from the aortic arch or carotid-vertebral arteries. Cardiac arrhythmias account for most instances of syncope or global cerebral ischemia among older persons. Furthermore, the statistical risk of future myocardial infarction in stroke patients is as great as or greater than the risk of a repeated cerebral event. Mitral valve prolapse, which can cause valvular or subvalvular thrombi, is found six times more frequently than normal among persons below age 45 with acute stroke. Similarly, a greatly increased incidence of focal stroke is associated with atrial fibrillation of whatever cause. Anterior wall myocardial infarction (MI) produces a high incidence of left ventricular thrombi; if not treated prophylactically with anticoagulants, as many as 40 per cent of such patients suffer stroke during convalescence from the MI. Table 116–4 lists common causes and manifestations of acute embolic stroke.

Neuropathology of Ischemic Brain Damage. The process of *cerebral infarction* damages or destroys all tissue elements, including neurons, glial cells, and blood vessels. Within a matter of hours after onset, osmotic gradients drag water into the ischemic-necrotic tissue, increasing the mass by edema. Tissue factors including excitatory-inhibitory imbalance at vulnerable synapses, tissue lactic acidosis, and free radical formation in the lesion may extend the damage. Infarction characteristically follows prolonged anoxia-ischemia such as occurs with vascular occlusion and can be focal or multifocal in nature depending on the pattern of affected vessels. Large infarcts involve the vascular territory of the major intracranial arteries. Small infarcts, 5 to 8 mm or so in diameter, sometimes called *lacunes*, result from occlusion of arteriolar branches. Lacunes may arise anywhere in the brain but especially result from occlusion of the terminal branches supplied by the middle cerebral and basilar arteries.

Hemorrhagic infarcts are marked by scattered areas of escaped red cells in the ischemic tissue, occurring most often at the periphery of an infarcted area. The mechanism is thought to represent reperfusion of damaged arterial endothelium, allowing diapedetic bleeding to occur.

Selective neuronal necrosis is damage restricted to specifically located nerve cells, sparing glial and vascular elements. When caused by anoxia, the process especially affects selectively vulnerable neurons located in the hippocampus, the deeper level of the cerebral cortex (laminar necrosis), and the cerebellar Purkinje cells. Selective neuronal death characteristically follows brief periods of acute cardiac arrest, prolonged status epilepticus, and profound hypoglycemia and has been attributed to a transient imbalance between excitatory and inhibitory neurotransmitters in the vulnerable area. Severe hippocampal damage represents the most frequent cause of memory loss following cardiac arrest, whereas Purkinje cell damage is a major factor in causing the distressing condition of postanoxic myoclonus.

Clinical Definitions of Stroke (Table 116–5)

Transient ischemic attacks (TIAs) are defined as periods of focal, acute neurologic insufficiency lasting from a few minutes to an hour or so, followed by complete functional recovery. Presumably, emboli composed of fibrin, platelets or, rarely, cholesterol crystals that arise in the heart or large cervical arteries are responsible for most TIAs. Less frequent sources include tiny fragments of cardiac valvular

---

TABLE 116–5. PRINCIPAL PATTERNS OF ACUTE STROKE

Transient Ischemic Attacks
Brief episodes of focal neurologic deficits lasting 2–3 minutes to at most a few hours; they leave no residual defects. The attacks may affect the distal distribution of either the retinal, internal carotid, middle cerebral, or basilar artery.

Completed Stroke
Acute, sustained functional neurologic loss lasting from days to permanently in the distribution of one or more branches of the intracranial arteries.

Minor strokes
Attacks that cause limited functional deficits and are usually of a small size by brain imaging.

Major strokes
Those that produce severe sensorimotor or cognitive impairments. Brain images typically show either a large lesion or one involving the paramedian distribution of the vertebrobasilar system.

Evolving stroke
An unusual condition in which a restricted neurologic insufficiency, usually motor, starts focally but spreads relentlessly over a matter of hours to involve adjacent functional areas supplied by the parent intracranial artery.

---

vegetations or hematogenous abnormalities within the affected vessels. Severe narrowing of greater than 75 per cent of a common or internal carotid artery in the neck may account for some cases on a hemodynamic basis. Magnetic resonance (MR) imaging discloses the presence of small areas of infarction in about half the cases.

Completed stroke refers to a sustained ischemic event sufficient to produce neuronal necrosis or infarction in at least part of the territory of the affected artery. The ensuing neurologic defect can last days, weeks, or permanently. Even after maximal recovery, at least minimal neurologic difficulties often remain. The clinical severity of completed strokes depends upon the particular arterial bed, the size of the associated infarct, and the functional neuroanatomy of the area affected by the lesion. Completed *minor strokes* involving only distal branches of the middle cerebral or basilar artery, for example, produce only restricted neurologic damage compared to *major strokes* that involve the main areas supplied by the middle cerebral or basilar arteries. A clinically important point is that minor strokes causing limited neurologic impairment in a vascular territory sometimes warn of impending thrombosis of the larger parent artery. This principle means that in the early hours following onset of neurologic damage it may be difficult or impossible to distinguish minor completed strokes from reversible ischemic neurologic deficits or even the beginnings of a more serious stroke in evolution.

Stroke in evolution refers to a condition wherein ischemic neurologic deficits begin in a focal or restricted distribution but spread gradually in a pattern reflecting involvement of more and more of the anatomic territory supplied by a middle cerebral or basilar artery. These early hours represent an important time period to attempt therapy. Occasionally, stroke can evolve for longer periods, up to a week or so, but such a pattern more often reflects ischemia or bleeding related to a neoplasm or arteriovenous malformation. The pathogenesis of most evolving strokes probably consists of extension of thrombus from an initial clot along the affected artery. Some may reflect hemodynamic instability with insufficiency spreading into the penumbral margin of ischemic zones at the edge of the initially hypoperfused area. Evolving stroke must be differentiated from the less specific and temporary neurologic worsening that sometimes results when cerebral edema complicates large, completed strokes (see below).

TABLE 116–6. MAJOR STROKE SYNDROMES

I. Anterior Circulation (ICA and tributaries)
  A. TIAs
  1. Retinal artery. Brief (10–30 sec), often repeated, unilateral graying-out of vision ipsilateral to propagating ICA. Pupil sluggish, retina pale, vessels underfilled, cholesterol emboli occasionally seen.
  2. MCA. Intermediate length (2–50 min) attacks, usually stereotyped, producing contralateral upper motor neuron (UMN) face-hand or hemiparetic weakness, sometimes aphasia or dysarthria. Sensory symptoms, seizures uncommon. Images show small lesions in approximately 50%.
  B. Completed strokes
  1. ICA-MCA distribution. Onset usually abrupt, a few evolve for 24 hr. Residua last days to indefinitely. Neurologic changes can include contralateral face, face-hand, hemiplegic, or sensorimotor weakness, attention-neglect, or aphasia if dominant hemisphere. Seizures affect 5%; brain edema plus large strokes can lead to stupor. Brain images rule out hemorrhages and almost always reveal infarction by 24 hr.
  2. ACA distribution. Incidence uncommon, some asymptomatic, others cause contralateral sensory–upper motor neuron weakness of leg-foot, occasionally Broca's aphasia.
II. Posterior Circulation (VA, BA, PCA)
  A. TIAs
  1. Duration 5–55 min. Attacks are often complex and symptoms may vary in different patients as well as in the same patient during different attacks, depending on whether the insufficiency involves paramedian or circumferential arteries (Fig. 116–1). Table 116–7 lists typical specific symptoms for each distribution.
  B. Completed Stroke
  1. VA. PICA syndrome: Headache, ataxia, vomiting, paralysis of swallowing and tongue, all ipsilateral; pain loss, ipsilateral face and contralateral body; Horner's Syndrome, ipsilateral.
  2. PICA, AICA, and SCA occlusions each can result in acute cerebellar infarction. Complete syndromes are described in the text.
  3. BA trunk:
  Lower (vertebrobasilar junction). Lower extremity paraplegia or tetraplegia, bizarre conjugate or disconjugate gaze paralyses, small pupils, breathing irregularities, often coma.
  Rostral (basilar apex–PCA junction). Variable: hemiplegia or diplegia; pupillary and oculomotor paralyses; stupor or coma; visual field defects.
  4. PCA. Distal branches: Quadrantic or hemianopic visual field loss. Proximal branches to thalamus: memory loss, sensorimotor hemiplegias.

Major Stroke Syndromes (Table 116–6)

Ischemia of the Internal Carotid Artery (Anterior Circulation) System. Both thromboses and emboli can occlude the anterior cerebral circulatory system. Emboli are especially common because of the large size of the system and the fact that so many emboli from the heart find their first escape up the large common carotid arteries.

Transient Ischemic Attacks Affecting the Internal Carotid Artery (ICA) Distribution. About one third of these events are associated with *stenosis-ulceration* or severe stenosis (>75 per cent) in the ipsilateral common or internal carotid artery, usually at its bifurcation. Thrombi from the heart or the proximal aorta cause most of the rest. A few carotid TIAs may be caused by hematogenous abnormalities producing small, spontaneously arising endovascular clots.

Anterior circulation TIAs almost entirely affect either the retinal artery or MCA circulation, with the two involved concurrently about 10 per cent of the time. Isolated ophthalmic artery TIAs have the least serious prognosis. Symptoms consist of a rapidly developing (10 seconds or so) unilateral graying-out of vision of one eye (*amaurosis fugax*). The episodes usually last for seconds, rarely for more than a few minutes, after which normal vision nearly always returns. Retinal examination during the attack may disclose conspicuous narrowing of both arteries and veins, sometimes with blood flow being so slow that venous filling appears segmented. Yellow, refractile, residual retinal arterial spots represent cholesterol crystals. Their presence implies cholesterol in an upstream arterial plaque and a greater potential risk for future irreversible embolic ischemia.

Symptoms of TIAs affecting the MCA distribution depend upon the functional neuroanatomy of the ischemic field. Peripheral branch occlusions characteristically cause transient, restricted hand-arm or face-hand-arm paresis with or without accompanying somesthetic sensory loss. Occlusions distal to the point where the lenticulostriate artery branches from the MCA in the dominant hemisphere can cause transient aphasia. More proximal occlusions produce transient motor hemiparesis with or without associated language defects. Neither altered consciousness nor confusion ordinarily accompanies ICA-MCA TIAs, most of which last less than 10 to 20 minutes. Seizures are rare.

ICA OCCLUSION. *Acute* occlusion of the previously fully patent vessel can result from atherosclerosis, immunologic-inflammatory disease, trauma arterial dissection, massive embolism, or surgical ligation performed in an effort to halt traumatic bleeding or entrap an intracranial aneurysm. Most spontaneous ICA occlusions develop at the site of a previously severe stenosis, either at the carotid bifurcation or, less frequently, in the intracranial siphon.

The neurologic effects of either severe stenosis or total ICA occlusion depend on the patient's age, the rate at which closure occurs, the presence or absence of ulcerated endothelial plaques, and the degree of intracranial anastomotic compensation. Stenoses less than 85 per cent usually cause little or no reduction in blood flow and few symptoms unless thrombi form on ulcerated plaques and break off as emboli. Plaques containing calcification are especially dangerous. Autopsy and arteriographic studies suggest that many ICA occlusions that evolve gradually cause neither symptoms nor structural brain damage. Neurologic injury with the remainder ranges from small, deep focal infarctions to massive strokes that involve the entire distribution of the ipsilateral middle and, sometimes, anterior cerebral arteries.

TIAs or small completed strokes precede symptoms of major acute stroke due to ICA occlusion in as many as 20 per cent of cases, usually reflecting progressive stenosis or plaque formation. If a major hemispheric lesion does occur, neurologic symptoms and signs affecting the MCA distribution characteristically develop rapidly, with their intensity depending on the size of the subsequent brain lesion. Ipsilateral or bitemporal headache may accompany the onset of occlusion. Focal motor or generalized seizures accompany the acute stage of about 5 per cent of large ICA-MCA distribution infarcts.

Diagnosis of an ICA-MCA distribution stroke usually is easily made on clinical grounds plus a confirming computed tomographic (CT) or MR image. Clinical diagnosis of internal carotid artery occlusion, by contrast, is not reliable and in most cases requires imaging studies by noninvasive methods (ultrasound or Doppler flow estimates) or arteriography.

External palpation of the neck is an unreliable sign in diagnosis of ICA occlusion, because internal and external carotid arteries cannot reliably be distinguished from one another. A total absence of cervical arterial pulsations in the region of the angle of the jaw or over the facial arteries suggests the uncommon event of common carotid or combined internal-external carotid artery occlusion. Bruits heard predominantly or entirely over the carotid bifurcation area below the angle of the jaw suggest an underlying stenosis of either the ICA or external carotid artery (ECA) or both. Generally, the harsher the bruit, the more likely that it reflects severe stenosis, especially if accompanied by a palpable thrill. Only bruits that disappear as auscultation moves down the neck from the angle of the jaw toward the clavicle can be regarded confidently as emanating from the carotid bifurcation.

MIDDLE CEREBRAL ARTERY (MCA) OCCLUSION. Embolism represents the most frequent cause of MCA occlusion. Other mechanisms include extension of clot from an occluded internal carotid artery, intrinsic atherosclerosis, and endovascular thrombosis. The onset of symptoms and signs usually is rapid, taking seconds or minutes to evolve, and commonly silent, producing no more than a sense of paralysis or "deadness" in contralateral body parts. Affected patients, if asleep at onset, may notice no difficulty until they attempt to arise after awakening. The immediate neurologic deficit, as with carotid occlusion or ICA-MCA TIAs, depends upon where along the MCA the occlusion rests. Major MCA strokes in either hemisphere tend to produce

contralateral hemiplegia. Those affecting the dominant hemisphere tend to cause aphasia, whereas those lying in the nondominant right hemisphere tend to produce confusional states, spatial disorientation, and various degrees of sensory and emotional neglect. Severe inattentiveness, stupor, or coma with unilateral cerebral stroke is limited to patients in whom acute, large, dominant-hemisphere lesions produce global aphasia or those who develop severe secondary brain edema and diencephalic compression-herniation.

ANTERIOR CEREBRAL ARTERY (ACA) OCCLUSION. The anterior cerebral artery has two major parts: (1) the basal portion extends from the ICA to join the anterior communicating artery, and (2) the interhemispheric portion supplies the ipsilateral medial frontal lobe as far posteriorly as the sensorimotor foot area. Occlusion of the interhemispheric branch produces an acute focal sensorimotor defect in the contralateral foot and distal leg. Proximal ACA occlusion may cause no neurologic deficits if a patent anterior communicating artery carries blood from the opposite carotid supply. Lacking such collateral, ischemia may affect deep frontal lobe nuclei to cause (in the dominant hemisphere) Broca's or anterior conduction aphasia. TIAs rarely affect the ACA distribution; recurrent paresthesias or weakness involving a single foot-leg is more consistent with cerebral seizures or, less often, recurrent ischemia in the vertebral-basilar system.

Ischemia of the Vertebral-Basilar (Posterior Circulation) System. The BA and two intracranial VAs are supplied rostrally by the posterior communicating arteries and caudally from the cervical VAs, which originate from the subclavians. Variation in the patency of these sources has several possible effects. With both ends of the double supply open, narrowing or even occlusion of a VA or even the BA sometimes can occur without causing symptoms. Emboli are less frequent in the posterior than the anterior circulation, whereas primary atherosclerotic occlusion affects the BA and VAs more frequently than the carotid systems.

Vertebral-basilar TIAs can produce complex and variable symptoms and signs, the nature of which depends upon the anatomic distribution of ischemia (Table 116–7). Often the neurologic changes vary from attack to attack in the same person. This variability contrasts with carotid TIAs, in which recurrent episodes in the same patient tend to remain stereotyped.

Occlusion of VA or BA and their main branches, the PICA, AICA, and SCA, can cause several different syndromes depending on the rostral-caudal brain level of the arterial stoppage, the point of occlusion along the length of the vessel, and whether or not the involvement includes the paramedian vessels, circumferential arteries, or both (Table 116–6).

PCA occlusions most often are due to atherosclerosis located at the basilar takeoff or from emboli that lodge more peripherally. Distal obstructions re-

TABLE 116-7. MOST COMMON SYMPTOMS OF VERTEBRAL-BASILAR TIAs

PARAMEDIAN ARTERIES (MIDLINE OF BA)	CIRCUMFERENTIAL ARTERIES (PICA, AICA, SCA, PCA)
Transient global amnesia	Nonpositional vertigo
Diplopia	Unilateral face or body
Episodic, paroxysmal drowsiness	paresthesias
Paraparesis or tetraparesis	Episodic hemianopia or
Ataxia	scintillations
Dysarthria	Unilateral posterior headache

sult in homonymous or quadrantic hemianopias, whereas more proximal stoppage produces infarction of the sensory thalamus and sometimes the lateral midbrain as well.

The effects of BA occlusion at the apex depend upon whether the obstruction includes the posterior cerebral arteries, the arteries supplying the overlying diencephalon, the vessels feeding the midbrain, or some combination thereof. Loss or reduction of consciousness is common and is often associated with a variety of pupillary, gaze, and oculomotor paralyses. If the cerebral peduncles are affected, decorticate or decerebrate motor posturing and paralysis ensue. Residua may include inattention, dementia, memory loss, visual field defects, gaze palsy, and sensory or motor impairments. More caudally placed occlusions of the BA, if they selectively affect paramedian vessels, impair consciousness and produce disconjugate eye movements, unequal pupils, and signs of bilateral upper motor neuron

TABLE 116-8. MAJOR CAUSES OF CEREBRAL VENOUS AND SINUS THROMBOSIS IN APPROXIMATELY DECLINING ORDER OF FREQUENCY

Late pregnancy and postpartum state
Contraceptive medication
Coagulant factors associated with malignancy, disseminated intravascular coagulation, thrombotic purpura
Idiopathic
Severe dehydration or intrinsic hyperviscosity
Septic extension from face, sinus, mastoid

TABLE 116-9. HYPERTENSIVE ENCEPHALOPATHY

Immediate cause:	Acute, severe hypertension
Associated illnesses:	Renal disease, eclampsia, abrupt withdrawal of antihypertensive drugs, pheochromocytoma
Manifestations:	Acute headache, nausea, vomiting, confusion or stupor, cortical blindness, convulsions, transient motor changes
Findings:	BP usually >200/130; retinal hemorrhages or papilledema; relatively normal renal function (BUN <100); MR shows disseminated small areas of acute leukoencephalopathy
Treatment:	Reduce mean BP deliberately by 30-40 mm Hg/hr, avoiding abrupt major declines (controlled nitroprusside drip most reliable). Treat seizures with diazepam IV.

dysfunction. Bizarre irregularities in breathing patterns often emerge.

Complete basilar occlusion affecting both paramedian and circumferential vessels usually produces incomplete ischemic transection of the brain stem. Affected patients usually are comatose and show pinpoint, irregular, or unequal pupils, bilateral conjugate gaze paralysis, or internuclear ophthalmoplegia and tetraplegia. Few survive more than a few days.

Unilateral VA occlusion occurs asymptomatically in about 50 per cent of cases. When symptoms do occur, they produce the syndrome of the posterior inferior cerebellar artery. Signs of mild ipsilateral cerebellar dysfunction are accompanied by ipsilateral lower motor neuron paralysis of cranial nerves IX, X, and XII, coupled with pain and temperature loss contralaterally on the body and ipsilaterally on the face. An ipsilateral Horner's syndrome usually is present.

Acute cerebellar infarction can occur when occlusion strikes any of the three main cerebellar arteries, principally the inferior branch. If the cerebellum swells from ischemic edema sufficiently to distort the brain stem and obstruct the normal CSF outflow, serious complications may occur. Symptoms initially include ipsilateral occipital headache and signs of mild cerebellar dysfunction followed by increasing occipital head pain, often vomiting, and the development of ipsilateral cranial nerve defects. Progression, if it occurs, usually develops within 12 to 36 hours and is marked by more severe headache and drowsiness or stupor. CT scans in such instances show an enlarged, hypodense cerebellar hemisphere with fourth ventricle obstruction and lateral ventricle enlargement. Lateral ventricular drainage can prevent further damage or death.

Spinal Stroke. Ischemic infarction due to atherosclerotic arterial occlusion rarely affects the spinal cord. More common is anoxic-ischemic injury associated with prolonged hypotension (shock) or compression by intraspinal mass lesions. Arterial lesions, when they occur, almost always involve the anterior spinal artery, atherosclerotic obstruction striking most often at the level of the cervical radicular artery or one or two segments below. Inflammatory and immune arteritides are, if anything, more frequent than atherosclerotic obstructions, especially in younger persons, and tend to occur at the T4 level. In both instances, neurologic damage develops acutely or rapidly, usually reaching a maximum within 24 hours of onset, and produces a transverse myelopathy affecting the anterior half of the cord. Lower motor neuron abnormalities sometimes can be detected at the level of the lesion combined with asymmetric, bilateral impairment of pain and temperature sensations beginning one or two dermatomes below. Injury to corticospinal pathways results in upper motor neuron dysfunction caudal to the level of occlusion. Dysfunction of bowel, bladder, and male sexual activities usually accompanies these abnormalities.

Cerebral Venous Thrombosis. Obstruction to the cerebral venous sinuses or their main tributaries has several potential causes (Table 116-8; see also

Chapter 120). Most spontaneous examples appear either during the postpartum period, as an idiopathic phenomenon related to little understood "physiologic" hypercoagulability, or as a complication of disease-related coagulopathy, especially that associated with cancer or infection.

Hypertensive Encephalopathy (HE). HE is an abnormal, dangerous state of multifocal cerebral ischemia induced by a severely, acutely, or subacutely elevated blood pressure (Table 116–9). The condition has become uncommon, thanks to the widespread use of effective antihypertensive drugs.

The pathogenesis of HE relates to the effect that the high systemic intravascular pressure has on the brain's arterioles. The elevated tension exceeds the upper limits of normal cerebral autoregulation, so that a combination of multifocal arteriolar vasodilatation and vasoconstriction occurs, producing diffusely distributed small zones of microhemorrhages and ischemia.

Differential diagnosis of HE includes acute uremia (BUN > 100 mg/dl), encephalitis (fever, no severe hypertension, usually slower course), cerebral venous sinus thrombosis, acute lead encephalopathy, disseminated intravascular coagulation, and acute bacterial endocarditis.

HE requires urgent treatment using intravenously regulated sodium nitroprusside to lower blood pressure promptly to levels within the upper range of autoregulation (mean 130 ± 10 mm Hg). Later, within 12 hours or so, systemic pressures can be reduced more gradually so as to allow arterioles to adapt and reduce the risk of inducing focal cerebral hypoperfusion. Long-term control of the underlying hypertension must be pursued vigorously.

Diagnosis and Differential Diagnosis in Ischemic Stroke

Clinical understanding plus judiciously chosen confirmatory laboratory tests give accurate diagnosis in nearly all instances. Age, mode of onset, the presence or absence of known risk factors or previous vascular events, and whether or not the neurologic deficit fits a known vascular distribution provide the chief clues. The first minutes or hours of observation show whether a stroke is a TIA, is progressing, or, for the moment, has completed its ravages. The general history and physical examination often disclose the presence or absence of stroke-causing systemic diseases (see Table 116–1), especially those of the heart or great vessels. These steps, combined with routine laboratory studies (urinalysis, CBC and smear, standard chemical and electrolyte screening, ECG, chest radiography) provide accurate diagnosis most of the time. A CT or MR head scan should be obtained for any first completed or progressive stroke, because about 4 per cent of such patients have other disorders such as a neoplasm, hematoma, vascular malformation, or abscess. CT or, if unavailable, lumbar puncture should be done before anticoagulants are administered. One should recall, however, that even large cerebral infarcts may not produce abnormalities on the CT scan until as late as 24 to 48 hours after onset.

Ischemic stroke seldom affects persons less than age 50 except in association with specific risk factors or identifiable toxic or systemic causes. Patients lacking such apparent antecedents deserve especially careful appraisal.

Differentiation among TIAs, progressive stroke, minor completed stroke, and severe completed stroke is implicit in their presentations. Several conditions, however, can be mistaken for stroke and vice versa (Table 116–10). Seizures usually are not difficult to distinguish from TIAs, because the latter rarely cause positive motor signs, are less long-lasting, and produce no postictal effects. Postictal paralysis usually can be distinguished from stroke by its association. Glaucoma or other local diseases of the eye, cranial arteritis, and migraine represent alternate potential causes of unilateral visual loss. Complicated migraine can produce symptoms suggesting acute stroke or vertebral-basilar TIA. The patient's age and past history usually are distinguishing. Benign positional vertigo differs from basilar TIAs by its strict link to positional stimuli and its lack of associated symptoms of brain stem dysfunction. Similar specific associations identify Meniere's disease as well as the nonspecific dizzy feelings experienced by many elderly persons. Cardiac arrhythmias rarely cause symptoms resembling TIAs, just as TIAs rarely cause syncope (page 744). Subdural hematomas or large, unruptured intracranial aneurysms sometimes produce brief attacks that are indistinguishable from carotid TIAs and that may have a similar embolic pathogenesis. Stroke almost always can be distinguished from deep cerebral hemorrhage or brain tumor by CT imaging. Afebrile brain abscesses or granulomas can similarly be identified. Cervical-cerebral angiography has little usefulness in evaluating acute stroke. Its place in managing aftercare is described below.

Etiologic diagnosis guides both acute and chronic management (see Tables 116–1 to 116–4). Echocardiography and cardiac wall motion studies can identify potential sources of emboli in patients with mitral prolapse, valvular stenosis, or anterior wall infarctions and detect the rare unsuspected atrial myxoma. EEGs and other clinical neurophysiologic studies seldom provide useful information. Noninvasive investigations, such as ultrasonic or Doppler flow studies, applied to the carotid systems are more useful in planning convalescent than acute manage-

TABLE 116–10. CONDITIONS MISDIAGNOSED AS STROKE

MISTAKEN FOR STROKE	MISTAKENLY DIAGNOSED AS STROKE
Focal seizures called TIAs	Complicated migraine
Glaucoma attributed to retinal artery occlusion	Subdural hematoma
Benign vertigo or Meniere's disease considered vertebral-basilar TIA	Occasional large aneurysms causing TIAs
Cardiac syncope regarded as minor stroke	Hemorrhage or infarction in neoplasms

ment. Generally speaking, the more restricted and reversible the initial neurologic injury, the more assiduously one searches for specific causes for which treatment might reduce the risk of future brain damage.

Management of Acute Stroke

Once ischemia has damaged the brain, no currently available treatment has been proved to reduce the injury, although several promising agents are undergoing early clinical trials. Thrombolytic agents such as streptokinase and tissue plasminogen factor have been found to reduce stroke damage as much as 50 per cent in preliminary, un-

TABLE 116–11. USE OF ANTICOAGULANTS IN STROKE

I. Acute Therapy
  A. Indications
    Repetitive TIAs clustered closely together within a single day or a few days. Acutely progressive weakness in stroke.
  B. Procedure
    Initiate with heparin. Start warfarin concurrently and discontinue heparin when prothrombin time reaches 1.5 × normal. Continue warfarin 3–4 weeks except in atrial fibrillation (AF). With acute stroke, start aspirin (ASA) therapy.
  C. Contraindications
    Hypertension, either systolic > 170 mm Hg or diastolic > 100 mm Hg; uremia; bleeding diathesis; intracranial bleeding (by CT or LP); LP within past 2 hours.
II. Prophylactic or Chronic Therapy
  A. Indications
    Acute anterior wall myocardial infarction with mural thrombus formation. Procedure: high-dose heparin continuing with warfarin until thrombi dissolve.
    Chronic atrial fibrillation with any or all of the following risk factors:
      1. Congestive heart failure within 3 months
      2. History of hypertension
      3. Previous thromboembolism
      4. Left ventricular dysfunction measured and/or enlarged left atrium measured by echocardiography
      5. Chronic cardiac valvular disease
    Atrial fibrillation with none of these risk factors is more safely treated with chronic ASA.
  B. Procedure: Initiate and maintain warfarin to maintain prothrombin time 1.5 × normal chronically.
  C. Contraindications:
    Same as in IC

TABLE 116–12. TREATABLE RISK FACTORS IN STROKE

Proven Benefits
Stop smoking.
Reduce systolic hypertension > 160 mm Hg by at least 20 mm Hg, if possible to below 150 mm Hg; reduce diastolic pressure > 90 mm Hg by at least 10 mm Hg, if possible to below 85 mm Hg.
Take daily aspirin, 0.6 gm, or ticlopidine, 0.5 gm/day as platelet antiaggregant.
Treat selected patients surgically for carotid stenosis.
Possible Benefits
Exercise
Lower cholesterol
Surgical endarterectomy
Use alcohol modestly
Control diabetes

controlled studies. A limitation of these drugs is that they carry a modest risk of precipitating cerebral hemorrhage. Also, to be effective they must be given within 2 hours or so of onset. Other potentially effective agents include drugs that block receptors for excitatory neurotoxins or nitric acid synthase as well as antioxidants and calcium channel blockers. Management consists of providing good general medical and nursing care, reducing hypertension or hyperviscosity if present, and taking steps to prevent acute or future worsening of the neurologic deficit. Acutely, one attempts to halt progressing stroke, to prevent recurring cerebral emboli, and to stabilize with the least possible deficit patients with fluctuating neurologic changes. In 24 hours or so after onset, the development of ischemic brain edema may require therapeutic attention.

The Use and Choice of Anticoagulants. Aspirin therapy has been sufficiently protective against recurrent thromboembolism that it can be recommended as immediate therapy in acute stroke. Anticoagulants have known value in protecting against certain well-documented risk factors in stroke. Their use in acute stroke is more controversial. Table 116–11 outlines widely accepted guidelines for using these agents in acute and chronic stroke. One reason for caution employing anticoagulants indiscriminately is that the treatment can cause dangerous bleeding of about 1 to 2 per cent per year, even in experienced hands. When indicated, heparin therapy is initiated at the time of admission to hospital: in patients describing repetitive, closely spaced TIAs; in those with progression of stroke signs during the immediately preceding hours or minutes; in those observed to have increasing neurologic deficits superimposed acutely on what at first appear to be minor strokes; and in patients demonstrating fluctuating signs and symptoms of vertebral-basilar, or carotid ischemia. In all such instances other than TIAs, either a CT scan or, when imaging is unavailable, a lumbar puncture must be performed to rule out hemorrhage. Heparin should be delayed for at least 2 hours after the lumbar puncture to reduce the risk of spinal epidural bleeding. As noted in the table, anticoagulation is contraindicated in the presence of uremia, any bleeding diathesis, and a diastolic blood pressure greater than 100 mm Hg.

Anticoagulation is stopped in most patients, except those with atrial fibrillation (AF), after 2 to 4 weeks. Anticoagulants have no demonstrated benefit for patients with completed acute stroke of more than 2 to 4 hours' duration. Their regimen immediately should proceed to the preventive measures listed in Table 116–12.

Ischemic Cerebral Edema. At least some degree of edema surrounds all cerebral infarcts. Ischemic edema generally becomes detectable within 12 to 24 hours following infarction and continues to increase for as long as 48 hours thereafter. Large, edematous hemispheric infarcts can produce sufficient brain swelling to cause transtentorial herniation. Similar enlargement in the cerebellum may compress the brain stem or obstruct CSF outflow pathways. Either can be fatal.

Cerebral edema produces hypodense areas detectable by brain imaging surrounding a more or less distinct region of recent infarction. Such changes usually cannot be imaged by CT until at least 48 hours after the ictus.

Unless postischemic edema produces serious shifts of the brain within the skull, the process produces few or no symptoms. Treatment of major degrees of swelling requires correcting or treating systemic medical complications and, if herniation threatens, giving intravenously a dehydrating agent such as mannitol in an effort to shrink the brain. Passive, sustained hyperventilation briefly reduces the intracranial volume by inducing 1 to 2 hours of arterial vasoconstriction. Diuretic drugs produce minimal benefit except as they treat systemic fluid overload. The induction of anesthetic coma has no therapeutic value. Corticosteroid drugs are contraindicated in the treatment of stroke; they do not benefit necrotic edema and may accentuate neurologic damage.

Medical Management of Stroke Patients and Risk Factors

Once past the acute phase of stroke, treatment consists of whatever rehabilitation is necessary, plus the initiation of measures designed to reduce the risk of future stroke, myocardial infarction, or other vascular complications (Table 116–12).

Aspirin and ticlopidine enjoy proven success in preventing recurrent stroke and myocardial infarction. Both drugs inhibit platelet aggregation but by different biochemical steps. Current evidence indicates that ticlopidine may be somewhat more effective than aspirin overall but is more expensive and produces severe neutropenia in about 1 per cent of those exposed. Neither dipyridamole nor sulfinpyrazone has proven value in stroke prophylaxis. Patients with atrial fibrillation who are less than 60 years of age and suffer none of the specific risk factors mentioned in Table 116–12 can safely and effectively be treated with aspirin rather than warfarin.

Surgical Treatment

A variety of vascular surgical approaches to treat or protect against acute stroke have been undertaken during the past 40 years. Of these, only carotid endarterectomy has withstood the tests of time and safety. Until recently, the indications and possible benefits of even that widely practiced operation remained debatable. Recent large population studies in Europe and North America now provide quantitative appraisals of the procedure's usefulness (Table 116–13).

Although the presence of any degree of carotid stenosis symbolizes the presence of atherosclerosis and a higher incidence of future strokes or myocardial infarctions, controlled population studies indicate that removal of the offending lesions improves future health only in certain highly selected instances. In the North American Study, only patients who had both arteriographically confirmed ICA stenosis of greater than 70 per cent and a history of an ipsilateral TIA or actual stroke within the 3 months

TABLE 116–13. CAROTID ENDARTERECTOMY AND STROKE PREVENTION*

INDICATIONS	CONTRAINDICATIONS OR UNCERTAINTIES
Good general health	Severe medical problems
If hypertensive, treated	No history of recent ipsilateral TIA or stroke
Internal carotid stenosis 70–99%	Inexperienced or unskilled surgeon
Ipsilateral stroke or TIA within 3–6 months	Internal carotid artery either completely or <70% occluded
Surgeon available with morbidity-mortality record <2%	

*Data from: Stroke 22:816–817, 1991; Lancet 337:1235–1243, 1991.

preceding surgery showed an improved longevity and freedom from stroke when compared with nonsurgical controls 18 months postoperatively. Similar qualifications marked in the European results: only persons with stenosis greater than 70 per cent who had suffered ipsilateral cerebral ischemic events during the antecedent 6 months did better with surgery. Outcomes up to 3 years indicate that surgical treatment was followed by a 2.8 per cent incidence of postoperative ipsilateral stroke, versus 16.8 per cent in controls. Rates for severe stroke or death were cut in half. No benefit from surgery was demonstrated in either study for patients with less than 70 per cent carotid stenosis, those who had not suffered recent preoperative events, or those with complete carotid occlusion. All evidence indicates that high surgical morbidity-mortality rates contraindicate carotid endarterectomy in patients with evolving strokes. Other contraindications include recent major strokes, myocardial infarction, uncontrolled hypertension, and severe systemic metabolic problems.

Prognosis in Stroke

About one fourth of patients with acute completed stroke die during hospitalization. Advanced age, severe brain stem dysfunction, coma, and serious associated heart disease all worsen the outlook. Among survivors, about 40 per cent of all patients with acute stroke make a good functional recovery. The degree and rate depend on the initial severity, the amount of improvement within the first 2 weeks, age, and how much language or cognitive difficulty persists. Few patients with pronounced Wernicke's aphasia or functional dementia regain full independence. Motor flaccidity or dense hemisensory defects persisting past the first weeks similarly reduce the chances for future independence.

Prognosis for patients with TIAs depends on the presence or absence of associated risk factors, especially cardiac. A variety of studies indicate a combined risk of about 12 per cent per year for either stroke, myocardial infarction, or death (from either) following the onset of these minor cerebrovascular events. The annual risk of such consequences climbs to about 20 per cent among patients with major strokes.

SPONTANEOUS PARENCHYMAL CEREBRAL HEMORRHAGE

Spontaneous (nontraumatic) cerebral hemorrhage may occur primarily into the substance of the brain (intracerebral or parenchymal) or over its surface (subarachnoid). Table 116–14 lists the major causes. Cerebral hemorrhage totals about 15 per cent of all clinically detectable strokes but assumes greater medical importance because of the serious consequences that often result. Table 116–15 lists the most characteristic manifestations.

Hypertensive-Atherosclerotic (H-A) Cerebral Hemorrhage. Roughly 90 per cent of spontaneous parenchymal cerebral hemorrhages fall into this category. Long-standing hypertension antedates the bleed in about two thirds of cases, with the incidence of bleeding generally paralleling the intensity and duration of that disorder. With or without hypertension, rupture reflects an area of weakening leading to hemorrhage from penetrating arterioles of approximately 100 to 150 μm in diameter. Sponta-

TABLE 116–14. NONTRAUMATIC CAUSES OF INTRACRANIAL HEMORRHAGE

I. Intracerebral Hemorrhage
  A. "Hypertensive" atherosclerotic hemorrhage: large; occurs mainly in basal ganglia, thalamus, cerebellum, pons. Often clinically catastrophic. Derives directly from degenerative-atherosclerotic vascular injury. Only 60% occur in hypertensives.
  B. Lobar hemorrhages. Usually smaller than A, arise in polar regions of frontal, temporal, or occipital-parietal lobes. More common in elderly and in association with amyloid angiopathy or small vascular malformation. Some are asymptomatic.
  C. Hemorrhage from vascular malformations, large and small. Many are cryptic lobar.
  D. Uncommon: Bleeding into brain tumors; accompanying blood dyscrasias or anticoagulants; from inflammatory vasculopathies; secondary to venous infarction.

II. Subarachnoid Hemorrhage
  A. 85% arise from congenital "berry" aneurysms; 10–15% penetrate brain parenchyma.
  B. 15% cause not found.

neous bleeding can affect almost any part of the brain, although the most common sites for H-A hemorrhages are into the deep cerebral regions of the internal capsule, basal ganglia, and thalamus, as well as into the central pons and the deep nuclear regions of the cerebellum (Figs. 116–2 and 116–3). Among patients over age 70, congophilic amyloid angiopathy becomes an increasing cause of cerebral hemorrhage, affecting most often the more peripheral or polar regions of the hemisphere. Such bleeds often produce few symptoms or cause mild symptoms that resemble ischemic stroke.

In contrast to ischemic stroke, which commonly occurs during sleep, most H-A cerebral hemorrhage begins during wakefulness, often associated with exertion. Sudden severe headache, "the worst in my life," often announces the onset, followed within minutes to hours by neurologic signs whose nature and severity reflect the site and extent of the bleeding. Characteristically, systemic examination discloses hypertension, sometimes to a temporarily severe degree, and, commonly, cardiac enlargement as well as hypertensive or atherosclerotic changes in the retinal arteries.

Basal Ganglia–Internal Capsular Hemorrhage. The onset headache commonly arises ipsilateral to the bleed and is followed shortly by a progressive contralateral hemiparesis, often accompanied by the eyes deviating toward the side of the lesion owing to damage to the adjacent frontal eye fields. Convulsions are common and can take either a generalized grand mal pattern or be focal and involve the body contralateral to the bleeding. In the latter case, the eyes often deviate away from the lesion during the seizure. Rupture into the lateral ventricle is frequent and precipitates autonomic symptoms of shivering, nausea, and vomiting. Large hemorrhages greater than 2.5 to 3 cm in diameter frequently cause coma within a few hours, and many such cases go on to develop transtentorial herniation followed by severe disability or death. Smaller hematomas cause proportionately less neurologic damage, and ultimate improvement may be considerable.

Thalamic Hemorrhage. Although serious, these often are smaller and less devastating than the ones discussed previously. Contralateral sensory loss,

TABLE 116–15. CHARACTERISTICS OF ACUTE, SPONTANEOUS, SEVERE CEREBRAL HEMORRHAGE

	HEADACHE	MOTOR-SENSORY SIGNS	GAZE PREFERENCE	CONSCIOUSNESS
Basal ganglia–internal capsule	Ipsilateral to bleed, generalized severe	Contralateral hemiplegia, convulsions	Eyes deviate toward lesion	Coma frequent
Thalamic	Either or both sides, moderate	Contralateral hemiparesis, hemianopia hemisensory defect, often	Eyes deviate down and contralateral to lesion	Drowsy to coma with large lesions
Pontine	Cataclysmic global	Stertorous breathing, bilateral posturing	Pupils pinpoint, bilateral lateral gaze paralysis, ocular bobbing	Coma within seconds to minutes
Cerebellar	Ipsilateral to bleed, occipital	Ipsilateral incoordination, dysarthria, facial weakness	Weakness, paralysis of ipsilateral conjugate gaze	Stupor or coma late, implies brain stem compression

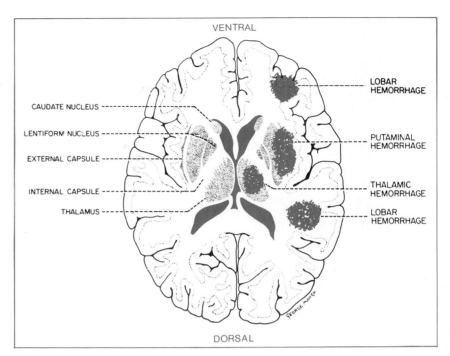

FIGURE 116–2. Horizontal section through the cerebral hemispheres illustrating frequent sites of thalamic, putaminal, and lobar hemorrhages.

Labels in figure: VENTRAL, CAUDATE NUCLEUS, LENTIFORM NUCLEUS, EXTERNAL CAPSULE, INTERNAL CAPSULE, THALAMUS, LOBAR HEMORRHAGE, PUTAMINAL HEMORRHAGE, THALAMIC HEMORRHAGE, LOBAR HEMORRHAGE, DORSAL

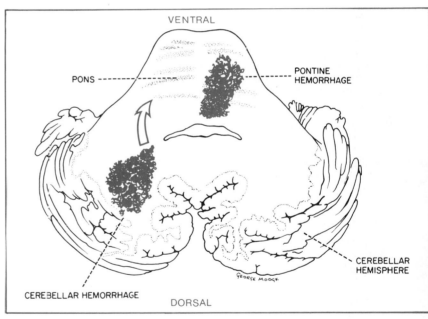

FIGURE 116–3. Horizontal section through pons and adjacent cerebellum showing common hemorrhage sites. The arrow shows a frequent line along which cerebellar hemorrhage can dissect into the pons.

Labels in figure: VENTRAL, PONS, PONTINE HEMORRHAGE, CEREBELLAR HEMISPHERE, CEREBELLAR HEMORRHAGE, DORSAL

hemianopia, and hemiparesis or hemiplegia are characteristic. Compression of the tectum-midbrain commonly induces drowsiness, which proceeds to coma only in rapidly fatal cases. Gaze palsies are common and include defects in upward gaze. Eyes cast down and laterally at rest provide an almost pathognomonic sign of bleeding in this area. Midbrain compression may transiently cause pupillary inequality or fixation.

Pontine Hemorrhage. The onset usually is cataclysmic, with sudden headache followed within seconds to minutes by coma accompanied by ster-

torous or irregular breathing, pinpoint pupils, bilateral conjugate gaze paralysis or ocular bobbing, tetraparesis and, often, decerebrate or decorticate rigidity. Most patients die, and those who survive usually are left quadriplegic and totally dependent.

Cerebellar Hemorrhage. Unilateral occipital headache often announces the onset followed by ipsilateral incoordination-ataxia of the extremities, slurred speech, and sometimes nausea and vomiting. Disequilibrium, ipsilateral facial weakness, and diplopia with ipsilateral conjugate gaze paralysis often follow within a matter of hours and may reflect either dissection of the hematoma into the lateral pons or only compression of that structure. The development of a reduced level of consciousness or of signs of upper motor neuron dysfunction affecting the extremities suggests the development of brain stem compression, due to direct enlargement of the hematoma or secondary to acute obstruction of the fourth ventricle, producing hydrocephalus.

Lobar Hemorrhage. These occur in peripheral distribution in the white matter of the cerebral or cerebellar hemispheres. They usually are smaller and produce fewer acute or permanent neurologic abnormalities than the deep hypertensive-atherosclerotic hematomas described above. Among younger persons, many arise from image-detectable arteriovenous malformations or sympathomimetic drug abuse. Cerebral amyloid angiopathy is the leading cause in the elderly.

Diagnosis

Only acute ischemic stroke represents a frequent source of potential diagnostic uncertainty, although hemorrhage into brain tumors occasionally may be indistinguishable. Headache, severe hypertension, acute prostration, nausea and vomiting, convulsions, autonomic signs, and loss of consciousness are all more characteristic of deep cerebral hemorrhage than of ischemia. If blood reaches the subarachnoid space or if downward or upward herniation threatens, the neck stiffens. CT scan is diagnostic for hemorrhage but not for the cause of bleeding. Patients who are not hypertensive, who are young, or who have less than devastating neurologic deficits deserve arteriography to seek a potentially treatable vascular anomaly. Lumbar puncture can precipitate fatal intracranial herniation and should be avoided unless brain imaging is unavailable and acute bacterial meningitis seems a strong possibility.

Treatment

Treatment consists of bringing the blood pressure to nearly normotensive levels and applying supportive measures. When clinical signs and CT examination suggest that a cerebellar hemorrhage is compressing the brain stem or causing acute hydrocephalus, lateral ventricular decompression, clot removal, or posterior fossa decompression may be lifesaving. Efforts to drain acute cerebral hemorrhages surgically usually remove viable brain in the process and tend to worsen rather than improve the eventual outcome.

Few patients in coma from cerebral hemorrhage survive, and those with extensive brain stem damage usually remain neurologically devastated. Considerable spontaneous neurologic recovery, however, often follows even moderately large hemorrhages in the peripheral parts of the cerebral or cerebellar hemispheres, because the blood dissects between much of the tissue rather than totally destroying it.

INTRACRANIAL ANEURYSMS

Intracranial aneurysms occur in three characteristic forms: fusiform, mycotic, and congenital "berry" aneurysms.

Fusiform aneurysms represent ectatic dilatations of the basilar or intracranial portion of the carotid artery. They develop a sausage-like or irregular bulbous shape, sometimes reaching a size of 5 to 10 cm in diameter. Usually they produce no symptoms, but sometimes their large size compresses adjacent

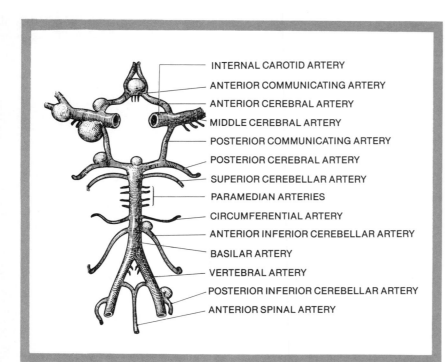

INTERNAL CAROTID ARTERY

ANTERIOR COMMUNICATING ARTERY

ANTERIOR CEREBRAL ARTERY

MIDDLE CEREBRAL ARTERY

POSTERIOR COMMUNICATING ARTERY

POSTERIOR CEREBRAL ARTERY

SUPERIOR CEREBELLAR ARTERY

PARAMEDIAN ARTERIES

CIRCUMFERENTIAL ARTERY

ANTERIOR INFERIOR CEREBELLAR ARTERY

BASILAR ARTERY

VERTEBRAL ARTERY

POSTERIOR INFERIOR CEREBELLAR ARTERY

ANTERIOR SPINAL ARTERY

FIGURE 116–4. The more common sites of berry aneurysm. The diagrammatic size of the aneurysm at the various sites is directly proportional to its frequency at that locus.

tissues or cranial nerves to cause local neurologic dysfunction. Large basilar artery aneurysms characteristically cause multiple bilateral asymmetric cranial nerve dysfunction extending anywhere from the third to the tenth nerve, while similar enlargements of the intracranial carotid artery can cause ipsilateral visual loss or contralateral hemiparesis, reflecting their parapituitary position. Such ectatic aneurysms seldom rupture, and they are rarely amenable to successful surgical therapy.

Mycotic aneurysms arise in the course of bacterial endocarditis when septic emboli lodge in a peripherally located cerebral vessel, producing endothelial ischemia at the embolic site. Infecting bacteria subsequently invade the arterial wall, and the resulting weakening invites aneurysmal blowout. Mycotic aneurysms are often multiple and characteristically arise peripherally on the cerebral arterial tree. Some resolve with antibiotic treatment, but those that remain after sterilizing the cardiosystemic infection should be treated surgically.

Congenital berry aneurysms arise at bifurcation points along the circle of Willis at the base of the brain (Fig. 116–4). In the anterior circulation they form especially at the junctions between the anterior cerebral and anterior communicating arteries; and between the middle cerebral and either the posterior communicating or carotid arteries (Fig. 116–4). Similar aneurysms can balloon out at one of the several major tributary points along the basilar-vertebral axis. Berry aneurysms vary considerably in size from a few millimeters to 1 to 2 cm or more in diameter. Those larger than 1.5 to 2 cm in diameter are commonly termed "giant" and carry a particular risk of rupture.

Berry aneurysms are thought to result from a congenital defect that affects adventitial tissue and muscle at arterial branch points along the base of the brain. The weak point allows aneurysmal formation and eventual rupture secondary to accumulated wear and tear. Similar aneurysms also occur in association with certain brain tumors, presumably owing to the release of an as yet undetected angiotrophic factor. Congenital aneurysms are more common in persons with long-standing hypertension, especially those suffering from coarctation of the aorta and polycystic kidney disease. Some persons have multiple intracranial aneurysms. Heredity creates a low but definite predisposition.

Most intracranial aneurysms are detected only when they rupture, an event that can affect any age but most commonly occurs between the ages of 40 and 65. Most ruptures take place during the waking hours, many occurring in association with vigorous physical activity.

Clinical Manifestations of Aneurysmal Rupture and Subarachnoid Hemorrhage (SAH)

These can be divided into five phases: onset, the first week of acute symptoms, the risk of secondary ischemic infarction, the development of communicating hydrocephalus, and the indications for and outcome of surgery.

The usual first symptom is sudden excruciating headache, sometimes followed by brief syncope, the latter resulting either from a neurogenically induced cardiac arrhythmia or from the brief concussion that accompanies the sudden rise in intracranial pressure. Subsequent effects depend on the locus and extent of the bleeding. Small warning leaks ("sentinel headaches") sometimes occur, causing a severe headache that then subsides over the following few days. Larger bleeds confined to the subarachnoid space produce more severe and sustained head pain, followed in 12 to 24 hours by signs of meningeal inflammation as red blood cells lyse and release irritating pigments into the CSF.

Stiff neck at onset implies a large hemorrhage either arising in the posterior fossa or producing acutely elevated intracranial pressure with descent of the cerebellar tonsils. Retinal hemorrhages can appear within minutes of the onset of the subarachnoid bleeding. Either focal neurologic signs or a reduced state of consciousness at onset imply that blood has dissected into the brain. Severe bleeds can immediately produce coma because bleeding dissects into the brain or ruptures into the ventricular system. Persistent coma implies transtentorial herniation and a poor prognosis. After the first day, the development of new focal motor or neurologic abnormalities reflects either rebleeding or cerebral infarction caused by secondary arterial vasoconstriction induced by the subarachnoid blood.

By a few hours after the onset of bleeding, a variety of systemic and secondary changes may complicate the picture. The initial bleed may stimulate the release of systemic catecholamines, which produce diffuse myocardial micronecrosis and abnormalities in the ECG. Acutely, systemic hyperglycemia, leukocytosis, and fever have a similar adrenergic pathogenesis. Subsequently, fever, leukocytosis, and delirium can last a week or more owing to a continuing blood-induced chemical meningitis. Most severely ill patients with acute SAH secrete inappropriately high levels of antidiuretic hormone, predisposing to hyponatremia. Late symptoms of lethargy, continued delirium, stupor, or diffuse, mild upper motor neuron abnormalities may reflect the development of communicating hydrocephalus secondary to blockage of CSF absorption pathways.

Diagnosis

The first principle is to respect thoroughly the development of sudden severe headache in a previously well adult. Although many such "thunderclap headaches" turn out to be benign, especially in persons of known hypochondriacal disposition, when serious doubt exists, one should obtain lumbar puncture, taking care to identify intrinsic bleeding by centrifuging bloody fluid and looking for a discolored supernatant.

For more obviously acutely ill patients with typical symptoms, CT scan is the laboratory procedure of first choice and detects an SAH large enough to threaten transtentorial herniation; if no blood is visualized, lumbar puncture can then be done to identify other potentially serious causes of sudden acute headache. CT scans also show the presence of large clots in the subarachnoid space or brain (they increase the risk of arterial spasm) and provide a baseline for future comparison in the event of subsequent unexplained worsenings. Contrast CT scans or MR images obtained with contemporary instruments often outline aneurysms of greater than 5 mm in diameter as well as arteriovenous abnormalities that may have caused the hemorrhage.

Acute subarachnoid hemorrhage is a highly dangerous illness that should be dealt with by specialized personnel, especially because time is an essential component of a good outcome. Once the condition is diagnosed, patients should be referred immediately to experienced neurosurgeons in a tertiary medical center. Arteriography is indispensable for identifying the presence and location of aneurysms and should be performed by skilled neuroradiologists as soon as possible. In poor-risk patients or when it is anticipated that surgery will be done elsewhere, no value is gained by adding the hazards of arteriography to the already precarious state.

Management and Prognosis

Optimal treatment for aneurysmal subarachnoid hemorrhage consists of surgical clipping of the leaking vessel as soon as possible after onset. Good-risk patients operated on within a day of acute bleeding enjoy the highest survival and the fewest neurologic complications. Prognosis is substantially worse in patients whose early course is complicated by reduced arousal, confusion, or severe somatic neurologic deficits. Despite statistically improved outcomes in surgically treated, good-risk patients, overall prognosis in acute SAH is poor. Of all such patients, two thirds die within 1 month (many without reaching a hospital), with about one fourth of the survivors being severely disabled. The first 2 weeks after onset carry the greatest risk of rebleeding, amounting to about 30 per cent. Among patients whose aneurysms cannot be treated successfully, rebleeding with a two thirds risk of mortality continues at a rate of about 3 per cent per year.

Medical therapy for acute SAH consists of bed rest, mild sedation, and nonopiate pain relief. The calcium channel blocker nimodipine lowers by one third the incidence of cerebral infarction after SAH and should be started immediately in all patients, employing oral doses of 60 mg every 4 hours for 21 days.

Surgery should be deferred or avoided in patients who are neurologically unstable, in those with major neurologic deficits, and in those who are stuporous or comatose. Similarly, most authorities avoid immediate surgery for patients whose arteriograms show arterial vasospasm. Continued obtundation not explained by focal damage but associated with CT evidence of progressive hydrocephalus sometimes can be relieved by ventricular shunting. It is not established whether operating on intracranial aneurysms more than 30 days following the bleed has any advantage over the natural history of the disease.

ARTERIOVENOUS MALFORMATIONS (AVMs)

In addition to congenital aneurysms, four types of vascular malformations can affect the brain. These include the following: (1) Capillary telangiectases, seldom a cause of clinical abnormalities. (2) Venous angiomas. One form constitutes the Sturge-Weber syndrome (p. 805); larger ones occasionally may rupture or, when in the spinal cord, can produce tissue compression. (3) Small vessel *cavernous angiomas*, which sometimes provide an occult source of intracerebral hemorrhage. (4) Arteriovenous malformations (AVMs) consisting of snakelike vascular tangles in which arteries connect directly with veins. AVMs can affect any part of the brain or spinal cord and can range in diameter from a few millimeters to 10 cm or more. Most arise from congenital abnormalities of the arterial wall at points where two or more major intracranial arteries conjoin, such as in the deep frontoparietal area where the distal branches of anterior, middle, and posterior cerebral arteries converge. Most AVMs gradually increase in size and characteristically produce their symptoms in persons over age 30 years.

AVMs can cause three kinds of neurologic disability: (1) As many as half leak intermittently, producing parenchymal or subarachnoid hemorrhages that usually are smaller and less dangerous than those resulting from hypertensive hemorrhage or ruptured berry aneurysms; (2) some cause focal epileptic seizures; and (3) others slowly enlarge, producing progressive neurologic deficits. A small percentage of AVMs are associated with unilateral headaches resembling classic migraines; among all migraines, however, this is a rare cause.

Surgical or angioplastic treatment of AVMs, although often successful, is technically difficult because many of the lesions reside in neurologically indispensable areas of brain. Moderate-sized AVMs discovered incidentally by CT scan or arteriography and causing no symptoms are best left alone. Similarly, patients with seizures as their only manifestation often are best treated with anticonvulsants alone. AVMs smaller than 3 cm in diameter often can be coagulated by proton beam or focused gamma ray radiation. The risk of neurologic damage or fatal bleeding in intracranial AVMs is relatively low, and cases should be judged individually in experienced neurologic centers.

REFERENCES

Kassell NF, Torner JC, Haley EC Jr, Jane JA, Adams HP, Kongable GL: The International Cooperative Study on the Timing of Aneurysm Surgery. Part 2: Surgical results. J Neurosurg 73:37, 1990.

Mendelow AD: Spontaneous intracerebral hemorrhage. J Neurol Neurosurg Psychiatry 54:193, 1991.

Pulsinelli WA, Levy DE: Cerebrovascular diseases. In Wyngaarden JB, Smith LH Jr, Bennett JC (eds): Cecil Textbook of Medicine. 19th ed. Philadelphia, WB Saunders Co, 1992, pp 2145–2170.

Recommendations on Stroke Prevention, Diagnosis and Therapy: Special Report from the World Health Organization. Stroke 20:1407, 1989.

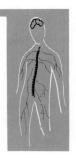

117 TRAUMA TO THE HEAD AND SPINE

The annual U.S. incidence of severe craniofacial and spinal injuries exceeds 100,000, almost half of whom die. Many of the survivors suffer chronic intellectual or motor-sensory limitations. Furthermore, most of the victims are in the younger, most productive decades of their lives. Emergency and early general medical care influences both mortality and morbidity, making an understanding of these disorders important to almost every physician.

HEAD INJURY

Pathophysiology of the Injury

Open, *focal brain injuries* caused by crush or penetrating objects affect specific regions, usually of the cerebrum. *High-velocity penetrating missiles* can emit shock waves that injure more remote areas of the hemispheres and brain stem. Most focal injuries produce relatively restricted problems requiring largely acute surgical treatment. *Closed head injury* is more frequent. Its consequences depend upon the intensity of impact, the direction of the resulting movement of the cranium, and whether or not complications arise. Heavy alcohol intake or illicit drug intoxication increases the incidence of accidental head trauma and worsens its subsequent severity and complications. Complicating systemic illnesses also influence management and outcome.

Most of the brain damage that comes from closed head injury results from impact-caused acceleration-deceleration forces. Inertia carries the gelatinous brain forward against the suddenly immobile skull, injuring structures both under the point of injury and 180 degrees away (contrecoup) (Fig. 117–1). In such circumstances, the presence or absence of a fracture is relatively irrelevant; it is the brain that suffers most.

Severity and Complications of Diffuse Head Injury

Whether or not consciousness has been lost, the presence or absence of associated neurologic abnormalities involving neuro-ophthalmologic, motor, and breathing functions provides the best index of severity. Later on, severity can be judged by the duration of coma and how long anterograde or retrograde amnesia lasts.

Mild injuries are those in which persons report feeling only dazed or syncopal and have normal neurologic findings. Neither hospitalization nor laboratory testing is needed so long as the patient can be depended upon to report potential complications. If doubt exists, conservative management includes obtaining a computed tomographic (CT) or magnetic resonance (MR) scan to rule out incipient extradural or parenchymal hematoma. When such are available, skull radiographs can be omitted.

Concussion is brief loss of consciousness with no immediate or delayed neurologic residua detectable by radiographic or clinical study. The boxer's knockout, which results from an abrupt sagittally delivered force, epitomizes the abnormality: for a few seconds awareness disappears, the pupils dilate and fix, breathing stops, the heart slows, and muscles become flaccid. Anterograde amnesia can last as long as an hour or so, but observable recovery begins within seconds to minutes and completes itself within hours. Psychosensory symptoms such as giddiness, anxiety, and apprehension may remain for days or longer. Brain imaging studies show no abnormality, and no treatment is indicated other than reassurance.

Intermediate diffuse brain injuries extend the length of unconsciousness to as much as an hour or so and are followed by a proportionately slower recovery of orientation and behavior. Permanent residua can follow. Associated drunkeness can make appraisal difficult, but in the earliest stages cautious evaluation requires that one attribute any neurologic changes directly to the trauma. Patients with moderate brain injuries often remain lethargic for a day to a week or more and many go through an agitated stage. Many are transiently disoriented, and others show mild or moderate focal neurologic abnormalities. Clinical signs of brain stem damage are lacking, but the cerebrospinal fluid (CSF) may be bloody, and CT or MR scans may show scattered petechiae or contusions (Fig. 117–1). Even with functionally severe closed injury, however, imaging studies can be normal. Patients with intermediate-level injuries require hospitalization to guard against complications and to control possible agitated behavior. More active treatment seldom is necessary in uncomplicated cases. Most patients younger than about age 40 years recover completely within days to weeks. Loss of consciousness for as little as 24 to 36 hours in older persons may be followed by permanent psychological and intellectual limitations.

Severe diffuse injury is judged by the patient's clinical response rather than the nature of the trauma. Serious neurologic damage usually is apparent from the start, although exceptions exist. For example, following seemingly mild to moderate

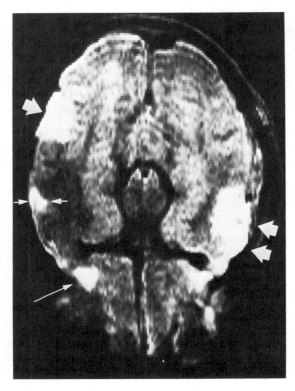

FIGURE 117-1. MR image of closed head injury showing cerebral edema-contusion at point of impact (*two large arrows*) and 180 degrees opposite (*one large arrow*) in a 22-year-old woman. An extradural hematoma had been removed at the impact site 6 days earlier. Small arrows indicate additional contusions. The patient recovered completely.

TABLE 117-1. AN ALGORITHM FOR MANAGING ACUTE HEAD INJURY

Patient Awake
Focal signs or severe headache.
   Absent: watch 1-2 hours, give phone number to call if symptoms arise.
   Present: watch but get brain image, observe until stable. If image negative, follow above.
Patient Unconscious, Obtunded, or Confused
At accident
   Place supine on flat carrying surface.
   Evaluate and clear airway.
   Seek and staunch hemorrhage.
     Await paramedics, who have antishock agents and transporting equipment.
   Give no opiates.
In emergency room, if possible a trauma center
   Intubate and deliver 30-50% oxygen.
   Assist ventilation as needed.
   Start IV line with large-gauge needle.
   Treat shock, avoid hyponatremia.
   Stop seizures; avoid steroids and opiates, give antibiotics as indicated.
   Obtain neurosurgical consultation; if delayed, complete systemic and neurologic examinations and obtain brain images.
   Assign to experts decisions about whether to treat systemic or neurologic injuries first.

head trauma, an occasional child or adolescent can develop within minutes to an hour or so massive and sometimes fatal brain edema. More commonly, in all age groups the development of severe brain edema or ischemic infarction can be delayed for several hours or more after injury. Even hemorrages can make a delayed appearance. Such patients who "talk and die" account for as many as 20 per cent of the fatalities in severe head trauma.

Excepting the above, most patients who suffer from severe brain trauma become deeply unconscious from the onset; many almost immediately develop decerebrate or decorticate posturing responses to noxious stimuli. Signs of systemic bodily trauma are common, and at least partial respiratory obstruction due to aspiration of vomitus or oral secretions is almost the rule. Evidence of brain stem damage indicated by bilateral pupillary fixation or impaired oculovestibular responses signifies severe injury and a poor prognosis, with fewer than 15 per cent making a satisfactory recovery. Almost half of all patients with such severe trauma show intracranial hemorrhages by CT scan; it is debatable whether early operative removal improves functional outcome in such instances.

Management of Acute Head Trauma and Its Complications

Emergency Management. Whether at the accident scene or hospital emergency room, proper immediate steps may save both lives and brains. The algorithm given in Table 117-1 outlines the general approach.

Hospital Management. This usually is best left to experts, but general principles can be emphasized. Patients with severe trauma should be treated in an intensive care setting. The level of consciousness, neuro-ophthamologic status, and motor responses should be monitored at 30- to 60-minute intervals in potentially unstable cases so that complications can be met quickly. Arterial blood gases and electrolytes need close attention. Unless specific complications evolve, care focuses on maintaining good physiologic balance and allowing the brain and systemic tissues spontaneously to recover their full potentials. Otherwise, standard critical care measures are the mainstay.

Pain can be a problem as patients recover consciousness, and if severe may require codeine to supplement milder analgesics. Opiates should not be given unless patients are on ventilators. Mild agitation is best controlled with diazepam, severe boisterousness with haloperidol. In alcoholics or those addicted to sedative drugs, delirium tremens or withdrawal seizures should be anticipated and counteracted with appropriate amounts of benzodiazepines at the first sign of tremulousness.

Management of Complications. *Cerebral edema* accompanies almost all severe head injuries, causing an increase in brain mass that interferes with the cerebral circulation and threatens to cause central or lateral transtentorial herniation. Brief periods of assisted hyperventilation coupled with infusions of hypertonic (20 per cent) mannitol solutions meet temporary crises. Most head injury centers use intracranial monitors and intraventricular cannulas to measure pressure and stabilize it by appropriate drainage of CSF.

Traumatic hematomas can arise acutely in either the subdural, extradural, or parenchymal regions, creating additional space-occupying lesions and producing further blood-induced irritation to the tissue. Such hemorrhages most often signify their presence with signs of increasing neurologic disability that begin at a time when improvement might otherwise be expected. CT or MR imaging can be invaluable in detecting and managing such complications. Few patients who require such acute surgical treatment make a fully satisfactory social-vocational recovery.

Where imaging is not available, skull radiographs must be done. Fractures have several potential complications that may demand attention. Bony breaks across the groove of the middle meningeal artery in the temporal bone can lacerate the artery, leading to delayed *extradural hematomas*. Typically, such clots enlarge progressively to produce signs of neurologic worsening beginning from a few hours to as much as 3 days following the initial injury. Unilateral headache followed by restlessness, agitation, or greater obtundation is characteristic. Such hematomas can be fatal unless surgically treated.

Basal skull fractures can open channels from the subarachnoid space into the paranasal sinuses or the middle ear. CSF rhinorrhea and secondary meningitis are risks. *Depressed skull fractures* displace pieces of skull to a level below the surrounding bone surface. Such lesions confer an increased risk of post-traumatic epilepsy and are best treated by surgical elevation.

Acute bacterial *infections* can follow open skull or spine injuries, infecting the subdural space or deeper tissues to cause meningitis or brain abscess. Diagnosis is suspected from the nature of the injury and is discussed, along with treatment, in Chapter 120.

Cranial nerve paralyses of the oculomotor and facial nerves commonly follow cranio-facial trauma, as does incurable anosmia. The management of more serious injuries often requires surgical facial reconstruction.

Carotid-cavernous fistulas result when basal skull fractures lacerate the artery within the cavernous sinus. Such abnormalities also may occur spontaneously or in association with intracavernous aneurysms or connective tissue diseases. Orbital chemosis, a painful semi-immobilized eye, and pulsating exophthalmos develop ipsilaterally to the fistula and occasionally contralaterally as well. Vision can decline in either eye associated with secondary glaucoma and stretching of the optic nerve. Treatment, often difficult, consists of surgical ligation or efforts to patch the vascular leak.

Post-Head Injury Problems (Table 117-2)

Postconcussion syndrome, sometimes called post-traumatic stress disorder, characteristically follows mild to moderate, often subconcussional head injuries as well as other forms of acute, psychologically threatening trauma, with or without direct cranial

TABLE 117-2. LATE COMPLICATIONS OF ACUTE BRAIN TRAUMA

SELF-LIMITED	SERIOUS
Postconcussion syndrome Benign, delayed post-traumatic encephalopathy	Intellectual, personality, and motor decline Post-traumatic epilepsy Chronic subdural hematoma Dementia pugilistica (boxers)

injury. Headache, giddy sensations, irritability, difficulty in concentration, and vague apprehension constitute the major symptoms. Physical and laboratory signs of biologically significant neurologic or systemic dysfunction usually are lacking, and the condition gradually passes with time, medication having no specific effect. No cause is known. Contrary to common opinion, compensation or psychological issues appear to have little influence on the incidence or duration of the disorder.

Delayed post-traumatic encephalopathy, an unusual syndrome affecting principally children or young adults, begins 15 minutes to 2 hours or more following usually minor head injuries. The young person becomes obtunded or stuporous, often with nausea or vomiting. Despite these potentially alarming early symptoms, most patients recover uneventfully, but focal neurologic deficits including cortical blindness sometimes can last for several hours or, very rarely, permanently. The cause is not known, although the visual loss may be secondary to posterior cerebral artery compression during transient edema-induced transtentorial herniation. Similarly unexplained are rare instances of parenchymal cerebral hemorrhage that can arise from hours to a matter of a week or more following relatively mild, initially uncomplicated cerebral trauma.

Incomplete intellectual and motor recovery affects many patients with severe head injury, including nearly all adults over age 30 who remain in coma for more than 1 week. Comprehensive rehabilitation efforts in specialized centers offer the best hope for social and vocational restoration.

Post-traumatic epilepsy, mainly with convulsive attacks, ranges in incidence from 50 per cent after penetrating brain injuries down to about 5 per cent following unconsciousness-producing closed head injury. Most authorities treat asymptomatic patients prophylactically with phenytoin or carbamazepine for up to 2 years following severe injury, adjusting medication accordingly if seizures appear. Antiepileptic medication is strengthened or treatment is lengthened according to the frequency and intensity of the attacks.

Chronic subdural hematomas can arise weeks to months after head injuries that are usually mild and sometimes so trivial as to have been forgotten. Age over 50, alcoholism, and the anticoagulated state are important predisposing factors. A sustained, new

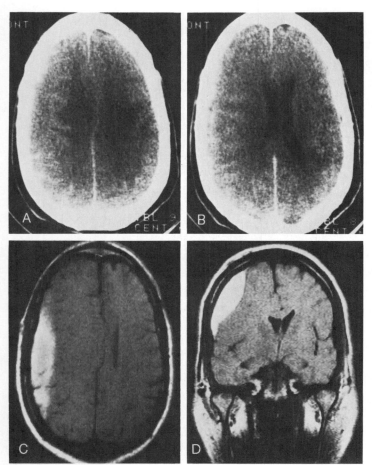

FIGURE 117–2. An isodense subdural hematoma invisible on CT scan (A and B) is readily disclosed by a concurrently obtained MR image (C and D). The patient had suffered from headache, loss of mental acuity, fatigue, and disequilibrium for 4 months. He was unable to tandem walk, but examination otherwise was unremarkable. He recovered completely following drainage of the hematoma.

headache and fluctuating mental dullness are the most common symptoms, often associated with hypersomnia and sometimes with hemiparesis. The varying symptoms presumably reflect small rebleedings or the development of transient intracranial pressure elevations associated with impaired cerebral arterial autoregulation. Diagnosis is best made by brain imaging, which in symptomatic cases shows brain shift or, with bilateral hematomas, smaller than normal ventricles and few sulci at the vertex. MR imaging is diagnostically superior because CT films obtained within a matter of a few weeks after injury may not distinguish the hematoma from the surrounding brain (Fig. 117–2). Small or moderate hematomas can be treated by observation with or without administering corticosteroids to relieve brain swelling. Larger clots, particularly those causing abnormal neurologic signs or symptoms, are best treated surgically.

Dementia pugilistica, the "punch drunk" syndrome, clinically affects former boxers older than age 55 years, although psychological tests may show a less serious degree of intellectual deterioration even before age 40. Victims develop progressive motor slowness, clumsiness, dysarthria, ataxia, memory loss, and incontinence. The syndrome relates directly to the number of former fights, with an incidence of about 20 per cent among those who box professionally 6 to 9 years or more. Brain images show cerebral atrophy and ventricular dilatation. Some victims improve after ventricular shunt procedures.

SPINAL CORD INJURY

Severe spinal cord injury is relatively uncommon but often is both devastating and prolonged in its consequences. Most affected persons are younger than 30 years of age. The intraspinal contents can be concussed, contused, lacerated, macerated, or sheared, depending upon the nature of the initiating injury. Road traffic accidents, domestic falls, and diving accidents are frequent causes. The levels most susceptible to trauma lie at the maximally mobile levels of the upper and lower ends of the cervical canal and the thoracolumbar junction. Any level, however, can be affected by injuries that strike the spinal column directly.

The principal mechanisms of spinal injury are dislocation with or without fracture at the atlas-axis junction, fracture-dislocations with or without bony fragmentation at other spinal levels, and penetrating missile or stab wounds. Less frequent causes derive from severe hyperflexion or hyperextension of the cervical spine in persons who suffer from an abnormally narrow spinal canal (stenosis) caused by congenital or age-related factors.

Patterns of Spinal Cord Injury and Their Resulting Disabilities

Complete versus partial cord injury can usually be discerned almost immediately following injury. Neurologic findings in complete injury reflect functional cord transection. With the occasional exception of priapism, flaccid motor paralysis develops below the level of damage accompanied by total anesthesia in the same distribution. Spinal shock generally lasts for at least days and sometimes weeks or more; extensor plantar responses ordinarily do not appear for several days. Bladder and bowel functions are lost, and prognosis for neurologic recovery is poor, irrespective of treatment.

Partial spinal injury is more common with cervical than thoracic cord trauma and can take several forms. Any discernible voluntary movement or sensory perception found distal to the injury at the time of accident means that the injured cord or nerve roots possess a capacity for recovery that only time will define.

Spinal concussion most often follows high-velocity missile wounds that pass close to the spinal canal but fail to damage the cord structurally. Distal neurologic loss never is complete, and recovery occurs within hours to days.

Central cord damage due to trauma affects primarily the lower cervical segments, usually with patchy hemorrhage centered along or adjacent to the spinal central canal (hematomyelia). Severe external blows or local fractures without serious canal displacement are the most common causes. The upper extremities become more paralyzed and insensate than the lower; sensory changes at and immediately below the cervical level affect pain and temperature more than touch; bladder and male sexual paralysis are common.

Cervical hyperextension injury typically produces mild or inconsequential paraparesis affecting legs more than arms, coupled with painful paresthesias in the arms and hyposensitivity to position and vibratory testing below the lesion. *Hyperflexion injury*, on the other hand, may simulate the effects of anterior spinal artery occlusion, producing tetraparesis or tetraplegia accompanied by bilateral pain and temperature impairment below the lesion. Acute urinary retention often ensues. Both hyperextension (posterior cord) and hyperflexion (anterior cord) injuries can vary widely in severity, and many patients enjoy considerable functional recovery. Mixed or unilateral injuries produce variants of the *Brown-Séquard syndrome* of hemicord damage.

Intraspinal damage at or distal to the first lumbar spinal level injures the *conus medullaris* or *cauda equina*. The result may produce various mixtures of flaccid paralysis, distal mixed sensory loss, and autonomic-sexual paralysis affecting the pelvic girdle and lower extremities.

Treatment

Management at the scene of the accident consists of maintaining ventilation, protecting against shock, and immobilizing the neck and spine to prevent further damage. Recent controlled studies show that methylprednisolone given intravenously in doses of 30 mg/kg of body weight within 8 hours after the onset of trauma and followed by 5.4 mg/kg infused hourly for 23 hours reduces the amount of eventual neurologic dysfunction. An additional, controlled study suggests that adding GM_1 ganglioside to the prednisone resulted in even greater recovery. Persons with severe spinal injuries are best cared for in experienced centers.

For most severe cord injuries, including all cases of functional transection, open surgical treatment confers little benefit and only adds another trauma. Acute and postacute management for quadriplegics or paraplegics requires elaborate attention to pulmonary, cutaneous, autonomic, musculoskeletal, and psychosocial problems.

REFERENCES

Bracken MB, Shepard MJ, Collins WF Jr, et al: Methylprednisolone or naloxone treatment after acute spinal cord injury: 1 year follow-up data. J Neurosurg 76:23–31, 1992.

Geisler FH, Dorsey FC, Coleman WP: Recovery of motor function after spinal cord injury—a randomized, placebo-controlled trial with GM-1 ganglioside. N Engl J Med 324:1829–1838, 1991.

118 EPILEPSY

Definitions

An *epileptic seizure* consists of an episode of uncontrollable, abnormal motor, sensory, or psychological behavior caused by repetitive, hypersynchronous, abnormal electrochemical activity of the central nervous system (CNS). *Epilepsy* is a chronic disorder characterized by recurrent seizures in which the attacks themselves become the target for specific therapy. Many seizures occur sporadically in conditions that are not part of the disease of epilepsy. These can result from a variety of causes such as electroconvulsive therapy, profound syncope, the ingestion or withdrawal of certain drugs or toxins, or any of several kinds of infections or acute injuries of the brain.

Seizure disorders fall into two general etiologic groups:

1. *Primary or idiopathic epilepsy*, most of which reflects genetic predisposition but whose exact cause remains largely or entirely unknown.

2. *Secondary or symptomatic epilepsy*, in which seizures result from a known structural or metabolic disease of the brain.

Incidence and General Etiology

Seizures can begin at any time of life (Table 118–1). Population studies in several developed countries worldwide indicate that 2 to 4 per cent of all persons suffer from recurrent seizures at some time during their lives. Third World areas show incidence rates almost twice as high.

Pathophysiology

Focal seizures produce abnormal unilateral movements or sensations as well as stereotyped behavioral patterns that express the pathologic excitation

TABLE 118–1. PRINCIPAL CAUSES OF SEIZURES BY AGE OF ONSET

Neonatal:	Developmental insufficiency or brain injury
Infantile:	Congenital malformations, perinatal injury, metabolic disorders
Children and adolescents:	Mainly genetic
Adults over 20:	Some genetic; otherwise, cerebral neoplasms, drug-alcohol withdrawal, brain injury by trauma, stroke, infection, or surgery

of specific parts of the cerebral hemispheres. Most often, they originate in association with anatomically restricted lesions of gray matter such as scars, tumors, arteriovenous malformations, or focal areas of inflammation. *Generalized seizures*, by contrast, express themselves with bilateral motor abnormalities usually accompanied by at least a brief loss of consciousness. They reflect either a diffuse hyperexcitable propensity of brain cells or the presence of deeply lying, cryptic epileptogenic abnormality that involves centrally located subcortical activating mechanisms. Focally originating ictal discharges can become generalized when they anatomically project bilaterally to widespread cerebral areas. Certain anatomic areas of the cerebrum are especially disposed to producing seizures. These include the frontal lobes, the medial temporal lobes (limbic system), the diencephalic reticular formation, and, to a lesser degree, the occipital lobes.

Genetic factors influence susceptibility to both generalized and focal epilepsy. Generalized epilepsies, such as petit mal absences and febrile convulsions, are usually transmitted as an autosomal dominant trait with variable penetration. The blood

TABLE 118–2. CLASSIFICATION OF EPILEPTIC SEIZURE PATTERNS

I. **Partial seizures** originate from a focal, usually structural lesion in brain and may express either a single symptom without altered consciousness (simple) or changing symptoms associated with altered consciousness (complex).
   A. Motor (includes monomyoclonic)
   B. Sensory
   C. Psychological
   D. Partial complex. Behavioral seizures with altered consciousness, usually of limbic-temporal lobe origin.
II. **Generalized seizures.** (All but some myoclonic attacks cause at least momentary loss of consciousness.)
   A. *Nonconvulsive*
      Absence (petit mal)
      Atypical absence
      Atonic
      Myoclonic
   B. *Convulsive*
      Tonic-clonic (grand mal)
      Tonic only
      Clonic only
III. **Atypical or unclassified seizures.** Consciousness usually remains intact.
   A. Paroxysmal tonic spasms
   B. Spinal myoclonus

relatives of patients with chronic focal seizures originating in the temporal lobe also show an above-normal incidence of seizure disorders of all kinds.

The specific brain mechanisms that cause seizure discharges to start, spread, or stop are poorly understood. Abnormalities that have been suggested include (1) intrinsic neuronal receptor and molecular channel changes that could induce abnormal ionic conductance; (2) abnormal neurotransmitter synthesis leading to deficiencies of inhibitory or excesses in excitatory neurotransmitters; and (3) deficiencies in genetically regulated intracellular enzymes that normally affect the capacity of the neurons or glial cells to pump ions and repolarize.

Clinical Seizure Patterns (Table 118–2)

Individual epileptic attacks can last from a few seconds to several minutes in duration, with the pattern of the symptoms often reflecting the functional anatomy of the seizure focus. Seizures and their effects can be divided into several stages: the *aura*, the first self-experienced symptom, usually reflects the anatomic focus where the seizure begins. The *attack* itself follows and subsequently gives way to the *postictal period*, during which headache, drowsiness, or focal neurologic abnormalities can remain, often for minutes, occasionally for hours or even days.

Partial Seizures

Partial seizures consist of attacks of repetitive, uncontrollable, focal neurologic dysfunction. The attacks are described as *simple* if only a restricted form of behavior or experience is expressed (equivalent to the aura) and consciousness remains intact. They are called *complex* if the pattern of neurologic symptoms and signs evolves or if consciousness is impaired or lost. The initiating signs and symptoms offer the best localizing evidence for the area of the brain that contains the epileptogenic lesion.

Partial motor seizures arise from epileptogenic foci in the primary motor or the premotor, supplementary motor, or prefrontal areas of either frontal lobe. Lateral prefrontal, supplementary motor, and premotor foci all cause adversive seizures, with only moderate differences distinguishing the respective movement patterns. Motor components in partial motor seizures can begin and remain as simple aversion of the head and eyes away from the side of the focus, can include extension or raising of the contralateral arm and turning of the trunk, and occasionally can include crude vocalizations or, in the dominant hemisphere, speech arrest. Because of abundant anatomic transcortical and thalamic interconnections, frontal seizure discharges can either produce contralateral motor activity or rapidly precipitate generalized convulsions. With lesions lying far anterior in the frontal lobes, consciousness may be lost concurrently with or even before any focal movements begin. Most patients with focal seizures arising from supplementary or premotor areas retain awareness for at least the beginning of the attack.

Primary motor (rolandic) seizures produce the

classic *jacksonian* epileptic attack, named for the English neurologist who first deduced the significance of the pattern. Rhythmic, clonic twitching begins in the contralateral thumb or corner of the mouth and slowly spreads to produce adjacent movements, most often from thumb to hand to arm to face, but sometimes jumping in the reverse direction. Spread to a generalized convulsion is common. Many jacksonian seizures are followed by transient or sustained postical *(Todd's) paralysis* of the limb affected by the seizure.

Partial sensory seizures produce the classic epileptic aura: a sensory presentiment that represents the time and place of the seizure onset. Most common are epigastric rising sensations that emanate from discharges affecting the insular cortex, followed in frequency by somatosensory tingling or numbness (postcentral gyrus), simple visual phenomena (mostly occipital), vertigo (superior temporal gyrus), or vague cephalic or generalized body sensations (no localizing value). Lesions in and around the temporal uncus cause foul smelling hallucinations that often blend into other temporal lobe symptoms.

Partial complex seizures of temporal lobe–limbic cortex origin represent the most frequent form of chronic epilepsy, amounting to about 40 per cent of total cases. About half begin before age 25 years, and most are associated with discernible structural lesions in the temporal limbic area. Frequent causes are developmental anomalies, residua of early life brain infection or severe febrile convulsions, head trauma, neoplasms, and in later life stroke or focal atrophy. Most partial complex seizures begin in foci that lie along the medial portion of the temporal lobe or the adjacent inferior frontal limbic area and spread posteriorly along the temporal lobe limbic cortex. They often project transcallosally to the opposite medial temporal area. Attacks also can spread into deep diencephalic structures to produce generalized convulsions. Consciousness and memory usually are severely dulled or lost during the evolution of the attack.

The aura of partial complex seizures is the first symptom of the attack (Table 118–3). It commonly reflects their anatomic origin and sometimes comprises the entire episode. More often, early, consciously perceived symptoms spread into stereotyped automatic movements that can take several forms (Table 118–4). Partial complex seizures usually last 1 to 2 minutes, seldom as long as 5, and are followed by slow reorientation accompanied by headache and drowsiness. Most affected patients show temporal lobe spikes or slow foci in interictal EEGs, provided that records during sleep are obtained. Sometimes, however, deep limbic discharges may go undetected altogether by skull surface electrodes.

Many patients suffering from temporal epilepsy display abnormal interictal behavior, including ruminative obsessiveness, religiosity, circumstantiality, hypersensitivity, and self-absorption, as well as hypergraphia.

Differential diagnosis of partial complex seizures includes mainly petit mal absences and psychiatric

TABLE 118–3. FREQUENT EARLY SYMPTOMS OF LIMBIC–TEMPORAL LOBE SEIZURES

SYMPTOM	LOCUS OF ORIGIN
Foul odor, "uncinate fit"	Temporal uncus-amygdaloid area
Micropsia or macropsia	Middle-inferior temporal gyrus
Déjà vu (intense familiarity)	Parahippocampal-hippocampal area
Jamais vu (environmental unfamiliarity)	
Fragments of voices, phrases, songs	Auditory association cortex
Lip smacking, abdominal pain, borborygmi, epigastric rising, cardiac arrhythmia	Insular, temporal-polar limbic cortex
Dreamy feelings, fear, pleasure, anger	Parahippocampal and septal areas

TABLE 118–4. COMMON ICTAL MANIFESTATIONS OF LIMBIC PARTIAL COMPLEX SEIZURES

Autonomic:	Flushing, pallor, tachypnea, nausea, eructation-borborygmi, sweating, cardiac arrhythmia
Cognitive:	Intense déjà vu (familiarity), jamais vu (spatial amnesia), forced thinking, dreamlike states, depersonalization
Affective:	Laughing, fear, rage, depression, elation
Sensory:	Olfactory hallucinations; macropsia, micropsia, familiar voice fragments, visualized objects or scenes, emotional experiences (dreamy states)
Motor:	Staring with lip smacking, chewing, semipurposeful rubbing; confused, bizarre behavior; walking or, occasionally, running; postictal confusion or drowsiness

fugue states. Absence attacks are abrupt in onset and offset, last only a few seconds, usually are unaccompanied by subjective self-awareness, do not produce auras or automatisms, and are associated with a diagnostic EEG abnormality. Psychiatric fugues can be more difficult to distinguish, especially from true psychomotor attacks in patients who have normal EEGs. Psychiatric states, however, include a past history of sustained psychiatric or behavioral aberration, they last longer than seizures, they lack the characteristic evolution from aura to attack to a drowsy and confused postictal state, and they often have a self-rewarding relationship to life situations that is lacking in true epilepsy. Partial complex seizures rarely offer a satisfactory explanation for unprovoked violence or planned crime.

Generalized Epilepsies

Secondary Generalization

As noted above, many partial seizures can evolve rapidly into generalized convulsions before the epileptic discharge burns itself out. Occasionally the generalized seizure explodes before any focal behavioral sign exposes itself. In such instances meticulous electroencephalographic (EEG) study, brain imaging, or detecting restricted postictal weakness may be needed to discover the focus and the lesion causing it.

TABLE 118–5. TYPES OF NONCONVULSIVE, GENERALIZED EPILEPSY

Absence seizures (petit mal): Common. Begin in childhood. High genetic influence. No structural brain abnormalities. Diagnostic EEG. Good cognitive prognosis.

Adult petit mal status: A rare middle-life disorder producing sustained dulled behavior; EEG resembles petit mal. Only some respond to standard anticonvulsants. Some deteriorate intellectually.

Myoclonus: Benign (juvenile) epileptic myoclonus. Fairly common. Begins in late childhood or adolescence. Autosomal dominant abnormality of chromosome 6. Clinically mild. EEG relates to petit mal.

Secondary myoclonic epilepsy: Several severe degenerative diseases of children and adults cause generalized or multifocal myoclonic attacks. Acquired causes include anoxia, encephalitis, and severe trauma.

Atonic-akinetic epilepsy and infantile spasms: Severe myoclonic or spasmogenic illnesses of infancy and young childhood.

Partial myoclonus: Is not myoclonus but a rhythmic 120/min tremor of the soft palate associated with brain stem–cerebellar disease.

Primary Generalized Epilepsies

These can take several forms depending upon the patient's age at onset and the extent and nature of any associated structural or metabolic disease of the brain. The generalized epilepsies can be divided conveniently according to whether or not they produce major convulsions.

Nonconvulsive Generalized Epilepsy
(Table 118–5)

Absence Seizures (Petit Mal). Absence seizures usually begin between ages 2 and 12 years, almost always before age 20. No structural or metabolic disease has as yet been identified as the cause, al-though genetic studies show an approximately 40 per cent incidence of EEG abnormalities among first-degree relatives. Neither intelligence nor other neurologic functions are impaired.

Simple absence attacks last no more than 1 to 2 seconds and are characterized by a blank stare, often accompanied by mild 3- to 4-Hz blinking of the eyelids. The child's head droops, the lids and sometimes the arms jerk rhythmically, and there may be brief motor automatisms and enuresis. In severely affected children, dozens to 100 or more such episodes can occur in a single day. More protracted, *complex absence attacks* can last for 15 to 30 seconds, rarely as long as a minute.

Both the clinical pattern and the EEG are typical (Fig. 118–1). The EEG contains repeated bursts and runs of symmetric 3.5-Hz activity. Overbreathing for 60 to 180 seconds often induces both the electrical abnormality and the seizures. Atypical seizures or EEG patterns that differ from the above suggest one of the less benign generalized childhood epilepsies. About half the children with petit mal seizures develop generalized tonic-clonic convulsions before the age of 20. Status epilepticus with petit mal seizures is described in a later section.

Myoclonus, a brief, unexpected, and uncontrollable jerk of the entire body or a focal portion of the trunk or one of the extremities, is a common, normal phenomenon that often occurs during presleep drowsiness. Diffuse, multifocal, or repetitive myoclonus, however, is abnormal and occurs in several degenerative toxic and infectious neurologic disorders as well as in several of the severe childhood epilepsies (Table 118–5).

Bilateral benign (juvenile) epileptic myoclonus consists of bilateral repetitive mild myoclonic jerks affecting girls more than boys and arms more than legs. The disease usually begins during early adoles-

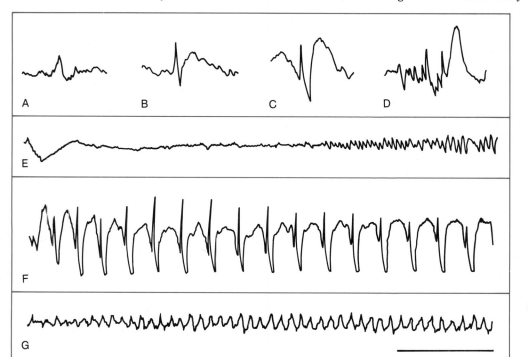

FIGURE 118–1. Electroencephalographic (EEG) patterns in seizure disorders. *A,* Interictal sharp wave. *B, C,* Interictal spike-and-wave complexes. *D,* Interictal polyspike-and-wave complex. *E,* Recruiting rhythm typical of the onset of a generalized convulsion. *F,* Repetitive spike-and-wave discharges typical of absence seizures. *G,* Rhythmic pattern seen with temporal lobe seizures. Line at the bottom right of the figure represents 1 second. (From Engel J: The epilepsies. In Wyngaarden JB, Smith LH, Bennett JC [eds]: Cecil Textbook of Medicine. 19th ed. Philadelphia, WB Saunders Co, 1992, p 2208.)

cence, and the symmetric jerks especially involve the shoulders and arms. Often, the EEG contains bifrontal 3.5- to 4-Hz sharp and slow activity similar to that found in absence seizures. The disorder pathogenetically and genetically lies close to petit mal and carries a similar modest risk of future tonic-clonic seizures. It responds to similar medication, especially sodium valproate, but may be so mild as to require no treatment. Table 118–5 describes other, less common forms of myoclonic attacks.

Generalized Convulsive Epilepsy

Generalized convulsive epilepsy can take either the tonic-clonic or tonic form.

Tonic-clonic (grand mal) seizures can begin at any age. Most produce loss of consciousness at onset, although patients occasionally report a brief rising epigastric sensation as the attack begins. Any focal manifestations in the evolution of the attack or in the postictal period suggest a localized structural cause rather than a generalized basis for the seizure. Prodromal warnings (not auras) sometimes precede the attacks by several hours and can include a change in mood, a sense of apprehension, insomnia, or loss of appetite. Sometimes clusters of repetitive myoclonus anticipate a convulsion. As the convulsion begins, patients may cry out unconsciously. They stiffen tonically in extension, usually with muscles contracted so tightly as to arrest breathing. Deep cyanosis follows before relaxation and a first post-tonic breath ensue. Such vigorously tonic phases seldom last as much as a minute but may be repeated several times over. Gradually, hyperextension gives way to a series of rapid successive clonic jerks of neck, trunk, and extremities. Finally, flaccid relaxation ensues, accompanied by stertorous breathing, pallor, and profuse salivation. Hypertension, tachycardia, and heavy perspiration accompany the motor changes. The pupils may be briefly fixed and moderately dilated during the tonic convulsions. Absent oculocephalic reflexes, hyperactive deep tendon reflexes, and extensor plantar responses can outlast the seizure for several minutes, but these changes usually disappear along with the reappearance of arousal 2 to 3 minutes after the relaxation phase begins. Many patients bite their tongues or lose sphincter control during attacks. Sometimes the tonic contractions are so strong that they compress dorsal or upper lumbar vertebrae. Other serious injuries are uncommon. Fatigue, muscle weakness and soreness, generalized headache, and drowsiness follow grand mal attacks. Occasionally, confusion can last for several hours. Most patients sleep postictally and awaken several hours later with only muscle soreness to remind them that a convulsion has occurred.

During the convulsive movement of generalized seizures EEG recordings disclose rapidly repeating spike discharges followed by sharp-slow activity as clonic contractions supervene. Postictally the record becomes abnormally slow, sometimes for several hours. The interictal EEG can be normal in about 20 per cent of instances but usually contains spike-slow complexes, bursts of abnormally slow activity, or mixtures of spike and slow activity in bursts or in short, 10- to 20-second runs appearing symmetrically over the scalp (Fig. 118–1).

Unusual Seizures and Other Conditions Responding to Antiepileptic Medication

In predisposed persons, a variety of sensory stimuli can precipitate *reflex epilepsy*. Photogenic seizures can be triggered by stroboscopic lights, driving past a stand of trees that filters the sun, or even waving the hand in front of eyes fixed upon bright illumination. The ensuing generalized seizure can take the form of myoclonus, an absence attack, or a tonic-clonic convulsion. Closely related are seizures elicited by looking at certain geometric patterns or, rarely, by reading. Polarized glasses may reduce the stimulus intensity of photosensitive attacks; valproic acid is the most effective anticonvulsant. Other rarer forms of responses to sensory stimuli consist of unduly violent, repetitive startle responses to noise as well as partial complex seizures triggered by particular musical themes.

Familial paroxysmal choreoathetosis is a rare disorder, inherited as an autosomal dominant or recessive trait and characterized by paroxysms of choreiform, dystonic, and athetoid body torsions occurring during full consciousness. Stress or sudden movement can precipitate the episodes. Phenytoin or carbamazepine relieves most cases.

Recurrent torsion spasms consist of episodic dystonic spasms affecting the face, trunk, and extremities in patients with multiple sclerosis. Body movement or startling stimuli can precipitate the attacks, which do not interfere with consciousness. The EEG remains normal, but phenytoin or carbamazepine treatment prevents the episodes.

Anticonvulsants also can favorably affect other disorders that result from an excess of central or peripheral excitation. Included are myokymia (p. 790) and *lightning pains*—episodic, severe, flashlike pains affecting the extremities, associated most often with neurosyphilis or diabetic neuropathy. Trigeminal neuralgia, a condition in which lightning pains affect one or more divisions of the fifth cranial nerve, is described on page 770. Relief by anticonvulsants is the common denominator that underlies all these difficulties.

Diagnosis

Given evidence that a seizure, automatism, or other brief episode of altered brain function has occurred, the major questions are whether it is epileptic and, if so, of what type and cause. Because the physician rarely can observe the attack, diagnosis usually derives from the history and supplementary, mostly inferential evidence.

The patient's description of his experience or a witness's accurate observation of an attack usually provides the most rewarding information. The setting of the attack often suggests acute causes such as drug withdrawal, CNS infection, trauma, or stroke; a history of recent-onset seizures in an adult suggests an intracranial mass lesion and a more chronically sustained or remote history of attacks suggests chronic epilepsy. Any focal feature reported either as an aura or during or following the seizure suggests a structural brain lesion demanding appropriate investigation. The pattern of an attack as well as the patient's age immediately delimits the possible types and causes (Table 118-6).

The physical and neurologic examinations are useful chiefly for identifying evidence of either systemic illness or structural neurologic disease. Laboratory studies should include lumbar puncture in children with acute-onset seizures as well as in any adolescent or adult suspected of developing CNS infection. Single seizures seldom affect the cerebrospinal fluid (CSF) content, but major motor status epilepticus temporarily can raise the protein concentration and generate up to 100 white cells mm³. Anyone in whom either the history, findings, or EEG suggests a focal abnormality, as well as all persons whose seizures begin after childhood, deserves an MR or CT scan with contrast enhancement. The older the patient, the higher the yield from such images.

TABLE 118-6. MAJOR CLINICAL FEATURES OF POSTINFANTILE EPILEPSY

AGE	MAJOR CAUSE	TYPES OF SEIZURES
Children <15 years	Idopathic and genetic epilepsy	Generalized (grand mal) Febrile convulsions Petit mal absence Adolescent myoclonus Partial complex attacks (uncommon)
	Developmental defects; birth trauma; inherited biochemical disorders; acute CNS infection-inflammation; post-traumatic or post-infectious	Generalized grand mal Partial motor, sensory, or psychological attacks, simple or complex Disseminated or multifocal myoclonus
	Brain tumors (uncommon)	Partial or generalized
Adults 15-25 + years	Idiopathic and genetic epilepsy	Generalized (grand mal) convulsions Polymyoclonus Partial complex seizures
	Acute CNS infection-inflammation; traumatic–post-traumatic; drug intoxication or withdrawal; brain tumor or arteriovenous malformation	Generalized or partial seizures
Adults >25 years	Brain tumor; CNS infection-inflammation; traumatic–post-traumatic; withdrawal; acute or post-stroke	Generalized or partial seizures

The EEG is particularly helpful in diagnosing the type of epilepsy and, therefore, its best therapy. The normal EEG contains fairly rhythmic, bilaterally symmetric potentials, with amplitudes ranging from about 20 to 200 mV (Fig. 118-1). The typical EEG frequencies recorded in healthy adults are 8.5 to 13 Hz, called alpha; 13 to 30 Hz, called beta; 4 to 7 Hz, called theta; and 0.5 to 4 Hz, called delta. Wakeful persons at rest typically show a dominant alpha rhythm, which accelerates into less rhythmic, faster frequencies during concentrated attention and after ingesting certain drugs. Frequencies of 8 Hz and slower occur normally during drowsiness or sleep; such slowing during wakefulness commonly reflects an abnormality of brain function. Regionally localized or asymmetric bursts of slowing, sharp waves, or spikelike waves characteristically reflect focal disturbances in brain function, whereas paroxysmal and symmetric slow, sharp, or sharp-slow activity is typical of primary epilepsy. One must recall, however, that as many as 20 per cent of patients with clinically typical epilepsy can have normal records, whereas 2 to 5 per cent of persons who never have a seizure can express occasional epileptic-like sharp waves or sharp-slow activity in the EEG. Most laboratories routinely employ hyperventilation and stroboscopic stimulation to activate potential EEG abnormalities. Atypical electrode placements, sleep studies, and telemetry are diagnostic tools utilized by specialists.

Chief to be considered in the differential diagnosis of epilepsy are syncope at all ages, pseudoseizures and other factitious attacks among adolescents and younger adults, and cerebral transient ischemic attacks in older patients.

Syncope (p. 744) provides the biggest problem, because one seldom can observe the attack and retrospective histories incline toward ambiguity. Furthermore, the disorder often recurs and, if severe, sometimes is punctuated at the maximum of hypotension by a brief, tonic seizure. As Table 118-7 indicates, however, syncope always occurs when sitting or standing except when associated with episodic cardiac arrest. Furthermore, attacks of syncope last a shorter time than seizures, produce characteristic changes in the patient's appearance and motor behavior, cause no postictal confusion or headache, and often are linked to emotional or visceral stimulation. Persons with syncope characteristically lack EEG abnormalities, and neither anticonvulsants nor other medications reliably improve the condition.

Factitious seizures or pseudoseizures provide a diagnostic challenge because they sometimes occur in persons who suffer from organic epilepsy as well. Most hysterical seizures occur in emotionally stressful settings or to achieve secondary gain. Certain features suggest pseudoseizures: rapidly rolling the head or body from side to side, an alternating thrashing of the extremities or pelvic thrusting. Few hysterics soil or injure themselves during attacks, whereas many epileptics do. Nevertheless, hysterics or malingerers can be good actors and their attacks can fool even experienced observers. A dependable but expensive way to differentiate organic from hysterical major motor seizures is to obtain a serum prolactin level immediately postictally: the level rises with true convulsions but not with hysteria. In most instances, however, observing the pattern of the attack coupled with obtaining a normal postictal EEG and employing diagnostic common sense yields the answer.

Episodic fugue states or attacks of behavioral dyscontrol sometimes become confused with partial complex seizures (p. 843). Most such episodes bear little resemblance to the stereotyped automatisms of temporal lobe epilepsy. As with major convulsion-like attacks, a strongly abnormal EEG inclines one toward a diagnosis of epilepsy. In difficult cases, telemetric monitoring of behavior concurrently with EEG recording can assist diagnosis.

Cerebral transient ischemic attacks (TIAs) (p. 825) only rarely produce symptoms resembling epilepsy, because their principal effects consist of ischemic hypofunction rather than epileptic hyperfunction. Occasionally, however, aphasic speech arrest can occur with TIAs, and a few TIA patients develop contralateral or generalized trembling of the extremities which may resemble epileptic phenomena. The recent development of symptoms, the vascular distribution of the changes, the lack of an epileptogenic lesion by clinical evaluation or brain imaging, and the presence of other signs of systemic or cerebral vascular disease almost always lead to the correct diagnosis.

Several other kinds of episodic events may briefly suggest seizures but can be dismissed by obtaining a careful history or description of the attack. These include breath-holding attacks in young children; migraine, which in children sometimes causes ataxia, vomiting, visual hallucinations or delirium, and stupor; narcolepsy-cataplexy; hyperventilation spells; and drop attacks in older adults. Nonepileptic causes of recurrent seizures include hypocalcemia, which can occur spontaneously in children and following parathyroidectomy in adults, hypoglycemia at any age, and recurrent alcohol or depressant drug withdrawal in adults.

Management

The initial management of recurrent seizures consists of efforts to halt the attacks completely. With symptomatic epilepsy this is followed by efforts to eradicate the cause, whereas in idiopathic seizure disorders antiepileptic therapy must be supplemented by efforts to help the patient adjust to a disease that brings fear to most and shame to many.

Control of Seizures

The ultimate goal is to achieve complete seizure control with minimal or absent antiepileptic drug toxicity. At present, in about 60 per cent of patients with chronic epilepsy, medication suppresses seizures completely and substantially improves another 15 to 20 per cent. Many of the uncontrollable patients suffer from a serious underlying disease of the brain, whereas others are psychologically unable to comply with therapeutic instructions. Certain principles can be listed that guide optimal pre-

TABLE 118–7. MAJOR DISTINCTIONS OF SYNCOPE FROM SEIZURES

SIGN	SYNCOPE	SEIZURES
Prodromes	Usually nausea, "swimming" sensation, faintness, sometimes none	Aura or epigastric rise. Often none
Onset	Sitting or erect	Any position
Self-awareness	Always present	Sometimes absent (petit mal absences)
Motor activity	Usually none, occasionally brief clonic. Rare convulsions with cardiac arrests	Focal, tonic, clonic, sustained
Duration	Seconds	0.5–2 min
Cardiovascular		
Appearance	Pulse slow, weak	Pulse fast, strong
Postictal	Pale, sweating	Flushed, salivating
	Oriented, sweaty, nauseated, sometimes vomiting, diarrhea	Confused, headache, drowsy
EEG	Normal	Abnormal

scribing of antiepileptic drugs and enhance the likelihood of their success.

1. Many persons have a single seizure with no recurrence. Accordingly, start long-term treatment on patients after a single, first attack only when a defined cause can be found that is likely to generate recurrences. Special social or vocational circumstances may override this rule. The principle of avoiding chronic treatment for only a single event also applies to uncomplicated febrile convulsions (see below).

2. Diagnose accurately the probable type of epilepsy and give the single preferred medication in full recommended therapeutic dose.

3. If a single drug does not control the seizures, even at toxic levels, try another. Similarly, if the first anticonvulsant causes serious side effects, withdraw it but immediately initiate the next most effective agent. If efforts at single drug therapy fail, most patients are best referred to a specialized center for consultation, because combined therapy is often difficult to regulate without producing toxicity. In any event, adjust medications gradually so as to accomplish maximal seizure control with minimal side effects.

4. Never stop anticonvulsant medications for generalized seizures abruptly. Status epilepticus may result.

Choice of Anticonvulsants. Table 118–8 lists the author's order of preference for effective anticonvulsants for the various types of chronic epilepsy. Table 118–9 summarizes some of the major toxicities of these agents. As with any potent medication, physicians and patients should read package inserts before prescribing. Notwithstanding these precautions, one must never forget that recurrent seizures constitute a physically dangerous, emotionally devastating, and intelligence-threatening risk. By comparison, the incidence of potential complications of antiepileptic therapy is almost trivial.

Use of Drug Levels in Management. The determination of blood levels can be a valuable adjunct to treatment. "Therapeutic" blood levels reflect empirically established values at which most patients acquire seizure control without toxic side effects. Many patients become well-controlled (or occasionally toxic) below the maximal therapeutic level, whereas others show no ill effects despite blood values above this point. In all instances the clinical response, not the blood level, defines the goal of the treatment.

Drug level determinations are especially useful within 2 to 3 weeks after beginning therapy so as to determine the patient's compliance, to judge his/her metabolic response to the medication, and to compare the pharmacologic and clinical effects. They also can be helpful when drug dosage is changed, because individual detoxification mechanisms can be saturated when antiepileptic drugs are increased or can overact to cause subtherapeutic ranges when the dose is reduced. Blood levels should be rechecked when patients are placed on an additional anticonvulsant or receive other medications that may influence hepatic enzyme systems.

An occasional blood level determination obtained during the course of chronic, effective therapy helps patients to understand the need for continued compliance. When seizures are well controlled, blood levels need be checked no more than annually.

Status Epilepticus

When seizures follow one another so rapidly that a new attack begins before the previous one has ceased, status epilepticus exists. Attacks that follow in close succession but with brief periods of reawakening between are designated *serial seizures*. Each condition can occur with either partial or generalized epilepsy. Status epilepticus is of special concern because the successive or continuous epileptic activity sometimes can damage the brain permanently. Without actually knowing that several seizures have occurred in rapid succession, however, the diagnosis cannot be made. Accordingly, if an accurate witness is unavailable, one must wait and be sure that epileptic attacks are still continuing before initiating the treatment outlined in Table 118–10.

Partial motor status, an uncommon condition sometimes known as *partial continuous epilepsy*, occurs in several forms and can last for hours, days, or even as long as a year or more. The seizure frequency can range from as little as one every 3 seconds to as many as several per second. The motor attacks can consist of as little as a highly focal, myoclonic, repetitively localized twitch to jerks that involve most of the limb or even half the body, not always affecting precisely the same muscles. In general, cerebral lesions cause partial motor seizures in the face or distal upper extremity, whereas brain stem or spinal lesions tend to cause proximal myoclonic activity. Large hemorrhagic or ischemic strokes cause about half the cases, whereas trauma, neoplasms, or encephalitic processes produce the rest. Sometimes the cause never becomes clear despite extensive searching. Furthermore, partial continuous epilepsy commonly resists any and all efforts at treatment.

Partial complex status produces a sustained state of confusion associated with stereotyped motor and autonomic automatisms as well as dull, slow, blunted behavior, often combined with semimuteness. Some attacks produce a schizophreniform or stuporous state, whereas others are marked by bizarre, detached activity. Patients may resist assistance in their fuguelike state, which can last for hours and sometimes days. The EEG usually shows continuous slow and spike activity predominating over one or both temporal areas, commonly in an asymmetric distribution. Occasionally, surface recordings may be only mildly abnormal, but epilepti-

TABLE 118–8. CURRENT BEST DRUGS FOR EPILEPSY

TYPE OF SEIZURE AND DRUG	USUAL TOTAL ADULT DOSE (gm)	DAILY DOSES	THERAPEUTIC BLOOD LEVELS (μ/ml)
Generalized tonic-clonic			
Carbamazepine	0.8–1.2	3–4	8–12
Valproate	1–4	4	50–100
Phenytoin	0.3–0.5	2	10–20
Phenobarbital	0.1–0.25	1	15–40
Absence seizures			
Ethosuximide	0.75–2.0	2	40–100
Valproate	Same as above		
Clonazepam	0.002–0.020	2	0.01–0.005
Partial epilepsies			
Carbamazepine	Same as above		
Phenytoin	Same as above		
Valproate	Same as above		
Phenobarbital	Same as above		
Clonazepam	Same as above		

TABLE 118–9. TOXICITY OF COMMON ANTIEPILEPTIC DRUGS

Carbamazepine
Dose-related: Mental slowing, nausea, drowsiness, ataxia, nystagmus
Idiosyncratic: Exanthema, inappropriate ADH secretion, leukopenia, aplastic anemia (rare), hepatic toxicity (rare)
Phenytoin
Dose excess: Tremor, vertigo, nystagmus, ataxia, drowsiness
Hypersensitivity: Gingival hyperplasia, hirsutism, coarse features, exanthema
Valproate
Dose-related: Increased appetite, hair loss, tremor, ataxia, drowsiness
Idiosyncratic: Toxic hyperammonemia, hepatic toxicity
Phenobarbital
Dose excess: Drowsiness, mental slowing, dysarthria, ataxia, nystagmus
Idiosyncratic: Exanthema
Primidone
Same as Phenobarbital
Ethosuximide
Dose-related: Dyspepsia, hiccup, headache, insomnia
Idiosyncratic: Psychotic behavior, aplastic anemia (rare)
Clonazepam
Dose-related (in up to 50 per cent): Sedation, muscular hypotonia, ataxia, oral and tracheobronchial hypersecretion

form activity can be detected on nasopharyngeal leads or from electrodes placed deep in the brain. Treatment should be initiated promptly, as the effects of prolonged seizures can permanently impair memory and intellect.

Absence status (petit mal status) occurs in two forms. The more common resembles partial complex status and consists of semiconfused automatic behavior accompanied by closely fused or continuous runs of 3- to 4-Hz spike and wave activity on the EEG. The condition occurs in patients with known petit mal and usually is confined to adolescents or occasionally young adults. Most episodes last less than 30 minutes. Similar behavioral attacks of prolonged (days to months) automatisms associated with confusion, EEG abnormality, and sometimes gradual interictal mental deterioration can occur in older persons with no history of epilepsy. Most but not all such attacks can be halted with diazepam given intravenously.

Major generalized motor status epilepticus with tonic-clonic convulsions creates a medical emergency, because continuation of the convulsions beyond an hour or so commonly produces residual brain damage. The most frequent cause is abrupt withdrawal of anticonvulsant medications from a known epileptic. Other precipitants include withdrawal of alcohol or drugs in a habitual user, cerebral infection, trauma, hemorrhage, or neoplasms. Treatment of the convulsions and protection of the brain are of immediate concern and should take the form outlined in Tables 118–8 and 118–10. Specific diagnostic steps to identify and treat the seizures must be undertaken as soon as possible after seizures have been controlled.

Special Management Problems

Febrile Convulsions. Convulsions caused by fever occur mainly in neurologically otherwise healthy children between the ages of 6 months and 5 years who recurrently develop single generalized seizures when affected by an acute, fever-producing illness. Factors that increase the chance of having a future chronic epileptic disorder include age less than 1 year at onset, convulsions lasting longer than 15 minutes or coming in clusters, any pre- or postictal sign of neurologic abnormality, or a family history of epilepsy. Present practice is to do everything possible to limit the course of the single convulsion but to place only children who have high risk factors on medication, usually phenobarbital.

Menstruation, Genetic Counseling, and Pregnancy. A number of women with epilepsy suffer an increase in seizures during the days immediately preceding and following the onset of menses. Acetazolamide, 250 to 500 mg daily, taken prophylactically or a modest increase in medication during the susceptible days often counteracts the problem.

Persons with seizure disorders should be advised about the hereditary risks to the fetus. Best evidence suggests that during their lifetime 4 to 10 per cent of the offspring of patients with generalized primary epilepsy suffer one or more seizures. This compares to an incidence of approximately 1.5 per cent of the

TABLE 118–10. TREATMENT OF ADULT STATUS EPILEPTICUS OR SERIAL SEIZURES

I. Convulsive tonic-clonic or complex partial status
1. Assure the airway, give O_2, check blood pressure and pulse. Establish a venous line and draw blood for glucose, calcium, hyper- or hypo-osmolar indicants. If indicated, measure pH, PaO_2, $PaCO_2$.
2. Promptly start infusion and give 50 ml of 50% glucose.
3. Infuse diazepam intravenously 5 mg/min until seizures stop or to total 20 mg. Also start phenytoin 50 mg/min to total 18 mg/kg.
4. If convulsions persist, give *either* (1) phenobarbital 100 mg/min or as loading dose to 20 mg/kg, or (2) 100 mg diazepam in 500 ml dextrose 5% run in at 40 ml/hr. Monitor ventilation closely.
5. If convulsions persist, start anesthesia with pentobarbital, intubation, and, if seizures persist, neuromuscular blockade.

II. Serial tonic-clonic or partial motor status
Steps 3 and 4 above but do not induce coma.

III. Petit mal status
Diazepam as in step 3 followed by oral ethosuximide, valproic acid, or both

general population. Rates in the partial epilepsies are less clearly different from the norm.

Chronic anticonvulsant medication often requires adjustment during pregnancy because blood volume increases and drug pharmacokinetics change. Blood level monitoring during the latter half of pregnancy can be useful in managing the difficult-to-control woman. During pregnancy, it is advisable to give vitamins and supplements, including folic acid and calcium. Vitamin K, 5 mg twice weekly, should be given orally during the final 6 weeks, with a parenteral supplement administered to the mother and infant at the time of delivery. Breast feeding is not contraindicated in women taking antiepileptics.

Teratogenic Effects. The overall incidence of important birth defects in children of mothers or fathers taking antiepileptic medication is two to three times higher than in the general population. The exact role of medication in these figures is uncertain. Seizures offer a greater risk to the mother and fetus than does the generally low rate of birth defects associated with antiepileptic drugs. Two agents, trimethadione and valproate, have been incriminated with especially high teratogenicity in experimental studies. Phenytoin, phenobarbital, or carbamazepine use during pregnancy, however, has been associated with development of the "fetal antiepileptic syndrome." Given all factors, phenobarbital probably has the least teratogenic effect.

Surgical Therapy. In addition to attempting to remove specific mass or destructive brain lesions that include seizures among their symptoms, several surgical treatments have been developed in efforts to halt or ameliorate medically intractable, chronic seizure disorders. Procedures include, for particular indications, local resection of seizure foci, anterior temporal lobe resections, section of the corpus callosum, and, rarely, subtotal hemispherectomy. Results can be favorable in as many as two thirds or more of cases, provided that meticulous preoperative evaluation and selection are carried out. The procedures are best conducted in large medical centers sponsoring specialized programs for determining the cause and best treatment of epilepsy.

Psychosocial Management. The presence of incompletely controlled epilepsy and its frequent association with other neurologic limitations often create large emotional problems for the patient. In addition, disorders that cause partial complex seizures may result in aberrant personality traits that intensify isolation. Outbreaks of frustration, depression, and suicide are more frequent among patients with epilepsy than in the general population. A reduced libido and hyposexuality have been noted in males with partial complex seizures. By contrast, in the absence of associated brain damage most persons with epilepsy score in the normal range on intelligence tests. Many persons with controlled epilepsy have performed superbly at every level of professional, governmental, artistic, and business life.

Patients with seizure disorders are helped most by bringing the attacks under control, but reassurance, empathy, and optimistic social guidance aid immeasurably. Once seizures are under control, affected persons should be encouraged to live a normal life using common sense as their guide. Body-contact and high-risk sports are best avoided unless seizures have been completely controlled for well over a year; high diving, deep water or underwater swimming, high alpine climbing, boxing, and head-contact football are ill-advised. Most states grant automobile driver's licenses to patients with epilepsy provided that no seizures have occurred for at least a year. Life and health insurance policies are available under special circumstances. The Epilepsy Foundation of America can assist patients with these and other social-vocational considerations.

Discontinuation of Medication. One considers stopping antiepileptic medication either (1) because seizures continue and all concerned believe the drugs are ineffective or (2) because seizures have been completely controlled for a long time. The first condition is uncommon and must be approached cautiously because of the dangers of precipitating status epilepticus. The latter decision can be considered between patient and doctor when absence seizures have been fully suppressed for 2 or 3 years and other types of seizures for 3 to 5 years. The patient's value system, economic and social factors, and knowledge of risks all should contribute to the decision. Between 20 and 50 per cent of those who discontinue treatment experience recurrent seizures, which may be more difficult to control than the original attacks. Particularly likely to relapse are persons whose initial seizures lasted longer than 6 months, were difficult to control, or were associated with any specific neurologic abnormality. A moderate or severely abnormal EEG represents an additional risk of recurrence if treatment stops. In general, we advise most socioeconomically stable, well-controlled adult epileptics to stop anticonvulsant medication only if they show drug toxicity. For most, the cost of relapse is just too high.

REFERENCES

Engel J Jr: Seizures and Epilepsy. Philadelphia, FA Davis Co, 1989.
Levy RH, Dreifuss FE, Mattson RH, et al: Antiepileptic Drugs. 3rd ed. New York, Raven Press, 1989.
Roger J, Dravet C, Bureau M, et al: Epileptic Syndromes in Infancy, Childhood and Adolescence. London, John Libbey Eurotext, 1985.

119 INTRACRANIAL NEOPLASMS, CNS COMPLICATIONS OF CANCER, AND STATES OF ALTERED INTRACRANIAL PRESSURE

INTRACRANIAL NEOPLASMS

Introduction and Definitions

Intracranial tumors can arise from any structure within the intracranial cavity. Most begin in the brain, but the pituitary, pineal region, cranial nerves, and leptomeninges are also sites of neoplastic degeneration. Furthermore, any of these structures may be the site of metastatic spread from tumors that arise outside the nervous system. Intracranial tumors are not rare; they are the second most common cancer in children, and in adults malignant brain tumors are more common than Hodgkin's disease. Brain lymphoma and malignant glioma appear to be increasing in incidence. Also, the incidence appears to be increasing as the population ages. Symptomatic metastatic intracranial tumors are equal to or greater in number than primary neoplasms (Table 119–1).

Intracranial tumors can be classified both by site of origin and by histologic type. Most arise from neuroectodermal elements (the precursor of both neurons and glia). The terms *benign* and *malignant* applied to brain tumors reflect histologic criteria that in turn reflect local growth rate rather than propensity to metastasize. Even highly malignant primary brain tumors rarely metastasize, although they may spread locally from the parenchyma to seed the leptomeninges and spinal cord. Many "benign" brain tumors recur despite treatment and eventually lead to the demise of the patient. Others may undergo "malignant degeneration" that alters their biologic potentiality.

Classification

Neuroectodermal Tumors. The most common neuroectodermal tumor is the *astrocytoma.* Astrocytomas can arise anywhere in the brain or spinal cord and infiltrate surrounding normal structures. Small nests of tumor cells often can be found several centimeters from the main bulk. In some instances, astrocytomas may have a multicentric origin or, more rarely, infiltrate the entire neuraxis (gliomatosis cerebri). Some, particularly cerebellar astrocytomas of childhood, may become quiescent for dec-

ades after only partial resection. About half of astrocytomas grow slowly. The others consist of rapidly growing tumors that include the anaplastic astrocytoma and the glioblastoma multiforme. In adults, benign astrocytomas have a prognosis of 4 to 7 years, anaplastic astrocytomas 1.5 to 2.5 years, and glioblastoma usually 1 year or less. *Oligodendrogliomas* usually grow more slowly than astrocytomas and tend to calcify. Glial tumors are often mixed, so that elements of oligodendroglioma may be found within a tumor that is primarily astrocytic in origin, and areas of benign astrocytoma may be found within a malignant glioblastoma. Because of the heterogeneity of such tumors, small biopsies may give misleading diagnostic and prognostic information. Primary lymphomas of the nervous system are increasing in frequency in both immunosuppressed and immunocompetent individuals. They are often multifocal in the brain and seed the leptomeninges. Common sites of *ependymomal* growth include the fourth ventricle in children and the spinal cord in children and adults. Malignant ependymomas of the fourth ventricle tend to spread to involve the leptomeninges. *Medulloblastomas* arise from a primitive neuroectodermal cell, usually in the cerebellum, and likewise may seed throughout the CSF. They are predominantly tumors of childhood and are highly malignant, but 50 per cent of children treated by surgery and radiation therapy now survive more than 5 years. In children, astrocytomas represent

TABLE 119–1. COMMON INTRACRANIAL TUMORS IN ADULTS

METASTATIC (50%)		PRIMARY (50%)			
		BRAIN TUMOR (70%)		OTHER INTRACRANIAL TUMOR (30%)	
Lung	40%	Glioblastoma	40%	Meningioma	80%
Breast	20%	Anaplastic astro-cytoma	20%	Acoustic neuroma	10%
Melanoma	20%	Astrocytoma	15%	Pituitary adenoma	5%
Miscellaneous	20%	Lymphoma	10%	Miscellaneous	5%
		Oligodendroglioma	5%		
		Miscellaneous	10%		

851

half of all cerebellar tumors, medulloblastomas and ependymomas making up the rest.

Mesodermal Tumors. The most common mesodermal tumor is *meningioma.* Meningiomas are usually benign and arise in certain favored sites: along the dorsal surface of the brain, the base of the skull, the falx cerebri, the sphenoid ridge, or within the lateral ventricles. Although these tumors are benign, they often reach a large size before they are discovered and may be difficult to remove. Furthermore, they may recur even after apparently complete surgical extirpation. The most common cranial nerve tumor is the *acoustic schwannoma* (neurilemoma, neuroma). Early discovery of such tumors has been possible in recent years because of the development of refined auditory tests and MR scans, thereby enabling these tumors to be removed frequently via a translabyrinthine approach. *Pituitary adenomas* may begin as intrasellar masses and extend into extrasellar locations, causing visual loss. *Microadenomas,* asymptomatic except for their hormone secretion, can now be identified by high-resolution computed tomographic (CT) or magnetic resonance (MR) scan of the pituitary. *Craniopharyngiomas* are developmental tumors derived from Rathke's pouch and may be intrasellar or suprasellar in location; they are frequently calcified and often cystic. *Pineal region tumors* occur primarily in children. They rarely truly originate from the pineal gland itself but instead are germinomas, often curable by chemotherapy and radiation. The benign *colloid cyst* usually grows in the anterior third ventricle. Vascular tumors include *arteriovenous malformations,* which are not truly neoplastic, and the *hemangioblastomas,* which are. The latter tumors, when located in the brain stem or cerebellum, may be part of the von Hippel–Lindau syndrome that includes hemangioblastomas elsewhere in the body. Congenital tumors include the craniopharyngiomas, *chordomas* (which arise at the base of the brain or the lumbosacral area from the primitive notochord), *dermoids,* and *teratomas.* Granulomas and parasitic cysts come from tuberculomas, cryptococcosis (toruloma), sarcoidosis, and cysticercosis.

Metastatic Tumors. These can spread to any part of the intracranial cavity and tend to exhibit growth characteristics similar to their parent neoplasm. Metastatic tumors, unlike primary tumors, tend to be well-circumscribed rather than infiltrative and are easier to remove in toto than are primary neoplasms.

Symptoms and Signs

Because they arise within the closed box of the skull, intracranial tumors tend to cause symptoms and signs while still relatively small. Symptoms may be caused by any of the four following factors (Fig. 119–1). (1) The tumor invades, irritates, or replaces normal tissue. This probably accounts for only a minority of symptoms in brain tumors but is particularly characteristic of low-grade infiltrating gliomas. (2) The tumor growth compresses normal tissues. As intracranial tumors grow, they compress surrounding tissues and cause shift of normal brain structures. Blood vessels are compressed as well, leading to ischemia of the surrounding tissue. (3) New vessels formed in the growing brain tumor do not possess a blood-brain barrier (that anatomic-physiologic structure that excludes proteins, ion-

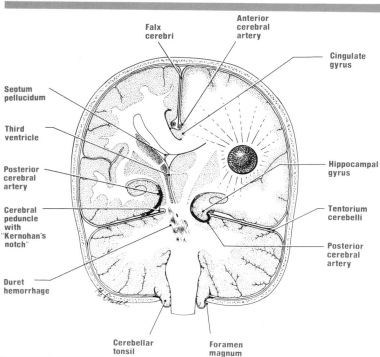

Falx cerebri
Anterior cerebral artery
Cingulate gyrus
Septum pellucidum
Third ventricle
Posterior cerebral artery
Cerebral peduncle with "Kernohan's notch"
Duret hemorrhage
Hippocampal gyrus
Tentorium cerebelli
Posterior cerebral artery
Cerebellar tonsil
Foramen magnum

FIGURE 119–1. Schematic representation of the pathophysiology of clinical symptoms caused by a brain tumor. A mass lesion (*black sphere*) and surrounding edema (*dashed lines*) enlarge the hemisphere, obliterating normal sulci and shifting normal structures caudally and across the midline. The tumor and surrounding edema destroy and displace normal tissue in the hemisphere, producing contralateral neurologic signs (e.g., weakness and sensory loss). Obliteration of subarachnoid spaces by the mass lesion raises intracranial pressure, producing generalized signs (e.g., headache and papilledema). Shifts of normal brain cause symptoms at a distance and may lead to cerebral herniation (see Chapter 112). (From Cairncross JG, Posner JB.) *In* Yarbro JW, Bornstein RS [eds]: Oncologic Emergencies. New York, Grune and Stratton, 1981; with permission.)

ized substances, and many water-soluble chemo-therapeutic agents from the normal CNS). The blood-brain barrier also breaks down in compressed tissue surrounding a brain tumor. As a result, edema forms both within and around the tumor, which adds to the mass in the brain. Furthermore, because the brain has no lymphatics, removal of edema is slow. That edema produces many of the symptoms of intracranial tumors is attested to by the dramatic response that most brain tumor symptoms show to corticosteroids. These drugs, which decrease brain edema by restoring the integrity of the blood-brain barrier, substantially ameliorate symptoms for most patients with brain tumors without having a biologically significant effect on the growth of the tumor. (4) Large or small strategically located tumors (third ventricular and fourth ventricular tumors, leptomeningeal tumors) obstruct cerebrospinal fluid (CSF) pathways, leading to hydrocephalus. The resulting inability of normally formed CSF to escape from the ventricular system or the subarachnoid space further adds unwanted mass and raises intracranial pressure.

The mass of a brain tumor plus the attendant edema and hydrocephalus all may lead to herniation of normal cerebral structures under the falx cerebri, through the tentorium or foramen magnum (Chapter 112).

The symptoms and signs caused by brain tumors depend on the location of the tumor and its histopathology (rapidity of growth). Sudden changes in tumor size resulting from hemorrhage, necrosis, or obstruction of CSF pathways can cause additional symptoms. Symptoms and signs may be divided into three major categories: (1) *generalized*, largely due to increased intracranial pressure; (2) *focal*, a result of ischemia and/or compression of normal brain at the site of the tumor; and (3) *false localizing*, a result of shifts of cerebral structures, causing neurologic abnormalities at a distance from the tumor.

Generalized Symptoms and Signs

The most common symptoms of increased intracranial pressure is *headache*. The head pain may be felt at the site of the tumor but more commonly is diffuse. In its early stages, the typical brain tumor headache is mild, tends to occur early in the morning when the patient first awakens, and disappears as the patient assumes an upright posture and breathes more deeply, thus lowering intracranial pressure. As the tumor enlarges, headaches become more constant and severe and are often exacerbated by coughing, bending, or sudden movement of the head. Later, headaches may awaken the patient at night. Headaches are common symptoms, only occasionally caused by brain tumors, but their onset in a patient not previously prone to headache or a recent change in headache pattern should alert the physician to the possibility of increased intracranial pressure. *Papilledema* occurs in about one tenth of patients with an intracranial neoplasm, probably as a result of obstruction of CSF pathways. Papilledema is much more common in children and young adults than it is in the elderly. *Vomiting*, with

or without preceding nausea, is a common symptom of intracranial hypertension in children but less so in adults. Vomiting usually occurs early in the morning before breakfast. It is often, but not always, accompanied by headache. Vomiting is more common in posterior fossa tumors but can occur with any tumor that raises intracranial pressure. *Mental changes* are also common. Patients first become irritable and then later quiet and apathetic. They retire to bed early, arise later (unless the early morning is accompanied by headache), and nap during the day. They are forgetful, seem preoccupied, and often appear psychologically depressed. Psychiatric consultation is frequently procured before the diagnosis of brain tumor is suspected. In patients with mass lesions and intracranial pressure, *plateau waves* are a common phenomenon. Plateau waves are increases in intracranial pressure that last between 5 and 20 minutes. They are caused by failure of normal cerebral vascular autoregulation so that an abrupt increase in cerebral blood volume occurs, causing the intracranial pressure to rise. Such pressure waves can increase an already high intracranial pressure by as much as 60 to 100 mm Hg. The wave may be asymptomatic but more commonly is accompanied by neurologic symptoms including headache, brief visual loss, altered consciousness, and sometimes weakness of the extremities. These episodic changes in neurologic function usually last only a few minutes and may be precipitated by a sudden rise from a lying position, by alterations in intracranial pressure associated with coughing, sneezing, or straining, or even by tracheal suctioning.

Focal Symptoms and Signs

The location of a brain tumor determines not only whether the growth is more likely to produce generalized or focal signs but also the type of focal signs it produces. Tumors arising in relatively silent areas of the brain (such as the frontal pole) may grow to large size, raise intracranial pressure, and cause severe signs of generalized brain dysfunction before focal signs are evident. Similarly, tumors arising in the ventricular system, particularly at the outflow of the third and fourth ventricles, also produce generalized signs before focal signs become evident. On the other hand, tumors arising in primary rather than association cortex are more likely at their outset to produce focal symptoms and signs. Tumors of the visual system cause visual loss or visual field deficits before generalized signs develop. Tumors of the sensorimotor cortex cause weakness and sensory change. In addition, because certain areas of the frontal lobe, temporal lobe, and sensorimotor cortex have a relatively low threshold for epileptic discharges, seizures are often an early symptom. If the tumor is in the sensorimotor cortex, the seizures take a focal sensory or motor pattern. Tumors arising in more silent areas can cause unrecognized focal epileptogenic discharges, which generalize to produce a grand mal seizure. Seizures are the most common presenting symptom of meningiomas and of low-grade infiltrating astrocytomas.

Cranial nerve tumors include trigeminal and acoustic schwannomas or meningiomas. Fifth nerve tumors are characterized by pain and sensory loss in the face, the pain sometimes resembling that of trigeminal neuralgia. Eighth nerve tumors are characterized by slowly progressive hearing loss with or without loss of balance. Both can be treated surgically.

A number of different tumors growing in the *pituitary fossa* and/or the *suprasellar cistern* lead to a combination of neurologic and endocrinologic abnormalities. The most common sellar tumor is the pituitary adenoma, a benign growth that often secretes excessive amounts of the hormone made by its parent cell. The tumors often remain very small, the only symptoms produced being those of hypersecretion of prolactin (amenorrhea-galactorrhea syndrome in women), growth hormone (acromegaly), or adrenocorticotropic hormone (Cushing's disease). Other adenomas, however, can grow to a large size, compressing and destroying the normal pituitary gland and leading to hypopituitarism and diabetes insipidus. As such tumors grow superiorly, they compress the diaphragma sella, a pain-sensitive structure, and cause headache. Immediately above the diaphragma sella lies the optic chiasm, compression of which leads to bitemporal hemianopsia. If the tumor grows laterally, it encounters the oculomotor nerves in the cavernous sinus, producing ocular palsies. Some pituitary tumors outgrow their blood supply. In this instance, patients suffer sudden hemorrhage or a necrosis into the tumor, producing the syndrome of *pituitary apoplexy*. A previously asymptomatic patient presents to the physician with acute headache plus visual changes (bitemporal hemianopsia or blindness), and sometimes oculomotor palsies. The patient is often febrile, with a stiff neck from spillage of blood and necrotic tissue into the subarachnoid space. A CT scan usually reveals a pituitary mass, often hemorrhagic. Emergency treatment with hormonal replacement and, often, decompression usually leads to a good outcome. Tumors arising in the *parasellar area* may cause visual loss simultaneous with or even before pituitary failure. The first sign of pituitary failure in these instances is usually diabetes insipidus; in children, failure of sexual development and obesity are common problems, probably resulting from compression of the hypothalamus. Craniopharyngiomas, optic gliomas, meningiomas, and sometimes large carotid aneurysms cause masses in this area, as do germinomas (ectopic pinealoma).

Most tumors arising in the *pineal area* are germinomas, teratomas, or other embryonal growths. These tumors are common in children, boys more than girls. They produce their symptoms by compression of the sylvian aqueduct, leading to hydrocephalus. Compression of fibers in the upper brain stem leads to loss of upward gaze and sometimes pupillary fixation, early signs of pineal region compression. Occasionally compression of the inferior colliculus causes deafness. A definitive diagnosis of pineal region tumor is important, because the germinomas are usually curable, whereas most of the others are not. *Leptomeningeal* tumors usually result from spread of a primary brain or systemic tumor to the leptomeninges; occasionally lymphoma or melanoma arises in the leptomeninges. Metastatic leptomeningeal invasion is common from lymphomas, leukemias, or solid tumors such as carcinomas of the breast or lung and malignant melanoma. Primary tumors of the nervous system that commonly seed the meninges include medulloblastomas, malignant ependymomas of the fourth ventricle, and germinomas. Symptoms of leptomeningeal involvement may occur before the primary tumor has declared itself. The first symptoms are often those of increased intracranial pressure from hydrocephalus (see Fig. 112–3). Additional symptoms include seizures from invasion of the cortex, cranial nerve palsies from infiltration of nerves passing through the subarachnoid space, and spinal root dysfunction, often involving the lower extremities and the bladder as a result of infiltration of the cauda equina. The diagnosis is suspected by the presence of diffuse or multifocal signs of CNS dysfunction and usually can be established by the identification of malignant cells in the CSF.

False Localizing Symptoms and Signs

Growing tumors mold the surrounding normal brain and displace adjacent and remote structures from their normal positions. When these structures are shifted, they may be compressed by nearby dura, by bone at the base of the skull, or by the bony foramina through which the cranial nerves pass. Compression of normal structures at a distance from the growing tumor leads to focal neurologic signs that may incorrectly localize the tumor. These false localizing signs usually occur with slow-growing tumors arising in relatively silent areas. Examples of well-recognized false localizing signs include diplopia as a result of displacement compression of the sixth nerve at the base of the brain, hemianopsia caused by tentorial herniation that compresses the posterior cerebral artery and produces ischemia to the occipital lobe, and tinnitus, vertigo, or hearing loss from compression of the eighth nerves as they pass through the internal auditory canal. False localizing signs rarely produce a diagnostic problem nowadays because of the availability of accurate imaging techniques. False localizing signs can also occur with pseudotumor cerebri or intracranial hypotension, in which their recognition is particularly important if one is to avoid unnecessarily exhaustive laboratory evaluation or inappropriate surgery.

Diagnostic Tests

In any patient clinically suspected of harboring an intracranial neoplasm, MR scan is the test of choice (Fig. 119–2). It can identify tumors sometimes missed by CT scan (low-grade gliomas and small posterior fossa lesions) and often helps differentiate tumor from arteriovenous malformations better than does CT. Meningiomas are often difficult to distinguish from normal structures by MR scan, unless the scan is enhanced by intravenous gadolinium. Radionuclide brain scan, skull radiographs, and electroencephalograms (EEGs) add nothing to the diagnosis. If a leptomeningeal tumor is suspected by the presence of unexplained hydrocephalus or a diffuse encephalopathy without focal abnormalities on a brain image, lumbar puncture should be performed to look for the typical changes of pleocytosis, malignant cells in the CSF, elevated protein, and hypoglycorrhachia (low glucose content). At times, contrast-enhanced MR scans or myelography identifies small tumors on the nerve roots.

Imaging techniques reveal the presence but not the exact nature of a lesion. Thus, neither CT nor MR can definitively distinguish between the histologic types of tumors, nor can they reliably differentiate between neoplasms and other tumors such as abscesses or granulomas. Angiography is useful primarily to assist the surgeon in defining the proximity of the tumor to nearby arteries and veins. If a lesion is present and cannot clearly be identified on clinical grounds, biopsy is necessary before treatment is undertaken. When the lesion is accessible, surgical excision not only establishes the diagnosis but also provides the first step in the treatment of the patient. If the lesion is not accessible, CT- or MR-directed stereotactic needle biopsy often can establish the diagnosis definitively.

Treatment

The treatment of intracranial neoplasms varies, depending on the nature of the neoplasm, its location, and the general condition of the patient. Certain general principles apply: When there is a single lesion and it is surgically accessible, it should be removed to whatever degree possible. Although some patients undergoing surgery of intracranial nec-

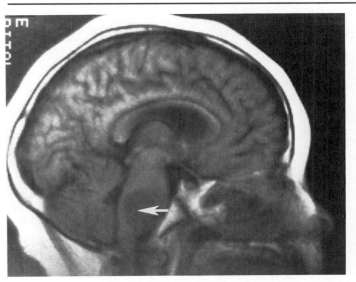

FIGURE 119–2. Magnetic resonance (MR) scan of an 18-year-old man with progressive cranial nerve symptoms suggesting a brain stem tumor. The computed tomographic (CT) scan was normal. Sagittal MRI reveals a mass (*arrow*) in the pons.

plasms suffer increased neurologic dysfunction, the majority improve after compression of brain structures is relieved. The advantages of surgery are that it cures some patients (pituitary adenoma, most meningiomas, cerebellar astrocytomas), it ameliorates symptoms in the majority of patients, and the debulking of a large malignant lesion allows time for other slower-acting therapeutic modalities to be effective. It also definitively establishes the diagnosis. An exception is the primary lymphoma of the brain, diagnosis of which should be established by stereo-

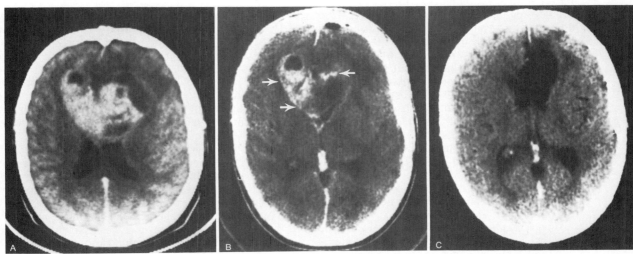

FIGURE 119–3. Results of treatment of glioblastoma multiforme. A 32-year-old man presented with headaches, seizures, and papilledema. A large contrast-enhancing bifrontal mass was partially extirpated and then treated with radiation therapy and chemotherapy. *A,* The mass prior to therapy. *B,* The mass shortly postoperatively, indicating that there had been a major but incomplete resection. A residual tumor is indicated by the arrows. *C,* CT scan 2.5 years later. The site of surgical extirpation is indicated by the lucent area. There is no evidence of contrast enhancement, suggesting that the residual tumor has been eradicated. The patient became asymptomatic.

tactic needle biopsy only. Treatment of that disorder is chemotherapy and radiation.

Most intracranial neoplasms cannot be cured surgically (Fig. 119–3). For them the second line of treatment is radiation therapy (RT). RT is delivered either to the site of the tumor, and to the entire neuraxis (e.g., with medulloblastomas), or to the whole brain (e.g., with multiple metastases). RT improves both survival and quality of life in most patients with malignant tumors. It probably also favorably affects the course of more benign tumors such as astrocytomas and recurrent meningiomas.

Chemotherapy, when added to RT, enhances both survival and quality of life of some patients with lymphoma and malignant astrocytomas, but its role in other intracranial neoplasms is not yet well established.

SPINAL NEOPLASMS

Spinal tumors originate from the same cell types as do intracranial tumors, and the same principles of diagnosis and treatment apply to them as to intracranial tumors. They are discussed in detail on pages 799 to 802.

PARANEOPLASTIC SYNDROMES

When patients with systemic cancer (i.e., cancer that arises outside the CNS) develop nervous system dysfunction, metastasis is usually the cause. However, cancer also exerts deleterious effects on the nervous system in the absence of direct metastatic involvement (paraneoplastic syndromes). Recognition of these nonmetastatic neurologic complications can prevent inappropriate and perhaps harmful therapy directed at a nonexistent metastasis. Since at times the nervous system symptoms precede the discovery of the cancer, they can also lead the physician to the diagnosis of an otherwise occult neoplasm. An almost bewildering variety of neurologic disorders have been ascribed to effects of systemic cancer (Table 119–2). Most patients with nervous system dysfunction not caused by metastases are eventually found to be suffering from systemic infections, from vascular or metabolic disorders that affect the nervous system secondarily, or from unwanted side effects of cancer therapy. This section discusses two types of nervous system damage related to cancer and not described elsewhere in this book: "remote effects" and radiation injury.

Remote Effects

Remote effects of cancer on the nervous system is a term used to describe nervous system dysfunction of unknown cause occurring either exclusively or with greater frequency in patients with cancer.

Remote effects are not common, probably affecting less than 1 per cent of patients with cancer. Circulating antibodies against the target nervous sys-

TABLE 119–2. REMOTE EFFECTS OF CANCER ON THE NERVOUS SYSTEM

A. Brain and cranial nerves
  1. Dementia
  2. Bulbar encephalitis
  3. Subacute cerebellar degeneration—opsoclonus*
  4. Optic neuritis—retinal degeneration
B. Spinal cord
  1. Gray matter myelopathy
    a. Subacute motor neuropathy
    b. "Autonomic insufficiency"
  2. Subacute necrotic myelopathy
C. Peripheral nerves and roots
  1. Subacute sensory neuronopathy (dorsal root ganglionitis)*
  2. Sensorimotor peripheral neuropathy
  3. Acute polyneuropathy, "Guillain-Barré" type
  4. Autonomic neuropathy
D. Neuromuscular junction and muscle
  1. Polymyositis and dermatomyositis (dermatomyositis in older men*)
  2. Lambert-Eaton "myasthenic" syndrome
  3. Myasthenia gravis (thymoma)
  4. Neuromyotonia
E. Metabolic encephalopathy
  1. Destruction of vital organs
    a. Liver (hepatic coma)
    b. Lung (pulmonary encephalopathy)
    c. Kidney (uremia)
    d. Bone (hypercalcemia)
  2. Elaboration of hormonal substances by tumor
    a. "Parathromone" (hypercalcemia)
    b. "Corticotropin" (Cushing's syndrome)
    c. Antidiuretic hormone (water intoxication)
  3. Competition between tumor and brain for essential substrates
    a. Hypoglycemia (large retroperitoneal tumors)
    b. Tryptophan (carcinoid)
  4. Malnutrition

*Neurologic disorders that may precede diagnosis of cancer and strongly suggest its presence.

tem organ can be found in some patients suffering from remote effects (Table 119–3). In a few instances, injection of the antibody or extracts of tumor into experimental animals has reproduced portions of the clinical syndrome, suggesting an autoimmune mechanism, with the antigen originating in the tumor. Not all patients harbor such antibodies, and other suggestions for causing remote effects have included viral infections, toxins secreted by the tumor, and nutritional deprivation.

A few neurologic syndromes are highly characteristic of remote effects. These include subacute cerebellar degeneration, subacute sensory neuronopathy, and the myasthenic syndrome. These are discussed in the paragraphs below.

Subacute cerebellar degeneration caused by cancer has a clinical picture sufficiently characteristic to suggest strongly that cancer is present even if the neurologic symptoms predate the appearance of the tumor. There is usually a subacute onset of bilateral and symmetric cerebellar dysfunction, the patient being equally ataxic in arms and legs. Severe dysarthria is usually present; vertigo, diplopia, and nystagmus are common. The CSF may have as many as 40 lymphocytes/mm³ and an elevated pro-

TABLE 119–3. AUTOANTIBODIES OF CLINICAL RELEVANCE IN PATIENTS WITH PARANEOPLASTIC SYNDROMES

NAME	HISTOCHEMISTRY	MOLECULAR WEIGHT	NEUROLOGIC FINDINGS	NEOPLASM
Anti-Yo also PCAb	Purkinje cell cytoplasm	62, 34 kDa	Cerebellar degeneration	Gynecologic cancer Breast cancer
Anti-Hu also ANNA	Neuronal nuclei	35–40 kDa	Sensory neuropathy Encephalomyelitis	Small cell lung cancer
Anti-Ri CAR	Neuronal nuclei Photoreceptors Retinal neurons	55, 80 kDa 26 kDa 65 kDa	Opsoclonus Visual loss	Breast cancer Small cell lung cancer Gynecologic cancer
LEMS	Neuromuscular junction	—	LEMS	Small cell lung cancer
Anti-Mag	Peripheral nerve myelin	70 kDa	Peripheral neuropathy	Lymphoma Waldenström's

Abbreviations: PCAb = Anti-Purkinje cell cytoplasmic antibody; ANNA = antineuronal nuclear antibody; CAR = carcinoma-associated retinopathy; LEMS = Lambert-Eaton myasthenic syndrome; MAG = myelin-associated glycoprotein.
Yo, Hu, Ri are the initials of the index patients.

tein and IgG concentration. The disease, which may be associated with any cancer, precedes the discovery of the neoplasm by a few weeks to 3 years in more than half the patients, and it tends to run a progressive course over weeks to months, rendering the patient severely disabled. Cerebellar atrophy may be seen on MR scan, particularly if done late in the course of the illness. Characteristic pathologic changes consist of diffuse or patchy loss of Purkinje cells in all areas of the cerebellum. There may be lymphocytic cuffs around blood vessels, particularly in the deep nuclei. This illness can be distinguished from cerebellar metastases by the symmetry of its signs and the absence of increased intracranial pressure. It differs from alcoholic-nutritional cerebellar degeneration because dysarthria and ataxia in the upper extremities are prominent in the carcinomatous cerebellar degenerations but are usually mild or absent in the alcoholic variety. The hereditary cerebellar degenerations rarely run so rapid a course. At times the disorder stabilizes or improves with successful treatment of the tumor. Antibodies to cerebellar Purkinje cells have been found in the serum of some patients.

Another, less common cerebellar syndrome is that of *opsoclonus* (spontaneous, conjugate, chaotic eye movements most severe when voluntary eye movements are attempted). Opsoclonus is frequently associated with cerebellar ataxia and myoclonus of the trunk and extremities. It is most common in children as a remote effect of neuroblastoma. In children, the neurologic symptoms respond to adrenocorticosteroid therapy and to therapy of the tumor.

Subacute sensory neuronopathy is marked by loss of sensation with relative preservation of motor power. The illness sometimes precedes the appearance of the carcinoma and progresses over a few months, leaving the patient with a moderate or severe disability. The CSF protein is usually elevated. Pathologically, there is destruction of posterior root ganglia with perivascular lymphocytic cuffing and wallerian degeneration of sensory nerves. Many of the patients have inflammatory and degenerative changes in brain and spinal cord as well. The entity is rare and there is no treatment. Some patients harbor an antibody that reacts with an antigen found in the nuclei of neurons throughout the CNS. Dorsal root ganglion cells also harbor the antigen.

The *myasthenic syndrome* (Lambert-Eaton syndrome) is associated with small cell lung cancer in about two thirds of patients; the other one third do not have cancer. It is discussed on page 817.

Injury from Therapeutic Radiation

When parts of the nervous system are included within an ionizing irradiation portal, adverse effects may result (Table 119–4). The likelihood of adverse effects is related to the total dose of radiation, the size of each fraction, the total duration over which the dose is received, and the volume of nervous sys-

TABLE 119–4. RADIATION INJURY TO THE NERVOUS SYSTEM

TIME AFTER RT	ORGAN AFFECTED	CLINICAL FINDINGS
Primary Injury		
Immediate (min to hr)	Brain	Acute encephalopathy
Early delayed (6–16 wk)	Brain	Somnolence, focal signs
	Spinal cord	Lhermitte's sign
Late delayed (mo to yr)	Brain	Dementia, focal signs
	Spinal cord	Transverse myelopathy
	Peripheral nerves	Paralysis, sensory loss
Secondary Injury (yr)	Several	Brain, cranial, and/or peripheral nerve sheath tumors
	Arteries (atherosclerosis)	Cerebral infarction
	Endocrine organs	Metabolic encephalopathy

tem tissue irradiated. Other factors such as underlying nervous system disease (e.g., brain tumor, cerebral edema), previous surgery, concomitant use of chemotherapeutic agents, and individual susceptibility make it impossible to define precisely a safe dose for any given individual. However, certain guidelines allow the radiation therapist to calculate generally safe nervous system doses. Adverse effects may involve any portion of the central or peripheral nervous system and may occur acutely or be delayed weeks to years following irradiation.

Clinical Manifestations

Acute encephalopathy may follow large radiation doses to patients with increased intracranial pressure, particularly in the absence of corticosteroid prophylaxis. Immediately following treatment, susceptible patients develop headache, nausea and vomiting, somnolence, fever, and occasionally worsening of neurologic signs, rarely culminating in cerebral herniation and death. Acute encephalopathy usually follows the first radiation fraction and becomes progressively less severe with each ensuing fraction. This disorder is believed to result from increased intracranial pressure and/or brain edema from radiation-induced alteration of the blood-brain barrier. It responds to corticosteroids. Acute worsening of neurologic symptoms does not occur after spinal cord irradiation.

Early delayed encephalopathy or *myelopathy* appears 6 to 16 weeks after therapy and persists for days to weeks. In children, the encephalopathy commonly follows prophylactic irradiation of the brain for leukemia and is called the "radiation somnolence syndrome." The disorder is characterized by somnolence, often associated with headache, nausea, vomiting, and sometimes fever. The EEG may be slow, but there are no focal signs. In adults, the syndrome usually follows whole-brain irradiation for brain tumors and is characterized by lethargy and worsening of focal neurologic signs. Both disorders usually respond to steroids, but if untreated they resolve spontaneously. In adults, the syndrome may be distinguished from recurrent brain tumor by MR scan. In children, lumbar puncture rules out the potential diagnosis of meningeal leukemia. *Early delayed myelopathy* follows radiation therapy to the neck or upper thorax and is characterized by Lhermitte's sign (an electric shock-like sensation radiating into various parts of the body when the neck is flexed). The symptoms resolve spontaneously. Early delayed radiation syndromes are believed to result from demyelination, possibly due to radiation-induced damage to oligodendroglia.

Late delayed radiation injury appears months to years following radiation and may affect any part of the nervous system. In the brain, there are two clinical syndromes. Diffuse injury may follow whole-brain irradiation either to patients without brain tumors (prophylactic irradiation for oat cell carcinoma) or to some patients with primary and metastatic brain tumors. The disorder is characterized by dementia without focal signs. There is cerebral atrophy on MR scan and pathologic changes are nonspecific; there is no treatment. Focal radiation damage affects patients who receive either focal brain irradiation during therapy of extracranial neoplasms or whole-brain irradiation for intracranial neoplasms. Neurologic signs suggest a mass and include headache, focal or generalized seizures, and hemiparesis. Brain MR scans reveal a hypodense mass, sometimes with contrast enhancement. Neuropathologic features include coagulative necrosis of white matter, telangiectasia, fibrinoid necrosis and thrombus formation, and glial proliferation and bizarre multinucleated astrocytes. The clinical and MR findings cannot be distinguished from those of brain tumor, and the diagnosis can be made only by biopsy. Corticosteroids sometimes ameliorate symptoms. The treatment, if the disorder is focal, is surgical removal. *Late delayed myelopathy* is characterized by progressive paralysis, sensory changes, and sometimes pain. A Brown-Séquard syndrome (weakness and loss of proprioception in the extremities of one side with loss of pain and temperature sensation on the other) is often present at onset. Patients occasionally respond transiently to steroids, and the disorder may stop progressing, but generally patients become paraplegic or quadriplegic. Pathologic changes include necrosis of the spinal cord. *Late delayed neuropathy* may affect any cranial or peripheral nerve. Common disorders are blindness from optic neuropathy and paralysis of an upper extremity from brachial plexopathy after therapy for lung or breast cancer. The pathogenesis is probably fibrosis and ischemia of the plexus. There is no treatment.

Radiation-induced tumors, including meningiomas, sarcomas or, less commonly, gliomas, may appear years to decades after cranial irradiation and may follow even low-dose radiation therapy. Malignant or atypical nerve sheath tumors may follow irradiation of the brachial, cervical, and lumbar plexuses. The CNS may also be damaged when radiation alters extraneural structures. Radiation therapy accelerates *atherosclerosis*, and cerebral infarction associated with carotid artery occlusion in the neck may occur many years after neck irradiation. Endocrine (pituitary, thyroid, parathyroid) dysfunction from radiation may be associated with neurologic signs. Hypothyroidism from radiation may also cause an encephalopathy.

NON-NEOPLASTIC ALTERATIONS OF INTRACRANIAL PRESSURE

Introduction and Definitions

Intracranial pressure is determined by rates of CSF formation and absorption and by cerebral venous pressure, the last a reflection of systemic venous pressure. Lumbar puncture pressure in the lateral decubitus position accurately reflects intracranial pressure in most instances. Depending on the patient's degree of relaxation, the normal CSF pressure ranges between 65 and 195 mm of CSF (5 to 15 mm Hg), although pressures as high as 250 mm of CSF have been reported in apparently normal individuals. Nevertheless, pressures above 170 are suspect, and pressures above 200 should be considered abnormal until proven otherwise. CSF pressure is not affected by obesity. Elevated CSF pressure measured at lumbar puncture does not necessarily reflect neurologic disease; e.g., elevation of the head of the bed can raise the lumbar CSF pressure, although it lowers intracranial pressure. Elevation of systemic venous pressure, such as occurs acutely with coughing, abdominal straining, crying or chronically with congestive heart failure or venous obstruction of the superior vena cava or jugular veins, raises intracranial pressure. Hypercapnia (e.g., pulmonary disease, excessive sedation) increases the cerebral blood volume and thus CSF pressure. Conversely, if the patient is positioned with the head down, lumbar puncture pressure is lower, although intracranial pressure becomes higher. The loss of CSF around the needle hole between the time the needle enters the subarachnoid space and the manometer is placed also lowers intracranial pressure. When all of these artifactual causes of altered intracranial pressure are eliminated, the most common cause of intracranial *hypertension* is intracranial tumor and the most common cause of intracranial *hypotension* is a CSF leak following lumbar puncture or myelogram. This section discusses several other disorders that can alter intracranial pressure.

Intracranial Hypertension

Pseudotumor cerebri, as the name suggests, is a disorder characterized by increased intracranial pressure in the absence of a tumor or obvious obstruction of CSF pathways. The cause is usually not established, although a number of CNS or systemic illnesses appear to play a role. Pseudotumor can follow head trauma, middle ear disease, internal jugular vein ligation, oral contraceptive use, pregnancy, and polycythemia vera, all conditions that suggest possible cerebral venous occlusion. In a few such patients, MR scans or angiograms show sagittal or lateral sinus occlusion. The disorder has also been reported in patients on prolonged corticosteroid therapy, after steroid withdrawal, with Addison's disease or hypoparathyroidism, and with ingestion of drugs such as vitamin A, nalidixic acid, and tetracycline. Most cases, however, are idiopathic.

The disorder usually affects young (ages 20 to 30), usually obese females, is characterized by headache, papilledema, and at times visual obscurations (sudden momentary, usually bilateral visual loss), and has a benign prognosis.

Most patients with pseudotumor present to the physician with headache and papilledema. In a few, headaches are absent and the disorder is discovered because of either brief visual losses (obscurations) or papilledema found on routine ophthalmologic examination. Sometimes there is no papilledema or only unilateral papilledema even though intracranial pressure is grossly elevated. Visual obscurations do not portend visual loss. However, whether or not

they occur, 10 to 15 per cent of patients lose some vision during the course of the disease, varying from small scotomata to, rarely, total blindness. Other clinical symptoms that are less common but that may concern the physician include vomiting, diplopia, vertigo, tinnitus, neck pain and stiffness, orbital pain, drowsiness, and dysesthetic sensation. These false localizing signs probably result from minor shifts of normal structures engendered by the intracranial hypertension. The disorder usually runs a benign course, with the headache and papilledema resolving in several weeks to several months, although in many patients intracranial pressure as measured at lumbar puncture remains elevated for months to years.

The diagnosis of pseudotumor is suspected clinically and established by the presence of elevated intracranial pressure in a patient with a normal MR or CT scan. The CSF pressure is usually above 300 mm and its composition is normal, although some patients may have a relatively low protein (below 15 mg/dl). Venous occlusions can usually be detected by MR. A few errors in diagnosis occur in patients with an anomalous elevation of the optic discs (pseudopapilledema) or, very rarely, in patients with diffuse infiltrating gliomas of the brain (gliomatosis cerebri). The first can be ruled out by appropriate ophthalmologic tests, including fluorescein angiography, and the second usually by MRI and time.

Treatment is symptomatic. Repeated lumbar punctures sometimes relieve the headaches, and some physicians believe that corticosteroids are helpful. Only if there is evidence of progressive visual loss is therapeutic intervention mandatory. In that instance, the best treatment appears to be shunting the CSF from the lumbar sac into the peritoneum.

Hydrocephalus refers to an enlargement of the cerebral ventricular system by an increase in the amount of ventricular fluid. Obstructive hydrocephalus can result from either stenosis or occlusion of CSF pathways within the ventricular system (noncommunicating) or from stenosis or occlusion of subarachnoid pathways outside the ventricular system (communicating). Nonobstructive hydrocephalus results from passive enlargement of the ventricular system because of atrophy of brain substance (hydrocephalus ex vacuo). Obstructive hydrocephalus is often but not always associated with intracranial hypertension and, when acute, may be rapidly fatal. The more chronic the hydrocephalus, the more likely the intracranial hypertension is to be either mild or undetectable (normal pressure hydrocephalus) and the more likely are the symptoms to be indolent.

Acute hydrocephalus, such as occurs with sudden obstruction of the ventricular system (e.g., colloid cyst of the third ventricle, subarachnoid or cerebellar hemorrhage), is characterized by sudden severe headache, vomiting, lethargy, and sometimes coma. If the ventricular system is not decompressed, herniation and death can occur. Subacute (subarachnoid hemorrhage, meningitis, leptomeningeal neoplasia) or chronic hydrocephalus (congenital aqueductal stenosis, spinal cord tumors, idiopathic normal pressure hydrocephalus) is usually characterized by progressive lethargy, apathy, and dementia, often associated with an unsteady gait and urgency incontinence of urine. There may be bilateral corticospinal tract signs, particularly in the lower extremities, with hyperactive knee and ankle jerks and extensor plantar responses. If the pressure is grossly elevated, patients may develop headache and papilledema, but these are uncommon.

The presence of enlarged ventricles is detected easily by MR or CT scan. Unfortunately, it is not always easy to distinguish on the scan between obstructive hydrocephalus and hydrocephalus ex vacuo unless the cause (e.g., tumor) can be identified. A lumbar puncture revealing an elevated intracranial pressure assists in the diagnosis, but because some patients with obstructive hydrocephalus have a relatively normal intracranial pressure, that test likewise may not give a definitive diagnosis. In patients with classic symptoms of chronic hydrocephalus (i.e., dementia, gait unsteadiness, and incontinence), removal of CSF at lumbar puncture sometimes relieves symptoms, indicating both that CSF obstruction is producing the symptoms and that ventricular shunting will be therapeutic.

Intracranial Hypotension

Intracranial hypotension usually follows lumbar puncture but occasionally results from spontaneous or traumatically induced tears of the dura, leading to leakage of subarachnoid fluid. The resulting low CSF pressure is characterized by headache beginning occipitally and radiating frontally when the patient assumes the erect posture. The headache is sometimes associated with nausea, vomiting, photophobia, and a stiff neck. Some patients develop diplopia from abducens nerve paralysis. Auditory symptoms such as tinnitus and vestibular dizziness also can occur. The symptoms probably result because the brain, unsupported by CSF, shifts downward when the erect posture is assumed. The diagnosis is easily made on clinical grounds if the patient has undergone a lumbar puncture or myelogram a few days previously, but can be established only by performing a lumbar puncture and noting the low CSF pressure if no such history is present. In some patients the MR scan reveals contrast enhancement of the cranial meninges. Symptoms usually resolve spontaneously but in a few instances may persist, in which case a search for the site of the leak should be made. Some investigators have recommended epidural injection of a few milliliters of the patient's blood to patch a dural leak following lumbar puncture. In a few instances of spontaneous or traumatic dural tears, surgical repair of the leak has been necessary.

REFERENCES

Apuzzo MLJ (ed): Malignant Cerebral Glioma. Park Ridge, IL, American Association of Neurological Surgeons, 1990.

Gutin PH, Leibel SA, Sheline GE (eds): Radiation Injury to the Nervous System. New York, Raven Press, 1991.

Patchell RA (ed): Neurologic complications of systemic cancer. Neurol Clin, Vol 9, 1991.

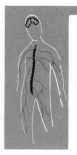

120 INFECTIOUS AND INFLAMMATORY DISORDERS OF THE NERVOUS SYSTEM

The central nervous system (CNS) is subject to attack by many of the same infectious agents and antigen-antibody reactions that affect the remainder of the body. As is true with systemic infections, bacterial, fungal, and parasitic diseases of the nervous system are particularly likely to occur when the body's resistive mechanisms have been breached. Viral infections of the nervous system are also common, especially in immunosuppressed hosts. Except for so-called slow viruses, discussed in this section, virus diseases of the nervous system are described in Chapter 97. Chapter 92 discusses factors that predispose to infections of the nervous system.

BACTERIAL INFECTIONS OF THE BRAIN

Bacterial infections of the CNS may be parenchymal, meningeal, or parameningeal. Parenchymal lesions include brain abscesses as well as some of the complications of bacterial endocarditis and venous thrombosis. The most common meningeal infection, acute bacterial meningitis, is discussed in Chapter 97. Less common *parameningeal infections* include brain and spinal epidural or subdural abscesses (subdural empyema).

Bacteria most often reach the nervous system from a prior site of infection in a systemic organ, exceptions occurring when abnormal pathways connect the CNS and the surface of the body. Examples may follow CNS trauma, surgical procedures, or the development of spontaneous CSF fistulas. Such pathways should be sought in patients with repetitive CNS bacterial infections. The offending organism is often *Streptococcus pneumoniae*.

Intracranial Abscesses

Intracranial abscesses consist of areas of acute bacterial inflammation (early in the course) or pus localized to one of the intracranial compartments (i.e., the epidural space, the subdural space, or the brain itself).

Epidural Abscess

Epidural abscesses usually arise by direct extension from adjacent osteomyelitis, mastoiditis, or infection of the paranasal sinuses. In the early stages, signs and symptoms amplify those of infection of the extracranial site from which they arose; e.g., head pain, local swelling, and redness commonly overlie epidural abscesses originating from frontal sinuses. Fever usually is present accompanied by leukocytosis with a preponderance of polymorphonuclear leukocytes. Focal neurologic signs are uncommon, and increased intracranial pressure is usually absent. In the early stages, the CSF usually contains at most a few lymphocytes with a slightly elevated protein; often the fluid remains normal. If the initial disorder is untreated, the infection may breach the dura to produce a subdural empyema, bacterial meningitis, or brain abscess. Alternately, if the epidural inflammation lies close to a large venous sinus, thrombophlebitis with sinus occlusion (page 862) often may complicate the infection. The extent of an epidural abscess is usually easily defined by brain images as a mass occupying the epidural space and compressing the underlying brain. Whether cranial or spinal, such abscesses in their early stages often can be treated successfully with appropriate antibiotics alone (the organism having been identified by culture of purulent material obtained from the ear or sinuses). In some instances, particularly when the abscess is large or when it fails to shrink rapidly with antibiotic therapy, surgical drainage is required.

Subdural Abscess

Most subdural abscesses (subdural empyemas) arise from infection of paranasal sinuses or the middle ear (otitis media). Organisms from the primary infection follow cranial venous channels, often producing thrombophlebitis as they go through the dura into the subdural space. Occasionally, traumatically induced subdural hematomas become secondarily infected to form subdural empyemas. The site of the empyema depends on the site of the primary infection. Those of the paranasal sinuses usually extend over the frontal lobe, whereas those from ear infections penetrate the skull posteriorly both above and below the tentorium. The inflammatory reaction excited by the organism may form a membrane that completely walls off the collection of pus.

Most patients with subdural empyema suffer the signs and symptoms of sinusitis or otitis prior to the onset of the empyema. As the intracranial abscess develops, the initial pain usually worsens and spreads more widely. Fever, if not already present, usually develops, the white count rises, and patients often become drowsy and may vomit. Secondary thrombophlebitis of the brain may ensue and cause focal neurologic signs of seizures or hemiparesis. Eventually the intracranial pressure rises, and a fulminant course may produce death within a few days if no treatment is undertaken. The diagnosis is suggested by a history of pre-existing infection combined with local physical abnormalities. Brain imaging defines both the site of primary infection and the subdural collection of pus. The cerebrospinal fluid (CSF), if obtained, is usually under increased pressure and may contain several hundred cells with an elevated protein but normal glucose concentration. Lumbar puncture, however, is ill advised in patients suspected of subdural empyema, because no organisms will be recovered and the rapidly increasing intracranial pressure threatens to produce cerebral herniation.

Subdural empyema almost always requires surgical drainage. If combined with appropriate antibiotic therapy, this step usually relieves the symptoms and cures the patient if the disease is detected in its earliest stages. Unfortunately, diagnosis is often delayed, resulting in a mortality of about 25 per cent. Most deaths result from venous sinus thrombosis with secondary cerebral infarction or meningitis. Heparin anticoagulant therapy may reduce the neurologic damage from such thromboses.

Brain Abscess

Brain abscess is the most common intracranial abscess. Like those of the epidural and subdural spaces, parenchymal abscesses of the brain can arise by direct extension along venous channels from infections in the paranasal sinuses or the ear. Currently, however, most arise by hematogenous spread from infections elsewhere in the body. Metastatic abscess probably originates from a transient bacteremia with organisms lodging in capillary vessels of the brain. The process begins as a focal inflammatory encephalitis, followed in days or weeks by encapsulation of pus to form a true abscess. Unlike epidural or subdural abscesses, in which one almost always can identify the primary site of the infection, with brain abscesses the systemic infection may already have resolved without having produced symptoms. Some patients with brain abscess give a history of dental manipulation or mild urinary tract infection several weeks earlier; others have had lung infections. Congenital cyanotic heart disease and arteriovenous shunts in the lungs increase the risk of brain abscess because the lungs normally filter out circulating bacteria. Immunosuppressed patients often develop multiple rather than the single brain abscesses that most often affect patients with normal immunity.

The primary site of the infection determines the offending organism. Common agents include an aerobic or microaerophilic *Streptococcus* as well as enteric bacteria. In traumatic brain abscesses, staphylococci are common; *Clostridium* occasionally is present. Many of the infections are mixed. Rarer causes of abscesses include *Actinomyces* and *Nocardia*. Tuberculous abscesses are uncommon in the United States but frequent in less developed countries.

The site of a brain abscess depends partly on its source. Those that originate in the middle ear generally invade the temporal lobe or cerebellum, those in the paranasal sinus penetrate the frontal lobe, and those from penetrating injuries involve the wound site. Hematogenous abscesses can affect any part of the brain, although most distribute themselves along the territory of the middle cerebral artery.

Most abscesses produce symptoms similar to but more rapidly progressive than those of a brain tumor. It is uncommon for patients to suffer from fever, substantial tenderness of the skull, or an elevated white blood cell count. Instead, patients present with headache, signs of increased intracranial pressure, and focal signs that depend on the site of the lesion. Focal or generalized seizures are common. Occasionally, the onset is strokelike.

Differential Diagnosis. This includes brain tumor and less often cerebral infarct. Abscess should be suspected if a patient suffers one of the predisposing causes (e.g., immune suppression, cyanotic heart disease, arteriovenous shunting in the lungs) or if a systemic bacterial infection has occurred in the recent past. A history of a draining ear or evidence of otitis media, particularly when clinical symptoms and signs point to a lesion in the temporal lobe or cerebellum, strengthens the likelihood of brain abscess, as does a history of purulent sinusitis. If fever exists or the white blood cell count is elevated (neither usually is the case), the diagnosis favors abscess. Lumbar puncture should not be performed because of the risk of cerebral herniation. Brain images are helpful but not always specifically diagnostic. Characteristically they show a hypodense lesion surrounded by a contrast-enhancing ring. Similar rings also can rim primary and metastatic brain tumors as well as recent cerebral infarcts. A thin, smooth-walled ring suggests an abscess, whereas a thick, irregular ring is more common with brain tumor (Fig. 120–1). In some instances surgical exploration is required to make the diagnosis.

Therapy. Brain imaging has revolutionized the diagnosis and treatment of brain abscess because early diagnosis often permits starting antibiotics before extensive pus formation and mass effect have

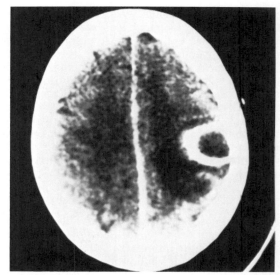

FIGURE 120–1. Computed tomographic (CT) scan showing a brain abscess. A woman presented to physicians after a focal seizure followed by headache and weakness of the arm. Dental work had been performed several weeks before. CT scan revealed a contrast-enhanced, ringlike mass surrounded by edema. It is not possible on this scan to differentiate tumor from abscess. At surgery a well-encapsulated abscess was encountered.

occurred. For abscesses 3 cm or smaller, antibiotics alone usually suffice, the choice depending on the suspected causal organism. If the organism is not known, a combination of penicillin and metronidazole in high doses for a period of about 6 weeks is usually effective. Serial imaging helps greatly in judging the effectiveness of antibiotic therapy and deciding when, if ever, surgical extirpation is necessary. Even after full recovery the contrast-enhancing ring may persist for many weeks and does not imply that the abscess is still active. Large abscesses, failure of antibiotic therapy to either shrink the lesion or improve the clinical course, or the presence of a doubtful diagnosis mandate surgical removal or, for surgically inaccessible lesions, stereotactic needle biopsy and drainage. With early detection and vigorous antimicrobial treatment, most patients do not need surgery and recover with few sequelae other than a tendency to seizures. These can be controlled by anticonvulsants. This approach has reduced the mortality from brain abscesses in some series to about 5 per cent.

Venous Sinus and Cortical Thrombophlebitis

Bacterial infections of the CNS may cause cerebral thrombophlebitis with secondary occlusion of the large dural sinuses. The most common sites of infective sinus occlusion are the lateral sinus (a complication of acute or chronic otitis media), cavernous sinus (a complication of orbital or nasal sinus infection), and the superior sagittal sinus, usually occluded by direct extension of infected clot from the first two. Cortical veins may be involved either by direct contact with an infection in the epidural or subdural space or by extension of infective clot from the sinuses.

The symptoms of lateral sinus occlusion depend on the rapidity of the occlusion and the importance of that sinus in draining the brain's blood. Because the two lateral sinuses are often of different sizes, slowly developing occlusion of the smaller one usually causes no symptoms at all. Occlusion of the dominant lateral sinus is often heralded by headache and papilledema. There are usually no focal signs unless the occlusion spreads to involve the jugular vein, in which case pain, swelling, and a palpable cord in the neck may develop. If the occlusion spreads to the inferior petrosal sinus, abducens and trigeminal nerve involvement (Gradenigo's syndrome) can be added and, if the jugular bulb is involved, dysarthria, dysphagia, and neck weakness (jugular foramen syndrome) ensue.

Cavernous sinus occlusion causes a florid picture, often resulting from staphylococcal infection of the face or sinus. Symptoms begin with fever, headache, nausea, vomiting, and seizures. Proptosis affects the ipsilateral eye with chemosis and ophthalmoplegia, to which sensory loss in the distribution of the first division of the trigeminal nerve sometimes is added (all result from the third, fourth, fifth, and sixth nerves passing through the cavernous sinus). Papilledema is a late event.

Sagittal sinus occlusion is characterized by headache and, often, papilledema. If acute in onset and involving the posterior distribution of the sinus, bilateral hemorrhagic infarction of the brain develops, sometimes producing bilateral hemiparesis more marked in the leg and proximal arm than in the hand and face.

The diagnosis of sinus occlusion or corticothrombophlebitis should be suspected in a patient with a head or neck infection who develops signs of increased intracranial pressure with or without focal neurologic signs. The diagnosis of sinus occlusion can easily be made by MR scan, which distinguishes clot from flowing blood in vessels, or by digital intravenous angiogram (Fig. 120–2); the tests do not distinguish between infective and noninfective thromboses.

Infective sinus thrombosis is usually successfully treated with appropriate antibiotics; sometimes despite treatment the clot propagates to cause severe cerebral infarction and even death. Recent evidence indicates that prompt diagnosis of sinus thrombosis, followed by heparin-warfarin therapy, substantially reduces mortality and prevents or reverses neurologic damage.

Bacterial Endocarditis

The disseminated emboli of subacute bacterial endocarditis affect the nervous system of a quarter to a third of patients with that disease (Table 120–1). The most common symptom is that of an embolic stroke characterized by the acute onset of focal motor weakness. Multiple small emboli may cause confusion, hallucinations, and lethargy with or without fleeting focal signs. Infected emboli lodged in cerebral blood vessels sometimes induce aneu-

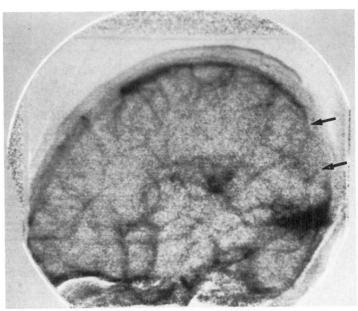

FIGURE 120–2. Digital venous angiogram (DIVA), lateral view, patient facing left, in a patient with sagittal sinus occlusion. The procedure is generally more effective in demonstrating the cerebral venous system than is an arteriogram, because the cerebral hemispheres are filled with contrast material simultaneously. The patient had a bland occlusion of the posterior sagittal sinus (*arrows*). Inflammatory sinus occlusions have a similar appearance.

rysm formation (mycotic aneurysm), typically located in the distal portion of cerebral arteries. The distribution differs from that of congenital aneurysms, which locate themselves more proximally. Mycotic aneurysms often rupture to cause severe cerebral or subarachnoid hemorrhage. Resolution of the aneurysms after antibiotic therapy has been reported, but the danger of rupture is so great that, once they are found, surgical clipping usually is performed. As in other disorders causing sepsis, brain abscesses can result from either acute or subacute bacterial endocarditis.

Spinal Infections

The spinal leptomeninges are bathed by the same CSF and suffer from the same kinds of meningeal

**TABLE 120–1. MAJOR NEUROLOGIC COMPLICATIONS OF
BACTERIAL ENDOCARDITIS***

Cerebral infarction
Multiple microemboli (diffuse encephalopathy)
Meningeal signs and symptoms
Seizures
Microscopic brain abscesses
Visual disturbances
Cranial or peripheral neuropathy
Mycotic aneurysm
Subarachnoid hemorrhage (with or without identifiable mycotic aneurysm)

*Signs of cerebral infarction or embolic encephalopathy affect as many as one third of cases, in many producing the first symptoms.

infections and inflammatory processes that affect the brain. Subdural and epidural collections of pus, however, can be localized to the spinal canal. Their clinical pictures differ from their counterparts in the intracranial cavity. Spinal cord parenchymal abscesses are exceedingly rare. They usually reach the spinal cord, as they do the brain, by hematogenous spread.

Spinal Abscess

Most *spinal epidural abscesses* arise at the cervical or lumbar levels and extend from an infected focus in an adjacent vertebral body (osteomyelitis) or soft tissues. *Staphylococcus aureus* is the most common organism. Other abscesses arise either by hematogenous invasion or by direct extension from a paravertebral infected focus. Depending on the virulence of the organism, clinical signs may develop either rapidly or slowly. In either case, neck or back pain is the most prominent symptom. The pain is usually severe and, in its early stages, well-localized. Tenderness of the spine surrounds the site of the infection. As the illness develops, pain may spread in a dermatomal distribution as nerve roots are irritated by the inflammatory process. Unless effective treatment is started at this stage, progressive weakness and sensory loss develop below the site of the lesion (myelopathy) and may lead to paraplegia in hours to days. Most patients with acute epidural abscesses are febrile and toxic, with an elevated white count. These findings may be less prominent with more chronic processes but the erythrocyte sedimentation rate is usually elevated. Radiographs of the vertebral body may not become abnormal for several weeks following the onset of symptoms. Magnetic resonance (MR) images of the spine, however, can detect the epidural lesion and are the diagnostic measure of choice. If MRI is unavailable,

computed tomographic (CT) scans are almost as useful. Percutaneous tapping of the abscess may enable bacteriologic diagnosis. If spinal imaging is unavailable, a myelogram can outline the epidural mass. CSF obtained at the time of myelography is characterized by pleocytosis (up to several hundred white cells), elevated protein, and a normal glucose concentration; organisms are rarely cultured. In more chronic processes the pleocytosis may be absent.

Spinal subdural empyemas, usually caused by *Staphylococcus aureus,* are more likely to be associated with meningitis and spinal cord infarction than are epidural abscesses but otherwise present with similar clinical changes. The diagnostic and therapeutic approaches are similar to those for epidural abscess.

With spinal epidural or subdural abscesses antibiotic therapy should be started as soon as one suspects the diagnosis. In the past, surgical drainage was considered imperative in acute abscesses. Recently, some of these lesions detected by imaging in their early stages have been cured with antibiotics alone. If signs of myelopathy or nerve root involvement develop, however, the patient should be surgically decompressed. The outcome is usually satisfactory in patients who are not already paralyzed when treatment is started.

Differential Diagnosis. Acute or subacute spinal abscesses must be differentiated from acute (subacute) transverse myelitis (see p. 868) and from spinal epidural or subdural hematomas (usually a disorder of patients with abnormal coagulation). Chronic spinal abscesses must be distinguished from tumor. In the acute disorder, fever, toxicity, and a history of prior infection support the diagnosis of abscess, and a carefully done myelogram or CT scan reveals the lesion to be extradural. Acute transverse myelopathy is associated either with a normal myelogram or with swelling of the spinal cord itself. With chronic abscesses, differentiation between tumor and infection may be more difficult. Both conditions can produce radiographic changes in the vertebral bodies, inflammation being more likely to affect two contiguous vertebral bodies across an intravertebral disc, whereas tumors are usually restricted to individual vertebral bodies. If the diagnosis is in doubt, biopsy of the vertebral body or decompression of the epidural space is necessary to make the differentiation.

Neurosyphilis and *tuberculosis* of the nervous system are discussed in Chapter 97.

SLOW VIRUS INFECTIONS OF THE NERVOUS SYSTEM

The term *slow virus infection* designates a group of transmissible disorders in which a long latent period separates the time between first inoculation and subsequent development of disease. Several such infections, not all attributable to true viruses, can selectively attack the human nervous system (Table 120–2). Two retroviruses, the human immunodeficiency virus type 1 (HIV-1) and the human T cell

TABLE 120–2. SLOW VIRUS INFECTIONS OF THE NERVOUS SYSTEMS

DISORDER	VIRUS	CLASSIFICATION
AIDS (see Ch. 108)	Human immunodeficiency virus I (HIV)	Retrovirus (RNA)
Japanese associated myelopathy (HAM); tropical spastic paraparesis	Human T-cell lymphotrophic virus Type I (HTLV-I)	Retrovirus (RNA)
Progressive multifocal leukoencephalopathy	JC virus	Papovavirus (DNA)
Subacute sclerosing panencephalitis	Measles virus	Paramyxovirus (RNA)
Progressive rubella panencephalitis	Rubella virus	Togavirus (RNA)
Creutzfeldt-Jakob disease, kuru, Gerstmann-Straussler-Scheinker syndrome	Prion	Protein, nature uncertain

lymphotrophic virus type 1 (HTLV-1), invade the nervous system of apparently healthy persons and require months to as much as several years to express their serious effects. Discussion of HIV-1 and its impact can be found in Chapter 108. *HTLV-1* recently has been identified as the cause of *tropical spastic paralysis* as well as a myelopathy occurring in the Kyushu district of Japan and termed HTLV-1/HAM. The virus has also been implicated in acute T-cell lymphoma/leukemia. The neurologic disorder is prevalent in tropical and semitropical belts worldwide and is encountered in the United States principally among Caribbean immigrants and Southeastern blacks. HTLV-1 can be transmitted sexually, by breastfeeding, and by transfusion. Usual age of onset is between 35 and 45 years, with an insidious onset and slow progression of spastic paraparesis followed by loss of bladder and bowel control. Peripheral or cranial nerves are sometimes affected. Diagnosis is made by detection of the virus as well as identification of high-level antibody synthesis and oligoclonal bands in the CSF. Treatment consists of immunosuppression or apheresis but at best brings modest improvements.

Subacute sclerosing panencephalitis, caused by measles virus, and a somewhat similar progressive panencephalitis caused by rubella viruses represent severely damaging brain disorders attributable to persistent defective viral replication. Both affect children fatally, usually beginning many months to several years after the initial viral infection and pursuing a slow course. Widespread measles and rubella vaccination have all but erased the diseases in the United States.

Progressive multifocal leukoencephalopathy (PML) results from the invasion of the papovavirus, JC virus, into the brain. Rare in its incidence, PML affects patients with AIDS or other disorders impairing T lymphocytes or macrophage-mediated immune responses. Gradually beginning but insidiously progressive cerebral demyelination produces signs of major sensory impairment coupled with characteristic white matter abnormalities on MR images. Occasionally the disease remits spontaneously but so far no useful treatment has been found.

Creutzfeldt-Jakob disease (CJD) is a rare form of midlife, rapidly progressive, transmissible dementia affecting patients worldwide with intellectual loss, signs of upper motor neuron impairment, ataxia, and myoclonus. The disease closely resembles or is identical with *kuru*, a clinically similar disorder discovered among members of a cannabalistic New Guinea tribe 40 years ago and found to be transmissible into the brains of animals with several years delay in appearance. CJD has been transmitted similarly to animals as well as between humans by the successive use of intracerebral electrodes, by cornea transplants, and by at least one batch of human pituitary gland growth hormone given to children for replacement therapy. An essentially identical clinical and pathologic condition exists as an autosomal dominant hereditary disease called *Gerstmann-Straussler-Scheinker syndrome (GSS)* or hereditary Creutzfeldt-Jakob disease. Both the hereditary and the sporadic disease are marked by the conversion

from normal to abnormal of a naturally occurring "prion" protein, the gene for which lies on chromosome 20. Presumably, the transmitted human agent, which is identical to the one that causes animal transmission in scrapie, a sheep disease, in some way denatures the recipient's normal prion protein, which then replicates in amounts that eventually become fatal to CNS cells. Several alleles of the prion protein have been found in the hereditary GSS syndrome. There is no treatment for CJD, almost all affected victims dying within 6 to 18 months after first symptoms appear. Risks to healthcare workers have been extremely small or absent.

DEMYELINATING AND OTHER CNS INFLAMMATORY DISORDERS OF PROBABLE IMMUNE CAUSE

Demyelinating Disorders

Disorders with a relative predilection for damaging CNS myelin are listed in Table 120-3. Those that have an immune basis are discussed here. Others, if they affect primarily adults, are described elsewhere in the text under appropriate headings.

Several disorders that are believed to operate via abnormal immune mechanisms cause CNS dysfunction by damaging the myelin sheaths covering axons. The conditions appear to have their primary effect on the oligodendroglial cells, which are responsible for the production and maintenance of the myelin sheaths. The acute lesions of these demyelinating disorders usually contain inflammatory infiltrates, particularly lymphocytes, at the site of subsequent demyelination. There is usually production of IgG within the CNS characterized by an elevated CSF-to-serum IgG ratio. In their severe forms, the disorders also can damage other structures in demyelinated areas, including axons and astrocytic cells.

Multiple Sclerosis (MS). This is by far the most common of the presumed immune demyelinating

TABLE 120-3. DEMYELINATING DISORDERS

A. **Unknown Cause**
   1. Multiple sclerosis
   2. Devic's disease
   3. Optic neuritis
   4. Acute transverse myelopathy
B. **Parainfectious Disorders**
   1. Acute disseminated encephalomyelitis
   2. Acute hemorrhagic leukoencephalopathy
C. **Viral Infections**
   1. Progressive multifocal leukoencephalopathy
   2. Subacute sclerosing panencephalitis
D. **Nutritional Disorders**
   1. Combined systems disease (vitamin B_{12} deficiency)
   2. Demyelination of the corpus callosum (Marchiafava-Bignami disease)
   3. Central pontine myelinolysis
E. **Anoxic-Ischemic Sequelae**
   1. Delayed postanoxic cerebral demyelination
   2. Progressive subcortical ischemic encephalopathy

disorders of the CNS. It usually causes its first symptoms between the ages of about 20 and 40 years and classically is characterized by remissions and exacerbations of neurologic dysfunction affecting several different sites in the CNS over many years (lesions disseminated in space and time). Typically, at onset an otherwise healthy person suffers an acute or subacute attack of unilateral loss of vision, true vertigo, ataxia, paresthesias, incontinence, diplopia, dysarthria, or paralysis (Table 120–4). The symptoms result from a focus of inflammatory demyelination (which later scars to form a "plaque") in the white matter of the brain (most frequently periventricular), brain stem, or spinal cord. The demyelination acts to slow or block conduction of nerve impulses thereby producing neurologic dysfunction. The symptoms usually are painless, remain for several days to weeks, and most often partially or completely resolve. After a period of relative freedom, new symptoms appear. Although individual frequencies vary widely, the average rate of exacerbations is about one every other year. In some patients, however, the clinical course consists of progressive neurologic dysfunction; this usually takes the form of a slowly progressive myelopathy characterized by spasticity and ataxia, predominantly of the lower extremities. In other instances

TABLE 120–4. SYMPTOMS AND SIGNS OF MULTIPLE SCLEROSIS LISTED IN DECLINING ORDER OF FREQUENCY

SYMPTOMS	SIGNS
Unilateral visual impairment	Optic neuritis
Paresthesias	Nystagmus
Ataxia or unsteadiness	Spasticity or hyperreflexia
Vertigo	Babinski sign
Fatigue	Absent abdominal reflexes
Muscle weakness	Dysmetria or intention tremor
Ocular disturbance, especially internuclear ophthalmoplegia	Impairment of central sensory pathways
Urinary disturbance	Labile or changed mood
Dysarthria or scanning speech	
Mental disturbance	

TABLE 120–5. CRITERIA FOR THE DIAGNOSIS OF MULTIPLE SCLEROSIS

Clinically Definite Multiple Sclerosis*: Evidence by history, neurologic examination, or both, of at least two distinct attacks separated in time and producing objective evidence of neurologic dysfunction involving separate areas of central white matter. A related laboratory abnormality such as abnormal visual evoked responses, MR-revealed white matter lesions, or CSF oligoclonal banding can be taken as one objective sign.

Clinically Probable Multiple Sclerosis: Two distinct, verified clinical neurologic attacks involving different areas of the nervous system plus existing clinical evidence of one relevant area of neurologic dysfunction or one of the laboratory abnormalities cited above.

* Reprinted with permission from Annals of Neurology, Vol 13, p 227, 1983.

one or two attacks may be the sole clinical expression of the disease for an entire lifetime. On average, about 60 per cent of MS patients remain fully functional 10 years after the first attack, and 25 to 30 per cent continue this way for 30 or more years after the onset. Statistically, the disorder does not greatly decrease life expectancy, although some middle-aged patients become severely disabled and die prematurely of complications.

ETIOLOGY. The etiology of MS is unknown, although most clues indicate immunologic and genetic factors. The disease is far more common in the northern and southern temperate latitudes than in more equatorial regions. Young children who move from a tropical to a temperate area increase their likelihood of contracting multiple sclerosis, and vice versa. The findings suggest an infective agent acquired early in life (a slow or retrovirus, or exposure to a childhood infection). An immune disorder is suggested not only by the inflammatory infiltrates sometimes seen in the perivascular areas of the demyelinated plaques but also by the fact that a decrease in suppressor lymphocytes in the serum usually precedes acute attacks. A relapsing encephalomyelitis resembling MS has been produced by injection of antigen into experimental animals. Genetic predisposition is suggested by the fact that haplotype DW2 is found in about 65 per cent of MS patients, compared with 15 per cent of control subjects, and there is a high coincidence in monozygotic twins. In addition, the disorder is uncommon in Orientals and African blacks, including those who are born in the United States.

DIAGNOSIS. The diagnosis depends upon identifying in persons of appropriate age clinical evidence of CNS lesions that have affected different areas of CNS white matter at intervals separated in time by at least 2 months (Table 120–5). When doubt exists, laboratory evidence of CNS immune dysfunction or of imaged white matter lesions should be sought. Clinically, however, otherwise healthy persons who suffer relapsing and remitting neurologic dysfunction over a long period of time (e.g., diplopia in year one, sensory loss in an arm in year three, urgency incontinence in year five) almost certainly have MS. Furthermore, evidence of more than one widely spaced lesion in the nervous system (e.g., optic neuritis plus internuclear ophthalmoplegia) strongly suggests disseminated sclerosis in a younger person who lacks evidence of other disease.

Certain symptoms strongly suggest the diagnosis of MS. These include bilateral internuclear ophthalmoplegia (see p. 779), Lhermitte's sign (electric shock-like sensation radiating to the extremities initiated by neck flexion), and an exacerbation of neurologic symptoms associated with acute febrile illness.

The laboratory examination is helpful but not definitive. Most patients have an elevated CSF gamma globulin level as well as discrete (oligoclonal) bands found in the gamma region on agarose or polyacrylamide gel electrophoresis. Multiple CSF oligoclonal bands (more than two) strongly support a diagnosis of MS in clinically appropriate cases, although other inflammatory diseases of the nervous system also

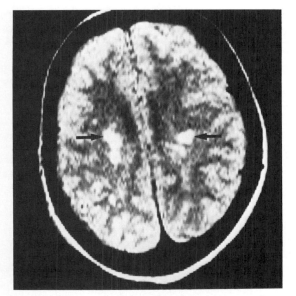

FIGURE 120–3. An MR image from a patient with MS. Multiple lesions of the white matter (arrows) with a predilection for periventricular areas strongly support the diagnosis of MS in a patient with an appropriate history and physical findings.

can produce oligoclonal bands. Spinal, auditory, or visual evoked responses can reveal additional subclinical lesions in doubtful cases. Most helpful from a laboratory standpoint is MR imaging, which usually reveals characteristic white matter lesions scattered through brain and/or spinal cord (Fig. 120–3). CT scanning provides less sensitive detection.

Early diagnosis can be difficult in some cases, particularly in the absence of the typical remitting and exacerbating history, and when neither CSF nor MR findings are as yet characteristic. Often, early symptoms are primarily sensory and sometimes appear to take bizarre and "nonanatomic" distributions, leading the physician to worry about a conversion reaction. Occasionally signs in MS may be severe and apparently unifocal, at first suggesting a brain or spinal cord tumor or vascular disease. Conversely, difficulty can arise with small brain stem structural abnormalities. Such lesions can give rise to a potentially misleading collection of cranial nerve, sensory, cerebellar, and motor signs that at first suggest demyelination. To prove a disseminated disorder in a patient with prominent brain stem signs requires evidence of dysfunction of structures not represented in the brain stem (e.g., optic neuritis, visual field deficit) or spinal cord. Visually evoked responses often help because MS-related optic nerve involvement is common and often causes abnormalities of conduction in the nerve without clinical symptoms. A difficult differential diagnosis in patients with prominent recurrent symptoms and signs of lower brain stem dysfunction lies between MS with remitting and exacerbating symptoms and small arteriovenous anomalies of the medulla or pons, which can produce recurrent symptoms by repetitive small hemorrhages. MR imaging usually solves the problem.

TREATMENT. One can treat the symptoms of MS,

but so far not the disease. Many physicians believe that acute bouts of neurologic dysfunction resolve more quickly when treated with short-term administration of corticosteroids. No evidence indicates that such treatment brings long-term benefit. Some therapeutic trials suggest the potential efficacy of immunosuppressive agents in chronic progressive MS, but firm evidence is lacking. Patients minimally affected by the disorder require no specific treatment. The illness understandably frightens patients, and sympathetic reassurance and follow-up supervision provide considerable support. Patients severely disabled by late symptoms, which generally include spasticity, and bladder and bowel dysfunction (see Table 120–4), often are best treated in multidisciplinary clinics or centers where physical therapy, psychological support, family counseling, and supportive medical therapy are all available.

Acute Disseminated Encephalomyelitis (ADE). This monophasic demyelinating inflammatory disorder can appear after viral infections or as a complication of vaccination. The condition usually produces multifocal brain and spinal cord symptoms but may be restricted to one area, particularly optic nerve (acute optic neuropathy) or spinal cord (acute transverse myelopathy). When related to an antecedent viral infection, ADE usually occurs 6 to 10 days after the appearance of the other systemic symptoms. When it follows vaccination, it usually begins 10 days to 3 weeks after the injections. At times a similar syndrome can appear in the absence of any identifiable exposure. The pathogenesis is believed to comprise an antigen-antibody response, the antigen being either the injected vaccination protein or the infecting virus. Clinically ADE typically produces acute headache, fever, and multifocal neurologic signs. The most severely affected patients develop delirium, stupor, or coma. Seizures are relatively common. The CSF is characterized by pleocytosis of 20 to 200 lymphocytes and usually an elevated gamma globulin. Protein concentration may be a little elevated, but glucose concentration is usually normal. Myelin basic protein can be identified in the CSF of some patients. The electroencephalogram (EEG) is usually diffusely abnormal, with widespread slowing, but does not have the characteristic focal slow and sharp wave activity of herpes simplex encephalitis.

ADE produces clinical and CSF manifestations similar to those of acute viral encephalitis and cannot be distinguished from that disorder by clinical findings. Since neither ADE nor acute viral encephalitis, save for herpes simplex, can be treated definitively, such a differentiation is not crucial. Despite its presumed immune mechanism, neither corticosteroids nor other immunosuppressive agents have been effective in treatment.

Acute hemorrhagic leukoencephalitis is a fatal, rare variant of acute encephalomyelitis. The illness usually occurs after an upper respiratory infection and is characterized by sudden headache, seizures, and rapid progression to coma. Patients often die within a few days. CSF often shows more polymorphonuclear leukocytes than lymphocytes. The brain at autopsy is swollen, with bilateral and asymmetric hemorrhages scattered throughout the white matter. There is no known treatment.

Acute Transverse Myelopathy (Myelitis). Acute transverse myelopathy is a clinical syndrome characterized by the rapid onset of ascending or transverse spinal cord dysfunction, usually involving primarily the midthoracic or high thoracic, low cervical cord. The disorder usually begins with abrupt, severe back pain and sometimes fever and malaise. In a matter of 12 to 24 hours, weakness and paresthesias appear in the lower extremities, sometimes with radicular pain at the level of the uppermost involved cord segments. Occasionally the disease is painless. In its severest form, complete paralysis and loss of sensation and autonomic function develop below the highest level of the lesion. In less severe forms there may be patchy loss of sensation with bilateral corticospinal tract signs predominating or a Brown-Séquard syndrome. In a few patients, the spinal cord signs ascend for hours to a week or two and reach a stable level, usually in the upper thoracic cord. About half the patients give a preceding history of banal infection, usually upper respiratory, or of a vaccination, the myelopathy presumably being a delayed immune response. Rarely, the illness is associated with an occult neoplasm. Late recurrences occasionally develop.

The CSF usually contains 50 to 100 white cells and a slightly elevated protein concentration. The diagnostic problem is to distinguish acute transverse myelopathy from parameningeal infection with secondary involvement of the cord. The history and findings in transverse myelopathy may mimic those of epidural or subdural infections. Accurate diagnosis can be established by MR imaging. If MRI is not available, myelography may be undertaken to rule out infection or hemorrhage. Sometimes, the spinal cord of patients with acute transverse myelopathy may be misleadingly swollen to produce a complete block to myelographic dye. Care must be taken to distinguish the swollen cord from an epidural or subdural block. There is no effective treatment for the disorder. About one third of patients recover spontaneously.

Other Demyelinating Disease. Devic's disease (neuromyelitis optica) is a clinical syndrome characterized by transverse myelopathy and optic neuropathy, usually bilateral. The two symptoms usually occur within days or weeks of each other. The disease is generally thought to be a variant of MS, but in many instances the spinal cord necrosis is considerably more intense than one finds in the demyelinating plaques of most cases of MS.

Acute optic neuritis can either occur as a symptom of MS or arise in isolation independently. This disorder is described on page 776.

Reye's Syndrome. Reye's syndrome is a parainfectious encephalopathy that usually follows influenza type A or B or varicella viral infections. The disease affects children far more frequently than adults. It is thought to involve heavy aspirin ingestion as a cofactor risk. Attacks damage several mitochondrial enzyme activities in liver and brain, producing serum hyperammonemia, lactic acidosis, and elevation of free fatty acids. The onset of Reye's syndrome usually occurs as signs of the initial flu-like disorder begin to subside and includes headache, intractable vomiting, and lethargy or stupor. Patients may rapidly become comatose. The diagnosis is confirmed by evidence of marked elevation of hepatic enzymes in the serum but without hyperbilirubinemia, and an elevated arterial ammonia level. In children, hypoglycemia may occur. The CSF is unremarkable. Mortality is high in comatose patients with mitochondrial abnormalities found in both liver and brain at autopsy. Careful control of increased intracranial pressure using hyperosmolar agents, as well as correction of hypoglycemia and electrolyte abnormalities, allows some persons to recover.

REFERENCES

Brown P, Goldfarb LG, Kovanen J, Haltia M, Cathala F, Sulima M, Gibbs CJ, Gajdusek DC: Phenotypic characteristics of familial Creutzfeldt-Jakob disease associated with the colon 178^{Asn} PRNP mutation. Ann Neurol 31:282, 1992.

Del-Curling O Jr, Gower DJ, McWhorter JM: Changing concepts in spinal epidural abscess. A report of 29 cases. Neurosurgery 27:185, 1990.

Hsiao K, Prusiner SB: Inherited human prion diseases. Neurology 40:1820, 1990.

Leys D, Christians JL, Derambure PL, Hladley JP, Lesoin F, Rosseaux M, Jomin N, Petit H: Management of focal intracranial infections. Is medical treatment better than surgery? J Neurol Neurosurg Psychiatry 53:472, 1990.

Mathews WB (ed): McAlpine's Multiple Sclerosis. 2nd ed. Edinburgh, Churchill Livingston, 1991.

Van Coster RN, Devivo DC, Blake D, Lombes A, Barrett R, Di Mauro S: Adult Reye's syndrome. Neurology 41:1815, 1991.

SECTION XIV

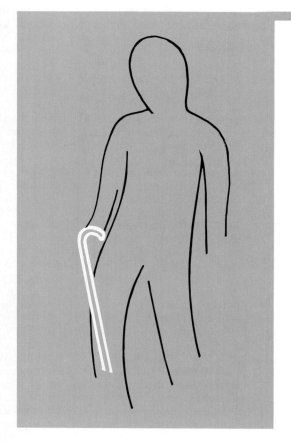

121 THE BIOLOGY OF AGING

THE AGING PATIENT

121 THE BIOLOGY OF AGING

A precise definition of normal physiologic aging remains elusive. Although probably regulated by intrinsic cellular mechanisms, the process of aging is modulated by a number of environmental influences. Because the lifetime experiences of each individual are unique and the combined effects of all environmental stimuli are impossible to calculate, it is frequently difficult to differentiate whether a measured alteration noted in older persons represents an inevitable consequence of the aging process or a potentially preventable disease. This issue has important clinical implications. It would be important to know, for example, how much of the physiologic decline seen with advancing age could be prevented by utilizing reasonable prophylactic measures.

The response of the whole organism to the aging process varies by organ system (Fig. 121–1, Table 121–1). Certain organs, such as the kidneys, lungs, and immune system, develop age-related declines in basal physiologic function. Many other organs, such as the heart, bone marrow, and liver, maintain a level of basal physiologic function comparable to that of the younger individual. However, the process of aging in most organ systems is characterized by a reduction in reserve capacity manifested by a blunted and more variable response to increased stimulation. This diminished reserve capacity renders older persons less able to maintain homeostasis when subjected to physiologic stress. As a consequence of these age-related changes, the elderly are more susceptible to disease and slower to recover from an injury or disease complication than is a younger person. For example, compared with younger individuals, the elderly are more susceptible to and less able to survive many infectious diseases because of an age-associated decline in their host defense mechanisms, particularly their cell-mediated immunity. These same alterations in immune function are also thought to contribute to the higher incidence of cancer seen in the elderly.

The intrinsic cellular mechanisms that cause aging have yet to be identified with certainty. However, a number of theories have been postulated. The **programmed aging theory** states that aging is programmed by genetic mechanisms. The resulting age-related alterations in cellular function become manifest as a decline in immunologic and neuroendocrine function that eventually contributes to susceptibility to disease and eventual death. An alternate theory states that aging is the consequence of an **accumulation of random genetic errors** that over time results in impaired protein synthesis and a deterioration in cellular function. Cells normally produce free radicals such as hydrogen peroxide and superoxide as by-products of metabolism. According to the **free radical theory**, aging is characterized by a progressive decline in the ability of cells to neutralize these metabolites rapidly, and this eventually results in irreversible cellular damage. A progressive decline in the **DNA repair capability** of cells has also been theorized to be the cause of aging. According to this theory, the decreased ability to repair damage to DNA results in errors in RNA and protein synthesis that eventually have an adverse effect on cellular function.

TABLE 121–1. AGE-RELATED DECLINE IN PHYSIOLOGIC FUNCTIONS

ORGAN SYSTEM	AGE-RELATED DECLINE IN FUNCTION
Special senses	Presbyopia
	Lens opacification
	Decreased hearing
	Decreased taste, smell
Cardiovascular	Impaired intrinsic contractile function
	Decreased conductivity
	Decreased ventricular filling
	Increased systolic blood pressure
	Impaired baroreceptor function
Respiratory	Decreased lung elasticity
	Decreased maximal breathing capacity
	Decreased mucus clearance
	Decreased arterial PO_2
	Impaired chemoreceptor regulation of respiration
	Increased risk of secondary infection
Immune	Decreased cell-mediated immunity
	Decreased T cell number
	Increased T suppressor cells
	Decreased T helper cells
	Loss of memory cells
	Decline in antibody titers to known antigens
	Increased autoimmunity
Endocrine	Decreased hormonal responses to stimulation
	Impaired glucose tolerance
	Decreased androgens and estrogens
	Impaired norepinephrine responses
Autonomic nervous system	Impaired response to fluid deprivation
	Decline in baroreceptor reflex
	Increased susceptibility to hypothermia
	Impaired gastrointestinal motility

As has been the case since the turn of the century, America is continuing to grow older. Between 1900 and 1980, the proportion of the population over the age of 65 grew from 4 per cent to approximately 12 per cent. By the year 2030, when most of the post-war baby boom generation will be over the age of 65, the elderly will constitute more than 20 per cent of the population. The largest percentage of increase will occur in subjects over the age of 85 (Fig. 121–2). This phenomenal aging of society is the consequence of improved life expectancy and a gradually falling birth rate. Because of differences in life expectancy, by the age of 75 there are twice as many females as males.

Advancing age is associated with a higher prevalence of both acute and chronic disease and an increasing risk of becoming functionally dependent. Roughly 5.3 per cent of adults between the ages of 65 and 75 require assistance with **basic activities of daily living** (bathing, dressing, walking, use of the toilet, and transferring from bed to chair). Slightly fewer than 6 per cent require assistance with **instrumental activities of daily living** (cooking, shopping, use of the telephone, household chores, and handling household financial matters). By the age of 85, these figures increase dramatically to 35 per cent and 40 per cent, respectively (Fig. 121–3). Functional dependence greatly increases the need for both acute and chronic health care and amplifies the risk of institutionalization.

The dramatic growth in the proportion of the population that is elderly has important economic consequences for the health care system and the nation. Because of the increasing need for health care with advancing age, the elderly are heavy consumers of health care resources. Although representing only 12 per cent of the population, the elderly account for

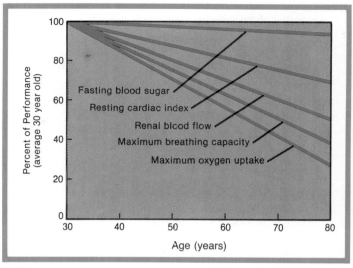

FIGURE 121–1. Percentage of decline, between ages 30 and 80, in a number of physiologic functions.

33 per cent of all hospital admissions, 44 per cent of all hospital days, and the vast majority of visits to physicians. Approximately 36 per cent of all health care dollars are spent on the elderly. A large proportion of these expenditures are incurred in the last year of life. Hospitalization accounts for 40 per cent of older persons' health care costs, with visits to physicians and nursing home care each contributing 20 per cent. Medicare is the major provider of health care for the elderly ($70 billion), with Medicaid contributing $20 billion and third party payers $10 billion.

Although high-technology acute care is readily available to most older persons, gross deficiencies exist in the delivery of primary and preventative

FIGURE 121–2. Panel *A* illustrates the absolute increase in the number of persons between the ages of 65 and 74 and over the age of 75 between 1910 and the current time. The projected increase to the year 2030 is also shown. Panel *B* shows that the percentage of the population over age 65 has significantly increased from 6 per cent of the total population in 1940 to 11 per cent at the current time. By the year 2030, it is projected that 16 per cent of the population will be over the age of 65. Thus, the increase in older persons is not merely a reflection of an overall rise in the total population.

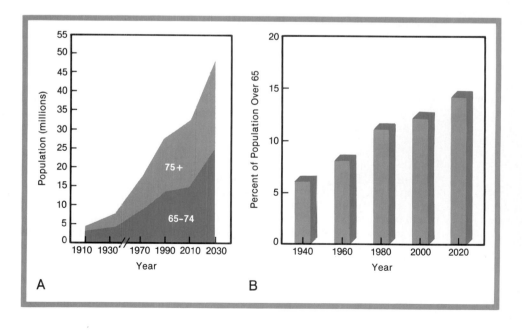

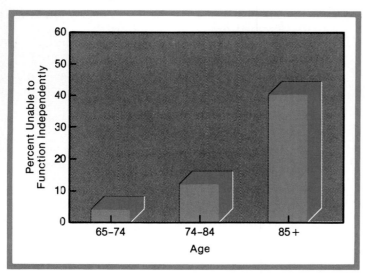

FIGURE 121–3. Percentage of the population with significant disabilities resulting in functional dependence and the need for assistance with activities of daily living.

care. There is a particular need for in-home care and social support services. Because of the increased prevalence of chronic disease and functional disability among the elderly, such specialized supportive services are needed to minimize the risk of nursing home placement. The continued rapid increase in the older population with chronic diseases and functional dependence will contribute significantly to the current health care crisis and will certainly affect priorities and the way medicine is practiced in the near future.

ASSESSMENT OF THE OLDER PATIENT

Disease Presentation in the Elderly

The elderly patient presenting for a diagnostic evaluation must be assessed carefully. Clinical signs and symptoms of disease in the older patient are often blunted, absent, or atypical. A good example is thyrotoxicosis. Compared with the younger patient, who typically presents with a variety of classic signs and symptoms such as nervousness, weight loss, tremor, and tachycardia, elderly patients are more likely to present with cognitive dysfunction, anorexia, muscle weakness, atrial fibrillation, or congestive heart failure. Even a carefully obtained history may fail to elicit expected diagnostic clues. The older patient may not report chest pain with an acute myocardial infarction, dysuria with a urinary tract infection, or cough and shortness of breath with pneumonia. Often, only subtle and nonspecific signs and symptoms, such as a change in mental status, increased lethargy, a diminished appetite, or an increased frequency of falls, suggest that an underlying acute illness is present. Although psychiatric symptoms such as depressed mood, personality change, or inattentiveness may indicate the presence of infection, congestive heart failure, or a metabolic disorder, a true psychiatric problem such as depression may manifest with constitutional symptoms such as headache or weakness and dizziness.

Medications often add to the diagnostic confusion. The side effects of drugs can either mimic or blunt the symptoms of acute illness. Difficulties in identifying the cause of an elderly patient's clinical deterioration can even result when the symptoms of a chronic disease mask those of a new illness. There may be a delay in diagnosing an acute septic arthritis, as, for example, when the patient has a history of chronic recurrent painful arthritis in the same joint. Potentially life-threatening diseases in the elderly can also present with initial manifestations that pose a diagnostic challenge for the clinician. For example, it is not uncommon for an older patient with pneumonia, urosepsis, or an intra-abdominal catastrophe to present with few identifying physical signs, a blunted or absent fever response, and a white blood cell count that is mildly elevated, in the normal range, or even low. A paradoxical fall in body temperature is usually a bad prognostic sign. The likelihood that disease will manifest atypically is increased in elderly patients who are cognitively impaired, malnourished, debilitated, or suffering from multiple chronic medical conditions. For this reason, these patients often present the greatest diagnostic challenge.

Assessment of Rehabilitation Potential

The sequelae of disease may be particularly devastating in older individuals. Even a relatively minor illness can cause a significant deterioration in the elderly patient's cognitive or physical functioning. Furthermore, compared with that in younger patients, recovery in the elderly is likely to be slower, requiring longer and more intensive periods of recuperation and rehabilitation if return to the premorbid state is to be achieved. Loss of functional independence from either physical or cognitive disability places the elderly patient at high risk for institutionalization. For these reasons, an assessment that includes an evaluation of functional and cognitive status and the development of a treatment plan that attempts to restore independence must be included in any medical evaluation of the elderly patient. In addition, selected patients require an in-depth assessment of their social support structure (family, friends, relatives), economic status, and home environment in order to determine what resources would be required to allow the patient to return to or remain at home safely. Such comprehensive assessments of the patient represent the cornerstone of geriatric care. These assessments require a **comprehensive interdisciplinary evaluation** that includes input from physicians, nurses, social workers, physical and occupational therapists, pharmacists, and, depending on the patient's needs, many other health care professionals (Fig. 121–4). In collaboration with the various team members, a

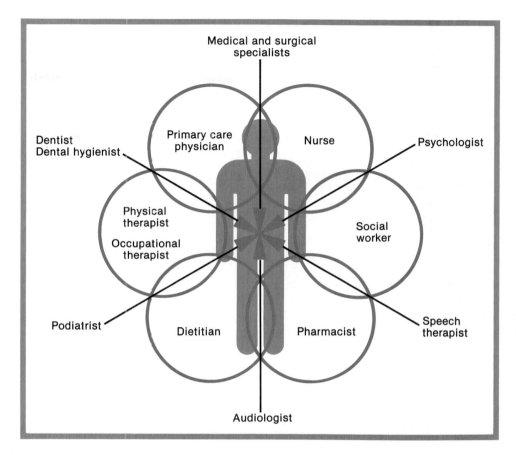

FIGURE 121–4. A diagrammatic illustration of health care professionals involved in the complex interdisciplinary assessment of frail elderly patients. The core health care team that should optimally evaluate every patient is shown in the circles. Consultative members of the team (shown outside the circles) contribute as needed. It must be emphasized that in many circumstances a consultant such as a dentist, psychologist, or medical subspecialist may be critically important in the development of a treatment and disposition plan.

treatment plan must be developed that includes optimal medical management, minimal medication use, and, as needed, a long-term strategy for physical, cognitive, or nutritional rehabilitation (Table 121–2). For elderly patients who are assessed to have a reasonable potential for rehabilitation, numerous studies have shown that such a comprehensive strategy of evaluation and care is cost-effective, improves functional status, and allows a large fraction of patients to return to or remain in their own home.

COMMON AND OFTEN INADEQUATELY ASSESSED MEDICAL PROBLEMS OF THE ELDERLY

Polypharmacy

The elderly are at high risk of developing medication-related problems. One reason for this is the fact that the elderly tend to take multiple pharmaceuticals. The average patient over the age of 70 takes 4.5 prescription and 3.5 over-the-counter medications. The risk of both adverse drug reactions and poor compliance increases in relation to the number of medications taken. The probability of ex-

TABLE 121–2. PRINCIPLES OF COMPREHENSIVE GERIATRIC ASSESSMENT

1. Identify treatable medical conditions
2. Screen for depression and memory loss
3. Minimize drug use
4. Avoid restraints if possible, both chemical and physical
   a. Discuss options with family or caregivers
   b. Consider nonrestraining alternatives
5. Assess functional status
   a. Activities of daily living (bathing, dressing, etc.)
   b. Instrumental activities of daily living (shopping, etc.)
6. Set rehabilitation goals
   a. Assess rehabilitation potential with consideration of the following:
      (1) Medical prognosis
      (2) Cause and duration of functional debilitation
      (3) The patient's and family's expectations or desires
   b. Develop rehabilitation program tailored to patient's needs
7. Develop a disposition plan
   a. Assess the patient's ability to return to work or remain at home. Include assessment of the following:
      (1) Family and informal community support networks
      (2) Financial resources and availability of private community services
      (3) Eligibility for sponsored programs or support services
   b. Evaluate need for short- or long-term placement in an institution
      (1) Geriatric rehabilitation center
      (2) Nursing home

periencing an adverse drug reaction, for example, increases from 2 per cent for patients taking two or fewer medications to more than 13 per cent for patients taking six or more. The often prohibitive cost of medications and the complexity of some treatment regimens contribute to poor compliance. The problem is compounded by the fact that elderly patients frequently see multiple physicians who are often unaware of medications prescribed by others. This leads to problems of overprescribing, duplicate prescriptions, and adverse drug-drug interactions.

In addition, medication-related problems often occur in the elderly owing to age-related alterations in both pharmacokinetics and pharmacodynamics. Compared with younger patients, the elderly take longer to clear many medications from their systems. They also are more likely to experience toxic manifestations of a drug even when the serum level is within a range considered normal for a younger patient. If prescribed dosages of certain medications are not reduced appropriately, an older patient can quickly develop a toxic reaction. The proper use of drugs, avoidance of unnecessary medications, and ensuring that medications do not aggravate existing disease are particularly important in the older patient.

Falls and Decreased Mobility

Difficulties with walking, gait, and balance occur frequently among older persons. As a consequence, approximately 30 per cent of subjects over the age of 70 fall once or more annually. This results in a high incidence of hip fracture and other injuries that confine patients to their beds, increasing the risks of developing other medical complications, such as dehydration, pneumonia, urinary retention, and infections. Usually, the etiology of falls is multifactorial and includes visual impairment, neurologic or vestibular disease, postural hypotension, decreased

muscle mass, joint disease, and various foot disorders. Falls often occur at night, are more common in dementia, and are increased in frequency by medication use. Recent reports have suggested that rehabilitation and strength training can improve muscle mass, balance, and gait and can decrease the risk of falls.

Delirium

Delirium is an acute confusional state that is commonly observed in hospitalized older persons. The diagnosis, which must be made clinically, should be suspected in any older person who has confusion that is of recent onset and is accompanied by a fluctuating level of consciousness. A decreased ability to maintain attention, daytime sleepiness, hallucinations, disorientation, and memory loss may all be part of the presenting clinical picture. Virtually any disorder can manifest with delirium in the elderly. Common causes include dehydration, congestive heart failure, myocardial infarction, pulmonary or urinary tract infections, and numerous drugs (Table 121–3). In addition to drugs that have known central nervous system effects, delirium has been reported with penicillin, digoxin, cimetidine, and nonsteroidal anti-inflammatory agents, such as aspirin and ibuprofen. In older persons, delirium may occur at a dose that would not usually be considered toxic.

Elderly patients can develop delirium even as a result of a change in their living environment, such as occurs with hospitalization or placement in a nursing home. Postoperative delirium is also very common in the elderly, occurring, for example, in 50 per cent of patients following hip surgery. In this setting, the etiology is multifactorial and often includes drugs and infection. Delirium is more common in patients who have baseline disorders of cognition. Because delirium is potentially reversible, it should not be ignored as "senile dementia" or "organic brain syndrome." Management involves accurate diagnosis and treatment of underlying diseases, stopping or changing all drugs that could be contributory, and aggressively treating dehydration. When agitation is severe, sedatives or tranquilizers may be required. Although not ideal, haloperidol is the drug of choice. The usual initial dose is 0.5 mg administered intramuscularly or orally and repeated at 30-minute intervals as needed. Although this drug is usually well tolerated, a rare but potentially fatal side effect is the development of the neuroleptic malignant syndrome, which is characterized by fever and extrapyramidal signs. In conjunction with haloperidol, benzodiazepines (e.g., lorazepam) have also been recommended as therapy for delirium. However, it is important to keep in mind that drugs themselves are often the cause of delirium. Sedatives should be avoided in the drowsy patient, and they should never be given for prolonged periods. Although pharmacologic and physical restraints are used commonly in patients with delirium, they are both associated with an increased risk of morbidity and should be avoided if at all possible.

TABLE 121–3. CAUSES OF DELIRIUM IN THE ELDERLY

Organ Failure	Drugs
Respiratory failure	Anticholinergics
Congestive heart failure	Antibiotics
Hepatocellular failure	Anticonvulsants
Infections	Digitalis
Acute bronchitis	Alcohol
Bronchopneumonia	Alcohol withdrawal
Bladder infections	**Neurologic Causes**
Septicemia	Subdural hematoma
Metabolic	Cerebrovascular accident
Dehydration	Raised intracranial pressure
Hyponatremia	Cerebral infections
Hypernatremia	**Miscellaneous**
	Postoperative delirium
	Sensory deprivation
	Recent institutionalization
	Change of living arrangement

Dementia is a global loss of intellectual function characterized by defects in memory, language, visuospatial function, cognition, and emotions or personality. Although minor changes in memory occur with aging (benign forgetfulness), defects that interfere with the ability to function independently are never caused by age per se and reflect a disease process. Dementia is very common among the elderly, occurring in 20 per cent of the population over the age of 85. The two most common causes are Alzheimer's disease and multi-infarct dementia. Because a number of conditions can present with a reversible clinical syndrome mimicking dementia, each patient with cognitive dysfunction of unknown etiology should receive a comprehensive medical and neuropsychological evaluation accompanied by an appropriate laboratory and radiologic investigation. This investigation should be focused specifically to rule out depression, chronic alcohol abuse, thyrotoxicosis, myxedema, vitamin B_{12} or folate deficiency, heavy metal intoxication, drugs, or normal-pressure hydrocephalus as causes of the cognitive disorder.

Alzheimer's disease and **multi-infarct or vascular dementias** account for the vast majority of cases of cognitive loss in elderly patients. Alzheimer's disease presents insidiously with progressive loss of memory. A common early feature is the development of language difficulties manifesting primarily with gradually worsening expressive and receptive aphasia. Patients frequently lose the ability to recognize common objects and often become lost in familiar environments. Later in the course of the disease, behavioral problems occur, including aggression, hallucinations, and delusions. Of particular concern to caregivers is late afternoon agitation (sundowning), wandering, and disordered sleep cycles.

Although a tentative diagnosis of Alzheimer's disease is often based on the clinical evaluation, the diagnosis may be confirmed by postmortem histologic examination of brain tissue. The histologic features diagnostic of Alzheimer's disease include the findings of multiple neurofibrillary tangles and beta-amyloid protein–containing neuritic plaques. Although both the neurofibrillary tangles, which are thought to represent degenerating neuron bodies, and the neuritic plaques are observed in conditions other than Alzheimer's disease, their presence in large numbers, together with a classic clinical history of progressive cognitive deterioration, weighs strongly in favor of a diagnosis of Alzheimer's disease. A brain biopsy may be justified in patients who have an atypical presentation or who present with the onset of symptoms early in life (<60 years). This procedure may allow the diagnosis of rare disorders and alleviate family concerns.

Multi-infarct dementia must be distinguished from Alzheimer's disease. The major pathology is multiple cerebral infarcts caused by atherosclerosis and thromboembolism. In contrast to the relentless progression seen in Alzheimer's disease, this disorder classically has a more abrupt onset and deteriorates in a stepwise fashion (Fig. 121–5A). Focal neurologic lesions and emotional lability are common, and the patient often has a history of hypertension and previous strokes. Multiple cerebral infarctions can usually be demonstrated by magnetic resonance imaging (MRI), which is very useful in the diagnosis of multi-infarct dementia.

Owing to the prevalence of dementia among the elderly, the primary care physician must be familiar with this syndrome and have a rational approach to work-up and referral. Costly diagnostic tests, particularly MRI and computed tomographic (CT) scans, should not be used indiscriminately. As a general rule, radiologic evaluation should be limited to those patients who have had symptoms of less than 2 years' duration or who have unexplained focal neurologic symptoms.

Once all potentially reversible causes of the patient's cognitive dysfunction have been excluded, management should focus on maintaining optimal

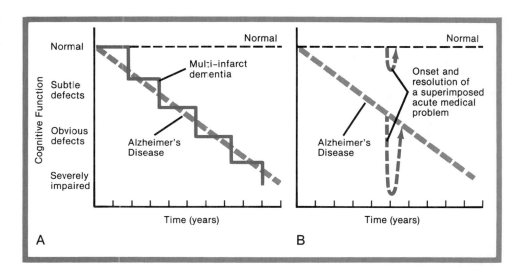

FIGURE 121–5. Panel A illustrates that normal aging is not associated with a significant decline in cognitive function and contrasts the progressive and steady decline in memory seen in patients with Alzheimer's disease with the stepwise decreases seen in patients with multi-infarct dementia. Panel B demonstrates that modest, temporary declines in cognitive function can occur in normal elderly subjects during periods of acute illness. In patients with Alzheimer's disease or other disorders associated with memory loss, an acute medical illness can result in a much greater loss of cognitive function, which may or may not return to the pre-illness level.

health through preventative care, identifying and treating complicating medical and psychiatric problems, education of the family and caregivers, referral to appropriate support groups, and the occasional use of sedatives or tranquilizers to treat aggressive or disruptive behavior. At the current time, there are no therapies that are of proven benefit for reversing the cognitive loss resulting from Alzheimer's disease or multi-infarct dementia. For the latter disorder, low-dose aspirin is recommended as prophylaxis against further strokes. Complicating medical and psychiatric problems should be identified and treated promptly. In older persons with or without a dementing illness, any acute or subacute medical illness can result in significant deterioration of the patient's cognitive and physical functioning. However, in most cases, with appropriate treatment of the complications, the patient can be expected to return to a baseline level of functioning after resolution of the acute disorder (Fig. 121–5B).

REFERENCES

Applegate WB, Blass, JP, Williams TF: Instruments for the functional assessment of older patients. N Engl J Med 322:1207–1214, 1990.

Francis J, Martin D, Kapoor WN: A prospective study of delirium in hospitalized elderly. JAMA 263:1097–1101, 1990.

Grisso JA, Kelsey JL, Strom BL, Chiu GY, Maislin G, O'Brien LA, Hoffman S, Kaplan F: Risk factors for falls as a cause of hip fractures in women. N Engl J Med 324:1326–1331, 1991.

Hazzard WR, Andres R, Bierman EL, et al (eds): Principles of Geriatric Medicine and Gerontology. 2nd ed. New York, McGraw-Hill Book Co, 1990.

Katzman R, Jackson JE: Alzheimer's disease: Basic and clinical advances. J Am Geriatr Soc 39:516–525, 1991.

Miller RA: Minireview. The cell biology of aging: Immunological models. J Gerontol 44:4–8, 1989.

Montamat SC, Cusack BJ, Vestel RE: Management of drug therapy in the elderly. N Engl J Med 321:303–309, 1989.

COMMONLY MEASURED LABORATORY VALUES

This appendix lists basic serum and urinary laboratory values measured commonly in clinical medicine. The values are presented in conventional units (CU) and standard international (SI) units. The table also includes conversion factors (CFs) for interchanging conventional and standard international units using the following formula:

$$SI\ units = CU \times CF$$

This collection of laboratory values is not intended to be exhaustive. Most of the laboratory values are from the following sources: Wyngaarden JB, Smith LH, Bennett JC, (eds): *Cecil Textbook of Medicine.* 19th ed. Philadelphia, WB Saunders Co, 1992, pp 2370–2377; and Henry JB (ed): *Clinical Diagnosis and Management by Laboratory Methods,* 18th ed, Philadelphia, WB Saunders Co, 1991, pp 1366–1382. These two sources also provide more comprehensive listings of laboratory measures. Laboratory values found in this appendix but not in either of the above references are from the clinical laboratories of University Hospital, University of Arkansas for Medical Sciences, Little Rock, Arkansas.

COMMONLY MEASURED LABORATORY VALUES

TEST	CONVENTIONAL UNITS	CONVERSION FACTOR	SI UNITS
ARTERIAL BLOOD GASES			
pH (37°C)	—	—	7.35–7.45
Oxygen (PO_2)	83–100 mm Hg	0.133	11–14.4 kPa
Oxygen saturation	95–98%	—	Fraction: 0.95–0.98
Carbon dioxide (PCO_2)	23–29 mEq/L	1	23–29 mmol/L
SERUM ELECTROLYTES			
Sodium	136–146 mEq/L	1	136–146 mmol/L
Potassium	3.5–5.1 mEq/L	1	3.5–5.1 mmol/L
Chloride	98–106 mEq/L	1	98–106 mmol/L
Bicarbonate	18–23 mEq/L	1	18–23 mmol/L
Anion gap [Na − (Cl + HCO$_3$)]	7–14 mEq/L	1	7–14 mmol/L
Calcium			
Total	8.4–10.2 mg/dL	0.25	2.1–2.55 mmol/L
Ionized	4.65–5.28 mg/dL	0.25	1.16–1.32 mmol/L
Magnesium	1.3–2.1 mEq/L	0.50	0.65–1.05 mmol/L
Phosphorus	2.7–4.5 mg/dL	0.323	0.87–1.45 mmol/L
COMMONLY MEASURED SERUM NONELECTROLYTES			
Urea nitrogen	7–18 mg/dL	0.357	2.5–6.4 mmol/L
Creatinine	M: 0.7–1.3 mg/dL	88.4	62–115 µmol/L
	F: 0.6–1.1 mg/dL	88.4	53–97 µmol/L
Uric acid	M: 3.5–7.2 mg/dL	0.059	0.21–0.42 mmol/L
	F: 2.6–6.0 ng/dL	0.059	0.15–0.35 mmol/L
Glucose	70–105 mg/dL	0.055	3.9–5.8 mmol/L
Osmolality	—	—	275–295 mOsm/kg
SERUM ENDOCRINE TESTS			
ACTH	0800 h: 8–79 pg/mL	1	8–79 ng/L
	1600 h: 7–30 pg/mL	1	7–30 ng/L
Aldosterone	Supine: 3–10 ng/dL	0.0277	0.08–0.28 nmol/L
	Upright: 5–30 ng/dL	0.0277	0.14–0.83 nmol/L
Chronic (β-hCG) gonadotropin	<5.0 mU/mL	1	<5.0 IU/L
Cortisol	0800 h: 5–23 µg/dL	27.6	138–635 nmol/L
	1600 h: 3–15 µg/dL	27.6	82–413 nmol/L
C-peptide	0.78–1.89 ng/mL	0.328	0.26–0.62 nmol/L
Estrogen	M: 20–80 pg/mL	1	20–80 ng/L
	F: Follicular phase, 60–200 pg/mL	1	60–200 ng/L
	Luteal phase, 160–400 pg/mL	1	160–400 ng/L
	Postmenopausal, ≤130 pg/mL	1	≤130 ng/L
Follitropin (FSH)	M: 4–25 mIU/mL	1	4–25 IU/L
	F: Follicular phase, 1–9 mU/mL	1	1–9 U/L
	Ovulatory peak, 6–26 mU/mL	1	6–26 U/L
	Luteal phase, 1–9 mU/mL	1	1–9 U/L
	Postmenopausal, 30–118 mU/mL	1	30–118 U/L
Gastrin	<100 pg/mL	1	<100 ng/L
Growth hormone	M: <2 ng/mL	1	<2 µg/L
	F: <10 ng/mL	1	<10 µg/L
Hemoglobin A_{1c}	5.6–7.5% of total Hg (whole blood)	0.001	Fraction: 0.056–0.075
Insulin (12-h fasting)	6–24 µIU/mL	7.0	42–167 pmol/L
Lutropin (LH)	M: 1–8 mU/mL	1	1–8 U/L
	F: Follicular phase, 1–12 mU/mL	1	1–12 U/L
	Midcycle, 16–104 mU/mL	1	16–104 U/L
	Luteal, 1–12 mU/mL	1	1–12 U/L
	Postmenopausal, 16–66 mU/mL	1	16–66 U/L
Progesterone	M: 0.13–0.97 ng/mL	3.2	0.4–3.1 nmol/L
	F: Follicular phase, 0.14–1.61 ng/mL	3.2	0.5–2.2 nmol/L
	Luteal phase, 2–25 ng/mL	3.2	6.4–79.5 nmol/L
Prolactin	Postmenopausal, 0–20 ng/mL	1	0–20 µg/L
Renin	Supine: 1.6 ± 1.5 ng/mL/h	1	1.6 ± 1.5 µg/L/h
	Standing: 4.5 ± 2.9 ng/mL/h	1	4.5 ± 2.9 µg/L/h

COMMONLY MEASURED LABORATORY VALUES *Continued*

TEST	CONVENTIONAL UNITS	CONVERSION FACTOR	SI UNITS
SERUM ENDOCRINE TESTS (*Continued*)			
Testosterone			
Free	M: 52–280 pg/mL	3.5	180.4–971.6 pmol/L
	F: 1.6–6.3 pg/mL	3.5	5.6–21.9 pmol/L
Total	M: 300–1000 ng/dL	0.035	10.4–34.7 nmol/L
	F: 20–75 ng/dL	0.035	0.69–2.6 nmol/L
Thyrotropin (TSH)	2–10 μU/mL	1	2–10 μU/L
Thyrotropin-releasing hormone (TRH)	5–60 pg/mL	1	5–60 ng/L
Thyroxine			
Free (FT$_4$)	0.8–2.4 ng/dL	13	10–31 pmol/L
Total (T$_4$)	5–12 μg/dL	13	65–155 nmol/L
Tri-iodothyronine resin uptake (T$_3$RU)	24–34%	1	24–34 AU (arbitrary units)
URINE ENDOCRINE TESTS			
Catecholamines	24 h: <100 μg/d	0.059	<5.91 nmol/d
5-Hydroxyindole-acetic acid	24 h: 2–6 mg/d	5.2	10.4–31.2 μmol/d
Metanephrines	24 h: 0.5–1.2 μg/mg creatinine	0.58	0.03–0.69 mmol/mol creatinine
Vanillylmandelic acid (VMA)	24 h: 2–7 mg/d	5.05	10.1–35.4 μmol/d
17-Hydroxycorticosteroids	24 h: M: 3–10 mg/d	2.76	8.3–27.6 μmol/d
	F: 2–8 mg/d	2.76	5.5–22.1 μmol/d
17-Ketosteroids	24 h: M: 9–22 mg/d	3.44	31–76 μmol/d
	F: 6–15 mg/d	3.44	21–52 μmol/d
SERUM MARKERS OF GASTROINTESTINAL ABSORPTION			
β-Carotene	10–85 μg/dL	0.0186	0.19–1.58 μmol/L
Vitamin B$_{12}$	100–700 pg/mL	0.74	74–516 pmol/L
Folate			
Serum	3–16 ng/mL	2.27	7–36 nmol/L
Red blood cells (RBCs)	130–628 ng/mL packed cells	2.27	294–1422 nmol/L
SERUM LIPIDS			
Cholesterol	Recommended: <200 mg/dL	0.026	<5.18 mmol/L
	Moderate risk: 200–239 mg/dL	0.026	5.18–6.19 mmol/L
	High risk: ≤240 mg/dL	0.026	≥6.22 mmol/L
Fatty acids, free	8–25 mg/dL	0.0356	0.28–0.89 mmol/L
HDL-Cholesterol	M: >29 mg/dL	0.026	>0.75 mmol/L
	F: >35 mg/dL	0.026	>0.91 mmol/L
LDL-Cholesterol	Recommended: <130 mg/dL	0.026	<3.37 mmol/L
	Moderate risk: 130–159 mg/dL	0.026	3.37–4.12 mmol/L
	High risk: ≥160 mg/dL	0.026	≥4.14 mmol/L
Triglycerides	M: 40–160 mg/dL	0.011	0.45–1.81 mmol/L
	F: 35–135 mg/dL	0.011	0.4–1.52 mmol/L
SERUM LIVER/PANCREATIC TESTS			
Alanine aminotransferase (ALT, SGPT)	—	—	8–20 U/L
Aspartate aminotransferase (AST, SGOT)	—	—	10–30 U/L
γ-Glutamyltransferase (GGT)	—	—	M: 9–50 U/L
			F: 8–40 U/L
Alkaline phosphatase	—	—	M: 53–128 U/L
			F: 42–98 U/L
Bilirubin			
Total	0.2–1.0 mg/dL	17.1	3.4–17.1 μmol/L
Conjugated	0–0.2 mg/dL	17.1	0–3.4 μmol/L
Amylase	—	—	25–125 U/L
Lipase	—	—	10–140 U/L
SERUM MARKERS FOR CARDIAC OR SKELETAL MUSCLE INJURY			
Aldolase	—	—	1.0–7.5 U/L
Lactate dehydrogenase (LDH)	—	—	208–378 U/L

COMMONLY MEASURED LABORATORY VALUES *Continued*

TEST	CONVENTIONAL UNITS	CONVERSION FACTOR	SI UNITS
SERUM MARKERS FOR CARDIAC OR SKELETAL MUSCLE INJURY *(Continued)*			
Isoenzymes (%)	Fraction 1: 18–33	—	0.18–0.33
	Fraction 2: 28–40	—	0.28–0.40
	Fraction 3: 18–30	—	0.18–0.30
	Fraction 4: 6–16	—	0.06–0.16
	Fraction 5: 2–13	—	0.02–0.13
Creatine kinase (CK)	—	—	M: 38–174 U/L
			F: 26–140 U/L
Isoenzymes (%)	Fraction 2 (MB): <4–6% of total	—	<0.04–0.06
Myoglobin	—	—	M: 19–92 μg/L
			F: 12–76 μg/L
SERUM MARKERS FOR NEOPLASIA			
Acid phosphatase	—	—	M: 2.5–11.7 U/L
Carcinoembryonic antigen (CEA)	Nonsmokers: <2.5 ng/mL	1	<2.5 μg/L
α-Fetoprotein	<10 ng/mL	1	<10 μg/L
Prostate-specific antigen (PSA)	0–4 ng/mL	0.001	0–4 μg/L
SERUM PROTEINS			
Albumin	3.5–5.0 g/dL	10	35–50 g/L
Immunoglobulins	IgA: 40–350 mg/dL	10	400–3500 mg/L
	IgD: 0–8 mg/dL	10	0–80 mg/L
	IgE: 0–380 IU/mL	1	0–380 KIU/L
	IgG: 650–1600 mg/dL	0.01	6.5–16 g/L
	IgM: 55–300 mg/dL	10	550–3000 mg/L
Protein			
Total	6.4–8.3 g/dL	10	64–83 g/L
Electrophoresis	α_1-globulin: 0.1–0.3 g/dL	10	1–3 g/L
	α_2-globulin: 0.6–1.0 g/dL	10	6–10 g/L
	β-globulin: 0.7–1.1 g/dL	10	7–11 g/L
	γ-globulin: 0.8–1.6 g/dL	10	8–16 g/L
COMPLETE BLOOD COUNT			
Hemoglobin (Hb)	M: 13.5–17.5 g/dL	0.155	2.09–2.71 mmol/L
	F: 12–16 g/dL	0.155	1.86–2.48 mmol/L
Hematocrit (Hct)	M: 39–49%	—	0.39–0.49
	F: 35–45%	—	0.35–0.45
Mean corpuscular Hb concentration (MCHC)	31–37% Hb/cell, or g Hb/dL RBC	0.155	4.81–5.74 mmol Hb/L
Mean corpuscular volume (MCV)	—	—	80–100 fL
Leukocyte count	4.5–11 × 10³ cells/μL	—	4.5–11 × 10⁹ cells/L

Differential count	%	Cells/μl	—	Fraction	Cells × 10⁶/L
Myelocytes	0	0	—	0	0
Neutrophils—bands	3–5	150–400	—	0.03–0.05	150–400
Neutrophils—segmented	54–62	3000–5800	—	0.54–0.62	3000–5800
Lymphocytes	23–33	1500–3000	—	0.25–0.33	1500–3000
Monocytes	3–7	285–500	—	0.03–0.07	285–500
Eosinophils	1–3	50–250	—	0.01–0.03	50–250
Basophils	0–0.75	15–50	—	0–0.0075	15–50
CD_4 (T_H) count	36–54	660–1500	—	0.36–0.54	660–1500
CD_8 (T_S) count	19–33	360–850	—	0.19–0.54	360–850
T_H/T_S ratio	1.1–2.9		—	1.1–2.9	
Platelet count	150–450 × 10³/μL (mm³)		—	150–450 × 10⁹/L	

ANEMIA TESTS			
Reticulocyte count	0.5–1.5% of erythrocytes	—	0.005–0.015
Iron	M: 65–175 μg/dL	0.179	11.6–31.3 μmol/L
	F: 50–170 μg/dL	0.179	9.0–30.4 μmol/L
Ferritin	M: 20–250 ng/mL	1	20–250 μg/L
	F: 10–120 ng/mL	1	10–120 μg/L
Total iron-binding capacity	250–450 μg/dL	0.179	44.8–80.6 μmol/L
Hemoglobin electrophoresis	HbA: >95%	—	>0.95
	HbA$_2$: 1.5–3.5%	—	0.015–0.035
	HbF: <2%	—	<0.02
	HbS: 0%		

COMMONLY MEASURED LABORATORY VALUES *Continued*

TEST	CONVENTIONAL UNITS	CONVERSION FACTOR	SI UNITS
COAGULATION TESTS			
Prothrombin time (PT)	9–13 sec	+9 sec	18–22 sec
Partial thromboplastin time (PTT)	—	—	60–85 sec
Activated PTT	—	—	25–35 sec
Bleeding time			
Ivy	—	—	Normal: 2–7 min
			Borderline: 7–11 min
Simplate			2.75–8 min
Clotting time (Lee-White)	—	—	5–8 min
Thrombin time	—	—	Time of control ±2 sec when control is 9–13 sec
DISSEMINATED INTRAVASCULAR COAGULATION TESTS			
Fibrinogen	200–400 mg/dL	0.01	2.0–4.0 g/L
Fibrin degradation products	<10 μg/mL	1	<10 mg/L
HEMOLYSIS TESTS			
Haptoglobin	26–185 mg/dL	10	260–1850 mg/L

INDEX

The colophon on the spine is an abstraction which symbolizes the universal aspects of medicine. The circle represents the world. The stylized triangle in the upper area is the classic image of positive and negative forces—the Law of Life. The vertical line with the upper right staff suggests the staff of Æsculapius and Hermes, and the horizontal bar connects all three symbols into the total summation of medicine as Art and Science.

ISBN 0-7216-3272-6

90069